Oxford Dictionary of
National Biography

Volume 20

Oxford Dictionary of National Biography

IN ASSOCIATION WITH

The British Academy

From the earliest times to the year 2000

Edited by
H. C. G. Matthew
and
Brian Harrison

Volume 20
Flattisbury–Freston

OXFORD
UNIVERSITY PRESS

OXFORD

UNIVERSITY PRESS

Great Clarendon Street, Oxford OX2 6DP

Oxford University Press is a department of the University of Oxford.
It furthers the University's objective of excellence in research, scholarship,
and education by publishing worldwide in

Oxford New York

Auckland Bangkok Buenos Aires Cape Town
Chennai Dar es Salaam Delhi Hong Kong Istanbul Karachi
Kolkata Kuala Lumpur Madrid Melbourne Mexico City Mumbai Nairobi
São Paulo Shanghai Taipei Tokyo Toronto

Oxford is a registered trade mark of Oxford University Press
in the UK and in certain other countries

Published in the United States
by Oxford University Press Inc., New York

British Library Cataloguing in Publication Data
Data available

Library of Congress Cataloging in Publication Data
Data available: for details see volume 1, p. iv

ISBN 0-19-861370-9 (this volume)
ISBN 0-19-861411-X (set of sixty volumes)

Text captured by Alliance Phototypesetters, Pondicherry
Illustrations reproduced and archived by
Alliance Graphics Ltd, UK
Typeset in OUP Swift by Interactive Sciences Limited, Gloucester
Printed in Great Britain on acid-free paper by
Butler and Tanner Ltd,
Frome, Somerset

LIST OF ABBREVIATIONS

1 General abbreviations

AB	bachelor of arts
ABC	Australian Broadcasting Corporation
ABC TV	ABC Television
act.	active
A$	Australian dollar
AD	*anno domini*
AFC	Air Force Cross
AIDS	acquired immune deficiency syndrome
AK	Alaska
AL	Alabama
A level	advanced level [examination]
ALS	associate of the Linnean Society
AM	master of arts
AMICE	associate member of the Institution of Civil Engineers
ANZAC	Australian and New Zealand Army Corps
appx *pl.* appxs	appendix(es)
AR	Arkansas
ARA	associate of the Royal Academy
ARCA	associate of the Royal College of Art
ARCM	associate of the Royal College of Music
ARCO	associate of the Royal College of Organists
ARIBA	associate of the Royal Institute of British Architects
ARP	air-raid precautions
ARRC	associate of the Royal Red Cross
ARSA	associate of the Royal Scottish Academy
art.	article / item
ASC	Army Service Corps
Asch	Austrian Schilling
ASDIC	Antisubmarine Detection Investigation Committee
ATS	Auxiliary Territorial Service
ATV	Associated Television
Aug	August
AZ	Arizona
b.	born
BA	bachelor of arts
BA (Admin.)	bachelor of arts (administration)
BAFTA	British Academy of Film and Television Arts
BAO	bachelor of arts in obstetrics
bap.	baptized
BBC	British Broadcasting Corporation / Company
BC	before Christ
BCE	before the common (*or* Christian) era
BCE	bachelor of civil engineering
BCG	bacillus of Calmette and Guérin [inoculation against tuberculosis]
BCh	bachelor of surgery
BChir	bachelor of surgery
BCL	bachelor of civil law
BCnL	bachelor of canon law
BCom	bachelor of commerce
BD	bachelor of divinity
BEd	bachelor of education
BEng	bachelor of engineering
bk *pl.* bks	book(s)
BL	bachelor of law / letters / literature
BLitt	bachelor of letters
BM	bachelor of medicine
BMus	bachelor of music
BP	before present
BP	British Petroleum
Bros.	Brothers
BS	(1) bachelor of science; (2) bachelor of surgery; (3) British standard
BSc	bachelor of science
BSc (Econ.)	bachelor of science (economics)
BSc (Eng.)	bachelor of science (engineering)
bt	baronet
BTh	bachelor of theology
bur.	buried
C.	command [identifier for published parliamentary papers]
c.	*circa*
c.	*capitulum pl. capitula*: chapter(s)
CA	California
Cantab.	Cantabrigiensis
cap.	*capitulum pl. capitula*: chapter(s)
CB	companion of the Bath
CBE	commander of the Order of the British Empire
CBS	Columbia Broadcasting System
cc	cubic centimetres
C$	Canadian dollar
CD	compact disc
Cd	command [identifier for published parliamentary papers]
CE	Common (*or* Christian) Era
cent.	century
cf.	compare
CH	Companion of Honour
chap.	chapter
ChB	bachelor of surgery
CI	Imperial Order of the Crown of India
CIA	Central Intelligence Agency
CID	Criminal Investigation Department
CIE	companion of the Order of the Indian Empire
Cie	Compagnie
CLit	companion of literature
CM	master of surgery
cm	centimetre(s)

Cmd	command [identifier for published parliamentary papers]
CMG	companion of the Order of St Michael and St George
Cmnd	command [identifier for published parliamentary papers]
CO	Colorado
Co.	company
co.	county
col. *pl.* cols.	column(s)
Corp.	corporation
CSE	certificate of secondary education
CSI	companion of the Order of the Star of India
CT	Connecticut
CVO	commander of the Royal Victorian Order
cwt	hundredweight
$	(American) dollar
d.	(1) penny (pence); (2) died
DBE	dame commander of the Order of the British Empire
DCH	diploma in child health
DCh	doctor of surgery
DCL	doctor of civil law
DCnL	doctor of canon law
DCVO	dame commander of the Royal Victorian Order
DD	doctor of divinity
DE	Delaware
Dec	December
dem.	demolished
DEng	doctor of engineering
des.	destroyed
DFC	Distinguished Flying Cross
DipEd	diploma in education
DipPsych	diploma in psychiatry
diss.	dissertation
DL	deputy lieutenant
DLitt	doctor of letters
DLittCelt	doctor of Celtic letters
DM	(1) Deutschmark; (2) doctor of medicine; (3) doctor of musical arts
DMus	doctor of music
DNA	dioxyribonucleic acid
doc.	document
DOL	doctor of oriental learning
DPH	diploma in public health
DPhil	doctor of philosophy
DPM	diploma in psychological medicine
DSC	Distinguished Service Cross
DSc	doctor of science
DSc (Econ.)	doctor of science (economics)
DSc (Eng.)	doctor of science (engineering)
DSM	Distinguished Service Medal
DSO	companion of the Distinguished Service Order
DSocSc	doctor of social science
DTech	doctor of technology
DTh	doctor of theology
DTM	diploma in tropical medicine
DTMH	diploma in tropical medicine and hygiene
DU	doctor of the university
DUniv	doctor of the university
dwt	pennyweight
EC	European Community
ed. *pl.* eds.	edited / edited by / editor(s)
Edin.	Edinburgh

edn	edition
EEC	European Economic Community
EFTA	European Free Trade Association
EICS	East India Company Service
EMI	Electrical and Musical Industries (Ltd)
Eng.	English
enl.	enlarged
ENSA	Entertainments National Service Association
ep. *pl.* epp.	*epistola(e)*
ESP	extra-sensory perception
esp.	especially
esq.	esquire
est.	estimate / estimated
EU	European Union
ex	sold by (*lit.* out of)
excl.	excludes / excluding
exh.	exhibited
exh. cat.	exhibition catalogue
f. *pl.* ff.	following [pages]
FA	Football Association
FACP	fellow of the American College of Physicians
facs.	facsimile
FANY	First Aid Nursing Yeomanry
FBA	fellow of the British Academy
FBI	Federation of British Industries
FCS	fellow of the Chemical Society
Feb	February
FEng	fellow of the Fellowship of Engineering
FFCM	fellow of the Faculty of Community Medicine
FGS	fellow of the Geological Society
fig.	figure
FIMechE	fellow of the Institution of Mechanical Engineers
FL	Florida
fl.	*floruit*
FLS	fellow of the Linnean Society
FM	frequency modulation
fol. *pl.* fols.	folio(s)
Fr	French francs
Fr.	French
FRAeS	fellow of the Royal Aeronautical Society
FRAI	fellow of the Royal Anthropological Institute
FRAM	fellow of the Royal Academy of Music
FRAS	(1) fellow of the Royal Asiatic Society; (2) fellow of the Royal Astronomical Society
FRCM	fellow of the Royal College of Music
FRCO	fellow of the Royal College of Organists
FRCOG	fellow of the Royal College of Obstetricians and Gynaecologists
FRCP(C)	fellow of the Royal College of Physicians of Canada
FRCP (Edin.)	fellow of the Royal College of Physicians of Edinburgh
FRCP (Lond.)	fellow of the Royal College of Physicians of London
FRCPath	fellow of the Royal College of Pathologists
FRCPsych	fellow of the Royal College of Psychiatrists
FRCS	fellow of the Royal College of Surgeons
FRGS	fellow of the Royal Geographical Society
FRIBA	fellow of the Royal Institute of British Architects
FRICS	fellow of the Royal Institute of Chartered Surveyors
FRS	fellow of the Royal Society
FRSA	fellow of the Royal Society of Arts

FRSCM	fellow of the Royal School of Church Music	ISO	companion of the Imperial Service Order
FRSE	fellow of the Royal Society of Edinburgh	It.	Italian
FRSL	fellow of the Royal Society of Literature	ITA	Independent Television Authority
FSA	fellow of the Society of Antiquaries	ITV	Independent Television
ft	foot *pl.* feet	Jan	January
FTCL	fellow of Trinity College of Music, London	JP	justice of the peace
ft-lb per min.	foot-pounds per minute [unit of horsepower]	jun.	junior
FZS	fellow of the Zoological Society	KB	knight of the Order of the Bath
GA	Georgia	KBE	knight commander of the Order of the British Empire
GBE	knight or dame grand cross of the Order of the British Empire	KC	king's counsel
GCB	knight grand cross of the Order of the Bath	kcal	kilocalorie
GCE	general certificate of education	KCB	knight commander of the Order of the Bath
GCH	knight grand cross of the Royal Guelphic Order	KCH	knight commander of the Royal Guelphic Order
GCHQ	government communications headquarters	KCIE	knight commander of the Order of the Indian Empire
GCIE	knight grand commander of the Order of the Indian Empire	KCMG	knight commander of the Order of St Michael and St George
GCMG	knight or dame grand cross of the Order of St Michael and St George	KCSI	knight commander of the Order of the Star of India
GCSE	general certificate of secondary education	KCVO	knight commander of the Royal Victorian Order
GCSI	knight grand commander of the Order of the Star of India	keV	kilo-electron-volt
GCStJ	bailiff or dame grand cross of the order of St John of Jerusalem	KG	knight of the Order of the Garter
		KGB	[Soviet committee of state security]
GCVO	knight or dame grand cross of the Royal Victorian Order	KH	knight of the Royal Guelphic Order
GEC	General Electric Company	KLM	Koninklijke Luchtvaart Maatschappij (Royal Dutch Air Lines)
Ger.	German	km	kilometre(s)
GI	government (*or* general) issue	KP	knight of the Order of St Patrick
GMT	Greenwich mean time	KS	Kansas
GP	general practitioner	KT	knight of the Order of the Thistle
GPU	[Soviet special police unit]	kt	knight
GSO	general staff officer	KY	Kentucky
Heb.	Hebrew	£	pound(s) sterling
HEICS	Honourable East India Company Service	£E	Egyptian pound
HI	Hawaii	L	lira *pl.* lire
HIV	human immunodeficiency virus	l. *pl.* ll.	line(s)
HK$	Hong Kong dollar	LA	Lousiana
HM	his / her majesty('s)	LAA	light anti-aircraft
HMAS	his / her majesty's Australian ship	LAH	licentiate of the Apothecaries' Hall, Dublin
HMNZS	his / her majesty's New Zealand ship	Lat.	Latin
HMS	his / her majesty's ship	lb	pound(s), unit of weight
HMSO	His / Her Majesty's Stationery Office	LDS	licence in dental surgery
HMV	His Master's Voice	*lit.*	literally
Hon.	Honourable	LittB	bachelor of letters
hp	horsepower	LittD	doctor of letters
hr	hour(s)	LKQCPI	licentiate of the King and Queen's College of Physicians, Ireland
HRH	his / her royal highness	LLA	lady literate in arts
HTV	Harlech Television	LLB	bachelor of laws
IA	Iowa	LLD	doctor of laws
ibid.	*ibidem*: in the same place	LLM	master of laws
ICI	Imperial Chemical Industries (Ltd)	LM	licentiate in midwifery
ID	Idaho	LP	long-playing record
IL	Illinois	LRAM	licentiate of the Royal Academy of Music
illus.	illustration	LRCP	licentiate of the Royal College of Physicians
illustr.	illustrated	LRCPS (Glasgow)	licentiate of the Royal College of Physicians and Surgeons of Glasgow
IN	Indiana	LRCS	licentiate of the Royal College of Surgeons
in.	inch(es)	LSA	licentiate of the Society of Apothecaries
Inc.	Incorporated	LSD	lysergic acid diethylamide
incl.	includes / including	LVO	lieutenant of the Royal Victorian Order
IOU	I owe you	M. *pl.* MM.	Monsieur *pl.* Messieurs
IQ	intelligence quotient	m	metre(s)
Ir£	Irish pound		
IRA	Irish Republican Army		

m. *pl.* mm.	membrane(s)
MA	(1) Massachusetts; (2) master of arts
MAI	master of engineering
MB	bachelor of medicine
MBA	master of business administration
MBE	member of the Order of the British Empire
MC	Military Cross
MCC	Marylebone Cricket Club
MCh	master of surgery
MChir	master of surgery
MCom	master of commerce
MD	(1) doctor of medicine; (2) Maryland
MDMA	methylenedioxymethamphetamine
ME	Maine
MEd	master of education
MEng	master of engineering
MEP	member of the European parliament
MG	Morris Garages
MGM	Metro-Goldwyn-Mayer
Mgr	Monsignor
MI	(1) Michigan; (2) military intelligence
MI1c	[secret intelligence department]
MI5	[military intelligence department]
MI6	[secret intelligence department]
MI9	[secret escape service]
MICE	member of the Institution of Civil Engineers
MIEE	member of the Institution of Electrical Engineers
min.	minute(s)
Mk	mark
ML	(1) licentiate of medicine; (2) master of laws
MLitt	master of letters
Mlle	Mademoiselle
mm	millimetre(s)
Mme	Madame
MN	Minnesota
MO	Missouri
MOH	medical officer of health
MP	member of parliament
m.p.h.	miles per hour
MPhil	master of philosophy
MRCP	member of the Royal College of Physicians
MRCS	member of the Royal College of Surgeons
MRCVS	member of the Royal College of Veterinary Surgeons
MRIA	member of the Royal Irish Academy
MS	(1) master of science; (2) Mississippi
MS *pl.* MSS	manuscript(s)
MSc	master of science
MSc (Econ.)	master of science (economics)
MT	Montana
MusB	bachelor of music
MusBac	bachelor of music
MusD	doctor of music
MV	motor vessel
MVO	member of the Royal Victorian Order
n. *pl.* nn.	note(s)
NAAFI	Navy, Army, and Air Force Institutes
NASA	National Aeronautics and Space Administration
NATO	North Atlantic Treaty Organization
NBC	National Broadcasting Corporation
NC	North Carolina
NCO	non-commissioned officer

ND	North Dakota
n.d.	no date
NE	Nebraska
nem. con.	*nemine contradicente*: unanimously
new ser.	new series
NH	New Hampshire
NHS	National Health Service
NJ	New Jersey
NKVD	[Soviet people's commissariat for internal affairs]
NM	New Mexico
nm	nanometre(s)
no. *pl.* nos.	number(s)
Nov	November
n.p.	no place [of publication]
NS	new style
NV	Nevada
NY	New York
NZBS	New Zealand Broadcasting Service
OBE	officer of the Order of the British Empire
obit.	obituary
Oct	October
OCTU	officer cadets training unit
OECD	Organization for Economic Co-operation and Development
OEEC	Organization for European Economic Co-operation
OFM	order of Friars Minor [Franciscans]
OFMCap	Ordine Frati Minori Cappucini: member of the Capuchin order
OH	Ohio
OK	Oklahoma
O level	ordinary level [examination]
OM	Order of Merit
OP	order of Preachers [Dominicans]
op. *pl.* opp.	opus *pl.* opera
OPEC	Organization of Petroleum Exporting Countries
OR	Oregon
orig.	original
OS	old style
OSB	Order of St Benedict
OTC	Officers' Training Corps
OWS	Old Watercolour Society
Oxon.	Oxoniensis
p. *pl.* pp.	page(s)
PA	Pennsylvania
p.a.	per annum
para.	paragraph
PAYE	pay as you earn
pbk *pl.* pbks	paperback(s)
per.	[during the] period
PhD	doctor of philosophy
pl.	(1) plate(s); (2) plural
priv. coll.	private collection
pt *pl.* pts	part(s)
pubd	published
PVC	polyvinyl chloride
q. *pl.* qq.	(1) question(s); (2) quire(s)
QC	queen's counsel
R	rand
R.	Rex / Regina
r	recto
r.	reigned / ruled
RA	Royal Academy / Royal Academician

RAC	Royal Automobile Club		Skr	Swedish krona
RAF	Royal Air Force		Span.	Spanish
RAFVR	Royal Air Force Volunteer Reserve		SPCK	Society for Promoting Christian Knowledge
RAM	[member of the] Royal Academy of Music		SS	(1) Santissimi; (2) Schutzstaffel; (3) steam ship
RAMC	Royal Army Medical Corps		STB	bachelor of theology
RCA	Royal College of Art		STD	doctor of theology
RCNC	Royal Corps of Naval Constructors		STM	master of theology
RCOG	Royal College of Obstetricians and Gynaecologists		STP	doctor of theology
			supp.	supposedly
RDI	royal designer for industry		suppl. *pl.* suppls.	supplement(s)
RE	Royal Engineers		s.v.	*sub verbo* / *sub voce*: under the word / heading
repr. *pl.* reprs.	reprint(s) / reprinted		SY	steam yacht
repro.	reproduced		TA	Territorial Army
rev.	revised / revised by / reviser / revision		TASS	[Soviet news agency]
Revd	Reverend		TB	tuberculosis (*lit.* tubercle bacillus)
RHA	Royal Hibernian Academy		TD	(1) *teachtaí dála* (member of the Dáil); (2) territorial decoration
RI	(1) Rhode Island; (2) Royal Institute of Painters in Water-Colours		TN	Tennessee
RIBA	Royal Institute of British Architects		TNT	trinitrotoluene
RIN	Royal Indian Navy		trans.	translated / translated by / translation / translator
RM	Reichsmark		TT	tourist trophy
RMS	Royal Mail steamer		TUC	Trades Union Congress
RN	Royal Navy		TX	Texas
RNA	ribonucleic acid		U-boat	*Unterseeboot*: submarine
RNAS	Royal Naval Air Service		Ufa	Universum-Film AG
RNR	Royal Naval Reserve		UMIST	University of Manchester Institute of Science and Technology
RNVR	Royal Naval Volunteer Reserve		UN	United Nations
RO	Record Office		UNESCO	United Nations Educational, Scientific, and Cultural Organization
r.p.m.	revolutions per minute			
RRS	royal research ship		UNICEF	United Nations International Children's Emergency Fund
Rs	rupees			
RSA	(1) Royal Scottish Academician; (2) Royal Society of Arts		unpubd	unpublished
			USS	United States ship
RSPCA	Royal Society for the Prevention of Cruelty to Animals		UT	Utah
			v	verso
Rt Hon.	Right Honourable		v.	versus
Rt Revd	Right Reverend		VA	Virginia
RUC	Royal Ulster Constabulary		VAD	Voluntary Aid Detachment
Russ.	Russian		VC	Victoria Cross
RWS	Royal Watercolour Society		VE-day	victory in Europe day
S4C	Sianel Pedwar Cymru		Ven.	Venerable
s.	shilling(s)		VJ-day	victory over Japan day
s.a.	*sub anno*: under the year		vol. *pl.* vols.	volume(s)
SABC	South African Broadcasting Corporation		VT	Vermont
SAS	Special Air Service		WA	Washington [state]
SC	South Carolina		WAAC	Women's Auxiliary Army Corps
ScD	doctor of science		WAAF	Women's Auxiliary Air Force
S$	Singapore dollar		WEA	Workers' Educational Association
SD	South Dakota		WHO	World Health Organization
sec.	second(s)		WI	Wisconsin
sel.	selected		WRAF	Women's Royal Air Force
sen.	senior		WRNS	Women's Royal Naval Service
Sept	September		WV	West Virginia
ser.	series		WVS	Women's Voluntary Service
SHAPE	supreme headquarters allied powers, Europe		WY	Wyoming
SIDRO	Société Internationale d'Énergie Hydro-Électrique		¥	yen
			YMCA	Young Men's Christian Association
sig. *pl.* sigs.	signature(s)		YWCA	Young Women's Christian Association
sing.	singular			
SIS	Secret Intelligence Service			
SJ	Society of Jesus			

2 *Institution abbreviations*

All Souls Oxf.	All Souls College, Oxford
AM Oxf.	Ashmolean Museum, Oxford
Balliol Oxf.	Balliol College, Oxford
BBC WAC	BBC Written Archives Centre, Reading
Beds. & Luton ARS	Bedfordshire and Luton Archives and Record Service, Bedford
Berks. RO	Berkshire Record Office, Reading
BFI	British Film Institute, London
BFI NFTVA	British Film Institute, London, National Film and Television Archive
BGS	British Geological Survey, Keyworth, Nottingham
Birm. CA	Birmingham Central Library, Birmingham City Archives
Birm. CL	Birmingham Central Library
BL	British Library, London
BL NSA	British Library, London, National Sound Archive
BL OIOC	British Library, London, Oriental and India Office Collections
BLPES	London School of Economics and Political Science, British Library of Political and Economic Science
BM	British Museum, London
Bodl. Oxf.	Bodleian Library, Oxford
Bodl. RH	Bodleian Library of Commonwealth and African Studies at Rhodes House, Oxford
Borth. Inst.	Borthwick Institute of Historical Research, University of York
Boston PL	Boston Public Library, Massachusetts
Bristol RO	Bristol Record Office
Bucks. RLSS	Buckinghamshire Records and Local Studies Service, Aylesbury
CAC Cam.	Churchill College, Cambridge, Churchill Archives Centre
Cambs. AS	Cambridgeshire Archive Service
CCC Cam.	Corpus Christi College, Cambridge
CCC Oxf.	Corpus Christi College, Oxford
Ches. & Chester ALSS	Cheshire and Chester Archives and Local Studies Service
Christ Church Oxf.	Christ Church, Oxford
Christies	Christies, London
City Westm. AC	City of Westminster Archives Centre, London
CKS	Centre for Kentish Studies, Maidstone
CLRO	Corporation of London Records Office
Coll. Arms	College of Arms, London
Col. U.	Columbia University, New York
Cornwall RO	Cornwall Record Office, Truro
Courtauld Inst.	Courtauld Institute of Art, London
CUL	Cambridge University Library
Cumbria AS	Cumbria Archive Service
Derbys. RO	Derbyshire Record Office, Matlock
Devon RO	Devon Record Office, Exeter
Dorset RO	Dorset Record Office, Dorchester
Duke U.	Duke University, Durham, North Carolina
Duke U., Perkins L.	Duke University, Durham, North Carolina, William R. Perkins Library
Durham Cath. CL	Durham Cathedral, chapter library
Durham RO	Durham Record Office
DWL	Dr Williams's Library, London
Essex RO	Essex Record Office
E. Sussex RO	East Sussex Record Office, Lewes
Eton	Eton College, Berkshire
FM Cam.	Fitzwilliam Museum, Cambridge
Folger	Folger Shakespeare Library, Washington, DC
Garr. Club	Garrick Club, London
Girton Cam.	Girton College, Cambridge
GL	Guildhall Library, London
Glos. RO	Gloucestershire Record Office, Gloucester
Gon. & Caius Cam.	Gonville and Caius College, Cambridge
Gov. Art Coll.	Government Art Collection
GS Lond.	Geological Society of London
Hants. RO	Hampshire Record Office, Winchester
Harris Man. Oxf.	Harris Manchester College, Oxford
Harvard TC	Harvard Theatre Collection, Harvard University, Cambridge, Massachusetts, Nathan Marsh Pusey Library
Harvard U.	Harvard University, Cambridge, Massachusetts
Harvard U., Houghton L.	Harvard University, Cambridge, Massachusetts, Houghton Library
Herefs. RO	Herefordshire Record Office, Hereford
Herts. ALS	Hertfordshire Archives and Local Studies, Hertford
Hist. Soc. Penn.	Historical Society of Pennsylvania, Philadelphia
HLRO	House of Lords Record Office, London
Hult. Arch.	Hulton Archive, London and New York
Hunt. L.	Huntington Library, San Marino, California
ICL	Imperial College, London
Inst. CE	Institution of Civil Engineers, London
Inst. EE	Institution of Electrical Engineers, London
IWM	Imperial War Museum, London
IWM FVA	Imperial War Museum, London, Film and Video Archive
IWM SA	Imperial War Museum, London, Sound Archive
JRL	John Rylands University Library of Manchester
King's AC Cam.	King's College Archives Centre, Cambridge
King's Cam.	King's College, Cambridge
King's Lond.	King's College, London
King's Lond., Liddell Hart C.	King's College, London, Liddell Hart Centre for Military Archives
Lancs. RO	Lancashire Record Office, Preston
L. Cong.	Library of Congress, Washington, DC
Leics. RO	Leicestershire, Leicester, and Rutland Record Office, Leicester
Lincs. Arch.	Lincolnshire Archives, Lincoln
Linn. Soc.	Linnean Society of London
LMA	London Metropolitan Archives
LPL	Lambeth Palace, London
Lpool RO	Liverpool Record Office and Local Studies Service
LUL	London University Library
Magd. Cam.	Magdalene College, Cambridge
Magd. Oxf.	Magdalen College, Oxford
Man. City Gall.	Manchester City Galleries
Man. CL	Manchester Central Library
Mass. Hist. Soc.	Massachusetts Historical Society, Boston
Merton Oxf.	Merton College, Oxford
MHS Oxf.	Museum of the History of Science, Oxford
Mitchell L., Glas.	Mitchell Library, Glasgow
Mitchell L., NSW	State Library of New South Wales, Sydney, Mitchell Library
Morgan L.	Pierpont Morgan Library, New York
NA Canada	National Archives of Canada, Ottawa
NA Ire.	National Archives of Ireland, Dublin
NAM	National Army Museum, London
NA Scot.	National Archives of Scotland, Edinburgh
News Int. RO	News International Record Office, London
NG Ire.	National Gallery of Ireland, Dublin

NG Scot.	National Gallery of Scotland, Edinburgh
NHM	Natural History Museum, London
NL Aus.	National Library of Australia, Canberra
NL Ire.	National Library of Ireland, Dublin
NL NZ	National Library of New Zealand, Wellington
NL NZ, Turnbull L.	National Library of New Zealand, Wellington, Alexander Turnbull Library
NL Scot.	National Library of Scotland, Edinburgh
NL Wales	National Library of Wales, Aberystwyth
NMG Wales	National Museum and Gallery of Wales, Cardiff
NMM	National Maritime Museum, London
Norfolk RO	Norfolk Record Office, Norwich
Northants. RO	Northamptonshire Record Office, Northampton
Northumbd RO	Northumberland Record Office
Notts. Arch.	Nottinghamshire Archives, Nottingham
NPG	National Portrait Gallery, London
NRA	National Archives, London, Historical Manuscripts Commission, National Register of Archives
Nuffield Oxf.	Nuffield College, Oxford
N. Yorks. CRO	North Yorkshire County Record Office, Northallerton
NYPL	New York Public Library
Oxf. UA	Oxford University Archives
Oxf. U. Mus. NH	Oxford University Museum of Natural History
Oxon. RO	Oxfordshire Record Office, Oxford
Pembroke Cam.	Pembroke College, Cambridge
PRO	National Archives, London, Public Record Office
PRO NIre.	Public Record Office for Northern Ireland, Belfast
Pusey Oxf.	Pusey House, Oxford
RA	Royal Academy of Arts, London
Ransom HRC	Harry Ransom Humanities Research Center, University of Texas, Austin
RAS	Royal Astronomical Society, London
RBG Kew	Royal Botanic Gardens, Kew, London
RCP Lond.	Royal College of Physicians of London
RCS Eng.	Royal College of Surgeons of England, London
RGS	Royal Geographical Society, London
RIBA	Royal Institute of British Architects, London
RIBA BAL	Royal Institute of British Architects, London, British Architectural Library
Royal Arch.	Royal Archives, Windsor Castle, Berkshire [by gracious permission of her majesty the queen]
Royal Irish Acad.	Royal Irish Academy, Dublin
Royal Scot. Acad.	Royal Scottish Academy, Edinburgh
RS	Royal Society, London
RSA	Royal Society of Arts, London
RS Friends, Lond.	Religious Society of Friends, London
St Ant. Oxf.	St Antony's College, Oxford
St John Cam.	St John's College, Cambridge
S. Antiquaries, Lond.	Society of Antiquaries of London
Sci. Mus.	Science Museum, London
Scot. NPG	Scottish National Portrait Gallery, Edinburgh
Scott Polar RI	University of Cambridge, Scott Polar Research Institute
Sheff. Arch.	Sheffield Archives
Shrops. RRC	Shropshire Records and Research Centre, Shrewsbury
SOAS	School of Oriental and African Studies, London
Som. ARS	Somerset Archive and Record Service, Taunton
Staffs. RO	Staffordshire Record Office, Stafford

Suffolk RO	Suffolk Record Office
Surrey HC	Surrey History Centre, Woking
TCD	Trinity College, Dublin
Trinity Cam.	Trinity College, Cambridge
U. Aberdeen	University of Aberdeen
U. Birm.	University of Birmingham
U. Birm. L.	University of Birmingham Library
U. Cal.	University of California
U. Cam.	University of Cambridge
UCL	University College, London
U. Durham	University of Durham
U. Durham L.	University of Durham Library
U. Edin.	University of Edinburgh
U. Edin., New Coll.	University of Edinburgh, New College
U. Edin., New Coll. L.	University of Edinburgh, New College Library
U. Edin. L.	University of Edinburgh Library
U. Glas.	University of Glasgow
U. Glas. L.	University of Glasgow Library
U. Hull	University of Hull
U. Hull, Brynmor Jones L.	University of Hull, Brynmor Jones Library
U. Leeds	University of Leeds
U. Leeds, Brotherton L.	University of Leeds, Brotherton Library
U. Lond.	University of London
U. Lpool	University of Liverpool
U. Lpool L.	University of Liverpool Library
U. Mich.	University of Michigan, Ann Arbor
U. Mich., Clements L.	University of Michigan, Ann Arbor, William L. Clements Library
U. Newcastle	University of Newcastle upon Tyne
U. Newcastle, Robinson L.	University of Newcastle upon Tyne, Robinson Library
U. Nott.	University of Nottingham
U. Nott. L.	University of Nottingham Library
U. Oxf.	University of Oxford
U. Reading	University of Reading
U. Reading L.	University of Reading Library
U. St Andr.	University of St Andrews
U. St Andr. L.	University of St Andrews Library
U. Southampton	University of Southampton
U. Southampton L.	University of Southampton Library
U. Sussex	University of Sussex, Brighton
U. Texas	University of Texas, Austin
U. Wales	University of Wales
U. Warwick Mod. RC	University of Warwick, Coventry, Modern Records Centre
V&A	Victoria and Albert Museum, London
V&A NAL	Victoria and Albert Museum, London, National Art Library
Warks. CRO	Warwickshire County Record Office, Warwick
Wellcome L.	Wellcome Library for the History and Understanding of Medicine, London
Westm. DA	Westminster Diocesan Archives, London
Wilts. & Swindon RO	Wiltshire and Swindon Record Office, Trowbridge
Worcs. RO	Worcestershire Record Office, Worcester
W. Sussex RO	West Sussex Record Office, Chichester
W. Yorks. AS	West Yorkshire Archive Service
Yale U.	Yale University, New Haven, Connecticut
Yale U., Beinecke L.	Yale University, New Haven, Connecticut, Beinecke Rare Book and Manuscript Library
Yale U. CBA	Yale University, New Haven, Connecticut, Yale Center for British Art

3 *Bibliographic abbreviations*

Adams, *Drama*　　W. D. Adams, *A dictionary of the drama*, 1: *A–G* (1904); 2: *H–Z* (1956) [vol. 2 microfilm only]

AFM　　J O'Donovan, ed. and trans., *Annala rioghachta Eireann / Annals of the kingdom of Ireland by the four masters*, 7 vols. (1848–51); 2nd edn (1856); 3rd edn (1990)

Allibone, *Dict.*　　S. A. Allibone, *A critical dictionary of English literature and British and American authors*, 3 vols. (1859–71); suppl. by J. F. Kirk, 2 vols. (1891)

ANB　　J. A. Garraty and M. C. Carnes, eds., *American national biography*, 24 vols. (1999)

Anderson, *Scot. nat.*　　W. Anderson, *The Scottish nation, or, The surnames, families, literature, honours, and biographical history of the people of Scotland*, 3 vols. (1859–63)

Ann. mon.　　H. R. Luard, ed., *Annales monastici*, 5 vols., Rolls Series, 36 (1864–9)

Ann. Ulster　　S. Mac Airt and G. Mac Niocaill, eds., *Annals of Ulster (to AD 1131)* (1983)

APC　　*Acts of the privy council of England*, new ser., 46 vols. (1890–1964)

APS　　*The acts of the parliaments of Scotland*, 12 vols. in 13 (1814–75)

Arber, *Regs. Stationers*　　F. Arber, ed., *A transcript of the registers of the Company of Stationers of London, 1554–1640 AD*, 5 vols. (1875–94)

ArchR　　*Architectural Review*

ASC　　D. Whitelock, D. C. Douglas, and S. I. Tucker, ed. and trans., *The Anglo-Saxon Chronicle: a revised translation* (1961)

AS chart.　　P. H. Sawyer, *Anglo-Saxon charters: an annotated list and bibliography*, Royal Historical Society Guides and Handbooks (1968)

AusDB　　D. Pike and others, eds., *Australian dictionary of biography*, 16 vols. (1966–2002)

Baker, *Serjeants*　　J. H. Baker, *The order of serjeants at law*, SeldS, suppl. ser., 5 (1984)

Bale, *Cat.*　　J. Bale, *Scriptorum illustrium Maioris Brytannie, quam nunc Angliam et Scotiam vocant: catalogus*, 2 vols. in 1 (Basel, 1557–9); facs. edn (1971)

Bale, *Index*　　J. Bale, *Index Britanniae scriptorum*, ed. R. L. Poole and M. Bateson (1902); facs. edn (1990)

BBCS　　*Bulletin of the Board of Celtic Studies*

BDMBR　　J. O. Baylen and N. J. Gossman, eds., *Biographical dictionary of modern British radicals*, 3 vols. in 4 (1979–88)

Bede, *Hist. eccl.*　　*Bede's Ecclesiastical history of the English people*, ed. and trans. B. Colgrave and R. A. B. Mynors, OMT (1969); repr. (1991)

Bénézit, *Dict.*　　E. Bénézit, *Dictionnaire critique et documentaire des peintres, sculpteurs, dessinateurs et graveurs*, 3 vols. (Paris, 1911–23); new edn, 8 vols. (1948–66), repr. (1966); 3rd edn, rev. and enl., 10 vols. (1976); 4th edn, 14 vols. (1999)

BIHR　　*Bulletin of the Institute of Historical Research*

Birch, *Seals*　　W. de Birch, *Catalogue of seals in the department of manuscripts in the British Museum*, 6 vols. (1887–1900)

Bishop Burnet's History　　*Bishop Burnet's History of his own time*, ed. M. J. Routh, 2nd edn, 6 vols. (1833)

Blackwood　　*Blackwood's [Edinburgh] Magazine*, 328 vols. (1817–1980)

Blain, Clements & Grundy, *Feminist comp.*　　V. Blain, P. Clements, and I. Grundy, eds., *The feminist companion to literature in English* (1990)

BL cat.　　*The British Library general catalogue of printed books* [in 360 vols. with suppls., also CD-ROM and online]

BMJ　　*British Medical Journal*

Boase & Courtney, *Bibl. Corn.*　　G. C. Boase and W. P. Courtney, *Bibliotheca Cornubiensis: a catalogue of the writings … of Cornishmen*, 3 vols. (1874–82)

Boase, *Mod. Eng. biog.*　　F. Boase, *Modern English biography: containing many thousand concise memoirs of persons who have died since the year 1850*, 6 vols. (privately printed, Truro, 1892–1921); repr. (1965)

Boswell, *Life*　　*Boswell's Life of Johnson: together with Journal of a tour to the Hebrides and Johnson's Diary of a journey into north Wales*, ed. G. B. Hill, enl. edn, rev. L. F. Powell, 6 vols. (1934–50); 2nd edn (1964); repr. (1971)

Brown & Stratton, *Brit. mus.*　　J. D. Brown and S. S. Stratton, *British musical biography* (1897)

Bryan, *Painters*　　M. Bryan, *A biographical and critical dictionary of painters and engravers*, 2 vols. (1816); new edn, ed. G. Stanley (1849); new edn, ed. R. E. Graves and W. Armstrong, 2 vols. (1886–9); [4th edn], ed. G. C. Williamson, 5 vols. (1903–5) [various reprs.]

Burke, *Gen. GB*　　J. Burke, *A genealogical and heraldic history of the commoners of Great Britain and Ireland*, 4 vols. (1833–8); new edn as *A genealogical and heraldic dictionary of the landed gentry of Great Britain and Ireland*, 3 vols. (1843–9) [many later edns]

Burke, *Gen. Ire.*　　J. B. Burke, *A genealogical and heraldic history of the landed gentry of Ireland* (1899); 2nd edn (1904); 3rd edn (1912); 4th edn (1958); 5th edn as *Burke's Irish family records* (1976)

Burke, *Peerage*　　J. Burke, *A general* [later edns *A genealogical*] *and heraldic dictionary of the peerage and baronetage of the United Kingdom* [later edns *the British empire*] (1829–)

Burney, *Hist. mus.*　　C. Burney, *A general history of music, from the earliest ages to the present period*, 4 vols. (1776–89)

Burtchaell & Sadleir, *Alum. Dubl.*　　G. D. Burtchaell and T. U. Sadleir, *Alumni Dublinenses: a register of the students, graduates, and provosts of Trinity College* (1924); [2nd edn], with suppl., in 2 pts (1935)

Calamy rev.　　A. G. Matthews, *Calamy revised* (1934); repr. (1988)

CCI　　*Calendar of confirmations and inventories granted and given up in the several commissariots of Scotland* (1876–)

CCLR　　*Calendar of the close rolls preserved in the Public Record Office*, 47 vols. (1892–1963)

CDS　　J. Bain, ed., *Calendar of documents relating to Scotland*, 4 vols., PRO (1881–8); suppl. vol. 5, ed. G. G. Simpson and J. D. Galbraith [1986]

CEPR letters　　W. H. Bliss, C. Johnson, and J. Twemlow, eds., *Calendar of entries in the papal registers relating to Great Britain and Ireland: papal letters* (1893–)

CGPLA　　*Calendars of the grants of probate and letters of administration* [in 4 ser.: England & Wales, Northern Ireland, Ireland, and Éire]

Chambers, *Scots.*　　R. Chambers, ed., *A biographical dictionary of eminent Scotsmen*, 4 vols. (1832–5)

Chancery records　　chancery records pubd by the PRO

Chancery records (RC)　　chancery records pubd by the Record Commissions

CIPM	*Calendar of inquisitions post mortem*, [20 vols.], PRO (1904–); also *Henry VII*, 3 vols. (1898–1955)
Clarendon, *Hist. rebellion*	E. Hyde, earl of Clarendon, *The history of the rebellion and civil wars in England*, 6 vols. (1888); repr. (1958) and (1992)
Cobbett, *Parl. hist.*	W. Cobbett and J. Wright, eds., *Cobbett's Parliamentary history of England*, 36 vols. (1806–1820)
Colvin, *Archs.*	H. Colvin, *A biographical dictionary of British architects, 1600–1840*, 3rd edn (1995)
Cooper, *Ath. Cantab.*	C. H. Cooper and T. Cooper, *Athenae Cantabrigienses*, 3 vols. (1858–1913); repr. (1967)
CPR	*Calendar of the patent rolls preserved in the Public Record Office* (1891–)
Crockford	*Crockford's Clerical Directory*
CS	Camden Society
CSP	*Calendar of state papers* [in 11 ser.: *domestic, Scotland, Scottish series, Ireland, colonial, Commonwealth, foreign, Spain* [at Simancas], *Rome, Milan,* and *Venice*]
CYS	Canterbury and York Society
DAB	*Dictionary of American biography*, 21 vols. (1928–36), repr. in 11 vols. (1964); 10 suppls. (1944–96)
DBB	D. J. Jeremy, ed., *Dictionary of business biography*, 5 vols. (1984–6)
DCB	G. W. Brown and others, *Dictionary of Canadian biography*, [14 vols.] (1966–)
Debrett's Peerage	*Debrett's Peerage* (1803–) [sometimes *Debrett's Illustrated peerage*]
Desmond, *Botanists*	R. Desmond, *Dictionary of British and Irish botanists and horticulturists* (1977); rev. edn (1994)
Dir. Brit. archs.	A. Felstead, J. Franklin, and L. Pinfield, eds., *Directory of British architects, 1834–1900* (1993); 2nd edn, ed. A. Brodie and others, 2 vols. (2001)
DLB	J. M. Bellamy and J. Saville, eds., *Dictionary of labour biography*, [10 vols.] (1972–)
DLitB	Dictionary of Literary Biography
DNB	*Dictionary of national biography*, 63 vols. (1885–1900), suppl., 3 vols. (1901); repr. in 22 vols. (1908–9); 10 further suppls. (1912–96); *Missing persons* (1993)
DNZB	W. H. Oliver and C. Orange, eds., *The dictionary of New Zealand biography*, 5 vols. (1990–2000)
DSAB	W. J. de Kock and others, eds., *Dictionary of South African biography*, 5 vols. (1968–87)
DSB	C. C. Gillispie and F. L. Holmes, eds., *Dictionary of scientific biography*, 16 vols. (1970–80); repr. in 8 vols. (1981); 2 vol. suppl. (1990)
DSBB	A. Slaven and S. Checkland, eds., *Dictionary of Scottish business biography, 1860–1960*, 2 vols. (1986–90)
DSCHT	N. M. de S. Cameron and others, eds., *Dictionary of Scottish church history and theology* (1993)
Dugdale, *Monasticon*	W. Dugdale, *Monasticon Anglicanum*, 3 vols. (1655–72); 2nd edn, 3 vols. (1661–82); new edn, ed. J. Caley, J. Ellis, and B. Bandinel, 6 vols. in 8 pts (1817–30); repr. (1846) and (1970)
DWB	J. E. Lloyd and others, eds., *Dictionary of Welsh biography down to 1940* (1959) [Eng. trans. of *Y bywgraffiadur Cymreig hyd 1940*, 2nd edn (1954)]
EdinR	*Edinburgh Review, or, Critical Journal*
EETS	Early English Text Society
Emden, *Cam.*	A. B. Emden, *A biographical register of the University of Cambridge to 1500* (1963)
Emden, *Oxf.*	A. B. Emden, *A biographical register of the University of Oxford to AD 1500*, 3 vols. (1957–9); also *A biographical register of the University of Oxford, AD 1501 to 1540* (1974)
EngHR	*English Historical Review*
Engraved Brit. ports.	F. M. O'Donoghue and H. M. Hake, *Catalogue of engraved British portraits preserved in the department of prints and drawings in the British Museum*, 6 vols. (1908–25)
ER	The English Reports, 178 vols. (1900–32)
ESTC	*English short title catalogue, 1475–1800* [CD-ROM and online]
Evelyn, *Diary*	*The diary of John Evelyn*, ed. E. S. De Beer, 6 vols. (1955); repr. (2000)
Farington, *Diary*	*The diary of Joseph Farington*, ed. K. Garlick and others, 17 vols. (1978–98)
Fasti Angl. (Hardy)	J. Le Neve, *Fasti ecclesiae Anglicanae*, ed. T. D. Hardy, 3 vols. (1854)
Fasti Angl., 1066–1300	[J. Le Neve], *Fasti ecclesiae Anglicanae, 1066–1300*, ed. D. E. Greenway and J. S. Barrow, [8 vols.] (1968–)
Fasti Angl., 1300–1541	[J. Le Neve], *Fasti ecclesiae Anglicanae, 1300–1541*, 12 vols. (1962–7)
Fasti Angl., 1541–1857	[J. Le Neve], *Fasti ecclesiae Anglicanae, 1541–1857*, ed. J. M. Horn, D. M. Smith, and D. S. Bailey, [9 vols.] (1969–)
Fasti Scot.	H. Scott, *Fasti ecclesiae Scoticanae*, 3 vols. in 6 (1871); new edn, [11 vols.] (1915–)
FO List	*Foreign Office List*
Fortescue, *Brit. army*	J. W. Fortescue, *A history of the British army*, 13 vols. (1899–1930)
Foss, *Judges*	E. Foss, *The judges of England*, 9 vols. (1848–64); repr. (1966)
Foster, *Alum. Oxon.*	J. Foster, ed., *Alumni Oxonienses: the members of the University of Oxford, 1715–1886*, 4 vols. (1887–8); later edn (1891); also *Alumni Oxonienses … 1500–1714*, 4 vols. (1891–2); 8 vol. repr. (1968) and (2000)
Fuller, *Worthies*	T. Fuller, *The history of the worthies of England*, 4 pts (1662); new edn, 2 vols., ed. J. Nichols (1811); new edn, 3 vols., ed. P. A. Nuttall (1840); repr. (1965)
GEC, *Baronetage*	G. E. Cokayne, *Complete baronetage*, 6 vols. (1900–09); repr. (1983) [microprint]
GEC, *Peerage*	G. E. C. [G. E. Cokayne], *The complete peerage of England, Scotland, Ireland, Great Britain, and the United Kingdom*, 8 vols. (1887–98); new edn, ed. V. Gibbs and others, 14 vols. in 15 (1910–98); microprint repr. (1982) and (1987)
Genest, *Eng. stage*	J. Genest, *Some account of the English stage from the Restoration in 1660 to 1830*, 10 vols. (1832); repr. [New York, 1965]
Gillow, *Lit. biog. hist.*	J. Gillow, *A literary and biographical history or bibliographical dictionary of the English Catholics, from the breach with Rome, in 1534, to the present time*, 5 vols. [1885–1902]; repr. (1961); repr. with preface by C. Gillow (1999)
Gir. Camb. opera	*Giraldi Cambrensis opera*, ed. J. S. Brewer, J. F. Dimock, and G. F. Warner, 8 vols., Rolls Series, 21 (1861–91)
GJ	*Geographical Journal*

Gladstone, *Diaries* — *The Gladstone diaries: with cabinet minutes and prime-ministerial correspondence*, ed. M. R. D. Foot and H. C. G. Matthew, 14 vols. (1968–94)

GM — *Gentleman's Magazine*

Graves, *Artists* — A. Graves, ed., *A dictionary of artists who have exhibited works in the principal London exhibitions of oil paintings from 1760 to 1880* (1884); new edn (1895); 3rd edn (1901); facs. edn (1969); repr. [1970], (1973), and (1984)

Graves, *Brit. Inst.* — A. Graves, *The British Institution, 1806–1867: a complete dictionary of contributors and their work from the foundation of the institution* (1875); facs. edn (1908); repr. (1969)

Graves, *RA exhibitors* — A. Graves, *The Royal Academy of Arts: a complete dictionary of contributors and their work from its foundation in 1769 to 1904*, 8 vols. (1905–6); repr. in 4 vols. (1970) and (1972)

Graves, *Soc. Artists* — A. Graves, *The Society of Artists of Great Britain, 1760–1791, the Free Society of Artists, 1761–1783: a complete dictionary* (1907); facs. edn (1969)

Greaves & Zaller, *BDBR* — R. L. Greaves and R. Zaller, eds., *Biographical dictionary of British radicals in the seventeenth century*, 3 vols. (1982–4)

Grove, *Dict. mus.* — G. Grove, ed., *A dictionary of music and musicians*, 5 vols. (1878–90); 2nd edn, ed. J. A. Fuller Maitland (1904–10); 3rd edn, ed. H. C. Colles (1927); 4th edn with suppl. (1940); 5th edn, ed. E. Blom, 9 vols. (1954); suppl. (1961) [see also *New Grove*]

Hall, *Dramatic ports.* — L. A. Hall, *Catalogue of dramatic portraits in the theatre collection of the Harvard College library*, 4 vols. (1930–34)

Hansard — *Hansard's parliamentary debates*, ser. 1–5 (1803–)

Highfill, Burnim & Langhans, *BDA* — P. H. Highfill, K. A. Burnim, and E. A. Langhans, *A biographical dictionary of actors, actresses, musicians, dancers, managers, and other stage personnel in London, 1660–1800*, 16 vols. (1973–93)

Hist. U. Oxf. — T. H. Aston, ed., *The history of the University of Oxford*, 8 vols. (1984–2000) [1: *The early Oxford schools*, ed. J. I. Catto (1984); 2: *Late medieval Oxford*, ed. J. I. Catto and R. Evans (1992); 3: *The collegiate university*, ed. J. McConica (1986); 4: *Seventeenth-century Oxford*, ed. N. Tyacke (1997); 5: *The eighteenth century*, ed. L. S. Sutherland and L. G. Mitchell (1986); 6–7: *Nineteenth-century Oxford*, ed. M. G. Brock and M. C. Curthoys (1997–2000); 8: *The twentieth century*, ed. B. Harrison (2000)]

HJ — *Historical Journal*

HMC — Historical Manuscripts Commission

Holdsworth, *Eng. law* — W. S. Holdsworth, *A history of English law*, ed. A. L. Goodhart and H. G. Hanbury, 17 vols. (1903–72)

HoP, *Commons* — *The history of parliament: the House of Commons* [*1386–1421*, ed. J. S. Roskell, L. Clark, and C. Rawcliffe, 4 vols. (1992); *1509–1558*, ed. S. T. Bindoff, 3 vols. (1982); *1558–1603*, ed. P. W. Hasler, 3 vols. (1981); *1660–1690*, ed. B. D. Henning, 3 vols. (1983); *1690–1715*, ed. D. W. Hayton, E. Cruickshanks, and S. Handley, 5 vols. (2002); *1715–1754*, ed. R. Sedgwick, 2 vols. (1970); *1754–1790*, ed. L. Namier and J. Brooke, 3 vols. (1964), repr. (1985); *1790–1820*, ed. R. G. Thorne, 5 vols. (1986); in draft (used with permission): *1422–1504*, *1604–1629*, *1640–1660*, and *1820–1832*]

IGI — *International Genealogical Index*, Church of Jesus Christ of the Latterday Saints

ILN — *Illustrated London News*

IMC — Irish Manuscripts Commission

Irving, *Scots.* — J. Irving, ed., *The book of Scotsmen eminent for achievements in arms and arts, church and state, law, legislation and literature, commerce, science, travel and philanthropy* (1881)

JCS — *Journal of the Chemical Society*

JHC — *Journals of the House of Commons*

JHL — *Journals of the House of Lords*

John of Worcester, *Chron.* — *The chronicle of John of Worcester*, ed. R. R. Darlington and P. McGurk, trans. J. Bray and P. McGurk, 3 vols., OMT (1995–) [vol. 1 forthcoming]

Keeler, *Long Parliament* — M. F. Keeler, *The Long Parliament, 1640–1641: a biographical study of its members* (1954)

Kelly, *Handbk* — *The upper ten thousand: an alphabetical list of all members of noble families*, 3 vols. (1875–7); continued as *Kelly's handbook of the upper ten thousand for 1878* [1879], 2 vols. (1878–9); continued as *Kelly's handbook to the titled, landed and official classes*, 94 vols. (1880–1973)

LondG — *London Gazette*

LP Henry VIII — J. S. Brewer, J. Gairdner, and R. H. Brodie, eds., *Letters and papers, foreign and domestic, of the reign of Henry VIII*, 23 vols. in 38 (1862–1932); repr. (1965)

Mallalieu, *Watercolour artists* — H. L. Mallalieu, *The dictionary of British watercolour artists up to 1820*, 3 vols. (1976–90); vol. 1, 2nd edn (1986)

Memoirs FRS — *Biographical Memoirs of Fellows of the Royal Society*

MGH — *Monumenta Germaniae Historica*

MT — *Musical Times*

Munk, *Roll* — W. Munk, *The roll of the Royal College of Physicians of London*, 2 vols. (1861); 2nd edn, 3 vols. (1878)

N&Q — *Notes and Queries*

New Grove — S. Sadie, ed., *The new Grove dictionary of music and musicians*, 20 vols. (1980); 2nd edn, 29 vols. (2001) [also online edn; see also Grove, *Dict. mus.*]

Nichols, *Illustrations* — J. Nichols and J. B. Nichols, *Illustrations of the literary history of the eighteenth century*, 8 vols. (1817–58)

Nichols, *Lit. anecdotes* — J. Nichols, *Literary anecdotes of the eighteenth century*, 9 vols. (1812–16); facs. edn (1966)

Obits. FRS — *Obituary Notices of Fellows of the Royal Society*

O'Byrne, *Naval biog. dict.* — W. R. O'Byrne, *A naval biographical dictionary* (1849); repr. (1990); [2nd edn], 2 vols. (1861)

OHS — Oxford Historical Society

Old Westminsters — *The record of Old Westminsters*, 1–2, ed. G. F. R. Barker and A. H. Stenning (1928); suppl. 1, ed. J. B. Whitmore and G. R. Y. Radcliffe [1938]; 3, ed. J. B. Whitmore, G. R. Y. Radcliffe, and D. C. Simpson (1963); suppl. 2, ed. F. E. Pagan (1978); 4, ed. F. E. Pagan and H. E. Pagan (1992)

OMT — Oxford Medieval Texts

Ordericus Vitalis, *Eccl. hist.* — *The ecclesiastical history of Orderic Vitalis*, ed. and trans. M. Chibnall, 6 vols., OMT (1969–80); repr. (1990)

Paris, *Chron.* — *Matthaei Parisiensis, monachi sancti Albani, chronica majora*, ed. H. R. Luard, Rolls Series, 7 vols. (1872–83)

Parl. papers — *Parliamentary papers* (1801–)

PBA — *Proceedings of the British Academy*

Pepys, *Diary*	*The diary of Samuel Pepys*, ed. R. Latham and W. Matthews, 11 vols. (1970–83); repr. (1995) and (2000)
Pevsner	N. Pevsner and others, Buildings of England series
PICE	*Proceedings of the Institution of Civil Engineers*
Pipe rolls	*The great roll of the pipe for . . .*, PRSoc. (1884–)
PRO	Public Record Office
PRS	*Proceedings of the Royal Society of London*
PRSoc.	Pipe Roll Society
PTRS	*Philosophical Transactions of the Royal Society*
QR	*Quarterly Review*
RC	Record Commissions
Redgrave, *Artists*	S. Redgrave, *A dictionary of artists of the English school* (1874); rev. edn (1878); repr. (1970)
Reg. Oxf.	C. W. Boase and A. Clark, eds., *Register of the University of Oxford*, 5 vols., OHS, 1, 10–12, 14 (1885–9)
Reg. PCS	J. H. Burton and others, eds., *The register of the privy council of Scotland*, 1st ser., 14 vols. (1877–98); 2nd ser., 8 vols. (1899–1908); 3rd ser., [16 vols.] (1908–70)
Reg. RAN	H. W. C. Davis and others, eds., *Regesta regum Anglo-Normannorum, 1066–1154*, 4 vols. (1913–69)
RIBA Journal	*Journal of the Royal Institute of British Architects* [later *RIBA Journal*]
RotP	J. Strachey, ed., *Rotuli parliamentorum ut et petitiones, et placita in parliamento*, 6 vols. (1767–77)
RotS	D. Macpherson, J. Caley, and W. Illingworth, eds., *Rotuli Scotiae in Turri Londinensi et in domo capitulari Westmonasteriensi asservati*, 2 vols., RC, 14 (1814–19)
RS	Record(s) Society
Rymer, *Foedera*	T. Rymer and R. Sanderson, eds., *Foedera, conventiones, literae et cuiuscunque generis acta publica inter reges Angliae et alios quosvis imperatores, reges, pontifices, principes, vel communitates*, 20 vols. (1704–35); 2nd edn, 20 vols. (1726–35); 3rd edn, 10 vols. (1739–45), facs. edn (1967); new edn, ed. A. Clarke, J. Caley, and F. Holbrooke, 4 vols., RC, 50 (1816–30)
Sainty, *Judges*	J. Sainty, ed., *The judges of England, 1272–1990*, SeldS, suppl. ser., 10 (1993)
Sainty, *King's counsel*	J. Sainty, ed., *A list of English law officers and king's counsel*, SeldS, suppl. ser., 7 (1987)
SCH	Studies in Church History
Scots peerage	J. B. Paul, ed. *The Scots peerage, founded on Wood's edition of Sir Robert Douglas's Peerage of Scotland, containing an historical and genealogical account of the nobility of that kingdom*, 9 vols. (1904–14)
SeldS	Selden Society
SHR	*Scottish Historical Review*
State trials	T. B. Howell and T. J. Howell, eds., *Cobbett's Complete collection of state trials*, 34 vols. (1809–28)
STC, 1475–1640	A. W. Pollard, G. R. Redgrave, and others, eds., *A short-title catalogue of . . . English books . . . 1475–1640* (1926); 2nd edn, ed. W. A. Jackson, F. S. Ferguson, and K. F. Pantzer, 3 vols. (1976–91) [see also Wing, *STC*]
STS	Scottish Text Society
SurtS	Surtees Society
Symeon of Durham, *Opera*	*Symeonis monachi opera omnia*, ed. T. Arnold, 2 vols., Rolls Series, 75 (1882–5); repr. (1965)
Tanner, *Bibl. Brit.-Hib.*	T. Tanner, *Bibliotheca Britannico-Hibernica*, ed. D. Wilkins (1748); repr. (1963)
Thieme & Becker, *Allgemeines Lexikon*	U. Thieme, F. Becker, and H. Vollmer, eds., *Allgemeines Lexikon der bildenden Künstler von der Antike bis zur Gegenwart*, 37 vols. (Leipzig, 1907–50); repr. (1961–5), (1983), and (1992)
Thurloe, *State papers*	*A collection of the state papers of John Thurloe*, ed. T. Birch, 7 vols. (1742)
TLS	*Times Literary Supplement*
Tout, *Admin. hist.*	T. F. Tout, *Chapters in the administrative history of mediaeval England: the wardrobe, the chamber, and the small seals*, 6 vols. (1920–33); repr. (1967)
TRHS	*Transactions of the Royal Historical Society*
VCH	H. A. Doubleday and others, eds., *The Victoria history of the counties of England*, [88 vols.] (1900–)
Venn, *Alum. Cant.*	J. Venn and J. A. Venn, *Alumni Cantabrigienses: a biographical list of all known students, graduates, and holders of office at the University of Cambridge, from the earliest times to 1900*, 10 vols. (1922–54); repr. in 2 vols. (1974–8)
Vertue, *Note books*	[G. Vertue], *Note books*, ed. K. Esdaile, earl of Ilchester, and H. M. Hake, 6 vols., Walpole Society, 18, 20, 22, 24, 26, 30 (1930–55)
VF	*Vanity Fair*
Walford, *County families*	E. Walford, *The county families of the United Kingdom, or, Royal manual of the titled and untitled aristocracy of Great Britain and Ireland* (1860)
Walker rev.	A. G. Matthews, *Walker revised: being a revision of John Walker's Sufferings of the clergy during the grand rebellion, 1642–60* (1948); repr. (1988)
Walpole, *Corr.*	*The Yale edition of Horace Walpole's correspondence*, ed. W. S. Lewis, 48 vols. (1937–83)
Ward, *Men of the reign*	T. H. Ward, ed., *Men of the reign: a biographical dictionary of eminent persons of British and colonial birth who have died during the reign of Queen Victoria* (1885); repr. (Graz, 1968)
Waterhouse, *18c painters*	E. Waterhouse, *The dictionary of 18th century painters in oils and crayons* (1981); repr. as *British 18th century painters in oils and crayons* (1991), vol. 2 of *Dictionary of British art*
Watt, *Bibl. Brit.*	R. Watt, *Bibliotheca Britannica, or, A general index to British and foreign literature*, 4 vols. (1824) [many reprs.]
Wellesley index	W. E. Houghton, ed., *The Wellesley index to Victorian periodicals, 1824–1900*, 5 vols. (1966–89); new edn (1999) [CD-ROM]
Wing, *STC*	D. Wing, ed., *Short-title catalogue of . . . English books . . . 1641–1700*, 3 vols. (1945–51); 2nd edn (1972–88); rev. and enl. edn, ed. J. J. Morrison, C. W. Nelson, and M. Seccombe, 4 vols. (1994–8) [see also *STC, 1475–1640*]
Wisden	*John Wisden's Cricketer's Almanack*
Wood, *Ath. Oxon.*	A. Wood, *Athenae Oxonienses . . . to which are added the Fasti*, 2 vols. (1691–2); 2nd edn (1721); new edn, 4 vols., ed. P. Bliss (1813–20); repr. (1967) and (1969)
Wood, *Vic. painters*	C. Wood, *Dictionary of Victorian painters* (1971); 2nd edn (1978); 3rd edn as *Victorian painters*, 2 vols. (1995), vol. 4 of *Dictionary of British art*
WW	*Who's who* (1849–)
WWBMP	M. Stenton and S. Lees, eds., *Who's who of British members of parliament*, 4 vols. (1976–81)
WWW	*Who was who* (1929–)

Flattisbury, Philip (*fl.* 1503–1526), antiquary, was the head of an important landowning family settled from the thirteenth century at Johnstown, near Naas, co. Kildare. A genealogy in Trinity College, Dublin, names his mother as Rose Boice or Boyse; his father may have been named Philip. In 1526 he calls himself 'lord of Johneston, captain of his nation' (PRO NIre., D.3078/1/18/13). He married Elizabeth, daughter of William Wogan of Rathcoffey, co. Kildare. Flattisbury was a retainer of Gerald FitzGerald, eighth earl of Kildare, and his son Gerald, ninth earl, governors of Ireland under Henry VII and Henry VIII, and frequently appears as a witness to their deeds. In 1503 he compiled for the eighth earl the chartulary known as the Red Book of the Earls of Kildare, a collection of documents bearing on the lands and possessions of the earls of Kildare and their ancestors. The original was acquired in 1984 by Trinity College, Dublin; the text has been edited by Gearóid MacNiocaill.

Flattisbury also transcribed for the ninth earl, in 1517, a collection of Anglo-Irish annals in Latin, terminating in 1370. To them he appended a few lines of additional matter, with a brief panegyric on the earl of Kildare. The work is preserved in a copy in MS 584 of Trinity College, Dublin. Some further annalistic notes in Flattisbury's hand are appended to the text of another version of the same annals in the British Library (Add. MS 40674, fol. 54) and yet more annals by Flattisbury are to be found in Cotton MS Vespasian D x (fols. 138–43) in the British Library. Campion and Stanihurst erroneously refer to Flattisbury as the author of the annals of which he was the transcriber. Another chronicle which an early annotator ascribed to Flattisbury is to be found in Cotton MS Domitian xviii (fols. 57*v*–104). This material, however, is nearly identical with that ascribed by Meredith Hanmer and Archbishop Ussher to James Grace of Kilkenny and printed as such in 1852, and it is likely that Grace was in fact only the transcriber, or even the owner, of the text. The original annals which Flattisbury transcribed were printed in 1607 by Camden, and, in a new edition from the original manuscripts, by Sir John Gilbert in 1885.

Flattisbury refers to himself in a deed of 1526, so was alive then. Stanihurst does not record the date of his death, but mentions that it took place 'at his town styled Johnstown' and observes that he was a 'worthy gentleman and a diligent antiquary' (Stanihurst, fol. 25). He seems to have been buried in the church of Johnstown, where a surviving slab with the arms of Flattisbury and of Wogan may mark his grave. His widow married, as her second husband, Maurice Keating.   K. W. NICHOLLS

Sources A. Vicars, 'The family of Flatesbury of Ballynasculloge and Johnstown, co. Kildare', *Journal of the County Kildare Archaeological Society*, 4 (1903–5), 87–94 • W. FitzGerald, 'The earl of Kildare's red book, 1503', *Journal of the County Kildare Archaeological Society*, 9 (1918–21), 461–2 • R. Flower, 'Manuscripts of Irish interest in the British Museum', *Analecta Hibernica*, 2 (1931), 292–340, esp. 325–9 • TCD, MS 1212, 11, 13, 14 • R. Stanihurst, 'Third booke of the Historie of Ireland, comprising the raigne of Henry the Eyght', *The chronicles of England, Scotlande and Irelande*, ed. R. Holinshed and others, 2 (1577), 76–115 • *DNB* • PRO NIre., D 3078/1/15, 18, 26 • K. W. Nicholls, 'The Geraldines of Allen', *Irish Genealogist*, 4 (1968–73), 93–

108, 194–200 • G. MacNiocaill, ed., *The Red Book of the earls of Kildare* (1964) • R. Butler, ed., *Jacobi Grace, Kilkenniensis, annales Hiberniae* (1852) • J. T. Gilbert, ed., *Chartularies of St Mary's Abbey, Dublin: with the register of its house at Dunbrody and annals of Ireland*, 2, Rolls Series, 80 (1884), appx

Archives PRO NIre., Leinster MSS, signature as witness, D 3078
Wealth at death probably quite high: Vicars, 'The family', 91

Flavel, John. *See* Flavell, John (1596?–1617); Flavell, John (*bap.* 1630, *d.* 1691).

Flavell, John (1596?–1617), writer on logic, was the son of a clergyman and a native of Bishop's Lydeard, Somerset. He was fourteen when he matriculated as a student of Trinity College, Oxford, in early 1611. He soon became 'the forwardest youth in that house, for his quick and smart disputations in logic and philosophy'. Having heard reports of 'the pregnancy of his parts', the founder of Wadham College 'made him one of her first scholars thereof, in 1613' (Wood, *Ath. Oxon.*, 2.207). He was admitted BA on 28 June 1614 and licensed MA on 23 June 1617. Again by recommendation of the Wadham College founder, he was made a probationer fellow on 24 March 1617 and a fellow on 30 June 1617. He apparently served as subdean of his college in 1615 and 1616.

Flavell's first published works were poems in university collections of verses. In 1613 he contributed a seventeen-line Latin poem to *Epithalamia* (1613), a collection honouring the marriage of Frederick V to Princess Elizabeth. In 1617 he contributed three poems—two in Latin, one in Greek—to *Jacobi ara*, a collection celebrating the return of James I from a trip to Scotland. Flavell's Greek poem is one of only two Greek poems in the collection. Shortly before his death he was made professor of grammar. Wood reports that he was 'esteemed a good Greek and Latin poet' and suggests that he may have written a textbook on Greek grammar (Wood, *Ath. Oxon.*, 2.207), but the textbook does not seem to have survived. Flavell died either in October 1617 (according to Robert Gardiner, citing the 'College MSS') or on 10 November 1617 (the date given by Anthony Wood); he was buried in the north part of the outer chapel of Wadham College.

As a baccalaureate of nineteen or possibly eighteen, Flavell composed a series of logic lectures for use in his teaching. After his death his colleague Alexander Huish, also of Wadham College and Somerset, decided to publish the lectures. In the absence of an autograph manuscript Huish had to reconstruct the whole work from the transcripts of Flavell's students, as he explained in his 'Lectori s[alutem]' (sig. fol. 3*r*). He divided the work into books, sections, and chapters; expanded the analysis; verified or supplied citations; compiled the indexes; and edited the prose for felicity. The result was a textbook of 144 pages, in four books, entitled *Tractatus de demonstratione methodicus et polemicus* (1619).

Flavell's and Huish's textbook is an up-to-date discussion of demonstration and scientific method, heavily influenced by the work of the Italian logician Jacopo Zabarella and ultimately the *Posterior Analytics* of Aristotle. The authors cite the Paduan Zabarella as frequently as they do Aristotle. Their other sources include Fortunatus

Crellius, Giulio Pace, Thomas de Vio Caietanus, Domingo de Soto, Pierre Tartaret, and Griffith Powell—all Renaissance commentators on Aristotle's logical works. Wood reports that the book 'hath been taken into the hands of all juniors' (Wood, *Ath. Oxon.*, 2.207), and contemporary book lists show that it was used, or at least purchased, by Oxford students throughout the seventeenth century. It was often bound with the 1618 edition of Robert Sanderson's *Logicae artis compendium*, the most popular British logic textbook of the seventeenth century. Later editions of the *Tractatus* were printed in 1624 and 1651. The 1651 edition has an added five-part *disputatio* on Aristotle's topics, but this is almost certainly not the work of Huish or Flavell. EDWARD A. MALONE

Sources Wood, *Ath. Oxon.*, new edn · R. B. Gardiner, ed., *The registers of Wadham College, Oxford*, 1 (1889) · J. W. Binns, *Intellectual culture in Elizabethan and Jacobean England: the Latin writings of the age* (1990) [incl. A. Huish's address to the reader of Flavell's lectures] · F. Madan, *Oxford books: a bibliography of printed works*, 3 vols. (1895–1931); repr. (1964) · *Reg. Oxf.*, vol. 2 · C. Schmitt, *John Case and Aristotelianism in renaissance England* (1983) · *ESTC* · Foster, *Alum. Oxon.* · *Hist. U. Oxf. 4: 17th-cent. Oxf.*

Flavell, John (*bap.* 1630, *d.* 1691), Presbyterian minister and religious writer, was born at Bromsgrove, Worcestershire, where he was baptized on 26 September 1630, the elder son of Richard Flavell (*d.* 1665), clergyman. His brother Phineas was sometime chaplain in the family of Edward Russell, earl of Orford.

In 1646, after being educated at home and in local grammar schools, Flavell was sent as a servitor to University College, Oxford, where he remained about two years. On 27 April 1650 Flavell was appointed assistant in the parish of Diptford, near Totnes in Devon. Shortly after ordination by the presbytery at Salisbury on 17 October 1650, he became minister of Diptford. His first wife, Joan Randall, died in childbirth on 15 November 1655 and he married Elizabeth Stapell on 18 November 1656. His second marriage produced a son, John, born on 23 December 1657. When Anthony Hartford, minister at Dartmouth, died in January 1656 Flavell was elected as his replacement, sharing parish duties with Allen Geare. The agreement settling Flavell and Geare at Dartmouth was drawn up by Major-General John Desborough on 7 August 1656. On Sundays Flavell ministered in St Clement's, Townstal, the ancient parish church overlooking Dartmouth, and on alternate Wednesdays he lectured in St Saviour's, a daughter church in the town. After 1656 he became a member of the Devon Association of Ministers. By all accounts he was a most effective preacher, one hearer remarking that a 'person must have a very soft Head, or a very hard Heart, or both, that could sit under his Ministry unaffected' (*Whole Works*, 1.4). Flavell and Geare both continued to preach in Dartmouth after they were ejected under the Act of Uniformity of 1662. After Geare's death in December 1662 Flavell taught in a small dissenting academy in the town.

The Five Mile Act of 1665 forced Flavell to move to Slapton, but he continued to visit Dartmouth secretly and a remarkable resourcefulness enabled him to sustain his ministry. On one occasion he rode to Totnes disguised as a woman in order to carry out a baptism. Another time, pursued by riders, he plunged his horse into the sea and escaped arrest by swimming round the rocks to Slapton Sands. He was also involved in meetings held on the Saltstone, a ledge in the middle of the Salcombe estuary accessible only at low water during spring tides. Between 1667 and 1671 Flavell's ministry extended beyond the South Hams. He leased property from the earl of Bedford at Landkey, near Barnstaple, and reputedly held midnight services in Hudscott Mansion, near Chittlehampton. On one occasion he narrowly escaped arrest while preaching in a wood near Exeter.

Following Charles II's declaration of indulgence in 1672, Flavell returned to Dartmouth, licensed as a Congregationalist minister. About this time his second wife died, and he married Agnes Downe with whom he had a son, Thomas. In 1674 Flavell sought to circumvent renewed persecution of nonconformists by continuing his ministry in print. Over the next ten years he published *A Token for Mourners* (1674), *The Seaman's Companion* (1676), *Divine Conduct* (1678), *Sea Deliverances* (c.1679), *The Touchstone of Sincerity* (1679), *The Method of Grace* (1681), *Navigation Spiritualized* (1682), *A Saint Indeed* (1684), and *Treatise on the Soul of Man* (1685). About 1682 Flavell retired to London, being 'in great Danger at *Dartmouth*, thro' the Malice of his Enemies' (Calamy, *Abridgement*, 2.221).

The night before Flavell took ship for London, he dreamed he was at sea in a great storm. Nearby sat a man busy writing. Beside the man was a cradle in which a child began to cry. The man struck the infant with a small whip saying: 'Child, be quiet; I will discipline, but not hurt thee' (*Whole Works*, 1.5). After a few days at sea Flavell also experienced a terrifying storm. Between two and three o'clock in the morning, as the ship neared Portland, it became clear that unless the wind changed direction immediately the vessel would be wrecked on the bill. Calling all available hands into his cabin, and bracing himself between two bulkheads, Flavell committed the ship's company to God. The moment he finished a voice on deck shouted: 'Deliverance! Deliverance! God is hearing Prayer! In a moment the Wind is come fair West!' (ibid.). These experiences undoubtedly influenced Flavell's deep concern for the spiritual welfare of mariners so powerfully expressed in *Navigation Spiritualized*, the work for which he is best remembered.

In late 1684, perhaps after his third wife died, Flavell returned to Dartmouth where he was soon placed under house arrest. In 1685 his antagonists burned his effigy in the streets, but despite extreme provocation, Flavell continued to preach in his own house, and resisted invitations to return to London. About this time he married Dorothy, the widowed daughter of George Jefferies, minister of Kingsbridge until his death in 1665. With the declaration of indulgence issued on 6 November 1687, Flavell resumed public preaching. However, Flavell delivered his last sermon in Ashburton, on 21 June 1691, after which he travelled to Topsham to preside as moderator in an assembly of the nonconformist ministers of Devon. On this occasion he strenuously advocated the heads of agreement under which the union of Presbyterians and Congregationalists in London had been effected by John Howe on 6 April 1691. Flavell obtained unanimous agreement to institute a similar union in Devon with the result that all future meetings of the Topsham assembly were combined. Sitting as Exeter assembly, this body resided over nonconformist affairs in Devon and Cornwall until 1753.

At supper in Totnes on 26 June 1691 Flavell suffered a stroke. He gradually became paralysed down one side of his body, and unable to speak. He died later that night. His body was later carried to Dartmouth, accompanied by several ministers and many others. Mourners from Newton Abbot, Ashburton, Totnes, and elsewhere rode out to meet the procession. The body was interred near the chancel in St Saviour's Church on the evening of 29 June. George Trosse of Exeter gave the address.

Flavell was said to have been an active man of middle stature. He was 'ready to learn from every Body, and as free to communicate what he knew', educating four young men for the ministry, one of whom he maintained entirely at his own expense (*Whole Works*, 1.8). By the time of his death he had achieved relative prosperity, probably through marriage, and in disposing of his effects he was generous to the poor. His influence over the inhabitants of Dartmouth and the esteem which his memory still commands in the town are perpetuated by the Flavel Methodist and United Reformed Church, erected in 1895. A contemporary brass tablet, placed originally in St Saviour's, is now preserved in the Flavel church. A proposed arts complex for the town is to be known as the Flavel Centre. Not least among Flavell's memorials are his voluminous writings. These printed sermons and reflections, through which the author identifies ingeniously with an absent congregation, form an integral part of a ministry which was widely admired by, among others, Cotton and Increase Mather. JAMES WILLIAM KELLY

Sources will, 12 July 1665, PRO, PROB 11/318/140 [Richard Flavell] · will, PRO, PROB 11/406/162 [John Flavell] · will, PRO, PROB 11/505/284 [Phineas Flavell] · Devon RO, L1258/16–18c, leases/24/1 [Landkey, Barnstable] · parish registers for St Clement's and St Saviour's, Devon RO, C. 1653–1848, M. 1653–1894, B. 1653–1876 · parish registers, Diptford, Devon RO, C. 1653–1908, M. 1653–1837, B. 1653–1886; bishop's transcripts, CMB 1596– · E. Calamy, ed., *An abridgment of Mr. Baxter's history of his life and times, with an account of the ministers, &c., who were ejected after the Restauration of King Charles II*, 2nd edn, 2 vols. (1713) · E. Calamy, *A continuation of the account of the ministers ... who were ejected and silenced after the Restoration in 1660*, 2 vols. (1727) · *The whole works of the Reverend Mr. John Flavel*, 2 vols. (1701) · *The select works of the Rev. John Flavel ... with an interesting account of his life* (1834) · Foster, *Alum. Oxon.* · Wood, *Ath. Oxon.*, new edn, vol. 4 · J. H. B. Andrews, 'Rolle of Hudscott and the will of Samuel Rolle', *Devon and Cornwall Notes and Queries*, 25 (1952–3), 26–8 · A. Brockett, *Nonconformity in Exeter, 1650–1875* (1962) · A. Brockett, ed., *The Exeter assembly: the minutes of the assemblies of the United Brethren of Devon and Cornwall, 1691–1717*, Devon and Cornwall RS, new ser., 6 (1963), 1–7 · W. Carr, *University of Oxford college histories: University College* (1902) · R. Freeman, *Dartmouth and its neighbours* (1990) · *Calamy rev.* · P. Russell, *A short account of the Congregational church in Dartmouth: founded under the leadership of John Flavell, 1662* (1950x59) · W. A. Shaw, *A history of the English church during the civil wars and under the Commonwealth, 1640–1660*, 2 (1900), 449 · A. Warne, *Church and society in eighteenth-century Devon* (1969) · E. Windeatt, 'John Flavell: a notable Dartmouth puritan and his bibliography', *Transactions of the Devonshire Association for the Advancement of Science, Literature, and Art*, 63 (1911), 172–89

Likenesses M. Vandergucht, line engraving, NPG · R. White, line engraving, BM; NPG · oils, DWL

Wealth at death leased property in Gloucester and north Devon (Landkey, Barnstaple); owned property in Dartmouth; assets in excess of £1000: will, PROB 11/406/162, 27 July 1686

Flavelle, Sir Joseph Wesley, first baronet (1858–1939), businessman and philanthropist in Canada, was born on 15 February 1858 in Peterborough, Canada, the fifth and youngest child of John Flavelle (1823–1882), a clerk, and his wife, Dorothea Dundas (1823–1908), a teacher, who on their marriage in 1847 emigrated from co. Cavan, Ireland, 'to seek ... fortune in the land of promise' (Bliss, 2). They did not prosper, but their three sons, including Joseph, became prominent merchants and leading Methodist laymen in the flourishing agricultural heartland of central Ontario. In 1887 Flavelle, having five years previously married Clara Ellsworth (1858–1932), a Peterborough woman whose father was a Methodist minister, moved his provision business to the regional metropolis of Toronto. In 1892 he agreed to become managing director and part owner of the William Davies Company, Canada's first modern meat-packing house. Displaying brilliant managerial flair and a methodistical passion for accounting, he presided over an immense increase in Davies's sales of sides of premium bacon to Britain. By 1900 the company boasted that it was the largest pork-packing house in the British empire, Toronto was acquiring its enduring nickname, 'Hogtown', and Flavelle had become a millionaire.

With a tightly knit network of businessmen, many from Peterborough and with Methodist connections, Flavelle became involved in a wide range of financial, railway, and retailing activities during Canada's prolonged turn-of-the-century boom. Most notably he was a principal owner of the Robert Simpson department store, the founder president of the National Trust Company, and a director and ultimately chairman of the board of the Canadian Bank of Commerce. He was a very generous and active supporter of the Methodist Church of Canada and the Conservative Party, a principal organizer of the rebuilding of Toronto General Hospital as a world-class institution, and chairman of an Ontario royal commission that led to the modernization of the University of Toronto. With only an elementary education, he was one of the most passionate supporters of higher education and cultural development among Canadian businessmen. He was also a fervent imperialist, and a member of the Round Table with many acquaintances in Britain.

In 1915 the British Ministry of Munitions appointed Flavelle chairman of the imperial munitions board, a small committee which was to administer all British munitions orders in Canada. As chairman he freed Canadian war production from earlier taints of scandal, and presided over the spending of $1250 million on Canadian-made shells, ships, and aeroplanes. The board's negotiation of significant loans from the Canadian government and its success in securing American contracts after 1917 were among the more imaginative aspects of a programme that was widely praised on both sides of the Atlantic.

Flavelle became a baronet in June 1917; his was considered an earned rather than a bought title. Four months later he was publicly pilloried in Canada as a 'baconet', 'baconeer', and several species of hog, when a government report misunderstood and mis-stated the William Davies Company's profit margins on its very large bacon and beef contracts with the War Office. The company had in fact earned record profits through low margins on huge volume. A popular myth that it had sold spoiled food to the troops was utterly without foundation. Flavelle's wartime philanthropies outweighed his wartime income and he was deeply hurt by the scandal. After this incident the Canadian government asked Britain not to grant hereditary titles to Canadians, and Flavelle thus became the last citizen domiciled in Canada to receive such a title.

In the inter-war years 'Holy Joe' Flavelle was an elder statesman of Canadian business and an unusually articulate exponent of market-orientated Conservative values. He was the last chairman of the board of the Grand Trunk Railway Company of Canada and a member of Ottawa's 1931–2 royal commission on railways and transportation. He was also chairman of the board of West China Union University and the Canadian Marconi Company. In 1919 he sold his interest in the William Davies Company.

On his death, from cancer, in Florida on 7 March 1939, Flavelle left three children, of whom Ellsworth inherited the baronetcy. His estate was valued at C$6 million. He was buried in Mount Pleasant cemetery, Toronto, and his splendid mansion in the city, Holwood, in Queen's Park, was given to the University of Toronto and eventually came to house its faculty of law. The Flavelle foundation continued its founder's philanthropic tradition. With the death of Ellsworth's son Sir David Flavelle in 1985 the baronetcy was extinguished.

While Flavelle's father had been overcome by life in America and by strong drink, his youngest son exemplified the North American rags-to-riches (or, in this case, sow's ear to silk purse) myth. 'In the end', a journalist noted, 'Sir Joseph touched the life of Canada at more points than any man of his time' (Bliss, 508). He had also served his empire in war.   MICHAEL BLISS

Sources M. Bliss, *A Canadian millionaire: the life and business times of Sir Joseph Flavelle, bart., 1858–1939* (1978) · Queen's University, Kingston, Ontario, Flavelle MSS · NA Canada, Flavelle collection

Archives NA Canada, MSS · Queen's University, Kingston, Ontario, MSS

Likenesses portrait, repro. in Bliss, *Canadian millionaire* · portrait, priv. coll.

Wealth at death C$6,053,038: probate

Flavius Claudius Constantinus. *See* Constantine III (d. 411).

Flavius Vespasianus, Titus. *See* Vespasian (AD 9–79) *under* Roman emperors (*act.* 55 BC–AD 410).

Flaxman, John (1755–1826), sculptor, decorative designer, and illustrator, was born on 6 July 1755 in York, the second son of three children of John Flaxman (1726–1795), a minor sculptor and producer of plaster casts and models,

John Flaxman (1755–1826), by George Romney, 1795 [modelling the bust of William Hayley]

and his first wife, formerly Miss Lee (d. c.1763); he was the younger brother of William [*see below*] and half-brother of Mary Ann [*see below*].

Early work and career The Flaxman family settled in London the year after John's birth and the boy was educated in the Covent Garden shop and studio of his father, who worked for leading London sculptors including L. F. Roubiliac and Peter Scheemakers. Sickly and slightly hunchbacked, young Flaxman was known for his drawing skills at an early age and, through his father's professional contacts, met several future patrons who played crucial roles in his career, notably the portrait painter George Romney and the potter Josiah Wedgwood. In 1767 the boy received his first commission from Mr Crutchley of Sunninghill for six black chalk drawings of subjects from classical literature; in the same year he began regularly to exhibit wax and plaster models at the Free Society of Arts in London.

From the early 1770s Flaxman exhibited portraits in terracotta and plaster, allegorical classical figures, and subjects from Ovid and Homer at the Royal Academy in London, where he won a silver medal in 1771. By 1775 he had begun to design decorative figures for the Wedgwood pottery factory, becoming arguably the most famous and skilful of all the artists employed by the potter. Flaxman's flowing, delicate lines, especially suited to the decorative reliefs on vases and plaques, also appeared in wax and terracotta portraits where accuracy was crucial to the production of popular medallions of contemporary luminaries produced by Wedgwood in the 1770s and 1780s. Examples include the oval blue and white jasper medallion of Captain Cook (c.1779; Wedgwood Museum, Barlaston, Staffordshire), the white jasper one of Sarah Siddons

(1782; Wedgwood Museum, Barlaston, Staffordshire), and the white relief likeness, on black jasper, of Dr Samuel Johnson (1784; Wedgwood Museum, Barlaston, Staffordshire). *The Apotheosis of Homer* (design 1778, vase 1786; BM), Flaxman's most famous moulded relief in white jasperware (a fine white clay), was given by Wedgwood to the British Museum and highly praised by Sir William Hamilton: 'I never saw a bas relief executed in the true and simple antique style half so well' (Bindman, 56). Flaxman also designed a set of medieval-styled chessmen for Wedgwood, objects which reflected the sculptor's growing enthusiasm for medieval art.

Flaxman met William Blake and Thomas Stothard at the Royal Academy and was inspired by Blake's semi-abstract, undulating line drawings. The young sculptor's own talents as a draughtsman made him particularly aware of contemporary fashions in graphic art. Two self-portraits (1778–9; Earls High School, Halesowen, and UCL, signed and dated 1779) demonstrate his interest in imitating in pen the techniques of copperplate engraving, while the figure with large eyes, long hair, and introverted expression betrays his admiration for similar, proto-romantic self-portraits by John Hamilton Mortimer and James Barry. Following the example of his fellow artists at the Royal Academy, Flaxman turned to medieval art as a means of exploring the flowing linear rhythms of a new vital and primitive style. He admired the tomb sculpture, decorative carving, and paintings in Westminster Abbey, York Minster, and Lincoln and Wells cathedrals. He never lost his taste for portraying images from antique poetry and Roman history, but he was also to play an important role in the development of the British Gothic revival, discovering the beauties of early English and native Gothic sculpture and architecture.

By 1780 Flaxman's principal ambition was to become a designer of funerary monuments and his later analysis of tomb sculpture in the lectures he gave to the Royal Academy reveals how important he considered British monumental sculpture in the history of artistic commemoration. He particularly admired the work of Thomas Banks (1735–1805), and in an address given to the Royal Academy in 1805 Flaxman revealed how far he had come under the influence of this major British sculptor. Flaxman's first tomb design was for a monument to Thomas Chatterton (exh. 1780) at the height of the posthumous craze in London for Chatterton memorabilia and biographical souvenirs. Flaxman made several drawings in connection with this tomb, which was never erected, and they reveal the artist's personal enthusiasm and reverence for the subject as well as the stylistic influence of contemporary 'sublime' masters such as Henry Fuseli (*c*.1775–85; FM Cam. and BM). Shortly after his marriage in 1782 to Ann Denman (*c*.1760–1820), Flaxman received his first major sculptural commission to design a monument for a Mrs Sarah Morley who had died in childbirth at sea, and the nature of the subject appealed to the sculptor's taste for the poetic and tragic. Erected in Gloucester Cathedral the Morley monument has a strong dramatic quality: its emotional appeal centres on the principal figure rising above realistically depicted stormy waves, deriving from the realism of earlier sculptors such as Roubiliac and Joseph Wilton. However, the attendant angels have the energy and grace of figures which the sculptor had studied in Westminster Abbey. The influence of Banks can be seen in the rhythmic quality of the contours and in the clever combination of antique and Gothic forms. Flaxman's first biographer, Allan Cunningham, alluded to the strength and energy of the design which he felt derived from a poetic sensibility: 'It elevates the mind, and not without tears' (Cunningham, 293). The uniqueness of this imagery in English sculpture at the time won Flaxman more commissions, but with the intention of enlarging his artistic repertoire with a visit to Italy he and his wife departed for Rome in 1787.

Italy, 1787–1794 Flaxman's seven-year sojourn in Rome changed his career and transformed him from an obscure British sculptor into a major international figure with proven ability in monumental and free-standing sculpture and in graphic design. His travel notebooks and sketchbooks (BL, FM Cam., UCL) reveal how meticulous were the records he kept of works of art seen in France and Italy. Sketches after Lorenzo Maitani's *Last Judgment* at Orvieto, works by Masaccio, the Pisani, Brunelleschi, Michelangelo, and Bernini as well as the masterpieces of antiquity demonstrate how profoundly this versatile scholar artist investigated the principal stylistic constituents of Renaissance and seventeenth-century art. Flaxman also made copies after early Italian masters and medieval carving, and his sketchbooks contain drawings which transform paintings and sculpture into brief, undulating silhouettes. His unusual enthusiasms brought him to the notice of several influential scholars, patrons, and fellow artists, notably W. Y. Ottley, who became the first keeper of prints and drawings at the British Museum; the neoclassical sculptor Antonio Canova; Guy Head, the Irish painter; and Thomas Hope, scion of the wealthy banking family.

Although his first year in Italy was not lucrative Flaxman continued sending designs to the Wedgwood factory and made a series of plaster casts for George Romney, who was one of the sculptor's closest admirers. Flaxman also worked on several highly original pieces of sculpture, including *Hercules and Hebe*, the figure of Hercules being a reconstruction based on the Torso Belvedere (plaster model, UCL), and the marble two-figure group *Aurora Visiting Cephalus on Mount Aurora* (1790–91; Lady Lever Art Gallery, Port Sunlight, Cheshire), a subject from Ovid, both of which were commissioned by Thomas Hope. Flaxman's group reveals the effect of the sculptor's new first-hand knowledge of antique sculpture: the figures of Aurora and Cephalus are based on a Nike or winged victory and the Apollo Belvedere, and illustrate Ovid's tragic story of the doomed love between mortal and immortal. Made for Hope's London house where Flaxman's marble group became the centrepiece for a special antique-styled room, this marble group attracted much attention and contributed to Flaxman's growing reputation as the foremost English sculptor of the period.

However, an even more original work produced in Rome resulted from a meeting which Canova arranged between Flaxman and the bishop of Derry, the earl of Bristol, who ordered a large free-standing marble group for the vestibule of his Suffolk manor house, Ickworth House. The resulting statue is one of the most important and influential to be produced in the late eighteenth century, initiating passion and violence into the sculptural portrayal of antique poetry and using Hellenistic imagery as source material in a way that few since the Renaissance had dared to contemplate. *The Fury of Athamas* (1790–93; Ickworth House, Suffolk) depicts another subject from Ovid's *Metamorphoses*, a text on which Flaxman often relied, but never portrayed before on so grand a scale. The story of the maddened king of Thebes killing one of his own children became the first occasion when a neoclassical sculptor had treated the subject of homicidal lunacy and was to set a precedent for Canova's monumental group of the maddened Hercules, *Hercules and Lychas* (1795–1815; Galleria Nazionale d'Arte Moderna, Rome). While Canova's sculpture is more dynamic and contains an erotic liveliness, Flaxman's figures express a strong sense of movement, elegance, and appropriate characterization which won him great esteem among many of his contemporaries. The earl of Bristol wrote in 1792: 'Flaxman will rise to be the first sculptor in Europe, the exquisite Canova not excepted' (Symmons, 64). And, as late as 1815, the architect C. R. Cockerell was to add: 'Canova is no poet; he has no severe and elevated idea of his art, at least in comparison with Flaxman' (Bindman, 33).

Athamas is a synthetic piece, deriving partly from the *Laocoön*, and partly from the *Gaul Killing his Wife and himself* which in Flaxman's day stood in the Villa Ludovisi (now in Rome, Museo dei Terme) and which the English sculptor copied several times during his Roman period. Flaxman himself attributed the achievement of his *Athamas* to the patronage he was able to obtain in Rome: 'Who would have employed me in England to make a group 7 feet high of a man and a woman, an infant and a larger child? I never yet heard of an English sculptor being employed on such a work', he wrote enthusiastically in 1790 (Symmons, 72). His delight over the uniqueness of the *Athamas* commission turned sour when the earl of Bristol failed to pay him adequately for the materials and labour: many of the sculptor's later financial problems derived mainly from this one professional disaster. However, in seeking out new commissions to remedy his monetary problems Flaxman rose to even greater heights of originality. The personal vision he had attained through his response to the works of art studied in England and on the continent reached fruition in a series of new and quite different masterpieces which won him international fame and made him posthumously one of the most influential of all British artists, with a reputation which remained intact well into the twentieth century.

The outline illustrations and their influence The poetic elements of Flaxman's sculpture may have suggested his potential talent as an illustrator. Before leaving England for Italy the artist had considered making cycles of illustrations to Sophocles, Milton, and the fake 'primitive' poetry of Thomas Chatterton. His interest in early British history coincided with that of Blake, who painted a number of British historical subjects, both factual and imaginary. In Rome Flaxman was recorded as spending many evenings drawing illustrations to his favourite texts. These were principally British, notably subjects from Bishop Percy's *Reliques of Ancient Poetry* and illustrations to the *Pilgrim's Progress* (UCL, FM Cam., and the Huntington Collection, San Marino, California). He hoped to interest prospective buyers in his drawings, but those who were prepared to commission sets of illustrations were mainly British with a taste for the classics. Although Flaxman proposed a set of illustrations to Milton in 1792, he was actually commissioned to produce outline illustrations to Homer by Mrs Hare Naylor, who later employed Flaxman's half-sister as governess to her children, while Thomas Hope commissioned 109 illustrations to Dante's *Divine Comedy*.

Both works seem to have been produced concurrently, and, according to Flaxman's wife, who kept a record of her husband's activities, the drawings were probably started some time in April or May 1792. The style of these drawings was new in Flaxman's repertoire. His early pre-Roman drawings had been washed in with contrasts backing up a linear style of figure drawing. The illustrations to Percy and Bunyan are pure outline with little depth. Mostly the figures emerge from a few inked lines, varying in width, and are set in a shallow space, analogous to sculptural relief, rather like the decorative, small-scale figures designed for Wedgwood. The numerous preparatory sketches Flaxman made for the illustrations to Homer's *Iliad* and *Odyssey* and to Dante show the stages he went through to achieve the power of each completed illustration. One sketchbook (Flaxman sketchbook 736* F, FM Cam.) consists of drawings for Dante's *Inferno* and contains thickly outlined figures probably made with a heavily loaded brush, and a strong sense of dramatic narrative as the figures move heavily across the page. By the time the final drafts were etched by the Italian engraver Tommaso Piroli they had been considerably refined and much of the original graphic energy lost. Nevertheless the unique effect produced by these illustrations probably came from the tension and clarity of Flaxman's lines and the way they seem to stretch across the blank paper, reducing expression and action to the minimum. The images anticipate strip cartoons; Flaxman would sometimes draw a before-and-after sequence of events, and the story emerges in flat, linear clarity without secondary considerations.

Enthusiasts who first saw the outlines compared Flaxman's Homer to the text by Alexander Pope, as if the sculptor were providing a new form of translation. Others thought the simplicity of the designs was analogous to the simplicity of figures from ancient vase paintings. As a lover of silhouette and side-angles, Flaxman was loath to make his figures face the spectator, but occasionally he was forced to adapt his imagery to suit both the patrons and the engraver. Finished plates have some curious fore-shortening and widely spread frontal views which make the blank white paper seem even heavier. The discrepancy between original drawings and the final engravings was noted by Flaxman's friends and by the artist himself, who occasionally complained about the interference of his patrons. He was recorded as saying that he did not think much of his designs and would have preferred to have illustrated Milton. Nevertheless the outlines have remained among his most enduring masterpieces.

In the plates to Dante's *Inferno*, in particular, Flaxman produced his most famous poetic images, ones which haunted paintings, illustrations, and even literature of the nineteenth century. His depiction of Paolo and Francesca in the whirlwind of the lustful (*Inferno*, canto 5) shows a solid white space peopled by thin vulnerable figures caught in the cold implacable damnation. The torments of adulterers are reduced to scratched, undulating lines reminiscent of the whorls of a thumbprint, and a few matchstick strokes summon up distant figures of other doomed souls, while the poet Virgil crouches isolated on the ground attempting to revive Dante who has fainted with horror at the scene. One reason for the effectiveness of Flaxman's graphic imagery is the way traditional observations of pictorial drama have been evaded. The damned cover their faces with their hands, the horrors of hell have become blank whiteness. Later illustrators of Dante, William Blake, for example, put the same scene into a forceful design with colour washes over the outlines, but Blake like many later portrayers of Dante owed a good deal to Flaxman's strikingly original example.

The distribution of Flaxman's illustrations was at first limited. The *Odyssey* appeared between February and April 1793 and the *Iliad* and Dante's *Divine Comedy* in July of the same year. Thomas Hope kept the copyright of the Dante illustrations and there was only a small first edition and no major distribution, but pirated copies appeared and a new edition came out in Rome and Paris in 1802. In 1795, the year after he returned from Italy to England, Flaxman completed another set of illustrations, thirty-one plates to the tragedies of Aeschylus, and he also published the first English edition of the *Iliad*. At this time Flaxman was particularly close to Blake, from whom he commissioned a set of illustrations to Thomas Gray's poetry in 1797, and the sculptor's interest in poetic illustration seems to have remained strong, perhaps because the growth of foreign admirers for his graphic works far outweighed the attention he received in England where he was still regarded primarily as a sculptor. In 1805 the London publisher Longman brought out new English editions of the *Odyssey*, *Iliad*, and Aeschylus, and Flaxman added eleven new plates to the Homer illustrations and five to the Aeschylus. In 1816 Flaxman negotiated a new contract with Longman for design to Hesiod which appeared in 1817 with stipple engravings by Blake.

Critics writing in the 1790s and early 1800s were fascinated by Flaxman's bold compositional brevity, and the power of these understated images became part of a Europe-wide experiment, as artists from Philip Otto Runge in Germany to Francisco Goya in Madrid copied and adapted the designs into their own work. In Italy Flaxman's close professional acquaintance with Canova also brought him into contact with one of Napoleon's principal designers, Charles Percier. After the treaty of Amiens in 1802 Percier was one of the first French artists to welcome the British sculptor to Paris where Flaxman went in order to view the Musée Napoleon. There he met pupils and associates of the neoclassical painter Jacques Louis David—notably J. A. D. Ingres, Anne-Louis Girodet, and Alexandre Lenoir, director of the Musée des Petits Augustins. Flaxman's passion for medieval antiquities as well as for the beauties of Greek and Roman sculpture would have made him sympathetic to the aims of these Frenchmen, and he gave copies of his illustrations to these new admirers. Ingres and Girodet made numerous studies after Flaxman's work. Ingres included a portrait of the English sculptor, copied from an illustration of John Jackson's portrait of Flaxman (*c*.1819) reproduced as the frontispiece to volume 3 of Allan Cunningham's *Lives of the Eminent British Painters, Sculptors and Architects* (1830–31). He figures among the élite in the fantastic pen drawing of *Homère déifié* (in or before 1827; Musée Ingres, Montauban), which shows the greatest artists of all time gathered together in a Greek temple to pay homage to Homer. The walls of the temple are decorated with precise copies of Flaxman's illustrations to the *Iliad*. David predicted that Flaxman's unique drawing style would inspire many paintings, and famous French artists, from Géricault to Degas and Seurat, continued the tradition of making copies after Flaxman's illustrations. The Parisian periodical *L'Artiste* (6/18, 1833, 209–10) recorded that the portfolios of French art students always contained copies after the greatest masters of graphic design, notably, Dürer, Rembrandt, Goya, and Flaxman.

In Germany, too, Flaxman was acclaimed as both sculptor and illustrator. His half-sister recorded seeing copies after his sculpture being sold in Hamburg, and in Weimar she met Goethe, who told her how much he admired her brother's art. The first published analysis of the outline illustrations, however, came from the writer and critic August von Schlegel. He had been given a rare first edition of the illustrations to Dante, and he published a detailed and very flattering critique in the Jena periodical *Athenaeum* in 1799. Although Flaxman himself wrote that his intention was to transfer his illustrations into decorative reliefs for both sacred and civil architecture, there is no doubt that his major contribution to the development of European art in the century following his death occurred when the strange new drawing style which he had started to develop at an early age was engraved. The many copies of Flaxman's designs available to art students caused his style to become accessible on a vast international scale and Schlegel was to prophesy that the outline illustrations would be immortalized as the nearest artistic approximation between painting and poetry.

The post-Italian career The capturing of mood and subtlety of expression in both engraving and sculpture was always considered to be among Flaxman's major qualities as artist and designer. The funeral monuments he produced after he returned from Italy, at the end of the eighteenth and in the first decade of the nineteenth centuries, are particularly striking in this respect. Known for the delicacy of his modelling techniques Flaxman built on his primacy in plaster and terracotta sketches established early in his career. The plaster sketch for the memorial to Agnes Cromwell (1799; UCL) is one of the few surviving plaster modelli of Flaxman's career. The image is formed from a constricted series of lines, rather similar to the artist's drawing style. The connection between plaster sketches, where movement and the palpable weight of figures are heavily modelled, and the drawings which professional engravers turned into illustrations, is here particularly relevant: the hardness of the finished marble version (Chichester Cathedral) becomes a less imaginative medium similar to the linear heaviness of engraving. Flaxman's admirers occasionally lamented the deadness of the engraved line imposed on his subtle drawings just as the small modelli which he created for sculpture have a lively, animated quality lost in the final cutting and enlargement of the model. Nevertheless the shallowness of the marble relief in the Cromwell monument, together with the surge of the upward movement showing the soul of the dead girl borne to heaven, gives this type of memorial immense rhythmic harmony, an originality which was adopted later by many Victorian tomb designers. Flaxman also transformed the neoclassical convention of the draped mourning girl in designs such as the monument to Barbara Lowther (1805–7; plaster modello, UCL; completed tomb in church of St Mary Magdalene, Richmond) which forms a subtle variation on a popular theme with the girl turning her head away from the spectator, a low viewpoint, and a full figure, none of which distorts the rhythm of the composition. Flaxman's female mourners are delicately grave and exercised immense influence on nineteenth-century tomb sculpture.

Small, hunchbacked, and bald, Flaxman was completely different from the mythical image of the heroic, muscular sculptor. His appearance and retiring, rather timid manner were to make him a conscientious worker but a bad self-publicist, and as he grew older his market declined. The general opinion of his admirers was that he was too unworldly. One of his most prestigious monuments, *Admiral Howe* (1803–11; St Paul's Cathedral, London), was criticized because Flaxman got the admiral's uniform wrong, adding incorrect pantaloons and putting the ribbon of his order over the wrong shoulder. C. R. Cockerell recorded the fuss made by the British navy over the sculptor's unfortunate blunder: 'An unpardonable historical error—this arose from Flaxman's living too little in the world,' he wrote (Bindman, 33). Nevertheless the impressive quality of Flaxman's best sculpture ensured that his work was on display in all the major cathedrals, municipal buildings, and galleries throughout Britain in the nineteenth century. Among his most memorable pieces are his monument to the lord chief justice, the first

earl of Mansfield (1795–1801; Westminster Abbey, London), the monument to Lord Nelson (1808–18; St Paul's Cathedral, London), and many touching images of women, such as the monument to Lady Fitzharris (1817; Christchurch Priory, Hampshire). Flaxman was often considered to achieve more feeling in intimate reliefs; his monument to Dr Joseph Warton, headmaster of Winchester College (1804, Winchester Cathedral), and the monument to the orientalist Sir William Jones (1798; University College, Oxford; exh. RA, 1801) have great feeling and immediacy. Less happy are the memorial statues to famous British figures such as Joshua Reynolds (1803–13; St Paul's Cathedral; model exh. RA, 1807) and Robert Burns (1822; Scottish National Portrait Gallery, Edinburgh), which are stiff and lifeless. Nevertheless, even towards the end of his career Flaxman could still infuse energy and passion into poetic subjects, and his over-lifesize marble group of a subject from Milton, *Satan Overcome by St Michael* (exh. 1822; Petworth House, Sussex), has the energy of the *Athamas* and was so admired that it was made the subject of a watercolour by Turner and described by Cunningham as 'a work of the highest merit—the conception is epic' (Cunningham, 355). Nevertheless, the sculptor's final years were comparatively unsuccessful as he competed for work with the larger studios of Francis Chantrey and John Rossi, who both owed much to the stylistic innovations of the older man's art but who virtually took over his market.

The artist's later years showed him to be no less versatile, however, than he had been in his youth. The clarity of Flaxman's linear designs which gave such gracefulness to his pottery decorations also enabled him to produce memorable work for the royal gold- and silversmiths Rundell, Bridge, and Rundell. The Trafalgar vase (V&A) was commissioned in order to set up a patriotic fund for casualties and their dependants in 1805 after the battle of Trafalgar: Flaxman's decorations for this work consisted of straightforward national symbols, lion, oak leaves, Britannia, and Hercules. This design contrasted strongly with the complexity of Flaxman's reconstruction of the shield of Achilles, described in the eighteenth book of Homer's *Iliad* (design exh. RA, 1805). Made in silver gilt in 1821–2 (Royal Collection) the work demonstrates the strength of Flaxman's hard-edged pattering and lively contours. Probably one of the first European sculptors to bring this constricted, undulating style into decorative relief work on popular patriotic ornaments and memorials Flaxman achieved in silver gilt a mastery no less striking than that of his marble and line drawing.

Arguably, the greatest public appreciation of Flaxman was bestowed on the artist by the Royal Academy when he was appointed the first professor of sculpture in 1810. Having been elected an associate of the academy in 1797 and a full member in 1800 he never ceased to exhibit modelli and sculptural designs at the annual exhibitions. His lectures were widely criticized by contemporaries for their gravity and scholarly earnestness. Shortly before he died Flaxman told a visiting German admirer, Ludwig Schorn:

It was the purpose of my lectures to the Academy to show that art in Christianity can rise higher than in paganism, since Christian ideas are more sublime than pagan ones, and the best that the art of Greece and Rome has produced is, to my mind, also contained in Christian ideas … and I maintain that there are more suitable artistic subjects to be found in the Old and New testaments than in pagan mythology. (Bindman, 31)

The contents of his lectures show Flaxman to have had extensive knowledge of the history of his medium, and his interest in strange new subject matter paralleled the enthusiasms of more radical art students on the continent such as the group known as *les Primitifs* in the studio of David. Nevertheless, as a retiring man who had little commercial success in the last twenty years of his life Flaxman was wary of promoting his remarkable ideas. 'As professor of the London academy I have also given lectures on art history but I do not dare, like Fuseli, Opie and Reynolds, to appear before the public with them' (Bindman, 31). In fact, Flaxman's lectures were published posthumously in 1829 with a number of lithographic illustrations after the artist's original drawings showing primitive figures and Egyptian, antique, and Gothic sculpture. His analysis of the sculpture on the west front of Wells Cathedral demonstrates his sensitivity to earlier styles, just as his enthusiasm for the early Christian art remained with him while he was imbibing classical Renaissance influences in Italy. His friendship with W. Y. Ottley continued throughout his life: when Ottley published one of the first English studies of early Renaissance art—*A series of plates engraved after paintings and sculptures of the most eminent masters of the early Florentine school* (1826)—he dedicated it to Flaxman. In the same year, on 7 December, the sculptor died in London. He was interred, as he wished, not in St Paul's Cathedral but in St Pancras cemetery.

Flaxman's posthumous reputation Innovative as both artist and craftsman Flaxman was one of the first great European masters to devote his talents to industry and adapt his austere vision of the art of the past to the beautification of household implements, decorative commercial objects, and the embellishment of public buildings. It is ironic that his adaptability and hard work never brought him financial security. After his death his studio and effects were seized by his creditors and many of his surviving models and effects were sold off. Admirers and benefactors, including Henry Crabb-Robinson and Edwin Field, set up an endowment designed to keep Flaxman's reputation alive and conserve his surviving works, many of which were given to University College, London. Here in 1851 the Flaxman Gallery opened and was celebrated with a banquet in memory of the artist. Significantly, this was an international affair, with artists and scholars from several European countries and toasts given in three languages, commemorating the sculptor's wide influence abroad. Prince Albert was one of the patrons of the whole enterprise and was numbered among the sculptor's admirers. Although Flaxman's reputation had become somewhat obscure by the end of the nineteenth and the beginning of the twentieth century, revival of interest in neoclassicism in the 1960s and 1970s and the first comprehensive retrospective exhibition of all aspects of Flaxman's art held at the Hamburger Kunsthalle, the Thorwaldsen Museum in Copenhagen, and the Royal Academy in London in 1979 have served to re-establish Flaxman's status as arguably the most widely celebrated British sculptor before Henry Moore. Nevertheless, much of his posthumous fame still turns on the novelty and power of his illustrations and his unique drawing style, so often compared with that of his greatest colleague, Blake. In 1874 a statue of him by Henry Weekes was erected on the façade of Burlington House in London, placed alongside eight further statues of great artists, including Michelangelo, Leonardo da Vinci, and Joshua Reynolds. Portrayed leaning on a bust of Homer, Flaxman is epitomized as a scholarly dreamer, dressed in an elegant suit, pantaloons, and a long-skirted jacket. His hair is also long and plentiful, as it is in the early self-portraits, and his chin rests on his hand in a thinker's pose. Thirty years later Flaxman's place within the history of British art was signalled by his inclusion as one of only six sculptors among the British artists represented on the façade of the Victoria and Albert Museum, London.

William Flaxman (*b.* 1753?), sculptor and woodcarver, was probably born in London in 1753, eldest of three children of John Flaxman the cast maker, and elder brother of John Flaxman the sculptor and designer. His earliest recorded work, a model of a Venus, was exhibited in 1768 at the Free Society of Arts and he went on to exhibit mainly portraits at the Royal Academy in the 1770s and 1780s, including a wax portrait of his brother John in 1781. His last recorded exhibit was in 1793 and he may have inherited the parental home in the Strand after his father's death in 1795. He probably carried on his father's cast business and may also have painted miniatures. The date and place of William Flaxman's death are not known.

Mary Ann Flaxman (1768–1833), artist, was the daughter of John Flaxman sen. and his second wife, Elizabeth Gordon, whom he had married on 27 February 1763 at St Anne's, Soho, London. Mary Ann was baptized on 31 July 1768 at St Martin-in-the-Fields, Westminster. At the age of four she sat to her half-brother, John, for a portrait in wax (V&A) in which she is figured sitting in a chair, her foot balanced on a mug, holding her doll. 'It is a piece of perfect observation with delicate touches within the rendering of the hair, the ruched lace bonnet and the drapery folds of her dress' (http://npg.org.uk/live/mirrc5.asp). Mary Ann exhibited at the Free Society of Artists, the Society of Artists, and the Royal Academy between 1786 and 1819. She showed miniature portraits and genre pictures including *Ferdinand and Matilda Playing Chess* (1819) and *Maternal Piety* (1819), and also drawings and designs; many of these were illustrations to poems. She also executed portraits in wax. For several years she lived as a governess with the Hare Naylor family, first in Italy and afterwards in Weimar. From 1810 she lived with John Flaxman and his wife in

Buckingham Street until the sculptor's death in 1826. Sidney Colvin noted that 'Her work in art was strongly influenced by his example, and shows both talent and feeling. She is best known by the six designs for [William] Hayley's *Triumphs of temper*', engraved by Blake, and published in 1803 (*DNB*). Mary Ann Flaxman died on 17 April 1833. Her obituary in the *Liverpool Mercury* (26 April 1833) stated that 'she was sister to the late eminent sculptor, and allied to him not more nearly by blood but by congeniality of character'. A miniature portrait attributed to Mary Ann as a self-portrait (*c*.1820; NPG) shows her aged about fifty in a white, lace-edged mob cap, ruff collar, and pale blue shawl over a purple dress. Her calm expression is described in the gallery's catalogue as 'smiling' (Walker, 1.189).

SARAH SYMMONS

Sources D. Bindman, ed., *John Flaxman R. A.* (1979) [exhibition catalogue, Royal Academy] · S. Symmons, *Flaxman and Europe: the outline illustrations and their influence* (1984) · D. Irwin, *John Flaxman, 1755–1826, sculptor, illustrator and designer* (1979) · R. R. Wark, *Drawings by John Flaxman in the Huntington Collection* (1970) · J. Flaxman, *Lectures on sculpture ... as delivered before the president and members of the Royal Academy, with a brief memoir of the author*, 2nd edn (1838) · A. Cunningham, *Lives of the most eminent British painters, sculptors and architects*, 2nd edn, 6 vols., 3 (1830–31) · J. T. Smith, *Nollekens and his times*, 2 vols. (1828) · N. Penny, *Church monuments in Romantic England* (1977) · freepages.genealogyrootsweb.com [*Liverpool Mercury* (26 April 1833)], 28 Oct 2002 [Mary Ann Flaxman] · *IGI* [Mary Ann Flaxman] · *DNB* [Mary Ann Flaxman] · E. Rideal, *Mirror, mirror: self-portraits by women artists* (2001) [exhibition catalogue, NPG, 24 Oct 2001 – 24 Feb 2002] · R. Walker, *National Portrait Gallery: Regency portraits*, 2 vols. (1985) · D. Foskett, *Miniatures: dictionary and guide* (1987) · www.npg.org.uk/live/mirrc5.asp, 28 Oct 2002 [Mary Ann Flaxman] · will, PRO, PROB 11/1720, sig. 17

Archives American School of Classical Studies, Athens, Gennadius Library, corresp. · Assay Office, Birmingham, corresp. · BL, corresp., Add. MSS 36652I 32491A, 37538B, 36540, fol. 50, 37309, fol. 220 · BL, sketches for casts of his monuments, Add. MS 39840 · BL, corresp., Add. MSS 36652, 39780–39792 · BL, notes on the history of sculpture, Add. MS 39790, fols. 104–b112 · BL, business books, Flaxman and executors, Add. MSS 39784A-CC · Bodl. Oxf., corresp., MSS Autog. D. 11 · Col. U., account book, special collection, D. 430 394-F. 61 · FM Cam., corresp. and literary papers · FM Cam., notebook 832/5 · FM Cam., notes and sketchbook, notebook 832/7 · FM Cam., notes on the decoration of St Paul's and other churches, and on classical architecture · FM Cam., MSS, journal in Italy (Florence and Rome) · Harvard U., corresp. · Hunt. L., corresp. · JRL, corresp., English MS 341 · Maine Historical Society, Portland, corresp. · Morgan L., corresp. · Museo Civico, Bassano, corresp., MS 5899-XII-1192 · NL Scot., corresp., MS 587, no. 1150; MS 590, no. 1742A; MS 685, fol. 20; MS 4947, fols. 114–16; MS 9819, fol. 104 · NYPL, corresp. · Swedenborg Society, London, corresp. · U. Edin., corresp., Laing, II, 641 and 426/170 · UCL, journal in Naples, notebook with lecture notes · UCL, notebook, drawings, and collection of plaster casts · UCL, journal and commonplace book · Yale U., corresp. · Yale U. CBA, Italian notebook | Art Institute of Chicago, L. H. Gurley collection, corresp., Mrs Flaxman · BL, address to the president of the Royal Academy, Add. MS 33610S · BL, corresp., Mrs Flaxman, Add. MS 39782 · BL, journal in Italy, Mrs Flaxman, Add. MS 39787 · BL, journal in Italy, Mrs Flaxman, Add. MS 39790, fols. 147 ff. · BL, journal in Italy, Mrs Flaxman, Add. MS 39792A · BL, journal on the way to Rome, Add. MS 39786 · Cornwall RO, letters to John Hawkins · DWL, corresp. relating to H. Crabb-Robinson · DWL, Henry Crabb-Robinson diaries [typescript and manuscript] · DWL, Flaxman Gallery MSS · Glos. RO, corresp. with Sir Rowland Winn · Keele University, Wedgwood Archive, corresp. and receipts, MSS 1330.2–1342.2 · Keele University, Wedgwood Archive, corresp. and receipts, MSS 30186-2–

30197-2 · Keele University, Wedgwood Archive, corresp. and receipts, MSS L. 204-1–L. 216-1 · Keele University, Wedgwood Archive, corresp., receipts, and lists, MSS L. 26272-I–L. 26273-1 · Keele University, Wedgwood Archive, Mosley collection, corresp. · Morgan L., corresp., Mrs Flaxman · RIBA, C. R. Cockerell diaries, drawings collection

Likenesses J. Flaxman, self-portrait, Wedgwood medallion, 1771, Birmingham Museums and Art Gallery · J. Flaxman, self-portrait, pen and wash drawing, 1778–9, Earls High School, Halesowen, Worcestershire · J. Flaxman, self-portrait, terracotta relief, 1778–9, V&A · J. Flaxman, self-portrait, pen, ink, and watercolour drawing, 1779, UCL · J. Flaxman, self-portrait, plaster relief, 1779, BM · W. M. Ottley, watercolour, *c*.1790, BM · J. Flaxman, self-portrait, plaster medallion, *c*.1790–1795, NPG · G. Head, oils, 1792, NPG · G. Romney, oils, 1795, NPG [*see illus.*] · G. Romney, oils, *c*.1795–1796, Yale U. CBA · G. Dance, drawing, 1796, RA · H. Howard, oils, *c*.1797, NPG · T. Cooley, pencil drawing, 1810, NPG · W. H. Lizars, pencil drawing, 1815, Scot. NPG · D. D'Angers, bronze medallion, *c*.1816, Musée des Beaux Arts, Angers, France · J. Jackson, oils, *c*.1819 · attrib. M. A. Flaxman, miniature, watercolour on ivory, *c*.1820 (Mary Ann Flaxman), NPG · W. Brockedon, chalk drawing, *c*.1824, Scot. NPG · J. Atkinson, watercolour drawing, 1826, NPG · E. H. Baily, marble bust, 1826, RA · J. A. D. Ingres, pen-and-pencil drawing, in or before 1827 (*Homère déifié*), Musée Ingres, Montauban · W. Brockedon, pencil and chalk drawing, 1830–38, NPG · H. Weekes, marble facade, 1873–4, Burlington House, London · J. Flaxman, self-portrait, plaster medallion, Royal Scot. Acad., Edinburgh · J. Flaxman, wax portrait (aged four; Mary Ann Flaxman), V&A · O. Humphry, crayon drawing, Walker Art Gallery, Liverpool · J. Jackson, oils, Althorp, Northamptonshire · W. M. Ottley, pen and wash drawing, BM · C. C. Vogel, drawing, Staatliche Kunstsammlungen, Dresden, Germany · H. Weekes, statue, Tate collection · engraving, repro. in Cunningham, *Lives*, frontispiece · oils, City Art Gallery, York

Wealth at death £1657 2s. 4d.—incl. studio contents: 30 Jan 1820, Symmons, *Flaxman and Europe*, 195; will, PRO, PROB 11/1720, sig. 17

Flaxman, Mary Ann (1768–1833). *See under* Flaxman, John (1755–1826).

Flaxman, William (*b*. 1753?). *See under* Flaxman, John (1755–1826).

Fleay, Frederick Gard (1831–1909), literary scholar, was born at Deptford Broadway, London, on 5 September 1831, the son of John Goss Fleay, linen draper, and his wife, Jane. Both parents were of Somerset families. Of their seven children, three—two sons and a daughter—alone lived to maturity.

According to family tradition, Frederick was able to read at twenty months old. At King's College School, which he entered in 1843 and where Frederic Harrison was one of his companions, he rose to be captain, distinguishing himself alike in classics and mathematics. In October 1849 he was admitted as a pensioner to Trinity College, Cambridge, his parents accompanying him in order to provide him with a home in the town. In his second year at Trinity he won an open mathematical scholarship, and after gaining several college prizes, graduated BA in 1853 as thirteenth wrangler, and sixth in the second class in the classical tripos. He was also placed third in the examination for Smith's prizes, and impressed the examiners with his aptitude for higher mathematics. The following year he obtained second place in the first class of the moral science tripos, and first place in the second class in the natural science tripos. Undergraduates dubbed him 'the industrious flea'. Despite the rare distinction of figuring in four tripos lists, Fleay just missed a fellowship at Trinity. He proceeded MA in 1856, and was ordained deacon, at Oxford, in that year and priest in 1857. On 14 January 1869 he married Mary Ann Kite who predeceased him in 1896.

Adopting a scholastic career, Fleay was from 1856 to 1859 vice-principal of the Oxford Diocesan Training College at Culham near Abingdon. From 1859 to 1865 he was second master and head of the scientific side at Leeds grammar school. After six months in 1865 as second master and head of the modern division at King Edward's School, Birmingham, he was headmaster of Hipperholme grammar school from 1868 to 1872, and filled a similar post at Skipton in Craven grammar school from 1872 to 1876. He had hoped to obtain a university position, but failing to do so he abandoned the teaching profession. He subsequently resided at Avondale Square, Old Kent Road, London. Although his teaching had been mainly devoted to mathematics and science, he was an efficient instructor in both classics and English and interested himself in educational theory. He wrote several pedagogical works including *Elements of English Grammar: Relations of Words to Sentences* (*Word Building*) (1859, 2 parts), *Hints on Teaching* (1874), and *Logical English Grammar* (1884).

Fleay also issued, while a schoolmaster, *The Book of Revelation* (1864), a collection of orthodox sermons. But his independent and speculative habit of mind gradually alienated him from the Church of England, and on 7 February 1884 he relinquished his orders. He had studied sympathetically Comte's philosophy without accepting the positivist religion. *Three Lectures on Education*, which show Comte's influence, were read at Newton Hall in November 1882, and published with a preface by Frederic Harrison in 1883. Fleay demonstrated his love of more recondite speculation in 1889 by privately circulating a highly complex mathematical study: *Harmonics of Sound and Colour: their Law Identical, their Use Convertible.*

Meanwhile Fleay was devoting himself to literary work. From an early date he had interested himself in phonetics and in spelling reform. In 1858 he won the Trevelyan prize for an essay on phonetic spelling, which convinced one of the examiners, Max Müller, of his philological promise. In 1878 his *English Sounds and English Spelling* was published, and in 1879 he joined the newly formed Spelling Reform Association and edited its journal, the *Spelling Reformer* (1880–81). He devised two alphabets, the 'Victorian form' for educational purposes, and the 'Elizabethan form' for literary purposes.

In 1874 Fleay joined the New Shakspere Society on its foundation by Frederick James Furnivall, and he applied much of his manifold industry for some twenty years to the elucidation of Shakespearian and Elizabethan drama. He contributed many papers to the *Transactions of the New Shakspere Society*, but resigned from the society's committee in July 1874 after a sharp disagreement with Furnivall over the validity of Fleay's use of a rhyme test in determining the chronology of Shakespeare's works. Undeterred he continued his investigations. His Shakespearian books began with an *Introduction to Shakespeare Study* (1877). There

followed his *Shakespeare Manual* (1878), with a few editions of Elizabethan plays, as well as two pamphlets, *Actor Lists, 1578–1642* (1881) and *History of Theatres in London* (1882). All these efforts were preliminary to his three imposing compilations: *A Chronicle History of the Life and Work of William Shakespeare* (1886), *A Chronicle History of the London Stage, 1559–1642* (1890), and *A Biographical Chronicle of the English Drama, 1559–1642* (2 vols., 1891).

Fleay's scholarship was Germanic in its mechanistic and quantitative methodology, which bordered on the statistical. He analysed with minuteness the changes in Shakespeare's metre and phraseology, and rigidly applied metrical and linguistic tests to a determination not only of the chronology of Shakespeare's and his fellow playwrights' acknowledged work but of the authorship of anonymous plays of the era. His arbitrary identifications of the writers of the anonymous Elizabeth drama were often startling and highly controversial. In 1874 in a letter to Furnivall, Tennyson reacted to Fleay's assertion that a part of *Timon of Athens* was not Shakespeare's: 'I have no doubt that in spite of all the Fleas in England the page you speak of is Shakespeare' (Benzie, 190). Fleay was no less dogmatic in his alleged detection of concealed topical or political allusions in text, plot, and character. And yet at the same time the immense care with which he traced the history of the playing companies in the Shakespearian period threw much new light on English dramatic and theatrical history.

From Shakespearian and Elizabethan themes Fleay finally turned to Egyptology and Assyriology, chiefly in their bearing on biblical criticism. His main results were collected in *Egyptian Chronology* (1899), dedicated to the memory of Edward White Benson. His final enquiry concerned the great pyramid, on which he published a paper in 1905.

Fleay died at his home, 27 Dafforne Road, Upper Tooting, London, on 10 March 1909, and was buried at Brookwood cemetery, Woking. His only child, John, survived him. Fleay's contributions to Shakespearian studies are in two distinct areas. His compilations on the history of Shakespeare's life and the theatre in London from 1559 to 1642 were major works that have formed a foundation for subsequent scholarship. His mechanistic and quantitative analyses of metre and phrase opened up new methodological approaches to the study of literature which have been more successfully employed in the late twentieth century through the use of computer technologies, but his questionable conclusions derived from these techniques diminished both the reception of his other works and his overall reputation.

SIDNEY LEE, *rev.* RICHARD W. CLEMENT

Sources A. Y. Stavisky, *Shakespeare and the Victorians* (1969) • W. Benzie, *Dr F. J. Furnivall: Victorian scholar adventurer* (1983) • Venn, *Alum. Cant.*, 2/2.517 • A. W. Ward, 'Frederick Gard Fleay', *The Athenaeum* (27 March 1909), 375–6 • F. Harrison, *Autobiographic memoirs*, 2 vols. (1911) • *The Observer* (11 March 1909)

Wealth at death £9850 19s. 7d.: resworn probate, 3 May 1909, *CGPLA Eng. & Wales*

Fleck, Alexander, Baron Fleck (1889–1968), chemist and industrialist, was born in Glasgow on 11 November 1889, the only son of Robert Fleck, coal merchant, and his wife, Agnes Hendry, daughter of James Duncan, coal clerk. He was educated at Saltcoats public school and Hillhead high school, but family circumstances compelled him to leave at the age of fourteen. By then, however, his heart was set on a scientific career and, undaunted by practical difficulties, he set about achieving his ambition in the only way open to him, by entering Glasgow University as a laboratory assistant. His keenness to learn brought him to the notice of Frederick Soddy. By attending the university, first at evening classes and then as a full-time student, he gained an honours degree in chemistry in 1911 at the age of twenty-two. Later, in 1916, he was awarded a DSc for a thesis entitled 'Some chapters on the chemistry of the radio elements'. In 1911 Fleck joined the university's teaching staff under Soddy, continuing his work on the chemistry of the radioactive elements, his findings contributing to the later conception of isotopes. Much later, he contributed the notice of Soddy (in addition to that of Sir W. A. Akers) to the *Dictionary of National Biography*. In 1913 he joined the staff of the Glasgow and West Scotland Radium Committee with his own laboratory for radiological work related to medicine. This kept him in touch with Soddy and he seemed set for an academic career.

The First World War changed Fleck's plans. In 1917 he went to Wallsend as chief chemist to the Castner Kellner Alkali Company, which was associated with Brunner, Mond & Co., and which manufactured a range of chemicals for wartime industry. The same year he married Isabel Mitchell (*d*. 1955), daughter of Alexander Kelly, a farmer. There were no children of the marriage. Fleck soon made his presence felt at Castner, both as an individual and as a chemist, and in 1919 he became works manager. With insatiable curiosity, he believed in seeing and trying for himself. A dispute about working conditions with the process men on the sodium plant gave an excellent example of this: the work was hot and arduous but Fleck spent a week on shifts doing the job to find out what was entailed. This won him the respect of the workmen.

The formation of Imperial Chemical Industries (ICI) in 1926, incorporating Brunner, Mond with Nobel Industries, the United Alkali Company, and British Dyestuffs Corporation, had a significant effect on Fleck's career, for it gave his talents wider scope. One result of the merger was to concentrate the activities of the Wallsend works, the Allhusen works at Gateshead, and the Cassel Cyanide works at Maryhill, Glasgow, on one new site at Billingham. This was later called the Cassel works and became one of the principal factories of ICI's General Chemicals Division. Fleck was transferred to Billingham with responsibilities for the planning and operation of the new works. Although there were many technical difficulties, the human problems were greater, for families had to be moved from Glasgow and Tyneside. The fact that most of those who were transferred settled happily, with no wish to return home, was clear evidence of Fleck's success in dealing with human problems.

Alexander Fleck, Baron Fleck (1889–1968), by Sir Lawrence Gowing, 1957

In 1931, following the reorganization of ICI, Fleck was appointed managing director of the General Chemicals Division with its headquarters in Liverpool. He returned to Teesside as chairman of the Billingham division in 1937; Billingham was by then one of the world's great centres of chemical manufacture. This was an important target during the Second World War and attracted well over a hundred high-explosive bombs. Fleck's daily meetings with his directors and works managers were an inspiration to all to keep the factory in operation, whatever the difficulties. In 1944 he was appointed to the ICI board but did not relinquish his highly successful chairmanship of the Billingham division until the war ended. As an ICI director, his other main responsibilities were Central Agricultural Control—the company's organization for marketing agricultural products—and the development of the new Wilton site on Teesside. He was chairman of Scottish Agricultural Industries from 1947 to 1951. He was appointed a deputy chairman of ICI in 1951 and, two years later, at the age of sixty-three, he was elected chairman, a post which he held until his retirement in 1960. During this period there were great advances in the manufacture of synthetic organic materials such as nylon and polythene.

In this high office Fleck remained unspoilt, always courteous and approachable, with a fine sense of humour and an engaging sense of the ridiculous. Wherever he went in the company—and he travelled widely—he was respected for his scientific acumen, his quietly firm leadership, but, above all, for his deep interest in people. He was always a great source of encouragement to the company's younger members, and liked to hear their views so that his own did not become outdated. Thus, as ICI's chairman, he was no distant figurehead; rather, he was looked upon as the wise father of a very large family. He was best in this role at the twice-yearly meetings of ICI's central council, when he presided over a gathering of some 500 representatives of the employees with a firmness moderated by geniality and understanding. He also initiated the practice of giving a full account of the company's fortunes in his opening addresses. The one cloud over this happy period of office was the death of his wife in 1955.

Despite Fleck's preoccupation with ICI he achieved much elsewhere. He was chairman from 1953 to 1955 of the Coal Board Organization Committee appointed by the minister for power; from 1957 to 1958 of the prime minister's committee on the Windscale accident (in which, it appeared, radioactive material had been released to the public danger); and from 1958 to 1965 of the Advisory Council on Scientific Research and Development. He chaired a government committee on the fishing industry which reported in 1961. In 1958 he was president of the British Association for the Advancement of Science—appropriately, the annual meeting was held in Glasgow, where Fleck unveiled a plaque commemorating the work of Soddy.

During Fleck's chairmanship of ICI his ties with the university world were re-established. Honorary degrees were conferred on him by several universities—LLD by Glasgow, and DSc by Durham (1953), Nottingham (1953), Oxford (1956), London (1957), and Trinity College, Dublin (1958). He was elected a fellow of the Royal Society in 1955, becoming treasurer and vice-president in 1960. He was elected an honorary fellow of the Royal Society of Edinburgh and of the Manchester College of Science and Technology in 1957. One of his most treasured honours was to be made a freeman of Saltcoats, his boyhood home.

Characteristically, Fleck marked his retirement by establishing four awards to be given to young people in ICI who showed promise. From 1960 to 1962 he was president of the Society of Chemical Industry, and he retained his directorship of the Midland Bank, to which he had been appointed in 1955. From 1960 to 1965 he was chairman of the nuclear safety advisory committee. In 1963 he became chairman of the International Research and Development Company and president of the Royal Institution. During Fleck's presidency Sir Lawrence Bragg, a Nobel laureate, retired from his post as the Royal Institution's director and Fleck was influential in securing Professor George Porter to succeed him. Fleck was awarded the Castner medal in 1947 and the Messel medal of the Society of Chemical Industry in 1956.

To the recognition Fleck gained in industry and in the academic world were added other high honours. He was appointed KBE in 1955—for services to the Ministry of Fuel and Power—and was created a baron in 1961. Fleck died on 6 August 1968 in Westminster Hospital, London.

C. M. WRIGHT, rev. FRANK GREENAWAY

Sources *Memoirs FRS*, 17 (1971), 243–51 · *The Times* (7 Aug 1968) · *Chemistry in Britain*, 4 (1968), 451 · *New Scientist* (22 Aug 1967), 20–22 [interview report] · *Daily Telegraph* (7 Aug 1968) · *WW* (1968) · d. cert.

Likenesses H. Coster, photographs, 1944–56, NPG · L. Gowing, oils, 1957, NPG [*see illus.*] · E. Halliday, portrait, 1960, Imperial Chemical House, 9 Millbank, London SW1 · W. Bird, photograph, 1964, NPG · W. Bird, photograph, repro. in *Memoirs FRS*, 242

Wealth at death £277,891: probate, 16 Oct 1968, *CGPLA Eng. & Wales*

Flecker, (Herman) James Elroy (1884–1915), poet and playwright, was born at Lewisham, London, on 5 November 1884. He was the elder son of the Revd William Herman Flecker DD (*b.* 1859), sometime headmaster of Dean Close School, Cheltenham, and his wife, Sarah Ducat. Both of his parents were of Jewish descent. He was educated first at Dean Close School; in January 1901 he went to Uppingham School, and in October 1902 to Trinity College, Oxford, on a classical scholarship. His time at Oxford was largely spent in writing poetry and in making some lasting friendships. He received a third-class degree in his BA examinations in 1906, which marked the beginning of considerable tension in his relationship with his parents, on whom he remained financially dependent until his death. In 1907 he went to London and taught in a school in Hampstead. His first book of verse, *The Bridge of Fire*, appeared in that year.

In 1908 Flecker resolved to enter the consular service. After passing the examination he went to Cambridge for the two-year special training at Gonville and Caius College, and studied oriental languages. In June 1910 he was sent to Constantinople, but in September a slight fever was diagnosed as tuberculosis and he returned to England to a sanatorium. He pronounced himself cured and spent his time writing or with Hélle Skiadaressi, whom he married on 25 May 1911 (an earlier engagement to Eleanor Finlayson having been broken in 1910). Skiadaressi came to provide a valuable stimulus and criticism for his poetry. He went back to Constantinople in March 1911, to be transferred in April to Beirut. Flecker was not a very efficient vice-consul, and was never altogether happy in the East, being increasingly anxious to obtain employment in England where he would not be cut off from the literary world. During this period his second book, *Thirty-Six Poems* (1910), was published; it was expanded to *Forty-Two Poems* in 1911.

Flecker's worsening state of health made it necessary, in May 1913, for him to move to Switzerland, where he spent the last twenty months of his life. Despite his illness, and increasing financial pressures, this period was very productive. He completed perhaps his best-known book of poetry, *The Golden Journey to Samarkand* (1913), in the preface to which he outlined his ideal of poetry which combined a disavowal of didactic purpose with the intention of expressing beauty with deliberate artistry. Flecker believed that a poet needed a definite theory to guide him in self-criticism, and he claimed to be a disciple of the French Parnassian school, which was, he wrote, 'a classical reaction against ... sentimentality and extravagance'. The characteristics of the Parnassians he understood to be a determination first and foremost 'to create beauty, a beauty somewhat statuesque, dramatic, and

Archives Bodl. Oxf., letters · Harvard U., Houghton L., letters · Ransom HRC, letters
Likenesses T. E. Lawrence, photograph, 1912, priv. coll. [*see illus.*]
Wealth at death under £30: administration, 26 Feb 1915, *CGPLA Eng. & Wales*

(Herman) James Elroy Flecker (1884–1915), by T. E. Lawrence, 1912

objective, rather than intimate'. It was sheer beauty and not 'the message' of poetry which mattered.

It was at this time that Flecker also wrote the poems which were posthumously published as *The Old Ships* (1915), and completed his novel, *The King of Alsander* (1914). He wrote his two plays, *Hassan* (published in 1922) and *Don Juan* (published in 1925), which mark the brief revival of poetic drama in English, and most vividly illustrate the influence of the Near East in Flecker's work. *Hassan* was performed to considerable critical acclaim in 1923, running for 281 performances to packed houses. However, Flecker's dramatic works were, like his poetry, radically divergent from contemporary trends. He died in Hans Baratelli Platz, Davos, Switzerland, on 3 January 1915 and was interred at Cheltenham after a first burial in the crypt of the Anglican church at Davos. His *Collected Poems*, edited by J. C. Squire, was published in 1916, and his *Collected Prose* followed in 1920.   SAYONI BASU

Sources J. Sherwood, *No golden journey* (1973) · S. Parry, introduction, in J. E. Flecker, *Poems: a new selection*, ed. S. Parry (1980) · *The Times* (6 Jan 1915) · J. C. Squire, 'Introduction', in J. E. Flecker, *The collected poems of James Elroy Flecker*, ed. J. C. Squire (1916) · G. Hodgson, *The life of James Elroy Flecker* (1925) · D. Goldring, *James Elroy Flecker: an appreciation with some biographical notes* (1922) · *Letters of J. E. Flecker to Frank Savery*, ed. F. Savery (1926) · C. E. Bosworth, 'James Elroy Flecker: poet, diplomatist, orientalist', *BJRL*, 69 (1987), 359–78 · J. M. Munro, *James Elroy Flecker* (1976) · DNB · *CGPLA Eng. & Wales* (1915)

Flecknoe, Richard (*b. c.*1605, *d.* in or after 1677), poet and playwright, is of unknown birth and parentage. Alexander Pope, in a note to *The Dunciad* (2.2), called him 'an Irish priest', but this is a misreading of Dryden's satirical reference in *Mac Flecknoe* to Shadwell as an Irish bard, and there is no evidence of an Irish origin for Flecknoe. On the contrary, Marvell (who met him) described him as 'an English priest', and the surname is found in Northamptonshire. Mayer (Mayer, cliii–cliv) suggests Little Harrowden, Northamptonshire, as a likely birthplace. Presumably Flecknoe came from a Roman Catholic family, for he appears to have attended the English College at St Omer, where his first book was published in 1626, a collection of pious verse called *Hierothalamium, or, The Heavenly Nuptialls of our Saviour*. It is this publication which provides an approximate date for his birth. It was probably on leaving the college that he was ordained to the secular priesthood.

Thereafter Flecknoe seems to have spent some time in fashionable circles in London, no doubt exercising his vocation, and published *The Affections of a Pious Soule unto our Saviour-Christ* in 1640. But as times became more unsettled, particularly for someone of Flecknoe's profession, he left for Flanders and the period of wandering which he would later describe in *A Relation of Ten Years Travells* (*c.*1656). His sojourn on the continent was passed in various aristocratic households (notably that of the duchess of Lorraine), where he was appreciated for his skill as a lutenist and as a maker of complimentary verses and witty entertainments. It was partly to avoid the war which was devastating Flanders, and partly to conduct a mission for the duchess, that Flecknoe travelled to Rome in 1644, where Marvell met him and wrote a satirical poem on his poor lodgings and emaciated appearance. Other journeys followed: to Lisbon, where he was arrested as a spy, but managed to prove his bona fides by displaying his skills on the lute to the king; to Rio de Janeiro; and finally back to England about 1653.

From this point on, the details of Flecknoe's life are elusive, but he evidently devoted considerable time to the composition of poems and plays, many of which were privately printed. The publication of *The Idea of his Highness Oliver* and the allegorical masque *The Marriage of Oceanus and Brittania*, both in 1659, seems to have made little impact. A collection of *Enigmatical Characters* in prose appeared in 1658, and a volume of verse *Epigrams*, modelled partly on Jonson, in 1669; both were repeatedly revised and reissued under varying titles, as were other volumes of miscellaneous trivia; but the continual republication of Flecknoe's work seems to have been prompted rather by the author's self-esteem than by public demand. His ventures into drama (under the patronage of the duke and duchess of Newcastle) achieved more attention, but not more success. *Loves Dominion*, 'Written as a Pattern for the Reformed Stage', was printed in 1654, and the tragicomedy *Erminia* in 1661; neither had been performed, and the preface to the latter criticized actors for the liberties which they took with a playwright's texts. When *Loves Dominion* was produced by Davenant and the Duke's Company in 1664 in a revised form as *Love's Kingdom*, 'it had the misfortune to be damn'd by the Audience' (Langbaine, 202). Republishing the play in the same year, Flecknoe blamed incompetent actors and an ignorant audience for its failure, and attached *A Short Discourse of the English Stage* which disparaged the elaborate sets and special effects which Davenant favoured. The *Discourse* is, however, important for a pioneering discussion of the relative strengths of Shakespeare, Jonson, Beaumont, and Fletcher in terms which anticipate Dryden's more influential criticism.

Flecknoe took revenge on Davenant after the laureate's death in *Sr William D'avenant's voyage to the other world: with his adventures in the poets Elizium* (1668). Nor were his relations happier with the other leading entrepreneur of the Restoration theatre, Thomas Killigrew, who turned down Flecknoe's play *Damoiselles à la mode*, causing Flecknoe to satirize him in *The Life of Tomaso the Wanderer* (1667). When Killigrew changed his mind, and staged the play in 1668, it was a failure: Pepys noted that it was 'so mean a thing, as when they came to say it would be acted again tomorrow, both he that said it … and the pit fell a-laughing—there being this day not a quarter of the pit full' (Pepys, 15 Sept 1668).

Flecknoe's death has usually been assigned to 1678, on the basis of two allusions by Dryden. However, the obscure reference in the 'Dedication' to Dryden's *The Kind Keeper* to 'a worse Poet remaining in the world than he of scandalous memory who left it last', while occurring in the same sentence as a reference to Flecknoe, may not refer to him; and while the play was staged in 1678, the 'Dedication' was not written until autumn 1679. Second, *Mac Flecknoe*, which casts Shadwell as Flecknoe's heir, was printed in 1682 but written and circulated in manuscript in 1676, and represents Flecknoe's retirement, not his death. Nevertheless, Flecknoe's last published work, *Seventy Eight Characters*, appeared in 1677, so one can assume that he died not long afterwards.

Flecknoe's true milieu seems to have been the world of aristocratic family entertainments; his ventures into the public domain—whether through incessant vanity publication or ill-judged drama—brought ridicule and a reputation as the archetypally bad poet. As Langbaine said, 'His Acquaintance with the Nobility, was more than with the Muses; and he had a greater propensity to Riming, than a Genius to Poetry' (Langbaine, 199). His apotheosis in *Mac Flecknoe* as the king who

> In Prose and Verse, was own'd, without dispute,
> Through all the realms of *Non-sense*, absolute;

may have been unkind, but not unjustified.

PAUL HAMMOND

Sources F. Mayer, ed., *The prose characters of Richard Flecknoe: a critical edition* (1987) · R. Flecknoe, *A relation of ten years travells* (c.1656) · 'Mac Flecknoe', *The poems of John Dryden*, ed. J. Kinsley, 1 (1958), 265–71 · G. Langbaine, *An account of the English dramatick poets* (1691) · Pepys, *Diary* · *The poems and letters of Andrew Marvell*, ed. H. Margoliouth, rev. P. Legouis, 3rd edn, 2 vols. (1971)

Fleet, Sir John (1647?–1712), sugar merchant and governor of the East India Company, was baptized on 18 March 1648, the son of Richard Fleet, innkeeper of Bourton, Buckinghamshire. He was apprenticed to a member of the London Coopers' Company in 1659 and became a freeman in 1667. On 20 June 1674 he married Elizabeth Arnold of St Andrew's, Holborn. After having set up as a sugar refiner, Fleet quickly became a highly successful London sugar importer during the Restoration heyday of West Indian sugar production. In one three-month period in 1681 he imported some 3000 hundredweight of brown sugar from Barbados, Nevis, and St Kitts. Fleet resided at Mark Lane, in Tower ward: he owned shipping and eventually possessed extensive warehouse and dockyard property. During his period of capital acquisition he remained aloof from civic and national affairs, despite the critical issues of the decade from 1678 to 1688. He declined offices and responsibilities in the Coopers' Company, for instance, and although he was elected to the Coopers' court of assistants in 1685, he was subsequently fined for non-attendance.

When James II restored the charter of the corporation of London in October 1688 Fleet achieved civic prominence, again somewhat against his own desire. He was chosen as one of the sheriffs for London and Middlesex at the common hall of 11 October 1688. Not permitted to fine for the office, Fleet was instead immediately knighted by James. He was also chosen as alderman by the householders of Langbourn ward and he sat on the court of aldermen for the next twenty-five years. Although he was new to office Fleet was nevertheless one of the principal magistrates of London during the revolutionary events of 1688–9. As sheriff he sought to restrain popular disturbances during the confrontation between James II and William of Orange. After James's flight Fleet joined other London aldermen and MPs from the Exclusion Parliaments in requesting William to assume the government until the meeting of the Convention Parliament. Yet Fleet was neither a revolutionary nor a militant whig. He had not been involved in the intense partisanship of the early 1680s, and he remained aloof from its renewal in the aftermath of the revolution of 1688. He co-operated with the London whigs during the establishment of their ascendancy in the city, but he sought to remain above the party fray until the financial and commercial implications of the revolution became clear.

Fleet was added to the London lieutenancy commission in March 1689, when that body was reconstructed in favour of the whigs. He remained a member of the civic lieutenancy for the next twenty years, eventually commanding one of the six militia regiments. He was a major contributor to the civic loans of 1689–90 and he sat on a corporation committee to advance them. He was one of the captains of a volunteer regiment of horse raised in the city in 1689, and in 1690 he also served on a city committee that raised a troop of horse for William III's Irish campaign. He served as master of the Coopers' Company in

1689–90. Fleet was one of two aldermen advanced by the whigs for the mayoralty in 1691 and he became lord mayor a year later, after the tory mayoral candidates were publicly denounced for their co-operation with Charles II. Transferring to the Grocers' Company as lord mayor, Fleet was then elected master. In March 1693 he prevailed in a poll over another whig alderman to replace a deceased city MP.

By the time of his mayoralty Fleet appears to have been withdrawing from active trade in favour of joint-stock investment. By April 1693 he had acquired £1100 of Royal African Company stock. He was chosen for the court of assistants of that company in 1693–4. He then became Royal African Company sub-governor in 1697–8 and he served again on the court of assistants in 1699–1702 and in 1704. In 1692 Fleet also joined the governing court of committees of the East India Company, and between April 1693 and April 1694 he tripled his shareholdings to about £13,000, thereby emerging as one of the company's principal stockholders. These investments also placed him in the company of such major civic tory leaders as Sir Thomas Cooke, Sir Samuel Dashwood, and Sir William Gore, whom Fleet unsuccessfully recommended for the London shrievalty during his mayoralty. Fleet succeeded Cooke as governor of the East India Company in 1694. He held that position in 1694–6, 1698–1700, 1702–4, and 1706–8; he also served on the court of committees for all other years between 1697 and 1709.

Fleet first became governor of the East India Company at a crucial time in its history. The company's critics, some of whom had been driven from the court of committees in the early 1680s, claimed that its capitalization was too small and that its monopoly had been utilized for the enrichment of a dominant clique of investors, Sir Josiah Child chief among them. Attacks within and without parliament had been staged by a syndicate of potential investors who sought either entry into the company on favourable terms or the creation of a new company. Although the company had secured a new royal charter in 1693, it had been forced to agree to future royal regulations and to an enlargement of its capital. As Fleet assumed leadership of the company its new charter was under attack in the House of Commons, which voted against the company's monopoly, and the company awaited the regulations that had been mandated the year before. In late summer 1694 Charles Talbot, duke of Shrewsbury and whig secretary of state, expressed disappointment about Fleet's reluctance to accept a delay in the issuance of new regulations during the king's absence on the continent. Fleet reportedly claimed that further negotiations about regulations for the company would 'be a great blow to their reputation' and that 'all people will be disheartened from coming into them'. Fleet thought it was better for the company 'to submit to any regulations [that] shall … be imposed upon them' by the date originally specified in the new charter than to enter into further discussions that might benefit the company's critics (*Buccleuch MSS*, 2.117, 133). When the regulations were issued, however, they proved more acceptable to the company's new subscribers than to the old shareholders whose interests had been defended by Fleet.

The enlargement of the East India Company in 1693–4 failed, however, to satisfy numerous London merchants seeking new investment opportunities. Many of them turned in 1694 to the initial capital subscription of the Bank of England. Fleet and some other East India Company magnates, on the other hand, were not particularly enthusiastic about the bank or about any of the other financial devices developed by the governing whig junto. As London whig merchants and investors became agents in the developing 'financial revolution' that would underwrite England's wars against Louis XIV, Fleet distanced himself from them. Macaulay may have exaggerated somewhat when he suggested that Fleet 'distinguished himself by the pertinacity with which he … opposed the financial and commercial policy of [Charles Montague] the first Lord of the Treasury' (Macaulay, 6.2844). Yet Fleet had clearly thrown in his lot with the opponents of whig war-financing. When Fleet entered the Commons in 1693 one observer had been uncertain whether to classify him as a court supporter or opponent. Fleet was re-elected as a city MP in the parliamentary election of 1695 with both whig and tory support. But in 1696 he voted against whig ministerial efforts to lower the price of guineas as part of a national recoinage. And in 1698, after the treaty of Ryswick, he was perceived as a probable supporter of army disbandment.

In the meantime criticism of the East India monopoly increased. Fleet's report to the Commons in 1698 that the East India Company would lend £700,000 to the government in return for a thirty-one year renewal of its monopoly was too little too late. Fleet's offer was 'knockt … on the head', when a rival syndicate successfully offered the government a £2 million loan in return for a new East India charter (R. Yard to A. Stanhope, Chevening MS 78, 17 May 1698). After 1698, then, Fleet was a leader of the old East India Company, which was forced to compete for profits with a new East India Company favoured by the whig parliamentary leadership. The division of the city between adherents of the old and new companies was quite apparent in the series of parliamentary elections between 1698 and 1702. In the London election of 1698 the whig ministry was embarrassed by the defeat of two new company leaders who challenged Fleet; but Fleet was the only tory returned for the city's four seats. Three years later, in the first parliamentary election of 1701, Fleet lost his seat in the electoral triumph of a London whig ticket of bank and new company directors. But when one of the successful whigs, Sir Gilbert Heathcote, was expelled by the house, Fleet defeated a whig alderman to take Heathcote's place. In the second parliamentary election of 1701 Fleet and other candidates of the 'church party' fell again to a ticket of bank and new company men; but Fleet re-entered the house as one of three old company men to secure city seats in the election for Queen Anne's first parliament in 1702.

By 1702 the two companies had come to an agreement for their amalgamation after an additional seven-year period of separate trading. Fleet served on the committee of old company representatives who negotiated the terms of this arrangement with their new company counterparts. Although he retained his leadership in the old company and also served as a director for the United East India Company in 1709–10 and 1711–12, Fleet played a less notable role in city affairs under Queen Anne. He was president of the city's Honourable Artillery Company in 1704–8, after serving two years as its vice-president; he was president of St Bartholomew's Hospital from 1705 until his death and he was a trustee for Sir Walter St John's School, Battersea. In 1705, he lost his London seat in the Commons when the whigs elected all four city MPs. He did not stand again for parliament. He had married the widow of Thomas Newcombe the younger (1651–1691), king's printer, after the death of his first wife. She also apparently predeceased him. Three of his four daughters had married into merchant families, the eldest being the widow of the old East India Company director Sir Rowland Aynsworth.

Fleet died on 6 July 1712 and was buried in the parish church of Battersea, where he had resided for some time. He bequeathed £3000 in cash to an unmarried daughter who had already received £500 of East India stock. He left the remainder of his estate to his only son, James Fleet.

GARY S. DE KREY

Sources W. Foster, 'Sir John Fleet', *EngHR*, 51 (1936), 681–5 · N. Luttrell, *A brief historical relation of state affairs from September 1678 to April 1714*, 1 (1857), 468–9, 556; 2 (1857), 289, 294, 569–70, 578, 581; 3 (1857), 47–8, 117, 123, 465, 538, 540, 542; 4 (1857), 376, 605, 721; 5 (1857), 29, 111, 193, 541; 6 (1857), 186 · J. R. Woodhead, *The rulers of London, 1660–1689* (1965), 70 · G. S. De Krey, *A fractured society: the politics of London in the first age of party, 1688–1715* (1985), 28, 31, 140–41, 241n., 250 · G. S. De Krey, 'Trade, religion, and politics in the reign of William III', PhD diss., Princeton University, 1978, 63–4, 305–6, 314, 318–20, 398–403 · H. Horwitz, *Parliament, policy and politics in the reign of William III* (1977), 233, 346 · *Report on the manuscripts of his grace the duke of Buccleuch and Queensberry … preserved at Montagu House*, 3 vols. in 4, HMC, 45 (1899–1926), vol. 2, pp. 117, 121–2, 133 · *CSP dom.*, 1698, 226–8, 289–91, 300, 309–10, 339, 369–71 · will, PRO, PROB 11/527, sig. 133 · London port books, imports from overseas, Dec 1680–Dec 1681, PRO, E 190/102/1 · Royal African Company journal, 1691–3, PRO, T70/188, fols. 113–21 [April 1693 stockholders] · R. Yard to A. Stanhope, CKS, Chevening MS 78, 27 Sept 1692, 9 Oct 1694, 22 Oct 1695 (bis), 5 Nov 1695, 17 May 1698, 9 Aug 1698 · H. G. Roseveare, 'The damned combination: the Port of London and the wharfingers' cartel of 1695', *London Journal*, 21/2 (1996), 97–111 · Home miscellaneous Series, Old East India Company, lists of adventurers, BL OIOC, vols. 1–2 (1693, 1694) · minutes of the court of committees of the old East India Company, BL OIOC, B/40, fols. 255–6 · minutes of the court of committees of the old East India Company, BL OIOC, B/41, fols. 272–3 · minutes of the court of committees of the old East India Company, BL OIOC, B/43, fol. 193 · T. B. Macaulay, *The history of England from the accession of James II*, new edn, ed. C. H. Firth, 6 vols. (1913–15), vol. 6, p. 2844

Likenesses Z. Alberstone, oils, 1693; at Coopers' Hall, London, in 1728 · portrait; at Grocers' Hall, London, in 1829

Wealth at death over £3500: will, PRO, PROB 11/527, sig. 133

Fleete, Henry (c.1602–1660/61), merchant and interpreter in America, was born at his family's estate of Chartham Court, Kent, the sixth child and fourth son of William Fleete (b. c.1571), lawyer and gentleman, and his wife, Deborah (d. 1651), daughter of Charles Scott of Edgerton in Godmersham, Kent. He was born into a prominent Kent family that traced its English roots to the Norman invasion and boasted a mention in the Domesday Book; however, as one of eleven children and the fourth of eight sons, Fleete could not expect sufficient lifelong support from his family's interests. He enjoyed the benefit of an education from private tutors at home but by 1621 had decided to seek his fortune in Virginia.

Fleete's father maintained a second home in London, where he mingled with the mercantile community, and, like many Kent gentlemen of the time, had invested in the Virginia Company (an initial £37 10s. in 1611). In 1621 Henry Fleete became part of the group of Kent gentry that assumed leadership of the colony, travelling to Virginia with his 'cousins' William Claiborne, George Sandys, Reverend Hawte Wyatt, and the colony's new governor, Sir Francis Wyatt. Soon after his arrival Fleete established a trading post on the present site of Georgetown with Captain Henry Spellman, who had arrived in Jamestown at the age of fourteen in 1609 and had promptly been sold by John Smith to Powhatan. Spellman was fluent in the region's Algonquian dialects and other Indian languages, which proved to be an enormous trading advantage. In March 1622 the Powhatan Indians and their allies turned against the white settlers, massacring about one-quarter of Virginia's white population. Spellman and Fleete, who were on the Potomac trading, were attacked. Of their party of twenty-six men, only five escaped, leaving Fleete alone and a captive of the Anacostan Indians. Fleete remained a captive for five years, learning the languages and customs of his captors. He was released in 1627 as a reward for his medical services during a severe plague that struck the Anacostan people.

After his captivity Fleete was well placed to pursue a lucrative trading career. Virginia was still recovering from the Powhatan uprising, and Fleete alone had intimate connections both with the elite London merchant community and their investors and with the American Indians. As such, he represented the trading interests of a number of London firms in North America and helped to pioneer the beaver trade. He has even been credited with teaching a number of the Chesapeake region's American Indian communities how to preserve the valuable pelts.

Fleete is perhaps best remembered for his role in the founding of Maryland. The Calvert family had long been interested in establishing another colony in America, and after a number of failed attempts, rivals' protests, and assorted other difficulties, Cecil Calvert, second Baron Baltimore, managed to secure a grant in the Chesapeake. In 1634 his brother Leonard, acting as the colony's first governor, led a party into the Potomac river to find a location for the colony's first settlement. There they met Fleete, who had established a trading post in the region. Fleete acted as an interpreter between the colonists and the natives, arranging for a suitable site for the settlement, named St Mary's City, and later a defensive alliance with the Piscataway against the Susquehannock. For his services Fleete was granted 4000 acres, and settled across the river from St Mary's, building West St Mary's manor.

He was active in the infant colony's development, serving on its assembly, advising on land grants, and developing the colony's trade with the American Indians.

Difficulties in arranging transportation of goods and increasing trade restrictions from Maryland's proprietor compelled Fleete to return to Virginia in 1638, where he continued his successful merchant interests and dealings with American Indians. Evidence of his abilities as an interpreter are best demonstrated by the fact that both Virginia and Maryland regularly called upon his services. This was despite the two colonies' intense rivalry that regularly flared into a quasi-war.

During a London business trip between 1646 and 1648 Fleete married Sarah Burden, a widow, with whom he had one son, Henry. In 1650 the Fleetes took up residence in what was then Northumberland county, where Fleete had been granted 1750 acres of land. He then left his merchant interests in favour of recruiting colonists in exchange for land grants. Through recruiting rewards and purchases he accumulated 13,197 acres of land in Virginia. He was active in the colony's government, assisting in the division of Northumberland into Rappahannock and Lancaster counties in 1653 and then serving as the latter's county court justice and representative in the House of Burgesses, Virginia's assembly. He was also called upon from time to time to deal with the American Indians, and by 1656 had reached the rank of lieutenant-colonel in the colony's militia. He died between 17 September 1660 and May 1661, and was buried at his home on Fleet's Island, Lancaster county, Virginia.   TROY O. BICKHAM

Sources B. Fleet, *Henry Fleete: pioneer, explorer, trader, planter, legislator, justice and peacemaker* (1989) · A. C. Land, *Colonial Maryland, a history* (1981) · T. W. Tate and D. L. Ammerman, *The Chesapeake in the seventeenth century: essays on Anglo-American society* (1979) · J. F. Fausz, 'Fleete, Henry', *ANB* · D. W. Jordan, *Foundations of representative government in Maryland, 1632–1715* (1987) · R. Semmes, *Captains and mariners of early Maryland* (1937) · L. G. Carr, P. D. Morgan, and J. B. Russo, eds., *Colonial Chesapeake Society* (1988)
Archives Maryland Historical Society, Baltimore, Calvert papers
Wealth at death substantial; owned 13,197 acres in Virginia: Fleet, *Henry Fleete* (1989), 68

Fleetwood [*née* Cromwell; *other married name* Ireton], **Bridget**, **Lady Fleetwood under the protectorate** (*bap.* 1624, *d.* 1662), daughter of Oliver Cromwell, was born in Huntingdon and baptized there on 5 August 1624 at St John's Church, the third of nine children and the eldest of four daughters of Oliver *Cromwell (1599–1658), the future lord protector, and his wife, Elizabeth *Cromwell (1598–1665), daughter of Sir James Bourchier. Although nothing is known of her childhood, she was almost certainly brought up in the family home at Huntingdon until 1631, St Ives from 1631 to 1636, and Ely from 1636. In 1646 she married Henry *Ireton (*bap.* 1611, *d.* 1651), commissary-general of the horse in the New Model Army and a confidant of Oliver Cromwell. Oliver signed the marriage settlement in April 1646, assigning Ireton the lease of a farm in Ely, and on 15 June the couple were married by Sir Thomas Fairfax's chaplain at the house of Lady Whorwood at Holton, near Oxford, where Ireton was then based. Cromwell wrote to Bridget four months later,

exhorting the newly-weds to seek the Lord: 'Dear Heart, press on; let not husband, let not anything cool thy affections after Christ. I hope he will be an occasion to inflame them. That which is best worthy of love in thy husband is that of the image of Christ he bears' (*Writings and Speeches*, 1.416). The couple had one son and three daughters, including Bridget *Bendish.

At the beginning of 1651 Bridget Ireton crossed to Ireland to join her husband, who was commanding parliament's army there. In April 1651 Thomas Patient, one of the preachers attached to Ireton's headquarters, assured Cromwell that 'I doe by good experience find, so far as I can discerne, the power of God's grace in her soul, a woman acquainted with temtations and breathing after Christ' (J. Nickolls, *Original Letters and Papers of State Addressed to Oliver Cromwell*, 1743, 6–7). She returned to England in the summer, and was in London when news reached her of Ireton's death at Limerick on 26 November 1651. In the following month the Rump Parliament voted her £2000. There were four children of the marriage, a boy and three girls (Henry, Elizabeth, Jane, and Bridget), all of whom survived into adulthood.

Bridget's widowhood was brief, for on 8 June 1652 she married another senior officer, Charles *Fleetwood (*c.*1618–1692), about to be appointed commander of the army in Ireland. It was the second marriage for both of them, Fleetwood's first wife, Frances, having died just a few days before Bridget's first husband. Lucy Hutchinson claims that the match resulted from a chance encounter in St James's Park, Fleetwood coming to the aid of the widowed Bridget when she was slighted by John Lambert's wife (Hutchinson, 291). Bridget was with Fleetwood in Ireland from September 1652 until September 1655. In 1652, soon after the couple crossed to Ireland, Cromwell asked Fleetwood to 'salute your dear wife from me. Bid her beware of a bondage spirit. Fear is the natural issue of such a spirit; the antidote is Love. The voice of fear is, If I had done this; if I had avoided that, how well it had been with me!—I know this hath been her vain reasoning' (*Writings and Speeches*, 2.602). In June 1655, shortly before Fleetwood left Ireland, Cromwell wrote sending his love 'to my dear Biddy, who is a joy to my heart, for what I hear of the Lord in her. Bid her be cheerful, and rejoice in the Lord' (ibid., 3.756).

Upon his return to London in autumn 1655, Fleetwood and his growing family were allocated lodgings at Derby House. As well as Bridget's children by her first husband, and his own by his first wife, Bridget and Charles Fleetwood had at least three children, a son and two daughters (Cromwell, Ann, and Mary), one of whom (Ann) died very young, and was buried at Westminster Abbey, but was exhumed at the Restoration. Fleetwood himself suffered nothing more than incapacity from public office in 1660 and he and Bridget continued to live quietly in London. She died in June 1662 and was buried at St Anne Blackfriars on 1 July. Her second husband survived her by thirty years and married a third time two years after her death.

PETER GAUNT

Sources *The writings and speeches of Oliver Cromwell*, ed. W. C. Abbott and C. D. Crane, 4 vols. (1937–47) · J. Waylen, *The house of Cromwell and the story of Dunkirk* (1897) · M. Noble, *Memoirs of the protectoral-house of Cromwell*, 2 vols. (1787) · A. J. Shirren, *The chronicles of Fleetwood House* (1951) · Thurloe, *State papers* · L. Hutchinson, *Memoirs of the life of Colonel Hutchinson*, ed. J. Hutchinson, new edn, ed. C. H. Firth (1906), 291
Archives BL, letter-book of H. Cromwell, Lansdowne MSS 821–823 · Bodl. Oxf., Thurloe state papers, MSS Rawl.
Likenesses Crosse, miniature, Royal Collection · oils, Chequers Trust · portrait (after P. Lely), BM; repro. in P. Young, *Oliver Cromwell and his times* (1962), pl. 13 · portrait (after C. Jonsen), BM · portraits, repro. in Shirren, *Chronicles*

Charles Fleetwood, appointed Lord Fleetwood under the protectorate (*c.*1618–1692), by unknown artist

Fleetwood, Charles, appointed Lord Fleetwood under the protectorate (*c.*1618–1692), army officer, was the third son of Sir Miles *Fleetwood (*d.* 1641) of Aldwincle, Northamptonshire, and Anne, daughter of Nicholas Luke of Woodend, Bedfordshire. The father was a prominent office holder, being receiver-general of the court of wards. Charles Fleetwood may have been at Emmanuel College, Cambridge, before entering Gray's Inn on 30 November 1638.

War and politics, 1642–1651 It was on the basis of the latter connection that in 1642 Fleetwood, in company with others from the inns of court, enlisted as a trooper in the life guards of the earl of Essex, parliament's commander. He first achieved prominence when Essex had him carry an offer of peace to the earl of Dorset in September 1642. By May 1643 he had been promoted to a captaincy, and he was wounded at the first battle of Newbury on 20 September 1643. In May 1643 he had been empowered to seize assets from the sequestered royalists in the eastern counties. Already he was associated in this task with such future comrades as Oliver Cromwell and John Desborough. His services secured him the reward from parliament in May 1644 of the receivership of the court of wards, formerly held by his father and recently removed from his royalist elder brother. He had secured command of a cavalry regiment in the eastern association under the leadership of the earl of Manchester. In this capacity he ran up against the hostility of the county committees of Norfolk and Suffolk. His regiment was soon noted for its large complement of sectaries whom he encouraged. Given the command of a regiment of horse in the New Model Army, he fought at Naseby on 14 June 1645. Thereafter he saw service in the west country and in the midlands around Oxford. On 26 April 1646 he received the surrender of Woodstock Manor.

In May 1646 Fleetwood was returned to parliament for the borough of Marlborough in a recruiter election. This confirmed his growing importance among the army officers as one, like Fairfax, Cromwell, and Ireton, whose role was not limited to fighting. In the unfolding crisis of 1647, in which the soldiery confronted a seemingly hostile parliament, Fleetwood and his regiment were to the fore. They unanimously declined to serve in Ireland, as the parliament had ordered. On 30 April 1647 he was selected as one of the four commissioners sent by parliament to explain its actions to the army. He joined with Cromwell in conveying the soldiery's response on 20 May. For the moment he concurred with the other grandees that an open rift between army and parliament was to be avoided if possible. On 1 July he was again one of those deputed by the army to set out its thinking to parliament. At the same time he may have been implicated in the intrigues which led soldiers from his regiment to seize the king at Holdenby, thus strengthening the army's hand in negotiations.

After the excitements of 1647 Fleetwood vanished from public view. He was compensated to the tune of £2250 when, with the abolition of the court of wards, his office as receiver disappeared. He is not recorded as fighting in the second civil war or as present at the king's trial in January 1649. However, on 14 August 1649 he was named as governor of the Isle of Wight. He had not accompanied Oliver Cromwell and his expeditionary force to Ireland that summer, but joined him the following year on his Scottish campaign. With many of the most experienced commanders detained in Ireland, his opportunity for rapid promotion had come. He now enjoyed the rank of lieutenant-general of the horse, in which capacity he fought at Dunbar in September 1650. His distinction and apparent closeness to Cromwell helped secure his election by the Rump Parliament to the council of state in February 1651. Recalled from Scotland, he was entrusted with command of the army in England. In this exposed position he had to prepare to repel Charles II's likely invasion from the north. On 24 August 1651 he rendezvoused with Cromwell at Warwick and together they planned the defensive campaign. He contributed materially to the royalists' defeat at Worcester in the following month. He was thanked formally by parliament and re-elected to the council of state. In parliament he associated with those members keen to provide better for preaching the gospel and to reform the law. Some time between September and December 1651 he participated in the discussions at the speaker's house on the future settlement of the country.

Governing Ireland Fleetwood's advancement continued in 1652. The post of commander in Ireland had been vacated when Ireton died at the end of November 1651. Parliament had intended as Ireton's successor John Lambert, but—in an excess of republicanism—withheld from him the title of lord deputy, which Ireton (in common with most English governors in Ireland) had enjoyed. Needing to find a substitute for the lordly Lambert, who refused the diminished post of commander-in-chief, on 8 July 1652 the council of state and parliament hit on Fleetwood. On 10 July Cromwell, as captain-general, commissioned him as commander-in-chief in Ireland, and the following month he was added to the parliamentary commissioners responsible for the civil government of the island. He landed near Dublin in September 1652, without previous experience of the troubled territory now devastated by warfare, pestilence, and famine. The rebellious country had been largely reconquered, with only a few outposts in the west still to be reduced. Thus, the tasks which faced him as commander were less military than political and administrative. There remained the threat of possible invasion by foreign powers sympathetic to the Stuarts and of domestic disturbances. A more urgent risk came from the occupying army itself. It contained radical veterans of the 1640s who, as campaigning slackened, grew restless. As in the past, their discontent related principally to material grievances: the accumulating arrears of pay; delays in allocating them confiscated Irish properties in lieu of that pay; and uncertainty when they would be free to return to England. In addition, some officers and men minded the religious and constitutional issues of the day. Those who adopted the tenets of the Independents, Baptists, and (after 1654) Quakers resented efforts to circumscribe their meetings for worship. Also, they acted aggressively towards their sectarian rivals, so threatening to disturb the fragile peace within the small but divided protestant communities of Ireland. Nor were radicals happy when they learned of the changes in England, with first the remnant of the Long Parliament expelled in April 1653 and then, at the end of the same year, Cromwell installed as protector. One high-ranking officer and parliamentary commissioner in Dublin, Edmund Ludlow, openly dissented from the alterations. Others were suspected of doing so. In addition, there were officers who took seriously their duties towards Ireland itself. Customarily this manifested itself in contempt and antagonism towards the native Irish and Catholics. The English, Scots, and Welsh who found themselves in or responsible for Ireland traditionally thought that its inhabitants needed to be brought into closer conformity with the religion and habits of Britain. By the 1650s this belief was overlaid by a wish to punish those Irish who had risen in 1641 and supposedly murdered many thousands of protestant settlers.

Fleetwood seems wholeheartedly to have subscribed to the hostile English view of the indigenous Irish. On the other questions which divided his army and administration he was more delphic. He was reluctant to upset partisans, hoping thereby to quieten the acrimonious controversies. In the event his passivity enabled numerous potentially subversive opinions to spread through protestant Ireland. Worries about the disruptive results of his approach reached England. In March 1654 the protector sent his younger son, Henry Cromwell, to investigate the nature and extent of disaffection in Ireland. The astringent analysis that followed did not spare Fleetwood, whose indulgence was felt to have worsened if not caused the difficulties. In practice, no governor in Dublin had much latitude to initiate or vary policies. The financial difficulties which let army pay fall heavily into arrear were hardly of Fleetwood's making. Furthermore, in regard to the main task which came to preoccupy him in the era of reconstruction, the confiscation and redistribution of lands, the essentials of the settlement had been decided by the Westminster parliament in a series of acts and ordinances between 1642 and 1654. In 1654 he and his fellow councillors authorized the surveys which formed the necessary preliminary to allocating estates to civilian creditors and the soldiery. However, it was a complex process unlikely quickly—or uncontentiously—to be completed. The impatience of likely beneficiaries to receive their Irish lands added to the agitation over Irish affairs. The government in Dublin, under Fleetwood's direction, was empowered to settle the details of how those involved in the Irish wars of the 1640s were now to be treated. The bulk were to be transplanted west of the River Shannon, where the lucky would be allocated small portions of generally poor land. This ambitious but vindictive scheme, approved by the authorities in England and Ireland, was backed by Fleetwood. A few in Ireland, however, did question its justice and wisdom. Such opposition angered the lord deputy, as it did most radical officers in the army. Fleetwood encouraged one of the latter, Richard Lawrence, to defend the transplantation project. Yet, as the time by which the transplanters were to uproot themselves approached, it had become clear that all would not do so. Also, the feeling had grown that such a measure would impoverish and unsettle the country.

In the face of local hostility to this proposed action Fleetwood had drawn yet closer to the sectaries and radical officers. This dependence, in turn, dismayed those who hoped that Ireland might revert to a more traditional system of government, in which those protestants settled before the outbreak of the wars would serve alongside newcomers and in which the more grandiose schemes of moving peoples would be abandoned. Moreover, as the protectorate preferred a more conservative approach to legal and religious issues, seeking to heal old wounds and reconcile former adversaries and to lessen the power of the army, Fleetwood's style of rule looked increasingly anachronistic. It could also be blamed for the slow and uncertain pace at which Ireland was recovering. Yet, despite the worrying reports emanating from Dublin, the protector was reluctant to dismiss him. Since the end of 1652 the two had enjoyed a closer relationship. Cromwell's daughter Bridget [see Fleetwood, Bridget (bap. 1624, d. 1662)], left a widow by the death of her first husband, Ireton, married Fleetwood as his second wife, following the death of Frances (née Smith) in November 1651. But for Cromwell, always anxious to avoid charges of dynasticism and nepotism, this new closeness was not of itself a reason to treat Fleetwood gently. It was clear that he was held in strong affection by the army and the godly congregations. Cromwell may have been wary about upsetting these groups further by sacrificing him. Already they were perturbed by the growing conservatism of the protectorate. Moreover, Cromwell shared some of his attitudes, although, in contrast to the latter, the protector was hostile to those who advanced worldly ambitions under cover of an assumed godliness.

Cromwell adopted an unsatisfactory compromise over the government of Ireland. Already, in August 1654, the parliamentary commissioners had been replaced as civil governors of Ireland by a lord deputy assisted by a council. At this date Fleetwood became lord deputy, so acquiring the dignity to which Lambert had vainly aspired. These dispositions indicated the more conservative tone of the protectorate. On 25 December 1654 Oliver Cromwell named his abrasive and energetic son Henry as a member of the Irish council and major-general of the Irish forces. He was sent to Dublin to discharge the offices only in August 1655. In September 1655 Fleetwood was recalled to England. Effectively, he had been superseded by his brother-in-law. But he kept his position as lord deputy, retaining it until his commission expired in September 1657. Then, after an interval of two months, Henry Cromwell replaced him. The awkward arrangement ensured that for two years between 1655 and 1657 there were rival rulers of Ireland. Henry Cromwell, on the spot, altered some of Fleetwood's priorities. Malcontents within the army and sects were handled more roughly; well-affected civilians in the local protestant communities were wooed. The scheme to corral the defeated Irish in Connaught and co. Clare was silently modified. Yet, Fleetwood, back in London, took his seat on the protector's council, to which he had been appointed in December 1654. He was henceforward deferred to as the resident expert on Ireland. Also, as lord deputy, he retained useful patronage. He listened patiently to the disgruntled, and relayed their grumbles about Henry Cromwell to the protector.

Later career Fleetwood, nominally still in charge of Ireland, gained extra responsibilities in England. He had accepted the largely honorific lieutenancy of Wychwood Forest in Oxfordshire, apparently as a substitute for the hereditary lieutenant who was a minor. When the system of major-generals was introduced in September 1655, he was given the care of the counties of Buckingham, Cambridge, Essex, Hertford, Norfolk, Oxford, and Suffolk, and the Isle of Ely. This unusually large territory, although one with which he was familiar through his service in the 1640s and where he had property, would have been a challenge for even the most assiduous. He hardly attempted to

reinvigorate the government of the region. Responsibility was largely delegated to two deputies. One, Hezekiah Haynes, had been a major in his regiment. The other was William Packer. The major-generals came to an end in 1656, and provoked a reaction in favour of more traditional civilian rule, which culminated in the kingship movement. Fleetwood was identified as one of three leading officers (with Desborough and Lambert) opposed to the plan. It was rumoured that they might incite disaffection in the army were Cromwell to become king. They also played on Cromwell's own doubts: in the end, successfully. Yet, Fleetwood meekly acquiesced in the settlement when 'The humble petition and advice' was adopted in June 1657. He swore the new oath required to continue as a councillor of state. In January 1658 he also accepted nomination to the 'other house', another innovation of the settlement. During the last year of the protectorate he was much involved in public duties, such as the reception of foreign ambassadors.

So long as Oliver Cromwell lived, Fleetwood was inhibited from any aggressively independent action. When an angry Cromwell decided to rid himself of the troublesome parliament on 6 February 1658, after it had sat for only sixteen days in its second session, Fleetwood tried to dissuade him. For his pains he was mocked by the protector as a 'milksop'. To a large degree his eminence, after Cromwell the senior officer in the army, had come about fortuitously. Potential competitors, like Lambert, Ludlow, and Harrison, had disabled themselves by their open dissent from the Cromwellian regime. Following the protector's death and the succession of Richard Cromwell in September 1658, he was suspected of encouraging the army to intervene in politics. How far he initiated and how far he simply acquiesced in the army's renewed activism is hard to ascertain. His residence at Wallingford House in London became a centre for the disaffected. Within the army and among sectaries he continued to be regarded as a powerful patron. Before the spring of 1659 he tended to exert himself on behalf of individuals rather than causes. Moreover, he seems to have restrained the headstrong in the army from offering violence to the parliament. Only in April 1659 did he join his junior officers in promoting 'the good old cause', an amalgam of religious liberty and army autonomy, against an apparently unsympathetic parliament and protector. In the resulting crisis the army was the stronger and parliament was dissolved on 22 April 1659. He still professed loyalty to his brother-in-law, the protector, but his inability to rein in the more outspoken republicans among his subordinates meant that he was soon overborne. The protectorate ended early in May 1659. Under the newly reinstated Commonwealth, he was appointed to the committee of safety and council of state. The following month he was made commander-in-chief. His powers derived from and were limited by the Rump Parliament, which had been recalled in May 1659. When his supporters within the army sought to free him of these restraints, parliament retaliated by cancelling his commission and instead vested control of the army in seven commissioners. Of these, he was to be one. But long-standing opponents were also included.

The growing tension between army and parliament led to the violent expulsion of the latter on 12 October 1659. Again Lambert, not Fleetwood, had been the principal in this act. Indeed, in the triumvirate which effectively directed the army—consisting of Fleetwood, Desborough, and Lambert—the temporizing Fleetwood looked the feeblest. But because he was malleable, he retained considerable popularity. Furthermore, in his concern with the causes of the godly and of reform, he saw the army and its allies still as the best custodian. On 18 October he was once more declared commander-in-chief. In practice he was merely one in a committee which now ran the forces. Left to oversee London while Lambert journeyed north, he played his favourite role as conciliator. But, as in past attempts, the jarring interests were too strong to be quietened. Once more, as in Ireland between 1652 and 1655, his indulgence may have created more problems than it solved. When, in the autumn of 1659, confusion enveloped the country, he stuck close to Lambert and the other officers. He repulsed the feelers extended by royalists, including his exiled elder brother. The restoration of the Rump on 24 December 1659 ended his commission as commander-in-chief, and his horse regiment was given to another. Out of favour with the returned parliament, he was likely to be in even worse odour with the restored king. Although not a regicide, he was originally designed to be among the twenty excepted from the benefits of the Act of Indemnity in June 1660. Thanks to the intercession of friends in the House of Lords, headed by the earl of Lichfield, he escaped this punishment. Instead he was simply disabled for life from holding any office of trust.

Fleetwood lived quietly thereafter. On 14 January 1664 he married his third wife, Mary (d. 1684), daughter of Sir John *Coke and widow of Sir Edward Hartopp. After 1664 he resided at Stoke Newington in Middlesex. His continuing sectarian affiliations were shown by his membership of Dr John Owen's congregation. Owen, whom he had known during the interregnum, in the 1680s expressed affection for Fleetwood and his family. In 1683, during the tory reaction, the Northamptonshire grand jury named him as one who should be required to give security for good behaviour. However, he did nothing to alarm the authorities, and so remained undisturbed for the rest of his life. His will, made on 10 January 1690, suggested comfortable circumstances and a lasting attachment 'to the poor distressed people of God', whose society he still kept. On 1 July 1652 he had purchased the Suffolk manor of Borrow (or Borough) Castle, which he later bequeathed to his eldest surviving son, Smith Fleetwood. He died on 4 October 1692 at Stoke Newington and was buried at Bunhill Fields.

Only the sectarian affiliation survived from his years of eminence in the 1650s. As an army officer he had regularly displayed courage and skill. Nevertheless, his eventual promotion to commander-in-chief owed much to chance, with the more experienced and senior unavailable. The same could be argued about his appointment to govern in Ireland: Lambert had been the first choice. Neither as lord deputy in Dublin nor as major-general of a large tract of East Anglia did he reveal particular dynamism or authority. In each place he was hampered by limited powers to initiate new measures. But in Ireland his hesitancy about disciplining the troublesome because they belonged either to the English army or to the religious congregations allowed too much energy to be dissipated in introspective quarrels when more urgent problems demanded attention. Finally, in 1659, the moment at which he enjoyed pre-eminence, he veered to whichever option his military companions inclined. Decisiveness was not his forte. TOBY BARNARD

Sources Thurloe, *State papers* · BL, Lansdowne MSS 821–823 · T. C. Barnard, *Cromwellian Ireland: English government and reform in Ireland, 1649–1660* (1975) · C. H. Firth and G. Davies, *The regimental history of Cromwell's army*, 2 vols. (1940) · B. Worden, *The Rump Parliament, 1648–1653* (1974) · PRO, PROB 11/412, fols. 51–2 [will of J. C. Fleetwood] · *The correspondence of John Owen (1616–1683)*, ed. P. Toon (1970), 159–60, 172–4 · R. L. Greaves, *Secrets of the kingdom: British radicals from the Popish Plot to the revolution of 1688–89* (1992), 207 · A. I. Suckling, *The history and antiquities of the county of Suffolk*, 1 (1846), 336 · M. Ashley, *Cromwell's generals* (1954), 181–98 · *The memoirs of Edmund Ludlow*, ed. C. H. Firth, 2 vols. (1894) · Greaves & Zaller, *BDBR*, 287–9 · *DNB*

Archives BL, corresp. and papers, Add. MS 4165 | BL, letters to Henry Cromwell, Add. MS 43724

Likenesses R. Dunkarton, mezzotint, pubd 1811 (after unknown artist), BM, NPG · R. Cooper, stipple (after R. Walker), NPG · J. Hoskins, miniature, repro. in Ashley, *Cromwell's generals* · J. Houbraken, line engraving (after R. Walker), BM, NPG; repro. in T. Birch, *Heads* (1740) · line engraving, BM · oils, S. Antiquaries, Lond. [see illus.]

Fleetwood, Charles (d. 1747), theatre manager, was the only son of Thomas Fleetwood of Gerard's Bromley in Staffordshire and Frances Gerard, the sister of Charles, sixth Baron Gerard. At the age of twenty-one he inherited (from Lord Gerard, through his mother) a landed estate valued at £6000 per annum. Described by Benjamin Victor as 'agreeable in his person' and 'affable and engaging in his address' (Victor, 1.33–4), the young Fleetwood enjoyed a highly extravagant lifestyle. His reputation for improvidence soon attracted the attention of a circle of gamblers, however, who quickly relieved him of his fortune. With his inheritance all but gone, he hit upon the idea of venturing into the theatre, and in the spring of 1734 he purchased John Highmore's share of the Drury Lane theatre patent. Knowing nothing of the mechanics of the stage, he appointed the actor Charles Macklin to take charge of his fellow players and supervise the artistic business of the theatre.

With Fleetwood overseeing the financial management of Drury Lane, the theatre thrived for several years. However, by the 1737–8 season Fleetwood appears to have grown tired of his day-to-day involvement. Leaving his treasurer, Pierson, in charge of financial affairs, he devoted his time to less salubrious amusements. In 1739 he began to referee boxing matches at Tottenham Court. He simultaneously renewed his passion for gambling, to which he devoted large sums of money taken from the profits at Drury Lane. Without the necessary funds for fresh scenes and costumes, the theatre suffered. Fleetwood responded by introducing a series of novelty acts, including physical freaks and rope-dancers, but their appearance served only to diminish box-office receipts still further.

Following the great success of Garrick's début season at Goodman's Fields in 1741-2, Fleetwood brought the young star to Drury Lane with an offer of £500 per year. However, his continuing abuse of the minor company actors, to whom he refused to grant a benefit night, soon prompted a rebellion among the players. In 1743 the leading actors formed a union and vowed that not one of them would agree individual terms with Fleetwood unless the other members of the company were satisfied with their own salaries. The manager responded by gathering together an alternative company of players, drawn principally from Giffard's disbanded troupe at Lincoln's Inn Fields. After several months of financial hardship, the majority of the rebels chose to make their peace with Fleetwood. However, despite a number of economies, the theatre continued to struggle. In a desperate attempt to raise money Fleetwood mortgaged the Drury Lane patent, and offered the theatre's store of costumes and props as security against a further £7000 loan.

On 17 November 1744 Fleetwood's decision to raise ticket prices provoked a riot among the audience, which the manager sought to quell by sending a number of men into the theatre armed with wooden clubs. A repetition of this incident, witnessed by Horace Walpole, appears to have sealed Fleetwood's disenchantment with the stage. In December 1744 he sold the Drury Lane patent to Richard Green and Morton Amber, who offered him a lump sum of £3200 and an additional annuity of £600.

In the spring of 1745 Fleetwood, suffering from 'excessive Gout' (Victor, 1.62), moved to France. He died, apparently bankrupt, at Chalon-sur-Saône in August 1747. He was survived by his wife, the actress and dancer Susanna Fleetwood, née Williams (b. 1714). They had two sons, Charles and John Gerard, both actors. The younger Charles Fleetwood made his London début in 1758, and spent two seasons at Drury Lane before moving to the Smock Alley Theatre in Dublin. He soon gave up the stage, however, and in 1769 emigrated to the East Indies; he died in 1784. John Gerard Fleetwood, the younger of the two brothers, made his first appearance at Covent Garden in April 1769. He then spent a season at the Haymarket before moving to Edinburgh in 1771. In 1773 he joined Tate Wilkinson's company at York, where he performed for three seasons. He died in Leeds in 1776.

CHARLES BRAYNE

Sources R. W. Buss, *Charles Fleetwood, holder of the Drury Lane Theatre patent* (1915) · B. Victor, *The history of the theatres of London and Dublin*, 1 (1761), 33–64 · *GM*, 1st ser., 49 (1779), 171 · *The thespian dictionary, or, Dramatic biography of the present age*, 2nd edn (1805) · *Queries to be answer'd by the manager of Drury Lane* (1743) · T. Wilkinson, *The wandering patentee, or, A history of the Yorkshire theatres from 1770 to the present time*, 1 (1795), 174–5, 218–19 · *The letters of Horace Walpole, fourth earl of Orford*, ed. P. Toynbee, 2 (1903), 61–2 · Highfill, Burnim & Langhans, *BDA* · A. H. Scouten, ed., *The London stage, 1660–1800*, pt 3: *1729–1747* (1961), xcii–xcvi · F. G. Stephens and M. D. George, eds., *Catalogue of prints and drawings in the British Museum, division 1: political and personal satires*, 3 (1877), 475–9 · W. S. Clark, *The Irish stage in the county towns, 1720–1800* (1965), 358 · GEC, *Peerage*

Likenesses group portrait, print, 1743 (*The theatrical contest*), repro. in *Catalogue of prints and drawings in the British Museum*

Wealth at death probably bankrupt: *GM*

Fleetwood, George [created Sir George Fleetwood under the protectorate], **Baron Fleetwood in the Swedish nobility** (*bap.* 1605, *d.* 1667), army officer in the Swedish service, was baptized on 30 June 1605 at Cople, Bedfordshire. He was the second son of Sir Miles *Fleetwood (*d.* 1641) of Cranford and Aldwincle, Northamptonshire, receiver of the court of wards, and his wife, Anne Luke (*b.* 1578), daughter of Nicholas Luke and his wife, Anne. His younger brother Charles *Fleetwood, the parliamentarian general, married Oliver Cromwell's eldest daughter, Bridget, in 1652. George's second cousin, also George *Fleetwood, was a regicide and a parliamentarian colonel.

In 1629 George Fleetwood raised a troop of horse for Swedish service in Germany during the Thirty Years' War and became a major in Colonel James Spens's regiment; and in 1630, after promotion to lieutenant-colonel, he recruited a regiment of infantry. He was present in November 1632 at the battle of Lützen, in which Gustavus Adolphus of Sweden was killed. George sent a detailed, if not entirely accurate, account of the battle to his father (getting the manner of the king's death wrong), in which he also noted the esteem in which he was held by the Swedish government. In 1633 he served as the commandant of a Swedish garrison in Prussia. The Swedish chancellor, Axel Oxenstierna, seeking a closer alliance with Charles I and further recruits, sent Fleetwood to the Stuart court in 1636 and 1637. En route to England in 1637 George, now a colonel, met Elizabeth of Bohemia. He obtained funds and permission to levy troops from Charles I. In 1639 he sailed with covenanters through the Danish sound to take up service first as commandant at Greifswald and then at Kolberg the following year.

On 22 April 1640 Fleetwood married Brita Gyllenstierna (1606–1653), lady in waiting to Queen Kristina, who was the daughter of Karl Gyllenstierna and his wife, Anna. They had four sons and two daughters. In 1646 he was rewarded with donations of land from the queen and three years later he was introduced into the Swedish house of nobility. George remained in active military service and in 1653 he was promoted major-general of the infantry. On 1 June 1654 he was made a baron and received the estate of Jälunda. His wife had died on 29 December 1653, leaving him homesick and lonely, for all his elevated social position and his appointment, with Colonel Hugh Hamilton, as a royal guard at the wedding of Karl X.

From 1655 to 1660 Fleetwood was the Swedish envoy-extraordinary in London, accompanied by his eldest son, Gustav Miles (1642–1705). There he worked for a confederation between Sweden and the English republic. George also obtained at least 3000 English and Scottish troops for Swedish service in Poland and against Denmark, and was accused of fomenting English attacks on

Danish ships in the Thames. He was knighted by Cromwell in September 1656 and attended his funeral in 1658, along with another Swedish commissioner. In Sweden Fleetwood was promoted lieutenant-general. He was still in London in May 1659, when Karl X requested an audience with the English council for him. After his return to Sweden he served on the council of war in 1665. He was noted as one of the three wealthiest men on the Swedish military staff.

Fleetwood died on 11 June 1667 at his Jälunda estate. He was buried first in Riddarholm church in Stockholm on 13 March 1668 before being moved to the family plot at Allhelgona church in Nyköping.   A. N. L. GROSJEAN

Sources G. Elgenstierna, *Den introducerade svenska adelns ättartavlor med tillägg och rättelser*, 2 (1926) · 'Svenska sändebuds till utländska hof och deras sändebud till Sverige', 1841, Riksarkivet, Stockholm · katalog öfver sköldebref, Riddarhusarkivet, Stockholm, Sweden · katalog öfver rullor 1638–40, 1641–43, Krigsarkivet, Stockholm · military muster rolls, Krigsarkivet, Stockholm · N. A. Kullberg, S. Bergh, and P. Sondén, eds., *Svenska riksrådets protokoll*, 18 vols. (Stockholm, 1878–1959) · S. Bergh and B. Taube, eds., *Sveriges ridderskaps ach adels riksdags-protokoll*, 17 vols. (1871) · *CSP dom.*, 1625–60 · *CSP Venice* · M. Roberts, ed., *Swedish diplomats at Cromwell's court, 1655–1656: the missions of Peter Julius Coyet and Christer Bonde* (1988) · E. Marquard, *Kancelliets brevbøger, 1637–39* (1949) · J. Kleberg, *Krigskollegii historia biografiska anteckningar, 1630–1865* (1930) · *The diary of Bulstrode Whitelocke, 1605–1675*, ed. R. Spalding, British Academy, Records of Social and Economic History, new ser., 13 (1990) · A. Stade, *Carl X Gustaf och Danmark, källkritik och krigshistoria* (1965) · G. M. Bell, *A handlist of British diplomatic representatives, 1509–1688*, Royal Historical Society Guides and Handbooks, 16 (1990) · *DNB* · 'Letter from George Fleetwood to his father', ed. P. de M. G. Egerton, *Camden miscellany, I*, CS, 39 (1847) · R. Spalding, *Contemporaries of Bulstrode Whitelocke, 1605–1675: biographies, illustrated by letters and other documents* (1990)
Archives Riksarkivet, Stockholm, Krigsarkivet, military muster rolls, 1629/11, 14, 16, 18–20; 1630/22, 24, 26–33; 1631/13, 15–21; 1632/10–21; 1633/11–22; 1634/12–23; 1635/1, 20–26, 28–30; 1637/15; 1638/21, 23, 26, 27; 1639/14, 16; 1640/6, 17–20; 1641/2, 3, 7, 19, 20, 22–5; 1642/6, 14–21; 1643/2, 3, 7; 1644/8; 1645/9, 21, 23, 24; 1646/7, 16, 17; 1647/8, 16; 1648/16, 20; 1649/13; 1650/4, 10; 1651/4; 1652/4; 1653/3; 1658/9 · Riksarkivet, Stockholm, Anglica, letters to King Karl X Gustav and replies, vols. 22–31
Wealth at death held over 250 farms in Sweden: Stade, *Carl X Gustaf och Danmark*

Fleetwood, George, appointed Lord Fleetwood under the protectorate

Fleetwood, George, appointed Lord Fleetwood under the protectorate (*bap.* 1623, *d.* in or after 1664), army officer and regicide, was the eldest son of Charles Fleetwood (*d.* 1628) of The Vache, Chalfont St Giles, Buckinghamshire, and his wife, Anne, daughter of Nicolas and Margery Watkins. He was baptized at Chalfont St Giles on 15 February 1623 and in 1628 on the death of his father he inherited the family estates while still a young boy. There is no record of his having attended either a university or an inn of court during the 1630s. He was twice married, his first wife being Katherine Oldfield, daughter of John Oldfield of Bow and St Katherine Creechurch, London; they had at least two children. His second wife, whom he married in 1651 or 1652, was Hester Smyth [*see* Fleetwood, Hester (*d.* 1714)], daughter of Sir Robert Smyth of Upton, Essex; they had two daughters and three sons, of whom two died young.

During the early part of the civil war, while still only in his early twenties, he raised a troop of dragoons for parliament and was active with them near his home in the Chiltern hills. By 1644 he had been named to the parliamentarian county committee for Buckinghamshire. In 1645 he was elected to the Long Parliament as recruiter MP for Buckinghamshire. During 1648 he sided with the New Model Army in its quarrel with the parliament and he was consequently allowed to retain his seat at Pride's Purge in early December of that year. Following the purge he was appointed one of the judges for the trial of Charles I. He attended only two of the court's sittings in January 1649, but was present when the sentence was passed and signed the king's death warrant [*see also* Regicides].

In 1650 Fleetwood was appointed colonel of the Buckinghamshire militia forces and during the last months of the Commonwealth at the end of 1652 and beginning of 1653 he served as a member of the republican council of state. Following the closure of the Rump by Cromwell, he was chosen to sit in Barebone's Parliament as member for Buckinghamshire. He was, however, one of the more moderate members of that assembly and took little active part in its proceedings. In 1654 he was elected to the first protectorate parliament as member for his native Buckinghamshire and the same year he was named one of the ejectors for that county. In the summer of 1655 he was appointed captain of the new horse militia for Buckinghamshire which was to be under the command of the major-general for Buckinghamshire, his distant kinsman Charles Fleetwood of Aldwincle in Northamptonshire. In the autumn of 1655 he was also appointed one of the commissioners for the securing of the peace of the Commonwealth in Buckinghamshire. The following February, William Packer succeeded Hezekiah Haynes as Charles Fleetwood's deputy in Hertfordshire, Oxfordshire, and Buckinghamshire; George Fleetwood was appointed as another deputy major-general, and was instructed to work with Packer in Buckinghamshire. In the autumn of 1656 he was the only major-general or deputy who was not returned to the second protectorate parliament. He was knighted by Cromwell on 15 September 1656. The following year the protector nominated him as a member of the new second chamber of parliament as George, Lord Fleetwood. In August 1659 the restored Rump authorized him to raise a troop of 'well affected volunteers' to resist Sir George Booth's rising in Cheshire. He subsequently refused to come to the aid of John Lambert and instead threw in his lot with Colonel George Monck, who put him in command of a regiment in February 1660.

Fleetwood proclaimed Charles II at York early in May 1660, but following the restored king's return several weeks later he was exempted from the Act of Indemnity as a regicide, put on trial, and sentenced to death. He subsequently petitioned parliament for a reprieve on the grounds that he had been appointed a commissioner to try the king without his knowledge, and had signed Charles I's death warrant only as a result of Cromwell's threats and intimidation. He also produced testimony from Monck and Lord Ashley that he had helped to bring about the restoration of the monarchy, and asked to be 'represented to his majesty as a fit object of his royal clemency and mercy'. In the event, the death sentence was commuted, but he remained in prison and his Buckinghamshire estates were confiscated and given to James, duke of York. In 1664 a warrant was issued for his transportation to Tangier. Whether he was actually sent to north Africa is unclear; some authorities claim that he died there in 1672, but others claim that the plan was abandoned after representations from his wife, Hester *Fleetwood (d. 1714), and that he was subsequently released from the Tower and allowed to emigrate to America. Care needs to be taken to distinguish him another George Fleetwood, the brother of Charles Fleetwood, who fought in Sweden.   CHRISTOPHER DURSTON

Sources M. Noble, *The lives of the English regicides*, 2 vols. (1798) · A. Woolrych, *Commonwealth to protectorate* (1982) · C. H. Firth and G. Davies, *The regimental history of Cromwell's army*, 2 vols. (1940) · *CSP dom.*, 1653–4; 1659–60 · C. H. Firth and R. S. Rait, eds., *Acts and ordinances of the interregnum, 1642–1660*, 3 vols. (1911) · *Seventh report*, HMC, 6 (1879) · *Mercurius Aulicus* (7 Dec 1643) · G. Lipscomb, *The history and antiquities of the county of Buckingham*, 4 vols. (1831–47) · *VCH Buckinghamshire* · *DNB* · GEC, *Peerage* · A. M. Johnson, 'Buckinghamshire, 1640–1660', MA diss., U. Wales, 1963
Likenesses S. Cooper, miniature, 1647, NPG

Fleetwood [*née* Smyth], **Hester** (d. 1714), compiler of recipes, was one of the seven children of Sir Robert Smyth (c.1594–1669) of Upton, Essex, barrister, and his wife, Judith (c.1605–1653), daughter of Nicholas Walmesley, esquire, of Dunkenhalgh, Lancashire. In 1651 or 1652 she married George *Fleetwood (bap. 1623, d. in or after 1664), a widower with two children, who had been a signatory of Charles I's death warrant and was now a militia commissioner for Buckinghamshire, commanding regiments of horse and foot. She lived with him at The Vache, a large house in Chalfont St Giles, Buckinghamshire. Their first two sons died young but a third son, Robert, was baptized in 1659 and lived until 1712. There were also two daughters, Hester and Elizabeth (bap. 1663).

Hester Fleetwood's life, and her children's prospects, changed dramatically when her husband, who had been knighted by Cromwell in 1656, was punished as a regicide following the Restoration. He was imprisoned in the Tower, and in 1664 a warrant was issued for his deportation to Tangier; it is uncertain whether he was in fact sent to Tangier or allowed to go to America. The Vache was confiscated and sold but the Fleetwoods were allowed to continue there during the lifetime of Hester's mother-in-law, Anne Fleetwood. Richard Baxter mentions that in 1665 three nonconformist ministers were at Mrs Fleetwood's house, David Clarkson, Samuel Cradock (Hester's brother-in-law), and Edward Terry, and that one person died of plague there. Upon the death of Anne Fleetwood on 29 May 1673 the household had to disperse. Hester Fleetwood, who had been bequeathed the contents of her bedchamber, including purple curtains, and the contents of her maid's room, was now homeless. It may have been then that she became a Quaker and went to live with the Russell family at Jordans, Chalfont St Giles. She is first recorded as attending a Quaker meeting in 1678, at Larkins Green. Her son Robert became, instead of a country gentleman, a glass-seller in London.

While at The Vache, Hester Fleetwood compiled an interesting little manuscript recipe book, which still survives. The legibly written book contains over 300 cookery and medical recipes, including 'plague water the Vache way' and a recipe for horse-dung water to prevent convulsions in children. A recipe for 'one that cannot make water' required live bees to be dried on a hot tile and then powdered. An experimental recipe for rheumatic eyes called for two snails, each placed with the open end to the eye, and tied on with a cloth to prevent them crawling away. A diet drink containing senna and rhubarb was taken by Hester's brother-in-law Cradock, spring and autumn. Of several recipes for melancholy, Hester tried at least one with success. The book also showed how to make pheasants lay, how to make French bread, and how to slay any worm which has crept into a man's ear, within five nights at most. She was adept at shorthand, which she occasionally used to complete a recipe. The book has a long shorthand note dated 23 April 1661 (Charles II's coronation day, an event of great significance in a regicide's family), recording a dinner conversation with her mother-in-law, Anne, regarding various relatives and their religious persuasions.

Hester belonged to the Upperside meeting of Quakers. She died on 9 February 1714 and was buried on the 14th at Tring, contrary to her will of 11 August 1712 (witnessed by Thomas Ellwood), which requested interment in the Quakers' burying-ground at New Jordans, under the supervision of her friends Mary Baker and Bridget Russell. The will mentions 'my loving friends William Russell and Bridget his wife, with whom I have long sojourned' (PRO, PROB 11/540, fol. 47). The recipe book passed into the hands of the Russell family at Jordans.   C. G. LEWIN

Sources recipe book of Hester Fleetwood, 1656, priv. coll. · will, PRO, PROB 11/540, sig. 94 · Greaves & Zaller, *BDBR*, 289–90 · A. Collins, *The English baronetage*, 3 (1741), 462 · parish register, Chalfont St Giles, 14 Feb 1714, Bucks. RLSS [burial] · 'The Fleetwoods and Milton's cottage', *N&Q*, 10th ser., 1 (1904), 422–4 · 'An unknown Fleetwood pedigree', *N&Q*, 9th ser., 9 (1902), 261–3 · *Reliquiae Baxterianae, or, Mr Richard Baxter's narrative of the most memorable passages of his life and times*, ed. M. Sylvester, 1 vol. in 3 pts (1696), pt 3, p. 2 · *CSP dom.*, 1693 · will, proved, 14 July 1673, Bucks. RLSS, D/A/WF/47/184 [A. Fleetwood of The Vache] · will, PRO, PROB 11/347, sig. 45 [Anne Fleetwood, eldest daughter of George Fleetwood] · B. S. Snell, ed., *The minute book of the monthly meeting of the Society of Friends for the upperside of Buckinghamshire, 1669–1690* (1937)
Archives priv. coll., recipe book
Wealth at death £130 in monetary bequests; plus mother-of-pearl purse, silver candlestick, looking-glass, tortoiseshell dressing box, silk cloak and mantle, childbed linen with child's cup, porringer and spoon, largest gold ring, little cabinet, wearing apparel, and household goods: will, PRO, PROB 11/540, sig. 94

Fleetwood, James (bap. 1603, d. 1683), bishop of Worcester, seventh son of Sir George Fleetwood of The Vache, Chalfont St Giles, Buckinghamshire, and his wife, Catherine, daughter of Henry Denny of Waltham, Essex, was baptized at Chalfont St Giles on 25 April 1603. In 1622 he went as a scholar from Eton College to King's College, Cambridge. He graduated BA in 1627, proceeded MA in 1631, and was a fellow from 1626 to 1634. Having been ordained deacon at Peterborough on 23 September 1632 Fleetwood attracted the patronage of Bishop Robert Wright of Lichfield, who made him his chaplain the same year, and presented him to the vicarage of Prees, Shropshire; subsequently, on 12 July 1636, he collated him to the prebend of Eccleshall in Lichfield Cathedral. Probably during the 1630s Fleetwood married Martha Mercer of Reading. The couple had four daughters and two sons, Arthur, probably born about 1638 and fellow of Queens' College, Cambridge, from 1661 to 1662, and John (c.1641–1705).

A fervent royalist, on the outbreak of the rebellion Fleetwood attached himself as chaplain to the regiment of John, Earl Rivers, and his services at the battle of Edgehill (though their nature is not clear) caused Charles I to command the University of Oxford to confer upon him the degree of DD on 1 November 1642. Fleetwood also became rector of the rich living of Sutton Coldfield, Warwickshire, but was subsequently ejected and sequestered in 1647. Thereafter he kept a school at Barnes, Surrey, attended in 1653 by Sir Ralph Verney's son. When this was closed in 1655 he became tutor to the children of the widowed duchess of Richmond and chaplain to Prince Charles.

At the Restoration Fleetwood's loyalty was rewarded with a royal mandate for the provostship of King's College, Cambridge, to which the fellows elected him in June 1660, in spite of the resistance of the Commonwealth provost, Dr Benjamin Whichcote, who had to be forced to depart with the aid of a letter mandatory from the king. Fleetwood was also incorporated DD at Cambridge and regained his living of Prees. From 1662 to 1671 he was rector of Anstey, Hertfordshire, and in 1669 became rector of Denham, Buckinghamshire. Although he was vice-chancellor of the university in 1663 and 1667, Fleetwood does not appear to have been active at Cambridge, and his promotion to the see of Worcester was clearly the final mark of royal gratitude rather than a sign of reward for abilities shown in his other posts.

Fleetwood was consecrated bishop of Worcester in the church of St Peter-le-Poer, Broad Street, London, on 29 August 1675. He did not prove an active prelate: his surviving diocesan records show him performing the minimum duties, and even the pamphlet *The Bishop of Worcester's Letter* (1679), published during the Titus Oates controversy and once attributed to him, proves to have been written by someone else. He will, however, be remembered for his major restoration of Hartlebury Castle, which occupied him for the greater part of his episcopate, and to which the only subsequent notable addition was Bishop Hurd's library room.

Fleetwood died on 17 July 1683 at Hartlebury Castle, and was buried in Worcester Cathedral, but the monument described by Wood as being placed over his grave in the lady chapel has vanished without trace. He was survived by his son John, who had become archdeacon of Worcester a few months after his father became bishop and remained so until his death nearly thirty years later in 1705.

B. S. BENEDIKZ

Sources Venn, *Alum. Cant.* · *Fasti Angl., 1541–1857*, [Ely], 108 · Foster, *Alum. Oxon.* · R. O. Walker, ed., *Hartlebury* (1986), 13 · Wood, *Ath. Oxon.* · Wood, *Ath. Oxon.: Fasti*, 1st edn, 2.51 · W. Stubbs, *Registrum sacrum Anglicanum*, 2nd edn (1897), 121 · *Walker rev.*, 304 · Bucks. RLSS, Chalfont St Giles parish register · Worcester Diocesan RO, Fleetwood's register
Archives Worcester Diocesan RO, bishop's register
Likenesses portrait, Hartlebury Castle, Worcestershire

Fleetwood, Sir Miles (*d.* 1641), administrator and politician, was the eldest son of Sir William Fleetwood (*d.* after 1610) of Ealing and Cranford, Middlesex, and of Cardington, Bedfordshire, receiver-general of the court of wards, and his wife, Jane (*d.* 1625×8), daughter of William Clifton of Brinton, Somerset, and widow of Hugh Coplestone. He was admitted to Gray's Inn on 9 January 1588. In January 1599 there were rumours of a marriage between 'the lord marquis daughter' and 'a youth under 18 son of Mr Fleetwood receiver of the court of wards' (*CSP dom.*, 1598–1601, 152), but Miles, probably by then of age, married Anne (*bap.* 1578), daughter of Nicholas Luke of Woodend, Cople, Bedfordshire. His eldest son, baptized on 8 January 1600, died in infancy. Fleetwood was knighted at Dublin by the lord deputy of Ireland in 1602.

On 6 September 1604 Fleetwood was granted the office of receiver-general of the court of wards and liveries in reversion after his father's death. Although Sir William was apparently sequestered from his office in 1609, Miles was granted it on 22 March 1610. Thereafter many warrants to him to pay moneys survive and there is evidence that by 1618 he was lending money to the crown. His father had died four years in arrears on his accounts, but Sir Miles delayed accounting until Charles I's reign. His basic fees had been raised in the accounting year 1609–10 because he kept more servants to protect the king's treasure and attended in vacations. In 1638 he received £278 13s. 4d. plus the attendant gratuities.

Fleetwood sat in every parliament from 1614, when he represented Huntingdon, until his death in 1641. In 1621 he represented Westbury, Wiltshire. Elected for Bletchingley, Surrey, in the parliament of 1624, he chose to sit for Launceston in Cornwall. In 1625 and 1626 he sat for Newton in Lancashire and in 1628 for Woodstock, Oxfordshire.

In 1621 Fleetwood was accused of fraud at the instigation of Sir Lionel Cranfield, master of the court of wards, part of a wider battle over the efficient management of the court (and of royal finances generally), delays in finalizing accounts, and the handling of money. Fleetwood attacked Cranfield over his instructions for the court of wards, arguing that they were injurious both to the king and to his subjects. At Cranfield's impeachment in 1624 Fleetwood—once it was clear that the duke of Buckingham and Prince Charles approved—accused him of obtaining unprecedented power and taking large bribes. Fleetwood was thought to be a client of Buckingham; in

1626 he opposed the attempted impeachment of the duke. Fleetwood also had ties with Charles, whom he assisted with his finances before his accession, taking up money at interest 'for the king's occasions' (*CSP dom.*, 1625–6, 378).

Fleetwood became involved in the crown's disafforestation schemes and estate policies. In 1626–7 he was a prime actor in negotiating the disafforestation of the forests of Leicester (for which he received fees of £950) and of Feckenham in Worcestershire. Fleetwood had been under-steward of the honour of Grafton, a crown estate which lay near his Northamptonshire seat of Aldwincle, since at least 1610. In the mid-1630s he negotiated additional leases to the honour's tenants to raise enough money in entry fines to pay back Sir Francis Crane, to whom the honour had been mortgaged in 1628. Fleetwood's scheme resulted in contracts worth £15,614. Crane's complaint that the renewed leases had been made too cheaply was partially upheld by a commission of inquiry in 1635, but Fleetwood's actions were approved the following year by the court of exchequer. In another case Fleetwood claimed that the manor of Haslope was part of the honour of Grafton, and without negotiating over Thomas Tyrrell's rights in it, disposed of the greater part of his estate. Fleetwood could, however, in other ways be a kind officer, helping Katherine Tothill in 1626 to free herself from the imputation of lunacy.

In parliament Fleetwood was an unyielding opponent of the Arminians. In 1625 he was a member of the Commons committee appointed to investigate the writings of Richard Mountague. In February 1629, warning against the threat posed to the church by Catholics and 'Arminian Sectaryes', he attacked Mountague's writings '1 for scisme and error in doctryne. 2 sedition in poynt of state: 3 an agravation resulting out of these 2'. Mountague's anti-Calvinism, Fleetwood urged, had introduced popery and faction into the Church of England, and used the slur of puritan against 'the Kings best subjects to bring them into jelosies with the King' (Notestein and Relf, 193–4). By contrast Fleetwood was the voice of compromise on constitutional issues. When he spoke during the Oxford session of the 1625 parliament against the immediate granting of supply and suggested first setting up a general committee of grievances he was probably acting as a spokesman of the duke as the latter offered placatory gestures towards the Commons. But it is also of a piece with the position of moderation and compromise which he displayed elsewhere: in 1628 in the debates which led to the petition of right and in 1629 over the issues of the king's right to levy customs dues without parliamentary consent and over MPs' privilege raised by John Rolle's case. Such moderation was motivated in part by his concern to defend his financial interests. When the payment of pensions was to be removed from the court of wards to the exchequer, Charles sent a soothing reply to Fleetwood, speaking of the latter's good service in advancing the revenue, promising recompense for lost income but arguing that the change was a matter of the 'public good' (*CSP dom.*, 1601–41, 344–5).

The trouble in wards went on into the 1630s. By this time the royal finances were so entangled, and Fleetwood in turn so entangled in them, that his exact position can hardly be determined and continued to be a problem long after his death. Fleetwood sat for Hindon, Wiltshire, in both the Short and Long parliaments. Sitting on the committee of privileges, and those on monopolies, Star Chamber, ship money, the charges against the earl of Strafford and Archbishop Laud, and several dealing with ecclesiastical abuses, he showed no sign of favouring the king. Nevertheless, as G. E. Aylmer has commented, 'To the last he continued to breathe fire and brimstone in matters of religion but to coo like a dove of peace on political questions' (Aylmer, 381). Fleetwood died on 8 March 1641.

SYBIL M. JACK

Sources *Northamptonshire Notes and Queries*, new ser., 1/4 (1906), 111, 112 · *Northamptonshire Notes and Queries*, new ser., 1/5 (1906) · G. E. Aylmer, *The king's servants: the civil service of Charles I, 1625–1642*, rev. edn (1974) · H. E. Bell, *An introduction to the history and records of the court of wards and liveries* (1953) · *CSP dom.*, 1598–1641 · M. Prestwich, *Cranfield, politics, profits under the early Stuarts* (1966) · D. Brunton and D. H. Pennington, *Members of the Long Parliament* (1954) · *Camden miscellany, I*, CS, 39 (1847) · *The obituary of Richard Smyth … being a catalogue of all such persons as he knew in their life*, ed. H. Ellis, CS, 44 (1849) · M. Jansson and W. B. Bidwell, eds., *Proceedings in parliament, 1625* (1987) · R. C. Johnson and others, eds., *Proceedings in parliament, 1628*, 6 vols. (1977–83) · W. Notestein and F. H. Relf, eds., *Commons debates for 1629* (1921) · C. Russell, *Politics and English parliaments, 1621–1629* (1979) · Keeler, *Long Parliament* · R. W. Hoyle, ed., *The estates of the English crown, 1558–1640* (1992) · W. J. Jones, 'Fleetwood, William III', HoP, *Commons, 1558–1603*
Archives PRO, WARDS 9 | Berks. RO, Packer MS 0/1/151, 234
Wealth at death over £1000

Fleetwood, Sir Peter Hesketh-, first baronet (1801–1866), founder of the town of Fleetwood, was descended from the ancient Lancashire families of Hesketh and Fleetwood; he was one of the three sons and one daughter of Robert Hesketh (1764–1824) of Rossall, Lancashire, and his wife, Maria (*d.* 1824), *née* Rawlinson. He was born at Wennington Hall, near Lancaster, on 9 May 1801. With the death of his elder brother, Edward, in 1820, which much affected him, he became heir to the considerable estates his father developed in the Rossall area. He was educated at Trinity College, Oxford, graduating BA in 1823 and MA in 1826. In 1826 he married (Eliza) Debonnaire (*d.* 1833), daughter of Sir T. J. Metcalfe; they had several children. He was high sheriff of Lancashire in 1830, and sat as MP for Preston from 1832 to 1847; initially a Conservative, by 1837 he was recorded by Dod as a Liberal. He was a strong advocate for the abolition of the death penalty, and in 1840 published *The Last Days of a Condemned*, a translation of Victor Hugo's pamphlet, to which he prefixed 'Observations on capital punishment'. He assumed the surname of Fleetwood by royal licence on 5 March 1831, and was created a baronet in June 1838. Hesketh-Fleetwood married precipitantly, in Belgium in 1837, Virginie Marie (*d.* 1900), daughter of Don Pedro Garcia of Spain.

Impressed by the poor facilities of Lancashire and by the opportunities of opening the country by railway construction, Hesketh-Fleetwood planned a new town, designed by Decimus Burton, on his estate at Rossall at the mouth of the River Wyre, in the Fylde, Lancashire. Burton's plan was ready in 1835, construction starting in 1836: it was one of the first towns to be planned around a railway. Shortage of capital and an underestimation of railway and building costs brought Hesketh-Fleetwood near to bankruptcy, and in 1844 he had to sell family estates at Blackpool and Rossall (as a result of which sale Rossall School was founded). Further land sales followed in 1850. The town prospered but its founder's family did not.

Hesketh-Fleetwood died at his residence, 127 Piccadilly, London, on 12 April 1866. His son, the Revd Sir Peter Louis Hesketh-Fleetwood, died in 1880, when the baronetcy became extinct. H. C. G. MATTHEW

Sources B. Curtis, *The golden dream: the biography of Sir Peter Hesketh-Fleetwood, bart.* (1994) · B. Curtis, *Fleetwood: a town is born* (1986) · *GM*, 4th ser., 1 (1866), 906 · C. R. Dod, *Electoral facts, from 1832 to 1853* (1853) · Boase, *Mod. Eng. biog.* · Burke, *Peerage* · Foster, *Alum. Oxon.*
Likenesses H. B. Burlowe, bust, Fleetwood, Lancashire · G. Hayter, group portrait, oils (*The House of Commons, 1833*), NPG
Wealth at death under £20,000: probate, 6 June 1866, CGPLA Eng. & Wales

Fleetwood, Thomas (1661–1717), owner and reclaimer of land, was the eldest son in the family of three sons and five daughters of Sir Richard Fleetwood, baronet, of Calwick, Staffordshire, who survived him, and his wife, Anne, daughter of Sir Edward Golding, baronet, of Colston Basset, Nottinghamshire. Fleetwood married Laetitia, daughter and heir of Christopher Bannister, of Bank Hall, Bretherton, Lancashire.

About 1690 Fleetwood bought the manor of Marton Grange, or Marton Sands, in Lancashire, from the Mainwaring family. The land was next to a large lake called Marton (or Martin) meer, occupying an area of 3132 acres, with a circumference of about 18 miles. Regular flooding of the mere damaged the meadows and made communications difficult, and Fleetwood decided to drain it by cutting a channel of 1½ miles from the mere to the sea. First he obtained a lease of rights in the mere for the duration of three lives and thirty-one years from the neighbouring landowners, and then in 1692 he procured an act of parliament allowing him to proceed in draining the land. The work began in the following year. At times there were as many as 2000 men working on the scheme. The result was fairly successful for about sixty years, but by 1755, five years after the lease had expired, it had become neglected, and the sea broke in, destroying all that had been achieved. In 1781 Thomas Eccleston of Scarisbrick, Lancashire, revived the drainage project, but it was not until the middle of the nineteenth century that Sir Peter Hesketh-Fleetwood managed to turn this large area of fertile land, crossed by good roads, to good use.

Fleetwood died on 22 April 1717 and was buried in North Meols church, Lancashire, where he was commemorated by a monument. His only daughter and heir, Elizabeth, married Thomas Legh, younger brother of Peter Legh, of Lyme in Cheshire.

C. H. DERBY, *rev.* ANNE PIMLOTT BAKER

Sources J. Thirsk, ed., *The agrarian history of England and Wales*, 5/1 (1984), 65–6 · J. P. Earwaker, *East Cheshire: past and present, or, A history of the hundred of Macclesfield*, 2 (1880) · E. Baines and W. R. Whatton, *The history of the county palatine and duchy of Lancaster*, 4 vols. (1836)

Fleetwood [Fletewoode], **William** (c.1525–1594), lawyer and antiquary, was the son of Robert Fleetwood, a cursitor in chancery, who was the third son of William Fleetwood of Hesketh in Lancashire. His name appears in the admissions register of Eton College, and in those of both Brasenose College and Broadgates Hall, Oxford (c.1538–43), although he did not take a degree. Having spent some time in Calais in the early 1540s, he enrolled at Clifford's Inn in 1543, proceeded to the Middle Temple in 1547, and was called to the bar there in 1551. He became freeman by patrimony of the Merchant Taylors' Company of London on 21 June 1557, was made steward of the company's manor of Rushbrook, Worcestershire, in 1564, and acted as counsel in their suit with the Clothworkers in 1565. He married Mariana, daughter of John Barley of Kingsey, Buckinghamshire.

Fleetwood sat as MP for Marlborough in the last parliament (1558) of Queen Mary, and served as an ecclesiastical commissioner for the dioceses of Oxford, Peterborough, and Coventry and Lichfield in 1559. Enjoying the patronage of Sir Ambrose Cave, chancellor of the duchy, he was MP for Lancaster in 1559 and 1563. Selected autumn reader (on termors and tenants at will) at the Temple for 1564, he was Lent reader (on liberties and franchises) in 1569. Thanks to the influence of the earl of Leicester he was elected recorder of London on 26 April 1571, and in the same year was made a commissioner to inquire into the customs, besides being returned to parliament for St Mawes. He became a serjeant-at-law in 1580 and was appointed commissioner for the reformation of abuses in printing in 1583, the same year in which he drafted a scheme for housing the poor and for preventing the plague in London by maintaining open spaces. On 27 April 1586 he was promised, but did not receive, the post of baron of the exchequer, apparently because Queen Elizabeth valued his service as recorder of London. He was elected MP for London in 1572, 1584, 1586, and 1589. He reported with the solicitor-general on proceedings to be taken against the Jesuits in 1588, and in 1589 on the right of sanctuary for criminals attaching to St Paul's Churchyard.

A member of the ecclesiastical court of high commission as well as recorder of London, Fleetwood also sat from time to time at quarter sessions in Middlesex, Surrey, and Buckinghamshire. As recorder he was famous for rigorously enforcing the laws against vagrants, masspriests, and papists, being committed to the Fleet prison for a short period in 1576 for breaking into the Portuguese ambassador's chapel under colour of the laws against recusants. A hard-working judge who once complained that he had 'not leisure to eat my meat' (HoP, *Commons, 1558–1603*, 2.137), he was 'sore wounded in the head' (*Lost Notebooks*, 367) at Charing Cross in 1577 by one of the queen's stablemen who was seeking revenge against

Fleetwood for having imprisoned him. Described as of a 'marvellous merry and pleasant conceit' (HoP, *Commons, 1558–1603*, 2.137), he was also a notable parliament man who served on innumerable committees and was known for his witty, if sometimes tedious, speeches. A committed protestant even during the reign of Queen Mary, Fleetwood had a lawyer's suspicion of clerical pretensions of any variety. He argued against the overly narrow interpretation of the Book of Common Prayer in cases of deprivation, but was unsympathetic to radical clergymen who claimed that temporal matters should be decided by religious censors, or who denied the queen the right to judge ecclesiastical causes. Although *Leicester's Commonwealth* dubbed him the earl's 'mad Recorder', he was a regular correspondent and friend of Lord Burghley and close to Thomas Sackville, Lord Buckhurst, with whom, according to his own account, he often discussed matters of state and shared a voracious interest in history.

Fleetwood collected his first manuscript year-book in the 1540s, some of his student notes survive from the 1550s, and he is reported on one occasion to have been reading a book during a debate in the Commons. Though their contents are now widely dispersed, he must have established large libraries at his country house as well as in London. Fifteen volumes from his collection of year-books and readings are in the Harley manuscripts at the British Library. Notebooks and manuscript treatises survive in various locations, and he was the likely owner of four well-known miniatures depicting the courts during the reign of Henry VII, which are now in the Inner Temple Library. A borrower of books from Archbishop Matthew Parker, he once noted that his love of history was inspired by the Greeks. Familiar with the works of, among others, Leland and Bale, he was able to quote the Frenchman Bodin in criticizing Polydore Vergil's use of historical evidence. Although he frequently lamented that pressure of work denied him the leisure to develop fully his own writings, he supplied commendatory verses for works by William Lambarde and Sir Thomas Chaloner. His own most sustained piece of historical research was an account of the forest laws based on the honour of Pickering, selected, he said, because of the incomparable quality of its surviving records. His overall interpretation—that forest courts enjoyed a jurisdiction outside the common law because the forests themselves had been allowed to kings as a source of recreation in return for their arduous labours—was remarkably similar to that published under the name of John Manwood in 1615. Despite the apparently narrow subject, the most complete version of Fleetwood's work placed the forest laws within the context of a thoroughly anti-papal account of the general history of English law, while another prefaces the subject with an investigation of the waves of immigration that had shaped the population of Britain since the time of the flood.

Fleetwood also produced professional works designed for law students and the wider public. He published an analytical index of the year-books from Edward V to Henry VIII, and another for Edmund Plowden's *Commentaries*, his aim being to make the law on any subject instantly retrievable. A guidebook for justices of the peace was widely circulated in manuscript but not printed until the middle of the seventeenth century. A general treatise on the laws of England, an account of the laws and customs of London, and a treatise on the criminal jurisdiction of the high court of admiralty, which was composed in the late 1560s and dedicated to Lord Cobham, remained in manuscript. Written as a response to the resistance he had met when attempting to execute a commission out of the admiralty in 1566, the latter work was garnished with quotations in equal measure from Bracton and the scriptures. It shows Fleetwood the systematizer setting out 'to prove what Jurisdiction or franchises the Admirall Courts hath and what matters it might determyn' (Prichard and Yale, 165), while at the same time calling for court officials to perform their functions strictly according to the letter of the law. According to a plausible early seventeenth-century attribution, Fleetwood was also the author of 'A brief treatise or discourse of the vallidity, strength, and extent of the charter of Bridewell [Hospital]'. Probably written in the 1580s and sometimes attributed to Sir Francis Bacon, this work criticized the discretionary powers exercised by the governors of the Bridewell in apprehending and punishing rogues, vagabonds, and other members of London's underclass. It argued that any non-parliamentary grant by the crown to inflict penalties without due process, including an indictment and a public hearing, was contrary to chapter 29 of Magna Carta, and therefore void.

Although it is unclear whether it is a literary invention or based on fact, Fleetwood's manuscript *Itinerarium ad Windsor* describes a conversation in 1575 between himself, Buckhurst, and Leicester, in which Fleetwood used the concept of the king's two bodies to prove that Queen Elizabeth, despite being a woman, ruled by the same laws as her predecessors, a point that he brought home by describing an incident during the reign of Queen Mary when one of her Spanish advisers allegedly produced a treatise suggesting that she should claim the throne by conquest and 'do as she list'. In 1563 Fleetwood admitted having read the notorious treatise by John Hales, which argued that the crown should descend to Lady Katherine Grey if Elizabeth died without a successor, and in 1573 he spoke often in parliament against the claims of Mary of Scotland. These circumstances, his connections with Burghley, and the resemblance to his of the handwriting of the corrected autograph copy suggest that Fleetwood may also have been the author of *Certaine errors upon the statute made the xxvth yeare of King Edward the Third of children borne beyond sea*. This lengthy and widely circulated work was almost certainly written in the mid-1580s, probably in connection with the government's plan that the queen should be protected by having her loyal subjects subscribe to bonds of association. Claiming that the common law prevented the succession of aliens to the throne, it proceeds to argue that the state, the laws, and the institutions of the crown continue to exist even after the death of the monarch. It was therefore perfectly logical for parliament to determine the succession in the event of a vacancy, just as urban corporations elected a new mayor when the existing one died.

Fleetwood resigned as recorder of London in 1591, whereupon the common council voted him a pension of £100. He was made queen's serjeant in 1592, and died at his house in Noble Street, Aldersgate, on 28 February 1594. He had formerly lived at Bacon House, Foster Lane, and at his death owned an estate at Great Missenden, Buckinghamshire, where he was buried. His elder son, Sir William, succeeded to Missenden, and the younger son, Sir Thomas, of the Middle Temple, was attorney to Henry, prince of Wales. One daughter, Cordelia, married Sir David Foulis, and another, Elizabeth, Sir Thomas Chaloner (d. 1615). CHRISTOPHER W. BROOKS

Sources HoP, Commons, 1509–58, 2.148–9 · HoP, Commons, 1558–1603, 2.133–8 · Reports from the lost notebooks of Sir James Dyer, ed. J. H. Baker, 2, SeldS, 110 (1994) · M. J. Prichard and D. E. C. Yale, eds., Hale and Fleetwood on admiralty jurisdiction, SeldS, 108 (1993) · J. H. Baker and J. S. Ringrose, A catalogue of English legal manuscripts in Cambridge University Library (1996) · DNB · 'Itinerarium ad Windsor', BL, Harley MS 6234 [W. Fleetwood] · CUL, MS Dd.9.17 · GL, MS 86 · GL, MS 9384 · Annalium tam regum Edwardi quinti, Richard tertii, & Henrici septimi (1579) · CUL, Add. MSS 9212 · Bibliotheca monastica-Fletewodiana (1744)
Archives BL, papers relating to London and to forests, Add. MSS 25249, 26047 · Folger, treatises in English law, MS V.B.9
Wealth at death considerable landed estate

Fleetwood, William (1656–1723), bishop of Ely, was born on 1 January 1656 in the Tower of London, the son of Captain Geoffrey Fleetwood (d. 1665), an ordnance official resident at the Tower, and his wife, Anne (d. in or before 1701), daughter of Richard Smith, protonotary of the poultry counter, of Little Moorfields, London. He was educated at Eton College between 1671 and 1675 before matriculating from King's College, Cambridge, in Michaelmas term 1675. He was made a fellow in 1678, graduated BA in 1679, and proceeded MA in 1683. On the death of the provost, John Coplestone, in 1689, the appointment of the next provost of King's College was claimed by the crown. Fleetwood and another fellow were deputed to assert the right of the college to elect their own provost, which was duly maintained. On 25 March 1689 he preached before the university in King's College chapel at the commemoration of the founder of the college, Henry VI. His sermon was printed, the first of many which found their way into print as his reputation as a preacher grew steadily. On 26 November 1689 he was installed as rector of St Augustine's, London, the same year he was made lecturer at St Dunstan-in-the-West. On 29 September 1690 Fleetwood, of St Benet Paul's Wharf, was licensed to marry Anne Smith (1663/4–1725), of St Giles Cripplegate. The marriage took place on 9 October at All Hallows, London Wall. In 1691 Fleetwood published his first work besides sermons, Inscriptionum antiquarum sylloge, a collection of pagan and Christian inscriptions. The vice-provost of King's College, Dr Henry Godolphin, secured a fellowship at Eton for Fleetwood on 13 October 1691, and he preached the Gunpowder Plot anniversary sermon before the House of Commons on 5 November, which attacked Catholic doctrine as the inspiration for wars of religion. Fleetwood

William Fleetwood (1656–1723), by John Simon (after Jonathan Richardson, 1702)

became a regular preacher before the king, both houses of parliament, the mayor and corporation of London, and other public bodies. He was named a chaplain to William III and Mary II, and gained a reputation as a whig clergyman. In 1701 Fleetwood published An Essay on Miracles from materials he had collected for the Boyle lecture which ill health had prevented him from delivering.

Shortly before William III's death Fleetwood was named a canon of Windsor by the king. Following the king's death Fleetwood's tory opponents tried to block his nomination, but Queen Anne confirmed it and on 2 June 1702 he was installed. In April 1705 he was made a DD during the queen's visit to Cambridge. On 8 April 1706 Fleetwood was instituted rector of Wexham, Buckinghamshire, a living worth only £60 per annum. This may have been provided as a scholarly retreat, for in 1707 Fleetwood published Chronicon pretiosum, on the value of money and the price of corn and other commodities for the previous six centuries. Queen Anne was deeply impressed by Fleetwood's sermons, 'my bishop' (DNB) as she called him, and he was the royal choice to succeed William Beveridge as bishop of St Asaph. Thomas Hearne remarked on Fleetwood's elevation to the see in late April 1708: 'a man of time-serving principles, plausible preacher, of some learning in antiquity' (Remarks, 2.104).

Fleetwood was duly consecrated bishop of St Asaph on 6 June 1708. He embarked on his primary visitation and this delayed his introduction into the House of Lords until 4 April 1709. Fleetwood's whig beliefs led him to vote against Henry Sacheverell during Sacheverell's trial for opposing the principles of the revolution settlement in March 1710. He delayed for as long as possible Dr

Sacheverell's institution to the rectory of Selattyn in Shropshire. He published his *Charge to the Clergy of the Diocese of St Asaph* in 1710, complete with a defence against accusations that he had been disloyal to the church. On 16 February 1711 he preached a sermon before the Society for the Propagation of the Gospel in Foreign Parts, which was widely circulated thereafter. His whiggish views were again revealed when William Nicolson, bishop of Carlisle, noted on 26 February 1711 that Fleetwood was 'much delighted with the *Medley* of this day by Mr [Arthur] Maynwaring' (*London Diaries*, 551); Maynwaring was a prominent whig pamphleteer. Fleetwood was opposed to the peace plans of the tory ministry. Henry Prescott described on 16 December 1711 a letter from Fleetwood 'wherein he triumphs upon the general vogue against peace, and on the access of Lord Nottingham [the former tory secretary of state Daniel Finch, second earl of Nottingham] to the Whig side' (*Diary of Henry Prescott*, 2.338). Nor was he willing to confine his views to private correspondence, for when Fleetwood was invited by the Lords on 22 December 1711 to preach on the fast day on 16 January 1712 his chosen text, 'the people that delight in war' (Bond, 3.440n.), which he wrote to defend the necessity of maintaining the war with France, caused his opponents to adjourn the house to prevent him actually delivering his sermon, although it quickly found its way into print albeit without some of its most critical paragraphs. In February and March 1712 he opposed the bill providing toleration for Scottish episcopalians. The publication of his *Four Sermons* in May 1712 (preached on the occasions of the deaths of Queen Mary, the duke of Gloucester, and William III, and on the accession of Queen Anne), complete with preface attacking the principle of non-resistance (also published as *The Spectator*, no. 384, 21 May 1712), caused such offence to the tory majority in the Commons that on 10 June the preface was voted by 119 to 54 as 'malicious and factious, highly reflecting upon the present administration of public affairs under her Majesty, and tending to create discord and sedition amongst her subjects' (*JHC*, 17.263), and was ordered to be burnt by the common hangman. Fleetwood was undeterred by this punishment, claiming that it merely increased the number of his readers. Fleetwood voted against the French commercial treaty in 1713 and the Schism Bill in 1714, thereby opposing both warmer relations with France and the abolition of dissenters' schools. Also in 1714 he was instrumental in passing the Mortuaries in Welsh Dioceses Act.

Fleetwood's political loyalty was rewarded after the Hanoverian succession when he was translated on 18 November 1714 to Ely, although he was not enthroned until 30 August 1715. He was appointed on 2 December 1715 to the third commission for building fifty new churches in London. In January 1716 he asserted his history of loyalty to the new dynasty by informing William Wake that for his sermon before George I in March he would deliver a sermon he had kept twenty years for that purpose. As bishop of Ely he was visitor of Trinity College, Cambridge, and inherited the case of Dr Richard Bentley,

master of Trinity, versus the fellows of the college, who accused Bentley of encroaching on their prerogatives. Fleetwood in effect favoured Bentley by at first threatening a general visitation, and when the quarrel broke out anew, declining to take action. In December 1718 Fleetwood voted for the repeal of the Occasional Conformity and Schism Acts.

Fleetwood died at Tottenham, Middlesex, on 4 August 1723, 'after a long illness, occasioned by apopletic and convulsive fits' (*Remarks*, 8.105), and was buried in Ely Cathedral on the 10th. In his will he placed his estate in Lancashire in the trust of two cousins for the use of his sister, Elizabeth, and after her death for the use of his son, Charles. Fleetwood's wife died on 5 May 1725 and was also buried in Ely Cathedral. Hearne summed up Fleetwood thus: 'he was a man of good learning and of a good style, and had many good qualities, tho' he was a great Whig in the latter part of his life, notwithstanding he was otherwise once' (ibid.). His nephew, Dr William Powell, dean of St Asaph's and prebendary of Ely, repaid his uncle's patronage by publishing a complete collection of his works in 1737. Manuscripts of his sermons are held by Yale University and by Lambeth Palace Library.

STUART HANDLEY

Sources Venn, *Alum. Cant.* • *Fasti Angl., 1541–1857*, [Ely] • *Fasti Angl.* (Hardy), vol. 1 • W. Sterry, ed., *The Eton College register, 1441–1698* (1943), 125 • *Remarks and collections of Thomas Hearne*, ed. C. E. Doble and others, 11 vols., OHS, 2, 7, 13, 34, 42–3, 48, 50, 65, 67, 72 (1885–1921), vols. 2–3, 5, 8 • W. Stevenson, *A supplement to the first edition of Mr Bentham's history and antiquities of the cathedral and conventual church of Ely* (1817), 114 • R. W. Buss, *The ancestry of William Fleetwood, bishop of St Asaph and Ely* (1926) • *IGI* • J. L. Chester and J. Foster, eds., *London marriage licences, 1521–1869* (1887), 492 • H. C. Tomlinson, *Guns and government: the ordnance office under the later Stuarts* (1979), 227 • *The diary of Henry Prescott, LLB, deputy registrar of Chester diocese*, ed. J. Addy and others, 3 vols., Lancashire and Cheshire RS, 127, 132–3 (1987–97) • *The London diaries of William Nicolson, bishop of Carlisle, 1702–1718*, ed. C. Jones and G. Holmes (1985) • will, PRO, PROB 11/592, fols. 234v–235v • G. S. Holmes, *British politics in the age of Anne*, rev. edn (1987), 435 • R. Steele and J. Addison, *The Spectator*, ed. D. Bond, 5 vols. (1965), vol. 3, p. 440n. • *JHC*, 17 (1711–14), 263 • Fleetwood to Wake, 24 Jan 1715, Christ Church Oxf., Wake MS 6/12 • G. Holmes, *The trial of Doctor Sacheverell* (1973) • *Tory and whig: the parliamentary papers of Edward Harley, third earl of Oxford, and William Hay, MP for Seaford, 1716–1753*, ed. S. Taylor and C. Jones, Parliamentary History Record Series, 1 (1998), 202–11 • *DNB*

Archives CUL, commonplace books • LPL, sermons • NL Wales, notebook • Yale U., Beinecke L., sermons | Bodl. Oxf., letters to Browne Willis

Likenesses B. Lens, two miniatures, NPG • attrib. J. Richardson, oils, LPL; version, Bishop's Palace, Ely • J. Simon, mezzotint (after J. Richardson, 1702), BM [*see illus.*] • R. White, line engraving, BM, NPG

Fleming, Abraham (*c*.1552–1607), author, literary editor, and Church of England clergyman, identified himself in his published works as 'London borne'. His elder brother, Samuel, having attended Eton College, matriculated at King's College, Cambridge, in 1565, aged seventeen. At about the same age Abraham became a sizar at Peterhouse, Cambridge, in 1570, from where he graduated early in 1582, although only after spending five or six years working in London publishing houses. Fleming identifies himself as a student in the dedications of his two earliest publications, English translations of Virgil's *The Bucolikes* (1575), and of John Caius's Latin treatise, *Of Englishe Dogges* (1576), so he probably went to London in 1576 or 1577, and quickly became well acquainted with the city's literary scene. During his early years in London, his commendatory verses graced publications by Barnabe Googe, Arthur Golding, Timothy Kendall, George Whetstone, and Reginald Scott, as well as Dionyse Settle's account of Frobisher's second voyage in pursuit of the north-west passage in 1577.

During his first ten years in London, Fleming was associated with at least fifteen printing houses, working principally as a translator, editor, indexer, and compiler. Among the fifty-seven works associated with his name are translations such as *A Registre of Hystories* (1576) from Claudius Aelianus; indexes for the *Zodiac of Life* (1576), Googe's translation of Palingenius; compilations such as *A panoplie of epistles, or, A looking glasse for the unlearned, containing a perfecte plattforme of inditing letters … used of the best and eloquentest rhetoricians* (1576); and devotional literature that ranged from accounts of marvellous events like *A strange and terrible wunder, wrought very late in the parish church of Bongay … in the yeere 1577 in a gret tempest* (1577) to elaborate collections of prayers and maxims, such as *The Diamond of Devotion, Cut and Squared into Six Severall Points* (1582). He also worked with Reginald Scott on the latter's *Discoverie of Witchcraft* (1584). His counsel to the readers of John Knox's *A Fort for the Afflicted* (1580) to 'exercise yourself in the good books of god's faithful', and his assurance that 'The benefite of this Booke belongeth to every particular member of Christes Mysticall bodie, and they onelie have the grace to use this', identifies Fleming's own religious position as firmly protestant, a quality that also marks the work for which he is best remembered, the 1587 edition of Raphael *Holinshed's *Chronicles*.

The first edition of Holinshed's *Chronicles of England, Scotland and Ireland* had been published in 1577. The second edition was printed at Henry Denham's printing house at the sign of The Star in Aldersgate. Denham placed the project in the hands of Abraham Fleming, who had been working extensively for him for the past three years. Donno has demonstrated that it was Fleming, and not John Hooker, alias Vowell (as the title-page claims), who served as the edition's general editor. Hooker revised and extended the Irish history, and Francis Thynne did the same for the Scottish, in an edition which was prepared with great care.

As general editor Fleming spent two years—1585 and 1587—fully engaged in the Holinshed revision. One of his most important tasks was extending the account of the reign of Elizabeth in the *Chronicles* of 1577 to 1586. Besides procuring annals from John Stow for the years following 1577, he also obtained further material for Elizabeth's entire reign, amending omissions that Holinshed had regretted. Throughout the revision of 1587 Fleming generally introduced amendments, and particularly his own, by

the symbol ¶ and concluded them with a bracket], using printed marginalia to identify the sources. Sometimes Fleming reproduced his source material verbatim; at other times he paraphrased. His prose style has been judged 'serviceable', despite its 'strong Protestant and anti-papal sentiments' (Donno, 205). It may have been the virulence with which he expressed those sentiments, however, that led in part to the censorship of the 1587 *Chronicles*. The censors called for heavy editing of Fleming's account of the Babington conspirators' trial and execution, which included such passages as 'these venomous vipers … hewne in peeces, their tigers hearts burned in the fire' (*Chronicles*, 1587, 1574, sig. A22–6, uncensored).

Most of Fleming's work on the *Chronicles*, however, was editorial: he imposed a more rational paragraph structure; he created an episodic structure by inserting editorial comments, Latin epigrams, and transitions; he extended and improved the 1577 edition's printed marginalia; and he created detailed indexes. When the privy council ordered a review and reform of the *Chronicles* in the edition of 1587, large portions of text were rewritten to accommodate castrations and to provide acceptable revisions. Since the latter show extraordinary familiarity with the text as well as a clear understanding of where and how text might be cut to fit the sizes of the cancel sheets, the actual 'reformations' produced in the printing house were surely Fleming's work. This is corroborated by the existence in 1722 of a number of Fleming's manuscripts relating to the censorship of Holinshed's *Chronicles* among papers that Francis Peck intended to publish in a second edition of *Desiderata curiosa*. Unfortunately Peck did not publish the volume and the manuscripts have been lost.

Perhaps one of the most remarkable tasks in which Fleming was engaged was the proof-reading of the 1587 edition. Although other hands appear in the proof copy of the *Chronicles* of 1587 now at the Huntington Library, it has been shown that the principal responsibility rested with Fleming, who was clearly intent on producing a typographically excellent text. That he should have done so is evidence for the book's importance, since only wealthy printing houses could afford 'learned correctors', and since correctors were usually employed only when subject matter as important as 'legal, theological, or Holy Writ' dictated it (Donno, 200).

The religious zeal displayed in his additions to Holinshed's English history clearly became more important to Fleming than his work in London publishing. On 2 August 1588 he was ordained deacon and priest, and he later became chaplain to Katherine Howard, Lady Howard of Effingham and, from 1597, countess of Nottingham. A further translation of Virgil, the *Georgicks* (1589), was dedicated to Archbishop John Whitgift, and on 19 October 1593 the latter collated him to the rectory of St Pancras, Soper Lane, London, which was a Canterbury peculiar. Between 1589 and 1606 Fleming preached eight times at Paul's Cross, and although none of his sermons was published, his devotional writings remained in print well into the seventeenth century. He died at Bottesford, Leicestershire, where his brother Samuel was rector, on 18 September 1607, aged about fifty-six, and was buried in the chancel of the church there.   CYNDIA SUSAN CLEGG

Sources E. S. Donno, 'Abraham Fleming: a learned corrector in 1586–87', *Studies in Bibliography*, 42 (1989), 200–11 · Venn, *Alum. Cant.*, 1/2.148 · *STC, 1475–1640*, vol. 1 · F. Peck, *Desiderata curiosa* (1722) · A. Patterson, *Reading Holinshed's 'Chronicles'* (1994) · Cooper, *Ath. Cantab.*, 2.489–64

Fleming, Alexander (1823–1875), physician, the son of Robert Fleming, a brewer, and his wife, Agnes Brown, was born on 10 September 1823 at Edinburgh. He studied medicine in his native town and graduated MD in 1844. His most notable work was his thesis, 'Physiological and medicinal properties of *Aconitum napellus*' (monkshood or wolfbane), for which he was awarded a gold medal by the university, and which was published in 1845. His researches led to the introduction of a tincture of aconite, a painkiller of uniform strength known as Fleming's tincture. After graduating he spent some time at the hospitals of Paris, Vienna, and Prague.

After his return from the continent Fleming began to practise in Edinburgh, where he was also editor of the *Edinburgh Monthly Journal of Medical Sciences*. He then moved to Cork in Ireland, where he spent some years as professor of materia medica in the Queen's College and was also one of the examiners of the Queen's University, Ireland.

Fleming next went in 1858 to Birmingham, where he held a similar post at the Queen's College, Birmingham, and was also the honorary physician to the Queen's Hospital until his retirement through ill health in 1873. In 1859 he had been elected a fellow of the Royal College of Physicians of London. He was also consulting physician to the Women's Hospital and to the Ear and Throat Infirmary. After the uniting of the two medical schools in Birmingham, Fleming became an active member of the council of Queen's College. He played an important part in the foundation and management of the Institute for Trained Nurses.

Fleming had built up a large and highly successful consulting practice in the west midlands. He was well known as both a teacher and a practitioner, and was chosen to give the address on medicine at the 1872 meeting of the British Medical Association. He was married to Mary Fleming. On retiring he spent some time in the south of France before returning to England, where he lived at Buxton in Derbyshire. He died at the Palace Hotel, Fairfield, Buxton, on 21 August 1875, and was survived by his wife.

   PATRICK WALLIS

Sources BMJ (28 Aug 1875), 286 · Munk, *Roll* · *Nomina eorum, qui gradum medicinae doctoris in academia Jacobi sexti Scotorum regis, quae Edinburgi est, adepti sunt, ab anno 1705 ad annum 1845*, University of Edinburgh (1846) · V. Skipp, *The making of Victorian Birmingham* (1983) · *CGPLA Eng. & Wales* (1875) · parish register (birth), St Cuthbert's, Midlothian, 10 Sept 1823 · *DNB*
Wealth at death £12,000: probate, 22 Sept 1875, *CGPLA Eng. & Wales*

Fleming, Sir Alexander (1881–1955), bacteriologist and discoverer of penicillin, was born on 6 August 1881, the

Sir Alexander Fleming (1881–1955), by Howard Coster, 1954

third of the four children of Hugh Fleming (d. 1888), farmer, of Lochfield, in the parish of Loudoun near Darvel, in Ayrshire, from his second marriage, to Grace Sterling Morton (d. 1928), the daughter of a neighbouring farmer. Hugh Fleming, whose ancestors probably came from the Low Countries, had four surviving children from his first marriage. He was sixty at the time of his second marriage, and died when Alexander (known as Alec) was seven.

Education and career Alec Fleming's early education was in a small country school at Loudoun Moor, then at Darvel School, and finally for eighteen months at Kilmarnock Academy. At fourteen Alec and his two brothers of the second marriage went to live with a doctor stepbrother in London, where he continued his education for two years at the Polytechnic Institute in Regent Street. The next four years were spent as a clerk in a shipping office in the City, but on the advice of his stepbrother, and with the help of a small legacy, Alec Fleming became a student at St Mary's Hospital medical school, London, in 1901. He won the senior entrance scholarship in natural science, and many other class prizes and scholarships during his student career. He took the conjoint qualification in 1906, and the degrees of MB, BS of London University in 1908, with honours in five subjects and a university gold medal. A year later he became FRCS, having taken the primary examination as a student, though he never practised as a surgeon. With a very good memory, learning was seldom a burden. However, his life was never all work and no play; both as an undergraduate and as a postgraduate he was an active and proficient member of the swimming, shooting, and golf clubs, and even took some part in the drama society. Fleming had a natural combativeness and urge to win which were very apparent in the games he played. This determination to succeed was also evident in his medical and laboratory work, where he took delight in using his technical skill and inventiveness to overcome difficulties.

Immediately after qualification, like many of his St Mary's contemporaries, Fleming became an assistant bacteriologist. He joined the inoculation department and began the association with its head, Almroth *Wright, which was to shape his whole career. Fleming also held for some years the post of pathologist to the London Lock Hospital. He worked with Wright in London and then in France during the First World War, and in 1920 he became lecturer in bacteriology in St Mary's medical school. Eight years later he was made professor of bacteriology in the University of London. He remained in the inoculation department, which eventually became the Wright-Fleming Institute of Microbiology, until he retired in 1948. He was made principal of the institute from 1946 to 1948, and remained an emeritus professor until 1954. Until 1942 Fleming was an accomplished metropolitan laboratory scientist whose career had been in the shadow of Wright. Then, at the age of sixty-one, he became an international celebrity because of his association with the development of penicillin. Over the next decade he was fêted across the world and received 189 honours, medals, decorations, and prizes, including sharing the Nobel prize for physiology and medicine with Ernst Chain and Howard Florey in 1945. While Fleming's name became synonymous with penicillin and the antibiotic revolution of the late 1940s and early 1950s, later assessments have given more weight to the work of other scientists, most notably Chain and Florey, and to the teams in the United States that produced penicillin on an industrial scale. There is also a fascination with what Fleming himself called the Fleming myth, that is, why and how a single scientist was ever made responsible for the discovery of penicillin, and how a reserved hospital bacteriologist became an international celebrity.

Laboratory medicine at St Mary's During his early postgraduate years at St Mary's, Fleming was research assistant to Almroth Wright, whose dominant character and fertile brain directed the general research of the inoculation department for many years. From the beginning the hallmark of Fleming's work was his technical ingenuity, especially his ability to devise apparatus of all types for tackling laboratory problems. His first published medical work, 'Acute bacterial infections', was published in *St Mary's Hospital Gazette*. This won him the Cheadle gold medal and led him to become an expert on skin infections, especially acne. About this time Paul Ehrlich, a leading German medical scientist, introduced chemotherapy for the treatment of syphilis. His drug was called Salvarsan and Fleming made a typical contribution by devising a simple micro-method for the serological diagnosis of this disease.

Soon after the outbreak of the First World War Wright was invited by the Medical Research Committee (later the Medical Research Council) to establish a laboratory in Boulogne to study the treatment of war wounds. Fleming, who had joined the Royal Army Medical Corps as a lieutenant (later he became a captain), was an important member of Wright's group. They worked on the bacteriology and treatment of septic wounds, showing the importance of *Streptococcus pyogenes* in wound infection and blood poisoning. Fleming advanced the view that the severity of wound infection was related to the presence of necrotic tissue in the wound and advocated early removal of this dead tissue. At the same time another Scot, Sir Henry Gray, had independently introduced surgical debridement to promote healing. Later, with A. B. Porteous, Fleming showed that most streptococcal infections usually occurred after the patient was admitted to the base hospital, indicating the importance of controlling hospital cross-infection. He also made a significant contribution to the knowledge of gas gangrene. Inevitably Fleming sided with Wright in the bitter public controversy over the treatment of war wounds, as their unfashionable advocacy of physiological methods (irrigating wounds with saline) went against mainstream opinion, which was in favour of antiseptic principles. On 23 December 1915 Fleming married Sarah (Sareen) Marion (1879/80–1949), daughter of a farmer, Bernard McElroy, of co. Mayo, Ireland, and herself a trained nurse. There was one son, who qualified in medicine and entered general practice.

Back at St Mary's after the war, Fleming discovered and named 'lysozyme', an anti-microbial substance produced by many tissues and secretions of the body, particularly in nasal mucus. He later suggested that lysozyme was his most important discovery, as it opened up the study of antibacterial substances that led to the discovery of the powers of penicillin and other chemotherapeutic agents. With V. D. Allison he showed its wide distribution in nature, its enzymic quality and remarkable stability, and the interesting phenomenon of the development of bacterial resistance to its action. He also developed new experimental techniques to demonstrate the diffusibility of lysozyme, which later proved useful in his studies of penicillin. Wright was encouraged by this work to propose Fleming for a fellowship of the Royal Society, though his nomination was unsuccessful. Fleming's own work on lysozyme continued for many years, but was limited by the chemical expertise available and his assumption, in line with Wright's immunological doctrines, that it was part of the body's complex immune system.

Fleming was generally acclaimed as the most skilled bench-worker among Wright's numerous colleagues and followers. He was his own technician to the end and was admired for his deft handling of glass slides and capillary pipettes. He was keenly interested in staining methods, and when Indian ink became unavailable after 1918 he introduced nigrosin in negative staining methods for demonstrating spores and capsules. He was probably the first to grow bacteria and moulds on paper or cellophane placed on top of nutrient agar, and he demonstrated the suitability of paper for bringing out the pigment of chromogenic bacteria. He left an interesting collection of 'coloured pictures', composed entirely of bacterial cultures, which he was fond of showing to royalty and other visitors to St Mary's.

Penicillin and other work In September 1928 Fleming made the world-famous observation of a mould inhibiting the growth of bacteria, which has been seen as the beginning of the antibiotic era in the treatment of infections. Fleming was studying colony variation in the staphylococcus, the germ that causes septic infections, for a chapter he was writing for the *System of Bacteriology*. On his return from a holiday he noticed on a discarded plate culture that the micro-organism was absent from an area around a contaminating mould. The contaminant was *Penicillium notatum*, a common mould found across the world. Fleming was more interested in the phenomenon than were his colleagues, not least because of its possible similarities with the action of lysozymes. He presumed that the contamination was accidental and that the mould had entered his laboratory through an open window. He worked with the mould and its 'juice' for the next six months, in the first instance determining the number of pathogenic germs that were affected. This turned out to be quite high and he hoped that he had found a natural antiseptic that was non-toxic to humans. He set two graduates to work out the chemistry of the active substance, while he explored bacteriological and clinical problems. His hopes that he had found a clinically useful natural antiseptic were not fulfilled. One problem was that the action of the mould juice was slow—it is now known that penicillin acts by affecting the formation of cell walls in developing bacteria rather than killing adult forms. Also, in animal experiments, Fleming had difficulties in maintaining high enough concentrations around infected areas before the juice lost potency or was excreted. This work suggested that penicillin had little potential as a systemic antibacterial, but would be of limited value in the treatment of local infections. Indeed, in his first recorded clinical trial with penicillin, Fleming irrigated an infected surgical wound, using methods similar to those developed by Wright in the First World War. Fleming first spoke on this work to the Medical Research Club on 13 February 1929, and submitted his first paper to the *British Journal of Experimental Pathology* on 10 May. It appeared a month later. The conclusions of this paper make it clear that Fleming regarded penicillin as a new natural antiseptic, whose main properties were its effects on septic and pneumonia germs. Its great advantage was that it did not interfere with white blood cell function, which Wright and his group thought was all-important in natural immunity. Fleming also discussed the use of penicillin in bacteriological laboratories, where he used it in culture media to prevent the growth of unwanted organisms. The paper was not received as being epoch-making at the time; it was cast within the tradition of Fleming's previous work on lysozyme, Wright's notions of immunity, general scepticism towards the use of antiseptics in anything other than local infections, and innovations in bacteriological techniques.

There has been much debate on why the therapeutic potential of penicillin was not recognized in 1929. Some early biographers, perhaps influenced by the Fleming myth, claimed that Fleming immediately saw the value of his mould juice and was prevented from developing it owing to a lack of support and the antagonism of colleagues. However, it now seems that Sir Henry Dale was correct when he wrote that 'neither the time when the discovery was made nor, perhaps, the scientific atmosphere of the laboratory in which he worked, was propitious to such further enterprise as its development would have needed' (*DNB*). Through the 1930s Fleming used penicillin in a small number of cases as a local antiseptic and as a laboratory reagent for selective culturing, as did a number of other clinicians. In 1931 he wrote a sceptical review on the value of intravenous germicides and, very significantly, chose not to mention penicillin in this context. However, in the late 1930s, when Chain and Florey began to test antibacterial substances, they used a culture of Fleming's mould that had been maintained at Oxford since 1929. By then, Fleming was preoccupied with other projects. One of his main tasks during the whole inter-war period was to oversee the production of therapeutic vaccines in the St Mary's laboratory, which were the source of most of its income. Its clinical and research programme was dominated by a commitment to exploiting natural immunity in the treatment of infections. Fleming continued to advocate and use vaccine therapy, which was controversial and mistrusted by many doctors. His continuing support of Wright's doctrines was typical of his constancy and loyalty to his friends and colleagues, to the inoculation department, to St Mary's, and to its staff and students.

The pivotal position of the St Mary's department in the treatment of infections in Britain was shown in 1936 when its staff, including Fleming, were pioneers in the assessment of the value of the new sulphonamide range of antibacterial chemicals. The initial expectation was that these would turn out to be another overrated product from the German chemical industry. However, Leonard Colebrook, formerly at St Mary's, had spectacular success at Queen Charlotte's Hospital with sulphonamides in the treatment of puerperal fever. The drug was also effective in pneumonia, and Fleming published on this in 1938, demonstrating his technical skill and ingenuity in devising micro-methods for measuring the concentration of these drugs in patients' blood. However, his overall assessment in 1939 was that the treatment of choice was a combination therapy of sulphonamides and vaccines.

The antibiotic revolution and the Fleming myth In 1938 and 1939 the Oxford group working on germicides began to home in on penicillin. The first experiments with intravenous injections of penicillin on infected mice began in May 1940, with their very promising results published in August. Fleming visited Oxford to catch up with the work in September, seemingly curious about the applications being made with 'his juice'. A year later, after publication of the results of the first extremely promising clinical trials, Fleming first made public his proprietorial claims to penicillin. He crossed swords in print with the Oxford group, claiming that as well as having discovered the antibacterial properties of the substance he had recognized its potential as a systemic antibacterial drug. This contretemps in the medical press brought media attention to penicillin, which was presented initially as an accidental discovery by Fleming that had been applied by a team of researchers at Oxford. Over the next twelve months work on penicillin continued at Oxford and the government began to take an interest in developing large-scale production. Soon the United States government, as well as universities and pharmaceutical companies, became involved. While relations between Fleming and the Oxford group were not cordial, they did not prevent Fleming's obtaining enough penicillin in August 1942 to treat a case, an employee of his brother's optical firm, who subsequently recovered from severe septicaemia.

Over the summer of 1942 press reports about penicillin and its powers increased in number. The differences between Fleming, and Chain and Florey—St Mary's and Oxford—continued to simmer below the surface. However, on 31 August differences became public when a letter from Wright was published in *The Times*. Never one to shirk controversy or hold back in promoting his St Mary's department, Wright claimed priority for Fleming as both the discoverer of penicillin and for recognizing its value in antibacterial therapy. The following day, a letter from Sir Robert Robinson, professor of chemistry at Oxford, was published, stating that if Fleming deserved a 'laurel wreath' for penicillin, then Howard Florey should be given a 'handsome bouquet'. The press descended on both St Mary's and Oxford, but found Fleming more accommodating, and his role in the penicillin story came to dominate. The therapy attracted press attention as it promised good news at a time when the war situation was uncertain. Fleming's life, with his humble background and long road to success, made a romantic story. Moreover, the idea of the mould blowing through a window by chance and the discovery by a lone, self-effacing scientist matched contemporary notions of scientific discovery and national pride. The alternative story of a group of researchers, led by an Australian and a German Jew, working on a planned programme of state-funded work, did not strike the same chords. In the post-war years penicillin became much more than an antibacterial drug. It stood as an icon for post-war reconstruction, improving welfare, and modernization. It was often included, with nuclear power and the jet engine, as one of the science-based technologies of tomorrow's world. There was a peculiarly British slant to this picture, which was cast around the notion that the Americans who developed the drug industrially had 'stolen' a British invention.

The high profile given to penicillin changed Fleming's standing in science and medicine. On 18 March 1943 he was elected a fellow of the Royal Society, a position he had sought for some twenty years. In 1944 he was made a fellow of the Royal College of Physicians and knighted, and in October 1945 he received with Florey and Chain the Nobel prize for physiology and medicine. Publicly, Fleming and Florey shared the credit for the revolutionary antibiotic drug, even appearing on the same platform at scientific meetings. However, tensions remained and were not eased when Fleming, who was almost at retirement age, toured the world as a modern hero, while the younger Florey returned to his laboratory. On Wright's retirement in 1946, Fleming became head of the newly named Wright-Fleming Institute, but he was more often than not away receiving many and varied accolades. He travelled widely in Europe and through the Americas, north and south, as further prizes were awarded, honorary degrees by the dozen were conferred, statues were unveiled, freedom of cities granted, and streets named in his honour. Among the most notable awards were: commander of the Légion d'honneur in France, member of the Pontifical Academy of Sciences, election as rector of the University of Edinburgh (1951–4), convocation member of the senate of the University of London from 1950, member of the Medical Research Council (1945–9), and president of the Society for General Microbiology (1945–7). Besides becoming an honorary citizen of numerous cities in Europe he was a freeman of the burgh of Darvel, where he was born, and of the London boroughs of Chelsea, where he lived, and of Paddington, where his work was done. In October 1949 Fleming's wife, Sareen, died. In the succeeding years Fleming continued to travel, becoming close to Amalia Vourekas, *née* Coutsouris (b. 1912/13), daughter of Harilaos Coutsouris, a physician. She was a medically qualified bacteriologist who had joined the institute in 1946. They eventually married on 9 April 1953. Fleming died suddenly from a heart attack at his home in Danvers Street, Chelsea, on 11 March 1955, in the middle of a busy schedule. He was cremated and his ashes interred in London in St Paul's Cathedral a week later.

The man and his achievements Physically, Fleming was short and stockily built with powerful square shoulders and a deep chest, a fresh-complexioned face with a fine broad forehead, intensely light blue expressive eyes, and for many years a good crop of snowy white hair. He had great powers of physical endurance and in the days when burning the midnight oil was a regular occurrence in the inoculation department, Fleming was always the first to appear, fresh and fit, the following morning. Later he seemed to stand up astonishingly well to the heavy journeyings and junketings he had to undergo, and he kept his freshness and jaunty step to the end. He was sensitive and sympathetic, enjoyed the simple things in life, and remained humble despite all the honours which were showered upon him. He was not an easy man to know well, partly because of his natural reluctance to talk and to express his feelings. He was not a conversationalist and awkward silences were sometimes broken by awkward remarks: as one visitor put it, talking with him was like playing tennis with a man who, whenever you knocked the ball over to his side, put it in his pocket. But this was shyness, not intentional rudeness, for he liked company and had many friends in various walks of life before he became famous. He was reserved with strangers, but very sociable in familiar company. A regular at the Chelsea Arts Club for many years, Fleming was also a freemason, rising to be a grand warden.

Sir Alexander Fleming remains one of the best-known British scientists of the twentieth century. He became important for two reasons: first, his role in the development of modern antibiotics, and second, his place as an iconic British scientist. The catalogue of Fleming's published work leaves little room for doubt that he had to an unusual degree an almost intuitive faculty for original observation coupled with a high degree of technical inventiveness and skill. He made significant contributions to medical research in several fields, but until the penicillin story broke in 1942 his peers did not regard his work highly enough to seal his reputation with election to the Royal Society. At St Mary's he was a pivotal figure in Wright's department, the influence of which was felt across the hospital and in medical science and clinical practice across the country. However, there is little doubt that Florey and Chain would have developed penicillin without Fleming's work in the period 1928–32. While not well known, its antibacterial properties had been noticed by other medical scientists and used clinically. Nevertheless, Fleming's work did aid the Oxford group. It enabled them to move more quickly and encouraged them to pursue specific lines of enquiry. Thus it was entirely appropriate that Chain, Fleming, and Florey shared the Nobel prize in 1945. Those who could have felt cheated by the award were the American workers who had made many breakthroughs in scaling up production, but then the Nobel prize itself, and science more widely, have tended to value pure research more highly than applied research, and both are held in much higher esteem than experimental development. Indeed, the Fleming myth, of a lone scientist making a chance discovery that allowed infectious diseases to be conquered, was an unhelpful representation of the scientific enterprise in the post-1945 world of 'big science'. Team work, organized research programmes, private and public research and development funding, and the growing economic importance of experimental development, would all feature in an accurate account of the development of penicillin. Ironically, these were all characteristics of Fleming's main career in the inoculation department at St Mary's in the thirty-five years before penicillin entered the public domain.

MICHAEL WORBOYS

Sources G. Macfarlane, *Alexander Fleming: the man and the myth* (1984) • *DNB* • R. Bud, 'Penicillin and the new Elizabethans', *British Journal for the History of Science*, 31 (1998), 305–33 • L. Colebrook, *Memoirs FRS*, 2 (1956), 117–27 • A. Maurois, *The life of Sir Alexander Fleming* (1959) • R. Hare, *The birth of penicillin and the disarming of microbes* (1970) • M. Weatherall, *In search of a cure: a history of pharmaceutical industry* (1990) • R. Hare, 'The scientific activities of Alexander Fleming, other than the discovery of penicillin', *Medical History*, 27 (1983), 347–72 • J. Ludovici, *Fleming: discoverer of penicillin* (1952) • R. W. Clark, *The life of Ernst Chain: penicillin and beyond* (1985) • G. Macfarlane, *Howard Florey: the making of a great scientist* (1979) • H. Swan, 'Mouldy case-notes and penicillin: a re-appraisal of Fleming's role', *Proceedings of the Scottish Society of the History of Medicine* (1988–90), 1–8 • J. Liebenau, 'The British success with penicillin', *Social Studies of Science*, 17 (1987), 69–86 • M. Wainwright, *Miracle cure: the story of penicillin and the golden age of antibiotics* (1990) • b. cert. • m. certs. • d. cert.

Archives BL, corresp. and papers, Add. MSS 56106–56225 • Medical Research Council, London, MSS • NRA, priv. coll. • St Mary's Hospital, London, Alexander Fleming Laboratory Museum, MSS • St Mary's Hospital, London, St Mary's Hospital Archives, MSS |FILM BFI NFTVA |SOUND BL NSA

Likenesses photographs, 1940–c.1955, Hult. Arch. • W. Stoneman, photograph, 1943, NPG • H. M. Campbell, pencil drawing, 1944, NPG • J. A. Grant, lithograph, 1944, NPG • E. J. Clark, bronze bust, c.1946, St Mary's Hospital, London, Wright-Fleming Institute • E. R. Bevan, bronze head, 1948, St Mary's Hospital, London, Wright-Fleming Institute • E. R. Bevan, bronze head, 1948, Scot. NPG • T. C. Dugdale, oils, c.1949, St Mary's Hospital, London, Wright-Fleming Institute • H. Coster, photographs, 1954, NPG [*see illus.*] • Y. Karsh, bromide print, 1954, NPG • F. Kovacs, bronze bust, c.1955, RCP Lond. • F. Kovacs, bronze medallion, 1955, NPG • P. N. Cardew, photographs, St Mary's Hospital, London, department of audio visual communication • E. Gabain, oils, IWM • A. Zinkeisen, portrait, St Mary's Hospital, London

Wealth at death £29,321 10s. 9d.: probate, 21 June 1955, *CGPLA Eng. & Wales*

Fleming, Alice [*née* Lady Alice Fitzgerald], **Lady Slane** (*b.* c.1508, *d.* in or after 1540), conspirator, was the daughter of Gerald *Fitzgerald, ninth earl of Kildare (1487–1534), chief governor of Ireland, and his first wife, Elizabeth Zouche (*d.* 1517). She was apparently the second of four daughters and a son—Thomas *Fitzgerald, known as Silken Thomas, the future tenth earl. She also had two half-brothers—the elder of whom, Gerald *Fitzgerald, later became eleventh earl of Kildare—and three half-sisters, the children of her father's second marriage, to Elizabeth Grey, following her mother's death in 1517. She was raised in the earl's lavishly furnished castle of Maynooth. Successive earls of Kildare all had large families, and some of her kinswomen also proved adept politicians, notably her aunts Margaret, countess of Ormond, and Eleanor, wife of MacCarthy Reagh and then Manus *O'Donnell, who harboured the future eleventh earl after the Kildare rebellion. Kildare practice was generally to marry their younger sons into the lordship's other leading families; but their daughters, including Alice's younger sisters, who married Brian *O'Connor and Ferganainm *O'Carroll [*see under* O'Carroll, Mulroney] respectively, were frequently matched with Gaelic chiefs to strengthen the family's influence in Gaelic Ireland.

Lady Alice Fitzgerald married her cousin James Fleming, ninth Baron Slane (1507/8–1573), son of Christopher Fleming, eighth Baron Slane, and her aunt Elizabeth Fitzgerald, probably in 1527 or 1528. James was nine when his father died in August 1517, and in January 1523 Kildare obtained his wardship from Henry VIII. Alice accompanied her father to court in December 1526, and they later stayed at the duke of Norfolk's house at Newington. Before his departure from Ireland, Kildare had arranged with his leading officials and advisers to use Alice as a 'prevy token' to indicate to them how well he was faring in the council's inquiries into his conduct as deputy. Accordingly, when Lady Slane, as she then was, arrived home without her father in August 1528, they knew the earl 'was not at his pleasour to come home' (PRO, SP 60/1, fol. 139). Allegedly, Kildare ordered her to procure his brothers and servants, O'Neill and O'Connor, to stir up war against the new deputy, the earl of Ossory; and 'upon hir arryvall, sche rod streth home to OConour is house, and had longe secrete comynycation' with her brother-in-law (*State Papers, Henry VIII*, 2.147). Immediately thereafter O'Connor recommended raids on the Englishry, and the earl's brother Sir Thomas Fitzgerald of Leixlip, captain in his absence, put up no resistance 'by reason of certain intelligence had with O'Conoghour, contrary to his allegiance' (*Calendar of Ormond Deeds*, 1509–47, no. 144). In the inquiries which followed, Lady Slane, together with the earl's steward, Sir Walter Delahide, and his wife, was commonly reputed the chief instigator of 'O'Connor's wars'. The king pardoned her of all treasons and conspiracies with Irish rebels in June 1529, but when the earl was posthumously attainted of treason by the Irish parliament in May 1536 for his role in the 1534–5 rebellion, the attainder took effect from 8 July 1528—the date on which he had dispatched Alice back home.

Neither Lady Slane nor her husband played a major role in the 1534–5 revolt, and so escaped attainder. Her date of death is not known, although she was still alive in May 1540, when granted the joint wardship of the future tenth Lord Slane. A Lady Slane was living in July 1561.

STEVEN G. ELLIS

Sources S. G. Ellis, *Tudor frontiers and noble power: the making of the British state* (1995) · M. A. Lyons, *Gearóid Óg, ninth earl of Kildare* (1998) · *LP Henry VIII*, 4, no. 5392 · *The statutes at large, passed in the parliaments held in Ireland*, 20 vols. (1786–1801) · *State papers published under … Henry VIII*, 11 vols. (1830–52), 2.147 · M. C. Griffith, ed., *Calendar of inquisitions formerly in the office of the chief remembrancer of the exchequer*, IMC (1991) · E. Curtis, ed., *Calendar of Ormond deeds*, 6 vols., IMC (1932–43) · GEC, *Peerage* · PRO, SP 60/1, fol. 139

Fleming, Amaryllis Marie-Louise (1925?–1999), cellist, was probably born on 10 December 1925, possibly in Switzerland, the daughter of the London socialite Evelyn Beatrice Ste Croix (Eve) Fleming, *née* Rose (1885–1964), whose husband, Major Valentine Fleming, was killed in the First World War. Her four half-brothers included the travel writer (Robert) Peter *Fleming and the novelist Ian *Fleming. Her mother told her she was adopted, and she did not learn until 1949 that the painter Augustus Edwin *John (1878–1961), who had been a regular visitor to her mother's residence, Turner's House in Cheyne Walk, Chelsea, was her father. Her mother—herself an amateur violinist—forbade her to learn the violin, and in 1934 she took up the cello. In 1937 she was sent away to school at Downe House, Berkshire, as a result of constant friction with her mother; the friction was transferred to the school authorities, who were eventually persuaded to allow her to travel to London every three weeks for cello lessons with John Snowden at the Royal College of Music. She made her first radio broadcast on the BBC *Children's Hour* in 1942, and in 1943 she won a scholarship to study full-time at the Royal College with Ivor James of the Menges Quartet. She made her public début in 1944 with the Elgar cello concerto at Newbury, and won all the college prizes. While at college Fleming met the sixty-year-

Amaryllis Marie-Louise Fleming (1925?–1999), by Thurston Hopkins, 1953 [at her promenade concert début]

old violinist André Mangeot, who introduced her to baroque music. At his house, which she often visited, she made the acquaintance of the Barbirollis, Eugene Goossens, Sándor Végh, and others. She purchased the house some years after Mangeot's death in 1970.

In 1946 Fleming heard the French cellist Pierre Fournier (d. 1985), and was overwhelmed by his playing. Fournier was fascinated by her, and offered her free tuition. She subsequently travelled with Fournier, with whom she had a passionate relationship, playing as second cellist in quintets with Mangeot and friends. At her mother's request, she then studied in Portugal with Guilhermina Suggia, the former wife of Pablo Casals, though this was not a success. After returning home she played with Artur Schnabel, Joseph Szigeti, and Pierre Fournier in six BBC concerts to commemorate the 150th anniversary of Schubert's birth. The discovery in 1949 of her true parentage had a traumatic effect, though she found a warm friend in Dodo, Augustus John's companion. Fryern, the painter's Wiltshire home, was to be a place of consolation for some thirty years.

Following lessons with Pablo Casals in Madrid, in 1949 Fleming joined the Loveday Trio, with Alan Loveday and Peggy Gray, and in 1951 she played with the Fidelio Ensemble for the first time. In 1952, after winning the queen's prize, she made her London début, accompanied by Gerald Moore, at the Wigmore Hall. Richard Capell described her in the *Daily Telegraph* as a 'dazzling young person [who] glowed with the sacred fire'. At her Promenade Concert début in 1953 she played the Elgar cello concerto with the Hallé Orchestra, conducted by Sir John Barbirolli; she gave the German première of the concerto in Hamburg later the same year. In 1955 she won the Munich international competition with the pianist Lamar Crowson, and formed the Paganini Trio with Loveday and Julian Bream (who was later replaced by John Williams). Ever the perfectionist, she endeavoured to improve her performance and posture, studying with the Italian cellist Enrico Mainardi and with Riccardo Mani in Bologna.

The beginning of Fleming's deep interest in baroque music arose in the late 1950s as the result of a meeting with the musicologist E. M. W. Paul, a Jewish-German refugee who, together with Norbert Brainin, the founder of the Amadeus Quartet, had been interned on the Isle of Man. Having trained in the post-war period as an instrument repairer and dealer, Paul assisted her in buying a Guarneri cello, followed by a 1717 Stradivarius cello and a rare cello made by the brothers Amati. She later had the Amati re-strung as a five-string instrument in order to play Bach's sixth suite. Although Paul was married, Fleming formed a deep attachment to him, which persisted until his death in 1966. It was through Paul that she was introduced to Basil Lam, the harpsichordist and BBC producer, and the musicologist Anthony Goldsborough, who, it is said, considered her BBC recording of the Bach suites for unaccompanied cello the finest he had heard. Her enthusiasm for baroque music did much to stimulate public and professional interest in the authentic performance of this repertory.

Fleming was praised by Sir William Walton for her interpretation of his second cello concerto, which she played all over Europe, but by the mid-1960s she could not compete with Jacqueline du Pré as a soloist, and concentrated instead on chamber music. In 1968, with Granville Jones (violin) and Kenneth Essex (viola) she formed the Fleming String Trio. For the film *Connecting Rooms* (1970), she played the cello, only her arms appearing on the screen: the cellist heroine was played by Bette Davis. She was appointed a professor at the Royal College of Music in 1974. In 1976 she formed a duo with Bernard Roberts (piano), which subsequently became a piano trio with the addition of Manoug Parikian (violin), but they disbanded on Parikian's death in 1987. In 1993 she suffered a stroke which left her unable to play the cello, though she was eventually able to resume teaching at both the Royal College of Music and the Wells Cathedral School. In her last years she was drawn to Eastern mysticism, meeting the Dalai Lama in the spring of 1999. She died, unmarried, at the Cromwell Hospital, Kensington, London, on 27 July 1999.

Amaryllis Fleming had a colourful, extrovert personality and preferred the company of men to that of women. Of a fiery disposition and 'gypsy-like appearance' with long red hair, she cut a flamboyant path through musical circles. A thoroughly professional musician, she was never satisfied with her own performances: as a result only a few recordings survive. A biography, written by her nephew Fergus Fleming with her co-operation, was published in 1993.   G. R. SEAMAN

Sources F. Fleming, *Amaryllis Fleming* (1993) · *The Times* (30 July 1999) · *The Guardian* (2 Aug 1999) · *Daily Telegraph* (30 July 1999) · *The Independent* (5 Aug 1999) · *The Scotsman* (10 Aug 1999) · d. cert. · M. Holroyd, *Augustus John*, 2: *The years of experience* (1974)
Likenesses A. John, drawing, 1950–59, repro. in *Daily Telegraph* · T. Hopkins, photograph, 1953, Hult. Arch. [*see illus.*] · photographs, 1953–65, Hult. Arch. · photograph, repro. in *The Guardian* · photograph, repro. in *The Times*
Wealth at death £2,437,664—gross; £2,429,978—net: probate, 8 Oct 1999, *CGPLA Eng. & Wales*

Fleming, Sir (John) Ambrose (1849–1945), electrical engineer and university teacher, was born at a house named Greenfield, in Lancaster, on 29 November 1849,

Sir (**John**) **Ambrose Fleming** (1849–1945), by unknown photographer, 1934

eldest of the seven children of James Fleming DD (d. 1879), a Congregational minister, and his wife, Mary Ann, daughter of John Bazley White of Swanscombe, Kent. Tutored early by his mother, the family's move to London in 1853 enabled Ambrose both to attend lectures by Professor Pepper at the London Polytechnic Institution and to enjoy learning to handle mechanical tools in grandfather White's Portland cement works in Kent. At University College School from 1863, Ambrose showed a great aptitude for mathematics, if not for Latin, and soon developed ambitions for engineering. Unable to muster the necessary pupillage fee, he resolved instead to pursue a career in science teaching, enrolling at University College, London (UCL), in 1867 to study experimental physics under George Carey Foster, chemistry under Alexander Williamson, and mathematics under Augustus De Morgan. During 1868, however, financial difficulties obliged him temporarily to discontinue his education, and he spent four unhappy months in a Dublin shipbuilder's drawing office. Easier life in a City stockbroker's office then enabled Fleming to study part time for the University of London BSc, in which he received first-class honours in 1870.

Following the recommendation of his father's friend Edward Frankland, Ambrose took a post teaching science at Rossall School in Lancashire. Saving enough to sponsor his chemical studies with Frankland at the Science

Schools in South Kensington from 1872, his growing interest in electrical science nevertheless drew Fleming towards the physics laboratory on the building's ground floor. There he observed experiments by Frederick Guthrie on the curiously asymmetrical behaviour of heated metals to electrical charges, a phenomenon Fleming later identified as the first observation of thermionic emission. Guthrie was so impressed by his young protégé that he invited Fleming to give the first paper at the inaugural meeting of the Physical Society of London in 1874. His scientific credentials thus established, Fleming was appointed as science master at Cheltenham College, where he became an effective and much respected teacher.

Researches into electricity Restless to continue electrical researches, Fleming read the works of Michael Faraday, and reported his results on electromagnetic induction in rivers to the British Association for the Advancement of Science (BAAS) in summer 1875. Fleming's greater ambitions to become involved with proposals for national standards of electrical resistance had already emerged, however, in his correspondence with James Clerk Maxwell at the new Cavendish Laboratory in Cambridge. After struggling with the mathematical intricacies of Maxwell's *Treatise on Electricity and Magnetism*, Fleming resolved to study under Maxwell. Supported by his savings, an examinership in the Department of Science and Art arranged by Guthrie, and an exhibition to St John's College, Fleming began to study for the natural sciences tripos in October 1877.

Determined not to be distracted by Cambridge undergraduate social life, the 28-year-old Fleming, unusually, lived outside the college. He was coached by W. H. Besant to refine his mathematical skills in preparation for Maxwell's lectures—and in several successful attempts to win college prizes. From January 1878 until May 1879, Fleming was one of only two students who attended Maxwell's lectures; at the time he found them paradoxical and allusive, but he drew much inspiration from them later in life. He also attended Maxwell's classes at the Cavendish, wherein he adapted Carey Foster's resistance bridge into an instrument known for many years as 'Fleming's banjo'. Somehow Fleming also found the time to pass the University of London DSc examination in the summer of 1879 as well as receiving first-class honours in the natural sciences tripos early in 1880. Fleming's father died in November 1879; Maxwell died in December 1880, and five days later Fleming was working for Professor James Stuart in the university's engineering workshop and lecturing on applied mechanics in order to support his widowed mother and family. Stuart encouraged Fleming's successful application for the professorship of physics and mathematics at University College, Nottingham, in summer 1881; Fleming was elected a fellow of St John's in the following year.

Teaching career As secretary for the Edison Telephone Company, his cousin Arnold White had called upon Fleming's commercial expertise in 1879; again at White's behest, in 1882 Fleming resigned his Nottingham post to take up a more remunerative consultancy position to the new Edison Lighting Company in London. After a patent dispute led to the merger of this business with the Swan lighting company in 1883, Fleming became electrician to the factory at Ponder's End which produced the first Ediswan filament bulbs. Fleming developed innovative photometric apparatus for the factory's quality control process and studied the intriguing pattern of blackening in early light bulbs known as the Edison effect. Continuing his Cavendish work on resistance measurement Fleming became known as the 'apostle of the potentiometer' and persuaded R. E. B. Crompton to market a commercial model. It was Crompton who in turn encouraged Fleming to give lectures to workmen, published as *Short Lectures to Electrical Artisans* (1886), and in 1884 Fleming received another invitation—to lecture on electrical technology at UCL. On the recommendation of his former teacher G. C. Foster, Fleming became professor of electrical technology at UCL in 1885, albeit equipped with just chalk and blackboard. In 1886 he acquired his own small college laboratory, supplementing its meagre equipment by apparatus borrowed from friends in electrical companies. Connections between this laboratory and the Edison company were strong, for not only did Fleming teach his students photometric analysis, but also compensated for the lack of heavy current equipment at UCL by taking them to lighting schemes on which he was a consultant. On 11 June 1887 he married Clara Ripley (1856/7–1917), daughter of Walter Freake Pratt, solicitor, of Bath.

After seeing Zipernowsky's transformer demonstrated at the Inventions Exhibition in 1885, Fleming became intensely interested in the potential of alternating current for long distance power transmission. Measurements of transformer efficiency and other a.c. parameters became a major preoccupation in his laboratory thereafter, students often being set the task of testing UCL's own lighting system. It was probably at this time that Fleming developed his eponymous 'right hand rule' which gave his students characteristically crystalline guidance in predicting the motion of a current-carrying body in a magnetic field. Fleming's important researches were embodied in *The Alternating Current Transformer* (2 vols., 1889–92), and with his reputation enhanced by a cogent analysis of the anomalous Ferranti effect in 1890–91, Fleming's book became a standard text for some years. It was, however, particularly for his continued researches on the Edison effect that Fleming was elected a fellow of the Royal Society in 1892.

From 1891 he campaigned with Foster and others for new laboratories to accommodate their expanding classes, purpose-built suites for which opened two years later. Fleming had then just commenced four years of collaborative research with James Dewar at the Royal Institution on the remarkable electrical and magnetic behaviour of materials at very low temperatures. In 1897 Fleming secured a benefaction from the estate of telegraph magnate, Sir John Pender, to build laboratories at UCL, Fleming thereafter occupying the retitled Pender chair of electrical engineering. As his congenital deafness worsened, however, Fleming devolved much of his laboratory teaching to his assistant, W. C. Clinton, and turned his attention to the production of a text on standardized class experiments, published in 1898 as *Laboratory Notes and Forms*. This was widely employed at educational institutions in Britain, Fleming's *Handbook for the Electrical Laboratory and Testing Room* (1901–3) receiving comparable usage at research establishments.

The thermionic valve In response to Marconi's famous invention in 1896, the Pender Laboratories saw much activity as Fleming sought to extend his expertise in alternate currents to the much higher frequency oscillations of wireless technology. Becoming scientific adviser to the Marconi Wireless Telegraph Company in 1899, Fleming assisted in designing and operating equipment for Marconi's plans for cross-channel transmission. At the BAAS meeting in Dover that summer, wireless signals from France were publicly heard for the first time in Britain at Fleming's celebrated lecture on the centenary of the electric current. Fleming was also closely involved in preparation for the company's transatlantic transmission in 1901, although he later felt slighted by Marconi's restrained acknowledgement of his limited contributions. Relations between Marconi and Fleming were in fact more delicate than many historians, with the notable exception of Hong, have admitted. Indeed, in an episode omitted from Fleming's autobiography, his embarrassing loss of expert credibility in the Maskelyne affair led Marconi to discontinue his advisory role in 1903. In that year Fleming became vice-president of the Institution of Electrical Engineers, but notably unlike professorial contemporaries, and several of his students, he never became its president.

Although Fleming claimed that his most famous invention came from a 'sudden very happy thought' in October 1904 (Fleming, 141), it stemmed from his expertise in a.c. technology, the Edison effect, and Guthrie's experiments thirty years previously—as well as a need to re-establish links with Marconi. On 16 November 1904 Fleming patented (no. 24,850) the thermionic valve as a device to facilitate measurements of the strength of wireless signals. His new device was revealed to the world in a paper read at the Royal Society on 9 February 1905, 'On the conversion of electrical oscillations into continuous currents by means of a vacuum valve', his cymometer for measuring wavelengths being shown at the same meeting. Marconi was persuaded to adopted the thermionic valve, and by adding a jigger circuit it was Marconi—not Fleming—who converted it into a robust detector of wireless signals.

Patent litigation The renewal of Fleming's consultancy contract required him to surrender all patent rights to the Marconi company, receiving only a retainer fee for his contributions. Nevertheless, Fleming took an active role in the company's many years of bitter litigation with the American de Forrest over the originality of the latter's 1906 patent for the three-electrode valve that was subsequently employed as an amplifier in many radio receivers.

As Hong points out, it was in defence of his patent that Fleming first claimed he had originally conceived his invention as a detector of radio waves. Fleming's apparent victory on this point in the American courts in 1917 was overshadowed, however, by the death of his wife. Ironically, two years before his own death, the American courts ruled that Fleming's patent had always been invalid.

Fleming meanwhile had embarked upon a substantial series of monographs that gave particular prominence to his own work in wireless telegraphy, telephony, lighting, mathematics, and mechanics. His many lucid and eloquent lectures, including four sets in the Christmas season at the Royal Institution in 1894–5, 1901–2, 1917–18, and 1921–2, sustained his high public profile in relation to the new electrical technologies. His populist volume *The Wonders of Wireless Telegraphy*, published for the Christian Knowledge Society in 1913, is one of only a few instances in which Fleming drew a direct link between his professional work and his latterly Anglican faith. Only after retirement from the secular institution of UCL in 1926 did he use pulpits and his presidency of the Victoria Institute (1927–42) as platforms to proclaim the historical accuracy of the Bible and attack the theory of organic evolution.

In retirement at Sidmouth from 1926, in a house shared with two of his sisters and equipped with a basement laboratory, Fleming nevertheless maintained active links with UCL as professor emeritus. Knighted in 1929, and elected president of the Television Society of London, Fleming enjoyed many honours which are related with great relish in his 1934 autobiography, *Memories of a Scientific Life*. On 27 July the previous year he had married the popular young singer Olive May Franks (*b*. 1898/9), of Bristol, daughter of George Franks, a Cardiff businessman. Fleming was slightly built with a brisk, unfanciful character and a ferocious energy for the hard work that furnished the grounds for his often unyielding opinions and his aversion to dissent. Generally helpful to those who sought general factual advice from him, commercial considerations nevertheless made his private research laboratory a domain of inviolable secrecy. His rare periods of leisure were given over to foreign travel, painting, and sketching, a convivial social life being largely precluded by his hearing difficulties. Even so, his chronic deafness was evidently not so great as to inhibit his love of music and especially not his appreciation of Lady Fleming's celebrated vocal talents. Outliving most fellow pioneers in electrical engineering, he was in a singularly congenial position to enjoy the legendary reputation of his accomplishments, especially his world fame as inventor of the thermionic valve. He died at his home, Greenfield, Manor Road, Sidmouth, Devon, on 18 April 1945. He was survived by his second wife.

J. T. MACGREGOR-MORRIS, *rev.* GRAEME J. N. GOODAY

Sources W. H. Eccles, *Obits. FRS*, 5 (1945–8), 231–42 · S. Hong, 'Forging the scientist-engineer: a professional career of John Ambrose Fleming', PhD diss., Seoul National University, Korea, 1994 · J. A. Fleming, *Memories of a scientific life* (1934) · J. T. MacGregor-Morris, *The inventor of the valve: a biography of Sir Ambrose Fleming* (1954) · S. Hong, 'From effect to artifact (II): the case of the thermionic valve', *Physis*, new ser., 33 (1996), 85–124 · S. Hong, 'Style and credit in early radio engineering: Fleming and Marconi on the first transatlantic wireless telegraphy', *Annals of Science*, 53 (1996), 431–65 · S. Hong, 'Forging scientific electrical engineering: John Ambrose Fleming and the Ferranti effect', *Isis*, 86 (1995), 30–51 · S. Hong, 'Syntony and credibility: John Ambrose Fleming, Guglielmo Marconi, and the Maskelyne affair', *Archimedes* (1996) · *Proceedings of the Physical Society*, 57 (1945), 581–3 · b. cert. · m. cert., 1887 · m. cert., 1933 · d. cert.

Archives Inst. EE, Archives, diary · RS, letters and papers to Royal Society · Sci. Mus., letters to Science Museum · UCL, corresp. and papers | PRO, corresp. with Sir Henry Dale, CAB 127/219 · St John Cam., letters to Sir Joseph Larmor

Likenesses two portraits, c.1890–1905, repro. in MacGregor-Morris, *Inventor of the valve*, frontispiece, 32 · W. Stoneman, photograph, 1923, NPG · W. Orpen, oils, exh. RA 1927, UCL · G. H. Paulin, bust, 1932, UCL · photograph, 1934, Sci. Mus. [*see illus.*]

Wealth at death £56,651: probate, 5 July 1945, *CGPLA Eng. & Wales*

Fleming [*née* Charteris], **Ann Geraldine Mary** [*other married names* Ann Geraldine Mary O'Neill, Lady O'Neill; Ann Geraldine Mary Harmsworth, Viscountess Rothermere] (**1913–1981**), society hostess, was born at Stanway, Gloucestershire, on 19 June 1913, the eldest daughter of Guy Lawrence Charteris (1886–1967), and his first wife, Frances Lucy Tennant (1887–1925). Her father was the second son of Hugo Charteris, ninth earl of Wemyss, and after her mother died, she spent long periods at Stanway, her grandparents' home in the Cotswolds. There she came under the benign influence of her grandmother Mary Constance *Charteris, countess of Wemyss, one of the last of the Souls, the group of intellectual aristocrats which had flourished at the turn of the century. In an atmosphere where plays were specially written for her and her siblings, Laura, Mary Rose, and Hugo Francis Guy *Charteris, by Sir James Barrie, Ann learned to prize conversation, conviviality, and literary prowess.

Unsuited for conventional schooling (she lasted one term at Cheltenham Ladies' College), Ann was educated at home by governesses. She was well grounded in English literature, but a poor speller. In 1931 she 'came out' as a débutante at a party given by her aunt, Kathleen Manners, duchess of Rutland. Always competitive with her sister Laura (later duchess of Marlborough), on 6 October 1932 Ann married one of her first real suitors—Shane Edward Robert O'Neill, third Baron O'Neill (1907–1944), a wealthy peer with a job in the City.

Settling into a conventional social life in London and Northern Ireland (where the O'Neills had a hereditary seat), Ann gave birth to two children, Raymond and Fionn. However, tiring of her husband's friends, she fell in love in 1936 with Esmond Cecil *Harmsworth (1898–1978), heir to Lord Rothermere, owner of the *Daily Mail*. She was also attracted to Ian Lancaster *Fleming (1908–1964), a young stockbroker. When Lord O'Neill went to war in 1939 Ann took a house in Gloucestershire. The following year Harmsworth succeeded his father, and Ann, attracted to his power, was regularly at his side at the Dorchester Hotel, London's wartime social centre. She continued to see Fleming, the influential assistant to the director of naval intelligence.

Ann was devastated when O'Neill was killed in Italy in

Ann Geraldine Mary Fleming (1913–1981), by Sir Cecil Beaton, 1950 [having her portrait painted by Lucian Freud]

October 1944. At the end of the war, she would happily have married Fleming, but settled for the second Viscount Rothermere, with whom she lived in great luxury at Warwick House, off Green Park, London, after their marriage on 28 June 1945. She fought post-war austerity with sumptuous parties, which mixed her husband's associates, the more interesting aristocrats, and a new generation of writers and artists—among them Lucian Freud, Frederick Ashton, Francis Bacon, and Peter Quennell. She enjoyed being the power behind the throne at the *Daily Mail*, where she found a job for her brother, Hugo, later a novelist. Hugo disapproved of her sybaritic lifestyle and was scornful of her continued attachment to Fleming who, while working at the *Sunday Times*, enjoyed three months' holiday every year in Jamaica. Pretending to visit her friend Noël Coward on this Caribbean island, she stayed with Fleming. In 1948 she gave birth to his daughter, Mary, who lived only a few hours. In late 1951 Rothermere tired of this set-up and divorced her. On 24 March 1952 she married Fleming; they had one son, Caspar.

Spurred by impending marriage Fleming wrote a novel, *Casino Royale*, featuring the secret agent James Bond and published to critical acclaim in April 1953. The Flemings bought a Regency house in Victoria Square, London, where Ann reinvented her social life, giving smaller lunch and dinner parties attended by new literary friends, including Evelyn Waugh, Cyril Connolly, and Patrick Leigh Fermor. She maintained her links to newspapers via a flirtatious relationship with Lord Beaverbrook, owner of the *Daily Express*. She also developed an interest in politics through the Conservative leader Sir Anthony Eden (who had married her friend Clarissa Churchill) and through his Labour opponent, Hugh Gaitskell, with whom she conducted a discreet romance.

Since Ann's husband preferred golf and bridge to literary gossip he was seldom at home. He spent increasing time in Kent (where the Flemings had a succession of houses) and in Jamaica, while she lobbied to live in the 'real countryside' of her childhood. Having become wealthy through his Bond books, he bought a house at Sevenhampton, near Swindon, Wiltshire, where the Flemings moved in 1962. In August 1964 Fleming died of a heart attack. Unhappy at the exploitation of the Bond franchise, Ann nevertheless welcomed the ensuing wealth. Her social gatherings metamorphosed into relaxed weekend house parties, attended by Oxford friends such as Maurice Bowra and John Sparrow. Despite right-wing views, she extended her political circle to include Labour Party spokesmen such as Anthony Crosland, Roy Jenkins, and the lawyer Arnold Goodman, with whom she was particularly close. In 1975 she experienced further tragedy when her depressive son, Caspar, killed himself.

Ann died of cancer at her home, Sevenhampton Place, on 12 July 1981, and was buried at Sevenhampton. Her intelligence is reflected in *The Letters of Ann Fleming*, posthumously edited by Mark Amory. Although seemingly hard she had a great capacity for friendship. At her memorial service Lord Annan noted that, unlike earlier hostesses, she was indifferent to celebrity and did not exist to please. He perhaps ignored her interest in power (one reason why she courted Labour politicians), but he was right that she brought out the best in an incongruous mix of people—and that she could do this 'because she was totally self-confident and cared not a jot for the opinion of others'.

ANDREW LYCETT

Sources *The letters of Ann Fleming*, ed. M. Amory (1985) · A. Lycett, *Ian Fleming* (1995) · Burke, *Peerage* (1999)
Likenesses C. Beaton, photograph, 1950, NPG [*see illus.*] · C. Beaton, photographs, priv. coll. · L. Freud, portrait, priv. coll.
Wealth at death £926,456: probate, 26 Oct 1981, *CGPLA Eng. & Wales*

Fleming, Sir **Arthur Percy Morris** (1881–1960), electrical engineer, was born on 16 January 1881 in Newport, Isle of Wight, the youngest of the three sons of Frank Fleming and his wife, Fanny Morris, a farming family of that locality. On completion of his education at the Portland House Academy, Newport, Fleming entered Finsbury Technical College, London, as a student of electrical engineering. Following short periods with the London Electric Supply Corporation and Elliott Brothers (electrical instrument manufacturers), he was selected in 1900 by the newly established British Westinghouse Company (later, from 1919, Metropolitan-Vickers) as one of the 'holy forty' to undergo a course of training with the American firm at its East Pittsburgh works. When he arrived at the company's British works at Trafford Park, Manchester, in 1902, he was engaged as a specialist on electrical insulation in the transformer department, of which he soon became chief engineer and, in 1913, superintendent. On 13 September 1905 Fleming married Rose Mary (1878/9–1948), daughter of the late William Ash, merchant, of Newport; they had two sons and one daughter.

Into his department Fleming soon began to introduce arrangements for the further education and systematic training of its schoolboy recruits. By 1908 he had extended these arrangements throughout the company; in 1914 he established a trade apprentice school; and in 1917 he became manager of the company's education department. He used often to say that the most important raw material of industry is its young people, and he took steps to ensure that his own young people, from the embryo craftsman to the university graduate, were recognized and treated as important. They came not only from the schools and universities of Britain but from all over the world, for in the sphere of industrial training the name of Fleming and Metropolitan-Vickers became known internationally. Fleming's influence and inspiration penetrated widely into the electrical industry as a whole and the benefits have been profound.

Fleming's views on engineering education were matched by his realization of the need for research within industry, especially research not bounded by the short-term problems of existing products. His plans were delayed by the First World War, in which he and a few colleagues made important contributions to submarine detection, for which he was appointed CBE in 1920. In that year the first buildings of his research department began to appear, and it was typical of his foresight and vigour that he arranged for these buildings to be used as the site for the transmitter and studios of the British Broadcasting Company's initial Manchester station—2ZY—which began to broadcast within a day of the opening of 2LO in London, in 1922. By 1929 the department contained one of the largest high-voltage laboratories in the world, and there were attracted to it a succession of men of ability, who made many notable contributions to both pure and applied science. Particularly important was the development of demountable high-power thermionic valves, which helped to make possible the installation just before the outbreak of war in 1939 of the first radar stations. In 1931 Fleming became the company's director of research and education, and so continued until his retirement in 1954.

Fleming's achievement was due to exceptional foresight, single-minded industry and tenacity, an extremely good memory, unlimited enthusiasm and vitality, and an ability to inspire and stimulate others. He was big enough to surround himself with men intellectually, perhaps, more gifted than himself, and to secure their willing co-operation and loyalty. He had the strength to ignore opposition as if it did not exist, and to persevere until eventually, on many matters, others came to think his way. He liked to quote with approval Drake's reflection that 'There must be a beginning of any great matter, but the continuing unto the end until it be thoroughly finished yields the true glory.'

Fleming's outside activities were manifold. He was a member of the council of the University of Manchester, of the governing body of the Imperial College of Science and Technology, of the delegacy of the City and Guilds of London Institute, of the Ministry of Education committee on the training of teachers and youth leaders, and of the war cabinet engineering advisory committee; chairman of the electrical engineering committee of the central register of the Ministry of Labour, of the Athlone Fellowship committee, and of the Federation of British Industries overseas scholarships committee; and president of both the education (1939) and engineering (1949) sections of the British Association, and of the British Association for Commercial and Industrial Education. He also played an important part in the establishment of the Department of Scientific and Industrial Research and of the Electrical Research Association.

Within all these interests, the Institution of Electrical Engineers occupied a place of special importance; Fleming became a member of its council (1932), vice-president (1935), president (1938), and an honorary member (1952), and was awarded the Faraday medal (1941). He received honorary degrees from Liverpool and Manchester and was awarded the Hawksley medal of the Institution of Mechanical Engineers. He was knighted in 1945.

Throughout his career, Fleming lectured frequently, both at home and abroad, about industrial research and training, and wrote many papers, the value of which lay in the widespread practices they did so much to stimulate. He was joint author of several books: *The Insulation and Design of Electrical Windings* (with R. Johnson, 1913); *Engineering as a Profession* (with R. W. Bailey, 1913); *The Principles of Apprentice Training* (with J. G. Pearce, 1916); *An Introduction to the Principles of Industrial Administration* (with H. J. Brocklehurst, 1922); *Research in Industry* (with J. G. Pearce, 1922); and *A History of Engineering* (with H. J. Brocklehurst, 1925). Fleming died in the Isle of Wight County Hospital, Ryde, on 14 September 1960; his remains were cremated.

JACKSON OF BURNLEY, *rev.*

Sources personal knowledge (1971) · private information (1971) · m. cert. · d. cert. · *Nature*, 188 (1960), 188–9 · *Electrical Engineering*, 79 (1960), 941 · *New York Times* (15 Sept 1960), 37 · *The Times* (15 Sept 1960), 18a · *The Times* (16 Sept 1960), 15a · *The Times* (19 Sept 1960), 10b
Archives Inst. EE, drafts of lectures, corresp., and working notes
Likenesses W. Stoneman, photograph, 1948, NPG · portrait, repro. in *ILN* (24 Sept 1960), 531 · portrait, repro. in *New York Times* (15 Sept 1960), 37 · portrait, repro. in *The Times* (15 Sept 1960), 18a
Wealth at death £202,947 18s. 11d.: probate, 30 Dec 1960, CGPLA Eng. & Wales

Fleming, Caleb (1698–1779), dissenting minister and religious controversialist, was born at Nottingham on 4 November 1698 and baptized at High Pavement Presbyterian Chapel on 10 November, the son of James Fleming, a respectable hosier, and Mary Buxton, a member of the Buxton family of Derbyshire, which possessed an estate and the lordship of the manor of Chelmerton. Fleming's career was far from typical of the dissenting ministry of the eighteenth century. Although he had the advantage of reasonably well-educated and moderately prosperous parents, who encouraged his early intellectual efforts, he seems to have been destined for a career in trade. However, at the age of sixteen he had the opportunity to study with the Revd John Hardy, a dissenting minister who subsequently conformed to the Church of England and who

Caleb Fleming (1698–1779), by Mason Chamberlin, 1772

ran a small academy at Nottingham. Here Fleming became proficient in mathematical subjects as well as theology, and it was probably here that he began to doubt the Calvinist principles of his upbringing.

In 1727 Fleming moved to London, where his theological position moved towards Socinianism, encouraged by his friend the Revd John Holt, who deepened Fleming's classical knowledge and who later served as a tutor at the Warrington Academy. Most biographical essays about Fleming by those who had known him personally state that about this time he acquired a knowledge of Hebrew from a rabbi. He had not yet determined to become a minister; instead he supported himself by unspecified commercial activity and by miscellaneous writing.

According to Palmer, Fleming was 'early married', presumably in the 1720s, to Mary, daughter of John Harris of Hardstaff, Derbyshire (*Sermon Preached at New-Broad Street*, 27–8). They had ten children, including at least one son. But only one child, his daughter Mary, survived him, as did his wife. She was credited by all Fleming's memoirists with consistent support during the years of relative poverty which marked his middle life.

During the early 1730s Fleming received, through the Revd William Harris, an invitation to write as a pamphleteer in defence of the ministry of Sir Robert Walpole. His characteristically vehement reply, 'that he would sooner cut off his right hand', not only acquired the status of a minor legend among dissenters, but established Fleming firmly within the 'commonwealth' tradition of radical whigs who regarded Walpole as irretrievably corrupt and a betrayer of the revolution of 1688. He responded in a similarly principled, if more courteous, manner to approaches from senior Anglican clergymen who offered him secure employment within the Church of England. About 1735 John Thomas, later bishop of Winchester, used his influence with Sir George Fleming (not a relative), bishop of Carlisle, to arrange for the living of Lazenby in Cumberland to be offered to him. Although he dedicated his *The Fourth Commandment Abrogated by the Gospel* (1736) to his namesake, Fleming had serious theological objections to the subscription to the Thirty-Nine Articles which Anglican ordination would have required; furthermore, as one convinced of the essentially voluntarist dissenting ethos, he strongly condemned the principle of an established church. He had already published (1732) a powerful attack on the Test and Corporation Acts, which took the form of a reply to Bishop Edmund Gibson's *The Dispute Adjusted*.

By this time Fleming's intellectual reputation had led to several invitations to preach from dissenting pulpits. He preached, for instance, for the Revd Thomas Mole at Rotherhithe, as well as at Oakingham in Berkshire, Guildford, Uxbridge, and Dorking. This preparation helps to explain why, on the death of John Munckley in 1738, Fleming was invited to succeed him as pastor of the Bartholomew Close Presbyterian congregation in London. On his acceptance, he was ordained in the same year at the age of forty. His statement, or confession, during that ceremony typified the rational dissent to which he belonged:

> That he believed the New-Testament writings to contain a revelation, worthy of God to give and of man to receive, and that it should be his endeavour to recommend them to the people in the sense in which he should, from time to time, understand them. He did not submit to the imposition of hands, which he considered as an unwarrantable mimicry of the apostles, and liable to misconstruction.   (Holden, 410)

His rejection of any form of priestcraft or patristic tradition as an intervening agency between the individual conscience and the authority of scripture was characteristic; so was his defence of revealed religion in the criticism of the deist position which he expressed in his *Remarks on Mr Thomas Chubb's Dissertation on Providence* (1738).

At first, Fleming served as joint minister at Bartholomew Close with William May. It was at about this time, according to his own account, that though previously an Arian, 'he became a Unitarian [and] preached a sermon from the first 14 verses of the 1st chap. of John to declare his change of opinion' (*Diary of Sylas Neville*, 33). This open avowal of Socinianism is reputed to have driven away some adherents from an already small flock, and the dwindling financial resources of the congregation meant that the 1740s were a time of poverty for him and his growing family. He continued, none the less, in his pamphleteering; he defended infant baptism in a tract of 1745 and in the same year issued *An Earnest Address to Britons* to coincide with the Jacobite rebellion. In 1749 he penned a riposte to William Warburton's *Alliance between Church and State* and in 1751 he wrote *The oeconomy of the sexes, or, The doctrine of divorce, the plurality of wives and the vow of celibacy freely examined*. This was a vindication of the institution of

marriage and was directed not only against the 'immorality' of the age but, even more pointedly, against the Catholic teaching of a celibate priesthood, a practice, Fleming averred, which had no biblical justification. Popery, he wrote, 'encourageth whoring and discourageth matrimony' (p. 58). The tract concluded with an anti-Catholic tirade which exemplified Fleming's view of the superstitious and tyrannical nature not only of the Catholic church but of its potential defenders in Anglican circles.

Fleming's opinions brought him to the attention of the group of commonwealth whigs who looked for inspiration to the republican Thomas Hollis and his family. In 1753, as a result of the temporary indisposition of the regular minister, James Foster, Fleming preached at the Pinner's Hall Independent Chapel. Here Timothy Hollis, cousin of Thomas Hollis, heard him with approval and recommended that he be appointed as Foster's assistant. After the appointment was confirmed, Fleming continued to conduct the afternoon service at Bartholomew Close. On Foster's death later in the same year, Fleming became sole minister at Pinner's Hall; the Bartholomew Close meeting was then closed, most of its surviving members joining Fleming's new congregation.

Fleming remained at Pinner's Hall until his retirement in 1777. He received financial support from several individuals who endorsed his Socinian theology; one such sympathizer was the Suffolk gentleman Richard Reynolds. An even more important source of succour was Thomas Hollis, whose diary reveals that throughout the 1760s he and Fleming were on terms of close friendship and political co-operation. Hollis repeatedly gave Fleming small sums of a few guineas, as the two men shared a common anti-Catholicism and commonwealth libertarianism, which they communicated to the press on every possible occasion. 'Venerable Dr Fleming', wrote Hollis in 1769, 'continues his labours in behalf of Truth and Liberty with unswerving diligence, and, indeed, to considerable public Benefit' (Bond, 146). The title reflects the conferment upon Fleming of the degree of DD by the University of St Andrews in that year; it was obtained for him, without his knowledge, by his heterodox friend William Dalrymple DD of Ayr. In his reply, Fleming asserted that his career had 'been ever devoted to the service of truth and liberty; never once resigning the right of private judgment to any human authority, nor consenting to sacrifice conscience upon the altar of human emolument' (Holden, 411–12). The award reflected Fleming's own interest in the anti-subscription moves within the Church of Scotland and his identification with the non-trinitarian tendencies of a small minority of its clergy. He regarded such clergy as natural allies in the campaign for relaxation of the Thirty-Nine Articles test for Anglican clergy, university undergraduates, and (in a more limited form) for dissenting ministers and schoolmasters. In 1773 he published *Religion not the Magistrate's Province, Occasioned by the Late Application to Parliament*, following the rejection of petitions for relief from the test both for Anglican clergy and undergraduates and for dissenting ministers and schoolmasters.

During his pastorate at Pinner's Hall, Fleming wrote some thirty separate tracts and confirmed his reputation as a fluent but highly partisan controversialist. Perhaps his best-known publication was *A Survey of the Search after Souls* (1758), a reply to a work which Fleming attributed to William Coward, but which is now attributed to Henry Layton. Fleming argued strongly for the existence of a separate soul and attacked the mortalist position. Among his other works were tracts on the eucharist (1763), on the authenticity of the first two chapters of St Matthew's gospel (1771), and on the 'alarming growth of Popery in this kingdom' (1768). On the latter theme he published in the London press numerous letters, under such pseudonyms as Old Milton.

One of Fleming's closest friends in these later years was the radical man about town and medical student Sylas Neville, whom he met in 1767. Their correspondence reveals a shared political outlook which involved support for the issues championed by the supporters of John Wilkes, although Fleming declared that Wilkes himself, 'being an enemy to every obligation of religion and morality cannot be a true friend to liberty' (*Diary of Sylas Neville*, 30). It also reflects a strong pro-Americanism in response to news of the growing conflict between Britain and her principal colonies. Fleming served as a kind of father figure to Neville, who was forty-three years his junior, giving him medical and financial as well as political guidance. On 30 April 1768 he introduced Neville to the circle of Catharine Macaulay, an event which Neville described in some detail in his diary.

Some members of Fleming's congregation at Pinner's Hall took offence at his radicalism and in particular at the oblique criticism of the monarchy which he insinuated into the traditional toasts at their annual dinner: 'May the reign of George the 3rd become glorious' (*Diary of Sylas Neville*, 116). Indeed, his flock dwindled in number and became extinct at his death. He was sustained in old age by legacies from sympathizers; one such legacy was a bequest of £100 from Thomas Hollis, who died in 1774. Subsidies of this sort help to explain why he was able to undertake quite lengthy tours in England to assist his health. Writers with an anti-Socinian bias, such as Walter Wilson, suggest that because of his 'uncommon itch for disputing', Fleming was 'neglected and discountenanced by the bulk of his brethren' (Wilson, 2.287). Yet he showed his collegiality by serving on the General Body of Dissenting Ministers and, from 1770 to 1779, as a trustee of Dr Williams's charity. He also formed a close friendship, as well as a theological affinity, with his neighbour in Hoxton Square, Nathaniel Lardner.

After retiring from his pastorate in 1777, Fleming died at his home in Hoxton Square, London, on 21 July 1779. He was buried in Bunhill Fields on 1 August. His will, with its bequests to several prominent Unitarians, including Theophilus Lindsey, was a final indication of the strength of his theological convictions. In many ways, however, Fleming represented an older tradition among rational dissenters, particularly in the vehemence of his anti-Catholicism: the next generation would have agreed with the comment of his sympathetic memoirist in 1818: 'Could the Doctor have had before him the more full, the repeated and able discussions, which have lately taken place on this subject, he might possibly have changed his opinion' (Holden, 411). Fleming's career as a whole is a lively demonstration of the close connection between theological heterodoxy and political radicalism in the eighteenth century.   G. M. DITCHFIELD

Sources L. Holden, *Monthly Repository*, 13 (1818), 409–13 · W. Wilson, *The history and antiquities of the dissenting churches and meeting houses in London, Westminster and Southwark*, 4 vols. (1808–14), vol. 2, pp. 283–90 · W. Turner, *Lives of eminent Unitarians*, 1 (1840), 275–98 · G. M. Ditchfield, 'Some aspects of Unitarianism and radicalism, 1760–1810', PhD diss., U. Cam., 1968, chap. 2 · G. M. Ditchfield, '"All truth, all righteous things": the correspondence of Caleb Fleming and Sylas Neville, 1769–1776', *Enlightenment and dissent*, 18 (1999), 84–123 · G. M. Ditchfield, 'Some literary and political views of Catharine Macaulay', *American Notes and Queries*, 12/5 (Jan 1974), 70–76 · *The diary of Sylas Neville, 1767–1788*, ed. B. Cozens-Hardy (1950) · C. Robbins, *The eighteenth-century commonwealthman* (1968) · Allibone, *Dict.* · W. H. Bond, 'Letters from Thomas Hollis of Lincoln's Inn to Andrew Eliot', *Proceedings of the Massachusetts Historical Society*, 99 (1987), 76–167 · *Protestant Dissenter's Magazine*, 4 (1797), 434–5 · *A sermon preached at New-Broad Street, August 1, 1779, occasioned by the death of the late Revd Caleb Fleming, D.D. … by John Palmer. With the oration delivered at the interment, by Joseph Towers* (1779) · J. Aikin and others, *General biography, or, Lives, critical and historical of the most eminent persons*, 10 vols. (1799–1815), vol. 4, pp. 132–3 · *IGI* · *DNB*

Archives DWL, MS sermons and notes, MSS 24.44, 24.45, 24.54 | BL, letter to T. Birch, Add. MS 4307, fol. 70 · DWL, John Disney Collection of letters on religious liberty from the newspapers, 87.6 · Harvard U., Houghton L., diary of Thomas Hollis · Norfolk RO, corresp. with Sylas Neville, MC 7/349 · Norfolk RO, MS diary of Sylas Neville, MC 7/1

Likenesses M. Chamberlin, oils, 1772, DWL [*see illus.*] · Hopwood, engraving (after oil painting attrib. M. Chamberlin), repro. in Wilson, *History and antiquities*, facing p. 283

Wealth at death household goods to wife; £1200 in government securities for daughter's maintenance; several hundred pounds in legacies to friends; plus books, rings, pictures: will, PRO, PROB 11/1056, fols. 91r–92v

Fleming, Christopher [*name in religion* Patrick] (1599–1631), Franciscan friar, was born on 17 April 1599 at Baile Atha Lagain (Lagan Bridge), co. Louth, the son of Captain Garrett (Gerald) Fleming and his wife, Elizabeth Cusack, daughter of Robert Cusack of Cushinstown and granddaughter of Christopher Nugent, heir to the barony of Delvin. He was nephew to Thomas Fleming OFM, archbishop of Dublin. He was baptized by William Jackson and in 1612 was sent to his uncle Christopher Cusack, president of the Irish College at Douai, to be educated there. He joined the Irish Franciscans at St Anthony's College, Louvain, on St Patrick's day 1617, and made his profession a year later to Anthony Hickey, taking the name Patrick, by which he is known. He was ordained a deacon on 18 December 1621 at Malines, and a priest presumably in 1622.

Fleming was chosen to accompany Hugh MacCaughwell OFM to Rome in 1623. On the way they met Hugh Ward OFM in Paris, and those three, together with Thomas Messingham, rector of the Irish College there, planned to publish the lives of the Irish saints to the glory of God and the honour of Ireland, and to refute the claims of the

Scottish priest Thomas Dempster on behalf of his home-land. Making his way to Rome, Fleming visited libraries, including Bobbio, Clairvaux, and Lyons, sent material through MacCaughwell to Messingham, and wrote letters to Ward about his findings. In Rome he stayed with Mac-Caughwell in the friary at Aracoeli, assisted him in his work on John Duns Scotus and sent what material he could get to Ward.

Fleming publicly defended theses as part of the proceed-ings of the general chapter of 1624, and in June 1625 was appointed the first lecturer in philosophy at St Isidore's College, Rome, founded that year. He composed a life of MacCaughwell, who was appointed archbishop of Armagh in 1626 but died the same year. It was used by Nicholas Vernulaeus, historiographer at Louvain Univer-sity, in his panegyric on MacCaughwell, which may sug-gest that Fleming was then at Louvain. Certainly he was teaching philosophy there in 1627. On his way there from Rome he had searched libraries in Italy, France, Germany, and the Spanish Netherlands making, for example, a sum-mary of the chronicle of the monastery of St Peter at Regensburg, where Irish monks had lived. At Louvain he worked on his collected lives of St Columbanus (or Colum-ban) and other Irish saints, and was preparing the manu-script for the printer when the Irish Franciscans obtained permission to start a college in Prague in 1629. On 17 December 1630 he was sent there as superior and lecturer in theology, making the long journey on foot, inspired by the example of St Columbanus.

There was much opposition to the new foundation from native Franciscans (Observants and Capuchins) and recourse was had to Rome through the prominent Francis-can Luke Wadding. A building was adapted, and on 6 July the chapel was solemnly opened. The address, written by Fleming, was declaimed by a young deacon named Mat-thew Hoare (a native of Dungarvan) whose parents were dead, and who became Fleming's travelling companion. Fleming began lecturing on sacramental theology. In August 1631 he journeyed to Vienna with Hoare to defend the fledgeling foundation. In Prague in October he again thought about publishing works on the saints of Ireland, as also on pilgrimages to Lough Derg, the latter for a princely benefactor, to be printed gratis in Prague. Instead the Thirty Years' War intervened, with the advance on the city of the army of the elector of Saxony, ally of Gustavus Adolphus of Sweden, and the friars decided to leave for safer places. On 7 November 1631, approaching the village of Benešov, on the way to the friary at Votice, Fleming and Hoare were attacked by a party of Hussites and killed. Fleming's body was reverently buried next day in the church of the Franciscans at Votice; Hoare's body was recovered in a wood on 11 November and was buried first at Benešov, then at Votice.

Fleming lived half his short life as a zealous Franciscan. A pioneer in the editing of Irish hagiography, he left behind a fine collection of annotated works on St Colum-banus, to whom he was devoted, and on some other Irish saints. Edited and added to by Thomas Sheeran (Sirinus)

OFM, it was published at Louvain in 1666 as *Collectanea sacra*, containing copies of some Bobbio manuscripts, sub-sequently lost.   IGNATIUS FENNESSY

Sources *R. P. F. Patricii Flemingi … Collectanea sacra, seu, S. Columbani Hiberni abbatis acta*, ed. T. Sirinus (1666) [incl. important biograph-ical information] · F. Matthews, 'Brevis synopsis provinciae Hib-erniae FF. Minorum', ed. B. Jennings, *Analecta Hibernica*, 6 (1934), 139–91 · B. Jennings, ed., 'Documents from the archives of St Isi-dore's College, Rome', *Analecta Hibernica*, 6 (1934), 203–47 · B. Jennings, ed., 'Documents of the Irish Franciscan college at Prague', *Archivium Hibernicum*, 9 (1942), 173–294 · B. Jennings, *Michael O Cleirigh, chief of the four masters, and his associates* (1936) · B. Jennings, ed., 'Irish names in the Malines ordination registers, 1602–1749 [pt 3]', *Irish Ecclesiastical Record*, 5th ser., 76 (1951), 128–40, esp. 139 · [F. Ó Briain], 'Irish Franciscan historians of St. Anthony's College, Louvain: Patrick Fleming', *Catholic Bulletin*, 18 (1928), 77–87 · A. Bruodinus, *Propugnaculum Catholicae veritatis* (Prague, 1669), 734–58 · N. Wright, 'Columbanus's *Epistulae*', *Columbanus: studies on the Latin writings*, ed. M. Lapidge (1997), 29–92 · B. Jennings, 'The Irish Franciscans in Prague', *Studies: an Irish Quarterly Review*, 28 (1939), 210–22 · [E. Hogan], 'Irish historical studies in the seven-teenth century', *Irish Ecclesiastical Record*, [new ser.], 7 (1870–71), 31–43, 56–77, 193–216 · W. Reeves, 'Irish library: no. 2, Fleming's *Collectanea sacra*', *Ulster Journal of Archaeology*, 2 (1854), 253–61 · R. J. Kelly, 'The Irish Franciscans in Prague, 1629–1768: their literary labours', *Journal of the Royal Society of Antiquaries of Ireland*, 6th ser., 12 (1922), 169–74 · H. Concannon, *Life of St. Columban* (1915), ix, xx–xxviii · P. A. Breatnach, 'An Irish Bollandus: Fr Hugh Ward and the Louvain hagiographical enterprise', *Éigse*, 31 (1999), 1–30 · R. Sharpe, *Medieval Irish saints' lives: an introduction to Vitae sanctorum Hiberniae* (1991) · *DNB*

Archives St Isidore's College, Rome, MSS W 11–14

Fleming, Christopher (1800–1880), surgeon, was born at Boardstown, co. Westmeath, Ireland, on 14 July 1800, the son of James Fleming, a country gentleman, and his wife, Catherine, daughter of B. Taylor of Castlepollard. From the lay college in Maynooth he entered Trinity College, Dublin, on 3 November 1817; he became BA in 1821, and proceeded MA in 1832 and MD in 1838. He was apprenticed to Richard Dease in 1818, and on the latter's death (from a dissecting-room wound) he transferred to work under Abraham Colles. He studied at the schools of surgery in the Royal College of Surgeons in Ireland, and took the LRCSI on 4 September 1824 and the MRCSI (equivalent to the later FRCSI) in 1826. He was surgeon to the Netterville Dispensary, lectured at the Park Street medical school, and in 1851 was appointed surgeon to the Richmond Hos-pital.

In 1856 Fleming was president of the College of Sur-geons. His fourteen contributions to the *Dublin Journal of Medical Science* dealt mainly with urinary problems; a selec-tion of them was edited by Sir William Thomson in *Clinical Record of Injuries and Diseases of the Genito-Urinary Organs* (1877). When chloroform became available Fleming pub-lished *Remarks on the Application of Chloroform to Surgical Pur-poses* (1851), which was favourably reviewed. He was appointed consulting surgeon to Dr Steevens' Hospital (an honorary position) on 4 December 1861, and joined its board of governors in 1870.

By birth and upbringing a Roman Catholic, Fleming later supported the Church of Ireland. His wife, Cather-ine, was a daughter of the Revd Stephen Radcliff. They had seven children (of whom a son and a daughter survived him) and lived at 6 Merrion Square North, Dublin, until his retirement; they then moved to 15 Brookfield Terrace, Donnybrook, co. Dublin, where he died on 30 December 1880, survived by his wife. He was buried in Mount Jerome cemetery. J. B. Lyons

Sources C. A. Cameron, *History of the Royal College of Surgeons in Ireland*, 2nd edn (1916) · T. P. C. Kirkpatrick, *The history of Doctor Steevens' Hospital, Dublin, 1720–1920* (1924) · *BMJ* (8 Jan 1881), 71 · *The Lancet* (8 Jan 1881) · *CGPLA Ire.* (1881)
Wealth at death under £16,000: probate, 11 Feb 1881, *CGPLA Ire.*

Fleming, Sir Daniel (1633–1701), antiquary, was born on 24 July 1633 at Coniston Hall, Furness, Lancashire, the eldest of six boys and one daughter of William Fleming (1608/9–1653) of Skirwith, Cumberland, and his wife, Alice (*d*. 1681), eldest daughter of Roger Kirkby, of Kirkby, Lancashire. As a boy Fleming experienced a succession of local schools and private tutors. He went to Queen's College, Oxford, for two years from July 1650, and then spent January to September 1653 at Gray's Inn. Fleming's father had attended Cambridge University, and his advice to his student son 'Apply your studdyes diligently for now is your Time to lay the foundations of all accomplishments hereafter' (*Le Fleming MSS*, no. 222) seems to have been acted on, in view of Fleming's later antiquarian interests, his continuing acquisition of books, and, for example, his familiarity with the publications of the Royal Society. But he also established valuable connections at the university with Thomas Smith his tutor, later bishop of Carlisle, and Sir Joseph Williamson, later a secretary of state, and met his future wife.

However, the committee for compounding with delinquents at London may have coloured Fleming's subsequent politics more than higher education. The recusant, royalist Fleming of Rydal family died out in the male line in 1649, leaving two heiresses. William Fleming of Skirwith claimed their estates by entail. Possession, disputed by the heiresses and their husbands, and complicated because parliament proposed to sell the sequestered lands, did not come to Daniel until 1654. A generation later when his own autobiography was finished, it still recorded that the civil war had been won by 'rebels', some of whom had confiscated Rydal. Fleming married on 27 August 1655 Barbara, eldest daughter of Sir Henry Fletcher, bt, of Hutton in the Forest, Cumberland, and his wife, Katherine, daughter of Sir George Dalston, bt, of Dalston, Cumberland. Barbara died from the birth of their fifteenth child on 13 April 1675, and he did not remarry.

At the Restoration Fleming was a safe sheriff of Cumberland, and soon a cavalier in purging Kendal corporation. He opposed and quickly attacked dissent, but as a supporter of the established church also proceeded against papists in the mid-1660s. He played a prominent role as a JP and deputy lieutenant for Westmorland, Lancashire, and Cumberland, and as an officer in the Westmorland militia. On one of his rare trips south he was knighted in 1681. He felt his large family a drain on his limited income, and that he could never afford to stand for parliament for the county (he was elected for Cockermouth, Cumberland, in 1685 under his brother-in-law's influence). An active tory alienated by James II, he became a moderate pursuer of Roman Catholics and Jacobites in the 1690s. Fleming's place in county society and politics was more prominent than his landed estate might suggest. For the order of the Royal Oak his income was put at £1800 p.a., but the family archive suggests less, nearer to a third than to half of that figure. His influence owed much to his personality and long pedigree, strengthened as the decades passed by his longevity and wisdom, which contrasted with the mortality, the absence, and the religious or financial problems of his more wealthy neighbours.

Fleming's reputation as an antiquary was acknowledged in Edmund Gibson's 1695 edition of Camden's *Britannia*, in the section on Westmorland. His antiquarian pursuits had developed in the 1660s and 1670s when he sent manuscripts and advice to Sir William Dugdale, and in 1677 he was known to Gregory King at the College of Arms. Fleming supplied information for Richard Blome's *Britannia* (1673), John Ogilby's *Britannia* (1675), and John Adams's *Index villaris* (1680). His knowledge of northern customs was valued by the circuit judges. Fleming's own works were not published until the nineteenth and twentieth centuries. His manuscript outline of Furness, Westmorland, and Cumberland, completed in 1671, paid homage to Camden and ancient antiquities, and gave useful contemporary detail of market towns and major families and estates, but also provided some documentary authority for their origins. His manuscript family history to 1684 was based on his archives, and gave supporting references to particular documents, which he had numbered, catalogued, and filed. He died on 25 March 1701 at Rydal Hall and was buried on 27 March at Grasmere. His eldest son, William, succeeded to the estates; another son, George *Fleming, bishop of Carlisle, inherited in 1736.

C. B. Phillips

Sources Cumbria AS, Kendal, Fleming of Rydal papers, WD/Ry [incl. MSS of Sir Daniel from the Senhouse family papers deposited at Cumbria AS, Carlisle] · *The memoirs of Sir Daniel Fleming*, ed. W. G. Collingwood, trans. R. E. Porter, Cumberland and Westmorland Antiquarian and Archaeological Society, Tract Series 11 (1928) · *The manuscripts of S. H. Le Fleming*, HMC, 25 (1890) · J. R. Magrath, ed., *The Flemings in Oxford*, 1, OHS, 44 (1904) · J. R. Magrath, ed., *The Flemings in Oxford*, 2, OHS, 62 (1913) · J. R. Magrath, ed., *The Flemings in Oxford*, 3, OHS, 79 (1924) · H. Maclean and H. Brierley, *The registers of the parish church of Coniston, 1599–1700*, Lancashire Parish Register Society, 30 (1907) · 'Sir Daniel Fleming's description of Cumberland, Westmorland and Furness, 1671', *Fleming-Senhouse papers*, ed. E. Hughes, 2 (1961) · *Catalogue of English books of the sixteenth and seventeenth centuries, the property of Richard le Fleming esq., removed from Rydal Hall* (1969) [sale catalogue, Christies, 1969] · M. L. Armitt, *Rydal*, ed. W. F. Rawnsley (1916) · G. Hampson and E. Cruickshanks, 'Fleming, Sir Daniel', HoP, *Commons, 1660–90*, 2.331–3 · *Camden's Britannia*, ed. and trans. E. Gibson (1695) · M. A. E. Green, ed., *Calendar of the proceedings of the committee for compounding … 1643–1660*, 5 vols., PRO (1889–92) · A. Macfarlane, *The justice and the mare's ale: law and disorder in seventeenth-century England* (1981)
Archives Bodl. Oxf., newsletters and papers · Cumbria AS, Kendal, corresp. and papers · Cumbria AS, Carlisle, MS historical notes, corresp., and antiquarian notes · Cumbria AS, Carlisle, description of Cumberland, Westmorland, and Furness · NRA, priv. coll., recipe book

Likenesses attrib. J. Bracken, portrait, 1665; known to be at Rydal Hall until 1970
Wealth at death approx. £700 p.a. in 1698: Cumbria AS, Kendal, WD/Ry, account book of Sir Daniel Fleming, 1688–1701

Fleming, Sir David (*d.* 1406), landowner and courtier, was the son of Malcolm Fleming (*d. c.*1390), lord of Biggar and Cumbernauld, and his wife, Christian. A middle-ranking baron, he rose to prominence in the service of David II and Robert III. His father had been a follower of David II, holding the office of sheriff of Dumbarton. David also entered royal service; he was termed 'our dear and faithful bachelor' by David II in 1362 (Thomson, no. 175) and married Jean, daughter of the king's adherent David Barclay of Brechin. After the death of the king in 1371 the Flemings may have given their support to John Stewart, earl of Carrick. According to the *Liber pluscardensis*, Fleming was the man responsible for arresting Robert II; if that is correct, the act probably occurred in 1384 when Carrick seized power from his father. By 1400 Fleming was 'luvit wel' by Carrick, now Robert III, and had established himself as an influential councillor of both the king and his younger brother, Robert Stewart, duke of Albany and earl of Fife (*d.* 1420).

Fleming's rise to a position of personal power came in 1404. The battle of Homildon Hill in 1402 had removed the major figures of southern Scotland into English captivity. Fleming himself had been captured in this clash, but he secured a quick release, and by early 1404 was employed in a major role in Anglo-Scottish diplomacy. His status in the kingdom is suggested by his place as first-named baron in the general council of April 1404. Along with his political allies, Henry Wardlaw, bishop of St Andrews (*d.* 1440), who was the guardian of the young heir to the throne, Prince James, and Henry Sinclair, earl of Orkney (*d.* 1418), Fleming sought to establish himself in the south. In 1405 they backed the rebellion in England of Henry Percy, earl of Northumberland, and after its collapse Fleming aided Percy's escape from Scotland before he could be exchanged for the captive Archibald Douglas, fourth earl of Douglas (*d.* 1424). This act, combined with Fleming's ambitions in the south, antagonized the Black Douglases, while his efforts to obtain control of the office of sheriff of Roxburgh from the heirs of George Douglas, first earl of Angus (*d.* 1403), brought the hostility of the Red Douglases. In an attempt to pressurize the Red Douglases, Fleming entered Haddingtonshire with Orkney, Prince James, and an armed following in early 1406. He overestimated his strength. Orkney and the prince escaped, but Fleming was killed on 14 February on Long Hermiston Moor, Edinburghshire, after a running fight by a force of Black Douglas adherents led by James Douglas of Balvenie (*d.* 1443), Archibald Douglas's brother. Faced by major magnates, the resources of a royal favourite such as Fleming proved to be insufficient for regional power.

Sir Malcolm Fleming (*d.* 1440), the son of David Fleming and his second wife, Isabel of Monycabock, also based his career on the backing of powerful patrons and suffered a similar fate to his father. Although he was worth 600 marks in 1424, he sought eminence by serving greater magnates. His marriage, before 1413, to Elizabeth, daughter of the duke of Albany, signalled his close association with the governor, and Fleming acted as his father-in-law's councillor and received of his patronage. The link with the Albany Stewarts continued into the 1420s, when Malcolm adhered to Albany's grandson Walter Stewart of Lennox. In 1424 he may have negotiated between Stewart and the newly returned king, James I, but his efforts only earned him James's mistrust. When Stewart was arrested at Edinburgh in May 1424, Fleming was also detained. Unlike Stewart, who was executed in 1425, Fleming was spared further punishment. Although in 1431 he exploited the fall of another of the king's victims, John Kennedy, to claim the lands of Lenzie, Fleming did not return to prominence until after the king's death. Again his importance was as the councillor of a great magnate, William, sixth earl of Douglas. The connection may have won both men the suspicion of James Douglas. On 24 November 1440 Earl William and Fleming were arrested in Edinburgh Castle at the so-called Black Dinner; William was executed that day, Fleming on the 25th.

Robert Fleming, first Lord Fleming (*d.* 1491), the son of Malcolm and Elizabeth, acted vigorously to reverse the sentence of forfeiture passed on his father. In 1442 he was restored as part of a settlement with James Douglas, now seventh earl of Douglas, whose daughter, Janet, Robert married (in or before 1451). In the 1440s Robert adhered to his in-laws, witnessing Douglas family documents, attending court with William, eighth earl of Douglas, in 1444, and leading an attack on their enemies in 1445. Unlike his father, however, when magnate kinsmen clashed with the crown, Robert took the king's side. In June 1452 he attended the parliament which exonerated James II for his murder of Douglas earlier that year, and was created a lord of parliament. By 1454 he was master of the king's household and an occasional councillor of James II. Lord Fleming retained links of service with magnates, acting as carver to William Sinclair, earl of Orkney (*d.* 1480), himself a royal councillor. His bond with Gilbert, Lord Kennedy (*d.* 1479), and Alexander Boyd in 1466 shows him dealing with two men of similar baronial rank, who were at that time heading the principal faction in James III's minority government. Though Fleming held no comparable influence, the fall of the great magnate houses nevertheless enabled him to act as an independent player in Scottish politics. After the death of his first wife in or before 1480 he married Margaret Lindsay. He died in 1491.   M. H. BROWN

Sources S. Boardman, *Robert II and Robert III* (1996) · M. Brown, *James I* (1994) · B. Seton, 'The provocation of James Douglas of Balvany', *SHR*, 23 (1925–6), 116–18 · C. McGladdery, *James II* (1990) · *Wigtown charter chest: charter chest of the earldom of Wigtown*, Scottish RS (1910) · J. M. Thomson and others, eds., *Registrum magni sigilli regum Scotorum / The register of the great seal of Scotland*, 2nd edn, 1, ed. T. Thomson (1912) · *Scots peerage*, 8.529–30 · W. Bower, *Scotichronicon*, ed. D. E. R. Watt and others, new edn, 9 vols. (1987–98), 61–3

Fleming, David Hay (1849–1931), antiquary and writer on Scottish history, was born at St Andrews on 9 May 1849,

David Hay Fleming (1849–1931), by Andrew Swan Watson, 1925

the third and youngest son of John Fleming, china and stoneware merchant, of St Andrews, whose ancestors were from Deeside, and his wife, Ann, daughter of David Hay, whose family came from St Andrews. Educated at Madras College, St Andrews, he entered the family business. Study of the civic records increased his existing taste for history, however, and following the successful prosecution of his mother's claim on an estate in Chancery, he was able to sell the business in 1883, and devote himself to the study of history.

In 1885 Fleming married Robina Agnes (*d.* 1909), daughter of James Hart, of St Andrews; they had no children. They lived for twenty years in St Andrews, where Fleming wrote a series of learned essays on the history of the burgh. His work gained him a reputation beyond the local area but, although much of it was embodied in the *Alphabetic Guide Book to St Andrews* (1881) which (as the *Handbook*) went through six further editions, much is preserved only in pamphlets and in contributions to the local press (chiefly listed in the bibliography in his biography). His knowledge of the antiquities of St Andrews was profound, and his last book, *St Andrews Cathedral Museum* (1931), describes an institution which he had done much to foster. Fleming's main interest was in ecclesiastical history. He was baptized into the Free Church of Scotland, but in 1899 he and his wife joined the Original Seceders: he ruled his life according to the strict practice of these churches and thought it his duty to justify their tenets upon historical grounds. Some of his criticism was acerbic, but Fleming was personally courteous. His rigid sabbatarianism did not prevent him being a good raconteur.

In 1891 a review in the *Original Secession Magazine* caught the eye of William Robertson Nicoll, and thereafter Fleming's contributions to the *British Weekly* and *The Bookman* made him known to a wide public as the champion of the Scottish Reformation and of the covenanters. He transcribed and edited for the Scottish History Society the *Register of the Ministers, Elders and Deacons of the Christian Congregation of St Andrews … 1559–1600* (2 vols., 1889–90), and in 1901 he produced a valuable edition of Patrick Walker's *Six Saints of the Covenant*. He also published *Mary, Queen of Scots, from her Birth to her Flight into England* (1897).

In 1905 Fleming moved to Edinburgh, where he became an active member of various learned societies. In 1907 he delivered at Princeton Theological Seminary the Stone lectures which were published in 1910 as *The Reformation in Scotland: Causes, Characteristics, Consequences*. He edited the second volume (1529–42) of the *Register of the Privy Seal of Scotland* (1921), and, although the hoped-for continuation of *Mary, Queen of Scots* and a life of John Knox never appeared, he produced pamphlets for the Knox Club and a steady stream of articles and reviews partly collected in *Critical Reviews Relating Chiefly to Scotland* (1912).

Fleming died in Edinburgh on 7 November 1931. He bequeathed to the city of St Andrews the residue of his estate for the foundation and maintenance of a public reference library of which his own great collection of books should be the core.

J. D. MACKIE, *rev.* H. C. G. MATTHEW

Sources H. M. Paton, *David Hay Fleming: historian and antiquary* (1934) [with bibliography]
Archives NL Scot., papers on Knox · NL Scot., corresp. · U. St Andr. L., collected MSS
Likenesses A. S. Watson, photograph, 1925, NPG [*see illus.*] · portraits, repro. in Paton, *David Hay Fleming*

Fleming, David Pinkerton, Lord Fleming (1877–1944), judge, was born at Rutherglen, near Glasgow, on 11 February 1877, the fourth son of John Fleming, writer to the signet, and his wife, Isabella Wark Pinkerton. He was educated at Glasgow high school and the universities of Glasgow (MA, 1895; LLB, 1896) and Edinburgh, where he took classes in evidence and procedure. He also studied technical subjects in electricity, engineering, and accountancy at the Heriot-Watt College, Edinburgh, and the knowledge there obtained stood him in good stead in his later forensic career. Determined by family tradition and personal inclination upon the law, he was admitted to the Faculty of Advocates in 1902. Unlike many who later achieve distinction, Fleming did not have long to wait before practice came his way and he early showed that he was competent to undertake it. He soon acquired by merit one of the best junior practices at the bar. In 1913 he married Beatrice Joan, daughter of James Swan, a well-known Scottish livestock dealer. There were no children of the marriage. Within six months of the outbreak of war in 1914 Fleming was commissioned in the Scottish Rifles (Cameronians). With them and later with the 13th Royal Inniskilling Fusiliers he saw much hard active service in France, was awarded the MC and the Belgian Croix de Guerre, and was mentioned in dispatches. He was seriously wounded at Tournai in October 1918 and returned to the bar in 1919. He rapidly regained his practice in the 'boom' years of litigation which followed and there were few commercial or Admiralty cases of any substance or importance in which David Fleming was not briefed on one side or the other. It is a characteristic of the Scottish bar that its members do not specialize as in England; consequently the range of practice of busy pleaders tends to be substantially wider than at the English bar.

In 1919 Fleming was appointed advocate depute by Lord Advocate (afterwards Lord President) Clyde and thus gained a wide experience in criminal matters as a responsible crown prosecutor. In 1921 he took silk and in the following year he was appointed solicitor-general for Scotland in Andrew Bonar Law's administration. He had no seat in the House of Commons and was unsuccessful in contesting Dunbartonshire in December 1923, but gained the seat at the general election of 1924, when Stanley Baldwin renewed his appointment as solicitor-general for Scotland. He was no stranger to party politics, for before 1914 he had been adopted as prospective Conservative candidate for Kilmarnock burghs. Fleming's political career, however, was brief, for in December 1925 came the announcement of his elevation to the Scottish bench, with the judicial title of Lord Fleming. Throughout his career as a pleader he had been distinguished by a breadth of outlook and moderation in argument which testified to his humanity and liberality of mind. In addition, he possessed the invaluable gift of common sense. These qualities, allied to a high measure of professional capacity and legal knowledge, were admirably combined with a natural patience and courtesy and excellently equipped him for the successful discharge of his high judicial office. He was brisk in expression, patient and receptive in argument, and possessed not only a firm grasp of legal principles but a determination to achieve a just decision. In every sense he was a wise and upright judge whose judgments, owing nothing to external graces or picturesque phrases, were of value for their plain, lucid, and accurate statements of apposite legal principle.

Fleming's personal activities and interests went outside the boundaries of his profession: his interest in youth showed itself in his presidency of the Boys' Brigade in Edinburgh and in his chairmanship of the departmental committee set up in June 1942 to consider means whereby the association between the English public schools and the general educational system of the country might be developed and extended. This committee, over which he presided with painstaking zeal and care, in its unanimous report outlined a plan for opening the doors of English public schools to children from all local authority schools. The Fleming report owed much to Fleming himself and bore the marks of his common sense and realistic outlook; it remains a notable contribution to educational thought and policy in this country. Fleming also served from May 1940 until appointed chairman of the public schools committee, as chairman of the London appellate tribunal for conscientious objectors, while his patriotic zeal took him on its formation into the Home Guard as a private. He was an honorary LLD of his own University of Glasgow (1938) and an honorary bencher of the Middle Temple (1940). As a member of an old Rutherglen family (his father, grandfather, and great-grandfather all having been provosts of the burgh) he received the freedom of that ancient and royal burgh on the celebration of its octocentenary in 1926.

Fleming died in Edinburgh after a very brief illness on 20 October 1944, survived by his wife. Genial and kindly in manner, in personal appearance Fleming was of middle height and good physique, and greatly attached to open-air life. Fishing, shooting, golf, and (in his earlier years) mountaineering all claimed his active pursuit in his leisure.   JOHN CAMERON, rev.

Sources personal knowledge (1959) · private information (1959) · *The Times* (21 Oct 1944) · *WWW* · *CGPLA Eng. & Wales* (1945)
Wealth at death £37,304 19s. 9d.: confirmation, 28 Dec 1944, *CCI*

Fleming [married name Stanley], **Fanny** (1792?–1861), actress, was probably born on 31 October 1792. She was said to be the granddaughter of West *Digges. In Liverpool and Manchester she played Lady Macbeth and Helen Macgregor. She married George Stanley, an actor who later died in America. A daughter, the actress Emma Stanley, was born on 13 November 1818 (or 1823). Mrs Stanley's first appearance in London took place at the Lyceum, probably in 1834 since her husband was billed there in October of that year. She moved to the Haymarket and, a tall, well-built woman, was known for her rendering of matronly characters. She died suddenly of bronchitis at her home, 20 Jermyn Street, London, on 17 January 1861 aged sixty-nine.   JOSEPH KNIGHT, rev. J. GILLILAND

Sources *Oxberry's Dramatic Biography* (1826) · *GM*, 3rd ser., 10 (1861), 234 · d. cert.

Fleming, Sir George, second baronet (1667–1747), bishop of Carlisle, was born at Rydal Hall, Westmorland, on 10 June 1667, fifth son of Sir Daniel *Fleming (1633–1701) of Rydal, and Barbara (d. 1675), daughter of Sir Henry Fletcher, baronet, of Hutton, Cumberland. Fleming was educated at Sedbergh School before entering St Edmund Hall, Oxford, on 14 July 1688; he graduated BA in 1692 and proceeded MA in 1694. Unlike his wayward brothers he was a pious and conscientious scholar, surviving in Oxford on an allowance of £20 a year. He displayed whig principles by composing verses of congratulation on the return of William III from Ireland in 1690.

In spite of a desire to be a lawyer, and though he had been rejected by his bishop for holy orders in 1692, Fleming was ordained priest in 1694. His father failed to obtain for him a chaplaincy to Lord Thanet and to the East India Company, but succeeded in persuading Bishop Thomas Smith of Carlisle to appoint him as his domestic chaplain in 1694. This was Fleming's route to preferment, and he declined the living of Penrith in favour of that of Aspatria, to which he was presented in 1695. However, Fleming remained in Oxford to study until 1696. He found Smith's successor, Bishop William Nicolson, with whom he shared an interest in historical scholarship, an equally generous patron, and received a prebend of Carlisle in 1701, the rectories of Kirkland and Stanwix in 1703, and

Sir George Fleming, second baronet (1667–1747), by John Faber junior (after John Vanderbank, 1738)

the archdeaconry of Carlisle in 1705. Fleming held a number of other livings in the diocese of Carlisle under successive bishops: Great Salkeld in 1705, Ullsby in 1719, and Grasmere—a family living—in 1729. About 1708 he married Catherine Jefferson (d. 1736), and they had one son and four daughters.

Fleming was an active archdeacon under Bishop Nicolson and was a JP in the commission for Cumberland from 1709, in which capacity he opposed the licensing of a number of dissenters' meeting-houses. He also supported Nicolson in disputes with the tory Dean Atterbury of Carlisle. In 1713, when the deanery of Carlisle fell vacant, Fleming, supported by his brother Sir William Fleming, was a strong, though unsuccessful, contender. It was perhaps inevitable, however, in view of his brother's influence in the county and his own reputation as an effective administrator, that Fleming should obtain greater preferment. In 1727 he was appointed dean of Carlisle, and in 1734 he was nominated bishop of Carlisle. He was consecrated bishop at Lambeth on 19 January 1735. Fleming owed his preferment to his friendship with Bishop Gibson, and the need for an uncontroversial appointment following the controversial appointment of Thomas Rundle to an Irish see.

Fleming was a conscientious and painstaking bishop who drew up detailed records of the livings in his diocese; his record of ordinations and institutions was exemplary. He also took care of the fabric of the bishop's residence, Rose Castle. In 1740 he sold wood from the episcopal lands to refloor and replumb the building and repair the chapel. He was generous in augmenting poor livings in the diocese; and he was a generous patron to both his son and

sons-in-law. In 1736 he succeeded his elder brother as baronet and owner of the Rydal estate, but in May that year his wife died, and seven years later his son also died.

During the Jacobite rising of 1745 Fleming was a staunch supporter of the Hanoverian regime. His reputation has been rehabilitated from suggestions of timidity: Fleming sent his chaplain out to obtain military intelligence, and the 78-year-old bishop took the saddle against the Pretender at Penrith. In the absence of the lord lieutenant, he was the principal authority within the county, and his horses dragged artillery to Carlisle from Whitehaven. Legend has it that the Stuart troops only refrained from sacking Rose Castle in 1745 because of the recent birth of Fleming's granddaughter.

Fleming was a pious man, often attending worship four times each day. His death at Rose Castle, on 2 July 1747, was marked in the *Gentleman's Magazine* as a loss to society of one of its valuable members and a loss to the Church of England of 'one of its chiefest ornaments' (*GM*, 326). He was buried in Carlisle Cathedral, where a marble memorial sculpture of him was erected at its east end.

WILLIAM GIBSON

Sources Foster, *Alum. Oxon.* • J. R. Magrath, ed., *The Flemings in Oxford*, 2, OHS, 62 (1913) • *The manuscripts of his grace the duke of Portland*, 10 vols., HMC, 29 (1891–1931), vol. 5 • *Fleming–Senhouse papers*, ed. E. Hughes (1961) • memorial inscription, Carlisle Cathedral • *GM*, 1st ser., 17 (1747), 324–6 • F. G. James, *North country bishop* (1958) • C. M. L. Bouch, *Prelates and people of the lake counties: a history of the diocese of Carlisle, 1133–1933* (1948) • Cumbria AS, Carlisle, Fleming papers • *DNB*
Archives BL, Add. MS 24120 • Bodl. Oxf., corresp. with his father • Cumbria AS, Carlisle • Cumbria AS, Whitehaven, corresp. and papers
Likenesses J. Faber junior, mezzotint (after J. Vanderbank, 1738), BM, NPG [see illus.] • J. Vanderbank, oils, Ponsonby Hall, Cumbria • marble monument; formerly at Carlisle Cathedral

Fleming, George (1833–1901), veterinary surgeon, born at Glasgow on 11 March 1833, was the son of a working shoeing smith there. Early in life he was taken by his father to Manchester, where both were employed in the farrier's shop of a veterinary surgeon. He subsequently entered the service of a well-known veterinary surgeon of Manchester, John Lawson, who sent him to the Edinburgh Veterinary College. He took several medals and prizes, and in 1855 obtained the certificate of the Highland and Agricultural Society of Scotland, which was then recognized as a veterinary diploma.

At the end of 1855 Fleming entered the army veterinary service, and he served in the Crimea until the end of the war. In 1859 he volunteered for the expedition to north China, and he was present at the capture of the Taku (Dagu) forts and the surrender of Peking (Beijing), receiving for his services a medal with two clasps. While in China he undertook an expedition beyond the Great Wall, which he described in *Travels on Horseback in Manchu Tartary* (1863). In 1866 he obtained the diploma of the Royal College of Veterinary Surgeons, and in 1867 he served with the army in Syria and Egypt. After his return he spent some years with the Royal Engineers at Chatham. In 1875

George Fleming (1833–1901), by unknown photographer, pubd 1901

Fleming who was described by a contemporary as being ambitious, impulsive, and somewhat dogmatic (*Veterinary Record*, 27 April 1901, 595), was a voluminous writer who contributed largely to professional journals and to general reviews. He translated from the French work by Alexandre Pierre Chauveau, *Comparative Anatomy of the Domesticated Animals* (1873; 2nd edn, 1891); and from the German work by Louis George Neumann, *Parasites and Parasitical Diseases of the Domesticated Animals* (1892; 2nd edn, 1905). Fleming's separately published works include: *Vivisection: is it Necessary or Justifiable?* (1866); *Animal Plagues: their History, Nature, and Prevention* (vol. 1, 1871; vol. 2, 1882); *Practical Horse-Shoeing* (1872; 10th edn, 1900); *Rabies and Hydrophobia* (1872); and *A Manual of Veterinary Sanitary Science and Policy* (2 vols., 1875). His library of 800 volumes of books on professional subjects was given by him in 1900 to the Royal College of Veterinary Surgeons.

Fleming died on 13 April 1901 at his home, Higher Lee, Berrynarbor, Devon.

ERNEST CLARKE, *rev.* LINDA WARDEN

Sources *Veterinary Journal*, 3 and 4 (1901), 284–94; 357–63; 383–7 · *Veterinary Record* (27 April 1901) · *Veterinary Record* (20 April 1901) · *The Times* (16 April 1901) · personal knowledge (1912) · d. cert. · register, Royal College of Veterinary Surgeons, London
Likenesses B. Hudson, oils, 1883, Royal College of Veterinary Surgeons · photograph, repro. in *Veterinary Record* (27 April 1901) [*see illus.*]
Wealth at death £3671 16s. 7d.: probate, 21 May 1901, *CGPLA Eng. & Wales*

he founded the *Veterinary Journal*; he retired from the editorship in 1894. In 1879 Fleming was appointed inspecting veterinary surgeon at the War Office, during which time he suggested the establishment of the army veterinary school at Aldershot, which he directed from 1883, when he became principal veterinary surgeon to the army. In 1887 he was made CB and in 1890 he retired from the army.

Fleming became a vice-president of the Royal College of Veterinary Surgeons in 1867, a year after his admission, and was a member of council from 1868 to 1892. He was elected president in 1880, when the agitation for an act of parliament to restrict the title of veterinary surgeon to the diploma holders of the college had become acute, and by his energy and pertinacity he was mainly instrumental in securing the passage through parliament of the Veterinary Surgeons Act 1881, which imposed a penalty upon unqualified persons who took or used the title of veterinary surgeon; the misuse of the title had become a public scandal. Fleming was in gratitude re-elected president for three years in succession (1881–4), and again in 1886–7. In 1883 he received the honorary degree of LLD from the University of Glasgow.

Fleming was married three times: first, to Alice, daughter of J. Peake of Atherstone, in 1863; second, to Susan, daughter of W. Solomon of Upchurch, Kent, in 1878; third, to Anna de Montmorency, daughter of Colonel R. D. Pennefather of Kilbracken, co. Leitrim, who survived him and afterwards remarried.

Fleming, Ian (1906–1994), artist and art teacher, was born on 19 November 1906 in Colvend Street, Glasgow, the younger son of John Fleming (*d.* 1939), a painter and decorator, of Byres Road, Glasgow, and his wife, Catherine, *née* McLean (*d.* 1970), a Gaelic speaker from Tiree. At birth he was given the name John, but he was always known as Ian. He was educated in Glasgow at Church Street primary school, where he first discovered he had a talent for drawing, and at Hyndland secondary school. From 1924 to 1929 he studied drawing and painting at Glasgow School of Art, where he also began printmaking. There he was taught lithography and colour woodcut by Chika McNab and Josephine Haswell Miller. He first exhibited at the Royal Glasgow Institute of the Fine Arts in 1927 and at the Royal Scottish Academy in 1930.

In 1929 Fleming spent his post-diploma year working with Charles Murray, who, recognizing his skill as a draughtsman, had earlier introduced him to engraving. His first engraving, in June 1928, was of the head of a girl, and he soon became obsessed with the medium. Murray, a great influence, taught him about mood and dynamic thrust in composition. At the end of 1929, as the recipient of a Glasgow School of Art travelling scholarship, he spent three months in London before travelling throughout France and Spain. In Paris he studied Degas and Jean-Emile Laboureur, a contemporary, at printsellers, and he also visited Stanley William Hayter in Atelier 17. In Spain, because of his fascination with El Greco, he visited the Prado in Madrid and Toledo. His most famous engraving,

Gethsemane (1931), was exhibited in Paris with works by the Society of Artist Printmakers, and the French government bought a copy for the Bibliothèque Nationale in Paris. Following his return to Scotland Fleming started using drypoint as he worked up drawings done abroad. He favoured the mood and tonality of drypoint and now found engraving too factual. In 1935 he tried his first etching.

Fleming spent the year 1930–31 at Jordanhill Teacher Training College, Glasgow. In 1931 he was appointed assistant lecturer at Glasgow School of Art, where he taught life drawing, painting, and art history. Through Adam Bruce Thomson he met the Edinburgh printmaker and stained glass artist William Wilson. The two became firm friends and shared ideas on printmaking, each influencing the other. Nominated in 1933 by Wilson, Fleming became an active member of the Society of Artist Printmakers. At Glasgow School of Art he taught Robert Colquhoun and Robert MacBryde, and his large oil portrait of these two young artists won the 1938 Guthrie award. His 1940 painting *Art Students Preparing a Still Life* was one of only a few works to survive a fire in his studio in 1942.

Fleming was at his most expressive in his printmaking with the blitz scenes in Maryhill, Glasgow, where he served from 1940 to 1943 in the police war reserve, Glasgow police F division. In 1943 he was commissioned as a second lieutenant in the Pioneer Corps, serving in Normandy, the Low Countries, and Germany. He was promoted captain in 30 corps in 1945 and left the army in 1946 as a major. Throughout the war he made sketches and watercolours drawn directly from his military experience. On 27 April 1943 he married Catherine Margaret Weetch (*b.* 1915), the daughter of Walter John Weetch. She, like Fleming, was an artist: they had met at Glasgow School of Art. They had two daughters, Elspeth (*b.* 1944) and Fiona (*b.* 1947), and a son, Alisdair (*b.* 1949).

Fleming rejoined Glasgow School of Art in 1946 as a senior lecturer, and in 1948 he was appointed warden at the Patrick Allan-Fraser Art College, Hospitalfield, Arbroath. While there he moved away from printmaking towards painting (in watercolours and oils) pastoral landscapes and fishing harbours; he also continued to paint very strong portraits. His skills as an administrator and teacher were used to the full during his term as principal from 1954 to 1971 of Gray's School of Art, Aberdeen. At the time of his appointment the school's premises were attached to Aberdeen Art Gallery and very limited. Fleming revived the department of printmaking, expanded the entire curriculum, and created a library. But his major achievement was the removal of Gray's to Garthdee and a purpose-built college that put Aberdeen on the map of national art education. He wanted to promote at Gray's the basic excellence of drawing, combined with emotional feeling. Colleagues recalled him as unpretentious, modest, enthusiastic, and full of energy. He visited every school in the Aberdeen area and gave talks about the opportunities at Gray's. From 1956 onwards he visited Shetland to teach in the summer schools at Jarlshof.

In his retirement, from 1973 to 1986, Fleming served as chairman of the Peacock printmakers' workshop in Aberdeen, acting as a leading figure in the revival of Scottish printmaking. He used Peacock premises to make his series *The Creation* in 1977 in response to the American artist Ben Shahn's book *Love and Joy about Letters* (1964). This led to the *Comment* series of prints, in which he experimented with abstraction. He had exhibitions at Aberdeen Art Gallery (and on tour, 1983), at Barclay Lennie in Glasgow (1985), and at the Fine Art Society in Glasgow and Edinburgh (1991). Fleming was a keen advocate of art for everyone. In 1955–6 he began a children's Saturday art class, and in 1958 he re-established the Aberdeen Artists' Society. He also worked from 1985 to 1994 on an art project with the Cyrenians.

Fleming was of medium build with a moustache, but in his later years he grew a neat beard and wore spectacles. He listed his recreation in *Who's Who* as 'anything Scottish', being an active member of the Scottish National Party and branch president of Aberdeen Ferryhill area. He was president of the Rotary Club and chairman of the Saltire Society in Aberdeen. He also served on the council and hanging committee of the Royal Scottish Academy. Towards the end of his life he spoke of his enduring love of light and circular movement in his prints and paintings. He was elected a member of the Royal Scottish Society of Painters in Watercolour in 1947, a Royal Scottish Academician in 1956 (associate in 1947), and a fellow of the Royal Glasgow Institute of the Fine Arts in 1986. He received honorary degrees from the University of Aberdeen in 1985 and Robert Gordon University in 1993.

Fleming died of kidney failure in Aberdeen on 24 July 1994 and was cremated on 28 July at Aberdeen crematorium. He was survived by his wife and three children. A commemorative plaque was placed on his house at 15 Fonthill Road, Aberdeen. In 1996 Aberdeen Art Gallery mounted a memorial exhibition. A posthumous bust by Gilbert Watt is in Aberdeen Art Gallery, which also holds the major collection of paintings and prints from his estate. Other collections holding works by Fleming include the Glasgow School of Art; the Glasgow Art Gallery; the Hunterian Art Gallery at the University of Glasgow; the Scottish National Gallery of Modern Art, the Scottish National Portrait Gallery, and the Royal Scottish Academy in Edinburgh; the Royal West of England Academy; the Laing Art Gallery, Newcastle; the Walker Art Gallery, Liverpool; and the Ulster Museum, Belfast.

FIONA PEARSON

Sources *Ian Fleming graphic works* (Peacock Printmakers, 1983) [exhibition catalogue, Aberdeen Art Gallery, 1983] · P. Ellis and D. Williamson, eds., *Debrett's distinguished people of today*, 3rd edn (1990) · R. Billcliffe, *Ian Fleming, RSA RSW REI* (1991) · *WWW*, 1991–5 · *The Scotsman* (3 Aug 1994) · *The Independent* (9 Aug 1994) · personal knowledge (2004) · private information (2004) · b. cert. · CCI (1995)

Archives priv. coll., MSS | FILM Aberdeen Art Gallery, film on print making

Likenesses I. Fleming, self-portrait, watercolour and pencil drawing, *c.*1928, priv. coll. · photographs, 1930–64, Hult. Arch. · I. Fleming, self-portrait, etching, 1937, Scottish National Gallery of Modern Art, Edinburgh · G. Watt, bronze bust, 1995, Aberdeen Art

Gallery · W. Crosbie, oils, priv. coll. · I. Fleming, self-portrait, pencil drawing, Scot. NPG · photographs, priv. coll.
Wealth at death £166,751.14: confirmation, 17 Feb 1995, *CCI*

Fleming, Ian Lancaster (1908–1964), writer, was born on 28 May 1908 at 27 Green Street, in London's Mayfair, the second of four sons of Valentine Fleming (1882–1917), a wealthy, conventional banker who in 1910 became Conservative member of parliament for South Oxfordshire, and Evelyn Beatrice Ste Croix, *née* Rose (1885–1964), the beautiful, flamboyant daughter of a Berkshire solicitor. The family lived in style in London and in Oxfordshire, where their house, Braziers Park, was close to that of Valentine's father, Robert *Fleming (1845–1933), who had risen from poverty in Dundee to found the eponymous bank. Fleming was educated (in the shadow of his brilliant elder brother, Peter *Fleming (1907–1971)) at Durnford preparatory school and at Eton College. While still at Durnford, in May 1917, he was devastated after his father was killed in action in France. At Eton he showed little academic potential, directing his energies into athletics, becoming victor ludorum two years in succession, and into school journalism, notably, editing an 'ephemeral' magazine, *The Wyvern*. Since he was deemed unlikely to follow Peter to Oxford, his widowed mother arranged for him to attend the Royal Military College, Sandhurst. However, he was not suited to military discipline and left without a commission in 1927, following an incident with a woman in which, to his mother's horror, he managed to contract a venereal disease.

Considered emotionally wayward, Fleming was sent to 'sort himself out' at a quasi-finishing school for men in Kitzbühel, Austria. There, while skiing and climbing mountains, he came under the benevolent tutelage of Ernan Forbes Dennis, a former British spy turned educationist, and his wife, Phyllis Bottome, an established novelist. Forbes Dennis brought out Fleming's aptitude for languages and introduced him to literature, while his wife encouraged him to write his first stories. With a career as a diplomat beckoning, Fleming studied briefly at Munich and Geneva universities, where he had a reputation as a playboy. However, he failed the competitive examination for the Foreign Office, and only his mother's entreaty to Sir Roderick Jones, head of Reuters News Agency, secured him an opening as a journalist. After reporting from Moscow on the 1933 'Metro-Vic' trial of six British engineers accused of spying, he was being groomed for higher things; however, bowing to family pressure, he opted to seek his fortune in the City. From 1933 to 1935 he worked for a small bank, Cull & Co. He then joined Rowe and Pitman, a leading firm of stockbrokers, where he was bored and ineffectual. In May 1939, with no obvious qualifications, he was invited to join the naval intelligence division as personal assistant to Admiral John Godfrey, the director of naval intelligence.

With his charm, social contacts, and gift for languages, Fleming proved an excellent appointment. Working from the Admiralty's Room 39, he showed a hitherto unacknowledged talent for administration, and was quickly promoted from lieutenant to commander. He

Ian Lancaster Fleming (1908–1964), by Sir Cecil Beaton, *c*.1960

liaised on behalf of the director of naval intelligence with the other secret services. One of few people given access to Ultra intelligence, he was responsible for the navy's input into anti-German black propaganda. He worked with Colonel Bill Donovan, the special representative of President Roosevelt, on intelligence co-operation between London and Washington before Pearl Harbor. In May 1941 he accompanied Admiral Godfrey to America, staying to help write a blueprint for the office of co-ordinator of information (the forerunner of the Central Intelligence Agency). In 1941–2 he oversaw operation Goldeneye, a plan to maintain vital intelligence if the Germans took over Spain. After Captain Edmund Rushbrooke became director in late 1942 Fleming's influence waned, though he controlled 30 assault unit, which operated behind German lines, retrieving scientific intelligence.

Already Fleming was telling friends of his ambition to write spy novels. (His brother Peter had enjoyed literary success in the 1930s with his travel books.) Instead, after being demobbed in May 1945, he joined the Kemsley newspaper group, which owned the *Sunday Times*, as foreign manager, responsible for its worldwide network of correspondents. He negotiated a favourable contract, allowing him to take three months' holiday every winter in Jamaica, an island with which he had fallen in love during a 1942 Anglo-American naval conference. In 1945 he acquired land at Oracabessa, on Jamaica's north coast; there he built a modest house, Goldeneye, named after his wartime exploit.

An early visitor was Fleming's long-time mistress, Ann Rothermere (1913–1981) [*see* Fleming, Ann Geraldine Mary], the steelily intelligent wife of the owner of the *Daily Mail*, the second Lord Rothermere. Born Ann Geraldine Mary Charteris in 1913, she was the eldest daughter of Guy Lawrence Charteris, son of the ninth earl of Wemyss. After the death of her first husband, the third Baron O'Neill, killed in action in Italy in 1944, she had been expected to become Fleming's wife, but he stuck to his bachelor status, and she married Lord Rothermere. However, she maintained her relationship with the saturnine Fleming, with whom she had a stillborn child in 1948. In 1951 she divorced Rothermere and married Fleming in Jamaica on 24 March 1952. Their only child, Caspar, was born in London in August that year.

The prospect of marriage inspired Fleming to attempt the spy novel he had discussed. Over two months in early 1952, he wrote his first book, *Casino Royale*, a taut tale of a British secret agent, James Bond (007), who challenges the Soviet operative Le Chiffre over the roulette table at Royale-les-Eaux. The book was published to critical acclaim in April 1953. Thereafter Fleming used his Caribbean holidays to write a James Bond story every year until his premature death in 1964.

Bond reflected much of Fleming: his secret intelligence background, his experience of good living, his casual attitude to sex. He differed in one essential—Bond was a man of action, while Fleming had mostly sat behind a desk. Fleming's news training was evident in his lean, energetic writing (with its dramatic set-piece essays on subjects that interested him, such as cards or diamonds) and in his desire to reflect contemporary realities, not only politically but sociologically. He was aware of Bond's position as a hard, often lonely professional, bringing glamour to the grim post-war 1950s. Fleming broke new ground in giving Bond an aspirational lifestyle and larding it with brand names.

A clear break in Fleming's writing career came in 1958, when after six years of writing what he considered entertainments, he was viciously attacked by the journalist Paul Johnson for his 'Sex, Snobbery and Sadism'. Harold Nicolson, commenting on *Goldfinger* in his diary in 1959, disliked 'the underlying atmosphere of violence, luxury and lust'. It was, for him, 'an obscene book, liable to corrupt' (N. Nicolson, ed., *Diaries and Letters*, 3 vols., 1966–8, 3.371). Fleming, who was experiencing marital difficulties, went into a personal and creative decline. His next book, a collection of inconsequential short stories, *For Your Eyes Only* (1960), was followed in 1961 by a novel, *Thunderball*, based on a screen treatment co-written with two film professionals, and in 1962 by the explicit *The Spy who Loved Me*. *Thunderball* became a nightmare after he was sued by his co-writers for stealing their plot. In April 1961 he suffered a heart attack, which has been linked to his worries over this case. At this stage his career took off again. Soon after his retirement from the *Sunday Times* (where he had latterly worked as the columnist Atticus) his books became best-sellers in the United States after President John F. Kennedy listed them among his favourites. In June 1961 he signed a film deal with the producers Cubby Broccoli and Harry Saltzman, whose *Dr No*, starring Sean Connery, opened in the autumn of 1962 and was an immediate box-office success. Now a worldwide celebrity, Fleming returned to more traditional Bond material in *On Her Majesty's Secret Service* (1963). However, he was unwell, and was smoking and drinking heavily. His death from heart complications in the Kent and Canterbury Hospital

on 12 August 1964 was not unexpected. He was buried at Sevenhampton, Wiltshire.

Fleming was a complex and often unhappy man, whose suave image was at variance with reality. He had a close circle of friends who enjoyed his quick wit. Yet normally he shied from company and relished simple, nursery food. He resented his wife's literary salon, attended by authors such as Cyril Connolly, Peter Quennell, and Evelyn Waugh, and would have preferred her in a more traditional role at their houses in London's Victoria Square, Sandwich (Kent), and later Sevenhampton (Wiltshire). As diversions, he liked motoring, golf, bridge, and swimming in the Caribbean. His collection of first editions of 'books that made things happen' (stimulating political or technological change) formed the nucleus of the 'Printing and the mind of man' exhibition (1963) in London.

Fleming wrote a book of his travel articles, a journalistic account of illicit diamond trading, a successful children's story (*Chitty Chitty Bang Bang*, which was filmed), and a short study of Kuwait which did not meet with official approval and was not published. But his enduring legacy is his James Bond stories with their understated mythic quality, representing the forces of good fighting evil, and their brilliantly imagined and carefully crafted world of menace, intrigue, and escape.

In total Fleming sold 30 million books during his lifetime—a figure that doubled in the two years after his death. Nine times he was presented with his paperback publisher Pan's Golden Pan award for sales of over 1 million softcover copies of his books. Half a century after *Dr No* was published, the entire James Bond *œuvre* remained in print. Few would deny, however, that this continuing success was a result of (and was overshadowed by) the even more phenomenal popularity of the James Bond films. Various actors—Sean Connery, George Lazenby, Roger Moore, Timothy Dalton, and Pierce Brosnan—portrayed Fleming's fictional secret agent, each in slightly different ways. In the movie business, Bond became the most successful 'franchise' of all time—not only in cinemas, but on video, laserdisc, and digital video disc. Up to the year 2000, Broccoli and Saltzman's Eon Productions had made nineteen Bond films, netting a reported $3.2 billion in box-office returns and $400 million in profits. In addition, two Bond feature films were produced outside the canon, while Fleming's own life was portrayed (both times in lacklustre fashion) in *Goldeneye*, starring Charles Dance (1989), and *Spymaker: the Secret Life of Ian Fleming*, starring Jason Connery (1990). ANDREW LYCETT

Sources A. Lycett, *Ian Fleming* (1995) · J. Pearson, *The life of Ian Fleming* (1966) · R. Benson, *James Bond bedside companion* (1988) · *The letters of Ann Fleming*, ed. M. Amory (1985) · I. Bryce, *You only live once* (1984)

Archives Indiana University, Bloomington, Lilly Library · U. Reading L., corresp. | HLRO, corresp. with Lord Beaverbrook **Likenesses** photographs, 1958–64, Hult. Arch. · C. Beaton, photograph, c.1960, NPG [*see illus.*] · A. Villiers, oils, priv. coll.; repro. in I. Fleming, *On her majesty's secret service*, limited edn (1968) **Wealth at death** £302,147: limited probate, 4 Nov 1964, *CGPLA Eng. & Wales* · £21,650: probate limited to literary estate, 24 Nov 1964, *CGPLA Eng. & Wales*

Fleming, James, fourth Lord Fleming (1533/4–1558), courtier and nobleman, was the elder son of Malcolm, third Lord Fleming (c.1494–1547), and his wife, Janet Stewart (d. 1560x64), an illegitimate daughter of James IV. Malcolm Fleming was chamberlain to James V by 1528 and remained high in the king's favour thereafter. A regular witness to charters under the great seal, he accompanied James to France in 1536. In 1542 he was captured in the defeat at Solway Moss and taken to London, where he was warded in the Tower until after Christmas, when he became one of the Assured Scots, pledged to support the policies of Henry VIII. It was a condition of his release that his elder son should be sent to England as a hostage, not necessarily an onerous or demeaning position. James Fleming remained in England until after the death of his father, killed at Pinkie on 10 September 1547; in the following June the second earl of Arran, the governor of Scotland, petitioned the English authorities for his return through Sir John Melville of Raith. No sooner was the new Lord Fleming back in Scotland, however, than he was assigned to accompany the young Queen Mary to France—his mother was Mary's governess, while his sister, Mary *Fleming (1542–c.1600) [see under Queen's Maries], was one of the group of little girls who became famous as 'the Queen's Maries'.

Having returned to Scotland, on 20 May 1549 Fleming was served heir to his father. In October 1550 he went back to France, this time accompanying the queen dowager, Mary of Guise, for her meeting with Henri II. On 12 November 1553 he was confirmed in his father's office of chamberlain and shortly afterwards, under a contract of 22 December, he married Arran's eldest daughter, Barbara, the widow of Alexander Gordon. They had a daughter, Jean *Fleming (1553/4–1609). On 10 October 1556 Fleming was made warden of the east and middle marches. He held office for only a few months, but the appointment was not inappropriate since his estates were centred on Clydesdale, while from 1552 he was acting sheriff of Dumfriesshire on behalf of his nephew, the sixth Lord Sanquhar. A man of acknowledged probity, on 8 December 1557 he was appointed by parliament to attend the marriage of Queen Mary to the dauphin François, which took place on the steps of Notre Dame, Paris, on Easter day (24 April) 1558. The French pressed the eight Scottish commissioners to recognize François as *roi dauphin* and to grant him the crown matrimonial, but they had to refuse, having no authority from parliament to do such a thing. Consequently King Henri requested that they return to Scotland and there obtain the necessary powers. Several of the party had serious reservations, and when three of them died before they could leave France, suspicions of poison abounded—quite possibly justified. Whatever the cause, Fleming was similarly afflicted. Having made his will at Dieppe on 8 November, he retired to Paris in hopes of medical treatment, but died on 15 December, aged twenty-four; he may have been buried there. His heir was his younger brother, John *Fleming (d. 1572).

MARCUS MERRIMAN

Sources *Scots peerage*, 8.542–3 · GEC, *Peerage*, 5.532–3 · J. Cameron, *James V: the personal rule, 1528–1542*, ed. N. Macdougall (1998) · T. I. Rae, *The administration of the Scottish frontier, 1513–1603* (1966)

Fleming, James (d. 1751), army officer, whose origins are unknown, was confused by the *Dictionary of National Biography* with Michael Fleming, captain in the earl of Derby's regiment and subsequently MP for Westmorland, who was wounded at the battle of Blenheim in 1704. According to the *Army List* of 1740, James Fleming was commissioned captain in 1706. However, little is known of his early military career. In 1722 he was made lieutenant-colonel of the Royal Fusiliers (7th foot) with whom he served for many years until promoted on 9 January 1741 colonel of the 36th foot, Herefordshire regiment. He became a brigadier-general in 1745, and was present at Falkirk and Culloden, where his regiment formed part of the 2nd line and played only a minor part. In 1747 his regiment served in Flanders, suffering serious losses at the battle of Laffeldt (Val). Shortly after he was promoted major-general. From 1749 his regiment was stationed at Gibraltar. He died probably at Bath on 23 March 1751.   JONATHAN SPAIN

Sources R. Cannon, ed., *Historical record of the thirty-sixth, or the Herefordshire regiment of foot* (1853) · *The army list of 1740*, Society for Army Historical Research (1931) · *GM*, 1st ser., 21 (1751), 141 · *Scots Magazine*, 13 (1751), 165 · K. Tomasson and F. Buist, *Battles of the '45* (1962); repr. (1978), 90, 100, 107, 151

Likenesses L. F. Roubiliac, medallion on monument, 1751, Westminster Abbey, London

Fleming, James (1830–1908), Church of England clergyman, was born at Carlow, south-west of Dublin, on 26 July 1830, the youngest son of the five children of Patrick Fleming (d. 1838) of Strabane, co. Tyrone, and Mary Kirkpatrick. In later life all three sons were ordained. Patrick Fleming was an army surgeon and while serving in Jamaica from 1831 to 1836 was accompanied by his wife and younger children. James attended Cavan College, Cavan, northwest of Dublin, where he came under the evangelical influence of the local curate. On the death of his father, the family moved to Bath: Fleming was educated at the grammar school from 1840 to 1846, and at Shrewsbury School from 1846 to 1849. He was awarded a Millington scholarship and matriculated on 15 November 1849 as a sizar at Magdalene College, Cambridge. He graduated BA in 1853, MA in 1857, and BD in 1865. At Cambridge he was influenced by William Carus, vicar of Holy Trinity Church, and he taught in the Jesus Lane Sunday school. On graduating, Fleming was awarded a fellowship and was a travelling bachelor for a year.

On 21 June 1853 Fleming married Grace Purcell (d. 1903); they had a family of three sons and three daughters. In the same year, he was ordained a deacon, and he entered the priesthood in 1854. As the curate of St Stephen's Church, Ipswich, 1853–5, his gifts as a speaker and preacher became evident. For the next eleven years he served in Bath, first as curate of St Stephen's Church (1855–6), and then as minister of All Saints' Chapel (1856–66). He possessed an outstanding voice and gave public readings and recitations to an estimated 54,000 people. Between 1860 and 1866, he was the professor of English literature and elocution at Somersetshire College. He supported missions to men in the army and navy, and was a lifelong advocate of the temperance movement. He was a keen teetotaller and a non-smoker, but did take snuff.

In 1866 Fleming became vicar of Camden church, Camberwell, moving to St Michael's, Chester Square, Belgravia, in 1873. Camberwell was an important centre for preaching, and Fleming maintained the reputation established by his predecessors, Henry Melvill (1798–1871) and Daniel Moore (1809–1899). His preaching was simple and direct, and he attracted large congregations. He made use of the 'electrophone' and his sermons were heard in hospitals within a 2 mile radius of St Michael's; some of his gramophone recordings are extant. Fleming was, like his predecessors, the Golden lecturer of St Margaret's Church, Lothbury, London. From 1876 he was also a royal chaplain to Queen Victoria and Edward VII, and frequently preached at the Chapel Royal and at Sandringham. Between 1880 and 1887, he was the first Whitehead professor of preaching at the London College of Divinity (also known as St John's Hall, Highbury, and now St John's College, Nottingham). His college lectures were published as *The Art of Reading and Speaking* (1896); his other publications included sermons and material used in his public readings.

According to his biographer, Fleming was preeminently 'a man of action' (Finlayson, 117). Throughout his ministry, he was a great fund-raiser for his numerous philanthropic and charitable activities: in Camberwell, he raised over £15,000 and at St Michael's—where his preaching attracted a large, fashionable, and wealthy congregation—nearly £35,000. His patron, the duke of Westminster, was particularly generous. At St Michael's, Fleming established numerous agencies to support the poor, and he oversaw the erection of the daughter church, St Philip's, which opened in July 1888. One member of the congregation gave £23,500 for the provision of a convalescent home for the poor at Birchington-on-Sea, Kent. Fleming also supported the work of Dr Thomas Barnardo, serving as a vice-president of his homes, and the Sunday hospital movement, for which he raised £32,675 at St Michael's.

Fleming was no scholar or theologian: he avoided involvement in the ecclesiastical politics of his day, and only once attended the church congress. A moderate evangelical churchman who opposed ritualism, he was a friend of Charles Haddon Spurgeon, and later identified with the protestant agitator John Kensit. He was a member of the Evangelical Alliance and of the council of Ridley Hall, Cambridge, and was an honorary secretary of the Religious Tract Society. During the course of his ministry he refused two deanships (Chester and Norwich), and two bishoprics (Rochester and Sydney, Australia); he was also considered for the bishoprics of Liverpool and Ripon. In 1877 he became a canon of York, and in 1882 a prebendary of the minster, spending three months a year in residence. Fleming died at St Michael's vicarage on 1 September 1908, and was buried next to his wife in Kensal Green cemetery on 4 September. A. F. MUNDEN

Sources A. R. M. Finlayson, *Life of Canon Fleming* (1909) · *The Times* (17 June 1879) · *The Times* (2 Sept 1908) · *DNB* · Venn, *Alum. Cant.* **Archives** SOUND BL NSA, London **Likenesses** W. & D. Downey, woodburytype photograph, NPG; repro. in W. Downey and D. Downey, *The cabinet portrait gallery*, 2 (1891) · Spy [L. Ward], caricature, chromolithograph, NPG; repro. in *VF* (29 June 1899) · engraving, repro. in Finlayson, *Life of Canon Fleming* · photographs, repro. in Finlayson, *Life of Canon Fleming* **Wealth at death** £6095 15s. 7d.: resworn probate, 25 Sept 1908, *CGPLA Eng. & Wales*

Fleming, Jean, countess of Cassillis (1553/4–1609), noblewoman, was the only child of James *Fleming, fourth Lord Fleming (1533/4–1558), and his wife, Lady Barbara Hamilton, the eldest daughter of James *Hamilton, second earl of Arran. The estates and title passed to her uncle, John *Fleming, fifth Lord Fleming, of whom Jean Fleming complained to the privy council in 1579 that he had failed to provide the 4000 merks promised for her marriage. She had a sixth part of the revenues of the lordship of Fleming assigned to her in September 1579 and was granted the lands of Thankerton and Biggar following her resignation as heir to her grandfather in 1583.

In January 1583 Jean married John *Maitland of Thirlestane (1543–1595), later James VI's chief minister, who became chancellor in 1587 and was elevated to the peerage as Lord Thirlestane in 1590. An English observer commented in 1589 that she was 'a wise woman and half chancellor when he is at home', although this was a rare comment on her involvement in politics (*Salisbury Papers*, 3.446–7). In 1590, the year of James's marriage to Anne of Denmark, she had a daughter, Anna (d. 1609). Two years later she incurred the queen's displeasure as a result of making indiscreet remarks about the latter's relationship with Francis Stewart, fifth earl of Bothwell, within Anne's hearing. This contributed to the friction between the queen and Maitland, and it was said in 1593 that Anne still 'cannot hitherto well brook his wife' (*CSP Scot.*, 11.233–4). The following year the Maitlands had a son, John.

Maitland died on 3 October 1595. Now a wealthy widow, Jean took a second husband, the much younger John *Kennedy, fifth earl of Cassillis (1574/5–1615), in November 1597; the marriage was conducted with some haste and excited attention at court as she was a woman 'of good years, not like to bear children' (BL, Cotton MS Caligula B. iv, fol. 244). Cassillis's union with a woman twice his age was a source of amusement and an embarrassment to the young earl's associates: one commentator at court declared Cassillis to be 'clengit out of credit both here and at home with his own friends' since his marriage (*CSP Scot.*, 13.I.329). By January 1598 King James owed the new countess 7000 merks and when he offered Cassillis the treasurership in spring 1599, it was rumoured that James's motive was that 'his wifes purse should be opened for her rose nobles' (*CSP Scot.*, 13.I.444). Although terms for his holding the office were agreed by mid-March, a fortnight later Cassillis had formally refused the job, worried by its financial implications and offended by the rumour. The matter was not resolved until spring 1600, but the couple entertained the king at Thirlestane Castle that February.

While Cassillis was with James in London in 1603, the countess and her brother-in-law, Hugh Kennedy, master of Cassillis, were captured, and the countess briefly imprisoned, by Kennedy of Drummurchie, one of the faction with whom the earl was feuding. In April 1604 Cassillis was ordered to be warded in Blackness Castle and find £5000 as surety for his wife's protection after assaulting her in the presence of the council and dragging her out of the council chamber; he was imprisoned again for the same offence later in the year.

In March 1609 the countess was 'havelie diseasit and under medicine', prescribed a diet which excluded fish, and granted permission to eat meat in Lent (*Reg. PCS*, 8.256–7). She died on 23 June 1609 aged fifty-five and was buried in St Mary's Church, Haddington, alongside her first husband. The Maitland family monument, erected by their son and heir, John Maitland, first earl of Lauderdale (1594–1645), depicts the recumbent effigies of Jean Fleming and Maitland of Thirlestane and also commemorates their daughter, Anna.   SHARON ADAMS

Sources CSP Scot., 1593–1603 · Reg. PCS, 1st ser. · Scots peerage · M. Lee, John Maitland of Thirlestane and the foundation of Stewart despotism (1959) · K. M. Brown, 'A house divided: family and feud in Carrick under John Kennedy, fifth earl of Cassillis', SHR, 75 (1996), 168–96 · GEC, Peerage

Fleming, John, fifth Lord Fleming (d. 1572), nobleman, was the second son of Malcolm, third Lord Fleming (c.1494–1547), and his wife, Janet Stewart (c.1510–1560x64), illegitimate daughter of *James IV and Agnes Stewart and sometime mistress of Henri II of France. Late in life he was described as having a pale and lean countenance, with a somewhat flat nose. He was granted the lands of Sunderland in Selkirkshire and Mossfennan in Peeblesshire by his father on 29 September 1541 and succeeded to the title following the death of his brother, James *Fleming, fourth Lord Fleming, probably from poisoning, in Paris on 15 December 1558. He was a cousin of Mary Stewart, and his sister Mary *Fleming was one of the four Maries, the queen's companions from her early childhood [see under Queen's Maries (act. 1548–1567)]. This familiarity drew him into Queen Mary's intimate circle after she returned from France in August 1561. Fleming entertained Mary at Cumbernauld Castle on 25 January 1562, the day before the hall fell down killing at least seven people, and when he married Elizabeth Ross (c.1545–1578), only child of Robert, master of Ross, and Agnes Moncrieff, at Holyrood on 10 May 1562, the queen and court attended their marriage banquet. The Flemings had five children: John, first earl of Wigtown [see below]; Margaret, who married Sir James Forrester of Carden; Elizabeth; Jean, wife of William Bruce of Airth; and Mary, married to James Douglas of Drumlanrig. Lord Fleming also fathered an illegitimate daughter, Lucrece. In January 1564 Fleming was awarded a generous French pension.

Although Fleming was numbered among the opponents of the earl of Lennox in February 1565, he gave his backing to Mary's marriage to Lord Darnley, Lennox's son, in June, probably seeking in return to be made earl of Wigtown.

Instead he was rewarded with the offices of great chamberlain of Scotland on 30 June and master usher of the queen's chambers on 25 July, both to be held for life. He was also appointed governor of Dumbarton Castle. He rode with Lord Darnley during the chaseabout raid, the unsuccessful rising of Lord Moray and the Hamiltons, and on 7 November received a commission of justiciary within the counties of Dumbarton, Forfar, Lanark, Peebles, and Stirling. A protestant, though with some Roman Catholic sympathies, Fleming declined to attend the celebration of Candlemas in Holyrood Chapel on 2 February 1566, a focal event for Catholics at court. He was within Holyrood Palace when David Riccio was murdered on 9 March 1566, but escaped to join the queen's supporters at Dunbar. In November he received a commission of justiciary in Liddesdale and Peebles. Fleming was not implicated in the murder of Darnley in February 1567, but signed the Ainslie Bond to advance the earl of Bothwell's marriage to the queen on 19 April. He remained loyal to Mary throughout the crisis which the marriage precipitated, but was sheltering in Edinburgh Castle when she took the field at Carberry on 15 June. After Mary was imprisoned in Lochleven Castle he responded at first to Bothwell's requests for assistance, but abandoned him when he was outlawed in July.

Following Mary's escape from Lochleven, Fleming joined her forces at Hamilton and on 13 May 1568 watched the fighting at Langside with her from a neighbouring hill. When they saw the battle lost they sought to reach Dumbarton Castle, but the route proving hazardous rode down into Dumfriesshire. Mary's party crossed the Solway in a fishing boat on 16 May and arrived at Workington in the evening. Two days later they were taken to Carlisle, from where on 30 May Mary dispatched Fleming to London with instructions to travel on to France if Elizabeth's assistance was not forthcoming. On 11 June Moray marched to Biggar and received the surrender of Boghall Castle. The castle was not cast down, ostensibly because Fleming was in England but principally because he controlled Dumbarton, the most likely point of entry for the French. For the same reason Elizabeth refused to allow Fleming to pass to France, but assented to his return to Scotland on parole. He brought the English queen's letters to Mary at Carlisle on 5 July and hastened on to Scotland, gathering with the earl of Argyll and other Marians at Largs on 28 July. On 16 August the regent Moray's parliament declared Fleming's forfeiture, though this was suspended a week later at Elizabeth's request.

Meanwhile, Fleming was besieging Glasgow Castle with Argyll. He returned to the queen, who was now at Bolton, in September and was one of her commissioners at the York conference. When this broke up he returned to Dumbarton Castle, hiring hagbutters for its defence and paying them out of the revenues of Paisley Abbey. His brother was captured in February 1569 during an assault by the Dumbarton garrison on Dunglass Castle. Fleming passed through Berwick in early August on his way to revisit Mary and in November his nephew John, master of Graham, was sent to persuade him to surrender Dumbarton. The regent, however, had antagonized Fleming by granting Whithorn Priory to his youngest brother Lord Robert Stewart following the death of the prior, Fleming's uncle Malcolm. Whithorn had been in Fleming hands since 1525 and was claimed by Lord Fleming's half-brother William. The sentence of forfeiture against Fleming was renewed on 17 November. It was rumoured in May 1570 that Lord Fleming would receive the French at Dumbarton, no idle fear, for later in the year he made a compact with his half-brother Henry, grand prior of France, to deliver the castle into the latter's hands. When Sir William Drury's invading army marched by Dumbarton on 3 June, Fleming and Archbishop Hamilton of St Andrews refused his invitation to parley and turned the castle's ordnance on him. Later in 1570 Fleming levelled Dumbarton church, which had been occupied as a fort by the besiegers, and used the masonry to extend the castle's fortifications.

The regency had lain vacant since Moray's murder in January, but when Lennox was elected regent in June he brought a new militancy into the conduct of the civil war. On 26 August he seized Cumbernauld Castle, in disregard of the abstinence, and throughout September raided the surrounding lands, slaughtering the deer and wild cattle in the forest of Cumbernauld and forcing Fleming's tenants to pay him their rents. Lennox continued to act against the Flemings in the new year, seizing the living of John Fleming of Boghall and sending Alexander Stewart of Garlies to reive Whithorn Priory. However, Garlies, who held a tack of the priory from Lord Robert Stewart, was captured in the ensuing fighting, during which three of Fleming's servants died. William Fleming continued to deprive Lord Robert of the priory until 1573. Despite this aggression Fleming agreed to keep the abstinence, though he saw little in all this diplomacy 'but spending of time and wasting of paper and ink' (*CSP Scot.*, 1569–71, 487).

In the early hours of 1 April 1571 Captain Thomas Crawford of Jordanhill led a daring ascent of Dumbarton Rock to surprise the garrison and seize the castle. Lord Fleming escaped by boat into Argyll, but Archbishop Hamilton of St Andrews was less fortunate, being taken and hanged by Lennox for his role in Moray's assassination. The execution served only to strengthen Fleming's resolve. He sailed for France in mid-September and by November was reported ready to re-embark with 300 Frenchmen, but in the end he remained on the continent seeking further aid, his primary need being money for supporters at home rather than men. In December he travelled with Lord Seton to Brussels, before returning to Paris where on 5 January he received 10,000 francs from Charles IX. Throughout the spring of 1572 Fleming was daily looked for on the western seas. In the borders William Trotter waited to join him with 100 horse. Fleming finally sailed from Brittany in May, arriving at Cruggleton on 20th. In early June Mary Fleming tried unsuccessfully to obtain a settlement for her brother through their nephew, now third earl of Montrose. Fleming and Lord Claud Hamilton were escorted into Edinburgh on 8 June, where Fleming delivered 2000 crowns to the garrison holding the castle in Queen Mary's name. A week later it was reported that he had agreed to loan the Hamiltons his mercenaries for a month. On 27 June he travelled from Blackness Castle to Edinburgh and on entering the city addressed the soldiers and townsmen, urging them to 'be of good cheer for all shall be well' (*CSP Scot.*, 1571–4, 339). He again passed to Edinburgh Castle with a French force on 5 July, but as they entered the soldiers fired a salute by shooting their hagbuts into the ground, in the process throwing up stones which wounded Lord Fleming in the knee. By 16 July his condition had greatly worsened and he sent word to the king's men at Leith requesting to speak to Montrose, presumably to seek the earl's protection for his family. He was removed on a litter to Biggar, where he died of his injuries on 6 September 1572 and was laid to rest with his ancestors in the parish church there. With his passing the queen lost one of her most consistent and active supporters. Fleming's widow was permitted to occupy some of their lands, while Montrose acted as chamberlain of the remainder of the forfeited estates.

Fleming's eldest son, **John Fleming**, first earl of Wigtown (*c*.1567–1619), nobleman, was restored by parliament as sixth Lord Fleming on 11 November 1579. He acted as an ambassador to Denmark in October 1590 and was created earl of Wigtown at Whitehall in London on 19 March 1607. Under a contract dated 12 and 13 January 1586 he married Lilias (*b. c*.1565, *d*. in or before 1611), only daughter of John Graham, third earl of Montrose, and Jean Drummond, daughter of David, second Lord Drummond. They had four sons and six daughters, including John *Fleming, second earl of Wigtown (*bap*. 1589?, *d*. 1650). Following his first wife's death the first earl married in 1611 Sarah Maxwell (*c*.1555–1636), wife of the late Sir James Johnston of Johnston and daughter of John Maxwell, Lord Herries of Terregles, and his wife, Agnes Herries, Lady Herries in her own right. He died in April 1619 and was also interred in Biggar parish church.   JOHN SIMMONS

Sources *CSP Scot.*, 1547–1603 · *Reg. PCS*, 1st ser., vols. 1–11 · *APS*, 1424–1625 · *The works of John Knox*, ed. D. Laing, 6 vols., Wodrow Society, 12 (1846–64) · GEC, *Peerage*, 5.532–3; 12.2, 634–6 · *Scots peerage*, 8.543–9 · G. Donaldson, *All the queen's men* (1983) · J. M. Thomson and others, eds., *Registrum magni sigilli regum Scotorum / The register of the great seal of Scotland*, 11 vols. (1882–1914), vols. 4–7 · *CSP for.*, 1558–95

Fleming, John, first earl of Wigtown (*c*.1567–1619). *See under* Fleming, John, fifth Lord Fleming (*d*. 1572).

Fleming, John, second earl of Wigtown (*bap*. 1589?, *d*. 1650), politician, was probably baptized on 7 December 1589, the eldest son of John *Fleming, first earl of Wigtown (*c*.1567–1619) [*see under* Fleming, John, fifth Lord Fleming], and his first wife, Lady Lilias Graham (*b. c*.1565, *d*. in or before 1611), daughter of John *Graham, third earl of Montrose (1548–1608). Styled from 1606 master of Wigtown and Lord Fleming, he married, by contracts dated 12 to 20 February 1609, Lady Margaret Livingstone (*d*. 1651?), younger daughter of Alexander *Livingstone, first earl of Linlithgow (*d*. 1621), and his wife, Eleanor or Helen *Livingstone (*d*. 1627). Following the death of his father in April 1619, he succeeded as second earl.

Wigtown played an active part in public life, becoming a member of the privy council immediately upon his father's death. He attended its meetings with some regularity and remained a member after Charles I's reform of the council in 1626. Although favoured by James VI and Charles I, Wigtown supported several of the dissident presbyterian ministers who would not conform to royal ecclesiastical policy, one of whom, John Livingstone, spent nearly two and a half years at Cumbernauld House, preaching on occasion to the family and their tenants. Wigtown initially supported the opposition to Charles I's liturgical innovations and was one of the nobles who signed an early protestation against the service book. His position was, however, somewhat ambiguous at this juncture since, as a member of the privy council, he was also responsible for suppression of the anti-prayer book activity and put his name to documents issued for that purpose.

Wigtown signed the king's covenant, Charles I's response to the national covenant, in 1638 and was one of the original signatories to the Cumbernauld bond, first subscribed at Wigtown's seat, Cumbernauld House, in August 1640. Although his relationship with the covenanting administration was initially ambivalent—he was a member of the committee of estates in 1640 and on the reconstituted privy council of 1641—Wigtown was increasingly identified as a supporter of the king and associated with his cousin, James Graham, marquess of Montrose. He received several letters from Charles I concerning support for the royalist cause in Scotland. While his eldest son, John, Lord Fleming, raised regiments in the first and second bishops' wars, Wigtown played little part in the covenanting wars and was less involved in public affairs after Montrose's defeat at Philiphaugh in 1645, after which time the family experienced greater difficulties with the covenanting regime and were subject to financial penalties. He died at Cumbernauld, Dunbartonshire, on 7 May 1650 and was succeeded as third earl by John (d. 1665), the eldest of his eight children.

SHARON ADAMS

Sources Scots peerage · W. Hunter, *Biggar and the house of Fleming* (1867) · 'Royal letters and instructions from the archives of the earls of Wigton', *Maitland Miscellany*, 2/2 (1840) · *Reg. PCS*, 1st ser. · *Reg. PCS*, 2nd ser. · J. Livingstone, 'A brief historical relation of the life of Mr John Livingstone', *Select biographies*, ed. W. K. Tweedie, 1, Wodrow Society, 7/1 (1845), 127–97 · GEC, *Peerage*
Likenesses G. Jamesone, portrait, priv. coll.

Fleming, John (1747–1829), surgeon and naturalist, may have studied medicine at the University of Edinburgh. He joined the Indian Medical Service (IMS) in Bengal as an assistant surgeon in August 1768 and was promoted surgeon in December 1771. He became a member of the medical board from May 1786, and its president in December 1800.

Fleming once described himself to Sir Joseph Banks as being 'a lover of natural history' (BL, Add. MS 33980, fols. 122–3). Francis Buchanan in a letter to Sir James E. Smith (3 March 1802) referred to 'my good friend Mr Fleming, a very great encourager and promoter of natural history'

(Linn. Soc., *Smith MSS, Letters*, 2.26). When Robert Kyd died in May 1793, Fleming took over the management of the Royal Botanic Garden, Calcutta until William Roxburgh was appointed superintendent later that year, and he acted as superintendent while Roxburgh was on sick leave in 1805–7. He was responsible for the presentation of a number of plants to the garden. Roxburgh allowed him to make copies for his personal use of some of the official collection of flower paintings. Fleming wrote the first published survey of Indian drugs, primarily for the use of European doctors newly arrived in the country. *A catalogue of Indian medicinal plants and drugs, with their names in the Hindustani and Sanscrit languages* appeared in *Asiatick Researches* (11, 1810, 153–96) and was reissued the same year as a separate publication with emendations and additions.

Fleming retired in November 1813. He became a fellow of the Royal Society in the same year, and of the Linnean Society in 1816. He became MP for Gatton near Reigate, Surrey, in 1818. He died at Gloucester Place, London, on 17 May 1829. William Roxburgh commemorated him in the genus *Flemingia*, a legume used as a dye. The entry in the *Dictionary of National Biography* confused him with another John Fleming, a doctor who died on 10 May 1815 and had nothing to do with India or botany.

RAY DESMOND

Sources J. Britten, 'John Fleming, M.D. (1747–1829)', *Journal of Botany, British and Foreign*, 54 (1916), 301–3 · D. G. Crawford, *A history of the Indian medical service, 1600–1913*, 2 (1914) · R. Desmond, *The European discovery of the Indian flora* (1992) · GM, 1st ser., 99/1 (1829), 475

Fleming, John (1785–1857), naturalist and Free Church of Scotland minister, was born on 10 January 1785 at Kirkroods, a farm near Bathgate, Linlithgowshire, the son of Alexander Fleming and his wife, Catherine Nimmo. He appears to have enjoyed natural history from an early age. He studied for the ministry of the Church of Scotland at the University of Edinburgh but while a student was also attracted to geology and zoology. At Edinburgh he became acquainted with the then fashionable controversy between the Huttonian and Wernerian theories of the formation of the earth, and through his contacts with the chemist Thomas Thomson he also acquired an interest in mineralogy. He left the university in 1805. In 1808 he became a founder member of the Wernerian Society of Edinburgh, and was an associate of its first president, Robert Jameson, a former student of Werner and the leading proponent of Wernerian geological theory.

Shortly after he left university Fleming was encouraged by Sir John Sinclair of the Scottish board of agriculture to visit Shetland and examine the mineralogy of the area. This journey indirectly led to his appointment to the parish of Bressay, Shetland, in April 1806, where he was ordained on 22 September 1808. In 1807 he published *Economical Mineralogy of the Orkney and Zetland Island*; this was followed by his *Description of a Small-Headed Narwal Cast Ashore on Zetland* (1808; 2nd edn, 1810). He was translated to Flisk, Fife, in 1810.

Fleming became a fellow of the Royal Society of Edinburgh in 1814, on the proposal of Robert Jameson, John Playfair, and David Brewster. By that point his position in the then current geological debates was sufficiently

Huttonian for him to favour the examination of contemporary shelly faunas as the key to understanding the ecology of fossil ones. By 1815 he was regarded as the premier zoologist in Scotland. This was his Wernerian period (1808–20).

The discrediting of Werner's and Jameson's neptunism about 1820 made Fleming sceptical of all theories and initiated his period of productivity and controversy (1820–32). One of his most important works during this period was *The Philosophy of Zoology* (1822), in which he put forward a dichotomous system of classification, in contradiction to Cuvier's system which was still influenced by the linear 'chain of being' theory (originally of Aristotle). Best remembered, however, is his controversy with William Buckland during the years 1824–6. Backed by Robert Jameson, he took issue with the catastrophist ideas set out in Buckland's *Reliquae diluvianae* (1823), which he believed to contradict both the Genesis account of the flood and the uniformitarian principle. His critique of Buckland was entitled *On the Geological Deluge as Interpreted by Baron Cuvier and Professor Buckland* (1826), and it is said that this attack led to the withdrawal of a new edition of Buckland's work.

Another dispute during this period was with William Conybeare in 1829–30. This argument centred on the question as to whether there had been a warmer climate in northern latitudes in the past as suggested by some fossils, which Fleming denied. He also had a disagreement with G. B. Greenough over his *Critical Examination of the First Principle of Geology* (1819). He was friendly with Lyell and Murchison, and was generally supportive of a uniformitarian approach, but appears to have held a low opinion of James Hutton. In 1813, probably at Cupar, Fleming married Melville Christie, second daughter of Andrew Christie, a banker of Cupar. They had two sons, one of whom, Andrew Fleming (1823–1901), was later to pursue notable palaeontological work in the Salt Range in India. Their other son did not survive into adulthood.

Despite his intensive work in natural history, Fleming did not neglect his pastoral work. In 1814 the University of St Andrews conferred on him the degree of doctor of divinity, but an application for the parish vacancy at Auchtermuchty was unsuccessful, possibly due to his not having the patron on his side. In 1832 he was appointed to the parish of Clackmannan and in 1834 appointed to the chair of natural philosophy at University and King's College, Aberdeen, rather against the wishes of his parishioners. The harmony of the kirk was disturbed in the years leading up to 1843 and Fleming joined the Free Church of Scotland in that year with, among others, his friend Brewster. As he was then considered to be no longer a minister of the established church he resigned from the Aberdeen University position and was appointed in 1845 to the newly established chair of natural history at the Free Church college, Edinburgh, set up by his one-time neighbouring minister, Thomas Chalmers. At the Free Church college he seems to have been motivated by what he saw as the need for divinity students to be familiar with the world of nature.

Among Fleming's writings in natural history was an important early zoological work, *The History of British Animals* (1828) which, curiously, left out insects but included information on fossil animal species. Encouraged by Chalmers he sought in this work to reconcile then current geology with a belief in the truth of scripture. He also did some interesting fieldwork. In 1831 he was the first to notice fish scales in the Old Red Sandstone rocks of Fife, and he was later to comment on fish remains in the Scottish Coal Measures at Clackmannan.

Fleming died at Edinburgh on 18 November 1857 after a short illness. His zoological thinking is broadly set out in his *The Lithology of Edinburgh*, published posthumously in 1859, in which he assumed that pre-Adamic life had been destroyed and that present-day plants and animals were post-Genesis. Nevertheless, throughout his life he broadly favoured a uniformitarian approach and was against catastrophic ideas. He was active in defending traditional Christian values against the rise of Lamarckian ideas of progress in nature, and was opposed to evolutionary theorizing. However, he shared the view that the scientist must be free to think without being hindered by a dogmatic interpretation of the scriptures. The Royal Society's *Catalogue of Scientific Papers, 1800–1863*, credits him with fifty-three papers on various zoological, palaeontological, and botanical topics. His name is commemorated in the Carboniferous gastropod *Flemingella*.   D. T. MOORE

Sources A. Bryson, 'Memoir of Rev. John Fleming', *Transactions of the Royal Society of Edinburgh*, 22 (1860–61), 655–80 · DNB · *The lithology of Edinburgh, by the late John Fleming*, ed. J. Duns (1859) · L. G. de Koninck, 'Faune du calcaire Carboniferous de Belgique: 3me partie, Gastropodes', *Annales de Musée Royal d'Histoire Naturelle de Belgique* [série palaeontologique, 4] (1881), 93–4 · J. Brookes Knight and others, *Mollusca 1: Mollusca—general features* (1960), pt 1 of *Treatise on invertebrate palaeontology* · L. E. Page, 'Diluvialism and its critics in Great Britain in the early nineteenth century', *Toward a history of geology*, ed. C. J. Schneer (1969), 257–71 · DSB · D. T. Moore, 'Geological collectors and collections of the India Museum, London, 1801–79', *Archives of Natural History*, 10 (1981–2), 399–428 · P. F. Rehbock, *John Fleming (1785–1857) and the economy of nature*, special publication of the Society for the History of Natural History, 3 (1985), 129–40

Archives NHM, MSS and specimens | GS Lond., letters to Sir R. I. Murchison · NL NZ, Turnbull L., letters to Gideon Algernon Mantell · Oxf. U. Mus. NH, letters to F. W. Hope · U. Leeds, Brotherton L., corresp. with John Wilson

Likenesses oils, U. St Andr., Fife · photograph, repro. in Rehbock, *John Fleming*, 10

Fleming, John (*d.* 1883), gardener, first came to public notice in 1850. His early life and antecedents have not been traced: the earliest detail offered in his obituaries was his residence with a Mr Aiton of Bardsea, Ulverston, Lancashire, about 1844. From there he went to the garden of the earl of Denbigh at Newnham Paddox, Warwickshire, and thence in 1850 to Harewood, Yorkshire, where the grounds were then in the course of transformation by Sir Charles Barry, whom Fleming assisted in the creation of the terrace garden. From 1853 to 1855 he was gardener to the earl of Southampton at Whittlebury Lodge, Towcester.

From 1855 Fleming was head gardener at Cliveden,

Buckinghamshire, initially to the second duke of Sutherland and then to H. L. Grosvenor, first duke of Westminster. At Cliveden he found himself working again with Barry, assisting him in the creation of a new terrace garden. By 1859 he could display the results of his experiments with the planting of bulbs in the parterre for a spring display. At this time there was much comment in the horticultural press about the excessive attention lavished on summer bedding at the expense of plants for the other seasons, and Fleming was the first gardener to become well known for 'spring gardening', though by the 1870s there was a coterie which pressed the claims to priority of William Ingram of Belvoir Castle. Fleming reported his experiments in the *Journal of Horticulture*, and published *Spring and Winter Flower Gardening* in 1864 (2nd edn, 1870).

In 1868, when a fashion for foliage came in, Fleming planted a bed of dwarf foliage plants and succulents, in the pattern of the countess of Sutherland's monogram. The *Gardeners' Chronicle*, reviewing the experiment, coined the name 'carpet bedding' for it, and recommended it for wider trial. Carpet bedding was to become a dominant fashion in England in the 1870s, and an international one in the 1880s. In 1870, with James Gray of Chelsea, Fleming erected new glasshouses at Cliveden, at the same time as he was engaged in landscaping a valley on the estate which was praised by William Robinson (1838–1935) as a fine example of wild gardening (*Garden*, 235).

From 1862 to 1864 Fleming served on the council of the Horticultural Society, and he was a member of the committee for the International Horticultural Exhibition of 1866. He died unmarried on 25 November 1883, and the administration of his estate was granted to a Canadian relative.   BRENT ELLIOTT, *rev.*

Sources *Gardeners' Chronicle*, new ser., 20 (1883), 701 · *The Garden* (1 Dec 1883) · *Journal of Horticulture* (6 Dec 1883)
Likenesses portrait, Royal Horticultural Society, London

Fleming, (William) Launcelot Scott (1906–1990), geologist and bishop of Norwich, was born on 7 August 1906 in Edinburgh, the youngest of four sons (the second of whom died at the age of five months) and fifth of five children of Robert Alexander Fleming MD LLD, surgeon, of Edinburgh, and his wife, Eleanor Mary, daughter of the Revd William Lyall Holland, rector of Cornhill-on-Tweed. Educated at Rugby School and at Trinity Hall, Cambridge, Fleming obtained a second class in part one and a first in part two of the natural sciences tripos (1927 and 1929), specializing in geology, and won a Commonwealth Fund fellowship to Yale University (1929–31). He then entered Westcott House, Cambridge, being ordained deacon in 1933 and priest in 1934, as chaplain and fellow of Trinity Hall (1933–49).

Having accompanied summer university expeditions to Iceland (1932) and Spitsbergen (1933), with his dean's encouragement Fleming joined the British Graham Land expedition to Antarctica (1934–7), as chaplain and geologist, and was one of the three-man dog-sledge party which explored the King George VI Sound (including the Fleming glacier), thus proving that Graham Land was a peninsula. Returning to Trinity Hall as dean in 1937, he contributed to the *Geographical Journal*'s accounts (April, May, and June 1938, and September 1940) of the expedition's scientific findings.

Commissioned as a chaplain in the Royal Naval Volunteer Reserve in 1940, Fleming's service included three years (of which 1941–2 were spent in the Mediterranean) in HMS *Queen Elizabeth*. In 1944 he became director of service ordination candidates. He returned to Cambridge in 1946 and became director of the Scott Polar Research Institute there in 1947. In 1949 he was appointed bishop of Portsmouth, and in 1959 bishop of Norwich. Struck by a rare spinal disorder, which seriously affected both legs, he resigned the see in 1971. The queen appointed him dean of Windsor and her domestic chaplain; he retired in 1976.

A great gift for friendship made him outstandingly effective pastorally; he genuinely cared about people. A remarkable rapport with young people led to his being made chairman of the Church of England Youth Council (1950–61). He helped plan the Duke of Edinburgh Award Scheme in 1954; was co-founder, with Dr Alec Dickson, of Voluntary Service Overseas in 1958; and played a part in inaugurating Atlantic College, the Prince's Trust, Project Trident, Outward Bound, and many similar projects to bring out young people's potential. The governor of numerous schools, he was much in demand for school confirmations.

Although Fleming became a bishop without parochial experience or any great gift for preaching, his unassuming friendliness and humility won over clergy and laity. Portsmouth became an exceptionally well-run diocese, with more than its share of young clergy and ordinands. Norwich, with 650 churches and a shortage of clergy, presented greater problems; he tackled them resolutely and imaginatively, developing rural group ministries and again attracting good clergy. He also played a significant part in planning the University of East Anglia (which, unusually, has its own university chapel). He was an uncanny judge of character, excellent in one-to-one situations. His desk might have looked chaotic, but he was a shrewd administrator with a clear grasp of priorities.

In 1968, most unusually for a bishop, Fleming piloted a bill (the Antarctic treaty) through the House of Lords. Well informed on environmental and ecological issues (he was a pre-war glaciologist of repute), he constantly urged responsible stewardship of the world (his maiden speech in the House of Lords was about cruelty to whales), and the need for international co-operation. He became vice-chairman (1969–71) of the parliamentary group for world government, and a member of the government Standing Advisory Committee on Environmental Pollution (1970–73). At Windsor, he consolidated the reputation of St George's House. His influence on church policy would have been greater but for synodical government: off-the-cuff debate was not his forte.

Private means, which made Fleming's polar exploration

possible, enabled him occasionally to inaugurate administrative improvements without waiting for official ecclesiastical sanction; and he was generous and hospitable. Proud of being a Scot, he loved the highlands, where his holiday home at Innerhadden welcomed many undergraduates and clergy. His other enduring love was Trinity Hall, especially its boat club. His degrees included the MS (Yale, 1931), DD (Lambeth, 1950), and honorary DCL (East Anglia, 1976). He became an honorary fellow of Trinity Hall (1956), FRSE (1971), and honorary vice-president of the Royal Geographical Society (1961), and was awarded the Polar medal (1940). In 1976 he was appointed KCVO.

Fleming was slightly built, wiry, alert, and energetic. He still played a good game of squash in his fifties: it was physical fitness as well as mental discipline that made his prodigious workload possible. He was fifty-eight when he married in 1965; it was a happy marriage which lasted for twenty-five years. His wife was Jane, widow of Anthony Agutter and daughter of Henry Machen, landowner. There were no children. Fleming retired to Dorset and died in Sherborne on 30 July 1990. He was cremated and his ashes were interred in the churchyard of All Saints' Church, Poyntington. GILES HUNT, *rev.*

Sources D. Lindsay, *Friends for life* (1981) · W. L. S. Fleming, 'Relic glacial forms on the western seaboard of Graham Land', *GJ*, 96 (1940), 93–100 · A. Stephenson and W. L. S. Fleming, 'King George the Sixth Sound', *GJ*, 96 (1940), 153–66 · *The Times* (1 Aug 1990) · *The Times* (26 Oct 1990) · *The Independent* (1 Aug 1990) · *The Independent* (8 Aug 1990) · *CGPLA Eng. & Wales* (1990) · *Eastern Daily Press* (Oct 1959–1971)
Archives Scott Polar RI, MSS | FILM Scott Polar RI, Grahamland expedition
Likenesses D. Poole, oils, 1988, Trinity Hall, Cambridge
Wealth at death £203,582: probate, 8 Oct 1990, *CGPLA Eng. & Wales*

Fleming, Malcolm, first earl of Wigtown (*d.* in or before 1363), magnate, was the elder son of Robert Fleming of Cumbernauld. He married, probably before *c.*1310, Marjorie (*d.* in or before 1361), a lady of unknown family. They had three known children: an unnamed son, for whose marriage in 1329 Fleming had a gift of money from the king and who died before 1351, leaving a son, Thomas [*see below*]; Marjorie, who married William Fawside; and Evota, who married John Ramsay.

Fleming rose in the service of the Bruce kings. Before 1321 he received Kirkintilloch from Robert I and properties in the Lennox, Ayrshire, and Wigtownshire, while before February 1327 he was appointed sheriff of Dumbarton and keeper of Dumbarton Castle. He was bailie of Carrick from at least February 1327 and steward of the royal household from August 1328 until June 1329. In 1324 his wife became nurse to the future David II, from whom, after 1341, she had various substantial grants of property in her own right.

One of the few important Scots to survive the battle of Halidon Hill on 19 July 1333, Fleming escaped to Dumbarton, which he held thereafter for the Bruce cause. He welcomed David II and his queen there and in May 1334 arranged their passage to France. Following David's return in May 1341 Fleming joined the king's inner circle

of councillors and was a regular charter witness. On 9 November 1341 his loyalty was rewarded by the grant of the lands of the sheriffdom of Wigtown and his creation as earl of Wigtown, with rights of regality and special judicial powers that were designed to enable him to re-establish Bruce control over this strongly pro-Balliol territory, a role for which his long-standing links with Carrick suited him.

In autumn 1346 Fleming took part in David's invasion of northern England, but on 17 October he was one of several leading Scots captured with the king at Nevilles Cross. Early in 1347, however, having escaped from the custody of Sir Robert Bertram, he was again at liberty. His escape was arranged by one of his captors, Robert Vale, whom Fleming repaid with properties in Lanarkshire and the Lennox. Apart from his attendance at the Dundee parliament of 1350, there is little evidence of further political activity until in 1357 he served as a commissioner in the negotiations leading to the treaty of Berwick that year. He then appears to have retired from political life—he had been replaced as sheriff of Dumbarton by 1359—and was dead before March 1363; he was probably buried in the Franciscan friary at Ayr, of which he had been a generous benefactor.

Malcolm Fleming was succeeded in his hereditary property and titles by his grandson, **Thomas Fleming** (*d.* in or after 1382). Thomas was named heir to the earldom as early as September 1351, when he was a hostage during David II's visit on parole to Scotland. Again a hostage under the treaty of Berwick from 1357, he suffered a prolonged captivity following David's suspension of ransom payments in 1360. The financial problems which dogged him thereafter probably stemmed from the expense of securing his release. In January 1367, by which time Fleming was free, he had a regrant of Wigtown, but was deprived of his rights of regality. Money difficulties and disputes with local lords, perhaps exacerbated by his own extended absences from the region, led him in February 1372 to sell the earldom lands to Archibald Douglas, lord of Galloway, and further finance was obtained through the grant of extended tacks or wadsets on other properties. Family possession of the residue of his estates was secured in November 1372, when his cousin Malcolm Fleming of Biggar received assignation of a wadset on the lands of Lenzie. On 20 September 1382 this Malcolm was given charters confirming the grant of Lenzie, which Thomas had resigned to the crown. There is no indication that Thomas Fleming ever married. The date of his death is unknown. RICHARD D. ORAM

Sources G. W. S. Barrow and others, eds., *Regesta regum Scottorum*, 5–6, ed. A. A. M. Duncan and B. Webster (1982–8) · *Scots peerage*, vol. 7 · *RotS*, vol. 1 · *CDS*, vol. 3 · A. Grant, *Independence and nationhood* (1984) · J. M. Thomson and others, eds., *Registrum magni sigilli regum Scotorum / The register of the great seal of Scotland*, 2nd edn, 1, ed. T. Thomson (1912) · T. Thomson, A. Macdonald, and C. Innes, eds., *Registrum honoris de Morton*, 2 vols., Bannatyne Club, 94 (1853) · F. C. H. Blair, ed., *Charters of the Abbey of Crosraguel*, 2 vols., Ayrshire and Galloway Archaeological Association (1886) · R. C. Reid, ed., *Wigtownshire charters*, Scottish History Society, 3rd ser., 51 (1960) ·

R. W. Cochran-Patrick, ed., *Charters of the Friars Preachers of Ayr*, Ayrshire and Wigtownshire Archaeological Association, 11 (1881) • R. Maitland of Lethington, *The history of the house of Seytoun to the year MDLIX*, ed. J. Fullarton, Maitland Club, 1 (1829)

Fleming, Sir Malcolm (d. 1440). *See under* Fleming, Sir David (d. 1406).

Fleming, (John) Marcus (1911–1976), economist and civil servant, was born on 13 March 1911 at Knockville, Balbardie Road, Bathgate, Linlithgowshire, the only child of John Fleming (1866–1962), shoemaker and owner of a shoe shop, and his wife, Helen McNeill McDonald (1884–1963). He was educated at Bathgate Academy and at Edinburgh University, where he received the degrees of MA (with honours) in history in 1932 and MA (with first-class honours) in political economy in 1934. He continued his education as a graduate research fellow (1934–5) at the Institut Universitaire des Hautes Études Internationales in Geneva, where he attended the seminar conducted by Ludwig von Mises, and then enrolled at the London School of Economics (LSE) for the academic year 1935–6. At the end of 1935, however, Fleming left the LSE and returned to Geneva, where he had been offered a job at the economic, financial, and transport department of the League of Nations, the department responsible for economic research, including the study of business cycles financed by the Rockefeller Foundation. Fleming's first assignment was to assist Professor Gottfried Haberler in writing *Prosperity and Depression: a Theoretical Analysis of Cyclical Movements* (1937). That study completed he worked for some time with Professor Jan Tinbergen on the successor project, to apply the then very new science of econometrics to the empirical testing of the wide variety of business cycle theories described by Haberler. In 1936 Fleming married Etta Leist (b. 1912), with whom he had two daughters; the marriage ended in divorce in 1958, and in 1959 he married Gloria Hile (1928–1998). Both his wives were economists.

After spending a year (1938–9) in the United States as a travelling fellow of the Rockefeller Foundation Fleming returned to the United Kingdom and entered government service, first in the Ministry of Economic Warfare (1939–42) and then in the economic section of the Cabinet Office (1942–51, from 1947 as deputy director), where he formed part of the small group of outstanding economists (which included Lionel Robbins and James Meade) that shaped the views of the UK government on the critical issues of wartime and post-war economic policy. A glimpse of Fleming's early views on trade policy is provided by two long letters written during the war (and available only because they were addressed to Maynard Keynes); in these Fleming attacks Keynes's advocacy of import restrictions as a permanent regime of commercial policy and presents a strong defence for reliance on the price system (*Collected Writings of John Maynard Keynes*, 291–7, 292–303). Fleming was a member of the UK delegation at the 1945 San Francisco conference that established the United Nations and the UK representative on the UN Economic and Employment Commission in 1951–2. He was appointed CMG in 1950.

In 1951 Fleming moved to the United States. He taught for three years at Columbia University and in 1954 he joined the research department of the International Monetary Fund, initially as chief of the special studies division, and, from 1964, as deputy director. He remained at the fund until his death from cancer, in Washington, DC, on 3 February 1976, a few weeks before his retirement, which he had planned to devote to the study of problems of ethics in his beloved Edinburgh. Later that year the IMF and Columbia University jointly honoured his memory by a two-day conference on the international monetary system, in which twenty-five of the world's leading academics and policy makers participated; the proceedings were published in 1977.

All Fleming's writings on economics, whether in journal papers, letters, or inter-office memoranda, share a common style: mastery of economics presented in rigorous argument, elegant drafting, and, occasionally, dry humour. His early published contributions to economics were mainly in the field of welfare economics, his later ones in that of international economics. They are assembled in two volumes: *Essays in International Economics* (1971) and the posthumous *Essays on Economic Policy* (1977). Some of the most interesting papers straddled both subjects, such as 'On making the best of balance of payments restrictions on imports', which introduced the concept of the 'second best'. His work in the IMF, most of it unpublished or published in anonymous reports, reveals his strong interest in applied welfare economics. That interest also guided his choice of policy priorities and recommendations. Thus he favoured exchange rate changes and floating exchange rates (in the 1960s a heretical view for an IMF official) and, to a lesser extent, incomes policies as the instruments for external adjustment, as against what he once called 'the sadism of IMF orthodoxy', to rely on demand management and unemployment. A confirmed internationalist he was also a devoted Keynesian, who wanted countries to have the freedom to make their own choices on how to balance the two economic 'bads', unemployment and inflation. In that vein he opposed the United Kingdom's joining the Common Market.

In the 1940s and 1950s the dominant models to describe the effects of a country's monetary and fiscal policies on employment and the balance of payments assumed fixed exchange rates and tended to neglect international capital movements. In a 1962 paper (reprinted in his *Essays in International Economics*, 1971) Fleming demonstrated that quite different effects would follow if one allowed for capital movements and floating exchange rates. Similar results were published at about the same time by Robert Mundell, who worked with Fleming in the research department of the IMF from 1961 to 1963, and their joint contribution is widely recognized as the Mundell–Fleming model. Fleming chose to work in the IMF rather than in academia because this gave him the closeness to action that was indispensable to having an influence on the complex mechanism of international trade and finance. He further contributed to the transformation of this mechanism as, usually, the only participant from the IMF in the so-called Bellagio Group, composed of both academic economists and officials from the central banks and treasuries of the main industrial countries, which met frequently between 1964 and 1975. The informality of this group permitted the open discussion of possible changes in the system, including the question of floating exchange rates, that were still taboo in official meetings, and thus prepared the ground for the changes in the system that took place in the early 1970s. Fleming's contributions to these meetings were described by their convener, Professor Fritz Machlup, as 'immensely valuable'.

Fleming's interests extended well beyond economics. He read widely in history, philosophy, and *belles lettres*, and he was a devotee of the theatre. In Washington he was an active member of the Theater Lobby, an amateur theatre group noticed for the professional level of its performances; he starred in a number of plays, including Sophocles' *Elektra* and Beckett's *Waiting for Godot*.

JACQUES J. POLAK

Sources J. M. Fleming, *Essays on economic policy* (1977) · J. M. Fleming, *Essays in international economics* (1971) · *The collected writings of John Maynard Keynes*, ed. D. Moggridge and E. Johnson, 26 (1980) · R. A. Mundell and J. J. Polak, *The new international monetary system* (1977) · WWW · b. cert. · private information (2004)

Fleming, Marjory (1803–1811), child diarist, was born on 15 January 1803 in Kirkcaldy, Fife, the third child of James Fleming (d. c.1840), accountant and magistrate, and Isabella Rae (d. 1850). Her mother was distantly connected to Walter Scott through her sister Marianne Rae who married William Keith, first cousin to Anne Rutherford, Scott's mother. In summer 1808, aged five, Marjory paid an extended visit to her Keith relatives at 1 North Charlotte Street, Edinburgh. Here she remained for three years, until the summer of 1811, under the irregular tutelage of her much loved teenage cousin Isabella (Isa) Keith. In July 1811 Marjory returned to her family home in Kirkcaldy, where she died on 19 December, just a month short of her ninth birthday, probably of meningitis following on from measles. She was buried in Abbotshall kirkyard.

Marjory Fleming's reputation as a child prodigy is based upon three manuscript journals, probably written between April 1810 and April 1811, in Edinburgh and on holidays at nearby Ravelston, the Keith family seat. A jumbled and colourful mix of copybook moralisms (extending to observations on sexuality, sin, and her own bad temper), childish enthusiasms about favourite animals and dolls, and quirkily humorous exercises in poetry, they were supervised and their wilder misspellings corrected by her cousin Isa. Almost fifty years after Marjory's death the journals, preserved by her sister Elizabeth Fleming, came to the attention of H. B. Farnie, who published in 1858 sentimentally embellished portions from them, coined the name Pet Marjorie, and began the mawkish Victorian construction of the child genius. The extracts were extended and the portrait further heightened by John Brown, reviewing Farnie in 1863. With no substantial evidence, Brown spun an account of a friendship between Marjory and the adult Walter Scott. Brown's full transcript of the journals eventually formed the basis of Lachlan

Marjory Fleming (1803–1811), by Isabella Keith

Macbean's edition of 1904, and it was Brown's fictitious account of the Scott–Marjory connection, a distasteful mixture of gush and coquetry, that authorized Leslie Stephen's *Dictionary of National Biography* entry of 1889 (in which he misnames her Margaret), and which fuelled the general turn-of-the-century fascination with Marjory, as references to her by R. L. Stevenson and Algernon Swinburne and a surprisingly hagiographic essay by the usually unsentimental Mark Twain attest.

Marjory Fleming's precocity is apparent in her inconsequential (to the adult mind) yoking of juvenile and maturer topics, and in her appetite for books (she records enjoying the poems of Pope and Gray, the *Arabian Nights*, Ann Radcliffe's 'misteris [sic] of udolpho', the Newgate calendar, and 'tails' by Maria Edgeworth and Hannah More). Her fragmentary prose style is vivid: 'and it was the very same Divel that tempted Job that tempted me I am sure but he resisted satan though he had boils and many many other misfortunes which I have escaped' (*Fleming*, ed. Sidgwick, 46); her poems deal with turkeys, a pet monkey known as pug:

O lovely O most charming pug
Thy gracefull air & heavenly mu[g],

the pleasure of sleeping at the foot of Isa Keith's bed:

Oft I embrace her feet of lillys
But she has goton all the pillies,

and an ambitious 205 lines on the imprisonment of Mary, queen of Scots, who in Edinburgh

was lodged in the castle
Which was as bad near as the bastile.
(*Fleming*, ed. Sidgwick, 148, 23, 141)

The manuscripts, published in facsimile (by A. Esdaile)

and as transcripts (by F. Sidgwick), both in 1934, were in 1930 deposited in the National Library of Scotland. A fictional biography, *Marjory Fleming* (1946), by Oriel Malet (pseudonym of Lady Auriel Rosemary Vaughan) prints extracts but is largely devoted to extending the legend. The general revaluation of juvenile and adult perceptions of childhood has led in the 1990s to a new consideration of Marjory as a socially situated early nineteenth-century child and Victorian mythic appropriation. Her status seems assured.   KATHRYN SUTHERLAND

Sources *The complete Marjory Fleming: her journals, letters and verses*, ed. F. Sidgwick (1934) · *The journals, letters and verses of Marjory Fleming*, ed. A. Esdaile (1934) · J. Brown, *Marjorie Fleming, a sketch: being the paper entitled Pet Marjorie, a story of child life fifty years ago* (1884) [first appeared in the *North British Review*, 1863] · H. B. Farnie, *Pet Marjorie: a story of child-life fifty years ago*, 2nd edn (1864) [first appeared in the *Fife Herald*, 1858] · M. Twain [S. L. Clemens], 'Marjorie Fleming, the wonder child', *Europe and elsewhere* (1923) [repr. from *Harper's Bazaar*, 1909] · M. Myers, 'The erotics of pedagogy', *Children's Literature*, 23 (1995), 1–30 · *DNB*
Archives NL Scot., diaries, corresp., and poems, MSS 1096–1100
Likenesses I. Keith, watercolour sketch, NL Scot. [*see illus.*]

Fleming, Mary (1542–*c*.1600). *See under* Queen's Maries (*act.* 1548–1567).

Fleming, Sir Oliver (*d.* 1661), courtier and diplomat, was a younger son of Sir Thomas Fleming MP (*c*.1572–1624) of Haseley and North Stoneham, Hampshire, and Dorothy (*bap.* 1582), fifth daughter of Sir Oliver Cromwell of Hinchinbrooke, Huntingdonshire, and grandson of Sir Thomas *Fleming (*c*.1544–1613); Oliver Cromwell was his first cousin. He seems to have gone to Italy as a 'gentleman' to Sir Isaac Wake, who was ambassador to Savoy from 1625 to 1630. By 1628 Wake had sent him to Zürich as his representative; in December that year he returned to London with the embassy of James Hay, earl of Carlisle, from Piedmont, and successfully solicited to be official English representative at Zürich, which he remained until 1642. In that post he sought to prevent the French levying Swiss mercenaries while they were at war with England, and to draw protestant cantons into assisting Sweden. Particularly friendly to Venice, Fleming was reckoned as aggressively anti-French. After his mission to the duke of Lorraine in 1635, his enthusiasm led the Venetian ambassador, Correr, to claim 'he writes rather like a servant of the duke than as a minister of His Majesty' (*CSP Venice, 1632–6*, 417). After reporting to the king at York in April 1639 Fleming married Elizabeth Reeve on 18 May at St Margaret's, Westminster, before returning to duty; he had by this time been knighted. In autumn 1641 he accompanied Sir Thomas Roe to Regensburg to negotiate with the emperor.

Political uncertainty at home impeded Fleming's effectiveness. 'Totally abandoned, great arrears due to me, no money transmitted for my subsistance' ('Humble narrative') he returned to England and met Charles at Windsor in January 1642, but obtained no compensation. His foreign languages and experience led to parliament's choosing him in October 1643 to show the French ambassador round London. The king's master of ceremonies, Sir

Charles Cotterel, having fled, on 2 November parliament chose Fleming as his successor at a salary of £200 per annum, forbidding the usual receiving of gifts. He was responsible for arranging the requisite 'public civilities' for ambassadors so as to maintain parliament's prestige, and for escorting them to audiences (*JHC*, 3.199). He retained the role under the Commonwealth, and in October 1649 informed the ambassadors that they must formally recognize the new regime before they could negotiate. He petitioned the council for a higher salary to avoid 'the temptation to do things dishonourable' (*CSP dom., 1651–2*, 334), his income being a fifth of his predecessor's, and for more personnel; in June 1652 the council commissioned Cromwell and Neville to approach parliament as Fleming's charges had 'reduced him to want and constrained him to contract debts'. In May 1652 Fleming dealt with the unofficial Venetian envoy Lorenzo Paulucci, sent to hire mercenaries to fight the Turks, warning that he 'had not escaped censure' for dealing with Paulucci at all (*CSP Venice, 1647–52*, 228); some Irish were eventually hired. Paulucci rated Fleming as 'very intelligent, expert in affairs, and enjoys the confidence of all the foreign ministers', but by October 1653 considered that his influence was waning owing to the 'jealousy' and mistrust of certain councillors (*CSP Venice, 1653–4*, 141, 126–8).

The establishment of the protectorate improved Fleming's position, largely owing to 'the confidence reposed in him by the Protector' (*CSP Venice, 1653–4*, 156), his cousin. Following Carolean precedents he escorted all arriving ambassadors by water from Greenwich to the Tower and thence by road to Whitehall. He acted as Cromwell's interpreter in the initial audiences with the French representatives Bordeaux and Baas (de Batz) in 1654; Baas believed him in Spanish pay. His other significant role was in the Venetian endeavours to secure English naval assistance against the Turks. Accompanying Paulucci and his successors to audiences with Cromwell, Fleming spoke glowingly of a crusade and denounced 'the private interests of a few merchants' but had to admit that Cromwell was 'really thwarted' by the Levant Company (ibid., 255). All he could do was promise indirect assistance from Robert Blake's naval expeditions. Although Fleming was spoken of as ambassador to Venice in 1656, his main function lay in smoothing over difficulties with ambassadors. Most notably, on 1 April 1656 he intervened when the Swedish ambassador, Count Bonde, kept waiting for an audience for an hour, threatened to walk out. Fleming 'did earnestly interpose with his persuasions', induced Bonde to stay, and made Cromwell come out; he 'plainly told him how unfit it was and how ill taken' (Whitelocke, *Memorials*, 624).

At Cromwell's installation on 26 June 1657 Fleming was sent to collect the ambassadors at a few minutes' notice. After Cromwell's death, he belatedly informed them on 17 September 1658 that they would need new credentials. At the funeral there were objections that only the three official ambassadors—those of France, Portugal, and the Dutch—were allowed to walk ahead of the barons.

Affronted envoys did not attend, and Fleming had to prevent a Swedish boycott by leaving his designated place and accompanying them between the ambassadors and the barons. In July 1659 he canvassed for the Constantinople embassy. He was dismissed as master of ceremonies in June 1660 when Cotterel was reappointed.

Owing £8000 and pursued by creditors, Fleming petitioned parliament for relief, claiming that he had been appointed in 1643 'without my seeking' and could not disobey a parliamentarian directive. He had served the regicides out of 'the duty that I owed to the honour of the nation' and 'a plain-hearted and sincere desire' to preserve England's reputation. He had acted out of 'lawless necessity', serving 'an irresistable tyrant' owing to debts, yet had only amassed more and had been told by some councillors that 'they needed no pedagogue to instruct them' ('Humble narrative'). He died intestate late in September 1661 and was buried on 26 September at St Margaret's, Westminster. Details of his family are unclear, but he had at least one son, Charles, and probably a second, John, and a daughter, Dorothy, who were living in London in the 1660s.

A conscientious and honest diplomat, Fleming did his best to maintain England's reputation in such a manner as to enhance foreign diplomats' assessment of its power and acceptability. Criticized by some Commonwealth leaders, he had an easier time as his cousin's government adopted more conventional trappings. His ineffectiveness on Mediterranean policy shows his restricted influence, but his strong opinions were apparent in both the 1630s and 1650s.

TIMOTHY VENNING

Sources 'The humble narrative of Sir Oliver Fleming, knight, shewing the manner how I came to execute the office of master of ceremonies, with my comportment and suffering therein, for the space of near eighteen years', *A collection of scarce and valuable tracts … Lord Somers*, ed. W. Scott, 2nd edn, 7 (1812), 499–505 • *CSP Venice, 1628–36; 1640–61* • *CSP dom., 1634–5; 1639–43; 1649–52* • state papers, French ambassador's papers, PRO, 31/3/93 and 31/3/101, SP 18/182, 183 • Thurloe, *State papers*, vols. 3, 7 • *Mercurius Politicus* (25 June–2 July 1657) • *Mercurius Politicus* (27 Aug–3 Sept 1657) • *Mercurius Politicus* (2–9 Sept 1658) • R. Sherwood, *The court of Oliver Cromwell* (1977) • B. Whitelocke, *Memorials of English affairs*, new edn, 4 vols. (1853), vol. 4 • *The diary of Bulstrode Whitelocke, 1605–1675*, ed. R. Spalding, British Academy, Records of Social and Economic History, new ser., 13 (1990) • *JHC*, 3 (1642–4) • *JHL*, 6 (1643–4) • *Parish registers of St Margaret's, Westminster, 1539–1660*, ed. A. M. Burke (1914) • H. F. Westlake and L. E. Tanner, eds., *The register of St Margaret's, Westminster, London, 1660–1675*, Harleian Society, register section, 64 (1935) • W. Berry, *County genealogies: pedigrees of the families of the county of Hants* (1833) • Foster, *Alum. Oxon.* • G. H. Gater and E. P. Wheeler, *The parish of St Martin-in-the-Fields*, 1: *Charing Cross*, Survey of London, 16 (1935) • P. Hyde, 'Fleming, Thomas I', 'Fleming, Thomas II', HoP, *Commons, 1558–1603*, 2.139–40 • M. Noble, *The illustrious house of Cromwell*, 1 (1787)

Archives PRO, state papers domestic, petitions to council of state • PRO, petitions to parliament, *Somers tracts*, vol. 7

Wealth at death governments owed him over £8000 in 1660 (for 1643–60): PRO, petitions to parliament; 'Humble narrative'

Fleming, (Robert) Peter (1907–1971), writer and traveller, was born on 31 May 1907 at 27 Green Street, Park Lane, London, the eldest of the four sons of Valentine Fleming (1882–1917), later Conservative member of parliament for

(Robert) Peter Fleming (1907–1971), by Howard Coster, 1935

South Oxfordshire, and his wife, Evelyn Beatrice Ste Croix (1885–1964), daughter of George Alfred Ste Croix Rose, solicitor and JP, of the Red House, Sonning, Berkshire. His grandfather Robert *Fleming (1845–1933), starting penniless in Dundee, had gone to London and made a fortune in the City. Peter's childhood was clouded by a mysterious and incapacitating illness that left him without sense of taste or smell, but he recovered in time to be an outstanding success at Eton College (1920–26). Although outdistanced in athletics by his younger brother Ian *Fleming, he became a member of Pop, the society of leading students, captain of the Oppidans (in effect, head of school), and editor of the school magazine. Most of his closest friendships were made at Eton. At Christ Church, Oxford (1926–9), he was equally successful—as president of the Oxford University Dramatic Society, a member of the Bullingdon Club, and editor of *Isis*. He obtained first-class honours in English.

Valentine Fleming had been killed in action in 1917 and Peter's family decided that he, the senior male heir, should carry on the flourishing family financial business, but a few months' apprenticeship in the New York office convinced him that his life's work lay elsewhere. 'My aversion to Business and all that it stands for grows almost hourly' (Hart-Davis, 68). He took a business excuse to go on a shooting expedition on the slopes of a volcano in Guatemala, after which he returned to Britain, and in the spring of 1931 joined, as assistant literary editor, the staff of *The Spectator*, with which he was to be associated for most of his life. Some months later he got leave to attend a conference of the Institute of Pacific Relations, and so obtained his first experience of Russia, the Trans-Siberian Railway, and especially China, where he was always to feel at home.

In April 1932 Fleming answered an advertisement in the agony column of *The Times*, which led him to take part in a crack-brained and amateurish expedition to the hinterland of Brazil, ostensibly to look for Colonel P. H. Fawcett, a missing explorer. Fleming persuaded *The Times* to appoint him their unpaid special correspondent. This mixture of farce, excitement, discomfort, and danger achieved nothing except to provide him with the subject matter for his first book, *Brazilian Adventure*, published in August 1933. In it he blew sky-high the excessive reverence and solemnity with which travel books had hitherto been treated, mocking the dangers and himself with infectious humour. People could not believe that a story of true adventure could be so funny, and the book had immense success at home and in America.

In June 1933 Fleming set out on his second journey to China, again as special correspondent of *The Times*, to report on the war between nationalists and communists. After reaching Mukden (Shenyang) in Manchuria and taking part in a sortie against local bandits, he travelled south, achieving an interview with Chaing Kai-shek, the commander-in-chief of the nationalist forces, entering communist-held territory, and finally returning home via Japan and the United States.

Again the excursion furnished Fleming with the material for a best-seller, *One's Company*, published in August 1934. 'One reads Fleming', wrote Vita Sackville-West, 'for literary delight and for the pleasure of meeting an Elizabethan spirit allied to a modern mind' (Hart-Davis, 126). The headline of her article, 'A modern Elizabethan', was how Fleming was often known for much of the 1930s.

At the end of August Fleming once again set off for the Far East with a far-ranging commission from *The Times*. After a brief shooting trip with friends in the Caucasus he travelled on to Harbin in Manchuria, where by chance he met the Swiss traveller Ella (Kini) Maillart. It transpired that they both wanted to walk and ride from China to India, and though they both preferred to travel alone, they agreed to join forces. This epic journey of some 3500 miles on foot or ponies, through the remote province of Sinkiang (Xinjiang), with many dangers, hardships, and holdups, took them seven months, from February to September 1935. This, the most arduous of Fleming's long journeys, he chronicled in fourteen long articles in *The Times* and later in his book *News from Tartary* (1936). On 10 December 1935 he married the actress Celia *Johnson (1908–1982). She was the daughter of John Robert Johnson, a physician.

In 1936 Fleming joined the staff of *The Times*, having declined the offer from J. L. Garvin of the editorship of *The Observer*. The editor of *The Times*, Geoffrey Dawson, was anxious that Fleming should eventually succeed him (as, post-war, was the then editor, R. M. Barrington-Ward), but Fleming's interest in politics was minimal, and the idea was gradually dropped.

In March 1938, taking Celia with him, Fleming made his fourth journey to China, to report on the Sino-Japanese War and on the completion of the Burma Road, the only remaining access to China from the west.

On the outbreak of the Second World War in September 1939 Fleming immediately joined the Grenadier Guards, on whose special reserve he had served for many years. In March 1940 during a week of German measles he wrote a short and very amusing fantasy of Hitler landing accidentally in England by parachute, with uproarious consequences. *The Flying Visit* was published in July, and when, less than a year later, Rudolf Hess arrived in Scotland by air, Fleming's joke began to look like prophecy. His one desire now was to see active service with his regiment, but for almost the whole war he was seconded to various intelligence and other jobs all over the world—first in Norway with Adrian Carton de Wiart, then training a post-invasion force of guerrillas in Kent, then in Cairo with General Sir A. P. Wavell, then in Greece, from where he was lucky to escape alive. Next he ran a street-fighting course in London until Wavell, now commander-in-chief in the south-west Pacific, summoned him to India and appointed him head of deception. From 1942 to 1945 he shuttled between Delhi and the Chinese capital at Chungking (Chongqing), besides making an unauthorized and almost disastrous glider flight into Burma with the Chindits under Orde Wingate. After the Japanese surrender in 1945 he returned to civilian life as a lieutenant-colonel, having been appointed OBE.

Now, with his desire to travel satisfied, Fleming settled down to the life of a literary squire at Merrimoles, the house he had built just before the war, near his grandparents' old home at Nettlebed in Oxfordshire, and in the middle of a 2000-acre estate which his uncle had given him. People had always imagined he was wealthy, but owing to muddled wills he never in fact had any money of his own except an allowance from his mother, until his books and journalism began to provide him with an adequate income.

Fleming continued to write amusing fourth leaders for *The Times*, and for many years contributed a column signed Strix to *The Spectator*. Then he found a new role as an extremely competent amateur historian. *Invasion 1940*, a clever analysis of Hitler's plans for the conquest of Britain, and British counter-measures, published in 1957, was a great success on both sides of the Atlantic and earned him more than any of his other books. There followed *The Siege at Peking* (1959), an account of the Boxer uprising in 1900; *Bayonets to Lhasa* (1961) on the 1903–4 expedition of Francis Younghusband; and *The Fate of Admiral Kolchak* (1963), concerning the White Russian commander in Siberia. At the time of his death he was engaged on the official history of strategic deception in the Second World War, which, but for several years of official obstruction, he would have had time to complete.

Apart from these major works, Fleming's essays from

The *Spectator* and elsewhere were published in five volumes: *Variety* (1933), *My Aunt's Rhinoceros* (1956), *With the Guards to Mexico!* (1957), *The Gower Street Poltergeist* (1958), and *Goodbye to the Bombay Bowler* (1961).

Fleming was slim, medium-tall, black-haired, very good-looking, and attractive. He habitually smoked a pipe. Shooting, at which he excelled, was the passion of his life, and he was at his happiest on long solitary patrols of his own acres with a gun and one of his beloved dogs. On every available day he walked or rode for miles. Every autumn he went to Scotland for a shooting holiday.

Fleming's persistent shyness with strangers was sometimes mistaken for arrogance: he was at his ease with contemporaries and old friends; those who served under him in peace and war would do anything for him; and he had a special relationship with men of his father's age—Carton de Wiart, Wavell, Geoffrey Dawson—to whom perhaps this dashing young man brought memories of their own youth. He was a man of courage and imagination, a faithful and generous friend. His literary style was compounded of clarity, a large vocabulary, and his own brand of incongruous and often self-deprecatory humour.

Fleming died at Black Mount, Argyllshire, on 18 August 1971, in exactly the way he would have chosen—a glorious summer's day, a grouse shoot on his beloved Scottish moors, a right-and-left, an instantaneous heart attack. He was buried in the churchyard of St Bartholomew's, Nettlebed. RUPERT HART-DAVIS, rev.

Sources *The Times* (20 Aug 1971) · D. Hart-Davis, *Peter Fleming* (1974) · I. McDonald, *The history of The Times*, 5 (1984) · H. Hobson, P. Knightley, and L. Russell, *The pearl of days: an intimate memoir of the Sunday Times, 1822–1972* (1972) · D. Griffiths, ed., *The encyclopedia of the British press, 1422–1992* (1992) · *WWBMP* · P. Fussell, *Abroad: British literary travelling between the wars* (1980) · *CGPLA Eng. & Wales* (1971)
Archives U. Reading L., corresp. and MSS | BL OIOC, corresp. with F. M. Bailey, MS Eur. F 157 · News Int. RO, MSS relating to work for *The Times* · U. Durham L., letters to William Plomer
Likenesses H. Coster, photograph, 1935, NPG [*see illus.*] · photograph, repro. in *The Times* · photographs, repro. in Hart-Davis, *Peter Fleming*
Wealth at death £439,628: probate, 13 Dec 1971, *CGPLA Eng. & Wales*

Fleming, Richard. *See* Flemming, Richard (*d.* 1431).

Fleming, Robert, first Lord Fleming (*d.* **1491**). *See under* Fleming, Sir David (*d.* 1406).

Fleming, Robert (1630–1694), Presbyterian minister in the Netherlands, was born in Yester, Haddingtonshire. His father, James Fleming (1590–1653), was the minister of Yester and a son of Bartholomew Fleming, an Edinburgh merchant. Robert's mother, Jean Livingston, his father's second wife, was a cousin of the famous presbyterian minister John Livingstone. Robert was a sickly child—and also survived a terrible blow from a club—and came to think of himself as 'God's Choice, and in a most singular way restored' (Burgess, 104). He possessed a religious bent from early childhood, and recorded 'that strange and extraordinary impression I had of an audible voice, in the church, at night; when, being a child, I had got up to the pulpit; calling to me; to make haste'. He studied first at the University of Edinburgh (MA, with distinction, 26 July 1649), then under Samuel Rutherford at St Andrews. He wrote later of:

> that solemn and memorable day of the Communion at Gray-Friars [Edinburgh], in the entry of the year 1648, where I had so extraordinary a sense of the Lord's presence; yea, whence I can date the first sealing evidence of my conversion, now 40 years past.

It was this religious experience, complete with manifestations of providence and dreams and voices, characteristic of contemporary evangelical presbyterianism, which would define his career as one of the leading Scottish divines of the day.

Fleming was present, apparently under arms, with the Scottish army at Dunbar (3 September 1650) and then in 1653 was called to the benefice of Cambuslang in the Clydesdale. Some time before 1660 he married Christian (*d.* 1674), daughter of Sir George Hamilton of Binny, Linlithgowshire, with whom he had seven children, two of whom survived him, including Robert *Fleming (*c*.1660–1716), his successor at Rotterdam. He was driven from Cambuslang following the Glasgow Act of 1662, which led to about 300 deprivations. He stayed in Scotland for about eleven years preaching as he was able. According to the *Dictionary of National Biography* he had the infeftment of the lands of Marbreck and Formontstoun in 1672. On 11 July 1672 he was cited by the privy council for attendance at conventicles in Perth. On 3 September following he was granted an indulgence to preach at Kilwinning, but he failed to settle there and on 5 September 1673 he was put to the horn. He fled to London, but his ministry there was hindered by his '[Scottish] idiotisms and accents'. He then returned to Scotland and in 1674 lived at West Nisbet in Roxburghshire in the borders. It was here that he had left his wife and that she died during the year.

Fleming published an array of theological treatises, beginning in 1669 when the first edition of *The Fulfilling of the Scripture* appeared, his most famous and enduring work. It is a handbook of evangelical presbyterianism's interest in defending the Bible and divine providence against sceptical philosophical tendencies; in demonstrating the Bible's authenticity appeal is made to historical examples of faith, including notices of renowned Scottish ministers such as John Welsh of Ayr, Robert Bruce, and Robert Blair. A second part, *The Faithfulness of God*, appeared in 1674. In 1675 he published *A Short and Plain Account of the Doctrine of the Romish-Church* (republished in 1678 as *The Truth and Certainty of the Protestant Faith*); in 1677 he published *A Survey of Quakerism*, in the next year *Scripture Truth Confirmed and Cleared*, and in 1679 *The One Necessary Thing to be Sought*, about practical religion.

In 1677 Fleming went to Rotterdam and succeeded Robert MacWard as colleague to John Hog (or Hoog), who minister of the Scottish church. His relations with MacWard were difficult owing to Fleming's readiness to welcome ministers who accepted the indulgences, whereas MacWard thought it a scandal to make such undertakings to the government. In 1678 Fleming returned to Edinburgh, intending to retrieve his children; he also preached there and was arrested and lodged in the tolbooth. As a result of a royal proclamation on 29 June 1679 he was released on condition that he would not preach at conventicles, but was sent back to prison when he refused to accept the conditions. When he was again released he returned to Rotterdam and in 1681 published *The Church Wounded and Rent by a Spirit of Division*, concerning the dissensions in the Church of Scotland. In 1683 Charles II named Fleming and Hog among those maintaining connections with the covenanters:

> The Rotterdam preachers permit rebels from Scotland to preach in the Scottish Church. They maintain the Covenant and have excluded from the Holy Communion persons who acknowledge His Majesty's government, and instead admit John Balfour, guilty of the murder of the Bishop of St Andrews. Finally, the two preachers have also prayed that God Almighty would give his blessing to Dutch arms against those of the King of Great Britain during the last war between the Netherlands and Great Britain. (Sprunger, 436)

Fleming was charged with harbouring some of Archbishop Sharp's murderers but vigorously defended himself from Rotterdam, denouncing Balfour and declaring that he had refused to serve him communion. He was first granted a delay in the proceedings owing to his ill health and inability to travel and then the charge was withdrawn on 17 April 1684.

More divinity followed in *The Confirming Worke of Religion* (1685); *An Epistolary Discourse on the Great Assistances to a Christians Faith* (1692); and *A Discourse of Earthquakes* (1693), whereby their occurrence was made to serve as 'supernatural and premonitory signs to a nation'. The revolution of 1688 allowed him the possibility of restoration to Cambuslang, but he chose to remain in Rotterdam. As was his custom he renewed his personal covenant with God on the first day of the new year—1 January 1694. Later that year he visited London but fell sick with a fever on 17 July and died on 25 July. Daniel Burgess, a renowned London Presbyterian minister, preached his funeral sermon. With the published version he included a brief life and also some excerpts from Fleming's journal. Fleming was an articulate evangelical, and while he was not the most intractable of his breed, his life reflected the experiences of many others, laity and clergy, who suffered imprisonment and exile and separation from family as a result of the Stuart regime's attempt at enforcing conformity.

DAVID GEORGE MULLAN

Sources D. Burgess, *The church's triumph over death: a funeral sermon preached upon the decease of blessed Mr. Robert Fleming, late pastor of a church in Rotterdam* (1694) · *Fasti Scot.*, new edn, 1.399; 3.236–7 · J. Morrison, *Scots on the Dijk: the story of the Scots church, Rotterdam* (1981) · *DNB* · *Reg. PCS*, 3rd ser. · K. L. Sprunger, *Dutch puritanism: a history of English and Scottish churches of the Netherlands in the sixteenth and seventeenth centuries* (1982)

Fleming, Robert (*c.*1660–1716), Presbyterian minister and religious writer, one of the seven children of Robert *Fleming (1630–1694) and his wife, Christian (*d.* 1674),

daughter of Sir George Hamilton of Binny, Linlithgowshire, was born at Cambuslang, Lanarkshire, where his father was minister. In October 1662 his father was ejected from his living and the family moved to Edinburgh. Fleming received his early education at the school of his uncle, John Sinclair, at Ormiston, near Edinburgh, and at the age of thirteen decided to devote himself to the ministry. In 1679 his father took his family to Rotterdam, where, since 1677, he had been a minister at the Scots Church. Here Fleming must have received his ministerial training, probably from his father. He was ordained at Rotterdam on 9 February 1688 and in the same year moved to England to become chaplain to a private family at Soham, Cambridgeshire. There he remained until 1692, when he accepted the invitation to become minister to the English Presbyterian congregation at Leiden and in August of that year he was admitted to the university there. On the death of his father in July 1694 Fleming accepted the invitation to succeed him at the Scots Church in Rotterdam. However, his congregation at Leiden advanced such strong objections that it was not until 1695 that he was able to take up the appointment.

On 19 June 1698 Fleming, partly at the wish of William III, succeeded Nicholas Blaikie as minister at the Scots Church, Founders' Hall, Lothbury, in the City of London, which he retained until his death. He proved to be a hardworking minister, gaining the respect of members of the established church as well as of dissenters. In particular he could count Thomas Tenison, archbishop of Canterbury, among his friends. His congregation became so numerous that a new meeting-house had to be opened for him about 1700. He was an erudite man, and a recognized authority both at home and abroad on the scriptures and on the classical and oriental languages. His scholarship led to his appointment on 15 May 1701 as Tuesday lecturer at Salters' Hall in succession to Vincent Alsop. He was also offered, but declined, the principalship of Glasgow University.

Fleming was noted for his liberal theology and championed freedom of enquiry. According to Joshua Oldfield he followed

> what he apprehended to be the meaning of [the scriptures], after prayer and serious consideration and enquiry, and allowed that everyone had a right to do so too ... he was always free in allowing others the liberty to differ from him. (Oldfield, 36–7)

Above all, Fleming pioneered the principle of nonsubscription to the Westminster confession, the statement of Calvinist orthodoxy. His views on subscription were first outlined in print in his *Christology*, the first of whose two volumes appeared in 1705; the second appeared in 1708. However, despite advocating nonsubscription and freedom of enquiry, Fleming remained orthodox on the doctrine of the Trinity. In politics he was an ardent supporter of the protestant and Hanoverian successions, and like many protestant dissenters of his day was deeply affected by what he considered to be the threats posed by the papacy, the king of France, and the Catholic Stuart claimant to the throne. Anxiety over the possibility of a Stuart restoration, made worse by his gloomy reflections on the divisions among protestants, brought on a bout of depression (*c*.1712–14) which necessitated a visit to the Netherlands in order to recover his health. By 1715 he had returned to England and was living at Homerton in Hackney.

Fleming wrote numerous religious works of which the most extensive, and perhaps most important theologically, was his *Christology*; its first volume was dedicated to Queen Anne and its second to Princess Sophia of Hanover. In this work, based on lectures delivered at Salters' Hall, Fleming 'indulges a liberty of thought that shows he was not fettered by any human system' (Wilson, 2.486). His *Discourses on Several Subjects* (1701) was republished in 1793 and 1848 as *Apocalyptical Key* and attracted attention on account of the striking coincidences between his conjectural interpretation of a prophecy in Revelation and events in France during the early period of the French Revolution and in Italy in 1848.

Fleming never fully recovered from his bout of depression. The threats posed by the Jacobite rising, coupled with the fact that several of his friends died within a short period, deepened his melancholy and destroyed what remained of his spirits and health. He died in London on 21 May 1716. His widow, Hannah, whom he had married about 1698, outlived him, together with several of their children, and died on 23 August 1733.   M. J. MERCER

Robert Fleming (1845–1933), by Francis Dodd, 1915

Sources J. Oldfield, *A funeral sermon upon the much lamented death of the pious, learned and reverend Mr. Robert Fleming* (1716), 29–45 · T. Thomson, *The rise and fall of Rome papal with a memoir of the author* (1848), xi–xx · W. Wilson, *The history and antiquities of the dissenting churches and meeting houses in London, Westminster and Southwark*, 4 vols. (1808–14), vol. 2, pp. 468–87 · A. Gordon, ed., *Freedom after ejection: a review (1690–1692) of presbyterian and congregational nonconformity in England and Wales* (1917), 265 · C. Surman, index, DWL · Chambers, *Scots.* (1855) · Anderson, *Scot. nat.* · *GM*, 1st ser., 3 (1733), 439 · *Protestant Dissenter's Magazine*, 6 (1799), 431 · E. Peacock, *Index of English speaking students at Leyden* (1883), 36 · J. Morrison, *Scots on the Dijk: the story of the Scots church, Rotterdam* (1981) · *DNB*

Archives Bodl. Oxf., letters, sermons, and papers · DWL

Likenesses R. White, line engraving, 1701 (after C. D. Gard), NPG · attrib. J. Closterman, oils, Bodl. Oxf.

Fleming, Robert (1845–1933), financier, was born on 17 March 1845 at Liff Road, Lochee, then a village about 3 miles to the north-west of Dundee. He was the fourth of seven children of John Fleming (1806–1873), an overseer in linen and jute mills in Lochee and Dundee, and his wife, Annie (1808–1860), the eldest of six children of James McIntosh, an itinerant tailor in Glen Shee, and his wife, Elspith. From such modest beginnings, Robert and John (1847–1925), the two surviving children of the marriage, went on to considerable success. John Fleming established a wood-importing firm in Dundee and Aberdeen, was elected to Aberdeen town council in 1893 and served as lord provost from 1899 to 1902, was knighted in 1908, and sat as Liberal member of parliament for South Aberdeen from 1917 to December 1918. Robert Fleming received a basic education at the Free Church of St David's School, Brown Street, Dundee. At eleven he was awarded a bursary that enabled him to study for a further two years

at Dundee high school. There he gained a thorough grounding in mathematics and bookkeeping, which proved of immense value to him in his career. He started work at thirteen as an office boy to James Ramsay jun., a merchant in Dundee's Cowgate, at an annual salary of £5. Within two years he had moved as a clerk to the mercantile office of Cox Brothers, the largest firm of jute spinners and weavers in the world; he then took up an appointment as bookkeeper to Edward Baxter, a prominent Dundee merchant, in 1866.

Investment trusts In his teens Fleming became fascinated by the stock market. The first half of the 1860s was a period of intense financial activity, following legislation permitting the formation of joint-stock companies, many of which were quoted on the London stock exchange. As the number of new companies mushroomed and share prices rose sharply, investors were increasingly driven by blind optimism. The inevitable crash came in 1866, when the major discount house Overend, Gurney & Co. stopped payment, bringing down a number of other companies and precipitating a major financial crisis. One of those companies was the Oriental Commercial Bank, in which a youthful Fleming had invested around £40 of the money he had saved from his salary of £100 per annum. However, the shares were only partly paid, and he was called on to pay a much larger sum. It was money he did not have and he was forced to compromise with the liquidator. Although not legally obliged to do so, Fleming vowed as a matter of honour to pay the calls in full as and when he could, and achieved this within five years. Despite having his fingers badly burnt, he was not put off investing. It was an episode that he never forgot and which shaped his lifelong investment philosophy of courage and caution.

It was during his time with Edward Baxter, who had

large holdings of overseas securities, that Fleming developed his investment ideas and in particular his interest in overseas stock markets. He realized that America, recovering from civil war, was a land of boundless opportunity, and that the mortgage bonds of railroads were the key to safe and profitable investment in that country. He also appreciated that British investors were anxious to obtain a greater return than could be earned from domestic securities, but that the vast majority of them were unwilling to risk investing overseas on their own. Fleming decided that the answer lay in promoting an investment trust—then a relatively new concept—which would be invested in American railroad bonds to yield 7 per cent, almost double the return on British government stocks. It says much about his personality and strength of character, his enthusiasm for investment, and his grasp of the complexities and pitfalls of the market in railroad securities that in 1873, aged twenty-seven, he was able to convince four of the most respected and influential businessmen in Dundee that his idea had merit and persuade them to act as trustees of the first investment trust to be formed in Scotland. The Scottish American Investment Trust encountered such an enthusiastic response from investors that the initial prospectus, seeking subscriptions of £150,000, had to be withdrawn and replaced by a prospectus for £300,000. Fleming was appointed secretary of the trust. Later that year he visited America for the first time—he was to cross the Atlantic a total of 128 times—supervising the investment of the trust's funds in railroad bonds. Almost immediately a financial panic hit America, following the collapse of the leading New York banking house of Jay, Cooke & Co., which triggered a severe economic depression that lasted until 1879. It was a testing time for Fleming and the trustees—the first of many—but the trust weathered the storm well. Its success led to the flotation of two further trusts over the next two years, both oversubscribed, increasing the total sum invested to £1.1 million, the bulk of the money raised in Dundee itself.

On 14 February 1881 Fleming married Sarah Kate (1857–1937), the second child of a son and three daughters born to Marshall Kirkland Hindmarsh, a senior official of the Inland Revenue in Scotland, and his wife, Mary Kirby Baylis. They had two sons and two daughters. Two of their grandchildren were Peter *Fleming (1907–1971), the writer and explorer, and his brother, Ian *Fleming (1908–1964), creator of James Bond.

Fleming was never a director of the three trusts, but in 1882 he was invited to join the board of the Dundee Land Investment Company Ltd and its sister company, the Dundee Mortgage and Trust Investment Company Ltd, later part of the Alliance Trust. For four years until his resignation (owing to pressure of other business) Fleming served as the companies' expert on American securities. Few transactions were undertaken without referral to him, and on his visits to the United States he was given wide discretion to acquire investments for the companies. He was closely involved also in negotiations for the transfer of the Matador Cattle Company to Scottish ownership, inspecting the ranch and signing the agreement in Texas on behalf of a syndicate of Dundee businessmen in 1882. The Matador, tightly controlled from Dundee, was one of the very few cattle companies floated during the ranching mania of the early 1880s to survive and prosper. Fleming went on to set up the Investment Trust Corporation in London in 1888 and the British Investment Trust in Edinburgh the following year. He helped establish the Northern American Trust Company in Dundee in 1896 and reorganized the Metropolitan Trust Company in London in 1899. For almost fifty years he exercised enormous influence in the field of investment, being a director of a number of investment trusts and acting as adviser or broker to many more.

American railroads It was as an investor and expert on American railroads that Fleming established an early international reputation. Railroads were America's first 'big business', but they were not for the unwary or faint-hearted. In addition to fraud and corruption, investors frequently had to contend with mismanagement and stock-manipulation on a grand scale. Superimposed on this was the business cycle of boom and bust. The often reckless over-expansion of the rail network during the good years brought disaster when economic depression set in, many railroads being forced into receivership more than once. In 1876, at the age of thirty, Fleming and a colleague were asked by Sir Edward Watkin MP to go to New York on behalf of the London bondholders' committee of the Erie Railway, then in receivership, to confer with representatives of the company. Their plan for the financial reorganization of Erie was largely adopted. Subsequently Fleming was involved in the restructuring of other railroads, including the Denver and Rio Grande (1884–6), the Mexican National (1886), the East Tennessee, Virginia, and Georgia (1885–6), the Atchison, Topeka, and Santa Fé (1894–6), and the Norfolk and Western (1895–6), of which he was also a director between 1886 and 1893. He was regarded in railroad and banking circles as a shrewd operator. He needed all his astuteness, perspicacity, and experience in 1886, when he assumed a central role in the battle with Jay Gould, the notorious railroad promoter and speculator, for control of the Texas and Pacific Railway. For a time it looked as if Gould, one of the most intelligent and artful operators of them all, would wrest control of the company from its bondholders and shareholders for next to nothing, but when Fleming arrived in New York and united the majority of the opposing parties behind his plan, Gould's attempt at 'daylight robbery' was foiled, though not without a fight.

London In 1884 Fleming turned down the offer of a lucrative partnership in the New York banking house of Jesup, Paton & Co. because he was unwilling to commit his family and himself to living in that city for the rest of his life. However, towards the end of the 1880s he became restless: he had been playing on an international stage and Dundee seemed to him rather restricting. In 1890 he decided to move his business to London, though retaining his Dundee office. He resigned as secretary of the three Scottish-American investment trusts, but, anxious to retain his expertise, the Dundee trustees appointed him their London correspondent. His family lived in Chislehurst for twelve years before Fleming purchased the Nettlebed estate in Oxfordshire, where he built a large mansion, Joyce Grove. He was high sheriff of Oxfordshire in 1909. He went on to acquire a town house in London, in Grosvenor Square. As a City financier for more than thirty years there were few ventures of any significance that he did not help to finance. He underwrote or placed issues of securities by companies in every corner of the world worth tens of millions of pounds using his network of British investment trusts, insurance companies, and other clients. Major commitments included supporting E. H. Harriman's restructuring of the Union Pacific Railroad in the early years of the twentieth century, financing Sir William van Horne in the construction of railways in Cuba, and underwriting issues amounting to more than £15 million by Anglo-Persian Oil Company, the forerunner of British Petroleum.

In 1904 Fleming engaged Walter Whigham, a young Scottish accountant, as his assistant. Although Fleming had admitted to working better 'in single harness', he needed help. Approaching sixty, his business was increasing and he was frequently away in Scotland or America. He also had a number of other commitments. For example, in 1906 he was appointed a member of the finance committee of King Edward's Hospital Fund for London, and the following year he was made an extraordinary director of the Royal Bank of Scotland. In 1909 he took his elder son, Valentine, and Whigham into partnership. His younger son, Philip, joined the firm in 1911. Tragically Valentine was killed in action in France in 1917. After the war the partnership went from strength to strength. It is said that Robert Fleming & Co. was one of only two City institutions that issuing houses would invariably consult before deciding on the terms of a new issue, the other being the Prudential.

Personality and reputation Fleming had an indefatigable energy for work. Above average in height, well-built, and erect, he presented a distinguished appearance. He was a serious, rather reserved man, who did not engage in idle conversation. Even to those who knew him he was a man of few words, these being delivered in a deep voice with a Scots accent. He could appear severe and intimidating, but by nature he was a kindly person and an adoring husband and father. He was very keen on outdoor pursuits—particularly, when he was young, rowing and walking; latterly his passion was stalking. With two exceptions, each year from 1892 until his death he rented a Scottish sporting estate where the family gathered in late summer. He was a fine shot, bagging two stags the same day at Black Mount in Argyll, in 1929, at the age of eighty-four.

Robert Fleming became a financier of international repute, establishing in London the investment bank that bore his name for more than a century until it was sold to Chase Manhattan Corporation in 2000. Throughout his life he was closely associated with investment trusts in Scotland and England. He is often referred to as the father of the investment trust, being largely responsible for establishing the principles of sound investment-trust management. A contemporary of J. Pierpont Morgan and a close business associate and friend of Jacob Schiff of the New York investment bank of Kuhn, Loeb & Co., Fleming was widely known and respected in financial circles on both sides of the Atlantic, a man of unquestioned integrity. He was among the shrewdest investors of his generation and an acknowledged expert on financing railways, particularly in the United States, Mexico, and Cuba. Despite his success and accumulated wealth, Fleming remained modest, unassuming, and very generous, his unostentatious benevolence supporting both national and local causes. He never forgot his birthplace, donating sums to University College, Dundee, and in 1929 donating £155,000 to the city to finance the building of houses for Dundee's workers. He received the honorary degree of doctor of laws from St Andrews University in 1928 in recognition of his gifts and of his advice to University College over many years. In 1929 he was made a freeman of the city of Dundee. Fleming died suddenly of heart failure at Black Mount, Bridge of Orchy, Argyll, on 31 July 1933, aged eighty-eight. He was buried at Nettlebed three days later.

W. N. SMITH

Sources W. Smith, *Robert Fleming, 1845–1933* (2000) · J. Fleming, *Looking backwards for seventy years, 1921–1851* (1922) · Fleming family archives, London · Dundee City Archives, Dundee · Dundee, Archives of the Alliance Trust PLC · *Commercial and Financial Chronicle* [New York] · C. Adler, *Jacob H. Schiff: his life and letters*, 2 vols. (1928) · D. R. Adler, *British investment in American railways, 1834–1898* (1970) · H. Burton and D. C. Corner, *Investment and unit trusts in Britain and America* (1968) · W. G. Kerr, *Scottish capital on the American credit frontier* (1976) · D. Hart-Davis, *Peter Fleming* (1974) · D. Kynaston, *The City of London*, 2 (1995); 3 (1999) · m. cert. · d. cert. · private information (2004) · *The Times* (Aug 1933) · gravestone, Nettlebed churchyard, Oxfordshire

Archives priv. coll., family archives | Alliance Trust PLC, Dundee, Dundee Mortgage & Trust Investment Co. Ltd · Dundee City Archives, Dundee, First, Second and Third Scottish American Trust Company Ltd

Likenesses F. Dodd, pencil drawing, 1915, priv. coll. [*see illus.*] · A. John, oils, priv. coll. · P. de Laszlo, oils, priv. coll.

Wealth at death £2,174,803 15*s.* 10*d.*: English probate certified in Scotland, 15 Sept 1933, *CCI*

Fleming, Sir Sandford (1827–1915), civil engineer in Canada, the second son of Andrew Greig Fleming, of Kirkcaldy, Fife, and his wife, Elizabeth, the eldest daughter of Sandford Arnott, was born at Kirkcaldy on 7 January 1827. After studying surveying in his native town he went to Canada in 1845. In 1855 he married Ann Jean (*d.* 1888), eldest daughter of James Hall MP, sheriff of Peterborough county, Ontario.

From 1852 onwards Fleming took a prominent part in the railway development of Upper Canada, and from 1855 to 1863 he was chief engineer of the Northern Railway. In 1864 he was appointed chief railway engineer by the government of Nova Scotia, and charged with the construction of a line from Truro to Pictou. The government policy of constructing the line by a series of small contracts did

Sir Sandford
Fleming (1827–
1915), by Edward
Lantéri, 1887

not work well, as the tenders received were so far above Fleming's estimate that he refused to entertain them. He was therefore requested by the government, in 1866, as the only method of getting them out of the imbroglio, to resign his position and carry out as contractor the work on which he had hitherto been employed as civil servant. This offer Fleming eventually accepted, and he completed the line by 31 May 1867, with profit to himself, at a great saving to the government, and to the entire satisfaction of the government inspectors.

Fleming early advocated a Canadian transcontinental railway, and when in 1867 the construction of a railway from the St Lawrence River to Halifax was made part of the federation pact, he was appointed by the newly formed dominion government as its chief engineer. He at once began the construction of the Inter-Colonial Railway, and carried it to completion in 1876. His difficulties were not only those of construction through a country which was in great part unsettled: he carried on a continual struggle with the governments of the day because they wished to award extravagant contracts to political favourites, while saving money on construction which Fleming considered essential. The great 'battle of the bridges', in which he insisted on iron bridges in places where the government desired wood, was finally won by Fleming. Meanwhile, in 1871, the construction of a Canadian Pacific Railway was made a part of the bargain by which British Columbia was induced to enter the new dominion, and Fleming was appointed engineer-in-chief. In 1872 he headed the ocean to ocean expedition, by which a practicable route was found through the Yellow Head Pass, but in 1880 the government changed its policy, abandoned the plan of government construction, and formed an agreement with the Canadian Pacific Railway Company. It was the hardest blow of Fleming's life. Over 600 miles of railway had been completed, the whole line surveyed, and most of the engineering difficulties overcome. All this work, together with vast subsidies of land and money, was handed over by the government to the new company, whose general manager, William Cornelius Van Horne,

was a little inclined to undervalue the work of his predecessor. But, beyond resigning his position as engineer-in-chief of the government railways, Fleming made little protest.

From that time forward Fleming's quiet, unceasing energy was occupied in promoting a series of good causes. He became a director of the Canadian Pacific Railway Company, and in 1883 he crossed the continent in its service and assisted in the survey of the main line through the Kicking Horse Pass. He and his party were the first white men to cross the Rockies by this route. The story is told by him in *Old to New Westminster* (1884). After protracted negotiations from 1879 onwards, he succeeded in persuading the Canadian, Australian, and imperial governments to co-operate in laying the Pacific cable, which was completed between Vancouver and Australia in 1902. From 1876 he had taken a prominent part in forcing the adoption of standard time, which greatly simplified travel in British North America and throughout the world. In 1880 he was appointed chancellor of Queen's University, Kingston, Ontario, a position to which he was continuously re-elected until his death. Though not a party man he was a devoted imperialist, was prominent in the Imperial Federation League, and in 1891 came forward as an opponent of reciprocity with the United States.

Fleming was tall and handsome, gentle in speech, but absolutely immovable once his mind was made up. Besides his numerous reports to the Canadian government on the Inter-Colonial and Canadian Pacific railways, Fleming wrote many pamphlets on time reckoning and on the Pacific cable, and published a series of small volumes of prayers and short services which grew out of those which he always provided for his engineering parties. During the summer he lived in Halifax, in the winter in Ottawa, though until late in life he travelled constantly. In 1877 he was created CMG, and KCMG in 1897. He died at Halifax, Nova Scotia, on 22 July 1915, survived by four sons and two daughters.   W. L. GRANT, *rev.*

Sources L. J. Burpee, *Sandford Fleming, empire-builder* (1915) · R. F. Legget, *Railways of Canada* (1973) · W. K. Lamb, *History of the Canadian Pacific Railway* (1977) · G. M. Grant, *Ocean to ocean, Sandford Fleming's expedition through Canada in 1872* (1873); rev. edn [1967] · S. Fleming, *The Inter-Colonial: a historical sketch, 1832–1876* (1876) · C. F. Hamilton, *Montreal Daily Witness* (20 Feb 1911) · personal knowledge (1927)

Likenesses E. Lantéri, terracotta bust, 1887, Scot. NPG [*see illus.*] · photograph, NA Canada; repro. in Lamb, *History of the Canadian Pacific railway* · portraits, repro. in Burpee, *Sandford Fleming*

Fleming, Thomas, **second earl of Wigtown** (*d.* in or after 1382). *See under* Fleming, Malcolm, first earl of Wigtown (*d.* in or before 1363).

Fleming, Sir Thomas (*c.*1544–1613), judge, was the son of John Fleming, mercer, of Newport, Isle of Wight, and his first wife, Dorothy Harris. He is said to have owed his advancement to Francis Walsingham, who in 1566 married a widow from the Isle of Wight. Destined for the law, he was admitted to Lincoln's Inn in 1567 and called to the bar in 1574. In 1570 he married Mary, daughter of Richard James of Newport, who was to be member of parliament

Sir Thomas Fleming (*c.*1544–1613), by unknown artist, 1596

for that borough (perhaps through Fleming's influence) from 1597 to 1604. (Foss's statement that Fleming married a daughter of Sir Henry Cromwell resulted from confusion with Fleming's son, another Sir Thomas, who died in 1624.) From as early as 1571 he was a reporter of queen's bench cases, and surviving fragments show that he continued reporting until at least 1600, though his work was never published. Throughout his life he lived in Hampshire, serving on the commission of the peace from about 1579 until his death. He set up home with Mary in Winchester, where he had a house in Chesil Street, was recorder from 1582, and represented the borough in parliament two years later; but in the early 1580s he bought the manor of North Baddesley, and somewhat later settled at Stoneham Park in the same county. He was to serve in seven parliaments between 1584 and 1604, for three Hampshire constituencies. Little is known of his parliamentary career, save that he helped to promote the Charitable Uses Act of 1601.

In 1590, three years after his election to the bench of Lincoln's Inn, Fleming delivered a reading on the statute of 1540 concerning the execution of debts (32 Hen. VIII c. 5); several copies of it survive. The eloquent prefatory speech began, 'Of all living creatures that God hath created there is none that hath more need of help one of another than man hath of man' (Baker, *Readers and Readings*, 577). He delivered a second reading in 1594, when he took the coif, and became recorder of London the same year. The patrons at his serjeant's creation ceremony were John Whitgift, archbishop of Canterbury, and Sir John Fortescue. In presenting the lord mayor of London in the exchequer

later in the year, he delivered a florid speech including the following remarks on judicial office:

> He that taketh upon him the office of a magistrate is like to a good man to whose custody a precious jewel is committed; he taketh it not to retain and challenge it for his own, nor to abuse it while he hath it, but safely to keep, and faithfully to render it to him that deposed it when he shall be required. He must do all things not for his private lucre, but for the public's good preservation and safe custody of those committed to his charge, that he may restore them to him that credited in a better and more happy state, it may be, than he received them. (Nichols, 3.254)

Only one year later Fleming was dispensed from the coif by patent in order to become solicitor-general, in succession to Sir Edward Coke and over the head of Francis Bacon, giving up the recordship of London at the same time. Returning to Lincoln's Inn, he served as its treasurer from 1595 to 1596. In 1601 he was appointed recorder of Southampton, though pressure of work compelled him to resign in 1603. As a law officer he was engaged in several treason prosecutions, including those against the Essex conspirators in 1601, and in the proceedings for blasphemy against the Jesuit John Gerard in 1597.

On the accession of James I, Fleming was reappointed solicitor-general and knighted, and on 27 October 1604 raised to the bench as chief baron of the exchequer. His most important judgment was that given in *Bates's case* (1605), concerning impositions, in which he supported—with some qualifications—the prerogative of the crown to impose customs: an opinion severely criticized by Hakewill and Whitelocke in the parliament of 1610, and by Coke in his *Second Institute*. On 25 June 1607 Fleming was promoted to be chief justice of the king's bench. After six years in that office, in Trinity term 1613 he was taken ill in the exchequer chamber during argument in the case of *Sutton's Hospital*, and on 7 August 1613 he died at Stoneham Park. According to Foster, he was created MA by the convocation of Oxford University on the day he died. There is an effigy in judicial robes in North Stoneham church, where he was buried.

Fleming did not leave much of a mark on the law, nor much of a stain. Campbell, with characteristic disregard for evidence, dismissed him as a 'poor creature' (Campbell, 1.237). But Bacon, even when his hopes of the solicitorship were defeated by Fleming in 1594, acknowledged that he was an 'able man' (Spedding, 1.365, 369), while Coke, who knew him intimately, said he had discharged all his offices 'with great judgment, integrity and discretion' and praised his 'sociable and placable nature and disposition' (Coke, 10.34). The latter judgement is borne out by his patronage of a bowling club at East Standen on the Isle of Wight, founded in 1609, and by the fact that he had been entertaining his tenantry on the day he died. According to the inscription on the monument, eight of fifteen children survived him. His descendants in the female line remained at Stoneham until the twentieth century. J. H. BAKER

Sources HoP, *Commons, 1558–1603*, 2.139–40 · B. B. Woodward, T. C. Wilks, and C. Lockhart, *A general history of Hampshire*, 3 vols.

[1861–9], vol. 2, pp. 110–12 • Baker, *Serjeants* • J. H. Baker, *Readers and readings in the inns of court and chancery*, SeldS, suppl. ser., 13 (2000) • Sainty, *King's counsel*, 61 • Sainty, *Judges*, 10, 95 • inquisition post mortem, PRO, C142/337/105 • *DNB* • J. F. Fraser, ed., *The tenth part of the reports of Sir Edward Coke* (1826) [10 Co Rep] • R. Strong, *Tudor and Jacobean portraits*, 2 vols. (1969) • J. Nichols, *The progresses and public processions of Queen Elizabeth*, new edn, 3 (1823), 254 • John, Lord Campbell, *The lives of the chief justices of England*, 3 vols. (1849–57) • Foster, *Alum. Oxon.* • *The letters and life of Francis Bacon*, ed. J. Spedding, 7 vols. (1861–74), vol. 1, pp. 365, 369 • monument, North Stoneham church, Hampshire

Likenesses oils, 1596, NPG [*see illus.*] • oils, 1608; Sotheby's, 6 July 1977, lot 5 • oils, 1609 • alabaster effigy, *c.*1613, North Stoneham church, Hampshire

Fleming, Thomas (1591/2–1651), Roman Catholic archbishop of Dublin, was probably born at Slane Castle, co. Meath, the third son of William Fleming, eleventh Baron Slane (1556/7–1611), and his wife, Eleanor (*d.* 1616), daughter and coheir of Thomas Fleming, tenth Baron Slane, and his wife, Catherine. He had three brothers: Christopher, the eldest, George, and James, and together with them he probably received his early education at home in Slane Castle. The Flemings of Slane were one of the most devoutly Catholic Old English aristocratic families of the pale with strong links to the observant Franciscans. Thomas Fleming himself entered the order in St Anthony's College, Louvain, on 19 April 1612, took minor orders on 1 April 1616, became a deacon on 28 May of the same year, and was ordained a priest on 31 March 1618. His nephew, also called Thomas, the heir to the barony, ultimately renounced the title in favour of his younger brother William and followed his uncle into the Franciscan order.

Fleming was a student both at Douai, where he probably completed a course in philosophy, and at the University of Louvain, where he evidently concentrated on theology to a greater extent. He ultimately lectured in both subjects at St Anthony's College and also seems to have lectured in Thomist philosophy in Cologne. It is likely, therefore, that he obtained at least a doctorate in divinity at Louvain, where he also acted as the guardian of St Anthony's. On 23 October 1623 he was made archbishop of Dublin and primate of Ireland and was consecrated two months later on 31 December, when he was aged thirty-one. This appointment was part of a pattern of episcopal provisions to sees in mostly Old English areas of Ireland which had been recommended by the exiled archbishop of Armagh, Peter Lombard, and which was intended to introduce a supply of relatively young residential Catholic bishops into Ireland, while creating the least amount of anxiety possible for the government. Fleming was the sixth such provision since 1618 and he embraced the responsibility with considerable reluctance. He was to become a well respected figure within the hierarchy, moderate in disposition but tenacious in his obedience to Roman authority. He was also strongly patriotic and this was reflected in his interest in Franciscan historical scholarship. He provided support both to the *Acta sanctorum* and to the annals of the four masters.

On his return to Ireland in 1625 Fleming seems to have lived with kin and friends in various houses within his diocese. Given the illegal nature of the Catholic church in Ireland, he was undoubtedly lucky that his aristocratic birth provided him with a network of wealthy and influential connections which enabled him to support the episcopal dignity with greater ease than many of his colleagues in the Irish hierarchy. As both a bishop and a Franciscan, however, Fleming rapidly found himself in the cockpit of a prolonged and often vicious conflict between members of the regular and the secular clergy which occurred in Ireland during the 1620s and 1630s. He was particularly unfortunate in that one of the most aggressive participants in these disputes, Paul Harris, was a priest in his own diocese. Harris, as well as denouncing Fleming in print, also lent support to two other priests, Luke Rochford and Patrick Cahill, against the archbishop's attempts to establish his authority. As a result one of Fleming's nominees to a Dublin parish was imprisoned and he himself ran the risk of being subjected to similar proceedings. In that context it was hardly surprising that in 1635 the bishop of Meath, Thomas Dease, was extremely reluctant to act on instructions from Rome to assist Fleming in disciplining Harris.

The outbreak of the Irish rising of 1641 had a massive effect on Fleming's life. He was represented by his procurator, Joseph Everard, at the synod of Catholic clergy in Kilkenny in May 1642 which effectively inaugurated the confederate Catholic association. Following the first general assembly of the association in October of that year he was elected to the supreme council of the confederates and served also on the next four councils until the Ormond peace of 1646. He was now a permanent exile from his diocese, which lay outside confederate quarters. In summer 1644 he was the solitary clergyman appointed by the general assembly to continue peace negotiations with Ormond. This aroused Ormond's strong opposition, not to Fleming personally, whom he accepted as an excellent choice, but because he was unwilling to treat with any of the Catholic clergy. The assembly, however, stood firm on his presence in the delegation although it remains doubtful whether he actually participated in any face to face meetings with the lord lieutenant.

Fleming was present at the meeting of the Catholic congregation in May 1645 which mandated as an essential part of any agreement the retention of the churches and the church livings by the Catholic party. Indeed, his vicar-general in Dublin, Edmund O'Reilly, was one of the theologians who prepared the most categorical statement in this respect. On 20 December 1645 Fleming was the first Irish signatory to a secret article prepared by the papal nuncio, Giovanni Battista Rinuccini, denouncing the proposed Ormond peace. When that peace was eventually rejected by the legatine synod of the Catholic clergy in August 1646 Fleming, who had himself convened a council of his metropolitan province during the previous May, was one of the group of eight clerics to which the authority of the synod was delegated to determine future action. He was not, however, a member of the supreme council created by the clergy in September 1646, his position as the prelate from the Dublin metropolitan province being taken by his suffragan and the rising star of the Irish hierarchy, Nicholas French, the bishop of Ferns. Neither was he selected as a councillor after the first general assembly of 1647 and he was not a resident but a supernumerary after the second assembly of that year. Fleming's absence from these councils can probably be attributed to a consciousness of failing powers. He had already requested the appointment of a coadjutor to assist him with his episcopal duties and his extreme corpulence evidently curtailed his activity and his enthusiasm.

The absence of French in Rome was in all probability one of the reasons for Fleming's greater activity in 1648. He signed the clerical denunciation of the Inchiquin truce in April of that year and was one of the four prelates deputized to confer with Rinuccini in the name of the clergy as a whole concerning any further action. In the event he was not present when the nuncio elected to censure the truce. Fleming may not have been particularly convinced concerning the wisdom of Rinuccini's actions but he loyally aligned himself with the nuncio, although he was unable to publish the censure within his own diocese which was under parliamentary control. He did not attend the general assembly which ultimately accepted the second Ormond peace in January 1649. Nevertheless in December he joined with Catholic prelates in Clonmacnoise to urge resistance to Cromwell and support for Ormond and the king. The lord lieutenant's helplessness in the face of the conquest however rapidly soured the attitudes of the Catholic hierarchy. In August 1651 they met in Jamestown in Leitrim and declared that he was no longer acceptable to Catholics as a leader in the war. Fleming was not present at this meeting, where the bishop of Ferns discharged the duty as his procurator, because he had died in Galway on 2 August and was probably buried in that city.   TADHG Ó HANNRACHÁIN

Sources B. O'Ferrall and D. O'Connell, *Commentarius Rinuccinianus de sedis apostolicae legatione ad foederatos Hiberniae Catholicos per annos 1645–1649*, ed. J. Kavanagh, 6 vols., IMC (1932–49), vols. 1–4 • D. F. Cregan, 'The social and cultural background of a Counter-Reformation episcopate, 1618–60', *Studies in Irish history presented to R. Dudley Edwards*, ed. A. Cosgrove and D. McCartney (1979), 85–117 • P. F. Moran, *History of the Catholic archbishops of Dublin since the Reformation* (1864), 294–411, 434–8, 463–5 • J. Linchaeo [J. Lynch], *De praesulibus Hiberniae*, ed. J. F. O'Doherty, 2 vols., IMC (1944), vol. 1, pp. 143f., 321f., 357; vol. 2, p. 292 • B. Jennings, ed., *Wadding papers* (Dublin, 1953) • M. Ó Siochrú, *Confederate Ireland 1642–1649: a constitutional and political analysis* (Dublin, 1999), 74, 174, 215, 222, 226, 232 • B. Millett, *The Irish Franciscans, 1651–1664* (Rome, 1964) • *Fourth report*, HMC, 3 (1874), 603 • *Irish Ecclesiastical Record*, fifth ser., 76 (1951), 138 • *Analecta Hibernica*, 6 (1934), 113, 126, 186 • T. Bourke, *Hibernica dominica, sive, Historia provinciae ordinis praedicatorum* (1970), 817, 897 • GEC, *Peerage* • DNB
Archives Franciscan House of Studies, Killinery, corresp.

Fleming, Thomas [*name in religion* Placid] (**1642–1720**), abbot of Regensburg, descendant of the earls of Wigtown, was born on 5 October 1642 at Kirkoswald, Ayrshire. He was educated in Edinburgh as a protégé of Sir George Lockhart until, in 1662 or 1663, he joined the navy. About 1665, when he was in Dublin, he became a Catholic. Subsequently, on his way to France he was captured by Moorish

pirates but after a month was freed by Spaniards. He was in the Scots College, Paris, for a time in 1667 and 1668 and from there went to the Scots Benedictine abbey at Regensburg.

Fleming received the monastic habit on 21 November 1668, taking the religious name Placid, and a year later, on 21 November 1669, made his vows. On 28 March 1671 he was ordained priest. On 5 December 1672, when just turned thirty, he was elected abbot of Regensburg, which also brought him control of the sister house at Erfurt. He was to hold the office for forty-seven years, working ceaselessly and single-mindedly, and transforming the entire situation of his community.

In 1672 the monastery was in a lamentable state, with an absentee abbot, the coffers empty, and only three professed monks in residence. Fleming began at once to improve the finances, tackling problems and defaulters with energy. At once he established relations with rulers and officials in church and state who could help him and protect the abbey. The British and French envoys to the imperial diet in Regensburg relied on his help and advice.

At Erfurt, where he appointed a prior answerable to himself, Fleming repaired and extended the buildings and secured two chairs of philosophy in the university to be held always by Scots monks. His greatest achievement, however, was to establish a seminary for Scots students in his own abbey. Finally opened in 1718 after thirty years of tireless lobbying and begging, it ensured a supply of novices and thus of missionary priests for Scotland.

In 1686 Fleming was the prime candidate to be bishop in Scotland but he firmly declined, seeing the Regensburg Abbey as his life's work. He died on 8 January 1720 at the abbey and was buried in the abbey church or cloister. When he died the monastic community and the Erfurt house were flourishing and twenty-eight students had entered the seminary. The results of his work endured: Scottish monks of Regensburg and Erfurt during the eighteenth century contributed significantly to the Scottish mission and to the cultural life of Germany.

MARK DILWORTH

Sources L. Hammermayer, 'Placidus Fleming (1642–1720)', *Lebensbilder aus der Geschichte des Bistums Regensburg, Beiträge zur Geschichte des Bistums Regensburg*, 29 (1989), 315–39 • M. Dilworth, *The Scots in Franconia* (1974) • P. J. Anderson, ed., *Records of the Scots colleges at Douai, Rome, Madrid, Valladolid and Ratisbon*, New Spalding Club, 30 (1906) • M. Dilworth, 'Two necrologies of Scottish Benedictine abbeys in Germany', *Innes Review*, 9 (1958), 173–203
Archives PRO, diplomatic corresp.
Likenesses photograph, Scot. NPG • portrait, Seminar St Jakob, Regensburg

Flemming [Fleming], **Richard** (d. **1431**), bishop of Lincoln, belonged to the Fleming family of Wath upon Dearne, Yorkshire, although the precise affiliation is unclear. His sister, Cecilia, died *c.*1422 as wife of Sir Robert Waterton (d. 1423) (the Waterton connection providing an undercurrent of actual or potential patronage at several points in Flemming's career). Robert *Flemming, later dean of Lincoln, was his nephew. Probably born in the early 1380s, Richard Flemming was reportedly in his eighteenth year in 1403, when he received a papal dispensation to hold a benefice with cure of souls; he was also mentioned as an Oxford MA in that year, and was old enough to become a priest in 1406.

Oxford was the focus of Flemming's early career. He was associated with University and Queen's colleges, and hired a school from Exeter College in 1407–8. He was identified as a scholar of theology in 1408 and 1411, and as bachelor by March 1414, in which year he incepted for his doctorate. In 1407–8 he was the university's northern proctor, and its envoy seeking support from the chapter of York Minster in the continuing conflicts with the townspeople of Oxford. Thomas Gascoigne, to whom Flemming was *episcopus famosus*, records him as an academic innovator, whose new method of disputation was still followed in Oxford in the mid-fifteenth century, and was a suitable basis for sermon construction.

Academic progress was matched by clerical advancement. Ordained acolyte and subdeacon on 22 December 1403 in Lincoln diocese, Flemming was priested on 16 December 1406, at London. His first known benefice, Slaidburn rectory in York diocese, had been acquired in November 1403. Other rectories followed, plus prebends in York and Lincoln.

On 20 November 1419 Flemming was appointed bishop of Lincoln by papal provision, following Philip Repingdon's resignation, and was consecrated at Florence on 28 April 1420. He received the temporalities on 23 May, spiritualities being granted following a profession of obedience made by proxy on the following day. (Archbishop Henry Chichele protested against the profession being made by proxy, lest it establish a precedent: Flemming repeated the profession in person on 1 December.) His diocesan administration was soon established, and Flemming was back in England by late June. His formal enthronement, attended by Henry V, was delayed until April 1421. His inheritance from Repingdon included the burden of an annual pension of 500 marks for his episcopal predecessor (presumably paid until Repingdon's death in 1424), and a cathedral chapter riven by discord between Dean John Macworth and the canons. He tried to resolve the latter by arbitration immediately after his enthronement, on 15 April 1421, but the resolution proved short-lived.

This first tenure of Lincoln was brief, although during it Flemming appears as a reasonably active bishop. Following the death in 1423 of Archbishop Henry Bowet of York, Pope Martin V on his own initiative provided Flemming to the archbishopric on 14 February 1424, quashing the election of Philip Morgan (bishop of Worcester). This was apparently done without consulting the English government, or perhaps even Flemming himself. (Flemming was then at the Council of Pavia–Siena, and immediately began to use the title of archbishop-elect and primate of England.) Flemming's Lincoln administration was supplanted by a *sede vacante* administration in June. The council that governed England during the minority of Henry VI would not permit the translation, invoking the Statute of Provisors and apparently issuing a writ of *praemunire*. York

and Lincoln were, however, technically vacant, the Lincoln temporalities having been seized by the crown. A solution was arranged at a council meeting on 21 October 1424. Flemming would withdraw all claims to York, support Philip Morgan's aspirations, and use his curial contacts to support Duke Humphrey of Gloucester (presumably in the dispute over the status of his marriage to Jacqueline of Hainault). Flemming would return to Lincoln (receiving the temporalities from the date of the appropriate papal bulls), the threats of the statutes would be withdrawn, and a formal pardon would be issued at the next parliament.

Despite this agreement the bull returning him to Lincoln was not issued until 20 July 1425, and did not end Flemming's difficulties. The vacancy administration functioned in Lincoln until late 1425. Restoration of spiritualities was delayed until early in 1426. The government still considered the see vacant, addressing summonses to parliament to a custodian of spiritualities. Desperate, Flemming petitioned parliament in 1426 for restoration of his temporalities, because of his dire financial straits. He had to wait until 3 August for the grant. Why Flemming's promotion to York was rejected is unclear, but in 1422–3 rumours were reportedly circulating in his diocese that he had recently fallen foul of the government, and been condemned for treason and imprisoned in the Tower of London. From the evidence of his register (admittedly incomplete), his second tenure of Lincoln was generally uneventful.

Flemming was closely involved in the contemporary difficulties produced by heresy and the great schism. He was an opponent of Wycliffism, although in autumn of 1409 he came under suspicion for a proposition in a theological disputation that reputedly savoured of heresy, and was duly referred to the committee of twelve recently appointed by Canterbury convocation (at the instigation of Archbishop Thomas Arundel) to restrain alleged heretical tendencies among Oxford's academics. He appealed against that committee to the wider regent body, and, when nothing was done, to the king. Archbishop Arundel became involved, delivering a verbal lashing, but the matter apparently subsided inconclusively after referral to another committee of eight. Flemming soon established his anti-heretical credentials, being on the university committee that in 1411 identified 267 errors in Wyclif's writings, and his orthodox standing was confirmed in March 1413, when Bishop Repingdon of Lincoln commissioned him to examine and license preachers within the University of Oxford.

From early 1417 Flemming acted on a wider stage, at the Council of Constance. Although officially a representative of Oxford University, he acted unofficially for Henry V. Six of his sermons have been identified, dating from 6 January (for which day two sermons survive) to 2 October 1417. Those of 21 June, 9 September, and 2 October were primarily funeral eulogies, for William Corfe (another member of the English group at Constance), Robert Hallum, bishop of Salisbury, and Cardinal Francisco Zabarella. Those for Epiphany and Passion Sunday (28 March) dealt primarily with the state of the church, including passionate calls for reform. The sermon of 9 September was particularly important, signalling a change in English policy, which had previously supported the emperor-elect, Sigismund, and calls for reform before a papal election; the new policy advocated adoption of reforms already agreed and a speedy papal election.

Following Martin V's election in November 1417 Flemming became a papal chamberlain. On 31 January 1418 the pope nominated him as envoy to England, presumably for negotiations on the English concordat. He was back at the curia by late August 1419, being involved in discussions about the promotion of John Langdon to the see of Lisieux. Diplomatic activity continued after his appointment to Lincoln. On 18 February 1421, following the treaty of Troyes, Henry V mandated him and Thomas Polton to receive the fealty of Normans and French at the curia; but there is no evidence that he went. Nor, apparently, did he respond to a papal summons to the curia on 6 November 1421. However, he was absent from his diocese from February to October 1422, as English envoy to Sigismund and the German princes to seek military assistance in the conquest of France. He was present at the Reichstag at Nuremberg from July, but the mission proved abortive. By the time he returned to England Henry V was dead.

Flemming again left England in March 1423, to attend the Council of Pavia–Siena. There he was president of the English nation, preaching to the assembly on 21 July 1423 and 23 January 1424. The latter oration was a notable defence of papal immunity from conciliar judgment save in cases of heresy, schism, and (perhaps) notorious crimes. From November 1423 to March 1424 he forcefully defended English claims to independent representation, against challenges from the French, Scots, and Spanish. His promotion to York was presumably intended to reward his papalist stance at the council. Precisely when he returned to England is not recorded, although he was still *in remotis* in May 1424.

Academic interests and a concern with heresy were major features of Flemming's episcopate. The evidence for heresy in his diocese is minimal, although some Lollard activity may be suspected. Presumably his activity as diocesan is obscured by the loss of appropriate sources: when tried in 1428 Richard Monk admitted he had earlier been arraigned before Flemming. Outside his diocese Flemming participated in the trial of William Taylor in February 1423, both as one of the panel of judges, and as a witness. He was involved in other heresy trials in 1428. In the most notorious action of his pontificate, in the spring of 1428, Flemming at last implemented the sentence proclaimed at the Council of Constance on 4 May 1415, and had the supposed remains of John Wyclif (d. 1384) disinterred from Lutterworth churchyard, burnt, and thrown into a nearby river.

Less controversial was his foundation of a new college at Oxford. On 13 October 1427 Flemming received royal licence to unite the Oxford parishes of All Saints, St Michael Northgate, and St Mildred, as the basis for the erection of 'the College of St Mary and All Saints, Lincoln'.

The union was actually implemented in April 1429, the foundation charter following on 19 December. Intended as a small foundation, it was explicitly a theological college (as Flemming's preface for the intended statutes explained), established as a bulwark against heresy. The foundation remained incomplete at Flemming's death; although statutes had been envisaged they had not been formally issued. He gave several books to the infant body, some of which are still in the college library. Among those known, theological texts predominate, including biblical glosses, Thomas Netter's *Doctrinale fidei catholicae* (significant for its anti-Wycliffite stance), and works by Aquinas and Bede. Other known volumes include works by Cicero and Horace. In the late 1420s he also planned to convert Boston church (where he had been rector) into a collegiate body. Draft royal letters patent were approved following an undated parliamentary petition; but seemingly nothing came of the proposal. Of his writings little record remains. Some of his sermons preached at the councils have been identified and edited; but the *Super Angliae etymologia* ascribed to him by Bale has not survived.

Flemming died at his episcopal residence at Sleaford on 25 January 1431. He was buried in Lincoln Cathedral, in a chantry chapel which he had constructed on the north side of the choir. The chapel and his tomb, with its double effigy of cadaver and vested bishop, still exist. His epitaph—which he had supposedly written himself—has disappeared from the structure, but was recorded by Anthony Wood in the seventeenth century. It had previously provided the basis for verses in praise of Flemming by a Carthusian monk.   R. N. Swanson

Sources *Snappe's formulary and other records*, ed. H. E. Salter, OHS, 80 (1924) · episcopal register XVI, Lincs. Arch., Lincoln diocesan archives [the first volume of a projected calendar of this register appeared as CYS, 73 (1984), ed. N. H. Bennett] · E. F. Jacob, ed., *The register of Henry Chichele, archbishop of Canterbury, 1414–1443*, 4 vols., CYS, 42, 45–7 (1937–47) · R. G. Davies, 'Martin V and the English episcopate', *EngHR*, 92 (1977), 309–44 · T. E. Morrissey, 'Surge, illuminare: a lost address by Richard Fleming at the Council of Constance [Clm 28433]', *Annuarium Historiae Conciliorum*, 22 (1990), 86–130 · W. Brandmüller, *Das Konzil von Pavia–Siena, 1423–1424*, 2 vols. (1968–74) · V. Mudroch, 'John Wyclif and Richard Flemyng, bishop of Lincoln: gleanings from German sources', *BIHR*, 37 (1964), 239–45 · W. K. Martin, *A history of the ancient parish of Wath-upon-Dearne, South Yorks.* (1920) · H. A. Hall, 'Some notes on the personal and family history of Robert Waterton, of Methley and Waterton', *Publications of the Thoresby Society*, 15 (1909), 81–102 · Emden, *Oxf.*, 2.697–9
Archives Lincs. Arch., episcopal register XVI
Likenesses oils, *c.*1638, Lincoln College, Oxford · J. Faber sen., mezzotint, BM, NPG · tomb effigy, Lincoln Cathedral

Flemming, Robert (1416–1483), ecclesiastic and humanist, was born in the diocese of York, probably the illegitimate son of Robert Flemming, esquire, of Wath, near Ripon (d. 1459); his uncle Richard *Flemming (d. 1431) was bishop of Lincoln, while his aunt Cecily (Cecilia) in 1407 married Robert Waterton, Henry IV's esquire and right-hand man. The fervent Lancastrianism of his family, and the bishop of Lincoln's standing in the church, determined Flemming's career. Bishop Richard obtained a papal dispensation, dated 20 January 1427, for his nephew to hold from his twelfth birthday a canonry and subdiaconal prebend at Lincoln Cathedral. On 2 April 1428 he was installed by proxy as prebendary of Farndon-cum-Balderton; two years later he transferred to Milton Ecclesia; in 1467 that was exchanged for Leighton Manor, and in 1478 this in its turn for Leighton Buzzard, still held at his death. From 1438 he held various benefices which, with the prebend, both funded his academic career and enabled him to form an exceptional library of mainly humanistic manuscripts and printed books.

During the year 1428–9 Flemming shared a room with one John Flemming as a commoner at University College, Oxford, as he did for the next two years. But from 1431–2 he rented there independently. By 1437–8 he had graduated MA at Oxford, and the next year was the university's junior proctor. Proceeding to holy orders (acolyte on 19 February 1439, he was ordained priest on 21 May 1440), he studied theology at University College until the summer of 1443, having become rector of the family living of Methley on 3 January that year. In the year of account which began on 12 April 1444, however, he rented his room in University College for only one term, a change doubtless dictated by his departure for the University of Cologne, a centre of theological excellence, where he matriculated some time between 28 June and 9 October following. By late January 1446 Flemming had left Cologne for the studium of Padua, receiving its BTh degree the following 4 September. His humanistic studies at this time are attested by his transcription in italic of Cicero's *De officiis*, an interest that probably motivated his move to Padua. Indeed the bent of his studies suggests that he already aspired to a career of royal service at the papal curia. Hearing Guarino da Verona lecture at Padua inspired Flemming to follow the master to the studium of Ferrara, where from 1447 to 1450 he attended Guarino's lectures and learned Greek; his personal Latin–Greek dictionary was known to Leland.

By October 1450 Flemming was back in England, and on 12 January 1452 he was collated by the archbishop of Canterbury to the vacant deanery of Lincoln; at the king's petition a papal dispensation of 3 February enabled him to hold three incompatible benefices, as against the two already dispensed. By February 1453 he was one of Henry VI's chaplains, essentially an honorific appointment, which he probably retained until Henry's deposition in 1461.

Lodovico Carbone's funeral oration for Guarino in 1460 claimed that it was humanistic learning that brought Flemming royal recognition, though his family's loyalty to the Lancastrian cause should not be overlooked. A commission dated 18 March 1455 named him royal proctor at the papal curia, with responsibility for ensuring that royal appointments to benefices and ecclesiastical offices were approved; he was reappointed on 4 February 1456. Though replaced as proctor by December 1456, Flemming remained in Rome, and a special commission dated 5 August 1457 appointed him and two English nobles (who were to join him) to renew the king's obedience to Pope Calixtus III—Flemming's humanistic learning meant that he was ideal for delivering orations.

The election of Pope Pius II in August 1458 led to Flemming's being appointed an apostolic protonotary the following 9 October. This position, which involved helping to draft provisions relating to higher appointments, was only conferred on those whose Latin proficiency was exceptional, and gave its holder considerable influence. Unsurprisingly, Flemming was again named as royal proctor in late October. Following the new pope's call for a crusade to recover Byzantium, Flemming was appointed one of the English envoys to attend the diet summoned to meet at Mantua on 1 June 1459. In spite of the outbreak of civil war in England in September, Flemming, with his fellow envoy Henry Sharp, travelled from Rome to Mantua, arriving there shortly before 7 September; the pope, deeming this contingent unworthy, refused to receive it. Out of favour in Rome, Flemming decided to return home the following spring, under a safe conduct issued on 26 April 1460. His family's Lancastrian associations meant that his royal appointments ceased at Edward IV's accession. Though dean of Lincoln, Flemming withdrew to University College, Oxford, presumably to continue his studies; perhaps there was friction with his bishop, John Chedworth, an outstanding diocesan, to whom Flemming's absenteeism was doubtless objectionable. In 1465 Flemming donated thirty-six manuscripts of classical and humanistic texts to Lincoln College, Oxford, founded by his uncle in 1427.

Flemming returned to Rome in 1473, probably at the invitation of Pope Sixtus IV (r. 1471–84), who made him a Lateran count palatine (with the right to legitimize bastards and create notaries and doctors). He studied in the Vatican Library, becoming a friend of its librarian, Platina, and probably acted at the curia as apostolic protonotary. In 1473 he began a neo-Latin hexameter poem in two books, *Tiburtinae lucubrationes*, in the pope's praise. Seemingly in England again by early 1474, functioning as dean of Lincoln, he stayed there until at least the summer of 1475 before returning to Rome. There his now-finished poem (differences in style suggest the two books were completed some years apart), whose Latin was exceptional for an Englishman, was printed by an 'English protonotary', with the colophon date 5 December 1477, almost certainly at the author's expense. Fourteen lines of the poem laud Edward IV and perhaps a presentation copy was sent to him, for one (now in the Bodleian Library, Oxford) was certainly given to Thomas Rotherham, Yorkist bishop of Lincoln from 1472—Roman-style decoration incorporating Rotherham's arms enhances the copy.

Back in Lincoln in 1478, Flemming finally returned to his duties as dean there, his influence with the papal curia bringing its reward in a large number of dispensations granted to the cathedral by Sixtus IV. Flemming died at Lincoln on 12 August 1483, destined for burial in the chapel and chantry on the north side of the cathedral's 'angel choir' that he had founded by the terms of his will for the souls of Bishop Richard and others, himself included. However in 1625 his tomb was reported to be beside that of his uncle, high in the wall of the cathedral's north aisle. His will, proved on 23 August, also left his extensive library to Lincoln College, Oxford, where many items remain in the library, stamped with his coat of arms. Leland mentions now lost works of his, including *carmina* and Latin letters.   CECIL H. CLOUGH

Sources Emden, *Oxf.*, 2.699–700 · R. Weiss, *Humanism in England during the fifteenth century*, 3rd edn (1967), 97–105, 191 · J. W. Walker, 'The Burghs of Cambridgeshire and Yorkshire and the Watertons of Lincolnshire and Yorkshire', *Yorkshire Archaeological Journal*, 30 (1930–31), 311–419, esp. 368–86 · *Fasti Angl., 1300–1541*, [Lincoln], 4, 66, 81, 84, 92 · J. Ferguson, *English diplomacy, 1422–1461* (1972), 142 (n. 6), 143, 151–2, 215 · M. Harvey, *England, Rome, and the papacy, 1417–1464* (1993), 10, 15, 29, 40–41, 196 · *CPR, 1452–61*, 227, 336, 424, 487 · C. W. Foster and A. H. Thompson, eds., 'The chantry certificates for Lincoln and Lincolnshire returned in 1548', *Reports and papers read at the meetings of the architectural societies … during the year 1921* (1922), 227 · *Commentarii de scriptoribus Britannicis, auctore Joanne Lelando*, ed. A. Hall, 2 (1709), 460–61, 486 · V. Green, *The commonwealth of Lincoln College, 1427–1977* (1979), 34–6, 49, 673–4 · A. C. de la Mare, 'Vespasiano da Bisticci and the Florentine manuscripts of Robert Flemmying in Lincoln College', *Lincoln College Record, 1962–63* (1963), 7–16 · F. Cairns, 'The *Lucubratiunculae Tiburtinae* of Robert Flemming (1477)', *Humanistica Lovaniensia*, 39 (1990), 54–66 · V. Pacifici, ed., *Un carme biografico di Sisto IV del 1477* (Tivoli, 1921) · *Account rolls of University College, Oxford*, ed. A. D. M. Cox and R. H. Darwall-Smith, 2 vols., Oxford Historical Society, 39–40 (1999–2001) · H. Keussen, *Die Matrikel der Universität Köln, 1389–1559*, 1 (1892), 361
Archives Lincoln College, Oxford, his library and papers

Flemyng, Malcolm (*c.*1700–1764), physiologist and writer, was born in Scotland. Nothing is known of his family, childhood, or early education. He was a pupil of Alexander Monro primus (1697–1767), the first professor of anatomy at the University of Edinburgh, and, from 1723 to 1724, heard lectures given by Hermann Boerhaave (1668–1738) of the University of Leiden. In correspondence with Albrecht von Haller (1708–1777), whom he may have met at Leiden, Flemyng described Boerhaave as 'mihi supra fidem amicus et beneficus' ('an incredible friend and benefactor to me'; *Epistolarum*, 10). On his return about 1724 or 1725, he practised in Scotland, but by 1738 at the latest had moved to Hull and at some stage acquired a wife and three children. Nothing is known about them. To avoid the ill health and excessive horse-riding provoked by country practice, in 1751 Flemyng moved to London to support his family by lecturing in physiology. Perhaps inspired by Monro, Flemyng reluctantly delivered lectures in English rather than Latin in order to attract pupils who had not been to universities and therefore had no Latin. He published a syllabus in 1752 and appears to have read one course of lectures; these provided the basis for his *Introduction to Physiology* (1759). Private medical lecturing in London was common in the period, especially in anatomy, but Flemyng was highly unusual in his choice of subject; no other lecturer taught physiology exclusively.

Within his modest and varied output, Flemyng is typical of the new breed of Enlightened medical practitioners that emerged in this period. His *Introduction to Physiology* was an accessible, thorough, and up-to-date course of lectures that used the latest authorities. Other physiological publications include *The Nature of the Nervous Fluid, or, Animal Spirits* of 1751, which engaged with Haller's work, a

paper on amniotic fluid in the foetus (1755), and a small work on respiration (1762). Yet he also wrote on nervous diseases, diagnostics, therapeutics, and general health. In 1740 he published *Neuropathia*, a Latin poem and treatise on hysteria, which he dedicated to Peter Shaw, Bacon scholar and English translator of Boerhaave and Stahl. It was translated into Italian in 1755. In *A Proposal for the Improvement of the Practice of Medicine* of 1748, first privately printed in 1742 and dedicated to Richard Mead, he considered the treatment of scurvy, the amelioration of smallpox using Peruvian bark, a cure for drowning, and the concept of the 'panacea' with reference to Bishop Berkeley's tar-water. It is the work of an innovative, independent, and dedicated mind; he drew on a Norwegian manuscript for his opinions on drowning, among the first published on the subject in English. A paper on Francis Solano's views on the pulse emerged in 1753; *A Proposal to Diminish the Progress of the Distemper among the Horned Cattle* in 1754; a paper on 'the nature, causes and cure of Corpulency', delivered at the Royal Society in 1757, was published in 1760, the same year as his *Dissertation on Dr James's Fever Powder*, a balanced and courteous evaluation of a powerful and controversial antinomial.

The combination of his wife's ailing health, which had responded badly to London air, and, probably, inadequate demand for his lectures, led Flemyng to find a practice in Brigg, Lincolnshire, in 1752 or 1753. In a letter of 1753 he hinted at the possibility of teaching physiology in Oxford and Cambridge, but nothing appears to have come of it. He remained in Lincolnshire thereafter, and died there on 7 March 1764.   L. A. F. DAVIDSON

Sources *Epistolarum ab eruditus ad Alb. Hallerum Scriptorum, pars I, Latinae*, 3 (1774) · S. Lawrence, 'Science and medicine at the London hospitals', DPhil diss., University of Toronto, 1985, chap. 4 · M. Flemyng, *A proposal for the improvement of the practice of medicine*, 2nd edn (1748) · [M. Flemyng], *A new critical examination of an important passage in Mr Locke's essay* (1751) · A. Goldgar, *Impolite learning: conduct and community in the republic of letters, 1680–1750* (1995) · M. Flemyng, *A syllabus … of a course of lectures* (1752) · M. Flemyng, *Adhesions, or, Accretions of the lungs to the pleura* (1762) · *GM*, 1st ser., 34 (1764), 146 · *Neuropathia* (1740) · M. Flemyng, *The nature of the nervous fluid* (1751) [preface] · M. Flemyng, *A dissertation on Dr James's fever powder* (1760), 5–6
Archives BL, letters to Thomas Birch, Add. MS 4307

Fleta (*fl.* 1290–1300) is the name sometimes used to designate the author of a Latin treatise on English common law written between 1290 and 1300, which is entitled *Fleta* and which updates and abridges an earlier treatise (*De legibus et consuetudinibus Angliae*) ascribed to Henry of *Bratton (*d.* 1268). The author of *Fleta* drew together scattered passages from the Bratton treatise into a more coherent order, omitted many of its digressions and citations of cases, and incorporated provisions of the legislation of Edward I.

The text of *Fleta* begins: 'Actions are either personal, real, or mixed'. The arrangement of the treatise, in six books with 277 chapters, follows this classification. The structure derives from Bratton's division of all law into the law of persons, of things (*res*), and of actions, which in turn derives from the elementary work on Roman law, Justinian's *Institutes*. Books 1 and 2 cover personal actions, first with a section on the law of persons (villeinage, wardship, and marriage), next with one on criminal actions, and finally, in book 2, with one on civil actions arising from obligations of debt and the courts that determine them. Book 3 begins the treatment of real actions with a section on the law of things (acquisition by gift). Books 4 to 6 deal with the complex procedures used in real actions, first in actions to recover possession of one's own or one's ancestor's land, then in actions to determine the ultimate property or ownership of land. *Fleta* ends, as Bratton's treatise ends, in the middle of a technical exposition of proceedings on the writ of right.

The author of *Fleta* certainly had a copy of Bratton's treatise at hand, and seems to have had access also to texts of Roman law and canon law, particularly the papal decretals. At the end of book 2, after dealing with the legal procedure for making stewards and bailiffs account to their lords, the author incorporated portions of two treatises on estate management, Walter of Henley's *Husbandry* and the anonymous *Seneschaucy*. *Fleta*'s author also gave detailed accounts of the royal household and officers, evidently from personal acquaintance.

H. G. Richardson and G. O. Sayles, the editors of the treatise, put forward no candidate for the authorship of *Fleta*. The treatise takes its name from a statement in its preface that it 'might well be called *Fleta* because in *Fleta* it was written'. This has long been taken to mean that its author resided in the Fleet prison at the time of its composition. The statement could also refer to the brevity of the treatise, playing on the word 'fleet' (Anglo-Saxon *fléot*), meaning both 'swift' and 'a watercourse', a word found in various place names in England. Noel Denholm-Young and Paul Brand put forward the case for authorship by one Matthew of the Exchequer (Matthew de Scaccario or Matthew Cheker). Matthew had been a yeoman of the royal household and a lawyer of broad experience when, in 1290, he was convicted of forgery and committed to the Fleet prison for two years. The case is plausible but not conclusive.

Fleta is preserved complete in only one medieval manuscript (BL, Cotton MS Julius B.viii), which collates with just a few passages in another manuscript collection (BL, Cotton MS Nero D.vi). The lack of other surviving manuscripts has been taken to establish that *Fleta* was never widely read by medieval lawyers. The treatise known as *Britton*, based on *Fleta* but written in Anglo-Norman French, survives in dozens of manuscripts and was probably much better known among fourteenth-century lawyers. *Fleta* received renewed attention in the early seventeenth-century writings of Sir Edward Coke, who regarded it as a work of authority. It was first printed in 1647, along with a learned dissertation by the legal antiquary John Selden. This imperfect text was reprinted in 1685 with some corrections, and a better text of the first book was published anonymously by Sir Thomas Clarke in 1735. A definitive text of *Fleta* with a full translation, prepared by Richardson and Sayles, was published by the Selden Society in 1953–83.

DAVID J. SEIPP

Sources H. G. Richardson and G. O. Sayles, eds. and trans., *Fleta*, SeldS, 72, 89, 99 (1953–83) · *Joannis Seldeni ad Fletam dissertatio* (1647); repr. with additions D. Ogg (1925) · N. Denholm-Young, *Collected papers of N. Denholm-Young* (1969) · P. Brand, *The origins of the English legal profession* (1992) · T. F. T. Plucknett, *Early English legal literature* (1958)

Archives BL, Cotton MS Julius B.viii · BL, Cotton MS Nero D.vi

Fletcher, Abraham (1714–1793), teacher of mathematics and medical practitioner, was born on 1 November 1714 at Little Broughton, Bridekirk, Cumberland, the eldest of seven children of Joseph Fletcher, a tobacco-pipe maker, and his wife, Elizabeth Palmer. He was largely self-educated, though he is said to have attended the village school for some months. He was intended to practise in his father's trade which, combined with some land that the family had inherited, offered a meagre income. In 1735 he married Mary Peat; they had one son and five daughters. About 1744 he decided to set up as a mathematical schoolmaster; his school was apparently of some repute in the neighbourhood. He was also interested in medical botany, and built up a successful practice dispensing herbal remedies. He was said to be particularly skilled in the relief of hypochondria. He reportedly also dabbled in astrology but it is not clear if he ever practised it commercially. By the time of his death he was worth £4000, of which £3000 was the result of his own earnings. In 1752 he published a compendium of basic problems in arithmetic, geometry, and practical mathematics (2nd part, 1753). Though not a particularly distinguished work, it appears to have been moderately successful, going through four editions in his lifetime (4th edn, 1784). Fletcher died on 1 January 1793. He was survived by his wife.

JOSEPH GROSS

Sources W. Hutchinson, 'Life of Fletcher', in W. Hutchinson, *The history of the county of Cumberland*, 2 (1794), 324–6; facs. edn (1974) · R. V. Wallis and P. J. Wallis, eds., *Biobibliography of British mathematics and its applications*, 2 (1986)

Wealth at death £4000: Hutchinson, 'Life of Fletcher'

Fletcher, Alexander (1787–1860), minister of the United Presbyterian church, was born on 8 April 1787 at Bridge of Teith, near Doune, Perthshire, the son of William Fletcher, Burgher minister at Bridge of Teith, and his wife, Jean, sister of the Revd Michael Gilfillan. He was educated in the village of Doune and at Stirling high school. At the age of eleven he was sent to Glasgow College; he ultimately became MA of the University of Glasgow, and from there passed to the Divinity Hall in 1802. Having been received into the Associate Synod on 23 December 1806 he became co-pastor with his father at Bridge of Teith. In November 1811 he went to London as minister of Miles Lane Chapel, Meeting-House Yard, London Bridge. Here he very soon gained popularity as a preacher. The church accommodation became too limited, and the congregation erected a new place of worship in London Wall under the name of Albion Chapel, which was opened on 7 November 1816. This building cost more than £10,000 and soon became crowded. Here Fletcher began his annual Christmas sermon to the young, a practice he kept up with unabating success to the last. In April 1824 he was prosecuted in the civil and ecclesiastical courts in a breach of promise case with Miss Eliza Dick. In the king's bench no verdict was given, but in the meeting of the United Associate Synod at Edinburgh he was suspended from the exercise of his office and from church fellowship. The trial and suspension provoked a spate of publications, including Fletcher's own *Appeal to the Public Against the Associate Synod of Scotland* (1824) and *The Injustice of the United Associate Synod Exposed* (1825). The result was his separation from the Secession church. He moved with the greater part of his congregation to Grub Street, and afterwards to a new and spacious building in Finsbury Circus, an edifice which cost about £13,000 and was, at the time, the largest chapel in London. Here for thirty-five years he continued to minister with acceptance and success. He married, on 13 January 1846, Lydia, daughter of Richard Baynes of Rayne Lodge, Essex. Fletcher was honoured with the degree of DD from America, and after a long separation was again welcomed as a minister of the United Presbyterian church in 1849. His last sermon was preached to nearly 3000 children in Surrey Chapel in February 1860, and from that time he gradually declined in health.

Fletcher's fame rested on his talent in preaching to children, and on his *Family Devotions* (1834), of which 50,000 copies were sold in England, besides numerous editions in the United States. His other main writings were devotional literature aimed at young people; they included *Sabbath School Preacher and Juvenile Miscellany* (2 vols., 1848–50) and the incomplete *Closet Devotional Exercises for the Young* (1859). He also wrote many introductions to theological works. Fletcher died of bronchitis and dropsy at 4 Portland Place, Lower Clapton, London, on 30 September 1860, and was buried in Abney Park cemetery on 8 October in the presence of 6000 people.

G. C. BOASE, rev. I. T. FOSTER

Sources J. MacFarlane, *Altar-light: a tribute to the memory of the Rev. Alexander Fletcher* (1860) · W. Blair, *The prince of preachers: being a memorial of the late Rev. Alexander Fletcher, DD* (1860) · J. F. Waller, ed., *The imperial dictionary of universal biography*, 3 vols. (1857–63) · Allibone, *Dict.* · Boase, *Mod. Eng. biog.* · Irving, *Scots.* · *Record* (1 Oct 1860)
Archives DWL, letters | NL Scot., letters to Charles Mackie
Likenesses J. Cochran, stipple (after H. Room), BM, NPG · W. Ridley, stipple (after N. Branwhite), BM, NPG; repro. in *Evangelical Magazine* (1811) · J. Rogers, stipple (after T. Wageman), NPG · G. Stodart, stipple and line engraving (after photograph), NPG · portrait, repro. in *The Christian Cabinet Illustrated Almanack* (1860), 31 · ; oil copy, Congregational Centre, Castle Gate, Nottingham

Fletcher, Sir Andrew, of Innerpeffer, Lord Innerpeffer (d. 1650), judge, was the eldest son of Robert Fletcher (d. 1622) of Innerpeffer and Beucleo, Forfarshire, merchant and burgess of Dundee, and his wife, Margaret Hume (d. 1623). He married a daughter of Peter Hay of Kirkland of Megginch, brother to George Hay, first earl of Kinnoul, a marriage which produced two sons and one daughter. Appointed a JP for Forfarshire in 1623, he succeeded Sir John Wemyss of Craigtoun as an ordinary lord of session

on 18 December 1623, with the title of Lord Innerpeffer, and retained his seat in 1626 when many of the lords were displaced. In 1630 he was placed upon a commission upon Scots law, and in 1633 was a member of the parliamentary commissions to revise the acts and laws of Scotland with a view to constructing a code (a project which was not proceeded with) and to report upon the jurisdiction of the admiral and chamberlain. He was also ordered to examine Sir Thomas Craig's *Jus feudale*, with a view to its publication. On 22 September 1638 the privy council appointed him one of the commissioners for the sheriffdom of Forfar to enforce subscription to the 1580 confession of faith. He was employed in 1639 in regulating the fees of writers to the signet and others and parliament adopted the scales which he laid down. On 13 November 1641 he was reappointed as an ordinary lord of session by parliament. His appointment was objected to by John Moncrieff of that ilk, one of the two Perthshire MPs, on the grounds that Fletcher was incapacitated by having purchased lands which were the subject of litigation before him. The matter was referred to the privy council, and as he retained his seat the charge was presumably disproved. On 15 November 1641 he was appointed a commissioner for the plantation of kirks and valuation of teinds. About this time he was elected a member of parliament for Forfarshire, but his election was voided for illegality. He was elected president of the court of session in January 1642.

Fletcher was a member of the exchequer commissions appointed on 29 July 1644 and 1 February 1645, and of a financial parliamentary interval committee, the committee of common burdens of 25 July 1644. He was one of the MPs for Forfarshire in the final session (3 November 1646 to 27 March 1647) of the first triennial parliament and played an active role in committee. He was named to the procedural committee for bills, ratifications, and losses (10 November), financial committees dealing with the excise (3 December) and the exchequer (25 March), as well as the 1647 committee of estates (20 March) and commission for plantation of kirks and valuation of teinds (24 March). His political role during the session extended to sounding out the political pulse of the shire and burgh members for defence of the king. Despite reporting an initial overall majority of thirty for the king's interest to the marquess of Hamilton, his advice was not fully exploited and the king's cause was lost in parliament. He was one of thirteen MPs who voted against the parliamentary decision of 16 January 1647 that Charles I should be left at Newcastle by the Scottish army, under the jurisdiction of the English parliament. He was a member of the committee of war for Haddingtonshire in 1647 and 1648, and was politically active in the parliamentary session of 1648. During the session of 2 March to 11 May he was appointed to the committee for dangers, remedies, and duties (10 March), which 'was a "close committee for the greatest affaires"' (J. R. Young, 198). He also served on the committee for preventing dangers (17 March), the committee anent the desires of the commission of the kirk to the engagement (22 March), and the committee of estates (11 May). At the close of the June session he was again appointed to the committee of estates (9 June) and to the commission for plantation of kirks and valuation of teinds (10 June). He supported the engagement, for which he had subscribed £8500 Scots (repaid by order of parliament to his son Robert in 1662), and as a result was purged from his offices of ordinary lord of session and exchequer commissioner in 1649. He died at his house in Haddingtonshire in March 1650. His son Sir Robert Fletcher was father of Andrew *Fletcher of Saltoun.

J. A. HAMILTON, *rev.* JOHN R. YOUNG

Sources G. Brunton and D. Haig, *An historical account of the senators of the college of justice, from its institution in MDXXXII* (1832) • APS, 1625–41; 1643–60 • *The historical works of Sir James Balfour*, ed. J. Haig, 4 vols. (1824–5) • *Reg. PCS*, 2nd ser. • *The diary of Mr John Lamont of Newton, 1649–1671*, ed. G. R. Kinloch, Maitland Club, 7 (1830) • J. Gordon, *History of Scots affairs from 1637–1641*, ed. J. Robertson and G. Grub, 3 vols., Spalding Club, 1, 3, 5 (1841) • *The memoirs of Henry Guthry, late bishop*, 2nd edn (1747) • J. R. Young, *The Scottish parliament, 1639–1661: a political and constitutional analysis* (1996) • M. D. Young, ed., *The parliaments of Scotland: burgh and shire commissioners*, 2 vols. (1992–3)

Fletcher, Andrew, of Saltoun (1653?–1716), Scottish patriot, political theorist, and book collector, was most probably born at Saltoun, in Haddingtonshire; a gap in the parish register between 1647 and 1660 leaves the precise date unknown, but 1653 is supported by a family record, and is more probable than 1655. He was the eldest son of Sir Robert Fletcher of Saltoun (1625–1665) and of Katherine (*d.* 1713), daughter of Sir Henry Bruce of Clackmannan; he had three brothers, Henry, Robert, and John, of whom the last two died young. The family was well established and well connected. On his mother's side Andrew was descended from the Haldanes of Gleneagles and related to the Campbells of Glenorchy. The Fletchers themselves were descended from an old Yorkshire family, and Sir Robert belonged to the sixth generation of the Scottish branch. From Tweeddale the family had moved to Dundee and acquired lands in Angus, including the estate of Innerpeffer. Sir Robert's father, Sir Andrew Fletcher, had risen in royal service; he became a lord of session as Lord Innerpeffer in 1623, and married Beatrix Hay, daughter to Peter Hay of Megginch, brother of George Hay, first earl of Kinnoul and lord chancellor of Scotland. It was Sir Andrew who acquired the estate of Saltoun in 1643. His support for the engagement led not only to loss of office in 1649 but to heavy fines, and on succeeding in 1650 Sir Robert sold the lands in Angus to pay off his father's debts.

Education and early travels Andrew Fletcher's early education is often ascribed to Gilbert Burnet, minister of the parish of Saltoun, but since Burnet took up the position only in 1665, the previous incumbent, Patrick Scougall, minister from 1658 until his appointment as bishop of Aberdeen in 1664, is likely to have been a more important influence. Scougall was a friend and Burnet a younger protégé of Robert Leighton, spiritual leader of a group of latitudinarian clergy who were not averse to episcopacy but who valued piety before dogma. One of Burnet's first acts as minister of Saltoun was to compose a funeral sermon in memory of Sir Robert Fletcher, who died in January 1665; Sir Robert was held up as a model of lay piety and Stoic

Andrew Fletcher of Saltoun (1653?–1716), by William Aikman, *c.*1707

morals, with a laudable interest in natural philosophy. The paths of Gilbert Burnet and Andrew Fletcher crossed on several later occasions, and on his death in 1713 the bishop of Salisbury left a bequest to found a school at Saltoun. Nevertheless, it seems that Fletcher had greater respect for the less worldly Scougalls, Patrick and his son Henry (1650–1678), whom Andrew would have known as a boy at Saltoun.

Andrew Fletcher was returned heir to his father in August 1665. In February 1667 he matriculated at the University of St Andrews, almost certainly accompanied by his brother Henry, and was admitted to the bachelor class at St Leonard's College. The choice of university was most probably determined by family tradition. There is no direct evidence as to what he studied, but he would have consolidated his knowledge of Latin, and the bachelor class was meant to concentrate on logic and ethics. Neither Andrew nor Henry graduated, however, and by August 1668 Andrew had left for London, with James Graham as his governor.

By the end of the year Fletcher was in the Netherlands, and he may well have been out of Scotland continuously between 1668 and 1678. The evidence of bills and receipts places him in Paris in 1670, in The Hague and Rotterdam in the summer of 1671 but back in Paris by October, in Paris in 1672 and 1673, and again in 1675. In December 1675 he was in London, but he had returned to Paris by May 1676 and was apparently there continuously until the second half of 1677, when he returned to London. In the course of these travels he learned French and acquired an abiding taste for the life of those cities, by then the largest and most developed in Europe. Most of all he took the opportunity to buy books, combining with the dealer James Fall to scour the back streets of Paris in the search for second-hand bargains.

Opposition and exile, 1678–1689 Fletcher was back in Scotland by 1678, when he was chosen a commissioner for Haddingtonshire in the convention of estates which met in June. He immediately made a name for himself by siding with the duke of Hamilton in opposition to the duke of Lauderdale, the high commissioner and chief minister of Charles II in Scotland. In the first of many episodes of parliamentary outspokenness Fletcher responded to the imprisonment of his brother Henry for smuggling himself into the convention, by identifying one of the high commissioner's servants and forcing Lauderdale to plead privilege to justify his presence. Following the convention he was punished by having soldiers quartered on him, to which he responded by joining in a petition challenging the legality of the privy council's action. He was in trouble with the council again in 1680, for obstructing the implementation of the council's decision to raise and use the militia against presbyterian dissidents. Elected to the new estates in 1681, he was equally forward in opposition to the new high commissioner, the duke of Albany and York (the future James VII and II). John Lauder of Fountainhall reported that he circulated anonymous letters to other members encouraging opposition to the Act of Succession in favour of the duke of York. He also openly opposed the Test Act, alongside the earl of Argyll, Viscount Stair, and Bishop Patrick Scougall. A year later, in April 1682, he was again arraigned by the privy council, this time for obstructing the provisioning of soldiers quartered in Haddingtonshire. By May he was in London, and by November in The Hague. Before he left he made an arrangement with William Fletcher of New Cranston to act as his factor and lift his rents.

Although he was not formally charged with an offence that would have obliged him to flee, Fletcher had effectively made himself a political exile, joining Argyll, Stair, and others in the Scottish exile community in the Netherlands. He certainly did not confine himself to plotting, and immediately resumed contact with James Fall in Paris to obtain news of book prices. But Thomas Chudleigh, English envoy at The Hague, reported to the earl of Sunderland on 10/20 August 1683 that he had been a close companion of William Carstairs during his visit to the Netherlands in April of that year, and was likewise frequently with Stair. A similar envoy's report placed him in Paris in October. Whether he then returned to England at the end of the year to make contact with the remnants of the Rye House plotters is unclear. When Fletcher was charged with high treason in 1685, the libel initially mentioned his part in the conspiracy of 1683, and a century later the historian Sir John Dalrymple suggested that Fletcher had come from the Netherlands to establish connections between the English plotters and potential Scottish allies. At all events Fletcher was back in the Netherlands in 1684, and by the end of that year was in Brussels, where, according to a witness at his trial in 1685,

he was often seen dining with the duke of Monmouth. Described by another as 'of low stature and slender', marked by small 'pocks', and wearing a peruke, he evidently cut a distinctive figure (depositions of Anthony Buÿse and William Williams, 19 Aug and 18 Nov 1685, high court of justiciary, NA Scot., JC 39/67/3, 5).

Trusted by Monmouth, Fletcher was privy to the discussions which preceded the attempts by the earl of Argyll and the duke to raise rebellions against James in Scotland and in England in 1685. According to Burnet, Fletcher doubted the success of both schemes, but 'resolved to run fortunes' with Monmouth out of personal loyalty. To Lord Grey's argument that Henry VII had landed with a smaller number, Fletcher responded that he had been sure of several of the nobility, 'who were little princes in those days' (*Bishop Burnet's History*, 2.310–11). Witnesses identified Fletcher among those gathered at Monmouth's lodgings in Thomas Dare's house in Amsterdam immediately before the duke set out, and he evidently continued to be one of the duke's closest advisers after the landing at Lyme in May. But Fletcher's participation in the rebellion itself was short-lived. In an episode notorious in his own day, he shot Thomas Dare dead after the latter had upbraided him for taking his horse in order to lead a scouting party. What particularly provoked Fletcher was Dare's striking him with a cane. Dare may have affronted a gentleman, but Fletcher had almost certainly deprived the expedition of its banker as well as its most important local contact. (A goldsmith who had previously served as banker to a number of exiles, including John Locke, Dare had already persuaded a number of Taunton men to join the rebellion.)

Monmouth saw no alternative to Fletcher's quitting the expedition, and he sailed for Spain in one of the frigates that had brought them from the Netherlands. Having put in at Santander, the ship was impounded, and Fletcher imprisoned. By the next morning he had mysteriously escaped, leaving behind, as the English consul, William Frankland, reported to Sunderland in July/August, two portmanteaus containing several rich suits, holsters for a horse embroidered with gold and silk, and a substantial credit note from an Amsterdam merchant. According to a later family memoir, he travelled incognito in Spain, and subsequently enlisted in the imperial army in Hungary, then pressing the Turk back beyond Buda. Both stories have been repeated and embroidered by Fletcher's biographers, but no contemporary evidence has come to light to support either of them, and bills and receipts suggest that Fletcher was back in the Netherlands or in Cleves (using the name Ebron) by 1687 if not 1686. In the meantime he was tried for treason by the high court of justiciary in Edinburgh, and on 4 January 1686 was condemned to death, with forfeiture of his estates, which were granted to the earl of Dumbarton. A life of exile was now essential, and for the next two years Fletcher was, for the historian as well as the authorities, more elusive than ever.

By contrast with his leading role in the events of 1685, Fletcher seems to have played little part in planning the invasion of 1688. In October he showed Carstairs a letter from Sir James Stewart of Goodtrees, suggesting it be passed to William of Orange, but Stewart was compromised by his dealings with James, and if anything the episode indicates Fletcher's exclusion from William's inner circle. His passage to England was delayed, and he crossed after the main force. Even so, his personal preparations were as fastidious and unstinting as in 1685. Detailed instructions were given to Andrew Russell, the faithful and patient Scottish merchant in Rotterdam, for the storage of his tent and swords, two trunks, and a valise containing a quill, a bolster, and boot skins, and for the stabling of four horses—instructions which Russell was doubtless not surprised to find were accompanied by requests for additional credit. Fletcher was even more particular in arranging for seven boxes of books and a sealed packet of papers to follow him to London and then to Scotland.

By January 1689 Fletcher was in London, where he attended the meetings of Scottish nobles and gentlemen summoned by William to arrange the transfer of power in Scotland. At this point he believed that there should be a union of parliaments between the two countries. On 8 January he wrote to Andrew Russell:

> For my owen part, I thinck we can never come to any trew setelment but by uniting with England in parliaments, and Traid. For as for our worship, & particular laws we certainly can never be united to them in thes.   (NA Scot., RH15/106/690, no. 7)

He was back in Scotland in March, but found himself on the outside of political developments. He was not elected a member of the convention which settled the succession on William, though others who had been forfeited were; he did not recover his estates until 1690. Instead he associated with 'The Club', an unofficial group led by Sir James Montgomery and Sir Patrick Hume, whom he encouraged to press for more radical limitations on the power of the crown. For all his record of opposition to James VII and II, Fletcher was regarded with much less favour by the new regime than many who had served James; there is little sign that he expected or would have wished it otherwise.

Saltoun, London, and publication, 1690–1702 Since the same parliament continued in existence throughout William's reign, Fletcher had no other opportunities to be elected a member. Without an institutional forum, he divided his time in the 1690s between Scotland and London. The management of his estates had suffered from exile as well as forfeiture, and required renewed attention. William Fletcher, his factor, had died in 1685, leaving unsatisfactory accounts, the pecuniary loss being aggravated by the additional loss of nurseries of trees, furniture, and books. Another source of difficulty was the Aberlady estate purchased by his uncle Sir Andrew Fletcher in 1668: following the deaths of Sir Andrew and his two sons, it was in the hands of a minor, and the Fletchers of Saltoun were responsible for its management. (Eventually ownership also passed to Saltoun in 1710, under the terms of an entail.) In practice it was Andrew's brother Henry who assumed responsibility for managing the estates. In 1688

Henry had married Margaret Carnegie, daughter of Sir David Carnegie of Pittarrow, who Andrew (who never married) apparently used to say was 'the woman who should have been my wife' (Saltoun papers, NL Scot., MS 17858, fols. 3–6). The resulting domestic arrangements at Saltoun are unclear: given Andrew's frequent absences, he may have become virtually a lodger in his own house. Even in his absence he continued to keep a close eye on the affairs of the estate, instructing Henry on matters ranging from the proper time to fix tenancies to the best methods of planting trees and enclosing fields. But the revenues of the estate were his to consume, and he spent them on travel and on the diversions of the city.

Throughout the 1690s Fletcher divided his time between Saltoun, Edinburgh, and London, often spending the winter months in lodgings in London. Among his closest friends in the south was John Locke, whom he is likely to have met when they were exiles in the Netherlands in the 1680s. Locke described Fletcher in 1694 as 'a person whose word I rely on', and presented him with a copy of the second edition of the *Essay Concerning Human Understanding* (1694). Fletcher helped Locke in finding a tutor for William Molyneux's son; in return he sought Locke's advice on several occasions about his mother's, his sister-in-law's, and his own health, though Locke cautioned that he was 'always very backward to prescribe at a distance'. The correspondence suggests that Fletcher occasionally visited Locke and Sir Francis and Lady Masham at Oates, but less than they might have wished: in 1695 Locke chided him in Lady Masham's name to spend 'a few days out of the chocolate house', if only 'to returne from us poore honest country folke, with the better stomach, to the Witts and the Braveries' (*Correspondence of John Locke*, 5.79, 82, 274–5). Evidently Fletcher enjoyed the company of the chocolate house. Other close acquaintances in London were Walter Moyle and Anthony Hammond, members of the circle of radical, republican-leaning whigs who met at The Grecian tavern. But Fletcher's pleasure in the attractions of the capital city did not mean that he neglected the affairs of Scotland. In 1692 he rallied the duke of Hamilton to resume his role as natural leader of opposition to the king's ministers. More substantially, Fletcher is credited by Sir John Dalrymple with taking the lead in urging the Scots to go it alone in supporting William Paterson's scheme for a trading company to Africa and India. He brought Paterson to Scotland to introduce him to his Haddingtonshire neighbour the marquess of Tweeddale, and in 1696 subscribed for £1000 worth of stock in the resulting Company of Scotland, on the day it opened its books. How much he was called upon to pay is unknown, but he was later to assign certificates for stock to the value of £604.

The relative leisure of his life in the 1690s also gave Fletcher the time and opportunity to write. All his published writings appeared within a period of eight years, between 1697 and 1704, and were posthumously collected in his *Political Works* (1732). The originals were separate pamphlets, those printed in Edinburgh almost certainly published by Fletcher himself, in several cases using a distinctive italic type which R. A. Scott Macfie suggested he may have obtained from abroad and supplied to the printer. The first three pamphlets were published in the space of twelve months in 1697-8, and were written in direct response to contemporary events.

A Discourse Concerning Militia's and Standing Armies was published in London in the autumn of 1697, as a contribution to the 'standing army controversy' which broke out on the announcement of the peace of Ryswick earlier that year. Led in print by John Trenchard and Walter Moyle, opposition whigs and tories seized on the end of war to demand a reduction in the size of William's army, on the grounds that maintaining a standing army in peacetime was the first step towards establishing a despotism. Fletcher's pamphlet advanced the same argument, but placed it within an altogether more sophisticated historical framework. In Fletcher's view the rise of standing armies was not 'the contrivance of ill-designing men', but the outcome of 'a total alteration in the way of living' which occurred about 1500. Adapting Bacon's trio of modern inventions unknown to the ancients—printing, gunpowder, and the compass needle—Fletcher explained that these had opened up overseas trade, creating new opportunities for consumption which encouraged the nobilities of Europe to dispense with retainers, and thus to give up the power of the sword. For their part the people had preferred to pay taxes rather than take up arms themselves, leaving it to princes to hire mercenary troops, with which in due course they established their arbitrary rule. Until now, Fletcher suggested, England had avoided this fate, but this was due merely to its geographical situation and early loss of continental possessions, not to its ancient constitution, as Trenchard and Moyle believed. The present situation was so dangerous because the war had given William the excuse his predecessors had lacked for maintaining a standing army.

The following year Fletcher republished the pamphlet in Edinburgh in a second edition, under the title *A Discourse of Government with Relation to Militia's*. There were two substantial changes. One was the inclusion of Scotland in his history of standing armies. In the 1550s the vigilance of the lesser barons (not the greater nobility) had frustrated the attempts of the regent, Mary of Guise, to hire mercenaries, but now Scotland had simply become the recruiting ground for armies which defended English and Dutch interests. Second, Fletcher added a detailed plan for a militia in both England and Scotland. He envisaged three camps in England and one in Scotland, in which all young men should be required to serve for one or two years, returning subsequently for summer exercises. Besides laying down detailed prescriptions for diet and exercise, and urging the youth to read histories in their spare hours, he would have all clergymen banned from the camps. Women too would be excluded, while men who abused their bodies would be punished with death. Well might he claim that such camps 'would be as great a school of virtue as of military discipline' (Fletcher, 3, 6, 29).

Fletcher's next work, *Two Discourses Concerning the Affairs of Scotland* (1698), addressed the increasingly severe economic and social crisis facing his country. It was written in June–July, as the first ships prepared to sail out of the Forth for Darien, the isthmus in Panama where the Company of Scotland hoped to establish a trading colony. In the 'First discourse' Fletcher underlined how much depended on the venture's success for a country 'which has been the only part of Europe which did not apply itself to commerce'. Suspicious that the crown's Scottish ministers were trying to obstruct a measure to which William and English ministers were firmly opposed, Fletcher urged the Scottish parliament to raise a land tax to support the company's venture. He was equally concerned about the effects of recruiting for the army in Scotland, as a drain on scarce resources and an encouragement to younger sons of the nobility to continue the tradition of becoming soldiers of fortune. The 'Second discourse' addressed an even more pressing crisis, the consequences of successive harvest failures in Scotland in the 1690s. Faced with what he believed to be a dramatic increase in the numbers of poor and vagabonds, Fletcher proposed drastic remedies: transportation of the worst vagrants to the Venetian galleys; the introduction of a system of domestic servitude for labourers and their families; and the imposition of a new regime of landownership, limiting the holdings of the nobility to what they could farm, and entrenching a class of small-holders who would pay rent to those who invested in their farms. The proposals were regarded as unacceptably draconian by Fletcher's contemporaries, and have been a source of embarrassment to later admirers of his patriotism. But they were characteristic of a utopian, exemplary streak in Fletcher's thinking, and are a measure of the extent to which he believed that the existing, noble-dominated structure of Scottish society was responsible for its present crisis. Even if his grasp of the economic implications of his proposals was shaky, the underlying analysis of Scotland's ills won widespread acceptance.

In the same month of July, Fletcher was also writing a third tract, this time in Italian, the *Discorso delle cose di Spagna*. Bearing the imprint 'Napoli', but printed in the same italic type as the *Two Discourses* and likewise published by Fletcher in Edinburgh, the pamphlet purported to offer a straight-faced analysis of the prospects of different European claimants to the Spanish succession, on the imminently expected death of the childless Carlos II. Fletcher began with the causes of the decline of Spain, which he attributed to its monarchs' neglect of trade and agriculture, and to the reduction in the population as a result of religious intolerance. But by reversing these policies, and by judicious territorial exchanges, a new ruler could still revive the monarchy's fortunes, and restore it to primacy in Europe. The *Discorso* has baffled many modern commentators, but Fletcher gave his readers plenty of clues, by his adoption of Naples as the place of publication, an allusion to Tommaso Campanella, the most extravagant proponent of Spanish universal monarchy, and by his extensive use of concepts and even phrases from Machiavelli. In case some still misunderstood, Fletcher added an 'Avviso' making explicit the work's ironic purpose. Informed contemporaries saw the point immediately, Walter Moyle expressing mock surprise that a 'surly patriot … should all of a sudden turn Projector for an Universal Monarchy' (Moyle, 243).

Three years later Fletcher published what was effectively a supplement to the *Discorso*, *A Speech upon the State of the Nation, in April 1701*. Supposedly a speech to the English parliament, the tract warned first against acceptance of a French successor to Carlos II as likely to destroy 'the balance of Europe'. But its author was also alarmed by the ambitions of William III. Were William to succeed in uniting the three kingdoms and the seventeen provinces of the Netherlands, he would be in a position to establish for ever 'the empire of the sea, with an entire monopoly of trade' (Fletcher, 123, 128).

Although each of these pamphlets was a *pièce d'occasion*, they were informed by a coherent set of political concepts, helpfully characterized by John Pocock as 'neo-Machiavellian' (Pocock, chap. 8). Fletcher is best understood as seeking to adapt the concepts of the Renaissance Florentine political thinker to the circumstances of the modern world of maritime commerce and great monarchies, and in particular to the predicament of small, outlying societies such as Scotland. It was this analytical purpose, and the historical perspective which supported it, that made Fletcher's writing original, and contemporaries appreciated this even if they found his prescriptions unacceptable. In Scotland in particular Fletcher had set a new intellectual standard in public political debate, just as discussion of closer union with England was beginning in earnest after 1700. At the same time Fletcher's writings also set a new standard in style, his nervous, clear, economical sentences demonstrating that Scots too could be polite authors.

Limitations and opposition to incorporating union, 1703–1707
With the death of King William in 1702, Fletcher finally had his political opportunity. He did not waste it. A new parliament had to be summoned in May 1703 to settle the succession after Anne: specifically, the Scots were to accept the Hanoverian succession provided for in the English Act of Settlement of 1701. But the presumption that the Scots had no alternative but to agree, combined with anger over what was seen as English subversion of the Darien venture, made the new parliament much more difficult to manage. Elected a member for Haddingtonshire, Fletcher quickly took the initiative. In a speech on 26 May he identified the dependence of Scots ministers on their English counterparts as the critical weakness of the Scottish parliament, and moved an act to have all office-holders chosen by parliament. Two days later he elaborated the argument in a longer speech, alleging that Scotland now appeared 'more like a conquered province, than a free independent people' (Fletcher, 133). A month later he drove home the message in further speeches accompanying his proposal of an act of security with limitations, under which any future monarch of Scotland who

was also ruler of England would be bound to accept parliament's independence and right to choose royal officers, and the arming of all 'fencible' men. In several respects the limitations reproduced the conditions imposed upon Charles I in 1641. Fletcher, however, was careful to distinguish his intentions from those of the covenanters in the previous century, scorning 'bigots of any sort'. Nor was his object the independence of Scotland: his proposals were designed to put the existing union of the crowns on a more strictly confederal footing. Again and again he insisted that the root of the problem was ministerial dependence: this was 'the band that ties up the bundle' (ibid., 135, 145).

Fletcher continued to speak regularly until the end of the session in mid-September, pressing the cause of his limitations in the face of ministers' refusal to adopt them, and shortly after the session closed he had his contributions printed as *Speeches by a Member of the Parliament* (1703). Characteristically, he then wintered in London. While there he composed a further (and, as far as is known, his last) published work, *An Account of a Conversation Concerning a Right Regulation of Governments for the Common Good of Mankind*, which he had printed in Edinburgh early in 1704. Written in the form of a letter to the marquess of Montrose and the earls of Rothes, Roxburghe, and Haddington, four young nobles who had supported him in the parliament, the conversation may have had a basis in fact, but the construction of the 'dialogue' (as Fletcher himself called it) was extraordinarily artful, showing every sign of authorial familiarity with the conventions and possibilities of the genre. The participants in the conversation were aptly chosen: Fletcher himself, the earl of Cromarty, a consistent advocate of incorporating union, and two English tories, the veteran country MP Sir Christopher Musgrave and the party's elder statesman Sir Edward Seymour, who played the part of Scotophobe with plausible relish.

Part of the *Conversation* was given over to a defence of the position taken by Fletcher and his young supporters in the previous session, which Fletcher gradually turned into an anticipatory discussion of the arguments for and against an incorporating union with England. Making clever comparative use of the case of Ireland, and specifically of arguments of William Petty and William Molyneux, Fletcher suggested that Scotland would be similarly vulnerable to England's inclination to draw resources to itself, and in particular to the area around London. At the prompting of Musgrave and Seymour, he proceeded to outline a solution to the problem of union in Britain which was but part of a more visionary scheme for a new political order throughout Europe. Requiring the arbitrary division of existing sovereign monarchies, including those of Scotland and England, the plan showed scant regard for the ideal of national independence. But its real target was the concentration of wealth and power in capital cities such as London. Beginning with praise of London's natural advantages and human pleasures, and ending with its condemnation as another Rome, the *Conversation* explores its author's deep ambivalence towards the city in which he spent so much of his time and fortune. Fletcher's solution was to spread its benefits more widely, by multiplying the seats of government in Britain and on the continent: as such his proposal, he admitted to Seymour, was the only way to render 'not only my own country, but all mankind as happy as the imperfections of human nature will admit' (Fletcher, 214).

Fletcher was back in Scotland in time for the second session of the parliament in the summer of 1704. He again spoke frequently, and moved a number of motions designed to embarrass ministers. But when the ministry finally accepted an Act of Security in August, it was without his limitations. As Fletcher had anticipated in the *Conversation*, free trade seemed to many a more valuable concession than guarantees of parliamentary independence. He no longer sought to publish his speeches, and though he later told Robert Wodrow that he had written them all out in order to memorize them, the drafts have not survived. As he lost the political initiative, Fletcher became more fractious, picking quarrels with individuals, even the duke of Hamilton, and treating them as matters of honour. In the autumn he again withdrew from Scotland, and in October was reported by a government agent to be in the Netherlands buying arms in pursuance of the clause in the Act of Security for arming.

The same pattern of behaviour was evident in the 1705 session, held under the shadow of the English Alien Act. Two episodes confirmed Fletcher's growing political eccentricity. On 12 July he proposed that John Law and Hugh Chamberlen should be ordered to attend the house to explain their economic proposals, whose language he described as 'gibberish'. When the earl of Roxburghe observed that in good manners parliament could not oblige Law to answer for his opinions, Fletcher assumed that he was being accused of ill manners and rounded on his erstwhile supporter, challenging him to a duel. Despite the efforts of the commissioner and their seconds to prevent it, the duel was on the point of occurring on Leith Sands when it was halted by a party of guards. In another intervention, on 31 July, he suggested that the Scots should offer their crown to the prince of Prussia, on the grounds that he was at least of their religion, whereas the Hanoverians maintained the absurd doctrine of consubstantiation. Fletcher was apparently oblivious to the oddity of suggesting that what Scots proudly supposed was the oldest continuously held crown in Europe should pass to the continent's newest royal dynasty, the Hohenzollerns.

As an incorporating, parliamentary union became ever more likely, Fletcher simply became more obstinate. He did not join in the increasingly vigorous public debate. (A pamphlet published at this time, the *State of the Controversy betwixt United and Separate Parliaments*, 1706, has been attributed to him, but its absence from his own lists of his works tells against his authorship.) When the treaty of union was published in the summer of 1706, he was adamantly confident that neither the Scottish nor the English parliament would accept it. Once parliament met to debate the treaty, he was quickly disillusioned. A series of

'studied speeches', in which he argued from history that under such unions weaker states were swallowed up and enslaved by greater kingdoms, had no impact. Soon he was embroiled again in personal exchanges. The house was remarkably indulgent of his temper, though it is unlikely that Fletcher appreciated Argyll's pleading on his behalf on the grounds that Saltoun was his kinsman. What redeemed him was his intelligence, and his friends' knowledge that after he had made his point, he would as readily fall to talking of books and the building of houses.

Last years, 1708–1716 Just a year after the union had been proclaimed, Fletcher was arrested on suspicion of involvement in an attempted Jacobite rising of 1708, and detained in Stirling Castle. Unlike some of his fellow prisoners, he made light of the inconvenience, and was soon released for lack of any plausible evidence. But the episode may well have reinforced his inclination to get away from Scotland. By September he was in London, and the following year he was in the Netherlands, with an excursion to Leipzig. He was back in London in time for the trial of Henry Sacheverell early in 1710, when the whig lords ignored his warnings against provoking the cry of 'the Church in danger'. Increasingly he seems to have found the company of Scots tories such as Lockhart and Henry Maule more congenial, and he strongly encouraged their efforts to move for the dissolution of the union. He was briefly back in Scotland in the winter of 1711–12, when he was caught up in 'the affair of the Scots' forage', about which he protested his innocence to Lockhart. Thereafter he returned to London, whence he could easily cross to the Netherlands.

From May 1715 Fletcher was on the continent, watching over his nephew and namesake Andrew Fletcher in Leiden before moving on to Paris in October. His letters from Paris to his nephew show that his relish for the city was undiminished, his appetite for books and eye for a bargain as keen as ever. The young Andrew received a stream of instructions and commissions, to be executed either by himself or by Alexander Cunningham (probably the former professor of civil law at Edinburgh, then resident at The Hague). Likewise undiminished was Fletcher's concern with appearances, his nephew also being given detailed advice on the cut of a new black suit. During the Jacobite rising of 1715 he was in Paris, from where he observed wryly to his nephew on 20 February 1716 that the care taken by the Pretender (James Stuart) to ruin his affairs 'convinces everybody who formerly did not believe it that he is of the family' (Saltoun papers, NL Scot., MS 16503, fols. 127–8). But while immune to Jacobitism, his bodily health was increasingly uncertain: he had been seriously ill in 1713, and during the summer of 1716 bouts of 'looseness' became increasingly prolonged. Much weakened, he was helped to make the journey from Paris to London by his nephew and Alexander Cunningham, but could go no further. His last coherent words, as reported by his nephew to his brother, were, 'Lord have mercy upon my poor countrey that is so barbarously oppressed' (Saltoun papers, NL Scot., MS 16503, fols. 173–4). Fletcher died in his old lodgings at Mrs Duras's in Charles Street, London, on 15 September. In a note scribbled a little earlier, he told his brother Henry that he desired to make no formal will, 'seeing what I have will naturally go to you', but he requested that £200 be employed to relieve Scots imprisoned after the late rebellion, and that 'for the love and favour I bear to Mr Alexander Cunningham', he be paid £100 at Martinmas next. This legacy was punctually paid by Henry, though he also told his son that Andrew had left the estate under 'a vast burden' (Saltoun papers, NL Scot., MS 16503, fols. 175, 186–7). He was buried at Saltoun parish church.

Library and place in Scottish intellectual life Over a lifetime of collecting, Fletcher built up a library of some 6000 books, almost certainly the largest private library in Scotland at the time. He left two manuscript catalogues of his books (one much fuller than the other), and since the books themselves were not dispersed until the 1960s, it has proved possible to reconstruct the library's contents (see Willems). In buying and arranging his books, Fletcher may have followed the advice of earlier bibliophiles such as Naudé, but the balance of the library clearly reflected personal interests. The largest categories were those of historians, poets, orators, and legislators; rather less space was taken by theologians, physicians, mathematicians, and jurists. Classical authors (often in several editions) were numerous, and he had an excellent collection of histories and modern political works. Protestant and Catholic authors co-existed under theologians, but alongside a disproportionate amount of heterodoxy. Although Galileo, Descartes, and Robert Boyle were represented, Fletcher evidently did not aim to keep up with the new natural philosophy: there was no work by Isaac Newton. There were books in Latin, Greek, English, French, Italian, and Spanish, though he is not known to have spoken Spanish. How well he knew Greek is also uncertain: Lord Hailes believed that he went late to its study, and Fletcher was in his forties when he confessed to his brother on 13 December 1699 that he would willingly exchange knowing it 'for all the knowledge I have of anything' (Saltoun papers, NL Scot., MS 16502, fol. 172).

Fletcher's interests were not confined to books. He liked drawing, and had a long-standing fascination with the design of buildings; through the good offices of David Gregory he obtained a favourable comment on one of his designs from Christopher Wren. Although his temper was notorious, he was respected and his company enjoyed by men across the political spectrum. The overriding impression is nevertheless one of remarkable self-sufficiency, intellectual as well as personal. His thinking is difficult to relate to the main currents in Scottish intellectual life at the time. Towards the end of his life his love of the classics and history was reciprocated by the Jacobite Latinist Thomas Ruddiman, whose preface to his new edition of George Buchanan acknowledged the loan of books from one he called 'Cato nostri seculi' (Ruddiman, xxi). But no similar intellectual fellowship had been possible with the great antiquary of the previous generation, Sir Robert Sibbald. Those whom Fletcher himself held in highest regard

among his Scottish contemporaries were the latitudinarian clergy and academics, such as the Scougalls and William Colvin, principal of Edinburgh University, yet there are few traces in his thought of the Stoic moral philosophy which they cultivated as an antidote to the dangers of Epicureanism. Fletcher's own, much more activist, neo-Machiavellian politics were unique in the Scottish context, even among those, like Sir Alexander Seton of Pitmedden, who shared his diagnosis of the ills of Scotland's noble-dominated society. But if his ideas were singular, his application of them was an inspiration: Fletcher not only showed his fellow Scots how to think analytically about their country's predicament, but taught them to do so in a broad historical and comparative perspective. In this Fletcher was the intellectual forebear of the Scottish Enlightenment.

The impression of intellectual self-sufficiency is reinforced by the obscurity—or discretion—of Fletcher's religious opinions. He made no secret of his hostility to bigots of any ecclesiastical stripe, nor of his sympathy for the tolerant eirenicism which Burnet found epitomized in his father. But much more radical views are suggested by his remark to Locke in 1695 that he was 'tracing priestcraft from its first original in Aegipt. Wheir I find lickways many other monsters but none so abominable' (*Correspondence of John Locke*, 5.275). Such anti-clericalism was characteristic of the republican circles Fletcher was then frequenting in London, but it seems unlikely that he followed John Toland all the way into Spinozism and atheism; Lord Hailes thought that Fletcher had once described Toland as 'a bigotted atheist' (Edinburgh University Library, Laing MS II 588). More probably Fletcher was a firm Erastian, sharing the conviction of many of the Scottish lay élite that church establishments should be subject to the civil powers. Such a position is compatible with the views Fletcher expressed in 1712 in conversation with Wodrow, when he argued that the power of the (clergy-dominated) presbyteries to choose new ministers should be curtailed.

Reputation Fletcher's reputation as a 'patriot'—albeit often a 'surly' one—was well established in his own lifetime, and has endured. But the significance attached to the designation has changed several times over the course of three centuries. An important early step in its consolidation was the collection of his pamphlets in a volume of *Political Works*, published in 1732 by three London booksellers; who or what prompted them to do so is unknown. There was a second edition in 1737, and a separate Scottish edition in 1749. The writings attracted the attention of several Enlightenment thinkers, including David Hume, who admired Fletcher's genius as well as his probity. Campaigners for a Scottish militia in the 1760s and 1770s invoked his name and arguments, and his proposal for domestic servitude also continued to be discussed, often critically. Another whose attention was caught was Jean-Jacques Rousseau, who offered to write Fletcher's life—and may have received family papers from the earl marischal to enable him to do so. (If he did, he is presumed to have lost them.) Failing Rousseau, anecdotes and family information about Fletcher were collected by his great-niece Elizabeth Halkett, who did her best to make him a good Presbyterian, favoured at critical moments by the intervention of Providence. Growing interest in the idea of a national biography encouraged Lord Hailes and David Steuart Erskine, earl of Buchan, to use and supplement these materials, but when Buchan wrote Fletcher's life he gave it a fresh twist, rendering the patriot an icon for the radical cause of the 1790s—literally so, the frontispiece reproducing Fletcher's portrait under a cap of liberty. His name was invoked in this spirit by Thomas Muir at the first national convention of the Scottish Friends of the People in 1792. As late as 1840 the Glasgow *Chartist Circular* celebrated Fletcher, with John Trenchard and Daniel Defoe, as having 'nobly contended for genuine political liberty' (no. 15, 4 Jan 1840).

As such company implied, the radicals' patriot was not a champion of Scottish independence. Nor was Fletcher's name invoked by the first movement to agitate on specifically national issues, the National Association for the Vindication of Scottish Rights in the 1850s. He was, however, taken up by the Scottish Home Rule Association of the 1880s. Drawing particularly on the *Account of a Conversation*, which the association republished as a pamphlet, John Morrison Davidson represented Fletcher as an exemplary proto-federalist, 'equally opposed to separation and incorporation' (Davidson, 15). Not until the twentieth century did the patriot become a full-blown nationalist. Not surprisingly he has occupied a prominent place in the historical pantheon of the Scottish National Party, whose publicists strive to present his opposition to the Act of Union as the destined climax of his political career. Perhaps equally important to his reputation as a national hero was his inclusion, as the subject of *The Patriot* (1982), in Nigel Tranter's series of popular Scottish historical novels. On the other hand, scholars have begun to get to grips with Fletcher's thought and intellectual connections, making possible a rather different assessment of his historical significance. As a result, Andrew Fletcher has become a prominent (though by no means the only) example of a Scottish hero whose popular and scholarly reputations are increasingly divergent.

JOHN ROBERTSON

Sources NL Scot., Saltoun MSS 16502, fols. 121–2, 152–3, 172, 193, 208–9; 16503, fols. 109–16, 127–30, 141–2, 156–9, 173–5, 186–7; 16809, fols. 10–11; 16831, fols. 9–56, 58–60; 16854; 17450; 17458, fols. 17–18; 17858, fols. 3–6; 17860 [family genealogy]; 17863, 17864 [library catalogues] · A. Fletcher, *Political works*, ed. J. Robertson (1997) · R. A. Scott Macfie, 'A bibliography of Andrew Fletcher of Saltoun', *Proceedings of the Edinburgh Bibliographical Society*, 4/2 (1901), 117–48 · P. J. M. Willems, *Bibliotheca Fletcheriana, or, The extraordinary library of Andrew Fletcher of Saltoun* (Wassenaar, 1999) · E. Halkett, 'Memoir of the family of Saltoun', 1785, U. Edin. L., MS La III.364 · G. W. T. Omond, *Fletcher of Saltoun*, Famous Scots Series (1897) · [G. Burnet], *A discourse on the memory of that rare and truly virtuous person Sir Robert Fletcher of Saltoun* (1665) · acta rectorum, U. St Andr. L., MS UY/305/3, p. 425 · NL Scot., Yester MS 14407 · J. Lauder, *Historical observes of memorable occurrents in church and state, from October 1680 to April 1686*, ed. A. Urquhart and D. Laing, Bannatyne Club, 66 (1840) · *The dispatches of Thomas Plott and Thomas Chudleigh, English envoys at The Hague*, ed. F. A. Middlebush, 22 (Rijks Geschiedkundige Publicatien, 1926) · *State trials*, vol. 11 · J. Dalrymple, *Memoirs of Great Britain and Ireland*, new edn, 3 vols. (1790) · NA Scot., high court of justiciary, processes in the trial of Andrew Fletcher of Saltoun for treason, JC 39/67/3, 5 · *Bishop Burnet's History of his own time*, ed. T. Burnet, another edn, 2 (1753) · PRO, state papers, Spanish consuls, SP 94/210 · G. Gardner, 'The Scottish exile community in the United Provinces, 1660–1690', DPhil diss., U. Oxf., 1998 · NA Scot., Andrew Russell papers, RH 15/106/648, nos. 22–5, and 15/106/690, nos. 7, 10 · *The correspondence of John Locke*, ed. E. S. De Beer, 5 (1979); 8 (1989) · J. S. Shaw, *The political history of eighteenth-century Scotland* (1999) · W. Moyle, *The whole works* (1727) · J. G. A. Pocock, *The Machiavellian moment: Florentine political thought and the Atlantic republican tradition* (1975) · R. Wodrow, *Analecta, or, Materials for a history of remarkable providences, mostly relating to Scotch ministers and Christians*, ed. [M. Leishman], 2, Maitland Club, 60 (1842) · *The Marlborough–Godolphin correspondence*, ed. H. L. Snyder, 1 (1975) · NA Scot., Montrose correspondence, GD 220/5/75, 220/5/800/13 · *The manuscripts of his grace the duke of Portland*, 10 vols., HMC, 29 (1891–1931), vols. 4, 8 · *Report on the manuscripts of the earl of Mar and Kellie*, HMC, 60 (1904) · NA Scot., letters of Andrew Fletcher to Henry Maule of Kelly, GD 45/14/337 · *Letters of George Lockhart of Carnwath, 1698–1732*, ed. D. Szechi, Scottish History Society, 5th ser., 2 (1989) · D. Dalrymple, Lord Hailes, letter to the earl of Buchan, 26 April 1787, U. Edin. L., MS La II.588 [copy] · T. Ruddiman, preface, in G. Buchanan, *Opera omnia* (1715) · D. S. Erskine, earl of Buchan, *Essays on the lives and writings of Fletcher of Saltoun and the poet Thomson* (1792) · *Chartist Circular*, 15 (4 Jan 1840) [Glasgow] · J. M. Davidson, *Scotia rediviva: home rule for Scotland* (1893) · N. Tranter, *The patriot* (1982)

Archives NL Scot., corresp. | NA Scot., Dalhousie muniments, GD 45/14/337, 361 · NA Scot., Andrew Russell papers, RH 15/106/648, 690, 708 · NL Scot., Saltoun papers

Likenesses W. Aikman, portrait, *c.*1707, priv. coll. [*see illus.*] · eleventh earl of Buchan, pencil and chalk drawing, 1794, Scot. NPG · oils (after W. Aikman), Scot. NPG · portrait, repro. in Erskine, *Essays*

Fletcher, Andrew, Lord Milton (1691/2–1766), judge, was probably born in 1692, but one source (Burke, *Gen. GB*) gives the year as 1691. He was the elder son among four children of Henry Fletcher (*d.* 1733) of Saltoun, Haddingtonshire, and his wife, Margaret (*d.* 1745), daughter of Sir David Carnegie of Pittarrow, bt (*d.* 1708), and his wife, Catherine, daughter of Sir Archibald Primrose, first baronet. His uncle was Andrew *Fletcher of Saltoun (1653?–1716), 'the Patriot', whom he accompanied on his last journey from Paris and tended on his deathbed in London. His mother, Margaret Carnegie, was both energetic and enterprising. She went on a mission of industrial espionage to the Netherlands, taking with her a weaver who procured the secrets of making the fine linen called holland and a millwright who found out a mechanical method of husking barley to render it fit for human consumption; production of both was started at Saltoun. Of her the Patriot said: 'My brother has got the woman that should have been my wife' (*Recollections*, 2).

Nothing is known of Fletcher's formal education before he matriculated to study law at the University of Leiden in 1714, though he had attended a private teacher of law in Edinburgh. Two years later he returned to Edinburgh and was admitted an advocate on 26 February 1717. On 4 June 1724, at an unusually young age, he became an ordinary lord of session, with the title of Lord Milton, and on 22

June 1726 a lord justiciary. By 1733 he had married Elizabeth (*bap.* 1710, *d.* 1782), daughter of Sir Francis Kinloch of Gilmerton (1676–1749) and his wife, Mary (*d.* 1749), daughter of Sir James Rocheid of Innerleith, with whom he had three sons and four daughters, including the scholar Elizabeth *Fletcher. About the time of his marriage, doubtless to please his bride, he bought Brunstane House, near Edinburgh, and transformed it into a classical villa to designs by William Adam.

On 21 June 1735 Milton succeeded as lord justice clerk, head of the criminal judiciary, in which post he continued until 1748. His resignation by no means marked the end of his public career. He had early on won wide political responsibilities in the service of Archibald Campbell, earl of Ilay, later third duke of Argyll. Sir Robert Walpole as prime minister favoured the Argathelian faction of Scottish whigs who thus rose to dominate the country, driving out the rival squadrone and completing the electoral ruin of the Jacobites. Ilay and Milton exploited official patronage to construct a national body of support and create an understanding of where power lay. Milton had 'the charge of superintending elections, which he considered as his masterpiece' (*Scotland and Scotsmen*, 1.89). For that purpose he also built up control of the royal burghs and their corporations. He made it equally his business to manage the general assembly of the Church of Scotland, with a view to orderly presentation of acceptable ministers, thereby extending his influence into the universities too. His regime showed a brutal resolve, unforgiving to beaten foes. But he took pains to find the right men for the right jobs, and in nominations to academic chairs displayed an enlightened (to his clerical opponents, deist) spirit.

The Argathelian regime was damaged by the Porteous riot of 1736 when it failed in what Walpole expected of it, that is to keep order in Scotland. Milton presided over the trial which acquitted Captain John Porteous of murder after the guard had fired on the mob at an execution in Edinburgh, and in 1737 he was summoned before the House of Lords to explain the subsequent unrest. Argyll's authority could not be restored and, after his death in 1743, Milton found himself working for his adversary of the *squadrone volante*, John Hay, fourth marquess of Tweeddale, in whom the dormant secretaryship of state for Scotland was revived. Ilay, now duke of Argyll, urged Milton to serve on though stripped of his wonted patronage. This proved sound advice, as their fortunes were soon reversed by Tweeddale's feebleness when faced with the Jacobite rising of 1745. Milton's contacts gave him some premonition of it, and he had befriended the English generals in Scotland, Sir John Cope and Joshua Guest. After witnessing Cope's defeat at Prestonpans on 21 September he fled into England. Having survived a purge of blameworthy Scottish officials early in 1746, his appointment in November as keeper of the signet gave him patronage still wider than before. In clearing up the Jacobite mess he became more than ever the government's man of business, writing to ministers, gathering intelligence, preparing evidence for trials, smoothing relations between military

and civil authorities, enforcing new laws against nonjurors, organizing transport of prisoners, and abolishing heritable jurisdictions.

Milton's confidence in his authority prompted him to personal initiatives pointing the way forward for an improving—if authoritarian—Scottish ruling class. The situation in the highlands now offered scope for nothing less than planning a new society. Supported by Argyll, Milton drew up in 1747 a scheme to annex estates of forfeited Jacobites to the crown and purchase further swathes of rebellious areas so as to create through the central highlands a stretch of territory owned by the government and ruled by a commission in Edinburgh. Its purpose was to destroy the power of the chiefs. In correspondence with Thomas Pelham-Holles, first duke of Newcastle, secretary of state, Milton stressed how the chiefs depended for security and prosperity on the number of fighting men at their command and thus had an interest in keeping their clansmen poor and ignorant. Not until that power was ended could there be hope of improvement—in education, dissemination of presbyterianism, and introduction of industry. Annexed estates might set an example for the whole of the highlands and produce permanent peace. Milton's plans were, however, watered down in the Annexing Act of 1752, and results fell short of his hopes.

A second initiative also relied on official sponsorship to make the Union of 1707 promote Scottish economic development. In 1727 Milton had helped to found the Royal Bank of Scotland, joined a commission for manufactures, and, following up his interest in textiles, established the Edinburgh Linen Co-partnery. This did well, but there remained ample room to improve quality and productivity in a scattered cottage industry with little finance, organization, or knowledge of superior continental technology. Milton wanted to make it national in scope and capable of exporting. To these ends he sought a royal charter for his British Linen Company, granted by George II on 5 July 1746. It proceeded by operating the putting-out system on a new scale, making loans to weavers and spinners, encouraging advanced techniques and the introduction of new cloths, bringing flax from the Baltic, and setting up warehouses for marketing in Scotland, England, and the colonies. All this required advances, financed by the company's own banknotes. Its banking at length grew more important than its textile business where, after the initial impetus, it was overtaken by entrepreneurs with better knowledge of markets. But Milton had succeeded in forming the only British bank with an industrial charter.

In the reign of George III the Argathelian regime carried on as usual under the ministry of John Stuart, third earl of Bute, Duke Archibald's nephew. Another scion of the clan, James Stuart Mackenzie, became Milton's correspondent in London. This promising partnership ended when Milton lapsed into senile dementia in 1764. In 1755 he had had a townhouse built in the Canongate, Edinburgh, by John Adam, but he died at Brunstane on 15 December 1766 and was buried at East Saltoun. He was succeeded in his estates by his eldest son, Andrew (*d.*

1799), and then by his second son, John. He had been a prime example of a new class of lawyer–landowners which emerged to run Scotland after 1707 and, if in utter political subservience, set out boldly, even ruthlessly, to make the nation an equal partner in Great Britain.

MICHAEL FRY

Sources J. S. Shaw, *The political history of eighteenth-century Scotland* (1999) · 'Letters of Andrew Fletcher of Saltoun and his family, 1715–1716', ed. I. J. Murray, *Miscellany … X*, Scottish History Society, 4th ser., 2 (1965), 143–73 · J. Home, *The history of the rebellion in the year 1745* (1802) · P. H. Scott, *Andrew Fletcher and the treaty of union* (1992) · S. Checkland, *Scottish banking, a history* (1976) · *Recollections of the family of Fletcher of Saltoun* (Edinburgh, 1803) · *Scotland and Scotsmen in the eighteenth century: from the MSS of John Ramsay, esq., of Ochtertyre*, ed. A. Allardyce, 2 vols. (1888) · J. S. Shaw, *The management of Scottish society, 1707–1764: power, nobles, lawyers, Edinburgh agents and English influences* (1983), 147–74 · A. Murdoch, 'The people above': politics and administration in mid-eighteenth-century Scotland (1980) · Burke, *Gen. GB* (1937) · *Edinburgh*, Pevsner (1984) · *Lothian, except Edinburgh*, Pevsner (1978) · *DNB*
Archives NL Scot., corresp. and papers | NA Scot., corresp. with Archibald Campbell of Stonefield · NL Scot., letters to Campbell · NL Scot., Saltoun papers · NL Scot., letters to marquess of Tweeddale · NL Scot., corresp., mainly with fourth marquess of Tweeddale
Likenesses A. Ramsay, oils, 1748, Scot. NPG; version, U. Edin. · R. Scott, watercolour drawing (after A. Ramsay), Scot. NPG

Fletcher, Archibald (1746–1828), advocate and political reformer, was born at Pooble in Glenlyon, Perthshire, the first of the six children of Angus Fletcher, a tacksman, and his second wife, Grace M'Naughton. He was educated at the grammar school of Kenmore, Breadalbane, and the high school of Perth, and at the age of sixteen he was placed in the office of an Edinburgh solicitor, Mr Grant, to train in law. This was followed by an apprenticeship with Mr Wilson of Howden, through the aid of the lord advocate, Sir James Montgomery, whom Fletcher had served as confidential clerk. Wilson afterwards took him into partnership, and he became a member of the Society of Writers to the Signet. During his early years in Edinburgh he attended Adam Ferguson's moral philosophy classes at the university (*c*.1763), and studied Greek in private. He was admitted to the Scottish bar in 1790, and he married Eliza Dawson (1770–1858) [*see* Fletcher, Elizabeth] on 16 July 1791. They had two sons and four daughters.

In 1778, soon after he had completed his initial legal training, Fletcher was asked to negotiate with the M'Cra highlanders, who were mutinying in Edinburgh against embarking for service in America. He nevertheless sympathized with the Americans during the War of Independence, and from then on he became involved in various liberal causes. He successfully attacked the proposal of the Faculty of Advocates to limit entrance to men aged twenty-seven and under, and he supported the evangelicals in their rejection of patronage in the Church of Scotland. He is said to have published pamphlets on both of these issues. He is best known, however, for his leadership of the campaign for the reform of the Scottish burghs. He was appointed secretary to the Edinburgh society for burgh reform in 1784, helped to draft a parliamentary bill

in favour of reform, and served as a delegate to a committee of the House of Commons in 1787, becoming acquainted in this way with leading London whigs.

Fletcher suffered for his political opinions during the 1790s, losing a considerable volume of legal business because of his resolute adherence to moderate reforming principles. He refused to join the radical Society of the Friends of the People, but he celebrated the anniversary of the fall of the Bastille every year. He acted voluntarily as counsel for the defence in the sedition trials of Joseph Gerrald, Charles Sinclair, and others, and he was one of a minority of thirty-eight who supported Henry Erskine in the vote that deposed him as dean of the Faculty of Advocates in 1796 for his opposition to the war with revolutionary France and to the repressive Two Acts of 1795. In 1797 he defended John Johnstone, printer and publisher of the *Scots Chronicle*, who had accused the soldiers who suppressed the Tranent crowds rioting against the militia ballot of deliberate murder. Fletcher was also a member of the Edinburgh committee for the abolition of the slave trade, and of the Society for the Improvement of the Highlands. His wife, a popular Edinburgh whig hostess, helped to establish the first female benefit society in Scotland in March 1798.

Despite his advancing years, Fletcher joined the Edinburgh Highland corps of volunteers during the Napoleonic wars, because of the threatened French invasion. After the war ended, he continued to take an active interest in political matters, though he retired from the bar in 1816. He was widely respected for his integrity and kindness, and he was cheered when he appeared at a reformist meeting held in 1818. Besides the two early publications noted above, he also wrote *A Memoir Concerning … the Reform … of the Royal Burghs of Scotland* (1819) and *A Dialogue between a Whig and a Radical Reformer* (1822). Archibald Fletcher died on 20 December 1828, surrounded by his family, at his home, Auchindinny House, near Penicuik, and he was buried four days later at Calton cemetery, Edinburgh.

EMMA VINCENT MACLEOD

Sources *Autobiography of Mrs Fletcher*, ed. M. R. [M. Richardson], 2nd edn (1875) · J. Kay, *A series of original portraits and caricature etchings … with biographical sketches and illustrative anecdotes*, ed. [H. Paton and others], new edn [3rd edn], 2 (1877), 445–7 · H. Cockburn, *Life of Lord Jeffrey, with a selection from his correspondence*, 1 (1852), 74–5 · A. Fletcher, *A memoir concerning the origin and progress of the reform proposed in the internal government of the royal burghs of Scotland* (1819) · H. Brougham, *Speeches … upon questions relating to public rights, duties and interests*, 4 vols. (1838), vol. 3 · H. W. Meikle, *Scotland and the French Revolution* (1912); repr. (1969) · *Memorials of his time, by Henry Cockburn*, new edn, ed. H. A. Cockburn (1909) · A. Fergusson, ed., *The Honourable Henry Erskine* (1882) · *Irving, Scots.*
Likenesses J. Kay, engraving, repro. in Kay, *Series of original portraits*, pl. 320

Fletcher, Banister (1833–1899), architect and surveyor, was the second son of Thomas Fletcher. He was privately educated, and then became a pupil of Charles James Richardson, architect and architectural author, before beginning, at the age of twenty, to practise as an architect at Newcastle upon Tyne. He designed and erected numerous wharves, warehouses, and other buildings there. In 1860 he was elected an associate of the Institute of British Architects, and in 1876 a fellow. On 23 April 1864 he married Eliza Jane, the only daughter of Charles Phillips, with whom he had two sons.

About 1870 Fletcher moved to London, and in the following year published a work on *Model Houses for the Industrial Classes* (1871), in which he reviewed the defects of existing model lodging-houses and which was praised by Lord Shaftesbury. He also published plans for new, more suitable, houses, and suggestions on how existing buildings could be modified. In 1875 he was appointed district surveyor of West Newington and part of Lambeth, and he was also one of the surveyors to the Board of Trade. His practice as a surveyor was very extensive, and his services were in constant demand as witness and arbitrator. In later life his sons, Sir Banister Flight *Fletcher (1866–1953) and Herbert Phillips Fletcher (1872–1916), were associated with him in his architectural practice. Alone or in conjunction with them he erected numerous chapels, schools, restaurants, shops, factories, flats, and model dwellings. He designed model houses at Pentonville, and Peckham, as well as large metropolitan estates at Hampstead, Hanwell, Kensington, Tulse Hill, and Manor Park. In addition to his architectural work, he was Liberal MP for north-west Wiltshire from 1885 to 1886.

In 1890 Fletcher was appointed professor of architecture and building construction at King's College, London, where his two sons also became lecturers. Together they published *A History of Architecture on the Comparative Method* (5th edn, 1905). Partly at his own expense he fitted up an architectural and building construction reference museum at the college, in which he placed his own collection of large architectural photographs of the principal buildings of the world. His work in Gothic furniture design enabled him to secure considerable support from the Carpenters' Company, of which he was master in 1889, obtaining casts, models, drawings, and photographs for the benefit of his students. In 1894 he was president of the tenth section of the international congress of hygiene and demography at Budapest, and of the engineering and building construction section of the British Association in the same year.

In addition to holding many positions within the building trade, Fletcher was also a member of the common council of the city of London, and a deputy lieutenant and JP for the county of London. It was said of him that 'all his life he did the work of two men' (Crook, 566). He wrote extensively on building matters, including a series of textbooks for surveyors which dealt with compensation, arbitration, quantities, and light and air, as well as two books on the Metropolitan Building Acts. With his son Banister Flight Fletcher he was responsible for the 1896 edition of *A History of Architecture for the Student, Craftsman and Amateur*. He died of tuberculosis at his home, Anglebay, Woodchurch Road, Hampstead, on 5 July 1899, and was buried at Hampstead. His wife survived him.

E. I. CARLYLE, *rev.* JOHN ELLIOTT

Sources *The Builder*, 77 (1899), 46 · *The Builder*, 77 (1899), 68 · R. Plumbe, A. Cates, and T. R. Smith, 'The late professor Banister Fletcher', *RIBA Journal*, 6 (1898–9), 522–4 · *Dir. Brit. archs.* · J. M. Crook, 'Architecture and history', *Architectural History*, 27 (1984), 555–78 · *CGPLA Eng. & Wales* (1899) · H. Meller, *London cemeteries: an illustrated guide and gazetteer*, 3rd edn (1994)

Archives RIBA, corresp.; nomination papers; notes · UCL, lectures, notes | BL, corresp. with Society of Authors, Add. MS 63240

Wealth at death £75,813 15s. 5d.: probate, 22 Aug 1899, *CGPLA Eng. & Wales*

Fletcher, Sir Banister Flight (1866–1953), architect and architectural historian, was born in Bloomsbury, London, on 15 February 1866, the elder son of the architect Banister *Fletcher (1833–1899) and his wife, Eliza Jane (May) Phillips. He was educated at the Norfolk county school, and at King's College and University College, London, and entered his father's office in 1884 but continued to study architecture also at the Royal Academy Schools, the Architectural Association, and the École des Beaux-Arts, Paris. He became an associate of the Royal Institute of British Architects (RIBA) in 1889 and a fellow in 1904. He was made a partner in his father's firm in 1889 and succeeded with his brother to the practice in 1899. During his early career he was regarded as a minor figure in the modernist movement; although little of his work was important, it did not lack character. It included a bank at Hythe, a church at Stratford East, flats in Harley Street and Wimpole Street, King's College School, Wimbledon Common (1899), and various shops, memorials, and houses. He also extended Morden College, Blackheath (1933). The firm continued under the style of Banister Fletcher & Sons after the death in 1916 of his brother H. Phillips Fletcher. Two large works done in later years were the Roan School, Greenwich (with Percy B. Dannatt, c.1926–8) and the Gillette factory, Osterley (c.1936). Fletcher was for many years surveyor to the Worshipful Company of Carpenters, and became its master in 1936. He was also director of its building crafts training school, St Marylebone.

Fletcher was much better known, however, as the author of *A History of Architecture on the Comparative Method*, which he published originally in 1896, jointly with his father. His wide travels provided the material and his knowledge of London in particular was extensive. The definitive edition during his lifetime was the sixth, published in 1921, with the text largely rewritten by Fletcher and his first wife, and with new plates brilliantly drawn by George G. Woodward and others. Major expansions and revisions have kept the book in continual demand; the twentieth edition was published in 1996. It has been translated into several languages. Fletcher also published the much criticized *Andrea Palladio* (1902) and several slighter studies. With his brother he produced two handbooks: *Architectural Hygiene, or, Sanitary Science as Applied to Building* (1899) and *Carpentry and Joinery* (1898), which were illustrated by his charming sketches. Other such sketches, in pencil and ink, are reproduced in the publication on his *Architectural Work* (1934).

On 30 July 1914 Fletcher married Alice Maud Mary, daughter of Edward Bretherton and widow of Sir John Bamford Slack. She died in 1932, and on 18 August 1933 he married Mary Louisa Hazell (1870/71–1949), a widow, daughter of Alfred Inman, a civil engineer. There were no children from either marriage. Fletcher was president of the RIBA (1929–31) and bore part of the cost of its library catalogue (2 vols., 1937–8). As a lecturer in his youth at King's College, following his father, and later on London University extension courses (1901–38), he did much to make his subject vivid and stimulating. Fletcher was called to the bar by the Inner Temple in 1908 and conducted arbitrations and advised on London Building Act disputes. He was for many years (1907–53) a common councillor of the City of London and the chairman at different times of the schools and library committees; in 1918–19 he was senior sheriff. He received a knighthood in 1919 and various foreign honours.

Fletcher was a man of great intellectual ability in certain fields, with a capacity for hard work and organizing acumen, but he was happier in his more historical activities. An autocrat, and patronizing even to his peers, he expected much of his staff and scenes were common, although he had, at heart, a kindly concern for their physical welfare. In manner and appearance he was 'sometimes genial, sometimes austere, but always dignified'. He died at his home, 4 Whitehall Court, Westminster, on 17 August 1953. He bequeathed much of his property (slides, lecture diagrams, and so on) and money to the University of London and the RIBA library, with the stipulation that the latter should be named the Sir Banister Fletcher Library. H. V. M. ROBERTS, rev. CATHERINE GORDON

Sources W. H. Smith, *The architectural work of Sir Banister Fletcher* (1934) · A. S. Gray, *Edwardian architecture: a biographical dictionary* (1985), 180–81 · A. K. Placzek, ed., *Macmillan encyclopedia of architects*, 4 vols. (1982) · *Architect and Building News* (27 Aug 1953), 238 · *The Builder*, 185 (1953), 310–11 · *RIBA Journal*, 60 (1952–3), 464–5 · *Architects' Journal* (27 Aug 1953), 251 · *The Times* (19 Aug 1953) · *Who's who in architecture* (1926) · J. A. Gotch, ed., *The growth and work of the Royal Institute of British Architects, 1834–1934* [1934] · personal knowledge (1971) · m. certs. · d. cert. · *CGPLA Eng. & Wales* (1953)

Archives BL, corresp. with Society of Authors, Add. MS 63240 · LUL, corresp. and drawings · RIBA BAL, corresp. and drawings; nomination MSS; sketchbooks and notes · UCL, lecture notes

Likenesses S. Lucas, oils, 1917, RIBA · G. H. Swinstead, oils, c.1920, RIBA · W. Stoneman, photographs, 1940, NPG · G. Philpot, oils, RIBA · portrait, repro. in *Architect and Building News*, 238 · portrait, repro. in *The Builder*, 310

Wealth at death £115,520 16s. 8d.: probate, 20 Oct 1953, *CGPLA Eng. & Wales*

Fletcher, Catherine, Lady Fletcher (1733–1816). *See under* Lintot, (Barnaby) Bernard (1675–1736).

Fletcher, Charles Montague (1911–1995), epidemiologist and broadcaster, was born in Cambridge on 5 June 1911, the son of Sir Walter Morley *Fletcher FRS (1873–1933), of Burrels Field, Cambridge, fellow of Trinity College and first secretary of the Medical Research Council (MRC), and Mary Frances, *née* Cropper, from a prominent Cumbrian family. Following early schooling in London and Horsham, Sussex, he entered Eton College in 1924, becoming captain of Conybeare House and a member of the Etonian society, Pop, success as an oarsman and hurdler contributing to his early distinction. His decision to follow in the mould of his father's medical career led him towards the

Charles Montague Fletcher (1911–1995), by Nick Sinclair, 1994

natural sciences, which he read between 1930 and 1934 at Trinity College, Cambridge, where his father had been a physiology don. He completed his second MB and took a first in physiology in 1934, electing to defer clinical studies in order to undertake research in the field of electrophysiology. He described this Cambridge period as the idyllic years, which included the continuation of a prominent family association with the Pitt Club, a rowing blue in 1933, and a growth of interest in amateur dramatics and music. The best and the worst of years he might have described them, with the premature death of his father in 1933 'the blackest of days'.

Fletcher began clinical studies at London's St Bartholomew's Hospital medical school in 1936, supported by a personal scholarship created in memory of his father, who had studied there. One of the most elegant young men about town, Fletcher combined a remarkably full social calendar and scholastic distinction with apparent ease, being awarded the Henry Brackenbury prize for medicine in his final year. The outbreak of war took him to Emergency Medical Service sector hospitals on the outskirts of London, knitting socks for the troops as part of his own war effort, before joining Professor Leslie Witts's team at Oxford's Radcliffe Infirmary, first as house physician then Nuffield research fellow. During this period he helped Professor Howard Florey with the first clinical tests of a new therapeutic agent known as penicillin. On 17 January 1941 he administered the first injection of 100 mg of penicillin to a human subject. The results, which he described as miraculous, paved the way for its use by the allied forces in the latter years of the Second World War.

In the calendar of Fletcher's life 1941 was a momentous year, including the onset of diabetes mellitus, which excluded him from the armed forces, and the beginning of a lifelong partnership with Louisa Mary Sylvia (*b.* 1912/13), daughter of John Edward Bernard *Seely, first Baron Mottistone (1868–1947), whom he married on 24 October. Soon afterwards he returned to St Bartholomew's (Barts) as registrar, transferring a year later to the Royal Postgraduate Medical School at Hammersmith Hospital, diagnostic investigations by gastroscopy forming the subject of his MD dissertation (1945). A strong supporter of the proposed national health service, his aspirations of becoming a staff physician at Barts were challenged by an invitation from the MRC to direct the ground breaking work of understanding the aetiology of pneumoconiosis within the mining valleys of south Wales. Twenty-five per cent of the coalminers were afflicted, with their lung capacity eroded. It was at Llandough Hospital, Cardiff, that Fletcher established, from scratch, a major research unit. Arguably his greatest achievement lay in recruiting an exceptionally able team, including Archie Cochrane, John Gilson, Philip Hugh-Jones, and Martin Wright, to the service of chest pathology and the unit's epidemiological surveys. Under his direction they achieved a new depth of understanding of pulmonary disease and its prevention. The unit also played a major role in drawing attention to the extent to which observer error plagued medical practice.

Regarding his period in Wales as a form of national service, compensating for lack of military service, Fletcher returned to the Hammersmith in 1952 as clinical lecturer in respiratory diseases. It did not prove the happiest of returns to mainstream medicine, seven years in Cardiff leaving him out of touch with clinical practice. He retreated increasingly into epidemiological surveys; it was a period of difficult adjustment and episodes of deep depression. It was, however, as a clinical epidemiologist that his career rose further, the great London smog of 1952–3 stimulating a wave of research options. He became secretary to the MRC's bronchitis research committee (1954–76), his own research including a major prospective study of bronchitis and emphysema among London's transport and Post Office workers. He also established a dialogue between North American and European physicians, who seriously lacked a consistent terminology. Until then doctors working in this field were not talking of the same diseases.

A skilled communicator himself, and undeterred by fierce opposition from members of the medical fraternity, Fletcher was already well known to the public through presentation of a range of television programmes on medical matters, notably *Hurt Minds* (1955) and *Your Life in their Hands* (1958–65). At the Royal College of Physicians, where he was elected vice-president in 1973, he drafted the first, ground breaking, report on smoking and health (1962) and was instrumental in founding the Council for Action on Smoking and Health (ASH). He continued to campaign for better communication in medicine, the topic of an inspiring Rock Carling lecture (1972) and future publications. In retirement he enjoyed gardening and beekeeping at his home on the Isle of Wight, remaining actively involved with a number of research charities and in the field of medical ethics, but no longer holding the strong religious beliefs of his youth inspired by his mother's moral crusading within the Oxford Group. Early in his career, following his pneumoconiosis studies in Wales, he was appointed CBE. Some have speculated that his outspoken lobbying against the tobacco industry, or his popular television image, denied him higher honours. Even his personal chair in clinical epidemiology (1973–6) may be regarded as rather delayed in arriving. But in advancing the public understanding of medicine more than any other physician of his generation and playing a leading role in unmasking tobacco, a lifetime feeling that he would never match his father's achievements turned out not to be justified. He died at his London home, 24 West Square, Kennington, on 15 December 1995, survived by his wife and three children. Friends and professional colleagues were among those who attended his memorial service at St Paul's Cathedral on 21 March 1996.

ELIZABETH BURROWS

Sources M. Blythe and C. Fletcher, series of unpubd biographical interviews on audiotape, 1982–8, priv. coll. · M. Blythe and C. Fletcher, interviews, Oxford Brookes University, Medical Sciences Video Archives, MSVA 001 (06.84); MSVA 001.1 (09.84) · 'Conversation with Charles Fletcher', Journal Interview 30, *British Journal of Addiction* (1992), 87, 527–38 · C. M. Fletcher, 'Medical research is reducing hazards of mining', *Municipal Journal* (29 July 1949), 1811 · C. M. Fletcher, *Communication in medicine* (1973) · C. M. Fletcher, ed., 'Terminology, definitions and classification of chronic pulmonary emphysema and related conditions: a report of the conclusions of a CIBA guest symposium', *Thorax*, 14 (1959), 286–99 · C. M. Fletcher, 'First clinical use of penicillin', *BMJ* (22–9 Dec 1984), 1721–3 · T. Jones and A. H. Willink, *James Cropper & Co. and memories of Burneside, 1845–1945* (1912) [repr. with additional notes by Westmorland Gazette Ltd, Kendal, 1945] · G. Scadding, *The Guardian* (27 Dec 1995) · *The Times* (2 Jan 1996) · G. Booth, *The Independent* (23 Dec 1995) · 'in memoriam', *Daily Telegraph* (23 March 1996) · *WW* (1955) · m. cert. · d. cert.
Archives Wellcome L., papers | CAC Cam., corresp. with A. V. Hill | FILM Oxford Brookes University, Medical Sciences, video archive recordings of interviews with Dr Max Blythe | SOUND priv. coll., unpublished audiotape recordings of interviews with Dr Max Blythe
Likenesses N. Sinclair, photograph, 1994, NPG [*see illus.*]

Fletcher, Charles Robert Leslie (1857–1934), historian, was born in London on 22 October 1857, the only child of Alexander Pearson Fletcher, an assurance company general manager, and his wife, Caroline Anna, daughter of the painter Charles Robert *Leslie and sister of Sir Bradford Leslie. He was a king's scholar at Eton College from 1868 to 1876, arriving, according to legend, in an Aberdeen version of an Eton jacket which had to be promptly discarded. In 1876 he went as a demy to Magdalen College, Oxford, obtained a first class in modern history in 1880, and won the chancellor's English essay prize and was elected a fellow of All Souls in 1881. In 1885 he married Alice Katharine (*d.* 1939), elder daughter of William Walter *Merry, rector of Lincoln College; they had three sons.

From 1883 to 1906 Fletcher was tutor and from 1889 fellow of Magdalen College. In that capacity he was one of a small group, including A. L. Smith, A. H. Johnson, Edward Armstrong, and Richard Lodge, which built up the history school at Oxford. As a tutor and lecturer he was extremely stimulating. Unconventional in his teaching methods, he never concealed his strong opinions: he was a fierce Protestant Anglican, a confirmed Conservative and imperialist, and an ardent opponent of liberalism and socialism. Although kind enough to individual women students, he refused to admit women to his lectures.

Fletcher was the founder at Magdalen of the undergraduates' history library which he ruled with a rod of iron. In 1905 he became a delegate of the Clarendon Press and was perpetual delegate from 1912 to 1927; until his death he took a lively interest in everything connected with it—its authors, its staff, and its workpeople. His main activity was in the promotion and criticism of books on modern history, and his acute and sympathetic comments were often of great value.

In his unpublished recollections Fletcher described himself as never really a loyal Magdalen man until his old age, disliking the vacuity of intellectual interests in the college. At the age of forty-nine he resigned his fellowship to concentrate on writing, becoming, according to *The Times* (2 May 1934), the greatest writer of short history since J. R. Green. His *Introductory History of England* (5 vols., 1904–23), with its famous description of the 'manor of Tubney' was written in an unusual, unconventional, and conversational style which set a fashion for some subsequent writers of popular history.

Fletcher's *School History of England* (1911) was viewed with misgivings by the Oxford University Press in light of his known prejudices but proved irresistible when Kipling was presented as co-author, contributing twenty-three new poems. In this book Fletcher gave full expression to his racial and political views, describing Spaniards as vindictive, West Indians as lazy and vicious, and the Irish as spoilt and ungrateful. His young readers were informed that democracy was still on trial in Britain and that it would be the duty of the king to dismiss any ministry which proposed to reduce the navy or surrender India or the colonies. The *School History* was hailed as the chief literary event of the coronation year by the *Church Family Times* and as a most pernicious influence on the minds of children by the *Manchester Guardian*. It remained in print and was to be found in the nurseries and schoolrooms of Britain for the next forty years, though banned in parts of the empire, to the author's bewilderment.

Among Fletcher's other works were a biography of Gustavus Adolphus (1890); *Edmond Warre* (1922); an annotated edition of Carlyle's *French Revolution* (3 vols., 1902); and *Historical Portraits* (1909–19), written in collaboration with H. B. Butler and Emery Walker. In 1914–15 and again from 1917 to 1919 he went back to Eton to help in the teaching of history, and proved an inspiring influence there. In 1915, at the age of fifty-seven, he joined the RNVR for anti-aircraft duties in London, but an attack of lumbago put an end to this enterprise. He died at his Oxford home,

Norham End, on 30 April 1934, and was survived by his wife and his eldest son, the two younger having been killed during the First World War.

Fletcher's intimate friends knew him as a racy, original, sparkling letter-writer; a glimpse of this he gave to the public in a collection of letters entitled *Mr Gladstone at Oxford 1890* (1908), a patronizing account of the statesman's conversation during a visit to All Souls in 1890.   C. H. K. MARTEN, *rev.* RICHARD SYMONDS

Sources *Oxford Magazine* (10 May 1934) · *The Times* (2 May 1934) · personal knowledge (1949) · private information (1949) · C. R. L. Fletcher, 'Recollections', Magd. Oxf. · P. Sutcliffe, *The Oxford University Press: an informal history* (1978) · Oxford University Press, archives · R. Symonds, *Oxford and empire: the last lost cause?* (1991) · CGPLA *Eng. & Wales* (1934)
Archives Bodl. Oxf., papers · Magd. Oxf., notebooks and recollections | All Souls Oxf., letters to Sir William Anson
Likenesses photograph, Magd. Oxf.
Wealth at death £28,244 19s. 11d.: probate, 1 June 1934, CGPLA *Eng. & Wales*

Fletcher, Elizabeth (1638?–1658), Quaker preacher, was probably born in October 1638 in Kendal, Westmorland. Though her parents remain unidentified, she was said to come from 'a considerable Famelly' (Penney, 258). She became a Quaker in 1652, after being 'convinced' by George Fox. She witnessed with Thomas Holme and Elizabeth Leavens (Heavens) in Cheshire and south Lancashire in early 1654. By June the two women were preaching to the scholars in Oxford, and Fletcher, though apparently 'a very modest grave young woman', went naked as a sign (ibid., 259). Public hostility from the crowd resulted in their being thrown into a pool. The vice-chancellor then ordered that the women be whipped.

Fletcher was one of the earliest Quakers to minister in Ireland. In 1655 she and Elizabeth Smith preached in Dublin and, though imprisoned there, they later set up Quaker meetings. Fletcher is next visible in the south of Ireland some time before March 1655, with Francis Howgill her companion in Cork. She made a second visit to Ireland in 1657 and travelled with Elizabeth Morgan. An account of her preaching in Youghal, co. Cork, indicates that she was opposed by Independent ministers and justified her prophetic output by speaking 'of the Lord's pouring forth his Spirit upon Sons and Daughters according to the prophet *Joel*' (Rutty, 93).

Fletcher wrote one pamphlet, *A Few Words in Season to All the Inhabitants of the Earth … to Leave off their Wickedness* (1660), a prophetic warning in which she describes herself as 'a servant of the Lord, who hath known his terror for sin' (Fletcher, 8). The text gives a flavour of her hortatory skills. She invokes the wrath and indignation of God against the proud and covetous, whom she believes must reform immediately or 'go down into the Lake that burneth for evermore' (ibid., 6). Fletcher died in July 1658 in Kirkby Lonsdale, and was buried in nearby Kendal aged about 19 years and 9 months. Her final illness was described as a 'weake and declineing Condition', and her early death attributed to her experience of persecution.

Thomas Camm, a fellow Quaker, blamed the 'schollers and rable' who attacked her for the fact that she 'was never so well againe in health' (Penney, 259–60).

CATIE GILL

Sources N. Penney, ed., 'The first publishers of truth': being early records, now first printed, of the introduction of Quakerism into the counties of England and Wales (1907) · J. Rutty, A history of the rise and progress of the people called Quakers in Ireland (1751) · E. Fletcher, A few words in season (1660) · R. Hubberthorne, A true testimony of the zeal of Oxford-professors and university-men who for zeal persecute the servants of the living God (1654) · M. R. Brailsford, Quaker women, 1650–1690 (1915) · W. C. Braithwaite, The beginnings of Quakerism, ed. H. J. Cadbury, 2nd edn (1955); repr. (1981) · P. Mack, Visionary women: ecstatic prophesy in seventeenth-century England, new edn (Berkeley, CA, 1994) · J. Besse, A collection of the sufferings of the people called Quakers, 2 vols. (1753) · 'Dictionary of Quaker biography', RS Friends, Lond. [card index] · M. Bell, G. Parfitt, and S. Shepherd, A biographical dictionary of English women writers, 1580–1720 (1990) · P. Kilroy, Protestant dissent and controversy in Ireland, 1660–1714 (1994)
Archives RS Friends, Lond., Swarthmore MSS

Fletcher [*married name* Wedderburn], **Elizabeth** [Betty] (*d.* **1758**), scholar, was the youngest of the eight children of Andrew *Fletcher, Lord Milton (1691/2–1766), lord justice clerk of Scotland, and his wife, Elizabeth Kinloch (*d.* 1782), daughter of Sir Francis Kinloch of Gilmerton. Generally known as Betty, the younger Elizabeth's birth date is unknown, and her life was brief. According to her only daughter, also Elizabeth, she married early and within a year she was dead in childbed (Wedderburn, 104–5).

Starkly summarized, Betty Fletcher's short existence and untimely end might seem tragic but unremarkable in an age of high maternal mortality. However, there was more to Betty than these brief facts suggest. Her father, Lord Milton, known for his shrewdness, leniency, and discretion, exercised these qualities not only as a judge but as confidential agent to Sir Robert Walpole's leading Scottish adviser, Archibald Campbell, Lord Ilay, later third duke of Argyll. The two men were friends as well as business associates, and so Betty spent several weeks each summer with her parents and sisters at Inveraray Castle, the duke of Argyll's principal residence. There she mixed with a stimulating group of clever young men. One of them was Robert Adam the celebrated architect, then at the start of his career. Proud and ambitious, he felt that Lord Milton's family were patronizing him when he met them at Inveraray in 1754. When Betty said that she envied his forthcoming opportunity of going to Italy, for she loved paintings, he commented to his own sisters: 'This from the stinkingest of mortals I look'd on as no small compliment, till [the] next disdainful look from her nizzety gab wipt entirely away all impression of it'. He went on to characterize her sister Mally as proud and overbearing and their amiable mother as 'virulent' (Lindsay and Cosh, 70).

Adam's reaction was not shared by others, for it seems that Betty was very popular with her contemporaries. More than that, she played an important role in the circle of young men who were to become the leading intellectuals of Scotland's Enlightenment. It was she who introduced William Robertson the historian, David Hume and Adam Ferguson the philosophers, Adam Smith the economist, and John Home the playwright to her father and so to the all-powerful Lord Ilay. 'They owe their rise to her—genius, taste and refinement of sentiment in no degree inferior to their own', her daughter wrote proudly, many years later, commenting that not one of them would disclaim it (Wedderburn, 104–5).

In the late 1750s Betty met Captain John Wedderburn of Gosford (1720–1793), who later changed his name to Halkett when he inherited the baronetcy of Pitfirrane. They fell in love, and married on 6 February 1758. A devoted couple, they hated being apart even for a few hours, but within months of the wedding Captain Wedderburn's regiment was posted to the West Indies. Betty was by now pregnant, and her friends urged her to use her influence to have her husband sent somewhere nearer home. She refused to interfere, and he set sail. She bore his absence with serenity, but she had always been delicate and 'Grief suppressed preys on the vitals' (Wedderburn, 104–5). She gave birth to a daughter, whom she named after herself, but died soon afterwards, on 18 December 1758, telling her friends, 'I have done my duty to my husband's honour, but my doing so has cost me my life' (ibid.).

Captain Wedderburn returned to Scotland, eventually remarried, and had fourteen more children, but he never forgot his first wife and he brought up their daughter on tales of her mother's modesty, discernment, and thirst for knowledge. At a time when women were increasingly developing scholarly interests, her short life demonstrates how, even without a formal education, intelligent women could play a full and influential part in intellectual society.

ROSALIND K. MARSHALL

Sources E. Wedderburn, 'A memoir of Fletchers of Saltoun', U. Edin. L., MS La. iii.364a, 104–5 · Edinburgh Register of Testaments, CC8/8/125/1 (Betty Fletcher), CC8/8/126/1 (Elizabeth Kinloch), NA Scot. · I. G. Lindsay and M. Cosh, Inveraray and the dukes of Argyll (1973) · The correspondence of Adam Ferguson, ed. V. Merolle, 2 vols. (1995) · GEC, Baronetage, 4.374
Archives NA Scot., MSS · probably NL Scot., Fletcher of Saltoun MSS
Wealth at death £100 of capital stock in British Linen Company: Edinburgh Register of Testaments 20 Dec 1780, NA Scot., CC8/8/125/1

Fletcher [*née* Dawson], **Elizabeth** [Eliza] (1770–1858), poet and autobiographer, was born on 15 January 1770 in Oxton, Yorkshire, the only child of a land surveyor named Dawson (*d.* 1798) and his wife (*d.* 1770), whose maiden name was Hill. Mrs Dawson died soon after the birth of her daughter, and Eliza was raised by her father and grandmother, who both doted on her, giving her considerable freedom and encouraging her to follow her own intellectual interests. Educated until she was eleven by her neighbour Mrs Brudenell, an unhappily married friend of her mother, Eliza then went to the Manor House School in York. Although the school library was poorly stocked (it contained only four volumes of *The Spectator*) she none the less managed to read widely in the English classics and contemporary European writing and to develop a passionate interest in literature. When she was given £20 to spend on books while she was still at school, her purchases included editions of Milton and Cowper and *The Sorrows of Young Werther*.

On 16 July 1791 Eliza Dawson married Archibald *Fletcher (1746–1828), an Edinburgh lawyer some twenty-five years her senior, whom she had met four years before. Mr Dawson initially disapproved of the marriage, but according to Eliza Fletcher's autobiography it was very happy. The Fletchers were politically active: Archibald Fletcher was a reformer who served as an unpaid counsel to the defendants during the Edinburgh sedition trial in 1793, and Eliza Fletcher apparently shared her husband's views. Before her marriage, she had gathered five hundred subscriptions for Ann Yearsley's poetry, and some years later she—along with Anne Grant and others—helped John Henning, a working-class Scottish artist, during his attempts to establish himself in London. By the early years of the nineteenth century, Eliza Fletcher had also established herself as one of the leading hostesses in the literary circles in Edinburgh, where her sympathies lay most fully with the whig writers of the *Edinburgh Review*. Her literary friendships crossed party lines, however; the ardent tory essayist and letter-writer Anne Grant, writing in 1810, placed Eliza Fletcher first among her Edinburgh friends, describing her as 'a Yorkshire lady, possessed of beauty and talents' whose 'enlightened, animated, and unaffected conversation' have made her 'the admiration of Edinburgh for years past' (*Memoir*, ed. Grant, 1.253). While Eliza spent most of her married life in and around Edinburgh or in the north of England, she became acquainted with writers from all across Britain. Her eldest daughter was educated by Anna Laetitia Barbauld, and Eliza Fletcher met many of her famous contemporaries during occasional visits to London. Despite her literary interests, Eliza Fletcher wrote relatively little herself, and during her lifetime, she was perhaps better known for her commitment to a number of benevolent causes than for her own writing. Aside from her posthumously published letters and autobiography, her only important publication was *Elidure and Edward*, blank verse 'historical sketches' printed in London in 1825. (Other poems and a journal of a tour she made to the highlands remained unpublished.) In addition, she wrote a brief memoir of her daughter Grace, who died in 1817 and who was, according to Anne Grant, 'the only one' of her six children who 'could be compared to her mother for talent' (ibid., 2.175). When her husband's health started to decline in 1816, Eliza Fletcher began to spend more of her time in the Stirlingshire countryside and at Auchindinny House, near Edinburgh, where Archibald Fletcher died in December 1828. During nearly thirty years as a widow, Eliza Fletcher continued to develop her literary interests and connections, particularly in the Lake District, where she settled in 1839; there she became a good friend of the Wordsworths. Following her death at Loughrigg, Grasmere, on 5 February 1858, her daughter Mary (then Lady Richardson) edited her letters and autobiography, which were published in 1875 and which are noteworthy for their vivid picture of early nineteenth-century Scottish literary society. PAM PERKINS

Sources *Autobiography of Mrs Fletcher*, ed. M. R. [M. Richardson], 2nd edn (1875) · *Memoir and correspondence of Mrs Grant of Laggan*, ed. J. P. Grant, 3 vols. (1844) · M. Wilson, *Jane Austen and some contemporaries* (1938) · J. G. Peters, 'An unpublished letter from M. Edgeworth to E. Fletcher', *ELN* (1993), 44–52 · Blain, Clements & Grundy, *Feminist comp.* · Anderson, *Scot. nat.* · M. Oliphant, *The literary history of England*, 3 vols. (1882)
Archives NL Scot., autobiography | NL Scot., letters, MSS
Likenesses J. Henning, porcelain medallion, 1802, Scot. NPG · G. Richmond, pencil drawing, 1850, Scot. NPG · plaster medallion (after J. Henning; after medallion in possession of M. Bell, 1892), Scot. NPG · two engravings, repro. in Richardson, ed., *Autobiography*
Wealth at death under £3000: probate, 29 March 1858, *CGPLA Eng. & Wales*

Fletcher, Sir Frank (1870–1954), headmaster, was born on 3 May 1870 at Atherton, near Manchester, the eldest son of Ralph Fletcher and his wife, Fanny Smith. The family were colliery owners known for the care of their employees and among the first to install life-saving apparatus and pithead baths. Frank was brought up to a simplicity of life and a sense of responsibility. At twelve he won a scholarship at Rossall School, then under H. A. James and afterwards C. C. Tancock. From Rossall, Henry Stuart-Jones and R. W. Lee won scholarships at Balliol and Fletcher followed them in 1889. He became the pupil of W. R. Hardie and won first classes in classical moderations (1891) and *literae humaniores* (1893), as well as the Craven (1890), Ireland (1891), and Derby (1894) scholarships. In his last year he played in the university hockey team against Cambridge; trained on the sands of Rossall as an individualist, he twice took the ball down the wing and scored a goal. He also acquired a passion for mountaineering, first in the Engadine and later in the southern Alps, and became a member of the Alpine Club.

In Fletcher's day the classics were supreme at Oxford and with his record he might well have chosen to become a don. His interest lay, however, in the teaching of boys and after two terms' tutoring at Balliol he accepted (in 1894) an offer from John Percival of a mastership at Rugby School. There he taught the classical sixth, among whom were R. H. Tawney and later William Temple, and also had the invaluable experience of teaching a low form. In 1902 he married Dorothy (d. 1958), daughter of William Pope, of Crediton; there were no children.

Fletcher was ambitious and stood for several headmasterships before he was elected in 1903 to be master of Marlborough College. As the first headmaster of a great public school who was not a clergyman, he was 'one lay apple in the clerical dumpling', as *The Times* put it (Hinde, 109). Fletcher's successes as a classical master at Rugby, as well as the fact that he was married, recommended him to the school's governing council. He loved the place, his life, and his teaching. Plato, St Paul, and Browning were his favourite subjects. As he set about curbing the philistine games cult which had grown up among the boys, and raising academic standards, Fletcher gained confidence in his capacity to rule. There were difficulties at first and mistakes; he was sometimes hasty, and his young wife's tact and charm were frequently needed to smooth out the resulting difficulties.

In 1911 Fletcher was invited to take on the headship of Charterhouse School and, pressed by the archbishop of Canterbury (Randall Davidson), he felt bound to accept. Under the mild regime of his predecessor, the scholarly G. H. Rendall, the housemasters had effectively run the school and games players (the bloods) had been allowed to exert excessive influence among the boys. It did not take Fletcher long to realize the problems or to start to deal with them and in consequence he was not at first popular. But masters and boys soon came to understand his aims and to recognize his fundamental kindliness and long before the end of his reign he was revered and loved. He tightened discipline (and was fierce with the cane), introduced new subjects to the curriculum, and had the school inspected for the first time (1913). His chief visible contribution to Charterhouse was the war memorial chapel, which was completed to the designs of Giles Gilbert Scott in 1927. During Fletcher's headmastership Charterhouse was restored to the forefront of public schools, and successfully rode out the depression which reduced pupil numbers at many other schools between the wars. He chose his assistant masters wisely and let them develop on their own lines. He was himself a man of high ideals which he felt that he could reach. The result was a kind of unconscious conceit which deceived those who did not know him well. Beneath it was a true humility arising from a naturally religious life which showed itself in his sermons and speeches.

Fletcher was not a great innovator, but his approach won admirers among his peers in the conservative educational climate of the 1920s and 1930s. He has been judged 'a schoolmaster's headmaster, decisive in judgement, conservative in approach and impressive in appearance and speech' (Quick, 108). He was many times chairman of the Headmasters' Conference and his knighthood in 1937 reflected his standing as one of the most prominent headmasters of his time. Balliol made him an honorary fellow in 1924. In 1935 he retired from Charterhouse and went to live near Dartmouth, where he did great service on the Devon education committee and on the governing bodies of several schools. Returning to his classical interests, he published an edition of the sixth book of the *Aeneid* (1941) and *Notes to the Agamemnon of Aeschylus* (1949), both admirable examples of the best sixth-form classical teaching. He was president of the Classical Association in 1946. In 1948 the Fletchers moved to Eashing near Godalming, where they could revisit Charterhouse and their many friends. Fletcher died in a nursing home at Hindhead, Surrey, on 17 November 1954.   CYRIL BAILEY, rev. M. C. CURTHOYS

Sources F. Fletcher, *After many days* (1937) · *The Times* (18 Nov 1954) · *The Carthusian* (March 1955) · private information (1971) · personal knowledge (1971) · T. Hinde, *Paths of progress: a history of Marlborough College* (1992) · A. Quick, *Charterhouse: a history of the school* (1990) · CGPLA Eng. & Wales (1955)

Likenesses G. Harcourt, oils, c.1915, Marlborough College, Wiltshire · photograph, c.1930, repro. in Quick, *Charterhouse*, 98 · J. Epstein, bronze bust, Charterhouse School, Surrey · bust (after J. Epstein), Rossall School, Lancashire · photograph, repro. in Hinde, *Paths of progress*, 109

Wealth at death £62,939 3s. 1d.: probate, 26 Jan 1955, *CGPLA Eng. & Wales*

Fletcher, George (d. 1855), reputed centenarian, was born, according to his own account, on 2 February 1747. However, according to baptismal records a George Fletcher was baptized on 15 October 1764, the son of Joseph Fletcher of Clarborough, Nottinghamshire. He was brought up a Wesleyan and was a farm labourer for some years. On 2 November 1785 he enlisted in the Royal Welch Fusiliers, from which regiment he deserted on 16 March 1792. Various accounts are given of his army service, and he seems to have taken advantage of an amnesty granted to deserters in 1793, and re-enlisted on 14 March 1793, stating that he had first joined the army in October 1773. He remained with the army for a further ten years. He was pensioned from Chelsea Hospital on 18 April 1803 at 1s. 2½d. a day. From 1803 to 1839 he served with the West India Dock Company and retired on a pension. He became a Wesleyan Methodist local preacher, and large congregations came to hear him owing to his great age; according to his own announcement, he was 108 in June 1854. In his sermons he gave sketches of his career, claiming that he had been present at the battle of Bunker Hill in June 1775 and that he had served with Abercromby in Egypt. His portrait, ostensibly aged 106, was extensively sold in 1853. He lived for another two years, and died at his home, 41 Wade Street, Poplar, London, on 2 March 1855, probably aged ninety-one.   G. C. BOASE, rev. J. GILLILAND

Sources *GM*, 2nd ser., 43 (1855), 440 · *GM*, 2nd ser., 44 (1855), 657 · *ILN* (10 March 1855), 221 · Boase, *Mod. Eng. biog.* · *The Times* (13 Feb 1855), 7g

Likenesses portrait, repro. in *ILN*

Fletcher, Giles, the elder (bap. 1546, d. 1611), diplomat and author, was baptized on 26 November 1546 in Watford, Hertfordshire, the second son of Richard Fletcher (c.1523–1586), Church of England clergyman of Bishop's Stortford, Hertfordshire, and subsequently of Cranbrook, Kent, and his wife, Joan (d. 1557?). His elder brother was Richard *Fletcher (d. 1596). His father was ordained by Nicholas Ridley, bishop of London, in 1550, and was deprived by Mary I.

Education and academic career, 1561–1580 About 1561 Giles Fletcher started at Eton College, where he seems to have shown early promise as a poet. He contributed eleven Latin verses to a manuscript presented to Elizabeth I when she visited the school in 1563, more than double the number written by any other pupil. On 27 August 1565 he was admitted as a scholar to King's College, Cambridge. He was made a fellow on 28 August 1568, and proceeded BA in 1569–70. Fletcher was made lecturer at King's College on 22 March 1572, holding this post until the following March, when he was appointed lecturer in Greek. On 3 July 1573 he commenced MA.

The best of Fletcher's poetic writing during this period includes three eclogues commenting on the state of religion in and outside Cambridge; they were later published in *Poemata varii argumenti* (1678). These eclogues are among the earliest Latin pastorals to be written in England.

Another poem, *De literis antiquae Britanniae*, is an allegorical narration of a distinctively protestant and Cambridge-centred history of British learning. Revised about 1594 it was eventually published by his son Phineas *Fletcher (1582–1650) in 1633. *De literis antiquae Britanniae* and two of the eclogues were included in a presentation manuscript of poems sent by Fletcher to Mildred Cecil, Lady Burghley, in the hope of preferment.

In 1576 Fletcher became involved in internecine quarrelling at King's College, joining other junior fellows, Robert Dunning, Stephen Lakes, Robert Johnson, and Robert Liles, in protest against the new provost, Roger Goad. Goad was accused of offences ranging from financial corruption to 'uncleanes of lief not to be named' (*English Works*, 11). The college's visitor, Thomas Cooper, bishop of Lincoln, handed the problem over to William Cecil, first Baron Burghley, lord treasurer, and when he found in Goad's favour Dunning and Lakes were imprisoned; Fletcher too may have been briefly detained. The fellows were required to write letters of submission to Burghley and Goad, and Lakes was ordered to make a public apology on behalf of all five. Fletcher continued, however, to gain promotion at Cambridge. He was appointed deputy public orator and examiner in 1577, senior fellow in 1578, and bursar in 1579. He was diverted into the study of civil law on 28 October 1579, and was appointed commissary to Dr Richard Bridgewater, chancellor of the diocese of Ely, on 3 July 1580. In autumn 1580 he gained his highest academic post, that of dean of arts.

Public life, 1580–1591 During 1580, however, Fletcher decided to marry, and was thus required to resign his fellowship. He married Joan Sheafe (1562–1614) in his father's church at Cranbrook on 16 January 1581. They had at least eight children, Phineas (*bap.* 1582), Anne (*bap.* 1584), Giles *Fletcher the younger (1585/6–1623), Elizabeth (*bap.* 1587, *d.* 1593), Joan (*bap.* 1588), Sarah (*bap.* 1590), Judith (*bap.* 1591), and Nehemias (*d.* 1596). On 23 June he was created LLD. After their marriage the Fletchers lived for some years at Cranbrook, but about 1585 moved to London, where three of their children were baptized. Although he left Cambridge on his marriage Fletcher seems to have retained links with his old college and later contributed a poem to a Cambridge volume published in honour of Sir Philip Sidney, *Academiae Cantabrigiensis lachrymae tumulo* (1587). He was JP for Sussex from 1582. In November 1584 he was elected MP for Winchelsea, Sussex, apparently through the influence of William Brooke, tenth Baron Cobham, lord warden of the Cinque Ports. Cobham's son, Maximilian, was a contemporary of Fletcher's at King's College, and Fletcher wrote a poem for Maximilian's coat of arms which was published in the 1587 edition of Raphael Holinshed's *Chronicles of England, Scotland, and Ireland*.

Fletcher gained his first permanent post as remembrancer to the city of London after the queen wrote to the mayor and aldermen on his behalf. He was formally confirmed in the appointment on 26 January 1586 and was admitted to the freedom of the city by redemption in the Haberdashers' Company. Fletcher seems also to have allied himself with the veteran diplomat Sir Thomas Randolph. In February he gained his first diplomatic experience, accompanying Randolph on his mission to Scotland. On 17 May Fletcher wrote from Edinburgh to Sir Francis Walsingham, principal secretary, saying that though he was 'not desirous to follow any ambitious course', he 'wouldbee very glad to bee employed … in soom honest service, that exceedeth not the measure and proportion of my mean qualitie' (*English Works*, 349). In May 1587 he was sent with Richard Saltonstall, governor of the Merchant Adventurers' Company, to negotiate with the senate of Hamburg. They conducted discussions for two months to little effect, and concluded a treaty with nearby Stade instead, securing the rights of the Merchant Adventurers' Company in the region for the next ten years. This was part of Elizabeth's efforts to find a vent for English overseas trade other than the Low Countries.

Fletcher's next mission was more prestigious, but also more dangerous. On 6 June 1588 he was sent as special ambassador to Moscow with orders to secure the privileges granted to the English merchants in Russia. This post was probably gained with the help of Randolph, who had himself been ambassador in 1568–9. Relations between the merchants and Feodor I had come under repeated strain in the 1580s, with various charges levelled against the Russia Company's agents. The difficulty of Fletcher's task was brought home to him immediately upon his arrival in Moscow; he later wrote to Burghley, 'my whole intertainment from my first arrival till towards the very end was such as if they had divised meanes of very purpose to shew their utter disliking both of the trade of the Marchants, and of the whole English nation' (*English Works*, 367). At length conditions improved; Fletcher gained an audience with the tsar on 19 December and was eventually able to negotiate a favourable settlement. He received permission to leave Feodor's court on 22 April 1589 but did not leave Russia until July or August. On his return to England, according to Thomas Fuller, 'he heartily exprest his thankfulnesse to God for his safe return from so great a danger; for the *Poets* cannot fansie *Ulysses* more glad to be come out of the *Den* of *Polyphemus*, than he was to be rid out of the power of such a *barbarious Prince*' (Fuller, *Worthies*, pt 2, sig. L3r).

Literary activities and civic duties, 1591–1601 Fletcher wrote an account of his travels, *Of the Russe commonwealth, or, The manner of government by the Russe emperor … with the manners, and fashions of the people of that country* (1591). It seems to have been suppressed at the request of the Russia Company, who were worried by his criticisms of the Russian tsar and state. There were no further single editions until 1643, although expurgated versions were included by Richard Hakluyt and Samuel Purchas in their anthologies of travel writing. The book is not wholly original; although Fletcher's reaction to what he perceived as Russian tyranny and his protestant inflected descriptions of the Russian church are distinctive, other parts of the tract draw on the accounts of English merchants, and on Baron

Sigismond von Herberstein's Latin description, first published in 1549. It was praised by his contemporaries: Purchas remarked that it was 'by men judicious which have in those parts enjoyed most honourable employment, and exactest intelligence, commended' (S. Purchas, *Purchas his Pilgrimes*, 4 vols., 1625, vol. 2, sig. R3*r*), and John Milton remarked that Fletcher's recollections 'being judicious and exact are best red entirely by themselves' (J. Milton, *A Brief History of Moscovia*, 1682, sig. H2*v*). The *Russe commonwealth* may have been written when Fletcher was prevented from writing a Latin history of Elizabeth's reign; he sent a letter to Burghley in November 1590 outlining the project and requesting access to public documents, but his request seems to have been turned down.

In 1593 *Licia*, Fletcher's most substantial poetic achievement, was published together with a first-person narrative poem, *The Rising to the Crown of Richard III*. The volume was published anonymously, but Phineas Fletcher attributes *Richard III* to his father in his *Piscatorie Eclogs* (1633), in which Giles Fletcher is characterized as the shepherd-poet Thelgon. Highly modish on its first publication, *Licia* comprised a sonnet sequence, elegies, and other short poems; the inclusion of *Richard III* can be compared to the inclusion of similar poems with the sonnet sequences of Samuel Daniel and Michael Drayton. Despite the accomplished nature of Fletcher's verse the volume is as notable for its preface, in which he echoes Sidney's *Apology for Poetry* in his defence of 'this trifling labor'.

In June 1596 Fletcher's brother Richard, bishop of London, wrote to Burghley and to Sir Robert Cecil, principal secretary, asking that Giles Fletcher be made extraordinary master of requests (a post he previously held while ambassador to Russia). Fletcher's post of remembrancer to the city of London was said to cause 'the mislyke & displeasure of great persons, for that he is inforced oftentymes to deliver unto them many unpleasing & denying messages [on] the cityes behalf' (BL, Lansdowne MS 82, no. 28). Fletcher had not ceased seeking patronage from various quarters. In 1596 he is first mentioned in connection with Robert Devereux, second earl of Essex; Fletcher was said to be 'intirelye devoted' to the earl (LPL, MS 658, fol. 202), and during the Cadiz expedition of June 1596 attempted to move the citizens of London and the city authorities in his favour.

On 15 June Richard Fletcher died suddenly, and Giles Fletcher was left to deal with his brother's heavily indebted estate and with bringing up his eight children, including the future dramatist John *Fletcher (1579–1625). As executor he was required to pay the debts owed to Elizabeth. In petitioning her on behalf of himself and his brother's children Fletcher was assisted by Essex, and it was through the latter's influence that the debt was eventually discharged in April 1597. Fletcher's appointment as treasurer of St Paul's Cathedral on 23 May probably also owed something to the earl's influence. Relations within the Fletcher family remained close until 1599–1600, when Giles Fletcher sued his brother-in-law, Nathaniel Pownell, regarding the sale of goods from the estate, and was in turn sued by Richard Fletcher's eldest son, Nathaniel.

In August 1597 Fletcher was employed with others (including the notorious government agent Richard Topcliffe) to examine the players—among them, Gabriel Spenser, Robert Shaa, and Ben Jonson—imprisoned in connection with performances of the allegedly seditious play *The Isle of Dogs*. This was the most notable among a variety of tasks he performed on behalf of the privy council about this time. He was sent on another diplomatic mission in May 1598, seeking a residency for the Merchant Adventurers' Company in the United Provinces, since their treaty with Stade had recently expired. The mission was successfully concluded in July.

The Essex revolt and final years, 1601–1611 Fletcher's association with Essex brought him into considerable danger after the abortive revolt of February 1601. On 14 February he was committed to the custody of a London alderman; on 3 March he testified that he had taken no active part in the revolt because Essex did not 'thinck so ill of mee as to judge mee a fitt man or safe for himself to impart with mee any suche ungodly practise knowing mee well that I would not indure to heer suche things, and not reveal them' (*English Works*, 406–7). During his imprisonment he complained that various people were trying to wrest his post as remembrancer from him, and in May 1601 one of the suitors, Clement Edmondes, was sworn in as his assistant; Edmondes took over the post when Fletcher finally resigned on 2 July 1605.

Fletcher was never favoured by James VI and I and never recovered financially from the blows dealt by inheriting his brother's debts and by his own imprisonment. In his last extant letter, dated 2 July 1609, he reminded the first earl of Salisbury (Robert Cecil) of his diplomatic service and complained of the 'unabillitie of my state to maintein the charge which God hath given mee' (*English Works*, 413). He seemed to have been made promises which were not kept: 'I am an humble suitor to his Majestie', he wrote, 'for his gratious help and supportation which at his entrance to this Kingdoom and long before hee voutchsafed to promise owt of his own meer goodnes and Princely grace withowt desert' (ibid.). In 1610 he returned to diplomatic life with a mission to meet Dr Jonas Charisius, the Danish ambassador, on behalf of the Merchant Adventurers' Company. His last piece of writing, 'The tartars or the ten tribes', a short treatise in the style of the *Russe commonwealth*, which conjectured that the Tartars were descended from the ten lost tribes of Israel, probably dates from this period. It was published in *Israel redux* (1677) by Samuel Lee, who claimed to have been given the manuscript by Fletcher's grandson.

Fletcher died in London on 11 March 1611, having made a nuncupative will in which he left all his property to his wife, who died on 14 August 1614. According to his son Phineas his last words were:

> had I followed the course of this World, and would either have given, or taken bribes, I might (happily) have made you rich, but now must leave you nothing but your education … But know certainly, that I your weak, and dying Father leave

you to an everliving, and All-sufficient Father, and in him a never fading inheritance; who will not suffer you to want any good thing, who hath been my God, and will be the God of my seed.   (P. Fletcher, *A Fathers Testament*, 1670, sig. B1v)

Poetry and protestantism In keeping with his family connections Fletcher maintained a commitment to English protestantism throughout his life. His pastoral poems of the 1570s focus on the need to maintain and protect the fragile Church of England, and he also contributed a commendatory poem to the 1576 edition of John Foxe's *Actes and Monuments*. Later Fletcher served on a parliamentary committee concerned with religious affairs, accused the Russian church of 'popish' practices in the *Russe commonwealth*, and was involved in the examination of priests and recusants in the 1590s.

Fletcher retains a quietly influential position in English literature, leaving to his sons and other poets such as Milton a tradition of religious commitment and poetic, especially pastoral, experimentation. His *Russe commonwealth* is still recognized as one of the most important foreign accounts of sixteenth-century Russia. Dependent as he was on patronage, especially after he left Cambridge, Fletcher's writing—poetic and non-poetic—cannot be separated from his public role, and his life in many ways typifies the possibilities and problems of the careers open to educated Elizabethan gentlemen.   LUCY MUNRO

Sources *The English works of Giles Fletcher, the elder*, ed. L. E. Berry (1964) · BL, Lansdowne MS 82, no. 28 · LPL, MS 658, fol. 202 · L. E. Berry, 'Giles Fletcher the elder: a bibliography', *Transactions of the Cambridge Bibliographical Society*, 3 (1961), 200–15 · S. H. Baron, *Explorations in Muscovite history* (1991) · G. McMullan, 'Giles Fletcher the elder (November 1546 – 11 March 1611)', *Sixteenth-century British nondramatic writers: second series*, ed. D. A. Richardson, DLitB, 136 (1994), 122–6 · L. Piépho, 'The ecclesiastical eclogues of Giles Fletcher the elder', *Acta Conventius Neo-Latini Hafniensis*, ed. R. Schnur, A. Moss, P. Dust, P. G. Schmidt, and J. Chomcrat (1994), 817–29 · L. E. Berry, 'Phineas Fletcher's account of his father', *JEGP: Journal of English and Germanic Philology*, 60 (1961), 258–67 · L. E. Berry, 'Five Latin poems by Giles Fletcher, the elder', *Anglia*, 79 (1962), 338–77 · L. E. Berry, 'Three poems by Giles Fletcher, the elder, in "Poemata varii argumentii" (1678)', *N&Q*, 204 (1959), 132–4 · R. Raymo, 'Three new Latin poems of Giles Fletcher the elder', *Modern Language Notes*, 71 (1956), 399–401 · P. Collinson, 'Cranbrook and the Fletchers: popular and unpopular religion in the Kentish weald', *Godly people: essays on English protestantism and puritanism* (1983) · parish register, London, St Katharine Coleman, 11 March 1611 [burial]

Archives BL, Royal MSS · Hunt. L. · PRO, state papers · Queens' College, Cambridge, MSS | BL, Lansdowne MSS · Hatfield House, Hertfordshire, Cecil papers

Wealth at death in a poor state financially in the fifteen years leading up to his death: letter to Robert Cecil, 14 March 1601; letter to Robert Cecil, 2 July 1609; nuncupative will, 11 February 1611; *English works*, ed. Berry, 48, 408–09, 413

Fletcher, Giles, the younger (1585/6–1623), poet, the son of Giles *Fletcher (*bap.* 1546, *d.* 1611), notable Elizabethan courtier and ambassador to Russia, and Joan Sheafe (1562–1614), of Cranbrook, Kent, was born in London; he was the brother of the poet Phineas *Fletcher and cousin to the dramatist John *Fletcher. According to Fuller, relying on the authority of John Ramsey, who married the poet's widow, Fletcher was educated at Westminster School. Encouraged and supported by Dr Thomas Neville, master

of Trinity College, Cambridge, he entered Trinity in September 1601; he was elected a scholar on 12 April 1605, proceeded BA in 1606, and became a fellow of the college on 17 September 1608 and university reader in Greek grammar in 1615.

Fletcher began writing poetry at a very young age, contributing some conventional elegiac verses 'Upon the Death of Eliza' to a commemorative volume on the death of Queen Elizabeth and the accession of James I (1603). His next and certainly principal work, after which he wrote almost nothing and on which his fame rests, appeared in 1610: this edition of *Christs Victorie, and Triumph in Heaven, and Earth, over, and after Death* was the only one published in his lifetime (there was a second edition in 1632, like the first printed in Cambridge). Fletcher dedicates his poem to Thomas Neville, in terms effusive even for the time; then he proceeds to his prefatory remarks 'To the Reader' in which he defends 'prophane Poetrie' that nevertheless may deal 'with divine and heavenly matters'. He invokes the names of Prudentius, St Bernard, Sannazaro, and especially DuBartas and Spenser—these two last having had, indeed, the greatest influence on Fletcher; yet Grosart perhaps justly describes Fletcher 'as the pioneer of England's religious poetry in epic or semi-epic form' (Grosart, 49).

Fletcher's 'epic' is very much in his own voice, imitative in a limited way of Spenser, and only incidentally instructive to such later writers as Edward Benlowes, Joseph Beaumont, and John Milton. The work itself is somewhat discontinuous, for it is actually four separate poems, each with its own title, in two parts, with two different title-pages: 'Christs Victorie in Heaven' (part 1/1); 'Christs Victorie on Earth' (part 1/2); 'Christs Triumph over Death' (part 2/3); and 'Christs Triumph after Death' (part 2/4). There is a further complication in that the first of the two title-pages is inclusive of the whole work, the second descriptive only of the last two parts. These four poems, which might also be called cantos, are very loosely related to each other. Grundy notes that:

> each poem pursues a different method from the rest: the first is similar to a mediaeval debate or psychomachia; the second is a Spenserian allegory; the third is a meditation on the Passion in the manner of the literature of 'Tears'; the fourth is a sustained Christian-Platonic beatific vision.
> (Grundy, 194)

Thus the four parts each illustrate a different literary genre.

Fletcher's poetry is often loosely described as baroque, a term notoriously difficult to define; in Fletcher's case it means that he manifests an Italianate sensuousness, characteristic, for example, of Giambattista Marino (1569–1625), 'the poet of the marvelous', whom both Giles and Phineas Fletcher, along with many of their contemporaries such as Richard Crashaw, read and admired. Stupefaction, astonishment, and unconditional wonder define their poetic vision:

> Wonder doeth call me up to see, O no,
> I cannot see, and therefore sinke in woonder,
> The man, that shines as bright as God, not so,

For God he is himselfe, that close lies under
That man, so close, that no time can dissunder
That band, yet not so close, but from him breake
Such beames, as mortall eyes are all too weake
Such sight to see, or it, if they should see, to speake.
('Christs Victorie', stanza 6, Boas, 1.41)

This vision, or the attempt to possess it, Fletcher combines with a copious use of rhetorical figures. He is intensely fond of antithesis, paradox, and contrasting patterns, above all of *antimetabole*, as in 'if any for love of honour or honour of love'. Sensuousness and rhetorical fancy, then, distinguish Fletcher's poem, which should be accorded a prominent place in the history of English epic writing.

The criss-cross nature of *antimetabole* forms a *chiasmus* (cross-patterning) and it may be observed in many stanzas throughout *Christs Victorie, and Triumph*. This cross-patterning shapes the structure of the whole poem, as Grundy shows, for the four books are disposed in the order heaven–earth–earth–heaven, a system of relationships that discloses the poem's theme. Through this theme, 'Fletcher expresses his awareness of the distance between earth and heaven, but also of the traffic between and temporary union of them brought about by the Incarnation' (Grundy, 197). The scene in heaven, with the debate between Justice and Mercy, closes after Mercy's speech (parts 1 and 2); for now the action moves to earth, where God is man, and the mystery of the incarnation is urgently conveyed (part 3). In the fourth part, Fletcher deals with the movement from earth to heaven, from the resurrection to the climax of the poem, the ascension. Christ is borne upwards on angels' wings, with the disciples looking up, an episode that parallels that of the first book where Justice and Mercy look down. Earth and heaven are separate, yet united, and Christ's triumph continues everlastingly. Yet there is more—an apocalyptic or beatific vision with the triumph of Christ and the joys of the New Jerusalem—in sustained, rapturous passages of extraordinary power and magnificence.

Much of Fletcher's poetry echoes Spenser—for example the debate of Justice and Mercy, which recalls the narrative of the 'Mutability Cantos'. But Fletcher's work is uniquely his own, and even the stanza form is original, an eight-line modification of Spenser's nine-line stanza. In the second part of his work Fletcher details the temptation in the wilderness, where Satan (a little like Spenser's Archimago) occurs in what becomes a new Eden, with voluptuous details and glorious sensuality—unashamedly a bower of bliss. Milton knew Fletcher's work but his account of the temptation in *Paradise Regained* is far more austere; also, Milton follows the order of temptations in Luke (4: 1–13), whereas Fletcher uses Matthew (4: 1–11).

Fletcher was ordained in the diocese of Peterborough to the diaconate on 18 September 1613, and to the priesthood on the following day. His patron Neville died in 1615, after which Fletcher sought some further outside preferment. He applied to Sir Roger Townshend, a friend and benefactor of his brother Phineas, whose uncle Sir Francis Bacon possessed a number of livings. Bacon subsequently presented Giles Fletcher to the rectory of Helmingham, Suffolk, early in 1617. Fletcher evidently found this benefice unsuitable, for he returned to Trinity College within the year, and in 1618 the university records show that he was appointed reader of Greek language, and in the following year he proceeded to his BD. Probably Townshend interceded again on his behalf with Bacon, and this time Fletcher secured a different living, in Alderton, a coastal village in Suffolk, where he remained until his death, only five years later. The air was bad, says Fuller, and his parishioners dismal, being 'clownish and low-parted … (having nothing but their shoes high about them)'. They did not value their pastor 'according to his worth, which disposed him to melancholy, and hastened his dissolution' (Fuller, *Worthies*, 372).

Fletcher wrote no more poetry after the publication of his epic work but there is a prose treatise, *The Reward of the Faithfull* (1623), which appeared just before his death, a compilation of likely sermon materials as well as a variety of reflections on his life at Alderton. Fletcher dedicated this book to Townshend and he writes in reference to Bacon, 'Your most noble and learned Uncle, the Right Honourable Francis Lord Verulam, Viscount Saint Albones my free and very Honourable Benefactor, whose Gift [that is, of the livings at Helmingham and Alderton], as it was worthy his bestowing, so was it speedily sent, and not tediously sued for'. In this prose work Fletcher firmly declares his already well-known royalist and protestant sympathies. He sets out his pastoral convictions—'a faithfull Minister is a great labourer … God himselfe compares him not onely to a husbandman, but to shew the greatnesse of his labour, to every calling indeed that is most sweated with industrie and toyle'. He condemns playhouses, and also the 'Country-Divels of drunkennesse, Blasphemy, Gaming, Lying, and Queaning'. But the work is most interesting in demonstrating Fletcher's theological views on grace and salvation, and revealing his essential protestantism. His views represent a 'middle' way, and they put him in the general tradition represented by John Jewel and Richard Hooker. On predestination, he writes:

If they shall be saved, let them live how they will, they know God will save them, but if he meanes not to have them, all the meanes they can use, they thinke but idle, and so they lie down in the secret decree of God which being imbrested in Gods owne bosome thoughts, they cannot possibly dive into; and never looke to the execution of Gods decree, which they may finde in the use of the meanes and in themselves, if by them the meanes be wisely applyed, and faithfully practised. (Holaday, 582–3)

A few verses are scattered throughout this book, principally translations from Boethius and a few Greek passages and epigrams.

Fletcher died at Alderton in November 1623 and was buried there. The registers of Alderton are not extant for this time, but there exist letters of administration given to his widow, Anne, whose surname is unknown, dated 12 November 1623.   P. G. STANWOOD

Sources J. Grundy, *The Spenserian poets* (1969) · W. B. Hunter, jun., ed., *The English Spenserians* (1977) · T. Fuller, *The worthies of England*, ed. J. Freeman, abridged edn (1952) · A. Holaday, 'Giles Fletcher and the puritans', *Journal of English and Germanic Philology*, 54 (1955), 578–86 · A. B. Langdale, *Phineas Fletcher: man of letters, science and divinity* (1937) · F. J. Warnke, *Versions of baroque* (1972) · J. V. Mirollo, *The poet of the marvelous: Giambattista Marino* (1963) · F. S. Boas, ed., *Poetical works of Giles Fletcher and Phineas Fletcher*, 2 vols. (1908) · *The complete poems of Giles Fletcher*, ed. A. B. Grosart (1876) · Venn, *Alum. Cant.*

Fletcher, Henry (*fl.* 1715–1744), engraver, lived in London but nothing is known of his background. Initially he worked for booksellers, and in 1715 produced a portrait frontispiece to Robert Nelson's *Works*. Later he also worked for printsellers, for instance making smaller duplicates of Bernard Baron's 1728 set of *Seven Acts of Charity*. In April 1729 Vertue noted that Fletcher had just published a *Story of Bathsheba* after Sebastiano Conca, 'this being the first public essay of his skill for himself' (Vertue, *Note books*, 3.38).

By that time, however, Fletcher was also working on the subjects from natural history for which he became best known. He engraved fifteen plates and the frontispiece (dated 1729) for the *Catalogus plantarum*, 'A catalogue of trees, shrubs, plants and flowers, both exotic and domestic, propagated for sale in the gardens near London by a society of gardeners' (1730). He was engraver and co-publisher of the *Twelve Months of Flowers* (1731), a set of twelve prints, each showing some thirty different flowers in bloom in each month of the year, after designs by Peter Casteels. The flowers themselves could be obtained from the Kensington nursery of the other co-publisher, the gardener Robert Furber. These plates, which cost the publishers some £500, were immediately copied by other printsellers; Fletcher gave evidence concerning these piracies to the parliamentary committee that was considering the question of copyright for prints prior to Hogarth's Act of 1735. Nevertheless *Twelve Months of Flowers* was a huge success and Fletcher engraved several of the plates for a second set, *Twelve Months of Fruit* (1733). He followed this with engravings for Charles Collins's *Twelve Prints of English Birds* (1736).

Much of Fletcher's later work was topographical. In 1739 he engraved a set of six views of Venice after Canaletto, published by Joseph Baudin, and he also engraved London views after Joseph Nichols. He was listed by Vertue (6.198) as an active engraver in 1744 but no work of later date is known. The British Library, the British Museum, and the Victoria and Albert Museum, London, hold examples of Fletcher's prints.   Timothy Clayton

Sources Vertue, *Note books*, vols. 3, 6 · D. Alexander, 'Canaletto and the English print market', *Canaletto and England*, ed. M. Liversidge and J. Farrington (1993), 39–40 [exhibition catalogue, Birmingham Gas Hall Exhibition Gallery, Birmingham, 14 Oct 1993 – 9 Jan 1994] · *Country Journal, or, The Craftsman* (17 April 1731) · *Engraved Brit. ports.* · T. Clayton, *The English print, 1688–1802* (1997)

Fletcher, Sir Henry, first baronet (1727?–1807), politician and director of the East India Company, was the seventh child of John Fletcher of Clea Hall, Cumberland, and his second wife, Isabella, daughter and coheir of John Senhouse of Netherhall, Cumberland. He joined the naval service of the East India Company, and commanded the *Stormont* and *Earl of Middlesex*, East Indiamen, from 1758 to 1766. On relinquishing his command in 1766, he turned his attention to politics and East India Company affairs. The family estate of Clea Hall had passed to him in 1759, and his marriage on 20 October 1768 to Catherine Lintot (1733–1816) [*see* Fletcher, Catherine, *under* Lintot, (Barnaby) Bernard (1675–1736)], daughter and heir of Henry Lintot, a London bookseller, brought him substantial property in the Horsham area. They had a son and a daughter. Through his Horsham interests Fletcher came into contact with the duke of Norfolk who became his 'great friend, patron and ally' (bishop of Carlisle to Lowther, 29 Oct 1806, Lowther MSS, quoted in HoP, *Commons, 1790–1820*). Fletcher also acquired Ashley Park, Walton-on-Thames, which became the family's main seat.

In the troubled company politics of the period Fletcher sided with the 'Indian interest' which was led by Laurence Sulivan and was supported by the Rockingham opposition party in parliament. Fletcher was elected to the company's court of directors in 1769 and remained a director more or less continuously until his resignation in 1783. He was chairman in 1782–3.

In 1768 Fletcher entered parliament for Cumberland, where, with the backing of the dukes of Norfolk and Portland, he had defeated the candidate of the influential Lowther family. By the late 1770s Fletcher had distanced himself from Sulivan, mainly it seems out of distaste for the governorship of Warren Hastings who enjoyed the support of the 'Indian interest'. As company chairman in 1782 he co-operated with the Fox government and received a baronetcy on 20 May 1782. In 1783 he supported the terms of the peace treaty with France, so far as it related to the territories of the East India Company. He helped Fox draft his India Bill and was nominated one of the seven commissioners proposed by the bill to take responsibility for East India affairs. Although he was respected for his integrity there were doubts about his abilities. Francis Baring, a fellow director and City merchant, blamed Fletcher for mistakes in the figures used by Fox and thought him 'neither capable of forming accounts himself or of digesting those which are formed by others' (Baring to Lord Shelburne, 20 Nov 1783, Lansdowne MSS, quoted in HoP, *Commons, 1754–90*). Fletcher declared in the House of Commons in 1783, during the second reading of Fox's bill, that it would have been much better for Britain, and for Europe in general, if

the navigation to the East Indies had never been discovered; but … he could not agree … that it would be right [for the British] to give up their possessions there; for were they to evacuate them, some other European nation would seize them.

Fletcher considered it absolutely necessary to establish 'regular and permanent government in India' (Cobbett, *Parl. hist.*). He resigned the company chairmanship to allow himself a freer hand in following his own views. After his resignation he 'lapsed into insignificance' (HoP,

Commons, 1754–90) in parliament and no known speech is recorded after 1790.

In 1796 Fletcher supported Fox's call for ministers to be censured on the grounds of having advanced money to the emperor of Germany and the prince of Condé without the knowledge or consent of parliament. He also supported Grey's motion on parliamentary reform in the following session. He continued to represent the county of Cumberland until declining health and the reduced influence of the duke of Norfolk in local politics forced his reluctant withdrawal from the seat at the general election of 1806. He died at his home, Ashley Park, on 30 March 1807, and was succeeded by his only son.

J. G. PARKER

Sources J. G. Parker, 'The directors of the East India Company, 1754–1790', PhD diss., U. Edin., 1977 · HoP, *Commons, 1754–90*, 2.439–40 · HoP, *Commons, 1790–1820*, 3.776–7 · L. S. Sutherland, *The East India Company in eighteenth century politics*, 2nd edn (1962) · Cobbett, *Parl. hist.*, 23.1301–5 · S. G. H. Freeth, I. A. Mason, and P. M. Wilkinson, eds., *A catalogue of the Horsham Museum manuscripts* (1995) · *GM*, 1st ser., 77 (1807), 385 · BL, Hastings MSS, Add. MSS 29132–29173, esp. Add. MSS 29159, fol. 351v; 29155, fol. 231; 29146, fol. 390v · Burke, *Peerage* (1939) · *DNB*
Archives Horsham Museum, West Sussex, his corresp. and papers and those of his family relating to Horsham; MSS | U. Nott., letters to duke of Portland
Likenesses oils, *c.*1770, NMM · J. Young, mezzotint (after J. Keenan), BM, NPG

Fletcher, James (1852–1908), botanist and entomologist, was born at Ashe, near Wrotham, Kent, on 28 March 1852, the second son of Joseph Flitcroft Fletcher and his wife, Mary Ann Hayward. His elder brother, Flitcroft Fletcher, was an artist who exhibited five pictures at the Royal Academy (1882–6) and died at the age of thirty-six. Fletcher was educated at King's School, Rochester, and joined the Bank of British North America in London in 1871 as a clerk, transferring to Montreal, Canada, in 1874. In 1875 he entered the Ottawa office of the bank but resigned in May 1876 in search of more interesting employment. He became an assistant in the Library of Parliament until 1 July 1887.

During his eleven-year stay at the library Fletcher was able to devote his leisure to the study of botany and entomology in which he became one of the leading Canadian experts. From 1884 he acted as dominion entomologist in the department of agriculture. Although his appointment was an honorary one, between 1884 and 1886 he did much work in establishing the practical foundations for Canadian economic entomology, developing a nationwide network of correspondents and informants including many farmers and gardeners. This activity led to his appointment in 1887 as the first permanent dominion entomologist and botanist, attached to the new Central Experimental Farm at Ottawa. He was responsible for pest control, and took part in drafting some of the early Canadian legislation on the subject. He founded Canada's national herbarium and what became the Canadian national collection of insects. After his first few years in the post his responsibilities were focused more on entomology than on botany; as a result of his activities he

became known as the father of economic entomology in Canada.

In 1879 Fletcher married Eleanor Gertrude Schreiber, the eldest daughter of Collingwood Schreiber, chief engineer of the Canadian Government Railways. They had two daughters. He was elected a fellow of the Linnean Society of London on 3 June 1886 and a member of the Entomological Society of America and other scientific societies, and he was one of the founders of the Ottawa Field Naturalists' Club. At his death he was president of the Entomological Society of Ontario, and honorary secretary of the Royal Society of Canada. In 1896 he received the honorary degree of LLD from Queen's University, Kingston.

Fletcher was a prolific writer. To the *Transactions* of the Ottawa Field Naturalists' Club he contributed a 'Flora Ottawaensis' (1880–87), and with George H. Clark he published *Farm Weeds of Canada* (1906). Valuable papers on injurious insects and on the diurnal Lepidoptera appeared at intervals. Seventeen species of butterflies bear his name. His friends remembered him as an indefatigable naturalist, an inspiring teacher, and a devoted Christian. He died at Montreal on 8 November 1908, and was buried in Beechwood cemetery, Ottawa. The Ottawa Field Naturalists' Club erected in his memory a drinking-fountain with bronze medallion at the experimental farm.

PELHAM EDGAR, *rev.* P. E. KELL

Sources *Ottawa Naturalist*, 22/10 (1908–9) [Fletcher memorial volume, including bibliography of publications and biographical notes] · private information (1912) · *DCB*, vol. 13 · Desmond, *Botanists*, rev. edn · *WWW, 1916–28* [Sir Collingwood Schreiber]
Archives NA Canada, MSS
Likenesses F. Brownell, oils, Ottawa Public Library, Canada · bronze medallion (on drinking fountain), Central Experimental Farm, Ottawa, Canada · photographs, repro. in *Ottawa Naturalist*, frontispiece and 202 (pl. 5 and 6) · portrait, repro. in *Canadian Entomologist*, 30 (1898) · portrait, repro. in *Canadian Entomologist*, 40 (1908) · portrait, repro. in *Canadian experimental farms report* (1909) · portrait, repro. in *Smithsonian miscellaneous collections*, 84 (1930)
Wealth at death £2775 14s. in England: Canadian probate sealed in England, 16 Jan 1909, *CGPLA Eng. & Wales*

Fletcher, John (1579–1625), playwright, was born on 20 December 1579 into a strongly protestant family in Rye, Sussex, the fourth of nine children of Richard *Fletcher (1544/5–1596) and Elizabeth Holland (*d.* 1592). His grandfather, also a Richard Fletcher, was friend to the martyrologist John Foxe, and his father, then dean of Peterborough, attended the execution of Mary, queen of Scots, exhorting her to renounce her Catholicism; he later became bishop of London, though at the time of John's birth he was minister at Rye.

A 'John Fletcher of London', who has generally been identified with the dramatist (though see the reservations of Taunton and of Kelliher), was admitted pensioner to Corpus Christi College, Cambridge, on 15 October 1591: this would make him eleven at matriculation, a young but not impossible age to go to university at the time (Francis Beaumont went to Oxford at twelve in 1597). The same John Fletcher became Bible clerk, reading the lessons in

John Fletcher (1579–1625), by unknown artist, c.1620

college chapel, which suggests that he was destined for a clerical career like the playwright's grandfather, father, uncle William Atkinson, elder brother Nathaniel, and cousin Phineas *Fletcher, the 'Spenserian' poet. In June 1596 Bishop Fletcher died in both disfavour and debt. A month after becoming bishop of London (he had previously held the sees of Bristol and of Worcester) and four years after the death of his first wife, he had married Mary Baker, a widow who was the subject of malicious gossip, to the extreme displeasure of Queen Elizabeth. His family became the responsibility of his brother, Giles *Fletcher the elder—diplomat, writer, and remembrancer of London—who within a few years was implicated in the Essex rebellion and was thus unable to provide either the financial support or the patronage needed to ensure a traditional career path for his brother's children.

Collaboration with Beaumont Nothing is known about Fletcher's life between his proceeding MA in 1598 (though he was probably still living with his uncle Giles in 1601) and his first involvement in writing a play, *The Woman Hater* (1606), with Francis *Beaumont. From this time until his death in August 1625, he wrote or had a hand in over fifty plays. There is no evidence that Fletcher, like Shakespeare and Jonson, began acting before writing plays. He and Beaumont both seem to have been part of Jonson's circle at the Mermaid by the time of *The Woman Hater*. According to the 1647 folio, Beaumont wrote a verse epistle to Jonson 'before he and Master *Fletcher* came to *London*, with two of the precedent Comedies, then not finisht, which deferred their merry meetings at the Mermaid' (sigs. Xxx3v–Xxx4r),

and Richard Brome's contribution to the prefatory material describes Fletcher as a 'son of Ben':

> Most knowing Johnson (*proud to call him* Sonne)
> In friendly Envy swore, He had outdone
> His very Selfe.
> (sig. g1r)

Fletcher's first plays were mostly written for the Children of the Queen's Revels, but about the time that the King's Company established the Blackfriars as their second playing space (they occupied the theatre in 1608 but probably did not start performing there until 1610), they seem to have acquired the services of both Beaumont and Fletcher. None of Fletcher's plays after 1614 can be shown to have been written for any other company.

Fletcher may have met Beaumont through Fletcher's patrons the earl and countess of Huntingdon or, more probably, vice versa; Beaumont and Henry Hastings, fifth earl of Huntingdon, were cousins, and the earl was closely connected to Beaumont's cousin, Sir Thomas Beaumont of Coleorton. Certainly, by 1609 Fletcher seems to have been part of the earl's circle, dedicating the published version of *The Faithful Shepherdess*, his first solo play, to Sir Walter Aston (who was already patron to the poet Michael Drayton) and Sir William Skipwith, who were both friends of the Hastings family. Philip Massinger, Fletcher's most frequent collaborator, notes in his 'Copie of a Letter written upon occasion to the Earle of Pembrooke Lo: Chamberlaine' that:

> Johnson much of what he has does owe
> To you and to your familie, and is never
> Slow to professe it, nor had Fletcher ever
> Such Reputation, and credit wonne
> But by his honord Patron, Huntington.
> (Massinger, ll. 51–5)

Among the Hastings papers is an extant verse-letter from Fletcher to Elizabeth, countess of Huntingdon, who was much the more dynamic and imaginative of the couple and seems to have been at least as much of a patron to the playwright as was her husband. It shows the closeness of Fletcher's relationship with this aristocratic family (he even names the Huntingdons' cook at their castle at Ashby-de-la-Zouch); it also shows that Fletcher's politics were in accord with the prevalent views at Ashby:

> Knights, and Lords
> praye by yor Leaves, I will not treate of you
> Ye are too teachy: nor whether ytt be true
> wee shall have warrs wth Spaine: (I wolde wee might:)
> nor whoe shall daunce i'th *maske*; nor whoe shall write
> those brave things done: nor summe up the Expence;
> nor whether ytt bee paid for ten yeere hence.
> (*Hastings MSS*, 2.58–9)

Fletcher seems to have shared both his patrons' protestant distaste for courtly extravagance and the desire of militant protestants to see James drop his pacific policies with regard to Spain and the Counter-Reformation—though the politics of the plays are rather more complex than the attitudes expressed here to war and to the masque.

The Woman Hater (entered in the Stationers' register on 20 May 1607 and performed by the Children of Paul's) and

Cupid's Revenge (first recorded performance by the Children of the Queen's Revels in January 1612, though probably first performed in 1607–8) are both effective plays—the former has an entertaining and grotesque sub-plot of a gourmand obsessed with a fish's head, the latter plays fast and loose both with classical representations of the god of love and with the category of revenge drama—but are both predominantly the work of Beaumont. The first major success for the team of Beaumont-and-Fletcher was (according to John Dryden) *Philaster*—subtitled *Love Lyes a-Bleeding* in reference to the protagonist's hysterical habit of stabbing his lovers at crucial moments in the action. This was Fletcher's third collaboration with Beaumont, an ironic, emotionally flamboyant play which seems to have initiated the fashion for what became the most significant dramatic genre of the century, romantic tragicomedy; it was entered in Stationers' register in 1610 and two markedly different quarto texts appeared in 1620 and 1622 respectively, the latter considered the more authoritative. *The Coxcomb*, *The Maid's Tragedy*, *A King and No King*, *The Captain*, *The Scornful Lady*, and *Thierry and Theodoret*, all collaborations with Beaumont, consolidated and extended the playwrights' reputations. The three best-known Beaumont and Fletcher collaborations—*Philaster*, *The Maid's Tragedy*, and *A King and No King*—were all written for the King's Company, and they have been performed and edited with reasonable regularity since: they focus (as, in a way, does the later *Henry VIII*) on royal intemperance and a fraught courtly environment. *The Maid's Tragedy*, in particular, remained popular right up to the closing of the theatres and continued to be a success after the Restoration: it is a tragedy (written in 1610 or 1611 and performed at court in late 1612) which shares in the unpredictable, excessive emotion of the tragicomedies and which offers several remarkable *coups de théâtre*—not the least of which is Evadne's assassination of the king after she has tied him to the bed in what he takes at first to be sexual playfulness. *A King and No King* was performed at court at Christmas 1611 and probably written earlier that year, but not entered in the Stationers' register until 1618: it is a romantic tragicomedy of tyranny, deposition, and incest, and is generally the play critics have in mind when deploring what they see as Fletcherian excess and amorality.

Fletcher's verse-letter to the countess of Huntingdon provides a key context for the late twentieth-century critical argument that, contrary to earlier views (beginning with Coleridge), these plays do not show symptoms of servile royalism, but instead ask questions, often oblique and ironic, of absolute values, sovereignty and nationalism, as well as of assumptions about gendered behaviour. It is the ironic way in which these questions are formulated that seems to have misled earlier critics, who tended to deplore what they saw as the plays' sexual immorality as well as their stylistic and structural inconsistencies. Certainly, the plots of the plays can be both unsubtle and fragmented to the modern critical eye. The often perfunctory last scenes, for instance, can be largely incidental: as Kathleen McLuskie observes, 'the pleasure' of these plays 'lies less in the happy and conventional conclusion than in the wit with which Fletcher holds potentially offensive material within the bounds of decorum while mocking decorum at every turn' (McLuskie, 230). There is little doubt that it was the exhilarating demonstrations of rapid-fire wit and plotting in plays such as *The Chances* and *The Wild Goose Chase*, as well as their tendency to test and contest definitions of appropriate social and sexual behaviour, that sustained audiences' enthusiasm for these plays; at the same time, a series of topical plays—most prominently *Sir John Van Olden Barnavelt*—demonstrate the close and at times controversial political engagement of many plays in the canon at the time of first production.

Of the other Beaumont and Fletcher collaborations, *The Captain*—a play which explores the struggle between virtue and superficiality and which is akin to Marston's *Dutch Courtesan* in its portrayal of a beautiful but morally depraved young woman—was performed at court for Christmas 1612, but was probably written a year or two earlier. Like Fletcher's solo play, *The Woman's Prize*, which dates from this time, *The Coxcomb* (performed at court by the Children of the Queen's Revels in November 1612 though perhaps performed as early as 1608) and *The Scornful Lady* (another Queen's Revels play, written probably in 1610 and first performed at that time) both explore the question of sovereignty within marriage and offer a radical assessment of the status of women, as do later plays such as *Women Pleased* and *The Wild Goose Chase*. Each of these plays offers a fast-moving, slightly repetitive plot in which one or more forthright, quick-witted, and playful women relentlessly trick the men who are the objects of their desire until these men, whose attitudes are dependent initially upon the patriarchal environments in which they have been educated, come to accept their inability to exert control over the women.

The Faithful Shepherdess and other solo plays Fletcher's first solo play, *The Faithful Shepherdess*, was a flop when first performed (by the Children of the Queen's Revels, probably in 1607–8) and it was published shortly afterwards with an apparatus designed to redeem it from failure on the stage. Jonson, in a sympathetic commendatory verse, laments that:

> The wise, and many-headed *Bench*, that sits
> Upon the Life, and Death of *Playes* …
> … had, before
> They saw it halfe, damd thy whole play.
> (Bowers, 3.492)

But the play's effect on readers seems to have been more positive: it served as a source both for Shakespeare in *The Tempest* and for Milton in *Comus*. Fletcher contributed a preface to the quarto in which, drawing on the theories of Giambattista Guarini, he provides a definition of tragicomedy which has been quoted repeatedly in discussions of the genre, though not always understood. As an ironic piece of writing, highly critical of the audience which rejected the play, it must be understood as a response to a particular theatrical moment (especially as Fletcher never again wrote a deliberately archaic pastoral of this kind), rather than as a prophecy of the form as it would develop over the next few decades. The play was revived at court by Queen Henrietta Maria in 1634 in a very different context from that in which it originally appeared, and its characteristic irony at the expense of a culture of chastity—which would have been apparent enough in 1610—seems to have been entirely submerged in the court's enthusiasm for 'innocent' pastoral.

There is no adequate evidence to suggest that Fletcher ever married. If one near-contemporary account is to be believed, his close professional relationship with Beaumont reflects an equally close personal attachment. Aubrey notes in his *Brief Lives* that '[t]here is a wonderfull consimility of phansey' between the two playwrights, 'which caused that dearnesse of friendship between them', and he adds that '[t]hey lived together on the Banke side, not far from the Playhouse, both batchelors; lay together ... had one wench in the house between them, which they did so admire; the same cloathes and cloake, &c., betweene them' (*Brief Lives*, 1.96). Aubrey reifies and domesticates the collaborative relationship, implying both sexual ambiguity and sexual rivalry. The prefatory material to the 1647 folio, written decades after the deaths of both playwrights, echoes this, emphasizing the writers' interdependence and describing their collaboration in marital terms (the plays are described poetically as the children of 'two Masculines espous'd' (sig. E2v). Beaumont, though, seems to have married a Kentish heiress, Ursula Isley, and to have ceased writing in 1613, probably after suffering a stroke; he died in March 1616.

Despite the failure of *The Faithful Shepherdess*, Fletcher continued to write plays without a collaborator both alongside his work with Beaumont and after the partnership ceased—*The Woman's Prize*, *The Night Walker*, *Bonduca*, *Valentinian*, and *Monsieur Thomas* date from 1611–13; *Wit without Money*, *Love's Pilgrimage*, and *The Mad Lover* from 1614–16; and *The Chances*, *Women Pleased*, *The Loyal Subject*, and *The Humorous Lieutenant* from between 1617 and 1619—but he seems always to have preferred working with collaborators, since he continued to do so throughout his career (as was standard practice for many early modern playwrights). None the less, he also wrote a number of very popular solo plays—the publisher of the 1647 folio, Humphrey Moseley, notes in a preface that he had considered printing 'Mr. *Fletcher's* workes by themselves, because single & alone he would make a *Just Volume*' (sig. A3v)—which broach a range of contemporary issues from sexual politics to the frustrations produced by James I's refusal to take England into war for the protestant cause. *The Woman's Prize* draws overtly on Shakespeare's *The Taming of the Shrew* to provide a humorous, radical mock-sequel to that play in which, after Katherine's death, Petruccio remarries but finds his new wife unwilling to submit to his control. A revival by the King's Men in 1633 created trouble with Sir Henry Herbert, master of the revels, who wished to remove 'oaths, prophaness, and publique ribaldrye' even from a twenty-year-old play (Adams, 21). *The Night Walker* was the first of four plays involving Fletcher at this time (when he was still not firmly established as a King's

Man) for the Lady Elizabeth's Company. *Bonduca* and *Valentinian* are Roman tragedies—both for the King's Men and both dating from 1610–11—which offer a metaphoric geography which invites the audience to see in the Roman culture of the plays a representation of the social instabilities produced by James's policy of non-intervention in continental religious conflict.

Monsieur Thomas and *Wit without Money* are both Lady Elizabeth's plays, written in 1613 and 1614 respectively: the latter provides a caustic portrait of the unrest provoked in his rural tenants by a gallant's mortgaging his estates to fund his leisure activities in London. *Love's Pilgrimage*, which is based on one of Cervantes' *Novelas exemplares*, can only be dated from internal evidence, since there are no contemporary records either of licensing or performance: it was most probably written in 1616. *The Mad Lover* was first produced in late 1616—Anne Clifford saw it performed at court in January 1617—and, revived in 1630, it became possibly the first play performed in the renovated Cockpit theatre. *The Chances* is one of the sharpest and funniest of Fletcher's comedies of male bonding; written probably in 1617 for the King's Men, it was regularly performed up to the end of the nineteenth century and had at least one significant revival in the twentieth. *Women Pleased* is based on Chaucer's *Wife of Bath's Tale* and once again explores the question of sovereignty within male/female relations. Sir George Buc, master of the revels, approved *The Loyal Subject*, which is set in Russia (about which Fletcher's uncle Giles had written in his travelogue *Of the Russe Commonwealth*), on 16 November 1618 in time for a court performance that day; it was revived in the mid-1630s. *The Humorous Lieutenant* was highly successful both in its day and after the Restoration, when Samuel Pepys saw it several times; it is a fast-moving comedy of manners which exists, unusually for a play in the Fletcher canon, in manuscript form (prepared by Ralph Crane, a regular King's Company scribe, for Sir Kenelm Digby), with the title *Demetrius and Enanthe*.

Collaboration with Shakespeare *The Woman's Prize*, with its humorous dependence upon a play in the Shakespeare canon, in a sense heralds the next significant phase of Fletcher's career. In 1612–13, he collaborated on three plays for the King's Company with William Shakespeare—*Cardenio*, *Henry VIII* (*All is True*), and *The Two Noble Kinsmen*. The first of these, *The History of Cardenio*, is not extant, although Lewis Theobald published a tragicomedy, based on the story of Cardenio from Cervantes' *Don Quixote*, called *Double Falsehood, or, The Distrest Lovers*, which he claimed to have 'revised and adapted' from the original, though there is no concrete evidence that this is the case. *Henry VIII* appeared last in the 'Histories' section in the Shakespeare first folio of 1623 without acknowledgement of Fletcher's involvement, but authorship analysis suggests that he wrote approximately half. There is unusually precise dating information about *Henry VIII* because it was the play which was being performed in June 1613 when the first Globe theatre caught fire and burnt down. According to accounts of the fire, the play seems to have been known by a different title when first performed—*All is True*—which reflects the play's habit of offering alternative versions of historical truth without resolving incompatibilities. *The Two Noble Kinsmen* was first published in quarto form in 1634 as 'Written by … Mr John Fletcher, and Mr William Shakespeare', and authorship analysis has confirmed this attribution: it is a remarkable, dark, complex tragicomedy—'a Jacobean dramatisation', as its Arden editor notes, 'of a medieval English tale [Chaucer's *Knight's Tale*] based on an Italian romance version of a Latin epic about one of the oldest and most tragic Greek legends' (*The Two Noble Kinsmen*, ed. Potter, 1)—which explores complex issues of same-sex intimacy and social coercion. These plays postdate the four plays—*Pericles*, *Cymbeline*, *The Winter's Tale*, and *The Tempest*—which are usually described as Shakespeare's 'late' or 'last' plays, and they serve to question the redemptive life structure traditionally created for Shakespeare—moving from the bleakest of tragedies into a final phase of hope invested in the young—since the tone of the two extant collaborations (especially *The Two Noble Kinsmen*) does not fit comfortably into this narrative.

The overlap of the careers of Fletcher and Shakespeare, despite producing only two surviving plays, has inevitably attracted disproportionate critical attention, arguably to the detriment of the rest of the canon; none the less, their collaboration was clearly highly significant for each playwright. Both wrote plays which were in the vanguard of the new genre of 'romantic tragicomedy' which would dominate the stage up to and beyond the English revolution. Shakespeare was not a regular collaborator, but he clearly worked with Fletcher for at least twelve months, and the influence was not entirely one-way. *The Woman Hater*, *Philaster*, and *Bonduca* draw on *Measure for Measure*, *Hamlet*, and *Cymbeline* respectively, and the success of *The Woman's Prize* depended upon the audience's knowledge of *The Taming of the Shrew*. Yet *The Tempest* echoes the structure of *The Faithful Shepherdess*, and the collaborations show influence going both ways: *The Two Noble Kinsmen* is a darker reworking of Chaucer's *Knight's Tale* than was *A Midsummer Night's Dream*, and *Henry VIII* draws not only on Shakespeare's earlier history plays but also on a scene from *The Maid's Tragedy*. The critical desire to demonstrate that one or other of the two (typically presumed to be Shakespeare) 'invented' the genre of romantic tragicomedy continues to misrepresent the mutual/competitive nature of the development of genre in the Jacobean theatre.

The King's Company playwright After 1613 Fletcher seems to have settled into Shakespeare's role as chief playwright for the King's Company. He appears to have sought a regular collaborator, initially working with Nathan Field on *The Honest Man's Fortune* and *Four Plays in One* in 1613 (both for the Lady Elizabeth's Men) and *The Jeweller of Amsterdam* (which is no longer extant), *The Queen of Corinth* (for which Fletcher probably contributed only act II) and *The Knight of Malta* between 1616 and 1618. Field, a boy-actor turned playwright, was a logical choice, since he had been a friend of Francis Beaumont from before the latter's playwriting days (see Kelliher); he died, however, in 1619 or

1620. *The Jeweller of Amsterdam*, *The Queen of Corinth*, and *The Knight of Malta* also involved Philip Massinger, who after Field's death became Fletcher's regular writing partner: they collaborated on approximately seventeen plays and, when Fletcher died, Massinger inherited his role as principal playwright for the King's Company. The collaborations with Massinger offer some of the best work in which Fletcher had a hand, despite the assumptions usually made about the superiority of the writing with Beaumont. Such assumptions stem partly from the royalist propaganda which accompanied the 1647 'Beaumont and Fletcher' folio, since Massinger would be a hard playwright to present as a royalist and his role in the canon is thus ignored by the publisher.

Fletcher's and Massinger's *Sir John Van Olden Barnavelt* (1619) is politically the most scandalous play in the canon: it was written in some haste to capitalize and comment upon contemporary events in the Low Countries. The play exists only in a unique manuscript held in the British Library, of particular importance not only because it is in the hand of Ralph Crane, a scribe associated with the King's Company and involved with the Shakespeare first folio, but principally because it contains the censoring marks of Sir George Buc, the master of the revels, and underlines the political nature of that censorship. Buc at one key point deletes a passage which shows the prince of Orange (whom James I supported) being rudely treated by his subjects, and he writes in the margin: 'I like not this: neith[r] do I think that the pr. was thus disgracefully used, besides he is to much presented' (T. H. Howard-Hill, 'Buc and the censorship of *Sir John van Olden Barnavelt* in 1619', *Review of English Studies*, 39, 1988, 39–63). *The Custom of the Country* (1619) was written shortly after the publication of an English translation of its main source, Cervantes' *Persiles y Sigismunda*, in 1619 and was first performed by the King's Men probably in that year: the 'custom' in question is the governor's exercise of his *droit de seigneur* and is treated with splendid indelicacy in the course of the play, leading to Dryden's objection that '[t]here is more Baudry in one play of *Fletcher's*, call'd *The Custom of the Country*, than in all ours together' (Dryden, sig. *D2v). There is no external evidence for a date for *The Double Marriage*, but internal references suggest 1621 or thereabouts; it draws on *Don Quixote*, on Thomas Danett's 1596 translation of *The History of Philip de Commines*, and on two of the elder Seneca's *Controversiae* for its extravagant tale of virtue and tyranny. *The Little French Lawyer* can be dated broadly between 1619 and 1623, though was most probably written in 1621.

The False One (late 1621) is the *Antony and Cleopatra* of the canon (or more precisely the 'Caesar and Cleopatra'), though it is very different in tone from Shakespearian tragedy, nearer to Fletcher's customary tragicomic form. *The Prophetess* is also a Roman play (licensed in May 1622) which, in its evocation of the supernatural, is the nearest in manner among Fletcher's later plays to *The Faithful Shepherdess* and a far cry from the insistent materiality of most of the canon: it was the basis for Henry Purcell's opera *Dioclesian*. *The Sea Voyage* (1622) is an entertaining tragicomedy which begins with a storm scene taken directly from

The Tempest and which draws on colonial narratives for its tale of islands, shipwreck, Amazons, and the threat of cannibalism (planned, in a typically cynical Fletcherian inversion of popular myth, by the shipwrecked Europeans, not by native islanders); it was licensed in June 1622 and acted at the Globe, and was revived in the Restoration with the title *The Storm*. *The Spanish Curate*, a comedy based on Leonard Digges's *Gerardo the Unfortunate Spaniard*, a translation of Gonzalo de Céspedes y Meneses's *Poema trágico del español Gerardo*, was probably written in late 1621 or early 1622: it was popular both before and after the closing of the theatres. *Beggars' Bush* was performed at Whitehall for Christmas 1622 by the King's Men and seems to have been popular at court, since there are records of further performances there in 1630, 1631, 1636, and 1639: one speech by a 'Knavish Beggar', curiously, parodies Cranmer's closing prophecy in the final, Fletcherian scene of *Henry VIII*.

The Christmas season for 1621 was a significant time for Fletcher, since he had no fewer than three new solo plays performed at court: *The Island Princess*, *The Wild Goose Chase*, and *The Pilgrim*. *The Island Princess*, along with *The Sea Voyage* of 1622, explores the topical issue of colonial enterprise, but where the later play creates a pair of islands in an unspecified, but broadly American, geographical location, *The Island Princess* offers a satirical vision of the effect of European occupation and trade competition on the inhabitants of the Moluccas. *The Wild Goose Chase* is one of the most effective plays in the canon, a remarkably fast-paced, almost surreal comedy of the sexes whose sustained popularity is indicated by Sir Henry Herbert's choosing it in 1632 as one of the two plays in a given year for which he received the proceeds of the second day after revival (the substantial sum of £15, in this case). *The Pilgrim*, based on Lope de Vega's *El peregrino en su patria*, was entered in the Stationers' register in September 1621 and seems to have been successful: it focuses on two assertive women orchestrating an apparently magical recognition scene to resolve a political and familial impasse. 1623–4 saw the creation of three more solo plays: *The Lovers' Progress*, *A Wife for a Month*, and *Rule a Wife and have a Wife*. A play entitled *The Wandering Lovers* by 'Mr Fletcher' was licensed for performance in December 1623 and is assumed to be the play called *The Lovers' Progress* in the 1647 folio: it is based on d'Audiguier's *Histoire tragecomique de nostre temps*. *A Wife for a Month* was licensed by Herbert in May 1624 and seems still to have been in the King's Company repertory in 1641. As so often in the Fletcher canon, the scene is a corrupt court: in the course of the play, the tyrannical ruler's presumptions about his absolute rights are reversed by the actions of a chaste couple and the return of the rightful king. Herbert also licensed *Rule a Wife and have a Wife* in October of the same year for court performance both the following month and again at Christmas: this witty battle-of-the-sexes play is based on one of Cervantes' *Novelas exemplares* and continued to be highly popular well into the nineteenth century. Fletcher also wrote *The Maid in the Mill* about this time in collaboration with William Rowley.

The sources for plays in the Fletcher canon are predominantly Spanish in origin: though he generally used translations, either into French or English, he does appear to have had at least rudimentary Spanish (see Wilson). He adapted work by Lope de Vega, de Céspedes, Calderon, and de Argensola, but his principal source was Cervantes. *Don Quixote* provided the basic material for *The Coxcomb*, *Cardenio*, *The Double Marriage*, *The Wild Goose Chase*, *The Prophetess*, and *The Noble Gentleman*; and Fletcher drew on *Persiles y Sigismunda* for *The Custom of the Country*. He seems also to have been particularly fond of the *Novelas exemplares*, which are the source for *Love's Pilgrimage*, *The Chances*, *The Queen of Corinth*, *Beggars' Bush*, *Rule a Wife and have a Wife*, and *The Fair Maid of the Inn*. Fletcher's dependence on the *Novelas exemplares* is perhaps underlined by the fact that the source for *The Island Princess* is a story appended by the French translator to his edition of the tales. Fletcher clearly worried that this enthusiasm for Spanish writing might be misinterpreted, and in his dedicatory verse to James Mabbe's translation of Alemán's *Guzmán de Alfarache* (1622), he is careful to differentiate literary interest from political alignment:

> I come no Spy, nor take
> A Factious part; No sound of Warre I make,
> But against sinne; I land no forraine mates;
> For Vertues Schooles should be Free in all states.
> (Mabbe, sig. A4r)

Despite his political antipathy to Spain, Fletcher seems to have found in his Spanish sources not only the kind of flamboyant plot he appreciated but also a self-conscious, anti-romantic quality correlative to his own generic experimentation in drama.

The authorship and dating of the remaining plays in the canon—*The Elder Brother*, *The Fair Maid of the Inn*, *The Noble Gentleman*, and *Love's Cure*—are highly problematic, although Fletcher's hand has been detected in each. The usual conclusion is that they were unfinished at Fletcher's death and required revision and additional work. According to Hoy, *The Elder Brother* (composed probably in early 1625, to judge from an apparent reference to Jonson's and Jones's *The Fortunate Isles*, the new year court masque for that year) is largely Fletcher's, with acts I and v rewritten by Massinger: the play is the source of the longstanding but inaccurate belief that Fletcher had no time for Holinshed's *Chronicles*, the major source for *Henry VIII* as well as for Shakespeare's earlier history plays, though this belief stems from an out-of-context reading of a speech by one snobbish character. *The Fair Maid of the Inn* (licensed in January 1626) is thought by Hoy to involve the work of Massinger, Webster, and Ford as well as Fletcher, which offers a unique blend of dramatic talent, if true. *The Noble Gentleman* (licensed by Sir Henry Herbert in February 1626 as 'by John Fletcher' and 'acted at the Blackfriars') is, according to Hoy, a Fletcher revision of an earlier Beaumont script, though Bentley saw it as one of Fletcher's very last plays; Finkelpearl argues for a date nearer 1611 on topical grounds. *Love's Cure*, according to both Bentley and Hoy, is a Massinger revision of an early Beaumont and Fletcher script; if so, it must have been begun before 1613 and possibly revised only after Fletcher's death. It is a remarkable play, comically exploring the nature/nurture issue in the formation of gender identity by way of a brother and sister each brought up, due to political machinations and the danger of revenge, in a manner appropriate to the opposite sex. Although the resolution is conventional (each discovers his/her 'true' sexual identity by falling in love with someone of the correct, that is other, sex), its very arbitrariness underlines the radical manner in which the play questions social and sexual assumptions.

Death and reputation Fletcher died in London on 29 August 1625. According to Aubrey:

> a knight of Norfolk (or Suffolke) invited him into the countrey. He stayed but to make himself a suite of cloathes, and while it was makeing, fell sick of the plague and dyed. This I had (1668) from his tayler, who is now a very old man, and clarke of St. Mary Overy's. (*Brief Lives*, 1.254)

Sir Aston Cockayne claimed that Fletcher and Massinger were buried together in the same grave, though the precise location of the grave within what is now Southwark Cathedral (formerly St Saviour) is unknown.

Alongside the Shakespeare and Jonson canons, the works of 'Beaumont and Fletcher' (more properly thought of as the works in the Fletcher canon, since only one play, *The Knight of the Burning Pestle*, is considered solely the work of Beaumont) make up, at least as far as the Restoration and eighteenth-century stage was concerned, the great triumvirate of Elizabethan and Jacobean drama. Yet the Fletcher canon remains, in Philip Finkelpearl's words, 'the vast unexplored Amazonian jungle of Jacobean drama' (Finkelpearl, 245), still awaiting even a small percentage of the attention that has been devoted to the other two component canons of the triumvirate. The plays are generically difficult for modern audiences: even when ostensibly comic or tragic, they provide a series of variants on the basic form of ironic tragicomedy, depending on and simultaneously mocking their sources in prose romance; they explore areas, both sexually and politically, that made them uncomfortable reading in the nineteenth and early twentieth centuries; and they are written in an unmetaphoric style which compares unfavourably, to post-Romantic eyes, with that of Shakespeare. Perhaps most importantly, the plays are irreducibly collaborative, impossible to divide definitively among the various playwrights reported to have been involved—as George Lisle's prefatory verse to the 1647 folio notes, the plays:

> are so wov'n and knit,
> Twas *FRANCIS-FLETCHER*, or *JOHN BEAUMONT* writ.
> (sig. b1r)

Hoy, for instance, outlines what he considers to be the standard pattern of collaboration between Fletcher and Massinger—Massinger writing the opening and closing scenes, Fletcher the central sections—and suggests that this pattern had a lastingly negative effect on Massinger's own work, thereby sustaining the critical notion that there is a marked difference between the collaborations with Beaumont and all of Fletcher's other work (see Hoy in Howard). But Hoy's methods, along with sociolinguistic

and other means for determining authorship, are subject to many caveats (see for example Masten; McMullan, 'Introduction' to Arden *Henry VIII*), and the 'Beaumont and Fletcher' canon offers the most substantial early modern challenge to Romantic assumptions about the centrality of individual creativity to the production of art. The nature of this canon, in a sense, makes the process of writing a biography of any early modern dramatist, and especially that of any of the playwrights involved in the Fletcher canon, an impossible task.

GORDON McMULLAN

Sources Hunt. L., Hastings papers · *The aristocracy, the state and the local community: the Hastings collection of manuscripts from the Huntington Library in California* (1986) [microfilm] · F. Bowers, ed., *The dramatic works in the Beaumont and Fletcher canon*, 10 vols. (1966–94) · G. E. Bentley, *The Jacobean and Caroline stage*, 7 vols. (1941–68), vol. 3 · C. Hoy, 'The shares of Fletcher and his collaborators in the Beaumont and Fletcher canon', *Studies in Bibliography*, 8 (1956), 129–46; 9 (1957), 143–62; 11 (1958), 85–106; 12 (1959), 91–116; 13 (1960), 77–108; 14 (1961), 45–67; 15 (1962), 71–90 · G. McMullan, *The politics of unease in the plays of John Fletcher* (1994) · *Report on the manuscripts of the late Reginald Rawdon Hastings*, 4 vols., HMC, 78 (1928–47), vols. 2, 4 · J. Q. Adams, ed., *The dramatic records of Sir Henry Herbert, master of the revels, 1623–1673* (1917) · R. Masters, *The history of the College of Corpus Christi and the B. Virgin Mary … in the University of Cambridge* (1753), pt 2, p. 285 · Venn, *Alum. Cant.*, 1/4.149 · *Brief lives, chiefly of contemporaries, set down by John Aubrey, between the years 1669 and 1696*, ed. A. Clark, 2 vols. (1898) · P. Massinger, 'Copie of a letter', in P. Simpson, 'Two poems of Philip Massinger', *The Athenaeum* (8 Sept 1906), 273–4 · J. Dryden, *Fables ancient and modern* (1700) · K. McLuskie, *Renaissance dramatists: feminist readings* (1989) · J. Hope, *The authorship of Shakespeare's plays* (1994) · W. H. Kelliher, 'Francis Beaumont and Nathan Field: new records of their early years', *English Manuscript Studies, 1100–1700*, 8 (2000), 1–42 · J. Mabbe, *The rogue, or, The life of Guzmán de Alfarache, written in Spanish by Matheo Alemán* (1622) · G. McMullan and J. Hope, eds., *The politics of tragicomedy: Shakespeare and after* (1992) · J. Masten, *Textual intercourse: collaboration, authorship, and sexualities in Renaissance drama* (1997) · W. Shakespeare and J. Fletcher, *King Henry VIII*, ed. G. McMullan (2000) · J. Savage, 'The date of Beaumont and Fletcher's *Cupid's revenge*', *ELH: a Journal of English Literary History*, 15 (1948), 286–94 · N. Taunton, 'Did John Fletcher the playwright go to university?', *N&Q*, 235 (1990), 170–72 · E. M. Wilson, 'Did John Fletcher read Spanish?', *Philological Quarterly*, 27 (1948), 187–90 · W. Shakespeare and J. Fletcher, *The two noble kinsmen*, ed. L. Potter (1997) · *The works of Beaumont and Fletcher*, ed. A. Dyce, 11 vols. (1843–6) · C. Hoy, 'Massinger as collaborator: the plays with Fletcher and others', *Philip Massinger: a critical reassessment*, ed. D. Howard (1985), 51–82 · P. J. Finkelpearl, *Court and country politics in the plays of Beaumont and Fletcher* (Princeton, NY, 1990)

Archives BL · Bodl. Oxf. | Hunt. L., Hastings papers · priv. coll.

Likenesses oils, *c*.1620 (after unknown artist), NPG; on display at Montacute House, Somerset · oils, *c*.1620, priv. coll.; on loan to Plymouth City Museum and Art Gallery [*see illus.*] · W. Marshall, line engraving, BM; repro. in F. Beaumont and J. Fletcher, *Comedies and tragedies* (1647) · engraving, repro. in Darley, ed., *The works of Beaumont and Fletcher*, 2 vols. (1840) · engraving, repro. in Dyce, ed., *Works of Beaumont and Fletcher*, vol. 1 · portrait, priv. coll.

Fletcher, John (d. 1848), Roman Catholic priest and religious writer, was born at Ormskirk, Lancashire. He was probably the son of Thomas Fletcher, who was descended from an old Lancastrian Catholic family. He was educated at Douai College from 1782 to 1791, and at the English seminary of St Gregory in Paris. When the seminary was dissolved he proceeded to the college at St Omer in France, of which his great-uncle, the Revd William Wilkinson, was for some time president. Fletcher was one of the professors at St Omer throughout the imprisonment of the members of the college at Arras and Dourlens. Upon their release in 1795 Fletcher accompanied them to England, and was ordained by Bishop Gibson, probably at York in April 1795. He was successively missioner at Hexham, Blackburn, and at Weston Underwood, where he was living in 1809. He was created DD by Pope Pius VII on 24 August 1821, in recognition of his missionary merit and excellent sermons. Fletcher became chaplain to the dowager Lady Throckmorton in 1833, and subsequently served the mission at Leamington. In 1844 he was transferred to the mission at Northampton, which he resigned in 1848, owing to his advanced age. He died shortly afterwards.

Fletcher was best known as the writer and translator of many religious works and devotional manuals. His translations included Bossuet's *The Catholic Manual* (1817), Fénélon's *On the Use of the Bible* (1837), and De Maistre's *Letters on the Spanish Inquisition* (1838). His own works included *The Prudent Christian* (1834) and *The Guide to the True Religion: a Series of Sermons* (1836), as well as polemical publications such as *A Comparative View of the Grounds of the Catholic and Protestant Churches* (1826) and *The Difficulties of Protestantism* (1829). The latter was a closely argued text which aimed to expose the divisiveness and inconsistencies of protestantism. Fletcher also wrote a topical response to the pressing issue of Catholic emancipation, *Thoughts on the rights and prerogatives of the church and state: with some observations upon the question of Catholic securities* (1823). The Roman Catholic lawyer and historian Charles Butler was much impressed by Fletcher's sermons; although he felt that they were 'less calculated for the pulpit than the closet', he compared them to the homilies of St Francis of Sales, and praised 'their mild, unambitious eloquence, their pure morality, and their persuasive reasoning' (2.321).

THOMPSON COOPER, *rev.* ROSEMARY MITCHELL

Sources Gillow, *Lit. biog. hist.* • P. R. Harris, ed., *Douai College documents, 1639–1794*, Catholic RS, 63 (1972), 400 • *Catholic Magazine and Review*, 3 (1833), 112 • C. Butler, *Historical memoirs respecting the English, Irish and Scottish Catholics, from the Reformation to the present time*, 2nd edn, 2 (1819), 321

Fletcher, John (1792–1836), physician and lecturer, was the son of Thomas Fletcher, merchant, of London. Finding work in his father's counting-house tedious, he began the study of medicine at Edinburgh after having heard some of the London lectures of John Abernethy and Charles Bell. He graduated MD in 1816. After making a start in practice at Henley-on-Thames, where his family had retired suddenly in reduced circumstances, he returned to Edinburgh and took private pupils in medicine. His Latin scholarship and systematic methods made him a popular teacher. In 1822 he published *Horae subsecivae, or, First steps to composing and conversing on medical subjects in the Latin language*. In 1828–9 he joined the Argyll Square school of medicine, having McIntosh, Argyle Robertson, and, for a time, James Syme, as his colleagues. He lectured on physiology, and afterwards on medical jurisprudence. His reputation as a lecturer was very high and in 1836 he gave a course of popular lectures on physiology to large audiences of the educated laity of both sexes, illustrated by preparations and diagrams of his own making. He died of a sudden illness the same year. His *Elements of Pathology*, published several years after his death (1842) by two of his pupils, John J. Drysdale and J. R. Russell, shows a certain leaning to the teaching of Hahnemann. A paper entitled 'Vieles Sprechen ist gesund' (in Behrend's *Wöchentl. Repert.* iv.175, 1837) is attributed to him. His other writings include *Rudiments of Physiology* (1835–7) and *Remarks on the Trial of R. Reid for the Murder of his Wife on 29 June 1835* (1835). His earliest publication *Rubi epistolae Edinburgenses* (n.d.) was quite different, providing a light-hearted satirical look at students and professors.

CHARLES CREIGHTON, *rev.* RACHEL E. DAVIES

Sources *British and Foreign Medical Review*, 2/3 (July 1836), 302–5 • R. Lewins, ed., *Rudiments of physiology* (1835–7)
Archives Royal College of Physicians of Edinburgh, lecture notes on physiology
Likenesses W. O. Geller, mezzotint, 1938, Wellcome L.

Fletcher, John William [*formerly* Jean Guillaume de La Fléchère] (*bap.* 1729, *d.* 1785), Church of England clergyman and Methodist writer, was baptized on 19 September 1729 in Nyon, Switzerland, the last of eight children of Jacques de La Fléchère (1678–1756), army officer and assessor to the bailiff in Nyon, and his wife, Suzanne Elisabeth, *née* Crinsoz de Colombier (*b.* 1693). Little is known of his childhood in Nyon except some incidents of brotherly rivalry and religious feelings, but enough to contradict the hagiographic tendencies of later biographers. At age eleven or twelve he went to complete his education in Geneva, which was preferred because of its openness to early Enlightenment thinking in comparison with Lausanne, where the Bernese government still imposed a strict reformed orthodoxy. For five or six years Fletcher was a pupil at the college, and once or twice won a prize for a dissertation on religious subjects, the *thèmes de piété*. In 1746 he entered the university at Geneva, where he studied classics for one or two years. Disappointed and feeling isolated by a split within a group of religiously interested students, he left university, abandoned the idea of taking religious orders, and turned instead towards the second alternative within his family: a military career. He tried several options, but when his high-ranking uncle Louis-Salomon resigned from his army post in the Netherlands in June 1750 John William decided to abandon military life too and fulfil his earlier wish to see England.

In summer 1750 John William arrived in England and went to a school in Hatfield, Hertfordshire, in order to improve his English and to find a suitable position in an aristocratic family. In the autumn of the following year he became tutor to the two sons of Thomas Hill, MP for Shrewsbury. He resided with them in London during sessions of parliament and at Tern Hall, their summer residence in Shropshire. During his first year as a tutor, amusements and sports became less important to Fletcher in comparison with his renewed quest for a religious life. He again studied manuscripts written by his uncle Théodore Crinsoz de Bionens, a reformed pastor

John William Fletcher (*bap.* 1729, *d.* 1785), by Jonathan Spilsbury, 1777

and student of biblical apocalyptic who had been dismissed from pastoral service for refusing the subscription and oath required by the Bernese government. On a journey from London to Tern Hall, probably in the spring of 1753, Fletcher started a religious conversation with a poor, pious woman. His actions were not well received by his employers. In a letter to Charles Wesley, Fletcher later recalled how members of the Hill family had feared that his actions would be interpreted as those of a Methodist preacher. Once aware of the character of the Methodists Fletcher spoke of his desire to 'be one of them if there was really such people in England' (Fletcher to Wesley, 10 May 1757, Streiff, *Fletcher*, 65).

Back in London in the autumn of 1753 Fletcher attended a Methodist service. The preaching of the Methodists, particularly Charles Wesley, did not confirm Fletcher's religious life, but did bring it to a crisis. All his confidence in religious achievements was destroyed. Fletcher recognized himself as the poorest, the proudest, and the most stubborn of sinners. He sought renewal of his life through the power of Christ. After severe internal struggles, he found relief and experienced some inner change in January 1754. On 24 August 1754 he signed a personal covenant with God in which he devoted himself wholly to God. He petitioned God as heavenly Father, divine Redeemer, and sanctifying Spirit to accept by grace alone his consecration and to pardon and renew him in His image. Fletcher revealed the faith he had discovered to his own family. His middle brother was soon converted, followed by his father

on his deathbed. Fletcher became a member of a Methodist class and a close friend of Charles Wesley, with whom he entertained an intensive personal correspondence.

On 6 and 13 March 1757 Fletcher was ordained deacon and priest of the Church of England, and on the 14th was installed as curate of Madeley, Shropshire. The first acts of his ministry were in support of John Wesley, who noted in his journal: 'When my bodily strength failed, and none in England were able and willing to assist me, he sent me help from the mountains of Switzerland! And an help meet for me in every respect' (20 March 1757, *Journal of John Wesley*, 4.199). As far as his duties as tutor permitted, Fletcher helped the Methodists in and around London. Part of his ministry was to the French. He became acquainted with the countess of Huntingdon, who appointed him as one of her chaplains alongside the likes of George Whitefield, Howel Harris, Thomas Maxfield, and John Berridge. Fletcher was held in high esteem, but drove himself to near despair because he demanded too much of himself. During the winter and spring of 1759 and 1760 Fletcher, Charles Wesley, and the countess of Huntingdon worked closely together in London. Uncertain as to his future, Fletcher sought to be guided passively by providence. In contrast Thomas Hill, whose sons had left for university, actively sought a parish living for Fletcher. After the refusal of one well-paid living, Fletcher accepted the poorer position of Madeley, where he had been curate. He was installed as vicar in October 1760 at the age of thirty-one and remained there until his death. Madeley was situated in a region of early industrial revolution at the time of his ministry.

John Wesley was upset and disappointed. He had hoped to find in Fletcher a capable young clergyman willing to itinerate with him and to oversee the 'united societies'. In summer 1761 he entreated Fletcher to leave Madeley, to join the Methodists, and to work with him as his partner. Wesley even offered to give the whole leadership over to Fletcher, who was twenty-six years his junior. In 1773 Wesley reiterated the invitation and designated Fletcher as his only possible successor. But Fletcher again refused. He later wrote to a friend: 'The snail does best in its shell: were it to aim at galloping like the race horse, it would be ridiculous indeed' (Fletcher to J. Ireland, 13 Sept 1784, Streiff, *Fletcher*, 462). On occasions Fletcher travelled to see Methodist societies or to attend the annual conference. Every time, his public speaking, coupled with his physical presence, left a strong impression, and John Wesley's hopes rose that Fletcher would at last serve as an itinerant preacher. Shortly before the 1784 conference, where Fletcher settled a dispute between Wesley and the preachers who were not among the legal hundred, Charles Wesley wrote to his friend: 'I trust you are reserved (after mine and my Brother's departure) to gather up the Wreck' (C. Wesley to J. Fletcher, 21 June 1784, Streiff, *Fletcher*, 462).

Despite his reluctance to accept Wesley's invitation, Fletcher always exercised his ministry as a firm supporter of Methodist principles. He was convinced that Methodism was destined to leaven the entire Anglican church. He worked together with the Wesleys as well as with the Calvinistic Methodists, with the itinerant lay preachers and with the ordained gospel ministers. In 1768 Fletcher agreed to superintend Trevecca College, Wales, on a non-residential basis, where ministerial students were to be trained in the Methodist spirit. The project of the college was initiated by Howel Harris and the countess of Huntingdon with a view to reuniting the different tendencies within the Methodist movement. When Fletcher resigned from the superintendency early in 1771 it was a preliminary to the great theological debate on salvation, free will and free grace, antinomianism and predestination. Fletcher was pushed against his will into a leading role in that controversy. The Calvinistic wing of Methodism was alarmed to see him writing in defence of Wesley and closed its pulpits to him. In 1773 the countess of Huntingdon again became more friendly towards Fletcher, allowed him to preach in one of her chapels, and acknowledged (in private only) the merits of his writing.

Prior to the controversy in the 1770s Fletcher had published only a single tract, a French sermon on the new birth, *Discours sur la régénération* (1759). What started in 1771 as *A Vindication of the Rev. Mr. Wesley's Last Minutes* became the first of five *Checks to Antinomianism* (1771–4), succeeded by the *Equal Checks to Pharisaism and Antinomianism* (1774–5) and the *Last Check to Antinomianism* (1775) on the related subject of Christian perfection. Two tracts against the Revd Augustus Toplady's philosophical understanding of necessity followed in 1776–7. The whole theological controversy was concluded with two smaller tracts, *The Doctrines of Grace and Justice* and *The Reconciliation* (both 1777), in which Fletcher attempted to reconcile the Arminian and the Calvinist wings of Methodism. Other works published in the same period included *An Appeal to Matter of Fact and Common Sense* (1772) and, in 1776, two tracts in defence of Wesley's position on the American War of Independence.

Fletcher was a prolific and meticulously detailed writer. He acknowledged the contribution made by his Calvinistic opponents to the development of his own theology, especially concerning prevenient grace and the doctrines of election and reprobation, and finally stressed the need to avoid both extremes of Arminianism and Calvinism by a doctrinal balance between grace and justice. He was convinced that 'Bible-Calvinists' as well as 'Bible-Arminians' observed that balance in spite of their different approaches to the gospel truth. He developed a view of the dispensations of the triune God as different degrees of the one revelation in both the history of mankind and the history of an individual person.

Fletcher wrote his tracts while ministering to a challenging parish. Weakened by an overload of work and signs of consumption, he was close to death in 1777. He was forced to leave his parish. During his illness, many of his former theological opponents came to see him and were ready for reconciliation. When Fletcher's health had partly recovered his friend and benefactor John Ireland took him to France and then to his native town, Nyon. In Switzerland Fletcher made a strong impression. He devoted his time to teaching children and to writing against French philosophers and practical atheism. He published a French poem on Psalm 148, *La louange* (1781), and, back in England, a shorter poem, *Essai sur la paix de 1783* (1784), as well as a revised and combined edition of the two works, *La grâce et la nature* (1785), dedicated to the queen.

Fletcher had taken up his pen in defence of John Wesley, who had been accused of heresy and had begun to publish Fletcher's letters; Charles Wesley read the manuscripts of most of Fletcher's later tracts and supervised the editing. Fletcher's writings, warmly commended by the Wesley brothers for their sound theological principles, sold primarily to those Methodists who were sympathetic to Arminianism. The only slight difference of opinion between Fletcher and John Wesley occurred in respect to Fletcher's pneumatology. He tended to minimize the importance of the gift and work of the Holy Spirit in every believer, and to stress the difference between 'babes in Christ' and the 'perfection' of mature Christian believers. He referred to some of Charles Wesley's hymns and tried to link Christian perfection and pneumatological expectations. Fletcher spoke of a 'baptism of the Spirit' which leads into the fullness of Christian life understood as perfect love. Unfortunately, the manuscript of his *An Essay on the Birth of the Spirit* (written about 1776–7) has not been discovered.

Back in England in 1781, Fletcher's health remained precarious. In a Methodist band meeting he witnessed to being altogether filled with love, dead unto sin, and alive unto God. His experience of Christian perfection was paralleled by his open declaration of love for Mary Bosanquet (1739–1815) [*see* Fletcher, Mary], whom he married in November 1781; the couple had no children. During his last years Fletcher's theological thoughts, similar to Charles Wesley's poems, focused increasingly on the unfathomable mystery of love of the triune God. Unpublished manuscript booklets with short spiritual meditations on love, the inner-Trinitarian life of love, and the outpouring of this love in creation and salvation give testimony to rich spiritual insights. Attacked by an epidemic fever, Fletcher died on 14 August 1785 at the vicarage at Madeley. He was buried three days later in the churchyard there. John Wesley preached a funeral sermon on Psalm 37 and concluded:

> Many exemplary men have I known, holy in heart and life, within fourscore years. But one equal to him I have not known—one so inwardly and outwardly devoted to God. So unblameable a character in every respect I have not found either in Europe or America. Nor do I expect to find another such on this side of eternity. (*Works*, 3.628)

Several of Fletcher's works were published posthumously, among them *The Portrait of St Paul*, translated from the French original written about 1780, and two tracts in defence of the traditional Trinitarian and Christological doctrines, *A Rational Vindication of the Catholic Faith* and *Socinianism Unscriptural* (both written about 1784–5 but not completed).

Fletcher became the theologian as well as the 'saint' of

Methodism. In the nineteenth century his works influenced generations of Methodist preachers on both sides of the Atlantic. In the post-civil war phase of the sanctification movement in the USA, interest in Fletcher's writings and saintly life grew again and gave rise to strong pneumatological, Pentecostal expectations. In the twentieth century interest in Fletcher as theologian weakened in mainstream Methodism, but remained strong among American Holiness churches and arose among Pentecostals and Charismatics.   PATRICK PH. STREIFF

Sources P. Ph. Streiff, *Jean Guillaume de la Fléchère / John William Fletcher* (Frankfurt, 1984) [in Ger., incl. list of primary and secondary sources; shortened, but updated, version in Eng., *Reluctant saint?* (2001)] • P. Ph. Streiff, 'Wie "methodistisch" war die Erweckung in der französischsprachigen Schweiz?', *Mitteilungen der Studiengemeinschaft für Geschichte der Evangelisch-methodistischen Kirche*, 16/2 (1995), 30–56 • P. S. Forsaith, 'Portraits of John Fletcher of Madeley and their artists', *Proceedings of the Wesley Historical Society*, 47 (1989–90), 187–201 • W. S. Gunter, *The limits of 'Love Divine'* (1989) • D. W. Dayton, *Theological roots of pentecostalism* (1987) • L. W. Wood, *Pentecostal grace* (1980) • *The journal of the Rev. John Wesley*, ed. N. Curnock and others, 8 vols. (1909–16) • *The works of John Wesley*, 3, ed. A. C. Outler (1986) • B. Coulton, 'Tutor to the Hills: the early career of John Fletcher', *Proceedings of the Wesley Historical Society*, 47 (1989–90), 94–103 • P. S. Forsaith, *John Fletcher, vicar of Madeley* (1994) • G. E. Milburn, 'Early Methodism and the Huguenots', *Proceedings of the Wesley Historical Society*, 45 (1985–6), 69–79 • H. D. Rack, 'Early Methodist visions of the Trinity', *Proceedings of the Wesley Historical Society*, 46 (1987–8), 38–44, 57–69 • P. P. Streiff, 'Der ökumenische Geist im frühen Methodismus', ed. M. Brecht, *Pietismus und Neuzeit*, 11 (1985), 59–77 • J. P. Tuck, 'Some pocket books in the Methodist archives', *Proceedings of the Wesley Historical Society*, 46 (1987–8), 32–7 • Taufregister, Archives cantonales vaudoises, Lausanne, Switzerland, Eb.91.4B
Archives JRL, Methodist Archives and Research Centre, corresp. | Archives Cantonales Vaudoises, Lausanne, Switzerland, family data • Bibliothèque Cantonale et Universitaire, Lausanne, family MSS • Cliff College, Calver, Sheffield, MSS of sermons and sermon outlines; prayer booklets • Duke U., Perkins L., letters, MSS • Emory University, Atlanta, Georgia, Robert W. Woodruf Library, letters, MSS • Ironbridge Gorge Museum Library and Archives, Ironbridge, MSS • John Wesley's Chapel, Bristol, letters, MSS • Shrops. RRC, letters, MSS • Wesley's Chapel, London, letters, MSS • Westminster College, Cambridge, Cheshunt Foundation, Cheshunt College MSS, corresp. with Selina, countess of Huntingdon
Likenesses J. Spilsbury, oils, 1777, John Wesley's Chapel, New Room, Bristol [*see illus.*] • J. Spilsbury, mezzotint, pubd 1786, BM • J. Jackson, oils, *c.*1805, Wesley's Chapel, City Road, London • J. Jackson, oils, Methodist Publishing House, London • W. J. White, stipple (after unknown artist), BM
Wealth at death est. to be low or non-existent in England • some income from parts of family vineyards around Nyon, Switzerland: 'Journal de Henry Louys Delafléchère', F 3639, département des manuscrits, Bibliothèque Cantonale et Universitaire, Lausanne

Fletcher, Joseph (1582/3–1637), poet, was the son of Thomas Fletcher, merchant tailor of London. He was entered at Merchant Taylors' School on 11 March 1594, and was elected to St John's College, Oxford, in 1600, matriculating on 23 January 1601, at the age of eighteen. He proceeded BA in 1604/5 and MA on 6 June 1608. He took part in a burlesque pageant called 'The Christmas Prince', played at Oxford in 1607, together with William Laud, also of St John's.

After leaving Oxford, he attracted the attention of the Wingfield family and was appointed household chaplain. In the autumn of 1609 he was presented to the rectory of Wilby, Suffolk, by Sir Anthony Wingfield, where in May 1610, he married Grace (1583–1618), daughter of Hugh Ashley, vicar of the nearby parish of St Margaret's, Ilkettshall. They had six children: Joseph (*bap.* 7 April 1611), William (*bap.* 13 April 1612), Grace (*bap.* 28 Dec 1613), Marie (*bap.* 27 Aug 1605), John (*bap.* 18 May 1617), and a sixth child, born in December 1618. Fletcher's first wife died in giving birth to the sixth child, and she was buried in Wilby church on 4 December 1618. Her husband, when entering her death in the burial register, added two elegiac poems, one in Latin and the other in English. These were printed by A. B. Grosart in his edition of Fletcher's poems in 1869. Fletcher's second wife (Anne) survived him, and to her he left all his property by a will dated 1 May 1630.

Fletcher was the author of a rare volume of poetry, entitled *The Historie of the Perfect, Cursed, Blessed Man* (1628). This is dedicated to the author's patron, Sir Anthony Wingfield. A long prose address to the reader precedes the poem, which is written throughout in heroic verse, and explores the degenerate state of man and the means of his redemption. Emblematical designs by Thomas Cecil are scattered through the volume.

Two further texts have been attributed to Joseph Fletcher. *A Sermon Preached at Ashby de-la-Zouch at the Funeral of the Lady Elizabeth Stanley* was delivered in February 1633 but printed two years later. The British Library catalogue, Grosart, and W. Carew Hazlitt accept the identification of I. F., the author of *Christes Bloodie Sweat, or, The Sonne of God in his Agonie*, by I. F. as Joseph Fletcher. But the authorship of the verse dedicated to William, earl of Pembroke, is very uncertain, and little of the fervour of the earlier work is discernible in the later. Modern scholarship tends, on the basis of internal, stylistic, and thematic evidence, to ascribe it to the dramatist John Ford.

Fletcher died at Wilby on 28 September 1637 and was buried in the church. A mural brass above his grave with verses inscribed upon it is still extant, and was transcribed by Grosart in his introduction to Fletcher's works.
                    SIDNEY LEE, *rev.* ELIZABETH HARESNAPE

Sources *Reg. Oxf.*, 2/2.245; 2/3.250 • Foster, *Alum. Oxon.* • J. S. Boas and W. W. Greg, eds., *The Christmas prince* (1922), 35 • *STC, 1475–1640* • W. C. Hazlitt, 'A guess at authorship', *N&Q*, 3rd ser., 8 (1865), 268 • A. B. Grosart, ed., *The Fuller Worthies' Library: the poems of Joseph Fletcher* (1869) • G. D. Monsarrat, 'John Ford's authorship of *Christes bloodie sweat*', *English Language Notes*, 9 (1971–2), 20–25 • M. J. Sargeant, 'Writings ascribed to John Ford by Joseph Hunter in *Chorus Vatum*', *Review of English Studies*, 10 (1934), 165–75 • R. Huebert, *John Ford: baroque English dramatist* (1977), 151, 231 n.28 • W. A. Ringler, 'The 1640 and 1653 Poems: by Francis Beaumont, gent. and the canon of Beaumont's nondramatic verse', *Studies in Bibliography*, 40 (1987), 120–40, esp. 125 • C. J. Robinson, ed., *A register of the scholars admitted into Merchant Taylors' School, from AD 1562 to 1874*, 2 vols. (1882–3)
Archives BL, transcription of sepulchral inscription at Wilby, Add. MS 32483, fol. 214
Wealth at death see preamble to will, Grosart, ed., *Fuller Worthies' Library*, xxv

Fletcher, Joseph (1784–1843), Congregational minister and theological writer, was born on 3 December 1784 at

Chester, where his father, Robert Fletcher, was a goldsmith. In his boyhood he was deeply impressed by the gospel, and, after attending the grammar school of his native city, prepared for the ministry in the Congregationalist church by studying, first at Hoxton Academy and then at the University of Glasgow, where he took the degree of MA in 1807. At about this time, he married Mary, *née* France. Receiving a call from the Congregational church of Blackburn, Lancashire, he began his ministry in 1807, and continued there until 1823, when he became minister of the Stepney meeting in London. In 1816 he added to his duties that of theological tutor in the Blackburn college for training ministers. While discharging both the pastoral and the academic duties with marked ability and success, Fletcher was also a voluminous writer. The *Eclectic Review* had just begun publication, and Fletcher was one of its regular contributors. His papers gave proof of ample stores of information, and of a scholarly and powerful pen. On particular subjects he published tracts and treatises that won considerable fame, notably his lecture collections *Principles and Institutions of the Roman Catholic Religion* (1817) and *Personal Election and Divine Sovereignty* (1825). A volume of poems (1846) was the joint production of himself and his sister, Mary Fletcher. In 1830 the senatus of the University of Glasgow conferred on him the degree of DD. He was chairman of the Congregational Union in 1837. Without reaching the first rank, he showed a combination of reasoning power and emotional fervour which made him an instructive preacher. As a writer who gave birth to all his literary offspring amid the whirl of constant practical work and endless engagements, he did little more than show what he might have done with leisure and other facilities for literary work. He died on 8 June 1843.

Joseph and Mary Fletcher's fourth son, **Joseph Fletcher** (1816–1876), Congregational minister, was born at Blackburn on 7 January 1816. He was educated at Ham grammar school, near Richmond, Surrey, and then, after working for some time in a Manchester counting-house, went in 1833 to study at Coward College, London. He was called to the Congregational church of Hanley in 1839, and was transferred to Christchurch, Hampshire, in 1849, in succession to Daniel Gunn. He kept a school for a time at Christchurch, but the death by drowning of seven of his pupils in May 1868 caused him to close it. He published *Memoirs* of his father in 1846, *Six Views of Infidelity* (1843), a *History of Independency*, an important work in four volumes (1847–9, reissued 1853), and a *Life of Constantine the Great* (1852). He is also credited with the libretto of an oratorio entitled *Paradise*, by John Fawcett the younger. Fletcher resigned his charge owing to paralysis at the close of 1873, and died at Christchurch on 2 June 1876.

W. G. BLAIKIE, *rev.* H. C. G. MATTHEW

Sources J. Fletcher, *Memoirs of the Rev. Joseph Fletcher* (1846) · *Congregational Year Book* · J. Waddington, *Congregational history*, 5 vols. (1869–80)
Archives DWL, letters
Likenesses Blood, stipple, pubd 1824 (after J. R. Wildman), NPG · T. Woolnoth, stipple, pubd 1831 (after J. R. Wildman), BM, NPG

Fletcher, Joseph (1813–1852), statistician and school inspector, was the third son of George Fletcher, of Rennes, France. Little is known of his background and early life, except that he was admitted to the Middle Temple in 1838 and called to the bar on 7 May 1841. As with contemporaries such as William Farr and George Richardson Porter, he turned his amateur interest in collecting facts about social and economic conditions into a successful career working for the expanding boards and inspectorates of the British government. He became an important figure in the early Victorian statistical movement, and shared its reformist sentiments. He sat on the council of the Statistical Society of London starting in 1839, edited its journal from 1842 until his death, and was a frequent secretary to the statistical section of the British Association. Between 1837 and 1841 he was secretary to the royal commission on hand-loom weavers, for which he wrote a report on the ribbon weavers of the midlands, and he performed the same job for royal commissions on the health of towns (1840) and children's employment (1843). From 1844 until his death he was a government school inspector, with jurisdiction over the British and Foreign School Society.

Fletcher compiled profusely. In the last ten years of his life he read thirteen papers at the London Statistical Society and five papers at the British Association, primarily on municipal administration, crime, and education. All but one of his papers on municipal topics concerned London, including its streets, markets, police, criminal courts, gas lights, and water. They all followed the formula of describing 'ancient' customs, listing various privileges granted by royal charter, and finally celebrating recent efforts to consolidate services and eliminate waste. In two long papers delivered in 1842 and 1844, he applied the same historical method to describe the diverse constitutional arrangements for local government both within London and in English towns.

A second theme in Fletcher's work was the connection between education and criminality. He first addressed education in his report to the commission on hand-loom weavers, where he claimed that weavers, once concentrated in towns, could transcend their depraved rural upbringing, but warned that they required inculcation in political economy and religion to avoid absorbing socialist ideas. His careful survey of criminal convictions in 1843, however, which revealed 'an excess of instruction greatly on the side of crime' ('Progress of crime', *Journal of the Statistical Society of London*, 6, 1843, 233), led him to question the efficacy of existing schools in abating class conflict. However, in a succession of papers on what he called moral and educational statistics, which he published after becoming a school inspector, he reaffirmed a strong link between elementary education (especially religious training) and social stability.

A lifelong Londoner who last lived in Savile Row, Fletcher died suddenly from heart disease on 11 August 1852, while visiting Chirk, Denbighshire, Wales. He was buried on 18 August at All Hallows, Tottenham, Middlesex.

TIMOTHY L. ALBORN

Sources M. J. Cullen, *The statistical movement in early Victorian Britain: the foundations of empirical social research* (1975) · A. Digby and P. Searby, *Children, school and society in nineteenth-century England* (1981) · *GM*, 2nd ser., 38 (1852) · J. Hutchinson, ed., *A catalogue of notable Middle Templars: with brief biographical notices* (1902) · parish register, All Hallows, Tottenham, London, LMA [burial]

Wealth at death left everything to sister: will, PRO, PROB 11/2157, sig. 630

Fletcher, Joseph (1816–1876). *See under* Fletcher, Joseph (1784–1843).

Fletcher, Sir Lazarus (1854–1921), museum director and mineralogist, was born at 11 Williamson Street, Salford, on 3 March 1854, the eldest child of six sons and two daughters of Stewart Fletcher of Salford and his wife, Betty, *née* Gregory. He was educated at Manchester grammar school (1865–72) and gained the gold medal for mechanics and the bronze medal for mathematics, as well as several certificates in other subjects, in the national examinations of the Department of Science and Art at South Kensington Museum in 1872. He won an open science scholarship, the Brackenbury, to Balliol College, Oxford, the same year. He took a distinguished first class in mathematical moderations in 1874 and in the final examinations in both the mathematical (1875) and natural science (1876) schools.

Fletcher was appointed a demonstrator in physics, under Professor R. B. Clifton, at the Clarendon Physical Laboratory (1875–7). He was elected to the Millard lectureship in physics at Trinity College, Oxford (1877–8), and in 1877 he was also elected to a fellowship at University College, Oxford. This last position he had to resign when, on 1 September 1880, at the parish church of Moorside, near Oldham, he married Agnes Ward Holme (*d.* 1915), the daughter of Thomas Holme, the vicar of Moorside. They had one daughter, Elizabeth Gregory Fletcher.

When at the Clarendon Laboratory, Fletcher read Groth's *Physikalische Krystallographie*. Thereafter Clifton drew Fletcher to the attention of Professor Story-Maskelyne, keeper of the mineralogy department at the British Museum. In 1878 Fletcher succeeded W. J. Lewis as assistant in that department. Upon Story-Maskelyne's resignation in 1880 he was promoted to keeper, a position he held until 1909. Shortly after his appointment he had to organize the moving of the collection of minerals and meteorites from Bloomsbury to the new buildings in South Kensington. This was a huge task owing to the vast number of specimens involved, to their value and fragility, and to their having to be completely rearranged. Fletcher also had to design new showcases, and he prepared guides and handbooks to the collections—deemed 'masterpieces of lucid and precise exposition'—not to mention some 17,000 labels for objects, printed labels now replacing the manuscript labels of old. Of particular note were his introductions to the study of meteorites (1881), of minerals (1884), and of rocks (1895). He also appointed guide-lecturers, but had difficulty appointing well-qualified assistants. He did, though, establish a well-equipped laboratory. He also travelled abroad, to Russia

(to the International Geological Congress) and Sweden in 1897 and to Switzerland and Italy in 1902.

In 1906 Fletcher developed a severe heart-related illness; he was never again fully to regain good health. However, in July 1909 he succeeded Sir Ray Lankester, who retired in December 1907, as director of the British Museum (Natural History). Fletcher had been overlooked as director when Sir W. H. Flower retired in 1898. This was largely through pressure brought about by certain members of the Royal Society, who, in addition to being strongly pro-Lankester, were against both a mineralogist and an internal candidate being promoted to the position, thereby overruling the museum's trustees. Fletcher was still able to carry out scientific research, particularly regarding meteorites and crystallography. Of greatest importance was his investigation of the transmission of light through crystals, published both in the *Mineralogical Magazine* (9, 1891, 278–388) and in book form (1892), which revolutionized the teaching of physical optics, bringing him international renown: 'This paper alone is sufficient evidence that he possessed unrivalled powers of elucidation and exposition which would have placed him in the front rank of teachers' (*Mineralogical Magazine*, 186). In his career Fletcher wrote over forty articles, most being read before the Mineralogical Society before appearing in the *Mineralogical Magazine*, as well as numerous contributions to other works. He also wrote the entry on meteorites in *Encyclopaedia Britannica* (11th edn, 1910–11). In 1911 he directed an exhibition on animals, plants, and minerals mentioned in the Bible, held to commemorate the tercentenary of the Authorized Version, and contributed an essay on biblical minerals, an area of personal interest. Illness often kept Fletcher away from the museum. He did not think too highly of his own tenure of the directorship. To Sir Frederic Kenyon, director of the British Museum, he wrote in 1919: 'as for the last ten years, there is nothing to show except the keeping of the peace, and keeping people at peace with each other so far as that is possible' (Stearn, 111).

Fletcher was an examiner in natural science at the Oxford public examinations in 1880, and for the Cambridge natural science tripos in 1882–3, 1889–91, and 1896–7. He was also a member of the boards of electors of Oxford and Cambridge universities to the professorships of mineralogy. In 1895 and in 1904 he gave a course of lectures on meteorites at the Royal Institution. He was elected a fellow of the Geological Society in 1879 and served as vice-president (1890–93); he was made a fellow of the Royal Society in 1889 and served on its council (1895–7 and 1910–12, for the latter period as a vice-president); and he was president of the Mineralogical Society (1885–8) and its general secretary from 1888 to 1909. His service to this society was rewarded by the presentation of his portrait, subscribed to by members, in 1912. He was also president of the geological section of the British Association at Oxford in 1894, to which he gave a notable address 'On the progress of mineralogy and crystallography'. He was a vice-president of the Physical Society (1895–7), and received numerous honours. He was made an honorary fellow of University College, Oxford, in 1910, and two years later was awarded the Wollaston medal of the Geological Society. He was a corresponding or honorary member of numerous societies and institutions, both abroad and at home. He also received honorary degrees from the universities of St Andrews (LLD) and Berlin (PhD).

In 1915 Fletcher's wife, for many years an invalid, died. The following year, on 15 August, he married her sister, (Martha Thomasina) Edith Holme, then aged fifty-two, at the parish church of Barnard Castle in co. Durham. He also received a knighthood in 1916. Upon his retirement in 1919 his reduced income necessitated moving from London, and he went to live in Ravenstonedale, a village near Kirkby Stephen, Westmorland. A particular interest was gardening. He also hoped to realize a long-held ambition to write a comprehensive treatise on the classification of minerals, but he did not live long enough. On 6 January 1921, while on a brief holiday in Grange over Sands with his family, he died of a heart attack at the Tents Hotel; he had also been suffering from arteriosclerosis and diabetes. He was buried in Ravenstonedale on 11 January.

ROBERT SHARP

Sources A. L., *PRS*, 99A (1921), ix–xii · *Mineralogical Magazine*, 19 (1920–22), 181–92 · *Nature*, 106 (1920–21), 636–7 · G. T. Prior, *Geological Magazine*, 58 (1921), 141–3 · R. D. Oldham, *Quarterly Journal of the Geological Society*, 77 (1921), lxvi–lxvii · *The Times* (10 Jan 1921), 15b–c · *WWW* · W. T. Stearn, *The Natural History Museum at South Kensington: a history of the British Museum (Natural History), 1753–1980* (1981) · b. cert. · m. certs. · d. cert. · *CGPLA Eng. & Wales* (1921)
Archives NHM, diaries, letter-books, and papers; historical notes | NHM, letters to C. E. Fagan · NHM, letters to Albert Gunther and R. W. T. Gunther
Likenesses Lafayette, photograph, repro. in *Mineralogical Magazine*, pl. v · oils, repro. in Stearn, *Natural History Museum* · photograph, repro. in *PRS*, facing p. ix
Wealth at death £5633 5s.: probate, 14 March 1921, *CGPLA Eng. & Wales*

Fletcher, Maria. *See* Manina, Maria (*fl.* 1712–1736).

Fletcher [*née* Bosanquet], **Mary** (1739–1815), Methodist preacher, was born on 12 September 1739 at Forest House, Leytonstone, Essex, the second of the four children of Samuel Bosanquet (*d.* 1767), merchant and lord of the manor of Leytonstone, and his wife, whose name is unknown, who also died in 1767. Her family was one of the most illustrious, wealthy, and well-connected Huguenot families in London, closely involved in financial trading in the City, where her younger brother Samuel was a director of the Bank of England and lived in a former residence of the earls of Norwich. Mary later testified that she had been conscious of 'the spirit of God striving with me and offering me salvation' from early childhood and that her confirmation at St Paul's Cathedral at the age of thirteen, following personal instruction in the catechism from her father, was 'a very rousing ordinance to me' (Moore, 13, 20). However, rejecting her family's fashionable lifestyle, she left home in 1760 and embraced Methodism, joining the London Foundery Society, where she experienced a deepening of her spiritual awareness during the revival of 1761–2. In 1763, with the help of a legacy from her grandmother and the support of her close friend

Mary Fletcher (1739–1815), by Jonathan Spilsbury, pubd 1812

Sarah Ryan, she established a Christian community at Leytonstone, providing for needy children and adults, and began to read the scriptures at Methodist class meetings, which were held regularly on Thursday evenings. Between 1763 and 1768 some thirty-four adults, including her co-workers Sarah Crosby and Ann Tripp, and thirty-five children, including Sally Lawrence, a four-year-old orphan, who remained devotedly attached to Mary for the rest of her life, joined the community. Notwithstanding her private means, Mary maintained an exceptionally frugal lifestyle from her youth and was 'always sparing of expense upon herself that she might have more to give "the household of faith"' (ibid., 417). Her portrait reveals a plainly attired, quietly determined, pious woman, with well-defined facial features, wide expressive eyes, an aquiline nose, slightly pursed lips, and hair neatly swept back under a white frilled bonnet, enveloped in a dark hooded cloak.

In June 1768, in order to establish the work on a more secure financial basis, the community moved to Cross Hall, Gildersome, Morley, near Leeds, where Mary faced the considerable challenge of managing an orphanage, school, dairy farm, and maltkilns without the assistance of Sarah Ryan, who died shortly after moving north. Undaunted, however, she initiated, with Sarah Crosby, regular Wednesday evening religious meetings, and the women were soon seeking advice from John Wesley, the founder of Methodism, about their call to preach. While recognizing women's importance to the Methodist movement, Wesley advised them 'never to take a text' nor 'speak in a continued discourse without some break'

(Wesley to S. Crosby, 18 March 1769, Burge, *Women Preachers*, 21). In February 1773, however, Mary, ignoring his advice, made her first explicit reference to a text, explaining later that she felt 'a greater approbation of what we call expounding, taking a part or whole of a chapter and speaking on it' (Burge, 'Impudent women', 97). Moreover, Wesley was evidently later impressed by her preaching, commenting that: 'her words are as fire, conveying both light and heat to the hearts of all that hear her … her manner is smooth, easy and natural, even when the sense is deep and strong' (*Journal*, 7.249). The demand for her as a preacher was such that in September 1776 she rode 20 miles across the moors to address 'such a rabble as I scarce ever saw', numbering around 2000, from a rock in Golcar, before conducting a cottage meeting in the village and then preaching from a horse-block to a roadside crowd in Huddersfield.

On 12 November 1781 Mary married at Batley parish church the saintly evangelical vicar of Madeley, John William *Fletcher (*bap.* 1729, *d.* 1785), who had written to her unexpectedly on his return from a period of convalescence in his native Switzerland, confessing that he had cherished a twenty-five-year regard for her. After the marriage Mary declared: 'I have such a husband as is in everything suited to me' (Moore, 148), while her husband confided: 'God has found me a partner, a sister, a wife who is not afraid to face the colliers and bargemen of my parish' (Burge, *Women Preachers*, 27). They exercised a remarkably effective joint ministry in the rural industrial parish, which had suffered considerable pastoral neglect during John Fletcher's recent absence. Mary Fletcher conducted regular class meetings and made frequent visits to the sick and infirm, dispensing natural medicines and recording details of her remedies in her commonplace books and in her annotated copy of John Wesley's *Primitive Physic*. The blissfully happy marriage was curtailed, Mary Fletcher ruefully recorded in her memoirs, after only 'three years, nine months and two days' by 'her heavenly minded' husband's untimely death from a fever on 14 August 1785 (Moore, 178). 'I have trodden deep waters', she recalled, 'but all my afflictions were nothing compared to this', when 'the sun of my earthly joys for ever set' (ibid., 165).

Mary was allowed by her husband's successor to continue to reside in the vicarage after her husband's death and even to advise on the appointment of curates, but, to avoid giving offence, Mary utilized the adjacent tithe barn for her religious meetings. In 1814, aged seventy-five, she was still preaching five times a week. She held her last religious meeting on 24 September 1815 and made her final entry in her journal on 26 October 1815. She had developed a suspected tumour in her left breast, but died on 9 December 1815 from a respiratory illness, which had caused her acute suffering in the last month of her life, when she was cared for by her faithful friend, companion, and executrix, Mary Tooth, who continued her work for almost another three decades after her death. The Fletchers thereby established an evangelical tradition at Madeley which lasted for three generations, and the census of religious worship reveals that the places of worship in Madeley were better attended than those in some neighbouring Shropshire parishes in 1851.

The epitaph on their shared grave in St Michael's churchyard, Madeley, records that during the long period in which Mary survived her husband 'she continued to tread the path in which he left her and ministered with ardent zeal and self denying beneficence to the spiritual and temporal wants of his flock', healing dissensions and preventing schism, endeavouring 'to induce all around her to dwell in unity and Godly love' (Burge, *Women Preachers*, 31).   JOHN A. HARGREAVES

Sources H. Moore, *The life of Mrs Mary Fletcher*, 13th edn (1851) · M. Edwards, *My dear sister* (1975) · P. W. Chilcote, *John Wesley and the women preachers of early Methodism* (1991) · E. K. Brown, *Women of Mr Wesley's Methodism* (1983) · Z. Taft, *Biographical sketches of the lives … of various holy women*, 2 vols. in 1 (1825–8); facs. edn (1992) · J. Burge, *Women preachers in community* (1996) · J. Burge, 'Impudent women', *Epworth Review*, 21/2 (May 1994), 93–102 · *The journal of the Rev. John Wesley*, ed. N. Curnock and others, 8 vols. (1909–16) · D. M. Valenze, *Prophetic sons and daughters: female preaching and popular religion in industrial England* (1985) · J. W. Laycock, *Methodist heroes in the great Haworth round, 1734–84* (1909) · G. E. Milburn, 'Early Methodism and the Huguenots', *Proceedings of the Wesley Historical Society*, 45 (1985–6), 69–79 · J. P. Tuck, '*Primitive physic*: an interesting association copy', *Proceedings of the Wesley Historical Society*, 45 (1985–6), 1–6 · *J. N. Fletcher, 1729–85* (1985) [exhibition catalogue, JRL, 1985]
Archives Ironbridge Gorge Museum, Ironbridge, Telford · JRL, Methodist Archives and Research Centre, corresp., diaries, journals, papers · Shrops. RRC
Likenesses oils, *c*.1790, Clive House Museum, Shrewsbury, Shropshire · J. Spilsbury, mezzotint, pubd 1812, NPG [*see illus.*] · portrait, repro. in Moore, *Life of Mrs Mary Fletcher*, frontispiece

Fletcher, Percy Eastman (1879–1932), composer and musical director, was born on 12 December 1879 in Handel Terrace, Curzon Street, Derby, the son of Alfred William Fletcher, professor of music, and his wife, Elizabeth Eastman. He was privately educated as a violinist, pianist, and organist, and having moved to London in 1899 he began a career as a composer. At the same time he worked his way towards a position as musical director, which he achieved at the Savoy Theatre in 1906–7. While there he composed the one-act musical farce *An Exile from Home*. Engagements followed at the Prince of Wales (1906–7), the Comedy (1907), the Queen's (1907 and 1910), the Apollo (1908), Terry's (1908–9), and the Comedy and the Criterion (1911–12); in 1913 he was at the Theatre Royal, Drury Lane, for Johnston Forbes-Robertson's farewell season. In May 1915 he was appointed musical director to Sir Herbert Tree at His Majesty's Theatre, where he remained until his death.

At His Majesty's Fletcher most notably was musical director for the record-breaking musical play *Chu Chin Chow* by Oscar Asche and Frederick Norton, which ran for five years and which he partially orchestrated. He then composed the music for Asche's spectacular successor, *Mecca*, which was first produced in 1920 in New York, in view of *Chu Chin Chow's* ongoing tenure of His Majesty's; when eventually it was staged at His Majesty's, in 1921, objections to the title from the lord chamberlain resulted in its being renamed *Cairo*. With Asche, Fletcher also composed for another musical spectacular, *The Good Old Days*, produced at the Gaiety Theatre in 1925. In 1918 he provided music for *The Pageant of Drury Lane*, to celebrate the twenty-first year of the management of Arthur Collins at the Theatre Royal, Drury Lane.

However, Fletcher's principal successes as a composer lay outside the theatre. He produced many pieces for piano and organ before making a mark in the light-music field with *Songe adoré* (1911) and *March of the Mannequins* (1911). In 1914 he achieved particular success with two light-orchestral pieces, the intermezzo *Demoiselle chic* and the waltz *Bal masqué*, which together made up his *Two Parisian Sketches*. Splendidly tuneful, elegantly scored, and wonderfully evocative, *Bal masqué* remained his most widely familiar work. It overshadowed his many other fine light-music compositions in similar vein, among them the *Three Light Pieces* (1918) and the suites *Rustic Revels* (1918), *Woodland Pictures* (1920), *Sylvan Scenes* (1921), *At Gretna Green* (1926), and *Famous Beauties* (1928).

Other original compositions were written for a wide range of audiences. There were ballads such as *Galloping Dick* (1911), *The Captain's Eye* (1912), and the beautiful *Valse lyrique* (1919). There were part-songs such as 'Dream Love' (1921) and also music for organ, such as the *Festival Toccata* (1915), dedicated to the celebrated concert organist Edwin H. Lemare. Fletcher's music for brass band included the tone poem *Labour and Love* (1913) and the *Epic Symphony* (1926); both were commissioned for Crystal Palace Brass Band festivals and both have survived as test pieces for brass band. They pointed the way towards other similar commissions from serious composers such as Edward Elgar, Gustav Holst, Ralph Vaughan Williams, and Harrison Birtwistle. The march *Spirit of Pageantry* also became a popular band composition.

Fletcher contributed to the choral repertory with *Choral Rhapsody on Welsh Airs* (1910) and the Elgarian sacred cantata *The Passion of Christ* (1922), of which the latter for some time enjoyed wide currency. He was hardly less prolific as an orchestrator and arranger. He orchestrated the suites *Hiawatha* (1919) and *Minnehaha* (1925) from the posthumous compositions of Samuel Coleridge-Taylor, and he provided orchestral versions of Amy Woodforde-Finden's *Indian Love Lyrics*, *A Lover in Damascus*, and *The Pagoda of Flowers*. He also arranged a fantasia for chorus and orchestra on themes from Richard Wagner's *Die Meistersinger von Nürnberg*.

Fletcher lived in Farnborough, Hampshire, and died in Holloway Sanatorium, Virginia Water, Surrey, on 10 September 1932, of a cerebral haemorrhage, survived by his wife, Marie, *née* St Paul. ANDREW LAMB

Sources P. L. Scowcroft, *British light music* (1997) • P. Gammond, *The Oxford companion to popular music* (1991) • K. Gänzl, *The British musical theatre*, 2 vols. (1986) • J. Parker, ed., *Who's who in the theatre*, 6th edn (1930) • b. cert. • d. cert. • *CGPLA Eng. & Wales* (1932)
Likenesses Yvonde, photograph, repro. in P. Pitt, *Music masterpieces*, 4 (*c.*1925), p. 53
Wealth at death £10,146 9s. 1d.: probate, 15 Nov 1932, *CGPLA Eng. & Wales*

Fletcher, Sir Peter Carteret (1916–1999), air force officer, was born on 7 October 1916 in Durban, South Africa, the son of Frederick Wheeler Trevor Fletcher (*d.* 1964), tobacco farmer, and his wife, Dora, *née* Clulee. Brought up in Southern Rhodesia, Fletcher was educated at the Jesuit school, St George's College, Salisbury, and subsequently read law at Rhodes University in Grahamstown, South Africa.

Having learnt to fly in his spare time, Fletcher was snapped up by the Southern Rhodesian air force at the outbreak of war in 1939 and qualified as a pilot. The Rhodesian air force was later absorbed by the RAF after Britain opened a number of training bases in the country, and Fletcher transferred to the RAF in 1941. In 1940 he had married Marjorie Isobel, daughter of Gilbert Percival Kotzé, a member of a distinguished legal family of Grahamstown, South Africa. They had two daughters.

From 1940 to 1942 Fletcher was commanding officer 135 fighter squadron and 258 fighter squadron, based in Colombo. On Easter day 1942, flying a Hurricane fighter, acting squadron leader Fletcher led an assault on a Japanese airborne attack on British bases in Ceylon. Having destroyed one enemy plane and damaged another, he was seriously wounded and bailed out. But for the action of Fletcher and his fellow officers, the Eastern Fleet might have suffered a similar fate to the American fleet at Pearl Harbor. For his bravery, Fletcher was awarded a DFC (1942).

After being shot down, Fletcher, on account of his wounds, returned to Southern Rhodesia to command a training establishment, a post he held through 1942 and 1943, after which he was dispatched on a course at the Haifa Staff College in Palestine where he made such a favourable impression that he was given a post on the directing staff. This move into management set the pattern for the rest of his career. From Haifa, Fletcher was assigned to the directing staff of the newly established Joint Services Staff College at Latimer, Buckinghamshire, a post he took up in 1946, having received a permanent commission in the RAF. The year before, he had been awarded the OBE for his work early in the war promoting Southern Rhodesia's war effort. In 1948 he became chief flying instructor at RAF Feltwell, where he was to win the AFC (1952) when testing an all-weather system for combat aircraft. In 1953 he was appointed air attaché at the British embassy in Oslo. Between 1956 and 1958 he was on the directing staff of the Imperial Defence College and from 1958 to 1960 he commanded RAF Abingdon.

From 1961 to 1973, when he retired from the RAF, Fletcher held a number of senior management posts. These included deputy director, joint planning staff (1960–61), and director of operational requirements (B) at the Air Ministry (1961–3), in which post he began negotiations to buy the American C-130 Hercules for the RAF. As assistant chief of the air staff (policy and planning) (1964–6), he weathered a long struggle with the Royal Navy over the future of aircraft-carriers, and emerged victor. He returned briefly to operations in 1966 as air officer commanding no. 38 group, transport command, but returned to Whitehall as vice-chief of the air staff (1967–70), where he was responsible for the operational efficiency of the RAF. He also introduced into service the Buccaneer low-flying bomber. Following a year (1970–71) as controller of aircraft, Ministry of Aviation Supply (formerly Ministry of Technology), Fletcher, as air systems controller, defence procurement executive, Ministry of Defence (1971–3), played a leading role in the restructuring of defence procurement.

Having been appointed OBE in 1945, Fletcher was made CB in 1965 and was advanced to KCB in 1968. He was also a fellow of the Royal Aeronautical Society. On retirement from the RAF, he became a director of Hawker Siddeley Aviation Ltd (1974–7); director of corporate strategy and planning, British Aerospace (1977–82); and was a member of the Airbus Industry Supervisory Board (1979–82).

Fletcher is best remembered as the man who fought many of the RAF's funding battles during the 1960s, which earned him the reputation of a 'Whitehall warrior'. As assistant chief and then vice-chief of the air staff (1964–70), he was seen by the Air Board as the most articulate advocate in the service and, on occasions, it seemed that Whitehall could not do without him.

A great reader, inveterate traveller, and a hospitable man with many friends outside the RAF, Fletcher died from pneumonia in Chelsea and Westminster Hospital, Chelsea, London, on 2 January 1999, survived by his wife and daughters.   BRIAN WIMBORNE

Sources *Daily Telegraph* (14 Jan 1999) · *Debrett's People of today* · *WW* (1990–98) · *The Times* (1 Jan 1968) · *The Times* (15 Jan 1999) · *LondG*, suppl. (Dec 1942), 5368 · d. cert.
Wealth at death under £200,000—gross; under £100,000—net: probate, 25 Feb 1999, *CGPLA Eng. & Wales*

Fletcher, Phineas (1582–1650), poet, was the elder son of Giles *Fletcher (*bap.* 1546, *d.* 1611), traveller and diplomat, and his wife, Joan Sheafe (1562–1614) of Cranbrook, Kent. He was born in Cranbrook early in April 1582 and baptized on 8 April in the parish church, where his grandfather Richard Fletcher was rector. Like his father, he was educated at Eton College, whence he proceeded to King's College, Cambridge, having been elected a scholar on 25 August 1600. His cousin, John *Fletcher the dramatist, had been admitted at Corpus Christi in 1591, and his younger brother Giles *Fletcher entered Trinity College in 1601. Phineas graduated BA in 1604, MA in 1608, and later BD, and was ordained to the priesthood in 1611, at about which time he obtained a fellowship in his college. He left Cambridge on 25 March 1615 for Risley in Derbyshire, the estate of his patron Sir Henry Willoughby, who retained Fletcher as his family chaplain and village priest. Probably late in 1615 he married Elizabeth Vincent of Risley; the first of their eight children, named Anne, was born in 1616. In 1621 Willoughby, who possessed the benefice of Hilgay in Norfolk, presented Fletcher to this living, where he remained for the rest of his life.

Fletcher wrote most of his poetry while still at Cambridge although its publication would wait for many years. His earliest work, like that of his brother Giles,

appeared in a Cambridge miscellany on the death of Elizabeth and accession of James, *Threno-thriambeuticon* (1603). It is more difficult to date *Brittain's Ida*, though it is probably very early. When the printer Thomas Walkley published this poem in 1628 he attributed it to Edmund Spenser, but this was a mere conjecture—Walkley or his advisers rashly concluded that an unclaimed poem written in a modified Spenserian stanza must be by Spenser. However, Boas has convincingly shown that Fletcher is its author, and the lushly erotic verse on the meeting of Venus with Anchises anticipates the exotic richness of Fletcher's later style (Boas, 2.xiii–xxiii). Also in his early Cambridge years Fletcher began his work in response to the Gunpowder Plot of November 1605, *The Locusts, or, Apollyonists*, which is preceded by its Latin companion piece, *Locustae, vel, Pietas*, printed in Cambridge by Thomas and John Buck (1627). Fletcher may have worked intermittently on these poems in Latin and English over a number of years; there are allusions to events around 1605, but also to the time of Charles's accession in 1625. It is difficult, indeed, to know whether Fletcher wrote first in Latin, then in English, or translated from one language into the other, while greatly expanding the materials in the English version.

The Locusts manages to describe a broad pattern of events, with many striking details. The poem is written in a unique nine-line stanza that combines the Spenserian stanza with ottava rima. Fletcher gives an English version of continental history from the Armada through the first quarter of the seventeenth century, which he sees, of course, through deeply patriotic and fiercely protestant eyes. Notable, especially for its probable influence on Milton's 'consult' in hell (*Paradise Lost*, bk 2), is Fletcher's depiction of the 'deepe Conclave' of Satanic figures in canto i, which he develops in the following canto about the inquisition and the founding of the Jesuit order. Moreover, though incidentally, Fletcher pauses in cantos iii and iv to recount the rise and death (in 1605) of Boris Godunov—knowledge he would have gained first-hand from his father. He refers also to the assassination of Henri IV in 1610, and to the Venetian uprisings from 1605 to 1607 against papal domination. In the fifth and last canto Fletcher focuses on the discovery of the nefarious gunpowder plotters, hiding amid their casks of powder, and at the end he writes in praise of God who rules the world with order and justice.

The years during which Fletcher wrote and revised *The Apollyonists* (as well as *Locustae*) contained further work, among which must be mentioned *Sicelides: a Piscatory*. This is a long and tedious comedy in five acts, a 'piscatory' equivalent of such pastoral dramas as Guarini's *Il pastor fido* (1585). The play was intended as an entertainment for the visit to Cambridge of King James and his entourage in March 1615 but the king left on the day that the play was performed, not staying to see it. Langdale believes that Fletcher had pinned his hopes for preferment and royal recognition on this work, and that his disappointment over the king's absence left him inconsolable. Therefore, as a broken man, he left Cambridge before the end of the month for Risley, never to return as a fellow of King's (Langdale, 70). Fletcher refers darkly to this or to other slights in the second of his *Piscatorie Eclogues* (especially stanzas 6–8 (Boas, 2.181–2), and undoubtedly he hoped for some kind of advancement through this and all of his writing; however, the fact that he wrote most of his poetry before leaving Cambridge, though he would continue to revise much of it, must cast a different light on his departure. Moreover, *Sicelides* was published in 1631 anonymously (probably, like *Brittain's Ida*, pirated), and Fletcher never claimed to own it.

Fletcher was greatly acclaimed for his most substantial achievement: *The Purple Island, or, The Isle of Man*, which he published in 1633, with *Piscatorie Eclogs and other Poeticall Miscellanies*. He writes modestly in his appreciative dedication to Edward Benlowes of his doubt about the value of *The Purple Island*:

> As some *Optick-glasses*, if we look one way, increase the object; if the other, lessen the quantity: Such is an *Eye* that looks through *Affection*; It doubles any good, and extenuates what is amisse. ... Such is that eye whereby you have viewed these raw *Essayes* of my very unripe yeares, and almost childehood. ... But since you please to have them see more *Day* then their credit can well endure, marvel not if they flie under your *Shadow*, to cover them from the piercing eye of this very curious (yet more censorious) age. (Boas, 2.3)

Edward Benlowes, some twenty years younger than Fletcher, was a wealthy patron of literature, especially of witty, picturesque, and ingenious poetry. From his estate at Brent Hall in Finchingfield, Essex, Benlowes could easily have visited Fletcher in Hilgay, Norfolk, but it is more likely that the friendship was conducted through correspondence.

Benlowes had been at St John's College, Cambridge, in the early 1620s, soon after Fletcher had left King's, and his knowledge and admiration of the poet's work, which already enjoyed some reputation, must have dated from that time. The author of *Theophila, or, Loves Sacrifice* (1652), Benlowes occupied himself not only with poetic composition but also with the generous encouragement of writers whose taste matched his own. *The Purple Island* was a poem that particularly appealed to him, for in it Fletcher worked out an extraordinarily elaborate (though highly traditional) allegorical conceit which represented the body of man as an island, whose good and moral inhabitants fiercely struggle against the evil attacks of the vicious world. Fletcher's carefully wrought poem (in twelve cantos) combines elements of Joshua Sylvester's translation of DuBartas's *His Devine Weekes and Workes* (1592, 1605), especially the first week, sixth day, and Spenser's House of Alma in *The Faerie Queene*, book 2, cantos ix and xi. The anatomical detail and moral earnestness of these popular works is greatly elaborated in *The Purple Island*. Benlowes may have been particularly attracted to the poem, Jenkins suggests, because of 'the astonishing ingenuity and minuteness with which the analogy of man and island was worked out and the didactic purpose which underlay the whole' (Jenkins, 70). Here was a kind of vision which could see the nose as a tower with a double-door open at its foot, and ultimately saw goodness being upheld in the

struggle for the possession of man's island in a climactic battle in which an evil dragon is destroyed through divine intervention.

Benlowes urged Fletcher to publish *The Purple Island* and it did at last appear, put forth by the Cambridge University printers. The poem was issued through Benlowes's very liberal patronage in a lavishly and beautifully printed edition, with some copies containing engravings, probably commissioned by Benlowes himself and perhaps even printed by him on his own rolling press at Brent Hall. These engravings were then inserted into the copies that Benlowes presented to his friends, for Benlowes regarded *The Purple Island* not merely as Fletcher's book, but also as his own. In a similar way Benlowes later sponsored Francis Quarles and was principally responsible for the publication of the *Emblemes* (1635).

Fletcher's lively inventiveness and his often fantastic and frequently repellent anatomical descriptions may be related to his fondness for medieval habits of mind, which he shared with his contemporaries DuBartas and Spenser. While DuBartas and Spenser are closest to him, Fletcher was working in a much older tradition which these contemporaries helped him to understand. The conceit of the body of man as castle (or island), a microcosm of the world, occurs in Robert Grosseteste (d. 1253), *Le château d'amour*; in the fourteenth-century homily *Sawles Warde*; and in the *Cursor mundi* (c.1300). It is elaborated also in such works as *Piers Plowman* (c.1362) and *The Castle of Perseverance* (c.1425), and in Lydgate's *Assembly of the Gods* (1498). Phineas Fletcher's special distinction lies in his ability to use traditional materials in a versatile and notably vigorous fashion. He was esteemed in his own time—Quarles is typical in calling him 'the Spencer of this age' (Boas, 2.8)—but later criticism has treated him less kindly, partly ignoring the tradition within which he wrote, but also shrinking before the richly grotesque details of his narrative. An anonymous writer in the *Retrospective Review* of 1820 is astonished by his 'gorgeous and fantastic' ornamentation. Gosse wrote that 'Of all the strange poems in existence, surely this is the strangest ... it is a strange anatomical ditty' (Gosse, 146–8).

Writing in 1912, H. E. Cory dismisses both Phineas and Giles Fletcher—the most representative of the followers of the 'school' of Spenser—as 'curious, half-diseased, half-divine poets' (Cory, 344). Even Langdale's mostly sympathetic book-length study largely misunderstands the literary tradition within which Fletcher lived and wrote. But Baldwin correctly describes the essential quality of *The Purple Island* which sees the world as textbook, wherein man is located in the divine scheme. Thus, one may recognize that 'several different allegorical traditions, ranging from description of the human body in microcosmic terms to the ready-made prophecy of the book of Revelation, mingle in Fletcher's account of the nature of man, the spiritual warfare in which he is engaged, and his apocalyptic expectations' (Baldwin, 471). Fletcher is certainly an earnest poet—a worthy successor of the 'sage and serious' Spenser—but his wittiness, his humour, and his obvious delight in unfolding a traditional story should not be overlooked. *The Purple Island*, written in seven-line stanzas, possesses an easy fluency and a strong narrative movement, and the extensive marginal notes clarify the often obscure though always inventive allegory.

Fletcher's years at Hilgay were marked by the regular publication of the poetry that he had completed while still in Cambridge, but apart from revising this work he seems to have composed very little during the many years of his ministry. Yet during this period Fletcher wrote a devotional treatise, with occasional poems interspersed at the end of chapters. This book was eventually printed posthumously by Henry Mortlock, a London bookseller, in 1670, some twenty years after Fletcher's death, as *A fathers testament. Written long since for the benefit of the particular relations of the authour*. In his preface 'To the Reader' Mortlock declares that Fletcher, '*growing towards Old-age*', had written the book for the 'private *Use only and Benefit of his own Children and Relations*' (Boas, 2.viii). The book is sombre and reflective, and the verses, including a number of translations from Boethius's *De consolatione philosophiae*, effusively moralistic. Fletcher drew up his will on 21 June 1649, leaving 20s. to each of his children and the remainder of his estate to Elizabeth, his wife. He died at Hilgay between 1 and 13 December 1650, and was buried there in the parish burial-ground.   P. G. STANWOOD

Sources A. B. Langdale, *Phineas Fletcher: man of letters, science and divinity* (1937) · J. Grundy, *The Spenserian poets* (1969) · R. G. Baldwin, 'Phineas Fletcher: his modern readers and his Renaissance ideas', *Philological Quarterly*, 40 (1961), 462–75 · F. S Boas, ed., *Poetical works of Giles Fletcher and Phineas Fletcher*, 2 vols. (1908) · W. B. Hunter, jun., ed., *The English Spenserians* (1977) · A. B. Grosart, ed., *The poems of Phineas Fletcher*, 4 vols. (1869) · H. Jenkins, *Edward Benlowes, 1602–1676: biography of a minor poet* (1952) · 'The purple island', *Retrospective Review*, 2 (1820), 341–2 · E. Gosse, *The Jacobean poets* (1894) · H. E. Cory, 'Spenser, the school of the Fletchers, and Milton', *University of California Publications in Modern Philology*, 2 (1912) · L. E. Berry, 'Phineas Fletcher's account of his father', *JEGP: Journal of English and Germanic Philology*, 60 (1961), 258–67 · Venn, *Alum. Cant.*

Fletcher, Ralph (*bap.* 1757, *d.* 1832), coal owner and magistrate, was born in Bolton, Lancashire, and baptized at St Peter's Church, Bolton, on 30 November 1757, the only son of John Fletcher (1727–1806), coal owner and farmer, and Mary Bolton (*d.* 1789). On 21 February 1805 Fletcher married Jane (*bap.* 1778, *d.* 1856), the third of four daughters of Edmund Grundy; between 1806 and 1817 they had one daughter and three sons. From his Bolton home, The Hollins, leased from Sir Orlando Bridgeman, Fletcher managed his coalmining affairs which stretched from Bolton south towards Salford and west towards Wigan. Many of his coalmines were leased from the Hulton family of Hulton Hall near Bolton.

Fletcher is best known for his public life. He was a major figure in the high-church tory oligarchy that dominated Bolton in the decades between the French Revolution and the 1832 Reform Act. He was an extremist in politics and consequently his contemporaries were rarely neutral in their opinion of him. Indeed, his public life evoked respect, loyalty, fear, and hatred from those whom he knew. The offices he held conferred local political and military power that he used to his advantage during periods of unrest, a fact which he was not slow to point out to the Home Office in his regular correspondence. From 1797 he was a magistrate and colonel of the Bolton Local Volunteers. His actions were driven by his reactionary political beliefs. He was a founder member of the Bolton Church and King Club, and, in the first decade of the nineteenth century, was a founder member of the English Orange order. By 1807 he was an official of the newly formed county grand lodge in Manchester. In 1808 he became deputy grand master of the newly formed English grand lodge. He actively recruited for the Orange order at all levels of society, including miners working in his pits and, in 1813, Lord Kenyon. The Orange order brought recognition for Fletcher from the highest levels of society and at an Orange meeting in Manchester in 1814 he was toasted along with the king and the prince regent, the duke of Wellington, the memory of Spencer Perceval, Lord Kenyon, and Robert Peel among others.

Fletcher was not afraid to put his political beliefs into practice. Indeed, in suppressing unrest he vehemently believed that he was defending the liberty of the nation. He is reported to have used spies extensively in order to secure information about dissident individuals. His suppression of Luddite attacks near Bolton in 1812 involved the use of spies; he deployed the militia to break up the riot and later, in his capacity as magistrate, arrested some of the chief suspects. In a parliamentary report several years later, a witness who was questioned about Fletcher and the suppression of Luddism, evasively, but provocatively, answered that, 'the [Orange] society was considered very useful by the magistrates' ('Select committee on Orange institutions'). Ralph Fletcher, along with his friend William Hulton of Hulton Hall, was one of the magistrates who took the decision to deploy the troops who carried out the Peterloo massacre in 1819.

Fletcher died in Bolton on 22 February 1832 and was buried at St Peter's Church, Bolton, on 28 February. Even in death he remained an important political icon and his political beliefs caused much antagonism between his allies and his opponents. The *Bolton Chronicle* reported that at the time of Fletcher's funeral 'the political feeling against the Colonel's opinions in this town was very strong' (*Bolton Chronicle*, 3 March 1832, 4). However, even by the 1840s the annual dinner to commemorate the birthday of Ralph Fletcher was still an important gathering of the tory elites. The *Bolton Free Press* reported that 'At one time this was a social gathering, but is now only a political club' (*Bolton Free Press*, 26 Nov 1842).   A. J. GRITT

Sources parish register, Bolton, St Peter's, 30 Nov 1757 [baptism] · parish register, Bolton, St Peter's, 18 March 1778 [baptism] · parish register, Bolton, St Peter's, 17 Dec 1789 [burial] · parish register, Bolton, St Peter's, 6 March 1806 [burial] · parish register, Bolton, St Peter's, 28 Feb 1832 [burial] · J. Watkins, 'The Hollins leases, 1756–1829, and reminiscences of the Hollins, 1830–1842', 1902, Bolton Central Library · *Bolton Chronicle* · F. Neal, 'Manchester origins of the English Orange order', *Manchester Region History Review*, 4/2 (1990–91), 12–24 · 'Select committee on Orange institutions in Great Britain and the colonies', *Parl. papers* (1835), vol. 17, no. 605 · Fletcher MSS, Bolton Central Library · *The blackfaces of 1812* (Bolton, 1839) · *Letters on the subject of the Lancashire riots, in the* *year 1812* (Bolton, J. Scholefield) • P. Taylor, *Popular politics in early industrial Britain: Bolton, 1825–1850* (1995) • J. Foster, *Class struggle and the industrial revolution* (1974) • H. Senior, *Orangeism in Ireland and Britain, 1795–1836* (1966) • E. P. Thompson, *The making of the English working class* (1963)

Archives Bolton Central Library, MSS

Likenesses portrait, Bolton Central Library, Watkins, 'The Hollins leases'

Wealth at death estate valued at under £14,000 when probate granted

Fletcher, Reginald Thomas Herbert, Baron Winster (1885–1961), politician, was born on 27 March 1885, the second son of Nicholas Fletcher (1848–1905) and his wife, Dinah Wright (*d.* 1912). His father, who had been twenty-fourth wrangler in 1873, was for many years professor of mathematics at the Royal Naval College, Greenwich. Rex, as he was always known, after early schooling privately and at Shirley House, Blackheath, chose the navy as a career and entered the Royal Naval College, Dartmouth, in 1899. On 13 October 1909 he married Elspeth, daughter of the Revd Henry Joshua Lomax, of Buxted, Sussex.

Fletcher served in the First World War in destroyers, seeing action at the Dardanelles, and serving in the Grand Fleet, the channel patrol, the light cruiser force, and the Royal Naval College, Dartmouth. After the armistice he served at the Admiralty on the naval general staff as head of the Near-Eastern section, intelligence division. He was promoted lieutenant-commander in 1922 and retired from the navy in 1924.

In the meantime Fletcher had turned to politics, and although his family background was Conservative he contested Basingstoke unsuccessfully as a Liberal in 1922. He was elected for the same constituency in 1923 with a majority of 348 but lost it at the general election of 1924. Selected as prospective candidate for Tavistock, he nursed it assiduously for three years, and at a by-election in 1928 lost it by only 173 votes to a Conservative VC. But for the intervention of a Labour candidate he would undoubtedly have won, and Fletcher began to wonder whether Labour was not destined to take the place of the Liberal Party. He joined the Labour Party in 1929, but did not stand as a candidate until 1935. Then, at Nuneaton, he turned a Conservative majority of 2464 into a Labour majority of 5237.

This notable success led some to think of Fletcher as one of the coming men of the Labour Party, but although in it, he was never really of it, and in the House of Commons he spoke almost with the detachment of an independent. He made his name chiefly on naval matters. When war broke out in 1939 he rejoined the navy and was posted to the London docks, where he worked arduously, supervising the fitting of guns to merchant ships. He next became chief staff officer at the Grimsby naval base, where he dealt with east-coast convoys. He now had the rank of commander. On the formation of the coalition government in 1940 A. V. Alexander became first lord of the Admiralty and invited Fletcher to be his parliamentary private secretary. Fletcher held the post until the end of 1941, when it was announced that he, with three other Labour members, was to be made a peer to strengthen the Labour Party in the Lords. Fletcher, who could trace his ancestry back to William Fletcher of Cartmel, at the end of the seventeenth century, in 1942 took the title Baron Winster of Witherslack, in the county of Westmorland. He soon found himself at ease in the House of Lords, where he spoke his mind, especially on naval matters, with even more independence than in the Commons. He was a joint author of a Penguin Special, *The Air Defence of Britain* (1938).

When the Labour government was formed in 1945 Attlee invited Winster to be minister of civil aviation, which made him a minister of cabinet rank (but without a seat in the cabinet), and he was sworn of the privy council. The post was in the circumstances important and controversial. Owing to the war, Great Britain had been able to pay little attention to civil air transport, and although Winster's Conservative predecessor, Lord Swinton, had formulated some plans Winster's task was virtually to recreate British civil aviation at a time of American world dominance and rapid technological development. To these inevitable difficulties there was added an unnecessary one—the pin-pricking opposition of the civil aviation group of the Parliamentary Labour Party led ironically by the member who had succeeded Winster at Nuneaton (F. G. Bowles) and had unfortunately marked out the Ministry of Civil Aviation for himself. They made it their aim to get Winster removed, and were in the end successful, but in the fourteen crucial months in which he held the post Winster's achievements were substantial and in most respects enduring. He decided to retain Swinton's proposed three airline corporations, but in view of the Labour victory at the polls thought it right to alter the balance of public and private elements in them. In the end the cabinet, yielding to the civil aviation group, insisted that they should be wholly public; but, while nationalizing all scheduled air transport operations, Winster was able to keep open a wide field for charter operators, and the machinery then devised was sufficiently flexible to permit changes according to the public mood.

Winster inherited a grave dispute with the United States about the right of airlines to pick up passengers freely, a dispute which was not merely hindering the growth of civil aviation but darkening the whole field of Anglo-American relations. The British policy, that of sharing out the traffic in equal proportions, had been called 'order in the air', but Winster agreed to a less doctrinaire and restrictive policy, produced at a conference in Bermuda which stood the test of time. He personally negotiated the agreements with Canada and Australia.

When Winster took office there were no British aircraft suitable for civil aviation and he skilfully relied on expedients—converted bombers and a limited number of American purchases—while laying with his colleagues sound plans for a new generation of British aircraft. He would have kept some flying-boats in service, but they were abandoned by his successors.

Heathrow had already been selected as the site of London airport but when Winster took office it consisted of only one runway. Within four months the first commercial service had begun from it, and before he left it had already become one of the busiest and best-equipped airports in the world. If his plans had not been subsequently modified, the need for a third London airport which caused so much controversy in the 1970s might have been avoided. Heathrow was state-owned, but Winster resisted the nationalization of all aerodromes and encouraged municipalities to build their own.

Winster's policy with regard to the airline corporations and aerodromes was embodied in the Civil Aviation Act (1946), a major statute whose piloting between Conservative advocates of private enterprise and Labour technocrats and malcontents required considerable skill. When it had received the royal assent, Attlee thought it politic to placate the civil aviation group by removing Winster, and in October 1946 it was announced that he was to be governor and commander-in-chief of Cyprus.

It was not a post Winster would have sought for himself, and he regarded his time in Cyprus as exile. But he did his duty conscientiously, and it was no fault of his that no constitutional progress could be made. Cyprus had been without a constitution since 1931, when the governor's house had been burnt, and it was Winster's task to make some progress towards agreement on a new constitution. But the Greek Cypriots would have nothing short of *enosis*, union with Greece, while the British government's attitude was that no change in the status of Cyprus could be contemplated. In the hope of reaching some agreement, the political exiles were allowed to return and the Greek Orthodox community was allowed to fill the vacant archiepiscopal see, the choice falling on Archbishop Makarios. A consultative assembly, drawn from representative elements in the island, was set up in 1947 to make recommendations for a form of constitution which would 'secure the participation of the people in the direction of internal affairs'. In reply to Greek Cypriot demands for fully responsible government a dispatch to Winster from the Colonial Office in May 1948 made specific proposals for a legislature consisting of 4 official members, 18 elected by territorial constituencies, and 4 by the Turkish community. The proposals were approved by 11 to 7 in the assembly, but when the seven dissentients refused to take any further part therein, progress became impossible; on 12 August 1948 Winster informed it that it was dissolved, although the British offer would remain open.

Constitutional failure should not conceal the considerable progress which was made economically, socially, and educationally. A ten-year programme of development had been announced in 1946, and Winster particularly interested himself in the improvement of agriculture. But with the breakdown of the constitutional talks he saw no point in remaining in Cyprus and he left in February 1949. He had been appointed KCMG in 1948.

Back in London, Winster took an even more independent line than ever before, and his strictures on left-wing members of his party were biting. He played no further great part in public life, however, and died at his home, Five Wents Way, Stone Cross, Crowborough, Sussex, on 7 June 1961. His wife, who survived him, was delicate and took little part in his public life. There were no children and the title died with Winster.

Short of stature with a ruddy, weather-beaten countenance, Winster enjoyed good wine and food. He was equally at home in the countryside and in the restaurants and clubs of London. He was not an orator, but in private he was excellent company with a rich treasure of anecdotes on which he could draw and a wit which could on occasion be mordant but seldom rankled.

IVOR BULMER-THOMAS, *rev.*

Sources personal knowledge (1981) · *The Times* (9 June 1961) · m. cert. · d. cert. · Burke, *Peerage* (1959)
Archives Bodl. RH, corresp. with Arthur Creech Jones · CAC Cam., corresp. with A. V. Alexander; corresp. with Sir E. L. Spears · HLRO, corresp. with Lord Beaverbrook | FILM BFI NFTVA, news footage
Likenesses W. Stoneman, photograph, 1945, NPG · H. Coster, photographs, NPG
Wealth at death £5622 11s. 3d.: probate, 24 Aug 1961, *CGPLA Eng. & Wales*

Fletcher, Richard (1544/5–1596), bishop of London, was born in Watford, Hertfordshire, son of Richard Fletcher (c.1523–1586), one of the first clergymen ordained according to the protestant ordinal, and his wife Joan (d. 1557?).

Early years and education The elder Fletcher, a Cambridge graduate from York diocese, was on 3 June 1550 ordained deacon (along with John Foxe) by Nicholas Ridley, bishop of London, and priested on 9 November following. Instituted vicar of Bishop's Stortford, Hertfordshire, in 1551 he was deprived for marriage in 1554 on Mary's accession. There is no evidence to support the tradition that he took his family abroad: indeed, in July 1555 father and son witnessed the martyrdom of Christopher Wade at Dartford, Kent, subsequently both signing an account which Foxe included in the second edition of *Actes and Monumentes* (1576).

After Elizabeth's accession both Richard Fletchers gained the patronage of Matthew Parker, archbishop of Canterbury, who in October 1561 collated the elder Richard to the vicarage of Cranbrook, Kent, and in 1566 to the nearby rectory of Smarden. His son was admitted pensioner at Trinity College, Cambridge, on 16 November 1562, and scholar in 1563, graduating BA early in 1566. In 1569 Parker, former master of Corpus Christi, nominated him to the first of four Norfolk fellowships which he had endowed at the college.

Fletcher proceeded MA from Corpus that year and, giving his age as twenty-four, was ordained deacon and priest on 9 September 1569 by Edmund Grindal, bishop of London. Incorporated at Oxford on 5 July 1572 he was on 30 September instituted prebendary of Islington in St Paul's on the presentation of Matthew Parker, the archbishop's son. According to Masters, the younger Parker secured the patronage for this turn in order to carry out his father's design of getting prebendal stalls annexed to his Norfolk fellowships by act of parliament.

Cranbrook, Rye, and the court, 1573–1583 In May 1573 Fletcher vacated his fellowship on his marriage, at Cranbrook, to Elizabeth Holland (d. 1592). He perhaps remained there as assistant to his father until in September 1574 he was engaged as town preacher of Rye, Sussex, where his four eldest children were born: Nathaniel in 1575, Theophilus in 1577, Elizabeth in 1578, and John *Fletcher, the dramatist, in 1579.

Under the guidance of Fletcher's predecessor, John Philpot, Rye had embraced protestantism. Preserved in the parish church is a collection of sermons on the Decalogue, traditionally attributed to Fletcher, which are forthright in their condemnation of images. Whether or not they were actually his, 'they reflect the uncompromising Protestantism in which he participated as minister of Rye' (Collinson, *Godly People*, 420).

Yet Fletcher was no nonconformist. Like his father, he appears to have subscribed unconditionally to the Elizabethan settlement. In 1575 he assisted his father in combating the activities of John Strowd, who was distributing copies of Thomas Cartwright's *Replye* to John Whitgift's *Answere to the Admonition* from his secret printing press. Thereafter the Rye authorities negotiated a concordat with Richard Curteys, bishop of Chichester, whereby the town preacher was to exercise ecclesiastical jurisdiction for the punishment of moral offences. Until his departure, probably in 1581, Fletcher co-operated with the magistrates in exercising 'an effectively unitary government, part spiritual, part secular, but inspired by the same principles of moral severity' (Collinson, *Protestants*, 173–4).

It was presumably also in 1575 that Parker introduced Fletcher to court, for in January 1596 the latter stated that it was twenty years since he had first enjoyed Elizabeth's favour. She was attracted by his handsome person, polished manners, and eloquent preaching. Partly for that reason his subsequent career has become thoroughly encrusted with legend. He has been generally portrayed as an elegant lightweight who cajoled Elizabeth into granting him ever more and better preferments, lived beyond his income in pursuing and supporting them, made the crashing error of contracting a second marriage, and died in both disgrace and debt.

In reality Fletcher's rise was far from rapid, his abilities considerable, and the preferments he secured in the 1580s unspectacular. Although he proceeded BTh in 1576 and DTh in 1580 it was not until 1583 that he was seriously considered for higher preferment when the new primate, John Whitgift, suggested him as a possible dean of Windsor should William Day become bishop of London.

The recommendation was astute: Fletcher proved one of the most successful preachers of his day 'and perhaps the closest any Elizabethan churchman came to the Jacobean model of a court preacher–prelate epitomized by Lancelot Andrewes' (McCullough, 120–21). The deanery of Windsor would have provided an ideal forum for his abilities but in the event Day remained in place until 1596.

Peterborough and Mary, queen of Scots On 15 November 1583 Fletcher was instead installed dean of Peterborough. It has been asserted that Elizabeth promoted him at his own petition, even though the post had been promised to Richard Howland. Elizabeth was not in the habit of taking such arbitrary decisions, relying always on the advice of the privy council, and a more plausible version of the story, given by John Strype, is that she parried Lord Burghley's recommendation of Howland on the grounds that he deserved something better than a junior deanery. If so Fletcher can only have regarded his appointment as a backhanded compliment. Other preferments conferred on him at this time seem to have owed nothing to Elizabeth. Rector of Algarkirk, Lincolnshire, by July 1585, he was on 22 January 1586 installed prebendary of Stow Longa in Lincoln Cathedral and later that year presented by Thomas Cecil, Burghley's eldest son, to the rectory of Barnack, Northamptonshire.

As dean of Peterborough Fletcher was intimately involved in the trial and execution of Mary, queen of Scots, at nearby Fotheringhay. He preached before the commissioners for her trial on 12 October 1586, drew up a report of her examination that month and officiated as chaplain at her execution on 8 February 1587, thereafter preaching at court. The report, both sermons, and descriptions of Mary's execution and funeral survive in a commonplace book at St John's College, Cambridge (MS I.30). Possibly written in Fletcher's own hand, the volume constitutes (if the Rye sermons be discounted) his only known body of writings. His exhortation to Mary on the scaffold and his prayer before her execution were printed respectively by John Strype and Symon Gunton.

Fletcher's part in Mary's destruction has been held against him even by historians unsympathetic to her cause, and his exhortation has been variously depicted as self-righteous, unfeeling, 'bad form', or downright brutal. To read between the lines of the surviving narratives is, however, to note that he did nothing that was not expected of him: until the last it was hoped that Mary might be persuaded to admit to treasonable activities and commit her soul to a protestant God. Only when the attempt proved futile did the earl of Shrewsbury order Fletcher to desist and lead the rest of the company in prayer, leaving Mary to her rosary.

That Fletcher acted not only under orders but also from deep conviction he demonstrated when he preached before Elizabeth at Greenwich, probably on 12 February. Braving the towering rage in which she had elected to cloak her overpowering sense of guilt Fletcher reminded her of the angel's command to Joseph in Matthew 2: 20: to return the holy family from Egypt to Israel, 'for they are deade that sought the chylde[s] Lyfe'. He rebuked her for lingering in the Egypt of remorse, exhorting her to remember her Christian duty and rejoice that in Israel God's providence had ensured that divine justice had been done. At one and the same time he stigmatized her guilty rage as 'politically dangerous' and 'morally culpable' (McCullough, 143) and sounded a clarion call for further action against her Catholic enemies.

It was an astounding performance during a week in which even Burghley was banished from Elizabeth's presence. It also gives the lie to the mean assumption that Fletcher's assiduity at Fotheringhay was a blatant bid for promotion. An unqualified attack on Elizabeth's deepest sensibilities as a crowned head was hardly a sure-fire method of securing it, and certainly it was not forthcoming.

The queen's immediate reaction is unknown but the sermon amply justifies the observation of Sir John Harington (a hostile witness) that Fletcher could 'preach well, and would speak boldly, and yet keep decorum. He knew what would please the queen, and would adventure on that though it offended others' (Harington, 2.45). If it was this sermon above all that Harington had in mind it would argue that Elizabeth took the lesson to heart even though 'others' supposed that Fletcher had strayed too far down the path of *lèse majesté*.

Higher preferment, 1587–1594 In September 1587 Fletcher petitioned the earl of Sussex in an attempt to secure the bishopric of Durham but further promotion came his way only in 1589 and again he was second choice for a second-rate appointment.

Since 1581 the modest revenues of Bristol had been enjoyed *in commendam* by John Bullingham, bishop of Gloucester, but it was now necessary to consecrate a bishop to the see in order that episcopal leases about to fall in might be legally renewed or reassigned. Burghley's first suggestion was the incumbent dean, John Sprint. Whitgift pronounced Sprint 'not meet for a bishopric' (BL, Lansdowne MS 61, fol. 5r) and on 14 December 1589 Fletcher was consecrated instead. The leases were duly passed and accordingly Harington castigated Fletcher for his compliance. Yet episcopal leases were not necessarily granted at unrealistic rentals and Fletcher was not treated with any obvious marks of favour by a grateful government. His temporalities were restored only with effect from Michaelmas 1589 and although like the occupants of all poorly endowed sees he was allowed to hold livings *in commendam* his warrant specified only Algarkirk and his Lincoln prebend. He resigned his other preferments.

Fletcher's star finally moved into the ascendant on 5 February 1591 when he became chief almoner, the most prestigious court appointment open to a bishop. Subsequent events suggest that he may have owed it less to Elizabeth than to the growing influence of Robert Devereux, earl of Essex. On 18 August he secured a royal warrant remitting Bristol's first-fruits because the revenues were small and in recognition of his service as almoner.

The almonership keeping him in attendance at court Fletcher lived principally at his private house in Chelsea. His eighth child, Mary, was baptized on 14 October 1592 in Chelsea parish church. His wife Elizabeth was buried there in December. Fletcher was translated to Worcester on 10 February 1593, possibly through the influence of Essex. In March, Burghley clashed angrily with Fletcher and Whitgift in the House of Lords when news broke that the separatists Henry Barrow and John Greenwood, whom Burghley had hoped to save, had been hurried to execution.

Fletcher conducted his primary visitation of Worcester in August 1593 but, retaining the almonership, continued to live at Chelsea. On 29 June 1594, following John Aylmer's death, he applied to Burghley for the bishopric of London. His letter suggests that despite their differences over Barrow and Greenwood, Burghley had been considering Fletcher's claims, but if so he now set them aside and espoused those of his old protégé, William Day. Whitgift undoubtedly pressed for Richard Bancroft, whose promotion he had urged in 1591 if Aylmer were translated to Worcester.

Fletcher secured Essex's backing. Whitgift made no headway in promoting Bancroft, thereafter supporting Essex, and Fletcher's promotion was announced by the queen in council on 1 December 1594. He immediately received from Robert Cecil a royal request for a lease in reversion of Bishop's Stortford and Broxbourne under the terms of the Act of Exchange (1559), by which episcopal leases were confined to twenty-one years or three lives unless the immediate beneficiary was the crown. The lease was earmarked for Cecil's kinsman and Hertfordshire neighbour, Sir Edward Denny. In a dignified refusal on 7 December Fletcher emphasized 'the scandal which such conditions of coming to dignities ecclesiastical' incurred and the prejudicial effect to the see of granting a lease for 100 years (*Salisbury MSS*, 5.31–2). Compromise was effected: on 21 December, whilst grieved that 'anything I spake in zeal and jealousy of my calling' should have provoked Elizabeth's displeasure, Fletcher agreed to pass the lease for twenty-one years only. His translation to London was confirmed on 10 January 1595.

Disgrace and rehabilitation In early 1595 Fletcher married Mary (*née* Gifford), widow of Sir Richard Baker of Sissinghurst, Kent, known to him since his days in Cranbrook. According to his own account Elizabeth had advised him, probably in November 1594, not to do so. At the time he had no such intention and said so. Afterwards Elizabeth chose to remember that he had promised her not to marry at all, 'where against', he confided to Cecil, 'because it pleaseth her Highness to propound it, I neither dare nor may contest. But … I remember it no farther than that I prayed that there might be no snare cast upon my conscience' (*Salisbury MSS*, 5.106–7).

On 23 February 1595 Whitgift informed Fletcher that he was formally suspended from his episcopal functions. Next day he begged Burghley, who seems to have advised against the suspension ('I know how much your L. approved') to intercede with Elizabeth (BL, Lansdowne MS 78, fol. 28r). On 15 April, informed that Fletcher and his wife had used insolent speeches against her, Elizabeth further suspended him from functioning as almoner on Maundy Thursday. His place was taken by Toby Matthew, bishop of Durham.

Whilst still forbidden Elizabeth's presence Fletcher's suspension from office was short. On 20 July he assisted at the consecration of William Morgan as bishop of Llandaff, thereafter vigorously engaging in diocesan affairs. He carried out his primary visitation in September and, although concerned to enforce uniformity and settle contentions in Maldon and Colchester, was favourably impressed with the general quality of the rural ministry. He preached eight times over three weeks, 'the confluence of the people and particular occasions requiring it'. Reporting all this to Cecil on 29 September he begged his further intercession with Elizabeth so that he might again enjoy her 'good pleasure from which I am fallen' (*Salisbury MSS*, 5.394).

Fletcher was Whitgift's principal coadjutor in drawing up the Lambeth articles, dated 20 November 1595, a full-scale Calvinist confession of faith which attempted to define the doctrinal position of the Church of England. Elizabeth took exception to them for several reasons but principally on the grounds that Whitgift had usurped her authority as supreme head. Only seven days later Fletcher was excusing himself to Cecil, who had evidently been told that Fletcher had again been making indiscreet remarks, some of them aimed at himself. Fletcher dismissed the report as 'malignant invention' (*Salisbury MSS*, 5.475) and nothing more is heard of the matter. He continued to press Burghley and Cecil to intercede with Elizabeth and in early April 1596 she relented, agreeing to visit him and his wife at his Chelsea house, which he had renovated for the purpose.

Fletcher's suspension was the only occasion on which the queen expressed public disapproval of the marriage of one of her bishops, and whilst Elizabeth may genuinely have convinced herself that he had broken a specific promise it seems more likely that others deliberately fuelled her anger—particularly since Lady Baker's reputation was sufficiently dubious for scurrilous verses and anecdotes to circulate freely. In a court increasingly under strain as the rivalry of Essex and the Cecils moved towards its climax, Fletcher had perhaps been caught in the crossfire. In May 1595, moreover, Essex himself fell into temporary disgrace when the queen learned of his liaison with Elizabeth Southwell and the existence of their child, Walter. He was thus in no position to protect Fletcher.

Death and debts On 13 June 1596 Fletcher assisted at the consecration of his successor at Worcester, Thomas Bilson. He sat in commission on 15 June until 6 p.m. and returned to Chelsea. Smoking a pipe of tobacco he suddenly exclaimed to his servant, 'Boy, I die', and did so. Probably just short of fifty-two years old he was buried in St Paul's without any memorial. He had made his will on 26 October 1593. A Calvinist confession of faith was followed by bequests to the poor of Watford (£10) and to those of Cranbrook, Rye, Peterborough, and Chelsea (all £5). His Chelsea house was to be sold to provide for his children's upbringing. His brother Giles *Fletcher, author of a celebrated account of Russia, was appointed one of his executors and his 'good and loving friends' Richard Bancroft and Richard Cosin overseers. Each received a ring, one a gift from Sir Francis Drake. Giles was granted probate on 23 June 1596.

Legend pursued Fletcher beyond the grave, thanks largely to Giles, who appeared at the exchequer on 20 June 1596 and acknowledged himself, as executor, indebted to the crown for £1000 owed for clerical taxes due from the bishopric. Thereafter a petition was submitted to Elizabeth 'to move her Majesty in compassion' towards Fletcher's 'poor orphans'. It was specifically stated that his death was 'an effect of his unhappy marriage' and that his personal debts were the result of payment of first-fruits

and tenths, he 'having paid into the Exchequer within 3 years the sum of £3000 or thereabouts'. He had also made 'gratifications out of London bishopric to divers of the Court by her highness' appointment to the sum of £2000 or thereabouts' (PRO, SP 12/259/47).

These figures were immediately conceded to be false. A revised petition stated that, translated from Worcester to London within two years, Fletcher had 'entered into new fruits before he had paid the old, having paid within three years into the exchequer for his first fruits, tenths and subsidies, the sum of £1458'. The 'gratifications' were now stated to have been £3000, his debts amounting to about £1400 and his sole assets his Chelsea property and goods worth £900 (*Salisbury MSS*, 7.533).

The figures are still incorrect. Fletcher had been excused the first-fruits of Bristol and in accordance with the terms of his warrant for Worcester his last three instalments were cancelled upon his translation. He had thus been required to pay only half of Worcester's first-fruits (£477) and had discharged two of his instalments for London (£510). Thus over seven years he had in fact paid less than £1000 in first-fruits.

Giles Fletcher secured Essex's backing in his efforts on behalf of the bishop's children. In December 1596 Essex told Anthony Bacon that he had frequently moved Elizabeth and Sir John Fortescue, chancellor of the exchequer, on the subject 'and so will still urge a good conclusion' (*Salisbury MSS*, 6.533). He succeeded. On 8 July 1597 Giles received a royal warrant stating that since he had discharged £600 of the see's £1000 debt the balance was remitted, as also the sum of £509 14s. 2d. owing for the third and fourth instalments of London's first-fruits, not due until after Fletcher's death. BRETT USHER

Sources J. Foxe, *Actes and monumentes*, 3rd edn, 2 vols. (1576) · P. Collinson, 'Cranbrook and the Fletchers: popular and unpopular religion in the Kentish weald', *Godly people: essays on English protestantism and puritanism* (1983) · P. Collinson, *The Elizabethan puritan movement* (1967) · P. Collinson, *The religion of protestants* (1982) · W. H. Frere, *The Marian reaction in its relation to the English clergy: a study of the episcopal registers* (1896) [ordination of Fletcher senior] · Venn, *Alum. Cant.*, 1/2.150 · *Registrum Matthei Parker, diocesis Cantuariensis, AD 1559–1575*, ed. W. H. Frere and E. M. Thompson, 3 vols., CYS, 35–6, 39 (1928–33) · *Fasti Angl., 1541–1857*, [St Paul's, London] · *Fasti Angl., 1541–1857*, [Lincoln] · *Masters' History of the college of Corpus Christi and the Blessed Virgin Mary in the University of Cambridge*, ed. J. Lamb (1831) · A. Peel, ed., *The seconde parte of a register*, 1 (1915), 116–20 [John Strowd] · *Tracts ascribed to Richard Bancroft*, ed. A. Peel (1953) · R. B. Manning, *Religion and society in Elizabethan Sussex* (1969) · W. P. M. Kennedy, ed., *Elizabethan episcopal administration*, 3 vols., Alcuin Club, Collections, 25–7 (1924) · J. Harington, *Nugae antiquae*, ed. T. Park and H. Harington, 2 vols. (1804) · will, PRO, PROB 11/87, sig. 50 · B. Usher, *Lord Burghley and episcopacy* [forthcoming] · F. Godwin, *A catalogue of the bishops of England, since the first planting of Christian religion in this island*, 2nd edn (1615) · E. H. Pearce, *Hartlebury Castle* (1926) [episcopal acts as bishop of Worcester] · F. O. White, *Lives of the Elizabethan bishops of the Anglican church* (1898) · J. Strype, *The life and acts of John Whitgift*, new edn, 3 vols. (1822) · J. Strype, *Annals of the Reformation and establishment of religion … during Queen Elizabeth's happy reign*, new edn, 4 vols. (1824) · P. E. McCullough, 'Out of Egypt: Richard Fletcher's sermon before Elizabeth I after the execution of Mary queen of Scots', *Dissing Elizabeth*, ed. J. M. Walker (1998), 118–49 · *Calendar of the manuscripts of the most hon. the marquis of Salisbury*, 24 vols., HMC, 9 (1883–1976), vols. 5–7 [letters to Robert Cecil, 1594–6] · PRO, state papers domestic, Elizabeth I, SP12/259/47 · BL, Lansdowne MSS 61, 78 · S. Gunton, *The history of the church of Peterburgh*, ed. S. Patrick (1686) · GL, MS 9535/1

Archives St John Cam., commonplace book, MS I.30 · Worcs. RO, visitation act book | BL, Lansdowne MSS, letters to Burghley · HMC, letters to Robert Cecil, Salisbury · St John Cam., papers relating to proceedings against Mary, queen of Scots

Wealth at death nil; private house in Chelsea; debts of approx. £1000

Fletcher, Sir Richard, first baronet (1768–1813), army officer, was the son of the Revd R. Fletcher (d. 1813). He entered the Royal Military Academy, Woolwich, on 7 October 1782, was gazetted second lieutenant in the Royal Artillery on 9 July 1788, and transferred to the Royal Engineers on 29 June 1790 as second lieutenant, advancing to first lieutenant on 16 January 1793. In 1794 he went to the West Indies and that year took part in the capture of Martinique, Guadeloupe, and St Lucia, where at the storming of the Morne Fortuné on St Lucia he was wounded in the head by a musket-ball. For a time he commanded the Royal Engineers at Dominica, and when he returned to England towards the end of 1796 he was appointed adjutant of the Royal Military Artificers at Portsmouth. On 27 November 1796 he married Elizabeth, daughter of John Mudge MD, of Plymouth. They had two sons and three daughters; Elizabeth predeceased her husband.

Promoted captain and lieutenant-captain on 18 August 1797, Fletcher continued to serve at Portsmouth until December 1798, when he was ordered to Turkey. On his way out he was shipwrecked off the River Elbe and had to cross 2 miles of ice to reach shore. He eventually arrived at Constantinople, on 28 March 1799, and in June accompanied the grand vizier on his march to Syria, after which he was employed on the defences of the Dardanelles. In January 1800, 'equipped as a Tartar', he left Constantinople on a special mission to Syria and Cyprus, returning in April, when he received a 'beniche' of honour from the sultan. Two months later he embarked for Syria again, landed at Jaffa, and helped to construct works of defence there and at al-ʿArish.

In December 1800 he sailed to Marmaris with dispatches for Lieutenant-General Sir Ralph Abercromby, whose expeditionary force was on its way to Egypt. Fletcher was then sent with Major McKerras to survey the coast of Egypt, for landing the troops. On arriving off Alexandria, they went in one of the *Peterel*'s boats to reconnoitre Abu Qir Bay, landing at the spot which appeared the most favourable for, and which was subsequently chosen as, the place of disembarkation. At dawn, as they were returning to *Peterel*, they were surprised by a French gunboat. McKerras was shot and Fletcher taken prisoner.

After the French surrender, Fletcher was released, and he received a gold medal from the sultan. A substantive captain from 18 April 1801, he returned to England in 1802 and was again stationed at Portsmouth, where he extended the Gosport lines of fortification. Subsequently appointed brigade major to Brigadier-General Everleigh, and promoted major on 2 April 1807, he joined the expedition to Copenhagen in July of that year. Then, in 1808, he

was ordered to the Peninsula, where Lieutenant-General Sir Hew Dalrymple was commander-in-chief; and he took over command of the Royal Engineers from Major George Thomas Landmann on 27 August, six days after the battle of Vimeiro. Following the convention of Cintra, Fletcher accompanied the army to Lisbon. On 24 June 1809 he was promoted lieutenant-colonel, having held that local rank, with extra command pay of 20s. a day, since 2 March.

On the appointment of Lieutenant-General Sir Arthur Wellesley as commander-in-chief, Fletcher joined his staff as commanding royal engineer, serving in the campaigns of 1809 and 1810 in Spain and Portugal. He took part in the battle of Talavera on 27–8 July 1809 and was complimented by Wellesley in his dispatch of 29 July. In October 1809 the duke of Wellington (as Wellesley had now become) withdrew to Portugal and Fletcher, as chief engineer, superintended the construction of the lines of the Torres Vedras until July 1810, when the defences were nearly complete. He then handed over the work to Captain John Jones and hastened to the scene of active operations on the River Coa. He was present at the battle of Busaco on 27 September, and Wellington in his dispatch of 30 September commended his conduct. The army now retired behind the lines of the Torres Vedras and Fletcher had the satisfaction of seeing the French effectively checked by them. In a dispatch to the secretary for war Lord Liverpool in November 1810, Wellington again noted Fletcher's services.

Fletcher was present at the battles of Sabugal (2 April 1811) and Fuentes d'Oñoro (5 May 1811), and at the evacuation of Almeida by the French on 10 May. During the first British siege of Badajoz in May, and at the second in June, he directed the siege operations, and afterwards was yet again mentioned in dispatches. In January 1812 he similarly directed the successful siege of Ciudad Rodrigo, and Wellington, in his dispatch of 20 January, stated that Fletcher's 'ability exceeded all praise' (*Dispatches*, 8.555). The third siege of Badajoz took place in March and April 1812, and Fletcher once more directed siege operations. On 19 March the garrison made a sortie, and Fletcher was struck in the groin by a musket-ball. His life was saved by a silver-dollar piece deflecting the blow, but a wound was inflicted which disabled him. Wellington, however, insisted that Fletcher should retain the direction of the attack, and still consulted him daily until his return to Britain.

The master-general of the ordnance had represented Fletcher's important services to the prince regent, and a pension had consequently been granted him of 20s. a day from 7 May 1811. Fletcher was awarded the gold cross for Talavera, Busaco, Ciudad Rodrigo, and Badajoz, and permitted to accept and wear the insignia of the Portuguese order of the Tower and Sword. In December 1812 he was created a baronet.

On his return to the Peninsula, Fletcher took part in the battle of Vitoria on 21 June 1813, and was mentioned in dispatches. He then made all the arrangements for the blockade of Pamplona, and, arriving at San Sebastian shortly after the start of the siege, he directed the investment under Lieutenant-General Sir Thomas Graham. In the final and successful assault on 31 August, however, he was killed by a musket-ball; he was aged forty-five. Lieutenant-Colonel Augustus Frazer wrote that Fletcher was 'one of the most amiable of men I ever knew, and one of the most solid worth. No loss will be more deeply felt, no place more difficult to be filled up.'

Fletcher was buried on the heights of San Bartolomé, opposite San Sebastian, and a tombstone marked his grave. A monument to his memory, designed by Edward Hodges Baily, was later erected in Westminster Abbey, at the west end of the north aisle, by the officers of the Royal Engineers. Fletcher's son Richard John Fletcher, second baronet (*b*. 1805), died in 1876 without issue, and the baronetcy became extinct.

R. H. VETCH, rev. JOHN SWEETMAN

Sources Army List · W. Porter, *History of the corps of royal engineers*, 1 (1889) · T. W. J. Connolly, *History of the royal sappers and miners*, 2nd edn, 2 (1857) · G. T. Landmann, *Recollections of my military life*, 2 (1854) · J. Kane, *List of officers of the royal regiment of artillery from the year 1716 to the year 1899*, rev. W. H. Askwith, 4th edn (1900) · *The dispatches of … the duke of Wellington … from 1799 to 1818*, ed. J. Gurwood, 4–6, 8, 11–12 (1835–8) · Burke, *Peerage* (1857) · Walford, *County families* (1875)
Likenesses J. Barwell, oils, *c*.1800, Royal Engineers Headquarters, Chatham, Kent · E. H. Baily, monument, Westminster Abbey, London

Fletcher, Robert (*fl.* 1581–1606), poet, published, in 1581, a version of St Augustine's *An Introduction to the Loove of God*, 'newlie turned into Englishe Meter' from the prose translation (1574) by Edmund Freake, then bishop of Rochester. Dedicated to Francis Knollys, its preface laments that works by such as 'professe Poetrie, and commit paltries' will 'be better sold twenty to one', and condemns the publication of sensational gossip 'never heard of, but at Billingsgate, or in Gravesende Barge'.

The reference suggests an acquaintance with London life incompatible with the career of Robert Fletcher of Merton College, Oxford (BA, 1564; MA, 1567), 'a Warwickshire man born', who in June 1569 'was for several misdemeanours turn'd out from his fellowship', thereafter became a schoolmaster in Taunton, Somerset, 'and at length became a godly minister and preacher of the word of God' (Wood, *Ath. Oxon.: Fasti*, 1.179). This man appears to have undertaken a series of rectorships in Cornwall between 1573 and 1591.

Wood confesses himself uncertain whether this was Fletcher the poet, among whose 'several translations' he lists the 1581 *Introduction* and an annotated verse translation of the Song of Songs (1586), no longer extant. The author is probably responsible for two Jacobean works by a Robert Fletcher, likewise anti-papist in tone. In *A Briefe and Familiar Epistle* (1603), a reflection on the succession in prose, verse, and prayer, Fletcher describes himself as resident 'neere Charing Crosse', a 'Yeoman Purveyor of Cariages for remooves' to Queen Elizabeth, 'under whose Table I have had … my nourishment almost fortie yeares of my life past'. *The Nine English Worthies* (1606) celebrates, in prose biographies and verse epitaphs, 'Eight famous Kings … Eight *Henries*' (p. 49), honouring Prince Henry as

the ninth, in the dedication to whom Fletcher describes himself as 'one of the meanest among the King your Fathers servants'.

NICK DE SOMOGYI

Sources Wood, *Ath. Oxon.: Fasti* (1815) · *Reg. Oxf.*, vol. 1 · Foster, *Alum. Oxon.* · R. Fletcher, *An introduction to the loove of God* (1581) · R. Fletcher, *A briefe and familiar epistle* (1603)

Fletcher, Thomas (1666–1713), poet, eldest son of John Fletcher of Winchester, was born at Avington, Hampshire, on 21 March 1666, and was educated at Winchester College. He matriculated from Balliol College, Oxford, on 9 April 1685, and on 12 September 1685 entered New College, Oxford, where he graduated BA on 10 April 1689, MA on 14 January 1693, and BD and DD on 25 June 1707.

In 1692 Fletcher published a small volume of verse entitled *Poems on several occasions and translations, wherein the first and second books of Virgil's 'Æneis' are attempted in English* (London, 8 vols.). A dedication to the Revd William Harris DD, 'school-master of the college near Winton', explains that the poems are chiefly juvenile exercises. The first book of the *Æneid* is translated in heroic couplets, part of the second and also part of the fourth in blank verse. The volume also contains a translation of the second epode of Horace, and of part of the first book of Boethius's *De consolatione philosophiæ*, some verses to Bishop Ken, a 'pastoral' on the birth of Christ, and some other pieces of a conventional stamp.

Fletcher became a fellow of New College, but resigned on his marriage to a daughter of William Master, fellow of New College, in 1702. They had three sons, Thomas, Philip, and William. He held the living of Fairfield, Somerset, in 1694, was prebendary of Barton David in the cathedral of Wells from 1696 until his death, and became an undermaster of Winchester College in 1701, and fellow of Winchester on 12 September 1711, resigning in 1712. Fletcher was an admirer of Bishop Ken, and wrote in youth some fulsome verses to him on his promotion to the see of Bath and Wells in 1685. Fletcher died in 1713, and was buried in Winchester Cathedral.

J. M. RIGG, rev. MATTHEW STEGGLE

Sources Foster, *Alum. Oxon.* · Wood, *Ath. Oxon.*, new edn, 4.559

Fletcher, Sir Walter Morley (1873–1933), physiologist and medical administrator, was born in Liverpool on 21 July 1873, the sixth and youngest son of the ten children of Alfred Evans Fletcher, civil servant, and his wife, Sarah Elizabeth, daughter of Richard Morley, of Leeds, cousin of the politician and philanthropist Samuel Morley and of the prime minister H. H. Asquith. Both parents were Congregationalists from Yorkshire.

Fletcher went in 1891 from University College School, London, to Trinity College, Cambridge, with a subsizarship to study physiology and with the auxiliary aim of medical qualification. There he was successful academically, socially, and in athletics. He graduated BA, obtaining first classes in both parts of the natural sciences tripos (1894, 1895). In 1897 he was elected to a fellowship at Trinity College and won an open scholarship to St Bartholomew's Hospital, London, which enabled him to complete the clinical studies for his medical training. During this period he remained at Trinity, working in the physiological laboratories under Michael Foster. He received his MA in 1898, MB in 1900, MD in 1908, and ScD in 1914. He was elected FRS in 1915 and was Croonian lecturer of the Royal Society in the same year.

In 1904 Fletcher married Mary Frances, second daughter of Charles James Cropper, of Ellergreen, Kendal; she was great-great-granddaughter of the philanthropist James Cropper and niece of Sydney Holland, second Viscount Knutsford. They had one son and one daughter; his wife survived him.

Between 1905 and 1914 Fletcher served as tutor at Trinity College, and administrative work for the college and the university progressively occupied him as much as did his laboratory research in physiology. But the latter was very fruitful. He had chosen the problems of the 'respiration' of frog's muscle, using an apparatus recently devised by the plant physiologist Frederick Frost Blackman for measuring the gaseous exchange of leaves. This enabled Fletcher to trace the discharge of small quantities of carbon dioxide during successive brief intervals of time, instead of simply measuring such accumulated end results as had alone been accessible to previous workers. He proved that there is no sudden discharge of carbon dioxide on the contraction of an isolated muscle, and that the main discharge occurs during the phases of recovery of power. This result was opposed to all the accepted teaching of the time. The next step, in collaboration with Frederick Gowland Hopkins, was to measure the cycle of changes in lactic acid during and after contraction, and to relate them also to the output of carbon dioxide and the muscle's ability for work. The entire group of experiments laid the foundation of the modern ideas of cellular activity that look on much of its material intake and output as never being raised to high levels of biochemical complexity, but as being used by the living cell protoplasm in relatively simple ways which are thereby individually accessible to analysis.

In 1914 Fletcher left Trinity and original research to take the post of secretary of the Medical Research Committee, created in 1913 by Lloyd George under the National Insurance Act of 1911. After the outbreak of war the committee concentrated on help for the services, and the speed with which Fletcher found himself free for action in arranging such work, combined with his policy of co-operation rather than intrusiveness, proved the value of an organization which could, without official delays, concentrate scientific workers on any urgent problem. The authority of the new committee became recognized everywhere, and Fletcher's services were acknowledged by the appointment as KBE in 1918. Civilian problems were not neglected and the proof, obtained by work which the committee had promoted during the war, that rickets is a deficiency disease, fully preventable by better feeding, seized Fletcher's imagination and made him eager to study and plan for improvements in human nutrition.

In 1920 Fletcher saw his committee, renamed the Medical Research Council, freed from any control by the Ministry of Health and placed under the privy council, with a charter of its own and direct financial support from the Treasury. This change and its high reputation were due in the main to Fletcher's administrative skill, his enthusiasm, and his wise use of scientific resources.

Fletcher's assistance was sought in other work. From 1919 to 1922 he was a member of the royal commission on the universities of Oxford and Cambridge. The buildings of the biochemical laboratories at Oxford and Cambridge and of the School of Hygiene and Tropical Medicine in London, together with considerable endowments for the medical sciences, were in large measure due to the confidence placed in his advice by the Sir William Dunn trustees and the Rockefeller Foundation. In 1928 he travelled to India as chairman of the Indian government committee for the organization there of medical research, and his visit was followed by the gift in memory of Lady Tata, the wife of Sir Dorabji Tata, of £250,000 for leukaemia research. He was appointed CB in 1929 and received honorary degrees from the universities of Leeds, Glasgow, Birmingham, Edinburgh, and Pennsylvania.

Fletcher recovered slowly from a serious attack of pneumonia in 1915–16 and a damaged lung led to occasional bouts of ill health. He died from a sudden infection in Brompton Hospital, Kensington, London, 7 June 1933, and was buried at Trumpington burial-ground, Cambridge.

T. R. ELLIOTT, *rev.* CAROLINE OVERY

Sources M. Fletcher, *The bright countenance: a personal biography of Walter Fletcher* (1957) · *DSB* · J. Crowther, 'Walter Morley Fletcher', *Scientific types* (1968), 307–32 · *The Times* (8 June 1933) · *Nature*, 132 (1933), 17–20 · *Cambridge Review* (13 Oct 1933) · T. R. E., *Obits. FRS*, 1 (1932–5), 153–63 · personal knowledge (1949)
Archives RS, MSS · Wellcome L., corresp. and papers | CAC Cam., corresp. with A. V. Hill · Nuffield Oxf., corresp. with Lord Cherwell · Wellcome L., letter to Edward Mellanby
Likenesses photograph, 1915, RS · W. Stoneman, photograph, 1917, NPG · D. Clarke, bronze bust, posthumous, National Institute for Medical Research, London · Elliott & Fry, photograph, NPG; repro. in *Obits. FRS* · photographs, repro. in Fletcher, *Bright countenance*
Wealth at death £4563 4s. 7d.: probate, 21 July 1933, *CGPLA Eng. & Wales*

Fletcher, William (*b.* 1773, *d.* in or after 1841), valet, was the son of John Fletcher (*c.*1750–1808), a farmer, and his wife, Mary (*c.*1750–1800). He was already a manservant at Burgage Manor, Southwell, Nottinghamshire, when Catherine Byron and her son arrived there in July 1803. On 23 July 1804 he married Sarah Bye (1783–1812), Mrs Byron's maid. She was his second wife, Susannah Mellers, a serving woman, whom he had married on 25 March 1794, having died childless. Fletcher and Sarah had two sons: William (*b.* 1805), and George (*b.* 1806), to whom Byron stood godfather. Fletcher was promoted to valet in October 1808, when his predecessor, Francis Boyce, was transported for theft. Accompanying Byron and Hobhouse abroad in July 1809 Fletcher was the 'staunch yeoman' of 'Childe Harold's Goodnight'. Having undergone many adventures in Portugal, Malta, Greece, Albania, and Turkey, including near shipwreck off Sicily, Fletcher re-entered England early in 1811, carrying important legal bonds. After re-employment on Byron's return in July, he informed the poet at Newport Pagnell of his mother's death on 1 August. Sarah Fletcher died in 1812, and on 12 January 1816 at St James's, Piccadilly, Fletcher married as his third wife Anne Rood, maid to Lady Byron. In July 1814 a relationship with another maidservant, Martha Willis, had produced an illegitimate son, also called William.

William and Anne Fletcher both sided firmly with Lord Byron in his 1816 separation crisis. On 25 April that year Fletcher again accompanied Byron abroad, abandoning his family to share his master's exile. Fletcher, like Byron, adapted well to Italian life, acquiring the language and taking a Venetian mistress called Tiretta. In July 1823 he returned to Greece, where he wrote his well-known letter to Augusta Leigh, dated 20 April 1824, describing Byron's death the previous day. Fletcher then supervised the return of Byron's body to England, attending his funeral at Hucknell Torkard, Nottinghamshire, on 12 July. Unfortunately Fletcher was not remembered in what was taken for Byron's final will. Although a promised £70 p.a. from Augusta Leigh was not forthcoming, he had sufficient savings to open a 'Macaroni Manufactory' near Brunswick Square, in partnership with Lega Zambelli, Byron's Italian secretary. This enterprise failed when the government lifted the duty on imported pasta, ruining Fletcher. By 1835, the year Anne Fletcher died, he was reliant on the charity of John Murray, J. C. Hobhouse, and others, who organized a subscription for his support. Despite their assistance in 1837 he was admitted to White Cross Street workhouse, where he proved unable to fulfil the required schedules.

The last record of Fletcher alive dates from March 1841, when Lady Byron wrote to Ada Lovelace that he had 'at last got a place'. Harold Nicolson appears to have been mistaken in imagining Fletcher living in the 1870s, probably confusing him with a son. Fletcher is often mentioned in Byron's letters and journals, sometimes ironically as 'the Learned Fletcher' (Lovelace MSS). Despite frequent quarrels, which led to Fletcher's being sacked and reinstated on three occasions, theirs was a remarkable master–servant relationship. Genuine grief, discretion, and honour always prevented Fletcher from revealing the myriad secrets of 'My late lamented lord and master', to the exasperation of Byron's biographer Thomas Moore.

RALPH LLOYD-JONES

Sources H. Nicholson, 'Mr William Fletcher', in H. Nicholson, *Small talk* (1937) · IGI · *Byron's letters and journals*, ed. L. A. Marchand, 12 vols. (1973–82) · parish registers, Southwell, Notts. Arch. · admissions to White Cross Street workhouse, 1837, LMA · Bodl. Oxf., Lovelace MSS, box 52, fol. 40
Archives BL, corresp., Egerton MS 2613, fols. 136, 143 · BL, Add. MS 31037 · BL, Add. MS 31038, fols. 36–9 · John Murray Publishers Ltd, corresp. · Morgan L., MS | Bodl. Oxf., Lovelace MSS · New York, MS
Likenesses stylized caricature, BL

Flete, John (c.1398–1466), prior and historian of Westminster Abbey, said his first mass in 1422–3, two years after entering the monastery, and was probably about twenty-four, the canonical age for ordination to the priesthood, at the time. The name may be a toponym adopted on entry into the monastery, or his family name; if the latter, membership of one of the London merchant families of this name is a possibility. Flete held no major office in the monastery for about fifteen years, but the onerous responsibilities of almoner, which he then assumed, would not have been given to an untried monk: in all probability he had proved himself in minor offices which have left no trace in the records. Subsequently he held all the major offices at Westminster except the abbacy itself. As prior (1456–66) he had the unusual experience of being second in command to two successive abbots, Edmund Kirton (d. 1466) and George Norwych (d. 1469), who were obliged to resign or retire on the grounds of incompetence. His historical interests, which he had time to cultivate as a young monk without heavy administrative cares, bore fruit in his *History of Westminster Abbey*. The title is modern and relates to a work in four parts: the story of the foundation of the abbey by, as Flete believed, King Lucius in 184 AD and later refoundations by King Sebert, St Dunstan, and St Edward the Confessor; an account of its privileges; lists of its relics and indulgences; and the lives of the abbots.

Flete conceived of the work as a whole and says in the preface that he intended it to extend to the twenty-second year of Henry VI's reign, which began on 1 September 1443. In 1444 Abbot Kirton's conduct occasioned the appointment of visitors whose report led to his suspension from office. 1443, therefore, was the last year that Flete could incorporate into his history without having to decide how to treat domestic scandal—a task not at all suited to a writer who preferred banalities to racy anecdotes. In the event, although evidently still at work on the lives of the abbots in the 1440s, he did not get beyond the death of Nicholas Litlyngton (1386), and there are indications in his account of the abbey's privileges that this, too, was unfinished. Flete may have been the first Westminster monk to put together a comprehensive list of the abbey's relics. With this exception, however, the first three parts of the history are scissors-and-paste work, containing very little beside verbatim transcriptions from narrative sources which include the writings of Sulcard, a work described as *Liber regius*, which has never been satisfactorily identified, and charters and papal letters. The lives of the abbots, a work not previously attempted at Westminster, contain more of Flete's own writing. His standard life includes details of the election of the abbot in question, his acquisitions of property, additions to the liturgical calendar, and other important acts, together with the date of death, the site of the tomb and the inscription; while after 1258 details of the ensuing vacancy, including the fate of the temporalities, are also included. Flete used, among other sources, the so-called Westminster Domesday (the monastery's principal cartulary), and pipe, originalia, and memoranda rolls: these were probably among the royal records kept at this time in the abbey precinct. Though not a distinguished work, the history exemplifies the deflection of monastic history, in its last phase, from national to local events and biography, and the appeal that this kind of writing sometimes had for monks of a practical disposition. Flete died in 1466, and was buried in Westminster Abbey.

BARBARA F. HARVEY

Sources Westminster Abbey, London, MS 29 · J. Flete, *The history of Westminster Abbey*, ed. J. A. Robinson (1909) · E. H. Pearce, *The monks of Westminster* (1916) · A. Gransden, *Historical writing in England*, 2 (1982) · B. Harvey, *Westminster Abbey and its estates in the middle ages* (1977) · B. Harvey, *The obedientiaries of Westminster Abbey and their financial records, c.1275 to 1540* (2002)
Archives CCC Cam. [copy] · LPL [copy] · TCD · Westminster Abbey, London, MS 29 · Westminster Abbey, London, obedientiary accounts

Flete, William [*known as* Brother William of England] (*fl.* 1352–1380), Augustinian friar and hermit, always called himself Brother William of England. He was first designated 'of Flete', which presumably refers to Fleet in Lincolnshire, when the prior-general of his order granted him conventual status at the priory of Lecceto, near Siena, in September 1359. His native connections were clearly with eastern England. He was licensed in February 1352 to preach for the diocese of Ely, and studied theology at Cambridge as a member of the Augustinian community there. A note in the manuscript of a sermon in commemoration of Catherine of Siena, perhaps dubiously attributed to him, says that he composed it around 1382 when he was 'about seventy' and that he survived the saint 'for several years'. More exact dates cannot be determined for his birth or for the landmarks of his early life.

Flete was known in Catherine's circle as *il baccelliere* ('the bachelor'). He had entered upon the stages preparatory to receiving the master's degree at Cambridge, but decided not to proceed and in July 1359 left England to spend the rest of his life at Lecceto, hallowed in Augustinian tradition as the very heart of the order and supposedly associated with Augustine himself. He thus detached himself totally from his native land, eschewing careerism and seeking spiritual perfection. At Lecceto he acquired a reputation for asceticism exceeding the requirements of the rule, and won the regard of two prominent holy men, Giovanni Colombini, founder of the Gesuati, and the Vallombrosan Giovanni dalle Celle. He has however attracted most attention as an associate of Catherine of Benincasa (St Catherine of Siena). On the evidence of a witness at the canonical process of investigation into Catherine's sanctity initiated in 1410, they knew each other already by early 1368, but another source intimates that they did not actually meet before January 1377, when Catherine visited Lecceto and Flete took down at her dictation a statement of her 'spiritual doctrine'. Benedict Hackett has argued for Augustinian influence on Catherine's early development and suggests that Flete may have been her guide.

There is some indication that Catherine thought Flete inclined to overvalue the ascetic's total seclusion. Perhaps influenced by her activist piety, he shared with her, between 1373 and 1375, in successful efforts to reform certain Sienese reprobates. His sole recorded excursion outside Lecceto was to attend the consecration of a conventual church founded by Catherine in the castle of Belcaro, donated to her by one of these penitents. In 1379, however, he refused to obey the summons to Rome which Urban VI (probably at Catherine's instigation) issued to him and other holy men in order to gain support in the early stages of the schism. Catherine was severely displeased, but at her death in 1380 she wished Flete none the less to share in the direction of her 'family' of devotees. It is not known where or when he himself died and was buried.

Flete's letters to Catherine do not survive; a handful of hers to him do. In 1377 he wrote to her confessor Raymond of Capua extolling her virtues, and he urged the public profession of obedience to Urban VI in letters to the rulers of Siena and to his Augustinian brethren in England; to the latter, breaking the silence of his self-imposed exile, he addressed other salutary spiritual counsels. The treatise *De remediis contra temptaciones*, which he may have composed before leaving England, achieved a considerable manuscript circulation, in England and elsewhere: Hackett lists twenty-one complete Latin and fourteen English extant manuscripts. Its influence has been detected on Walter Hilton and also perhaps on Thomas More.

DIANA WEBB

Sources A. Gwynn, *The English Austin friars in the time of Wyclif* (1940) [fundamental account] · B. Hackett, *William Flete, OSA, and Catherine of Siena*, ed. J. E. Rotelle (1992) [incl. trans. of all extant writings] · B. Hackett, 'William Flete and the *De remediis contra temptaciones*', *Medieval studies presented to Aubrey Gwynn*, ed. J. A. Watt, J. B. Morrall, and F. X. Martin (1961), 330–48 · M. H. Laurent, 'De litteris ineditis Willelmi de Fleete, 1368–1380', *Analecta Augustiniana*, 18 (1942), 303–27 · E. G. Gardner, *Saint Catherine of Siena* (1907)

Flett, Sir John Smith (1869–1947), geologist, was born on 26 June 1869 at Kirkwall, Orkney, the second son of James Ferguson Flett, merchant and bailie, and his wife, Mary Ann (*née* Copland). From the Kirkwall burgh school he went to George Watson's College, Edinburgh. In 1886 he entered Edinburgh University, graduating in arts and science (MA, BSc) in 1892 and medicine (MB CM) in 1894. He won many prizes and scholarships, and briefly practised medicine, but increasing deafness led him, in 1895, to switch to geology. His interest in the subject had been stimulated by Professor James Geikie who recruited him as an assistant, and soon promoted him to lecturer in petrology. In 1897 Flett married Mary Jane, daughter of David Meason of Kirkwall. They had two sons and daughters, including Martin Flett.

Flett's early researches dealt with rocks from the midland valley of Scotland and also focused on the stratigraphy of the Old Red Sandstone of Orkney and the remarkable alkaline dyke-rocks there. He described the latter under the splendid title of 'The trap dykes of the Orkneys', research for which he gained his DSc in 1899.

In 1901 the petrographer to the geological survey, Jethro

Teall (1849–1924), was promoted to the position of director and Flett was appointed to fill the vacancy. For ten years he had a prolific output of first-rate research, including petrological contributions to some thirty survey memoirs, particularly those of the Scottish highlands, Edinburgh, and south-west England including Land's End and the Lizard.

Sponsored by the Royal Society, Flett was chosen to go in 1902 with Tempest Anderson to investigate the disastrous volcanic eruptions of Soufrière in St Vincent and Mont Pelée in Martinique. Their investigations contributed an early account of the *nuée ardente* type of eruption, an eruption comprising a pyroclastic flow with accompanying ash cloud. In 1911 Flett returned to Scotland as assistant director (Scotland), continuing his petrological work for English and Scottish memoirs. During the First World War he was responsible for many contributions to the *Special Reports on the Mineral Resources of Great Britain*.

The crowning stage of Flett's career began in 1920 when he became director of the Geological Survey and Museum in London. The production of maps, memoirs, and scientific accounts of the highest quality were produced under Flett's direction and arrears of publication resulting from the war were overtaken. Under pressure for geological work on the nation's coalfields Flett established district offices in Newcastle upon Tyne, Whitehaven, Cumberland, York, and Manchester, although their advantages were sometimes outweighed by the shortness of their useful lives and the isolation of their staff.

Flett was the driving force in achieving the move of the survey headquarters and museum from Jermyn Street, central London, to South Kensington, and it fulfilled his greatest ambition. With the curator William McLintock (1887–1960), Flett visited the principal museums in Europe and incorporated the latest thinking in the new museum. Flett arranged that the displays in the museum should be complemented by eighteen published handbooks on the regional geology of Great Britain, and these proved to be very popular. The new museum was opened in 1935 in the centenary year of the geological survey, and Flett retired the same year. The museum was transferred in 1985 to form part of the adjacent Natural History Museum but an education block and lecture theatre opened in 1976 bearing Flett's name, and his portrait was hung there in the foyer.

After his retirement Flett kept up his interest in geology, publishing a definitive history of the geological survey in 1937, and he worked on a second edition of the *Geology of the Lizard and Meneage* which was in the press when he died.

Flett was an imposing, forceful man, a fluent and immensely knowledgeable speaker who travelled widely and was well known to geologists throughout the world. His deafness sometimes allowed him not to hear views which did not coincide with his own, but his often blunt manner concealed his goal of always furthering good science, a characteristic that came to be much appreciated by those closest to him.

Flett received many honours including the Neill prize of the Royal Society of Edinburgh (1901), the Bigsby medal of the Geological Society of London in 1909 and its highest award, the Wollaston medal, in 1935, and the Bolitho medal of the Royal Geological Society of Cornwall (1917); he was elected FRSE in 1900 and FRS in 1913; he was awarded an honorary LLD from Edinburgh in 1912; and he was created OBE in 1918 and KBE in 1925. He was three times president of the Edinburgh Geological Society, president of the geological section of the British Association in 1921 and of the Mineralogical Society in 1930, and a member or correspondent of numerous overseas societies. He died in the garden of his home, The Cottage, 24 May Hill, Ashdon, Essex, on 26 January 1947, and was survived by his wife.   PETER A. SABINE

Sources DNB · H. H. Read, *Obits. FRS*, 5 (1945–8), 688–96 · M. M., *Quarterly Journal of the Geological Society of London*, 103 (1947), li–liv · J. S. Flett, 'Memories of an Edinburgh student, 1886–1894', *University of Edinburgh Journal*, 15 (1949–51), 160–82 · *Nature*, 159 (1947), 326 · E. B. Bailey, *Geological survey of Great Britain* (1952) · private information (2004) · *Year Book of the Royal Society of Edinburgh* (1948–9), 17–19 · *Mineralogical Magazine*, 28 (1947), 192–3

Archives BGS, corresp. and papers | BGS, letters to Herbert Thomas

Likenesses W. Stoneman, photograph, 1917, NPG · F. B. Craig, oils, c.1935, NHM · photograph, repro. in *Obits. FRS* · photograph, repro. in *Mineralogical magazine* · photograph, repro. in *Quarterly journal of the Geological Society* · photograph, repro. in *Nature*

Wealth at death £3756 0s. 3d.: probate, 25 Aug 1947, CGPLA Eng. & Wales

Fleure, Herbert John (1877–1969), geographer and anthropologist, was born in Guernsey on 6 June 1877, the only son and younger child of John Fleure (1803–1890), accountant to the States, Guernsey, and a member of an old family of Guernsey, Alderney, and Sark ancestry, and Marie Le Routegel (1841–1914) of Jersey.

Fleure's childhood was marked by periods of ill health and developing blindness in one eye. He could attend the States Guernsey intermediate school only intermittently and ceased to attend at fourteen. He was a devoted reader, however, and was dedicated to furthering his education to research the idea of evolution as related to humanity. Having passed the London matriculation examination in 1894 he won a scholarship to study geology, botany, and zoology at the University College of Wales, Aberystwyth, in 1897. He graduated in zoology with first-class honours in 1901 and became a research student at Aberystwyth. After studying zoology and anthropology at the Zoological Institute, Zürich University, in 1903–4, he returned to Aberystwyth and graduated DSc of the University of Wales in 1904. Research in zoology and geology was precluded by his failing eyesight and consequent inability to use microscopes so he moved towards the discipline of geography. He held various teaching positions at Aberystwyth between 1907 and 1917 but in the latter year was delighted to secure appointment to the newly created Gregynog chair of geography and anthropology. He served as professor at Aberystwyth until 1930 when he became first professor of geography at Victoria University, Manchester, a post which he held until his retirement in 1944. In 1910 Fleure married Hilda Mary, daughter of the Revd C. H. Bishop, a

Guernsey Methodist minister, and Lucy Johnson. They had two daughters and one son. Fleure shared his wife's Methodist background but was not himself religious.

Through geography Fleure was able fully to articulate his childhood aim of examining people, societies, and their environments in holistic and evolutionary relationship. Between 1905 and 1916 he attempted, with T. C. James, to classify and uncover the geography of Welsh physical types through measuring the head shape and facial characteristics of approximately 2500 people. In this way he connected prehistoric Wales to other parts of Europe through migration. One notable type was a neolithic survival found in remote upland areas; local legend in Cardiganshire has it that he persuaded one of these, one of two farming brothers, to sell him his head—for which the farmer, naturally, demanded payment in advance! For this anthropometric work Fleure was elected fellow of the Royal Society in 1936, the first geographer to receive that honour. During his active retirement he developed research, with Elwyn Davies, on the distribution of blood groups in the United Kingdom, particularly Wales. While the scientific basis of his anthropometric work has been superseded, it illustrates vividly a branch of geographical and anthropological science that was significant for much of the twentieth century.

More lasting, perhaps, are the socio-cultural insights of this work which make Fleure an important figure in the radical, humanist tradition of geography. He was a committed anti-racist who explicitly challenged the notion of a single national physical type; in the 1930s he attacked the Nazis' 'Nordic myth' of racial purity. He also criticized those eugenicists who claimed that certain physical types were essentially 'unfit' and should be suppressed. Fleure argued to the contrary, in what has been identified as a form of 'biological socialism' (Campbell), that these types had been disadvantaged by industrialization and that social reform and town planning should work to ameliorate their condition. Fleure attacked the materialism of modern industrial society which, he argued, damaged the personalities of places and peoples. He was a passionate advocate for cultural diversity and continuity, and felt that his Guernsey bilingualism had made him sensitive to the Welsh cultural tradition when he moved to Aberystwyth. His research stressed the character and continuing relevance of folk traditions throughout Europe, and his reminiscences of fieldwork in Wales are dotted with encounters with a gentle and learned people:

> A humble farm kitchen may have some of the masterpieces of religious literature on the bookshelf. And these simple folk will lead the Sunday school in Wales or Cornwall and tell the Bible stories with a dramatic form that might shock English folk if they understood. (Fleure, 'The Celtic West', *Journal of the Royal Society of Arts*, 88, 1940, 884)

He argued during the 1920s that urban civilization's one hope of avoiding collapse was to have a stream of people from the remote corners, and especially from the 'Celtic West', to impart their cultural and sociological heritage. The broader educational and political aims of this study of locality were to create a 'humane geography', aware of the strengths and weaknesses of the home region and able to place it within a global continuum of regions. This would 'spread the feeling that in addition to being citizens of our region we are citizens of civilisation' (Gruffudd, 'Countryside as educator', 418). In this Fleure directly challenged geography's imperial past, and as a supporter of the League of Nations he also argued for the right to political expression of Europe's small nations and historic regions.

Humble and unselfish, Fleure was an inspiring teacher, active in adult education and a prolific author of elegant prose. His first book, *Human Geography in Western Europe*, was published in 1918, and among his other major publications were the ten volumes of *The Corridors of Time* series, published with H. J. E. Peake between 1927 and 1956, and *A Natural History of Man in Britain* (1951). From 1917 until 1947 Fleure was honorary secretary and honorary editor of the publications of the Geographical Association, the society which engages university teachers in the promotion of geographical teaching in schools. He was its president in 1948; he transformed the status and role both of the association and of the discipline of geography. He served as president of three sections of the British Association for the Advancement of Science and was also president of the Cambrian Archaeological Association (1924), the Manchester Literary and Philosophical Society (1940–44), the Royal Anthropological Society (1945–7), and the Folklore Society (1948). He was awarded honorary degrees by the universities of Bowdoin, Maine (1945), Edinburgh (1950), and Wales (1954), was an honorary member of the Italian Anthropological Society and the Hungarian Geographical Society, and was a commandeur de l'ordre de Léopold (Belgium). He was awarded the gold medal of the Royal Scottish Geographical Society and the Victoria medal of the Royal Geographical Society, and was elected to an honorary fellowship of the latter in 1965. After an unexpected and short attack of bronchitis he died at his home, Corner House, 66 West Drive, Cheam, Surrey, on 1 July 1969, survived by his wife and children.   PYRS GRUFFUDD

Sources T. W. Freeman, 'Herbert John Fleure, 1877–1969', *Geographers: biobibliographical studies*, 11, ed. T. W. Freeman (1987), 35–51 [incl. complete bibliography] · *Transactions of the Institute of British Geographers*, 49 (1970), 201–10 · P. Gruffudd, '"Back to the land": historiography, rurality, and the nation in inter-war Wales', *Transactions of the Institute of British Geographers*, new ser., 19 (1994), 61–77 · P. Gruffudd, 'The countryside as educator: schools, rurality, and citizenship in inter-war Wales', *Journal of Historical Geography*, 22 (1996), 412–23 · *DNB* · J. A. Campbell, 'Some sources of the humanism of H. J. Fleure', research paper no. 2, U. Oxf., school of geography and the environment, 1972 · *The Times* (3 July 1969) · *The Times* (17 July 1969) · A. Garnett, *Memoirs FRS*, 16 (1970), 253–78 [incl. complete bibliography] · *WWW* · *CGPLA Eng. & Wales* (1969)
Archives BLPES, papers on race · NL Scot., corresp. · NL Wales, corresp. and papers · Royal Anthropological Institute, London, anthropometric survey of Wales, bibliography of his writings · U. Wales, Aberystwyth, papers relating to fishery experiments | Bodl. Oxf., corresp. with Sir John Myres · JRL, letters to the *Manchester Guardian* · Keele University Library, LePlay Collection, corresp. · NL Scot., letters to Patrick Geddes · NL Wales, letters to John Glyn Davies · NL Wales, letters to Thomas Iorwerth Ellis · NL Wales, corresp. with Thomas Jones

Likenesses L. Garnett, oils, Geographical Association, Sheffield · photograph, repro. in *Geography*, 54 (1969) · photograph, repro. in *Memoirs FRS*

Wealth at death £17,789: probate, 14 Nov 1969, *CGPLA Eng. & Wales*

Fleury, Abbo of. See Abbo of Fleury (945x50–1004).

Fleury, Maria de (*fl.* 1773–1791), religious controversialist and hymn writer, was based in Cripplegate, London, but little is known of her family and background, other than that she had a brother who married about 1773. An active member of a circle of moderate Calvinist Baptists and other dissenters, she published several pieces on the theological and political controversies of the day. She was a Baptist but the Independent minister John Towers records that she was also a member of his congregation in Clerkenwell for many years.

De Fleury was a member of the anti-Catholic Protestant Association and wrote in their praise and defence in her *Poems, Occasioned by the Confinement and Acquittal of the Right Honourable Lord George Gordon* (1781) and in her versified account of the Gordon riots, *Unrighteous Abuse Detected and Chastised* (2nd edn, 1781), in which she claimed that the Roman Catholics were to blame for the violence. Her anti-Catholic allegory *Henry, or, The Triumph of Grace* (1782), dedicated to Lord George Gordon, went into three editions.

De Fleury was a close friend of the Baptist minister John Ryland (1753–1825) and joined with him in his paper war against the flamboyant and high Calvinist minister William Huntington. Her popular *Letter to the Rev. Mr. Huntington* (2nd edn, 1787) was the first of several attacks she made on Huntington's religious beliefs and practices. She criticized his alleged antinomianism again in *Antinomianism Unmasked and Refuted* (1791). In a response of 1792 to de Fleury's criticisms, *An Answer to Fools*, Huntington claimed that Ryland had co-written *Antinomianism Unmasked*. He also made the scandalous claim that the address given by de Fleury in her prefaces was false and that he had eventually found her home by enquiring at a gin shop, where he maintained she was well known. Huntington's claim seems unlikely; the address, 31 Jewin Street, London, was given in some of her publications as a sale outlet, and other references to her poverty would suggest that her writing was an important source of income.

De Fleury's writing suggests that she was defensive of her poor education and her independence as a writer; Huntington's allegation that she collaborated with Ryland was clearly not new. Her collection *Divine Poems and Essays* (1791) has recommendatory prefaces by Ryland and two other evangelical ministers, John Towers and Thomas Wills, in which Towers contends that her theologically assertive style is due to the amount of time she has spent conversing with ministers and is not a sign that her work is by another, more educated person. The ministers all stress her commitment to the protestant church, and although she explained in her *Letter* of 1787 that she was not then an official member of the ecumenical evangelical association she emphasized that her friendships within that circle had confirmed her belief in the great value of their activities. She justified the publication of her poetry and controversial tracts by the need for protestant and Trinitarian evangelism at a time that she felt was one of crisis because of the spread of arianism and socinianism. Her poetry reflects her evangelical mission, and it is perhaps not surprising that she also published *Hymns for Believer's Baptism* in 1786. It is not known when or where de Fleury died.

EMMA MAJOR

Sources ESTC · D. M. Lewis, ed., *The Blackwell dictionary of evangelical biography, 1730–1860*, 2 vols. (1995) · J. Mee, *Dangerous enthusiasm* (1992), 60 · W. T. Whitley, *A history of British Baptists* (1923), 231 · Allibone, *Dict.*

Wealth at death poor: T. Wills, preface, in M. de Fleury, *Divine poems* (1791), vii

Flew, (Robert) Newton (1886–1962), Methodist minister and theologian, was born on 25 May 1886 in Holsworthy, Devon, the elder son of the Revd Josiah Flew (1859–1925), Wesleyan Methodist minister, and his wife, Florence Jones (1863–1964). The family's home was originally in Portland, Dorset, but Wesleyan ministry took them to Wiltshire and Warwickshire before they settled finally in London suburbs. In 1897 Flew won a scholarship to Christ's Hospital, from where he was awarded a classical postmastership at Merton College, Oxford. Here he had a distinguished academic career, reading both classics and theology and subsequently being awarded several theological prizes. In 1909 he spent a term studying in Bonn and Marburg, where he came under the influence of Wilhelm Herrman and Adolf Jülicher.

During his Oxford course Flew had decided to follow his father into the Wesleyan Methodist ministry. He was invited to act as assistant tutor in theology and classics at Handsworth College, Birmingham, while completing his own training for ministry. In 1913 he began a five-year circuit ministry in Winchmore Hill in north London. During this time he was given leave of absence to use a travelling scholarship to make two extended study visits (despite the war) to Switzerland and Italy, where he made his first ecumenical friendships with Roman Catholics. Before the war ended in 1918 he had volunteered to undertake a naval chaplaincy. The armistice had already been signed when he set sail for Mesopotamia, where he remained for eighteen months. From there he moved to India to teach at the United Theological College in Bangalore for another eighteen months.

In July 1921, a few weeks after his return home, Flew married Winifred Garrard (1887–1982), a teacher and Wesleyan Methodist. The couple had a son, and Flew spent the following six years in circuit ministry in London. During these years the foundations of his ecumenical commitment were laid, through both friendship and scholarship. In the London Society for the Study of Religion he met the Roman Catholic theologian Baron von Hügel, who encouraged him in the study of spirituality which was to result in *The Idea of Perfection in Christian Theology* (1934), a work which earned him the Oxford DD in 1930; he was the first nonconformist to gain this degree by examination.

In 1927 Flew's academic achievements had already led

(Robert) Newton Flew (1886–1962), by Frank O. Salisbury, c.1955

to his being appointed to the Greenhalgh chair of New Testament language and literature at Wesley House, Cambridge, a college founded in 1921. Its new buildings had just been opened in 1926. Cambridge was to be Flew's home for the rest of his life. After ten years as tutor, he was appointed principal of Wesley House, a post he held until his retirement in 1955, exercising a profound influence on a whole generation of students. From the outset Wesley House had accepted Primitive and United Methodists as well as Wesleyan Methodist students, and Flew helped the new united Methodist church after 1932 to deepen its understanding of the church and churchmanship. His book *Jesus and his Church* (1938) was based on the Fernley–Hartley lecture delivered to the Methodist conference in 1938, and went through several editions. He was a respected and influential member of the Cambridge faculty of divinity.

Flew's influence spread far beyond Cambridge. He was elected moderator of the Free Church Federal Council for the year 1945–6, and president of the Methodist conference in the year immediately following. While firmly rooted in Wesleyan Methodism, he grew to love and appreciate other Christian traditions and to long for a deeper unity with them, and the main focus of his scholarly work moved from spirituality to the doctrine of the church. He was a member of the Friends of Reunion and a firm supporter of the proposed Church of South India. He was one of the group of nonconformists appointed to respond to Archbishop Fisher's Cambridge sermon of November 1946 calling for new moves towards unity. He chaired the group which produced *The Catholicity of Protestantism* (edited jointly by Flew and Rupert Davies, 1950) in

response to an Anglo-Catholic work entitled *Catholicity*; both were intended to aid ecumenical conversations.

At the same time Flew was active on the international ecumenical stage. In 1934 he was appointed as a Methodist member of the World Faith and Order Continuation Committee set up at the Lausanne conference in 1927; this led to his being appointed as a delegate to both the life and work conference in Oxford and the faith and order conference in Edinburgh in 1937 (both forerunners of the World Council of Churches). After the war he was appointed vice-chairman of the provisional committee of the World Council of Churches, and he was recognized as a leading figure at the inauguration of the council in Amsterdam in 1948. As chairman of the faith and order commission on the church, he edited a volume entitled *The Nature of the Church* in preparation for the second meeting of the World Council of Churches at Lund in 1952. During all these years he maintained his lifelong interest in sport, especially cricket.

Flew remained in Cambridge in retirement, editing the *London Quarterly and Holborn Review* and preparing his book *Jesus and his Way*, published posthumously in 1963. One of his last public acts was to support the inauguration of Anglican–Methodist conversations at the Methodist conference in 1955. He died in Addenbrooke's Hospital, Cambridge, after a fall, on 10 September 1962, his mother's ninety-ninth birthday.   ELAINE KAYE

Sources G. S. Wakefield, *Robert Newton Flew* (1971) · *Methodist Recorder* (13 Sept 1962) · *Methodist Recorder* (20 Sept 1962) · *The Times* (11 Sept 1962) · W. B. Brash, *The story of our colleges* (1935) · A. Hastings, *A history of English Christianity, 1920–1985* (1986) · H. Davies, *Worship and theology in England*, 5 (1965) · private information (2004) [Professor Antony Flew] · *CGPLA Eng. & Wales* (1963)
Archives Wesley House, Cambridge, lecture notes
Likenesses F. O. Salisbury, portrait, c.1955, Wesley House, Cambridge [*see illus.*]
Wealth at death £8840 9s. od.: probate, 24 Jan 1963, *CGPLA Eng. & Wales*

Flexman, Roger (1708–1795), Presbyterian minister and indexer, was born on 22 February 1708 at Great Torrington, Devon. Nothing is known of his parents or family except that his father was a manufacturer. He demonstrated an early desire to enter the ministry, and entered the Presbyterian academy of John Moore at Tiverton at the age of fifteen. He declined an offer from Moore to be his assistant in 1728, and applied to the Exeter Assembly the same year to gain admission to the ministry. Though only twenty he was successful, for he had already become noted for his learning and there were few ministers in the area. He began his ministry that year at Great Torrington, and was ordained in 1730.

In the following year Flexman became minister at Crediton, moving in 1735 to Chard and in 1739 to Bradford, Wiltshire. He soon came into wider notice and in 1747 was appointed minister of the Presbyterian congregation at Jamaica Row, Rotherhithe, London. In the same year he married Miss Yerbury, the daughter of a leading member of the Bradford congregation. She predeceased him.

Flexman's early ministry proved acceptable, but his studious interests did not make him a popular preacher.

However in 1754 he was made the Friday lecturer at Little St Helen's, Bishopsgate, an office which he retained to extreme old age. He was affected by the religious doubts of the period and became Arian and heterodox in his theology. Perhaps he was more appreciated outside his congregation than within. In 1770 he was made DD by Marischal College, Aberdeen, and it is said he was offered preferment in the established church. He lived a distance from his church, which could have contributed to the long, slow decline of Jamaica Row. A nineteenth-century critic of evangelical views puts it more sharply:

> Dr Flexman devoted his extensive learning to the work of undermining the faith of the Gospel. ... He was greatly out of place as pastor of a Christian Church, and left only a nominal society at Jamaica Row to prove the withering influence of error. (Waddington, 150)

Flexman was notable for his historical expertise, and especially for his detailed knowledge of the constitutional history of England. He was often consulted by members of both houses of parliament. A remarkable memory led him towards index-making, and his services were in increasing demand as he was noted for his accuracy. George Steevens, in conversation with Samuel Johnson, happened to mention Flexman's 'exact memory in chronological matters'. Johnson impatiently characterized him as 'the fellow who made the index to my *Ramblers*, and set down the name of Milton thus: Milton, *Mr. John*' (J. Boswell, *Life of Johnson*, ed. P. Rogers, 1980, 1784). He also prepared bibliographies and published religious works and collections of sermons. He wrote religious poems, many of which were used as hymns; one was included in Andrew Kippis's *Collection* of 1795. Flexman's love and concern for books was recognized in his appointment as librarian of Dr Williams's Library from 1786 to 1792. His main pleasure was the study of the New Testament in Greek.

The work for which Flexman is chiefly known is as a compiler of the general index to the journals of the House of Commons, an office to which he was appointed in 1770. He was assigned the period 1660–97, which he began in 1776 and completed in 1780. These were published in four volumes (8–11), for which he was paid generously. This great task has proved a lasting monument to his skill and dedication.

When Flexman retired from his ministry at Jamaica Row in 1783, the congregation disbanded and 'the managers sold the lease of the chapel, and presented the money realised by the transaction to their minister' (Waddington, 150). During his last years Flexman was subject to a painful and distressing disorder which seems to have weakened his mind. He died on 14 June 1795 at the house of his daughter in Prescot Street, Goodman's Fields, London, and was buried in Bunhill Fields.

ALAN RUSTON

Sources *Protestant Dissenter's Magazine*, 2 (1795), 264, 399–400 · J. Waddington, *Surrey Congregational history* (1866), 150 · W. Wilson, *The history and antiquities of the dissenting churches and meeting houses in London, Westminster and Southwark*, 4 vols. (1808–14), vol. 4, pp. 361–6 · *DNB* · *GM*, 1st ser., 65 (1795), 534 · J. A. Jones, ed., *Bunhill memorials* (1849), 49 · E. E. Cleal, *The story of congregationalism in Surrey* (1908), 33–4 · J. Murch, *A history of the Presbyterian and General Baptist churches in the west of England* (1835), 67–8 · C. Surman, index, DWL · H. McLachlan, *English education under the Test Acts: being the history of the nonconformist academies, 1662–1820* (1931), 14
Likenesses J. Yeatherd, mezzotint, pubd 1795, BM, NPG · line engraving, pubd 1796, NPG · engraving, repro. in *Protestant Dissenter's Magazine*, 3 (1796)

Flexmore, Richard (1824–1860), clown, whose real name was Richard Flexmore Geatter, was born on 15 September 1824, at Kennington, London, the son of Richard Flexmore Geatter (d. in or before 1849), a comic dancer, and his wife, Ann (1781–1869). He commenced his theatrical career in 1832 when he danced at the Victoria Theatre, and later became a grotesque clown. Between 1844 and 1845 he appeared at such venues as the Grecian Saloon and the Olympic Theatre. He was then engaged by the Princess's Theatre, where he remained for several seasons. On 28 July 1849, at St Mary's Church, Lambeth, he married Francisca Christophosa, the daughter of Jean Baptiste Auriol, the famous French clown. He acted with his wife in several European cities before appearing at the Strand and the Adelphi, and by 1860 had graduated to Covent Garden and Drury Lane. As a clown, he made his mark by introducing the costume with tights and short frilled trunks that became the standard outfit used by his successors. He was also noted for his imitations of leading dancers of the day, such as Perrot, Carlotta, Grisi, Taglioni, Cerito, and others. Although chiefly renowned as a dancing clown, he could, when required, take the part of clown à la Grimaldi, signifying his versatility within the profession. One observer described him, among other things, as 'agile, humorous and quick at the innovation' (Adams, 525).

Flexmore died on 20 August 1860 at his home, 66 Hercules Buildings, Lambeth, at the age of thirty-four of consumption 'brought on by the violent exertion he underwent in his professional duties' (*The Era*, 26 Aug 1860, 10). Accordingly, 'his physical strength and activity were remarkable and he so severely taxed his powers to obtain the plaudits of the public that he may be truly said to have purchased his popularity at the cost of his life' (ibid.). He was buried at Kensal Green cemetery on 27 August. Since Flexmore had left 'little or nothing behind', a fund for his family was proposed among members of the profession. However, his wife 'beg[ged] to say that no such thing was sanctioned ... Happily I have no need of any assistance at present. As regards, my mother-in-law, I have settled an allowance that will keep her comfortably' (*The Era*, 2 Sept 1860, 10). She married a cousin, and died in Paris in 1862. After Flexmore's death, Harry Payne took over the role of principal clown at Covent Garden.

G. C. BOASE, rev. BRENDA ASSAEL

Sources Boase, *Mod. Eng. biog.* · Adams, *Drama*, 1.525 · D. Pickering, ed., *Encyclopaedia of pantomime* (1993) · *The Era* (26 Aug 1860), 10 · *The Era* (2 Sept 1860), 10
Likenesses C. Baugniet, double portrait, lithograph, 1848 (with Mlle Auriol), BM · C. N. G., lithograph, Harvard TC

Fliccius, Gerbarus. See Flicke, Gerlach (d. 1558).

Flicke, Gerlach [Garlick, Garlicke] (*d.* **1558**), portrait painter, was probably a native of Osnabrück in Germany, and was working in England by about 1545. Nothing is known of his parentage, early life, or training. An inscription on his portrait of Archbishop Thomas Cranmer (NPG) is the earliest record of his presence in England: 'Gerlacus Flicus / Germanus / faciebat' and 'Anno etatj 57 Julij 20'. Cranmer was born on 2 July 1489, and so the painting must date from either 1545 or 1546, depending on whether the inscription is taken to mean that Cranmer was fifty-seven years old or in his fifty-seventh year. The portrait, although in some respects rather stiff and flat, is an interesting and decorative work, containing a number of references to Cranmer's protestant doctrinal beliefs, and reflecting Flicke's awareness of Hans Holbein's earlier portrait of the Catholic Archbishop Warham, as well as knowledge of fashionable French prints of the Fontainebleau school.

Although the commission of a portrait of the archbishop of Canterbury suggests that Flicke was an important and highly regarded artist, few of his paintings have survived. A portrait of an unknown gentleman (NG Scot.) is signed and dated 1547. Three portraits by Garlicke (the form of his name used in Flicke's will) are recorded in the inventory of John, Lord Lumley (1534?–1609), made in 1590. These are of Queen Mary (now in Durham Cathedral Library); of Thomas, third duke of Norfolk; and a full-length portrait of Thomas, first Lord Darcy of Chiche, which was recorded in the mid-nineteenth century at Irnham Hall, Lincolnshire, but is now lost. Although the condition of his surviving paintings is uneven, they generally testify to his being one of the more able artists in the generation after Hans Holbein the younger.

Flicke was for a time incarcerated in the Tower of London: it is not known for what crime, or for how long. The evidence of his imprisonment is a tiny double portrait (NPG), showing the artist himself with a well-known pirate, Henry Strangwish or Strangways, who is known to have been in the Tower in March 1555. Flicke depicted himself with a palette, and Strangwish with a lute, recorded the date 1554, and inscribed lines in English and Latin recording the identity of the sitters and the fact that they were prisoners, in a beautiful and minute hand above each portrait. He described himself in Latin as 'a painter in the City of London'.

Although he lived for a time in the parish of St Mary Woolnoth in London (he is recorded there in 1549), when Flicke died in 1558 (between 24 January, when he made his will, and 11 February, when it was proved) he was living in the parish of St Giles Cripplegate. At this time he had a wife, Katherine, but apparently no children. He left property in Osnabrück to a servant, which, along with the fact that he indicated on two of his portraits that his nationality was German, suggests that this was his native town.

CATHARINE MACLEOD

Sources K. Hearn, ed., *Dynasties: painting in Tudor and Jacobean England, 1530–1630* (1995), 48–9, 120 [exhibition catalogue, Tate Gallery, London, 12 Oct 1995 – 7 Jan 1996] · M. S. Hervey, 'Notes on a Tudor

Gerlach Flicke (*d.* 1558), self-portrait, 1554

painter: Gerlach Flick - 1', *Burlington Magazine*, 17 (1910), 71–9 · E. Auerbach, *Tudor artists* (1954) · PRO, PROB 11/40, sig. 7

Likenesses G. Flicke, self-portrait, oils, 1554 (with Henry Strangwish, or Strangways), NPG [*see illus.*]

Wealth at death property in London and Osnabrück: will, PRO, PROB 11/40, sig. 7

Flight, Benjamin (1764/5–1846), organ builder, was born in London, the son of Benjamin Flight, of the organ-building firm of Flight and Kelly. About 1800 he formed a partnership with Joseph Robson. Between 1812 and 1817, with his son John Flight and Robson, and at a cost of £10,000, he constructed the Apollonicon, a large orchestrion with five manuals (detachable so as to accommodate five players, all facing the public), forty-five stops, and three barrels. From June 1817 it was exhibited at the firm's London showrooms, the Apollonicon Rooms, in St Martin's Lane, but although it attracted much attention it was not a financial success and was demolished about 1840. A smaller version was built for Viscount Kirkwall. The partnership with Robson was dissolved in 1832, but Flight continued to interest himself in certain inventions and improvements in the mechanism of organs. He died on 7 May 1846, aged eighty-one, at 16 King William Street, Charing Cross; his son carried on the business until 1885.

L. M. MIDDLETON, *rev.* JOHN WARRACK

Sources *New Grove* · M. Wilson, *The English chamber organ* (1968) · S. Marcuse, *Musical instruments: a comprehensive dictionary* (1966) ·

A. Rees and others, *The cyclopaedia, or, Universal dictionary of arts, sciences, and literature*, 45 vols. (1819–20) · d. cert.

Flight, (Walter) Claude (1881–1955), linocut artist and art teacher, was born on 16 February 1881 at 12 Clairville Grove in South Kensington, London, son of Dr Walter *Flight FRS (1841–1885), mineralogist and authority on meteorites at the British Museum, and his wife, Katherine Fell (1847–1942), daughter of Dr Fell of Ambleside. Flight's interest in art was a relatively late development; after he left school he worked in an engineer's office for two years, took up librarianship for eighteen months, and then spent seven years farming and bee-keeping in Sussex at Little Bines, Burwash, as a neighbour of Rudyard Kipling. In 1912, aged thirty-one, Flight enrolled as a full-time student at the Heatherley School of Fine Art in London, where he met (Helena) Clare James, whom he married on 20 May 1915 in the parish church of St John, Hampstead; they had two daughters. At the outbreak of the First World War he volunteered as a farrier and subsequently became a captain in the Army Service Corps in France, being awarded the Mérit Agricole medal by the French government for his three and a half years' service. After demobilization he spent a year at the Paris art schools and purchased for 300 francs a neolithic chalk cave by the Seine at Chantemesle, 40 miles from Paris. He made the cave his regular summer retreat, declaring in an interview: 'it is here that I cook, sail my canoe, sketch and dream' (Flight, 'Golders Green artist's life', 1).

Following his marriage break-up Flight met in 1922 **Edith Lawrence** (1890–1973), an artist working in various media, including textile design and linocut, who moved into his studio at St John's Wood in 1925 and thereafter became his lifelong companion and artistic partner. Born on 22 March 1890 at Walton-on-Thames, Surrey, youngest daughter of George Adams Lawrence, the founder of Jackson's, the fashionable grocery store in Piccadilly, Lawrence trained at the Slade School of Fine Art, London (1910–14), where she was a prizewinning student. Before meeting Flight she had already embarked on her career: in 1916 she exhibited paintings at the Royal Academy and the New English Art Club and from 1917 was teaching art at Runston Hill School. In 1927 Flight and Lawrence set up an interior decoration business from their new studio at 5 Rodmarton Mews, off Baker Street, London, designing murals and utilitarian decorative objects, many of them in textile. A joint exhibition of their embroidered work, mostly designed by Flight and executed by Lawrence, that included fire screens, pictorial door curtains, cushion covers, and even a bedroom hot water cosy, was shown at the Embroiderers' Guild, London, in 1937.

Although Flight's geometrically constructed oil paintings and watercolours were regularly shown at the progressive Seven and Five Society (1922–8) and were widely reproduced during this period in the leading art magazines, including *The Studio*, *Colour*, and *Artwork*, his importance rests on his championship of the colour linocut as the modern medium for the modern age. Inspired by the machine-age aesthetic of F. T. Marinetti and the Italian futurists (whose work he knew from their well-publicized

(Walter) Claude Flight (1881–1955), by unknown photographer, 1931 [with Edith Lawrence at the entrance to his cave at Chantemesle, Seine-et-Oise, France]

visit to London in 1912), Flight sought to express the vitality, speed, and movement of modern life through the twentieth-century linocut, which, he claimed, 'has no tradition of technique behind it, so that the student can go forward without thinking of what Bewick or Rembrandt did before' (Flight, *Art and Craft*, 63). From 1926 to 1930 Flight gave weekly instruction in linocut technique at the Grosvenor School of Modern Art, founded at 33 Warwick Square, Pimlico, London, in 1925 by the enlightened teacher and wood-engraver Iain Macnab. Among Flight's numerous students were Cyril E. Power and Sybil Andrews, Eileen Mayo, the Swiss Lill Tschudi, and the Australians Dorrit Black, Ethel Spowers, and Eveline Syme, all of whom helped to disseminate his ideas abroad. Syme wrote at the time of his success as a teacher:

> Sometimes in his classes it is hard to remember that he is teaching so complete is the camaraderie between him and his students. He treats them as fellow-artists rather than pupils, discusses with them and suggests to them, never dictates or enforces. At the same time he is so full of enthusiasm for his subject, and his ideas are so clear and reasoned, that it is impossible for his students not to be influenced by them. (Syme, 3)

Flight's book *Lino-cuts* (1927) was the first monograph on the subject and became the standard manual for artists and teachers; it was illustrated with examples of his prints that showed the combined influence of futurism and art deco. His second textbook, *The Art and Craft of Lino Cutting and Printing* (1934), expressed many of his ideas on art education, particularly for children. He wrote several children's books illustrated with his linocuts, including three with Edith Lawrence written in Basic English in 1938: *A Little about Art*; *A Little about Geography*; *A Little about History*. In 1929 Flight organized the first exhibition devoted exclusively to the linocut in Britain; its success at the Redfern Gallery, London, led to a series of eight annual exhibitions which he arranged, initially at the Redfern and then at the Ward Gallery, London, until 1937. Flight also introduced the linocut to a diverse international audience through exhibitions toured by the Redfern to the United States (1929 and 1934), China (1931), Australia (1932 and 1937), and Canada (1935–6). Flight viewed the modern linocut, with its bold colour, geometric design, and rhythmic expression, as the new democratic art medium that would furnish homes with contemporary decorative designs at affordable prices. With utopian fervour he looked forward to the day when this 'art of the people for their homes' (Flight, *Lino-cuts*, 12) might sell 'at a price … paid by the average man for his daily beer or his cinema ticket' (ibid., 4).

Until the late 1930s Flight conducted regular classes at his cave in France during the summer as well as occasional sketching tours in Dorset. In June 1940 Flight and Lawrence, to escape the threat of aerial attack, moved to a small cottage in Donhead St Andrew, Wiltshire, taking with them their prints and watercolours; the studio at Rodmarton Mews was destroyed during the blitz in 1941, with the loss of all their lino printing blocks and larger oil paintings and screens. In April 1947 Flight suffered a stroke, which left him paralysed. He was nursed by Lawrence at Donhead St Andrew until his death on 10 October 1955. By this date his reputation had declined, with little interest after the war being shown in his work and in that of the linocut movement he represented; it was not until the 1970s that his achievements as an artist and teacher began to receive their proper due. Principal holdings of his prints are in the British Museum and the Victoria and Albert Museum, London, and the National Gallery of Australia, Canberra.

Flight's pupil Dorrit Black described him as:

a small man with very bright eyes, little bits of side-curls, and one feels instantly at one's ease with him. During the summer he lives in a cave in France … and in the winter he comes out of his cave to teach lino-cutting to students of the Grosvenor School. (Black)

This light-hearted vignette encapsulates the paradoxical qualities of Flight's character: as an artist he openly embraced metropolitan life with its speed and complexity and yet felt compelled to return each year to a caveman simplicity.

In 1955 Lawrence, who had become almost blind during Flight's last years, was able to paint again after a cataract operation. In 1961 she moved to Worth Matravers, Dorset, where she continued to work with the use of one eye for the next twelve years. An exhibition of her work was held at the University of Hull a few months before her death on 2 October 1973, at the Maristow Nursing Home, Bourne Avenue, Salisbury. A joint memorial exhibition of the work of Flight and Lawrence was held at the Parkin Gallery, London, in November 1973, a show which marked the start of their artistic rehabilitation.

STEPHEN COPPEL

Sources S. Coppel, *Linocuts of the machine age: Claude Flight and the Grosvenor School* (1995) · C. Flight, *Lino-cuts* (1927) · C. Flight, *The art and craft of lino cutting and printing* (1934) · E. Syme, 'Claude Flight and his teaching', *The Recorder*, 3 (Sept 1929), 3–4 · D. Black, 'London letter', *Undergrowth* (Jan–Feb 1928) · C. Flight, 'Golders Green artist's life as "Caveman"', *Golders Green Gazette* (3 June 1927) · C. Flight and E. Lawrence, *A little about art* (1938) · C. Flight and E. Lawrence, *A little about geography* (1938) · C. Flight and E. Lawrence, *A little about history* (1938) · *The Times* (11 Oct 1955) · *The Times* (6 Oct 1973) · B. Denvir and M. Parkin, *A memorial exhibition of oils, watercolours and linocuts by Claude Flight, 1881–1955 and Edith Lawrence, 1890–1973* (1973) [exhibition catalogue, Parkin Gallery, London, 2–24 Nov 1973] · *CGPLA Eng. & Wales* (1956) · *CGPLA Eng. & Wales* (1974) · b. cert. · m. cert.
Likenesses double portrait, photograph, 1931 (with Edith Lawrence), Michael Parkin Gallery, London; copy, priv. coll. [*see illus.*]
Wealth at death £11,518 10s. 4d.: probate, 4 Jan 1956, *CGPLA Eng. & Wales* · £31,928—Edith Lawrence: probate, 19 April 1974, *CGPLA Eng. & Wales*

Flight, Walter (1841–1885), mineralogist, was born in Winchester on 21 January 1841, fourth in the family of five boys and three girls of William Pyke Flight of Winchester, and his wife, Elizabeth, *née* Jeffery. He was educated at Queenwood College, Hampshire, where Heinrich Debus (1824–1915) then taught chemistry and Professor John Tyndall physics; Debus remained his constant friend. After coming of age Flight proceeded to Germany and spent the winter session of 1863–4 studying chemistry under Professor Heintz at the University of Halle. He passed the next two years at Heidelberg and acquired a thorough knowledge of chemistry. His studies in Germany were completed at Berlin, where he acted for some time as secretary and chemical assistant to Professor Hofmann. In 1867 Flight returned to England and obtained his DSc at London University. In 1868 he was appointed assistant examiner there in chemistry under Professor Debus. On 5 September 1867 he became an assistant in the mineralogical department of the British Museum under Professor N. Story-Maskelyne. In the laboratory, which was now specially fitted up, he devised new methods by which to investigate the mineral constituents of meteorites and their occluded gases, which rapidly brought him into notice. He was appointed examiner in chemistry and physics at the Royal Military Academy, Woolwich, in 1868, and in 1876 examiner to the Royal Military Academy, Cheltenham. He also acted for several years as a member of the committee on luminous meteors appointed by the British Association. In 1880 he married Katherine (Kate) (1847–1942), daughter of Dr Fell of Ambleside.

Flight wrote twenty-one papers on scientific subjects, of which the first three, all on chemical subjects, appeared in German periodicals between 1864 and 1870. The later papers were chiefly on meteorites, dealing in detail with the recorded circumstances of their fall, and with their mineralogical and chemical constituents; several, written in conjunction with Story-Maskelyne, give accounts, published in the *Philosophical Transactions*, of the meteorites which fell at Rowton in Shropshire, at Middlesbrough, and at Cranbourne in Australia. Flight's last paper was on the meteorite of Alfianello in Italy. Between 1875 and 1883 he contributed a series of twenty-three papers to the *Geological Magazine*, entitled 'A chapter in the history of meteorites' (published in book form in 1887). Flight was elected a fellow of the Royal Society on 7 June 1883. In 1884 he became mentally incapacitated; he was compelled to resign his post in the British Museum and died at his home, 4 Wildwood Terrace, North End, Hampstead, on 4 November 1885, leaving a widow and three young children, including his son (Walter) Claude *Flight, the linocut artist and teacher.

W. J. HARRISON, rev. ANITA MCCONNELL

Sources *Geological Magazine*, new ser., 3rd decade, 2 (1885), 575–6 · L. Fletcher and H. Woodward, 'In memoriam', in W. Flight, *A chapter in the history of meteorites*, ed. L. Fletcher and H. Woodward (1887), vii–viii · d. cert. · *CGPLA Eng. & Wales* (1885)
Archives NHM, diaries and papers
Likenesses photograph, repro. in 'In memoriam', frontispiece
Wealth at death £1839 10s. 6d.: probate, 11 Dec 1885, *CGPLA Eng. & Wales*

Flindell, Thomas (1767–1824), newspaper editor and printer, was born at Helford, in the parish of Manaccan, Cornwall, one of the six children of Thomas Flindell, victualler, and his wife, Alice Williams. He was apprenticed to a printer, probably Philip Elliot of Falmouth, his father's friend. Following Elliot's death in 1787 he moved successively to Bath, Edinburgh, and London.

In 1790, when twenty-three years old, Flindell became the editor of the *Doncaster Gazette*, substantially increasing its circulation. On 2 June 1794 he married Mary Brunton of Doncaster. Four years later he returned to Cornwall, establishing the Stannary Press in Helston, where three of Thomas and Mary's children were born. One of Flindell's first publications at Helston was Alexander Pope's *Essay on Man*. He printed numerous pamphlets by local authors of note, including the Methodist writer Samuel Drew and Dr Robert Hawker, vicar of Charles Church, Plymouth, who conducted a public debate with Richard Polwhele, vicar of Manaccan and Cornish historian.

Flindell's greatest work at Helston was, however, the printing of the Bible, the only known Cornish edition, with Richard Polwhele as editor and with an introduction by the erudite Cornish cleric John Whitaker. Its publication in fortnightly parts made possible the purchase of a bible by almost every family, and also avoided substantial publishing costs. In 1800 Flindell moved to Falmouth, occupying rooms at the rectory, and although a few more parts of the Bible were produced he never completed its publication, partly because of the rise in the duty on paper, but partly also because of personal financial problems.

In March 1801 Flindell founded the *Cornwall Gazette and Falmouth Packet*, a weekly paper, which survived only to October 1802, when it ceased through the bankruptcy of his partners. Flindell was imprisoned at Bodmin for debt.

By 1803, however, he had attracted financial support from a number of influential local gentry and clergy. He moved to Truro, where seven more children were baptized, and where, from his new house in Lemon Street, he was able to establish a larger newspaper called the *Royal Cornwall Gazette and Western Advertiser* under the patronage of the duke of Cornwall. Flindell was both proprietor and editor of this, the first successful newspaper to be produced in Cornwall. Its first number appeared on 2 July 1803. Although the *Gazette* was at first probably politically impartial, by 1809 it had become decidedly tory. A rival newspaper, the *West Briton*, was established in 1810 with whig support and with Edward Budd as its editor. A bitter pamphlet war ensued and the two editors engaged in a fierce controversy in the columns of their respective newspapers. Gradually the *West Briton* gained influence and circulation and, although Flindell remained in Truro to publish three of the seven volumes of Richard Polwhele's *History of Cornwall*, by 1818 he had sold his interest in the *Gazette* and moved to Exeter. The *Gazette* survived until 1951, when ironically it was amalgamated with the *West Briton*.

Flindell's next venture was the *Western Luminary*, a weekly newspaper with tory leanings, which he established in 1813. It prospered for some years, but in 1820 it described Queen Caroline as 'notoriously devoted to Bacchus and Venus' and, following a debate in the House of Commons in July of that year, Flindell was prosecuted. On 19 March 1821 he was sentenced to nine months in Exeter gaol. During his imprisonment he wrote a pamphlet entitled *Prison recreations: the philosophy of reason and revelation attempted, with a view to the restoration of the theory of the Bible on the ruins of infidelity*, which discussed in controversial terms the nature of the Trinity. Flindell's health deteriorated during his imprisonment. He was also unhappy at what he considered had been unfair treatment of his comments in the press, others who had been equally outspoken having received no punishment. After several years of illness he died at Exeter on 11 July 1824, aged fifty-seven, survived by his wife and most of his children. Publication of the *Western Luminary* continued under the proprietorship of his widow. 'A man of strong understanding, though by no means polished or refined' was Polwhele's estimate of Flindell's character.

CHRISTINE NORTH

Sources *DNB* · R. Potts, 'Early Cornish printers', *Journal of the Royal Institution of Cornwall*, new ser., 4 (1961–4), 264–323 · G. C. Boase, *Collectanea Cornubiensia: a collection of biographical and topographical notes relating to the county of Cornwall* (1890), 251 · Boase & Courtney, *Bibl. Corn.*, 1.151, 3.988, 1406 · R. Polwhele, *Traditions and recollections; domestic, clerical and literary*, 2 (1826), 778–81 · R. Polwhele, *Reminiscences in prose and verse*, 1 (1836), 125–6 · R. Polwhele, *Biographical sketches in Cornwall*, 1 (1831), 57 · C. Redding, *Yesterday and to-day*, 3 vols. (1863) · Lease to T. Flindell of a newly built house in Lemon Street, Truro, Sept 1804, Cornwall RO, WH 1179 · *IGI*
Archives Wilts. & Swindon RO, corresp.

Flinders, Matthew (1774–1814), naval officer and hydrographer, the eldest son of Matthew Flinders (1750–1802) and his first wife, Susannah, *née* Ward (1752–1783), was

Matthew Flinders (1774–1814), by Helena G. de Courcy Jones, 1919 (after unknown artist, 1801?)

born on 16 March 1774 at Donington, near Boston in Lincolnshire, where his father and grandfather had practised as surgeons.

Early life and voyages He was intended for the same profession, and attended Donington Free School from 1780 and John Shinglar's Grammar School at Horbling from 1785 until 1788; but was in his own phrase, 'induced to go to sea, against the wish of friends, from reading *Robinson Crusoe*', and applied himself, with some assistance from his father, to the study of geometry, trigonometry, and navigation and gained a competent knowledge of them.

His opportunity came when his cousin Henrietta, who was governess in the family of Captain Thomas Pasley, brought his name before her employer. Pasley was sufficiently impressed by what she had to say to offer Flinders a vacancy in his ship the *Scipio*, then at Chatham, which he joined in May 1790. Pasley received Flinders kindly, placed him on the quarter-deck, and took him with him to the *Bellerophon* during the Spanish armament (1790). The following year, on Pasley's personal recommendation he joined the *Providence* under Captain William Bligh, who was on the point of sailing to the south seas on his second and successful attempt to transplant the breadfruit tree from Tahiti to the West Indies. His earlier study of navigation now proved useful and, according to his father, he was entrusted by Bligh with a greater share of the navigation and chart-drawing than was due to his few months' service at sea. On his return to Britain in 1793 he rejoined the

Bellerophon, now flying the broad pennant of Commodore Pasley, and in her took part in the battle of the Glorious First of June.

Australian exploration On returning to Portsmouth after the battle, Flinders was appointed to the *Reliance* under Captain Henry Waterhouse, formerly a lieutenant of the *Bellerophon*. The *Reliance* was then being fitted out for a voyage to New South Wales, in order to carry out Captain John Hunter, the newly appointed governor.

The *Reliance* arrived at Port Jackson in September 1795, and for the next five years Flinders devoted all the time that he could be spared from his ship duties to exploring and surveying the adjacent parts of Australia. In this he was associated with the surgeon of the *Reliance*, George Bass, with whom he carried out two boat expeditions to the south of Port Jackson. Between December 1797 and February 1798, while Flinders was detained on board, Bass made an extended coasting voyage by himself in a whale-boat, during which he entered and named Western Port. The strong westerly seas and swell which he encountered convinced Bass that a strait existed between New South Wales and Van Diemen's Land (later Tasmania), until then believed to be connected with it. Shortly before Bass returned to Port Jackson, Hunter sent Flinders in the 44 ton colonial schooner *Francis* to the Furneaux group, where the *Sydney Cove* had been wrecked, to complete the salvage of its cargo, thus enabling Flinders to carry out his first independent survey. In September 1798 Hunter appointed Flinders to command the *Norfolk*, a 25 ton sloop, and sent him, with Bass as his assistant, to examine behind the Furneaux Islands, with instructions, if he found a strait, to pass through it, sail round Van Diemen's Land, and return by its south and east coasts, making such examinations and surveys as circumstances would permit. This was happily done in a voyage extending from 7 October 1798 to 12 January 1799, and the existence of the strait being thus demonstrated the governor, acting on Flinders's suggestion, gave it the name of Bass's Strait. Between 7 July and 20 August 1799 Flinders made a final voyage in the *Norfolk*, during which he examined the coast to the north of Port Jackson as far as Hervey Bay.

When the *Reliance* returned to Britain, Flinders published the result of his surveys in 1801 under the title *Observations on the coasts of Van Diemen's Land, on Bass's strait and its islands and on part of the coasts of New South Wales*, which brought his name to the attention of Sir Joseph Banks. As a result, a more systematic examination of the coasts of New Holland was called for. Banks was a keen advocate and, mainly at his instigation, an expedition for that purpose was resolved on. Flinders had already been promoted lieutenant on 31 January 1798, and was now, on Banks's recommendation, appointed to command the *Xenophon*, receiving the rank of commander a few weeks later, on 16 February 1801. Also appointed to the *Xenophon*, mainly at the instigation of Banks, was a talented scientific staff, comprising Robert Brown, naturalist, Ferdinand Bauer, botanical artist, William Westall, topographical artist, John Crosley, astronomer, who left the expedition at the Cape of Good Hope because of ill health, Peter

Good, gardener, who died at Sydney in 1803, and John Allen, miner. The *Xenophon*, a north-country ship of 334 tons which had been bought into the navy in 1798 was now renamed the *Investigator*, and was liberally equipped, the East India Company also granting the officers £600 for their outfit. Meanwhile, on 17 April 1801, Flinders married Ann Chappelle (1770–1852).

The instructions for the new expedition, dated 22 June 1801, prescribed the survey of New Holland, beginning with the south coast from King George's Sound to Bass Strait. Provided with these, with all relevant existing charts and books of voyages, and with a passport from the French government (as Britain and France were then at war), the *Investigator* sailed from Spithead on 18 July 1801. Touching first at Madeira and then calling at Simon's Bay, from which she sailed on 4 November, on 6 December she was off Cape Leeuwin, and on the 8th arrived in King George's Sound. This had already been examined by Captain George Vancouver in 1791, and was now more carefully surveyed by Flinders, after which he examined, in more or less detail, the whole coastline eastward as far as Cape Howe. The greater part of this was new ground, and the names given by Flinders to the different bays, gulfs, headlands, and islands still call attention to the names of the officers of the *Investigator*, to some of the incidents of the voyage, and to the fact that the captain, his brother Samuel, the second lieutenant, and a midshipman named John Franklin were natives of Lincolnshire. Cape Catastrophe commemorates the loss of the cutter with her crew and two officers, whose names, Thistle and Taylor, were given to two neighbouring islands. Hard by is Memory Cove, and a few miles further are Port Lincoln, Cape Donington, Boston Island, Spalding Cove, Grantham Island, and Spilsby Island, one of the Sir Joseph Banks group. On Kangaroo Island they found many kangaroos, and killed thirty-one, shooting some and knocking others down with sticks.

On 8 April 1802, off Encounter Bay, they met the French exploring ship *Le Géographe*, under the command of Captain Nicolas Baudin, with whom they exchanged information. Possibly because of the delay caused by meeting Baudin, Flinders did not enter Encounter Bay and so failed to discover the mouth of the Murray, Australia's longest river. With this exception he seems to have compiled a chart of the coast which, under the circumstances of a running survey—and, for the most part, it was nothing more—was remarkably accurate, and remained the basis of Admiralty charts for most of the nineteenth century. From Port Phillip, which Flinders surveyed, the coast eastward had first been explored by Bass and then been examined more closely by Lieutenant Grant of the *Lady Nelson* in 1800—a priority of discovery and survey which was disputed by the French, who, ignorant of Grant's work, also surveyed the coast in 1802, naming afresh a number of features, not only in that part but also further west, which had been examined by Flinders (F. Péron and L. de Freycinet, *Voyage de découvertes aux terres australes*, 2 vols. and atlas, 1807–16). On 9 May 1802 the *Investigator* arrived at Port Jackson, where she found the *Lady Nelson*, ordered to act as her tender during the further progress of the survey. While the ship was refitting, an observatory was established on shore under the charge of Lieutenant Flinders and Franklin. The ship's company was badly in need of fresh provisions, but the price of fresh meat was so prohibitive that it was impossible for Flinders to consider purchasing it on the public account. However, he managed to obtain a quarter of beef for the ship's company in exchange for salt meat, while the governor sent some vegetables from his own garden. All that could be done was to pay the men what savings' allowance was due, so that they might buy some for themselves. When *Le Géographe* came in in a very distressed state, owing to the ravages of scurvy, out of a complement of 170 not more than 12 were capable of doing their duty. All the resources of the colony were at once put at their disposal, and some few cattle which the governor had as breeding stock were slaughtered for them.

On 22 July the *Investigator* sailed from Port Jackson, with the *Lady Nelson* in company. The tender proved, however, of little use; she was so bad a sailer that she delayed the work, and, after having run aground and lost her main sliding keel, was worse than ever. She was accordingly sent back to Sydney, and the *Investigator*, rounding Cape York on 31 October and passing through Torres Strait, proceeded with the survey of the Gulf of Carpentaria. The ship, however, was leaking badly; it was found that many of her timbers were rotten, and the examining officers reported that if she had fine weather she might last six months without much risk. Flinders was naturally very disappointed. He had hoped 'to make so accurate an investigation of the shores of Terra Australis that no future voyage to this country should be necessary'. This was now impossible. He spent the next three months completing the survey of the Gulf of Carpentaria. Then, finding his men sickly he broke off his survey in Arnhem Bay and went to Timor for refreshments. On returning to Port Jackson on 9 June 1803 the *Investigator* was officially surveyed and pronounced incapable of being repaired. Flinders therefore, in consultation with the governor, decided to go home as a passenger in the *Porpoise*, the former Spanish prize *Infanta Amelia*, attached to the colony. Robert Fowler, the first lieutenant of the *Investigator*, was appointed to command her. Thirty-eight of the ship's company of the *Investigator* completed the complement of the *Porpoise*, while twenty-two of her officers and men were appointed to the *Porpoise* as supernumeraries for passage to Britain. The rest of the ship's company stayed at Port Jackson to await Flinders's return with another vessel.

The *Porpoise* put to sea on 10 August in company with the East India Company's ship *Bridgewater* and the *Cato* of London; and standing to the north, on the 17th the *Porpoise* and *Cato* both struck on Wreck Reef. The *Porpoise* stuck fast, but the *Cato* rolled over and sank in deep water, her men having barely time to scramble ashore. The *Bridgewater* sailed away, leaving them to their fate; and after earnest deliberation, it was determined that Flinders should attempt to reach Port Jackson in one of the boats. This he succeeded in doing, and the governor at once engaged the *Rolla*, bound to China, to relieve the party and to carry them on to Canton (Guangzhou). Two schooners accompanied her, the *Francis* to bring back to Port Jackson those who preferred it, and the *Cumberland* (29 tons), with Flinders in command, to proceed to Britain to obtain another vessel to complete his survey. At the wreck the master, the boatswain, and eight men agreed to accompany Flinders on this risky voyage. After parting from the *Rolla* on 11 October, the *Cumberland* passed safely through Torres Strait, enabling Flinders to add to its survey.

In crossing the Indian Ocean the *Cumberland* proved very leaky; her pumps were worn out and the labour was excessive; so much so that Flinders determined to call at Mauritius in the hope of finding some more convenient way of getting home. According to his last news from home, France and Britain were at peace; and even if not, he believed that the passport given him by the French government before he left Britain would meet the case. Unfortunately, as the instructions given him by Governor King, on leaving Port Jackson, did not clearly warrant his touching at Mauritius, he considered it prudent to state his reasons in his journal. While stressing the leaky condition of the schooner and the fact that her pumps were worn out, he also mentioned that it would afford him the opportunity to obtain information on the state of the colony and its possible usefulness to Port Jackson. He anchored on 15 December in Baie du Cap, from where he was directed to take the schooner round to Port Nord Ouest (Port Louis) and to call on the governor, General Decaen. Decaen at once objected that the passport was for the *Investigator*, and had no mention of the *Cumberland*. Flinders was therefore detained, his men were made prisoners, and his books and papers taken for examination. The last entry in his journal was sufficient to excite suspicion; and Flinders, anxious to get to Britain and renew his survey, appears, even from his own account, to have acted with considerable lack of prudence and tact. After reading Flinders's journal Decaen was convinced that the neutrality of Flinders's passport had been violated by his intention to obtain information on the state of the colony. Flinders was accordingly kept in close confinement. Although, after nearly two years, he was allowed to reside in the country with permission, under his word of honour, not to venture more than 6 miles from the house, his imprisonment continued for five more years. All exchanges were refused; instructions for his release were sent out from France, but Decaen chose to consider them not sufficiently explicit, and still detained him; nor did he release him until 7 June 1810, when he gave him permission to return to Britain, via Bombay, on parole not to serve against France during the course of the war. Accordingly, on 13 June Flinders left Mauritius in a cartel bound for Bombay, but meeting with the blockading squadron off the island he transferred to the *Otter* which was bound to the Cape, where he found a ship going to Britain. He arrived at Portsmouth on 24 October 1810. As soon as his release was known in Britain, he had been promoted to post rank, with seniority dated back to 7 May 1810, the date of the patent appointing Yorke first lord of the Admiralty. It was admitted that had Flinders succeeded in reaching Britain in the *Cumberland* in 1804, he would have been promoted then, but it was impossible to backdate his commission without an order in council, which the board was unwilling to undertake.

Last years and achievements A few months after his return Flinders began to prepare an account of his voyage under the supervision of Banks, to which task he steadily devoted himself for the next three years. The sedentary employment may have aggravated the symptoms of a disease due possibly, in its origin, to the hardships to which he had been exposed, and which had become more developed during the term of his long imprisonment. He lived to complete his work, but died, on 19 July 1814, at 14 London Street, Fitzroy Square, London, the day after it was published, a copy having been delivered to his lodgings on that day. He was buried in St James's burial-ground, Hampstead Road, London. He was survived by his wife and one daughter, Anne, a child two years old. She later married William Petrie and their son William Matthew Flinders *Petrie became a distinguished Egyptologist.

Flinders appears to have had an extraordinary natural gift as a surveyor, so that with little or no training he became one of the best of the British naval hydrographers. His survey of much of the Australian coast, though carried out under great disadvantages, stood the test of time, and formed the basis of Admiralty charts for most of the nineteenth century. He was also one of the first to investigate the error of the compass due to the attraction of the iron in the ship, carrying out experiments in various ships in 1812 at the instigation of the Admiralty, which he described in a 21-page appendix in his *Voyage*. One of his suggestions for overcoming this problem, a vertical bar of soft iron placed on the binnacle, was introduced many years later as the Flinders bar.

In a letter to Banks in 1804 Flinders first suggested the name Australia for the southern continent, and continued to use it himself for the next seven years. But in 1811, owing to official unwillingness to accept this name, he reverted to the name Terra Australis for the continent, which was the name he reluctantly used in the title of his *Voyage*. However, his small-scale chart of the entire continent was titled *General Chart of Terra Australis or Australia*. The first use of the name Australia by a government office in London was made by the Admiralty in 1824, when the charts of Phillip Parker King, who completed Flinders's survey of the continent, were published under the name of Australia in their titles with no mention of the name Terra Australis. There is a memorial tablet to Flinders in Donington parish church erected by instructions given in his will, and other memorials to him in Britain. He also became a popular hero in Australia. Statues were erected in Sydney, Melbourne, and Adelaide; Flinders River, Flinders Island, and other places, as well as Flinders University, were named after him, and he was the subject of popular biographies.

J. K. LAUGHTON, rev. ANDREW C. F. DAVID

Sources G. C. Ingleton, *Matthew Flinders: navigator and chartmaker* (1986) · E. Scott, *The life of Matthew Flinders Captain, R.N.* (1914) · J. D.

Mack, *Matthew Flinders, 1774–1814* (1966) · M. Flinders, *A voyage to Terra Australis*, 2 vols. (1814) · *Matthew Flinders: private journal 1803–1814* (1986) [facs. of the MS journal held in Mitchell Library with an introductory note by G. C. Ingleton] · M. Flinders, *Observations on the coasts of Van Diemen's Land, or Bass's strait and on part of the coasts of New South Wales* (1801) · *Matthew Flinders' narrative of his voyage in the schooner Francis, 1798*, ed. G. Rawson (1946) · *Matthew Flinders' narrative of Tom Thumb's cruise to Canoe rivulet*, ed. K. Bowden (1985) · J. S. Clarke, 'Biographical memoir of Captain Matthew Flinders', *Naval Chronicle*, 32 (1814), 177–91

Archives American Philosophical Society, Philadelphia, corresp. and papers [mainly copies] · CUL, Board of Longitude MSS, memoir explaining the construction of charts of Australia; log, corresp., and observations · Hydrographic Office, Taunton, MSS relating to Australia; MS charts · Lincs. Arch., family corresp. · Mitchell L., NSW, journals, letter-books, and corresp. · NMM, corresp. and papers · PRO, logbooks; MSS relating to Australia; official corresp. · State Library of Victoria, Melbourne, La Trobe manuscript collection, MSS and corresp. | BL, letters to Sir Joseph Banks, etc., Add. MS 32439 · BL, Robert Brown MSS · BL, St Vincent's letter-book · Ministry of Defence, London, oil paintings by William Westall · Mitchell L., NSW, Brabourne Collection, Banks MSS · Mitchell L., NSW, King MSS · Mitchell L., NSW, journal kept by Samuel Smith on board *Investigator* · NHM, botanical drawings by Ferdinand Bauer · NHM, journal kept by Robert Brown and his zoological collection · NHM, journal kept by Peter Good, gardener · NL Aus., landscape and topographical drawings by William Westall

Likenesses coloured miniature, 1801?, State Library of New South Wales, Sydney, Australia; repro. in Ingleton, *Matthew Flinders* · T. A. de Chazal, portrait, 1807, repro. in Ingleton, *Matthew Flinders* · silhouette, 1812, repro. in Scott, *Life of Matthew Flinders*; formerly in possession of W. F. Petrie · print, *c.*1814, BM, NPG; repro. in Clarke, 'Biographical memoir' · H. G. de C. Jones, miniature, watercolour, 1919 (after original, 1801?), NPG [*see illus.*] · W. R. Colton, statue, 1925, Sydney, Australia · W. Gilbert, statue, 1925, Melbourne, Australia · B. Hitch, statue, 1934, Adelaide, Australia · stained-glass window, 1980, Donington parish church · Blood, engraving, repro. in Clarke, 'Biographical memoir' · C. Webb, stained-glass window (with Bass), Lincoln Cathedral

Wealth at death £3498 16s. 1d.: Mack, *Matthew Flinders*

Flint, Frank Stuart (1885–1960), writer and civil servant, was born on 19 December 1885 at 117 Barnsbury Road in Islington, London, one of several children of William Thomas Flint, a commercial traveller, and his wife, Hannah Alice Tricker. He grew up in a working-class area of London and attended local schools until the age of thirteen, when his family's financial circumstances forced him to seek a variety of unskilled jobs. A tall, gangly, bespectacled youth, he soon began a programme of independent reading, and through classes in typing and shorthand at a working men's night school qualified for a secretarial job in the civil service in 1904. His particular interests in poetry, history, and philosophy, however, combined with a gift for languages, encouraged him to move rapidly beyond his neighbourhood and class. His fluency in French and knowledge of European literature, coupled with his special focus on the French symbolist poets, placed him at the vanguard of early English modernism.

Flint began his career as a literary critic in 1908 writing articles and reviews in A. R. Orage's *New Age*. Through his work for this journal, and later for *The Egoist* and for Harriet Monroe's *Poetry* in Chicago, he introduced British and

then American readers to a range of new avant-garde writers, among them the French author Rémy de Gourmont and the Belgian poet Emile Verhaeren. He also initiated at this time important correspondences with a myriad of younger writers publishing in Paris in the *Mercure de France* and the *Nouvelle Revue Française*, among them Vildrac, Romains, Duhamel, Fort, and the Italian futurist Marinetti. He began to publish his own verse in Ford Madox Hueffer's *English Review* in 1909. On 20 November of that year he married Violet Maude Fisher (1883/4–1920), daughter of John Fisher, a school attendance officer, and published his first volume of poetry, *In the Net of Stars*, which featured both conventional love lyrics and experimental free verse, often on urban subjects and influenced by the poetic theories he was developing in the weekly conversations of the informal poetry club which included T. E. Hulme, Frances Tancred, Florence Farr, Edward Storer, and occasionally Ezra Pound.

Flint's reputation as an authority on modern French literature led in 1912 to his influential essay 'Contemporary French poetry' for a special issue of Harold Monro's *Poetry Review*. Here he described several schools of post-symbolist writing and emphasized both the importance of free verse as a prosodic mode and the image as a vital element in perception and literary expression. In 1913 he joined Hulme in a second, more formal poetry club and continued to publicize French verse in his column, 'French chronicle', in *Poetry and Drama*. He was also a member of Pound's circle of promising young writers, becoming particularly close friends with Richard Aldington and Hilda Doolittle (H. D.) and championing their new literary movement, imagism, in which he participated.

Flint contributed poems to Pound's anthology *Des imagistes* (1914) as well as to the three subsequent imagist anthologies edited by Richard Aldington and Amy Lowell (1915–17). In 1915 he published his second book of poems, *Cadences*, in which he experimented further with free verse, exploring the tensions between the beautiful and the squalid in modern life. The First World War interrupted his literary career, however, as many of his contemporaries entered the military, while his socialist sympathies were sharpened by the unrest both at home and abroad. His family obligations, which by this time included two children, Ianthe (*b.* 1911) and Oliver (*b.* 1914), pressed heavily upon him, and he clung to his civil service position, now in the Post Office, until conscripted in 1918. He served in the army for eleven months in primarily clerical capacities, remaining in home service, until demobilized in 1919. His most intimate friend during this period was Richard Aldington, who dedicated his poem 'The Walk' (1920) to Flint, revealing a deep affection echoed by Flint in his third and last book of verse, *Otherworld* (1920), in which he addressed the title-poem as well as 'Soldiers' 'To R. A.'.

When Flint's wife died in childbirth in 1920, he was devastated. Desperate for help in caring for his children, he married Violet's sister Ruth Ellen Fisher (*b.* 1884/5) within a few months, on 18 August 1920, a domestic arrangement which ended in their divorce in 1928, several years after they had ceased to live together. He became increasingly involved with socialist causes and with his new post in the overseas section of the statistics division of the Ministry of Labour. His influence on literary modernism consequently diminished. Unlike his fellow imagists he chose finally not to be a poet: he continued to translate (from French, German, and Russian) throughout the 1920s and wrote literary essays, notably for T. S. Eliot's *Criterion*, into the early 1930s, but his subjects grew increasingly topical as his early translation of literary works gave way to books about current events and general biography. His position as an authority on French literature passed to Aldington, and by the late 1920s he had turned his attention primarily to popular German non-fiction, which he translated with D. F. Tait, including René Fueloep-Miller's *Lenin und Gandhi* (as *Lenin and Gandhi*, 1927), *Die heilige Teufel: Rasputin und die Frauen* (as *Rasputin: the Holy Devil*, 1928), and *Macht und Geheimnis der Jesuiten* (as *The Power of the Jesuits*, 1930), and Arthur Polzer-Hoditz's *Kaiser Karl* (as *The Emperor Karl*, 1930). He concluded his writing career with two privately printed pamphlets: *Economic Equilibrium* (1940) and *Paying for War and Peace* (1948).

When Flint retired from the civil service in 1951 as chief of the overseas section of the Ministry of Labour's statistics divison, he was awarded the ISO. For the last years of his life, a burly and often cranky man with thick white hair, he lived in quiet isolation first in Highbury, London, then at West View, Harwell, Berkshire, where he died of a stroke on 28 February 1960; he was later cremated.

CAROLINE ZILBOORG

Sources M. M. Zajdel, 'Flint, F. S.', *British poets, 1880–1914*, ed. D. E. Stanford, DLitB, 19 (1983), 172–4 · *Richard Aldington and H. D.: the early years in letters*, ed. C. Zilboorg (1992) · C. N. Pondrom, *The road from Paris: French influence on English poetry* (1974) · G. Hughes, *Imagism and the imagists* (1931) · J. B. Harmer, *Victory in limbo: imagism, 1908–1917* (1975) · N. T. Gates, 'Richard Aldington and F. S. Flint: poets' dialogue', *Papers on Language & Literature*, 8 (winter 1972), 63–9 · C. Doyle, *Richard Aldington* (1989) · H. Underhill, 'F. S. Flint: zeppelin into moon', *Helix*, 13–14 (1983), 31–44 · H. Carpenter, *A serious character: the life of Ezra Pound* (1988) · F. S. Flint, autobiography, Ransom HRC · C. Pondrom, ed., 'H. D.'s letters to Flint', *Contemporary Literature*, 10 (autumn 1969), 557–86 · N. T. Gates, *Richard Aldington: an autobiography in letters* (1992) · *The poetry of Richard Aldington: a critical evaluation and an anthology of uncollected poems*, ed. N. T. Gates (1974) · b. cert. · m. certs. · *CGPLA Eng. & Wales* (1960) · private information (2004) [Oliver Flint]
Archives Ransom HRC · Yale U., Beinecke L. | Ransom HRC, Aldington MSS · Ransom HRC, H. D. MSS · Yale U., Beinecke L., T. S. Eliot MSS · Yale U., Beinecke L., H. D. MSS · Yale U., Beinecke L., Ezra Pound MSS
Likenesses group portrait, photograph, *c*.1914, repro. in Doyle, *Richard Aldington* · photograph, *c*.1920, repro. in Zajdel, 'Flint, F. S.'
Wealth at death £441: probate, 6 May 1960, *CGPLA Eng. & Wales*

Flint, George (*fl.* **1714–1750**), printer and political writer, was descended from a family resident in Newcastle upon Tyne, though no further details of his parentage and upbringing are known. By his own account he received his education in a custom house, in a bank, and by travel. He claimed that he 'threw up a very handsome fortune to take the pen in hand', paying 'the whole expense of printing &c. out of my own pocket' (letter of George Flint to the

earl of Mar, 18 June 1718, *Stuart Papers*, 6.551). He was a convert to Roman Catholicism and was greatly assisted in his religion and in his Jacobite activities by his wife, Mary (*fl.* 1715–1750), about whom further details are unknown. Flint claimed to have been involved in trying to organize a rising against George I in 1714, but was seriously ill at the time of the 1715 rising. His most significant contribution to the Jacobite cause was the production of notoriously treasonable newspapers between 1715 and 1717.

Flint began his *Weekly Remarks and Political Reflections, Upon the Most Material News Foreign and Domestick* in 1715, and it continued into 1716. *Robin's Last Shift* first appeared in February 1716, became the *Shift Shifted* later that year, and re-emerged as the *Shift's Last Shift* in February 1717 as it sought to evade government persecution. The printer Isaac Dalton was fined, gaoled, and pilloried for producing the *Shift Shifted*, but it was continued by James Alexander, the churchwarden of Robert Orme's nonjuring meeting-house. Flint himself was arrested, fined, and imprisoned in 1716, but continued to write and publish.

Flint's own accounts of his propaganda efforts while in gaol, admittedly written later in order to plead for financial support from the Jacobite leadership, gave a graphic account of his activities:

> When not quite recovered, I betook myself to those labours which had like to have ended at Tyburn, and in prison, when sick and in bed unable to wield a pen, I caused my wife to write by me, and when shut up from the sight & hearing of mankind other than the jailers, I caused them by my wife's means, unknown to themselves, to fetch and carry my papers, had in spite of them pen, ink and paper and wrote from 1 to 5 or 6 in the morning … our enemies oft said and still say I did them more harm than all the rest of their enemies. (Flint to Mar, *Stuart Papers*, 6.551)

Flint claimed that 'during his first three months in prison he caused forty or fifty thousand Papers against the Government to circulate every week throughout the three Nations' (petition of George Flint, [1729], Royal Stuart MS 131/46). The Flints retained a very high estimation of the importance of their work even in 1745, with Mary Flint writing to James Edgar, the secretary of the Old Pretender (James Stuart), 'The same Government, that in 1715 boasted It self everywhere settled for ever, trembled before the End of 1716. What wrought this change but the Pen?' (Mary Flint to James Edgar, 2 Aug 1745, Royal Stuart MS 266/161). These accounts were to some extent confirmed by contemporary writers of different political persuasions and by members of the Jacobite court in exile. Flint was recognized by both the earl of Mar and the Old Pretender's mother, Queen Mary of Modena, as a worthy candidate for financial aid when he arrived at Calais in 1717. He was commissioned by Mar to write further Jacobite pamphlets to be sent back into Britain. He received a small sum of money on the orders of 'James III' in 1729, and he was later assisted by the Roman Catholic Jacobite landowner John Baptiste Caryll.

In his various writings Flint portrayed the Hanoverian regime as illiberal, arbitrary, and often illegal in its actions. His newspapers included praise of the Old Pretender's personal qualities, encouragement for moderation in the treatment of the Jacobite rebels, and increasingly virulent attacks on Britain as a military state, with a standing army safeguarding a severe and cruel administration and an illegally perpetuated parliament. His writing seems to fit into the canon of so-called 'whig Jacobites' who, whether through conviction or opportunism, sought to use contract theory arguments to embarrass the Hanoverians (Chapman, 36, 242).

Flint's imprisonment in 1716 had seen him confined to Newgate. A charge of high treason was levelled against him and he was due to be tried in the week after Easter. Anticipating a death sentence he contrived to escape, disguised 'in a Footman's Habit'. He remained

> undiscover'd till two or three Days after, his Wife having told the Keeper who came to ask for him, That he was dangerously sick in Bed, and not fit to be disturb'd: For which Fidelity to her Husband, who is now beyond the Seas, she was put into the Condemn'd Hold, and us'd after the most barbarous manner, to extort a Confession. (*The History of the Press Yard*, 1717, 137)

He fled to France, where his wife was eventually able to join him. According to one source sympathetic to the government, 'Mary Flint's Fine was adjusted, and her Fees paid out of the Popish Fund for Sufferers: Which is a fresh Proof how Libels against the Government are carried on' (*The Secret History of the Rebels in Newgate*, 2nd edn, 1717, 46).

In exile Flint tried hard over many months to persuade Jacobite leaders to support him in further propaganda attempts. He felt that, far from encouraging him, 'much pains have been taken to keep me silent' (George Flint to Captain Booth, [1718], *Stuart Papers*, 6.480), though, as noted, he did receive limited support through the mediation of the earl of Mar in 1718. However, this was insufficient to sustain the sort of propaganda campaign that Flint envisaged, and it was short-lived. In February 1719 Nathaniel Mist's *Weekly Journal, or, Saturday's Post* reported that Flint had been forced to leave Calais for Dunkirk, and had been arrested on his return. On 7 March 1719 he wrote to the earl of Mar from a Calais gaol, apparently having visited England for recruitment purposes. He was released on condition that he left Calais again. At some point in 1720 he wrote from Rheims to the keeper of Newgate to threaten legal action if his plays, papers, and books were not returned. Also in 1720 he was imprisoned for debt in Calais, where he languished for twenty months. In 1729 he petitioned the Old Pretender, emphasizing his zeal in 'begging for many years, as if it had been for the salvation of his Soul, to have the Pen imploy'd in Yr Service'. However, he found, 'every where branded him a Madman, stamp'd him a dreaded Bugbear even to his own party, avoided, hated, despised, ridiculed, himself and his family perishing unpitied' (petition of George Flint, [1729], Royal Stuart MS 142/141). He was still writing to proffer seemingly unwanted propaganda advice in 1744 and 1745. Some assistance was had from the Roman Catholic church, and Flint also wrote theological tracts during his long exile.

Flint's career seems to typify the dedication and endurance of many committed Jacobites, together with the ingenuity and courage of several resourceful Jacobite publicists like Mist, Francis Clifton, James Alexander, and John Purser. His story also shows the frustration that many felt at the lack of effective leadership and direction from the exiled Stuart court and the supposed Jacobite leaders in Britain. A letter from his wife to John Caryll (BL, Add. MS 28231/60) confirms that Flint was alive in July 1750; however details of his date and place of death are unknown.

PAUL CHAPMAN

Sources P. M. Chapman, 'Jacobite political argument in England, 1714–66', PhD diss., U. Cam., 1983 · Bodl. Oxf., Nichols newspapers · Royal Arch., Royal Stuart MSS, 131/46; 142/141; 266/161 · *Calendar of the Stuart papers belonging to his majesty the king, preserved at Windsor Castle*, 7 vols., HMC, 56 (1902–23), vol. 6 · BL, Add. MS 28231, fol. 60
Archives Bodl. Oxf., Nichols newspapers · Royal Arch., Royal Stuart MSS, letters

Flint, Robert (1838–1910), philosopher and theologian, born at Applegarth, near Dumfries, on 14 March 1838, was the son of Robert Flint, a farm overseer, and his wife, Grace, *née* Paterson. His first school was at Moffat. In 1852 he entered Glasgow University, where he distinguished himself in arts and divinity. He won a number of prizes but did not graduate, preferring not to concentrate his studies on preparation for exams. Having been employed as a lay missionary by the Elders' Association of Glasgow, he was licensed to preach in 1858, and for a short time acted as assistant to the prominent Presbyterian minister Norman Macleod (1812–1872) at the Barony Church, Glasgow. He was minister of the East Church, Aberdeen (1859–62), and of Kilconquhar, Fife (1862–4), a country parish, which gave him time for study and for visits to Germany.

On the death of James Frederick Ferrier in 1864 Flint was elected to succeed him in the moral philosophy chair at St Andrews University, despite T. H. Green's presence among the competing candidates. He held this chair until 1876, when he succeeded Thomas Jackson Crawford in the divinity chair of Edinburgh University. On this appointment he was made LLD of Glasgow and DD of Edinburgh. Flint was Baird lecturer (1876–7), Stone lecturer at Princeton (1880), and Croall lecturer (1887–8). He became a fellow of the Royal Society of Edinburgh on 1 March 1880, and on 21 May 1883 he was elected corresponding member of the Institut de France (Académie des Sciences Morales et Politiques). Fellowship of the British Academy followed in 1901. Further honours came from the universities of Princeton (DD, 1896), Yale (LLD, 1901), Glasgow (DD, 1901), Edinburgh (LLD 1903), and Aberdeen (DD, 1906). He resigned his chair in 1903 to devote himself to writing and lived at Musselburgh for some time. He was appointed Gifford lecturer for 1908–9, but was unable to deliver his lectures owing to ill health. He died, unmarried, at 5 Royal Terrace, Edinburgh, on 25 November 1910 and was buried in Liberton churchyard.

Slightly built and of pale complexion with a dark moustache, Flint had few intimates, though his relations with his parents and sister Margaret were close. He lived much of his life apart, a devoted student and an ardent researcher. These qualities are especially in evidence in his *The Philosophy of History in France and Germany* (1874) and *History of the Philosophy of History* (1893). His interest in the philosophy of history is further exemplified in his book on the Italian philosopher *Vico* (1884). He had no taste for amusements, and country walks were his only recreation. As a teacher he was popular, for he was patient and kind; yet of those whom he taught only two were ever privileged to accompany him in his walks. His students were stimulated to the exercise of their own minds and to the attainment of a high intellectual standard. In church matters he kept aloof from many current controversies, though in *The Duties of the People of Scotland to the Church of Scotland* (1882) he argued strongly for the maintenance of the national church on a basis of 'mutual understanding, conciliation and peace'. In 1895 he declined to serve as moderator of the general assembly of the Church of Scotland.

Flint's methods were deliberate, his composition slow and sure in a small and neat handwriting, his speech measured and with some peculiarities of enunciation, such as 'awtoms' or 'know-ledge'. All his work was planned on a large scale; the cycle of his divinity lectures extended to seven sessions; his best-known books, complete in themselves, were parts of wider schemes; his sermons, examples of which are in his *Sermons and Addresses* (1899), were once described as of 'magnificent length and toughness'. As a thinker, his characteristic was the confidence with which he brought all matters to the test of reason, trusting it as a guide to positive conclusions, and resting nothing on sentimental or prudential grounds. He welcomed every advance of physical science and speculative thought as enlarging the field for critical investigation. Flint was an early student of *Socialism* (1894). He welcomed its emphasis upon fraternity, but questioned its more revolutionary (as opposed to evolutionary) expressions. He found it opposed to Christianity in so far as it is allied with atheism or materialism and is exclusively this-worldly. He felt that it thought more of socio-economic conditions than of moral character, and threatened the individual's rights. His papers *On Theological, Biblical and other Subjects* (1905) clearly reveal his awareness of other current intellectual trends.

It is as one who offered an intellectual defence of the faith—an apologist—that Flint is best remembered. In connection with the Edinburgh University tercentenary in 1884, in a series of professorial portraits by William Hole he is etched in knightly armour as champion of the common faith. Here, as elsewhere, his constructive work is strongly rooted in the history of the discipline (see, for example, his 'Theism' in the ninth edition of the *Encyclopaedia Britannica*, to which he also contributed the article on 'Theology'). His Baird lectures of 1876 and 1877, republished respectively in 1889 and 1879 as *Theism* and *Anti-Theistic Theories* (including a critique of materialism and

pantheism) and his Croall lectures, published as *Agnosticism* (1903), comprise an impressive, if not finally satisfying, trilogy in which he argues for the existence of God and for the reasonableness of belief in him, while opposing contrary positions. His case, which turns initially upon the conviction that in the absence of a priori knowledge of God we must argue inferentially, places him in the line of Butler and Paley; and while he did not believe that a coercive proof of God's existence could be adduced, he thought that the cumulative effect of the cosmological, teleological, and moral arguments was intellectually persuasive, and preferable to alternative views, whether supportive of belief grounded in feeling rather than intellect, or materialistic, or agnostic. While he believed that his favoured arguments both proved God's existence and indicated his nature, he granted that apologetics leaves us only at the threshold. It does not yield the holiness or the love of God; it does not prescribe the antidote to sin; it does not provide the impetus to newness of life. For these we need God's revelation in scripture.

Although alive to current thought, Flint was by no means bowled over by it. Thus, although he could accommodate evolutionary theory (as indicative of the divine method, not as an account of origins) within his theological perspective, he did not capitulate to the idealism of his contemporaries John and Edward Caird at Glasgow, which was then in the ascendant. Nevertheless, his conviction that at the end of our apologetic journey we come to the a priori conviction that this is how things must be prompted such critics as James Lindsay and Alfred Caldecott to wonder why Flint did not go over to the fully transcendentalist position. It would appear that like the idealists themselves, Flint believed more than could readily be contained by his apologetic method.   ALAN P. F. SELL

Sources D. Macmillan, *The life of Robert Flint, DD, LLD* (1914) • A. P. F. Sell, *Defending and declaring the faith: some Scottish examples, 1860–1920* (1987) • *The Scotsman* (26 Nov 1910) • *The Times* (26 Nov 1910) • *Fasti Scot.* • W. I. Addison, *A roll of graduates of the University of Glasgow from 31st December 1727 to 31st December 1897* (1898), 198 • *WWW* • *Life and Work* (Jan 1911), 18–19 • S. R. Obitts, 'The thought of Robert Flint', PhD diss., U. Edin., 1962 • A. Caldecott, *The philosophy of religion in England and America* (1901) • J. Dickie, *Fifty years of British theology* (1937) • J. K. Mozley, *Some tendencies in British theology* (1951) • B. M. G. Reardon, *From Coleridge to Gore: a century of religious thought in Britain* (1971)
Archives U. Edin., MSS and notebooks; lectures, MSS, and sermons | NL Scot., corresp. with Blackwoods
Likenesses G. Reid, oils, 1903, U. Edin. • W. Hole, etching, NPG; repro. in W. Hole, *Quasi Cursores* (1884) • oils, U. St Andr. • portraits, repro. in Macmillan, *Life of Robert Flint*
Wealth at death £3229 8s. 10d.: confirmation, 8 Feb 1911, CCI

Flint, Sir William Russell (1880–1969), artist, was born on 4 April 1880 in Edinburgh, one of three children of Francis Wighton Flint, a graphic designer and watercolourist, and Jane Purves, a civil servant. The Flints' two sons, William Russell and Robert Purves (1883–1947), both became artists and a daughter, Charlotte Elisabeth, a pianist. Flint was a pupil at Daniel Stewart's College for Boys and the Royal Institution School of Art, Edinburgh. He then served an apprenticeship with Banks & Co. as a lithographer and designer for six years, beginning in 1894. He travelled to London in 1900 for a post with Messrs Bale, Sons, and Danielsson as a medical illustrator recording the effects of leprosy, eye disease, and Second South African War wounds. He then took part-time work so that he could enrol at Heatherley's Art School. From 1903 to 1907 he was an illustrator for the *Illustrated London News*. His first big success was a commission from Cassell to illustrate Rider Haggard's *King Solomon's Mines*.

At Heatherley's Flint met another budding young artist named Sibylle Sueter (*b.* 1875?), the daughter of fleet-paymaster J. T. Sueter RN and sister of Admiral Sir Murray Sueter CB RN. The couple were married on 12 August 1905 in the Presbyterian church in George's Street. Their first residence was in Eyot Gardens, St Peter's Square, Hammersmith. They shared a love of travel, art, and lively discussion. In 1912 the Flints settled in Rome for a year, taking a studio in the famous bohemian artistic community at the Villa Strohl-Fern where the painter John William Godward (1861–1922) befriended them and whose influence is clear in Flint's aestheticist interiors such as *Silver and Gold* (1930; City of Birmingham Art Gallery). The Flints toured Italy, visiting the natural and historical sites which often appear in his watercolours: the fountains at Tivoli, the canals of Venice, the temples of Paestum and Montegufoni, and the salons held at Sir Osbert Sitwell's Florentine villa attended by artists and ballerinas such as Moira Shearer who became one of Flint's favourite models. In 1915 the marriage produced a son, Francis Russell Flint, who also became an artist. During the First World War Flint first served as a lieutenant in the Royal Naval Volunteer Reserve, designing and inspecting rigid airships, and later as a captain in the RAF. The family settled in Peel Cottage, west London, in 1925, where Flint was to live and work for the rest of his life.

Characterized by Charles Wheeler, president of the Royal Academy, as an artist of 'a steady hand, keen eye and gay spirit in a shaky world' (*Exhibition of Works by Sir William Russell Flint*, 4) Flint himself stated he was inspired by 'many sorts of beauty' (ibid.) and a determination to address both populist and artistic milieus with his artwork. A pragmatist as well as an aesthete, Flint's father had ensured that his son was educated (and as such employable) through both industrial apprenticeships and academic studios. Flint's illustrations encompassed both medical journals and artistic book illustrations. His watercolours inspired numerous appreciative articles in the *Studio Magazine* and reached a huge popular audience as affordable prints. The breadth of Flint collectors includes influential patrons such as Marcus B. Huish, who also commissioned Whistler's Venetian etchings, and the American newspaper magnate William Randolf Hearst, as well as the general public and over forty public museums.

Flint's membership in many leading artistic societies reflected both the critical acclaim accorded to him by the London art world during his own lifetime and the breadth of media in which he excelled. First an associate in 1914, then a member in 1919, Flint was elected president of the Royal Society of Painters in Water Colours and served in

that post for twenty years. *Castanets* (1933; RA) was accepted as Flint's diploma work when he was made a Royal Academician and he was honoured with a one-man retrospective held in the Royal Academy's diploma gallery in 1962, a privilege accorded to only five other contemporary artists. His election as a member by the Royal Society of Painter-Etchers and Engravers and a silver medal at the 1913 Paris Salon for his edition of Mallory's *Morte d'Arthur* recognized his gifts as an illustrator. Both Flint's institutional recognition and broad popularity were underlined by his ennoblement as a knight bachelor in 1947.

Flint's nudes have dominated his reputation. He clothed an unchanging perfectly proportioned female type in various exotic guises, most frequently as romanticized Spanish Gypsies as in *Four Singers of Vera* (undated; Kelvingrove Art Gallery, Glasgow), reminiscent of Sargent's *El Jaleo*, and rococo fantasies. The arresting linearity of his illustrations for Homer's *Odyssey* (1924; Medici Society) and the oil painting *Artemis and Chione* (undated; Harris Museum and Art Gallery, Preston) capture Flint's participation in art deco's stylization of classical precedents. Spaces of creativity such as the artist's studio and the ballet rehearsal room were also a favourite theme. His commitment to life drawing was matched by a love of *plein-air* technique; he always declared that landscape was his favourite subject. Regrettably, these works remain less well known, as they are principally held in private collections. The atmospheric effects of Flint's watercolours infuse the distinctive terrain and architecture of the continent and his beloved Scotland, which the Flint family toured annually, not only with a sensitivity of mood but also a vibrancy of colour and freedom of wash which both emulates and modernizes the achievements of British topographical watercolour painting. He created dynamic relationships between subtle colour washes or vigorous chalk or pencil line and the rich colours and textures of the antique supporting papers he often used.

'Somewhere between the art of striptease and the art of painting and drawing' (Newton, 5), Flint's personal formula of idealized, eroticized, unindividualized female anatomy has become more problematic in light of the women's movements of recent decades. He began his artistic career recording the atrocities enacted upon the human body by war or disease. In a private fantasy world transcribed with consummate draughtsmanship, Flint imagined away all signs of the ravages of the twentieth century and perhaps lost sight of the individual and natural imperfections which make a woman's body unique and beautiful. Flint died in Paddington Hospital on 27 December 1969.   CLAIRE I. R. O'MAHONY

Sources K. S. Gardner and N. D. Clark, *Sir William Russell Flint, 1880–1969: a comparative review of the artist's signed limited edition prints* (1986) · C. I. R. O'Mahony, *An exhibition of watercolours and drawings by Sir William Russell Flint RA, PRWS* (1997) [exhibition catalogue, Richard Green Gallery, 1997] · R. Lewis, *Sir William Russell Flint, 1880–1969* (1980) · A. Palmer, *More than shadows: a biography of W. Russell Flint RA, PRWS* (1942) · E. Newton, *The Guardian* (19 Oct 1962) · W. R. Flint, *Drawings* (1950) · W. R. Flint, *Models of propriety*

(1951) • W. R. Flint, *Minxes admonished, or, Beauty reproved* (1955) • *Pictures from the artist's studio* (1962) [exhibition catalogue, RA] • *Exhibition of works by Sir William Russell Flint RA, PRWS* (1962) [exhibition catalogue, RA] • W. R. Flint, *Shadows in Arcady* (1965) • W. R. Flint, *The lisping goddess: a figurehead fantasy* (1968) • W. R. Flint, *Breakfast in Perigord* (1968) • W. R. Flint, *In pursuit: an autobiography* (1970)

Archives NL Scot., corresp. • V&A, corresp., diaries, and MSS; notebooks | Richard Green Gallery, London, catalogue of all works and MSS in his picture collection • V&A NAL, letters to Dame Hildelith Cumming | SOUND NSA, BBC radio interview with Flint, BBC LP 152

Likenesses W. Stoneman, photograph, 1947, NPG • photograph, 1962, RA • photographs, NPG • photographs, Sir Russell Flint Galleries Ltd, Bristol

Wealth at death £140,766: probate, 13 Feb 1970, *CGPLA Eng. & Wales*

Flinter, George Dawson (*d.* 1838), army officer in the Spanish service, by birth an Irishman, entered the British army in 1811 as an ensign in the 7th West India regiment, and was promoted lieutenant on 22 July 1813. He went with his regiment to Curaçao in the West Indies in 1812, and in 1815 visited Caracas, then suffering a bloody civil war which gave rise to many terrible atrocities. There he acted as interpreter to the British embassy. In 1816 he was placed on the half pay list, and, seeing no prospect of promotion in the British service, he resided at Caracas, where he was treated as someone of distinction by the captain general, Cagigal, and obtained employment as interpreter between the Spaniards and the English and Americans. He afterwards travelled in the West Indies and South America, married a Spanish American lady, through whom he acquired much land and many slaves, and obtained a commission in the Spanish army as a staff officer, although remaining on the British half pay list until 1832.

On the outbreak of the Carlist war in 1833 Flinter declared for Isabella, and in 1834–5 he served under Mina and Valdez in their unsuccessful operations against Zumalacarregui in the Basque provinces. In 1836, while organizing the militia in La Mancha, he was surprised by some of the troops of Gómez and Cabrera at Almaden, and taken prisoner. He escaped, with the connivance of his gaoler, made his way to Madrid, and was placed in command of Toledo; from there on 18 February 1838 he made a sortie, defeating the Carlists under Jara and Peco, who were in great force in the neighbourhood. On his return to Toledo on 20 February he was welcomed by the municipal authorities as the liberator of the province, and on 22 February the Cortes thanked him.

On 16 March, though outnumbered by two to one, Flinter drove Basileo García out of Valdepeñas, but he was prevented by lack of reinforcements from exploiting this. His conduct was censured by the Spanish government, and he was removed from his command. On 9 September 1838, maddened by disappointment and disgust, he committed suicide in Madrid by cutting his throat. Flinter was a knight of the royal order of Isabella the Catholic, and the author of several works on the Spanish empire in Latin America.　　　　　J. M. RIGG, *rev.* CHARLES ESDAILE

Sources *Army List* (1812) • *Army List* (1813) • *Army List* (1816) • *Army List* (1832) • *GM*, 2nd ser., 9 (1838) • A. Pirala, *Historia de la guerra civil y de los Partidos Liberal y Carlista*, ed. J. Arostegui, 6 vols. (1984)

Flintoft, Luke (*c.*1680–1727), clergyman and composer, was a native of Yorkshire. He was admitted a sizar at Queens' College, Cambridge, on 6 July 1697 and took his BA in 1700. He was appointed a chorister at Trinity College in May 1698, chaplain of King's College in 1700, ordained deacon at Lincoln in 1701, and priest in 1702. He was a priest vicar-choral at Lincoln Cathedral, 1704–14, and was sworn a gentleman of the Chapel Royal on 4 December 1715. He held the living of Inkberrow, Yorkshire, from 1713. On 9 July 1719 he was appointed reader in Whitehall Chapel, and was subsequently made a minor canon of Westminster. He died in London on 3 November 1727 and was buried in the cloisters of Westminster Abbey.

To Flintoft is attributed the composition of a double chant in G minor, which (against the claims of William Morley's double chant in D) is probably the earliest known example of the form. In 1866 the music antiquary Edward Rimbault claimed to be in possession of a manuscript album containing the chant, dating from not later than 1725.　　　　　　　　　　　　　　　K. D. REYNOLDS

Sources Venn, *Alum. Cant.* • W. Shaw, 'Flintoft, Luke', *New Grove* • *DNB* • *N&Q*, 3rd ser., 10 (1866), 206 • *N&Q*, 3rd ser., 11 (1866), 267, 391, 445

Flitcroft, Henry (1697–1769), architect, was born on 30 August 1697, the son of Jeffery Flitcroft, a labourer at Hampton Court, and was apprenticed as a joiner to Thomas Morris of London from November 1711 to November 1718. His rise from this humble start was the result of a happy accident. The story that he came to the notice of Richard Boyle, third earl of Burlington, when he fell off a ladder while working on the reconstruction of Burlington House, Piccadilly, appears to be supported by payments for medical care of an injured workman in the earl's accounts in late 1719.

The patronage of Lord Burlington provided the recent apprentice with a thorough education in architecture. Initially Flitcroft showed skill as a draughtsman and his clinical pen-and-wash style, sometimes enlivened with a thick flourish in the title, characterizes many of his drawings for Burlington's buildings. In addition he made copies of the earl's newly acquired drawings of Palladio and Jones, many of which were published by William Kent in 1727 as the *Designs of Inigo Jones*. At the same time Flitcroft provided drawings or on-site attendance for architectural commissions on which Burlington was engaged, such as Tottenham House, Wiltshire, for his brother-in-law Lord Bruce. Flitcroft's wide competence having been proved, Burlington ensured his appointment as clerk of works at Whitehall, Westminster, and St James's palaces in 1726. From this Flitcroft proceeded through the office of works as master carpenter in 1746, then master mason and deputy surveyor in 1748, and finally comptroller from 1758 until his death. By 1733 Flitcroft was already thought too busy to supervise the day-to-day work on the new Treasury building in Whitehall and during thirty years as a stalwart member of the office of works he is estimated to have attended over 1100 meetings of the board.

The indirect influence of Lord Burlington, as well as his

own good conduct of business, ensured Flitcroft a considerable private architectural practice. His first commissions in the late 1720s were two small houses in Essex, and he was successful in the competition against James Gibbs and others for the design of St Giles-in-the-Fields, the first purely Palladian church in London. But a succession of important aristocratic commissions—such as Montagu House, Whitehall, for John, second duke of Montagu, in 1731, the completion of the east front of Wentworth Woodhouse, Yorkshire, from 1735 for Thomas Watson-Wentworth, earl of Malton, of Wimpole, Cambridgeshire, from 1742 for Philip Yorke, Baron Hardwicke, and finally Woburn, Bedfordshire, from 1748—is evidence of growing repute. When William Pultney, earl of Bath, fell out with him in 1742 and hoped to have him removed from the board of works, he found that 'this Flitcroft had many great Supporters' (Pultney to Z. Pearce, Westminster Abbey Muniments, 64662), including the duke of Cumberland, whose architectural tutor he had been between 1733 and 1737. Although work for his grander patrons is better documented, Flitcroft also provided designs for much more humble figures, such as his friend William Stukeley or the Yorkshire gentleman Thomas Yarborough of Campsmount.

The building operations at Wentworth Woodhouse and at Woburn were carried out on a large scale, and the fact that in both he took over from another architect suggests that Flitcroft was regarded as a trusted manager of such building campaigns. Robert Morris's *Art of Architecture* (1742) suggested (p. 32) he was well qualified to

> correct your Plan,
> [And] freely, when you err, instruct the Man
> In what's amiss, with Judgement, and with Care,
> Where needful add; and where profusive; spare.

The architectural result of Flitcroft's interventions was rarely innovative. Established Palladian motifs were deployed on elevations, with a combination of two canonical window types, the Palladian and the Diocletian, placed one above the other over a rusticated door as a central emphasis. This astylar arrangement, introduced at Wimpole in 1732 and found at Milton, Northamptonshire, in 1750 and elsewhere, suggests deliberate avoidance of the central portico which may have endeared him to careful clients in a period of economic stringency. But following the injunction of Inigo Jones, who had made a distinction between solid and unaffected external architecture and imaginative internal design, the reticence of Flitcroft's exterior work contrasts with the extravagance of his interiors. Even small early works such as Boreham Hall, Essex, of 1729 exhibit the richness of Palladian wood-and plasterwork, but the full range of Flitcroft's versatility can be seen in the apartments of Woburn Abbey (1748–61), reconstructed for John Russell, fourth duke of Bedford. Orthodox Palladianism is varied with French rococo and designs taken from Robert Wood's recently published *Ruins of Palmyra* (1753), with strict regard to the appropriateness of each form of decoration to the function of the rooms. Flitcroft is now best seen as a decorator of interiors

and few garden buildings survive, of which the most interesting, including a temple of Apollo indebted to Wood's *Ruins of Balbec* (1757), were designed for Henry Hoare at Stourhead, Wiltshire.

On 4 June 1724 Flitcroft married Sarah Minns and they had one son, Henry (1742–1826), a barrister. By the 1740s he was living in Hampstead, where he built himself a house called Frognal Grove. The decade which opened with Morris's repeated commendation in the *Art of Architecture* saw the height of his reputation. Speculative building in London, often in conjunction with the mason and statuary John Devall, would have made Flitcroft prosperous, but the source which first refers to him by the sobriquet of Burlington Harry also remembers him as a 'formal, good kind of man' (Hardcastle, 2.243). Flitcroft died on 25 February 1769, in Hampstead, and his son erected a monument in his memory at Teddington, Middlesex, where he was buried. He was also survived by his wife.

T. P. CONNOR

Sources Colvin, *Archs.* · H. M. Colvin and others, eds., *The history of the king's works*, 6 vols. (1963–82) · W. A. Littledale, ed., *The registers of St Bene't and St Peter, Paul's Wharf, London*, 2, Harleian Society, register section, 39 (1910) · E. Hardcastle [W. H. Pyne], *Wine and walnuts, or, After dinner chit-chat*, 2nd edn, 2 vols. (1824) · H. Flitcroft, letter to W. Stukeley, c.1723–1724, Bodl. Oxf., Gough maps 229, fol. 139 · T. Friedman, 'Baroque into Palladian: the designing of St. Giles-in-the-Fields', *Architectural History*, 40 (1997), 115–43 · G. Worsley, 'Woburn Abbey, Bedfordshire', *Country Life*, 187/16 (22 April 1993), 51–5 · M. Draper, 'The houses of the Russell family', *Apollo*, 127 (1988), 387–92 · J. Allen, 'Wentworth Woodhouse', *Archaeological Journal*, 137 (1980), 393–6 · K. Woodbridge, *Landscape and antiquity: aspects of English culture at Stourhead, 1718 to 1838* (1970) · J. Park, *History of Hampstead* (1818), 337–8 · R. Morris, *Art of architecture* (1742) · Westminster Abbey Muniments, 64662 · J. Roberts, *Royal landscapes: the gardens and parks of Windsor* (1997) · D. Lysons, *The environs of London*, 3 (1795), 507 · apprenticeship ledger of Joyners Company, GL
Archives Beds. & Luton ARS, accounts relating to work at Woburn Abbey · Woburn Abbey, papers relating to Woburn Abbey | Bedford estate office, London, Russell MSS · Bodl. Oxf., Gough maps 229
Likenesses attrib. B. Dandridge, oils, RIBA

Flood, Sir Frederick, baronet (1741–1824), lawyer and politician, was the younger son of John Flood (*d.* 1774), landowner and politician, of Farmley, co. Kilkenny, Ireland, and his wife, Jane Crompton. He was the nephew of Warden Flood, chief justice of the court of king's bench in Ireland, and thus a cousin of Henry Flood (1732–1791), politician. He was educated at Trinity College, Dublin, where he proceeded BA in 1761, MA in 1764, LLB in 1766, and LLD in 1772. He trained at the King's Inns, Dublin, and was made KC in 1768 and a bencher of the King's Inns in 1770. He was called to the Irish bar in 1764 and soon attained a sizeable legal practice; in the social circles of Dublin he was immensely popular. He married first, on 31 May 1765, Juliana Donovan (*d.* 1768), daughter of Richard Donovan of Camolin Park, co. Wexford, and second, on 15 May 1769, Frances Cavendish, daughter of Sir Henry Cavendish, first baronet, of Doveridge, Derbyshire.

Flood succeeded to considerable estates from both his

parents, and in 1776 was elected to the Irish House of Commons as member for Enniscorthy. He sat for that constituency until 1783. From 1783 to 1790 he was MP for Ardfert, and in 1796–7 for Carlow borough. He purchased his return for all three constituencies. On 3 June 1780 he was created a baronet of Ireland 'of Newton Ormonde, co. Kilkenny, and Banna Lodge, co. Wexford'. He was made a placeman by the earl of Buckingham's administration. This position ultimately separated him from his cousin Henry Flood. In 1783 he did not support his cousin's famous motion for a reform of the Irish parliament. He lost office probably because he deserted the administration during the regency crisis of 1788–9. He took a prominent part in the volunteer movement and was elected colonel of the Wexford regiment. In many debates which preceded the abolition of the Irish parliament Flood was a frequent speaker. Barrington called him an ostentatious blunderer, whose 'bulls' did not contain the pith of sound sense which underlay the mistakes of Sir Boyle Roche. He added that Flood would rashly accept any suggestions made to him while speaking, and one day, just after he had declared 'that the magistrates of Wexford deserved the thanks of the lord-lieutenant', he added, on some wit's suggestion, 'and should be whipped at the cart's tail' (Barrington, i.111). Even though he was neither in office nor an MP, he steadily opposed the Act of Union, but when that measure was carried he did not retire from politics.

In 1801 Lord Ely, a political rival in Wexford, declared that Flood wished to stand in the Catholic interest at the next general election and to act as an independent. Ely's intention was to prejudice the government against Flood. Lord Mountnorris, who commanded a major political interest in the county, declared his support for Flood. Privately, the government was assured of Flood's support should he be returned, but in the event, however, he was persuaded not to stand. In the 1806 general election he rendered his support to two government candidates and in return he was appointed *custos rotulorum* for Wexford. In 1812 he was returned as MP for co. Wexford without a contest, yet he did not fulfil his ambition of becoming a privy councillor, largely because he was deemed unreliable by the Richmond administration at Dublin Castle. He sat as MP until 1818 but did not seek re-election. In order to dispel the image of him as a place-hunter, he set about displaying his independency at the castle and at Westminster. The result was that he became one of the most colourful MPs in the house. Yet, in common with most 'independent' Irish members, he generally supported the ministry of the day. He had a particularly close understanding with Peel, the Irish secretary.

Flood's only son died unmarried in 1800. It was proposed to perpetuate the title by creating Flood a baronet of the United Kingdom, with remainder to his only surviving child, Frances, daughter of his second wife, who was married to Richard Solly. Flood died on 1 February 1824, before the patent for this new honour had passed the great seal, and he left his estates to his grandson, Richard Solly, who took the name of Flood in addition to his own.

H. M. STEPHENS, *rev.* THOMAS P. POWER

Sources P. J. Jupp, 'Irish parliamentary representation, 1800–1820', PhD diss., U. Reading, 1966 • Burke, *Gen. Ire.* (1904) • Burtchaell & Sadleir, *Alum. Dubl.*, 2nd edn • E. Keane, P. Beryl Phair, and T. U. Sadleir, eds., *King's Inns admission papers, 1607–1867*, IMC (1982) • J. Barrington, *Personal sketches of his own times*, 3 vols. (1827–32) • H. Grattan, *Memoirs of the life and times of the Rt Hon. Henry Grattan*, 5 vols. (1839–46) • F. Hardy, *Memoirs of the political and private life of James Caulfeild, earl of Charlemont* (1810)
Archives BL, corresp., Add. MS 19349 | BL, corresp. with Robert Peel, Add. MS 40218

Flood, Henry (1732–1791), politician, was born out of wedlock to Warden Flood (1694–1764), solicitor-general, attorney-general, and chief justice of the king's bench in Ireland, and Isabella Whiteside (*d.* 1778) at Donnybrook, co. Dublin. Following instruction from private tutors and Mr Butler, a Dublin schoolmaster, he was admitted, aged fifteen, to Trinity College, Dublin, as a fellow-commoner in December 1747. After three years he left Trinity for Christ Church, Oxford, where his tutor was William Markham, the future archbishop of York, under whom he studied very assiduously, in contrast to his former indolence at Trinity College. He graduated MA in 1752. He was admitted a member of the Inner Temple on 19 January 1751, but he did not seek admittance to the King's Inns in Dublin and never practised law in Ireland.

Patriot politician Flood's first public act following his return to Ireland in the mid-1750s was to support Thomas Sheridan's proposal for a Hibernian academy of education. He became a member of the academy's committee of guardians, but his election to represent co. Kilkenny in a by-election in November 1759 focused his energies thereafter on politics. He contested but did not retain the county seat in the 1761 general election. However, he overcame the formidable challenge posed to his family's interest on the corporation of Callan to secure the representation for the borough in January 1762 following the House of Commons' invalidation of the return made at the behest of his rival, James Agar of Ringwood, in 1761. In the same year, on 13 April 1762, he married Lady Frances Maria Beresford (1731–1815), the sixth daughter of Marcus Beresford, first earl of Tyrone (1694–1763), and his wife, Katherine Power (*d.* 1769). It was at this time also that Flood moved from the Dublin Castle benches, on which he had elected to sit in 1759–60, to those of the opposition, and it was from there that he made his maiden speech in 1762. This speech does not survive, but it is clear from the series of combative and well-crafted piece orations and extempore interventions he made during the 1763–4 session that the time he devoted to practising and to familiarizing himself with the forms and procedures of the House of Commons before he took the floor was well spent as he made an immediate impression. Indeed, he was soon being described in some quarters as a more capable leader of the patriot opposition than Edmund Sexten Pery. This was premature, but his exceptional oratorical skill combined with his readiness to proffer motions and to propose legislation on issues as varied as the reduction of the pension list, the duration of parliaments, and the establishment of a militia secured for him the reputation of

Henry Flood
(1732–1791), by
Hugh Douglas
Hamilton

being the most forthcoming and effective critic of 'tyranny and oppression' in the House of Commons by 1765 (Rosse MS F/21).

To many of those who admired Flood he was the epitome of what a patriot was supposed to be—principled, vocal, and in opposition. What they failed to take cognizance of was that Flood also had heroes and ambitions and that opposition was not the best place to emulate or achieve these. His political beau ideal was William Pitt, earl of Chatham, and George III's invitation to him to become prime minister in 1766 aroused Flood's hopes that he could become part of a reformist Irish administration responsible to Chatham. Indeed, such was his enthusiasm that this should happen that he arranged to meet Chatham at Bath on 7 January 1767 to inform him that his price for supporting the administration was a septennial act, a habeas corpus act, the recognition of the independence of the Irish judiciary, and the reform of the pension list. Chatham proved elusive, but despite this and Flood's abrogation of his search for a parliamentary seat at Westminster, Flood did not give up the idea of supporting a reform-minded Irish administration. He entertained expectations of Lord Townshend, who was made lord lieutenant in August 1767, and declined to take his place at the head of the opposition at the opening of the 1767–8 session for this reason. The fact that his septennial bill was allowed progress encouraged him, but his increasingly poor opinion of the lord lieutenant was a serious obstacle which the British privy council's transformation of his septennial bill into an Octennial Act did little to ease. Flood swallowed his dislike of the modifications made to the measure and helped ensure that the bill reached the statute book in 1768, but his decision to publish a number of critical commentaries in the *Freeman's Journal* under the pseudonym Philadelphus attested to his dissatisfaction with Townshend's leadership and the state of Irish politics.

One of the objectionable measures which Flood wrongly attributed to Townshend was the provision in the Octennial Act that a general election should take place in 1768. Because of the increasing tenuousness of his authority on Callan corporation Flood did not want to have to go to the polls at this time. His uncles and he had managed, through a combination of legal and illegal means, to keep one step ahead of their rivals, the Agars, since the late 1750s, when battle for control of the borough was joined, and he was to do so again in 1768, when his cousin John Flood of Floodhall and he were returned to represent the constituency. James Agar appealed against the return unsuccessfully, which intensified the hostility with which Flood and he now regarded each other. They had already engaged in a non-fatal duel at Holyhead in 1765. They met again in September 1769 at Dunmore in co. Kilkenny, and in the course of their meeting Agar was shot dead. Since Flood had conducted himself impeccably on and off the duelling field there was never any question but that a verdict of manslaughter in his own defence would be returned when the case was heard, which was at the Kilkenny assizes in April 1770. One cannot, at the same time, claim that Flood escaped scot-free, since the fall-out over the affair caused Lord Townshend to postpone inviting him to join the administration. The lord lieutenant at this time was endeavouring to construct a castle connection strong enough to relieve him of the need to appeal ever again to the parliamentary undertakers whose opposition had consigned to defeat his plan to augment the army towards the end of the 1768 session.

Flood did not favour the augmentation of the army in 1768 but he did not campaign actively against it. Electoral complications ensured he was not in the House of Commons in November 1769 when it was finally ratified. He was not present either when the privy council money bill was defeated, but, appalled by Townshend's decision to respond to this reversal by proroguing parliament, which he regarded as a despotic act, Flood went into unconditional opposition. In the absence of parliament written propaganda was one of the few practical means open to him, and, stimulated by the success of his Philadelphus letters, he adopted the more aggressive *nom de plume* of Sindercombe, taken from Miles Sindercombe, who had plotted to assassinate Oliver Cromwell, as a cover to relay to the public in the spring of 1770 his perception that Townshend was seeking deliberately to undermine Ireland's liberties. Flood was, as Lecky remarked, no Junius, but he and the other contributors to what are known as the Baratariana letters ensured that the political temperature remained high. Indeed, he reinforced his argument by writing the introduction to a new edition of William Molyneux's *Case of Ireland*, in which he attributed the historic failure to grant 'the blessings of liberty' to Irish protestants to the 'weak or wicked councils of English ministers' (Molyneux, vi–viii). This was the prelude to two years of intense political activity, centred largely on the parliamentary session, in which Flood repeatedly demonstrated just how skilful a parliamentarian he was by spearheading the opposition's resistance to Townshend's attempt to vest political power in Ireland firmly in the castle executive. He registered a significant number of triumphs in the division lobbies during the 1771–2 session when the separation of the customs and revenue functions of the revenue board was at issue, but he was unable to deflect the lord lieutenant, who overcame all opposition to achieve his aim of breaking the undertaker system.

Negotiating office The appointment of Earl Harcourt as lord lieutenant of Ireland in September 1772 was a matter of transcendent importance to Flood because he had not allowed the experience of Lord Townshend to destroy his hopes of establishing a productive relationship with the Irish administration. Through his former tutor, William Markham, whom he used to communicate on his behalf with leading figures in the British establishment, he let it be known to the new lord lieutenant that he was well disposed. Although this was not an intimation of his readiness to take office, both Harcourt and his chief secretary, Sir John Blaquiere, concluded that he could be won over if they offered him the lead in the House of Commons and an office commensurate with his abilities. The first position they identified was the chancellorship of the Irish exchequer, but its incumbent, William Gerard Hamilton, withstood all attempts to persuade him to accept an equally remunerative pension in exchange. As a result Flood did not act on the administration's behalf in the House of Commons in the 1773–4 session, but Harcourt's endorsement of an absentee tax, until opposition in Britain obliged him to do otherwise, ensured that Flood behaved with discretion. He was not happy with what he perceived as the administration's failure to deliver on its promise to provide properly for him, but his unwillingness to spell out his terms allied to the unavailability of a suitable office meant that the session passed without any offer being made. Worse, when on the death of Francis Andrews, the elderly provost of Trinity College, in the summer of 1774 Harcourt offered Flood the minor office of alnager, he refused it 'with no small contempt of mind' (H. Flood to W. Markham, 20 June 1774, Rosse MS C/2/20). He felt 'grossly abused' that he had been made such an 'inferior offer' when he had been promised 'the first great employment which should become vacant' (H. Flood to W. Markham, 21 and 25 June 1774, Rosse MS C/2/21, 22) and when the administration had seen its way to offer the plum position of provost to John Hely-Hutchinson, whom Flood regarded with a hostility bordering on contempt.

Conscious now that they had to offer Flood an appropriately prestigious office if they were to win his support, Harcourt and Blaquiere targeted the vice-treasurership. This proved extremely complex because of the antipathy of Lord North and George III to the implication, which was what attracted Flood to the position, that this would result in a net transfer of crown patronage from Britain to Ireland. However, Blaquiere's industry and Harcourt's insistence enabled them to negotiate all obstacles with the result that they were in a position to offer Flood the vice-treasurership by August 1775. They anticipated that he would seize the opportunity, but to their dismay Flood prevaricated. Of the points he adduced, the concern he articulated that Harcourt's viceregal successors might 'dismiss him from an employment of a very precarious

tenure without ceremony' was the most consequential (Lord Harcourt to Lord North, 13 Aug 1775, Gilbert MS 93, fols. 242–3). Harcourt gave him time to consider his position and, while one cannot be absolutely sure because the documentary record of their contacts is incomplete at this crucial point, it appears that the combination of Flood's ability to hold out until his price was met and Harcourt's eagerness to bring him on side produced an agreement on the eve of the new session. As well as accepting the vice-treasurership during pleasure, Flood secured a commitment that he would be advanced to another major office for life and supported in his political aspirations in Callan and co. Kilkenny. This was an exorbitant price to pay for the support of one man, but it mirrored Harcourt's assessment of Flood's 'great abilities' and of 'how more than ordinarily valuable' he was likely to be during 'difficult times' (Harcourt, *The Harcourt Papers*, 9.361). Certainly, the demoralization his recruitment caused the patriot opposition in the Commons during the 1775–6 session, when the subjects of an embargo on Irish exports and the provision of 4000 troops to aid the war effort against the American colonies dominated the agenda, was helpful to the administration.

Office-holder Although Flood made a number of incisive contributions, he did little enough during the 1775–6 session to warrant the extraordinary effort the Irish administration had made to secure his services, or to repay his appointment to the Irish privy council on 28 October 1775. This was due in part to his wish for a more 'permissive' empire, which he expressed in a draft of a pamphlet entitled 'An answer to *Taxation no tyranny*' in 1775 (Rosse MS C/3), but it was also informed by the realization that his admission to office did not result in the embrace by the Irish administration of the patriot policies he favoured. To compound matters, he was soon at odds with both the Irish administration and the British government because of his expectation that he would be raised to the British privy council and his wish to become an MP at Westminster. The former request was conceded eventually, but the tensions it occasioned were intensified by Flood's perception that the administration did not honour its commitment to support him electorally in 1776. He won in Callan in controversial circumstances, but the outcome was still under appeal to the House of Commons when Harcourt was replaced as lord lieutenant by the second earl of Buckinghamshire.

Flood's relationship with Buckinghamshire got off on the bad note on which it was to continue when the lord lieutenant rejected his nominee for the shrievalty of co. Kilkenny. Buckinghamshire's object was to demonstrate that his good will could not be assumed, but instead of persuading Flood to support the administration in the House of Commons, Flood interpreted it as evidence of Buckinghamshire's unwillingness to implement the agreement into which Harcourt and he had entered in 1775. He was strengthened in this conclusion by the failure of the administration to support him when his petition against the return for co. Kilkenny and the petition against his election for Callan were heard in November

1777. This does not explain why the result went against him in both instances, but Flood was angry that the outcome meant that he had to buy a seat for the borough of Enniskillen, and he was little inclined in consequence to support the administration, which badly needed good advocates in the House of Commons. He had no intention, at the same time, of reverting to opposition, with the result that when he had important contributions to make—and his cautionary observations about the rise of the volunteers and the wisdom of not allowing Catholics influence in the political process in the spring of 1778 fit this category—his was a lone and uninfluential voice. Buckinghamshire did offer him an opportunity to escape isolation in June 1779, when he sought his observations on the merits of 'free trade', and in the following December, when he invited him to the meeting at Dublin Castle at which he made Lord North's decision to concede free trade known, but Flood spurned the opportunities. Demonstrating the self-righteousness for which he became well known, Flood concluded that there was no reason for him to modify his conduct as long as the administration did not honour the terms of the 1775 agreement. Inevitably, his conduct during the 1779–80 session, when he supported free trade, a six months' money bill, a Mutiny Bill, and other popular measures, caused Buckinghamshire to recommend his dismissal. Lord North was unwilling to do so at this time because he wanted to remove Buckinghamshire, but Flood's hold on office was extremely tenuous. As he prepared for the 1781–2 session the new lord lieutenant, the earl of Carlisle, let it be known that he expected office-holders to support the administration, so when Flood took a contrary view on the issue of trade relations with Portugal on 1 November 1781 Carlisle responded decisively. Flood was summarily dismissed from the vice-treasurership and the British privy council.

Independent radical Flood's dismissal from office gave him political freedom once more, and true to his patriot principles he wasted no time reverting to active opposition. He was not welcomed back by those such as Henry Grattan, Hussey Burgh, and Barry Yelverton who had taken his place as the leading lights of opposition, but, ostensibly unbothered by the cool reception, he was indefatigable in debating procedural points, proposing motions, and, most significantly, in agitating the major constitutional issues—Poynings' law, the Declaratory Act, and the Mutiny Act—that now dominated the political agenda. Some of the resentment he engendered in the Commons derived from the more radical analyses and solutions he advanced as to how constitutional grievances should be redressed, but it won him immediate credit with the volunteers, whose support he welcomed, and with political activists. As a result, Flood's standing with the public improved sharply. Lord Charlemont observed this with some interest. Although Flood had rejected his advice when he had taken office, the two men had remained friendly, and, convinced that the united oratory of Flood and Grattan must overcome official resistance to the concession to Ireland of increased constitutional freedom, Charlemont encouraged them to co-operate. The two men regarded each other warily, but as their joint preparation of resolutions for the volunteer convention at Dungannon in February and their readiness to support each other's motions in the House of Commons attest, they were prepared to co-operate in support of the cause of legislative independence in the spring of 1782. However, when the fall of Lord North's government in March created the conditions which enabled Grattan, Yelverton, and Charlemont to advance their essentially moderate programme of constitutional reforms, Flood declined to play any further part. He was obliged by the simple weight of numbers to accede to their stand on Poynings' law, but his argument that the 'simple repeal' of the Declaratory Act did not represent a renunciation by Britain that it had the right to legislate for Ireland was well received by the public. As a result Flood was able to displace Grattan as the most popular politician of the moment before the end of 1782 and oblige the Westminster parliament to ratify a short act recognizing the legislative independence of Ireland early in 1783. For Grattan, who did not believe this legislation was necessary, the loss of popularity was a bitter pill. Eager to expose his rival's flaws and failings, he waited until Flood took his seat for the borough of Kilbeggan in the House of Commons towards the end of October 1783 to commence what proved one of the most deliberate exercises in political character assassination ever attempted in the Irish parliament. He did not achieve his object, partly because of the able defence Flood mounted, but his depiction of Flood's political career as successively 'intemperate', 'corrupt', and 'seditious' was not without effect, as Flood proved by challenging his rival to a duel, which was only prevented by the intervention of the authorities (*The Parliamentary Register*, 2.35–43).

Had Grattan's malicious attack achieved its purpose it would have damaged the campaign for parliamentary reform as well as Flood's reputation, since reform was the political issue that most occupied him at this time. Flood joined this campaign at the invitation of the Ulster Volunteers, though his failure to attend their convention at Dungannon in September indicates that he did not share all their goals. He was opposed in particular to the suggestion that Catholics should be admitted to the political process. At the same time it was his vision and skill that produced a coherent plan of moderate reform out of the welter of conflicting proposals presented to the Grand National Convention of volunteer delegates which met at Dublin in November 1783. This plan was repulsed by the Irish House of Commons on 28 November on the grounds that it originated with another body, but this was largely an argument of convenience. When Flood presented the bill once more in March 1784 and cited petitions from twenty-two counties and eleven towns in its favour it was still rejected.

Despite these reversals, and another in March 1785, Flood remained committed to the cause of reform. However, his involvement in Irish politics diminished greatly from 1783 following his election to the Westminster parliament for the duke of Chandos's borough of Winchester. A seat at Westminster was a lifelong ambition of

Flood. But if the combination of poor preparation on his part and the resolve of his many enemies to cut him down to size accounted for the failure of his maiden speech, his failure to prosper subsequently was largely a product of his refusal to adapt to the intensifying party divisions in that assembly. To compound his problems, his failure to secure his re-election for Winchester in the 1784 general election, which provoked a bitter dispute with Chandos, deprived him of a parliamentary seat for two years. This freed him to devote his attention to the Irish parliament and enabled him to take the lead in that assembly against William Pitt's plan for a commercial union of Britain and Ireland in 1785. It was to be the last session in which his voice was to dominate that assembly. After a sustained struggle he secured a Westminster seat for the constituency of Seaford, and he devoted the rest of his political life to the Westminster stage. He never made more than an occasional impression, but his speech against the treaty of commerce with France on 15 February 1787 and, in particular, his speech for leave to introduce a bill for the reform of parliament on 4 March 1790 indicate that he retained his fabled oratorical and political skills to the last. At the general election in 1790 Flood was not returned for either parliament.

Flood retired to his seat at Farmley, co. Kilkenny, where he died from pleurisy on 2 December 1791. He was buried in Burnchurch graveyard, co. Kilkenny. He was survived by his wife, who died at Clifton on 18 April 1815; they had no children. By his will, he left the bulk of his property, valued at £5000, to Trinity College, Dublin, after his wife's death, for the establishment of a professorship of Irish, for the maintenance of a prize fund for composition, and for the purchase of Irish books and manuscripts. However, the will was challenged by his cousin John Flood of Floodhall, with whom he had argued during his lifetime, and declared invalid on the grounds that John Flood was the legitimate heir, and the lands passed to him.

Flood was a man of high intelligence as well as ample wealth. The habits of scholarship which he embraced at Oxford remained with him throughout his life. While at Oxford his verse in English on the death of Frederick, prince of Wales, was published in *Epicedia Oxoniensa* (1751). The classics were his main enthusiasm, however, but his translations from Demosthenes and others were incinerated along with the majority of his papers after his death. A surviving example of his literary endeavour—*An Ode on Fame and the First Pythian Ode of Pindar* (1775)—shows him to have possessed but moderate literary skill. He was more adept as a political propagandist, but his Philadelphus and Sindercombe letters (*Baratariana: a Collection of Fugitive Political Pieces*, 1772) and his *Letter to the people of Ireland on the expediency and necessity of the present associations in Ireland in favour of our own manufactures, with some cursory observations on the effects of a union* (1779) are not classic illustrations of the genre. He was in the first instance a politician who was at his most effective when he had the floor of the House of Commons because, as well as being a talented orator, he was a superb debater. His reputation in this respect has remained constant, but his larger political reputation suffered in comparison with that of Henry Grattan in the nineteenth century. Later, as Grattan's limitations became apparent and Flood's more acute political mind was acknowledged, he experienced partial rehabilitation. He was certainly one of the most consequential figures on the Irish political landscape and one of the most powerful voices of eighteenth-century Irish protestant patriotism during the 1760s and early 1770s, when he dominated patriot politics, and during the early 1780s, when he was the most provocative patriot spokesman.   JAMES KELLY

Sources J. Kelly, *Henry Flood: patriots and politics in eighteenth-century Ireland* (1998) · Birr Castle, Birr, Offaly, Rosse MSS · entrance book, 1725–8, TCD, MUN V/23/3 · examination returns, 1750–70, TCD, MUN V/27/1 · BL, Flood MSS, Add. MS 22930 · W. Flood, *Memoirs of the life and correspondence of Henry Flood* (1838) · W. Molyneux, *The case of Ireland's being bound by acts of parliament in England, stated*, new edn (1770) · *The manuscripts and correspondence of James, first earl of Charlemont*, 2 vols., HMC, 28 (1891–4) · J. Caldwell, *Debates relative to the affairs of Ireland in the years 1763 and 1764*, 2 vols. (1766) · J. Porter, P. Byrne, and W. Porter, eds., *The parliamentary register, or, History of the proceedings and debates of the House of Commons of Ireland, 1781–1797*, 17 vols. (1784–1801) · *Correspondence of William Pitt, earl of Chatham*, ed. W. S. Taylor and J. H. Pringle, 4 vols. (1838–40) · Dublin Public Library, Harcourt MSS, Gilbert MS 93 · E. W. Harcourt, ed., *The Harcourt papers*, 14 vols. (privately printed, London, [1880–1905]), vol. 9 · L. Parsons, *Observations on the bequest of Henry Flood esq.* (1795) · NA Ire., Langrishe MSS

Archives BL, political and general corresp., Add. MS 22930 | Birr Castle, Birr, Offaly, Rosse MSS · BL, Liverpool MSS, Add. MSS 38206, 38211, 38306 · Hunt. L., Chandos MSS · NA Ire., Langrishe MSS · Royal Irish Acad., letters to Lord Charlemont

Likenesses line engraving, *c*.1770, NG Ire. · line engraving, pubd 1785, NG Ire. · G. C. Stuart, group portrait, stipple and print, pubd 1795 (*The Rt Hon. Henry Grattan's answer to the Roman Catholic address*), NG Ire. · J. Heath, stipple, 1811 (after J. Comerford), BM, NPG; repro. in J. Barrington, *Memoirs* (1811) · B. Clayton, engraving (after oil painting, TCD), repro. in Flood, *Memoirs* · H. D. Hamilton, portrait, priv. coll. [*see illus.*] · B. Stoker, line print and etching, NG Ire. · etching (*Flood of corruption*), BM · oils, TCD · portrait, Birr Castle, Birr, Offaly

Wealth at death £2200 in legacies; plus estate valued at approx. £5000 p.a.: will; contemporary estimates

Flood, Valentine (1800/01–1847), anatomist, was born in Dublin, where his father, Henry Flood, practised as a barrister. At the age of fourteen he entered Trinity College, Dublin, as a pensioner on 4 July 1815, taking the degrees of BA (1820), MB and MA (1823), and MD (1830). After serving an apprenticeship, at that time necessary for becoming licensed by the Irish College of Surgeons, to Richard Carmichael, he took out the letters testimonial of the college, of which he ultimately became a fellow, and in 1828 or 1829 was appointed demonstrator of anatomy in the school of medicine connected with the Richmond Hospital. His increasing reputation as an anatomist led to his being chosen a lecturer on anatomy in the Richmond school about 1831–2.

For a few terms Flood gave his undivided attention to anatomy and became a favourite with the students. As a private teacher he eventually commanded one of the best classes in Dublin. Had Flood continued to concentrate on anatomy it is certain that he would have enjoyed a highly prosperous career. But an ambition to become a successful general practitioner led him, about 1835, to become attached to one of the Dublin dispensaries, where he worked incessantly among the poor of the district in which he lived. Flood's work in general practice led to his neglecting his anatomy classes; students first complained, then rebelled, and finally deserted him. Having lost his positions both as a lecturer and a private teacher, Flood was at length obliged to leave Dublin. He went to London, and became associated with a medical school in Charlotte Street, Fitzroy Square; but he did not succeed. Ill health forced him to return to Ireland in 1846. He was then appointed by the board of health to some fever sheds at Tubrid, co. Tipperary, where he contracted the epidemic typhus, of which he died on 18 October 1847. A stone was erected to his memory by the clergy of both denominations and the principal members of the relief committee at Tubrid.

As early as 1828 Flood published at Dublin the first volume of a work never completed, entitled *The Anatomy and Physiology of the Nervous System*, which, though not without merit, lacked lucidity, and attracted little attention. In 1839 he issued the treatise upon which his reputation rests, *The surgical anatomy of the arteries, and descriptive anatomy of the heart: together with the physiology of the circulation in man and inferior animals* (1839, new edition by John Hatch Power, 1850). During Flood's connection with the Richmond school he brought out a work on *The anatomy and surgery of femoral and inguinal hernia. Illustrated with eight folio plates, drawn on stone by Mr. William Lover, from dissections and designs by Dr. Flood* (1843). Flood was a member of the Royal Irish Academy.

GORDON GOODWIN, rev. MICHAEL BEVAN

Sources *Dublin Quarterly Journal of Medical Science*, 5 (1848), 282–5 · Burtchaell & Sadleir, *Alum. Dubl.* · *London Medical Directory* (1845)

Florence (V), count of Holland (1254–1296), claimant to the Scottish throne, was born at Leiden in 1254, perhaps in July, the son of William (II), count of Holland and king of the Romans (1227–1256), and Elisabeth of Brunswick (1228–1266), and grew up in an atmosphere of intrigues under changing regentships and during the early years after his coming of age in 1266. In 1268 or 1269 he married Béatrice de Dampierre (1253/4–1296), daughter of Gui, count of Flanders (d. 1305), with whom he probably had nine children, of whom seven died in infancy. He also fathered at least seven bastards. At the start of his reign Florence was in free and undisputed possession of only a relatively small part of his territory and he considered it his main task to remedy this situation. In 1283 the southern part of Holland was freed from its feudal ties with Brabant. After a disastrous campaign against the rebellious West Frisians in 1272, a more successful one in 1282 formed the beginning of the subjection of the north of his territory, completed in 1289. And from 1278 onwards, by a shrewd but unscrupulous policy, the count managed to gain considerable power over the adjacent prince-bishopric of Utrecht and to extend his own territory at the bishop's expense. But Florence's authority over the Zeeland Islands, where an unruly nobility stood in his way, remained uncertain, and in 1290, after a short war, he was forced to recognize the suzerainty of the count of Flanders over the isles.

From about 1280 Edward I of England acted as a mediator in several of Florence's conflicts with his neighbours. The king's interest in the strategically important county of Holland, as well as his influence on Florence, are apparent from two contracts concluded in 1281 and 1285, arranging the marriage of the count's daughter with the king's son Alphonso (d. 1284), and of Florence's son and heir, John (Jan), born in 1284, with Edward's daughter Elizabeth respectively. In 1291, after the death of Margaret, the Maid of Norway, the count was among the principal claimants to the Scottish throne. He asserted that his great-great-great-grandmother Ada, a sister of King William the Lion, had been recognized as heir to the throne after her other brother, David, earl of Huntingdon (d. 1219), from whom the other main contenders were descended, had either relinquished his own claim in return for the lordship of Garioch, or lost it through forfeiture as a felon. Court proceedings were delayed to allow Florence time to produce the relevant documents, but though it is certain that in 1291 a (forged) relinquishment by Earl David existed in Scotland, Florence never produced it, but withdrew his claim at the last moment in 1292. It is unclear who or what influenced his actions, but it may be significant that in June 1292 he struck a deal with Robert (V) de Brus (d. 1295), another claimant, for their mutual advantage should either of them succeed to the Scottish throne, and that in 1290 and 1291 he had received large sums under the treaty of 1285 from Edward I, with whom he had come to Norham for the opening of the Great Cause in May 1291.

Florence's relationship with Edward I remained unchanged for the time being, and in 1294 he acted as the king's main negotiator over a treaty with the king of the Romans. In 1295, however, while Edward was building up a coalition against France which included the count of Flanders, Florence entered upon a new war with that county. Edward reacted with measures damaging to the economic interests of Holland, and Florence then concluded a treaty with the king of France (January 1296). A conspiracy of nobles from his own county, aimed at kidnapping the count and delivering him into the hands of the English king, miscarried disastrously and ended in Florence's murder near Muiden Castle (east of Amsterdam) in June 1296; he was buried at Rijnsburg Abbey.

JOHANNA KOSSMANN-PUTTO

Sources A. C. F. Koch and J. G. Kruisheer, eds., *Oorkondenboek van Holland en Zeeland tot 1299*, 3 vols. (1970) · E. L. G. Stones and G. G. Simpson, eds., *Edward I and the throne of Scotland, 1290–1296*, 2 vols. (1978) · G. G. Simpson, 'The claim of Florence, count of Holland, to the Scottish throne, 1291–2', *SHR*, 36 (1957), 111–24 · J. A. Kossmann-Putto, 'Florence V, count of Holland, claimant to the Scottish throne in 1291–2: his personal and political background', *Scotland and the Low Countries, 1124–1994*, ed. G. G. Simpson (1996), 15–27 · F. W. N. Hugenholtz, *Floris V*, 2nd edn (1974) · J. G. Kruisheer, *De oorkonden en de kanselarij van de graven van Holland tot 1299*, 2 (The Hague, 1971), 299 [Regesten] · A. W. Dek, *Genealogie der graven van Holland*, 4th edn (1969), 16–17 · Ph. C. van den Bergh, ed., *Oorkondenboek van Holland en Zeeland*, 2 (1873), no. 950 · D. E. H. de

Boer, E. H. P. Cordfunke, and H. Sarfatij, eds., *Wi Florens … de Hollandse graaf Floris V in de samenleving van de 13de eeuw* (1996) **Archives** Nationaal Archief, The Hague, Rijksarchief Zuid-Holland, archief van de graven van Holland

Florence, Alix Sargant- (1892–1973). *See* Strachey, Alix, *under* Strachey, James Beaumont (1887–1967).

Florence, Philip Sargant (1890–1982), economist, was born on 25 June 1890 at Nutley, New Jersey, USA, the son of Henry Smythe Florence and his wife, Mary Sargant-Florence. He was an American citizen, but spent most of his life in Britain. Alix *Strachey [see under* Strachey, James Beaumont] was his sister. After attending Rugby School, he entered Gonville and Caius College, Cambridge, in 1909 as a history scholar, and obtained a first-class degree in economics in 1914. He then studied at Columbia University, New York, where he took his PhD degree with a thesis on the effects of fatigue on the productivity of workers. He married an American, Lella Faye Secor, in New York in 1917, and she became his close companion until her death in 1966. They had two sons.

After committee work in Britain and the USA, Sargant Florence returned to Cambridge University as a lecturer in economics in 1921 and stayed there until 1929, when he was appointed professor of commerce at the University of Birmingham. He was dean of the faculty of commerce and social science at Birmingham from 1947 to 1950, and retired in 1955. He remained active in retirement, taking visiting professorships in the United States, at Johns Hopkins University and the University of Rhode Island, and serving on a number of committees. From 1972 until his death he was a vice-president of the Royal Economic Society. He was appointed an honorary CBE in 1952.

Sargant Florence was a lively Cambridge undergraduate, much influenced by his contemporary C. K. Ogden, who interested him in words and their meaning. This was later reflected in Florence's *Basic English for the Social Sciences* (1962). At Cambridge he was a founder of the Heretics Society, and served as its secretary until 1914. He also helped to found the *Cambridge Magazine* and served on its editorial committee. His mother, Mary, was one of its contributors.

Sargant Florence was much interested in social as well as economic questions, having served on the British Association committee on fatigue from the economic standpoint (1913–15), and as investigator to the Health of Munitions Workers Committee (1915–16). In the USA he was an investigator for the US public health service (1917–21), and lecturer for the bureau of industrial research and bureau of personnel administration, New York (1919–21). His first book, published in 1918, was *Use of Factory Statistics in the Investigation of Factory Fatigue*. The title of this book displayed another of his main interests—the statistical study of industrial problems. This was reflected directly in his *Statistical Method in Economics and Political Science* (1929), and in his many works on the economics of industry. For example, his *Ownership, Control and Success of Large Companies, 1936–51* (1961) was a pioneering and detailed study of the concentration of ownership in British industry,

including details of directors, ownership, dividend policy, financial success, and an analysis of very large companies. Perhaps his best-known work, again involving many statistical comparisons, was his *Logic of British and American Industry* (1953, revised 1971). His width of interests was reflected not only in his books, but also in articles published in sociological, statistical, and psychological, as well as economic, journals.

Sargant Florence soon became well known in the midlands, and became an influential figure both in the university and in midlands industry. These interests were temporarily suspended by the Second World War, when he and his wife, both American citizens, were evacuated to the United States, where he acted for a while as consultant to the national resources planning board. On returning to Britain during the war he joined the staff of the American ambassador, John Winant.

After the war Sargant Florence resumed his university duties, and undertook wide-ranging investigations in the midlands connected with post-war reconstruction, especially town and country planning. He published, among other works, *Country Town* (1946), a study of Worcester; *English County* (1947), an inquiry into the industries of Herefordshire; and *Conurbation*, a report on regional planning in Birmingham and the Black Country. From 1957 to 1963 he presided over the Greater Birmingham employment committee, and remained active as an author, academic, and committee member well into old age. His work for Birmingham University was recognized by his honorary degree of DSocSc (Birmingham), and his reputation in America was recognized by his honorary LittD (Humanities) (Columbia).

Sargant Florence was a man of many and varied interests, who infected all around him with his lively mind, his *joie de vivre*, and his delightful and witty personality. He was no theoretical economist, though he did develop an interest in macroeconomics in his old age, but he made many contributions, both academically and practically, through his extensive work in the midlands, to improving industry and the conditions of its workers. He was always interested in local and national politics, and was a member of the Labour Party, at least for a time. But he was no enemy of capitalism, believing that its strength may lie in its very variety and balance of power, allowing the fittest for the given circumstances to dominate. Florence died on 29 January 1982, probably in Birmingham.

AUBREY SILBERSTON

Sources *WW* · *WWW* · *The Times* (3 Feb 1982) · J. Eatwell, M. Milgate, and P. Newman, eds., *The new Palgrave: a dictionary of economics*, new edn, 4 vols. (1998) · P. S. Florence and J. R. L. Anderson, eds., *C. K. Ogden: a collective memoir* (1977) · *CGPLA Eng. & Wales* (1982) **Archives** Birm. CA, corresp., diaries, and papers | BLPES, corresp. with editors of the *Economic Journal* · University of East Anglia, Norwich, corresp. with J. C. Pritchard **Wealth at death** £192,940: probate, 13 May 1982, *CGPLA Eng. & Wales*

Florey, Howard Walter, Baron Florey (1898–1968), experimental pathologist and bacteriologist, was born in

Howard Walter Florey, Baron Florey (1898–1968), by Walter Bird, 1960

Adelaide, Australia, on 24 September 1898, the youngest child and only son of Joseph Florey (d. 1918), an Oxfordshire shoemaker who had emigrated in 1885, and his second wife, Bertha Mary Wadham, an Australian, with whom he had two daughters and a son. Joseph's first wife had died in 1886, leaving two daughters. By 1906 he had built up a shoe manufacturing business with branches throughout Australia. Howard Florey went to Kyre College and St Peter's Collegiate School, Adelaide, where he was nicknamed Floss. He was clever, hard-working, and determined, winning six scholarships and many prizes. He was also good at games, representing his school (and later his university) at tennis, at football, and in athletics. He first wanted to study chemistry at the university but his father had been told that there would be little scope for this subject in Australia and in 1916 he entered Adelaide University medical school. There he was usually first in his class, winning three scholarships. He qualified as MB BS in 1921. In 1918 his father died suddenly, his business was found to be insolvent, and the Florey family was translated from wealth to poverty. Florey's medical studies were secured by his scholarships, but his earlier ambition for research rather than a well-paid clinical post in Adelaide was maintained with some personal misgivings. In 1921 he was awarded a Rhodes scholarship and, having qualified in medicine, he worked his passage to England as a ship's surgeon, arriving on 24 January 1922.

Move to England In Oxford, Florey enrolled in the department of physiology under Sir Charles Sherrington, and at Magdalen College. Sherrington recognized his drive and creative independence of mind, and became his most influential guide and friend. In 1923 Florey obtained a first class in the honour school of physiology, then stayed on, at Sherrington's invitation, to study the blood flow in the capillaries of the brain. He made some discoveries and devised a method for inserting transparent windows in living tissues which he later used in various parts of the body to answer questions by direct, simple observation. In October 1924 he moved to Cambridge as John Lucas Walker student in the pathology department under Professor H. R. Dean, who, with Sherrington, felt that a more experimental approach to pathology could be achieved by an active young physiologist. Florey had spent the summer vacation with the third Oxford University Arctic expedition as medical officer, and, though it provided no major excitements, he never forgot this experience of human comradeship and of the colourful beauty of the Arctic. In Cambridge he continued his study of blood flow changes in inflammation and thrombosis—problems which remained a major interest for the rest of his career. He submitted this work for an Oxford BSc in 1925, and was congratulated by his examiners. In the same year he was awarded a Rockefeller fellowship to go to the United States to learn microsurgical techniques. He spent three months with Dr A. N. Richards in Philadelphia and then went to Chicago to work out methods for the study of mucus secretion. Since his Arctic expedition Florey had suffered bouts of indigestion. Investigation had revealed a mucous gastritis and, experimenting on himself, he became interested in mucus, the mechanism of its secretion, and its importance in protecting the mucous membranes. It was a line that led by logical stages to his work on penicillin.

Cambridge and early work on lysozyme While in America, Florey accepted the offer of a Freedom research fellowship at the London Hospital. He took up this post in June 1926, but it proved not entirely congenial since the laboratories were more concerned with routine than research. But he found a collaborator in Paul Fildes, with whom he experimented on a treatment for tetanus, and he often slipped away to work for a few days in Oxford or Cambridge. In 1926 he married Dr Mary Ethel Hayter (d. 1966), a pathologist, the daughter of John Hayter Reed, an Adelaide bank manager, whom he had known as a medical student in Adelaide; they had one son and one daughter. London life suited neither of them, and when Florey was offered the Huddersfield lectureship in pathology at Cambridge he returned eagerly in October 1927 to the same room which he had occupied before going to America. He now had a new laboratory boy—the fourteen-year-old Jim Kent, who was to stay as his indispensable and devoted assistant for the next forty-one years, and who contributed so much to the success of his research projects. Florey had become a fellow of Gonville and Caius College and its director of medical studies, but he had (or made) ample time for research. He had embodied work on the flow of blood and lymph in a thesis for a Cambridge PhD which was conferred in 1927. During the next four years he began several fruitful lines of study and with various collaborators published twenty scientific papers. One of these lines in particular had momentous consequences. In 1922 Alexander Fleming had accidentally discovered an agent in mucoid secretions which dissolved certain bacteria. He called it 'lysozyme' and supposed that it might normally prevent infection. It proved, however, to act on only relatively harmless bacteria, and little further work was done on it. Florey took up lysozyme in 1929 because he thought that its presence in mucus might explain an antibacterial action he had observed and also the natural immunity of some animals. He studied lysozyme in animals, publishing two papers in 1930. Though the results did not suggest that lysozyme was necessary to natural immunity, Florey retained a determination to discover its nature and mode of action.

In 1932 Florey was appointed Joseph Hunter professor of pathology at Sheffield University, a choice which surprised orthodox pathologists who still considered him a physiologist. However, there were experienced pathologists in the department who could maintain the routine work while Florey infused vitality into the teaching and research. One of his projects was on the control of the spasms in tetanus by curare combined with mechanical artificial respiration—the basis of the modern treatment. He made important advances in the field of gastrointestinal function. Lysozyme remained a major interest, although one constantly frustrated by the lack of adequate biochemical collaboration.

Chair of pathology in Oxford and the development of penicillin
In 1934 the chair of pathology in Oxford became vacant on the death of Georges Dreyer. Florey was appointed in 1935, being strongly supported by Edward Mellanby, secretary of the Medical Research Council. The Sir William Dunn school of pathology, designed by Dreyer himself on a grand scale, had become something of a mausoleum. Florey came into this partial vacuum with Beatrice Pullinger (from Sheffield) and Jim Kent. The three of them brought the department to life at all levels—teaching, research, and technical assistance. They were hampered by lack of money and Florey had to spend much time in fund-raising. The Medical Research Council and the Rockefeller Foundation were his main benefactors, but the sums obtained now seem absurdly small. There was little to be had from the university, and Florey was disappointed that pre-clinical departments like his own did not receive any substantial help from the £2 million Nuffield benefaction which was mostly spent on clinical research and teaching at the Radcliffe Infirmary.

Florey brought his department to life largely by attracting young postgraduates who had their own grants. The quality of their research and his own work attracted others and within a few years the Oxford school of pathology was among the best laboratories of its kind in the world. Florey expanded his own lines of research to include these new recruits, forming teams in which each contributed some special expertise, and over which he kept a general but not authoritarian control. One such project was the study of the lymphocyte, another was gastrointestinal function, a third was the study of the microcirculation by cine-photography. But the most productive of all was the work which established the clinical value of penicillin.

In 1935 Florey finally obtained the help of a chemist, E. A. H. Roberts, who partly purified lysozyme by 1937. He had also engaged a young refugee biochemist, Ernst B. Chain, and asked him to discover how lysozyme dissolved bacteria. Chain found it to be an enzyme which attacks a specific bacterial structure. While reviewing the literature on lysozyme, Chain came across the paper by Fleming, published in 1929, describing the chance discovery of a *Penicillium* mould that apparently dissolved pathogenic bacteria in its vicinity. Fleming gave the name 'penicillin' to filtrates of broth cultures of the mould. Chain also found a culture of Fleming's mould in the school of pathology, with which he did a few tentative experiments in 1938. Florey had been well aware of many cases in which one micro-organism inhibited another. However, he had not been particularly interested in penicillin, even though Dr C. G. Paine at the Jessop Hospital in Sheffield had tried it locally, with some success, on eye infections. Florey noted the fact that Harold Raistrick and his colleagues had abandoned an attempt at the London School of Hygiene to purify this labile substance, but he agreed with Chain that a study of antibacterial substances produced by micro-organisms might widen a research which now seemed to be reaching a dead end in lysozyme as a therapeutic agent, and they decided to work together on three such products, including penicillin. The project was mentioned to the Medical Research Council in January 1939, and again in September, when a request for a special grant yielded £25 and the possibility of £100 later. However, the Rockefeller Foundation granted $5000 (£1200) per annum, for five years, a considerable sum at the time. Experiments showed that penicillin was the most promising of the substances chosen for study, and might have therapeutic as well as scientific importance. Thereafter the project became a team one. N. G. Heatley undertook the production of the mould filtrate; Chain, later joined by E. P. Abraham, worked on the purification and chemistry, while Florey and Margaret Jennings (who later became his second wife) carried out the animal work and, with Professor A. D. Gardner, the bacteriology.

On Saturday 25 May 1940 there was enough penicillin, still less than 1 per cent pure, to discover if it could protect mice from an otherwise lethal infection—a crucial test. Eight mice were injected with virulent streptococci, and an hour later four of these had injections of the crude penicillin. All four untreated mice were dead in a few hours; all the treated mice were alive and well the next day. Florey's remark, 'It looks promising', was a typically laconic assessment of one of the most important experiments in medical history. The results of a large series of such experiments, published in August 1940, completely confirmed the initial promise. Florey tried to persuade British drug firms to produce enough penicillin to treat human cases, but they were already hard-pressed by wartime needs and damage and when he failed he turned his own department into a small factory. All that can be said here of the physical, chemical, biological, and administrative difficulties is that they were overcome by collaborative perseverance and ingenuity, and by Florey's energy, determination, and personal example. Beginning in January 1941, there was a limited trial under his direction by C. M. Fletcher on patients at the Radcliffe Infirmary, Oxford. The cases chosen were mostly those of otherwise hopeless infection. Though only six could be treated systematically, and even these with restricted doses, the results were practically conclusive. Penicillin had been shown to overcome infections which were beyond any other treatment.

In June 1941, with Mellanby's approval, Florey and Heatley went to the United States to try to enlist commercial help. Florey's old friend A. N. Richards promised government support for firms prepared to develop large-scale methods of production, and three accepted. While Heatley remained to assist, Florey returned to Oxford to direct an even greater production effort in his department. This allowed a completely conclusive trial on 187 cases in 1942, largely carried out by Florey's wife. In the summer of 1943 Florey and Hugh Cairns went to north Africa to find out how a small amount of penicillin could be used most efficiently for the treatment of war wounds. Six months later Florey went to Russia with information on the new results. Meanwhile commercial production had, at last, begun in Britain, and this revealed that certain technical methods had been patented in America. Florey was criticized for having given away a valuable commercial asset. The information which Florey gave in America had been freely offered earlier in Britain. But in America he learned that much larger amounts of penicillin might be obtained by deep fermentation in large aerated vessels and this was to change the whole outlook on penicillin production. It was then considered unethical in Britain for those in medical research to patent medical discoveries. Soon after the end of the war the official attitude to patenting changed completely. When, in 1953, G. F. Newton and E. P. Abraham in the school of pathology isolated the first of the therapeutically useful cephalosporin antibiotics Florey gave them strong encouragement and confirmed himself its curative value in mice. This was his last personal involvement in the field of antibiotics. In 1949 a complete account of the Oxford work at that time was published as a two-volume book, *Antibiotics*, by Florey and six of his collaborators. In all, he was also the author or co-author of thirty-two scientific papers and more than thirty published lectures and reviews on the subject.

Recognition and its rewards In scientific and medical circles the Oxford achievement had been recognized and applauded. Florey had been elected a fellow of the Royal Society in 1941, before the true value of penicillin had been established. Thereafter many other honours followed. He was knighted in 1944, and in 1945 he shared the Nobel prize for medicine with Chain and Fleming. The general public, however, tended to regard Fleming as the creator of penicillin therapy. He had, of course, discovered by chance the antibacterial power of a *Penicillium* mould, shown that the 'mould broth filtrate' was nontoxic to animals, and had used it, without much success, as a local antiseptic in a few cases. He had also suggested that it might be injected locally. But he had not during the next ten years developed his discovery or aroused interest in it, and, in any case, in the 1930s sulphonamides, which were easy to make, had captured medical interest. Fleming had taken no part at all in the Oxford work, although his cultures had prompted it. When the astonishing success of penicillin therapy became popular news, 'so gratifying as to be at times almost unbelievable', Florey was unwilling to talk to reporters. Fleming had less reserve, and articles appeared in which he was portrayed as the hero of a long struggle to harness his discovery, producing large amounts of penicillin at St Mary's Hospital, London, for use there or at Oxford under his direction. Such distortions, continuing uncorrected for many years, created a general impression that only Fleming's name should be associated with penicillin.

After a period of work on the use of antibiotics in tuberculosis, Florey returned in the mid-1950s to his early research interest. He used electron microscopy and marker techniques in new studies of mucus secretion and of vascular changes which can cause thrombosis. As always, he encouraged young workers to participate, and because his interest in the leucocytes was leading into the wider fields of immunology and cytogenetics, his department was ready to move into another new era. Florey, always the best animal surgeon in the department, regularly did long experiments undistracted by his emergence as a public figure. In this latter role he surprised those who had known him as something of a firebrand, since he accepted high official responsibilities with patience and even pleasure. He was concerned with the foundation of the Australian National University, paid many visits to Canberra, and was personally involved with the design, building, and organization of the John Curtin School of Medical Research. He refused to become the school's director and wrote to the vice-chancellor of the university in 1957: 'I have all my life struggled against becoming merely an administrator because I like doing experiments' and he believed that detailed bureaucratic control could stifle the essential function of an academic institution. However, he retained his association with the university and was its chancellor in 1965. In 1960 Florey was elected president of the Royal Society, and he brought to it a vitality which rejuvenated what was rather a staid organization and made of its officers and staff a team with a new sense of purpose. A major change was the move from the society's elegant but cramped quarters in Burlington House to the far more spacious Carlton House Terrace. He also widened the society's interests to include applied science and demography, and he opened its doors to lively discussion meetings and study groups which extended its already great influence.

In 1962 Florey became provost of Queen's College, Oxford, and relinquished his chair of pathology. The move puzzled some colleagues who thought that, after a life concerned with the clear objectives of science and scientists, he would find it tiresome to preside over a college with a then difficult governing body. For a time, it seems, he did, but mutual adjustments led to a pleasant working relationship and he was able to contribute practical improvements, as he had done before in other appointments. The college gained European studentships and the Florey Building, and something of a new outlook; he received the pleasure of a gracious style of living. He had always appreciated the college system in Oxford and Cambridge, and had much enjoyed the fellowship of Lincoln College which he had held since 1935 (he was made honorary fellow in 1962). In 1965 he was created a life peer as Baron Florey of Adelaide and Marston and a member of the Order of Merit. He had become a commander of the Légion d'honneur, and had received the US medal for merit, the royal and the Copley medals of the Royal Society, honorary degrees from ten British and eighteen foreign universities, and other worldwide honours, medals, and prizes. But he always spoke of his achievements with a modesty that was undoubtedly sincere. He went out of his way to claim that what had been done in Oxford with penicillin was due to the work of a small group of people and to see that they received recognition.

In 1966 Ethel Florey died after some years of disabling ill health. In 1967 Florey married Margaret Augusta Jennings (1904–1994), daughter of Thomas Fremantle, third Baron Cottesloe, and formerly wife of Denys Arthur Jennings. She had worked in fruitful collaboration with Florey at the school of pathology since 1936. For some years Florey had suffered from angina, unknown to his colleagues, and it was from a heart attack that he died suddenly in Oxford on 21 February 1968.

Qualities and personality As a scientist, Florey had an extraordinary flair for choosing expanding lines of research; the ability to reduce a problem to simple questions answerable by experiment; great industry and determination; and an honesty that allowed of no self-deception. Equally important, he could inspire others to work almost as hard and well as himself. He published more than 150 scientific papers (excluding reviews and lectures) but the vast amount of experimental work entailed is revealed only by his notebooks. *General Pathology* (1954), the textbook edited by Florey and published in four editions, reflects the progressive teaching at his school. As a person, despite his outward geniality and humour, he was a man of profound reserve. He did not show his deeper feelings and he had few, if any, close friends. Ethel Florey's ill health and, in particular, her progressive deafness, had from the first marred the happy companionship which both had hoped for from their marriage. Yet she had charm, if not tact, and made a supreme effort to overcome these physical handicaps in her work on penicillin. Outside his own laboratory, Florey's main enjoyment was in travel, which in later years became worldwide. From his first arrival in Oxford in 1922 he took every opportunity to go abroad, working in foreign laboratories, learning languages, and, above all, appreciating the history, art, architecture, and music of the countries he visited. His letters to Ethel before their marriage are full of these experiences, and they reveal him as sensitive, lonely, unsure of himself, and deeply concerned for human troubles—a picture of himself very different from the one he presented to the world. 'I don't think it ever crossed our minds about suffering humanity' he said publicly of his reasons for starting work on penicillin. But in 1923, in a letter to Ethel, he wrote of 'the appalling thing of seeing young people maimed and wiped out while one can do nothing'. He was referring to untreatable infections. He, perhaps more than anyone before him, helped to achieve their defeat.

R. G. MACFARLANE, *rev.* E. P. ABRAHAM

Sources G. Macfarlane, *Howard Florey: the making of a great scientist* (1979) · L. Bickel, *Rise up to life* (1972) · E. P. Abraham, *Memoirs FRS*, 17 (1971), 255–302 · personal knowledge (1981) · personal knowledge (2004) · *CGPLA Eng. & Wales* (1968) · 'Margaret Florey', *The Independent* (24 Nov 1994)

Archives Australian National University Library, Canberra, Noel Butlin Archives Centre, corresp. and papers · Harvard U., Countway Library of Medicine, lectures · Medical Research Council, London, corresp. and papers · RS, corresp., notebooks, and papers | Nuffield Oxf., corresp. with Lord Cherwell · Rice University, Houston, Texas, Woodson Research Center, corresp. with Sir Julian Huxley · Wellcome L., corresp. with Sir Ernst Chain

Likenesses W. Stoneman, photograph, 1943, NPG · W. Bird, photograph, 1960, NPG [*see illus.*] · H. Carr, oils, 1965, RS · H. Carr, oils, Queen's College, Oxford · W. Dargie, portrait, St Peter's Collegiate School, Adelaide · F. Deane, portrait, Sir William Dunn School of Pathology, Oxford · J. Dowie, bronze head, Prince Henry Gardens, Adelaide · A. Gwynne-Jones, portrait, University of Adelaide

Wealth at death £30,554: probate, 6 June 1968, *CGPLA Eng. & Wales*

Florio, John (1553–1625), author and teacher of languages, was born in London, the son of a Tuscan former Franciscan friar, Michael Angelo *Florio (*d.* 1566x71), and of an Englishwoman whose identity has not been determined. His father, like the famous Italian reformers and preachers Bernardino Ochino and Pietro Martire Vermigli (known as Peter Martyr), had escaped the Inquisition and had fled to London, which during the reign of Edward VI was a haven for refugees of many nationalities. After his arrival in London in 1550 Michael Angelo began preaching in a newly constituted Italian protestant church, but disagreements with other members of the church led him to turn to Italian language teaching for a living. Two of his pupils were Henry Herbert, second earl of Pembroke, and Lady Jane Grey, to each of whom he dedicated an Italian grammar, 'Regole de la lingua thoscana' (1553) and 'Institution: de la lingua thoscana' (undated) respectively, two manuscripts that remained unpublished in his lifetime.

Early years In March 1554, following Catholic Mary Tudor's elevation to the throne and the proclamation of the edict that foreign exiles were to leave the realm, Michael Angelo Florio abandoned England with his English wife and infant son, John. After a year spent in Strasbourg the family settled in the Grisons canton of Switzerland, in the town of Soglio in the Val Bregaglia, just

En virtute suâ contentus, nobilis arte ,
Italus ore, Anglus pectore, vterâ opere
Floret adhuc, et adhuc florebit; floreat vltra
FLORIVS, hâc specie floridus, optat amans .
GuilHole sculp: *Tam fœlix vtinam .*

John Florio (1553–1625), by William Hole, 1611

beyond the Italian border. John Florio spent his early childhood in Soglio, where a number of other Italian religious refugees also made their home, and where his father became pastor of the local reformed church. There is no evidence that John ever set foot in Italy during these years. At the age of ten he was sent by his father to Tübingen to study under the distinguished Italian refugee Vergerio, formerly bishop of Capodistria. He remained there until probably 1565. According to Yates (p. 25), Michael Angelo Florio died in Soglio, and by 1576 John had returned to London.

First writings In England, John Florio followed in his father's footsteps by making language teaching his principal source of income. In 1578 he published his first manual for teaching Italian, aptly called *Florio his Firste Fruites*, which he dedicated to Jane Grey's brother-in-law, Robert Dudley, earl of Leicester, whom his father had previously served. At the outset Florio made contact with the patrons previously frequented by his father and saw himself as his father's successor in attempting to satisfy the thirst that people in high places had for a knowledge of the Italian language, which in Elizabethan England was considered an essential gateway to Renaissance culture. The *Firste Fruites* contains forty-four chapters of graded phrases, dialogues, proverbs, and borrowed prose extracts, arranged in Italian and English in two columns, and followed by an

Italian grammar and by rules to help Italians learn English. Despite Florio's apologetic declaration in the preface that it was not his profession to write a language textbook, the volume makes interesting reading in its lively glimpses of contemporary London life and for the variety of topics that it treats. The occasional appearance of Italian regional vocabulary in the text betrays his familiarity with the northern Italian vernacular that he must have acquired in his childhood in the Val Bregaglia.

Some time after 1578 and until 1583 Florio lived in Oxford, where he taught Italian to university scholars and made the acquaintance of the poet Samuel Daniel, whose sister he married *c*.1580. A daughter of this union, Joane Florio, was baptized in Oxford in 1585; a son, Edward, was baptized in 1588 and another daughter, Elizabeth, in 1589. While at Oxford Florio published in London *A shorte and briefe narration of the two navigations and discoveries to the northweast partes called Newe Fraunce* (1580), a translation into English of Ramusio's Italian version of the work by Jacques Cartier.

In 1583 Florio returned to London, and for two years was employed in the French embassy as tutor to Katherine Marie, the daughter of the French ambassador, Mauvissière, while at the same time apparently serving as a spy for the statesman Sir Francis Walsingham. It was at the embassy that Florio met the Italian philosopher Giordano Bruno, who, while residing there during the same period, wrote and published in London his six most celebrated moral dialogues, including the *Cena delle ceneri*, in which Florio is mentioned as Bruno's companion. Florio in the meantime was busy translating several Italian newsletters that had been dispatched from Rome to France, from where they probably reached the French embassy in London. The Rome correspondent provided news of events surrounding the papacy as well as other gossipy items from various parts of the world. The resulting pamphlet, entitled *A letter lately written from Rome, by an Italian gentleman to a freende of his in Lyons in Fraunce*, was published in London in 1585.

In 1591 Florio compiled a second dialogue manual, entitled *Florios Second Frutes*, together with a collection of 6000 Italian proverbs, the *Gardine of Recreation*, the largest proverb list to be published in the sixteenth century. This bilingual manual, dedicated to Nicholas Saunder of Ewell of the well-known Surrey family, was aimed, as before, at the educated upper classes among whom Florio moved, but now the earlier moralizing tone of the *Firste Fruites* was replaced by a more joyous celebration of life. The *Second Frutes* contained a wealth of popular phrases and proverbs set into dialogues depicting everyday genteel activities, such as playing tennis or chess or attending a banquet, presented in a way that would enable the student of Italian speedily to develop colloquial and graceful conversation skills, and at the same time learn of the more refined manners and customs of the Italians.

Florio's dictionary Seven years later, in 1598, Florio published the first edition of what would be one of his major achievements. *A Worlde of Wordes, or, Most Copious, and Exact*

Dictionarie in English and Italian far surpassed the only previous Italian–English dictionary, a modest volume by William Thomas published in 1550. Florio dedicated his work to his pupils Lucy, countess of Bedford, and Roger, fifth earl of Rutland, and to Henry, third earl of Southampton, in whose 'paie and patronage' he had lived for some years (sig. a 3r). Half of the six-page introductory 'Address to the reader' consisted of an invective against H. S., originally thought to refer to Shakespeare, but since shown convincingly by Yates to be Hugh Sanford, tutor and secretary in the Pembroke family, who had publicly criticized Florio's previous work. Whereas William Thomas had assembled just 6000 words, Florio, according to the titles that he listed at the beginning of his *Worlde of Wordes*, consulted seventy-two works by mainly sixteenth-century writers to provide no fewer than 44,000 Italian entries. A major source of words, not acknowledged in his list of titles probably because the volume was a well-known contemporary lexicon, was the third edition of Thomas Thomas's Latin–English dictionary of 1592. Florio turned many of Thomas's Latin entries into their Italian equivalent and borrowed many of his elaborate English definitions.

Detached from the linguistic debate taking place in Italy at the time regarding the priority to be given to fourteenth-century Florentine, Florio indiscriminately included in his list words from all parts of Italy (including Italian slang), with the result that his dictionary provided his English contemporaries with a valuable resource for understanding the many Italian plays, poems, treatises, encyclopaedic collections, and scientific and historical works that were then reaching England. Throughout the volume he displayed his erudition not just in his ability to understand such an extensive range of Italian vocabulary but also in his ability to provide an impressive spread of formal, colloquial, and occasionally vulgar English equivalents—for example, '*Sbattuto*, trampled, crossed, vext, dasht, beaten, shaken, rouzed, striken, tugged, touzed, tossed, turmoiled, confounded, affrighted, tumbled, driven away in a quandrie, thrashed, weatherbeaten, weathershaken' (sig. 2F5v; p. 346). At a time when interest in languages was at its peak in cosmopolitan London and particularly among the ruling class, Florio offered the Elizabethans a vehicle for discovering Italy, its language, and its Renaissance culture without necessarily travelling to the continent.

The translation of Montaigne Florio's greatest fame as a manipulator of English and as a translator was achieved through his English version of Montaigne's *Essais*, which he published in 1603 as *The Essayes, or, Morall, Politike and Militarie Discourses*. Florio by now had numerous aristocratic patrons, many of them women, as attested by the names of the people to whom he dedicated the three parts of the translation: Lucy, countess of Bedford; her mother, Lady Anne Harington; Elizabeth, countess of Rutland; Lady Penelope Rich; Lady Elizabeth Grey; and Lady Mary Neville. In the dedication Florio explained that he sought 'to repeate in true English what you read in fine French' (sig. A2r). Although he received assistance from his brother-in-law Samuel Daniel, his Welsh friend Dr Mathew Gwinne, and the Italian protestant Theodore Diodati, Florio's style is clearly visible throughout the translation. His extraordinary skill in the use of alliteration, his ability to embroider and amplify the French original through the addition of English synonyms, his sense of rhythm, his art of turning French proverbs and expressions into idiomatic English equivalents, and his experimentation with new-formed English words (such as 'conscientious', 'endeare', 'efface', 'facilitate') made his Montaigne one of the great translations of the Elizabethan age. The work was a source of inspiration for such as Ben Jonson, Sir Walter Ralegh, John Webster, and Shakespeare. Despite the fact that, as a translation, it was occasionally inaccurate, 'Florio's Montaigne' was reprinted both in his lifetime and over subsequent centuries.

The *New World of Words* Florio's reputation was now at its peak. The following year, 1604, he was appointed groom of the privy chamber, and reader in Italian and private secretary to Queen Anne. He translated into Italian James I's *Basilikon Doron*, but did not publish it; a manuscript copy survives in the British Library. Apart from tutoring the royal family in Italian and French, he devoted considerable time to revising his Italian–English dictionary, which he republished in 1611 as *Queen Anna's New World of Words*. The new edition, dedicated to Anne of Denmark, wife of James I, contained over 70,000 entries, for the compilation of which he claimed to have consulted as many as 252 Italian publications. His list of book titles now included a vast assortment of works dealing with history, travel, religion, astrology, philosophy, artillery, mechanics, and medicine, as well as the London publications of Giordano Bruno and numerous comedies, tragedies, and pastorals. His aim was to capture the 'complete' corpus of Italian words, so that he could interpret for his English contemporaries the huge variety of vocabulary—including regionalisms, archaisms, and exoticisms—that were present in sixteenth-century Italian literature. The dictionary included Florio's portrait, engraved by William Hole, and a short Italian grammar. He made no attempt to provide an English–Italian word-list, an addition that was inserted by Giovanni Torriano when he published the manuscript of Florio's third edition in 1659.

Last years Florio remarried on 9 September 1617, taking Rose Spicer (*d.* in or after 1626) as his new wife; they had a daughter, Aurelia *Molins [*see under* Molins, James (*c.*1580–1638)]. When Queen Anne died in 1619 Florio lost his position at court. A year later an English version of Boccaccio's *Decameron* was published in London. While it is uncertain whether the unnamed translator was Florio, it is not hard to imagine the indefatigable and 'resolute' John Florio, as he elsewhere often signed himself (for example, *Worlde of Wordes*, sig. b2r), taking on such a task at court in the years following the completion of his *New World of Words*. If the work was indeed his, however, it certainly did not provide him with any financial reward, because in 1619 he was already residing in poverty at Fulham, where, despite his attempts, he was unsuccessful in extracting a pension from the lord treasurer. We know that at Fulham he worked on the third edition of his dictionary, translated into English parts of Traiano Boccalini's *Ragguagli di Parnaso*, destined to be published after his death as *The New-Found Politicke*, and compiled ten dialogues in Italian and English, most of which found their way into Torriano's *The Italian Tutor* (1640).

Florio died about October 1625, a victim of the plague. Beneficiaries of his will, which was dated 20 July 1625, included his wife and daughter Aurelia. Florio named Theophilus Field, bishop of Llandaff and a member of the earl of Pembroke's circle, and Richard Cluet, vicar of Fulham, as his executors; however, they renounced their position in this regard, and on 1 June 1626 Rose was issued with a commission to act as executor. Aurelia, the only offspring mentioned in the will, married James Molins, a surgeon; they had at least six sons and three daughters.

Florio and Shakespeare Since Florio was a contemporary of Shakespeare, it has always been tempting to seek connections between the two. It seems certain that they knew each other, since both had as patrons the earls of Southampton and Pembroke. Shakespeare gives evidence of familiarity with Florio's work: in *Love's Labour's Lost* he has Holofernes the schoolmaster utter the precise proverb from Florio's *Firste Fruites* 'Venetia, Venetia, chi non ti vede non ti pretia', indicating that he had read Florio's language manuals; he included in *The Tempest* (act II, scene i) a passage from Florio's translation of Montaigne; and, given Florio's skill as a word-gatherer and word-expositor, Shakespeare no doubt consulted the vast store of Italian and English vocabulary contained in his *Worlde of Wordes*.

Over a dozen plays by Shakespeare feature Italy or Italian names. This, coupled with the fact that a few theorists during the past two centuries have suggested that Shakespeare's plays could not have been written by the less-than-aristocratic Stratford-born son of a glover, has encouraged the occasional dilettante researcher to give Shakespeare an Italian identity. The theory that Shakespeare was, after all, the cultured Italian Florio was first advanced in Italy in the 1920s during the fervently nationalistic fascist regime. In recent times the same unsubstantiated and anachronistic case has again been made that Michael Angelo Florio was born in Messina, the son of Giovanni Florio and Guglielma Crollalanza (Shake-spear in English), and, being a Calvinist, as a young man fled to England, where he assumed the identity of a deceased cousin who had Anglicized his surname. However, if this Shakespeare were in fact Italian-born, he should surely have known that Milan and Padua were not by the sea, as *The Tempest* and *The Taming of the Shrew* would have it.

The real John Florio, teacher, translator, writer, interpreter, grammarian, and paroemiologist, with his excellent language skills, his knowledge of Italian Renaissance literature, and his elegant style, contributed to the regeneration of English humanism in the latter part of the sixteenth century and to its consolidation at the beginning of the seventeenth century. As the leading language teacher of his day he understood the needs of the inquisitive spirit of his contemporaries. He lacked the inspiration and originality of the poet and playwright, and did not hesitate to borrow, as necessary, his predecessors' material for the compilation of his own works, but he far surpassed the linguists who came before him in the range and size of his productions, in his clever manipulation of the English word, and in his success in providing the impetus, and the passion, for the study of Italian language and culture in his own and in later generations.

DESMOND O'CONNOR

Sources F. A. Yates, *John Florio: the life of an Italian in Shakespeare's England* (1934) · C. Longworth Chambrun, *Giovanni Florio: un apôtre de la Renaissance en Angleterre à l'époque de Shakespeare* (Paris, 1921) · D. O'Connor, *A history of Italian and English bilingual dictionaries* (Florence, 1990) · S. Policardi, *John Florio e le relazioni culturali anglo-italiane agli albori del XVII secolo* (Venice, 1947) · V. Spampanato, 'Giovanni Florio: un amico del Bruno in Inghilterra', *La Critica* [Buenos Aires], 21 (1923), 56–60, 113–25, 189–92, 313–17; 22 (1924), 56–61, 116–24, 246–53 · S. Rossi, *Ricerche sull'umanesimo e sul Rinascimento in Inghilterra* (Milan, 1969) · R. C. Simonini, *Italian scholarship in Renaissance England* (1952) · S. Gamberini, *Lo studio dell'italiano in Inghilterra nel '500 e nel '600* (Messina - Florence, 1970) · D. T. Starnes, 'Bilingual dictionaries of Shakespeare's day', *Publications of the Modern Language Association of America*, 52 (1937), 1005–18 · D. T. Starnes, 'John Florio reconsidered', *Texas Studies in Literature and Language*, 6 (1965), 407–22 · G. Pellegrini, *John Florio e il 'Basilikon doron' di James VI: un esempio inedito di versione elisabettiana* (Milan, 1961) · G. Pellegrini, 'Le regole della lingua thoscana di Michelangelo Florio', *Studi di Filologia Italiana* [Florence], 12 (1954), 77–184 · DNB · R. Owens, 'Shakespeare? He's one of us, say Italians', *The Times* (8 April 2000) · will, PRO, PROB 11/149, sig. 97 · G. Stein, *The English dictionary before Cawdrey* (1985), 378–409
Likenesses W. Hole, line engraving, BM, NPG; repro. in J. Florio, *Queen Anna's new world of words* (1611) [see illus.]
Wealth at death died in poverty: Yates, *John Florio*, 312–15

Florio, Michael Angelo (*d.* 1566×71), Reformed minister, author, and translator, was probably born in Florence or Siena, into a family of converted Jews. He joined the Franciscan conventual order under the name Paolo Antonio, but about 1541 converted to the reform movement, and started a wandering career as a preacher in several Italian cities. In 1548 he was arrested, tortured, and detained in Rome for twenty-seven months. However, he managed to escape on 4 May 1550, and after an adventurous journey arrived in London in November. At this time the English government welcomed continental reformers, hoping that they would contribute to the reform of the English church. Florio formed part of an influx of Italian protestants, who had been officially invited to come over.

Earlier in 1550 a foreign protestant congregation had been set up in London, headed by the Polish reformer John à Lasco. Under the protection of Archbishop Cranmer and Sir William Cecil, Florio was quickly accepted into the ministry of this church, preaching in Italian. He was provided with a royal annuity of £20, while the Italian community in London was to provide him with lodging and a yearly salary. Some prominent Italian merchants, however, refused to contribute. Florio complained bitterly to Cecil, and denounced several wealthy Italians as papists, but without effect. Instead, Florio himself was soon deposed from his ministry, sent out of Cecil's house, and threatened with banishment, as the result of an act of fornication. In addition to this, he entangled himself in a dispute about predestination, which caused suspicions among evangelical leaders about his position on doctrine.

Florio's ministry in London was a failure, but he seems never to have lost favour in court circles. He started a second, and more successful, career as a tutor of Italian. He taught Lady Jane Grey, and perhaps also Princess Elizabeth. His work resulted in two manuscripts about Italian grammar, the 'Regole de la lingua thoscana', and the 'Institution: de la lingua thoscana'; one dedicated to the earl of Pembroke (CUL, MS Dd.xi.46), the other to Lady Jane Grey (BL, Sloane MS 3011). Florio was a close and compassionate eyewitness of Lady Jane's rise and fall in 1553, which he describes in his *Historia de la vita e de la morte … Signora Giovanna Graia*, written in 1561 and published in 1607, in Middelburgh, Zeeland, by the Dutch merchant and scholar Johan Radermacher the elder (Bostoen, 40, 53–5).

Mary Tudor having become queen, Florio, like all foreign protestants, was forced to leave England, departing in the spring of 1554 along with his 'little family'. This probably indicates that his misstep had been regularized by marriage. The family would certainly have included his son John *Florio, who was born in 1553. Michael Angelo Florio went to Strasbourg, where in the middle of 1555 he was invited to minister to the Reformed congregation in Soglio, a tiny village in Val Bregaglia in the Grisons canton of Switzerland. This region was the nearest safe haven for Italian protestants. Here he wrote his *Apologia*, published in 1557, which is the main source of data about his early life and career. In his new office Florio brought trouble upon himself again by defending Bernardino Ochino, who by this time was out of line with Genevan protestantism, and accused of anti-Trinitarianism. The Reformed synod of Chur in 1561 interrogated Florio and two colleagues on this subject, and they were forced to retract their opinions. In spite of his recantation Florio stayed in contact with anti-Trinitarian circles, a fact which only became evident after his death.

In 1563 Florio produced an Italian translation of George Agricola's work on metallurgy, *De re metallica*, and dedicated it to Queen Elizabeth. In the same year he managed to send his promising son John to the Italian reformer Pier Paolo Vergerio, who was working in Tübingen for the duke of Württemberg. He died 'some years before 1571' (Yates, 25), the last written reference to him dating from 1566.

Michael Angelo Florio was a minor, but fervent and outspoken theologian, who was closely in touch with Italian anti-Trinitarianism. His reputation rests principally on his activities as tutor of, and translator into, the Italian language. His son John inherited his father's interest and ability in this field, to become an outstanding linguist and author in that same England where his father's career had been so short and unhappy.　　　　　　　OWE BOERSMA

Sources [M. A. Florio], *Apologia di M. Michel Agnolo Fiorentino, ne la quale si tratta de la vera e falsa chiesa, de l'essere, e qualità de la messa, de la vera presenza di Christo nel sacramento, de la cena, del papato, e primato di S. Piero, de concilii & autorità loro, scritta contro a un' heretico* (1557) • [M. A. Florio], *Historia de la vita e de la morte de l'illustris. signora Giovanna Graia, gia regina eletta a publicata d'Inghilterra* (1607) • F. A. Yates, *John Florio: the life of an Italian in Shakespeare's England* (1934); repr. (1968) • D. Cantimori, *Italienische Haeretiker der Spätrenaissance* (1949), 270ff, 274ff, 282, 290, 292, 466, 468 • O. Boersma and A. J. Jelsma, *Unity in multiformity: the minutes of the coetus of London, 1575 and the consistory minutes of the Italian Church of London, 1570–1591*, Huguenot Society, 59 (1997) • L. Firpo, 'La chiesa italiana di Londra nel cinquecento e i suoi rapporti con Ginevra', *Ginevra e l'Italia* (1959), 309–412 • J. Strype, *Memorials of the most reverend father in God Thomas Cranmer*, new edn, 2 vols. (1812) • J. Strype, *Ecclesiastical memorials*, 3 vols. (1822) • A. M. Ghisalberti and others, eds., *Dizionario biografico degli Italiani*, 56 vols. (Rome, 1960–) • K. Bostoen and others, *Bonis in bonum: Johan Radermacher de Oude, 1538–1617; humanist en koopman* (Hilversum, 1998), 40, 53–5

Florry, Sarah (1744–1832), businesswoman, was born in co. Meath, Ireland, the only surviving child of four children of John Florry (*d.* 1788), ironmaster, and his wife, Anne (*d.* 1799). She was taken to Birmingham as a child and lived in the town for the rest of her life. It is not known how or where she acquired training in running a business. Literate, articulate, and energetic, Sarah Florry applied herself assiduously to building up her enterprise as well as to helping her father in his business on an occasional basis. She set up on her own, at premises at 25 Moor Street, Birmingham, when she was twenty-five years old; this initiative apparently coincided with her parents' move to Shropshire.

Like many eighteenth-century businesspeople Sarah Florry had multiple interests. In the early years she took boarders as well as selling wine. She was principally a metal factor, taking on boys as apprentices and employing men as travellers. One of her travellers, William Walker, became her business partner from about 1784 and thereafter they traded as Florry and Walker. They moved their premises to 6 Easy Row in 1785 and to Congreve Street in 1790. The production and distribution of metalwares in the town was controlled increasingly by intermediaries, such as factors, who grew rich in the process. Operating in this way Florry's partnership with Walker prospered and they apparently used the proceeds of this venture to build up further commercial interests. They were among a group of men and women who, in June 1789, formed a partnership to manufacture brass at a foundry in Smethwick, near Birmingham. Their shareholdings guaranteed them a supply of the metal at a fixed price when the demand for it was growing rapidly in the town, and undoubtedly contributed to their financial success. Sarah Florry retired from business on 31 December 1798, when she and Walker dissolved their partnership.

Sarah Florry had amassed a sufficient fortune during the thirty years of her working life to provide for the remaining and longest part of her life, the time she spent in retirement. She had hoped to settle in Bristol with her mother at the home of her friend Lady Holte, the widow of Sir Charles Holte, MP for Birmingham, but she had to abandon this plan when both women died in 1799. She remained in Birmingham and, in common with other members of the town's wealthy and retired middle classes, she moved to Edgbaston, a cleaner and less crowded suburb on the outskirts of the town. During her retirement she occupied herself in genteel sociability, making calls, drinking tea, dining with friends, and visiting the theatre. She travelled widely for pleasure, and visited many of the favourite tourist destinations in England of the affluent and leisured: London, spas such as Bath and Cheltenham, and country houses of the aristocracy to which respectable sightseers were admitted. She was a regular attender at Anglican churches in Birmingham and on her travels.

Sarah Florry, who never married, died on 15 April 1832, probably aged eighty-eight, at her home at Five Ways, Edgbaston, and was buried on 23 April 1832, in the same vault as her father and mother, at St Philip's Cathedral, Birmingham. Her estate, valued at £4000 for legacy duty purposes, was divided among her female friends and included small bequests to her servants and a distant male relative in Ireland.   CHRISTINE WISKIN

Sources S. Florry, autobiography, 1744–1812, Birm. CA, MS 259854 · *Rotton v. Davis*, Birm. CA, MS 211/11 · *The New Birmingham Directory* (1774) · *Pye's Birmingham Directory* (1785) · *Aris's Birmingham Gazette* (16 April 1832) · parish register, Birmingham, St Philip, 23 April 1832 [burial]
Archives Birm. CA, autobiography, MS 259854 | Birm. CA, *Rotton v. Davis*, MS 211/11
Wealth at death £4000: PRO, death duty registers, IR 26/1288/374; will, PRO, PROB 11/1165/243

Flower, Benjamin (1755–1829), political writer, was born in London, the son of George Flower, a prosperous tradesman and puritan dissenter. One of his brothers, Richard, was the father of the brewer Edward Fordham Flower. Flower inherited a share of his father's business but lost his inherited wealth through unfortunate speculations which he candidly described in his *Statement of Facts* (1808). He worked for a while as a private tutor and in 1785 accepted an engagement to travel in Europe on business for half the year, spending the other six months in the service of a firm at Tiverton. He thus had opportunities of visiting the Netherlands, Germany, and Switzerland, and spent six months in France in 1791, during what he described as 'the most innocent part of the revolution'.

Flower's experience in France inspired him to write a treatise on the French constitution (1792), which is, however, much less an account of the French political system than an attack on the alleged defects of the English. It contributed to his being selected to edit the *Cambridge Intelligencer*, which his brother Richard, a farmer and staunch liberal, had a considerable share in establishing. It was almost the only provincial newspaper in Britain that denounced the war with France as 'absurd and wicked', and advocated the removal of the grievances of the dissenters on the broad grounds of religious liberty. It thus attracted considerable attention and Flower became notorious as a leading anti-government publicist. This hostility to the war was vigorously expressed in his *National Sins Considered* (1796).

In 1799 Flower was summoned before the House of Lords for an alleged libel upon Bishop Watson, whose political conduct he had censured. After a very short hearing he was judged guilty of a breach of privilege, and sentenced to six months' imprisonment in Newgate prison and a fine of £100. The proceedings seem to have been of a very arbitrary nature, but Flower's attempts to obtain their revision by application to the court of king's bench were unsuccessful. His captivity was alleviated by the visits of Eliza Gould (1770–1810), the eldest daughter of John Gould of Dodbroke, a schoolteacher who had herself suffered for her liberal opinions. They married probably in 1800, shortly after his release; the marriage produced two daughters: Eliza *Flower (1803–1846), radical Unitarian and composer, and Sarah Flower *Adams (1805–1848), poet and hymn writer.

Flower relinquished his newspaper and established himself as a printer at Harlow in Essex, where he printed the works of his favourite divine, Robert Robinson, and carried on a monthly magazine, *The Political Register*, from 1807 to 1811. He was a Unitarian, and he edited some works on religious toleration by William Penn and John Milton. Flower's other publications included a pamphlet (1810) justifying dissent from the Church of England, a preface to his brother Richard's *Letters from Illinois*, and some pamphlets on family affairs. His wife died in 1810, and in his latter years he retired to Hackney, where he died on 17 February 1829.

Circumstances have given Flower a more important place in the history of English journalism than was merited by his literary or political abilities. Throughout his life he showed consistency of thought and was a determined publicist for radical causes. Though an advocate of the French republic, he was not in favour of republicanism in Britain.

RICHARD GARNETT, rev. ADAM I. P. SMITH

Sources B. Flower, *A statement of facts, relative to the conduct of … J. Clayton, senior … J. Clayton, junior … and … W. Clayton in the proceedings on the trial of an action brought by N. Flowers against J. Clayton, junior, for defamation, with remarks* (1808) · *Monthly Repository*, new ser., 3 (1829), 210–12
Archives NL Wales, corresp. with his wife
Likenesses J. Baldrey, stipple, pubd 1799 (after J. Bunn), BM, NPG · A. Birrell, stipple, pubd 1799 (after S. Harding), BM, NPG

Flower, Charles Edward (1830–1892), brewer and benefactor, was born on 3 February 1830 at 2 Payton Street, Stratford upon Avon, the eldest of the three sons of Edward Fordham *Flower (1805–1883) and his wife, Selina, *née* Greaves (d. 1884). Educated first by governesses and briefly at the free school in Stratford, he was sent to Edgbaston preparatory school, returning to Stratford when his master, John Atkinson, was transferred to the King Edward VI School. Sir William Henry *Flower, the eminent zoologist, was his brother.

In June 1845 Flower entered the family brewing firm in Stratford, where he learned all aspects of the trade. In October 1846, while his father travelled for six months in America, he managed the Flower brewery, of which he was made a partner in 1852. Marrying Sarah, youngest daughter of Peter Martineau of Islington, on 13 May the same year, he moved to London and for a year managed the export trade of the newly named Flower & Son brewery from a small store in James Street, Adelphi, before returning to Stratford, where he and his wife lived at the brewery. In 1867 he built Avonbank, their home for the remainder of their lives.

On his father's retirement in 1863 Flower became head of Flower & Sons and with his brother, Edgar, modernized and expanded the enterprise. In 1870 a new brewery, incorporating the latest brewing technology, was built and oriented to rail, rather than water transport. In 1888 the firm became a limited liability company, whereupon Charles resigned his active involvement with the business, nevertheless remaining a brewery director and active in Stratford.

Besides having been one of the founders of the Stratford Volunteers, together with his father Flower organized the Stratford Tercentenary in 1864. His greatest achievement, however, was establishing the Shakespeare Memorial Theatre, which was begun in 1879 on land donated by him. Despite constant criticism, the project, which included a gallery and a library, was completed in 1883, funded primarily by Flower. An interest in Shakespeare also led him to contribute to the literature concerning the playwright. In *Shakespeare on Horseback* (1887) and *Shakespeare No Dog Fancier* (1890), Flower discusses the bard's knowledge of horses and dogs as expressed in his plays. His only other publication, *Algerian Hints for Tourists*, was compiled in 1889 after visiting Algiers, and served as a guidebook for many years.

Although a passion for travel took him to remote destinations, including America and Africa, Flower travelled less in his later years. In 1875 he purchased an estate of 11,000 acres at Glencassley in Sutherland, of which county he became a JP. Although he frequently visited his property in Scotland, his other civic duties kept him rooted in Stratford.

His leading role in Stratford involved Flower in many committees and led him to undertake numerous civic and public duties. He served on the town council from 1876 to 1888, and was mayor from 1878 to 1880. He was chairman of the land and buildings committee, the Birthplace Trust executive committee and the records committee which, under his leadership, arranged for the conservation of the hitherto neglected town records. He was a JP for Warwickshire, and for Stratford upon Avon. He was a governor of the Edward VI School, and funded its restoration in 1892. After retiring from the town council, Flower was elected to the Warwickshire county council, on which he served until 3 May 1892, dying of apoplexy during one of their meetings at the court house, Warwick; he was buried four days later at the cemetery, Evesham Road, Stratford upon Avon.

In his will Flower left a bequest to the Memorial Theatre Fund and the Edward VI School, the latter of which was used to establish a scholarship. He also generously supported his nieces and nephews, as well as brewery managers. Having no children of his own, Flower bequeathed nearly his entire estate to his wife. On her death on 21 July 1908 it was distributed among family members and the various hospitals, committees, and organizations which they had supported throughout their lives.

JONATHAN REINARZ

Sources S. Flower, *Great Aunt Sarah's diary, 1846–1892*, ed. E. F. L. Flower (1964) · draft history of the Flower & Sons firm, Shakespeare Birthplace Trust RO, Stratford upon Avon, DR 227/140 · *Stratford Herald* (6 May 1892) · Burke, *Gen. GB* · M. J. Pringle, *The theatres of Stratford-upon-Avon, 1875–1992: an architectural history* (1994) · will, Shakespeare Birthplace Trust RO, Stratford upon Avon, PR 95 · Sarah Flower's will, Shakespeare Birthplace Trust RO, Stratford upon Avon, UR 35/165 · 'Charles Flower's burial', *Stratford Herald* (13 May 1892) · C. E. Flower, 'Shakespeare on horseback': paper read at the Union Club, Stratford-on-Avon (privately printed, Stratford upon Avon, [1887]) · [C. E. Flower], 'Shakespeare no dog fancier', *'Shakespeare on horseback' and 'Shakespeare no dog fancier': papers read before the Stratford-upon-Avon Shakespeare Club* [1892] · C. E. Flower, *Algerian hints for tourists* (1889) · CGPLA Eng. & Wales (1892)
Archives Shakespeare Birthplace Trust RO, Stratford upon Avon, Flower family MSS; records of the firm of Flower & Sons Ltd
Likenesses two photographs, 1864–90, Shakespeare Birthplace Trust RO, Stratford upon Avon · P. Morris, oils, 1891, Royal Shakespeare Theatre, Stratford upon Avon
Wealth at death £156,705 5s. 0d.: resworn probate, Jan 1893, CGPLA Eng. & Wales (1892)

Flower [*née* de Rothschild], **Constance**, **Lady Battersea** (1843–1931), philanthropist and author, was born on 9 December 1843, the daughter of Sir Anthony Nathan de *Rothschild, baronet (1810–1876) [*see under* Rothschild, Nathan Mayer], banker and landowner, and Louisa Montefiore (1821–1910) [*see* Rothschild, Louisa de, Lady de Rothschild], philanthropist. She was educated at home by private tutors in mathematics, English literature, philosophy, drawing, music, French, and Hebrew, but most of her religious instruction came from her mother, who would remain the greatest intellectual and emotional influence of her life. Lady de Rothschild instilled in her most of the traits which would characterize her adult life: her love of reading and of foreign travel, her philanthropic drive and spiritual curiosity and uncertainty. It was her mother who schooled her—to a degree unusual for a Jewish child—in the New Testament, who encouraged her to visit the rural poor in the Rothschild heartland of south Bedfordshire, who brought her into the poor Jewish community of east London, where she began teaching in the Jewish Free School in 1861, and who guided her on her elaborate and educative European travels. Her young adulthood spent with her mother set the pattern for her entire life, and her relatively late marriage to Cyril *Flower (1843–1907), whom she had known for thirteen years, on 22 November 1877, would not disturb this pattern.

Though 'radiantly happy. I love and am beloved' (C. Flower, journal, 21 May 1875, BL, Add. MS 47932, fol. 9), Constance de Rothschild made it a condition of the marriage that she and Cyril should live with her mother at Aston Clinton, her family home since 1853. In return the two women endeavoured to promote Cyril's political career after his adoption as Liberal candidate for Brecon in 1878, cultivating the constituency and even attempting to learn Welsh. Lady de Rothschild was a committed Liberal, but Constance thought politics 'very disgusting' (Cohen, 186–7) and feared the populist potential of democracy. She considered the voting qualification for the boroughs to be too low, but was happiest in a small borough such as Brecon, where it was still possible to know virtually the entire electorate. However, the borough of Brecon was abolished in the redistribution of 1885, and Cyril took refuge in the county seat of South Bedfordshire, where the Rothschilds had for many years selected tenants with Liberal views. Constance Flower would never again involve herself in political work with the commitment that she had shown in Brecon: 'Politics', she wrote in 1884, 'means expediency instead of justice' (C. Flower, 'Jottings', 20 Sept 1884, BL, Add. MS 47938, fol. 11); specifically she found political remedies inadequate for the social problem of drunkenness which now exercised her. Perhaps influenced by the Bacchanalian conduct of the 1880 campaign in Brecon, which she described in some detail in her journal, she took the pledge in 1884 and set up a temperance mission in the town. Her involvement with the temperance cause convinced her that political action could not adequately address pressing moral issues. Her disenchantment with politics was accentuated by Cyril's failure to gain more than a junior lordship of the Treasury in Gladstone's third ministry of January 1886, and above all by the Liberal split over Irish home rule in 1886. Cyril's decision to remain loyal to Gladstone strained relations between him and many close political friends, including several of the Rothschilds, and Constance herself remained uneasy about home rule. 'The division of party is doing its cruel separating work in my case as in so many others' she recorded in 1892 (C. Flower, journal, review of 1892, BL, Add. MS 47940, fol. 71). The home-rule split clouded the cross-party salons which had offered her intellectual stimulation at the Flowers' London home, and Constance found little compensating moral earnestness in Cyril's surviving political circle, 'thoroughly agnostic, neither Jews nor Christians' (ibid., fol. 72).

This stringent tone was characteristic of Constance Flower's journal entries in these years. She noted with veiled contempt Cyril's response to the stagnation, at best, of his political career, in the more vigorous pursuit of pleasure—art collecting, political conviviality, and field sports. Her asceticism reflected unease about her own moral worth, which was in turn rooted in a deeper spiritual crisis. Louisa de Rothschild had interested herself intellectually in Unitarianism and Quakerism as well as Judaism; in Constance, more fervent than her mother, this theological eclecticism transformed itself into a sometimes corrosive spiritual restlessness. Frustrated by the fastidious and archaic nature of her orthodox training, she had once aspired to 'purify and revive' Judaism (Cohen, 182). With her sister Annie (1844–1926) she had published in 1870 *The History and Literature of the Israelites*, conveying the essence of Judaism in two volumes of erudition aimed optimistically at children. By 1884, though, she had convinced herself that Judaism was doomed, and embarked upon the quest to satisfy her complex spiritual

demands, a quest which led her not so much to abandon Judaism as to augment it with other spiritual stimuli. Finding her native faith 'so limited, so narrow, so racial' (C. Flower, journal, 31 Dec 1890, BL, Add. MS 47940, fol. 11), she sought consolation in 'the vivifying breath of Christianity' (ibid., 1891, fols. 47–48). One of six Rothschild women in ten years to marry out of the faith, she never felt out of place at Anglican services, but hers was more than social Christianity. 'There are times when I wd give everything I possess to have been born a Xtian', she noted in her review of 1890. The yearning tone suggests an awareness already of what had become clear to her by 1904, that she stood 'only at the very outer gates of Christianity [which] I shall never enter although it attracts me' (ibid., review of 1904, BL, Add. MS 47944, fol. 17). The Anglican church certainly provided some of the beauty of holiness that she thought lacking in Jewish ceremony. Such emotional stimuli were important to a woman whose greatest secular pleasure derived from Wagner's operas, but they did not resolve her intellectual crisis of faith. In consequence she became susceptible to the heterodox influences of guru figures more confident in their faith than she was—the itinerant American evangelist Moody in 1884, Mary Ward in 1892, and above all the theist Frances Power Cobbe, a close friend from 1876 to her death in 1904. Theism appealed to her for its integrity, its 'having no absurdities to get rid of' (ibid., 5 Aug 1894, BL, Add. MS 47941, fol. 50), but it denied her the experience of collective worship.

Increasingly uncertain about doctrine, Constance Flower clung to her essentially Jewish belief in the redemptive power of good works. In 1885, noting that she cared less for 'society' than before, she began rescue work among London's Jewish community, creating with her sister the Jewish Association for the Protection of Girls and Young Women. Five years later she joined the British Women's Temperance Association. She stepped up her visitation work, begun in the 1870s, in the homes of the London poor. Though a substantial contributor to the organizations which she patronized, her interest lay in active philanthropy rather than in donations alone. Despite her family's wealth, her financial position after marriage was sporadically precarious and was presumably compromised by Cyril's connoisseurship and other expensive pursuits. The construction of the Lutyens-designed house at Overstrand, near Cromer, in 1888 certainly pushed the Flower finances into temporary deficit in 1891. Cyril's conspicuous consumption contrasted with Constance's moral earnestness. 'Why did we not begin modestly in a small house with few servants', she asked her journal (14 Jan 1891, BL, Add. MS 47940, fol. 14). She admired the sturdy virtues of the English middle class—'men who have their day's work not their day's play to attend to' (ibid., review of 1898, BL, Add. MS 47942, fol. 63)—and became increasingly frustrated by her husband's idle life. Cyril, for his part, disapproved of her growing public role. The tension came to a head in 1893. The Liberals' return to power in 1892 had brought Cyril a peerage, as Lord Battersea, rather than office; in the following year he was offered the governorship of New South Wales. The appointment would have ended Constance's philanthropic enterprises in Britain, forced her back into a life of political hostessing, and separated her from her septuagenarian mother. After several sleepless nights and a tearful session with her cousin's widower, Lord Rosebery, she vetoed the move.

With her husband thus confined to the redundant role of a Liberal peer, Lady Battersea developed her own public life. In 1894 she became a prison visitor in the women's prison at Aylesbury, close to Aston Clinton, and from the late 1890s she involved herself in the National Union of Women Workers (NUWW), serving as its national president in 1901–2 and 1902–3. Her public work now became something of a compulsion for her: she made 26 speeches in 1899, while in 1901 she recorded 7 temperance gatherings, 4 city visits, 14 prison visits or prison board meetings, 2 meetings of the National Society for the Prevention of Cruelty to Children, a prize-giving, and an address to pupil teachers. Privately she was troubled by the guilt that had set in almost as soon as she had blocked the move to New South Wales. In 1904 she recorded in her journal that Cyril was spending more time with his relations and less with hers, but the diagnosis of his diabetes in that year began a decline in his health that prevented further estrangement. His death in 1907 genuinely distressed Lady Battersea, who dabbled in the Edwardian fad of spiritualism in the hope of making contact with him. She was more deeply affected, though, by the death of her mother in 1910. Her public work diminished from this date: she lost touch with the NUWW—its industrial lobbying had always interested her less than rescue work and individual visiting—and attended her last prison board meeting in 1918, though she continued her prison visits until 1925. Her last major philanthropic work was the establishment of a hospital at Cromer for Belgian and other allied soldiers in 1914.

Constance Flower's journals in the British Library, though much mutilated and erased, depict in unusual depth a familiar late Victorian and Edwardian type: a highly educated woman, frustrated by the role of political wife, spiritually restless, childless against her wishes, and increasingly unhappy in her marriage, who found her métier in philanthropic activism. Such figures became rarer after 1918. By 1923 Constance, almost eighty, had withdrawn from public work, and, in failing health, she spent her last years alone at Overstrand, 'a useless, helpless old female' in her own eyes (C. Flower, journal, 29 April 1926, BL, Add. MS 47947, fol. 14). She died on 22 November 1931 at Overstrand, and was buried at the Jewish cemetery at Willesden, London.   JOHN DAVIS

Sources C. Flower, journal, BL, Add. MSS 47909–47964 · C. Flower, *Reminiscences* (1922) · L. Cohen, *Lady de Rothschild and her daughters, 1821–1931* (1935) · 'Jewish women's work in philanthropy and education', *Jewish Chronicle* (4 April 1902) · *Jewish Chronicle* (27 Nov 1931) · d. cert. · *Rothschild family tree, 1450–1973* (privately printed, London, 1973)
Archives BL, corresp. and diaries, Add. MSS 47909–47964 | BL, corresp. with Macmillans, Add. MS 55047

Likenesses Mrs Robertson, double portrait, *c.*1844 (with her mother), repro. in Cohen, *Lady de Rothschild and her daughters*, frontispiece · O. E. Galsworthy, photograph, *c.*1923, repro. in Cohen, *Lady de Rothschild and her daughters*, 336 · double portrait (with her sister Annie), repro. in Cohen, *Lady de Rothschild and her daughters*, 118
Wealth at death £200,000: probate, 1931, *CGPLA Eng. & Wales*

Flower, Cyril, Baron Battersea (1843–1907), politician, was born on 30 August 1843, probably at Tooting, the third child and second son of Philip William Flower, West India merchant, of Furzedown, Tooting, and his first wife, Mary, daughter of Jonathan Flower of Feltwell, Norfolk. He was educated at Harrow School and Trinity College, Cambridge, where he matriculated in the Michaelmas term, 1863. After taking his BA in 1867 he was admitted to the Inner Temple. Called to the bar in April 1870, he succeeded immediately as a special pleader, earning £365 in his first year, but the death of his father in February 1872 obliged him to devote himself to the family estate in Battersea. He married Constance (1843–1931) [*see* Flower, Constance], the eldest daughter of Sir Anthony Nathan de Rothschild, first baronet, of Tring Park, Hertfordshire, on 22 November 1877, thirteen years after meeting her through her cousin Leopold, a contemporary of his at Cambridge.

Admission to the Rothschild circle brought Flower into public life and reinforced his interest, expressed to his wife soon after their marriage, in a political career. Adopted Liberal candidate for Brecon in December 1878, he captured the seat from the tories in the 1880 general election. An Englishman and a churchman, whose political friends Constance Flower considered 'thoroughly agnostic and unbelieving', he none the less won this largely nonconformist Welsh constituency by fifty-nine votes. He owed his victory to eighteen months' cultivation of the electorate—he claimed to have met every voter in the borough. The Brecon parliamentary borough was abolished in 1885 and Flower moved to South Bedfordshire (Luton), winning comfortably in 1885, 1886, and 1892. He served as junior lord of the Treasury in Gladstone's 1886 government. Simultaneously he became a Liberal whip in the Commons, a position which he occupied for six difficult years, encompassing the Irish home-rule split and the Parnell scandal. Although Lady Frances Balfour believed, after the 1885 election, that 'in his heart of hearts he will be thankful that the country has not declared for Chamberlain's revolution', his public statements reflected 'advanced' Liberalism. In Brecon he advocated improved industrial injury compensation and the equalization of the borough and county franchises, in South Bedfordshire the abolition of entail and primogeniture. Though friendly with many of the whig defectors in 1886, Flower, whose political life, Lady Balfour believed, 'may be said to be the creation of the personal magnetism of Mr Gladstone', declared for home rule. Gladstone rejoiced that a Rothschild connection had remained loyal. Nevertheless, the 'overwhelming element of bitterness' which his wife attributed to home rule tainted the bipartisan political salon world in which the Flowers had flourished.

Cyril Flower, Baron Battersea (1843–1907), self-portrait, 1890s

Flower did not return to office; after the 1892 election he was promoted to the House of Lords as Baron Battersea of Battersea and of Overstrand. He served Gladstone's purpose of augmenting the diminished Liberal presence there but Vicary Gibbs considered him 'not one of [Gladstone's] most successful efforts to adorn the upper house' (GEC, *Peerage*, 2.33). In February 1893 he declined the governorship of New South Wales, apparently in deference to Lady de Rothschild's reluctance to lose her daughter, and effectively withdrew, demoralized, from public life.

The Flowers were very rich. Flower shared his wife's philanthropic interests, becoming president of the People's Entertainment Society and a governor of the Battersea Polytechnic. He built model housing for the working class in Battersea, though by 1900 the Flower estate was occupied, according to Charles Booth, by 'the upper-grade artisan and lower-grade salaried classes'. His private life combined hunting and riding (he won the first House of Commons steeplechase in 1889 on a horse rechristened Home Rule) with an adventurous aestheticism. He patronized the painters Watts, Tissot, and Millais, and the sculptor Alfred Gilbert (who exhibited a bust of him at the Royal Academy in 1886) and decorated his homes, Surrey House at Marble Arch and Overstrand, near Cromer, so lavishly as to burden his estate. He took up motoring in 1905, but ill health—diabetes was diagnosed in 1904—restricted this pleasure. He died of pneumonia at the Royal Pier Hotel, Ryde, on 27 November 1907, and was buried at Overstrand; he left no heir. His wife survived him.

JOHN DAVIS

Sources C. Battersea, *Reminiscences* (1922) · L. Cohen, *Lady de Rothschild and her daughters, 1821–1931* (1935) · F. Balfour, *Ne obliviscaris: dinna forget*, 2 vols. [1930] · GEC, *Peerage* · *The Times* (28 Nov 1907) · *Daily News* (28 Nov 1907) · *Daily Telegraph* (28 Nov 1907) · *Westminster Gazette* (28 Nov 1907) · C. Booth, *Life and labour of the people in London*, 3rd ser., 5 (1902) · Venn, *Alum. Cant.* · *Brecon County Times* (1880) · *Luton Times and Bedfordshire Advertiser* (1885–6)
Archives BL, corresp. and papers, Add. MSS 47909–47964
Likenesses A. Gilbert, portrait, exh. RA 1886 · C. Flower, self-portrait, photograph, 1890–99, NPG [*see illus.*] · Sandys, crayon · G. F. Watts, sketch · photograph, repro. in *ILN*, 101 (1892), 300 · photograph, repro. in *ILN*, 106 (1895), 131 · photograph, repro. in *VF* (19 Aug 1882), pl. 408
Wealth at death £186,747 8s.: probate, 8 Feb 1908, CGPLA Eng. & Wales

Flower, Sir Cyril Thomas (1879–1961), record scholar, was born on 31 March 1879 at Warminster, Wiltshire, the only child of Thomas Flower, who practised medicine there, as his father had done. Thomas Flower, cousin of Henry Fawcett, the blind politician, married Jessie Susan, daughter of William Pope, of Biggleswade, Bedfordshire; he died in 1881. Cyril Flower won a scholarship at St Edward's School, Oxford, and entered Worcester College, Oxford, as senior scholar; he obtained a first in classical moderations (1899) and a second in *literae humaniores* (1901), and entered the Public Record Office in 1903. His first nine years were spent mainly in the legal search room; he joined the Inner Temple and was called to the bar in 1906.

In 1910 Flower began the work on the *curia regis* rolls which he was to continue for fifty years. In 1912 he moved to the secretary's office to assist R. A. Roberts and later A. E. Stamp. Flower married in 1910 Helen Mary Harding, daughter of David William Thompson, an Irishman and a retired inspector of schools in the Punjab; they had one daughter. On his marriage Flower moved from his mother's house in Ealing to the house next door.

In November 1914 Flower went to the War Office as a private secretary to the director of contracts; a year later he was commissioned in the Royal Garrison Artillery and went with his battery to France in August 1916. In October he was severely wounded; and, on 'light duty', he returned to army contracts in 1917 and remained there until he was demobilized in June 1919. For his services in contracts he received the Croix de Guerre.

After returning to his former post at the Public Record Office, Flower also became the legal member and secretary of the inspecting officers' committee which arranged, with the departments concerned, schedules of the records that were to be preserved or destroyed. In 1926 he became secretary of the PRO when Stamp succeeded Sir Henry Maxwell Lyte as deputy keeper; on Stamp's death in March 1938 Flower was appointed deputy keeper by the master of the rolls, the statutory keeper of the records. In October the office celebrated the centenary of the Public Record Act of 1838. Flower was made CB in the following January.

His nine years as deputy keeper included the six wartime years. The dominating problem in 1938 was the safety of the records and the protection of the PRO in the event of air attacks. Flower could not bring himself to believe that war was imminent or inevitable, but plans were made for evacuating records to several temporary repositories in the country, and for instructing staff in air-raid precaution (ARP) services. Evacuation of the records began apace in late August 1939 and continued with breaks until 1942; some 2000 tons of records were dispatched from Chancery Lane and the repository for modern records at Canterbury to seven centres in the country ranging from the gaol at Shepton Mallet in Somerset to Belvoir Castle in Leicestershire. Flower kept in touch with the office custodians there and visited most of them. The records remaining at Chancery Lane were assembled on the lower floors. With this large-scale dispersal of the records, the closing of the literary search room, and the departure of many members of the staff to military service or to other government offices, the staff remaining at Chancery Lane were organized mainly on an ARP footing. Flower took more than his share in this arduous business, patrolling the vast building during 'alerts' and spending at least one night a week on this duty.

Although situated in a heavily bombed area, the Public Record Office escaped serious damage throughout the war; and the records remaining there and those in the country repositories were intact. Flower was unwilling to reassemble them before Japan was out of the war. The work began in earnest in September 1945, and in June 1946 he was able to report to the master of the rolls that the records had returned safely to the strongrooms at Chancery Lane; the modern records formerly at Canterbury were lodged temporarily in some of the wartime 'deep shelters' in the London area.

As chairman of a depleted inspecting officers' committee Flower co-operated with departments under pressure from the paper shortage committee in preparing new schedules to shorten the periods for retention of documents. On the other hand, as the executive member of the Historical Manuscripts Commission and chairman of the British Records Association's council, he was much involved in their efforts to prevent documents of historical importance in private hands from being swept away in the drive for salvage. Another of his official activities was his membership of the committee for the control of official histories of the war; and he succeeded R. A. Butler, then president of the Board of Education, as chairman of the editorial board of the official medical history of the Second World War.

Another institution under Flower's charge during the war was the Institute of Historical Research of which he was honorary director from 1939 until 1944, arranging for the several compulsory wartime moves of the institute, its library, and stocks of the Victoria History of the Counties of England.

Flower's connections with learned societies were many: fellow of the Society of Antiquaries from 1921 and vice-president from 1939 to 1943; secretary of the Canterbury and York Society in 1906; treasurer of the Pipe Roll Society from 1938. He served on the council of the Selden Society from 1937 and was president from 1949 to 1952; for the society he edited *Public Works in Mediaeval Law* (vol. 32, 1915;

vol. 40, 1923) and prepared an *Introduction to the curia regis rolls, 1199–1230* (vol. 42, 1943).

Flower's major contribution to scholarship was his transcription and editing of the *curia regis* rolls. The first volume, *Curia regis rolls, Richard I.–2 John*, delayed by the first war, was published in 1922, the fourteenth (1230–32) in 1961. There remained in manuscript his transcripts (with assistance latterly from former colleagues) for a further twenty years, already indexed. Medievalists over the decades welcomed this important series and reviewers were particularly appreciative of the elaborate indexes. Flower was a first-rate compiler of indexes, especially of subject indexes.

Flower was knighted in 1946 and elected FBA in the following year. He retired in 1947 on his sixty-eighth birthday, after forty-four years in the PRO, of which the last nine were the most strenuous.

A churchwarden and a manager of the local Church of England schools for forty years, Flower was in politics as in outlook unshakeably conservative. He played rugby for school and college, and for Middlesex from 1904 to 1906: a 14-stone forward, over 6 foot 2 'and fast for a big man'. Despite his severe wounds and some deafness he continued to live an active life, retained an equable temper and remarkably good health up to the end. He died peacefully in his sleep at his home, 2 Lammas Park Gardens, Ealing, London, on 9 August 1961.   DAVID L. EVANS, *rev.*

Sources D. L. Evans, 'Sir Cyril Flower, 1879–1961', *PBA*, 48 (1962), 387–96 · personal knowledge (1981) · *CGPLA Eng. & Wales* (1961)
Likenesses W. Stoneman, photograph, 1946, NPG
Wealth at death £12,381 16s. 8d.: probate, 25 Oct 1961, *CGPLA Eng. & Wales*

Flower, Edward Fordham (1805–1883), brewer, was born on 31 January 1805, at Marden Hall, near Hertford, Hertfordshire, the eighth son of Richard Flower (d. 1829), a brewer, banker, and well-known agriculturalist. One of his uncles was Benjamin Flower, a celebrated political writer and newspaper editor, who was imprisoned on more than one occasion for his beliefs. In 1817, when Edward was twelve, the family emigrated to the United States, where Richard Flower founded the settlement of Albion, Illinois. Edward Flower abruptly returned to England in 1824 after threats were made on his life on account of his involvement in the campaign to abolish slavery in Kentucky. With capital of £2000 from his father, he settled in Stratford upon Avon and began working in the corn trade, and later went into partnership with James Cox to found a timber merchants' firm. In 1827 he married Selina Greaves (d. 1884) of Barford, the eldest daughter of John Greaves of Radford House, near Leamington Spa; they had three sons. Upon the death of his father in 1829 Flower inherited a modest sum from the proceeds of his estate, which he invested in the building of a brewery in Stratford in 1831. The brewery proved very successful: in 1833 sales figures amounted to £3423, and by 1866 the company was turning over £100,000 in sales per year.

By this date Flower had already retired from the brewing business for at least three years, but he continued his interest in local affairs, which began in his thirties when he became an overseer of the poor. He was four times chosen mayor of the borough of Stratford, the last occasion being in 1864, when he organized the tercentenary celebrations of Shakespeare's birth. He was well known for his hospitality to all visitors to Shakespeare's birthplace, especially Americans, many of whom stayed with him at his residence, The Hill, built in 1855. He was a magistrate for Warwickshire. As a Liberal he contested Coventry in 1865, and at the 1868 general election he unsuccessfully contested the northern division of the county.

In 1873 Flower retired to London, and devoted the rest of his life to the advocacy of more humane treatment of horses. In *A Few Words about Bearing Reins* (1875), *Bits and Bearing Reins* (1875), and *Horses and Harness* (1876) he proposed the abolition of equestrian harnesses and gag-bits. The improvement of road construction was the subject of another pamphlet, entitled *The Stones of London, or, Macadam v. Vestries* (1880).

Flower died at his home, 35 Hyde Park Gardens, London, on 26 March 1883, aged seventy-eight. His widow Selina survived him, but died on 2 March 1884. Their eldest son, Charles Edward *Flower, joined his father as a partner in the brewery in 1852, but will be remembered as the founder of the Shakespeare Memorial Theatre at Stratford upon Avon, which later became the base of the Royal Shakespeare Company. Their second son was Sir William Henry *Flower, Hunterian professor of comparative anatomy at the Royal College of Surgeons, and president of the Zoological Society of London. The youngest son, Edgar Flower (d. 1903), became a partner in the family brewery in 1854, when the company became E. F. Flower & Sons. Edgar was later chairman of the Shakespeare Birthplace Trust.   FIONA WOOD

Sources *Stratford upon Avon Chronicle* (30 March 1883) · *The house of Whitbread* (1961), 25–8 · H. Jones, 'Flowers breweries', Whitbread Archives, London · B. McVie, 'Stratford upon Avon Flowers brewery', *Brewing in Warwickshire*, ed. A. Kir [n.d.] · *Brewers' Journal* (15 April 1883), 116–17 · *Guide to Flower's ales in Shakespeare's country* (1935) · obituary files, Brewers' Society, London
Archives Brewers' Society, London, obituary files · Whitbread, London, Flowers Brewery
Wealth at death £51,726 4s. od.: probate, 9 May 1883, *CGPLA Eng. & Wales*

Flower, Eliza (1803–1846), radical and composer, was born at Harlow in Essex on 19 April 1803, the eldest daughter of Benjamin *Flower (1755–1829), a Cambridge printer, and his wife, Eliza, *née* Gould (1770–1810), a schoolteacher, the eldest daughter of John Gould of Dodbroke. Benjamin Flower was, like several members of his family, well known as a radical and closely connected with Unitarian circles. He was editor of the *Cambridge Intelligencer* from 1793 to 1800 and of the *Political Review* from 1807 to 1811. He was sent to prison in 1799, accused of libelling Bishop Watson. In prison he later met Eliza's mother, who, on being told she had to choose between her boarding-school in South Molton and her radical political beliefs, had travelled to London to meet Flower. They married in 1800, upon Flower's release from prison.

Eliza Flower senior died in 1810 after giving birth to a short-lived baby boy, and Eliza and her sister, Sarah, were brought up unconventionally by their father. In 1820 Flower and his daughters moved to Dalston near Hackney where they became acquainted with the Unitarian writer Harriet Martineau. Martineau was immediately struck by the Flower girls, and particularly Eliza, and they apparently were the models for the Ibbotson sisters in her 1839 novel *Deerbrook*. By 1823 the Flowers were moving at the heart of an extremely unconventional, radical Unitarian circle presided over by the minister of South Place Chapel, William Johnson Fox. This brought them into contact with many of the aspiring writers and reformers of the day, including Robert Browning, Thomas Southwood Smith, Harriet Taylor (with whom Eliza Flower began to develop an intense friendship), William Bridges Adams (whom Sarah married in 1834), Vincent Novello, and John Stuart Mill.

In 1829 Benjamin Flower died and his daughters went to live with their guardian, W. J. *Fox (1786–1864), and his family. Eliza Flower grew increasingly intimate with Fox, whom she assisted greatly with his literary work. Tensions between Fox and his wife mounted, and in 1832 they decided upon a separation, although they continued to live in the same house. In 1834 Fox left his wife and went on to set up a new home with Eliza Flower and his two eldest children, Eliza and Florance (a deaf mute), at Craven Hill. Although a minority of the South Place congregation left Fox's ministry and he was obliged to resign from the Unitarian body, Fox continued as preacher at the increasingly radical South Place Chapel.

Eliza Flower was instrumental in cultivating the radical salon at Craven Hill, to which such figures as William James Linton, Thomas Wade, the Gillies sisters, and the Howitts were attracted. It was this circle which proved to be so important to the development of the radical and feminist ideas which found expression in the *Monthly Repository*, of which Fox was the editor and Flower his assistant. Flower appears to have had a remarkable impact upon all whom she met. Extremely beautiful and highly charismatic, she seems to have been possessed of a rare spiritual quality, earning her the name Ariel among many contemporaries, and entirely captivating such men as John Stuart Mill, William James Linton, and also the writers Robert Browning and John Forster, who often sought her literary advice. Contemporary observers often claimed that Fox's fame was largely due to Eliza's influence.

Eliza Flower was also a gifted musician. Although largely untrained, by 1831 she had published her first musical composition, *Fourteen Musical Illustrations of the Waverley Novels*. This was followed by *Songs of the Seasons* in 1834. She worked closely with the musical director of South Place Chapel, the radical Collet Dobson Collet, to raise the priority of music at the chapel by training choirs and organizing lectures and meetings. Her organ concerts were enormously popular and frequently involved her sister, Sarah Flower *Adams, a gifted singer whose verses, including the famous 'Nearer, my God, to thee', she often set to music. Flower wrote a musical service for the congregation of South Place, *Hymns and Anthems*, which was arranged in five parts, of which four were published. Sixty-three of the hymns were composed by Flower and many others adapted or arranged by her. A reform anthem, written to words by Harriet Martineau, became a popular song with contemporary political reform unions. Flower also composed music sung at the funeral of the reformist Hindu divine Raja Rammohun Roy. Although Flower's compositions subsequently fell into obscurity, many contemporary reviewers believed that she was the greatest female composer the country had yet seen, particularly praising her gift of harmonic arrangement.

The last years of Flower's life do not appear to have been happy. While she became a central figure to Eliza and Florance Fox, her relationship with W. J. Fox was often difficult. Some of her contemporaries believed this was because the couple felt constrained to maintain it as a platonic relationship, although it is obviously difficult to evaluate such claims. The situation deteriorated following their decision to move to London in 1839, which enabled Fox to participate more fully in political life. They lived for a time with Flower's beloved sister and brother-in-law, but Flower always hated the noise and bustle of London and residence there appears to have exacerbated her poor health. From 1842 she often had to spend periods in the countryside. She died on 12 December 1846 from consumption while at Hurstpierpoint near Brighton. Eliza Flower was buried in the family grave at the Baptist cemetery at Harlow in Essex. Congregants remembered for years later her emotional memorial service which took place at South Place Chapel on the 20 December, presided over by Fox.   KATHRYN GLEADLE

Sources H. W. Stephenson, *The author of Nearer, my God, to thee* (1922) · R. Garnett and E. Garnett, *The life of W. J. Fox, public teacher and social reformer, 1786–1864* (1910) · M. D. Conway, *Centenary history of the South Place Society* (1894) · *Westminster Review*, 37 (1842), 496 · K. Gleadle, *The early feminists: radical Unitarians and the emergence of the women's rights movement, 1831–51* (1995) · M. D. Conway, *Autobiography: memories and experiences*, 2 vols. (1904) · F. E. Mineka, *The dissidence of dissent: the Monthly Repository, 1806–1838* (1944) · *The Reasoner* (7 Feb 1849), 95 · W. J. Linton, *Memories* (1895) · E. F. Bridell Fox, *Sarah Flower Adams: a memoir and her hymns* (1894) · *Mary Howitt: an autobiography*, ed. M. Howitt, 2 vols. (1889)

Likenesses E. Bridell Fox, portrait, repro. in Garnett, *Life of W. J. Fox*, 70

Flower, John (*b.* 1623/4), Church of England clergyman, was born at Cubley, Derbyshire, the son of William Flower, gentleman, of Cubley. He attended Oxford University, matriculating at New Inn Hall on 17 June 1640, aged sixteen. He graduated BA on 2 April 1647 and MA on 14 April 1648. It seems likely that he was the Mr Flower who on 28 September 1648 was ordered to be examined for the ministry by the Westminster assembly; in 1652 he became a preacher at Ilmington, Warwickshire, remaining there until 1656. On 15 February that year Flower was instituted to the sequestered rectory of Staunton, Nottinghamshire, perhaps on the presentation or through the influence of

Colonel Edward Whalley, a moderate Independent and major-general in the east midlands. *Several Queries Concerning the Church of Christ upon Earth*, issued by 'John Flowre MA, preacher at Staunton in the County of Nottingham', was hostile to the gathering of churches in England and sympathetic to the reformed churches of Europe. Its preface to Whalley, dated 2 February 1658, recalls 'the countenance and many respects I have received from you'; a second preface is directed to 'my much esteemed friends and neighbours the inhabitants of the town and parish of Staunton'. On 23 July 1660 a successor was instituted at Staunton on presentation of the crown. Flower conformed after the Restoration, and was probably the man ordained deacon and priest in the diocese of Galloway on 28 March 1661. He was instituted to the rectory of Leigh in Essex on 11 January 1662, after which nothing is known of him. The admission of William Secker to the living on 30 August 1667 may indicate the approximate date of Flower's death.   STEPHEN WRIGHT

Sources *Calamy rev.* · *Walker rev.* · J. Flowre [J. Flower], *Several queries concerning the church of Christ upon earth* (1658) · Foster, *Alum. Oxon.* · A. F. Mitchell and J. Struthers, eds., *Minutes of the sessions of the Westminster assembly of divines* (1874) · R. Newcourt, *Repertorium ecclesiasticum parochiale Londinense*, 2 (1710)

Flower, Robin Ernest William (1881–1946), scholar of Irish literature and poet, was born on 16 October 1881 at Meanwood, Leeds, the son of Marmaduke Clement William Flower, a portrait painter who had fought on the Confederate side in the American Civil War after being disowned by his family, and his wife, Jane Lynch. Both parents were of Irish extraction: Jane Lynch came of a Galway family, and the Flowers were English settlers in Ireland. Marmaduke's father was the son of the Revd William Bambro' Flower, a patristic scholar who translated St Bernard of Clairvaux. Robin Flower was educated at Leeds grammar school and from 1900 at Pembroke College, Oxford, where he gained a double first in classics (1904). After a period of recuperation from ill health spent in the Orkneys and at Cologne, he took up appointment in 1906 as assistant in the department of manuscripts in the British Museum, where he was to become deputy keeper of manuscripts in 1929. Soon after starting at the British Museum he was commissioned to complete the catalogue of the museum's Irish manuscripts which had been started by Standish Hayes O'Grady in 1886.

In 1906 Flower began with dedication and spectacular success to learn Irish in its three forms: Old Irish (which he studied briefly in Dublin in 1910 with the great Norwegian Celticist Carl J. S. Marstrander, who was to be godfather to Flower's eldest daughter), Middle Irish (defined by Flower himself as extending from the twelfth century to the seventeenth), and modern spoken Irish, on which he was to become a major authority. In 1910 he made the first of many visits to the Blasket Islands off west Kerry, where he stayed (as Marstrander had in 1907) on the Great Blasket with Pádraig Ó Catháin, the rí ('king') of the island. He became known to the islanders as Bláithín ('little flower'), and his correspondence with them over the next thirty years is a significant holding in the department of Irish folklore in University College, Dublin. In 1911 he married Ida Mary Streeter, daughter of John Soper Streeter, a solicitor from Croydon, and the youngest sister of Flower's university friend Canon B. H. Streeter. They had three daughters and one son; the eldest daughter, Barbara, was a scholar who died in 1945. At the outbreak of the Second World War in 1939 Flower was sent to the National Library of Wales in Aberystwyth, to take charge of the British Museum manuscripts in safe keeping there. He resigned from the British Museum in 1944 because of illness, and he died at the North Middlesex Hospital, Edmonton, on 16 January 1946.

Flower's volume 2 of the *Catalogue of Irish Manuscripts in the British Museum* appeared in 1926, along with his updating of O'Grady's volume 1; his projected third volume, which was intended to comprise introduction, indexes, and some commentary, never appeared, such was his activity on several other fronts. He was elected fellow of the British Academy in 1934, and was also a member of the Royal Irish Academy, a corresponding fellow of the Mediaeval Academy of America, and a leading member of the Irish Texts Society, of which he was chairman of the council, and the Early English Text Society, of which he became honorary acting director in 1940. He was an honorary lecturer in Celtic at University College, London, and lecturer in Irish at University College, Dublin. He was a fellow of the Royal Historical Society and a DLitt of both the National University of Ireland and Trinity College, Dublin, where he gave the Donnellan lectures in 1938. He was 'above all a medievalist', in the words of Séamus Ó Duilearga in his Radio Éireann obituary for Flower, prefaced to Flower's important collected essays *The Irish Tradition* (1947; repr., 1994), with a knowledge of Anglo-Saxon (as well as German, Welsh, Latin, and Greek); in 1933 he collaborated in editing the facsimile of the Exeter book, one of the codices of the greatest Old English poetry. His models were Kuno Meyer and W. P. Ker, whom Flower idolized; they were the godfathers of his other two daughters.

Robin Flower's principal significance lies in his shaping of an Irish tradition, in reaction against the misty Celticism of Renan and Arnold, especially in his 1927 Sir John Rhŷs memorial lecture for the British Academy, 'Ireland and medieval Europe' (reprinted as chapter 5 of *The Irish Tradition*). He was a skilful poet in two forms: the elegant quatrains into which he translated Old Irish poetry, and a quiet, free-verse plainstyle for his original poems, the most significant of which are on Blaskets subjects and included in his delightful memoir *The Western Island, or, The Great Blasket* (1944). A volume of his post-Renaissance translations, *Love's Bitter-Sweet*, was published by Elizabeth Yeats's Cuala Press in 1928, and collected in the complete *Poems and Translations* (1931; repr. 1994). He declared that 'to translate poetry by less than other poetry is a sin beyond absolution' (Conghaill, xvi). Perhaps his most important friendship (and literary achievement) was with

Tomás Ó Criomthain, whose *An tOileánach* Flower edited and translated as *The Islandman* (1936). Through his recording of such writers and storytellers as Ó Criomthain and Peig Sayers, Robin Flower was the founder of the Blaskets literary tradition of Irish autobiography.

BERNARD O'DONOGHUE

Sources H. I. Bell, *PBA*, 32 (1946), 353–74 · *DNB* · S. Ó Duilearga, *In memoriam*, Radio Éireann, 1946 [radio broadcast]; transcribed as introduction to R. Flower, *The Irish tradition* (1947) · M. M. Conghaill, 'A note on the author', in R. Flower, *Poems and translations* (1994) · *CGPLA Eng. & Wales* (1946)

Archives BL, corresp. with Sir Idris Bell, Add. MS 59510 · Somerville College, Oxford, letters to Percy Withers and family **Likenesses** W. Stoneman, photograph, 1934, NPG · D. Bell, pencil drawing, priv. coll. · W. Bennett, watercolour drawing, priv. coll. **Wealth at death** £2123 17s. 3d.: probate, 4 May 1946, *CGPLA Eng. & Wales*

Flower [Flore], **Roger** (*d.* 1427), administrator and speaker of the House of Commons, was the son of William Flower (*d. c.*1405), a wool merchant who was member of parliament for Rutland in October 1382, and his wife, Ellen. Like his father, Roger was involved in the wool trade, working in partnership with William Dalby of Oakham, whose daughter Katherine he married by 1398 (and whose foundation of the hospital of St John the Evangelist and St Anne, Oakham, he effected as Dalby's executor and heir). Flower followed his father, too, in administrative duties in the royal manor of Oakham, and also in the forests of Rutland and Northamptonshire under Edward, earl of Rutland, later duke of York (*d.* 1415). It was probably through the latter's patronage that he was first elected to parliament for Rutland in January 1397, and again in 1399; the duke later appointed him an executor. Presumably he had received legal training before 1397, since he enjoyed an expanding practice thereafter.

The course of Flower's career was only briefly disturbed by Henry IV's seizure of the throne in 1399. He was entrusted with a commission against sedition in 1402, and returned to parliament in that year (and in October 1404), later becoming sheriff of Rutland in 1407–8 and 1412–13. In 1416 Henry V made Flower steward of the duchy of Lancaster's estates north of the Trent (and so also justice of the peace in no less than ten counties), with a salary of £40 plus 5s. per day worked; early in the following year he also became steward of Lancashire and Cheshire. In his will of 1417 the king nominated Flower as a possible replacement for any of the duchy's panel of trustees who should die during his absence in France. Flower was again returned for Rutland to the seven parliaments from 1414 to 1419, and for a twelfth time in 1422. He was also speaker an unprecedented three times running (October 1416, 1417, 1419). In 1422 he was appointed speaker yet again, immediately after a hurried election, which suggests that his experience was needed for the first parliament of Henry VI's minority. The parliaments in which Flower was speaker of the Commons were gratifyingly generous to the crown; if the Agincourt effect was largely responsible, it was also to his credit as a Lancastrian servant. It is possible that his personal concern with the impact of Lollardy in the east midlands influenced the petition presented in the parliament of 1417 for the speedy execution of Sir John Oldcastle. Flower continued to exert influence on Rutland elections after his retirement, and he attended the parliaments of 1425 and 1426 as the abbot of Crowland's proxy.

Flower died in 1427 before November, leaving land in Rutland, Lincolnshire, and Leicestershire, and over £550 in legacies. By 1412 he had married as his second wife, Cecily Samon, who outlived him. There were seven surviving children of his two marriages; his heir, Thomas, followed him as member for Rutland (1432, 1445) and as sheriff, and also assumed his father's Lancastrian mantle, which proved increasingly detrimental to his position and prospects.   JULIAN LOCK

Sources C. Rawcliffe, 'Flore, Roger', HoP, *Commons* · J. S. Roskell, 'Roger Flore of Oakham', *Leicestershire Archaeological and Historical Society Transactions*, 33 (1957), 36–44; repr. in *Parliament and politics in late medieval England*, 3 (1983), 255–63 · J. S. Roskell, *The Commons and their speakers in English parliaments, 1376–1523* (1965) · J. S. Roskell, *The Commons in the parliament of 1422* [1954] · F. J. Furnivall, ed., *The fifty earliest English wills in the court of probate, London*, AD 1387–1439, EETS, original ser., 78 (1882); repr. (1964), 55–64 · G. L. Harriss, *Cardinal Beaufort: a study of Lancastrian ascendancy and decline* (1988) · J. C. Wedgwood and A. D. Holt, *History of parliament*, 1: *Biographies of the members of the Commons house, 1439–1509* (1936)
Wealth at death £550—legacies in moveables: Furnivall, *Fifty earliest English wills*, 55–64

Flower, William (1497/8–1588), herald, was probably the son of John Flower, tailor and corn merchant of York. He married Helen Davyes and had two sons and three daughters, of whom Elizabeth married Robert Glover, Somerset herald, and after his death a Mr Woolward. Little is known of Flower until he was appointed an officer of arms, beginning as Guînes pursuivant-extraordinary in 1536. As an officer he was often employed on overseas missions, which led him to complain that he was not able to furnish himself with his colleagues' heraldic treatises at their deaths, including those he would eventually need as Norroy king of arms. It has been claimed that he held an appointment as Calais pursuivant-extraordinary, but this seems to be confusion between Flower and Nicholas Fellow. Flower received his patent as Rouge Croix pursuivant in 1544, with his salary from Lady day 1543. His patent as Chester herald passed the great seal in 1547, though he drew his salary in that office from Michaelmas 1545. In 1555 he deputized for Thomas Hawley as Clarenceux and served as his marshal. In 1562 he became Norroy king of arms.

As Norroy, Flower was caught up in the strife that characterized the Elizabethan College of Arms. Responding to the earl marshal's orders of 1568 that attempted to consolidate the heralds' books as well as to regulate grants of arms, Flower as Norroy and Robert Cooke as Clarenceux were still defending their right to grant arms in 1585, in a document that may have been written by Flower's son-in-law, Robert Glover, Somerset herald—it is remarkably similar to the latter's treatise of 1587, 'The gyving of

armes no wayes hurtfull to the commonweale', which also draws on Sir Thomas Smith's *De republica Anglorum*. The document defends the two kings of arms in their right to grant arms to 'worthy' petitioners.

In addition to these problems, Flower and Cooke also had to fend off the attempts of Sir William Dethick as Garter to encroach on their rights to make visitations to record arms and pedigrees, and even to grant arms himself. Presumably because of Flower's advancing years, his defence against Garter seems largely to have fallen to Glover, who was not only defending Flower as Norroy but also his own future office. In 1580, when Flower was eighty-two, he obtained a new patent as Norroy granting the reversion of his office to Glover. This undoubtedly explains not only Glover's defence of the rights of Clarenceux and Norroy, but also his arguments against promotion in the College of Arms by mere seniority. Norroy's attempt to secure the reversion of his office to Glover foundered when his son-in-law died shortly before him.

Either by Glover as his deputy or in person, Flower visited virtually all of his northern province. Mark Noble is warm in his praise of Flower, claiming that 'Few have been more assiduous in the duties of their profession, than this Norroy, as the visitations of his province evince' (Noble, 172), though he seems to be mistaken that a relative, Robert Flower, briefly held the post of Somerset. This may be a confusion with Robert Glover, married to Elizabeth Flower. Flower adopted what Wagner calls Glover's 'modern rectilinear tabular form' (Wagner, *Records and Collections of the College of Arms*, 58) for his visitation of Cheshire of 1566, and it was under his aegis that Glover began the modern practice of using records as evidence for the arms and pedigrees he entered. With Clarenceux, Norroy gave a commission to visit Wales.

Flower became one of the Poor Knights of Windsor, and in his will of 1588 calls himself their governor. He died at Windsor in 1588, leaving little in his will aside from clothing and furniture. Flower's visitations have been published by the Harleian Society. As well as these, his ordinaries and pedigrees, he was also responsible for a report from France in 1559 that Mary, queen of Scots, had quartered her arms with those of England, thereby claiming the English throne.   J. F. R. DAY

Sources W. Flower, 'Report on the royal escutcheon brought by [Flower] out of France', 1559, BL, Add. MS 25247, fol. 304 · 'Clarenceux [Cooke] and Norroy [Flower] their answer delivered to the erle marshall in defence of their authorite to graunt arms, 1585', BL, Cotton MS Faustina E.i., fol. 166ff. · R. Glover, 'The gyving of armes no wayes hurtfull to the commonweale', BL, Cotton MS Faustina E.i., fol. 161ff. · R. Glover, 'A brief rehearsall of the cause of the disorder in the office of arms and the means shewed how the same may be reformed', BL, 'Officers and office of arms', Harley MS 6591, fol. 63ff. · W. H. Godfrey, A. Wagner, and H. Stanford London, *The College of Arms, Queen Victoria Street* (1963) [incl. list of officers of arms] · M. Noble, *A history of the College of Arms* (1804) · T. Smith, *De republica Anglorum*, ed. M. Dewar (1982) · A. Wagner, *Heralds of England: a history of the office and College of Arms* (1967) · A. R. Wagner, *The records and collections of the College of Arms* (1952)
Archives BL, MS of visitation of Chester, Add. MS 39925 · BL, MSS · Bodl. Oxf., arms and pedigrees from visitations [copies] · Coll. Arms · PRO

Likenesses T. Dawes, engraving, *c.*1578 (Rouge croix, procession of the order of the Garter), repro. in Wagner, *Heralds of England* · M. Gheeraerts, engraving (after engraving by T. Dawes)

Flower, Sir William Henry (1831–1899), zoologist and museum curator, was born on 30 November 1831 in Stratford upon Avon, the second son of Edward Fordham *Flower (1805–1883) and his wife, Selina Greaves (*d.* 1884). His father, a businessman, established Flowers brewery. His elder brother, Charles Edward *Flower, entered the family brewing firm in 1845. He was educated at University College, London, followed by Middlesex Hospital, where he studied medicine and surgery. Graduating MB at London University in 1851, he won both a gold medal in physiology and a silver in zoology. He married, in 1858, Jane Georgiana Rosetta, daughter of Admiral William Henry Smyth; she survived him with three sons and three daughters.

Museum work and public lectures After several years' work in surgery, including from 1854 medical service in the Crimean War, Flower was appointed curator of the surgical museum of Middlesex Hospital, a post which he combined in 1858 with a lectureship in comparative anatomy. In 1861, on the recommendation of 'intimate scientific friends' (Lydekker, 10) including Thomas Henry Huxley, he was appointed conservator of the Hunterian Museum of the Royal College of Surgeons; to this he added in 1870 the Hunterian chair of comparative anatomy and physiology, vacated by Huxley, with its responsibility for delivering lecture courses on annually varying subjects. Flower's third and most elevated museum position came in 1884 with his election, again facilitated by Huxley, to the prestigious new post of director of the British Museum (Natural History) at its splendid new South Kensington site.

From the unconventional springboard of museum work Flower attained extraordinary social and professional advancement. Besides receiving numerous academic and official honours in Britain and overseas, which culminated in a knighthood in 1892, he gained a string of scientific presidencies topped by that of the Zoological Society, of which he was president for twenty of his thirty-seven years of involvement; he was also president of the British Association for the Advancement of Science (1889), as well as its biological section (1878) and anthropological section (1881, 1894), the Anthropological Institute (1883–5), and the Museums Association (1893). He was elected a fellow of the Royal Society in 1864.

Flower's success was noteworthy in the context of widespread calls in Britain for the higher professional status of science. In museums he found the means to assert particular zoological and anthropological theories by which artefacts were ordered, and also a corresponding idea of the way in which the natural order displayed should be translated into social and political order. However, by using rhetorical and persuasive techniques to evade specific acknowledgement of theories informing his arrangement, Flower defied challenges to either the theory behind the presentation, or the implied socio-political scheme. Thus he declared 'that in future museums Nature

Sir William Henry Flower (1831–1899), by C. Schmid, 1868

should … illustrate its own story, subject only to the intervention of man as *Naturae minister et interpres*' (Cornish, 54).

At both the Hunterian and the Natural History museums Flower was commended for his painstaking work towards the preservation, augmentation, and display of the zoological collections, especially those of the vertebrates. His integration of living and fossil specimens corresponded with his aim of illustrating the 'facts' of comparative anatomy and evolution. A famous advocate of the 'new museum idea', whereby separate collections were maintained for the purposes of research and education, Flower endeavoured to make his arrangements accessible not only to scientific researchers, but to many members of the newly enfranchised artisan and lower-middle classes. At the Hunterian Museum Flower was involved in a 'wider diffusion of knowledge, by the visits which have been organised on summer Saturday afternoons by various associations of artisans' to whom he would give a 'popular demonstration' of some part of the museum's contents (*Essays on Museums*, 1898, 93); on these occasions, it was reported, 'large gatherings of working men … flocked' to the galleries (Lydekker, 153). Like the sequences of human artefacts displayed in the 'working-class' museum of his colleague A. H. Pitt Rivers, Flower's evolutionary sequences of skulls and other bones from various peoples, manifesting what appeared to be a gradual physical development over time, could be seen as presenting the message that social evolution was necessarily slow, and not to be upset by premature demands for social reform. Moreover, in 'A practical lesson from biological studies', Flower urged members of the Newcastle upon Tyne Working Men's Trade Societies individually to give 'full liberty' to the inequality which he claimed existed naturally in all areas of human life. He insisted that:

> if you are to have progress there must be no attempt whatever to keep down the capacities of the superior to the level of the inferior. Any man who gets a little rise above his fellows helps on the progress of the world, and brings all the others on with him.   (*Essays on Museums*, 137)

At the same time Flower reassured all his audience, including many members of the new professional and educated classes, of the superiority of the European 'race', in contrast to the 'inferior races' of mankind which were the objects of his study, and therefore appropriate museum pieces. Indeed, of Flower's Hunterian lectures 'Perhaps the most important and certainly the most voluminous … was the series on the Comparative Anatomy of Man' (Lydekker, 51), published in 1870 as *Osteology of the Mammalia*. He also gave many public science lectures on this subject, notably in 1878: a Friday Evening lecture at the Royal Institution, 'The native races of the Pacific Ocean'; one of the Manchester Science Lectures for the People, 'The Aborigines of Tasmania, an extinct race'; and, to the Glasgow Scientific Lectures Association, 'The races of men'. His particular focus on exterminated or dwindling races corresponded to 'a favourite dictum' of his, that contact with Europeans 'must inevitably lead, sooner or later, to the disappearance of the inferior, or "non-adaptive" races of mankind' (*Essays on Museums*, 154). Predicting—though taking no steps to arrest—the imminent extinction of 'the Australians, the Melanesians, the Maories, and most of the Polynesians', he energetically collected osteological specimens of such races, and appealed to the British nation, responsible 'by its commercial enterprise and widespread maritime dominion' for these peoples' demise, to fulfil its duty of 'gathering together every fragment of knowledge that can still be saved, of their languages, customs, social polity, manufactures, and arts' as well as 'evidence of their physical structure' ('Native races of the Pacific Ocean', *Proceedings of the Royal Institute*, 8, 1878, 606). Whereas Darwin, in his *Descent of Man*, had not explicitly placed racial characteristics on a comparative scale of value, Flower's highlighting of the decline of the indigenous populations of New Zealand, Australia, southern Africa, and North America before the advance of European colonists suggested the operation of natural selection on mankind, in determining the survival or extinction of races.

Anthropology and evolutionary theory As regards Flower's own research, one of his most significant innovations derived from his work of the later 1870s comparing the capacities of different human crania. The first volume of his *Catalogue of … the osteology and dentition of vertebrate animals … in the museum of the Royal College of Surgeons*, devoted to man, comprised not just a listing but a 'manual of the methods employed in human craniology'. Specifically, Flower's was one of the earliest post-*Descent of Man* revivals of proposals of the 1860s for empirical research into anthropology from an evolutionary perspective, from the accumulated data of which could be drawn

social laws, to be disseminated through popular education. Earlier efforts had abandoned detailed craniological work owing to the problems of individual variation and racial intermixture which impeded the search for specific racial divisions. Acknowledging these problems, Flower presented the solution of statistical averaging as a way of accurately identifying 'the various groups into which the human species is divided, and thereby in throwing light upon their relations to one another, their history, and their origin' ('On the cranial measurements as characteristic of race', *Catalogue … of the RCS*, 250). Accordingly he drew up comparative tables of 'alveolar', 'nasal', 'orbital', and other indices for the cranial measurements of different races, wherein the values for the 'Mixed Europeans', and the English in particular, invariably lay at the top of the scale; those for the newly extinct Tasmanians frequently lay at the bottom. Clearly laid out at the end of the Hunterian Museum catalogues, the 'evidence' of these tables was substantiated by what was the most comprehensive and well-ordered collection of materials for the study of vertebrates in existence; conversely, by providing even the untutored eye with a means of discerning 'racial characteristics', the system of indices made the collections themselves more accessible. Through his lectures and demonstrations, and papers in a broad range of journals, Flower made this facility available to a wider audience than just the specialist readers of the catalogues, thus establishing the reliability of quantitative anthropometric techniques as a basis for the future study of race and society.

Flower has perhaps chiefly been commended to historians as one of the coterie that assisted T. H. Huxley in his self-styled Darwinian crusade against Richard Owen. On behalf of this group of claimants who sought professional and political advancement as scientifically qualified civil and imperial servants, Flower was able to utilize not only the physical resources of the Hunterian Museum to substantiate his theoretical contentions, but also the rhetoric of scientific objectivity and fact-finding to lend added authority to his claims. Most famously, an extensive study performed by Flower in 1861 on the brains of the quadrumana clinched Huxley's highly publicized victory over Owen in the so-called 'Hippocampus controversy'. Claiming for his work the objective quality of 'purely anatomical' research, 'undertaken without reference to any theory as to the transmutation of species, or origin of the human race' ('On the posterior lobes of the cerebrum of the quadrumana', *PTRS*, 152, 1862, 187), Flower disputed Owen's claim that certain cerebral features distinguished all humans from simians. The climax, however, came at the 1862 British Association meeting in Cambridge when, according to *The Times*, it was a case in which seeing was believing: following Huxley's attack on Owen, 'a Mr. Flower, one of the audience, rose up and said, "I happen to have in my pocket a monkey's brain," and produced the object in question' (Cornish, 66). The sensational display of this pocket museum piece, allegedly manifesting the characteristics which Owen had claimed as unique to man, established Huxley's interpretation as an evolutionary 'fact' which Owen had apparently ignored.

In 1868 Flower joined in another highly personal attack on Owen, expressing doubts about the carnivorous habits attributed by him to the so-called 'marsupial lion', *Thylacoleo carnifax*: the aggressive reaction this elicited from Owen, however, tended only to strengthen the sympathy of Royal Society referees for the Huxleyan camp. Again, in 1877, Flower enlisted the support of the Royal Society against Owen by appealing to the standards of gentlemanly conduct: he emphasized the 'gross discourtesy' (London, University College, Huxley MSS, 16.120) with which Owen had reproduced for a publication certain plates Flower had himself published in the *Philosophical Transactions of the Royal Society*.

Besides his anthropological studies, Flower was noted for his work on the zoology of many different mammals, which was published most prodigiously in the proceedings and transactions of the Royal and Zoological societies. He was an expert particularly on the order Cetacea, and was intimately involved in the establishment of a whale room at the Natural History Museum, with an impressive series of skeletons and plaster casts.

Having retired from the museum in 1898 with failing health, Flower died on 1 July 1899 at his home, 26 Stanhope Gardens, London; he was cremated at Woking on the 5th and his remains interred at Stone, Buckinghamshire.

KATE FLETCHER

Sources R. Lydekker, *Sir William Flower* (1906) · C. Cornish, *Sir William Henry Flower KCB* (1904) · A. E. Gunther, *The founders of science at the British Museum, 1753–1900* (1980) · N. A. Rupke, *Richard Owen, Victorian naturalist* (1994) · H. D. Rushing, 'The gorilla comes to Darwin's England', MA diss., U. Texas, 1990 · W. T. Stearn, *The Natural History Museum at South Kensington: a history of the British Museum (Natural History), 1753–1980* (1981) · E. Miller, *That noble cabinet: a history of the British Museum* (1973) · D. A. Lorimer, *Colour, class and the Victorians* (1978) · G. W. Stocking, *Victorian anthropology* [1987] · J. Lester, *E. Ray Lankester and the making of modern British biology*, ed. P. J. Bowler (1995) · D. K. van Keuren, 'Human science in Victorian Britain …, 1863–1908', PhD diss., University of Pennsylvania, 1982 · W. R. Chapman, 'Ethnology in the museum', DPhil diss., U. Oxf., 1981 · *CGPLA Eng. & Wales* (1899)

Archives NHM, corresp. as director of the natural history departments; notebooks, drawings, and papers · RCS Eng., papers · RS | American Philosophical Society, Philadelphia, letters to J. T. Gulick · ICL, college archives, letters to T. H. Huxley · NHM, letters to C. E. Fagan · NHM, letters to A. C. L. G. Gunther and R. W. T. Gunther · Oxf. U. Mus. NH, letters to Sir E. B. Poulton · Yale U., Sterling Memorial Library, letters to Othniel March

Likenesses C. Schmid, oils, 1868, RCS Eng. [*see illus.*] · F. S. Baden-Powell, silhouette, 1898, NPG · Schmidt of Berlin, portrait, priv. coll. · bust, NHM · photograph, repro. in Gunther, *Founders of science* · photograph, RS

Wealth at death £36,925 0s. 10d.: probate, 1 Aug 1899, *CGPLA Eng. & Wales*

Flowerdew, Edward (d. 1586), judge, was the fourth son of John Flowerdew of Hethersett, Norfolk, and Katherine, daughter of William Sheres of Ashwellthorpe in the same county. The family background was modest—Thomas and William Flowerdew of Hethersett had been scriveners in 1502—and Edward was probably not very well off when he was admitted to the Inner Temple in 1552. However, he soon built up an extensive practice with corporate and private clients in Norfolk, and after only fifteen years became a bencher of his inn, giving his first reading in 1569. His second reading, in 1577, was on the statute 32 Hen. VIII c. 28, concerning leases. He was elected as member of parliament for Castle Rising in 1572, and was active in legal committee work that year. Although he was replaced by Sir William Drury while sick, and was himself returned to represent Norwich when its sitting member became ill, these elections were held void in 1581 and in consequence Flowerdew remained in law the member for Castle Rising.

Flowerdew married Elizabeth, daughter of William Foster of Wymondham. Through the earl of Leicester's influence he was elected recorder of King's Lynn in 1577, and he became steward of Norwich the following year. He took the coif in 1580, his patrons at the ceremony being the earl of Arundel and Lord Burghley, and in the same year became recorder of Norwich and steward of Yarmouth. On 23 October 1584 he was appointed third baron of the exchequer, and on 26 June 1585 second baron. He rode the Oxford circuit twice in 1585 as a justice of assize, but in March 1586 while on the western circuit he contracted gaol fever at Exeter, from which he died on 31 March. His body was taken to Hethersett for burial in the church there in April.

In 1564 Flowerdew had purchased Stanfield Hall in Wymondham from his wife's former paramour, John Appleyard, whose half-sister Amy Robsart had married Robert Dudley in 1550. His reputation in Norfolk was not uniformly genial. After acquiring Wymondham Abbey he caused considerable local resentment by removing the lead and freestone which the parishioners thought they had purchased from the crown, and he was also involved in a long-standing feud with Sir Arthur Heveningham. He directed a monument to be placed in his chapel called Stanfield chapel in Wymondham church, but this was not done, and 'for want of a gravestone of his friends' cost' was 'covered with one from another man's grave' (Blomefield, 5.30). His will also contained a provision for a new great bell to be installed in Hethersett church, accompanied by a declaration that he utterly condemned in his conscience the superstitious ringing of bells. He left no issue, and his property was divided between his wife and brothers.

J. H. BAKER

Sources HoP, *Commons, 1558–1603*, 2.142–3 · Baker, *Serjeants*, 173, 434, 512 · Sainty, *Judges*, 122 · F. Blomefield and C. Parkin, *An essay towards a topographical history of the county of Norfolk*, 5 vols. (1739–75), vol. 1, pp. 721, 724, 734; vol. 5, p. 30 · J. S. Cockburn, *A history of English assizes, 1558–1714* (1972), 53, 266 · All Souls Oxf., MS 156, fol. 150 · BL, Hargrave MS 373, fol. 185v · PRO, CP 40/959, m. 113 · inquisition post mortem, PRO, C 142/210/132 · will, PRO, PROB 11/69, sig. 23 · Cooper, *Ath. Cantab.*, 2.5

Flowers, Frederick (1810–1886), police magistrate, was born at Boston, Lincolnshire, the third son of the Revd Field Flowers, rector of Partney, Lincolnshire, from 1815 to 1818. His brothers included George French *Flowers, composer and musical theorist. He was educated at Louth grammar school, Lincolnshire. Admitted a student of Lincoln's Inn on 10 November 1828, he was called to the bar on 18 November 1839, joined the midland circuit, and for many years practised as a special pleader. In 1841 he married Ann, daughter of R. Kirby; they had one son. In 1862 he was appointed recorder of Stamford, and was for some time revising barrister for the northern division of Nottinghamshire. He was police magistrate at Bow Street, London, from 6 July 1864 until his death. He also acted as a magistrate for Middlesex, Kent, Surrey, Hertfordshire, and Essex. As a police magistrate he was well known and respected. His common sense, combined with a sound knowledge of the law, prevented him from making many mistakes in his decisions. He possessed kindness, tact, and discrimination, and a strong sense of justice, especially towards those who were poor and weak. He died at his home, Holmesdale, Tottenham Lane, Hornsey, London, on 26 January 1886, and was buried on 30 January at Partney where was erected a memorial brass in the church. He was survived by his wife.

G. C. BOASE, rev. CATHERINE PEASE-WATKIN

Sources *Law Times* (13 Feb 1886), 275 · *Solicitors' Journal*, 30 (1885–6), 225 · *Law Journal* (30 Jan 1886), 79 · *The Graphic* (8 Jan 1881), 32 [sketch at Bow Street police court] · *Saturday Review*, 61 (1886), 145–6 · *CGPLA Eng. & Wales* (1886)
Likenesses sketch, repro. in *The Graphic*
Wealth at death £4978 5s. 2d.: probate, 8 March 1886, *CGPLA Eng. & Wales*

Flowers, George French (1811–1872), composer and musical theorist, was born on 28 June 1811 in Boston, Lincolnshire, the fourth son of Field Flowers, later rector of Partney. He studied music with C. H. Rinck and Schnyder von Wartensee in Germany, and went on to graduate BMus from Lincoln College, Oxford, in 1839, and DMus in 1865. In the meantime he was organist of the English Chapel in Paris (1836–7), of St Mark's, Myddelton Square, and St John's, Paddington, Middlesex, of Beverley Minster, and of St Marie, High Barnet.

Flowers founded the Contrapuntists' Society in 1843, became music critic of the *Literary Gazette* at about the same time, and was author of an analysis of John Goss's *Harmony* in the *Fine Arts Journal* (1847, 445ff.). His *Essay on the Construction of Fugue with … New Rules for Harmony* appeared in London in 1846, followed by the *Pictorial Representation of the Science of Harmony*, a translation of Basler's *Reisekarte*, in 1850, and a poem on *Muscular Vocalisation* in 1861. He introduced and developed the Abbé Vogler system of twelve progressive cadences (see his papers in the *Musical World*, 23, 1848, 501–2 and 554–5), and contributed opinions on musical matters for many years to the *Musical Examiner* and the *Musical World*. It is claimed (Brown & Stratton, *Brit. mus.*) that he was an unsuccessful candidate for the music professorship at Oxford in 1848 and also for that of Gresham College in 1863.

In 1850 Flowers announced his determination to cultivate and bring forward English vocal talent by means of a British school of vocalization for the teaching of singing on new principles. His attempt was justified in 1851 by some measure of success, with acclaimed performances by his young pupils in St James's Hall, but the institution did not last long: Mrs Howard Paul was perhaps its most distinguished member. Flowers demonstrated the influences of J. S. Bach and Vogler in his *Six Fugues for the Organ*, *Pastoral Chorus* (1852), and *Choral Fugue*. His elaborate first mass (1860?) perhaps marks the date of his reception into the Roman Catholic church. He died of cholera in London on 14 June 1872.

L. M. MIDDLETON, rev. DAVID J. GOLBY

Sources W. H. Husk, 'Flowers, George French', Grove, *Dict. mus.* (1954) · Foster, *Alum. Oxon.* · W. G. Gorman, *Converts to Rome* (1910) · J. D. Brown, *Biographical dictionary of musicians: with a bibliography of English writings on music* (1886) · Brown & Stratton, *Brit. mus.*

Flowers, Thomas Harold (1905–1998), engineer, was born on 22 December 1905 at 160 Abbott Road, Poplar, in London's East End, the son of John Thomas Flowers, bricklayer, and his wife, Mabel Emily, formerly Richardson. One sister was born in 1910. Tommy, as her brother was nicknamed, complained at the time that he would have preferred a Meccano set. Flowers gained a scholarship enabling him to attend technical college until he was sixteen. From there he served a four-year mechanical apprenticeship at the Royal Arsenal in Woolwich, while at the same time he attended evening classes, gaining a London University degree in engineering. In 1926 Flowers joined the Post Office as an electrical engineer, and in 1930 he moved to its Dollis Hill laboratory, located in north-west London.

During the 1920s work at Dollis Hill focused on the application of electronic techniques to telephony. Flowers built up considerable experience and expertise in the use of valves, in particular developing systems of valve amplifiers and switches that by 1939 enabled long-distance calls to be made without the intervention of an operator. On 31 August 1935 Flowers married Eileen Margaret, daughter of John James Richard Green, a conveyancing clerk. The couple had two sons, Kenneth and John.

Flowers continued to work at Dollis Hill as the pace and urgency of the laboratory increased with the outbreak of war. Forty miles to the north the codebreaking effort was under way at the Government Code and Cypher School at Bletchley Park. After the 1970s, when security restrictions were partially lifted, historians had cause to reassess their accounts of the Second World War due to knowledge of Bletchley Park's considerable achievements. Most famous was the breaking of Morse messages encrypted by the Enigma machine used by the German navy, army, air force, railways, and *Abwehr* (secret intelligence service of German high command). The attack on Enigma involved the development of statistical techniques and the application of machines, in particular the electromechanical 'bombes', but also relied considerably on inspired guesswork and an industrial-scale bureaucracy. The decoded messages provided vital information on the movements of the German armed forces.

Less well known than, but as important as, the breaking of Enigma was the decryption of non-Morse messages, which the British recorded and labelled 'Fish'. Fish messages were encoded with a machine called the Lorenz SZ,

Thomas Harold Flowers (1905–1998), by unknown photographer

using a 32-letter Baudot alphabet. While Enigma machines were capable of 159 trillion settings, the number of the combinations possible with the Lorenz SZ was estimated at 5,429,503,678,976 times greater. This level of security was deemed necessary for long messages passed between the highest levels of the German command. In particular a variant of Fish used by the German army, named Tunny, was of growing importance as the theatre of war turned from the north Atlantic back to the European continent. The techniques used against Enigma were relatively ineffective against Fish. Max Newman, a member of hut F, which was responsible for the attack on Fish, persuaded the director of Bletchley Park that high-speed machinery was needed for the job of comparing two enciphered messages. The first machines, called Heath Robinsons after the cartoonist of outlandish machines, entered service in May 1943. A combination of mechanics and a handful of electronics, they were designed by C. E. Wynn-Williams at the Telecommunications Research Establishment assisted by electrical engineers, including Flowers, at Dollis Hill.

However, it was clear to Newman that the work of the Heath Robinsons would be considerably speeded up if some way could be found of storing electronically the contents of one, or both, of the messages. Many senior staff at Bletchley Park were sceptical, assuming that any machine with such capabilities would need so many valves as to be unreliable. Flowers believed differently: if the valves were never disturbed or turned off, their lifetimes could be vastly increased. Largely as a self-supported sideline at Dollis Hill, Flowers and his team began in February 1943 to design and construct a prototype machine. The Colossus, containing 1500 thyratron valves, was demonstrated on 8 December 1943, running for eight hours without fault.

The project was vindicated when a tightening of German security in February 1944 meant that only such high-speed techniques were effective and threw the task of code-breaking Fish almost entirely on to the machines. A full-scale version, Colossus mark II, employing 2500 valves and built by Flowers's team, was ready only five days before D-day. F. H. Hinsley has estimated that the availability of decrypted Fish messages tipped the balance in operation Overlord. Ten Colossi were in operation by the end of the war, after which all but one (possibly two) were destroyed. The survivors ended up at GCHQ, Cheltenham. Flowers received £1000 compensation—less than he spent—and an MBE (1943).

After an intelligence-gathering trip to Germany Flowers returned to Dollis Hill and telephony in 1945, where he was head of the section developing electronic switching, forerunner of the subscriber trunk dialling (STD) system introduced in the post-war decades. He also assisted the National Physical Laboratory's project to build the ACE, an early stored-program computer. As Post Office chief engineer Flowers designed an electronic random-number generator, ERNIE, operational from 1957, to pick winners among holders of premium bonds. This was a public success.

The work at Bletchley Park and the development of the Colossus was not public knowledge until the 1970s. In 1977 Flowers's role was recognized, after groundbreaking historical research by the computer scientist Brian Randell, in the award of an honorary degree by Newcastle University. He was the first recipient of the Post Office's Martlesham medal, in 1980. Flowers died at his home, 8 Holland Court, Page Street, Mill Hill, London, on 28 October 1998.   JON AGAR

Sources G. O. Hayward, *The Independent* (14 Nov 1998), 10 a–e · T. H. Flowers, 'Pioneers of computing', 1976, Sci. Mus. [audio tape, no. 16 in a series of recorded interviews] · *The Times* (10 Nov 1998) · *Daily Telegraph* (10 Nov 1998) · J. Fineberg, *The Guardian* (13 Nov 1998), 24 a–f · M. R. Williams, *A history of computing technology* (1985) · A. Hodges, *Alan Turing: the enigma* (1983) · B. Randell, 'The Colossus', *A history of computing in the 20th century*, ed. N. Metropolis (1980) · F. H. Hinsley and A. Stripp, eds., *Codebreakers: the inside story of Bletchley Park* (1993) · *New York Times* (8 Nov 1998) · CGPLA Eng. & Wales (1998) · b. cert. · m. cert. · d. cert.
Archives BT archives, London · PRO
Likenesses photograph, 1980, repro. in *Daily Telegraph* · photograph, Universal Pictorial Press Agency Ltd, London [*see illus.*]
Wealth at death under £200,000—gross; under £100,000—net: probate, 1 Dec 1998, CGPLA Eng. & Wales

Floyd [Lloyd], **Edward** (*fl.* 1588–1621), lawyer, was probably the Edward Lloyd of Berth-lwyd, Montgomeryshire, who, as second son of David Lloyd Jenkin, sheriff of the county in 1587, was admitted to the Inner Temple in 1588–9 and called to the bar in 1598. He may have been the same Edward Flud or Lloyd who signed Star Chamber pleadings in the Easter term of 1616, and he was certainly a barrister who became steward in Shropshire to Lord Chancellor Ellesmere and the earl of Suffolk. At an unknown date he married Joane, whose other name is unknown.

Like many other contemporary members of the inns, Floyd remained a Roman Catholic in religion. In 1621 he was a prisoner in the Fleet prison by order of the privy council. During an examination of the warden of the Fleet on charges of misdemeanour, the House of Commons became aware of the allegations against him. In January that year Floyd had apparently remarked on the defeat of the protestant cause at the battle of the White Mountain in 1620 in language insulting to the king's son-in-law, the elector palatine, and daughter, referring to them as 'goodman' and 'goodwife'. Motivated partly by members' concerns about the fate of the Palatinate, and extending their jurisdiction beyond its hitherto accepted scope, on 20 April 1621 the Commons acted independently of the Lords and impeached Floyd. On 1 May they sentenced him to pay a fine of £1000, to stand in the pillory in three different places for two hours each time, and to be carried from place to place on an unsaddled horse, facing towards the horse's tail and holding it in his hand.

Floyd's immediate appeal to the king resulted on 2 May in a stay of execution and a request that the Commons clarify their precedents for acting as a judicial body in a cause not directly concerning their privileges and membership or the general grievances of the kingdom. On 5 May the Lords, sensing an infringement of their right of judgment as a court of record, insisted in a joint conference with the Commons that the lower house's claims to jurisdiction be examined by the king's counsel and judges. Ultimately on 10 May a parliamentary subcommittee recognized the Lords' jurisdictional competence and declared that the Commons' actions in condemning Floyd should not be drawn into precedent. Under pressure from the Lords as well as the king, lacking strong historical precedents, Sir Edward Coke and the Commons backed down and referred the matter to the Lords, although the lower house remained divided. The Lords increased Floyd's sentence on 26 May, adding degradation from the state of a gentleman, branding, whipping, a £5000 fine, and life imprisonment in Newgate. At the behest of Prince Charles the Lords spared Floyd the lash but the rest of his sentence was carried out. He was, however, liberated on 16 July 1621 when the duke of Buckingham and Lord Keeper Williams prevailed on the king for a liberal use of his prerogative of mercy with regard to political prisoners. In response to a petition from his wife, on 6 December the Lords ordered Floyd's trunk and writings to be delivered to her, once the clerk had removed 'such popish beads and popish books' (*JHL*, 3.183) as were among them.

Details of Floyd's later life are unknown. He may have been the 'Mr Fludd (an honest recusant), my old acquaintance' that Richard Smyth of the Poultry Compter, London, recorded as having died about July 1648 (R. Smyth, *The Obituary of Richard Smyth*, ed. H. Ellis, CS, 44, 1849, 26).

D. A. ORR

Sources C. Russell, *Parliaments and English politics, 1621–1629* (1979), 104, 117–18, 126–7, 179 · W. R. Prest, *The inns of court under Elizabeth I and the early Stuarts, 1590–1640* (1972), 183 · W. R. Prest, *The rise of the barristers: a social history of the English bar, 1590–1640* (1986), 67 · W. H. Cooke, ed., *Students admitted to the Inner Temple, 1571–1625* (1868), 121 · C. G. C. Tite, *Impeachment and parliamentary procedure in early Stuart England* (1974) · *DNB* · S. Lambert, 'Procedure in the House of Commons in the early Stuart period', *EngHR*, 95 (1980), 753–81 · J. S. Hart, *Justice upon petition: the House of Lords and the reformation of justice, 1621–1675* (1991), 15–63

Floyd, Henry (*c*.1560–1641), Jesuit, older brother of the Jesuit controversialist John *Floyd, was born in Norfolk; some Jesuit catalogues claim Cambridgeshire—the diocese of Ely—for his birthplace, but records from Seville and Valladolid state the diocese of Norwich. At some unspecified date he arrived at the English College then situated in Rheims and on 24 September 1588 he was ordained deacon at Soissons. On 8 May 1589 he was sent with other students by Richard Barret, president of the college, to assist in establishing the new English college founded by Robert Parsons at Valladolid. There he was ordained, probably in 1590. In 1592 he was one of the first students at the English College in Seville where on 20 February 1593 he and Richard Walpole publicly defended theological theses to great acclaim. Shortly thereafter Floyd departed for Lisbon where, as superior of the residence, he worked among English exiles and on behalf of the Inquisition until his return to England in 1597 as chaplain to John Southcote, son and heir of the judge Sir John. In 1599 he applied for the Society of Jesus. Because Floyd was needed on the mission Henry Garnet allowed him to complete his noviceship in England.

During his fourth year in England (about 1601), Floyd was captured by pursuivants and thrown into Newgate prison. One of his fellow prisoners was Francis Page, and Floyd somehow arranged to celebrate mass with Page on the night before his execution on 20 April 1602. Floyd was transferred to Framlingham Castle, Suffolk, before his banishment following the accession of James I in 1603. Despite Anthony Rivers being one of Floyd's aliases it is unlikely that he was the same Anthony Rivers who, as Henry Garnet's secretary, wrote newsletters between 1601 and 1603. By 1606 Floyd was back in Lisbon as English confessor. He returned to England some time before 6 December 1618 when he was professed of the four vows in London. From 1621 until 1623 he was superior of the Jesuit mission in Suffolk. In 1623 he moved to the house of probation of St Ignatius, London.

Captured some time in 1627 or 1628 Floyd was imprisoned first in the Clink and then in the Fleet. Through the intercession of Queen Henrietta Maria he successfully petitioned to be released in 1633 on grounds of age and ill health. Other petitions in the late 1630s sought to end the harassment by the pursuivants. Floyd died in London on 7 March 1641.

THOMAS M. MCCOOG

Sources T. M. McCoog, *English and Welsh Jesuits, 1555–1650*, 1, Catholic RS, 74 (1994), 172 · T. M. McCoog, ed., *Monumenta Angliae*, 2: English and Welsh Jesuits, catalogues, 1630–1640 (1992), 314 · H. Foley, ed., *Records of the English province of the Society of Jesus*, 1 (1877), 503–13; 7/1 (1882), 267–9 · E. Henson, ed., *The registers of the English College at Valladolid, 1589–1862*, Catholic RS, 30 (1930), 5 · G. Anstruther, *The seminary priests*, 1 (1969), 120 · M. Murphy, *St Gregory's College, Seville, 1592–1767*, Catholic RS, 73 (1992), 67 · *The Elizabethan Jesuits: Historia missionis Anglicanae Societatis Jesu* (1660) of Henry More, ed. and trans. F. Edwards (1981) · F. Edwards, 'Identifying Anthony Rivers', *N&Q*,

239 (1994), 62–3 • M. E. Williams, 'The origins of the English College, Lisbon', *Recusant History*, 20 (1990–91), 478–92 • R. Macaulay, *They went to Portugal* (1946) • R. Macaulay, *They went to Portugal too*, ed. L. C. Taylor (1990) • T. F. Knox and others, eds., *The first and second diaries of the English College, Douay* (1878), 220, 244 • B. Nurse, 'A chapter in the recusant history of Cheam in Surrey: Henry Floyd, S. J., and Bartholomew Fromond Versus the Pursuivants', *London Recusant*, 3 (1973), 102–14 • R. Persons, 'Annals of the English College, Seville', ed. J. H. Pollen, *Miscellanea, IX*, Catholic RS, 14 (1914), 1–24, esp. 16

Archives Archives of the British province of the Society of Jesus, Stonyhurst College, Lancashire • Archivum Romanum Societatis Iesu, Rome | Westm. DA, archives of the London Clergy Chapter ('Old Brotherhood')

Floyd, John (1572–1649), Jesuit and religious controversialist, was the younger brother of Henry *Floyd (*c.*1560–1641) and was born on 14 October 1572 at Badlingham, Cambridgeshire. Jesuit records give no details of his parentage. After studying at the Jesuit school at Eu in Normandy he proceeded to the English College, Rheims, in March 1588, then to the English College, Rome, in October 1590. There he entered the Society of Jesus in November 1592 and went on to study theology partly at the Roman College, partly at the English College, Valladolid, being ordained priest at Rome in 1599.

Sent on the English mission, Floyd was visiting his fellow Jesuit Edward Oldcorne, imprisoned at Worcester for alleged complicity in the Gunpowder Plot, when he was himself arrested and held in prison for a year. He was then sentenced to perpetual banishment. From 1607 to 1616 he was at the English College, Louvain, with a high reputation both as preacher and as professor of theology, being 'a person excellently learned, as well in philosophy as in theology' (Wood, *Ath. Oxon.*, 3.483). After being professed of the four vows in July 1609 he returned for a year to England, where he was partly responsible for the conversion to Rome of the protestant minister Theophilus Higgons, who publicly recanted the following year.

On returning to Louvain, Floyd took up the cudgels of controversy with William Crashaw and Sir Edward Hoby, who had sponsored Higgons's reconversion, publishing his *Overthrow of the Protestants Pulpit-Babels* over the initials I. R. in 1612. Sir Edward responded in 1613 with *A Counter-Snarle for Ishmael Rabshacheh* (referring to the railing Assyrian in 2 Kings 18). Floyd retaliated in the same year with his *Purgatories Triumph over Hell*, prompting a further response from Sir Edward.

From 1617 until his death (apart from the year 1629, when he was instructor of tertians at Ghent) Floyd remained at the Jesuit college of St Omer for more convenient access to the printing press there. From that time he stands out as the Jesuit champion in a series of major controversies, being described as 'the brain behind the St Omer's publications' and as 'a shrewd, desiccated theologian' (Basset, 204). The first of these controversies was with the apostate archbishop of Spalato, Marc'Antonio de Dominis, who had embraced the Anglican religion in 1616. In response to Marc'Antonio de Dominis's *Manifestation of the Motives* (1616), Floyd brought out under the

pseudonym of Fidelis Annosus Verimentanus his *Synopsis apostasiae* (later translated into English) in 1617. Floyd produced two further books in response to de Dominis under the same pseudonym, *Hypocrisis Marci Antonii De Dominis detecta* in 1620 and *Monarchiae ecclesiasticae … demonstratio* in 1622, in which year the archbishop made his counter-recantation.

At the same time Floyd ventured to cross swords, if indirectly, with the king himself. This was in response to the anonymous Latin dialogue *Deus et rex* which had appeared in 1615 from the pen of the archbishop of Canterbury's chaplain, Richard Mocket, 'with special privilege of his royal majesty', to justify the oath of allegiance. What Floyd wrote was a witty parody in Latin, similarly entitled *Deus et rex*, in 1619 (translated 1620).

A third major controversy also involved Floyd, again indirectly, with the king, in support of another fellow Jesuit, John Fisher. This initially took the form of a series of three conferences held at the request of the countess of Buckingham, mother of the king's favourite, between Fisher and two Anglican divines, Francis White, dean of Carlisle, and William Laud, then bishop of St David's, in May 1622—with the king himself presiding at the last two conferences. Floyd, who had already assisted Fisher in a related controversy, now helped him to answer a royal note, 'Nine points of controversy'. Whereas Fisher presented his provisional *Answer* within a month, Floyd added 'a learned commentary' which was published in 1626 after James's death.

In the new reign Floyd was soon caught up in a hardly less important controversy with the English Catholic bishop of Chalcedon, Richard Smith, who was no friend of the Jesuits. This arose out of a book by the president of Douai, Matthew Kellison, published in 1629 ostensibly against 'the anarchie of Calvin' but really against the papalism of the Jesuits. In the flurry of publications which followed Floyd defended the Jesuits with *An Apology of the Holy Sea Apostolicks Proceeding* (translated into Latin in 1631) under the new pseudonym of Daniel of Jesus. Condemned both by the theological faculty of the Sorbonne and by the French bishops, Floyd defended himself under the further pseudonym of Hermannus Loemelius in three Latin works and wittily but imprudently applied to the apostles' creed the method used by the Sorbonne in their censures. The controversy was brought to an end by a papal brief of 9 May 1631 imposing silence on both sides, while deciding against Smith.

A further controversy pitted Floyd against the celebrated Anglican divine William Chillingworth (once a convert of Fisher's), who published his famous book *The Religion of Protestants* in 1638 under the influence of his godfather William Laud. Floyd answered him in 1638 with *The Church Conquerant over Humane Wit* (as part 1) and in 1639 with *The Total Sum* (as part 2), observing a common controversial method of refuting one's opponent by showing him up in self-contradiction.

Floyd died suddenly at the college in St Omer on 16 September 1649. 'He was', Gillow says, 'a man of great talents, remarkable for the success with which he taught philosophy and theology, and greatly distinguished as a preacher' (Gillow, *Lit. biog. hist.*, 2.301–2).

PETER MILWARD

Sources A. F. Allison, 'Richard Smith's Gallican backers and Jesuit opponents [pt 1]', *Recusant History*, 18 (1986–7), 329–401 • B. Basset, *The English Jesuits, from Campion to Martindale* (1967), 168–9, 204–8 • T. H. Clancy, *A literary history of the English Jesuits: a century of books, 1615–1714* (1996), 53–65 • H. Foley, ed., *Records of the English province of the Society of Jesus*, 1 (1877), 8–53; 4 (1878), 237–8; 6 (1880), 185 • Gillow, *Lit. biog. hist.*, 2.301–6 • P. Milward, *Religious controversies of the Jacobean age* (1978), 118–19, 161–3, 174, 188–91, 212–13, 220–27 • A. F. Allison, 'The later life and writings of Joseph Cresswell, SJ (1556–1623)', *Recusant History*, 15 (1979–81), 79–144 • Wood, *Ath. Oxon.*, new edn, 3.483 • T. M. McCoog, *English and Welsh Jesuits, 1555–1650*, 1, Catholic RS, 74 (1994), 173

Floyd, Sir John, first baronet (1748–1818), army officer, was the eldest son of Captain John Floyd (1707–1758) of the 1st or King's dragoon guards (killed in Germany during the Seven Years' War) and his wife, Mary (1713–1782), daughter of James Bate, rector of Chilham, Kent. He was born on 22 February 1748 and entered the army on 5 April 1760 as a cornet in Eliott's light horse, afterwards called the 15th or King's Royal Hussars. Floyd received his commission without purchase in recognition of his father's service. After distinguishing himself at the battle of Emsdorf, Floyd was absent from the regiment for two years while he completed his education at Utrecht. He was promoted to lieutenant on 20 April 1763 and appointed riding master of his regiment. His skill in this capacity brought him under the notice of the authorities and he was 'lent' to the 1st dragoons, the Royals, in order to improve their riding. He was promoted, without purchase, captain-lieutenant on 20 May 1770, and captain on 25 May 1772 in the 15th hussars, and on 5 May 1779 major in the newly raised 21st light dragoons.

In 1781 the court of directors of the East India Company requested the loan of a regiment of cavalry, and on 24 September Floyd was gazetted lieutenant-colonel of the newly raised 23rd (later the 19th) light dragoons. He reached Madras in 1782, was promoted colonel on 18 November 1790, and served as a cavalry commander in Lord Cornwallis's campaigns against Tipu Sultan of Mysore (1790–92). During the siege of Bangalore in March 1791 he drew Cornwallis's displeasure when he disobeyed orders and attacked one of Tipu's columns, which resulted in a heavy loss of British horses. Wounded in this encounter, Floyd carried a bullet in his neck for the rest of his life. He distinguished himself at the battle of Arikera in May 1791, and served in the general action in May 1792 near Seringapatam, which led Tipu to sue for peace. Floyd was promoted major-general on 5 October 1794. When the Fourth Anglo-Mysore War broke out in 1799, Floyd again commanded the cavalry, and acted as second in command to General Harris. He led the advance into Mysore, and the charges of his cavalry did much to win the battle of Malavalli. When the siege of Seringapatam was begun, he commanded the covering army and brought the Bombay column, under Major-General James Stuart, safely into camp. Following the company's victory, he was chairman of the prize committee which distributed the booty taken at Seringapatam.

Floyd himself accumulated great wealth from his lucrative appointments and prize money, and returned to England in 1800. He was appointed colonel of the 23rd light dragoons on 11 September 1800 and was promoted lieutenant-general on 1 January 1801. He spent some years on the staff in Ireland, commanding the Limerick division from 1803 to 1806 and the Cork division from 1809 to 1812. Floyd was transferred to the colonelcy of the 8th light dragoons on 13 September 1804, promoted general on 1 January 1812, and in 1813 was appointed to the sinecure office of governor of Gravesend and Tilbury. On 30 March 1816 he was created a baronet and a special crest of a lion rampant, bearing the standard of Tipu Sultan in its paws, was granted to him.

Floyd was twice married: first, on 29 January 1791, to Rebecca Juliana, daughter of Charles Darke, a free merchant of Madras. They had a son and three daughters before her death from scarlet fever on 3 February 1802 (which had claimed their youngest daughter Flavia two days earlier). He married, second, on 29 July 1805, Anna (*d.* 1844), daughter of Crosbie Morgell of Tullilease, co. Cork, and widow of Sir Barry Denny, bt, of Tralee Castle. Floyd died suddenly at his home in London, 10 Mansfield Street, of 'gout in the stomach', on 10 January 1818. His remains were placed in a vault in St James's Church, Hampstead Road, London, and a marble monument to his memory existed until the church was demolished in 1964. Floyd was succeeded in the baronetcy by his son, Henry, an army officer who served in the Peninsular War and at Waterloo. His eldest daughter, Miranda, married Sir Joseph Fuller, and her sister Julia married Sir Robert Peel, second baronet, the prime minister.

H. M. STEPHENS, *rev.* ENID M. FUHR

Sources W. Floyd, *A memoir of General Sir John Floyd, Bart. K.P.* (1880) • D. Forrest, *Tiger of Mysore: the life and death of Tipu Sultan* (1970) • H. C. Wylly, 'Sir John Floyd', *Tradition*, 5/30, 9–12, 37 • *Correspondence of Charles, first Marquis Cornwallis*, ed. C. Ross, 3 vols. (1859) • R. MacKenzie, *A sketch of the war with Tipu Sultan*, 2 vols. (1793–4) • A. Dirom, *Narrative of the campaign in India* (1793) • A. Beatson, *A view of the origin and conduct of the war with Tippoo Sultan* (1800) • S. Lushington, *Life of General Lord Harris* (1840) • *The despatches, minutes and correspondence of the Marquess Wellesley … during his administration in India*, ed. M. Martin, 5 vols. (1836–40) • J. Philippart, *East India military calendar*, 1 (1823) • Burke, *Peerage* (1939)
Archives Wilts. & Swindon RO, corresp. with the tenth and eleventh earls of Pembroke

Floyd, Thomas (*fl.* 1589–1603), author, a Welshman, entered New Inn, Oxford, as a commoner in 1589. He graduated BA on 9 February 1593 and afterwards transferred himself to Jesus College; he took the degree of MA on 5 February 1596. He supplicated for the BCL on 18 July 1599. He was the author of *The picture of a perfit common wealth, describing as well the offices of princes and inferior magistrates over their subjects, as also the duties of subjects towards their governors* (1600), dedicated to Sir Thomas Egerton, the lord keeper. It was a conventional study of the three classical forms of government, which concluded that monarchy was the best and examined the virtues that it required in both rulers and subjects. Floyd also wrote some Latin verses in *Academiae Oxoniensis Pietas erga serenissimum … Jacobum … Regem* (1603).

J. M. RIGG, rev. SARAH E. TROMBLEY

Sources Foster, *Alum. Oxon.* · T. Floyd, *The picture of a perfit common wealth, describing as well the offices of princes and inferiour magistrats over their subjects, as also the duties of subjects towards their governours* (1600); facs. edn (1973)

Floyer, Ernest Ayscoghe (1852–1903), explorer, born on 4 July 1852 at Marshchapel, Lincolnshire, was the eldest surviving son of the Revd Ayscoghe Floyer (*d.* 1872) and his wife, Louisa Sara. **Louisa Sara Floyer** (1830–1909), promoter of needlework in schools, was the elder daughter and eldest surviving child of the three children born to the Hon. Frederick John Shore (1799–1837) of the Bengal civil service and his wife, Charlotte May (*d.* 1883), second daughter of George Cornish of Salcombe Hill, Devon. Mrs Floyer was the granddaughter of John *Shore, first Baron Teignmouth. On 12 April 1849 she married. She saw needlework and knitting as the mainstay of the curriculum for girls in elementary schools. She maintained that, as well as acquiring the skill itself, girls in needlework lessons learned cleanliness, obedience, caution, concentration, and other virtues. Other subjects could be integrated into the teaching of needlework. Spelling, for example, could be learned by copying such words as 'herringbone' or 'cross-stitch'; essay writing could be practised by describing the execution of complex stitches or patterns. Mrs Floyer was the first needlework examiner to be appointed by the London school board, and was the founder of the London Institute for the Advancement of Plain Needlework; she wrote eight textbooks on the subject, as well as instructions for examiners of needlework. Her methods were satirized by Clara Grant, a teacher in London elementary schools in the 1890s. Grant argued that in general the teaching of plain needlework was of less benefit to the pupils who performed it than to the local gentry, who got their needlework done free. Grant particularly attacked Mrs Floyer, suggesting that the worst effect of her ministry was the enthusiasm she inspired everywhere for the senseless drills by which classes of fifty or sixty children would practise putting on thimbles or manipulating knitting needles for an hour at a time. Eventually the London county council banned such drills from infant classes, but as late as 1911 manuals describing intricate drills were still being published. Mrs Floyer died in 1909.

Ernest Floyer was educated at Charterhouse from 1865 until 1869, and then served for seven years in the Indian telegraphic service, being stationed on the coast of the Persian Gulf. Between January 1876 and May 1877 he explored the interior of Baluchistan. His observations and surveys, published as *Unexplored Baluchistan* (1882), describe a journey from Jask to Bampur, a tour in the Persian Gulf, and a journey from Jask to Kerman via Angohran. There are appendices on dialects of western Baluchistan and on plants collected. The volume met with praise from contemporary reviewers and established his reputation as an explorer. It was republished in a new edition as recently as 1980.

In January 1878 Floyer was appointed inspector-general of Egyptian telegraphs, a post which he held until his death, turning the department's annual loss into a substantial annual surplus. He persuaded the government to spend part of this on experiments in the cultivation of trees and plants in the desert. He took charge of these experiments in the capacity of director of plantations, state railways, and telegraphs of Egypt. He cultivated successfully cactus for fibre, casuarina for telegraph poles, *Hyoscyamus muticus*, which yields the alkaloid hyoscyamine, and other plants. Having discovered nitrate of soda in a clay in Upper Egypt, he was appointed by the government to superintend its extraction.

At the same time Floyer engaged in exploration. In 1884 he travelled from Halfa to Debba, and in 1887 surveyed two routes between the Nile and the Red Sea about lat. 26° N. In 1891 he was appointed by the khedive commander of an important expedition in a more southern part of the same desert (about lat. 24° N). In this expedition he rediscovered the abandoned emerald mines of Sikait and Zabara, which had been worked at various epochs from early times. As the result of Floyer's report these mines were reopened. The outcome of this expedition is described in his *Étude sur la Nord-Etbai entre le Nil et la mer rouge* (1893). For services to the military authorities Floyer received the British medal 'Egypt, 1882', with clasp 'The Nile, 1884–5', and the khedive's bronze star. Floyer, who was popular with his Egyptian employees, knew Arabic well enough to discern minute differences of dialect.

Floyer married in 1887 Mary Louisa, eldest daughter of William Richards Watson, rector of Saltfleetby St Peter's, Lincolnshire. They had three sons. He died at the Planter's House, El Katta, Cairo, on 1 December 1903.

Floyer was a fellow of the Royal Geographical Society, and contributed three articles to its publications (1884, 1887, and 1893) on the geography of Egypt. He was a fellow of the Linnean Society, and wrote on botanical and agricultural matters for the journal of the Institut Égyptien (1894–6). He published other papers on geology. His contribution lay in his intelligent and well-informed descriptions of Egypt and particularly of Baluchistan, then little known to Europeans.

VAUGHAN CORNISH, rev. ELIZABETH BAIGENT

Sources personal knowledge (1912) · V. Cornish, 'Ernest Ayscoghe Floyer', *Journal of the Royal Asiatic Society of Great Britain and Ireland* (1904), 381–6 · *CGPLA Eng. & Wales* (1904) · Allibone, *Dict.*, suppl. · C. Dyhouse, *Girls growing up in late Victorian and Edwardian England* (1981) · C. E. Grant, *Farthing bundles* (1931)
Wealth at death £3485 18*s*. 9*d.*: resworn probate, 18 Feb 1904, *CGPLA Eng. & Wales*

Floyer, Sir John (1649–1734), physician, was born on 3 March 1649 at Hints Hall, Staffordshire, the third child of Richard Floyer (1603–1679), barrister of the Inner Temple, and his second wife, Elizabeth (1618–1680), daughter of William Babington of Curborough, near Lichfield. His grandfather Ralph Floyer, descended from a mercer of Stafford, acquired the manor house and estate, Hints Hall, in the village of Hints, in 1601. The Staffordshire Floyers were probably an offshoot of the Floyer family long established at Floyer Hayes near Exeter, but the link remains to be proved. John Floyer is likely to have received his early education from a tutor, along with his elder brother; his two younger brothers attended the grammar school in Tamworth. At the age of fifteen he matriculated at Queen's College, Oxford, and was 'entered on the physic line'. He became BA (1668), MA (1670), BM (1674), and DM (8 July 1680). For his doctorate he responded to three questions relating to digestion, arguing in the affirmative that food was dissolved in the stomach by fermentation.

By 1675 Floyer was living in Lichfield, the city with which he remained closely identified and where he practised as a physician for over half a century. In April 1680 he married Mary, widow of Arthur Fleetwood, and daughter of Sir Henry Archbold, chancellor of the diocese of Lichfield; with her he had two sons. By his marriage he became connected to Lord Dartmouth, to whom he dedicated his first book. His second wife, whom he married on 15 June 1706, was surnamed Whitehall. Floyer was knighted on 24 January 1684 by Charles II, for local political services. In 1686 he was among the party which welcomed James II to Lichfield, and in the same year he was appointed justice of the peace. It was Floyer who recommended that Michael and Sarah Johnson should take their ailing infant son, Sam, to London to be touched by Queen Anne for the 'evil'. Michael Johnson published four of Floyer's books. Dr Samuel Johnson, Floyer's former patient, recalled many years later that, though a sufferer from asthma, Floyer 'panted on to ninety'.

During Floyer's years of residence in Oxford, much was happening 'to infuse life into the dry bones of Galen and Hippocrates' (Gunn), so that his youthful curiosity was heightened by the discoveries and ideas of 'Oxonian sparkles' (Sinclair, 378), such as Robert Boyle, John Locke, and John Mayow. Floyer took with him into the life of a practising physician a spirit of research and enquiry, while at the same time retaining the highest respect for the ancients. In his first book, *The Touchstone of Medicines* (2 vols., 1687–90), his declared purpose was to classify medicines for their usefulness in different conditions, according to their tastes and smells. His next work, concerning the animal humours, was an attempt to reinterpret Galenic notions in the context of new discoveries. Floyer then played an important role in stimulating public interest in wells and waters, enthusiasm for which had been growing since the Restoration. He was not averse to the therapeutic use of temperate and warm baths on occasions, but his special predilection was for cold-water bathing. To provide local facilities, he persuaded 'worthy and obliging' gentlemen of Lichfield to contribute towards the construction of cold baths at Abnalls, a mile from the city, where he had found by thermometer readings that the spring water was the coldest in the district. St Chad's baths became the prototype for other small bathing spas. Underlying the promotion of cold-water bathing was a concern that, because of the growing popularity of tea, coffee, and other importations from hot countries, body-warming processes were

becoming more common. Floyer's *The ancient Psychrolousia revived, or, An essay to prove cold bathing both safe and useful* (1702), which reached six editions, was the most published of his works.

In his preface to *A Treatise of the Asthma* (1698) Floyer mentioned that he had:

> suffered under the tyranny of the asthma at least thirty years … and since I have made many trials for the relieving and the preventing of the fits … I design to relate what I have found useful both to myself and others.   (3rd edn, 1745, 2)

As a result of observations on himself and on his patients, he was able to define bronchial asthma sufficiently to separate the condition from other pulmonary disorders, to deduce that constriction resulting from muscular contraction in the walls of bronchi was the likely mechanism, and to recognize numerous factors which could initiate or exacerbate attacks in individual sufferers. In a postscript Floyer described the dissection of a broken-winded mare, noting the analogy of the condition with human emphysema; he observed 'the rupture or dilation of the lungs, by which the air is too much retained in the bladders (of the lungs) or their intersticies' (203). The originality and validity of many of Floyer's observations on asthma later tended to be underestimated, conveyed as they were in the idiom of Galenic medicine.

The significance of Floyer's *The Physician's Pulse Watch* (2 vols., 1707–10) lies in his insistence on the value of accurate measurement of pulse rates, so that 'we may know the natural pulse and the excesses and defects from this in diseases' (*The Physician's Pulse Watch*, 1, 1707, 23). Pulse-timing became a routine procedure for Floyer, and enabled him to make scores of observations, in which he endeavoured to establish relationships between pulse rates and other measurements, such as the rate of respiration, temperature, and barometric readings, age, sex, and season, and even the latitude where readings were taken. To begin with his timing device was the minute hand of a pendulum clock or a sea-minute glass. He then commissioned Samuel Watson, a clockmaker in Coventry, to make a watch for the purpose of timing the pulse. The physician's pulse watch, the first instrument designed for bedside clinical measurement, incorporated a second hand, as well as a lever for stopping the mechanism. Though most of his search for the clinical relevance of pulse-timing proved futile, in Haller's words, Floyer introduced a practice which is now universal. He also produced some of the first reports made in English concerning Chinese pulse lore and acupuncture, news of which had recently been conveyed to the west by Jesuit missionaries.

In his later years Floyer's involvement in medical subjects declined, in favour of theological enquiries and commentaries, particularly those concerning prophecies. These included *The Sibylline Oracles, Translated from the Greek* (1713), *Two Essays on the Creation and on the Mosaic System* (1717), and *An Exposition of the Revelations* (1719). He returned to medical topics with his *Medicina gerocomica, or, The Galenic Art of Preserving Old Men's Healths* (1724). On the last page of this book he listed the manuscripts he had deposited in the library of Queen's College. The most interesting of these is 'Advice to a young physician', written for a grandson, in which he gave his recommendations on the education, conduct, and practice of a physician. When Floyer was aged over eighty, a friend wrote that he remained 'of a happy temper, not to be moved by what he cannot remedy' (Wilmot, 282). He died in Lichfield on 31 January 1734 and was buried on 1 February within the shadow of Lichfield Cathedral; no memorial remains.   D. D. GIBBS

Sources J. A. Gunn, 'British masters of medicine: Sir John Floyer, 1649–1734', *Medical Press and Circular* (3 Oct 1934), 297–9 · L. Lindsay, 'Sir John Floyer (1649–1734)', *Proceedings of the Royal Society of Medicine*, 44 (1951), 43–8 · D. D. Gibbs, 'Sir John Floyer (1649–1734)', *BMJ* (25 Jan 1969), 242–5 · D. D. Gibbs, 'The physician's pulse watch', *Medical History*, 15 (1971), 187–90 · D. D. Gibbs, 'Recommendations of Sir John Floyer on the education of a physician', *Proceedings of the 23rd International Congress of the History of Medicine*, 1 (1972), 367–70 · G. L. Townsend, 'Sir John Floyer (1649–1734) and his study of pulse and respiration', *Journal of the History of Medicine and Allied Sciences*, 22 (1967), 286–316 · G. L. Townsend, 'Sir John Floyer (1649–1734) and the discovery of pulmonary emphysema', *Mayo Clinic Proceedings*, 44 (1969), 484–8 · A. W. Franklin, 'Clinical medicine', *Medicine in seventeenth century England: a symposium held … in honor of C. D. O'Malley* [Berkeley 1974], ed. A. G. Debus (1974), 113–45 · A. Sakula, 'Sir John Floyer's *A treatise of the asthma* (1698)', *Thorax*, 39 (1984), 248–54 · A. Sakula, 'A history of asthma', *Journal of the Royal College of Physicians of London*, 22 (1988), 36–44 · P. Hembry, 'Cold-bathing at the minor spas', *The English spa, 1560–1815: a social history* (1990), 159–78 · B. Szczesniak, 'John Floyer and Chinese medicine', *Osiris*, 11 (1954), 127–56 · J. Rosenbloom, 'The history of pulse timing with some remarks on Sir John Floyer and his physician's pulse watch', *Annals of Medical History*, 4 (1922), 97–9 · D. E. Bedford, 'The ancient art of feeling the pulse', *British Heart Journal*, 13 (1951), 423–37 · J. Wilmot, *The life of the Rev. John Hough, DD* (1812), 282 · *A catalogue of all graduates … in the University of Oxford, between … 1659 and … 1850* (1851) · H. M. Sinclair, 'Oxford medicine', *Medicine in seventeenth century England: a symposium held … in honor of C. D. O'Malley* [Berkeley 1974], ed. A. G. Debus (1974), 371–91 · M. Jenner, 'Bathing and baptism: Sir John Floyer and the politics of cold bathing', *Refiguring revolutions: aesthetics and politics from the English Revolution to the Romantic Revolution*, ed. K. Sharpe and S. N. Zwicker (1998), 197–216 · A. Hamilton, *The apocryphal apocalypse: the reception of the second book of Esdras (4 Ezra) from the Renaissance to the Enlightenment* (1999), 279–84
Archives Lichfield Cathedral Library · Queen's College, Oxford, medical notes
Likenesses C. E. Stringer, pen-and-ink sketch, Bodl. Oxf. · portrait, priv. coll.

Floyer, Louisa Sara (1830–1909). *See under* Floyer, Ernest Ayscoghe (1852–1903).

Fludd, Robert (*bap.* 1574, *d.* 1637), physician and writer on the occult, was born in Milgate House, Bearsted, Kent, and baptized on 17 January 1574 in Bearsted parish church, the seventh of twelve children of Sir Thomas Fludd (*d.* 1607), who served the crown in various senior administrative appointments, and his wife, Elizabeth (*d.* 1592), daughter of Philip Andrews (or Andros) of Wellington, Somerset.

Education and work as a physician Nothing is known of Fludd's early schooling. He entered St John's College, Oxford, as a commoner on 10 November 1592 and took his BA on 3 February 1596 and his MA on 8 July 1598. While at Oxford he came into contact with George Abbot, later archbishop of Canterbury, Richard Andrewes, whose

Robert Fludd (*bap.* 1574, *d.* 1637), by Matthäus Merian the elder, pubd 1626

medical career was to remain closely linked to that of Fludd, and Sir William Paddy, later the physician of James I. It seems that Fludd was in contact with occult circles which were active in Oxford at that time; he records in a later work an incident involving the use of astrology to discover the whereabouts of a stolen object for a tutor. He alludes also to his extensive study of music. From the typographical presentation of his later writings, it is clear that he was trained in Ramist method. The entry recording his graduation as MA mentions that he was 'going over sea'; he says himself that he spent six years abroad (presumably between 1598 and 1604–5), travelling in France, Italy, Germany, and Spain. The suggestion in Zedler's *Universallexikon* that he spent some time in an army is not confirmed by him, but in the second volume of his *Utriusque cosmi … historia*, published in 1618, there is a long and well-informed section on the art of warfare. In 1601–2 he certainly visited Lyons, Avignon, and Marseilles (where he became the tutor in mathematics to two prominent members of the Guise family) and went from there by way of Leghorn to Rome and Venice. He reports also a stay in Augsburg, but the suggestion that he visited the courts and learned circles of Heidelberg and Kassel, where there were scholars who may have influenced his later work, is conjectural. It seems likely that he was exposed to hermeticism and Paracelsianism during these years, during which he composed the sections of later works on arithmetic, geometry, perspective, and the art of warfare. After his return to Oxford (this time to Christ Church), he supplicated for his MB and MD on 14 May 1605, and was granted these two days later, together with a licence to practise medicine. Before continuing with his career, he travelled abroad again at least once, in August 1606, to meet French and Italian medical colleagues somewhere in France.

After leaving Oxford, Fludd set up house in Fenchurch Street in London and applied to the College of Physicians on 8 November 1605 for a licence to practise. Apparently suspected as a Paracelsian, he failed to obtain this at his first attempt on the grounds that he was not well enough versed in Galenic medicine, but was admitted to the college by the grudging grant of a licence on 7 February 1606. He was secretly denounced as an anti-Galenist on 2 May 1606, and failed in his attempts to be admitted to candidature for fellowship on 1 August, 9 October, and 22 December 1607. On 21 March 1608 he even had his licence withdrawn for his allegedly arrogant support of anti-Galenic opinions, but was eventually admitted candidate on 25 June, and made a fellow on 20 September of the following year. Thereafter he played a full part in the activities of the college, being censor in 1618, 1627, 1633, and 1634, and participating in the inspection of the London apothecaries in 1616. His name was among those who as fellows authorized the *Pharmacopoeia Londoniensis* in 1618; from this it is reasonable to conclude that, even if he offered other forms of treatment, he subscribed also to the mostly traditional therapies set out in that volume. On 27 June 1620 he gave the annual anatomy lecture; this again suggests that the unorthodox beliefs about anatomy expressed in his *Anatomiae amphitheatrum* of 1623 were combined with a prudent public conformism. Fludd was later to show his attachment to the college by making a gift of his published works to it, and by having his fellowship recorded on the monument erected to him in Bearsted church. One of his friends in the college was William Harvey. Fludd joined the Barber–Surgeons' Company on 12 June 1634, possibly to legitimize his activity as a surgeon. It seems that the early suspicions of him as a Paracelsian and astrologer were dispelled, and that his practice in London was well respected and secure. It was certainly quite profitable: he was able not only to employ a secretary to whom to dictate his voluminous works, but also an apothecary and at one point a French technician–metallurgist.

Fludd is reported by Fuller as being very successful as a healer, inducing in his patients a 'faith-natural' which helped his prescriptions to be effective. It appears also that he administered chemical remedies, although without necessarily subscribing to the elaborate theory constructed by the followers of Paracelsus to justify their use. A near-contemporary anecdote attributed to Nicholas Culpeper by Peter Cole has Fludd admitting that he found traditional Galenic remedies more effective than therapy of a chemical or sympathetic nature. All this suggests that his practice was successful and largely orthodox—an orthodoxy matched by that of his religion, which he protests in his 'Declaratio brevis' to the king of 1617–19 to be loyally Anglican. His association with Archbishop Abbot and two other bishops, John Thornborough of the see of Worcester, and John Williams, bishop of Lincoln, also indicates that his broad-based protestantism was seen as acceptable to the Anglican hierarchy of his day. He later described all three churchmen as his patrons.

In his establishments at Fenchurch Street and later at Coleman Street, Fludd engaged in experiments and in the mechanical arts. By his own account he constructed automata (a wooden bull which bellowed, an automatic dragon, and a self-performing lyre), and sought from the privy council a patent for making steel, after it had received complaints from competitors of his unlicensed activity; the patent was granted on 27 September 1620. However, his most remarkable products were his writings. Of the major works, *Utriusque cosmi* was published as five parts in two volumes (1617–21), and the *Medicina catholica* in four parts (1629–31). Most of these were published on the continent, at Leiden, Frankfurt, and (posthumously) Gouda. One reason for this was expense: had Fludd wished to have his typographically complex and copiously illustrated books printed in London, he would have had to pay the printers a very large sum, whereas, as he records, the celebrated Frankfurt and Oppenheim printer Theodor De Bry not only agreed to publish them gratis (having had them refereed by a number of scholars including Jesuits in Frankfurt), but gave Fludd sixteen free copies and a generous fee. De Bry's successors Johann Theodor De Bry and William Fitzer continued loyally to publish his works. It was unusual for English scholars to be printed on continental presses at this time; Fludd confirmed that his work was brought to De Bry's attention through the good offices of a German, although it now seems likely that this was not the Rosicrucian doctor Michael Maier, as had been previously thought.

From the time of their first publication, Fludd's works were well known and respected on the continent, even by traditional doctors such as Gregor Horst, but Thomas Fuller, Anthony Wood, and even Fludd himself, are unanimous in declaring that he was not much read in England. It seems therefore that Fludd had two almost completely separate existences, one as an ambitious universal philosopher and writer in the neoplatonist and occult tradition, the other as a respected and successful London gentleman and physician. There can be no doubt but that he was well connected in the society of the capital and at court. He had several attested meetings with James I, with whom he discussed his medical and philosophical ideas; Charles I made him a grant of land in Suffolk; and he retained his early links with Archbishop Abbot and Sir William Paddy. He was also a member of the learned circle of John Thornborough, William Camden, John Selden, and Sir Robert Cotton.

The Rosicrucian debate Fludd was perhaps the Englishman most involved in the debate about the Rosicrucians, which was unleashed in Europe in 1614, with the publication of an anonymous pamphlet entitled *Fama fraternitatis*. There it was claimed that an international brotherhood with hermetic and occult connections, and possibly with political ambitions as well, existed in Europe. It is difficult to gauge how fraudulent or satirical these claims were, or how genuine are the visionary beliefs expressed in the various documents supporting the existence of the brotherhood of the rosy cross. It was vigorously denounced on the continent, among others by the famous iatrochemist Andreas Libavius. Fludd decided to write in defence of the brotherhood, by refuting Libavius's tract in a short *Apologia compendiaria* in 1616; this appeared in the following year in an expanded version, entitled *Tractatus apologeticus*. Both texts include an apparently sincere appeal by Fludd to be admitted to the brotherhood. Fludd's defence of Rosicrucians does not mean necessarily that he had met any of them during his travels abroad; in fact, he specifically denies this, claiming not to have heard of the brotherhood until 1614 or 1615. But that he should defend the order seems to have alarmed James I, who summoned him to give account of his tracts.

Fludd reports that the king was satisfied by Fludd's account of himself, but urged him to set down his position in writing; this he did in a 'Declaratio brevis', followed by a 'Philosophical key', both written at some time between 1617 and 1619. From these some of the personal and intellectual reasons which attracted Fludd to the brotherhood can be gauged. Fludd himself knew that one requirement for initiation into hermetical lore was that one should abstain from all sexual activity, and he duly declared himself to be 'virgo immaculata'. Intellectually, the combination of a stress on Christian virtue with a broadly neoplatonist theory of cosmic mystical harmony in Rosicrucian writings is very close to Fludd's own convictions. It is less clear that he shared the political ambitions of the brotherhood, if indeed they harboured these. Given the orthodox nature of Fludd's practice as a doctor and a believer, it would seem safest to assume that his interest in Rosicrucians was aroused by the remarkable coincidence of their recorded beliefs and his own intellectual convictions.

Scientific disputes The first of Fludd's philosophical works to appear was the account of the macrocosm and the microcosm, entitled *Utriusque cosmi … historia*. It consists in two massive folios which are copiously illustrated with remarkable mystical emblems representing relationships between man, the cosmos, and the godhead. It is very likely that Fludd himself was the draughtsman of these illustrations with their recurrent geometrical motifs of concentric circles, triangles, pyramids, hemispheres, blazing suns, and the interplay of areas of dark and light.

The significance of the emblems is revealed in accompanying texts, which bring together quotations from the Bible and hermetic lore. In these volumes Fludd expresses both his adherence to a Judaeo-Christian interpretation of world history based on the text of the Bible and his hostility to the learning of the universities in the form of Aristotelian natural philosophy and Galenic medicine. Fludd's originality lay in his revival of the fifteenth-century neoplatonism of Ficino and Pico and their sources in the *corpus hermeticum*, and his uniting of these with an alchemical account of the creation based on a literal reading of the book of Genesis. The major explanatory mechanism of the workings and order of the world is the parallel between macrocosm and microcosm. Man is revealed to be the 'ape of nature', imitating and completing her work through the exercise of geometry, music, memory, astrology, physiognomy, chiromancy, and the mechanical arts, including cosmography, painting, and the art of warfare; all of these are in some sense founded on number. Fludd's metaphysics postulates a complex and all-embracing correspondence between the world of spirits and the physical world; this entailed opposition to Copernicanism. For Fludd the sun, source of heat, light, and spirit, goes round the earth and vivifies it, just as the Holy Spirit vivifies man. This theory led him to the view (expressed later in the *Anatomiae amphitheatrum* of 1623) that the blood circulates in the body, thus prefiguring in a general sense the work of his friend William Harvey's *De motu cordis*, whose conclusions Fludd supported shortly after its publication in the second volume of his *Medicina catholica*, entitled *Pulsus*, which appeared in 1629. But as in the case of the weather-glass (a primitive barometer) and the monochord (a single-stringed musical instrument), both of which he invokes for various explanatory purposes, Fludd's apparent agreement with the new science derives from a fundamentally different attitude to experiment and observation.

Fludd's theories were attacked by a number of emerging or established scholars of his day, testifying to the fact that what he had to say was perceived as potent and serious enough to warrant refutation. The French mathematician and physicist Marin Mersenne rejected Fludd's neoplatonist metaphysics in his *Quaestiones celeberrimae in Genesim* of 1623, and accused him of being a heretical 'cacomagus'. Fludd defended himself in a pamphlet in 1629, which drew a response from Mersenne's colleague Pierre Gassendi, to which Fludd replied in turn. These replies to Catholic thinkers show that Fludd thought of himself as being in a solid protestant tradition, remote from the illicit forms of magic with which he was associated by his adversaries.

He was attacked also by the astronomer Johann Kepler, who challenged his ideas on celestial correspondence in an appendix to his *Harmonices mundi* of 1619. This also led to an exchange of pamphlets. Like Fludd, Kepler was an enthusiastic exponent of neoplatonist mathematics; where his approach differs is over the two issues of the authority of holy writ in natural philosophy and the nature of celestial correspondences. For Kepler, a correspondence between the heavens and man, or a description of the nature of celestial motion, would have to be more than an arbitrary alignment; he insisted on its being subject to empirical confirmation in some way. For Fludd, the authority of holy writ determined the nature of evidential proof, not vice versa. Part of his reply to Kepler is drawn from his work on music, and is entitled the *Monochordum mundi* (1622); in it he argues for the unity of the spiritual and physical worlds, and illustrates exhaustively the correspondences between the numerical proportions of the monochord, the parts of the human body, and the disposition of the stars.

Medical writings Fludd's longest work is his *Medicina catholica* of 1629–31; it is not clear why it was left unfinished. The book is an attempt at a universal account of medicine from a characteristically wide range of sources: some elements of the Galenic system (notably the theory of the humours); the Old Testament; the neoplatonist theory of demons and spirits; occult and cabbalistic philosophy; and a theory of disease as wind-borne. For Fludd, all disease has its origin in sin. Because of the unbroken chain of being in the universe linking the deity with celestial and terrestrial spirits, the physical elements, and the humours of the body, God is said to be responsible for both illness and cure. Evil spirits who control the winds excite lesser spirits in the air; these enter the body through the pores or through respiration. Health is portrayed as a fortress, assailed by disease-bearing winds and defended by angelic powers inside the human being. If these are for any reason impaired, an imbalance of humours (or disease) results in the patient, and may only be cured by sympathetic means. The text is set out in Ramist dichotomies, and is illustrated, although less copiously than earlier volumes.

Among other contested remedies, Fludd had supported the use of the weapon-salve in his *Anatomiae amphitheatrum*; this was the Paracelsian doctrine that a wound could be cured by anointing the weapon which caused it with a mixture of the patient's blood, moss grown on a human skull, and mummy (human flesh from the body of a hanged man). The cure is based on the theory that there is a magnetic or sympathetic relationship between the weapon and the wound which allows for action over distance to occur; the wound itself needs only to be disinfected with the patient's own urine. Fludd was vigorously attacked by the clergyman William Foster, who went so far as to nail a copy of the title-page of his tract (entitled *Hoplocrisma-spongus, or, A Sponge to Wipe Away the Weapon-Salve*) to Fludd's door in 1631. Foster alleged that the cure was not only ineffective but also inspired by the devil. Fludd duly replied with a spirited and cogent pamphlet of his own, his only work to be published in the vernacular. He associates Foster's attack with Mersenne's and Gassendi's criticisms (many of which were repeated by Foster), and goes on to vindicate his public reputation, citing his patrons and the signs of approval which his written work had attracted (mainly from abroad). He quotes examples of the efficacy of the cure, including one

performed by himself on one of his brother-in-law's servants, and argues that the cure is neither superstitious nor magical, but natural. He argues for the unity of the spiritual and physical worlds, for which he was able to cite much evidence in common experience (quoting liberally from Gilbert's recent work on the magnet), and does so in a traditional (syllogistic) way; as a result, the tract reads as sober, reasonable, and often witty. His defence of his position was later translated into Latin and published in Gouda after his death.

Likenesses, death, and reputation There are two original engravings of Fludd in works published by him in his lifetime. The first is in the *Philosophia sacra* of 1626, and was engraved by Matthäus Merian, presumably from a drawing or miniature; it is made to function as an emblem (of Fludd's inspiration from the God-sun), but also carries a coat of arms with twelve quarterings, indicating Fludd's sense of gentlemanly status. Fludd is shown as bareheaded and bald, but both features may be conventional. He is not wearing a doctor's cap, presumably to show that his gentle birth takes precedence over his profession: and in his remarks on physiognomy, he claims that baldness is a sign of subtlety of mind and astuteness. This is the basis of another contemporary portrait in Boissard's *Bibliotheca sive thesaurus virtutis et gloriae* of 1630. This unsigned engraving is much more lifelike and depicts a balding gentleman of serious demeanour, with no doctor's cap, and the clothes of a Stuart courtier. He ordained in his will that a bust be erected after his death in Bearsted church in the style of that of Camden in Westminster Abbey; this was installed at Bearsted on 10 August 1638 by his nephew and executor Thomas Fludd. The face, with its naval beard, fuller head of hair, and almost jovial expression, has little in common with the engraved portraits.

Fludd never married; he died in his house in Coleman Street, London, on 8 September 1637, and was interred in Bearsted parish church. His career may be seen as consisting in two parts: his activities in London as a practising doctor and member of scholarly circles, well connected at court, reasonably prosperous, and well respected; and his literary career, which, apart from the debate about the weapon-salve, took place principally in the continental arena. By the first he earned a place in Fuller's *Worthies*; by the latter, he was remembered for rather longer as one of the last in line of synthetic Renaissance universal philosophers of neoplatonist, alchemical, and hermetic persuasion. The tradition he represents attempted a unitary explanation of the cosmos and of man's place in it by the mystical linking of the physical world with the spiritual. Fludd's synthesis unites this tradition with a protestant-inspired syncretic exposition of the accounts of creation and redemption in the Bible, whose authority is taken to be absolute. Even though Fludd refers to experiment and observation, had recourse to mathematical demonstration, and indeed was a practitioner of several of the mechanical arts, these are adduced to confirm the pre-existing theory; Fludd was clearly out of sympathy with the new science. His last work, the *Philosophia moysiaca*, published posthumously in 1638, shows him not to have modified any of the views which he expressed in his first publications. It is for this ambitious and all-embracing vision of the world that Fludd was remembered on the continent into the eighteenth century. IAN MACLEAN

Sources W. H. Huffman, *Robert Fludd and the end of the Renaissance* (1988) · *Robert Fludd: essential readings*, ed. W. H. Huffman (1992) · J. Godwin, *Robert Fludd* (1979) · A. G. Debus, *The English Paracelsians* (1965), 105–27 · B. Vickers, ed., *Occult and scientific mentalities in the Renaissance* (1984), 73–95, 177–230 · [P. Cole], *Mr Culpepper's ghost* (1656), 5–9 · Fuller, *Worthies* (1662), 2.78–9 · Wood, *Ath. Oxon.* · J. H. Zedler, *Universallexikon* (1732–50) · Munk, *Roll* · *Reg. Oxf.*, 2/1.191; 2/2.193; 2/3.194 · A. Libavius, *Wolmeinendes bedencken* (1614) · M. Mersenne, *Quaestiones celeberrimae in Genesim* (1623) · J. Kepler, *Harmonices mundi* (1619) · P. Gassendi, *Epistolica exercitatio* (1630) · W. Foster, *Hoplocrisma-spongus* (1631) · will, PRO, PROB 11/175, fols. 18r–19v · parish register (baptism), 17/1/1574, Bearsted parish church, Kent · memorial stone, Bearsted parish church, Kent **Likenesses** marble bust on monument, 1638, Bearsted parish church, Kent · line engraving, 1650, BM, NPG; repro. in J. J. Boissard, *Bibliotheca chalcographica* (1650) · M. Merian the elder, etching, BM, NPG; repro. in R. Fludd, *Philosophia sacra* (1626) [*see illus.*] · engraving, repro. in R. Fludd, *Integrum morborum mysterium* (1631) · oils, priv. coll. · portrait, repro. in J. J. Boissard, *Bibliotheca sive thesaurus virtutis et gloriae*, 2 (1630), 197 **Wealth at death** reasonably prosperous: will, PRO, PROB, 11/175, fols. 18r–19v

Fludyer, Sir Samuel, first baronet (1704/5–1768), clothier and merchant, was born in 1704, or possibly in 1705, the first son of Samuel Fludyer and Elizabeth de Monsallier, his wife. The elder Fludyer was a Somerset clothier who had moved his business from Frome to London. Young Samuel was trained in his father's business and for a time attended the great trains of packhorses that brought cloth from the west country to London.

In partnership with his brother Thomas, the younger Samuel Fludyer established a London firm of his own, which became a major force in the English, particularly the west-country, cloth trade. In the London directories from 1738 to 1796 the partners were described as 'warehousemen', though in legal documents they were termed 'Blackwell Hall factors' (this building housing the woolcloth exchange) and 'merchants'. As factors, they received from country clothiers consignments of woollen cloth to be sold on commission; as warehousemen (wholesalers), they sold cloth bought from other factors or directly from country clothiers; as merchants they exported such cloth and ventured in trade to the Americas. In a trade characterized by long credits on sales, great pressure arose from the need of clothiers for prompter payment. Samuel Fludyer pointed the way for other factors by issuing personal bearer notes. According to a contemporary writer:

> Sir Samuel Fludyer, who was factor to most of the great clothiers, used to send them their balances in his own notes instead of money, which circulated in Gloucestershire, and the parts adjacent, for two, three, and four years, without returning to him to be liquidated in bank bills or specie. (Isaac de Pinto, *An Essay on Circulation and Credit*, trans. S. Baggs, 1774, 6)

Fludyer's market standing was recognized by his election as director of the Bank of England from 1753, and deputy governor, 1766–8. He was also alderman for Cheap

ward from 1751, sheriff in 1754–5, and lord mayor in 1761–2. He failed to obtain election as member of parliament for the City in 1761, but sat in the Commons for Chippenham, a Wiltshire cloth centre, from 1754 until his death. As a member of parliament, he was better able to obtain lucrative government victualling and remittance contracts. As a contractor, he normally supported the government of the day, despite the difficulties created by the frequent ministerial changes of the 1760s. He was knighted in 1755 and was made a baronet in 1759.

Fludyer's first wife was Jane Clerke of Westminster. After her death on 20 March 1757, he married, on 2 September 1758, Caroline, daughter of the Hon. James Brudenell MP, brother of George, third earl of Cardigan. Fludyer died in London on 18 January 1768 and was buried at Lee, in Kent, on the 24th. At his death he was reported to have left a fortune of £900,000. His heir, the son of his second marriage, was Sir James Brudenell Fludyer MP. The succeeding baronets in the next century were substantial country landowners, particularly in Rutland.

ROBERT HARRISON, *rev.* JACOB M. PRICE

Sources HoP, *Commons* · J. de L. Mann, *The cloth industry in the west of England from 1660 to 1880* (1971) · J. M. Price, *Capital and credit in British overseas trade: the view from the Chesapeake, 1700–1776* (1980) · GEC, *Baronetage*, 5.117–18 · IGI · will, PRO, PROB 11/936/59 · W. Musgrave, *Obituary prior to 1800*, ed. G. J. Armytage, 6 vols., Harleian Society, 44–9 (1899–1901) **Archives** Royal Bank of Scotland, London, business papers relating to his partnership with John Drummond **Likenesses** oils, Bank of England, London **Wealth at death** £900,000: HoP, *Commons*

Flügel, John Carl (1884–1955), psychologist and psychoanalyst, was born in Brompton House, Livingston Drive South, Toxteth Park, Liverpool, on 13 June 1884, the only child of Karl Rudolf Dietrich Flügel, a wealthy German merchant, and his wife, Mary, *née* Eccles. Flügel was privately educated, a congenital foot defect preventing school attendance. In 1902 he went to Balliol College, Oxford, graduating BA in Greats (1906). Here he displayed wide-ranging, often heretical, interests (for example, psychical research), came under William McDougall's influence, and began a lifelong friendship with fellow student Cyril Burt. A spell at Würzburg, studying psychology under Oswald Külpe, followed. After returning to Oxford in 1908 he won a John Locke scholarship in mental philosophy. In 1909 he became C. Spearman's first assistant at University College, London, as demonstrator in the psychology laboratory. Flügel remained at University College until his death, being appointed senior lecturer (1920), assistant professor (1929) and special lecturer following his official retirement (1944).

Flügel is best remembered as virtually the only British psychologist of his day successfully to straddle academic psychology and psychoanalysis, between which he always strove to mediate. His first experimental work (with McDougall, on perception), appeared in 1909; several further papers (often cited by Spearman) on perception and hearing appeared into the 1920s. The experimental work culminated in *Practice, Fatigue and Oscillation* (1928). This established his orthodox scientific credentials but, while long continuing to be involved in teaching experimental psychology, his creativity lay elsewhere. After marrying Sophie Mabel Ingeborg, daughter of Richard Theodore Klingberg, merchant, on 20 December 1913, Flügel sought psychoanalytic help for some personal problems. By this time he was already on his way to becoming a convert and practitioner; in October 1913 he co-founded the London Psycho-Analytical Society with Ernest Jones, and later, in 1919, the British Psycho-Analytical Society. He became secretary of the International Psycho-Analytic Association (1919–24) and assistant editor of the *International Journal of Psycho-Analysis*. His *Psycho-Analytic Study of the Family* (1921) was the first book by a British author in the International Psycho-Analytic Library series. While theoretically orthodox, Flügel's psychoanalytic interests often displayed originality, with papers on the Esperanto movement, Henry VIII, the 'Tannäusser Motif', and a book entitled *The Psychology of Clothes* (1940). His wife shared his interests, and her 'Some psychological aspects of a fox-hunting rite' appeared in *Men and their Motives* (1934). The early influences of McDougall and Herbert Spencer, plus his cosmopolitan background, added a social and internationalist dimension to Flügel's concerns, most evident in the highly regarded *Man, Morals and Society: a Psychoanalytical Study* (1945) and the neo-Malthusian *Population, Psychology and Peace* (1947). *A Hundred Years of Psychology* (1933; rev. D. J. West 1957) was also for many years the only history of psychology written by a Briton. From 1920 until his death Flügel taught psychoanalysis on the University College undergraduate course, the academic co-existence of this alongside Spearman's psychometric factor approach being facilitated by a territorially convenient theoretical demarcation between emotional ('orectic') and cognitive processes. This enabled him to collaborate harmoniously with Spearman and, from 1931, Burt (Spearman's successor), on the jointly taught introductory course.

Meanwhile Flügel played central roles in the British Psychological Society, as honorary secretary (1911–20), honorary librarian (1921–32) and president (1932–5), combined with memberships of the Society for Psychical Research (dating from undergraduate days), the University of London Council for Psychical Investigation (1934), the Royal Anthropological Institute, and the Folklore Society. He received the University of London Carpenter medal (1931) and delivered the 1941 Conway memorial lecture ('The moral paradox of peace and war'). In 1950 he became president of the psychology section of the British Association. Additionally, he received an honorary fellowship of the British Psychological Society and honorary membership of the Indian Psychological Association.

Temperamentally Flügel was, by general consensus, original, humorous, diplomatic, and a fine lecturer. Socially, his forte was as a mediator in potentially conflict-ridden situations (for example, chairman of the programme committee for the 1948 International Congress on Mental Health) and as a calm, rational exponent of new ideas. In some respects, however, he spread himself too widely, pursuing very diverse intellectual interests, while fulfilling numerous and varied administrative commitments.

This, combined with an apparent light-heartedness, could give the impression of dilettantism, and renders Flügel's long-term significance difficult to weigh, the considerable legacy of forty-five years' inspirational teaching at one of Britain's major psychology departments being particularly elusive. His most enduring publications are *The Psychology of Clothes* (as one of the earliest texts on the topic) and *Man, Morals, and Society* (an ambitious integration of psychoanalytic and sociological perspectives), but his more ephemerally visible achievements as one of British psychology's great popularizers, fixers, teachers, and diplomats contributed in equal measure to the discipline's fortunes.

Flügel died as a result of a coronary thrombosis at his home, 20 Merton Rise, Hampstead, London, on 6 August 1955. His wife survived him.   GRAHAM RICHARDS

Sources E. Jones, *International Journal of Psycho-Analysis*, 37 (1956) · T. H. Pear, *British Journal of Psychology*, 47 (1956), 1–4 · B. Edgell, 'The British Psychological Society', *British Journal of Psychology*, 37 (1946–7), 113–31 · *Calendar* [University College, London] (1919–20) · *Calendar* [University College, London] (1954–5) · b. cert. · m. cert. · d. cert.

Likenesses W. Stoneman, photograph, repro. in J. C. Flügel, *Man, morals and society* (1955), jacket

Wealth at death £112,040 15s. 2d.: probate, 23 Nov 1955, *CGPLA Eng. & Wales*

Flürscheim [Flurscheim]**, Bernhard Jacques** (1874–1955), organic and theoretical chemist, was born at Baden-Baden on 27 November 1874, the son of Michael Flürscheim (*d.* 1904), an engineer and socialist who published several books on economics in English, and Marie-Amélie Heilbronne (*d.* 1891). His mother was French; his parents had met during the Franco-Prussian War. His maternal grandmother had been attached to the court of Louis-Philippe and it was the inheritance of her French estates that made him and his sister, Helen, financially independent. He received a classical education at schools in Baden-Baden and at Arnold College, Bournemouth, in England, before, at the age of seventeen, studying metallurgy and engineering at Winterthur, Switzerland, and Brunswick in Germany. At the age of twenty he switched to chemistry, studying successively at the universities of Zürich, where he took his first degree with Alfred Werner (1866–1919), Geneva, Heidelberg (with F. Kehrmann and E. Knoevenagel), where he obtained the PhD in 1901, and finally at Strasbourg with Johannes Thiele (1865–1918).

In 1902, while in Strasbourg, Flürscheim married Nora Kathleen Marie (*d.* 1973), a talented painter and the only daughter of Henry Northover, farmer, of Fonthill, Wiltshire. They had a son, Cedric Harold, an electrical engineer, and a daughter. In 1905 the couple settled at Crookham, Fleet, Hampshire, where he built a house and separate laboratory in woodland that reminded him of his boyhood in the Black Forest. He joined the Chemical Society in 1906, publishing his work both in English and German journals. He spent the remainder of his life in Fleet apart from a period in America during the First World War, and two periods as a visiting unpaid research worker in the Davy–Faraday laboratories at the Royal Institution, London, 1905–7 and 1925–8.

Flürscheim was described by C. K. Ingold as 'the last of the great pre-electronic builders of the theory of organic chemistry' (Ingold, *Journal of the Chemical Society*, 1087). In a German paper of 1902, which was inspired by Werner's and Thiele's ideas on the divisibility of affinity among atoms in a compound, Flürscheim speculated that a substituent in a carbon compound caused the distribution of affinities to alternate through a chain of carbon atoms such that different positions became vulnerable to attack by other substituents. He developed a symbolism of thick and thin lines (bonds) to indicate strengthened and weakened affinities, and over the following decades showed how the theory explained the mechanisms of many familiar reactions. In 1904, while engaged in work directed at proving the theory, or resolving its difficulties, he discovered the explosive tetranitroaniline, which he patented as TNA in 1910 (patent nos. 3224, 3907). In 1915, at Lord Moulton's request, Flürscheim went to America to supervise the manufacture of his explosive by Aetna, but came to regret that the discovery, which further increased his wealth, had forced him into commerce. During the 1920s he was active in debates over the emerging electronic theory of chemical reactions. While glad of Ingold's support for his theoretical insights, which Ingold thought superior to those of Robert Robinson, Flürscheim stubbornly refused to accept the shared electron theory of the chemical bond. Realizing that the electronic theory of valency had replaced his theoretical insights, he abandoned research in 1932.

As a private research worker in an era dominated by academic and industrial science, Flürscheim remains an enigmatic figure; nevertheless he was an individual who had an important influence on twentieth-century theoretical chemistry. He took English nationality, but was not very sociable outside his family circle, though he loved travelling and alpine climbing. He was well read and retained a love of classical languages. Although politically Conservative, in the 1930s he spoke out concerning the Nazi threat, and advocated a military alliance with the Russians. He died at the Trimmers Hospital, Farnham, on 15 June 1955.

W. H. BROCK

Sources C. K. Ingold, *JCS* (1956), 1087–9 · *Nature*, 176 (1955), 191 · C. H. Flürscheim, typescript life, Dec 1979, Open University, Centre for History of Chemistry ['to be deposited'] [author subject's son] · *The Times* (24 June 1955), 13 · C. K. Ingold, *Structure and mechanism in organic chemistry* (1953) · M. Flürscheim, *Rent, interest, and wages* [n.d., *c*.1891]; 2nd edn (1892); 3rd edn (1895) · M. Flürscheim, *Clue to the economic labyrinth* (1902)

Likenesses photograph, repro. in *Natural Products Reports*, 4 (1987), 62

Wealth at death £16,191 9s. 1d.: probate, 25 July 1955, *CGPLA Eng. & Wales*

Flux, Sir Alfred William (1867–1942), economist, statistician, and civil servant, was born in Portsmouth on 8 April 1867, the only son of John Flux, a journeyman cement maker, and his wife, Emily, daughter of Alfred Prince, dairy farmer, of Newport, Isle of Wight. Educated at Portsmouth grammar school and St John's College, Cambridge, where he was a minor scholar, he was bracketed as senior wrangler in the mathematical tripos of 1887, and was elected a fellow of his college in 1889. His focus turned rapidly to economics under the influence and encouragement of Alfred Marshall, also a fellow of St John's. Flux was awarded Cambridge's Marshall prize for political economy in 1889, and in 1893 he left Cambridge for Owens College, Manchester, where he became Cobden lecturer in political economy. The title of Stanley Jevons professor was added in 1898 and he served as president of the Manchester Statistical Society in 1900. He married, in 1895, Emilie, daughter of Wilhelm Hansen, a businessman, of Copenhagen; there were no children.

Finding limited scope in Manchester for the expansion of economic teaching and research, Flux emigrated to Canada in 1901, to become William Dow professor of political economy at McGill University, Montreal, where a considerable expansion of economics teaching was under way. He remained there until 1908, when he abandoned his academic career and returned to Britain. Although considerable, his academic success had not entirely fulfilled his early promise, but he was to find his métier, and full scope for his strong empirical bent, in the task of constructing and improving British economic statistics.

The Board of Trade was organizing in 1908 the first census of production; Flux was brought in as statistical adviser and, although not given the titular position of director until 1911, was responsible for the final report. He also supervised, in close collaboration with Henry Macrosty, the censuses of production inquiries of 1912 and 1924. Upon a reorganization of the board in 1918 he became an assistant secretary in charge of an expanded statistical department. He retired in 1932.

The early years of the twentieth century had seen a greatly increased interest in economic statistics. The inspiration and organizing ability of Sir Robert Giffen and later Sir Hubert Llewellyn Smith had already done much to extend and improve the statistical information published by the Board of Trade. But official statistics were still in the main a by-product of administration. Flux arrived at a time when the scientific collection of economic data with no immediate and specific administrative object had become politically possible. He had not the dynamic qualities of Giffen and Llewellyn Smith; but his technical competence and academic prestige, added to his personal qualities of candour, devotion to his subject, and complete freedom from party feeling, admirably fitted him to take advantage of the opportunity they had created. He played a chief part in a revolution in official statistics. The census of production made possible the quantitative study of the structure and interrelations of British industry. This was followed by an adequate index of prices (1921), indexes of industrial activity (1927), and an estimate of national income on the basis of product, which supplemented earlier estimates made by aggregating individual incomes (1929).

As Board of Trade representative on interdepartmental committees Flux contributed to the wider improvement of official statistics, and he served effectively as British representative on many intergovernmental committees and conferences concerned with statistical issues. After retirement he served, often as chairman, on a series of committees through which the League of Nations was developing uniform classifications and common standards for economic statistics. His knowledge of languages and wide experience made him an admirable agent in this work.

During the academic phase of his career Flux published a considerable number of articles, notes, and reviews, mainly in the *Economic Journal*. His contributions were predominantly applied in character, the most significant analysing trends in international trade. Issues of pure economic or statistical theory failed to attract him, although he is still remembered for an elegant clarification of marginal productivity theory in the course of a book review (1894). His textbook *Economic Principles* (1904; rev. edn, 1923) is clear and sound, but not markedly original, and the same can be said of his Newmarch lectures, published as *The Foreign Exchanges* (1924). A revision of Jevons's *Coal Question* (1906) and *The Swedish Banking System* (1910), a study undertaken for the US monetary commission, also have roots in the academic phase of his career.

His official position after 1908 did not debar Flux from scholarly publication and debate. He became closely involved in the activities of the Royal Statistical Society, and served as an honorary secretary from 1910 to 1928, when he became president. He was awarded the society's gold Guy medal in 1930. The new developments in his official work were presented to the world in a series of papers to the society; and its meetings provided an outlet, denied to him as a civil servant, for lengthy and formal oratory, in which he delighted. No member of the society was more respected or held in greater affection.

As an economist Flux was sound rather than original and his chief service to economics was to inculcate and assist a quantitative approach to its problems. His services were recognized by appointment as CB in 1920 and by a knighthood on the occasion of the Royal Statistical Society's centenary in 1934. For some years after his retirement Flux and his wife lived in Denmark, where he died, of pneumonia, at Ladeplatts, Zealand, on 16 July 1942. His wife survived him.

HENRY CLAY, *rev.* JOHN K. WHITAKER

Sources S. J. Chapman, *Economic Journal*, 52 (1942), 400–403 · H. Leake, *Journal of the Royal Statistical Society*, 105 (1942), 144–7 · V. W. Bladen, 'Sir William Flux, 1867–1942', *Canadian Journal of Economics and Political Science*, 9 (1943), 74–5 · Venn, *Alum. Cant.* · American Economic Association, *Index of economic journals*, 1 and 2 (1961) [provides references to most of Flux's professional articles] · private information (1959) · personal knowledge (1959)

Fockart, Janet (d. 1596), merchant and moneylender, was probably descended from the Fockarts found as Edinburgh burgesses from the fifteenth century, who may themselves have been descended from the Fockarts of Lesmahagow parish, Lanarkshire. Having outlived three husbands, Janet became a well-known figure in the merchant community of late sixteenth-century Edinburgh. Little is known about her first husband, John Todd. About 1560 she married William Fowler, a successful merchant and magistrate who traded in luxury cloths and accessories,

mainly with France. He and his wife drew income from burgh property and had a substantial house in Fowler's (now Anchor) Close on the north side of Edinburgh High Street. When Fowler died in 1572 Janet faced considerable problems, including the collection of debts due to him, a court action by a French creditor, and the need to carry on business for the sake of her seven children. Trade suffered during the civil wars of 1567–73, and the volume of business which she carried on during the two and a half years it took to complete Fowler's executory affairs was not extensive. In order to reduce expenditure she cancelled a contract between Fowler and his neighbours for the enlargement of the family house. The date of her marriage to her third husband, James Hathoway, is unknown. Hathoway committed suicide in 1579. To avoid crown confiscation of his assets Janet bought his escheat two days after his death.

Thereafter Janet Fockart increasingly took to moneylending, which she had begun to practise during Fowler's lifetime. In 1580 she and three other merchants contracted with Robert Stewart, earl of Orkney, to purchase large quantities of his rents, at the same time lending him £5340 Scots on security of part of his grain rent. Her own clients, who pledged jewellery, silverware, and richly embroidered garments for loans, included lairds, nobles, and their wives. The regent James Douglas, fourth earl of Morton, and later James VI himself borrowed regularly from her. Annual receipts for interest payments, in Janet's own bold handwriting, survive in the archives of some landed families. She continued to draw rents from burgh property and she rented lodgings. James VI's second cousin Esmé Stewart, who briefly provided a focus for the opponents of Morton, lodged with her when he arrived from France in 1579. The court of exchequer met in her house in 1593.

Janet had four sons and three daughters: William Todd, William Fowler senior, who became a merchant like his father, William junior, who attended St Andrews University and became a poet in the literary circle of King James VI, John (William junior's twin), Barbara, Janet, and Susannah. The last, who married John Drummond, son of the laird of Carnock, Stirlingshire, became the mother of the family's second poet, William Drummond of Hawthornden, born in 1585. Both William Fowler senior and John Drummond, who was for some time Janet's business partner, quarrelled with her over family property and financial affairs, both taking her to court.

Janet Fockart died at High Street, Edinburgh, in May 1596. The testamentary inventory drawn up after her death (she did not leave a will) suggests a comfortable home and a considerable income. The booth, which had been stocked with luxury goods when William Fowler died in 1572, was almost empty, but Janet held a long list of gold and silver items, clothes, and jewellery pledged by her debtors, who included many notable figures of the day. She had over £500 Scots in ready money, and household goods worth over £700. Her net estate was valued at £22,467 3s. 9d. Scots (about £1873 sterling), compared with William Fowler's £7900 Scots, putting her in a small minority of the richest Edinburgh merchants, who left more than £1000 sterling. Perhaps it was the memory of family quarrels, or the wish to suppress the presence in the family of a 'wad wyfe' or pawnbroker, however prosperous, that caused her great-grandson John Fowler to eradicate her name from his family tree when applying for a birth brieve in the late seventeenth century. At any rate, he named his great-grandmother on his father's side as 'Janet Fischer of the English family of Fischer' (*Registrum magni sigilli*, 11.98).

MARGARET H. B. SANDERSON

Sources M. H. B. Sanderson, 'Janet Fockart, merchant and moneylender', *Mary Stewart's people: life in Mary Stewart's Scotland* (1987), 91–102 · William Fowler's testament, NA Scot., Edinburgh commissary court, registers of testaments, CC8/8/3, fol. 360v · Janet Fockart's testament, NA Scot., Edinburgh commissary court, registers of testaments, CC8/8/29, fol. 399v · NA Scot., Edinburgh burgh register of deeds, B22/8/2, fols. 29v–30r · M. Livingstone, D. Hay Fleming, and others, eds., *Registrum secreti sigilli regum Scotorum / The register of the privy seal of Scotland*, 7 (1966) · J. M. Thomson and others, eds., *Registrum magni sigilli regum Scotorum / The register of the great seal of Scotland*, 11 vols. (1882–1914), vol. 11 · NA Scot., register of the privy council of Scotland, PC 1/7, fol. 173
Wealth at death £22,467 3s. 9d. Scots. [£1873]: NA Scot. Edinburgh commissary court, registers of testaments, CC8/8/29, fol. 399v

Foden, Edwin (1841–1911), vehicle manufacturer, was born on 5 August 1841 in Smallwood, near Sandbach, Cheshire, the son of William Foden, a grocer, and his wife, Martha, *née* Goodall. He left school at thirteen, and after two years as a village post-boy he took up an apprenticeship with the agricultural engineering firm of Platt and Hancock, at Elworth, near Sandbach, walking the 3 miles from Smallwood daily. He then widened his experience at Crewe railway workshops and at another workshop in nearby Kidsgrove before returning to Elworth, where by the age of nineteen he was shop foreman.

By 1866, when he was twenty-five, Foden had risen to be a partner in the firm, now Hancock and Foden. He worked closely with his staff, readily sharing his engineering expertise. He earned their respect and loyalty, despite his tendency to criticize what he regarded as poor workmanship. He was known to peer over the shoulder of an employee, then take the tool from the man's hand and do the job himself, saying, 'Do it this way, lad, then tha'lt do it reet' (Kennet, 33).

In the mid-1860s Foden married Sophia Scragg (1841–1893); they had two sons and two surviving daughters. In 1868 their first son, William *Foden, was born. In 1870 Foden's partner, George Hancock, retired from Foden and Hancock, as it now was, though remaining as adviser. In 1876 Foden took sole control and renamed the firm Edwin Foden & Sons, anticipating a family concern. At first he built mainly traction engines and mechanical threshers powered by horse-drawn 'portable' steam engines. Such machines were cumbersome and costly, however, and he sought to improve them. Most traction engines were then of the single-cylinder type and designed for agricultural use, since the legislation of the day severely limited the haulage of freight by road. When restrictions on the use of engines on roads began to be lifted from the 1870s, Foden saw that the way lay ahead for a much more efficient engine, and that it could attract a healthy market. However, it would need to economize on fuel, since all the coal would have to be carried by the vehicle instead of being left in a heap at the worksite.

Foden's answer was a traction engine powered by a twin-cylinder, compound steam engine. It took him three years to develop this and early trials were not always successful. Finally, he produced a reliable, marketable engine and was so pleased with its performance that he entered it for the Royal Agricultural Society trials at Newcastle in 1887. Driven by his second son, Edwin Richard *Foden (b. 1870) [see under Foden, William], it won a gold medal, thanks to its low fuel consumption (only 1.84 lb of coal per horsepower per hour) and versatility. Even so, it was still designed for agricultural use, and it was only in 1896, when the Locomotives on Highways Act was passed, allowing heavy machines to travel on the road, that Foden was finally free to develop his road engines.

Building on the success of his agricultural model, Foden and his sons concentrated their efforts on the production of a road steamer. The first four prototypes were built by 1900, the last of which, a 3 ton vehicle with horizontal boiler, defeated ten other engines in trials by the War Office in 1901, again gaining praise for its performance and manoeuvrability.

Despite such acclaim Foden was aware that his family business was inadequate to cope with the necessary expansion and modernization. To raise capital, in 1901 he formed a new company, Fodens Ltd, with himself as managing director and a business colleague, Cecil Brunner, as chairman. His two sons were joined on the board by two more brothers, former Elworth customers. Over the next ten years the firm's profits rose fivefold. Foden's first wife died in 1893, and several years later he married Annie Cowap (1868–1939). There were two daughters and one surviving son from the second marriage.

By 1910 Edwin Foden's health was in steady decline, and he died from cancer on 31 August 1911 at his home, Elworth House, Bradwall, near Sandbach, Cheshire. His cortège was led by the Foden Motor Works Band, which he had helped to found, playing his favourite Methodist hymns. His younger son, Edwin Richard Foden, founded ERF, the truck manufacturers, in 1933.

ADRIAN ROOM

Sources P. Kennet, *The Foden story: from farm machinery to diesel trucks* (1978) · H. Nancollis, *Foden: my life with the company* (1995) · P. Foden, *60 years on: the story of ERF, a British commercial vehicle manufacturer* (1993) · b. cert. · d. cert. · *CGPLA Eng. & Wales* (1911) · C. Gulvin, 'Foden, William, and Foden, Edwin Richard', *DBB*
Likenesses photograph, c.1880, repro. in Nancollis, *Foden*
Wealth at death £70,683 16s. 5d.: resworn probate, 24 Oct 1911, *CGPLA Eng. & Wales*

Foden, Edwin Richard (1870–1950). *See under* Foden, William (1868–1964).

Foden, William (1868–1964), vehicle manufacturer, was born on 23 September 1868 at Bradwall Green, near Sandbach, Cheshire, the elder son of Edwin *Foden (1841–1911), engineer and vehicle manufacturer, and his wife, Sophia Scragg (1841–1893). His father was a partner, later proprietor of an agricultural engineering business at Sandbach which, as Edwin Foden & Sons (later Fodens Ltd), became a noted manufacturer of steam-powered goods vehicles. Educated at Sandbach grammar school, William shared his father's engineering skill, as also did his younger brother, **Edwin Richard Foden** (1870–1950), who was born at Bradwall Green on 28 March 1870. They both joined the business and assisted their father. On 5 January 1892 William Foden married Ellen Arden Davies (*b.* 1870?), daughter of Thomas Davies, a hotel keeper; they had three children. Edwin Foden married in 1896 Elizabeth Alice Devonport, and they also had three children; Elizabeth died in 1912, and in 1929 Edwin married Mary Cooke, with whom he had a further child.

During the period from the late 1880s to the early years of the twentieth century the family firm successfully developed a steam vehicle for the road, in the form of the 'overtype' steam wagon, which carried its payload rather than pulling it as the traction engine did. The Foden overtype wagon, in its 5 ton form, provided Fodens' main product line into the mid-1920s. By this time the model had dated and a successor was introduced, with an improved cab, better driving visibility, and, most important, more powerful brakes.

In 1924 William Foden, who had largely run the commercial side of the business, retired to Australia with his family. This move was brought about by the brothers' major differences with their stepmother, a major shareholder since their father's death in 1911. More general factors lay behind the upheaval: the depressed market in commercial vehicles as a result of the availability of military stock, and an increasing preference for the internal combustion engine with its greater ease of operation.

William, by correspondence, helped to convince Edwin of the future of the diesel engine, and limited production was in place at Fodens by 1932. Edwin retired in 1932, but after a period of recuperation he returned to the development of a diesel lorry on his own account. With the collaboration of his son Dennis, William's son Ted, and several key figures dismissed by Fodens, Edwin went on to establish in 1933 a rival concern, which became ERF Ltd.

Two years later William returned from retirement, at the age of sixty-seven, and took over again as managing director of Fodens. The firm was by then in dire straits, with an order book of three vehicles and a file of unsettled warranty claims. William eased liquidity problems by introducing sharper accounting methods and greater manufacturing economy. His son Ted also joined the firm, which now concentrated on diesel lorry manufacture, the first Foden diesel lorry having been built in 1931, powered by a Gardner engine. The introduction of a new series of diesel-engined lorries subsequently restored the viability of Fodens. By the end of 1937 the tide of decline had been turned, placing the company in a strong position to develop its war production of military lorries, and also of tanks and shells.

ERF's war production concentrated on military lorries, mostly for the Royal Army Service Corps, with some vehicles for essential civilian users. Edwin Foden died on 23 December 1950, having remained active in the firm until the end of his life and having seen some development of what was to be the post-war model range. He had an interest in all forms of transport: he was successful in cycle racing and progressed to motorcycles and cars, being reserve driver for the Vauxhall works' team in the 1914 Isle of Man motor car TT races. He was also an enthusiastic owner of motor cruisers and interested in flying. Active in charity, Edwin Foden was particularly involved with the Foden Motor Works Band, which had been established by his father. Edwin remained its patron even after setting up ERF. Under such distinguished conductors as William Rimmer and Fred and Harry Mortimer, it played a major role in the life of Fodens in the inter-war period, and it also achieved national prominence through broadcasting.

Diversification helped to carry Fodens through a difficult period after the war. With William Foden as governing director, and assisted by his two sons as managing directors, the firm applied the new two-stroke diesel to industrial and marine uses and developed a rugged dumper-truck range. William's long involvement with the family company came to an end only with his death from heart failure on 2 June 1964, at Knowlton House, Parson Street, Congleton, Cheshire. He was described by Fodens' historian as 'a firm, insistent but sympathetic boss' (Kennett, 155).

The Fodens, William and Edwin Richard, take their place alongside the Dennis, Jensen, and Rootes brothers, as examples of fraternal co-operation in the development of successful motor-manufacturing concerns, but with a significant difference: the Foden brothers finished their working lives as proprietors of competing companies.

RICHARD A. STOREY

Sources C. Gulvin, 'Foden, William, and Foden, Edwin Richard', *DBB* · P. Kennett, *The Foden story* (1978) · P. Kennett, *ERF*, World Trucks, 1 (1978) · M. Seth-Smith, *The longhaul: a social history of the British commercial vehicle industry* (1975) · b. cert. [Edwin Richard Foden] · m. cert. · d. cert. · *CGPLA Eng. & Wales* (1964)
Archives Ches. & Chester ALSS, DFO
Wealth at death £25,301: probate, 30 Nov 1964, *CGPLA Eng. & Wales* · £97,396—Edwin Richard Foden: *DBB*

Fogartach mac Néill (*d.* 724), high-king of Ireland, was the son of the leading dynast Niall mac Cernaich (*d.* 701) and a member of Síl nÁeda Sláine, an Uí Néill dynasty afflicted by regular internecine conflict both during and after Fogartach's lifetime. It is not known when he was born, but he seems to have reached adulthood by 697, for one 'Focortoch' appears as a signatory to the law of Adomnán which was enacted that year; his father was certainly a signatory.

Fogartach first appears in the chronicles in 704, when an alliance of southern Uí Néill rulers was defeated by the king of Leinster: the kings of Meath and of Cenél Lóegairi were killed, and 'Fogartach grandson of Cernach' (*Ann. Ulster*, 704.4 (s.a. 703)) fled. Some regnal lists show him as king of Tara (the formal title of the high-kings of Ireland) from about this time, either on his own or in co-regency with the northern Uí Néill's Congal mac Fergusa, while most lists say that he was not king of Tara until after the reign of Fergal (*d.* 722). An error may have arisen from an annalistic mistranscription in the entry for 704—the annals of Ulster has *fuit* ('was') instead of *fugit* ('fled') and a compiler of regnal lists could have taken such a reading to be a mistake for the common expression *uictor fuit* ('was victor') and presumed from this that Fogartach had achieved overlordship of the Uí Néill and consequently the kingship of Tara.

In 714, 'Fogartach grandson of Cernach was expelled from the kingship; he went to Britain' (*Ann. Ulster*, 714.4 (s.a. 713)). The chronicles do not name the kingship from which he was expelled; it was probably that of the southern Uí Néill. The only chronicle to say who had forced him into exile is the late and untrustworthy annals of the four masters, which name Fergal mac Máele Dúin, king of Tara, as the person responsible. This may be based on an anachronistic view of the powers of the king; more likely candidates are the two other leading members of the southern Uí Néill at this time, Murchad mac Diarmata of Clann Cholmáin and Fogartach's brother Conall Grant mac Néill. Murchad won a victory against Síl nÁeda Sláine in the year of Fogartach's expulsion and in 715 he was himself killed by Conall Grant. In 716 Fogartach resumed his kingship, now clearly supreme among the southern Uí Néill.

The following year Fogartach was responsible for a disturbance at the fair of Tailtiu (Teltown). This was the royal fair of the kings of Tara, and Fogartach's action may well have been intended as an act of defiance against Fergal mac Máele Dúin; however, not enough details are given to be certain of Fogartach's objectives. Fergal himself then seems, intentionally or otherwise, to have done Fogartach a series of good turns.

In 718 Fergal killed Conall Grant, who was becoming an increasingly prominent ruler in Brega, Fogartach's homeland. Three years later, this territory was assaulted by the kings of Leinster and Munster, and Fergal, probably in retaliation, invaded Leinster and compelled its submission. The following year the high-king of Ireland invaded Leinster again with a great force, but he was defeated and killed in the battle of Allen, north of Kildare. Fogartach does not seem to have participated in this battle, but at some point thereafter he took the high-kingship. His reign was short, however: he was killed in battle at 'Cenn Deilgden' on 7 (or 30) October 724, by his cousin and successor Cináed mac Írgalaig. He is said to have been buried in Clonard (Meath).

Fogartach's sons included Flann Foirbthe (*d.* 716 or 748), Cernach (*d.* 738), Fergus (*d.* 751), Fínsnechta (*d.* 761), Cumascach (*d.* 797), and Coirpre (*d.* 771); and he had a daughter, Dúnflaith (*d.* 774).   PHILIP IRWIN

Sources *Ann. Ulster* • W. Stokes, ed., 'The annals of Tigernach [8 pts]', *Revue Celtique*, 16 (1895), 374–419; 17 (1896), 6–33, 119–263, 337–420; 18 (1897), 9–59, 150–97, 267–303, 374–91; pubd sep. (1993) • M. Ní Dhonnchadha, 'The guarantor list of Cáin Adomnáin, 697',

Peritia, 1 (1982), 178–215 • *AFM*, 2nd edn • R. Thurneysen, 'Baile in Scáil', *Zeitschrift für Celtische Philologie*, 20 (1933–6), 213–27, esp. 227

Fogerty, Elsie (1865–1945), founder and principal of the Central School of Speech and Drama, was born at Sydenham, London, on 16 December 1865, the daughter of Joseph Fogerty (*d.* 1899), engineer and architect, of Dublin, and his wife, Hannah Cochrane (*d.* 1910), of Limerick. An only child, she travelled widely with her parents and was educated privately at Sydenham. In 1883 she studied for some time at the Paris conservatory under Coquelin aîné and Delauney, and with Hermann Vezin in London.

Following her father's incapacitating illness, Fogerty began giving elocution lessons and, at the invitation of Russell Wakefield (the future bishop of Birmingham), she taught elocution at the Crystal Palace School of Art and Literature from 1889. In the 1890s she extended her teaching to various girls' private schools and then most notably at Roedean from 1908.

In 1898 Fogerty took over existing speech classes at the Royal Albert Hall and further built up her clientele. At the same time she appeared as an actress both commercially in London and with William Poel's Elizabethan Stage Society. In 1903 she encountered Frank Benson at his Stratford season. Benson decided to open a school in London to prepare actors for his company—as Herbert Tree had just done in creating the future Royal Academy of Dramatic Art (RADA). Fogerty taught diction for Benson at his school in Hampstead but on its only limited success she took the surviving pupils back to her Albert Hall classes. This was the origin of the Central School of Speech and Drama formed in 1906 with Benson as president.

Whereas RADA was closely linked with the actor–manager grandees of the commercial West End, Fogerty made the Central distinctive by reaching out in more diverse directions. There was a strong interest in the physiological and medical aspects of voice production in the work of Dr H. H. Hulbert. Fogerty taught classes in voice for London county council (LCC) teachers resulting in the important LCC speech conference in 1912. She also started a speech clinic in the same year at St Thomas's Hospital dealing with stammering and speech defects, shortly afterwards treating children literally struck dumb by Zeppelin air raids. For the bishops of London and Birmingham she coached clergymen in the delivery of sermons. She also sought to revive Greek dancing (by studying vases in the British Museum) and ran slum party-entertainments for children of the London poor. In these ways Fogerty both in her school and outside sought to relate narrow drama training and elocution to the wider worlds of medicine, physiology, education, the church, speech therapy, and social work. The school taught teachers and therapists as well as actors.

The 1920s saw a remarkable drive to raise the status of the theatre as part of the national culture and to increase awareness of the importance of good, even beautiful, speech. In all these Elsie Fogerty played a significant role. The formation of the British Drama League in 1918 (of which she was a lifelong council member), and the Stratford summer school in the same year were followed by

Elsie Fogerty (1865–1945), by Reginald Grenville Eves, 1937

John Masefield's annual Oxford recitations from 1923 and Barry Jackson's Malvern festival from 1928. Elsie Fogerty was a ubiquitous figure in committees, Oxford lecture rooms, and on lawns at Stratford and Malvern. Most of the supporters of these movements were, like Fogerty herself, keenly working for a national theatre at this time. In this context London University, largely at the instigation of Elsie Fogerty, started its two-year diploma in dramatic art in 1923, intended to be more challenging than the practical studies of RADA and the Central School and taken by the more academically inclined of both drama schools.

In addition to her public life and her work with the school Elsie Fogerty was a private consultant in voice production to many leading actors, including Laurence Olivier and Peggy Ashcroft (her former pupils at the Central), John Gielgud, Edith Evans, various clergymen, and even royalty. In person she was short and plump but impressive in her deportment and in her energy and sense of commitment. She was an indefatigable 'networker' of contacts and creator of conferences and organizations necessary to advance her causes. She remained unmarried and was a women of genuine Anglican religious beliefs. She was appointed CBE in 1934 and retired as principal of the Central School in 1942 when the school returned to London after a brief evacuation to Exeter. Her last years were saddened by losing all her possessions in the bombing of her flat in 1944 and thereafter she lived in a South Kensington hotel. But the chief joy of this last year was Olivier's film of *Henry V* in which she saw her leading pupil bringing Shakespeare and fine speech to popular audiences as she

had hoped. She finally died in a nursing home at 51 Lillington Road, Leamington Spa, on 4 July 1945, a major influence in the creation of drama training, speech therapy, elocution in schools, and the acceptance of serious theatre as part of the national culture.

Michael Sanderson

Sources DNB · M. Cole, *Fogie: the life of Elsie Fogerty, CBE* (1967) · W. Fortescue, *There's rosemary … there's rue* (1939) · M. Sanderson, *From Irving to Olivier* (1984), chaps. 2 and 9 · *Viva Voce* [Central School of Speech and Drama magazine] · *CGPLA Eng. & Wales* (1945)
Archives Bodl. Oxf., corresp. with Gilbert Murray | FILM BFI NFTVA, 'A speech pioneer: recollections of Elsie Fogerty', T190W Woman's Hour
Likenesses photograph, c.1900 (with her mother), repro. in Cole, *Fogie* · photograph, 1911, repro. in Cole, *Fogie* · photograph, 1934 (with G. B. Shaw), repro. in Cole, *Fogie* · R. G. Eves, portrait, 1937, Central School of Speech and Drama, London [see illus.] · photograph (with B. Jackson), repro. in Cole, *Fogie*
Wealth at death £3106 1s. 6d.: probate, 16 Nov 1945, *CGPLA Eng. & Wales*

Fogg, Laurence (c.1630–1718), dean of Chester, was born at Darcy Lever, Lancashire, the son of Robert Fogg (d. 1676), who was ejected from the rectory of Bangor Is-coed, Flintshire, in 1661. Educated at Bolton grammar school, Laurence Fogg was admitted to Emmanuel College, Cambridge, on 28 September 1644 and migrated to St John's College on 2 August 1645. He matriculated in 1645, graduating BA in 1649 and proceeding MA in 1652; in 1650 he was made a fellow of St John's. He was created BD in 1659 and DD in 1679. While at St John's he held the office of 'taxor', in which he acted for the university in legal matters. On 30 October 1657 he was admitted to the rectory of Hawarden, Flintshire. He was ordained first by the Cambridgeshire Association in 1658, but on 28 February 1661, like his brother, he took Anglican orders. In the interval, he was married to Mary Harrison (1630/31–1718) of Merstham, Surrey. Although he resigned his living in July 1662 he subsequently conformed and resumed his career in the church. He was curate of Prestwich, Lancashire, in 1666 and later obtained the curacy of Plemondstall, worth some £80 per annum, which was in the gift of the chief justice, Sir Orlando Bridgeman. He held this living for fifty years. In 1672, the same year that his father was licensed to keep a presbyterian meeting-house, Fogg was presented as vicar of St Oswald's, Chester, and served there until 1699. He evidently attracted attention for his capacities as an administrator—for instance, in 1680 Bishop Wilkins wrote that Dr Fogg 'hath bin most acquainted with the business' of the disputed rectory of Bradeley, Staffordshire (MS Tanner 144, fol. 9)—and on 2 November 1692 he was instituted dean of Chester, remaining in this office until his death there on 27 February 1718. He was buried in St Mary's Chapel, Chester Cathedral.

Fogg gained respect on both sides of the divide between conformity and dissent. Writing to Edmund Calamy, he sought to correct the impression that he was ever a nonconformist, stating that he had been among the first to restore the public use of the prayer book in 1660. Instead he had refused to take the oath against resistance to the government required by the Act of Uniformity, and left the ministry until 1665, when Justice Bridgeman interpreted the Oxford oath in terms acceptable to him. One of his sermons, given about 1698, found favour with the nonconformist Matthew Henry, who described it as 'very much to the purpose, pressing home the necessary duty of beating down sin and wickedness'. Henry declared that such preaching would 'heal differences among those who fear God' and forgave 'all that the Dean has at any time said against Dissenters, and against me in particular' (Gastrell, 1.136). In later years Fogg engaged in controversy over Calvinist doctrine, publishing *Theologiae speculativae schema* (1712) and *God's Infinite Grace in Election and Impartial Equity in Preterition Vindicated* (1713). After old age left him 'disabled for Publick Performances', he expressed his concern for the spiritual welfare of his flock at Plemondstall in two introductory treatises on the Christian faith 'adapted to Vulgar Capacity', *Two treatises: a general view of the Christian religion … [and] An entrance into the doctrine of Christianity* (1714).   JOHN D. RAMSBOTTOM

Sources F. Gastrell, *Notitia Cestrienses, or, Historical notices of the diocese of Chester*, ed. F. R. Raines, 1, Chetham Society, 8 (1845) · *Calamy rev.* · G. Ormerod, *The history of the county palatine and city of Chester*, 2nd edn, ed. T. Helsby, 3 vols. (1882) · *The diary and correspondence of Dr John Worthington*, ed. J. Crossley, 1, Chetham Society, 13 (1847) · *DNB* · Venn, *Alum. Cant.*
Likenesses portrait, St John Cam.

Fogge, Sir John (*b.* in or before **1417**, *d.* **1490**), administrator, of Repton, near Ashford, Kent, was the son of John Fogge, esquire, the second surviving son of Sir Thomas Fogge (*d.* 1407). He was born *c.*1417, since he was of legal age in 1438, but he only came to prominence when he inherited the lands of the senior line on the death of Sir Thomas's grandson and heir, William. This had occurred by February 1447, and John was an esquire of the king's household by 1450, when he was involved in the military activity against the rebel Jack Cade. In November 1453 he was made sheriff of Kent. Despite this background in the king's service, Fogge joined the Yorkists in June 1460, and was rewarded with the grant of Tonford and Dane, Kent, of which he had claimed the reversion.

After the Yorkist victory at Towton in March 1461, Fogge emerged as a leading royal associate in Kent, heading all commissions named in the county. His possession of Tonford and Dane was confirmed, and he was given the custody of Rochester Castle. His interests were not, however, purely local. He was treasurer of the household from the beginning of Edward IV's reign until 1468, and was also a royal councillor. With other royal associates he received the custody of the forfeited earldom of Oxford in March 1462. His prominence at court was recognized in 1469 when he was denounced by the rebels as one of those whose 'covetous rule and gydynge' had brought the king and his realm to great poverty and misery (Warkworth, 46). Fogge features on none of the readeption commissions and may have gone into exile with Edward IV. He was certainly well rewarded on Edward's return, receiving further land and a grant of the gold and silver mines in Devon and Cornwall.

During Edward's second reign Fogge also built up links with the prince of Wales, helped by his recent marriage to the queen's cousin Alice Haute, the daughter of Joan Woodville and Sir William Haute. The Woodville connection proved dangerous in 1483, when Richard, duke of Gloucester, made himself protector of the young Edward V and accused the Woodvilles of conspiring against him. Fogge, according to Sir Thomas More, took sanctuary, but was offered the favour of Richard III. If so, it was an offer Fogge did not accept, and he rebelled against the new regime in October 1483. He was attainted and much of his forfeited land granted to Richard's ally Sir Ralph Ashton, who was already in dispute with Fogge over some of the Kyriell inheritance. By the winter of 1484-5, however, Richard was moving towards a *rapprochement* with the Woodvilles and their circle, and in February 1485 Fogge, having bound himself to future good behaviour, was pardoned and granted four of his confiscated manors. Fogge played little role in national affairs after the accession of Henry VII, presumably because of his age rather than any loss of favour, since he was granted the marriage of the son and heir of Sir Humphrey Stafford. He made his will on 9 July 1490 and was dead by 9 November. He was buried in Ashford church, of which he had been a notable benefactor.

Fogge's first wife, who was the mother of his heir, John, was Alice, the daughter of Thomas Kyriell (*d.* 1460). They were married by the early 1440s (since John was associated with his father in a land transaction in 1465), which means that Alice was Kyriell's daughter with an unknown first wife, rather than with Cecily Hill, whom he married in 1437. Alice was still alive in February 1462 but Fogge had remarried by 1468. It was his second wife, Alice Haute, who was the mother of his son Thomas, and he was of full age by 1490, when he received an extensive land grant in his father's will, along with all Fogge's musical instruments except a clavichord and a clavicembalo, which went to John junior. Fogge also had three daughters— Anne, Elisabeth, and Margaret—who, as they were still unmarried at his death, were probably also children of his second marriage.   ROSEMARY HORROX

Sources PRO · Chancery records · A. J. Pearman, *History of Ashford* (1868) · T. G. F. [T. G. Faussett], 'Family chronicle of Richard Fogge, of Danes Court, in Tilmanstone', *Archaeologia Cantiana*, 5 (1862-3), 112-32 · J. Warkworth, *A chronicle of the first thirteen years of the reign of King Edward the Fourth*, ed. J. O. Halliwell, CS, old ser., 10 (1839) · St Thomas More, *The history of King Richard III*, ed. R. S. Sylvester (1963), vol. 2 of *The Yale edition of the complete works of St Thomas More* · R. Horrox, *Richard III, a study of service*, Cambridge Studies in Medieval Life and Thought, 4th ser., 11 (1989) · A. R. Myers, ed., *The household of Edward IV: the black book and the ordinance of 1478* (1959) · will, CKS, PRC 32/3, fols. 280 – 281v [Fogge's will]
Wealth at death see will, CKS, PRC 32/3, fols. 280-281v

Foggo, George (1793-1869). *See under* Foggo, James (1789-1860).

Foggo, James (1789-1860), portrait and history painter, was born in London on 11 June 1789. His father was a native of Fife, a reputable watchmaker, and a republican who, fearing persecution after advocating emancipation of black slaves in repeated visits to North and South America, took his wife and family to France in 1799. With his younger brother **George Foggo** (1793–1869), history painter, who was born in London on 14 April 1793, he studied at the École des Beaux-Arts in Paris under the instruction of Jean-Baptiste Regnault (1754–1829). They were influenced by and emulated the work of the French historical painters. In 1815 James Foggo returned to England and set up a studio in Frith Street, Soho, London. In 1816 he exhibited *Jane Shore* at the Royal Academy, and in 1818 *Hagar and Ishmael* and a study, *An Assassin's Head*, at the British Institution. In 1819 when his father went on a journey to Brazil, James Foggo's mother and his brother George joined him in London. For the next forty years the two brothers lived and worked together, painting on the same canvas, and devoting themselves to grand-manner, historical compositions despite the unfashionable status of this style in England. They spent about three years painting a very large work, *The Christian Inhabitants of Parga Preparing to Emigrate* (1819; lithograph, BM). When completed the painting measured 26 feet by 16 feet and was too large for exhibition in ordinary galleries, so the Foggos had to exhibit it separately at their own expense. This and subsequent works obtained the praise of Sir Thomas Lawrence, Sir Henry Fuseli, William Hilton, and John Flaxman. The monumentality of their paintings meant that few sold. They collaborated on many historical pictures including *The Martyrdom of Anne Askew* (exh. RA, 1852), *Napoleon Signing the Death-Warrant of the Duc d'Enghien* and *General Williams among the Inhabitants of Kars* (exh. Society (later Royal Society) of British Artists 1857 and 1858 respectively). In 1837 the brothers founded the National Monuments Society, which advocated free public access to museums, monuments, and works of art, as they were keen to encourage a national appreciation of art. In 1844 George Foggo published *The National Gallery: its Pictures and their Painters, with Critical Remarks*, which ran into several editions. This catalogue was the first attempt to render the collection intelligible to the public. The brothers lost patronage by openly advocating a more liberal system of education in art than that provided by the Royal Academy, a subject on which George Foggo published several pamphlets. They entered the competitions for fresco designs for the new Palace of Westminster between 1840 and 1843, but without success. They exhibited their works with Haydon and others at the Pantheon, Oxford Street, where in 1852 they undertook the arrangement and care of exhibitions until 1855.

James Foggo supported himself financially by teaching and occasionally painting portraits including one of James Thomas Holloway DD, vicar of Stanton upon Hine Heath and minister of Fitzroy Chapel (1780–1855) (lithograph, also by J. Foggo, BM). By producing lithographs the brothers embraced the most popular nineteenth-century print medium and found a way of popularizing and selling images of their work. Examples include *Dog Days* (exh. 1829; British Institution; lithograph, BM), *The Orphan's Prayer*, *The Gout*, *The Sailors' Farewell*, and *True Courage* (lithographs, BM). All illustrate the rise in Victorian sentimental

subject matter. In 1828 George Foggo published by himself a set of large lithographs from the cartoons by Raphael.

By sketching accessories to architectural and sculptural designs the brothers became acquainted with the architect Francis Goodwin, who advised them to paint pictures suitable for altarpieces in churches. They produced *The Pool of Bethesda* for the Bordesley Chapel at Birmingham; *Christ Blessing Little Children* for St Leonard's Church, Bilston; *Christ Confounding the Rulers of the Synagogue*, (exh. RA, 1825); *Nathan Reproving David* for Macclesfield town hall; and *The Entombment of Christ*, presented by Mr Edward Moxhay to the French protestant church, St Martin's-le-Grand, London.

Both brothers were much esteemed in their private lives for many excellent qualities, and their friends were numerous and sincere. James Foggo died in London on 14 September 1860 and was buried in Highgate cemetery. George Foggo died at his home at 29 Grafton Street, Fitzroy Square, London, on 26 September 1869. Both brothers were apparently unmarried.

L. H. Cust, rev. Lucy Dixon

Sources Wood, *Vic. painters*, 3rd edn · J. Turner, ed., *The dictionary of art*, 34 vols. (1996) · Bénézit, *Dict.* · F. Lewis, *A dictionary of British historical painters* (1979) · Bryan, *Painters* (1866) · B. Stewart and M. Cutten, *The dictionary of portrait painters in Britain up to 1920* (1997) · *Engraved Brit. ports.*, vol. 2 · Graves, *Brit. Inst.* · J. Johnson, ed., *Works exhibited at the Royal Society of British Artists, 1824–1893, and the New English Art Club, 1888–1917*, 2 vols. (1975) · Graves, *RA exhibitors* · R. Billcliffe, ed., *The Royal Glasgow Institute of the Fine Arts, 1861–1989: a dictionary of exhibitors at the annual exhibitions*, 4 vols. (1990–92) · *CGPLA Eng. & Wales* (1870) [George Foggo]
Wealth at death under £100—George Foggo: administration with will, 1870, *CGPLA Eng. & Wales*

Foillan [St Foillan] (*d.* 653x5), holy man, was the uterine brother of *Fursa. Both were of noble Irish background, the sons of Gelges, daughter of Áed Find, though whether Foillan was also the son of Fursa's father, Fintan, son of Findloga, is unknown. Foillan left Ireland *c.*637, along with Fursa and two other brothers, one of them named Ultan. The brothers made their way to the kingdom of the East Angles where, according to Bede, Fursa founded the monastery of Cnobheresburg (Burg Castle, Suffolk). When Fursa went off to join his brother Ultan as a hermit, Foillan was left in charge of the monastery. Following 'pagan invasions' into East Anglia, probably in 648, Fursa left for Francia, where soon afterwards he died and was eventually interred in the monastery of Péronne (on the River Somme, east of Amiens). Shortly after this, Foillan and Ultan also left England for Francia and were received there by Fursa's patron and protector, the mayor of the palace, Erchinoald, who put Péronne in their charge. But soon Erchinoald had a change of heart and expelled the Irish from Péronne. Why he did this is not clear, but it is possible that he had lost control over Fursa's cult to local bishops, and consequently no longer wished to support the Irish holy men.

Foillan and Ultan travelled due eastwards from Péronne and arrived at the monastery of Nivelles, which was the principal foundation of the illustrious Pippinid family, the family which would eventually produce the Carolingian dynasty. Under the protection of the Pippinid sister and brother, Geretrud and Grimoald, Foillan and Ultan founded another monastery at Fosses, near Nivelles. Some time after 652, and before 656, Foillan set out from Fosses on business which concerned his monastery; but he and three companions were murdered by brigands along the way. According to the martyrology of Oengus, Foillan died on 31 October, and the violent manner of his death meant that he was accorded the status of martyr. His body was not found until the following January, when it was buried at Fosses.

The source for Foillan's life and death in Francia is the late seventh-century 'Nivelles supplement to the *Vita Fursei* concerning Foillan'. This has been of great interest to historians who study later Merovingian Francia, not for what it tells about Foillan, but because of the information it holds on the Pippinid family, and in particular, on the background to the so-called 'Grimoald coup'. About the year 656, the Pippinid Grimoald, mayor of the palace in Austrasia, tried to displace the Merovingian kings in Austrasia by exiling the rightful heir to the throne, Dagobert II, and substituting his own son as king. Dagobert's place of exile was Ireland and it may have been contact with Foillan which led Grimoald to choose that destination. When the coup took place, it was Dido, bishop of Poitiers, who had Dagobert conducted to Ireland. It is the 'Supplement' which tells how Grimoald and Dido were meeting at Nivelles when they received news that Foillan's body had been found, a detail construed as evidence that Dido and Grimoald had indeed planned this coup together, perhaps well in advance of the death of Dagobert's father. Foillan has thus been noticed not for what he did in Ireland, England, or even in Francia, but because an account of his death quite incidentally happens to be the vehicle for evidence vital to the political and constitutional history of Francia. PAUL FOURACRE

Sources Bede, *Hist. eccl.*, 3.19 · *Félire Óengusso Céli Dé | The martyrology of Oengus the Culdee*, ed. and trans. W. Stokes, HBS, 29 (1905) · P. Fouracre and R. A. Gerberding, 'The Nivelles supplement to the *Vita Fursei* concerning Foillan', *Late Merovingian France: history and hagiography, 640–720* (1996)

Folbury, George (*d.* 1540), college head, was perhaps a younger son of the Richard Fowberry, gentleman, of Fowberry, Northumberland, who died between 1509 and 1513. He was educated at Cambridge University, graduating from Pembroke College as bachelor of arts in 1514 and as MA in 1517. In 1515 he was a fellow of Clare College, and he was also a fellow of Pembroke. He was preacher to the university in 1519, graduating bachelor of theology in 1524. He is believed to have taken his doctorate of divinity from Montpellier.

Writing in 1748 Thomas Tanner, bishop of St Asaph, claimed that Folbury was for a time tutor to Henry Fitzroy, duke of Richmond, only illegitimate son of Henry VIII. Folbury had been a contemporary of Richmond's former tutor, Richard Croke, at Cambridge, and it is possible that he was the new schoolmaster referred to by Richmond, on 27 October 1527, after Croke's departure on the king's business. The royal grant of the canonry and prebend of North Newbald, Yorkshire, dated 16 March 1531 (admitted 24 March 1531) was perhaps in reward for Folbury's services in this capacity. On 20 February 1534 he was presented to the parish of Maidwell in Northamptonshire, where he served as rector until his resignation on 15 January 1538. From 1537 he was master of Pembroke College, Cambridge, with the benefit of the college living of Tilney, Norfolk, from 10 February 1539. Although widely reputed to have been a poet, orator, and epigrammatist, no examples of his work can be traced.

In Folbury's will, dated 14 July 1540, he bequeathed more than £45 among his fellows, servants, and relatives. He was dead by 22 October 1540, when an inventory of his goods listed possessions worth £52 2s. 4d. He was buried at the church of St Mary-the-Less, Cambridge.

BEVERLEY A. MURPHY

Sources Tanner, *Bibl. Brit.-Hib.*, 290 · *Fasti Angl., 1066–1300*, [York], 70 · N. Cantalupus and R. Parker, *The history and antiquities of the University of Cambridge* (1721), 55 · Northants. RO, MSS BH (K) 178; BH (K) 179 · *LP Henry VIII*, 5/1, nos. 79(31), 166 · Bale, *Index*, 83 · Cooper, *Ath. Cantab.*, 1.76 · Venn, *Alum. Cant.* · M. Bateson, ed., *Grace book B*, 2 (1905), 55 · W. G. Searle, ed., *Grace book Γ* (1908), 113, 143, 213 · Northumbd RO, MSS NRO 3635/29 2J14 [Fowberry Pages from Percy Hedley's notes] · will and inventory, Pembroke Cam., Archives · M. Wren, 'Masters of Pembroke College to 1589', Pembroke Cam., Archives, MS C delta, 76–77

Wealth at death monetary bequests of over £45: will, 14 July 1540, Pembroke Cam. · value of goods £52 2s. 4d.: inventory, 22 Oct 1540, Pembroke Cam.

Folcard (*d.* after 1085), monk, musician, and hagiographer, was a Benedictine of St Bertin's, at St Omer in Flanders, who became acting abbot of Thorney (*c.*1069–85). He can be compared with Goscelin of St Bertin. All that is known of him comes from some, mostly cryptic, autobiographical remarks in the prefaces to his few extant works and a brief notice in Orderic Vitalis's *Historia ecclesiastica* concerning Thorney Abbey. Folcard notes that he was educated at St Bertin's under Abbot Bovo (1042–65), a fine teacher, and offers, probably *c.*1050, his refashioning of the existing lives of their patron saints as an atonement for his idleness as a pupil. In the preface to his life of St John of Beverley, commissioned by Ealdred, archbishop of York (1061–9), he explains that he had been expelled from his monastery owing to internal feuds and jealousy. The house could have been St Bertin or, possibly, Sherborne, Bishop Hermann of Wiltshire's cathedral priory, although Christ Church, Canterbury, and even Thorney have been advocated. He had been rescued by the queen, a woman of outstanding qualities and joined by God to the king so that, through her vigilant care, she could be useful to 'this our kingdom' (J. Raine, *Historians of the Church of York and its Archbishops*, 3 vols., Rolls Series, 1879–84, 1.239–40). She had put him under Ealdred's protection; and for him he had composed responsories for St John's feast day and now offered a life of the saint. According to Orderic, Folcard also wrote in honour of St Oswald of Worcester, doubtless likewise for Ealdred (1046–69). The queen was either Edith (*d.* 1075), wife of Edward the Confessor, or

Matilda of Flanders, William the Conqueror's wife, who crossed from Normandy to England for her coronation by Ealdred in May 1068 with an ecclesiastical suite that included Gui, bishop of Amiens, the author of *Carmen de Hastingae proelio*. Although an ascription to Matilda is attractive, it would drastically shorten Folcard's association with Ealdred; and the description also suits Edith better. Hence Folcard is a candidate for the authorship of *Vita Ædwardi regis*, an anonymous work dedicated to Edith. It is possible that he had travelled with, or followed, Goscelin to join Hermann, bishop of Wiltshire, about 1061, but had, or chose, to move on.

About the time of Ealdred's death, at Christmas 1069, the king, when beset by widespread native revolts and a Danish invasion, appointed Folcard to replace Siward, a Dane, as abbot of Thorney in the Cambridgeshire fens. And, perhaps shortly after, Folcard wrote a life of the abbey's patron, St Botwulf. This, significantly, he dedicated not to his diocesan, Remigius of Lincoln, but to Walkelin, bishop of Winchester (1070–98). Orderic says that Folcard had several quarrels with Remigius, and, like Siward, was never consecrated abbot. According to the Thorney annals he was deposed at a royal ecclesiastical council held at Gloucester at Christmas, probably in 1085. The sequel is unknown. Orderic only says, 'he went away' (*Ordericus Vitalis, Eccl. hist.*, 6.150). But, since it appears that he had some connection with Christ Church, Canterbury—some manuscripts of his life of St John have a seventeenth-century ascription to Folcard, monk of Canterbury, who flourished there in 1060—it is possible that Archbishop Lanfranc charitably offered him a home.

Orderic describes Folcard as a friendly, genial, and charitable man. Erudite, and a most accomplished writer and musician, he bequeathed to posterity many monuments to his literary skill and also delightful and melodious responsories (*historiae*) to be sung on the feast days of saints born in Albion. With so few of Folcard's works, even if *Vita Ædwardi regis* is added, now extant, he must be judged by the homage of his contemporaries. That Ealdred, a sophisticated connoisseur of the arts, should have chosen him to contribute to the embellishment of Beverley Minster, on which he was lavishing so much treasure, was a compliment indeed. Folcard stands with Goscelin, two Flemish monks, as major contributors to the transmission of the English devotional heritage into the Anglo-Norman era.   FRANK BARLOW

Sources F. Barlow, ed. and trans., *The life of King Edward who rests at Westminster*, 2nd edn, OMT (1992), lii–lix · *Ordericus Vitalis, Eccl. hist.*, 2, 6 · Folcard, 'Vita S. Bertini', *Patrologia Latina*, 147 (1853), 1089–98 · Folcard, 'Vita S. Iohannis', *The historians of the church of York and its archbishops*, ed. J. Raine, 1, Rolls Series, 71 (1879), 239–60 · Folcard, 'Vita S. Botulfi', *Acta sanctorum: Junius*, 3 (Antwerp, 1701), 402–6 · T. D. Hardy, *Descriptive catalogue of materials relating to the history of Great Britain and Ireland*, 1, Rolls Series, 26 (1862), 373

Foldsone, John (d. **1784**), portrait painter, became known as a painter of small conversation pieces and oval portraits. He visited his sitters in the morning and finished his work before evening. He received commissions from notable families such as that of Sir Archibald Edmonstone, a series of whose portraits are in Duntreath Castle, Stirlingshire. Two portraits by him of the Haffey children were engraved in mezzotint by Robert Laurie, and a picture by him, entitled *Female Lucubration*, was similarly engraved by P. Dawe in 1772. Foldsone exhibited at the Society of Artists in 1769 and 1770, and afterwards at the Royal Academy from 1771 to 1783. In 1777 he exhibited *Cymon and Iphigenia* at the Royal Academy, as well as several Madonna and child compositions which show the influence of Romney and Reynolds. He lived at 52 Little Castle Street, Oxford Market, London, and later at 91 Newman Street, London. Foldsone died in 1784, leaving a wife and family; his eldest daughter became a successful miniature painter [*see* Mee, Anne].

L. H. CUST, rev. NATASHA EATON

Sources B. Stewart and M. Cutten, *The dictionary of portrait painters in Britain up to 1920* (1997) · Waterhouse, *18c painters* · E. Edwards, *Anecdotes of painters* (1808); facs. edn (1970) · Redgrave, *Artists*, 2nd edn · D. H. Solkin, *Painting for money: the visual arts and the public sphere in eighteenth-century England* (1993) · Graves, *RA exhibitors*, vol. 2 · J. C. Smith, *British mezzotinto portraits*, 4 vols. in 5 (1878–84) **Archives** BM, department of prints and drawings · Hewitt Picture Archive, London **Likenesses** J. Foldsone, self-portrait, Witt Picture Library, London, Foldsone box

Foley family (*per. c.*1620–1716), ironmasters and government contractors, traces its origins to **Richard** [ii] **Foley** (1579/80–1657), baptized on 28 March 1580 at Dudley, Worcestershire. His father, Richard [i] Foley, was a nailer, an occupation which at this date provided a decent living and in which Richard [ii] continued. The name of Richard's first wife is unknown but on 31 October 1621 he married as his second wife Alice Brindley (1587/8–1663), of Hyde, near Kinver, Staffordshire. He had eleven children in all; six daughters and two sons from his first marriage and three sons from his second. He had land outside Dudley and a house in the town, where he was active in local government and was mayor in 1616. He was responsible for placing the town grammar school on a sound administrative and financial footing and he became by far the wealthiest property owner in Dudley.

The charcoal iron industry By 1624 Richard [ii] was taking leases of local iron mills, including Hyde mill, Kinver, which by 1626 was using waterpower for the slitting of iron rod, the basic raw material of the nailmakers. Richard [ii] was at one time credited with having introduced the slitting mill from Sweden, but the process was not new; his real achievement was the successful organization and exploitation of water-powered charcoal iron furnaces, forges, and slitting mills, leasing them from landowners who, having built or converted them, found them difficult to manage. He established a business structure which combined centralized control with dispersed plant, thus spreading his risk.

Between 1624 and 1633 Richard [ii] acquired leases of five furnaces, nine forges, and other ironworks, either on his own or in partnership with local ironmasters or

Thomas Foley (1617–1677), by William Trabute, 1670

gentlemen. His sons Richard [iii] (d. 1678), **Thomas** [i] **Foley** (1617–1677), and Robert [i] (bap. 1626, d. 1676), were among his partners. By 1638 they had a warehouse in London adjoining Leadenhall and were competing with the London ironmasters and ironmongers, addressing a national market.

Richard [ii] bought property in the neighbouring parish of Oldswinford and by 1631 had moved to a brick house in High Street, Stourbridge. Though of puritan sympathies he and his son Thomas [i] supplied iron ordnance, shot, pikeheads, and nails to the king's armies in 1642–5. He was active in Stourbridge local government and a feoffee of Stourbridge grammar school. Richard Foley died in July 1657 at the age of seventy-seven and was buried in St Mary's Church, Stourbridge. Four of his five sons continued in the development of the iron business, and his daughters and sons-in-law were also actively involved. Capital was raised by a series of interlocking partnerships between family members and close associates, while one-quarter and one-sixth shares in the business were subdivided among other investors. Iron mills were added or disposed of according to their profitability and value as contributors to the whole enterprise.

Expanding enterprise Richard [iii], the eldest son of Richard [ii] and his first wife, extended Foley interests to north Staffordshire. In 1651 he bought the manor of Longton, north Staffordshire, where there were coal and ironstone mines, and in 1661 he leased Meir Heath furnace in that manor. By 1666 there was an associated warehouse for slit rod at Normacote Grange. With Consall and Oakamore forges these formed a group known as the Moorland

works, supplying rod and bar to north Staffordshire iron-mongers. These were operated by Richard [iii] in partnership with his younger stepbrother Philip [i] (d. 1670). He also brought together Lawton furnace and the forges of Cranham and Warmingham in Cheshire. Both the Moorland and the Cheshire works supplied rod and bar to north Staffordshire ironmongers. Henry Glover of Stourbridge was brother-in-law to the Foley sons and was their agent. From 2 June 1675 to 15 July 1676 more than 1000 tons of iron were cast at Meir Heath. Richard [iii] died in 1678, and the north Staffordshire works passed to his son Richard [iv] (d. 1684).

Civil war opportunities Meanwhile, Thomas [i] Foley, born on 3 December 1617 at Witley Court, Worcestershire, the second son of Richard [ii], worked with his father from an early age and married (before 1641) Anne Browne (b. c.1619) of Spelmonden, Kent, whose father, John, was a gun-founder with iron furnaces in the Weald at Hawkhurst and Bedgebury. Of their four sons, Thomas [ii] (c.1641–1701), Paul *Foley (1644/5–1699), Nathaniel (1647–1663), and **Philip** [ii] **Foley** (bap. 1648, d. 1716), three took part in the iron business, and all but Philip [ii] had a university education. In 1651 Thomas [i] bought the manor of Kinver, on which lay several watermills in addition to Hyde mill, and in 1661 the manor of Harborne. He was managing the Stour works from about 1640 and in 1665 he was living at Compton, Kinver, where his house was assessed at 15 hearths. The civil war brought problems in the transport of iron, but it also provided opportunities for sale. Although the partnership supplied the king's armies it was able to remain neutral and after the war secured valuable naval ordnance contracts for Cromwell's government.

In the aftermath of the war, between 1648 and 1675, Thomas [i] acquired ninety-seven leases and partnerships, expanding in particular into the Forest of Dean where the furnaces produced exceptionally high grade iron from local ores. By 1670 the family had under its control mines, woodlands, furnaces, forges, slitting mills, a wire works, and warehouses, located in Worcestershire, south and north Staffordshire, Shropshire, the Forest of Dean, Kent, and Sussex. Furnaces, chafery and finery forges, and slitting mills were grouped to form production units of furnaces and forges, but some work was put out to other iron-masters. The Foley mills produced bar iron, rod iron, wire, cast pots, and anvils. The River Severn was an important line of communication and transport connecting the Stour valley, Shropshire, and Forest of Dean mills with each other as well as with the seaport of Bristol and the river port of Bewdley. Thomas [i] was also a governor of the Society of Mines Royal and of the Society of Mineral and Battery Works.

Thomas's house in Austin Friars, London, was an important assertion of his role on the national market, but Worcestershire remained his main centre. In 1667 he founded Oldswinford Hospital, which provided food, clothes, education, and apprenticeships for sixty poor boys. His contracts with Cromwell's government led to his being drawn into public affairs and in 1656 he was high sheriff for Worcestershire. In the previous year he had bought the manors of Great and Little Witley in Worcestershire and other properties for £2600. In 1669 Thomas [i] reorganized control of the ironworks, grouping the mills on a broadly geographical basis. He handed them over to be managed by his sons, though he continued to supervise and arbitrate between them: Paul became responsible for the Forest works, Philip [ii] for the Stour works, and Richard [iv] (his nephew, son of Richard [iii]) for the north Staffordshire works. Thomas [i] Foley died on 1 October 1677 and was buried at Witley.

Managing the enterprises The ironworks partnerships were becoming even more widely dispersed as more ironworks were leased, and new partners were brought in. Raw materials, pig iron, and wrought iron were moved greater distances in the course of production, and the numerous customers expected extended credit and paid mainly by means of bills of exchange. This presented problems of management, logistics, and accounting, which required sophisticated solutions.

Richard [iv] was trained by his father and inherited the north Staffordshire works on his father's death in 1678. Philip [ii] and other interested parties made an agreement to resolve the outstanding debts and enabled Richard [iv] to establish his ownership. However Richard died in 1684 and his heir was his uncle, John Foley (1631–1684), the youngest son of Richard [ii] Foley. When John Foley died in November of the same year the ironworks were inherited by Henry Glover senior, his brother-in-law, who had long been manager of the Stour works. For a short period the Cheshire works were transferred to the Yorkshire ironmasters, but they had returned to Foley hands by 1696. John Wheeler of Wollaston, Stourbridge, took over the Moorland works, with Obadiah Lane as manager, the partners being Wheeler, Lane, and Philip [ii] Foley. These works were in a favourable location between the expanding industrial areas of north and south Staffordshire where most of the bar and rod iron was sold.

Presence in parliament Thomas [ii] (c.1641–1701), the eldest son of Thomas [i], was educated at Pembroke College, Cambridge, where he was admitted in 1657 aged sixteen; he entered the Inner Temple, London, in the same year. He married Elizabeth (d. 1686), daughter of Edward Ashe, a draper of Heytesbury, Wiltshire, and London. Thomas [ii] held the Longhope and Tintern furnaces and Whitbrook and Wilden forge mills in the Forest of Dean. He too was a governor of the Society of Mines Royal and of the Society of Mineral and Battery Works. As eldest son, Thomas [ii] was increasingly preoccupied with building up a landed estate and a political career in the House of Commons. In 1683 he bought the Jacobean manor house of Great Witley from the Russell family, and added long wings to it. He was very active in the House of Commons, a member of all three Exclusion parliaments, supported the revolution, and sat in all the parliaments of William III. He was appointed to 177 committees of the house. In 1685 Thomas's daughter, Elizabeth (d. 1691), married Robert *Harley, first earl of Oxford and Mortimer. His eldest son,

Thomas *Foley, first Baron Foley (1673–1733), was one of the twelve new peers created by Robert Harley in January 1712.

Meanwhile the younger sons of Thomas [i], Paul *Foley and Philip [ii], had become the principal managers of the family works, bringing the partnerships to their widest extension in 1692. Paul was educated at Magdalen Hall, Oxford, from 1662, and possibly at the Inner Temple in London from September of that year. Between 1668 and 1670 he married Mary, daughter of John Lane, a clothworker, of St Lawrence, Poultney Lane, London, and bought the estate of Stoke Edith in Herefordshire. Not long before his death he completely rebuilt the house. He was a dissenter, and employed an ejected minister as tutor for his children. Like his elder brother Thomas [ii] he was a governor of the Society of Mines Royal from 1666 to 1678 and the Society of Mineral and Battery Works from 1666 to 1687.

Rifts and recombinations In 1669 the numerous but interlocking partnerships and semi-dependent enterprises of the ironworks had been divided into three segments. Paul purchased the king's works in the Forest of Dean in 1674 and these remained the main base of his power and responsibilities within the ironworks partnership. The Forest of Dean works were mainly furnaces producing high-quality iron from local ores. Eventually Paul held seven blast furnaces including Redbrook furnace and two forges at Lydbrook, Gloucestershire. He also had a half-interest in St Weonard's furnace, and the Pontrilas, Peterchurch, and Llansillo forges in Herefordshire.

The Stour works were controlled by the youngest of the brothers, Philip [ii] Foley, baptized on 12 May 1648 in the parish of St Peter le Poer in London. He married Penelope, daughter of William Paget, in 1670, bringing the Cannock group of forges into the family, and his father settled Prestwood estate in Kingswinford parish on them. They had two sons and five daughters. At the age of nineteen Philip took over the Stour valley and south Staffordshire works, then comprising four furnaces, thirteen forges, and the Bewdley warehouse, the stock and debts of which were estimated as £68,830. Philip entered into a bond to pay £60,000 to his father. There was a thorough assessment in 1667–8 of each and every mill in respect of its productivity and profitability, and the workmen were appraised in detail in respect of their skills, diligence, and reliability.

In 1674 there was a rift between Paul and Philip [ii]. Philip was both Paul's chief customer and his main competitor. Paul had expanded his output of pig iron in the Forest works and needed to expand his market in the midlands, but he also raised the price of the best quality Forest iron. Their father, Thomas [i], had to intervene in what threatened to become a bitter quarrel between the brothers. An agreement was drawn up which gave Philip one third of the Forest works but ensured Paul access to the midland market for iron. The partnership was, however, always strained and Paul was never satisfied that he was receiving support from his brother nor a full return from his mills. There were constant shifts and changes in the arrangements and although Paul received a steady profit from the Forest works he was by 1685 anxious to persuade Philip and other ironmasters to buy him out. This may have been a negotiating ploy, for Paul continued to operate the Forest works in close association with Philip.

At the same time Philip [ii] was establishing links with other partners in the Stour valley and in Shropshire, strengthening his own position and making himself less dependent upon Paul for bar iron. His agent and partner John Wheeler of Wollaston became important both in the practical management of the Stour valley and of the north Staffordshire works, and in his personal support for Philip. By 1691 Wheeler was also active in the Forest works. The partnerships included other ironmasters who held shares of one-sixth, or one-quarter, contributing to the large capital required, and they also created an active link with partnerships in other parts of the country.

As the leases of the ironworks were usually for short periods, and without right of survivorship, there was a continual need for adjustment and change of personnel. In 1692 Paul and Philip [ii] Foley together with John and Edward Wheeler and Richard Avenant drew up a new agreement for seven years which created a supervisory group of six partners. This brought together once more the Forest, Stour, and Staffordshire works. Paul and Philip paid in cash; the others were deemed to have put in the stock and debts from the mills which they had been operating for some years. The Stour ironworks were similarly reorganized with five partners. John Wheeler was the chief agent and salaried cash-holder for both partnerships.

Closing years Although this episode marked the climax of the process of expansion it did not halt the process of continuous renewal and reorganization of capital. It was a flexible arrangement and new mills continued to be brought within the network while others passed into other hands. Philip [ii] briefly made agreements which brought mills in Derbyshire (only between 1695 and 1698) and Nottinghamshire (from 1696) into the partnership. The organization was called in the accounts 'The Ironworks in Partnership'. Although other ironmasters held shares in the partnerships, Paul and Philip retained control of capital and the leadership in decision making. The day-to-day running of the units of production was in the hands of salaried clerks. These were educated men of modest background, who organized the sales and purchases along with the movement of raw materials and iron, and who hired and fired the workmen. The highly skilled men commanded high wages; their competence was monitored by the management, and they moved from mill to mill. In addition the ironworks required local unskilled labourers and large numbers of carriers by land and water. The enterprise was documented and controlled by a single set of annual accounts which were derived from detailed and regular records of daily transactions, wages, stock, debts, buildings repairs, and customers.

Such attention to financial detail was remarkable for the period, but the Foleys had long been concerned with county and national finance as well as business accounting; in the House of Commons Paul was respected as a good financier and lawyer, and he was one of the main organizers of the Land Bank proposed by Robert Harley. Philip [ii] was less involved in politics than his brother but was elected MP for Bewdley in 1679, for Stafford in 1689, 1695, and 1698, and for Droitwich in 1690 and 1701. There were five Foley cousins in the House of Commons, including the speaker in 1698, and all of them were notable members. In politics as in business the Foley brothers both supported and competed with each other.

The skills of public administration and private business in the Foley concern combined to make possible the effective co-ordination of more than fifty mills located in England and Wales. The enterprise was a landmark in the development of management techniques, but, perhaps as important, it also developed the selection, training, and control of local agents and managers at the sites. Many of the family members who had built up the business to its greatest extent died between 1699 and 1716. Paul Foley died of gangrene on 13 November 1699, and was buried at Stoke Edith, leaving an estate reputed to be worth £4000 a year. Thomas Foley [ii] died in 1701 and Philip [ii] in 1716. Their sons made aristocratic marriages and entered the peerage. From 1710 the Foleys gradually disposed of many of the works, retaining mainly those at the Forest of Dean and the Bewdley warehouse, and domination of the industry thus passed to other families.

Throughout the seventeenth century the Foley family were outstanding in the business of the production and sale of cast and wrought iron. They developed systems of management which enabled them to co-ordinate a multiplicity of units of production spread over a wide geographical area. Their achievement lay in the development of a business which was at once based on a multiplicity of units of production and local salaried management, a sophisticated system of central controls, and an elaborate unified accounting system. At the level of middle management the clerks of two or three related units worked to a uniform pattern throughout the enterprise. At the centre Henry Glover of Stourbridge and John Wheeler were of great importance both as managers and partners, but the Foleys were directly and personally creating policies and enforcing the routines which held together the whole enterprise, and demanding accountability from all those involved. They were also active in local and county government and in the second half of the century in the House of Commons. The two spheres of action were closely linked, not least in providing access to large government contracts and the experience of the management of money. There were other partnerships of ironmasters with whom they both competed and associated, but for six generations they were the leaders of a dynamic sector of industrialization. With the profits they founded three landed estates, namely Great Witley in Worcestershire, Stoke Edith in Herefordshire, and Prestwood in Staffordshire.   M. B. ROWLANDS

Sources B. L. C. Johnson, 'The charcoal era in the midlands 1690 to 1720', MA diss., U. Birm., 1950 · B. L. C. Johnson, 'The Foley partnerships: the iron industry at the end of the charcoal era', *Economic History Review*, 2nd ser., 4 (1951–2), 322–40 · B. L. C. Johnson, 'New light on the iron industry in the Forest of Dean', *Transactions of the Bristol and Gloucestershire Archaeological Society*, 72 (1953), 129–43 · B. L. C. Johnson, 'The iron industry of Cheshire and north Staffordshire, 1688–1712', *Transactions of the North Staffordshire Field Club*, 83 (1954), 32–55 · B. L. C. Johnson, 'The charcoal iron industry in the early eighteenth century', *GJ*, 117 (1951), 167–77 · R. G. Schafer, 'Genesis and structure of the Foley "Ironworks in partnership" of 1692', *Business History*, 13 (1971), 19–38 · R. G. Schafer, ed., 'A selection from the records of Philip Foley's Stour valley ironworks, 1668–74', *Worcestershire Historical Society*, new ser., 9/1 (1978) · B. G. Awty, 'Charcoal ironmasters of Cheshire and Lancashire, 1600–1785', *Transactions of the Historic Society of Lancashire and Cheshire*, 109 (1957), 71–124 · P. Riden, *A gazetteer of charcoal-fired blast furnaces in Great Britain in use since 1660* (1987) · G. F. Hammersley, 'The history of the iron industry in the Forest of Dean region, 1562–1660', PhD diss., U. Lond., 1972 · M. B. Rowlands, 'Two Worcestershire ironmongers', *West Midlands Studies*, 7 (autumn 1974), 18–22 · *VCH Staffordshire*, 2.108–33 · E. Rowlands, 'Foley, Paul', HoP, *Commons, 1660–90* · E. Rowlands and G. Jagger, 'Foley, Philip', HoP, *Commons, 1660–90* · P. Watson, 'Foley, Robert', HoP, *Commons, 1660–90* · M. W. Helms, E. Rowlands, and G. Jagger, 'Foley, Thomas I', HoP, *Commons, 1660–90* · E. Rowlands and G. Jagger, 'Foley, Thomas II', HoP, *Commons, 1660–90* · P. Lead, 'The north Staffordshire iron industry, 1600–1800', *Journal of the Historical Metallurgy Society*, 11 (1977), 14 · T. Nash, *Collections for the history of Worcestershire*, 2nd edn, 2 (1799), 464–6 · H. E. Palfrey, 'Foleys of Stourbridge', *Transactions of the Worcestershire Archaeological Society*, new ser., 21 (1944), 1–15 · P. McGrath, ed., *Merchants and merchandise in seventeenth-century Bristol*, Bristol RS, 19 (1955), 17, 229 · J. S. Roper, *Parish register of St Edmund's Dudley*, 1: (1540–1611), ser. 2 (1961) · H. R. Schubert, *History of the British iron and steel industry from c. 450 BC to AD 1775* (1957) · PRO, C 10 51/153, C 6/133/88 [Robert Foley] · J. S. Roper, *Dudley: the seventeenth century town*, transcripts from Dudley Archives, 5 (1965) · R. E. Sherwood, *Civil strife in the midlands, 1642–1651* (1974), 29 · G. P. A. Mander, *History of Wolverhampton to the early nineteenth century*, ed. N. W. Tildesley (1960), 82 · M. B. Rowlands, *Masters and men in the West Midland metalware trades before the industrial revolution* (1975)
Archives Herefs. RO, accounts, corresp., and papers | PRO, lawsuits · Staffs. RO, Heathcote MSS
Likenesses W. Trabute, oils, 1670 (Thomas Foley), repro. in Nash, *Collections*; copyprint, NPG [*see illus.*]

Foley, Alice (1891–1974), trade unionist and autobiographer, was born at 22 Back Shaw Street, Bolton, Lancashire, on 28 November 1891. She was the youngest of six children—two sisters and three brothers—of a 'big, intelligent but unruly' Irish Catholic father, Thomas Foley (*c.*1850–*c.*1906), who worked sporadically, between bouts of drinking, gambling, and Fenian activities (Foley, 8), and his wife, Alice, *née* Mort. At the time of her birth her father was described as a boiler stoker in a cotton mill. Her mother, who was illiterate, was known as Meg. Born prematurely, after what she described as a 'moonlight flit' (ibid., 3), Alice was not expected to survive, and so her sister took her immediately to the priest at St Patrick's Catholic Church for baptism. Her childhood was frugal and austere, the family, who lived in Milk Street, existing mainly on the money earned by her mother as a washerwoman. When Alice was three the family moved to a better house in Rankin Street, and in 1896 she began her education at St Peter's and St Paul's Catholic Infant School, taking her first holy communion and confirmation in due course. At twelve, unlike many of her classmates, Alice escaped the effects of the half-time factory system, as her father thought it an exploitation of child labour. She stayed at school for a final year, during which she was voted 'the most popular girl in the school'. While still at school she fell ill, distressed by the death of her sixteen-year-old brother Jimmie from appendicitis. On her recovery, in August 1904, she was taken on a four-day holiday to Morecambe by her eldest sister, Cissy, the first time Alice had left Bolton.

Shortly afterwards, helped by the older children's wages, the Foley family moved to Noble Street. In 1905, after fruitless searching for other work, Alice, aged thirteen, joined Cissy in rising at 5 a.m. to dress in clogs and shawl for work at the cotton mill. She first worked in Gibraltar Mill as a 'knotter', and then with the firm Hodgkinson and Gillbrands at Moor Mill on Derby Street, as a 'tenter', a 'cloth fettler', and finally in the preparation department. Always an avid reader, she continued her education, attending evening classes at her old school, and proceeding to secondary education at the municipal school in Great Moor Street.

Encouraged by Cissy, a suffragette and member of the Labour church, and by family readings and discussion of the weekly *Clarion* and the socialist Robert Blatchford's publications, Alice Foley developed an interest in socialism. Her father's death broke her last link with the Catholic church, and she and her younger sister, Emily, joined the Labour church and the newly established Socialist Sunday School. She also became a member of the Bolton Social Club and the socialist-run Clarion Cycling Club, and, through her activity in the weavers' trade union, a spokeswoman for her fellow workers. Lloyd George's 1911 National Insurance Act enabled her to find an outlet for her social idealism when, after seven years of factory work, she was appointed as sick visitor by the Bolton Weavers' Association for the supervision of scheduled benefits.

During the First World War, when her two brothers enlisted (the elder was killed on the Somme), Alice Foley served on the Women's Conscientious Objectors Tribunal and the War Savings Committee. She established the first Women's Labour Group in Bolton and also became governor of Bolton Girls' School. In 1917 she became a clerk in the Bolton weavers' trade union office at a wage of 30s. a week and by 1920 she and her now invalid mother had moved to Chip Dean Road, in Dean, a new estate on the edge of the town.

Foley's long involvement with the Workers' Educational Association (WEA) began in 1918, when she attended a summer school in Bangor, north Wales. In 1923 she won the WEA Cassel scholarship to attend Manchester University for a year. Over the next fifty years she served at every level of the WEA; in the Bolton branch, on the north-western district executive committee, as vice-chair of the north-western district, and on the national central council, later the national committee. Her work for adult education in the WEA and on the Manchester University joint committee for adult education was recognized by the award of an honorary MA degree in 1962.

Foley's career as a trade union official culminated in her secretaryship of the Bolton and District Weavers' and Winders' Union from 1949 to 1961, for which she was appointed MBE in 1951. During 1956–7 she was president of the Bolton united trades council. She was a long-standing JP, having first been appointed in 1931, and served on the Bolton education committee.

Foley's autobiography, *A Bolton Childhood*, published in 1973, described her childhood and early adult life. In narrating her own rise from factory floor to clerk in the Bolton weavers' office up to her involvement with the WEA, she referred to her purpose of helping her fellow workers 'left behind in the weaving sheds' (Foley, 76). She never married, but instead devoted her life to trade unionism and the WEA in a career which bore out the altruistic claims of her autobiography. A modest, public-spirited woman, Alice Foley died on 30 June 1974 at Bolton District General Hospital, Farnworth, after a long illness. Her memorial service was held at Bank Street Chapel, Bolton.

CAROL JENKINS

Sources A. Foley, *A Bolton childhood* (1973) · Alice Foley collection, archives, Bolton Central Library, ref. 22 ZFO-C · 'A Bolton childhood', *Destiny obscure*, ed. J. Burnett (1982), 90–99 [extract from A. Foley, *A Bolton childhood*] · b. cert. · d. cert.
Archives Bolton Central Library, political papers, incl. speeches
Likenesses photograph, 1907, repro. in Foley, *A Bolton childhood* · photograph, *c*.1920, repro. in Foley, *A Bolton childhood*
Wealth at death £18,074: probate, 8 Oct 1974, *CGPLA Eng. & Wales*

Foley, Daniel (*c*.1815–1874), philologist, was born at Tralee, co. Kerry, the son of Timothy Foley, a merchant. His parents were poor, and he never wore shoes until he was employed in the shop of Patrick Grey in Tralee. Under the influence of a local clergyman he left the Roman Catholic church, and in 1838 was sent to study theology for ordination in the then established Church of Ireland at Trinity College, Dublin. He gained his degrees of BA in 1843, MA in 1852, BD in 1854, and DD in 1858.

After ordination Foley obtained the prebend of Kilbragh, in the cathedral of Cashel, and from 1852 the rectory of Templetuohy. Irish was his first language, and in 1849 he was appointed professor of Irish in the University of Dublin, a post he held until 1861. He wrote a preface to a small Irish grammar by C. H. H. Wright, and *An English–Irish Dictionary, Intended for the Use of Students of the Irish Language* (1855). This work is based upon an earlier dictionary by Thaddeus Connellan, published without date and issued in Dublin from time to time with a variety of false title-pages. Foley, who does not refer to this source, altered some of the Irish interpretations, and made additions. Many of the Irish words are inventions of his own, as *fuam-ainm* (sound-name) for onomatopoeia; or paraphrases, as *duine* (person) for microcosm and *eudaigh*

(clothes) for caparison; or simply errors, as *ainis* (anise) for caraway. The University of Dublin made a grant towards the publication, but the work lacked authority. Foley's *The People and Institutions of the United States of America* (1858) has interesting observations on New York, the American Irish, and slavery.

Foley took an active part in opposition to disestablishment of the church in Ireland, and lectured on the subject in England and Scotland. He died at Blackrock, near Dublin, on 7 July 1874, and was buried in the cemetery of Kill o' the Grange. NORMAN MOORE, *rev.* JOHN D. HAIGH

Sources A. J. Webb, *A compendium of Irish biography* (1878) · Boase, *Mod. Eng. biog.* · private information (1889) [J. Manning] · D. Foley, *An English–Irish dictionary* (1855), preface, iii–iv · Burtchaell & Sadleir, *Alum. Dubl.*, 2nd edn · D. Foley, *The people and institutions of the United States of America* (1858) · Allibone, *Dict.*, suppl.

Foley, Francis Edward [Frank] (1884–1958), intelligence officer, was born on 24 November 1884 at 7 Walrow Terrace, Highbridge, Somerset, the third of six children of Andrew Wood Foley (*c*.1850–1932), engineer, and his wife, Isabella Turnbull. Foley's father was of Irish descent; his mother was a Scottish Catholic. Foley was educated at St Joseph's Roman Catholic School, Burnham, and at Stonyhurst College before studying at St Joseph's College, a Roman Catholic seminary in Poitiers, France. His early ambition to become a priest did not survive a period at Poitiers University reading classics and, in 1908, he began travelling around Europe. At the outbreak of the First World War Foley was in Hamburg. He escaped to Britain disguised as a Prussian officer on his way to the front and took a commission in the Hertfordshire regiment. He was attached to the North Staffordshire regiment before moving into military intelligence.

At the end of the First World War Foley was recruited by the British Secret Intelligence Service (later commonly known as MI6) to be its head of station in Berlin. His cover was as passport control officer, responsible for issuing visas for anyone wanting to go to Britain or its empire, a useful method of keeping track of Bolshevik agents. During his time in the army he had met Katherine Eva Lee (1897–1979), the daughter of a hotelier from Dartmouth. They were married in Dartmouth on 21 June 1921, and their only child, Ursula Margaret, was born in Berlin on 25 August 1922.

Foley was remarkably successful in his professional life, recruiting Jonny X, the Bolshevik agent Johann deGraff, who kept the British informed in great detail of Soviet intelligence operations in the West and is still regarded as one of the most successful agents ever recruited by MI6.

When Hitler came to power in 1933 Foley was inundated with requests from Jews wishing to travel to Palestine. He blatantly ignored the strict rules governing the issuance of visas to ensure that large numbers of Jews who might otherwise have gone to the gas chambers were assisted to safety in Palestine and the United Kingdom. Short, balding, and with his spectacles giving him an owlish appearance, Foley made an unlikely hero. Yet he went into the concentration camps to get people out, helped them obtain false passports and hid them in his own home, despite the fact that he had no diplomatic immunity and that the Germans, who were aware he was a spy, might arrest him at any time. Benno Cohn, president of the German Zionist Organisation, told the trial of Adolf Eichmann in 1961 that Foley had been the 'Pimpernel of the Jews' adding: 'In my opinion, he was one of the greatest among the nations of the world. He rescued thousands of Jews from the jaws of death' (Eichmann trial, session 14, 25 April 1961).

Foley left Berlin on the eve of the Second World War and was posted to Oslo, which was thought to be the ideal base to run his agents in Germany. These included Hans Mayer, the author of the Oslo report, which gave the British details of the Nazis' secret technology, and Paul Rosbaud, who provided information on German lack of progress in atomic research. When Germany invaded Norway, Foley was the only link between London and the Norwegian armed forces and was subsequently awarded the knight's cross of St Olav (7 August 1943). On returning to Britain he was appointed commander in the Order of St Michael and St George for his work in Germany (1 January 1941) and was allocated to interrogate Rudolf Hess, the deputy Führer, who had flown to Britain on a lone peace mission. Foley always said Hess was mad and should never have been put on trial.

For the rest of the war Foley was in charge of the MI6 contribution to the double cross system, under which Nazi spies caught attempting to gather intelligence on Britain were used to feed false information to the Germans. He retired in 1949 to Stourbridge, Worcestershire, and died at his home, 32 Eveson Road, Norton, Stourbridge, of heart failure on 8 May 1958. He was buried at Stourbridge borough cemetery on 13 May. On 25 February 1999, Yad Vashem, Israel's Holocaust Memorial Centre, belatedly named him Righteous Among the Nations, the highest award the Jewish people can grant to a gentile.

MICHAEL SMITH

Sources M. Smith, *Foley: the spy who saved 10,000 Jews* (1999) · H. Pollack, 'Captain Foley, der Mensch und andere Berichte', Yad Vashem, Jerusalem, YVS01/17 · H. Pollack, 'Personal and confidential note on the late Major Francis E Foley', Central Zionist Archives, Jerusalem, CZA K11/391 · British Army record of Capt F E Foley, PRO, WO374/24816 · U. Leeds, Brotherton L., Margaret Reid MS 708 · N. Shepherd, *Wilfred Israel: German Jewry's secret ambassador* (1984) · A. Kramish, *The griffin* (1986) · M. Reid and L. C. Rolstad, *April 1940: en krigsdagbok* (1980) · A. J. Sherman, *Island refuge: Britain and refugees from the Third Reich, 1933–39* (1994) · CGPLA Eng. & Wales (1958) · b. cert. · baptism cert. · WW (1952) · m. cert. · d. cert. · d. cert. [Katherine Foley] · *County Express* [Stourbridge] (17 May 1958)
Archives U. Leeds, Brotherton L., Margaret Reid MSS, MS 708
Likenesses photographs, U. Leeds · photographs, repro. in Smith, *Foley*
Wealth at death £3937 2s. 11d.: probate, 18 July 1958, CGPLA Eng. & Wales

Foley, John Henry (1818–1874), sculptor, was born on 24 May 1818 in Dublin, the son of Jesse Foley, a grocer. Following the example of his brother, Edward, he was educated at the Royal Dublin Society's art schools (1831–4) and the Royal Academy Schools, London (1835–8), winning prizes at both institutions. Like Edward Foley, he also served as a

studio assistant to the sculptor William Behnes (c.1835–c.1838). Success came rapidly to Foley, earned by Royal Academy exhibits such as *Ino and Bacchus* (1840; plaster, Royal Dublin Society), *Youth at the Stream* (1844; V&A), and *Innocence* (1847; Royal Collection, Osborne House, Isle of Wight). These 'ideal' sculptures represent a stylistic transition from neo-classicism to Victorian realism and, as with all Foley's work, are sensitively executed and graceful in contour. The *Art Union* considered *Youth at the Stream* to be the finest exhibit at the 1844 Royal Academy and in 1860 commissioned a bronze statuette version.

Following these successes, Foley was commissioned to execute marble statues of two seventeenth-century statesmen, *John Hampden* (1847) and *John Selden* (1855), for the palace of Westminster. Numerous portrait commissions ensued, both historical and contemporary, to the virtual exclusion of imagined subjects. However, Foley presented a Miltonic theme, the *Elder Brother from Comus* (1860), to the Royal Academy as his diploma work, following election to full membership in 1857. After 1861 Foley stopped exhibiting there in protest against what he believed were the poor display conditions accorded to sculpture. His evidence to the royal commission on the Royal Academy (1863) nevertheless took the form of constructive criticism rather than hostility.

At a time when sculpture was widely considered to have reached a low point in vision and quality, the work of Foley was seen as an exception. This is evident in his critical press, whether from contemporaries such as Francis Turner Palgrave and William Michael Rossetti, or from the younger Edmund Gosse, who saw Foley's achievements as smoothing the path for the New Sculpture. Particularly admired were the technical excellence, versatility, and the lifelike qualities of his work. Foley avoided over-reverence towards antiquity, stating that he placed 'no greater value on acquaintance with the best works of ancient times than with those of modern times' (*Royal commission … Royal Academy*, 221). He was, however, mindful of historical precedents. *Ino and Bacchus* has a mild eroticism, influenced by the French rococo sculptor Étienne Maurice Falconet, and *Sir Charles Barry* (1860; palace of Westminster) portrays the architect dressed in a loose gown, perhaps inspired by the precedent of Jean-Antoine Houdon's *Voltaire Seated*. The meditative qualities of Foley's bronze statue of the politician Sidney Herbert (1867; Waterloo Place, London) distinguish it from its neighbours. Also much admired was the equestrian statue of Henry, first Viscount Hardinge (1858; priv. coll., Kent), which formerly stood outside Government House, Calcutta. It was described in the *Art Journal* as 'a triumph of British art' (20, 1858, 232) and Rossetti claimed that it stood 'markedly at the head of British equestrian statues of any period' (Rossetti, 360).

Foley's best-known works are his sculptures for the Albert Memorial (1864–76; Kensington Gardens, London). The marble group *Asia* flanks the monument and portrays the voluptuous allegorical figure of India, mounted on an elephant, unveiling herself. This action alludes to the subcontinent's display of products at the Great Exhibition of

1851, in which Prince Albert played a central role. Other figures in the group show Foley's careful attempt to convey accurate racial types and costumes. His most significant contribution to the memorial is the 14 foot gilt-bronze figure of Prince Albert seated under the central canopy. Foley was commissioned to execute the statue following the death of Carlo Marochetti in 1867. Unfinished at the time of Foley's death, the statue was completed by his principal assistant, Thomas Brock. In his representation of the prince, Foley aimed at an image that was at once humane and monumental. Prince Albert is portrayed in his Garter robes, holding the Great Exhibition handbook which, given the shrine-like setting, is invested with biblical authority.

A further major commission was for Foley's native Ireland, his monument to Daniel O'Connell (1864–82; O'Connell Street, Dublin). At first there were protests that Foley's long residence in London had somehow rendered him less Irish and therefore less suited to execute such a monument. While there is no obviously Irish stylistic element to the work, such was the admiration for his design when it was exhibited in model form in 1867 that this was overlooked and the end result vindicated his choice as sculptor. Over 39 feet tall, the monument comprises a statue of O'Connell, a drum relief of fifty figures led by Erin, and four seated winged victories, the last revealing Foley's admiration for the early nineteenth-century German sculptor Christian Daniel Rauch. Another major Irish work was Foley's bronze statue of Oliver Goldsmith (1864; Trinity College, Dublin), a fine example of Victorian sartorial realism. Foley remembered his Irish links with the bequest of original plaster models to the Royal Dublin Society, many of which have unfortunately been destroyed.

John Henry Foley died on 27 August 1874 at his home, The Priory, Upper Terrace, Hampstead; an attack of pleurisy contracted in 1871 while at work in uncomfortable conditions on the Albert Memorial sculpture had seriously weakened him. His death came three months after that of his sculptor brother, Edward, who had committed suicide. Foley's burial on 5 September 1874 in the crypt of St Paul's Cathedral, London, and the publication of two monographs on his work confirm Benedict Read's view that he was 'recognised as the master of public statuary' in mid-Victorian Britain (Curtis, 38). Yet for much of the twentieth century Foley's reputation was overshadowed by that of his close contemporary Alfred Stevens. While Foley might have lacked Stevens's creative genius, his tangible achievements and influence were far greater. Temperamentally, he shared some of Stevens's perfectionism: his biographer, Cosmo Monkhouse, described him as 'a very conscientious and fastidious workman, consulting his friends as to his designs, and altering them continually in the course of execution' (DNB). According to Samuel Carter Hall, editor of the Art Journal, Foley was 'pensive almost to melancholy ... all his sentiments and sensations were graceful: so in truth were his manners. His leisure was consumed by thought' (Art Journal, 36, 1874, 306). Foley left behind him an impressive body of students, including

Brock, who completed most of the works that were unfinished at the time of his death, C. B. Birch, Francis John Williamson, Albert Bruce-Joy, and Mary Grant.

MARK STOCKER

Sources R. Gunnis, *Dictionary of British sculptors, 1660–1851*, new edn (1968) • B. Read, 'John Henry Foley', *The Connoisseur*, 186 (1974), 262–71 • B. Read, *Victorian sculpture* (1982) • W. C. Monkhouse, *The works of John Henry Foley, R. A.* (1875) • M. Stocker, 'Foley, John Henry', in J. Turner, *The dictionary of art* (1996) • S. Bayley, *The Albert Memorial: the monument in its social and architectural context* (1981) • P. Murphy, 'The O'Connell monument in Dublin: the political and artistic context of a public sculpture', *Apollo*, 143 (March 1996), 22–6 • S. A. [S. Atkinson], *Arts and industries in Ireland*, 1: *John Henry Foley* (1882) • *DNB* • C. Avery and M. Marsh, 'The bronze statuettes of the Art Union of London: the rise and decline of Victorian taste in sculpture', *Apollo*, 121 (1985), 328–37 • W. M. Rossetti, *Fine art, chiefly contemporary* (1867) • J. Sankey, 'Thomas Brock and the Albert Memorial', *Sculpture Journal*, 3 (1999), 87–92 • 'Royal commission to inquire into ... the Royal Academy', *Parl. papers* (1863), 27.1, no. 3205; 27.587, no. 3205-I • *Art Journal*, 11–39 (1849–77) • *Art Union*, 5–10 (1844–8) • J. Blackwood, *London's immortals: the complete outdoor commemorative statues* (1989) • E. Gosse, 'The new sculpture, 1879–1894 [pt 1]', *Art Journal*, new ser., 14 (1894), 138–42 • S. Beattie, *The New Sculpture* (1983) • P. Curtis, ed., *Patronage and practice: sculpture on Merseyside* (1989) • J. Physick, 'Victorian mantelpiece found', *Antique Collector*, 55 (1984), 72 • *CGPLA Eng. & Wales* (1875) • Graves, *RA exhibitors*

Archives BL, corresp. with A. H. Layard, Add. MSS 38993–38996 • City Hall, Dublin, archives, material relating to O'Connell monument • Royal Arch., MSS relating to Albert Memorial, Add. MSS

Likenesses C. B. Birch, plaster medallion, 1876, NPG • C. B. Birch, wax relief, 1876, NG Ire. • J. Gamble, statue, c.1905, V&A; repro. in Read, 'John Henry Foley' • C. B. Birch, pencil, NG Ire. • E. Edwards, photograph, NPG; repro. in L. Reeve, ed., *Men of eminence*, 1 (1863) • C. V. Foley, watercolour, NG Ire. • T. Mogford, portrait, NG Ire. • G. Stodart, stipple (after bust by T. Brock, 1873), NPG • engraving, repro. in *Art Journal*, new ser., 11 (1849), 49 • wood-engraving (after photograph by J. Watkins), NPG; repro. in *ILN* (2 May 1857) • wood-engraving (after photograph), NPG; repro. in *ILN* (12 Sept 1874)

Wealth at death under £14,000: probate, 23 Nov 1875, *CGPLA Eng. & Wales*

Foley, Paul (1644/5–1699), speaker of the House of Commons, was the second son of Thomas *Foley (1617–1677) [see under Foley family] of Witley Court, Worcestershire, and Anne, daughter and heir of John Browne, esquire, of Spelmonden, Kent, a gun-founder. Foley's father, elder brother, Thomas, and younger brother, Philip, were all members of parliament and active in the iron business, as was Paul; all were conforming presbyterians. Richard Baxter considered Thomas Foley senior his 'Worthy Friend' (R. Baxter, *The Crucifying of the World*, 1658, dedication) and Paul and his brothers 'religious worthy men' (Manning, 395). Paul Foley matriculated at Magdalen Hall, Oxford, 19 June 1662, aged seventeen, and may have entered the Inner Temple in September 1662. He was called to the bar on 22 November 1668. In March 1668, he took out a licence to marry Mary, daughter of John Lane of London, a freeman of the Clothworkers' Company. In 1670 their eldest son, Thomas, was born in London, and Foley engaged a presbyterian tutor for his education. Foley retained a London residence in Essex Street and continued to study if not practise law, ascending to the bench in 1687 and becoming a reader at the Inner Temple in 1690.

Foley also became a squire and patron in Herefordshire. In 1667 he purchased the church livings of Tarrington and Solers Hope and in 1670 he bought Stoke Edith estate outside Hereford from the widow of the influential royalist Sir Henry Lingen. His fellow presbyterian Colonel John Birch and others advanced Foley as an anti-court candidate for an intended Leominster by-election in 1670, although his candidacy was unpromising and he never made real preparations. In December 1675 an opponent disapproved of a meeting of the 'close designing party' at Stoke Edith, which 'cantoned out' the county for an ensuing parliament. At the meeting Foley's chaplain reportedly decried local MPs as court pensioners and thought the 'Bishops should be excluded … [as] they are a dead weight' (*CSP dom.*, 1675-6, 460-61). Foley himself established his influence in Hereford city by purchasing the living of St Peter's there and, in 1677, presenting the corporation with a new sword and cap of maintenance (and a type of fire engine). He successfully stood as burgess for the city in February 1679, even though opponents circulated a manuscript libel 'A Public Vindication of Paul Foley Esq.' (Herefs. RO, Hereford city records, quarter sessions, May 1679).

Foley represented Hereford and was active during all three Exclusion parliaments. He voted for the first Exclusion Bill, 21 May 1679, declaring 'I shall rather exclude the duke of York from Succession, than lose the Protestant Religion' (Grey, 7.255-6). In the second Exclusion Parliament he served on perhaps fifty committees, including that about the Popish Plot. Foley's speeches attacked popery and arbitrary principles. His 15 December 1680 speech is memorable. 'The Danger of the Papists is that the Government should take their parts, or should have foreign assistance to support them', he noted. Besides banishing Papists, he would also 'enable the Protestants to defend themselves' (ibid., 8.158-70). He called for an armed protestant association, and such a bill passed. Foley recited a litany of Catholic inroads into the country—'the duke's interest', the Catholic majority in Ireland, Catholics in the standing army, local Catholics protected by the marquess of Worcester—but the greatest threat came from revived conflicts within protestantism:

> And will not the divisions they carry on amongst us, as to churchmen and fanatics, Plot or no Plot, be very useful to [the Papists]; but especially their arraignments of parliaments, and all that speak against popery, as [16]41 men, and enemies to the government? (Cobbett, *Parl. hist.*, 4.1245-7)

Foley censured the Anglican bishops for their active opposition to exclusion and protestant unity.

Foley's whiggery stemmed not only from his pan-protestantism, but also from his concern, as a common lawyer, for precedent. About 1681 Lord Keeper Francis North had discovered Foley combing 'musty old repositories' to prove the ancient powers of the Commons (Manning, 397) and in January 1681, Foley asked:

> is not the Order about Printing a King of an act of State, to serve instead of Law? Is not the use of Grand-Juries a very essential part of this Government? And is not the dismissing of them, as [Chief Justice Scroggs] did, a way to render them

useless? (*An Exact Collection of the most Considerable Debates*, 228)

The arch-tory North claimed that his brother-in-law's cousin, Foley, was less concerned with the law than with rebellion and that he had heard him state 'things would never go well till forty heads flew for it' (North, 1.292-3). Foley had been at the forefront of those calling for an armed protestant association and, when the earl of Shaftesbury met with the Herefordshire representatives after the third Exclusion Parliament to establish a protestant militia, Foley approved and, among others, was nominated a captain. In any case, the government and local tories sought to silence him and he was removed from the commission of peace in January 1680. In 1682 the remodelling of Hereford corporation temporarily destroyed Foley's electoral interest there and, when the new charter was brought to the city in May the new steward, Lord Worcester, replaced the sword and cap of maintenance given by Foley in 1677 with new ones, thus symbolizing the transfer of power. During the Rye House Plot scare in 1683 Foley, Sir Edward Harley, and others were confined at Hereford for almost a month. After being imprisoned again during Monmouth's rebellion, Foley left Stoke Edith, rented out his ironworks, and retired to Oxford for several years. He corresponded with Harley throughout the 1680s and the obvious political and religious ties between the families were cemented when Sir Edward's eldest sons each married one of Foley's nieces, Robert Harley in 1685 and Edward Harley two years earlier. Indeed, in 1687 Foley channelled funds for the Huguenots through the younger Edward Harley in London. When James II's agenda forced the king to seek new allies he returned Foley to the bench and licensed him to empark Stoke Edith. Foley prepared for elections. In October 1688, Robert Harley reported 'as to Hereford city Paul Foley seems secure' (Rowlands, 'Black as Hell', 49). Foley quickly swung to support the revolution, however. In December 1688, Robert met his father, Sir Edward, at Stoke Edith and the Harleys and Foleys rode to Worcester with a newly raised troop of horses in support of the prince of Orange. Foley gave liberally (£50) to the Herefordshire subscription for the prince.

In the Convention, Foley again represented Hereford (and would do so until he died). He was again very active, being appointed to 128 committees, and chairing seven. In 1689 he helped manage the conference between the two houses which led to the settlement of the succession. He was also active on committees concerning legal precedent and those on religious comprehension and toleration. He was among those ordered to prepare a bill regarding the corporations and, when Hereford refused to elect another whig 'without money' (HoP, *Commons*, 2.337), he sought as revenge to exclude the city from the bill to restore corporations. He spoke on abuses in the provisioning of the Irish army and the victualling of the fleet. On 14 December 1689 he asked 'why Ireland was not relieved in proper time … [?] As for the ministers, they have done the same things as in Charles 2's time, which makes me think them pensioners to France still' (Cobbett, *Parl. hist.*, 5.373), apparently forgetting that Barillon had allowed him 300 guineas for service to France during the first Exclusion Parliament.

During the next parliament, from 1690 to 1695, Foley's anti-court position became more pronounced and he and his nephew Robert Harley led whig backbenchers towards a new political grouping with tories as the 'new country party'. In early 1690 he worried publicly about settling 'such a Revenue as that the King [William] should have no need of a Parliament' (Grey, 10.10). From December 1690, when Foley and Harley were appointed among the nine commissioners of accounts, he increasingly censured court administration and pushed for 'good management' (Horwitz, 98). Backbenchers tended to support his criticism of the management of the war, which was open from summer 1691, but were quick to find fault with Foley when he appeared to criticize the war itself. Foley did not confine his critique of war management to accounts but at times attacked the entire army structure, for example demanding in November 1692 that English soldiers be commanded by English officers; backbenchers were quick to point out Foley's own lack of direct experience of war. By December 1692 Foley's and Harley's combined opposition with churchmen brought arch rumours that 'the Jacobites and Commonwealthmen [had] joined together' (Horwitz, 109). The fear that Foley had 'turned' (ibid., 214) perhaps explains the whig Bishop Burnet's assessment of him about 1693 as:

> a man of virtue and good principles, but morose and wilful, and he had the affectation of passing for a great patriot, by his constant finding fault with the Government, and venting and ill humour, and a bad opinion of the court. (Manning, 397)

Foley continued a Commonwealthsman critique of court influence and pushed for frequent parliaments. In April 1694 he retained a seat on the commission of accounts after a ballot. Early the next year he helped gather signatures to a petition against the whig Bank of England (and he would later be appointed a trustee to one of the three private land banks established in opposition to the bank). In March he chaired the committee to inspect the books of the East India Company and the City of London. His report brought down the speaker, Sir John Trevor, for accepting a bribe.

On 14 March 1695 the Commons chose Foley as speaker. When Wharton, the comptroller of the household, recommended Sir Thomas Littleton, this was opposed as seeming too much in the court's interest, and Foley was elected instead. The next day, after his first speech as speaker, Foley had a private hour-long talk with King William, and on 20 March he was re-elected to the commission of accounts. At the meeting of the new parliament in November Foley was again chosen speaker. He personally reformed the fees for private bills and seems to have been an even-handed speaker, but his political dealings with the government led to criticism as trade declined. In May 1697 a Hereford mob threatened to pull down his house, and jeered his family. He was not chosen speaker for the new parliament in December 1698, and he spent his last years building a new house at Stoke Edith (built between 1697 and 1699, it burned down in 1927) and compiling notes on various subjects. His eldest son, Thomas (d. 1737), entered parliament after a double return at Weobley by-election in 1691 and remained active in the Commons, and his younger son, Paul, became a barrister.

Foley died of gangrene in the foot on 13 November 1699, at Stoke Edith, and was buried in the church there. His will established trustees for tithes gathered from Herefordshire and Gloucestershire lands to dispense to ministers in need and particularly to the vicar of St Peter's Church in Hereford. Many of his papers survive, including voluminous notes on parliamentary history as well as on scripture, the millennium, and church history (for example, 'Of toleration in religion', Herefs. RO, E12/IV/25–9); these papers appear to have been written (and collected) between 1694 and 1697. Portraits of Foley and his wife remain at Stoke Edith, where the Foley family still lives.

NEWTON E. KEY

Sources HoP, *Commons, 1660–90* · J. A. Manning, *The lives of the speakers of the House of Commons*, 2nd edn (1851) · H. Horwitz, *Parliament, policy and politics in the reign of William III* (1977) · J. Duncumb and others, *Collections towards the history and antiquities of the county of Hereford*, 1 (1804); 3–5 (1882–97) · A. Grey, ed., *Debates of the House of Commons, from the year 1667 to the year 1694*, new edn, 7–8 (1769) · Cobbett, *Parl. hist.*, vols. 4–5 · R. North, *The life of the Right Honourable Francis North, baron of Guilford*, 2nd edn, 2 vols. (1808) · D. R. Lacey, *Dissent and parliamentary politics in England, 1661–1689* (1969) · T. Rowlands, '"As black as Hell to my own people": James II's reputation in Herefordshire', *Midland History*, 14 (1989), 43–52 · N. Key, 'Comprehension and the breakdown of consensus in Restoration Herefordshire', *The politics of religion in Restoration England*, ed. T. Harris, P. Seaward, and M. Goldie (1990), 191–216 · N. Lyde, *A narrative of the life of Mr. Richard Lyde of Hereford* (1731) · *An exact collection of the most considerable debates in the honourable House of Commons* (1681) · Foster, *Alum. Oxon.* · *Herefordshire*, Pevsner (1963) · W. C. Metcalfe, ed., *The visitation of the county of Worcester* (privately printed, Exeter, 1883) · T. Rowlands, 'Robert Harley's parliamentary apprenticeship', *British Library Journal*, 15 (1989), 173–86

Archives Herefs. RO | BL, Harley MSS

Likenesses portraits, Stoke Edith estate, Herefordshire

Foley, Philip (bap. 1648, d. 1716). *See under* Foley family (*per.* c.1620–1716).

Foley, Richard (1579/80–1657). *See under* Foley family (*per.* c.1620–1716).

Foley, Samuel (1655–1695), Church of Ireland bishop of Down and Connor, eldest son of Samuel Foley (d. 1695), a wealthy gentleman of Clonmel and Dublin, and his wife, Elizabeth Richards, was born at Clonmel on 25 November 1655. He attended the school of Edward Jones at Kilkenny, and gained admission to Trinity College, Dublin, on 8 June 1672. He graduated BA in 1675, and, having been elected to a fellowship in 1677, proceeded MA in 1678, the year he was ordained as a deacon and priest in the Church of Ireland; he served in the chapel at Trinity College from 16 March 1679.

Foley became vicar of Finglas in 1681. In 1683, when he published a sermon preached in 1681 at the consecration of three bishops, as well as a visitation sermon he had preached in 1682 before Francis Marsh, archbishop of Dublin, he was described as 'Chaplain to His Grace'. In this latter sermon he argued against extremes in religion, whether Calvinist or Catholic, but also counselled caution in the handling of both, especially in light of 'our present Circumstances'. He and his close friend William King, future archbishop of Dublin, were acutely aware of the dangers which would arise in the event of a Catholic succession to the crown of Ireland, and together they collected manuscripts to help prepare against the day when the protestant settlement came under attack. As well as exploring the prospects for a reconciliation with Presbyterian dissenters, they even went so far as to rehearse the argument that either church or state might dissolve their formal partnership if necessity demanded. The two men were appointed to administer the diocese of Dublin when Archbishop Marsh fled to England in February 1689. Foley was installed as chancellor of St Patrick's Cathedral on 14 February. He was among those attainted by the patriot parliament shortly afterwards. He survived the furore of the next two years, and was appointed dean of Achonry and precentor of Killala on 4 April 1691. His patent for the bishopric of Down and Connor was dated 31 August 1694, and he was consecrated on 2 September and enthroned on 4 October following.

Foley wrote an account of the Giant's Causeway which was published in *Philosophical Transactions* the same year. His brief episcopacy was marked by an evident sensitivity to the special needs of his diocese, where nonconformity was rife and the material means to combat it largely unavailable. In an *Exhortation* to his flock concerning the education of their children, he urged that they not learn from their parents 'little scoffs or by-words against any person's way of worshipping God, who differs from that way in which they are brought up' (Greaves, 154).

Foley died of a fever on 22 May 1695 at Lisburn, and was buried there. At an unknown date he had married Honora, daughter of Roger Moore, of Johnstone, near Dublin, and his wife, Elizabeth, apparently the granddaughter of Murrough O'Brien, Lord Inchiquin. Samuel and Honora had a son, Roger, who became chaplain to Archbishop King. Another son, Samuel, was under the archbishop's guardianship until he came of age.   SEAN KELSEY

Sources DNB · S. Foley, *Two sermons* (1683) · H. Cotton, *Fasti Ecclesiae Hibernicae*, 5 vols. (1848), vol. 1, p. 270; vol. 2, p. 118; vol. 3, p. 208; vol. 4, pp. 84, 105 · J. B. Leslie and H. B. Swanzy, *Biographical succession lists of the clergy of the diocese of Down* (1936), 9–10 · *The correspondence of Jonathan Swift*, ed. F. E. Ball, 6 vols. (1910–14), vol. 1, p. 302 · A. Carpenter, 'William King and the threats to the Church of Ireland during the reign of James II', *Irish Historical Studies*, 18 (1972–3), 22–8 · A. Ford, J. McGuire, and K. Milne, eds., *As by law established: the Church of Ireland since the Reformation* (1995) · R. Greaves, *God's other children: protestant nonconformists and the emergence of denominational churches in Ireland, 1660–1700* (1997)
Archives University of Ulster at Magee, Londonderry, Derry Diocesan Library, portion of a diary

Foley, Thomas (1617–1677). *See under* Foley family (*per. c.*1620–1716).

Foley, Thomas, first Baron Foley (1673–1733), politician, born on 8 November 1673, was the grandson of the ironmaster Thomas *Foley (1617–1677) [*see under* Foley family] and the eldest son of Thomas Foley (*c.*1641–1701) of Witley Court, Worcestershire, and his wife, Elizabeth (*d.* 1686),

the daughter of Edward Ashe, a draper of Fenchurch Street, London, and Heytesbury, Wiltshire. He was educated at Sheriffhales dissenting academy (1689) and the university at Utrecht (1689–93), as befitted the scion of a family still noted for its Presbyterianism. However, although he inherited an interest in the iron industry from his father, his calling was that of an educated country gentleman. Thus, within weeks of turning twenty-one, he entered parliament, having been able to call on his uncle Philip Foley to ensure his return for Stafford in a fortuitous by-election in November 1694. He retained his seat until his elevation to the peerage.

Foley quickly joined his Foley and Harley relatives in the new country party and began his assimilation into the ranks of the tories. Parliamentary politics did not preclude him from entering Lincoln's Inn in 1695 or from being elected a fellow of the Royal Society the following year. Having succeeded to a considerable fortune on his father's death in 1701, on 18 June 1702 he married Mary (1671/2–1735), the daughter of Serjeant Thomas Strode of Lincoln's Inn and Beaminster, Dorset, an heiress worth £30,000. In Queen Anne's reign he continued to follow the lead of his brother-in-law, Robert Harley, who in 1685 had married his sister, Elizabeth (*d.* 1691). Although he voted with the tories in the opening years of Anne's reign, Harley's acceptance of office in 1704 saw Foley join the ranks of the court. However, he joined Harley in opposition in 1708, and reverted to the court in 1710 when Harley became head of a predominantly tory ministry.

As early as 1705 Foley's wealth had marked him out as a potential recruit to the peerage, but he had to wait until 1 January 1712 to be created Baron Foley of Kidderminster. Consistent with a creation owing much to political necessity, he supported the tories in the Lords, although he paid some heed to his nonconformist roots in voting against the Schism Bill in 1714. He remained loyal to the tories after the Hanoverian succession, and was a member of Lord Cowper's opposition in 1720–23. Although he lost heavily in the South Sea Bubble he remained a wealthy man. He died on 22 January 1733 at his London house in Hanover Square, and was buried in Great Witley church, which he had been responsible for rebuilding. He allowed his only surviving daughter, Elizabeth, a portion of £15,000; his title and estate went to his only surviving son, also named Thomas.   STUART HANDLEY

Sources 'Foley, Thomas', HoP, *Commons* · will, PRO, PROB 11/657, sig. 89 · R. G. Schafer, 'Genesis and structure of the Foley "Ironworks in partnership" of 1692', *Business History*, 13 (1971), 19–38 · T. Nash, *Collections for the history of Worcestershire*, 2 (1782), 464, 468 · R. C. Hoare, *The history of modern Wiltshire*, 1 (1822), 118 · A. Boyer, *The political state of Great Britain*, 45 (1733) · C. Jones, 'The new opposition in the House of Lords, 1720–1723', *HJ*, 36 (1993), 309–29 · letters of Thomas Foley to Robert Harley, BL, Add. MS 70227
Archives Worcs. RO, letters and papers | Herefs. RO, Foley MSS
Wealth at death wealthy; title and estate to son; £15,000 to daughter: will, PRO, PROB 11/657, sig. 89

Foley, Sir Thomas (1757–1833), naval officer, was the second of three sons of John Foley, a landowner of Ridgeway, Narberth, Pembrokeshire, a nephew of Thomas Foley, a captain in the navy, who had been round the world with

Anson in the *Centurion*. The younger Thomas entered the navy on the sloop *Otter* in 1770 and served on the Newfoundland station. By February 1774 he was serving in the West Indies on the *Antelope*, the flagship of Rear-Admiral Clark Gayton, and in the following year he was transferred to the sloop *Racehorse*, in which he was employed in the Windward passage protecting trade against American privateers.

During the American War of Independence he served on the American station. Promoted lieutenant on 25 May 1778, he took part in Keppel's action against the French fleet in July of that year. In 1779 he was given command of the frigate *San Bueno* (28 guns), a prize, and ordered to take her to Sheerness. Off Beachy Head he encountered a convoy, escorted by the brig of war *Ranger* and a small armed vessel, under attack by two French frigates. Foley immediately joined in to assist and helped drive off the frigates. Subsequently he rejoined the *Prince George* and went with her to North America in 1781, and the West Indies where he was present at both the attempted relief of St Kitts and the engagements between fleets under Sir George Rodney and De Grasse off Dominica on 9 and 12 April 1782. In December Foley was promoted commander and appointed to the *Britannia*, which cruised between New York and Quebec until 1785 when she returned to England and was paid off. From December 1787 until September 1790 he commanded the sloop *Racehorse*, cruising off the northeast coast of England. On 21 September 1790 he was promoted post captain but, not being appointed to a ship, went on half pay.

Following the outbreak of war with revolutionary France, Foley was appointed flag-captain of the *St George* (98 guns) under Rear-Admiral John Gell. *En route* to the Mediterranean to join Admiral Samuel Hood's fleet, Gell's squadron captured the French privateer *General Dumourier* and a Spanish vessel, the *San Iago*, which the privateer had taken earlier. The prizes were found to be carrying an enormously valuable cargo. When they were condemned as prizes, the squadron received the net value of £166,609, with the crews of the *Ganges* and *St George* alone sharing £42,006. When Gell was subsequently superseded by Rear-Admiral Hyde Parker, Foley continued as his flag-captain. In March 1795 the *St George* was part of Admiral William Hotham's fleet during an engagement with the French fleet off Toulon, during which two French ships of the line were captured. During that year Foley began to receive his prize money from the *Dumourier* and *San Iago*, and purchased the estate of Abermarlais Park, near Llangadog in south Wales, where he erected a new house.

In February 1797 Foley, now flag-captain to Vice-Admiral Sir Charles Thompson in the *Britannia*, took part in the battle of St Vincent, following which he was awarded a gold medal and transferred to command the *Goliath* (74 guns). In July 1797, in an attempt to provoke the Spanish fleet to leave Cadiz, Admiral John Jervis ordered the bomb-vessel *Thunderer* to moor close in shore and bombard the town. After several shots it was realized that the *Thunderer's* mortar was faulty and the vessel had to be withdrawn. As she did so a flotilla of gunboats sallied out to attack her. Foley in the *Goliath* together with the frigate *Terpsichore* (Captain Richard Bowen) sailed in to protect her, despite heavy fire from the shore.

In May 1798 the *Goliath* was sent to reinforce Horatio Nelson's fleet and on 1 August it was Foley who led the attack against the French fleet in Abu Qir Bay at what became known as the battle of the Nile. It may have been Foley's suggestion that the British ships should sail inside the anchored French fleet to attack them from the landward side, in the belief that the guns facing the shore would be unprepared. Within ten minutes the *Goliath* had shot away the masts of the *Conquerant* and by the end of the battle the *Goliath* had suffered 21 killed and 41 wounded.

Following the battle the *Goliath* continued on the Mediterranean station until the end of 1799, when she was sent home. On 6 January 1800 Foley was appointed to command the *Elephant* (74 guns) blockading Brest and Lorient, taking with him his nephew Richard as midshipman. Then, in March 1801, the *Elephant* was attached to Hyde Parker's fleet bound for the Baltic in pre-emptive operations against the Danes. Before entering the sound to advance against Copenhagen, Nelson transferred his flag to the *Elephant*, which was a lighter, more manoeuvrable ship. On the night before the battle Foley and Edward Riou dined with Nelson and spent the remainder of the night arranging the order of battle, and drawing up each ship's instructions. During the ensuing battle Nelson told Foley that he was unable to see Hyde Parker's signal ordering his squadron to disengage. Following the battle Nelson returned to the *St George* and the *Elephant* continued in the Baltic until she returned to be paid off in the autumn.

On 31 July 1802 Foley married Lady Lucy Anne *Fitzgerald (1771–1851), youngest daughter of the duke of Leinster and Lady Emily Lennox, daughter of the duke of Richmond. The couple resided mainly at Abermarlais, where they concentrated on laying out the parkland and plantations. Nelson was a regular visitor whenever they were in London and became a close friend. When, in 1803, Nelson was given command in the Mediterranean and Foley's brother Richard died, Nelson wrote to condole him saying that he would be happy to have Foley with him in the Mediterranean 'and to have frequent opportunities of personally assuring you how much I am, my dear Foley, your faithful and affectionate friend' (Herbert, 75). However, Foley was now suffering from poor health and was unable to serve.

In 1807, perhaps to ease his financial position, Foley was appointed a colonel of marines, a sinecure often awarded as a recognition of services. Then on 28 April 1808 he was promoted rear-admiral, and in March 1811 he became commander-in-chief of the Downs station, based at Deal.

In February 1814 a horseman arrived at Foley's headquarters, Walmer Castle, claiming to have urgent news of the death of Napoleon. Foley's coachman became suspicious of the messenger and Foley refused to telegraph the message, sending it by ordinary mail instead. In making this decision Foley unconsciously defeated a conspiracy to defraud the stock exchange by creating a sudden rise in the value of stocks and shares. However, another famous naval officer, Lord Cochrane, was implicated and dismissed from the navy.

On 12 April 1815, at the end of the war, Foley was made KCB and terminated his command at Deal, preferring to return to the peace of Abermarlais. Five years later he was promoted GCB and in 1830 he was appointed commander-in-chief at Portsmouth, taking up residence at Government House in Portsmouth High Street, opposite the George Hotel, where his friend Nelson had spent his last night in England.

Foley died on 9 January 1833 while in post at Government House; he was buried in the garrison chapel at Portsmouth on 16 January. The coffin in which his body was interred was made from oak saved from the *Elephant* when she was broken up. Lady Foley remained at Portsmouth until 1836 when she moved to Arundel where it was thought the climate might suit her health. However, her health declined further and in 1841 she moved to the south of France, and lived at the Château Belle Vue above Marseilles. She died there on 21 January 1851, aged eighty, leaving £1000 in her will to the Portsmouth sailors' home. The Foleys had no children.   TOM WAREHAM

Sources O'Byrne, *Naval biog. dict.* · J. Marshall, *Royal naval biography*, 1/1 (1823), 363–72 · J. B. Herbert, *The life and services of Admiral Sir Thomas Foley, GCB, rear-admiral of Great Britain* (1884) · C. Oman, *Nelson* (1950) · D. Syrett and R. L. DiNardo, *The commissioned sea officers of the Royal Navy, 1660–1815*, rev. edn, Occasional Publications of the Navy RS, 1 (1994) · *Debrett's Peerage* (1834) · correspondence of Sir Thomas Foley and his wife with Lord Holland, 1799–1839, BL, Add. MS 51803 · correspondence, 1797–1832, NMM · private information (2004)
Archives NMM, corresp., mainly relating to patronage · priv. coll., family corresp. | BL, corresp. with Lord Holland, Add. MS 51803
Likenesses W. Bromley, J. Landseer and Leney, group portrait, line engraving, pubd 1803 (after R. Smirke, *Victors of the Nile*), BM, NPG · Worthington and Parker, group portrait, line engraving, pubd 1803 (*Commemoration of 14 Feb 1797*; after R. Smirke, *Naval victories*), BM, NPG · H. Edridge, pencil-and-watercolour drawing, 1807, NPG · portrait (after W. Beechey), Hanbury Hall, Worcestershire

Folger, Peter (1617–1690), interpreter and public official in America, was born in Norwich, the son of John Folger and Meriba Gibbs. Little is known of Folger until 1635, when he and his widower father moved to Massachusetts. During the voyage Folger met Mary Morrill, an indentured servant, and apparently fell in love for he spent the next nine years of his life working as a weaver, miller, surveyor, and shoemaker to raise the £20 to buy out her contract and marry her in 1644. The couple had nine children that survived infancy. During the 1640s the family moved to Martha's Vineyard, an island settlement that was effectively ruled by the senior and junior Thomas Mayhew. There Folger began a long and prosperous career as an interpreter and cultural intermediary with the American Indian population. At the Mayhews' puritan mission he evangelized the native inhabitants and mastered Algonquian, a major Amerindian language family that would have enabled communication with the vast majority of American Indians in New England. About 1648 the younger Thomas Mayhew extended the mission to nearby Nantucket Island, part of the Mayhew proprietorship, which was home to several thousand American Indians. In 1659 Folger, who was by then familiar with the island through his missionary work, aided a group of white settlers who had purchased the island from the younger Thomas Mayhew in surveying Nantucket. That same year Folger also publicly declared himself a Baptist at a Martha's Vineyard town meeting, which undoubtedly agitated the puritan Mayhews and prompted Folger to move to the more tolerant colony of Rhode Island.

In 1663 Folger returned to Nantucket at the request of the island's proprietors in order to soothe worsening tensions with the native population that had arisen mainly from the interference of the white settlement's cattle with Amerindian crops. As an enticement he was awarded a half share in the proprietorship (full shares were reserved for families of original white settlers). Nantucket was something of an anomaly in the puritan New England context in that established religion did not gain a substantial foothold among the whites until the eighteenth century. The only churches on the island in Folger's time, therefore, were found among the American Indians. In such tolerance Folger comfortably settled his family, acted as an intermediary with the American Indians, and continued his highly successful evangelizing efforts. He also worked as a teacher, surveyor, miller, and farmer, and even served as the clerk of courts.

Folger's greatest triumph as chief diplomat to the American Indians came in 1665, when Metacom 'King Philip', arrived with a number of his warriors in pursuit of John Gibbs. Gibbs, an Amerindian from Nantucket who had recently finished his studies at Harvard, had insulted the powerful Pokanoket sachem by publicly speaking his father's name, Massasoit, which was an offence punishable by death. Gibbs was most likely a close friend of Folger, who had baptized the American Indian and given him the Christian name John Gibbs, which was the name of Folger's maternal grandfather. Neither the Amerindian nor the white population (about 100 people) was in a position to thwart Metacom through force, but Folger intervened to save Gibbs, offering his pursuer a ransom in exchange for Gibbs's life. Metacom agreed, but the people of Nantucket were only able to raise £11—significantly less than he wanted. An angry Metacom threatened to destroy the settlement, but the islanders called his bluff, threatening to attack him unless he departed, which he promptly did. A decade later Metacom led a coalition of Amerindians against New England in what became known as King Philip's War. The brutal fighting saw extensive slaughter and murder on both sides, but did not touch Nantucket.

Folger died on Nantucket Island in 1690. He was survived by a substantial family that would produce a number of prominent American scientists, merchants, and politicians, the most famous of whom was Benjamin *Franklin, Folger's grandson.   TROY O. BICKHAM

Sources N. Philbrick, *Away off shore: Nantucket Island and its people, 1602–1890* (1994) · E. Byers, *The nation of Nantucket: society and politics in an early American commercial center, 1660–1820* (1987) · S. F. Beegel,

'Folger, Peter', *ANB* • B. Franklin, *The autobiography of Benjamin Franklin*, ed. L. W. Labaree, R. L. Ketcham, H. C. Boatfield, and H. H. Fineman (1964) • F. B. Anderson, *A grandfather for Benjamin Franklin* (1940)

Wealth at death substantial property on Nantucket

Foli, Allan James [*real name* Allan James Foley] (1835–1899), singer, was born Allan James Foley on 7 August 1835 at Cahir, co. Tipperary. After working as a carpenter he went to America, where he sang in church choirs, then studied in Naples with Bisaccia. He made his début as Elmiro in Rossini's *Otello* in Catania in December 1862, going on to sing in Turin, Modena, Milan, and, in 1864, at the Théâtre Italien in Paris. In 1865 he joined Mapleson's company at Her Majesty's Theatre, singing Saint-Bris in Meyerbeer's *Les Huguenots* (17 April), the Second Priest in *The Magic Flute* (6 July), and the Hermit in *Der Freischütz* (28 October). He appeared at Drury Lane and Covent Garden until 1887, performing at least sixty roles: these included Daland in the first English performance of Wagner's *Der fliegende Holländer* in 1870. He was also much in demand in oratorio and at festivals. His oratorio début was on 25 April 1866 in Handel's *Israel in Egypt* at the National Choral Society, singing the duet 'The Lord is a man of war' with Charles Santley, though his first real success came with a performance of Haydn's *The Creation* at the Sacred Harmonic Society. His festival appearances included roles at Norwich (1869), Birmingham (1870), and Gloucester (1871). He also sang Jacob in the first performance of George Macfarren's *Joseph* at the Leeds Festival on 21 September 1877 and Herod in the first English performances of Berlioz's *L'enfance du Christ* in Manchester under Hallé on 30 December 1880 and in London on 26 February 1881. In Russia he sang Caspar (*Der Freischütz*), Rossini's *Mosè* and Pietro in Auber's *La muette de Portici* with great success; he also visited Vienna and toured America. In 1892 he toured South Africa, and in 1893 Australia, and in 1896 he sang again in London. He was a popular ballad singer, and for this repertory he billed himself as Signor Foli; his operatic and concert appearances were as A. J. Foli. His voice was described as 'a rich powerful bass of more than two octaves from E below the line to F' (Grove, *Dict. mus.*, 1st edn). Bernard Shaw, however, complained of his poor articulation. He died at the Royal Hotel, Southport, on 20 October 1899. JOHN WARRACK

Sources Grove, *Dict. mus.* • *The Mapleson memoirs: the career of an operatic impresario, 1858–1888*, ed. H. Rosenthal (1966) • H. Rosenthal, *Two centuries of opera at Covent Garden* (1958) • Brown & Stratton, *Brit. mus.*

Likenesses portrait, repro. in *ILN* (1899)

Wealth at death £1690 4s. 8d.: probate, 15 March 1900, *CGPLA Eng. & Wales*

Foliot, Gilbert (*c*.1110–1187), Benedictine monk and bishop of London, was the son of Agnes de Chesney, sister of Robert de Chesney, bishop of Lincoln, 1148–66, and her husband, who was possibly Robert Foliot, steward of David I, king of Scots, when David was earl of Huntingdon.

Family, youth, and education The identification of his father has been challenged, but Gilbert was undoubtedly

Gilbert Foliot (*c*.1110–1187), seal

related to this and other branches of the Foliot family, which may have sprung from the Cotentin, and was established in England before 1100. Gilbert's mother was probably a daughter of Roger de Chesney (from Le Quesnay, Seine-Maritime, Normandy) and Alice de Langetot, whose father, Ralph de Langetot, was a Domesday tenant under Walter Giffard in 1086. Gilbert was also related to Miles, constable of Gloucester and earl of Hereford (*d*. 1143), to the two Richards de Belmeis (of Beaumais-sur-Dives, Calvados, Normandy), bishops of London (1108–27, 1152–62), and to Richard of Ilchester, a Somerset man who ended his life as bishop of Winchester. Although the exact pattern of relationships cannot be established, he was certainly one of a very large extended family, with cousins spread far and wide over the Anglo-Norman world. Miles helped him to his first major office, as abbot of Gloucester (1139), and his Belmeis relatives doubtless smoothed his path to London in 1163. In his turn he helped his many clerical relatives to canonries and dignities at Hereford and London.

In early life Foliot acquired considerable expertise in the liberal arts, especially (it seems) in rhetoric, and in Roman law and theology. It is not certain where he acquired his learning: nothing further is known of his early teachers, Master Adam and Ranulf de Turri, than their names. But it has been conjectured that he studied Roman law in Bologna and theology in the cathedral school at Exeter; it is reasonably certain that he was a pupil of Master Robert Pullen, who taught in Paris, Exeter, and perhaps in Oxford—probably in Exeter in the 1120s, when Foliot is most likely to have sat at his feet.

In witness of Foliot's learning there have survived a large collection of letters—between 250 and 300: the figure is imprecise because the borderline between letters and *acta* or charters is hard to define; letters and charters combined bring the total to nearly 500, including many letters of business and some of friendship; often the two were combined. He was also the author of sermons, and commentaries on the Song of Songs and the paternoster, which survive; and other biblical commentaries which have perished.

Abbot of Gloucester Foliot's career in the schools lasted long enough for him to be called, when abbot of Gloucester, a 'master of scholars' as well as 'father of monks' by one Odo, author of a theological tract (Morey and Brooke, *Gilbert Foliot and his Letters*, 53–4 and note). Yet he was still a young man when he became a monk at Cluny, perhaps about 1130. Thereafter promotion came rapidly: he was soon one of the priors of Cluny, then prior of the Cluniac house at Abbeville; and in 1139 he became abbot of the Benedictine house of St Peter at Gloucester—now Gloucester Cathedral. This is a largely Romanesque structure, much of it earlier than Foliot's time, and it is not certain whether any of it was built during his abbacy. He was personally ascetic in manner of life; but it may be presumed that the young man to whom Cluny herself had been so attractive admired also the grandeur of Gloucester—and perhaps contributed to it. Gloucester had had a good reputation for monastic observance since the days of the first Norman abbot, Serlo and this it retained under Foliot. But it had also acquired wide territories and a number of dependent houses not only in its own region but deep into Wales; and the breakdown of authority in Stephen's reign set the energetic young abbot many problems. A long-standing dispute with the archbishops of York over possession of a group of manors was resolved with the aid of some remarkable forgeries. There are strong grounds for believing Foliot to have been implicated in the forgery—an activity notoriously common in English Benedictine houses in this period.

Foliot became abbot in the same year in which the Empress Matilda landed in England, under the protection of her half-brother Robert, earl of Gloucester, illegitimate son of Henry I. Foliot was fervent in her cause in the early and mid-1140s. His letter no. 26, to a leading lay supporter of the empress, Brian fitz Count, lord of Wallingford, is the most elaborate manifesto which survives of the issues between Matilda and Stephen, and of exceptional interest for the arguments in political theology in the empress's favour. One strand of the entangled issues was the question of whether a woman could succeed.

> Let us hear what the divine law answers to this. In the Book of Numbers, the last chapter, you will find a passage which we have often heard the earl of Gloucester bring to our attention: Zelophehad was a Jew of the tribe of Manasseh, who had daughters but no son.   (Morey and Brooke, *Gilbert Foliot and his Letters*, 116)

Bishop of Hereford Until the empress's withdrawal from England in 1148, it was a divided country; and the political involvement of King Stephen's brother, Henry de Blois, bishop of Winchester (*d.* 1171), tended to enhance the divisions by extending them to the church. But it is evident that Theobald, former abbot of Bec, after he became archbishop of Canterbury in 1139, set himself to preside over a united English church. Although his attempt to win back primacy over York was ultimately unsuccessful, in his own province, in spite of great difficulties, he secured a substantial measure of unity and prestige. Gloucester's

extensive lands and connections in the west of England—in the region owing allegiance to the empress—made its abbot an important power in the politics as well as the religious life of the region. In the 1140s Foliot rapidly won the attention and friendship of Theobald, and became a major ally: he helped Theobald to keep in communication with, and some measure of influence over, the regions that owed allegiance to the empress.

In 1148 Foliot had his reward. 'Gilbert, abbot of Gloucester, was elected [*electus*] bishop of Hereford by the advice and direction of the archbishop of Canterbury' (Morey and Brooke, *Gilbert Foliot and his Letters*, 96). This was a period of great tension between Theobald and Stephen, and Foliot was consecrated overseas, at St Omer, by Theobald and a group of French bishops, on the pope's orders, on 5 September 1148. By now Matilda's claims had fallen to her son, the future Henry II, who tried to secure an oath of allegiance from Foliot. The matter has been disputed, but it seems most probable that Foliot stopped short of an oath—and proceeded, on the archbishop's instructions, to do fealty to Stephen, as part of the archbishop's measures towards peace. This brought difficulties with Prince Henry, which were eventually smoothed over, and Foliot was to rise high in Henry II's favour after Henry became king in 1154.

Bishop of London: the beginnings of the Becket dispute In April 1161 Theobald died; and Thomas *Becket, who had been close to both king and archbishop—as royal chancellor and archdeacon of Canterbury—was chosen by the king to succeed him. After a surprisingly long interval the royal messengers reached Canterbury in May 1162 with instructions to see Becket elected. The monks complied, and at a meeting soon after in London, the bishops joined in confirming the election, Gilbert Foliot alone (according to the sources) objecting. He was thought to covet the office himself; he certainly had grounds for thinking Becket a worldly and unworthy successor to Theobald. Becket was duly consecrated; and he and the king evidently felt that some compensation was owed to Foliot. His reward was the see of London. The chapter of St Paul's contained many of his relatives, and the whole chapter was, so Ralph de Diceto records, in favour of his election. Diceto was himself a canon and archdeacon, and later dean. Canon law and custom were still opposed to the translation of bishops, and papal approval was needed. He was postulated in the king's presence on 6 March 1163, and Pope Alexander III, then in Paris, confirmed and gave dispensation for him to be translated on 19 March; on 28 April he was enthroned in St Paul's Cathedral—and he remained bishop of London until his death in 1187.

Henry II had need of Foliot: Becket was not proving the compliant archbishop he had looked for, and the pope and the king saw Foliot as a potential mediator. In 1163 he evidently stood high with pope, king, and archbishop alike, and at the height of his prestige. Something of this he was to forfeit by persistent and eloquent opposition to Becket. In one sense he was a moderating influence. He had accepted the royal statement of customs, the constitutions of Clarendon, in 1164—as had Becket himself—

but he acted as a check on the king's efforts to enforce the more radical of them; in particular the attempt to curb appeals to Rome foundered on Foliot's own insistence on appealing to the pope in the cause against Becket. There were even moments when Henry bared his teeth on Foliot. But most of the time they valued each other's support too much to quarrel. After Becket fled into exile late in 1164, Foliot was one of the chief spokesmen before the pope at Sens in Henry's first attempt to have the archbishop deposed; Foliot's excessive advocacy won only a sharp rebuke from Alexander.

Leading the opposition to Becket Through the years that followed Foliot was the leader, with Roger de Pont l'Évêque, archbishop of York, of those bishops who were steadfast in opposition to Becket, and he reckoned to be safe from the archbishop's censures only by constant appeals to the pope against Becket's past and future actions. But in 1168 the pope at last freed Becket from this restraint—though still hoping that the endless negotiations would bring peace. On Palm Sunday, 13 April 1169, at Clairvaux, Becket solemnly excommunicated Foliot, and the bishop of Salisbury and others, for their contumacious resistance to the archbishop's will and commands. At first Foliot attempted to ignore or circumvent the ban. But on Ascension day, 29 May 1169, a brave messenger delivered the letter of excommunication on the high altar of St Paul's, and Foliot could ignore it no longer. After some months of negotiation with legates in the north of France, he set off for Rome at the turn of the year in search of absolution, choosing to go via Montpellier and St Gilles to avoid the threat of danger in Burgundy, and on to Milan. There he was informed that the archbishop of Rouen and the bishop of Exeter had been commissioned by the pope to absolve him; and so he set off north again. At Rouen on Easter day (5 April) 1170 he was duly absolved.

But Foliot showed how little his attitude to Becket had changed by joining the archbishop of York and others in crowning the young king Henry, Henry II's son, on 14 June. This treasured scheme of the old king was carried through against fervent opposition from Becket—who saw it as a flagrant breach of the privileges of Canterbury—supported by the pope. In September the pope became fully aware of the facts of the coronation, and excommunicated the bishops of London and Salisbury, and suspended the archbishop of York. But meanwhile Henry II had patched up a peace with Becket, and the archbishop was due to return to England. On the day before he set sail he forwarded the letter of excommunication to Foliot, and this provocative act (as it was reckoned by the king and the English bishops who fell under the ban) provided the worst of omens for the archbishop's reception in England. Henry II was himself in Normandy, and the news of Becket's measures, brought by the excommunicate bishops, and of his activities in England, roused Henry's fiercest anger. It was this anger that inspired the four barons to set off to Canterbury, where, on 29 December 1170, they murdered the archbishop.

Foliot's intellectual armoury The aftermath of the murder was perhaps the lowest point of Foliot's fortunes: although he was formally relieved of excommunication, he had to recognize the growing cult of his old rival—even to the point of asking for the martyr's help in a dangerous illness about the time of his absolution.

In the course of his disputes with Becket, Foliot tried to wield three particular weapons against the archbishop. It had been the original intention of Pope Gregory the Great (r. 590–604), in sending the mission of St Augustine, to make London the centre of the southern province, as one or two of Foliot's predecessors had reminded the archbishops of their day. Foliot made the strongest attempt to revive the claim that at least the bishop of London should be an archbishop, or perhaps even replace Canterbury as primate—a claim which won him few friends at the time and made little headway. In his efforts to ward off any sentence the archbishop might try to launch against him, he developed the technique of the appeal *ad cautelam*—against the archbishop's future actions. His enemies laughed him to scorn; but the pope did not challenge the principle, and may even (within limits) have welcomed any move which helped to check the archbishop's more extreme measures. Foliot's third weapon was rhetoric: in a series of letters in 1166 he laid out the case against Becket's actions with vigour and venom. Two of the letters, to the pope and to Becket, were written in the name of the English bishops and clergy at large (*Letters and Charters of Gilbert Foliot*, nos. 166–7). John of Salisbury's verdict that they were drafted by Foliot is probably correct—he reckoned nothing more likely 'than that it [the letter of Becket] was dictated by counsel of Achitophel … and written by the hand of Doeg the Edomite'—one or both of whom represented Gilbert (John of Salisbury, *Letters*, 2.152–3). To Becket's personal rebuke in response to this, Foliot's letter *Multiplicem nobis* of late 1166 was a shattering rejoinder (*Letters and Charters of Gilbert Foliot*, no. 170). Once commonly regarded as a forgery, it is full of special pleading and sets every event in the most unsympathetic possible light; but the twists and turns of Becket's career left him open to attack, and many or most of the facts were probably correctly stated. As to whether Becket or Foliot suffers more in the reading of it, scholars have differed; it can hardly be doubted that it was the work of an angry, unforgiving man.

Foliot as diocesan Foliot, meanwhile, had been for many years an active and conscientious diocesan bishop. Over 60 *acta* survive from his period as bishop of Hereford (1148–63), and about 150 from his London episcopate (1164–87), which makes him perhaps the most prolific bishop of the mid-twelfth century after Theobald. He evidently took a serious interest in many aspects of diocesan administration: he was active in the affairs of the cathedral chapters, in fostering the religious houses of his two sees—a natural activity for a monk turned bishop—and in keeping in touch with his archdeacons and rural deans. His involvement in the chapters and in his archdeacons was not wholly disinterested: Foliots were to flourish at Hereford for seventy years after his departure, and the only archdeacon he appointed there was one of them. All the archdeacons he appointed in London were his nephews or somehow related to him—and there were other relatives, probably many of them, at St Paul's. But he took pains to ensure sound training for these men: two of them at least he sent to Bologna to study canon law under the eye of Master David of London (d. 1189), the most considerable canonist in Foliot's household. He clearly expected his archdeacons to be professionals: they included no persistent absentees.

Foliot's interest in Bologna and his patronage of Master David may have sprung partly from his own early training—doubtless also in part from his appreciation of the greatly enhanced role of canon law in the life and ordering of the church in his time. He was in some demand as a papal judge-delegate throughout his middle and later years. In the 1170s his colleagues Roger, bishop of Worcester (1164–79), and Bartholomew, bishop of Exeter (1161–84), were the leaders in this field in the English church; and it was perhaps partly for that reason that Master David transferred his allegiance from Foliot to Roger. In his early years Foliot had been recognized as an authority on Roman law and its application to the procedures of the canon law courts; as canon law itself matured he seems to have been a little left behind—but he was active in church courts until near the end of his life.

Death and reputation Gilbert Foliot died, aged perhaps about eighty, on 18 February 1187. Any final judgement on him must comprehend an array of qualities and activities not easily reconciled. He was a scholar and a monk, much admired as a leader among monks and as diocesan bishop; yet he played his part in the fashionable monastic forgery of his day, and in his dispute with Thomas Becket he showed every quality except charity. However, the satirist Walter Map, who had enjoyed Foliot's patronage and passed on to higher things, spoke with a respect and affection rare in his work of the old bishop in the 1180s, blind yet still actively at work on his biblical studies. 'No longer with your bodily eyes, but with such as angels use to see the Lord, may you view and contemplate him and his works' (Map, 312–15).   C. N. L. BROOKE

Sources *Letters and charters of Gilbert Foliot*, ed. A. Morey and others (1967) · A. Morey and C. N. L. Brooke, *Gilbert Foliot and his letters* (1965) · D. Knowles, *The episcopal colleagues of Archbishop Thomas Becket* (1951), 37–49, 115–27, and *passim* · D. Knowles, *The monastic order in England*, 2nd edn (1963), 293–6 · J. Barrow, ed., *Hereford, 1079–1234*, English Episcopal Acta, 7 (1993), xl–xli, 54–76 · F. Neininger, ed., *London, 1076–1187*, English Episcopal Acta, 15 (1999) · D. N. Bell, 'The commentary on the Lord's prayer of Gilbert Foliot', *Recherches de Théologie Ancienne et Médiévale*, 56 (1989), 80–101 · G. Foliot, *Expositio in cantico canticorum*, ed. P. Junius (London, 1638); repr. as G. Foliot, 'Expositio in cantica canticorum', *Patrologia Latina*, 202 (1855), 1147–1304 · *The letters of John of Salisbury*, ed. and trans. H. E. Butler and W. J. Millor, rev. C. N. L. Brooke, OMT, 2: *The later letters, 1163–1180* (1979), esp. nos. 173–5, 187, 236, 292, 295, 304 [Lat. orig. with parallel Eng. text] · *The Historia pontificalis of John of Salisbury*, ed. and trans. M. Chibnall, rev. edn, OMT (1986), 47–9 · W. Map, *De nugis curialium / Courtiers' trifles*, ed. and trans. M. R. James, rev. C. N. L. Brooke and R. A. B. Mynors, OMT (1983), 36–7, 80–81, 202–3, 312–15 · F. Barlow, *Thomas Becket* (1986) · *Fasti Angl., 1066–1300*, [St Paul's, London] · *Radulfi de Diceto … opera historica*, ed. W. Stubbs, 2 vols., Rolls Series, 68 (1876) · C. Clay, review of *Gilbert Foliot and his letters*, *Antiquaries Journal*, 47 (1967), 124–5 · Odo, 'Ysagoge', *Écrits théologiques de l'école d'Abélard*, ed. A. Landgraf (Louvain, 1934), 61–298 [esp. 287–9]
Archives Bodl. Oxf., corresp. [copies]
Likenesses seal, BL; Birch, *Seals*, 1901 [*see illus.*]

Foliot, Robert (d. 1186), bishop of Hereford, was of uncertain origins. He was related to Gilbert Foliot, successively bishop of Hereford and of London, though the exact degree of kinship is unclear; Robert's immediate family may have been the line of Foliots who held Warpsgrove in Oxfordshire, since he confirmed a grant by Ralph Foliot of Warpsgrove of land there to his son, suggesting that he might have been Ralph's brother or uncle. It is probable that he received a good education, but there is no evidence of where he studied, and Bale's attributions to Robert of various scholarly works are misplaced, Foliot having been confused with his predecessor as bishop of Hereford, Robert de Melun.

Robert Foliot owed his early promotion to Bishop Alexander of Lincoln, who made him a canon of Lincoln Cathedral at some point before 1142. After Alexander's death in February 1148, when Bishop Henry of Winchester was trying to secure the election of one of his nephews to the vacant see, Lincoln Cathedral chapter sent Robert to the Council of Rheims in April 1148 to receive instructions from Pope Eugenius III (r. 1145–53) as to the episcopal succession: Eugenius blocked Henry's wishes. The successor was the chapter's own choice, Robert de Chesney, who made Foliot one of his clerks and then, before January 1152, archdeacon of Oxford. This office would have opened excellent opportunities for acquiring expertise in canon law, for Oxford, being easy of access, was one of the places most often chosen to hear serious ecclesiastical disputes. Doubtless it was legal expertise that led Thomas Becket to choose Foliot as one of his circle of *eruditi* ('men of learning') once he became archbishop in 1162. In this position Foliot acted as mediator between his kinsman Gilbert Foliot and his patron. Later Gilbert repaid him by urging his election to the see of Hereford in 1173, when Henry II, having made peace with the church, had to fill several vacant bishoprics, among them Hereford. Robert was elected after Easter 1173, but was not consecrated until 6 October 1174. He occurs holding a prebend at Hereford Cathedral in 1173, but it is not certain whether he had acquired this while Gilbert was still bishop of Hereford (1148–63), or through royal patronage during the seven-year vacancy of the see (1167–74).

The public occasions that Robert Foliot is known to have attended are mostly ecclesiastical. Much of his time was taken up with papal commissions—he is known to have received about forty papal mandates and letters of advice. He was also one of only four English bishops to attend the Third Lateran Council in 1179. The letters of advice, which would have been elicited by specific queries on his part, show that he was seriously worried about how he could eliminate clerical marriage in his diocese without alienating too many of his clergy in the process; several of the cathedral clergy were married, including at least one of Foliot's own relatives. He obtained Alexander III's approval for not proceeding against priests already married, on the grounds that the people in the diocese were 'barbarous', but for combating instead clerical concubinage and the practice of priests passing on churches to their sons. He was also concerned with the need to protect the burial rights of parish churches against the hospitallers (evidently the newly founded house at Dinmore in Herefordshire). Burial disputes between parish churches occur frequently in Foliot's charters, showing how old minster parishes in his diocese were steadily being subdivided. Nearly forty of Foliot's charters survive; the collection as a whole shows that he employed a sizeable body of household clerks to assist him, and that they were developing different types of document for particular purposes.

Robert Foliot had a taste for fine objects, manifested in his choice of secret seal—an antique gem—and also in his gifts to churches; he gave a purple and gold cape to the Augustinian canons of Wigmore Abbey when he dedicated their new church in 1179, and many gifts, including a church on one of the episcopal manors, books and altar vessels, to his cathedral chapter. Furthermore, he must have commissioned the fine timber hall that survives in the episcopal palace at Hereford, and whose construction can be dated on dendrochronological evidence to 1179. He died on 9 May 1186, perhaps after a long illness, for he had a physician in his household while he was bishop. He was buried in Hereford Cathedral.   JULIA BARROW

Sources J. Barrow, ed., *Hereford, 1079–1234*, English Episcopal Acta, 7 (1993), 42–3, 54–6, 72, 80–88, 104–5, 111–12, 115, nos. 82–126, 314–15 · J. Barrow, 'Hereford bishops and married clergy', *Historical Research*, 60 (1987), 1–8 · A. Morey and C. N. L. Brooke, *Gilbert Foliot and his letters* (1965), 44–5, 70, 199, 270 · *Fasti Angl., 1066–1300*, [Lincoln], 35, 74 · *Letters and charters of Gilbert Foliot*, ed. A. Morey and others (1967), nos. 75, 204, 224 · J. C. Robertson and J. B. Sheppard, eds., *Materials for the history of Thomas Becket, archbishop of Canterbury*, 7 vols., Rolls Series, 67 (1875–85), vol. 3, pp. 46, 524; vol. 6, 607–10 · M. G. Cheney, *Roger, bishop of Worcester, 1164–1179* (1980), 73, 95, 129, 131–2, 142, 205, 222, 247, 261, 274, 288–92, 296, 303, 343, 351, 355, 361, 363, 367, 370–1, 373 · D. Haddon-Rees, D. Miles, and J. Munby, 'Tree-ring dates', *Vernacular Architecture*, 20 (1989), 46–7 · J. Blair, 'The twelfth century bishop's palace at Hereford', *Medieval Archaeology*, 31 (1987), 59–72 · *Fasti Angl., 1066–1300*, [Hereford], 4, 120 · *Ann. mon.*, 1.53; 4.385 · Dugdale, *Monasticon*, new edn, 6.344–7 · *Radulfi de Diceto ... opera historica*, ed. W. Stubbs, 1: 1148–79, Rolls Series, 68 (1876), 392 · R. W. Eyton, *Court, household, and itinerary of King Henry II* (1878), 175

Archives Bodl. Oxf., corresp. [copies]

Folkes, Martin (1690–1754), antiquary and natural philosopher, was born on 29 October 1690 in Queen Street in the parish of St Giles-in-the-Fields, Westminster, the elder of two sons of Martin Folkes (*d.* 1705), one of the benchers of Gray's Inn, and his wife, Dorothy, second daughter of Sir William Hovell of Hillington Hall, near Lynn in Norfolk. His mother's older sister Etheldreda married William Wake, who later became archbishop of Canterbury. Martin was educated privately for seven years by James Cappel, who had been professor of Hebrew at Saumur University until its suppression in 1695. The belief that Folkes himself was a student there as has been variously suggested is a mistake. Shortly after the death of his father

Martin Folkes (1690–1754), by William Hogarth, 1741

in February 1705 he was sent to Clare College, Cambridge, where he was admitted in July 1706. He inherited a substantial estate from his father, estimated by his friend William Stukeley to be worth nearly £3000. This wealth allowed him to live an easy life of leisure and study from a young age. In December 1713, apparently while still a student, he was proposed as a candidate to become a fellow of the Royal Society. According to obituary notes made by the society's secretary, Thomas Birch,

> The progress he made there [at Cambridge], & after he left the University, in all parts of Learning, & particularly Mathematical & Philosophical, distinguish'd him at so early an age, that when he was but three & twenty years old, he was ... worthy of a seat in the Royal Society.   (BL, Add. MS 4222, fol. 22r–v)

He was soon elected to the society's council and in January 1723 was appointed as a vice-president; the president at that time was Sir Isaac Newton. Folkes made various communications to the society, largely on astronomical subjects, and a number were published in the *Philosophical Transactions*; he also gave advice to Robert Smith FRS, Plumeian professor of astronomy at Cambridge University, in his *A Compleat System of Opticks in Four Books* (1738) and is acknowledged there for his 'curious remarks' on vision, astronomy, and optics. On 17 February 1720 he was elected to the Society of Antiquaries, and was a member of the Spalding Gentlemen's Society, then one of the liveliest groups exchanging information on and contemplating the progress of the sciences. He was also a freemason, and became a deputy grand master by 1725.

Folkes's wife, whom he married on 18 October 1714 at St Helen's, Bishopsgate, was the actress **Lucretia Bradshaw** (*d. c.*1755). Supposedly the daughter of a Drury Lane box-keeper, she first appeared on the stage as early as 1696, but her career took off in 1706, when she appeared as Mrs Bradshaw at the new Queen's Theatre in the Haymarket. Playing both comic and tragic roles, she was hailed as the successor to Mrs Barry, and migrated from the Queen's Theatre to Drury Lane from 1707, and appeared there again from November 1710 to 1713. According to a short 'history of the English stage' published in 1741, 'It was the opinion of a very good Judge of Dramatical Performers' that she 'was one of the greatest, and most promising *Genij* of her Time'. The same source recorded that she 'was taken off the Stage, for her exemplary and prudent Conduct, by *Martin Folkes*, Esq; a Gentleman of a very considerable Estate, who married her; and such has been her Behaviour to him, that there is not a more happy Couple' (*The History of the English Stage*, 62). Stukeley (who in error called her Mrs Bracegirdle, confusing her with another contemporary actress, Anne Bracegirdle) wrote that Folkes's mother 'grievd' at this match 'so much that she threw her self out of a window & broke her arm' (*Family Memoirs*, 1.99–100). They had two daughters, Dorothy and Lucretia, and a son, Martin, who while a student at the academy in Caen, Normandy, died in 1740 following a fall from his horse.

On Newton's death in 1727 Folkes participated in a heated contest for the presidency with the other vice-president, Sir Hans Sloane, which he lost, and was dismissed from the society's committee. James Jurin, the society's secretary and a supporter of Folkes's candidature, addressed the thirty-fourth volume of the *Philosophical Transactions* to him, concluding his dedication with the observation, 'It is sufficient to say of him, that he was Sir Isaac Newton's Friend' (Nichols, *Lit. anecdotes*, 2.580). Sloane subsequently appointed Folkes as one of his vice-presidents on 8 February 1733. But Stukeley directly associated Folkes's defeat with his decision in March 1733 to leave with his family for a tour of Germany and Italy, and he spent some time in Venice, Rome, and Florence. Stukeley noted that while in Rome Lucretia Folkes 'grew religiously mad' (*Family Memoirs*, 1.99–100). After their return to England in September 1735, she was confined to a lunatic asylum in Chelsea. After his tour Folkes's interests took an increasingly antiquarian turn. By examining various collections in Italy he was able to write 'an excellent Dissertation on the Weights & Values of the antient Coins' (BL, Add. MS 4222, fol. 24) which was read at the Society of Antiquaries, as well as papers on the Trajan and Antonine columns in Rome. He became a member of the short-lived Egyptian Society, which met in London between 1741 and 1743, and sponsored the publication of plates of Egyptian antiquities by the Danish explorer Frederick Ludvig Norden. He published at his own expense *A Table of English Silver Coins from the 18th Year of King Edward III* (1736) and *A Table of English Silver Coins from the Norman Conquest to the Present Time* (1745). Nevertheless, he continued to retain an interest in scientific subjects. At a Royal Society council meeting on 10 November 1736 it was Folkes who proposed that the interest from Sir Godfrey Copley's £100 donation

of 1709 should be converted 'into a Medal or other honorary Prize … by which means he apprehended a laudable emulation might be excited among men of genius to try their inventions, who in all probability may never be moved for the sake of lucre' (Lyons, 172). When news of Abraham Trembley's discovery of the freshwater polypus reached Britain, Folkes made his own studies in microscopy, which were published in *Philosophical Transactions*.

As Folkes had not visited France on his first European tour, he travelled with his son to Paris in May 1739, 'chiefly with a view of seeing the Academies there, and conversing with the learned men' (BL, Add. MS 4222, fols. 25–6). When Sloane resigned his position as president of the Royal Society for health reasons in 1741, Folkes was unanimously chosen to succeed him, and shortly afterwards donated £100 as a gift. Following the death of Edmond Halley in January 1742 he was elected a foreign fellow of the Académie Royale des Sciences in Paris. Various other honours followed: in July 1746 Oxford University conferred on him the degree of doctor of laws, and shortly afterwards Cambridge did likewise.

In 1743 a number of fellows established the Club of the Royal Philosophers (known from 1795 as the Royal Society Club), an exclusive dining society that met at the Mitre tavern on Thursday evenings. The practice of dining before or after society meetings had a long tradition but this was the first time it was formalized; in 1747 Folkes became the club's first recorded president. On the death of his friend Charles Lennox, duke of Richmond, Lennox, and Aubigny, in August 1750 Folkes was unanimously elected on 22 November to succeed him as president of the Society of Antiquaries, a position he held until his own death in 1754. As president, he led the petition to the king for the society to receive a royal charter, which would allow the society, which at that stage was only a voluntary body, to hold property in perpetuity and to receive benefactions. Acquiring the charter, though, would be an expensive judicial process; an alternative would have been integration into the Royal Society. A conflict arose in which Folkes was accused by several antiquarians of instigating a Royal Society plot when trying to incorporate them. These principal critics were George North, Ducarel, and George Vertue. On 15 March 1751 Vertue wrote to North complaining that the president and other 'Royal Society schemers' were leading the campaign for incorporation with the aim of lining their own pockets (Nichols, *Lit. anecdotes*, 2.712). Incorporation was granted by the king in November 1751, and it is only after this date that members of the Society of Antiquaries may be termed fellows. Nothing survives to reveal Folkes's own attitude to these divisions within the Society of Antiquaries and it is unknown whether he genuinely wanted to unite the two societies. Given the time and space he allowed to antiquarian matters in the Royal Society, it might have made sense. The only indication of his feelings is posthumous. In his will he bequeathed £100 to the Royal Society, together with a seal and a portrait of Francis Bacon. But Nichols subsequently noted, 'It has been thought somewhat singular, that this gentleman, who at the time of his death was President of the Society of Antiquaries, should not have left them the smallest token of his regard' (Nichols, *Lit. anecdotes*, 2.589–90).

Folkes's religious views verged on deism, if not actually atheism. In 1747 he explained to his friend da Costa, who was Jewish, that 'we are all citizens of the world, and see different customs and tastes without dislike or prejudice, as we do different names and colours' (Nichols, *Lit. anecdotes*, 5.635). William Stukeley later described him as

> In matters of religion an errant infidel & loud scoffer. Professes himself a godf[athe]r to all monkeys, believes nothing of a future state, of the Scriptures, of revelation … He thinks there is no difference between us & animals; but what is owing to the different structure of our brain, as between man & man.   (*Family Memoirs*, 1.99–100)

Folkes's presidency of the Royal Society had other critics, by far the most tenacious of whom was his former friend the polymath writer John Hill, who attacked Folkes in his *A Dissertation on Royal Societies* (1750) and *A Review of the Works of the Royal Society* (1751). Hill described Folkes as

> upon the whole … a Man of great Abilities in many Branches of Knowledge, but unluckily in no one that has any Connection with, or Relation to, the Business of the Royal Society; indeed, that he is utterly unacquainted with all the Sciences in which his Office in this Body requires a discerning and critical Judgment. (J. Hill, *A Dissertation on Royal Societies*, 35–6)

The period after his retirement from the Royal Society certainly saw a number of necessary procedural reforms, particularly of the *Philosophical Transactions*.

However, by this stage Folkes's health was failing. At a meeting of the Society of Antiquaries some time in autumn 1750 George Vertue noted that Folkes, 'lately not been very well in health[,] appeard to be heavy & low spirited much different from his usuall looks'. Vertue thought that this might have been 'occasiond by reflection of the loss of his good & noble Friends lately. Earl of Pembroke [,] the Duke of Montague & lastly the Duke of Richmond— these were noble worthy Friends … such as gave life & spirit to his Studies his amusements and conversation' (BL, Add. MS 23096, fol. 23v). According to Thomas Birch's account, on 26 September 1751 Folkes was 'seiz'd … with a Palsy, which depriv'd him of the use of his left side' (BL, Add. MS 4222, fol. 30r), which prevented him from presiding in person either at the Society of Antiquaries or the Royal Society. He resigned the presidency of the Royal Society on 30 November 1753 and never regained his health. He died after a second attack of 'palsy' at 4 a.m. on 28 June 1754 at his home in Ormond Street. He instructed before his death that his papers should be destroyed, and this was duly enacted. The published posthumous accounts of his life are politely positive in their accounts of his intellectual achievements and contributions to the republic of letters. According to Birch's posthumous assessment, 'The Generosity of his Temper was no less remarkable than the Civility & Vivacity of his Conversation' (BL, Add. MS 4222, fol. 32).

In appearance Folkes was a large man, and if Hill's satirical attacks are to be believed, he was often more interested in food than natural philosophy; Stukeley records

that he lost his teeth, and 'he speaks so as not to be understood' (*Family Memoirs*, 1.99). He was buried in the chancel of Hillington church, Norfolk, and in 1792 a memorial to him was erected on the south side of the choir in Westminster Abbey. His widow, who had never recovered her sanity, and was still living in the Chelsea asylum, was bequeathed an annuity of £400 for life in Folkes's will, and died *c*.1755.   DAVID BOYD HAYCOCK

Sources BL, Add. MS 4222, fols. 22–56v · D. B. Haycock, '"The cabal of a few designing members": the presidency of Martin Folkes, PRS, and the society's first charter', *Antiquaries Journal*, 80 (2000), 273–84 · G. S. Rousseau and D. A. B. Haycock, 'Voices calling for reform: the Royal Society in the mid-eighteenth century, Martin Folkes, John Hill, and William Stukeley', *History of Science*, 37 (1999), 377–406 · *The family memoirs of the Rev. William Stukeley*, ed. W. C. Lukis, 3 vols., SurtS, 73, 76, 80 (1882–7) · Nichols, *Lit. anecdotes* · H. Lyons, *The Royal Society, 1660–1940: a history of its administration under its charters* (1944) · J. Hill, *A dissertation on royal societies* (1750) · C. R. Weld, *A history of the Royal Society*, 2 vols. (1848) · J. Evans, *A history of the Society of Antiquaries* (1956) · T. Betterton, [W. Oldys and others], *The history of the English stage* (1741) · *DNB* · Highfill, Burnim & Langhans, *BDA*

Archives BL, corresp. and papers, Add. MSS 1783–1835, *passim* · Bodl. Oxf., journal while in Venice and Rome, MS Eng. misc. c. 444 · Norfolk RO, memoranda book, rent roll, etc. · RS, corresp. · Wellcome L., MSS 2391–2392, 5403 · Wellcome L., letters and papers sent to RS of London | BL, Sloane MSS, letters to Sir Hans Sloane · CKS, corresp. with Lord Stanhope

Likenesses J. Richardson, portrait, 1718, S. Antiquaries, Lond. · J. Smith, mezzotint, 1719 (after J. Richardson), BM · B. Lens, watercolour miniature, *c*.1720, NPG · J. Vanderbank, portrait, 1736 · J. Faber junior, mezzotint, 1737 (after J. Vanderbank), BM, NPG · A. Dassier, medal, 1740, BM · W. Hogarth, oils, 1741, RS [*see illus.*] · J. Faber junior, mezzotint, 1742 (after W. Hogarth) · J. McArdell, mezzotint, *c*.1748–1750 (after T. Hudson), BM, NPG · L. F. Roubiliac, marble bust, 1749, Wilton House, Wiltshire; plaster model, BM · G. P. Harding, pencil drawing, NPG · drawing, FM Cam.

Wealth at death £400 p.a. to wife; £12,000 to each of two daughters; £3090 5s. 0d. from sale of library; £100 bequest to Royal Society, London, together with a seal and a portrait of Francis Bacon: will, BL, Add. MS 4222, fols. 22–56v

Follett, Sir William Webb (1796–1845), lawyer and politician, was born on 2 December 1796 at Topsham, near Exeter, the second and eldest surviving son of Benjamin Follett (1762–1833), a timber merchant of Topsham and formerly a captain in the 13th regiment of foot, and his wife, Anne (1772–1840), daughter of John Webb of Kinsale, co. Cork. His sister Elizabeth married the physician Richard *Bright in 1826. He was educated at Exeter grammar school under Dr Lemprière, and privately by Mr Hutchinson, the curate of Heavitree, near Exeter, before going up in 1813 to Trinity College, Cambridge, where he took a BA degree without honours in 1818 and an MA in 1830. In 1836 he was appointed counsel to the university. In Michaelmas term 1814 he joined the Inner Temple, and read in the chambers of Robert Bayly and Godfrey Sykes. He became a special pleader in 1821, was called to the bar on 28 May 1824, and joined the western circuit in the following summer. His first notable case was *Garnett* v. *Ferrand* in May 1827, before the full court of king's bench. From the time of his arrival in London his political opinions were tory, and he formed a close friendship with John Wilson Croker, though at Cambridge he was apparently a whig.

Sir William Webb Follett (1796–1845), by George Raphael Ward, pubd 1842 (after Frederick Richard Say, exh. RA 1835)

On 11 October 1830 he married Jane Mary (1808–1847), eldest daughter of Sir Ambrose Hardinge *Giffard (1771–1827), chief justice of Ceylon, who was a ward of Croker and a cousin of Mrs Croker. They went to live in Duke Street, Westminster, where their first three children were born. They had five sons and two daughters. In his first four years at the bar Follett's income grew from 308 to 2853 guineas. He quickly overtook Coleridge and all the other members of the western circuit, apart from the leader of the circuit, Sjt. Wilde, the future Lord Chancellor Truro. In November 1828 he was briefed with Brougham in the great Cornish mining case, *Rowe v. Brenton*, and when Brougham became lord chancellor in November 1830 Follett was one of the first barristers to whom he offered a silk gown, but he declined. The years 1831–3 brought Follett an election petition practice of unprecedented magnitude; when the privy council was reorganized in 1833 he built up a large practice there; he had a House of Lords practice second only to Pemberton and far ahead of Campbell and his other rivals; and he had a very heavy practice in the court of king's bench.

In 1832 Follett contested the borough of Exeter unsuccessfully against Buller and Divett. When Sir Robert Peel formed his administration in November 1834 Follett became solicitor-general after Pemberton declined on grounds of health. At the same time he was appointed a king's counsel and received a knighthood. In January 1835 he was returned for Exeter, heading the poll with 1425 votes, ahead of Divett with 1161. He succeeded well in the House of Commons, speaking mainly on legal topics, but also in important debates on foreign affairs. His first major speech was on 31 March 1835 on Lord John Russell's Irish church motion. On 23 June of the same year he moved an amendment to clause 9 of the Government Corporation Bill to preserve the rights of freemen to the parliamentary franchise, and was only defeated by 278 to 232. When, later in the year, the House of Lords, on Lyndhurst's advice and against Peel's, recast the bill, and so produced a conflict between the two Houses, there were suggestions among the high tories of dispensing with Peel and coming in with Lyndhurst as prime minister, with Follett and Praed leading the Commons. In 1837 Follett was re-elected at Exeter without a contest, and in 1841 he headed the poll with 1302 votes, ahead of Divett with 1191, a much reduced majority. In Peel's second administration in the same year he again became solicitor-general, and in April 1844, when Pollock became chief baron, Follett succeeded him as attorney-general, winning the contest when his re-election was opposed with 1293 votes and a massive majority.

While Follett was solicitor and attorney-general he retained his private practice, especially in the House of Lords and the court of king's bench, and received special retainers to appear at assizes from one end of the country to the other. Exeter was neglected: he did not visit the city between March 1842 and September 1843, or ever again thereafter. This combination of law and politics ruined his health: he was first ill, briefly, in December 1835, and then again in April 1836. In February 1839 he collapsed and did not return to work until November. His health seemed to have recovered, but in April 1844 he again collapsed. When he addressed the House of Lords for the crown on O'Connell's appeal, he was obliged to do so sitting on a high chair. He spent some months on the continent, but soon fell ill again on his return home to Park Street, Westminster, in March 1845. He died on 28 June 1845 at Croker's house, 9 Cumberland Terrace, Regent's Park, and was buried in the Temple Church on 4 July. Towards the end of his life he had bought a large estate at Coombe Davy, Hemyock, and Coombe Pyne, Clayhidon, in northeast Devon, which had been connected with the family of Foliot in the middle ages, but he never resided there.

Follett left behind him the reputation of having been the greatest advocate of his generation. His best-known cases at the bar were his defence of Lord Cardigan for his duel with Captain Tuckett in 1841, in which he obtained an acquittal on technical grounds, and the action of Norton against Lord Melbourne in 1836, in which he appeared for the unsuccessful plaintiff. The speech of Sjt. Buzfuz on behalf of Mrs Bardell in the *Pickwick Papers* (1837) is a parody of Follett's speech on behalf of Norton. He had a sharp eye for technical detail. 'Perhaps no man ever defeated a greater number of important cases by unexpected objections of the most technical character' (*Blackwood's Magazine*, 59, 1846, 9). In person he was tall and slim, with a fine brow, large mouth, and grey eyes. 'In every qualification of intellect and grace of manner, he was as nearly perfect as man can be' (Lord Hatherley, *Life*, i.270).

J. A. HAMILTON, *rev.* DAVID PUGSLEY

Sources D. Pugsley, *Follett, our great lawyer* (1991) · [J. Grant], *Random recollections of the House of Commons* (1836) · [H. T. Ryall], ed., *Portraits of eminent conservatives and statesmen*, 2 vols. [1836–46] · [J. Grant], *The bench and the bar*, 2nd edn, 2 vols. (1838) · *Fraser's Magazine*, 32 (1845), 165–74 · H. Brougham, *Works*, 11 vols. (1872–3), 4.296–311 · *Life of John, Lord Campbell, lord high chancellor of Great Britain*, ed. Mrs Hardcastle, 2 vols. (1881) · *The Croker papers: the correspondence and diaries of … John Wilson Croker*, ed. L. J. Jennings, 3 vols. (1884) · B. J. S. Coleridge, *The story of a Devonshire house* (1905) · B. Coleridge, *This for remembrance* (1925) · A. Follett, notebooks, priv. coll. · UCL, Brougham MSS · J. Coleridge, journals, BL, Add. MS 47533

Archives Devon RO, legal opinions, letters patent · priv. coll., MSS | BL, corresp. with Sir Robert Peel, Add. MSS 40416–40567

Likenesses M. A. Shee, oils, *c.*1820, NPG · F. R. Say, oils, exh. RA 1835, Royal Albert Memorial Museum, Exeter · E. B. Stephens, marble bust, exh. RA 1842, Devon and Exeter Institution, Exeter · G. R. Ward, mezzotint, pubd 1842 (after F. R. Say, exh. RA 1835), NPG [*see illus.*] · J. Doyle, pen and pencil sketch, 1845, BM; repro. in J. Doyle, *HB sketches* (1830–48), no. 842 · W. Behnes, marble statue, 1849, Westminster Abbey, London · S. F. Diez, drawing, Staatliche Museen zu Berlin, Germany · H. T. Ryall, stipple (after A. E. Chalon), BM, NPG; repro. in Ryall, *Portraits of eminent conservatives and statesmen* · F. Stone, pencil and chalk drawing, Scot. NPG

Wealth at death under £160,000—personal property: *GM*, 1 (1848), 100–01

Folley, (Sydney) John (1906–1970), biochemist, was born at 92 Broad Street, Swindon, Wiltshire, on 14 January 1906, the younger child and only son of Thomas John Folley, an engine fitter in the Great Western Railway running shed at Swindon, and his wife, Katie, née Baggs. Folley's parents were anxious to make it possible for their children to take full advantage of every educational opportunity and they must have felt well rewarded for their sacrifices for Folley's scholastic career was brilliant. For six years he attended the Swindon and North Wilts. Secondary School and Technical Institution, being awarded an exhibition at Hulme Hall, Manchester University, in 1924. In 1927 he obtained a first-class honours degree in chemistry, coming out at the head of the list.

Folley's first research was in colloids, under D. C. Henry, from which he obtained an MSc. He then changed to biochemistry, and joined the biochemical laboratory of H. S. Raper, Brackenbury professor of physiology at Manchester. In 1931 he was awarded a PhD (Manchester) for a thesis on plastein and was then appointed assistant lecturer in biochemistry in the University of Liverpool. In 1932, on Raper's recommendation, he was appointed research assistant in the physiology department at the National Institute for Research in Dairying at Shinfield, Reading. He stayed in this department, becoming its head in 1945, working almost entirely on the physiology of lactation, until his death.

Folley's work on lactation developed along three main lines: the metabolic aspects of milk formation, the endocrinological aspects of mammary growth and milk secretion, and the neurophysiology of milk secretion. The early work of the physiology department was necessarily confined to small laboratory animals, mainly rats and guinea-pigs, and to such cows as could be made available by other departments. About 1937 Folley realized the value of goats

as prototype ruminants for lactational research, and during 1938 and 1939 he started to build up a herd of British Saanen goats, which played a major part in the department's work on the mammary gland.

The work on the metabolic aspects of lactation started immediately after Folley's arrival in Shinfield, first, on the relation between blood electrolytes and the lipid constituents of milk; secondly, on the alkaline phosphatase of the mammary gland, and later on endocrinological aspects of lactation in which his interest had been aroused by contact with Alan S. Parkes. The outbreak of war in 1939 kept applied research of this kind in the forefront for many years. In the late 1940s, however, Folley studied the respiratory metabolism of slices of mammary gland from ruminants and non-ruminants using ^{14}C. The results contributed significantly to knowledge of mammary metabolism.

He was twice married, first, on 9 February 1935, to Madeline (*b.* 1907), a psychologist and the daughter of Francis James Kerr, barrister, of Altrincham, Cheshire, and, then, after a divorce, he married, on 18 June 1947, Mary Lee (*b.* 1902/3), the divorced wife of F. A. I. Muntz and daughter of Canon William Lee Harnett, of Wolverton. There were no children of either marriage.

Folley's first work on the endocrinology of lactation arose from the finding in laboratory animals that oestrogen inhibited lactation, but he discovered that in cows the inhibition was only temporary and was accompanied by very prolonged increase in the concentration of milk solids, a phenomenon which he called the 'enrichment' effect. The preparation by E. C. Dodds and his colleagues of di-ethylstilboestrol and related artificial oestrogens, soon to be available in large quantities, enabled observations on oestrogenized cows to be carried out on a much larger scale as a wartime project. However, the work did not get beyond the pilot experiment stage.

Another wartime project arose from Folley's work on the effects of thyroxine and iodinated casein in increasing milk production, but, as with the oestrogen work, no worthwhile results in terms of overall milk supply were obtained. Folley's interest in the hypophysial lactogenic hormone prolactin arose from his meeting with F. G. Young, the first fruit of which was the idea that lactogenesis involved a complex of anterior hypophysial hormones, of which prolactin and adrenocorticotrophin were the most important. Much of the work at Shinfield in the 1960s dealt with prolactin secretion and the milk-ejection reflex involving oxytocin, the secretion of which was found to be stimulated by suckling or other stimulation of the udder and, in conditioned animals, by auditory and visual signals associated with milking time.

In his undergraduate days Folley was something of an athlete, representing Manchester University at cross-country running and being secretary of the swimming club. It is a sad irony, therefore, that for much of his life he had to struggle with physical disabilities—attacks of tuberculosis in 1931 and 1938, and in 1946 a severe deterioration in vision. By April 1959, following a disastrous operation, he became almost totally blind at the age of fifty-three. This stunning blow would have incapacitated many people permanently, but his dogged resolution and fortitude enabled him to carry on to a surprising extent.

Folley had wide interests outside science, mainly in the arts. In his own words:

> For many years I have been interested in the arts, particularly music, painting, ballet, cinema, architecture, etc. and I have formed collections of drawings and paintings by contemporary French and English painters and of gramophone records for the reproduction of which I have assembled a fine electrical reproducer.

There can be no doubting Folley's intellectual capacity and the value of his contributions to science. When he joined the institute in 1932 the newly established department of physiology at Shinfield was housed in a converted back bedroom of the old manor house. By the time of his death it occupied a prominent place in world research on the physiology of lactation.

Among Folley's many honours were his fellowship of the Royal Society (1951) and his honorary doctorate of the University of Ghent (1964). He was a member of many learned societies and advisory bodies—for example, the Medical Research Society's committee on human fertility (1945–7) and the World Health Organization's scientific group on lactation (1963). He wrote numerous scientific papers and reviews.

Folley's devotion to his department and his colleagues was wholeheartedly reciprocated. Yet he was in no sense insular or introverted. His wide travels included three visits to the USA and he also welcomed overseas visitors at Shinfield. Although he was unable to handle anything with a light touch, his colleagues outside the department regarded him with respect and admiration, as witness the symposium on lactogenic hormones planned by the Ciba Foundation to honour him on his retirement but perforce dedicated to his memory. He died in the Royal Berks Hospital, Reading, on 29 June 1970, survived by his second wife. ALAN S. PARKES, *rev.*

Sources A. S. Parkes, *Memoirs FRS*, 18 (1972), 241–65 · personal knowledge (1981) · *The Times* (1 July 1970), 13g · *WWW* · b. cert. · m. certs. · d. cert. · *Nature*, 227 (1970), 1070
Wealth at death £32,269: probate, 11 Nov 1970, *CGPLA Eng. & Wales*

Follows [*née* Alcock]**, Ruth** (**1718–1808**), Quaker minister, was born on 7 January 1718 at Weston, Nottinghamshire, the sixth of the seven children of Richard Alcock (d. 1757) and his wife, Ruth Noble (1686/7–1738). Although brought up as a Quaker, she rebelled for a while after her mother's death, keeping worldly company and taking 'a large swing at vanity' (*Memoirs*, 14). However she soon realized her fault, returned to the fold, and aged about twenty-three married George Follows (1716/17–1803) a Quaker of Castle Donington, Leicestershire. Together they worked hard to gain a basic living at George's trade of rush-basket making; they had four sons.

Gradually it became clear to Follows that she was being called to become a travelling minister, as her mother had been before her, and after some struggle she accepted this responsibility at the age of thirty. For much of the next forty years she travelled extensively throughout Britain, often leaving her children in the care of her husband and writing long and affectionate letters home. She usually travelled with younger women ministers who derived much support from her company. In 1761–2 and again in 1782–3 she visited Ireland and was particularly troubled by what she saw as Friends' excessive worldliness there. In 1764 she laboured in Wales and visited Scotland in 1788. Ruth's ministry sometimes lay in silence, directing her congregants back within themselves to dependence on Christ the inward teacher. On other occasions, when she perceived a fault, Ruth spoke out as 'a sharp instrument in the Lord's hand' (*Memoirs*, 10), although she was always encouraging to the faithful.

Follows's sons George (1742–1766) and Joseph (1751–1809) gave her considerable cause for anxiety by their youthful wildness, bad company, and heavy drinking. However, both reformed under the steadying influence of Friends, George before his early death and Joseph after three years working for a Quaker master in Newfoundland. On his return to England Joseph settled down in the family business and in 1793 accompanied his mother on one of her last journeys in the ministry. Towards the end of her life Ruth became increasingly infirm, and after a journey to the yearly meeting in London in 1795 she remained at her home at Castle Donington, where she received visiting Friends and faithfully attended local meetings. Following her husband's death on 6 July 1803 she lived alone at Castle Donington until her own death there on 3 April 1808. She was buried in the Quaker burial-ground at Castle Donington seven days later. Her spiritual autobiography and letters were published twenty years after her death as the *Memoirs of Ruth Follows*, edited by Sarah Stansfield. James Jenkins, not known for his charitable judgements on his fellow Quakers, described Ruth as 'highly esteemed both as a minister and as a woman extremely amiable in private life'; he also described her as 'one of the most musical preachers I have ever heard—even in old age she used to exalt a clear strong voice into strains of delightful melody' (Jenkins, 469). GIL SKIDMORE

Sources *Memoirs of Ruth Follows*, ed. S. Stansfield (1829) · RS Friends, Lond., Follows papers, temp MS 127 [2 boxes] · J. Jenkins, *Records and recollections*, ed. J. W. Frost (1984) · *Memoirs of the life, travels and religious experience of Martha Routh* (1824)
Archives RS Friends, Lond., personal and family corresp., family papers

Folston, Alice (*fl. c.*1386–1395). *See under* Women in trade and industry in York (act. c.1300–c.1500).

Folville, Eustace (d. 1346), gangster and soldier, was the second of the seven sons of John Folville (d. 1310), lord of Ashby Folville in Leicestershire, and his wife, Alice. He came of an established gentry family. The John Folville who was a king's banneret in 1286, and was knight of the shire for either Leicestershire or Rutland, or both together, six times between 1298 and 1306, was probably his father; the Ralph Folville who was knight of the shire for Leicestershire in 1315 was doubtless a relative. There is no unequivocal evidence linking the Folville family with criminality before Eustace's generation, but it is at least interesting that in 1284 John Folville appealed one Gillian Crumbaud of involvement in the killing on 30 November 1276 of her husband, Eustace de Folville, who was also his father; Gillian, who was presumably John's stepmother, was acquitted, though a man was outlawed for the crime. Then in 1292 John was himself accused by an approver at Reading of having harboured his own brother Robert, killed in the company of thieves. But again the charge was dismissed—Robert had been killed by, not with, thieves.

Of Eustace Folville's own involvement in felony there can be no doubt. On 19 January 1326, with his brothers Robert and Walter, and perhaps fifty other men, he committed one of the most sensational crimes of an exceptionally disorderly decade, when they waylaid and murdered Sir Roger *Beler, a baron of the exchequer, at Rearsby, Leicestershire. The context of the deed was political: Beler was a former Lancastrian who had become a leading agent of the Despensers, and had made many bitter enemies as a result. Among those enemies were members of the Zouche family, one of whom struck the fatal blow, and apparently also the Folvilles themselves. But once the deed was done, perhaps because they were outlawed in consequence, Eustace and his followers became full-time criminals. A series of pardons—one early in 1327, another in 1329—made no difference; they continued to kill, kidnap, and rob. Eustace himself was said to have been implicated in three or four murders, a rape, and three robberies between 1327 and 1330. Then, on 14 January 1332 he led what was now a criminal band (one that included four of his own brothers) in an exploit as startling as the murder of Beler, when they kidnapped Sir Richard *Willoughby, a justice of the court of common pleas, and allegedly notorious for corruption, and held him to ransom for 1300 marks (£866 13s. 4d.).

In this and some of his other misdeeds Folville co-operated with the gang led by James Coterel, which was based in Derbyshire but was prepared to engage in crime elsewhere; and the Coterels, in their turn, gave Folville shelter when necessary. Folville also had friends among the ostensibly law-abiding, who may have hired him and his company to commit acts of violence on their behalf—precisely this charge was brought against a group that included a canon of Sempringham Priory, Lincolnshire, and the cellarer of Haverholm Abbey, also in Lincolnshire. Their pardons in the late 1320s suggest that the Folvilles could look for support somewhere in the regime of Mortimer and Isabella. More specifically, Eustace and two of his brothers wore the robes of Sir Robert Tuchet, lord of Markeaton, Derbyshire, and Ashwell, Rutland, and they numbered the constable of Rockingham Castle, Northamptonshire, among their associates. The activities of the Folvilles helped to inspire a government campaign against criminals in 1332, which as far as Eustace was concerned had very little effect. He was brought back into the ranks of the law-abiding in a manner characteristic of the later middle ages, by a pardon granted in 1333 in consideration of military service in Scotland. His skills in violence were called upon again for campaigns in Scotland in 1337,

and in Flanders in 1338. In the following year he became a member of the abbot of Crowland's council, receiving 20s. per annum for life in return for aid and advice. Whether his services were genuine is unknown, and it is possible that the fee represented a form of protection money—in either 1340 or 1341 his brother Richard was killed as a criminal resisting arrest outside the parish church of Teigh, Rutland, of which he was rector.

Eustace Folville died unmolested in 1346. His passing was noticed by the chronicler Henry Knighton, who described him simply as 'Eustace de Folville, who slew Robert [sic] Bellers' (Knighton's Chronicle, 77). To present-day eyes Folville's career provides a perfect illustration of the weakness of authority and the ineffectiveness of law enforcement in the first half of the fourteenth century. To his own contemporaries, aware of the ill repute of his principal victims, he presented a more ambiguous image. Consequently he was remembered as an enforcer of rough justice as well as a lawbreaker. In William Langland's Piers Plowman, written over thirty years after the gangster's death, part of the process of setting the world to rights consists of what has been unrighteously taken being forcibly recovered, 'fro fals men with Foluyles lawes' (Langland, 1.564).   HENRY SUMMERSON

Sources E. L. G. Stones, 'The Folvilles of Ashby-Folville, Leicestershire, and their associates in crime', TRHS, 5th ser., 7 (1957), 117–36 · J. Bellamy, Crime and public order in England in the later middle ages (1973) · M. Keen, The outlaws of medieval legend, 2nd edn (1977) · J. C. Holt, Robin Hood (1982) · gaol delivery rolls, PRO, JUST/3/91 m 7d · W. Langland, Piers the Plowman, ed. W. W. Skeat, 2 vols. (1886), vol. 1, p. 564 · Knighton's chronicle, 1337–1396, ed. and trans. G. H. Martin, OMT (1995), 77 [Lat. orig., Chronica de eventibus Angliae a tempore regis Edgari usque mortem regis Ricardi Secundi, with parallel Eng. text] · N. Denholm-Young, The country gentry in the fourteenth century (1969), 31 n.2 · P. Heath, Church and realm, 1272–1461 (1988), 324 · rolls of justices in eyre, PRO, JUST/1/463, m. 10d

Fonblanque, Albany William (1793–1872), political journalist and journal editor, was born in London, the third and youngest son of John *Fonblanque (1759–1837), distinguished lawyer and MP for Camelford (1802–6), who in 1828 changed his surname by royal licence to de Grenier Fonblanque, and Frances Caroline (1760–1844), daughter of Colonel John Fitzgerald. When aged fourteen he was sent to the Royal Military Academy, Woolwich, to prepare for the Royal Engineers, but he withdrew following a serious illness and studied law under the eminent special pleader Joseph Chitty the elder. In 1812, aged nineteen, Fonblanque abandoned law for journalism. He became known as a contributor to The Times and the Morning Chronicle, where John Black, later its editor, was then a leading reporter. Black and Fonblanque became members of the circle of radical thinkers and writers with Owenite views who gathered around James Mill and were known as the Co-operative Society. In 1820 Fonblanque married Caroline, daughter of the late Captain Keane, of co. Meath, Ireland. Beginning in 1824 he contributed nine articles to the Westminster Review, mainly on literary or theatrical subjects. Following its founding in May 1826 he briefly wrote

Albany William Fonblanque (1793–1872), by Alfred, Count D'Orsay, 1838

for *The Atlas*, but he left later that year to become chief political writer of *The Examiner*.

By 1821 Leigh Hunt and his brother John, who had founded and edited *The Examiner* and made it known for fearless radical views, had both resigned. When Fonblanque arrived the paper's ebbing fortunes revived, and in 1830 he was made editor by the new owner, the Revd Dr Robert Fellowes. Fonblanque was later, after 1832, to own the paper. During the 1830s he also contributed to the *New Monthly Magazine* and the *Monthly Chronicle*, in each case a single article, and published *England under Seven Administrations* (1837), three volumes of his *Examiner* leaders. In 1846 he wrote political leaders for Dickens's *Daily News*. During this period he was offered the governorship of Nova Scotia but declined, fearing the abrupt break with old habits. However, in 1847 he accepted Lord John Russell's offer of the post of statistical secretary to the Board of Trade and resigned his editorship. He retained ownership of the paper until 1865 and contributed occasional articles.

Fonblanque's period of greatest influence as a journalist was from 1826 to 1837, when he was a prominent 'philosophic radical'. He was strongly opposed to the aristocratic principle, a fierce champion of suffrage extension, and thus a leading supporter of the 1832 Reform Bill. John Stuart Mill commented on 'the ardour of his sympathy with the hard-handed many' (*Collected Works*, 6.360) and praised his 'verve and talent, as well as fine wit … [He] was zealous in keeping up the fight for radicalism against the Whig ministry' (ibid., 1.179, 205); Thomas Carlyle, from a different political perspective, considered that Fonblanque's journalism made him 'the cleverest man living of that craft at present' (*Collected Letters*, 9.151).

Mill nevertheless recognized that Fonblanque 'was always divergent from us on many important points' (*Collected Works*, 1.107), being more the 'constitutional' than the 'philosophic' radical and believing that the form of government, however traditional, did not matter if people loved freedom and liberty. Throughout the 1830s Fonblanque became steadily more whiggish, opening up an ideological gap between himself and his earlier radical associates that was never to close. As Mill wrote sadly, regarding Fonblanque's support of Melbourne's ministry: 'We did not expect that he would so soon fall behind those whom he formerly ran so far before' (*Collected Works*, 6.379). Carlyle stated bluntly and with typical overstatement that Fonblanque had 'dwindled virtually into a nonentity and diner at Holland House' (*Collected Letters*, 9.364), that bastion of whig opinion.

Although his views changed Fonblanque was not accused of dishonest compromise. His journalism was always distinguished by its principled plain-speaking, regardless of the consequences. Before 1832 his bitter attacks on Wellington made enemies, and his strong views on reform were said to have lost *The Examiner* 200 subscribers. His articles were always carefully considered, for he was a meticulous writer who wrote slowly, re-wrote constantly, and was obsessed with accuracy. He was famous for his devastating wit, often expressed through satirical analogies, as when he commented that 'The sign of the fool with his finger in his mouth, and the sentiment, "Who'd have thought it?" is the precise emblem of English jurisprudence' (A. W. Fonblanque, *England under Seven Administrations*, 1837, 1.284). Indeed, during the period leading up to the Reform Bill 'an epigram, an illustration, a witticism in *The Examiner* … went off like a great gun, echoing all over the country' (Fonblanque, 38).

Leigh Hunt considered that Fonblanque was 'the genuine successor … of the Swifts and Addisons themselves; profuse of wit even beyond them, and superior in political knowledge' (Bourne, 2.37); to John Stuart Mill he was 'a great writer, who happens accidentally to be a journalist' and whose *Examiner* articles would 'take a place among English classics' (*Collected Works*, 6.351). Such opinions are overstated for Fonblanque's work, for all its force and wit, also demonstrates the limitations of journalism: invariably he was critical and negative, 'obliged', wrote Carlyle, 'to turn all his fine spirit into contemptuous bitterness' (*Collected Letters*, 6.213). As for *England under Seven Administrations*, Fonblanque's only book, the truth of Macaulay's comment has been confirmed by the test of time: that when newspaper articles are reprinted they 'would be compared, not with the rant and twaddle of the daily and weekly press, but with Burke's pamphlets, with Pascal's letters, with Addison's Spectators and Freeholders. They would not stand this new test a minute' (*Letters of Thomas Babington Macaulay*, 4.41).

Fonblanque was a great editor whose own writing and that of numerous distinguished contributors made *The*

Examiner 'the principal representative, in the newspaper press, of radical opinions' (*Collected Works*, 1.179), and a leading commentator on literature, the theatre, and the fine arts. He brought the paper safely through crises, particularly in 1833, when grave financial problems were solved by enlisting the support of Sir Henry Bulwer, John Stuart Mill, Benjamin Disraeli, and others, for a subscription list that paid for new printing machinery to reduce running costs. His honesty and fearless integrity did much for the status of journalism, as did his election as a corresponding member of the French Imperial Academy of Moral and Political Science.

During the 1820s the Fonblanques lived at 19 Edgware Road, London, and later at 9 Pine Apple Place, Kilburn Road; Thomas Carlyle, visiting in 1831, saw 'a long, thin, flail of a man, with wintry zealous looking eyes; lank, thin hair, wide, small-chinned mouth, *baggy*, wrinkly care-accustomed face; greatly the air of a Radical. I observed that he had a high forehead, and low crown' (*Collected Letters*, 6.32). By 1838 they had moved to Connaught Square. Carlyle also described Mrs Fonblanque as 'a "beautiful ideal"', but the marriage—there were three sons and a daughter—was unhappy. Matters were not helped by financial difficulties caused by Fonblanque's extravagance, and by his poor health. Domestic unhappiness may explain his inveterate dining out and frequent after-dinner appearances in London drawing-rooms: he was often at Holland House, had links with the Carlyles, William Macready, and the Dickens circle, and had a reputation for seeking the company of cultivated women. N. P. Willis met him at Lady Blessington's salon at Gore House in 1830, and described him thus:

> sallow seamed and hollow, teeth irregular, skin livid, straight black hair uncombed and straggling over his forehead. A hollow, croaking voice, and a small fiery black eye, with a smile like a skeleton's. ... He sat upon his chair very awkwardly and was very ill-dressed; but every word he uttered showed him to be a man of claims very superior to exterior attraction.   (Connelly, 171)

Fonblanque loved to play cards and chess, and could be a brilliant conversationalist. He was a regular theatregoer and an occasional continental traveller. Despite his poor health his great enthusiasm was yachting with the Royal Thames Yacht Club; Dickens joined him on two occasions. His health was further taxed, it was said, through studying classics, philosophy, and literature for six hours each day, though Mill regarded him as having 'no systematic or solid acquirements' (*Collected Works*, 12.126).

Fonblanque's life changed abruptly when he became the Board of Trade's statistical secretary in 1847; he retained the post until shortly before his death. It was said that he found the work uncongenial and took unhappy refuge in inaccessibility, but there is no evidence of incompetence, even though, for a man who gave such witty and vigorous support to the 1832 Reform Bill, the compiling of such statistics as the acreage of land under potatoes might fail to prove exciting. Fonblanque represented England in 1854 at the International Statistical Congress in Paris. His *Agricultural Returns for 1870*, which

included figures for potatoes, was praised as 'very able' (*The Times*, 15 March 1871).

Although Fonblanque was occasionally seen in the Athenaeum Library or playing chess at the St James's Club, during his last decade he was seen less and less in society, becoming virtually a recluse. He died on Sunday, 13 October 1872, at 64 Connaught Square, and was buried on 19 October at Kensal Green cemetery. On 26 September 1873 a letter in *The Times* appealed for help for Fonblanque's youngest son, Berkeley, who was both consumptive and an epileptic: he and his young wife were destitute and starving. It can only be speculated what this might say about Fonblanque's domestic unhappiness.

JAMES A. DAVIES

Sources E. B. de Fonblanque, *The life and labours of Albany Fonblanque* (1874) · *The collected works of John Stuart Mill*, ed. J. M. Robson and others, 33 vols. (1963–91), vols. 1, 2, 6, 12–13, 17 · H. R. Fox Bourne, *English newspapers: chapters in the history of journalism*, 2 vols. (1887) · *The collected letters of Thomas and Jane Welsh Carlyle*, ed. C. R. Sanders and K. J. Fielding, 6 (1977); 9 (1981); 12 (1985) · *The Times* (17 Oct 1872) · *The Examiner* (19 Oct 1872) · *DNB* · private information (2004) [E. S. M. Hemming] · *The letters of Charles Dickens*, ed. M. House, G. Storey, and others, 1–4 (1965–77), 203n. · *The diaries of William Charles Macready, 1833–1851*, ed. W. Toynbee, 2 vols. (1912) · *The letters of Thomas Babington Macaulay*, ed. T. Pinney, 4 (1977) · *Wellesley index*, vol. 3 · J. A. Davies, *John Forster: a literary life* (1983) · W. Connelly, *Count D'Orsay* (1952) · D. Griffiths, ed., *The encyclopedia of the British press, 1422–1992* (1992) · S. E. Koss, *The rise and fall of the political press in Britain*, 2 vols. (1981–4)

Archives BL, Add. MSS 33546, 35149, 37949, 38110, 38524 · Princeton University Library, corresp. and papers · UCL, Huguenot Library | Bodl. Oxf., letters to Lord and Lady Lovelace · Herts. ALS, corresp. with Lord Lytton · Hunt. L., Dickens corresp. · Hunt. L., Dickens MSS; Forster collection · Morgan L., Dickens corresp. · NL Scot., Carlyle corresp. · NYPL, Berg collection MSS · U. Hull, Brynmor Jones L., T. P. Thompson MSS · U. Nott., D'Orsay MSS · UCL, Huguenot Library · UCL, Bentham MSS · UCL, corresp. with Edwin Chadwick

Likenesses Count D'Orsay, drawing, 1838, repro. in *Graphic*, 6 (1872), 442; in possession of J. P. Hennessey, 1952 · Count D'Orsay, lithograph, 1838, BM, NPG [*see illus.*] · J. Doyle, pen-and-pencil drawing, 1851, BM

Wealth at death under £3000: probate, 28 Oct 1872, *CGPLA Eng. & Wales*

Fonblanque, Florence Gertrude de [*née* Florence Gertrude Sparagnapane] (1864–1949), suffragist, was born on 22 July 1864 at 142 Bishopsgate Street in the City of London, a younger daughter of Gaudente Sparagnapane (*c*.1816–1877), an Italian immigrant wholesale confectioner, and his wife, Aurelia Williams (*c*.1832–1915). She was educated in Brussels and at Brighton. Tall, dark, and elegant, she became an actress. On 17 October 1891, at St George's Bloomsbury, giving her age falsely on her marriage certificate as twenty-one and her father's profession as 'gentleman', she married a young actor, Robert Edgar De Grenier de Fonblanque (*c*.1869–1932), the son of a barrister. Her husband later acquired the titles marquess of Juliers, comte de Hautserve, and comte de Fonblanque. Nothing is known of the couple's early married life except that they apparently had no children and by 1906 had taken up residence in Duncton, a small Sussex village.

At this time, with her sister, Maud Arncliffe Sennett, Florence became interested in the movement for women's suffrage, belonging successively to both constitutional and militant societies. By 1912 she was a member of the committee of the west Sussex branch of the Conservative and Unionist Women's Franchise Association. It was in this year that she originated the idea of a 'Woman's March' to draw the country's attention to the woman's cause. She felt that the constitutional arm of the movement should be seen to enact a heroic feat to emulate the daring deeds of the militants. Her first idea was that women should march from London to Edinburgh, but she was soon convinced by more experienced publicists that the direction of the march should be changed to culminate in London. Maud Arncliffe Sennett wrote of her sister, 'She dressed her little army in warm autumnal brown and bright emerald green brazzards and rosettes, and she secured a splendid Press—London as well as the provinces' (Arncliffe Sennett, 70).

The 'army' was indeed 'little'. Although invitations were sent in early September to all the suffrage societies, only six women set off from Edinburgh on 12 October, a few others joining the march *en route*. Despite the small numbers taking part, the report of the march in the *Suffrage Annual and Women's Who's Who* (1913) was exhaustive—a result, no doubt, of the sisters' ability to activate the publicity machine. It appears from this report that the character of the march was distinctly more religious and spiritual than political, and that the suppression of sweated labour and of the white slave trade were of concern as well as the enfranchisement of women. The marchers reached London on 16 November, having held as many as three meetings a day along the route. Maud Arncliffe Sennett co-ordinated the arrival into London, the women being accompanied at this stage by such male suffragists as Cecil Chapman and Israel Zangwill. A large meeting was held in Trafalgar Square, at which Charlotte Despard was one of the speakers, and a petition praying 'the Government to bring in a bill for Women's Suffrage this Session' and containing thousands of signatures garnered during the course of the march was presented by Florence de Fonblanque to a representative of the prime minister. 'Mr Asquith promised to give it his consideration; and later, informed Mrs de Fonblanque that he had nothing to add to his previous statement' (*Suffrage Annual*, 149). Although the march achieved no political success it provided an outlet for active women who could not condone militancy.

Florence de Fonblanque founded and became leader and honorary organizer of what was originally called the Marchers 'Qui Vive' Corps, later the Qui Vive Corps. This group, although not militant, was distinctly militaristic, dressing, as they had done for the march, in a brown and green uniform. Perhaps it was Florence de Fonblanque's stage experience that gave her a penchant for such dressing up. The idea was that the Qui Vive Corps should offer its services to different suffrage services impartially whenever extra workers were required. Although intended as a national movement, with the aim of showing that the women of England were as capable of organization, comradeship, and discipline as the men, its influence does not appear to have spread beyond Sussex. However, although the main constitutional society, the National Union of Women's Suffrage Societies, had refused to take part in the Women's March, it obviously recognized the value of the idea, and shamelessly adopted it, organizing its own Pilgrimage the next year.

Florence de Fonblanque died of cardiac failure at her home, The Cottage, in Duncton, on 2 January 1949. Her gravestone in the tiny parish churchyard carries the epitaph 'Originator and leader of the women's suffrage march from Edinburgh to London 1912', wording she specified in her will. One might conclude from this evidence that she felt that her contribution to the suffrage cause represented the highlight of her life.

ELIZABETH CRAWFORD

Sources E. Crawford, *The women's suffrage movement: a reference guide, 1866–1928* (1999) · A. J. R., ed., *The suffrage annual and women's who's who* (1913) · M. Arncliffe Sennett, *The child* (1938) · b. cert. · m. cert. · d. cert. · will of F. G. de Fonblanque
Likenesses photograph, repro. in *Votes for Women* (22 Nov 1912)
Wealth at death £11,329 17s. 2d.: probate, 2 March 1949, CGPLA Eng. & Wales

Fonblanque, John de Grenier (1759–1837), jurist, was a descendant of a noble Huguenot family of Languedoc and the second son of Jean de Grenier Fonblanque, banker, and his wife, Eleanor, daughter of Thomas Bagshaw. The father had been sent to England by his own father to receive a protestant education and had subsequently settled in London. John was educated at Harrow School, and matriculated at St John's College, Oxford, on 18 November 1780. He was admitted to the Middle Temple in September 1777 and was called to the bar on 4 January 1783, and thereafter he established a good equity practice. On 30 May 1786 he married Frances Caroline (1760–1844), daughter of Colonel John Fitzgerald.

Fonblanque won fame in the legal profession for his edition of the *Treatise on Equity* ascribed to Henry Ballow, which was published in 1793 and which reached a fifth edition in 1820. Fonblanque's extensive notes contained both an elaboration of the general principles of equity discussed in the text and a valuable commentary on case law at a time when equity was nearing completion as a body of doctrine. The book became an instant classic, and Fonblanque, whose reputation was made by the book, was complimented on his achievement by Lord Thurlow.

Fonblanque was also successful in practice. He was leading counsel at the bar of the House of Commons in 1790 on behalf of the merchants of London in opposition to the Quebec Bill, and was said to have caused a sensation by disputing the then established, but later exploded, doctrine in the law of real property of *scintilla juris* (a mere spark of right). Such was his brilliant early reputation that he was spoken of as a future whig lord chancellor. He was made king's counsel on 28 April 1804 and received a patent of precedence on 24 June 1804, and he became a bencher of his inn on 1 June of the same year. In Lent term 1808 he became a reader of the Middle Temple and in 1815 he was appointed treasurer.

Fonblanque took an early interest in politics, joining the Whig Club in January 1786, and writing in 1790 *A Serious Exhortation to the Electors of Great Britain*. He was returned as MP for Camelford in 1802 under the patronage of the duke of Bedford. In parliament he was listed as one of the prince of Wales's 'friends', and was credited with having drafted the prince's letters to his father that protested at his exclusion from the army. However, as a result of his financial difficulties he lost Bedford's support, and he had to give up his seat at the dissolution of 1806. Although he wrote another pamphlet, *Doubts as to the Expediency of Adopting the Recommendation of the Bullion Committee* (1810), his political career was effectively over.

A vain man described by Thomas Creevey as 'a dolorous fop of a lawyer', Fonblanque's income never matched his extravagant tastes. In 1807–8 financial problems led him into a dispute with Jeremy Bentham, the landlord of his chambers at Lincoln's Inn, and by 1809 he had been subjected to imprisonment for debt, living within 'the rules' of the king's bench prison. This term referred to the area outside the prison where debtors were allowed to settle, though still under the jurisdiction of the prison, and which they were not supposed to leave. Fonblanque's social decline continued, and in January 1812 Joseph Jekyll noted that he kept 'a little whore at Kingston' (HoP, *Commons*, 3.784). Problems with money continued to hound Fonblanque and his family for the rest of his life. By the 1830s he was reduced to writing letters to Lord Henry Brougham, describing his state of destitution and asking both for professional patronage and personal loans to stave off his creditors. In 1834 he was back within the rules of the king's bench, where he ended his days. His marriage had by then broken down, his wife having left him. She, too, was reduced to straitened circumstances.

Although Fonblanque remained active in the legal profession for fifty years and became the senior practising barrister, his professional career suffered as a result of his problems, and towards the end of his life he stayed away from his chambers to avoid his creditors. As his financial situation worsened, so his expectations became more modest. In 1823 he unsuccessfully solicited Lord Liverpool's patronage to obtain a vacant Welsh judgeship, and by the time he was seventy-two he told Brougham that there was 'no occupation or appointment which, if not disgraceful, I would not, however humble, thankfully accept' (Brougham MSS). Nevertheless, his legal reputation remained high. He advised Baron de Bode in the early 1830s in his dispute with the crown which sought compensation for lands seized in France during the revolution, and his advice was published by the baron in 1834. After Fonblanque's death Lord Lyndhurst wrote to one of his sons: 'I have known jurists as profound as your father, but I have known no one who was so perfect a master of the philosophy of law' (HoP, *Commons*, 784).

On 14 May 1828 Fonblanque took the additional surname de Grenier. He died on 4 January 1837 and was buried in the Temple Church. He had one daughter and three sons, John Samuel Martin de Grenier *Fonblanque, a lawyer and commissioner of bankrupts, Albany *Fonblanque, the celebrated journalist, and Thomas Fonblanque, who became a consul in Serbia.

MICHAEL LOBBAN

Sources HoP, *Commons* · *GM*, 2nd ser., 7 (1837), 325 · Foster, *Alum. Oxon.* · W. Thomas, *The philosophic radicals: nine studies in theory and practice, 1817–1841* (1979), 309 · *The correspondence of Jeremy Bentham*, 7, ed. J. R. Dinwiddy (1988) · H. A. C. Sturgess, ed., *Register of admissions to the Honourable Society of the Middle Temple, from the fifteenth century to the year 1944*, 1 (1949), 385 · E. B. de Fonblanque, *The life and labours of Albany Fonblanque* (1874) · UCL, Brougham MSS
Archives UCL, corresp. with Brougham
Wealth at death in debtor's prison during lifetime

Fonblanque, John Samuel Martin de Grenier (1787–1865), legal writer, eldest son of John de Grenier *Fonblanque (1759–1837) and his wife, Frances Caroline (1760–1844), daughter of Colonel John Fitzgerald, was born in Brook Street, Grosvenor Square, London, in March 1787. Albany *Fonblanque was his brother. He was educated at Charterhouse and at Gonville and Caius College, Cambridge, where he was one of the founders of the Union Debating Society. He also kept terms at Lincoln's Inn. At college he burst a blood vessel and was advised change for his health, whereupon he obtained a commission in the 21st fusiliers and served with the regiment in Cadiz and Gibraltar, and in Italy under Lord William Bentinck, by whom he was appointed deputy judge advocate-general. He took an active part in the Anglo-American War of 1812–14 between Britain and the United States. He was present at the taking of Washington, the battle of Baltimore, and the disastrous attempt to capture New Orleans, where he was taken prisoner. After the battle of Waterloo in 1815, he served in France with the army of occupation.

On returning to England, Fonblanque was called to the bar on 26 November 1816 and appointed a commissioner of bankruptcy by Lord Eldon the following year. On the institution of the bankruptcy court, he was appointed one of the original commissioners. He married Caroline, daughter of John O'Connell of Cork; they had at least one daughter.

In 1823 Fonblanque and John Paris published their *Medical Jurisprudence*, which was awarded the first Swiney prize, and remained almost the only book on the subject for many years. Fonblanque was also one of the founders of *The Jurist*.

Fonblanque died at 24 Marine Parade, Brighton, on 3 November 1865.

FRANCIS WATT, *rev.* JONATHAN HARRIS

Sources *GM*, 3rd ser., 19 (1865), 801 · R. L. Arrowsmith, ed., *Charterhouse register, 1769–1872* (1974), 143 · *County Courts Chronicle and Bankruptcy Gazette* (1 Feb 1866), 44 · *CGPLA Eng. & Wales* (1865)
Wealth at death under £7000: probate, 28 Dec 1865, *CGPLA Eng. & Wales*

Fonnereau, Thomas George (1789–1850), writer and artist, was born at Reading on 25 August 1789, the second and posthumous son of Thomas Fonnereau (d. 1788) and his wife, Harriet (d. 1832), the daughter of John Hanson. Thomas George Fonnereau's grandfather was Zachary Philip Fonnereau, the descendant of an ancient family from the neighbourhood of Rochelle; the family settled in England at the edict of Nantes and realized a fortune in the linen trade. Fonnereau's parents married on 19 October 1786.

After practising as an attorney in partnership with John Gregson at 8 Angel Court, Throgmorton Street, London, from 1816 to 1834, Fonnereau succeeded, by the death of a relative, to a good property and he devoted himself to his books and his friends for the rest of his life. His political opinions leaned to Conservatism and he published in 1831 a *Practical View of the Question of Parliamentary Reform*, which, unlike most of the swarm of pamphlets issued at that crisis, passed through two editions. It was written mainly to prove that a purely democratic government is inapplicable to the circumstances of England and that the existing system was 'founded on a concentration of the various interests of the country in the House of Commons'. While still a lawyer he occupied chambers in the Albany and as a 'great lover and liberal patron of art' he entertained a distinguished set of artists and wits at 'choice little dinners' which are commemorated in the pages of J. R. Planché's *Recollections* (1872). With one of these friends, Clarkson Stanfield, Fonnereau travelled in Italy and France between 26 August 1838 and 18 March 1839. On his return there were printed for private distribution, at the expense of D. Colnaghi, a few copies of *Mems. of a tour in Italy, from sketches by T. G. F., inspired by his friend and fellow-traveller, C. S., esq., R.A.* containing thirteen sketches of scenery.

Fonnereau had printed for private circulation in 1849 a few copies of *The Diary of a Dutiful Son, by H. E. O.*, H. E. O. being the second letters of his three names. A copy fell accidentally into the hands of J. G. Lockhart, who inserted numerous extracts from its pages into the *Quarterly Review* (86, 1850, 449–63). The introduction to the volume sets out that Fonnereau's father had urged him to keep a diary of the remarks that he heard in the house of a distant relative, 'a literary man in affluent circumstances', and that some little time afterwards he had shown the diary as a proof that he had adopted the suggestion. A concluding paragraph reveals that this was a fabrication, as the conversations were the product of his own inventive powers. They contained many original and acute observations, from a thinker inclined to a conservative viewpoint, on poetry, philosophy, and political economy, and they present in style and substance an accurate representation of his talk.

On inheriting his fortune Fonnereau had built with the assistance of Decimus Burton, to whom Stanfield had introduced him in 1839, 'a bachelor's kennel'—his own depreciatory designation of 'an Italian villa with colonnade and campanile'—at Haydon Hill, near Bushey in Hertfordshire. Fonnereau died there on 13 November 1850 and was buried in a vault in Aldenham churchyard with many members of the family of Hibbert, his nearest relatives. His *Diary of a Dutiful Son* was published posthumously by John Murray in 1864.

W. P. COURTNEY, rev. M. CLARE LOUGHLIN-CHOW

Sources *GM*, 1st ser., 56 (1786), 907 · *GM*, 1st ser., 58 (1788), 1183 · *GM*, 2nd ser., 35 (1851), 107 · J. E. Cussans, *History of Hertfordshire*, 3/1 (1881), 268; 3/2 (1881), 179 · J. R. Planché, *The recollections and reflections of J. R. Planché*, 1 (1872), 233 · [T. G. Fonnereau], 'Preface', *Diary of a dutiful son, by H. E. O.* (1864) · D. C. A. Agnew, *Protestant exiles from France in the reign of Louis XIV, or, The Huguenot refugees and their descendants in Great Britain and Ireland*, 2nd edn, 3 (1874), 234 · P. van der Merwe, 'Theatres and spectacles in Italy: an Englishman on tour, 1838–9', *Theatre Research International*, 10 (1985), 46–58 · will, PRO, PROB 11/2123, sig. 887

Fonseca, Alvaro da [Jacob Jessurun Alvares] (1657?–1742), diamond merchant, was born in Lisbon, the second of three children of Manuel Alvares and Brites Gomes. His full name was probably Alvaro da Fonseca Alvares. The family were New Christians from Trancoso in northern Portugal. In 1667 his uncle and namesake was arrested by the Coimbra Inquisition and convicted of Judaizing. Fear of the Inquisition forced the family to leave Portugal. Fonseca converted to open Judaism, probably in Amsterdam, and took the name of Jacob Jessurun. In 1673 he settled in London as a merchant, using the name Jacob Jessurun Alvares; he paid the synagogue £4 10s. in consulage or *imposta*, which, at 1s. per £100, implies a trading turnover of £9000. On 6 May 1674 he married Sarah, daughter of Isaac Henriques Faro, at the Portuguese Synagogue in Amsterdam. They had one son, Isaac Jessurun Alvares (c.1675–1711). In 1675 Fonseca was endenizened as an English subject. In 1676 he was the fourth highest contributor to the synagogue *imposta*, paying £32 4s. 7d., which implies a year's turnover of £64,400. The ledger of Manuel Levy Duarte of Amsterdam shows that Fonseca bought polished diamonds from Amsterdam for resale in London. He is listed in the *Little London Directory* of 1677 as Jacob Jesrum Alvarez in St Mary Axe. In 1677 he was elected treasurer of the Portuguese Synagogue in London and acquired the copyhold of their cemetery at Mile End, which he held as a trustee until 1736. From 1675 to 1679 he figures in the port books as one of the seven most active London Jewish merchants. In 1680 he was in partnership with Abraham do Porto.

In that year the East India Company sought to monopolize the diamond trade. This induced Simon Henriques and Alfonso Rodrigues, diamond importers in London, to open a branch house in India outside the company's jurisdiction. In 1682 they sent their brother Bartholomew Rodrigues, their brother-in-law Domingo do Porto, and Fonseca out to India on the interlopers' ships. Fonseca left his wife and son in London and was not to see them again for nineteen years. After an unsuccessful attempt to enter Masulipatam, they settled at Covelong, 20 miles south of Madras. The East India Company's directors reacted quickly to this well-organized competition. They threw open the trade in diamonds, pearls, and other 'fine goods', and instructed the council in Madras to allow the Jewish merchants to settle and trade at Fort St George, which they did. In 1686 the Dutch East India Company responded by allowing Abraham do Porto and two other Portuguese Jewish merchants to settle at Surat. The English company reacted by reducing their 'permission' rates for aliens and by setting up the corporation of Madras with an English mayor and 120 burgesses and twelve aldermen: three Englishmen, three Hindus, three Portuguese Catholics, and three Jews. Fonseca was sworn as an alderman of Madras in 1690, in succession to Domingo do Porto, who had died. He traded to Bengal, Burma, and the Philippines, and finally returned to London in 1700.

On first meeting him then, Sir John Chardin wrote to his brother Daniel in Madras that Fonseca seemed to him to be an honest man of good commerce. Thomas Pitt, the governor of Fort St George, was of the same opinion, referring to him as 'Mr Alvares', and addressed him cordially as 'Dear Sir and Friend'. When Pitt's famous 426 carat diamond was sent to London, Fonseca refused to accept its consignment, but advised Robert Pitt on how to have it cut and polished and to market its offcuts. In London he traded in partnership with Roger Bradyll and became a leading London importer of Indian diamonds. In 1709 the company fined them for smuggling. He served six times as a warden of the Portuguese Synagogue in Bevis Marks (in 1702, 1707, 1712, 1716, 1720, and 1726). He died in London in 1742 at the age of eighty-five and was buried on 16 November next to his wife, Sarah (d. 1723), in its old cemetery at Mile End. Fonseca was a prominent member of the group of Jewish diamond merchants who were forced to flee Portugal and who diverted this profitable trade from Lisbon to London.   EDGAR SAMUEL

Sources G. Yogev, *Diamonds and coral: Anglo-Dutch Jews and eighteenth-century trade* (1978) · E. R. Samuel, 'The diamond trade in the late seventeenth century, with special reference to London', MPhil diss., U. Lond., 1978 · M. Woolf, 'Foreign trade of London Jews in the seventeenth century', *Transactions of the Jewish Historical Society of England*, 24 (1970–73), 38–58 · W. J. Fishel, 'The Jewish merchant-colony in Madras (Fort St George) during the 17th and 18th centuries', *Journal of the Economic and Social History of the Orient*, 3 (1960), 78–107, 175–95 · L. D. Barnett, trans., *El libro de los acuerdos: being the records and accompts of the Spanish and Portuguese synagogue of London from 1663 to 1681* (1931) · A. S. Diamond, 'The cemetery of the resettlement', *Transactions of the Jewish Historical Society of England*, 19 (1955–9), 163–90 · [S. Lee], *A collection of the names of the merchants living in and about the City of London* (1677); repr. as *The little London directory of 1677* (1863) · A. M. Hyamson, *The Sephardim of England: a history of the Spanish and Portuguese Jewish community, 1492–1951* (1951) · D. Verdooner and H. J. W. Snel, *Handleiding bij de index op de Ketuboth van de Portugees-Israëlietische gemeente te Amsterdam van 1650–1911* (Netherlands, 1990) · M. Woolf, 'Notes of entries in the London port books … relating to Jewish merchants between 1600 and 1680', Jewish Museum [see Woolf, 'Foreign trade'] · will, PRO, PROB 11/722, sig. 345 · E. Samuel, 'Diamonds and pieces of eight: how England won the rough diamond trade', *Jewish Historical Studies*, 38 (2003) [2003]
Archives Arquivo Nacional de Torre do Tombo, Lisbon, Coimbra Inquisition Processo 9297 · BL, corresp. of Thomas Pitt, Add. MSS 22842–22856 · Gemeentearchief, Amsterdam, ledger of Athias and Levy · Yale U., Beinecke L., letters to Daniel Chardin

Fontaine, Jacques [James] (1658–1728), Reformed minister and diarist, was born on 7 April 1658 at Jenouillé, near Pons, in Charente, France, the tenth and youngest child, and fourth son, of Jacques Fontaine (1603–1666), Reformed minister at Vaux and Royon, and the fifth child of his father's second marriage, to Marie Chaillon (1616/17–1680). The family sprang from minor nobility. As an infant, the younger Jacques was dropped by his nurse

and permanently lamed. He gained admittance to the Collège de Guyenne, where he graduated MA in 1680. Shortly thereafter his mother died and he succeeded to her estates. He chose, however, to live with his sister Marie and her husband, Pastor Pierre Forestier of St Mesme, in Angoumois. In 1684 the St Mesme Temple was closed by order of Louis XIV, and Forestier was forced into exile. Fontaine then conducted clandestine prayer groups and was arrested for allegedly officiating at an open-air service. He was first incarcerated at Saintes, then transferred to the Tower of Pons for having organized inmate prayer meetings. Convicted and fined 100 livres, and prohibited from engaging in religious activity, he successfully appealed for acquittal to the *parlement* of Guienne. In 1685, in an attempt to force him to abjure protestantism, royal dragoons occupied and ransacked his home. He managed to flee and went into hiding for several months, sheltering at 'safe houses' of fellow protestants. When, on 17 October 1685, Louis XIV issued the edict of Fontainebleau, revoking the edict of Nantes and stripping Calvinist protestantism of its legal status, Fontaine decided to go into exile. He secured passage from La Tremblade for himself, his fiancée, Anne Elizabeth Boursiquot, her sister, and his niece Jeanette Forestier, and—after near detection—they landed, destitute, in England at Appledore, near Barnstaple, late in 1685.

At Barnstaple Fontaine eked out a marginal living teaching French and Latin and engaging in grain smuggling from England into France until he and his partners had a falling out. His financial situation was rendered more precarious by his refusal to conform to the formulae for worship required by the Church of England. Declining to accept holy communion from Church of England priests made him ineligible for assistance from the government's French refugee relief funds. He was, however, ordained as a minister by the presbyterian congregation at Barnstaple. There, on 24 February 1686, he married Anne Elizabeth Boursiquot (d. 1721). In November of 1688 he received his first ministerial appointment, at the former Pesthouse in London, which had been converted to a refugee almshouse. However, he shortly thereafter became pastor of the French church at Taunton, in Somerset. At Taunton he started a cloth manufactory and dabbled in retail sales enterprises.

In 1694 Fontaine moved his family to Ireland, where he assumed the post of minister of the Huguenot church at Cork city, establishing a broadcloth manufactory. The contention that he initiated the first woollen manufactories in Cork is unsupported. By 1699 much had apparently gone awry: bills passed by the British parliament restricting the export of Irish products had bankrupted his businesses, and his uncompromising stance as a nonconformist had embroiled him in controversy with the bishop of Cork and the lord justice, the earl of Galway. He resigned his pastorate and left for Berehaven, co. Cork, to set up a herring fishery. His house and family were twice attacked by Irish Catholic tories and French privateers (1704 and 1708), and on the second occasion he was captured and held until ransom was paid. The Fontaine family moved to

Dublin, where he bought a house at St Stephen's Green and ran a private school. Anne Boursiquot Fontaine died on 29 January 1721. Afterwards, apparently at his children's request, Fontaine wrote *Memoires d'une famille huguenote, victimes de la revocation de l'édit de Nantes* (1877; first printed in English translation in 1838), which is one of the few surviving refugee accounts of the Huguenot dispersion. He died in Dublin in 1728.

RAYMOND PIERRE HYLTON

Sources [J. Fontaine], *Memoirs of a Huguenot family*, ed. A. Maury (1872) • E. J. Lefroy, 'The Reverend James Fontaine', *Proceedings of the Huguenot Society*, 21 (1965–70), 11–14 • S. Smiles, *The Huguenots: their settlements, churches and industries in England and Ireland* (1867; repr. (1972) • D. C. A. Agnew, *Protestant exiles from France in the reign of Louis XIV, or, The Huguenot refugees and their descendants in Great Britain and Ireland*, 2nd edn, 2 (1871) • J. de C. Ireland, 'Maritime aspects of the Huguenot immigration into Ireland', *The Huguenots in Ireland: anatomy of a migration*, ed. C. Caldicott, H. Gough, and J.-P. Pittion (1987), 333–75 • R. D. Gwynn, *Huguenot heritage* (1985) • R. D. Gwynn, 'The distribution of Huguenot refugees in England', *Proceedings of the Huguenot Society*, 21 (1965–70), 404–36 • [J. Fontaine], *Memoirs of the Reverend Jacques Fontaine, 1658–1728*, ed. D. W. Ressinger (1992)
Wealth at death minimal; possessions had been dispersed to children long since; left remainder to daughter: *Memoirs*, ed. Maury, 222

Fontenelle, Louisa [*known as* Mrs Williamson] (**1769–1799**), actress and singer, was born on 31 August 1769 in the parish of St Margaret, Lothbury, London, the daughter of John Fontenell and his wife, Ann. After receiving a boarding-school education designed to fit her for the life of a respectable tradesman's wife, the lively girl became set on a stage career and made her début at Covent Garden on 6 November 1788, as Moggy in the première of John O'Keeffe's comic opera *The Highland Reel*. The *European Magazine* commented that her face and figure were attractive and her eyes expressive and that she performed 'with great spirit, vivacity, and comic effect' (p. 373). Later in the season she created Sophia in O'Keeffe's *The Toy*, sang the highwayman Macheath in John Gay's *The Beggar's Opera*, and, at her own benefit, played Priscilla Tomboy in T. A. Lloyd's afterpiece *The Romp*. Her high spirits pleased at first, but audiences grew tired of 'too much liveliness, and too many gestures' (Haslewood, 2.307) and the Covent Garden management did not retain her beyond her first season. Miss Fontenelle appeared at the Theatre Royal, Edinburgh, in winter 1789–90, playing soubrette roles in plays and musical afterpieces, and after this performed in London only in the lightweight pieces of the Haymarket summer seasons of 1790–93. In Scotland she also appeared at Glasgow and at the newly opened theatre in Dumfries in 1792 and 1793, where Robert Burns admired 'her personal charms, amiable manner & gentle heart' (*Complete Letters*, 683). He wrote a prologue, *The Rights of Woman*, for her benefit in November 1792 and asked that she should include the afterpiece *The Spoiled Child*, in which she played the mischievous boy, Little Pickle. He also wrote the verses *On Seeing Miss Fontenelle in a Favourite Character* ('Sweet naïveté of feature …') and a new prologue for her 1793 benefit. The actor John Brown Williamson (*d.* 1802) was a fellow performer at the Haymarket, in Edinburgh, and at Dumfries. She joined his company of English actors

on an unsuccessful tour of Germany, and in 1795 they emigrated together to the USA, where Fontenelle acted as Mrs Williamson, although it is unclear whether they married or whether Williamson's first wife was still alive. They made their American début at the Federal Street Theater, Boston, Massachusetts, on 25 January 1796, with John in the title role of *Othello* and Louisa as Little Pickle in the afterpiece. Her performance was described by one critic as 'the most astonishing and brilliant display of theatrical genius ever exhibited in America' (Hornblow, 1.236–7). Williamson was appointed manager of the company in May 1796, but sustained disastrous losses in his first season. The couple acted in New York in summer 1797 and that autumn made their first appearances at Charleston, South Carolina, where Williamson became senior manager of the theatre company the following year and where Louisa's appearances in her three favourite roles, Moggy, Priscilla Tomboy, and Little Pickle, drew crowded houses. In December 1797 she played Rosalind in *As You Like It*, a performance described as 'impressive, gay, touching and pointed' (Willis, 372), and she was later to play Portia and the breeches role of Sir Harry Wildair. She died after three days' illness in Charleston, South Carolina, on 31 October 1799; the Charleston theatre was closed until 4 November as a mark of respect, and John Williamson did not act again for almost two months. He died on 28 March 1802.

OLIVE BALDWIN and THELMA WILSON

Sources C. B. Hogan, ed., *The London stage, 1660–1800*, pt 5: *1776–1800* (1968) • [J. Haslewood], *The secret history of the green rooms: containing authentic and entertaining memoirs of the actors and actresses in the three Theatres Royal*, 2 (1790), 2 • 'Theatrical journal', *European Magazine and London Review*, 13 (1788), 372–3 • *The complete poetical works of Robert Burns, 1759–1796*, ed. J. A. Mackay, rev. edn (1993) • *The complete letters of Robert Burns*, ed. J. A. Mackay (1987) • J. Jackson, *The history of the Scottish stage* (1793) • E. Willis, *The Charleston stage in the XVIII century: with social settings of the time* (1933); repr. (1968) • W. Dunlap, *History of the American theatre*, 1 (1833), 1 • J. Bernard, *Retrospections of America, 1797–1811*, ed. B. Bernard (1887) • J. N. Ireland, *Records of the New York stage, from 1750 to 1860*, 1 (1866) • G. O. Seilhamer, *History of the American theatre from 1774 to 1797*, 3 vols. [1888–91], vol. 3 • A. Hornblow, *A history of the theatre in America*, 1 (1919) • *The thespian dictionary, or, Dramatic biography of the eighteenth century* (1802) • T. Bellamy, 'The London theatres: a poem', *Miscellanies in prose and verse*, 2 vols. (1794–5) • M. J. Young, *Memoirs of Mrs Crouch*, 2 vols. (1806), 2 • parish register, London, St Margaret Lothbury, 1 Oct 1769 [baptism]
Likenesses J. Barlow, engraving (as Moggy in *The highland reel*), Harvard TC • print (after engraving by J. Barlow), repro. in *Portraits of actors* (1893) • watercolour drawing (as Moggy in *The highland reel*), BM

Fonteyn, Dame Margot [*real name* Margaret Evelyn Hookham; *married name* Margaret Evelyn de Arias] (**1919–1991**), ballerina, was born on 18 May 1919 at 49 London Road, Reigate, Surrey, the younger child and only daughter of Felix John Hookham (*b.* 1889), civil engineer, and his wife, Hilda Acheson, formerly Fontes (1894–1988). Fonteyn claimed to have inherited her enthusiasm and response to music and rhythm from her half-Irish, half-Brazilian mother, and from her father the tenacity and perfectionism to exploit those qualities so as to become one of the great dancers of all time.

First dancing classes and the Vic-Wells School From the age of four Peggy attended dancing classes with Grace Bosustow in Ealing, where the family had moved. Bosustow luckily gave her not only a proper grounding but was able to tell her mother (the prime mover of her career) how to choose good teachers when Mr Hookham's new job with the British–American Tobacco Company necessitated moving to the United States and then China. At first the liveliness of character-dancing attracted Peggy more than the pure classicism that later brought her fame, and she had no real ambition until inspired, on a visit home in 1931, by seeing Alicia Markova (the finest English ballerina before Fonteyn) in *Les sylphides*. The Hookhams were then living in Shanghai, where luckily they found an exceptionally talented teacher, the Russian émigré George Goncharov. He already had another English girl, June Brae (later Fonteyn's colleague at Sadler's Wells), as a pupil, whose seriousness fired Peggy to try harder, having grown used to being the best in her class. (Goncharov's partner Vera Volkova later became one of Fonteyn's most influential teachers in London.) After two years her mother brought her back to England, and she studied first with Markova's teacher Seraphine Astafieva before joining the Vic-Wells School. Within a few weeks she was performing with the Vic-Wells Ballet, and before the year was out had her first solo role, acting not dancing as the child in Ninette de Valois's *The Haunted Ballroom*, under an interim version of her stage name, Margot Fontes. She then took the name Fonteyn; her brother, Felix, a photographer specializing in dance, adopted it too. Before Fonteyn was sixteen Frederick Ashton gave her the surprisingly voluptuous leading part of the Creole girl in his *Rio Grande*; when Markova left the company soon afterwards, Fonteyn was one of the young dancers who shared the ballerina's roles among them. It did not take long for her (despite her own feelings of inadequacy) to emerge as the pick of the bunch, and by the time she was twenty Fonteyn had danced the lead in three of the great classics: *Giselle*, *Swan Lake* and *The Sleeping Beauty*. She had also created roles in a series of ballets by Ashton: the Fiancée in *Le baiser de la fée*, the captivating Woman in Ball-dress in *Apparitions*, the poor duped Flower-seller in *Nocturne*, forlorn Julia in *A Wedding Bouquet*, and the Young Woman in *Horoscope*. Ashton, whose muse had hitherto been Markova's more brittle precision and delicacy, wrote later (in *The Art of Margot Fonteyn*) of her innate musicality and wonderful physical proportions, her sense of line and beautiful arm movements, and that:

> Never once did she make a gesture which was not completely true; one that did not come from the heart. … Along with her other attributes she has a feminine warmth which readily communicates itself to an audience. … Had I not been able to work with Margot, I might never have developed the lyrical side of my work. (Money)

Fonteyn was fortunate in the colleagues under whose professional influence she found herself. De Valois, directing the young company, had a far-sighted grasp of strategy in repertory and casting. Ashton not only developed Fonteyn's interpretative gifts but advised her how to dress and behave off-stage. Robert Helpmann, her most frequent partner, set the example of his keen theatrical flair, and the company's music director, (Leonard) Constant *Lambert, a man of wide culture, took her particularly under his wing. Lambert and Fonteyn became lovers, but he ended their relationship gracelessly when he remarried, which perhaps explains why in her autobiography she failed to mention his artistic influence.

Wartime and post-war ballet The outbreak of the Second World War brought a more urgent tempo to the company's work. Instead of only two or three performances a week, they began dancing nightly, with matinées besides, to entertain war workers and troops on leave; long, gruelling tours were made between short London seasons. The

Dame Margot Fonteyn (1919–1991), by Alan Bergman, 1972 [on the opening night of *Raymonda* by Marius Petipa at the Metropolitan Opera House, New York]

company, renamed Sadler's Wells Ballet, was in the Netherlands when the Germans invaded, and escaped with nothing more than what the dancers stood up in. Fonteyn by now was, at twenty, the undisputed ballerina, with a consequent demand for her to appear as often as possible. And there were new roles to add, notably two by Ashton which extended her range with the passion of *Dante Sonata* and the glitter of *The Wanderer*, besides another classic, *Coppélia*, to which she brought a distinctive sense of humour.

This wartime experience helped develop the stamina that made Fonteyn's later career possible, but at the time it did more to consolidate her talent than to advance her artistry. The way she danced in *The Sleeping Beauty* when the company moved to Covent Garden in 1946 seemed impressive by the standards of the time. Luckily Ashton immediately created in *Symphonic Variations* a work showing Fonteyn's lyrical gifts to supreme advantage. Further important roles were as the Miller's Wife in *The Three-Cornered Hat* (dancing with its choreographer, Léonide Massine) and in Ashton's creation of the austerely evocative *Scènes de ballet*. Another turning point came in 1948, when she went to Paris to create the role of Agathe, the cat-woman (Fonteyn loved cats) in Roland Petit's *Les demoiselles de la nuit*. The frank admiration of this glamorous young choreographer, and being treated as a star, added a new assurance and crispness to everything she did on returning to London. The acclaim Fonteyn received in New York in the following year, opening the Sadler's Wells Ballet's first season there with *The Sleeping Beauty*, completed the transformation into a ballerina of international quality.

Before the American tour an injury during the first night of Ashton's *Don Juan* had kept Fonteyn from the stage for several months and prevented her from dancing in the première of his first three-act ballet, *Cinderella*. When she took over, however, she made the work specially her own, bringing out its qualities of humour and romance. This was soon followed by two of Fonteyn's greatest roles: the emotional depth and richness of *Daphnis and Chloë*, the drama, comedy, and classic display of *Sylvia*. Both were by Ashton but they were as different as could be.

Fonteyn's career was subsequently interrupted more than once by serious injury or illness that might have precipitated other dancers into early retirement, but she returned each time apparently stronger than before, and went on successfully long past the age when a dancer's powers usually decline. In Fonteyn the physical loss was compensated for by continually developing expressiveness and artistic maturity.

Marriage and wider recognition In 1955 Fonteyn married Dr Roberto Emilio de Arias (1918–1989), son of Harmadio Arias, president of Panama from 1932 to 1936, and his wife, Rosario Guardia de Arias. He was a sweetheart of Fonteyn's girlhood who had married and had a family before re-entering her life. A lawyer and politician in his native Panama, he was immediately after their wedding appointed ambassador to the court of St James. Fonteyn managed to combine the duties of an ambassador's wife with her already demanding career, although she revealed otherwise little concern for politics (she was criticized for dancing in South Africa during a dancers' union ban over apartheid, and she happily accepted invitations from Imelda Marcos, wife of the right-wing Philippine president). When Arias fell from political favour she supported his attempts to regain power in Panama, even to the point of being arrested and deported during one of his attempted coups, an experience she bore with calm dignity, as she did also an occasion in 1967 when she and Rudolf *Nureyev were held in custody in San Francisco after attending a party where some of the guests had used drugs.

Shortly before Fonteyn's wedding Ninette de Valois told her that she had been chosen to become president of the Royal Academy of Dancing (an international body responsible for teaching standards in ballet) in succession to its founder president, Adeline Genée. When she found her reluctance to accept the post firmly overruled, Fonteyn refused to treat it as a sinecure, and to her other responsibilities she added frequent meetings, oversight of a new syllabus, and the organization of annual fund-raising galas.

In 1956 Fonteyn, having been created CBE five years earlier, was promoted to DBE. That same year, seeing the Russian ballerina Galina Ulanova as Juliet during the Bolshoi Ballet's first London season was a stimulus for Fonteyn; at last she could understand what Ashton had always said about the extraordinary speed of Anna Pavlova, and try to emulate it. Another Russian former ballerina much admired by Ashton, Tamara Karsavina, also helped from 1954 by coaching her in *The Firebird* and other roles. But during the later 1950s, troubled by a painful left foot, Fonteyn began to think longingly of retirement, and more so when Michael Somes, her most regular partner since Helpmann's retirement ten years earlier, and well suited to her by his musicality, relinquished all his parts needing strong technique. Fonteyn even for a time gave up her most demanding ballet, *Swan Lake*, with its double role for the ballerina. She was worried that this might lead to a general decline in her ability, although reassured when Ashton created another long ballet for her, *Ondine*, a fluent role that gave her special pleasure.

Nureyev The most vital impetus to extending Fonteyn's career came in 1962 when de Valois invited Rudolf Nureyev, newly settled in the West, to dance with what had by now become the Royal Ballet, and offered Fonteyn the opportunity of dancing with him in *Giselle* for his début. She had reservations because of the difference in age (she forty-two, he only twenty-three) but decided she must accept to maintain her pre-eminence. In fact they went wonderfully together, each inspiring the other and able to learn from the experience. Thus began possibly the greatest of all ballet partnerships: two dancers, both individually superb, who raised each other to new heights. Their immediate rapport, the chemistry between them on stage, and the unanimity of purpose in preparation gave their performances together a uniquely satisfying quality.

Besides, both learned so much from the other in matters of style, emotional understanding, and presentation that their work with other partners benefited too. Nureyev's analytical understanding of technique and its physical basis also helped Fonteyn to overcome difficulties she had experienced, for instance with fouettés.

Fonteyn's long career on stage was made easier because her dancing never depended primarily on virtuosity, although her technique was stronger than was often said—by herself among others. It was she who introduced the long, sustained balances now expected of Aurora in the 'Rose adagio' of *The Sleeping Beauty*. Notably, too, when younger dancers took over some of the roles created for Fonteyn, they revealed unexpected difficulties, apparently because they lacked her gift of phrasing steps to the music. Certainly Fonteyn never lacked the technique for any role in which she was cast. These covered a vast range. Besides the many ballets created for her by Ashton, other choreographers who made roles for her were as varied as de Valois in her seriously dramatic *Don Quixote*; John Cranko, whose *Poème de l'extase* with the Stuttgart Ballet was inspired by Scriabin's music, the paintings of Klimt, and a Colette novel to show Fonteyn the mature woman; Peter Darrell, who presented her as a Beardsley seductress in *Scarlet Pastorale* with the Scottish Ballet; and even the American contemporary dance pioneer Martha Graham, who mounted *Lucifer* for Nureyev and Fonteyn.

The greatest dramatic experience of the Fonteyn–Nureyev partnership was *Marguerite and Armand*, where Ashton adapted the story of Marguérite Gautier into a series of flashbacks to a Liszt sonata. Fonteyn's role in this ranged, within a few minutes, from the smiling cynosure of all male eyes at a party, through her sickness, her happiness in the country, her self-sacrifice, the bitterness (shown in the inimitably painful dragging of her feet) of rejection and insult, to the final reconciliation coming tragically too late; all set against the feverish intensity of Nureyev's Armand and the stubborn dignity of Somes as the father.

Fonteyn and Nureyev were, against her wishes and those of the choreographer, but at the insistence of the Royal Ballet's American impresario, the first to play the title roles in Kenneth MacMillan's *Romeo and Juliet*, which had been meant for two of MacMillan's previous collaborators. Mostly, however, it was the old classics in which Fonteyn and Nureyev repeatedly played together. Both, for instance, were unmatched in giving theatrical point to Petipa's sublime dances for *The Sleeping Beauty* (although, surprisingly, she claimed it was the ballet she least liked). In *Swan Lake* she amazingly got better and better, not by elaborating but by simplifying so as to strip the role down to its essence. When Nureyev added unfamiliar classics to the Royal Ballet's repertory (the Shades scene from *La bayadère*, *Raymonda*, the *pas de deux* from the *Corsair*) and invented his own *Swan Lake* in Vienna, he insisted that Fonteyn had to be the ballerina, and deliberately gave her solos she would find difficult, to spur her to new discoveries.

With the Royal Ballet Fonteyn occupied a position of complete supremacy. It was sometimes suggested that her presence held back the progress of other dancers, but there was never among her contemporaries or juniors anyone to equal her. By 1959 the demand for seats when she appeared was such that special prices were charged, and in that same year she began to be billed as a guest artist so that she would be free to accept more of the other engagements she was offered worldwide. Nevertheless the Royal Ballet remained her base until Ashton, who had succeeded de Valois as director, retired in 1970, although she also danced with more than thirty other companies and specially assembled groups.

Final performances From 1964, when Dr Arias was shot and paralysed by a colleague whom he was alleged to have cuckolded, Fonteyn had an extra incentive to go on working for his medical bills; she remained devoted to his well-being and took him in a wheelchair on most of her journeys. To mark her sixtieth birthday in May 1979 the Royal Ballet gave a gala in her honour, including a *Salut d'amour* by Ashton which he danced with her. She also danced with her old partner Helpmann in the 'Tango' of Ashton's *Façade*, and at the end of the performance the Royal Ballet gave her, uniquely, the official title of prima ballerina assoluta. This had been widely assumed to be her farewell, but after that she took on another new role as the leading nymph in Nijinsky's *L'après-midi d'un faune* during Nureyev's 1979 summer season, for which he also persuaded her to resume the Girl in *Le spectre de la rose*. From time to time thereafter she appeared on special occasions, but only in parts that required no steps; her last time on stage was as the Queen in *The Sleeping Beauty* with Birmingham Royal Ballet in Miami in February 1986.

In later years Fonteyn settled in a small house with no telephone in a remote village in Panama, where Arias had a farm, and that remained her home after his death on 22 November 1989. She had few comforts, having spent most of her money on caring for him, but she found a real interest in cattle farming. She fell ill with cancer, but still undertook some teaching and coaching. She also continued visiting England each year, for the assembly of the Royal Academy of Dancing and to attend the degree ceremony at Durham University, which had elected her its chancellor in 1982. This honour was offered unexpectedly and she said that she accepted with awe, but she threw herself wholeheartedly into its duties, astonishing the academics with the fluency and passion for education revealed in her speech, delivered without notes, at her installation in Durham Cathedral.

Fonteyn's own general education had been repeatedly interrupted by putting dance first, but that did not prevent her writing several books. The most ambitious was based on a six-part television series which she wrote, introduced, and starred in, called *The Magic of Dance* (1980; BBC television series 1979). There were also an autobiography (1975), a study of Pavlova (1984), and *A Dancer's World* (1978), explaining the nature of a ballet career.

Because Fonteyn was known to have exhausted her savings on hospital bills for her husband and then for herself, Covent Garden gave a gala for her benefit in May 1990 at which the tenor Placido Domingo volunteered to sing, and Somes and Nureyev took small parts in *Romeo and Juliet*, before an audience determined to demonstrate its admiration and affection for the guest of honour. She died in Panama City nine months later, on 21 February 1991, and was buried near her village home. A memorial service was held in Westminster Abbey on 2 July 1991.

Many dancers excelled Fonteyn in virtuosity or their theatrical intensity in dramatic roles. Her special gift was for grasping completely the intention and balance of the dance and the music and bringing them to life for the audience. She never lost the joyousness which marked her dancing from childhood, and the ability to communicate that was perhaps the supreme secret of her art. During an extraordinarily long career she brought her gifts to ever wider audiences in many parts of the world on stage; millions more saw her on television or in films. Consequently, even more than Anna Pavlova in the early years of the century, Fonteyn awakened a love of dance in untold thousands of spectators.   (*The Times*)

JOHN PERCIVAL

Sources *Margot Fonteyn: autobiography* (1975) · *The Times* (22 Feb 1991) · K. Money, *The art of Margot Fonteyn, photographed by Keith Money; with a commentary contributed by Ninette de Valois, Frederick Ashton, Keith Money, and Margot Fonteyn herself* (1965) · b. cert. · *WWW* · F. Holliday, *Daily Telegraph* (23 Feb 1991)
Archives Tate collection, corresp. with Lord Clark
Likenesses photographs, 1937–79, Hult. Arch. · A. Bergman, photograph, 1972, NPG [*see illus.*] · K. Money, photographs, repro. in Money, *The art of Margot Fonteyn* · portraits, NPG
Wealth at death £241,739—in England and Wales: administration with will, 29 March 1994, *CGPLA Eng. & Wales*

Fontibus, John de. *See* Fountains, John of (*d.* 1225).

Foord, Arthur Humphreys (1844–1933), palaeontologist and scientific illustrator, was born on 14 September 1844 at Brixton, Surrey, together with his twin brother, Alfred Stanley Foord (1844–1934), also an illustrator of scientific papers, and secretary of a mining company. Arthur was the fourth, and youngest, son of John Bromley Foord of Bexleyheath, Kent, who was secretary (in London) of the General Mining Association of Nova Scotia, and his wife, Sarah Stanley Hooper. From a preparatory school, where he studied from 1853 to 1856, he went in 1857 to Chatham House School, Ramsgate, Kent. He held a post in commercial business in London from 1861 until 1871 and during this period his ability in natural history illustration was quite well recognized, in particular by Henry Woodward, keeper of the geological department of the British Museum and co-editor of the *Geological Magazine*.

At the end of 1871 Foord went to Montreal with letters of introduction to Sir William Edmond Logan, first director of the geological survey of Canada, to his successor, Alfred Richard Cecil Selwyn, and to John William Dawson, principal of McGill University. Early in 1872 the geological survey of Canada appointed him as a natural history artist, a post he held until 1883. During these eleven years he came under the influence of such eminent palaeontologists as Elkanah Billings, John J. Frederick Whiteaves, and Henry Alleyne Nicholson. He worked in the survey mainly as artist, but gained much experience as a collector in the field

and as a museum curator. While in Montreal he took Dawson's courses (in 1875–6) in zoology and palaeontology at McGill University. When the survey moved to Ottawa in 1883 he was appointed assistant palaeontologist, but in the summer of the same year he resigned his position and returned to England. In London he worked as a volunteer at the British Museum (Natural History) and studied privately geology under Thomas Rupert Jones, editor of the *Geological Magazine*, and practical zoology and comparative anatomy under George Bond Howes and T. Johnson, professors at the Royal School of Mines. After his first publication, 'Contribution to the micro-palaeontology of the Cambro-Silurian rocks of Canada' (1883), five other papers on fossil corals were published between 1884 and 1886 in the *Annals and Magazine of Natural History*, while collaborating with Robert Etheridge junior and Henry A. Nicholson.

In 1886 Foord was charged with the preparation of his most famous work, the *Catalogue of the Fossil Cephalopoda in the British Museum* (*Natural History*), of which he completed the first two volumes (1888, 1891) and the third (1897) with George Charles Crick. In connection with this research he also studied type collections in Brussels and Munich. Several papers on nautiloids and reviews were also published by him at about this time in the *Geological Magazine*. In 1888 the Geological Society of London, of which he was a fellow, awarded him one half of the Lyell geological fund in recognition of his work as a palaeontologist and illustrator. In 1891 he moved to Dublin to take up the position of librarian and editor of scientific publications of the Royal Dublin Society until his retirement in 1920. During these years he worked on cephalopod material in the National Museum of Ireland and geological survey of Ireland collections as well as compiling a considerable personal collection. He obtained a doctorate from the University of Munich in 1896 by submitting a thesis to the distinguished palaeontologist Karl Alfred von Zittel. This work was later published as part of his 5-volume monograph of the Palaeontographical Society, *Carboniferous Cephalopoda of Ireland* (1897–1903). The monograph, together with the catalogue cited above, form an indispensable reference for cephalopod workers, and Foord's taxonomic work ranks alongside those of Alpheus Hyatt and Laurent Guillaume de Koninck. He was apparently married as he translated in 1899, together with his wife, a work in German by Edmund von Mojsisovics on Himalayan fossils. However, nothing is known of his family life. In 1930 Foord moved to Hove, Sussex, where he died at his home, Red Cottage, Hove Street, on 12 August 1933.

KATHLEEN HISTON and EZIO VACCARI

Sources A. H. Foord, Curriculum vitae, 1892, Munich University Archives, sig. OC-I-23p · A. H. Foord, 'List of books and papers of my own, and others with collaborators', 1896, Munich University Archives, sig. OC-I-23p · A. H. Foord, Testimonials, 1883–92, Munich University Archives, sig. OC-I-23p · *Quarterly Journal of the Geological Society of London*, 90 (1934), lii · J. W. Judd, 'Award of the Lyell geological fund', *Quarterly Journal of the Geological Society*, 44 (1888), 39 · R. J. Cleevely, *World palaeontological collections* (1983) · M. Zaslow, *Reading the rocks: the story of the geological survey of Canada, 1842–1972* (1975) · S. Sheets-Pyenson, *Index to the scientific correspondence of John William Dawson* (1992) · W. A. S. Sarjeant, *Geologists and the history of* *geology: an international bibliography from the origins to 1978* (1980), vol. 2 · R. L. Praeger, *Some Irish naturalists: a biographical note-book* (1949) · *BL cat.*, vol. 111 · d. cert.

Archives Archiv der Ludwig-Maximilians-Universität München, papers on A. H. Foord's doctorate, Signatur · National Museum of Ireland, Dublin, collections of fossil specimens · NHM, collections of fossil specimens

Likenesses W. J. Topley, two photographs, 1883, NA Canada

Wealth at death £2315 2s. 8d.: probate, 27 Sept 1933, *CGPLA Eng. & Wales*

Foord, Joseph (1714–1788), land surveyor and hydraulic engineer, was born on 13 July 1714 at Fadmoor, near Kirkbymoorside in Yorkshire, the third of the four children of Matthew Foord (*bap.* 1682, *d.* 1744), Quaker farmer and land agent of the Duncombe Park estate, and his wife, Leah (1678–1752), daughter of William and Jane Pilmoor, Quakers, of Fadmoor.

Foord moved to Skiplam with his parents in 1734, and continued to farm at Skiplam Grange after his father's death in 1744. At twenty-nine Foord's strong Quaker affiliation was disrupted when Kirkbymoorside meeting concluded, after exhaustive inquiry, that he was the father of a child, Joseph, born at Fadmoor late in 1743 (perhaps on 31 October) to Sarah Pilmoor (*bap.* 1713, *d.* 1778). The Society of Friends formally denied unity with Foord in March 1744. On 16 January 1746 he married Mary Anderson (*bap.* 1713, *d.* 1779) of Kirkbymoorside; of their six children only two attained adulthood. He inherited his father's copyhold farms and water cornmills and a lease in Ankness moorland coalfield. A practical understanding of hydrology, supplemented by an intimate working knowledge of the geology of his native landscape, led him to construct an experimental water race about 1747. It ran 5 miles from moorland springs to Gillamoor and Fadmoor and was extended about 1757 to the market town of Kirkbymoorside. Between 1759 and 1768 open cuts to Carlton, Nawton, Pockley, Old Byland, and Rievaulx townships completed Foord's gravity-fed water system of some 70 miles in length. He was 'a self-taught engineer of great ingenuity' (Marshall, 1.166) whose races, starting in distant moorland valleys, supplied running water to nine villages and 'to ponds in all the fields' (Tuke, 241) of a large tract of dry limestone uplands. They functioned for much of the twentieth century. Their uniqueness as a rural water supply system has ensured their recognition by English Heritage.

As well as being skilled in fixed-level surveying over long distances, Foord became an accomplished land surveyor. He was surveyor and commissioner for seven enclosure awards between 1763 and 1776. Between 1780 and 1785 he carried out a general survey and valuation of the 29,000-acre Duncombe estate. In 1786 Foord hired a London attorney when Charles Slingsby Duncombe refused to pay, in full, his bill for £564. The case never came to court, Duncombe being advised that Foord was an 'honest man' and as 'eminent' a surveyor as James Brindley (Duncombe, 2v). No personal documents survive but four court cases initiated by Foord indicate an assertive temperament.

In 1765 he moved to farm at West End in Kirkbymoorside, where his wife died in 1779. Foord seems to have visited America in 1787. A later local source described him visiting 'the wilds of America' and dying 'when setting his foot upon the English shore' (Parker). The sea voyages must have taxed the old man's strength. He died on 23 January 1788 at Fawdington, near Thirsk, Yorkshire, in the farmhouse of his Quaker daughter Mary Flower. The record of his burial on 25 January 1788 in the Quaker burial-ground at Thirsk (then sited in an area called Barbeck, on the edge of the town) stated that he was not a member of the society. His goods were valued at under £73, including his surveying instruments at £5; his house was his only immovable property. His telescopic level and brass theodolite are preserved at Ryedale Folk Museum.

Foord's natural son, Joseph Pilmore (also Pilmoor) (1743–1825), baptized on 13 April 1747, was sent to America by John Wesley in 1769 to further the Methodist cause. Ordained in 1785, Pilmore served as an Episcopalian rector in New York (1794–1804) and Philadelphia (1804–21). The man he called 'my father' (*Journal of Joseph Pilmore*, 15) was William Sleightholme of Fadmoor, who married Sarah Pilmoor in 1754.   ISABEL ANNE MCLEAN

Sources I. McLean, *Water from the moors: the life and works of Joseph Foord* [forthcoming] · W. Marshall, *The rural economy of Yorkshire*, 2 vols. (1788) · J. Tuke, *A general view of the agriculture of the north riding of Yorkshire* (1800) · C. S. Duncombe, draft brief to counsel in *Foord v. Duncombe*, 1786, N. Yorks. CRO, ZEW VI 8 · T. Parker, 'History of Kirkdale', 1, 1858, Ryedale Folk Museum, 1380 · *The journal of Joseph Pilmore, Methodist itinerant*, ed. F. E. Maser (Philadelphia, 1969) · Guisborough monthly meeting of the Society of Friends, birth, submissions, and reports, 1716–50, N. Yorks. CRO, R/Q/G 3/1 · minute book, Kirkbymoorside preparative meeting, 1702–81, U. Hull, Brynmor Jones L., DQR 5/1 · Duncombe Park estate rentals, 1730–86, N. Yorks. CRO, ZEW IV 5/4–16 · probate, 1744, Ryedale deanery, Borthwick, vol. 89, fol. 200 · I. Cooper, *Helmsley 100 years ago* (1887) · B. English, *Yorkshire enclosure awards* (1985) · digest of registers of Yorkshire quarterly meeting (Society of Friends), U. Leeds, Brotherton L., entries 1412/38; 1412/19; 1307/8 · Kirkdale parish registers, N. Yorks. CRO, PR/KRD 1/3 [baptism of Matthew Foord] · Nunnington parish registers, N. Yorks. CRO, PR/NU 1/2 [baptism of Joseph Pilmore]

Wealth at death £72 13s. 6d.; also house in Kirkbymoorside: administration, 28 Feb 1788, Borth. Inst.

Foot, Sir Dingle Mackintosh (1905–1978), politician and lawyer, was born on 24 August 1905 in Plymouth, the eldest child in the family of five sons and two daughters of Isaac *Foot (1880–1960), MP and solicitor, and his wife, Eva Mackintosh (1878–1946). She was a Scot of Cornish descent and he was given her father's family name. He was educated at Bembridge School, Isle of Wight—whose headmaster, the pacifist Howard Whitehouse, was a family friend—and at Balliol College, Oxford, where he took a second in modern history in 1927. He was president of the University Liberal Club in 1927 and of the Oxford Union one year later, before becoming secretary to his father in the House of Commons after the latter's election in 1929. Foot shared his father's political influences—Methodism and west country radicalism—in equal doses. Aside from politics, his lifelong vocation was the law, and he was

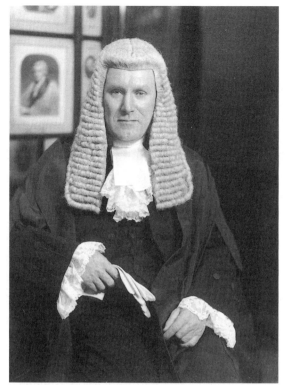

Sir Dingle Mackintosh Foot (1905–1978), by Elliott & Fry, 1954

called to the bar at Gray's Inn in 1930, joining the western circuit.

Brought up in an intensely political household—three of his brothers, Hugh Mackintosh *Foot (Baron Caradon), John, and Michael, were to become parliamentarians—Foot contested Tiverton as a Liberal in the 1929 general election before topping the poll at Dundee in 1931. He sat alongside his father until Isaac Foot's defeat in 1935; both were firmly on the side of Herbert Samuel and free trade during the crises which rent the Liberal Party asunder during that parliament. He married, in 1933, Dorothy Mary Elliston, a staunch Conservative and formidable political hostess, daughter of William Rowley Elliston, at one time recorder of Great Yarmouth. There were no children of the marriage.

At the outbreak of war in 1939 Foot was unable to enlist because of a tubercular right arm, and instead joined the Royal Observer Corps. He was recalled by Churchill in 1940 to become parliamentary secretary to the Ministry of Economic Warfare, a post he held for the duration of the conflict, working under Hugh Dalton. He was engaged in several missions abroad regarding the blockade of the axis powers and was also, in 1945, a member of the British delegation to the San Francisco conference which framed the United Nations charter.

Foot lost his Dundee seat in the Labour landslide of 1945. He prevaricated during repeated attempts by the city's Liberals to re-adopt him as their parliamentary candidate, sensing that the party's position there was irredeemable.

Instead, he was adopted for North Cornwall, losing narrowly in 1950 and somewhat less narrowly in 1951. Facing, in effect, the end of his political career, Foot began to distance himself from the Liberal leadership. Although he had run in tandem with the Conservative Florence Horsbrugh for the two-member constituency of Dundee, Foot was increasingly aligned with the radical wing of the Liberal Party, alongside his close friend Lady Megan Lloyd George, and in opposition to Clement Davies, perceived as right-wing. He resigned as a vice-president of the Liberal Party, and from being prospective candidate for North Cornwall, in 1954, before following Lady Megan into the Labour Party in July 1956.

Out of parliament, Foot's legal career advanced. He became a bencher of Gray's Inn in 1952 and took silk two years later. He was a member of the royal commission on justices of the peace from 1946 to 1948, was appointed a member of the committee on intermediaries in 1949, and chaired the Observer Trust from 1953 to 1955. It was at this time that Foot cultivated his links with legal practice in the Commonwealth, being admitted as an advocate in the Gold Coast, Ceylon, Nigeria, Northern Rhodesia, Sierra Leone, India, Bahrain, Malaysia, and Southern Rhodesia. He specialized in constitutional and civil liberties cases, defending Dr Hastings Banda, then leader of the Nyasaland African Congress Party, when he was jailed in Southern Rhodesia, and Shaikh Muhammad Abdullah, the former chief minister of Kashmir, in the Kashmir conspiracy case. He was expelled from Nigeria in 1962 while challenging the Emergency Powers Act on behalf of the western Nigerian premier, Alhaji D. S. Adegbenro, and was refused entry the next year when he sought to represent Chief Enaharo on a treason charge after his expulsion from the United Kingdom. Lord Diplock described him as 'an ambassador of common law throughout the Commonwealth' (The Times, 20 June 1978) and, passionate for the cause of racial equality, he established one of the first multiracial chambers in the Temple.

By this time Foot was re-established in the House of Commons. He was returned for Ipswich at a by-election in 1957 after the death of Richard Stokes, ironically heading off a Liberal revival in the process. He was chairman of the Society of Labour Lawyers from 1960 to 1964 and when Labour returned to power, in 1964, he was appointed solicitor-general, accepting a knighthood at the same time. He was a quietly efficient law officer, but his learned academic radicalism was out of sympathy with the labour movement. He remained a liberal in all but name, struggling to find a niche for himself in the Parliamentary Labour Party. He resigned his post in 1967, claiming age as the reason, although his disagreement with the government's Rhodesian policy was a more significant influence. He was subsequently sworn of the privy council. His election address in 1970 differed from the Labour Party manifesto on several points, notably immigration policy, and possibly contributed to his defeat by just 13 votes.

Foot again turned to his legal career after he left the government. He was treasurer of the bar in 1968 and was called to the Northern Ireland bar in 1970; in the previous year he had defended Bernadette Devlin (later McAliskey), MP for Mid-Ulster. He continued to practise extensively throughout the Commonwealth, particularly in Malawi and Hong Kong. In 1974 he was awarded an honorary LLD from Dundee University and two years later published *British Political Crises*, which offered some autobiographical insights in a narrative which dwelt on the decline of the Liberal Party as a major political force. These were not happy years for Foot—he has been described as 'virtually an alcoholic' at this time (Jones, 287). He died on 18 June 1978, during a case in Hong Kong, by choking on a sandwich in his hotel room. His remains were cremated in Hong Kong. ROBERT INGHAM

Sources *The Times* (20 June 1978), 1a · *DNB* · D. Brack and M. Baines, eds., *Dictionary of liberal biography* (1998) · M. Jones, *Michael Foot* (1994) · D. Foot, *British political crises* (1976) · S. Hoggart and D. Leigh, *Michael Foot: a portrait* (1981) · *The Times* (20 June 1978), 7d · *The Times* (21 June 1978), 5f · *The Times* (27 June 1978), 19g · *WWW, 1971–80* · Dundee RO, Dundee Liberal Association MSS · private information (2004) · *CGPLA Eng. & Wales* (1979)
Archives BLPES, corresp. and papers · CAC Cam., corresp. and papers | Dundee Central Library, letters to Sir Garnet Wilson · Dundee RO, Dundee Liberal Association MSS · King's Lond., Liddell Hart C., corresp. with Sir B. H. Liddell Hart | FILM BFI NFTVA, documentary footage · ITN archive, London · Reuters, London | SOUND BL NSA, 'The political clans', M5582W BD1
Likenesses ACME, group portrait, photograph, 1945, Hult. Arch. · Elliott & Fry, photograph, 1954, NPG [*see illus.*] · photograph, repro. in Foot, *British political crises* · photograph, repro. in *The Times* (20 June 1978)
Wealth at death £14,916: probate, 21 March 1979, *CGPLA Eng. & Wales*

Foot, Hugh Mackintosh, Baron Caradon (1907–1990), colonial administrator and diplomatist, was born on 8 October 1907 in Plymouth, the second son and second child in the family of five sons and two daughters of Isaac *Foot (1880–1960), solicitor and Liberal MP for Bodmin, Cornwall, and his wife Eva (1878–1946), daughter of Dr Angus Mackintosh DPH of Fincastle, Perthshire. Isaac Foot's life centred on Liberal politics and Methodism. His children were brought up in a devout Christian home, over-brimming with books and the scholarship of radical philosophy. Hugh was the tallest and strongest of the children and the only one to win a scholarship to his school (the Quaker Leighton Park School in Reading). Unlike his father and three of his brothers, he did not enter the law, and whereas Dingle [*see* Foot, Sir Dingle Mackintosh], John, Michael, and Christopher studied at Oxford, Hugh went to St John's College, Cambridge, where he rowed and played cricket. Politics and public speaking were a busy part of his life and, following his father's radical Liberalism, he became president of the Liberal Club at Cambridge. Michael wrote of him later:

> He had acquired strange tastes and was ready to indulge in pastimes which the rest of us wouldn't be seen dead at—such as rowing, playing polo, dressing up in Goering-like uniforms and enjoying it, and occasionally even—at a pinch—placing some trust in the word of Tory Prime Ministers.

Four of the Foot brothers, including Hugh (1929), became presidents of their university unions. Hugh Foot obtained

Hugh Mackintosh Foot, Baron Caradon (1907–1990), by Elliott & Fry, 1957

a second class (division one) in part one of the history tripos (1927), and a second class (division two) in part two of the law tripos (1929).

In 1929 Foot joined the colonial service and was posted to Palestine. He became an Arab linguist and learned about the stresses and strains of the Middle East, developing an understanding which was invaluable when in later years he worked at the United Nations. In 1936 he married, in Haifa, (Florence) Sylvia (*d.* 1985), daughter of Arthur White Millar Tod OBE, director of the Steam Navigation Company of Baghdad. They had three sons, one of them the writer and journalist Paul Foot, and a daughter. Foot was back in London in the Colonial Office in 1938–9. On the outbreak of the Second World War he was appointed assistant British resident in Transjordan, where he stayed until 1942. In 1943 he became lieutenant-colonel in charge of military administration in Cyrenaica and later in the same year was sent as colonial secretary to Cyprus, which was dangerously near to German-occupied Greece, Rhodes, and Crete. In 1945 he went happily to Jamaica as colonial secretary and in 1947 he was posted to Nigeria as chief secretary. The preparatory work he did there contributed to Nigerian independence in 1962. He returned to Jamaica in 1951 as governor and captain-general. He was disappointed that plans for a federation of the West Indies were unsuccessful, Jamaica (which attained full independence in 1961) preferring to proceed alone.

Foot left the Caribbean in 1957 to become governor of the violent, riven island of Cyprus, which had changed dramatically since 1943. Greece and the Greek Cypriots wanted Enosis (union), Turkey and the Turkish Cypriots desired partition, and the British government insisted on holding on to all of Cyprus. By 1960, after years of difficult diplomacy, independence was attained, with Britain retaining two sovereign bases on the island. The Conservative colonial secretary paid tribute in the House of Commons to Foot's 'unfailing imagination, courage and leadership'. Cyprus was Foot's last colony. For over thirty years he had moved with authority in lands of daunting complexity and engineered their metamorphoses from colonies into free countries, working as a mediator rather than a ruler. He believed that the only way to teach people responsibility was to give it to them. Everywhere he respected the individual dignity of his subjects, never patronizing them, and never remote from their human condition.

Foot's next move to the United Nations was consistent with his experience and his passionate belief that the UN was the only alternative to the division and destruction of the world. In 1961 he became the British representative on the Trusteeship Council, with special responsibility for Africa. However, Foot could not support the Conservative government's policy on Rhodesia. Deeply troubled, he resigned in 1962, writing: 'I do not feel able to speak in the UN or elsewhere in defence of our position in this matter. I simply cannot do it'. Foot was well aware that this might end his UN career. Yet his international reputation and popularity were such that he was invited by the UN to remain in charge of its own development programme.

After the Labour Party's victory in 1964 Harold Wilson appointed Foot minister of state at the Foreign Office, and ambassador to the UN (1964–70). He was created a life peer as Baron Caradon (1964) and spoke on occasion forcefully in the House of Lords, particularly on the role of the UN charter in dealing with the world's dilemmas of violence and poverty. His efforts produced resolution 242 which formed the basis of the Egyptian–Israeli peace treaty. In New York his energy and robust optimism could be demanding and sometimes colleagues and staff could not keep up with the speed of his thinking and vision of his arguments. He certainly tried to implement the ideals of the charter. From 1971 he was consultant to the UN Development Programme, a post from which he retired in 1975, but he continued to advise in the troubled places of the world. He had a rare adaptability to peoples and places, which he happily shared with his talented, dedicated wife.

Foot was appointed OBE (1939), CMG (1946), KCMG (1951), and GCMG (1957). He became an honorary fellow of St John's College, Cambridge, in 1960 and was sworn of the privy council in 1968. Foot was often regarded as a colonial governor who ran out of colonies. He rejoiced that every colony he governed became independent. He was at the axis of an old empire swinging through conciliation to freedom and independence, enfranchising more than 6 million people in twenty years. Caradon died on 5 September 1990 in Plymouth.   LENA M. JEGER, *rev.*

Sources H. Foot, *A start in freedom* (1964) • *The Times* (6 Sept 1990) • *The Times* (25 Sept 1990) • *The Independent* (12 Sept 1990) • private information (1996) • personal knowledge (1996) • *CGPLA Eng. & Wales* (1990)

Likenesses Elliott & Fry, photograph, 1957, NPG [*see illus.*]
Wealth at death £115,000: probate, 6 Dec 1990, *CGPLA Eng. & Wales*

Foot, Isaac (1880–1960), politician, was born in Plymouth on 23 February 1880, the fourth son of Isaac Foot (1842–1926), builder and undertaker, and his wife, Eliza Ryder (*d.* 1922). He was educated at the Plymouth public school and then at the Hoe grammar school. After a brief spell in London, where he went to prepare for the civil service examination, Foot returned to Plymouth to train as a solicitor. He qualified in 1902, and in 1903 founded the enduring legal partnership of Foot and Bowden. On 22 September 1904 he married Eva (1878–1946), daughter of Angus Mackintosh MD, a granddaughter of William Dingle of Callington in Cornwall.

With a measure of financial security behind him, Foot entered politics. His upbringing had been staunchly Methodist, and his political and religious beliefs were ever closely intertwined. He first learned the skills of oratory when preaching in his local chapel and he entered politics as, and always remained, a Liberal. After two unsuccessful contests in ward elections in Plymouth he became a councillor for the Greenbank ward in 1907 and remained a member of the city council for some twenty years.

The focus of Foot's ambitions and the field of his talents was, however, to be the House of Commons. He fought the Totnes division in January 1910 and was well beaten by the Conservative candidate, F. B. Mildmay. In December 1910 he fought the South-East Cornwall (Bodmin) division and was defeated by only forty-one votes by Sir Reginald Pole Carew. He justly hoped to win the seat at the next attempt, but this proved to be the 1918 'coupon' election, when his support for Asquith against Lloyd George in the schism affecting the Liberal Party told heavily against him. He lost by more than 3000 votes. In 1919 in the Sutton division of Plymouth he was beaten by Lady Astor—with whom thereafter he had a lifetime's fast friendship. He was finally successful in 1922 for the Bodmin division at a by-election, and was returned again in 1922 and 1923.

Foot lost his seat in the Liberal collapse of 1924 but won it back in 1929, when his vigorous campaigning helped the Liberals to victory in all five Cornish seats. In the crisis of 1931 he gave conditional support to the National Government of Ramsay MacDonald, and accepted the junior ministerial post of secretary for mines. He was elected unopposed at Bodmin at the ensuing general election. Foot was a member of the round-table conference on India in 1930–31 and on Burma in 1931, and also served on the joint select committee on India. His championing of the rights of the poor on the subcontinent earned him the title 'the member for the Depressed Classes'.

Foot made a great impression during his brief time in office, but when faced with the government's protectionist measures, brought about by the Ottawa conference of 1932, he resigned instantly. The decision cost him the whole of his political future, as he must have known it would, but it was a decision that he made without hesitation and which he never regretted. He remained in the mainstream of traditional Liberalism and refused to contemplate the prospects of continued office as a national or Simonite Liberal. In the 1935 general election he lost at Bodmin to the Conservative candidate.

In 1937, the year that he was sworn of the privy council, Foot accepted the invitation of St Ives Liberals to contest the by-election that followed when Walter Runciman, the National Liberal member, succeeded to his father's peerage. Foot had helped Runciman to win the seat in 1929 and he was indignant that his former colleague should now seek, with Conservative support, to establish its reversion to the National Liberals. Foot's campaign attacked the ethical basis of such hybrid politics and aimed, too, at the National Government's policy of appeasement. The St Ives Labour Party stood aside in Foot's favour, and he narrowly lost the contest by 210 votes. He would later reflect that his eight electoral defeats—he contested Tavistock in 1945—meant more to him than his five victories, and he remembered particularly the lost battles of 1935 and 1937.

Out of office and out of the House of Commons, Foot devoted himself to the two other great enthusiasms of his life, the collection and reading of thousands of books and the study and practice of public speech. At their home, Pencrebar, some 3 miles out of Callington, he and Eva Foot brought up a remarkable family. There were two daughters and five sons: Dingle Mackintosh *Foot, who became solicitor-general, with a knighthood, in the Labour government of 1964; Hugh Mackintosh *Foot, who became Baron Caradon, and as Sir Hugh Foot was the last governor of Cyprus; Michael, the left-wing rebel, former editor of *Tribune*, member of parliament for Ebbw Vale in succession to his friend Aneurin Bevan, and Labour Party leader in 1980–83; John, a solicitor and chairman (later president) of the United Kingdom Immigrants Advisory Service (1970–78), who received a life peerage in 1967; and Christopher, who carried on the family law practice in Plymouth. A formative influence on them all was undoubtedly the merciless cut and thrust of political and literary debate in that lively household.

Over the years Foot built up at Pencrebar a famous library of more than 70,000 books, which formed the basework of the remarkable photographic memory with which he so astounded his contemporaries and obliterated his opponents. All his life he was a voracious reader, waking at five or earlier every morning for the purpose. He taught himself Greek at an advanced age in order to read his New Testament in the original. His lay sermons, like his speeches, were famous and remembered for years by his listeners. They were framed and composed with admirable clarity, and lapped round and incensed with that rich Devon speech which he never lost.

Foot had been chosen as deputy mayor of Plymouth in 1920 and during his year of office he visited the United States as Plymouth's representative at the *Mayflower* tercentenary. His gift for memorable oratory was by this time so well developed as to produce an indelible impression upon all those who heard him. In 1945 he was chosen by unanimous vote to be lord mayor of the city of Plymouth,

an honour very rarely accorded to one not at the time a member of the city council. During his mayoralty his acute sense of history lent unusual distinction to the office. He made a point of visiting every school in the city in full robes to bring local history and civic pride to life in the minds of the children.

One of Oliver Cromwell's greatest disciples in the twentieth century, Isaac Foot was president of the Cromwell Association for many years until his death, and always enjoyed taking part in the annual services held beside Cromwell's statue outside parliament. Cromwell and Lincoln were his great sources of inspiration, and the subjects of a comparative biography by him, published in 1946. The Methodist church made Foot its vice-president in 1937–8, and he was also a leader of the temperance movement, holding 'the somewhat severe opinions associated with his puritanical sympathies' (*The Times*, 14 Dec 1960). He was president of the Liberal Party Organization in 1947. In 1945 he was appointed deputy chairman of Cornwall quarter sessions; and in 1953 he was appointed chairman, serving until 1955, a very rare distinction for a solicitor. In 1959 he was given the honorary degree of DLitt by Exeter University. Following the death of Eva Foot, he married on 11 August 1951 Catherine Elizabeth Taylor, the daughter of Frederick Dawe, of Liskeard, Cornwall.

Foot died at Callington on 13 December 1960, at the age of eighty, when his powers had hardly begun to fade. In the west country the Foot name had a magic about it which is easily understood by his countrymen but difficult to describe. Isaac Foot was the last of the great orators, and Lord Samuel said of him: 'He was a natural orator, drawing fresh inspiration from Milton and Cromwell, and many of his speeches in Parliament and in his own county touched rare heights of eloquence.' He was survived by his second wife and by his seven children.

STANLEY GOODMAN, rev. MARK POTTLE

Sources personal knowledge (1971) · private information (1971) · J. Foot, biographical note, *The dictionary of liberal biography*, ed. D. Brack (1998) · S. Foot, *My grandfather: Isaac Foot* (1980) · *The Times* (14 Dec 1960)

Archives Plymouth and West Devon RO, corresp. and papers, incl. MS sermons · priv. coll., papers | FILM BFI NFTVA, documentary footage | SOUND Plymouth Public Library Service, recorded talks

Likenesses W. Stoneman, photograph, 1931, NPG

Wealth at death £63,118 12s. 1d.: probate, 2 Aug 1961, CGPLA Eng. & Wales

Foot, James (d. 1776), poet, studied under the remarkable Philip Doddridge (1702–1751) at his dissenting academy at Northampton, leaving in 1737. In 1743 he became minister at Chard, Somerset, and from 1759 until his death he was minister at the Grove Chapel, Bradford-on-Avon, Wiltshire. Already a 'widower', Foot married Ann Pike on 18 August 1755, and their son James was baptized on 23 March 1758.

Foot's long blank verse poem in six books, *Penseroso, or, The Pensive Philosopher in his Solitudes*, which appeared in May 1771, reflects his liberal dissenting principles, recommending 'piety, the social virtues, and a love of liberty'

(Foot, iii), and passionately defending religious toleration. Particularly striking is his expression of devotion to 'Nature' as revelation of God. 'Christianity', the poet declares in his extensive notes, recalling the full title of Matthew Tindal's deistical treatise *Christianity as Old as the Creation* (1730), 'seems to be a republication of the religion of nature, which mankind had grossly corrupted, as the most learned divines have unanswerably proved' (ibid., 200).

Foot was buried at Holy Trinity, Bradford-on-Avon, on 22 July 1776; an obituary notice in the *Bath Chronicle* (1 August 1776) describes him as 'a man of the most benevolent and amiable disposition, beloved, respected, and lamented by all who knew him'.   Robert Inglesfield

Sources J. Foot, *Penseroso, or, The pensive philosopher in his solitudes* (1771) · *The correspondence and diary of Philip Doddridge*, ed. J. D. Humphreys, 5 (1831) · H. M. Gunn, *History of free churches in Chard and the neighbourhood* (1867) · G. F. Nuttall, 'Morgans Hill Congregational Church, Bradford-on-Avon', *Transactions of the Congregational Historical Society*, 14 (1940–44), 40–47 · *Bath Chronicle* (9 May 1771) · *Bath Chronicle* (1 Aug 1776) · *GM*, 1st ser., 41 (1771) · *GM*, 1st ser., 46 (1776) · marriage register, Combe St Nicholas · register of births and baptisms belonging to the congregation of protestant dissenters of Ilminster · parish register, Holy Trinity, Bradford-on-Avon, 22 July 1776 [burial], 1776

Foot, Jesse (1744–1826), surgeon and biographer, is thought to have been born at Charlton, Wiltshire. He was trained in London, possibly at the Middlesex Hospital, and became a member of the Company of Surgeons. Foot spent the years 1766–9 on Nevis in the West Indies, where he presumably practised on a plantation, as he later boasted of being responsible for the 'care of 2,000 negroes annually' (Foot, *A Defence*, 31). After leaving the West Indies, Foot travelled to St Petersburg, where he became 'a privileged practitioner of the College of St Petersburg'. On his return to Britain he was house surgeon at the Middlesex Hospital between 1774 and 1775. He then established a practice in Salisbury Street, Strand, before moving to fashionable Dean Street in Soho. He published works on a number of medical topics, his first being *A critical inquiry into the ancient and modern manner of treating diseases of the urethra, and an improved method of cure* (1774).

However, Foot is now chiefly remembered as the author of the *Life of John Hunter* (1794), an unremittingly hostile biography of the famous surgeon. His harshness towards Hunter has usually been explained as originating in the jealousy of a less talented professional rival. True as this may be, Foot's hatred of Hunter had its roots in their involvement in the tumultuous relationship of Mary Eleanor Bowes, countess of Strathmore (1749–1800) and her second husband, Andrew Robinson Bowes (1747–1810), whose former name was Stoney. Bowes, a coward and a bully who had already mistreated one wife, schemed at making the wealthy and recently widowed countess break off her engagement with someone else and marry himself. Part of the plot required Bowes to defend the countess's honour, which had been questioned in the *Morning Post*, by fighting a duel against the paper's editor,

Jesse Foot (1744–1826), by William Ward (after John Opie)

the notorious 'Fighting parson', the Revd Henry Bate. It appears that the whole episode was a sham designed to make the countess think well of Bowes. Bowes acquired some minor injuries during the fight, which took place in a room in the Adelphi tavern on 13 January 1777, and was attended by Foot who had been summoned from his house in nearby Salisbury Street. This appears to be the first time the two met, but thereafter they were in fairly constant communication over the years. The countess married Bowes four days after the duel, and John Hunter, her surgeon, visited their house soon after. There then followed a series of unsavoury events between the countess and Bowes, culminating in her abduction in Oxford Street, his imprisonment, and their divorce.

These events were caused solely by Bowes's desire to get his hands on his wife's considerable fortune, which was hampered by her making a settlement of the estates left to her by her father so that the rents and produce of the estates were at her own disposal. Foot's view, one probably shared by Bowes, was that this was an 'obnoxious settlement' (Foot, *Lives*, 144) and under pressure from Bowes it was soon revoked. Given that Foot was considered a friend of Bowes, and that Hunter had some concern for the countess's well-being, it appears that Foot's hatred of Hunter stemmed from his relationship with Bowes rather than from any professional differences. Foot published his account of the episode in *The Lives of Andrew Robinson Bowes, Esq., and the Countess of Strathmore* (1810) where, while he is correct in portraying Bowes as a scheming coward, he shows little loyalty to the man whom he had known for over thirty years, whom he willingly visited in prison, and for whom he had carried out numerous tasks. It seems fair to say that his *Life of John Hunter* was not an isolated production but typical of 'the offspring of a narrow and envious mind' (*GM*, 1017).

Foot had published *A Defence of the Planters in the West Indies* in 1792; his assertion that one of the benefits enjoyed by slaves in the Caribbean was that they 'live in a climate where the sun always shines' (p. 32) indicates the level of argument in this pamphlet. He also produced a biography of his friend, the actor Arthur Murphy (1727–1805), in 1811. Foot died in Ifracombe, Devon, on 27 October 1826.

Foot's nephew, **Jesse Foot** (1780–1850), surgeon, practised for many years in Clarendon, Jamaica. On his return to Britain about 1819 he lived with his uncle in Dean Street, Soho, and married a Miss Foot (presumably a cousin) on 4 September 1819. He succeeded to his uncle's practice in 1826 and in the same year brought out a new edition of his work on the urethra. He became surgeon to the Royal Westminster Ophthalmic Hospital, published *Ophthalmic Memoranda* (1838), and contributed a number of papers to *The Lancet* and *The London Medical and Surgical Journal*. He also published *The Medical Pocket Book for 1835* (1834). Foot died at Ilfracombe, Devon, on 5 January 1850.

MICHAEL BEVAN

Sources J. Foot, *The lives of Andrew Robinson Bowes, esq, and the countess of Strathmore* (1810) · DNB · R. Arnold, *The unhappy countess and her grandson, John Bowes* (1957) · J. Foot, *The life of John Hunter* (1822) · *GM*, 1st ser., 64 (1794), 797–8 · *GM*, 1st ser., 64 (1794), 1017–23 · J. Foot, *A defence of the planters in the West Indies* (1792)
Likenesses pencil and sanguine drawing, 1798 (after G. Dance), RCP Lond. · W. Ward, mezzotint (after J. Opie), BM, NPG [*see illus.*]

Foot, Jesse (1780–1850). *See under* Foot, Jesse (1744–1826).

Foote, Sir Edward James (1767–1833), naval officer, was born on 20 April 1767, probably at Charlton House, Bishopsbourne, near Canterbury, Kent, the youngest son of Catherine, third daughter of Robert Mann of Linton, and Francis Hender Foote, who, after a career as a barrister, had taken holy orders and purchased Charlton House from his relatives. He was never the rector of Bishopsbourne, and did not serve there as a curate. Catherine, who was the sister of Sir Horace Mann, also gave birth to three daughters.

Edward James entered the Royal Naval Academy at Portsmouth in 1779, and the following year he joined the *Dublin* (74 guns), under Captain Samuel Wallis, the circumnavigator. In November he was moved into the frigate *Belle Poule* (Captain Philip Patton) and in her he was present in the action on the Dogger Bank on 5 August 1781. He shortly afterwards joined the frigate *Endymion* (Captain James Gambier), in which he was present at the battle of Dominica on 12 April 1782. After the peace he was appointed to the *Europa*, bearing the flag of Gambier (now a vice-admiral), on the Jamaica station. He subsequently served as acting lieutenant of the *Swan*, the *Antelope*, and the *Janus*, and was confirmed in the rank on 12 August 1785. In September 1788 he was appointed to the *Crown*, before going out to the East Indies with the broad pennant of

Commodore William Cornwallis, by whom, in the summer of 1791, he was made commander of the sloop *Atalanta*. He was afterwards transferred to the *Ariel*, which he brought home and paid off in October 1792.

On 7 June 1794 Foote was advanced to post rank, and appointed to the frigate *Niger*, in which for the next two years he was employed in the channel and on the coast of France. He then joined the Mediterranean Fleet under Sir John Jervis. It was Foote who, early on 14 February 1797, brought the first positive intelligence of the immediate proximity of the Spanish fleet, and, a few hours later, assisted in its defeat. The *Niger* shortly afterwards returned to England, and attended the king at Weymouth during the autumn; on going back to Spithead, Foote was at the king's request appointed to the *Seahorse* (38 guns), and ordered to the Mediterranean. He was on his way to join the detached squadron under Sir Horatio Nelson, when, off the coast of Sicily on 26 June 1798, he fell in with and captured the French frigate *Sensible* (36 guns), carrying General Baraguay d'Hilliers and his staff. From his prisoners Foote learned the destination of the expedition. He immediately changed course for the Egyptian coast, and in company with the *Terpsichore* arrived off Alexandria on 20 July. After seeing the French ships there and in Abu Qir Bay the frigates made a fruitless search for Nelson's squadron. Returning to Egypt on 17 August, they found that the French fleet had been destroyed.

Foote remained attached to the blockading squadron, but rejoined Nelson at Palermo in the spring of 1799 before being sent with Captain Thomas Troubridge into the Bay of Naples, where, on Troubridge's departure in May, he became the senior officer. In this capacity, on 22 June, he signed the capitulation of the forts Uovo and Nuovo—a capitulation which Nelson, on arriving in the bay two days later, pronounced invalid, and refused to carry into effect.

Nelson's treatment of the Neapolitan democrats which the capitulation was supposed to protect, was the darkest episode of his career. Foote did not present any remonstrance against the capitulation being annulled. On the contrary, until he was ordered home in September, he continued to address Nelson in terms of gratitude and devotion, which in J. K. Laughton's view went far beyond the submission required from a junior officer. After Nelson's death, however, he published a *Vindication* of his own conduct which strongly criticized Nelson's actions.

On his return to England in the early part of 1800, Foote, still in the *Seahorse*, was again sent out to the Mediterranean, with the army officer Sir Ralph Abercromby, and his staff, as passengers. He once more attended the king at Weymouth during the summer of 1801, and was then sent to India in charge of convoy. While there he undertook the difficult task of salvaging the masts and stores of the frigate *Sensible* which had been wrecked and was flooded to the gun-deck. In October 1802 the *Seahorse* was paid off, and on the king's orders Foote was appointed to the royal yacht *Princess Augusta*, in which he remained until he was promoted to flag-rank in August 1812. Two years later he hoisted his flag as second in command at Portsmouth, but he struck it at the peace, and had no further service, becoming in due course a vice-admiral in 1821. He was nominated a KCB in 1831. Foote was twice married: first, to Nina, daughter of Sir Robert Herries, and second, to Mary, daughter of Vice-Admiral Philip Patton. There were children from both marriages. Foote died at his Southampton residence on 23 May 1833.

J. K. LAUGHTON, rev. NICHOLAS TRACY

Sources J. Marshall, *Royal naval biography*, 1/2 (1823), 559–68 · J. Ralfe, *The naval biography of Great Britain*, 4 vols. (1828) · E. Hasted, *The history and topographical survey of the county of Kent*, 2nd edn, 9 (1800) · Bishopsbourne baptismal records, and archdeacons' transcripts, Canterbury Cathedral Archives
Archives BL, Sir Walter Hamilton's MSS, letters and MSS, Add. MS 37077 · BL, Nelson MSS, letters and MSS, Add. MSS 34911–34912 · BL, Sinclair collection, letters and MSS, Add. MS 36873
Likenesses J. Hoppner, oils, Tel Aviv Museum of Art, Israel · portrait (probably posthumous), NMM

Foote, George William (1850–1915), radical journalist and secularist, was born at 2 How Street Cottages, Plymouth, on 11 January 1850, the son of William Thomas Foot, customs officer, who died when he was about four. He was brought up an Anglican by his mother, Ann Foot, *née* Winzar, but joined the Unitarians when he was fifteen. In January 1868 he went to London to work in a West End library, and was soon involved in radical freethought, starting both the secular Sunday school and the Young Men's Secular Association at the Old Street Hall of Science in 1869, and contributing to Charles Bradlaugh's *National Reformer* from 1870. He also served as secretary of the London Republican Club (1870) and National Republican League (1871). In 1876 he opposed Bradlaugh's domination of the secularist movement, starting his own paper, the *Secularist*, and the following year, with G. J. Holyoake and Charles Watts, formed the British Secular Union as an anti-Bradlaughite organization.

Bradlaugh's exclusion from the House of Commons in 1880 brought an indignant Foote back to mainstream secularism. Abandoning his hitherto mild and literary approach to freethought, in May 1881 he started the monthly *Freethinker* (weekly from September), in which he attacked Christianity with barbed wit and a series of infamous cartoons for which he was twice prosecuted for blasphemy. Tried at the Old Bailey before Mr Justice North in March 1883, he received a year in Holloway prison, but on an earlier charge subsequently heard before Lord Chief Justice Coleridge at queen's bench the jury was divided. Coleridge's liberal summing up, that there was a distinction between the manner and the substance of an alleged blasphemy, remained the basis of the blasphemy law in England until 1979.

As Bradlaugh became increasingly involved in parliamentary affairs, Foote emerged as the principal organizer of secularism at a time when the movement was declining in popularity. He founded the London Secular Federation in 1888 and succeeded Bradlaugh as president of the National Secular Society in 1890. As a leading member of the Metropolitan Radical Federation (founded 1886) Foote was primarily an individualistic champion of free expression, opposed to socialism and increasingly disillusioned

with democratic mediocrity. In 1887 he debated the question 'Is socialism sound?' with Annie Besant at the Old Street Hall of Science. In the long run his defence of liberalism alienated many former supporters who were attracted to socialism, and he faced increasing criticisms for his failure to recreate the success which secularism had enjoyed under Bradlaugh. With declining support came financial difficulties, quarrels with other leaders, and a period of bankruptcy from 1901 until 1905. He nevertheless was largely responsible for the survival of secularist radicalism into the twentieth century.

Foote ran his own publishing business from 1882 under various titles, latterly the Pioneer Press, and edited the *Freethinker* until his death, as well as the more ephemeral *Secularist* (1876), *Liberal* (1879), *Progress* (1883–7), *Radical Leader* (1888), and *Pioneer* (1903–4). He wrote over eighty publications, mostly pamphlets of a polemical nature. Some of his best writing came in the form of weekly editorial essays in the *Freethinker*, published as *Flowers of Freethought* (1893–4). His ambitions beyond religious controversialism remained literary, and behind the public image was a cultured scholar with a wide knowledge of English literature, a devotee of Shakespeare, and a friend and admirer of George Meredith.

Foote's first marriage, to Henriette Mariane (*b.* 1850/51), daughter of Adolph Heimann, a professor of German, on 20 March 1877, ended with her death in October of the same year. His second wife, Rosalia Martha (*b.* 1862/3), daughter of Leopold Angel, a silversmith, supported his work but remained in the background. They were married on 12 April 1884, and had four children, including a son, Francis, and two daughters, Helen and Florence. In later years Foote suffered from bronchitis, which led the family to move out of London to Westcliff-on-Sea in 1903. He died at his home there, 39 Meteor Road, on 17 October 1915 and was cremated at the City of London crematorium, Ilford, on 21 October.

EDWARD ROYLE

Sources *The Freethinker* (31 Oct 1915); (7 Nov 1915); (14 Nov 1915); (12 Dec 1915) · *Literary Guide* (Nov 1915), 165 · *Literary Guide* (Dec 1915), 189–90 · *Republican* (April 1883), 481–2 · A. B. Moss, 'Famous freethinkers I have known: George William Foote', *The Freethinker* (2 May 1915) · J. M. Wheeler, 'George William Foote', *The Freethinker* (1 July 1883) · H. T. Law, 'George William Foote', *Secular Chronicle* (17 March 1878) · F. J. Gould, 'Literary chats. VII: with George William Foote', *Literary Guide* (Aug 1895), 9–11 · E. Royle, *Radicals, secularists and republicans: popular freethought in Britain, 1866–1915* (1980) · D. Tribe, *100 years of freethought* (1967) · J. Herrick, *Vision and realism: a hundred years of the 'Freethinker'* (1982) · b. cert. · m. certs. · d. cert.
Likenesses engraving, repro. in Law, 'George William Foote' · engraving, repro. in *Republican*, 481 · photograph, repro. in *The Freethinker* (31 Oct 1915)
Wealth at death £1355 14s. 6d.: administration, 13 Jan 1916, CGPLA Eng. & Wales

Foote, Lydia [*real name* Lydia Alice Legg] (1843–1892), actress, born on 8 May 1843 at 8 Tavistock Street, London, was the daughter of Arthur Wellington Legg, a coachbuilder, and his wife, Sarah Judith Legg, *née* Goward, and a niece of the actress Mary Ann Keeley. According to a contemporary writer, Clement Scott, she took the name Foote because 'she preferred a foot to a leg'. She made her début

Lydia Foote (1843–1892), by unknown photographer

at the Lyceum on 1 April 1852 as Edward, a child, in *A Chain of Events*, by Charles Mathews and Slingsby Lawrence. At the age of sixteen she played Amanthis in Elizabeth Inchbald's *The Child of Nature*, but she did not make any particular impression, although she was already regarded as beautiful. She later appeared at Sadler's Wells, at the Victoria, and at Manchester, and made her first appearance at the Olympic on 31 August 1863, replacing Kate Saville as May Edwards in Tom Taylor's *The Ticket-of-Leave Man*. She played original roles—Enid Gryffydd in *The Hidden Hand* (*L'Aïeule*) and Miss Hargrave in *Settling Day*, both by Taylor— and enhanced her reputation with Maria in *Twelfth Night*, Clara Vernon in Wilkie Collins's *Frozen Deep*, and, her great triumph, Esther Eccles in T. W. Robertson's *Caste* in 1867. Further original parts followed, notably as Lady Selina Raffleticket in Boucicault's *How she Loves him* and as Amanda in Robertson's *Play*. She played twin sisters in H. J. Byron's *Blow for Blow*, the lead in his *Minnie*, and the heroine of Robertson's *Progress*. Thereafter she appeared at the Holborn, the Gaiety, the Prince of Wales's, the Princess's, and the Adelphi, where she was Smike in *Nicholas Nickleby* in March 1875. She was much in demand for original roles and was the first Anna in Lord Newry's *The Danischeffs* (1877) and the first Midge in Boucicault's *Rescued* (1879). During the next two years she created further original parts in *O'Dowd* and in *Pluck*. She also took part in many revivals at the Adelphi. Her acting was said to be possessed

of remarkable pathos. She died of cancer at 18 Osborne Road, St Peter's, Ramsgate, on 30 May 1892 and was buried at Kensal Green cemetery, London.

JOSEPH KNIGHT, *rev.* J. GILLILAND

Sources C. E. Pascoe, ed., *The dramatic list* (1879) · *The life and reminiscences of E. L. Blanchard, with notes from the diary of Wm. Blanchard*, ed. C. W. Scott and C. Howard, 2 vols. (1891) · Adams, *Drama* · D. Cook, *Nights at the play* (1883) · C. Scott, *The drama of yesterday and today*, 2 vols. (1899) · H. B. Baker, *The London stage: its history and traditions from 1576 to 1888*, 2 vols. (1889) · J. Hollingshead, *Gaiety chronicles* (1898) · H. Morley, *The journal of a London playgoer from 1851 to 1866* (1866) · A. Davies and E. Kilmurray, *Dictionary of British portraiture*, 4 vols. (1979–81) · d. cert. · b. cert.

Likenesses Album Portrait Co., carte-de-visite, NPG · A. Bean, carte-de-visite, NPG · London Stereoscopic Co., carte-de-visite, NPG · C. B. Walker, carte-de-visite, NPG · photograph (in T. Taylor, *The ticket-of-leave man*, 1863), repro. in Scott, *Drama of yesterday and today* · photograph, NPG [*see illus.*]

Foote, Maria [*married name* Maria Stanhope, countess of Harrington] (**1797–1867**), actress, was born at Plymouth on 24 July 1797, the daughter of Samuel T. Foote, a theatre manager, and his wife, a Miss Hannington, of Twyford, Hertfordshire. In July 1810 she appeared at her father's Plymouth theatre as Juliet, and on 26 May 1814 she made her début at Covent Garden as Amanthis in *The Child of Nature* (adapted by Elizabeth Inchbald from the French of Madame de Genlis). In this part, which was particularly suited to her abilities, she was widely acclaimed. She performed in every season at Covent Garden until 1825, and in 1826 made her first appearance at Drury Lane. Indefatigable in touring, she is said to have performed in the English provinces, Scotland, and Ireland every year for five years. She was, however, more notable for her beauty than her talents: Macready recorded that, for the original production of Sheridan Knowles's *Virginius* (17 May 1820), 'the lovely Miss Foote' played Virginia, and that, 'thankfully accepting my tuition, [she] produced the most pleasing effect by aiming at none' (*Macready's Reminiscences*, 1.209). John Genest wrote that 'she was a very pretty woman and a very pleasing actress, but she never would have travelled about as a star if it had not been for circumstances totally unconnected with the stage' (Genest, 9.358–9).

In 1815 Maria Foote had become the mistress of Colonel William Berkeley, later Earl Fitzhardinge (1786–1857), 'a sort of tenth-rate Rochester' (GEC, *Peerage*), with whom she had two children. A promise of marriage was given, but, when it did not occur, in June 1824 Maria broke off the relationship. She then received an offer of marriage from Joseph 'Pea-Green' Hayne of Texon Hall, Staffordshire; she ended her theatrical contract, but Hayne too eventually refused to marry her, claiming not to have known of her relationship with Berkeley until Berkeley, in a fit of pique, told him about it. Maria Foote sued Hayne for breach of promise on 22 December 1824, and secured £3000 in damages, having proved that Hayne had renewed his offer of marriage after his interview with Berkeley and after Maria had given custody of her children to her former lover. The case caused a sensation, and was taken up by pamphleteers. Following the failure of her matrimonial scheme,

Maria Foote returned in January 1825 to the stage at Covent Garden, where the notoriety of her personal life ensured full houses. She made her last appearance in Birmingham on 11 March 1831. On 7 April 1831 she married Charles *Stanhope, fourth earl of Harrington (1780–1851), at his family seat, Elvaston Hall, Derbyshire. They had a son, who died at the age of four, and a daughter, who lived to marry the third Marquess Conyngham. Unable to move in society, Lady Harrington lived in virtual seclusion at Elvaston Hall. She died from bronchitis at her home, 2 Richmond Terrace, Whitehall, London, on 27 December 1867.   JOSEPH KNIGHT, *rev.* K. D. REYNOLDS

Sources *DNB* · GEC, *Peerage* · *GM*, 1st ser., 94/2 (1824), 638 · *N&Q*, 7th ser. (1886), 54 · *Macready's reminiscences, and selections from his diaries and letters*, ed. F. Pollock, 2 vols. (1875) · Boase, *Mod. Eng. biog.* · Genest, *Eng. stage* · Burke, *Peerage* · *Facts illustrative of the evidence on the late trial of Foote v. Hayne* (1825) · *Oxberry's Dramatic Biography*, 1/3 (1825), 33–46 · M. Girouard, *The return to Camelot: chivalry and the English gentleman* (1981)
Likenesses R. Cooper, stipple, pubd 1817 (after R. E. Drummond), NPG · C. Picart, stipple, pubd 1822 (after G. Clint), BM, NPG · T. Lupton, mezzotint, pubd 1824 (after G. Clint), BM · thirty-eight prints, Harvard TC
Wealth at death under £6000: probate, 22 Jan 1868, *CGPLA Eng. & Wales*

Foote, Samuel (*bap.* **1721**, *d.* **1777**), actor and playwright, was baptized on 27 January 1721 at St Mary's, Truro, the fourth son and fifth child of Samuel Foote (1678–1754), a lawyer and magistrate and MP for Tiverton, and his wife, Eleanor Dinely, the daughter of Sir Edward Goodere, bt, of Hereford. Two of Samuel's siblings, Eleanor (*b.* April 1712) and Samuel (*b.* November 1715), had died in infancy. His elder surviving brother, Edward, baptized on 5 November 1716, was educated for the clergy but did not flourish as a minister. Although there is no definite information on his second brother, John, baptized on 14 August 1718, he may have gone to Jamaica. Samuel Foote attended the grammar school at Truro and Worcester College, Oxford, but was dismissed from Oxford on 25 February 1740 'after a course of many irregularitys' (cited in P. Fitzgerald, *Samuel Foote: a Biography*, 1910, 17–18). He entered the Inner Temple, presumably to study law, but failed to register.

Early career About 1740 or 1741 Foote published *The Genuine Memoirs of the Life of Sir John Dinely Goodere, Bart.*, an account of the murder of his maternal uncle, Sir John Dinely Goodere, by his brother, Captain Samuel Goodere; young Foote received only £20 for his efforts. His next business venture, a partnership with a Mr Price to make and sell small beer, failed. On 10 January 1741, at St Clement Danes in London, Foote married Mary Hickes (*bap.* 1724), the daughter of John and Chastity Hickes. A pretty neighbour of sixteen or seventeen from Truro, she brought a good dowry, which Foote quickly squandered. Besieged by creditors, including his mother and Frances Wandesford, Viscountess Castlecomer (the sister of Henry Pelham and the duke of Newcastle), he was confined in the Fleet debtors' prison on 13 November 1742, where his wife joined him—although thereafter she disappears from his life. Released after a few months, he was soon

Samuel Foote (*bap.* 1721, *d.* 1777), by Jean-François Colson, 1769

recommitted on the same charges until finally released on 7 September 1743, following the passage of the bill for the relief of insolvent debtors.

After receiving instruction from the veteran actor Charles Macklin, Foote appeared at the Haymarket on 6 February 1744, as Othello, to 'Universal Applause' (*Daily Advertiser*, 21 Feb 1744). Foote performed the role five additional times at the Haymarket (13, 20, 23 February, 2 March, 26 April) and once at Drury Lane (10 March). He completed the season acting Lord Foppington in Sir John Vanbrugh's *The Relapse* at the Haymarket on 6 and 9 April and at Drury Lane on 13 April.

At Dublin's Smock Alley Theatre, Foote acted Bayes in *The Rehearsal* by George Villiers, second duke of Buckingham, on 25 October 1744 and Lord Foppington on 15 November, performances that Robert Hitchcock grants were 'well received' (Hitchcock, 1.147). An enthusiastic unknown letter writer maintained that Foote played Wildair, Bayes, and Pierre five times each at the Capel Street Theatre 'to as crowded Audiences as ever were known' (Highfill, Burnim & Langhans, *BDA*, 5.327). Surviving notices document his appearances as Wildair in George Farquhar's *The Constant Couple* (28 January), Tinsel in Joseph Addison's *The Drummer* (8 February), Pierre in Thomas Otway's *Venice Preserv'd* (9 February), and Fondlewife in *The Credulous Husband* (authorship unknown; probably an adaptation of Congreve's *The Old Batchelor*; 9 February). On his return to London, Foote played significant comic roles at Drury Lane during the 1745–6 season: Wildair, Tinsel, Bayes, Sir Novelty Fashion in Colley Cibber's *Love's Last Shift*, Dick in Vanbrugh's *The*

Confederacy, Young Loveless in *The Scornful Lady*, by Beaumont and Fletcher, and Sir Courtly Nice in Crowne's play of that name. Throughout his career he added other roles, including Brazen in Farquhar's *The Recruiting Officer*, Hartop in his own *The Knights*, Lady Pentweazle in *Taste*, also his own play, Myrtle in *The Conscious Lovers*, by Richard Steele, Sir Paul Plyant in William Congreve's *The Double Dealer*, Gomez in John Dryden's *The Spanish Fryar*, the Scotchman in *The Register Office*, by Joseph Reed, and Don Lewis in Cibber's *Love Makes a Man*, but he seemed unable to captivate an audience. After watching Foote perform Sir Paul Plyant and Buck in his own *The Englishman Return'd from Paris* on 1 November 1756, the prompter Richard Cross could only note in his diary: 'Mr. Foote brings sad houses' (Stone, pt 4, 2.562). Thomas Davies thought his playing 'despicable' (Davies, 1.228), but granted that his performances were better in parts he himself wrote. Essentially, because Foote did not excel in standard repertory roles he could not obtain a permanent position with either company, and, on account of that, he assumed an entrepreneurial role and devised innovative theatrical modes.

Chocolate, tea, and pictures: a successful satirist The resourceful Foote rented the Haymarket, assembled an acting company during the 1746–7 season, and created the dramatic form that became the staple of his career, the satirical revue effected through mimicry of well-known persons. His first entertainment was *The Diversions of the Morning, or, A Dish of Chocolate* on 22 April. To conform to the Licensing Act, the performance was given gratis, following a concert. To avoid conflict with the patent theatres Foote soon scheduled performances for 12 noon. *Diversions* met with immediate success and was acted thirty-five times, drawing great crowds through its exaggerated imitations of popular performers such as James Quin, Dennis Delane, Lacy Ryan, Peg Woffington, Charles Macklin, and David Garrick. On 1 June Foote retitled his work *Tea*, more appropriate for his new performance time of 6 p.m.

The next season Foote performed *Tea* only thirteen times at Covent Garden because, according to Genest, the play 'having now lost its novelty, had in a great degree lost its attraction' (Genest, *Eng. stage*, 4.247). On 18 April 1748 Foote retitled his revue *An Auction of Pictures*, exploiting the current popularity of auctions. The new orientation allowed him to pretend to auction detailed portraits of his favourite satiric targets. The *Auction* attained thirty-six performances by 16 June 1748. Foote began his next season of the piece on 1 December 1748. Despite the fact that virtually all his properties for the production were destroyed in a riot, unrelated to him, at the Haymarket on 16 January 1749, the resilient satirist was back on stage nine days later, auctioning his wares on 25 January. By 18 February he had achieved eighteen performances. On 3 April he introduced his own two-act comedy, *The Knights*, featuring a duet of Italian cats, an overt attack on Italian opera.

Following a continental sojourn Foote returned to London with another of his own plays, a farce, *Taste*, which he maintained in the 'Preface' was genuine comedy. Even with Garrick dressed as an auctioneer, delivering his Prologue, the play failed on 11 January 1752 at Drury Lane, but, slightly altered, it was successfully brought back the following week. Foote's *The Englishman in Paris* was unsuccessful at Covent Garden on 24 March 1753, with Charles Macklin as Buck, but when the author took that role at Drury Lane the following season, the play achieved great popularity.

Foote again produced *Tea* during the 1753–4 season, and on 3 February 1756 he brought out *The Englishman Return'd from Paris*, a sequel to his *Englishman in Paris*, having stolen the idea from Arthur Murphy, who had confided in him that he was working on such a play. Foote's next play, *The Author*, which satirized an uncle of Foote's friend Francis Delaval, a Mr Apreece, was soon withdrawn from the repertory after pressure exerted on Garrick by the influential Apreece.

Foote, still without a permanent position at either theatre, tried to invigorate his career by using life-size puppets in place of actors during a performance of *Diversions* in October 1758, thereby earning the anger of London performers. His ingenuity not exhausted, he set out, with Tate Wilkinson, for Edinburgh, using £100 that Wilkinson had borrowed from Garrick. The Scots received him with enthusiasm at the Canongate theatre, where he put on *The Author*, *The Diversions of the Morning*, and *The Englishman Return'd from Paris*. In addition he performed the roles of Shylock, Gomez, Bayes, Sir Paul Plyant, and the Earl of Essex. Back in London he appeared at the Haymarket on 9 November 1759, promising *Comic Lectures*, but angered the audience by presenting only himself on a darkened stage reading aloud parts of his next play, *The Minor*. He quickly left for Dublin, where *The Minor* failed at Crow Street, probably because Henry Woodward gave a poor performance. When Foote returned to London he succeeded with the play, which he enlarged from two acts to three and brought out at the Haymarket on 28 June 1760, with a group of virtually unknown performers. An uncompromising satire on George Whitefield and the Methodists, *The Minor* was both a theatrical and personal success for Foote, who played three roles—those of Shift, Smirk, and Mother Cole. As a virulent paper war of letters, essays, and tracts, both for and against the Methodists, flooded London, Garrick's interest was aroused, and the play, with excisions made by the lord chamberlain under pressure from the archbishop of Canterbury and George Whitefield's patroness, Selina Hastings, countess of Huntingdon, opened at Drury Lane on 22 November 1760.

Unable to lease the Haymarket during the summer of 1761, the ever-resourceful Foote rented Drury Lane from Garrick and went into partnership with Arthur Murphy. Each man promised to write three new plays for the summer season. Murphy fulfilled his contract, producing *All in the Wrong* on 15 June 1761, and *The Citizen* and *The Old Maid*, both on 2 July 1761, but Foote failed to write any new plays. The season ended with performances on only twenty-three of the projected forty-eight nights; nevertheless, it was profitable for the co-managers, who made over £300 each.

Early in the 1761–2 season Foote's career went into temporary eclipse, with only a single performance of *The Minor*, on 10 November 1761, and the failure of his comedy, *The Lyar*, on 12 January 1762, which lasted only four performances. But by 28 April 1762 he had leased the Haymarket to institute a 'Course of Lectures on English Orators'. *The Orators* exploited his considerable talent in topical satire and mimicry for thirty-eight performances. Two of Foote's most successful satiric attacks were on Thomas Sheridan and George Faulkner, the one-legged Dublin printer whom Foote mocked as Peter Paragraph. In January he printed in the *Gentleman's Magazine* 'An address to the public', a mock suit for libel by Peter Petros against Aristophanes, capitalizing on his nickname 'the English Aristophanes'.

On 20 June 1763 Foote played Major Sturgeon in his new comedy, *The Mayor of Garratt*. During the following summer he introduced his three-act comedy *The Patron*, on 13 June 1764, taking the roles of Sir Thomas and Sir Peter Pepperpot. On 10 June 1765, as Zachary Fungus in his new comedy *The Commissary*, Foote brought his career to its high point: he had finally attained theatrical recognition and financial independence.

Feuding in fashion: Foote and his foes But, however successful, Foote's career had always been marked by his continual feuding with London personalities, among them Henry Fielding, Henry Woodward, Charles Macklin, and Arthur Murphy. As far back as 1748, after Foote targeted Fielding in his 18 April *Auction*, the latter responded by presenting, in Panton Street, a satiric puppet show, which he called *Madam de la Nash's Breakfasting Room*. Foote and Fielding continued their quarrels through broadsides for several months, to the delight of Londoners. The next year Foote reignited a feud with Woodward, which had been simmering since March 1748, when both actors were performing in Dublin. Woodward, at the Crow Street theatre, had written *Coffee*, an obvious satire on Foote's *Tea*. During a performance of *Auction of Pictures* at the Haymarket on 7 January 1749 Foote mimicked Woodward's performance in *Lethe*, which he was acting at Drury Lane. The contentious Foote further publicly twitted Woodward in the *General Advertiser* of 10 March. Woodward retaliated with his own afterpiece *Tit for Tat, or, One Dish of his Own Chocolate*, on 18 March at Drury Lane. He drew a large crowd and enjoyed 'uncommon applause' (*General Advertiser*, 21 March 1749) at Foote's expense; *Tit for Tat* was performed five more times at Drury Lane through 26 April. To counter, Foote inserted Woodward once again into his *Auction of Pictures* on 8 April, referring to his rival as Harry the Smuggler. Although Foote left England and lived on the continent for the next two years, Woodward kept the feud brewing, announcing that he would mimic the playwright in the role of Malagene in Otway's *Friendship in Fashion*, to be performed in January 1750. From the continent Foote protested to Garrick at Drury Lane, to no avail. In an open letter to Woodward placed in the *Daily Advertiser*, Foote argued 'the dignity of the stage' and hinted darkly to Woodward about 'my future vengeance' (Stone, pt 4, 1.169). Woodward persisted and played the role of

Malagene on 22 January 1750, but the audience was not amused, and the feud died.

In December 1754 Foote initiated another feud, this one with his one-time teacher, Charles Macklin, who, in his retirement, had established a school of oratory in the Great Room at Hart Street. Not only did Foote visit the Great Room and personally heckle Macklin, interrupting his performance, but on 16 December, in the rented Haymarket Theatre, Foote produced a comic lecture obviously aimed at Macklin. Meanwhile, Macklin was attacking Foote in the Great Room in Hart Street under the name of Sam Smatter, 'alias Mimic, alias Buffon'. Fortunately, the venture seems to have been profitable for Foote and did little damage to his friendship with Macklin. And on 6 April 1761, in a performance of *Taste* at Drury Lane, Foote retaliated against Charles Churchill and Robert Lloyd for recent public criticism of him, presenting them as puppets.

An actor–manager upon two sticks Foote's life—acting, writing, and feuding—was irrevocably changed in February 1766, when he was a guest of John Savile, first earl of Mexborough, and his countess, Sarah Delaval, at Cannon Park in Hampshire at a reception honoring Edward, duke of York, the brother of George III. The Delavals and the duke of York shared a passion for the theatre, and the countess's father was the dedicatee of *Taste*. Foote allowed himself to be teased by several of the socially renowned guests about his horsemanship and to be challenged to ride the duke of York's spirited horse. He accepted the challenge and in a very short time was thrown from the horse, fracturing his leg in two places; it was soon clear that his leg had to be amputated. Refusing to allow this tragedy to dominate his life, the resilient and practical-minded Foote requested that the duke of York obtain for him a patent for the Haymarket Theatre. The patent was granted on 5 July 1766, allowing Foote to operate the Haymarket from 15 June to 15 September. Although Foote had requested a patent for year-long performance, he accepted the shorter summer one and proceeded to have two wooden legs crafted, one a simple stick and the other decorated with a silk stocking and a gold-buckled polished shoe, to be used on stage. He also obtained a gold crutched cane to aid his walking.

Foote returned for his first performance since the accident to a large and enthusiastic audience on 18 June 1766, acting Mother Cole in *The Minor*. Soon he performed in *The Orators*, *The Commissary*, and *The Credulous Husband*, proudly advertising his theatre as 'the Theatre Royal' on the bills and describing his company as 'His Majesty's Company of Comedians'. John O'Keeffe recalled in his *Memoirs* how Foote 'looked sorrowful' as a servant attached his stage leg before a performance, but then how he 'hobbled forward, entered the scene, and gave the audience what they expected—their plenty of laugh and delight' (O'Keeffe, 1.328). On 15 July Foote rode a hobby horse onto the stage in the role of Zachary Fungus. On 20 August he acted in *The Minor* at the King's, but he ended his season abruptly the next day, on 21 August 1766. In 1767 Foote purchased the Haymarket from the executors of John Potter, the original builder, and improved and enlarged it by adding an upper gallery. He also purchased a house on Suffolk Street which he used for living and wardrobe space. In May the following year his satire on the medical profession, *The Devil upon Two Sticks*, in which he played a lame devil, was very successful at the Haymarket and later at Smock Alley, where he brought it in November.

In November 1770 Foote took his Haymarket company to Edinburgh, where he had leased the Theatre Royal from David Ross for three years. He presented *The Commissary*, Garrick's *The Lying Valet*, and *The Minor*, the last of which upset the local clergy with its satire on George Whitefield; Foote also acted the roles of Shylock and Fondlewife. James Boswell wrote to Garrick, 'We have been kept laughing all this winter by Foote, who has made a Very good Campaign of it here' (*Letters*, no. 628, 2.733 n. 2). Despite the fact that he reported to Garrick that he made upwards of £1000 in Edinburgh, in 1771 Foote sold his lease at a loss to the actors West Digges and James Bland and returned to London. On 26 June 1771 he presented his own *The Maid of Bath* at the Haymarket and ended the season with a £3700 profit. That winter he renovated the Haymarket, doubling the size of the stage. In 1772, after the successful run of *The Nabob*, his satire on the East India Company, he petitioned the king for permission to operate the Haymarket all year but received no answer. Despite this, he produced the *Primitive Puppet Shew* on 15 February 1773, with life-size puppets manipulated by wires or strings. The *Morning Chronicle* of 16 February was enthusiastic about the puppets, which were 'managed with great adroitness'. The puppet show, somewhat altered, was produced an additional sixteen times by 16 April. Foote also introduced *The Bankrupt* on 21 July 1773. He travelled to Dublin in November and acted in *The Maid of Bath*, *The Nabob*, and other pieces before going to Edinburgh for three weeks in February, where he performed for seven nights for £250. During the 1774 season at the Haymarket he brought out *The Cozeners* on 15 July, acting the part of Aircastle. Weary, he went to the continent for vacation after the 1774 season but returned to London in December 'in great Spirits' (*Letters*, no. 873, 3.971).

Foote's next play, originally titled *The Siege of Calais*, was an overt attack on Elizabeth Chudleigh, duchess of Kingston, an influential figure who was currently facing trial on charges of bigamy. Foote dramatized Chudleigh as Lady Crocodile, but the lord chamberlain rejected his play during the summer of 1775. The feud between Foote and the duchess heated up as Foote first threatened to publish the play, then rejected a bribe from her, and later claimed he had lost £3000 by the work's suppression. Determined to silence the persistent and obstreperous Foote, William Jackson, publisher of the *Public Ledger* and a supporter of the duchess, initiated and printed rumours that Foote was homosexual. Although Foote hurriedly tried to clear his name, the attacks continued: in August 1775 the duchess declared in the public press that she would 'prostitute the term of manhood by applying it to Mr. Foote' (*Public Advertiser*, 16, 18 Aug 1775). On 8 July, John Sangster, a servant of Foote, charged the actor with an attempted homosexual

attack, a capital offence. Foote's sense of personal security collapsed under the repeated and vicious attacks. His case came to trial on 9 December 1776 and he was quickly acquitted, but his spirit was broken. His biographer noted that, when Arthur Murphy, who acted as Foote's attorney, visited the actor to tell him he had been acquitted, Foote collapsed on the floor 'in strong hysterics' (Cooke, 1.231–2).

Unable to continue his professional life with vigour and enthusiasm, Foote leased his patent at the Haymarket to George Colman. The announcement was made in January 1777 that Foote would receive an annuity of £1600 in quarterly payments, and £500 for his unpublished plays, which included *The Trip to Calais*, *The Nabob*, *The Capuchin*, *The Maid of Bath*, *The Devil upon Two Sticks*, and *The Cozeners*. Foote agreed to perform for six nights at the Haymarket in 1777 and to act nowhere else. He fulfilled his agreement, appearing on stage at the Haymarket in 1777, but he was then shrunken in appearance and almost inanimate in personality.

In an effort to regain his health, Foote planned to spend the winter in southern France. All seemed well when he arrived at Dover on 20 October before sailing to Calais, but a shivering fit and chills overcame him, and he died on 21 October 1777. His body was taken to his house on Suffolk Street by his friend William Jewell, treasurer of the Haymarket, who announced the funeral for Monday 3 November. Foote was buried in Westminster Abbey; although no monument was erected to him in the abbey, Jewell had a memorial tablet installed in St Mary's Church, Dover, 'plac'd here by his Affectionate Friend'.

Foote's will had been drawn up in 1768, and, although some of its provisions were invalidated by changing circumstances, it demonstrated the depth of his regard for Jewell and his concern for his relatives. To Jewell he bequeathed 'my Theatre Royal in the Haymarket and all my buildings thereto belonging' and various privileges pertinent to the theatre. To others he made several small sentimental gifts. The remainder of the estate was bequeathed to his two illegitimate sons, Francis and George Foote, equally upon their reaching their majority. Foote also made provision for his mother (by then deceased) and his brother Edward.

Foote died as a controversial and celebrated public figure, an actor, playwright, wit, and brilliant conversationalist. The usually urbane Garrick commented that he 'had much wit, no feeling, sacrific'd friends & foes to a joke, & so has dy'd very little regretted even by his nearest acquaintance' (*Letters of David Garrick … Countess Spencer*, 39). Dr Johnson once said of him, 'Foote is quite impartial, for he tells lies of everybody' (Boswell, *Life*, 2.434), but he later wrote to Mrs Thrale that 'he was a fine fellow in his way' (ibid., 3.185). Though often brusque and abusive in public, Foote maintained close friendships with Jewell, Francis and James Delaval, and Arthur Murphy.

As an actor Foote fared best in roles he wrote for himself, as Thomas Davies noted, for here he fully exploited his theatrical gifts: mimicry, exuberant energy, the acute observation of character, and the ability to render witty dialogue. Unfortunately, poor judgement often led him to overact and allow his instinct for farce to degenerate into buffoonery and his satiric energy to malign his enemies. Mimicry was his most natural approach to acting, for he had much to overcome in physical appearance: he was short and corpulent and visually unconvincing in many tragic roles.

Foote, as a writer, has been largely undervalued because his critical writing, which is clear, logical, and forcible, is often unread and because his subjects are usually topical, holding little interest for succeeding generations. In *The Roman and English Comedy Considered and Compared* he claimed the object of comedy is 'the Correction of Vices and Follies of an inferior sort'. In his prologue to *Tea*, on 21 January 1748, he praised the personal satire of Aristophanes as a significant contribution to Greek virtue (Genest, *Eng. stage*, 4.248). And Foote is a distinct forerunner of Goldsmith's 'Essay on laughing comedy' in his 'Dedication to Francis Delaval' prefaced to *Taste* (1752), when he identifies himself as 'a Rebel to this universal Tyrant [Love]' that has subjected both tragedy and comedy to its power. Arthur Murphy recognized the power of Foote's attack on sentimental comedy, noting that he 'brought that species of composition into disrepute' (Murphy, 2.52). A minor but important playwright of the Garrick era, Foote made a significant contribution to English drama, deriving his form from the *petit pièce* developed by Fielding, writing in the tradition of old comedy, and anticipating the return of laughing comedy.

PHYLLIS T. DIRCKS

Sources A. H. Scouten, ed., *The London stage, 1660–1800*, pt 3: *1729–1747* (1961) · W. Cooke, *Memoirs of Samuel Foote*, 3 vols. (1805) · M. Belden, *The dramatic work of Samuel Foote* (1929) · Genest, *Eng. stage* · Highfill, Burnim & Langhans, *BDA*, vol. 5 · Boswell, *Life* · *The letters of David Garrick*, ed. D. M. Little and G. M. Kahrl, 3 vols. (1963) · *Letters of David Garrick and Georgiana, Countess Spencer, 1759–1779*, ed. Earl Spencer and C. Dobson, Roxburghe Club, 226 (1960) · T. Davies, *Memoirs of the life of David Garrick*, 2 vols. (1780) · A. Murphy, *The life of David Garrick*, 2 vols. (1801) · R. Hitchcock, *An historical view of the Irish stage from the earliest period down to the close of the season 1788*, 2 vols. (1788–94) · S. Trefman, *Sam. Foote, comedian, 1720–1777* (1971) · J. O'Keeffe, *Recollections of the life of John O'Keeffe, written by himself*, 2 vols. (1826) · H. Tapley-Soper, ed., *The register of marriages, baptisms and burials of the parish of St Mary, Truro, co. Cornwall, AD 1597 to 1837*, 2, Devon and Cornwall RS, 22 (1940), 391 · G. W. Stone, ed., *The London stage, 1660–1800*, pt 4: *1747–1776* (1962) · C. B. Hogan, ed., *The London stage, 1660–1800*, pt 5: *1776–1800* (1968)

Archives V&A, corresp. with David Garrick

Likenesses J.-F. Colson, oils, 1769, NPG [*see illus.*] · F. Cotes, chalk drawing (as Mrs Cole in *The minor*), BM · J. Roberts, drawing (as Fondlewife in Congreve's *Old batchelor*), BM · T. Worlidge, miniature, V&A · J. Zoffany, portrait (in *Devil upon two sticks*), Castle Howard, North Yorkshire · portrait (after Reynolds), Knole, Kent; version, Garr. Club · theatrical prints, BM, NPG

Wealth at death over £1700; plus two houses on Suffolk Street and house in North End Village, Fulham: Highfill, Burnim & Langhans, *BDA*, 5.344, 348

Forannán [St Forannán, Farannán] (*d.* **982**), bishop of Donaghmore and abbot of Waulsort, was born in Ireland. He became bishop of Donaghmore, Tipperary, but left Ireland as a *peregrinus* (a person who took an ascetic vow to live as an exile) and, having possibly heard about the Irish

connections of Waulsort in Lotharingia, decided to settle there. During the tenth century, several monasteries in this area were centres of a movement which attempted to stimulate and revive both spiritual and intellectual life. This initiative began in Gorze, a monastery reformed by the abbot, John of Vandières (959–74), at the request of Adalbero I, bishop of Metz (929–62). It soon extended to the provinces of Trier and Cologne. Although this reform developed thanks to the support of the princes and bishops, the contribution of the Irish was significant.

In the first half of the tenth century, following a movement started in the seventh century, many Irishmen undertook travels on the continent, among them St Maccalan (*d.* 978) and St Catroe (*d.* 971), who were the two first abbots of Waulsort. About 945 the noble Eilbert and his wife, Heresinde, founded first the monastery of St Michel-en-Thiérache, and then, somewhat later, Waulsort. Maccalan, who had received his clerical education in Gorze under Abbot Einold (933–59) and ruled the abbey of St Michel-en-Thiérache, was nominated first abbot of Waulsort. But after a while, probably finding the management of two monasteries too difficult, he retired to St Michel and let Waulsort be ruled by one of the most famous Irishmen, Catroe, who was schooled in Fleury-sur-Loire under Abbot Archambald (943–50). On one of his frequent journeys Catroe had the opportunity to meet Frederick, duke of Upper Lotharingia, and to become a close friend of Adalbero I. About 953 this bishop appointed Catroe abbot of St Félix of Metz (renamed St Clément in the eleventh century). In Waulsort Catroe's successor was Godefroid, a monk of St Rémi at Rheims. But such was the lack of discipline under Godefroid that, about 969, Eilbert had to appoint a new head to the convent. He chose Forannán; the decision was confirmed by Pope John XIII and under Forannán's administration, the monastery flourished again. It was then that Eilbert bestowed the abbey on Theodoric, bishop of Metz (964–84), who united it with the neighbouring abbey of Hastières. Forannán died in Waulsort on 30 April 982 and was buried in the church.

The few things that are known about Forannán come mainly from a chronicle of the abbey written in the middle of the twelfth century, the biography of St Catroe written by a monk of St Clément in 982 or 983, and Forannán's life, said to be based on oral traditions only and written by Robert, a monk of Waulsort, between *c.*1130 and 1135; some charters also exist. Contradictions between these sources and problems of authenticity affecting the charters have raised many difficulties, in particular about the chronology of the abbots. The period between 1080 and 1130 was disastrous for Waulsort and required it to attract pilgrims and so to develop Forannán's cult more widely. His life was written, presenting him as the first abbot. At about the same time, another monk of Waulsort wrote the *Translatio* of St Eloquius (a saint said to have come from Ireland together with St Fursa and St Foillan and who died *c.*651); although Eloquius's relics were transferred to Waulsort in 946, the writer attributes their translation to Forannán. From the twelfth century onwards a piece of linen said to have been Forannán's stole was venerated in the church on the grounds that it cured rabies, an attempt by the then abbot of Waulsort, Godescalc (d. c.1100), to compete with the fame of his widely known neighbour, St Hubert, a great healer of rabies.

NATHALIE STALMANS

Sources 'Vita Forannani', *Acta sanctorum: Aprilis*, 3 (Antwerp, 1675), 807–22 · 'Vita Kaddroae', *Acta sanctorum: Martius*, 1 (Antwerp, 1668), 468–80 · P. Ó Riain, ed., *Corpus genealogiarum sanctorum Hiberniae* (Dublin, 1985), 15, 93 · D. Misonne, *Eilbert de Florennes: histoire et légende, la geste de Raoul de Cambrai* (Louvain, 1967), 67–80 · D. Misonne, 'L'éloge de Forannan, abbé de Waulsort', *Anciens Pays et Assemblées d'États*, 38 (1966), 49–60 · M. Coens, 'L'étole de S. Forannan, abbé de Waulsort, et la rage', *Mélanges courtoy* (1952), 257–63 · J. Semmler, 'Iren in der lothringischen Klosterreform', *Die Iren und Europa im früheren Mittelalter*, ed. H. Löwe, 2 (Stuttgart, 1982), 941–57 · M. C. Chartier, 'Les moines irlandais en Lotharingie aux Xᵉ–XIᵉ siècles', MA diss., University of Paris X, 1975 [Mémoire de maîtrise, Université de Paris X Nanterre] · G. Despy, *Les chartes de l'abbaye de Waulsort* (Brussels, 1957), 2–8, 52–7

Forber. For this title name *see* Claypon, Janet Elizabeth Lane- [Janet Elizabeth Forber, Lady Forber] (1877–1967).

Forbes family (*per. c.*1400–*c.*1490), nobility, took its name from Forbes in Aberdeenshire. It had been long established there by the end of the fourteenth century, when it was represented by Sir John Forbes, who married Margaret Kennedy of Dunure. Sir John died in 1405 and was succeeded by his eldest son, **Alexander Forbes**, first Lord Forbes (d. 1448), who appears on 20 November 1406 as witness to a charter given by Robert Stewart, duke of Albany and governor of Scotland. Wyntoun names Forbes as one of the participants in a knightly tournament held in England in 1408; as serving his feudal superior, Alexander Stewart, earl of Mar, on the latter's expeditions abroad between 1406 and 1408, when he fought in the army of the duke of Burgundy; and as joining with Mar at the battle of Harlaw in 1411 against the lord of the Isles. On 16 October 1423 Forbes had a charter from Murdoch, duke of Albany, for the lands and barony of Forbes, situated in the sheriffdom of Aberdeen, on the boundary of the provincial earldom of Mar, thereby enhancing and underlining his position in the north-eastern political community. That he was anxious to maintain his new privileges is shown by the undertaking he received from his brother-in-law, William *Douglas, second earl of Angus, on 4 November 1423, in which Angus promised that he would not sell or alienate any of his lands or possessions to the prejudice of his sister, Elizabeth Douglas (Forbes's wife), or their heirs.

Forbes's wider ambitions included royal service; in 1423 and 1424 he received letters of safe conduct from the English king to go to Durham to treat for the ransom of James I. Following the return of the king in 1424, Forbes served as a royal councillor, and when the king went north to Aberdeen in August 1426, he used Forbes, familiar with the politics of the area, as one of his advisers. Forbes's support was also courted by Robert Erskine, another influential member of the north-eastern nobility, who entertained aspirations to the earldom of Mar, while in May 1432 Forbes entered into an agreement with Alexander Lindsay, earl of Crawford, who, as sheriff of Aberdeen, was able to offer him the office of deputy sheriff.

In 1435, following the death of the earl of Mar in that year, Forbes was made bailie of Mar by the king, thus acquiring an office which rendered his support vital for those who sought influence in Mar; it was for this reason that, on 17 November 1435, Forbes made an indenture with Erskine, offering the latter help in recovering the earldom of Mar and Garioch in return for 100 marks or lands in Mar, subject to Erskine's success. In the event, the king claimed the earldom himself. However, in 1438, following the death of James I, the consequent turmoil was exploited by the politically ambitious nobility of the north-east, with Forbes, as deputy sheriff of Aberdeen, backing Robert Erskine's continued claim to the earldom of Mar in defiance of the government. In doing so Forbes demonstrated the extent to which he was giving his local interests precedence over royal service, in consequence of the unpopularity created by the royal annexation of Mar. On 26 June 1439 Forbes received a charter from Erskine, styling himself earl of Mar, for half of the lordship of Strathdee.

Recognition of Forbes's influence probably led to concerted efforts by the minority government to court his support, and the ultimate failure of Erskine to achieve his ambitions in Mar seems to have had no adverse affect on Forbes, who had been raised to the peerage as a lord of parliament by 1 July 1445, when he appears as Lord Forbes. On 4 July 1440 the house of Drumynour (in Strathbogie, Aberdeenshire) is first mentioned as the chief residence of the Forbes family, and the status afforded by its acquisition, and by the peerage title, argues that Forbes had come to enjoy the patronage of Chancellor William Crichton, seeking to advance a man whose local influence would facilitate the effective administration of the north-east during the royal minority. Before 1423, Forbes married Elizabeth, daughter of George *Douglas, first earl of Angus, through whom their children were heirs of entail to the earldom of Angus. Forbes died in 1448 and was succeeded by his son, James.

James Forbes, second Lord Forbes (d. in or before 1462), was granted a licence by James II on 4 May 1456 to fortify the tower of Drumynour, and he was one of the lords of session appointed to sit at Aberdeen in 1457. He married Egidia (*fl.* 1450), second daughter of William *Keith, first Earl Marischal [*see under* Keith family], so linking the family to another important north-eastern family, recently elevated to the ranks of the higher nobility. He died before 30 July 1462, being succeeded by his son William, third Lord Forbes, who sat frequently in the parliaments which met between 1467 and 1488, and further consolidated the family's position, again in the arena of local as well as national politics, by marrying Christian Gordon, third daughter of Alexander, first earl of Huntly. He died before 5 July 1483.

Alexander Forbes, fourth Lord Forbes (d. 1491), succeeded his father and, on 5 July 1483, was ordered to pay 2000 marks to Margaret, Lady Dirleton, for failing to fulfil his agreement to marry her daughter. Instead, Forbes married Margaret Boyd, the daughter of Mary Stewart—the king's sister—and Thomas *Boyd, earl of Arran [*see under*

Boyd, family]; this royal connection may have been a factor in making Forbes one of James III's staunchest and most consistent supporters. He was present with the king at Aberdeen in April 1488 during the crucial latter stages of the king's confrontations with the rebels in that year. He accompanied James to Blackness early in May, and remained with him in Edinburgh between the 18th and the 28th, but seems almost certainly to have accompanied John Ramsay, Lord Bothwell, and the bishop of Moray in early June on a commission to enlist support for James III from fugitive Scots in Northumberland. The effort came too late, and the king was defeated and killed at Sauchieburn on 11 June 1488.

On 16 August 1488 Ross herald was sent north with a summons for treason to Lord Forbes. In the following spring, after he received further letters concerning the raising of a tax in the north-east, according to the sixteenth-century chronicler George Buchanan, Forbes rode through Aberdeen and the neighbouring towns carrying James III's bloodstained shirt on a spear, in an effort to incite revolt against the government. Forbes and the Earl Marischal had joined the leaders of the southern uprising against James IV in the castle of Dumbarton by September 1489, but after the defeat of the rebels in October, Forbes was pardoned. He took little further part in politics, and had died before 6 May 1491. He was succeeded by his brother Arthur, as fifth Lord Forbes.

C. A. McGLADDERY

Sources J. Robertson, ed., *Illustrations of the topography and antiquities of the shires of Aberdeen and Banff*, 4, Spalding Club (1862) · J. M. Thomson and others, eds., *Registrum magni sigilli regum Scotorum / The register of the great seal of Scotland*, 11 vols. (1882–1914), vol. 2 · *APS*, 1424–1567 · G. Burnett and others, eds., *The exchequer rolls of Scotland*, 7 (1884) · [T. Thomson], ed., *The acts of the lords auditors of causes and complaints*, AD 1466–AD 1494, RC, 40 (1839) · M. Brown, *James I* (1994) · C. McGladdery, *James II* (1990) · N. Macdougall, *James III: a political study* (1982) · N. Macdougall, *James IV* (1989) · *Scots peerage*, vol. 4

Forbes, Alexander, first Lord Forbes (d. 1448). *See under* Forbes family (*per. c.*1400–*c.*1490).

Forbes, Alexander, fourth Lord Forbes (d. 1491). *See under* Forbes family (*per. c.*1400–*c.*1490).

Forbes, Alexander (1564–1617), bishop of Aberdeen, was the son of John Forbes of Ardmurdo, from the Brux branch of the Forbes family, and his second wife, Helen Graham, a daughter of Graham of Morphie. He graduated MA from the University of St Andrews in 1585 and was appointed to his first pastoral charge as minister of Fettercairn, Kincardineshire, in May 1588. Evidently able, conscientious, and enthusiastic, Forbes soon began to play a conspicuous role in the activities of the higher church courts. In 1594 he was included in a committee of eminent ministers commissioned by the general assembly to investigate the claims made by the crown against the outspoken preacher, John Ross. The following year he was one of the commissioners chosen to undertake a visitation of the Scottish universities. Between 1593 and 1602

he was a member of eight out of the ten general assemblies, and seems to have consistently supported the king's endeavour to restore Erastian episcopacy in the Church of Scotland.

On 22 November 1604 Forbes was advanced to the bishopric of Caithness. However, to the consternation of his presbyterian detractors he was permitted to retain his benefice at Fettercairn. He was one of the bishops who, 'clothed in silk and velvet', rode in procession between the earls and lords at the opening of the parliament at Perth in 1606. In December that year the Linlithgow assembly appointed him constant moderator of the presbytery of Caithness. In an attempt to forestall prospective presbyterian opposition to this perpetual office the privy council issued an injunction to the presbytery on 17 January 1607 to receive him as such within twenty-four hours on pain of rebellion. Forbes was actively involved in the Linlithgow assembly of 1608, and in May 1609 was part of the episcopal delegation which met with presbyterian malcontents at Falkland Palace in an attempt to end the factionalism and bitterness within the church.

Not surprisingly Forbes took part in the famous Glasgow assembly of 1610 which restored full ecclesiastical authority and jurisdiction to bishops. He was consecrated in Brechin Cathedral in 1611 by the archbishop of St Andrews and the bishops of Brechin and Dunkeld, after episcopal succession was reintroduced from England at the king's bidding. His name was included among those eligible to sit and adjudicate in the newly instituted court of high commission of 1610 and again in 1615 when the two provincial courts were amalgamated and the commission renewed. In the latter year he incurred the opprobrium of the Scottish church for allegedly granting consent in the name of the Scottish hierarchy to the king's request that the Roman Catholic marquess of Huntly receive absolution from the archbishop of Canterbury while there at court. Forbes's apparent duplicity probably paved the way for his translation to the see of Aberdeen on 16 July 1616, where Huntly's influence was paramount. He was evidently a very ambitious man. Among his seven published letters is one to Sir Robert Carr on 3 May 1615 suggesting to the king's favourite that he and not John Spottiswode was the right man to succeed Gladstanes in the metropolitan see (*Original Letters*, 2.437). Forbes was officially installed as bishop of Aberdeen at St Andrews on 23 February 1617 and also became chancellor of King's College, Aberdeen, that same year.

Forbes had married Christian Straton of Crigie; they had seven sons and three daughters: William; Colonel Alexander; John, minister of Auchterless; Robert; Captain Arthur; George; Bernard; Margaret or Marjory who married Andrew Straton of Warburton; Isobel who married George Forbes of Allathan; and Jean who wed Robert Leighton, the son of Lord Usan. Forbes died in Leith on 14 December 1617.

David Calderwood, the presbyterian historian and polemicist, wrote that on his deathbed Forbes 'fain would … have spoken with the Bishop of St Andrews, but he being loathe to leave his play at cards, howbeit it was the Lord's day, the other departed before he came to him' (Calderwood, 7.287). He added that Forbes 'was impudent and shameless. He was not ashamed, when the Lords of Session and advocats came out of the Tolbuith at twelve houres, to follow them into their houses uncalled, and sitt down at their tables; therefore he was nicknamed Colie' (ibid.). By contrast, it should be recognized that Forbes was well respected throughout his locality and among his episcopalian contemporaries.

JAMES COOPER, *rev.* A. S. WAYNE PEARCE

Sources *Fasti Scot.*, new edn, 7.329–30 • D. Calderwood, *The history of the Kirk of Scotland*, ed. T. Thomson and D. Laing, 8 vols., Wodrow Society, 7 (1842–9), vols. 5–7 • *Original letters relating to the ecclesiastical affairs of Scotland: chiefly written by … King James the Sixth*, ed. D. Laing, 2 vols., Bannatyne Club, 92 (1851) • J. Spottiswoode, *The history of the Church of Scotland* (1655) • *The autobiography and diary of Mr James Melvill*, ed. R. Pitcairn, Wodrow Society (1842) • *DNB*
Archives NL Scot., Advocates MSS

Forbes, Alexander, fourth Lord Forbes of Pitsligo (1678–1762), philosopher and Jacobite army officer, only son of the third lord, Alexander Forbes (*c.*1655–1690), and Lady Sophia Erskine (*fl.* 1676–1734), third daughter of John, twentieth earl of Mar, was born on 24 May 1678. He succeeded to the estates and title on the death of his father in 1690. Forbes married first, in 1713, Rebecca (*d.* 1731), daughter of John Norton, a London merchant, with whom he had one son, John, master of Pitsligo (*c.*1713–1781); and secondly, in 1731, his wife's companion, Elizabeth Allen (*d.* 1759), in a match which produced no children. In his youth he travelled to France, where he received some education and made the acquaintance of Fénelon, and was introduced by him to Mme Guyon and other quietists. These were very influential in forming his religious ideas, which, although he remained a lifelong episcopalian, were resolutely ecumenical. He returned to Scotland in 1700. After the deposition of George Garden from his living for Jacobitism in 1701, Forbes gave him a house at Rosehearty, where an ecumenical religious community was set up 'where persons of different religious persuasions lived together in the love of God and the practice of self-abnegation' (Henderson, 18): Chevalier Andrew Ramsay was one of those who sought to join it. In the Scottish parliament Forbes sought what was 'consistent with the honour and independence of Scotland' (Forbes, *Thoughts*, 1829, iv), opposed steps leading to the union with England, and withdrew from the consideration of the articles to Pitsligo Castle.

In 1715 Forbes joined the Jacobite rising under his first cousin the earl of Mar, commanding a troop of horse at Sheriffmuir. Following the collapse of the rising, he was forced to flee to France. Subsequently he made his way via Rotterdam, Leiden, Vienna (where he may have acted as James's agent), Venice, and Munich to the Jacobite court in Italy, where he kept a diary of events, published in 1938 as *The Jacobite Court at Rome in 1719*. In 1720 he went to Paris, where he discussed Jacobite schemes with the financier John Law. Having not been attainted, he borrowed money

Alexander Forbes, fourth Lord Forbes of Pitsligo (1678–1762), by Alexis-Simon Belle, 1720 [detail]

from a Roman banker and returned to Scotland in the same year; living in retreat at Pitsligo Castle, he corresponded with other quietists and wrote philosophy, publishing *Essays Moral and Philosophical* in 1734. *Thoughts Concerning Man's Condition and Duties in this Life, and his Hope in the World to Come*, also composed at this time, was not published until 1763: this work proved to be even more of a success, going through several editions and remaining in print well into the nineteenth century. Elsewhere, he explored the question of the legitimacy of the state in his unpublished 'On government' and 'A letter on governments', composed about 1720 (which interestingly contradict some of the arguments of his published work). In them he appears to move some way towards a contractualist whig position. His thought combines a benign Christian ecumenism—'Every Body knows 'tis accident, for the most part, that makes us of one Religion, rather than another' (Forbes, *Essays*, 170)—with a kind of providential version of legitimacy and ideas of the centrality of popular consent, which can be held to hint towards the arguments of utilitarianism. He also (in his *Essays*) showed some sympathy with the position of women, whom he thought 'more active, more foreseeing and better managers than we' (McLynn, *The Jacobites*, 157).

In 1745 Forbes 'weighed and weighed again' the prospect of joining the rising, as he discusses at length in his complex 'Apologia' ('Memsie apologia', Aberdeen University Library, Pitsligo MS 1/16), but when he did so he entered on it with enthusiasm: 'Did you ever know me absent at the second day of a wedding?' he asked his friends (Forbes, *Thoughts*, 1854, xvii); to his soldiers he simply said 'Oh Lord, Thou knowest our cause is just. Gentlemen, march' (Tayler and Tayler, *Jacobite Letters*, 2). By the end of September 1745 Forbes was in Aberdeen, whence he marched south with around 130 horse and two companies of Banffshire infantry, later incorporated in the duke of Perth's regiment. On arrival at Edinburgh on 8 October, he was appointed general of horse by Prince Charles (Charles Edward Stuart), with the rank of full colonel. In England, where his cavalry were often used as scouts or forward patrols, he was in the thick of the action. Pitsligo's horse was the first body of Jacobite troops to enter Manchester, where Forbes threatened a reluctant constable with his sword; on 1 December he commanded the building of the bridge at Gatley ford and engineered the crossing of the Mersey by pontoon.

In the first stage of the fight at Clifton on 18 December, Pitsligo's horse was put to flight by government cavalry and dragoons, and retired to Penrith. At Falkirk in January 1746 the horse was stationed in the third line with the Royal Scots and the rest of the cavalry. On the retreat north, Forbes entered Aberdeen on 7 February: on the disorder of the further retreat, all or nearly all his horses were lost. At the battle of Culloden, the men of Pitsligo's horse thus stood in the rear and took little part in the action. Their leader, however, was still at this stage (and beyond) a zealous recruiter: Adam Hay later claimed to have been held by Forbes as a pressed man in the days immediately before Culloden, while in the aftermath of the battle he was still trying to raise men, despite acknowledging over 2000 dead on the field. Eventually accepting the inevitable, Forbes went into hiding on his own estates for the rest of his life, where his exploits became a local legend. During the day he lay in the mosses at Craigmaud, 9 miles up-country from Fraserburgh, or hid 'in a hollow place in the earth, under the arch of a small bridge' (Forbes, *Thoughts*, 1829, xxi). On other occasions he called at his own castle in the guise of a beggar, ordered searching soldiers breakfast in the house in which he was hiding, or guided a search party to his own hiding place in the Cave of Cowshaven (still known as Lord Pitsligo's Cave) on the Buchan coast, 2 miles from Rosehearty. His attainder named him as Lord Pitsligo (rather than Lord Forbes of Pitsligo), and on this technicality and the basis of similar mistakes made in attainders after the 'Fifteen, it was reversed by the court of session in 1749. This decision was, however, overturned by the House of Lords in the following year. Government troops continued to search sporadically for the ageing philosopher (who went under the name of Mr Brown in his correspondence with the countess of Erroll, carried by the laird of Udny's fool as go-between) until the later 1750s, by which time he was almost eighty years old. His dignity and resignation under this treatment were remarkable: in 1752 he could still write that 'We have nothing to depend upon but the Goodness of God every moment, we are sure he can do us no Injustice' (Aberdeen University Library, Pitsligo MS 1/6). He died at Auchiries on 21 December 1762.

By all accounts Lord Forbes was a man of extraordinary moral qualities: the personification of 'Virtue and Justice' to William Hamilton (Forbes, *Thoughts*, 1829, lvii); 'the best father … best friend and the best subject in Britain' to John Murray of Broughton (Forbes, *Jacobite Court*, 33). His character forms the basis for that of Baron Bradwardine in Sir Walter Scott's *Waverley*. In the judgement of William King, Forbes was the 'one person' known to him who spoke no evil 'of any man living' and found good to say of all (King, 143–5).   MURRAY G. H. PITTOCK

Sources DNB · Lord Forbes of Pitsligo [A. Forbes], *Essays moral and philosophical on several subjects* (1734) · Lord Forbes of Pitsligo [A. Forbes], *Thoughts concerning man's condition*, 3rd edn (1829) · Lord Forbes of Pitsligo [A. Forbes], *Thoughts concerning man's condition*, 4th edn (1854) · U. Aberdeen, Pitsligo MSS 2740/4/1B/1/1–29, 2740/4/1B/2/1–18 · W. King, *Political and literary anecdotes of his own times*, ed. [P. B. Duncan] (1818) · H. Tayler, ed., *The Jacobite court at Rome in 1719*, Scottish History Society, 3rd ser., 31 (1938) · A. Tayler and H. Tayler, eds., *Jacobite letters to Lord Pitsligo* (1930) · A. Tayler and H. Tayler, *Jacobites of Aberdeen and Banffshire in the Forty-Five* (1928) · M. G. H. Pittock, 'The political thought of Alexander, Lord Forbes of Pitsligo', *Northern Scotland* (1996) · M. G. H. Pittock, 'Jacobitism in the north-east: the Pitsligo Papers in Aberdeen University Library', *Aberdeen in the Enlightenment*, ed. J. Carter and J. Pittock (1987) · F. J. McLynn, *The Jacobite army in England, 1745: the final campaign* (1983) · B. G. Seton and J. G. Arnot, eds., *The prisoners of the '45*, Scottish History Society, 3rd ser., 13–15 (1928–9) · S. Reid, *1745: a military history of the last Jacobite rising* (1996) · H. Tayler, ed., *Jacobite epilogue* (1941) · F. McLynn, *The Jacobites* (1985) · GEC, *Peerage* · A. Tayler and H. Tayler, *Jacobites of Aberdeenshire and Banffshire in the rising of 1715* (1934) · A. Livingstone, C. W. H. Aikman, and B. S. Hart, eds., *Muster roll of Prince Charles Edward Stuart's army, 1745–46* (1984) · G. D. Henderson, *Chevalier Ramsay* (1952) · *Scott in carnival: selected papers from the fourth International Scott Conference, Edinburgh, 1991*, ed. J. H. Alexander and D. S. Hewitt (1993)

Archives NL Scot., corresp. and papers · U. Aberdeen L.

Likenesses A.-S. Belle, portrait, 1720, priv. coll. [*see illus.*] · J. Pettie, group portrait (*Bonnie Prince Charlie entering the ballroom at Holyrood*), Royal Collection

Forbes, Alexander Penrose (1817–1875), bishop of Brechin, was born on 6 June 1817 at York Place, Edinburgh, the second eldest of the ten children of John Hay *Forbes, Lord Medwyn (1776–1854), judge of the court of session, and his wife, Louisa Cumming Gordon (1779–1845), daughter of Sir Alexander Cumming Gordon of Altyre, Elgin. His parents were both Scottish and he was baptized in St Paul's Chapel of the Scottish Episcopal church in York Place, Edinburgh, on 9 July 1817. Forbes's father and grandfather, the banker Sir William *Forbes of Pitsligo, bt, were leading laymen in the Scottish Episcopal church. A few years later his family moved to the more fashionable Edinburgh address of 17 Ainslie Place and, after tutoring at home, Forbes attended the Edinburgh Academy from 1825 to 1832. To prepare for the civil service of the East India Company, Forbes was coached by the Revd Thomas Dale at Beckenham in Kent between August 1832 and September 1833. After attending Glasgow University for the 1834 session, he began his studies at the company's Haileybury College from July 1834 for the standard two-year course. Excelling as a student, especially in languages, he contracted as a writer in the company in September 1836. At Madras he was posted in July 1837 to the district of Rajahmundry as assistant collector, and then became assistant to the registrar of the Sudderand

Alexander Penrose Forbes (1817–1875), by Valentine

foujdari. Recurrent fever forced him to return to Britain in January 1840 and he left the company's service in June 1844. He went up to Oxford as a gentleman commoner in Brasenose College in May 1840. At university he embraced the Oxford Movement through the acquaintance of John Henry Newman, Charles Marriot, and especially Edward Pusey. Pusey remained a lifelong mentor to his younger friend, and his commitment to fostering Tractarian communities of single priests in urban areas shaped Forbes's future ministry and celibate life.

Graduating with a fourth-class pass in 1844 Forbes was ordained deacon in that year by Bishop Richard Bagot of Oxford. Following a short rural curacy in Aston Rowant, Oxfordshire, he was ordained priest by Bishop Bagot in 1845 and became assistant curate to Thomas Chamberlain, the early Tractarian vicar of St Thomas's, West Oxford. During this time he contributed to Chamberlain's journal *The Ecclesiastic* and wrote a novella, *The Prisoners of Craigmacaire* (1852), which demonstrated his sympathies for non-juring Scottish Episcopacy. He resigned his curacy in February 1846. After taking temporary charge of the Episcopalian congregation at Stonehaven from June 1846 he became, in May 1847, vicar of the advanced Tractarian parish of St Saviour's, Leeds, of which Pusey was the founder and patron. In September 1847 he was elected bishop of Brechin in succession to Bishop David Moir, owing to his family's prominence in Episcopalian circles and the support of leading English churchmen, especially W. E. Gladstone and Bishop Samuel Wilberforce of Oxford. Forbes was the first adherent of the Oxford Movement to become a bishop.

Consecrated bishop of Brechin on 28 October 1847, Forbes also succeeded to the charge of St Paul's congregation, Dundee. One of the most industrialized cities of nineteenth-century Britain, Dundee's workforce, mainly women, lived in dark, dank, crowded tenements in the city centre. Forbes chose to live and work among these tenements of the labouring poor, thus setting an example of slum ministry unique among Anglican bishops in the United Kingdom and rare even among Episcopalian and Anglican clergy, but for which his English Tractarian experience had helped to prepare him. He became extensively involved with the social concerns of Dundee and his diocese, where he facilitated church extension and rising standards of clerical professionalism as Scottish Episcopalians began to feel the effects of a generally rising population and a more public position after their eighteenth-century penal obscurity. He built a new cathedral in Dundee, designed by Gilbert Scott, on the highest point of the city, where its spire was easily visible. It was a testimonial both to Forbes's belief in the greater prominence of the Episcopal church in his country and to the importance of the city compared with the historic centre of the diocese at Brechin. His ardent support for the diocesan library, as well as for congregational schools, were only the most obvious illustrations of his concern for raising the educational levels of the clergy and the laity, down to the poorest social level.

A cautious ritualist, Forbes's major concern was with doctrine, because he believed that a more specific and explicit Tractarian doctrine could remedy the growing doubt about Christianity in mid-Victorian Britain. This concern catalysed the eucharistic controversy in the Scottish Episcopal church when Forbes, in his primary charge of 1857, defended the real corporeal presence of Christ in the eucharist as Anglican doctrine. Forbes was acting in concert with Pusey and John Keble in a Tractarian defence of Archdeacon George Denison, then on trial for this doctrine in the Church of England. The charge created intense division among Episcopalians as Forbes's Tractarian doctrine, with its Roman Catholic associations, collided with traditional Episcopalian high-church teaching and hostility to Rome. Forbes was eventually presented for heresy in October 1859 by one of his clergy, to be tried before the other Scottish bishops. At the trial in March 1860 Forbes was found guilty of erroneous teaching, but only cautioned. His ministry among the Dundee poor, as well as his national Tractarian connections, had brought him powerful support, and the bishops were concerned lest a more severe sentence led to Tractarian schism.

In the early 1860s, using Gladstone's powerful political support, Forbes led a successful campaign to save the use of the Scottish communion office, the non-juring liturgy still used by a minority of Episcopalians, from being repudiated in favour of the English Book of Common Prayer. The attempt at repudiation was an Anglicizing move by the Episcopal church in a campaign to have legal disabilities on Episcopalian clergy serving in the Church of England removed by parliament. The parliamentary support of English evangelical bishops hostile to the Scottish communion office was deemed necessary for the campaign's success. Forbes's backing for the communion office restored his credibility among traditional Episcopalians sympathetic to the non-juring tradition but previously alienated by Forbes's Tractarian eucharistic doctrine. However, the eucharistic controversy and the threat to the Scottish communion office undermined Forbes's confidence in the catholicity of his own church and he seriously considered secession to the Roman Catholic church during the 1860s.

Forbes's Anglicanism revived as a consequence of the failure of Pusey's campaign for Anglican reunion with Rome. He had been an early adviser to the Association for the Promotion of the Unity of Christendom, formed in 1857; this concern continued with his support for Pusey's campaign which began with the publication of Pusey's *Eirenicon* in 1865 and ended with the First Vatican Council in 1871 (he was often called 'the Scottish Pusey'). Forbes canvassed his extensive European Catholic contacts, including the German historian Ignaz von Döllinger. His major scholarly works were contributions to Victorian hagiography and liturgy, including the *Lives of S. Ninian and S. Kentigern* (1874) and his editing of the *Kalendars of Scottish Saints* (1872) and the Arbuthnott missal (1864) with his brother George Hay *Forbes. But he also wrote, for the reunionist cause, his major theological work, *Explanation of the Thirty-Nine Articles* (1867-8), exegeting the articles to show their congruence with Roman doctrine. Ultimately Forbes could not tolerate the Vatican council's adding papal infallibility to the deposit of truth given to the early church, thereby making Christianity increasingly difficult for the educated to accept.

In the final years of his life Forbes demonstrated renewed Tractarian energies. He also returned to the toryism of his family, which he had previously relinquished under the influence of Gladstone. He successfully opposed in 1870 the introduction of laity into synods of the Scottish Episcopal church. His long interest in the vowed religious life came to fruition when he founded in 1871 his own Community of Saint Mary and Saint Modwenna for women in Dundee. A severe gastric illness caused Forbes's unexpected death on 8 October 1875 at the Bishop's House, Castlehill, Dundee, and he was buried in his cathedral on 15 October.   ROWAN STRONG

Sources R. Strong, *Alexander Forbes of Brechin* (1995) · W. Perry, *Alexander Penrose Forbes* (1939) · D. J. Mackey, *Bishop Forbes* (1888) · Dundee University Archives, A. P. Forbes MSS · Pusey Oxf., Forbes papers · BL, Gladstone MSS · NA Scot., Register of College of Bishops · U. St Andr. L., special collections department, George Hay Forbes MSS · BL, East India Company MSS · Pusey Oxf., Pusey papers · Pusey Oxf., Keble papers · W. Perry, *The Oxford movement in Scotland* (1939) · *Scottish Guardian* (22 Oct 1875), 219 · baptismal cert.

Archives LPL, corresp. · NRA, priv. coll., corresp., notebooks, and papers · Pusey Oxf., MSS · University of Dundee, corresp. and papers | BL, corresp. with W. E. Gladstone, Add. MS 44154 · LPL, letters to Cecil Wray · NA Scot., Scottish Episcopal Church MSS · Pusey Oxf., De Buck MSS · Pusey Oxf., Keble MSS · Pusey Oxf., Pusey MSS · Scottish Catholic Archives, Edinburgh, corresp. with James Kyle · U. Newcastle, letters to Sir Walter Trevelyan · University of Dundee, corresp. with A. F. Kinnaird

Likenesses Valentine, photogravure, repro. in Mackey, *Bishop Forbes* [see illus.] · engraving, repro. in Perry, *Alexander Penrose Forbes* · photograph, Dundee University Library

Wealth at death £2179 12s. od.: probate, 1876, Dundee

Forbes [*née* St Clair-Erskine], **Lady Angela Selina Bianca** (1876–1950), wartime catering organizer, was born at 8 Grafton Street, Mayfair, London, on 11 June 1876, the fifth of the five children of Robert Francis St Clair-Erskine, fourth earl of Rosslyn (1833–1890), and seventh child of his wife, Blanche Adeliza Fitzroy (d. 1933), daughter of Henry Fitzroy and widow of the Hon. Charles Maynard. Angela St Clair-Erskine was the youngest of five beautiful sisters, the most outstanding of whom was her half-sister Daisy, countess of Warwick, mistress of Edward VII. Angela's childhood was spent between Dysart, near Kirkcaldy, Fife, and Lady Anne's House, near Stamford, Lincolnshire. She was educated by governesses, but her father was the strongest influence in her early life and shared with her his love of horses, hunting, and good food.

Angela was nearly 6 feet tall with a turned-up nose, not beautiful like her sisters but full of vitality, with a gift for repartee and the vocabulary, it was said, of a stable boy. Hunting was her passion and she recounts in her autobiography *Memories and Base Details* (1921) how, when James Stewart (Jim) Forbes (1872–1957), a soldier, asked her to marry him, she replied 'yes, if I may have your chestnut horse' (p. 84). They married on 27 April 1896 and had two daughters. In 1907 they divorced.

After the divorce, and short of money, Angela Forbes wrote four novels which she later described as pot-boilers, though the first and most autobiographical, *The Broken Commandment* (1910), still reads well. By 1912 she was the acknowledged mistress of Lord Elcho, later ninth earl of Wemyss (1857–1937), sharing his passion for gambling and dividing her time between her house at Le Touquet, France, and Gosford, the Wemyss house in East Lothian, while Mary Elcho lived at Stanway, Gloucestershire.

At the outbreak of the First World War, Angela dumped her children at Stanway and went out to Dr Haden Guest's Hospital in Paris. There, although quite unqualified, she took notes for the surgeons in the operating theatre. She was in Boulogne when she saw trains of wounded coming in, the soldiers being left on the quay for hours with no food or drink. She went straight back to London, spent £8 on provisions at Fortnum and Masons, and in November 1914 started a canteen for the soldiers in the station waiting-room. It was an immediate success. Unlike the official canteens, the British Soldiers' Buffets, commonly known as Angelinas, met every train of wounded as it arrived and were often open twenty-four hours a day. Although Angela and her volunteers, who were mainly her friends and relatives, never knew if there would be 1000 or 4000 to feed, food never ran out.

At first Angela and then Lord Wemyss, who became treasurer, raised money successfully through appeals in the press; then in 1915 the Red Cross canteens started charging the soldiers for food. The British Soldiers' Buffets also began to charge and—unlike the Red Cross—made a profit, which Angela used after the war to help pay for her training scheme for disabled soldiers. In 1916 she opened another canteen, in the biggest house in Étaples, for the workmen who were building the British army training camp there, and another in 1917 for the 10,000 soldiers who were drilled there. From her canteen profits she built fourteen recreation huts. The buffets also operated in the station at Étaples, serving men on their way to the front line. On 9 September 1917 rioting occurred in the camp; the description of the near-mutiny in *Memories and Base Details* throws an interesting sidelight on an incident that was hushed up at the time.

A few days after the riot Angela was ordered to leave France. The excuse given was that her conduct was unseemly: she had been heard to say 'damn' and she had washed her hair in the canteen. She was astonished and furious, and made an appeal, but the army was adamant. With her abrasive manner and her disregard for red tape she had made enemies, and her dislike of the commander-in-chief, Sir Douglas Haig, was well known. It has been suggested that there was a connection between her witnessing the 'mutiny' and her departure. She was denied an inquiry, but her case came before the House of Lords, and both Lord Ribblesdale and Lord Wemyss spoke eloquently in her defence. As the whole house knew they were, or had been, her lovers, the scene must have caused some quiet mirth, but her name was cleared.

After the war Angela Forbes started a training scheme for disabled soldiers, but it soon faded out, as did a dress shop, an attempt at journalism, and a scheme to run Gosford as a hotel. She reverted to her maiden name by deed poll in 1929. She travelled widely, describing her adventures in *Fore and Aft* (1932). Angela St Clair-Erskine died on 22 October 1950 in Jersey, and her funeral took place at Roslin Chapel, Midlothian, on 2 November.

CLAYRE PERCY

Sources A. Forbes, *Memories and base details* (1921) · Burke, *Peerage* (1959) · *Lady Cynthia Asquith: diaries, 1915–1918* (1968) · *The letters of Arthur Balfour and Lady Elcho, 1885–1917*, ed. J. Ridley and C. Percy (1992) · W. Allison and J. Fairley, *The monocled mutineer* (1978) · *Hansard 5L* (1918), vol. 28 · A. Forbes, *Fore and aft* (1932) · private information (2004) · b. cert. · A. Lambert, *Unquiet Souls: the Indian summer of the British aristocracy, 1880–1918* (1984)
Likenesses photographs, *c*.1894–*c*.1920, repro. in Forbes, *Memories*

Forbes, Ann (1745–1834), portrait painter, was born in Inveresk, Scotland, on 31 May 1745, the daughter of Hugh Forbes, advocate, and Margaret Forbes, *née* Aikman, and granddaughter of the Scottish portraitist William Aikman. In 1768 she left Edinburgh to study art in Rome, accompanied by her widowed mother as chaperone. The trip was sponsored by a family friend, Robert Chalmers, who had been sufficiently impressed by her ability in pastel (then known as 'drawings in crayon') to arrange for her family and friends to subscribe to the cost of the journey. There was an expectation that she would then be able to

support her family from her improved skill, and she herself hoped to achieve success as great as that already enjoyed by the Scottish artist Katharine Read (1723–1778), who also specialized in pastels. Forbes had arrived in Rome by March 1768. She took instruction and advice from (among others) the artist and antiquary Gavin Hamilton and the artist James Nevay, her connection with the latter producing unfounded rumours of plans for their marriage; she was also visited by most of the British residents and by the envoy to Naples, Sir William Hamilton. While in Rome she determined on working in oil, an important development, considering her intention to earn her living as a professional painter in potential competition with Read. Her stay was not, however, an easy one; she suffered from the heat and found the Italian language difficult.

Forbes returned to Britain in March 1771. She visited Edinburgh, where she received commissions that she undertook in London, where she established a studio. At this period she had more than enough work, with further commissions from Scots in London and people she had met in Italy. In 1772 she exhibited at the Royal Academy, and she could have enjoyed success in the longer term had she been able to start in London with enough connections in society, but the lack of a personal base on which to build, together with slow production, made for an uphill struggle. She became overwhelmed and exhausted, and by October 1772 had fallen ill. In 1773 she returned to Scotland, where she regained her health and resumed her production of portraits; in 1788 she was appointed portrait painter to the Society of Antiquaries of Scotland. She continued to make a living as a painter. Her paintings are good, solid productions—for example, her portraits of Lady Anne Stewart (National Gallery of Scotland, Edinburgh), which shows the influence of Allan Ramsay, and of Baron Ord (*c*.1775, Royal College of Physicians, Edinburgh)—but she never rose to artistic prominence. She died, unmarried, in Edinburgh in 1834, aged eighty-eight.

PATRICIA R. ANDREW

Sources K. Sloan, 'Forbes, Anne', *Dictionary of women artists*, ed. D. Gaze (1997) · J. Ingamells, ed., *A dictionary of British and Irish travellers in Italy, 1701–1800* (1997) · D. Macmillan, *Scottish art, 1460–2000* (2000) · artist's file, archive material, Courtauld Inst., Witt Library · b. cert. · will, PRO, SC 70/1/50, 768–78
Archives NL Scot., corresp. MSS, Acc. 3081 · Scot. NPG, artist's folder, cuttings, MSS notes, photocopies, and photographs | NA Scot., inventory of Ann Forbes's personal estate, 17 June 1834
Likenesses D. Allan, oils, 1781, Scot. NPG · A. Forbes, self-portrait, pastels, priv. coll.

Forbes, Archibald (1838–1900), journalist, the son of Lewis William Forbes DD (*d*. 1854), minister of Boharm, Banffshire, and his second wife, Elizabeth, *née* Leslie, was born in Morayshire. He attended the parish school, then, intended by his father for the ministry, King's College, Aberdeen, from 1853 to 1855. He was a wild youth and, as he later wrote, 'follies and extravagance abruptly terminated my university career' (*Souvenirs*, 48); he left King's College without graduating. His next movements are not known with certainty, but he apparently squandered his

Archibald Forbes (1838–1900), by Sir Hubert von Herkomer, 1881

inheritance and was penniless when, influenced by a lecture on the Crimean War, given by William Howard Russell, he enlisted in the 1st (Royal) Dragoons. He served uneventfully from 1859 to 1864, in his spare time reading military theory and publishing pseudonymous articles on military subjects. He was always proud that he had been a private of dragoons, and later attributed to it much of his success as a war correspondent.

Forbes became a struggling journalist in London, writing for the *Morning Star* and *Evening Star*, and editing and largely writing an unprofitable weekly, the *London Scotsman*. He also wrote for the *Morning Advertiser*, edited by James Grant, and published a melodramatic novel, *Drawn from Life* (1871). In 1870 Forbes's chance came when Grant sent him as war correspondent to the Franco-Prussian War. To economize, Grant soon sacked Forbes, but the latter's reports had attracted the attention of J. R. Robinson, general manager of the *Daily News*, who hired Forbes and sent him back to the war, where he again accompanied the German forces. There his ability to write dramatic copy quickly, and to expedite its dispatch to London—by ingenuity, subterfuge, exceptional rides, and the American reporters' practice of telegraphing—sometimes scooping his rivals (who included W. H. Russell of *The Times*), won him outstanding success. He hurriedly compiled from his war correspondence his book *My Experiences of the War between France and Germany* (2 vols., 1871) and then reported the end of the Paris commune. The Franco-Prussian War established his reputation as a

leading war correspondent and launched his career as the *Daily News* leading special correspondent, which continued until he retired.

In the 1870s Forbes reported the Carlist wars, Serbo-Turkish War, and the Russo-Turkish War, in which he again enhanced his reputation. He returned to England 'the lion of the season and the hero of the hour' (G. A. Sala, quoted in the *Daily News*, 3 Dec 1877, 2), and lectured on the war. He added to his celebrity by a controversial article condemning the Bulgarians, in the November 1877 *Nineteenth Century*, which was denounced by Gladstone, and other 'atrocitarian' pro-Bulgarians. In 1878 Forbes reported the occupation of Cyprus and exposed the sickness and mortality of the garrison, to the annoyance of Sir Garnet Wolseley, the high commissioner, and of the Conservative government. In 1878–9 he reported the first part of the Anglo-Afghan War, accompanying the Peshawar valley field force to Jalalabad. On the Bazar valley punitive expedition he bandaged wounded soldiers under fire and was mentioned in dispatches; he also went to Burma to interview King Thibaw. Later in 1879 he reported the Anglo-Zulu War, describing the advance to Ulundi and the battle there, and criticizing Lord Chelmsford. After the battle of Ulundi (4 July 1879) Chelmsford decided not to send dispatch riders that evening; Forbes rode alone through hostile territory to Landmann's Drift, and his telegram was the first news of the battle received in Britain. By this 'ride of death' he achieved his greatest fame. However, this was his last campaign; his health failed and in 1883 he described himself as an invalid. Yet his fame continued; in 1883 his old university awarded him the LLD.

In the 1870s, while primarily a war correspondent, Forbes was also used by the *Daily News* as a peacetime special correspondent, reporting, besides various disasters, manoeuvres, and shipwrecks, the Vienna exhibition and several royal visits, among them the prince of Wales's tour of India. He also functioned as an investigative and crusading journalist. In 1872 he reported sympathetically on English agricultural trade unionism, travelling with and praising its leader, Joseph Arch. His emotive comments stimulated public support for the agricultural workers; Arch wrote that Forbes had 'helped to turn the scale in our favour at a critical time' (Arch, 84). Yet privately Forbes was more cynical: he later wrote that he had been 'inventing Joseph Arch, and describing the situation of the clods' (quoted in H. Lucy, *The Diary of a Journalist*, 1920, 69).

In 1882 Forbes married Louisa, daughter of General Montgomery Cunningham Meigs of the USA; they had no children. In the 1880s and 1890s, retired from war reporting, Forbes exploited his earlier experiences, studies, and writings: he gave public lectures in Britain, Australia—there reportedly gaining some £12,000—New Zealand, and the United States. As a reporter he had been well paid, but he lost money, presumably through unwise investments; his financial situation probably motivated his later mediocre 'pot-boiling' books. He wrote articles and short stories, and compiled and wrote books, fiction and non-fiction, of varied quality. These included derivative biographies, histories, and *Czar and Sultan* (1894), a largely autobiographical novel of the Russo-Turkish War. In 1895 he published a collection of autobiographical and other articles, *Memories and Studies of War and Peace*, possibly his best book.

William Howard Russell had established the role of the war correspondent as military pundit and controversialist. Forbes was proud of his profession and his military expertise; truculent and dogmatic, he continued, in articles in the reviews and in books, to pronounce on military issues and on war correspondents, whom he defended. Despite having worked for a Gladstonian paper he was, he insisted privately, the reverse of a Gladstonian Liberal. His views on the army and war were toughminded and bellicist. The Franco-Prussian War was apparently the formative influence on his military thinking, establishing his Prussocentric 'continentalism' and admiration for German military theory and practice. He became the most widely read popularizer of continentalist doctrine. An effective polemicist, he pronounced on military controversies, criticized commanders and caused offence. Forbes resented the apparent failure of the British authorities to share his good opinion of himself. He was awarded fourteen continental decorations, including the Iron Cross, but craved British medals. In public and in correspondence with the War Office, he claimed campaign medals for the Anglo-Afghan and Anglo-Zulu wars, but without success.

After a long illness and painful operations, Forbes died at his London home, 1 Clarence Terrace, Regent's Park, on 29 March 1900. It is indicative of his reputation that he was commemorated by a tablet in St Paul's Cathedral, unveiled by Lord Wolseley.

Forbes in his prime was a large, strong, handsome man, physically and mentally tough. He was brave—repeatedly risking death—determined, and energetic, and a good horseman. All these qualities contributed to his success as a correspondent, as did his vivid writing and his ability to get his copy through by whatever means were available. He seized the new opportunities in a period exceptionally favourable to war correspondents. Proud, pugnacious, critical, and 'a good hater' (obituary, *Daily News*, 31 March 1900), he was a controversial figure. To himself and his other admirers he was a hero, but his enemies saw him as a bad-tempered, arrogant braggart, who faked war reports and claimed for himself other correspondents' feats. Yet even if he may have sometimes exaggerated, embroidered, and made dubious claims—and the truth is now probably unascertainable—there remained an indubitable achievement. His writings were widely read and helped to shape British perceptions of war. 'With a halo of journalistic romance' (J. Hatton, *Journalistic London*, 1882, 58), he became the archetype of the adventurous war correspondent, and among Victorian war correspondents, he was second only to Russell, who called him 'that incomparable Archibald' (quoted in Thomas, 173).

ROGER T. STEARN

Sources R. T. Stearn, 'Archibald Forbes, special correspondent', *Journal of Newspaper and Periodical History*, 8/2 (1992) · R. T. Stearn, 'War images and image makers in the Victorian era: aspects of the British visual and written portrayal of war, c.1866–1906', PhD diss., U. Lond., 1987 · A. Forbes, *Memories and studies of war and peace* (1895) · A. Forbes, *Souvenirs of some continents* (1885) · A. Forbes, *Barracks, bivouacks and battles* (1891) · A. Forbes, *Camps, quarters and casual places* (1896) · A. Forbes, reports and articles, *Daily News* · F. L. Bullard, *Famous war correspondents* (1914) · *Fifty years of Fleet Street: being the life and recollections of Sir John R. Robinson*, ed. F. M. Thomas (1904) · J. Arch, *Joseph Arch: the story of his life*, ed. countess of Warwick (1898) · *Daily News* (31 March 1900) · *The Times* (31 March 1900) · Gladstone, *Diaries*
Archives BL, T. H. S. Escott MSS · BL, Gladstone MSS · Hove Central Library, Sussex, Wolseley MSS
Likenesses H. von Herkomer, oils, 1881, Kunsthalle, Hamburg, Germany [*see illus.*] · medallion portrait on tablet, 1900, St Paul's Cathedral, London · Ape [C. Pellegrini], chromolithograph caricature, NPG; repro. in *VF* (5 Jan 1878) · F. Villiers, pencil drawing, NPG · photograph, repro. in Forbes, *Memories and studies* · photograph, repro. in Bullard, *Famous war correspondents* · woodcut, NPG
Wealth at death £10,908 6s. 11d.: probate, 14 June 1900, CGPLA Eng. & Wales

Forbes, Sir Archibald Finlayson (1903–1989), industrialist and banker, was born on 6 March 1903 in Johnstone, Renfrewshire, the elder child and only son of Charles Forbes, chief constable of Johnstone, and his wife, Elizabeth, daughter of James Robertson, slater and plasterer, also of Johnstone. He was educated at Paisley grammar school, and then joined the Glasgow firm of accountants Thomson McLintock, and as part of his training attended Glasgow University. In 1927 he qualified as a member of the Scottish Institute of Chartered Accountants; his incisive brain, rapid grasp of detail, and capacity for hard work soon attracted the notice of Sir William McLintock, and marked the start of a close working relationship that continued for eight years. In 1930 he moved to the London office as McLintock's assistant.

In 1935 he was offered a partnership, but instead of taking this significant promotion he elected to accept an invitation to join Spillers, one of the milling clients, as finance director. This decision to leave the profession was an important milestone in his career, and was prompted partly by a realization that exceedingly able and more senior partners would succeed Sir William, and partly by his attraction to the challenge of and, at that time, more lucrative life in industry. Between 1939 and 1953 the food industry was under close operational control, and the scope for the able and ambitious young finance director in Spillers was therefore very limited. In 1940 Forbes was seconded to the Air Ministry as director of capital finance, but soon afterwards he joined the first Baron Beaverbrook, who, with a small hand-picked team, was charged by Winston Churchill with cutting through bureaucracy and red tape to speed up the production and repair of Spitfires and Hurricanes. He became first deputy secretary at the Ministry of Aircraft Production, where the stimulating and unorthodox life fully extended his talents. From 1943 until 1945 he was controller of repair, equipment, and overseas supplies and from 1942 to 1945 a member of the Aircraft Supply Council.

In 1946 Forbes was appointed chairman of the Iron and Steel Board, which was disbanded on nationalization in 1949. After returning to office in 1951, the Conservatives denationalized steel, recreated the board, and reappointed Forbes as chairman for a further six years (1953–9). He was president of the Federation of British Industries from 1951 to 1953, and on decontrol in 1953 returned to more active participation in Spillers' affairs, playing a major role in its growth and diversification; he became deputy chairman in 1960, chairman (1965–8), and president (1969–80). His financial acumen and experience were much in demand by other companies, and between 1954 and 1964 he variously served as a non-executive director on the boards of Shell, English Electric, and Dunlop. From 1959 to 1964 he was chairman of the Central Mining and Investment Corporation. In 1959 he was appointed to the board of Midland Bank, whose deputy chairman he became in 1962. This signalled the final phase of his business career, which was to be devoted to the banking world. In 1964 he became chairman, but he suffered a minor heart attack in 1966 and was advised to cut back his activities. He gave up his other directorships, including in 1968 the chairmanship of Spillers.

As chairman of the Midland Bank, Forbes changed the traditional role of the office to one of a more executive character, while bringing the board much more closely in touch with the management. He was a strong advocate of diversification and between 1967 and 1974 played a direct personal part in negotiating some major deals. From his retirement in 1975 until 1983 he was president, an honorary office. While chairman of the Midland he served as chairman of the Committee of London Clearing Bankers and president of the British Bankers' Association (both 1970–72). He also sat on several government review bodies and committees, and was on the governing body of Imperial College, London (1959–75), and president of Epsom College (from 1964). He was knighted in 1943 and appointed GBE in 1957.

Forbes was urbane, courteous, and immaculately dressed, with a slim figure and iron-grey hair always in place; with a ready smile and at times acerbic wit he had great charm, particularly for women, who also found his soft Scottish accent an attraction. Occasionally he could infuriate his business colleagues by being indecisive or over-playing the role of devil's advocate, but his even temper ensured that this did not lead to bitterness. By no account mean, he had few extravagances and, despite his proclaimed enjoyment of golf, fishing on the River Test, and playing bridge at Brooks's, his work was his paramount interest in life.

In 1937 Forbes married Bina, daughter of Major Ronald Elliott, of Krickenbeek. They had no children. The marriage was dissolved in 1943, and in the same year he married Angela Gertrude, daughter of Horace Ely, of private means, of Arlington House, London. They had two daughters and a son. His second wife brought him a happy social life that could otherwise so easily have been subordinated to his demanding career activities. Her sudden and untimely death in 1969 was a great blow to him. He continued to lead an active life until about 1987, when he was confined increasingly to his flat at 40 Orchard Court, Portman Square, London, where he had lived for over fifty years. He died there on 2 June 1989, from a heart condition.   W. MICHAEL VERNON, rev.

Sources *The Times* (6 June 1989) · *WWW* · private information (1996) · personal knowledge (1996) · *CGPLA Eng. & Wales* (1989)
Archives CAC Cam., mainly relating to iron and steel boards · U. Warwick Mod. RC, papers as president of Federation of British Industries
Wealth at death £1,246,784: probate, 1989, *CGPLA Eng. & Wales*

Forbes, Arthur, first earl of Granard (1623–1695), politician and army officer, was the eldest son of Sir Arthur Forbes, baronet (*d.* 1632), of Corse in Aberdeenshire, and Jane (*d.* in or after 1642), widow of Sir Alexander Hamilton of Killeshandra, co. Cavan, and daughter of Sir Robert Lauder of the Isle of Bass. His father went to Ireland in 1620 with the master of Forbes's regiment, of which he was lieutenant-colonel, and was granted large estates in co. Leitrim and co. Longford by James I. However, Sir Arthur was killed in a duel in 1632, and his eldest son succeeded to his title and was thereafter brought up entirely in the care of his mother. During the Irish rising of 1641 she was besieged in Castle Forbes, the family seat, for nine months, and Forbes raised men for her relief, though only eighteen years old. He is next heard of in Scotland serving under Montrose in the cause of Charles I. On the defeat of Montrose in 1645 he was taken prisoner, and for two years confined in Edinburgh Castle. On his release he still embraced every opportunity to aid the fallen fortunes of the Stuarts until cowed into capitulation in 1651. In 1653 he quickly joined Seaforth and Balcarres in the retraction of their allegiance to the new British Commonwealth. But defeated in arms by Major-General Robert Lilburne's forces, and eventually captured by Major-General Monck's, he returned to Ireland in 1655, where, by the terms of his articles of surrender, he enjoyed his Leitrim and Longford estates unmolested. About this time he married Catherine (*d.* 1714), widow of Sir Alexander Stewart, bt, and daughter of Sir Robert Newcomen, bt, of Mosstown, co. Longford. The couple had five sons and one daughter.

In 1660 Forbes was sent to Charles II at Breda to assure him that if he would only go over to Ireland the whole kingdom would declare for him. At the Restoration he was appointed a commissioner of the court of claims in Ireland, and received additional grants of land in co. Westmeath. In 1661 he entered the Irish privy council and sat in parliament as member for co. Tyrone, having been elected also for St Johnstown, co. Longford. In 1663 he did good service in the north of Ireland by nipping in the bud efforts there in support of Blood's plot. Honours now flowed rapidly in on him. In 1670 he was sworn of the Irish privy council, and appointed marshal and commander-in-chief of the army. In 1671 he was one of the lords justices during the absence of the lord lieutenant, Lord Berkeley, and held the same post in 1675–6 and 1685–6. He has been described as the Restoration regime's troubleshooter in the north of Ireland. In 1672 he was the means of rendering to the presbyterian church of Ireland, of which he was an attached member, an important service, by procuring for it the first grant of *regium donum*, which that body continued to enjoy until the passing of the Irish Church Act in 1869, with the exception of a short interval. One historian gives an account of his action in this matter, which, he says, came 'from Sir Arthur Forbes's own mouth', to the effect that he (Forbes) being in London, the king enquired of him as to the welfare of the Irish presbyterian ministers, of whose loyalty and sufferings in his cause he had often heard. Forbes having told him that 'they lived in no great plenty', the king said 'that there was 1,200l. a year in the settlement of the revenue of Ireland which he had not yet disposed of, but designed it for a charitable use, and he knew not how to dispose of it better than by giving it to these ministers'. It subsequently appeared that only £600 was available for the purpose, and at this figure the grant was made to Forbes (Kirkpatrick, 384).

In 1672 the lord lieutenant, the earl of Essex, warmly commended Forbes to Charles II, calling him 'as worthy a man and as faithfull a servant to you as any person I have ever known' (*Second Report*, HMC, 211). Essex nominated him one of the lords justices to officiate in his absence in England in 1675. The same year Forbes was created Baron Clanehugh and viscount of Granard. In 1684 he raised the 18th regiment of foot, and was made its colonel, and in the same year was advanced to the dignity of earl of Granard. His appointment as one of the lords justices after the recall of the lord lieutenant, the duke of Ormond, was reassuring to protestants in Ireland when James II came to the throne in 1685. But Granard was subsequently replaced by Tyrconnell at the head of the Irish army, a move heralding the launch of the king's ill-fated Catholic coup. The blow was not softened by Granard's appointment to the somewhat superfluous position of president of the Irish council, which dubious honour he declined. When James's Dublin parliament passed the acts of repeal and attainder in 1689, Granard boldly remonstrated with the king. Finding his arguments in vain he went to the House of Lords, entered his solemn protest against these measures, and retired to Castle Forbes. There he was besieged by the Irish, but in vain. When William of Orange went over to Ireland no one welcomed him more heartily than Granard. He was placed by the king in command of a force of 5000 men for the reduction of Sligo, the surrender of which he secured. He entered William and Mary's privy council in 1690, and sat in the Irish parliament in 1692. His closing years were spent quietly at Castle Forbes. He died on 1 November 1695 and was buried at Newtown Forbes. Much given to the improvement of his lot in Ireland, he was a keen bog drainer and has been credited with the cultivation of Ireland's first plane tree. His widow was buried with him at her death in 1714. The couple's eldest son, Arthur, succeeded to the titles.

SEAN KELSEY

Sources R. Lascelles, ed., *Liber munerum publicorum Hiberniae … or, The establishments of Ireland*, 2 vols. [1824–30] · J. Forbes, *Memoirs of the earls of Granard*, ed. G. A. Hastings [earl of Granard] (1868) · GEC,

Peerage, 6.54–5 · GEC, *Baronetage*, 2.360 · T. W. Moody and others, eds., *A new history of Ireland*, 3: *Early modern Ireland, 1534–1691* (1976) · F. D. Dow, *Cromwellian Scotland, 1651–1660* (1979) · J. Kirkpatrick, *An historical essay upon the loyalty of presbyterians in Great-Britain and Ireland from the Reformation to this present year, 1713* (1713) · *Second report*, HMC, 1/2 (1871); repr. (1874) · A. Vicars, ed., *Prerogative wills of Ireland, 1536–1810* (1967), 201

Archives BL, Add. MSS, letters and papers · Hunt. L., corresp. · NRA, priv. coll., corresp. | BL, letters to earl of Essex, Stowe MSS 200–212

Forbes, Sir Charles, first baronet (1773–1849), politician, was the third of the eleven children of the Revd George Forbes of Leochel (*d.* 1799) and his wife, Katherine, daughter of Gordon Stewart of Drumin, Banff. He was born on 3 April 1773. He was a descendant of Alexander Forbes of Kinaldie and Pitsligo, and was in 1833 served heir male in general to Alexander, third Lord Forbes of Pitsligo, father of Alexander, fourth Lord Forbes, attainted in 1745. Forbes was educated at Aberdeen University, of which, late in life, he was elected lord rector. Shortly after leaving the university he went out to India to join the family firm then being run by his uncle John Forbes in Bombay. In due course Charles Forbes became head of Forbes & Co., Bombay. His name ranked high in the commercial world for ability, foresight, and rectitude of character.

On returning to England, Forbes was elected for the borough of Beverley in 1812, 'independent of every party' and opposed to the East India Company's monopoly; he was especially authoritative in the debates in 1813 on the renewal of the company's charter. In 1818 he was returned for Malmesbury, supported by Joseph Pitt, and represented it until the passing of the Reform Bill in 1832. In the Commons he spoke authoritatively and frequently on India and opposed the introduction of Christian missions there: 'He had translated the gospels [into Hindi], but he left the Hindoos to do with them what they pleased' (HoP, *Commons*). Though a tory of the tories, he 'never allowed his political creed to cloud his fine judgment and keen sense of right and wrong, and his manly spirit was readily engaged in favour of the poor, the weak, and the persecuted'. He supported Catholic emancipation and Wellington's handling of the question. Forbes was one of the earliest to advocate the claims of women to the franchise. In the session of 1831 he asked upon what reasonable grounds they could be excluded from political rights, pointing out that women had the power of voting for directors of the East India Company, and maintaining that if the right of voting was grounded on the possession of property, there ought to be no distinction of sex. He was a strong opponent of the Reform Bill of 1831–2. During the debates in the former session he spoke of the measure as 'the vile Reform Bill, that hideous monster, the most frightful that ever showed its face in that house'. Despite Forbes's opposition, Malmesbury's two members were reduced to one and he was squeezed out; in 1832 he vainly contested Middlesex against Joseph Hume. He continued charitable work in India, especially improving the Bengal water supply, and a statue of him by Sir Francis Chantrey was placed in the town hall of Bombay in 1839, paid for by public subscription, probably the first instance of the people of India raising a statue to anyone unconnected with the civil or military service of the country. An address, signed by 1042 inhabitants of Bombay, expatiated upon his services to the commercial development of the country and the improvement in the position of Indians. Forbes was also a munificent contributor to the leading public charities of Scotland. He was of a bluff but kindly nature, diffident as to his own merits, of a straightforward character. On the death of his uncle John in 1821 he succeeded to the entailed estates of the Forbeses of New. He rebuilt New Castle and changed its name to Newe (it was demolished in 1931). He was created a baronet in 1823. He married in 1800 Elizabeth, daughter of Major John Cotgrave, of the Madras army, widow of William Ashburner and already the mother of three children, one of whom, Mary, was kidnapped to the USA in 1809, but was subsequently retrieved. Forbes and his wife, who died on 14 April 1861, had one son (d. 1840) and five daughters. Forbes died in Fitzroy Square, London, on 20 November 1849 and was succeeded by his nephew, Sir Charles Forbes (1832–52). G. B. SMITH, rev. H. C. G. MATTHEW

Sources GM, 2nd ser., 33 (1850), 208–9 · Aberdeen Journal (28 Nov 1849) · HoP, Commons · A. Tayler and H. Tayler, eds., The house of Forbes, Third Spalding Club, 8 (1937) · E. Lodge, Peerage, baronetage, knightage and companionage of the British empire, 81st edn, 3 vols. (1912)
Archives BL OIOC, corresp., MS Eur. D 100 · Bodl. Oxf., corresp.
Likenesses F. Chantrey, statue, exh. RA 1842, Bombay Town Hall · F. Chantrey, pencil drawing, NPG

Forbes, Sir Charles Fergusson (1779–1852), army surgeon and ophthalmic physician, the son of William and Elizabeth Forbes, was born on 22 March 1779, and was baptized at the Independent Chapel, Great Coggeshall, Essex, on 21 May. He received his medical education in London and joined the army medical staff as surgeon's mate in Portugal in 1798. In the following year he was gazetted assistant surgeon to the 2nd battalion of the 1st regiment of foot. He went on the expedition to The Helder in 1799, and was present at the attack on Ferrol in 1800. The following year he served with the army in Egypt under Sir Ralph Abercrombie, and subsequently at Malta and Gibraltar. In 1803 he was present at the capture of St Lucia and Tobago. He was appointed surgeon to the forces in July 1808, and served in Galicia. In this same year he received the MD of Edinburgh University.

Forbes served in the Peninsular War, and in February 1813 was appointed deputy inspector-general of hospitals. He retired with that rank, and was awarded the war medal with five clasps. In 1814 he became a licentiate of the Royal College of Physicians, and settled in practice at Argyll Street, London. In 1816 he was appointed physician to the Royal Westminster Infirmary for Diseases of the Eye, in Warwick Street, Golden Square, which he jointly founded with George James Guthrie, his surgical colleague.

In 1827 Guthrie and Forbes became involved in a notable controversy. Initially a dispute over the treatment and administration of cases at the infirmary, it became instead a matter of etiquette and professional values. In March 1827 Forbes informed the committee of the infirmary that he had overheard complaints from pupils and patients regarding the hurried treatment of cases. At this time Forbes made it known to Guthrie that he believed 'stimulating applications to the eyes of the patients were too indiscriminately used' (The Lancet, 15 March 1828, 881). On 26 May 1827 a paragraph critical of the care given to patients at the infirmary appeared in The Lancet, which prompted Guthrie to begin libel action against the journal, although the action was withdrawn when Guthrie discovered that Forbes was to be subpoenaed as a witness.

Forbes was subjected to intense criticism and insults from his colleagues, and in particular Guthrie's pupils at the infirmary. He was berated for unprofessional conduct in that he was willing to make a private disagreement over treatment a public issue, to the detriment of the medical profession as a whole, and the infirmary in particular. In correspondence though, Forbes repeatedly claimed that he was unwilling to testify, not wishing to criticize his colleagues. He complained that Guthrie had interfered with treatment which Forbes had prescribed for patients, thereby undermining his authority within the infirmary.

Having been insulted by Hale Thomson, a young surgeon at the infirmary, Forbes challenged him to a duel, which was fought with pistols on Clapham Common at 3.30 p.m. on 29 December 1827. Each man fired three times without inflicting injury, and the seconds then declared the duel at an end, against the combatants' wishes. Forbes then resigned his appointment at the infirmary, taking a number of its subscribers with him. A complete record of the correspondence regarding the dispute between Forbes and Guthrie was published in The Lancet on 8 March 1828. During the dispute no opportunity was missed by Thomas Wakley, editor of The Lancet, to ridicule Guthrie, an esteemed member of the Royal College of Surgeons, an institution much despised within the pages of the journal.

Forbes maintained a considerable practice among the nobility, and was greatly esteemed, in spite of his dispute with Guthrie. His only writings are two small pamphlets of correspondence, published in 1828, regarding the dispute at the infirmary, and a brief record of a case of fatal thrombosis of the thigh veins appearing in the Medico-Chirurgical Transactions in 1827. He was a knight of the Crescent; in 1842 he was made a knight of the Royal Guelphic Order, and in 1844 a knight bachelor. He died at Argyll Street on 22 March 1852. CLAIRE E. J. HERRICK

Sources A. Peterkin and W. Johnston, Commissioned officers in the medical services of the British army, 1660–1960, 1 (1968), 119 · Munk, Roll · Medical Times and Gazette (3 April 1852), 355 · 'Statement of Dr Forbes respecting Mr Guthrie's action against The Lancet—the late duel etc', The Lancet (8 March 1828); (15 March 1828) · J. G. Humble and P. Hansell, Westminster Hospital, 1716–1974 (1974), 58 · H. Grimsdale, 'George James Guthrie, FRS, founder of the Royal Westminster Ophthalmic Hospital', British Journal of Ophthalmology, 3 (1919), 148 · N. Cantlie, A history of the army medical department, 2 (1974), 391 · The Lancet (27 March 1852), 321 · BMJ (31 March 1852), 184 · London and Provincial Medical Directory (1853), 550 · P. J. Wallis and R. V. Wallis, *Eighteenth century medics*, 2nd edn (1988) · *GM*, 2nd ser., 37 (1852) · *IGI*

Archives NL Scot., lecture notes

Forbes, Sir Charles Morton (1880–1960), naval officer, was born at Colombo, Ceylon, on 22 November 1880, the second son of James Forbes, broker, and his wife, Caroline Delmege. Educated at Dollar Academy, Clackmannanshire, and Eastman's school, Southsea, he joined the Royal Navy as a cadet in the *Britannia* in 1894. On passing out two years later he obtained five first-class certificates and gained twelve months' seniority. After serving in the flagships of the channel and Pacific fleets he was promoted lieutenant in 1901 and in the following year became a specialist in gunnery. For the next eleven years he served as gunnery officer in various cruisers and battleships, and at the gunnery schools, until his promotion to commander in 1912, at which time he was serving as first lieutenant and gunnery officer of the battleship *Superb* in the Home Fleet.

Soon after the outbreak of the First World War Forbes was appointed to the newly commissioned battleship *Queen Elizabeth* which bombarded the Gallipoli forts in the initial attack on the Dardanelles in 1915. Later in the same year he joined the staff of Sir John Jellicoe, commander-in-chief of the Grand Fleet, as flag commander in the *Iron Duke*. He was present at the battle of Jutland and was appointed to the DSO. After Sir David Beatty succeeded to the command of the fleet in 1916 Forbes was appointed to the staff of the second in command, Sir Charles Madden, where he continued in the same duties until his promotion to captain in 1917. He was then appointed to the command of the cruiser *Galatea*, in which he was present at the surrender of the German high seas fleet in November 1918. He thus served afloat throughout the whole war and shortly before its end he was awarded the Russian order of St Stanislaus.

Thereafter, Forbes's service life alternated between appointments at the Admiralty and staff college and in one of the two main fleets—Home or Mediterranean. His first Admiralty appointment was as naval member of the ordnance committee in 1919, to which duty he returned in 1925–8 as director of naval ordnance. On the staff side, he was deputy director of the Naval Staff College, Greenwich, from 1921 to 1923. The remainder of his service in the rank of captain was spent in seagoing appointments, first as flag captain to the commander-in-chief, Atlantic Fleet, Sir John De Robeck, in the *Queen Elizabeth*, and second as flag captain to the second in command, Mediterranean Fleet, H. D. R. Watson, in the *Iron Duke*.

Forbes was promoted rear-admiral in 1928 and in 1930–31 commanded the destroyer flotillas of the Mediterranean Fleet. He then returned to the Admiralty as third sea lord and controller—an appointment generally recognized as one calling for exceptional qualities of technical knowledge and ability in committee. He was promoted vice-admiral in 1933.

In 1934 Forbes was again appointed to the Mediterranean, as vice-admiral commanding the 1st battle squadron, and second in command, Mediterranean Fleet; it was

Sir Charles Morton Forbes (1880–1960), by Walter Stoneman, 1932

during this period of his service that the Abyssinian crisis occurred and a period of such strained relations with Italy that in preparation for hostilities the fleet transferred from Malta to Alexandria. In 1935 Forbes was appointed KCB and in 1936 promoted admiral.

In April 1938 Forbes was appointed commander-in-chief, Home Fleet, with his flag in *Nelson*, at a time of increasing international tension culminating in the outbreak of the Second World War in September 1939. The fleet was ready but the bases were not, and Forbes had the anxiety and responsibility of maintaining constant vigil and readiness for action with bases lacking anti-aircraft defence or anti-submarine protection. Their vulnerability was quickly demonstrated by a German air attack on Rosyth on 16 October, the sinking of the *Royal Oak* by a U-boat which penetrated Scapa Flow on 14 October, and the damage sustained by the flagship *Nelson* herself in December from a mine laid by a U-boat in Loch Ewe. Nevertheless, under Forbes's capable command, the fleet carried out its duty successfully during those testing months of 1939 and 1940 when the full effects of mass air power in modern war were being learnt the hard way. Opportunities for offensive action were few, but they came with the German invasion of Norway in April 1940, and with it the successful destroyer battles of Narvik. But this campaign also included the ill-fated military expedition for the defence of Norway, which started too late to be effective, and after only two months had to be withdrawn, after considerable loss. During these operations,

Forbes's temporary flagship, *Rodney*, was damaged by air attack. The fleet suffered a number of losses, the principal ones being the aircraft-carrier *Glorious* and nine destroyers; the German losses and damage were very much greater. It was this fact which rightly convinced Forbes that they would not attempt a seaborne invasion of Britain that year in the face of the overwhelming superiority of the British fleet and the failure of the German air force to defeat the RAF.

In December 1940, seven months after being promoted admiral of the fleet and GCB, Forbes was succeeded in the command of the Home Fleet by Sir John Tovey, and in May 1941 he was appointed commander-in-chief, Plymouth, which the enemy was then making a target for most savage air attacks. Nevertheless, the operational work of the command was prosecuted with vigour by the cruisers, light forces, and coastal craft under Forbes's orders. Chief among these were the many successful attacks in co-operation with Coastal Command on U-boats leaving and returning to their base at Brest; the interception of enemy armed merchant-vessel raiders trying to get back to Germany; and raids on the enemy destroyers and shipping passing along the French coast. The gallant and successful attack on St Nazaire was also mounted.

During the final months of Forbes's command preparation for the reception and disposition of the American naval and military forces which would take part in the invasion of France in 1944 was well advanced, but Forbes's period of command terminated before their arrival. His flag was hauled down for the last time on 24 August 1943.

An officer of great experience of the world and of men, Forbes was a master of his profession and had the very great faculty of recognizing instantly all the factors in any problem with which he was faced, and in grappling competently with all difficulties. No man ever saw him rattled: he had full confidence in himself and he inspired it in those under him. His reserves of power, clear vision, sound judgement, and strong sense of proportion were a tower of strength to those who, working under him, shared his burdens though not his responsibilities. Modest and unassuming in demeanour, and with an attractive, dry sense of humour, he never feared to speak his mind, even though in conflict with the views of his superiors.

Forbes was twice married: first, in 1909, to Agnes Millicent (d. 1915), younger daughter of J. A. Ewen JP, of Potters Bar, with whom he had one daughter and one son. Second, in 1921, he married Marie Louise, daughter of Axel Berndtson, of Stockholm, and they had one daughter.

In his younger days Forbes was fond of horses and hunting. He was also a keen golfer and played on several occasions in the 'Admirals v. Generals' match. He was most generous in his hospitality, and never failed to impress by the courtly grace and charm with which he habitually welcomed his guests.

After relinquishing his last appointment Forbes returned to live at his home, Cawsand Place, Wentworth, Surrey. From 1946 until shortly before his death Forbes was a member of the councils of the Association of Retired Naval Officers and the National Association for the Employment of Regular Sailors, Soldiers, and Airmen, in whose work he was keenly interested. He died in the Queen Alexandra Military Hospital, Millbank, London, on 28 August 1960.   CLIFFORD CASLON, *rev.*

Sources *The Times* (30 Aug 1960) · *WWW* · private information (1971) · personal knowledge (1971) · S. W. Roskill, *The war at sea, 1939–1945*, 3 vols. in 4 (1954–61) · *CGPLA Eng. & Wales* (1960)
Archives BL, papers, Add. MS 52565 | FILM BFI NFTVA, news footage
Likenesses W. Stoneman, two photographs, 1932–43, NPG [*see illus.*] · O. Birley, oils, *c.*1945–1948, Royal Naval College, Greenwich
Wealth at death £79,757 17s. 6d.: probate, 26 Sept 1960, *CGPLA Eng. & Wales*

Forbes, David (1777?–1849), army officer, was the son of a Scottish minister of religion in Morayshire, and entered the army when still a boy as an ensign in the 78th highlanders, or Ross-shire Buffs, raised by Francis Humberstone Mackenzie (afterwards Lord Seaforth) in March 1793. He was promoted lieutenant on 3 May 1794, and in the following September the 78th joined the army in the Netherlands, under Lieutenant-Colonel Alexander Mackenzie Fraser.

Forbes served with distinction in the disastrous retreat before Pichegru, and was especially noticed for his conduct at Geldermalsen on 5 January 1795. Later that year he was present at the affair of Quiberon and the attack on Belle Île, and in 1796 he went with the 78th to the Cape and then to India, where he remained for more than twenty years, seeing much service. In 1798 the 78th formed the escort of Sir John Shore when he advanced into Oudh to dethrone the nawab, and it was engaged throughout the Maratha campaign of 1803, and especially at the storming of Ahmednagar. For his services in this campaign Forbes was promoted captain on 25 June 1803, and he remained in garrison until 1811, when the 78th took part in the expedition against Java under Sir Samuel Auchmuty.

Forbes was placed in command of the flank companies of the various British regiments, and at their head led the assaults on the lines of both Waltevreede and Cornelis, and was to the front in every engagement with the Dutch. For these services he was five times thanked in general orders, received the gold medal for Java, and was promoted major on 29 August 1811. In May 1812 he commanded the grenadiers of the 59th regiment and the light companies of the 78th in an expedition against the sultan of Djojo-carta, and in May 1813 he suppressed the insurrection among the Malays at Probolingo in the east of Java. In this action Lieutenant-Colonel Fraser of the 78th was killed, and Forbes, as major, received the step in promotion on 28 July 1814.

In 1817 Forbes returned to Scotland, the only officer to return out of forty-two, and he brought with him only thirty-six out of 1200 rank and file. He went on half pay and settled in Aberdeen, where he lived without further employment for the rest of his life. On 10 January 1837 he was promoted colonel, in 1838 made a CB, and in 1846 promoted major-general. He died in Aberdeen on 29 March

1849. According to the *Gentleman's Magazine* he had 'that genuine humanity which rendered him the soldier's best and kindest friend' (*GM*, 543).

H. M. STEPHENS, rev. ROGER T. STEARN

Sources *GM*, 2nd ser., 31 (1849), 542–3 • *Hart's Army List* • *Military Panorama*, 3 (Feb 1814) • A. Harfield, *British and Indian armies in the East Indies, 1685–1935* (1984) • P. Moon, *The British conquest and dominion of India* (1989) • T. C. W. Blanning, *The French revolutionary wars, 1787–1802* (1996)
Likenesses J. H. Foley, bust, 1858, Calcutta mint

Forbes, David (1828–1876), geological chemist and mining engineer, was born at Douglas, Isle of Man, on 6 September 1828, one of the eight surviving children and fifth son of Edward Forbes (*b*. 1786) of Oakhill and Croukbane, near Douglas, a Manx banker and businessman, and Jane (*d*. 1836), eldest daughter and heir of William Teare of the same island. He was younger brother of the biogeographer Edward *Forbes (1815–1854), whose sense of humour and cosmopolitanism he shared and who encouraged his boyhood interest in science. Following education at Athole Academy, Douglas, he attended a boarding-school at Brentwood in Essex until 1844 when he entered Edinburgh University and studied chemistry with the extramural lecturer George Wilson, whose assistant he became. He also attended natural philosophy classes at the university in 1845–6, but did not take a degree.

In 1846 Forbes spent some months in a metallurgical laboratory which John Percy had opened in order to supplement his meagre salary as physician in Birmingham's Queen's Hospital. Percy, who was then developing a new method for extracting silver from its ores, and who was interested in geology, brought Forbes to the attention of the Birmingham nickel-cobalt refiner Brook Evans (1797–1862). In 1848 Evans took Forbes on a tour of nickel mines he owned at Espedal, Norway. Forbes was made superintendent of the mining and metallurgical colony there, and charged with the construction of further mining and smelting works. He spent ten years in Norway, receiving royal favours for arming miners in support of the king of Sweden in the revolutionary year of 1848. For his many contributions to, and knowledge of, Norwegian geology he was elected FRS on 3 June 1858.

Forbes was made a partner in the firm of Evans and Askin in 1856 and in the following year he was sent to Chile (where he became a close friend of Frederick Field), Peru, and Bolivia in search of exploitable nickel and cobalt ores, spending three years on horseback and sleeping under the stars while gaining an unrivalled knowledge of the geology and mineralogy of South America. On Forbes's return to England from Bolivia in 1860 efforts were made to persuade Lord Russell, the prime minister, to give him an official post in South America to counter advances being made by German traders there. Following the failure of this proposal, Forbes made further extensive travels in Chile and the south sea islands, whose volcanic origins and mineralogy he studied.

In 1866, following further travels in Africa and Europe,

Forbes settled in London as a mining consultant for overseas metallurgical enterprises, including those of the Japanese government. He had become an associate of the Institution of Civil Engineers in 1853 and served on its council in 1872–3. On the foundation of the Iron and Steel Institute in 1869, he became its conscientious foreign secretary, in which capacity he wrote half-yearly reports on the progress of metallurgy abroad, which appeared in the institute's journal from 1871 to 1876. He also participated in the social activities of the chemists' B Club and the deliberations of the Ethnological Society, to which he contributed a paper on the Aymara Indians of Bolivia and Peru. From 1871 until his death he was also a senior secretary of the Geological Society, which he had joined in 1853. He described himself to Francis Galton as restless in temperament and religious but without commitment to revealed Christianity (Hilts, 48).

While in Norway, Forbes took advantage of the metallurgical operations he directed to submit various rocks to high temperatures and pressures in order to investigate chemical and physical actions in the production of foliations in metamorphic rocks. With his global experience of petrology and metallurgy he not surprisingly became one of the first geologists to support Henry Sorby's use of microscopy in the elucidation of geological phenomena, becoming Sorby's 'close friend, disciple and vigorous champion' (Higham, 43). With his chemical training, Forbes took especial interest in the bearings of chemistry on geology, a field which he believed was unduly neglected in Great Britain. He helped to lay the methodological foundations of geochemistry in 1867–8 during a strenuous public debate with the American geologist Thomas Sterry Hunt (1826–1892) over whether it was more important to be a geological chemist (as Hunt advocated) or, as Forbes believed, a chemical geologist.

During his worldwide travels Forbes had amassed a large fund of geological information, of which only a part appeared in his sixty-odd published papers. He had intended to write a large-scale systematic work on petrology, but left it too late. He had always neglected his health, and the death of his young wife, Julia Elizabeth Camilla (*b*. 1848/9), from peritonitis on 28 March 1876, was a heavy blow. His constitution already weakened by a recurrent malarial fever caught in Peru, Forbes succumbed and died on 5 December 1876, at his home, 11 York Place, Portman Square, London. He was buried at Kensal Green cemetery on 11 December 1876.   W. H. BROCK

Sources J. M. [J. Morris], *Geological Magazine*, new ser., 2nd decade, 4 (1877), 45–8; repr. in *Journal of the Iron and Steel Institute* (1876), 516–24 • P. M. Duncan, *Quarterly Journal of the Geological Society*, 33 (1877), 41–8 • *PICE*, 49 (1876–7), 270–5 • F. Field, *Chemical News* (15 Dec 1876), 260–61 • *Nature*, 15 (1876–7), 139 • *JCS*, [31] (1877), 496–9 • *The Times* (12 Dec 1876), 6 • V. L. Hilts, *A guide to Francis Galton's English men of science* (1975), 48–9 • W. H. Brock, 'Chemical geology or geological chemistry?', *Images of the earth*, ed. L. J. Jordanova and R. Porter (1979), 147–70 • D. Forbes, *Correspondence with Lord John Russell* (1861) • N. Higham, *A very scientific gentleman* (1963) • d. cert. [Julia Elizabeth Camilla Forbes] • d. cert.
Archives JRL, chemistry notebook

Wealth at death under £40,000: probate, 5 Jan 1877, *CGPLA Eng. & Wales*

Forbes, Duncan (*b.* in or after **1643**, *d.* **1704**), genealogist and politician, was the eldest son of John Forbes (*d. c.*1688) of Culloden, Inverness-shire, provost of Inverness, and Anna, daughter of Alexander Dunbar of Grange. His parents were married in 1643, and Forbes was probably born soon afterwards. He entered Marischal College, Aberdeen, in 1656, and attended the arts course there for at least a year. He was further educated at Bourges and elsewhere on the continent, where he travelled extensively, at one point visiting Paris. When he returned to Scotland is unknown. In 1668 he married Mary, daughter of Sir Robert Innes of Innes, bt. The marriage produced seven daughters and two sons, the younger of whom, Duncan *Forbes (1685–1747), later became lord president of the court of session and a major figure in early eighteenth-century Scottish politics.

Forbes took an active role in Scottish political affairs. He was commissioner to the convention of estates for Nairn-shire in 1678, and commissioner to parliament, also for Nairnshire, in 1681. In 1689 he was commissioner to the convention of estates for Inverness-shire. A staunch presbyterian and whig, Forbes was a dedicated promoter of the revolution of 1688. He signed the act declaring the 1689 convention a lawful meeting of the estates, and also the letter of congratulation to King William of the same year. He also proposed the revival of a law of 1641 for appointing office holders with consent of parliament, and firmly supported the establishment of Presbyterianism in Scotland in 1689. He continued to serve as commissioner to parliament for Inverness-shire from 1689 to 1702, and in 1696 signed the association for the defence of King William. William II and III remained grateful to Forbes for his services. He later appointed Forbes's brother John to a majority in one of his regiments, although powerful figures like Secretary Melville and General Mackay wanted the post for candidates of their own.

In the tumults arising from the revolution, Forbes's political position naturally made him anathema to the Jacobites. In 1689 the family estates of Ferintosh and Culloden, to which Forbes had succeeded on the death of his father about 1688, were ravaged by the Jacobite forces of Buchan and Cannon. The resulting damage amounted to £54,000 Scots, or £4500 sterling. Forbes claimed compensation from the Scottish parliament, which responded by granting him, in perpetuity, the privilege of distilling whisky in the barony of Ferintosh without being subject to the normal excise regulations. An act confirming this was passed on 22 July 1690.

Forbes was interested in the genealogy of his wife's family, and in 1698 he compiled 'Ane account of the familie of Innes', which was used as a source by Thomas Pennant in his *Tour in Scotland*. It was later privately printed for the duke of Roxburghe in Edinburgh in 1820, and in 1864 was edited for the Spalding Club by Cosmo Innes, from Forbes's original manuscript at Culloden.

Forbes was known as a highly pious Presbyterian, conducting regular family worship; often, in the absence of a chaplain or minister, he performed the necessary offices himself. He continued to take an interest in political matters, being particularly concerned, as his more famous son Duncan later was, with the potentially dangerous state of the highlands, where Jacobite and episcopalian sympathies were marked. He addressed this problem in a short 'Plan for preserving the peace of the highlands', which is included in the *Culloden Papers*. He also continued to serve in parliament, and was commissioner for Nairn-shire from 1703 until his death on 24 June 1704. His wife survived him, and was still alive in 1716.

ALEXANDER DU TOIT

Sources J. H. Burton, *Lives of Simon, Lord Lovat, and Duncan Forbes of Culloden* (1847), 272–5 · G. Menary, *The life and letters of Duncan Forbes of Culloden, lord president of the court of session, 1685–1747* (1936), 3, 22 · M. D. Young, ed., *The parliaments of Scotland: burgh and shire commissioners*, 1 (1992) · [H. R. Duff], ed., *Culloden papers* (1815), ii–xliv · *Memoirs of the life of the Right Honourable Duncan Forbes esq. of Culloden, lord president of the court of session in Scotland* (1748), 9–10
Archives NL Scot., corresp. and papers | BL, Mackenzie papers · NL Scot., Macphail collection · NL Scot., Culloden papers
Wealth at death estates of Culloden and Ferintosh

Forbes, Duncan (**1685–1747**), politician and judge, was born near Inverness on 10 November 1685, the fifth of nine children and the younger of two sons of Duncan *Forbes (*b.* in or after 1643, *d.* 1704), of Culloden, Inverness-shire, member of the Scottish parliament and genealogist, and his wife, Mary, daughter of Sir Robert Innes of Innes, second baronet. His brother, John (*c.*1673–1734), inherited the family estates of Culloden, Bunchrew, and Ferintosh in 1704 but, having died childless, was succeeded by Forbes.

It was observed of Forbes in his obituary in the *Scots Magazine* (1747) that he was 'pleased with popular applause' and 'susceptible too of flattery' (p. 557). In these terms his career was a glowing success, such was the praise heaped upon him in his lifetime—although not from all quarters—and in later biographies. However his public and political life was marred by thwarted ambitions. Its course was ultimately dictated not by his considerable talent and his good relationship with his patron, the soldier John Campbell, second duke of Argyll—whose commissioner in Scotland he became—but more pertinently by his determination to act independently of and at times to frustrate the latter's brother Archibald, earl of Ilay (third duke of Argyll, 1743), Scotland's political manager under Walpole from 1725. It is also likely that Forbes suffered from his closeness to the soldier duke in that relations between the latter and Ilay were bad, despite their common political cause until 1740. Finally Forbes undermined his own credibility through an inability to keep things in proportion. Thus there was his campaign of 1730 against the consumption of brandy in Scotland—much of which was smuggled—and another campaign in the early 1740s—which badly damaged his reputation in élite political circles—against the drinking of tea, a habit which he deplored because of its deleterious effects on the revenues and the economy.

Duncan Forbes (1685–1747), by Jeremiah Davison, *c*.1737

Early career In choosing the law as a career Forbes took a path well trodden by younger sons of Scottish landed families. Aspects of his education are obscure. After his schooldays in Inverness he attended Marischal College, Aberdeen, from 1699 to 1702; it is also said that he studied 'at the different seminaries' of Edinburgh (*Culloden Papers*, viii). In November 1704 his uncle David Forbes of Newhall, a leading advocate, found a writing chamber for him in Edinburgh and insisted upon him attending John Spottiswoode's Scots law classes. From 1705 to 1707 Forbes studied civil law at Leiden. He married Mary, a daughter of Hugh Rose of Kilravock (marriage contract 21 October 1708); she died some time before 13 July 1717. They had a single child, John. On 26 July 1709 Forbes became a member of the Faculty of Advocates. The sedate impression of him to that point is enlivened by reference to the reputations that he, as a young man, and his brother are said to have had as 'the greatest bouzers in the North' (*Memoirs*, 11).

Forbes established himself quickly as a leading advocate, being regularly employed in appeals from the court of session to the House of Lords, in the course of which he became acquainted with Philip Yorke, the future Lord Chancellor Hardwicke. Forbes and his brother, John, were intent upon advancing Forbes's prospects, and John's electoral ambitions, in another way, through political patronage. With John taking the lead they cultivated the two ambitious London-based politicians Argyll and Ilay, for whom there were also political benefits in the connection—in drawing support from the Forbeses' network of friends and relatives among the landed gentry of the north-east of Scotland. Forbes seems to have benefited

from Argyll's patronage when appointed to his first legal office, as sheriff depute of Edinburghshire, in November 1714, from which he rose to the post of sheriff in 1716.

During the Jacobite rising of 1715 Forbes, a strong presbyterian supporter of the Hanoverian succession, was deputy lord lieutenant of Inverness-shire. On 13 November 1715 Rose of Kilravock, the Forbes brothers, and Simon Fraser, twelfth Lord Lovat (better known as a Jacobite but at that time supporting the government), having gathered together a substantial force, obtained the surrender of the town of Inverness from the Jacobites. Forbes was appointed lord advocate depute on 12 March 1716, with the responsibility of deputy public prosecutor. Despite his zealous conduct he was compassionate and politically astute in seeking moderation towards the Jacobites and their families at the end of the rising and he resented the removal of Jacobite prisoners to Carlisle, in the north of England, for trial. He was also anxious in these difficult times to support Argyll, who faced criticism in ruling circles in London for not hunting down the Jacobites with sufficient vigour after the inconclusive battle of Sheriffmuir on 13 November 1715. A bitter military rival, William Cadogan, replaced Argyll as commander-in-chief in Scotland to complete the mopping-up operation against the Jacobites. Cadogan also mounted a propaganda campaign against Argyll. Against this background Forbes was chosen ruling elder from the presbytery of Inverness to attend the general assembly of the Church of Scotland in May 1716. He managed the assembly in such a way that, to the delight of Argyll, 'A congratulatory Address to the King, upon suppressing the Rebellion' lauded the victorious Argyll, while reference to Cadogan and his exploits was excluded from the address.

Lord advocate Argyll and Ilay were out of political favour from June 1716 until February 1719. In September 1721 Forbes entered parliament, with Argyll's support, as member for the Ayr burghs. From October 1722 until June 1737 he represented the Inverness burghs, where his family had a strong interest. All seemed set fair therefore when on 29 May 1725 he replaced Robert Dundas—of the Squadrone faction bitterly opposed to Argyll and Ilay—as lord advocate. Indeed Forbes made an immediate impact on events after the enforcement in June 1725 of the malt tax in Scotland. Following problems in Glasgow—non-cooperation by the maltsters in the implementation of this measure, public disturbances (including the gutting of the house of Daniel Campbell of Shawfield, MP for the Glasgow burghs), and a lack of zeal by the magistrates (the provost and other leading burgh councillors)—Forbes took extreme action in having the magistrates arrested and taken to Edinburgh. He also persuaded the court of session to threaten the brewers in Edinburgh with imprisonment when they stopped production in opposition to the tax. But these steps by Forbes, praised though they were in London, did not tend towards stable government in Scotland and undermined the political strategy of Ilay, who had been painstakingly building up his brother's political interest in Scotland for years, latterly with Sir Robert Walpole's backing. Matters were all the more acute in that the Squadrone regime then in government, led by John Ker, first duke of Roxburghe and third secretary of state for Great Britain (in effect Scottish secretary)—a regime that was in its death throes—encouraged the dissent against the tax. Ilay travelled from London to Edinburgh to impose himself on events; the Edinburgh brewers were persuaded to be sensible, and the prosecution of the Glasgow magistrates was deferred and later dropped. Ilay had the support of Walpole, who believed that 'more gentle means' (such as Ilay used) leave 'lesse rancour and determined resentment against the government'. Walpole was anxious nevertheless not to upset Forbes: 'he must not know I write in this manner', said Walpole to Ilay, who was 'to do what is right, and at the same time, not distaste him' (Coxe, 2.455).

At the very point, therefore, at which Ilay took on the role of Scottish political manager in alliance with Walpole (without the position of third secretary, which was left vacant) it became clear that Forbes did not entirely share the political imperatives of these two. This presaged his futile long-term preoccupation with thwarting Ilay. In general Forbes was to become engaged, while safely under Argyll's protective wing, in a fight against what he saw as abuses in the administration of Scotland and its revenues. An example, combining the various strands of Forbes's campaigning zeal, was the attention that he directed in the 1730s and 1740s towards the dominant role of Ilay's henchman in Scotland, Andrew Fletcher, Lord Milton (lord justice clerk from 1735 to 1748), on the board of trustees for manufactures in Scotland. Forbes did not consider that the advancement of the manufactures—primarily through the management of funds to encourage the linen industry—was best served by those in control of the board. He was a trustee himself, and one with influence, but he could not bend the board to his will in the face of the number of votes that Milton could call upon there. Not long after becoming lord president he mounted a ferocious campaign, including a petition to an old friend, John Scrope, secretary to the Treasury, concerning an agreement between the board of trustees and the Royal Bank of Scotland, whose governor until 1737 and deputy governor were, respectively, Ilay and Milton. Ilay, in the course of checkmating Forbes, wrote from London to Milton in November 1738 that 'I will in the meantime tip my friend Duncan with two new Trustees who will not be ruled by him' (Shaw, 131). Forbes's last act at the end of his parliamentary career, before taking up his lord president's post on 21 June 1737, was to complement what Argyll had done in the Lords, by leading fierce and successful opposition in the Commons to the bill of pains and penalties against the city of Edinburgh following the Porteous affair of 1736. His opposition was in spite of his position as a member of the government, as lord advocate.

Later career The historical significance of Forbes's position as lord president of the court of session lies in the status that it gave him in Scottish society rather than in his work at the court. His notable achievement in the legal world was to tackle interminable delays in the process of justice at the court. Towards the end of his career came a

more dramatic opportunity in the political arena to make a mark on society. Walpole and Ilay fell from power in February 1742. Argyll was at that time an ally of the new, Wilmington, administration and with John Hay, fourth marquess of Tweeddale (a friend of Carteret and from the remnant of the old Squadrone group), having been given the revived post of third secretary of state on 20 February, Forbes received an invitation from Tweeddale three days later. This was to travel to London with a long-standing foe of Forbes, Robert Dundas, now the judge Lord Arniston, to join in concerting a plan for the government of Scotland. It is relevant in this respect that Tweeddale's undersecretary was Forbes's close friend Andrew Mitchell, later a leading diplomat. After a delay by Forbes, and then Argyll's sudden break with the new regime on 10 March 1742, Forbes signalled at the beginning of April that he could not fraternize so blatantly with the old enemy. He considered that 'att present, I am affraid the coall is too hot to be toutched' (*Culloden Papers*, 180). At the start of the Jacobite rising of 1745 Tweeddale, prompted by the commander-in-chief, John Dalrymple, second earl of Stair, gave Forbes another invitation, which he accepted. This was to distribute blank commissions for raising twenty independent companies in the highlands. He stayed on in the north of Scotland during the rising and worked on this scheme with zeal and fair success, despite the erratic supply of money and arms from the government. His influence faded in January 1746. In that month came the resignation of Tweeddale and the return—as Scottish political manager for the Pelham administration—of Ilay, now third duke of Argyll. On 22 January Forbes was sent dismal tidings from Edinburgh by General Joseph Wightman: Lord Milton, in Edinburgh, was 'once more Vice Roy' to Argyll, and 'Generalissimo' in Army matters, governing all and 'drunk with Power' (ibid., 266). Wightman could at least look forward to Forbes returning to his old role of hindering Milton, but it was not to be. In a letter of July 1746 Forbes accepted that his own 'knighterrantry' was over, that he had been ridiculed, and that his suggestions for the long-term pacification of the highlands after the battle of Culloden were being ignored (Allardyce, 1.329). Nor did he receive recompense for the large sums that he spent in the public service during the rising.

Among Forbes's illustrious friends and acquaintances in London was the Scottish poet James Thomson. Forbes helped Thomson by recommending him to friends, particularly valuable among them being the painter William Aikman, who mixed in influential circles. Thomson, who became a close friend of Forbes's son, John, eulogized Forbes in 'Autumn'. An allusion in Thomson's 'Castle of Indolence' to a 'joyous youth' who

> whilst he stay'd, kept in a gay uproar,
> Our madden'd Castle all

is believed to refer to John. Forbes also had a lively interest in mathematics. He enjoyed a warm friendship with Professor Colin Maclaurin; Patrick Murdoch, author and mathematician, was former travelling tutor and a friend to Forbes's son. The author of the important anonymous biography of Forbes published in 1748 refers to Maclaurin, 'the darling of the sciences', as 'my great master' (*Memoirs*, 61–2). There is strong evidence that this biography is by Andrew Henderson, author, bookseller at Long Acre, and a former mathematics teacher.

The biographer of 1748 described Forbes thus:

> above six foot high, very streight and genteel in his body, which much enclined to slenderness; his face was smooth and majestick, his forehead large and graceful, his nose high; his eyes were blue and full of sweetness, and tho' very quick, yet rather grave than sparkling; the pupilla was charmingly intermixed with the white; his cheeks and chin were finely proportioned, his hands and arms were every way delightful. (*Memoirs*, 73–4)

The biographer mentioned a foible in the character of Forbes the lawyer: Forbes 'had frequently observed the cunning and falshood of petty-foggers, messengers, and hackney-writers; when any of these had come before him, and were found guilty of imposing upon their Employers, he appeared in a particular manner severe' (ibid., 54).

One of Forbes's enthusiasms, following from his admiration of the works of John Hutchinson, author of *Moses's principia*, was the study of the Old Testament in Hebrew. He wrote three short tracts, published in 1732, 1735, and posthumously, the last being incomplete; in these he commented on Hutchinson's views and championed Christianity against freethinkers. Another enthusiasm, described with a mathematician's eye by the biographer of 1748, was golf. When in Edinburgh during the summer session Forbes would proceed on Mondays to Leith from his home, Stoneyhill, in Musselburgh, to play golf. He took it very seriously:

> He struck the ball full, and having a long nervous arm, upon a well pois'd body, he generally drove very far; when nigh the hole, he tipped with so much circumspection, that even a lesson might be learned from his innocent amusements.

These amusements by his example discouraged 'the idle and insinuating recreations that entirely depend upon chance' (*Memoirs*, 60).

Forbes died in Edinburgh on 10 December 1747 and was buried in Greyfriars kirkyard. He left a heavily encumbered estate. In his last words to his son, a cavalry officer, which were written down, he observed: 'You have come to a very poor fortune, partly by my own extravagance and the oppression of power' (*Culloden Papers*, xxxviii).

JOHN S. SHAW

Sources [H. R. Duff], ed., *Culloden papers* (1815) • *Memoirs of the life of the late Right Honourable Duncan Forbes, esq; lord-president of the court of session in Scotland* (1748) • D. Warrand, ed., *More Culloden papers*, 5 vols. (1923–30) • W. Coxe, *Memoirs of the life and administration of Sir Robert Walpole, earl of Orford*, 3 vols. (1798) • J. H. Burton, *Lives of Simon, Lord Lovat, and Duncan Forbes of Culloden* (1847) • J. Allardyce, ed., *Historical papers relating to the Jacobite period, 1699–1750*, 2 vols., New Spalding Club, 14, 16 (1895–6) • J. S. Shaw, *The management of Scottish society, 1707–1764: power, nobles, lawyers, Edinburgh agents and English influences* (1983) • G. W. T. Omond, *The lord advocates of Scotland from the close of the fifteenth century to the passing of the Reform Bill*, 1 (1883) • *The works of Mr James Thomson* (1802–3) • R. R. Sedgwick, 'Forbes, Duncan', HoP, *Commons, 1715–54* • G. Harris, *The life of Lord Chancellor Hardwicke*, 3 vols. (1847) • NL Scot., Culloden papers • IGI

Archives NL Scot., corresp. and papers · NL Scot., session papers | BL, corresp. with Lord Hardwicke, Add. MSS 35446, 35586, 36137–36138 • Hunt. L., letters to earl of London • NL Scot., Culloden papers • NL Scot., corresp. with Erskine family • NL Scot., letters to John McFarlane • NL Scot., corresp. with fourth marquess of Tweeddale • U. Edin. L., letters to William Forbes

Likenesses J. Davison, oils, *c*.1737, Advocates Hall, Edinburgh [*see illus.*] • J. Campbell, watercolour drawing, 1746, Scot. NPG • J. Faber junior, mezzotint, 1748 (after J. Davison, *c*.1737), BM, NPG • L. F. Roubiliac, statue, 1752, Advocates Hall, Edinburgh • attrib. J. Davison, oils, Scot. NPG • oils (after J. Davison), NPG

Wealth at death see testamentary records, Inverness Commissary Court, 20 April 1748, 8 April 1749, 8 Sept 1768, NA Scot., vols. CC11/1/5 and 6

Forbes, Duncan (1798–1868), orientalist, was born of humble parentage at Kinnaird in Perthshire on 28 April 1798. His parents emigrated to America in the spring of 1801, taking only their youngest child with them, while Duncan was consigned to the care of his paternal grandfather in Glenfernate. His early schooling was very basic; he spoke only Gaelic until he was about thirteen years old, but he soon showed intellectual independence and plain common sense. When barely seventeen years old he was chosen as village schoolmaster of Straloch, and soon after began to attend Kirkmichael School as a student. In October 1818 he entered Perth grammar school, and two years later he matriculated at the University of St Andrews, where he obtained an MA in 1823. In the summer of the same year he accepted an appointment in the newly established Calcutta Academy, and arrived at Calcutta in the following November. Ill health, however, forced him to return to England early in 1826. Soon after his arrival in London, he became assistant to Dr John Borthwick Gilchrist, teacher of Hindustani, and afterwards to Dr Sandford Arnot. In 1837 he was appointed professor of oriental languages in King's College, London, a post which he held until 1861, when he was elected to an honorary fellowship of the college. From 1849 to 1855 Forbes was employed by the trustees of the British Museum to make a catalogue of the collection of Persian manuscripts. This work is contained in four large volumes of manuscript in the department of oriental manuscripts. Forbes's work is now replaced by the printed *Catalogue of Persian MSS*, the preface to which states that 'the use of Dr. Forbes's catalogue was practically confined to the help it afforded in the preliminary classing of the MSS' (*British Museum Catalogue of Persian MSS*, 3.xxviii).

Forbes was a successful teacher, and writer of useful publications. His interest in chess resulted in two books. One was on the theory and practice of the game in India and the Arab and Persian worlds. The second was on the history of the game and its establishment in the West. Some portions of this book were severely criticized by Dr van der Linde in his *Geschichte des Schachspiels*. Forbes, who was a member of the Royal Asiatic Society, was created honorary LLD of St Andrews University in 1847. He died at his home, 58 Burton Crescent, Middlesex, on 17 August 1868.

With Sandford Arnot, Forbes was joint author of grammars of Persian and Hindustani. He also wrote several manuals and dictionaries of Hindustani alone, as well as Bengali and Arabic grammars, and made translations from Persian and Hindustani. In the *Gentleman's Magazine* he discussed Celtic dialects and initiated a warm controversy by denying that Welsh was one such.

Forbes's books show little original research. Although Forbes wrote on many and varied subjects, from Arabic to Bengali, he did not have a thoroughly scholarly knowledge of any of them.   [ANON.], *rev.* PARVIN LOLOI

Sources *Journal of the Royal Asiatic Society of Great Britain and Ireland* (May 1869), vii–viii · *St Andrews University calendar, 1800–53*, 24, 70 · *Calendar of the King's College, University of London* · *British Museum catalogue of printed books* · *Catalogue of the Persian manuscripts in the British Museum*, Department of Oriental Printed Books and Manuscripts, 3 vols. (1879–83); repr. (1966) · T. H. Jamieson and J. A. Hjaltalín, eds., *Catalogue of the printed books in the library of the Faculty of Advocates*, 3 (1874), 206–7 · private information (1889) · Boase, *Mod. Eng. biog.* · Allibone, *Dict.*
Archives UCL, Society for the Diffusion of Useful Knowledge, MSS
Wealth at death under £6000: probate, 8 Oct 1868, *CGPLA Eng. & Wales*

Forbes, Edward (1815–1854), natural historian, was born on 12 February 1815 in Douglas, Isle of Man, the oldest of eight surviving children of Edward Forbes (*b*. 1786), banker, and his wife, Jane Teare (*d*. 1836). He was the elder brother of David *Forbes. Educated at home, then in a local grammar school, he was sent to London in 1831 to become a painter, but was refused by the Royal Academy and went later the same year to Edinburgh to study medicine. During his childhood years he had shown a deep interest in natural history, including marine life, botany, and geology. In Edinburgh these, rather than medicine, occupied his time. He attended the natural history lectures of Robert Jameson and the philosophically orientated anatomy lectures of Robert Knox, collected plants and animals, and became deeply involved in student affairs and scientific societies. The death of his mother, and his natural inclinations, led him to abandon medicine in 1836 and to take up natural history as his full-time occupation, living at first on a stipend from his father.

Natural historian, 1835–1854 As a student, Forbes travelled to Norway in 1835, to France in 1835 and 1836 to study in the Jardin des Plantes (in Paris he heard the lectures of Prévost, Beaudant, Blainville, and Geoffroy Saint-Hilaire), and to France and Algeria in 1837. With his friend John Goodsir (1814–1867) he visited Shetland in 1839 to collect plants and marine invertebrates. This was the prelude to Forbes's role in stimulating, co-ordinating, and compiling the results of dredging by local groups all over Britain, much of the work funded by the British Association for the Advancement of Science (BA).

Forbes's link with the BA began in 1836, at its third meeting, in Bristol. In 1839 he and more senior colleagues were granted £60 'for researches with the dredge with a view to the investigation of the marine zoology of Great Britain, the illustration of the geographical distribution of marine animals, and the more accurate determination of the fossils of the Pleiocene Period' (*Report of the British Association for the Advancement of Science*, 1839), subjects that would occupy much of the rest of his life. During this period, too, his books on Manx molluscs (*Malacologia Monensis*, 1838)

Edward Forbes (1815–1854), by David Octavius Hill and Robert Adamson, 1844

and British starfishes (*A History of British Starfishes*, 1841) were published.

By 1841 Forbes was established as a recognized natural historian, but without any paid employment; he had applied without success for the chairs of natural history in Aberdeen and St Andrews and was still dependent on income from his father. When the opportunity arose early in 1841 to join a Royal Navy surveying and archaeological expedition to the eastern Mediterranean, he accepted without hesitation.

Forbes's experience of the Mediterranean strengthened his views, published during the late 1830s, that marine animal species were arranged in discrete depth zones from the intertidal into deep water, that this zonation could yield information about the habits and habitats of fossil species, and that distribution in depth and in latitudinal range were correlated. He described eight zones of animal life in the Mediterranean, and wrote tentatively of life becoming more and more sparse with depth until it disappeared at the greatest depths (below about 300 fathoms according to a later publication). He thought that modern distributions threw new light on the fossil record, including the changes that occurred each time ancient fauna were replaced by newer species, or as climatic changes such as the glaciations occurred in higher latitudes. With justification Forbes regarded his work in the Mediterranean as a key to new principles in geology and the study of marine life, but it was cut short by his father's bankruptcy. He returned to England in 1842, responsible for the support of his family, to take up the ill-paid chair of botany at King's College, London, a position arranged by friends during his absence.

Forbes's London career was the busiest and most troubled period of his life. Plagued by financial insecurity and ill health (he contracted recurrent malaria in the Mediterranean and had suffered from bouts of depression all his life), he was forced to take extra jobs, such as curator of the Geological Society's collections in 1843, and to write prolifically for *The Athenaeum*, *The Lancet*, the *Literary Gazette*, and other periodicals. Some stability came in 1844 when he resigned his job with the Geological Society to become palaeontologist to the fledgeling Geological Survey of Great Britain under Henry De la Beche. For the next decade his life centred on lectures at King's College and the annual field seasons of the geological survey in England and Wales. On 31 August 1848 he married Emily Marianne Ashworth (d. 1909); she accompanied him into the field even after their children were born.

Forbes's geological survey fieldwork was the foundation of monographs on Palaeozoic, Mesozoic, and Tertiary fossils. It fostered indirectly his important monograph of 1846, *On the connexion between the distribution of the existing fauna and flora of the British Isles, and the geological changes which have affected their area*, invoking glaciations (to British naturalists these were ice-infested inundations by the sea) and land bridges between Europe, Ireland, and Britain to account for the modern distributions of plants and animals. In a preliminary account he described five groups of British plants of different geographic origins, neglecting to acknowledge the prior work of Hewett Cottrell Watson. Although the oversight was corrected in the long essay of 1846, Forbes's dispute with Watson was never resolved. In succeeding years he continued to write faunal monographs, including the important series, co-written with Sylvanus Hanley (1819–1900), *A History of British Mollusca and their Shells* (4 vols., 1848–53), and began to prepare his well-known *A Natural History of the European Seas* (1859; finished after Forbes's death by his geological survey colleague Robert Godwin-Austen). When the survey's Museum of Practical Geology was enlarged in 1851 to become part of the Government School of Mines (later the Royal School of Mines), Forbes was appointed lecturer in natural history in the new school, reducing even further his ability to complete the zoological and palaeontological work that he loved.

Forbes became a member of the Geological Society at the end of 1844 and was elected a fellow of the Royal Society in February 1845. A clubbable and humorous man, he had an active social life which revolved around several small dining societies of like-minded individuals. Among them were the Maga Club of his university, Edinburgh (the club described itself as a 'Universal Brotherhood of the Friends of Truth'), a Red Lions Club which he started at the British Association's Birmingham meeting in 1839, a University Club which he founded in the same year, and a Metropolitan Lions Club which he started in London in the mid-1840s. His conversation, his humorous songs, and his physical contortions all contributed to his reputation among friends for the love of good fellowship.

Forbes had longed for years to replace his mentor Robert Jameson in the regius chair of natural history in Edinburgh and when the aged Jameson died in April 1854 Forbes was appointed to replace him. With characteristic energy he tried to finish his work in London, began lecturing in Edinburgh, reorganized Jameson's museum, and undertook a strenuous series of field trips. His recurrent illness returned; within a few days, on 18 November 1854, he died, to the shock and distress of most of the British natural-history community. On 23 November he was buried in Dean cemetery, Edinburgh, where his gravestone bears the simple inscription 'Edward Forbes. Naturalist'.

Character and philosophy Tall and thin, with long, lank hair, Forbes (who pronounced his name 'fourbees') was regarded by many who knew him as the kindest and most genial of colleagues. Professionally, he was one of the most distinguished and certainly the most enigmatic of pre-Darwinian British natural historians. The facts of his life conceal problems in placing him in early- and mid-nineteenth-century natural science. Even to the many colleagues who admired his accomplishments in zoology and palaeontology, his abstract philosophical thought was a puzzle. Modern scholarship has thrown a little light on his system of thought, especially on his views of how species originated in space and time, but the loss of many of his papers makes definitive interpretation difficult. By background and inclination he was a high Anglican and a tory. Philosophically he shows a strain of Platonism that appears to be partly of his own development, partly from his teachers Jameson and Knox, partly derived from the Cambridge Platonists (especially Henry More), and modified by some strains of German philosophical idealism, mediated by the work of Coleridge.

Forbes's approach to zoology, geology, and biogeography was unashamedly creationist. Species were originated by acts of divine creation, in specific centres, from which they migrated to the limits set by their conditions of existence. Where environments were similar, closely similar 'representative species' had been created, accounting for the close similarity, but not identity, of fauna in broad latitudinal groupings ('homoiozoic belts'). The species themselves could, in a sense, be regarded as epiphenomena; behind them lay generic ideas. Genera were, in Forbes's words, 'God-born thoughts that become manifest in living shapes' (*The Relations of Natural History to Geology and the Arts*, 1851). In contrast to Lamarckian evolutionists he saw no evidence of an increase in faunal complexity during the ages, claiming that, if there were, the most simple animals would replace the most complex plants in the fossil record. This was manifestly not so.

Also manifest to Forbes was the fact that fossil fauna of the Palaeozoic and of Recent strata were the most complex generically; between these, in Mesozoic strata, were found depauperate (or 'impoverished') fauna. It appeared that generic development was arranged along axes of time and structure, not from simple to complex, but often from complex through simpler to complex again, showing a bipolar nature. In his presidential address to the Geological Society in 1854, shortly before his death, he presented and elaborated the idea of polarity before a bemused audience, defining it as 'a manifestation of force of development at opposite poles of an ideal sphere', explaining that it resulted in 'contrasting development in opposite directions'. Polarity was a manifestation of the divine plan of creation. As a result, genera were created in groups and were different and characteristic of their time and location.

Forbes's philosophical thought, uncharacteristically abstract even in his own time, was rapidly eclipsed by the success of Darwin's theory of evolution and the controversies that arose around it after 1859. Darwin himself was scathing in his views of polarity, regarding it as akin to spiritualism. Alfred Russel Wallace in 1855 also reacted against Forbes's ideas, and sought to explain the origin of representative species, not by polar creative forces working through generic ideas, but by their relationship to preexisting, closely allied species. According to Wallace the 'polarity' of species in time could best be explained by changes of climate and land area, which led to decreased fossilization and increased extinction. However, it would be a mistake to categorize Forbes as a failed pre-Darwinian, or as an arbitrarily idiosyncratic thinker. He was undoubtedly the pre-eminent British naturalist of his era, and his thought is representative of the fecundity of ideas prevailing in Britain and on the continent during the early decades of the nineteenth century. He was one of many who attempted to make sense of the distribution of living organisms and the patterns of the fossil record by invoking idealistic notions of powers immanent in nature, God-derived or not, which united and made comprehensible the facts of natural history. During the first decades of the nineteenth century his Neoplatonic approach, consistent with his personal mysticism and religiosity, provided an alternative cosmology to materialism, English Kantianism, and empiricist natural theology. That all were eclipsed by the renewed topicality of evolutionary theory after 1859 does not reduce the importance of Forbes's scientific work, nor his significance as a formulator of ideas about the origin and history of organisms in accordance with the range of views current in his time.

ERIC L. MILLS

Sources G. Wilson and A. Geikie, *Memoir of Edward Forbes, F.R.S., late regius professor of natural history in the University of Edinburgh* (1861) • E. L. Mills, 'A view of Edward Forbes, naturalist', *Archives of Natural History*, 11 (1982–4), 365–93 • E. L. Mills, 'Edward Forbes, John Gwyn Jeffreys, and British dredging before the *Challenger* expedition', *Journal of the Society of the Bibliography of Natural History*, 8 (1976–8), 507–36 • P. F. Rehbock, 'Edward Forbes (1815–1854): an annotated list of published and unpublished writings', *Journal of the Society of the Bibliography of Natural History*, 9 (1978–80), 171–218 • P. F. Rehbock, *The philosophical naturalists: themes in early nineteenth-century British biology* (1983) • J. Browne, *The secular ark: studies in the history of biogeography* (1983) • A. Desmond, *The politics of evolution: morphology, medicine and reform in radical London* (1989) • J. Browne, 'The making of the *Memoir* of Edward Forbes', *Archives of Natural History*, 10 (1981–2), 205–19 • L. Reeve, 'Biographical sketch', *Literary* papers by the late Professor Edward Forbes, F.R.S. (1855), v–xiv • *Literary Gazette* (25 Nov 1854), 1016–18

Archives American Philosophical Society, Philadelphia, papers • BGS, notebook • Institute of Geological Sciences, London • Linn. Soc., letters and papers • Manx Museum, Isle of Man, letters and papers • NHM, notebooks and letter to James Scott Bowerbank; notes on plants in Turkey • NL Scot., letters and papers • Royal Botanic Garden, Edinburgh, papers relating to Isle of Man • Royal College of Physicians of Edinburgh, lecture notes • RS, corresp. and papers; letters and papers • U. Edin. L., journal and papers | American Philosophical Society, Philadelphia, letters to Sir Charles Lyell • ICL, letters to Thomas Huxley • ICL, letters to Lyon Playfair • ICL, letters to Sir Andrew Ramsay • Manx Museum, Isle of Man, letters to William Thompson • NHM, corresp. with Joshua Alder and Alfred Merle Norman • NHM, corresp. with Richard Owen and William Clift • RBG Kew, letters to Sir Joseph Hooker • U. Edin. L., letters to Sir William Jardine, etc. • U. Newcastle, Robinson L., letters to Sir Walter Trevelyan

Likenesses D. O. Hill and R. Adamson, calotype, 1844, Scot. NPG [see illus.] • T. H. Maguire, lithograph, 1851, BM, NPG; repro. in T. H. Maguire, *Portraits of honorary members of the Ipswich Museum* (1852) • D. O. Hill, photograph, *c*.1854, Scot. NPG • C. Cook, stipple, pubd 1855 (after daguerreotype by Claudet), BM • J. G. Lough, marble bust, exh. 1856, Geological Museum, London • N. N. Burnard, marble bust, Douglas, Isle of Man • J. Steell, plaster bust, Linn. Soc., Scot. NPG • L. C. Wyon, bronze medallion (after bust by J. G. Lough), NPG • L. C. Wyon, silvered glass medal (after J. G. Lough), Scot. NPG • engraving, RS • portrait, repro. in Reeve, 'Biographical sketch'

Forbes [*née* Armstrong], **Elizabeth Adela** (1859–1912), artist, was born on 29 December 1859 near Ottawa, Canada, the youngest of three, and only daughter of William Robertson Armstrong (*d*. *c*.1873), civil servant, and his wife, Frances, *née* Hawksley (1816–1897). Following drawing tutorials at home, at the age of fourteen Elizabeth attended South Kensington Art Schools, London. The latter studies were 'almost a pity', she believed, for one so young (Birch, 57). Living with her widowed mother at her uncle's home on Cheyne Walk, London, was intensely inspiring, however, to Elizabeth's already fertile imagination. The progressive medical practitioner and philanthropist Thomas Hawksley (1821–1892) was a constant support to his sister and niece throughout their lives. Next door lived the painter Dante Gabriel Rossetti, and, though Elizabeth never met him, her Pre-Raphaelite leanings developed early. She was a voracious reader, and the seeds for later book illustrations and paintings, pastorals, and idylls were planted deep in the literary references she absorbed in her youth.

It was during 'three winters' with the New York Art Students League (1878–81) that Armstrong met her most influential mentor, the American impressionist William Merritt Chase. Concurrently she recorded an interest in the peasant paintings of Bastien Lepage such as '*Jean, Jeanne, Jeannette*' (City Art Gallery, Manchester), which anticipate the subject of some of her own later work. At Chase's suggestion, Armstrong travelled to Munich (1882), later recalled as her unhappiest time, due to the 'perpetual disadvantage' of her gender (Birch, 61). A lasting benefit was help from Frank Currier, who initiated her to the 'felicitous use of charcoal in landscape work' (ibid., 61). That 'most ductile of mediums' became a hallmark of her future art, especially when boldly combined with water-colour (Forbes, *King Arthur's Wood*; original illustrations, private coll.).

A fortuitous move to Pont Aven, Brittany, placed Armstrong in a lively artistic set who regularly worked towards exhibitions. 'Tiny watercolours' (1882; Birch, 62), sold at the Royal Institute, were her first success. From 1883 she established a London studio at 18 Lupus Street, Victoria, and her exhibiting career escalated. Joining Chase and Art League friends in Zandvoort, the Netherlands (1883), she was introduced to etching by the drypoint method. Nurtured in etching by Mortimer Menpes and Robert Blum, she discovered a skill which won her admission to the Royal Society of Painter-Etchers and Engravers, and new friends, including Whistler and Sickert.

With her mother as chaperone, Armstrong led a cosmopolitan working life, employing a variety of media, travelling and exhibiting frequently. It was at this period that she painted *Zandvoort Fisher Girl* (1884, oil on canvas; Penlee House Gallery and Museum, Cornwall). Hearing that both Newlyn and St Ives in west Cornwall were home to 'colonies' of painters, who gathered there from Brittany and Paris, the Armstrongs visited and with intermissions stayed. From 1883 until her marriage to the painter Stanhope Alexander *Forbes (1857–1947) on 7 August 1889, Armstrong participated in sixty-three major London exhibitions, with a 'speciality' noted as 'Domestic'.

Her marriage, though happy, served to diminish Elizabeth Forbes's independent growth and standing to that of 'wife of' a Royal Academician and acknowledged leader of the Newlyn colony [*see also* Newlyn school]. Marriage removed her from the Whistler set, and from etching, neither of which her husband understood or approved. Her lively, even lyrical, play with colour and line, treating classical, literary, rural, and mythological themes and portraits, continued to receive notice, however, for Mrs Stanhope Forbes, E. A. Forbes, or Elizabeth Stanhope Forbes (the names by which she was known). Often implied in these reviews was an understanding of 'a somewhat prosaic male artist with a brilliant wife' within the 'Newlyn brotherhood of the palette' (Cook, Hardie, and Payne, 22).

Elizabeth Forbes exhibited widely, achieving recognition and medals from Paris (1889) to Chicago (1893; gold medallist, painting), and from Whitechapel (1902) to St Louis (1904). The Newlyn Art Gallery opening in 1895 inaugurated a venue for the exhibition and sale of work, before and after major shows elsewhere, and here she was acknowledged 'queen' (*Pall Mall Gazette*, 2). The Forbeses opened their school of art in Newlyn in 1899 which attracted pupils internationally. Election to the Royal Watercolour Society (1898–9) followed Elizabeth's production of a collection of mixed-media paintings to illustrate an original fairytale for their only child, Alec (1893–1916). Published as *King Arthur's Wood* (1904), this is a central work in her *œuvre* and demonstrates her startling versatility and engaging imagination. Among many large works in oil her *School is Out* (exh. RA, 1889; Penlee House Gallery and

Museum) demonstrates her success in painting subjects including children. Elizabeth Forbes died on 16 March 1912 at Higher Faughan, Newlyn, the home the Forbeses had built in 1904–5 to include both indoor and outdoor studios. She was interred on 21 or 22 March at Sancreed church, near Newlyn. Her watercolours are occasionally confused with those of a former pupil at the Forbes's school, Maudie Clayton, daughter of Edward Hume Palmer of Bexhill, whom Stanhope Alexander Forbes married in 1915.   MELISSA HARDIE-BUDDEN

Sources J. Cook, M. Hardie, and C. Payne, *Singing from the walls: the life and art of Elizabeth Forbes* (2000) [incl. catalogue raisonné] • Mrs L. Birch, *Stanhope A. Forbes, A.R.A., and Elizabeth Stanhope Forbes, A.R.W.S.* (1906) • M. Hardie, *A hundred years in Newlyn: diary of a gallery, 1895–1995* (1995) • A. K. Sabin, 'The dry-points of Elizabeth Adela Forbes, formerly E. A. Armstrong (1859–1912)', *Print Collectors Quarterly*, 9 (Feb 1922), 75–100 • E. Forbes, *King Arthur's wood* (1904) • M. Hardie, 'Painting with their eyes wide open: women painters in Cornwall', *Women artists in Cornwall, 1880–1940*, ed. C. Wallace (1996) • J. Colenbrander, *Portrait of Fryn* (1984) • *Letters of Frances Hodgkins*, ed. L. Gill (1993) • A. Wormleighton, *A painter laureate: Lamorna Birch and his circle* (1995) • *Pall Mall Gazette* (18 March 1912) • *Cornishman* (18 March 1912) • *Cornishman* (21 March 1912) • personal information record, National Gallery of Canada

Archives National Gallery of Canada, Ottawa, papers • Penlee House Gallery and Museum, Penzance, papers • Tate collection, papers and letters, archive no. TGA9015 • West Cornwall Art Archive, Penzance, collection [incl. Newlyn Art Gallery collection]

Likenesses E. Forbes, self-portrait, charcoal, repro. in Cook, Hardie, and Payne, *Singing from the walls* • E. Forbes, self-portrait, drypoint etching, Penlee House Gallery and Museum, Penzance • S. A. Forbes, oils, Newlyn Art Gallery, Penlee House, Penzance; repro. in Cook, Hardie, and Payne, *Singing from the walls*

Wealth at death £5341 15s. 11d.: probate, 13 June 1912, CGPLA Eng. & Wales

Forbes, Eric Gray (1933–1984), historian of astronomy, was born on 30 March 1933 at Linskill Villas, St Andrews, Fife, the only child of Robert James Forbes (1904–1952), railway clerk, and Christina Pearson, *née* Gray (1906–1978), a nanny and teacher. He was educated at Madras College, St Andrews, from 1939 to 1951, and then took a degree in astronomy and mathematics at the University of St Andrews, graduating in 1954. He subsequently began work for a PhD in solar astronomy at St Andrews under E. Finlay-Freundlich. His supervisor had many contacts in Europe, so Forbes spent much of the latter half of the 1950s working at observatories in Florence, Italy, and Göttingen, Germany. During these years he learned both Italian and German, the latter, in particular, proving important for his later career. At Göttingen he was involved in the discovery of archive papers left by the eighteenth-century Göttingen astronomer Tobias Mayer. This stimulated his interest in the history of astronomy.

Having received his PhD Forbes moved, in 1961, to St Mary's College, Twickenham, where he lectured in physics and mathematics. At the same time he registered as a part-time MSc student in the history and philosophy of science at University College, London. As part of that course he began to study material on eighteenth- and nineteenth-century astronomy and navigation contained in the board of longitude papers at the Royal Greenwich Observatory. He was awarded his MSc in 1965, and almost immediately took up a post as lecturer in the history of science at the University of Edinburgh. There he concentrated initially on Tobias Mayer, being awarded a London PhD for a thesis on Mayer's contributions to astronomy. Further work led to a number of books on this topic in the early 1970s. Since Mayer was particularly known for his work on navigational astronomy this led to a wider study of the latter field. The preparation of a book to celebrate the Royal Observatory tercentenary in 1975 stimulated an especial interest in the work of John Flamsteed, the first astronomer royal, and he began to make a definitive collection of all Flamsteed's correspondence.

During the 1970s Forbes was promoted first to reader, then, in 1978, to professor of the history of science at Edinburgh. Shortly after the latter appointment he also became director of the history of medicine and science unit. The unit was especially involved in tracing the backgrounds of fellows of the Royal Society of Edinburgh to which he himself was elected in 1984. When he was first appointed to Edinburgh he had feared that history of science would prove marginal to the interests of the history department. However, by 1982 he had established his standing in the department so well that he became its chairman. The appointment reflected both his organizational skills and his unfailing good humour. These, together with his linguistic abilities, made him a natural leader in national and international activities. From the 1960s onwards, he served on bodies concerned with the history of science in the United Kingdom. Then, in 1977, he organized a successful international congress in Edinburgh for the International Union of the History and Philosophy of Science. The following year he became secretary of the union's division of the history of science. He was very soon promoted to the onerous post of secretary-general for the union as a whole. In 1981 he was made vice-president.

Forbes was now clearly poised to become a person of great influence in the realm of the international history of science. However, he had always had problems with high blood pressure, and he suffered a major heart attack from which he died, at Edinburgh's Royal Infirmary on 21 November 1984. He was cremated at Mortonhall crematorium, Edinburgh, five days later. He had married Maria Sibilla Lürken (b. 1936), a talented linguist, on 25 March 1966, and they had two children, Edgar and Andrea. After his death his wife worked for many years to ensure that his collection of Flamsteed's correspondence should be published with appropriate annotation. The resultant volumes represent a memorial to his life and work.

A. J. MEADOWS

Sources personal knowledge (2004) · private information (2004) [Maria Forbes] · J. Meadows, *Annals of Science*, 42 (1985), 547–8 · H. T. Dickinson and D. Hay, *Year Book of the Royal Society of Edinburgh* (1984–5), 184–5 · *Archenhold-Sternwarte Berlin-Treptow*, 29 (1985) · b. cert. · d. cert. · register of births and deaths, Leuchars and St Andrews, Fife · City of Edinburgh certificate of cremation, 27 Nov 1984

Likenesses photograph, U. Edin. · photographs, Tobias Mayer Museum, Marbach am Neckar, Germany · three photographs, Royal Museum of Scotland, Edinburgh

Forbes, Sir Francis (1784–1841), lawyer and colonial official, was born at Bermuda, eldest son of Francis Forbes MD (c.1740–1814) and his second wife, Mary Tucker. Parental education preceded schooling in St George's. He then read law under Bermuda's Chief Justice Leonard, an English loyalist expelled from America. Sent to Lincoln's Inn, Forbes from 1806 read with Edward Sugden, later lord chancellor, and attained his qualifications, but returned home before being called to the bar. He was specially admitted to practise in Bermuda's courts from 1809 and specialized in vice-admiralty cases, Judge Territt having an 'exalted opinion' of him. Governor John Hodgson so trusted Forbes's advice that he caused him to be appointed attorney-general in 1810.

In 1812 Forbes went to England, to be called to the bar and to marry a long-standing friend, Amelia Sophia, daughter of Dr David Grant, formerly of Jamaica. Forbes sought a more lucrative crown colonial appointment, preferably at Jamaica. Instead he was offered the chief justiceship of Newfoundland, where, since 1791, only one of several appointees had been a lawyer and the legal system was moribund. Attracted by the Admiralty connection, Forbes accepted. Commissioned on 24 August 1816, at £1000 annually, he was sworn in on 15 July 1817. Governor Pickmore, who commended Forbes, soon yielded place to Admiral Sir Charles Hamilton, an autocrat unversed in any rule of law but naval command. Hamilton frequently clashed with Forbes, while demeaning him in dispatches—accusing him of courting popularity, of being predisposed towards America because of travels there, and of having 'political tendencies of the freest tendency' (Hamilton to Bathurst, 28 Feb 1819, PRO CO 194/62, fol. 19a). The reverse was the truth. Forbes took a paternal, not populist, part in seeking to better the community; his inflexibly English attitudes were strengthened by recollections of family estates confiscated in America; and he never trespassed from the judicial to the political domain. Newfoundlanders widely admired his probity and judiciousness.

Weary of Hamilton and of St John's severe climate, Forbes sought leave. Hamilton first ignored, then refused, him. Forbes submitted medical certificates. 'Studious life and too long and laborious attendance in the Court house' (Dr W. Carson to Hamilton, 4 May 1822, Newfoundland Archives, GN 2/1/31, 401) had caused infirmities. If the governor would not grant leave, Forbes would achieve it by resignation. Hamilton gave way, ungraciously, and Forbes departed in May 1822 to a tumultuous citizens' farewell. Despite intolerable executive interference, he had transformed and made regular Newfoundland's legal system.

In England, convalescing, Forbes strengthened a friendship with Robert Wilmot-Horton, under-secretary for the colonies, and was well received by Henry, Earl Bathurst, who sought his return to Newfoundland or his acceptance of the new chief justiceship of New South Wales. Forbes resigned the former office, reflected on the latter, and contemplated some Indian judicial appointments. His wife rejected India's climate, but would go to New South Wales. He was commissioned on 13 October 1823 at £2000 per year and, with his wife, reached Sydney on 5 March 1824. Forbes had, before departure, helped draft the act of 1823 known as the New South Wales Act, on which depended the colony's metamorphosis from convict penitentiary to free community with inadequate, but improved, constitutional, legislative, and judicial institutions.

Forbes opened the supreme court of New South Wales on 17 May 1824. Using Newfoundland experience, he temporized with informal court procedures suiting colonial circumstances. Nevertheless, the criminal calendar overwhelmed him. Until August 1825 he was the colony's only judge.

The peculiar status of New South Wales evoked much litigation in constitutional and public law. Forbes's pellucid pronouncements offended the landed gentry ('exclusives') in their class war against ex-convicts and convict offspring. Forbes's essential resort to reason in legal interpretation was lost upon the exclusives who railed on him when he prevented their subverting the law to suit themselves. Thus he was improperly characterized as a leader of convicts, a republican, and an enemy of the exclusives. His *ex officio* place in the executive and legislative councils added, falsely, to a perception of partisanship. Whispering campaigns, denigrating him, were stimulated by the exclusives who also used Downing Street connections to attack him *ex parte*. Those personalities were aggravated when General Ralph Darling arrived as governor late in 1824. Like Hamilton in Newfoundland, Darling lacked a constitutional governor's temperament or ability. He was a military man, prickly, officious, and cold, who desired his 'orders' to be obeyed unquestioningly by all subordinates, including judges, as if commands.

Forbes was not the governor's subordinate: friction was inevitable. Throughout years of controversy, Forbes refused to revile, but patiently explained himself in courteous, rational language. He was consistently right, but rarely understood. Notably he was vindicated in refusing his required certificate of legality for Darling's bills to curb outspoken newspapers. And, although the exclusives tried to stifle it, he introduced a limited right to trial by jury through a bold interpretation of the New South Wales Act in a characteristically robust judgment.

Assistant judges, who equally deplored Darling's meddling incompetence, gradually augmented the bench. But Forbes's health had already suffered from the stress of being sole judge, from the governor's onslaughts, and from the exclusives' attacks. Only his friendship with Wilmot-Horton, with whom he corresponded privately, sterilized his enemies' determination to unseat him. In spite of them, and at great personal cost, he secured the rule of law in Australia.

The arrival of Governor Richard Bourke, in 1831, transformed relations between executive and judicial arms of government. Bourke and Forbes worked in great harmony. But Forbes was so physically reduced that he could barely continue. Granted sick leave in 1834, he would not, because of disagreements over his locum tenens, depart until their resolution in 1836. He travelled in a shattered

state to England, where he was lauded at the Colonial Office and, on Bourke's recommendation, knighted in April 1837.

Granted leave to retire on a pension, Forbes did so on 1 July 1837, returning to Sydney too ill to resume any public life. His closing years were spent in seclusion at Leitrim Lodge, Newtown, near Sydney, where he died on 8 November 1841, survived by Lady Forbes and their two sons. He was buried in the Devonshire Street cemetery, Sydney, on 11 November.					J. M. BENNETT

Sources C. H. Currey, *Sir Francis Forbes* (1978) · H. C. Wilkinson, *Bermuda from sail to steam*, 2 vols. (1973) · A. H. McLintock, *The establishment of constitutional government in Newfoundland* (1941) · D. W. Prowse, *A history of Newfoundland from the English, colonial, and foreign records*, 2nd edn (1896) · J. M. Bennett, *A history of the supreme court of New South Wales* (1974) · R. Therry, *Reminiscences of thirty years' residence in New South Wales and Victoria*, 2nd edn (1863) · Lady Forbes [A. S. Forbes], 'Sydney society in crown colony days', Mitchell L., NSW · D. G. Forbes, *Memoir of Sir Francis Forbes* (1875) · P. O'Flaherty, 'Forbes, Sir Francis', *DCB*, vol. 7 · PRO, CO 194/62, fol. 19 at 19a · Newfoundland Archives, Colonial Secretary's Department, GN 2/1/31, 401

Archives Derbys. RO, letters to Sir R. J. Wilmot-Horton · Mitchell L., NSW · PRO, CO 37/68, 70, 71, 73; 38/20, 28; 40/25; 194/58–60, 62–5, 69; 195/17; 201/188, 195, 215 · State Archives of New South Wales, Sydney, supreme court letter-book | Mitchell L., NSW, Bourke MSS · Provincial Archives of Newfoundland and Labrador, colonial secretary's MSS

Likenesses oils, *c*.1837, Sydney grammar school, Australia · attrib. J. Backler, oils, Supreme Court of New South Wales, Australia · monochrome portrait, Historical Monuments Trust, Bermuda · portrait, State Library of New South Wales, Sydney

Wealth at death widow, who long survived him, had eventually to supplicate for pension from New South Wales government, having exhausted what little provision Sir Francis had been able to make: Currey, *Sir Francis Forbes*, chap. 54

Forbes, George, third earl of Granard (1685–1765), naval officer and diplomatist, was born in Ireland on 21 October 1685, the son of Arthur Forbes, second earl (*c*.1656–1734), army officer, and his wife, Mary (1661–1724), daughter of Sir George Rawdon, baronet, of Moira, co. Down. Forbes was for a time at the grammar school at Drogheda. His grandfather Arthur *Forbes, first earl, died in 1695.

After moving to London with his grandmother in 1702 Forbes introduced himself to Admiral George Churchill, then first of the council to the lord high admiral, Prince George of Denmark, and sought to enter the navy. Churchill got him a lieutenancy in one of the new marine regiments and he served as a marine under Rooke at the capture of Gibraltar, 20–24 July 1704, where he was employed onshore as aide-de-camp to the prince of Hesse-Darmstadt, and in the *St George* (96 guns) in the great sea-fight off Malaga on 13 August. In the same year he became heir to the earldom, styled Viscount Forbes, on the death of his elder brother, Lord Forbes, a captain in the Scots Royals, from wounds received at Blenheim.

Between 1702 and 1704 Forbes served for 18 months as volunteer per order and then midshipman on the *Britannia* and *Torbay*, before qualifying as a naval lieutenant on 13 January 1705, 'the time prescribed by her Majesty's order in Council to qualify him for a Lieutenant [being] dispensed with by his Royal Highness's Command' (PRO,

ADM 107/2, fol. 40). Three days later he was appointed fifth lieutenant of the *Royal Anne* at Portsmouth, and, on 15 August 1705, second lieutenant of the frigate *Triton*, one of the most active cruisers in the navy, which was responsible for capturing twenty-three French privateers in the channel in fifteen months from January 1705. He was in her at the siege of Ostend in 1706, where he served onshore, and first became known to his future friend John Campbell, duke of Argyll, who commanded in the trenches.

On returning home Forbes found his commission awaiting him as captain of the frigate *Lynn* (16 July 1706), in which he served, convoying the Baltic trade. He was transferred on 3 January 1707 to the *Leopard* (50 guns), and then to the *Gosport* on 5 March 1707. On the following day he was appointed brigadier in the 4th troop of Horse Guards, of which the duke of Argyll was captain and colonel. Forbes did duty with his troop until appointed to command the *Sunderland* (60 guns) on 18 May 1708, part of the western squadron under Lord Dursley (afterwards third Earl Berkeley). In the same year Forbes became exempt of his troop and a brother of Trinity House.

In May 1709 Forbes left his ship to do duty with his troop at Windsor, where 'his sprightliness of genius and politeness of manner recommended him to Queen Anne' (Forbes, 86), at whose instance he was appointed to the *Grafton* (70 guns) on 22 July 1709. In the same year he married Mary (1672/3–1758), eldest daughter of William Stewart, first Viscount Mountjoy, and widow, with two children, of Phineas Preston of Ardsallagh, co. Meath; they had three children.

Forbes sailed for the Mediterranean in the *Grafton* with Sir John Norris in 1710. Charles III of Spain then had his court at Barcelona, and Norris stationed some ships off the coast of Catalonia, the command of which was assigned to Forbes, who was directed to co-operate as much as possible with the Spanish court, and was permitted to reside onshore. Two Genoese ships of war, of 50 and 70 guns respectively, were at Cadiz taking in specie, alleged to be for the use of the French faction in Italy. The Spanish king proposed that Forbes should put out to sea and seize the vessels on their return voyage. Forbes explained that England was at peace with the Genoese republic; but he was pressed by the king, and the queen provided for his indemnification, and so, with his own ship and the *Chatham* (50 guns, Captain Haddock), he took the Genoese ships into Port Mahon, discharged the officers and crews to shore, landed the specie, and returned with the ships to Barcelona. Charles III, greatly pleased, made Forbes a grant of the duty on coinage, and urged him to retrieve the specie. Forbes, doubting the legality of the capture, excused himself until he should receive instructions from home, or from General Stanhope, the British ambassador and commander-in-chief in Spain, and set out to confer with Stanhope.

After joining part of the allied army under Marshal Staremberg he was slightly wounded in a charge with Brigadier Lepell's regiment at the battle of Villaviciosa, on 10 December 1710. On Forbes's return to Barcelona he found orders from home forbidding the disposal of the Genoese treasure, which sorely disconcerted the Spanish court. Forbes returned to England bearing a signed letter from Charles III to Queen Anne, and eventually the British government, decided to retain the capture and indemnify the Genoese republic. In the end Forbes accepted £6000 in lieu of what had once seemed likely to prove a large fortune.

In January 1711 the duke of Argyll was appointed to command in Spain. He set out in the spring, leaving Forbes, who was to serve with him, in London to solicit supplies for the army, which was short of money. Obtaining an order for 800,000 dollars of the Genoese treasure, Forbes travelled through the Netherlands, Germany, the Tyrol, and Italy to Genoa, where he boarded a ship for Barcelona. He served with the army in Spain during 1711, at the head of 300 cavalrymen drafted from home, whom Argyll intended to form into a new cavalry regiment under Forbes's command, but the regiment was never completed as peace negotiations were too far advanced. In the same year he left the army after Argyll had dissuaded him from paying 10,000 guineas for the command of the 4th troop of Horse Guards. From this date his military career was linked to the navy. On 21 August 1712 Forbes was appointed to the *Greenwich* (50 guns); he then became cornet and major in his cavalry troop. After the peace of Utrecht in 1713 he commanded a small squadron of vessels in the Mediterranean, and took up residence with his wife and eldest child in Minorca, from where he returned home in 1716. In 1717 he was appointed lieutenant-governor of the castle of St Phillipa, Minorca, and in 1718 he acted as governor of the island during the brief hostilities with Spain. He is credited with introducing better order in the island, and abolished trials for witchcraft.

On his return home in 1719 Forbes was asked by George I to proceed to Vienna and attempt to carry into effect the long-cherished plan of Charles III (now emperor Charles VI) to form a naval power either in Naples and Sicily or on the Adriatic; for this purpose Forbes received the rank of vice-admiral in the imperial service with a salary of 12,000 florins a year, and unlimited powers of organization. But the imperial ministers looked coldly on the scheme, and adopted a policy of tacit obstruction, which at the end of two years led Forbes to resign his appointment; the emperor presented him with a diamond ring in recognition of his services.

On 13 April 1726 Forbes was given command of the *Canterbury* (60 guns) on the Mediterranean station; thereafter he was employed on shore at the defence of Gibraltar against the Spaniards. Between 1723 and 1727 he was MP for Queenborough, Kent, and in September 1727 he was given an Irish peerage, under the title Baron Forbes. In 1729 he was appointed governor and captain-general of the Leeward Islands, a post he resigned at the end of a year.

In 1730 Forbes made a proposal to the government that he set up a colony on Lake Erie, one which would form a barrier against French encroachments from Canada. He was to be fettered by 'no restrictions beyond the ten commandments', and wanted an annual grant of £12,000 for the use of the colony for seven years. If the government at the end of that time chose to take over the settlement, Forbes was to be created an English peer, with a perpetual pension of £1,000 a year out of the revenues of the Post Office. If the government declined the offer of the colony a grant of the sum was to be made to Forbes and his heirs, with a palatine jurisdiction, similar to that of Lord Baltimore in Maryland, in which case Forbes was to repay the £84,000 advanced; he was ready to pledge his family estates as security for the amount. Sir Robert Walpole, who disliked Forbes, regarding him as 'too busy and curious' (Forbes, 292), admitted the fairness of the terms, but the project was not carried out. On 13 May 1731 Forbes was appointed to the *Cornwall* (80 guns); he commanded her in the Mediterranean under Sir Charles Wager, this being the last time he served afloat.

In 1733 Forbes was appointed envoy-extraordinary and minister-plenipotentiary to the Empress Anne of Russia. He negotiated and concluded a treaty—the first entered into by the court of St Petersburg with any European state—for the better regulation of the customs, and for favouring the introduction of British woollen goods. After his return to England in 1734 the empress, with whom he was a favourite, offered him supreme command of the imperial Russian navy, which he declined. He obtained his flag rank, rear-admiral of the white, on 4 May 1734, and succeeded to the title of earl of Granard on the death of his father in August.

Granard, who was a member of the Irish Linen Company, and took much interest in political economy, was instrumental in 1737 in making improvements to the Irish currency. When the popular outcry against Spain, which led to the War of Jenkins's Ear, arose in 1739, he was offered the command of 'a stout squadron' for the West Indies, but declined the offer, doubting the ministry's commitment. Nevertheless when his senior, Admiral Edward Vernon, was sent out, Granard considered himself superseded, and refused to serve again. His name was retained on the flag list, and half pay was issued for him for some time, but on 31 December 1742 his resignation was finally accepted.

By Argyll's interest Granard was returned to the House of Commons for the Ayr burghs in 1741; he took a very active part in the stormy discussions which drove Sir Robert Walpole from office on 3 February 1742, in consequence of which he was appointed one of the committee of inquiry into the conduct of the ex-minister. But he subsequently separated from his colleagues in disgust, and retired from public life, resigning his seat in 1747. He was sworn of the privy council of Ireland, and held the governments of Westmeath and Longford.

Granard was a spare figure, of average height, with a dark complexion and strongly marked features. In his habits he was very active and extremely abstemious, eating little and drinking nothing but water, customs to which he attributed his good health. He was a great reader, with a very retentive memory, and a quick, intelligent observer. The family manuscripts contain several treatises by him on subjects connected with political economy, geography, and the naval resources of different countries. He died in Dublin on 19 June 1765, and was buried at Newtown Forbes. He was survived by his three children: George, fourth earl of Granard (1710–1769), an army officer who served in the Mediterranean, raised the 76th infantry regiment, which was disbanded in 1763, and died a major-general and colonel of the 29th infantry regiment in 1769; John *Forbes (1714–1796), naval officer; and Mary (d. 1797), who married James Irvine of Kingcaussie.

H. M. CHICHESTER, rev. RANDOLPH COCK

Sources commission and warrant books, PRO, ADM 6/8, 9, 10, 11, 13, 14 · lieutenants' passing certificates, PRO, ADM 107/2, fol. 40 · J. Forbes, *Memoirs of the earls of Granard*, ed. G. A. Hastings [earl of Granard] (1868) · HoP, *Commons, 1715–54* · GEC, *Peerage* · GM, 1st ser., 35 (1765), 346–7 · PRO, Army and Foreign Office MSS
Archives NRA, priv. coll., corresp. and papers incl. those as ambassador to Russia | BL, Egerton MSS · NA Scot., letters to Sir Andrew Mitchell

Forbes, George, sixth earl of Granard (1760–1837), army officer, was born on 14 June 1760 at Great Marlborough Street, London. He was the eldest son of George Forbes, fifth earl of Granard (1740–1780), and his first wife, Dorothea (1738–1764), second daughter of Sir Nicholas Bayley, baronet, of Plas Newydd, Anglesey, and great-grandson of Admiral George, third earl of Granard.

Forbes was educated at Armagh. On 10 May 1779 he married Lady Selina Frances (1759–1827), youngest daughter of George Rawdon, first earl of Moira, and his third wife, Lady Elizabeth Hastings, eldest daughter of the ninth earl of Huntingdon. Forbes and Lady Selina, who was also the sister of the first marquess of Hastings, had five sons and four daughters. After succeeding to the Irish title on 15 April 1780 he made a long tour of the continent. He met Cardinal York in Rome, attended one of Frederick the Great's reviews in Silesia, and stayed in France and at Vienna. On his return home he devoted himself to politics, and, following the example of Lord and Lady Moira, adopted liberal opinions, supporting the policy of Charlemont, Grattan, Curran, and other leaders of the liberal party in Ireland. The marquess of Buckingham referred to him as the most uncompromising opponent of his administration.

Granard was appointed lieutenant-colonel in the army on 17 May 1794, and lieutenant-colonel commandant of the 108th foot, an Irish regiment which he raised in November 1794 but which was broken up at Gibraltar in 1796. Granard also raised the Longford militia, and commanded it at the battle of Castlebar in August 1798, when the regiment, allegedly disaffected, ran away, thus making it easier for the French invaders to rout General Lake's force. Lord Cornwallis praised Granard's bravery in trying to rally his regiment. He was also present at Ballinamuck, where the French, under General Joseph Humbert, surrendered to Cornwallis.

Granard strongly opposed the union, despite the lavish inducements offered by government, and he was one of the twenty-one Irish peers who protested against it. Without a seat in the House of Lords after the union, he took little part in politics; he devoted himself to the management of his estates, and is said to have been a popular landlord. On 24 February 1806, during the brief 'ministry of all the talents', Granard, a whig, was made a peer of the United Kingdom, Baron Granard of Castle Donington, Leicestershire (the seat of his father-in-law); he was also appointed clerk of the crown and hanaper in Ireland (1806–7, 1815–36), a most lucrative office. He became a colonel in the army in 1801, major-general in 1808, and lieutenant-general in 1813; after this he resided chiefly in France, but he came to England to support both Roman Catholic emancipation and the Reform Bill. After the passing of the latter he was offered a promotion in the peerage; this he declined, as he had previously refused the Order of St Patrick.

Granard was made full general in July 1830. He died at his residence, the Hotel Marboeuf, Champs-Elysées, Paris, on 9 June 1837, at the age of seventy-six, and was buried in the family resting-place at Newtown Forbes, Longford, Ireland.   H. M. CHICHESTER, rev. ROGER T. STEARN

Sources J. Forbes, *Lives of the earls of Granard* (1858) · *GM*, 2nd ser., 8 (1837) · GEC, *Peerage* · Burke, *Peerage* (1959) · T. Pakenham, *The year of liberty: the story of the great Irish rebellion of 1798* (1969) · R. F. Foster, *Modern Ireland, 1600–1972* (1989)
Archives priv. coll., corresp. and papers
Likenesses J. Heath, stipple (after T. Wright; after J. Comerford?), BM; repro. in J. Barrington, *Historic anecdotes and secret memoirs* (1815)

Forbes, George (1849–1936), electrical engineer and inventor, was born in Edinburgh on 5 April 1849, the younger son—there were also three daughters—of James David *Forbes (1809–1868) and Alicia Wauchope (d. 1885). His father was later principal of St Andrews University and was an expert in the field of glacier flow. Forbes was educated at Edinburgh Academy, the University of St Andrews, and at Christ's College and St Catharine's College, Cambridge. He graduated BA in 1871. In 1872 he succeeded Alexander Herschel as professor of natural philosophy at Anderson's University, Glasgow (later the Royal Technical College and then the University of Strathclyde). He retained this post until 1880. Significantly, in view of his later work, his lectures included the advocacy of electricity as a means of traction. His chief work at this time was research into the velocity of light with James Young; however, their results, published in 1882, showed a higher velocity than was later accepted. In 1880 he predicted the existence of a trans-Neptunian planet, fifty years before the discovery of Pluto. In 1874 Forbes led a British expedition to Hawaii to observe the transit of Venus. He then returned to Scotland via Peking (Beijing) and St Petersburg, crossing the Gobi Desert and Siberia in 1875. As a result of the contacts he made on this journey, Forbes was able to become the only British war correspondent with the Russian army in the Russo-Turkish War of 1877–8, reporting for *The Times*.

In 1880 Forbes resigned from Anderson's and moved to London; for the next two decades he worked extensively in the field of electrical power engineering. He was commissioned to report on how the City and South London Railway should be powered, and recommended electricity, a significant conclusion for the future of the London underground. In 1881 he served as a juror at the Paris Exposition Internationale d'Eléctricité. In the following year he became manager of the British Electric Light Company, manufacturers of carbon filaments and arc lamps, and at this time began to apply himself to improvements in products and processes. The growing use of electricity made some form of metering essential. Forbes was one of several who invented machines for metering alternating current, though his was never adopted. Of far greater significance was his idea that the brushes in electric motors should be made of carbon rather than the wire or gauze which was then employed. In 1885 he took out a patent for the 'improved means for establishing electric connection between surfaces in relative motion applicable to the collectors of dynamo machines' in which he advocated the use of carbon as a current collector for rotating electrical machines. His suggestion would prove outstandingly successful and the practice was still almost universal a century later. This invention could have made him a very rich man, but he sold his American patent rights to the Westinghouse Company for £2000 and there is no evidence that he received any British royalties.

From 1891 to 1895 Forbes was consulting engineer on the Niagara Falls hydroelectric scheme, reporting to a panel chaired by Lord Kelvin. He initiated a number of design innovations, though this consultancy was not without some technical controversy with Ferranti and C. E. L. Brown, who were also employed on the project. He also advised on other schemes, in India (1893), southern Africa (1895), New Zealand (1896), and Upper Egypt (1897–8). He recommended to Lord Kitchener the use of electric locomotives on the railway then being built across the Nubian Desert, and he made similar proposals with respect to the Nile region. In southern Africa he consolidated his friendship with Sir David Gill, the astronomer.

After the turn of the century, Forbes turned his attention to military work, studying techniques of gunnery and qualities of ballistics. He invented an infantry rangefinder which was used successfully in the Second South African War in 1902, and between 1903 and 1906 he worked with the Admiralty on rangefinders and related matters. The gunsight he developed was still in use by the navy at the outset of the Second World War. During the First World War he was involved in devising methods of signalling for submarines.

In 1906 Forbes built a home near Pitlochry to house the books and memorabilia of his father. This house, which he liked to call 'The Shed', was a large wooden structure with an observatory on the upper storey overlooking Loch Faskally and the hydroelectric scheme which he had first proposed in the early 1900s. He now returned to an earlier interest, from 1906 to 1930 delivering the David Elder lectures on astronomy at the Royal Technical College in Glasgow. Forbes received many honours, including the Russian order of St George (for his services during the Russo-

Turkish War) and the French Légion d'honneur. He was elected FRS in 1887. He was also FRSE, FRAS, and a member of the Institution of Civil Engineers, the Vienna Astronomiches Verein, the Franklin Institute of Philadelphia, and the American Philosophical Society. He was elected a member of the Institution of Electrical Engineers in 1881, served on its council 1885–9, and was its vice-president in 1894–5. He received an honorary LLD from St Andrews.

Forbes did not marry and, in his last years, became something of a recluse. Though he was described in his obituaries as a man with a stern code of honour who thought much of his work and little of his reward, he seems to have been disillusioned that his obvious talents had earned him neither fame nor fortune (there is evidence that he had hoped at one point for a knighthood). He lived in increasing poverty, though in 1928 friends did successfully petition a variety of organizations for assistance on his behalf. His politics were Conservative and he is unlikely to have been comfortable with the developments of the Ramsay MacDonald era: indeed, in the 1920s he complained to a colleague that 'even the Tories are all damn socialists' (Duthie, 66).

Forbes published extensively. Titles included *The Transit of Venus* (1874), *Lectures on Electricity* (1888), *Alternating and Interrupted Electric Currents* (1895), *History of Astronomy* (1909), *Star Talks to Boy Scouts* (1911), *David Gill, Man and Astronomer* (1916), and *The Wonder and the Glory of the Stars* (1926), plus numerous contributions to the *Transactions* and *Proceedings* of the Royal Society, the Royal Astronomical Society, the Royal Society of Edinburgh, the Royal Society of Arts, the British Association, and various professional bodies. He died in an accident at his home, 13 New Parade, Worthing, on 22 October 1936. In 1987 the University of Strathclyde honoured his memory by naming a new student hall of residence after him.

JAMES McGRATH

Sources *WWW* · F. Duthie, 'Long life brushes—100 years', *Proceedings of the International Coil Winding Association* (1985), 65–76 · J. A. Fleming and D. W. Thompson, *Obits. FRS*, 2 (1936–8), 283–6 · G. L. Addenbrooke, *Proceedings of the Physical Society*, 49 (1937), 698–700 · *Nature*, 138 (1936), 830–31 · *Journal of the Institution of Electrical Engineers*, 79 (1936), 693 · *DNB* · *Worthing Gazette* (28 Oct 1936)
Archives RAS, letters to Royal Astronomical Society · U. St Andr. L., corresp. and papers | CUL, letters to Sir George Stokes · U. St Andr. L., James David Forbes MSS
Likenesses photograph, Strathclyde University Archives, Glasgow

Forbes, George Hay (1821–1875), Scottish Episcopal clergyman and liturgical scholar, was born on 4 August 1821 in York Place, Edinburgh, the ninth child in a family of four sons and six daughters of John Hay *Forbes, later Lord Medwyn (1776–1854), judge of the court of session, and his wife, Louisa (1779–1845), daughter of Sir Alexander Cumming Gordon of Altyre. His brother was Alexander Penrose *Forbes, the bishop of Brechin. In 1825 George became permanently disabled, probably due to poliomyelitis. With no formal schooling, he was tutored privately,

spending some years in France under orthopaedic specialists. He read extensively in the classics and became an accomplished linguist.

Forbes's family were leaders in the Scottish Episcopal church, and in 1846 he was a founder member of the Gaelic Tract Society in the church. He was ordained deacon in 1848 and priest in 1849. In 1848 he began his life's work—the mission in Burntisland, Fife. There he opened a day school in 1849 and built a parsonage in 1854. He planned a very large church, but only the baptistery was completed (in 1856). In 1869 he was elected to the Burntisland town council and he was later chosen as provost.

In 1852 Forbes began the Pitsligo Press as a vehicle for his own scholarship and for high-church theological views. He edited two series of periodicals aimed at Scottish Episcopalians, wrote a number of works on liturgical theology, contributed articles to the *Encyclopaedia Britannica* (1874–5), and produced editions of several medieval missals. He translated and edited a number of works, including those of St Gregory of Nyssa and Bishop Thomas Rattray. A frequent traveller to Europe, he corresponded with leading European scholars, including Cardinal Jean-Baptiste Pitra (the Vatican librarian), Charles de Montalembert (a leading French liberal Catholic), and Jacques Migne (the editor and publisher of patristic literature). In 1853 he married Eleanor Maria Irby, daughter of James Wemyss of Cariston, a major in the Scots Greys. It was a happy but childless marriage. They lived simply, most of their income going towards the building of the Burntisland church or the support of the printing press.

Forbes devoted much energy to championing the Scottish communion office, the eucharistic liturgy deriving from the 1637 Scottish Book of Common Prayer; he was one of the instigators and revisers of the controversial edition of 1850, issued by Patrick Torry, bishop of St Andrews. The edition was repudiated by a majority of the Scottish bishops as lacking the authority of the Scottish Episcopal church. Forbes's advocacy of the 1850 prayer book derived from his support for the liturgical and theological standards of the eighteenth-century non-juring Scottish Episcopal church. These he regarded as superior to the English Book of Common Prayer, and to the Tractarianism of his brother Bishop Forbes. He believed that lack of knowledge and support for the native non-juring traditions of the Scottish Episcopal church by contemporary Episcopalian clergy exposed the church to Anglicization and Tractarianism. These views also caused Forbes to oppose his brother when the latter was tried for heresy in 1860 over the corporeal presence of Christ in the eucharist. When in 1862 the general synod of the Scottish Episcopal church removed the Scottish communion office from its primacy of authority over the English Book of Common Prayer, Forbes took the Episcopal bishops to court, appealing as far as the House of Lords; he defended his case himself, but lost the action in 1867.

Forbes was the most knowledgeable liturgical scholar of his day in the Scottish Episcopal church, but his published work, and hence his influence, was reduced by an overstrained attention to detail and other scholarly opinion. A man of great personal charm, he was nevertheless stubborn and pugnacious towards those with whom he disagreed. He was one of the most important scholarly forces upholding Scottish traditions in the Scottish Episcopal church against the prevailing Anglicization of the nineteenth century.

Forbes died at the parsonage, Burntisland, on 7 November 1875 and was buried in the Warriston cemetery, Edinburgh, alongside his parents.   ROWAN STRONG

Sources W. Perry, *George Hay Forbes* (1927) · St Andrews UL, Forbes (George Hay) MSS · R. Strong, *Alexander Forbes of Brechin* (1995) · J. Wordsworth, *The episcopate of Charles Wordsworth, bishop of St Andrews* (1899) · J. B. Primrose, 'The Pitsligo Press of George Hay Forbes', *Edinburgh Bibliographical Society Transactions*, 4 (1960–74), 53–89 · W. Forbes, *Narrative of … Dame Christian Forbes* (1875) [Forbes genealogy] · parish register (baptism) Sts Paul's and George's Church, Edinburgh, 25 Sept 1821 · m. cert.
Archives NA Scot., corresp., literary and historical papers · U. St Andr. L., corresp. and papers | University of Dundee, Brechin diocesan archives
Likenesses engraving, repro. in Perry, *George Hay Forbes*, frontispiece
Wealth at death £19,150 6s. 9d.: confirmation, 3 Feb 1876, *CCI*

Forbes, George William (1869–1947), prime minister of New Zealand, was born at Norwich Quay, Lyttelton, New Zealand, on 12 March 1869, the third son of Robert Forbes, a sail maker and ship's chandler, and his wife, Annie Adamson. He attended the Lyttelton borough school and Christchurch Boys' High School (1882–3), after which he worked for a merchant in Christchurch and then in his father's business. In his spare time he studied the political history of Britain, joined a debating society, and took part in local Liberal politics.

A landmark in New Zealand settlement history was the subdivision of the 84,000 acre Cheviot Hills estate by the government in 1893–4. Forbes drew two sections, and family and neighbours helped him to become successfully established. On 12 December 1898 he married Emma Serena Gee.

Forbes took a leading role in local affairs. In 1902 he stood for the Cheviot electorate but was defeated by the official Liberal candidate. Nevertheless, he was appointed to the 1905 royal commission on crown lands, thus gaining a wider reputation. In 1908 he was elected as Liberal member for Hurunui. His enduring local popularity enabled him to hold the seat continuously until 1943.

As a back-bencher Forbes, the state leasehold Cheviot settler, was the embodiment of the Liberal tradition of the 1890s. However, in 1908 he was one of a diminishing group of leasehold Liberals opposing the freehold policy of W. F. Massey, leader of the Reform Party, who came to power in July 1912. In the course of the changeover Forbes was elected Liberal whip, which office he held until 1922.

After the war the Liberal Party was in retreat, caught between Reform and rising Labour, and without its long-time leader Sir Joseph Ward. In 1922 Forbes supported a change of name back to Liberal-Labour. His leader, T. M. Wilford, favoured fusion with Reform, and in 1925 Forbes led the Liberal delegation to an abortive joint conference.

Wilford announced that his party would take the name National, and then resigned.

The new party was hardly more than a Liberal rump, and there was no obvious successor to Wilford. Forbes was elected on 13 August 1925. His first electoral venture as party leader was a failure: in November 1925 National fell to eleven members and Forbes lost the leadership of the opposition to Labour. The party appeared to be in terminal decline.

The turnaround in Forbes's political fortunes during the next five years has few parallels in New Zealand or any other politics. He was the beneficiary of a remarkable succession of events. The sensational Reform victor of 1925, J. G. Coates, was by 1928 leading a seriously divided party. Labour scented victory but persisted in unpopular policies. In this developing political vacuum there reappeared the aged and ailing Ward as leader of the United Party, a revivified form of National. Forbes was elected as one of two deputy leaders. An unexpected election result gave United more seats than Reform or Labour.

United took office with Labour support, and Forbes became minister of lands and agriculture. Ward soon became seriously ill but would not give up the leadership. Forbes presided informally over cabinet. At last, in May 1930, Ward resigned. The United caucus narrowly elected Forbes as leader in preference to E. A. Ransom, and he was sworn in as prime minister on 28 May.

By this time New Zealand was in the grip of depression. Forbes supervised orthodox deflationary measures, waiting for something to turn up. In his absence at the 1930 Imperial Conference the ministry put through with Labour support an Unemployment Act which promised relief payments. On his return in 1931 Forbes abruptly announced that there would be no payout without work, thus precipitating a crisis with Labour. The break was complete when wages were cut by 10 per cent and the arbitration court was given power to lower award rates.

Paradoxically, Forbes was now kept in power with reluctant Reform support. Yet he had achieved a kind of popularity among business and farming leaders as Honest George, the courageous announcer of unpalatable truths. Coates had at least two opportunities to dislodge him by provoking a general election, but procrastinated.

An inter-party conference initiated by Coates attempted to draw up an agreed policy. Forbes bluntly announced that he was not prepared to commit political suicide as implementer of hard proposals, and he demanded a coalition to share responsibility, following the recent British example (August 1931). Forbes had driven Coates into a corner by sheer doggedness and use of his office; Coates now had no alternative but to go along with him.

The coalition government was formed on 22 September 1931. In revenge, Coates drove a hard bargain. Forbes sacrificed nine of his cabinet colleagues and Reform took over most of the chief portfolios—but not the chief office. This forced union, presented as national solidarity, was endorsed at the general election in December 1931.

Forbes supported the cautious policies of W. D. Stewart,

now minister of finance, but the downward spiral of unemployment and social misery continued. In April–May 1932 there were brief urban demonstrations and riots. Coates now put forward new and bolder solutions, especially the raising of the exchange rate, which would improve farmers' incomes. In January 1933 Coates got his way. Stewart resigned, though Forbes parted with him reluctantly.

From this point Coates, as minister of finance, was *de facto* head of government. Forbes continued to preside, but it was in Coates's shadow. He was overseas for long periods: in 1933 he attended the International Monetary and Economic Conference and in 1935 the dominion prime ministers' meeting during the silver jubilee celebration of George V.

In the landmark election of November 1935 Forbes's following was reduced to nineteen. For the first time he was elected in Hurunui on a minority vote. Defeat had a welcome side for him, as he was heartily sick of unpopular leadership. He was elected leader of the opposition and the New Zealand National Party (formed in May 1936), but only because a permanent new leader could not be agreed on. Forbes resigned from the leadership at the end of the 1936 session, though he retained his seat until 1943. He died at Crystal Brook, his Cheviot farm, on 17 May 1947, survived by his wife, two daughters, and a son, and was buried three days later at Homeview cemetery, Cheviot.

Stop-gap party leader three times, stop-gap prime minister twice, Forbes may qualify as the most unlikely head of government in New Zealand history. Power was not so much thrust upon him as acquired by default. Yet, if he did not have the qualities for the highest office, he had some political skills which made him a useful minister. He was an effective debater with a capacious memory who could marshal arguments on his feet. Once he had made a decision he stuck to it and remained imperturbable under attack. He could switch off from politics with a frequent cigarette or a visit to the cinema. Privately, he was a man of integrity and good humour, courteous and approachable both to fellow members and to constituents. However, his public image was severely tarnished by the depression policies which he approved and defended. By the 1930s he was a long way from the spirit of classic liberalism, being especially influenced by what he saw of British Conservative policies. New Zealand required a leader of vision and initiative in the depression of the 1930s, and Coates went some way towards fulfilling that need. Forbes was quite incapable of rising to the challenge: his stolid, slow-moving figure was completely outpaced by the speed of events.   W. J. GARDNER

Sources W. J. Gardner, 'Forbes, George William', *DNZB*, vol. 3 · A. H. McLintock, ed., *An encyclopaedia of New Zealand*, 3 vols. (1966) · M. Bassett, *Coates of Kaipara* (1995) · B. Farland, *Coates' tale* (1995) · M. Bassett, *Sir Joseph Ward: a political biography* (1993) · M. Bassett, *Three party politics in New Zealand, 1911–1931* (1982) · R. M. Chapman, *The political scene, 1919–1931* (1969) · B. Gustafson, *The first fifty years: a history of the New Zealand national party* (1986) · J. Wilson, *Cheviot: kingdom to county* (1993) · d. cert. · m. cert.

Archives Archives New Zealand, Wellington, governors' MSS · Archives New Zealand, Wellington, prime ministers' papers · University of Otago, Dunedin, Hocken Library, W. Downie Stewart MSS | FILM BFI NFTVA, news footage · Film Archive, Wellington, New Zealand | SOUND BL NSA, news recording · Radio New Zealand, archives
Likenesses F. O. Salisbury, charcoal and white chalk drawing (in court dress), NL NZ, Turnbull L. · photographs, NL NZ, Turnbull L.
Wealth at death £39,593 0s. 2d.: National Archives New Zealand, Christchurch

Forbes, Henry (1804–1859), organist and composer, was born in London. He studied with George Smart, Hummel, Ignaz Moscheles, and Henri Herz. He conducted the Società Armonica from 1827 to 1850, and was for some years organist of St Luke's, Chelsea. He published songs and a collection of four-part psalm tunes, *National Psalmody* (1843), containing some original numbers. His only opera, *The Fairy Oak*, was produced at Drury Lane on 18 October 1845 and condemned by the critics, but lasted for a week or two before being withdrawn. His oratorio *Ruth* was performed at the Hanover Square Rooms in 1847. He frequently gave concerts with his brother, George (1813–1883), organist of St Mary's, Bryanston Square, and composer of songs and organ and piano pieces. He died at his home, 3 Upper Belgrave Place, Pimlico, on 24 November 1859, leaving a widow, Ann Mary.

L. M. MIDDLETON, *rev.* JOHN WARRACK

Sources *New Grove* · Brown & Stratton, *Brit. mus.* · *CGPLA Eng. & Wales* (1860)
Wealth at death under £3000: probate, 7 Jan 1860, *CGPLA Eng. & Wales*

Forbes, James, second Lord Forbes (d. in or before 1462). See under Forbes family (*per. c.*1400–*c.*1490).

Forbes, James [Jacob] (1580–1656), merchant and army officer in the Swedish service, was the eldest son of Henry Forbes (d. 1605), a soldier, of Thainstone and Margaret Forbes, eldest daughter of William Forbes of Corse and Susanna Stauchan. James was born in Thainstone, Aberdeen and probably arrived in Sweden with his father and brother Peter (also known as Patrick) about 1600. Henry Forbes served in the Swedish army under Karl IX and was killed in September 1605 at the battle of Kirkholm in Livonia. Peter moved to Schönewalds in Prussia where, in 1634, he served as the factor for the Swedish forces in Germany. James Forbes remained in Sweden after his father's death and went on to become a merchant for Gustav II Adolf. By August 1624 he received all the privileges of a burgess of Stockholm when he became a citizen there.

Perhaps surprisingly for a man of forty-six, James Forbes (who was known as Jacob in Sweden) decided to enter military service. The motivation behind the career change remains unclear. None the less he enlisted as a private in the Narke–Värmlands regiment in 1626 and in the following year he was promoted lieutenant. This rapid rise in rank is suggestive of some earlier military experience although there is as yet no evidence for this. Forbes's progress through the ranks continued and by 1628 he became a captain for a company of Värmlanders before transferring to the Södermanlands regiment in 1628 or 1629. During this period Forbes had occasion to undertake business with the Riksråd (the Swedish state council) in his capacity as a burgess of Stockholm. These matters, which showed that he maintained his civic and trading interests, included inquiries regarding shipping and complaints against the overvaluation of Swedish currency.

Forbes applied to Charles I for evidence of his noble origins which would allow him to become ennobled in Sweden. A letter from Charles I authenticating the nobility of 'Jacob and Patrick Forbes de Thainstone' dated 1629 still survives in the library in the city of Lund. James's application for ennoblement in Sweden proved successful. In 1630 the Riksråd prepared an open letter on Forbes's behalf and the year 1631 saw him naturalized, ennobled and introduced into the Swedish nobility. Things progressed at a slower pace for Peter Forbes, who did not become naturalized as a Swedish nobleman until March 1651.

Despite his elevation in Swedish society there is some evidence to suggest that James Forbes found himself in conflict with Colonel Alexander Forbes, master of Forbes. A letter of recommendation for Alexander Forbes addressed to Queen Kristina in January 1636 contains reference to a dispute between Alexander and a James Forbes already in Swedish service. The details are not given, only that the dispute is a private matter which the master of Forbes hoped the queen could help resolve. No evidence has been found that there was any other James Forbes of sufficient status to warrant a request for royal intervention.

James Forbes remained active in the Swedish army despite his increasing years. In 1647 he served as a colonel for one of the few recruited Scottish regiments still in Swedish service, probably that of his kinsman William Forbes. The peace of Westphalia in 1648 reduced the need for military commanders within Sweden. By the time of renewed hostilities against Poland in 1655 Forbes was well beyond his military prime. He died on 17 June 1656 in Lund after a distinguished civic and military career. A tomb decorated with his coat of arms was erected for his body in Funbo church in Lund. James married Lillieram Chesnecopherus although the date of their wedding has not been established. Their children included Peter, Olof, Jacob and Henrik (twins), Johan, Nils, and at least four daughters. They in turn had children, and the military muster rolls and university matriculation records of Sweden and Finland are replete with the names of the progeny of James Forbes of Thainstone.   STEVE MURDOCH

Sources G. Elgenstierna, *Den introducerade svenska adelns ättartavlor med tillägg och rättelser*, 9 vols. (1925–36), vol. 2 · A. Tayler and H. Tayler, eds., *The house of Forbes*, Third Spalding Club, 8 (1937), 402, 470 · N. A. Kullberg, S. Bergh, and P. Sondén, eds., *Svenska riksrådets protokoll*, 18 vols. (Stockholm, 1878–1959), vols. 1–2 · *Rikskansleren Axel Oxenstiernas skrifter och brefvexling*, 15 (Stockholm, 1956), 23 · T. A. Fischer [E. L. Fischer], *The Scots in Sweden* (1907), 128, 215

Forbes, James (1628/9–1712), nonconformist minister, was born in Scotland of unknown parents. He was educated at King's College, Aberdeen, where he graduated MA in 1648. According to later evidence he probably left Scotland in 1653, and his degree was incorporated at Oxford University on 31 May 1654. After preaching for several Sundays in a parish which wanted him to become its minister, but which he did not name, Forbes wrote:

> I could not accept the call to be a parochial minister, for if I received the parish maintenance from all, all would expect to have me baptize their children, and administer the Lord's Supper to all according to long custom. This was against my conscience. (*Pastoral Instruction*, 7)

Fortunately, on 25 August 1654 he was appointed preacher or lecturer in Gloucester Cathedral, an employment which carried no parochial charge and which was paid for by the state out of the cathedral revenues plus the revenues from St Mary Crypt. However, within a year of his arrival in Gloucester he was approached by several people to become their pastor. Eventually Forbes relented and became pastor of a congregational church which met in the great hall of Edward Fletcher's house near the little cloister in the cathedral precincts. It was in his capacity as a minister that in 1657 he signed a remonstrance from Gloucestershire churches asking Cromwell not to accept the crown. He was confirmed as preacher at the cathedral by order of council on 18 September 1657 and in the following year was present at the Savoy conference which he later described as 'a kind of heaven upon earth, I think, to all who were present' (Nuttall, 'George Whitfield's "Curate"', 371). Forbes invited Increase Mather to Gloucester, and he stayed there with Forbes in 1659–60. In 1660 Fletcher's will left the reversion of his house in trust to Forbes and five members of the congregation.

Forbes was ejected from the cathedral in 1660, although Dean Frampton, later bishop of Gloucester, 'courted him to conformity in vain' (*Nonconformist's Memorial*, 2.250). He continued to preach in Gloucester and suffered two spells of imprisonment. With the consent of his congregation he then left for London. In January 1664 he was reported to be living as a shoemaker in Clapham, Surrey, and collecting money to finance the publication of a work by Ralph Wallis, 'the cobler of Gloucester'. Following his arrest, he was examined on 1 October 1664, when he had to explain away the presence in his home of such works as *Sufferers' Catechism*. He remained in London during the plague and the great fire.

Forbes had returned to Gloucester by 25 May 1672 when a licence was issued for a congregational meeting at the house of Samson Bacon. A further licence was issued in February 1673 for Forbes to teach in the barn of Charles Eliot of Stinchcombe. When persecution resumed he was able to find a niche (possibly at Stinchcombe) where he remained for five years. With the more propitious circumstances of the later 1670s he again returned to Gloucester, where his congregation was over a hundred strong, and in 1677 he wrote of it being 'marvellously preserved' (*Calamy rev.*, 205). The tory reaction again led to his imprisonment, but the first earl of Anglesey wrote on his behalf to the mayor of Gloucester to try to ensure that after his six-month term of imprisonment he would not be prosecuted again. According to Bishop Frampton of Gloucester, Forbes, 'once a Presbyterian, afterwards an Independent, but always a sectary, in Cromwell's time, and ever since' (ibid.), was released and moved outside the city to preach at a house owned by Lord Craven, presumably Elmbridge Court, but Craven intervened to prevent him. However, Frampton still could not silence Forbes, calling him 'the source of all the schisms that we have had in and about Gloucester' (ibid.). Forbes and his family moved back to Gloucester in 1687 to take advantage of James II's religious policies. His wife, Mary, was buried in St Michael's Church on 17 August 1687. In the early 1690s Forbes was training students for the ministry (including two of his grandchildren), supported the Happy Union of Independents and Presbyterians, and was the moderator of an association of ministers in Gloucestershire, Somerset, and Wiltshire. He also became engaged in a pamphlet controversy with local Quakers, who denounced him as a false witness.

In 1699 Barton Street meeting-house was built for Forbes, and he continued to preach there until his death. His last sermon to ministers in Gloucestershire was delivered at Stroudwater on 19 June 1711, but he continued to preach until shortly before his death. He died in Gloucester on 31 May 1712, aged eighty-three, and was buried on 3 June under the communion table of Barton Street meeting-house. His funeral sermon was preached by Isaac Noble, a congregational minister in Bristol. Forbes bequeathed his large library of 1300 printed books, 300 pamphlets, and other manuscript material in trust for the benefit of dissenting ministers in Gloucestershire.

STUART HANDLEY

Sources Calamy rev., 204–5 · VCH Gloucestershire, vol. 4 · The nonconformist's memorial … originally written by … Edmund Calamy, ed. S. Palmer, [3rd edn], 2 (1802), 249–51 · A. Gordon, ed., Freedom after ejection: a review (1690–1692) of presbyterian and congregational nonconformity in England and Wales (1917) · P. Heyworth, James Forbes, nonconformist: his library (1968) · Pastoral instruction: being some remains of the Reverend James Forbes (1713) · W. Lloyd, A brief account of the foundation and history of the protestant dissenting meeting-house in Barton Street, Gloucester (1899) · [T. G. Crippen], 'Origin of the Congregational Fund Board', Transactions of the Congregational Historical Society, 5 (1911–12), 134–48 · G. F. Nuttall, 'George Whitfield's "Curate": Gloucestershire dissent and the revival', Journal of Ecclesiastical History, 27 (1976), 369–86 · CSP dom., 1663–4; 1680–81 · Original letters and papers of state addressed to Oliver Cromwell … of Mr. John Milton, ed. J. Nickolls (1743), 139–41 · A. T. S. James, 'The Forbes Library Southgate Chapel, Gloucester', Transactions of the Congregational Historical Society, 10 (1927–9), 100–04 · G. F. Nuttall, 'Assembly and association in dissent, 1689–1831', Councils and assemblies, ed. G. J. Cuming and D. Baker, SCH, 7 (1971), 289–309 · Foster, Alum. Oxon.
Archives University of Toronto, Thomas Fisher Rare Book Library, sermons, letters, and notebooks

Forbes, James (1749–1819), author and traveller, was born on 8 May 1749, the eldest of five children of Timothy Forbes, merchant, of Coleman Street in the City of London. After a three-year course in 'common figures and merchants' accounts', at Hadley, Middlesex, Forbes sailed in March 1765 for Bombay as an East India Company writer. In 1772 he was appointed member of council at

Anjengo. In 1775 he officiated as chaplain, later secretary, attached to British forces sent to assist Raghunath Rao in the Maratha civil wars. For his health he embarked for England on 1 December 1775. He returned to India in 1777, having been promised the first vacancy at Broach. A beloved sister, Elizabeth (1753–1812), accompanied him, and in that same year married his intimate friend and colleague John Dalton (b. 1748). Dalton's sudden death in 1785 was an enduring grief. As collector at Dabhoi, Forbes became entranced with the region. To his mortification, following the 1782 treaty of Salbai, the East India Company evacuated Gujarat and in Forbes's words, 'the peasants on her luxuriant plains were abandoned to Mahratta despotism' (Forbes, Oriental Memoirs, 3.347). Although he complained that 'no compensation nor place of emolument was offered to the civil servants exiled from Guzerat' (ibid., 404), he appears to have retired with a fortune. Forbes and the Daltons travelled to the Malabar coast, then embarked for England, where they landed at Portsmouth on 17 July 1784.

During his Indian career James Forbes wrote lavishly illustrated letters, in line or colour, describing the flora, fauna, manners, religions, and archaeology of the west coast of India. These, which included places touched at on his voyages, were later to form the basis of Oriental Memoirs, a remarkable source book for the west coast of India, published at his own expense in four volumes between 1813 and 1815. A fervent Anglican, he had already published separately what became the last chapter of Oriental Memoirs, Reflections on the Character of the Hindoos (1810), in which he favoured the conversion of the Hindus to Christianity, thereby entering the current evangelical debate. He settled in Great Stanmore, Middlesex, where Dalton's brother was rector, and married, on 31 May 1787 at St Marylebone, Middlesex, Rosée (1757–1809), daughter of Joseph Gaylard of Stanmore. Their only child, Elizabeth Rosea, was baptized there on 27 April 1788. He also had a house in Albemarle Street, London. Forbes enlarged their house, Stanmore Hill (built by the duke of Grafton), in the Palladian style. He improved the gardens and built a small temple to Friendship to display the Hindu sculptures which, to the Brahmans' surprise, but with their acquiescence, he had retrieved from the ruins in Dabhoi. They are almost certainly the earliest known collection of Hindu deities in England. (Remains of the temple were rediscovered in 1992.)

Forbes travelled extensively in Britain, writing illustrated descriptive letters. In 1796–7 with a 'learned and intimate friend', probably the bookseller and bibliographer James Edwards, he travelled to Italy through Germany. In Rome he was elected to the whimsical literary society, the by now cosmopolitan Arcadi, and commissioned from his friend Angelica Kauffman Religion, a large allegorical painting. In 1800 he completed a six-year task, the collection of all his manuscripts and art works, which were bound into 150 volumes, comprising 52,000 folios, dedicated to his daughter. (The collection was dispersed in 1966.) In 1801 he was elected to the Society of Antiquaries and in 1803 was made a fellow of the Royal Society (sponsored by William Hamilton, James Rennel, John Townley, and William Marsden). During the peace of Amiens he set off for the Netherlands and France with his wife and daughter, intending to complete the latter's education. On arrival in Paris, war having been resumed, he found English residents already prisoners of war, but they were permitted to visit his only brother, Charles, who was staying near Tours, before being interned with their compatriots at Verdun. His *Letters from France* (2 vols., 1806), although stilted, are of considerable interest, especially in the descriptions of his less than arduous captivity. After a year the family was released when Sir Joseph Banks, president of the Royal Society, appealed to the president of the Institut National. Forbes's passport at this time detailed his high white forehead, aquiline nose, and full oval face.

In 1809 Forbes's daughter, Elizabeth, married Major Marc René de Montalembert, member of an old Poitou family, who, escaping the terror, had joined the British army. Their son Charles Forbes Montalembert (the future liberal Catholic writer) was born the following year. While his mother followed the flag and her husband, the infant was left in the care of his grandfather, who devoted himself to his upbringing. On 6 March 1815, following the death of his sister Elizabeth Dalton, and for reasons partly financial, the widowed Forbes sold Stanmore Hill. From 1816 he and his grandson spent almost two years in Paris with the Montalemberts. In 1819, when Montalembert was appointed French ambassador to Württemberg, they set out for Stuttgart. However, at Aix-la-Chapelle, where his daughter had come to meet them, James Forbes sickened and died of a 'lingering and painful illness' on 1 August 1819. He was buried on 31 August at St John's, Stanmore. His estate, although depleted by loans to his daughter and other relations and by the purchase for £6000 of an extinct Montalembert title for his son-in-law, provided £4000 for the education of his eldest grandson as well as annuities for all his relatives.   ANNE BULLEY

Sources J. Forbes, *Oriental memoirs*, 4 vols. (1813–15) · J. Forbes, *Letters from France with a particular account of Verdun and the situation of the British captives*, 2 vols. (1806) · J. Forbes, *Ricordanza: memoir of Elizabeth Dalton* (privately printed, London, 1813) · J. Forbes, 'The campaign on behalf of Ragonath Row 1775', BL OIOC · J. Forbes, 'Journal of an European tour, 1796–7', McGill University, Montreal, dept. of rare books · M. Oliphant, *Memoir of count de Montalembert: a chapter of recent French history*, 2 vols. (1872) · *London Ambulator* (1820), 292 · J. Ingamells, ed., *A dictionary of British and Irish travellers in Italy, 1701–1800* (1997) · P. Rohatgi, R. J. Godrej, and R. Mehrotra, eds., *Bombay to Mumbai: changing perspectives* (1997) · J. Fisch, 'A solitary vindicator of the Hindus: the life and writings of General Charles Stuart', *Journal of the Royal Asiatic Society of Great Britain and Ireland* (1985), 35–57 · F. Gerard, *Angelika Kauffman* (1892) · writers' petitions, BL OIOC, J/1/5, fol. 258 · will, PRO, PROB 11/1620, sig. 418 · *GM*, 1st ser., 89/2 (1819), 179 · parish register, 1819, Stanmore, Middlesex · *Company of musicians* (1865)
Archives BL OIOC, journal · McGill University, Montreal, rare books and special collections division, journal of European tour · Oscott College, Birmingham, Oriental memoirs · priv. coll. · University of Rochester, New York, Rush Rhees Library · Yale U. CBA
Likenesses Bate, stipple, 1812 (after D. B. Murphy), BM, NPG; repro. in Forbes, *Oriental memoirs* · J. Blood, engraving, repro. in *European Magazine* (1816) · J. Murphy, portrait (after engraving by J. Blood, 1816), NPG, Heinz Library · plaster medallion (after J. Tassie), Scot. NPG
Wealth at death legacies and annuities to all relatives and servants, incl. £4000 in trust for grandson's education: will, proved, 16 Sept 1819, PRO, PROB 11/1620, sig. 418

Forbes, James (1779–1837), military surgeon and physician, was born at Aberdeen, and received his MA at Marischal College, Aberdeen. He then studied medicine at the University of Edinburgh, where he graduated MD in 1803. In the same year he entered the army as assistant surgeon to the 30th regiment, and subsequently to the 15th hussars. He became surgeon to the 95th regiment in 1809, and staff surgeon in the same year. In that capacity he participated in the retreat from Corunna, and immediately after accompanied the expedition to Walcheren, where he was commended for his abilities and zeal during the disastrous outbreaks of intermittent fever and other camp sickness. He then returned to service in the Peninsula, and, after being praised by the duke of Wellington, received the rank of physician to the forces.

After the peace Forbes was appointed by the director-general of the Army Medical Service to take charge of the large hospital built at Colchester for the sick and wounded from the field of Waterloo. He then became superintendent of the Chelsea Hospital and, later, medical director at Chatham. In 1822 he was promoted to the rank of deputy inspector-general of hospitals and returned to foreign service in the West Indies. He was then transferred to Nova Scotia, and later to Canada, where he was principal medical officer. In 1829 he was appointed principal medical officer in Ceylon, from which he returned to England in 1836 in a state of bad health. He was then promoted to the rank of inspector-general of hospitals, and later appointed superintendent of the army medical department in India. However, ill health made it impossible for him to take this post.

Forbes died on 7 November 1837 at Maddox Street, Regent Street, London. On 22 November he was buried in Rochester Cathedral. Forbes was remembered by contemporaries as a 'remarkable man', who had 'quickness of perception, sound judgement and a great knowledge of human nature, combined with mild and conciliatory manners, and a high sense of honour' (*GM*, 211).

CHARLES CREIGHTON, *rev.* JEFFREY S. REZNICK

Sources *GM*, 2nd ser., 9 (1838), 210–11
Likenesses T. Brisley, relief bust, Rochester Cathedral

Forbes, James David (1809–1868), physicist and geologist, was born on 20 April 1809 at 86 George Street, Edinburgh, youngest son and sixth child of Sir William Forbes of Pitsligo, seventh baronet (1773–1828), banker, and Williamina Belsches (1777–1810), sole child and heir of John Belsches of Invermay, Perthshire, afterwards Sir John Belsches Stuart of Fettercairn, Kincardineshire. Forbes was a delicate child and had the misfortune to have his mother die when he was little over eighteen months old. The result was an isolated and overprotected early education, which was carried on at home and from April 1818 also partly by private tuition from Robert Hunter, parish schoolmaster at Colinton. This, together with his tory,

James David Forbes (1809–1868), by Thomas Faed

Episcopalian, and aristocratic family background, laid the foundation of his later Conservative, superior, aloof, but also responsible and high-minded attitudes and opinions.

In November 1825 Forbes entered Edinburgh University to take most of the subjects of the standard course, which comprised both arts and sciences, although he did not attend in session 1826/7, which he spent with his family touring abroad, mostly in Italy. At university he showed a particular aptitude for physics, in which he twice, in 1828 and 1829, gained the class medal. In 1828 he also gained the class medal in moral philosophy. After completing his arts course (like the majority of his contemporaries he did not bother to fulfil the formality of graduation), he turned to the study of law and in July 1830 he was admitted to the Faculty of Advocates. But he was never to practise because meanwhile his real interest was being demonstrated in a series of scientific articles derived from his Italian tour, which he contributed from 1827 to the *Edinburgh Journal of Science*. These so impressed the editor, David Brewster, that he proposed Forbes in 1829 for the fellowship of Edinburgh Royal Society. His election was delayed until January 1831, after he had reached the minimum age of twenty-one.

By this time Forbes had determined on a scientific career and he became a keen and enthusiastic figure in the movement towards the foundation of the British Association for the Advancement of Science, which he actively supported to the end of his life. In April 1831 he went to London to meet and make himself known to the scientific

establishment and in May and June he visited Cambridge and Oxford. The Cambridge visit, where he met Whewell, Sedgwick, Airy, and Peacock, had a profound effect on his future thinking and interests and he formed particular friendships with Whewell and Airy.

In September, at the inaugural meeting at York of the British Association, Forbes undertook to prepare a report on the progress of meteorology for the next (Oxford) meeting, having already begun a personal meteorological diary in January 1827 and published several papers on the subject. In July 1832 he was elected FRS, having left for his first major scientific journey to the continent, travelling up the Rhine to Switzerland with Professor Louis Necker and armed with a large number of introductions to Italian scientists. The sudden death, in November, of John Leslie, the Edinburgh professor of natural philosophy, brought him immediately home to find that his brothers and uncle had already taken up the canvass on his behalf. His only real opponent was his scientific patron, David Brewster, but political influence counted for more than scientific achievement and Forbes was elected in a tory triumph as professor of natural philosophy by twenty-one votes to nine. Forbes's ill-judged and largely unavailing attempts to rally scientific support lost him friends including Brewster, but the two men were later reconciled.

Forbes prepared for his first course of lectures, which he delivered in session 1833/4, by taking lessons in elocution from Mrs Siddons, and he entered on a period of prodigious activity, lecturing and researching. Some of his researches entailed travelling over much of Britain and a great deal of western Europe. In the course of these travels he performed many pedestrian and mountaineering feats, including ascents of Sgurr Alasdair in the Cuillins of Skye in 1836 and of the Jungfrau in the Alps in 1841. His teaching and research were both influenced heavily by his Cambridge visit and contacts. He greatly increased the mathematical content of his courses and introduced written examination papers into a system which had relied largely on oral examination. Although he had to argue hard for his exams against colleagues such as Sir William Hamilton, who contended that the new system passed students who would never have passed the oral test, Forbes won the day and the new examinations became universal. In compliment to his advocacy Forbes was made dean of the faculty of arts in 1837. Forbes took great pains with his teaching and ensured that his department was furnished with an excellent collection of scientific apparatus, but does not appear to have been particularly interested in individual students. He could however spot promising ones—he retained among his papers exercises by three of them, James Clerk Maxwell, Peter Guthrie Tait, and Alexander Carnegie Kirk.

Although Forbes published on a range of geophysical topics, the chief research of his early years, on the polarization of heat, was inspired by the Cambridge advocates of Fresnel's wave theory. He had begun to investigate radiant heat phenomena in 1830 and after contact with Macedonio Melloni, who had detected the refraction of thermal radiation, he acquired in 1833 with Melloni's assistance a thermopile for his own use. With this instrument in November 1834 Forbes discovered the polarization of radiant heat and later he demonstrated the double refraction of thermal radiation and in 1836 he found that heat could be circularly polarized. He thus demonstrated the identity of the laws that regulate the phenomena of radiant heat and light, making an important contribution to the development of the concept of a continuous radiation spectrum. For these discoveries he received the Keith medal of the Royal Society of Edinburgh and in 1838 the Rumford medal of the Royal Society of London. From November 1840 until his resignation in November 1860 he served as general secretary of the Royal Society of Edinburgh.

After the Glasgow meeting of the British Association of 1840 Forbes met Louis Agassiz and agreed to visit the Aar glacier with him the following summer. This gave his interests a new turn. Immediately after his return from the Aar he wrote the first of his papers on glaciers, plunging into a controversy which was to continue beyond his lifetime. Agassiz felt that Forbes had not only withheld credit for his previous work but had published Agassiz's ideas as his own and had also purloined the work of Louis Rendu, an earlier writer on the subject. Forbes's confrontational approach did him little good especially as the whole subject became tied up with scientific disagreements about glacier theory, where Forbes's chief British opponent was John Tyndall. Forbes spent four months the following year conducting experiments on the Swiss glaciers to be followed by further visits in subsequent years and in 1851 a tour of the glaciers of Norway. The result was a stream of some forty publications on the subject over the next twenty years. The chief of these were *Travels through the Alps of Savoy* (1843), *Norway and its Glaciers* (1853), and a collection of his most important glacier papers, *Occasional Papers on the Theory of Glaciers* (1859). His reputation as a mountain man is commemorated in the naming of the Aiguille Forbes in the Alps and of Mount Forbes in both Canada and New Zealand.

Between 1841 and 1851 Forbes made detailed observations of glacier ice velocities across the surface, and at depths, and at different times of the day and different seasons of the year, and proposed what he called the viscous or plastic theory of glacier motion. He claimed that his data demonstrated that glaciers flowed as if they were composed of viscous fluids. He also explained the veined or ribboned structure of the ice, now called foliation, as created by stresses within the glacier. Forbes used the terms viscous, plastic, and semi-fluid indifferently, and did not resolve the question of how a brittle substance such as ice could flow viscously, but simply asserted on the basis of his observations that it did. Tyndall, who, in 1853, had already demolished a very inaccurate early piece of work by Forbes on the vibration of heated metals, in 1856 turned his attention to glaciers and dismissed Forbes's viscosity as apparent not real. Instead he proposed a theory of fracture and regelation to explain glacier motion, and he repeatedly accused Forbes of taking credit which belonged to Rendu. The argument between the two men and their respective supporters spread over many publications, displayed much more polemic than scientific argument should do, and only closed with the reprinting of Rendu's *Memoir* in 1874 by Forbes's son George. According to Rawlinson the modern view of glaciers is closer to that of Forbes than to that of Tyndall, and later experiments have shown that ice does display that genuine molecular plasticity or continuous deformation under stress ascribed to it by Forbes. However, as fracture and regelation undoubtedly occur in glacier flow, and other factors also contribute to glacier motion, neither man was wholly right or wrong.

Forbes says of the period from 1832 to 1842

> I travelled extensively at home and abroad ... those years were the very happiest of my life. The age of conscious physical power in pedestrian journeys and of mental power in connection with teaching and investigation filled the cup of worldly happiness and left me then nothing to wish for. I never for a moment thought of marriage, all my interests being preoccupied. (St Andrews University Library MS Deposit 7 Box 2.30)

On this evidence he married immediately he thought about it, asking, on 18 May 1843, Alicia (d. 1885), daughter of George Wauchope, a Leith merchant, to marry him and having the ceremony on 4 July. They had two sons and three daughters. George *Forbes (1849–1936) became a professor of physics and an electrical power engineer, and Edmund Batten (1847–1924) a civil engineer for South American railways. The latter was father of Air Chief Commandant Dame Katherine Jane Trefusis (Forbes) Watson-Watt (1899–1971). A spell of ill health shortly after his marriage caused Forbes to spend most of the period from July 1843 until September 1844 abroad. This episode, with his new responsibilities, seems to have caused him concern about his future and with an energy little characteristic of the seriously ill he mobilized influence to back an application for a civil-list pension. Although this was refused in 1844, £200 a year was granted in 1845 by Sir Robert Peel, whom he had visited in 1839.

Forbes was unwell in the early autumn of 1850, but it was in November of 1851 after his return from Norway that he began spitting blood and his health seriously declined. For the next two and a half years he was mainly at Clifton with his family to be under the care of Dr John Addington Symonds. He continued writing and in June 1853 received an honorary DCL at Oxford. Although he returned to Edinburgh in July to do some teaching, his health continued poor and the work of his chair was mostly carried out by assistants: James Sime, at first with help from Professor Philip Kelland, until 1856; Balfour Stewart until April 1859; and William Keith during his final session. Forbes had by now proved himself an original, able, accurate, and eloquent researcher, but he was greedy for recognition and put himself forward for some of the honours he received, indulging in a fit of pique at failing to get a second royal medal from the Royal Society in 1846 though he had already received it in 1843. Despite by this time being unable to do further research, Forbes continued to work at publishing his earlier results and as late as 1866 he received the Keith medal for the third time for a paper on the thermal conductivity of iron.

In October 1859 Forbes became a candidate for the supposedly less demanding post of principal of United College in the University of St Andrews, vacant by the translation of Sir David Brewster to be first principal of the newly reorganized University of Edinburgh. With the same dedicated exercise of influence applied in obtaining his chair he was successful in opposition to a unanimously supported local candidate and he was inducted on 10 December 1859. He did not resign his Edinburgh chair until the end of the teaching year in April 1860, when he received an honorary LLD.

Forbes was not a man to treat his new post as a sinecure. He took a minute interest in the business affairs of the college, and each session while he was able gave a number of gratuitous lectures. One student describes him as 'looking like an icicle', another as 'an arresting figure with his tall gaunt form, quick searching eyes, austere aspect and swift moving steps' (St Andrews University muniments M310), but there was little direct contact and many of his actions were inept. In 1862 Forbes led the successful majority to annul the matriculation of Elizabeth Garrett, who wished to take medical classes. His accusation against the professor of medicine, George Edward Day, that he had not acted like a gentleman in the matter was not calculated to make a friend. He annoyed the parishioners of St Leonards, who used the college chapel as their church, by initiating moves to make it look less like a Presbyterian kirk, and he did not mollify the students by trying to suppress the rowdy pageant which marked the end of their studies and which lampooned the professors. He failed when the disguised student he physically selected for discipline was revealed as Lord Haddo.

The main project of Forbes's principalship was the College Hall, opened in session 1861/2, a residential institution created with the explicit purpose of attracting back to St Andrews the sons of 'persons of the higher ranks' of Scottish society. This scheme prospered so well as a result of Forbes's aristocratic contacts that in 1867 it was decided to proceed with a new building. But by this time Forbes's health had declined so far that his presence at the ceremonial laying of the foundation stone on 20 April 1867 was the last official act of his principalship. He left St Andrews immediately thereafter and never returned. He went to the continent and finally to Clifton to be under the care of Dr Symonds. He resigned from the United College principalship on 15 November 1868; he died at 8 Princes Buildings, Clifton, on 31 December and was buried in the Dean cemetery, Edinburgh, on 5 January 1869.

R. N. SMART

Sources J. C. Shairp, P. G. Tait, and A. Adams-Riley, *Life and letters of James David Forbes* (1873) [incl. bibliography] · St Andrew's University, J. D. Forbes, corresp. and MSS, deposit 7, especially box 30 [brief summary of main events in life, 1822–66] · F. Cunningham, *James David Forbes: pioneer Scottish glaciologist* (1990) · St Andrew's University, muniments, senatus minutes, United College minutes, student reminiscences, UY 452; UC 400; M310 · J. Morrell and A. Thackray, *Gentlemen of science: early years of the British Association for the Advancement of Science* (1981) · D. B. Horn, *A short history of the University of Edinburgh, 1556–1889* (1967) · R. G. Cant, *The University of St Andrews: a short history*, 3rd edn (1992) · J. Tyndall, *Principal Forbes and his biographers* (1873) · *Theory of the glaciers of Savoy* by M. le Chanoine Rendu, translated by Alfred Wills, to which are added the original memoir and supplementary articles by P. G. Tait and John Ruskin, ed. G. Forbes (1874) · D. B. Wilson, 'The educational matrix: physics education at early Victorian Cambridge, Edinburgh, and Glasgow universities', *Wranglers and physicists: studies on Cambridge physics in the nineteenth century*, ed. P. M. Harman (1985), 12–48 · R. N. Smart and E. J. Hill, *An index to the correspondence and papers of James David Forbes (1809–1868): and also to some papers of his son, George Forbes* (1968) · J. S. Rowlinson, 'The theory of glaciers', *Notes and Records of the Royal Society*, 26 (1971), 189–200 · B. Hevly, 'The heroic science of glacier motion', *Osiris*, 2nd ser., 11 (1996), 66–86 · d. cert. · *St Andrews Gazette* (9 Jan 1869)

Archives NL Scot., family corresp. · U. Edin. L., lecture notes · U. St Andr. L., corresp. and papers | Alpine Club, London, letters to A. Goutier · Alpine Club, London, corresp. with Alfred Wills · BL, letters to Charles Babbage, Add MSS 37186–37200, *passim* · CUL, corresp. with Sir George Airy · CUL, corresp. with Lord Kelvin · CUL, letters to Sir George Stokes · GS Lond., letters to Sir R. I. Murchison · NL Scot., letters to John Lee · RS, corresp. with Sir John Herschel · Trinity Cam., corresp. with William Whewell · U. Edin. L., corresp. with Sir Charles Lyell · U. Edin. L., letters to Thomas Jameson Torrie

Likenesses J. G. Tunny, photograph, c.1855, U. St Andr. L. · J. Watson-Gordon, oils, 1860, Royal Society of Edinburgh · J. Adamson, photograph, c.1864, U. St Andr. L. · J. Wilson, oils, 1870, U. St Andr. · T. Faed, wash drawing, Scot. NPG [*see illus.*] · photographs, U. St Andr. L.

Forbes, James Ochoncar, eighteenth Lord Forbes (1765–1843)

Forbes, James Ochoncar, eighteenth Lord Forbes (1765–1843), army officer, the eldest son of James, seventeenth Lord Forbes (c.1725–1804), and his wife, Catherine (d. 16 April 1805), only daughter of Sir Robert Innes, sixth baronet, of Ortoun, was born on 7 March 1765. The lands of Forbes in Aberdeenshire had been held by this ancient family since the reign of William the Lion (1165–1214). Forbes entered the army as ensign in the Coldstream Guards on 13 June 1781; he became lieutenant and captain on 21 April 1786, captain and lieutenant-colonel on 23 August 1793, and colonel on 3 May 1796, major-general on 29 April 1802, lieutenant-general on 27 March 1808, and general on 12 August 1819.

Forbes served in Flanders with his regiment, and was at the battles and sieges of St Amand, Famar, Valenciennes, Durkirk, Lincelles, Tournai, Vaux, Cateau, Nijmegen, and Fort St André. He accompanied the expedition to The Helder, and was at nearly every action. He was appointed second in command of the troops in the Mediterranean in March 1808, and that year sailed for Sicily. He was colonel, 3rd garrison battalion, 1807–9, 94th foot on 14 April 1809, 54th foot on 23 September 1809, and 21st foot from 1 June 1816 until his death.

Forbes married at Crailing, on 2 June 1792, Elizabeth (1775–1830), eldest daughter and heir of Walter Hunter, of Polmood, Peeblesshire, and Crailing, Roxburghshire, and Lady Caroline Mackenzie, fourth daughter of George Mackenzie, third earl of Cromarty; they had ten children. Forbes succeeded his father on 29 July 1804, and was chosen a representative peer, a tory, in 1806. He was a baronet of Nova Scotia, and a knight of St Januarius of Sicily.

From 1825 until 1830 Forbes was high commissioner of the Church of Scotland. He died on 4 May 1843 at Bregenz, on Lake Constance, Austria, and was succeeded by his second son, Walter *Forbes, nineteenth lord. His eldest son, the Hon. James Forbes, master of Forbes (b. 1796), an officer in the Coldstream Guards in the Peninsula and at Waterloo, had died, unmarried, in February 1835.

RICHARD HOOPER, rev. ROGER T. STEARN

Sources GEC, *Peerage* · *Colburn's United Service Magazine*, 2 (1843) · private information (1889) · A. J. Guy, ed., *The road to Waterloo: the British army and the struggle against revolutionary and Napoleonic France, 1793–1815* (1990) · T. C. W. Blanning, *The French revolutionary wars, 1787–1802* (1996)
Archives NA Scot., corresp. and papers | BL, corresp. with Sir Robert Peel, Add. MSS 40230–40611
Likenesses J. Brown, stipple, pubd 1837 (after B. R. Faulkner), BM, NPG

Forbes, James Staats (1823–1904), railway administrator and art connoisseur, was born at Aberdeen on 7 March 1823, the eldest of the six children of James Staats Forbes, a member of a Scottish family long settled in England, and his wife, Ann Walker. A brother, William, became manager of the Midland Great Western Railway of Ireland, and was father of William, who was general manager of the London, Brighton, and South Coast Railway, and of the painter Stanhope Alexander *Forbes RA. Educated at Woolwich, Forbes showed early skill as a draughtsman, and in 1840 entered the office of Isambard Kingdom Brunel, who was then constructing the Great Western line. He joined the Great Western Railway (GWR) as a booking clerk at Paddington the following year and achieved rapid promotion in its service, reaching by successive steps the post of chief goods manager at Paddington. Forbes married on 20 August 1851 Ann (d. 1901), daughter of John Bennett. They had two daughters and two sons. Their sons were Duncan, who went on to work for the Great Indian Peninsula Railway, and William Alexander *Forbes (1855–1883), the zoologist.

In 1857 Forbes left the GWR to join the staff of the Dutch-Rhenish Railway in the Netherlands, then under British management, and soon rose to the post of general manager, bringing the line, then on the verge of bankruptcy, into a state of comparative success. On his retirement at the end of his five-year contract the directors partly retained his services as their permanent adviser until the railway's concession expired in 1890. In 1861 the directors of the London, Chatham, and Dover Railway (LCDR)—which had been formed by amalgamation in 1859 and was then in the hands of the receiver—appointed him general manager. By this time he had been offered, and had twice refused, the post of general manager of the Great Western Railway at a salary of £10,000.

Debt, confusion, pressing creditors, and lack of money menaced the London, Chatham, and Dover Railway, which was fighting for its very existence against two powerful neighbours, the South Eastern and the London, Brighton, and South Coast railways. Under Forbes's skilful and daring leadership the LCDR held its own, and in 1871 he joined the board of directors, succeeding in 1873 to the post of chairman, which he held jointly with that of

general manager until 1 January 1899. On the amalgamation, at that date, of the LCDR with the South Eastern, Forbes declined the chairmanship of the joint board, but acted as its adviser. In his management of the finances of his own company, his tact in presiding at meetings of shareholders, and the exceptionally good terms which he secured for the LCDR in the amalgamation, Forbes proved himself a skilled diplomatist of great ability.

He also restored the fortunes of another near bankrupt concern, the Metropolitan District Railway; he joined its board on 6 October 1870, was chairman from 28 November 1872 to 5 September 1901, and subsequently acted as advisory director until 17 February 1903. For twenty-five years (1870–95) the rivalry between Forbes, of the LCDR and the Metropolitan District Railway, and Sir Edward Watkin, of the South Eastern and the Metropolitan railways, was a source of anxiety to the shareholders on both sides, while yielding much profit to lawyers. This antagonism caused considerable damage to the railways concerned, and the communities they served, through the effects of wasteful, confusing, and inefficient competition. Forbes was at a great disadvantage, his opponent having control over two concerns which were solvent and successful and being himself a railway strategist of a high order. But for Forbes's suavity of temper and charm Watkin would probably have succeeded in crushing the two younger and poorer companies.

Forbes was connected with several other railways, most of them needing help to bring them out of difficulties. He was director and at one time deputy chairman of the Hull and Barnsley Railway, and financial adviser to the financially tottering Didcot, Newbury, and Southampton Railway; he was chairman of the Whitechapel and Bow Railway, and of the planned, but never built, Regent's Canal City and Docks Railway. His financial ability was widely in request, and at the height of his career he was chairman of three important electric light companies, a director of the Lion Fire Insurance Company, and president of the National Telephone Company; from many of these boards he retired towards the end of his life.

Although generally as parsimonious as his fellow railway managers, Forbes showed himself more ready than most to introduce improvements when convinced that they were worth their cost. He was prepared to invest in improved brakes and signalling on his railways, and produced a marked enhancement of the LCDR's cross-channel ferry services. Forbes excelled as an administrator on broad lines and in boldly taking an initiative, but had no taste for details. He was a frequent witness before parliamentary committees, and was a talented after-dinner speaker. In September 1873, at a by-election, he unsuccessfully contested Dover in the Liberal interest, but this was his sole effort in the political arena.

Forbes was much interested in art and, though his judgement was sometimes criticized by contemporaries, he enjoyed a considerable reputation as a collector. His large collection of works of nineteenth-century artists included many examples of the Barbizon school of mid-nineteenth-century Romantic landscape painters and works by contemporary Dutch artists. A selection was exhibited at the Grafton Gallery in May 1905, and a smaller exhibition, of which a printed catalogue appeared, was held in July 1908 at the Brighton Library and Art Gallery.

Forbes died on 5 April 1904 at his residence, Garden Corner, 13 Chelsea Embankment, London, and was buried on 10 April in the churchyard of West Wickham, Kent, where he had formerly lived.

CHARLES WELCH, *rev.* RALPH HARRINGTON

Sources *The Times* (6 April 1904) · *The Engineer* (8 April 1904) · *Railway Times* (9 April 1904) · T. R. Gourvish, 'Forbes, James Staats', *DBB* · T. R. Gourvish, 'The performance of British railway management after 1860: the railways of Watkin and Forbes', *Business History*, 20 (1978), 186–200

Likenesses H. von Herkomer, oils, 1881 · W. Orpen, oils, 1900, Man. City Gall. · G. C. Beresford, photograph, 1902, NPG · G. C. Beresford, two photographs, NPG · H. Furniss, pen-and-ink sketch, NPG · Pet, chromolithograph caricature, NPG; repro. in *Monetary Gazette* (24 Jan 1877), suppl. · Spy [L. Ward], chromolithograph caricature, NPG; repro. in *VF* (22 Feb 1900) · Trentenoir?, marble bust

Wealth at death £135,367 11s.: probate, 2 July 1904, *CGPLA Eng. & Wales*

Forbes, Dame (Katherine) Jane Trefusis [*married name* Dame (Katherine) Jane Watson-Watt] **(1899–1971)**, businesswoman and director of the Women's Auxiliary Air Force, was born on 21 March 1899 in the Chilean desert, the youngest of three children, and the second daughter, of Edmund Batten Forbes (1847–1924), civil engineer, and his wife, Charlotte Agnes Wauchope (*d.* 1958). Little is known about her schooling, except that part of it was conducted in London, but, whether it was learned or inherited, Jane Trefusis Forbes combined a lively and creative mind with formidable and tireless powers of organization and leadership, which served her well in both business and military environments. Her business career was successful and varied. A breeder of prize-winning Dandie Dinmont terriers, in the 1920s she founded Bell Mead kennels and canine nursing home. In the 1930s she combined work as managing director of this enterprise—by now a company—with managing a housing trust, Caroline Trust Ltd Estates. After the Second World War she revived her interest in housing as chairman of Draydonne Properties, and she branched out into the dry-cleaning industry, retiring as managing director of Davis Dry Cleaners in the 1960s.

However, it was in the military sphere that Jane Trefusis Forbes was particularly celebrated. Her military career started in 1916 when she joined the Women's Volunteer Reserve as a driver. The women's voluntary services were disbanded at the end of the war, but in 1934 German rearmament prompted women who had served in the First World War to prepare for a revival of their wartime role. In 1935 Jane Trefusis Forbes joined the Emergency Service, a voluntary Officers' Training Corps formed to train women for service in the event of a national emergency, and as senior cadet she played a key organizational role. The Emergency Service was renamed the Auxiliary Territorial Service (ATS) on receiving Army Council recognition in May 1938, and Trefusis Forbes served as chief

Dame (Katherine) Jane Trefusis Forbes (1899–1971), by Thomas Cantrell Dugdale, 1941

instructor at its school of instruction until, when the Air Council requested that some ATS companies be attached to RAF stations, she became company commander of no. 20 RAF (County of London) company, ATS. On 28 June 1939 the RAF finally took the plunge and formed its own independent women's service—the Women's Auxiliary Air Force (WAAF); two days later Jane Trefusis Forbes was appointed as its first, non-executive, director. The outbreak of war saw a distracted Air Ministry largely unencumbered by a coherent strategy for the organization and administration of the WAAF, and Trefusis Forbes needed all her powers of tact, diplomacy, and, on occasion, no small degree of cunning, to see that the service-women were clothed, accommodated, and trained, and to reconcile a host of often conflicting interests and needs while establishing the service on a firm organizational footing. The remarkable expansion of the service from 1734 at its mobilization to 181,835 at its peak in July 1943 stood as testament to her success. She firmly believed that the WAAF could only contribute to the war effort to the fullest extent and with the greatest efficiency if airwomen served on equal terms with airmen as an integral part of the RAF. In an atmosphere not always conducive to such an egalitarian agenda she worked tirelessly, and doggedly when need be, to expand the employment of service-women into skilled, technical trades, and into positions of authority and responsibility. She also looked beyond a purely wartime agenda: her 'progressive training' scheme to enhance airwomen's sense of themselves as citizens displayed an exceptional and creative long-term vision of women's role in the post-war world, and she gave considerable and detailed consideration to the problems that both service-women and -men might encounter on demobilization. She resigned as director in October 1943, convinced (incorrectly) that Air Ministry plans for the decentralization of the WAAF would diminish its overall efficiency. It was a further year before she retired from the service, however, having conducted a fact-finding mission to North America, India, Gibraltar, Ceylon, the Middle East, and the Far East. Her role as deputy director and then director of welfare services for the Allied Control Commission for Germany from 1946 to 1948 called on many of the skills she had displayed as director of the WAAF, and her work producing a welfare handbook, increasing the scope of leave centres in the British zone, and organizing cultural and sporting competitions did much to ease the difficulties faced by civilian staff in unfamiliar surroundings.

Slim, tall, a little plain, but always immaculate in uniform, Trefusis Forbes's austere appearance belied a charming manner. An impressive speaker with a commanding presence, she could inspire the loyalty and boost the morale of service-women of every rank, while those with whom she worked closely praised her colossal energy and drive, her originality of thought, and her outstanding organizing ability. Her interest in, affection for, and readiness to serve the RAF never diminished: after her retirement from the service she was vice-president of the WRAF Officers' Association and of the RAF Association (RAFA), deputy chairman of the RAFA executive, and a member of the RAFA council, the RAF Benevolent Fund council, and of numerous subcommittees. Her charitable interests included the national advisory council for the employment of the disabled, and the disabled advisory committee, Hammersmith. She was appointed CBE in 1941 and DBE in 1944, and in 1968 was awarded an honorary LLD by St Andrews University. On 10 March 1966, in a quiet ceremony at Kensington register office, she became the third wife of Sir Robert Watson-*Watt (1892–1973), the developer of radar, with whom she had worked during the war. She survived a coronary thrombosis in 1970, but died at their home in London, 7 Crescent Place, Brompton Road, Kensington, following a second heart attack on 18 June 1971.　　　　　　　　　　　　　　　TESSA STONE

Sources RAF Museum, department of research and information services, Hendon, London, K. J. Watson-Watt files, AC 72/17 · d. cert. · m. cert. · *The Times* (21 June 1971) · *The Times* (25 June 1971) · *WWW*, 1971–80 · *The Times* (11 March 1966) · *The Guardian* (27 June 1960) · B. E. Escott, *Women in air force blue: the story of women in the Royal Air Force from 1918 to the present day* (1989) · K. B. Beauman, *Partners in blue: the story of women's service with the Royal Air Force* (1971) · Air Ministry (AHB), *The women's auxiliary air force* (1953) · Burke, *Peerage* (1967)
Archives Royal Air Force Museum, Hendon, files, AC 72/17
Likenesses T. C. Dugdale, oils, 1941, Royal Air Force Museum, Hendon, London; on loan to RAF, Linton-on-Ouse [*see illus.*]
Wealth at death £211,765: probate, 1971

Forbes, John (*c.*1565–1634), Church of Scotland minister, was the third of seven sons of William Forbes of Corse, Aberdeenshire (*d.* 1598), an early protestant, and his wife, Elizabeth Strachan, daughter of Alexander Strachan of Thornton. Of his brothers, Patrick *Forbes, the eldest, became bishop of Aberdeen, William Forbes, the second, founded the family of Craigievar, and Arthur Forbes, the sixth, was father of the first earl of Granard.

John Forbes was educated at the University of St Andrews, where he graduated MA in 1583. In 1593 he was ordained minister of Alford, Aberdeenshire. He soon rose to distinction in the church, and when the privy council interfered with the proceedings of the synods of Aberdeen and Moray against the Catholic marquess of Huntly, the synods sent Forbes to London to seek redress from the king. In their letter to James they stated that Forbes had been specially chosen because of 'his fidelity and uprightness, and his sincere affection borne to the kingdom of God, his majesty's service and peace of the land' (*Original Letters*, 1, no. 7). He went to court in March 1605, was warmly received by the king, and succeeded in the object of his mission.

In July 1605 Forbes was elected moderator of the Aberdeen assembly, which was held in defiance of a royal command. When he and others were summoned before the privy council to answer for their disobedience they declined its jurisdiction, insisting that as the matter was spiritual it should be judged by the courts of the kirk. For this Forbes and five others were imprisoned in Blackness Castle, tried for high treason, found guilty by a packed jury, and banished from the king's dominions for life. They sailed from Leith for Bordeaux on 7 November 1606.

On reaching France, Forbes visited Boyd of Trochrig at Saumur, and then went to Sedan. He travelled much, visiting the reformed churches and universities in which many Scots then held professorships. In 1611 he was settled as pastor of a British congregation at Middelburg, and in the following year he and his brother Arthur, then an officer in the Swedish service, spent several weeks at Sedan with their kinsman Andrew Melville. Soon after this Forbes was offered release from banishment on conditions which he could not accept. In 1616 he was in London for several months and saw the king, who promised to revoke his sentence of exile, but this was not fulfilled. After a ministry of ten years at Middelburg, where he was greatly respected, he became pastor of the British church at Delft. In 1628 Charles I began to interfere with the worship and discipline of the English and Scots churches in the Netherlands, and Forbes was removed from his charge. He died and was buried in the Netherlands in 1634, aged about sixty-nine. He had married Christian, daughter of Barclay of Mathers. Two of his sons were colonels in the Dutch service, one of whom afterwards fought on the side of the covenanters. A third, Patrick *Forbes (*d. c.*1680), became bishop of Caithness, and a fourth, minister of Abercorn. His three daughters married in Scotland.

He was the author of *The Saint's Hope, and Infallibleness Thereof* (Middelburg, 1608); *Two Sermons* (Middelburg, 1608); *A Treatise Tending to the Clearing of Justification* (Middelburg, 1616); *A Treatise how God's Spirit may be Discerned from Man's Own Spirit* (London, 1617); *Four Sermons on 1 Tim. Vi. 13–*

16 (1635); *A Sermon on 2 Tim. Ii. 4* (Delft, 1642); *Certaine Records Touching the Estate of the Kirk in the Years MDCV & MDCVI* (Edinburgh, Wodrow Society, 1846).

G. W. SPROTT, rev. ALAN R. MACDONALD

Sources J. Forbes, *Certaine records touching the estate of the kirk in the years MDCV & MDCVI*, ed. D. Laing and J. Anderson, Wodrow Society, 19 (1846) · *Fasti Scot.*, new edn, 6.117–18 · *The autobiography and diary of Mr James Melvill*, ed. R. Pitcairn, Wodrow Society (1842) · D. Calderwood, *The history of the Kirk of Scotland*, ed. T. Thomson and D. Laing, 8 vols., Wodrow Society, 7 (1842–9) · M. Lumsden, *Genealogy of the family of Forbes*, ed. W. Forbes (1883) · T. M'Crie, *The life of Andrew Melville*, 2nd edn, 2 vols. (1824) · *Original letters relating to the ecclesiastical affairs of Scotland: chiefly written by … King James the Sixth*, ed. D. Laing, 2 vols., Bannatyne Club, 92 (1851) · A. R. Macdonald, *The Jacobean kirk, 1567–1625: sovereignty, polity and liturgy* (1998), 109–10, 116–17, 125–6

Forbes, John [*name in religion* Archangel] (**1570/71–1606**), Capuchin friar, was probably born at Druminnor, Aberdeenshire, the fifth child of John (1542–1606), master of Forbes and son of William, seventh Lord Forbes, and his first wife, Margaret Gordon (*c.*1544–1606), daughter of George, fourth earl of Huntly. Events during his early life are uncertain, although there was a long-standing and well-attested feud between the lords Forbes and the earls of Huntly, as each vied for supremacy in the north-east, aggravated by the Huntly Gordons remaining basically Catholic while John Forbes's father became a protestant protagonist. In addition, when her husband was imprisoned Margaret Gordon entered an adulterous liaison; he, granted a divorce in 1574, married again. At some point John's elder brother William went to Flanders and, after service with the duke of Parma, became a Capuchin in 1590 with the religious name of Archangel, but died in Ghent on 13 March 1592.

John Forbes went to Flanders in his early twenties and also entered the Capuchins, receiving the habit at Tournai on 2 August 1593 and taking the religious name Archangel. Political agents thought Forbes's flight was assisted by Huntly, and very possibly the Jesuit James Gordon, uncle of both Huntly and John Forbes, influenced the young man's Catholic commitment.

After his noviciate John made his religious vows at Tournai on 23 August 1594 and was sent to Lille, where he studied philosophy and theology. In November 1596 he petitioned Rome for release from his vows in order to support his mother in Scotland. This was refused, but about this time the pope granted leave for him to return to Scotland to help reconcile the Forbes and Gordon families. He did not go, but John's mother joined him at Lille; she accompanied him when in 1601 he was appointed vicar of the friary at Antwerp. In 1602 Forbes went to Dendermonde as guardian and was also *diffinitor* (assistant to the provincial superior). He did not, however, disappear entirely from the Scottish scene. Scottish Catholics wanted him to return and papal permission was obtained for this. His Capuchin superiors intended to send him as a missionary. Other, less friendly attempts were made, or at least feared; there were rumours of his imminent return and at least one impostor claiming to be Forbes arrived in Scotland. About 1603 he wrote to James VI, whom he had attended at

V. P. ARCHANGELVS. Scotus Capucinus Predicator. Viæ ejus viæ pulchræ, et omnes Semite illius pacificæ P....) Obijt anno Dñi 1606. Ætatis Suæ 36. conuerf. 13. die 2 Augusti.
J. Picart incidit.

John Forbes (1570/71–1606), by J. Picart, pubd 1623

court and in the field, urging him to embrace Catholicism.

On 1 January 1606 Forbes's mother died and was buried in the Capuchin church at Ghent, where William had been buried. When Scottish mercenaries arrived at Diksmuide in west Flanders, Forbes converted many to Catholicism. Plague broke out at Waasmunster, some miles distant from Dendermonde; Forbes tended the sick there and himself caught the plague. Taken back to Dendermonde he died on 4 August 1606, in his thirty-sixth year. He was buried at the Capuchin church there, though his body was later transferred to a Capuchin common grave.

In January 1594, when his father succeeded as eighth Lord Forbes, John became master of Forbes but apparently ceded his rights of inheritance to Arthur, son of his father's second marriage. Lord Forbes in 1598 made over the lordship to Arthur, who was subsequently named in documents as master of Forbes. In 1600 Arthur and John corresponded amicably about religious matters. Their father died on 29 June 1606, and Arthur succeeded as ninth lord. Peerage lists, with one exception, showed this until in 1907 John was inserted as ninth lord, being shown as holding the title for five weeks. Some see this as the wrong application of English law to a Scottish peerage.

Forbes's religious life exemplified two Capuchin characteristics of the time: zeal to combat protestantism and the fearless tending of plague victims. He had gained a reputation for holiness and already by 1612 a biography had been drafted by a fellow friar. Another friar, however, Faustinus of Diest, collected information for a new biography and sent it to the civic authorities in Antwerp, and it was proposed to take steps to have Forbes beatified by Rome. This came to nothing, but the biography, which received approval in 1614, was published in Latin in 1620; in 1623 an English translation by Robert Rookwood was included in a book of other lives. The work, though marred by the usual hagiographical faults, was based in part on personal knowledge and reliable sources. Its title was *Alter Alexius* (a second Alexis), Alexis being a fifth-century saint who, to escape an imminent marriage, fled the parental home. According to Faustinus, a marriage had been arranged for Forbes but he and his fiancée agreed that they were too young. He fled in disguise, reached Antwerp, and after dramatic dangers and hardships, became a Capuchin. Faustinus dramatized John and his mother as heroes suffering exile and penury for their Catholic faith. The book was translated into other languages and, not surprisingly, the story of John and his legendary Scottish namesake, Archangel Leslie, appeared together in some works.

MARK DILWORTH

Sources A. Tayler and H. Tayler, eds., *The house of Forbes*, Third Spalding Club, 8 (1937) · Faustinus Diestensis, *Alter Alexius* (Cologne, 1620) · *The life of … Fa. Angel of Joyeuse* (Douai, 1623) [Eng. trans. of *Alter Alexius*] · T. G. Law, 'The bibliography of the lives of two Scottish Capuchins', *Papers of the Edinburgh Bibliographical Society*, 1 (1890–91), 1–12 · *Scots peerage* · Father Cuthbert, *The Capuchins*, 2 (1928) · *CSP Scot., 1588–1603* · *Reg. PCS*, 1st ser., vols. 4, 6 · A. Bellesheim, *History of the Catholic Church in Scotland*, ed. and trans. D. O. H. Blair, 3 (1889), 408–10, 476–7 · P. Hildebrand, *De Kapucijnen in de Nederlanden en het Prinsbisdom Luik*, 10 vols. in 11 (Antwerp, 1945–56), vol. 7, p. 89; vol. 8, p. 584; vol. 9, pp. 779–82
Likenesses Audran, line engraving, NPG · J. Picart, line engraving, BM; repro. in *The life of … Fa. Angel of Joyeuse*, frontispiece of section on Forbes [*see illus.*] · portrait, Castle Forbes, Aberdeenshire; repro. in Tayler and Tayler, *House of Forbes*, facing p. 141

Forbes, John, of Corse (1593–1648), theologian, was born on 2 May 1593, the second son of Patrick *Forbes (1564–1635), laird of Corse and bishop of Aberdeen, and Lucretia, daughter of David Spens of Wormiston, Fife. He entered King's College, Aberdeen, in 1607. In 1612 he went to the continent, studying at Heidelberg under David Pareus; in 1615 he moved to Sedan where he studied under his kinsman Andrew Melville; he attended other continental universities also. About 1618 he went to Middelburg, where he quickly established a place in the community. He was licensed to preach in 1619 and on 23 July 1619 he married Soetjen (Zoetken) Roosboom (1599–1640), daughter of a Middelburg magistrate. The officiant and witness was his uncle John *Forbes of Alford, then minister of the Middelburg English congregation. He later married a certain Janet Turing (*d.* in or after 1654).

Forbes was subsequently ordained in Aberdeen, presumably by his own father, and on 27 April 1620 he became the first incumbent of the chair of divinity at King's College; he was created DD that same year. From November 1634 to November 1635 he was a minister at St Nicholas's Church in Aberdeen. He succeeded to his father's lairdship in 1635 and contributed a sermon and verses to *Funerals of a Right Reverend Father in God Patrick Forbes of Corse, Bishop of Aberdeen* (1635); it is likely that he also edited the volume.

Forbes was learned in Christian doctrine and history, and in classical and Hebrew scholarship. Beyond his academic qualifications he gained a reputation for his pious character, revealed in his diary 'Spirituall exercises', which he kept from 3 January 1624 until 22 July 1647. His prayerful and introspective piety was similar to that of his presbyterian antagonists, typified by a cycle of emotional highs and lows. The diary chronicles his 'fearful wrestlings and comfortable victories through Christ' and records a number of personal covenants with God: 'the Covenant serveth to waken me to the careful avoyding of sin'. His spiritual counsel was valued by his students. One came to him on 3 February 1624 concerned about his hardness of heart and 'intreated me for some word of comfort'.

Located in 'Scotland's conservative north' (Donaldson), Aberdeen stood apart theologically and ecclesiastically from the university centres of the south. It welcomed episcopacy, accepted the liturgical practices of the five articles of Perth (1618), and embraced the ministry of William Forbes, who sought a middle way between Christian camps, based upon an acceptance of patristic theology and precept. If John Forbes did not go so far as William he had a deep knowledge of patristic authors and was favourable to the practices of antiquity, as he revealed in his *Irenicum amatoribus veritatis et pacis in ecclesia Scoticana* (1629). Here he defended episcopacy as part of the *melius esse* of the church, and affirmed that in matters of indifference, such as kneeling at communion, the church must obey the dictates of the magistrate. In his *A Peaceable Warning, to the Subjects in Scotland* (1638) he urged that to follow the dictates of presbyterianism entailed the condemnation of 'the Doctrine and Practise of sound Antiquitie' (p. 19). He appealed for mutual charity 'in these oeconomicall and rituall controversies' (ibid., 20), and in February 1637 he had engaged in John Durie's scheme for church union among Lutherans and the reformed (see *De pace inter evangelicos procuranda, eminentiorum in ecclesia Scoticana theologorum sententiae*, Frankfurt, 1643). However, if it may be said that he anticipated the modern ecumenical spirit (Torrance, 90), it must also be recalled that he could be impatient with those who refused their obedience to the commands of James VI, 'one who surpassed all the Christian princes of the world's history in knowledge of, and devotion to, true and pure Christianity' (J. Forbes, *The First Book of the Irenicum*, trans. E. G. Selwyn, 100).

When the national covenant was promoted, from 28 February 1638, Forbes refused to sign, and continued his opposition to the end of his life. In July, Montrose, Alexander Henderson, David Dickson, and Andrew Cant, among others, came to Aberdeen to dispute. Forbes and five other 'Aberdeen doctors' initiated a pamphlet war with their

Generall demands concerning the late covenant: propounded by the ministers and professors of divinity of Aberdene. The covenanters countered with *The answeres of some brethren of the ministerie, to the replyes of the ministers and professours of divinitie in Aberdene.* This was followed by *Duplyes of the ministers and professors of Aberdene.* The doctors argued against the covenant both in principle and because it abjured episcopacy and the five articles of Perth, to which they had sworn obedience at their ordinations. Subsequently a number of residents of the city, including the doctors, fled to escape reprisals.

Forbes was an enigma to the covenanters. His Augustinian theology was unobjectionable in the point of grace. In a work against Pelagianism he wrote that belief follows upon election, and in his diary he recorded more than once: 'I learned by experience that faith is not of our selves' (Forbes, 'Spirituall exercises'). Robert Baillie hoped, vainly, that he might be won over to the cause, and when the general assembly met in Aberdeen in July and August 1640 Forbes was called in to face a committee: 'efter sum quereis and ansueris, no more process past aganes him at this tyme, bot wes continewit upone good hoipes of his incuming' (Spalding, 311). However, his intractability resulted in deposition from his chair on 20 April 1641 'to the gryte greif of the youth and young studentis of theologie' (Spalding, 2.57); he was also forced from his residence, which he had failed to reserve to his own use for life. He was among those prohibited from taking communion, but he ignored the ban (20 June 1641). His opposition to the solemn league and covenant (August 1643) obliged him to leave Scotland, sailing for Campvere in the Netherlands on 5 April 1644, in the company of his son George, the only one of his nine children to survive him, his wife having died on 19 January 1640. There he preached and worked on his greatest work, *Instructiones historico-theologicae de doctrina Christiana.* In 1645 Baillie urged his cousin William Spang, minister of the anglophone congregation in Campvere, to expedite its publication.

Forbes returned to Aberdeen in July 1646, and spent the remainder of his life in seclusion at Corse, where in 1647

I did often preach at home in the hall of Corse to my domesticks and tennants, there being no sermon at the kirk of Lochell by reason of the bodilie infirmitie of Mr Thomas Forbes, ordinar pastor of that congregation, and it pleased the Lord to be graciouslie present with us and to comfort us. Blessed be God. Amen.

This is the final entry in the diary. He died at Corse Castle on 29 April 1648 and was interred in the Leochel kirkyard, upon the refusal of the presbytery of Aberdeen to allow his burial with his father and first wife in St Machar's Cathedral grounds. His collected works, *Opera omnia*, were edited by George Garden and published in two volumes in Amsterdam in 1702 and 1703, and included a Latin translation of his 'Spirituall exercises'. Forbes has been described as 'one of the ablest and most learned theologians whom Scotland produced between the Reformation and the Disruption' (Torrance, 79). DAVID GEORGE MULLAN

Sources T. F. Torrance, *Scottish theology: from John Knox to John McLeod Campbell* (1996) · J. Forbes, *Opera omnia*, ed. G. Garden, 2 vols. (1702–3) · G. D. Henderson, 'The ordination of John Forbes of Corse', *Scottish Notes and Queries*, 3rd ser., 10 (1932), 33–5 · G. D. Henderson, 'The wife of John Forbes of Corse', *Scottish Notes and Queries*, 3rd ser., 6 (1928), 178–80 · D. Stewart, 'The Aberdeen doctors and the covenanters', *Records of the Scottish Church History Society*, 22 (1984–6), 35–44 · J. D. Ogilvie, 'The Aberdeen doctors and the national covenant', *Papers of the Edinburgh Bibliographical Society*, 11 (1921), 73–86 · *DNB* · J. Forbes, 'Spirituall exercises', NA Scot., CH 12/18/6 · J. Forbes, 'Spirituall exercises', King's College, Aberdeen, MSS 635, 635A · D. G. Mullan, *Scottish puritanism, 1590–1638* (2000) · G. Donaldson, *Scottish church history* (1985) · J. Spalding, *Memorialls of the trubles in Scotland and in England, AD 1624 – AD 1645*, ed. J. Stuart, 2 vols., Spalding Club, [21, 23] (1850–51) · A. Tayler and H. Tayler, eds., *House of Forbes* (1937)

Archives NA Scot., diary, 'Spirituall exercises', CH 12/18/6 · U. Aberdeen, King's College, diary, 'Spirituall exercises', MSS 635, 635A

Forbes, John (1707–1759), army officer, was born on 5 September 1707 in Edinburgh, the son of Lieutenant-Colonel John Forbes of Pittencrieff, Fife, and his wife, Elizabeth Graham. His father died before he was born. Although 'bred to the profession of physic' (*Pennsylvania Gazette*, 15 March 1759), Forbes chose a military career by purchasing a cornetcy in the 2nd Royal North British Dragoons, or Scots Greys, dated 16 December 1735. His regiment saw six years of service in the War of the Austrian Succession, during which Forbes gained rapid promotion. He first served as captain and aide-de-camp to Sir James Campbell, who commanded the British cavalry at Fontenoy in May 1745. Promoted the same year to major and lieutenant-colonel in the army, he was recalled to Scotland to help suppress the Jacobite rising of 1745 and participated in the battle at Culloden. After returning to Flanders he was present with his regiment at Laffeldt in 1747, serving as aide-de-camp to Sir John Ligonier, and as quartermaster-general on the duke of Cumberland's own staff the following year. He was made lieutenant-colonel in the Scots Greys in 1750.

Forbes was given the colonelcy of the 17th regiment of foot on 25 February 1757 and soon afterwards was sent to Halifax, Nova Scotia, as adjutant-general to Lord Loudoun. Through his service and friendship with Ligonier, who recommended Forbes 'with great warmth' (Middleton, 53), he was appointed brigadier-general by Pitt on 28 December 1757. In the plan of operations for 1758 he was charged with the capture of Fort Duquesne (later Pittsburgh), which the French had built on the Ohio, and against which Braddock had failed so disastrously in 1755. He arrived at Philadelphia at the end of April, but had to wait there for troops and stores until the beginning of July. His force consisted of Montgomery's Highlanders, reckoned at 1400 men, 400 men of the Royal Americans, and forty artillerymen, with about 5000 provincials.

Although he had trouble with his Native American allies, whom he called 'the most imposing Rogues that I have ever had to deal with' (*Writings*, 205), and in handling his provincial troops, whom he described as, with a few exceptions, 'an extream bad Collection of broken Innkeepers, Horse Jockeys, and Indian traders … a gathering from the scum of the worst of people' (ibid., 226), he quickly adapted to North American ways of war, confessing that, 'in this country, wee must comply and learn the Art of Warr, from Ennemy Indians or anything else who have seen the Country & Warr carried on in itt' (ibid., 125). Despite the remonstrances of George Washington, commander of the Virginia troops, whose behaviour Forbes regarded as 'noways like a soldier', he decided not to follow Braddock's route, but to cut a fresh road through western Pennsylvania, across the Alleghenies. Trying to learn from Braddock's mistakes, Forbes formed a plan to advance by steps, making a stockaded camp and blockhouse at every 40 miles, and bringing up a fortnight's supplies to it before he moved on. Forbes's Road, as it came to be known, constituted a permanent conquest and a highway for western expansion.

Forbes's plans were initially and extensively delayed by difficulties in gathering men and supplies for the attack. Intercolonial squabbling over the financing of the project, and over whether it should be launched from Virginia or Pennsylvania, also caused delays. Local inhabitants along the route were reluctant to help, fearing they would not be compensated for offered supplies, leading Forbes to conclude that they seemed 'rather bent upon our ruin, and destruction, than give the smallest assistance' (*Writings*, 224–5). He also made a treaty with the Cherokees but many of the Native Americans, impatient with the slow preparations, deserted before the campaign was finished. Forbes reached Carlisle with his main body about 10 July, and moved on to Raystown (later Bedford), where a fort was built by the advance party under Colonel Henry Bouquet. The road across the Alleghenies proved feasible, but its difficulties and the bad weather made progress very slow. Forbes himself was so reduced by a 'cursed flux'—probably a severe case of camp dysentery— that he had to travel on a hurdle slung between two horses.

Forbes was not inactive during this period of delay, but spent the lost time wisely. Indeed, he may have purposely delayed the attack to accommodate a gathering of Shawnee, Delaware, Mingo, and other Ohio valley and western tribes in September and October at Easton. Over 500 Native Americans from as many as fifteen different tribes met with British emissaries and negotiated a neutrality that deprived the French of many of their key alliances in the Ohio valley. Although a major skirmish early in September between a detachment under Major James Grant within 40 miles of Fort Duquesne resulted in the loss of 283 officers and men and temporarily jeopardized negotiations, the treaty of Easton was formalized, and the way was clear for the British.

Forbes with the main body now advanced quickly, to finish the campaign before the onset of winter and the expiration of service of his colonial troops at the beginning of December. By 2 November the entire expedition was congregated at Loyalhannon, where captured enemy revealed that the fort was weakly defended, and that many of the Ohio valley tribes with the French had moved off under the influence of the treaty of Easton. On 18 November a force of 2500 men, lightly equipped, set out for Duquesne, which was reached on the 25th, and was found to have been abandoned by the French. Forbes wrote to Pitt on 27 November: 'I have used the freedom of giving your name to Fort Du Quesne, as I hope it was in some measure the being actuated by your spirits that now makes us masters of the place.' Leaving a garrison of 200 provincials, Forbes returned along his 193-mile road to Philadelphia in a prostrate condition. He died there on 11 March 1759, aged fifty-one, and was buried with military honours in the chancel of Christ Church on 14 March.

Forbes was described as 'just and without prejudices, brave without ostentation, uncommonly warm in his friendship and incapable of flattery; … well bred, but absolutely impatient of formality and affection. … steady in his measures, but open to information and council' (*Pennsylvania Gazette*, 15 March 1759). According to Colonel Henry Bouquet, the success of the expedition was entirely due to him: 'in all his measures he has shown the greatest prudence, firmness, and ability.' Washington also recognized his 'great merit'. Forbes's success against Fort Duquesne in 1758, which secured the Ohio valley for the British, was of immense strategic significance in the Seven Years' War in America. In weakening powerful alliances between many Native American tribes and the French and opening a secure route to New France from the south-west, his actions, together with the simultaneous successful siege of Louisbourg, have been described by one modern historian as constituting the 'pivotal campaign of the entire war in North America' (Leach, 444), clearing the way for a decisive full-scale assault on Quebec in 1759.

E. M. LLOYD, rev. MICHAEL A. MCDONNELL

Sources *Writings of General John Forbes relating to his service in North America*, ed. A. P. James (1938) · *Correspondence of William Pitt, when secretary of state, with colonial governors and military and naval commissioners in America*, ed. G. S. Kimball, 2 vols. (1906) · *The papers of Henry Bouquet*, ed. S. K. Stevens and others, 2: *The Forbes expedition* (1951) · *The writings of George Washington from the original manuscript sources, 1745–1799*, ed. J. C. Fitzpatrick, 39 vols. (1931–44) · *Pennsylvania Gazette* (15 March 1759) · *DAB* · *DCB*, vol. 3 · D. E. Leach, *Arms for empire: a military history of the British colonies in North America, 1607–1763* (1973) · R. Middleton, *The bells of victory: the Pitt–Newcastle ministry and the conduct of the Seven Years' War, 1757–1762* (1985) · J. Titus, *The old dominion at war: society, politics, and warfare in late colonial Virginia* (1991) · L. H. Gipson, *The great war for the empire: the victorious years, 1758–1760* (1949) · N. Anderson, 'The general chooses a road: the Forbes campaign of 1758 to capture Fort Duquesne', *Western Pennsylvania Historical Magazine*, 42 (1959), 110–24 · E. Almack, *The history of the second dragoons, 'royal Scots greys'* (1908)

Archives PRO, corresp. and MSS, CO 5/50; WO 34/44, 34/76 · University of Virginia, Charlottesville, corresp. and papers | BL, corresp. with Bouquet, Add. MSS 21630–21660 · Hunt. L., Loudoun MSS, letters to James Abercromby · NA Scot., Dalhousie muniments, corresp. and papers, military papers, GD 45/2 [microfilm]

Likenesses portrait, repro. in James, ed., *Writings of General John Forbes*

Wealth at death equally divided between two brothers: *Writings*, ed. James, 299–300

Forbes, John (1714–1796), naval officer, was born at Minorca on 17 July 1714, the second son of George *Forbes, third earl of Granard (1685–1765), naval officer, and Mary, née Stewart (1672/3–1758), eldest daughter of William, first Viscount Mountjoy. On 31 May 1726 he entered the *Burford* as a volunteer under the command of his maternal uncle, the Hon. Charles Stewart. After service in the Mediterranean, Forbes followed Stewart to the *Lion* and went with him in 1729 to the West Indies. While on that station Stewart promoted Forbes lieutenant. His first commission noted in the Admiralty commission register was as third lieutenant of the *Kingston* (60 guns) on 13 January 1733. On 15 February of the following year he became fourth lieutenant on the *Edinburgh* (70 guns). On 21 July he was appointed sixth lieutenant on the *Britannia* (100 guns) and by May 1735 he had risen to third lieutenant. The *Britannia* was now the flagship of Sir John Norris, who led an expedition to Lisbon to support the Portuguese in the face of a Spanish threat.

On 7 March 1737 Norris appointed Forbes captain of the *Poole* (32 guns) and he sailed back to England in company with Norris and the *Britannia*. On 3 October he was given command of the *Port Mahon* (20 guns) in which he served on the Irish station. On 10 August 1739, war with Spain imminent, he was appointed to command the *Severn* at Plymouth. He was moved to the *Tiger* on 30 June 1740. The ship was not a happy one: she had been a sickly vessel and the crew had outstanding grievances over their claim to prize money. Forbes had no time to find a solution before, on 10 August, he was moved to the new ship *Guernsey* (50 guns), which was launched at Chatham on the following day. By 15 September Forbes had the *Guernsey* at the Nore, where he was busy recruiting seamen. After voyages to the Netherlands and Ireland, Forbes sailed with a convoy for the Mediterranean in February 1741. Sickness plagued the voyage, but Forbes continued to serve on convoy duty to and from Gibraltar and the Mediterranean squadron.

In 1742 Admiral Thomas Mathews appointed Forbes to the *Norfolk* (80 guns). In this ship Forbes took part in the battle off Toulon on 11 February 1744. The *Norfolk* was immediately ahead of Mathews in the *Namur* in the line of battle, and bore down on the enemy as soon as he saw his admiral doing so. After nearly two hours the *Norfolk* drove her opposite number out of the line of battle, but Forbes did not pursue, holding instead to the line of battle. By August 1744 Forbes had been in poor health for some time and Mathews gave him permission to resign his command and seek medical relief at the baths at Montferrat. After his return to England he was called upon to give evidence against Vice-Admiral Richard Lestock in the court martial between March and June 1746 that followed the parliamentary inquiry into the battle.

On 15 July 1747 Forbes was promoted rear-admiral of the blue and sent to be second in command to Vice-Admiral John Byng in the Mediterranean. He rose to rear-admiral of the white on 12 May 1748 and on 8 August took over command of the Mediterranean squadron on Byng's departure for England. Forbes returned to England after the peace. Suffering from persistent ill health, he rejected an offer to command in the East Indies in 1754. He was not to serve at sea again, but his political and professional ambitions did not end at this point. He was promoted vice-admiral of the blue on 6 January 1755. He had been elected to the Irish parliament for St Johnstown in 1751 and for

Mullingar in 1761, but unlike his father he did not take up a seat in the Westminster House of Commons. His father's political connection had been with the duke of Argyll, who had been an important figure in the opposition to Walpole. Lord Granard continued to distrust the old corps whigs, and his son John became associated with the Grenvilles and William Pitt. Pitt formed his first ministry in November 1756 and Forbes was appointed to the Admiralty board in the following month. He left the board after Pitt's dismissal in April 1757 and returned to it when the Pitt–Newcastle ministry was formed in June. The most significant event for Forbes during his time on the board was the execution of Vice-Admiral John Byng. Despite the opinion of twelve judges Forbes was convinced of the illegality of the judgment and refused to sign the death warrant.

On 5 February 1758 Forbes became admiral of the blue; he continued to sit on the Board of Admiralty, where he shouldered a heavy workload and was well respected, until April 1763. On 1 May 1763 he received the sinecure of general of marines. He became admiral of the white on 18 October 1770 and admiral of the fleet on 24 October 1781, after the death of Lord Hawke. Forbes had married Lady Mary Capel (1722–1782), the daughter of the third earl of Essex, on 2 September 1758 and with her had twin daughters in January 1761. His wife died on 9 April 1782 and was buried in the Essex family vault in the parish church of St Mary's, Watford.

Forbes's long life and service gave him a wealth of knowledge of the Hanoverian navy, which he passed on to the naval antiquary William Locker. He lived on until 10 March 1796 and was buried next to his wife on 18 March.

RICHARD HARDING

Sources DNB · J. Forbes, *Memoirs of the earls of Granard*, ed. G. A. Hastings [earl of Granard] (1868) · PRO; captains' letters, 1722–38, ADM 1/1779; 1739–41, ADM 1/1780; 1741–4, ADM 1/1781; letters from Vice-Admiral Byng and Rear-Admiral Forbes to the secretary of state, SP 42/99; warrants and commissions, ADM 6/13; ADM 6/14; ADM 6/15; seniority list, ADM 6/424; admiralty minute book, ADM 3/65 · parish register, Watford, St Mary, 18 March 1796, Herts. ALS [burial] · D. Syrett and R. L. DiNardo, *The commissioned sea officers of the Royal Navy, 1660–1815*, rev. edn, Occasional Publications of the Navy RS, 1 (1994) · J. Charnock, ed., *Biographia navalis*, 4 (1796), 338–43 · H. Walpole, *Memoirs of King George II*, ed. J. Brooke, 3 vols. (1985), vol. 2 [1754–7], 213

Archives CKS, notebook · priv. coll., corresp. and papers | priv. coll., letters to Lord Shelburne

Likenesses G. Romney, oils, 1778, NMM

Forbes, John, of Skellater [John Forbes-Skellater] (1732×4–1808), army officer in the French and Portuguese services, was the second son of George Forbes of Skellater (d. 1767) and Christian (d. 1784), daughter of the Jacobite general John Gordon of Glenbucket. The Forbeses of Skellater, Aberdeenshire, were staunch supporters of the Stuart cause. During the rising of 1745 George Forbes held a commission as lieutenant-general in the Jacobite army. After Culloden he escaped to France and obtained a captain's commission in a regiment in the French service commanded by David, Lord Ogilvy.

John Forbes attended school in Glengarin, a Gaelic-speaking Roman Catholic area with strong Jacobite sympathies. It was here that he acquired the Gaelic name Ian Roy (Red John), on account of the colour of his hair.

By the age of fifteen Forbes had left Scotland and joined his father's regiment in the French service and was present at the siege of Maastricht (1748), which brought to a close the War of the Austrian Succession. In September 1754 he returned to Scotland and was given leave by David Inglis, the bailie of Edinburgh, to visit his home so long as he was not recruiting. By then he was a lieutenant. He continued to serve in the French army during the Seven Years' War in the campaigns in Flanders. In August 1763 he is recorded as a captain in the royal Écossais—the Royal Scots, or 103rd regiment of French infantry. Ogilvie's regiment was disbanded by then.

During 1763 Forbes achieved public notoriety in both Paris and London when he attempted a duel with John Wilkes, who had provoked Forbes's animosity with his campaign of abuse against the Scots in the *North Briton*. Forbes challenged Wilkes when the latter visited Paris in mid-August, but Wilkes declined with the ingenious plea of a prior claim to a duel with Charles Wyndham, second earl of Egremont, and placed himself under police protection. Forbes was brought before Marshal Noailles, head of the French police, but released after undertaking not to fight a duel in France. Forbes arrived in London by mid-September, where rumours began to spread of a duel. Meanwhile Egremont had died suddenly and Wilkes made it known that he was now prepared to meet Forbes outside France, although there was a suspicion that Wilkes was not serious. The matter became a subject of comment in the London press, generating much sympathy for Forbes within Jacobite circles. In order to prevent a breach of the peace the secretary of state, Lord Sandwich, instructed Forbes to quit London and on 27 September he sailed on the sloop *Bastinado*, bound for Grenada, in the West Indies.

It is not likely that Forbes ever reached that island for opportunities for military employment presented themselves in Portugal, where the count of Lippe-Bückeburg, the sovereign of a small German state and commander of a British auxiliary force during the Seven Years' War, was busy reorganizing the Portuguese army. In late 1763 Forbes was appointed captain in the foot regiment of Praca de Peniche, which was officered by Scots. Seven months later he was made major, and became lieutenant-colonel of the regiment in June 1766. In 1767 he was promoted to colonel of the 2nd infantry regiment of Elvas, and in 1772 was made colonel of the cavalry regiment of Almeida. He achieved the rank of brigadier of cavalry in June 1775. Such rapid promotion was aided by his marriage to Anna Joaquina d'Almeida (1746–1797), of the family of the counts d'Almeida, where his cavalry regiment was based, whom he married probably before 1775.

In 1787 Forbes was appointed field marshal of the Portuguese armies by Maria I (a rank between brigadier and lieutenant-general). In the royal order of appointment he was called Forbes de Skellater (the 'de' was later dropped).

He also received the first of several pensions which would descend to his surviving family.

The nature of Forbes's character and his position in Lisbon society is suggested by the journals of William Beckford (1759–1844), the author and dilettante, who travelled to Portugal in 1787–8. Beckford became a regular guest at Forbes's house and described him as a man of 'excellent sense and much experience … who speaks his mind with a manly openness that comforts my heart and gives me the soundest disinterested advice I receive in this cursed country' (*Journal*, 101, 212). Robert Walpole, the British minister in Lisbon, had refused to receive Beckford on account of the sexual scandal surrounding him, and as such Beckford could not be presented at the Portuguese court. Forbes, the Jacobite exile, would not have thought himself obliged to deny Beckford social acceptance, and may have taken his side—although he may have used his influence to dissuade Beckford from pushing his attendance at court to the point of public embarrassment. During some political conversation Forbes made it clear to Beckford that he considered 'like the land of Egypt this Kingdom is a broken reed' (*Journal of William Beckford*, 101), and feared Spanish subjugation.

Forbes's rise continued. In 1790 he was granted the order of Christ and appointed adjutant-general. In 1793 he was made lieutenant-general and when Portugal decided to join the war against revolutionary France he was given command of the force sent to assist the Spanish army in Roussillon. Forbes succeeded in bringing the bulk of his force across the Pyrenees and joined the attack upon the French army at Cerat (26 November 1793), which forced their retreat. This early success was not to be repeated. The situation deteriorated during the winter and in April 1794 Forbes requested the withdrawal of his forces across the Pyrenees. The eventual evacuation of the Spanish–Portuguese army, which Forbes commanded, was successful but further victories by the French forces in Catalonia during 1794 led the Spanish to conclude a separate peace in July 1795. The only creditable feature of the campaign was the conduct of Forbes and the Portuguese troops—the Spanish commanders being often at variance—and he returned to Lisbon, with honours from the Spanish court, in December 1795.

Forbes's wife died on 29 March 1797 and soon afterwards Forbes paid a last visit to Skellater, accompanied by his eldest daughter, Christina. In 1801 he commanded the Portuguese forces in the region south of the Douro River, in the face of a combined French–Spanish invasion. After a short campaign lasting four months the Portuguese were beaten. A peace was concluded in June. In October 1803, aged about seventy, Forbes was made a councillor of the council of war and a general of cavalry soon after, but he was now too old for active military service. Following a further Spanish invasion under the command of the French marshal Junot in 1807, Forbes embarked with the queen, the prince regent, and the court in a squadron commanded by Sir Sydney Smith and sailed for Rio de Janeiro, his last exile. Upon his arrival in November 1807, Forbes was appointed military governor of the city, only to die there on 4 April 1808. He was buried in Rio de Janeiro at the convent of St Anthony. In the *Gentleman's Magazine* of September 1808 he was described as a 'virtuous and honourable man, and as a soldier possessed undaunted courage, indefatigable activity, promptitude and decision' (*GM*, 851). Of his three daughters the eldest, Christina, married Brigadier-General Henry David Fraser of Fraserfield, who took service in the Portuguese army and later became governor of Rio de Janeiro. His second daughter, Joanna Victoria, married the Portuguese duc d'Alburquerque. The third, Anna Benedicta, married Don Joas de Mello, of an old and well-established Lisbon family.

JONATHAN SPAIN

Sources J. Neil, *Ian Roy of Skellater, a Scottish soldier of fortune, being the life of General John Forbes of the Portuguese army* (1902) · A. Tayler and H. Tayler, *Jacobites of Aberdeenshire and Banffshire in the forty-five* (1928) · Burke, *Gen. GB* (1894) · *Scottish Notes and Queries*, 2nd ser., 3 (1901–2), 43–4, 60 · *GM*, 1st ser., 78 (1808), 851 · H. V. Livermore, *A new history of Portugal* (1966) · J. Grant, *The Scottish soldiers of fortune* (1889) · *The journal of William Beckford in Portugal and Spain, 1787–88*, ed. B. Alexander (1954) · A. Williamson, *Wilkes, 'a friend to liberty'* (1974) · L. Kronenberger, *The extraordinary Mr Wilkes* (1974) · A. Tayler and H. Tayler, eds., *The house of Forbes*, Third Spalding Club, 8 (1937)
Archives NA Scot., family MSS · NL Scot., corresp. and papers
Likenesses portrait, repro. in Neil, *Ian Roy of Skellater*, frontispiece · portrait, Castle Forbes, Aberdeenshire · print, repro. in C. de Chaby, *Exceptos historicos ... relativos á guerra ... do Roussilon e Cataluna*

Forbes, John (1750–1797), politician and colonial governor, the second son and youngest of the four children of John Forbes (1703–1757), barrister, and Sophia Curtis, was born possibly at the family seat at Newstone, co. Meath, Ireland. He was educated at Trinity College, Dublin, to which he was admitted on 8 July 1764 and from where he graduated BA in 1769. From 1770 he read law at the Middle Temple, and he was called to the English bar in 1776. He was torn between his father's profession of the law and politics, but the death of his uncle, Alderman William Forbes, a successful Dublin merchant, while travelling from Holyhead in October 1775, put sufficient funds at his disposal to enable him to purchase a seat for the borough of Ratoath in 1776. His entry to the Irish bar the following year suggests that he took to heart the advice of an acquaintance, William Glascock, that he should make the law his 'sheet anchor', but politics proved more tempting (W. Glascock to J. Forbes, 29 March 1775, Forbes MS 10713).

Having established a working relationship with Henry Grattan and carved out a niche for himself as a patriot spokesman on financial issues, Forbes joined with Grattan and others in advancing a six-month money bill as the patriots successfully pursued 'free trade' in the winter of 1779–80. Forbes's role was primarily supportive at this time, but he was 'a useful speaker' in his own right, and he was adept at pulling strings behind the scenes (Sayles, 262). This is illustrated by his attempt in January 1780 to induce Henry Flood to take charge of the fast-emerging demand for legislative independence in order to ensure it did not give rise to 'jealousy in Great Britain' (Rosse MS C/1/13). Forbes's concerns on this point at this time were

such that he informed a whig acquaintance in Great Britain, James Adair, that it was hardly possible for the political oppositions in Britain and Ireland to co-operate, but it did not prompt him to moderate his advocacy of constitutional reform. He was among the most forthright and vocal proponents of legislative independence in the House of Commons in 1780 and 1781, and on 4 December 1781 he urged Irish MPs to take advantage of the opportunity provided by the humiliation of the crown's forces at Yorktown to secure the amendment of Poynings' law. These were hardly the sentiments of a potential officeholder, yet within six months, as the legal and constitutional changes that constituted legislative independence were being implemented by a whig administration headed in Ireland by the duke of Portland, speculation was rife that Forbes would be made solicitor-general. This did not come to pass, but he did have the satisfaction of introducing the bill 'for securing the independence of the judges', which was one of the four 'causes of complaint' specified by MPs on 16 April 1782 when Henry Grattan successfully introduced an amendment to an address to the king asserting that the Irish parliament was the 'sole legislature' of the kingdom of Ireland (*The Parliamentary Register*, 1.338–9).

Forbes was one of the Irish MPs whom Portland hoped would constitute 'the nest egg of a real Whig party' in Ireland in 1782 (BL, Add. MS 38716, fols. 154–73). This was frustrated by, among other factors, the lord lieutenant's early recall, but Forbes's preparedness to work with the new viceroy, Lord Northington, in 1783 suggested that Portland's hopes were not unfounded, and this conclusion was reinforced by speculation that Forbes would take office in the whig-patriot administration that Northington sought initially to construct. However, Forbes was too disquieted by the trust reposed in John Fitzgibbon, whom he regarded as anti-whig, and too committed to the cause of parliamentary reform, which the administration was under instructions to oppose, to find the prospect congenial. Unwilling, as one contemporary report put it, to vote 'for the ministry on every occasion right or wrong' (*Volunteer Journal*, Dublin, 15 Dec 1783), he reverted to the independent opposition with which he was comfortable. He continued thus until the summer of 1785, when the shared eagerness of the patriots in Ireland and the opposition whigs in Britain to defeat William Pitt's plan to bring a commercial union between the two kingdoms into being prompted a further attempt to found an Irish whig party. As one of their main points of contact with the whigs and the key figure in promoting unity within the divided ranks of the Irish opposition, Forbes was at the heart of this, though his priority was to defeat the proposed commercial settlement because it 'involved ... the very existence of the Irish parliament, as an independent legislature' (*The Parliamentary Register*, 5.243). When this was achieved, Forbes had consolidated his position as one of the leading and most respected figures on the Irish opposition benches. Possessed also of a safe parliamentary seat in Drogheda, which constituency he represented between 1783 and 1796, he was one of the most prominent reforming voices in the House of Commons in the late 1780s. He was particularly active in resisting the administration's disposition to favour a coercive response to Whiteboyism, and was a strong advocate of the reform of the pension list. His efforts in respect of the latter were reinforced as a consequence of the Regency crisis.

As an Irish whig with close contacts with the duke of Portland, Forbes was well disposed to the idea of an unlimited regency if it would facilitate the accession of the whigs to power. The intervention of the Irish whigs proved counterproductive in this respect, but the establishment in June 1789 of an Irish Whig Club, of which Forbes was a founder member, was a most positive outcome as far as he was concerned as it gave new impetus to the demand for economic reform with which he was identified. Successive place and responsibility measures proposed by him in the early 1790s to disallow pension- and office-holders from sitting in the Commons were lost until the 1793 session, when he secured a diluted Place Act, a Pensions Act capping the pension list at £82,000, and a Consolidated Fund Act that made important changes in the way public finances were managed. In addition, Forbes supported Catholic enfranchisement, although he would have been more content if the act that was approved in respect of this in 1793 had set a higher franchise qualification. This, in practice, brought the curtain down on his political career in Ireland. He did speak on a number of occasions between then and October 1796, when it was announced that he had 'accepted the government of the Bahama Islands'. This represented a new departure for Forbes, but by the mid-1790s both his finances and his health had deteriorated to such an extent that he needed to secure remunerative employment. Unable, despite the help of his long-time mentor, the duke of Portland, to find a suitable position in Ireland, he accepted the lieutenant-governorship of the Bahamas. Appointed in the expectation that he would quickly eradicate the peculation that was rife in all branches of government there, he was frustrated by the delay in the departure of the outgoing governor by adverse weather. However, the lengthy reports he sent to London in the eight months that he was in office indicate that he identified both the problems and the means by which they might be alleviated. Forbes was struck down with yellow fever and died on 3 June 1797 in Nassau; he was buried the following day with full honours in Christ Church, Nassau.

JAMES KELLY

Sources NL Ire., Forbes MSS, 978, 10713 · PRO NIre., Forbes MS, T 3391 · T. J. Kiernan, ed., 'Forbes letters', *Analecta Hibernica*, 8 (1938), 313–71 · J. Porter, P. Byrne, and W. Porter, eds., *The parliamentary register, or, History of the proceedings and debates of the House of Commons of Ireland, 1781–1797*, 17 vols. (1784–1801) · J. Kelly, *Prelude to Union: Anglo-Irish politics in the 1780s* (1992) · G. O. Sayles, ed., 'Contemporary sketches of the members of the Irish parliament in 1782', *Proceedings of the Royal Irish Academy*, 56C (1953–4), 227–86 · J. Kelly, *Henry Flood: patriots and politics in eighteenth-century Ireland* (1998) · A. P. W. Malcomson, *John Foster: the politics of the Anglo-Irish ascendancy* (1978) · R. B. McDowell, *Ireland in the age of imperialism and revolution, 1760–1801* (1979) · Birr Castle, Birr, Offaly, Ireland, Rosse MS, J. Forbes to H. Flood, 20 Jan 1780, C/1/13 · Burtchaell & Sadleir, *Alum. Dubl.* · PRO, colonial MSS, Bahamas · BL, Add. MS 38716

Archives NL Ire., political corresp., MS 978 [transcript in PRO NIre.] · NL Ire., corresp., MS 10713 | Birr Castle, Offaly, Rosse MSS · BL, corresp. with James Adair, Add. MS 53802 · PRO, colonial MSS, Bahamas, 17967

Likenesses platinotype photograph, NL Ire.

Forbes, Sir John (1787–1861), physician and medical journalist, was born and baptized on 17 December 1787 at Cuttlebrae, near Cullen, Banffshire, the fourth son of Alexander Forbes (1750–1842), a tenant farmer, and his wife, Cicilia Wilkie (1755–1831). The family later moved to Dytac, near Fordyce, where Forbes attended Fordyce School (1793–1801), where he met his lifelong friend James Clark (1788–1870), later also a fellow physician. When he was fifteen Forbes spent a year at Aberdeen grammar school before entering Marischal College, Aberdeen. He attended classes for two years between 1803 and 1805 but there is no record that he ever graduated.

During the Napoleonic wars Forbes decided to enlist in the Royal Navy. He took tuition in Edinburgh and obtained the diploma of the College of Surgeons, Edinburgh, in February 1806. The following year he entered the medical service with the rank of temporary assistant surgeon, assigned to HMS *Royal George* at Plymouth. He was confirmed full surgeon on 27 January 1809. He served on the West Indian station, then in various ships and shore establishments, including Haslar Royal Naval Hospital. His last position was under Rear-Admiral Sir Philip Charles Durham in HMS *Venerable*, on the Leeward Islands station. When the war ended in 1816 Forbes returned to Edinburgh and studied at the medical school and university as a mature student, receiving his MD in August 1817, on the same day as James Clark.

While pursuing his medical studies Forbes had attended lectures in geology given by Professor Robert Jameson. When Jameson was asked to recommend an Edinburgh physician with an interest in geology for a medical practice in Penzance, Cornwall, Forbes's name was put forward. He was duly appointed and moved to Cornwall in September 1817. Alongside his general practice Forbes was also physician to the Penzance Public Dispensary. During these years he acquired a knowledge of the newly invented stethoscope of René Laënnec, which Clark had brought back from his visit to the Necker Hospital in Paris in 1818. In particular Forbes described the stethoscopic signs of pulmonary tuberculosis, then common among Cornish miners. Clark was enthusiastic about Laënnec's *De l'auscultation médiate* (1819) and urged Forbes to translate it into English. The resulting work, *A Treatise on Diseases of the Chest* (1821), while it was criticized for rearranging and shortening the original, and especially for altering Laënnec's terminology in describing the lung sounds found at auscultation, was a great success. In 1823 Forbes wrote to Laënnec, apologizing for the liberties he had taken in his translation and explaining that a more concise version made a greater impact on British readers. Further editions were published in 1827, 1829, and 1834.

On 19 May 1820 Forbes married, at Great Torrington, Devon, Eliza Mary (1787–1851), born in Calcutta where her father, John Burgh (d. 1793), had been a banker. Forbes took a keen interest in local affairs and was the first honorary librarian of the Penzance Public Library in 1818. His interest in meteorology and natural history was aired before the Penwith Agricultural Society and he published on the subject in 1821. He also served as secretary of the Royal Geological Society of Cornwall and contributed to the society's *Transactions* of 1822 on local geology, and 'On the temperature of mines', which concerned the working conditions and health of Cornish tin and copper miners.

In 1822 Forbes and his wife moved to 21 North Street, Chichester, where their only child, Alexander Clark Forbes, was born on 18 April 1824. Forbes built up a large and profitable practice and became involved with local non-medical groups. In 1831 he founded the Chichester Literary and Philosophical Society, to which he later contributed, and he published two articles concerning diseases in Cornwall in the *Transactions of the Provincial and Surgical Association*, the association which was the forerunner of the British Medical Association. He became acquainted with John Conolly (1794–1866), an Edinburgh graduate who also practised at the Chichester Public Dispensary. Its building was very out of date by the time of Forbes's arrival, and it was largely through his fundraising efforts that it was replaced by a new infirmary which admitted its first patients in 1826. (This became the Royal West Sussex Hospital in 1913.)

At Chichester, Forbes wrote *Original cases with dissections and observations illustrating the use of the stethoscope and percussion in the diagnosis of diseases of the chest* (1824), to which he appended commentaries translated from continental authors, some of which had not previously been available in English. The cases were those of thirty-nine patients whom he had treated at Chichester, with the physical signs verified by autopsy in fatal cases. This comparison of the vital signs with post-mortem findings was another importation of Laënnec's teaching into British practice. *The Lancet*, in a favourable review, commented 'It is the first of the kind published in the country, and reflects no small credit on the author for the pains he has taken to make these discoveries generally known' (*The Lancet*, 5, 1824, 180).

Forbes and Conolly were persuaded by a third Edinburgh graduate, Alexander Tweedie (1794–1884), to collaborate on a *Cyclopaedia of Practical Medicine*, in four volumes (1832–5). Forbes was the main editor for this work, which was issued monthly in London, Edinburgh, Dublin, and also in the USA. It proved a popular forum for the best medical writers in the British Isles and made a handsome profit for the publisher. Forbes's creation of *A Manual of Select Bibliography* (1835) for the *Cyclopaedia* remedied the absence of references in the original articles. His arrangement in chronological and alphabetical order was the first of its kind and set a standard for subsequent medical literature.

In 1829 Forbes was elected fellow of the Royal Society.

He applied unsuccessfully in 1830 for the London University post of professor of the nature and treatment of diseases, but two years later was appointed physician-in-ordinary to the duke of Cambridge. In 1836 Forbes and Conolly embarked on a new venture in medical journalism, the *British and Foreign Medical Review, or, A Quarterly Journal of Practical Medicine*, issued from 1836 to 1847. It was read widely in Europe and America, the articles helping to promote more rational methods of treatment than the bleeding and purging still prevalent, and it did much to enhance the reputation of British medicine. Even before Conolly withdrew in 1839 Forbes was undertaking most of the editorial work.

His decision in 1840 to move to 12 Old Burlington Street, Westminster, was a turning point in Forbes's career. In 1841 he was appointed court physician to Prince Albert and the royal household. Fellowship of the Royal College of Physicians was conferred on him in 1844, and in 1845 honorary fellowship of the Imperial Society of Physicians at Vienna. He was a member of numerous academic and medical societies across Europe and in America. The *Review* established his reputation in the world of medical journalism, and he soon built up his consultant practice. Unfortunately his success was marred by the chronic ill health of his wife, who died in 1851.

The *Review* of 1846 published an unsigned article, ostensibly reviewing various British and foreign articles dealing with homoeopathy, entitled 'Homoeopathy, allopathy and "young physic"'. The author, almost certainly Forbes, set out a case for the curative force of nature and the shunning of polypharmacy. The practice of medicine, he said, must combine science and art, and this required a substantial improvement in teaching. The medical establishment considered this view iconoclastic and its impact was to be reflected in an unflattering obituary notice nearly sixteen years later in *The Lancet*. Forbes's general reputation was, however, unharmed; in the same year (1846) he was appointed one of the first two consulting physicians to the Brompton Hospital for Consumption and Diseases of the Chest. Before resigning as editor of the *Review* Forbes was able to write on the new technique of operating under anaesthesia. At University College Hospital, London, on 21 December 1846 he witnessed Robert Liston amputate the thigh of a man who had been anaesthetized by ether vapour. The operation was painless and the patient quickly recovered consciousness.

After his retirement from medical practice in 1848 Forbes remained at Old Burlington Street, where he was joined by his elder brother Alexander who had for many years lived in Mexico. Forbes enjoyed the theatre and would treat actors without charging a fee. In appreciation of these services the managers of Covent Garden Theatre presented him with a handsome silver cup in 1849. In 1852 the University of Oxford conferred on him the degree of DCL, and in 1853 he was knighted. A walking holiday in Switzerland led to the first of several travel books. In 1852 he visited Ireland to see for himself the state of the country after the famine years. He was a prolific letter-writer;

Sir Walter Scott, Florence Nightingale, and Charles Dickens were among his correspondents. Forbes's final publication, *Of Nature and Art in the Cure of Disease* (1857), was a philosophical little book on his favourite subject.

In 1859, after suffering several mild strokes, Forbes went with his brother to live with Forbes's son at Swanston House, Whitchurch-on-Thames, Oxfordshire. He donated his library, consisting of 2500–3000 volumes, to Marischal College, Aberdeen. Resigning from the *comitia* of the Royal College of Physicians he explained 'I am a poor chair-ridden invalid, having totally lost the power of self-locomotion' (archives, RCP Lond.). He died on 13 November 1861 at Whitchurch and was buried in St Mary's churchyard there six days later; in December the body of his wife was exhumed from Kensal Green cemetery and laid alongside his.   R. A. L. AGNEW

Sources E. A. Parkes, 'Memoir of Sir John Forbes, Kt', *British and Foreign Medico-Chirurgical Review*, 1 (1862), 7–70 • P. J. Bishop, 'The life and writings of Sir John Forbes (1787–1861)', *Tubercle*, 42 (1961), 255–61 • A. Sakula, 'Sir John Forbes, 1787–1861: a bicentenary review', *Journal of the Royal College of Physicians of London*, 21 (1987), 77–81 [incl. complete bibliography] • A. A. Cormack, 'Two royal physicians: Sir James Clark, Bart., 1788–1870, Sir John Forbes, 1787–1861: schoolmates at Fordyce Academy', *Banffshire Journal* (26 June 1965) • J. Craig, 'A general dispensary practice 150 years ago', *Aberdeen University Review*, 44 (1971–2), 358–67 • R. A. L. Agnew, 'John Forbes (1787–1861), in memoriam: from Cuttlebrae to Whitchurch', *Journal of Medical Biography*, 2 (1994), 187–92 • A. Sakula, 'Laënnec's influence on some British physicians in the nineteenth century', *Journal of the Royal Society of Medicine*, 74 (1981), 759–67 • P. J. Bishop, 'Evolution of the stethoscope', *Journal of the Royal Society of Medicine*, 73 (1980), 448–56 • F. W. Steer, *The Royal West Sussex Hospital: the first hundred years, 1784–1884*, The Chichester Papers, Chichester City Council, 15 (1960) • W. F. Bynum and J. C. Wilson, 'Periodical knowledge: medical journals and their editors in nineteenth-century Britain', *Medical journals and medical knowledge: historical essays*, ed. W. F. Bynum, S. Lock, and R. Porter (1992) • *BMJ* (23 Nov 1861), 561–2 • *The Lancet* (23 Nov 1861), 512 • *Medical Times and Gazette* (16 Nov 1861), 504–7 • *Medical Times and Gazette* (23 Nov 1861), 534–5 • *PRS*, 12 (1862–3), v–xi • Munk, *Roll* • bap. reg. Scot. • d. cert.
Archives W. Sussex RO, letters to duke of Richmond
Likenesses J. Andrews, portrait, c.1830–1839, Postgraduate Medical Centre, Chichester, West Sussex • J. Partridge, oils, c.1847, RCP Lond. • T. H. Maguire, lithograph, 1848, BM, Wellcome L. • W. Walker, mezzotint, 1852, NPG, Wellcome L.; repro. in *ILN*, 39 (1861), 590 • daguerreotype (in old age), repro. in Parkes, 'Memoir of Sir John Forbes' • wood-engraving, NPG; repro. in *ILN* (1861)
Wealth at death £8000: resworn probate, Nov 1862, *CGPLA Eng. & Wales* (1861)

Forbes, John (1799–1823), botanical collector, was a pupil of John Shepherd (c.1764–1836), the first curator of the Liverpool Botanic Garden. The Horticultural Society of London dispatched him to the east coast of Africa, and for this he left London in February 1822, in the expedition commanded by Captain William Owen. He sent home to the society considerable collections from Lisbon, Tenerife, Madeira, Rio de Janeiro, the Cape of Good Hope, and Madagascar. He then determined to ascend the Zambezi River to the Portuguese station Zoumbo, 300 leagues from its mouth, and then proceed southwards to the Cape of Good Hope. However at Sena, Mozambique, in August 1823, he died from heat and fatigue before completing

half the distance. The genus *Forbesia*, a group of South African lilies, was constructed in his honour by Christian Friedrich Ecklon, author of *Enumeratio plantarum Africae Australis extratropicae* (1835–7). *Forbesia* was subsequently subsumed into the genus *Empodium*, named by Richard Anthony Salisbury (1761–1829). He is also commemorated by a tablet in Chiswick churchyard.

B. D. JACKSON, *rev.* P. E. KELL

Sources [J. C. F. Hoefer], ed., *Nouvelle biographie générale*, 18 (1856), 146 • A. Lasègue, *Musée botanique de M. Benjamin Delessert* (1845), 376 • Desmond, *Botanists*, rev. edn • J. Britten and G. S. Boulger, eds., *A biographical index of British and Irish botanists* (1893)
Archives Royal Horticultural Society, London, corresp. and journal

Forbes, John Hay, Lord Medwyn (1776–1854), judge, was born in Edinburgh, the second son of Sir William *Forbes, baronet (1739–1806), banker and author, and his wife, Elizabeth (d. 1802), daughter of Sir James Hay of Smithfield, baronet. He was admitted advocate in March 1799. Forbes married Louisa (1779–1845), daughter of Sir Alexander Cumming Gordon of Altyre, Elgin. Their children included Alexander Penrose *Forbes, bishop of Brechin, and George Hay *Forbes, episcopalian clergyman and scholar. Forbes was appointed sheriff-depute of Perthshire in May 1807, and was made lord of session in January 1825, when he assumed the courtesy title of Lord Medwyn, from his estate near Perth. In December 1830 he was made a lord of justiciary. He edited a new edition of *Thoughts Concerning Man's Condition and Duties in this Life, and his Hopes in the World to Come* by Alexander Forbes, fourth Baron Forbes of Pitsligo (1678–1762), with a life of the author (1835). He was a strong episcopalian, and did much to promote the interests of his church in the Scottish capital, giving support to the construction of St Paul's Episcopal Church, in York Place, Edinburgh. Forbes resigned as lord of justiciary in May 1849, retired from the bench in October 1852, and died in Edinburgh, on 25 July 1854.

FRANCIS WATT, *rev.* ERIC METCALFE

Sources Irving, *Scots.* • *GM*, 2nd ser., 42 (1854), 300 • Anderson, *Scot. nat.*, 232 • J. Kay, *A series of original portraits and caricature etchings … with biographical sketches and illustrative anecdotes*, ed. [H. Paton and others], new edn [3rd edn], 2 (1877), 99 • Gladstone, *Diaries*
Archives NL Scot., letters to his father | BL, corresp. with W. E. Gladstone, Add. MS 44258 • LPL, letters to A. C. Tait
Likenesses A. Robertson, watercolour on ivory miniature, Scot. NPG • A. Robertson?, watercolour on card, Scot. NPG

Forbes, Katherine, Lady Rothiemay (c.1583–1652/3), noblewoman, was probably born at Castle Forbes, Aberdeenshire, daughter of John, eighth Lord Forbes (1542–1606), and his second wife, Janet (d. 1616), daughter of Walter Seton, and half-sister of John *Forbes (1570/71–1606). She was educated in the burgh of New Aberdeen, and in the winter of 1603 to 1604 was married to William Gordon of Rothiemay (d. 1630). They had at least two sons and four daughters.

Rothiemay was a scion of the powerful house of Gordon, headed by the earls of Huntly. The Forbeses were in a state of constant feud with the Huntly family and its adherents, and the marriage may have formed part of a truce between the two houses. The Gordons of Rothiemay were, in their turn, feuding with the Crichtons of Frendraught, and this feud later precipitated a long period of tragedy and crisis in Lady Rothiemay's life. Although at one time a justice of the peace, Rothiemay fell foul of the law in the course of his feud with the Crichtons. In late December 1629 the sheriff of Banff led a party to Rothiemay with the aim of arresting the laird, and in the ensuing skirmish Gordon was fatally wounded by a Crichton in the sheriff's entourage, and died on 7 January 1630. Under the mediation of the marquess of Huntly, Crichton agreed to pay compensation of 50,000 marks Scots (approximately £2777) to Lady Rothiemay and her children. However, the feud was reignited in October 1630 by the suspicious deaths in a fire of Lady Rothiemay's son John Gordon, who had succeeded his father as laird of Rothiemay, and his kinsman the Viscount Aboyne, heir to the marquess of Huntly, while the pair were guests of the Crichtons in the tower house of Frendraught. These deaths, like that of Lady Rothiemay's husband, were commemorated by the poet Arthur Johnston.

These events had two profound consequences for Lady Rothiemay. The first was that the loss of two consecutive heads of house left her, her lands, and her children vulnerable to the predatory interests of kinsmen. Her house was taken over for a time in 1631, her lands and stores plundered, and she and her children kept prisoners in their own home. Finally, her nine-year-old son James Gordon, heir to the lands of Rothiemay, was forcibly removed from her care by John Gordon of Invermarkie. When the case came before the privy council in the spring of 1632 the lords ordered that Invermarkie should have curatorship of the boy and administration of his estate, but that the young Rothiemay should be educated in Aberdeen under the auspices of the bishop, with Lady Rothiemay bearing the expenses.

The second major consequence was that Lady Rothiemay became deeply involved in the quest of the Gordons for revenge on the Crichtons. In 1632 Crichton complained to the privy council of 'certain oppressions, heirships, depredations and bloodsheds committed upon his lands and tenants and servants … by some broken Hieland men at the command of Katherine Forbes, Lady Rothiemay' (Reg. PCS, 4.241). Matters came to a head in 1635, when the lords of the privy council declared, 'in all the disorders and troubles quhilks hes of lait fallin out in the north pairtes of this kingdome Katherine Forbes, Ladie Rothiemay, hes had a speciall hand', and went on to list her activities in turning her house into a stronghold for the Gordon rebels (Reg. PCS, 5.515). The sheriff of Banff was charged to take control of the castle of Rothiemay and have the lady conveyed as a prisoner to Edinburgh, to answer for her crimes. It was not until February 1637 that the king ordained she should be released.

During the civil wars the Rothiemay family was royalist, and their lands were plundered by the covenanting forces under Argyll in 1644. Lady Rothiemay's daughter Elizabeth was married to James *Gordon, the minister of Rothiemay, who was antipathetic to the covenant, her son's wife was suspected of popery, and she herself was a

reluctant communicant in the covenanting period. However, she seems to have lived quietly in the last decade of her life. In June 1642, she had made a mortification—gift in perpetual trust—of £1000 Scots to the burgh of Aberdeen for the maintenance of a schoolmistress in the burgh to teach girls and young women reading, writing, sewing, and 'any other art or science whairof they can be capable' (Aberdeen City Archive, council register of the burgh of Aberdeen, vol. 52/1, 733). She took an active interest in the selection of the schoolmistress up until at least 1651, and characteristically sought the removal of any she thought incompetent. Lady Rothiemay died some time shortly after October 1652.   SHONA MACLEAN VANCE

Sources Reg. PCS, 2nd ser., vols. 3–6 · J. Spalding, The history of the troubles and memorable transactions in Scotland and England, from 1624 to 1645, ed. J. Skene, 2 vols., Bannatyne Club, 25 (1828–9) · J. Spalding, Memorialls of the trubles in Scotland and in England, AD 1624 – AD 1645, ed. J. Stuart, 2, Spalding Club, [23] (1851), 426 · A. Tayler and H. Tayler, eds., The house of Forbes, Third Spalding Club, 8 (1937) · council register of the burgh of Aberdeen, Aberdeen City Archive, vols. 52/1, 53/1 · W. D. Geddes, ed., Musa Latina Aberdonensis, 1–2: Arthur Johnston, New Spalding Club, 9, 15 (1895–1910) · GEC, Peerage · D. Shearer, Notes, historical and ecclesiastical, on the parish of Rothiemay [n.d.] · private information (2004)
Archives Aberdeen City Archives, council register of burgh of Aberdeen

Forbes, Nevill (1883–1929), Slavonic scholar, was born on 19 February 1883 at Forbes's (later Ashbee's), Godden Green, Seal, near Sevenoaks, Kent, the younger child of Francis Augustine Forbes (1844–1911), stockbroker, and his wife, Jessie Mary, née Carrick (1842–1925). His mother's family was resident in Kronstadt, Russia, but both his parents were of Scottish descent. Nevill was educated at home by a governess until he was eight or nine, when he was sent as a weekly boarder to a local preparatory school. In January 1897 he entered Marlborough College, but left prematurely owing to tuberculosis. As his mother's brother George was a specialist on the koumiss remedy for this disease and had a sanatorium near Orenburg, in southern Russia, it was decided to send him there for treatment. After two separate summer visits to the sanatorium in 1900 and 1901, during which he studied Russian, he travelled with his mother to the Caucasus and the Crimea (autumn 1901 to spring 1902). He made a full recovery and his tuberculosis never recurred.

In October 1903 Forbes entered Balliol College, Oxford, as a commoner, and in his first term won the Taylorian scholarship in Russian. A pupil of William Richard Morfill, he graduated BA (first class) in modern languages in 1906, being the first candidate at Oxford ever to offer Russian in finals. Morfill intended him to continue his studies under Vatroslav Jagić in Vienna, but Forbes's other teacher, Joseph Wright, insisted on the University of Leipzig, where he himself had studied nearly twenty years earlier. Considering Wright the more influential of his two patrons, Forbes registered at Leipzig in autumn 1908. His research there, supervised by (Johann Heinrich) August Leskien, resulted in his dissertation Der Gebrauch der Relativpronomina im Altrussischen (1910), for which he gained the degree of doctor of philosophy. Morfill died in

November 1909 and in 1910 Forbes was appointed as his successor at Oxford, at first only as reader, but from November 1921 as professor of and reader in Russian and the other Slavonic languages. Additionally (from 1920) he was lecturer in Russian at the Queen's College. During the First World War he was unfit for active service but became a lieutenant in the Royal Naval Volunteer Reserve, worked in the intelligence department of the Admiralty, and in 1918 was serving in Salonica.

The importance of Forbes's contribution to Slavonic studies in Britain lies primarily in the influence of his introductory grammars and textbooks, of which there had previously been very few, on generations of students. His *Russian Grammar* (1914), which for a long time was unrivalled, remained in print throughout most of the twentieth century, the third edition (revised and enlarged by John Dumbreck) being last reissued in 1990. Forbes also edited several elementary Russian readers and collaborated with Dragutin Subotić in publishing a *Serbian Grammar* (1915) and an English grammar (*Engleska gramatika*, 1920) for Serbs. His interest in the south Slavs was further reflected in the chapters on Bulgaria and Serbia he contributed to *The Balkans* (1915), and in his pamphlet entitled *The Southern Slavs* (1915). With C. Raymond Beazley and G. A. Birkett he published *Russia: a History from the Varangians to the Bolsheviks* (1918). Though a poor lecturer, he was an excellent tutor and not short of pupils.

Forbes was a homosexual and never married. He was fond of children and translated a series of Russian children's stories which were published with illustrations by his cousin Valery Carrick as *Picture Tales from the Russian* (1913), *More Russian Picture Tales* (1914), and *Still More Russian Picture Tales* (1915). He was a great traveller: in addition to many European countries he had, before the First World War, visited India. He had a gentle disposition, was thin and delicate in appearance, and, being short-sighted, wore glasses. A tendency to hypochondria was revealed in his habit of enquiring, before kissing his nieces, whether they had colds. A skilled amateur pianist with a large repertory known by heart, he was devoted to music and liked concerts. His artistic temperament was also revealed in a love of the theatre and, above all, of bright colours. From 1919 until his death he resided in a house overlooking the River Thames at 17 Botley Road, Oxford, known as Bridge House (later the River Hotel), where he spent much time cultivating his garden. His sister, visiting Oxford in the spring of 1926, saw him 'happy in his lot and content' and noted 'it is evident that wherever he goes he is liked and welcomed' (Ashbee, 90). Early in 1929 Forbes became concerned about the condition of his teeth. His dentist sent him to a bacteriologist, whose report worried him. Fears about his health preyed on his mind and on 9 February 1929 he was found in his bath, semi-conscious and bleeding from self-inflicted wounds. His doctor was called and attempts were made to save his life, but he died the same day. A member of the Church of England, he was buried in the churchyard of the parish church of St Peter and St Paul, Seal, near Sevenoaks, in the Forbes family grave.

GERALD STONE

Sources private information (2004) · F. Ashbee, 'Nevill Forbes, 1883–1929: some family letters from Russia', *Oxford Slavonic Papers*, new ser., 9 (1976), 79–90 · 'Professor Forbes's death', *The Times* (12 Feb 1929) · *Slavonic and East European Review*, 7 (1928–9), 699–702 · *The Times* (11 Feb 1929) · *The Times* (12 Feb 1929) · *The Times* (20 Feb 1929) · R. Filipović, 'Nevill Forbes', *Englesko-hrvatske književne veze* (Zagreb, 1972), 190–92, 212–14 · N. Forbes, *Der Gebrauch der Relativpronomina im Altrussischen* (1910) [incl. mini-autobiography] · C. Firth, *Modern languages at Oxford, 1724–1929* (1929) · b. cert. · d. cert.
Archives U. Oxf., Taylor Institution, papers
Likenesses photographs, 1890–1929, priv. coll. · photograph, 1909, priv. coll. · photograph, c.1918, U. Oxf., Taylor Institution · V. Carrick, caricature drawing, priv. coll.
Wealth at death £38,043 12s. 11d.: probate, 3 April 1929, CGPLA Eng. & Wales

Forbes, Patrick, of Corse (1564–1635), bishop of Aberdeen, was born at Corse Castle, Aberdeenshire, on 24 August 1564, the eldest son of William Forbes (d. 1598), laird of Corse, and Elizabeth Strachan, and brother of John *Forbes of Alford. After attending the high school of Stirling under Thomas Buchanan, from about 1581 he studied at the universities of Glasgow and St Andrews, where he was taught by his second cousin Andrew Melville. He accompanied Melville and other presbyterian stalwarts in their flight to England in 1584 arising from opposition to the Black Acts, which asserted the royal supremacy over the church and maintained the episcopal estate. Late in 1585 he returned to Scotland and to his theological studies. He was offered a lectureship at St Andrews, but this he declined in deference to paternal wishes.

Forbes then went to live near Montrose. In 1589 he married Lucretia Spens, daughter of David Spens of Wormiston, Fife. They had two daughters and three sons, including the celebrated theologian John *Forbes of Corse (1593–1648). In 1598 Forbes moved to Corse when he inherited the estate on the death of his father.

Forbes resisted the promptings of bishop and clergy to enter the ministry formally, but did take it upon himself to preach in his parish church, one of twenty-one vacant churches in two local presbyteries. However, the king and George Gledstanes, then archbishop of St Andrews, insisted that he must accept ordination in order to continue, and Forbes immediately desisted, curbing any activities beyond ministering to his own household. What finally moved him was the suicide in 1611 of John Chalmers, minister of Keith. Forbes had given him pastoral care in his last suffering, and Chalmers urged Forbes to succeed him. He received ordination and took up the charge in 1612.

Forbes's treatises, all written before 1618, reflect the unquenchable anti-Catholicism of the reformed theological mind, and the realities of his own struggle against the enemy in the north-east. His divinity was of an unexceptionable puritan strain, emphasizing preaching and maintaining the doctrines of election and effectual calling. In his earliest publication, *An Exquisite Commentarie upon the Revelation of Saint John* (1613; another edn, *A Learned Commentarie upon the Revelation of Saint John*, Middelburg,

Pectoris indicio data frons est, quæq; profund
Corde latent, tacitis reddit imago notis.
Hoc vultu pietas, probitas, constantia, candor,
Sinceri referunt archetypos animi.
                                        R. G. Sculp.

Patrick Forbes of Corse (1564–1635), by R. G., pubd 1635

1614), he contrasted 'the Primitive Apostolike Church, glorious in the cleare light of the sunne of righteousnesse' (Forbes, *Exquisite*, 105) with the decay which had set in even before Constantine and was much increased as the first Christian emperor stoked the 'fire of ambition' among bishops (ibid., 64). This permitted the entry of corruption in worship 'in manifold rites and superstitious ceremonies'. The apocalyptic beast was fully unleashed about 1300, during the reign of Pope Boniface VIII, but at that same time 'the woman', that is, the true church, began to return, suffering terrible persecution.

In his *Short Discovery of the Adversarie* (1614) Forbes stated that episcopacy was not a necessary institution in and for the church, but by this time he was certainly moving away from earlier presbyterian loyalties. In 1616 he preached at the opening of the general assembly and was among the commissioners appointed to revise the confession of faith, liturgy, and rules of discipline. That same year he was proposed for the vacant see of Aberdeen, but the bishopric went on this occasion to Alexander Forbes. Then, in 1618, upon the latter's death, he was at the king's bidding elected to the see on 24 March 1618 and consecrated at St Andrews on 17 May 1618.

James Melville described Forbes as 'guid, godlie, and kynd' (*Autobiography and Diary*, 1842, 18), but he did not live to see Patrick become a bishop, and other presbyterians who did were less flattering. The controversialist David

Calderwood wrote that Forbes had become a hypocrite. Andrew Melville was reported to have expressed his sorrow over Forbes's apparent defection (*Original Letters*, 2.621), while William Scot alleged that Forbes accepted the bishopric *nolens volens*, pretending that he did not want it, but entered the ministry only when such prestigious positions became available, hoping to prop up the parlous condition of 'his decaying estate' (Scot, 254). There is no evidence to support these bitter outbursts. Forbes wrote, in the midst of the affair, that he had first declined to accept (Calderwood, 7.291), but when another letter came he was placed in a very difficult position, 'eyther to accept, or to incurre the King's indignation, which to a subject is the messenger of death' (*Original Letters*, 2.553). In fact Archbishop Spottiswood urged him on, not to succumb to 'the malice of the wicked'. More encouragingly the chapter and other ministers who elected him wrote that they had done so with a joyful unanimity.

In his letter of 16 February 1618, explaining his desire not to rise to the episcopate, he declared

> I am so farre from disallowing the office and degree of a bishop … that they being conjunctlie elected, rightlie defyned, in such moderation of place and power as may putt restraint to excessive usurpation, and practising accordinglie, I thinke it not onlie a tolerable and a carefull, but even a lawfull and expedient policie in the church, and verie weill consisting with God's written Word. (Calderwood, 7.291–2)

Thus Forbes, the obedient subject, accommodated himself to episcopacy and also defended the liturgical revisions of the five articles of Perth on grounds of indifference, despite his reservations about their disruptive effect.

Presbyterian critics notwithstanding, he was highly regarded for his piety and attention to the pastoral duties of the episcopate, apologizing to the king that 'the great and dayly task of my calling' prevented him from performing other obligations elsewhere, presumably in Edinburgh. Among the tasks he took up with diligence was that of chancellor of the Aberdeen colleges. In particular he instituted major reforms of the finances and instruction at King's, with a rigour which entailed both 'ruthless and even unscrupulous' action (Stevenson, 88). In 1620 Forbes's son John was appointed professor of divinity and awarded the DD, newly revived. In 1628–9 the bishop took steps to replace the regenting system of instruction with specialist instructors who would in due course leave the college and fill pastoral charges. The strengthening of the church was his ultimate goal, and he advanced the study of divinity at King's to that purpose.

His final sickness began in 1632, when

> Forbes, sitting in his awin chear in the Oldtoun wes … suddantlie strikin in ane apoplexie and his richt syd clein takin away, and wes forsit to lerne to subscribe with his left hand: He wes careit in menis armes sumtymes to provinciall assemblies and sumtyms to sermons; and contyneuit so whill the 28th of Marche anno 1635. (Spalding, 1.31)

He was buried in his cathedral. Upon his death a volume of

tributes, *Funerals of a Right Reverend Father in God*, was published in Aberdeen, testifying to the esteem in which he was held.   DAVID GEORGE MULLAN

Sources D. Stevenson, *King's College, Aberdeen, 1560–1641: from protestant Reformation to covenanting revolution* (1990) · W. G. S. Snow, *The times, life and thought of Patrick Forbes, bishop of Aberdeen, 1618–1635* (1952) · D. Calderwood, *The history of the Kirk of Scotland*, ed. T. Thomson and D. Laing, 8 vols., Wodrow Society, 7 (1842–9) · *Original letters relating to the ecclesiastical affairs of Scotland: chiefly written by … King James the Sixth*, ed. D. Laing, 2 vols., Bannatyne Club, 92 (1851) · *Funerals of a right reverend father in God Patrick Forbes of Corse, bishop of Aberdeen, 1635* (1845) · *The autobiography and diary of Mr James Melvill*, ed. R. Pitcairn, Wodrow Society (1842) · W. Scot, *An apologetical narration of the state and government of the Kirk of Scotland since the Reformation*, ed. D. Laing, Wodrow Society, 19 (1846) · J. Spalding, *Memorialls of the trubles in Scotland and in England, AD 1624 – AD 1645*, ed. J. Stuart, 1, Spalding Club, [21] (1850), 31 · P. Forbes, *An exquisite commentarie upon the Revelation of Saint John* (1613); new edn (1614) · P. Forbes, *Short discovery of the adversarie* (1614) · *Fasti Scot.*
Likenesses R. G., line engraving, pubd 1635, BM, NPG [*see illus.*] · portraits, repro. in R. Lippe, ed., *Selections from Wodrow's biographical collections: divines of the north-east of Scotland* (1890)

Forbes, Patrick (*d. c.*1680), bishop of Caithness, was the third son of John *Forbes (*c.*1565–1634), the minister of Alford banished from Scotland for his defiant stance against the royal supremacy at the Aberdeen assembly of 1605, and Christian, the daughter of George Barclay of Mathers. He was also the nephew of Patrick *Forbes, the bishop of Aberdeen who was also chancellor of King's College, Aberdeen, where he completed his education, graduating MA in 1631. After returning to the Netherlands, where his father was pastor to the English-speaking church at Delft, he was ordained an army chaplain.

Although extant accounts vary Forbes allegedly returned to Scotland to take part in the famous Glasgow assembly of November 1638, where he signed the national covenant and with it pledged his commitment to a presbyterian ecclesiology. In 1641 he was called to his deceased father's former charge at Delft. Correspondence between Robert Baillie, one of the Scottish commissioners to the Westminster assembly in the mid-1640s, and William Spang, minister of the Scots congregation at Campveere (Veere) in the Netherlands, recorded for posterity by Baillie in his *Letters and Journals*, confirms that Forbes's influence transcended his congregation in Delft. He appears to have taken a keen interest in the affairs of the Westminster assembly and was an able apologist for the Reformed faith. In particular Spang, himself a pivotal figure linking Scottish and continental thought, was urged to persuade Forbes to employ his pen against Anabaptism and Antinomianism. Although the exact date remains unknown, in the mid-1640s he appears to have resumed his post as army chaplain, probably to the Scots brigade on the continent, and he continued in this capacity until after 1660. During the 1650s he firmly adhered to the resolutioner party within the Church of Scotland. In 1658 he was appointed chaplain to Andrew Rutherford, the earl of Teviot, who was governor-general of Dunkirk.

Notwithstanding his earlier animosity to Erastian episcopacy King Charles made Forbes bishop of Caithness on 19 March 1662. He received episcopal consecration in the royal chapel at Holyrood Palace, Edinburgh, on 7 May that year at the hands of the archbishops of St Andrews and Glasgow and the bishop of Galloway. Little is known of Forbes's episcopal oversight and ecclesiastical effectiveness in Caithness, although from an account in Robert Wodrow's *Analecta* it would appear that he gained the notorious epithet of 'the swearing bishop' (Wodrow, 3.315) for his alleged all too common use of intemperate or profane language among those under his jurisdictional competence. As a member of the Scottish episcopate he played a conspicuous role in the secular work of the Scottish parliament, where he enjoyed the privilege as a lord of the articles of selecting and scrutinizing the legislative agenda placed before the parliament. He married twice: first the daughter of Colonel Erskine, whose name has gone unrecorded, and after her death Katherine, the daughter of Patrick *Scougal, bishop of Aberdeen and the widow of William Scougal, bishop of Argyll, with whom he had one son and two daughters. Their son, John, became commissary of Caithness but predeceased his father when he died unexpectedly at Craigievar, Aberdeenshire, in October 1668. Jacobina Henrietta, or Hendrina, later married William Buchanan of Russland and after his death James Fea of Whitehall, Orkney. The name of their younger daughter is unknown but she married Alexander Skene, minister to the second charge in Perth and later provost of St Salvator's College, St Andrews. Forbes died about 1680 and was interred in Kirkwall Cathedral, Orkney.   A. S. WAYNE PEARCE

Sources DNB · *Fasti Scot.*, new edn, vols. 6, 7 · *APS, 1661–86* · *The letters and journals of Robert Baillie*, ed. D. Laing, 2 (1841) · R. Wodrow, *Analecta, or, Materials for a history of remarkable providences, mostly relating to Scotch ministers and Christians*, ed. [M. Leishman], 3, Maitland Club, 60 (1843), 315 · R. Keith and J. Spottiswoode, *An historical catalogue of the Scottish bishops, down to the year 1688*, new edn, ed. M. Russel [M. Russell] (1824), 218 · G. Grub, *An ecclesiastical history of Scotland*, 4 vols. (1861), vol. 3, p. 197

Forbes, Robert (*bap.* 1708, *d.* 1775), Jacobite annalist and Scottish Episcopal bishop of Ross and Caithness, was baptized on 4 May 1708 at Rayne, Aberdeenshire, the second child and only son of Charles Forbes (*d.* 1715?), schoolmaster, and his wife, Marjory Wright, a domestic servant. He was educated at the parish school and, from the age of fourteen, at Marischal College, Aberdeen, where he graduated AM in 1726. Aberdeenshire was at that time predominantly Episcopalian, and therefore Jacobite, and this was to mean for Robert Forbes a lifetime of involvement with the Stuart cause. In 1735 he was ordained minister by David Freebairn, bishop of Edinburgh, and soon afterwards became assistant to the Revd William Law at Leith. He was arrested at St Ninians on 7 September 1745 on his way to join the rising, and was imprisoned in the castles of Stirling and Edinburgh until 29 May 1746. His first wife, Agnes Gairey, whom he had married probably in 1736, died in 1750, and in early August 1751 he married Rachel Houston (*d.* 1776?) who actively shared his Jacobite principles. He became bishop of Ross and Caithness in 1762 and, with William Falconer, bishop of Moray, published a definitive version of the Episcopal communion liturgy

(1762–5). His political activities attracted government surveillance and required constant vigilance. On 5 August 1764 a party of dragoons appeared at his morning service in Leith and he was summoned before the military authorities for failure to pray for King George III. On 22 September he fled to London following a warning to his wife that 'some things may happen should he stay at home, that may be very, very troublesome to him … the sooner he set out the better' (*Journals*, 30).

Forbes was elected in 1765 to the bishopric of Aberdeen, a key position since, after nearly a century of persecution, it was the last real bastion of the church. The college of bishops, however, looking to eventual accommodation with the state, vetoed his appointment. In August 1769 he met secretly with Bishop Robert Gordon, head of the English nonjurors, and 'Mr and Mrs Lyon' (Laurence and Margaret Oliphant of Gask) at Moffat, where they laid plans for a protestant marriage for Charles Edward in the hope of producing an acceptable Stuart heir.

Forbes's miscellaneous writings, usually pseudonymous, include articles for the *Edinburgh Magazine* (dating from 1760) and meticulously detailed travel journals (published posthumously, edited by J. Craven, in 1886). He may also be the author of *Ajax his Speech to the Grecian Knabbs, Attempted in Broad Buchans* (1742), a lively contribution in north-east Scots to the eighteenth-century vernacular revival. But his life's work was *The Lyon in Mourning*, Forbes's history of the 1745 Jacobite rising in which the lion symbolized the Scottish nation. He began soon after Culloden

> to make up a collection of papers relative to the affairs of a Certain Young Gentleman and of those who followed his fortunes … establishing the truth both as to facts and men … for a strict and impartial examination, that so they may be carefully recorded and transmitted to posterity according to truth and justice. (*Lyon in Mourning*, 2.44)

By interview and correspondence he sought first-hand accounts of every detail of the rising of 1745, from the landing of Charles Edward Stuart to the lengthy military and political aftermath. The collection included letters regarding the prisoners after Culloden, last speeches and eyewitness accounts of executions, correspondence with those who had gone into hiding, records of clandestine meetings and plots, and regular news of the prince and the Jacobites in exile. Facts were scrupulously cross-checked and examples of humane behaviour on the part of the authorities were carefully noted as well as details of atrocities. He worked urgently, aware of the perishable nature of such testimony, declaring 'Now is the time or never' (*Lyon in Mourning*, 1.186). The material had to be assembled covertly, in circumstances entailing a high degree of integrity and trust. Forbes wrote to the Revd James Hay in 1749:

> where giving of names may be a point of delicacy and danger, I do assure you of the utmost secrecy, and that they shall not be mentioned by me in any shape till a safe and proper opportunity appears of publishing dangerous truths—and when that may happen—God only knows. (*Lyon in Mourning*, 2.352)

Within five years Forbes had produced eight manuscript volumes, each more than 200 pages. By 1761 the ninth was begun, and in 1775 volume ten, which was unfinished at his death. In 1834 Robert Chambers published substantial extracts in *Jacobite Memoirs of the Rebellion of 1745*. The full text was published in 1895, edited by Henry Paton for the Scottish History Society.

The Lyon in Mourning is an exhaustive source book of contemporary history, an attempt to take a cross-section through a whole society at a time of crisis, based upon the principle that either everybody matters or nobody does. It is one of a series of Scottish works of scholarship during the eighteenth century which sought to establish a new empirically based historiography and social science, including the work of Thomas Innes in the field of early history, Robert Wallace in demography, and Sir John Sinclair in the field of social statistics. As such it stands in the central tradition of the Scottish Enlightenment.

Forbes did not live to see his church's formal declaration of severance from the Stuart cause in 1788 upon the death of Charles Edward. He died at Leith on 18 November 1775 and was buried in the maltman's aisle in South Leith church.   WILLIAM DONALDSON

Sources *Journals of the episcopal visitations of the Right Rev. Robert Forbes*, ed. J. B. Craven (1923) · R. Forbes, *The lyon in mourning, or, A collection of speeches, letters, journals … relative to … Prince Charles Edward Stuart*, ed. H. Paton, 3 vols., Scottish History Society, 20–22 (1895–6) · G. T. S. Farquhar, *Three bishops of Dunkeld: Alexander, Rose and Watson, 1743–1808* (1915) · G. Grub, *An ecclesiastical history of Scotland*, 4 vols. (1861) · *Jacobite memoirs of the rebellion of 1745 edited from the manuscripts of the Right Rev. Robert Forbes*, ed. R. Chambers (1834) · W. Donaldson, *The Jacobite song: political myth and national identity* (1988) · F. McLynn, *The Jacobites* (1985) · W. Stephen, *History of the Scottish Church*, 2 vols. (1896) · bap. reg. Scot.
Archives NL Scot. · U. Edin. L.

Forbes, (Joan) Rosita (1890–1967), traveller and writer, was born on 16 January 1890 at Riseholme Hall, near Lincoln, the eldest of the six children of Herbert James Torr (1864–1935), landowner, and his wife, Rosita, daughter of Duncan Graham, of Lydiate, Willaston, Cheshire. Her childhood and upbringing were conventional, leaving her with few recollections beyond an early familiarity with horses and an enjoyment of reading. Her marriage on 5 October 1911 to Colonel Ronald Foster Forbes, which took her to India and Australia, ended in divorce in 1917.

Rosita Forbes's first book, *Unconducted Wanderers* (1919), describes a journey round the world with a woman friend which terminated in north Africa. There she made her first contact with the Arab world, in the ferment in which the Middle East had been left by the defeat of Turkey in the war. She met leading personalities in Cairo, Damascus, Beirut, and elsewhere, and laid the foundation of her life-long interest in Arab affairs. She also planned the adventure on which rests her claim to be taken seriously as an explorer: her journey in the winter of 1920–21 across the Libyan desert to the oasis of Kufra, which lay beyond the frontiers of Italian occupation and within the territory of Sayed Idris el Senussi (later King Idris of Libya). Only one European expedition, that of Gerhard Rohlfs in 1879, had previously visited Kufra.

Rosita Forbes disguised herself as a Muslim, taking the

name of Khadija and inventing a Circassian mother to account for imperfections in her Arabic. She had introductions to the Italian authorities, who tried to prevent her moving outside the zone they controlled, and to the sheikhs of the Senussi. She had, too, the good fortune to travel with Ahmad Hassanein Bey, the Egyptian scholar and explorer. Their journey by camel across the desert to the oasis, reached on 15 January 1921, was arduous and at times difficult, the return through Egypt by the Siwa oasis hardly less so, and Hassanein Bey's knowledge of the terrain and personalities concerned was vital to the success of the venture. Rosita Forbes's *The Secret of the Shahara: Kufara* (1921) decidedly underplayed her companion's share in the expedition and gave rise to resentments which long persisted.

After her second marriage, to Colonel Arthur Thomas McGrath (*d.* 1962), on 22 October 1921, she continued to use Rosita Forbes as her professional name and to travel as energetically as before. In 1922 she visited the Yemen, again disguised as Khadija, and made plans with H. St J. Philby for a traverse of the Rub' al-Khali, the then unexplored 'empty quarter' of southern Arabia. The plan was left in abeyance while she undertook a commission to write the life of al-Raisuni, the Moroccan brigand chief notorious for his kidnapping exploits in the early 1900s, whom she visited in his Atlas Mountains retreat. *El Raisuni, the Sultan of the Mountains* was published in 1924, by which time Rosita Forbes was on her way to join Philby for the Rub' al-Khali crossing, with a valuable commission from the *Daily Telegraph* in her pocket. When the British authorities in Aden refused the necessary permits, owing to unrest in the region, she undertook instead an ambitious trek through Ethiopia, accompanied by Harold Jones, a photographer with whom she made a film; *From Red Sea to Blue Nile* (1925) was one of her most successful books. Another visit to the Middle East produced *Conflict: Angora to Afghanistan* (1931); and in 1931 a tour of South America with her husband revealed new horizons. In 1936 she took off from Kabul on a journey through Afghanistan to Samarkand. A judicious combination of social introductions in high places, and spontaneous friendships *en route*, was the typical pattern of this as of other journeys.

Rosita Forbes's travels, recorded in a series of lively books, were interspersed with lecture tours on both sides of the Atlantic, and by rounds of visits in Europe, accompanied by her husband, to the kings, presidents, and other notables. She herself went more than once to India, disturbing the traditional routines of government houses and enjoying the anachronistic splendours of the princely states. In London the McGraths kept house in style, entertaining widely. She was a strikingly handsome woman, affecting the bright colours which suited her dark hair and eyes; as far afield as Aden, British officials had heard of her huge Ascot hats, and librarians of learned societies were amazed by her high heels and sophisticated make-up.

Rosita Forbes played her part in two world wars: she was twice decorated for driving ambulances in France in the first, and in the second she lectured in support of the war effort in Canada, the United States, and Great Britain. In her later years she was attracted to the Caribbean, and in 1939–40 the McGraths built Unicorn Cay on Eleuthera in the Bahamas, which became their permanent home and where her husband died in 1962. Rosita Forbes died at Warwick, Bermuda, on 30 June 1967. She left a vivid and highly personal account of her life in numerous travel books, and in two autobiographies, *Gypsy in the Sun* (1944) and *Appointment with Destiny* (1946), which were abridged and reissued as *Appointment in the Sun* (1949).

Although she made no major discoveries, Rosita Forbes was a bold and successful traveller. Her courage and resource were extraordinary, as was her extreme toughness in the exacting conditions of desert travel, and her range was world wide. Her achievements were recognized by the award of the gold medals of the Royal Antwerp (1921) and French (1923) geographical societies and of the silver medal of the Royal Society of Arts (1924).

DOROTHY MIDDLETON, *rev.*

Sources R. Forbes, *Gypsy in the sun* (1944) · R. Forbes, *Appointment with destiny* (1946) · A. M. Hassanein Bey, *The lost oases* (1925) · H. St J. Philby, *Forty years in the wilderness* (1957) · Burke, *Gen. GB* (1937) · personal knowledge (1981) · private information (1981) **Archives** St Ant. Oxf., letters to H. St J. B. Philby | FILM BFI NFTVA, documentary footage · BFI NFTVA, news footage **Likenesses** S. Bowen, oils, priv. coll. · H. Coster, photographs, NPG

Forbes, Stanhope Alexander (1857–1947), genre painter, was born in Dublin on 18 November 1857, the younger son of William Forbes, manager of the Midland Great Western Railway in Ireland, and his French wife, Juliette de Guise. His uncle James Staats *Forbes, an important art collector, particularly of the French Barbizon and Dutch Hague schools, his cousin William Alexander *Forbes, and his elder brother, Sir William Forbes, all followed careers as railway managers, but Stanhope Forbes showed a talent for drawing which was encouraged by his art master at Dulwich College, John Sparks. Later, when Sparks became master of Lambeth School of Art, he prepared Forbes for entry to the Royal Academy Schools in 1874. In 1880 Forbes moved to Paris to become a pupil of Léon Bonnat and shared a studio with Arthur Hacker. In Paris, Forbes was much influenced by the work of Jules Bastien-Lepage, the leading rustic naturalist painter in the Paris Salon. Following Bastien's advice that young painters should find their own *coin de terre* Forbes spent the summer months of each of the following three years working in coastal villages in Brittany (1881–3), first at Cancale and later in the area around Quimperlé. Paintings produced during this period included *A Street in Brittany* (1881), which was sold to the Walker Art Gallery, Liverpool, in 1882, and *Preparations for the Market, Quimperlé*, exhibited at the Royal Academy in 1883 (Dunedin Public Art Gallery, New Zealand).

Fired by enthusiasm for painting *en plein air* Forbes sought out a similar setting when he returned to England in 1884. In that year he visited Cornwall and was attracted by the little village of Newlyn, a sort of 'English Concarneau' (Fox and Greenacre, 8) where there were already a number of painters in residence, including Walter Langley. Forbes immediately began work on a large painting, *A Fish Sale on a Cornish Beach* (Plymouth City Museum and Art Gallery), shown at the Royal Academy in 1885. This picture, painted on the beach, with canvas and easel anchored by ropes to the sand, signalled to its London audience the new 'naturalism' of what was later dubbed the *Newlyn school. Within a short time Forbes was joined at Newlyn by Frank Bramley, Chevalier Tayler, Fred Hall, Thomas Cooper Gotch, and Henry Scott Tuke. Over the next five years this group established itself as a major force in British painting. Its members were associated with the first exhibition at the New English Art Club in 1886 although Forbes and his colleagues quickly became disenchanted with the club. It was clear from the beginning that he saw the main outlet for his major works as the Royal Academy and from 1886 onwards he produced a series of large multi-figure compositions portraying village life which entered municipal and colonial collections. The most important of this sequence was *The Health of the Bride* (1889; Tate Collection), which was purchased for £600 by Henry Tate for the collection of British art he intended to gift to the nation. This scene of a village wedding celebration was produced in the year of Forbes's own marriage to the painter Elizabeth Armstrong [see Forbes, Elizabeth Adela (1859–1912)], on 7 August. The daughter of William Robert Armstrong, a civil service official in Ottawa, she had studied in New York under William Merritt Chase. Other village scenes included that of an auction in *By Order of the Court* (1890; Walker Art Gallery, Liverpool), for which Forbes was complimented by the critic of the *Saturday Review* as having 'narrowly escaped producing a great work' (Fox, 29). The depiction of a smoke-blackened smithy in *Forging the Anchor* (1892; Ipswich Borough Council), shown in the year of Forbes's election as associate of the Royal Academy, drew critical comment from George Moore for its 'seam by seam, patch by patch' realism (Moore, 116). In these large academy pieces, it was clear that Forbes was seeking patronage from the newly formed municipal art galleries which favoured contemporary works that could be interpreted by the general public. Now regarded as the principal exponent of 'democratic' painting and leader of the Newlyn painters, Forbes established an art school at Newlyn with his wife in 1899. In 1915 Forbes married a former pupil, Maud Clayton Palmer.

A sequence of paintings of Cornish Gypsy encampments, such as *Round the Camp Fire* (1903; Laing Art Gallery, Newcastle upon Tyne), took Forbes's art in a new direction, and in the early years of the century Forbes's technique broadened and he began to embrace impressionistic effects. The Newlyn fishermen who had been portrayed with photographic exactness in a tonal palette were now seen in bright sunlight. Forbes's compositions, including such works as *The Seine Boat* (1903; priv. coll.), became simpler and his figures more heroic. He was elected a Royal Academician in 1910 and, although not an official war artist, he produced large pictures of the steelworks at Rotherham manufacturing munitions during the First World War. Typical of this group is *The Munition Girls* (1918; Sci. Mus.). During the inter-war period Forbes continued to produce smaller pictures of Cornish village life and landscape for the Royal Academy. He also continued to take pupils until the Second World War and in his teaching stuck rigidly to his naturalist principles. His last pupil, Adrian Heath, recalled being taught by the aged Forbes in studio sessions which involved an old fisherman posing with a tankard of ale, mimicking compositions which Forbes might have tackled fifty years earlier. Forbes died at his home, Higher Faughan, Newlyn, on 2 March 1947, aged eighty-nine, of heart disease.

KENNETH MCCONKEY

Sources S. A. Forbes, 'The treatment of modern life in art', *Transactions of the National Association for the Advancement of Art and its Application to Industry, Birmingham Meeting, MDCCCXC* (1891), 123–30 · M. H. Dixon, 'Stanhope A. Forbes', *Magazine of Art*, 15 (1891–2), 181–4 · N. Garstin, 'The work of Stanhope A. Forbes, ARA', *The Studio*, 23 (1901), 81–8 · F. Dolman, 'Illustrated interviews: Mr Stanhope Forbes ARA', *Strand Magazine*, 22 (1901), 483–94 · Mrs L. Birch, *Stanhope A. Forbes, ARA, and Elizabeth Stanhope Forbes, ARWS* (1906) · C. Lewis Hind, 'Stanhope A. Forbes', *Christmas Art Annual* (1911) [Christmas no.] · *The Times* (3 March 1947) · C. Fox and F. Greenacre, *Painting in Newlyn, 1880–1930* (1985) [exhibition catalogue, Barbican Art Gallery, London, 11 July – 1 Sept, 1985] · C. Fox, *Stanhope Forbes and the Newlyn school* (1993) · T. Cross, *The shining sands: artists at Newlyn and St Ives* (1994) · G. Moore, *Modern painting* (1893) · m. cert. · d. cert. · *CGPLA Eng. & Wales* (1947)

Archives Tate collection, corresp., record book of sales of works

Likenesses S. A. Forbes, self-portrait, 1889, Newlyn Art Gallery, Penlee House, Penzance · S. A. Forbes, self-portrait, oils, 1891, Aberdeen Art Gallery, MacDonald collection · R. Bolitho, oils, 1896, priv. coll. · E. S. Forbes, c.1900, repro. in Fox, *Stanhope Forbes*, 57 · bronze medallion, Passmore Edwards Art Gallery, Newlyn, Cornwall · photograph, NPG

Wealth at death £24,238 15s. 6d.: probate, 30 June 1947, *CGPLA Eng. & Wales*

Forbes, Walter, nineteenth Lord Forbes (1798–1868), army officer, was born on 29 May 1798 at Crailing, Roxburghshire, the second son of James Ochoncar *Forbes, eighteenth lord (1765–1843), and his wife, Elizabeth (1775–1830), daughter and heir of Walter Hunter, of Polmood, Peeblesshire, and Crailing, Roxburghshire. He served in the navy, then in 1814 joined the Coldstream Guards, of which his father had been for twenty-six years an officer, and in which his elder brother, the Hon. James Forbes, then held a commission. He was present with his regiment at Waterloo, being one of the youngest British officers there. Though only a junior ensign, Forbes commanded a company at Hougoumont, for his senior officers were ill or absent. He retired from the army in 1825, having married, on 31 January, Horatia (1799–1862), seventh daughter of Sir John Gregory Shaw, bt, of Eltham, Kent; they had seven children. His elder brother James having predeceased their father, Forbes succeeded as nineteenth lord and premier baron of Scotland on 4 May 1843.

Forbes was much concerned with church affairs, and was greatly attached to the episcopal church in Scotland. He was one of the founders and greatest benefactors of St Ninian's Cathedral, Perth. He married, secondly, on 4 April 1864, Louisa (d. 26 Jan 1921), daughter of James Ormond of Abingdon, Berkshire; they had two sons.

Forbes died on 1 May 1868 at Richmond, Surrey. There was a beautiful memorial window in the guards' chapel at Wellington barracks, given by his widow, and also a memorial tablet to him, his father, and elder brother, but this was destroyed by enemy action on 18 June 1944.

RICHARD HOOPER, rev. JAMES LUNT

Sources private information (1889) · *Royal Military Chapel, Wellington Barracks* (1882) · Fortescue, *Brit. army*, vol. 10 · E. Longford [E. H. Pakenham, countess of Longford], *Wellington*, 1: *The years of the sword* (1969) · *The reminiscences and recollections of Captain Gronow*, 2 vols. (1892) · Burke, *Peerage* · GEC, *Peerage* · *Dod's Peerage* (1858)
Wealth at death under £14,000: probate, 8 July 1868, *CGPLA Eng. & Wales*

Forbes, William (1585–1634), bishop of Edinburgh, was born in Aberdeen, the son of Thomas Forbes, a burgess descended from the Forbeses of Corsindae, and his wife, Janet Cargill, sister of Dr James *Cargill. He was educated from 1597 at Marischal College, graduating MA in 1601, and was soon after appointed a regent (lecturer) in the same college, where he defended Aristotle against Ramus. He resigned in 1606 and travelled through Poland, Germany, and the Netherlands. He studied at several universities, delving into the fathers and mastering Hebrew; he also acquired the friendship of Scaliger, Grotius, and Vossius.

Returning after five years to Britain, Forbes was invited to become professor of Hebrew at Oxford, but always inclined to ill health, he accepted advice to return to his homeland. Here at some point he married a kinswoman, Elizabeth Forbes, sister of John Forbes of Corsindae; they had four sons. Ordained, probably by Bishop Blackburn of Aberdeen, he was minister successively of two Aberdeenshire parishes, Alford (c.1614) and Monymusk (October 1615). On 29 October 1616, pursuant to a nomination by the general assembly, he was appointed one of the ministers of Aberdeen, and in 1617 he was made DD by St Andrews University.

At the Perth assembly in 1618 Forbes was selected to defend the lawfulness of kneeling at communion, and in the same year, in a formal dispute with Principal Aidie of Marischal College, he maintained the lawfulness of prayers for the dead. Such doctrines would scarcely have been tolerated elsewhere in Scotland, but in Aberdeen they were received with favour, and on Aidie's forced resignation in 1620 the town councillors, who were patrons of Marischal College, appointed him principal on condition 'that he continew his ministerie in teacheing twa sermonis everie weik as he dois presentlie' (*Extracts from the Council Register*, 2.370).

On 21 March 1622 Forbes was transferred to St Giles', Edinburgh. He went reluctantly, and soon ran into trouble with some of the outspoken presbyterian laity. His zeal for the observance of the Perth articles was distasteful to many, and when he taught that the doctrines of Romanist and reformed could in many points be easily reconciled, discontent was succeeded by disorder. Five ringleaders were dealt with by the privy council, but Forbes felt that his ministry at Edinburgh was a failure, and he gladly availed himself of an opportunity in 1626 to return to his former charge in Aberdeen, where the townspeople welcomed him.

Forbes himself published nothing, but in 1658 a posthumous work, *Considerationes modestae et pacificae*, which Baillie referred to as his 'wicked dictates' (*Letters and Journals*, 3.406), was published from his manuscripts by Thomas Sydserf, bishop of Galloway. He also wrote animadversions, now lost, on Bellarmine's works (*Considerationes* likewise has much about Bellarmine), and some of Forbes's writings were found in Aberdeen in 1640 in the house of Dr Robert Sibbald, which did that divine no good (Spalding, 1.312). G. D. Henderson said that Forbes was 'an avowed Arminian' (Henderson, 494), but in fact Forbes attempted to walk a 'via media' (Forbes, 2.507), which brought him sometimes closer to Catholicism, sometimes to moderate protestantism, but almost always away from 'the more rigid Protestants' (ibid., 2.545). He believed that reverence for Christian antiquity would bring about peace in the church, and used this measure against Romanists and puritans alike. He was ambiguous on the question of predestination, and refused to conform to the radical Augustinianism of his detractors. He also rejected the puritan quest for certainty of salvation which he feared led to 'incredible griefs and torments in the most pious minds, as sad experience daily witnesses' (ibid., 1.258). On the other hand he was unstinting in his criticism of Romanists for their assertion of the intrinsic worth of good works.

In 1633 Forbes preached before Charles I at Holyrood, to the king's great satisfaction. Shortly afterwards, when the see of Edinburgh was erected, Forbes was nominated to it, and was consecrated on 28 January 1634. In early March he sent an injunction to his clergy to celebrate the eucharist on Easter Sunday according to the manner prescribed, that is, kneeling. When Easter came he was very ill, and just able to celebrate in St Giles' Cathedral. He died in Edinburgh on the following Saturday, 12 April 1634, aged forty-nine, 'efter taking of sum phisick, sitting in his owne chear suddantlie' (Spalding, 1.45), and was buried in his cathedral; his monument was afterwards destroyed, but a copy of the inscription is in William Maitland's *The History of Edinburgh* (1753).

Forbes had been effectively the founder of the Scottish equivalent of English Laudians; Robert Baillie wrote that Laud was Forbes's 'father and patron' (Baillie, *Canterburians*, C1r). Forbes's reputation among presbyterians may be gleaned from a verse epitaph:

Here lyes Bishop Forbes who never did good,
A degenerat gentleman of no great blood,
A traitor to Christ and souldier of Rome,
Here lyes his corpse till the day of doom.
(Lippe, 263)

However, Sir Thomas Urquhart thought him the ablest Scottish philosopher and divine since Scotus Subtilis, and Bishop Gilbert Burnet offered an encomium based upon recollections provided by his father's personal knowledge of him, that Forbes made him think of the biblical words 'Did not our hearts burn within us, while he yet talked with us, and opened to us the scriptures?' Burnet added:

He preached with a zeal and vehemence, that made him forget all the measures of time; two or three hours was no extraordinary thing for him; those sermons wasted his strength so fast, and his ascetical course of life was such, that he supplyed it so scantly that he dyed within a year after his promotion. (Burnet, preface)

JAMES COOPER, rev. DAVID GEORGE MULLAN

Sources W. Forbes, *Considerationes modestae et pacificae*, 2 vols. (1850–56) • R. Lippe, 'Collections on the life of Mr William Forbes', *Selections from Wodrow's biographical collections: divines of the north-east of Scotland*, New Spalding Club, 5 (1890) • J. Spalding, *Memorialls of the trubles in Scotland and in England, AD 1624 – AD 1645*, ed. J. Stuart, 2 vols., Spalding Club, [21, 23] (1850–51) • D. Calderwood, *The history of the Kirk of Scotland*, ed. T. Thomson and D. Laing, 8 vols., Wodrow Society, 7 (1842–9) • D. Irving, *Lives of Scotish writers*, 2 (1839) • D. G. Mullan, *Scottish puritanism, 1590–1638* (2000) • R. Baillie, *A large supplement of the Canterburians self-conviction* (1641) • *The letters and journals of Robert Baillie*, ed. D. Laing, 3 vols., Bannatyne Club, 73 (1841–2) • J. Stuart, ed., *Selections from the records of the kirk session, presbytery, and synod of Aberdeen*, Spalding Club, 15 (1846) • J. Stuart, ed., *Extracts from the council register of the burgh of Aberdeen, 2: 1570–1625*, Spalding Club, 19 (1848) • R. Keith and J. Spottiswoode, *An historical catalogue of the Scottish bishops, down to the year 1688*, new edn, ed. M. Russel [M. Russell] (1824) • G. D. Henderson, 'Arminianism in Scotland', *London Quarterly and Holborn Review*, 157 (1932), 493–504 • *DNB* • T. Urquhart, *The jewel*, ed. R. D. S. Jack and R. J. Lyall (1983) • G. Burnet, *Life of William Bedell* (1685) • *Fasti Scot.*, new edn, 7.341
Likenesses eleventh earl of Buchan, pencil and chalk (after G. Jamesone), Scot. NPG • G. Jamesone, portrait, Marischal College, Aberdeen; repro. in J. Pinkerton, *Iconographia Scotia* (1797) • portrait, Scot. NPG
Wealth at death £8183 14s. 6d.—incl. library worth approx. 4000 merks; other goods £466 13s. 4d.: NA Scot., CC 8/8/57, fols. 74r–76v

Forbes, Sir William, of Craigievar, first baronet (*d.* 1648), politician, was the eldest son of William Forbes (*d. c.*1627), of Menie, later of Craigievar, Aberdeenshire, and his wife, Margaret Udward or Edward, daughter of the provost of Edinburgh; his parents had married in 1603. His father, known as Merchant Willie or Dantzig Willie, was a younger brother of Patrick Forbes of Corse, from 1618 bishop of Aberdeen and uncle of the eirenicist John Forbes of Corse. William was served heir to his father for his lands of Craigievar on 24 March 1629. His inheritance included Craigievar Castle, begun in the Flemish style by the Mortimer family but sold to Merchant Willie in 1610 and only completed in 1626. On 30 April 1630, ostensibly for his loyalty but more probably for his money, Charles I created William a baronet of Nova Scotia. In 1635 Forbes married Bathia (*d.* after 1649), second daughter of Sir Archibald Murray of Blackbarony; they had two sons and three daughters.

Sir William had been appointed a justice of the peace for Aberdeenshire in 1634, but it was through the civil strife that engulfed Scotland over the signing of the national covenant of 1638 that he became a figure of importance, not just in local but also in national affairs. From an early stage of the dispute, in spite of his earlier favour with the king and the Episcopalian tendencies of his kinsmen of Corse, Sir William took the side of the covenanters against the supporters of the king. In 1638, for instance, he used his patronage of the wealthy parsonage of Kincardine to secure the submission to the Glasgow assembly of his younger brother John Forbes, whose

opposition to the covenant was driving him to leave Scotland for Ireland. From 1641 onwards Sir William was prominent on the committees through which the covenanters sought to govern Scottish affairs. In that year he was appointed a commissioner for receiving brotherly assistance from the parliament of England and for conserving the treaty, and a commissioner for manufactures. In 1643 he was appointed to the committee for the loan and tax, and to that for war, also serving on the latter in 1644, 1646, and 1648. In 1644 he was also appointed to the committees for the north, for propositions of peace, and for negotiating with Sweden. He served on the committee of estates in 1644–5. He was on the committee on losses in 1645 and the commission of visitation to Aberdeen University in 1645–6, was a commissioner for re-evaluation of Aberdeenshire in 1647, and was appointed sheriff of Aberdeen in 1647. He was granted £10,000 Scots in reparation for war-related losses in 1647 and had the barony of Logiefintray ratified to him by parliament in 1648, but he appears soon afterwards to have suffered a downturn in fortune and favour. Despite his being elected a commissioner of parliament for Aberdeenshire in 1648, another commissioner took his place.

An eighteenth-century descendant claimed that Forbes, ultimately sickened by the depredations of the covenanters, sought to distance himself from them and, gathering his wealth, planned to put it and himself at the service of the king. The covenanters forestalled this by stripping him of his assets on the pretext of acting for the public good. So affected by this turn of events was Sir William that he died soon afterwards, between 19 June and 13 September 1648, allegedly of a broken heart. His wife survived him, and his twelve-year-old son and heir, John, became liable for payment of significant debts when, in 1653, Alexander Lindsay succeeded in having the family patrimony apprized to the value of £44,612 Scots.

SHONA MACLEAN VANCE

Sources M. D. Young, ed., *The parliaments of Scotland: burgh and shire commissioners*, 1 (1992) • A. Tayler and H. Tayler, eds., *The house of Forbes*, Third Spalding Club, 8 (1937) • J. Spalding, *Memorialls of the trubles in Scotland and in England, AD 1624 – AD 1645*, ed. J. Stuart, 2 vols., Spalding Club, [21, 23] (1850–51) • J. Gordon, *History of Scots affairs from 1637–1641*, ed. J. Robertson and G. Grub, 3 vols., Spalding Club, 1, 3, 5 (1841) • M. Ellington, *Craigievar Castle* (1985)
Likenesses G. Jamesone, oils, Craigievar Castle, Aberdeenshire • engraving (after G. Jamesone), repro. in Tayler and Tayler, eds., *House of Forbes*
Wealth at death various lands apprized at the instance of Alexander Lindsay for payment of £44,612 Scots owed to Lindsay (1653); stripped of cash by the covenanters, for the public good, shortly before death: Gordon, *History of Scots affairs*, vol. 3, p. 202 n. 1; Young, ed., *Parliaments of Scotland*, vol. 1, p. 246

Forbes, William (1668x71–1745), lawyer and jurist, was born possibly in 1668 or between November 1670 and January 1671, the elder of two children of Thomas Forbes (1629–1687) and his wife, Isabel (1635–1715), daughter of David Edgar of Keithock, Forfarshire, and widow of James Pitcairn. Thomas Forbes was of an old Aberdeenshire family with good connections in the burgh and university of

Aberdeen. He studied at Leiden and Padua and was professor of philosophy in the University of Pisa from 1658 to 1659 and of medicine there from 1659 to 1662, before returning to Scotland.

Details of Forbes's early education are unknown; however, he did graduate AM from a university, probably St Andrews as a William Forbes matriculated at St Salvator's College there in 1685 and Thomas Forbes moved to St Andrews between January 1684 and May 1685, but the evidence is circumstantial. On 28 October 1688 a William Forbes, noted as a Scot aged twenty, matriculated at the University of Leiden. In 1690 Forbes prepared to compete for the position of regent in philosophy at Edinburgh, but was frustrated by ill health. He may then have remained in Edinburgh or returned to the Netherlands to study law; he was certainly in Edinburgh in 1694, when he prepared his mother's poll tax return. On 15 February 1696 he was admitted as a member of the Faculty of Advocates.

On 25 January 1700 Forbes married Margaret, the daughter of Alexander Lindsay, an Edinburgh wool merchant. The couple had two children: Thomas (*bap.* 1702), who became an advocate, and Janet (*bap.* 1708), who married Alexander Carmichael, a landowner in Leith. By February 1700 Forbes had been appointed an examinator of the Faculty of Advocates. He was clerk of faculty from January 1702 to January 1703, and joint clerk from November 1705 until the end of 1714. In 1705 the faculty agreed that Forbes should collect court of session decisions (eventually published as *A Journal of the Session* in 1714) and he was appointed joint keeper of the faculty library.

Following his marriage, financial pressure on Forbes may have led him to turn to writing: *A Methodical Treatise concerning Bills of Exchange … according to the Analogy of the Scots Law* appeared in 1703. The dedications and contents of the works show how Forbes tried to demonstrate his abilities not only to his colleagues but to politicians who he thought might be useful to him. *A Treatise of Church Lands and Tithes* (2 vols., 1705) and *The Duty and Powers of Justices of the Peace in this Part of Great Britain called Scotland* (2 pts, 1707–8) were dedicated respectively to Sir Hew Dalrymple of North Berwick, lord president of the court of session, and his brother Sir David Dalrymple of Hailes, then solicitor-general. The latter work devoted special attention to the extended duties of justices regarding customs and excise following the union with England, and appeared at the same time as Forbes was seeking the new post of auditor of the exchequer to deal with excise-related questions. A further work concerned with the consequences of the union was *The Law of Election of Members of Parliament* (1710).

In 1708 Forbes had decided upon his major task, the writing of a:

> complete body of the law of Scotland, containing the harmony thereof with, and differences from the civil and feudal laws; and shewing how far the Scots and English law do agree and differ; with incident comparative views of the modern constitutions of other nations in Europe. (*Minute Book of the Faculty of Advocates*, 1.277)

This book, 'The great body of the law of Scotland', was never published; the manuscript is in Glasgow University Library. However, Forbes's interest in comparing Scots with English law was well known and was a factor in his subsequent appointment at Glasgow.

In December 1713 Queen Anne assigned income in the sum of £90 for the establishment of the chair of civil law at the University of Glasgow. Soundings about suitable candidates resulted in the report that 'Mr. William Forbes, Advocat … is Esteem'd a man very well skill'd in the Civil Law and Capable to teach the same, and … thought the fittest for that post' (minutes of meetings of faculty, 1701–1717, 28 Jan 1714, U. Glas., Archives and Business Records Centre, MS 26632, 113). Among his strongest supporters at Glasgow was the rector, Sir John Maxwell of Pollock. Forbes was elected the university's first professor of civil law in February 1714. His teaching remit was identified as civil, feudal, canon, and Scots law.

On 18 February 1714 Forbes gave his inaugural lecture, on 'the nature, fortune, dignity, utility, and authority of the civil law'. He followed this with a series of classes on 'the civil and Scottish laws', comparing Scots law with Roman law and explaining the contrast with English law. These were the first classes on Scots law to be taught in a university; previously Scots law, less prestigious than Roman law, had been taught privately by advocates in Edinburgh. His teaching on Scots law led to *The Institutes of the Law of Scotland*, published in two volumes in 1722 and 1730, the first dealing with private, the second with criminal law. However, attendance at his classes in Scots law seems to have been low; in 1716 he offered only civil law, and he had almost certainly given up Scots law by the 1730s.

Forbes's commitment to Scots law cannot be doubted but his professorship was controversial. He did not always teach at times required by the university, demanded full payment for teaching law to divinity students, and for some time feuded with his patron, Pollock, and the principal who had appointed him, John Stirling. He changed political allegiance several times, but by the 1730s had become an ally of Principal Neil Campbell and his patron, Archibald Campbell, earl of Ilay and manager of Scotland for Walpole. This possibly followed Campbell's appointment of Forbes's son, Thomas, as college advocate in 1728. Forbes was dean of the faculty from 1732 to 1734, and as library quaestor from 1736 to 1738 he acquired many Dutch and English texts. He represented the University of Glasgow at the general assembly of the Church of Scotland in Edinburgh in 1740. He died intestate at Glasgow on 27 October 1745, leaving £4145, and 14,800 marks in bonds.

MICHAEL P. CLANCY

Sources J. W. Cairns, 'The origins of the Glasgow law school: the professors of civil law, 1714–61', *The life of the law*, ed. P. Birks (1993) • F. J. Grant, ed., *The Faculty of Advocates in Scotland, 1532–1943*, Scottish RS, 145 (1944) • W. Macfarlane, *Genealogical collections concerning families in Scotland*, ed. J. T. Clark, 2 vols., Scottish History Society, 33–4 (1900) • public register of arms and bearings in Scotland, Lyon Office • H. Paton, ed., *The register of marriages for the parish of Edinburgh, 1595–1700*, Scottish RS, old ser., 27 (1905) • *Reg. PCS*, 3rd ser., vol. 3 • G. du Rieu, ed., *Album studiosorum academiae Lugduno Batavae, MDLXXV–MDCCCLXXV: accedunt nomina curatorum et professorum per* *eadem secula* (The Hague, 1875) • J. M. Pinkerton, ed., *The minute book of the Faculty of Advocates*, 1: *1661–1712*, Stair Society, 29 (1976) • C. Innes, ed., *Munimenta alme Universitatis Glasguensis / Records of the University of Glasgow from its foundation till 1727*, 4 vols., Maitland Club, 72 (1854), vol. 2 • U. Glas., Murray MSS • W. Fraser, ed., *Memoirs of the Maxwells of Pollok*, 2 vols. (privately printed, Edinburgh, 1863), vol. 2, p. 366 • D. M. Walker, *The Scottish jurists* (1985) • register of Glasgow testaments, NA Scot., CC 9/7/59, 23262 • Watt, *Bibl. Brit.* • private information (2004) [J. W. Cairns] • NA Scot., B 22/2/14, fols. 67v–68v

Archives NL Scot., Advocates' Library, MSS • U. Glas., MSS
Likenesses engraving, repro. in W. Forbes, *Institutes of the law of Scotland* (1722)
Wealth at death £4145; plus 14,800 marks in bonds

Forbes, Sir William, of Pitsligo, sixth baronet (1739–1806), banker and benefactor, was born on 5 April 1739 at Edinburgh, the eldest surviving son of Sir William Forbes, fifth baronet (1706/7–1743), advocate, and Christian Forbes (1705–1789), daughter of John Forbes and Susan, *née* Morison. Both his parents were descended from branches of the Forbes family of Monymusk, Aberdeenshire, whose lands had been sold by his great-grandfather. His father inherited a Nova Scotia baronetcy, created in 1626. His paternal grandmother, Mary Forbes, was a sister of Alexander, Lord Forbes of Pitsligo, attainted after the Jacobite rising of 1745. Forbes was to become obsessed by the task of restoring the title and estate.

When Forbes was four years old his father died, aged thirty-six, and soon afterwards his younger brother also died. Christian Forbes, who moved to Aberdeen, was for many years reduced to a state of dignified penury which, following her death at the age of eighty-four, excited the written admiration of her son, followed by Victorian biographers. Forbes's formal education was placed in the hands of four senior members of the family, while his mother introduced him to the disciplines of the Scottish Episcopal church. In later life he never wavered from its teaching, being called 'one of the most perfect specimens of the Christian character which Great Britain has ever produced' (Chambers, *Scots.*).

In 1753 his mother moved to Edinburgh, and Forbes was introduced by a family friend, Francis Farquharson of Haughton, to the Coutts brothers, in whose banking house he was articled on Whitsunday 1754, aged fifteen. Despite hard treatment both during and after his apprenticeship (which had allowed him only one night out of Edinburgh in five years), he always paid tribute to the Coutts family as the architects of his success. It was timely for him that the death of John Coutts, and a change of emphasis to London banking, meant that new blood was needed in the Edinburgh partnership soon after he had completed his training. It was not, however, until 1763 that he was fully admitted. Joining him in the Scottish bank, which traded another ten years as John Coutts & Co., were James Hunter (later Sir James Hunter Blair), who had been a fellow apprentice, and (briefly) Robert Herries, who was soon to establish his own firm in London.

Forbes was a prudent and influential banker who soon became a leading member of the Merchants' Company of Edinburgh, and advised the lord advocate in 1772 on the wording of a new bankruptcy act. His career produced two secondary virtues: it gave him significant wealth, as a platform for his benefactions, and resulted in his autobiographical *Memoirs of a Banking-House*, originally written for his eldest son, William, in 1803 and eventually published in 1860. This book gives useful insight into the early mercantile and banking concerns of the Coutts family, and describes the origins of the London Exchange Banking Company of Robert Herries, in which both Forbes and Blair were to have a short-term interest.

As a benefactor, Forbes was exceptionally generous: he put aside an annual proportion of his income and 'for the last thirty years of his life … was either at the head, or actively engaged in the management of all the charitable establishments of Edinburgh' (Chambers, *Scots.*). The charity workhouse, Orphans' Hospital, Maidens' Hospital, Watson's Hospital, Gillespie's Hospital, Royal Infirmary, lunatic asylum, asylum for blind people, and Royal High School all benefited by him, as instigator or money raiser. He gave relief to impoverished individuals, especially those of high birth, and supported a fund for indigent clergy, in which (as in certain other schemes) he pamphleteered. He was responsible for the Cowgate Episcopal Chapel and promoted, with Sir James Hunter Blair, the Edinburgh South Bridge scheme, one of his few controversial activities. When Forbes succeeded to the title and arms of Pitsligo following the death, without heirs, of John Forbes in 1781, Aberdeenshire began to share his largesse. He laid out the village of New Pitsligo, encouraging agriculture, building chapels, a school, and linen works, and improving communication with the seaports of Peterhead and Banff.

Forbes was a close friend of the poet and philosopher James Beattie, and also of James Boswell, who introduced him to Samuel Johnson in 1773. Urbane and welcoming, with refined tastes in music, dancing, and drawing, Forbes gravitated towards London, where he made his mark in two ways. At one level he was a conversationalist, accepted in West End society, a member of Johnson's Literary Club, and a friend of Sir Joshua Reynolds (for whom he sat); at the other level he was a wise banker, introduced by Lord Melville to William Pitt the younger, who took his advice in monetary matters. In 1799 Forbes declined the offer by Pitt of an Irish peerage; he had also refused parliamentary seats. At home in Edinburgh, he was no less of a socialite. In 1770 he had married Elizabeth Hay (d. 1802), eldest daughter of Sir James Hay MD, baronet, of Haystoun, Peeblesshire, and they entertained in grand style, receiving visiting foreigners. Four sons and five daughters were born of the marriage.

No inkling of Forbes's conviviality can be inferred from the ponderous literary style of his three main books. As the *Memoirs* and the *Narrative of the Last Sickness and Death of Dame Christian Forbes* (published in 1875) were not written for publication, some allowance can be made for the long-winded arrangement of the former and the lugubriousness of the latter. But Forbes's principal work, *An Account of the Life and Writings of James Beattie, including Many of his Original Letters* (2 vols., 1806; 2nd edn, 3 vols., 1807), though successful, exercised the patience of the *Edinburgh Review*, who found it 'a great deal larger, and a great deal duller, than we are bound to tolerate' (*EdinR*, 10, 172). One of Beattie's letters, published by Forbes, refers to a natural difficulty among the Scots in writing readable English: 'We are … continually afraid of committing *gross* blunders; and, when an easy, idiomatical phrase occurs, dare not adopt it … for fear of Scotticisms' (Forbes, *An Account of the Life … Including many of his Original Letters*, 2.164).

In winter 1792–3 Forbes and his wife, for the sake of the latter's health, made a rare trip abroad, staying mainly in Rome and Naples. His wife died in 1802, and he wrote, as he had of his mother's, a narrative of her death. He was called to London in 1806 as a witness in Lord Melville's impeachment, and never recovered from the journey. He died in Edinburgh on 12 November 1806, aged sixty-seven, of 'water in the chest', and was buried there; he was mourned by Sir Walter Scott in the introduction to the fourth canto of *Marmion*. His eldest son, William Forbes, who succeeded to the baronetcy, was Scott's lifelong friend and beat him to the hand of Williamina Belsches Stuart. James Skene, another intimate friend of Scott, married Jane, Forbes's youngest daughter. John Hay *Forbes, Forbes's second son, became the judge Lord Medwyn. In 1838 the banking house still known as Sir William Forbes & Co. was affiliated with the Glasgow Union Banking Company, which absorbed the firm totally in 1843 on becoming the Union Bank of Scotland.

JOHN BOOKER

Sources W. Forbes, *Memoirs of a banking-house*, ed. [R. Chambers], [2nd edn] (1860) · Chambers, *Scots.* (1835), vol. 2 · J. Paterson, *Kay's Edinburgh portraits: a series of anecdotal biographies chiefly of Scotchmen*, ed. J. Maidment, 1 (1885) · J. C. Shairp, P. G. Tait, and A. Adams-Riley, *Life and letters of James David Forbes* (1873) · *Boswell's journal of a tour to the Hebrides with Samuel Johnson*, ed. F. A. Pottle and C. H. Bennett (1936) · W. Scott, 'Introduction to canto fourth', *Marmion: a tale of a Flodden field* (1808), 161–82 · W. Forbes, *An account of the life and writings of James Beattie*, 2nd edn, 3 vols. (1807) · review of *An account of the life and writings of James Beattie*, *EdinR*, 10 (1807), 171–99 · W. Forbes, *Narrative of the last sickness and death of Dame Christian Forbes*, ed. A. P. Forbes (1875) · C. C. Abbott, *A catalogue of papers relating to Boswell, Johnson and Sir William Forbes found at Fettercairn House* (1936) · G. Galloway, *Elegy on Sir W. Forbes* (1806) · R. Carmichael, *Extempore, on seeing Sir W. Forbes' funeral* (1806) [poem]
Archives Coutts & Co., London, letters, MSS, 9694, 17918–17922 · NL Scot., corresp. and papers · NL Scot., journal of a continental tour | NA Scot., letters to Hugh Hamilton of Pinmore · U. Aberdeen L., corresp. with James Beattie · U. Aberdeen L., corresp. with G. Ogilvie · Yale U., Beinecke L., corresp. with James Boswell and others
Likenesses P. Batoni, oils, 1776, Lochinch Castle · J. Reynolds, oils, *c.*1786, Scot. NPG · J. Tassie, paste medallion, 1791, Scot. NPG · J. Henning, porcelain medallion, 1802, Scot. NPG · J. Kay, caricature, etching, 1806, NPG · J. Kay, caricature, etching, BM · H. Raeburn, oils, Glasgow Art Gallery and Museum · H. Raeburn, oils, unknown collection · W. S. Watson, group portrait, oils (*The inauguration of Robert Burns as poet laureate of the Lodge Canongate, Kilwinning, 1787*), Scot. NPG · T. Woolnoth, stipple (after A. Skirving), BM · J. Zoffany, oils, priv. coll.

Forbes, William Alexander (1855–1883), zoologist, was born at 16 Pittville Villas, Cheltenham, on 25 June 1855,

the second son of James Staats *Forbes (1823–1904), chairman of the London, Chatham, and Dover Railway Company, and Ann (*d.* 1901), daughter of John Bennett. He was educated at Kensington School and Winchester College (1866–72). He went on to study German at Aix-la-Chapelle in 1872, and after a year became a student of medicine at Edinburgh University (1873–5) and then at University College, London (1875–6). Early in his studies he showed great interest in (and a talent for) biology, to which he finally devoted himself.

Through the influence of his friend Alfred Henry Garrod, the zoologist, Forbes entered St John's College, Cambridge, in 1876. Here he gained a first class in the natural sciences tripos of 1879, and was subsequently elected a fellow of his college. In the same year he was appointed prosector to the Zoological Society of London on the death in October of the previous incumbent, Professor Garrod, whose literary executor he became. (A collection of Garrod's scientific papers was published in 1881, edited by Forbes with a biographical notice.) In addition to his zoological work he lectured on comparative anatomy at Charing Cross Hospital medical school.

Between 1879 and 1882 Forbes's work at the Zoological Society's gardens yielded some original and valuable papers. Those on the muscular structure and voice organs of birds were most notable, including 'On the anatomy of the passerine birds' (*Proceedings of the Zoological Society*, 1880–82), 'On the contributions to the anatomy and classification of birds made by Professor Garrod' (*The Ibis*, 1881), and 'On the anatomy of the petrels collected during the voyage of H.M.S. *Challenger*' (*Zoology of the Challenger*, 4, pt 11, 1882).

In the summer of 1880 Forbes made a short excursion to the forests of Pernambuco, in Brazil, and published an account of the trip in *The Ibis* in 1881. He also travelled in the United States and, on 19 July 1882, sailed from Liverpool to investigate the fauna of tropical Africa, starting from the mouth of the Niger delta. However, owing to the non-arrival of a steamer, he was prevented from continuing upriver from Shonga. He decided to return home to England immediately, but shortly after Christmas he was seized with a fever and dysentery, and died on 14 January 1883 in Shonga. His remains were brought to England and buried, on 1 April 1884, in the churchyard of Wickham in Kent.

Forbes was an excellent worker, popular with his contemporaries, and had the potential to be one of the leading zoologists of his time. His collected papers and last journals (published in *The Ibis* in 1883) were issued as a memorial volume edited by Frank Evers Beddard, Forbes's successor as the Zoological Society's prosector, in 1885.

G. T. BETTANY, *rev.* YOLANDA FOOTE

Sources *The collected papers of the late William Alexander Forbes*, ed. F. E. Beddard (1885) · *The Ibis*, 5th ser., 1 (1883) · J. B. Wainewright, ed., *Winchester College, 1836–1906: a register* (1907) · Venn, *Alum. Cant.* · Boase, *Mod. Eng. biog.* · b. cert.

Forbes-Robertson. For this title name *see* Robertson, (Mary) Gertrude Forbes-, Lady Forbes-Robertson (1874–

1950) [*see under* Robertson, Sir Johnston Forbes- (1853–1937)].

Forby, Robert (1759–1825), philologist, was the son of Thomas Forby, a grocer at Stoke Ferry, Norfolk. He was educated at King's Lynn Free School under David Lloyd LLD, and from 1776 at Gonville and Caius College, Cambridge, where he obtained a fellowship (BA, 1781; MA, 1784). He became deacon in September 1781 and priest in September 1785. Sir John Berney, bt, persuaded him to leave the university and to become tutor of his sons, and presented him in 1787 to the small living of Horningtoft, Norfolk. Afterwards he lived at Barton Bendish, where he took pupils; when their number increased he removed to Wereham near King's Lynn. In 1789, by the death of his uncle, the Revd Joseph Forby, he became incumbent of the valuable rectory of Fincham, Norfolk. He moved there in 1801, and continued to live in his parish until his death. He was a keen student of botany, and was elected a fellow of the Linnean Society in 1798. In 1803 he was justice, deputy lieutenant, and commissioner of land tax. At one time he was resident at Aspall, Suffolk, as tutor to the children of a Mr Chevallier.

Forby's important philological work, left unfinished, was *The vocabulary of East Anglia: an attempt to record the vulgar tongue of the twin sister counties, Norfolk and Suffolk, as it existed in the last twenty years of the eighteenth century, and still exists, with proof of its antiquity from etymology and authority* (2 vols., London, 1830; new edn, 1840). This was edited by the Revd George Turner of Kettleburgh. A supplementary volume by the Revd W. T. Spurdens was published in 1858.

Forby assisted Mannings in his *Pursuits of Agriculture*, and in 1824 wrote the prospectus of a continuation to the new edition of Francis Blomefield's *Norfolk*. He died at the rectory, apparently of a fainting fit, while he was taking a warm bath, on 20 December 1825, aged sixty-six.

THOMPSON COOPER, *rev.* JOHN D. HAIGH

Sources D. Turner, 'Memoirs of the Rev. Robert Forby', in R. Forby, *The vocabulary of East Anglia*, ed. G. Turner (1830), 1.xiii–xlvii · Venn, *Alum. Cant.* · *GM*, 1st ser., 96/1 (1826), 281 · *BL cat.* · J. Britten and G. S. Boulger, eds., *A biographical index of British and Irish botanists* (1893), 247, 446, 448, 1344
Likenesses line engraving, 1830 (after W. Sharp), BM; repro. in Turner, 'Memoirs' · portrait, Norwich Castle Museum, Norfolk

Forcer, Francis (*bap.* 1649, *d.* 1705), organist and composer, the son of Thomas Forcer, was baptized in Durham on 1 December 1649. He was a chorister at Durham Cathedral and then organist to John Cosin, bishop of Durham, until he ran away from the bishop's London household in 1669. From 1669 until 1671 he was organist at Dulwich College in London, and by 1673 he had moved to St Bartholomew by the Exchange, London, marrying Jane Taylor at St Bartholomew's on 30 July that year. He served as organist at St Giles Cripplegate from either 1674 or 1675 until 1676, and then at St Sepulchre, Holborn, possibly until his death. He may also have served as organist at St Bride's, Fleet Street, from 1693 until 1696. Forcer was a member of the burgeoning musical scene of London and a colleague of Henry Purcell. In 1684 he served as one of four stewards in the performance of John Blow's ode in celebration of St

Cecilia's day at Stationers' Hall. Two years later he joined Blow, Purcell, and John Moss in appraising the new organ at St Katharine Cree and selecting its new organist.

Forcer composed a variety of music, including songs and dances for theatre. He wrote music for plays such as Aphra Behn's *Abdelazer*, performed at the Dorset Garden Theatre in 1676, and Charles Hopkins's *Boadicea, Queen of Britain* and Mary Pix's *The Innocent Mistress*, both performed at Lincoln's Inn Fields theatre in 1697. His songs were included in contemporary collections such as *Choice Ayres, Songs and Dialogues*, published by John Playford in 1679, 1681, and 1683, and *Theater of Music*, published in 1685, 1686, and 1687 by Henry Playford and Richard Carr. Forcer also composed for the harpsichord and used a number of his pieces for teaching. He was the main scribe of two manuscripts in the Filmer collection, one of which contains pieces by Forcer and others, and appears to have been used in the instruction of Amy Filmer. Compositions by Forcer also appear in *The second part of musick's handmaid: containing the newest lessons, grounds, sarabands, minuets, and jiggs, set for the virginals, harpsichord, and spinet*, published by Henry Playford in 1689 and reissued in 1700 as *A choice collection of lessons, being excellently sett to the harpsichord, by the two great masters Dr. John Blow and the late Mr. Henry Purcell*. Although most of the pieces appear anonymously, an allemande and courante are probably by Forcer.

Forcer has long been believed to have been a proprietor of Sadler's Wells, in partnership with either Richard Sadler, who discovered the well in 1683, or James Miles, who was the subsequent proprietor until his death. However, during Forcer's lifetime the site was known alternately as Sadler's Wells and Miles' Musick House, and there is no contemporary evidence to support the idea that Forcer was involved.

Forcer died at Cross Street, St Andrew's parish, Holborn, on or after 20 January 1705 and was buried at St Andrew's, Holborn, on 26 January. He left his property in Durham and London to his son Francis Forcer [*see below*] and a few items of silver to his daughter, whom he identified in his will only as the wife of Mr Raynton. He made no mention in the will of his wife or of Sadler's Wells.

Posterity has not been kind to Forcer's musical abilities. His compositional skills were not particularly strong; his 'Hark how Noll and Bradshaw's heads above us', composed in honour of the uncovering of the Rye House plot and published in *A Choice Collection of 120 Loyal Songs* in 1684, has been described as 'so awful that it must have made Whigs of any sensitive musician present' (I. Spink, *English Song, Dowland to Purcell*, 1974, 78). However, his contemporaries recognized his skill as a performer; when he was appointed organist at Dulwich College in 1669 it was on the recommendation of the archbishop of Canterbury, who stated, 'I have heard a very good report of … Mr. Forcer, both of his skill in Musick, which may render him very fitt to be your organist and of his civill demeanor and sobriety of life' (Dawe, 98).

Francis Forcer (*bap.* 1676, *d.* 1743), lawyer and theatre manager, baptized at St Bride's, Fleet Street, London, on 14

January 1676, was the son of Francis Forcer and Jane Taylor. He attended the Merchant Taylors' School, London, from 1687 to 1696 and was admitted to Lincoln College, Oxford, in 1696. He entered Gray's Inn in 1696 and was called to the bar in 1703. At some point before 1724 Forcer married Frances Tompkins (d. 1726), the daughter of James Miles, proprietor of Sadler's Wells, with whom he had his only child, a daughter also named Frances. James Miles died in 1724, and Forcer was granted the lease to Sadler's Wells in 1730, after which he improved the tone of the place significantly. Although he continued the usual rope-dancing and tumbling, he replaced the more indelicate attractions of Miles's day, such as the Hibernian cannibal—whose act consisted of jumping on tables and eating live chickens—with more sophisticated entertainment, including opera.

Forcer died at Sadler's Wells on 9 April 1743 after a few days' illness. He left his property to his second wife, Catherine, and his daughter, Frances, and requested that his lease to Sadler's Wells be sold to cover his debts and provide for his family.

By all accounts Forcer was a decent and well-respected man. In his poem *New-River* (1728), William Garbott praised Forcer for the improvements brought to Sadler's Wells, describing him as a genteel and educated man. Forcer's obituary in the *London Evening-Post* described him as:

> a kind and indulgent husband, a tender and loving father, a generous friend and a good Master: In short, he had all the qualifications necessary to render a person a complete gentleman, which makes his death lamented by all those who had the pleasure of his acquaintance. (*London Evening-Post*, 7–9 April 1743)

ELIZABETH SCHOALES

Sources D. Dawe, *Organists of the City of London, 1666–1850* (1983) · *New Grove*, 2nd edn. · C. Day and E. Murrie, *English song-books, 1651–1702* (1940) · C. Price, *Music in the Restoration theatre, with a catalogue of instrumental music* (1979) · will, PRO, PROB 11/481, sig. 68 · PRO, PROB 11/726, sig. 158 [will of Francis Forcer, son] · R. Percival, ed., *Collections related to Sadler's Wells*, 1: *1683–1786* (1975) [microfilm] · *Records of the great playhouses; series one, part one: the Sadler's Wells* (1988) [archives from the Finsbury Central Library, London, microfilm] · D. Arundell, *The story of Sadler's Wells* (1978) · *DNB* · *London Evening-Post* (7–9 April 1743) · B. Crosby, *Come on choristers! A history of the chorister school, Durham* (1999) · T. Ormiston, ed., *Dulwich College register, 1619–1926* (1926?) · Mrs E. P. Hart, ed., *Merchant Taylors' School register, 1561–1934*, 1 (1936) · Foster, *Alum. Oxon.* · *IGI* · J. Harley, *British harpsichord music*, vol. 1: *Sources* (1992); vol. 2: *History* (1994) · R. Ford, 'The Filmer manuscripts: a handlist', *Notes*, 34 (1977–8), 814–25 · T. Dart, ed., *Musick's hand-maid*, vol. 2, rev. H. Purcell (1969)

Wealth at death property in Durham; left two houses in London (to son Francis); silver items to daughter and her son: will, PRO, PROB 11/481, sig. 68

Forcer, Francis (*bap.* 1676, *d.* 1743). *See under* Forcer, Francis (*bap.* 1649, *d.* 1705).

Ford. *See also* Forde.

Ford, Ann. *See* Thicknesse, Ann (1737–1824).

Ford, (Richard) Boris (1917–1998), educationist and literary editor, was born on 1 July 1917 in Simla, India, son of Brigadier Geoffrey Noel Ford CBE and his Russian wife,

Ekatarina. He was first educated as a chorister at King's College School, Cambridge. Music was a lifelong passion: he sang, latterly as counter-tenor, was a good pianist, and built a harpsichord. He attended Gresham's School, Holt, a progressive public school in Norfolk, especially strong in the humanities. Its pupils included W. H. Auden and Benjamin Britten, whose work was always close to Ford's heart: his last book, *Benjamin Britten's Poets* (1994), was an edition of verse set to music by Britten. His English master at Gresham's, Denys Thompson, sent him to be taught by F. R. Leavis at Downing College, Cambridge, where he took both parts of the English tripos (1938, 1939). While still an undergraduate he published an essay in Leavis's journal *Scrutiny*. He was active among the undergraduates in the English Club who were determined, under Leavis's influence, to reform the English curriculum.

Ford was a wartime educator: from the army education corps he moved up to become by 1946 officer commanding the Middle East School of Artistic Studies and then chief editor and director of the Army Bureau of Current Affairs (ABCA). ABCA gave officers and men a critical account of Britain, so critical that Ford attracted the attention of MI5. ABCA pamphlets helped the emergence of the welfare state: Ford believed that the Labour Party came to power in 1945 as a result of the democratizing influence of ABCA seminars. His first book was *Discussion Method* (1949).

In 1951 Ford became information officer of the technical assistance board of UNESCO. In 1953 he was invited by W. E. Williams, a former ABCA man, to edit a multi-authored seven-volume *Pelican Guide to English Literature* (1954–61; revised, 1982–8). It was a significant initiative in English studies. Ford wrote in the 'General introduction' that earlier manuals had 'a take-it-or-leave-it attitude about them', but the *Pelican Guide* was intended to be evaluative, concerned 'first and foremost, with value for the present', in the spirit of F. R. Leavis—and perhaps it was created at Leavis's expense. Leavis closed *Scrutiny* in 1953, remarking bitterly that Ford had 'approached my main people', and rightly considering that some of the *Pelican Guide* essays were derivative. None the less, the overall plan was successful: the *Pelican Guide* did provide a 'contour-map of the literary scene' with accompanying social history. The first volume, *The Age of Chaucer*, was unique to the series because it included a 200-page anthology of non-Chaucerian medieval poetry in original texts which gave early English poetry a presence for contemporary poets.

In his *Pelican Guide* period Ford also wrote and administered in the educational field. He was secretary to an inquiry into liberalizing technical education, publishing *Liberal Education in a Technical Age* in 1955, when he became editor of *Universities Quarterly* (until 1983; later known as *New Universities Quarterly*), and also head of schools broadcasting for the television company Associated Rediffusion. His tenure was abbreviated by patrician comments on the quality of the network's advertising output. However, Ford received encouragement from the company for Benjamin Britten's opera for children *Noye's Fludde*. In

1957–8 Ford was education secretary at Cambridge University Press, initiating its schools books committee which enabled the press to carry university-level English studies into the school curriculum. He brought David Holbrook and Sybil Marshall to the press. From 1963 to 1965 he was chairman of the National Association for the Teaching of English.

Ford's torrent of post-war proposals and commissions flowed into an academic professional career as educationist, first as professor of education and director of the Institute of Education, then from 1960 to 1963 at Sheffield University, and then from 1963 to 1973 at Sussex University, where, as dean to the school of culture and community studies, with Vice-Chancellor Asa Briggs as ally, he put music on the map in the university. His last chair was at Bristol (1973–82). At a time when teacher training colleges were closing, his *Changing Relationships between Universities and Teachers' Colleges* (1975) was timely.

Ford never really retired. He edited for Cambridge University Press the seven-volume *Cambridge Guide to the Arts in Britain* (1988–91), which resembled the *Pelican Guide*. He disliked being called an entrepreneur: he was an opportunist with ideas which he nurtured with persistent gentleness, a gentleness that made him a friend to women, though not always to their husbands. He was married twice, first on 7 March 1950 to a schoolteacher, Noreen Edna Auty, *née* Collins (1921/2–1995), the cheery companion of his Yorkshire and Sussex years, with whom he had three children. This marriage was dissolved about 1973, and he married on 21 July 1977 Inge (originally Enid) Inglis, *née* Evans, a fund-raiser and exhibitions organizer; their marriage was dissolved in 1984. Boris Ford died in the Whittington Hospital, Islington, London, on 19 May 1998.   IAN MACKILLOP

Sources *The Times* (21 May 1998) · *The Guardian* (22 May 1998) · *The Independent* (27 May 1998) · *The Independent* (29 May 1998) · WWW · m. certs. · d. cert.
Likenesses photograph, repro. in *The Times* · photograph, repro. in *The Guardian* · photograph, repro. in *The Independent* (27 May 1998)

Ford, Sir (Richard) Brinsley (1908–1999), art connoisseur, was born on 10 June 1908 at The Elmes, Wisborough Green, Petworth, Sussex, the only son of Captain Richard Ford (1860–1940), officer in the rifle brigade, and his first wife, Rosamund Isabel (1872–1911), daughter of Sir John Ramsden, fifth baronet. He was a direct descendant of Richard Brinsley Sheridan, after whom he was named, and a grandson of Sir (Francis) Clare *Ford, diplomatist. He was educated at Eton College, and at Trinity College, Oxford, graduating with a third-class degree in modern history in 1930.

A significant portion of the remarkable collection formed by Benjamin Booth (including the largest collection of paintings and drawings by the eighteenth-century landscape artist Richard Wilson) and enriched by his grandson (Ford's great-grandfather) Richard Ford, author of *The Handbook for Travellers in Spain*, was left to Ford by his

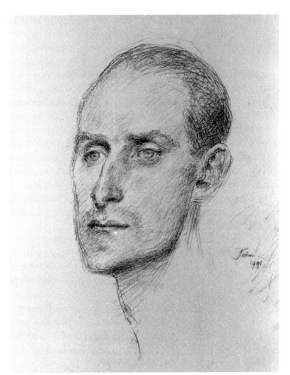

Sir (Richard) Brinsley Ford (1908–1999), by Augustus John, 1941

uncle in 1917. This remained in his father's keeping until the latter's death and came to Ford in 1941, but from his coming of age in 1929 he received the 'handsome income' of a legacy from his maternal grandfather. His career as a serious collector commenced with purchases of contemporary works. He became a member of the Burlington Fine Arts Club and developed close friendships with kindred spirits, notably Villiers David, Charles Prescott, and James Byam Shaw. His purchases of the 1930s ranged widely, from Henry Moore and Toulouse-Lautrec to Fuseli, Ingres, the Venetians, and, most spectacularly, Michelangelo, whose study of the *Risen Christ* he secured for £3570 in the Oppenheimer sale of 1936. On 27 April 1937 he married his third cousin, Joan Mary (*b*. 1910), daughter of Captain (William) Geoffrey Vyvyan, officer in the Royal Welch Fusiliers. They settled at 14 Wyndham Place, Bryanston Square, Westminster, and had two sons and a daughter.

As the shadows cast by Hitler's Germany lengthened, Ford joined the Territorial Army as a gunner in the Royal Artillery in April 1939, and by the outbreak of the Second World War he had been promoted to lance-bombardier. He delighted to recall that, because of his loud voice, he became a troop sergeant in November. In 1941 he was transferred to military intelligence (MI9), in which, after a brief transfer to MI6 under Airey Neave in 1944—during which he made one sortie to the coast of occupied Brittany—he was promoted to major, running the MI9 bureau in Brussels. On 11 April 1945, shortly after its liberation, he visited Buchenwald: he never forgot the horror of the experience.

After the war 14 Wyndham Place became the perfect setting for Ford's expanding collection. In 1952 he extended the house by acquiring two adjacent properties and knocking through the walls on the first floor. Post-war additions to his collection included a significant number of Italian *seicento* and *settecento* pictures, among which were masterpieces by such artists as Cavallino, Cozza, and Batoni, and pictures of other schools, including Subleyras's *Endymion*. In later years Ford was particularly assiduous in his patronage of younger representational artists. In 1976 he sold a first edition of Goya's *Tauromachia* and with the proceeds established the Richard Ford award enabling young artists to travel to Spain. He was generous in allowing scholars and students access to his collection, and the arrangement of this, with its elegantly patterned hang, was in advance of conventional taste.

Ford was a trustee of the National Gallery from 1954 to 1961 and of the Watts Gallery, Compton, from 1955 until 1995, serving as chairman from 1974 to 1984. He derived much enjoyment from his membership of the Society of Dilettanti—the world of whose founders he understood so well—of which he was secretary from 1972 until 1988 and whose move from the St James's Club to Brooks's in 1975 he oversaw. He supported the Georgian Group, of which he was a founder member in 1937, and the National Trust, on the arts panel of which he served until 1996. He was a leading spirit in the National Trust's foundation for art, under the auspices of which contemporary works were commissioned for many houses in the trust's care. But the charity with which he was most publicly associated was the National Art Collections Fund, which he joined in 1927: he sat on the executive committee from 1960 until 1988, was vice-president in 1974–5, and chairman from 1975 to 1980. The range of his interest in the arts meant that he was exceptionally well qualified for the role. As chairman he was responsible for extending the remit of the fund so that grants could be made towards acquisitions for National Trust houses, and presided over a dramatic increase in activities which helped to prepare the ground for the subsequent increase in membership. His contribution to the arts was recognized by the award of a knighthood in 1984.

Ford did not think of himself as an art historian—protesting that he was 'merely an aesthete' (personal knowledge)—but his publications set a high standard. An article of 1939 on Ingres's portrait drawings of British sitters was the first of many contributions to the *Burlington Magazine*, of which he was a resourceful director from 1952 until 1986. *The Drawings of Richard Wilson* (1951) became the standard monograph, while his six essays in a special number of *Apollo* of 1974 demonstrated his empathy with the world of grand tour patronage. His sustained study of the grand tour led to the preparation of a biographical dictionary, work on which proceeded in the 1970s: it was a source of much gratification to him that when the project was revived, his material was edited with masterly efficiency by John Ingamells and published as *A Dictionary of British and Irish Travellers in Italy, 1701–1800* (1997). This was followed in 1998 by *The Ford Collection*, edited by Luke

Hermann, the sixtieth volume of the Walpole Society, of which Ford had become president in 1986; he himself wrote with charm and authority about the history of the collection he had inherited and about his own career in the field. He kept journals from 1946 until 1975: drawn on in National Trust guide books to Hinton Ampner and Felbrigg, these constitute a significant record of his world. He was also a committed writer of letters, punctilious in his response to a steady stream of scholarly enquiries, and ever ready to entertain his friends. The letters, generally typed, had the timbre of his conversation, erudite and teasing by turn: his style of speaking was once described as uniting 'the measured cadences of Edward Gibbon with the humorous sparkle of Horace Walpole' (*The Independent*).

Tall and distinguished looking, and bearing a strong resemblance to his great-grandfather Richard Ford, he was described by one obituarist as possessing 'an unmalicious wit, with an element of foolery thrown in' (*The Times*). Another wrote that 'no one was more modest, more given to humorous self-deprecation or more sensitively kind-hearted' (*The Guardian*). He died at his home on 4 May 1999 following a heart attack, leaving an estate valued at £16,742,280 net. He was survived by his wife and their three children.   FRANCIS RUSSELL

Sources G. Jackson-Stops, 'The Apollo portrait, Sir Brinsley Ford', *Apollo*, 125 (1987), 363–9 · *The Times* (7 May 1999) · *The Independent* (8 May 1999) · *Daily Telegraph* (8 May 1999) · *The Guardian* (12 May 1999) · WWW · Burke, *Peerage* · personal knowledge (2004) · private information (2004) · b. cert. · m. cert. · d. cert.
Archives Paul Mellon Centre for Studies in British Art, London, Brinsley Ford collection · priv. coll., journals
Likenesses A. John, drawing, 1941, priv. coll. [*see illus.*] · photograph, 1976, repro. in *The Independent* · P. Procktor, sketch, line drawing, repro. in *The Guardian* · photograph, repro. in *The Times*
Wealth at death £16,786,670: probate, 5 June 2000, *CGPLA Eng. & Wales*

Ford, Charles Bell (1784–1860), insurance company manager, was baptized on 24 May 1784 at Pitcombe, Somerset, the ninth child of John Ford, barrister of the Middle Temple, and Margaret Ford. His father was a man of considerable means, a benefactor of charities in Bath and probably a director of Bath Fire Office. His brothers, John and William, went up to Oxford and followed their father into the Middle Temple. However, nothing is known of Charles's early career. He was appointed secretary to the Sun Fire Office in 1814 at the age of thirty. Unlike most of Sun's salaried officers, he had not come up through the ranks of clerical staff, nor, like previous secretaries, did he belong to the closed circle of existing managers. He was brought in to fill the vacancy left by the death of Philip Bewicke only after no internal volunteer for the onerous post of secretary could be found. One of the terms of his appointment, and what marked him as an outsider, was that he had to relinquish his seat on Sun's self-electing management committee if he gave up the post of secretary. Although Ford never married, his family did in time become 'insiders': his nephew Harry, son of his sister Eliza and Sir Robert Chester, was a Sun manager from 1835 to 1868.

At the time of Ford's appointment, Sun was the largest fire insurer in Britain, but had entered a difficult stage in its history. The new offices of the 1800s had eroded its market share, particularly in the north of England. One of Ford's principal achievements was to reverse this decline, so that the office continued to dominate British fire insurance long after his death. Ford proved ruthless in pursuit of market power. Particularly during the period of intensified competition in the late 1820s and 1830s, he undercut the premium rates of weaker opposition in a range of markets, and forced the other major offices to follow suit. The company take-over, however, proved to be his most potent device for maintaining Sun's competitive position. In seventeen successful take-overs during his term as secretary, including an extraordinary average of one each year between 1835 and 1848, he revealed himself as a great tactician, and a shrewd and tough negotiator. He would keep a close eye on the movements of his competitors, would carefully gauge the probability of persuading a majority of shareholders to sell, and would make great efforts to win the loyalty, sometimes through financial enticements, of a key insider—a director or manager—in the company targeted for purchase. In three, ultimately successful, attempts to buy the Bath Fire Office, Ford even recruited his father, his elder sister, and the family physician, all resident in Bath, to collect information and canvas support on Sun's behalf.

To his counterparts in other insurance offices, Ford could seem somewhat cold and aloof. He had a rather caustic sense of humour and did not tolerate fools gladly, but he clearly had a taste for the corporate battlefield, as well as a sense of fairness. A late convert to the cause of co-operation between insurers, he drafted the plan of the London Fire Engine Establishment in 1833, and he was the regular chairman of the Fire Offices' tariff committee from 1842. In 1836 he rather belatedly took Sun into foreign underwriting. The frequent generous bonuses awarded to Ford by Sun's board marked the high regard in which they held his managerial skills. He was appointed deputy chairman in 1845 and held this post, as well as the chairmanship of the Sun Life Office, until his death. He retired from the post of secretary in 1856 on an annual pension of £1000, though he retained his title of manager. He died on 2 April 1860, aged seventy-six, at his home, 18 Grafton Street, Piccadilly, London, and was buried in Highgate cemetery. ROBIN PEARSON

Sources P. G. M. Dickson, *The Sun Insurance office, 1710–1860* (1960) · R. Pearson, 'Taking risks and containing competition: diversification and oligopoly in the fire insurance markets of the north of England in the early 19th century', *Economic History Review*, 2nd ser., 46 (1993), 39–64 · general committee minutes, GL, Sun Fire Office, MS 11931/9 · take-over papers, GL, Sun Fire Office, MS 11935E · C. Walford, *The insurance cyclopaedia*, 4 (1876) · H. A. C. Sturgess, ed., *Register of admissions to the Honourable Society of the Middle Temple, from the fifteenth century to the year 1944*, 3 vols. (1949) · Foster, *Alum. Oxon.* · IGI

Archives GL, Sun Fire Office, take-over papers, MS 11935E

Wealth at death under £60,000: probate, 21 April 1860, *CGPLA Eng. & Wales*

Ford, Charles Edmund (1912–1999), cytogeneticist, was born on 24 October 1912 at Eversleigh, Fairfield Road, Latchford Without, Runcorn, Cheshire, the eldest of the six children of Charles Ford (b. 1884), a commercial clerk, later works manager for the St Helens Cable and Rubber Company, and his wife, Ethel Eubornia Fawcett (b. 1887), who was secretary in the same company before their marriage in 1910. Charles's two sisters, Kathleen and Marjorie, were also born in Cheshire, but in 1924 the family accompanied the Cable and Rubber Company on its move to Slough, where three further sons, Peter, Richard, and Michael, were born. Before leaving Cheshire, Charles had been awarded a scholarship to Manchester grammar school, and this was transferred to Slough grammar school, where he showed a keen interest in the local flora and fauna. His interest was extended when, in 1928 at the age of sixteen, he went to King's College, London, to read botany. Although he commuted daily from Slough, he participated fully in college activities, showing a range of talents from chess to rugby union football. On graduating in 1931 he enrolled for a PhD with Professor R. R. Gates at King's to work on the cytogenetics of the evening primrose. He obtained his higher degree in 1935 and was appointed university demonstrator in the botany department at King's in 1936. In 1938 he moved to Ceylon to work as a geneticist for the Rubber Research Scheme, and in 1940 he married Jean Ella (b. 1912), one of the six children of Edith and Frank Dowling of Slough. They had four sons—Peter, Michael, Christopher, and Brian—the first three going on to read for biological degrees and the fourth becoming an architect. Over almost sixty years of marriage, Jean afforded Charles tremendous care and support.

Ford's time in Ceylon was interrupted by the Second World War, and from 1942 to 1943 he served as a lieutenant in the Royal Artillery. Post-war, following his return to Britain, he worked for the Ministry of Supply at Chalk River, Ontario, Canada, his brief as a cytogeneticist to investigate the chromosome-damaging effects of radiation on the dividing cells of broad bean root tips. Meanwhile, in Britain, concern about radiation hazards had become the remit of the Medical Research Council, and in 1949 Ford was appointed head of cytogenetics at their newly formed radiobiology unit at Harwell. The appointment led to the most fruitful period in his career, since a fortunate switch from plants to developing technical methods of observing mammalian chromosomes led to a worldwide interest that could be described as the launch of the human gene mapping project. This began in 1956 with Ford's involvement in determining the correct human diploid chromosome number as 46, followed by an increasing awareness of the relationship between aberrant chromosomes and clinical syndromes. Ford also convened a study group to resolve observational disagreements; their conclusions, in the Denver report (1960), remained the model for updates published beyond the end of the twentieth century.

Ford, Sir (Francis) Clare (1828–1899), diplomatist, was born in London, the son of Richard *Ford (1796–1858), author of the *Handbook for Travellers in Spain*, and his first wife, Harriet Capel (d. 1837). He spent much of his boyhood in Spain, for which country he inherited his father's affection. He was appointed a cornet in the 4th light dragoons on 8 May 1846, was promoted lieutenant on 20 April 1849, but sold out on 9 June 1851 and entered the diplomatic service in the modest position of unpaid attaché. To climb to the position of secretary of legation took him fifteen years, during which he lived in Naples (1852), Munich (1855), and Paris (1856), became paid attaché in Lisbon on 9 March 1857, and was transferred from there to Brussels, Stuttgart, Karlsruhe, and finally (on 25 June 1864) Vienna. He served as secretary of legation at Buenos Aires, Copenhagen, and Washington, DC, where he was acting chargé d'affaires during the winter of 1867–8.

In March 1871, having already begun to acquire a reputation as a specialist in affairs where economic and commercial interests were concerned, Ford was promoted to secretary of embassy and proceeded to St Petersburg, from where he was transferred to Vienna on 26 October 1872. On 26 July 1875 he was appointed agent to represent the British government before the international commission created for the purpose of estimating the amount of compensation which should be paid by the United States for the fishery rights acquired under articles 22 and 23 of the Washington treaty of 8 May 1871. The commission sat in Halifax, Nova Scotia, from June until November 1877, when it was decided that the United States should within a year pay $5.5 million. For his services in preparing the British case Ford was made a CB on 3 January and a CMG on 24 January 1878. He was promoted to envoy-extraordinary and minister-plenipotentiary to the Argentine republic on 9 February 1878 and undertook some rather delicate negotiations for renewing diplomatic relations between Uruguay and Great Britain, which ended in his being made British minister in Montevideo as well as in Buenos Aires. In June 1879 he was appointed to Brazil, and in March 1881 to Athens.

On 15 December 1884 Ford was appointed minister in Madrid, and when the legation there was raised to the rank of an embassy he became ambassador on 8 December 1887. He felt at home in Spain, the art treasures of which country appealed to him both as a connoisseur and as a collector. During his eight years' tenure of office there he acted in 1884 and 1885 as British commissioner in Paris for the settlement of the Newfoundland fisheries dispute, a subject which he had studied with minute care. Unfortunately the conventions which he drew up, and with which he got his French fellow commissioners to concur, were never carried out. He was more successful in the negotiations which terminated with the signature of the Anglo-Spanish commercial convention of 26 April 1886. For these services he was made KCMG in 1885 and GCMG in 1886, was sworn privy councillor on 10 August 1888, and was promoted GCB on 29 April 1889.

In January 1892 Ford was transferred from Madrid to Constantinople. The promotion was unsought by him,

Charles Edmund Ford (1912–1999), by Godfrey Argent

The laboratory mouse featured prominently in the Harwell radiation research. This work produced insights into many aspects of genome unbalance and genetic risk; it also produced an easily recognized marker chromosome which proved invaluable in monitoring the progression of donor cells in experiments designed to 'rescue' lethally irradiated mice and to determine the basic principles of tissue transplantation. Ford's success led to the expansion of cytogenetics at Harwell but to a drift away from radiobiology; hence the Medical Research Council cut both budget and space, and in 1971 Ford and a much-reduced group moved to the Dunn School of Pathology in Oxford, where he remained until his retirement in 1978—an event commemorated by the publication in his honour of a special issue of the journal *Cytogenetics and Cell Genetics*.

Ford was elected fellow of the Royal Society in 1965 and honorary fellow of the Royal College of Pathology in 1988. After his retirement he spent a year as Boerhaave visiting professor at the University of Leiden. He suffered a stroke in 1996 which left him severely disabled, but survived a further two years and died at his home, 156 Oxford Road, Abingdon, Oxfordshire, on 7 January 1999. He was buried in Oxford on 12 January. EDWARD P. EVANS

Sources M. F. Lyon, *Memoirs FRS* [forthcoming] · T. Evans, *The Independent* (16 Jan 1999) · A. Gropp, P. L. Pearson, and H. P. Klinger, 'Charles E. Ford', *Cytogenetics and Cell Genetics*, 70 (1978), v–vii · M. Kent-First, 'Charles Edmund Ford PhD, FRS: in loving memory of my mentor and friend', *Cytogenetics and Cell Genetics*, 85 (1999), 193–5 · d. cert.
Likenesses G. Argent, photograph, Godfrey Argent Studio [see illus.] · photograph, repro. in Gropp, Pearson, and Klinger, 'Charles E. Ford', frontispiece

and he soon found himself unequal to the strain of so difficult a position. In December 1893 he procured his transfer to Rome, where he remained until he was superannuated in 1898. He received the Jubilee medal in 1897.

In 1857 Ford married Annie, daughter of the marqués de Garofalo, of Naples. They had at least two sons, one of whom, John Gorman Ford, was also a diplomatist. Ford died at the Hôtel Impérial, Paris, on 31 January 1899.

THOMAS SECCOMBE, rev. H. C. G. MATTHEW

Sources The Times (1 Feb 1899) · FO List (1899) · Kelly, Handbk · census returns, 1881
Archives Bodl. Oxf., corresp. with Lord Kimberley · Lpool RO, corresp. with fifteenth earl of Derby
Likenesses R. T. & Co., wood-engraving, NPG; repro. in ILN (30 Jan 1892)
Wealth at death £35,979 17s. 4d.: resworn probate, Nov 1899, CGPLA Eng. & Wales

Ford, David Everard (1797–1875), Congregational minister and composer, was born on 13 September 1797 at Long Melford, Suffolk, where his father, David Ford, was Independent minister. After an apprenticeship in London he entered Wymondley College, London, in 1816, where Thomas Binney was a fellow student. While still a student Ford missioned and then opened a chapel at Wood End. In October 1821 he became minister at Lymington, where he served until December 1841. At Lymington he wrote several books of psalm and hymn tunes and other works on the subject of sacred music: perhaps surprisingly his name does not appear in Julian's Dictionary of Hymnology. He also published a number of evangelistic sermons and tracts which enjoyed a wide circulation: Decapolis, Chorazin, Damascus, Laodicea, and Alarm in Zion were particularly well known. Between 1842 and 1843 he served the British Mission (the Home Missionary Society) of the Congregational Union, visiting many causes throughout the country. In October 1843 he went as minister to a new church at Greengate, Salford, which had recently separated from Chapel Street Congregational Church. He inspired his congregation to erect Richmond Chapel, of which he was pastor until May 1858. A man of striking appearance and powerful voice, he was a firm evangelical and a foe of liberal thinking; in November 1856 he fired the opening shots in the campaign against Samuel Davidson of Lancashire Independent college. After retirement he continued to preach until he finally retired to Bedford in June 1875. He died on 23 October of that year, and was buried in Harpurhey cemetery, Manchester. His wife, Jane Elizabeth, survived him; his distinguished son, Gerard Nonus Ford (1849–1934), Manchester businessman and Congregationalist, was cast very much in the paternal mould.

JOHN BROWN, rev. IAN SELLERS

Sources Congregational Year Book (1876) · newspaper cuttings, Man. CL · 'The autobiography of D. E. Ford', Transactions of the Congregational Historical Society, 11–12 (1930–36) · The story of Richmond Chapel: centenary, 1843–1943 (1943)
Archives DWL, corresp. · King's AC Cam., diaries, MS autobiography, corresp., household accounts, registers of sermons, papers, and cuttings

Wealth at death under £6000: probate, 22 Nov 1875, CGPLA Eng. & Wales

Ford, Edmund Brisco (1901–1988), geneticist, was born on 23 April 1901 in Dalton, near Ulverston in Lancashire, the only child of the Revd Harold Dodsworth Ford, curate at Dalton in Furness, and his wife, Gertrude Emma Bennett. His interest in butterflies started as a boy, when he and his father observed each season a colony of the marsh fritillary butterfly in Cumberland. The numbers fluctuated greatly and in periods of rapid increase there was an extraordinary outburst of variability in pattern. When the population decreased again the common form was recognizably distinct from that which had prevailed before the period of abundance. An opportunity for evolution had occurred and the insect had made use of it. Ford was educated at St Bees School in Cumberland and then as an undergraduate at Wadham College, Oxford, where he gained a second class in zoology in 1924. He became a demonstrator in zoology and comparative anatomy at Oxford in 1930, then lecturer and later reader (1939) in genetics.

From 1952 to 1969 Ford was director of the genetics laboratory, and from 1963 to 1969 professor of ecological genetics at Oxford. He was president of the Genetical Society of Great Britain from 1946 to 1949, and was elected to the Royal Society in 1946. From 1958 to 1971 he was a fellow of All Souls College, Oxford (serving two terms as senior dean); this was the first occasion for almost a century that an All Souls man had been a fellow of the Royal Society.

Ford devised elaborate techniques of mark–release–recapture, which enabled his team to estimate changes in frequency of particular forms of moths and butterflies, and of the genes controlling them, and to assess migration. This was classic work, done with Sir Ronald Aylmer *Fisher, and had a far-reaching effect on population genetics. The surveys were, however, characterized by a famous controversy with the American geneticist Sewell Wright over natural selection versus genetic drift—a chance process which can occur particularly in small populations. The moths provided an excellent example of Ford's conception of balanced polymorphism applied to the study of ecological genetics and of evolution in the wild. He was the first to predict that the human blood group polymorphic systems would influence susceptibility to disease. The association of cancer of the stomach and group A, and of duodenal ulcer and group O, bore this out. In the sickle cell haemoglobinopathy the dictum of the advantage of the heterozygote was excellently demonstrated, as this genotype protected children against malaria.

Ford was an inspiring teacher and his influence on genetics was worldwide. He had a particular gift for picking good research workers and then giving them their heads. Philip Sheppard, with C. A. Clarke, applied Ford's suggestion about the human blood groups to the Rh (rhesus) system, and with other researchers in the department of medicine at Liverpool University devised a successful method of preventing Rh haemolytic disease of the newborn. It was for this type of research that the Nuffield Foundation, of which Ford was a trustee, set up the Unit of Medical Genetics in Liverpool: Ford himself (he was always most generous) made a large personal contribution to this. It was a nice quirk that in the Rh polymorphism, when the mother is Rhesus negative, her heterozygous baby does not obey the rules, for it is always at a disadvantage. In his later years Ford became interested in the genetics of the Gypsy moth, *Lymantria dispar*, in relation to pest control. Using the heteropyknotic body technique, he and C. A. Clarke showed that R. B. Goldschmidt was wrong in thinking that unusual sex ratios in race crosses of the moth were the result of complete sex reversal. In fact the all-male broods were fully fertile and the result of the Haldane effect. Goldschmidt had thought his explanation would mean that these males were sterile and therefore would be useful in combating the pest, but this was not the case.

Known as Henry to his friends, Ford had very wide interests that included heraldry and archaeology. He contributed much to the Prehistoric Society, and with J. S. Haywood produced *Church Treasures in the Oxford District* (1974). The titles of his genetics books also demonstrate his versatility—*Mendelism and Evolution* (1931), *The Study of Heredity* (1938), *Genetics for Medical Students* (1942), *Butterflies* (1945), *Moths* (1955), *Ecological Genetics* (1964), *Genetic Polymorphism* (1965), *Genetics and Adaptation* (1976), *Understanding Genetics* (1979), and *Taking Genetics into the Countryside* (1981). Several went into many editions and each is characterized by lucid prose. *Butterflies*, much to his surprise, proved a bestseller.

Ford travelled widely, but in spite of this he knew virtually nothing about the wider political world, and cared for it even less. He would not allow radio and television in his house, and he did not look at newspapers. In some respects time stood still for him and he regarded molecular geneticists as incomprehensible interlopers. He had a prickly manner and a feline skill in making his disapproval felt. Lecturing to an audience of mixed sex, he always began 'gentlemen'; once, when only women were present, he is said to have walked out.

In 1954 Ford was awarded the Darwin medal of the Royal Society. He won the Weldon memorial prize at Oxford University in 1959, and the medal of Helsinki University in 1967. He became an honorary fellow of the Royal College of Physicians of London in 1974 and was elected an honorary DSc of Liverpool University in the same year. He was also an honorary fellow of Wadham College (1974) and, from 1977, senior dean and distinguished fellow of All Souls. He was a homosexual and misogynist, and he never married. He died in Oxford, in his rooms at All Souls, on 21 January 1988.   CYRIL CLARKE, *rev.*

Sources Munk, *Roll*, vol. 8 · R. Creed, ed., *Ecological genetics and evolution: essays in honour of E. B. Ford* (1971) · *The Independent* (25 Jan 1988) · *The Times* (23 Jan 1988) · b. cert. · CGPLA Eng. & Wales (1988) **Archives** Bodl. Oxf., corresp. and papers · Oxf. U. Mus. NH, corresp. and papers | Bodl. Oxf., corresp. with Sir C. A. Clarke relating to joint paper · Rice University, Houston, Texas, Woodson Research Center, corresp. with Sir Julian Huxley · Wolfson College, Oxford, corresp. with H. B. D. Kettlewell **Wealth at death** £302,236: probate, 22 July 1988, CGPLA Eng. & Wales

Ford, Sir Edward (*bap.* 1605, *d.* 1670), royalist army officer and inventor, was born at Up Park, in the parish of Harting, Sussex, and baptized in the parish church of Harting on 22 April 1605. He was the eldest son of Sir William Ford (*fl.* 1605–1646), knight, of Harting, 'the soape projector', and Anna Caryll, daughter of Sir Edmund Caryll, knight, of West Harting (Blaauw, 45). The Carylls were a Catholic family, though no evidence survives which suggests that Sir Edward Ford was not an Anglican (and indeed his wife's family were puritan). Ford became a gentleman commoner of Trinity College, Oxford, in 1621, but left the university without taking a degree; in 1629 he became a 'virtuoso' student of the Inner Temple. He developed an interest in hydraulic engineering, and by 1641 offered to undertake, at his own expense, construction of a canal from Rickmansworth to St Giles-in-the-Fields that would alleviate London's water shortage and be navigable as well.

Ford served as an officer in the king's army from the beginning of the first civil war. In 1642 Charles I made him high sheriff of Sussex. According to the parliamentarian polemicist John Vicars, Ford offered the king 'a thousand men, and to undertake the conquest of the whole county of Sussex, though sixty miles in length' (J. Vicars, *Gods Arke*, 1646, 123). Accordingly on 14 November 1642 he issued a warrant in obedience to the king's commission of array enjoining the county to come in with their arms to Arundel. On 15 November parliamentarians in Chichester seized control of the town, but on 16 November Ford, with a hundred horse and several hundred foot, and the aid of royalist gentry in the town, occupied it. However, in the face of local caution and indifference he was unable to sustain a drive into east Sussex, and by 20 December Sir William Waller had brought his army to besiege Chichester. Beset by heavy bombardment, a weak defensive position, and disaffected townspeople, Ford surrendered on 27 December. On 28 December Waller sent him a prisoner to London. Meanwhile on 18 November the House of Commons had declared his warrant summoning to Arundel illegal and ordered that Ford be apprehended as a delinquent. Ford obtained his release, perhaps through the interest of his wife, Sarah, with her brother Henry Ireton, the future commissary-general of the New Model Army.

In June 1643 the king commissioned Ford to raise a regiment of horse, and in September he was with royalist forces threatening Southampton. On 4 October 1643 he was knighted by Charles I at Oxford, and on 6 December he and Sir Edward Bishop, acting under Hopton's command, took the town of Arundel and besieged the castle, which fell on 9 December. Ford was appointed governor, but although well supplied with men failed to make adequate preparations to withstand a siege. On 20 December Waller retook the town and besieged the castle. His heavy bombardment shattered the walls, and on 6 January 1644 the garrison surrendered. Clarendon judged that Ford had insufficient experience of war although 'a man of honesty and courage' (Clarendon, *Hist. rebellion*, 3.334). Ford and Bishop served as hostages for the delivery of the castle, both thus becoming Waller's prisoners for the second time, and Ford was sent to Windsor. They were declared by parliament on 9 October 1644 to be incapable of any employment. Ford was imprisoned in the Tower of London, from which he escaped in December. He was again a hostage in surrender negotiations in October 1645 at Winchester. At some later point he retired to the continent.

In 1647 the queen sent Ford to England to prepare the way for Sir John Berkeley's futile negotiation with the army. Between August 1647 and April 1648 he sent letters of intelligence from London to Hopton and Sir Edward Hyde. On 12 November 1647 he with others had been ordered by the House of Commons into safe custody upon suspicion of being privy to the king's escape from Hampton Court. On 21 March 1649 parliament included him in the list of delinquents who were to pay one full third of the value of their estate. On 9 July 1649 the House of Commons belatedly admitted him to the benefits of the Oxford articles of 1646 and made an order for remitting the remainder of his fine and discharging his sequestration. In 1651 Ford remained an object of suspicion and was believed to be ready to aid royalist designs in Sussex, but in 1656 Cromwell approved his exemption from the decimation tax levied against the royalists.

In the same year Ford was employed, with Cromwell's encouragement, and at the request of the citizens of London, in devising an engine for raising the water of the Thames into all the higher streets of the city, a height of 93 feet. This he accomplished in a year, and at his own expense; and the same 'rare engine' was afterwards employed in other parts of the kingdom for draining mines and lands, which it did better and more cheaply than any former contrivance (Wood, *Ath. Oxon.*, 3.905). After the Restoration he remained an active entrepreneur and projector, whose interests ranged from technology to monetary theory. He extended his hydraulic projects, and, in conjunction with Thomas Toogood, constructed the great water-engine near the Strand Bridge for the neighbourhood, but on 31 July 1664 the king, at the urging of Queen Catherine, ordered its removal on the ground that it was a 'nuisance', its 'inconvenient height' obstructing the view from Somerset House (*CSP dom.*, 1663–4, 55; 1664–5, 72). However, Ford and Toogood obtained a royal licence to erect other waterworks at Wapping and Marylebone, and between Temple Bar and Charing Cross.

Ford invented a mode of coining farthings that could not be counterfeited: each piece was to differ minutely from another to prevent forgery. Ford argued for the development of the herring trade as a means of increasing national wealth. After the fire of London he proposed the introduction of paper money on the security of taxation, and he also allowed a place for 'Banks of Loan upon Pawns, truly called Mounts of Piety' (Ford, *Experimented Proposals*, 3). He had, he claimed, a method to protect 'Bill-Money' too from counterfeiting (ibid.). He argued that his proposal would facilitate the rebuilding and improvement of London, and lower taxes by providing a source of income for the king.

Ford failed, through the obstruction of Prince Rupert, to procure a patent for his farthings in England, but obtained one for Ireland. He died in Ireland on 3 September 1670 before he could carry out his design. His body was taken to England and interred in the family burial-place at Harting. 'He was a great virtuoso of his time, yet none of the Royal Society, and might have done greater matters, if he had not been disintrigued for those things he had done before', was Wood's judgement (Wood, *Ath. Oxon.*, 3.906). Ford's wife had died before him. By the marriage of his only surviving daughter, Catherine, to Ralph Lord Grey of Warke, Up Park became the property of the earls of Tankerville until it was sold in 1745.　　BARBARA DONAGAN

Sources Wood, *Ath. Oxon.*, new edn, 3.905 • M. A. E. Green, ed., *Calendar of the proceedings of the committee for compounding … 1643–1660*, 5 vols., PRO (1889–92) • *JHC*, 2 (1640–42), 854 • *JHC*, 3 (1642–4), 657, 730 • *JHC*, 5 (1646–8), 356 • *JHC*, 6 (1648–51), 169, 257 • *CSP dom.*, 1649–50, 46; 1659–60, 97; 1663–4, 55, 396, 655; 1664–5, 72; 1665–6, 170; 1666–7, 127, 439 • [E. Ford], *A designe for bringing a navigable river from Rickmansworth in Hartfordshire, to St Gyles in the Fields* (1641) • E. Ford, *Experimented proposals how the king may have money* (1666) • *Sixth report*, HMC, 5 (1877–8), 330–31 • *Ninth report*, 2, HMC, 8 (1884), 393 • *The manuscripts of his grace the duke of Portland*, 10 vols., HMC, 29 (1891–1931), vol. 1, p. 578 • *Calendar of the Clarendon state papers preserved in the Bodleian Library*, 1: *To Jan 1649*, ed. O. Ogle and W. H. Bliss (1872), 381–419 • Thurloe, *State papers*, 4.257, 285 • A. Fletcher, *A county community in peace and war: Sussex, 1600–1660* (1975) • W. H. Blaauw, 'Passages of the civil war in Sussex', *Sussex Archaeological Collections*, 5 (1852), 36–63 • Foster, *Alum. Oxon.*, 1500–1714 [Sir Edward Forde] • will, PRO, PROB 11/335, fols. 146r–147r • IGI • DNB
Archives Bodl. Oxf., Clarendon state papers, letters of intelligence • PRO, 'Proposals for maintaining the fleet and rebuilding London', state papers, domestic, Charles II, vol. 171
Wealth at death Up Park; estate in Tatford(?), Hampshire; other lands and money; appears to have made money through lottery licence and waterworks; forgave a debt of £6000 owed to him by son-in-law; also gave him £300–£400 p.a. on his daughter's marriage: *CSP dom.*, 1663–4, 396; will, PRO, PROB 11/335, fols. 146r–147r

Ford, Edward (*fl.* 1638–1660), ballad and verse writer, whose birth date, place of birth, and parentage are unknown, dedicated his verse *Fair Play in the Lottery* (1660) to Sir Edward Ford of Uppark House, which suggests that he may have been a native of Sussex. Ford is likely to have been resident in London, then the centre of the ballad trade, and must have acquired a considerable reputation for his signature to be appended to his ballads—an uncommon occurrence at the time and afforded only to authors with a popular following.

Ford's principal publisher was Francis Coles or Coules, a prominent bookseller who specialized in the ballad and who helped launch the pro-parliament news periodical the *Perfect Diurnal*. To judge from the content of his ballads, Ford's sympathies lay with parliament and its army, although he later appeared to flirt with the more radical religious and political agenda of the sectarians. Ford's work is permeated by a note of disapproval at contemporary immorality, combined with an intensely personal awareness of the providential presence of God, beginning with the satirical *Impossibilities, or, A Matter of Nothing* (1638), with its promise of a divine renewal of corrupt society. His *Wine and Women, or, A Brief Description of the Common Courtesie of a Curtezan* (1647) was dedicated to the MP and regicide Robert Wallop, and denounces drunkenness, 'immoderate affections, chambering and wantonnesse', from which the author, apparently displaying the passion of the convert, says he had at one time been delivered (Ford, *Wine and Women*, 'Epistle Dedicatory'). Ford introduces a note of apocalyptic urgency in *An Alarm to Trumpets* (1651), published with reference to the republic's otherwise successful campaigns in Ireland and Scotland, which he implies were being undermined by worldliness and vanity and an insufficient sense of the living presence of God. Ford's *Fair Play in the Lottery*, dedicated to the author's namesake the royalist soldier and inventor Sir Edward Ford, is a collection of witty verses which suggest that the real lottery winner is he who experiences spiritual contentment.

In addition to the *Impossibilities*, three broadside ballads are extant in the Roxburghe collection, probably dating from about 1640, but which allude to events about 1625: *A Merry Discourse 'twixt him and his Joane*, which warns of the dangers of keeping evil company; *A Merry Discourse between Norfolke Thomas and Sisly Standtoo't, his Wife*, which extols the simple, religious, life; and *A Dialogue between Master Guesright and Poore Neighbour Needy*, describing the disastrous effects of a love of money. Typically, these ballads are critical of the moral turpitude of metropolitan England and display Ford's characteristic blend of droll mockery of contemporary mores and confident expectation of national spiritual regeneration.   GEOFFREY BROWELL

Sources E. Ford, 'Epistle dedicatory', *Fair play in the lottery* (1660) • E. Ford, *Wine and women, or, A brief description of the common courtesie of a curtezan* (1647), esp. 'Epistle dedicatory' • E. Ford, *An alarm to trumpets, or, Mounte Chival to every defeated, remisse, and secure trumpet in England, Scotland, and Ireland* (1651), 5–6, 8–10, 17–21 • W. M. Chappell, ed., *The Roxburghe ballads* (1878); repr. (New York, 1966), 1.230–33, 248–53, 492–8, 2.169–76 • J. O. Halliwell, *The Norfolk anthology: a collection of poems, ballads, and rare tracts relating to the county of Norfolk* (1852), 149–57 • Arber, *Regs. Stationers*, 4.387

Ford, Edward (1746–1809), surgeon, was the son of Thomas Ford, prebendary of St Decuman, Wells, and vicar of Banwell and Wookey, Somerset, who died on 29 August 1746. He received his medical training under John Ford, then in practice at Bristol. At an early age he settled as a surgeon in London, succeeding to the practice of his brother James. He was admitted a member of the court of assistants of the Company of Surgeons, acquired an excellent practice, and became extremely popular. In 1780 he was appointed surgeon to the Westminster General Dispensary, holding the post until he resigned on 16 July 1801. At this time the finances of the dispensary being in a precarious state, Ford generously presented it with the arrears of his salary, amounting altogether to 400 guineas; his example was followed by the physicians to the institution, Foart Simmons and Robert Bland.

Not long after his appointment to the Westminster Dispensary, Ford became involved in a dispute that led to the publication of *Original letters that passed between Mess. Brand and Ford, surgeons, on account of Mr Ford's conduct relative to Mr Paterson, and afterwards on Sheldrake* (1784). Ford himself was author of *Observations on the disease of the hip joint; to which are added some remarks on white swellings of the knee … illustrated by cases and engravings* (1794), of which revised

editions were published in 1810 and 1818 by his nephew and successor, Thomas *Copeland (1781–1855). Ford was elected a fellow of the Society of Antiquaries on 3 May 1792. He was twice married. His first wife, Sarah Frances, daughter of Hugh Josiah Hansard, died in 1783, and was buried at Hillingdon, Middlesex. In 1785 he married Mrs Hunt, of Percy Street, London, widow of Charles Hunt, an attorney. Ford died at Sherborne, Dorset, on 15 September 1809, while on his way from Weymouth to Bath. He bequeathed his house in Golden Square, London, and a considerable legacy, to his nephew, Thomas.

GORDON GOODWIN, rev. MICHAEL BEVAN

Sources *GM*, 1st ser., 55 (1785), 664 • Venn, *Alum. Cant.* • *GM*, 1st ser., 79 (1809), 984, 1168 • *GM*, 1st ser., 16 (1746), 496 • *GM*, 1st ser., 71 (1801), 661 • *Original letters that passed between Mess. Brand and Ford, surgeons, on account of Mr Ford's conduct relative to Mr Paterson, and afterwards on Sheldrake* (1784) • Watt, *Bibl. Brit.*, 257d, 377e • D. Lysons, *An historical account of those parishes in the county of Middlesex which are not described in 'The environs of London'* (1800), 161 • [D. Rivers], *Literary memoirs of living authors of Great Britain*, 1 (1798), 191

Ford, Emanuel (*fl.* 1585–1599), romance writer, matriculated from Trinity College, Cambridge, in Lent term 1585. He was the author of *Parismus, the Renoumed Prince of Bohemia*, which was entered in the Stationers' register to Thomas Creede on 22 November 1597 and printed in London in 1598. The dedicatee was Robert Radcliffe, the earl of Sussex, Viscount Fitzwaters, Lord Egremond and Burnell. At the end is a recommendatory epistle by L[azarus] P[yott], a pseudonym of the writer Anthony Munday. The matter of the book imitates the Spanish romances then popular in England (most of them translated by Munday), and its style is euphuistic. A second part was licensed on 25 October 1598 and published in 1599 under the title *Parismenos: the second part of the most famous, delectable, and pleasant historie of Parismenos, the renowned prince of Bohemia*. It was dedicated to the countess of Essex.

The works were often reprinted. Over twenty further editions appeared in the seventeenth century, and eight in the eighteenth century; the romance was also published as a chapbook. References to *Parismus* in six surviving seventeenth-century comedies bear witness to its popularity: allusions occur in Thomas May, *The Heire* (1622, sig. B3r); the anonymous comedy *The Ghost, or, The Woman Wears the Breeches* (1653, p. 9); Sir Aston Cockayn, *The Obstinate Lady* (1657, p. 16); Thomas May, *The Old Couple* (1658, p. 4); Richard Fanshawe, *Querer por solo querer: To Love Only for Love Sake* (1671, p. 84); and the third part of Thomas d'Urfey's *The Comical History of Don Quixote* (1696, p. 23).

Another of Ford's romances is titled *The most pleasant historie of Ornatus and Artesia: wherein is contained the unjust raigne of Thaeon, king of Phrygia*. It was published about 1599. This too proved extremely popular with nine more editions before the end of the century; some of these, such as those of 1683 and 1700, were abridged. A chapbook adaptation appeared under the title *The most Excellent History of Antonius and Aurelia* in 1682. In 1598 Francis Meres included *Ornatus and Artesia* in his list of romances which are 'hurtfull to youth' (*Palladis tamia*, 268v). A third romance by Ford is called *The famous history of Montelyon, knight of the Oracle, and sonne to the renowmed Persicles, king of Assyria*. The earliest extant edition is dated 1633, but a reference to Henry Chettle's *Piers Plainness* (1595) in the preface suggests that *Montelyon* was originally published nearer to the beginning of the century. Twelve further editions were published in the seventeenth century, and seven in the eighteenth; it also continued to be read into the nineteenth century in chapbook format. In the preface to this romance, Ford notes the favour bestowed on his books of *Parismus* and *Parismenos*, and hopes that *Montelyon* will find a similarly warm reception (sig. A3v).

The title of 'Montelion, knight of the Oracle' was the pseudonym adopted by John Phillips, one of Milton's nephews, who issued a spoof almanac under that name in 1660. Thomas Flatman also employed the name in his mock almanacs of 1661 and 1662, and in his mock romance *Don Juan Lamberto, or, A Comical History of the Late Times* (1661 and 1665), which is directed against Sir Henry Vane the younger. HELEN MOORE

Sources STC, 1475–1640 · ESTC · Arber, *Regs. Stationers*, 3.98, 129 · Venn, *Alum. Cant.* · E. Ford, *Montelyon, knight of the oracle*, ed. A. Falke (1981) · H. Bornheim, 'Emanuel Forde: *Ornatus and Artesia*', *Anglia*, 90 (1972), 43–59 · V. E. Neuburg, *Chapbooks: a bibiography of references to English and American chapbook literature of the eighteenth and nineteenth centuries* (1964), 40 · J. Simons, ed., *Guy of Warwick and other chapbook romances: six tales from the popular literature of pre-industrial England* (1998) · J. L. Gaunt, 'The most excellent history of Antonius and Aurelia: an unusual Restoration abridgement', *Studies in Short Fiction*, 14 (1977), 399–401

Ford, Ford Madox [*formerly* Ford Hermann Hueffer] (1873–1939), writer and editor, was born on 17 December 1873 at 5 Fair Lawn Villas, Merton, Surrey, the first among the three children of Francis *Hueffer (1845–1889), musicologist and author, and Catherine (1850–1927), painter, daughter of Ford Madox *Brown (1821–1893) and his second wife, Matilda (Emma) Hill (1829–1890). His father was German and his mother English. His father (Franz Hüffer before he Anglicized his name) emigrated to England in 1869, and later became music critic for *The Times*. His grandfather, the painter Madox Brown, was associated with the Pre-Raphaelites. Ford considered becoming a composer—a hoard of song manuscripts has survived—but he soon settled on a literary career, publishing his first book, a fairy story, *The Brown Owl* (1891), at the prodigious age of seventeen. When his father died prematurely in 1889, Ford and his brother Oliver *Hueffer went to live with their grandfather at 1 St Edmund's Terrace, Regent's Park, London. Both the boys adored Madox Brown, and introduced a 'Madox' into their own names.

The two brothers were sent to an advanced primary school in Folkestone, then to University College School (in Gower Street, London). They never went to university, but moved through important bohemian, musical, and intellectual circles. Dante Gabriel and Christina Rossetti were their uncle and aunt. Ford later recalled being overwhelmed as a child by the 'Middle Victorian, tumultuously bearded Great' (Ford, 264), such as Ruskin, Carlyle, and Holman Hunt. One of his most vivid childhood memories was of offering Turgenev a chair. Ford's Rossetti

Ford Madox Ford (1873–1939), by Emil Otto Hoppé, *c*.1915

cousins were precocious anarchists. Through them he met Russian political émigrés such as Prince Kropotkin. Dr Richard Garnett, keeper of printed books at the British Museum, was a neighbour; his daughter Olive became a close friend; also his son Edward Garnett, later an influential critic and publisher's reader, who married Constance, famous for her Russian translations.

In 1894 Ford eloped with his school girlfriend Elsie Martindale (1877–1949), the daughter of Dr William Martindale (1840–1902), an eminent analytical chemist, who opposed her marrying someone with such unreliable financial prospects. Ford and Elsie married in Gloucester on 17 May 1894. They left London, and settled in Bonnington, on the Romney Marsh; in 1901 they moved to The Bungalow, Winchelsea. They had two daughters, Christina (1897–1984) and Katharine (1900–1978). Ford befriended the authors living nearby: Henry James, Stephen Crane, and H. G. Wells. It was also during this period that he met the sceptical tory mathematician Arthur Marwood (1868–1916), on whom he based many fictional characters. In 1898 Edward Garnett had introduced Ford to Joseph Conrad—the writer who had the deepest influence on him. They decided to collaborate on a novel about pirates. It was the beginning of a decade of apprenticeship, intimacy, and frustration. When *Romance* was published in 1903, the faint praise of reviewers damned the collaborators' high hopes after working on the book on and off for five years. His marriage under strain—he is thought to have had an affair with his sister-in-law Mary Martindale—Ford had a severe agoraphobic breakdown in 1904. He was sent to Germany for a 'nerve cure' near some of his German family. He later recreated the regime of such resorts in his best pre-war novel, *The Good Soldier* (1915).

After his return to England, Ford began at last to find success. He spent more time in London, and his study *The Soul of London* (1905) was 'boomed' in the papers. This was followed by two other volumes to make up a trilogy, *England and the English* (1907). At the same time he wrote a trilogy of historical romances about Henry VIII's wife Katherine Howard: *The Fifth Queen* (1906), *Privy Seal* (1907), and *The Fifth Queen Crowned* (1908). He now defined himself (with James, Crane, and Conrad) as an 'impressionist' writer; this for him entailed not only a psychological emphasis on the processes of perception, but a provocative freedom with fact reminiscent of the decadent movement.

As Ford became increasingly prominent in London literary life, and further estranged from his wife, he moved to a flat at 84 Holland Park Avenue. From there he founded and edited the *English Review*, and consolidated the classic canon of early modernist literature virtually single-handed, publishing established writers like James and Hardy alongside more modern figures such as Conrad, Bennett, and Wells. But it is also for his new discoveries that he is considered one of the century's greatest editors: writers such as Ezra Pound, D. H. Lawrence, and Wyndham Lewis. Wells recalled him:

> with distraught blue eyes, laying his hands on heads and shoulders, the Only Uncle of the Gifted Young, talking in a languid, plangent tenor, now boasting about trivialities, and now making familiar criticisms (which are invariably ill-received), and occasionally quite absent-mindedly producing splendid poetry. (H. G. Wells, *Boon, The Mind of the Race, The Wild Asses of the Devil, and The Last Trump*, 1915, 123–4)

Ford remained a lifelong friend of Pound, who not only received Ford's criticisms well, but thought him the best critic in England, and became one of his fiercest champions, arguing that modernist *vers libre* was made possible by Ford's insistence that poetry should be as well written as prose. The *Review* lost money, however, and Ford was ousted as editor (though he continued to contribute) after fourteen monthly issues.

Ford became involved with the novelist and socialite (Isabel) Violet *Hunt (1862–1942), and went to live fairly openly with her at her Kensington house, South Lodge on Campden Hill Road. Though he had been received into the Roman Catholic church in 1892, Ford was rarely a practising Catholic, and attempted to divorce his wife. When she refused, Ford and Hunt conceived the dubious idea of his going to live in Germany and becoming a German citizen in order to secure a divorce there. The divorce probably never happened, but they claimed it had. When Hunt was reported in the press as being 'Mrs Ford Madox Hueffer', Elsie Hueffer sued for libel, and won. The case was a society scandal from which Ford's reputation only gradually recovered. The strain of the episode took its toll on Ford and his relationship with Hunt, but unleashed some of his best writing, in *The Good Soldier*. He began dictating it to Brigit Patmore, with whom he had become infatuated. The novel is a masterpiece of modernist technique, using an unreliable narrator to piece together a complex plot of sexual intrigue and betrayal through elaborate time-shifts.

Ford joined the army in 1915 and served as an officer in the Welch regiment. It was an escape from a life that had become intolerable, and he appears to have wanted to die. When he was sent to the Somme in July 1916, only two weeks into the bloodiest battle in British military history, he nearly did die: a shell explosion concussed him, and he lost his memory for three weeks, forgetting even his own name for a few days. He was sent back to the front, this time in the Ypres salient. But he became ill again, suffering from pneumonia, probably exacerbated by having been gassed. His wartime experiences went into his other masterpiece, the four novels known collectively as *Parade's End* (1924–8), now increasingly seen as one of the greatest literary works about the First World War. Ford was sent to convalesce in the south of France, but when he returned to the front he had to be invalided home. He served for the rest of the war mostly in the north of England, attached to the staff and lecturing troops. While staying with Violet Hunt on leave he had met Esther (Stella) Bowen (1893–1947), a young Australian painter who had arrived in London to study at the Westminster School of Art under Sickert. They started corresponding, and in 1919 became lovers.

When Ford was demobilized in 1919 he and Stella set up house together in a picturesque Sussex cottage auspiciously called Red Ford, in Hurston, Pulborough. He wanted to get back to the land and start a new life, becoming a self-sufficient farmer. His bricolage was ramshackle, and his pigs died. But the experiment worked. He regenerated himself and changed his name by deed poll, metamorphosing into Ford Madox Ford, and beginning to write once more. He needed to change his name now that he had two scorned partners fighting for the right to be Mrs Hueffer.

Ford and Bowen moved to a larger and more comfortable cottage before their daughter Esther Julia (Julie; 1920–1987) was born. But they found the Sussex winters depressing. The poet Harold Monro offered them his house on Cap Ferrat in 1922. Ford wrote a wry fantasy poem, *Mister Bosphorus and the Muses*, dramatizing his need to turn from a cold and philistine north to the Latin-based civilization of the Mediterranean. It was his credo, but also a farewell to England. He began *Parade's End*. The sequence is more expansive than *The Good Soldier*, following its intelligent protagonist, Christopher Tietjens, through the traumatic changes in recent British society: Edwardian unrest, the war, post-war reconstruction. It is also another major work of European modernism, continuing Ford's experiments with presentation: exploring mental multiplicity, time, memory, and stream of consciousness.

In 1923 Ford and Stella Bowen moved to Paris, and settled into a cottage in the artists' colony known as the 'Cité Fleurie' at 65 boulevard Arago. There he was once again at the centre of another literary revolution, and acted as uncle to the next generation of the avant-garde. With

Pound's help, he founded the *Transatlantic Review*, and published James Joyce, Gertrude Stein, and the young Ernest Hemingway, whom Ford took on as a sub-editor. One of his latest discoveries was Jean Rhys, with whom he had a brief affair. When Conrad died in 1924, Ford wrote a memoir, *Joseph Conrad: a Personal Remembrance* (1924), one of his most moving books, combining reminiscence and criticism.

Ford was a large, tall man, fair-haired and with a drawling, omniscient manner. Whether he inspired passionate loyalties or animosities, the artists he met frequently felt impelled to record the figure he cut. Wyndham Lewis called him: 'a flabby lemon and pink giant, who hung his mouth open as though he were an animal at the Zoo inviting buns—especially when ladies were present' (W. Lewis, *Rude Assignment*, 1951, 121–2). To Herbert Gorman he appeared 'a behemoth in grey tweeds' and 'the Leviathan of the Quartier Montparnasse' (H. Gorman, 'Ford Madox Ford: the personal side', *Princeton University Library Chronicle*, 9, April 1948, 119–22). But the striking impression was as much due to what Lewis called Ford's 'vivid and theatrical imagination'; to his mischievous brilliance as a raconteur; and to his mesmerizing openness to other personalities. Gorman found him 'the most receptive intellectual' he had ever known. And D. H. Lawrence called him 'a really fine man, in that he is so generous, so understanding, and in that he keeps the doors of his soul open, and you may walk in' (*Letters of D. H. Lawrence*, ed. J. T. Boulton, vol. 1, 1979, 141).

As *Parade's End* began to appear, Ford found himself successful again, this time particularly in America. He made lecture tours there in the late 1920s, and took a flat in New York. He and Bowen separated in 1928. When he was back in Paris in May 1930, he met Janice Biala (originally Janice Tworkovski, 1903–2000), an American painter, with whom he spent the rest of his life. They never had money—the depression severely damaged his sales—and he was rarely in good health. Yet they managed to live their truly bohemian life travelling between New York, Paris, and Provence (especially at the Villa Paul, Cap Brun, Toulon), growing vegetables, encouraging writers with talent, and working tirelessly at their arts. He continued to write novels throughout the 1930s, becoming particularly preoccupied with the motif of the double. *The Rash Act* (1933) is the best of these. He also turned to autobiography, producing brilliant but partly fictionalized memoirs of his pre-war world—*Return to Yesterday* (1931)—and of his post-war life in Sussex and France—*It was the Nightingale* (1934). His writing rarely confined itself to narrow genres: in his last phase he fused history, reminiscence, cultural criticism, and travel-writing into the charming books *Provence* (1935) and the *Great Trade Route* (1937)—his personal 'impression' of the process of civilization. His last published book was *The March of Literature* (1938), an immense comparative survey 'From Confucius to Modern Times', a vivid, idiosyncratic testament to his faith in literature as an international republic of letters. On most days Ford got up early, and wrote a thousand words or two. He produced nearly eighty books, some of which changed the course of modern literature. He died in Deauville, France, on 26 June 1939, and was buried there on 1 July.

The younger writers and critics Ford befriended—Douglas Goldring, William Carlos Williams, Allen Tate, Caroline Gordon, Robert Lowell, John Crowe Ransom, and Graham Greene—ensured his reputation as a writer's writer. The American new critical school valued his technique, especially in *The Good Soldier* (which was filmed by Granada Television in 1981, starring Jeremy Brett). Later criticism has also focused on *Parade's End* (which was filmed by the BBC in 1964, starring Ronald Hines and Judi Dench) for its treatment of war, shell-shock, and social change. His major novels have rarely been out of print, and Carcanet Press in Manchester and the Ecco Press in New York have been bringing the best of his prolific other work back into print since the 1980s. A Ford Madox Ford Society was founded in 1997, numbering among its members Malcolm Bradbury, Gore Vidal, Ruth Rendell, A. S. Byatt, and Julian Barnes. MAX SAUNDERS

Sources M. Saunders, *Ford Madox Ford*, 2 vols. (1996) · F. M. Ford, *Mightier than the sword* (1938) · D. D. Harvey, *Ford Madox Ford, 1873–1939: a bibliography of works and criticism* (1962) **Archives** Cornell University, Ithaca, New York, Carl A. Kroch Library, literary papers and MSS · Indiana University, Bloomington, Lilly Library, literary papers and MSS · Northwestern University, Evanston, Illinois, literary papers and MSS · NYPL, literary papers and MSS · Princeton University Library, New Jersey, literary papers and MSS · Ransom HRC · University of Virginia, Charlottesville, literary papers and MSS · Yale U., Beinecke L. | Forbes Magazine, corresp. with John Galsworthy · HLRO, letters to Catherine Hueffer · HLRO, letters relating to legal action by his wife for restitution of conjugal rights · Hunt. L., letters, mainly to his agent James Brand Pinker · NRA, priv. coll., corresp. with John Galsworthy |SOUND Museum of Broadcasting, New York **Likenesses** E. O. Hoppé, photograph, c.1915, NPG [*see illus.*] · S. Bowen, three portraits, priv. coll. · F. M. Brown, portrait (*Tell's son*), FM Cam. · A. Cohen, charcoal and gouache · A. Cohen, drawings · photographs, repro. in Saunders, *Ford Madox Ford*

Ford, Sir Henry (*bap.* 1617, *d.* 1684), politician, was baptized at Littleham, Devon, on 19 January 1617, the posthumous son of Henry Ford (*d.* 1616), of Bagtor, Ilsington, in the same county, and his wife, Catherine (*d.* in or after 1657), daughter and heir of George Drake of Sprathayes, Exmouth, Devon. In November 1621 his mother married John Cloberry (*d.* 1657), of Bradstone, Devon. Ford matriculated from Exeter College, Oxford, on 21 November 1634. On 25 February 1641 he married Eleanor (*bap.* 1619, *d.* 1673), daughter of Sir Henry Rowe of Shacklewell, Hackney, Middlesex. They had three sons (two of whom predeceased their father) and four daughters. The early years of Ford's majority were taken up with legal suits with his stepfather, who clearly did not have an easy relationship with his mother; Cloberry noted in his will that she had failed in her duty as 'a religious Christian wife' (PRO, PROB 11/273, fol. 367). Ford's royalist sympathies may be deduced from his appointment as a Devon JP in 1644. In 1649 he purchased Nutwell Court in Woodbury, Devon, for £6050, but he seems to have been chiefly known before the Restoration as one of the 'topping' Devonian 'wits' (Hartmann, 19), much in the company of Thomas Clifford, the future lord treasurer. By 1659 he was a member of the Rota Club in London.

Ford twice failed to gain a seat in the House of Commons, at Lostwithiel in 1660 and Newport in 1662. On 22 July 1663 he was elected a fellow of the Royal Society, of which he remained a member until 1682. In April 1664 he was returned to parliament for Tiverton in a by-election. In 1669 he was appointed secretary to Lord Robartes, lord lieutenant of Ireland, and he returned with him to England following his recall in 1670. Ford was 'an excellent orator, and spoke every thing he had to say with a graceful presence, both of mind and body' (Prince, 315), usually on the side of the court. By February 1672 he was acting as a commissioner for sick and wounded, and on 20 July he was knighted. This honour coincided with his second stint as secretary to the lord lieutenant of Ireland, the earl of Essex, and by August he was in Dublin. While in Dublin Ford's wife died, on 3 February 1673. Essex did not trust Ford, describing him in May 1673 as 'perfectly my Lord Treasurer's [Clifford's] spy upon me' (Airy, 85–6), and merely awaited a suitable opportunity to replace him. Ford was duly dismissed for leaking information in December 1673.

Ford remained a government supporter, telling in the spring 1675 session against the first article of impeachment against the earl of Danby and earning the reward of an unpaid pension. During the duke of Albemarle's visit to Exeter in 1675 Ford was made a freeman. However, he was now in financial difficulties and by May 1677 could no longer be relied upon as a court supporter. Although classed as 'vile' by the earl of Shaftesbury, Ford was able to win election to the exclusion parliaments, no doubt because of his strong support for the Devonian wool industry. He duly opposed exclusion. Ford made his will on 11 September 1684 and died the same day or on the 12th, when he was buried at Woodbury. His eldest son, Henry (d. 1679), having married without a portion, Ford was forced to place most of his lands in trust to provide £1000 each for his four daughters (three of them unmarried). Nutwell was sold by his trustees (including his son Charles) for £6318. Litigation concerning the rights of his grandson (Henry's son) was still continuing in 1693.

STUART HANDLEY

Sources M. W. Helms and J. P. Ferris, 'Ford, Henry', HoP, *Commons, 1660–90*, 2.341–4 · J. L. Vivian, ed., *The visitations of the county of Devon, comprising the herald's visitations of 1531, 1564, and 1620* (privately printed, Exeter, [1895]), 350 · Foster, *Alum. Oxon.* · J. Prince, *Danmonii orientales illustres, or, The worthies of Devon* (1701), 314–16 · M. Hunter, *The Royal Society and its fellows, 1660–1700: the morphology of an early scientific institution* (1982), 186–7 · O. Airy, ed., *Essex papers*, CS, new ser., 47 (1890), 85–6 · IGI · *The manuscripts of the House of Lords*, new ser., 12 vols. (1900–77), vol. 1, pp. 10–12 · will, PRO, PROB 11/380, fols. 259v–261r · will, PRO, PROB 11/273, fol. 367 [John Cloberry] · *CSP dom.*, 1672–3 · A. Jenkins, *Civil and ecclesiastical history of the city of Exeter*, 2nd edn (1841), 175 · C. H. Hartmann, *Clifford of the cabal* (1937), 19 · H. F. Russell Smith, *Harrington and his Oceana* (1914), 103

Wealth at death see will, PRO, PROB 11/380, fols. 259v–261r

Ford, Isabella Ormston (1855–1924), socialist propagandist and suffragist, was born on 23 May 1855 at St John's Hill, Clarendon Road, Headingley, Leeds, the eighth and youngest child of Robert Lawson Ford (1809–1878), solicitor and landowner, and his wife, Hannah (1814–1886), the daughter of Thomas Benson Pease of Darlington and Martha Whitelock. When Isabella was ten the family moved to Adel Grange, a large property on the outskirts of Leeds, which was to be home for her and two of her sisters, Elizabeth Helen (Bessie; 1848–1919) and Emily Susan (1850–1930), until shortly before Isabella's death.

The Ford children were brought up in a Quaker household immersed in radical Liberal politics, women's rights campaigns, and humanitarian causes. The girls were educated at home by governesses and were taught a wide range of subjects. Isabella's mother encouraged her to take an interest in the employment conditions and education of working women and at sixteen she was expected to teach in a night school for mill girls set up by her parents and a local shoemaker. A family friend, Emma Paterson, president of the Women's Protective and Provident League, suggested that she should become involved in trade union organization and during the mid-1880s Isabella Ford helped to establish two short-lived societies for women workers in Leeds. It was the labour unrest of 1888–90, however, which brought her to prominence as a trade union organizer. She assisted in disputes among female textile workers and took a leading role in the lengthy Leeds tailoresses' strike of 1889. She also took part in the Manningham mills dispute in Bradford in 1890/91 and became a lifelong friend of Ben Turner, leader of the Textile Workers' Union.

The labour unrest also marked the beginning of Isabella Ford's commitment to socialist politics and she was a founder member of the Leeds Independent Labour Party (ILP). From then on she argued that trade union organization, the vote, and socialism were all necessary for women's emancipation, although her priorities shifted over time. During the 1890s, as president of the Leeds Tailoresses' Union, she was most active in day-to-day organizing work among clothing workers and in speaking for the Textile Workers' Union in its drive to recruit more female members in the West Riding. She was a member of the executive committee of the Women's Trade Union League and after 1895 attended international textile workers' congresses where she translated from French and German for the English delegates. Isabella Ford tried to draw the attention of middle-class women to the work conditions of female workers by speaking at meetings of women's organizations, such as the Women's Liberal Federation, and by writing numerous pamphlets on the subject.

Isabella Ford also carried out propaganda work for the Leeds ILP, speaking at meetings all over the West Riding and writing a column in the *Leeds Forward*. She was one of the 'new life' socialists who gathered around the Yorkshire writer Edward *Carpenter (1844–1929). She was attracted by his vision of a socialism which would transform all areas of life, including the relationship between the sexes, and which would bring love, truth, and beauty into people's lives. Adel Grange became a centre for anyone interested in socialism and women's rights and attracted visitors from all social classes. Isabella Ford had a wide range of interests. She wrote three novels, *Miss Blake of Monkshalton* (1890), *On the Threshold* (1895), and *Mr Elliott* (1901), and was a member of the Leeds arts club, the Humanitarian League, and the Leeds Women's Suffrage Society. In 1895 she was elected to the parish council of Adel cum Eccup.

After 1900, despairing of her lack of success in organizing women workers, Isabella Ford concentrated on propaganda work for socialist and feminist politics at a national level. Between 1903 and 1907 she was elected to the national administrative council of the ILP and embarked on a punishing schedule of meetings which took her all over the country. She was excited by the revival of the women's suffrage movement and was one of a small number of socialist women, neglected in both suffrage and labour histories, who tried to link feminism and socialism, never putting one before the other. She took every opportunity to persuade the labour movement to support a limited franchise and spoke on this subject at the annual conferences of the Labour Representation Committee in 1903 and 1904, which she attended as a delegate of the ILP. In 1904 she took part in a debate with the adult suffragist Margaret Bondfield and was described by Sylvia Pankhurst as 'a plain, middle-aged woman, with red face and turban hat crushed down upon her straight hair, whose nature yet seemed to me … kindlier and more profound than that of her younger antagonist' (Pankhurst, 178). Isabella Ford also reminded the Hungarian suffragist Rosika Schwimmer of 'a caricature of an English spinster', and yet when she began to speak her wit and depth of knowledge about her subject soon captured an audience's attention (R. S., 'Women's age of innocence').

Isabella Ford's writing style was also full of wit and humour and her output reached a peak between 1903 and 1906 both in quantity and quality. Articles and letters appeared regularly in the ILP journal, *Labour Leader*, varying from commentaries on recent political events to more discursive pieces which analysed women's social position. Her ideas were explored more fully in an important pamphlet, *Women and Socialism*, published by the ILP in 1904, in which she attempted to develop a theory which would link the labour movement and the women's movement together. As the demand for the suffrage grew more urgent after 1907, and a rift developed between the Labour Party and the militant suffragettes, Isabella Ford decided to join with other committed suffragists in giving priority to the vote. Between 1907 and 1915 she served on the executive committee of the constitutionalist National Union of Women's Suffrage Societies (NUWSS), led by her close friend Millicent Fawcett. She used her speaking talents to good effect at meetings all over the country and was described as the 'raciest' speaker in the NUWSS: 'she speaks with equal success to an audience of 5,000 working men or 25 clergymen—they laugh and weep as she chooses, and they all love her' (*Common Cause*, 3 Oct 1913). Her speeches referred constantly to the problems faced by working women. She made a special effort to gain the support of labour groups and played a role in bringing about the alliance for electoral purposes in 1912 between the Labour Party and the NUWSS.

In this, as in most of her activities, Isabella Ford acted as a conciliator. She was described by one contemporary as:

> broad and well balanced, and even for Suffrage … refuses to be a fanatic … she swims in the mainstream, she belongs to the centre … Sweet humour puts a twinkle in her eye and on her lips a laugh, at herself maybe, with no bitterness. (Mallon)

On the other hand she was not afraid to express intense indignation against injustice, in particular on behalf of the weak.

During the First World War Isabella Ford was a pacifist and resigned with other friends in 1915 from the executive of the NUWSS in order to work for peace, as usual speaking at meetings all over the country. She served on the executive of the British section of the Women's International League. She was also a member of the Union for Democratic Control and the 1917 Club and established a Leeds branch of the Women's Peace Crusade.

In the post-war period, age and ill health curtailed her public activities, but Isabella Ford continued to work wherever she could for women's rights, international peace, and socialism. In 1919, for example, she attended an international congress of women in Zürich and in 1922 she was a delegate to the international peace conference at The Hague. She was asked on a number of occasions to stand for parliament as a Labour Party candidate, but declined because of her health. None the less she continued to work for the Labour Party and campaigned for her old friend Philip Snowden at the 1923 election which saw the return of a Labour government.

Isabella Ford never fully recovered from the death in 1919 of her sister Bessie, who had always provided emotional support, and wrote to Edward Carpenter that 'a piece of myself is gone' (I. Ford to E. Carpenter, 2 Aug 1919). In 1922 she moved with Emily to Adel Willows, a small property near the Grange, and it was here that she died in her sleep on 14 July 1924 after several months of ill health caused by a weak heart. Her funeral took place at the Quaker burial-ground, Adel, and a memorial gathering organized by the Women's International League and the National Union of Societies for Equal Citizenship was held at the Guildhouse, London, on 28 July. She left an estate valued at £24,540, which, apart from a legacy to her parlourmaid, was shared among her relatives.

JUNE HANNAM

Sources J. Hannam, *Isabella Ford, 1855–1924* (1989) · J. Arnott, 'In memoriam: Isabella O. Ford', *Leeds Weekly Citizen* (19 July 1924) · *Woman's Leader* (1 Aug 1924) · *Yorkshire Evening Post* (15 July 1924) · *The Friend* (1 Aug 1924) · J. J. Mallon, 'Isabella Ford', *Woman Worker* (7 Aug 1908) · 'Some eminent trade unionists: no. 8, Miss Isabella Ford', *Leeds Weekly Citizen* (12 June 1914) · E. E. Crossley, 'Isabella O. Ford', *Leeds Weekly Citizen* (28 June 1929) · E. S. Pankhurst, *The suffragette movement: an intimate account of persons and ideals* (1931) · G. Beith, ed., *Edward Carpenter: in appreciation* (1931) · J. Liddington and J. Norris, *One hand tied behind us: the rise of the women's suffrage movement* (1978) · A. Wiltsher, *Most dangerous women: feminist peace campaigners of the First World War* (1985) · B. Turner, 'Miss I. O. Ford:

an appreciation', *Yorkshire Factory Times* (24 July 1924) • R.S. [R. Schwimmer], 'Women's Age of Innocence', NYPL, Humanities and Social Sciences Library • I. O. Ford, letter to E. Carpenter, 2 Aug 1919, Sheff. Arch., Carpenter collection

Archives U. Leeds, Brotherton L., MSS • Women's Library, London, corresp. files | BLPES, corresp. with the independent labour party • L. Cong., Walt Whitman MSS • Man. CL, suffrage MSS • NYPL, Schwimmer Lloyd collection • Sheffield Central Library, corresp. with Edward Carpenter

Likenesses photograph, repro. in *Yorkshire Factory Times* (1 Nov 1989) • photograph, repro. in Mallon, 'Isabella Ford' • photograph, repro. in *Common Cause* (Oct 1913) • photograph, repro. in *Leeds Weekly Citizen* (7 May 1915) • photograph, repro. in *Common Cause* (June 1910)

Wealth at death £24,540 5s. 7d.: probate, 29 Aug 1924, *CGPLA Eng. & Wales*

Ford, James (1779–1850), antiquary and benefactor, born at Canterbury on 31 October 1779, was the eldest son of the Revd James Ford (d. 1824), minor canon of Durham and afterwards minor canon of Canterbury, and his wife, Dorothy, third daughter of William Spearman of Durham. He entered the King's School, Canterbury, in 1788, matriculated from Trinity College, Oxford, in 1797, became a scholar in 1798, and was a fellow of his college from 1807 to 1830. He graduated BA in 1801, proceeded MA in 1804 and BD in 1812, and was junior proctor of the university in 1811. He held the perpetual curacies of St Laurence, Ipswich, and of Hill Farrance, Somerset. He was presented by his college (28 October 1830) to the vicarage of Navestock in Essex, and married shortly afterwards (19 November 1830) Laetitia (d. 1848), youngest daughter of Edward Jermyn, bookseller, of Ipswich. His wife, who was the author of *The Butterfly Collector's Vade Mecum* (1827), cultivated wide literary tastes.

Ford was a collector and compiler on antiquarian subjects. His materials for a new edition of Philip Morant's *History of Essex* are in Trinity College, Oxford, and his manuscript collections for a history of bishops from the revolution of 1688 onwards were purchased by the British Museum. His collections on Suffolk are in the Bodleian Library and the Cambridge University Library. He was also a contributor to the *Gentleman's Magazine* and to John Nichols's *Literary Illustrations* (vols. 6 and 7), and was the author of *The Devout Communicant*, which was first published in 1815 and reached a sixth edition in 1830, and of *A Century of Christian Prayers* (2nd edn, 1824). Ford died at Navestock, Essex, on 31 January 1850. His quaint directions for a funeral of great simplicity were carried out when he was buried in Navestock churchyard.

Ford left no children but, by his will dated 5 February 1849, made extensive bequests, reserving a life interest for his surviving brothers and sisters. He also left £4000 to Trinity College, Oxford, for the purchase of advowsons, as well as £4000 for the endowment of four Ford's studentships, two of which were to be confined to boys educated at King's School, Canterbury. In 1869 the University of Oxford received his bequest of £2000 to endow a Ford's professorship of English history, which was to come into being when a sum sufficient to produce £100 a year had accumulated. When that figure was reached in 1894 it was no longer regarded as adequate to sustain a professor and

James Ford (1779–1850), by William Mineard Bennett, 1844

the position was instead constituted, after some debate, as an annual lectureship, with the lecturer, chosen by a board of electors, giving the prestigious Ford lectures (usually a series of six lectures) in Hilary term. The first lecturer, S. R. Gardiner, was appointed in 1896.

W. W. WROTH, rev. M. C. CURTHOYS

Sources J. S. Sidebotham, *Memorials of the King's School, Canterbury* (1865), 95–8 • *GM*, 1st ser., 94/1 (1824), 91 • *GM*, 2nd ser., 30 (1848), 330 [obit. of Laetitia Ford] • Oxf. UA

Archives BL, Suffolk Garland and Index Episcopalis, Add. MSS 23965–23966, 24272 • Suffolk RO, Ipswich, antiquarian and historical notes relating to Suffolk; index to Harleian and Cottonian MSS relating to Suffolk, genealogical papers relating to the Bacon family • Trinity College, Oxford, antiquarian notebooks and papers | Bodl. Oxf., Suffolk collection • CUL, Suffolk collection

Likenesses W. M. Bennett, pencil-and-watercolour drawing, 1844, Trinity College, Oxford [*see illus.*]

Ford, John (*bap.* 1586, *d.* 1639×53?), playwright, was baptized on 12 April 1586 at Ilsington, near Newton Abbot, Devon, the second son of Thomas Ford (d. 1610), a Devon landowner and justice of the peace. The Fords were a prosperous and well-established gentry family, and Ford's mother was niece to Sir John Popham, lord chief justice under both Elizabeth and James (1592–1607); she was probably the Elizabeth Popham (*bap.* 1564) who married a Thomas Ford on 2 April 1580 at North Petherton, Somerset.

Oxford and the Middle Temple Like most younger sons of his class, Ford was destined for a professional career: he seems to have spent a period at Exeter College, Oxford, where a 'John Ford Devon Gent.' (usually identified with the dramatist) matriculated on 26 March 1601, before moving to the London inns of court to pursue a legal education. On 16 November 1602 he joined his paternal cousin Thomas Ford at the Middle Temple, of which Popham (who probably sponsored him) was treasurer. Ford was twice in trouble with the authorities at his inn: in the Hilary term of 1605 he was expelled from his inn for failure to pay his buttery bill—a punishment not rescinded until 10 June 1608—and in 1617 he was among a group of forty members who were disciplined for an organized protest against the requirement to wear lawyers' caps in hall. While there is no evidence of his ever being called to the bar, the dramatist probably earned his livelihood from some branch of the law, since he seems to have remained in chambers at the Middle Temple for the whole of his working lifetime: as late as 1638 Edward Greenfield's encomiastic verses on *The Fancies, Chast and Noble* address him as 'John Ford of the Middle Temple'.

Very little else is known about Ford's biography. On the death of his father in 1610 he received an inheritance of £10, which was followed by another small bequest of £20 (in exchange for the surrender of some Devon property) when his elder brother died in 1616. Although his *Fames Memorial* (1606) alludes to an unrequited love affair with 'cruel Lycia', the two-line portrait of Ford as an icon of love-melancholy in William Heminges's satiric *Elegy on Randolph's Finger* (c.1632):

> Deepe In a dumpe Jacke forde alone was gott
> W^th folded Armes and Melancholye hatt

is probably no more than a witty allusion to his tragicomedy *The Lovers Melancholy* (licensed 1628), and more generally to the recurrent preoccupation of his plays with crossed and frustrated loves. Beyond these few details there remain only the publication record and a few scraps of theatrical information.

Ford's residence at the Middle Temple linked him to one of the more important centres of Tudor and Stuart culture, for the inns of court, regarded as 'the third university of England', were a significant focus of intellectual activity and artistic production. Attended by members of the gentry and nobility as often 'for fashion's sake' as for professional training, the inns nurtured a number of literary talents, including several members of the rising generation of gentlemen playwrights—among them John Marston and Francis Beaumont. Also at the Middle Temple, Ford is likely to have encountered his maternal kinsman Sir John Stradling, a major contributor to the dissemination of neo-Stoic moral philosophy in England. With *Two Bookes of Constancie* (1594) Stradling had produced an elegant translation of Justus Lipsius's *De constantia* (1584), a book that probably did more than any other to popularize the sixteenth-century European revival of Stoic thought. *De constantia*, interestingly enough, is among a small group of texts cited in the marginalia to Ford's *The Golden Meane* (1613), and it seems probable that it was Stradling who introduced his younger cousin to the ideas that not only permeate *The Golden Meane* and its successor, *A Line of Life* (1620), but also give a distinct neo-Stoical colouring to his plays.

Ford's residence at the Middle Temple was also of some material importance for an aspiring writer. Above all the inns of court were an important source of patronage for players and playwrights: not only did they support a strong tradition of amateur theatre and make regular use of professional companies in their entertainments, but they provided an influential segment of the play-going public, especially at the élite 'private theatres' for which Ford's plays were almost exclusively written. Ford's own gratitude to the support of this fraternity was signalled by the dedication of his first published independent play, *The Lovers Melancholy*, to a group of friends from 'the Noble Society of *Grayes* Inne'; the outlines of the intellectual circle to which he belonged may be discerned through the substantial list of later dedicatees and encomiasts whose names can be linked to one or other of the inns.

Literary career: non-dramatic works A writer could not depend solely on the support of his peers, however, and Ford launched his literary career in 1606, during his rustication from the Middle Temple, with the publication of two non-dramatic works, evidently designed to secure aristocratic patronage. *Honor Triumphant*, the later of the two, is a prose scenario aimed at the festivities for James's brother-in-law, Christian IV of Denmark, in the summer of 1606; it provides elaborate glosses on four paradoxes of chivalric love which the gallant earls of Lennox, Arundel, Pembroke, and Montgomery had offered to defend in a tournament before the two kings. *Fames Memorial*, the earlier of the two, is a long verse elegy for Charles Blount, earl of Devonshire and Lord Mountjoy, to whom Ford paid a further tribute with his contribution to Giovanni Coperario's *Funerall Teares for the Death of the Earl of Devonshire*. Like Sir John Stradling, who had composed a set of Latin verses celebrating the earl's prowess in completing the Elizabethan conquest of Ireland, Ford was no doubt attracted by the glamour of Mountjoy's personality, which had been somewhat ambiguously enhanced by his prolonged affair with Penelope Rich, sister of Elizabeth's rebellious favourite Robert Devereux, earl of Essex, and well known as the Stella of Sir Philip Sidney's love sonnets. Penelope's scandalous divorce from Lord Rich and marriage to Mountjoy in 1605 led to the couple's banishment from court in a disgrace that perhaps contributed to Mountjoy's untimely death in April 1606; but Ford's romantic sympathy for their plight is registered in his greatest tragedy, *The Broken Heart* (published 1633), whose plot remembers their story.

Of course Ford's early publications also had a more worldly motive: taken together, they suggest a writer anxious to secure patronage from an important court faction with whom Ford could claim ties through the well-connected Stradling family. Not only was *Fames Memorial* dedicated to the widowed Penelope Blount, but *Honor Triumphant* was jointly offered to Susan Herbert (*née* de Vere), countess of Montgomery, and her sister-in-law, Mary Herbert (*née* Talbot), countess of Pembroke, whose husband, William, was a personal friend of Essex and Mountjoy. Despite the misfortunes of several of its members, this remained a powerful grouping. Nevertheless, Ford's choice of patrons must have seemed controversial in certain court circles, as well as being peculiarly provocative to some members of his own family—in the course of the Essex rising Penelope Rich had somewhat presciently urged the execution of Ford's great-uncle, Chief Justice Popham, whom she regarded as a potentially dangerous enemy; it was Popham who subsequently passed sentence of death upon Essex himself.

This evidence of sympathetic links to the Essex circle is reinforced by the dedications of Ford's next two published works, a Calvinistic devotional poem entitled *Christes Bloodie Sweat, or, The Sonne of God in his Agonie* and the handbook of neo-Stoical ethics entitled *The Golden Meane*. Both were printed in 1613, *Christes Bloodie Sweat* being offered to Essex's friend William Herbert, earl of Pembroke, and *The Golden Meane* to the imprisoned Henry Percy, earl of Northumberland, husband of Essex's sister Dorothy. An enlarged edition of this tract was published in the following year and again in 1638, while a second Lipsian treatise, entitled *A Line of Life*, elaborating Ford's neo-Stoical position, appeared in 1620, dedicated this time to Northumberland's loyal son-in-law, Viscount Doncaster, who was working for the earl's release. Not only is Northumberland himself saluted in *The Golden Meane* as the perfect type of Ford's theme 'The Noblenesse of perfect vertue in extreames' (sig. B, fol. 3r), but Essex is approvingly cited among the historical exempla in both tracts as a man 'propt up in honours, and cast downe by envie', who was nevertheless able 'to preserve ... his happinesse with a Resolution that depends upon the guard of innocencie & goodnes' (*A Line of Life*, sig. E, fol. 3v).

The readiness to align himself with controversial causes that is suggested by these dedications is equally apparent in Ford's stance on the scandal surrounding the murder of his fellow Middle Templar Sir Thomas Overbury in 1613. Once again the Essex family was involved: Overbury was poisoned for speaking out against the cooked-up annulment of Frances Howard's marriage to Robert Devereux's son, the third earl of Essex, and her espousal to Overbury's own patron, the royal favourite Robert Carr, earl of Somerset. Ford's account of the affair in *Sir Thomas Overbury's Ghost* (licensed 1615) was a conspicuous shot in the propaganda campaign that ultimately resulted in the disgrace of the Somersets and the execution of their hirelings. The tract itself has not survived, but Ford, along with John Webster and other prominent literary figures, also contributed to *Sir Thomas Overbury his Wife*, an assembly of theophrastan 'characters' published as a memorial to Overbury in the year of Somerset's fall, 1616.

Ford's participation in the Overbury collection is itself a sign that by this time he had achieved a position of some prominence in the London literary world. Further evidence of this can be discovered in the string of encomiastic poems he published, beginning with the verses for Barnabe Barnes's neo-Stoical *Four Bookes of Offices* (1606). The majority of these belong to the 1620s and 1630s and are attached to works by leading fellow dramatists, including Webster (*The Duchess of Malfi*, 1623), Massinger

(*The Roman Actor*, 1629; *The Great Duke of Florence*, 1636), Shirley (*The Wedding*, 1629), and Brome (*The Northern Lass*, 1632); he also contributed verses to prose works by Cockeram (1623) and Saltonstall (1636); and he has been credited with encomiastic lines printed with *Dia poemata* (1655), as well as with a verse anagram entitled 'A Contract of Love and Truth', written for the marriage of Sir Erasmus de la Fountaine to the daughter of Viscount Camden. Most importantly, perhaps, in 1638 he was among the large group of literary admirers included in Ben Jonson's memorial volume, *Jonsonus virbius*. Shirley in turn wrote an encomium on *Loves Sacrifice* (1633), the tragedy which attracted an equivocally admiring epigram from the poet Crashaw:

> Thou cheat'st us *Ford*, mak'st one seeme two by Art.
> What is *Loves Sacrifice* but *the broken Heart*?

Recent evidence suggests that one more poem should be added to the Ford canon: the lengthy 'A Funeral Elegy' (1612) dedicated to the memory of the murdered Oxford scholar John Peter. Privately published and signed 'W. S.', the elegy was for a time attributed to William Shakespeare; but it shows so many similarities in both style and theme to Ford's other work that (despite its puzzling subscription) it is almost certainly his. Ford is quite likely to have known Peter (*b.* 1582), who was the dramatist's near contemporary and a fellow Devon man, from Bowhay, near Exeter.

Dramatic career: collaborations and early works When exactly Ford began writing for the stage remains a matter for conjecture. A lost play entitled *A Bad Beginning Makes a Good Ending*, staged by the King's Men in 1612–13, may well have been the same as *An Ill Beginning has a Good End*, assigned to Ford by the Stationers' register in 1660, but though the allusiveness of his own work reveals extensive familiarity with the work of his Elizabethan and Jacobean predecessors, there is no certain record of Ford as a dramatist on his own account before he emerges as a collaborator with a number of well-established playwrights in the early 1620s. The earliest of his collaborations was probably *The Witch of Edmonton*, a domestic tragedy written with Thomas Dekker and William Rowley in 1621. Ford is generally thought to have worked with Dekker again on the latter's pseudo-historical *Welsh Ambassador* (*c.*1623), before further known collaborations in 1624 on a 'moral masque', *The Sun's Darling*, and on three lost plays, including *The Bristow Merchant* and *The Fairy Knight*. In the same year, with the further assistance of Webster and Rowley, the two worked together on the sensationally entitled *Late Murder of the Son upon the Mother* (1624). In this very active period Ford also seems to have contributed scenes to *The Spanish Gipsy* (1623), a tragicomedy by Middleton and Rowley, and to a tragicomedy and a comedy from the John Fletcher canon—*The Laws of Candy* (1619–23) and *The Fair Maid of the Inn* (1626)—as well as writing on his own a (now lost) comedy, *The London Merchant* (*c.*1624).

Ford's most important work as an independent dramatist, however, belongs entirely to the reign of Charles I, beginning with *The Lovers Melancholy* in 1628 and ending a decade later with *The Ladies Triall* (1638). Between the staging of these two tragicomedies Ford published three tragedies, *Loves Sacrifice*, *'Tis Pitty shee's a Whore*, and *The Broken Heart* (all in 1633), a chronicle history, *Perkin Warbeck* (1634), and a romantic comedy, *The Fancies, Chast and Noble* (1638). The precise performance dates for this group of plays remain a matter of conjecture, but another lost work, *Beauty in a Trance*, was performed in 1630 by the King's Men, the same company who had staged *The Lovers Melancholy* at the Blackfriars two years earlier, and it seems reasonable to suppose that these two plays, together with *The Broken Heart* (also assigned on its title-page to the Blackfriars), belong to a period when Ford was working for Shakespeare's old company; he later transferred his allegiance to the Queen's Men, at whose Phoenix playhouse the remainder of his plays were performed. There are no substantive indications as to the probable date of *The Queen*, a tragicomedy published anonymously in 1653. The record is equally blank about its place of performance (if any) and the company that owned it, but its rather inert subservience to the Fletcherian tradition is consistent with its being an early work. The fact that its publisher, Alexander Gough (who, as a boy actor with the King's Men, had taken part in the first performance of *The Lovers Melancholy* in 1628), was apparently ignorant of its authorship suggests that it probably predates his first appearance on the London stage.

The imitative aspects of *The Queen*'s design—the fondness for paradox, sudden reversals of expectation, and elaborate symmetry of design that mark its Fletcherian antecedents, together with its incidental borrowings from the jealousy plot in *Othello*—are characteristic of a compositional technique that reflects Ford's years of apprenticeship with the leading professional dramatists of his day, as well as the self-conscious theatrical connoisseurship of a dedicated inns of court playgoer. For a popular dramatist Ford was unusually self-conscious in his use of sources, and one of his plays, *The Lovers Melancholy*, was even printed with marginalia acknowledging (in a fashion reminiscent of Ben Jonson's court masques) his debt to Burton's *Anatomy of Melancholy* and highlighting his graceful imitation of a late Latin lyric by Strada (itself imitated from Claudian). From his theatrical predecessors—especially Shakespeare, whose love-tragedies *Othello* and *Romeo and Juliet* provided him with a particularly rich source of inspiration—he borrowed not only tricks of style, but characters, episodes, and sometimes entire plots. While these borrowings reveal a certain anxious belatedness, they are seldom merely parasitic, however: Ford's characteristic preference is to defamiliarize the appropriated material by exposing it to disconcerting switches of tone and context, combining it in unexpected ways with adaptations from quite disparate sources, or exposing it to strange generic dislocations. Thus *The Lovers Melancholy* yokes the transvestite confusions of *Twelfth Night* and *As You Like It* to the world-weary pathos of *King Lear* and the anti-court satire of Marston's *Malcontent*, within a tragicomic framework borrowed from the romantic extravagance of Beaumont and Fletcher but modulated by a detailed awareness of Burtonian psychological theory. Furthermore, by consigning most of the story's intrigue to its imagined past, and concentrating on what would constitute the catastrophe of a conventional Fletcherian design, Ford diverts attention from the external excitements of plot to their inward consequences, and, by recalling the more improbable conventions of romantic tragicomedy only to discard them, makes an implicit criticism of the extravagant pseudo-ethics on which Fletcher's plots depend.

Loves Sacrifice* and *'Tis Pitty shee's a Whore *Loves Sacrifice*, in its turn, transposes elements borrowed from the main plot of *Othello* into an ambience of Italianate corruption and courtly intrigue that repeatedly flags its debts to Webster's *The White Devil* and *The Duchess of Malfi*. Ford's Iago figure, D'avolos, remains a monster of diabolic malice, yet paradoxically acts as the guardian of orthodox morality; Shakespeare's hero, by contrast, becomes the passion-driven tyrant Caraffa, shorn of the Moor's martial *virtú*, but justified in his suspicions of his wife and friend. Biancha and Fernando, the Desdemona and Cassio of the play, remain innocent only by virtue of an absurd platonic technicality, yet they nevertheless invite sympathy in a world dominated by lust, malevolence, and arbitrary injustice. In the later *The Ladies Triall* audience response is further confused by re-imagining Othello (Auria) as a model of patience and trust, while presenting Iago (Aurelio) as a genuinely devoted friend, driven only by excessive zeal, and transforming Cassio (Adurni) into a cynically lecherous nobleman who is restored to the path of goodness only by the unassailable virtue of the central couple.

Even more disorienting is the treatment of *Romeo and Juliet* in Ford's best-known play, *'Tis Pitty shee's a Whore*. Ford had already reworked the disastrous end of Shakespeare's star-crossed lovers in the scene of eroticized self-immolation that gave *Loves Sacrifice* its title; in *'Tis Pitty* he relocated the entire romantic action in the corrupt bourgeois world of Middletonian satire, and reinvented the lovers as a mutually infatuated brother and sister, Giovanni and Annabella, whose fatally intense passion is protected from the audience's instinctive condemnation by its contrast with the cynical opportunism and thoroughgoing Italianate viciousness that characterize the society whose norms they defy. The play carries to its logical extreme the romantic individualism that justifies Shakespeare's lovers, making of the hero an atheistical Marlovian overreacher; turning the good-natured Nurse into a 'tutress' named Putana ('Whore'), a female Pandarus whose amoral encouragement exposes the libertine grossness underlying the lovers' metaphysical flourishes; and transforming Shakespeare's benignly paternalistic Friar Lawrence into the ironically named Friar Bonaventura ('Good Fortune'), whose hellfire sermons alternate with shameless doctrinal equivocation. Like *Romeo and Juliet*, *'Tis Pitty* ends in a scene of erotic sacrifice in which both lovers are destroyed, but in Ford's version Giovanni is both celebrant and executioner, making his spectacular final entry with Annabella's heart impaled on his own dagger, in a bizarre literalization of the traditional emblems of love's cruelty. Even more than in *Loves Sacrifice*, the effect of this disconcerting palimpsest is to leave the audience uneasily poised between habitual sympathy for rebellious young lovers and moral revulsion at the extremes of self-consuming desire to which the incestuous couple have been driven.

Perkin Warbeck and The Broken Heart If *Loves Sacrifice* and *'Tis Pitty* rewrite Shakespearian love tragedy in the idiom of Jacobean revenge drama, *Perkin Warbeck* re-views the chronicle history play—a genre belonging substantially to the 1590s—through the contrasting prisms of late humanist historiography, post-Fletcherian romance, and the courtly ideals propagated by Castiglione's *The Courtier* (1528; transl. 1561). Turning for his principal sources from the officially sanctioned Tudor chronicles of Hall and Holinshed to Thomas Gainsford's much less reverential *True and Wonderful History of Perkin Warbeck* (1617) and Francis Bacon's neo-machiavellian *History of the Reign of Henry VII* (1622), Ford produced a sequel to *Richard III* that turns many of Shakespeare's assumptions on their head. The play is full of self-conscious homages to his great predecessor's historical cycle, beginning with an elaborate pastiche of the king's opening speech in *1 Henry IV*, and taking as a structural model *Richard II*, with its elaboration of the player–king motif and carefully developed contrasts between opposing styles of monarchy. It shows the new Tudor dynasty, under a coolly calculating Henry VII consolidating its power, as the internecine butchery of the Wars of the Roses gives way to small-scale provincial revolts and the largely ineffectual scheming of pretenders like Lambert Simnel and Warbeck himself. But, inspired perhaps by the studied ambivalence of Massinger's pretender drama, *Believe as you List* (1631), Ford reverses the valencies of Shakespeare's play, to make the legitimate monarch a crafty master of realpolitik, while endowing the would-be usurper with the courtly graces and histrionic flair that Shakespeare gave to his annointed king, Richard. The effect is ultimately to hollow out the rhetoric of legitimacy through which Henry mounts his propaganda war against the 'counterfeit', making the balancing of ancient rights against power and efficiency—so crucial to Shakespeare's tragic effect—seem an ideological distraction. Instead (in an uncanny anticipation of Marvell's judgement on Charles I and Cromwell) Perkin's 'pageant majesty', his ability to command the demeanour and 'language of a king', and Henry's machiavellian 'providence' are shown to belong to incompatible discursive realms. Perkin, however, claims the sympathy of the audience through a constancy in performance that not only is conspicuously absent in his quixotic patron, the Scottish King James, but commands the unquestioning love and loyalty of the one unambiguously admirable character in the play, the pretender's wife, Katherine Gordon.

This style of theatrical Stoicism—which, by consecrating Perkin's claim to be a 'King ... o'er death', establishes his paradoxical claim to the 'Strange Truth' of the play's subtitle—is equally conspicuous in what many regard as Ford's finest play: often described as a 'tragedy of manners', *The Broken Heart* celebrates the power of social artifice to impose a semblance of harmony upon the 'chaos' of fate and the wild disorder of human emotion. Unlike the histrionic villain–heroes of Elizabethan and Jacobean drama, creatures of flux who delight in the multiplication of their own identities, Ford's tragic actors are tormented beings who see in performance a stratagem against flux, imposing a role on the refractory and divided inner self that enables them to fix their being in postures of marmoreal constancy. Though the closing scene, with its stately dance of death, is modelled on the spectacular episode of Biancha's brawl in Marston's *The Malcontent*, and though its characterization of the maniacally jealous Bassanes clearly owes something to the frantic Corvino in Jonson's *Volpone*, *The Broken Heart* is less marked by specific borrowings and adaptations than most of Ford's plays: instead its power to disturb audience expectations depends on its striking refashioning of a familiar genre. The plot, triggered by Ithocles' enforced marriage of his already betrothed sister Penthea to the possessive Bassanes, is substantially that of a revenge tragedy: Penthea is consumed by grief and shame at this moral rape, and her suicide by starvation (like the suicide of Lucrece, or of Antonio's wife in *The Revenger's Tragedy*) is construed by her lover, Orgilus, as an invitation to revenge. Orgilus's ensuing murder of Ithocles is avenged in turn by Bassanes, acting under the direction of Ithocles' bereaved mistress, Princess Calantha, whose own death ensues in the spectacular final scene. The dramatic effect of this characteristically brutal sequence is transformed, however, by the extraordinary formality and self-restraint with which it is conducted: so the executions of Ithocles and Orgilus become carefully matched exhibitions of courtesy-in-killing and constancy-in-dying, as victims and killers gravely exchange compliments and forgiveness, while the deaths of Penthea and Calantha are each played out to music designed as a studiously artificial substitute for the inward harmonies that passion has destroyed. Indeed Calantha's death, from the broken heart that gives the tragedy its title, is self-consciously played out in the elegant patterns of a dance into whose successive 'changes' the violent symmetries of revenge are triumphantly absorbed.

Later plays It is generally agreed that Ford's later plays, *The Fancies, Chast and Noble* and *The Ladies Triall*, show a considerable falling-off in dramatic power. Combined with the somewhat defensive tone of the introductory material attached to *The Broken Heart* and *Perkin Warbeck*, the gap between *The Fancies* (*c*.1636) and the earlier independent plays (all of which must have been performed by 1633) suggests that Ford may have temporarily turned away from the stage after one or more failures in the early 1630s. The prologue to *The Fancies* announces a new direction of sorts in its claim to include

> Nothing, but what our author knows his own
> Without a learned theft,

and the plot, such as it is, appears to be entirely of Ford's invention. It concerns the efforts of a group of Sienese gallants to establish the true nature of the 'Bower of Fancies', in which the aged and apparently impotent Marquess Octavio presides over the education of a group of aristocratic young women. The resulting amalgam of romantic comedy and court satire amounts to little more than an elaborate theatrical riddle in which opposing genres are manipulated to produce teasingly conflicting views of the Bower as either fashionable Neoplatonic academy or private bordello. *The Ladies Triall*, Ford's last reworking of the *Othello* story, offers a series of variations, tragicomic and comic, on the theme of justice. The most important of these involve the supposed adultery of Spinella and Adurni; Spinella's denunciation by an essentially benign Iago-figure named Aurelio; the repudiation by her husband, Auria, of the arbitrary punishments of revenge in favour of the judgement of reason; and the would-be seducer's submission to the bar of his own conscience. In its systematic subversion of both revenge convention and the contrived excitements of tragicomic plotting, *The Ladies Triall* follows the familiar Ford prescription, upsetting generic decorum in order to unsettle the audience's formal expectations and moral assumptions. But by now the exercise, largely uncomplicated by the psychological subtleties of the best work, has come to seem mechanical, and, because it relies so extensively on an orchestrated sequence of anticlimax, dangerously undramatic.

Like most of the details of his life, the circumstances, and even the date, of Ford's death remain shrouded in obscurity: he must still have been active in 1639, when *The Ladies Triall* was published with a dedication signed by the poet and a title-page adorned with the same anagrammatic motto, *Fide Honor* (Iohn Forde), that he had attached to three earlier plays. Gifford claimed to have uncovered 'an indistinct tradition amongst his neighbours' that, having retired to Ilsington, the dramatist married and produced children. As we have seen, he has been credited with the authorship of a commendatory poem published as late as 1655, but, given the close personal interest he seems to have taken in the publication of his own plays, it seems likely Ford was dead by 1653, when *The Queen, or, The Excellency of her Sex*, now generally accepted as his, was issued anonymously.

Reputation Because of the plangently lyrical emotionalism of his finest verse and the striving for sensational effect that marks plays like *'Tis Pitty* and *Loves Sacrifice*, Ford's drama has often been linked with the work of Fletcher and his Caroline successors as an early example of the baroque idiom that reached its apogee in the tragedies of the Restoration period. But in his evident fascination with the erratic moment-to-moment psychology popularized by Montaigne he is as much the heir of Shakespeare and Webster as the precursor to Otway and Lee, and in his recurrent promotion of a theatricalized version of Stoicism, in which the violent and unpredictable emotions of the Montaignean psyche are overlaid with a veneer of impeccable self-control, he recalls the icy restraint

and elegance of Bronzino's mannerist portraiture. Mannerist too is the formal reflexiveness that marks his restless play with generic convention, and his ingenious reworkings of material borrowed from his predecessors. It was this conspicuous artfulness, pitched (as it explicitly was) at the knowing coterie public from which he himself came, that gave Ford's plays much of their interest for twentieth-century critics, but it also reflected a highly localized literary-historical dimension that helps to account for their lack of success on the modern stage. Significantly, though both *The Broken Heart* and *Perkin Warbeck* have been revived to some critical acclaim, only *'Tis Pitty*, whose debt to the most popular of Shakespeare's tragedies is too conspicuous to be missed, has proved attractive enough to be revived with any frequency, making its way even to the cinema screen.   MICHAEL NEILL

Sources *The selected plays of John Ford*, ed. C. Gibson (1986) • J. Ford, *'Tis pity she's a whore, and other plays*, ed. M. Lomax (1995) • *The works of John Ford*, ed. W. Gifford, rev. A. Dyce (1869) • *John Fordes Dramatische Werke / John Ford's dramatic works*, ed. W. Bang and H. de Vocht, 2 vols. (1908–27) • L. Hopkins, *John Ford's political theatre*, Revels Plays Companion Library, 7 (1994) • M. Neill, ed., *John Ford: critical revisions* (1988) • R. Huebert, *John Ford, baroque English dramatist* (1977) • *IGI*

Ford, Michael (d. 1765), painter and printseller, was a native of Dublin and a pupil of the mezzotint engraver and printseller John Brooks. Ford, who styled himself 'painter', commissioned a handful of prints in the mid-1740s from Andrew Miller and published them from an address in Ann Street, Dublin. When Brooks left Dublin about 1747 Ford took over his shop on Cork Hill, where he worked under the sign of Vandyke's Head. He engraved a few mezzotints himself, including historical portraits such as that of William III and portraits of contemporary royalty and nobility. Ford also engraved some of his own portrait paintings, notably those of Henry Boyle, speaker of the House of Commons of Ireland, and Henry Singleton, lord chief justice of Ireland, and he copied from Kneller the heads of William III and Field Marshal Schomberg, which he composed as a dual portrait. He published prints of local interest, such as *The Earl and Countess of Kildare*, by MacArdell from paintings by Reynolds, and copies of prints that had been successful in London, such as *Mr Garrick in the Character of Richard III*, after Hogarth, some of them in rivalry with Miller, who had another print shop on Hog Hill. In the Dublin press he advertised that he made annual visits to London in order to purchase stock, and he invited Irish collectors to place orders with him for London-published prints. The story retailed in the *Dictionary of National Biography* that Ford was among the passengers on the *Dublin Trader* which was shipwrecked in October 1758 is now discounted. He died on 6 March 1765.

TIMOTHY CLAYTON and ANITA McCONNELL

Sources W. G. Strickland, *A dictionary of Irish artists*, 1 (1913); repr. with introduction by T. J. Snoddy (1989), 367–72 • J. T. Gilbert, *History of Dublin*, 3 vols. (1854–9); repr. (1972), vol. 2, p. 21, appx 4; vol. 3, p. 361 • T. Dodd, 'History of engravers', BL, Add. MS 53400, fol. 487 • C. Lennox-Boyd and others, *Theatre: the age of Garrick. English mezzotints from the collection of the Hon. Christopher Lennox-Boyd* (1994) [exhibition catalogue, Courtauld Inst., 1994] · J. C. Smith, *British mezzotinto portraits*, 2 (1879)

Ford, (Edward) Onslow (1852–1901), sculptor, was born in Islington, London, on 27 July 1852, the son of Edward Ford (*c*.1820–1864), a businessman, and his wife, Martha Lydia Gardner (*b*. *c*.1830, *d*. after 1902). After his school education in Blackheath, he went on to Antwerp with his widowed mother, where he studied painting at the Koninklijke Academie voor Schone Kunsten (*c*.1870–71). During his subsequent sojourn in Munich (*c*.1871–4), where he attended the Akademie der Bildenden Künste, he was encouraged to take up sculpture by the sculptor Michael Wagmüller, who greatly influenced his early work. Ford shared a studio with Roscoe Mullins, who later became a major figure in British architectural sculpture.

On his return to London (*c*.1874), Ford specialized in portraiture. His first public commission, a bronze statue of Sir Rowland Hill (1881; King Edward Street, City of London), immediately established him as a forerunner of the New Sculpture. Benedict Read contrasts this statue with its duller, mid-Victorian predecessors: 'no longer a flat, bland expanse of bronze … but a subtler handling of the material, a more variegated treatment of mass in general and in detail, to give a livelier effect of reflected light and texture' (Read, 292). This was soon followed by Ford's life-sized marble portrait of Sir Henry Irving as Hamlet (1883; Guildhall Art Gallery, London), whose meditative qualities reflect the influence of Michelangelo.

Ford came into close contact from 1884 with Alfred Gilbert, who occupied a neighbouring studio in The Avenue, Fulham Road. There was an edginess to their friendship, based on what Gilbert later called Ford's 'powers of assimilation' (McAllister, 94). Ford's downward-gazing portrait head *A Study* (1886; Aberdeen Art Gallery) unmistakably echoes Gilbert's *Study of a Head* (1883; National Museum and Gallery of Wales, Cardiff). Likewise, a late work, the *Queen Victoria* statue (1901; Piccadilly, Manchester), owes much to Gilbert's counterpart (1885–1912; Hampshire county council, Winchester). Ford also assisted Gilbert in his experiments with lost-wax casting, and went on to establish his reputation with statuettes in this medium. Yet Ford was more than a mere Gilbert imitator. Indeed, his works are often more impressive, with a better sense of abstract form and possessing greater human sympathy. The latter was conveyed in Marion Hepworth Dixon's description of *A Study* as 'not simply a young girl, it is *the* young girl, soft-breathing in her fugitive grace, her exquisite unconsciousness' (Dixon, 'Onslow Ford', *Magazine of Art*, 15.326).

Ford built on these qualities in two major works, the statuette *Folly* (1886; Tate collection) and the life-sized *Peace* (1887; Walker Art Gallery, Liverpool). Both of these lost-wax bronzes explore the female adolescent nude. *Folly* is a thin, spiky figure who stands precariously on a rock 'and points onward with careless glee to some other adventure more precarious still' (Spielmann, *British Sculpture*, 55). Though criticized for extreme naturalism, it was precisely this, together with its enigmatic theme, that

(**Edward**) **Onslow Ford** (1852–1901), by Ralph W. Robinson, pubd 1891

established *Folly* as a New Sculpture classic. M. H. Spielmann described the more melancholic *Peace* as 'a figure of great beauty with a dash of "the beauty of ugliness"—a natural quaintness—in the leg and stride' (ibid.). In *Echo* (1895; Lady Lever Art Gallery, Port Sunlight), Ford revisited the attenuated adolescent figure and moved further towards subjectlessness.

Ford's art related closely to the arts and crafts movement, particularly when and where it crossed traditional boundaries between sculpture and precious metalwork. He was the first British New Sculptor to exhibit mixed-media works, and was thus an important precursor to George Frampton, William Reynolds-Stephens, and Gilbert Bayes. Ford's earliest and best-known work of this type is *The Singer* (1889; Tate collection). This bronze statuette portrays an Egyptian girl wearing turquoises and garnets in her circlet, holding a harp decorated with imitation enamelling. Ford also executed architectural sculpture, large cast medals, and, in 1891, submitted designs for the British coinage.

Ford's masterpiece is his memorial to Percy Bysshe Shelley, the most ambitious Victorian figure sculpture in Oxford. Originally intended for the protestant cemetery in Rome, it proved too large for its site. Following its acclaim at the 1892 Royal Academy, it was accepted by University College, Oxford, where Shelley had briefly been an undergraduate. The specially commissioned top-lit, domed pantheon (1893) designed by Basil Champneys, in which the memorial sculpture is situated, forms part of the Shelley memorial and part of the celebrated roofline of Oxford High Street. In the memorial Ford tellingly combines white marble for the androgynous nude figure representing the drowned poet, bronze for the mourning figure and lions below, and coloured marble for the base. Equally eclectic were Ford's sources, which included Stefano Maderno's effigy of St Cecilia (1600; Sta Cecilia in Trastevere, Rome) and Henry Wallis's Pre-Raphaelite painting *The Death of Chatterton* (1856; Tate collection). Ford recycled the marble figure of the memorial with relatively minor alterations in his last major carving, *Snowdrift* (1901; Lady Lever Art Gallery, Port Sunlight). Other large-scale monuments by Ford include the *Major-General Charles George Gordon on a Camel* (1887–90; Gordon's School, Woking, Surrey; replica at Royal Engineers' Museum, Chatham) and *Hugh Rose, First Baron Strathnairn* (1895; formerly Knightsbridge, London; now Foley Manor, Liphook, Hampshire).

Spielmann admired Ford's portrait busts as much as his ideal sculptures: 'they are speaking likenesses: in every instance the man himself (or the lady) is before you' (Spielmann, *British Sculpture*, 63). Though Ford was less prolific in this area than Edgar Boehm and Thomas Brock, his busts surpassed theirs in sympathy towards their sitters' personalities and in vividness of modelling. Poignantly, towards the end of his own life, Ford modelled the last busts executed in their lifetimes of John Everett Millais (bronze, 1897; RA) and Queen Victoria (marble, 1899; Royal Collection). The latter was originally intended as a study for Ford's Manchester statue, but so pleased the elderly queen that she commissioned several replicas.

Onslow Ford died at his home, 62 Acacia Road, St John's Wood, London, on 23 December 1901 and was buried on 27 December at East Finchley. He was survived by his wife, Anne Gwendoline von Kreuzer (*d.* after 1905), whom he had married in 1873, and by four sons and a daughter. Although Ford had suffered from heart disease in 1900, his premature and sudden death shocked the art world. Suggestions that he committed suicide carry some credibility. When he died, Ford was in debt and chronically overworked. Of a nervous, perfectionist temperament, he was experiencing creative problems in his later sculpture, in which, as Spielmann stated, 'his highest excellence is not always maintained' (Spielmann, 'E. Onslow Ford', 181).

During his lifetime Ford had achieved high artistic status, reflected in his membership of the Royal Academy (he was elected an associate in 1888 and Royal Academician in 1895), his election to the Art Workers' Guild (1884; master, 1895), and his extensive coverage, greater even than that accorded to Gilbert, in Spielmann's book *British Sculpture and Sculptors of To-day* (1901). Meticulous in his appearance and dress, Ford was affectionately recalled by Gilbert as 'certainly a dandy … proud of his beautiful moustache' (McAllister, 95). Ford was popular with his contemporaries, 'the gentlest and kindest of human beings', according to Spielmann (Spielmann, 'E. Onslow Ford', 181). He was particularly admired by his two most significant assistants, A. C. Lucchesi and the medallist Frank Bowcher. Lucchesi modelled the portrait roundel for the monument to Ford near his studio (1903; Grove End Road

and Abbey Road, St John's Wood, London). Ford's art-historical neglect in subsequent years is largely due to two factors: first, the dearth of personal papers—most were probably destroyed by his family shortly after his death—and second, the more spectacular sculptural achievements and greater longevity of Alfred Gilbert.

MARK STOCKER

Sources M. H. Spielmann, *British sculpture and sculptors of to-day* (1901) • S. Beattie, *The New Sculpture* (1983) • M. H. Dixon, 'Onslow Ford', *Magazine of Art*, 15 (1891–2), 325–30 • M. H. Dixon, 'Onslow Ford', *Art Journal*, new ser., 18 (1898), 294–7 • A. Brook, 'Ford, Edward Onslow', *The dictionary of art*, ed. J. Turner (1996) • M. H. Spielmann, 'E. Onslow Ford: in memoriam', *Magazine of Art*, 26 (1901–2), 181–4 • M. H. Dixon, 'Onslow Ford: an imaginative sculptor', *ArchR*, 8 (1900), 257–63 • W. Armstrong, 'E. Onslow Ford, A.R.A.', *The Portfolio*, 21 (1890), 67–71 • B. Read, *Victorian sculpture* (1982) • F. Haskell, 'The Shelley memorial', *Oxford Art Journal*, 1 (1978), 3–6 • F. Rinder, 'Edward Onslow Ford', *Art Journal*, new ser., 22 (1902), 59–62 • J. Darke, *The monument guide to England and Wales* (1991) • I. McAllister, *Alfred Gilbert* (1929) • A. Bluhm, *The colour of sculpture, 1840–1910* (1996) [exhibition catalogue, Van Gogh Museum, Amsterdam, 26 July – 17 Nov 1996, and Henry Moore Institute, Leeds, 13 Dec – 6 April 1997] • *DNB* • H. W. Janson, *Nineteenth-century sculpture* (1985)
Archives RA, Spielmann MSS
Likenesses J. M. Hamilton, oils, 1893, NPG • Brown, Barnes & Bell, photograph, NPG • Elliott & Fry, photograph, NPG • G. Grenville Manton, group portrait, watercolour (*Conversazione at the Royal Academy, 1891*), NPG • S. P. Hall, group portrait, chalk and wash (*The St John's Wood Arts Club, 1895*), NPG • S. P. Hall, two pencil sketches, NPG • J. M. Hamilton, pencil study for oil painting, NPG • C. Holroyd, oils, Art Workers' Guild, London • A. C. Lucchesi, relief bronze medallion on stone obelisk, Grove End Road and Abbey Road, London • R. W. Robinson, photograph, NPG; repro. in *Members and associates of the Royal Academy of Arts* (1891) [*see illus.*] • J. M. Swan, unfinished oil sketch, City of Bradford Art Gallery
Wealth at death £10,568 8s. 6d.: resworn probate, Aug 1902, CGPLA Eng. & Wales

Ford, Patricia. *See* Fisher, Patricia (1921–1995).

Ford, Patrick (1837–1913), journalist and politician, was born in Galway on 12 April 1837, the son of Edward Ford and his wife, Anne, *née* Ford. In 1841 Ford's parents emigrated to the United States; they settled in Boston, and he was educated at public school and at the Boston Latin school. He served his apprenticeship as a compositor in the Boston printing office of William Lloyd Garrison, the militant anti-slavery campaigner. Ford began to write for newspapers in 1855, and from 1859 to 1860 was editor and publisher of the *Boston Sunday Times*, which proved unsuccessful. He was editor of the *Charleston Gazette* in South Carolina from 1864 to 1866. During the civil war he served in the Union army. In 1863 he married Odele McDonald.

Ford saw that the Irish immigrant community was disorganized and losing its links with Ireland. In 1870 he founded the *Irish World* to gather Irish and Roman Catholic news, both from Ireland and from the Irish diaspora in America. Initially the newspaper was not interested in Irish nationalism, but it was drawn into active politics, partly through articles by Jeremiah O'Donovan Rossa, who in 1876 first advocated a 'skirmishing fund' in the *Irish World* to finance acts of terrorism in England. When the Land League was founded in 1879, Ford promoted the organization of over 2000 branches in North America, and *Irish World* publicity was crucial for the collection of money to aid both the constitutional and the paramilitary movements in Ireland. Ford was accused of advocating dynamite and assassination as political weapons, and association with him was one of the charges brought at the special commission hearing against the Irish leaders Parnell, Dillon, and Davitt, all of whom on their visits to America had been welcomed by Ford. Davitt, in defence, protested that Ford was never a member of any secret society. In later years Ford unreservedly supported the constitutional movement. After the split in the Irish Parliamentary Party, Ford supported John Redmond, and in 1912 backed the terms of the Home Rule Bill for Ireland's future government.

Ford was a man of quiet and unassuming manners, slightly built and of medium height. He was a Roman Catholic. He wrote two books, on British and Irish foreign relations. He died in Brooklyn on 23 September 1913, and was buried at Holy Cross cemetery, Brooklyn, two days later. On his death Redmond described him as 'one of the purest patriots and best men he had ever known'. His obituary in *The Times* was less complimentary, describing him as 'an advocate of dynamite', but this was widely refuted. The *Freeman's Journal* drew attention to his conversion to moderate constitutional reform, and the *Irish World* quoted the *Newspaper World of London*, which described Ford as 'more the scholar and student than the agitator', and claimed that he was an 'authoritative student of Shakespeare' (*Irish World*, 11 Oct 1913).

MARIE-LOUISE LEGG

Sources *Irish World* (4 Oct 1913) · *Irish World* (11 Oct 1913) · *Irish World* (18 Oct 1913) · *The Times* (25 Sept 1913) · *Freeman's Journal* [Dublin] (25 Sept 1913) · D. J. Hickey and J. E. Doherty, *A dictionary of Irish history* (1980); pbk edn (1987)
Archives NL Ire., Michael McDonagh MSS
Likenesses T. Fleming, cartoon, repro. in *Irish World* (11 Oct 1913), 1

Ford, Sir Richard (1758–1806), police magistrate, was the fourth son of James Ford and Ann Hole of Albemarle Street, Piccadilly. His father, a personal friend of George III, was physician-extraordinary and accoucheur to Queen Charlotte. He was educated at Westminster School from 1765 to 1774, where he was a contemporary of Thomas Pelham, the future home secretary. He entered Lincoln's Inn in 1777, was called to the bar in 1782, and practised on the western circuit. Since 1776, his father had been a principal shareholder with Richard Brinsley Sheridan in the Drury Lane Theatre, and this association led to Ford's meeting Dorothy *Jordan (1761–1816), who was then acting at the theatre. Dorothy Jordan became his mistress, and they had three children: Dorothea Maria (Dodey; *b.* 1787), a son stillborn in 1788, and Lucy Hester (1789–1850). James Ford lost his entire fortune by the failure of Sheridan's theatre management, leaving Richard only a private box and free tickets to offset continuing financial disputes with Sheridan. In 1790 Mrs Jordan transferred her affections to Prince William, duke of Clarence. Ford subsequently married, on 7 April 1794, Marianne Booth (1767–1849), an exceptionally talented amateur artist, whose father, Benjamin Booth, director of the East India Company, was a connoisseur collector. They had three children, Richard *Ford (1796–1858), connoisseur and authority on Spain, James, and a daughter.

Ford served briefly as member of parliament for East Grinstead from 1789 to 1790, and for Appleby from 1790 to 1791, but financial straits forced his resignation. Appointed as a stipendiary police magistrate in January 1793, he began his career as third magistrate simultaneously at Bow Street and Shadwell police offices. He was called by Henry Dundas to the Home Office, where he carried out the examinations of arrested members of the London Corresponding Society in 1794. For this, and other work as acting magistrate at the Home Office, the duke of Portland recommended him for a salary of £500 per annum in addition to his magistrate's salary of £400. In 1795 he was sent to Dover to oversee immigration under the Alien Act.

Ford's dedicated efficiency brought him promotion to chief magistrate at Bow Street and superintendent of aliens in 1800, and he was granted a knighthood on 16 December 1801. In 1805 he revived Fielding's horse patrols to promote law and order on London's streets and approach roads. Consisting of two inspectors and fifty-two men armed with pistols, cutlasses, and truncheons, they were the first branch of the infant Metropolitan Police to have a proper uniform.

Ford's correspondence covered every aspect of policing the metropolis, from apprehending a horse thief, Ferguson, nicknamed Galloping Dick, in the Haymarket, to writing orders for the commanding officers of horse and foot guards to provide protection for magistrates reading the Riot Act at a 'riotous, unlawful and tumultuous assembly' in St George's Fields (PRO, HO 65/11, 29 June 1795). A police magistrate's duties also included making arrests. On 20 September 1800, with only one constable to assist, he took three men from a mob in Clare Market, Westminster. To overcome footpads, he went to Hounslow Heath disguised as an old man riding alone. When attacked, his patrol duly rescued him and apprehended the men. In an example of surveillance of persons suspected of treasonable practices, in June 1802 Ford, using the alias William Bruce, took over the management of John Moody, alias Notary, a warehouseman of Carnaby Street, who supplied information on the Despard conspiracy. His other duties included the treatment of state prisoners and relief payments for wives and families, as well as responsibility for royal security. On the king's visits to Weymouth, Ford accompanied the selected Bow Street constables. His work leading to the arrest of persons forging Danish and Russian banknotes in London earned him the gratitude of Christian VII of Denmark and Alexander I of Russia, who each presented him with a diamond-studded enamel snuff-box.

Ford died of a fever on 3 May 1806 at his house, 129 Sloane Street, London, and was buried on 10 May 1806 at St Luke's, Chelsea.

ELIZABETH SPARROW

Sources PRO, C 234/25, 36; HO 36/9/59, 36/11/378, 38/8/455; PC 1/23 A38, 1/40 A129, 1/3117, pt 1; FO 95/615 · BL, Add. MSS 33115, 33122 ·

Mrs Jordan and her family: the unpublished correspondence of Mrs Jordan and the duke of Clarence, later William IV, ed. A. Aspinall (1951) • F. C. Ford, *The Ford family* (1878), 12–14 • R. Paley, 'The Middlesex Justices Act of 1792: its origins and effects', PhD diss., U. Reading, 1983, 262–6, 287–92 • M. M. Drummond, 'Ford, Richard', HoP, *Commons* • W. Stokes, 'Ford, Richard', HoP, *Commons* • Metropolitan Police memorandum no. 143A, Mrs Bell of Scotland Yard Museum to PRO, 18 June 1973 • *The later correspondence of George III*, ed. A. Aspinall, 5 vols. (1962–70), vol. 2, nos. 1369, 1373, 1512, 1596; vol. 3, no. 2245; vol. 4, nos. 2663, 2679, 2699, 2706, 2708 • L. Radzinowicz, *A history of English criminal law administration from 1750*, 2: *The clash between private initiative and public interest in the enforcement of law* (1956), 407 • L. Radzinowicz, *A history of English criminal law and its administration from 1750*, 3: *Cross-currents in the movement for reform of the police* (1956), 229 • private information (2004) • *Annual Register* (1806), 531 • C. Tomalin, *Mrs Jordan's profession* (1994)

Archives BL, Add. MSS 33115, 33122 • PRO, FO 27/56; 95/615; 74/4; 97/242/7 • PRO, HO 36/9; 36/11; 65/1 • PRO, MEPO 5/9 • PRO, PC 1/23/A38; 1/40/A129; 3117

Likenesses oils, 1800–05, priv. coll. • E. M. Booth, oils, priv. coll.; photograph, Courtauld Inst. • attrib. H. Edridge, pencil sketch (as a young man), priv. coll.; photograph, Courtauld Inst.

Ford, Richard (1796–1858), art connoisseur and author, was born at 129 Sloane Street, Chelsea, London, on 21 April 1796. He was the eldest of the three legitimate children of Sir Richard *Ford (1758–1806), police magistrate, and Marianne (1767–1849), a talented artist, the daughter of Benjamin Booth (1732–1807), a director of the East India Company, from whom she inherited an important collection of pictures, including sixty-eight paintings by Richard Wilson. Ford was educated at Winchester College, and at Trinity College, Oxford (BA, 1817; MA, 1822), before entering the chambers of Thomas Pemberton Leigh and Nassau William Senior. In 1822 he was called to the bar at Lincoln's Inn, but never practised. Of cultivated tastes and independent means, he made four European tours between 1815 and 1819, travelling as far afield as Naples and Vienna (where he met Beethoven) and collecting engravings and paintings. On 18 October 1824 he married Harriet Capel (1807–1837), natural daughter and only child of George, fifth earl of Essex, and, like Ford, a skilful amateur artist.

In October 1830 Ford and his young family sailed for southern Spain, hoping the climate might improve his wife's delicate health. They spent the next three winters in Seville and the intervening summers in the Alhambra at Granada, leaving Spain in October 1833, just before the outbreak of the First Carlist War. During his three years in Spain, Ford made numerous excursions throughout Andalusia, and three longer expeditions: in spring 1831 to Madrid, Talavera, and Badajoz; in autumn 1831 via Valencia, Barcelona, and Saragossa to Madrid and back; and in summer 1832 on horseback via Mérida, Yuste, and Salamanca to Santiago de Compostela, Oviedo, León, Burgos, and Bilbao. While on these journeys, of which he remarked that a riding expedition for civilians in Spain was 'almost equivalent to serving a campaign'—referring to those of the Peninsular War, several battlefields of which he visited—many notebooks were filled with descriptions of the monuments and works of art he saw, and he also made over 500 drawings and watercolours, largely devoted to Seville and Granada. Some of them

were to be the basis of more finished paintings and gouaches completed a decade later. The artist John Frederick Lewis stayed with the Fords in Seville for several months during the winter of 1832–3. On several occasions Ford was the guest of Henry Unwin Addington, the British minister at Madrid. In the Prado there Ford saw the work of Velázquez 'in all his protean variety' and in 1843 he wrote a life of that artist for the *Penny Cyclopaedia* (reprinted in Sutton and Ford). He is also credited with 'rediscovering' in 1851 the whereabouts in England of the *Rokeby Venus*. Among paintings he acquired while in Spain were Zurbarán's *San Serapion* (later in the Wadsworth Atheneum, Hartford, Conn.), Ribalta's *The Vision of Father Simón* (National Gallery, London), and Murillo's *Two Franciscans* (National Gallery of Canada, Ottawa). Many of these paintings were sold at Rainy's Rooms in June 1836. As Ford remarked, those 'which encumber other people's houses, give me no pleasure and much expense and trouble. The pleasure is in the *acquisition, not in possession*'.

Early in 1834 Ford separated from his wife, and settled at Southernhay, Exeter, to be near his younger brother, the Revd James Ford (1797–1877). He later purchased a house at nearby Heavitree, which was to shelter the valuable collection of Spanish books that he started to make in Spain and to which he continued to add, notably at the Heber and W. B. Chorley sales (1834–6 and 1846 respectively), but which were largely dispersed at Sothebys in 1861. Several of them, some in the British Library, contain his annotations. Ford amused himself by laying out gardens, building a summer-house in a Moresque style, and writing on the cob walls of Devonshire for the *Quarterly Review* (April 1837), in which he compared them to Spanish *tapia*. The house, sold by Sir Clare Ford in 1898, was demolished in 1958 and the gardens built over.

In May 1837 Harriet died suddenly in London, leaving Ford to bring up their two daughters, Georgina and Mary Jane, and a son, Francis Clare *Ford (1828–1899). Margaret Henrietta (1840–1899) was the only child of his second marriage, on 24 February 1838, to Eliza Linnington (d. 1849), elder daughter of the ninth Lord Cranstoun. On 12 June 1851 Ford married Mary Molesworth (1816–1910), the sister of Sir William Molesworth. Among his descendants was Sir (Richard) Brinsley *Ford.

The piece on cob walls was the first of a series of some fifty substantial articles and book reviews, largely on Spanish subjects, which Ford wrote during the next two decades, mainly for the *Quarterly Review*. These and his anonymous 76-page pamphlet, *An Historical Enquiry into the Unchangeable Character of a War in Spain* (1837)—a vigorous reply from a tory point of view to one written in defence of Lord Palmerston's 'The policy of England towards Spain'—brought him to the notice of their publisher, John Murray. In 1839 Murray invited Ford to write a *Handbook for Travellers in Spain* for the growing series of guides he was publishing. Ford started work in the autumn of 1840 on his return from a prolonged visit to Italy, where in Rome he acquired a torso of a Venus in Greek marble (British Museum), and some important maiolica. It was during the four-year period of gestation of his *Handbook* that he first met George Borrow. Murray had submitted the manuscript of Borrow's *The Zincali* to Ford, who recommended its publication and later advised and encouraged Borrow in the writing of *The Bible in Spain* (both works sympathetically reviewed by Ford) and *Lavengro*.

In deference to Addington's advice, Ford decided in February 1845 to cancel (at some cost) three-quarters of the *Handbook* as already printed, the so-called 'Suppressed Edition', as it contained many passages likely to offend Spanish and French susceptibilities. An example of this cancelled edition which has survived—for Ford retained some twenty-five copies for presentation to friends—contains his confirmatory inscription that it was 'rare from the almost entire destruction of the whole impression'. It was not until late July 1845 that the first published edition appeared. Within days, Ford was being lionized as the perceptive and articulate author of a most comprehensive and accurate account of that country, and one unlikely to be ever superseded. Although opinionated and occasionally acerbic, his perennially fresh descriptions and observations appear here at their most spontaneous, and stimulating. As later affirmed by Sir William Stirling Maxwell, 'So great a literary achievement had never before been performed under so unpretending an appellation', which 'took its place among the best books of travel, humour, and history, social, literary, political, and artistic, in the English language' (*The Times*, 1858), and that judgement holds. The influence of this masterpiece, reprinted in 1966, has been profound. The second edition (1847) was reduced in length by one third, having been pruned of the eminently readable introductory articles contained in the first edition, which, with new material, had been published late in 1846 as *Gatherings from Spain*, written 'to offer a few hours' amusement, and may be of instruction, to those who remain at home'.

Ford's later years, mainly spent between Heavitree and 123 Park Street, London, the family home, were occupied in part with the compilation of the third edition of the *Handbook* (1855), the last in his lifetime, in which much of the excised material was reincorporated. Although the product of his maturer years is a more factually complete guidebook, twenty years had passed since Ford himself had left 'well-beloved' Spain. All later editions were emasculated, and have been compared to 'Niagara passed through a jelly-bag'.

By 1855 Ford's eyesight was beginning to fail, and he was suffering from Bright's disease, which was to cause his death on 31 August 1858 at Heavitree, where he was buried. His tombstone was fitly inscribed 'Rerum Hispaniae indigator acerrimus': he was indeed the most ardent explorer of the *Cosas de España*, the 'Things of Spain'.

IAN CAMPBELL ROBERTSON

Sources *The letters of Richard Ford*, ed. R. E. Prothero (1905) • F. C. Ford, *Documents and memorials of the Ford family* (privately printed, 1878) • B. Ford, introduction, in R. Ford, *Gatherings from Spain* (1970) • W. I. Knapp, *Life, writings and correspondence of George Borrow*, 2 vols. (1899) • I. Robertson, *Los curiosos impertinentes*, revised edn (1988), chaps. 19, 23 • B. Ford, *Richard Ford in Spain* [1974] [exhibition catalogue, Wildenstein Gallery, London, 1974; incl. introduction by D. Sutton] • I. Robertson, introduction, in R. Ford, *A hand-book for travellers in Spain and readers at home*, ed. I. Robertson, new edn, 1 (1966), xiii–xviii • I. Robertson, introduction, in R. Ford, *Gatherings from Spain* (2000) • B. Ford, 'Richard Ford's articles and reviews', *Book Handbook*, 7 (1948), 369–80 • A. Gámir, introduction, in R. Ford, *Granada: escritos con dibujos inéditos del autor Granada* (Granada, 1955) [an account illustr. with unpubd orig. drawings] • B. Ford, introduction, *Richard Ford en Sevilla*, trans. X. de Salas (1963) [a collection of his drawings with notes by D. A. Iniguez] • R. Ford, *Letters to Gayangos*, ed. R. Hitchcock (1974) • T. J. Bean, *Proceedings of 1991 George Borrow Conference* [Norwich 1991], ed. G. Fraser (1992) • N. Glendinning, 'A collector's passion for Spain: Richard Ford, 1796–1858', *Country Life*, 155 (1974), 1550–51 • W. Stirling-Maxwell, *The Times* (4 Sept 1858) • T. Hughes, *Fraser's Magazine*, 58 (1858) • *Walpole Society*, 60 (1998) [2 pts; *The Ford collection*, ed. L. Herrmann] • I. Robertson, *Richard Ford, 1796–1858: Hispanophile, connoisseur, and critic* [forthcoming]

Archives John Murray Archives, London, MSS • priv. coll., collected papers and corresp. • T. J. Bean collection, MSS | BL, letters to Macvey Napier and others • Bodl. Oxf., letters to Lord Lovelace and Lady Lovelace • Hispanic Society of America, New York, letters to George Borrow • Mitchell L., Glas., Glasgow City Archives, letters to Sir Edmund Head and Sir William Stirling Maxwell

Likenesses J. Gutierrez de la Vega, portrait, 1831, priv. coll. • José Domínguez Bécquer, three portraits, 1832, priv. coll. • J. F. Lewis, portrait, 1833, priv. coll. • A. Chatelain, portrait, 1840, priv. coll.; copy, oils, NPG • H. W. Phillips, portrait, posthumous

Wealth at death under £25,000: resworn probate, May 1878, *CGPLA Eng. & Wales* (1858)

Ford, Simon (1618/19–1699), Church of England clergyman, was born at East Ogwell, Devon, the son of Richard Ford of East Ogwell. Educated at Exeter and Dorchester grammar schools, he entered Magdalen Hall, Oxford, at the age of seventeen in 1636. He graduated BA in 1641 but was expelled from Oxford soon after on account of his puritan leanings. After the parliamentary visitation of delegates in 1647 he returned and was received with honour. He proceeded MA in 1648 and was created BD in 1650 'by dispensation of the delegates', of whom he was one. He was appointed to a senior studentship of Christ Church, Oxford, by the dean, Edward Reynolds, but removed in 1651 after a sermon against the engagement. In 1645 he had been given the sequestered living of Puddletown, Dorset, and in 1651 he became vicar of St Lawrence, Reading. Presumably while there or through links then established he married Martha Stampe of Reading (*d.* 1684).

Ford was engaged in a good deal of local controversy, primarily about an assize sermon in which he denounced the people of Reading for their support of extravagant religious views. He was also in dispute with Thomas Speed, a Bristol Quaker. Against Speed, Ford and Christopher Fowler, the vicar of St Mary's, Reading, wrote *A Sober Answer to an Angry Epistle* in 1656. In places a vituperative work, it starts by attacking the Quakers for some of their more extreme teachings: their attack on tithes would force orthodox ministers to 'live as the sparrows do' (S. Ford and C. Fowler, *A Sober Answer*, 20); their insistence on the second person singular and other quirks is 'pedantry' and will 'destroy civility and good manners' (ibid., 43). Some of their behaviour brings them close to the Ranters. Their emphasis on the inner light leads them to heretical doctrines on the godhead and Christology, and gives them the liberty of 'tearing up all the professed religion of England' (ibid., 50). Against this Ford and Fowler insist on the scriptures, 'the rule, ground and foundation of faith' as interpreted and 'drawn out' through the ages (ibid., 60). In 1659 Ford moved to All Saints, Northampton. He conformed in 1662 and proceeded DD at Oxford in 1665. He moved to London in 1670, first to Bridewell and then to St Mary Aldermanbury. Failing health compelled him to move in 1676 to the rectory of Old Swinford, Worcestershire, to which he was presented by Thomas Foley. He died there on 7 April 1699, and was buried at Old Swinford parish church.

Ford's most considerable work was *The Spirit of Bondage and Adoption* (1655). The spirit of bondage is the ministry of the law whereby, through fear of the wrath of God, the Holy Spirit brings sinners to conversion. The minister has the duty of preaching on the wrath of God, even if this may 'rub up old sores' in the converted (*Spirit*, 80). The second, much longer, section of the book is in fact a treatise on assurance for the converted. It is muddled, repetitious, and unconvincing. After advising various taxing expedients to establish assurance, Ford warns against 'overscrupulousness and sceptical questionfulness' (ibid., 276). Again, when he describes the signs of assurance through complicated self-examination, he immediately warns that they may be the snares of the devil. His final 'thesis' is 'that one principal work of the spirit of adoption in the soul that hath received it is to embolden and enlighten it in prayer' (ibid., 511). Yet at once he comments 'facility and fluency of expression in prayer, what evils it often occasions … Better a humble acknowledgement of your own impotency to pray' (ibid., 527). On the other hand there is such a thing as 'sinful modesty' (ibid., 557). He ends 'how shall I know whether my actual boldness and fervency be from God's spirit or from Satan'—and provides no answer (ibid., 576). As much as any book of the time Ford's work illustrates the agonizing of the Christian over his election.

Another contemporary controversy into which Ford plunged was that on infant (or paedo-) baptism. He produced two 'dialogues' against John Tombes, the Baptist minister of Leominster, Hereford. These were *Concerning the Practical Use of Infant Baptism* in 1654 and 1656, the first of which had reached its third edition by 1657. Ford bases his defence of infant baptism on the concept of God's covenant with Abraham and his descendants (Genesis, 17: 7). Through it the child of believing parents enters into this covenant, which is sealed by God. He thereby joins the church in which salvation is found. Ford makes extravagant claims for infant baptism. It is 'the most lively representation and obsignation of election and justification' (*Infant Baptism*, 1657 edn, 40). Even if the child does not grow up a believing Christian, God's covenant remains with him. Finally there is the wider influence of infant baptism: 'I conceive it morally impossible to rivet Christian religion into the body of a nation, but by way of infant baptism' (ibid., 77).

Between the first and second dialogues Ford wrote with a list of queries to Baxter, who had earlier at Bewdley engaged in a lengthy verbal debate on baptism with Tombes. Baxter replied: 'I verily believe you have taken a righter way to prevent the growth of anabaptistery than any of us all … truly I am myself unsatisfied'—a reference probably to his suspending the practice of infant baptism for some years at Kidderminster (Keeble and Nuttall, 1.195). Ford's *Second Part of the Dialogue* was intended to clarify and amplify the first. For instance, it guarded against the danger of presuming that baptism was equivalent to election; it is 'only the covenant of grace as made with the church visible' (p. 71). Ford recognized that infant baptism laid on the church and the family the solemn duty of catechizing. *A Sermon on Catechising* was annexed to the first dialogue. Catechizing is the core of the Christian community; 'by this means a plantation of churches may be erected. People talk of gathering churches, but their way (generally) is scattering them, as many precious ministers have found by sad experience' (*Catechising*, 27). In practice, in children this is the 'learning age', not to be missed: 'catechising in youth is a great security against apostasy in age' (ibid., 30, 16). Ford followed this up in his own ministry. In 1657 he produced a *Short Catechism* to drive home his teaching on infant baptism. Back in the Church of England he wrote for his parish at Old Swinford, and published in 1684 two expositions of the church catechism, one for 'adult children and the elderly in need of it' and a very short one broken into memorable phrases 'for the younger sort of catechumens' (Green, 154n., 246f., 650f.). Ford had a sideline in poetry concerning contemporary events such as the fire of London. This was in Latin hexameters, often translated into heroic couplets.

To summarize: throughout his life Ford showed himself to be a courageous (though confused) moderate minister caught in the fierce religious currents of his time. He lost his Christ Church studentship for his sermon against the engagement; he preached against extravagant religious views at Reading and was called before a grand jury for his pains; he wrote against Quakerism and Anabaptism. In a sermon at the Restoration he called for moderation 'by abating voluntarily our heretical heights and heats' and urged the king to consult the 'most moderate and least biased men of all sides', and decide the remaining differences by calling an 'indifferent synod'—the quintessential moderate platform (*Loyal Subject's Exultation*, 1660, 48). It is no surprise that he conformed. In 1671 Baxter classed him, along with Stillingfleet and others, as 'among the best and ablest of the conforming ministers' (*Reliquiae Baxterianae*, part 3, 19, 87; Keeble and Nuttall, 2.105).

BARRY TILL

Sources DNB · *Walker rev.* · I. Green, *The Christian's ABC: catechisms and catechising in England, c.1530–1740* (1996) · *Calendar of the correspondence of Richard Baxter*, ed. N. H. Keeble and G. F. Nuttall, 2 vols. (1991) · *Reliquiae Baxterianae, or, Mr Richard Baxter's narrative of the most memorable passages of his life and times*, ed. M. Sylvester, 1 vol. in 3 pts (1696) · Wood, *Ath. Oxon.: Fasti*, new edn

Ford, Stephen (*d.* 1695/6), Independent minister, is of unknown parents and background. Nothing is known of his early years or education and he first appears in Oxford in the early 1650s, but not as a student. Ford seems to have served one of the college heads, probably Thankful Owen, then president of St John's College, by whom he was also reported to be employed in 1669. But it was as chaplain of New College, Oxford, that Ford officiated at Deddington in 1655. On 14 March 1656 he was admitted vicar of Chipping Norton, Oxfordshire, having been commended by John Owen in his role as a trier. There had been three better offers and according to Ford himself 'one of them was worth near twenty times as much as this poor vicarage'. But, as he informed his new parishioners, 'I found my heart more inclined towards you than towards any of the said places; and through grace, I refused them all for your sakes' (Wilson, 472). In or before 1656 he married Catherine, whose surname is unknown. They had at least two children: Mary, baptized at Chipping Norton on 5 September 1656, and Stephen, buried there on 18 January 1661.

Ford was named as an assistant to the commissioners into the ministry in Oxfordshire (29 September 1657) and in Gloucestershire (24 October 1657). But after the Restoration he found his living increasingly uncomfortable. The House of Lords heard on 30 May 1660 that:

> insolent Persons came into the church of Chipping-Norton … and when Mr Stephen Ford, the minister of the said parish, was going to exercise the duty of his place by prayer and preaching, they fell violently upon him, pulled him by the neck and throat, and by the hair of the head, and wounded him and pulled him out of the Church, calling him 'rogue and rascal', and other opprobious and odious words without any cause or provocation of the said Mr Ford, and afterwards proudly and insolently said, 'Let the Justices of the Peace relieve him, or do any thing herein for him at their peril.' (*JHL*, 11, 1660–66, 49)

The house ordered an investigation and punishment of the offenders, but Ford had left Chipping Norton by the end of the year. He continued to preach in the area, but was 'sadly harassed; and at length some of his Enemies threaten'd his Life, and he was forc'd to fly to London, where he often preach'd in the Time of the Plague' (*Calamy rev.*, 206). In 1669 'one Ford a servant to Thankfull Owen' was reportedly preaching in London at a brewer's malthouse in Mill Lane, in the parish of St Olave Southwark (ibid.). On 2 April 1672 he was licensed as a congregational teacher at a house near Miles Lane, off Cannon Street, London.

Ford was one of the twenty-one divines who subscribed the expanded edition of John Faldo's *Quakerism No Christianity* (1675). He took his pastoral duties with the utmost seriousness: 'I could have sit down (as others do) with preaching to you twice every Lords day, and one lecture in the week days', but disdaining such laxity he had instituted a 'Lords day fortnight lecture' and a 'monthly lecture' (Ford, preface). Later he inaugurated a catechetical lecture for young men in Miles Lane. Ford signed his will, as of London, on 9 April 1683. His last public duty was as messenger of the Congregational Fund Board, undertaken at its foundation on 17 December 1695. He died between that date and the probate of his will on 14 May 1696. He was able to leave £1000 to his widow, and many legacies to friends and relations. Anticipating wrangles, he stipulated that if any should 'trouble or molest' his

widow and executrix, Catherine, in pursuit of their portion, or fail to sign a declaration averring their satisfaction of what was on offer, they would receive nothing (PRO, PROB 11/431, fol. 186v).   STEPHEN WRIGHT

Sources *Calamy rev.* · A. Gordon, ed., *Freedom after ejection: a review (1690–1692) of presbyterian and congregational nonconformity in England and Wales* (1917) · PRO, PROB 11/431, fol. 186v · W. Wilson, *The history and antiquities of the dissenting churches and meeting houses in London, Westminster and Southwark*, 4 vols. (1808–14) · *JHL*, 11 (1660–66) · S. Ford, *A gospel church* (1675)

Wealth at death approx. £2000: PRO, PROB 11/431, fol. 186v

Ford, Thomas (*d.* 1648), composer and viol player, of unknown family and origin, published in 1607 *Musicke of Sundrie Kindes, Set Forth in Two Bookes*. The first book, containing eleven songs, among which are the celebrated 'Since first I saw your face' and 'There is a lady sweet and kind', is dedicated to Sir Richard Weston, and the second, containing eighteen lyra viol duets, to Sir Richard Tichborne.

At Christmas 1610 Ford was appointed a musician to Henry, prince of Wales, at a salary of £30 p.a. He continued to serve the prince, at a salary raised to £40 at Christmas 1611, until his master's death in 1612. In 1614 he contributed to Sir William Leighton's *Tears and Lamentacions of a Sorrowfull Soule* two anthems, 'Almighty God, which hast me brought', for four voices with lute and treble viol, and 'Not unto us' for five voices.

From 25 March 1617 Ford served as musician to Prince Charles, continuing in office after the latter's accession. On 11 July 1626 the king appointed him additionally to a position formerly held by John Ballard, so that he was both a viol player among the lutes and voices and also a composer. On 1 January 1627 Ford was among thirty-one musicians who received as new year gifts 5 ounces in gilt plate from the king. The charter of the Corporation of Musick in Westminster, dated 15 July 1635, which gave the king's musicians authority over the training and performance of musicians in the capital and its immediate environs, lists Ford as one of the corporation's first two wardens (the second being Jerome Lanier) with the authority to administer the 'corporall oathes' (Ashbee, 5.246–8).

At his death in November 1648 Ford was still receiving a combined yearly salary of £80 plus liveries for service as 'composer to the private musick' and as 'a viall, among the lutes and voices' (Ashbee, 1.2). Under the terms of his will, dated 12 November 1648, several persons received bequests, including the musicians Walter Porter and Henry Cooke; a total of £105 was bequeathed. Ford was buried in St Margaret's, Westminster, on 17 November 1648. There is no evidence that he married.

An authoritative assessment of the significance of Ford's music in the context of his time must await wider dissemination and study of his work than have occurred thus far. It is possible to say that the music merits better than its present relative obscurity. Of the anthems—perhaps the least well known of his works—it has been written that some show such 'mastery of compositional techniques and … high level of inspiration' that they 'are equal to the works of the most eminent composers of the period' (Hsieh, 145, 143). The lute songs and lyra viol duets included in his one published book are more accessible: the former, for instance the delicately elegant 'Since first I saw your face', rank with the best in a genre not lacking in great works; the latter are so finely idiomatic as to suggest Ford must have been a fine performer, and the depth of expression and originality of, for example, 'Pavin, M. Maynes Choice' show him to have been a composer of true inspiration.   FRANK TRAFICANTE

Sources T. Ford, *Musicke of sundrie kindes* (1607); facs. edn (1971) · A. Ashbee and D. Lasocki, eds., *A biographical dictionary of English court musicians, 1485–1714*, 2 vols. (1998) · A. Ashbee, ed., *Records of English court music*, 1 (1986) · A. Ashbee, ed., *Records of English court music*, 3 (1988) · A. Ashbee, ed., *Records of English court music*, 4 (1991) · A. Ashbee, ed., *Records of English court music*, 5 (1991) · O. Timofeyev, 'The lyra viol duets by Thomas Ford: a critical edition of instrumental pieces from Thomas Ford's "Musicke of sundrie kindes"', MA diss., University of Southern California, 1993 · F. Hsieh, 'The anthems of Thomas Ford', PhD diss., Louisiana State University, 1989 · F. Traficante, 'Music for the lyra viol: the printed sources', *Lute Society Journal*, 8 (1966), 7–24 [repr. in *Journal of the Viola da Gamba Society of America*, 5 (1968), 16–33] · private information (2004) [A. Ashbee] · Burney, *Hist. mus.*, new edn
Archives Christ Church Oxf., MSS 56–60, 736–738
Wealth at death £105—bequests

Ford, Thomas (1598–1674), clergyman and ejected minister, was born at Brixton, Devon. He attended school at Plympton and matriculated at Magdalen Hall, Oxford, in 1621, graduating BA in 1625, proceeding MA in 1627, and becoming a fellow of his college. He was ordained deacon at Salisbury on 6 March 1631 and priest at Bristol on 12 May 1632. As a result of a sermon at Oxford on 12 June 1631, when he attacked the innovations creeping into the church, turning communion tables into altars, making the eucharist a sacrifice, and magnifying tradition, he was summoned before the vice-chancellor, who on 25 June sealed up Ford's study. A subsequent search through his books and papers revealed nothing the vice-chancellor could use against him. Laud, as chancellor, now ordered Ford's punishment and on 23 August brought the matter before the king in his council at Woodstock. After questioning by the king Ford was ordered to quit the university within four days. He was escorted out of the city, with honour, by a crowd of scholars in their gowns. He returned to Devon, where the magistrates of Plymouth proposed to elect him their lecturer and appoint him vicar when the living became vacant, but on 12 September the king forbade this.

The next stages of Ford's career were associated with the Fleetwood family. As chaplain to Colonel George Fleetwood, then in the service of Gustavus Adolphus, he spent some time in the garrisons of Stode and Elbing and was offered the position of minister to the English merchants of Hamburg but preferred to return to England, where on 18 October 1637 he was presented to the living of Aldwincle All Saints, Northamptonshire, by Sir Miles Fleetwood (1576–1641), father of his former colonel. By licence dated 21 June 1638 he married at St Mary Staining, London, Bridget (d. 1675), described as the daughter of one Fleetwood, esquire, of Gray's Inn; various members of the

Lancashire, Buckinghamshire, and Middlesex branches of the family entered the inn in the late sixteenth and early seventeenth centuries, but Ford's bride may have been the Bridget, daughter of Henry Fleetwood, baptized at St Martin Ongar or St Clement, Eastcheap, in 1608, who perhaps may be identified as a daughter of the former MP and Gray's Inn bencher of that name, and thus as a granddaughter of Thomas Fleetwood of Vache, Buckinghamshire, and Bridget Spring. Thomas and Bridget Ford had a son and a daughter who reached adulthood.

In 1640 Ford served as one of the representatives of the diocese of Peterborough at convocation; his first publication, *Reformation Sure and Steadfast*, based on a sermon delivered on 15 June 1641 and issued that year by order of the House of Commons, reveals his ecclesiological position. On 23 May 1644 he added St Peter's Aldwincle to his original living but, having been plundered there, he left and from at least November that year until the following spring was chaplain to the regiment of Sir Samuel Luke, parliamentarian governor of Newport Pagnell and a first cousin of George Fleetwood. In March 1645 he became a member of the Westminster assembly, and that year was also minister of St Faith's under St Paul's, London. He preached fast sermons before the Commons in July 1645 and April 1646, but does not seem to have stayed long in the City. In 1647 he published his *The Times Anatomiz'd* in London but relinquished his Northamptonshire livings. By January 1648, when, as 'minister of Puddletown, Dorset', he was elected a possible successor to John White, the eminent vicar of Dorchester, he had already departed for Exeter, where he became vicar of St Lawrence.

Later that year Ford showed his presbyterianism by signing *The Joint Testimonie of the Ministers of Devon* in support of the solemn league and covenant. He was one of the presbyterians preaching in the cathedral, empty since the dispersal of the dean and chapter in 1646; the building was also being used by the Independents. According to Edmund Calamy, Ford was temporarily excluded from the cathedral by Major-General Desborough for not taking the engagement. This may be connected with orders from the council of state to the justices of the peace to take action against some preachers, Ford being one of the most active, whose 'intemperate declarations and seditious invectives' might endanger the safety of the Commonwealth (*CSP dom.*, 1650, 1 April). However, this did not affect the respect with which Ford was held in Exeter and the influence he had with the clergy of the city. He persuaded them to arrange a Tuesday lecture with each of them taking his turn, and also to hold a communion service once a fortnight, alternating among the churches with members of any of the congregations allowed to communicate. 'These Methods prevented all Jealousies among them, and united the people firmly among themselves' (Calamy, *Abridgement*, 2.212).

In 1654 Ford became one of the assistants to the Devon commission of triers and ejectors. The following year he collaborated with George Hughes in calling a meeting at Exeter of ministers from all over the county to form an association on the pattern of the Worcestershire association started by Richard Baxter. In accordance with an act of parliament of 4 September 1656, which gave the mayor and commonalty of the city control over the parishes and parish churches, St Lawrence was one of thirteen parishes whose churchwardens were ordered, on 11 August 1657, to hand over their keys to the mayor. On the same day the chamber presented ministers to the four remaining parishes, enlarged at the others' expense, and to St Peters East, and decreed that Thomas Ford, bereft of St Lawrence, should continue with his Wednesday lectures in West Peters, even though this was the Independent end of the cathedral. Ford was also to assist the other ministers 'as he find strength and opportunity which is lefte to his owne freewill' (chamber act book, fol. 90v). The chamber also decided that the cathedral should be divided by a brick wall but this did not stop a public dispute between Ford and Lewis Stuckley of West Peters when Stuckley excommunicated two women for attending presbyterian services.

Ford remained in Exeter after the Restoration and preached a farewell sermon at St Mary Major on 13 August 1662 before being ejected for refusing to accept the Act of Uniformity. When the Five Mile Act of 1665 was passed he petitioned the Exeter justices of the peace to accept a revised form of the oath; this was rejected so he retired to Exmouth. Here he occupied himself at least partly by writing. His *Logos autopistos, or, Scriptures Self-Evidence* (1667) described itself as 'a plea for Protestants in the defence of their profession, and intended only for the use and instruction of the vulgar sort'. He had lost none of his vigour or his zeal for the presbyterian cause. In *Aytokatakritos, or, The Sinner Condemned of himself* (1668) he argued that the ungodly were guilty of their own destruction, while in *Felo de se, or, The Bishops Condemned out of their Own Mouthes*, published the same year, he aimed to reveal the dire consequences of restored episcopal government. He cast himself as 'a mourner for the poor nations, that are enslaved under prelatical tyranny … one that was once of this black fac'd hierarchy (as Luther was of the Popish) but is now wonderfully delivered from them'.

Ford returned to Exeter after the 1672 declaration of indulgence, under the terms of which he was licensed to minister and his house in Exeter was licensed as a meeting-place, but he only preached there twice, owing to ill health. He died in 1674 and was buried in St Lawrence Exeter on 28 December. **MARY WOLFFE**

Sources E. Calamy, ed., *An abridgement of Mr. Baxter's history of his life and times, with an account of the ministers, &c., who were ejected after the Restauration of King Charles II*, 2nd edn, 2 vols. (1713) • *The nonconformist's memorial … originally written by … Edmund Calamy*, ed. S. Palmer, [3rd edn], 2 (1802) • *CSP dom.*, 1631–3; 1671–2 • W. J. Harte, 'Ecclesiastical and religious affairs in Exeter, 1640–1662', *Report and Transactions of the Devonshire Association*, 69 (1937), 41–72 • R. N. Worth, 'Puritanism in Devon and the Exeter assembly', *Report and Transactions of the Devonshire Association*, 9 (1877), 250–91 • A. Laurence, *Parliamentary army chaplains, 1642–1651*, Royal Historical Society Studies in History, 59 (1990), 127 • P. W. Jackson, 'Nonconformists and society in Devon, 1660–1689', PhD diss., Exeter University, 1986 • *Calamy rev.* • E. Calamy, *A continuation of the account of the ministers … who were ejected and silenced after the Restoration in 1660*, 2 vols.

(1727) • A. Brockett, *Nonconformity in Exeter, 1650–1875* (1962) • Wood, *Ath. Oxon.*, new edn, 3.1096 • Foster, *Alum. Oxon.* • *VCH Northamptonshire*, vol. 3 • R. S. Paul, *The assembly of the Lord: politics and religion in the Westminster assembly and the 'Grand debate'* (1985) • J. T. Cliffe, *Puritans in conflict* (1988) • J. Prince, *Danmonii orientales illustres, or, The worthies of Devon* (1701) • I. Gowers, 'The clergy in Devon, 1641–62', *Tudor and Stuart Devon … essays presented to Joyce Youings*, ed. T. Gray, M. Rowe, and A. Erskine (1992), 200–26 • J. Foster, *The register of admissions to Gray's Inn, 1521–1889, together with the register of marriages in Gray's Inn chapel, 1695–1754* (privately printed, London, 1889) • *ESTC* • Exeter chamber act book, 9 March 1651–30 June 1663, Devon RO, B1/10

Ford, William (*b.* **1559**, *d.* in or after **1616**?), Church of England clergyman, was born at Bury St Edmunds, perhaps a relative of the zealous protestant iconoclast of the same name who had been schoolmaster of Winchester College in the 1530s. He graduated BA from Trinity College, Cambridge, in 1578, and was ordained priest by Thomas Cooper, bishop of Lincoln, on 21 February that year. Elected a fellow of Trinity in 1581, he proceeded MA in 1582 and BTh in 1591. One William Ford, presented by Lord St John of Bletso to the rectory of Thurleigh, Bedfordshire, in 1594, was in 1604 stated to be doctor of divinity: this was surely the same man. On 24 September 1606 the bishop of Lincoln was informed that he was 'very conformable'; he had not preached against the canons, or 'the surplice, whood, with other ceremonyes and orders of the church' (Foster, cxvii). His—perhaps reluctant?—conformity may have been a factor in his decision to seek preferment abroad.

By 1611 Ford had become chaplain to the Levant Company, for on 31 July that year he petitioned the company court to augment his salary. On 11 October the court assented to an increase from about £30 to £50, acknowledging that he was 'well spoken of for paines and merits in his charge'. Ford's *Sermon Preached at Constantinople, in the Vines of Perah* on the occasion of the funeral of Anne, wife of Sir Thomas Glover, the English ambassador to the Porte, attracted an audience which included persons of French, Dutch, German, and Italian nationality, along with 'Papists, Hungarians, Russes, Greeks, Armenians, Bedoins, Turks and Jews'. What they made of Ford's lengthy exposition in English of Genesis 23: 2–4 (the death and burial of Abraham's wife, Sarah), is not recorded. The sermon was published in 1616 and dedicated to Lady Wentworth, a patron of the deceased Lady Glover. Ford meanwhile petitioned, on 1 September 1613, to be allowed to relinquish his post, but was asked to stay a year longer, receiving permission to leave only on 6 July 1614. After this date nothing certain is known of him, but it seems likely that he was still alive when his sermon was published, and he may have been the William Ford BD who became vicar of Bristow, Herefordshire, in 1615.

STEPHEN WRIGHT

Sources Venn, *Alum. Cant.*, 1/2.158 • J. B. Pearson, *A biographical sketch of the chaplains to the Levant Company, maintained at Constantinople, Aleppo and Smyrna, 1611–1706* (1883) • C. W. Foster, ed., *The state of the church in the reigns of Elizabeth and James I*, Lincoln RS, 23 (1926) • W. Ford, *A sermon preached at Constantinople, in the vines of Perah* (1616) • J. Strype, *Ecclesiastical memorials*, 3 vols. (1822)

Ford, William (1771–1832), bookseller and print dealer, was born in Manchester, the son of Ann and John Ford, a tin man, brazier, and brass-founder. He was baptized on 8 February 1772 in the Cannon Street Independent Chapel in Manchester, and educated at Manchester grammar school. It is said that he was destined for the medical profession but it would appear that he joined his parents and brother Thomas in their manufacturing business. He had a considerable collection of pictures and engravings which temporary financial hardship forced him to sell in 1802, but he continued to accumulate a large and valuable personal library, and in 1805 began printing a catalogue of it. It contained many rarities, the most notable being the unique copy of Shakespeare's *Venus and Adonis*, bound with Giles Fletcher's *Licia, or, Poems of Love* (1593). The *Venus and Adonis* was sold to Malone and is now in the Bodleian Library, Oxford. The *Licia* was bought by Richard Heber. The 1805 catalogue was followed by others in 1807, 1808, 1811, and 1814, all of which were characterized by their full bibliographical descriptions.

Ford's 1814 catalogue had included 'A small, but choice collection of Oriental Manuscripts', and by 1815 he was describing himself as an 'English and Foreign Bookseller', the range of his stock fully justifying his claim. In 1805 he was one of the founder members of the Portico Library in Manchester and was one of several suppliers of books and periodicals. His range of stock was expanded to include prints and engravings, and these were listed in his catalogues. Such was his reputation, which extended far beyond Manchester, that among his customers were Sir Walter Scott, Richard Heber, and Sir M. M. Sykes, and he also corresponded with Thomas Frognall Dibdin, who praised his catalogues for their complete and accurate bibliographical descriptions.

In 1816 Ford suffered a set-back in his business and a large part of his stock was sold at auction. In 1817 his household furniture was also put up for auction, together with pictures, drawings, and prints. By 1818 he was once again in business, and no fewer than three catalogues were issued, one of which included 'A … collection of manuscripts and printed books in the Persian, Arabick, Turkish and other oriental languages'. *Bibliographiana* (1817), a volume comprising articles which had originally appeared in Aston's *Manchester Exchange and Herald* in 1815 and 1816, was published in a small print run of twenty-four copies. Ford was one of its principal contributors, along with F. R. Atkinson and Nathan Hill. The series was later continued in the *Stockport Advertiser* and reprinted in only ten copies. Also 'Compiled expressly for the *Stockport Advertiser*' was a *Chronological Series of Events in Manchester* beginning in 1301 and ending in 1822. Ford was also an early contributor to the *Retrospective Review*. In 1822 he was selling books to the earl of Stamford at Dunham Massey and undertaking binding of books from that library. He also advised on the arrangement of this and other country-house libraries.

The evidence of Ford's print dealing is shown in a series of letters from John Britton in 1806 on the subject of his *Beauties of England and Wales*, in which Ford is offered a commission of 10 per cent of the list price of any prints purchased by Britton. An unpublished manuscript, 'Character of the different picture collectors in and about Manchester', is preserved in the Manchester Central Library and consists of short, not always complimentary, verses about the artists, who were originally identified only by their initials but have since been fully identified.

In 1820 Ford's eldest son, John, joined the business. Between then and 1825 four catalogues were issued, the 1825 being the last one from his Manchester premises, his business then being transferred to Liverpool, where he had for some time been selling both books and prints. Only two catalogues were issued from Liverpool, both in 1832, the later one being posthumous. William Ford died in Cheetwood, Manchester, on 3 October 1832 and was buried in St James's cemetery, Liverpool. An obituary notice appeared in the *Liverpool Mercury* on 9 November 1832.

BRENDA J. SCRAGG

Sources Chetham's Library, Manchester, Ford MS MUN.A.4.27 · letters, Chetham's Library, Manchester · book catalogues, Chetham's Library, Manchester · letters to William Ford, Man. CL, BRq 091F5 · commonplace book, Man. CL, BR 091F4 · Man. CL, Farrer collection, L1/49/16 · 'Character of the different picture collectors in and about Manchester', Man. CL, MS 827.79 F1 · register of shareholders, Portico Library, Manchester · invoice books, Portico Library, Manchester · Ford's book catalogues, JRL · Dunham Massey MSS, JRL · J. F. Smith, ed., *The admission register of the Manchester School, with some notes of the more distinguished scholars*, 2, Chetham Society, 73 (1868), 79–81 · *Palatine Note-Book*, 1 (1881) · *Palatine Note-Book*, 2 (1882) · *Palatine Note-Book*, 3 (1883) · *Pigot's Manchester and Salford directory* (1794) · A. Lister, 'William Ford (1771–1832) "the universal bookseller"', *Book Collector*, 38 (1989), 343–71 · R. W. Proctor, *Memorials of bygone Manchester with glimpses of the environs* (1880), 36–7, 341–2 · J. P. Earwaker, ed., *Local gleanings relating to Lancashire and Cheshire*, 2 vols. (1875–8) · *Local notes and queries from the 'Manchester Guardian'* (1874–7) · W. E. A. Axon, ed., *The annals of Manchester: a chronological record from the earliest times to the end of 1885* (1886) · T. F. Dibdin, *Reminiscences of a literary life*, 2 vols. (1836), 317 · C. H. Timperley, *Encyclopaedia of literary and typographical anecdote*, 2nd edn (1842), 927 · Ford letters, *Manchester Review* [Manchester public library magazine] (spring/summer 1967) · *Liverpool Mercury* (9 Nov 1832)

Archives Chetham's Library, Manchester, corresp. with book collectors · Man. CL, Manchester Archives and Local Studies, corresp. · NL Scot., album of letters to and printed items collected by Ford through his involvement in the Edinburgh book trade | JRL, Dunham Massey MSS, corresp. relating to earl of Stamford's library

Likenesses H. Wyatt, engraving, Chetham's Library, Manchester

Ford, William Justice (1853–1904), writer on cricket, was born in Paddington, Middlesex, on 7 November 1853, the eldest of seven sons of William Augustus Ford, a solicitor, and Katherine Mary Justice. Educated at the Eagle House, Wimbledon, and at Repton School, he entered St John's College, Cambridge, as a minor scholar in 1872. He won his cricket blue in 1873 and was awarded a major scholarship in 1874. He obtained a second in the classical tripos (1876) and graduated BA in 1876, proceeding MA in 1879. He was a master at Marlborough College from 1877 to 1886, principal of Nelson College, New Zealand, from 1886 to 1889, and headmaster of Leamington College in Warwickshire from 1890 to 1893. While in New Zealand he married Katherine Macey Browning in 1887; they had no children.

Ford's career predated the modern county cricket championship (1890). He played in the amateur milieu of his day, representing his school and university, with such excursions for Middlesex and the MCC as his teaching career would permit. Five of his brothers followed him to Repton and Cambridge, two of them also gaining cricket blues. He was probably not as good a player as his brother Francis Gilbertson Justice Ford (1866–1940), who played for England, though they were similar players, both being slow bowlers and big hitters. Although he once (1881) scored 250 for the MCC against Uxbridge and made a fifty in difficult conditions in his first innings in the varsity match, his principal feats on the field consisted of big hitting and fast scoring. A man of formidable physique (he stood 6 feet 3 inches tall and weighed 17 stone), he hit the ball out of many of the great cricket grounds of England. His largest measured hit was just under 144 yards. At Maidstone in August 1885 he scored 44 runs in 17 minutes against Kent in the first innings and 75 in 45 minutes in the second.

Ford retired at the early age of forty, to a life of sports writing and peripatetic examining. It is, perhaps, typical that when he retired he left Leamington College in financial difficulties but with a new gymnasium. He wrote regularly on public school cricket in Wisden's *Cricketer's Almanack*; his brother Lionel George Bridges Justice Ford (1865–1932) became headmaster of Harrow. He also contributed articles on cricket to the *Encyclopaedia of Sport* (1897–8), edited by the earl of Suffolk, and the *Encyclopaedia Britannica*. His *History of Cambridge University Cricket Club, 1829–1901* (1902) became a classic work. Apart from cricket, Ford wrote also on forms of billiards, and contributed to both William Broadfoot's book on the subject and to the volume in the Badminton Library series. Although not himself in the front rank of cricketers, Ford made a significant contribution to British life through his part in the development of a written culture of sport in the late nineteenth century. He died of pneumonia at his home, 36 Abingdon Mansions, Warwick Street, Kensington, London, on 3 April 1904, and was buried at Kensal Green cemetery.   LINCOLN ALLISON

Sources *DNB* · B. Green, ed., *The Wisden book of obituaries* (1986) · Venn, *Alum. Cant.* · *Cambridge Review* (28 April 1904), 258 · *WWW*
Archives Warks. CRO, Leamington College archive
Wealth at death £681 0s. 1d.: administration, 18 May 1904, *CGPLA Eng. & Wales*

Forde, (Cyril) Daryll (1902–1973), anthropologist, was born on 16 March 1902 at 38 Manchester Road, Tottenham, Middlesex, the son of the Revd John Percival Daniel Forde, schoolmaster, and his wife, Caroline Pearce Pittman. He went to Middlesex county school at Tottenham and then to the geography department of University College, London, from where he graduated in 1922. There in 1923 he was appointed a lecturer in geography, and in 1928 was awarded a PhD in prehistoric archaeology. At this period both geography and anatomy at University College had research interests in ethnography and archaeology, and

Forde found himself welcome in both disciplines. He was also in the student set associated with the Bloomsbury group. Though he was intellectually closer to the archaeologist Gordon Childe, it was through Sir Grafton Elliot Smith in anatomy that Forde met both the psychologist W. H. R. Rivers (for whose posthumously published books Forde drew the maps) and the distinguished Californian anthropologist R. H. Lowie. Forde spent 1928–30 as Commonwealth fellow in anthropology with Lowie at Berkeley, working on American Indian economies. The twenty-eight-year-old Forde was recognized as *the* up-and-coming geographer, and at a time when air travel was still unusual, he was flown over from California to be offered the chair of geography and anthropology at the University of Aberystwyth.

Forde's academic career falls into four periods. The first, from 1923 to 1934, culminated in the publication of his major general text, *Habitat, Economy and Society* (1934). He was already recognized as an innovative archaeologist with his study on Welsh megaliths; at Aberystwyth he pioneered 'anthropology at home' by initiating ethnographic studies of Welsh villages and towns. But his reading had shown him how little was really known about African economies. With the recently established International Institute for African Languages and Culture sending out researchers like Meyer Fortes to an acephalous community in northern Gold Coast, and S. F. Nadel to a complex state in northern Nigeria, in 1935 Forde opted instead for something in between—a 'village' of 10,000 Yakö in south-eastern Nigeria, whose kinship system ('double unilineal descent') was particularly interesting for lineage theorists. Forde's second period (1935–43) was interrupted by the Second World War. His curtailed fieldwork on Yakö marriage was none the less published in 1941. In the same year he was posted to the Foreign Office research department (then in Oxford), heading the section on the USA. He returned to Aberystwyth in 1943.

The third period, from 1944 to 1956, saw Forde appointed in 1944 to the post of part-time director of the renamed International African Institute in London; in 1945 was added the chair of the newly established department of anthropology at University College, London. He held both posts until 1969. As director he had to rebuild an institute crippled by war. The need for an up-to-date understanding of the societies of post-war Africa was obvious, especially with the new emphasis on economic development and calls for self-government. In 1946 Forde wrote, with R. Scott, *The Native Economies of Nigeria*. He devised an extended practical programme of research and publication (in English and French), and negotiated funding from government and from UNESCO. In nearly sixty volumes, the *Ethnographic Survey* under Forde's direction systematized existing ethnographic data, region by region; a similar, smaller series, Handbooks of African Languages, was produced; ethnographic monographs were published; *African Abstracts* regularly summarized the periodical literature; and the institute's quarterly journal, *Africa*, which Forde edited, again became the leading journal in the field. Of the symposia from this period,

African Systems of Kinship and Marriage (1950) and *African Worlds* (1954) remain outstanding.

In his fourth period (1957–69) Forde analysed Yakö ritual and belief, publishing *Yakö Studies* (1964). More importantly, he raised funds from the Ford Foundation for a series of international seminars, bringing together in different African countries scholars from America, Europe, and Africa. With new universities established in Africa and with independence near, these nine seminars (and the resulting volumes) were path-breaking, assembling the latest ideas and research in key subjects. Only Daryll Forde, with his network of contacts, his administrative skills and geniality, his intellectual energy and openness, could ensure success.

The department of anthropology that Forde started in 1945 reflected his broad vision. Based on the American model, it was the only department in Britain to combine archaeology and material culture with both social and biological anthropology. Forde's vision and intellectual generosity attracted, by the 1950s, some of the best postgraduates of the day; posts in his department were the starting-point for a talented new breed of anthropologists (including west Africans); new directions, for example in African history or medical anthropology, were warmly encouraged. Forde created not so much a school of anthropology as a style; and he developed the field of African anthropology less by his own writings than by his dissemination of new knowledge—through international seminars, monographs, bibliographic aids, and the journal he edited, *Africa*. A crucial element in the expansion of African studies which he stimulated was breadth: the Forde style of anthropology included archaeology, genetics, technology, history, ecology, demography, and linguistics, as well as social anthropology. He fostered intellectual exchange and, over a period of twenty-five years, gave support, intellectually or financially, to an extraordinary number of scholars in Britain, Europe, and Africa.

Forde was twice married. In 1930 he married Joyce Marion Stock, and they had two sons. This marriage was dissolved in 1947, and in the following year he married Evelyn Harty Singer, a medical practitioner. After a brief semi-retirement, Forde died at his home, 8 The Boltons, Kensington, London, on 3 May 1973.   MURRAY LAST

Sources M. Fortes, 'Cyril Daryll Forde, 1902–1973', *PBA*, 62 (1976), 459–81 · N. A. Barnicot, 'Daryll Forde, 1902–1973', *Africa*, 43 (1973), 283–7 · M. G. Smith, 'Foreword', *Man in Africa*, ed. M. Douglas and P. Kabeny (1969) · I. M. Lewis, 'Professor Daryll Forde, FBA', *Proceedings of the Royal Anthropological Institute* (1973), 56–8 · private information (2004) · b. cert. · *CGPLA Eng. & Wales* (1973) · WWW
Archives Bodl. RH, corresp. and papers | CUL, corresp. with Meyer Fortes
Likenesses photograph, repro. in Fortes, 'Cyril Daryll Forde'
Wealth at death £73,355: probate, 13 Aug 1973, *CGPLA Eng. & Wales*

Forde, Florrie [*real name* Flora May Augustus Flanagan; *married name* Flora May Augustus Barnett] (**1876–1940**), music-hall entertainer, was born in Fitzroy, Melbourne, Australia, on 14 August 1876, the daughter of Francis Lott Flanagan, monumental mason, and his wife, Phoebe. She first appeared on stage at a concert at Sydney Polytechnic

Florrie Forde (1876–1940), by Elliott & Green

in 1893, singing 'He kissed me when he left me and told me to be brave'. The following year she joined Dan Tracy's Variety Company, appearing as William in *Black-Eyed Susan* and Pat in *The Work Girl*. In 1895 she appeared in pantomime at the Theatre Royal, Sydney, and was at once invited to return the following year. She was to make a long career as principal boy in pantomime; these early appearances attracted the attention of actor and manager C. B. Westmacott, who billed her in his touring company as the Australian Marie Lloyd. Her first British appearance was on the 1897 August bank holiday, when she appeared (as was typical of music-hall artistes at that time) at the London Pavilion, the Oxford, and the South London Palace on the same night.

Like many successful principal boys, Forde was well built, her size a stock joke on the halls: fellow comedian Harry Weldon used to follow her act by stepping gingerly onto the stage and then announcing 'If it'll stand Florrie Forde, it'll stand me'. Rather than exploiting a comedy of self-deprecation, however, Forde used her size to convey both glamour and authority. Her costumes glittered with sequins and embroidery, and she made herself even wider and taller with ostrich plumes, capes and trains, and high-heeled shoes. She used the freedom of wearing tights rather than skirts to march about the stage vigorously, and a characteristic prop was a jewelled cane with which she would conduct the audience in the choruses of her songs; her style was that of a benevolent sergeant-major addressing raw recruits. Signed photographs of Forde show a signature full of confident and energetic flourishes.

While memories of Forde herself faded, she lodged her songs firmly in popular memory. 'Oh, oh, Antonio', 'Down at the Old Bull and Bush', and 'She's a Lassie from Lancashire', which featured in the royal command performance of 1912, became staples of any music-hall revival. She reached the height of her fame during the First World War: 'It's a long way to Tipperary' was not written for her, but Forde transformed the song of a homesick Irishman into one of the most poignant anthems for British troops. 'Goodbye-ee', 'Pack up your troubles', and 'Take me back to dear old Blighty' symbolized the bouncy confidence with which the nation covered its anxieties about the realities of trench warfare.

Forde was one of the few women to launch her own touring revue company, Flo and Co. (which included Chesney Allen), and for thirty-six summers she performed on the Isle of Man, entertaining tourists with 'Has anyone here seen Kelly?' and 'They're All Single by the Seaside'. Her *Times* obituarist remarked that her bank-holiday début back in 1897 had been prophetic: 'If ever there was an artist who seemed to personify the spirit of a holiday crowd, it was she' (*The Times*, 19 April 1940). Her energy never seemed to flag, and she appeared in the 1935 royal variety show. However, the critic James Agate wrote wistfully that her performance as principal boy in *Ali Baba* at the London Lyceum that same year (she was nearly sixty) was perhaps a mistake: she could no longer sustain the illusion of youth, her voice was weakening, and her weight was no longer a sign of her abounding energy. Her celebrated efficiency in marshalling her audience, however, was longer lived, and the affection with which she was regarded by fellow professionals (she was widely known as Aunt Flo) ensured that she was able to take a full part in entertainment activities as the Second World War broke out. Indeed, she seemed to acquire a new following among the younger generation who had missed her prime. She died suddenly on 18 April 1940 at 21 Albyn Place, Aberdeen, where she had gone to entertain wounded soldiers in a military hospital. Her husband, Laurence Barnett (*b.* 1875/6), a fine art and antique dealer, had died in 1934. Her likeness appears on the sign of the Bull and Bush, Hampstead, which also boasts a Florrie Forde bar. Louis MacNeice wrote an epitaph for Florrie Forde, 'Death of an Actress' (*85 Poems*, 1959), in which he celebrated her style: ageing, sometimes vulgar, sometimes sentimental, but expressive of a kind of innocence lost to newer forms of popular entertainment:

> she stood
> For an older England, for children toddling
> Hand in hand while the day was bright. Let the wren and
> robin
> Gently with leaves cover the Babes in the Wood.

FRANCES GRAY

Sources R. Busby, *British music hall: an illustrated who's who from 1850 to the present day* (1976) · B. Green, ed., *The last empires: a music hall companion* (1986) · *New York Herald Tribune* (19 April 1940) · *The Era* (20 March 1909) · L. Senelick, D. Cheshire, and U. Schneider, *British music-hall, 1840–1923: a bibliography and guide to sources, with a supplement on European music-hall* (1981) · *The Times* (19 April 1940) · d. cert. · d. cert. [Laurence Barnett]

Archives FILM BFI NFTVA, documentary footage · BFI NFTVA, performance footage |SOUND BL NSA, 'Mistress of the music hall', BBC Radio 4, 10 Sept 1995, H5668/2 · BL NSA, documentary recording · BL NSA, performance recording
Likenesses Elliott & Green, photograph, priv. coll. [*see illus.*]

Forde, Francis (*c.*1718–1770?), army officer in the East India Company, was the son of Matthew Forde (*c.*1675–1729), politician, of Seaforde, co. Down, and his wife, Anne, daughter of William Brownlow of Lurgan. He attended Trinity College, Dublin, and received a BA degree in 1738. On 12 August 1747 he married Margaret, *née* Bowerbank (*d. c.*1779), at St Mary's, Portsea, Hampshire. In April of the previous year Forde was appointed a captain in the 39th foot and in September 1754 the regiment arrived in Madras, the first King's regiment to be sent to India. In November 1755 he was promoted to the rank of major, and in 1757 commanded the expedition which unsuccessfully attacked Nellore. In that same year the 39th foot was recalled to England, but Forde was invited to take charge of the East India Company's army in Bengal following the death of James Killpatrick. The prime mover in this invitation appears to have been Robert Clive, who had a few months previously defeated the nawab of Bengal, Siraj ud-Daula, at Plassey. Clive had met Forde in the Carnatic in 1756 and his high opinion of his military abilities was shared by others. Following his arrival in Bengal, Forde rejected the invitation and only accepted it after compensation of £5000 for loss of the commission and rank he held in the king's service had been agreed to. Forde's secretary was a fellow Irishman and friend from the 39th foot, John Carnac.

In October 1758 an expedition which included a large proportion of the European troops in Bengal sailed from Calcutta under Forde's command with the intention of striking at the French presence in the Northern Circars, an eastern coastal district between the Carnatic and Bengal. Clive, now governor of Bengal, perceived that the expedition, if successful, could prevent support from the Deccan reaching the French forces in the Carnatic, thereby helping to safeguard Madras. On 7 December 1758 Forde was successful against the marquis de Conflans at Condore but was subsequently hampered by a lack of the support that had been promised by a raja who had rebelled against the French. By early March 1759 Conflans and his now enlarged force were entrenched in the fort at Masulipatam, which was besieged by Forde. The latter's position was weak; his army was outnumbered, short of supplies, and virtually surrounded. The European troops mutinied, but Forde was able to persuade them to return to their posts. In the face of this adversity he devised a strategy to attack the fort, which on 7 and 8 April succeeded. The Northern Circars were now no longer in French control, and Forde's expedition had contributed to the failure of the siege of Madras which had been raised in February. Clive described Forde's achievement to a friend as 'one of those extraordinary actions which we seldom hear of in these modern times, and must gain him great honour when it comes to be known at home' (J. Malcolm, *The Life of Robert, Lord Clive*, 3 vols., 1836, 2.23).

Forde's successes against the French were repeated against the Dutch. In November 1759 a force dispatched by the latter landed near Calcutta. According to Clive's biographer Sir John Malcolm, Forde sent Clive a note asking for permission to attack. Clive, who received the request while playing cards, is said to have scribbled a reply—'Dear Forde, fight them immediately'—and dispatched the instruction (J. Malcolm, *The Life of Robert, Lord Clive*, 3 vols., 1836, 2.96–7). Forde successfully attacked the Dutch garrison at Chinsura, and then in a brief but bloody encounter won a victory over the remaining forces at Badara. Despite these successes, he saw no more service in Bengal. The directors of the East India Company disapproved of his appointment and dismissed him from their employment, appointing in his place, to Clive's dismay, Eyre Coote.

In 1760 Forde returned to England, where he was reunited with his wife and his children. Disgusted with the treatment he had received from the directors, he settled in Ireland at Johnstown, co. Meath. In 1769 he was one of three individuals appointed to a supervisory commission which was designed to improve the administration of the company's affairs in India. Together with another of Clive's supporters, Luke Scrafton, and the third supervisor, Henry Vansittart, he sailed in September that year on board the *Aurora*, but they were not heard from again following their departure from the Cape of Good Hope on 27 December. The ship seems to have been lost in heavy seas after a decision to navigate the Mozambique Channel in bad weather. H. M. STEPHENS, *rev.* D. L. PRIOR

Sources V. C. P. Hodson, *List of officers of the Bengal army, 1758–1834*, 4 vols. (1927–47) · L. Forde, *Lord Clive's right-hand man: a memoir of Col. Francis Forde* (1910) · K. K. Datta and others, eds., *Fort William–India House correspondence*, 2 (1957) · M. Bence-Jones, *Clive of India* (1974) · P. Mason, *A matter of honour: an account of the Indian army, its officers and men* (1974) · Burke, *Gen. GB* · Burtchaell & Sadleir, *Alum. Dubl.* · D. L. Prior, 'The career of Robert, first Baron Clive, with special reference to his political and administrative career', MPhil diss., U. Wales, 1993 · correspondence with John Carnac, BL OIOC, F 128/32 · BL OIOC, MS Eur. Orme

Archives BL OIOC, corresp., MSS Eur. Orme | BL OIOC, Clive MSS · BL OIOC, Sutton Court collection · JRL, letters to Samuel Bagshawe

Forde [Ford], **John of** (*c*.1150–1214), abbot of Forde and religious writer, was probably born in the west of England. His parents are unknown, and the course of his early life can only be deduced from his writings. These show a competent Latinist well read in the church fathers and in Cistercian authors, but suspicious of the approaches to these authorities currently being made in the schools. This suggests that most of his intellectual formation occurred at Forde (then in Devon, now in Dorset). He entered that monastery *c*.1170, when Baldwin (*d*. 1190), later archbishop of Canterbury, and abbot of Forde from *c*.1173 to 1180, and his former pupils made it a centre of learning. John became prior at Forde, and then between *c*.1187 and 1191 was abbot of Forde's first daughter house, Bindon, Dorset. He returned thence to serve as abbot at the mother house where he died on 21 April 1214. Forde Abbey flourished under his rule, establishing another daughter house

at nearby Dunkeswell in 1201, founded by that formidable Devonian servant of the Angevins, William Brewer (*d*. 1226).

John of Forde's legal knowledge and conciliatory skills resulted in service as a papal judge-delegate and delegate for the archbishop of Canterbury, and often, too, for the Cistercian general chapter. He caught the attention of Archbishop Hubert Walter by 1195–7, and through him became confessor and alms-giver to King John from 1204 to 1207. The king's interest in Forde Abbey went back to 1195, but in 1210 the abbot could not persuade him to reduce the fine of 750 marks he levied on it, after the Cistercian order had refused to grant him an aid. This episode emerges from sermons 41 and 76 (among 120) which John wrote upon the Song of Songs, completing the commentary begun by Bernard of Clairvaux and continued after his death by another English Cistercian, Gilbert of Holland. John's literary reputation had been made earlier by his life of a local anchorite, Wulfric of Haselbury (*d*. 1154). Four manuscripts, all contemporary with their author, exist, and the life was later used by Roger of Wendover and Matthew Paris. It is notable for its lively portraits of Wulfric and those who knew him. An isolated sermon for Palm Sunday also survives, and there are some indications that John wrote other works no longer extant.

There is only one, early thirteenth-century, manuscript surviving of John of Forde's commentary, although at least two other copies existed at the dissolution. It had few readers in the middle ages or later, until it was edited in 1970, and subsequently translated. Its completion during the interdict may have limited its circulation, but its type of leisurely rumination upon the spiritual meaning of the Song of Songs—reading the bride as the church, or the individual soul, occasionally as the Virgin Mary, or the Jews—may have seemed old-fashioned. John's concern for the welfare of his monks is evident, as is his anguish at his frequent absences from them. He is a rare critic from within of the effects of prosperity on the life of a monastery, but also shows that spiritual enthusiasm and discernment were still alive among English Cistercians in the early thirteenth century.

CHRISTOPHER HOLDSWORTH

Sources H. Costello and C. Holdsworth, eds., *A gathering of friends: the learning and spirituality of John of Forde* (1996) · John of Ford, *Sermons on the final verses of the Song of Songs*, trans. W. M. Beckett, 1 (Kalamazoo, MI, 1977) · *Wulfric of Haselbury, by John, abbot of Ford*, ed. M. Bell, Somerset RS, 47 (1933) · *Ioannis de Forda Super extremam partem Cantici canticorum sermones CXX*, ed. E. Mikkers and H. Costello, 2 vols. (Turnhout, 1970) · D. Knowles, C. N. L. Brooke, and V. C. M. London, eds., *The heads of religious houses, England and Wales*, 1: *940–1216* (1972) · C. R. Cheney and E. John, eds., *Canterbury, 1193–1205*, English Episcopal Acta, 3 (1986) · *Balduini de Forda opera*, ed. D. N. Bell (Tournai, 1991) · C. R. Cheney, *Hubert Walter* (1967) · *Ann. mon.*, 2.281

Forde [Ford], **Roger of** (*fl. c*.1182), Cistercian monk and religious writer, was a member of his order's house at Forde in Devon. It is not known when he entered that house, but the seventeenth-century writer Angelo Manrique, following Leland and Pits, names him as a pupil of Baldwin (*d*. 1190), abbot of Forde from *c*.1173 to 1180, and afterwards archbishop of Canterbury, and like Pits gives him a floruit of *c*.1182. Roger's reputation was not monastic but scholastic, and it seems that he left Forde to pursue his studies *ad Belgas* (perhaps in the Rhineland) at an unspecified date: it is unlikely, and certainly unrecorded, that he ever returned to England.

Roger of Forde is known for having collected in two books the Revelations of Elisabeth of Schönau, along with a sermon on the 11,000 virgin martyrs of Cologne and an encomium of the Virgin. These writings survive in two Oxford manuscripts (Bodl. Oxf., MS Bodley 83; St John's College, Oxford, MS 149, nos. 8 and 9). Elisabeth, who died in 1165 at the age of thirty-six, was the ecstatic contemporary of Abbess Hildegard von Bingen, and was herself abbess of the women's house of Schönau (Trier), in partnership with her brother Egbert, who was abbot of the male house. Roger's account of her was dedicated to 'his abbot' Baldwin, and produced with great help from Guillaume de Toulouse, abbot of Savigny in the early 1160s, who was himself renowned for his learning. How Roger was able to abandon his monastic vocation, what his connection was with Guillaume de Toulouse, and whether he went to Schönau are all unknown. As Manrique noted, Roger is apt to be confused with his English contemporary, Roger, the learned and saintly first abbot of Cistercian Élant, in the diocese of Rheims, who also wrote on the virgins of Cologne.　　　　　　　　　　　　　DEREK BAKER

Sources A. Manrique, *Cisterciensium, seu, Verius ecclesiasticorum annalium a condito Cistercio*, 4 vols. (Lyons, 1642–59), vol. 3, pp. 121–2 · *Acta sanctorum: Januarius*, 1 · D. de Sainte-Marthe and others, eds., *Gallia Christiana in provincias ecclesiasticas distributa*, 16 vols. (1715–1865) · D. Knowles, *The monastic order in England*, 2nd edn (1963) · J. Leclercq, F. Vandenbroucke, and L. Bouyer, *La spiritualité du moyen âge* (1961) · C. J. Holdsworth, 'Christina of Markyate', *Medieval women*, ed. D. Baker, SCH, Subsidia, 1 (1978), 185–204 · G. Constable, 'Aelred of Rievaulx and the Nun of Watton: an episode in the early history of the Gilbertine order', *Medieval women*, ed. D. Baker, SCH, Subsidia, 1 (1978), 205–26 · D. Baker, 'Heresy and learning in early Cistercianism', *Schism, heresy and religious protest*, ed. D. Baker, 9 (1972)

Archives Bodl. Oxf., MS Bodley 83 · St John's College, Oxford, MS 149

Forde, Samuel (1805–1828), painter, was born in Cork on 5 April 1805, the second son of Samuel Forde, a tradesman, who, owing to business failures and general discontent, went to America, abandoning his family. Samuel's elder brother, William, was a talented musician, earning enough to send young Samuel to school, where he learned Latin and French. A friend, Mr Aungier, gave him lessons in Italian free of charge, while he studied Greek from books. Forde very soon displayed a talent for art, and his taste for literature and painting nourished the high aspirations which were manifest even in his very early sketches. He copied, from prints, Charles Le Brun's 'passions' (his system for painting the passions and the engravings he produced to illustrate his lectures of 1668 at the Académie Royale) and Sir Charles Bell's *The Anatomy of Expression as Connected with the Fine Arts* (1806), and transcribed sections from the *Discourses* of Sir Joshua Reynolds (1797). A rather solitary character, Forde avoided crowds

and was known to steal away on occasion to a chapel in Carey's Lane, which housed a fine copy of Guido Reni's *Crucifixion*. He became a student in the Cork Society school of art and drew from the collection of casts of antique sculpture in the Vatican which Lord Listowel had obtained for Cork from the prince regent in 1818. Chalmers, the master at the Cork school, was a scene painter, and taught Forde to work in distemper, which enabled him to find employment in theatres, houses, and shops. Among his fellow students and friends were the painter Daniel Maclise and the sculptor John Hogan. Both family responsibilities and the influence of friends prompted him to become a mezzotint engraver, and he taught himself the art without any professionally made materials or implements. He soon relinquished any further practice, however, and became a teacher of architectural drawing, and subsequently master, in the Cork Mechanics' Institute. Up to about twenty years of age, Forde was principally engaged on decorative works painted in distemper, including the ceiling of the Cork theatre, and pen-and-ink drawings for works which were never executed. However, in 1826 he undertook the first commissions of his own invention, and was at last presented with the opportunity to realize some of the grand projects which had occupied his mind. The first of these was the *Vision of Tragedy* (*c*.1825; Victoria and Albert Museum, London, watercolour study), an idea taken from Milton, which was a large work, also painted in distemper, in grisaille. Forde continued to conceive and plan ambitious projects, including designs for monuments and paintings of biblical, historical, and literary subjects. Of his drawings for a monument for the architect James Pain, Sir David Wilkie remarked, allegedly, that 'he would have thought they were made by some of the old Masters' (Strickland, 1.373–4). His portraiture was of unpredictable quality, but otherwise his work was greatly admired by patrons, critics, and artists alike. In October 1827 Forde was first affected by the lung complaint which later claimed his life, but nevertheless in November managed to complete a triptych altarpiece, *The Crucifixion*, for the Catholic church in Skibbereen, co. Cork. Early in 1828 he began a large picture, *Fall of the Rebel Angels* (Crawford Municipal Art Gallery, Cork), having been guaranteed a weekly stipend of 30*s*. by the architect Sir Thomas Deane, but although he found a buyer for the picture, he was destined never to complete it. His physical condition deteriorated rapidly and he was confined to bed. He died, unmarried, in Cork on 29 July 1828, aged twenty-three, and was buried at St Fin Barre's Cathedral in Cork.　　　　　L. H. CUST, *rev.* BRENDAN ROONEY

Sources 'Memoir of Samuel Forde—a Cork artist', *Dublin University Magazine*, 25 (1845), 338–57 · P. Murray, *Illustrated summary catalogue of the Crawford Municipal Art Gallery* (Cork, 1991), 198–207 · W. G. Strickland, *A dictionary of Irish artists*, 1 (1913), 372–5 · T. C. Croker, 'Recollections of Cork, *c*.1833', TCD, MS 1206 · H. Mangan, 'Samuel Forde: an Irish artist admired by Davis', *Irish Book Lover*, 29 (1943–5), 137–8 · A. Crookshank and the Knight of Glin [D. Fitzgerald], *The watercolours of Ireland: works on paper in pencil, pastel and paint, c.1600–1914* (1994), 102–6 · 'Gleanings on old Cork artists [pt 1]', *Journal of the Cork Historical and Archaeological Society*, 2nd ser., 6 (1900), 104–11, esp. 109–11

Archives TCD, T. C. Croker, 'Recollections of Cork, c.1833', MS 1206
Likenesses S. Forde, self-portrait, oils, Crawford Municipal Art Gallery, Cork, Ireland

Forde, Thomas (d. 1582), Roman Catholic priest and martyr, was born in Devon and educated at Trinity College, Oxford, where he graduated BA on 13 May 1563 and was elected to a fellowship a year later; he was admitted MA on 21 April 1567. Forde showed early Catholic tendencies during a college debate, where he objected to mockery of the pope: 'I cannot submit to such insulting language towards so good and holy a father,' he exclaimed, and 'commenced to argue' (Pollen, 251). After becoming a Roman Catholic he helped Cuthbert Mayne to flee the country and later left Oxford himself. He made his way to Douai, where he was received at the English College in 1570. One of the first graduates of the college to be presented for holy orders, he was made a priest together with Richard Bristow and Gregory Martin at Brussels on 23 March 1573. Forde graduated BD at Douai University on 14 November 1573, and was sent to England on 2 May 1576, using the aliases of Harwood and Saltwell in order to work in the mission in Oxfordshire and Berkshire.

Staying at Lyford, Berkshire, together with John Colleton, Forde was betrayed by George Eliot during Edmund Campion's stay there and was captured on 17 July 1581. 'On that occasion he wanted to give himself up to save Campion, but the latter altogether refused' (Pollen, 251). He shared Campion's ignominious journey to London where he was ordered to be tortured on 30 July, 14 August, and 29 October. He was accused of having been involved in the conspiracy of Rheims and Rome, although he had never been in either city. He was condemned to death together with Campion on 21 November 1581 and was hanged, drawn, and quartered at Tyburn with two other priests, John Shert and Robert Johnson, on 28 May 1582. He is described as having been 'above the average height' (ibid.) and wearing a red beard.

Forde was beatified in 1886 by Pope Leo XIII.

J. ANDREAS LÖWE

Sources [J. Gibbons and J. Fenn], *Concertatio ecclesiae catholicae in Anglia adversus Calvinopapistas et puritanos* (1583), 85b, 86b · Foster, *Alum. Oxon.* · T. F. Knox and others, eds., *The first and second diaries of the English College, Douay* (1878), 3–6, 25, 104, 181, 188, 272 · R. Challoner, *Memoirs of missionary priests*, ed. J. H. Pollen, rev. edn (1924), 45–7 · W. Allen, *A briefe historie of the glorious martyrdom of XII reverend priests, executed within these twelve monethes for confession and defence of the Catholicke faith* (1582); repr., ed. J. H. Pollen (1908), 10, 57–64, 109 · J. H. Pollen, ed., *Acts of English martyrs* (1891), 251 · E. Simpson, *Life of Campion*, 22off. · beatification records, Jesuit archive, London · PRO, KB 9/656, II, 41 · *CSP dom.*, 1579–80, 329
Likenesses portrait, 17th cent. (*Convent in Bruges*), Archives of the British Province of the Society of Jesus, London; repro. in beatification records

Forde, Thomas (fl. 1647–1661), writer and playwright, described himself as being from the neighbourhood of Maldon, Essex, and of the same kindred as John Udall, the puritan (Forde, 'Faenestra', *Virtus rediviva*, 135). He was an educated man whose works reveal him as pious and serious-minded with a good knowledge of the classics. He was also a loyal royalist.

An early work of Forde's was *The Times Anatomized in Several Characters*, published in London in 1647, when, according to a note in the British Library copy, he was 'servant to Mr. Sam. Man'. The work revealed his concerns about the troubles of the times with essays on such topics as 'A good subject', 'A soldier of fortune', and 'Religion'. Two years later his *Lusus fortunae, The Play of Fortune, Continually Acted by the Severall Creatures on the Stage of the World* was published. It is a collection of moral essays, illustrated by quotations from classical and near contemporary writers, such as Edmund Spenser, Abraham Cowley, John Donne, Francis Bacon, and Thomas Fuller.

Forde's major work, *Virtus rediviva*, was published after the restoration of the monarchy. The work is in five sections, each with its own title-page dated 1660 and its own pagination. The collective title-page is dated 1661.

Section 1, *Virtus rediviva, or, A Panegyrick on the Late King Charles I*, consisted of a prose tract and two elegies in verse, written on the anniversaries of Charles I's execution in 1657 and 1658 respectively. Section 2, 'Love's Labyrinth, or, The Royal Shepherdess', a tragi-comedy in blank verse, presents the affairs of Domocles, king of Arcadia, Agenor, king of Thessaly, his daughter, Euriphyla, and Maximus, prince of Cyprus, who married Sephestia. The play has borrowings from Robert Greene's *Menaphon* and Robert Gomersall's *The Tragedie of Ludovick Sforza, Duke of Milan*. The title-page has 'Philothal' after Forde's name, an abbreviation for 'Philothalassios', indicating that he liked to be thought of as a lover of the sea. Section 3, 'A theatre of wits ancient and modern', provides a collection of pithy maxims and basic truths. Section 4, 'Faenestra in pectore', gives a selection of letters from Forde's correspondence with his father, a friend in Barbados, E.B., and others. One letter (p. 135) is addressed to Thomas Fuller and praises his *Church History*. Another (p. 166) includes a translation of Martial's 'Non amo te Sabidi' as 'I do not like thee, Nell', a forerunner of the more widely known 'I do not like thee, Dr Fell'.

Section 5, 'Fragmenta poetica, or, Poetical diversions with a panegyrick upon his sacred majestie's most happy return on the 29 May 1660', provides a collection of poems, with that to the king ending:

While others their rich Presents bring,
All I can give's God save the King.

The collection includes sacred poems as well as verses to George Herbert and Thomas Bastard.

SIDNEY LEE, rev. F. D. A. BURNS

Sources J. E. Bailey, *The life of Thomas Fuller, D.D.* (1874) · T. Forde, *Virtus rediviva* (1661) · T. Forde, *The times anatomized in several characters* (1647) · T. Forde, *Lusus fortunae* (1649)

Forder, Henry George (1889–1981), mathematician, was born on 27 September 1889 at Shotesham All Saints, Norfolk, the eldest of the four sons and two daughters of Henry Forder and his wife, Mary Ann, *née* Chilvers. Both his parents had been born in the same village, where his paternal grandfather was the blacksmith. Henry Forder senior left school at eleven and was trained as a craftsman, as joiner, blacksmith, farrier, and wheelwright; by 1900 he was working at Worstead, where he had bought the blacksmith shop, and neighbouring villages. At Worstead village school the schoolmaster noticed the young Forder's gifts, and gave him special tuition; when, in 1902, county scholarships were introduced, Forder was among the first to benefit, attending Paston School, a grammar school founded in 1604, in North Walsham. There he became a leading figure, according to his youngest brother, the Ven. Archdeacon Charles R. Forder, who wrote the history of Paston School. In 1907 Forder founded, with another boy, the school debating society. In the same year he went up to Sidney Sussex College, Cambridge, as a sizar, with a Norfolk county council scholarship of £65 per annum, another £20 per annum from the governors of Paston School, and, after he had passed the Cambridge 'Little-go', a further £27 per annum from the college. In 1908 he was awarded a college scholarship after gaining a first class in part one of the mathematical tripos; in 1910 he was one of the twenty-three wranglers in the tripos part two.

Forder then embarked on a career as mathematics master, at Hulme grammar school in Oldham, Lancashire, until 1913, then at Cardiff high school, St Olave's School in London, and finally at Hymer's College in Hull, Yorkshire. He was, by all accounts, a successful and highly regarded teacher. His brother Charles wrote: 'When I was vicar in Hull, 1947–57, I met many of his former pupils from Hymer's College, and all remembered him with affection' (private information). In 1921, during his time in Hull, he married his cousin Dorothy Whincup (d. 1970) of Bingham, Nottinghamshire; they had no children.

In 1933 Forder was invited to apply for the professorship of mathematics at the University College of Auckland (later the University of Auckland), one of the six constituent colleges of the University of New Zealand; he took up the appointment in 1934, and remained in Auckland for the rest of his life. His main works were several books on geometry: *The Foundations of Euclidean Geometry* (1927), *A School Geometry* (1930), *Higher Course Geometry* (1931), *The Calculus of Extension* (1941), *Geometry* (1950), and *Co-ordinates in Geometry* (1953). Most of these were reprinted, several went to a second edition, and some were translated into Romanian and Turkish. Most of his original research was published in thirty-six fairly short notes in the *Mathematical Gazette*, though he also published in a number of other journals. Forder was an inspiring teacher for gifted students. In Auckland he was greatly appreciated as a man of learning, as well as a brilliant conversationalist and wit. He was elected a fellow of the Royal Society of New Zealand in 1947 and awarded its Hector medal in 1946. The University of Auckland conferred on him the honorary degree of DSc in 1959, and a Festschrift for his eightieth birthday. *A Spectrum of Mathematics* (published by the Auckland University Press) and special issues of New Zealand mathematical journals marked his eightieth and his ninetieth birthdays. When the New Zealand Mathematical Society, founded in 1974, held its first annual general meeting, Forder was elected an honorary member. He

died at his home, Lichfield, Selwyn Village, Port Chevalier, Auckland, on 21 September 1981.

Forder donated his extensive mathematical library to the University of Auckland, and a substantial sum of money to the London Mathematical Society, of which he was a member for sixty years; this now supports an H. G. Forder lectureship that biennially sends a prominent British mathematician on a lecture tour of New Zealand.

B. H. NEUMANN

Sources J. C. Butcher, *Bulletin of the London Mathematical Society*, 17 (1985), 162–7 · *WWW*, 1981–90 · private information (2004) · *Newsletter of the New Zealand Mathematical Society* [various issues] · C. Forder, *A history of the Paston School*, 2nd edn (1975) · personal knowledge (2004)
Archives University of Auckland, MSS
Likenesses P. Brown, drawing, repro. in *Newsletter of the New Zealand Mathematical Society*, 19 (1980), centrefold · photograph, repro. in Butcher, *Bulletin of the London Mathematical Society*, facing p. 162
Wealth at death considerable bequest to London Mathematical Society

Fordham, George (1837–1887), jockey, son of James Fordham, was born at Cambridge on 24 September 1837. He was apprenticed to Richard Drewitt, for whom his uncle was travelling head lad, and went from Middleham, Yorkshire, to Lewes, Sussex, when Drewitt moved south. He had his first mount at the age of thirteen, at Brighton, where, with heavy clothing and a large saddle making up his 3 stone 8 lb to the required 5 stone, he trailed in last. A year later, in October 1851, he gained his first victory, in the trial stakes at the Brighton autumn meeting. His first big race win was in the Cambridgeshire in 1853 on Little David. From 1855 to 1869 Fordham headed the list of winning jockeys in every year except 1864 and 1866, his best record being 165 wins in 1862. In 1859 he won his first classic, the One Thousand Guineas, the first of seven successes in that race. He also won five Oaks, but surprisingly for a jockey of his calibre, had only two wins in the Two Thousand Guineas, a solitary Derby victory, and no St Leger triumphs.

Known as The Demon, Fordham was famous for his 'kidding', in which he would pretend that his horse was distressed but then suddenly attack. His seat was ungainly with very short leathers and his body skewed to one side, but he was a fine judge of pace and had a light touch, which made him ideal for two-year-olds. He frequently rode in France, but did not speak the language; this led on one occasion to a Gallic barber's virtually shaving his head, and may have contributed to his being conned by a French financier. Fordham himself was scrupulously honest and refused to ride again for both William Day and Captain Machell when they accused him of not trying.

Fordham eschewed the high life and enjoyed hunting, shooting, cricket, a round of whist, and the occasional practical joke. Alcohol was his weakness. In 1875 he retired from the turf but when he suffered heavy financial losses in continental stocks he sought refuge in the gin bottle. However, Sir George Chetwynd persuaded him to dry out and ride again—which he did, riding a further 482 winners. His last win was in Leopold de Rothschild's colours on Brag in the Brighton Cup of 1883, and his last race was the Park Stakes at Windsor in August 1884.

Fordham was twice married: first to Miss Hyde of Lewes, who died in 1879, and then to her cousin Lydia Leith. After the loss of his first wife he moved from Slough to west Brighton. There he was concussed in a riding accident that left him in a serious condition for several weeks, but from which he eventually recovered. At the end of 1884 he returned to Slough, where he died at his home, the Villa Montrose, The Grove, on 12 October 1887. He was buried at Upton, near Slough. In a letter to a fellow jockey, Charlie Wood, Fordham expressed appreciation for his few 'fair friends, considering all others gave me up'. A silver plate on his coffin proclaimed "Tis the pace that kills'.

WRAY VAMPLEW

Sources M. Tanner and G. Cranham, *Great jockeys of the flat* (1992) · R. Mortimer, R. Onslow, and P. Willett, *Biographical encyclopedia of British flat racing* (1978) · W. Vamplew, *The turf: a social and economic history of horse racing* (1976) · *The Times* (13 Oct 1887) · *The Sportsman* (13 Oct 1887) · G. Plumptre, *The fast set: the world of Edwardian racing* (1985)
Archives York Racing Museum, letter
Likenesses Spy [L. Ward], caricature, watercolour study, NPG; repro. in *VF* (22 Sept 1882) · Sturgess, wood-engraving, NPG; repro. in *ILN* (7 June 1879)
Wealth at death £19,903 8s. 6d.: probate, 22 Nov 1887, *CGPLA Eng. & Wales*

Sir Herbert George Fordham (1854–1929), by unknown photographer

Fordham, Sir Herbert George (1854–1929), writer on cartography, the eldest son of Herbert Fordham, brewer, of Odsey, Ashwell, Hertfordshire, and his wife, Constantia Elizabeth, daughter of his uncle, Edward George Fordham, of Odsey, was born at Odsey on 9 May 1854. He was educated at home, at private schools, and at University College, London, where he early showed an ability for scientific research, and became a member of the Geological Society at nineteen and a life member of the British Association at twenty-one. Between 1874 and 1892 he published several papers on the geology, natural history, and botany of Cambridgeshire and Hertfordshire. After leaving university he entered the family brewery at Ashwell, of which his father was managing partner, and in 1877 he married Fanny Osler, third daughter of William Blake, of South Petherton, Somerset. She died in 1911, and in 1914 he married Ethel Maud Elizabeth (d. 1917), daughter of the Revd Thomas Brodbelt Berry and widow of Commander Stewart Carnac Weigall RN. There were two sons and three daughters of the first marriage.

In 1882 Fordham left the family business, and in 1885 was called to the bar by the Inner Temple, joining the south-eastern circuit. The legal side of local government soon began to interest him, and in 1887 he published *Rural Municipalities and the Reform of Local Government*. Ill health led him to move with his family to Switzerland but he returned to England on the death of his father in 1891, to run the family business and to live at the family seat at Odsey. He also found time to serve in local government, chairing the Cambridgeshire county council from 1904 to 1919, and being rewarded with a knighthood in 1908.

Around the turn of the century Fordham began seriously to collect old maps and road books, initially from England and later from continental Europe, especially France. From this time on he began to publish on maps in his own collection and in those of others, often printing his works himself when unable to find another outlet. In his collected *Studies in Carto-Bibliography* (1914) he coined the term for the new systematic study of maps. He found time also to write many articles, letters, and pamphlets on Cambridgeshire antiquities, rural education, parish councils, and district midwifery, and took an energetic part in opposing the creation of a county borough of Cambridge. In 1918 he contested West Fulham as a Liberal, but was defeated, partly because of his opposition to conscription.

After 1920 Fordham, though active as a deputy lieutenant of Cambridgeshire and a magistrate of Cambridgeshire and Hertfordshire, devoted himself more and more to the study of cartography against a background of economic difficulties caused by the agricultural and manufacturing depression. For his pioneering books and articles he was awarded the gold medal of the Brussels Geographical Society in 1929. His frequent lectures, generally illustrated by exhibits from his collections, to the British Association and to other learned bodies, at home and in France and Belgium, established his reputation as one of the foremost authorities in Europe on cartography and allied subjects and brought a recognition of the importance of historical geography in school and university education. Fordham presented some rare maps and atlases to the British Museum and to Cambridge University Library, and bequeathed some 1300 volumes, including many rare road books and itineraries, to the Royal Geographical Society, to which he had been elected fellow in 1924. To the same institution he gave, in 1928, £200 to provide a fund for the encouragement of carto-bibliography.

Fordham died in a nursing home in Cambridge on 20 February 1929. His work foreshadowed modern interest in the history of cartography. His methods of cataloguing maps have been widely adopted and the Fordham collection at the Royal Geographical Society remains one of the most important in the country.

E. Lynam, rev. Elizabeth Baigent

Sources M. J. Freeman and J. Longbotham, *The Fordham collection: a catalogue* (1981) · M. J. Freeman and J. Longbotham, 'The Fordham collection: an introduction', *GJ*, 146 (1980), 218–31 · J. A. Henshall, 'Sir H. George Fordham: carto-bibliographer', *Map Collectors' Series*, 51 · *CGPLA Eng. & Wales* (1929)
Archives Letchworth Museum and Art Gallery, corresp. and papers · RGS, corresp. and papers · University of Bristol, corresp. and papers | King's AC Cam., letters to Oscar Browning · U. Birm. L., letters to R. P. L. Booker
Likenesses photograph, RGS [*see illus.*] · photograph, repro. in Freeman and Longbotham, 'The Fordham collection: an introduction'; priv. coll.
Wealth at death £33,017 19s. 1d.: probate, 24 May 1929, *CGPLA Eng. & Wales*

Fordham, John (*c*.1340–1425), administrator and bishop of Ely, was born in Fordham, Cambridgeshire, to a family of no obvious distinction. His only certain kinsman, John Kirkby, worked for him in later years, as did John Fordham, who was a squire (*scutifer*), and Thomas Fordham. Employed first by Edward III, he rose under Edward, the Black Prince, and became the latter's secretary in 1375 and an executor of his will in 1376. From 1 January 1377 he was receiver and keeper of the privy seal to the Black Prince's young son, Richard, prince of Wales, and on the latter's accession to the throne, Fordham at once (on 26 June 1377) became keeper of the king's privy seal. At that time this office was doubtless regarded as less significant than under an adult king, and Fordham was no politician, but proximity to the boy king and his household soon proved more important than had been intended. The insurgents in London in 1381 called for Fordham's death, but in the event he suffered no more than damage to his house and wine cellar.

Fordham could sustain this, for the royal household had brazenly looked after its own. Having secured the deanship of Wells in 1379 by royal request, and the prestigious archdeaconry of Canterbury in 1380–81, Fordham secured election on 30 May 1381 to the mighty see of Durham. The temporalities were restored on 23 October, and on 12 December he resigned the privy seal (as was conventional). He was consecrated at Lambeth on 5 January 1382. Fordham went north in the summer and stayed there. Problems over the Anglo-Scottish border he could not avoid, but, that apart, his days in royal service seemed done. However, Richard II and his government were lurching towards an angry showdown with their critics. With the crisis already well in motion, the beleaguered king recalled his family's loyal servant to become treasurer of the realm on 17 January 1386.

This was a hapless task, and inevitably Fordham could not survive the general onslaught on the chief ministers in the Wonderful Parliament. He resigned on 24 October 1386 with the rest. Even so, he remained with the king in 1387 as Richard prowled the midlands seeking to regain control. When the opposition took to arms to break the king's affinity, Fordham was among those banished from court. Still, he was not arrested or forced to flee, and could attend the Merciless Parliament in February 1388 without fear of being among those indicted. In March he was ordered with other northern lords to hasten to defend the border against Scottish invasion. There, like others, he left the Percys to suffer from their rashness at the battle of Otterburn. Already though, on 3 April, he had been translated by the pope (at the opposition's request) to Ely, as part of an unprecedented political reshuffle of the episcopate. Yet, if Durham had special strategic and political features that made Fordham unacceptable there in the eyes of the crown's opponents and of key northern lords, Ely was notoriously the rich neo-sinecure of English bishoprics, and for Fordham a homecoming. He took to it at once after the bull arrived in September 1388. Probably he was not sorry, and never wanted to be recalled to secular politics again.

Fordham attended parliaments fairly regularly until late in life, and once (in 1406) agreed to help settle Baltic trade disputes. That apart, he came to live almost permanently at his episcopal manor of Downham. His longevity exasperated contenders for episcopacy, particularly his perennial ability to fail then rally. His will, dated 3 October 1425, is an attractive picture of an old man at peace in a little world of cathedral, household, and staff, for all of whom he made careful provision in a modest, surprisingly austere account. It would seem natural that from the outside world only Edward III, the Black Prince, and Richard II entered his final thoughts. Even at the end he clung to life for seven weeks more. He died on 18 November 1425 and was buried, as he requested, not in the nave but in the lady chapel of Ely.

R. G. Davies, rev.

Sources E. F. Jacob, ed., *The register of Henry Chichele, archbishop of Canterbury, 1414–1443*, 2, CYS, 42 (1937), 327–9 · R. G. Davies, 'The episcopate in England and Wales, 1375–1443', PhD diss., University of Manchester, 1974 · R. G. Davies, 'The episcopate and the political crisis in England of 1386–1388', *Speculum*, 51 (1976), 659–93

Fordun, John (*d*. in or after **1363**), chronicler, was a compiler of historical works relating to Scotland which, after circulating for some eighty years, came to be incorporated in the 1440s in the more extensive *Scotichronicon* of Walter *Bower. It has been assumed at least since a statement of William Camden in the early seventeenth century that Fordun took his name from the parish of Fordoun in the Mearns, Kincardineshire; however, contemporary evidence for this is non-existent, and he may equally well have taken his name rather from the lands of Fordun near Auchterarder in Perthshire. No family or local connections are known with others of the same surname who are found *c*.1330 either at Dundee or in the royal household.

Bower (who knew an older man who had known Fordun) records that he was an undistinguished priest, not a product of any of the schools. A scribe copying Bower's book in the early 1450s describes Fordun as a chaplain of the church of Aberdeen; as such he was of too humble status to have left his name on any record there. His literary achievement was thus all the more remarkable. The explanation may lie in his putative Perthshire birthplace, which would have made it more possible for him to have had an upbringing that included some understanding of Gaelic than if he had belonged to the Mearns. Perhaps he even had inherited knowledge of Gaelic traditions as the descendant of a hereditary Gaelic learned professional kindred.

Bower suggests that Fordun was stimulated by the comparative lack of chronicles and records with information about Scotland's past (supposedly the result of Edward I's deliberate policy of destruction), and believes that Fordun travelled extensively throughout Britain and Ireland, making notes from books of annals which he found in many different places and recording his discussions with historians and chroniclers. Fordun certainly preserves factual information on a larger scale than in any earlier surviving Scottish chronicles, and embellishes his writing with literary references in a way that is remarkable in a self-educated man.

To W. F. Skene in 1871 belongs the credit for a successful effort to identify the manuscripts which contain Fordun's writings without the changes and additions made by Bower. Skene's edition (in which all but one of these manuscripts are described) has, however, come to be regarded as untrustworthy in the detail of many readings, in the uneven collation of the various texts, and in its misleading pattern of presentation—he had to relegate three long sections to appendices since they would not fit this pattern. The problems are formidable, and no revised text has yet been produced, not least because none of the seven surviving manuscripts date from Fordun's lifetime, so that all of them appear to contain elements of corrections and additions made by copyists as they decided in various ways how to combine the different elements which they found in manuscripts to which Fordun's name was attached.

Fordun gave no titles to his writings. (Eighteenth-century editors caused two centuries of bibliographical confusion by attaching the title *Scotichronicon* to his work, when that title belongs only to the work of Bower.) Following the lead of Skene we can identify two separate works. One he called *Gesta annalia* and the other *Chronica gentis Scotorum*. The annals comprise a single series of 231 notes on items of relevance to Scottish history from the time of King Alfred of Wessex (*c*.900) to 1363 (or 1385 in some manuscripts). Each note is an assertion of fact, with only the occasional more expansive passage of argument or explanation, usually without indication of the sources being used. The chronicle is quite elaborately constructed: each of its five books is divided into numbered chapters with rubrics. Mentioning many sources as it goes along, this much more literary work starts with the age-old myths of Scota and Gaythelos as the eponymous founders of the kingdom of the Scots and runs down to the death of King David in 1153. In two manuscripts there is a tailpiece of fifteen chapters in similar style, on the Saxon lineage of St Margaret (*d*. 1093) from Cedric of Wessex in 495, to round the chronicle off (probably identified wrongly by Skene as part of an intended sixth book left incomplete).

Two copyists who did not include this tailpiece attempted instead to join the chronicle and annals into one by deleting the first forty-one items in the annals relating to the period before 1153, presumably on the grounds that Fordun had already adapted them for incorporation in the chronicle; but the other scribes kept the two works distinct. Four of the manuscripts came to contain in addition a collection of documentary texts of historical importance for the Scots in their struggle against English domination (including a version of the famous declaration of Arbroath of 1320). There are no allusions to these texts in the annals for the period, and so it is an open question whether Fordun was responsible for collecting them or whether it was later copyists who attached them in different ways to manuscripts containing his two genuine works.

These are difficult to date. The annals may have been collected over an extensive period. If Fordun did travel extensively south of the border, it is likely to have been in the years following 1357, when after a long period of hostility the English government was willing to grant safe conducts to ordinary Scottish visitors. Then it is noteworthy how, having given detailed information in the annals about dramatic events in the spring of 1363, Fordun fails to mention David II's visit to Westminster in November of that year. This suggests that he had given up work by then and that the mere five extra items covering the events of the next twenty years which are found in some of the manuscripts of the annals were the work of later copyists, as were certainly some items inserted at earlier periods.

On balance it is likely that the chronicle, which overlaps chronologically with the annals, was the more developed work, ranging as it does over a much wider spread of sources. When it reaches back to the origin-myths, it may well have been constructed partly from sources surviving in both Ireland and Scotland. It is a matter of debate how far Fordun included materials which had already (perhaps long before) been synthesized into the form in which he presents them and how far it was he who was the synthesist. But there is nothing in the chronicle to suggest when Fordun worked on it. It seems best to abandon Skene's view that he lived until between 1384 and 1387, and to prefer 1363 or soon afterwards as his date of death.

As a man of his time Fordun illumines the cultural heritage of mid-fourteenth-century Scotland in the way that he supports the authority of duly established kings, provided they took the trouble to heed advice. The internal quarrels of the magnate families he regarded as disastrous. He revels in the freedom that the Scottish nation had won from hostile English aggression. This is seen in the story that he chooses to tell and in the way he tells it. For this he deserves the respect of historians for the eleventh century onwards, if not before, and also for his presentation of the origin-myths to back up his point of view. His work needs to be read as a whole to understand his approach. His attitude was one that was welcome in the Scotland of his day and for at least 150 years afterwards, for his works were not regarded as superseded by Bower's grander enterprise of the 1440s. At least three and perhaps more of the manuscripts containing them were copied later in the fifteenth century. Though modern scholars who study the early centuries of Scottish history are understandably cautious to the point of scepticism regarding his version of events long before his time and have to bear his prejudices in mind, they often have little or nothing else to go on. Early Scottish history without Fordun is literally unimaginable.   D. E. R. WATT

Sources Johannis de Fordun Chronica gentis Scotorum / John of Fordun's Chronicle of the Scottish nation, ed. W. F. Skene, trans. F. J. H. Skene, 2 vols. (1871–2) • W. Bower, Scotichronicon, ed. D. E. R. Watt and others, new edn, 9 vols. (1987–98) • G. Camdeno [W. Camden], Britannia, sive, Florentissimorum regnorum, Angliae, Scotiae, Hiberniae, later edn (1607), 712 • RotS, 1.808ff. • M. Drexler, 'Attitudes to nationalism in Scottish historical writing from Barbour to Boece', PhD diss., U. Edin., 1979 • D. Broun, The Irish identity of the kingdom of the Scots (1999) • H. Utz, 'Traces of nationalism in Fordun's Chronicle', Scottish Studies, 4 (1986), 139–49 • R. Mason, 'Kingship, tyranny and the right to resist in fifteenth-century Scotland', SHR, 66 (1987), 125–51 • R. J. Goldstein, 'The genealogy of Scotland: John of Fordun's Chronica gentis Scotorum', The matter of Scotland: historical narrative in medieval Scotland (1993), 104–32 • G. Burnett and others, eds., The exchequer rolls of Scotland, 1 (1878)

Fordyce, Alexander (*bap.* **1729**, *d.* **1789**), banker, youngest son of George Fordyce (1663–1733), provost of Aberdeen, and his second wife, Elizabeth Brown (1688–1760), was born at Eggie in the parish of Belhelvie, where he was baptized on 7 August 1729. He was the brother of David *Fordyce, James *Fordyce, and William *Fordyce, and was educated under Thomas Blackwell the younger. After an apprenticeship to Baillie John Dingwall of Aberdeen in stocking manufacture, he found local trade insufficiently challenging and moved to London, where he obtained employment as an 'out-door clerk' in the bank of Boldero & Co. The duties of such clerks included obtaining acceptances and payments on bills of exchange. Proficiency in such work and his intelligence attracted attention and by 1759 he had become a junior partner in the bank of Roffey, Neale, James and Fordyce, rising to managing partner in its post-1768 successor, Neale, James, Fordyce and Down. Apart from his activity in the bank, Fordyce engaged in heavy private speculation in the stock market. His greatest successes there are believed to have been based on early knowledge of the conclusion of the preliminaries of peace in 1762 and on the sudden rise in the price of East India Company shares in 1764–5. With the proceeds of these and other speculations, Fordyce purchased an estate in Scotland and built a fine residence at Roehampton, Surrey, where he entertained in great magnificence. He spent nearly £14,000 at Colchester in 1768 in an unsuccessful effort to obtain election to the House of Commons. He

subsequently continued to cultivate the electors there, but was defeated more decisively when he next stood as a candidate in 1780. In 1770 he married Lady Margaret Lindsay, second daughter of the earl of Balcarres. At the height of his prestige in 1770–71, he was twice elected rector of Marischal College, Aberdeen.

The tide of fortune then turned. In 1771–2 Fordyce lost heavily on the stock market, particularly by selling short in anticipation of a fall (unrealized) in the price of East India shares. He had to use the resources of his bank to cover his 'short' positions and quarrelled seriously with his partners. The final blow came from the Bank of England in early June 1772. The directors were alarmed at the decline in that bank's gold reserves and, instead of raising the discount rate, announced suddenly that they would no longer discount bills of exchange for most Scots and for Jews with Amsterdam connections (both elements that used discounts to obtain gold for shipment out of London). Unable to obtain cash by discounting at the bank, Fordyce could not pay his accepted bills of exchange when due or cover his immediately pressing short positions in the stock market. Cornered, he fled from London early on the morning of 10 June. His partners struggled on for another week but were then declared bankrupt. Since the firm had a great volume of acceptances outstanding, news of their failure created acute panic in London and Edinburgh on 22–3 June, with all private banks now suspect, and a number failing. In Scotland, the greatest disaster was the failure of Fordyce's major correspondents, the Ayr Bank. As most payments between businesses in different parts of Great Britain were then effected by bills of exchange on London, it was imperative for the new Scottish banks, particularly the very ambitious Ayr concern, to have in London helpful correspondents, such as the Fordyce firm, who would accept their bills and obtain gold for them when needed, if necessary by having other bills discounted at the Bank of England. The 1772 failures of Neale, James, Fordyce and Down and their Scottish correspondents were therefore felt as a serious setback to north British enterprise.

In London, this financial crisis was considered the worst since the Bubble year of 1720. Lord North's government was forced to intervene and persuaded the Bank of England to resume discounting for less suspect Scots. Fordyce returned to London shortly thereafter and testified in September before the commissioners in bankruptcy, placing his personal shortfall at over £75,000. He died on 8 September 1789 at George Street, Portman Square, London. In 1812 his widow married Sir James Bland Burges.

JACOB M. PRICE

Sources 'An account of the examination of Mr. Alexander Fordyce, banker in London, before the commissioners of bankruptcy', Scots Magazine, 34 (1772), 473–80, 529–35 • 'Memoirs of a late celebrated banker', Scots Magazine, 34 (1772), 421–7 • 'Some account of the present stagnation of public credit', Scots Magazine, 34 (1772), 311–18 • London Magazine, 41 (1772), 292, 313–14, 431–3 • GM, 1st ser., 42 (1772), 292–3, 296, 310–11, 434–5 • A. Dingwall Fordyce, Family record of the name of Dingwall Fordyce in Aberdeenshire (1885) • J. M. Price, 'The Bank of England's discount activity and the merchants of London, 1694–1773', in I. Blanchard and others,

Industry and finance in early modern history (1992) · H. Hamilton, *An economic history of Scotland in the eighteenth century* (1963) · *Morning Chronicle* (1772) · *HoP, Commons* · R. L. Emerson, *Professors, patronage, and politics: the Aberdeen universities in the eighteenth century* (1992) · *IGI*

Fordyce, David (*bap.* 1711, *d.* 1751), university teacher and writer on education, was born at Broadford, near Aberdeen, and baptized there on 1 April 1711, the second son of George Fordyce (1663–1733), merchant, farmer, and sometime provost of Aberdeen, and his second wife, Elizabeth (1688–1760), daughter of the Revd David Brown, Church of Scotland minister, of Neilston, near Perth. He was the brother of Alexander *Fordyce, James *Fordyce, and William *Fordyce. He entered Aberdeen grammar school in 1720 and Marischal College, Aberdeen, in 1724; there he studied philosophy and mathematics. In the early eighteenth century it was not unusual to go to university at the age of thirteen (he was one of nine of similar age who went from the school at the same time), as there was no developed form of advanced secondary education. He graduated MA in 1728 and, being intended for the ministry, proceeded to study for his BD, which he obtained in 1733, under James Chalmers. He received a licence to become a preacher in Scotland but not a call to a specific ministry; this is likely to have been due to hesitancy on his part, as he was considered an able young man. It was at this time that he developed a taste for travelling—in Scotland, England, and Europe. In 1735 he was joining in the academic debates of the time in Glasgow, with the support of Professor Thomas Blackwell (described by the *Dictionary of National Biography* as uncle to the Fordyce brothers). In 1736 he had to take charge of the family business, and, on the death of his elder brother, the estate at Eggie, near Belhelvie.

During 1737 and 1738 Fordyce travelled in England, associating with leading English Presbyterians and considering a ministerial appointment. Philip Doddridge, who was clearly on friendly terms with Fordyce, wrote of him:

> The people at Newport [Pagnell] were so charmed with a gentleman who preached the other day with them that I believe they will be joining in a unanimous Invitation. His name is Fordyce, a Scotchman, Educated at Aberdeen, A very learned and worthy person. (letter to Samuel Clark, 23 Sept 1738, *Calendar*, ed. Nuttall, 521)

Fordyce conducted a short ministry at Newport but this was terminated in November 1739, when he was appointed to the post of private chaplain to John Hopkins of Brettons, near Romford, Essex. By the middle of 1741, after a short period in France, he was in Edinburgh assisting the minister at the Tron Kirk, a collegiate church. Fordyce states that he was looking for a ministerial charge but on 9 September 1742 he was appointed professor of moral philosophy at Marischal College, in place of Alexander Innes. The position was probably obtained through the influence of Thomas Blackwell.

Fordyce proved a successful lecturer on general and natural philosophy, including mechanics, optics, and astronomy. He published his first work in 1745, entitled *Dialogues Concerning Education*, which met with immediate success. It appeared anonymously, as did all his books published in

his lifetime. The dialogue format was much appreciated in the mid-eighteenth century but was new in Scotland at that time. His book expressed the essential values of the Enlightenment on education and is seen by some commentators as a precursor of the ideas of Rousseau's *Émile*. The work was recommended by Doddridge in his lectures and was on the book list of dissenting academies. His *Elements of Moral Philosophy* (1754), which originally appeared in the *Modern Preceptor* in 1748, was also a success, reaching its fourth edition by 1769, and was translated into German in 1757. His other main work, completed in 1750, was published after his death in 1752 and entitled *Theodorus: a Dialogue Concerning the Art of Preaching*; it was often reprinted with his brother James's *Sermon on Eloquence: an Essay on the Action of the Pulpit*. This same brother, who exercised a prominent Presbyterian ministry in London, kept Fordyce's memory alive and his name before the public.

Fordyce's books were secular in content and his theology is difficult to determine, which may explain why he never entered the ministry, except on a temporary basis. His works sold well in the eighteenth century, although he was forgotten by later generations. His style was lively—some saw it as dilettante—but little of the content was original; some of his work could be seen as essentially part of an educational textbook. He played an important role in the early Scottish Enlightenment through his contacts in Europe and England and with the leaders of English dissent.

Fordyce never married. In the summer of 1750 he started on a grand tour through Europe, during which he stayed mostly in Italy, where he spoke the language fluently. He was returning home to Leith from Rotterdam on the *Hopewell* in September 1751 when the boat foundered off the Dutch coast and he was drowned. His memory was perpetuated by his brother James, who published Fordyce's *Temple of Virtue: a Dream*, with additions of his own, which went to at least three editions. James wrote a florid poem on his brother in one of his *Addresses to the Deity* (1785), which contains the following:

> Was he thy friend? Yet grieve not. The friendly wave, which wrapt him up from pain and sorrow, washed his soul from earth to heaven, where his desire of knowledge will ever be satisfied, and his virtues abundantly rewarded.

ALAN RUSTON

Sources A. Chalmers, ed., *The general biographical dictionary*, new edn, 14 (1814), 468–70 · W. T. Steven, 'Life and work of David Fordyce', PhD diss., U. Glas., 1978 · *Calendar of the correspondence of Philip Doddridge*, ed. G. F. Nuttall, HMC, JP 26 (1979) · J. V. Price, 'Fordyce, David', *The dictionary of eighteenth-century British philosophers*, ed. J. Yolton, J. V. Price, and J. Stephens (1999) · *London Christian Instructor, or, Congregational Magazine*, 1 (1818), 666 · J. Bull, *Memorials of William Bull*, 2nd edn (1865), 41–2 · *GM*, 1st ser., 21 (1751), 515 · *GM*, 1st ser., 66 (1796), 1052–3 · *DNB*
Archives DWL, letters · JRL, Unitarian College collection, letters · U. Aberdeen, lecture notes [transcriptions] | NA Scot., Clerk of Penicuik papers · NA Scot., letters to Sir Archibald Grant

Fordyce, George (1736–1802), physician, was born in Aberdeen on 18 November 1736, posthumous son and only child of George Fordyce, owner of a small landed estate at Broadford, near Aberdeen. His father was one of a large family of twenty, and several of his brothers became well known: Alexander *Fordyce (*bap.* 1729, *d.* 1789), banker; David *Fordyce (*bap.* 1711, *d.* 1751), professor of philosophy; James *Fordyce (1720–1796), Presbyterian divine; Sir William *Fordyce (1724–1792), physician; and John Fordyce, also a physician. Fordyce's mother remarried after his father's death and he was sent to school at Fouran and to Aberdeen University, where he graduated MA in 1750 at the age of fourteen. He then spent four years as assistant to his uncle John Fordyce, physician at Uppingham, Rutland, where he learned the basics of medical practice before entering the medical school at Edinburgh University in 1754. One of William Cullen's earliest and most favoured pupils, he graduated MD in 1758 with a thesis entitled 'De catarrho', in which he already showed a good knowledge of chemistry.

Fordyce next moved to London, where he attended John Hunter's lectures on anatomy and studied medical botany at the Chelsea Physic Garden. In the autumn of 1759 he went to Leiden, where he studied anatomy with Bernard Albinus. Returning to London, he settled in Essex Street, the Strand, and began to give a course of lectures on chemistry to a class of nine pupils. In 1762 he married a daughter of Charles Stuart, conservator of the Scotch privileges in the united Netherlands. There were two sons: George died in infancy and William drowned in the Thames near his home at the age of eleven, an event which afflicted his father all his life. There were also two daughters: Maria, who married Samuel Bentham, a brigadier-general in the Russian service, inspector-general of naval affairs, and brother of Jeremy Bentham; and Margaret (who remained unmarried).

Always a hard worker, Fordyce added lectures on materia medica and the practice of physic to his chemistry courses in 1764. He would lecture from 7 a.m. to 10 a.m. six days a week, devoting one hour to each subject. Each course lasted four months and was repeated three times in the year. His classes became very popular and he continued them for thirty years, during which time several thousand pupils passed through his hands.

In 1765 Fordyce became a licentiate of the Royal College of Physicians and five years later, following the death of Mark Akenside, was chosen physician to St Thomas's Hospital after a very close contest with William Watson. Friend of men such as Joshua Reynolds, David Garrick, Richard Brinsley Sheridan, and Edward Gibbon, Fordyce was elected to the Literary Club in 1774, proposed by Oliver Goldsmith and Samuel Johnson. He published several papers in the *Philosophical Transactions* and in 1776 was elected FRS. The clearest evidence of the high regard in which he was held in the medical profession came in 1787, when he was admitted to the fellowship of the Royal College of Physicians (*speciali gratia*), despite his Scottish origins and his activities in the disputes in the 1760s between licentiates and fellows. The college was preparing a new edition of the *Pharmacopoeia Londinensis*, and there was no one among the members better acquainted with pharmaceutical chemistry than Fordyce, who played a leading

role in preparing the new edition. He was responsible for abandoning the more bizarre items of materia medica, such as dried vipers, or elk's hoof as a remedy for epilepsy. Fordyce was censor in 1787, 1792, and 1800, Goulstonian lecturer in 1789, and Harveian orator in 1791.

In 1793 Fordyce assisted John Hunter to establish the Society for the Improvement of Medical and Chirurgical Knowledge, the members of which included Matthew Baillie, Edward Jenner, and Everard Home; he continued to attend the meetings until shortly before his death. By 1802 the society had published two volumes of the *Medico-Chirurgical Transactions*. Fordyce was also involved in founding the Lyceum Medicum Londinense (1785), which promoted meetings of medical students and young doctors at Hunter's lecture rooms in Castle Street, Leicester Square, London. John Abernethy, Gilbert Blane, and the young Astley Cooper were among the members.

Fordyce published several books including notably *Elements of Agriculture and Vegetation* (1765); *Elements of the Practice of Physic* (1770); *A Treatise on Digestion and Food* (1791); and four volumes of *Dissertations on Fever* between 1794 and 1802. A fifth volume was published posthumously by Fordyce's friend and colleague Charles Wells in 1803. Fordyce made some fine clinical observations on fever and studied muscular motion and digestion. With Charles Blagden he made important observations on temperature control in the human body in rooms heated to temperatures up to that of boiling water. Fordyce also published important experiments on the increase in weight during calcination, the results of which challenged the phlogiston theory.

Fordyce had a remarkable memory, on which he relied heavily. He is said to have given all his lectures without notes; and although he never kept memoranda of his engagements, he was almost always punctual in observing them. He read widely, remembered what he read, and so became more knowledgeable in the sciences connected with medicine than any of his contemporaries. In lecturing his delivery was slow and hesitant, with frequent long pauses, yet this did not prevent him from attracting large numbers of pupils, on the expectation of receiving fuller and more accurate information from him than they could obtain elsewhere.

Fordyce is said to have been handsome in his youth. He conceived the notion of eating only one meal a day and he regularly dined at 4 p.m. on a heavy meal, including half a chicken or a similar quantity of fish, followed by a large joint of beef, and accompanied by ale, brandy, and port wine. In the evening he would often drink more brandy, and after continuing this mode of living for many years he gradually became florid and full of face, developing a coarseness which was reflected in his manners and careless dress. Consequently he was less refined than was usually considered appropriate for a physician, a fact which may have contributed to his slowness in building up a practice. He made it a habit never to spend longer with a patient than was absolutely necessary to make a judgement and he did not resort to flattery to attract patients.

He therefore never made as good a living as many of his contemporaries. According to Astley Cooper, Fordyce 'was a coarse man, a bad lecturer, got drunk every evening', while his method of examining patients was '"put your tongue out—there, now let me feel your pulse,—that will do", and then he prescribed' (Cooper, 303–4).

Fordyce was not a good conversationalist, yet he was fond of the pleasures of society and loved to be where people met and talked. To allow for this as well as giving time to his pursuit of knowledge, he slept very little. His vigour enabled him to pursue this debilitating mode of life for many years, but at length he was attacked by gout, which later became regular and gave him excruciating pain. His feet and ankles swelled and shortly before his death he recognized the symptoms of water in the chest, but knowing his condition to be hopeless he ignored them, attributing all his physical problems to gout. He died at his house in Essex Street, London, on 25 May 1802, attended by his daughter Margaret. His remains were interred privately at St Anne's Church, Soho, on 1 June 1802.　　　　　　　　　　　　　　　　　N. G. COLEY

Sources GM, 1st ser., 72 (1802), 588–91 • R. G. Howell, St Thomas's Hospital Gazette, 46 (1948), 120–21 • J. Winstanley, St Thomas's Hospital Gazette (1981), 96–9 • Munk, Roll • F. G. Parsons, The history of St Thomas's Hospital, 2 (1934), 226–7 • D. T. Bird, Catalogue of the printed books and manuscripts in the library of St Thomas's Hospital Medical School (1984), 145, 414–15 • B. B. Cooper, The life of Sir Astley Cooper, 1 (1843), 303–4

Archives McGill University, Montreal, Osler Library of the History of Medicine, lecture notes • Northwestern University, Chicago, medical school library, lecture notes • Royal College of Physicians of Edinburgh, dissertation on inflammation • RS, papers • Som. ARS, lecture notes • U. Glas. L., papers relating to minerals • Wellcome L., lecture notes • NA Scot., letters to Sir Archibald Grant • V&A NAL, letters to David Garrick

Likenesses G. Kenting, mezzotint, 1795 (after T. Phillips), Wellcome L. • S. Phillips, engraving, 1796 (after T. Phillips) • J. Greenwood, Indian ink and pencil, BM • T. Phillips, oils, St Thomas's Hospital, London; copy, RCP Lond. • plaster medal (after J. Milton), Scot. NPG

Fordyce [née Cumming], **Henrietta** (1734–1823), governess, was born in Scotland, lost her father at an early age, and was educated at home by her mother. From the age of twelve, when the death of her mother left her orphaned (and 'tocherless' without a dowry; Memoir of the Late Mrs. Henrietta Fordyce, 8), she lived with an aunt in Edinburgh. In 1761 she attracted the notice of Anne Dalrymple, countess of Balcarres, wife of James Lindsay, the fifth earl of Balcarres, who offered her a position as governess. Residing at Balcarres in Fife, Cumming served as governess to Anne, Margaret, and Elizabeth Lindsay for ten years, developing close ties to Margaret, who would later become her sister-in-law. In 1771 she married the Scottish clergyman James *Fordyce (1720–1796), who is perhaps best remembered for his enormously popular Sermons to Young Women (1765). The couple had no children. They lived in London until the early 1780s, then moved briefly to Southampton before finally settling at Bath.

While most eighteenth-century governesses lived and died in obscurity, Henrietta Fordyce achieved a modest degree of fame or notoriety. She was, in the opinion of the antiquarian scholar James Ramsay of Ochtertyre, 'the 1st Scottish [governess] that got a great name' (Ramsay, 'Strictures', fol. 194), and the details of her life would be recorded and embellished in the hagiographical and somewhat unreliable Memoir of the Late Mrs. Henrietta Fordyce (1823). According to the Memoir's anonymous author, Fordyce accepted a small pension from Queen Charlotte in return for the present of an embroidered silk, but declined an invitation to serve as governess to the royal household. The fact that Fordyce was remembered well into the nineteenth century owes less to this Memoir than to her correspondence with Alison Cockburn (1712–1794) and to the reminiscences of her eldest pupil.

Fordyce enjoyed a warm friendship with Alison Cockburn, the celebrated Edinburgh hostess and friend of David Hume, who looked upon the governess of Balcarres as both confidante and protégée. In letters addressed to 'my little Sylph' Cockburn expressed a lively interest in the younger woman's romantic fortunes, and lavished praise upon her 'Noble Mind' and 'luminous fancy'. Writing at the height of the famous quarrel between Hume and Rousseau, Cockburn once suggested that her friend write to the French philosopher as 'an Admirer' of Hume who could testify to 'the Simplicity of David's character' (Cockburn to H. Cumming, 19 Oct 1766, Edinburgh University Library, Laing MS 2, 81/2/5).

While Cockburn saw her 'dear Henny' as a paragon of feminine virtue and accomplishment, a rather different portrait emerges from the unpublished memoirs of Lady Anne Lindsay Barnard (1750–1825), which are cited extensively in Alexander Crawford's Lives of the Lindsays (1849). Referring to Henrietta Fordyce as 'a young woman, or rather, a young lady, to whom I dare hardly, even at this moment, give the title of our governess', Barnard described her as a 'wild' and 'perfectly fantastic being' that possessed a 'variety of uncultivated talents', along with uncommon 'powers of attaching, [and] of injuring, … of genius, magnanimity, obstinacy, prejudice, romance, and occasionally enthusiastic devotion' (Crawford, 2.312–14). According to Barnard, Fordyce would not consider herself a governess, and starved herself until she was permitted to eat with the family (rather than, as was usual, with the upper servants) and even refused remuneration: 'The proposal to give her £20 per annum nearly cost Henrietta her life—as an act of friendship she was ready to take care of us, but her soul spurned emolument' (ibid., 313–14). Although her account reveals a certain admiration and even affection, in satirizing her former governess Barnard adopted the stance of a social superior. Her perspective may have been coloured by the unhappy fate of her sister Margaret, who married James Fordyce's brother Alexander, only to be deserted by her husband when he fled to the continent after a spectacular banking failure from which many, including James and Henrietta Fordyce, suffered serious financial losses. In the hands of later commentators Barnard's ironic depiction of

Fordyce's attempts to assert her gentility provided grounds for a harsher, and more earnest, condemnation. In several nineteenth- and early twentieth-century sources Fordyce's hunger strike and refusal to accept a salary were cited as evidence of the unsuitable class aspirations of a 'vain', 'unscrupulous' (*Letters and Memoir*, 33), and 'hysterical creature' (Graham, 191). A more sympathetic account would acknowledge the difficult predicament of the eighteenth-century governess, who was expected to be at once a servant and a gentlewoman during a period in which paid employment for women was increasingly stigmatized as shameful and degrading. Although she married a Presbyterian, Henrietta Fordyce remained an Episcopalian throughout her life. She died at Bath in 1823.

MARY CATHERINE MORAN

Sources *Memoir of the late Mrs. Henrietta Fordyce, relict of James Fordyce, D.D.* (1823) · *Letters and memoirs of her own life, by Mrs. Alison Rutherford or Cockburn*, ed. T. Craig-Brown (1899) · Lord Lindsay [A. W. C. Lindsay, earl of Crawford], *Lives of the Lindsays*, [new edn], 3 vols. (1849) · H. Graham, *A group of Scottish women* (1908) · S. Tytler and J. L. Watson, *The songstresses of Scotland*, 2 vols. (1871) · J. Ramsay, 'Strictures on female education', NL Scot., Ochtertyre MS 1644 · Chambers, *Scots.* (1835) · *DNB*
Archives U. Edin., Laing MSS

Fordyce, James (1720–1796), Church of Scotland minister and moralist, was born on 5 June 1720 in Aberdeen, the fourth son of George Fordyce (1663–1733) and his wife, Elizabeth (1688–1760), daughter of the Revd David Brown, minister of Neilston, near Perth. His father was a farmer, landowner, and leading merchant in Aberdeen and had served as provost. It is said that George and Elizabeth had twenty children. Five of their sons became eminent figures: David *Fordyce, Alexander *Fordyce, James, Sir William *Fordyce, and Robert, a leading Aberdeen manufacturer. James Fordyce had a classical education at Aberdeen high school, after which he attended Marischal College, Aberdeen, where he trained for the Scottish Presbyterian ministry. In February 1743 he was licensed to preach by the Aberdeen presbytery, and in September 1744 was presented by the crown as second minister at Brechin. His appointment was resisted and, although ordained as a Church of Scotland minister in August 1745, he did not get on well with his colleague or the congregation.

In October 1753 Fordyce moved to Alloa where he began a successful ministry, soon becoming noted as an excellent preacher. In the 1750s he published some of his sermons dealing with moral and social issues. His address to the general assembly of the Church of Scotland in 1760, 'The folly, infamy and misery of unlawful pleasures', was a great success, and he was recognized as an outstanding preacher. It was generally agreed that 'nothing of its kind had been heard before in Scotland' (Chalmers, 14.471). The University of Glasgow made him a DD the same year. His thoughts turned to London, where his brothers were making names for themselves, and they pressed him to come south. A visit the previous year gave him the taste for a wider and more urbane society than he had experienced in his native Scotland. It was during this visit that an

James Fordyce (1720–1796), by James Tassie

unsuccessful attempt was made to secure him the pastorate at Carter Lane Chapel. In June 1760 he was appointed as colleague to Samuel Lawrence, minister to the Presbyterian congregation meeting at Monkwell Street. Lawrence died a few months later and Fordyce became sole pastor, though Thomas Toller, Lawrence's son-in-law, continued to preach in the morning.

Fordyce soon became one of the most celebrated and fashionable preachers in London, and the famous and well known flocked to hear him. He had the natural talents of a preacher:

> Tall beyond the common standard ... [his] features displayed a great variety of expression and understanding ... With respect to his theological sentiments, he appears to have possessed that general liberality which is civil to all systems without being attached to any ... Morality seems to have been his chief object; and as to the manner, he evidently studied a polish and a spirit which is seldom met with in English pulpits. (Chalmers, 14.471–2)

He was what was termed a sentimental preacher, speaking to the emotions and not delving into religious topics, especially those that were in dispute. His effect in the pulpit must have been striking:

> His elocution, which he studied with care and practised with success; by the figure of his person which in the pulpit was particularly dignified and by the expression of his countenance which was animated at all times ... His eye was particularly bright and penetrating, and he carefully attended to the effect that an orator may produce on an audience. (Lindsay, 48–9)

Fordyce presented himself as a moralist in the pulpit, and it was his addresses to young people for which he became particularly well known both in his own time and later. He 'saw himself surrounded by multitudes of genteel people and especially of young gentlemen and ladies of the first respectability in the city. To them he considered it his business to preach' (Bogue and Bennett, 2.607). His *Sermons to Young Women* (1765) went to numerous reprints and was translated into several European languages. This was perhaps his most famous work, although his *Addresses to Young Men* (1777) also enjoyed a wide appeal.

Fordyce was welcomed into many salons of the London intelligentsia in the 1760s; his manners and address were noted to be impeccable. James Boswell recalls that he met Fordyce at a gathering at Dr Johnson's chambers at Inner Temple Lane on 24 May 1763. The subject of discussion, which had been introduced by Fordyce, was a recent translation of Ossian. Boswell concluded in 1784: 'Nay, though Johnson loved a Presbyterian the least of all, this did not prevent his having a long and uninterrupted social connection with Rev Dr James Fordyce' (Boswell, 1388). Fordyce was also said to be a friend of Oliver Goldsmith. On 2 May 1771 Fordyce married Henrietta Cumming (1734–1823) [see Fordyce, Henrietta], governess: they had no children.

In the early 1770s Fordyce's popularity declined sharply. Walter Wilson concluded on his decline that 'Hearers will change their preachers as they change their dress, to be with others who admire' (Wilson, 3.209–14). A cause of his decline was the spectacular bankruptcy of his brother Alexander, which ruined some of his warmest supporters and alienated many friends. In 1775 Fordyce and Toller had an argument, and Fordyce, not to his credit, secured Toller's dismissal. This led to a split in the congregation, and Fordyce became the sole preacher at Monkwell Street.

The congregation declined sharply in the 1770s, a fact which preyed on Fordyce's health. He resigned his ministry at Christmas 1782, when he retired to a country house near Christchurch, Hampshire. In 1792, on the death of his brother Sir William Fordyce, he moved to Bath. It is said that as he got older his views became more liberal and even tended towards deism. Fordyce did not sit securely in any denomination, so that after he died suddenly at his home in Bath on 1 October 1796 he was 'buried at his parish church at Bath, in a private manner attended by a few respectable friends. The service was read by the Revd Mr Whitby' (*Protestant Dissenter's Magazine*). A detailed description of the last day in Fordyce's life, written by his widow, is included as an appendix to James Lindsay's *A Sermon Preached … 16 October, 1796*.   ALAN RUSTON

Sources A. Chalmers, ed., *The general biographical dictionary*, new edn, 14 (1814), 470–73 · J. Lindsay, *A sermon preached … October 16th, 1796, on the occasion of the death of Dr J. Fordyce* (1797) · W. Wilson, *The history and antiquities of the dissenting churches and meeting houses in London, Westminster and Southwark*, 4 vols. (1808–14), vol. 3, pp. 209–19 · *Fasti Scot.*, new edn, 4.293; 8.386 · D. Bogue and J. Bennett, *History of dissenters, from the revolution in 1688, to … 1808*, 2nd edn, 2 (1833), 606–9 · *Protestant Dissenter's Magazine*, 3 (1796), 399–400 · J. Boswell, *Life of Johnson*, ed. R. W. Chapman, rev. J. D. Fleeman, rev. edn (1980), 1388 · *GM*, 1st ser., 66 (1796), 1052–3 · C. E. Surman,

index to dissenting ministers, DWL, card F.551 · *DNB* · *IGI* · Anderson, *Scot. nat.*, 2.245–6 [poem] · J. V. Price, 'Fordyce, James', *The dictionary of eighteenth-century British philosophers*, ed. J. W. Yolton, J. V. Price, and J. Stephens (1999) · will, PRO, PROB 11/1280, fol. 499
Likenesses J. Tassie, Wedgwood medallion, Scot. NPG [*see illus.*] · attrib. Tassie, Wedgwood medallion, Wedgwood Museum, Barlaston, Staffordshire
Wealth at death value of estate not ascertained; estate left to wife: will, PRO, PROB 11/1280, fol. 499

Fordyce, Sir William (1724–1792), physician, was born at Aberdeen, the son of George Fordyce (1663–1733), provost of Aberdeen, and his wife, Elizabeth Brown (1688–1760). He was the brother of Alexander *Fordyce, the banker, James *Fordyce, the divine, and David *Fordyce, professor of moral philosophy at Marischal College, Aberdeen. William was educated at Marischal College and served a medical pupillage with a local practitioner, and with his brother John, at Uppingham in 1743, as did his nephew George Fordyce a few years later. It has been inferred that he qualified at Edinburgh from the fact that he was admitted a member of the Royal Medical Society there, in 1744; but it is more probable that he left Edinburgh without qualifying.

Fordyce volunteered for the army during the war with France, which ended in 1748, and he obtained an appointment as surgeon to the guards, with whom he served in three campaigns. Probably after the peace he travelled and studied in France. He was at Turin in 1750, but returned to London in the same year. While retaining for many years his connection with the army, he set up in general practice in London, and this and the growing note of his brothers introduced him to the best circles. In 1770 Fordyce was created MD at Cambridge by royal mandate, and he was admitted licentiate of the College of Physicians in 1786. He became a fellow of the Royal Society in 1787 and was knighted in the same year.

Fordyce's publications, especially *A New Inquiry into the Causes, Symptoms, and Cure of Putrid and Inflammatory Fevers* (1773, translated into German in 1774), extended his fame, and he was sent for from as far afield as Naples and Switzerland, becoming one of the most wealthy physicians of his time. His medical skill and knowledge were considerable, as testified by his works, some of which went through numerous editions. The Society of Arts voted him a gold medal for his work, *The Great Important and Proper Method of Cultivating and Curing Rhubarb in Britain for Medical Uses* (1784).

Fordyce was a man of great generosity and hospitality. He aided his brother Alexander in his rise to fortune, and suffered great financial loss when he failed. Fordyce died at Brook Street, Grosvenor Square, London, after a long illness, on 4 December 1792. At the time of his death he was lord rector of Marischal College, Aberdeen, to which he left his medical library, and where he founded the lectureship on agriculture.

G. T. BETTANY, *rev.* CAROLINE OVERY

Sources *GM*, 1st ser., 62 (1792), 1218–19 · Munk, *Roll* · P. J. Anderson and J. F. K. Johnstone, eds., *Fasti academiae Mariscallanae Aberdonensis: selections from the records of the Marischal College and University,*

MDXCIII–MDCCCLX, 3 vols., New Spalding Club, 4, 18–19 (1889–98), vol. 2, pp. 17–18
Likenesses A. Kauffmann, portrait, probably U. Aberdeen, Marischal College · bust, probably U. Aberdeen, Marischal College
Wealth at death see will repr. in *Fasti academiae Mariscallanae Aberdonensis*, ed. Anderson, vol. 1

Fores, Samuel William (*bap.* **1761**, *d.* **1838**), publisher and printseller, was baptized on 29 March 1761 at St Benet Fink, Threadneedle Street, London, the son of Samuel Fores (*b.* 1738), a stationer and bookseller of the Savoy, Strand, and his wife, Mary, *née* Allington. In 1783 S. W. Fores founded a business as a printseller specializing in hand-coloured, singly-issued satirical prints or caricatures 'at the City Arms, No. 3 Piccadilly near the Hay Market', in the heart of London's West End, and soon came to dominate the trade in such prints alongside William Holland (who started business almost concurrently), Hannah Humphrey, and a number of other minor competitors. The Fores–Holland–Humphrey triumvirate thrived during the era of the French Revolution when James Gillray, Thomas Rowlandson, and Isaac Cruikshank were at the peak of their activity, a period considered the 'golden age' of English graphic satire. The prolific Fores and Holland, the latter of whom was more radically inclined politically, were particular rivals, and both frequently resorted to hyperbolic notices on their prints advertising exhibitions and new prints. In 1789 Fores announced an exhibition that was 'the largest in the kingdom' and later a 'Grand Caricatura Exhibition … Containing the most complete Collection of Humorous, Political and Satirical Prints and Drawings, Ever exposed to public view in this kingdom'. Fores even advertised lurid attractions to outdo Holland such as a 6 foot working model of the guillotine and the 'head and hand of the unfortunate Count Struenzee, who was beheaded at Denmark' (perhaps only a death mask).

In 1795 Fores moved to larger premises at no. 50 Piccadilly, on the corner of Sackville Street. The number was changed to 41 about 1820, presumably as a result of the Regent Street development planned by John Nash. A watercolour painted in 1853 by Thomas Hosmer Shepherd shows the premises. Fores outlasted Holland, who died in 1815, but he experienced major new competition from the likes of Rudolph Ackermann, who sold various satirical prints alongside topographical aquatints to a fashionable clientele; Thomas Tegg, who went downmarket and drastically reduced the price of his prints; and later Thomas McLean, who embraced lithography, and published William Heath and John 'HB' Doyle. Fores, it seems, was particularly innovative in marketing his prints, selling them wholesale and retail, and was one of the first to hire out folios of caricatures for the evening. Notably Fores started selling large collections of caricatures, and those prints stamped with the initials 'S. W. F.' probably derive from such collections or are those prints that were hired out. There are collections with the 'S. W. F.' stamp in the Reform Club, London, and the Anthony de Rothschild collection, Ascott, Wing, Buckinghamshire. A surviving handbill now in the department of prints and drawings of the British Museum headed 'Roxburgh Collection of Caricatures' advertises for sale a collection 'bound in 24 uniform Volumes' at 250 guineas. Prints were also available to buy ready prepared for screens, assorted for folios, and arranged for scrapbooks.

Fores also offered other services such as frame-making and teaching etching, and he kept a large stock of art supplies. He published drawing books and had a drawing library 'where prints and drawings are lent to copy'. Fores's business at this stage has echoes of Ackermann's luxurious Repository of the Arts in the Strand and he was clearly looking to diversify as a result of competition and waning caricature sales. Some of the best prints that Fores published were by Gillray between 1787 and 1791, before his monopoly by Humphrey, and his imprint is found on Gillray's *Monstrous Craws*, *A March to the Bank*, and *The Hopes of the Party*. Fores also published Gillray's portrait of the prime minister William Pitt, but surviving correspondence reveals that this resulted in some acrimony. Although most of Fores's output was not unsympathetic to the Pitt regime, Fores was nevertheless briefly arrested in 1796 for selling Gillray's *The Presentation, or, The Wise Men's Offering*—actually published by Humphrey—which was deemed a blasphemous libel, reminding him of the limits of acceptable subject matter and the risks involved in publishing satirical material. The period is notable for its severe censorship and the gagging of radical expression.

Fores published work by numerous artists but seems to have dealt most consistently with Isaac Cruikshank and in 1797 he also had brief dealings with the youthful and talented Richard Newton, publishing together at least five prints. Fores's address is also found on a number of prints relating to the Queen Caroline affair of 1819–20, which provoked a great outpouring of satirical material. Fores probably deserves the distinction of being the most prolific publisher of singly-issued satirical prints and also as the founder of one of London's longest running firm of printsellers.

Fores married twice and had numerous children (either fourteen or seventeen), some with curious patriotic names: following Trafalgar a son was christened Horatio Nelson and in 1814 another was called Arthur Blücher, in honour of the conquerors of Napoleon. His first wife, Elizabeth (*b.* 1758/9), died in 1797. His second wife, Jane (1772/3–1840), actively looked after the shop and was apparently popular with the customers (who included such notables as the duke of Queensberry, Sir Francis Burdett, Nelson, and the exiled duke of Orléans, Louis Philippe). In addition to his publishing and printing work, Fores also published *Fores's New Guide for Foreigners* (*c*.1790) and wrote a treatise entitled *Man-Midwifery Dissected* under the pseudonym John Blunt in 1793. Fores died on 3 February 1838, and was buried in the family vault on the Jermyn Street side of St James's, Piccadilly.

The business continued as Messrs Fores after Samuel William's death and his sons George Thomas Fores (1806–1858) and Arthur Blücher Fores (1814–1883) took over, quickly replacing satirical prints with sporting prints. The will of Arthur Blücher, who never married and accrued considerable wealth, states that the business was being carried on by his nephew George Thomas Byron Fores, but it seems that it was in fact another son of George Thomas, George Philip Byron Fores (1831–1916), who mainly oversaw production. The latter's son George Poole Fores (1865–1950) was next to run the firm which remained *in situ* until 1938 when Fores & Co. moved to no. 123 New Bond Street. Fores Ltd, 'specialists in sporting engravings', moved to 29 Bruton Street and relocated again in 1980 as Fores Gallery Ltd to 15 Sicilian Avenue. Although no longer family-run, the business continued to operate as Fores into the twenty-first century. SIMON TURNER

Sources F. G. Stephens and M. D. George, eds., *Catalogue of political and personal satires preserved … in the British Museum*, 5–11 (1935–54) • A. M. Broadley, *Napoleon in caricature*, 2 vols. (1911) • D. Hill, *Mr Gillray the caricaturist* (1965) • D. Donald, *The age of caricature: satirical prints in the reign of George III* (1996) • R. Godfrey, *James Gillray: the art of caricature* (2001) • IGI
Archives NYPL, letters to Gillray
Likenesses R. Cruikshank, hand-coloured etching, 1823, BM • Appleton, portrait, 1825, priv. coll.
Wealth at death see will, PRO, PROB 11/1902

Forest, John (c.1470–1538), Franciscan friar and martyr, is of unknown origins, nor can any trace of him be found in the records of the universities, though he was repeatedly referred to as 'doctor' by contemporaries. By 1512 he had joined the Observant Franciscans at their Greenwich convent, and in 1525 at Paul's Cross he announced the excommunication of nineteen of his brethren who had fled the convent rather than submit to Cardinal Wolsey's visitation of the house. By the early 1530s he was a senior figure in the Greenwich community, a regular preacher at Paul's Cross, and reportedly a favourite of the king and the duke of Norfolk, though there is no reliable evidence for the tradition that he was Katherine of Aragon's confessor. Like a number of his confrères he emerged as an opponent of the king's divorce, and was denounced in a series of letters to Cromwell by two fellow Observants, John Lawrence and Richard Lyst. In consequence the provincial minister of the order, Francis Faber, exiled Forest to one of the northern convents (probably Newark or Newcastle) in May 1533. Later tradition suggests that Forest was in prison in 1534, when he was said to be about sixty-four years old, but it is impossible to verify this. A series of letters between the incarcerated Forest and Katherine of Aragon printed by Thomas Bourchier, in his martyrology of the Observants first published in 1582, has been accepted as genuine by a number of authorities, including David Knowles, but it is likely that these were Bourchier's invention.

By early 1538 Forest was in London, based at the house of the Conventual Franciscans, and his conservative teaching in the confessional brought him again to the attention of Cromwell. By March or early April he was under arrest, and a decision was made to try him for heresy. The principal charge against him was that of identifying the Catholic church of the creed with the Church of Rome. He was convicted and ordered to abjure his opinions at Paul's Cross. However, while incarcerated in Newgate with the

Carmelite Laurence Cooke and the Carthusian William Horne, Forest's resistance stiffened. At Paul's Cross on 12 May he refused to read the recantation, laying himself open to the fate of relapsed heretics, death by burning. This took place at Smithfield on 22 May, in the presence of a crowd of thousands, including Cromwell, Cranmer, the dukes of Norfolk and Suffolk, the earls of Sussex and Hertford, and the bishop, mayor, and sheriff of London. A sermon was preached by Bishop Hugh Latimer, and extra fuel for the pyre was provided by the 'abused image' of Dderfel Gadarn, a great wooden statue from the pilgrimage site of Llandderfel in north Wales. The claim has often been made that a Welsh prophecy stating that Dderfel Gadarn would one day set a forest on fire prompted the authorities to burn Forest. However, heresy proceedings had begun before Cromwell knew of the existence of the image, and the earliest reference to any prophecy comes in Edward Hall's *Chronicle*, published in 1548. According to Bourchier, Forest wrote a book entitled *De auctoritate ecclesiae et pontificis maximi*, but no trace of this survives, and it was not mentioned at the trial.

Forest was unique among Tudor and Stuart papalists in being burnt as a heretic, rather than hanged, drawn, and quartered as a traitor. It is possible that his fate was connected with fears over the recent papal summoning of the Council of Mantua. Henrician propaganda in the mid-1530s stressed that it was heretical for the pope to believe himself to be superior to a general council, and one of the charges against Forest was that he had impugned the Council of Nicaea for lacking papal authorization. His notoriety among contemporaries, however, owed more to his admission that when swearing the oath of supremacy 'he had denied the bishop of Rome by an oath given by his outward man but not in th'inward man' (*LP Henry VIII*, 13/1, no. 1043 (i))—an early case of the casuistical technique of 'mental reservation' which was to bedevil later Tudor governments in their dealings with Catholic recusants. Forest was beatified by the Roman Catholic church in 1886. PETER MARSHALL

Sources *LP Henry VIII*, vols. 5–6, 13 • P. Marshall, 'Papist as heretic: the burning of John Forest, 1538', *HJ*, 41 (1998), 351–74 • K. Brown, 'The Franciscan Observants in England, 1482–1559', DPhil diss., U. Oxf., 1986 • C. Wriothesley, *A chronicle of England during the reigns of the Tudors from AD 1485 to 1559*, ed. W. D. Hamilton, 1, CS, new ser., 11 (1875) • T. Bourchier, *Historia ecclesiastica de martyrio fratrum ordinis diui Francisci* (Ingolstadt, 1583) • D. Knowles [M. C. Knowles], *The religious orders in England*, 3 (1959) • B. Camm, ed., *Lives of the English martyrs declared blessed by Pope Leo XIII in 1886 and 1895*, 1 (1904) • M. A. S. Hume, ed. and trans., *Chronicle of King Henry VIII of England* (1889) • *Hall's chronicle*, ed. H. Ellis (1809) • Bishop Tunstall's register, GL, MS 9531/10, fol. 157v

Forester, Cecil Scott. See Smith, Cecil Lewis Troughton (1899–1966).

Forester, Frank. See Herbert, Henry William (1807–1858).

Forester, James (c.1560–1622?), separatist apostate and Church of England clergyman, was born in Cambridge of unknown parents. He matriculated at Clare College, Cambridge, in Easter term 1576, graduating BA in 1580 and MA in 1583. Forester was ordained deacon on 21 July 1585, aged twenty-five, by the bishop of London, and as priest the following year. Probably soon after this, he became the curate of Rayleigh in Essex.

Before the end of 1589 Forester had become associated with the London separatist church led by Henry Barrowe and John Greenwood. As witnesses claimed three years later, he had 'expounded' to them 'in a garden house by Bedlam' in December 1589 or January 1590 (*Writings*, 336). Soon after, Forester and forty-two others were arrested; in February he was among those held in Newgate, but was moved before April to the Bridewell. Here, as it later emerged, he had played an important role in preparing for the press Barrowe's *A Brief Description of the False Church*. He had been commissioned to correct the text and to prepare a fair copy for the printer. By the means of the future separatist elder Daniel Studley, 'as one sheet was written the same was taken away, with the copy thereof, and [another] new brought' (ibid., 310).

In April 1590 Forester was one of those who petitioned Burghley for their release. This seems to have been granted, but he was arrested again and examined on 19 March 1593 by chief justices John Popham and Edmund Anderson; Thomas Egerton, the attorney-general; and Edward Stanhope, chancellor of the bishop of London and a member of high commission. In an effort to dissociate himself from his former friends and their separatist ideas, the accused admitted only that he had 'began to incline that way, but hath sithens seen, he thanketh God, their great error', further claiming in his defence that he had sought to soften 'the sharp manner of writing' of Barrowe's book (*Writings*, 310). In April Thomas Mitchell claimed he had been drawn towards his separatist convictions 'by conference with one Forester, who now cometh to church [Church of England]' (ibid., 370). Neither Forester nor another apostate, Robert Stookes, was arraigned with the other separatists.

Forester now turned to medicine. In 1594 he published an edition of *The Pearle of Practise, or, Practisers Pearle, for Phisicke and Chirurgie* by John Hester of St Paul's Wharf, adding observations of his own. An exponent of 'Paracelsicall Physicke', Forester argued for simple, well-prepared medicines and against making exaggerated claims for their curative powers. He signed his epistle to the reader from 'my studie in the Blackefriers, 19 January'. Revealing that he had recently purchased from Hester's 'survivor' very many of the apothecary's medicinal preparations, Forester provided a long list of herbs, oils, and spices now available from his house.

This foray into medicine appears to have been a temporary recourse. Venn tells us that Forester became a chaplain to Henry Clinton, the earl of Lincoln. In 1606 he became rector of Mavis Enderby in Lincolnshire, and in that capacity, on 8 January 1611, he signed his book *The Marrow and Juice of Two Hundred and Sixtie Scriptures*. By this time, he had so far gained the establishment's favour as to be able to claim for himself the dignity of 'chaplaine to the Queene's most excellent majesty'. In an epistle dedicated to King James, the 'defender of the true ancient and catholicke faith', he attacks 'seditious and factious conventicles' who 'inveigle the unlettered, ignorant, yonglings with their siren songs'. The author's former mentor, Henry Barrowe, had derided the Book of Common Prayer as 'a peece of swine's flesh' (Forester, sigs. A3, A4). Forester makes angry reference to this phrase, attacking Barrowe by name in the epistle to the reader. We may wonder with Leland Carlson whether it was in reaction to his extreme earlier convictions that Forester had become equally zealous in the cause of the official church. Little is known of him after this date, but he held his rectory of Mavis Enderby until 1622, and it may be that this was the year of his death.   STEPHEN WRIGHT

Sources *The writings of John Greenwood and Henry Barrow, 1591–1593*, ed. L. H. Carlson (1970) • J. Forester, *The marrow and juice of two hundred and sixtie scriptures* (1611) • J. H. [John Hester], *The pearle of practise, or, Practisers pearle, for phisicke and chirurgie*, new edn (1594), epistle to the reader • Venn, *Alum. Cant.* • *The writings of Henry Barrow, 1587–1590*, ed. L. H. Carlson (1962) • *The writings of John Greenwood, 1587–1590*, ed. L. H. Carlson (1962) • C. W. Foster, ed., *The state of the church in the reigns of Elizabeth and James I*, Lincoln RS, 23 (1926)

Foresythe, Reginald Charles (1907–1958), jazz pianist and composer, was born on 28 May 1907 at 15 Hetley Road, Shepherd's Bush, London, the son of Charles Albert Foresythe, a Yoruba (Nigerian) barrister, and his wife, Charlotte Annie Falk, an Englishwoman of German descent. The family lived in the small west African community in the Shepherd's Bush area of London. Foresythe received a public school education, and studied piano and composition. Throughout his life Foresythe used his upper-class British accent to achieve some measure of acceptance in an otherwise racially segregated world. In the 1930s in Britain he won respect in jazz circles for such bold and dazzling compositions as 'Serenade for a Wealthy Widow', 'Garden of Weed', 'Berceuse for an Unwanted Child', 'The Autocrat before Breakfast', 'Greener the Grass', 'Melancholy Clown', and 'Dodging a Divorcee'. In *Just Jazz 3* Charles Fox says: 'Foresythe's music frequently possessed wit as well as sophistication, charm as well as ingenuity, and certainly nobody in this country worked harder to expand the boundaries of jazz' (Traill and Lascelles, 30).

On a visit to New York in 1937 Foresythe composed the music for some of the songs in that year's *Cotton Club Parade*, a lavish revue with a cast headed by Ethel Waters and Duke Ellington. With lyrics by Andy Razaf, Foresythe contributed the rhumba 'Chile: a South American Fantasy', performed by Duke Ellington's vocalist, Ivie Anderson, and 'Taps is Tops', performed by the Nicholas Brothers. In America in the 1930s, jazz giants such as Louis Armstrong and Fats Waller admired Foresythe and recorded his compositions. Earl Hines used Foresythe's 'Deep Forest' as a signature tune on his first radio series. Charles Fox recorded:

> When I spoke to Hines about Foresythe he remembered him well, and agreed that if he had only stayed in the United States, instead of returning to Britain, he might easily have become an influential and important figure in jazz. Over here, of course, his ideas were considered to be 'too far out' even by many musicians; he was looked on, in fact, as

Reginald Charles Foresythe (1907–1958), by unknown photographer

something of a musical eccentric. The result was that a very talented jazz composer failed to live up to his early promise. (Traill and Lascelles, 30)

When the American singer Elisabeth Welch made London her home in 1933, she began looking for an accompanist. She recalls in *Brief Encounters: Lesbians and Gays in British Cinema, 1930–71*:

When I arrived in London I was offered cabaret and variety engagements, but I didn't know anyone who could accompany me. I was given Reggie's name and of course I'd heard about him in America and Paris. He was a sweet, simple, charming person. His appearance was always immaculate and elegant. He loved good food and talked with that wonderful English upper-class accent. When we made fun of his accent, he didn't mind at all. He had a great sense of humour about himself. We all loved him. I used to go almost two or three times a week to see him perform his famous 'New Music' at the 400 Club, a very chic place in Leicester Square. Reggie was a 'confirmed bachelor'. I do not recall a woman ever being associated with him. I know he had liaisons with men, but they were always very discreet. (Bourne, 41)

At the height of his popularity Foresythe made several guest appearances in British films, including *Calling the Tune* (1936), for which he composed 'Evergreen Restaurant' and performed it as a piano solo in the film. On his return to London from New York, Foresythe worked in Mayfair clubs until the outbreak of the Second World War. Over age for active service, he volunteered for the RAF anyway. In 1941 he became an intelligence officer in the RAF and served in north Africa.

In the 1930s Foresythe had been ahead of his time, but after the war time seemed to have passed him by. He was soon leading bands in obscure west country hotels and playing solo piano in drinking clubs in London's Soho and Kensington. His career ended in obscurity and alcoholism. He died, aged fifty-one, on 23 December 1958 from heart failure after a fall at his home at 174 Sussex Gardens, Paddington, London.   STEPHEN BOURNE

Sources J. Chilton, *Who's who of British jazz* (1997) · S. Traill and G. Lascelles, *Just jazz 3* (1959) · S. Bourne, *Brief encounters: lesbians and gays in British cinema, 1930–71* (1996) · b. cert. · d. cert.

Archives FILM BFI NFTVA, performance footage | SOUND BL NSA, performance recordings
Likenesses photograph, priv. coll. [*see illus.*]

Forfait, Pierre Alexandre (1752–1807). *See under* Industrial spies (*act. c.*1700–*c.*1800).

Forfar. For this title name *see* Douglas, Archibald, first earl of Forfar (1653–1712); Douglas, Archibald, second earl of Forfar (1692–1715).

Forggus mac Muirchertaig (*d. c.*566), joint high-king of Ireland, appears to be one of a group of northern Uí Néill kings who established a hegemony in the years after the death of Diarmait mac Cerbaill (*d.* 565). His generation lies on the edge of the annalistic record, Iona, the home of the earliest Irish annals, having been founded in 563. The annalistic references to his career partially overlap with similar, but not identical, references in Adomnán's life of St Columba. What was remembered in the annals was a series of battles, beginning in 547 (or, in an alternative dating, 543) and ending in what appears to have been the year of Forggus's death, 566. Although Forggus and his brother (and joint high-king of Ireland), Domnall, were sons of *Muirchertach, also known as Mac Ercae (*d.* 534), of Cenél nEogain, they were allied with rulers of Cenél Conaill, another branch of the Uí Néill and the one to which Columba and Adomnán belonged. Not only were their careers entwined with those of kings of Cenél Conaill, but they also belonged to the immediate context of Columba's *peregrinatio* (voluntary exile) to Britain, which Adomnán dates by reference to two of their battles. Partly for this reason, the annals contain much more about the kings of the northern Uí Néill than about Diarmait mac Cerbaill, high-king of Ireland for a much longer period, but himself of the southern Uí Néill.

Forggus's battles began with the battle of the River Sligo in 547 (or 543) fought against Éogan Bél who belonged to the Uí Fhiachrach, the most powerful kindred within the Connachta apart from the Uí Néill and particularly strong in what is now northern Connacht, in the counties of Sligo and Mayo. This may well have been the area from which the Uí Néill mounted their expansionary drive in the fifth and early sixth centuries; and Éogan Bél's grandfather, Ailill Molt (*d.* 482), is included within the lists of kings of Tara (the formal title of the high-kings). Forggus and his brother Domnall appear then as enemies of a rival group within the Connachta, very possibly one which had previously been closely allied with the Uí Néill. The prize was overlordship among the Connachta. At the River Sligo they defeated and killed Éogan Bél and followed up this success in 550 by defeating and killing two of his sons, Ailill Inbanda and Áed Fortobol, much further west, close to Clew Bay.

Forggus's next recorded battle was in 561: the battle of Cúl Dreimne became wrapped up in legends about Columba's exile in Britain, but even in the bare annalistic record it represents a clear change of direction for Forggus and his brother Domnall. They were now allied with Ainmire mac Sétni and Nainnid mac Duach of Cenél Conaill and with Áed mac Echach of the Uí Briúin, another branch of the Connachta, later centred principally in what is now co. Roscommon. Their opponent was the current high-king, Diarmait mac Cerbaill, ruler of Mide and Brega. This battle represented an attack by northern and western elements within the Connachta upon the king, who had taken the greatest prize within the grasp of the Uí Néill, domination of the midlands. The battle did not, however, give the victors the high-kingship of Ireland; that came to Forggus and his brother Domnall only in 565 after Diarmait mac Cerbaill had been killed by a Cruithnian prince. They began their reign promisingly enough, with a victory in 566 over the principal enemies of the Uí Néill, the Leinstermen, but Domnall died in the same year and his brother appears, from the fragmentary record, to have died at about the same time. They were, however, succeeded by other members of the northern Uí Néill alliance which they had built up, Ainmuire mac Sétnai of Cenél Conaill and then Domnall's brother Báetán and his son Eochaid as joint kings.

T. M. CHARLES-EDWARDS

Sources Adomnán's Life of Columba, ed. and trans. A. O. Anderson and M. O. Anderson, rev. edn, rev. M. O. Anderson, OMT (1991) · W. Stokes, ed., 'The annals of Tigernach [8 pts]', Revue Celtique, 16 (1895), 374–419; 17 (1896), 6–33, 119–263, 337–420; 18 (1897), 9–59, 150–97, 267–303, 374–91; pubd sep. (1993) · Ann. Ulster · G. Murphy, 'On the dates of two sources used in Thurneysen's Heldensage: 1. Baile Chuind and the date of Cin Dromma Snechtai', Ériu, 16 (1952), 145–56, esp. 145–51 · M. C. Dobbs, ed. and trans., 'The Banshenchus [3 pts]', Revue Celtique, 47 (1930), 283–339; 48 (1931), 163–234; 49 (1932), 437–89 · W. M. Hennessy, ed. and trans., Chronicum Scotorum: a chronicle of Irish affairs, Rolls Series, 46 (1866) · M. A. O'Brien, ed., Corpus genealogiarum Hiberniae (Dublin, 1962) · K. Meyer, ed., 'The Laud genealogies and tribal histories', Zeitschrift für Celtische Philologie, 8 (1910–12), 291–338 · F. J. Byrne, Irish kings and high-kings (1973)

Forglen. For this title name see Ogilvy, Sir Alexander, first baronet, Lord Forglen (d. 1727).

Forman family (per. 1784–c.1870), ironmasters, lived during the first half of the eighteenth century at Waltham on the Wolds in Leicestershire. **Thomas Forman** (1692–1768) was a local landowner married to Jane, née Houton, but three of his sons, **Anthony Forman** (1725–1802), **Henry Forman** (bap. 1741), baptized on 14 January 1741 at Waltham, and **Richard** [i] **Forman** (bap. 1733, d. 1794), baptized on 11 January 1733 at Waltham, left the county to take up employment in the ordnance department of the army. The brothers probably owed their appointments to the patronage of John Manners, marquess of Granby (1721–1770), eldest son of John, third duke of Rutland (1696–1779); the Rutlands were the most important landowners in the Waltham on the Wolds area. Granby was a soldier of note and became a lieutenant-general and colonel of the Royal Horse Guards. After distinguished service in the Seven Years' War he became master-general of the ordnance on 1 July 1763.

The turbulent period of the Seven Years' War and the American War of Independence saw a great expansion in the ordnance trade. As a clerk in the Board of Ordnance Richard [i] Forman witnessed this increase in trade and the effects it had on the iron industry. He spent his working life at the Tower of London, where he became proof master during the American War of Independence. He married twice; his first wife was Mary Baines, his second, Elizabeth Crewe, and his six children were baptized in the church of St Peter ad Vincula, within the Tower precincts.

Through his work for the Board of Ordnance Richard [i] Forman became associated with the *Homfray family, who had been involved in casting cannon at the Calcutts ironworks in Shropshire, and at Cyfarthfa, Merthyr Tudful, in south Wales. In 1784 Forman advanced more than £10,000 to the Homfrays to assist in funding the Penydarren ironworks at Merthyr Tudful, and he became a partner in the concern. By 1796 the Penydarren partnership included members of the Homfray family, Henry Forman of Woolwich, and Richard [i] Forman's son William. Henry Forman had by this time risen to become first secretary of the royal laboratories under Colonel Congreve.

Richard [i] Forman's sons and grandson also became employees of the Board of Ordnance. His son **Richard** [ii] **Forman** (bap. 1763, d. 1830), baptized on 15 September 1763 at St Peter ad Vincula, was employed at the Tower of London before moving to the naval branch of the office. He married on 5 June 1786 Martha Skey of Harpenden. Their son, **Richard** [iii] **Forman** (1795–1880), worked at his father's office at Chatham and later became chief storekeeper at Gibraltar, which ranked third in the garrison. He married Mary Heath (1810–1880) and died on 5 May 1880 at his home at Langley Road, Watford, Hertfordshire.

Richard [i] Forman's fourth son, **William Forman** (bap. 1767, d. 1829), baptized on 6 June 1767 at St Peter's, also combined the family's interests in the ordnance trade and the Welsh iron industry. After the Homfray family withdrew their business interests from Merthyr Tudful, William Forman became co-owner of the Penydarren ironworks with Alderman William Thompson of London, who had set up a merchant house in London in 1798 with the Homfray and Forman families. During the 1820s William Forman considerably expanded his iron-making interests, and on his death in 1829 he held a three-eighths share in the Penydarren ironworks along with shares in the Aberdâr, Tredegar, Bute, and Rhymni ironworks. Part of the capital for this expansion had been acquired through his marriage on 8 September 1789 to Mary Seaton, the daughter of a Doncaster landowner. He died at Cornwall Terrace, Regent's Park, London, on 23 July 1829.

After William's death the family's interest in the iron trade was continued through his sons, **Thomas Seaton Forman** (1791–1850), **Richard** [iv] **Forman** (d. 1882), and **William Henry Forman** (1794–1869). The brothers presided over the Forman financial empire at a time of great expansion within the Welsh iron trade. In 1830 the south Wales ironworks produced no less than 40 per cent of all the iron manufactured in Britain. Furthermore, all the Forman ironworks were to be successful producers of wrought-iron rails during the boom period from 1840 to

1860. Thomas Seaton Forman's business career encouraged him to become involved in politics, and he sat as MP for Bridgwater in Somerset from 1841 until 1847. His wealth also allowed him to purchase Pippbrook House, Dorking, in 1849, and then to indulge fully in his hobby of collecting antiques and *objets d'art*. He died in 1850 at Pisa, while on a collecting trip to Italy. He left a widow, Elizabeth, *née* Moore (*d.* 1889); they had no children and the majority of the family's wealth became concentrated in the hands of his unmarried brother, William Henry Forman, who wisely withdrew from the ownership of the Penydarren ironworks in 1859 and sold the mineral property to the Dowlais ironworks. At this time his fortune was assessed at several million pounds, some of which he contributed to church restoration. In 1853 a fire had destroyed St George's Church, Doncaster, and because of his family's connections with the town Forman offered to rebuild the south chapel at his own expense. George Gilbert Scott was employed as the architect and the rebuilt chapel became known as the Forman Chapel. Forman also engaged the Scott office to rebuild and extend Pippbrook House. He was a great collector of antiques and a private museum was built within the house. During the 1860s Forman also paid for the rebuilding of the chancel of St Martin's Church, Dorking. He died at his home, Fonthill House in Tunbridge Wells, on 28 August 1869, after three and a half years' suffering from paraplegia.

Throughout the 1860s the Forman family continued to operate their iron merchant's business in London and to hold a major share in the Tredegar ironworks. However, the family's long-standing connection with the south Wales iron trade came to an end soon after the death of William Henry Forman in 1869. An indication of the important position that the family held in the south Wales iron industry is that his will was later proved at just over £1 million. The family had been actively involved in the iron trade of south Wales for nearly ninety years, and members of the Forman family had been founding partners in three of the largest ironworks in the area.

LAURENCE INCE

Sources L. Ince, *The south Wales iron industry, 1750–1885* (1993) · J. Lloyd, *The early history of the old south Wales ironworks, 1760–1840* (1906) · *GM*, 1st ser., 99/2 (1829), 92 · *GM*, 2nd ser., 35 (1851), 335 · private information (2004) · d. cert. [William Henry Forman] · d. cert. [Richard [iv] Forman] · *CGPLA Eng. & Wales* (1869) [William Henry Forman] · *IGI* · *CGPLA Eng. & Wales* (1880) [Richard [iii] Forman] · parish register (baptisms), Doncaster, St George's, 11 Oct 1791 [Thomas Seaton Forman] · *CGPLA Eng. & Wales* (1882) [Richard [iv] Forman] · parish register (marriage), Doncaster, St George's, 8 Sept 1789 [William Forman]

Wealth at death under £1,100,000—William Henry Forman: resworn probate, Feb 1878, *CGPLA Eng. & Wales* (1869) · £19,046 7s. 5d.—Richard [iv] Forman: probate, 6 April 1882, *CGPLA Eng. & Wales*

Forman, Alfred William (1840–1925), translator, was born on 13 September 1840 at Camden Place, Southampton Street, Camberwell, the fourth of the eight children of George Ellery Forman (1800–1867), naval surgeon, and his wife, Maria Courthorpe (1805–1888). The family soon moved to Teignmouth in Devon where Alfred went to Thorn Park School (*c.*1850–1854), and then moved to the Royal Naval School at New Cross, London, in 1854. He left in 1857 and never settled to a career. He started at a colonial broker's office in Mincing Lane, followed that with some ten years as a paper merchant with two different firms, from 1890 to 1891 he was secretary to the New English Art Club, then worked for four years for Robert Cocks & Co., music publishers; he finally ended with a menial job in the General Post Office telephone service. On 30 September 1876 he married Alma (1856–1945), daughter of Leigh Murray, a well-known character actor of the 1840s. Alma Murray gained a reputation for undertaking challenging roles, appearing in the Shelley Society's production of *The Cenci* in 1886 and creating Raina Petkoff in Shaw's *Arms and the Man* in 1894. They had one child, Elsa (1878–1966), who never married and was for many years secretary of the Keats–Shelley Association.

Forman heard one of Edward Dannreuther's Wagner concerts in 1873 and concluded that there had 'been given to the world something so new and so great that it would be at my own spiritual risk if I deferred for a moment longer the attempt to come to an understanding with it' (Forman, 'Pioneer', 463). He privately printed his translation of *Die Walküre* in 1873 and sent a copy to Wagner, who encouraged him. By 1876 all four parts of his translation of The Ring had been printed and Forman went to Bayreuth to present them to Wagner. This was during the first complete performance, to which Forman contributed the stage animals, ordered from Richard Keene of Wandsworth, a well-known maker of pantomime props. In 1877 Wagner visited England and Forman was lent the manuscript of *Parsifal* overnight; just before this, he was sent the libretto of a scene from *Die Walküre* which was later acquired by his brother Henry (Harry) Buxton *Forman (1842–1917) (it was lot 890 in the first part of the sale of his library). Alfred Forman's other Wagner translations appeared in 1891 (*Tristan*), 1899 (*Parsifal*), and posthumously in 1928 (*Tannhäuser*). He was Wagner's first translator, but his style was very stilted, and he was superseded by H. and F. Corder, Margaret Glyn, J. P. Jackson, Ernest Newman, and others. In *Parsifal*, for instance, his knights urge Amfortas to 'unmuffle the grail'.

Forman, like his brother, was a friend of John Payne, translator and writer of verse, and was for some ten years secretary of the Villon Society. This was initially formed to print Payne's translations of Villon, and in due course all of Payne's work. Forman produced a number of other translations (Dante, Victor Hugo, Grillparzer, Aeschylus), but most remained in manuscript. Like his brother he had poetical leanings and he produced a volume of sonnets in 1886. He was a neat, fastidious man with a short pointed beard in later life. He was never well off, though he received a small pension from 1916 in recognition of his Wagner work, and his family was left in somewhat straitened circumstances. Unlike his brother he remained a churchgoer to the end of his days. He died on 19 December 1925 at 49 Comeragh Road, Baron's Court, London, where he had lived for many years.

J. F. R. COLLINS

Sources J. Collins, 'A short note on Alfred William Forman, 1840–1925', *Book Collector*, 23 (1974), 69–76 · J. Collins, *The two forgers: a biography of Harry Buxton Forman and Thomas James Wise* (1992), 285 [note from W. C. Forman] · W. C. Forman, 'A pioneer of Richard Wagner in England', *Cornhill Magazine*, [3rd] ser., 62 (1927), 462–6, esp. 463 · private information (2004) · b. cert. · m. cert. · d. cert. · parish register, Camberwell, St George's, 14 Oct 1840 [baptism]
Likenesses G. D. Hammond, pencil sketch, 1912, priv. coll.
Wealth at death under £1000: private information

Forman, Andrew (*c.*1465–1521), diplomat and archbishop of St Andrews, was probably the son of Nicholas Forman of Hatton, Berwickshire, and his wife, Janet Blackadder. He had at least two brothers. A determinant at St Andrews University in 1481, he graduated there two years later, when he was probably about eighteen; he does not appear to have proceeded MA. In the late 1480s he was employed by Archibald Douglas, fifth earl of Angus, but by October 1489 had also entered the service of the crown, and in 1490 he was James IV's procurator in Rome, where he was made an apostolic protonotary. In 1495–6 he had the task of escorting Perkin Warbeck during James's temporary espousal of the pretender's cause as a means of putting pressure on Henry VII, and received £69 8s. for Perkin's expenses. He was subsequently heavily engaged in efforts to make peace between England and Scotland. By 3 June 1497 he had been rewarded with the commendatorship of Pittenweem, and in the following year he was given an annual pension of 1000 crowns, to continue until his promotion to a bishopric or abbacy. In May 1501 Henry VII granted him the Yorkshire rectory of Cottingham, and on 26 November he was provided to the see of Moray. To these were added the commendatorships of Dryburgh (1509) and Kelso (1511), the lease of Dunbar Mains, the keepership of Darnaway Castle, and the posts of chamberlain of Moray and custumar north of the Spey.

Essentially a career diplomat, Forman owed his position entirely to royal service. In 1502 he was regarded as the principal architect on the Scottish side of that year's 'perpetual peace' with England. In 1508 he stated that he was opposed to the renewal of Scotland's alliance with France, but his position was always liable to change as royal policy dictated, and in this he may just have been following the king's lead. He travelled to Blois in 1510 to urge Louis XII to make peace with the pope, and to Italy in 1511 to try to reconcile Louis to the Venetians. These embassies were ostensibly undertaken in aid of James's plans for a crusade, but more truly reflected his policy of trying to influence continental affairs by acting as a mediator between the major European powers. Louis sent Forman back to Scotland empowered to make any terms that would prevent Scotland's joining the Holy League against France. Forman also used his embassies to press for personal advancement and rewards, but with varying success. He hoped that a further mission to the papal and French courts in 1513 would bring him a cardinal's hat, hinted at by Pope Julius II, but this eluded him with the latter's death and the succession of the less favourably disposed Pope Leo X. Greater success attended Forman's mission to France, for on 15 July Louis XII secured his provision to the archbishopric of

Bourges. His elevation reflected Louis's eagerness to persuade the Scots to go to war against the English, and Forman was certainly one of the principal supporters of the Franco–Scottish alliance, and of the campaign which was to culminate so disastrously at Flodden.

The Flodden campaign, ending as it did with the death of King James and the destruction of his army, dealt a severe blow to Forman, who was denounced by his enemies (and by later chroniclers) as the 'evil counsellor' whose malign advice had lured the king to disaster. Such a reputation did not help Forman's candidacy, late in 1513, for the vacant primatial see of St Andrews, particularly as he had a number of powerful rivals, led by Cardinal Innocenzo Cibo, Leo X's nephew, whom his uncle provided on 13 October. Forman had some influence on the continent, however, with the support, at least at first, of John Stewart, fourth duke of Albany, who was shortly to become governor of Scotland, and also through his own position as archbishop of Bourges. In April 1514 Leo and Albany worked out the eventual solution to the problem, whereby Forman would be translated to St Andrews while resigning Bourges in favour of Cibo, who would in turn abandon his claim to the Scottish primacy. But although he was formally provided to St Andrews on 13 November, and granted the coveted title of *legatus a latere* on 11 December, Forman also had to face no fewer than three rivals in Scotland itself. The most distinguished of them, the aged William Elphinstone of Aberdeen, was nominated by the Scottish council in October 1513 but died a year later. Forman's bulls of provision were published in Scotland in January 1515, by which date he had been opposed by John Hepburn, prior of St Andrews, who had been elected by the convent late in 1514. Hepburn had the support of magnates hostile to Queen Margaret, but this was insufficient to secure him the archbishopric, and eventually he renounced his claim. A more substantial opponent was Gavin Douglas, provost of St Giles, Edinburgh, who received the crown nomination after Elphinstone's death, and was able to occupy St Andrews Castle. However, Douglas was unable to withstand the pope's support for Forman, and in 1515 he accepted the see of Dunkeld.

Forman nevertheless found it difficult to win acceptance in Scotland. The council accused him of having caused the war of 1513, and also of infringing crown privileges by purchasing bulls for St Andrews and for the commendatorships of Dunfermline and Arbroath. Such was the strength of feeling against him that Albany returned to Scotland in May 1515 without him, and when Forman sailed for Scotland later that month Albany had him detained in Pittenweem Priory until the end of the year. By July Albany had secured grudging agreement to Forman's appointment from the lords of council, but only around the beginning of February 1516 did he hand over the temporalities of the see. Forman was principally involved in secular business thereafter, but he did not entirely neglect his diocese, which he administered through vicars-general. Early in his tenure he held a number of diocesan synods, and issued constitutions dealing with such matters as clerical non-residence and concubinage, wills, and the holding of ecclesiastical courts.

Following Albany's departure for France in June 1517 Forman was one of seven vice-regents appointed to exercise the governor's authority during his absence. To the crisis precipitated on 17 September by the murder near Duns of Antoine d'Arces, seigneur de la Bastie, Albany's principal deputy, was added extensive unrest caused by threats to vested territorial interests and the personal antipathy between the earls of Arran and Angus. Forman and his fellow councillors tried to reconcile the earls, but the intransigence of Angus, who resented Arran's lieutenancy of the Merse, led to a hardening of the council's attitude towards him, and in 1518 Forman had little choice but to concur in the council's attacks on the interests of the Douglases, even though they were his own former patrons. Another victim of those attacks was Forman's erstwhile rival for St Andrews, Gavin Douglas, who was Angus's brother. Forman obtained papal briefs against him, while at the same time effectively denying him a licence to go to Rome to defend himself. Such partisanship implies that Albany's return to Scotland was expected, despite the determination of Henry VIII to prevent it, but in 1519 it came to look increasingly unlikely, and on 26 February Angus rejoined the council. Angus was concerned for his political position in the face of the threat of divorce from Queen Margaret, whom he had married as her second husband in 1514, and appealed to Forman as legate to make Margaret live with him as his wife or show reasonable cause why she should not.

Angus's return to the council did not lead to an easing of tension, and by the end of the year the government was divided into clear Angus and Arran factions. Most of the surviving regents now supported Angus, including Forman, but the primate continued to seek compromise and the avoidance of conflict, for instance in the dispute of November 1519 over the provostship of Edinburgh, from which Arran had been ousted by the burgesses in favour of Archibald Douglas of Kilspindie. Forman also continued to play a part in diplomacy, though here too his efforts might suffer from factional politics. When an English embassy arrived in Edinburgh in December 1520 Forman was there to greet them, but nothing could be done because Chancellor Beaton and the earls of Arran and Lennox stayed away. Some four months later, on 18 April 1521, negotiations for an Anglo-Scottish truce were postponed until June, for reasons which included Forman's death at Dunfermline on 11 March. Forman was buried in his cathedral at St Andrews. He had an illegitimate daughter, Jane, recorded in 1519, but his heir and executor was his brother Robert, to whom he had earlier transferred the commendatorship of Pittenweem.

C. A. McGLADDERY

Sources N. Macdougall, *James IV* (1989) · W. K. Emond, 'The minority of James V, 1513–1528', PhD diss., U. St Andr., 1988 · J. Herkless and R. K. Hannay, *The archbishops of St Andrews*, 5 vols. (1907–15), vol. 2 · J. Dowden, *The bishops of Scotland ... prior to the Reformation*, ed. J. M. Thomson (1912) · D. E. R. Watt, ed., *Fasti ecclesiae Scoticanae medii aevi ad annum 1638*, [2nd edn], Scottish RS, new ser., 1 (1969) · *LP Henry VIII*, vols. 1–3

Forman, Anthony (1725–1802). *See under* Forman family (*per.* 1784–c.1870).

Forman, Charles (d. **1739**), political pamphleteer and translator, was an Irishman by birth, educated as a Roman Catholic, and a Jacobite. Before 1709 he married a woman named Mary in Ireland, where at least one of their sons was born. By December 1710 he was in London; by December 1713 he was an army agent (salary £40 p.a.) and soon afterwards was also first clerk in the war office.

In November 1715 Forman delayed orders to the English force opposing Jacobite rebels in Lancashire; when the rebellion failed he fled to France with his wife and two daughters, sending three sons to Ireland. The younger daughter, Charlotte *Forman, born on 23 October 1715, was 'nursed in the palace of the Trianon' (BL, Add. MS 30869, fol. 165). In April 1718 the Pretender granted Forman a pension of 45 livres a month—perhaps discontinued by 1720, when Forman became secretary to John Law (1671–1729), comptroller-general of the finances in France. Forman shared the disgrace when Law's 'Mississippi scheme' crashed in that year and was heavily fined by the French government. In May 1721 he made the first of several unsuccessful attempts to obtain a pension or employment from the English government.

Forman's earliest traced publication is a *Letter* to William Pulteney, dated Amsterdam 24 October 1724, warning of dangers to British commerce from the Austrian imperial trading company at Ostend. In following years Forman wrote a dozen meddlesome self-important pamphlets on politics and commerce, containing frequent obscure references to persecution he had suffered on both sides of the channel. These were printed in London, but mostly dated from Amsterdam, Rotterdam, or (after April 1731) Paris. One of his four pamphlets addressed satirically to Walpole (Pulteney's antagonist) has literary pretensions: this is *Protesilaus, or, The Character of an Evil Minister* (1730), an allegorical paraphrase of the tenth book of Fénelon's *Telemachus*. Forman's most successful work was *A Defence of the Courage, Honour, and Loyalty of the Irish Nation*, dated Paris 14 April 1731, of which there were successively enlarged fifth and sixth editions in 1735 and 1736, and a reprint as late as 1767.

In August 1734 Forman made his peace with Walpole, hitherto his chief enemy, and returned to London, but he was still known as a Jacobite and was soon charged with seditious libel for having, in the *Daily Post* on 2 and 20 December 1735, insinuated that the treaty of Seville (1729) contained a secret article restoring Gibraltar to Spain. He was arrested in January 1736, and, unable to find bail of £400, was confined until May of that year, when charges were dropped and he was released.

Forman turned to hack translations from the French, including *The Adventures of Malouka, the Beautiful Arabian* (August 1738), *An Historical Account of the Antient Parliaments of France* (1739), and an abridged version of Crousaz's commentary on epistle 1 of Pope's *Essay on Man* (1739). The last was published by Edmund Curll and advertised as 'a critical Satire' (*Public Advertiser*, 25 Nov 1738), but it is in fact friendly to Pope. Forman's complaint in the preface to *Malouka* that Dangervilliers, a French secretary of state, was plotting to abduct or assassinate him prompted another libel charge, which, like the first, did not come to court. He died in London on 28 April 1739.

JAMES SAMBROOK

Sources *Calendar of the Stuart papers belonging to his majesty the king, preserved at Windsor Castle*, 7 vols., HMC, 56 (1902–23), vol. 2, pp. 321; vol. 3, p. 2; vol. 4, pp. 265, 275; vol. 6, pp. 126, 142, 172, 297–9, 412, 464; vol. 7, p. 154 · R. Wodrow, *Analecta, or, Materials for a history of remarkable providences, mostly relating to Scotch ministers and Christians*, ed. [M. Leishman], 3, Maitland Club, 60 (1843), 233 · *GM*, 1st ser., 9 (1739), 272 · C. Forman, *Mr Forman's letter to the Right Honourable William Pulteney* (1725) · C. Forman, 'Mr Forman's letter to a friend in Paris, 23 September 1734', *A letter to the author of a pamphlet, intitled, a letter to a friend* (1734) · C. Forman, *A defence of the courage, honour, and loyalty of the Irish nation* (1731) · PRO, SP 36/33, fols. 33–8, 130, 139, 150, 156, 263 · PRO, TS 11/157, fols. 533–4 · BL, Add. MS 22521, fols. 52–7 · C. Dalton, *George the First's army, 1714–1727*, 1 (1910), 234 · W. A. Shaw, ed., *Calendar of treasury books*, 29, PRO (1957–9), 167 · J. Redington, ed., *Calendar of Treasury papers*, 5, PRO (1883), 85 · B. Rizzo, 'Forman, Charlotte (1716–1787)', *A dictionary of British and American women writers, 1660–1800*, ed. J. Todd (1984) · BL, Add. MS 30869, fols. 165–6 · C. Forman, *A letter to the Right Honourable Sir Walpole concerning the election of a king of Poland* (1733) · C. Forman, *A letter to the Right Honourable Sir Robert Sutton* (1728) · G. C. Gibbs, 'Britain and the alliance of Hanover, April 1725–February 1726', *EngHR*, 73 (1958), 419–20

Archives BL, letters to Sir Robert Sutton and Lord Carteret, Add. MS 22521, fols. 52–7 · PRO, letters to an unknown, highly placed Frenchman, complaining about Forman's treatment in France, SP 36/33, fols. 33–8 · PRO, letters to George Tilson (under-secretary in Lord Harrington's office), concerning Forman's confinement and release, SP 36/38, fols. 150, 156, 263 · PRO, warrant to apprehend Forman and notes concerning his bail, SP 36/38, fols. 130, 139 · PRO, draft information by the attorney-general concerning libel charges against Forman, TS 11/157, fols. 533–4

Forman, Charlotte [*pseud.* Probus] (**1715–1787**), journalist and translator, was born on 23 October 1715, perhaps in England, one of five children of Charles *Forman, an Irish Jacobite and pamphleteer, and his wife, Mary. Charles was a clerk in the English war office at the time of the Jacobite rising of 1715; he delayed sending orders to the English general Charles Wills, who was fighting the Jacobites, then fled to France with his wife and two daughters. Three sons remained in Ireland. Charles Forman continued in exile on the continent until 1734, supporting himself and his family with a pension from the Jacobite court, work as a secretary to John Law, and the writing or translating of political pamphlets. Much later, Charlotte wrote that she had been genteely bred and 'nursed in the palace of the Trianon' (BL, Add. MS 30869, fol. 165).

Charlotte Forman was virtually unknown in her lifetime, yet her career as a newspaper journalist has significance because of the light it sheds on the history of journalism and because she was one of the few women of the period who wrote successfully about subjects conventionally considered masculine. She is not known to have published anything under her own name and she almost certainly published some works anonymously that cannot now be attributed to her.

Forman was the author of a long series of topical political essays that first appeared in the *Gazetteer and London Daily Advertiser* between 1756 and 1760, then continued in the *Public Ledger, or, Daily Register of Commerce and Intelligence* in 1760. Both newspapers were designed to appeal to London merchants, traders, and shopkeepers. Their columns were filled with shipping news and offers of wholesale and retail goods, as well as with foreign, London, and provincial news. They printed some letters from readers, like our modern letters to the editor, but they also featured letters addressed 'To the printer' from more regular correspondents, like Forman, who were paid.

Forman's essays in *The Gazetteer* and the *Public Ledger*, all signed Probus, were written in the months leading up to the declaration of the Seven Years' War in 1756 and during the war. A large number of these roughly 200 surviving Probus essays comment upon the diplomatic news, offering historical background relevant to understanding the interests of the contending nations, weighing the credibility of various news reports, and analysing the interests of England, Prussia, France, Holland, Austria, Russia, Spain, Sweden, and Denmark. Probus consistently supports the English war effort, reassures readers that England has the capacity to defeat France, defends Frederick the Great and William Pitt from critics, and argues against a premature peace that would make unnecessary concessions to France.

Probus's second major subject, equally unfeminine, is political arithmetic, including state finance of the war, but also more general matters of political economy like trade regulation, taxation, and the finance of public works. Probus worries repeatedly about the level of national debt (although he accepts a well-managed national debt of 30 million pounds as good for commerce), insists that flourishing commerce and knowledge of the arts of peace are as essential to national welfare as are the arts of war, and proposes such fiscal measures as more equal assessments for the land tax and a tax on houses.

Given the pseudonym Probus and the style and content of the essays, it is hardly surprising that contemporary readers responding to Probus assumed they were responding to a 'gentleman'. Indeed, the author of an excellent monograph on *The Gazetteer* also assumed they were written by a man and singled them out as 'a particularly well-written series … obviously written by a professional connected with or paid by the *Gazetteer*' (Haig, 38). Were it not for the fact that John Almon, who was associated with *The Gazetteer*, in 1805 identified Charlotte Forman as Probus, there would be no reason to imagine that these essays were written by a woman. Almost none of them even touches on subjects associated with women. One rare exception enthusiastically greets the publication of Charlotte Lennox's magazine, the *Lady's Museum*. Creating ironies that could only have been appreciated by insiders at the newspaper, Probus comments:

> Though by nature inclined to dry investigations and serious contemplations, and partly by accident led into political disquisitions and speculations, I am nevertheless a great admirer of the literary productions of the fair sex, and, as often as I have time to spare, fly to them for relaxation, being

always charmed with their easy, graceful, delicate sentiments, the pure language of nature, which they never lose sight of. (*Public Ledger*, 16 Feb 1760)

The Probus essays were popular enough to be reprinted in other newspapers including *Lloyd's Evening Post* and the *London Chronicle*, yet the surviving biographical information about Forman emphasizes her often desperate poverty. Never married, until 1764 she received £50 per annum, probably from her brother Charles. When that income ceased, she began to translate for John Meres, publisher of the *London Evening-Post*. She was arrested for debt in 1766 and, probably briefly, confined to the Marshalsea prison. In 1768 and 1769 she was translating the foreign news, first for John Meres and then for Charles Say, publisher of *The Gazetteer*. Fearing another arrest for debt in June 1768 and eviction from her rented London room, she appealed for patronage to a stranger most distressed gentlewomen would not have considered a likely protector: the radical John Wilkes, himself then incarcerated in the king's bench prison. Her letter to Wilkes relates that her 'sallary for translating is but nine shillings a week', a sum so small that she reasonably says it makes her 'like the day labourer' (Gold, 41). Wilkes did assist her. In March 1769 Say, who was already behind in paying her wages, informed her that her services as a translator for *The Gazetteer* would no longer be needed. Her letters to Wilkes written between 12 June 1768 and 9 April 1770 describe her grinding poverty, a solitary life in a rented room 'where I am obliged to stop the chasms of the old casements with rags to keep out the wind' (ibid.). So little hope did she have of substantially bettering her condition by selling her writing that she told Wilkes, 'I may as well hope, that in time, I shall become Queen of England, as expect to get a competency by the pen, and clear off old scores' (ibid.).

It is possible that Forman was also the author of about two dozen letters, also signed Probus, that appeared in London newspapers from 1773 to 1775. However, these letters, expressing a Wilkite view of liberty in the years leading up to the American War of Independence, cannot be securely attributed to her. Forman died on 23 December 1787 and was buried at St Bride's Church in London.

SUSAN STAVES

Sources *Gazetteer and London Daily Advertiser* (Jan 1756–Dec 1760) · *Public Ledger, or, Daily Register of Commerce and Intelligence* (Jan–June 1760) · J. Gold, '"Buried alive": Charlotte Forman in Grub Street', *Eighteenth-Century Life* (1982), 28–45 · R. L. Haig, *The Gazetteer, 1735–1797: a study in the eighteenth-century English newspaper* (1960) · B. Rizzo, 'Charlotte Forman', *Dictionary of British women writers*, ed. J. Todd (1989) · R. Rea, *The English press in politics, 1760–1774* (1963) · *Calendar of the Stuart papers belonging to his majesty the king, preserved at Windsor Castle*, 7 vols., HMC, 56 (1902–23)

Archives BL, Add. MS 30867, fol. 165; Add. MS 30870, fols. 52–3, 66–8, 82–3, 99, 117–18, 179–80, 216, 238–9, 239; Add. MS 30871, fol. 26

Forman, Henry (*bap.* 1741). *See under* Forman family (*per.* 1784–*c*.1870).

Forman, Henry Buxton [Harry] (1842–1917), bibliographer and forger, was born on 11 July 1842 at Camden Place, Southampton Street, Camberwell, the third son

Henry Buxton Forman (1842–1917), by unknown photographer [detail]

and fifth child of the eight children of George Ellery Forman (1800–1867), naval surgeon, and his wife, Maria Courthorpe (1805–1888). He was baptized Henry but was always known as Harry and this name appears on all his books and on his death certificate. The family soon moved to Teignmouth in Devon and Harry had a happy childhood playing on the beach and being educated at Thorn Park School, which he left in 1860 to go to London and become a supplementary clerk in the Post Office. Three years later Edmund Gosse was a pupil at the same school, which he describes in *Father and Son*. In addition to his literary work, Forman was to remain at the Post Office all his life, retiring in 1907 with a CB, which he was awarded in the Diamond Jubilee honours in 1897. He produced a report on European parcel post in 1882 (in preparation for the introduction of the same in the United Kingdom) and became the acknowledged overseas expert at the Post Office headquarters at St Martins-le-Grand. He was appointed surveyor of British post offices in the Mediterranean in 1883, was a delegate at four international postal congresses, and ended his career, as controller of packet services, in charge of the Post Office contracts for carrying overseas mail.

On 16 February 1869 Forman married Laura (1841–1932), daughter of William Selle, the organist at Hampton Court. Their three children were Eliot Buxton (1870–1931), Gwendolen Buxton (1871–1930), and Maurice Buxton (1872–1957). The youngest took a job in the South African post office and also followed his father as editor and forger.

In his spare time Forman wrote a great deal, leaving an unpublished verse epic on Devon of 10,000 lines. His first published work was a story in *Aunt Judy's Magazine* in 1867, and his first published book *Our Living Poets* (1871). This was respectfully reviewed, and his treatment of the Rossettis brought him to the attention of that family. His literary interests crystallized round Keats and Shelley. He channelled a general enthusiasm into a minute study of textual details, for which his careful and exacting temperament was ideally suited. His patient application produced impressive editions of Shelley (8 vols., 1876–80) and Keats (4 vols., 1883). His most controversial piece of scientific editing was *The Letters of John Keats to Fanny Brawne* (1876), as there was thought to be something improper in the publication of such frank letters. After the fuss had died down, Forman's insistence on what the author wrote was seen to be correct, and his editions became standard and his methods widely adopted. He produced many later and improved editions, his popular position culminating in the Oxford Standard Authors edition of Keats (1907), reprinted many times in many hundreds of thousands of copies. His son Maurice inherited his father's role, his last contribution being the fourth edition of Keats's letters, in 1952. Forman's researches on other writers connected to his major interest and led to other books, including editions of Charles Jeremiah Wells's *Joseph and his Brethren* (1876) and Edward Trelawny's letters (1910). He had a lifelong interest in Elizabeth Barrett Browning and William Morris; he edited *Aurora Leigh*, and some unpublished poems, and produced *The Books of William Morris* (1897), still considered the standard bibliography one hundred years after its publication. He was much impressed by Morris, whom he knew for twenty-five years; yet his bibliography is a flawed tribute which includes a number of his own forgeries. He patronized J. D. Hosken, the postman poet of Cornwall, and arranged for the printing of his *The Betrothal of Venus* (1903). Forman was the literary executor of R. H. 'Orion' Horne and inherited his library; when he sold much of this in 1884, one lot included the first creative forgery. This was Horne's 'Galatea secunda', a four-page pamphlet with the imprint 'Melbourne, 1867' but actually printed in London about 1881. Forman was printing a piece which plausibly could have appeared at that time and place but in fact did not. It is not a literary forgery—the poem is certainly by Horne—and since there is no original for comparison, that method of detecting a forgery is ruled out. 'Galatea secunda' may have been no more than a literary conceit, to please a dying poet. However, the concept of a creative forgery was to be exploited by a team consisting of Forman himself and his acquaintance Thomas James *Wise.

Forman and Wise first met in 1886, a connection made through the Shelley Society, and its publication programme of reprints and new works on the poet. In the next year they jointly printed a piracy from Dowden's *Life of Shelley* (1886) with a false imprint and an imaginary editor (Shelley's *Poems and Sonnets*, edited by 'Charles Alfred Seymour' [probably T. J. Wise] and printed in 'Philadelphia' [London, Richard Clay]). This was the forerunner of a clandestine publishing programme of some hundred piracies and forgeries, of which some sixty creative forgeries were the most novel. In broad terms, Forman was the editorial director, and Wise the production manager and sales director. This programme falsified the bibliography and thus the publishing history of Swinburne, Morris, Kipling, Lewis Carroll, Rossetti, Tennyson, Wordsworth, George Eliot, Ruskin, Matthew Arnold, Thackeray, Dickens, Meredith, and the Brownings. Its most remarkable achievement was to rewrite the literary history of Elizabeth Barrett Browning's *Sonnets from the Portuguese*, which was supposed to have appeared as a pamphlet privately published in Reading in 1847, rather than in the second edition of her collected poems three years later. The two conspirators gained both financially and in being able to announce new discoveries, often in their own bibliographies. In many cases these are still the standard works, being otherwise sound, so that the forgeries have had a very long life, and some may remain as yet undetected.

Forman seems to have repented of the partnership, but he was not able to free himself. He died on 15 June 1917 at 46 Marlborough Hill, St John's Wood, London, his home for many years. Wise supervised the disposal of his extensive and interesting library (most of which was sold in three sales in New York in 1920) and wrote the *Dictionary of National Biography* article on Forman, his fellow conspirator. Forman was a tall, somewhat gangling man with a large and flowing beard. Determined and very knowledgeable in his own fields he was a rather daunting figure to meet socially and was never much at ease with small talk. In his early years he was a convinced positivist and follower of Comte, but this enthusiasm seems to have waned. He left funeral instructions in verse; he was cremated, and his ashes scattered on Dartmoor in the River Teign, which runs down to the sea at Teignmouth.

J. F. R. COLLINS

Sources J. Collins, *The two forgers: a biography of Harry Buxton Forman and Thomas James Wise* (1992) · J. Carter and G. Pollard, *An enquiry into the nature of certain nineteenth century pamphlets*, 2nd edn (1983) · N. Barker and J. Collins, *A sequel to an enquiry* (1983) · b. cert. · m. cert. · d. cert. · parish register, Camberwell, St George's, 10 Aug 1842 [baptism]
Archives BL, corresp. with James Dykes Campbell, Add. MS 49525 A, *passim* · BL, letters to T. J. Wise · Keats House, Hampstead, London, corresp. with Fanny Keats · University of Delaware, Newark, papers relating to John Keats · University of Western Ontario, London, Ontario, D. B. Weldon Library, letters to Richard Maurice Bucke
Likenesses photograph, repro. in *St Martins-le-Grand: the Post Office Magazine*, 15 (1908) · photograph, University of Western Ontario, London, Canada · photograph, Keats House, London [see illus.]
Wealth at death £27,509 15s. 11d.: probate, 28 Aug 1917, CGPLA Eng. & Wales

Forman, Richard (*bap.* **1733**, *d.* **1794**). *See under* Forman family (*per.* 1784–*c.*1870).

Forman, Richard (*bap.* **1763**, *d.* **1830**). *See under* Forman family (*per.* 1784–*c.*1870).

Forman, Richard (**1795–1880**). *See under* Forman family (*per.* 1784–*c.*1870).

Forman, Richard (*d.* **1882**). *See under* Forman family (*per.* 1784–*c.*1870).

Forman, Simon (**1552–1611**), astrologer and medical practitioner, was born in Quidhampton, Wiltshire, on 31 December 1552, the fifth of the eight children of William Forman (1524–1564) and his wife, Mary (*c.*1505–1602), daughter of John Ratewe and Marion Hallam. His grandfather Richard Forman was governor of Wilton Abbey before the suppression of the monasteries. Forman began school at the St Giles's Priory when he was eight. He then spent two years at school in Salisbury, but when he returned home for Christmas in 1563 his father died (1 January 1564). For a short time his mother made him do manual labour, but he was soon able to return to school in Salisbury.

On 8 February 1567 Forman apprenticed himself to Matthew Commin, a hosier and grocer, from whom he learned to sew and make hose, as well as the 'knowledge of all wares and drugs and howe to buy and selle'. He 'grue soe apte and had such good fortune that in shorte tyme his master committed all to his charge' (Bodl. Oxf., MS Ashmole 208, fol. 138v). A condition of the apprenticeship was that he be allowed to attend the free school for the first three years of the ten. This was not fulfilled, and his master confiscated his Latin books to discourage him from studying in the evenings. He was none the less able to maintain his previous learning by engaging a schoolboy who lodged with his master to teach him by night all he had learned by day. Forman was on good terms with his master, but was forced to break the apprenticeship on 24 June 1572 after a serious quarrel with his mistress.

Forman returned to Quidhampton and attended the free school for two months, until his mother refused to maintain him further. He then became a schoolmaster himself at the St Giles's Priory, and over the next six months saved 40 shillings. On 20 May 1573 he went to Oxford with Thomas Ridear. He entered Magdalen College as a poor scholar, and studied at the school attached to the college. John Thornborough, a demy of the college (ultimately bishop of Worcester), and Robert Pinkney of St Mary Hall took him into their service. Forman was unable to study as much as he would have liked, frequently accompanying these gentlemen hunting and on visits to court the daughters of Dr Lawrence of Cowley.

Forman left Oxford on 12 September 1574, and until midsummer 1578 taught at several schools in Wiltshire. During this time he began to study astronomy, physic, magic, philosophy, and surgery 'wherein he profited and professed mightily' (Forman, MS Ashmole 208, fol. 225). In 1579 he was imprisoned by a sheriff of Salisbury, Giles Estcourt, for a year, the first of several such sentences. He had another encounter with Estcourt in 1587 when he was imprisoned for having been found in possession of a number of magical books (*CSP dom., 1581–90*, 394). After Forman's release from his first prison sentence in 1580 he moved to Greenwich where he worked as a carpenter and continued practising physic. In August he claimed to have cured a Henry Jonson of a consumption, and the two travelled to the Low Countries, including the Netherlands, where they stayed at The Hague for a fortnight.

Forman was home again in October, and spent a year in Quidhampton where he treated lame and sick people, including a man who had a severe case of the king's evil. He was bound over at the Lent assizes, and lived by manual labour until October 1581, when he moved to Salisbury, took a house on the ditch by the skinnery, and practised astrology, physic, and surgery. About this time he began to keep a diary of the weather and prices. In June 1582 he became acquainted with Anne Young (d. 1600), his

first mistress, with whom he had at least one child, Joshua Walworth (1585–1603), before the relationship ended in June 1588. In September 1582 he went to sea with Robert Grey, and was captured by pirates at Studland. He returned to Salisbury in October, and became schoolmaster to John Penruddock's children.

Throughout 1583 Forman frequently travelled from Salisbury to London 'in business' with Mrs Penruddock. By 1584 he was able to support himself through his medical and astrological practice and left the Penruddocks. In 1585 he travelled around the country, engaged in a number of legal disputes over payment of medical fees and other matters, and copied a number of alchemical manuscripts. In the summer he was imprisoned by the bishop of Salisbury. The lawsuits continued through 1586, though he was discharged from the assizes, and was 'made friends' with the bishop of Salisbury by Lord Anderson and Sir John Danvers. In March 1587 he spent another month in prison.

In August 1588 Forman began to call angels and spirits and to practise necromancy. In 1589 he was impressed into the navy but within a month he was in prison in Hampton. The next few years were very troublesome for him. He moved frequently throughout London, Surrey, and Wiltshire, often staying with friends, and suffered from venereal disease. Much of his time seems to have been spent in pursuit of the philosophers' stone.

On 10 April 1591 Forman went to London and stayed with Emery Molyneux whom he taught his method for finding longitude (but who rejected it). That summer Forman's only printed work, *The Groundes of Longitude*, was published by Thomas Dawson. In it Forman advertises that Robert Parkes (a merchant with whom he had stayed the previous year) received this method through divine revelation, and that the method could be learned from either Parkes or himself. Forman vilified some of London's most prominent mathematical practitioners for rejecting this method, including Molyneux, Thomas Hariot, and Thomas Hood, who responded with a pamphlet attack on Forman which is now lost.

In 1592 Forman's fortunes changed. He moved to Stone House in Philpot Lane, London, in February, and in the summer he caught what he called the plague, from which he suffered for twenty-one weeks. He cured himself by lancing his boils and taking a special drink. Having discovered this method, Forman used it to cure others of the plague, and thereby established a strong reputation as a medical practitioner. He soon began to clear his debts. During this time he began what was to be a rather tumultuous relationship with a recusant, a married woman called Avis Allen, which lasted intermittently until her death on 13 June 1597.

By 1595, despite periodic imprisonment, Forman's astrological medical practice was thriving. He was consulted more than 8000 times between March 1596 and 1603. Most of his consultations were for medical questions; others concerned lost or stolen property, missing persons, preferment, and the prospects for various journeys and voyages. He was popular with women, and was consulted frequently by some members of the gentry. In 1596 he began his most substantial treatise, *The Astrologicalle Judgementes of Phisick and other Questions* (Bodl. Oxf., MSS Ashmole 363, 389, 403), a vernacular guide to astrological medicine, which was to undergo numerous revisions, and which he planned to have printed in 1599 with a prefatory defence of judicial astrology by Richard Napier, to whom Forman had taught astrology in 1596. This work failed to materialize. In autumn 1597 he moved to Lambeth, perhaps to escape the jurisdiction of the College of Physicians. In summer 1598 he moved back to London.

Forman's success as a medical practitioner and his magical techniques attracted attention from the regulatory authorities of London as they had from the authorities in Wiltshire and Salisbury. In February 1593 he was called before the Barber–Surgeons for the first and only time. In March 1595 he was called before the College of Physicians. According to the college, he confessed that he had practised medicine in England for sixteen years, but in London for only two, claimed to have effected many cures, stated that the only medical authors he had studied were 'Corkes and Wainefleet', and boasted that he needed no other help than the ephemerides to know diseases. ('Corkes' is Johan Cockys, a fourteenth-century Oxford medical master and the author of a manuscript which Forman had purchased in Oxford in 1578, now in King's College, Cambridge, as MS 16.) He did not believe that a disease could be diagnosed by taking the pulse or inspecting urine. On subsequent occasions the college examined Forman on astrology and medicine and found him laughably ignorant, a conclusion which is difficult to reconcile with the scholarly pursuits recorded in his papers. On the first interview Forman was fined, and in November and December 1595 and September 1596 he was fined and imprisoned. In November 1600 the college summoned Forman again, but to no avail, presumably because he was in Lambeth; on 25 June 1601 Forman was singled out as the most obnoxious of the 'unlearned and unlawful practitioners, lurking in many corners of the City' beyond the college's jurisdiction (annals, RCP Lond., fol. 149a).

As Forman established a reputation as an astrologer and practitioner of physic in London in the second half of the 1590s, he began to earn a considerable income, and to realize his aspirations to become a member of the gentry. William Lilly recorded that Forman had gathered a fortune of £1200. In early 1599 Forman returned to Lambeth, where he was to stay for the rest of his life. On 23 July 1599, when he was forty-six, he married the sixteen-year-old niece of Sir Edward Monnings, Anne (or Joan) Baker. Forman always referred to her as 'Tronco', but her own use of two names gave rise to some reports that he was twice married. As a result of his marriage, and the birth of legitimate children, Dority (*b*. 1605) and Clement (*b*. 27 Oct 1606), Forman became interested in genealogy, beginning in one account with the year 1028 and linking himself with the nobility of Scotland and England. These interests were the occasion for Forman's autobiographical writings.

From 1599 until his death Forman stayed in Lambeth and continued his astrological and medical practice. His feud with the College of Physicians continued, and at one point Forman thought the college was planning to murder him. In an attempt at reconciliation, Forman challenged them to a debate in 1603. The college declined, and Forman interpreted this as an acknowledgement of his superior judgement. In another attempt to end the confrontations Forman went to Jesus College, Cambridge, for several months in 1603 and obtained a doctorate in physic and astronomy and a licence to practise medicine from the university. The physicians remained unappeased, and made several further attempts to curtail his activities.

During the last decade of his life Forman's astrological and medical practice continued. The dubious nature of his employment by several court ladies is spelled out in the accounts of his association with Frances Howard and Anne Turner which emerged during their trials for the murder of Sir Thomas Overbury, four years after Forman's death. A very familiar letter was produced in court, written by Frances Howard to Forman, in which she asked him to prepare magical philtres to alienate the love of her husband, the earl of Essex, and to draw towards her the love of the earl of Somerset. Indecent wax images were brought into the court by Forman's widow. A book in his handwriting was also produced, purportedly containing the names of his female clients and accounts of their intrigues with gentlemen about the court. In the pamphlets that surrounded this case Forman is portrayed as

> that fiend in human shape,
> that by his art did act the devil's ape.
> (R. Niccols, *Sir Thomas Overbury's Visions*, 1616)

This episode added 'magician', and even 'murderer', to the College of Physicians' appellation of Forman as a 'quack'.

Forman died on 8 September 1611, and was buried four days later in the church of St Mary, Lambeth. William Lilly relates the curious circumstances of Forman's death which Forman's widow reported to him. On the previous Sunday Forman's wife had asked him whether he or she should die first, and he answered that she would bury him on the following Thursday. On the Monday, Tuesday, and Wednesday Forman was in his usual health, and his wife teased him about the falseness of his prophecy. But on Thursday after dinner he took a boat at Southwark to cross the Thames to Puddle Dock, and having rowed into midstream, fell down dead. A storm arose immediately after his death.

None of Forman's astrological treatises was published, but his personal notoriety, his pugnacious defence of his art in his manuscripts, and his eventual material success ensured that he was not forgotten by his astrological successors. Seventeenth-century practitioners of astrology who were concerned with establishing the respectability of their profession saw him as an interesting predecessor. His papers were given to the astrologer Richard Napier, who in turn left them to his nephew, Sir Richard Napier. William Lilly claims that he first became interested in astrology because of accounts of Forman, and writes that 'had Forman lived to methodize his own papers, I doubt not but he would have advanced the Iatromathematical part thereof very completely' (Lilly, 17). Elias Ashmole shared Lilly's respect for Forman and collected more than forty volumes of his papers. In the nineteenth century, when William Black discovered Forman's accounts of Shakespeare performances from 1610 and 1611, and J. O. Halliwell prepared an edition of his diary and autobiography (which was found unsuitable for publication and cancelled) interest in his colourful persona was revived. In the later twentieth century Forman's casebooks and autobiographical writings have been used by social historians of the family, youth, and medicine, and literary critics have drawn on his accounts of Shakespeare and identified several notable authors, namely Emilia Lanier and possibly Robert Burton, in the pages of his casebooks.

Forman's widow married a Northamptonshire gentleman, a Mr Neal, and they had a son. A single trace of Forman's son Clement is a letter dated 1628 which he sent to Richard Napier from St Kitts, West Indies.

LAUREN KASSELL

George Formby (1904–1961), by A. J. Tanner, 1953

Sources S. Forman, diary and autobiographies, Bodl. Oxf., MS Ashmole 208 · S. Forman, astrological casebooks, 1596–1603, Bodl. Oxf., MSS Ashmole 234, 226, 195, 219, 236, 411 · S. Forman, 'Forman his repitition of the troble he had with the doctors of phisick in London', Bodl. Oxf., MSS Ashmole 240, art. 2; 802, art. 6 · annals, RCP Lond., vol. 2 · W. Lilly, *Mr William Lilly's history of his life and times* (1715) · B. H. Traister, *The notorious astrological physician of London: works and days of Simon Forman* (2000) · D. B. Quinn and J. W. Shirley, 'A contemporary list of Hariot references', *Renaissance Quarterly*, 22 (1969), 9–26 · A. L. Rowse, *Simon Forman* (1974) · B. Traister, 'New evidence about Burton's *Melancholy*', *Renaissance Quarterly*, 24 (1976), 66–70 · *CSP dom.*, rev. edn, 1581–90 · *DNB* · parish register (burial), St Mary Lambeth, 12 Sept 1611

Archives BL, papers · Bodl. Oxf., autobiography and papers · King's Cam., papers · St John's College, Oxford, papers · Trinity Cam., papers

Likenesses R. Godfrey, line engraving, pubd 1776 (after Bullfinch), BM, NPG · drawing, priv. coll. · engraving, repro. in Rowse, *Simon Forman* · engraving (after drawing), repro. in Rowse, *Simon Forman* [for *Antiquarian repertory*, 1 (1720), 275]

Wealth at death approx. £1200: Lilly, *Life and times*, 23

Forman, Thomas (1692–1768). *See under* Forman family (*per.* 1784–c.1870).

Forman, Thomas Seaton (1791–1850). *See under* Forman family (*per.* 1784–c.1870).

Forman, William (*bap.* 1767, *d.* 1829). *See under* Forman family (*per.* 1784–c.1870).

Forman, William Henry (1794–1869). *See under* Forman family (*per.* 1784–c.1870).

Formby, George [*real name* George Hoy Booth] (1904–1961), music-hall entertainer and actor, was born at 3 Westminster Street, Wigan, Lancashire, on 26 May 1904, the eldest of the seven surviving children (four girls and three boys) of James Lawler Booth (1875–1922), music-hall entertainer, and his wife, Eliza Hoy. George was born blind but gained his sight after a few weeks when a coughing fit, while he and his mother were crossing the Mersey, dislodged an obstructive caul. His father, born poor and illegitimate, learned his trade as a singing beggar and despite persistent ill health achieved success in the music halls under the name of George Formby. He created the

character of John Willie, the archetypal gormless Lancashire lad in baggy trousers, tight jacket, and bowler hat, slow-talking, hen-pecked, accident-prone, but muddling through.

The young George was educated only to the age of seven at Notre Dame School, Wigan, after which he was sent to train as a jockey, first in Yorkshire and later in Ireland. As a result he remained barely literate all his life. While serving his apprenticeship he made his screen début at the age of ten, playing a stable boy who outwits a criminal gang in the film *By the Shortest of Heads* (1915). In 1922 his father died, at the age of forty-six, and his mother launched him on a stage career, coaching him in George senior's songs and routines and putting him into the John Willie costume. He made his début as George Hoy at the Hippodrome, Earlestown, but was soon calling himself George Formby junior.

On 13 September 1924, at Wigan, Formby married champion clog dancer Beryl Ingham (*d.* 1960), and she became the driving force behind his career, negotiating contracts, controlling the money, and managing the act. They had no children. They put together their own show, with which they toured the country, and under his wife's influence Formby abandoned the John Willie costume while retaining the character. He also mastered the banjulele which, along with a toothy grin, became his trademark.

The revue format and the John Willie character formed the basis of two films, *Boots! Boots!* (1934) and *Off the Dole* (1935), in which Formby made his adult screen début, co-starring with his wife. Made on tiny budgets in a one-room London studio by John E. Blakeley's Mancunian Films, the films were hugely successful. They attracted the attention of Basil Dean, the Liverpool-born head of Ealing Studios, who had already signed up Gracie Fields and saw in Formby the makings of a similar success. He signed Formby to a seven-year contract which resulted in eleven highly profitable films. When this contract expired Formby set up his own company, Hillcrest Productions, and signed in 1941 with Columbia Pictures to produce his own films for them; this resulted in seven more films in similar vein to the Ealing productions.

There was no attempt to play down Formby's Lancashire character and Dean engaged the Salford-born author of *Love on the Dole*, Walter Greenwood, to script Formby's first Ealing film, *No Limit* (1935). This and *Keep your Seats, Please* (1936) were both directed by Monty Banks, who later married Gracie Fields. After this a special Formby unit was set up at Ealing, headed by writer and director Anthony Kimmins, to produce his films. These usually conformed to a set pattern; at their centre is Formby, a shy, innocent, gauche, accident-prone Lancashire lad; frequently he is in a skilled trade (photographer, typesetter, gramophone engineer) and lives in the south, either in the suburbs or the countryside, thus nationalizing his appeal; he has a bashful courtship with a brisk, sensible heroine with an upper-class accent; he is put through a succession of comic humiliations but he eventually wins the girl and achieves success in his job or in sport or, later, in war. The point of universal identification was that if Formby could win through against adversity, then anyone could. His eternal optimism was summed up by his catch-phrase 'Turned out nice again, hasn't it'.

It was thus partly by becoming a universal symbol that Formby achieved his success. He was northern and working-class but, more important, he was the little man who wins through against all the odds, as Chaplin had been on the silent screen, and as Norman Wisdom was to be in the 1950s. He was, as Colin MacInnes observed, Everyman, 'the urban "little man" defeated—but refusing to admit it' (*Sunday Times*, 13 Jan 1963). *Mass-Observation* recorded that the fantasy sequence in *Let George do it* (1940), in which Formby landed at Nuremberg and knocked out Hitler, was one of the biggest cultural morale-boosters of the early war years, the visual encapsulation of the people's war with the English Everyman flooring the Nazi Superman. The popularity of his character is indicated by the fact that from 1937 to 1943 inclusive Formby was the top British male star at the cinema box office, and from 1938 to 1942 the highest-paid entertainer in Britain.

There was an innocence about Formby that was essentially childlike, which explains why he was as popular with children as with adults. The cry 'Ooh, mother' which he emitted whenever in danger, and the gleeful 'Aha, never touched me' when he escaped his pursuers, were the reactions of a child. He even put his tongue out at pursuers on occasion. It was this innocence and the sunny outlook that neutralized the potential offensiveness of some of his songs. His songs—he recorded 189 in all—were a vital part of his appeal. Many of them dealt with sex but in a way which stressed shyness, voyeurism, caricature, and saucy innuendo: 'My Auntie Maggie's remedy', 'My grand-dad's flannelette nightshirt', 'My little stick of Blackpool rock', 'When I'm cleaning windows', 'In my little snapshot album'. In their approach and their themes—honeymooners, nudists, fat ladies, underwear—they all recall the comic seaside postcards of Donald McGill and they served the same function—the harmless defusion of

a major source of tension in a deeply repressed and conventional society.

Formby maintained his popularity through the Second World War both in films and on the ENSA tours he undertook, entertaining the troops frequently in close proximity to the front line. It was estimated that he had sung to 3 million service personnel by 1946, and in that year he was appointed OBE in recognition of his morale-boosting activities. However, his final film, *George in Civvy Street* (1946), was a box-office failure as the public turned to new film idols for the new post-war world, although his stage career continued. In the late 1940s he toured Canada, Australia, South Africa, and Sweden, raising thousands of pounds for charities. In 1951 he achieved a major West End stage success in the musical *Zip Goes a Million*, but during the run of the show he suffered a heart attack and thereafter his career was dogged by ill health. Despite this, he still packed in audiences to see him in pantomime and summer shows.

Formby's wife Beryl, who had been suffering from pernicious anaemia and cancer, died on Christmas day 1960, and six weeks later Formby announced his engagement to a young schoolteacher, Pat Howson. However, shortly before the planned wedding he suffered another heart attack and died on 6 March 1961 at St Joseph's Roman Catholic Hospital in Preston. By projecting in his thirty-year career a spirit of good nature, good humour, and good will, George had been able to embody simultaneously Lancashire, the working classes, the people, and the nation, and his passing was genuinely and widely mourned. He was buried next to his father in Manchester Road Catholic cemetery, Warrington.

JEFFREY RICHARDS

Sources A. Randall and R. Seaton, *George Formby* (1974) · J. Fisher, *George Formby* (1975) · J. Walley, *George Formby complete* (1973) · J. Richards, *The age of the dream palace: cinema and society in Britain, 1930–1939* (1984) · D. Bret, *George Formby: a troubled genius* (1999) · *Sunday Times* (13 Jan 1963) · *The Times* (7 March 1961) · CGPLA Eng. & Wales (1961)

Archives FILM BFI NFTVA, *South Bank Show*, ITV, 8 Nov 1992 | SOUND BL NSA, documentary recordings · BL NSA, performance recordings

Likenesses A. J. Tanner, photograph, 1953, Sci. Mus., Science and Society Picture Library [*see illus.*] · photographs, Hult. Arch.

Wealth at death £135,142 5s. 9d.: administration, 14 Aug 1961, CGPLA Eng. & Wales

Forres. For this title name *see* Williamson, Archibald, first Baron Forres (1860–1931).

Forrest, Alexander (1849–1901). *See under* Forrest, John, first Baron Forrest (1847–1918).

Forrest, Arthur (d. **1770**), naval officer and planter; details of his parents and upbringing are unknown. Prior to his joining the Royal Navy he was a petty officer who traded to Cartagena as a mate or master of a merchantman and who volunteered as a pilot. By December 1740 he had passed his lieutenant's examination and was appointed to command the sloop *Pilot*, with orders to train the squadron's officers in the pilotage of Port Royal. Forrest distinguished himself during the expedition against Cartagena, being skilled in pilotage, under Edward Boscawen, who was attached to the expedition in command of the *Shoreham* in the attack on the Baradera battery on shore on 17 and 18 March 1741. On 25 May Forrest was promoted by Edward Vernon to the command of the bomb *Alderney*. In November 1742 he was appointed to the sloop *Hawk*, in which, and afterwards in the *Success*, he was employed on the home station and in convoy service to America. In 1745 he was posted to the command of the *Wager*, in which he took out a large convoy to Newfoundland. In November he was at Boston, where, by pressing some seamen contrary to colonial custom, he got into a troublesome dispute, ending in a serious fray, in which two men were killed. The boatswain of the *Wager* was arrested on a charge of murder, was convicted, and sentenced to death; the sentence, however, does not appear to have been carried out.

Forrest afterwards went to the West Indies, where, in 1746, he captured a Spanish privateer of much superior force. In 1755 he commanded the *Rye*, in which he was again sent to the West Indies, and in 1757 was moved into the *Augusta* (60 guns). In October he was detached, with two other ships—*Dreadnought* and *Edinburgh*—under his command, to cruise off Cap François, and on the 21st he fell in with a powerful French squadron of four ships of the line and three heavy frigates, bent on liberating the large convoy waiting in the port. After conferring briefly with captains Suckling and Langdon, Forrest bore down on the enemy. While he has been criticized for 'irresponsible zeal' (Pares, 281), it remains true that 'few pluckier' actions 'have ever been fought' at sea (Clowes, 3.166). Nelson, through his uncle Suckling, drew inspiration from Forrest's audacity, and Lord Glenbervie later wrote of 'a very brave, sensible and candid man' (*Diaries*, 1.12). After a sharp combat for upwards of two hours, the two squadrons parted, each disabled. The French returned to Cap François, where they refitted and then proceeded on their voyage, and Forrest went back to Jamaica. On 24 December, being detached singly off Petit Guave, he cleverly bagged the whole of a fleet of eight merchant ships, capturing in the night the sloop of war which was escorting them, and using her as a tender against her own convoy.

In August 1759 Forrest took the *Augusta* to England, and on paying her off, in April 1760, commissioned the *Centaur*, one of the ships taken by Boscawen off Lagos in the preceding year. After a few months with the Grand Fleet in the Bay of Biscay, he went out to Jamaica, where, by the death of Rear-Admiral Charles Holmes in November 1761, he was left senior officer. On this he moved into the *Cambridge*, hoisted a broad pennant, and took on himself both the duties and privileges of commander-in-chief, until Sir James Douglas, coming from the Leeward Islands in April 1762, summarily dispossessed him. He returned to England, passenger in a merchant ship, where, on reporting himself to the Admiralty, he was told that his conduct in constituting himself commodore was most irregular and unjustifiable, and that the officers whom he had promoted would not be confirmed. This led to a long correspondence in which the Admiralty so far yielded as to order

him to be reimbursed for the expenses he had incurred, though without sanctioning the higher rate of pay. In 1769, however, he was sent out to Jamaica as commander-in-chief, with his broad pennant in the *Dunkirk*. In Jamaica he bought land for cultivation and became a wealthy and well-known figure. He married a daughter of Colonel Lynch of Jamaica, with whom he had a family. Forrest enjoyed his appointment for only a short time, and died at Jamaica on 26 May 1770. He was survived by his wife, who died in 1804 at the age of eighty-two.

J. K. LAUGHTON, *rev.* RUDDOCK MACKAY

Sources W. L. Clowes, *The Royal Navy: a history from the earliest times to the present*, 7 vols. (1897–1903); repr. (1996–7) • N. A. M. Rodger, *The wooden world: an anatomy of the Georgian navy* (1986) • R. Pares, *War and trade in the West Indies, 1739–1763* (1936) • *The Vernon papers*, ed. B. McL. Ranft, Navy RS, 99 (1958) • PRO, Adm, 1/235 • PRO, Adm, 1/1787 • PRO, Adm, 1/1789 • *The diaries of Sylvester Douglas (Lord Glenbervie)*, ed. F. Bickley, 2 vols. (1928)
Archives NMM, corresp., UPC/2 and UPC/3 • PRO, ADM, MSS 1/235, 1/1787, 1/1789 • PRO, CO 142/31, fol. 15
Likenesses R. Page, stipple (after unknown artist), BM, NPG; repro. in *Naval Chronicle* (1811) • R. Purcell, mezzotint (after van Diest), BM • line engraving (after Fouquet), BM, NPG • line engraving (after van Diest), BM, NPG

Forrest, Ebenezer (*bap.* **1700**, *d.* **1793**), lawyer and writer, was baptized on 13 October 1700 at St Dunstan and All Saints, Stepney, Middlesex, the son of John and Mary Forrest. He resided at George Street, York Buildings, London, and was intimate with William Hogarth and John Rich, proprietor of the Lincoln's Inn Theatre. With Rich, Hogarth, and twenty-two other friends, he was a founder member of the Sublime Society of Beefsteaks on 6 December 1735, and was also a member of the same masonic lodge as Hogarth. He was married to a woman named Theodosia and was the father of Theodosius *Forrest (*c.*1728–1784), also an attorney and an artist and playwright. Ebenezer's opera entitled *Momus Turn'd Fabulist, or, Vulcan's Wedding*, a translation from the French of Marc Antoine Legrand and L. Fuzelier, was performed at the Lincoln's Inn Theatre on 3 December 1729 and some subsequent nights. He is now best-known for his *Account of what seemed most remarkable in the five days' peregrination of … Tothall, Scott, Hogarth, Thornhill, and F.* (1782, illustrated with plates by Hogarth). This was edited by Charles Mitchell and reprinted as *Hogarth's Peregrination* in 1872, along with W. Gostling's versified account of the trip. Nichols incorporated it into his *Anecdotes of Hogarth*. Ebenezer Forrest died in 1793.

J. M. RIGG, *rev.* REBECCA MILLS

Sources IGI • D. E. Baker, *Biographia dramatica, or, A companion to the playhouse*, rev. I. Reed, new edn, rev. S. Jones, 1/1 (1812), 251–3 [Theodosius Forrest] • *GM*, 1st ser., 94/1 (1824), 410, 581–2 • *GM*, 1st ser., 54 (1784), 877–8 • R. Paulson, *Hogarth*, 3 vols. (1991–3)

Forrest, Edwin (**1806–1872**), actor, was born on 9 March 1806 on George Street, Old Southwark, Philadelphia, the sixth of the seven children of William Forrest (1758–1819), a Scottish-American bank messenger, and his wife, Rebecca Lauman (1763–1847). As a young man he took elocution lessons and performed with an amateur acting society, the conventional route to an acting career in a profession still dominated by English theatrical traditions. He persona, his performances in the 1830s and 1840s induced hero worship from lower- and middle-class males in American cities. His fame increased after a successful London début in 1836; the London press disliked his prize plays, but praised his passionate sincerity. While in England, on 23 June 1837, Forrest married Catherine Norton Sinclair (1819–1891), the daughter of a professional singer and actress. He seriously considered an offer from the New York democrats to run for Congress in 1838. By 1840 his identification with workers and Jacksonian democrats led most elite playgoers in America to disdain him.

Upper-class antagonism to Forrest continued through the 1840s, reaching a climax in the bloody Astor Place Opera House riot of 1849. The riot derived from a feud between Forrest and the English star William Charles Macready that began in London in 1845. Forrest believed that Macready had hired a spectator to hiss his Macbeth (a charge never proved) and returned this affront by hissing Macready's Hamlet in Edinburgh (where he was joined by others in the audience). Public exchanges of letters kept the actors' rivalry simmering in the newspapers on both sides of the Atlantic, where both stars had their advocates. When Macready went to New York in 1849, workers claiming Forrest as their hero vowed vengeance. To them, Macready and the opera house where he was scheduled to perform were symbols of English and American aristocratic oppression. In the midst of the riot on 10 May, the state militia opened fire, killing twenty-two and wounding scores of others. Although he probably welcomed the show of support, Forrest took no part in the rioters' plans and actions. The Astor Place riot had begun as a dispute between two actors, but it went far beyond their rivalry to engage nationalistic and class-based antagonisms that sharply divided the pro-English elite who cheered for Macready from the working-class fans of Forrest.

The breakup of Forrest's marriage and a scandalous divorce trial in 1851 kept the star's name in the headlines. With little evidence, Forrest accused his wife of infidelity, gained a legal separation, and finally sued for divorce. Catherine Forrest brought suit on the same grounds; her lawyers easily proved that Forrest had frequented a house of prostitution and committed adultery with an actress while on tour. The jury upheld Catherine's innocence and Forrest's guilt on every count, and she won her divorce suit, ending their childless marriage. Seeking consolation from his fans, Forrest acted his starring roles at the Broadway Theatre in New York for sixty-nine performances, a record at the time. The Forrest divorce case served as a lightning rod for social antagonisms; it dramatized the division between those who held to traditional patriarchal values regarding family honour and others who favoured notions of mutual responsibility in marriage.

Beginning in 1857, Forrest cut back on his touring to rest for increasingly long periods at his home in Philadelphia. But the star continued to perform, even after an attack of sciatica in 1865 slowed his still powerful body. He last appeared as a platform speaker shortly before his death, which occurred in Philadelphia on 12 December 1872. He

Edwin Forrest (1806–1872), by Thomas Sully, 1836–9

also trained his body by practising acrobatics, a regimen he continued throughout his life. Soon after his début in 1820, he went west with a travelling troupe and finally arrived in New Orleans, where he performed for two years. In Albany, New York, in 1825 he played several supporting roles for Edmund Kean. His own performance of Othello in New York city the following year boosted Forrest to stardom, the first native-born American to achieve this status. By 1828 he was touring the country with a repertory that included Macbeth, Mark Antony, and major roles in John Banim's *Damon and Pythias* and Otway's *Venice Preserv'd*.

The young star was 5 feet 10 inches tall, with a muscular build and a clear, melodious voice that ranged easily from a low growl to rafter-shaking power. In acting style he combined Kean's passionate outbursts with the deliberate declamation of the Kemble tradition. His powerful performances generally gravitated between long passages of rhetorical restraint with little movement and moments of quick action and emotional release.

To increase his starring roles, Forrest held the first play competition in America in 1828. John Augustus Stone won the contest with *Metamora, or, The Last of the Wampanoags*, a heroic melodrama featuring a Native American hero. In the eight competitions that followed over the next nineteen years, Forrest awarded prizes to three other plays that he turned into successful star vehicles: *The Gladiator* (1831), by Robert Montgomery Bird; *The Broker of Bogota* (1834), also by Bird; and *Jack Cade* (1841), by Robert T. Conrad. Most of these prize plays featured a hero of primal strength and virtue fighting aristocratic oppression to gain the freedom of his people.

Because of Forrest's charismatic appeal and republican

was buried four days later in St Paul's churchyard in Philadelphia. His will established his former residence as the Edwin Forrest Home for retired actors.

BRUCE MCCONACHIE

Sources B. A. McConachie, *Melodramatic formations: American theatre and society* (1992) • R. Moody, *Edwin Forrest, first star of the American stage* (1960) • M. Moses, *The fabulous Forrest: the record of an American actor* (1929) • D. Grimsted, *Melodrama unveiled: American theatre and culture, 1800–1850* (1968) • W. R. Alger, *Life of Edwin Forrest, the American tragedian* (1877) • L. Barrett, *Edwin Forrest* (1882) • J. Rees, *The life of Edwin Forrest* (1874)
Archives Harvard TC • NYPL • University of Pennsylvania
Likenesses T. Sully, portrait, 1836–9, Garr. Club [*see illus.*] • twenty-four portraits, repro. in Moody, *Edwin Forrest*

Forrest, George (1873–1932), plant collector, was born at Graham's Road, Falkirk, Stirlingshire, on 13 March 1873, the youngest child of George Forrest, a draper's assistant, and his wife, Mary (*née* Bain). After attending a school in Falkirk, in 1887 he moved with his family to Kilmarnock, where his father set up in business. Completing his education at Kilmarnock Academy, he then went to work in a chemist's shop with a view to qualifying as a pharmacist. Though that came to nothing, it gave him a smattering of medical knowledge, which he was later to put to good use, and introduced him to botany.

Receipt of a small legacy gave Forrest the opportunity to travel. Abandoning his training, he visited relatives in Australia, where he worked on a sheep station and in the goldfields before returning to Scotland, by way of South Africa, in 1902. He went to live with his mother, now widowed, on the outskirts of Edinburgh, and obtained a post in the herbarium of the Royal Botanic Garden, thanks to an acquaintance with its regius keeper, Isaac Bayley Balfour. Through his menial work there he acquired some understanding of the practices in use in professional taxonomy and a reputation for asceticism—he disdained the use of a chair all day, and regularly walked 6 miles to work and 6 miles home. These qualities attracted the notice of Bayley Balfour and led him to recommend Forrest to the wealthy Liverpool cotton broker and horticulturist A. K. Bulley who, in 1904, was looking for someone to collect on his behalf in the mountains of south-west China.

Forrest's first expedition (out of seven in all) was both richly productive and hair-raisingly adventurous. The Younghusband incursion into Tibet the previous year had provoked the Batang lamas into a ferocious campaign to eradicate all foreign influence. Forrest's party was set upon and all except him were murdered. Relentlessly hunted for eight days and nights, his foot pierced through by a bamboo stake, starving and delirious with fatigue, his belongings and that summer's collections and field notes all lost, he finally reached safety only to learn that he had been reported dead.

After returning to Edinburgh in 1907 Forrest married Harriet Clementina Mary Wallace Traill, to whom he had become engaged before leaving for the East. She was a herbarium assistant and the only daughter of G. W. Traill, an authority on Scottish seaweeds. Three of Forrest's plant introductions were to be named after her and the

couple had three sons. However, over the next quarter of a century Forrest was to spend less time at home than in China.

After three years back in his humdrum, ill-paid post in the herbarium Forrest needed no persuading to make a second expedition, on behalf of a syndicate put together by his previous backer, Bulley. The latter's failure to reply to Forrest's letters, however, led to the two falling out and his transfer on the next occasion to Bulley's rival, J. C. Williams. In doing so Forrest created a rival of his own—Frank Kingdon-Ward, whom Bulley promptly took on in his place. Jealously territorial, regarding Yunnan as 'his' and fiercely resenting anyone else intruding into it, Forrest was always to keep Kingdon-Ward and that other member of the trio of 'greats', Reginald Farrer, at a distance, refusing their offers to collaborate and denigrating their efforts. Reserved by nature and with a reputation for touchiness, he did not encourage companionship, his one experiment to that end quickly proving irksome and, to his relief, short-lived. Away from the field, though, it was a different matter: when relaxing with friends his bristly manner would drop away and a keen sense of humour and a rich store of anecdotes would appear in its place.

Whereas Kingdon-Ward was as much an explorer as a botanist, Forrest was a plant collector first and last, content to keep to just one region and work it steadily year after year. It was a strategy that proved amply justified, for he continued to turn up novelties, many of them of high horticultural potential. He also made valuable collections of birds, mammals, butterflies, dragonflies, and ethnographical material, his bird collections alone yielding thirty species new to science. While these went to a variety of museums in Britain, it was the Edinburgh Royal Botanic Garden that was the prime recipient of his torrent of plant specimens, eventually over 31,000. These were almost invariably of the highest quality and impeccably annotated (in contrast to Kingdon-Ward's, which were too often scrappy). In the words of his *Journal of Botany* obituarist, 'it is probable that in quality and richness his herbarium material has never been surpassed. He had developed the technique of plant-drying to a fine point.' The key to this was his policy of training local hillmen as collecting assistants, who came to develop great skill in this delicate craft. Like Farrer, but again in contrast to Kingdon-Ward, Forrest felt an affinity with the Chinese, taking much interest in their customs and dialects (of which he mastered several).

The climate in Edinburgh proved well suited for raising alpines from seeds brought back by Forrest. This encouraged the garden to specialize in the study of the flora of the 'roof of the world', giving its research programme a helpfully unifying direction. Forrest himself had no feel for taxonomy and hated working through his collections, content to leave that side largely to his original mentor, Bayley Balfour, with whom he forged a close personal as well as working relationship. Devastated by Bayley Balfour's death in 1922, Forrest was fortunate to find in his successor, Professor William Wright Smith, a scarcely less sympathetic collaborator.

An excellent photographer, latterly a fluent and popular lecturer, capable of vivid prose and profusely informative letters, Forrest nevertheless had a blockage when it came to publication. Despite repeated urgings by his friends, all he produced were a few, mostly short, articles. The one book he did intend to write he reserved for the retirement he was ultimately never to enjoy. His death came very suddenly, on 5 or 6 January 1932, just as he was about to return home after what he had accepted was his last expedition. He was nearly sixty by then and had had an operation for cataracts in both eyes shortly before leaving home; his friends had thought the trip inadvisable, but he had always had a strong constitution. While relaxing with a final spot of duck-shooting near his main base at Tengchung (Tengchong), he collapsed from a heart attack and never recovered consciousness. He was buried on 7 January in the foreign cemetery just outside the city.

Many honours came to Forrest in his later years, most notably the two highest awards of the Royal Horticultural Society, the Victoria medal of honour in 1920 and the Veitch memorial medal in 1927. In 1924 a volume of *The Garden* magazine was dedicated to him, and in 1930 he received the rhododendron cup in tribute to his discovery of over three hundred new species in that genus. *Rhododendron forrestii*, a product of his very first expedition, is one of numerous plants, as well as a warbler and a squirrel, that bear his name. In addition, an annual George Forrest medal awarded by the Scottish Rock Garden Club preserves his memory. D. E. ALLEN

Sources J. Keenan, 'George Forrest, 1873–1932', *Journal of the Royal Horticultural Society*, 98 (1973), 112–17 · G. Forrest, jun., 'George Forrest, "The Man"', *Journal of the Scottish Rock Garden Club*, 13 (1973), 169–75 · J. T. Aitken, 'George Forrest—the man and his work', *Journal of the Scottish Rock Garden Club*, 13 (1973), 185–96 · J. M. Cowan, ed., *The journeys and plant introductions of George Forrest* (1952) · W. W. Smith, *Rhododendron Society notes*, 3/5 (1932) [repr. in *Journal of the Royal Horticultural Society*, 57 (1932), 356–60] · R. E. Cooper and others, *Man hunts and plant hunts, being the adventures of George Forrest* (1935) · A. M. Coats, *The quest for plants* (1969), 123–7 · G. Taylor, *Journal of Botany, British and Foreign*, 70 (1932), 79–81 · CCI (1932)
Archives NHM, insects collection from south-west China · Royal Botanic Garden, Edinburgh, MSS and specimens | Royal Botanic Garden, Edinburgh, corresp. with John Charles Williams
Likenesses photograph, repro. in *Gardeners' Chronicle*, 1 (1932) · photograph, repro. in E. Nelmes, *Curtis's Botanical Magazine: dedications, 1827–1927, portraits and biographical notes* (1931) · photograph, repro. in *Transactions and Proceedings of the Botanical Society of Edinburgh*, 31 (1932) · photograph, repro. in Cowan, ed., *Journeys and plant introductions*, frontispiece · photograph, repro. in Forrest, 'George Forrest'
Wealth at death £3520 18s. 9d.: confirmation, 30 April 1932, CCI

Forrest, Sir George William David Stark (1845–1926), historian, was born at Nasirabad, near Ajmer, India, on 8 January 1845, the second son of Captain George Forrest (1803/4–1859), of the Bengal artillery, and his wife, Ann Edwards (*b.* 1816/17). Captain Forrest was one of three surviving officers awarded the Victoria Cross for the defence of the Delhi magazine on 11 May 1857; he died from his wounds in November 1859, whereupon his widow and children returned to Britain. The elder son, Robert Edward Trexton Forrest (1835–1914), did twenty-one years'

service in the irrigation branch of India's public works department before retiring to write Indian potboilers, including *Eight Days* (1891) and *The Bond of Blood* (1896).

George Forrest was educated privately until he entered St John's College, Cambridge, as a pensioner in 1866. He gained a BA in mathematics in 1870 and afterwards read law, but although admitted to the Inner Temple in 1872, he was never called to the bar and in December 1872 he became headmaster at Surat high school. It was a career switch perhaps dictated by limited finances, for Forrest did not like teaching and moreover suffered perennial ill health in the land of his birth. He was home on sick leave from June 1874 to August 1876 and again in 1877, when he married Emma Georgina (*b.* 1850/51), daughter of Thomas Viner of Broadfield, Crawley, Sussex, on 6 August. In June 1879 he was appointed professor of mathematics at Deccan College, Poona. In 1882 he was additionally given charge of the Bombay census office, but writing was his first love and throughout these years he poured out a stream of journalism. He later recalled how, as correspondent for *The Times*, he had been the first to alert London to Britain's defeat at Maiwand in Afghanistan in July 1880.

In 1884 Forrest entered upon the real work of his life with the publication of *Selections from the Official Writings of Mountstuart Elphinstone*, Bombay's paternalistic governor from 1819 to 1827, after which he was seconded to examine the records preserved in the Bombay secretariat—a task which bore fruit in a Maratha (1885) and a home (1887) series of state papers. In April 1888, after some months as professor of English and history at Elphinstone College, Forrest was finally freed from teaching duties to become the first director of records at Bombay. Shortly afterwards he was summoned to investigate the official records at Calcutta, a duty from which he produced his first volume of *Selections from the State Papers in the Foreign Department* (1890). Under Lord Lansdowne's viceregal patronage, Forrest went on to create and preside over the Imperial Record Office at Calcutta. He was acutely aware of the bureaucracy's resistance to his brainchild and took every opportunity to press upon Lansdowne examples from the past that would illuminate contemporary conundrums. While in Calcutta, he also worked in the patents branch (1894–1900) and as assistant secretary to the government (1898).

Although superficially successful, Forrest often felt his work to be undervalued. Inevitably his journalism got him into trouble, as in 1889, when the governor of Bombay, Lord Reay, christened him 'the Liar', and accused him of maligning the provincial administration because he had been refused promotion. This was unfair: Forrest was certainly not self-denying but he never wrote out of pique. To him history was brimming with relevance and he was convinced of its utility in preventing the repetition of past mistakes. Accordingly, his pamphlet *The Famine in India* (1897) shows the imperial administration on a whiggish learning curve, imbibing new truths from old administrative failures.

In 1900 ill health forced Forrest to retire. He was bitterly disappointed at missing Lord Curzon's viceroyalty and from England urged him on with plans for the Victoria Memorial. He continued to write histories, including *The Life of Field-Marshal Sir Neville Chamberlain* (1909), *Selections from the State Papers of the Governors-General of India: Warren Hastings* (2 vols., 1910), and a time-consuming documentary *History of the Indian Mutiny* (3 vols., 1904–12). Craving recognition for his work, Forrest was a better judge of a dead subject than a living one: his *Life of Lord Roberts* (1914) lacks the distance and impartiality of his mutiny studies. By contrast, in *The Life of Lord Clive* (2 vols., 1918) Forrest allows his subject's letters to speak for themselves, with little authorial intervention.

Forrest was knighted in 1913 and lived to see government record offices all over India undertake ambitious publishing programmes. In his latter years he enjoyed a reputation in Oxford and at the Savile Club in London as a convivial, amusing companion—a sign perhaps that he had outgrown his early insecurities. He died on 28 January 1926 at his home, Iffley Turn House, near Oxford, and was buried at Iffley church, on 30 January. Among the mourners were his widow, a son, Viner Forrest, and a daughter, Mrs Harlow. It was fitting that a last work, *Selections from the State Papers of the Governors-General of India: Lord Cornwallis* (2 vols., 1926), appeared posthumously. In his commentaries Forrest always celebrated imperial advance. Nevertheless, in making so many documents available to the public he had opened the way for a new type of history of British India, one that broke with the privileged narratives of inside men such as J. W. Kaye: it was a lasting achievement. KATHERINE PRIOR

Sources *History of services of gazetted officers … in the Bombay presidency* (1890) · *The Times* (29 Jan 1926), 14 · *The Times* (1 Feb 1926) · letters from Forrest to Lord Curzon, BL OIOC, Curzon MSS · letters from Forrest to Lord Lansdowne, BL OIOC, Lansdowne MSS · ecclesiastical records, BL OIOC · *WWW* · Venn, *Alum. Cant.* · m. cert. **Archives** Bodl. Oxf., papers | BL OIOC, Curzon MSS · BL OIOC, Lansdowne MSS **Wealth at death** £368 3s. 5d.: probate, 28 April 1926, *CGPLA Eng. & Wales*

Forrest, Henry (*d.* 1533?), protestant martyr, is identified with the student of that name who appears fleetingly on record as a determinant, designated 'pauper', in St Leonard's College at St Andrews University in 1526. There, in all probability, he imbibed the Lutheran beliefs circulating in the university and may well have witnessed Patrick Hamilton's execution for heresy in St Andrews in 1528. Certainly Forrest hailed from Linlithgow, where Hamilton's brother, Sir James of Kincavil, the sheriff of Linlithgow, was delated for heresy in 1532 and forfeited in 1534. Forrest's involvement in inchoate, underground protestantism, where academic and familial ties afforded contact and a measure of protection, preceded the rise of a network of organized protestant communities. Calderwood, citing Foxe, describes Forrest as 'a young man, born in Linlithquo, who a little before, had received the orders of Bennet and Collet', from which he is understood to have been a Benedictine monk (Calderwood, 1.96). The main Benedictine house in Scotland was Dunfermline in Fife, some 40 miles from St Andrews.

Forrest's conviction for heresy resulted from his possession of a copy of the New Testament in English and from his approving Patrick Hamilton's doctrine. Imprisoned by James Beaton, archbishop of St Andrews, on suspicion of heresy, Forrest is said to have been betrayed to the archbishop by Friar Walter Laing, who heard Forrest's confession and to whom he declared that he 'thought Master Patrick to be a good man and wrongfully to be put to death, and that his articles were true and not heretical'. After degradation from holy orders he taunted the clergy present to remove his Catholic baptism. He was burnt for heresy, apparently in 1533, at the stile on the north side of the Augustinian church in St Andrews, so that heretics in distant Angus 'might see the fire' (*History of the Church*, 1.129–30). The suggestion that he may have been the son of Thomas Forrest in Linlithgow, who received payment from the crown in 1505 for building a wall around Linlithgow Palace, is no more than conjecture. JAMES KIRK

Sources *The works of John Knox*, ed. D. Laing, 6 vols., Wodrow Society, 12 (1846–64) · D. Calderwood, *The history of the Kirk of Scotland*, ed. T. Thomson and D. Laing, 8 vols., Wodrow Society, 7 (1842–9) · J. Spottiswood, *The history of the Church of Scotland*, ed. M. Napier and M. Russell, 3 vols., Bannatyne Club, 93 (1850) · A. I. Dunlop, ed., *Acta facultatis artium universitatis Sanctiandree, 1413–1588*, 2 vols., Scottish History Society, 3rd ser., 54–5 (1964)

Forrest, John, first Baron Forrest (1847–1918), explorer and politician in Australia, third son of the ten children born to William Forrest (1819–1899), farmer and millwright, of Preston Point, near Bunbury, Western Australia (who had migrated from Stonehaven, Kincardineshire), and his wife, Margaret Guthrie (1821–1895), daughter of David Hill, of Dundee, was born on 22 August 1847 at Preston Point. After attending the government school in Bunbury and Bishop Hale's School, Perth, and having been apprenticed as a surveyor from 1863, he entered the survey department of the colony in 1865. He soon showed conspicuous skill at exploration: first in 1869, when he led a search for the remains of the lost Ludwig Leichhardt; then in 1870, when he travelled overland from Perth to Adelaide, establishing a reliable overland telegraph route; and, most notably, in 1874, by his expedition from Geraldton to the overland telegraph line between Adelaide and Port Darwin, a distance of 2000 miles through the central desert country. He was fêted in Australia and London, received a freehold grant of 5000 acres and the founder's medal of the Royal Geographical Society, and was appointed deputy surveyor-general in 1876. On 29 February 1876, at St George's Cathedral, Perth, he married Margaret Elvire (1844–1929), daughter of Edward Hamersley of Guildford, Western Australia. Wealthy and well connected, she proved a great asset to his political career, although the couple were childless.

In 1883 Forrest was promoted surveyor-general and commissioner of crown lands with a seat in the executive and legislative councils. He proved as thorough and thoughtful an administrator as he had been an explorer, although he was not immune from the endemic quarrels

John Forrest, first Baron Forrest (1847–1918), by unknown engraver

in the administration. When the colony was granted responsible government in 1890, he formed its first ministry, as treasurer with the unofficial title of 'premier'. In ten years Forrest's administration oversaw the construction of almost 2000 miles of railway and many important public works including Freemantle harbour and the 350 mile pipeline supplying 6 million gallons of water daily to the Coolgardie–Kalgoorlie goldfields, discovered in 1892–3. These projects increased colonial debt sevenfold, but, helped by the gold, Forrest transformed a huge pastoral expanse with a few transitory miners into a prosperous colony with settled rural, mining, and urban populations. His Homestead Act (1893) instituted free land grants of 160 acres to those wanting to settle, and he founded the Agricultural Bank in 1894 to extend credit to agriculturists for improvements. He improved the rights of industrial, mining, and shop workers, and of women in general, abolished state aid to religion, and tightened the restrictions on immigration from Asia. He represented Western Australia at the colonial conferences in London in 1887 and 1897, playing a prominent part in each. He worked steadily for Australian federation, and although his caution looked to some like reluctance, he finally led the campaign for popular acceptance of the federal constitution.

In February 1901 Forrest left state politics to join the first commonwealth administration. He held office in three non-Labor governments, before resigning in 1907 from a ministry which had become dependent on Labor support

in parliament. Having been active in discussions among non-Labor members, he returned as treasurer in the new Liberal Party 'fusion' administration, and negotiated improved financial arrangements between the commonwealth and the states. He was narrowly defeated four times in party elections for leader, and thereby for prime minister, but was treasurer again in 1913–14 and 1917–18, before cancer forced his resignation in 1918. Already appointed a KCMG in 1891 and a GCMG in 1901, in 1918 he was created Baron Forrest of Bunbury, the first peerage bestowed on an Australian politician; but while bound for England to take his seat in the House of Lords and to seek medical advice, he died at sea on 3 September 1918 off Sierra Leone. He was buried in the Karrakatta cemetery, Perth. He left an estate worth £45,000.

Although by 1918 Forrest's political style seemed outmoded in the era of national party politics, he left a lasting legacy of social and economic advances and physical infrastructure. His achievements at Perth were not matched by those in federal politics, but within and beyond Australia he won lasting renown as an explorer and practical geographer, convinced that rational resource exploitation based on accurate survey and mapping was the only scientific and coherent means to develop a new nation.

Alexander Forrest (1849–1901), surveyor and entrepreneur, John Forrest's brother, was born on 22 September 1849 at Preston Point, near Bunbury, in Western Australia. He attended the same schools as his brother and also trained as a surveyor. Not so accomplished a surveyor as John, he was the more adventurous explorer. He accompanied John in his expeditions of 1870 and 1874 and himself led a party past Coolgardie and south to Esperance Bay in 1871, forming an overfavourable opinion of that district. In 1879 he led a brilliant expedition in the north of Western Australia, with a party which included his brother Matthew, when he discovered and named the Kimberley district and a huge tract of well-watered grazing lands on the Fitzroy and Ord rivers. Having, like John, already been criticized for profiting from his discoveries, he resigned his government appointment to become an extremely successful land agent in the south-west and particularly in the Kimberleys, attracting investment, settlement, and railway construction, and himself setting up a number of concerns and becoming very wealthy. There were complaints against some of his business practices, but he was never found to have broken the law. On 15 January 1880 he married Amy-Eliza (1852–1897), daughter of Edward Thomas Barret-Lennard; they had four sons and a daughter.

An ardent supporter of responsible government and protectionism, Forrest represented Kimberley in the legislative council from 1887. After responsible government was granted he sat in the assembly from 1890 to 1901, strongly opposing federation. As mayor of Perth in 1892–5 and in 1897–1900 he used his connections with his brother to win government subsidies for public works in the city, although in general he was a firmer believer in private enterprise than John, who increasingly advocated government planning in developing public lands. Appointed a CMG in May 1901, Alexander died on 20 June, in Perth, from a kidney disease; he was buried in Karrakatta cemetery, Perth, on the 21st. He left an estate worth £195,000, but also a lasting legacy in the settlements and landholdings he laid out in the north-west of Australia.

ELIZABETH BAIGENT

Sources *AusDB* · J. M. Powell, 'John Forrest 1847–1918 and Alexander Forrest 1849–1901', *Geographers*, 8 (1984), 39–43 · F. K. Crowley, *Forrest 1847–1918* (1971) · J. S. Battye, *Western Australia* (1924) · S. Glynn, *Government policy and agricultural development* (1975) · J. Forrest, *Explorations in Australia* (1875) · F. K. Crowley, 'The statesman: Sir John Forrest', *Western portraits*, ed. L. Hunt (1979), 78–91 · G. C. Bolton, *Alexander Forrest* (1958) · T. Staunage, *The people of Perth* (1979)
Archives NL Aus., corresp. with Alfred Deakin · NL Aus., corresp. with Viscount Novar · University of Western Australia, Perth, MSS · Western Australia Lands and Survey Department, Perth
Likenesses E. P. Fox, oils, 1915, Art Gallery of Western Australia, Perth · B. Mackennal, bronze statue, 1926, King's Park, Perth · Imp, chromolithograph caricature, NPG; repro. in *VF* (7 Oct 1897) · double portrait, statue (with Alexander Forrest), St George's Terrace, Perth · lithograph?, RGS [*see illus.*]
Wealth at death £45,160—in Australia · £195,238—Alexander Forrest: probate, Western Australia

Forrest, Robert (1790–1852), sculptor, was born on 28 June 1790 at Braidwood, Carluke, Lanarkshire, the son of Robert Forrest and Helen Hamilton. He trained as a stonemason in the quarries of Clydesdale, and began carving figurines and animals in 1810 after visiting the collections of various local noblemen. In 1817 he was discovered working in a remote quarry by an army officer who had become lost while out hunting. Forrest subsequently moved his workshop to the village of Orchard, near Lanark. His first public work was a colossal statue of William Wallace, which was erected in a niche in the steeple of Lanark parish church in 1817. During the inaugural celebration of this work, he was carried in triumph through the streets of Lanark. Numerous prestigious commissions followed, including the statue of the first Viscount Melville (1822) on a column in St Andrew Square, Edinburgh, which he carved from a design by Francis Leggatt Chantrey, and the *Monument to John Knox* (1825) in Glasgow necropolis. Despite his secure reputation as a sculptor, in 1823 he began attending classes in drawing, modelling, and anatomy in various private studios and schools, including the Trustees' Academy in Edinburgh and Warren's Academy in Glasgow. His education continued in 1837 when he visited France and Italy. In 1832 he was given permission by the committee of contributors to the national monument to set up a temporary exhibition hall beside the national monument on Calton Hill, Edinburgh. Initially the exhibition consisted of four colossal equestrian statues of historical figures including Robert the Bruce, Mary, queen of Scots, the duke of Marlborough, and the duke of Wellington, each carved from a single block of sandstone weighing approximately 20 tons. The collection was subsequently extended to about thirty groups, and also included an ante-room containing many

of his early 'characteristic' studies. Although the exhibition was well received, and did much to enhance his reputation as Scotland's 'national sculptor' (*Descriptive Catalogue of Statuary from the Chisel of Mr Robert Forrest*, appendix, 2), it was not a financial success, and eventually proved ruinous. His most ambitious project was the design for a statue of the duke of Wellington, commissioned by Lord Elgin for the summit of Arthur's Seat, Edinburgh. This was to be 80 feet tall, but remained unexecuted after Lord Elgin's death in 1841. His statue of Mr Ferguson of Raith was erected at Haddington in 1843. Forrest died, apparently unmarried, at Edinburgh, after an illness of about six weeks' duration, on 29 December 1852.

L. A. FAGAN, rev. RAY MCKENZIE

Sources 'The Lanarkshire sculptor', *Chambers' Edinburgh Journal*, 1 (1832), 357–8 · *Descriptive catalogue of statuary from the chisel of Mr Robert Forrest* (1835) · R. Forrest, *Descriptive account of the exhibition of statuary, national monument, Calton Hill* [n.d., after 1842] · R. Forrest, *Descriptive account of the exhibition of statuary, national monument, Calton Hill, Edinburgh* (1846) · *The Builder*, 11 (1853), 32 · R. L. Woodward, 'Nineteenth century Scottish sculpture', PhD diss., U. Edin., 1979 · R. Gunnis, *Dictionary of British sculptors, 1660–1851* (1953); new edn (1968) · *IGI*

Forrest, Theodosius (*c.*1728–1784), lawyer and songwriter, was born in London, the son of Ebenezer *Forrest (*bap.* 1700, *d.* 1793), the writer of the opera *Momus Turn'd Fabulist* and a friend of William Hogarth and the impresario John Rich, and his wife, Theodosia. Theodosius Forrest studied drawing under George Lambert but then entered his father's legal practice. As solicitor to the Covent Garden Theatre, Forrest was able to maintain close ties with the arts, 'the mistress of his affection' (Tyers, 54.877). He exhibited annually at the Royal Academy until a few years before his death. He also sat with his friend the antiquarian Francis Grose, both dressed as monks, for a portrait by Nathaniel Hone. A passion and a talent for music led him to compose a number of popular songs, including 'I made love to Kate' and his own musical afterpiece 'The Weathercocks', produced at Covent Garden on 17 October 1775. The work was not well received and later described as 'poor stuff' (Genest, 5.512). Forrest also listed a number of prominent dramatists among his friends. In his early life Gay, Pope, and Swift were said to think of Forrest as 'their playfellow and companion' (Tyers, 877). He was later a regular and much-liked member of the Beefsteak Club, where he associated with David Garrick and George Colman. Known for his generosity, intelligence, and integrity, Forrest was also a highly sensitive individual prone to insomnia and vulnerable to the criticisms which greeted his musical entertainment. His condition worsened to a 'nervous disorder, attended with a black jaundice' (ibid.), and in the summer of 1784 he travelled in Ireland in the hope of easing his condition. On 5 November of that year Forrest, aged about fifty-six, committed suicide at his lodgings in York Buildings, George Street, London.

G. B. SMITH, rev. PHILIP CARTER

Sources T. Tyers, 'Biographical sketch of the late Mr Theodosius Forrest', *GM*, 1st ser., 54 (1784), 877–8 · *GM*, 1st ser., 94/1 (1824), 582 · Genest, *Eng. stage*, 5.512

Archives BL, papers and drawings relating to tour of Paris, Add. MS 42232
Likenesses N. Hone, mezzotint (with F. Grose), BM, NPG

Forrest, Thomas (*fl.* **1580**), translator, of unrecorded family, is known for a single published work. On 4 January 1580 Thomas Purfoot paid for a licence to print Forrest's English translations of Isocrates, and an edition emerged that year. In *A Perfite Looking Glasse for All Estates* Forrest translated three speeches: 'Ad Demonicum', 'Ad Nicoclem', and 'Nicocles'. By 1580 these speeches had already been translated many times into Latin and the European vernaculars, and Forrest's own versions were made from the Latin of Hieronymus Wolf. He does not seem to have known the English version of 'Ad Nicoclem' by Thomas Eliot (1534), or that of 'Ad Demonicum' by John Bury (1559). Forrest's is the first printed English rendering of 'Nicocles'. He dedicated this collection to the new lord chancellor, Sir Thomas Bromley, and it appears from the dedication that Forrest had previously received some assistance from the chancellor's mother. He prefaced his work with a verse encomium to Sir Thomas and received commendatory poems from 'I. D.' and 'S. Norreis'.

Forrest's apparatus in this volume is substantial. Besides the dedication and the commendatory poems, each speech has its own preface. The first attacks the moral decay of the clergy. In the second he condemns the traffic in benefices, and there seems to be an element of personal frustration in his complaint that livings intended to maintain scholars are being given to more worldly men. Forrest's translations are supplied with an extensive marginal commentary, drawn in part from Wolf's edition. Forrest's marginalia provide historical exempla taken primarily, although not exclusively, from classical literature. There are a few digressions. He complains, for example, of a contemporary preference for amorous poetry instead of works of moral instruction (fol. 28*v*). He also complains of the theatre of his day: 'You maye come to a play now and neither understand the beginning nor ending, for it containeth not any example of well living, but onely a fardell of gibes cobled together by an ignoraunt Idiot' (fol. 29*r*).   P. BOTLEY

Sources T. Forrest, *A perfite looking glasse for all estates* (1580) · Arber, *Regs. Stationers*, 2.363 · H. B. Lathrop, *Translations from the classics into English from Caxton to Chapman, 1477–1620* (1933); repr. (1967), 206–7

Forrest, Thomas (*c.*1729–*c.*1802), navigator, appears to have served for some time in the Royal Navy, and to have been a midshipman in 1745, which suggests a birth date of about 1729. It was probably after the peace in 1748 that he entered the service of the East India Company, and his writings show that he was employed in Indian seas from 1753 almost continuously, though he implies that during part of the Seven Years' War he was on board the *Elizabeth*, (64 guns) in the squadron under Admiral Steevens. His name, however, does not appear in the *Elizabeth's* pay book. In 1762 he had command of a company's ship, from which he seems to date his experience when, writing in 1782, he spoke of himself as having been more than twenty years in 'the country trade'; and as having made fifteen voyages from Hindustan to the East, and four voyages from England to India. Having thus gained some knowledge of the winds, weather, and sailing routes of the station, though not of the Persian and Red Sea gulfs which he had never visited, he published *A Treatise on the Monsoons in East India* (Calcutta, 1782; 2nd edn, London, 1783), a little book of interesting experiences and exploded theories.

In 1770 Forrest was engaged in forming the new settlement at Balambangan, which had been recommended by Alexander Dalrymple, and in 1774, when the council, in accordance with their instructions and with a view to developing new sources of trade, wanted to send an exploring party in the direction of New Guinea, Forrest offered his services, which were readily accepted. He sailed on 9 December in the *Tartar*, a native boat of about 10 tons burden, with two English officers and a crew of eighteen Malays. In this, accompanied part of the time by two small boats, he pushed his explorations as far as Geelvink Bay in New Guinea, examining the Sulu archipelago, the south coast of Mindanao, Mandiolo, Batchian, and especially Waygiou, which he was the first to chart with any degree of accuracy, and returned to Achin in March 1776. The voyage was one of examination and enquiry rather than of discovery, and the additions made to geographical knowledge were corrections of detail rather than startling novelties; but the tact which Forrest had shown towards the local inhabitants and the amount of work done in a small boat in a poor state of repair deservedly won him credit. He published a detailed account of the voyage, under the title *A Voyage to New Guinea and the Moluccas from Balambangan … during the Years 1774–5–6* (1779).

In December 1782 Forrest was employed by the governor-general, Warren Hastings, to gain intelligence of the French fleet, which had left the coast of India, and evaded the observation of Sir Edward Hughes, the English commander-in-chief. It was believed that it had gone to Mauritius. Forrest found it at Achin, and bringing back the information to Vizagapatam, just before the return of the French, saved many country vessels from falling into their hands. In the following June he sailed again to survey the Andaman Islands, but falling to leeward of them passed through the Preparis Channel to the Tenasserim coast, which he examined southwards as far as Quedah; the account of the voyage, under the title *A Journal of the 'Esther' Brig, Capt. Thomas Forrest, from Bengal to Quedah, in 1783*, was edited by Dalrymple, and published at the expense of the East India Company in 1789. In 1790 he made a fuller examination of the same coast and of the islands lying off it, in, as he discovered, a long row, leaving a sheltered passage 125 miles long between them and the mainland, which he named Forrest Strait. It and the Forrest Passage still bear witness to his exploits, in the twenty-first century. The results of this voyage were published as *A Voyage from Calcutta to the Mergui Archipelago* (1792), with which were included some other minor essays. This volume is dedicated to William Aldersey, president of the board of trade in Bengal, by his 'most affectionate cousin', which is the only information known about his family. Some letters to Warren Hastings in 1784–5 (BL, Add. MSS 29164, fol. 171; 29166, fol. 135; 29169, fol. 118) show that before 1790 he had already examined the Mergui Islands. Forrest is said to have died in India about 1802. J. K. LAUGHTON, rev. ELIZABETH BAIGENT

Sources T. Forrest, *A treatise on the monsoons in East India* (1783) · T. Forrest, *A voyage to New Guinea and the Moluccas* (1779) · T. Forrest, *A journal of the 'Esther' brig, Capt. Thomas Forrest* (1789) · T. Forrest, *A voyage from Calcutta to the Mergui archipelago* (1792) · BL, Add. MSS 29164, fol. 171; 29166, fol. 135; 29169, fol. 118

Archives Wellcome L., papers

Likenesses W. Sharp, line engraving, 1779 (after J. K. Sherwin), BM, NPG; repro. in Forrest, *Voyage to New Guinea*

Forrest, William (*fl.* 1530–1576), poet, the date of whose birth is unknown, was a close kinsman and possibly the nephew of John Forest, the Franciscan friar who was chaplain to Katherine of Aragon, wrote against the breach with Rome, and was burnt for heresy by Henry VIII in 1538. William Forrest was a student at Cardinal College, and possibly its successor, King Henry VIII College, Oxford. He himself says that in 1530, while 'attending upon a certain good man' (Forrest, 75), he was present in Oxford when the university gave its opinion on the king's marriage. He was ordained priest, and appointed a petty canon at the cathedral for the bishopric of Oxfordshire which was established at Osney in 1542. When that cathedral was dissolved in 1546 he was awarded by the court of augmentations an annual pension of £6, which was still being paid in 1556, and this argues that he held no benefice at the new cathedral that was created in what replaced his old college at Christ Church. He also writes critically in one of his works of Richard Cox, successively dean of Osney and of Christ Church, which might support such a view.

Forrest was a prolific poet, almost all of whose works have remained in manuscript. He was a skilled calligrapher and several of his poems exist in autograph, decorated with something of the care of the medieval copyist. One of his influences as a poet was Alexander Barclay, the Benedictine, to whom Forrest refers as a friend. Forrest's first major poem was an epic, the *History of Joseph the Chaste*, which he wrote in 1545 and dedicated to William Parr, earl of Essex, brother of the queen. The dedication suggests a search for influential patronage. His next work appeared in manuscript in 1548 when he completed a very free translation of Aegidius Romanus's *De regimine principum*, which he entitled *The Pleasant Poesie of Princelie Practise*. This work was a long piece in, as he says, 'metre royal' (Herrtage, lxxxiii), written after the fashion of the Commonwealthsmen, the social commentators and reformers who were active around the duke of Somerset, to whom Forrest presented his work. Forrest, like the other writers in this genre, expressed concerns about unemployment, poverty, enclosures, inflation, the decay of the yeomanry, and problems of the cloth trade. In dedicating his work to both Protector Somerset and the king, Forrest expressed the hope that it might be used, as the original Latin text had been intended, as a means of educating the young Edward VI. An illustration in his own

hand in a manuscript copy of this work shows Forrest giving a copy of his book to the king. In 1551 Forrest completed a metrical translation of fifty psalms, which he also dedicated to Somerset. His translations of the psalms were intended, as he says, as a continuation of the work of his fellow collegian at Oxford, Thomas Sternhold, who died in 1549, and were he says 'metred by crosse ryme … by eight and six' (Forrest, 176). It is quite clear from these two major poetic productions that Forrest was happy to associate himself with Somerset, one of the leading protestant laymen of his period, and this suggests a pliability in religious matters. Still, to dedicate a book to Somerset in 1548 looks like sycophancy, but to persist in doing so in 1551, after the duke had fallen from power, is a mark of constancy.

The translation of the psalms may also reflect the musical side of Forrest's character in that good metrical translations might serve some liturgical purpose under the new dispensation. It was thanks to him that a very important collection of Tudor masses has been preserved. When John Taverner was appointed at Cardinal College, a manuscript collection of contemporary masses by Taverner himself and a number of other north-country composers was started for use in the chapel. The 1530s and 1540s witnessed a tragic destruction of such collections as the church was purged of idolatry. Forrest seems to have quietly hidden away this collection of six manuscript books. With the accession of Queen Mary, Forrest himself added to the collection, copying in his own hand a further six more recently composed masses into the books. The compilation as a whole is described as 'one of the three great collections of early Tudor festal Masses which have survived' (Bergsagel, 248), and after Forrest's death it came eventually into the new library of the Oxford music school.

Forrest's career improved under Queen Mary. He greeted her accession by composing 'A New Ballad of the Marigold', a loyal paean of fourteen eight-line verses, which was printed in London. The queen was inspired to make him one of her chaplains in 1555 because of their shared interest in music, and doubtless also to reward him for his poetry and perhaps also for the bravery of his kinsman, the martyred friar. Forrest published in 1555 two further short poems of praise to her: one cast in the form of a version of the Lord's prayer; the other of the Te Deum. John Foxe took such great exception to the mixture of spiritual and temporal themes involved in this that he reprinted them in his 1563 edition of *Acts and Monuments* with a hostile gloss; this has helped consolidate Forrest's later reputation as a good Catholic. In 1558 Forrest completed his major work of thanks to the queen, a long metrical account of the life of her mother, Katherine of Aragon, which he called *The History of Grisild the Second*. This presented Katherine as a tragic heroine, but at the same time succeeded in preserving Henry VIII from too much criticism. It contains some interesting historical details, drawn from Forrest's own experience, for instance on attitudes to the divorce in Oxford, which are not to be found elsewhere.

The accession of Elizabeth did not adversely affect Forrest who seems to have adapted yet again to a change in religious emphasis. He had been appointed parson of Bledlow in Buckinghamshire on 1 July 1556, and continued to hold this post for the next twenty years, despite the change of religion. Many of his later manuscript verses are on Catholic themes, especially connected with the life of the Virgin Mary. He lamented the lack of respect with which the Virgin had been treated since the beginning of the Reformation and attacked Luther by name; but at the same time he suggested that the papacy was responsible for the schism, and put forward the idea that each national church in Christendom should be under the control of its own clerical patriarch. He also referred to Elizabeth as 'our noble Queen' (Forrest, 187). He carried on writing, reworking in 1572 his early poem the *History of Joseph*, and now, after the death of the earl of Essex, to whom it had originally been dedicated, presenting it to the duke of Norfolk, who was executed that very year.

When Forrest formally resigned his living at Bledlow on 13 November 1576, he did so before an official in Oxford. This, and the fact that Oxford was the final resting place of his priceless musical collection, may suggest that his last years were spent in his old university town. There is no clear reference to him after 1576 and it is safe to assume that he died shortly afterwards.   PETER HOLMES

Sources DNB · Emden, *Oxf.* · W. Forrest, *The history of Grisild the Second*, ed. W. D. Macray (1875) · *Prose and poetry: Sir Thomas North to Michael Drayton* (1909), vol. 4 of *The Cambridge history of English literature*, ed. A. W. Ward and A. R. Waller (1907–27) · Wood, *Ath. Oxon.*, new edn, 1.297–300 · [W. Forrest], *Extract from the 'Pleasaunt poesye of princelie practise'*, ed. S. J. Herrtage, in T. Starkey, *England in the reign of King Henry VIII*, 1, EETS, 32 (1878), lxxix–xcix · Gillow, *Lit. biog. hist.* · C. Dodd [H. Tootell], *The church history of England, from the year 1500, to the year 1688*, 1 (1737), 515–16 · *LP Henry VIII*, 21/1, no. 778 · J. D. Bergsagel, 'The date and provenance of the Forrest–Heyther collection of Tudor masses', *Music and Letters*, 44 (1963), 240–48 · G. Lipscomb, *The history and antiquities of the county of Buckingham*, 4 vols. (1831–47), vol. 2, p. 118 · A. Hughes, *Medieval polyphony in the Bodleian Library* (1951), 43–4 · *The acts and monuments of John Foxe*, ed. J. Pratt, [new edn], 7 (1877), 124–5 · C. W. Foster, ed., *Lincoln episcopal records, in the time of Thomas Cooper … bishop of Lincoln*, CYS, 11 (1913), 295 · T. Warton, *The history of English poetry*, new edn, ed. W. C. Hazlitt, 4 vols. (1871), vol. 4, pp. 229–31 · A. Wood, *The history and antiquities of the University of Oxford*, ed. J. Gutch, 2 (1796), 46–9 · *Literary remains of King Edward the Sixth*, ed. J. G. Nichols, 1, Roxburghe Club, 75 (1857), cccxxxiv–cccxxxv · W. Oldys and T. Park, eds., *The Harleian miscellany*, 10 (1813), vol. 10, pp. 253–4

Archives Bodl. Oxf., music collection, Mus. Sch. e. 376–81

Likenesses W. Forrest, self-portrait, BL, Royal MS 17.D. iii, p. 8

Forrester family (*per. c.*1360–*c.*1450), administrators, illustrates the growing importance of burgess families in Scottish politics during the late fourteenth and fifteenth centuries. **Sir Adam Forrester** (*d.* 1405) combined a mercantile career with royal service. A merchant by 1363, he became clerk of the rolls in 1366, then served as exchequer auditor, deputy chamberlain, chamberlain of the queen's household, sheriff of Lothian, keeper of the great seal, and ambassador to England and Europe. He was custumar of Edinburgh from 1375 to 1405. In the 1380s he supervised fortification work at Edinburgh Castle. He lent large sums of money to the crown, and was financial

agent for the earl of Caithness, the bishop of Aberdeen, and others. As a burgess of Edinburgh, he represented the town in parliament in 1370 and was alderman in 1373 and 1378. In 1387 he was party to a contract to enlarge St Giles's Church. Forrester came to possess extensive lands, including Niddrie and Drylaw near Edinburgh, Traquair in Peeblesshire, and Fingask in Aberdeenshire; Fingask was granted to him by the bishop of Aberdeen as a reward for his services. In 1376 he acquired Corstorphine in Edinburghshire, which became the family seat; he probably built Corstorphine Castle. He also held lands in Edinburgh, including property in Forrester's Wynd, where he lived for a time.

Forrester's first wife was probably Agnes (*d.* before 1405), daughter of John Dundas of Dundas, who held Fingask in Perthshire. His second wife, Margaret (*d.* after 1429), was possibly a Forrester. Adam and Margaret had at least three children, John [see below], Marie (*d.* after 1439), and Thomas (*d.* after 1431), who held the lands of Drylaw. Marie married first Andrew Leper, an Edinburgh burgess, and second, *c.*1402, Alan Farnlie, custumar of Edinburgh with John from 1406 to 1425.

Forrester was knighted by 1403, perhaps because of service at the battle of Hamildon Hill in 1402, where he and his son John were taken prisoner. He endowed three chaplains in the chapel of St John the Baptist which he founded in Corstorphine, beside the parish church. He was probably also a benefactor of St Machar's, Aberdeen, where his obit was recorded. He died on 13 October 1405, probably at Corstorphine Castle, and was probably buried either in St Giles's or in his chapel at Corstorphine. A tomb and a burial slab at St John's are traditionally associated with him, although their identification is not certain.

Walter Forrester (*b. c.*1355, *d.* before 1426), bishop of Brechin, son of Marion Forrester (*b.* before 1353, *d.* before 1391) and brother of Patrick Forrester (*d.* after 1406), burgess of Dundee, was probably kin to Adam Forrester. The link cannot be established conclusively, but the two men moved in similar circles, and Walter witnessed documents of family interest to the Forresters of Corstorphine, and also served on peace commissions with Adam's eldest son, John. Walter's career embraced both Scottish royal service and university life in Paris. He studied at the University of Paris in the 1370s, graduating BA in 1375. In 1379 he returned to Scotland and by 1384 he was a canon of Aberdeen. He was royal wardrobe clerk (1380–93), and also served as keeper of the privy seal, king's clerk, and auditor of the exchequer. In August 1390 he helped to arrange Robert II's funeral and Robert III's coronation, and in the same year he resigned his lands of Inverdovet in Fife to his brother Patrick. About 1393 he went back to Paris to graduate MA, and became involved in university affairs; he supported the withdrawal of obedience from the Avignon pope Benedict XIII (*r.* 1394–1417) in 1398.

After returning to Scotland Forrester served on the duke of Rothesay's governing council, and acted as exchequer auditor (1399–1404), king's secretary (1402–5), and clerk of the rolls (*c.*1403–25). He was rewarded for his service to Robert II and Robert III, and for his future service to Prince

James, with a life annuity from 1406. In 1405 he went to France, possibly to arrange for Prince James's proposed stay. He remained abroad, and in 1407 was made bishop of Brechin by Benedict XIII, to whose allegiance he had returned. His royal service in Scotland resumed under the duke of Albany after 1408. He participated in embassies to discuss James I's release from captivity in England, and was also influential in Scottish policy towards the papal schism. Forrester was abroad again from 1422 to 1424, and during this period visited the curia in Rome, presenting a petition there. He died before April 1426.

Sir Adam Forrester's eldest son, **Sir John Forrester** (d. 1448x50), had been knighted by 1406. He was deputy chamberlain (1406–22), master of the king's household, custodian of the great seal, auditor of the rolls, and custumar of Edinburgh (1405–31). He helped to negotiate James I's release from England, and became his trusted servant; he was appointed chamberlain in 1424 and was on the king's council in 1437. In 1425 Corstorphine and adjacent lands were erected into a barony. After James I's murder in 1437 the earl of Douglas became Forrester's patron. Chancellor William Crichton (d. 1454) burnt his Corstorphine lands in 1445 because the family had aided Douglas in an attack on the Crichtons at Barnton, Edinburghshire. Forrester last served as chamberlain in 1448; whether he retired owing to waning Douglas influence or to infirmity is unclear. In 1448 the pope allowed Forrester and his wife, Marion, 'old and stricken in years', a private confessor. Forrester was patron to St Giles's, where he founded an altar c.1425, and St Machar's. He and his mother endowed two more chaplains in St John's Chapel at Corstorphine in 1429; he obtained papal recognition of it as a collegiate church in 1444, and it became the family's burial place.

Forrester married first Margaret (d. c.1408); second Jean St Clair (d. before 1422), daughter of the earl of Orkney; and third, c.1422, Marion Stewart (c.1380–c.1448) of Dalswinton, Dumfriesshire, widow of Sir John Stewart of Garlies, Kirkcudbrightshire. From either his first or second marriage he had four children: Elizabeth (d. after 1408), who married Sir Alexander Lauder of Halton; John, his heir (b. before 1425, d. c.1456), who married into the Edinburgh family of Wigmer; Henry (b. before 1425, d. c.1473), who married Helen, daughter of John Farnlie of Braid; and Jonet (d. c.1488), who married Robert, Lord Maxwell (d. 1485). John Forrester (d. c.1437), who held Kirkmahoe benefice in Dumfriesshire, was probably an illegitimate son. Forrester died between 20 September 1448 and 20 September 1450; he was buried in St John's Church, Corstorphine. A tomb near the altar is assumed to be that of Sir John and one of his wives. The Forresters were among the most successful of those fourteenth-century mercantile families who used their financial talents in royal service to rise into the gentry. ELIZABETH EWAN

Sources G. Burnett and others, eds., *The exchequer rolls of Scotland*, 2–6 (1878–83) • *CDS*, vol. 4 • *RotS* • J. M. Thomson and others, eds., *Registrum magni sigilli regum Scotorum / The register of the great seal of Scotland*, 11 vols. (1882–1914), vols. 1–2 • D. E. R. Watt, *A biographical dictionary of Scottish graduates to AD 1410* (1977) • D. Laing, ed., *Registrum cartarum ecclesie Sancti Egidii de Edinburgh*, Bannatyne Club, 105 (1859) • C. Innes, ed., *Registrum episcopatus Aberdonensis*, 1, Spalding Club, 13 (1845) • C. McGladdery, *James II* (1990) • A. S. Cowper, *Historic Corstorphine and roundabout*, pts 1 and 2 (1991–2) • P. Chalmers, J. I. Chalmers, and C. Innes, eds., *Registrum episcopatus Brechinensis*, 2 vols., Bannatyne Club, 102 (1856) • D. Laing, ed., *Registrum domus de Soltre*, Bannatyne Club, 109 (1861) • C. Innes, ed., *Registrum episcopatus Glasguensis*, 2 vols., Bannatyne Club, 75 (1843); also pubd as 2 vols., Maitland Club, 61 (1843) • *CEPR letters*, vols. 7–8, 10 • C. Innes, ed., *Registrum monasterii de Passelet*, Maitland Club, 17 (1832) • J. D. Marwick, ed., *Charters and other documents relating to the city of Edinburgh*, Scottish Burgh RS, 7 (1871) • M. Brown, *James I* (1994) • *Scots peerage*, vol. 4
Archives NL Scot., Adv. MS 80.4.15, fol. 112
Likenesses double portrait, tomb effigy (probably Sir John Forrester; with one of his wives), St John's Church, Corstorphine, Edinburgh • tomb effigy (possibly Adam Forrester), St John's Church, Corstorphine, Edinburgh

Forrester, Sir Adam (d. 1405). *See under* Forrester family (*per. c.*1360–*c.*1450).

Forrester, Alfred Henry [*pseud.* Alfred Crowquill] (1804–1872), illustrator and writer, was born in London on 10 September 1804, the second son of Robert Forrester of 5 North Gate, Royal Exchange, London, a wealthy City of London notary. He was educated at a private school in Islington, London. His elder brother, Charles Robert *Forrester (1803–1850), was a lawyer and writer, and both brothers collaborated on literary ventures under the name Alfred Crowquill (literally the quill taken from a crow for writing and drawing). Alfred assumed the pseudonym for himself before his brother's death.

Crowquill began to draw caricatures before 1822, and as a talented amateur fully entered into the great age of the separately issued print. After literary contributions to *The Hive* in 1822, and to the editor John Timbs's *The Mirror* in 1823, he studied drawing, wood-engraving, and etching on steel and collaborated with George Cruikshank as engraver on a *Freischütz* travesty (1824) by Septimus Geobus (J. A. Apel) and on W. F. von Kosewitz's *Eccentric Tales* (1827). He achieved some fame with his single prints *Beauties of Brighton* (1825) and *Dover Coach 5 O'Clock Morning*, which show strong characterizations. He explored the follies of fashion and the court in *A Trump, a Court Card* (1828), satirizing the duchess of St Albans; *The Great Humming Top* (1829), featuring Baron M. A. Rothschild; and *Bull Broke Loose* (August 1832), a Reform Bill print, which was unusually a lithograph. Elsewhere he showed a liking for grammatical personifications and puns. On 10 March 1838 he married Mary Saunders at St Dunstan and All Saints, Stepney, London.

With the shift from the printseller to pictorial journalism in the 1840s, Crowquill found work on *Bentley's Miscellany* (1840–41) and in *Punch*'s early numbers from 1842 to 1844, including some cartoons. But M. H. Spielmann says that his appearance in *Punch* was 'sought after at a time when comic artists were few' (Spielmann, 450). He was very soon outclassed by the likes of John Leech and John Tenniel. He contributed full-page figure subjects to the *Illustrated London News* Christmas supplements between 1844 and 1870, but not regularly. Although not a first-rate artist, he drew competent genre subjects, filling sketch-books and exhibiting four pen-and-ink works at the Royal Academy in 1845 and 1846. He was also an occasional painter in oils.

During the 1840s Crowquill issued a number of comic books written and illustrated by himself, of which good examples are *A. Crowquill's Guide to the Watering Places* (1839), *Sketches of Pumps, Handled by R. Cruikshank with some Temperate Spoutings by A. Crowquill* (1846), *A Missile for Papists!* (1850), and *A bundle of crowquills, dropped by A. Crowquill in his eccentric flights over the fields of literature* (1854). He illustrated works by Henry Cockton and Cuthbert Bede and was 'understudy' in works illustrated by the great names John Leech and H. K. Browne (Phiz), notably the former's *Comic Latin Grammar* (1840) and the latter's *Merry Pictures* (1857). He collaborated with both Richard Doyle and Leech in *The Book of Ballads by Bon Gaultier* (1845).

After 1860, when burlesque books were less popular, Crowquill devoted much of his time to children's books, which he both wrote and illustrated. *The Times* obituarist noted that 'Among other things he could dash off a little tale with much humour, infuse spirit into a song, and win all the attention of children by such works as the *Careless Chicken* and *Fairy Footsteps*' (31 May 1872). Basing his anthropomorphic animals on the styles and themes of his great French contemporary Grandville, he brought to scenes a particularly British element, even if his illustrations were less incisive. But contemporary audiences applauded him—'Human arrogance scowled in his lions, feminine conceit strutted in his ostriches, impertinent coxcombry appeared in his monkeys, craftiness governed the expression in the eye of his wolves and foxes to a remarkable degree' (ibid.). He issued nearly thirty of these delightful titles between 1839 and 1870, and one, *The Pictorial Grammar*, was reprinted posthumously in 1875.

Forrester's versatility extended to stage scenery and many pantomimes and transformation scenes were enlivened by his inventions. He was also a skilled modeller, producing a statuette of the duke of Wellington in 1851, which he presented to Queen Victoria a fortnight before the duke's death. That same year he exhibited at the Great Exhibition a porcelain statuette of a child leading a lion on a floral halter. He turned his virtuosity to designing book covers for Messrs Routledge in the 1860s and adapted himself to the new trade and fashion for Christmas cards in the 1870s. A frame of his drawings was shown at the important exhibition 'English humorists in art', at the Royal Institute of Painters in Water Colours in June 1889 (no. 1384). Examples of his works on paper, including the watercolour for the *Beauties of Brighton* (1825), are in the Victoria and Albert Museum, London.

Crowquill suffered from heart disease for eight years and died on 26 May 1872 at his home, 3 Portland Place North, Clapham Road, London. He was buried at Norwood cemetery, London, on 31 May. His wife survived him. A surviving photograph shows a powerful man with a rather Roman head and fine beard. A contemporary wrote of Forrester: 'If not a genius, the man was talented and clever—a universal favourite. He could draw, he could write, he was an admirable vocalist, setting the table in a roar with his medley of songs' (Everitt, 370). SIMON HOUFE

Sources G. Everitt, *English caricaturists and graphic humourists of the nineteenth century*, 2nd edn (1893) • M. H. Spielmann, *The history of 'Punch'* (1895) • R. L. Patten, *George Cruikshank's life, times, and art*, 1 (1992), 258–9 • *Exhibition of the works of the English humorists in art* (1889) [exhibition catalogue, Royal Institute of Painters in Water Colours, London] • S. Houfe, *The dictionary of 19th century British book illustrators and caricaturists*, rev. edn (1996) • *English caricature, 1620 to the present: caricaturists and satirists, their art, their purpose and influence*, V&A (1984) [exhibition catalogue, Yale U. CBA, L. Cong., the National Library of Canada, Ottawa, and the V&A, London, 1984] • J. I. Whalley and T. R. Chester, *A history of children's book illustration* (1988) • M. Bryant and S. Heneage, eds., *Dictionary of British cartoonists and caricaturists, 1730–1980* (1994) • *CGPLA Eng. & Wales* (1872) • d. cert. • *The Times* (31 May 1872) • 'Forrester, Charles Robert', *DNB* • parish register (marriage), Stepney, St Dunstan and All Saints, 10 March 1838

Archives Hunt. L., drawings, letters, and literary MSS | V&A NAL, letters to W. Lee and sketches

Likenesses C. Baugniet, three lithographs, 1843, BM, NPG • C. Baugniet, lithograph, 1850, BM • photograph, repro. in Spielmann, *History of 'Punch'*, 349 • woodcut (after photograph by J. Watkins), NPG; repro. in *Illustrated Review* (15 June 1872)

Wealth at death under £200: probate, 3 Sept 1872, *CGPLA Eng. & Wales*

Forrester, Charles Robert (1803–1850), lawyer and writer, son of Robert Forrester, public notary, of 5 North Gate, Royal Exchange, London, was born in London and succeeded his father as a notary, having his place of business at 5 North Piazza, Royal Exchange; he afterwards moved to 28 Royal Exchange, where he remained until his death. His profession made him a wealthy man, and he used his money and leisure time to write. Under the pseudonym 'Hal Willis, student at law' he brought out in 1824 *Castle Baynard, or, The Days of John*, and in 1827 a second novel, *Sir Roland: a Romance of the Twelfth Century* (4 vols.). In 1826–7 he contributed to *The Stanley Tales, Original and Select, Chiefly Collected by Ambrose Marten* (5 vols.). *Absurdities in Prose and Verse, Written and Illustrated by Alfred Crowquill* appeared in 1827, the illustrations being by his brother Alfred Henry *Forrester (1804–1872), so that in this instance, as well as on succeeding occasions, the two brothers were conjointly using the same name.

On 17 March 1830 Charles Forrester married Ann Garratt at St Bartholomew's, London. He also wrote for the *Ladies' Museum* and for Louisa Henrietta Sheridan's *Comic Offering*. Under the editorship of Theodore Hook he was on the staff of the *New Monthly Magazine* in 1837 and 1838, where he used the name of Alfred Crowquill. At the end of 1839 he became connected with *Bentley's Miscellany*, in which magazine his writings are sometimes signed A. Crowquill and at other times Hal Willis, the former being illustrated by his brother. In 1843 a selection of his articles in those two magazines was brought out in two volumes under the title of *Phantasmagoria of Fun*. He was also the author of *Eccentric Tales, by W. F. von Kosewitz* (1827), *The Battle of the Annuals: a Fragment* (1835), and *The Lord Mayor's Fool* (1840), the last two of which were published anonymously. He was also well acquainted with Latin, French, German, and Dutch.

About 1843 Forrester retired from literary life, and his brother continued to use the pseudonym Alfred Crow-quill, so that, eventually, he became known as its sole originator. Forrester died of heart disease at his home in Beaumont Square, Mile End, London, on 15 January 1850. He was survived by his wife and four children.

G. C. BOASE, rev. REBECCA MILLS

Sources IGI · will, PRO, PROB 11/2107, sig. 113 · GM, 2nd ser., 33 (1850), 545 · Ward, Men of the reign, 328
Wealth at death exact sum unknown; all bequeathed to wife: will, PRO, PROB 11/2107, sig. 113, fol. 99

Forrester, David (1588–1633), Church of Scotland minister, was the second son of John Forrester of Garden, burgess of Stirling, and his wife, Margaret Cornwall of Bonard. He was probably educated at Stirling's grammar school before entering the University of St Andrews, from where he graduated MA on 22 July 1608. Owing to the influence of his kin, who were frequently represented on the kirk session of the town, Forrester was admitted to the exercise at Stirling and was presented to the parish of Denny on 3 April 1610. He was translated to north Leith, Edinburgh, on 16 December 1613. He married, on 30 January 1614, Margaret Paterson, daughter of Duncan Paterson, burgess of Stirling, and Marion Alexander, a sister of Sir William Alexander of Menstrie. The couple had three sons, the eldest of whom, Duncan, was later a regent at the University of Edinburgh.

Raised according to presbyterian principles Forrester was soon involved in the controversy which accompanied the imposition of the five articles of Perth in 1618. In particular he refused to implement the king's instruction that communicants should kneel at the receiving of the sacrament. Consequently his kirk at Leith became a haven for those 'inhabitants [of Edinburgh] who travelled abroad to seek the Communion where it was administered in puritie' (Calderwood, 7.380). On the insistence of Archbishop John Spottiswood of St Andrews that he conform, Forrester explained that he could not 'be persaudit of the lawfulnes' of kneeling, 'for I was brought up under that reverend [minister of Stirling] Mr Patrick Simson, from whom I sucked the contrarie from my childhood' (Calderwood, 7.407).

Forrester was ordered to remove himself to Aberdeen, where Bishop Patrick Forbes admitted him to the parish of Rathven on 20 April 1620. The sentence of exile did not bring about a change of heart, and Forbes noted with some apprehension Forrester's determination to 'stand on his own conscience'. Nevertheless, the bishop thought him 'als modest, and [as] subject to heare reason, as the youngest scholler in Scotland' (Calderwood, 7.408). But Forrester's energetic pursuit of northern 'papists' brought him into conflict with the Catholic marquess of Huntly, and eventually rendered him equally troublesome to the bishopric of Aberdeen. Thus Forbes did not contest the intervention of his wife's uncle, Sir William Alexander, who procured the minister's restoration to the parish of Leith on 20 September 1627.

At some date after his return to Edinburgh Forrester remarried, probably because of the death of Margaret Paterson. His second wife was Margaret Hamilton, a daughter of Robert Hamilton of Preston. The couple had two children, James and Margaret. Forrester's continuing nonconformity ensured that he did not accumulate wealth during the last years of his life. His immediately realizable assets in 1633 amounted to £180 Scots, while he was owed £3790 in unpaid stipend and other debts, which were notoriously difficult to collect. He died at Leith in June 1633.

VAUGHAN T. WELLS

Sources D. Calderwood, The history of the Kirk of Scotland, ed. T. Thomson and D. Laing, 8 vols., Wodrow Society, 7 (1842–9) · Fasti Scot., new edn, 1.154, 6.294 · C. Forrester, The Forresters: a lowland clan and its lands (1988) · J. Row, The history of the Kirk of Scotland, from the year 1558 to August 1637, ed. D. Laing, Wodrow Society, 4 (1842) · W. R. Foster, 'Ecclesiastical administration in Scotland', PhD diss., U. Edin., 1963 · Stirling presbytery register, Scottish Central Region archives, CH2/722/4 · Stirling kirk session register, Scottish Central Region archives, CH2/1026/1 · R. Renwick, ed., Extracts from the records of the royal burgh of Stirling, AD 1519–1666 (1887) · Scots peerage, vol. 8
Wealth at death £3953 Scots: Foster, 'Ecclesiastical administration'

Forrester [née McColl], **Isobel Margaret Stewart** (1895–1976), ecumenist, was born on 30 June 1895 at Glenlyon Free Church manse, Perthshire, the first of the two children of John McColl (1849–1921) and his wife, Jane Mary (Jeannie) Baillie. Her father was a minister of the Free Church of Scotland, and the family lived in a rural highland glen until 1904, when a House of Lords ruling awarded the properties of the Free Church to the small minority which refused to join the 1900 United Free Church ministers. John McColl lost his charge and manse, and the family moved to Edinburgh. During her early years Isobel was educated at home. In Edinburgh she attended St George's School to 1913, winning a scholarship to study English at Lady Margaret Hall, Oxford, which she attended 1913–16, graduating BA with third-class honours in English. After returning to Edinburgh in 1917 she taught at her old school and also at the Edinburgh Academy. Her eighteen-year-old brother was killed at the front, and Isobel developed a lifelong loathing of war.

In 1920 Isobel was appointed educational secretary with the United Free Church Girls Auxiliary—a national organization for women aged fifteen to thirty in support of the church's Women's Foreign Mission. Isobel herself considered a missionary career, but on 21 November 1922 she married the Revd William Roxburgh Forrester MC (1892–1985). They lived for six years in the small Midlothian mining community of Roslin, and then moved to Gorgie, an inner-city working-class area of Edinburgh. During these years Isobel gave birth to four children—John, Anne, David, and Jean—and fulfilled the traditional supportive role expected of a minister's wife, but also edited the Primary Quarterly, a teachers' guide for Sunday schools.

In 1935 W. R. Forrester was appointed to the chair of practical theology and Christian ethics at St Andrews University. A fifth child, Duncan, was born, and the family settled at 54 South Street. In St Andrews for twenty-five years Isobel led a full and active life, offering warm hospitality and lively discussions on the issues of the day to students, colleagues, and visitors from all over the world. She was a leading member of the St Andrews Women's Debating Society; she led retreats at the university; and she even preached at a service in Aberdeen University Chapel. Her ability to work well in a team was discerned in many situations. In 1940 she led a student mission at Edinburgh University with the Revd Dr George MacLeod (founder of the Iona community) and the Revd Mervyn Stockwood (later bishop of Southwark). She 'went quietly among the students, listening, sharing her own experiences and insights, doing so ever so gently, so that they were prepared to travel in their thinking with her' (I. Fraser, *Salted with Fire*, 1999, 152). The Forresters had a special concern for refugees, and a German family lived with them for fifteen months after the Second World War. They sheltered refugees from political persecution in Malawi, and were close to ex-president Orton Chirwa and his wife, Vera, during their years of imprisonment. Isobel's commitment to a global, inclusive, and challenging vision of Christianity also found expression in her presidency of the Church of Scotland Women's Foreign Mission.

Isobel Forrester was a creative advocate and pioneer of ecumenism. She was one of the instigators of the Dollarbeg Group, established in 1946 to participate in a World Council of Churches study concerning the life and work of women in the church. It continued to meet in conference for several years as an unprecedented interchurch forum, engaging with all the major contemporary social, political, and religious issues. She described how the original group had been 'shaken and convicted and profoundly grateful for the new relationship with one another, and their committal to a common task' (Small, 20).

For the next three decades Isobel Forrester played a pivotal role, inspiring and supporting the development of ecumenical relationships, dialogue, and organization in Scottish church life—at local and national levels, and within a global context. She served the Scottish Churches Ecumenical Association in different capacities, including chairman. But her enthusiasm went beyond institutions, and was especially fired by the dynamic connections made at the interfaces between religious, civic, and political life. She was a passionate supporter of women's ordination.

Isobel Forrester was a tiny woman, with clear skin, a low and gentle voice, but with an inner steel of conviction and wisdom. She died on 30 August 1976 in York. At the funeral service on 4 September Archie Craig recalled that her 'intellectual vigour, edged with wit and made lustrous by poetical feeling, shone through her platform addresses, committee work and everyday conversation ... She was always probing, always questing'. She would be remembered especially for the 'width and depth and patience of her affections' (private information). She was cremated in Edinburgh on 4 September 1976.

LESLEY ORR MACDONALD

Sources private information (2004) · M. Small, *Growing together: the ecumenical movement in Scotland, 1924–64* (1964) · *Life and Work* (Oct 1976) · J. Horsman and W. S. Landale, *Footprints of faith* (1988) ·

C. Avent and H. Pipe, eds., *Lady Margaret Hall register, 1879–1990* (1990) · b. cert. · m. cert.
Likenesses photographs, priv. coll.
Wealth at death £29,547.16: confirmation, 15 Oct 1976, *CCI*

Forrester, James. See Grimston, James Brabazon, fifth earl of Verulam (1910–1960).

Forrester, Sir John (d. 1448x50). See under Forrester family (*per. c.*1360–*c.*1450).

Forrester, Joseph James (1809–1861), wine merchant and topographer, was born at Kingston upon Hull on 27 May 1809, the only son of Patrick Forrester (1772–1846), jeweller and goldsmith, and his wife, Sarah, *née* Weddell (1777–1856). Nothing is known of his early years, but in 1831 he went to Oporto to join his uncle, James Forrester (1775–1840), who had entered the port wine firm of Campion Offley Hesketh in 1803. On 10 May 1836 Joseph married Eliza Cramp, whose brother Francis became a partner in the firm of Offley, Cramp, and Forrester in 1848. When Eliza died on 3 August 1847, their six surviving children were confided into the care of relatives in England, though Joseph was a devoted father and saw them as frequently as his visits to the company's London office at 76 Mark Lane allowed. After Joseph's own death, Francis Cramp invited Joseph's two eldest sons to enter the family firm in Oporto, where they had offices at Rua dos Inglezes 80.

Portugal at the time of Joseph Forrester's arrival was in the throes of civil war, and in January 1832 Forrester took part in the defence of the British port wine lodges at Vila Nova de Gaia on the south bank of the Douro, and so witnessed the closing stages of the siege of Oporto by the forces of Dom Miguel. When not engaged in the complex business of port wine production and export, Forrester, a keen amateur cartographer and painter, undertook a survey of the entire River Douro within Portugal, with a view to making it safer for boats by blasting, or otherwise diminishing, the many rapids and obstructions along its course. His map, completed in 1843, was published by Weale of London in 1848. It measured 116 by 24 inches, with English and Portuguese texts explaining its origins and the astronomical bearings upon which it was based, a declaration of the Portuguese government's approval of the map, and was embellished with vignettes depicting typical river craft and the more notorious of the rapids. Forrester dedicated and signed a coloured copy, which he presented to the London Geographical Society of which he was also a member. A smaller map of the demarcated port wine district of the Upper Douro, published by Wyld in 1843, was republished by Weale, and was included in a parliamentary committee report of 1852 on import duties on wines. The same map illustrated Forrester's prize essay on *Portugal and its Capabilities* (1853), describing several aspects of the country and its commercial potential, with which he had won a 50 guinea prize offered by Benjamin D'Oliveira MP. In 1855, the regent, Dom Fernando, conferred on Forrester the title of barão (baron) for life.

Forrester had already acquired notoriety in 1844 by the

publication in Oporto of a pamphlet entitled *One or Two Words about Port Wine*, written anonymously, but easily traceable to him. In it he exposed with some vehemence what he considered to be the fortification and adulteration of port wine by the addition of brandy, and of elderberry to give it extra colour. This caused a furore among the interested British shippers, and their antagonism took several years to subside. As an exponent of the 'pure wine' school, Forrester practised what he preached, producing wines which were neither of the type that his customers were used to and expected, nor to their taste. This was hardly acting in the best interest of the firm, and it caused constant concern among his partners in London. The result was that in 1851 Forrester withdrew from active participation in Offley, Cramp, and Forrester, although he continued to write articles defending his views. He also wrote on allied subjects such as the *oïdium Tuckeri* vine disease, and on the chemical changes which took place in port when stored in England; a sequel to his earlier pamphlet, *A Word or Two More on Port-Wine*, appeared shortly before his death.

Forrester, described by one of his descendants as 'a dynamic Scot, an energetic Victorian whose portrait revealed a firm strong jaw and an obstinate expression of the mouth' (Delaforce, 92), had a high opinion of himself. Forrester had reason to be proud of the numerous honours, awards, and decorations showered on him in acknowledgement of his efforts to improve communications in his adopted country, and in maintaining the distinction of its port wine, although some people considered that he pursued his controversial campaign obsessively, even to the point of eccentricity. He was a member of many learned academies and societies. In London alone (where he spent more time in his later years) he was a fellow of the Royal Geographical Society, the Society of Arts, the Geological Society, the Royal Astronomical Society, and the Royal Agricultural Society.

In Portugal, Forrester would frequently sail up country in his luxuriously appointed *barco rabelo*; he claimed to have been the first, in 1841, to reach the Salto da Sardinha by boat. On that occasion he was accompanied by Auguste Roquemont, a Swiss artist, who had lived in Portugal since 1828 and who taught Forrester painting. Forrester became a talented amateur artist. As early as 1834 he painted a detailed watercolour depicting the top-hatted British shippers congregating to talk shop in the Rua Nova dos Inglezes, Oporto, near the mansion he later called 'the so-styled British Factory House', which was home to an association or club of which, even before he became *persona non grata* in 1844, he appears never to have courted membership. A series of ten views in the vicinity followed, lithographed in London in 1835, and entitled *Portuguese Scenery with Illustrative Notes*; a further ten views, of the Douro valley, were reproduced on his large map of 1848. Several oil paintings, watercolours, and sepia drawings have also survived, together with portraits, dated largely between 1848 and 1851, including eighteen of Portuguese personalities, hung in the British Club at Oporto.

Forrester, like his contemporary in Oporto, Frederick William Flower (1815–1889), was also a pioneer in photography, and through his friendship with Dr Hugh Diamond became a member of the Photographic Exchange Club. In the mid-1850s he experimented with portraiture and in photographing peasant groups, which he later used to illustrate his *Journeyings in the Minho Province*, published in Oporto in 1855. He also formed an extensive collection of earthenware figures representing regional costumes.

In Portugal, when visiting his numerous friends in their port wine *quintas*, or estates, Forrester would usually sail up the Douro; and it was when returning downstream, after lunching at the Quinta de Vesúvio on 12 May 1861, that the boat carrying Forrester and his party capsized in the rapids of the Cachão de Valeira, below the village of São João da Pesqueira. Although the ladies were saved by the buoyancy of their crinolines, Forrester, a powerfully built man, not quite fifty-two years of age, was swept away and drowned. Stories circulated to the effect that he had been weighed down by a belt full of gold sovereigns with which to pay farmers; that his high boots had filled with water, and so on. Whatever the reason, his body was never recovered from the river to which he had devoted so much of his life.

IAN CAMPBELL ROBERTSON

Sources J. Delaforce, *Joseph James Forrester: baron of Portugal* (1992) · *DNB* · A. D. Francis, *The wine trade* (1972) · R. Macaulay, *They went to Portugal* (1946) · G. Robertson, *Port* (1978) · G. Seiberling, 'The photographs of Joseph James Forrester', *History of Photography*, 7 (1983), 51–61 · S. Bradford, *The story of port*, revised edn (1983) · A. Berkeley and S. Lowndes, *English art in Portugal* (1994) · *Journal of the Royal Geographical Society*, 31 (1861), cxxiii–cxxiv · J. J. Forrester, 'Map of the Douro', 1848, RGS [pubd map] · *CGPLA Eng. & Wales* (1861)

Archives RGS, signed and ded., 'Map of the Douro', 1848

Likenesses A. Roquemont, oils, *c*.1835, Instituto do Vino do Porto, Oporto · H. Diamond, photograph, *c*.1854, National Museum of Photography, Film and Television, Bradford, Royal Photographic Society collection · photograph, *c*.1854, repro. in Delaforce, *Joseph James Forrester*, frontispiece · photograph, *c*.1854, repro. in Bradford, *Story of port*, 60 · engraving, repro. in J. Delaforce, *The factory house at Oporto* (1990), 96 · portrait, Romantic Museum, Oporto · two portraits, repro. in Berkeley and Lowndes, *English art in Portugal*

Wealth at death £4000: probate, 5 July 1861, *CGPLA Eng. & Wales*

Forrester, Thomas (*c*.1588–1642), Church of Scotland minister and satirist, is of unknown parentage. He graduated MA at the University of St Andrews on 22 July 1608, but nothing is known of his career until he was recommended, on 10 March 1623, by the archbishop of Glasgow for appointment to the ministry in Ayr, the previous minister of the parish having been deposed in 1622 for his opposition to the king's religious policies. The kirk session of Ayr, 'after they had convocated the haill body of the town', represented to the archbishop that Forrester was not suitable to be their minister (*Fasti Scot.*, 2.187), and, though James VI signed a presentation to the parish for him on 10 April, his predecessor continued to preach in the parish until 1624 and Forrester never took up the post. He was instead appointed minister of Melrose, perhaps in 1623, certainly by 1627, as he represented the parish at a meeting of commissioners of the church in Edinburgh in July that year. He was an enthusiastic supporter of royal policies in religion, and when these were overthrown by the covenanters in 1638 'This monster was justlie deposed' (*Letters and Journals of Robert Baillie*, 1.165–6) after the general assembly heard allegations against him on 11 December. While the surviving evidence is obviously biased it suggests that as well as supporting royal policies Forrester was an eccentric who had enjoyed taunting his opponents with outrageous statements and actions, such as denouncing the great reformer John Knox, great-uncle of Forrester's predecessor at Melrose (also called John Knox).

Forrester's reaction to deposition was, according to Henry Guthrie (writing in the 1650s), the vigorous satiric verses entitled *The New Litany*, which comprehensively denounced the covenanters and all their deeds—not forgetting 'the knock doune race of Knoxes'. This became well enough known for an 'old Gentlewoman' in Melrose to be able to recite parts of it a century later (Milne, 39), though it was not published until 1847. Forrester's own experience is reflected in the litany's plea to be saved 'From Presbyteriall inquisitione, / Queherin I was once toss'd amaine / I houpe neuer to come ther againe' (Maidment, 52, 55). The attribution to him in 1743 of an epitaph on the earl of Strafford, otherwise ascribed to John Cleveland, has been dismissed as 'late, putative and uncorroborated' but the admissions that it is 'unlike any of [Cleveland's] genuine poems' and that it should be seen only as 'at least possibly Cleveland's' (J. Cleveland, *Poems*, ed. B. Morris and E. Witherington, 1967, xxxiii–xxxiv) suggest that Forrester's claim to it may not be entirely lost.

Forrester died in 1642, when he is said to have been aged about fifty-four. He was survived by his wife, Agnes Kennedy, who died in 1666.   DAVID STEVENSON

Sources *Fasti Scot.*, new edn, vol. 2 · *DNB* · A. Milne, *A description of the parish of Melrose* (1743) · *The letters and journals of Robert Baillie*, ed. D. Laing, 3 vols. (1841–2) · J. Gordon, *History of Scots affairs from 1637–1641*, ed. J. Robertson and G. Grub, 3 vols., Spalding Club, 1, 3, 5 (1841) · *The memoirs of Henry Guthry, late bishop*, ed. G. Crawford, 2nd edn (1748) · 'A satire relating to public affairs', *Scots Magazine and Edinburgh Literary Miscellany*, 69 (1807), 117–22 · J. Maidment, ed., 'The new litany', *A book of Scottish pasquils* (1868) · D. Laing, ed., *The Bannatyne miscellany*, 3, Bannatyne Club, 19b (1855) · Anderson, *Scot. nat.*

Forrester, Thomas (c.1635–1706),

Church of Scotland minister, was born at Stirling and was the eldest son of David Forrester (*d.* in or before 1686), local politician, and his first wife, Mary Erskine, possibly the illegitimate daughter of John Erskine of Balgorie. Forrester's father was the laird of Denovan, provost of Stirling in 1653–4, and a supporter of the royalists in the civil war. Forrester was admitted as minister of Alloa, Stirlingshire, under the restored bishops in 1664. However, by 1672 and perhaps earlier, influenced by John Brown's *Apologetical Relation of the Sufferings … of the Church of Scotland* (1665) and other works, he turned against episcopacy and began to boycott meetings of the Stirling presbytery. When warned about his conduct he replied on 26 August 1673 that the then form of church government was 'ultimately referrable unto the magistrate's civil power, which frame I judge to be contrary to the word of God, the confessions of Reformed Churches and our own church's judgement'; meetings of the presbytery were merely 'a badge of acknowledgement of the lawfulness of this frame' (Wodrow, 1.377). Accused of schism, he asked 'how can they be schismatics from the church of Scotland who own and walk according to her principles vows and engagements' over many decades (Wodrow, 1.159). Forrester was ejected from his Alloa ministry. The following February he was discovered by the Stirling magistrates at 'a numerous conventicle kept in the house of Patrick Thomson, merchant'. He was taken under guard to Edinburgh and there imprisoned. After petitioning the privy council, Forrester was released under the indemnity of March 1674, but he was deposed by the diocesan synod of Dunkeld on 29 April 1674, an order ratified by Bishop Henry Guthrie on 4 May.

Forrester now threw in his lot with the underground presbyterian preaching movement of 'field preachers', and had much 'success in conversion in Stirlingshire, Dunbartonshire and other places' (Wodrow, 1.378). In 1678 he was involved in a controversy over church government with James Ramsay, bishop of Dunblane, and by June 1681 he was being sheltered by Archibald Edmonstone, laird of Duntreath, in which vicinity he preached at a conventicle. On 5 May 1684 Forrester was proclaimed a fugitive and settled at Killearn, where he continued to preach. At some point in the 1670s he married Anne (*d.* in or before 1733), daughter of John Govan, minister of Muckart; one of their fourteen children was born in 1678. Forrester may also have had an illegitimate son. Forrester's father, who died some time before 10 June 1686, disinherited him for his whig politics, and Forrester's eldest son, David, therefore succeeded as laird of Denovan. In November 1687 Forrester was one of several persons to whom King James granted remissions of treason.

Following the revolution of 1688 the Church of Scotland was reformed, and in 1689 representatives of the parishes of Killearn and of Kincardine appeared before the ministers of Edinburgh in order to secure Forrester's services; it was decided that 'the paroch of Killearne had greatest interest in the petitioner and ordained him to continue minister thereat', though he seems to have maintained a connection with Kincardine. His post was confirmed by the privy council in 1691. In 1690, concerned that 'the books in the bibliotheque of Dumblaine … may during the present troubles of the kingdom be either imbazled [embezzled] or destroyed', the privy council had appointed Forrester and John Bruce, chamberlain of the bishopric, to go to Dunblane and compile an inventory of the collection, prior to its transfer under guard to Stirling Castle for safe keeping (*Reg. PCS*, 3rd ser., 15.341–2). Forrester became minister of St Andrews in May 1692 and on 26 January 1698 was appointed principal of St Mary's, the new college at St Andrews University. In this capacity he issued *The Hierarchical Bishops Claim to a Divine Right* (1699). He died at St Andrews on 2 November 1706 and was buried there on 7 November.

W. G. BLAIKIE, *rev.* STEPHEN WRIGHT

Sources R. Wodrow, *The history of the sufferings of the Church of Scotland from the Restauration to the revolution*, 2 vols. (1721–2) · J. K. Hewison, *The covenanters*, 2 vols. (1913) · *Reg. PCS*, 3rd ser., vols. 4, 12–15 · C. D. I. G. Forrester, *The Forresters: a lowland clan and its lands* (1988) · J. C. Gibson, *Lands and lairds of Larbert and Dunipace parishes* (1908) **Archives** NL Scot., journal and notes · U. Edin., New Coll. L., letters and papers

Forrester, Walter (*b. c.*1355, *d.* before 1426). *See under* Forrester family (*per. c.*1360–*c.*1450).

Forret, Thomas (*d.* 1540?), protestant martyr, was the son of Thomas Forret, master stabler to James IV. He had travelled abroad and studied at Cologne, where he matriculated in 1515, before entering the Augustinian abbey of Inchcolm in the Firth of Forth. The Augustinians were active in the world and Forret became vicar of Dollar in Clackmannanshire. His activities and death are recorded in detail by Calderwood (1.125–9). Forret's enthusiasm for preaching was such that he preached each Sunday 'showing the mysteries of the Scriptures to the vulgar people in English', and was critical of onerous clerical exactions, teaching 'not to take the cow and not to wear uppermost cloth as the churchmen do'. His change in outlook, by which he 'came to the knowledge of the truth', he attributed to reading the works of St Augustine. By applying himself to studying the scriptures, he began to convert some of the younger canons to his ideas. But the 'old bottles', he used to say, 'would not receave the new wine'. When his abbot warned him to keep his thoughts to himself if he wished to avoid punishment, Forret is reported to have replied 'I thanke your lordship, ye are a freind to my bodie, but not to my soule'. At Dollar, he taught his flock the ten commandments and 'shew them the way of their salvation to be onlie by the blood of Jesus Christ'. When visiting, he was apt to take some bread and cheese, as well as silver, for the sick and needy. He prepared a little catechism 'to allure the hearts of the hearers to embrace the truthe'. Much of his day was spent in study, reading in particular the epistle to the Romans in Latin, so that 'he might dispute against the adversaries'. He committed three chapters of the Bible to memory each day and made his servant Andrew Kirkie hear him repeat them at night. Condemning pardoners, offering indulgences, who came to his church, Forret explained 'parochiners, I am bound to speake the truthe to you: this is but to deceave you: there is no pardoun for our sinnes that can come to us frome Pope, or anie other, but onlie by the blood of Christ'.

Forret's stand attracted criticism from the archbishop of St Andrews and from the bishop of Dunkeld, who, it was said, knew neither the Old nor the New Testament, considered the novelty of weekly preaching unnecessary, 'for we are not ordeaned to preache', and so was content to rely on his breviary and pontifical. With the ascendancy of Cardinal Beaton, however, by 1538, Forret was summoned for trial. He declined to profess belief in the Virgin Mary, admitted instructing parishioners to recite the Lord's prayer and ten commandments in English and to using the English New Testament. He taught that in communion 'as the bread entereth into your mouth so sall Christ

dwell by livelie faith into your hearts'. He also affirmed it not to be lawful for:

> kirkmen to spend the teinds and the patromeney of the kirk as they do on harlattis and houris and deliecat clething, ryottous bancating and wantoun playing at cairttis and dice, and the kirk rewin and the pullpit doun and the pepill nocht instructit in godis word, nor the sacramentis trewlie ministrat to thame as the scriptour of Christ commandis. (*Historie and Cronicles*, 1.348–9)

Forret was a participant, too, at the wedding of Thomas Cocklaw, vicar of Tullibody, and was one of the group, whose numbers included George Buchanan, who at the bridal ate meat in Lent. Condemned to death as a heretic in Holyrood Abbey, he was burnt on Castle Hill in Edinburgh, in the king's presence, with four other heretics.

There are discrepancies in the various sources as to the year in which Forret was executed, perhaps arising from differences in dating the start of the calendar year. Knox and Calderwood assign his death to 28 February 1539, but Buchanan, himself associated with this circle of heretics, places it firmly in late February 1540, as does Foxe and also (though with some contextual confusion) the *Diurnal of Remarkable Occurrents*. The issue is incapable of final resolution, but 1540 seems the likelier date.   JAMES KIRK

Sources *John Knox's History of the Reformation in Scotland*, ed. W. C. Dickinson, 2 vols. (1949) · D. Calderwood, *The history of the Kirk of Scotland*, ed. T. Thomson and D. Laing, 8 vols., Wodrow Society, 7 (1842–9), vols. 1, 7 · J. Foxe, *Acts and monuments*, 8 (1857) · *The historie and cronicles of Scotland … by Robert Lindesay of Pitscottie*, ed. A. J. G. Mackay, 3 vols., STS, 42–3, 60 (1899–1911) · G. Buchanan, *Opera omnia* (1725) · T. Thomson, ed., *A diurnal of remarkable occurrents that have passed within the country of Scotland*, Bannatyne Club, 43 (1833) · R. Pitcairn, ed., *Ancient criminal trials in Scotland*, 7 pts in 3, Bannatyne Club, 42 (1833) · *APS*, 1424–1567 · J. M. Aitken, *The trial of George Buchanan* (1939)

Forsdyke, Sir (Edgar) John (1883–1979), museum director, was born at 63 Upper Grange Road, Bermondsey, on 12 September 1883, the second son of Frederick Palmer Forsdyke, commercial traveller, of Hasketon, Suffolk, and his wife, Mary Eliza Sainsbury. The family moved to Bushey, Hertfordshire, and Forsdyke entered Watford grammar school but transferred on a scholarship to Christ's Hospital. He then won a scholarship to Keble College, Oxford, and received a second class in Greats in 1906. In the following year he joined the British Museum as an assistant keeper in the department of Greek and Roman antiquities. While at Oxford he had joined the Oxfordshire yeomanry but on the outbreak of the First World War he was commissioned into the Royal Field Artillery, and served in France, Macedonia, Egypt, and Palestine, rising to the rank of captain.

Not a remarkable scholar, Forsdyke edited the *Journal of Hellenic Studies* from 1912 to 1923 and was for some time secretary of the Hellenic Society. In 1925 he published a catalogue of the museum's Aegean pottery—a lucid and important book—and with H. B. Walters wrote three fascicules of *Corpus vasorum antiquorum*. His only other book was published after his retirement, *Greece before Homer* (1956), an excursus into the relationship between archaeology and Homeric myth and legend. In 1927, at the behest of Sir Arthur Evans, he was sent to Crete to complete the excavation of the Bronze Age cemetery near Knossos, a task that he completed swiftly and published promptly.

Forsdyke, through seniority, had become keeper of Greek and Roman antiquities in 1932, at a time when Lord Duveen had agreed to fund a gallery at the British Museum to house the Parthenon sculptures. Duveen was a difficult man but Forsdyke seemed to be able to work with him and, perhaps for this reason, the trustees in 1936 appointed him (against all the odds, though it was a weak internal field) as director and principal librarian (he was created KCB in 1937). He was seen as the person most able to complete the successful transfer of the marbles to the new gallery and also to sort out the difficulties with the benefactor that had been experienced by his predecessor and by the trustees. These he did, but the removal of the marbles and their subsequent cleaning provoked an outcry which still haunts the museum. British Museum staff, employed at Duveen's behest to clean the marbles, had started to use rather crude methods. Forsdyke discovered the cleaning (unfounded stories that he had himself approved it are clearly untrue) and stopped it. A trustees' committee issued a public statement in May 1939 which admitted (with some degree of obfuscation) that the marbles had indeed been cleaned but not that they had been damaged. The ensuing row was familiar to the British art establishment of the time (who had been through a similar controversy at the National Gallery) and was about to cause controversy internationally. Forsdyke, never popular in the museum, was unjustly accused of scapegoating two members of the departmental staff and escaping censure himself. However, the outbreak of war meant that more important matters had to be considered, and the issue subsided.

Forsdyke came into his own as a wartime director. From 1933 he had been deeply involved with government in preparing for the evacuation of the museum's treasures. It is largely due to him that the evacuation was carried out so successfully and that, long before a single bomb fell on the building, the major treasures had been moved to safe storage, either in the London Underground or outside London. During the blitz that followed Forsdyke personally directed fire-fighting and salvage work in the museum. Though the building was badly damaged (including serious damage to the newly completed Duveen gallery) and a major section of the library was destroyed it was possible after the war to return to a partially functioning building and to restore many of the library losses with confidence. Forsdyke had been an early exponent of the use of microfilm, and immediately after the war, with the aid of a grant from the Rockefeller Foundation, he established a microfilm studio at the museum's newspaper library at Colindale. The survival of the museum through the war was his greatest memorial, for an autocratic and fearless manner in the middle of the bombing brought out his true qualities of leadership and kept damage to a minimum. He retired in 1951.

Forsdyke was a small, dapper man with a caustic tongue and an almost total inability to delegate, save with regard to the library departments of the museum. His view of himself is perhaps indicated by the fact that his official portrait, by his friend Gerald Kelly, shows him in full civil service uniform (the only director so depicted) but with a quizzical twinkle in his eye. He had strong opinions and was not afraid to air them. He married twice. The details of his first marriage have largely been expunged from the printed record, but in 1910, he married aged twenty-six, Frances Beatrice Mumford, daughter of the Revd Joseph Gifford, a forty-eight-year-old widow, to fulfil a promise it is said, to a dying friend that he would marry his mother. She died in the late 1930s. In 1942 he married Amadea Leonie (Dea), daughter of Dr Karl Gombrich of Vienna and sister of the art historian Sir Ernst Gombrich, with whom he had two daughters. On 3 December 1979, aged ninety-six, he died at his home, 13 Sandringham Road, Golders Green, of bronchopneumonia and senile myocardial degeneration.   DAVID M. WILSON

Sources WWW · R. Hood, *Faces of archaeology in Greece* (1998) · P. R. Harris, *A history of the British Museum library* (1998) · *The Times* (8 Dec 1979) · D. M. Wilson, *The British Museum, a history* (2002) · b. cert. · m. cert. [Frances Beatrice Mumford] · d. cert.
Archives AM Oxf. · BM | Bodl. Oxf., corresp. with J. L. Myres; corresp. relating to Society for Protection of Science and Learning
Likenesses P. de Jong, caricature, priv. coll. · G. Kelly, oils, BM
Wealth at death £54,106: probate, 31 Oct 1980, *CGPLA Eng. & Wales*

Forsett, Edward (1553/4–1629/30), government official and political writer, was a younger son of Richard Forsett (d. *c*.1561), of Gray's Inn, and his wife, Margaret. He matriculated from Christ's College, Cambridge, on 22 February 1564, aged ten. A scholar at Trinity College from 1571, he graduated BA in 1572, became a fellow in 1574, and proceeded MA in 1575. In 1578 Forsett wrote a long commendatory letter in Latin appended to the Latin translation by William Whitaker of a work by Bishop John Jewel, *Ioannis Ivelli … adversus Thomam Hardingum volumen alterum*. Whitaker was 'a divine of immense learning, a moderate puritan, and recognised as the champion of English protestantism against Bellarmine' (Moore Smith). Forsett's authorship of the first commendation to the work has been taken as an indicator of his own reputation as a scholar by the time he was no more than twenty-five. The Latin comedy 'Pedantius' which was performed at Trinity early in 1581, shortly before Forsett vacated his fellowship there, has been attributed to him, to the satisfaction of its modern editor.

After leaving Cambridge, Forsett entered royal service, apparently under the patronage of either Sir William Cecil, the future Lord Burleigh, or else Gilbert Gerrard, the queen's attorney-general. Both men received bequests in the will of Forsett's father, who commended to them his three sons, Henry, William, and Edward, asking that they might find gainful employment for one of them. William was later described as a gentleman of Stonham Parva, Suffolk, and Edward is the only one known to have undertaken public service. In 1583 he obtained letters patent granting him a 21-year lease of the manor of Tyburn in Middlesex, which his family already controlled as the grantees of the existing tenant, Sir Henry Sidney. The lease took effect in 1598, at an annual rent of £16 11s. 8d., on expiry of Sidney's own. On 24 April 1587, at the church of St Clement Danes, Westminster, Forsett married Elizabeth (*bap.* 1565), daughter of Robert Carr of Hillingdon, Middlesex. They had a son, Robert, and a daughter, Frances, who eventually married Matthew, afterwards Sir Matthew Howland, gentleman pensioner. By 1606 Forsett was employed in the office of works, apparently at the Tower of London to judge from reports he made in February and March regarding conversations among some of the Gunpowder Plot prisoners which had been overheard there.

Probably at some point that summer, Forsett was elected to the parliamentary seat for Wells, Somerset, vacated by the death of Sir Robert Stapleton. He was active in both of the last two sessions of parliament, in 1606–7 and 1610, being named several times to committees for considering bills after their second reading. Twice during that period he was entrusted with safeguarding the Tower during the temporary absence of the lieutenant. In 1606 he published *A comparative discourse of the bodies natural and politique: wherein … is set forth the true forme of a commonweale, with the dutie of subjects, and the right of the soveraigne*, which exhibits a particular interest in theories of a natural law inscribed by God in the hearts of men, discoverable by reason, and superior to any human law. In one of the potent political debates of the day, what Forsett conceded to the power of royal prerogative he took back with the counsel that it be used not wilfully, but in the public interest. The tract also made the case for union with Scotland, and has been described as 'an idiosyncratic and rather foolish work which had no discernible influence' (Sommerville, 49). On 19 May 1609 Forsett made a report on 'inconveniences likely to ensue in the Office of Works from refusal of the paymasters to comply with the regulations', which is preserved in the state papers. The following day he had a warrant for £200 for repairs undertaken at the royal palace of Oatlands. In May he was occupied in providing an estimate for the construction of a new barn at Nonsuch. On 8 June 1611 Forsett obtained a grant of the manor of Tyburn, for the sum of £829 3s. 4d.; after this he lived for some years at the manor house, which remained in the family until it was sold in 1710.

Forsett was a member of the county bench, and is known to have been active as a justice in 1620 and 1621. In 1624 he published *A defence of the right of kings; wherein the power of the papacie over princes is refuted, and the oath of allegiance justified*, which was probably written in 1609 in response to the advocacy of papal authority over temporal authorities by Robert Parsons. It is distinguished by little but the hackneyed nature of its claims for the patriarchal nature of kingly authority. Forsett made his will on 13 October 1629, directing in it that he be buried in the vault he had had made in Marylebone church. He died within the next few months, probably in his chamber in Charing Cross House, London: probate was granted to his son and heir, Robert, on 25 May 1630. SEAN KELSEY

Sources G. C. Moore Smith, ed., *Pedantius: a Latin comedy formerly acted in Trinity College, Cambridge* (1905) · J. P. Sommerville, *Politics*

and ideology in England, 1603–1640 (1986) · G. Burgess, *The politics of the ancient constitution: an introduction to English political thought, 1603–1642* (1992) · Venn, *Alum. Cant.* · *CSP dom., addenda, 1580–1625*, 516 · *DNB*

Wealth at death see will, PRO, PROB 11/157, sig. 46

Forshall, Josiah (1795–1863), museum administrator, was born at Witney, Oxfordshire, on 29 March 1795, the eldest son of Samuel Forshall. His mother may have been Martha Matthews, whose marriage to a Samuel Forshall is recorded in Ulverston, Lancashire, in 1790. As his father moved from Witney to Devon, to Cheshire, and then to Wales, Josiah was at the grammar schools at Exeter (*c.*1804–1805) and Chester (*c.*1806–1810), and then remained at home for four years before entering Exeter College, Oxford, in 1814. After graduating in 1818, with a first class in mathematics and a second in *literae humaniores*, he was elected a fellow in 1819, took his MA in 1821, was ordained, and was tutor from 1822 to 1824, when he became the assistant librarian in the department of manuscripts of the British Museum. He vacated his fellowship in 1826, when at Edgbaston, Warwickshire, on 13 July he married Frances (1795–1865), the only daughter of Richard Smith of Harborne Heath. They had four sons and one daughter.

In January 1828 Forshall was promoted under-librarian (keeper) of the department of manuscripts, and in February he was in addition appointed secretary of the British Museum. In the same year he was elected a fellow of the Royal Society. Henry Ellis, who became principal librarian of the British Museum at this time, was not an effective administrator, and Forshall increasingly took charge of the museum, aided by the support of William Howley, archbishop of Canterbury, the senior of the museum's three principal trustees. Forshall also ran the department of manuscripts (with the able assistance of Frederic Madden), adding considerably to its collections (almost 3500 items between 1828 and 1835) and supervising catalogues of the Arundel (1834), Burney (1840), and Syriac (1838) manuscripts. He opposed attempts to popularize the museum.

The select committees of the House of Commons which investigated the museum in 1835 and 1836 recommended that the secretary should not also be keeper of a department, so in 1837 Forshall resigned his keepership of the department of manuscripts to concentrate on the secretaryship. His dominant position during the next decade provoked much resentment on the part of the keepers of departments, although Ellis, the person whose position was most affected, with his usual good nature did not complain. Forshall controlled the proceedings of the board of trustees by arranging the agenda of its business as he wished, by summoning to meetings such trustees as he thought appropriate, and by being the only official who normally attended such meetings. Neither the principal librarian nor the keepers of the departments, except in extraordinary circumstances, were permitted to be present.

When a royal commission sat from 1847 to 1849 to consider the affairs of the museum, its members were so shocked by this situation that they recommended in their report that the post of secretary should be abolished. The problem of what to do with Forshall was solved by using his two long periods of sick leave because of mental illness from July to November 1847 and during 1849 (he had suffered a similar illness in 1841). After taking medical and legal advice, the trustees retired Forshall on grounds of ill health in August 1850. On quitting his residence in the museum in October 1851, Forshall sent a letter of thanks to the trustees for their consideration towards him. But his attitude towards the commission was embittered. He considered that his appointment had been made for life and then unjustly revoked. In 1850 he published a pamphlet fiercely attacking the proceedings of the royal commission, *Misrepresentations of her Majesty's Commissioners Exposed*.

The remainder of Forshall's life was devoted mainly to his work as chaplain of the Foundling Hospital, a post to which he had been appointed in 1826. His duties involved reading prayers in the chapel on Sundays and baptizing the foundlings. He also spent much time supervising their education. When he gave up this post in 1861 because of ill health, the authorities of the Foundling Hospital rewarded his faithful service of nearly thirty-five years by a gift of 200 guineas.

Forshall's major publication, produced in association with Madden, was an edition of Wycliffe's version of the Bible, to which he devoted much of his leisure time for over twenty years: *The holy Bible … in the earliest English versions made … by John Wycliffe and his followers* (4 vols., 1850). He also published editions of the gospels, some sermons, and a work on the Lord's prayer.

Despite his bad relations with a number of his colleagues in the museum, Forshall was regarded as having a kind nature. He died at his home, 49 Woburn Place, London, on 18 December 1863 after some days' great suffering following the failure of a prostate operation, and was buried on 24 December in the vaults below the chapel of the Foundling Hospital. (In 1927, when the Foundling Hospital was demolished, the remains in the vaults were moved to the catacombs of Kensal Green cemetery.)

P. R. HARRIS

Sources BM · LMA, Foundling Hospital archives · *The Times* (24 Dec 1863) · R. Cowtan, *Memories of the British Museum* (1872) · E. Miller, *That noble cabinet: a history of the British Museum* (1973) · 'Select committee on … the British Museum', *Parl. papers* (1835), vol. 7, no. 479 · 'Select committee on … the British Museum', *Parl. papers* (1836), vol. 10, no. 440 · 'Royal commission to inquire into … the British Museum', *Parl. papers* (1850), vol. 24, no. 1170 · C. W. Boase, ed., *Registrum Collegii Exoniensis*, new edn, OHS, 27 (1894) · parish registers, St George, Bloomsbury, LMA · census returns, 1841, 1851, 1861 · *CGPLA Eng. & Wales* (1864) · parish register (baptism), Witney, 15 May 1795
Archives CUL, letters to Royal Society of Literature · LMA, Foundling Hospital archives · Lpool RO, letters to Royal Society of Literature | Auckland Public Library, letters to Sir George Grey · BL, corresp. with A. H. Layard, Add. MSS 38977–38979, *passim* · BL, corresp. with Sir Frederic Madden, Egerton MSS 2839–2844, *passim* · BL, corresp. with Sir Robert Peel, Add. MSS 40300–40600, *passim* · Bodl. Oxf., corresp. with Sir Thomas Phillipps · Lpool RO,

letters to Lord Stanley · NL NZ, letters to Gideon Algernon Mantell
Wealth at death under £14,000: probate, 30 Jan 1864, *CGPLA Eng. & Wales*

Forster [Foster], **Agnes** (*d.* 1484), wealthy widow and prison reformer, came from Kent and was married for about twenty years to the London shipowner, merchant, and MP Stephen Forster, who was mayor in 1454–5. He came from Somerset and maintained close links with the Canynges family of Bristol. At his death in 1458 he left 5500 marks for his widow and their four children, and fifty legacies in London and Bristol totalling some £600. Agnes and the eldest son, John, were appointed executors, assisted by four overseers who included William Canynges, the most prominent member of his family, and Master William Cliff, the city of London surveyor.

During Forster's mayoralty there had been a serious fire at Ludgate, and the prison for citizen debtors there had been damaged (Newgate prison was for criminals). The rebuilding and improvement of the prison began soon after Forster's death and was supervised by William Cliff and Agnes herself. By 1463 a new quadrangular prison had been built which included an 'exercise yard' measuring 13 yards by 10, lodgings on the first floor, and 'faire leades to walk upon, well imbattailed, all for fresh ayre and ease of prisoners'. The administration of the prison was overhauled, and new rules were drawn up to prevent gaolers charging the inmates extortionate prices for the necessities of life such as food, bedding, fuel, and candles. A committee of four prison visitors was appointed and all this was done at the 'request, praier and desire of the weldisposed, blessed and devote woman Dame Agnes Foster' (*Calendar of Letter-Books*, L.40). John Stow recorded the execrable verse engraved on a plaque fixed to Ludgate:

> Devout soules that passe this way,
> for Stephen Forster late Maior, heartily pray,
> And Dame Agnes his spouse, to God consecrate,
> that of pitie this house made for Londoners in Ludgate
> So that for lodging and water prisoners here nought pay,
> as their keepers shal all answere at dreadful doomes day.
> (Stow, 1.40)

The rebuilding and reform of Ludgate prison appears to have exhausted Agnes Forster's charity, if not her resources. Most unusually, part of her business archive has survived, probably because it passed to her daughter Agnes and her second husband, the lawyer Robert Moreton. Agnes lent large sums of money (for example, £700 to Margaret, Lady Hungerford, in 1464 and £250 to Lord Hastings, the king's chamberlain, in 1470) and carried out business deals in her own name with a wide range of London merchants, particularly drapers, between 1460 and her death in December 1484. In 1463 Agnes received as her 'house guests' two French knights from Normandy who had been captured fighting for the Lancastrian army in the north. By 1476, when Agnes handed the two knights over to her son Robert in gratitude for his 'tender love and filial service', the ransoms were still outstanding (Jones, 106). If Agnes had 'bought' the prisoners they proved a poor investment, for in 1482 Robert Forster had to pay 20 pence to the churchwardens of his parish of St Stephen

Walbrook for the burial of 'the French knight' (Milbourn, 345).

Agnes Forster appears to have remained close to all her children: she lent Robert money and acted as his executor; her third son, Stephen, was a priest and appears to have lived with his mother. She is mentioned five times in his will as his 'dearest mother', and was appointed his sole executor (Harley charter, 58.G.11). When Agnes drew up her very modest will (her total bequests amounted to £300) in 1484, she made legacies to the servants of the households of her remaining two children, John and Agnes. She displayed particular concern for the orphan daughters of her son Robert, and she committed them to the care of their uncle and aunt. She also remembered her two other granddaughters, Dorith and Lettice, the children of her daughter Agnes. In contrast to the expansive and charitable will of her husband, Stephen Forster, Agnes made no charitable bequests, although she provided for prayers for the souls of her husband and their dead children. She asked for burial not with her husband in the church of St Botolph, Billingsgate, but in St Stephen Walbrook where she had been a parishioner, living in her son Robert's house.

In the troubled political climate of the third quarter of the fifteenth century, Agnes had been able to trade independently, to execute three family wills, to educate and marry her children well, to hold the family together as an effective and affective unit, and to see through to completion the rebuilding and reform of one of the city's prisons. CAROLINE M. BARRON

Sources BL, Harley charters · will, PRO, PROB 11/7, sig. 9, fols. 65–6 · F. W. Weaver, ed., Somerset medieval wills, 1, Somerset RS, 16 (1901), 181–5 · J. Stow, A survay of London, rev. edn (1603); repr. with introduction by C. L. Kingsford as A survey of London, 2 vols. (1908); repr. with addns (1971) · R. R. Sharpe, ed., Calendar of letter-books preserved in the archives of the corporation of the City of London, [12 vols.] (1899–1912), vol. L · P. E. Jones, ed., Calendar of plea and memoranda rolls preserved among the archives of the corporation of the City of London at the Guildhall, 6: 1458–1482 (1961) · S. L. Thrupp, The merchant class of medieval London, 1300–1500, pbk edn (1962) · M. Albertson, London merchants and their landed property during the reigns of the Yorkists (1932) · M. L. Kekewich and others, eds., The politics of fifteenth-century England: John Vale's book (1995) · T. Milbourn, 'The church of St Stephen Walbrook', Transactions of the London and Middlesex Archaeological Society, 5 (1876–80), 327–402
Archives BL, Harley charters
Wealth at death minimum of £300 in goods and chattels: will, PRO, PROB 11/7, sig. 9, fols. 65–6

Forster, Anne (1797–1873). See under Forster, William (1784–1854).

Forster, Benjamin (1736–1805), Church of England clergyman and antiquary, was born in Walbrook, London, on 7 August 1736, the third son of Thomas Forster (1698–1743), merchant and a descendant of the Forsters of Etherston and Bamburgh, and his wife, Dorothy (1710–1763), daughter of Benjamin Furly and granddaughter of Benjamin Furly, the friend and correspondent of Locke. His eldest brother was the antiquary Edward *Forster (1730–1812). He was educated at Hertford School and at Corpus Christi College, Cambridge, where he had as friends and fellow students the antiquaries Richard Gough, Edward Haistwell, and Michael Tyson. After matriculating in 1753 he graduated BA in 1757, becoming MA and fellow of his college in 1760, and BD in 1768. Having taken orders, 'though he was never very orthodox', he became in succession curate of Wanstead and of Broomfield and Chignall Smealy in Essex (1760), Lady Camden lecturer at Wakefield (1766), and rector of Boconnoc, Broadoak, and Cherichayes in Cornwall (1770).

Forster was somewhat eccentric, surrounding himself with multifarious pet animals, to whom he was much attached; but his letters show him to have been a man of taste and learning, and a skilful antiquary. He and his brother Edward corresponded for many years with Gough (a number of their letters were privately printed at Bruges, in 1845–50, by his great-nephew, Thomas Ignatius Maria Forster), and with Haistwell they made a number of antiquarian tours together. Gough was later to claim that Forster had taught him to make antiquarian notes (Forster, 203). Among his other friends were the poets William Mason and Thomas Gray.

Forster died, unmarried, at Boconnoc parsonage on 2 December 1805; his tomb, by his orders, was merely inscribed 'Fui'. In his will he made detailed provisions as to which members of his family should receive which books from his library.

G. S. BOULGER, rev. R. H. SWEET

Sources F. [T. Forster], Epistolarium, or, Fasciculi of curious letters ... as preserved among the MSS of the Forster family, 2 vols. (privately printed, Bruges, 1845–50) · Nichols, Lit. anecdotes, 7.138, 567; 9.648–50 · Nichols, Illustrations, 5.280–328 · Venn, Alum. Cant. · IGI · will, PRO, PROB 11/1436, sig. 32
Archives BL, corresp. with Lord Camelford and Lady Camelford, Add. MS 69303
Wealth at death books, manuscripts, and music bequeathed to members of family: will, PRO, PROB 11/1436, sig. 32

Forster, Benjamin Meggot (1764–1829), mycologist and inventor of scientific instruments, was born in Walbrook, London, on 16 January 1764, the second son of Edward *Forster the elder (1730–1812) and his wife, Susanna Furney (d. 1823). His brothers were Thomas Furly *Forster (1761–1825) and Edward *Forster the younger (1765–1849). Benjamin Forster was educated with his brothers at Walthamstow and became a member of the company of Edward Forster & Sons, Russia merchants, but spent little time at the firm.

Forster's whole life was devoted to the study of science, especially botany and electricity. He produced many fine drawings of fungi, communicated various species to Sowerby, and in 1820 published, with initials only, An Introduction to the Knowledge of Fungusses. He contributed numerous articles to the Gentleman's Magazine under various signatures and on various subjects. Forster made eight contributions to the Philosophical Magazine, listed in the Royal Society's catalogue. They dealt with fungi, the electric column, and atmospheric phenomena. He invented the sliding portfolio and the atmospherical electroscope, and attempted to create an orrery of perpetual motion.

Forster was one of the earliest advocates of emancipation, and one of the first members of the committee of 1788 against the slave trade. He joined the societies for the suppression of climbing chimney-sweepers, for diffusing knowledge about capital punishments, for providing refuge for the destitute, and for repressing cruelty to animals. He was conscientiously opposed to field sports. He never married, living with his father and mother until their death. He then took a cottage called Scotts, at Hale End, Walthamstow, where he died on 8 March 1829.

G. S. BOULGER, *rev.* ALEXANDER GOLDBLOOM

Sources Desmond, *Botanists*, rev. edn · *GM*, 1st ser., 99/1 (1829), 279 · Nichols, *Illustrations*, 8.553 · F. [T. Forster], *Epistolarium, or, Fasciculi of curious letters … as preserved among the MSS of the Forster family*, 2 (privately printed, Bruges, 1850), xiii–xv
Archives Essex Field Club · Linn. Soc. · Trinity Cam.

Forster, Edward, the elder (1730–1812), merchant and antiquary, was born on 11 February 1730 in London, eldest of the four sons of Thomas Forster (1698–1743), merchant, and his wife, Dorothy (1710–1763), daughter of Benjohan (Benjamin) Furly, a Rotterdam merchant of Colchester Quaker forebears. Forster was educated at Felsted School in Essex. As a child, he was thought to be consumptive, which may have been the reason he was sent to the Netherlands to his Furly grandparents. The philosopher John Locke had stayed with Edward's great-grandfather Benjamin Furly during his exile, and his letters to Furly were given to Forster, and were later to be published by Forster's grandson, Thomas Forster, in 1830.

Thomas Forster senior died in Paris in 1743. By 1755 Dorothy Forster had moved to Walthamstow with her two younger sons, Benjamin *Forster (1736–1805) and Richard (1739–1819), Edward and his brother Thomas Furly being then in London, where Edward had established himself as a Russia merchant, in business at St Helen's Place, Bishopsgate. Edward married, on 2 September 1756, Susanna Furney (*d.* 1823), from an old Somerset family. At first they continued to live at St Helen's Place but after the birth of their first child they moved to Bond Court, Walbrook, in the City of London. Four of their children died in infancy but they raised three sons, Thomas Furly *Forster (1761–1825), Benjamin Meggot *Forster (1764–1829), and Edward *Forster (1765–1849), known as 'the younger', all of whom became noted botanists, and a daughter, Susannah Dorothy (1757–1822), who married the Revd J. Dixon of Bincombe in Dorset.

After Forster's mother died in 1763 he moved to Walthamstow, his brother Thomas taking the house in Bond Court. Forster was by this time a man of influence. His firm of Edward Forster & Co. was profitable; he was a member of the Mercers' Company; for thirty years he was a governor of the Corporation of the Royal Exchange Assurance Company; he was twenty-nine years in the Russia Company, rising to governor; and he was deputy governor of the London docks. In 1773 he addressed the House of Commons committee on the linen trade with Russia, a matter with which he would have been extremely familiar, as his company imported flax and cheap linen, in order to satisfy demand for hammocks, tents, and suchlike, besides clothing for the poorer classes, and he exported other textiles and goods to Russia. Forster persuaded the committee that the Russia trade did not harm the domestic industry and that the balance of trade and duties paid was in England's favour.

By this time Forster's prosperity allowed him to seek pleasure in his rural surroundings, searching out antiquities, sketching, drawing, and writing verse. In 1782 he moved to a seventeenth-century house in Hoe Street, Walthamstow, and there assembled a considerable collection of herbaceous plants, his sons being responsible for their cultivation. He enjoyed a wide circle of friends, among them Thomas Gray (1716–1771), Michael Tyson (1740–1780), William Gilpin (1724–1804), and the antiquary Richard Gough (1735–1809), who dedicated poems to him and bequeathed £500 to Forster and £100 to each of his four children. Forster's advice to the government concerning the matter of paper currency led to his being offered a baronetcy, which he however declined.

In his placid old age Forster confided to Gilpin, 'I have always had reason to thank God, for an uninterrupted state of good health, though not capable of exertions of any kind; from the age of 14, when I was supposed to be consumptive, to that of 72, which I have now attained' (Forster to Gilpin, 12 Aug 1802, Bodl. Oxf., MS Bodley 42485, fols. 130*v*–131*r*). He died at his house in Hoe Street, Walthamstow, on 20 April 1812; his wife died in 1823. John Nichols wrote of him: 'Few men possessed a sounder judgement or more capacious mind; and as these were combined with piety the most sincere and manners the most amiable, he was eminently successful in the discharge of every duty, both public and private' (Nichols, 6.616–17).

ANITA MCCONNELL

Sources R. H. Jeffers, 'The Forsters of Walthamstow', *Essex Journal*, 3 (1968), 119–42 · *GM*, 2nd ser., 32 (1849), 431 · *GM*, 1st ser., 82/1 (1812), 487–8 · Nichols, *Lit. anecdotes*, 6.616–17 · Forster's letters to William Gilpin, 1802, Bodl. Oxf., MS 42485, fols. 130*v*–131*r* · F. S. Moller and others, eds., *Alumni Felstedienses: being a list of boys entered at Felsted School, May 1564 – September 1931*, 6th edn (1931), 21
Archives BL, corresp. with earl of Liverpool, Add. MSS 38220–38234, 38309, 38376, 38471, *passim* · Bodl. Oxf., letters to William Gilpin, MS 42485, fols. 130*v*–131*r* · PRO, letters to William Pitt, PRO 30/8
Likenesses C. Turner, mezzotint, pubd 1810 (after J. Hoppner), BM, NPG

Forster, Edward, the younger (1765–1849), botanist, was born at Wood Street, Walthamstow on 12 October 1765, the third and youngest son of Edward *Forster the elder (1730–1812), and his wife, Susanna Furney (*d.* 1823). He received his commercial education in Holland, and entered the banking house of Forster, Lubbocks, Forster, and Clarke. He began studying botany in Epping Forest at the age of fifteen. Later in conjunction with his two brothers, Thomas Furly *Forster and Benjamin Meggot *Forster, he cultivated in his father's garden almost all the herbaceous plants then grown, and contributed the county lists of plants to Gough's edition of *Camden* (1789).

In 1796 he married Mary Jane, the only daughter of Abraham Greenwood. She died in 1846 leaving no surviving children.

In 1800 Forster was elected fellow of the Linnean Society, founded in 1788; he was elected treasurer in 1816 and vice-president in 1828. He was elected to the Royal Society in 1821. With his brothers he was one of the chief founders of the Refuge for the Destitute in Hackney Road. He died at home of cholera, on 23 February 1849, two days after inspecting the refuge during an outbreak of the disease. He was buried in the family vault at Walthamstow. Forster was methodical, shy, taciturn, and exclusive, rising early to work among his extensive collections of obscure British plants before banking hours, and devoting his evenings to reading and to his large herbarium. He lived chiefly at Hale End, Walthamstow, but at the time of his death was living at Ivy House, Woodford, Essex.

In 1817 Forster had printed a catalogue of British birds, *Catalogus avium in insulis Britannicis habitantium cura et studio Eduardi Forsteri jun.*, but seems subsequently to have devoted his attention to plants exclusively. He printed various papers on critical species of British plants in the proceedings of the Linnean Society, the *Annals and Magazine of Natural History*, and the *Phytologist*, and collected material towards a flora of Essex. He described several species in the *Supplement to English Botany* (1834). At his death his library and herbarium were sold by Sothebys, the latter being purchased by Robert Brown and presented to the British Museum.

G. S. BOULGER, *rev.* ALEXANDER GOLDBLOOM

Sources Desmond, *Botanists*, rev. edn · *GM*, 2nd ser., 32 (1849), 432 · Nichols, *Illustrations*, 8.554 · *Proceedings of the Linnean Society of London* (1856–7), xxxix · F. [T. Forster], *Epistolarium, or, Fasciculi of curious letters … as preserved among the MSS of the Forster family*, 2 (privately printed, Bruges, 1850), xv · G. S. Gibson, *Flora of Essex* (1862), 448

Archives Linn. Soc. · NHM, notebooks · Passmore Edwards Museum, London · RS · Trinity Cam. | Linn. Soc., letters to Sir James Smith · RBG Kew, letters to Sir William Hooker

Likenesses C. Baugniet, lithograph, 1850, BM · E. U. Eddis, oils, Linn. Soc. · Miss Turner, engraving, RS · engraving, RS

Forster, Edward (1769–1828), writer, born at Colchester, Essex, on 11 June 1769, was the only son of Nathaniel *Forster (1726–1790), the rector of All Saints in that town. After receiving some basic education at home, he was sent to Norwich grammar school, then presided over by his father's close friend Samuel Parr (1747–1825). On 5 May 1788 he matriculated at Balliol College, Oxford, where he studied medicine and law. In late 1790 he married Elizabeth, the widow of Captain Addison and the youngest daughter of Philip Bedingfeld of Ditchingham Hall, Norfolk, but she died four years later. In order to renew his acquaintanceship with Parr, Forster resided at Hatton, Warwickshire, for a while and ultimately became a member of St Mary Hall, Oxford. He graduated BA in 1792, and entered himself at Lincoln's Inn on 15 June of the same year. On deciding, however, to become a clergyman, he was ordained priest by Beilby Porteus, bishop of London, in 1796. He proceeded MA in 1797. On 3 August 1799, while he was living at Weston, Oxfordshire, he married as his second wife, Lavinia, the only daughter of Thomas *Banks (1735–1805), the sculptor.

Forster at this time made an agreement with a bookseller, William Miller of Old Bond Street, subsequently of Albemarle Street, to edit the works of selected standard authors for expensive illustrated editions. His first venture was an edition of Jarvis's translation of *Don Quixote*, which was published in 1801. Several works of less significance followed, while Forster prepared for the press a new translation (from French) of the *Arabian Nights* (1802), with twenty-four engravings designed by Robert Smirke. During the same year Forster also published an edition of *Anacreon*, for which the printer, William Bulmer, produced a fine Greek type; the title-plate and vignette illustrations were by Forster's wife. Various editions of dramatic authors followed (under the titles of British Drama, New British Theatre, and English Drama), some of which were illustrated.

In 1803 Forster was presented to the rectory of Aston Somerville, Gloucestershire, by an old friend, Lord Somerville, who had also procured for him the appointment of chaplain to the duke of Newcastle in 1796. As there was no vicarage, the residence requirement was dispensed with, and Forster settled in London, where his sermons were in demand. Between 1800 and 1814 he served successively as morning preacher at Berkeley and Grosvenor chapels, and at Park Street and King Street chapels, where he divided the duty alternately with Sydney Smith, Stanier Clarke, T. F. Dibdin, and other popular preachers. In 1805 Forster began a correspondence with Walter Scott on the subject of a projected edition of Dryden, subsequently abandoned. Forster later planned to publish an 'Essay on punctuation', of which he had made a special study. An elegant illustrated quarto edition of Samuel Johnson's *Rasselas* was published by Forster in 1805; it was followed in 1809 by a small privately printed volume of verse, entitled *Occasional Amusements*, which appeared without his name. But his major publication was *The British Gallery of Engravings*, a series of highly finished prints of line drawings from paintings in private and royal collections. Descriptions in English and French accompanied each engraving. The first number of this work appeared in 1807; by 1813 the first volume only was completed, and as the project was running at a loss, it was abandoned.

After peace was made in 1815 Forster and his family moved to Paris, his finances having suffered from his publishing schemes. Forster began publishing an edition of Plautus; three volumes were already completed when it was stopped by the sudden death of the printer. About a year after he had settled in Paris Forster began to preach in the French protestant church of the Oratoire, and eventually obtained a grant from the consistory for the use of the church when it was not required for French service. Here he officiated until the autumn of 1827, when ill health forced him to resign. In 1818 he was appointed to the post of chaplain to the British embassy, which he continued to hold until his death. In 1824 the earl of Bridgewater made him his chaplain. Forster died at Paris on 18 March 1828, after a long illness, and was buried in Père Lachaise cemetery in that city. He left a widow and three daughters, for whose benefit an edition of his sermons, with a memoir, was published in 1828. Forster had been elected FRS on 10 December 1801, and FSA previously. He was also an active supporter of the Royal Institution from its establishment, was appointed honorary librarian by the directors, and was engaged to deliver lectures there during three seasons.

GORDON GOODWIN, *rev.* NILANJANA BANERJI

Sources *GM*, 1st ser., 98/1 (1828), 566 · *GM*, 1st ser., 69 (1799), 716 · Foster, *Alum. Oxon.* · Burke, *Gen. GB*
Archives BL, letters to George Cumberland, Add. MSS 36499–36501

Forster, Edward Morgan (1879–1970), novelist and essayist, was born on 1 January 1879 at 6 Melcombe Place, Marylebone, London, the only child of Edward Morgan Llewellyn (Eddie) Forster (1847–1880), an architect, and his wife, Alice Clara (Lily) Whichelo (1855–1945); they were married on 2 January 1877. Forster's partly Irish paternal grandfather, Charles Forster (1789–1871), was a clergyman whose wife, Laura, twenty years younger than himself, was descended from members of the Clapham Sect, that 'industry in doing good' (Cowper, 10.31); Henry Whichelo, his maternal grandfather, was an artist, from a family of artists originally from Spain. From one side came the affluence and self-confidence that permitted social conscience, from the other unpretentiousness and knowledge of struggle.

Lily Whichelo was 'taken up' by Eddie Forster's aunt Marianne Thornton (1797–1887), but the family never forgot that she was the daughter of a Stockwell drawing-master who died suddenly and improvidently, that her mother took in lodgers, and that she had been a governess. In October 1880 Eddie Forster died of tuberculosis leaving £7000 which, prudently invested, would mean that his small family would always be comfortably off. When Marianne Thornton died in 1887 she left £2000 to Lily and £8000 in trust. This ensured that mother and son would be much more than merely comfortable; but his affluence was something about which Forster dissembled.

Childhood The widowed 'head of the family, occupation gentlewoman' (1881 census) now devoted herself to 'the Important One', Morgan or Morgie as Forster was known to his family and friends. As an adult Forster accused his mother of smothering him; however, she undeniably gave him great self-confidence and in early photographs he looks noticeably at ease with himself; it was only later, when human relations became complicated and painful, that he started to become gawky, his clothes ill-fitting, and his beautiful musician's hands held awkwardly. When, in 1883, mother and son moved to Rooksnest near Stevenage, Hertfordshire, a modestly beautiful house which was the model for Howards End, it was the start of a decade which was, in retrospect, a paradise: he enjoyed his closeness to his mother and played in the fields with

Edward Morgan Forster (1879–1970), by Dora Carrington, 1920

local boys. Holidays were spent with his uncle Willie Forster in Northumberland, or Maimie Aylward at Salisbury, or with Laura Forster at West Hackhurst, near Abinger Hammer, Surrey, the only house designed by his father; with Rooksnest and with the Thornton family home, Battersea Rise, it was the third in an almost sacred trinity of houses. When the time came to leave Rooksnest, Forster went reluctantly: 'If I had been allowed to stop on there, I should have become a different person, married, and fought in the war' (unpublished paper, 'Memory', early 1930s, E. M. Forster archive, King's Cam.).

Tonbridge and Cambridge In 1890 Forster was sent to board at Kent House, an Eastbourne preparatory school with a liberal reputation. Then, in September 1893, he and his mother moved to Dryhurst, Dry Hill Park Road, Tonbridge, so that he could be a day boy at the school. In later years he claimed that he was unhappy at Tonbridge. It is not clear that he was; nevertheless, public schools came to represent what he most hated in English life: philistinism, snobbery, the assumption of racial and class superiority, Englishmen going forth into the world 'with well-developed bodies, fairly developed minds, and undeveloped hearts' ('Notes on the English character', 1926, *Abinger Harvest*, 15). Yet he began to develop his great love of classics at Tonbridge; and he had friends, for example Reginald Elliott Tiddy, who died on the Somme in August 1916. When Forster left in summer 1897, he had won both the Latin verse and the English essay prizes.

In the autumn Forster went up to King's College, Cambridge; it had a radical reputation and 'an unconquerable faith in the value and interest of human beings' (John

Sheppard, Apostles paper 'King's or Trinity', 5 Dec 1903, King's Cam.). For the first year he lodged in rooms in Market Square. In October 1898, his mother having moved to 10 Earls Road, Tunbridge Wells, he took possession of two rooms at W7 Bodley's, overlooking the Backs. 'With a sigh of joy he entered the perishable home that was his for a couple of years' (*The Longest Journey*, 58). Now, as he wrote later about one of his mentors, Goldsworthy Lowes Dickinson: 'Body and spirit, reason and emotion, work and play, architecture and scenery, laughter and seriousness, life and art—these pairs which are elsewhere contrasted were there fused into one' (*Goldsworthy Lowes Dickinson*, 29). The 'cynical, aggressive, Mephistophelian' Nathaniel Wedd, his supervisor, was another influence; it was, Forster claimed, to Wedd 'more than to anyone – that I owe such awakening as has befallen me' (ibid., 61).

In 1900, having gained a second in the classics tripos (but won a Latin verse prize and an English essay prize) and his college exhibition having been renewed, Forster decided to stay on for a fourth year. He lived at 12 King's Parade and read history; and also started to write essays for the King's magazine *Basileon* and began 'Nottingham Lace', a novel about a young man who encourages another to spurn conventional thinking. In the following year he was elected to the Conversazione Society, a self-selecting group of Apostles who met in secret to discuss each other's papers on philosophical and moral questions. He replaced G. E. Moore and joined Desmond MacCarthy, Austin Smyth, G. H. Hardy, A. R. Ainsworth, Ralph Hawtrey, and H. O. Meredith; now he could truly start to shed some of his ancestral values and embrace truth, beauty, and personal relations. But some weeks later any thoughts he might have had about remaining in Cambridge came to an end when he was again awarded a second. He had no idea what to do next, yet was in the unfortunate position of not needing to earn his living. Lily put their possessions in store, and they set out for Europe.

Travels in Italy and Greece Forster and his mother arrived in Florence at the end of October 1901, staying at the Pensione Simi on the ground and first floor of 2 lungano alle Grazie. *A Room with a View*, inspired by the vista from this hotel, was begun in Rome, in December, 'Nottingham Lace' having been abandoned. Then, in spring 1902 Forster wrote two short stories, including in Ravello 'The Story of a Panic'; he

> would bring some middle-class Britishers to picnic in this remote spot. I would expose their vulgarity. I would cause them to be terribly frightened they knew not why and I would make it clear by subsequent events that they had encountered and offended the Great God Pan. ('Three countries', 1959, *The Hill of Devi*, 290)

After some weeks in northern Italy and Austria the Forsters returned to London in October 1902. They settled into a hotel in Bloomsbury, but apart from teaching a weekly Latin class at the working men's college in Great Ormond Street (with which he had connections for some years to come), Forster was no closer to knowing what to do. Then, in the following spring, he went with other Kingsmen on a three-week cruise round the Greek islands.

This turned out to be a time of supreme happiness, so much so that the loss of King's now came to matter as much as the loss of Rooksnest: Forster had begun to realize that the companionship of male intellectual equals was what he longed for more than anything else. When, during the previous winter of 1902-3, he and Meredith had an intense if chaste love affair, 'it was, he felt, as if all the "greatness" of the world had been opened up to him. He counted this as the second grand "discovery" of his youth—his emancipation from Christianity being the first' (Furbank, 1.98). He had not yet confronted his homosexuality, but like Ralph in the unpublished fragment 'Ralph and Tony' written at this time: 'he did not need health or self-confidence or success … He merely needed human love, and then without argument or effort all his doubts and weaknesses and unhappiness would disappear' (*Arctic Summer*, 76).

Weybridge, 1904–1912 Settled once more in a hotel in Bloomsbury, Forster applied to be taken on by the Cambridge University local lectures board: during the years 1903–11 he gave eleven courses entitled 'The republic of Florence' at places such as Harpenden, Lowestoft, and Harrow. A piece about Greece appeared in print, and a short story; the quiet success of these gave him the impetus to return to the early draft of *A Room with a View*; he also began working on a new edition of the *Aeneid*. During spring 1904, when he and Lily were living at 11 Drayton Court, in South Kensington, London, he went on writing his novel; then, in July, he abandoned it again and started *Where Angels Fear to Tread*. By the time they had bought and moved into Harnham (now Revard), 19 Monument Green, Weybridge, Surrey, in September 1904, this, his first published novel, was close to being finished; and here all his six novels were completed or written.

In spring 1905 Forster went to Germany to be tutor to the daughters of the writer Elizabeth von Arnim (the aunt of his friend Sydney Waterlow) at Nassenheide in Pomerania. During that summer three instalments of a long short story appeared in the *Independent Review*, and by the time he returned to England in September 1905 his career as a writer was a reality: *Where Angels Fear to Tread* was published in October. 'The object of the book', Forster told R. C. Trevelyan (28 October 1905, *Where Angels Fear to Tread*, 161) 'is the improvement of Philip', a young Englishman whose sister-in-law marries the son of an Italian dentist; after she dies in childbirth he travels to Italy from Sawston/Tonbridge, 'a joyless, straggling place, full of people who pretended' (ibid., 113), in order to return the baby to England and English values. The novel's brevity, humour, and insight were quite unlike those of any contemporary fiction, as reviewers recognized: 'This is a book which one begins with pleased interest and gradually finds to be astonishing' (Gardner, 43). 'What Mr Forster has done with a refreshing and brilliantly original touch in his novel is … to expose Sawston's ideals and ways of life in the glare of the vertical Italian sun' (ibid., 50).

During winter 1905–6 and all through the next year Forster was at work on *The Longest Journey*, a novel with strongly autobiographical elements (it was his own favourite) about Rickie Elliott, who is idyllically happy at Cambridge but then stumbles into marriage and a life teaching at an English public school. Its themes are truth and loyalty versus convention and self-interest, the English countryside versus suburbia, the constrictions of bourgeois marriage, the aesthetic impulse versus the worldly, the tragic result of ignoring the defining or 'symbolic' moment. It was published in April 1907. 'Critics approve,' wrote its author, 'except the *Queen* & the *World*. All say "jerky", "too many deaths"' (notebook journal, 12 June 1907, E. M. Forster archive).

The pattern of Forster's life was now set—living with Lily in Weybridge and going to stay with Whichelo or Forster relations, or with friends from Cambridge; writing in his room while the domestic life of the household went on downstairs; occasionally giving a lecture or course of lectures; taking long solitary walks; playing the piano; and paying visits in London. His circle was expanding fast and he was getting to know people such as Edward Marsh, Rupert Brooke, Forrest Reid, Edward Garnett, and Lady Ottoline Morrell, and deepening his friendship with members of the Bloomsbury group (particularly Leonard Woolf) and with friends from Cambridge such as George Barger, Edward Dent, and Hilton Young. They were beginning to marry ('the astonishing glass shade had fallen that interposes between married couples and the world'; *Howards End*, 177) and Forster had begun to see that it was unlikely he would ever do the same, noting 'I'm going to be a minority if not a solitary, and I'd best make copy out of my position' (notebook journal, 21 March 1904, E. M. Forster archive). But two years later he met a young Indian named Syed Ross Masood (1889–1937), to whom he gave Latin coaching before he went up to Oxford, and a close friendship developed; eventually Forster believed himself to be in love, even though he knew, as he wrote in his diary, 'He is not that sort—no one whom I like seems to be' (ibid., 22 Nov 1908).

In summer 1907 Forster went back to his drafts of *A Room with a View*. He had already written the first part, showing the effect of sunny, uninhibited Italy on the chilly suburban English, and was now at work on the second, in which Lucy, the heroine, returns to England and resumes the kind of life he knew so well; she too escapes from 'daily life' through playing the piano, and if she 'ever takes to live as she plays, it will be very exciting—both for us and for her' (*A Room with a View*, 52). When the novel was published in autumn 1908 the reviews were spread over the usual spectrum from perceptive (C. F. G. Masterman, in *The Nation* wrote that although each of his characters 'approves of the orderly comfort of the "room", there is within all of them some wild or exultant element which responds to the high calling of the "view"'; Gardner, 112), to crass ('an irresponsible work about people who never act or talk sanely'; Gardner, 116).

There are two alternatives for Lucy—an unconventional life with the bohemian George, or a conventional one with suburban Cecil. To Forster either was beginning to seem unattainable. 'Am anxious not to widen a gulf that must always remain wide,' he noted; 'there is no doubt

that I do not resemble other people, and even they notice it' (notebook journal, 31 Dec 1907, E. M. Forster archive). But a few days later (ibid., 27 Jan 1908) he had a unique vision: the news had come that a man had briefly flown in an air machine.

> It's coming quickly, and if I live to be old I shall see the sky as pestilential as the roads. It really is a new civilization. I have been born at the end of the age of peace and can't expect to feel anything but despair. Science, instead of freeing man … is enslaving him to machines. Nationality will go, but the brotherhood of man will not come … The little houses that I am used to will be swept away, the fields will stink of petrol, and the airships will shatter the stars … such a soul as mine will be crushed out.

Later in the year Forster wrote 'The Machine Stops', a short story describing man as he might become after the machine has finally triumphed. It was one of the first of the twentieth century's anti-utopias, written in part as a reaction to H. G. Wells. This vision was also the impetus for *Howards End* (1910), which contrasts the ideals and preoccupations of the Schlegels and the Wilcoxes and their attempts to connect (the words 'Only connect' appear on the frontispiece), to build 'the rainbow bridge that should connect the prose in us with the passion' (*Howards End*, 187). It explores themes such as business and imperialism versus the intellect and the imagination; that 'England and Germany are bound to fight' (ibid., 74); the intertwining of money and death because of inherited wealth, exile, and rootlessness; Mr Wilcox's belief that 'one sound man of business did more good to the world than a dozen of your social reformers' (ibid., 38); and the Schlegel sisters' credo that 'personal relations are the important thing for ever and ever, and not this outer life of telegrams and anger' (ibid., 176).

This key sentence links directly with Forster's next novel, *Maurice* (written in 1910–13). The hero may have been partly based on a King's man named Ernest Merz (1881–1909) who took his own life, and the book seems to have been inspired by Forster's admiration for Edward Carpenter, the author of *The Intermediate Sex* (1906). We see Maurice's life at Cambridge, his platonic love for Clive, his thoughts of suicide when Clive marries, and his happiness when his love for the gamekeeper Alex is requited; although 'by pleasuring the body Maurice had confirmed … his spirit in its perversion, and cut himself off from the congregation of normal man' (*Maurice*, 199). One of the few novels about homosexual love to have been written in the years before gay liberation, it could not, of course, be published; but it was revised and quietly circulated among Forster's friends for the next fifty years. It was finally published after his death in 1971 (when some criticized his decision not to publish once it had become legally possible to do so).

After eight intensely creative years Forster was beginning to feel that he had lost his way as a novelist. 'Weariness of the only subject that I both can and may treat—the love of men for women & vice versa' ('Locked journal', 16 June 1911, E. M. Forster archive). But he began to write stories on homoerotic themes (published posthumously as *The Life to Come* in 1972), as well as starting a novel called

'Arctic Summer' in which he tried to imagine, using two characters called Martin and Venetia, what married life would have been like. And now Masood's words two years before—'You know my great wish is to get *you* to write a book on India, for I feel convinced from what I know of you that it will be a great book' (Furbank, 1.194)—were to take effect: with Goldsworthy Lowes Dickinson and R. C. Trevelyan he went on a passage to India.

India, Alexandria, and India again, 1912–1924 Forster arrived in October 1912, staying initially with Masood and his family at Aligarh, and then travelling to Delhi, to Lahore (his first encounter with real Anglo-India), to the Khyber Pass, Simla, Chhatarpur, Bhopal, and Indore (where he was appalled by the English Club). He spent Christmas with his King's friend Malcolm Darling and his wife at Dewas, then went to Allahabad and Benares and visited Masood at Bankipore (Chandrapore in *A Passage to India*). It was here he finally accepted that he and Masood would never be lovers; that his novel began to germinate; and from where, on 28 January 1913, he went to the Barabar caves. He did a great deal more travelling, before returning to England in April 1913.

In Weybridge Forster managed to write the first seven chapters of *A Passage to India* and several articles for the *New Weekly*. But he felt that 'I am leading the life of a little girl so long as I am tied to home' (Forster to Florence Barger, 10 Aug 1913, *Selected Letters*, 1.229) and that he spent 'his time in rowing old ladies upon the river' (V. Woolf, 31 Aug 1915, *Letters*, 63). He started working part-time in the cataloguing department of the National Gallery, to some extent as an escape; he was reviewing seriously (he considered Virginia Woolf's *The Voyage Out* a masterpiece); and he began a book on Samuel Butler. When the First World War broke out his attitude towards it was ambivalent and he was glad to have an excuse to go abroad; in October 1915 he set out for Alexandria, to be a Red Cross searcher tracing missing soldiers. He enjoyed the work, because he felt useful, but the war dismayed him: '"We must fight again as soon as we are strong enough" is all I expect the war to teach Europe' (Forster to Dickinson, 5 April 1916, E. M. Forster archive).

One of the friends Forster made was the poet C. P. Cavafy, and possibly because of him—Cavafy was an active homosexual—he now had his first sexual encounter, and then began an affair with a young tram conductor named Muhammad al-Adl. As well as working for the Red Cross he published short pieces in the *Egyptian Gazette* and *Mail* and wrote a guidebook to Alexandria (published in 1922). When he returned to England in January 1919, a few days after his fortieth birthday, the pattern of the rest of his long life was set: he was trying to finish *A Passage to India*, and wrote the occasional short story; and his intellectual and emotional maturity meant that he was now becoming a respected man of letters. As Virginia Woolf wrote at this time, 'he says the simple things that clever people don't say; I find him the best of critics for that reason' (V. Woolf, 6 Nov 1919, *Diary*, 1.311).

In 1921 Forster accepted an invitation from the maharaja of Dewas to take up the post of private secretary, partly in the hope that a return to India would give impetus to his novel. He was content in a world which 'can have no parallel, except in a Gilbert and Sullivan opera' (*The Hill of Devi*, 6), and wrote detailed letters home (published in *The Hill of Devi* in 1953). Upon leaving he went to Egypt to visit al-Adl, who was seriously ill with tuberculosis and died a few weeks later, and returned to England, according to Virginia Woolf,

> depressed to the verge of inanition. To come back to Weybridge, to come back to an ugly house a mile from the station, an old, fussy, exacting mother, to come back having lost your Rajah, without a novel, & with no power to write one ... The middle age of b[—]s is not to be contemplated without horror. (V. Woolf, 12 March 1922, *Diary*, 2.171)

Forster himself could foresee that his life would be literary, companionable, yet without love, just as it was before. 'I want to love a strong young man of the lower classes and be loved by him' (28 Aug 1920, 'Locked journal', E. M. Forster archive) he had written—but he meant permanently. Yet he saw something of writers such as Thomas Hardy, D. H. Lawrence, T. E. Lawrence, Walter de la Mare, Desmond MacCarthy, and Naomi Mitchison; a great deal of others such as Siegfried Sassoon, Sebastian Sprott, and William Plomer; and was intimate with members of the Bloomsbury group such as the Bells, Duncan Grant, Maynard Keynes, and Roger Fry, and with Lytton Strachey and Dora Carrington. Indeed Leonard and Virginia Woolf counted him among their closest friends; and it was only with their active encouragement that he managed to finish his novel.

A Passage to India describes Adela Quested going out to India with the intention of marrying an Englishman whose 'self-complacency, his censoriousness, his lack of subtlety, all grew vivid beneath a tropic sky' (*Passage to India*, 96). Through her attempts to see the 'real India', her encounter with the Indian Aziz and the English Fielding, and her reaction to what happens in the Barabar/Marabar caves, Forster explores themes such as the importance of personal relations, imperialism, Adela's dislike of institutions and the machinery of power, and the impossibility of accord between English and Indian given that the former are 'associated with a system that supported rudeness in railway carriages' ('Reflections in India', 21 Jan 1922, *The Prince's Tale*, 243): 'One touch of regret—not the canny substitute but the true regret from the heart—would have made [Ronny Hislop] a different man, and the British Empire a different institution' (*Passage to India*, 70). The last third of the book, over which Forster had had such difficulty, explores the Hindu ethos, and was more 'philosophical and poetic' (*The Hill of Devi*, 298) than anything he had ever written before as it leads to the final, pessimistic conclusion:

> 'Why can't we be friends now?' said [Fielding], holding [Aziz] affectionately. 'It's what I want. It's what you want.'
> But the horses didn't want it—they swerved apart; the earth didn't want it ... (*Passage to India*, 316)

It was this abyss of separation between the English and the Indians which became fertile ground for post-colonial studies when they emerged in the 1970s: was Forster imposing on the Indians the limitations and prejudices of his English imagination, or was he a pioneer in recognizing an independent Indian identity, whether that of the Westernizing Aziz or of the eternal rhythms of the Hindu masses?

Abinger Hammer, 1925–1945 Early in 1925 Forster and his mother moved to West Hackhurst, Abinger Hammer, Surrey; and a *pied-à-terre* in London (at Brunswick Square, Bloomsbury) gave Forster some independence and a place to meet the male acquaintances with whom he had casual relationships. He was by now writing for publications such as the *Atlantic Monthly*, the *New Leader*, and *The Criterion*. Early in 1927 he gave the Clark lectures at Trinity College, Cambridge, published as *Aspects of the Novel* later that year; he was also elected to a supernumerary fellowship at King's College and started to spend six weeks a year in Cambridge. *A Passage to India* was translated into French by Charles Mauron, with whom he became close friends. A collection of his short stories was published as *The Eternal Moment* (1928). He also actively promoted Cavafy's poetry and enjoyed a revival of interest in his early novels.

But apart from some hasty sexual encounters, and an affair with a young policeman named Harry Daley in mid-1926, Forster was still lonely. 'Famous, wealthy, miserable' was how he described himself ('Locked journal', 2 Jan 1925, E. M. Forster archive), for the huge success of *A Passage to India* (17,000 copies sold in Britain by the end of 1924 and 54,000 in the USA; 1 million by the time he died in 1970) meant that he was indeed famous. Then, in April 1930, at J. R. Ackerley's house in Hammersmith, he met a young policeman named Robert Joseph (Bob) Buckingham; it was a relationship that lasted until his death. For the last two years 'I have been happy', he wrote in 1932, 'and would like to remind others that their turns can come too. It is the only message worth giving' (*Commonplace Book*, 94); and, later, 'I am happier now than ever in my life' (7 Oct 1934, 'Locked journal', E. M. Forster archive). Even after Buckingham's marriage in 1932 the two men continued to be close; eventually Forster became deeply fond of both his wife, May, and of his son Robert Morgan. It was accepted by now that there would be no new novels, and over the years many reasons were put forward about why this was so: his authorized biographer P. N. Furbank suggested that it was because:

> he received his whole inspiration—a vision, a kind of plot, a message—all at once, in early manhood. He became an artist because of that early experience, an experience of salvation, and his inspiration as a novelist always harked back to that moment of enlightenment. (Furbank, 2.132)

In the 1930s Forster emerged as a public figure representing the liberal conscience. His clear insights, his compassion, his accessibility, and his direct, unaffected tone of voice coalesced with his beautiful prose style and he became a highly respected commentator and broadcaster. In 1928 he had protested publicly against the banning of the lesbian novel *The Well of Loneliness*. In 1934 he was elected the first president of the National Council for Civil Liberties and in 1939 he sat on the lord chancellor's committee on defamatory libel. He wrote articles, sat on committees, and signed letters on individual liberty, censorship, penal reform, and the rise of fascism (but was never tempted to become a communist). Stephen Spender, who considered Forster, T. S. Eliot, and Virginia Woolf to be the only older writers 'who made themselves *present* to contemporaries twenty years younger' (*The Thirties and After*, 1978, 257) wrote:

> When during the thirties E. M. Forster appeared on *front populaire* platforms he did so because the time demanded that he should assume a role in which he had no confidence and for which he felt little enthusiasm. His presence at Congresses of the Intellectuals during the anti-fascist period, and that of young English poets, was an exceptional action produced by exceptional times. (ibid., 187)

When the Second World War was imminent he wrote 'Two cheers for democracy', later called 'What I believe', an essay which included the famous credo: 'I hate the idea of causes, and if I had to choose between betraying my country and betraying my friend, I hope I should have the guts to betray my country' (*Two Cheers*, 76). During the war huge audiences listened to his broadcasts on the BBC, as he argued for the importance of the individual and of personal freedom, and above all for tolerance: the post-war world should be based on 'the negative virtues: not being huffy, touchy, irritable, revengeful' (ibid., 55).

Cambridge again, 1945–1970 Lily died in March 1945 and, to add to Forster's despondency, some months later the West Hackhurst landlord decided not to renew his lease. However, King's were able to offer him an honorary fellowship as well as the room that had been Wedd's. He arrived in Cambridge in November 1946, taking lodgings at 3 Trumpington Street before, in 1953, moving to King's permanently; here he became a familiar and much-loved figure, a symbol of the civilized, liberal values that he had always held so dear. One aspect of these was an antipathy to the showy, a lack of worldliness, which was reflected even in his personal appearance. William Plomer wrote in the 1940s:

> In appearance he was the reverse of a dandy. Incurious fellow passengers in a train, seeing him in a cheap cloth cap and a scruffy waterproof, and carrying the sort of little bag that might have been carried in 1890 by the man who came to wind the clocks, might have thought him a dim provincial of settled habits and taken no more notice of him. (Plomer, 107)

During his last quarter of a century Forster travelled, went to stay with the Buckinghams, saw friends (many old ones, but also each new generation of undergraduates, including P. N. Furbank), wrote articles, and dealt with a vast correspondence—all the accoutrements of the successful elder statesman's literary life. He was translated into numerous languages and, especially after Lionel Trilling published his critical book in 1944, began to be taken seriously by literary critics. He refused permission for his books to be made into films, perhaps fearing the simplifications and nostalgic glow of the widely acclaimed films of David Lean and Merchant–Ivory made after his death.

With Eric Crozier he wrote the libretto for Benjamin Britten's opera *Billy Budd* (1951). *Abinger Harvest*, a collection of his essays and reviews, had been published in 1936 and a second collection, *Two Cheers for Democracy*, appeared in 1951. His biography of Marianne Thornton appeared in 1956. In 1960 he was a defence witness in the case brought by the crown against Penguin Books after the publication of *Lady Chatterley's Lover*. But it was at about this time that there were muttered attacks by contemporaries on Forster's public reticence on the subject of his homosexuality: Angus Wilson was one of those who criticized what he saw as his lack of moral courage for not openly declaring his sexual orientation. Yet Forster, who was by then nearly eighty, gave a large donation to the Homosexual Law Reform Society in the 1960s and wrote the occasional article quietly championing reform of the law.

Forster refused a knighthood in 1949 ('I seem to be a Great Man', he said wearily to J. R. Ackerley (Ackerley, 12), but in 1953 became a Companion of Honour and on his ninetieth birthday received the Order of Merit. He received eight honorary degrees. Honours such as these recognized that Forster was not only one of the most important novelists of the twentieth century but also, in the words of Lord Annan, that 'he spoke for liberal humanism':

> No one wrote with greater simplicity or originality in defence of such well-worn concepts as liberty, democracy, and tolerance. He was unafraid of the contradictions in life which he believed liberals ought to face: that friendship may mean being hard on friends; that freedom and art depended on money and inequality; that racial prejudice was iniquitous but that it was folly to deny that chasms between cultures and races existed and that the bridges between them were flimsy; that his working-class friends needed houses but the new housing estates meant the death of rural England and destroyed man's healing contact with nature. But if a choice had to be made he would make it. He distrusted size, pomp, the Establishment, empires, politics, the upper classes, planners, institutions. He put his trust in individuals, small groups and insignificant people, the life of the heart and mind, personal relations. *(DNB)*

It was at King's in May 1970 that Forster had a stroke, after a succession of smaller ones during the previous months. He was well enough to be moved to the Buckinghams' house at 11 Salisbury Avenue, Coventry, and here he died on 7 June. He was cremated and his ashes scattered on the rose bed in Coventry's crematorium.

In the thirty years after Forster's death the huge success of the Merchant–Ivory films has made a new generation familiar with the novels, most of which continue to be available in paperback. However, the average high street bookshop finds room for only one or two of them, and then only if they are texts for schools; neither of the two biographies is in print. Yet E. M. Forster is one of the greatest English novelists of the twentieth century and his remark, in an interview in 1959, that 'I am quite sure I am not a great novelist' will one day be seen as far too modest.

NICOLA BEAUMAN

Sources King's AC Cam., E. M. Forster archive • P. N. Furbank, *E. M. Forster*, 1 (1977); 2 (1978) • J. H. Stape, *An E. M. Forster chronology* (1993) • *Selected letters of E. M. Forster*, ed. M. Lago and P. N. Furbank, 2 vols. (1983–5) • M. Lago, ed., *Calendar of the letters of E. M. Forster* (1985) • F. King, *E. M. Forster and his world* (1978) • N. Beauman, *Morgan: a biography of E. M. Forster* (1993) • L. Trilling, *E. M. Forster* (1944) • *E. M. Forster's commonplace book*, ed. P. Gardner (1978); new edn (1988) • B. J. Kirkpatrick, *A bibliography of E. M. Forster* (1965) • F. P. W. McDowell, *E. M. Forster: an annotated bibliography of writings about him* (1976) • P. Gardner, ed., *E. M. Forster: the critical heritage* (1973) • J. Stape, *E. M. Forster: interviews and recollections* (1993) • E. M. Forster, *Abinger harvest* (1936); Penguin edn (1974) • E. M. Forster, *The longest journey* (1907); Penguin edn (1989) • E. M. Forster, *Goldsworthy Lowes Dickinson* (1934); new edn (1973) • E. M. Forster, *Marianne Thornton* (1956) • E. M. Forster, *The hill of Devi*, ed. E. Heine (1983) • E. M. Forster, '*Arctic summer' and other fiction*, ed. E. Heine (1980) • E. M. Forster, *Where angels fear to tread* (1905); Penguin edn (1976) • E. M. Forster, *Howards End* (1910); Penguin edn (1989) • E. M. Forster, *A room with a view* (1908); Penguin edn (1979) • E. M. Forster, *A passage to India* (1924); Penguin edn (1989) • [E. M. Forster], 'The prince's tale' and other uncollected writings, ed. P. N. Furbank (1998) • E. M. Forster, *Maurice* (1971) • *The letters of Virginia Woolf*, ed. A. O. Bell, 2 (1980) • *The diary of Virginia Woolf*, ed. A. O. Bell and A. McNeillie, 5 vols. (1977–84), vols. 1–2 • L. Woolf, *Sowing* (1960) • E. M. Forster, *Two cheers for democracy* (1951); Penguin edn (1965) • W. Plomer, *At home* (1958) • J. R. Ackerley, *E. M. Forster: a portrait* (1970) • W. Cowper, 'In memory of the late John Thornton esq', *Works*, 10.31 [Nov 1790] • *DNB* • d. cert.

Archives King's AC Cam., corresp., literary MSS, journals, other papers • NRA, letters • University of San Francisco, Richard A. Gleeson Library, letters and literary MSS | BL, letters to S. S. Koteliansky, Add. MS 48974 • BL, corresp. with the Society of Authors, Add. MS 56704 • BL, corresp. with Marie Stopes, Add. MS 58502 • Bodl. Oxf., corresp. with Sibyl Colefax • Bodl. Oxf., letters to E. J. Thompson • CUL, letters to V. N. Datta • CUL, letters to Lord Kennet and Lady Kennet • Hunt. L., corresp. with Christopher Isherwood • King's AC Cam., letters to Sir George Barnes • King's AC Cam., letters to Vanessa Bell • King's AC Cam., corresp. with the Buckingham family • King's AC Cam., corresp. with A. E. Felkin • King's AC Cam., corresp. with J. M. Keynes • King's AC Cam., letters, postcards, and telegram to G. H. W. Rylands • King's AC Cam., letters to W. G. H. Sprott • King's Lond., Liddell Hart C., corresp. with Sir B. H. Liddell Hart • Lpool RO, corresp. with James Hanley • NL Scot., letters to Naomi Mitchison • Ransom HRC, letters to Hugh Walpole • Tate collection, corresp. with Lord Clark • Trinity Cam., letters to Elizabeth Trevelyan • U. Durham, letters to William Plomer • U. Sussex, letters to Kingsley Martin • U. Sussex, corresp. with *New Statesman* magazine • U. Sussex, corresp. with Leonard Woolf • U. Sussex, corresp. with Leonard Woolf and Virginia Woolf • University of Bristol Library, corresp. and statements relating to the trial of *Lady Chatterley's lover* • University of Victoria, British Columbia, McPherson Library, letters to Sir Alex Randall | SOUND BL NSA, performance recordings

Likenesses R. Fry, portrait, 1911, Evert Barger collection • D. Grant, pencil, 1919, NPG • D. Carrington, oils, 1920, NPG [*see illus.*] • W. Rothenstein, chalk drawing, 1923, King's Cam. • E. Kapp, drawing, 1930, King's Cam. • E. Kapp, drawing, 1930, Barber Institute of Fine Arts, Birmingham • H. Coster, photographs, 1930–39, NPG • M. Beerbohm, caricature, drawing, 1940, King's Cam. • B. Brandt, photograph, 1947, NPG • F. Topolski, pen-and-ink, c.1960, NPG • D. Bachardy, pencil, 1961, NPG • F. Topolski, oils, 1961, U. Texas • C. Beaton, photograph, NPG • photographs, Hult. Arch. • photographs, King's Cam.

Wealth at death £68,298: probate, 6 Nov 1970, *CGPLA Eng. & Wales*

Forster, Frances Egerton Arnold- (1857–1921), ecclesiastical historian, was born on 7 August 1857 at Dharmsala, Punjab, India, the fourth child of William Delafield *Arnold (1828–1859), director of public instruction in the Punjab, and his wife, Frances Anne Hodgson (d. 1858). Her grandfather was Thomas *Arnold of Rugby. Following the death of their mother in India in 1858, Frances, her sister, Florence Mary, and her brothers, Edward Penrose and Hugh Oakeley Arnold-*Forster, were sent to England. Their father died at Gibraltar in 1859 before their arrival. They were adopted and brought up by their maternal aunt, Jane Martha Arnold, daughter of Thomas Arnold, and her husband, W. E. *Forster, at their home at Burley in Wharfedale, in the West Riding of Yorkshire. They took the surname Arnold-Forster in adult life. Frances was initially educated at home, then at a private girls' school. As an active member of the Church Missionary Society and the Society for the Propagation of the Gospel, she was involved in the work of the school and mission connected with the Anglican church of St James-the-Less, Lillington Street, west London. Most of her published several works, notably *Heralds of the Cross* (1882), containing stories of missionary work abroad, and *The King's Business* (1909), also a biographical compilation based on missionary society reports, were intended for young readers. However, her *Studies in Church Dedications, or, England's Patron Saints* (3 vols., 1899) was the product of independent scholarly research in diocesan and county records. It stemmed from her interest in a topic she pioneered: the significance of church dedications for local history. It was the first systematic study of its subject, on which it long remained the standard authority. The book combines statistical analysis with pious but lively commentaries on the lives of the saints and church fathers. It was written in conditions of considerable domestic difficulty while the author was nurse and companion to her widowed aunt and looking after her sister's young children. She herself suffered from mental stress and had often to lay her work aside. Frances Arnold-Forster died unmarried at Belmont Grove, Leeds, on 8 July 1921. R. J. FAITH

Sources M. Trevor, *The Arnolds: Thomas Arnold and his family* (1973) · *Florence Arnold-Forster's Irish journal*, ed. T. W. Moody and others (1988) · *CGPLA Eng. & Wales* (1921)

Archives TCD, corresp., MSS 5004–5006

Wealth at death £26,790 13s. 2d.: probate, 4 Oct 1921, *CGPLA Eng. & Wales*

Forster, (Johann) Georg Adam (1754–1794), traveller and naturalist, was born on 27 November 1754 in Nassenhuben near Danzig in Polish Prussia, the eldest of the six children of Justina Elisabeth, *née* Nicolai, and **(Johann) Reinhold Forster** (1729–1798), the local Lutheran pastor. Forster's family appears to have been of British origin, though long settled on the Baltic coast. Forster's father, a somewhat reluctant cleric, sought opportunities to prove his abilities as a man of science to a wider world. In 1765 he travelled to St Petersburg in search of suitable employment, accompanied by Georg, then aged only eleven, who learned Russian and later attended school there. Reinhold Forster was commissioned to undertake an extensive tour of southern Russia during which his son assisted him in scientific observations for the Imperial Academy of Sciences and in the preparation of maps. In the following year the pair travelled to London in a further search for an appropriate position. On their arrival, the elder Forster established contact with other German-speaking clergy

(**Johann) Georg Adam Forster** (1754–1794), by Daniel Beyel (after John Francis Rigaud, exh. RA 1781) [right, with his father, Johann Reinhold Forster]

and intellectuals in London, and especially with Carl Gottfried Woide, the Lutheran preacher and man of letters, who helped them find lodgings in Denmark Street. (The rest of the family rejoined them only later.) Georg quickly mastered English to add to his knowledge of Russian; his translation work, though mostly attributed to his father alone, was probably the family's principal source of income while Reinhold Forster sought regular employment, built his reputation, and established contacts within the British scientific and scholarly communities. The latter was engaged from 1768 as a tutor at the nonconformist Warrington Academy, which Georg also attended briefly as a student, but returned to London in 1770 in pursuit of a more challenging post. In 1772 he was engaged as naturalist on James Cook's second circumnavigation of the globe in the *Resolution*, again taking his son along as his assistant.

The voyage took the Forsters round the Cape of Good Hope to New Zealand, Tahiti, Tonga, and south beyond the Antarctic circle. Georg Forster's later reputation was based largely on the descriptions of the voyage he published after their return in 1775. The first of these was a botanical work, *Characteres generum plantarum, quas in itinere ad insulas maris Australis, collegerunt, descripserunt, delinearunt, annis MDCCLXXII–MDCCLXXV*, published together with his father, which earned him election to the fellowship of the Royal Society. *A Voyage Round the World, in His Britannic Majesty's Sloop, Resolution* (1777), which Forster published after his father had been denied the opportunity to write the official account of the voyage, had much greater impact. In particular Forster's German translation (*Reise um die Welt*, Berlin, 1778) not only introduced the newly discovered, almost utopian cultures of the south Pacific to the German reading public but was acclaimed for a prose style of great freshness and clarity. In his preface to the German edition, Forster emphasized the subjective nature of description and evaluation in travel writing. The work was praised by many of the leading German literary figures of the day and was held by Alexander von Humboldt, for example, to be the first truly modern account of scientific exploration. Following the publication of the London edition, the Forsters were embroiled in much controversy about the expedition and the role of its members, which gave rise to a minor pamphlet war. Georg's *Reply to Mr. Wales's Remarks* is an elegant riposte to a pamphlet attack by William Wales, the astronomer to Cook's expedition. *A letter to the right honourable the earl of Sandwich, first commissioner of the Board of Admiralty* (1778) sets out his father's case. From 1775 to 1778 the family lived in Percy Street near Tottenham Court Road. In 1780 Reinhold was invited to Halle as professor of natural history and inspector of the botanic garden, and as this post was connected with the faculty of medicine he was made MD. The early death of his son Georg affected him deeply and early in 1798 he described himself as a dying man. He died at Halle on 9 December 1798.

In October 1778 Georg Forster moved to Germany, presumably seeking advantage from his literary celebrity there. In the following year he was appointed professor of natural science at the Collegium Carolinum in Kassel. He married Therese (1764–1804), the daughter of Christian Gottlob Heyne, professor of rhetoric and university librarian at Göttingen, on 3 September 1785. Forster took up a post at the University of Vilna, then in Poland, in 1784, but after several unhappy years accepted an appointment by the elector of Mainz as university librarian in 1788. From April to June 1790 he undertook a further journey, accompanied by Alexander von Humboldt, this time along the Rhine, through the Low Countries, and on to London, returning through revolutionary France. Forster's account of the journey (*Ansichten vom Niederrhein, von Brabant, Flandern, Holland, England und Frankreich*, Berlin, 1791) was held in almost as much esteem by contemporaries as *Reise um die Welt* itself.

Forster remained in Mainz after the occupation of the city by French revolutionary forces in 1792, becoming active in Jacobin circles. A supporter of the incorporation of the west bank of the Rhine into the French republic, in early 1793 Forster was elected deputy for Mainz to the national convention in Paris. His writings about the revolution were significant, if highly contentious, contributions to its reception in the German-speaking world. He died suddenly in Paris on 10 January 1794; the failure of his marriage had caused him much personal unhappiness towards the end of his life, adding to the strain of continual financial difficulties.

Although he was of somewhat unpersonable appearance, contemporaries nevertheless testified to Forster's attractive and open personality and considerable moral courage. Despite his birth in Polish Prussia and upbringing in Russia and England, he clearly felt a close affinity with the German language and culture. Nevertheless he maintained quite close ties with England after his move to Germany in 1778. He was invariably referred to in contemporary English sources as George Forster, a style which has occasionally led to his being confused with the contemporary traveller–writer of the same name, an East India Company servant. His regular correspondents included Sir Joseph Banks and, in the 1790s, Charles Heydinger (presumably Charles William Heydinger (*b.* 1769), the son of the London-based German bookseller Carl Heydinger). Heydinger supplied Forster with English books and maps, apparently sent via Heyne, his father-in-law at Göttingen, with the diplomatic mails of the Hanoverian legation in London. Neither his familiarity with the country nor mastery of the language appear to have made Forster particularly well disposed towards the English themselves. In a letter to Heyne written during his last visit to London and dated 24 May 1790, he wrote: 'The English are, however, too guarded, too mistrustful, too indifferent towards anything from abroad, or indeed any foreign undertaking, for me to have achieved anything during my short sojourn that might further my literary undertakings'. Despite these reservations, Forster should be regarded as a key figure in the reception of English culture and sensibility in eighteenth-century Germany, especially through the English influence on his prose style and approach to scientific writing. The lack of a significant modern biography of Forster in English is unaccountable.   Graham Jefcoate

Sources *Georg Forsters Werke: Sämtliche Schriften, Tagebücher, Briefe* (1958–93) · C. V. Klenker, ed., *Georg Forster in interdisziplinärer Perspektive: Beiträge des Internationalen Georg-Forster-Symposions in Kassel* (1994) · J. Aikin and others, *General biography, or, Lives, critical and historical of the most eminent persons*, 10 vols. (1799–1815) · G. Steiner, 'Forster, Johann Georg(e) Adams', *Neue deutsche Biographie*, ed. Otto, Graf zu Stolberg-Wernigerode (Berlin, 1953), 301–2 · R. Mahlke and R. Weiss, *Faszination Forschung: Johann Reinhold Forster* (Berlin, 1998)
Archives Bodl. Oxf., account of travels | NL Aus., letters to Sir Joseph Banks
Likenesses J. H. Tischbein, oils, 1782, Museum für Völkerkunde, Frankfurt am Main, Germany · D. Beyel, engraving (after J. F. Rigaud, exh. RA 1781), NL Aus. [*see illus.*]

Forster, George (*c.*1752–1791), traveller and writer, was a civil servant of the East India Company appointed to the Madras establishment. The precise date and place of his birth, and details of his parentage, are unknown. From 1782 to 1784 he made a remarkable overland journey from Calcutta to Europe, travelling through Jammu to Kashmir, Kabul, Herat, Persia, across the Caspian Sea, and thence to Russia. This journey traced back, to a large extent, the route of Alexander in his pursuit of Bessus. It also took Forster through districts of considerable commercial and political interest to the British. Adopting various disguises on his route, including those of a Georgian and a Mughal, he travelled in the company of local merchants. This clandestine mode of travel, through regions completely unfamiliar to contemporary Europeans, made it impossible for him to use any instruments to survey his route, although he was later described as an acute observer with a good knowledge of the languages of central Asia. Notwithstanding the absence of accurate measurements in his account of this journey, Forster's contribution to the revision of existing European maps of the region (notably that of the French cartographer J. B. B. d'Anville) was acknowledged by James Rennell, who illustrated his route from the banks of the Ganges to the Caspian Sea in the *Memoir of a Map of Hindoostan* (1788).

On his return to England in 1784 Forster became acquainted with Henry Dundas, who, impressed by his knowledge, encouraged him to write about the general political state of India. In 1785 he published *Sketches of the Mythology and Customs of the Hindoos*, a work which attracted considerable attention. Having returned to India, Forster was employed in 1787 by the governor-general and commander-in-chief Lord Cornwallis to conclude a defensive alliance with Mudhoji Bhonsla and the Nizam Shah against Tipu Sultan, ruler of Mysore. He was accompanied on the journey from Kalpi by the surveyor J. N. Rind, eventually reaching Nagpur on 15 July 1788. This combination of diplomacy and the business of surveying was not unusual: in fact, much of the British cartographic knowledge of the interior of India during this period was gained by officers attached to various political missions. Forster remained in Nagpur until he was recalled to Madras in February 1789. In June 1790 he returned to Nagpur as resident to the court of Raja Raghoji Bhonsla, and on this occasion his route from Cuttack to Nagpur was surveyed by James Davidson, the commander of his escort. He died at Nagpur on 5 January 1791.

The first volume of Forster's best-known work, *A Journey from Bengal to England*, was published in Calcutta in 1790. The second volume of his *Journey* (published posthumously in London in 1798 with another edition of the first volume) was apparently compiled from papers found in his possession. The work appeared in a French translation in 1802. It was valued by contemporaries for its contribution to the geographical knowledge of central Asia, though in other respects (notably its historical narratives) it was said to be less reliable. In the words of a contributor to the *Monthly Review*, 'The late Mr. Forster was endowed with an inquisitive mind, and a good, though not a highly cultivated, understanding' (vol. 27, December 1798, 361). George Forster has often been confused with (Johann) Georg Adam *Forster, traveller and naturalist, who accompanied Captain Cook on his second voyage to the south seas in 1772–5 and who was generally referred to in contemporary British sources as George Forster.

LUCIANA DE LIMA MARTINS

Sources biographical file 5, BL OIOC, OIR.920.054 · R. H. Phillimore, ed., *Historical records of the survey of India*, 1 (1945) · G. Forster, *Voyage du Bengale à Pétersbourg*, trans. L. Langlès, 1 (1802) · J. Rennell, *Memoir of a map of Hindoostan, or the Mogul empire* (1788) · letters to Henry Dundas, 1785, BL OIOC, IOR: H/Misc/685 · C. E. Buckland, *Dictionary of Indian biography* (1906) · *Monthly Review*, new ser., 27 (1798), 361–73 · *Monthly Review*, new ser., 28 (1799), 120, 479 · *DNB* · G. Forster, 'Forster's route from Jumboo to Astracan', 1785, BL, MS Eur. B.14 · G. Forster, *A journey from Bengal to England, through the northern part of India, Kashmire, Afghanistan, and Persia, and into Russia, by the Caspian sea*, 2 vols. (1798)
Archives BL OIOC, home misc. series

Forster, Henry Pitts (c.1766–1815), orientalist, entered the Bengal service of the East India Company on 7 August 1783 and was therefore probably born in or about 1766. He held a succession of company posts until 1798: second assistant to the collector of Jessore (1787), registrar to the Calcutta court of circuit (1791), collector of Tippera (1793), and registrar of the *diwani adalat* (civil court) of the twenty-four *parganas* (1794). In 1803 he re-entered company employ as acting mint-master, and became mint-master on 1 August 1804.

Forster was the first British scholar to publish a lexicon of the Bengali language, *A Vocabulary in Two Parts, English and Bongalee, and Vice Versâ* (2 pts, 1799–1802). It is evident from the introduction that the work was undertaken primarily on political and practical grounds. Bengali at that time was, officially at least, an unrecognized vernacular, and Forster highlighted the absurdity and inconvenience of continuing to use Persian in courts of law, appealing to the company to replace it with Bengali. It is not clear how great a part Forster's work played in the eventual adoption of Bengali as the official language of the Bengal presidency; similar appeals had come from William Carey, Joshua Marshman, and other Baptist missionaries based in the Danish enclave of Serampore, as well as from the native Bengali scholar and reformer Rammohun Roy and his circle.

Forster also directed his attention to Sanskrit. In the *Calcutta Gazette* of 26 August 1802 he stated that he had finished an *Essay on the Principles of Sanskrit Grammar*, the first such work in English. This was submitted, according to its introduction, to the council of Fort William College, Calcutta, in 1804, but the first part was not published until 1810, by which time the Sanskrit grammars of Carey, Henry Thomas Colebrooke, and Charles Wilkins had already appeared. The second part, which was to have included a translation of Vopadeva's popular grammar, the *Mugdhabodha*, seems not to have been published at all. The *Essay* never enjoyed great popularity, partly because it relied heavily on the traditional Indian presentation of the material and was thus less accessible to non-scholarly Europeans. Forster died in India on 10 September 1815, leaving a son, Henry Forster (1793–1862), who pursued a military career in India.

R. S. SIMPSON

Sources Dodwell [E. Dodwell] and Miles [J. S. Miles], eds., *Alphabetical list of the Honourable East India Company's Bengal civil servants, from the year 1780 to the year 1838* (1839), 182–3, 600–01 · C. E. Buckland, *Dictionary of Indian biography* (1906) · S. Sen, *History of Bengali literature* (1960), 178–80 · Muhammad Abdul Qayyum, *A critical study of the early Bengali grammars: Halhead to Haughton* (1982), 16–19, 149–50, 217 · *Calcutta Gazette* (26 Aug 1802) · H. P. Forster, 'Introduction', in H. P. Forster, *A vocabulary in two parts, English and Bongalee, and vice versâ* (1799–1802) · H. P. Forster, 'Introduction', in H. P. Forster, *An essay on the principles of Sanskrit grammar* (1810) · DNB

Forster, Hugh Oakeley Arnold- (1855–1909), politician and author, was born at Dawlish, Devon, on 19 August 1855, second son and third child (a second sister, Frances

Egerton Arnold-*Forster, was born later) of William Delafield *Arnold (1828–1859), director of public instruction in the Punjab province of India, and Frances Anne (d. 1858), daughter of General J. A. Hodgson (who became surveyor-general of India). His father was a younger son of Thomas *Arnold, headmaster of Rugby School, and brother of Matthew Arnold, the poet, critic, and inspector of schools. Oakeley (as he was known to family and friends) Arnold was thus born into the academic purple of the 'intellectual aristocracy' of Victorian imperial Britain. Among his widely ramifying cousinhood were Francis Cranmer Penrose, architect and archaeologist, and his daughter Emily Penrose, the principal of Somerville College; and on his mother's side Mary Augusta Ward, known as Mrs Humphry Ward, the novelist and mother-in-law of G. M. Trevelyan, and Julia Frances Huxley, daughter-in-law of T. H. Huxley, and mother of Julian and Aldous Huxley. All his life Arnold bore the stamp of this élite. He had a justifiably high opinion of his intellectual abilities and a corresponding sense of obligation to employ them worthily in social and public service. His high-mindedness was of an uncompromising integrity, redolent somewhat of his famous grandfather's schoolmasterly manner. He worked intensely as a scholar, writer, and controversialist, and then as a politician, to instruct and improve the world about him.

Early life and education When Arnold was four months old his parents returned with him to India, where his early years passed with the family at Dharmsala and the hill station at Kangra. It was at this latter place that his mother died in 1858. His father decided to send the children back to England, but, while following them, died at Gibraltar on 9 April 1859. The orphaned children were taken in to the home of their aunt Jane Martha, their father's elder sister, who had married in 1850 the Quaker-bred Bradford woollen master and liberal politician William Edward *Forster. The Forsters were childless, and the match between them and the Arnold orphans proved to be entirely happy and affectionate.

Arnold's early schooling was in his maternal family country at Exmouth, under John Penrose, a relation of his late mother. In 1869 he entered Rugby School, scene of his grandfather's renown, but was later withdrawn by Forster on the ground that the standard of discipline had declined. After preparation under a private tutor Arnold matriculated at University College, Oxford, on 24 January 1874. At Oxford he proved receptive to the influence of Ruskin's social, national, and imperial ideals, much as was the case with his near contemporary Cecil Rhodes. He graduated in 1877 with a first-class degree in modern history. On leaving Oxford Arnold, along with his siblings, adopted the name of Arnold-Forster.

Early career On 5 November 1879 Arnold-Forster was called to the bar at Lincoln's Inn, after having read at the chambers of R. A. McCall. 'In all that he did', McCall later recalled, 'he was ever *thorough*' (Arnold-Forster, 29). A promising career as a barrister seemed in prospect, but Forster's appointment by Gladstone in April 1880 to the

chief secretaryship at the Irish Office opened up a much more spacious opportunity. Arnold-Forster took on the position of private secretary to his foster father at one of the most critical times in Britain's relationship with Ireland. As Forster grappled with the Irish revolution inspired by Parnell and the Land League his adopted son was initiated into the great world of high politics. Arnold-Forster commenced his voluminous career as a controversialist with the anonymous publication in 1881 of *The Truth about the Land League*. Forster's break with Gladstone, and his resignation over the so-called Kilmainham treaty and Parnell's release from prison in May 1882, followed by the murder of Lord Frederick Cavendish in Dublin a few days later, left foster father and adopted son united in hostility to Gladstone's Irish policy. Released from official secretarial duties, Arnold-Forster engaged himself assiduously in a variety of public activities. He became involved in social work projects in association with Octavia Hill, Canon Barnett, and other leading philanthropists. He wrote extensively for the reviews, soon establishing himself as an expert in the field of naval, military, and imperial affairs. He joined his foster father among the founders of the Imperial Federation League in 1884, and became its secretary. He became political editor of *The Statist*, which platform he used in the mid-1880s to criticize Gladstone for the want of a definite and constructive Egyptian policy. He travelled extensively, particularly in eastern Europe and Russia, often in Forster's company. Arnold-Forster had an insatiable love of the sea and seafaring: there was many a cruise in his Thames barge as well as, later, an immersion in the higher concerns of naval policy. His most notable exploit in this earlier period was his role in conspiracy with Captain John Arbuthnot Fisher RN, then director of the Portsmouth gunnery school, and the 'sensational' journalist William Thomas Stead to get up very successfully the 'navy scare' of the autumn of 1884. In 'The truth about the navy', published in Stead's *Pall Mall Gazette*, Arnold-Forster accused Gladstone's government of neglecting Britain's imperative duty to assure command of the seas.

Amid the stir of these activities in 1884 Arnold-Forster married Mary, eldest daughter of Mervyn H. N. Story-Maskelyne, professor of mineralogy at Oxford. In order to put his marriage on a secure financial footing (there were eventually four sons of the union) Arnold-Forster entered the publishing firm of Cassells in 1885, and commenced on an extensive programme of writing books designed to instruct children in (in his foster father's words) 'what ought to be the principles which should actuate them as patriotic citizens' (Arnold-Forster, 62). Of his historical and geographical texts, a piece for *Murray's Magazine*, 'In a conning tower' (1888), was admired by Rudyard Kipling for the authenticity of its depiction of naval warfare. Arnold-Forster was a critic of Edward Cardwell's army reforms of the 1870s, and in 1892 and 1898 made two books out of his indefatigable letters to *The Times* on the subject. In all, the list of Arnold-Forster's books and 'principal articles' in reviews extends to forty-four items. Sir

Michael Grant-Duff remarked that 'Arnolds seem to write as naturally as they learn to breathe or walk' (ibid., 40).

Like his uncle Matthew, Arnold-Forster found Gladstone's summoning of the 'masses' increasingly indigestible. He disliked also what he saw as the pointless brawling of party politics. At the time of debate about the third Reform Bill in 1884 he collaborated with Sir John Lubbock on *Proportional Representation*. His reservations about Liberalism led to his declining an offer of nomination to contest Oxford City in the Liberal interest in 1881. In 1883 he was nominated to contest Devonport, but withdrew in 1885, following Forster's repudiation of Gladstone's appeal to the country in the general election of that year. It was after the Liberal split over Irish home rule in 1886 that Arnold-Forster found a more congenial role as a Liberal Unionist. He stood unsuccessfully at Darlington in 1886 and at Dewsbury in 1888. In these years he continued to write copiously on questions of imperial defence and inter-service collaboration, as raised particularly by the Hartington commission's work between 1888 and 1890. It was George Robert Parkin, the educationist and imperialist, who commented on Arnold-Forster's intolerance of dissent and his 'brusque manner which sometimes exposed him to criticism' (Arnold-Forster, 41).

Parliament and the Admiralty At the general election of 1892 Arnold-Forster was successful as a Liberal Unionist in the West Belfast division, which he continued to represent until 1906. He entered the House of Commons as one of Joseph Chamberlain's followers, though characteristically he was at pains to insist upon his independent standing. One of his first acts as an MP in 1893 was to be instrumental in having the union flag flown over the Palace of Westminster while parliament was in session, when existing protocol dictated that the royal standard alone be raised over a royal palace. Official employment could not be found for Arnold-Forster in the construction of the Conservative and Liberal Unionist coalition government in 1895. He was never a popular House of Commons man, nor was he at ease in the clubs. In his advocacy of Chamberlainite policies such as imperial federation and tariff reform Arnold-Forster was ever the stiff and austere intellectual. Chamberlain, now colonial secretary, asked him in August 1900 to go to South Africa as chairman of a land settlement commission to report on the prospects of settling discharged British soldiers in that country after the Second South African War. Arnold-Forster fulfilled his task in highly difficult circumstances with characteristic dispatch and efficiency. On his return later in 1900 Lord Salisbury invited him to take on the parliamentary secretaryship of the Admiralty in the reconstructed Unionist government, and to answer for that department (Lord Selborne being the new first lord) in the House of Commons.

This was a post well suited to so enthusiastic a navalist as Arnold-Forster. With accustomed energy and single-mindedness he launched himself into a programme of reforms 'modern and scientific'. A characteristic concern was to optimize the efficiencies to be got by standardization of dimensions of equipment and materials. He worked to this end with Sir Joseph Whitworth, having already (in 1899) published *The Coming of the Kilogram*. He worked also once more with the new second sea lord, Sir John Arbuthnot Fisher, in revolutionizing the system of entry and training of naval officers to meet the exigent demands of a new era of technology. He worked too with the 'back-room' eminence and royal confidant Lord Esher and with Sir George Sydenham Clarke at the War Office on the beginnings of what became the committee of imperial defence. As the journalist James Louis Garvin remarked of Arnold-Forster, 'no man knew more about public affairs as a whole' (Arnold-Forster, vii). If such knowledge, combined with unsparing application and athletic dynamism (he was a keen cyclist), were the essential prerequisites of political success, Arnold-Forster's public career seemed by 1903 to be poised on the brink of expansive good fortune.

In 1903 A. J. Balfour, who succeeded his uncle Lord Salisbury as prime minister in 1902, was in great difficulties following Chamberlain's resignation of the Colonial Office in order to further his campaign for tariff reform in an imperial *Zollverein*, and the consequent counter-resignation of the chief of the free traders, the duke of Devonshire. In his reconstruction Balfour moved St John Brodrick from the War Office to the India Office. Brodrick had not been a convincing reformer of the army, which the Second South African War had exposed as the most imperative requirement among the great institutions of the British state. On paper Arnold-Forster was his obvious replacement at the War Office. Balfour's difficulty was that he knew Arnold-Forster's great weakness: that he was an over-rigid theoretician and an intellectual perfectionist, unwilling to accept that (in Clarke's words) 'curiously … illogical institutions' could answer for Britain's needs more effectively than ones founded on dialectic impeccability (Tucker, 100). In a subordinate office, as at the Admiralty, these considerations were not disabling for Arnold-Forster. But the War Office notoriously required a tactful handling of personalities and a sureness of parliamentary touch. It was thus that Balfour's offer of the War Office and cabinet rank came to Arnold-Forster only after the refusal of five more favoured candidates (the king first wanted Esher, Balfour first wanted Aretas Akers-Douglas).

The War Office Hence Arnold-Forster was reluctantly appointed to an office widely regarded as a graveyard of political reputations, at a time when Balfour's ministry was beginning to crumble under the pressures of the division in the Unionist Party over the fiscal question. It was unfortunate also that shortly before taking over at the War Office Arnold-Forster strained his heart severely in a riding accident, from which he never fully recovered. He none the less set about confidently scrapping the Cardwell and Brodrick reforms. Linked battalions and regimental depots were set to be abolished, with 'large depots' established for recruitment and supply. Brodrick's army corps system was abandoned. Arnold-Forster wanted a perfectly logical dual-system army: a short-service (two-year) home army to build up a reserve for expansion in time of war, and a long-service (nine-year) army to garrison the empire. His primary aim was to create a real striking force of all arms able to take the field without cumbersome delays of mobilization. In order to fit into this system the militia would be scrapped and integrated into the short-service home army, liable for foreign service in time of war. The commandership-in-chief was abolished and an army council established on the model of the Board of Admiralty. Arnold-Forster set in train plans for a general staff and an inter-service defence committee composed of the intellectual élite. He 'lectured the generals of the army council as if they were schoolboys and treated the House of Commons with scarcely more respect' (Hamer, 230).

This ruthless frontal assault on well-entrenched professional interests created for Arnold-Forster many enemies. Eminent and influential people with whom he had collaborated when at the Admiralty, and who were initially sympathetic to root and branch military reforms, found his personality and his methods at the War Office counterproductive. The militia colonels in parliament were especially active in stirring up hostility to his plans. Balfour defended Arnold-Forster to Esher as the 'best of good fellows, [but] he is at once unconsciously inconsiderate of other people's feelings, and unduly sensitive in his own,—a rather unfortunate combination' (Hamer, 231). Esher thought Arnold-Forster 'not quite a gentleman' (Lees-Milne, 147), and likened his policies to his lack of prowess at shooting: 'He knows all about guns, but he can't hit a haystack' (ibid., 231). It was he who played the decisive part in undermining Arnold-Forster's reforming plans at the War Office. Avoiding responsible office, and adept and feline in intrigue, Esher used his connections with the court and his place on the War Office reconstruction committee to work to subordinate the War Office to the policy decisions of the newly formed committee of imperial defence. Esher challenged Arnold-Forster directly on such issues as disposition of militia battalions in what his biographer has described as 'a bold stance for an independent peer to take up against an accredited Secretary of State for War' (Lees-Milne, 152). Arnold-Forster 'never forgave Esher for his interference in military affairs'. He felt he had cause also to condemn Brodrick as a 'false friend' (Hamer, 227). Fisher also in his own way became a 'false friend' by his resistance to Arnold-Forster's plan to make the Admiralty subject to inter-service co-operation. Esher clandestinely arranged for the formation in January 1905 of a secret subcommittee of the committee of imperial defence, chaired by Balfour and backed by Joseph Chamberlain, to settle matters behind Arnold-Forster's back.

The impasse into which Arnold-Forster got himself in any case hardly mattered in the context of the general disintegration of the position of Balfour's government in 1905. Balfour's resignation in December of that year ended any chance of Arnold-Forster's achieving substantial results for his 'dual army' scheme. At the general election called by the new prime minister, Campbell-Bannerman, in January 1906 Arnold-Forster retired from his Belfast constituency and was adopted at more convenient Croydon. This division he successfully held amid the collapse of the unionist parties under the Liberal landslide. In the new parliament he conducted a futile campaign against his successor at the War Office, Richard Burdon Haldane.

Death and reputation During 1907 Arnold-Forster suffered severely from his heart condition. A visit to Jamaica, accompanied by his wife and a son, on the invitation of Sir Alfred Jones to attend the conference of the Imperial Cotton Growing Association was intended as a relaxing diversion, but unfortunately coincided with a devastating earthquake which wrecked Kingston and destroyed Port Royal. He and his family were lucky to survive. He returned to Britain in shock, his health in unrelieved decline, and died at 27 Hereford Square in South Kensington on 12 March 1909. He was buried at Wroughton, Wiltshire, the parish of his wife's family home.

Arnold-Forster's career illustrated vividly the strengths and limitations of pure intellect as applied to the impure world of parliamentary politics and ministerial intrigue. He was constitutionally inhibited from making concessions or compromises in policy or from cultivating popularity. He was an easy target for enemies such as Campbell-Bannerman, who could take advantage of Arnold-Forster's superb unwillingness to ingratiate himself and mock his allegedly 'metallic voice, sour visage, and dogmatic egotism' (Hamer, 256). 'His patriotism', as J. L. Garvin judged, 'was a religion which possessed him from head to foot. He was a pioneer of all the imperial causes through their darkest days' (Arnold-Forster, vii). Balfour paid accurate tribute to Arnold-Forster: no man was 'more absolutely absorbed in a great and unselfish desire to carry out his own public duty' (*DNB*).   R. T. SHANNON

Sources M. Arnold-Forster, *H. O. Arnold-Forster: a memoir* (1910) · *DNB* · BL, Arnold-Forster MSS, Add. MSS 50275–50357 · W. S. Hamer, *The British army: civil–military relations, 1885–1905* (1970) · A. Tucker, 'The issue of army reform in the unionist government, 1903–5', *HJ*, 9 (1966), 90–100 · J. Lees-Milne, *The enigmatic Edwardian: the life of Reginald, 2nd Viscount Esher* (1986) · J. Luvaas, *The education of an army: British military thought, 1815–1940*, new edn (1965) · Foster, *Alum. Oxon.* · N. G. Annan, 'The intellectual aristocracy', *Studies in social history: a tribute to G. M. Trevelyan*, ed. J. H. Plumb (1955), 241–87 · WWW · *The Times* (13 March 1909) · Hansard · Kelly, *Handbk* · d. cert. · *CGPLA Eng. & Wales* (1909)

Archives BL, papers, incl. diaries, Add. MSS 50275–50357 · TCD, family corresp. · Wilts. & Swindon RO, corresp., political papers | BL, corresp. with Arthur James Balfour, Add. MSS 49722–49723 · BL, corresp. with Sir Charles Dilke, BL MSS 43893, 43916 · BL, corresp. with Herbert Gladstone, Add. MS 46053 · BL, corresp. with E. T. H. Hutton, Add. MS 50085, *passim* · BL, letters to R. J. Marker, Add. MS 52277 · Bodl. Oxf., corresp. with Lord Selborne · CAC Cam., corresp. with Lord Esher · NA Scot., corresp. with A. J. Balfour · NAM, letters to Earl Roberts · NRA Scotland, priv. coll., corresp. with Sir John Ewart

Likenesses B. Stone, two photographs, 1899, NPG · Elliott & Fry, photograph, NPG · S. P. Hall, pencil drawing, NPG · R. P. Harris-Brown, oils, Athenaeum, London · Spy [L. Ward], chromolithograph caricature, NPG; repro. in *VF* (24 Aug 1905)

Wealth at death £13,764 2s. 4d.: probate, 14 April 1909, *CGPLA Eng. & Wales*

Forster [*née* Mackenzie], **Jacqueline Moir** [Jackie] (1926–1998), journalist and campaigner for homosexual rights, was born on 6 November 1926 at the Royal Northern Hospital, Upper Holloway, London, the only daughter and eldest of two children of Kenneth Pirie Mackenzie, a doctor and major in the Royal Army Medical Corps, and his wife, Margaret Rutherfurd Alexander (*d.* 1961). She spent her early years in India, where her father was stationed, then moved to Scotland, and was educated at St Leonard's School, Fife, and Wycombe Abbey, Buckinghamshire. She gained theatrical experience touring in repertory (1945–50) and had a brief film acting career before moving into television. There she worked with Gilbert Harding as a reporter and was soon recognized for her spirited presentation. In 1956 she won a prix d'Italia for her coverage of the marriage of Grace Kelly to Prince Rainier of Monaco; her own series followed. She returned to acting in the television sitcom *Trouble for Two* (1958), but reportage was her forte and she graduated to the news programmes *Tonight*, *Panorama*, and *Late Night Extra*.

On 15 February 1958 she married Peter Currie Forster (*b.* 1925/6), an author and journalist. She began travelling to the USA to make television programmes, and it was there, in 1958, that she had her first lesbian experience. This clandestine relationship, with an American journalist, lasted until 1961.

Following her divorce in 1962, Jackie Mackenzie travelled to Canada where, on a lecture tour in 1964, she met Barbara Mary (Babs) Todd, *née* Thomas (*b.* 1933), an actress. They lived together in Toronto, Massachusetts, and London with Todd's two daughters whom they raised together. They separated in 1975 but the daughters continued to regard Mackenzie as their stepmother.

Although she returned to journalism, working for Border Television and writing regular columns for *She* and the *Sunday Express*, MacKenzie became increasingly incensed at the prejudice which forced gays and lesbians into a 'closet' existence. She was soon active in the movement for homosexual equality and (now using the name Jackie Forster) 'came out' in 1969 when she made an impassioned speech at a Speakers' Corner meeting of the reformist Campaign for Homosexual Equality.

As the gay liberation movement developed, Forster switched her allegiance to the more radical Gay Liberation Front, and in 1971 she took part in the first Gay Pride march. An involvement with *Arena-3*, the first British lesbian magazine of the modern era, developed into her founding, with Todd, the networking lesbian organization Sappho with its eponymous magazine, which she edited for ten years (1971–81).

As a member of Women in Media, Forster acquired techniques of lobbying for change at the side of fellow journalists Anna Raeburn, Mary Stott, and Jill Tweedie. Such action was inspired by trade-union tactics rather than by lesbian bar culture, although the latter remained a vital sector of Forster's constituency: it was at Sappho's monthly meetings that, with glass in hand and a willing ear, she provided friendship and guidance to women who kept a low profile by choice and those who were forced to

keep a low profile through circumstances. Sappho's guest speakers were impressive, ranging from Helena Kennedy and Maureen Duffy to Lord Longford, and members debated issues as apparently removed from lesbian cultural concerns as the death penalty and nuclear disarmament.

Her early forays into the arena of debate with the Campaign for Homosexual Equality, Kenric (the lesbian support and social organization), and the Minorities Research Group made Forster a natural recruit for the Greater London council's women's committee in the 1980s; there she provided a constant, prodding presence and was never afraid to speak her mind even when her opinions clashed with the socialist *status quo*. Later she took part in direct action, participating in sit-ins at homophobic pubs and radio stations and aligning herself with Outrage, the gay and lesbian pressure group.

Forster was at the forefront of many campaigns. When she organized help for lesbians to conceive children via artificial insemination by donor she was vigorously attacked by some elements of the press. She remained a champion of lesbian motherhood and, with Gillian E. Hanscombe, co-authored a book on the subject, *Rocking the Cradle* (1981). Hanscombe called her 'a rare individual. She has noble instincts and the noblest of them is to fight for justice of any kind, not just for lesbians' (Woodis).

In confrontational situations Forster's earthy humour often carried the day. She persisted in engaging publicly in the fight against injustice, whether discussing the London lesbian and gay policing initiative or drawing attention at a civic reception to the sexist differential affecting the pay of the men and women employed there as waiters. She campaigned for the Sex Discrimination Act (1975) and the creation of the London Women's Centre (of which she was a director, 1992–6), was a curator of the Lesbian Archives, and was involved with gay medical and social workers' organizations. She also taught drama in prison.

A founder member of the Women's Broadcasting and Film Lobby, Forster became the archetypal 'rent-a-dyke' whenever a 'lesbian quote' was required (Woodis). She featured in London Weekend Television's *Speak for Yourself* (1974), the first lesbian and gay access television programme, and 'From High Heels to Sensible Shoes' (1997) in the BBC series *The Day that Changed my Life*; the same year the National Film Theatre devoted an evening to her work at which she appeared in conversation with the writer Rose Collis.

For over two decades MacKenzie's slogan, 'What about the women?' was as familiar as her gold cigarette-holder and the sound of her rich, fruity voice. She had once been a prospective Liberal candidate for Cheltenham, but she abandoned conventional politics in favour of lesbian feminist activism and, furthermore, did so at a time when lesbian concerns were still marginalized by an emerging women's movement. By establishing Sappho, the magazine and the organization, she provided an important forum and 'probably saved a lot of isolated lesbians under plain brown wrappers' (Wilmer, 'Visions of liberty').

In 1993 Forster was diagnosed with breast cancer but

recovered and, typically, campaigned to raise awareness of the disease. She remained active in journalism as a voluntary editor with Talking Newspapers for the Blind while earning a living working in London for the British School in Rome. In 1995 she founded Daytime Dykes, a social group whose focus—visiting historical buildings and museums—contrasted somewhat with that of her carousing days but which nevertheless continued to perpetuate lesbian solidarity. In 1993 she began a relationship with an actress known as Lace, which lasted until her death. She died on 11 October 1998 at Guy's Hospital, London, from emphysema.   VAL WILMER

Sources C. Woodis, *The Independent* (31 Oct 1998) • S. McLean and others, 'Remembering Jackie', *Diva* (Dec 1998) • J. Cassidy and A. Stewart-Park, *We're here: conversations with lesbian women* (1997), 57–66 • V. Wilmer, 'A salute to Sappho', *Spare Rib*, 116 (March 1982), 31–2 • V. Wilmer, 'Visions of liberty', *City Limits* (5–11 March 1982), 53–4 • *The Times* (28 Oct 1998) • D. Northmore, *The Guardian* (19 Oct 1998) • V. Wilmer, *The Guardian* (27 Oct 1998) • J. Mackenzie, 'How to stay in television', *Television Annual* (1958), 77–80 • L. Carolin, 'Waiting for the red light', *Everywoman* (July 1996) • b. cert. • m. cert. • d. cert.
Archives Glasgow Women's Library, 109 Trongate, Glasgow | FILM BFI NFTVA, documentary films | SOUND Glasgow Women's Library, oral history items
Likenesses J. P. Goodchild and A. Stewart-Park, photograph, *c.*1977, priv. coll. • V. Wilmer, photographs, 1981, priv. coll.

Forster, Sir John (*c.*1515–1602), administrator and soldier, was the second son of Sir Thomas Forster (*d.* 1526), administrator, of Adderstone, Bamburgh, Northumberland, and Dorothy (*d.* 1582), daughter of Robert, fourth Baron Ogle. He had three brothers and at least six sisters, but when his mother married Sir Thomas Grey of Horton in 1529 and had six more daughters and a son, his immediate kindred was comparatively large. As most of these siblings and step-siblings married, Forster was related to most of the greater landed families of Northumberland. He first made his mark as an ambitious younger son exploiting the dissolution of the monasteries when he bought the Bamburgh lands and tithes belonging to Nostell Priory in 1541. He thereafter designated himself as Forster of Bamburgh. He may have borrowed the money for this purchase from his elder brother, Thomas, and the latter's wife, Florence, a sister of the first Lord Wharton. He continued to purchase former monastic land throughout his life, such as Alnwick Abbey (from Sir Ralph Sadler in 1557), and he later controlled much of Hexham Abbey and Hulne Priory. He also accumulated substantial non-monastic lands at Spindlestone, Bamburgh, Hexham, Alnwick, Corbridge, Middleton Hall, Belford, Easington, and Elwick in Northumberland. Added to these were various tithes, fishings, and coal-pits, and the lay rectorships of Alnmouth, Lesbury, Longhoughton, Lucker, Shilbottle, and Warkworth churches.

Forster captained 100 light horse at Fenton between 1544 and 1549 during the Anglo-Scottish wars. He may have been wounded at the battle of Ancrum Moor in February 1545, though he was not killed as French reports suggested. His military prowess was rewarded by a knighthood *c.*1548, probably on the suggestion of Sir Ralph Sadler who admired Forster's bravery. Sir John then settled back into gentry life after hostilities ceased in 1549: he was chosen as sheriff of Northumberland in 1550. In 1555 he was awarded the captaincy of Bamburgh Castle, and he began acting as a deputy warden of the English middle march in 1556. He was described as 'a man of great servyce on the Borders' in 1558 (*APC*, 6.270–71). However, Forster was dismissed from office by the newly restored seventh earl of Northumberland. The earl had been enraged by the Forsters' success in the county at the expense of his family's traditional influence.

The accession of Elizabeth I signalled Sir John's return to the office of deputy warden, for the earl of Northumberland was forced to retreat from the frontier. Forster became warden of the middle march in his own right in November 1560 and remained in this office until 1596, with a small break during 1587–8. He was much trusted for his good service and now openly supported the protestant cause, while many local gentlemen remained Catholic. He even became a puritan, probably through the influence of the earl of Bedford. His years as warden were difficult, but he handled the deteriorating conditions on the marches with tenacity, effectiveness, and pragmatism. His local knowledge was invaluable, making him more successful in this post than strangers. He gained even more wealth, influence, and offices by assisting the defeat of the northern uprising of 1569–70. He then took every opportunity he could to aggrandize his homes at the expense of the earls of Northumberland and their followers. While warden, Sir John had also been a long-serving JP (1562–1601), a councillor of the north, *custos rotulorum* for Northumberland, a border commissioner, and a frequent commissioner for the crown, exchequer, chancery, and the church. He was widely respected, though he ultimately lost power through old age and alleged incompetence. He died on 13 January 1602 at Spindlestone. His funeral at Bamburgh parish church befitted his rank and cost £454 11*s.* 7*d.*, an exceptional sum by Northumbrian standards.

He was by far the most successful younger son of any sixteenth-century Northumbrian gentry family, but the Forsters of Bamburghshire were notorious for their infidelities and Sir John was no exception. He had a son, Nicholas, with Janet Buicks before his first marriage in the 1540s to the widow of his cousin Robert, fifth Lord Ogle, namely Jane Radcliffe of Dilston. This marriage produced a daughter, Juliana, who in 1571 married Sir Francis Russell, a younger son of the first earl of Bedford. By quirk of fate, she was the mother of the third earl of Bedford, since both her husband and his brother, the second earl of Bedford, died within hours of each other in July 1585. Sir John was very proud to be the earl's grandfather. His second marriage, by 1597, was to his long-standing mistress Isabel Sheppard. She was the mother of Matthew Sheppard alias Forster, and Mary, who were legitimized by their parents' marriage. Mary married Henry Stapleton of Wighill, Yorkshire, in 1599. As he had no son to succeed him, Sir John went to the church courts at Durham in July 1596 to have Nicholas legitimated as his son and heir. The outcome of this case is unclear, but Nicholas did succeed his father in

1602. Sir John's other illegitimate children, of unknown maternity, included a son, John, and a daughter, Mary, who married Ralph Salkeld of Hulne Park, Alnwick.

MAUREEN M. MEIKLE

Sources M. M. Meikle, 'A godly rogue: the career of Sir John Forster, an Elizabethan border warden', *Northern History*, 28 (1992), 126–63 · E. Bateson and others, eds., *A history of Northumberland*, 15 vols. (1893–1940) · U. Durham L., archives and special collections, Durham probate records, wills, 1602 · [J. Raine, W. Greenwell, and others], eds., *Wills and inventories from the registry at Durham*, 4 pts, SurtS, 2, 38, 112, 142 (1835–1929) · APC, 1556–8 · PRO, E 310/21/107 · M. M. Meikle, 'Northumberland divided: anatomy of a sixteenth-century bloodfeud', *Archaeologia Aeliana*, 5th ser., 20 (1992), 79–89 · M. M. Meikle, 'Lairds and gentlemen: a study of the landed families of the Eastern Anglo-Scottish Borders, *c.*1540–1603', PhD diss., U. Edin., 1989
Archives BL, Cotton MSS, corresp. and papers
Wealth at death £1020 5*s.* 8*d.*: inventory, Bateson and others, eds., *A history*, I.158–9

Forster, John (1812–1876), writer and literary adviser, was born on 2 April 1812 at Fenkle Street, Newcastle upon Tyne, the second of four children of Robert Forster (*d.* 1836), butcher and cattle dealer, and Mary (*c.*1780–1852), the daughter of a Gallowgate dairy farmer. The family, which was Unitarian, was not well off: Forster's uncle John enabled him to attend the Newcastle Royal Grammar School, where he became head boy. During his schooldays he wrote a vigorous defence of theatre-going to answer the objections of a friend's mother. In 1828 his melodrama *Charles at Tunbridge, or, The Cavalier of Wildinghurst* was performed at Newcastle's Theatre Royal. Later in 1828 he went to Jesus College, Cambridge, but after only a month he moved to London to study law at University College with Thomas Chitty, the eminent special pleader. Forster showed brilliant potential but 'flung away his chances at the Bar—for which Mr Chitty never forgave him' (Davies, 9). Although he never practised, he was called to the bar in 1843, a step which he took with an eye to government preferment: this eventually came in 1855, when he became secretary to the lunacy commission at a salary of £800 per annum. The abandoning of Cambridge and a legal career—the latter later regretted—reflected his youthful determination to make his way in the literary world.

There Forster rose 'not rapidly but by degrees' (Davies, 12). He contributed to the *New Monthly Magazine*, and edited the short-lived *Reflector*. In 1832 he published *Rhyme and Reason*, a volume of undistinguished verse, and became drama critic of the *True Sun*. His essays in the *Englishman's Magazine* on Commonwealth leaders attracted attention—parts were reprinted in *The Times*—and he was commissioned to contribute biographies of leading seventeenth-century figures under the title *Lives of Eminent British Statesmen* (1836–9) to the Cabinet Cyclopaedia.

In 1833 Forster became drama critic, and, soon after, literary critic, of *The Examiner*, the weekly edited by Albany Fonblanque that was, as J. S. Mill later wrote in his *Autobiography* (1867), 'the principal representative, in the newspaper press, of radical opinion' (quoted in Davies, 12). He moved to 58 Lincoln's Inn Fields—described in *Bleak House* (1853) as Mr Tulkinghorn's chambers—where

he lived until 1856. Here, in 1844, Dickens read *The Chimes* to his friends, an occasion sketched by Daniel Maclise. Forster entertained frequently, presiding over what Longfellow described as the 'brave world in No. 58, Lincoln's Inn Fields … the fire-light, wine-light, and, friend-light indoors' (quoted in Davies, 93), becoming a central figure in London literary life.

Forster reviewed regularly for *The Examiner* until 1855, succeeding Fonblanque as editor in 1847. He wrote political articles, edited and contributed to the *Foreign Quarterly Review*, wrote for Dickens's *Daily News* (which he also edited following Dickens's withdrawal), published *The Life and Adventures of Oliver Goldsmith* (1848), which was republished in an extended version in 1854, contributed articles to Dickens's *Household Words*, and literary essays to the *Edinburgh Review* and the *Quarterly Review*. He was also literary adviser to the publishing firm of Chapman and Hall.

Forster's main contribution to nineteenth-century literary life was made through his friendships. He gave practical help to many writers and actor–managers, among them Thomas Hood, Alfred, Lord Tennyson, Elizabeth Gaskell, Longfellow, and Samuel Phelps, advising on their work, recommending them to publishers, supporting them in reviews. By 1836 he had been or had become the close associate of six important figures: Leigh Hunt, Charles Lamb, Bulwer-Lytton, Walter Savage Landor, William Charles Macready, and Robert Browning. Lamb died in 1834; the friendships with Hunt, Bulwer-Lytton, Landor, Macready, and Browning were long-lasting and complex. That with Bulwer-Lytton, who died in 1873, in its ramifications and intimacy rivalled that with Dickens. Forster was involved in almost every area of Bulwer's literary, theatrical, and personal life: he read and commented on Bulwer's manuscripts, often placed them with publishers or actor–managers and negotiated terms, corrected proofs, and reviewed or obtained reviews of the published works. In Bulwer's complicated personal life Forster was even, for a period, a caring surrogate father—and later literary adviser—to Bulwer's neglected son, the diplomat–poet Robert Lytton, who became viceroy of India. The friendship with Robert Browning was notable for Forster's early support of Browning's work; Browning contributed to Forster's biography of Strafford, work that led to Browning's own play *Strafford*, which Macready staged. Forster encouraged Browning's career as a playwright which, though unsuccessful and soon abandoned, aided the development of the dramatic sense that informs his finest poetry.

Leigh Hunt, Forster recalled, 'influenced all my modes of literary thought at the outset of my life' (Davies, 22); Lamb was idealized by Forster as the model literary man. He regarded Hunt and Landor as literary martyrs, whose lack of adequate recognition and financial reward drew attention to writers' needs. Both Bulwer-Lytton and Macready were obsessed with the status and dignity of their professions. These relationships, and the later one with Thomas Carlyle—who prized Forster's sociability and business acumen and, as the author of 'The hero as man-of-letters' shared similar views—shaped and nourished

Forster's intense concern for the dignity of literature and drama, a burning desire that writers and actors should receive the respect and rewards which they deserved. Such feelings informed all his literary activities, even his reviewing, which attacked excess and praised moderation and respectability, and his biographies of writers, which sought to present a socially acceptable idea of the literary man. Even his work as a historian, with its stress on individual rights and the popular cause, can be seen as grist to the 'dignity' mill.

The most famous of Forster's friendships is that with Charles Dickens. It began in 1837 and lasted until Dickens's death in 1870, following a pattern similar to that of the friendship with Bulwer. In particular, Forster represented Dickens in negotiations with publishers, always in command of his brief and driving hard bargains, and ensuring that Dickens worked his copyrights by means of new editions and translations. He enabled Dickens to contribute reviews and articles to *The Examiner*. Further, from October 1837, as Forster wrote, 'There was nothing written by him … which I did not see before the world did, either in manuscript or proofs' (Davies, 166). His hard-headed advice, generally concerned to prune excesses, remove impieties, and strengthen the moral force of narrative, reflected firm critical principles and an understanding of the mid-Victorian readership. Most famously, or infamously, he claimed credit for persuading Dickens to end *The Old Curiosity Shop* with the death of Little Nell. Forster's influence on the young Dickens was great, an important aspect being the widening of Dickens's social and literary circle through introductions to his friends. From 1850 onwards Dickens increasingly associated with younger and more bohemian companions, including Wilkie Collins and G. A. Sala. The consequent gap between Forster and Dickens was widened by Forster's marriage and by his strong disapproval—invoking the 'dignity of literature'—of Dickens's public readings. However, that gap was never unbridgeable: Dickens continued to consult Forster about all important literary and personal matters. In 1859 he chose Forster to represent him in the arrangements relating to his separation from his wife. In 1870 Forster was an executor of Dickens's will and was left his remaining manuscripts.

Forster, wrote W. M. Thackeray, is 'Great and Beneficent like a Superior Power … whenever anyone is in a scrape we all fly to him for refuge. He is omniscient and works miracles' (quoted in Davies, 93). His sociability was also valued. Many could say, with Dickens, 'you are a part, and an essential part, of our home, dear friend' (ibid., 174), and welcomed him to numerous family occasions. He was often a godfather—he was a devout Christian—always the bachelor 'uncle' and usually good company. Though he had forthright opinions and was often difficult, rude, bad-tempered, bullying, and pompous—qualities caught by Dickens in the character of Podsnap in *Our Mutual Friend* (1865)—and so made enemies or disrupted friendships with fierce quarrels, Forster's friends knew that, essentially, he was tender-hearted, affectionate, loyal, convivial, and generous. His servants thought the world of him.

Bulwer summed him up as 'A most sterling Man … He may be irritable, sometimes bluff to rudeness—But these are trifling irregularities in a nature solid & valuable as a block of gold' (quoted in Davies, 267). When young he was of medium height, dark-haired, with forceful, handsome features conveying great drive, and something of a dandy. His health was poor: he suffered greatly from bronchitis and from rheumatism, constant pain from the latter contributing to his fierce manner and short temper. He became thickset, his determined, aggressive, side-whiskered features increasingly lined with pain. He was always formally dressed and used an eye-glass. To the end he retained his northern accent.

In 1833 Forster had been on the point of marriage to the poet Letitia Elizabeth Landon (L.E.L.), but he withdrew when he heard rumours about her other liaisons. Seemingly a confirmed bachelor, in 1856 he astonished his friends by becoming engaged to Eliza Ann Colburn (1819–1894), the widow of the publisher Henry Colburn and the daughter of the late Captain Robert Crosbie RN. 'After I knew it (from himself) this morning', wrote Dickens, 'I lay down flat, as if an Engine and Tender had fallen upon me' (Davies, 108). They were married at All Saints' Church, Upper Norwood, on 24 September 1856. Eliza Forster was wealthy: the couple moved first to 46 Montague Square before building Palace Gate House in Kensington. The marriage proved happy, though childless.

From 1861 to 1871 Forster was a commissioner in lunacy at a salary of £1500 per annum. His poor health made the constant travelling to inspect asylums an increasing burden, particularly since he was busily publishing volumes of Commonwealth history, notably *The Arrest of the Five Members by Charles I* (1860), *The Debates on the Grand Remonstrance, November and December, 1641* (1860), and *Sir John Eliot: a Biography* (1864), and, in 1869, *Walter Savage Landor*, a two-volume literary biography. After 1871 came *The Life of Charles Dickens* (1872–4) and *The Life of Jonathan Swift*, volume 1 (1875).

As both editor and reviewer, Forster's honesty and clear principles did much to improve the status of journalists, as did his government appointment and, in 1864, an honorary doctorate from Trinity College, Dublin. His historical studies, however, were soon superseded. He worked hard, used original sources, on occasion wrote with verve, but lacked objectivity: in Gardiner's words he was 'an advocate, not a judge' (Davies, 241). Most of his literary biographies have suffered the same fate. The exception is *The Life of Charles Dickens*, a fascinating account of his close friend. Forster was cavalier in his use of documents, most of which have not survived, yet, as Madeline House and Graham Storey have noted, though 'the *Life* contains numerous small distortions of fact … paradoxically these distortions were in the interest of a larger, or ideal, truth' (Davies, 250). This last, however, does not mean that Forster simply sanitized his material: though constrained by the inhibitions of his time, he makes use of revealing juxtapositions to offer unique insights into Dickens's sometimes troubled private life.

After 1871 Forster's deteriorating health kept him

housebound for long periods. He outlived most of his friends and died at Palace Gate House on 1 February 1876. He was buried at Kensal Green cemetery five days later; his wife survived him. From 1864 he had destroyed many of his papers; his literary executor, Whitwell Elwin, destroyed more, thus obscuring his contribution to his literary friendships. What remained, together with his magnificent library, including his incomparable collection of Dickens's manuscripts, Forster left to what is now the Victoria and Albert Museum.   JAMES A. DAVIES

Sources J. A. Davies, *John Forster: a literary life* (1983) · *The Dickensian*, 70/3 (1974) [J. Forster issue; incl. A. Burton, ed., 'The greatest man I know', 192–204] · J. J. Fenstermaker, *John Forster* (1984) · *DNB* · R. Renton, *John Forster and his friends* (1912) · W. L. Harle, 'John Forster: a sketch', *Monthly Chronicle of North-Country Lore and Legend*, 2 (1888), 50–54 · *The Times* (22 Sept 1856) · *The Times* (7 Sept 1876) · Venn, *Alum. Cant.*
Archives Baylor University, Waco, Texas, collection · BL, letters to Royal Literary Fund · Hunt. L., corresp. · NL Scot., corresp. · University of Iowa Libraries, Iowa City, corresp. · V&A NAL, corresp. and papers, incl. literary and historical MSS | BL, letters to Leigh Hunt, Add. MSS 38109–38111, 38523–38524, *passim* · BL, letters to Macvey Napier, Add. MSS 34624–34626 · Herts. ALS, letters to Julian Fane · Herts. ALS, corresp. with Lord Lytton · Hunt. L., Dickens MSS · Morgan L., Dickens MSS · NL Scot., letters to John Burton · NL Scot., corresp. with Thomas Carlyle and Jane Carlyle · NYPL, Dickens MSS, Berg collection · Trinity Cam., letters to Lord Houghton · UCL, letters to Lord Brougham
Likenesses T. Warrington and D. Maclise, oils, 1830, V&A · D. Maclise, two pen-and-ink sketches, 1840, V&A · C. Stanfield, group portrait, water and body-colour, *c.*1842 (*The Logan Rock, Cornwall, climbed by Charles Dickens, John Forster, Daniel Maclise and the artist*), V&A · pen-and-ink caricature, 1842, V&A · D. Maclise, group portrait, pencil sketch, 1844, V&A · D. Maclise, group portrait, oils, exh. RA 1848, V&A · E. M. Ward and E. N. Downard, oils, *c.*1850, V&A · photograph, *c.*1860, Dickens House Museum, London · C. E. Perugini, oils, *c.*1867, Dickens House Museum, London · Elliott & Fry, carte-de-visite, *c.*1870, V&A · R. Doyle, three pen sketches, BM · C. H. Jeens, stipple and line engraving, NPG
Wealth at death under £30,000: probate, 22 March 1876, *CGPLA Eng. & Wales*

Forster, John Cooper (1823–1886), surgeon, the son of John Forster (1795–1870), and his wife, Catherine Matilda, *née* Cooper, was born on 13 November 1823 in Mount Street, Lambeth, where both his prosperous father and grandfather were medical practitioners. The house had a large garden which Forster tended as a boy, gaining a lifelong love for flowers and ferns. From King's College School Forster entered Guy's Hospital in 1841. There he was captain and trainer of the boat club, and had great success. He became MRCS in 1844, MB (London) in 1847, gaining the gold medal in surgery, and FRCS in 1849. In 1850 he was appointed demonstrator of anatomy at Guy's, and married Adela, a lady of great musical talent, the only daughter of Munden Hammond of Kennington. They had seven children, of whom two died of diphtheria, one after a tracheotomy by Forster. In 1855 he was appointed assistant surgeon, and in 1870 full surgeon. In 1880, when senior surgeon, he resigned his appointment, at the same time that Samuel Habershon resigned the senior physicianry, as a mark of disapproval of the conduct of the governors and treasurer of the hospital in disregarding the opinions of the medical staff on questions relating to the nursing staff. After their resignation over 400 Guy's men subscribed to a testimonial and presentation of silver plate to both. After long service on the council of the College of Surgeons and as examiner in surgery Forster was in 1884 president of the college, and did much to facilitate the starting of the combined examination scheme of the colleges of physicians and surgeons. On the termination of his year of office he retired from practice, having long ceased to extend it after inheriting a fortune in 1859. After a stay at Cannes and Nice in January and February 1886 he returned home prostrated by the cold of travelling, and died at his home, 29 Upper Grosvenor Street, Greenwich, of an obscure disease on 2 March 1886. He was buried in his father's grave at Kensal Green cemetery, and was survived by his wife, one son, and three daughters.

Forster was a good practical surgeon, prompt and decisive in the wards, and bold when operating. He was the first to perform gastrostomy in England in 1858, and went to Aberdeen to study Pirrie's procedure of acupressure in 1867. His various papers in the Pathological and Clinical Society's *Transactions* and his reports of surgical cases in *Guy's Hospital Reports* showed keen observation. His clinical lectures were terse, emphatic, and full of common sense. His only published volume was *The Surgical Diseases of Children* (1860). There is no doubt that Forster would have done more as a surgeon but for his easy circumstances. Over 6 feet tall, with bushy black hair, he was a good practical horticulturist, a very skilful oarsman, had a very wide and complete knowledge of English waterways, and was a devoted fly-fisher. A gourmet, he was also noted for his cheery and well-planned hospitality.

G. T. BETTANY, *rev.* ROGER HUTCHINS

Sources V. G. Plarr, *Plarr's Lives of the fellows of the Royal College of Surgeons of England*, rev. D'A. Power, 2 vols. (1930) · *BMJ* (13 March 1886), 525 · W. H. A. Jacobsen, 'John Cooper Forster', *Guy's Hospital Reports*, 3rd ser., 29 (1887), 39–57 · *IGI* · Z. Cope, *The Royal College of Surgeons of England: a history* (1959)
Likenesses H. J. Brooks, group portrait, oils (*Council of the Royal College of Surgeons of England, 1884–85*), RCS Eng. · portrait, RCS Eng.
Wealth at death £25,084 16s. 4d.: probate, 13 April 1886, *CGPLA Eng. & Wales*

Forster, Josiah (1782–1870). *See under* Forster, William (1784–1854).

Forster, Leonard Wilson (1913–1997), German scholar, was born in London on 30 March 1913, the son of Edward James Forster, businessman, and his wife, Linda Charlotte, *née* Rogers. After Marlborough College, he read modern and medieval languages at Trinity Hall, Cambridge, from 1931 to 1934, little imagining when he attended the funeral of the first Schröder professor of German, Karl Breul (1860–1932), that thirty years later he would occupy this chair himself. Missing a first through, he claimed, spending too much time on Italian, he resolved to take a doctorate in Germany. After serving as English Lektor at Leipzig (1934–5) and Königsberg (1935–6), and having witnessed how the eminent Renaissance scholar Paul Hankamer was ruthlessly dismissed by the Nazis at Königsberg, Forster quit Germany for Switzerland, working again as

Lektor at Basel and receiving his doctorate there in 1938 for his thesis (published in 1944) on the polyglot poet and diplomat Georg Rudolph Weckherlin (1584–1653).

In 1939, now a fellow of Selwyn College, Cambridge, and assistant university lecturer in German, Forster married Jeanne Marie Louise Billeter, daughter of Dr Charles Otto Billeter, of Basel, with whom he had a son and two daughters. The outbreak of the Second World War temporarily halted his academic career. Initially attached to the Admiralty, from 1941 until 1945 he was engaged on codebreaking at Bletchley Park. In 1945–6 he was on special duties, partly in Germany, with the rank of lieutenant-commander in the Royal Naval Volunteer Reserve.

Forster returned to Cambridge in 1947, and quickly showed that he had not let the grass grow under his feet by publishing *German Poetry, 1944–1948* (1949). In 1950 he succeeded Leonard Willoughby as professor of German at University College, London. His masterly inaugural lecture, published as *The Temper of Seventeenth-Century German Literature* in 1952, in which he explored the paradox of *vanitas* and *Lebensfreude* underlying the period, and his electrifying reading of Paul Celan's newly published *Todesfuge*, confirmed his reputation as a spellbinding teacher. In 1961 he was embraced again by Cambridge, succeeding Walter Bruford as Schröder professor. Here he threw himself into a dizzying round of activities, impelled by a genuine sense of responsibility for the whole subject and becoming one of Britain's best-known and best-loved Germanists. Even after his retirement in 1979, he was tireless in promoting his subject at home and abroad, showing himself unstintingly generous in assisting young scholars, not least by encouraging them to publish in *German Life and Letters* and *Daphnis*, journals he co-edited for many years. Even though final years were dogged by ill health, his scholarly enthusiasms remained undiminished and his spirit indomitable.

A consummate linguist, Forster's knowledge of German (including 'Baseler Düütsch') was astonishing, his command of Dutch earned him a compliment from the queen of the Netherlands, and he was at home in Czech, French, and Italian too. His facility with Renaissance Latin ensured his reputation as a leading neo-Latinist. Like the humanists he studied, he demonstrated that literatures and cultures cannot fruitfully be studied in nationalistic isolation.

Forster represented all that was best in British scholarship: he was a man of fearsome intellect and immense erudition, yet he wore his learning lightly, and in his scholarship as in his life he was a model of urbanity, elegance, and sheer style. Small wonder, then, that he was much in demand, whether as a regular consultant at the Herzog August Bibliothek, Wolfenbüttel, or as visiting professor at Toronto, McGill, Heidelberg, Otago, Utrecht, Kiel, and Basel. He attained the pinnacle of his international reputation when as president of the Internationale Vereinigung für Germanische Sprach- und Literaturwissenschaften he hosted the world congress of Germanists at Cambridge in 1975, easing tensions over methods and future directions with sovereign eirenicism. He was

president of the English Goethe Society from 1986 to 1990. Among the many honours which came his way were the grand cross of the order of merit of the Federal Republic of Germany (1976), the gold medal of the Goethe Institut, Munich (1966), the Friedrich Gundolf prize of the Deutsche Akademie für Sprache und Dichtung, Darmstadt (1981), the Comenius medal (Czechoslovakia, 1992), and fellowships of academies at Leiden, Amsterdam, and Ghent. As well as the Cambridge LittD, he held honorary doctorates from Leiden, Bath, Strasbourg, and Heidelberg. He was elected a fellow of the British Academy in 1976.

To the general public Forster was best-known for *The Penguin Book of German Verse* (1957), with his own prose translations of poetry from the *Hildebrandslied* to Celan. But his outstanding achievement was to have helped give baroque studies a firm international foundation. Alive to the continuities and connections on which civilization is built, he was supremely qualified to write a monumental synoptic study of the European baroque, but he consistently preferred the briefer compass. The most significant among his many concise books was *The Icy Fire: Five Studies in European Petrarchism* (1969; enlarged German version, *Das eiskalte Feuer: sechs Studien zum europäischen Petrarkismus*, 1976), in which he opened up new critical vistas. His engagement with the work of Günter Grass enabled him to combine his love of contemporary literature with his passion for the baroque period. A selection of his essays on baroque poetry was published as *Kleine Schriften zur deutschen Literatur im 17. Jahrhundert* (1977).

Forster died at Cambridge on 18 April 1997. His ashes were interred at Selwyn College, and the spot was marked by a Latin epitaph composed by Vivian Nutton. A monument of a different kind is his vast collection of papers and extensive correspondence with scholars and writers, deposited in the Deutsches Literaturarchiv at Marbach. He was survived by his wife and three children.

JOHN L. FLOOD

Sources L. Forster, 'Leonard Forster: persönliches Bekenntnis', *Wie, warum und zu welchem Ende wurde ich Literaturhistoriker?*, ed. S. Unseld (Frankfurt, 1972), 79–84 · *The Independent* (26 April 1997) · *The Times* (1 May 1997) · *Publications of the English Goethe Society*, new ser., 66 (1997), 1–2 · *German Life and Letters*, 40 (1997), 589–91 · personal knowledge (2004) · private information (2004) · WWW [forthcoming] · *From Wolfram and Petrarch to Goethe and Grass: studies in literature in honour of Leonard Forster*, ed. D. H. Green and others (1982), 633–42 [bibliography to 1980]

Archives CUL, papers, Add. MS 9252 · Deutsches Literaturarchiv, Marbach, Germany, Nachlass

Likenesses photograph, repro. in Green and others, eds., *From Wolfram and Petrarch to Goethe and Grass*

Forster, Mark Arnold- (1920–1981), journalist and author, was born on 16 April 1920 at Cheriton Nursing Home, Westcott Road, Swindon, the only son of William Edward Arnold-Forster (1886–1951), painter, publicist, and gardener, and his wife Katharine (Ka) Laird, née Cox (1887–1938). Though nothing in his low-keyed adult manner was to advertise it, his parents' families included leading politicians and writers, among them Matthew Arnold and W. E. Forster; his mother had been close to Rupert Brooke and his group as well as to Virginia Woolf. Shortly after his birth his parents went to live in a picturesque Cornish house, Eagle's Nest, Zennor, Cornwall. Seared by their experiences in the First World War, they saw a paramount need for international understanding; they therefore placed their son, aged seven, in a boarding-school in French Switzerland, and at nine in Kurt Hahn's school at Salem in Germany. When Hitler's coming to power in 1933 drove Hahn into exile, Arnold-Forster was one of two British boys who followed the headmaster to a new school in Scotland at Gordonstoun, Moray, and he stayed on until 1937. This upbringing made him fluent in French and German; Hahn's stress on hard living and ethical aspiration rather than on academic achievement meant that he had to cram at a technical college to win a place in mechanical engineering at Trinity Hall, Cambridge (which he never took up), but it also prepared him for the war just ahead.

After a year's apprenticeship (1938–9) with the Blue Funnel Line, involving a voyage to Manchuria, Arnold-Forster went into the Royal Navy. He served on a destroyer on the Murmansk convoy and then (1942–4) on motor torpedo boats in the channel; ultimately a lieutenant in command of a flotilla, he won the DSO, DSC, and three mentions in dispatches—awards essentially for leadership, earned by a very young man who at the time looked about sixteen. His tasks included engaging the *Scharnhorst*, *Gneisenau*, and *Prinz Eugen* and their enemy boat escort; torpedoing a tanker; limping home from a battle with a broken-down engine and enemy boats for a time (as he radioed) 'still in company'; being nearly rammed by a German destroyer; laying mines under fire off the French coast; and working for naval intelligence. These experiences shaped his personality. The humorously understated wartime manner clung to him; to experience his kindness and sense of responsibility in peacetime—a later colleague wrote—made one 'understand why he was a great commander in war' (*The Guardian*, 28 Dec 1981). As a reservist (holder of a seagoing mate's ticket and an inland waters captain's ticket) he was, for a few months in the mid-1950s, to undertake 'special duties' in the Mediterranean. Did his wartime experiences somehow burn him out, not then but after a lapse of years? His own view was that he enjoyed the war, especially its absurd side, and learned the need for prudence and self-control.

After an awkward interlude spent lecturing to German prisoners of war, Arnold-Forster in 1946 joined the editorial staff of the *Manchester Guardian*, then about to add to its international prestige a growing circulation in London and the south such as to make it by the 1960s a national newspaper. He worked first in Manchester and then in Germany, where he wrote sensitively about the miseries of the immediate post-war period and about the Berlin blockade; the well-researched account of the blockade which he wrote much later (*The Siege of Berlin*, 1979) shows his respect for the Social Democratic and Christian Democratic leaders who did much to uphold morale. In 1949 he became labour correspondent, a key job he did for eight years, at a time when trade unions were an estate of the realm as well as a pillar of the Labour Party; in 1955–7 he doubled this with deputizing for the London editor, in charge of the small office where most of the specialist writers and the few London reporters worked, covering what on other papers required large staffs.

This was Arnold-Forster's finest period as a journalist. His coverage not only of industrial disputes but of the Bevanite split in the Labour Party showed enterprise, knowledge, and insight; his distrust of the Bevanites (anyhow less than that of the editor, A. P. Wadsworth) hardly showed in his sober reports. Colleagues held him in deep respect and affection as a man of utter integrity, personal and professional, considerate, soft-spoken, yet determined to get the best out of himself and others. His personality was bound up with a physique slight but wiry, high forehead, pointed chin and nose, subdued colouring; he looked almost as if he had been pressed between the pages of a book. He dressed anyhow; new clothes looked rumpled as soon as he put them on. On 12 January 1955 he married Valentine Harriet Isabella Digne Mitchison (*b.* 1930), also a journalist, daughter of the Labour politician G. R. Mitchison and the novelist Naomi Mitchison. Both were descended from the 'intellectual aristocracy' (Annan, 269) and kin to successive secretaries of state for war, H. O. Arnold-Forster and R. B. Haldane. They had five children; their house, large and much lived-in, was a place of hospitality and warmth.

Many colleagues thought Arnold-Forster a potentially ideal editor of the *Manchester Guardian*, but when the editorship fell vacant in 1956 it went to his exact contemporary Alastair Hetherington. Partly because of this, Arnold-Forster agreed to join the then new Independent Television News as deputy to the editor, Geoffrey Cox; more impelling reasons were his interest in the new medium and, with a growing family, a need for more money. Cox, however, wanted Ian Trethowan (not at once available) and sacked his deputy after a year. Arnold-Forster then worked for *The Observer* as chief reporter, later as news editor and political correspondent. He won some scoops (one, characteristically, because the Liberal leader Jo Grimond liked him and said more than he had intended) but disliked the weekly rhythm of production; he raged when he correctly forecast Lord Home as the next leader of the Conservative Party and the editor, David Astor, inserted R. A. Butler's name instead. In 1963 he and Astor agreed to part.

After an anxious, uncertain period Hetherington offered Arnold-Forster a way back to the *Guardian* as chief leader writer, later as diplomatic editor. Here, as on *The Observer*, Arnold-Forster did serious investigative work, particularly on defence and on the European Economic Community. He was 'a thorn in the flesh of the Foreign Office' (*The Times*, 28 Dec 1981); though not ultimately opposed to Britain's joining 'Europe', he concentrated, like many others, on the detailed absurdities he uncovered in the common agricultural policy and in Brussels directives, and easily gave the impression of niggling rather than of having made a fundamental choice. He took time off to write *The World at War* (1973), a lucid account of the Second World War to accompany the award-winning television series; it became a best-seller.

When Hetherington retired in 1975, Arnold-Forster, though aware that he might be thought too old for the editorship, was hurt not to be consulted, let alone considered. This sidelining, which grew under the next editor, Peter Preston, probably contributed to the persistent ill health which he suffered in his fifties, a series of minor strokes in particular. In 1979 he developed cancer of the upper colon; he died of it at his home, 50 Clarendon Road, Notting Hill, London, on Christmas day 1981, and was cremated at West London crematorium on 5 January 1982.

JOHN ROSSELLI

Sources personal knowledge (2004) • private information (2004) • G. Taylor, *Changing faces: a history of The Guardian, 1956–1988* (1993) • *The Guardian* (28 Dec 1981) • *The Times* (13 Jan 1955) • *The Times* (28 Dec 1981) • D. Ayerst, *Guardian: biography of a newspaper* (1971) • A. Hetherington, *'Guardian' years* (1981) • P. Scott, *The battle of the narrow seas, 1939–1945* (1945) • H. L. Brereton, *Gordonstoun* (1968) • H. Röhrs and H. Tunstall-Behrens, eds., *Kurt Hahn* (1970) • B. Sendall, *Origin and foundation, 1946–62* (1982), vol. 1 of *Independent television in Britain* (1982–90) • P. Delany, *The neo-pagans* (1987) • N. G. Annan, 'The intellectual aristocracy', *Studies in social history: a tribute to G. M. Trevelyan*, ed. J. H. Plumb (1955), 241–87 • b. cert. • d. cert. • Burke, *Peerage*
Archives JRL, *Guardian* archives, communications with editor and other members of *The Guardian* • priv. coll., journalist's notes
Likenesses W. Arnold-Forster, oils, c.1925–1945, priv. coll. • W. Arnold-Forster, pencil sketches, c.1925–1945, priv. coll. • photographs, c.1942, repro. in Scott, *Battle of the narrow seas* • P. Scott, pencil sketch, c.1943, repro. in Scott, *Battle of the narrow seas*; priv. coll. • J. Bown, photographs, c.1960, priv. coll. • G. Hermes, bronze bust, c.1970, priv. coll. • photograph, c.1975, repro. in *The Guardian*

Forster, Sir Martin Onslow (1872–1945), chemist, was born in Lambeth, London, on 8 November 1872, the fourth and youngest child of Martin Forster (d. 1908), a clerk in the Bank of England, and his wife, Ann Hope Limby (d. 1916). He was educated from 1882 at Dane Hill House (known as Boulden's), Margate, where he showed a leaning towards chemistry, and in October 1888 entered Finsbury Technical College intending to train for the chemical industry. He obtained his certificate after only two years, being bracketed first. Then followed a year's research under Raphael Meldola and a further year under Emil Fischer at Würzburg where in July 1892 he obtained his PhD.

On returning to England Forster was appointed research assistant to W. A. Tilden at Mason College, Birmingham. Two years later he decided upon a career as a university teacher and, recognizing the necessity for a British university degree, went as a research student to the laboratory of H. E. Armstrong at the Central Technical College, South Kensington, where he was soon awarded the first Salters' Company research fellowship. Although he spent only one year in the laboratory this period profoundly influenced the whole of his future research. Armstrong suggested to Forster that he should investigate the action of fuming nitric acid on camphor and Forster's main contributions to chemistry were to deal with the reactions of camphor and its derivatives.

In 1895 Tilden, who had moved from Birmingham to the Royal College of Science, offered Forster the post of demonstrator in chemistry, which he accepted. Forster obtained his DSc, and with it the Granville scholarship, from the University of London in 1899. In 1902 he became assistant professor of chemistry, a post which was virtually a professorship of organic chemistry. Forster took full advantage of the opportunities which it offered, and built up a research group which included a number of Swiss students; the most distinguished of them, H. E. Fierz, later held a chair in Zürich. While the main publications from the laboratory dealt with the chemistry of camphor, an important series of papers was devoted to triazo- compounds.

After Tilden's retirement from the Royal College of Science in 1909 organic chemistry lost its prominence. Disappointed at not having been appointed to a full professorship, Forster retired in 1913, intending to enter politics. At the outbreak of war in 1914 he returned to chemistry as a consultant to the dye-using industries, which had formerly bought their dyes abroad and were now cut off from their supplies. In 1915 he became chairman of the technical committee of British Dyes Ltd, and in 1916 director. Amid controversy, he and his colleagues resigned in 1918, and he was then appointed first director of the Salters' Institute of Industrial Chemistry, a post which left him sufficient leisure to return to experimental work in the Davy–Faraday Laboratory, in Albemarle Street.

Forster was essentially an experimentalist and had little interest in theory. The value of his original work was recognized by his election as FRS in 1905 and by the award in 1915 of the Longstaff medal of the Chemical Society. Nearly all Forster's papers were published by the Chemical Society, of which he was elected a fellow in 1892. He served on the council (1901–4), was honorary secretary (1904–10), vice-president (1910–13), and treasurer (1915–22). He was twice vice-president of the (Royal) Institute of Chemistry and a convocation member of the senate of London University (1914–22). He was prime warden of the Dyers' Company (1919–20), president of the chemistry section of the British Association meeting at Edinburgh, 1921, and president of the Indian Science Congress in 1925. Forster married on 1 January 1907 Madeleine, daughter of William Henry Nichols, manufacturing chemist, of New York; they divorced in 1916. In 1925 he married Elena Josefina (d. 1941), daughter of William Hall Haynes of Cadiz, and widow of Horace P. Parodi, a barrister, of Gibraltar. There were no children of either marriage.

Despite his influential position within British chemistry and his impressiveness as a public speaker, Forster was not a remarkable leader. He seemed aloof, with an air of superiority which made him unpopular, and, except in his own research, he tended to avoid difficulties. He was more successful in India where he went in 1922, on the recommendation of Sir W. J. Pope, as director of the Indian Institute of Science, Bangalore. There he established excellent relations with both staff and students. Although unable to continue his own experimental work, his social and administrative activities helped the advancement of science in India. He was due to retire in 1927 but remained until 1933, when he was knighted on his retirement. He did not return to England, but settled in Mysore, where he died on 24 May 1945.

J. L. SIMONSEN, rev. K. D. WATSON

Sources E. F. Armstrong and J. L. Simonsen, *Obits. FRS*, 5 (1945–8), 243–61 • *The Times* (25 May 1945), 4e • *The Times* (29 May 1945), 6e • *The Times* (14 June 1945), 7d • *Nature*, 156 (1945), 13–14 • *WWW*
Archives ICL, staff file • RS, MSS • Salter's Institute of Industrial Chemistry, London, MSS
Likenesses photograph, repro. in *Obits. FRS*
Wealth at death £52,331 16s. 8d.: probate, 18 Sept 1945, *CGPLA Eng. & Wales*

Forster, Mary (*c.*1619–1686), religious writer, is of unknown birth and parentage, but her date of birth can be inferred from her approximate age at death. She married Thomas Forster (*d.* 1660), a lawyer, and they had eight children.

A Quaker for more than two decades, Forster was one of the people who followed the movement from its inception as a sect for religious enthusiasts to the establishment of formal structures of organization. Mary Forster played a part in this process. In 1659 she headed the Quaker women's petition against tithes: a radical document to which approximately 7000 women put their names. After the Restoration, Quakerism became increasingly bureaucratic, so women's contributions changed. Forster was involved in meetings concerning discipline, printing, and poor relief in her capacities within the London six weeks meeting (of which she was a member from its inception in 1671), the morning meeting, and the women's meeting. During Forster's lifetime, therefore, Quakerism rose from its origins as a sect of radical prophets to become an organized, though possibly 'hermit like', society (Braithwaite, 309).

Forster's changing attitudes can be traced through her published works. In her 1659 preface to *These Several Papers*, Mary Forster grudgingly acknowledges that it is 'strange' for women to enter the public sphere, yet she also argues that God chose 'the foolish things of the World to confound the wise, weak things to confound the Mighty' (here echoing 1 Corinthians 1: 27; Forster, *Several Papers*, Preface). Clearly, her own sense of personal salvation informs her assertion that: '[God] is risen in us … to cast out all our enemies' (ibid.).

Mary Forster's political imperatives gradually changed, arguably like the movement more generally, from activism to greater quietism. By 1669 Forster's advice to Friends urges them to be content with their worldly achievements and, by implication, focus on inner revelation. She represents her own relationship to a beneficent God who, like the breadwinner she now lacks, provides her with bread and drink. She advises others of 'low estate … having many depending on thee' to trust in God 'and assuredly thee and thine shall be fed' (Forster, *Declaration*, 10).

In *Some Seasonable Considerations* (1684) Forster again uses her personal sadness as the index. Advising others on matters of conduct, she depicts a corrupt society—one increasingly guided by Satan. She writes of her 'sad experience' of grief and despair at the torments of the 'enemy', and urges Friends to remain morally upright in contrast to the 'perverse and crooked generation' (Forster, *Seasonable Considerations*, 4). That this encodes political quietism ('give no occasion to the Enemy to blaspheme or speak Evil of that holy Profession') and moral conservatism ('deny Ungodliness and worldly Lusts and live Soberly, Godly and Righteously in this present World') goes without saying (ibid., 4, 10).

In the 1680s Forster's writing is structured by her experience in the women's meetings. The collectively written statement of policy issued by the London women's meeting in 1685 is the creation of self-termed 'Aged Women in the Truth'. Mary Forster aligns herself with co-writers Mary Elson, Anne Travice, Ruth Crowch, Susannah Dew, and Mary Plumstead. Even at its most conservative, this text makes visible the web of patriarchal opposition to female agency. It is incumbent on the women to address 'unruly Spirits [who have] printed and written so many slanderous and reproachful Books against us'. Their activities are not autonomous, since they accept the right of men to direct them to 'proper' tasks (*Living Testimony*, 5, 7).

Forster also contributed short texts to larger works, such as Anne Whitehead's memorial *Piety Promoted* (1686) and Thomas Forster's *A Guide to the Blind* (1671). Her work is an index of the changing patterns of women's activism over a period of more than twenty-eight years.

Mary Forster died of phthisic (possibly tuberculosis, but certainly some sort of lung, throat, or chest infection) on 25 December 1686 at All Hallows, Lombard Street, London, aged about sixty-seven years. Most of her money and property she left to named family members, with her son Luke to act as executor should the will have to be proved in court. But companions in the London women's meetings Mary Elson and Rebecca Travers also benefited, while Forster left her Quaker kinswoman Hester *Fleetwood a memorial ring. Money was also bequeathed to the poor.

CATIE GILL

Sources W. C. Braithwaite, *The beginnings of Quakerism*, ed. H. J. Cadbury, 2nd edn (1955) • 'Dictionary of Quaker biography', RS Friends, Lond. [card index] • M. Forster, *These several papers* (1659) • M. Forster, *A declaration of the bountifull loving kindness of the Lord, manifested to his hand-maid Mary Harris* (1669) • M. Forster, *Some seasonable considerations* (1684) • M. Forster and others, *A living testimony from the power and spirit of our lord Jesus Christ* (1685) • M. Forster, 'Mary Forster: her testimony concerning Ann Whitehead', *Piety promoted by faithfulness manifested by several testimonies concerning that true servant of God, Ann Whitehead* (1686) • M. Forster, 'Testimony', in T. Forster, *A guide to the blind pointed to, or, A true testimony to the light within, wherein some men are reproved, others counselled … to the path of life*, ed. M. Forster, another edn (1671) • will, PRO, PROB 11/386, sig. 21
Archives RS Friends, Lond., Swarthmore MSS
Wealth at death *c.*£370—bequests; also personal goods: will, PRO, PROB 11/386, sig. 21

Forster, Mary (1786–1873). *See under* Forster, William (1784–1854).

Forster [*married name* Lofthouse], (**Emma Judith**) **Mary** (1853–1885), watercolour painter, was born at 20 Marlborough Buildings, Bath, on 6 December 1853, the daughter of Thomas Barton Watkin Forster (1822–1887) and his wife, Emma Stewart Galbraith (d. 1882). Until her marriage she lived at Holt Manor, near Bradford-on-Avon, Wiltshire, the seat of her father, an amateur landscape painter. Father and daughter painted in Wales and France as well as locally, and Mary Forster also exhibited scenes of Yorkshire, Norfolk, and Hampshire. She may have visited Switzerland with her father and probably knew Scotland, her mother being a Galbraith from Macrihanish, Argyll. From the age of twenty Mary Forster exhibited in the annual general exhibitions at the Dudley Gallery, London; she also showed at the Royal Academy in 1876, 1878, and 1880. In early 1884 she was elected an associate of the Royal Society of Painters in Water Colours, but her art, in J. L. Roget's words, was:

> too delicate and refined to attract the attention which it deserved during the two years only in which her landscapes were accorded a place in the gallery. But they afforded fair ground for anticipation that had she lived longer they would have become a much more important feature in the annual gatherings. (Roget, 2.426)

On 3 June 1884, at Bradford-on-Avon, Mary Forster married Samuel Hill Smith Lofthouse (b. 1841), a barrister, who had himself exhibited a winter landscape at the Society of British Artists in 1874. For her final exhibits she used her married name. She died in childbirth at their home, Elmbank, Lower Halliford, Walton-on-Thames, Surrey, on 2 May 1885, during the summer exhibition of the Royal Watercolour Society, at which her *Pembroke Castle* was attracting very favourable attention. A collection of twenty-six frames of her studies and sketches was hung in the society's winter show that year as a memorial.

HUON MALLALIEU

Sources *The Times* (5 May 1885) · J. L. Roget, *A history of the 'Old Water-Colour' Society*, 2 vols. (1891); repr. (1972) · b. cert. · m. cert. · d. cert. · Walford, *County families* (1883) · *DNB* · *CGPLA Eng. & Wales* (1885)
Wealth at death £138 5s. 11d.: administration, 26 June 1885, *CGPLA Eng. & Wales*

Forster, Nathaniel (1718–1757), classical and biblical scholar, born on 3 February 1718 at Stadscombe, in the parish of Plymstock, Devon, was the son of Robert Forster, Church of England clergyman, and Elizabeth Tindal, daughter of the Revd John Tindal, vicar of Cornwood, Devon, and Elizabeth Prideaux. His mother was the niece of Matthew Tindal, author of *Christianity as Old as the Creation*. After his father, who had been minister at Plymstock, became lecturer of St Andrew's Church, Plymouth, he was educated at home there, and then at Plymouth grammar school under the Revd John Bedford. After 'gaining the first place' before he was thirteen, he was sent to Eton College in 1732 and was simultaneously enrolled as an exhibitioner at Pembroke College, Oxford, from where he matriculated on 16 March 1732, thereby entitling him to £40 a year (Nichols, 289). After about sixteen months at Eton he went to Pembroke. He was admitted as a scholar of Corpus Christi College, Oxford, on 13 June 1733, from where he graduated BA (1735), MA (1739), BD (1746), and DD (1750). He was elected a fellow of the college, ordained deacon in 1739, and ordained priest in 1742.

In 1743 Forster published his first work, *Reflections on the natural foundation of the high antiquity of government, arts, and sciences in Egypt*, and in 1745 his popular edition of five of Plato's dialogues appeared. In 1746 he printed a sermon on Mark 7: 13, and *Appendix Liviana*. On 6 July 1749 he was offered the rectory of Hethe, Oxfordshire, by the Lord Chancellor Hardwicke, on the recommendation of Thomas Secker, then bishop of Oxford. While at Hethe he published anonymously *A dissertation upon the account ... of Jesus Christ by Josephus: being an attempt to show that this ... may be esteemed genuine* (1749).

In 1750 Forster published the first Hebrew Bible in Britain, in two volumes. The same year he became Bishop Joseph Butler's domestic chaplain on his translation from Bristol to Durham. Butler, who appointed him executor of his estate and bequeathed £200 to him, 'absolutely died in his arms at Bath' on 16 June 1750 (Nichols, *Lit. anecdotes*, 292). After his friend's death Forster returned to Corpus Christi until, in July 1752, Thomas Herring, archbishop of Canterbury, made Forster one of his chaplains, and in autumn 1754 appointed him vicar of Rochdale, Lancashire. Although 'his character ... was that of much discernment, mildness, and benevolence' and his skill as both classicist and preacher was such that Benjamin Kennicott used both his edition of Plato and his sermon, Forster was not popular in the parish (ibid., 301). Thus, in spite of the good stipend, he left the living soon after. The lord chancellor made him a prebendary of Bristol on 1 February 1755. On 15 May 1755 he was elected a fellow of the Royal Society, and that year printed *Remarks* on Henry Stebbing's *Dissertation on the power of states to deny civil protection to the marriages of minors*. On 12 May 1756 he was sworn a chaplain to George II.

In the summer of 1757, through the interest of Lord Royston, Forster succeeded Dr Terrick as preacher at the Rolls Chapel. On 3 August that year, he married Susan Balls in Norwich. She was the widow of John Balls of Norwich, who had left her a generous estate; they took a house in Craig's Court, Charing Cross, London. He died there on 20 October 1757, supposedly as a result of 'excessive study', and was buried in St Martin's Church, Westminster; he and his wife had no children (Nichols, *Lit. anecdotes*, 300). His widow, who later married Philip Bedingfield of Ditchingham, Norfolk, erected a monument to him in Bristol Cathedral, the epitaph of which was written by his friend Bishop Hayter of Norwich.

THOMPSON COOPER, rev. ADAM JACOB LEVIN

Sources Nichols, *Lit. anecdotes*, 9.289–303 · Foster, *Alum. Oxon.* · Watt, *Bibl. Brit.* · *GM*, 1st ser., 86/1 (1816), 537
Archives BL, corresp., Add. MSS 9815–9816, 11275

Forster, Nathaniel (1726–1790), writer on political economy, was baptized on 20 July 1726 at Crewkerne, Somerset, the son of the Revd Nathaniel Forster and his wife, Catherine Petvin. He was a cousin of the Oxford Plato scholar Nathaniel Forster. He matriculated at Balliol College, Oxford, in 1742 and migrated to Magdalen College, graduating BA in 1745 and MA in 1748. Returning to Balliol as a fellow, he proceeded BD and DD in 1778. The living of All Saints, Colchester, in Essex was the gift of Balliol College and he made his residence there in 1762, exercising his duties diligently and also becoming chaplain to the countess dowager of Northington. At Colchester in 1777 he engaged the services of Dr Samuel Parr as master of the Colchester School and curate of Trinity Church and St Leonard's.

At Balliol in 1762 Forster met the young Jeremy Bentham and the two remained friends, meeting at Colchester and at the home of their mutual acquaintance John Lind in the 1770s. Forster was not a strict utilitarian, though the principle of utility appears in several of his works. The published work for which Forster is best-known was his *Enquiry into the Causes of the Present High Price of Provisions* (1767). Dozens of works with similar titles appeared as responses to the rise of food prices and resulting popular commotion after 1756 and, especially, the food riots of 1766, but Forster's work stood out as an original contribution then and since, appealing to such divergent nineteenth-century commentators as J. R. McCulloch, who regarded it as 'perhaps the ablest of the many treatises published about this period' (McCulloch, 193) and Karl Marx: 'this good book' (Marx, 886).

Although published as a *pièce d'occasion*, it was also marked by a deeper concern and interest in the problems of commercial society, and by a familiarity with Enlightenment thought and the fledgeling discipline of political economy, notably the writings of Rousseau, Montesquieu, and Hume. Declaring himself an 'advocate for the poor' (N. Forster, *Enquiry into the Causes*, 1767, 62), Forster criticized the growth of inequality and its display in the form of excessive luxury consumption, praised the policy of a bounty on exported corn (other than in times of scarcity), and advocated a system of political economy which had the well-being of the population at large as its principal object. He opposed the then still widely held doctrine that it was necessary to keep the labouring poor in a state of near penury in order to excite industry from them and he favoured higher wages. Convinced of the validity of free trade arguments, he made an exception, however, in the question of subsistence goods. He also supported a theory of the natural harmony of interests quite similar to that which underlay the work of Adam Smith. Later work by Forster suggests a more protectionist bias in his orientation. A pamphlet of 1782 attacked proposals for a loosening of the regulations governing the exportation of raw wool to France and elsewhere.

As well as publishing four sermons, Forster also wrote on the political controversies around the Wilkes and Liberty affair of the period 1763–8, vindicating the decision of the House of Commons not to allow the election of John Wilkes following the Middlesex election of 1768. In 1786 he played a leading role in establishing Sunday schools in the county of Essex and delivered 'A discourse on the utility of Sunday schools' in which he espoused the benefits of free education for the children of the poor.

Forster died at Colchester on 12 April 1790, aged sixty-three, leaving a son, Edward *Forster (1769–1828), and a daughter, Catherine (d. 1796). His widow, Rhoda, died in 1805 at Witney, Oxfordshire.   R. D. SHELDON

Sources *VCH Essex*, vol. 9 · J. B. Butt, 'Notes on Colchester Society', Essex RO, Colchester, C905 · J. R. McCulloch, *The literature of political economy: a classified catalogue* (1845) · K. Marx, *Capital*, trans. B. Fowkes, 3 vols. (1976), vol. 1 [with introduction by E. Mandel] · *The works of Jeremy Bentham*, ed. J. Bowring, [new edn], 11 vols. (1843–59), vol. 10 · correspondence with Peter Forster, BL, Add. MS 11277 · correspondence with Sir Robert Smyth, Essex RO, Chelmsford, D/DFg Z1 · will, 1790, PRO, PROB 11/1195 · *DNB* · *IGI*
Archives BL, letters to his cousin, Peter Forster, Add. MS 11277 · Essex RO, corresp. with Sir Robert Smyth, D/DFg Z1
Wealth at death collection of books worth £2500, left to son: will, 1790, PRO, PROB 11/1195

Forster, (Johann) Reinhold (1729–1798). *See under* Forster, (Johann) Georg Adam (1754–1794).

Forster, Richard (*c*.1546–1616), physician, son of Laurence Forster, of Coventry, was educated at All Souls College, Oxford, graduating BA 1563, MA 1567. He became a fellow of All Souls in 1562. He graduated BM and DM at Oxford, both in 1573. He became a fellow of the College of Physicians, London, about 1575, but his admission is not mentioned in the annals. In 1583 he was elected one of the censors, he was treasurer in 1600, and was the first Lumleian lecturer in 1602. He was president of the college from 1601 to 1604, and was again elected in 1615, and held office until his death. He had considerable medical practice, and was also esteemed as a mathematician. When recording his death William Camden described him as 'Medicinae doctor et nobilis Mathematicus'. William Clowes, the surgeon, praised him, and in 1591 spoke of him as 'a worthie reader of the surgerie lector in the Phisition's college' (Clowes, 46).

It is thought that Forster lectured in London on Wednesdays and Thursdays between 10 and 11 a.m., covering the whole of anatomy over a period of six years. Forster had been introduced to Robert, earl of Leicester, by Sir Henry Sidney, and dedicated to the earl his only published work, *Ephemerides meteorographicae Richardi Fosteri artium ac medicinae doctoris ad annum 1575 et positum finitoris Londini emporii totius Angliae nobilissimi diligenter examinatae* (1575). Besides the prose dedication, in which astronomy is said to be the handmaid of medicine, twenty lines of Latin verse on Leicester's cognizance, the bear, precede the tables of which the book is made up. Forster died in London on 27 March 1616.   NORMAN MOORE, *rev.* RACHEL E. DAVIES

Sources Munk, *Roll* · W. Clowes, *A prooved practise for all young chirurgians* (1591) · Wood, *Ath. Oxon.* · H. Spencer Robinson, 'The Lumleian lectures before Harvey', *Medical Life*, 35 (1928), 583–9 · G. Lewis, 'The faculty of medicine', *Hist. U. Oxf.* 3: *Colleg. univ.*, 213–56 · Foster, *Alum. Oxon.*

Forster, Sir Richard [alias Mr Johnson], **first baronet** (1585?–1661), courtier and financier, was probably born in Earswick, Yorkshire, the only son of William Forster of Earswick (d. in or before 1618) and his second wife, Isabel Langley (d. 1585). Heralds' visitations of the sixteenth and seventeenth centuries record many branches of gentry families called Forster or Foster deriving their origin from Adderston, Northumberland. The Forsters of Earswick were strongly Roman Catholic. One of Richard's grandfathers was Richard Langley of Millington, co. Durham, hanged at York in 1586 for harbouring priests; the other, John Forster, third son of Thomas Forster of Adderston, was imprisoned for recusancy before 1580 at York Castle and later died there with his wife and daughter-in-law Isabel. Richard's father was also imprisoned at York in 1606. However, Richard himself conformed for a time to the established church. In 1607 he married Joan, daughter of Charles and Alice Middleton of Leighton, Lancashire, and soon afterwards returned to Roman Catholicism. Forster and his wife had five children: Henry, Anna Christina, Richard, Charles, and another son unnamed in the records.

About 1622–3 Forster purchased the manor, estate, and forest of Stokesley in the North Riding of Yorkshire from William, Lord Eure, a recusant whose family had long connections with the Forsters of Adderston. The neighbourhood contained many Roman Catholic families including the Calverts at Danby Wiske. Forster was later recorded as holding other land in co. Durham, including Pulford Manor, and a colliery at Benwell, Northumberland. He, his wife, or their servants were presented as recusants three times in the years 1623–4 at the local quarter sessions and the lack of subsequent presentments was probably due to his moving to London. He compounded for a fine of £40 in 1630 but, after a petition, his composition was reduced. In 1635 it was further reduced from £20 to £5 and in 1636–7 the manor of Stokesley, having been seized by the crown for arrears of fines, was leased back to Forster and his heir, Henry, at an annual rent of £5.

Forster was probably introduced into the royal service by George Calvert, who, though he came from a Yorkshire Roman Catholic family, had conformed in religion and become a secretary of state. However, the main influences on Forster's early career were Richard, Lord Portland (lord high treasurer, 1628–35), and Sir Francis Cottington (chancellor of the exchequer, 1629–42), who both had strong Roman Catholic family connections. From 1625 to 1640 Forster was a courier between the courts of London and Paris and was noted in 1640 as 'a very busy fellow' (Collins, 2.666). About 1635 he entered the queen's household as sewer; he was then cupbearer and became treasurer-general in 1642. He assisted Sir Kenelm Digby, Walter Montagu, and Father George Conn in the queen's scheme to raise funds from the Roman Catholic gentry for the Scottish campaign of 1639, and during the civil war, as Mr Johnson, he was the queen's emissary in raising arms and money in France and the Netherlands. During her exile he was appointed her treasurer-general in France on 3 November 1644. On 18 September 1649 Forster was created a baronet by Charles II at St Germain. About this time he became keeper of the king's privy purse and managed the pension secured from the French government. He had to keep the impoverished exiled court going by appeasing landlords, tradesmen, and servants with promises, eked out by payments as far as possible in arrears. During 1655, however, he apparently retired.

Curiously, despite the extreme poverty of the court in exile, Forster amassed large sums of money. In 1652 some English Benedictine nuns were sent from their convent at Ghent to start a new community, first at Boulogne and then at Pontoise. Among them was Forster's daughter, Anna Christina, who became abbess in 1656. In 1653 and 1655 Forster gave substantially towards the new convent: indeed he and Walter Montagu, a fellow contributor and now commendatory abbot of St Martin's, Pontoise, were revered as founders. Forster's munificence continued and, in all, as Abbess Anne Neville later recorded, he gave 41,000 livres (worth in November 1653 about £24,000) besides goods and assignments of debts amounting to £10,000. Forster died on 27 January 1661, possibly in Paris, and was buried at St Martin's, Pontoise.

MICHAEL FOSTER

Sources M. Foster, 'Sir Richard Forster (?1585–1661)', *Recusant History*, 14 (1977–8), 163–74 · [T. Birch and R. F. Williams], eds., *The court and times of Charles the First*, 2 (1848), 482–7 · CSP dom., 1625–6; 1635–7 · *Calendar of the Clarendon state papers preserved in the Bodleian Library*, ed. O. Ogle and others, 5 vols. (1869–1970), vol. 1, p. 81; vol. 2, pp. 136, 138, 161, 162, 165, 201, 210, 220, 276, 382; vol. 3, pp. 10, 18, 24 · 'Registers of the English Benedictine nuns at Pontoise, now at Teignmouth, 1680', *Miscellanea, X*, Catholic RS, 17 (1915), 248–326, 252, 254 · J. Foster, ed., *The visitation of Yorkshire made in the years 1584/5 … to which is added the subsequent visitation made in 1612* (privately printed, London, 1875), 618 · GEC, *Baronetage*, 3.11 · *Letters of Queen Henrietta Maria*, ed. M. A. E. Green (1857), 155 · H. Sydney and others, *Letters and memorials of state*, ed. A. Collins, 2 (1746), 666 · M. A. E. Green, ed., *Calendar of the proceedings of the committee for compounding … 1643–1660*, 5 vols., PRO (1889–92), 3193, 3215 · H. Aveling, *Northern Catholics: the Catholic recusants of the North Riding of Yorkshire, 1558–1790* (1966), 238

Wealth at death gave most of money (excl. English estates) to women's Benedictine abbey, Pontoise

Forster, Robert (1791–1873). *See under* Forster, William (1784–1854).

Forster, Sir (Samuel Alexander) Sadler (1900–1973), regional planner, was born on 9 September 1900 at 6 Southfield Road, Middlesbrough, Yorkshire, the only son of Frederic John Forster, chartered accountant, of Middlesbrough, and his wife, Annie Elizabeth, *née* Hoskins. Educated at Middlesbrough high school, he qualified as a chartered accountant and became a partner in his father's firm in 1926, practising until 1935. On 12 September 1928 he married Edna Violet (1901/2–1930), only daughter of Michael Henry Potts, ironworks foreman, of Middlesbrough; they had one daughter. Following his first wife's death in 1930, Forster married Kathleen Bulmer (*b.* 1902/3), schoolteacher, and daughter of Harold Bulmer, mines deputy, of Great Ayton, Yorkshire, on 8 September 1932. There was one son of this second marriage.

Forster took on the job of secretary of the Teesside chamber of commerce in 1929, and was appointed secretary of the Tees District Development Board in 1933. As the recession worsened he became concerned about the effects of rising unemployment in the north-east, where the traditional heavy engineering and shipbuilding industries of the Tyne and Wear were particularly badly affected. In 1930 he was one of the first to put forward the idea of government financed industrial trading estates in the depressed areas in order to attract new industry, an idea that was also being promoted by the new development boards. He became obsessed with the idea, making repeated journeys to London over the next five years to try to persuade senior civil servants to act, but there was no mention of trading estates in the 1934 Special Areas Act, which was designed to encourage the location of new factories in areas of high unemployment. *The Times* printed a letter from Forster on 26 July 1935, in which he set out his arguments, pointing to the success of trading estates in the new towns of Letchworth and Welwyn Garden City, where in order to attract light industry ready built factories were leased to small manufacturers. Pressure also came from the North-East Development Board, set up in 1935, and in October 1935 the commissioner for the special areas was given the authority to build trading estates. In 1936 North-East Trading Estates Ltd, a non-profit making company, was set up to provide factory sites for industry, and work began in 1936 on the first government trading estate, the Team Valley trading estate, near Gateshead, which went on to attract a large number of light industries to the area, and was employing 12,000 workers by 1939.

Forster left Middlesbrough in 1936 to take up the position of industrial development manager for the Welwyn Garden City Company Ltd in Hertfordshire. Welwyn Garden City (1919) was the second garden city to be founded by Sir Ebenezer Howard, whose vision, set out in *Garden Cities of Tomorrow* (1902), included the building of factories to make the garden cities self-sufficient. Forster was responsible for building more factories on the existing trading estate. After five years he returned to the northeast as regional controller of the Board of Trade in Newcastle upon Tyne, in charge of factory and storage premises. The concept of the diversification of industry in the special areas, which he had done so much to promote, was incorporated into the 1945 Distribution of Industry Act, which replaced the special areas legislation of the 1930s, and extended the boundaries of the special areas, which were renamed development areas. The Board of Trade took over their administration from the commissioners for the special areas. From 1945 to 1948 Forster was head of the new directorate for industrial estates in the development areas at the Board of Trade. In 1948 he was appointed chairman of North-East Trading Estates, based at Team Valley. He found this post frustrating, as he had little opportunity to influence regional industrial policy because the new Labour government attached great importance to the creation of employment in the former depressed areas and took over full control. He clashed frequently with the Board of Trade, but remained at North-East Trading Estates until 1960, when it was absorbed into the English Industrial Estates Corporation. He was chairman of the latter from 1960 until his retirement in 1970.

Forster was also one of the first to call for the creation of new towns in the north. Peterlee, Britain's seventh new town, was founded in 1948 on land owned by the National Coal Board in the mining area of south-east Durham, to house some of the population from congested areas of the Tyne and Wear. Forster served on the Peterlee New Town Development Corporation from 1950 to 1959, trying unsuccessfully in 1952 to get Harold Macmillan, minister of housing and local government, to authorize the building of advance factories, purpose-built factories which would be leased to manufacturers. It was not until the 1960s that a high proportion of new industries came to Peterlee, which in the 1950s had had to depend on coalmining for employment, and was prevented from diversifying into light industry.

Highly respected in the north-east, Forster served many regional organizations. He was a member of the executive council of the North-East Industrial and Development Association from 1952 to 1961, and its vice-president from 1957 to 1961, and a member of the Northern Economic Planning Council from 1965 to 1969. In 1965 he published, for the European Coal and Steel Community, *Location of Industry Policy in Britain*. He was made CBE in 1956, received an honorary DCL degree from Durham University (where he was a member of the appointments board) in 1958, and was knighted in 1966. An enthusiastic gardener, he enjoyed only a few years of retirement before his death on 24 June 1973, from colonic cancer, at his home, 29 Osbaldeston Gardens, Newcastle upon Tyne. He was survived by his second wife and two children.

ANNE PIMLOTT BAKER

Sources H. Loebb, *Government factories and the origins of British regional policy, 1934–1948* (1988) · M. Fogarty, *Plan your own industries: a study of local and regional development organisations* (1947) · A. A. L. Caesar, *A survey of industrial facilities of the north-east region* (1942), 105–9 · J. M. Cousins, 'Aspects of contradiction in regional policy: the case of north–east England', *Regional Studies*, 8/2 (1974), 133–44 · G. Philipson, *Aycliffe and Peterlee new towns, 1946–1988* (1988) · R. Prestwich and P. Taylor, *Introduction to regional and urban policy in the United Kingdom* (1990) · *The Times* (25 June 1973) · *The Times* (27 June 1973) · *The Journal* [Newcastle upon Tyne] (25 June 1973) · *WWW, 1971–80* · b. cert. · m. certs. · d. cert.
Likenesses photograph, repro. in *Journal*
Wealth at death £44,790: probate, 25 Sept 1973, *CGPLA Eng. & Wales*

Forster, Simon Andrew (1801–1870). *See under* Forster, William (1739–1808).

Forster, Thomas (*b.* 1676/7), portrait draughtsman, is of unknown origins. Vertue reported seeing 'the head of Mr Foster done by himself on Vellum. Aeta. 31. 1708' (Vertue, *Note books*, 4.114), which implies a birth date of 1676 or 1677, but this is the only surviving biographical information on him. C. F. Bell still provides the best account of Forster's work and patronage in 'English seventeenth-century portrait drawings in Oxford collections' (*Walpole Society*, 14, 1925–6, 73–80). Bell speculated on the possibility that Forster had some connection with Northumberland because his surname was particularly common there but no definitive link has been made. Bell also pointed out that 'The statement made in the account of the artist in Thieme and Becker's *Allgemeines Kunstler-lexikon* … that Forster's miniatures in black lead were generally copied from oil pictures by Kneller and other painters is completely mistaken' (Bell, 73). An example of a rare copy is a portrait of William III (1650–1702) dated 1074 (presumably 1704; Goulding, catalogue 144, plate 21).

Forster's portraits are mostly in the *ad vivum* tradition and are rarely of people who were then famous or are historically significant today; instead they seem to have had 'a considerable vogue amongst people in a private station of life' (Bell, 73). According to the list of Forster's work drawn up by Bell one portrait was dated as early as 1690 (*Dorothy Yates*, belonging in 1889 to Mrs Keightley, shown in the Burlington Fine Arts Club exhibition, XXIX, 54). If Vertue's dates for Forster are correct Forster would have drawn this portrait as a precocious thirteen-year-old. The date, however, may have been read incorrectly and it seems significant that the next known dated work is from five years later, in 1695, and that the majority of his works date from between 1696 and 1712. None of his drawings, which include a number of portraits of members of the Bulteel family, bears a date after 1712, although a number are undated.

These works are known as plumbagos (black lead) because graphite was long believed to be lead-based. The true chemical nature of graphite was discovered in the late eighteenth century, when it was named graphite to honour its role in the graphic arts. The art of small portraiture in graphite on vellum was continental in origin and developed in the early seventeenth century out of the book trade. In England the art became fashionable with the return of artists from exile on the continent at the time of the Restoration. These artists, such as David Loggan and Robert White, were primarily engravers who engraved versions of their own plumbagos. Forster in contrast was not an engraver, and few of his plumbagos have been reproduced. The taste for this refined art was also given a fillip in England in the third quarter of the seventeenth century with the opening up of rich deposits of exceptionally pure graphite in Borrowdale in Cumberland; hitherto graphite had been imported.

Forster's works are particularly delicate, virtuoso pieces. Bell identified a strong link in terms of patronage:

> it is noticeable that a considerable number of his drawings are portraits of persons who were associated either officially or personally with the second Duke of Ormonde. Perhaps this is especially true of the group of miniatures preserved in the Holburne Museum at Bath. (Bell, 74)

Other examples of Forster's work are in the Victoria and Albert Museum, London; the British Museum; and the City of Liverpool Museums. Bell lists Forster's work known in 1926, and Goulding lists examples of works known in 1916 (Goulding, 28). The British Museum holds an engraving after a putative self-portrait but this has long been discounted, since it is of a man of about thirty or forty and is inscribed 'T. [or I] Foster 1689 from a pencil Drawing by himself in the possession of G. Walker Esq., published by A Bengo June 12, 1803' and signed 'G W 1797'. Thomas Forster would have been twelve or thirteen in 1689.

KATHERINE COOMBS

Sources C. F. Bell and R. L. Poole, 'English seventeenth-century portrait drawings in Oxford collections, pt 2', *Walpole Society*, 14 (1925–6), 49–80, esp. 73–80 · Vertue, *Note books* · J. Murdoch, *Seventeenth-century English miniatures in the collection of the Victoria and Albert Museum* (1997), 345 · R. W. Goulding, 'The Welbeck Abbey miniatures', *Walpole Society*, 4 (1914–15) [whole issue] · private information (2004)

Likenesses G. Walker, etching, pubd 1803 (after T. Forster; after drawing), BM

Forster, Thomas (*bap.* 1683, *d.* 1738), politician and Jacobite army officer, was the eldest son of Thomas Forster (1659–1725) of Adderstone, Bamburgh, Northumberland, and his wife, Frances, the daughter of Sir William Forster of Bamburgh, and was baptized at Bamburgh on 29 March 1683. He graduated from St John's College, Cambridge, in 1700. Forsters had sat for Northumberland in the House of Commons, representing the high-church tory interest, since the revolution of 1688, and he was returned in succession to his father in 1708 and re-elected in 1710 and 1713; he was on the Jacobite wing of the party and was drawn into the planning of the rising in 1715 because of the significance of his constituency in Jacobite strategy. The plan, formulated by the earl of Mar and Colonel Henry Oxburgh, envisaged the assembly of an Anglo-Franco-Scottish army in Northumberland on or about 10 October which would seize Tyneside unopposed, and thus gain control of London's fuel supplies, then sweep south to take the capital and restore Prince James Edward Stuart to the throne usurped from his father. The role of the Northumbrian Jacobites was to facilitate the landing of the French seaborne insurgents, to receive the Scottish troops, and to sustain the force with horses, wagons, and victuals.

The project was entrusted to two tory Jacobite MPs, Forster and Sir William Blackett (member for Newcastle), and the Catholic lords Derwentwater and Widdrington, all four of whom were industrial capitalists on Tyneside and expected to mobilize their tenants and employees. The plan became known to the government and the arrest of the leaders was ordered; they went into hiding but, finding it increasingly difficult to evade capture, they were forced into arms prematurely on 6 October. At a council of war Forster, despite his lack of military expertise, was appointed general officer in command until the arrival of the main body of French and Scottish troops; this was decided primarily to avoid placing a Catholic in command, but it was also thought that his connections with Lord Crewe, bishop of Durham, whose wife was Forster's aunt, could be useful in recruiting the Anglican gentry and securing high-church and nonjuring clerical backing. But support did not materialize as the leaders had hoped: Blackett was scared off and did not rise, and the miners and keelmen did not follow their employers. Only 200 Northumbrian gentlemen and their retainers assembled at Lesbury, near Warkworth, joined by about a hundred Scottish borderers under Lord Kenmure. Meanwhile the leadership at St Germain changed the landing place of the French to south-west England, but the Northumbrians and Scots were not informed and were left exposed and in confusion. Without French reinforcements or the Scottish cavalry, which had been prevented from reaching England, the Jacobites lacked any substantial fighting capability, offensive or defensive, and they were fortunate to avoid an engagement with government forces which managed to garrison Newcastle before an assault could be attempted. The Jacobites decided to march north to combine with the main body of Scots, under Brigadier William Mackintosh, laird of Borlum, to raise their Lancastrian allies, and to march on London from the north-west instead; the Scots complied but with misgivings. The Jacobites marched south, encouraged by the retreat before them of the militia at Penrith, Lancaster, and Preston, but dismayed at how few Lancastrians turned out in support. They entered Preston on Wednesday 9 November, some 3000 to 4000 strong, and rested, anticipating an easy capture of Manchester in due course. But General Carpenter was in hot pursuit from the north with three regiments of dragoons, and General Wills was moving up from the south with six regiments of dragoons and horse and one of foot. On the afternoon of Saturday 12 November Wills brought the Jacobites to action; street fighting continued until nightfall and government forces were repulsed, but large numbers of Jacobites deserted during the following night. Carpenter came up on Sunday morning and the town was encircled by midday; Mackintosh and Derwentwater proposed a break-out but, unknown to them, on the advice of Widdrington, Oxburgh, and others, Forster had sought terms because of the overwhelming odds against them. On Monday 14 November the Jacobites laid down their arms, bringing the rising in England to an end.

Forster was gaoled in Newgate and indicted for high treason, but, having obtained the appropriate keys, he made his escape on 10 April 1716, four days before his trial, and, to considerable popular acclaim, got clean away to the continent with his servant in a small boat from Rochford, Essex. The beheading in February of lords Derwentwater and Kenmure had swung public opinion against further executions and the government spared the lives of many convicted Jacobites thereafter, but a reward of £1000 was offered for Forster's recapture; he was excepted from the Act of Grace (3 Geo. I c.19), and his Northumbrian estates worth £530 a year were forfeited. His royal master did not blame Forster for capitulating at Preston but appointed him steward of his household at Urbino, and afterwards at the Palazzo Muti, Rome. Forster kept out of Jacobite politics, hoping to be pardoned and eventually allowed to return home. His correspondence at this time shows that he liked opera and hunting; he was asthmatic and visited spas and the French coast; he had always spoken with the Northumbrian burr, and did not learn to speak French. He died in Boulogne in October 1738, aged fifty-four, and was buried at Dover on 27 October. His remains were removed on 23 November and reinterred in the chapel of Bamburgh Castle on 7 December.

LEO GOOCH

Sources L. Gooch, *The desperate faction? The Jacobites of north-east England, 1688–1745* (1995) · S. Hibbert Ware, *Lancashire memorials of the rebellion*, 2 pts in 1, Chetham Society, 5 (1845) · *A history of Northumberland*, Northumberland County History Committee, 15 vols. (1893–1940), vol. 1 · HoP, *Commons, 1715–54* · R. Patten, *The history of the late rebellion*, 2nd edn (1717) · parish registers, Bamburgh, Northumberland · parish registers, Dover, Kent · *GM*, 1st ser., 8 (1738), 604

Archives NRA, priv. coll., corresp.
Likenesses G. Kneller, oils, repro. in Gooch, *Desperate faction*, 38 · J. T. Wedgewood, line engraving (after R. Carriera), BM, NPG

Forster, Thomas Furly (1761–1825), botanist, was born in Bond Street, Walbrook, London, on 5 September 1761, the eldest son of Edward *Forster the elder (1730–1812) and his wife, Susanna Furney (d. 1823). His father moved to Walthamstow in 1764, and, being a great admirer of Rousseau, brought up his son according to his principles. From his uncle Benjamin Forster he early acquired a taste for antiquities, coins, prints, and plants. He was introduced to the Linnaean system of classification, to which he always remained a firm adherent, by the Revd John Dixon. He was encouraged further in his studies by a number of others, including Michael Tyson (1740–1780), and between 1775 and 1782 he made many drawings of plants. A list of additions to Warner's *Plantæ Woodfordienses* was printed in 1784; it was attributed by Dryander to Thomas Forster.

In 1788 Forster married Susanna, daughter of Thomas Williams of West Ham. He was one of the first fellows of the Linnean Society, founded in that year. In conjunction with his brothers, Benjamin Meggot *Forster and Edward *Forster, the younger, he drew up the county lists of plants in Gough's *Camden* (1789), and communicated various plants to the *Botanical Magazine* and to *English Botany*. From 1796 to 1823 he lived mainly at Clapton and devoted himself to greenhouse exotics, giving much assistance to Messrs Loddiges in establishing their nursery at Hackney. A list of the rare plants of Tunbridge Wells, probably published in 1800, is attributed to him by Dryander, and in 1816 he published a *Flora Tonbrigensis*, having visited Tunbridge Wells every year since 1788. The work was reissued by his son in 1842. His fondness for animals made him refuse to prepare an account of the fauna. Following the death of his mother in 1823 he returned to Walthamstow where he died on 28 October 1825, leaving two sons, including Thomas Ignatius Maria *Forster, writer on science and phrenology, and three daughters.

Forster contributed two papers to the Linnean Society's *Transactions*, and left an extensive hortus siccus of algæ, as well as of flowering plants, together with collections of fossils, music, and more than a thousand drawings of churches and other ancient buildings. His natural history journals, which included weather prognostics, were published by his son in 1827 as *The Pocket Encyclopædia of Natural Phenomena*. He was a member of many scientific and philanthropic societies. Among his friends were the botanists J. E. Smith, Joseph Banks, Dryander, Dickson, Robert Brown, and Afzelius of Uppsala.

G. S. BOULGER, *rev.* ALEXANDER GOLDBLOOM

Sources Desmond, *Botanists*, rev. edn · S. T. Jermyn and J. K. Adams, *Flora of Essex* (1974), pl. 16 · *GM*, 2nd ser., 32 (1849), 431 · Nichols, *Illustrations*, 8.553 · F. [T. Forster], *Epistolarium, or, Fasciculi of curious letters … as preserved among the MSS of the Forster family*, 1 (privately printed, Bruges, 1845), 33–41
Archives Linn. Soc. · Merseyside Museum, Liverpool · Trinity Cam. | Linn. Soc., letters to Sir James Smith
Likenesses Miss Turner, lithograph, BM, NPG

Forster, Thomas Ignatius Maria (1789–1860), writer on science and phrenologist, was born on 9 November 1789 in London. He was the eldest son of the botanist and antiquarian Thomas Furly *Forster (1761–1825), and his wife, Susanna Williams. He was a nephew of Edward and Benjamin Meggot Forster, and great-nephew of Benjamin Forster the antiquary. His life was eccentric from the start. According to his autobiography he was born in the confines of the Bank of England, Threadneedle Street, London, and his distinguished family line provided many early introductions to famous men and unusual lines of thought. He was brought up by Rousseau's principles mainly at the family seat at Hale End, Walthamstow, Essex, acquiring great facility with ancient and modern languages and a pronounced love of animals. He had no formal schooling.

As a boy Forster accompanied relatives to meetings of the Linnean Society and Sir Joseph Banks's conversaziones. Benjamin Meggot Forster explained to him the rudiments of astronomy and mechanics, which became the basis of his first scientific writings, a *Journal of the Weather* and a *Liber rerum naturalium* in 1805. In 1808 he published an article in the *Philosophical Magazine* under the pseudonym Philochelidon, on the migration of swallows, later expanded into a book with a catalogue of British birds. He became a fellow of the Linnean Society in 1811.

A lengthy illness in 1810, coupled with the comet of 1811, turned Forster's attention to atmospheric phenomena, especially in relation to health. From that time on he wrote a succession of learned papers describing meteorological phenomena and the atmospheric conditions that induce disease, particularly cholera, and which influence insanity. He distinguished epidemics, which he thought were caused by cometary disturbances of the atmosphere, from contagions, propagated by infectious contact. At the same time he studied Pythagorean and Hindu philosophy, becoming an ardent vegetarian and a believer in the immortality of animal souls. In a paper of 1812 on the evils of alcohol he proposed that mankind was not naturally carnivorous. Most of these articles were published in the *Philosophical Magazine* or *The Pamphleteer*, and were expanded or collected into books afterwards.

In 1812 Forster's father allowed him to enter Corpus Christi College, Cambridge, to study law. He changed to medicine, and despite constant illness and a number of recuperative tours in Europe, graduated MB in 1818. John Abernethy accepted him as a student at St Bartholomew's Hospital, London, in 1815. He never practised. During one tour in France in 1814 he began climbing mountains to study thin air at the summit. During another, he collected and translated German folk songs. He also issued an annotated edition of the *Diosemia* of Aratus, then suppressed it, and wrote a number of poems in dialect. His medical studies were marked by an interest in mental function, especially phrenology. Claiming to have been attracted to Gall's doctrines as early as 1806, he met Spurzheim in London in 1814 and became an enthusiastic convert. He studied brain anatomy under Spurzheim, introduced him to Sir Joseph Banks, and accompanied him on a lecture tour.

The following January, in an article in the *Philosophical Magazine*, he coined the term phrenology. He spoke on the subject at the Cambridge Philosophical Society and on 15 April 1816 delivered a paper to the Wernerian Society of Edinburgh. A note in the minute book observes that this was the first paper on phrenology read before a learned society in Scotland. The text was expanded for printing in 1817. He dedicated the second edition of his book on insanity (1819) to Spurzheim and was elected an honorary member of the London Phrenological Society in 1825.

Forster was unwilling to use phrenology to attack traditional thought, apart from educational reform. In the dispute over mental function between William Lawrence and Abernethy he stated that spirit was not solely a function of the brain's physiology. A short pseudonymous tract, *Somatopsychonoologia* (1823), written after a visit to Gall in Paris, does not clarify his views. His only book of practical medicine, *Medicina simplex* (1829), followed Abernethy's teachings. Some time afterwards he proposed an organ of supernaturality, or mystery, and argued with Spurzheim over its existence. His interest in phrenology subsided, probably because of his conversion to Roman Catholicism in 1824. In the end he regarded Spurzheim as an intellectual thief.

On 11 February 1817 Forster married Julia, daughter of Colonel Henry Beaufoy FRS, and moved to Hartfield, Sussex, then to Spa Lodge, Tunbridge Wells. There he collected plants and made astronomical observations. In 1818 their only child, Selena, was born. He published an edition of Catullus and on 3 July 1819 discovered a comet. Having become a fellow of the Royal Astronomical Society he established a short-lived meteorological society around 1823 in conjunction with Sir Richard Philips. On his father's death in 1825 he inherited a noted herbarium and a fine collection of manuscripts. In 1827 he moved to Boreham, near Chelmsford, close to his daughter's school, and published many medical and atmospherical works, in connection with which he made an ascent in a balloon on 30 April 1831 from the gardens of the Dominican friary, Moulsham, watched by his wife through a telescope. The flight was conducted by George Green, the most experienced balloonist of the era. Forster intended making electrical and physiological experiments but inadvertently leaving his instruments behind managed to observe only the effect on his ears at 6000 feet. His pamphlet describing the ascent provides a thorough summary of flight and mountaineering, which he called aerostatics. He also published an edition of letters between Locke, Shaftesbury, and Algernon Sydney, inherited from Benjamin Furly, with a preface on metaphysics.

From 1833 Forster mostly lived abroad on independent means, first moving the family to Brussels, and then roaming through Europe until May 1837 when he took a house in Schaerbeek. During these years he acquired several dogs, later publishing eulogies of the best loved ones and reflections on animal souls and animal phrenology. *Philozoia* (1839), a work on the Pythagorean doctrine of *sati*, or universal immortality, was inspired by the death of a favourite poodle. Forster experienced difficulties in reconciling Roman Catholicism with the non-Christian elements of his Pythagoreanism. In 1833 he joined Lewis Gompertz in setting up the Animals' Friend Society after Gompertz resigned from the Society for the Prevention of Cruelty to Animals over alleged Pythagorean sympathies. Forster, honorary foreign secretary of the society, continued advocating animal immortality and vegetarianism long after it failed in 1846. These interests drew him into a friendship with Shelley.

In 1836, after publishing articles on refraction and other astronomical phenomena, Forster became involved in controversy with Arago about the influence of comets on terrestrial events. Bad health returned in 1840, and at one point he was given up for dead. The family moved him to Tunbridge Wells from August 1841 to April 1842 to recuperate, where he reissued his father's *Flora Tonbrigensis* with a biographical memoir. He contributed several papers to the Linnean Society at this time.

From 1842 the family lived in Bruges, a centre for English Roman Catholics. Forster thereafter published poems, songs, and literary studies, the most well known being 'Pan', in which he discussed Christianity. He composed various pieces for violin and collected choice instruments. His edition of family letters, privately printed at Bruges, is valuable, and his autobiography, *Recueil de ma vie*, gives a colourful account of his life. He died on 2 February 1860 in Brussels. Thomas Bell rightly remembered him as 'a man of eccentric habits and views, and an accomplished linguist' (Bell, xxiii). Disliking some of the rules, Forster declined fellowship of the Royal Society in 1816.

JANET BROWNE

Sources T. I. M. Forster, *Recueil de ma vie*, 3rd edn (1837) · R. Cooter, *The cultural meaning of popular science: phrenology and the organization of consent in nineteenth-century Britain* (1984) · Gillow, *Lit. biog. hist.* · T. Bell, *Proceedings of the Linnean Society of London* (1859–60), xxiii · F. [T. Forster], *Epistolarium, or, Fasciculi of curious letters … as preserved among the MSS of the Forster family*, 2 vols. (privately printed, Bruges, 1845–50)
Archives Bodl. Oxf., corresp. and collection of Forster and Pitt family papers · NHM
Likenesses T. I. M. Forster, self-portrait, repro. in T. I. M. Forster, *Anecdotes and eulogies of favourite dogs* (1848), frontispiece

Forster, William (*fl.* 1627–1673), mathematician, was perhaps the William Forster who entered Trinity College, Cambridge, in the Easter term of 1627. He received his BA in 1631 and his MA three years later. Few details of his life are known.

Forster was given tuition in mathematics by William Oughtred and passed some time with him at his house at Albury in Surrey. During the summer of 1630 he was with Oughtred, who showed him two of the instruments of his own devising. These were a circular slide rule and the horizontall instrument (a tool for demonstrating astronomical principles and for laying out sundials on any kind of plane). Finding that Oughtred had written some rules for their use in Latin Forster asked leave to translate these into English and to publish them. *The Circles of Proportion and the Horizontall Instrument* appeared in 1632, and embroiled both Forster and Oughtred in a dispute with

Richard Delamain over the authorship of the instruments. This book gave Forster's address as 'at the Red Bull over against St Clements churchyard without Temple bar'; it appears that Forster had set himself up in this residence as a teacher of mathematics and of the use of mathematical instruments. He also undertook some surveying and produced some almanacs. A protractor of his design was described by William Leybourn during the 1650s.

In 1667 Forster published an arithmetic, simply called *Forster's Arithmetick*. He intended it for the use of merchants and accountants, and aimed to provide a clear method for demonstrating the principles. It provided basic teaching on the four main operations of arithmetic, the use of fractions and the application of rules of proportion to various business transactions. Apart from the inclusion of both old and new methods of division it was very similar to other arithmetics being produced at the time. It was republished in 1673 and again in 1686, the latter edition being amended by Henry Coley, suggesting that Forster died in the years between the second and third editions.

H. K. HIGTON

Sources E. G. R. Taylor, *The mathematical practitioners of Tudor and Stuart England* (1954) · W. Oughtred, *The circles of proportion and the horizontall instrument*, trans. W. Forster (1632) · Venn, *Alum. Cant.*

Forster, William (1739–1808), musical instrument maker and publisher, was born at Brampton, Cumberland, the son of a spinning-wheel maker and repairer and maker of violins. He made his way southward as a cattle-drover and reached London in 1759. At home he had been carefully taught music and the making of instruments, and the violins with which he subsequently supplied the London shops were accepted and sold without difficulty. His talent won him employment from Beck, a music-seller of Tower Hill, until Forster started his own business in Duke's Court, St Martin's Lane, from where he moved, as 'violin maker to the Prince of Wales and Duke of Cumberland', to 348 Strand about 1785. From the early 1770s his instruments (originally copies of Stainer models and later based on Cremonese examples) were in demand and great attention was paid to their characteristic thick, dark red varnish. The earlier 'Forsters', especially the cellos and double basses (he made three of the latter at the command of George III), have remained highly regarded to the present day. Perhaps his most famous instrument is the 'Royal George' cello of *c.*1782, which bears the prince of Wales's coat of arms. As a publisher and music-seller Old Forster (as he was known) was also significant, issuing music by J. S. Bach and G. M. Cambini, among others. However, it is through his connection with Haydn that he is best known. Forster made an agreement with Haydn in 1781 for the publication rights in England of over one hundred of his works, which in turn helped to popularize orchestral and chamber music generally. Among the letters published in *The History of the Violin*, by W. Sandys and S. A. Forster, are several of interest from Haydn, referring to the purchase of his compositions by the Forsters. Old Forster was married, possibly to Margarett; he died in London on 14 December 1808.

Forster's son, **William Forster** (1764–1824), followed

him in the business. He was born on 7 January 1764, and if he was the person of that name baptized at St Mary, Whitechapel, on 5 February of that year, then his mother can be identified as Margarett Forster. He made instruments of a fair quality from about 1779. He worked with his father for many years and, following his marriage to Elizabeth Fraser on 16 July 1786, took over the publishing and music-selling business. As music-seller to the prince of Wales and duke of Cumberland, he continued the Forster connection with the royal family. He died on 24 July 1824. His eldest son, **William Forster** (1788–1824), was born in London on 14 December 1788. He made relatively few instruments. He became a cellist in theatre orchestras and died shortly after his father, on 8 October 1824. It was a younger son, **Simon Andrew Forster** (1801–1870), born in London on 13 May 1801, who carried on the violin- and cello-making tradition, in Frith Street, and later at 13 Macclesfield Street, Soho. With William Sandys he was the author of *The History of the Violin* (1864), which provides much information about his family and other English instrument makers. He died at his home, 13 Macclesfield Street, on 2 February 1870, leaving his sister Octavia as executor of his will.

L. M. MIDDLETON, rev. DAVID J. GOLBY

Sources B. W. Harvey, *The violin family and its makers in the British Isles: an illustrated history and directory* (1995) · C. Beare and P. Ward Jones, 'Forster', *New Grove* · Brown & Stratton, *Brit. mus.*, 149–50 · W. Sandys and S. A. Forster, *The history of the violin* (1864) · V. Walden, *One hundred years of the violoncello: a history of technique and performance practice, 1740–1840* (1998) · IGI

Wealth at death under £800—Simon Andrew Forster: probate, 21 March 1870, *CGPLA Eng. & Wales*

Forster, William (1764–1824). *See under* Forster, William (1739–1808).

Forster, William (1784–1854), philanthropist and Quaker minister, was born at Tottenham, Middlesex, on 23 March 1784, the second of the ten children of William Forster (1747–1824), schoolmaster and later land surveyor, and Elizabeth (1759–1837), daughter of Robert and Mary Hayward of Kelvedon, Essex. William senior's father, Josiah (1693?–1763), who hailed from co. Durham, settled in 1752 in Tottenham, a village which was to become a Quaker stronghold and, until 1880, the home of members of the family.

After education at the village schools and with private tutors, William junior learned land surveying in Sheffield with his uncle William *Fairbank (c.1730–1801) [*see under* Fairbank family]. On returning to Tottenham he joined his father, but in 1806 he was released from business responsibilities and devoted himself to working for the Society of Friends and his various philanthropic concerns. Before he was twenty he had begun to take a vocal part in Quaker worship, and his gift in the ministry was acknowledged by Tottenham monthly meeting in August 1805. Next month he received the meeting's support for the first of a succession of religious visits in Britain, including (1812) the Hebrides. Like other itinerant ministering Friends his concern was not only domestic and pastoral but also to reach a wide audience through specially appointed meetings, often where there was no Quaker presence. This was particularly true of his extensive visit to Ireland (1813–14).

Forster's head and hands were huge and his frame unwieldy; his whole body would shake with emotion and his voice deepen as he gave expression to his feelings. His ministry was evangelical, but his sense of awe was such that he felt it almost profane to talk of religion, and his humanitarian zeal transcended the doctrinal. His intellectual capacity was considerable, but it was the manner of his ministry that was remembered rather than the content. Forster accompanied the American Quaker Stephen Grellet (1773–1855) in visiting London prisons in January 1813, and went with him to Elizabeth Fry to report the appalling conditions on the women's side of Newgate. Her first visit, next day, with clothing for the children was (as were later visits) with Anna Buxton (1784–1855), whom Forster married on 3 October 1816. She was the daughter of Thomas Fowell and Anna (*née* Hanbury) Buxton of Earls Colne, Essex, and sister of Sir Thomas Fowell *Buxton, first baronet, the anti-slavery protagonist. For two decades they lived at Bradpole, Dorset, but in 1837 moved to Norwich, which was their home until his death.

Forster travelled extensively in North America in 1820–25, viewing with increasing misgiving the growth among Friends there of what he considered unitarian views. His and concurrent visits by George Withy (1763–1837) in 1821, Elizabeth Robson and her brother Isaac Stephenson (1765–1830) in 1823, and Anna Braithwaite in 1824 had the cumulative effect of giving the suspect Elias Hicks (1748–1830) and his many adherents the impression that they were being preached at rather than listened to, and may well have hastened the American Quaker separations of 1827–8.

Forster's second visit to America (1845–6) was with his brother Josiah [*see below*], George Stacey (1786–1857), and John Allen (1790–1859), following a breach in Indiana yearly meeting over the slavery issue: it was perhaps ironic that the anti-slavery militants whom the deputation condemned for separating were, in effect, closer to the views of British Quakers on slavery than the main body, who received the deputation's support.

Irish Quakers, following the 1846 failure of the potato crop, set up on 13 November a central relief committee. Forster spent over four months visiting the worst-stricken districts, especially in Connaught. His knowledge from 1813–14 stood him in good stead, and his reports and contacts, not least with Catholic parish priests, were crucial to the relief committee's work. His son William Edward *Forster accompanied him for part of the time, as also did James Hack Tuke. For each it was an introduction to a lifetime's concern. Forster and his brothers Josiah and Robert [*see below*] also served on a committee of British Friends to arouse awareness of the need and to raise funds.

In 1849 British Quakers drew up a memorial against the continuance of the slave trade: from then until 1852 Forster was on a number of deputations to continental rulers. In 1853, with his brother Josiah, John Candler (1787–1869), and William Holmes (1805–1867), he paid his third American visit. After seeing the president, Franklin Pierce

(1804–1869), they travelled through many of the southern and mid-western states, securing interviews with the governors of thirteen of them. Forster died at the home of Samuel Low, near the Holston River, Knox county, East Tennessee, on 27 January 1854, his body being interred in the Friends' burial-ground, Friendsville, Tennessee.

Of William Forster's nine brothers and sisters, one died in childhood. The others remained single except for **Josiah Forster** (1782–1870), who in 1808 married Rachel Wilson (1783–1873), daughter of John Wilson (1748–1801) and Sarah, *née* Dillworth (1754–1788) of Kendal: there was one child, who died aged eleven weeks. In 1805 Josiah opened a school at Southgate, which moved to Tottenham in 1820 and closed in 1826. He had a reputation for naïvety—as when, confiscating fireworks as dangerous toys, he threw them on the fire to ensure their destruction. But with his adult fellow Quakers, so far from being naïve, he could be stentorian and unyielding. He was from 1820 to 1831 clerk (presiding officer) of the yearly meeting of British Quakers, a body he consistently attended from the late eighteenth century until his death, and in which he was an ever more frequent speaker. His wife was recorded as a minister in 1810. In 1811 he was appointed to the meeting for sufferings (the representative committee of the yearly meeting) and in 1817 he became an elder: both offices he held until his death. He frequently accompanied ministering Friends visiting the continent and was an indefatigable correspondent. He was for many years on the committees of the British and Foreign Anti-Slavery Society and of the British and Foreign Bible Society.

Another brother, **Robert Forster** (1791–1873), carried on the family land surveying business. For many years steward to the earl of Darnley, he managed the Kentish estates during the young earl's minority and built a great part of Northfleet, Kent. Perhaps his most notable Quaker service was as a member of deputations to present to European governments 'A plea for liberty of conscience', drawn up by the yearly meeting of 1856: that year he visited Paris, in 1857 the Netherlands and Germany, and in 1858 Russia and northern Europe. He served as an elder and for many years on the meeting for sufferings. He was a member of the committee of the British and Foreign School Society from 1817 until his death. He was also on the committee of the Quaker school at Croydon, and he and Josiah were longtime members of the London committee for Ackworth School. They were lifelong trustees, and active in the management, of Grove House School, Tottenham, established in 1828 and notable for the part that science had in the curriculum.

In his later years Robert, who suffered a decline of mental powers, was tended by his sister **Anne Forster** (1797–1873), whose philanthropic interests extended to the animal kingdom if the ascription to her of the broadside *To Butchers, their Men and Boys* (Norwich, n.d.) be correct. **Mary Forster** (1786–1873) was with relatives in Plymouth from 1810 to 1834; on her return to Tottenham she devoted herself to visiting women prisoners and in 1837 was appointed an elder. Sarah (1799–1880), who was recorded a minister in 1848, was granted minutes for religious service on

seventeen occasions. Most of the sisters' activities were local rather than national, and the family home in Philip Lane, Tottenham Green, was noted for its warm hospitality.

Josiah Forster died on 27 June 1870; and the year 1873 saw the deaths of his widow on 5 March, of Mary on 24 February, Robert on 11 October, and Anne on 14 October. Elizabeth died on 29 March 1879 and Sarah on 14 September 1880. The bodies of all were interred in Tottenham Friends' burial-ground.   EDWARD H. MILLIGAN

Sources B. Seebohm, ed., *Memoirs of William Forster*, 2 vols. (1865) · *Annual Monitor* (1871), 191–216 [Josiah] · *Annual Monitor* (1875), 49–62 [Mary; Robert; Anne] · *Annual Monitor* (1881), 57–60 [Sarah] · *Transactions of the central relief committee of the Society of Friends during the famine in Ireland in 1846 and 1847* (1852); facs. edn with new introduction, and index by R. Goodbody (1996) · J. T. Mills, *John Bright and the Quakers*, 2 vols. (1935) · T. Compton, *Recollections of Tottenham Friends and the Forster family* (1893) · M. A. Collie, *Quakers of Tottenham, 1775–1825* [typescript dissertation, publ. in abridged form] · *Biographical catalogue: being an account of the lives of Friends and others whose portraits are in the London Friends' Institute*, Society of Friends (1888), 211–30 [Josiah; Robert; William] · W. Robinson, ed., *Friends of a half century* (1891), 114–26 [Josiah; William] · London and Middlesex digest of births to 1837, RS Friends, Lond. · digest registers (marriages to 1837), RS Friends, Lond. [Dorset and Hampshire quarterly meeting]

Archives RS Friends, Lond., letters and memoranda

Likenesses pencil sketch, 1835, repro. in Robinson, ed., *Friends* · Maull & Polyblank, photograph, *c*.1860 (Robert Forster), RS Friends, Lond. · Maull & Polyblank, photograph, *c*.1860 (Josiah Forster), repro. in Robinson, ed., *Friends* · B. R. Haydon, group portrait, oils (*The Anti-Slavery Society convention, 1840*), NPG · S. Lucas, group portrait, oils (*London yearly meeting about 1840*), RS Friends, Lond. · S. Lucas, group portrait, oils (*William Forster with Josiah Forster; London yearly meeting about 1840*), RS Friends, Lond. · silhouette, RS Friends, Lond.

Forster, William (1788–1824). *See under* Forster, William (1739–1808).

Forster, William Edward (1818–1886), politician, born at Bradpole, Dorset, on 11 July 1818, was the only son of William *Forster (1784–1854), Quaker philanthropist and minister, and his wife, Anna (1784–1855), daughter of Thomas Fowell Buxton, gentleman, and sister of Sir Thomas Fowell *Buxton, first baronet, the philanthropist. Anna Forster was actively involved in prison reform with Elizabeth Fry. Forster was taught at home, and at Quaker proprietary schools in Fishponds, Bristol (1831), and Grove House, Tottenham (1832–5), and later by a private tutor in Norwich. His taste for politics was whetted early through helping his uncle, Buxton, in his anti-slavery campaigning.

The model employer Forster sought a career in law leading to politics, but his father insisted on a business apprenticeship in textiles and banking. Using funds provided by the wealthy Quaker friends of his father (notably J. J. Gurney), Forster joined T. S. Fison in his wool-stapling business in Bradford during the winter of 1840–41, and became the partner of Fison's brother, William Fison, as a woollen worsted manufacturer, a year later. Trade expanded rapidly, with spinning being added, and in 1852 the works moved to Greenholme Mills at Burley in

William Edward Forster (1818–1886), by Henry Tanworth Wells, 1875

Wharfedale at a cost of £33,500. The workforce grew from 532 to 1200 between 1851 and 1870, and Forster's share of the fixed capital totalled £88,000 by 1872. This had fallen to £41,000 by the time of his death. Forster's personal income peaked at £36,000 in 1871. Thereafter it declined rapidly, and his business interests traded at a loss in some years between 1872 and 1886. Nevertheless Forster remained a rich man and, from his entry into parliament in 1861, was able to leave the daily running of the business to his partner.

Fison and Forster were regarded as model employers, establishing a mill school in 1854 and a local board of health five years later. A public lecture hall was built in Burley in 1868, along with other improved public utilities. After a period in lodgings Forster bought a house at Rawdon in 1846, before building Wharfeside at Burley in 1852, which was to remain his Yorkshire home. In 1863 Forster took a lease on 80 Eccleston Square, London SW1, which he retained until his death.

Friendships and marriage From the start, Forster was set on a public as well as a manufacturing life. Later he would be characterized as the blunt and unsophisticated Yorkshire manufacturer in politics, and he possibly played up this side of his character. Through Quaker connections Forster met John Sterling and, through him, F. D. Maurice and Thomas Carlyle. The last was a most important influence, Forster describing him as 'the deepest mind of his age', while Carlyle, in return, commented on Forster's 'locomotive energy'. He also formed a lifelong friendship with Richard Monkton Milnes, and developed close links

with Robert Owen and Thomas Cooper, the Chartist leader. Forster was also introduced to the family of the late Thomas *Arnold, and in the summer of 1850 he married Arnold's eldest daughter, Jane Martha (1821–1899).

The marriage was a happy one, and Jane Forster, an intelligent, pious woman interested in public affairs, provided Forster with a solid domestic foundation. Though childless, Forster and his wife created an extended family for themselves in 1859 by adopting the four children of Jane Forster's brother, William Delafield *Arnold (1828–1859). The children, who included the later unionist politician Hugh Oakeley Arnold-*Forster, Florence Arnold-Forster, and Frances Egerton Arnold-*Forster, were brought up as the Forsters' own. In 1873 Forster acquired Fox Ghyll, near Ambleside, adjacent to the Arnold family home at Fox How.

Through marriage to a non-Quaker Forster was required by law to leave the connexion. This move coincided with a period of religious doubt, and he never again acquired a defined denominational membership, although he attended Anglican services in Burley and London, most notably those of F. D. Maurice. But he remained unbaptized, and his burial was marked by a simple Quaker ceremony. Little is known of his religious development before his marriage. He accepted the liberal Anglican tradition of Thomas Arnold, later defending the established status of the Church of England and the national value of the parochial system.

Social reform and local politics In 1846 Forster travelled to the west of Ireland to observe the famine conditions, staying with Daniel O'Connell. He published an account of his impressions, which he later claimed had made an indelible impact. He supported public works for the relief of Irish distress, along with state-aided emigration, and returned to Ireland in 1849, accompanied by Carlyle and Sir Charles Gavan Duffy.

Prompted by the Ten Hours Movement, Forster supported some of the aspirations of the moral force Chartists, including the extension of the franchise and the idea of national workshops as a remedy for unemployment. He visited Paris in 1848, returning the following year with Thomas Cooper. Forster's economic ideas, which owed much to John Stuart Mill, were brought together in three lectures, published as *Pauperism and its Proposed Remedies* (1848). He condemned unbridled *laissez-faire* as ignoring the moral responsibilities of individuals and governments, urging working-class restraint as the only answer to the destructive cycle of Malthusian overpopulation and impoverishment. The state should assist, through emigration, public works, and the provision of education. Two years later, in letters to the co-operative newspaper *The Leader*, Forster advocated the creation of state farms and workshops, operating under market conditions, in which managers and workers would be paid by results. He was also attracted to industrial partnership, supporting the idea of workers becoming small shareholders in their employers' enterprises, and introducing profit sharing among his own senior employees.

Forster quickly became involved in Bradford's electoral

politics, supporting Colonel Perronet Thompson, the radical candidate in the 1847 general election. In 1848 he worked to unite the middle classes and moderate Chartists, chairing a public meeting attended by 2000 Chartists on 25 April. Although failing to become a town councillor, Forster was elected to the board of guardians in 1849, becoming its chairman the following year. He had to wait until 1861 to realize his parliamentary ambitions. For this the strongly nonconformist nature of West Riding politics was largely responsible; his belief that the state had a responsibility to educate the poor offended the voluntarists, and Edward Baines, editor of the *Leeds Mercury*, in particular. In 1857 Forster twice failed to secure the Liberal parliamentary nomination for Leeds, decisions which led him to establish a rival newspaper, the *Leeds Express*. By 1859 these damaging disputes had been resolved, and both men were selected, with Forster representing the radical interest. He was again unsuccessful in the parliamentary election, being pushed into third place by twenty-two votes by the Conservative candidate, George S. Beecroft (1809–1869).

At the same time Forster was developing views on foreign and colonial affairs which were to remain fundamental for the rest of his life. In 1854 he criticized the government's handling of the 'native question' in the Cape. He supported the Crimean War as a legitimate response to Russian tyranny, and was involved in the public debates on Indian finance. He was also an enthusiast for the popular patriotism of the volunteer movement, seeing it as a means of uniting the middle and operative classes. He established his own corps at Burley in 1859.

MP for Bradford Forster finally secured election unopposed for Bradford at a by-election in February 1861, supported by his Christian socialist friend Viscount Goderich and by William Byles (1807–1891), editor of the *Bradford Observer*. In parliament he was a vigorous defender of non-intervention in the American Civil War, most notably over the *Trent* affair in November 1861. A passionate supporter of the north, he established a close friendship with Charles Adams, the American minister in London, and later criticized the government for failing to stop the *Alabama* sailing from Liverpool in March 1863. Forster also favoured non-intervention in European affairs. In 1864 he chaired the select committee on foreign trade, which led to the establishment of the commercial affairs section of the Foreign Office. On the domestic front he supported reform of the game laws, criticized the 1862 revised education code, and supported franchise extension.

Returned unopposed at the general election in 1865, Forster became under-secretary for the colonies in the ministry of Earl Russell in November of that year. He had little chance to make an impact during his few months of office (November 1865 to June 1866), but he supported the government's decision not to prosecute Governor Eyre in Jamaica, believing that he had acted in good faith. After the fall of Russell's government he supported the movement for parliamentary reform at the great meeting at Woodhouse Moor in Leeds on 8 October 1866, and in 1867 contributed to the detailed debates on Disraeli's Franchise Bill.

Education and the 1870 act Forster was also increasingly involved in the education question, building on an earlier interest as a member of the Leeds Education Society, an interdenominational group including W. F. Hook, the vicar of Leeds. He sympathized with the aims of the Manchester and Salford Educational Aid Society, founded in 1864. On the divisive question of religious teaching he supported non-denominational biblical instruction in his own school at Burley. This was the form advocated by the British and Foreign Bible Society, of which his uncle had been an active member, and of which Forster himself was to become a vice-president. He was later a member of Sir John Pakington's select committee in 1865.

Among leading Liberals, Forster joined H. A. Bruce, G. J. Goschen, and De Grey (as Goderich had become) in trying to find an acceptable legislative framework for elementary education. They were encouraged by the abandonment of the voluntary principle by leading nonconformists in October 1867, and by Gladstone's declaration of interest in the education question in December. Forster had given his name to Bruce's enabling bill during the 1867 session, and announced its reintroduction early in 1868 following a major conference at Manchester at which he had been a prominent presence. The 1868 bill included compulsory powers for the first time. On the formation of Gladstone's first government in early December 1868 Forster became vice-president of the council (with responsibility for education) under De Grey. He was made a privy councillor, but did not join the cabinet.

Forster first introduced legislation to reform the endowed schools. A member of Lord Taunton's royal commission, he had hoped to establish a ladder of scholarships out of the schools' historic endowments, as well as a permanent regulatory mechanism in the face of opposition from the newly founded Headmasters' Conference. The latter had to be dropped, and the battle with local vested interests slowed the pace of reform considerably. Nevertheless, the Endowed Schools Act (1869) had a significant impact on secondary education in England and Wales, establishing a cadre of boarding and day schools, below the Clarendon élite, providing an academic education for the children of the professional classes.

In preparing an elementary education bill, most notably in his cabinet paper of 21 October 1869, Forster wanted to build on earlier legislative efforts. A pragmatist on matters of detail, he had three main aims. First, to establish a mandatory and comprehensive national system of elementary education, publicly funded from locally raised rates. Secondly, to ensure that such a system should include religious teaching on the basis of regular biblical instruction as a minimum. Thirdly, that such legislative provision should extend, and not destroy, the existing voluntary system. The bill would require borough and parish authorities to report to the education department on the provision of elementary education in their area. Where there was a shortfall local voluntary agencies would be given a period of grace to meet it, but if they did not do so school boards would be set up to provide new rate-funded schools. Forster expected board schools to be the norm in urban areas, while many rural districts would continue to be served by church schools. He accepted that there would need to be a conscience clause, and that funds would be required for poor scholars. He also wished attendance to be compulsory, once adequate numbers of places were available. In making specific proposals he adapted an earlier model of Robert Lowe, rejecting the schemes proposed by the Birmingham Education League, the National Education Union, and his former collaborator, Henry Bruce.

Initial cabinet discussion focused on the question of religious teaching in board schools. Gladstone opposed non-denominational instruction, with the result that the bill, as introduced on 17 February 1870, left this matter to local decision. This and other changes made to Forster's original proposals opened the way to significant nonconformist opposition, led by the National Education League, which portrayed Forster as the evil genius behind a bill designed to protect and extend the influence of the voluntary (and mainly Anglican) schools. On 13 May 1870 Forster and De Grey pressed Gladstone to accept that religious instruction should be given only at the beginning and the end of the school day, that non-denominational religious instruction should be the norm in the new board schools, and that rate support for voluntary schools should be confined to secular subjects. A cabinet impasse continued for some weeks, until Gladstone was persuaded by Forster to accept a cross-party amendment of Cowper-Temple: that catechetical and denominational religious instruction should be excluded from board schools, but that no other official guidance should be given.

Gladstone agreed to this concession only in return for an agreement to rate aid voluntary schools compulsorily. In a naïve attempt to lessen the hostility of nonconformists to such a change, the cabinet accepted a proposal of Lowe that the voluntary schools should be funded directly by the Treasury, thereby creating unintentionally the dual system of elementary education in England and Wales. Forster also accepted later amendments which reduced the period of grace given to the voluntary agencies to six months, but insisted, against the views of the House of Lords, that school boards should be able to provide free schooling. In procedural terms the bill was also innovative in allowing female ratepayers a vote in school board elections, and in its introduction of voting by secret ballot in London and of proportional representation. The bill received the royal assent on 9 August 1870, just three weeks after Forster had joined the cabinet. The 1870 Elementary Education Act, rightly known as Forster's Act, was his greatest political and legislative achievement.

The Education Act gave Forster national fame and notoriety, later confirmed by his taking charge of the legislation to introduce the secret ballot for parliamentary elections in 1871 and 1872, and by his support for international arbitration over the *Alabama* payment. But he faced political difficulties in his Bradford constituency, where the emerging Liberal caucus led by Alfred Illingworth tried to bind him exclusively to the policies endorsed by the Liberal Association. Forster absolutely refused to be so bound, arguing that he was no delegate but the representative of all Liberals in Bradford. He was vindicated in the 1874 general election, coming top of the poll.

In opposition, 1875–1880 By early 1875 Forster was seen as the leading front-bench radical. He supported the extension of the franchise to the rural householder, the introduction of representative county government, and a reform of the land laws. Only on church and education questions did he remain resolutely opposed to the aspirations of radical nonconformists. On Gladstone's retirement in January 1875 Forster emerged as the rival candidate to Hartington for the party leadership in the House of Commons, but stood down in the interests of party unity, perhaps realizing that his moral seriousness jarred with some of his more Olympian colleagues.

For the next five years Forster was an extremely energetic member of the opposition front bench, especially in relation to foreign and colonial affairs. His concern over slavery and the rights of indigenous peoples led him to see the Anglo-Saxon race as having a special mission in the colonial sphere—ideas that took political shape in the concept of imperial federation, and that were outlined in his speech in Edinburgh on 5 November 1875, entitled 'Our colonial empire'. Making the queen empress of India, on the other hand, he regarded as a dangerous constitutional precedent. On Europe, Forster confused some of his radical colleagues by not fully endorsing Gladstone's moral outrage over the Bulgarian atrocities. His approach, though strongly critical of Turkey, was closer to that of Hartington and the foreign secretary, Lord Derby. As the Eastern question unfolded, he was able to rejoin his colleagues in opposing any military support for Turkey. He was critical of the settlement agreed at the Congress of Berlin, and in particular of the British acquisition of Cyprus, which he saw as a move underpinning Turkish misrule.

Chief secretary for Ireland, 1880–1882 Gladstone appointed Forster chief secretary for Ireland on 30 April 1880. Forster was not well prepared, despite a visit to Ireland in 1878, and needed time to assess the condition of the Irish countryside. He recommended that coercion should not be renewed immediately, nor any decision made about the land question, but that the existing tory relief policy be continued. Increasing agrarian disorder, linked to a rising number of eviction processes, compelled Forster to act. He established a royal commission, under the earl of Bessborough, to report on the working of the 1870 Land Act. In early June he introduced legislation to compensate evicted tenants under certain limiting conditions. The bill was poorly drafted, and whiggishly inclined members, fearful of Gladstone's radicalism, were dismayed at the apparent threat to property rights. It got bogged down in debate and the tory opposition cast doubt on the government's eviction figures. Fearing a possible defeat in the Commons, ministers were relieved that the bill reached the House of Lords, where it was overwhelmingly rejected on 3 August. It was not an auspicious beginning.

The period of Forster's chief secretaryship proved to be the most challenging of the century. He was joined in Dublin by Earl Cowper as lord lieutenant, an inexperienced whig grandee inclined to indolence. Forster quickly found himself shouldering a double burden in London and Dublin. Despite his rugged exterior Forster, a sensitive man subject to considerable fluctuations of mood, found it increasingly distressing to be unable to help the innocent victims of agrarian intimidation and violence, and to be almost wholly identified with coercionist policies, earning himself the nickname Buckshot Forster.

Even with a promising harvest, agrarian disorder continued to rise during the autumn of 1880, and Forster recommended that the Land League leadership should be prosecuted for incitement. This was never a credible posture but by the end of October Forster had become convinced that parliament should be immediately recalled in order to suspend habeas corpus in Ireland and to introduce greater arms control. By locking up local troublemakers for short periods without trial, he believed that disturbed districts could be quietened down in the short term, before the introduction of a measure of land reform. He was opposed not only by Chamberlain and Bright but also (and most persistently) by Gladstone, who suggested (but never actually recommended) that action ought to be taken against the Land League directly. A major cabinet split developed in mid-November, differences resolved only through a compromise whereby parliament would be summoned at the usual time but with coercion as its first item of business. It was not a happy outcome for Forster, now identified as coercionist among radicals and as irresolute among whigs.

At the same time Forster was pressing for a comprehensive land bill, even before the Bessborough commission had reported. Again he faced weighty cabinet opposition, not only from the whigs led by the duke of Argyll but also from Gladstone. Strongly influenced by Ulster opinion and by Irish Liberal friends from co. Limerick, Forster was convinced that the principles known as the three Fs (fixity of tenure, fair rents, and free sale) should become part of Irish land law. Without this change Land League power and Parnell's political authority would remain undiminished. Gladstone proved very resistant to so extensive a change, favouring at first a complicated scheme of compensation for eviction. Forster argued that farmers wanted security from eviction, not compensation.

At two cabinet meetings, on 30 and 31 December 1880, it was finally agreed to introduce coercion immediately, and that the land legislation should build upon the 1870 Land Act. This was a narrower basis than Forster would have liked. Thereafter responsibility for Irish policy was divided, Forster taking charge of the passage of the coercive legislation while Gladstone slowly fashioned a new land bill. Forster faced ferocious Parnellite opposition in the Commons, thereby becoming almost wholly identified publicly as a coercionist minister, while more privately he was persuading Gladstone to adopt a more extensive land

reform measure. Despite the unprecedented obstruction, the Protection of Persons and Property Bill became law on 2 March 1881 and was immediately followed by the Arms Act on 21 March. Forster and his Dublin colleagues used their powers sparingly, and only fifty men were arrested initially. He had much less impact on the final shape of the Irish land legislation, though Gladstone later acknowledged his contribution to the second Irish Land Act.

Forster became depressed in May 1881 as a result of the dual pressures from parliamentary intimidation by Parnellite members and the weight of executive work in Dublin, and requested that Cowper be replaced. Gladstone took no action, although O'Hagan was persuaded to retire as Irish lord chancellor. Forster was increasingly dogmatic on questions of law and order during the autumn of 1881, ultimately putting himself at odds even with those cabinet colleagues who generally supported coercion. This divergence was not immediately obvious. Parnell's policy of testing the Land Act in carefully selected cases, and the subsequent 'no rent' manifesto, equally angered Gladstone. Consequently, Forster was fully supported by all his cabinet colleagues in arresting Parnell on 13 October 1881 and in his later unilateral proclamation of the Land League itself. But, implicitly, the arrest of an elected parliamentary leader suggested future negotiation and a conditional release. Forster could not accept this. When Parnell offered to negotiate terms for an acceptance of the Land Act in return for the release of himself and the other Kilmainham prisoners, Forster did not attach the same significance to the offer as did the majority of the cabinet. In part this was because he distrusted Parnell's initial emissary, Captain O'Shea, husband of Parnell's mistress. He was prepared eventually to accept the settlement of the arrears question by gift rather than loan, but would not compromise on law and order. Failing to understand fully the political pressure to which Parnell was subject, Forster would consent to his release only if additional powers were already operational, or if the country was wholly quiet (neither possible in the short term), or if Parnell made an open declaration in support of public order.

At the same time as these negotiations were beginning in the spring of 1882, sections of the radical press, led by Chamberlain's close associate John Morley, editor of the *Pall Mall Gazette*, launched a bitter attack on Forster, arguing that his policies had failed and that he should be replaced. Officially inspired or not, all these uncertainties led to much speculation about a new departure in the government's Irish policy during the Easter recess.

Resignation Although wounded by the press attacks and deeply shocked by the murder of Mrs Smythe, a well-known figure in Dublin society, in co. Westmeath on 3 April 1882, Forster did not contemplate resignation before the last days of April, and was looking forward to working with Earl Spencer as Cowper's replacement as lord lieutenant. But he continued to see the negotiations with Parnell as misconceived, as reversing policies just at the moment they were succeeding, and as giving Parnell a representative status that previously had been vigorously denied. After receiving a letter from Parnell to O'Shea of 28 April, which apparently offered future parliamentary co-operation between the Irish members and the government, Gladstone decided to bring the negotiations to a rapid conclusion. In return for the settlement of the arrears question, and the non-renewal of the existing measures of coercion, Parnell agreed to end all opposition to the Land Act, and also promised the prospect of future co-operation with the Liberal government in parliament and in the Irish countryside. The question of future exceptional law and order powers was left deliberately vague. It was a price that Forster was not prepared to pay, and he threatened resignation at the cabinet on 1 May. Convinced of the immediate political value of an agreement, Gladstone and his colleagues, including coercionists, made no serious efforts to change his mind. There was no cabinet crisis, and Forster was allowed to resign on 2 May. The impression of a new departure was significantly increased as a result.

The reasons behind Forster's resignation, followed as it was, three days later, by the murder of his successor, Lord Frederick Cavendish, and the under-secretary, T. H. Burke, in Phoenix Park, were much debated, both at the time and by historians. Gladstone argued consistently that it arose from a failure in understanding, and that the government had no choice but to release Parnell once he had finally accepted the Land Act. On the other hand, Forster claimed that the negotiations and the agreement now gave Parnell a representative status, and that it constituted a great step towards home rule. Others saw him as physically and emotionally exhausted, and anxious to quit. C. S. Roundell (1827–1906), a friend of Spencer, believed that Forster

> had committed himself to a kind of antagonism to Parnell etc., and being an obstinate man, and a man of cumbrous, and in a certain sense narrow morale, he made a point of honour to give in to P[arnell] in nothing. (Althorp MS K.218)

Forster's later attitudes confirm Roundell's view. Continuing to support Irish reform in respect of franchise extension and the introduction of representative county government, Forster never changed his view about Parnell. On 15 May he challenged O'Shea to read to the Commons a fuller text of Parnell's letter of 28 April, which had apparently offered collaboration with the Liberal government. In the highly charged atmosphere it seemed as though Gladstone and his colleagues had thereby colluded unconsciously in the murder of their own representative in Ireland. Again, on 22 February 1883, Forster launched an emotional and personally abusive attack on Parnell as a man content to derive political advantage from the men of violence.

Forster remained politically active, supporting domestic reform but becoming a strong-minded critic of the government's colonial policies, often in association with G. J. Goschen. Two of Forster's lifelong concerns came together here. First, that the government was betraying the trust of indigenous peoples in the Transvaal in trying to seek a rapprochement with the Boer republics, and second that the British, as an Anglo-Saxon people, had a unique and historically grounded national destiny in the shape of their empire, which required fuller recognition and development. Forster was closely involved in the formation of the Imperial Federation League, presiding at its first meeting on 29 July 1884. Not surprisingly he became an astringent critic of Gladstone's handling of the crisis in Egypt and the Sudan, the government's 'candid friend', as Dilke put it. In the Commons on 13 May 1884 he accused Gladstone of self-delusion, and he finally voted against the government in the censure debate, following the death of Gordon, on 27 February 1885. Later in the year he chaired the committee examining the legislation concerning the Manchester Ship Canal.

Death and assessment Forster's criticism of the government reopened the tensions within his local Liberal Party, and it was not until October 1885 that he was formally adopted as the candidate for the new Central division of Bradford. By then he was terminally ill, and took no part in the election in November 1885, although he was returned by a majority of 1500. Despite recuperative trips to Baden-Baden and Devon his health continued to deteriorate, and, on returning to London, he died at 80 Eccleston Square on 5 April 1886. A funeral service was held at Westminster Abbey on 9 April, and he was buried the following day at Burley in Wharfedale; his widow died on 21 October 1899. Statues were later erected in Forster Square, Bradford, and in the Victoria Embankment Gardens in London.

Forster was a tall, ungainly man, careless of dress and poorly co-ordinated in his movements, presenting a rugged and hairy appearance, which earned him the nicknames the Bear and, less flatteringly, the Gorilla. He had a directness of speech and action that could be interpreted as stubborn inflexibility. Paradoxically this proved not unattractive to women, including the leading Liberal political hostesses, the Countess Waldegrave and the duchess of Manchester. He became a favourite minister of the queen. But beneath this rough exterior was an emotional, sentimental, and moral nature, which was expressed, for instance, in his passionate hostility to vivisection, his hatred of slavery, and his commitment to indigenous peoples.

Although coming from outside the political class, Forster became part of the governing establishment without compromising his antecedents: he never showed any interest in acquiring a landed estate nor in following country pursuits. His political career and attitudes were underpinned by his religious upbringing, and his business and political career were rooted in the West Riding. An untutored intellectual, he admired the poetry of Henry Vaughan in particular. He spent his summers climbing and scrambling in the Alps, and was elected to the Alpine Club in 1859. More leisurely pursuits included playing whist, at times noisily, with Anthony Trollope at his club.

Forster has not been well served by historians. For over a hundred years, after the publication of the official biography by T. Wemyss Reid in 1888, he received little scholarly attention. As a result his contribution was usually seen from the perspective of his political opponents, most notably Chamberlain and Parnell. Inevitably any assessment rests on his periods at the education and Irish offices. While later commentators may regret the shape of the English elementary school system after 1870, there is little doubt that Forster made a significant contribution to the debate on the issue from the mid-1860s and to its legislative resolution. Some historians have seen him simply as an opportunist, but a more balanced assessment is that he found a narrow area of political and denominational common ground on which a legislative settlement could be built, and then forced others to accept what was their own least worst option.

In Ireland Forster's achievements have to be more qualified. Not a coercionist by inclination, he recognized that law and order needed to be maintained while new legislative remedies were found. Left to him the 1881 Land Bill would probably have been more comprehensive than that eventually introduced by Gladstone. More negatively, Forster failed to recognize the significance of Parnell and the forces he was trying to lead and control, never seeing him as more than a political agitator. Consequently he could not accept, as governments had been able to do in the case of O'Connell, that Parnell's political stature was a factor in the politics of governing Ireland. His straightforward approach proved to be simplistic in the confused and complicated politics of April 1882, and he failed to understand that it was the very ambiguity of the Kilmainham negotiations that gave them their political strength. Forster was right in his assessment that the release of Parnell would be a step in a home-rule direction, but was wrong in assuming that Parnell could be discredited totally by being kept in gaol. It was a misunderstanding he never overcame. Even so, Forster managed to combine strong moral convictions with considerable abilities as a minister, and, unlike his radical contemporaries Bright or even Chamberlain, he left a living national memorial in the system of elementary education.   ALLEN WARREN

Sources P. Jackson, *Education Act Forster: a political biography of W. E. Forster, 1818–1886* (1997) · T. W. Reid, *Life of the Right Honourable William Edward Forster*, 4th edn, 2 vols. (1888) · M. R. Temmel, 'W. E. Forster and liberal politics, 1847–1875', PhD diss., University of Maryland, 1974 · D. Roland, 'The struggle for the Elementary Education Act and its implementation, 1870–73', BLitt diss., U. Oxf., 1957 · D. G. Wright, 'Politics and opinion in nineteenth century Bradford, 1832–1880', PhD diss., U. Leeds, 1966 · A. Warren, 'Forster, the liberals and new directions in Irish policy, 1880–1882', *Parliamentary History*, 6 (1987), 95–126 · Gladstone MSS, BL · Gladstone, *Diaries* · *Florence Arnold-Forster's Irish journal*, ed. T. W. Moody and others (1988) · *Wellesley index* · Althorp MSS, BL · *DNB* · private information (2004)

Archives NL Ire., memoranda on Ireland · TCD, corresp., speech notes, etc. | BL, corresp. with W. E. Gladstone, Add. MSS 44157–44160 · BL, letters to Sir A. H. Layard, Add. MSS 38983, 39101–39118, *passim* · BL, corresp. with Lord Ripon, Add. MSS 43536–43537 · Bodl. Oxf., letters to Lord Kimberley · Bodl. RH, corresp. with T. F. Buxton · Chatsworth House, Derbyshire, letters to Lord Hartington · PRO, corresp. with Lord Granville, PRO 30/29 · Trinity Cam., letters to Lord Houghton · U. Birm. L., corresp. with Joseph Chamberlain · University of Sheffield Library, letters to A. T. Mundella · W. Yorks. AS, Bradford, letters to W. S. Nicholas and other Bradford reformers

Likenesses H. T. Wells, oils, 1875, NPG [*see illus.*] · H. R. Hope Pinker, statue, 1889, Victoria Embankment Gardens, London · J. H. Thomas, bronze statue, exh. RA 1890, Forster Square, Bradford · Ape [C. Pellegrini], caricature, watercolour study, NPG; repro. in *VF* (6 March 1869), pl. 5 · Appleton, carte-de-visite, NPG · M. Bowness, carte-de-visite, NPG · Burton, etching, NPG · Elliott & Fry, two cartes-de-visite, NPG · H. Furniss, pen-and-ink sketch, NPG · Lock & Whitfield, woodburytype photograph, NPG; repro. in T. Cooper, *Men of mark: a gallery of contemporary portraits* (1878) · London Stereoscopic Co., carte-de-visite, NPG · prints, NPG

Wealth at death £81,574 2s. 11d.: resworn probate, Sept 1886, CGPLA Eng. & Wales

Forsyth, Alexander John (1768–1843), inventor, son of James Forsyth, minister of Belhelvie in Aberdeenshire, and Isabella, daughter of Walter Syme, minister of Tullynessle, was born on 28 December 1768 in his father's manse. He attended King's College, Aberdeen, from 1782 to 1786, and in 1790 was licensed as a preacher. After his father died suddenly on 1 December 1790, a presbytery meeting held in Aberdeen on 24 August 1791 chose Alexander John to be his successor. He devoted to chemistry and mechanics the time which he could spare from his duties as minister and one of his amusements was to make knives from ironstone. He was fond of wildfowl shooting, and as the birds often escaped by diving at the flash of his flintlocked fowling piece, he constructed a hood over the lock of his gun. He took an interest in inventions, especially those connected with steam and electricity, and, having contacted Dr Jenner, he inoculated his parishioners against smallpox. His ingenuity also found an outlet in developing an ignition system for firearms. The French were unsuccessfully attempting to substitute chloride of potash for nitrate in gunpowder, and Forsyth began experiments on the known detonating compounds. His first plan was to use the new powders, either on their own or mixed with gunpowder, as the propellant charge, but he soon found that these mixtures were so powerful, unstable, and irregular in their action that they were unsuitable for this purpose. He next tried using the fulminating powders as priming, and found that while they were readily ignited by a spark, the rate of burning was so fast that they would burn without igniting the gunpowder. However it was at this stage that he made an observation which was the very essence of his whole invention: he realized that fulminating powder acted more powerfully when ignited by percussion than by fire.

Using a short, heavy iron tube with a touch-hole of very small diameter and a flash pan, Forsyth found that fulminating powder placed in the pan and ignited by a stroke with a hammer would set fire to the main charge of gunpowder provided that this was held in place with a wad. Without the wad, there was a tendency for the powder to be thrown forward unignited. He then constructed a suitable lock, and during the season of 1805 shot with a fowling piece made on his plan. In the spring of 1806 he took it to London and showed it to some sporting friends. Lord Moira, then master-general of the ordnance, saw the gun and invited Forsyth to make some experiments at the Tower of London. Here he remained for some time, Moira providing for the discharge of his pastoral duties meanwhile, and after patient effort a lock that answered all requirements was produced. He had to undertake the dangerous task of preparing the detonating powder for himself, the workmen being ignorant and unwilling. The new principle was then applied to a carbine, and to a 3-pounder, which were approved by the master-general of the ordnance.

Moira proposed that Forsyth should receive as remuneration for his invention an amount equivalent to the value of the saving of gunpowder obtained by the use of the new lock, and it was agreed that this should be over a two-year period. Furthermore, he stipulated that Forsyth must not take out a patent as the benefit of the invention would be reserved for the government. It was at this stage on 30 March 1807 that Lord Chatham succeeded Lord Moira as master-general of the ordnance, and early in April Forsyth was told to stop his experiments. He was also asked to send in an account of his expenses, to deliver to the Tower property of the department in his possession, and to remove his own.

Before leaving London for Belhelvie, Forsyth obtained permission from Lord Chatham to patent his invention, the specification being drawn up by his friend, the engineer James Watt. He also went into partnership with his cousin James Brougham and in June 1808 the Forsyth Patent Gun Company was formed to make firearms with locks on Forsyth's principle. In October 1809 the name was changed to Forsyth & Co. Patent Gunmakers. From the time of his return home until 1819 Forsyth took the greatest interest in this work and sent many letters to James Brougham with information and advice.

Forsyth lived on quietly and cheerfully, apportioning his time, as before, among his various pursuits. Starting in 1834 he had correspondence with Lord Brougham concerning a reward from the government for his invention, and in 1841 he wrote to Sir George Murray, the master-general of the ordnance, stating his case and the fact that the percussion lock was in use in Queen Victoria's service. As a result, in April 1842 he received a gratuity of £200. Lord Brougham considered this inadequate and ultimately in June 1843 a sum of £1000 was approved, but Forsyth died on 11 June; he never knew of this award, and in December the money was divided among three of his relatives. JAMES BURNLEY, rev. D. H. L. BACK

Sources A. J. F. Reid and M. F. Reid, *The Reverend Alexander John Forsyth and his invention of the percussion lock: from information collected mostly by M. F. Reid* (1909) · M. F. Reid, Notes on the life of Rev. A. J. Forsyth, c.1877 · W. K. Neal and D. H. L. Back, *Forsyth & Co.: patent gunmakers* (1969) · *Fasti Scot.*, vol. 3/2 · *Aberdeen Daily Journal* (26 March 1902) · *Aberdeen Daily Journal* (12 July 1843) · *Aberdeen Herald and General Advertiser* (19 Oct 1839) · *Aberdeen Herald and General Advertiser* (18 July 1840) · Belhelvie kirk records, NA Scot., vols. 8, 9 (Ch 2/32) · *LondG* (8 Oct 1841) · *Supplement to the Votes and Proceedings* (1840) · Presbytery records, Aberdeen, NA Scot., vol. 11 · private information (2004)
Archives Cumbria AS, Kendal, MSS · PRO, WO 44/625, 47/2595; C 13 659/50, 729/15, 733/1, 733/5 | UCL, letters to James Brougham
Likenesses bronze tablet, U. Aberdeen, King's College; version, Tower of London · photograph, Gunmakers' Company, London

Wealth at death £572 10s. 5d. £1000 grant from government authorized and paid after death

Forsyth, Andrew Russell (1858–1942), mathematician, was born in Glasgow on 18 June 1858, the only child of John Forsyth, whose family had come from Campbeltown, and his wife, Christina Glen, of Paisley. When Forsyth was in his sixth year his mother died and in January 1868 his father, who was then engaged as a marine engineer in a Liverpool boat trading with the Mediterranean, entered him at Liverpool Collegiate Institution where he remained for eight years. In March 1875 his father died, and it was only by overcoming great financial difficulties that Forsyth was able in April 1877 to compete for the entrance scholarships at Trinity College, Cambridge, which he entered the following October. Although the Cambridge professors at the time were of unsurpassed eminence—Arthur Cayley in pure mathematics, G. G. Stokes and James Clerk Maxwell in mathematical physics, and J. C. Adams (the discoverer of Neptune) in celestial mechanics—they did not teach undergraduates, and Forsyth obtained most of his instruction from his coach, E. J. Routh. However, he had the audacity to attend a course by Cayley, where he was the only auditor under the standing of MA.

Forsyth graduated as senior wrangler and first Smith's prizeman in 1881, and in October of the same year won a Trinity fellowship with a dissertation on the theory of the double theta functions. This subject is almost incredibly rich in identities of all kinds, great numbers of which were already known: what Forsyth did was to show that practically all of them can be obtained by specialization from a single theorem of immense generality, which includes 4096 particular cases. On the basis of this theorem he developed the whole subject systematically. In October 1882 he left Cambridge to become the first professor of mathematics in the newly established University College at Liverpool; in January 1884 Trinity called him back as a college lecturer and at the end of 1885 appeared his well-known *Treatise on Differential Equations*. A number of original papers followed and in 1886, at the age of twenty-seven, he was elected a fellow of the Royal Society. By 1890 he had come to be recognized generally as the most brilliant pure mathematician in the British empire.

Forsyth had for some time realized, as no one else did, the most serious deficiency in the Cambridge school, namely its ignorance of what had been and was being done on the continent of Europe. He determined to reform this state of things, and with this aim published in 1893 his *Theory of Functions*, a book which exercised considerable influence on British mathematics. From the day of its publication, the face of Cambridge was changed: most of the pure mathematicians who took their degrees in the next twenty years became function-theorists. The subject of this book was complex function theory as it had been developed by Cauchy, Riemann, and Weierstrass. Forsyth was praised internationally for being one of the first to try to bring these three approaches together, but his way of doing this was also subject to criticism. His book was marred by numerous failures to establish analytic sense:

here as later in his life Forsyth's formal skill blinded him to deeper questions. Not long after publication of his *Theory of Functions*, which despite the criticisms levelled at it secured for Forsyth a place of outstanding honour in the record of British university studies, his own reputation as a mathematician began to decline. The fact was that, although he was the initiator of the new developments, he himself belonged essentially to the old order. His special gift was a wonderful dexterity and generalship in operations involving a great number of symbols. In discovering formulae expressive of relations and identities, or structural forms invariant under transformations, he was supreme, but he arrived at his results by a combination of manipulative skill and intuition rather than by conscious logical processes, and he was not fitted by nature to excel in the types of problem which then came into fashion, such as those concerning the range of validity of equalities involving limit-processes.

In 1895 Forsyth was elected to succeed Cayley in the Sadleirian chair of pure mathematics. As head of the Cambridge school he was conspicuously successful, and many of the wranglers of the period 1894–1910 became original workers of distinction. British mathematicians were already indebted to him for the first introduction of many theories which had originated on the continent, and the importation of novelties continued to occupy his attention. A great traveller and a good linguist, he loved to meet eminent foreigners and invite them to enjoy Trinity hospitality.

In 1910 Forsyth married Marion Amelia (*d.* 1920), daughter of Henry Pollock, master of the supreme court of justice, and the recently divorced wife of C. V. Boys. He then resigned his chair and his fellowship (although this was his for life) and left Cambridge for ever. In April 1913 he was appointed to a chair in the Imperial College of Science and Technology, South Kensington, at that time an institution of comparatively recent origin, where his organizing ability did great service. His wife died in September 1920, and he retired, sooner than he needed to, in 1923. Forsyth died on 2 June 1942 at Bailey's Hotel, South Kensington, where he was living, after a long and unhappy retirement. He was cremated at Golders Green four days later.

E. T. WHITTAKER, *rev.* J. J. GRAY

Sources E. T. Whittaker, *Obits. FRS*, 4 (1942–4), 209–27 • personal knowledge (1959) • J. J. Gray, 'Mathematics in Cambridge and beyond', *Cambridge minds*, ed. R. Mason (1994), 86–99 • *CGPLA Eng. & Wales* (1942)
Archives CUL, corresp. • ICL, papers • RS, papers | BL, corresp. with Macmillans, Add. MS 55197 • CUL, corresp. with Sir George Stokes, etc. • UCL, letters to Karl Pearson
Likenesses Barraud, photograph, *c.*1885, RS • Maull & Fox, photograph, 1892, RS • W. Stoneman, photographs, 1917–31, NPG • Brown, Barnes & Bell, photograph, RS • photograph, repro. in Whittaker, *Obits. FRS*, facing p. 209
Wealth at death £30,465 4*s.* 6*d.*: probate, 28 July 1942, *CGPLA Eng. & Wales*

Forsyth, David (1844–1934), headmaster and educationist, was born in October 1844 at Coatbridge, Glasgow, the son of David Forsyth, a master engineer, and his wife, Agnes

Laidlaw. He began his teaching career at the age of thirteen as a pupil teacher in Ayrshire. In 1862, at the age of eighteen, he won a first-class queen's scholarship to the Church of Scotland Training College in Glasgow. He entered the University of Glasgow in 1864 and gained his MA degree in 1870, the year in which, on 5 July at Cambridge Street, Glasgow, he married Christina Cairns (1845–1922) of Darlington, daughter of Andrew Cairns, a foreman cabinet-maker, and his wife, Mary Ann Brand. By this time he had already served for one year as headmaster of Green Street School, one of the largest elementary schools in the east end of Glasgow.

In 1875 Forsyth was appointed to a lectureship at the Church of Scotland Training College, having spent the previous three years as headmaster of its practising school. During his time at the college he developed a specialist interest in geology; he gained a BSc degree at the University of Glasgow in 1884 and became a DSc by examination in the same subject in 1890. He also travelled extensively throughout Scotland, lecturing on a variety of subjects, and wrote a book on the teaching of perspective (1883). He later edited a volume of Shakespeare's *Julius Caesar* (1899), and provided an introduction to a successful chemistry textbook (1899) written by one of his staff.

In 1889 Forsyth was appointed headmaster of the higher grade school in Leeds. Here, as in most major towns and cities, the expenditure of ratepayers' money by the school board on higher grade education, which was secondary in all but name, was a major political issue. Strongly opposed to the class system that shaped secondary education in England, Forsyth sought to promote higher grade (post-elementary) education as the English equivalent of the practice, more common in Scotland, of educating in the parochial schools pupils drawn from very different classes within society. He played a major role in establishing an Association of Headmasters of Higher Grade and Organized Science Schools and, as its president, appeared before the royal commission on secondary education in 1894. He saw the future of higher grade schools in making the great mass of the people aware that they offered, at a very moderate cost, an education which would open the doors of the professions and the universities to children from poorer, as well as from more prosperous, families. Under his leadership the Leeds higher grade school, which had opened in temporary premises in 1885 with over 500 pupils, developed to become by the end of the century an institution with a distinguished academic record and a recognizable tradition that attracted favourable national and international attention.

In the closing decades of the nineteenth century public funds for education were available—subject to inspection, success in examinations, or both—for public elementary education and for courses and classes which met the very different requirements of the Department of Science and Art. These funding arrangements were complex and lacked co-ordination but Forsyth exploited them to the full to construct a senior-school curriculum at the Leeds Central higher grade school that included English, Latin, mathematics, French, German, science, geography, history, art, commercial subjects, and drawing. Pupils from the school were outstandingly successful in a range of public examinations, securing prizes for their work in the examinations set by the Department of Science and Art and gaining a stream of passes in the important matriculation examination of the University of London. In addition, between 1894 and 1903, they won over £8000 in scholarships and bursaries, and sixty-five former pupils gained university degrees.

Equally committed to the democratic control of the governance of schooling, Forsyth advocated a national system of directly elected school boards responsible for the provision of education on behalf of the community. Although a different model of educational governance was embodied in the Education Act of 1902, his vision of the role of higher grade schools had a pioneering quality, and their work can be seen both as a response to the political and educational aspirations of a rapidly growing organized labour movement and as an important element in the emergence of a lower middle class within late-nineteenth-century society. If higher grade schools necessarily fell somewhat short of accommodating all classes within society, there is no doubt that they provided an advanced academic education for many children belonging to a class that had hitherto had no such opportunity. Forsyth's own school was particularly important in educating the sons of Jewish immigrants who had settled in Leeds from about 1880 onwards; children from Jewish homes accounted for about 40 per cent of the boys in the senior classes at the school by the end of the First World War.

A firm disciplinarian deeply committed to the academic and professional improvement of his teaching staff, Forsyth was a familiar figure in a frock coat and silk hat, walking each day to school with short brisk steps. In the re-organization of post-elementary education that followed the legislation of 1902, his school became the Leeds Central high school, under the control of the newly created Leeds local education authority. He seized the opportunity provided by the events of 1902, and the subsequent establishment of an adjacent secondary school for girls, to develop the Central high school into a highly successful boys' grammar school, with its own Latin motto, and organized into houses that competed academically and on the sports field. The school continued to recruit pupils, on the basis of a scholarship examination, on an unusually wide social and geographical basis.

Forsyth remained headmaster until 1918, when he finally retired at the age of seventy-four. In 1915, accepting the award of an honorary degree of LLD from the University of Leeds, he expressed his gratitude that the university had acknowledged 'his type of school' and the work he had done to promote the cause of popular higher education and the 'cultivation of a University spirit among the democracy' (Forsyth to M. E. Sadler, 20 March 1915, University of Leeds archive, microfilm 107, fol. 116). He was to do more, campaigning vigorously throughout the 1920s for funds for the institution which had honoured him. He died on 6 August 1934, two months short of his

ninetieth birthday, at the home of his son, Dr J. A. Cairns Forsyth, in Fairholm, Alloway, Ayrshire. He was buried at Lawnswood cemetery, Leeds.   EDGAR W. JENKINS

Sources *David Forsyth: in memoriam* (1934) · E. W. Jenkins, *A magnificent pile: a centenary history of the Leeds Central high school* (1985), chap. 2 · 'Royal commission on secondary education: minutes of evidence', *Parl. papers* (1895), 45.161ff., C. 7862-II · G. McCulloch, 'David Forsyth and the Leeds Central higher grade school', *Yorkshire studies in education*, ed. K. Fenwick (1983), 15–19 · m. cert. · d. cert.

Likenesses oils, 1919, City of Leeds School, Leeds, West Yorkshire

Wealth at death £12,205 6s. 10d.: probate, 15 Sept 1934, *CGPLA Eng. & Wales*

Forsyth, Sir (Thomas) Douglas (1827–1886), administrator in India, was born at Birkenhead on 7 October 1827, the tenth child of Thomas Forsyth, a Liverpool merchant of Scottish descent, and his wife, Jane Campbell, daughter of John Hamilton. Educated at Sherborne and Rugby schools, in 1846 he entered East India College, Haileybury, to take up a writership in the Bengal civil service. Having topped the class for the Bengal list, Forsyth arrived in Calcutta in March 1848 and was sent up-country as an assistant to the magistrate of Saharanpur. In March 1849, Henry Lawrence selected him for duty at Pakpattan in the Punjab; barely five months later, however, ill health forced a retreat to the hills, whereupon Lord Dalhousie appointed him assistant commissioner at Simla. On 23 February 1850 Forsyth married Mary Alice, elder daughter of Thomas Hall Plumer, of Canons Park, Edgware, to whom he had become engaged before leaving England. In 1851 he was appointed assistant commissioner to the hill district of Kangra.

At the outbreak of the uprising in May 1857, Forsyth, as deputy commissioner of Ambala, promptly secured grain and carriage for the Delhi relief force. Proud of his ability to nip rebellion in the bud, he recounted in his autobiography that he was one of the first officers to convict and execute a rebel—a Sikh who had advised the townspeople of Rupar not to pay their revenue. After the relief of Delhi, Forsyth was appointed one of the special commissioners to hunt down rebels—a job he relished. In May 1860 he was created CB for his mutiny services.

In February 1860 Forsyth was posted to Lahore as officiating commissioner, and was confirmed in the post in March 1861. In December 1865 he was transferred to Jullundur, which included his old district of Kangra. Keen to further trading contracts with central Asia, he travelled to Leh, the capital of Ladakh, in 1867 to persuade the local Kashmiri officials to lift restrictions on trade between eastern Turkestan and the Punjab, and on his return instituted an annual fair at Palampur to which he invited traders from Turkestan.

In 1869, with Lord Mayo's blessing, Forsyth undertook a mission from London to St Petersburg and won from the Russians an agreement on the extent of the amir of Kabul's territories. In the summer of 1870 he embarked on a more arduous mission to Yarkand in Turkestan, 2000 miles distant from Lahore, to gauge the friendliness of the amir, Yakub Beg, towards the British. Yakub Beg, however, was absent throughout Forsyth's visit, causing him considerable diplomatic embarrassment and irritation.

In February 1872, shortly after Forsyth had been appointed commissioner of Ambala, a small millenarian sect of reformist Sikhs called the Kukas murdered several butchers in the neighbouring princely state of Maler Kotla. Forsyth instructed the junior officer on the spot, Lambert Cowan, not to proceed with any trials or executions until he got there, but upon arriving found that Cowan had already blown forty-nine Kukas from cannons—a form of punishment much favoured in the Indian mutiny but long since regarded by the British as an oriental barbarity. Reasoning that the rulers must not appear divided before the natives, Forsyth not only approved Cowan's actions, but proceeded to try sixteen remaining Kukas and have them also blown from guns. Forsyth's understanding of British-Indian relations had barely advanced beyond 1857 and he failed to comprehend the abhorrence with which the government of India would greet his mode of execution. Cowan's dismissal from the service he thought fair, but he was devastated to find himself demoted to the commissionership of Fyzabad in Oudh.

In December 1872 the incoming viceroy, Lord Northbrook, salvaged Forsyth's career by appointing him plenipotentiary to Yarkand. This second expedition, begun in the summer of 1873, established the amir's commercial friendliness towards the British and amassed useful geographical, botanical, and ethnological information on the region. On his return in 1874 Forsyth was made KCSI and was subsequently elected a fellow of the Royal Geographical Society. During the next two years he was engaged intermittently in discussions concerning the Nepal–Oudh border and in negotiations with Burma on the independence of the Karenni States. In 1876 he returned to England and resigned from the civil service.

In 1878, after a flirtation with tory politics, Forsyth joined the Sind and Punjab railway board and in the following year became chairman of the Great Indian Peninsula Railway Company, charged with constructing a harbour at Marmagao in Portuguese India and a railway to connect it with the southern Maratha and Deccan countries. He died on 17 December 1886, after a short illness, at Elsing Lodge, Grange Road, Eastbourne, and was buried in the town. He was survived by his wife and three daughters, who erected a tablet in his memory in the Palampur church, Kangra district. In 1887 his eldest daughter, Ethel Mary, published a volume of his reminiscences and travel writings.   KATHERINE PRIOR

Sources *Autobiography and reminiscences of Sir Douglas Forsyth*, ed. E. Forsyth (1887) · G. R. Elsmie, *Thirty-five years in the Punjab, 1858–1893* (1908) · Fauja Singh Bajwa, *Kuka movement: an important phase in Punjab's role in India's struggle for freedom* (1965) · BL OIOC, Hailey-bury MSS · *The Times* (21 Dec 1886), 7 · G. W. de Rhé-Philipe, ed., *Inscriptions on Christian tombs or monuments in the Punjab*, 2 (1912) · B. P. Pick, *The Sherborne register, 1550–1950*, 4th edn (1950) · *CGPLA Eng. & Wales* (1887)
Archives Balliol Oxf., corresp. with Sir Robert Morier · BL OIOC, Montgomery MSS · BL OIOC, Northbrook MSS · CUL, corresp. with Lord Mayo

Likenesses group portrait, photograph, *c.*1857, BL OIOC · J. Ewing, photograph, 1884, repro. in Elsmie, *Thirty-five years* · G. J. Stodart, engraving (after photograph by J. Ewing), repro. in Forsyth, ed., *Autobiography and reminiscences*
Wealth at death £18,154 1s. 7d.: probate, 25 Jan 1887, *CGPLA Eng. & Wales*

Forsyth, James (1838–1871), administrator and traveller in India, entered the civil service after receiving a university education in England and taking the degree of MA. He went to India as assistant conservator and acting conservator of forests. In a short time he was appointed settlement officer and deputy commissioner of Nimar, and served with distinction under Sir Richard Temple, chief commissioner of the Central Provinces. Forsyth acquired a wide reputation as a hunter and in 1862 published a comprehensive treatise entitled *The Sporting Rifle and its Projectiles*. Forsyth, who was attached to the Bengal staff corps, made a complete tour of the Central Provinces of India in 1862–4, penetrating to Amarkantak, near the sources of the Narbada, the Mahanadi, and the Son. He thence travelled across the plain of Chhattisgarh to the *sál* (*Shorea robusta*) forests in the far east.

Forsyth returned to England in 1870, but died at 38 Manchester Street, Manchester Square, London, on 1 May 1871 leaving his book *The Highlands of Central India* to be published posthumously in November that year. Originally intended as a guide and general description, its value in the late twentieth century lies in its description of forests, particularly their extent, species diversity, and management practice, as the contribution of the Indian forest service to early conservation is more fully appreciated.

G. B. SMITH, *rev.* ELIZABETH BAIGENT

Sources review of *The highlands of central India: notes on their forests and wild tribes, natural history, and sports* by Capt. J. Forsyth, *The Athenaeum* (25 Nov 1871), 681–2 · Boase, *Mod. Eng. biog.* · R. H. Grove, *Green imperialism: colonial expansion, tropical island Edens, and the origins of environmentalism, 1600–1860* (1995) · E. P. Stebbing, *The forests of India*, 4 vols. (1922–62)

Forsyth, Joseph (1763–1815), writer on Italy, born at Elgin, Scotland, on 18 February 1763, was the son of Alexander Forsyth, merchant in Elgin and a friend of Isaac Watts, and his second wife, Ann Harrold, daughter of a farmer who fought for Prince Charles at Culloden, was taken prisoner, and died on board ship while being carried for trial to England. From Elgin grammar school Forsyth went at the age of twelve to King's College, Aberdeen, whence he graduated MA in 1779. Too diffident to enter the church as his parents had hoped, he went to London and became assistant master at an academy at Newington Butts; he soon bought the establishment and carried it on successfully for thirteen years until failing health led him to give it up and return to Elgin. He now had the leisure and the means to realize his dream of visiting Italy. Just a few days after learning of the peace of Amiens he set off, to spend the next eighteen months in Italian cities, where he had access to literary circles. He was well read in Italian history, literature, and architecture and had a keen eye.

Forsyth was at Turin on his way home when war was

renewed, and on 25 May 1803 he was arrested and imprisoned at Nîmes. Caught trying to escape, he was marched in midwinter 600 miles to Fort de Bitché, in north-east France, where his confinement was at first strict. It was, however, gradually relaxed; after two years he was moved to Verdun, where he remained for five years. In 1811 he was briefly permitted to reside in Paris but four months later had to return to detention, this time at Valenciennes. He spent his time studying Italian literature and art, and, hoping to secure his release by appealing to Napoleon as a patron of the arts, he wrote *Remarks on Antiquities, Arts, and Letters, during an Excursion in Italy* (1813). The book failed in its practical objective and he was not freed until the allies entered Paris in March 1814. After a year in London Forsyth returned to Elgin, intending to settle there; but, his health weakened by thirteen years of exile, he died on 20 September 1815, and was buried in his parents' tomb in Elgin Cathedral churchyard. His book went to several editions, one (1820) issued at Geneva. Although he apparently regretted its publication, it was widely regarded as one of the better written and more useful books on Italy at the time.

JAMES COOPER, rev. ELIZABETH BAIGENT

Sources I. Forsyth, memoir, in J. Forsyth, *Remarks on antiquities, arts, and letters*, 2nd edn (1816) · private information (1888)
Archives Moray District RO, papers, incl. some of his brother Isaac
Likenesses vignette, repro. in Forsyth, *Remarks*, 4th edn (1835), title-page

Forsyth, Peter Taylor (1848–1921), Congregational minister, was born on 12 May 1848 at 100 Chapel Street, Aberdeen, the eldest child in the family of two sons and three daughters of Isaac Forsyth, from the Cabrach, a bookseller and later postman, and a deacon at the Blackfriars Street Congregational Church, Aberdeen, and his wife, Elspet McPherson, a crofter's daughter from Kingussie, Inverness-shire. Forsyth was educated from 1859 at Aberdeen grammar school, and entered Aberdeen University in 1864. After graduating MA with first-class honours in classical literature in 1869, he spent one year as a private tutor, and then from 1871 to 1872 was an assistant to Professor Black in the department of humanities at King's College, Aberdeen.

Following a period of study in Göttingen in 1872 under Albrecht Ritschl, Forsyth started theological studies in September 1872 at Hackney Theological College, Hampstead, but did not complete the course, leaving in 1874. The writings of F. D. Maurice were an early influence on him. In London he became a member of the congregation of James Baldwin Brown, a liberal Congregational minister in Brixton, and in 1876 he was ordained minister at the Congregational church in Shipley, Yorkshire. On 4 April 1877 he married Maria Hester (Minna), *née* Magness (1850/51–1894). They had one daughter. After his wife's death, he married on 25 September 1897 Emily Bertha, *née* Ison (*b.* 1866/7), of Oxford. For twenty-five years Forsyth held a series of appointments as minister: St Thomas's Square, Hackney (1880–85); Cheetham Hill Congregational Church, Manchester (1885–8); Clarendon Park, Leicester (1888–94); and Emmanuel Church, Cambridge (1894–1901).

During this period Forsyth began to publish, starting with *Pulpit Parables for Young Hearers* in 1886. *Religion in Recent Art* appeared in 1889, based on lectures on Pre-Raphaelite paintings and Richard Wagner's *Parsifal*. His early leanings towards socialism were evident in articles he wrote under a pseudonym from 1885 to 1889 for the *Manchester Examiner*.

In 1889 Forsyth was one of the delegates to the International Congregational Council in Boston, and he made several further trips to North America, including one in 1907 to give the Lyman Beecher lectures at Yale University. In 1901 he became principal of Hackney College, Hampstead, and in 1905 he was elected chairman of the Congregational Union of England and Wales. In 1911 he was appointed dean of the faculty of theology at London University. Aberdeen University awarded him an honorary DD in 1895. Forsyth was very distressed at the outbreak of the First World War, for he loved Germany and German literature, and had been greatly influenced by German theologians such as Jakob Boehme; but he was not a pacifist, and in *The Justification of God* (1916) he supported the war.

Forsyth came to be regarded as the greatest Congregational theologian of his day. Reacting against his early liberalism, he adopted views that some have seen as anticipating those of Karl Barth and Emil Brunner. While he was an enthusiastic supporter of biblical criticism, he denounced much contemporary theology as no more than a shallow humanitarianism: 'The liberal theology finds Christ's centre of gravity in what he has in common with us; a positive theology in that wherein he differs'. This issue was what divided him from R. J. Campbell, then minister of the City Temple in London, during the sustained New Theology controversy of 1907–10. Deeply influenced by the philosophical idealism of the day, Campbell claimed that deity and humanity were fundamentally one. Forsyth contended that to reduce the power of the gospel to a merely 'human' Jesus, without the cross as the heart of the Christian message, would be fatal. The heart of Forsyth's theology was that the holiness of God needed to deal drastically with the sin of humanity; his sermon on the Holy Father (first published in the *Christian World Pulpit* in 1896) marked a focal point in his life. In *The Person and Place of Jesus Christ* (1909), a book often regarded as his best, he found the two-nature doctrine of Christ deficient, inclining to the kenotic theory, which he modified by thinking of a 'pleroma' following the resurrection and exaltation of Jesus.

Forsyth's writing is that of a passionate preacher, but his epigrammatic style is not to everyone's taste. It is also true that to wrestle with his thought demands a rethinking of the gospel: that his students found him so witty and stimulating a teacher is understandable. Forsyth died on 11 November 1921 at his home at Hackney College, Finchley Road, Hampstead, survived by his wife.

JOHN HUXTABLE, rev.

Sources H. Escott, *P. T. Forsyth and the cure of souls: an appraisement and anthology of his practical writings* (1970) • W. L. Bradley, *P. T. Forsyth: the man and his work* (1952) • T. Hart, ed., *Justice the true and only mercy: essays on the life and theology of Peter Taylor Forsyth* (1995) • A. Peel, *The Congregational two hundred* (1948), 241–2 • J. Forsyth Andrews, memoir, in P. T. Forsyth, *The work of Christ*, 2nd edn (1938), vii–xxviii • H. Escott, *A history of Scottish Congregationalism* (1960) • G. O. Griffith, *The theology of P. T. Forsyth* (1948) • private information (1993) • m. certs.
Likenesses portrait, repro. in A. Peel, *These hundred years: a history of the congregational union of England and Wales, 1831–1931* (1931), facing p. 288
Wealth at death £4738 17s. 11d.: probate, 21 March 1922, *CGPLA Eng. & Wales*

Forsyth, Robert (1766–1845), writer, was born on 18 January 1766 in Biggar, Lanarkshire, the only son of Robert Forsyth, shoemaker, and his wife, Marion, *née* Pairman. His parents were poor but they gave him a good education with a view to making him a minister. When he was fourteen he entered Glasgow College; he says of himself that he 'had slow talents, but great fits of application' (Forsyth, xii). After the usual course of study he obtained licence as a preacher of the Church of Scotland. As he spoke without notes and was somewhat vehement and rhetorical in his style he gained considerable popularity but, having no influence, he grew tired of waiting for a parish.

Forsyth then turned his attention to the law; he studied Roman law on his own and attended civil law classes, where he met Sir Walter Scott, but the fact that he was a preacher and from a poor family prevented him from being admitted to the bar. Refused by the Faculty of Advocates he petitioned the court of session for redress; there were various delays and Forsyth was forced to resign his office of preacher but the faculty eventually gave way, and in 1792 he was admitted an advocate. Disappointment again awaited him. He had joined the reformist Society of Friends of the People and was looked on with suspicion as a revolutionary; this marred his prospects.

Forsyth then turned to literature and managed to make a living by writing for booksellers. In 1802–3 he contributed articles to the *Encyclopaedia Britannica*, including 'Agriculture', 'Asia', and 'Britain'. He also wrote other pieces and re-published some of these in *Principles and Practice of Agriculture* (2 vols., 1804). Eventually he obtained a successful practice at the bar, where he was noted for his dogged industry, blunt honesty, and dry humour. However, he found time to collect and edit some essays he had written when he was a student, which appeared as *Principles of Moral Science* in 1805. In 1806 he married Jacobina, daughter of Dr John Carson, from Philadelphia, USA. But the work by which he was best-known is *The Beauties of Scotland* (5 vols., 1805–8), which was admired not only for its valuable information but for its many engravings of towns and places of interest.

Forsyth, who had always adhered loyally to his church, published in 1843 *Remarks on the Church of Scotland*. This brought him under the lash of Hugh Miller, then editor of *The Witness*, who not only reviewed the pamphlet (14 January 1843) with merciless severity but also recalled some of Forsyth's speculations in philosophy, which he covered with ridicule and scorn. It is curious that in these speculations Forsyth seems to have had an inkling of opinions largely current half a century later: 'whatever has no tendency to improvement will gradually pass away and disappear for ever'. There Forsyth hinted at the 'survival of the fittest' (*Remarks on the Church of Scotland*) and interpreted it in a religious context. Until his death, in Edinburgh on 30 September 1845, he continued to write sermons and articles on religious questions.

WILLIAM FORSYTH, rev. S. R. J. BAUDRY

Sources R. Forsyth, *A memoir of the author* (1846) • F. J. Grant, ed., *The Faculty of Advocates in Scotland, 1532–1943*, Scottish RS, 145 (1944) • bap. reg. Scot.

Forsyth, William (1722–1800), merchant, was born at Cromarty, the eldest of three sons and two daughters of James Forsyth (*d.* 1739), formerly a builder from Morayshire, who had recently married Katherine Morrison and set up as a shopkeeper in the prosperous herring port of Cromarty. William attended the local school under the tutelage of David Macculloch, whose curriculum included the classics, besides the usual subjects. At sixteen he left for London, where it is thought he worked in a counting-house, but his father died the following year and he was recalled to take over his father's business and support his mother and her four young children.

The herring fishery had by this time declined, and with it Cromarty's former prosperity. Forsyth realized, however, that the town had good access to the surrounding settlements via the Dornoch, Cromarty, and Moray firths, and by road, making it a good base for general trading. He therefore set out to supply the entire district with its needs, an undertaking which he carried out successfully for many years. He bought a cargo boat to serve the firths and hired a large sloop to trade with the north-east ports and across the North Sea to the Netherlands, whence he imported Swedish iron, Norwegian tar and spars, and Dutch delftware, glass, and tiles. The uprising of 1745 disrupted his trade and on one occasion his sloop was seized and plundered, but on the whole, despite his known support of the government side, he suffered little from the Jacobite troops.

Local industry flourished on the back of Forsyth's own prosperity. On the suggestion of a former schoolfellow, a Dr Hossack, he introduced the process of kelp burning, the ash being sold for soap and glass making. About 1749 he became the first agent in the north of Scotland for the British Linen Company, established in 1746. Through this agency Baltic flax was supplied to local people for spinning and weaving in their own homes, and their products were bought at an agreed price. He established his brothers in business, one in Dingwall in the highlands, the other in Newcastle. When he could afford his own sloops, they were built locally. He was the first to import coal, about 1770, as a fuel to relieve the regional shortage of peat and wood.

In 1752 Forsyth married Margaret Russell of Earlsmill, but she died within the year, in childbirth. It was eleven years before he remarried, his second wife being Elizabeth (d. 1808), daughter of the Revd Patrick Grant of Nigg, Ross-shire; they raised nine children. Forsyth held an honoured place in his community, being popularly referred to as 'the maister'. A generous benefactor to Cromarty, he was seen as having largely restored its prosperity, and as always willing to help its young men to make their way in the world. When hereditary justices were replaced he became the sole magistrate; in his thirty years' tenure no appeal was made against any of his decisions. He was an elder of the kirk for forty years. In his later years he became interested in agriculture. He bought a farm and built a fine house and garden. In old age his sight failed and he became weak in body. He died at home in Cromarty on 30 January 1800 and was buried at Cromarty. His wife, son, and two daughters survived him. Miller's *Memoir* (1839) depicts an energetic, far-sighted, caring, and pious man, his conversation solid rather than sparkling, wise rather than witty, but one who brought real prosperity to his community. ANITA McCONNELL

Sources H. Miller, *Memoir of William Forsyth Esq.: a Scotch merchant of the 18th century* (1839) · IGI

Forsyth, William (*bap.* 1737, *d.* 1804), horticulturist, the son of John Forsyth, was born at Old Meldrum, Aberdeenshire, and baptized there on 25 March 1737. He probably served his apprenticeship in the gardens of Lord Aberdeen at Haddo House, before going to London to work under Philip Miller at the Chelsea Physic Garden. In 1763, on Miller's recommendation, he was appointed head gardener to the duke of Northumberland at Syon House, Brentford, returning to Chelsea to succeed Miller in 1771. He was active in reorganizing and restocking the Chelsea garden.

In 1784 Forsyth was appointed superintendent of the royal gardens of St James and Kensington. Here his interest in the improvement of diseased and decayed fruit trees led him to develop and promote his own 'plaister', a paste whose application would, he asserted, cause new wood to grow and bind to the old. His invention came to the notice of those charged with procurement of sound wood, particularly oak, for naval use, and after preliminary investigation he was paid £1500 to reveal the composition of this mixture. A second payment, to follow successful trials, was, however, never made. In 1791 Forsyth published *Observations on the Diseases, Defects, and Injuries of Fruit and Forest Trees*, and in 1802 his *Treatise on the Culture and Management of Fruit Trees*, which reached a seventh edition in 1824.

A modest and unaffected man with many friends, Forsyth was a significant figure in horticultural affairs. He was a fellow of the Linnean Society and of the Society of Antiquaries. He played an important part in bringing about the establishment of the Horticultural Society in 1804. The attack by Thomas Knight in 1802 on Forsyth's claims for his paste, which Knight asserted was neither a new invention nor an effective one, led to a long and bitter debate which severely damaged Forsyth's reputation. The

date of his marriage to Sarah, who died on 21 November 1799, aged sixty-two, is not known. Forsyth died on 25 July 1804 at his official residence at Kensington.

B. D. JACKSON, *rev.* RUTH STUNGO

Sources Desmond, *Botanists*, rev. edn, 256–7 · A. Simmonds, *A horticultural who was who* (1948), 52–62 · G. Meynell, 'The personal issue underlying T. A. Knight's controversy with William Forsyth', *Journal of the Society of the Bibliography of Natural History*, 9 (1978–80), 281–7 · [A. Simmonds], 'The founders: William Forsyth, 1737–1804', *Journal of the Royal Horticultural Society*, 66 (1941), 319–24 · *Cottage Gardener*, 4 (1850), 233 · H. Field, *Memoirs of the botanic garden at Chelsea belonging to the Society of Apothecaries of London*, rev. R. H. Semple (1878), 112–13 · *GM*, 1st ser., 74 (1804), 787 · *GM*, 1st ser., 75 (1805), 431 [incorrectly numbered 341] · 'Early writers on English gardening, no. 17', *Journal of Horticulture, Cottage Gardener and Country Gentleman*, 31 (1876), 147 · A. Coats, 'The duke's gardeners', *Gardeners' Chronicle*, 3rd ser., 163 (1968), 15–16 · *Cottage Gardener*, 7–9 (1852–3) · *GM*, 1st ser., 69 (1799), 1005 · bap. reg. Scot.

Archives RBG Kew, corresp. and papers · RCS Eng., notes
Likenesses Freeman, stipple, NPG

Forsyth, William (1812–1899), writer and politician, was born at Greenock on 25 October 1812, the eldest son of Thomas Forsyth of Birkenhead and his wife, Jane Campbell, of Hamilton. After education at Sherborne School he entered Trinity College, Cambridge, as a pensioner, on 9 December 1829. He was admitted scholar on 4 May 1832, minor fellow on 2 October 1835, and major fellow on 4 July 1837. He took his BA degree in 1834, being third senior optime, third in the first class of the classical tripos, and second chancellor's medallist; he proceeded MA in 1837. He became a student at the Inner Temple on 10 April 1834, was called to the bar on 22 November 1839, and went the midland circuit, where he had considerable success as an advocate. In 1841 he published his first legal treatise, *On the Law of Composition with Creditors*. This was succeeded by several other treatises, among which a careful and trustworthy study, *The History of Trial by Jury* (1852), was quoted with high commendation in Lieber's *Civil Liberty and Self-Government* (1856) and, many years later, by *Cases and Opinions on Constitutional Law … with Notes* (1869).

On 23 February 1843 Forsyth married Mary (d. 1864), youngest daughter of George Lyall MP of Findon, Surrey. In 1849 he dedicated to Lord Denman his scholarly and original sketch of the office and functions of a fictitious advocate, entitled *Hortensius*, a historical survey of the bar from earliest times, of which a second edition was called for in 1874. The book laid the foundation of a friendship with Lord Brougham, who came to call Forsyth Hortensius; sections of their correspondence were privately printed by Forsyth in 1872. *Hortensius* was followed by the *History of the captivity of Napoleon at St Helena, from the letters and journals of the late Sir Hudson Lowe* (1853; French translation, 1855), in which Forsyth concludes that 'by mere force of facts he had proved that neither the British government nor Lowe were in fault as regards the treatment of Napoleon at St Helena' (p. x). Forsyth became a senior barrister on 6 July 1857 and a bencher of the Inner Temple on 24 November of the same year.

In 1859 Forsyth was appointed standing counsel to the

secretary of state for India, and this appointment he held until 1872, when he was made treasurer of his inn at the Inner Temple. He was also a member of the Council of Legal Education from 1860. But there was in fact much more of the student and the fellow of Trinity about Forsyth than of the politician or the parliamentary hand; he was commissary of Cambridge University (in 1868) and was made an LLD by the University of Edinburgh in 1871. He appeared as a lecturer on the platforms of many literary institutions in England, and several of his lectures were printed. His claims as a writer were recognized not only by his appointment as editor of the *Annual Register* (1842–68) but by his being urged repeatedly to write both for the *Edinburgh Review* and the *Quarterly Review*. To the former he contributed essays on Brougham and on criminal procedure, and to the latter 'The kingdom of Italy' (1861) and a cordial review of Foss's *Judges of England* (1866), while to *Fraser's* he sent his interesting 'Literary style'. Sixteen of his articles were reprinted in *Essays Critical and Narrative* (1874). Reverting to his earlier course of study, he dedicated to Brougham in 1863 his *Life of Marcus Tullius Cicero* (1867), a conscientious attempt to steer between eulogy and unforgiving erudition.

Forsyth's interest in politics led him to stand for parliament, and he was elected for the borough of Cambridge for the Conservative Party in July 1865, but he was unseated on the ground that the office of standing counsel was one of profit under the crown and disqualified him from sitting in parliament. After he had relinquished this office he was an unsuccessful candidate for Bath in 1873, but he was elected for Marylebone at the general election of 1874 and held the seat until 1880. Though a clear and forcible speaker, he spoke infrequently in the house and the high expectations formed of him when he first entered parliament came to nothing. Men of far less knowledge and experience, but with greater command over the house, easily passed him in the race. Following the death of his wife, Forsyth married, second, on 3 July 1866, Georgiana Charlotte, daughter of Thomas Hall Plumer and granddaughter of Sir Thomas Plumer.

Meanwhile the results of another branch of Forsyth's studies appeared in 1871, when he published *Novels and Novelists of the Eighteenth Century*, illustrating the manners and morals of the period. The following year saw the publication of his dramatic essay 'Hannibal in Italy', a historical drama in verse, and of his *History of Ancient Manuscripts*, being the substance of a lecture given before the benchers of the Inner Temple. In 1876 he published some travel papers under the title *The Slavonic Provinces South of the Danube*.

Forsyth, who spent several months each year in foreign travel, took a philanthropic interest in prison life at home and abroad, visiting the prisons of France, Italy, Russia, the United States, and Turkey. In 1873 he made an inspection of prison life at Portland and gave the results of his investigations in an article in *Good Words* (October 1873). He died at his home, 61 Rutland Gate, London, on 26 December 1899 and was survived by his wife. At the great

age of eighty-seven he 'had outlived not only nearly all his contemporaries but the reputation that his talent and industry had built up' (*The Times*).

THOMAS SECCOMBE, rev. S. R. J. BAUDRY

Sources Venn, *Alum. Cant.* • J. Foster, *Men-at-the-bar: a biographical hand-list of the members of the various inns of court*, 2nd edn (1885) • *The Times* (27 Dec 1899) • *Daily News* (27 Dec 1899) • *Annual Register* (1899), 186 • Allibone, *Dict.* • H. R. Luard, ed., *Graduati Cantabrigienses*, 7th edn (1884) • *Selections from the correspondence of … Macvey Napier*, ed. M. Napier (1879) • S. Smiles, *A publisher and his friends: memoir and correspondence of the late John Murray*, 2 vols. (1891) • *CGPLA Eng. & Wales* (1900)
Likenesses Faustin, chromolithograph caricature, NPG • wood-engraving, NPG; repro. in *ILN* (6 March 1875)
Wealth at death £18,667 0s. 8d.: probate, 26 Jan 1900, *CGPLA Eng. & Wales*

Forsyth, William (1818–1879), poet and journalist, son of Morris Forsyth and Jane Brands, was born at Turriff, Aberdeenshire, on 24 October 1818. He was educated at Fordyce Academy and the universities of Aberdeen and Edinburgh. For some years he studied medicine, becoming assistant to a country doctor and twice acting as surgeon on a Greenland whaling ship, but he never took a medical degree, and ultimately abandoned medicine for literature. In 1854 he married Eliza Duff Fyfe.

In 1842 Forsyth became sub-editor of the *Inverness Courier*, edited by Dr Robert Carruthers (1799–1878), whom he assisted in the preparation of *Chambers's Cyclopaedia of English Literature* (1843–4). In 1843 he became sub-editor of the *Aberdeen Herald*, to which he contributed in prose and verse for several years. In 1848 he joined the staff of the *Aberdeen Journal*, one of the oldest and most influential of Scottish newspapers; he was eventually appointed editor, an office which he held for about thirty years.

Politically Forsyth was a reformist, interested in a wide range of measures. During the American Civil War he stood almost alone among Scottish journalists in advocating the cause of the North. On church questions his articles were much respected, and Bishop Charles Wordsworth (1806–1892) of St Andrews and Alexander Ewing (1814–1873), bishop of Argyll, corresponded with him privately. Forsyth also wrote two pamphlets on Scottish church matters, entitled *A Letter on Lay Patronage in the Church of Scotland* (1867) and *The Day of Open Questions* (1868). In the first of these he discussed the issue which had provoked the Disruption of 1843; the pamphlet may have paved the way for the Act for the Abolition of Church Patronage of 1874.

Forsyth rendered valuable services to Aberdeen, where, at Bonnymuir, Maryville, Friendville, Gordondale, and Richmondhill, his successive homes, he spent more than thirty years. The establishment of the Association for Improving the Condition of the Poor was mainly due to him, and he not only served as an active member of the managing committee but for six years gratuitously performed the duties of secretary. In 1877 he read a paper to the Social Science Congress entitled 'The province and work of voluntary charitable agencies in the management of the poor', which was based on his own experience. Forsyth was elected a member of the first Aberdeen school board. He also took a warm interest in the volunteer movement, and was chosen captain of the citizens' battery, an appointment he held for eighteen years, retiring with the rank of major. Some of his martial songs were very popular. He also took much interest in everything connected with the army, and made some useful suggestions to the War Office relating to practical gunnery and the use of armed railway carriages in warfare, a tactic which was in fact employed during the Egyptian campaign of 1882.

Forsyth's major works were two collections of his poetry: *The Martyrdom of Kelavane* (1861) and *Idylls and Lyrics* (1872). The latter volume contained 'The Old Kirk Bell' and several other pieces published for the first time, but consisted mainly of reprints from magazines. Of these the best was 'The River', which originally appeared in the *Cornhill Magazine*. The moving 'The Piobrach o' Kinreen' (an old piper's lament for the clearance of Glentannar) was first published in *Punch*. During the last ten years of his life Forsyth suffered from a disease of the tongue, which became cancerous. He died on 21 June 1879 at Aberdeen and was buried in the cemetery of Allenvale on the Dee. He was survived by his wife. After his death, selections from his unpublished writings were published, with a memoir, edited by his friend Alexander Walker of Aberdeen, in 1882.

WILLIAM FORSYTH, *rev.* NILANJANA BANERJI

Sources *Selections from the writings of William Forsyth* (1882) [incl. memoir by A. Walker]

Wealth at death £549 2s. 9d.: confirmation, 18 July 1879, *CCI*

Fortes, Meyer (1906–1983), anthropologist, was born in Britstown, Cape Colony, on 25 April 1906, the eldest child in the family of four sons and two daughters of Nathan Fortes. His grandfather left Russia as an adolescent to escape being drafted into the army and settled in Leeds, where he worked in the clothing industry with his two sons. One son, Nathan, left for South Africa. There he met and married Bertha Karbel, of Yamshik in Lithuania, Meyer Fortes's mother, and settled down as an innkeeper. Meyer Fortes attended the South African Collegiate High School at Cape Town, which was dominated by Scottish teachers, and then with the aid of various scholarships took the degree of MA in English and psychology at the University of Cape Town in 1926. In 1928 he married Sonia (d. 1956), daughter of N. Donen, of Worcester, South Africa, with whom he had one daughter.

On the basis of two scholarships and strong recommendations from the University of Cape Town, Fortes was accepted as a postgraduate student in psychology at University College, London, where he carried out research for a PhD (1930) on non-verbal intelligence tests for interracial use under C. E. Spearman. From 1930 he held the Ratan Tata research studentship at the London School of Economics working with Emanuel Miller at the first child guidance clinic in the East End of London on the effects of sibling order on adolescent behaviour. His association with the clinic and his contact with J. C. Flugel led to a permanent interest in psychoanalytic theory, especially as it affected interpersonal interaction within the family.

It was through Flugel that Fortes met the influential anthropologist Bronislaw Malinowski in 1931 and was invited to join his seminar at the London School of Economics. As a result he got to know E. E. Evans-Pritchard and through him the other professor of anthropology at the school, C. G. Seligman, both of whom were somewhat critical of Malinowski's functional theories as well as his style of functioning. But his seminars were the prevailing intellectual feature in the field and he was the dominant patron. He it was who backed Fortes for a fellowship (1934–8) with the newly founded International African Institute, financed by the Laura Spellman Rockefeller Foundation, which enabled a body of talented, established, scholars from many countries to undertake intensive field research in Africa over an extended period of time. He was Rockefeller fellow in 1933–4, and a fellow of the institute in 1934–8.

Advised by the administrator and anthropologist R. S. Rattray, Fortes left to carry out fieldwork among the Tallensi of the northern territories of the Gold Coast in December 1933. The initial direction of his research was towards 'the psychological approach to the study of African societies', with particular reference to the family. Under the influence of Malinowski's seminars the project became more sociological and in his major accounts of his research, *The Dynamics of Clanship among the Tallensi* (1945), but largely written in 1938) and *The Web of Kinship among the Tallensi* (1949), he explored the nature of tribal social organization. This was largely based upon kin groups and kin relationships, to the comparative study of which he made major contributions, especially in his L. H. Morgan lectures, *Kinship and the Social Order* (1969). At the same time he was deeply interested in the link between the family, morality, and religion; in these studies, notably the Frazer lecture of 1957, entitled *Oedipus and Job in West African Religion* (1959), and in his essays *Religion, Morality and the Person*, published posthumously in 1987, his psychological and psychoanalytic interests came to the fore.

When his fellowship came to an end, Fortes took a temporary lectureship at the London School of Economics (1938–9), then moved to Oxford to join Evans-Pritchard and A. R. Radcliffe-Brown, who had taken up the chair of social anthropology in 1937. There he held a research lectureship for the first two years of the war. In 1941–2 Fortes carried out research in Nigeria under a project organized by Margery Perham, remaining in west Africa to carry out intelligence work. In 1944 he became head of the sociological department in the West African Institute, Accra, a forerunner of the new University of the Gold Coast. There he directed the Asante social survey (1945–6), one of the first major socio-economic enquiries in an oral culture carried out in conjunction with a geographer and economist, and making use of modern data processing methods. On returning to Britain in 1946, he joined Evans-Pritchard and became reader in social anthropology. The two of them had long planned for a 'new' anthropology, less functionalist, more structuralist, than the Malinowskian variety and they built up a strong department. In 1950 Fortes moved to the William Wyse chair at

Cambridge, a position which he held until his retirement in 1973.

Fortes was one of the leading members of that outstanding generation of British scholars who followed Malinowski and Radcliffe-Brown at a time when social anthropology in the United Kingdom was at the peak of its reputation. They were an international group of scholars who gave 'British' social anthropology a pre-eminence throughout the world. Fortes made important advances in the field, merging empirical enquiry with wider theoretical concerns in a profitable if unobtrusive manner. He had wide interests in social theory, using demographic techniques and automatic data processing, as well as being an excellent linguist. He will be particularly remembered for his work in the field of interpersonal relations, that is, of kinship and the family in relation to ritual and political concerns, not only among the patrilineal Tallensi and the matrilineal Asante of Ghana, but also on a broader, comparative, canvas. He had honorary degrees from Chicago and Belfast, was an honorary fellow of the London School of Economics (1975), and was elected FBA (1967). Following the death of his first wife he remarried in 1960; his new wife was Doris Yankauer Mayer MD, a psychiatrist, daughter of David Sigmund Yankauer, wholesale textile dealer, of New York. Fortes died on 27 January 1983 in Cambridge and was cremated there. His second wife survived him.   JACK GOODY

Sources personal knowledge (2004) · archives of the International African Institute · private information (2004) [Dr Doris Fortes, Professor Raymond Firth, Professor Isaac Schapera, Professor M. N. Srinivas and Professor J. A. Barnes] · *The Times* (29 Jan 1983) · *WWW* · *CGPLA Eng. & Wales* (1983)
Archives CUL, corresp. and papers; papers relating to Asante social survey · Ghana National Archives, Accra, MSS · Royal Anthropological Institute, London, report on Gold Coast fieldwork and paper on African cultural values and intellectuals · SOAS, International African Institute, archives · U. Cam., faculty of archaeology and anthropology, MSS | BLPES, corresp. with C. G. Seligman and B. Z. Seligman, MSS | FILM U. Cam., department of social anthropology
Likenesses D. Fortes, portrait · photographs, U. Cam., department of social anthropology
Wealth at death £62,578: probate, 18 April 1983, *CGPLA Eng. & Wales*

Fortescue. For this title name *see* individual entries under Fortescue; *see also* Aland, John Fortescue, first Baron Fortescue of Credan (1670–1746).

Fortescue, Sir Adrian (*c*.1481–1539), landowner and alleged traitor, was the second son of Sir John Fortescue (*d*. 1500) of Punsborne, near Hatfield, Hertfordshire, and Alice, daughter of Sir Geoffrey Boleyn (and great-aunt of Anne Boleyn). Sir John had arranged for Adrian's marriage to Anne Stonor, his ward, by 1499. The couple took possession of the ample Stonor inheritance when Anne's elder brother John (married to Adrian's sister Mary) died in 1499, and Stonor Park in Oxfordshire became their family seat. Anne also inherited a share of the lands of her grandfather John Neville, Marquess Montagu. Her estate (worth about £200 a year in the 1520s) assisted Adrian's entry into public life. He was made a knight of the Bath when Henry

VII's second son, Henry, became prince of Wales in 1503, and thenceforward appeared regularly on county commissions for Oxfordshire. Under Henry VIII, he appeared occasionally at court, on such great occasions as Henry VII's funeral and the Field of Cloth of Gold. He saw action with Henry VIII in France in 1513, as well as in the French campaigns of 1522 and 1523. However, his career faded after 1515, when he dropped out of the commission of the peace. The coincidence of his decline with the rise of Cardinal Wolsey is suggestive, as are the facts that Sir Adrian was granted the stewardship of some of the fallen cardinal's former lands in 1529, and briefly returned to the bench in 1531–2.

The two daughters born to Fortescue and his first wife made advantageous marriages: Mary, the elder, to Sir Thomas Wentworth of Nettlestead (later first Baron Wentworth); and Frances, the younger, to Thomas Fitzgerald, 'Silken Thomas', heir of the tenth earl of Kildare. Anne Stonor died on 14 June 1518, and Sir Adrian took as his second wife (probably towards 1530, certainly by 1531) Anne Rede (1510–1585), daughter of Sir William Rede of Boarstall, who bore him three sons and two further daughters: John *Fortescue (later chancellor of the exchequer), Thomas, Sir Anthony *Fortescue, Mary, and Elizabeth (who married Sir Thomas Bromley, later lord chancellor). After Fortescue's death his widow married Sir Thomas Parry.

After the death of Anne Stonor in 1518, Sir Adrian's title to the Stonor lands was contested by Sir Walter Stonor, the son of her uncle Thomas (*d*. 1512), and a protracted legal dispute ensued. Fortescue might have hoped for a revival of his fortunes in the 1530s, thanks to his relationship to Anne Boleyn: his account book records a payment to the messenger who brought news of the birth of Anne's daughter, Elizabeth, in 1533. However, Walter Stonor had attached himself to the rising star of Thomas Cromwell, and was suitably grateful to him when, just after Easter 1534, Henry VIII entailed Stonor Park and its manors upon the Stonors of the male line. Fortescue's position deteriorated still further in the summer, when his son-in-law, Silken Thomas, launched his ill-fated rebellion in Ireland. Fortescue was arrested as a precaution in August 1534, and spent the winter in the Marshalsea. In February 1535 he was moved to the Tower of London, and there was a rumour that he would be executed, but he survived and was eventually released. He was certainly at liberty by late 1536, as he was ordered to raise troops against the Pilgrimage of Grace.

Sir Adrian's remaining years were spent in doubtless reduced circumstances at Brightwell in Oxfordshire, until his mysterious arrest in February 1539 and his still more mysterious inclusion in the act of attainder of 1539 (31 Hen. VIII c. 15). Condemned to death for unspecified treasons, Sir Adrian Fortescue was executed at Tower Hill on 9 July 1539. In the seventeenth century he came to be venerated as a martyr for the Catholic church (and was declared beatified in 1895), and it has been conjectured that he denied Henry VIII's claim to be supreme head of the Church of England, and that this was also the reason for his original arrest in 1534. However, as a cousin of Anne Boleyn he is unlikely to have opposed Henry's divorce, and there is no reason to believe that he refused the oath to the succession in 1534. Moreover, his missal and book of hours show that he not only dutifully deleted the papal title from the liturgy, but also used bidding prayers describing Henry as supreme head. It is impossible to be certain as to why Sir Adrian was condemned for treason, but it may well have owed something to another family tie, also by way of his first wife, Anne Stonor, this time to the Poles, who were descended like her from the Nevilles. The 1539 act of attainder, passed against the background of the 'Courtenay conspiracy', was among other things concerned to destroy the Pole family, whose leading representative, Cardinal Reginald Pole, was a key figure in the papacy's manoeuvres against Henry VIII.

The seventeenth-century cult of Sir Adrian was fostered by the knights of Malta, as it was then believed that Sir Adrian had been a knight of that order. This confusion originated in the fact that he was executed in company with Sir Thomas Dingley, who really was a knight of Malta. Lax drafting and editing in some seventeenth-century chronicles contrived to suggest that both men were members, but sixteenth-century records furnish no evidence for Sir Adrian's membership, nor is it consistent with the fact that he was twice married. The seventeenth-century 'portraits' of Sir Adrian which survive on Malta can therefore be characterized as devotional representations rather than authentic likenesses.

Sir Adrian Fortescue was a man whose first marriage brought him social and financial standing far above what he might have expected as a younger son. Ironically, exalted family connections entangled him in the dangerous world of Tudor high politics and brought down upon this conventionally devout and loyal knight, perhaps thanks to some unguarded words, the wrath of the prince. RICHARD REX

Sources R. Rex, 'Blessed Adrian Fortescue: a martyr without a cause?', Analecta Bollandiana, 115 (1997), 307–53 · CIPM, Henry VII, 2, no. 118 · Missale secundum usum insignis Ecclesie Sarum, 1510, Law Society Library, Mendham Collection [housed in Canterbury Cathedral Library on behalf of the University of Kent at Canterbury, R438] · J. Fortescue, A history of the family of Fortescue, ed. T. Fortescue, 2nd edn (1880) · LP Henry VIII · HLRO, statutes 31 Henry VIII c. 15 · M. De Goussancourt, Le martyrologe des chevaliers de S. Iean de Hierusalem, dits de Malte (1643) · C. Wriothesley, A chronicle of England during the reigns of the Tudors from AD 1485 to 1559, ed. W. D. Hamilton, 1, CS, new ser., 11 (1875) · M. St C. Byrne, ed., The Lisle letters, 6 vols. (1981), vol. 2 · CPR · B. Camm, ed., Lives of the English martyrs declared blessed by Pope Leo XIII in 1886 and 1895, 1 (1904)

Fortescue, Sir Anthony (b. c.1535, d. in or after 1611), conspirator, was the third son of Sir Adrian *Fortescue (c.1481–1539), of Punsbourne, Hertfordshire, and Stonor Park, Oxfordshire, and his second wife, Anne (1510–1585), daughter of Sir William Rede. Sir Adrian had been condemned with Margaret Pole, countess of Salisbury, and others in 1539 for reasons that are still unknown, and executed the same year. Anthony Fortescue also associated with the Poles, again with disastrous consequences. After studies at Winchester College he married Katherine Pole, daughter of Sir Geoffrey *Pole (d. 1558) and granddaughter of Margaret Pole. They had three sons, Anthony, John, and George. Fortescue became comptroller of the household of his wife's uncle, Reginald Pole, cardinal archbishop of Canterbury and papal legate during the reign of Mary I, who knighted him.

Soon after the deaths of Mary and Cardinal Pole on 17 November 1558 Fortescue and his brothers-in-law, Arthur and Edmund Pole, sought out John Prestall and a man named Kele to cast a horoscope and deduce the remaining years of Elizabeth I. They were discovered by the privy council, which on 22 November ordered the apprehension of Fortescue and his fellow intriguers. They were later released, though the council ordered Edmund Bonner, bishop of London, to prosecute Fortescue in an ecclesiastical court for practising astrology.

In September 1562 Fortescue and the Poles again conspired against Elizabeth. Under the direction of Arthur, they again consulted the astrological expertise of Prestall and that of Edward Cosyn to discover the queen's remaining lifespan. Believing the days left to Elizabeth to be few, they and several others planned to take ship to Flanders where Arthur Pole would claim the title of duke of Clarence. They would then travel to France, where they would beseech the aid of Catherine de' Medici, the Guise family, and the papacy. Assisted by these parties, they planned to marry Edmund to Mary, queen of Scots, proclaim her queen of England, and in May 1563 land in Wales with an army of 6000. They would overthrow Elizabeth, crown Mary, and restore Roman Catholicism in England. Fortescue sought the aid of the Spanish and French ambassadors, who were highly doubtful of the scheme and declined to support it.

The plot was discovered in October 1562, and the conspirators were arrested. Tried for high treason on 26 February 1563, Fortescue pleaded guilty, and the Poles and other conspirators not guilty. All were found guilty and condemned. Fortescue and the Poles were not executed, perhaps due to the intercession of Sir John *Fortescue, Sir Anthony's brother and keeper of the great wardrobe. They were imprisoned in the Tower, where Arthur and Edmund probably died about 1570, but it appears that Sir Anthony was released at some point and exiled. Apparently he was alive in 1611 when his brother Thomas died; Thomas's will of 10 May 1608 stated 'that all suche plate, householld stuffe, and bookes as are belonginge unto Anthony Fortescue my brother, be safely kept, and delyvered to the use of my said brother'. Sir Anthony Fortescue's end is therefore as enigmatic as much of his life: one may only surmise the reasons, whether religious or familial devotion, that drove him to seek the overthrow of Elizabeth I with the aid of astrology.

WILLIAM WIZEMAN

Sources Report of the Deputy Keeper of the Public Records, 4 (1843), appx 2, 263–4 · J. Strype, Annals of the Reformation and establishment of religion … during Queen Elizabeth's happy reign, new edn, 1/1 (1824), 9,

555–8 • J. Fortescue, *A history of the family of Fortescue*, ed. T. Fortescue, 2nd edn (1880), 255, 263, 426–9 • will of Thomas Fortescue, PRO, PROB 11/117, sig. 7

Fortescue, Chichester Samuel Parkinson- [Chichester Samuel Fortescue], **Baron Carlingford and second Baron Clermont** (1823–1898), politician, was born at Glyde, co. Louth, on 18 January 1823. He was the youngest child of Lieutenant-Colonel Chichester Fortescue of Glyde Farm, co. Louth, MP for Hillsborough in the last Irish parliament, and his wife, Martha, daughter of Samuel Meade Hobhouse, barrister, of Muckridge House, co. Cork.

Education, travel, art Fortescue was educated privately and at Christ Church, Oxford, where he matriculated on 26 May 1841, being elected to a studentship (fellowship) in 1843 (which he held until 1856), gaining a first in *literae humaniores* in 1844, and graduating BA in 1845 and MA in 1847. In 1846 he won the chancellor's essay prize with an essay published as *Effects of the Conquest of England by the Normans* (1846). Christ Church elected him to an honorary studentship in 1867. Handsome, but shy and with a slight stutter, he was happy to move in academic and artistic circles. He studied German in Dresden and Italian in Rome, winning the affections of Edward Lear there in 1845. He travelled to Greece and Albania in 1846–7. He was friendly with Millais, Ruskin, Monckton Milnes, and Watts. About 1847 he formed a liaison with Polly Fleming, a horseback performer with Astley's Amphitheatre. As a youth he was an interesting combination of the intellectual and the bohemian.

Politics and love Fortescue's eldest brother, Thomas, a hypochondriac, bullied him into politics in the family's interest and in 1847 he was elected as a Liberal for co. Louth; he retained the seat until he was defeated in 1874. In July 1847 he met Frances, Countess Waldegrave, who was then married to G. G. V. Harcourt [*see* Fortescue, Frances Elizabeth Anne Parkinson- (1821–1879)]. His ensuing love affair with her—a passion which became an obsession—determined his private, and to an extent his public, life until her death in 1879. He became her fourth husband in 1863. Shortly after meeting her he began to keep a daily diary, maintained almost to the end of his life, which is principally focused on her doings, as well as giving a valuable account of the politics of the day. Almost all of it is now in the British Library. Lady Waldegrave brought him wealth which was soon supplemented by his inheritance of the estate of his aunt, Anna Maria (*d.* 1863), daughter of Thomas Fortescue and widow of William Parkinson Ruxton of Ardee, co. Louth, on condition that he added Parkinson to his surname. The Irish estates of Parkinson-Fortescue and his brother were 23,265 acres, worth £18,086 a year. His relationship with Lady Waldegrave and her salon at Strawberry Hill brought Parkinson-Fortescue to the heart of the Liberal establishment. This fitted the cast of his mind. His maiden speech in the Commons (4 May 1848) supported the removal of Jewish disabilities. He moved smoothly, though not speedily, towards the cabinet, being junior whip in the final year of the Aberdeen coalition (March 1854 to March 1855) and under-secretary

Chichester Samuel Parkinson-Fortescue, Baron Carlingford and second Baron Clermont (1823–1898), by Bassano, 1894

for the colonies under Palmerston in 1857–8 and 1859–65. In the latter term he was subordinate to the duke of Newcastle, also enamoured of Lady Waldegrave. He was a competent administrator but a dry, repetitive, and prosy speaker in the Commons. He was sworn of the privy council on 7 April 1865.

Ireland When, in November 1865, Russell formed his administration following Palmerston's death, he appointed Parkinson-Fortescue chief secretary for Ireland. He held this post until July 1866, and again from December 1868 until January 1871 in Gladstone's first government. In 1866–8 he was not in the cabinet, despite Lady Waldegrave's best efforts. The couple cut a dash in Dublin society and partially restored the Liberals' popularity, spoilt by Parkinson-Fortescue's predecessor, Sir Robert Peel (1822–1895). In February 1866 he sent Gladstone, with whom he was increasingly associated, a large 'budget' of possible Irish legislation, and from this Gladstone encouraged him to develop a land bill (Carlingford MSS, CD 1.4). His chief initiative was thus the introduction of a Land Bill in 1866 which reversed, but not retrospectively, the presumption of law that, in the absence of agreement to the contrary, improvements were the landlord's property. This modest measure of tenants' compensation for improvement raised Irish expectations but was withdrawn when the Liberals' Reform Bill took precedence. Reappointment in December 1868 as chief secretary (even with the cabinet added) was a disappointment, for

Parkinson-Fortescue and Lady Waldegrave had schemed for the Colonial Office. But with Spencer, the lord lieutenant, not in the cabinet, Parkinson-Fortescue expected a freer hand. In fact, he immediately found himself working for Gladstone on details of the Irish Church Bill, which was enacted in 1869, the prime minister rather than the chief secretary handling the bill's passage. Lady Waldegrave seems to have resented this more than Parkinson-Fortescue, whose strength and speaking capacity would both have been inadequate.

It was also Gladstone who determined on a substantial Land Bill in 1870, as a counter to Fenianism. Whereas Parkinson-Fortescue had had no significant difference with Gladstone on disestablishment, he had on land, where his position was more cautious. While Gladstone supported the extension of the principle of Ulster tenant right to the whole of Ireland, Parkinson-Fortescue argued for a further measure to grant compensation for disturbance. Combat by correspondence, with the whigs in cabinet supporting Parkinson-Fortescue, led to a more limited bill than Gladstone had hoped for. Again the prime minister handled the parliamentary passage of the bill, and Parkinson-Fortescue's success was unknown. The absence of credit given to Parkinson-Fortescue infuriated Lady Waldegrave. In the reshuffle following the death of the foreign secretary, Lord Clarendon, in 1870, Parkinson-Fortescue and his wife again hoped for the Colonial Office unavailingly, even though he believed he had an assurance from Gladstone that he would get it. Parkinson-Fortescue was left to introduce, later in the 1870 session, the Peace Preservation Bill, a bill deeply unpopular in his native Ireland, but one which followed from the coercionist line he had taken in cabinet. In January 1871 Gladstone appointed him president of the Board of Trade (succeeding John Bright), Lord Hartington replacing him as chief secretary. In this post he improved railway safety. Against his inclinations, he spoke for the government's abortive Irish University Bill in 1873. Like many Irish Liberals, he lost his seat in 1874 to a home-ruler; he had insisted on standing despite offers of a safe English seat. He was created Baron Carlingford in the resignation honours on 27 February 1874. His title occasioned this lyric by Edward Lear:

O! Chichester, my Carlingford!
O! Parkinson, my Sam!
O! S. P. Q., my Fortescue!
How awfully glad I am!

Later career Carlingford's years of influence, though not of office, at the summit of politics were over, though this was not immediately apparent. The essential relationship—that with Gladstone—had soured, though for no explicit reason. Out of office, Carlingford travelled much on the continent, fulfilled his duties as lord lieutenant of Essex (from August 1873), worked to re-establish Horace Walpole's library and to solve the authorship of the Junius letters, and attended the Philobiblon Club. Roulette was played at his Irish house parties. He attended the exiled Orleanist court at Twickenham. Lady Waldegrave's death in 1879 prematurely aged Carlingford and left him

obsessed with her memory. His diary recorded daily visits to her grave and chronic mourning. He was not included in Gladstone's second government in 1880, but was made lord privy seal on 2 May 1881 to enable him to help with the Land Bill in the Lords, where he was a considerable asset—despite his reservations about the bill—when he was well enough to speak. He visited Ireland in the spring of 1882 and was asked by Gladstone to help in the arrangements following the Kilmainham 'treaty' and the Phoenix Park murders in May 1882. On 19 March 1883 he added the lord presidency of the council to the privy seal. In 1884 he refused to become ambassador to Constantinople so as to vacate a cabinet post for Rosebery. His joint offices gave him responsibility for education and agriculture and he resisted Gladstone's proposals for both. He felt, with justification, that Gladstone had treated him cavalierly and he dug in his heels, refusing explicit requests to resign. In May 1885 he eventually ceded the privy seal to Rosebery, retaining the lord presidency until the government's fall in June 1885. On the formation of Gladstone's home-rule government in January 1886, he was abroad and was not invited to join, having showed unionist tendencies. He was hostile to the home-rule proposals and became president of the Liberal Unionist Association of Somerset. On 29 July 1887 he succeeded his brother Thomas as second Baron Clermont.

Lady Waldegrave had left to him for life (and afterwards to the Waldegrave family) the Waldegrave property which she had inherited absolutely from her husband, Lord Waldegrave: Strawberry Hill, near Twickenham, Chewton in Somerset, and Dudbrook in Essex. These estates were 13,287 acres, worth £21,193 a year. Carlingford sold Strawberry Hill soon after her death and Dudbrook shortly before his own. He had no children and the Chewton property reverted to the Waldegrave family.

Carlingford's final years were unhappy. Squeezed in his prime between the dominant personalities of Frances Waldegrave and W. E. Gladstone, his political promise had been only partially fulfilled. Although he is thought to have been the dashing model for Trollope's *Phineas Phinn, the Irish Member* (1869), he ended his days bitter and resentful. He died from influenza at Marseilles on 30 January 1898 and was buried at Chewton Mendip. Carlingford was remembered for half a century only as Lady Waldegrave's fourth husband, but studies by Wyndham Hewett of him and his circle in 1956 and 1958 reawakened interest in him, and the availability of his copious diary, one year of which was published in 1971, ensures him some presence in the history of later Victorian politics.

H. C. G. MATTHEW

Sources O. W. Hewett, '… and Mr. Fortescue' (1958) · O. W. Hewett, *Strawberry fair: a biography of Frances, Countess Waldegrave, 1821–1879* (1956) · Carlingford Diaries, BL · *Lord Carlingford's journal: reflections of a cabinet minister, 1885*, ed. A. B. Cooke and J. R. Vincent (1971) · Gladstone, *Diaries* · E. D. Steele, *Irish land and British politics: tenant-right and nationality, 1865–1870* (1974) · H. C. G. Matthew, *Gladstone*, 2 vols. (1986–95) · K. T. Hoppen, *Elections, politics, and society in Ireland, 1832–1885* (1984) · J. P. Parry, *Democracy and religion* (1986) · GEC, *Peerage*

Archives BL, diaries, Add. MSS 63654–63704 · Som. ARS, corresp. and papers | BL, letters to Sir Charles Dilke, Add. MSS 43874–43913 · BL, corresp. with W. E. Gladstone, Add. MSS 44121–44123 · BL, Spencer MSS · Bodl. Oxf., letters to Sir William Harcourt · Bodl. Oxf., corresp. with Lord Kimberley · Broadlands, Romsey, Hampshire, Palmerston MSS · NRA, priv. coll., letters to John Hamilton · PRO, corresp. with second Earl Granville · PRO, corresp. with Lord John Russell, PRO 30/22 · PRO NIre., corresp. with Lord O'Hagan · U. Nott. L., letters to duke of Newcastle

Likenesses J. Tissot, oils, 1871, Examination Schools, Oxford · Bassano, photograph, 1894, NPG [*see illus.*] · Ape [C. Pellegrini], chromolithograph caricature, NPG; repro. in *VF* (14 Aug 1869) · W. & D. Downey, carte-de-visite, NPG · Lock & Whitfield, woodburytype photograph, NPG; repro. in T. Cooper, *Men of mark: a gallery of contemporary portraits* (1883) · F. M. Taubman, monument, Waldegrave Chapel, Chewton Mendip, Somerset · carte-de-visite, NPG · group portrait, lithograph (*The cabinet council, 1883*), NPG; repro. in *VF* · photograph, repro. in Hewett, '… and Mr. Fortescue' · photograph, repro. in Hewett, *Strawberry fair* · sepia print, NPG · two stipple engravings, NPG

Wealth at death £41,808 1s. 7d. effects in England: Irish probate sealed in London, 25 June 1898, *CGPLA Eng. & Wales*

Fortescue, Sir Edmund (*bap.* 1610, *d.* 1647), royalist army officer, the eldest child of the five sons and two daughters of John Fortescue (*bap.* 1586, *d.* 1650) of Fallapit, in the parish of East Allington, Devon, and his wife, Sara Prideaux (*d.* 1628), daughter of Sir Edmund Prideaux of Netherton, was baptized on 15 July 1610. He married Jane Southcott (*d.* 1642), daughter of Thomas Southcott of Mohun Ottery, on 8 November 1633 and they had two sons and three daughters.

On 14 February 1642 Mr Edmund Fortescue was thanked by the House of Commons for capturing a barque at Salcombe which was taking Irish from France to Ireland; the house also asked the lord keeper to put him on the commission of the peace for Devon. This request was immediately complied with and Fortescue was appointed to the bench on 24 February. He was an active JP and in August, with his brother-in-law Sir Popham Southcott, presented the petitions, seeking peace, from quarter sessions to parliament and later to the king at York. This was probably the occasion for Fortescue's knighthood, which was certainly conferred some time in 1642.

Fortescue was not on the commission of array at the outbreak of the war, nor did he respond to the efforts of the commissioners to raise Devon for the king. However, on his appointment as sheriff he fulfilled the traditional duty of the sheriff and summoned the *posse comitatus* to Tavistock on 27 November 1642, though with such little success that he made a fresh summons to Modbury on 6 December when about 3000 responded but few were equipped for war. During the night a parliamentarian force from Plymouth under Colonel Ruthven attacked the raw recruits, dispersed them, and captured Fortescue, his brother Peter, and other officers including Sir Edward Seymour and his son Edward, a close friend of Fortescue. The prisoners were dispatched by sea to London and the Commons recorded their arrival and their committal to Winchester House. They were all accused of high treason for actual levying of war against the king and parliament. Fortescue was later transferred to Windsor Castle where his incarceration was recorded by an inscription on the wall of a small chamber, close to the Round Tower, consisting of his name with a rude cut of his coat of arms and the words *Pour le Roy C* and the date 22 May 1643.

Sir Edmund Fortescue's escape was mentioned in a September newsletter, and on 10 September he and Colonel Edward Seymour were sent a warrant from Prince Maurice to summon Dartmouth to surrender. While Seymour became governor of Dartmouth, Fortescue was active as one of the commissioners for the royal army in Devon. He had held the command of the fort of Salcombe when he had captured the Irish barque; now he proposed that he should refortify and man it and on 9 December 1643 he received a commission from Prince Maurice to do so. Repairs started immediately and an attack was repelled in July 1644, though Fortescue does not seem to have been in the fort at this time. During 1644 and 1645 he commanded a trained regiment of foot and horse of the stannaries. He served with Prince Maurice in the siege of Lyme Regis, in Exeter, at Lostwithiel, and in the siege of Plymouth.

In January 1646, when the New Model Army moved into south Devon, Fortescue dispatched his regiment to join the garrison of Dartmouth and he retired into the fort at Salcombe, which he had renamed Fort Charles. The fort stands on a rock at the entrance of Salcombe harbour, approachable from the land at low tide, but completely surrounded by the sea at high water. Details survive of the cost of rebuilding, fortifying, and victualling the fort showing that nothing needed for the support of the garrison during a long siege was neglected. Some of this expense was met by martial rates but more came from Fortescue himself, who supplied beds, chairs, tables, and all other sorts of household equipment. The relief of Plymouth and the capture of Dartmouth freed parliamentarian troops and guns for an attack on Fort Charles later in January 1646. A battery of three guns was erected in a commanding position on the mainland, exactly opposite and slightly above the small promontory on which the fort is situated.

The effectiveness of the strengthened defences was sufficient for Fortescue to reject the summons sent about 23 January. There is little evidence of action during the siege; only three were wounded and none killed out of the garrison of sixty-five men and two laundresses. After Charles's surrender to the Scots in April further resistance was pointless and articles of surrender were agreed on 7 May between Fortescue and Colonel Ralph Weldon, governor of Plymouth. Fortescue obtained favourable terms for the garrison who were allowed to march out with all the honours of war and proceed in safety to their own homes. Fortescue and his officers were allowed to remain at home unmolested for three months and then either make their peace with parliament or go abroad. Fortescue went to Delft where he remained until his death late in 1647 at the age of thirty-eight; he was buried in the 'New Church' of Delft.   MARY WOLFFE

Sources DNB · *The works of Sir John Fortescue*, ed. T. Fortescue, 2: *A history of the family of Fortescue* (1869) · M. J. Stoyle, *A history of Fort Charles, Salcombe, Devon*, Exeter Museums Archaeological Field

Unit • Devon RO, QS 1/8, 7 Oct 1642 • Devon RO, QS 28/1, 2 • Devon RO, QS Box 46 • Devon RO, Seymour MS 1392M/L1643-45 • C. E. H. Chadwyck-Healy, ed., 'Sir Ralph Hopton's campaign in the west 1642–1644', *Somerset RO*, 18 (1902) • appointment as colonel of Stannary regiment, BL, Harley MS 6804, fol. 31 • *Kingdomes Weekly Intelligencer* (27 Dec 1642–3 Jan 1643) [Thomason tract E 84(4)] • *The petition of the rebells in New-Gate* (1642) [Thomason tract E 141(4)] • *Mercurius Aulicus* (24 April 1644) • *The Weekly Account, Containing Certain Speciall and Remarkable Passages* (6 Sept 1643) [Thomason tract] • P. Q. Karkeek, 'Sir Edmund Fortescue and the siege of Fort Charles', *Report and Transactions of the Devonshire Association*, 9 (1877), 336–50 • *JHL*, 5 (1642–3) • *JHC*, 2 (1640–42), 430–31 • I. R. Palfrey, 'Devon and the outbreak of the English civil war, 1642–3', *Southern History*, 10 (1988), 29–46 • J. L. Vivian, ed., *The visitations of the county of Devon, comprising the herald's visitations of 1531, 1564, and 1620* (privately printed, Exeter, [1895]) • A. Hawkins, *Kingsbridge and Salcombe* (1819) • Som. ARS, WO 56/6/52.6 • PRO, C231/5 [appointment as JP] • parish register, East Allington, Devon [baptism]
Archives Devon RO, letters to Edward Seymour
Likenesses H. Danckerts, line engraving, 1647, NPG • Dutch engraving; in Bodl. Oxf. in 1869 • portrait; in possession of William Blundell Fortescue in 1889

Fortescue, Sir Faithful (*b.* in or before **1581**, *d.* **1666**), royalist army officer, was the second son (there were also two daughters) of John Fortescue (*d.* 1604) of Buckland Filleigh, Devon, and his second wife, Susannah, daughter of Sir John Chichester, of Raleigh, Kent. He was a fifth-generation descendant of Sir John *Fortescue (*c.*1397–1479), chief justice of king's bench.

Almost nothing is known of Fortescue's youth; on his own admission he left school at an early age. The foundation of his advancement lay in his association with his maternal uncle, Sir Arthur (later Lord) *Chichester, with whom he went to Ireland (probably in 1598), where Chichester commanded a regiment of infantry and later became lord deputy (1604–15). In 1604 Fortescue was left a mere £50 in his father's will, but in 1606 he was appointed joint (later sole) constable of Carrickfergus, the main English garrison in Ulster. The post provided him with a salary of £120 per annum, lodgings in the castle, a share of the port customs dues, and a tenth of the fishing catch. Soon afterwards he married Anne (*d.* 5 Sept 1634), daughter of Gerald (or Garret) Moore, later first Viscount Moore; they had ten sons and six daughters (five of the children died young).

In 1610 Fortescue obtained a patent granting him a share in the fines from unlicensed alienations and concealed wardships in co. Cork. Another patent (27 January 1612) gave him the wardship of Charles O'Connor, of Sligo; Fortescue's activities on his behalf caused the countess of Desmond to write a letter of complaint to the lord deputy on 29 May 1613 about their effect on her jointure. By 1613, finding Carrickfergus and his manor in co. Antrim too far from the seat of government in Dublin, Fortescue was residing at the castle of Dromiskin, 5 miles south of Dundalk, co. Louth, which he held on a long lease from the archbishop of Armagh; he later bought a considerable freehold estate around the castle. In the Irish parliament of May 1613 to 1615 Fortescue sat for Charlemont, co. Armagh, one of the places beyond the English pale

which returned an MP for the first time. He acquired (1614) the prestigious position of commander of the lord deputy's troop of horse. Although, in common with other Chichester relations, Fortescue failed to secure any lands in the plantation of Ulster (1614), as recompense his uncle made him one of the original grantees in the Wexford plantation. It is no surprise that, in a short memoir of Chichester, Fortescue showed his esteem for his patron by portraying his career in glowing terms.

Although Chichester was recalled in 1615 Fortescue continued in his posts. In 1617 he was in England, where he was knighted by James I. His landed estate in Ireland continued to increase. On 30 May 1618 he received a crown grant of extensive territory around Galgorm, co. Antrim, formerly possessed by the Irish chieftain, Rory Oige MacQuillane; much of this he sold in 1624, but he gained further territory in co. Antrim, at Gortfadda, and lands near Scarva, co. Down, which he soon planted heavily with Scotsmen. In 1624 Chichester, by then lord treasurer of Ireland and a member of the council of war, wrote two letters to Secretary Conway (4 September and 3 November), pressing Fortescue's case for a foot company among the troops then being raised for Ireland; when he was instead given command of a company in the contingent to serve under Count Mansfeld in the Netherlands against the Habsburgs, a third Chichester letter (11 November) seems to have achieved Fortescue's transfer to the Irish service, in a regiment then being enlisted in Cumberland and other northern counties. (There is a list of fifty men levied for him, dated 16 March 1625, by the deputy lieutenants of Cumberland.)

On 1 January 1632 Thomas, Viscount Wentworth (later earl of Strafford), was appointed lord deputy, and before his arrival in Ireland he commissioned Fortescue to raise him a troop of horse. But when in July 1633 Wentworth finally reached Dublin, where Fortescue had leased a house in Wood Quay in order to be of more immediate service, the lord deputy dismissed forty of the troop without pay and replaced them with his English entourage. Later that year Fortescue was sent to inspect the garrisons and military stores in the province of Leinster. His relations with Wentworth were strained. He complained, in his 'Relation of passages of the earle of Strafford, concearning himselfe' (1645) that he received no promotion from the lord deputy, nor any settlement of arrears due to him, despite a letter from the king to Wentworth (5 March 1639), asking him to consider the latter. Fortescue also alleged that, after his eldest son, Chichester, was given command of his foot company at his suggestion, requests to be granted the companies of two deceased commanders, Sir Robert Loftus and Lord Caufield, elicited no effective response.

Fortescue felt the final insult to be Strafford's attempt, from the Tower in 1640–41, to secure his dismissal from the command of his troop, as if he had been 'his Mercinary servant or Scullion, of his kitchen (and not the King's officer) to bee throwne owt by the tounge of his Steward' (*Works*, 2.106). Chichester Fortescue succeeded his father as MP for Charlemont in 1634; Sir Faithful was instead elected for Dungannon (17 June) and then for co. Armagh (14 July). In 1635 he failed to be elected, despite Wentworth's recommendation, MP for Dundalk, where he commanded the fifty-strong garrison, but in 1639 he was again returned for co. Armagh. Fortescue did not spend all his time in Ireland: in 1637 he was in Breda, in the United Provinces, 'to see what doings are there' (*CSP dom.*, 1637, 391). By 1637 he had married his second wife, Eleanor, daughter of Sir Marmaduke Whitechurch and widow of John Symonds, who had left her lands in counties Antrim and Monaghan; they had no children.

In April 1640 Fortescue appears, attached to the lord-general's regiment of horse, in a list of army officers appointed for an expedition to Scotland, under the earl of Ormond; but it never took place. On 27 January 1641 his petition for promotion to the rank of lieutenant-colonel on the Irish establishment was read in the House of Commons, and the house recommended the appointment, 'being very well satisfied, that he is a Man of Honnour and Experience, and worthy of such an Employment' (*JHC*, 2, 1640–42, 398). In April Fortescue offered to finance the pay of the troops at Armagh until the relevant subsidies were collected. His diligent attendance in the Irish parliament between May and August 1641 included sitting on sixteen committees in its fourth session and twenty in its fifth.

In the summer of 1641 Fortescue was appointed governor of Drogheda. When, in October, revolt broke out in Ulster and the insurgents threatened Drogheda, the only fortified town between them and Dublin, it was ungarrisoned, and defended solely by a small reinforcement hurriedly raised by his brother-in-law, Viscount Moore. Fortescue, after vainly appealing to the lords justices for aid, resigned his command and went to London to urge the government to send supplies to Ireland and to engage in raising men himself. Dean Bernard, who was in Drogheda during the ensuing siege, caustically complained that Fortescue 'gave us over, being willing to hazard his life for us, yet loth to lose his reputation also' (Bagwell, 1.352). Fortescue's two eldest sons were present during the siege: in 1642 Chichester, a major in Lord Moore's regiment, died, and John was killed by the rebels. On 31 December 1641 Sir Faithful was again recommended for employment by the House of Commons, and in 1642 he was appointed by the parliamentary commissioners to serve as colonel of the third troop of horse under Lord Wharton, lord-general of Ireland; Fortescue helped to raise this force, in addition to a company of foot.

After the raising of the royal standard at Nottingham in August 1642, Fortescue's troops were, without consultation, drafted into the parliamentarian army and, while waiting at Bristol to embark for Ireland, his troop of horse was placed under the command of the earl of Essex. On the eve of the civil war Fortescue had been dismissed by parliament as governor of Carrickfergus in favour of a Scottish garrison. With extreme pay arrears and his estates overrun by the Irish rebels, he had no love for the parliamentarian cause, and on the eve of the battle of Edgehill on 23 October, when acting as a major in William Waller's regiment, Fortescue sent his lieutenant to Prince Rupert with a promise to change sides, the signal being a discharge of pistols into the ground. Unfortunately there was no time for Rupert to notify his subordinate commanders. When some of Fortescue's troops failed to remove their orange scarves (Essex's colours) as they deserted, at least eighteen out of his troop of sixty were killed or wounded by the cavalry they had joined. Fortescue was also a company commander in the earl of Peterborough's regiment of foot, captured by the royalists at Banbury a few days later. Much play was made by parliament's pamphleteers, especially John Vicars, of 'Faithless Fortescue'. In contrast, Fortescue's own colours proclaimed an image of resolute chivalry: a shield and scabbard, the former bearing the punning motto 'La Fort' (*Works*, 2.113).

Soon after Edgehill, Fortescue was appointed lieutenant-colonel of the 10th regiment of royal infantry, and he served in the royalist army, based at Oxford, for the remainder of the civil war. By 1643 he had lost a third son in royal service, and on 25 May the king granted his petition that his eldest son Chichester's commands should go to his next surviving son, Captain Thomas Fortescue. Fortescue was again in Ireland in September 1646. On parliament's capture of the king, the marquess of Ormond handed over the Dublin garrison to parliament with special terms to protect Fortescue from parliamentarian resentment over his desertion at Edgehill. But Fortescue, doubting their efficacy, fled to the Isle of Man soon after 28 July 1647 'to avoyd offenceive souldiers, & to live quiet & cheape' (*Works*, 2.114–15). Finding the island a barren place, and aiming to join Ormond in London, he then crossed to Anglesey, where he was arrested by the parliamentarian commander at Beaumaris in November and imprisoned, by order of the House of Commons. He was held first at Caernarfon Castle (for nine months, despite Ormond's remonstrances) and then, from 2 August 1648, at Denbigh Castle, mainly because he was 'very obnoxious to … all their partie for an action done soe unlike a Gent in deserting his Colours upon the Feild att Edgehill, & running to the Enemy' (*Works*, 2.116). The length of his confinement is unclear, but in April 1651 he was able to join Charles II at Stirling, and he took part, as a full colonel, in the campaign which ended in the royalist defeat at Worcester on 3 September.

Fortescue then retired to the continent, where he remained, first in France, and afterwards in the Netherlands, until the Restoration. Charles II restored him to his constableship of Carrickfergus (21 August 1660), allowing him to resign it a few months later in favour of his son Thomas. On 14 October 1661 Fortescue was appointed a gentleman of the privy chamber, a post he held until his death. This kept him at court, and the king also gave him some sinecure appointments, including that of water-bailiff and searcher of rivers in England, and a grant of £100, 'to contribute to his pressing wants' (*CSP dom.*, 1664–5, 73). At the outbreak of the great plague of London in 1665 he retired to the Isle of Wight, where he occupied the manor house of Bowcombe, near Carisbrooke. Here he died between 24 and 28 May 1666; he was buried at Carisbrooke church on 29 May.   BASIL MORGAN

Sources *The works of Sir John Fortescue*, ed. T. Fortescue, 2: *A history of the family of Fortescue* (1869), 95–123 · *DNB* · J. McCavitt, *Sir Arthur Chichester* (1998) · *CSP dom.*, 1624–5; 1637; 1639; 1664–6 · C. Falls, *The birth of Ulster* (1973) · *APC*, 1613 · M. Perceval-Maxwell, *The outbreak of the Irish rebellion of 1641* (1994) · R. Bagwell, *Ireland under the Stuarts*, 3 vols. (1909–16) · P. Young, *Edgehill, 1642* (1967) · *JHC*, 2 (1640–42) · *JHC*, 6 (1648–51) · P. Morrah, *Prince Rupert of the Rhine* (1976) · P. R. Newman, *The old service: royalist regimental colonels and the civil war, 1642–1646* (1993) · H. Kearney, *Strafford in Ireland, 1633–41: a study in absolutism*, 2nd edn (1989) · M. Bennett, *The civil wars experienced: Britain and Ireland, 1638–61* (2000)

Fortescue, Frances Elizabeth Anne Parkinson- [*née* Frances Elizabeth Anne Braham; *other married name* Frances Elizabeth Anne Waldegrave, Countess Waldegrave] (1821–1879), political hostess, was born on 4 January 1821 at 3 Tavistock Square, London, the third child and eldest daughter of John *Braham (1777?–1856), singer, and his wife, Frances Elizabeth, *née* Bolton (1799–1846). She had four brothers and a sister. She was baptized at St Pancras church in the following August: Braham had long forsworn his Jewish background. She was allowed to run wild as a child, but her mother had high ambitions for her. John Braham made a fortune as a singer, but lost it as a theatre manager, and Frances was to redeem the family by a prosperous marriage. In fact, the fair-haired, exuberant Fanny Braham married four times. Her first husband was John James Henry Waldegrave (1814–1840), the illegitimate son of the sixth Earl Waldegrave. They married on 25 May 1839; eleven months later he was dead from a combination of *delirium tremens* and epilepsy. Five months later, on 28 September 1840, she married George Edward Waldegrave, seventh Earl Waldegrave (1816–1846), her first husband's legitimate brother. They spent six months of the first year together in the queen's bench prison, whence Waldegrave had been committed for assaulting a policeman before the marriage. In 1842 Waldegrave put up for auction the contents of Horace Walpole's Gothic villa, Strawberry Hill, Twickenham, which he had inherited from his aunt, and took his countess to live in Switzerland for two years. On their return to England he manifested signs of liver disease and mental breakdown, and he died from cirrhosis of the liver on 28 September 1846. Like his brother, he left all his estates to his widow.

Lady Waldegrave (she retained the title throughout her life, formally styling herself Frances, Countess Waldegrave) married for the third time on 30 September 1847; her new husband was George Granville Vernon Harcourt (1785–1861), a widower of sixty-two, with a daughter five years Frances's senior. This was a very different proposition from the Waldegrave marriages: the brothers were typically wild young men, their family socially marginal despite their estates and titles, and Frances had had little to do with aristocratic society while they lived. Harcourt, by contrast, was the very acme of respectability: a Peelite MP, son of an archbishop of York, and cousin of the duke of Sutherland. Under his tutelage, Frances acquired polish, and soon became an accomplished hostess at his

Frances Elizabeth Anne Parkinson-Fortescue (1821–1879), by Camille Silvy, 1861

houses, Nuneham Park, Oxfordshire, and in London (initially in St James's Place, then at 5 Carlton House Terrace, and, from 1853, at 7 Carlton Gardens), making a feature of amateur theatricals. Harcourt was not an easy man to live with, for although he rejoiced in his wife's social success, he was snobbish, jealous, and insecure, and never wholly put aside the role of tutor. The diplomatist Robert Morier described their relationship as belonging to a Louis XV vaudeville, with Harcourt 'the old Marquis, heir to palaces and broad acres, a genealogy "as long as my tail", and an ungovernable temper', and Frances the young wife, 'with immense fortune, beauty, accomplishments, whims without end, gigantic animal spirits, the world-spoiled child, with every denomination of admirer flitting about her, really fond of the old "Marquis" but determined to stand no humbug' (Wemyss, 115). It was at least in part to give herself a refuge from him that Frances decided to restore Strawberry Hill. She carried out extensive building works, bought items which had previously been in Walpole's collections, and began a portrait gallery of her friends in imitation of Walpole's. From 1856 'Friday to Monday' parties at Strawberry Hill were a regular feature of the London season, and as time passed they took on a more pronouncedly political character.

Frances Waldegrave had been interested in politics

from the time of her second marriage. Waldegrave had been a tory in so far as he had political opinions, and Harcourt was a follower of Sir Robert Peel. That Frances developed into one of the most prominent whig-Liberal political hostesses stemmed in some measure from the fluidity of party allegiances in the 1850s; Frances herself became and remained more of a whig than a Liberal. Until 1865 the pre-eminent political hostess was Lady Palmerston, who entertained on behalf of her husband's coalitions with verve and enthusiasm. Frances's guests were more eclectic than those of most London hostesses: alongside politicians, aristocrats, royalty, and diplomats were to be found artists, journalists, musicians, and actors. She had her critics, who thought that her parties lowered the tone of society by admitting such lesser mortals, but she also inspired deep attachments. Her admirers included most of the members of her husbands' families, the duke of Newcastle (whom she aspired to make prime minister), Lord Chelsea, the duc d'Aumale (son of the deposed Orleanist king, Louis Philippe) and his duchess, who lived near Strawberry Hill at Orleans House, Lord St Germans, the marquess of Lansdowne, Edward Lear, and a bevy of young men and women including Julian Fane, William Vernon Harcourt (Harcourt's nephew), Mary Bulteel (later Lady Ponsonby), and the young Irish MP Chichester Samuel Fortescue, later Parkinson-*Fortescue, from 1874 Baron Carlingford (1823–1898). It was not just as a hostess that Frances was in demand: her advice was widely sought by her adherents, who gave her drafts of speeches to comment on, brought their articles for publication to her for approval, and came daily to discuss debates in parliament and events in the political world. Her contacts with the press made her especially useful to aspiring authors, and she did not hesitate to encourage her friends to write on particular issues for the editors who were also among her guests, notably J. T. Delane of *The Times* and J. D. Cook of the *Saturday Review*.

Chichester Fortescue was obsessively in love with Lady Waldegrave from 1850, and preferred the often uncomfortable position of being the confidant of both husband and wife to the alternative of shunning her company. There was always gossip about Lady Waldegrave, and she enjoyed her reputation as a matchmaker, but despite her worldliness and pleasure in the admiration of men, she was also genuinely religious and was shocked by sexual immorality and infidelity. When Harcourt died five days after the prince consort, on 19 December 1861, speculation was rife about who would succeed him as Lady Waldegrave's husband. Like her first two husbands, Harcourt left everything he could to Frances (Nuneham was entailed), along with a glowing commendation of his wife in his will, advising her to remarry. The duke of Newcastle was widely thought to be the favourite, but it was the faithful Fortescue—Newcastle's junior at the Colonial Office—whom she married on 20 January 1863. (Shortly afterwards Fortescue changed his name to Parkinson-Fortescue, on inheriting land in Ireland from his aunt.)

Lady Waldegrave devoted the next twenty years to promoting Parkinson-Fortescue's political career and the interests of the Liberal Party to which he belonged. Like the political hostesses of earlier generations, she used her phenomenal energy, her personal tact and sympathy, her hospitable instincts, her considerable wealth, and her open houses to drum up and maintain support for the party, and to find support for her husband's career. When Parkinson-Fortescue was sent to Ireland as chief secretary (1865–6, 1868–71), Frances accompanied him; her entertainments in Dublin were on a lavish scale not seen for years as she set about wooing support for the ministry. She made at least one enemy, Lord Kimberley, who was lord lieutenant, and whose wife was completely outshone by Lady Waldegrave. With Parkinson-Fortescue's chief, W. E. Gladstone, Frances had a difficult relationship: he frequented her parties in the 1860s, but they came into conflict over policy, as Frances and Parkinson-Fortescue were always more conservative than Gladstone. She was determined that Parkinson-Fortescue should shine and felt aggrieved when Gladstone first took over the development of policy on the disestablishment of the Irish church and the Irish Land Act of 1870. She threatened to bring down the government, which vastly overestimated both her influence with the party and Parkinson-Fortescue's necessity to it; but she was not a negligible figure, and her social influence had to be taken into account as a factor promoting the cohesion of the Liberal Party. The real difficulty was that Parkinson-Fortescue had probably been promoted beyond his capacities; unlike Lady Palmerston, Frances threw her weight behind a man who fatally lacked ambition and had no more than moderate talents.

Throughout the 1870s Lady Waldegrave and Baron Carlingford (as Parkinson-Fortescue became in 1874) continued their relentless round of entertaining, at Strawberry Hill, at Dudbrook House in Essex, at Chewton Priory in Somerset, and at 7 Carlton Gardens. The prince and princess of Wales kept up the royal connections, especially after the Aumales (who had been such frequent guests as to become a positive menace) returned to France in 1871. She had never been politically exclusive: Conservatives as well as Liberals and whigs were welcomed to her parties—Disraeli was a regular guest, slipping into Carlton Gardens from the neighbouring Carlton Club. Late in June 1879 Frances was taken ill, initially with a cold, but she began having heart problems and congestion of the lungs. She died at 7 Carlton Gardens on 5 July 1879 and was buried at Chewton Mendip parish church, Somerset. Carlingford was devastated by his wife's death, and spent his remaining twenty years mourning her, his political career effectively ended by the passing of her ambition.

Frances, Countess Waldegrave, was an extraordinary figure in Victorian society. With her origins in the theatre, she was herself an intensely theatrical, larger-than-life individual: no truly satisfactory portrait of her was ever taken. She aroused strong emotions; many adored her, others considered her an upstart adventuress. She was widely supposed to have been the model for Anthony Trollope's Madame Max Goestler in the Palliser novels; Phineas Finn owed much to Carlingford. The Somerset and

Essex estates that had come to her from her first marriages returned to the Waldegrave family under the terms of her will. Carlingford could not bear to live at Strawberry Hill without her, and in 1888 a second Strawberry Hill auction took place.   K. D. REYNOLDS

Sources Som. ARS, Strachie MSS • O. W. Hewett, *Strawberry fair: a biography of Frances, Countess Waldegrave* (1956) • O. W. Hewett, '… and Mr Fortescue' (1958) • K. D. Reynolds, *Aristocratic women and political society in Victorian Britain* (1998) • E. D. Steele, *Irish land and British politics* (1974) • *Letters of Edward Lear to Chichester Fortescue, Lord Carlingford, and Frances, Countess Waldegrave*, ed. Lady Shirley (1907) • *Later letters of Edward Lear*, ed. Lady Strachey (1911) • *CGPLA Eng. & Wales* (1879) • V. Wemyss, ed., *Memoirs and letters of the Right Hon. Sir Robert Morier from 1826 to 1876*, 2 vols. (1911)
Archives BL, diaries, Add. MSS 63705–63727 • Som. ARS, corresp. and papers | Bodl. Oxf., letters to Disraeli
Likenesses L. E. Dubute, oils, 1849, repro. in Hewett, '… and Mr Fortescue'; priv. coll. • M. Noble, statuette, 1858, repro. in Hewett, '… and Mr Fortescue'; priv. coll. • C. Silvy, photograph, 1861, NPG [*see illus.*] • Desanges, group portrait, 1865 (*Strawberry Hill: the drawing room*), repro. in Hewett, *Strawberry fair* • Ercole, portrait, 1871, repro. in Hewett, *Strawberry fair* • A. Maclure, lithograph, BM; repro. in *Whitehall Review* (1876) • J. A. Vinter, lithograph (after M. Tekusch), BM • lithograph (after J. K. Swinton, 1850), repro. in Hewett, *Strawberry fair* • lithograph, BM • photographs, repro. in *Later letters of Edward Lear*, ed. Strachey
Wealth at death under £70,000: probate under certain limitations, 25 Aug 1879, *CGPLA Eng. & Wales*

Fortescue, George (*c*.1588–1659), essayist and poet, was born in London, the only son of John Fortescue (*fl.* 1570–1614), officer of the queen's wardrobe, and his wife, Ellen, daughter of Ralph Henslow of Barrald, Kent. His father, who sheltered Catholics at his house in Blackfriars, London, was the second son of Sir Anthony *Fortescue and a grandson of Sir Geoffrey *Pole. Having probably attended the English College at Douai, George was at the English College at Rome from October 1609 to April 1614.

Fortescue was the author of *Chori inter publicas disputationes auditi* (1612) and perhaps of *The Soule's Pilgrimage to Heavenly Hierusalem* (1650). Dedicatory verses by him appear at the start of the *Poems* of Sir John Beaumont, his brother-in-law, of whom he writes therein: 'my Pen was taught to move by thee'. He also has lines prefixed to Sir Thomas Hawkins's translation of the *Odes of Horace* (1625), Rivers's *Devout Rhapsodies* (1628), and *The Tongue's Virtuis*. An adamant recusant, Fortescue was associated with the circle of Counter-Reformation writers that included Beaumont, Hawkins, and Walter Colman. Others with whom he corresponded in Latin were: Cardinal Franceso Barberini, nephew of Urban VIII; Gregorio Panzani, Urban VIII's messenger to the English Catholics; Famiano Strada, the historian of the Spanish wars in Flanders; and Thomas Farnaby, the critic and grammarian.

Published in Douai in 1630, Fortescue's *Feriae academicae* is a collection of elegant Latin essays on diverse subjects. The exercises frequently display the author's artistic sensibilities, whether in passages praising the palaces and gardens of noble Roman families or in descriptions of paintings by his friend Sir Nathaniel Bacon. That his erudition extended far beyond the arts is demonstrated in chapters such as 'Astrologorum concessus' ('A meeting of astronomers'; *Feriae*, 122ff). Moreover, he was asked by Galileo

Galilei for his opinion on the nature of the tides in a letter addressed 'Eruditissimo viro' ('to a most learned man'; Fortescue, 439). It was probably through a combination of his learning and his Catholicism that Fortescue appeared on Edmund Bolton's list of proposed 'essentials' of the Royal Academy.

Until 1642 Fortescue had served as the duke of Lorraine's ambassador to Pope Urban VIII, and was secretary in London to his cousin Anthony Fortescue, the duke's resident at the English court, at the time of his dismissal by the houses of parliament in 1644. George Fortescue was arrested and imprisoned for sixteen weeks, then ordered to quit the kingdom with his principal. He died in London in 1659, his will being dated on 17 July that year, and may have been buried at St Andrew's, Holborn.

ROSS KENNEDY

Sources J. Fortescue, *A history of the family of Fortescue*, ed. T. Fortescue, 2nd edn (1880), 254, 429, 436–44 • J. Mitford, 'Retrospective review', *GM*, 2nd ser., 28 (1847), 382 ff. • W. Kelly, ed., *Liber ruber venerabilis collegii Anglorum de urbe*, 1, Catholic RS, 37 (1940), 156 • E. H. Burton and T. L. Williams, eds., *The Douay College diaries, third, fourth and fifth, 1598–1654*, 2, Catholic RS, 11 (1911), 439, 442–3 • A. F. Allison and D. M. Rogers, eds., *The contemporary printed literature of the English Counter-Reformation between 1558 and 1640*, 1 (1989), 75 • J. Nichols, *The history and antiquities of the county of Leicester*, 3/2 (1804), 656 • J. Hunter, 'An account of the scheme for erecting a Royal Academy in England in the reign of King James I', *Archaeologia*, 32 (1847), 144 • [J. Beaumont], *The shorter poems of Sir John Beaumont*, ed. R. D. Sell, 49 (1974), 8–9, 21, 63

Fortescue, George Knottesford (1847–1912), librarian, was the fourth of six sons (and one daughter) of Edward Bowes Knottesford Fortescue (*d.* 1877), provost of St Ninian's Cathedral, Perth, and his wife, Frances Anne (*d.* 1868), daughter of William Spooner, archdeacon of Coventry and rector of Elmdon, Warwickshire. He was born at Alveston Manor, Warwickshire, 2 miles from Stratford upon Avon, in October 1847. During 1862 and 1863 he was educated at St Mary's College, Harlow, an Anglo-Catholic school, where his high spirits got him into trouble. He then entered the merchant service and served for a time as a midshipman in the *St Lawrence*, a Blackwall frigate. For most of 1868 he worked for Lucius Spooner, a land agent in Westminster, and then for T. & W. Smith of Crosby Square, shipowners, whose vessels included the *St Lawrence*.

After failing to obtain a post in the British Museum in 1869, Fortescue entered the department of printed books in 1870, on the nomination of A. C. Tait, archbishop of Canterbury, his mother's brother-in-law. Though not a scholar he had great abilities and contemporaries saw in him a sailor's quickness and versatility. He soon made his mark and became an expert on the French Revolution, as a result of cataloguing the museum's collection of pamphlets from the period (to which he published a summary guide in 1899). From 1877 to 1884 he had the responsible post of 'placer', which involved arranging the books on the shelves in subject order, and exercising overall control of accommodation in the book stacks. In December 1884 he succeeded Richard Garnett as superintendent of the reading-room, where he was very popular with the readers, but found the work tiring and worrying. He promptly began, mainly in his private time, to compile a subject index of the modern books acquired since the titles of accessions were first printed (instead of transcribed) in 1880. He grasped at once the doctrine, which he continually preached, that headings must be chosen to fit books, not books classified under headings previously selected to cover the whole of human knowledge. His *Subject-Index* to the acquisitions of 1880–85, published by the trustees of the British Museum in 1886, met the wants of readers, and its continuation in successive five-yearly volumes to 1910 was his main achievement. (The series continued until the publication in 1986 of the volumes covering the period 1971–5.) This task left him little energy for literary work, but he wrote the lives of eight of his ancestors for the *Dictionary of National Biography*, besides a few articles and papers.

In May 1899 Fortescue became keeper of printed books, and held this office (despite much ill health) until his death. As keeper, his good nature gained for him the affectionate devotion of his staff. In 1907 he dealt ably with the problems arising from the closure for six months of the reading-room so that it could be redecorated and its collection of reference books reorganized. In 1908 he edited a catalogue of the books and newspapers relating to the civil war and the Commonwealth, collected by George Thomason and given to the museum by George III, and became almost as much interested in these as in the French Revolution pamphlets. He was president of the Library Association (1901) and of the Bibliographical Society (1909–10). In 1906 he received an honorary LLD from the University of Aberdeen.

Fortescue was married twice; first, in 1875, to Eliza (known as Ida), daughter of the Revd William Blatch, minister of St John's Episcopal church, Perth; and (after her death in 1896) second, in 1899, to Beatrice (d. 1936), widow of H. Webster-Jones MD. By neither of his marriages had he any children. He died on 26 October 1912, four days before he was due to retire, at Residence 4, the British Museum, and was buried in St Pancras cemetery, Finchley, on 31 October. A. W. POLLARD, rev. P. R. HARRIS

Sources H. Jenner, *George Knottesford Fortescue: a memory*, reprinted from *The Library* (1913) · *The Times* (28 Oct 1912) · *Library Association Record*, 15 (1913), 48–50
Archives BL, MSS
Likenesses photograph, BL; repro. in Jenner, *George Knottesford Fortescue*
Wealth at death £883 9s. 11d.: probate, 15 Nov 1912, CGPLA Eng. & Wales

Fortescue, Henry (d. c.1460), justice, was the eldest son of Sir John Fortescue (d. c.1435) of Holbeton, Devon, and his wife, Eleanor Norris; Henry would inherit the manor of Wood Barton in Woodleigh from his mother. The family had links with the Courtenays, earls of Devon, and Henry Fortescue is recorded as an esquire of Earl Hugh before March 1419. But like his younger brother John *Fortescue, Henry trained as a lawyer, and was a member of Lincoln's Inn by 1420. In December 1421 he was returned as a knight of the shire for Devon. His career as a lawyer brought him promotion in Ireland rather than England, for on 25 June 1426 he was appointed chief justice of king's bench in Dublin. His salary was at first to be £40 per annum, but on 8 November following this was increased to a fee of 3s. 4d. a day. Payments fell into arrears, and perhaps for this reason on 4 April 1427 he was granted the custody of lands in Rathmore, Kildare, and elsewhere in Ireland. His tenure of office was not without controversy; twice a spokesman for the Irish parliament in making representations to Westminster, in November 1428 it was alleged that he and Sir Thomas Strange had been assaulted in the course of one of these missions. Fortescue received a new patent on 10 June 1428, but was replaced as chief justice by Stephen Bray on 18 February following.

The rest of Fortescue's career was spent in England, though he did not at once sever all links with Ireland—in March 1430 he acted as a feoffee for the fourth earl of Ormond. Consistently overshadowed by his brother John, he was one of the Devon notables sworn to keep the peace in 1434, but was only occasionally appointed to judicial commissions. Perhaps because he was from time to time said to be involved in acts of disorder—an alleged assault at Dodbrooke in 1421, a dispute over land in Nethercombe some ten years later, in the course of which he was said to have deployed a troop of Irishmen and Scots against his adversaries—he was not appointed to the Devon bench until November 1447, at the end of a year in which he served as sheriff of the county. He was sheriff of Cornwall in 1447–8, and of Devon again in 1452–3—all appointments that he probably owed to his brother. In 1454 Fortescue was a commissioner of array to defend the coasts of Devon, and in 1457 he was appointed to levy 284 archers in the county. Though last appointed a JP on 21 September 1458, Fortescue was among the feoffees to whom Joan Penells conveyed lands in Bowden and Georges Teign on 28 May 1460, and he was apparently believed to be still alive on 31 October following. But further references are wanting, and he probably died at about this time.

Henry Fortescue married three times. With his first wife, named Katherine, whom he had married before 4 February 1421, he appears to have had a son, John. Katherine was dead by 1424, when Fortescue is recorded as married to Joan Bosom of Bosomzeal. His third wife, whom he had married before 20 November 1437, was Margaret, daughter and heir of Nicholas Fallapit, with whom he had another son, Richard. Margaret outlived Fortescue and died in 1465, having married Ralph Strode of Newnham-Strode. HENRY SUMMERSON

Sources HoP, *Commons, 1386–1421*, 3.108–9 · Chancery records · J. Fortescue, *A history of the family of Fortescue*, ed. T. Fortescue, 2nd edn (1880), 44–9 · E. Tresham, ed., *Rotulorum patentium et clausorum cancellariae Hiberniae calendarium*, Irish Record Commission (1828) · R. Lascelles, ed., *Liber munerum publicorum Hiberniae … or, The establishments of Ireland*, 2 vols. [1824–30] · A. Hughes, *List of sheriffs for England and Wales: from the earliest times to AD 1831*, PRO (1898); repr. (New York, 1963) · CClR, 1454–61, 448 · CPR, 1452–61, 620

Fortescue, Hugh, second Earl Fortescue (1783–1861), politician, was born on 13 February 1783 at the Army Pay Office, Whitehall, the eldest son of Hugh Fortescue, third

Baron and first Earl Fortescue (1753–1841), and his wife, Hester (1760–1847), daughter of the statesman George Grenville. He had two brothers and six sisters. When his father, one of the largest landowners in Devon, received an earldom from Pitt in 1789, Fortescue took the courtesy title of Lord Ebrington, by which name he was known for most of his career. He was educated at Eton College and at Brasenose College, Oxford. He was returned to parliament for Barnstaple in 1804, and acted with the 'new' opposition to Pitt led by his uncle, Lord Grenville [see Grenville, William Wyndham, Baron Grenville], whose own administration he supported. He was re-elected for Barnstaple in 1806, but defeated there as an opponent of the Portland ministry in 1807. Another uncle, the first marquess of Buckingham, returned him for St Mawes in July; but two years later he took a half-pay army commission, vacated his seat, and went to follow the Peninsular campaign.

In 1812 Ebrington re-entered parliament—again thanks to his uncle—as MP for Buckingham. He was an evangelical in religion and in his maiden speech, on 27 June 1814, he supported a call for suppression of the slave trade. He had two audiences at Elba with Bonaparte (whom he admired) in December of that year (*Memorandum of Two Conversations*, 1823). Already disenchanted with the Grenvillites' conservatism, he deplored the renewal of war, and in 1816 began to vote with the advanced wing of the whigs. He vacated Buckingham to contest Devon in May, and was defeated; but he was returned again for Buckingham through his cousin, the second marquess of Buckingham. Ebrington's final, though amicable, political break from his relatives occurred in 1817, when he opposed the suspension of habeas corpus and voted for parliamentary reform before surrendering his seat.

Ebrington headed the poll for Devon in 1818, was beaten in 1820 and in 1826, but won a spectacular victory in 1830. He had meanwhile been accommodated at Tavistock by the influence of the sixth duke of Bedford. He was unopposed in Devon in 1831, as he was in its northern division in 1832, 1835, and 1837. In the 1820s he attained an influential position in the whig party as one of its younger generation of noblemen who actively promoted a liberal agenda, including parliamentary reform, in an attempt to wrest the initiative from the radicals. He had no office in the Grey ministry, but played a prominent part in rallying support for it in the reform crises of October 1831 and May 1832. Ebrington, who provided a valuable link between the aristocratic and country strands of whiggism, subsequently mustered back-bench support for the appropriation of surplus Irish church revenues, thereby helping to commit the party to practical reform while remaining undefiled by radicalism. Le Marchant wrote of him in 1833: 'He is not a man of powerful mind or extensive information, but he is integrity personified, and all his views are liberal and enlightened' (Aspinall, 366). In 1839 Ebrington was summoned to the Lords in his father's barony and appointed viceroy of Ireland, where he remained until the fall of the Melbourne government in 1841, shortly after he succeeded as second Earl Fortescue. Partly

to publicize free-trade doctrines, he published in 1844 *A Selection from the Speeches and Writings* of his brother-in-law, the seventh Lord King. A promoter of public health and educational reform, Fortescue was lord steward of the household in Russell's ministry, from 1846 to 1850.

Ebrington was twice married: first, on 4 July 1817, to Lady Susan Ryder (1796–1827), daughter of the first earl of Harrowby; they had three sons, including the politician Hugh *Fortescue, before her premature death. His second marriage, on 26 July 1841, was to Elizabeth, widow of Sir Marcus Somerville, and daughter of Piers Geale of Clonsilla, co. Dublin; they had no children. Fortescue, who was lord lieutenant of Devon from 1839 and was made a KG in 1856, died at Exeter on 14 September 1861. His widow died in 1896, aged ninety-one.   D. R. FISHER

Sources HoP, *Commons, 1790–1820*, 3.791–3 · J. Saunders, *Saunders' portraits and memoirs of eminent living political reformers* (1840), 135–7 · *Eton portrait gallery* (1876), 348–52 · *The Times* (17 Sept 1861) · R. Brent, *Liberal Anglican politics: whiggery, religion, and reform, 1830–1841* (1987) · I. Newbould, *Whiggery and reform, 1830–41* (1990) · P. Mandler, *Aristocratic government in the age of reform: whigs and liberals, 1830–1852* (1990) · A. Aspinall, ed., *Three early nineteenth-century diaries* (1952) [extracts from Le Marchant, E. J. Littleton, Baron Hatherton, and E. Law, earl of Ellenborough] · GEC, *Peerage*
Archives Bodl. Oxf., memoranda on visits to Napoleon Bonaparte · Devon RO, corresp., diaries, and papers · TCD, letters | BL, letters to George Fortescue, Add. MS 69364 · Hunt. L., letters to Grenville family · PRO, corresp. with Lord John Russell · Sandon Hall, Staffordshire, Harrowby Manuscript Trust, corresp. with Lord Harrowby · U. Durham, corresp. with second and third earls Grey · UCL, corresp. with Sir Edwin Chadwick · W. Sussex RO, letters to duke of Richmond · Woburn Abbey, corresp. with duke of Bedford
Likenesses W. Hull, engraving, 1833 (after portrait by G. Hayter), NPG
Wealth at death under £50,000: probate, 17 Sept 1862, *CGPLA Eng. & Wales*

Fortescue, Hugh, third Earl Fortescue (1818–1905), politician, was born on 4 April 1818 in Upper Brook Street, London, the eldest son of Hugh *Fortescue, second Earl Fortescue (1783–1861), and his first wife, Lady Susan (1796–1827), eldest daughter of the Dudley *Ryder, first earl of Harrowby. A younger brother, Dudley Francis Fortescue (1820–1909), was MP for Andover (1857–74) and a commissioner in lunacy (1867–83). Known until his grandfather's death in 1841 as the Hon. Hugh Fortescue, and thenceforth until 1859 as Viscount Ebrington, he was educated first at Harrow School and from 1836 at Trinity College, Cambridge; he did not take a degree. He left the university in 1839 to become private secretary to his father, then lord lieutenant of Ireland, and in 1840–41 he was private secretary to Lord Melbourne, the prime minister. Elected MP for Plymouth as a whig in 1841, he held the seat until 1852; in 1846 he easily defeated Henry Vincent, the Chartist, but in 1847 was almost defeated by Roundell Palmer, the Peelite. In 1852 he unsuccessfully contested Barnstaple, the constituency being disfranchised for bribery two years later. In 1854 he was returned for Marylebone.

Ebrington was a serious whig of religious bent. He supported free trade and the repeal of the corn laws and was appointed lord-in-waiting in 1846 by Russell. He formed an important friendship with Sir Edwin Chadwick, and supported Chadwickian initiatives in a variety of areas. From 1847 to 1851 he was secretary to the poor-law board. He was also a member of the Metropolitan Consolidated Commission on Sewers from 1847, and its chairman from 1849 (unpaid), during the period of Chadwickian reform. He resigned from the chairmanship in 1851 following a row over London sewers. 'The Commission did indeed make a sorry hash of its work, and everyone was discredited—except the engineers' is Chadwick's biographer's view (Finer, 441). He supported Chadwick's view of the future administration of public health during a sharp row in 1850–52, and the legislation of 1852 was a defeat for both of them. He lectured and wrote on these subjects voluminously, publishing among other works *Unhealthiness of Towns* (1846) and *Representative Government in the Metropolis* (1854). In the 1880s he frequently recommended a knighthood for his friend Chadwick, which was eventually forthcoming just before the latter's death.

On 11 March 1847 Ebrington married Georgiana Augusta Charlotte Caroline (1826–1866), eldest daughter of the Hon. George Lionel Dawson-Damer and his wife, Mary Georgiana Emma, *née* Seymour. They had thirteen children before his wife died in childbirth on 8 December 1866. She had earlier refused an offer of marriage from Louis Napoleon, her father rejecting him as a penniless Frenchman.

Though he was regarded by some as a promising whig leader for the future, Ebrington, perhaps because of his strong association with Chadwick, could not find a place in Aberdeen's government in 1852 or in Palmerston's in 1855. He pursued his reforming views, however, and his interest in public health led him to inspect soldiers' conditions in the Crimea in 1856; while doing so he contracted ophthalmia, lost an eye, and seriously injured his health. He was unopposed at the election in 1857 and retired from his seat in February 1859. On 5 December 1859 he was given a peerage as fifth Baron Fortescue through his father's barony of Fortescue; on his father's death on 14 September 1861 he succeeded to the earldom and the family estates, chiefly in Devon but also at Waterford, Ireland. Once in the Lords, he took no great part in political life.

Fortescue remained a moderate reformer, active in writing pamphlets and addresses, including *Public Schools and the Middle Classes* (1864), an address to the British Association at Plymouth (1877) and to the Sanitary Congress in Exeter (1880). He increasingly differed rather angrily with Gladstone, as leader of the Liberal Party, on Irish church disestablishment and many other issues between 1868 and 1874 and on the Eastern Question from 1876. He told the Lords he was not willing to join the Conservatives—'I am not yet Revolutionary enough for that'—but he ceased on most questions to support his former party (Parry, 323). He cautioned against further political reform in 'Our next leap in the dark' (*Nineteenth Century*, March 1881) and in 1886 he opposed home rule for Ireland. He was a strong supporter of the establishment of elected county councils in 1888, however, and he supported the establishment of a university in Devon. He worked with Frederick Temple, when bishop of Exeter, in setting up the diocesan conference and was a noted benefactor in the county. He encouraged stag-hunting on Exmoor and was a good horseman, being the last man habitually to pay calls in London and make his way to the Lords on horseback. He died at his seat, Castle Hill, near South Molton, Devon, on 10 October 1905 and was buried at Filleigh on 14 October, a monument being erected in Filleigh church. He was succeeded by his eldest son, Hugh (1854–1932); several of his sons went into the forces; Sir John William *Fortescue, the military historian, was his fifth son.

H. C. G. MATTHEW

Sources DNB · *The Times* (11 Oct 1905) · GEC, *Peerage* · J. P. Parry, *Democracy and religion* (1986) · *Disraeli, Derby and the conservative party: journals and memoirs of Edward Henry, Lord Stanley, 1849–1869*, ed. J. R. Vincent (1978) · Venn, *Alum. Cant.* · S. E. Finer, *The life and times of Sir Edwin Chadwick* (1952)

Archives Devon RO, letters and papers | Arundel Castle, letters to Charles Wentworth George Howard · Devon RO, letters to Sir Thomas Dyke Acland · Glos. RO, letters to Sir Michael Hicks Beach · NL Scot., corresp. with Lord Rutherfurd · U. Durham, letters to third Earl Grey · UCL, corresp. with Edwin Chadwick

Likenesses E. U. Eddis, oils, *c*.1850, priv. coll. · E. B. Stephens, bust, 1861, Barnstaple Infirmary · Bassano, four photographs, 1895, NPG · F. C. Lewis, stipple (after G. Richmond), BM, NPG · T. [T. Chartran], chromolithograph caricature, NPG; repro. in *VF* (17 Sept 1881)

Wealth at death £9510 12*s.* 5*d.*: resworn probate, 7 April 1906, *CGPLA Eng. & Wales*

Fortescue, James (1716–1777), Church of England clergyman and writer, was born at Ford, Milton Abbot, Devon, and baptized in Milton Abbot on 21 July 1716, the son of George Fortescue and Mary, daughter of John Barrett of St Tudy, Cornwall. He matriculated from Exeter College, Oxford, on 9 February 1733, graduating BA on 14 October 1736. He was elected to a Petrie fellowship in 1737, and proceeded MA on 22 June 1739 before being appointed subdean of his college the following year. He was appointed curate of St Swithin's, Merton, near Bicester, a benefice within the gift of Exeter College, on three occasions: 29 September 1738, 5 October 1743, and 27 December 1746. He held this office concurrently with his fellowship at Exeter. He never married.

Fortescue commenced his modest literary career with *An Epistle with some Odes on Love, Virtue, and other Subjects*, published anonymously in London in 1746. A prefatory advertisement claims that the author composed the verses 'by way of Amusement, under sickness, or Diversion from Business'. The first ode in this charming miscellany, a heartfelt complaint to Chloe on the eve of her marriage to an older, wealthy, suitor, might suggest that Fortescue had been crossed in love. His second venture into print, *The Expedition*, was a patriotic poem in heroic couplets celebrating William Augustus, duke of Cumberland, on his departure for the ill-fated martial expedition to Flanders in 1747. Fortescue was elected senior proctor of the University of Oxford on 20 April 1748 and the gravitas of his appointment seems to be reflected in his next published work, *A View of Life in its Several Passions: with a Preliminary Discourse on Moral Writing*, which appeared in the following year. He graduated BD in 1749, and DD on 20 January 1751.

In 1752 Fortescue published the first part of *Essays Moral and Miscellaneous* which was noticed in the *Monthly Review* (January 1752), and a second part followed two years later. *Pomery-Hill*, an anonymous poem dedicated to the prince of Wales, also appeared in 1754. The lengthy preface to *Pomery-Hill*, which is almost more remarkable than the poem itself, demonstrates the author's formidable classical erudition, and his expert knowledge of prosody. Fortescue signed his final publication, *Dissertations, Essays and Discourses, &c. in Prose and Verse*, which appeared in two volumes in 1759. It received a contemptuous notice in October's *Monthly Review*. On 29 June 1764 he was appointed to the rectorship of St George's parish in Wootton, Northamptonshire, by Exeter College, on the last day of the two calendar months within which the presentation was to be made. Fortescue resigned his fellowship of Exeter College in 1775 and he died at Wootton, intestate, two years later. He was buried in Wootton on 24 September 1777. His widowed sister Mary Venning was granted administration of his effects in November 1777, and his library was sold in 1779.

Fortescue revels in his entrenched position as an implacable ancient, pouring scorn on archetypal moderns: 'O critics, at a distance I feel the terrors of your presence. I tremble at the very thought of your black, your formidable wigs, your rhadamanthean looks, dread inquisition … with reverence I bow myself to your whole divan' (Fortescue, *Pomery-Hill*, xix–xx). He asserts deep misgivings about the moral consequences of literary innovations emanating from the continent: 'all that Cargoe of Farces, Novels, and Romances daily imported from *France* … highly improper for an *English* Taste, and *English* Constitution' (Fortescue, *View of Life*, vi). Although his poetry has some merit, Fortescue's admission of his peripheral literary importance expressed in 'Castle Hill', wherein he describes himself as 'wandr'ing round the verge / Of steep *Parnassus*' (Fortescue, *Dissertations*, 1.i), is a realistic assessment.   JAMES WILLIAM KELLY

Sources parish register, Wootton, Northants. RO, 374P/2 · administration, PRO, PROB 6/153, fol. 125r · register, Milton Abbot, Devon, 1653–1723, Plymouth and West Devon Record Office, Plymouth, acc. no. 797/1 [baptism, marriage, death; microfiche] · [J. Fortescue], *An epistle with some odes on love, virtue, and other subjects* (1746) · [J. Fortescue], *The expedition: a poem, on the duke's going to Flanders* (1747) · [J. Fortescue], *A view of life in its several passions: with a preliminary discourse on moral writing* (1749) · [J. Fortescue], *Science: an epistle on its decline and revival with a particular view to the seats of learning, and a virtuous, philosophical life* (1750) · [J. Fortescue], *Science: a poem (in a religious view) on its decline and revival. With a particular regard to the mission of Moses, and the coming of the messiah* (1751) · J. Fortescue, *Essays, moral and miscellaneous*, 2 parts (1752); (1754) · [J. Fortescue], *Pomery-Hill, a poem: humbly addressed to his highness the prince of Wales, with other poems, English and Latin* (1754) · J. Fortescue, *Dissertations, essays, and discourses, &c. in prose and verse*, 2 vols. (1759) · C. W. Boase, ed., *Registrum Collegii Exoniensis*, new edn, OHS, 27 (1894), 141 · Foster, *Alum. Oxon., 1715–1886*, 2.480 · S. Kelly, *The Fortescue family* (1840) · S. Y. R., 'James Fortescue', *N&Q*, 3rd ser., 5 (1864), 354–5 · *VCH Northamptonshire*, 4.294–5 · Watt, *Bibl. Brit.* · A. Wood, *The history and antiquities of the colleges and halls in the University of Oxford*, ed. J. Gutch (1786); appx (1790), 170 · *GM*, 1st ser., 47 (1777), 507 · *Monthly Review, or, Literary Journal*, 6 (Jan 1752), 78 · *Monthly Review, or, Literary Journal*, 21 (Oct 1759), 291–6

Fortescue, Sir John (*c*.1397–1479), justice and political theorist, was the second of the three sons of Sir John Fortescue (*d. c*.1435) of Holbeton in Devon, and Eleanor, daughter and heir of William Norris of North Huish, Devon. His date of birth is unknown. His father was a client of the Courtenays who would later fight at Agincourt, hold a number of military posts in France, and be knighted by the duke of Bedford about 1426. There is no ground for the conjecture that John the younger studied at Oxford, but both he and his elder brother, Henry *Fortescue, were on the books of Lincoln's Inn by 1420. Henry held the post of chief justice of the king's bench of Ireland between 1426 and 1429, and John became a serjeant-at-law in July 1438.

Early life and legal career   Estimating John Fortescue's date of birth is difficult because of confusion with his father and ambiguities in his own writings. Training for the law normally began in the mid-teens and the conventional birth date for Fortescue of *c*.1385 is based on reading autobiographical references as indicating that he started his legal education *c*.1402. This, however, means that he was passed over for appointment as a serjeant in 1425 and not promoted until his mid-fifties, each of which is highly unlikely. Read differently, the references in his writings can indicate a start to training in the early 1420s, and this interpretation is supported by the evidence for his legal practice only becoming plentiful towards the end of that decade.

Fortescue must, however, have begun his studies late because he was undoubtedly the John Fortescue elected MP for Tavistock in May 1421, which would mean that he was born not later than 1399–1400. If it was he and not his father who was appointed in 1418 to the commission of the peace for Devon, the latest date becomes *c*.1397. The probable explanation for this late start in the law is that although he had been entered at Lincoln's Inn by 1420, he was actually absent at the war in France. This was certainly the case with his brother Henry.

In 1423 John Fortescue married Elizabeth, daughter and coheir of Robert Brytte of Doddiscombe in Devon, but she died a minor on 26 April 1426, leaving him no children and none of the expected property. His second marriage (before 1436) was to Isabel, daughter of John James of Norton St Philip near Bath and was altogether more fruitful—property there and a son, Martin, and two daughters. Martin predeceased him (dying in 1471) but left two sons from whom came the earldom of Fortescue and four other eighteenth- and nineteenth-century peerages in the United Kingdom and Ireland.

Fortescue first served as a governor of Lincoln's Inn in 1424–5 (which probably indicates that in the preceding Lammas vacation he had given his first law reading and joined the inn bench). He served as governor again in

1425–6 and 1428–30 (probably reading a second time at Easter 1430). In November 1436 he was one of the benchers involved in regularizing the attendance of senior men at the inn's readings, while on being called to become a serjeant in 1438 he probably read for a third time. None of the readings has so far been identified. Fortescue's growing reputation as a lawyer is shown by his involvement in property transactions for a wide range of clients. In 1429 he was retained by the corporation of Canterbury, and in 1432 by the duchy of Lancaster. This latter entry into royal employment may have been helped by Fortescue's personal position as counsel to Walter, Lord Hungerford, treasurer of the exchequer (1426–32). Between 1430 and 1432 Fortescue was comptroller of the stannaries and certainly benefited from a number of crown grants and wardships. His increasing status ensured that after sitting for a Devon borough—variously Tavistock, Totnes, and Plympton—in each of the parliaments from 1421 to 1432, he was elected in 1437 as county member for Wiltshire (possibly with Hungerford influence), and his wealth is indicated by his loaning the crown £40 to support military initiatives in France in 1436.

Royal lawyer Immediately on promotion to the coif, Fortescue was commissioned on the Norfolk circuit, and on 26 January 1441 he was retained as a king's serjeant, moves that secured his professional services for the crown. He was not, however, immediately promoted to the bench and only after four chief justices had retired or died in a matter of three years was Fortescue raised to lead the king's bench on 20 January 1442. One of his early actions as chief justice was to preside (in 1443) when the bench again rejected an attempt to have a defendant on bail counted as still being in custody, but in 1452 his court did adopt this crucial interpretation, so putting the king's bench on course to expand its jurisdiction and become the dominant court for civil suits until the nineteenth century.

Chief Justice Fortescue was, however, principally notable as one of the most reliable supporters of the troubled Lancastrian government. Although he moved (as convention dictated) to the home circuit, in 1443 he was back in Norwich, sorting out local disturbances on behalf of the king's council, which sent him a special letter of thanks. He is frequently noted as present in council, and took on a wide range of legal and quasi-legal tasks in addition to his regular judicial work. Loyalty and energy brought Fortescue considerable rewards. He was a knight by October 1442, and in 1443 was granted an annuity of 40 marks (in addition to the normal emoluments of his office, plus two extra tuns of wine a year), and he received a further annuity of £40 from 1447. He benefited from the farms of several valuable estates in crown hands, and was able to purchase considerable property in Gloucestershire, Herefordshire, and Wiltshire.

Fifteenth-century justices knew nothing of any separation between an executive and a judiciary. They were sworn to do justice without fear or favour, but in practice this meant exploiting due process to achieve what the king wanted. Fortescue may, as was claimed in the letters of fraternity issued by Christ Church, Canterbury, to himself and his wife in 1447, have been personally 'vir equidem iustus quem omnes diserti iustum discernunt obsequuntur venerantur et diligunt' ('a truly just man, whom all wise men perceive to be just, and whom they defer to, venerate and love'; Fortescue, *Governance*, 48)—although he is known to have accepted at least one large bribe (from Sir John Fastolf)—but he was certainly not independent of government. Historians have noted that in 1447 he refused royal orders to release a pardoned traitor from prison at Wallingford, but this was merely because he did not have the proper authority, and an appropriate signet instruction arrived in days. His support for the Lancastrian government soon made his name a byword. The Kentish rebels in 1450 accused him of being 'fals to beleve' (Gairdner, 98); in January 1451 he was holed up in his house for a week for fear of assault and later that year Kent again complained about him. In 1450 when the justices were consulted by the Lords about the accusations brought by the Commons against the king's favourite, the duke of Suffolk, Fortescue led his colleagues to advise that the charges were not serious enough to justify custody, and the proviso exempting him from the subsequent act resuming royal grants possibly represents his reward. In 1453 when consulted about the imprisonment at the suit of the duke of York of another royal partisan, Speaker Thomas Thorpe, Fortescue explained on behalf of the justices that though they could not rule on the power of parliament, precedent was clearly on the side of releasing Thorpe.

Lancastrian partisan Throughout the 1450s Fortescue was clearly, in his own words, 'a partial man' (*Works*, 532), acting on commission after commission against local unrest. His younger brother, Richard, fought for the king and was killed at the first battle of St Albans in 1455, and when Henry VI and his queen, Margaret of Anjou, recovered power Sir John appears to have taken a leading role in securing the attainder of the Yorkists at the Coventry parliament of 1459. He was also named an executor of Henry VI's will. Fortescue nevertheless appears not to have thought himself to be in immediate danger when the Yorkists turned the tables at the battle of Northampton in July 1460. He continued to preside at Westminster, and in October is listed among the justices consulted on the claim of Richard of York to the throne.

Two months later the defeat and death of the duke of York at Wakefield forced men to take sides openly. Fortescue witnessed his last document at Westminster in January 1461, settled property on his wife in her own right (using as his agent the Yorkist lawyer Thomas Yonge) 'bicause of the trouble and Joperde that [he] was and stode in' (Scofield, 323), and went to join Queen Margaret in the north. On 29 March 1461 he was present at Towton where the new Yorkist claimant, Edward IV, and his ally the earl of Warwick won a decisive victory. Fortescue took immediate refuge in Scotland with the royal party, but then returned to help lead a Lancastrian counter-attack in June, only to be defeated at Ryton and Brancepeth in co. Durham.

Back in Scotland, Fortescue was appointed chancellor to Henry VI (and also helped to finance him for a time). In 1462 he visited France to seek support from her new king, Louis XI, and in July 1463, with Queen Margaret and the prince of Wales, he left Scotland (and Henry VI) for the last time, settling eventually at St Mihiel in the duchy of Bar. There he tutored the adolescent prince of Wales, badgered Louis XI for support, and attempted to recruit other continental powers to the Lancastrian cause. His activities made him something of a bogeyman for the Yorkist regime. In 1462 he was rumoured to be about to land at Sandwich with a Franco-Spanish force, part of a three-pronged Lancastrian invasion. More realistic were his ultimately successful efforts to bring about the alliance in 1470 between Margaret and the now dissident earl of Warwick that restored Henry VI to the throne. Warwick, however, was defeated and killed at Barnet on 14 April 1471, the day on which Margaret, Prince Edward, and Fortescue landed at Weymouth, and three weeks later the prince was killed at the battle of Tewkesbury, and Margaret and Fortescue were captured.

The popular expectation was that Sir John would lose his head at last, but Edward IV required him instead to produce a refutation of the writings he had published attacking the Yorkist claim to the throne. He was pardoned and reinstated as a royal counsellor, and once the refutation was complete his attainder was reversed and his property restored. He lived for nearly six more years, dying shortly before 18 December 1479. A painted stone tomb effigy survives in St Eadburga's Church, Ebrington.

Political propagandist Edward's assessment of the relative value of Fortescue's pen as against his neck is a clear measure of his importance as a writer. With the possible exception of Sir Thomas More, Fortescue is the English common lawyer who until the days of Coke and Bratton had most to say of importance to a reading public outside his own profession. He was the author of nine literary works still extant, and at least five others are known to have been lost (one of them a book of devotion); there is one conjectural work, and in addition the possibility that Fortescue was responsible for the *Dialogue between Understanding and Faith*, a translation of Alain Chartier's *Traité de l'esperance*. There are also four attributed items, probably spurious. Fortescue was fluent in both Latin and French and had an easy familiarity with the standard apparatus and ideas of the late medieval scholar, including the Bible, Aristotle (quoted very frequently), Vincent of Beauvais, Boethius, St Augustine, and St Thomas Aquinas. In some cases he had the texts at first hand, but more often he used one of the compendia of knowledge that were in common circulation. He also knew works by Poggio Bracciolini and Leonardo Bruni. Less surprisingly, Fortescue had a close acquaintance with Roman and canon law. His mental world was also deeply informed by his common-law background, and some of his thinking can be paralleled elsewhere in the profession.

Ten of Fortescue's pieces were Lancastrian propaganda tracts: *De titulo Edwardi comitis Marchie*; *Of the Title of the House of York*; *Defensio juris domus Lancastrie*; *A defence of the title of the house of Lancaster, or, A replication to the claim of the duke of York*; *Opusculum de natura legis nature et eius censura in successione regnorum suprema*; the ascribed *Somnium vigilantis, or, A Defence of the Proscription of the Yorkists*, and lost works on the succession in English and Latin, a genealogy of the house of Lancaster, and a related genealogy of James II of Scotland. Of the extant works, *De titulo* was written not earlier than the coronation of Louis XI on 15 April 1461 and the remainder before July 1463. An eleventh political item is the refutation demanded by Edward IV, *Declaration upon certayn wrytinges sent oute of Scotteland ayenst the kynges title to the roialme of Englond*, written between the defeat at Tewkesbury and 6 October 1473.

The Yorkist claim to the crown rested on descent from Edward III through the female line, and Fortescue based part of his propaganda case on the history of various countries, which showed that women did not inherit or transmit rights to the crown. He also pointed to the strength of the Lancastrian title by prescription. However, his principal argument (worked out in detail in *Opusculum de natura legis nature*) was that women were excluded from ruling by natural law, a principle that had also been specifically endorsed by scripture. When it came to recanting these views, the historical precedents presented Fortescue with few problems. He trumped the natural law difficulty by arguing that since 'ther is now noo kingdome in erthe of Cristen men of which the Kynge is not subjecte [to the pope] also welle in temporaltes as spirituelles', the Yorkist claims via the female line did not violate the principle of ultimate male supremacy (*Works*, 535). The unanswerable Lancastrian claim by prescription was quietly ignored.

Writings on government Fortescue's propaganda skills saved his neck in 1471, but the interest of history is in his remaining three works, which deal with English government and the constitution. *De laudibus legum Angliae*, written in the last years of Fortescue's exile (1468–71), ostensibly to instruct the young prince of Wales, is an exposition of the advantages of English common law over the Roman law of the continent, and contains a uniquely valuable description of the inns of court and the legal profession. The *Articles Sent from the Prince to the Earl of Warwick* (December 1470–March 1471) is a short blueprint for a council to control the senile Henry VI. In the years immediately after Tewkesbury, elements of this were incorporated in a second and much more substantial assessment of the problems facing the country, written in English but known from the title of its first chapter as *De dominio regale et politico* (alternatively *The Difference between an Absolute and a Limited Monarchy*).

Fortescue's analysis of the problems of his day has had a significant influence on later historical interpretations of the period. He argued that poverty was the root cause of the collapse of royal authority, a poverty caused by the alienation of the royal estate. This had destroyed the king's freedom to act, and had denied him the means to maintain an image of magnificence and to exercise a proper degree of patronage. The beneficiaries had been 'ouer myghtye subgettes'—a memorable term perhaps coined by Sir John (Fortescue, *Governance*, 127). The landed wealth of such magnates allowed them to eclipse the power of the king and to focus loyalty on themselves. Fortescue's answer was to re-endow the king by a parliamentary resumption of land grants, together with a one-off subsidy to buy the loyalty of those who lost by it, coupled with an exploitation of the custom duties. He also advocated a significant reduction of the influence of the magnates on the council, and their replacement by salaried officials, and particular caution over the future exercise of patronage.

Beyond this analysis of the problems of his own day, Fortescue's importance lies in his writing on the nature of political authority. He distinguished three kinds: regal dominion, political dominion, and a combined form: regal and political dominion. Fortescue took the original distinction from St Thomas Aquinas, who had postulated the third form to accommodate the government of imperial Rome which exhibited both regal and political features. Sir John's originality was to realize that other states fell into that category, including England. Its king ruled by hereditary right, and had full regal authority over his subjects. His duty was that imposed by the law of nature on every king—to do justice. On the other hand he was not absolute. His power derived from the body politic, and the laws he had to administer were only such as he and the people assented to. What is more, that limitation on regality was institutionalized in parliament, and enforcement was by judges sworn to uphold those laws, not the king's will.

Later influence Fortescue's authority on constitutional law was widely recognized in his own day and increasingly thereafter. This particularly applied to the *De laudibus*, of which the first printed edition appeared in 1545–6, and eight further editions were published before the century was out. Interpretation, however, became increasingly anachronistic. When Sir John wrote that in England 'the regal power is restrained by political law' (Chrimes, 27), he had in mind the contrast between the absolutism of French kings and English kings who exercised royal authority within political parameters. However, by the seventeenth century the maxim was being regularly used to justify the imposition of constitutional restrictions on the crown. Fortescue was substantially cited by the lawyers representing John Hampden; Edward Coke said that the *De laudibus* was 'worthy to be written in letters of gold for the weight and worthiness thereof' (Coke, report no. 8, fol. xiv). After the civil war the whigs interpreted the term *dominium politicum et regale* as a constitutional formula for the protection of liberty, while in 1778 the philanthropist Granville Sharp claimed Fortescue's authority for colonial resistance to the absolutist pretensions of the Westminster parliament. In the next century interest in Sir John became more scholarly. A respectable edition of the judge's writings was published in 1869 by a distant descendant, Thomas Fortescue, Lord Clermont, supported by an archive-based family history,

and in 1885 Charles Plummer produced a modern text of the *De dominio regale et politico* under a somewhat misleading title, *The Governance of England*. In 1942 an authoritative edition of the *De laudibus legum Angliae* by Stanley B. Chrimes set modern scholarship on the soundest of bases.   E. W. IVES

Sources J. Fortescue, *De laudibus legum Anglie*, ed. and trans. S. B. Chrimes (1942) · J. Fortescue, *The governance of England*, ed. C. Plummer (1885) · *The works of Sir John Fortescue*, ed. T. Fortescue, 2 vols. (1869) · HoP, *Commons, 1386–1421*, 2.108–11 · S. B. Chrimes, *English constitutional ideas of the fifteenth century* (1936) · F. Gilbert, 'Sir John Fortescue's *dominium regale et politicum*', *Medievalia et Humanistica*, 2 (1944), 88–97 · P. E. Gill, 'Politics and propaganda in 15th-century England: the polemical writings of Sir John Fortescue', *Speculum*, 46 (1971), 333–7 · W. P. Baildon, ed., *The records of the Honorable Society of Lincoln's Inn: the black books*, 1–4 (1897–1902) · Baker, *Serjeants* · Sainty, *King's counsel* · Sainty, *Judges* · S. E. Thorne and J. H. Baker, eds., *Readings and moots at the inns of court in the fifteenth century*, 1, SeldS, 71 (1954) · N. Davis, ed., *Paston letters and papers of the fifteenth century*, 2 vols. (1971–6) · *The Paston letters, 1422–1509 AD*, ed. J. Gairdner, new edn, 3 vols. (1872–5); repr. in 4 vols. (1910) · M. Blatcher, *The court of king's bench, 1450–1550: a study in self-help* (1978) · M. S. Blayney, 'Sir John Fortescue and Alain Chartier's *Traité de l'esperance*', *Modern Language Review*, 48 (1953), 385–90 · R. A. Griffiths, *The reign of King Henry VI: the exercise of royal authority, 1422–1461* (1981) · C. L. Scofield, 'Sir John Fortescue in February 1461', *EngHR*, 27 (1912), 321–3 · J. Gairdner, ed., *Three fifteenth-century chronicles*, CS, new ser., 28 (1880) · G. Wilson, ed., *The reports of Edward Coke*, 7 vols. (1777) · G. Sharp, *An address to the English people* (1778) · E. Fortescue, *Fortescutus illustratus* (1663) · A. Davies, *Dictionary of British portraiture*, 1 (1979)

Likenesses W. Faithorne, line engraving, BM, NPG; repro. in Fortescue, *Fortescutus illustratus* · tomb effigy, St Eadburga's, Ebrington, Gloucestershire

Fortescue, Sir John (1533–1607), administrator, was the eldest of three sons of Sir Adrian *Fortescue (*c*.1481–1539), landowner and alleged traitor, of Shirburn and Stonor Place, Oxfordshire, and his second wife, Anne (1510–1585), daughter of Sir William Rede of Boarstall, Buckinghamshire. One of his younger brothers was Sir Anthony *Fortescue (*b*. *c*.1535, *d*. in or after 1611). Their father was executed for alleged treason on 9 July 1539, probably because of his kinship with Anne Boleyn [see Anne (*c*.1500–1536)] and because of his connection with the Poles. Fortescue's mother married Sir Thomas *Parry (*b*. in or before 1515, *d*. 1560), administrator, about 1540. In 1551, following his restitution in blood by act of parliament, Fortescue took possession of his father's estate. About 1555 he entered Princess Elizabeth's household, assisting his stepfather at Woodstock, Oxfordshire, and becoming clerk of the library in 1559. About 1556 he married Cecily (*d*. 1570), daughter of Sir Edmund Ashfield of Ewelme, Oxfordshire, and his wife, Eleanor. They had four sons, including the MPs Francis (*b*. before 1562, *d*. 1624), William (*c*.1562–1629), and Thomas (*b*. *c*.1566, *d*. after 1593), and two daughters. On 20 November 1558, three days after Elizabeth's accession, Parry was appointed comptroller of the royal household and sworn of the privy council. Most likely at his instigation, on 22 July 1559 Fortescue was made keeper of the great wardrobe, a post he held until his death. As keeper, Fortescue was responsible for the care of royal attire, 'cloths and stuff', armour, state documents, and the occasional detention and interrogation of prisoners (*CPR*, *1558–60*, 354).

During summer 1559 Parry granted Fortescue the lease of the manor of Salden in Buckinghamshire. In 1560 Fortescue was made ranger of Wychwood Forest and Cornbury Park, Oxfordshire. He progressively acquired more property in the two counties, purchasing the manors of Drayton Parslow and Tickford in Buckinghamshire and leasing from the queen the manor of Swyncombe in Oxfordshire. In 1599 Fortescue bought the manor of Spelsbury as well as the town of Burford, Oxfordshire, for £2500 and is said to have spent in excess of £33,000 on the construction of a house at Salden. He also acquired the manor house at Hendon in Middlesex and, in addition to his official residence in Blackfriars, owned a house in Westminster. In 1598 he negotiated with Sir Robert Cecil over the purchase of another house in Chelsea.

Before his move to Salden in 1559, Fortescue probably still lived on Parry's estates in Wallingford, Berkshire. Fortescue's first wife died in 1570 and he married Alice (*d.* after 1607), daughter of Christopher Smythe of Annables, Hertfordshire, and his wife, Margaret. They had one daughter. Parry was MP for the borough of Wallingford and his stepson succeeded to the seat in 1559. Fortescue was MP there again in 1572. In 1567 he was appointed steward of Charlbury in Oxfordshire and two years later he was named of the quorum for Buckinghamshire. In 1584 he was appointed steward of the town of Buckingham and was returned as its MP in 1586. He was knight of the shire for Buckinghamshire three times (1589, 1593, and 1597). His influence in the county was extended further when, in late autumn 1586, he was appointed a commissioner of array for Buckinghamshire and Bedfordshire to recruit troops for deployment to the Low Countries.

On 10 February 1588 Fortescue's hitherto loyal yet undistinguished service at court was rewarded with his appointment as a privy councillor. This was typical of the queen's habit of advancing long-standing servants. The parliamentary commissions he sat on before his preferment were merely concerned with routine subjects such as gamekeeping (18 February 1581), the leases of his local diocese (13–15 March 1581), or the learned ministry (8 March 1587). As a privy councillor and, from 1589 to 1603, in his capacity as under-treasurer and chancellor of the exchequer, Fortescue gradually became closely involved in the daily administration of the realm, although his role in parliament remained marginal. As a parliamentary commissioner, he contributed to matters of ecclesiastical discipline, such as the plurality of benefices (20 March 1589), and was noted for his pragmatism and his frequent appeal to tradition.

Despite the pressure of work in the exchequer, Fortescue still presided over an impressive number of lawsuits. These ranged from 'howshold cases', to the indictment of 'lewd and badd people', Middlesex property disputes, grievances of London guilds, or a suit concerning a 'garden plott' in the Tower of London (*APC*, *1590*, 324; *1591*, 51; *1597–8*, 363). His close involvement, early in 1593, in the examination of a number of recusant seminarians in London led to the setting up of two privy council committees on the matter.

Later in 1593 Fortescue was appointed keeper of Hatfield House, Hertfordshire, and *custos rotulorum* for Buckinghamshire. By the following year he had been named *custos rotulorum* for Middlesex. His local influence was buttressed by the return of his brother Thomas Fortescue (1534–1611) as MP for Wallingford in 1593, 1597, and 1601, and the election of his eldest son, Francis Fortescue, as MP for Buckingham in 1589, 1593, and 1597, and for Buckinghamshire in 1601. Fortescue was rather fastidious about protocol and on the first day of business, 27 October 1597, 'moved and admonished that hereafter no member of the House should come into the House with their spurs on, for the offending of others' (D'Ewes, 550). His defeat in the 1604 Buckinghamshire elections by the puritan Francis Goodwin prompted a minor constitutional crisis for the crown and the House of Commons, raising in turn the important question as to whether parliament or the courts had jurisdiction over electoral matters. At the instigation of the court of chancery, Goodwin's election was declared void on the basis of a prior charge of outlawry. A hearing of both candidates by the Commons in March 1604, however, led to the approval of Goodwin by MPs. James VI and I, as arbiter, is said to have displayed considerable indifference in the matter, since Fortescue 'was a councillor not brought in by himself' (PRO, C 142/305/132). The king decided to return both parties as MPs for Buckinghamshire, but Fortescue sat for Middlesex instead, where, by virtue of his London residence, he had been a lord lieutenant since 1596 and had been MP in 1601 (having stepped down from his Buckinghamshire seat to make way for his heir).

Fortescue's contributions to parliamentary debate on the whole remained insignificant. In addition to his regular reports from the subsidy committee of the privy council, he attended minor parliamentary committees, among them discussions on Aylesbury (20 December 1598) and the improvement of attaining a reliable seven mile mark from Great Yarmouth (23 January 1599). At the 1601 parliament he left it to Cecil to defend government policy on the subsidy. Fortescue merely 'spake … to the like effect'. He appealed to parliament in support of increased subsidies: 'I beseech you, remember that the Great Turk when he conquered Constantinople found therin three hundred millions of gold; if they, quoth he, had bestowed three millions in defence of the city, he could have never gotten it. From this blindness, I pray God defend us' (D'Ewes, 685).

Fortescue was chancellor of the duchy of Lancaster from 24 September until 3 October 1601, and then again from 4 November 1601 until his death. For two months, from 23 October 1607, he held the office in conjunction with his half-brother, Sir Thomas *Parry (1544–1616). Early in July 1602 Fortescue was asked to give up his new residence, Duchy House in the Savoy, to accommodate his successor as chancellor of the exchequer, Sir George Home.

Fortescue protested in a letter to Cecil: 'the loss would be a great touch to my reputation' (*Salisbury MSS*, 16.171).

While Fortescue held a number of key offices, his contribution to English political life remained marginal. His loyalty to the crown is paralleled by his loyalty to his wider family. During the trial of his distant relative Robert *Devereux, second earl of Essex (1565–1601), with whom he was on close terms, he is said to have given his charges so quietly as to be inaudible. In 1603 Essex's uncle, Sir George Devereux, reflected that Fortescue had shown the earl 'more benevolent favour [... than his other] friends and kindred' (*Letters of John Chamberlain*, 1.48). Later commentators single out Fortescue's learning, and in particular his aptitude for classical languages, alongside his trustworthiness and his ability to foster lasting friendships. He conducted extensive private correspondence with personal friends such as Francis and Anthony Bacon, Sir Wiliam Cecil, Essex, and Sir Walter Ralegh, much of which survives.

Fortescue died without the provision of a will on 23 December 1607. John Chamberlain commented: 'he left no will, which is thought strange for a man of his years and state: so that his wife carries away all the goods, and her daughter ... the house, land and furniture here at Hendon in Middlesex' (*Letters of John Chamberlain*, 1.248). A friend of Sir Thomas Bodley, during his lifetime Fortescue donated manuscripts and books to the Bodleian Library. He is buried in the parish church of St Mary the Virgin, Mursley, Buckinghamshire.   J. ANDREAS LÖWE

Sources Chancery, patent rolls, PRO, C 66/1421 · Chancery, inquisitions post mortem, series II, PRO, C 142/305/132 · *CPR, 1558–60*, 90, 118, 354, 426; *1569–72*, no. 1878, 3121; *1578–80*, no. 1030 · *APC*, *1586–7*, 115; *1588–9*, 76, 186; *1590*, 21, 208, 324, 338; *1591*, 51, 242; *1592–3*, 145; *1597–8*, 363 · *CSP dom.*, *1595–7*, 4, 566; *1598–1601*, 252 · *Statutes at large* (1619), 5.xiv · W. Camden, *Annales: the true and royall history of the famous Empresse Elizabeth*, trans. A. Darcie (1625), 2.27 · S. D'Ewes, ed., *The journals of all the parliaments during the reign of Queen Elizabeth* (1682), 549, 550, 553–62, 664–8, 685 · D. Lloyd, *State worthies, or, The state men and favourites of England since the Reformation* (1670), 556 · *The letters of John Chamberlain*, ed. N. E. McClure, 1 (1939), 48, 248 · R. Somerville, *History of the duchy of Lancaster, 1265–1603* (1953) · *HoP, Commons, 1558–1603*, 2.147–52
Archives BL, Add. MS 4119 · BL, Harley MSS, corresp. · BL, expenses of coronation of James I, Add. MS 34321 · E. Sussex RO, financial papers · HMC Hatfield, xvi. 171 94f. · Leics. RO, abstract accounts | Hunt. L., letters to Temple family
Likenesses S. Hunt, oils, 1879 (after contemporary portrait), Bodl. Oxf.

Fortescue, Sir John William (1859–1933), military historian, was born on 28 December 1859 in Madeira, the fifth son (and ninth of thirteen children) of Hugh *Fortescue, third Earl Fortescue (1818–1905), and his wife, Georgiana Augusta Charlotte Caroline (1826–1866), eldest daughter of Colonel George Lionel Dawson-Damer, third son of the first earl of Portarlington, and his wife, Mary Georgiana Emma Seymour. He was descended from the fifteenth-century chief justice Sir John *Fortescue. Brought up in country surroundings at Castle Hill, near Barnstaple, he developed a great love of country life, as was later demonstrated in his children's book *The Story of a Red Deer* (1897).

Sir John William Fortescue (1859–1933), by William Strang, 1909

Fortescue was educated at Harrow School (1873–8) and Trinity College, Cambridge (1878–80), receiving a pass degree in 1884. He had wished to follow two elder brothers into the army but his father ruled this out on grounds of expense, so the only practical outlet for his love of the service and its traditions was as an officer in the Royal North Devon yeomanry.

Fortescue left Cambridge intending to read for the bar but, finding the law uncongenial, he became private secretary successively to Sir William Robinson, governor of the Windward Isles (1880–82), and to Sir William Jervois, governor of New Zealand (1886–90). These experiences deepened his interest in military history and the publication of some essays by him on the subject suggested that he might make a career as a writer. In 1895 he published a history of the 17th lancers (the regiment of his elder brother Lionel, who was subsequently killed in the Second South African War), followed by a study of *Dundonald* in Macmillan's English Men of Action series (1896). The same publisher then commissioned him to write a popular one-volume history of the British army, and thus, somewhat fortuitously, he began the Herculean labour which was to occupy him virtually for the rest of his life.

Quickly appreciating that he had embarked upon a huge and largely unresearched subject, Fortescue obtained his publisher's assent to a four-volume work. According to his own memoirs, the first two volumes, published in 1899 and carrying the narrative to 1713 and 1763 respectively, 'fell flat', and the third fared little better. Only the author's dedication to his subject could have sustained him through these years of self-imposed drudgery, and he clearly drove himself to the brink of physical collapse. With volume 4 (published in 1904), however, the importance of his work began to be recognized, and late in the following year, by a stroke of great good fortune, he was appointed librarian at Windsor Castle, a post he retained until 1926. On 30 April 1914 he married Winifred [see Fortescue, Winifred], eldest surviving daughter of the Revd Howard Beech, then rector of Barlavington, Sussex; there were no children. Her dress-making and house-decorating business was to prove vital to the completion of his history.

Fortescue's work as the royal librarian is described in interesting detail in his Author and Curator (1933). It was not a sinecure or part-time occupation, intended to allow him ample leisure for his magnum opus. On the contrary, he found that large collections of books, prints, and documents had been gathering dust since the death of the prince consort, or even longer. While many of the changes he made were overdue and beneficial, some of the steps he took to raise funds for new library acquisitions and improvements were later deemed to be unfortunate. In particular, he sold off some of what he mistakenly considered to be less important drawings from the print room collections, as well as some duplicates of other prints and drawings. No list appears to have been made of the items sold. In recent years some of these drawings have been repurchased, notably those of the early seventeenth-century Roman collector, Cassiano dal Pozzo, which had originally been acquired in 1762. Another of his fund-raising projects, from 1909 onwards, was to arrange for facsimile reproductions to be made of some of the more famous drawings, particularly the portrait drawings of Holbein. Editions of 1000 each of eighty-three drawings were published and marketed by J. Manley, printseller of Windsor, and (from 1920) by Cintra, his wife's dress shop in Hampstead. In both cases the king received half of the income. As the king's librarian, Fortescue accompanied the royal family to India in 1911 for the coronation durbar, of which he published the official account in 1912. At the castle he frequently acted as guide to the library and art collections, his visitors ranging from cabinet ministers and generals (Foch was bored by the tour, Weygand very interested), to convalescent soldiers during the war.

Fortescue's publications were not confined to military history. Before becoming the royal librarian he supplemented his income by compiling the Calendar of State Papers, Colonial Series for the years 1677 to 1698 (7 vols., 1896–1905). Later he edited County Lieutenancies and the Army, 1803–1814 (1909), and six volumes of the Correspondence of King George the Third (1927–8).

C. T. Atkinson, fellow of Exeter College, Oxford, and compiler of the Dictionary of National Biography entry, described Fortescue from personal knowledge as 'an excellent lecturer with a good presence and delivery'. He attracted, and retained, a large undergraduate audience for his Ford lectures at Oxford in 1911 (published as British Statesmen of the Great War, 1793–1814). He also delivered the Lees Knowles lectures at Cambridge in 1914 and the Romanes lecture at Oxford in 1929. He was elected an honorary fellow of Trinity College, Cambridge, in 1920, received honorary degrees from Oxford and Edinburgh, and was awarded the Chesney gold medal of the Royal United Service Institution.

Ironically, the unhappiest assignment of Fortescue's career as an author was concerned with military history; namely his appointment in 1916 to prepare a history of the First World War for the general public. Confident of eventual victory from the outset, and a fervent patriot, he was happy to lend his pen to the recruiting effort by praising the virtue of the regimental system and the value of tradition, which he did successfully in his pamphlet The Foot Guards. But only at the third request from the War Office in February 1916 did he reluctantly agree to write the interim official history. However, Kitchener's death in June deprived him of the expected guidance and support and he became increasingly frustrated. Official material was sifted for him but a great deal remained inaccessible, and his draft interpretations were diluted by officials anxious to muffle references to blunders in the field. During the years 1916–19 he wrote about 1800 pages covering operations on the western front only up to May 1915; but his heart was never wholly committed to the thankless task. For him 'the great war' remained the struggle against Napoleon and he found it difficult to empathize with the war of attrition waged by a nation in arms that he was living through. When his critical review of Sir John French's book 1914 caused his removal from the official history project, he expressed joy at getting back to the old history again. He returned with relief to the British army's achievements in the final year of the Napoleonic Wars, but now brought to the subject critical views—on such matters as political interference in operations and the delay in introducing compulsory service—reinforced by his recent experience as an official historian.

By the end of the First World War, Fortescue had published eight volumes of his History of the British Army. Between 1920 and 1929 he published a further five volumes bringing the chronological coverage up to 1870. He found the post-war atmosphere less congenial to his great enterprise: the gentry's purchasing power had declined sharply and at 4 guineas per volume the final works in the series achieved neither the sales nor the influence he had hoped for. Indeed his writings became to a large extent a 'patriotic offering' funded by his wife's business. Consequently Fortescue completed his work in a different spirit from Edward Gibbon, who, with sober melancholy, took leave 'of an old and agreeable companion'. It had haunted every moment of his leisure for thirty years, and only contempt for those who abandon a self-imposed task had caused him to persevere. Knighted in 1926, he did not long survive the completion of his life's work; he died, after an operation, on 22 October 1933, at Cannes in France.

It would be pleasant, but untruthful, to record that Fortescue's history shows signs of enduring interest and appeal. It was the product of indefatigable research in original documents, a determination to present a clear, accurate, and readable narrative of military operations, and a close personal knowledge of the battlefields, which enabled him to elucidate his account with excellent maps. Most important, however, was his motivation: namely, a lifelong affection for the old, long-service, pre-Cardwell army, the spirit of the regiments of which it largely consisted, and the value of its traditions to the nation. An important part of his task was to distil and inculcate these soldierly virtues which, in his conservative view, contrasted sharply with the unedifying character of politicians who habitually meddled in military matters.

Fortescue's most successful volumes were probably those on the eighteenth century, whose style of warfare best exemplified his own personal interests, closely followed by those on the wars against France between 1793 and 1814. He was least convincing on the nineteenth-century campaigns in India, mainly because he had not explored either the battlefields or the archives there. He was in fact one of the last, and most thorough, exponents of a somewhat narrow conception of military history, which was largely concerned with campaigns, battles, and tactics, and for which the regiment was the all-important unit. Even contemporaries noted critically that Fortescue paid comparatively little attention to the important roles of the Royal Artillery and Royal Engineers—which were organized as corps rather than regiments—and to the significance of naval power and economic blockade. Since 1945 his limitations have become ever more apparent as the definition of 'military history' has steadily broadened to embrace the whole process of war-making, including weapons production, logistics, manpower, and the interrelationship between the home and military fronts. But perhaps his work is most obviously dated by his partisan commitment to defending the army against political interference and incompetence. For example, he described the blunders in organizing national resources for war in the years 1803–14 as 'one and all sad proof of the unteachable ignorance of our Governors'.

It would, however, be unjust to dismiss Fortescue's *magnum opus* on the British army, which has never been surpassed in its scope, operational detail, and wealth of documentation. The work still provides a goldmine for historians, and the early volumes, especially, continue to be quite frequently cited. It is a tribute to Fortescue's industry and determination that no single scholar would today attempt to write a history of the British army on such a grand scale; indeed teams of specialists have been engaged in revising Fortescue's work by producing more rounded histories which place war in its full social, political, and economic context. For all its faults and limitations, Fortescue's *History of the British Army* can now be seen to constitute one of the great achievements of his generation.   BRIAN BOND

Sources J. W. Fortescue, *Author and curator* (1933) · *The Times* (23 Oct 1933) · *DNB* · private information (2004) · GEC, *Peerage* · Venn, *Alum. Cant.* · *WWW* · K. Grieves, 'Early responses to the Great War: Fortescue, Conan Doyle and Buchan', *The First World War and British military history*, ed. B. Bond (1991), 15–39 · W. Fortescue, *There's rosemary, there's rue* (1939)
Archives Devon RO, family and literary papers · NAM, notebooks and transcripts | BL, corresp. with Macmillans, Add. MSS 55064–55065 · BL, corresp. with Sir Sydney Cockerell, Add. MS 52715 · Harvard U., Houghton L., letters to E. H. Wells · King's Lond., Liddell Hart C., Edmonds MSS · King's Lond., Liddell Hart C., corresp. with Sir B. H. Liddell Hart
Likenesses W. Strang, drypoint etching, 1909, NPG, Royal Collection [*see illus.*] · E. Gill, pencil drawing, 1927, Trinity Cam. · photographs, Royal Collection
Wealth at death £1135 8s. 4d.—in England: probate, 9 Jan 1934, *CGPLA Eng. & Wales*

Fortescue, Sir Nicholas (1575?–1633), exchequer official, was the eldest son of Ursula and William Fortescue (*d.* 1607), and grandson of Sir Nicholas Fortescue (*d.* 1549), groom porter to Henry VIII, who in 1542 had been granted former nunnery lands at Cookhill, Worcestershire. The young Nicholas did not attend university but is probably the person of that name admitted as a student to the Inner Temple in November 1591.

The ecclesiastical property at Cookhill included part of the original nunnery, of which much was demolished and rebuilt by the time of Fortescue's birth. The estate formed the bedrock of the Fortescue family's prosperity and status. It is therefore ironic that Nicholas Fortescue, grandson and namesake of the grantee, was a zealous Roman Catholic. On 14 December 1601 he wrote to Robert Cecil on behalf of unnamed persons threatened by the 'malice of the puritans' (*Salisbury MSS*, 11.519). In 1605 he was suspected of complicity in the Warwickshire circle of the gunpowder plotters. In the month of that attempt he wrote to Cecil protesting that he employed no recusant servants, that the armour found at his house had been there for many years, and that the conspirator Robert Winter had not visited his house for a year. Ominously in March 1606, Chief Justice Anderson wrote complaining that Fortescue had evaded a summons to attend an examination before them. However, one of Cecil's secretaries reported that his own investigations in the area had exonerated Fortescue from any disloyalty.

In 1607 Fortescue's father William died intestate and was survived by his wife, Ursula, and by his children, Nicholas, John, and Dorothy. Nicholas succeeded, following a *post mortem*, though his brother John also inherited property at Cookhill. By this time Nicholas had married Prudence, daughter of William Whetely esquire, of Holkham, Norfolk. The marriage produced seven children. William, the eldest son (1603–1649), married Joan Wilde of Glasely, Shropshire, and appears in the composition papers as 'a popish recusant' and Nicholas *Fortescue (*c.*1605–1644) became a knight of Malta. In 1608 a Benedictine monk, David Baker, is known to have sheltered at Cookhill and may have lived there for several years.

The progress of Fortescue's career may perhaps have been held back by suspicions aroused by his religious sympathies. However, before 18 June 1618 he was appointed a commissioner of the navy. At Whitehall on 2 February 1619 he was knighted by James I, and was described at the time as a great friend of the powerful Sir Thomas Lake. A few days later, by letters patent of 26 February, he was appointed Maduit chamberlain of the exchequer for life, a post with responsibilities in both the receipt and audit sections of the department. On 4 July 1622 he was made commissioner under the great seal for inquiring into defective titles to lands granted by the crown in Worcestershire; on 3 March 1623 he was named with Cranfield and others to a special commission into piracy; two further commissions followed on 9 May of the same year, into the governments of Ireland, and of Virginia and the Somers Islands. In 1625, however, his brief period of public prominence came to a close. On 30 May 1625 the chamberlaincy, vacant through his resignation, was granted to Sir Edward Bash, and by 22 September he had resigned to his son Edmund the position of surveyor of the king's lands in Worcestershire.

Fortescue, however, seems to have stayed for part of the year in London. He was friendly with one of his colleagues on the piracy commission, Sir William Pitt of Hartley Waspell to whom he wrote from his house in Fetter Lane in August 1627. It was here that he died on 2 November 1633. His body was taken back to Worcestershire, and buried in the chapel attached to the house at Cookhill on 20 November 1633.   G. K. FORTESCUE, *rev.* STEPHEN WRIGHT

Sources J. Fortescue, *A history of the family of Fortescue*, ed. T. Fortescue, 2nd edn (1880) · *CSP dom.*, 1603–10; 1625–6 · Rymer, *Foedera*, 3rd edn, vol. 7 · *APC* · J. C. Sainty, ed., *Officers of the exchequer: a list* (1983) · *VCH Worcestershire*, vol. 3 · J. Nichols, *The progresses, processions, and magnificent festivities of King James I, his royal consort, family and court*, 3 (1828), 526 · *Calendar of the manuscripts of the most hon. the marquis of Salisbury*, 11, HMC, 9 (1906); 17 (1938) · P. Salvin and S. Cressy, *The life of Father Augustine Baker*, ed. D. J. McCann (1997), xxi–xxii, 73 · *The letters of John Chamberlain*, ed. N. E. McClure, 2 (1939), 210 **Wealth at death** substantial: administration, PRO, PROB 6/16, fol. 24r; *VCH Warwickshire*, 3.173–4; *VCH Worcestershire*, 3.419–25

Fortescue, Sir Nicholas (*c.*1605–1644), royalist army officer, was the fourth son of Sir Nicholas *Fortescue (1575?–1633), of Cookhill, Worcestershire, chamberlain of the exchequer, and Prudence, daughter of William Wheteley of Holkham in Norfolk, in a prominent Roman Catholic family. It is unclear if Nicholas was the Fortescue from Worcestershire who attended the English College at St Omer about 1613. Nor is it certain how he became involved in the project to re-establish the order of St John in England—a possible influence may have been Sir Adrian *Fortescue who became a member of the order in 1532. In 1637 Nicholas Fortescue went to Malta, according to Pozzo, the historian of the order, carrying a commission from Queen Henrietta Maria, who was anxious to revive the order in England; he became a knight of Malta in 1638. His project, lodged on 21 February 1639, was favourably reported upon to the grand master, the pope, and Cardinal Barbarino, protector of the order, by a commission appointed to investigate the proposal. The chief difficulty, which proved insuperable, was to raise the sum of 12,000 scudi needed. Negotiations lasted some years, during which time Fortescue travelled to and from England several times. On 30 October 1638 he was a guest at the English College at Rome, where, as the strangers' book

shows, he dined with John Milton, like himself travelling abroad.

In 1642 the scheme was finally abandoned, owing to the outbreak of civil war. Fortescue joined the royal army and rose to become lieutenant-colonel in Sir John Mayney's horse regiment. Mayney commanded a brigade at Marston Moor and it was there that Fortescue was mortally wounded. Three days later, on 5 July 1644, he was buried at Skipton parish church. The biographer of royalists, David Lloyd, said of Fortescue:

> [his] worth is the more to be regarded by others, the less he took notice of himself; a person of so dextrous an address that when he came into notice he came into favour; when he entered the court he had the chamber, yea the closet of a prince; a gentleman that did much in his person, and, as he would say, let reputation do the rest.   (Lloyd, 669)

G. K. FORTESCUE, *rev.* MALCOLM GRATTON

Sources P. R. Newman, *Royalist officers in England and Wales, 1642–1660: a biographical dictionary* (1981) · parish register, Skipton, 1617–53, N. Yorks. CRO, PR/SKP (HT) 1/2 [burial] · *A list of officers claiming to the sixty thousand pounds etc. granted by his sacred majesty for the relief of his truly loyal and indigent party* (1663) · *The royal martyrs* (1663) · *A catalogue of the lords, knights, and gentlemen (of the Catholick religion) that were slain in the late war* (1660) · G. Holt, *St Omers and Bruges colleges, 1593–1773: a biographical dictionary*, Catholic RS, 69 (1979) · A. Mifsud, *Knights hospitallers of the ven. tongue of England in Malta* (1914) · D. Massun, *The life of John Milton* (1881), vol. 1 · H. S. Grazebrook, *The heraldry of Worcestershire* (1873) · *VCH Worcestershire*, vol. 3 · D. Lloyd, *Memoires of the lives ... of those ... personages that suffered ... for the protestant religion* (1668)

Fortescue, Richard (*d.* 1655), parliamentarian army officer, was of Heckfield, near Southampton. His parents and education are unknown, but when he made his will in July 1648 he owned estates at Bray in Berkshire, and houses in Broad Street, Reading. He had a wife, Mary (who outlived him), and two daughters, both minors.

On 22 November 1642 Fortescue was discharged from his office of town attorney at Reading. Around that time he joined the parliamentarian army and was commissioned major in Henry Bulstrode's regiment of foot. By the spring of 1644 he was lieutenant-colonel of the regiment in the earl of Essex's army formerly commanded by Charles Essex. Fortescue was present when the earl's army surrendered at Lostwithiel in August 1644 and commanded a regiment of foot at the second battle of Newbury in October. He was named a colonel of foot in the New Model Army by March 1645. On 8 May 1645 he joined Colonel Ralph Weldon's brigade which relieved Taunton three days later. Subsequently he served at Bridgwater, and at the storming of Bristol, where his men suffered 'by reason of the height of the works ... and the shortness of the Ladders' (Sprigge, 116).

On 19 January 1646 Fortescue captured Tunstall church during the storming of Dartmouth, Devon. In March he was appointed commander-in-chief under Fairfax in Cornwall, commanding two regiments of foot and three troops of horse. He captured Pendennis Castle on 17 August, later taking St Michael's Mount and receiving the surrender of the Isles of Scilly. He became prominent among the presbyterian faction within the New Model command. Most of the men in his regiment were willing to follow their colonel and volunteered for Ireland; they elected only one officer-agitator. Fortescue was among the six colonels who seceded to Westminster from the increasingly radicalized army at the end of May 1647. By 19 July Fairfax had stripped Fortescue of his command and sent him to Plymouth where the garrison, threatened with disbandment, almost killed him during their mutiny on 18 February 1648.

In 1651 Fortescue journeyed to Scotland to intercede with Cromwell for the life of Christopher Love, and himself became involved in presbyterian conspiracy. He was captured by moss-troopers and eventually returned to London where he was arrested on 13 August and examined 'concerning the reports which he has made in the North of the greatness of the Scots' army' (*CSP dom.*, 1651, 325). After Cromwell's victory at Worcester, Fortescue was discharged on security of £400 on 6 September. In 1654 he accepted Cromwell's offer of a colonelcy on his 'western design', the campaign against Spanish power in the Caribbean, upon Cromwell's promise to pay his arrears and protect his family from his debts. He embarked his regiment in December 1654, under the command of General Robert Venables and Major-General Heane.

Fortescue was promoted major-general when Heane was killed in the failed attack on Hispaniola on 25 April 1655. After sailing on to Jamaica, Fortescue signed the articles of surrender of the Spanish there on 17 May, and warned Don Francisco de Carvajal 'that God had no need of the service of idolaters' (Taylor, 58). On 24 June he succeeded the ailing Venables as commander of land forces on Jamaica. His diligence won Cromwell's praise:

> I doe commend in the midst of others miscarriages your constancy and faithfulness to your trust ... and takeing care of a company of poore sheepe left by their shepheards; and be assured that as that which you have done hath been good in itselfe, and becomeinge an honest man, so it hath a very good saviour here with all good Christians and all true Englishmen, and will not be forgotten by me as opportunity shall serve. (Thurloe, 4.633)

On 20 July Fortescue wrote to Thurloe asking him to remind Cromwell of his promise and pointed that his arrears were over £2674. The next day Fortescue wrote to remind Cromwell of his wife's trouble with lawsuits, and added 'I have great cause to bles God for the large interest I have in the affections of the army' (Thurloe, 3.675). He experienced difficulties with one of the commissioners, appointed to the expedition for managing its affairs, Captain Gregory Butler, whom he reproached: 'much of his business having been to engender strife and create factions amongst the officers' (ibid., 3.674).

Fortescue stocked the two plantations assigned him with sugar and cocoa and in 1661 his widow petitioned that they be granted to her and her child. He remarked that Jamaica was 'a fruitful and pleasant island and a fit receptacle for honest men' (Taylor, 77). However, by the end of October fatal sicknesses had halved his regiment, and Fortescue himself then contracted a fever, perhaps similar to yellow fever. He died in Jamaica four or five days later, probably ultimately of dysentery, caused by neglect of sanitation, and was buried there.

ANDREW J. HOPPER

Sources Thurloe, *State papers*, vols. 3–4 · S. A. G. Taylor, *The western design: an account of Cromwell's expedition to the Caribbean*, 2nd edn (1969) · C. H. Firth and G. Davies, *The regimental history of Cromwell's army*, 1 (1940) · will, PRO, PROB 11/266, sig. 276 · CSP dom., 1651; 1655–6 · J. Sprigge, *Anglia rediviva* (1647) · I. Gentles, *The New Model Army in England, Ireland, and Scotland, 1645–1653* (1992) · *The Clarke papers*, ed. C. H. Firth, 4 vols., CS, new ser., 49, 54, 61–2 (1891–1901), vols. 1 and 2 · S. R. Gardiner, *History of the Commonwealth and protectorate, 1649–1656*, new edn, 4 vols. (1903), vol. 4 · CSP col., vol. 5 · *Reading records: the diary of the corporation*, 4 vols. (1892–6), vol. 4 (1641–1654) · DNB

Archives BL, Add. MS 34326, fol. 28

Wealth at death portions of £200 to his two daughters; two houses in Broad Street, Reading; house and lands at Bray; £50 p.a. rents from St Giles parish, Reading: will, PRO, PROB 11/266, sig. 276, fols. 128v–129

Fortescue, Thomas (*b.* in or before **1545**, *d.* **1602**), translator and alleged sorcerer, was born probably at Fallapit in Devon, one of six sons and four daughters of Lewis Fortescue (*d.* 1545), baron of the exchequer, and his wife, Elizabeth Fortescue, daughter and heir of John Fortescue of Fallapit. On 17 October 1557 Thomas Fortescue became a fellow at Exeter College, Oxford: he resigned on 10 February 1558, and was re-elected on 2 December 1561. He was made a full fellow on 20 March 1563, and was left in charge of the college during the plague of 1564. In 1566 his fellowship was renewed, and he was granted permission 'to travel in France and elsewhere for four years to study medicine or law, with an allowance of £6 13s. 4d. and the rent of his rooms' (Boase, 69). He resigned his fellowship in 1569.

Fortescue's travel in France was disrupted by civil disorder, and he busied himself translating. In 1571, he published *The Forest, or, Collection of Histories*, a translation of Pedro Mexia's prose collection *Silva de varia lecion* (1540) via the French translation of Claude Gruget, *Les diverses leçons de Pierre Messie* (1552). *The Forest* is dedicated to Sir John Fortescue, master of the queen's great garderobe, and enjoyed some contemporary success, being reissued in 1576. The account of Tamburlaine it contained was long thought to have been the main source used by Christopher Marlowe, although, as Thomas Izard pointed out, Marlowe is more likely to have been using George Whetstone's 1586 translation of Mexia. The following extract indicates Fortescue's style: Tamburlaine

> answered in most furious wrath and ire, his face red and firy, all flaming with burning Sparcles, as it were blasing out on every side. Thou supposest me to be a man, but thou too much abusest me, for none other I am, but the wrathe and vengeance of God, and the mine of the world. (Marlowe, 295)

About 1576 Fortescue returned to his native Devon, and became somehow involved with Mary Hext (*née* Pomeroy) and her son Edward Sharpham. Hext later accused Fortescue of returning from his travels 'a Rype exquysite and perfect scholar' in black magic (Eccles, 119). In particular, she alleged, he had used enchantments to cause the death of her husband Richard Sharpham in 1581, and then he had used love charms to make himself irresistible to Mary: '(as nill she will she) greate adoe she had to withstande the often assaulte of his lewde and shamefull desieres' (Eccles, 119). Legal actions and counter-actions arising from this case started in 1592 and ran for some years with further accusations coming from a doctor, Dr Saule, who alleged that Fortescue had made a wax effigy of Richard and killed him by warming it by the fire once a day. Saule further accused Fortescue of plotting to do the same to Edward Sharpham, and of having caused the death of Mary's second husband, Alexander Hext. Pretesa Sparry, the sister of Sir Thomas Bodley, also accused Fortescue of having bewitched her continuously for a fortnight.

Fortescue had been married, although nothing is known of his wife except that her family name was Grenfyldes, and that neither she, nor any children they may have had, were living by 1595. Fortescue himself died in 1602, and his will includes a bequest to Exeter College and mentions property Dr Saule held of him on the New Quay of Dartmouth: evidently the accusations of witchcraft had not entirely soured their business relations.

MATTHEW STEGGLE

Sources M. Eccles, *Brief lives: Tudor and Stuart authors* (1982), 54 · J. Fortescue, *A history of the family of Fortescue*, ed. T. Fortescue, 2nd edn (1880) · C. W. Boase, ed., *Registrum Collegii Exoniensis*, new edn, OHS, 27 (1894) · T. C. Izard, 'The principal source for Marlowe's *Tamburlaine*', *Modern Language Notes*, 58 (1943), 411–17 · C. Marlowe, *Tamburlaine*, ed. U. Ellis-Fermor (1939)

Wealth at death cash bequests and some property

Fortescue, Thomas (1780–1872), administrator in India, son of Gerald Fortescue (*d.* 1780) and his wife, Elizabeth, daughter of John Tew, was born, probably in Dublin, on 13 November 1780. In 1798 Henry Dundas, president of the Board of Control, obtained a writership for him in the East India Company's service in Bengal. Initially in the secretariat in Calcutta, from 1805 until 1807 he officiated as collector variously at Dacca, Murshidabad, and Midnapore. From 1807 until 1810 he was secretary to the commissioners engaged in the settlement of the western districts of Oudh, including Delhi, that had been prised from the nawab of Oudh between 1801 and 1803. In January 1819, after several other postings including a three-year stint as judge of Allahabad, Fortescue returned to Delhi as civil commissioner and in this capacity produced his detailed and voluminous *Report on the Revenue System of the Delhi Territories* (1820), which almost instantly became a standard source for the economic and social history of the region.

Fortescue left India in 1821 and subsequently resigned the company's service. On 19 March 1859 he married Louisa Margaret, daughter of Thomas Russell. He died at his home at 10 Eaton Square, London, on 7 September 1872.

KATHERINE PRIOR

Sources H. T. Prinsep and R. Doss, eds., *A general register of the Hon'ble East India Company's civil servants of the Bengal establishment from 1790 to 1842* (1844) · BL OIOC, Haileybury MSS · *DNB* · *CGPLA Eng. & Wales* (1872)

Archives BL OIOC, reports on disputed boundaries, MSS Eur. F 87–89 · Glos. RO, papers | BL, Henry Wellesley MSS

Wealth at death under £70,000: probate, 15 Oct 1872, *CGPLA Eng. & Wales*

Fortescue, William (*bap.* 1687, *d.* 1749), judge, was baptized at Buckland Filleigh, Devon, on 26 June 1687, the only son of Henry Fortescue (1659–1691), gentleman, and his wife, Agnes, daughter of Nicholas Dennis of Barnstaple. After his father's early death his mother married Dr Gilbert Budgell, who was the father of the minor writer Eustace Budgell. Fortescue, who was descended from the eminent medieval jurist Sir John Fortescue, attended Barnstaple grammar school where he first made the acquaintance of his lifelong friend the poet John Gay, a bond that was further strengthened by the marriage of Fortescue's half-brother to Gay's sister Joanna. In 1705 he matriculated at Trinity College, Oxford.

Already squire of the estate at Buckland Filleigh, Fortescue ensured a future addition to his estates when he married at East Allington, Devon, on 7 July 1709 a distant cousin, Mary (1690–1710), the daughter and coheir of Edmund Fortescue of Fallapit, near Totnes, Devon. However, her death on 1 August 1710, aged only twenty, shortly after giving birth to their daughter, Mary, seems to have spurred Fortescue to embark on a professional career at the bar. He was accordingly admitted at the Middle Temple in September that same year, though in 1714 removed to the Inner Temple where he was called to the bar in July 1715. During his pupillage in London, Fortescue's friend Gay introduced him to several literary acquaintances, most notably the poet Alexander Pope, and in 1713 he became a founder member of the Scriblerus Club. Fortescue was said to have assisted Pope and Jonathan Swift in one of the club's productions, a humorous parody of a legal report entitled *Stiles versus Stradling* which was eventually published in 1727. His friendship with Pope, who naturally drew on Fortescue for legal and financial advice, endured over many years as testified by the poet's numerous surviving letters to him; and it was to Fortescue that Pope addressed his 'Imitation' of the first satire of the second book of Horace published in 1733.

Fortescue was a sound and businesslike barrister and by the early 1720s his practice was based at Harcourt Buildings at the Inner Temple. His involvement in politics first appears about 1724, when Robert Walpole selected him to act as his secretary in his capacity as chancellor of the exchequer. The appointment is sometimes said to date from 1715, the beginning of Walpole's first period as chancellor, though there appears to be no proper foundation for this. Fortescue's exchequer accounts, preserved among Walpole's papers, commence in 1724, which, indicatively, was the year in which Walpole's eldest son, Robert, Lord Walpole, married Fortescue's distant relative Margaret Rolle. Fortescue retained the post until 1736. At the 1727 general election he was elected on the government's interest for the borough of Newport, Isle of Wight, and unlike most of Pope's political friends was an

William Fortescue (*bap.* 1687, *d.* 1749), by John Faber junior, 1741 (after Thomas Hudson)

unwavering supporter of Walpole's ministry. He maintained his legal practice which sometimes took him on circuit; Pope ruminated with him on the attractions of this situation in 1728: 'what an advantageous circumstance is it … to be a grave and reputable rambler? You travel the round of the earth and behold all the iniquities under the heav'ns' (Sherburn, 2.521).

In the House of Commons, Fortescue was not a figure of distinction and is on record as having given just one or two pro-government speeches at the beginning of the 1730s. His services to Walpole, both in parliament and at the exchequer, were acknowledged in May 1730 by his appointment as a king's counsel, and in the same year he became attorney-general to Frederick, prince of Wales. Within a few years his suitability as a future judge was the subject of public comment, and in February 1733 the *London Evening-Post* was reporting a rumour that he might soon be given the court of common pleas. Promotion did not come until 9 February 1736, however, when, resigning from the prince's household, he was raised to the judicial bench as a baron of the exchequer, thereupon relinquishing his parliamentary seat. Fortescue's continuing loyalty and friendship towards Walpole, who appears to have regarded him as a family member, and his expeditiousness in courts of law ensured his swift advancement to higher judicial office; on 7 July 1738 he was transferred to the court of common pleas, and on 5 November 1741 was appointed master of the rolls in succession to Hon. John Verney, taking the oath of a privy councillor on 19 November. He remained in this office until his death in London on 16 December 1749, having for a number of years suffered from 'gravel'. He was buried at the Rolls Chapel in Chancery Lane, London. His only daughter, Mary, the wife of John Spooner of Beachworth, died in 1752, her only child, a daughter, having died an infant.

A. A. HANHAM

Sources Foster, *Alum. Oxon.* · HoP, *Commons, 1715–54*, 2.46–7 · Foss, *Judges*, 8.123–4 · Sainty, *King's counsel*, 92 · Sainty, *Judges*, 80, 129, 151 · *The correspondence of Alexander Pope*, ed. G. Sherburn, 2–5 (1956) · will, PRO, PROB 11/776 · P. Rogers, 'Pope and the social scene', *Alexander Pope*, ed. P. Dixon (1972), 131–2 · P. F. Gaye, *John Gay: his place in the eighteenth-century* (1938), 31, 59, 80 · H. A. C. Sturgess, ed., *Register of admissions to the Honourable Society of the Middle Temple, from the fifteenth century to the year 1944*, 3 vols. (1949) · J. L. Vivian, ed., *The visitations of the county of Devon, comprising the herald's visitations of 1531, 1564, and 1620* (privately printed, Exeter, [1895])

Archives CUL, Cholmondeley (Houghton) MSS, letters to Sir Robert Walpole

Likenesses J. Faber junior, mezzotint, 1741 (after T. Hudson), BM, NPG [*see illus.*]

Wealth at death Buckland; Fallapit; Devon lands at Ford, Milton Abbot, South Sydenham, Somerton, Ilfracombe, etc.: will, PRO, PROB 11/776

Fortescue [*née* Beech], **Winifred**, **Lady Fortescue** (1888–1951), author, was born on 7 February 1888 at the rectory, Great Bealings, near Woodbridge, Suffolk, the daughter of Howard Beech, rector of Great Bealings, and his wife, Henrietta Mildred Godden. She had two elder brothers, Mervyn and Guy, and a sister, Marjory, born in 1892. She was educated at home, mainly by her mother, until the age of nine, and then went with one of her brothers to a boys' school, St Augustine's, Cliftonville, an experience that made her independent and plain-speaking all her life. At sixteen she went to Old Cedar House School in Slough, which, soon after her arrival, transferred to London and became Wentworth Hall, Mill Hill. In 1905 she broke the mould and persuaded her parents, initially reluctant, to allow her to train as an actress at one of the first drama schools. For the daughter of a Victorian rectory to enter what was still a barely respectable profession took considerable strength of character on her part, and considerable tolerance on the part of her parents. She was a minor success playing the West End and, in the years up to 1914, touring Britain and Ireland.

In 1911 she met John William *Fortescue (1859–1933), thirty years her senior and the king's librarian and archivist at Windsor. He was also working on his history of the British army, which occupied the rest of his life. Despite the difference in their ages it was, she insisted, love at first sight. They were married in April 1914. During the First World War, Winifred Fortescue worked with wounded servicemen in Windsor and in London, while John worked on an 'interim' official history of the war. However, at the end of the war it became clear to them both that John Fortescue would not be able to finance himself and finish his history of the British army. To Winifred, convinced as many were of the importance of his work, this was another challenge. In 1921 she set up her company, Cintra, in a flat in Knightsbridge dealing with imported clothes from southern Europe. Her business was successful, but in 1925, partly as a result of the strain of her work, she became ill and was forced to sell it. As soon as she recovered she began writing, publishing features in several London papers and in *Punch*; she was briefly women's editor of the *Morning Post*.

In 1926 John Fortescue was knighted, and in 1929 he finished his history of the British army. He earned a little from writing, as did Winifred, but it became clear to both of them that their finances and his health meant that they would need to find somewhere cheaper to live. They found the answer in Provence, which dominated the rest of her life. The Provence of 1930 was remote, poor, and even bleak, especially in winter. Its economy was based on cheap wine and olives, but housing was inexpensive. However, the devaluation of the pound and Sir John's continuing ill health brought them near to the edge of financial calamity. Yet they loved the land they had found. Unlike many visitors (and colonizers) Lady Fortescue spoke French well and was accepted by her neighbours.

When Sir John Fortescue died in 1933 Winifred's friends and family urged her to return to England, but she refused. Provence had become her home, and she now wrote about it. In 1935 she published *Perfume from Provence*, a witty account of her life in France with Sir John. It foreshadows many later popular accounts of the English in France and has contributed more than a little to their ideas. Through the friendship of an American exile, Elisabeth Starr, she grew to know Provence and its surrounding *départements* in a way few English of her period did. In *Sunset House*, published in 1937, she wrote of her trips with Starr through Provence, the Alps, and the fashionable coast. It is in many ways a lighter and happier book than her first and is full of an exuberance which reminds the reader she was once a young actress.

The idyll was short-lived. The collapse of France in 1940 found Winifred back in England, although Elisabeth Starr remained in Provence. However, Winifred's love of France did not fail. At a time when France and the French were deeply unpopular in Britain she became one of the first organizers of the Amis des Volontaires Français, a group of English sympathizers and supporters of the Free French. Her accounts of those years, *Trampled Lilies* (1941) and *Beauty for Ashes* (1948), are important and moving records of the 'little history' of those who stood by France in her darkest days.

As the war progressed, news from Provence and from Elisabeth Starr got worse. In the terrible winter of 1943–4 Starr died from malnutrition, and on the day Paris was liberated Winifred Fortescue decided that as soon as the south was liberated she would return and continue the medical work begun by her 'beloved companion' among the poor and especially the children of Provence. She began collecting clothes, food, and money, and in May 1945 she returned to France and found a desperate situation. What she had brought with her seemed, as she wrote, 'pitifully small and inadequate', but in the devastated land of Provence it seemed massive. She continued her fund-raising and her trips, and at Christmas 1945 she arranged that every child in her area should have something to hang on the *arbre de Noël*. As a result she became

known as Maman Noël. Her final triumph was to see, in 1947, the tiny hospital built by Elisabeth Starr rebuilt and opened for the care of disabled orphans.

After the end of the war Winifred settled again in Provence. She wrote one more book, *Laughter in Provence*. In many ways it may be her best. It laughs at herself, her friends, and her neighbours, especially the new rich. On these she comments wryly, and usually generously, but the book is imbued with a sense of the end of an era.

Winifred Fortescue died on 9 April 1951 at Fort Escu (Sunset House), Opio, Alpes-Maritimes, France, and was buried in the cemetery at Opio where her friend Elisabeth already lay. On her tombstone is carved the cross of Lorraine, a mark of honour for those who fought for 'la France libre', and the name Maman Noël. The tombstone and the simple but powerful tributes are fitting for an Englishwoman who not only took inspiration and love from Provence but also paid for them in equal measure.

LINDA MERRICKS

Sources W. Fortescue, *Perfume from Provence* (1935) · W. Fortescue, *Sunset house: more perfume from Provence* (1937) · W. Fortescue, *There's rosemary, there's rue* (1939) · W. Fortescue, *Trampled lilies* (1942) · W. Fortescue, *Beauty for ashes* (1948) · W. Fortescue, *Laughter in Provence* (1950) · L. Merricks, 'Lady Winifred Fortescue', *France Magazine* (spring 1996) · WWW · b. cert. · CGPLA *Eng. & Wales* (1951)
Archives priv. coll., MSS
Likenesses photographs, priv. coll.; repro. in Merricks, 'Lady Winifred Fortescue'
Wealth at death £7587 13s. 2d. in England: probate, 8 Aug 1951, CGPLA *Eng. & Wales*

Forteviot. For this title name *see* Dewar, John Alexander, first Baron Forteviot (1856–1929).

Forth. For this title name *see* Ruthven, Patrick, earl of Forth and earl of Brentford (d. 1651); Drummond, George Henry Charles Francis Malcolm, Viscount Forth (1834–1861).

Fortibus, Isabella de. *See* Forz, Isabella de, *suo jure* countess of Devon, and countess of Aumale (1237–1293).

Fortibus, William de. *See* Forz, William de, count of Aumale (1191x6–1241); Forz, William de, count of Aumale (b. before 1216, d. 1260).

Fortnum, Charles (1738–1815), royal servant and grocer, is presumed to be the son of William Fortnum, of Berkeley Street, Portman Square, London. He had a brother and a sister. His grandfather William Fortnum is said to have become a footman to Queen Anne in 1707, although the name is absent from the records of the lord steward's department. About the same time, William Fortnum senior had reportedly founded a grocery business in Duke Street, London, jointly with his landlord, **Hugh Mason** (*fl.* 1707–1734), owner of a shop in nearby St James's Market. In 1734 a Hugh Mason was appointed as porter at 'His Majesty's Royal Palace of Somerset House', while John Mason esquire, a 'gentleman of his majesty's Chapel Royal' since 1715, was in 1744 made 'gentleman sewer in ordinary', the traditional job description of an attendant at the royal table. No documentary evidence of the Fortnum and Mason business appears to exist before 1756, when it moved to premises in Piccadilly that had been leased from Bethlem Hospital.

In August 1761 Charles Fortnum, then aged twenty-three, became footman to Sophie Charlotte, princess of Mecklenburg-Strelitz, shortly before her marriage to George III. The meagre salary of 40 guineas a year was amply supplemented by perquisites. Thus while his grandfather (so it was said) had been entitled to candle ends and any left unburned in candlesticks, Fortnum was allowed to help himself to coal, house linen, food, and wine. No doubt he succeeded in combining his duties with the running of the grocery because he worked at the former every alternate fortnight. In 1767—on 26 December, after the last Christmas hamper had been sent on its way—he married, at St James's Church, Westminster, Mary (1738–1805), daughter of Edward and Mary Monday, of Wendover, Buckinghamshire. Two sons and a daughter survived him.

Fortnum's work at court helped him to build up an extensive clientele of wealthy and influential customers of his 'celebrated Italian warehouse'. In addition to Italian goods such as fruit and olive oil the shop sold tea, coffee, and spices, most being imported through the agency of some Fortnum cousins employed in the East India Company. It was also famous for delicacies such as portions of poultry and game in aspic jelly, Scotch eggs, mince pies, fresh fruit in season, and dried fruits during the rest of the year. Goods were always dispatched in attractive hampers, baskets, and boxes; as a slightly later advertisement put it, 'Owing to the handsome packages, the above are particularly adapted for presents' (*The Times*, 30 Dec 1817).

During the fraught period of George III's so-called madness, at the turn of the year 1788–9 Fortnum is reported to have begged to resign owing to ill health, and also to allow him to concentrate on his grocery business. At that time the current Mason in the firm, John, who later became a partner, was only eighteen. Fortnum's wish to resign was mentioned in her journal by Mrs Charlotte Papendiek, wife of a colleague at court. The dramatist Alan Bennett used Fortnum as a character in his play *The Madness of George III* (1992), the subsequent film version showing him, quite ahistorically, sweeping out in anger at having to carry chamber pots containing the royal purple-tinged water.

In reality, his service in the queen's household remained unbroken for the rest of his life. In 1805 his wife died, but he did not marry again. Two years later, designated as 'Mr Charles Fortnum', he was appointed a page of the queen's presence chamber, the annual salary being slightly lower at £40. He handed over his 75 per cent share of the grocery to his second son, Richard, then aged twenty-seven, John Mason owning the other 25 per cent. The *Court and City Register* shows him, from 1810 onwards, as the queen's groom of the privy chamber, perhaps an honorary post to give him additional status.

The Napoleonic wars, especially after the opening of the peninsular campaign in 1808, yielded much business to the grocery, which was kept busy in sending foodstuffs to army officers and civilian officials overseas. The younger

Fortnum and Mason worked hard to expand the firm, and about 1811 rebuilt the premises at 181–3 Piccadilly, the design being copied from a mansion in Padua. Still in the queen's service, Charles Fortnum died early in 1815. His salary ceased on 5 April, and two days later his will was proved. He described himself as of St Giles parish, Reading, but the rate books mention only a Joseph Fortnum, and he was not buried in the town.   T. A. B. CORLEY

Sources A. Tanner, 'The last of the Fortnums', *Journal of the History of Collections*, 11 (1999), 147–57 · Treasurer's accounts of Queen Charlotte, 1761–1816, BL, Add. MSS 17870–17892 · will, 7 April 1815, PRO, PROB 11/1567 · value of estate, 1815, PRO, IR 26/640/205 · PRO, LC 1–2, 3/62–70 · PRO, LS 13/199–266 · *Court and City Register* (1810–13) · *Royal Kalendar* (1814–15) · rate books, Piccadilly ward, LMA, WR/PLT/357–80 · W. Macqueen-Pope, *Goodbye Piccadilly* (1960), 44–56 · 'BAM' [A. M. Broadley], *Piccadilly, 1686–1906, for a century and a half the home of Fortnum and Mason* (1906) · A. Bennett, *The madness of George III* (1992) · H. B. Wheatley, *Round about Piccadilly and Pall Mall* (1870) · *Court and private life in the time of Queen Charlotte, being the journals of Mrs Papendiek*, ed. V. D. Broughton, 2 (1887), 28

Wealth at death under £3500: PRO, death duty registers, IR 26/640/205

Fortnum, Charles Drury Edward (1820–1899), art collector and art historian, was born on 2 March 1820 in Holloway, London, the son of Charles Fortnum (1770–1860), merchant, and his second wife, Laetitia Stephens (1782–1853), widow of Lieutenant Robert Basden RN (d. 1810). He was baptized Charles Edward, but by 1840 had adopted the middle name Drury, by which he was subsequently known. Fortnum had a younger brother who died in infancy and two elder half-brothers: Charles Fortnum (b. 1803), his father's son by his first wife, Sophia King, and Charles Stuart (1812–1891), his mother's illegitimate son, born before she married his father. Fortnum's father had been made bankrupt in 1804. In an autobiographical sketch, Fortnum wrote that his education had been:

> under private tuition, his health having been enfeebled by severe illness when young, it was thought that the rough life of a public school, in those days, would be too severe; other subsequent circumstances prevented his going to either of the Universities. By his Father's wish he entered a merchant's house in the City, but found, after a fair trial, that he disliked in practice what he had objected to in theory, his tastes leading him rather to the natural sciences, Chemistry & Entomology being his chief studies. (*Journal of the History of Collections*, 269–70)

In 1840 Fortnum emigrated to Australia, where his half-brother Charles Stuart was already settled; the two shared a land order in the new colony of South Australia. From there he sent back natural history specimens to the Revd F. W. Hope, and others to the British Museum; several Australian insects published by Hope were given the specific name *fortnumi*. In 1845 Fortnum returned to England and on 7 March 1848 married his second cousin Fanny Matilda Keats (1808–1890), who had recently inherited wealth from the profits of Fortnum and Mason of Piccadilly. Thereafter, Fortnum's interests shifted from science to art and he could live as a gentleman collector and scholar. In 1852 the Fortnums bought the Hill House, Great Stanmore, Middlesex, which was to be his home for the rest of his life.

Fortnum and his wife travelled abroad and his first recorded art purchases were made in Italy in 1848. His principal areas of collecting were sculpture, bronzes, maiolica, and rings; the collections were of wide chronological range, with a bias towards the arts of Renaissance Italy. Fortnum was a ground-breaking enthusiast in England for Renaissance applied arts. In the 1850s he was among a group of collectors whose guiding lights were A. W. Franks of the British Museum and J. C. Robinson of the South Kensington (later Victoria and Albert) Museum. He lent to the 'Special exhibition of works of art' mounted by Robinson at South Kensington in 1862 and to exhibitions of the Burlington Fine Arts Club. After various disputes led to Robinson's dismissal from South Kensington in 1867, Fortnum acted as 'Art Referee', advising on acquisitions and making purchases for the museum on the continent; he received fees but, insisting he was an 'amateur', not a dealer, accepted no commission. Parts of his collection were lent to South Kensington, but he came to have a low opinion of its management.

Fortnum was invited to undertake South Kensington catalogues renounced by Robinson, who wrote to him that 'Catalogues of any kind would be entirely useless and superfluous in the state of disgraceful confusion, which reigns at present in that institution' (Robinson to Fortnum, 5 March 1869, Fortnum MSS, AM Oxf.). In 1873 appeared Fortnum's *Descriptive Catalogue of the Maiolica, Hispano-Moresco, Persian, Damascus, and Rhodian Wares in the South Kensington Museum*, and in 1876 his *Descriptive Catalogue of the Bronzes of European Origin in the South Kensington Museum*. His later writings on maiolica include *Maiolica* (1896) and a catalogue of his own collection (1897). Articles in *Archaeologia* include two on the diamond signet of Henrietta Maria, which he discovered, acquired, and in 1887 presented to Queen Victoria. His writings show a characteristically South Kensington concern with technique, together with the careful observation, meticulous data accumulation, and classificatory skill of a scientist; they remain landmarks in the study of their subjects.

Fortnum was characterized in *The Times* (11 March 1899) as the 'second founder' of the Ashmolean Museum. In 1868 he discussed with J. H. Parker, keeper of the Ashmolean from 1870 to 1884, the possibility of supporting a broadly conceived 'archaeological' museum in Oxford. In 1882 he approached the vice-chancellor, Benjamin Jowett, about giving his collections, but felt slighted by the response. In 1884 Arthur Evans, the newly appointed keeper of the Ashmolean, won Fortnum's confidence, and received parts of his collection on loan. These became a gift in 1888, and in 1889 Fortnum was made a 'visitor' of the Ashmolean and DCL. In 1891 he offered an endowment of £10,000 to enable the fast growing collections in the old Ashmolean to be rehoused in new buildings adjoining the University Galleries. After tortuous negotiations the offer was accepted, and the collections were moved in 1894. In his will he left most of his remaining collections to Oxford, and porcelain to the British Museum (to which he had previously given some important objects), with endowments to both institutions.

Fortnum was elected FSA in 1858 and was a vice-president of the Society of Antiquaries and of the Royal Archaeological Institute. He was elected a trustee of the British Museum in 1889, and was also an alderman and deputy lieutenant of Middlesex. After his first wife's death, he married, on 22 October 1891, Mary Fortnum (1822–1899), another second cousin. Fortnum had no children. He died at the Hill House, Great Stanmore, on 6 March 1899, and was buried in Highgate cemetery.

TIMOTHY WILSON

Sources AM Oxf., Fortnum MSS · AM Oxf., Evans MSS · *DNB* · private information (2004) [Elizabeth Warburton] · d. cert. · *Journal of the History of Collections* [ed. B. Thoma and T. Wilson], 11/2 (1999),

Charles Drury Edward Fortnum (1820–1899), by Charles Alexander

127–277 [C. D. E. Fortnum issue] · N. B. Penny, 'The Fortnum collection', *Catalogue of European sculpture in the Ashmolean Museum, 1540 to the present day*, 1 (1992), xvii–xxx · J. P. Warren, *Renaissance master bronzes from the Ashmolean museum, Oxford: the Fortnum collection* (1999) [exhibition catalogue, Daniel Katz, Ltd, St James, London, June 7 – July 16, 1999] · J. V. G. Mallet, 'C. D. E. Fortnum and Italian maiolica of the Renaissance', *Apollo*, 108 (1978), 396–404 · J. V. G. Mallet, 'Storico e storicismo: Fortnum, Cantagalli e Castellani', *Faenza*, 64 (1978), 37–47 · C. Lloyd, 'Two large plaquettes in Oxford from the collection of C. D. E. Fortnum', *Italian plaquettes*, ed. A. Luchs (1989), 207–24 · T. Wilson, 'La collezione Fortnum all'Ashmolean Museum di Oxford', *CeramicAntica*, anno 5, no. 8 (1995), 38–53 · R. F. Orenell, *The Ashmolean Museum, 1683–1894* (1986) · D. Scarisbrick, 'Sir John Evans and Charles Drury Fortnum: two Victorian ring connoisseurs and their collections', *Finger rings from ancient Egypt to the present day*, ed. G. Taylor and D. Scarisbrick (1978), 5–21 · J. P. Warren, 'Bode and the British', *Jahrbuch der Berliner Museen*, new ser., 38 (1996), 121–42 · Islington registers, LMA **Archives** AM Oxf., art collection | AM Oxf., corresp. with A. J. Evans, papers, pedigree · V&A NAL, corresp. with Sir Henry Cole **Likenesses** J. F. Jacquemart, graphite and watercolour drawing, 1878, AM Oxf. · H. J. Brooks, group portrait, oils, 1889 (*Private view, the Old Masters exhibition, Royal Academy, 1888*), NPG · C. Alexander, oils, AM Oxf. · C. Alexander, oils, AM Oxf. [*see illus.*] · Cirilotti, cameo, AM Oxf. · photographs, AM Oxf. **Wealth at death** £41,246 19s. 8d.: probate, 1 Aug 1899, *CGPLA Eng. & Wales*

Fortnum [née King], **Sophia** (b. 1781/2, d. in or after 1805), writer, was the daughter of Jonathan King, born Jacob Rey (1753–1824), moneylender and radical writer known in London society as Jew King, and his wife, Deborah, née Lara. In 1798 Sophia, with her sister Charlotte [see Byrne, Charlotte (1782?–1825)], dedicated to him *Trifles of Helicon*, to show 'the education you have afforded us has not been totally lost'. Later in the year she published a melodramatic novel, *Waldorf, or, The Dangers of Philosophy*, in which sceptical doctrines propel all the main characters through unauthorized sexual behaviour to madness and death.

In 1799 *Cordelia, or, A Romance of Real Life* was published at the Minerva Press; *The Victim of Friendship*, 'a German romance', followed in 1800. *The Fatal Secret, or, Unknown Warrior* (1801) again links sex and death in the figure of a destructive demon lover. In the preface Sophia King describes herself as a 'weak sapling of nineteen years growth' and complains about the 'extortionate' mechanics of the book trade (the book was printed 'for the author'). She also mocks her own love of the Gothic formulae developed by Ann Radcliffe. On 19 July 1801 she married Charles Fortnum. As Sappho she wrote newspaper verse, some of which was republished in *Poems, Legendary, Pathetic and Descriptive* (1804) alongside pieces from *Trifles of Helicon*. In the preface she celebrates Matthew Lewis's *Tales of Wonder* and espouses 'the fairy world of ghosts, and of magic' where 'the fantastic imagination roves unshackled'. The volume was dedicated to a Miss Sawbridge. There were sixty-five subscribers, including many aristocrats; John Penn, the MP to whom her sister dedicated her *Hours of Solitude* (1805), subscribed £20. Sophia Fortnum's last known work was *The Adventures of Victor Allen* (1805). Nothing is known of her after this date.

PAUL BAINES

Sources Blain, Clements & Grundy, *Feminist comp.*, 613 · J. Todd, ed., *A dictionary of British and American women writers, 1660–1800* (1984) · J. Todd, ed., *Dictionary of British women writers* (1989) · W. S. Ward, *Literary reviews in British periodicals, 1798–1820: a bibliography*, 2 (1972), 355 · A. H. Jones, *Ideas and innovations: best sellers of Jane Austen's age* (1986), 224–49

Fortrey, Samuel (1622–1682?), writer on economics, was born on 11 June 1622, the eldest son of Samuel Fortrey (d. in or before 1647), London merchant, and his wife, Katherine (d. in or before 1642), daughter of James de Latfeur of Hainault, Southern Netherlands. The Fortrey family had been forced to flee Flanders to escape religious persecution, and had quickly established itself in Elizabethan London. Samuel senior was included in the heraldic visitation of 1633–5, and gained sufficient wealth as a London merchant to create a notable retreat at Kew, which became known as the Dutch House. The erection of this impressive Flemish-styled mansion has been dated to 1631, but the family's earlier presence in Surrey is suggested by Samuel junior's baptism at Richmond church on 20 June 1622. By 1647 the house at Kew had passed to Samuel junior, and he appears to have shown little interest in following his father into the City. However, his business instincts led him to become one of the original investors in the corporation draining the Bedford Level, a scheme which promoted an increasing interest in the fen region. On 23 February 1647 he married Theodora (b. 1612), daughter of Tyrell Josceline of Holywell, Cambridgeshire, an advantageous match which provided him with an interest in several East Anglian properties. The couple had at least three sons and four daughters, whose baptisms suggest that Fortrey was resident in Cambridgeshire from the early 1650s. He built his own 'commodious habitation' at Mepal, near Ely, which reportedly received 'the admiration of the time', and he also possessed a substantial property at Oakington (Lysons and Lysons, 236).

During the interregnum Fortrey busied himself as one of the conservators in the Bedford corporation, drawing an annual salary of £150. At the Restoration he achieved greater personal prominence, for he can be confidently identified as the Samuel Fortrey who published *England's interest and improvement, consisting in the increase of the store and trade of this kingdom* (1663). Fortrey's familial background and business interests accorded with the subject matter of this tract, and his subsequent career bespeaks the court connections prized by its author. The dedication acknowledged that the Stuarts had bestowed an 'excess of … goodness' upon him, perhaps in reference to the Bedford Level scheme, and Fortrey styled himself a gentleman of the privy chamber, even though official records do not corroborate this claim (Carlisle). The treatise patriotically argued for the vigorous promotion of native industries and commerce, but personal advantage may well have been behind arguments in favour of enclosure and the production of livestock, while Fortrey's heritage was reflected in support of more liberal laws of naturalization. However, rather than as a bible of economic improvement, his work was destined to be remembered for its emphasis on the country's trade deficit with France, which was said to cost England at least an annual £1.6 million. He duly castigated his countrymen's attachment to French fashions and luxuries, and called upon the king to set an example by using English goods. His stress on the balance of trade echoed that of Thomas Mun during the great economic difficulties of the 1620s, but his provision of a set figure for national losses ensured him a ready audience during subsequent commercial debates. Fortrey provided no hard evidence for his claim, but it is possible that he was influenced by a petition from a group of merchants in 1659, which had suggested that England lost an annual £1 million by its trade with France. While accepting that England did not enjoy a favourable balance of trade with France, modern historians seriously doubt the accuracy of these figures, although there remains little evidence on which to form any precise picture. Contemporaries with more immediate agendas seized upon Fortrey's figures to press for more protectionist policies towards France, and the tract was duly reprinted in 1673, 1713, and 1744 at times of heightened Anglo-French tension.

Fortrey's views thus enjoyed wide publicity, and personal advancement followed with his appointment in November 1670 to the office of clerk of deliveries of the ordnance. He retained this post until his death, and in this capacity supervised the equipping of the fleet during the Third Anglo-Dutch War. His duties required him to have a base at Salisbury Court in London, which was the address he gave in his last will, written in March 1680. His fame was attested later that year when 'Mr. Fortrey' was cited as one of the experts who might advise parliament on the improvement of the nation's commerce (*CSP dom.*, *1680*, 93). He probably died in January or February 1682; he was replaced as clerk on 2 February 1682, and his will was proved fourteen days later. He was survived by his wife, while his eldest son, Samuel, duly succeeded him as conservator in the Bedford corporation, and served as sheriff of Cambridgeshire and Huntingdonshire in 1684–5. More notably, his third son, James, served as groom of the bedchamber to James II, and would have gone into exile in 1688 but for the express orders of his royal master. Although these Jacobite connections probably conspired to halt the rise of the family in the eighteenth century, both the houses at Kew and Mepal survive as testimony to its short-lived prominence. PERRY GAUCI

Sources W. C. Metcalfe, 'Pedigrees of Cambridgeshire families [pt 2]', *The Genealogist*, 3 (1879), 296–314, esp. 297–8 • D. Lysons and S. Lysons, *Magna Britannia: being a concise topographical account of the several counties of Great Britain*, 2 (1808); repr. (1978), 236 • M. Priestly, 'Anglo-French trade and the unfavourable balance controversy', *Economic History Review*, 2nd ser., 4 (1951–2), 37–52 • will, PRO, PROB 11/369, sig. 17 • will, Samuel Fortrey (*d.* in or before 1647), PRO, PROB 11/202, sig. 231 • W. M. Palmer, ed., 'The fen office documents', *Proceedings of the Cambridge Antiquarian Society*, 38 (1936–7), 64–157 • N. Carlisle, *An inquiry into the place and quality of the gentlemen of his majesty's most hon. privy chamber* (1829) • BL, Add. MSS 5520, fols. 5–6, 5849, fol. 91v • *The visitation of London, anno Domini 1633, 1634, and 1635, made by Sir Henry St George*, 1, ed. J. J. Howard and J. L. Chester, Harleian Society, 15 (1880), 284 • J. O. Appleby, *Economic thought and ideology in seventeenth-century England* (1978) • *VCH Surrey*, 3.484 • *VCH Huntingdonshire*, 2.352 • *VCH Cambridgeshire and the Isle of Ely*, 9.195 • *CSP dom.*, *1680–81*, 93 • H. C. Tomlinson, *Guns and government: the ordnance office under the later Stuarts*, Royal Historical Society Studies in History, 15 (1979), 88, 225 • J. Nichols, *History and antiquities of Leicestershire* (1798), vol. 2, esp. p. 446

Archives BL, family MSS, Add. MS 26082 | BL, departmental accounts when clerk at the ordnance, Add. MS 38158

Wealth at death see will, PRO, PROB 11/369, sig. 17

Fortune, Robert (1812–1880), traveller and botanist, was born at Kelloe in the parish of Edrom, Berwickshire, on 16 September 1812, the son of Thomas Fortune, hedger, and his wife, Agnes, *née* Ridpath. After education in the parish school and apprenticeship in local gardens, he entered the Edinburgh Botanical Garden, and became subsequently superintendent of the indoor-plant department in the Royal Horticultural Society's garden at Chiswick.

In 1843 Fortune was sent as collector to the society to China, charged with collecting both ornamental and useful plants, and with gathering information about Chinese horticulture and gardening, the climate of the country, and its influence on vegetation. He spent three years in China, exploring nurseries and gardens in towns and inland areas little known to foreigners. He spoke some Chinese, and was generally able to pass himself off as a native of a part of China other than that which he was visiting. He disguised himself in Chinese dress to visit Soochow (Suzhou), then closed to Europeans, and through his resourcefulness and determination was able to survive shipwreck, attack by pirates, thieves, and bandits, as well as fever. He visited Java on his way out in 1843 and Manila in 1845, where he collected orchids, returning to England in May 1846. Among the many beautiful and interesting plants which he sent back to Britain were the double yellow rose and the fan palm (*Chamoerops fortunei*) that bear his name, the Japanese anemone, many varieties of the tree peonies, long cultivated in north China, the kumquat (*Citrus japonica*), *Weigela rosea*, *Daphne fortunei*, *Jasminium nudiflorum*, *Skimmia japonica fortunei*, *Berberis japonica*, and *Dicentra spectabilis*, besides various azaleas and chrysanthemums.

In 1846 Fortune was appointed curator of the Chelsea Physic Garden, but had to resign in 1848 on his return to China to collect plants and seeds of the tea shrub on behalf of the East India Company. In 1847 he published *Three years' wanderings in the northern provinces of China, including a visit to the tea, silk, and cotton countries, with an account of the agriculture and horticulture of the Chinese*, a lively account of his adventures. In 1851 he successfully introduced 2000 plants and 17,000 sprouting seeds of tea into the North-Western Provinces of India, as described in his *Report upon the Tea Plantations in the North-West Provinces* (1851), *A Journey to the Tea Countries of China* (1852), and *Two Visits to the Tea Countries of China and the British Plantations in the Himalayas* (2 vols., 1853).

In 1853 Fortune visited Formosa (Taiwan) and described the manufacture of rice-paper carried on there, and about the same time paid several visits to Japan, from where he introduced *Kerria japonica*, *Aucuba japonica*, *Lilium auratum*, and the golden larch (*Larix koempferi*), with many other species which rapidly became popular in British gardens. In 1857 he published *A Residence among the Chinese*, describing the culture of the silkworm, and in the same year was commissioned to collect tea shrubs and other plants in China and Japan on behalf of the United States patent office. The story of this journey was told in his last work, *Yeddo and Peking* (1863), written after his retirement, when he engaged for a time in farming in Scotland. He died at his home at 1 Gilston Road, South Kensington, London, on 13 April 1880, leaving a widow, Jane, of whom nothing more is known.

Fortune was a skilled gardener and botanist. In his lifetime he was also known as an entomologist and as a travel writer, as his books are full of lively incident and perceptive accounts of inland China, then little known to Europeans. His introduction of tea plants to British India was of long-term commercial importance, but he is chiefly remembered as one of the earliest of a line of plant hunters, starting with his forerunner William Kerr and later including E. H. Wilson, George Forrest, and Frank Kingdon-Ward, to visit China and bring back new plants capable of cultivation in Britain. Fortune's success was in part due to fortunate timing, since he was sent to China very soon after it became more accessible to Europeans and after the invention in 1833 of the Wardian case, a sealed glass case which greatly increased the chances of bringing back plants alive from distant countries and which he used to particularly good effect. His fame was in part assured because his journeys coincided with an unprecedented demand in Britain for colourful flowering shrubs and ornamental trees as gardening gained popularity with the middle classes and as formal gardening styles were abandoned. But his successes were also due to his intelligence, perseverance, courage, and determination, which saw him rise from humble parentage to a position of considerable scientific success and the status of 'gentleman' (*CGP*), and allowed him to enjoy a peaceful and prosperous old age, in marked contrast to the unpleasant deaths met by many other plant hunters.

G. S. BOULGER, rev. ELIZABETH BAIGENT

Sources *Gardeners' Chronicle*, new ser., 13 (1880), 487–9 · *The Garden*, 17 (1880), 356 · Desmond, *Botanists*, rev. edn · H. Field, *Memoirs of the botanic garden at Chelsea belonging to the Society of Apothecaries of London*, rev. R. H. Semple (1878) · *The Athenaeum* (17 April 1880), 507 · K. Lemmon, *The golden age of plant hunters* (1968) · C. Lyte, *The plant hunters* (1983) · b. cert. · *CGPLA Eng. & Wales* (1880)
Archives Royal Horticultural Society, London, papers relating to his botanical mission to China
Likenesses photograph, Carnegie Mellon University, Pittsburgh, Hunt Botanical Library; repro. in Lyte, *Plant hunters*, facing p. 128
Wealth at death under £40,000: probate, 3 May 1880, *CGPLA Eng. & Wales*

Forwood, Sir Arthur Bower, first baronet (1836–1898), politician, was born on 23 June 1836 at Edge Hill, Liverpool, the eldest of the four sons of Thomas Brittain Forwood (1810–1884), shipbroker, and his wife, Charlotte (1814–1861), daughter of William Bower, cotton broker.

Sir Arthur Bower Forwood, first baronet (1836–1898), by Brown, Barnes & Bell

His paternal grandfather, George, the son of a royal naval lieutenant from Plymouth who was killed in action, was the first to establish the Forwoods in Liverpool, and in 1812 was a partner in the Otterspool oil works. Arthur's father joined Leech, Harrison & Co. (founded in 1785), commission merchants, at the age of fourteen and became a partner in 1837. During Forwood's childhood, the family moved home several times, to Marsh Lane, Bootle, and to Crosby Road, Seaforth, both then sylvan suburbs commanding marine views, to escape the spreading city. Based on the port's prosperity, Liverpool grew in population from 210,000 in 1831 to 685,000 in 1901. This made it the second city in Britain after London in size, 'the second city of the Empire', Liverpudlians boasted. One of Arthur Forwood's political designs was to register that weight in national affairs.

Absorption in business precluded Forwood's forebears from much involvement in public life, though his grandfather published pamphlets on economic and social questions, and his father was active in the chamber of commerce and on the Mersey Docks Board. When he retired from business and bought Thornton Manor, Cheshire, Thomas Forwood became a county magistrate and chairman of the building restoration committee of Chester Cathedral. Arthur, locally schooled at Liverpool Collegiate, started work in his father's firm, as did his three brothers after him. One, William *Forwood (1840–1928; knighted 1883), wrote that their father refused to send them to Oxbridge, arguing that 'a university training would spoil' them for business. In 1862 Arthur and William bought out their father and took over the management. Already, Arthur Forwood demonstrated in business that hard-headedness and perspicacity which later were hallmarks of his politics. Visiting America in 1861, he was sure that civil war was coming. He backed his judgement by buying cotton heavily, on which the firm made substantial profits. He also moved Leech, Harrison, and Forwood into steamship ownership, trading to the West Indies, so successfully that he forced their competitors to amalgamate with them in a new company, the West Indian and Pacific Company. Forwood managed this company for nine years, before turning to politics. He had not done with business, however: the premium the Forwoods received for surrendering their interest in the West Indian and Pacific Company enabled them to found the Atlas Company, running steamers between New York and the West Indies; and Arthur gave time to this even as his political interests expanded.

Forwood joined Liverpool's municipal council in 1871. He served as councillor or alderman for twenty-seven years, and was mayor in 1878–9. He was secretary of the Constitutional Association from 1868 and chairman from 1880, in effect head of the Liverpool conservative caucus. The decisive year was 1875 when Irish nationalism first seriously disturbed municipal politics, leading to the election ten years later as MP for Liverpool Scotland of the only Irish nationalist ever to win a parliamentary seat on the British mainland, T. P. O'Connor. Forwood marshalled the non-Catholic Irish electors to resist the subordination of Liverpool interests to Irish separatism. Constitutionally, Forwood was orthodox, a resolute champion of the union and empire, monarchy and church, Lords and Commons; but he was alarmed that Conservative leaders nationally were too faint-hearted or stuck up to promote this creed in urban centres and to invest traditional institutions with a democratic seal. Forwood also encountered timidity in the Liverpool merchant plutocracy. He won support for the establishment of an episcopal see (1880) and University College (1881); but the merchants were unnerved by his advocacy of universal household suffrage and redistribution of seats, temperance reform and comprehensive employers' liability legislation, old age pensions and adventures in municipalization, including council housing as well as public utilities and transport. Forwood broadcast his ideas in a pamphlet in 1883 on housing the working classes, and in articles in the *Contemporary Review* (1883–4) on democratic toryism and single-member constituencies. He encouraged popular political organization in the Liverpool Working Men's Conservative Association, the largest such body in the country; moreover, he courted the Orange order and abetted campaigns to enforce church discipline against ritualism. His ambition of representing Liverpool in parliament was dashed in 1882 in a by-election defeat when his candidature was undermined from within the Conservative establishment. Undaunted, he spearheaded the assertion of urban Conservative leaders in the national union in 1884–5 and, though disappointed by Lord Randolph Churchill's

errancy, he won the mind of Lord Salisbury during the franchise crisis, whose settlement emerged on lines he advised.

At the general election held under the new arrangements in December 1885, Forwood was returned for Ormskirk: wisely, he did not divide his supremacy in Liverpool by representing one of its constituencies. Salisbury appointed him financial secretary to the Admiralty, a post he held from 1886 to 1892, during a period of agitation for fleet re-equipment. Forwood was the first shipowner to become an Admiralty minister and, in 1892, the first serving town councillor to become a privy councillor. His superior at the Admiralty, Lord George Hamilton, reckoned Forwood a 'hustler', with 'a rare driving power as an administrator and reformer, but not the knack of making himself popular' (*Parliamentary Reminiscences and Reflections, 1886–1906*, 1922, 35). The sense of a man who had risen above his proper station was apparently confirmed when, in a slip during a parliamentary debate, Forwood called the speaker 'Mr Mayor'. When the Conservatives resumed office in 1895, Forwood was denied preferment and scarcely mollified by a baronetcy (5 September 1895). He was rich—at his death, his effects were probated at £87,321 19s. 7d.—and his heir, Dudley (1875–1961), was educated at Harrow School. Though no man below cabinet rank did more to promote tory democracy in the country than Forwood, his unvarnished manner was as unappealing to the aristocratic élite who dominated the Conservative Party as it was to his party opponents in Liverpool who likened his rule to the ruthlessness of an American city boss. The Liberal leader, the merchant shipowner, Sir Robert Holt, wrote that 'he is certainly short of the instincts of a Gentleman and carries his political bias too far so as to be unjust to others' (Waller, 153). Holt acknowledged Forwood's effectiveness, however: 'What he decided to do he worked at till he did it' (ibid., 166). The foundations he laid, of a popular Conservatism pursuing both progressive and protestant causes, were tended by his immediate successors, Sir Archibald Salvidge and Sir Thomas White, and sustained the Conservative ascendancy in Liverpool until 1955. Forwood's political creed and style created acrimony but did not break down the interconnection of the provincial élite. He himself twice married into Liberal families, marrying first on 26 October 1858 Lucy, daughter of Simon Crosfield, who died aged thirty-six from jaundice on 5 November 1873, and second on 1 September 1874 Mary Anne Eliza (Lizzie), daughter of Thomas *Baines, who survived him. Forwood died at his home, The Priory, Gateacre, on 27 September 1898, from colitis leading to heart failure.

PHILIP WALLER

Sources P. J. Waller, *Democracy and sectarianism: a political and social history of Liverpool, 1868–1939* (1981) • W. B. Forwood, *Recollections of a busy life: being the reminiscences of a Liverpool merchant, 1840–1910* (1910) • Boase, *Mod. Eng. biog.* • d. cert.
Archives Hants. RO, corresp. and papers | Hatfield House, Salisbury MSS, letters • Lpool RO, letters to Robert Holt
Likenesses Brown, Barnes & Bell, photograph, NPG [*see illus.*] • portrait, repro. in *ILN*, 107 (1895), 166 • portrait, repro. in *ILN*, 113 (1898), 507 • portrait, repro. in *VF* (16 Aug 1890), pl. 572 • portrait,

repro. in B. J. Orchard, *Liverpool's legion of honour* (1893), pl. 9 · statue, St John's Gardens, Liverpool
Wealth at death £87,321 19s. 7d.: probate, 2 Jan 1899, *CGPLA Eng. & Wales*

Forwood, Sir William Bower (1840–1928), merchant and politician, was born on 21 January 1840 in Edge Hill, Liverpool, the second son of Thomas Brittain Forwood (1810–1884), Liverpool merchant, and Charlotte (d. 1861), daughter of William Bower, Liverpool cotton broker. Arthur *Forwood was his brother.

Thomas Forwood was senior partner in Leech, Harrison, and Forwood, and was also a notable civic figure: he was vice-president of the Liverpool chamber of commerce, a long-serving member of the dock board, a Cheshire magistrate, and involved in the restoration of Chester Cathedral. His eldest sons, Arthur and William, continued and widened these concerns. William was educated at Liverpool Collegiate, and at Dr Heldenmier's Pestalozzian school in Worksop. After leaving school he temporarily joined the cotton brokers, Salisbury, Turner, and Earle. In late 1857 his father sent him on a voyage around the world, and before he was eighteen he had visited the Australian goldfields, learned to helm and navigate an ocean-going ship, and gone aloft to break out frozen sails south of Cape Horn.

William Forwood entered the family business in late 1859. Almost immediately the American Civil War disrupted the cotton trade. Thomas Forwood retired in 1862, leaving Arthur and William in charge. They rapidly made their fortunes, first from wartime speculation and blockade running, and then from exploiting telegraph and cotton futures. William Forwood had a keen analytical mind—he was elected president of the Liverpool Philomathic Society in 1868 and fellow of the Statistical Society in 1871—and he later claimed that the firm had adjusted more quickly than most. He wrote in his autobiography (almost certainly exaggerating) that 'Futures trading … was very profitable, and for some time we had it all to ourselves' (Forwood, *Recollections*, 74).

The firm established branches in New York, New Orleans, and Bombay. Forwood visited the southern United States regularly, but his major contribution was in Liverpool. The new methods progressively reduced commissions and set merchants against brokers. Forwood had already served as president of the American chamber of commerce (in 1872) and of the Liverpool chamber of commerce (in 1871 and 1878–81). He claimed that in 1877 he brought the merchants and brokers together, and became 'President of the United Cotton Association, the promoters of the Liverpool Cotton Association' (Forwood, *Incidents*, 3). The Cotton Association managed the Liverpool cotton exchange, which became one of the world's leading commodity markets. While Forwood's narrative does not match Thomas Ellison's detailed contemporary account of the formation of the association in 1882, it is likely that, as mayor of Liverpool in 1880–81, he did play some important mediating role.

The Forwood brothers also became shipowners, against strong competition successfully running a small fleet to the West Indies, Costa Rica, and New York. By the early 1880s both were rich men, and they reduced their business interests. Leech, Harrison, and Forwood continued as general merchants into the next century. The Forwoods' shipping line was absorbed by the Royal Mail Steam Packet Company in 1908. Arthur Forwood became an MP in 1885 and quickly gained national as well as local influence. William Forwood, on the other hand, despite retiring from trade in 1890, specialized in civic affairs and retained important business interests. He organized the Liverpool docks' overhead railway in 1887—the first electric railway in the world. He served as a director of Cunard from 1888 to 1923, and as its deputy chairman from 1906 to 1909—when the *Lusitania* and *Mauretania* were built; he was also director of the Bank of Liverpool from 1887 to 1928, and its chairman from 1898 to 1901.

William Forwood had demonstrated political flair as a sixteen-year-old by collecting 60,000 signatures in support of Wavertree Park. He was elected to the city council in 1868 and served for more than forty years. His main interests were the watch committee and the libraries' committee—he persuaded Andrew Carnegie to give £50,000 to build new libraries. He was knighted in 1883 for his mayoral work in opposing the Fenians. As a leading Liverpool Conservative he successfully managed the election campaign against W. E. Gladstone, in 1868, and he persuaded George Nathaniel Curzon to stand for parliament in 1883. He represented Liverpool's commercial interests against the Lancashire railway companies in 1872–3, and against the Manchester Ship Canal in 1883–5. He served on the royal commission on motor cars in 1905, advocating tight speed-limits. His last important service, in 1921, was to win over the Liverpool chamber of commerce, and the public generally, to the concept of a Mersey road tunnel.

Forwood also sat on the Liverpool borough bench from 1873 to 1925 and was JP for Lancashire from 1882. As a magistrate he attempted to moderate Liverpool's notorious alcoholism by sensible licensing. He became deputy lieutenant for Lancashire in 1902, and high sheriff in 1905. He was invited to stand for several Lancashire constituencies, 'but always considered my native city had the first claim on me' (Forwood, *Incidents*, 16). Elected an honorary freeman of the city in 1902, Forwood was created KBE in 1917. His Conservatism included sympathy for social problems and labour, and he was proud that when he retired Liverpool was no longer 'the black spot on the Mersey' that he had observed in 1860. He refused to support Chamberlain on imperial protection, but in 1920 he denounced the Labour Party for ignoring economic realities.

Forwood married in 1862 Mary Miles Moss, only daughter of William Miles Moss, a Liverpool shipowner; they had three sons and seven daughters. After Mary died in the mid-1890s, he married in 1898 Elizabeth, daughter of General le Fleming of Rydal House. Forwood was a great traveller, visiting North and Central America many times.

In 1861 he was arrested in New York city, suspected of carrying money and dispatches to the Confederacy. After his release Abraham Lincoln offered to meet him, an invitation he rejected. Forty years later he did finally dine at the White House, after which President Theodore Roosevelt insisted on a bout of ju-jitsu. He also met and negotiated railroad contracts with President Diaz of Mexico. At home he was an active canoeist, gardener, and yachtsman. He became commodore of the Mersey and Windermere yacht clubs, and was a co-founder of the Yacht Racing Association. He claimed that he was never happier than at the Windermere regattas.

A committed Anglican, Sir William was chairman of the committee which financed and built Liverpool Cathedral. Bishop Chavasse wrote to him, 'You are really the Father of the Cathedral. ... If it had not been for your wonderful energy and enthusiasm ... the Cathedral would never have been built' (Forwood, *Incidents*, 14). In 1925 Forwood published a survey of the cathedral, entitled *The Liverpool Cathedral: the Story of its Foundation, 1850–1914*.

Forwood documented his views and experiences in a number of works. He kept a journal of his voyage on the *Red Jacket* to Australia. Although he was too busy to write during his early years in business and politics, he presented lengthy written and oral evidence in the debates about water, railways, and the Manchester Ship Canal. In the 1890s and early 1900s he wrote pamphlets on art, technical education, and free trade. In 1912 he was lucky to survive a severe fall, which dislocated his back. Thereafter he had to wear a steel corset and rest much of the time, but he continued writing, including pamphlets on the war effort and the Mersey Tunnel as well as his autobiographical *Reminiscences of a Liverpool Shipowner, 1850–1920* (1920).

Sir William Forwood died after a short illness on 23 March 1928 at Reids Palace Hotel, Funchal, Madeira. He was buried in the war memorial chapel, which he had built, at Bowness-on-Windermere. His obituaries emphasized his positive, optimistic, and helpful contribution to Liverpool.

J. R. KILLICK

Sources ING Barings, London, Barings archives · Hants. RO, Forwood of Liverpool papers, 19M62 · catalogues, Liverpool Public Library · W. B. Forwood, *Recollections of a busy life: being the reminiscences of a Liverpool merchant, 1840–1910* (1910) · W. B. Forwood, *Reminiscences of a Liverpool shipowner, 1850–1920* (1920) · W. B. Forwood, *Incidents in my public life, 1840–1925: compiled for his children on his 86th birthday* (1926) · W. B. Forwood, *The Liverpool Cathedral: the story of its foundation, 1850–1914* (1925) · *Liverpool Post* (24 March 1928) · *Liverpool Post* (26 March 1928) · *Liverpool Post* (2 April 1928) · *Liverpool Post* (4 April 1928) · *Liverpool Post* (5 April 1928) · B. G. Orchard, *Liverpool's legion of honour* (1893), 72, 304–9 · F. E. Hyde, *Liverpool and the Mersey: an economic history of a port, 1700–1970* (1971) · S. Mountfield, *Western gateway: a history of the Mersey docks and harbour board* (1965) · J. Smith-Hughes, 'Forwoods of Liverpool and London', *Sea Breezes*, 42 (1968), 150–53 · P. J. Waller, *Democracy and sectarianism: a political and social history of Liverpool, 1868–1939* (1981) · E. C. Woods, 'A voyage on the *Red Jacket* in 1857–8', *Transactions of the Historic Society of Lancashire and Cheshire*, 95 (1943), 57–91 · T. Ellison, *The cotton trade of Great Britain* (1886) · d. cert. · *CGPLA Eng. & Wales* (1928)

Archives Liverpool Central Library, journals

Likenesses photograph portraits, 1872, Liverpool Public Library · photograph, 1880–81, Liverpool Public Library · R. E. Morrison, oils, c.1919, Merseyside County Art Galleries · F. May, caricature, repro. in *Cunard Magazine*, 6 (1921), 90 · Medrington, photograph, repro. in Forwood, *Recollections*, 261 · R. E. Morrison, portrait, Walker Art Gallery, Liverpool · G. H. Neale, portrait, Walker Art Gallery, Liverpool · E. W. Smith, bust, Walker Art Gallery, Liverpool · four cartoons, repro. in *Liverpool Review* (9 Jan–26 Dec 1891) · photograph, repro. in Orchard, *Liverpool's legion of honour*, 73

Wealth at death £356,090 8s. 11d.: probate, 14 May 1928, *CGPLA Eng. & Wales*

Forz [Fortibus], **Isabella de**, *suo jure* countess of Devon, and countess of Aumale (1237–1293), magnate, was the elder daughter of Baldwin de Revières, earl of Devon (d. 1245), and Amicia (d. 1284), eldest daughter of Gilbert de *Clare, earl of Gloucester and Hertford (d. 1230). Born in July 1237, when she was eleven or twelve she became the second wife of William de *Forz (or de Fortibus), count of Aumale (d. 1260), whose lands lay in three blocks based on Holderness and Skipton in Yorkshire, and Cockermouth in Cumberland. Most of what is known of Isabella de Forz's life comes from the time of her long widowhood.

When William de Forz, the last count of Aumale, died, the surviving children of his marriage with Isabella were all under age. The wardship of the heir and of the estates passed to the king. Countess Isabella was granted her dower lands and the custody (but not the marriage) of her sons Thomas and William. The remaining two-thirds of the estates, and the marriage of the heir, were granted to the Lord Edward (later Edward I). Her dower lands were principally a third of Holderness and half the barony of Cockermouth including the castle; she was also granted the honour and castle of Skipton.

In 1261 Isabella combined with her mother, Amicia, the dowager countess of Devon, to buy the marriage of the Aumale heir and the remaining two-thirds of Holderness. The two women and the Forz children lived in the same household, chiefly at Burstwick, and administered Holderness together for four years until they quarrelled, seemingly because the younger countess supported the baronial cause while the older adhered to the king. Their dispute, about income from the family estates, was taken to the king and later to the exchequer court, but no decision was reached, and at Easter 1274 the two countesses were formally reconciled, without however living together again. Meanwhile, in 1262 Countess Isabella's brother, Baldwin de Revières, earl of Devon, died, and as his sister and heir she was in August 1263 admitted to his lands in Devon, Hampshire, the Isle of Wight, and Harewood in Yorkshire, subject to the dower rights of his widow and his mother. She subsequently called herself countess of Aumale and of Devon, or on some occasions countess of Devon and of Aumale, and lady of the Isle (of Wight). Her surviving charters regularly call her de Fortibus (whereas her husband had sometimes used the surname Forz, and sometimes Fortibus). Still in her mid-twenties, she was now one of the richest heiresses in England.

After the battle of Evesham in 1264 Simon de Montfort's son, the younger Simon de Montfort (d. 1271), acquired the rights to her remarriage. The countess tried to hide from Montfort in Breamore Priory, Hampshire, and although the prior informed on her, she bribed him into letting her escape. Simon de Montfort continued to pursue her until she found refuge in Wales. In November 1268 (perhaps after the death of her last surviving son) her marriage was granted to Henry III's son Edmund, earl of Lancaster (1245–1296); she never remarried, but her daughter was to marry the earl. Isabella's children all died young. Two sons, John and Teron, died in their father's lifetime, and Thomas, William, and Avice died before April 1269, when the only surviving child, Aveline (who had been born in January 1259 at Burstwick in Holderness), married the earl of Lancaster in Westminster Abbey. In 1273 Aveline was declared of age, but in the following year, on 10 November 1274, she died childless, and was buried in Westminster Abbey on the north side of the presbytery. The king's escheator once more took the Aumale lands, save the dower, and Isabella de Forz lived on alone, having survived all her children, until 1293.

The administration of the countess of Aumale's estates has been the subject of several studies, based on a long series of accounts covering her widowhood. From 1260 to 1262 the countess received income mainly from her northern estates, especially Cockermouth and Holderness. After 1262 the administrative centre moved to Carisbrooke on the Isle of Wight and from this time the countess lived mainly at Carisbrooke Castle, with one visit to Paris to try to reclaim the long-lost *comté* of Aumale. Her finances were organized from the 1270s by the royal clerk and moneylender Adam of Stratton (*d.* 1292x4), using the Riccardi of Lucca as her bankers. Stratton also acted for the countess as one of the two hereditary chamberlains of the exchequer. In the 1260s Countess Isabella's net income was about £1500 a year, rising later to £2500. Isabella was much involved in litigation, pursuing dozens of civil and criminal cases through the royal courts; it is interesting that she or her advisers appear to have had their own copy of statutes of the realm.

Edward I planned over a number of years to acquire Isabella's great estates. After the heir, Aveline de Forz, died, the northern (Forz) lands (apart from the dower lands), all rights to the *comté* of Aumale and associated lands in England and Normandy were quitclaimed to the crown in 1278 by John of Eston, who was found by a jury, against probabilities, to be the next heir. The king had proposed in 1276 that Countess Isabella should sell the southern (Revières) lands to him. This arrangement appears to have been void; but in 1293 negotiations were reopened. Travelling from Canterbury, Isabella was taken ill, and halted at Stockwell, near Lambeth. Emissaries of the king hurried to her and there, in a garden, Edward's leading councillor Walter Langton (*d.* 1321) wrote the charter which confirmed the sale of the Isle of Wight to the king. It was read to the dying countess, who ordered her lady of the bedchamber to seal it. She made her will and received the last sacrament, dying between midnight and dawn on 10 November 1293. She was buried at Breamore Priory, Hampshire.   BARBARA ENGLISH

Sources N. Denholm-Young, 'Edward I and the sale of the Isle of Wight', *EngHR*, 44 (1929), 433–8 · N. Denholm-Young, 'The Yorkshire estates of Isabella de Fortibus', *Yorkshire Archaeological Journal*, 31 (1932–4), 389–420 · N. Denholm-Young, *Seignorial administration in England* (1937) · K. Ugawa, *Lay estates in medieval England* (1966) · B. English, *The lords of Holderness, 1086–1260: a study in feudal society* (1979) · H. Hall, ed., *The Red Book of the Exchequer*, 3 vols., Rolls Series, 99 (1896) · *Ann. mon.* · H. Jenkinson and B. E. R. Fermoy, eds., *Select cases in the exchequer of pleas*, SeldS, 48 (1932) · W. Farrer and others, eds., *Early Yorkshire charters*, 12 vols. (1914–65), vols. 3, 7 · A. Beanlands, 'The claim of John de Eston', *Miscellanea*, Thoresby Society, 24 (1919), 227–44 · V. H. Galbraith, 'Statutes of Edward I: Huntingdon Library MS HM 25782', *Essays in medieval history presented to Bertie Wilkinson*, ed. T. A. Sandquist and M. R. Powicke (1969), 176–91

Archives BL · Bodl. Oxf. · East Riding of Yorkshire Archives Service, Beverley | PRO, chancery rolls · PRO, special collections, SC 6

Forz [Fortibus], **William de**, count of Aumale (1191x6– 1241), magnate, raised one of the most serious threats to the stability of England during the minority of Henry III.

Parentage and inheritance His title and lands in England and Normandy were inherited through his mother, *Hawisa, countess of Aumale (*d.* 1213/14), a royal ward who married first William de Mandeville, earl of Essex (*d.* 1189); second, in 1190, Forz's father, William de Forz (or Fors; *d.* 1195), a Poitevin naval commander who accompanied Richard I on crusade; and finally the Fleming Baldwin de Béthune (*d.* 1212). The surname Forz (used on the seals of both father and son) was derived from one of two places named Fors in Poitou. He is sometimes called 'earl of Albemarle', but incorrectly: he did not hold an English earldom, but, like his mother, took his title from Aumale, a small *comté* in north-eastern Normandy.

Nothing is known of William de Forz as a young man. After his mother's death in 1214 he came to England (perhaps from Poitou) under safe conduct, to speak with the king about his inheritance; his journey was the result of petitions by Robert de Ros (*d.* 1227). In September or October 1214 John gave back to William de Forz all the lands in England of his mother's inheritance, with the proviso that he should have no receipts or profits until he had married Aveline, daughter of Richard de Montfichet of Stansted, Essex. The young man was first addressed as count of Aumale in royal charters of November 1214. His English lands consisted principally of the honours of Holderness and Skipton in the East and West Ridings of Yorkshire, Cockermouth in Cumberland, lands in Lincolnshire around Barrow-on-Humber in the north and Castle Bytham in the south, and a number of manors elsewhere. The Norman *comté* was lost to the French before he inherited; he had some Poitevin lands and a connection with the Île d'Oléron.

Shifting allegiances in the civil war, 1215–1217 William de Forz arrived in England amid the ferment of northern discontent leading to Magna Carta and civil war. He may have been influenced in his political choice by Robert de Ros (a leading northern baron), Richard de Montfichet his brother-in-law, and Fulk d'Oyry (steward for the counts and countesses of Aumale for many years), all of whom opposed King John. The count joined the rebel barons in time to become one of the committee of twenty-five executors of Magna Carta, to which he was the second witness in June 1215. He rapidly changed sides, however, and by August was with the king, attesting charters and being granted rebel lands. He was also admitted, at the king's command, to Scarborough Castle. When, in December 1215, King John set off on a punitive expedition to the north, Forz accompanied him; and he gained many lands in this and the following year from the dispossessed, together with the castles of Rockingham, Sauvey, and Bytham. Although William de Forz deserted John briefly in June 1216, he returned to royal service by the autumn. At the beginning of Henry III's minority Forz was an active supporter of the young king. He sealed the reissue of Magna Carta in 1216 (and was to do so again in 1225). During 1217 he was sent a stream of royal orders concerning the confiscation and restoration of lands. He was present throughout the main events of the war between the king's party and Prince Louis.

The war of Bytham After the war successive government attempts were made to reclaim from William de Forz the additional possessions he had acquired: prisoners, hostages, lands and manors seized unlawfully (including the Edenham manor of Gilbert de Gant, the royal castles of Rockingham and Sauvey, and the castle of Bytham, Lincolnshire, whose ownership was in dispute). These moves, especially in relation to the castles, were resisted by the count, and he compounded his disobedience by taking part in a forbidden tournament at Brackley. During 1218 his daughter's intended marriage to the son of William (I) Longespée, earl of Salisbury, was broken off; the earl wrote to the justiciar Hubert de Burgh (d. 1243) disowning any acquaintance with Forz's plans. On 30 November 1219 the sheriffs of six midland and northern counties received letters listing the count's offences and warning the men of the shires not to aid him in any way. In spite of this he managed to keep the castles until May 1220, when Rockingham and Sauvey, threatened with siege, surrendered to the king in person. Bytham, however, he retained. In the south-western corner of Lincolnshire, it had been in the possession of the counts of Aumale since their arrival in England in the eleventh century, and there had been a castle there since at least 1141. It was part of, and probably the *caput* of, the Aumales' southern Lincolnshire demesne, but nevertheless it had been alienated to the Coleville family by William de Mandeville, earl of Essex, the first husband of Hawisa, the Aumale heir, who was William de Forz's mother. The count was granted Castle Bytham in time of war in 1215, and although in 1217 William de Coleville regained the lands outside the castle gate by legal process, the count continued to refuse him the castle and attempted for many years to overthrow the decision of council and court.

In addition to the trouble over Castle Bytham, in 1220 William de Forz was baulked in his proposed appointment as seneschal of Poitou and Gascony. He was passed over a second time at the Christmas council of 1220, and, without seeking the king's permission, he left the court at Oxford during the night to raise rebellion in Lincolnshire.

The Worcester annalist gives a number of reasons for the rebellion, and modern historians have suggested others, including the government's general resumption of former royal demesne; the central problem seems, however, to have been Bytham, and Forz's brief rebellion was known to contemporaries as 'the war of Bytham'.

Forz unsuccessfully attacked the castles of Newark, Sleaford, and Kimbolton, but was successful in taking Fotheringhay Castle, Northamptonshire, in January 1221. He was excommunicated by the papal legate Pandulf (for the second time) and the council ordered the assembly of an army at Northampton. Forz, meanwhile, garrisoned Fotheringhay and Bytham, and from there issued letters of protection to the mayors of the cities of England, as if he were king. The royal army, collecting a number of siege engines, master carpenters, and miners, threatened his midland castles, and at the end of January 1221 he went north, where most of his estates lay, and ultimately claimed sanctuary in Fountains Abbey, Yorkshire. The desperate journey to the north, including the abandonment of foundered horses, and even some of his conversation with his wife, was recorded by a government spy who rode with Forz. The government was lenient to him: although Castle Bytham was razed and its site returned to Coleville, Forz and his men were pardoned. This leniency, was, as Wendover wrote, a bad example to others. Forz was, however, in company with other barons of England, charged with scutage on his knights' fees for the campaign of Bytham against himself. He made one further attempt through the courts, in 1236, to regain Castle Bytham, but failed.

Later career, death, and legacy William de Forz was at odds with the government again in 1223, in a group who made an armed demonstration against the Tower of London, demanding the removal of Hubert de Burgh. In 1224 his loyalty was suspected in the campaign against Falkes de Bréauté (d. 1226). His actions at this time may have been driven by his dislike of Hubert de Burgh, and also by his association with 'foreigners'—other Poitevins, as opposed to the Anglo-Normans. After Bréauté's defeat, however, Forz played a more statesmanlike role in government. He received lands and favours and was sent abroad on diplomatic and military missions. In 1227 he went to Antwerp to treat with the envoys of the emperor. He went to Poitou in 1230 with the king, and then to Brittany where the barons, who were supposed to be on campaign, amused themselves 'as though they were at a Christmas party' (Powicke, 183). He attended the colloquium in 1237 to deal with Llywelyn ab Iorwerth, prince of Gwynedd (d. 1240); and in the same year was made custodian of the lands of the late earl of Chester (to which Forz's son had a claim). His last political involvement was in 1241, when he was twice summoned to Gregory IX's projected council against the emperor, Frederick II.

During the autumn of 1239 Forz's wife, Aveline, died, and she was buried at Thornton Abbey, Lincolnshire. In the spring of 1241 Forz set out for Jerusalem; after being unable to eat for eight days, he died on the voyage, at the end of March 1241. His place of burial is unknown. He was succeeded by his son William de *Forz (d. 1260). Forz continued his family's patronage of existing religious houses, but did not make any new foundations. Almost all of his surviving charters were confirmations of earlier gifts by his predecessors or his tenants.

Forz was a man of mercurial temperament, who, in years of conflicting loyalties, changed sides more quickly than most. Both contemporaries and modern historians remark upon his turbulence, lack of resolution, and impulsiveness. The rapidity with which he was pardoned his successive offences suggests that he had some genuine grievances, perhaps connected with the threats to his inheritance posed by both King John and the regents for Henry III. In addition to the penalties he incurred through his inconstancy, he, or his officers, were incompetent administrators; free of family debt on inheritance, by 1226 he owed money to Jewish financiers and he was heavily indebted to the exchequer by 1231—these debts he left to his son. Of his many recorded lawsuits he lost all save one (which ended in a fine), and most were lost by carelessness or recalcitrance, as neither Forz nor his attorney came to court, so that the cases went by default.

William de Forz's seal depicts him on horseback, in armour and brandishing a sword; the counterseal shows his shield of arms, a cross patonce vair, both giving his surname and title as 'De Forz Comitis Albemarlie'.

BARBARA ENGLISH

Sources R. V. Turner, 'William de Forz, count of Aumale: an early thirteenth-century English baron', *Proceedings of the American Philosophical Society*, 115 (1971), 221–49 · D. A. Carpenter, *The minority of Henry III* (1990) · B. English, 'The counts of Aumale and Holderness, 1086–1260', PhD diss., St Andrews, 1977 · B. English, *The lords of Holderness, 1086–1260: a study in feudal society* (1979) · G. J. Turner, 'The minority of Henry III, pt 1', *TRHS*, new ser., 18 (1904), 245–95 · G. J. Turner, 'The minority of Henry III', *TRHS*, 3rd ser., 1 (1907), 205–62 · *Chancery records* · J. C. Holt, *The northerners: a study in the reign of King John*, new edn (1992) · F. M. Powicke, *Henry III and the Lord Edward: the community of the realm in the thirteenth century*, 1 (1947) · W. W. Shirley, ed., *Royal and other historical letters illustrative of the reign of Henry III*, 1, Rolls Series, 27 (1862) · J. C. Holt, *Magna Carta* (1965) · R. C. Stacey, *Politics, policy and finance under Henry III, 1216–1245* (1987) · R. Eales, 'Castles and politics in England, 1215–1224', *Thirteenth century England: proceedings of the Newcastle upon Tyne conference* [Newcastle upon Tyne 1987], ed. P. R. Coss and S. D. Lloyd, 2 (1988), 23–43 · *Pipe rolls, 5 Henry III* · *Paris, Chron.*
Likenesses seal, repro. in English, *Lords of Holderness*, pl. 10

Forz [Fortibus], **William de**, count of Aumale (b. before 1216, d. 1260), magnate, was the son of William de *Forz, count of Aumale (d. 1241), and his wife, Aveline, daughter of Richard de Montfichet of Stansted, Essex. His title of count of Aumale was derived from the *comté* of Aumale in Normandy; the family name evolved from Forz to Fortibus, but both forms are found. He was born before 17 December 1216, when his father gave the king his eldest son, William, as a hostage; he was probably one of the little boys who had been sent with their mother to Devizes Castle some months earlier. Nothing is known of his early life until his marriage, before 1234, to Christiana, one of the daughters of Alan of Galloway and his wife Margaret, the eldest sister of John the Scot, later earl of Chester. Christiana de Forz became in 1235 coheir of her father's

lands in Galloway, and in 1237 coheir to her mother's interest in the earldom of Chester.

Neither the Galloway lands nor the Chester inheritance, however, were to be retained by the Forz family. When Christiana died in 1246 without surviving children, her Galloway lands returned to her surviving sister, Dervorguilla, wife of John de Balliol (d. 1269). On the death of the earl of Chester without male heirs in 1237, William de Forz claimed that Chester was, as a palatinate, impartible, and that he should by right of his wife, the senior coheir, be both earl of Chester and the holder of all the lands of the earldom. The court allowed Forz the title, but decided that the lands of the honour should be divided. The king, however, persuaded the coheirs and their husbands to give up their claims, in exchange for lands elsewhere. William and Christiana de Forz finally quitclaimed their rights to the earldom in October 1241, in return for an insignificant amount of property elsewhere. William de Forz's father died in March 1241 and the king had taken the son's homage by 18 September 1241, when the escheator was ordered to give William de Forz, son of William de Forz, all lands, tenements, and castles that he held in chief, that is, honours based on the castles of Cockermouth, Cumberland, Skipton in Craven, and Skipsea in Holderness, both in Yorkshire. In 1242 and 1245 William de Forz, count of Aumale, accompanied Henry III on his campaigns in Poitou and Wales. After Christiana's death in 1246, in 1248 or 1249 the count married again. Isabella de *Forz (1237–1293), his second wife, was another great heiress, born Isabella de Revières, the daughter of the earl of Devon.

His northern property and his Scottish connections through his first wife made William de Forz a useful mediator with the Scots, and in 1231 when the king of England and the king of Scots made a treaty at York, he was one of the pledges for the Scottish king. He was appointed justice of the forest for Cumberland in 1251, and was sent on an embassy to Scotland in 1255; in the same year he was appointed sheriff of Cumberland and keeper of Carlisle Castle, offices he held until his death. In 1257 he was called to the army of Wales but paid scutage instead, because he was ill. The count of Aumale took a prominent part in the events of 1258, being appointed one of the king's counsellors under the provisions of Oxford. He was one of the escorts chosen to ensure that the Lusignan brothers left England safely. In March 1259 he was a member of Gloucester's reactionary party, and was one of those who made a pact with the Lord Edward. He went to France with the king in the autumn, was at Paris from December 1259 to January 1260, and at St Omer with the king in February. Later in the year he was again in France, on legal business, and died there on 23 May 1260, at Amiens. His body was buried in Thornton Abbey, Lincolnshire, at the feet of his mother, and his heart was buried at Meaux Abbey, Yorkshire, in the presbytery next to his daughter. With his second wife William de Forz had numerous children, but only one, Aveline, lived into adult life, to marry Henry III's younger son Edmund, earl of Lancaster; she died without any children in 1274.

As a great landowner William de Forz, the last count of Aumale, was inevitably involved in government and diplomacy, yet his personality is shadowy and as an individual he remains the least interesting of his line.

BARBARA ENGLISH

Sources B. English, 'The counts of Aumale and Holderness, 1086–1260', PhD diss., St Andrews, 1977 · B. English, *The lords of Holderness, 1086–1260: a study in feudal society* (1979) · cartularies, published and unpublished · W. Farrer and others, eds., *Early Yorkshire charters*, 12 vols. (1914–65), vols. 3, 7 · *Chancery records* · *Pipe rolls* · H. R. Luard, ed., *Flores historiarum*, 3 vols., Rolls Series, 95 (1890) · Paris, *Chron.* · GEC, *Peerage* · R. Eales, 'Henry III and the end of the Norman earldom of Chester', *Thirteenth century England: proceedings of the Newcastle upon Tyne conference* [Newcastle upon Tyne 1985], ed. P. R. Coss and S. D. Lloyd, 1 (1986), 100–13 · *CIPM*, 2, no. 44
Likenesses seal, repro. in English, *Lords of Holderness*, pl. 11

Fosbroke [Fosbrooke], **Thomas Dudley** (1770–1842), antiquary, was born Thomas Dudley Fosbrooke on 27 May 1770, the only son of the Revd William Fosbrooke (1734–1775) and his second wife, Hesther (1746–1832), daughter of Thomas Lashbroke of Southwark. His mother later married James Holmes (*d.* before 1821), adjutant of the West Essex militia. Until his father moved to London the family had been settled at Diddlebury, Shropshire, from about 1580. He attended St Paul's School, London, from 1779 and entered Pembroke College, Oxford, in 1785 (BA, 1789; MA, 1792). He was ordained in 1792 and, disappointed of an expected benefice, took the curacy of Horsley, Gloucestershire, in 1794. He married Mary Howell (1775–1850) of Horsley on 11 April 1796; they had four sons and six daughters (three of whom died in infancy). He later frequently complained of the financial hardship caused by his large family and lack of preferment.

Fosbrooke's literary pursuits offered some relief. In 1795 the *Gentleman's Magazine* reviewed his poem 'The economy of monastic life', and in 1799 he was elected a fellow of the Society of Antiquaries. His well-received major work, *British Monachism, or, Manners and Customs of the Monks and Nuns of England*, followed in 1802 (rev. edns, 1817, 1843). Influenced by the Maurists and encyclopaedic in character, it is based on a wide range of cited prime sources, a formula he variously repeated in his subsequent historical works. It opened a fruitful friendship with the printers John Nichols and his son (John) Bowyer Nichols which is recorded in a business correspondence more lively than Fosbrooke's published writings. Although in 1801 John Nichols would not let him edit Ralph Bigland's unfinished *Collections* on Gloucestershire history and Thomas Rudge forestalled him in 1803, he persevered with his innovative *Abstracts of Records and Manuscripts Respecting the County of Gloucester* (1807).

Finding Horsley too opulent for his circumstances, in 1810 Fosbrooke accepted the curacy of Walford, near Ross, Herefordshire, with the neighbouring parochial chapelry of Ruardean, Gloucestershire; he moved to Walford in 1811. For eighteen years he had studied for eight hours or more a day and his publications now included *An Original History of the City of Gloucester* (1819), incorporating some of Bigland's papers; *Berkeley Manuscripts* (1821), containing extracts from John Smyth's 'Lives of the Berkeleys' and

appending biographical anecdotes of Fosbrooke's friend, Edward Jenner; and his largest work, the *Encyclopaedia of Antiquities* (1825; 2nd edn, 1840), the first English publication of its kind, with its sequel, *Foreign Topography* (1828). He also wrote tourist guides, the most popular being *The Wye Tour* (1818; 6th edn, 1841). Between 1816 and 1833 he contributed monthly reviews to the *Gentleman's Magazine*. After tracing his family's Staffordshire and Northamptonshire origins he changed the spelling of his surname to Fosbroke in April 1820.

Despite this literary activity Fosbroke carried out parochial duties conscientiously: he founded Sunday schools and in 1810 paid for the inoculation of 600 Horsley parishioners. In 1815 he published *Key to the Testament, or, Whitby's Commentary Abridged*, and as a freemason he was provincial grand chaplain for Herefordshire, Monmouthshire, and Gloucestershire between 1815 and 1818. He undertook genealogical work for the duke of Newcastle in 1826–8 in the (unfulfilled) hope of being rewarded with a benefice. Eventually, in 1830, he was presented to the vicarage of Walford, though too late to restore his fortunes. From 1826 he suffered increasingly from gout, which finally incapacitated him, putting him in 1839 to the expense of engaging curates for his two parishes. In his last letters he begged Bowyer Nichols for financial help. Fosbroke died, intestate and insolvent, on 1 January 1842 at Walford vicarage, and was buried on 8 January at Walford, where there is a memorial to him in the church. His portrait, obituary, and family's history are conveniently published together in *British Monachism* (3rd edn, 1843). His family sold his papers to the Bristol bookseller William Strong. Many were acquired at auction in 1847 by Sir Thomas Phillipps and are now dispersed.

BRIAN S. SMITH

Sources DNB · T. D. Fosbroke, *Companion to the Wye tour. Ariconensia, or, Archaeological sketches of Ross, and Archenfield*, 2nd edn (1821), 168–83 [notes on the Fosbroke family] · J. B. N. [J. B. Nichol], 'Memoir of the author', in T. D. Fosbroke, *British monachism, or, Manners and customs of the monks and nuns of England*, 3rd edn (1843), 9–13 · GM, 2nd ser., 17 (1842), 214–16 · T. D. Fosbroke, 'Memoir of the family of Fosbroke', *British monachism, or, Manners and customs of the monks and nuns of England*, 3rd edn (1843), 14–23 · P. Ripley, introduction, in T. D. Fosbroke, *An original history of the city of Gloucester* (1819); repr. (1976) · I. Gray, 'Thomas Dudley Fosbroke, 1770–1842', *Antiquaries of Gloucestershire and Bristol*, Bristol and Gloucestershire Archaeological Society Records Section, 12 (1981), 87–90 · R. Austin, 'Letters of Thomas Dudley Fosbrooke', *Transactions of the Bristol and Gloucestershire Archaeological Society*, 37 (1914), 135–84 [incl. bibliography] · letters from T. D. Fosbroke and family to J. Nichols and J. B. Nichols, 1796–1847, Gloucestershire Public Library, Gloucestershire collection, 8208 · T. D. Fosbroke, 'Biographical account of the author', *Encyclopaedia of antiquities and elements of archaeology, classical and mediaeval*, 1 (1825), vii–xi · parish register, Horsley, 1794–1810, Glos. RO, P181 · parish records, Walford, 1810–42, Herefs. RO, AO19 · death duty record, 1842, PRO, IR 26/255, fols. 176r–176v
Archives Bodl. Oxf., antiquarian collections, notes and transcripts, MSS Eng. misc. e. 712–718, fol. 419; MS Top. Gen. d. 61; MS Top. Glouc. c. 10–12; MSS Phillipps/Robinson e. 141, 143 · Bodl. Oxf., Gloucestershire collections and notes · Glos. RO, corresp. and MSS · NRA, priv. coll., pedigree of Dobyns family · Yale U., Beinecke L., Osborn collection, notebooks | Bodl. Oxf., corresp. with Sir Thomas Phillipps · Glos. RO, corresp. with Nathaniel Clifford · Gloucester Public Library, Gloucestershire collection, Fosbroke–

Nichols corresp., 8208 · U. Nott., Clumber MSS, MSS relating to Clinton family
Likenesses engraving, 1816, repro. in Fosbroke, 'Biographical account of the author'
Wealth at death insolvent: PRO, death duty registers, IR 26/255, fols. 176r–176v

Foscolo, Ugo (1778–1827), poet and Italian patriot, was born on 6 February 1778 on the Ionian island of Zante, then under the control of Venice, the eldest of the four children of Andrea Foscolo (1754–1788), an Italian physician, and his wife, Diamantina Spatis (1747–1817), who was Greek. Following the death of his father he moved to live with his mother in Venice, where he completed his studies and began to make his way in literary circles. His enthusiasm for the Napoleonic cause received a setback in 1797 when the emperor ceded Venice to the Austrians and the young poet fled to Milan. Out of this experience grew his popular epistolary novel *Ultime lettere di Jacopo Ortis* (1802), which features a youthful hero who flees from Venice to escape the Austrian occupation and commits suicide in despair at the loss of his fatherland and the woman he loves. Foscolo, however, did not commit suicide but joined the Italian forces fighting against the Austrians and was wounded on several occasions. He continued to write poems, tragedies, and various political and literary works, including an Italian translation of Laurence Sterne's *Sentimental Journey* (1813). His best-known poem, *I sepolcri*, a 300-line celebration of tombs as mediators between the dead and the living and spurs to patriotic action, was published in Verona in 1807. With the defeat of Napoleon, Foscolo, as a leading and outspoken dissident, chose to go into exile, first to Switzerland and then to England; he arrived in London in September 1816, famous but penniless.

Foscolo was warmly welcomed in whig circles, and at Holland House he gained an entrée into polite society which led him to adopt a lifestyle beyond his means. His attempts to earn his living with his pen were inhibited by his imperfect knowledge of English, but Francis Jeffrey accepted a number of his articles for the *Edinburgh Review*, two of which, on Dante (February and September 1818), are recognized as landmarks in the development of a serious historical criticism of the *Divine Comedy*. Other articles for the *Edinburgh Review* included an exposure of the papal government in Rome (April 1819) and of the fate of the inhabitants of the Ionian island of Parga (October 1819), which the British government had recently ceded to the Turks; Foscolo was instrumental in getting the case raised in the Commons. However, under the constraint of the Aliens' Act he subsequently confined himself to literary and historical subjects, writing for the *Quarterly Review*, the *New Monthly Magazine*, the *London Magazine*, the *Retrospective Review*, and the *Westminster Review*. In 1821 a volume of his masterly *Essays on Petrarch* was privately printed in London; in 1825 he provided a scholarly *Discorso* for an edition of Boccaccio's *Decamerone*, and in 1826 the critically important *Discorso sul testo della 'Commedia' di Dante* intended for an edition of the *Divina commedia*.

Foscolo was also largely responsible for an 'Essay on the present literature of Italy', which appeared under the name of his friend John Cam Hobhouse in the latter's *Historical Illustrations to Childe Harold, Canto IV*, published in 1818 in explanation of the background to Byron's poem. The essay, with its forthright comments on living Italian writers, caused some offence in Italy, to the embarrassment of Hobhouse but the delight of Byron. Foscolo also wrote a 'Dissertation on an ancient hymn to the graces', which appeared in English as an appendix to a volume privately printed for the duke of Bedford describing the sculptures in his newly constructed gallery at Woburn Abbey. This included the duke's replica of Antonio Canova's famous group *The Three Graces* (*Outline Engravings and Descriptions of the Woburn Abbey Marbles*, 1822). Canova's acceptance of the original commission in 1812 from Empress Josephine had stimulated Foscolo to take up a long-cherished project, a *carme* or hymn to the graces, which he then addressed to the Italian sculptor. The poem which emerged, *Le grazie*, although never completed or published in the poet's lifetime, is regarded by many as Foscolo's best work, and the dissertation forms an interesting English coda to this masterpiece.

During these years, when Foscolo was alternately hobnobbing with the gentry and dodging his creditors, his spirits were variously lifted and depressed by a series of attachments to a number of well-born ladies: Lady Caroline Lamb, Caroline Russell, Lady Barbarina Wilmot, and others. Foscolo was a striking-looking man, with fiery red hair, piercing deep-set eyes, and a furrowed brow: Walter Scott said he was 'ugly as a baboon' (*Journal*, 12). He was of a passionate, excitable disposition, capable of great charm and exceptional eloquence, but also of fits of temper which alienated most of his friends and acquaintances; only the most patient supported him to the end. Reputedly he fought two duels—one in England, in which he threw his pistol at his opponent's head to demonstrate his contempt. Throughout his exile in England he fell repeatedly into debt and was subject to frequent periods of ill health, but his final years were cheered by the arrival of a young daughter, Mary Hamilton (Floriana), the fruit of a brief liaison in France in 1804 with an Englishwoman, Sophia St John Hamilton, the illegitimate daughter of Lady Mary Walter and granddaughter of Alexander, seventh earl of Melville. The inheritance she brought was mismanaged, and the poet died in extreme poverty, at Turnham Green, Middlesex, on 10 September 1827. He was buried in Chiswick cemetery on 18 September, but his remains were disinterred in 1871 and transferred to Santa Croce in Florence to lie alongside Italy's hallowed dead.

PETER BRAND

Sources A. M. Ghisalberti and others, eds., *Dizionario biografico degli Italiani*, 49 (Rome, 1997) · *Ugo Foscolo: opere*, ed. F. Gavazzeni, 2 vols. (1974) · *Edizione nazionale delle opere di U. Foscolo*, ed. M. Fubini, 1 (1933) · E. R. Vincent, *Ugo Foscolo esule fra gli inglesi* (1954) · E. R. Vincent, *Byron, Hobhouse and Foscolo* (1949) · W. Binni, *U. Foscolo: storia e poesia* (1982) · U. Renda, P. Operti, and V. Turri, eds., *Dizionario storico della letteratura italiana* (1952) · GM, 1st ser., 97/2 (1827), 566–9 · *The journal of Sir Walter Scott*, ed. [J. G. Tait and W. M. Parker] (1950)
Archives Biblioteca Nazionale Centrale, Italy · Livorno Library, Italy · University of Pavia, Italy

Likenesses A. Fabre, oils, Biblioteca Nazionale Centrale, Florence, Italy; repro. in A. Caraccio, *Ugo Foscolo: l'homme et le poète, 1778–1827* (1934) · F. Pistrucci, oils, Biblioteca Braidenze, Milan, Italy; repro. in E. R. Vincent, *Ugo Foscolo: an Italian in regency England* (1953)

Wealth at death nil: E. R. Vincent, *Ugo Foscolo: an Italian in regency England* (1953)

Foskett, Bernard (1685–1758), Particular Baptist minister and college head, was born in North Crawley, Buckinghamshire, on 10 March 1685, the son of William Foskett, the local justice of the peace. Educated at home, he subsequently trained in London to be a physician. It was in London on 7 October 1708 that he was baptized and joined Little Wild Street Church. Three years later he accepted a call to pastor the Baptist church in Henley in Arden, Warwickshire. He served there until October 1720, when he moved to Bristol to be the tutor at the Bristol Baptist Academy and to assist Peter Kitterell, the pastor of Broadmead church and president of the academy. When Kitterell died in 1727 Foskett succeeded him as both pastor and president.

The work at the academy had languished prior to Foskett's arrival in Bristol. It began to grow significantly when Hugh Evans, baptized by Foskett on 13 September 1730, was called as his assistant in 1734, a position that Evans accepted on 9 January 1735. Despite a difference in age—Evans was twenty-seven years younger than Foskett—and personality—Evans was vivacious while Foskett could be somewhat austere—the two men experienced a deep harmony in their work at the academy. From four students in the 1720s the numbers grew to a peak of twenty-nine in the 1740s. Among the ministers trained by Foskett and Evans were John C. Ryland, John Ash, Benjamin Beddome, and Benjamin Francis, who became key leaders among the English Particular Baptists in the second half of the eighteenth century.

Foskett also had a significant impact upon the Welsh Baptist community; half of the seventy or so men whom he trained over the course of his time as president were Welsh. Imbued with the ethos and theology of Foskett's evangelical Calvinism, a number of these students led the Particular Baptist cause in Wales when it experienced revival in the latter half of the eighteenth century.

Foskett played a key role in helping the Baptist churches of the Western Association to resist the inroads of Arianism and Socinianism, both of which threatened more than one Baptist cause in the west country after the London Salters' Hall controversy of 1719. The association had rested upon an inadequate doctrinal basis that laid the churches open to theological influences foreign to their tradition. Cognizant of this danger Foskett began urging the association leadership in the early 1720s to affirm its commitment to the second London confession of faith, which had been ratified by the Particular Baptists in 1689 as the doctrinal standard for their communities. He was not successful in this endeavour until 1732, when he and Evans sent a letter in the name of the Broadmead church inviting the churches to form a new association based on this confession. Foskett's dogged insistence on a confessional basis for the association bore rich dividends in the decades to come, as a considerable portion of the vitality of English Baptist life in the late eighteenth century can be traced to the west country Baptists. Further involvement in the life of the association included his encouragement of hymn singing and the catechizing of children.

Foskett never married. He died at the home of John Beddome, in the castle precincts at Bristol, on 17 September 1758 and was buried in Bristol burial-ground. Hugh Evans, who succeeded him as both senior pastor of the Broadmead church and president of the academy, well summed up his character when he said of him:

> though he was strenuous for what he apprehended to be the truth, yet was he fond of no extreme. While he strongly asserted the honours of free grace, he earnestly contended for the necessity of good works … recommending holiness as the only way to happiness. (Rippon)

MICHAEL A. G. HAYKIN

Sources R. Hayden, 'Evangelical Calvinism among eighteenth-century British Baptists with particular reference to Bernard Foskett, Hugh and Caleb Evans and the Bristol Baptist Academy, 1690–1791', PhD diss., University of Keele, 1991 · R. Hayden, 'The contribution of Bernard Foskett', *Pilgrim pathways*, ed. W. H. Brackney, P. S. Fiddes, and J. H. Y. Briggs (Macon, Georgia, 1999), 189–206 · J. Rippon, *A brief essay towards an history of the Baptist academy at Bristol* (1795) · S. A. Swaine, *Faithful men* (1884) · N. S. Moon, *Education for ministry* (1979)

Archives Bristol Baptist College | Bristol RO, Broadmead church records · DWL, Wilson MS · Regent's Park College, Oxford, sermons in MS book of Broadmead sermons

Likenesses oils, Bristol Baptist College

Wealth at death £130 in bequests: Bristol RO; will, PRO, PROB 10/2236, CC44/66

Foskett [née Kirk], **Daphne** (1911–1998), art connoisseur and writer, was born on 23 December 1911 at Shoddesden, Kimpton, Hampshire, the daughter of John William Carnegie Kirk, a captain in the Duke of Cornwall's light infantry, and his wife, Agnes Maud Haynes. Her paternal grandfather was Sir John *Kirk, the noted botanist and physician, who was David Livingstone's chief assistant and photographer on his second Zambesi expedition (1858–63). Proud of this Scottish ancestry, in the early 1980s Foskett arranged for her grandfather's archive to be placed on long-term loan at the National Library of Scotland (which has since acquired it).

Daphne Kirk had a peripatetic childhood centred mainly on Sevenoaks in Kent. She was educated at St Ives School in Bexhill, Sussex, but left with no formal qualifications. After a period in the mid-1930s as matron at a Kent preparatory school, she married on 7 April 1937 Reginald Foskett (1908/9–1973), then a curate, the son of Albert Ernest Foskett, a technical engineer. Daphne was the driving force behind her husband's career as curate and as vicar in the Nottinghamshire parishes of Rainworth (1937–43) and Ordsall (1943–7), and then at Ilkeston in Derbyshire (1948–56). In 1956 Reginald Foskett was appointed provost to St Mary's Cathedral in Edinburgh, where the couple stayed for the next eleven years.

It was during this period that Daphne Foskett developed her love for and expertise in portrait miniatures. For several years she assisted Arthur Tite, a dealer in miniatures,

Daphne Foskett (1911–1998), by Heather O. Catchpole, 1990

at the annual Grosvenor House art fair. As her immense knowledge of the subject increased, she was encouraged to publish her research. Her first book was published in 1963, the lavishly illustrated *British Portrait Miniatures: a History*. In the following year she produced the first ever monograph on the outstanding but hitherto under-appreciated eighteenth-century miniaturist John Smart. For this book she was able to draw on Arthur Jaffé's extensive unpublished research on Smart. In 1965 Foskett was invited by the Scottish committee of the Arts Council for Great Britain to curate a major exhibition, 'British Portrait Miniatures', to coincide with the Edinburgh international festival. Held at the Arts Council gallery in Rothesay Terrace, this major exhibition presented more than 400 miniatures from public and private collections across the world.

In 1967 Reginald Foskett was appointed bishop of Penrith, a suffragan bishopric in the diocese of Carlisle. The Fosketts lived at Brathay, near Ambleside, but after Reginald retired on account of ill health in 1970 they moved to Field Broughton, also in Westmorland. Daphne became a governor of St Ann's School in Windermere.

In 1972 Foskett published her massive research in the two-volume *A Dictionary of British Miniature Painters*, which recorded biographical information on more than 4500 portrait miniaturists. This publication superseded and expanded Basil Long's landmark dictionary *British Miniaturists* (1929). Foskett's dictionary has been in print since 1987, when it was republished together with a new edition of her book *Collecting Miniatures* (1979) to form the one-volume *Miniatures: Dictionary and Guide*.

Reginald Foskett's death at Field Broughton in 1973 was a considerable blow to Daphne, but she had two monographs and an exhibition catalogue published in the following year. Her book on the greatest of all British miniaturists, Samuel Cooper, was accompanied by her catalogue to the exhibition 'Samuel Cooper and his Contemporaries', which she curated for the National Portrait Gallery, drawing together nearly 250 outstanding seventeenth-century miniatures from across the world. In addition she produced her significant monograph on the Lakeland artist John Harden of Brathay Hall. In 1983 Foskett was involved as a consultant on the ground-breaking exhibition 'Artists of the Tudor Court', held at the Victoria and Albert Museum. She left an unpublished but completed manuscript on this key period of the portrait miniature. Foskett published numerous articles on miniatures and portrait miniaturists throughout her career.

Arguably more than anybody since the end of the Second World War, Foskett succeeded in bringing the art of the portrait miniaturist closer to collectors and connoisseurs, as well as to the wider public. Her prolific and popular output of writings compares well with the major scholarly contributions made by a series of curators and conservators who worked at the Victoria and Albert Museum, principally Graham Reynolds, Roy Strong, Jim Murrell, and John Murdoch. Foskett's knowledge was generously shared across the world with museum curators and private collectors, as well as with dealers and auctioneers. On her regular visits to London or elsewhere, such as during two punishing tours of the United States, she would leave behind a re-enthused curator or a budding cataloguer much the wiser and the keener. She conducted a very wide international correspondence and built up a substantial photographic archive; these were the building blocks of her painstaking research.

Foskett also received numerous visitors and students at her home in Field Broughton. There her razor-sharp memory was deployed in honing the eyes of younger specialists. This was often in discussion over some of her own exquisite collections. Apart from portrait miniatures, these included ivories, porcelain, and pottery, as well as Georgian furniture. Such close training in minute connoisseurship was a bracing experience, but it was mediated by her twinkling sense of humour. She was indefatigable, sometimes formidable, but always generous. After her death her photographic archive and a major part of her collection of portrait miniatures were placed on long-term loan at the Scottish National Portrait Gallery in Edinburgh, where the miniatures were catalogued and exhibited in 2003.

Daphne Foskett died on 15 June 1998 in the Solihull Parkway Hospital. She had moved to Solihull ten years earlier to be closer to some of her family, and is buried there. She was survived by her two daughters. Foskett's numerous publications and significant exhibitions reached a wide audience, while her writing was driven by a keen eye and by a desire to make miniature painting more accessible to amateurs and specialists alike, while also furthering existing knowledge. She did a great deal to popularize this much-loved but often hidden mode of portraiture.   STEPHEN LLOYD

Sources S. Lloyd, *The Scotsman* (18 July 1998) · b. cert. · m. cert. · d. cert.
Archives Scot. NPG, photographs, articles, MSS, slides, corresp., notebooks, proof and annotated copies of books and catalogues
Likenesses H. O. Catchpole, miniature, watercolour on ivory, 1990, Scot. NPG [*see illus.*] · photograph, repro. in Lloyd; priv. coll.
Wealth at death £862,913, gross; £858,141, net: probate, 18 Dec 1998, *CGPLA Eng. & Wales*

Foss, Edward (1787–1870), legal writer and biographer, eldest son of Edward Smith Foss (*d.* 1830), solicitor, of 36 Essex Street, Strand, London, and Anne, his wife, daughter of Dr William Rose of Chiswick, was born in Gough Square, Fleet Street, on 16 October 1787. He was educated under Dr Charles Burney, his mother's brother-in-law, at Greenwich, and remained there until he was articled in 1804 to his father, whose partner he became in 1811. In 1822 he became a member of the Inner Temple, but never proceeded further towards a call to the bar, maintaining instead a highly successful solicitor's practice. In 1814 he married Catherine, eldest daughter of Peter Martineau, with whom he had one son, who died in infancy. On his father's death in 1830 he moved to Essex Street, and carried on the practice alone until 1840, when he retired, leaving his business in the hands of H. M. Clark. During his professional career he had, owing to his literary tastes and connections, been especially concerned with questions relating to publishers and literary figures. Among his clients were the trustees of the Baldwin estate, whom he served during their protracted disputes with the Society for the Diffusion of Useful Knowledge over the right to publish the Society's editions.

Throughout his career and after his retirement, Foss devoted his leisure to literary pursuits. While still a very young man he contributed to the *Monthly Review*, *Aikin's Athenaeum*, the *London Magazine*, the *Gentleman's Magazine*, and the *Morning Chronicle*. In 1817 he published *The Beauties of Massinger*, and in 1820 he produced an abridgement of Blackstone's *Commentaries*, begun by John Giffard and published under his name, which was later translated into German. On retiring from professional practice he devoted himself to collecting materials for his history of the legal profession, which he lent to Lord Campbell for his *Lives of the Chancellors*. In 1843 he published *The Grandeur of the Law*, and in 1848 the first two volumes of his *Judges of England* appeared. The latter work was at first unsuccessful, owing to the obscurity and unpopularity of the subject of the first volumes—judges of the Norman period; but as further volumes progressed, the work rose in favour, until it became established as the standard authority in its field. In recognition of his labours, Lord Langdale, to whom the first two volumes were dedicated, procured for him a grant of the entire series of publications of the record commission. The third and fourth volumes appeared in 1851, the fifth and sixth in 1857, and the seventh, eighth, and ninth in 1864. In 1865 Foss published *Tabulae curiales*.

Foss was an original member of the Archaeological Institute and helped to found the Kent Archaeological Association. He was elected a fellow of the Society of Antiquaries in 1822 and was a member of the council of the Camden Society from 1850 to 1853 and from 1865 to 1870. He was also a member of the Royal Society of Literature from 1837, and was on the council of the Royal Literary Fund. Until 1839 he was secretary to the Society of Guardians of Trade, and he was also a regular contributor to *Archaeologia* and to *Notes and Queries*.

Foss held a number of other offices during his life. In 1827–8 he served as under-sheriff of London. He was connected with the Law Life Assurance Society from its foundation in 1823, first as auditor and afterwards as director, and was active in founding the Incorporated Law Society, of which he was president in 1842 and 1843. In 1844 he moved from Streatham to Canterbury, where he proved himself a useful chairman of the magistrates' bench; he later became deputy lieutenant for Kent. In 1859 he moved to Dover, and in 1865 he went on to Addiscombe. Following the death of his first wife, Foss married Maria Elizabeth, eldest daughter of William Hutchins, in 1844; they had six sons and three daughters. The eldest son, Edward, a barrister, assisted in the preparation of the *Biographia juridica*, an abbreviation of Foss's *Judges of England*, the printing of which was far advanced when Foss died of an apoplexy on 27 July 1870 at Frensham House, Croydon.   MICHAEL LOBBAN

Sources J. C. Robertson, memoir, in E. Foss, *Biographia juridica: a biographical dictionary of the judges of England … 1066–1870* (1870), xii–xv · *Law Times* (24 Sept 1870) · *N&Q*, 4th ser., 6 (1870), 126 · A. W. B. Simpson, ed., *Biographical dictionary of the common law* (1984) · Boase, *Mod. Eng. biog.* · review, *Solicitors' Journal*, 15 (1870–71), 268–9
Archives BL, corresp., Add. MS 40166 · UCL, letters to Society for the Diffusion of Useful Knowledge
Wealth at death under £45,000: probate, 22 Aug 1870, *CGPLA Eng. & Wales*

Foss, Hubert James (1899–1953), music publisher and composer, was born on 2 May 1899 at Woodcroft, Park Hill Road, Croydon, Surrey, the thirteenth and youngest child of Frederick Foss (1850–1908) and his wife, Anne Penny Bartrum (1853–1924). His father, a solicitor, served as a JP and was mayor of Croydon from 1892 to 1893, his grandfather was Edward *Foss (1787–1870); Josephine *Foss (1887–1983) was his sister.

Foss showed linguistic and musical ability at an early age and was sent to Stanley Roper, a notable organist and composer, for specialist teaching. He received his general education at St Anselm's School, Croydon, and at Bradfield College, near Reading, where he had a senior classical foundation scholarship. The college offered opportunities for developing his artistic interests, which included not only music and literature during these years, but also drama. After leaving Bradfield in December 1917, Foss enlisted in the 5th Middlesex regiment as a second lieutenant and served until his discharge in 1919. He then undertook a range of jobs, including teaching in a preparatory school, writing his first pieces of freelance journalism, and working as assistant editor on G. K.

Chesterton's journal *Land and Water*. In 1920 he married Kate Frances Carter Page (1900–1952), and they had two daughters.

Foss and his wife—from whom he separated about 1923—moved to Eynsford, Kent, where he became close to the artistic community that centred on Philip Heseltine, better known as the composer Peter Warlock, with whom he shared a deep interest in the revival of Elizabethan music and in contemporary English song. Indeed, Foss not only was a fine accompanist, but also made a significant contribution to the repertory during the inter-war years, publishing over fifty songs and song arrangements with firms such as Boosey (later Boosey and Hawkes), Curwen, and Oxford University Press (OUP). Of these, songs such as 'Clouds', 'As I walked forth', 'Infant Joy', and the *Seven Poems by Thomas Hardy* seem to be most characteristic. Other notable inter-war compositions include the *Newcastle Dances* for two pianos and two masques, *The Masque of the Manuscript* and *The Masque of Perusal*, written in collaboration with the poet Charles Williams.

In April 1921 Foss took a post as a sales representative and senior assistant to the educational manager of OUP in London. His new job gave him vital experience of the education and publishing worlds at a time of rapid expansion in the wake of post-war education reforms. Foss's energy and vision were soon evident, and in 1923 Humphrey Milford founded OUP's music department, appointing Foss as its first head. Initially the department specialized in educational sheet music and books aimed at the musical appreciation market. However, it was not long before Foss led the department through an extraordinary period of expansion. In 1925 he began to publish the music of Ralph Vaughan Williams and William Walton, as well as individual works by Frederick Delius, Ethel Smyth, and Gustav Holst. Foss had a remarkable ear for the work of a new, younger generation, and soon the department was also publishing the latest works by Constant Lambert, Bernard van Dieren, John Gardner, Ernest (Jack) Moeran, Alan Rawsthorne, Edmund Rubbra, and Peter Warlock. Meanwhile he also built an impressive catalogue of books on music, including studies by his friend and mentor, William Henry Hadow, Michel Calvocoressi, Cecil Gray, and, most notably, Percy Scholes and Donald Tovey. Foss published some of Benjamin Britten's early works but then, in a decision later much regretted by OUP, decided not to continue as his publisher. Foss's second marriage, to the singer Dora Maria Stevens (1893–1978), took place in 1927. The couple had a son and a daughter.

By the outbreak of the Second World War, Foss had established OUP's music department as one of the foremost music publishers in Britain. However, he suffered throughout the later 1930s from bouts of serious ill health which were exacerbated by his punishing lifestyle. He also became increasingly frustrated by financial constraints on his work at OUP. Matters came to a head in 1941, and he resigned to pursue a freelance career as a music journalist and broadcaster. Foss had already published *Music in my Time* (1933) and given occasional broadcasts on contemporary English music for the BBC, but it was during the war and post-war years that he established a significant reputation as a music critic. During the war itself, he gave hundreds of talks for the Council for the Encouragement of Music and the Arts, the Entertainments National Service Association, and the BBC, spanning the whole range of its services. He also began writing *Ralph Vaughan Williams: a Study*, which, when it was published in 1950, was the first large-scale study of the composer to appear. It proved to be his most enduring critical achievement, intertwining his own personal insights with a view of the composer that spoke for a whole generation. In the following years Foss began preparing a number of other studies, most notably concerning Walton and Lambert. Tragically, however, his sudden death on 27 May 1953 at his home, 60 Corringham Road, London, caused by a severe stroke during a period of post-operative rehabilitation, meant that they were never completed; nor could he take up his forthcoming appointment as editor of the *Musical Times*. He was cremated at Golders Green crematorium on 30 May 1953.

Although Foss is remembered chiefly for his work as founder editor of the OUP music department and for his study of Vaughan Williams, these achievements represent only two facets of his extraordinary and highly creative personality. In addition to his musical accomplishments he wrote short stories, was a skilled versifier, and achieved distinction as a typographer and printer.

DUNCAN HINNELLS

Sources DNB · D. Hinnells, *An extraordinary performance* (1998) · [P. A. Mulgan], *Oxford music: the first fifty years, '23–'73* (1973) · P. Foden and P. Nash, 'The wet grass of bookishness: Hubert J. Foss as book designer', *Matrix: a review for printers and bibliophiles*, 14 (1992), 139–47 · C. G. Mortimer, 'Leading music publishers: Oxford University Press, music department', *Musical Opinion*, 63 (1939–40), 187 · b. cert. · *CGPLA Eng. & Wales* (1953) · family papers, priv. coll. [in possession of Diana Sparkes, daughter] · *The Times* (28 May 1953)
Archives priv. coll., family papers | BBC WAC, files · BL, corresp. with G. K. Chesterton, Add. MS 73231A, fols. 34–57 · Oxford University Press, files | SOUND BL NSA
Likenesses photograph, repro. in Hinnells, *An extraordinary performance* · photograph, Oxford University Press, London

Foss, Hugh Rose (1902–1971), cryptanalyst, was born on 13 May 1902 in Kobe, Japan, one of five children of Hugh James Foss (1848–1932), Anglican bishop of Osaka, and his wife, Janet Ovans (b. 1870). He was educated at Hoylake, at Marlborough College, and at Christ's College, Cambridge. In December 1924, shortly after leaving Cambridge, he joined the Government Code and Cypher School (GCCS), then situated in Queens Gate, Knightsbridge, London. The public role of GCCS was 'to advise as to the security of codes and ciphers used by all Government departments and to assist in their provision'. But it also had the secret role of breaking the codes and ciphers of other nations.

The success of the British military and naval codebreakers during the First World War led a number of nations to adopt machine ciphers, which were seen as more difficult to break. It is commonly assumed that the difficulties encountered by the British in breaking the German Enigma machine cipher stemmed from the fact that they made no attempt to break it between the wars.

This was not the case. At some time in 1927 Foss was asked to examine a commercial Enigma machine to see if it was suitable for use by the Admiralty. He concluded that it had a high degree of security but nevertheless managed to break it, recording how this could be done. On 16 April 1932 he married Alison (1908–1979), daughter of Walter Armstrong Graham. They had a daughter and a son.

One legacy of Foss's childhood in Kobe was a fluency in Japanese. This proved extremely useful in his code-breaking career. Japan was rapidly becoming a major military power capable of threatening British interests in the Far East and was adopting machine ciphers for important diplomatic communications. Working with Oliver Strachey, Foss broke the machine cipher used by Japanese naval attachés at its embassies abroad in September 1934. Foss and Strachey are also believed to have been responsible for another major British code-breaking success only two months later, the solution of the 'Type A' diplomatic cipher machine (also known as the Red machine) used by the Japanese for all their major diplomatic communications. By now GCCS had moved to the offices of the Secret Intelligence Service, located in Broadway, Victoria, London. It was during this time that Foss developed an interest in Scottish country dancing and he became a leading member of the Chelsea Reel Society.

Despite Foss's earlier efforts there was no real British attempt to break the German Enigma machine ciphers until the Spanish Civil War in 1936. On 24 April 1937 an Enigma machine given by the Germans to the Italians and Spanish was broken by Dillwyn Knox, using an improved version of the system recommended by Foss ten years earlier. During this period, and in the early years of the war, Foss was also heavily involved in the British efforts to break the more complicated versions of the machine which were in general use in the Wehrmacht. These incorporated a plugboard, greatly increasing the difficulty involved in breaking them. GCCS failed to do so throughout the 1930s but fortunately Polish code-breakers enjoyed more success. During the months leading up to the war Foss was involved, along with Knox and Alastair Denniston, the operational head of GCCS, in the urgent discussions with the Poles on how to break the Wehrmacht ciphers. The information the Poles supplied led to the successful British wartime breaks into a number of different Enigma ciphers.

After the code-breakers moved in September 1939 to their wartime home at Bletchley Park, Buckinghamshire, Foss worked in the German naval Enigma section, Hut 8. He played a prominent role in the efforts to break the principal German navy Enigma cipher in use in the early years of the war, the home waters cipher, known to GCCS as Dolphin.

With the advent of the war in the Far East in December 1941, Foss was made head of the Japanese naval section, Hut 7. He also taught a regular class on Scottish country dancing. A number of the original code-breakers were renowned for their eccentricities and Foss was no exception. A cousin, who also worked at Bletchley Park, recalled that his domestic life was dominated by his desire for efficient organization. Crockery and cutlery were washed up in a strict order whereby saucers were cleaned first, on the basis that they were least contaminated by contact with the human mouth. She recalled:

> Then teaspoons; then side-plates; then pudding plates; soup bowls; main course; knives; glasses; cups; forks; pudding and soup spoons; and finally saucepans. If one tried to help there would be shrieks of: 'Oh you mustn't do the cups yet. Saucers first'. There was also in theory some weird arrangement so that things Hugh was supposed to put away were located at distances appropriate to his great height and long arms, while [his wife] Alison, who was small and dumpy, had a shorter range. (Smith, *Emperor's Codes*, 146)

In December 1944 Foss was sent as a liaison officer to Washington, where his distinctive red hair and beard, and a penchant, common among the British code-breakers, for wearing sandals, led to his being dubbed affectionately Lend-lease Jesus. He continued after the war to work for GCCS and its successor organization, government communications headquarters. He retired in 1953, and in 1955 moved to Dalry, near Castle Douglas, Kirkcudbrightshire, where he continued his interest in Scottish country dancing, composing, compiling, and publishing a number of popular and regularly performed dances. Hugh Foss died at his home, Glendarroch, Dalry, on 23 December 1971. He was survived by his wife.   MICHAEL SMITH

Sources H. R. Foss, 'Reminiscences of Enigma', PRO, 25/10 [brief record of Foss's 1927 examination of the Enigma machine] · H. R. Foss, 'The reciprocal Enigma', PRO, 25/14 [paper believed written in 1928, describing how to break the commercial Enigma machine] · M. Smith, *The emperor's codes: Bletchley Park and the breaking of Japan's secret ciphers* (2000) · M. Smith and R. Erskine, eds., *Action this day: Bletchley Park from the breaking of the Enigma code to the birth of the modern computer* (2001) · E. Nave, 'An Australian's unique naval career', Australian War Memorial, MS 1183 [unpublished memoir] · private information (2004) · m. cert. · d. cert. · CCI (1972)
Likenesses portraits, repro. in Smith and Erskine, eds., *Action this day*
Wealth at death £17,623.40: confirmation, 4 Sept 1972, CCI; NA Scot., SC 16/41/98/104–9

Foss, Josephine (1887–1983), missionary teacher and welfare worker in Asia, was born on 19 March 1887 at Eastleigh, Dingwall Road, Croydon, the seventh child of Frederick Foss (1850–1908), solicitor, and his wife, Anne Penny Bartrum (1853–1924). Hubert James *Foss (1899–1953) was a younger brother. After training as a teacher at the Froebel Institute, specializing in science subjects, she taught for seven years in London and Lancashire before training to become a missionary at St Denys College, Warminster. Early in 1914 she was appointed by the Society for the Propagation of the Gospel (SPG) to teach elementary science, nature study, and craft at two schools in Peking (Beijing). She travelled from Berlin to Vladivostok by the Trans-Siberian Railway, having to show her baptism certificate in tsarist Russia because of their current persecution of Jews. Once in China she had to learn to speak and read Mandarin. After a year of intense tuition and much practice with the children in her hostel, she was able to teach elementary physics in Chinese to the boys. Having survived a virulent strain of tuberculosis, she struggled to open kindergartens and clinics in rural areas, carrying bones and crusts of bread in her pockets for the pariah dogs that were at first set on her as 'a blue-eyed Devil'.

Foss returned on furlough to Europe in 1919 and had to be treated in Switzerland for her tuberculosis. Peking was judged too unhealthy for her and she was sent to Natal (1921–4), to teach English and teaching method to Zulu boys, including the future bishop of Zululand. In 1924 the SPG sent her to St Mary's Anglican School in Kuala Lumpur. In the backstreets of Kuala Lumpur she discovered a primitive school for the children of the Chinese poor, run over shop fronts by an elderly, frail English lady, Miss Gage Brown. Josephine Foss took over when Miss Brown went back to England to die and immediately found herself struggling for government backing for her Pudu English School for Girls. 'But money, how much I wanted and how little I got' (memoirs, 30). She was allowed to move the site of the school to undrained wasteland near an old tin mine crater and, thanks to donations from the local Chinese, the first kindergarten, primary, and secondary classes for girls in Malaya began. She also established a boarding-house for rural girls—Chinese, Indian, Ceylonese, Dutch, and English—though not Malay Muslims because of their dietary restrictions. They were not all Christians, but Miss Foss did not think that mattered. She also initiated a Girl Guide movement, did local welfare work among lepers and battered children, and found herself the *de facto* adoptive mother of several abandoned illegitimate little daughters of prostitutes. In 1937 she was made MBE for services to education. Her girls became the first women doctors, nurses, matrons, accountants, therapists, teachers, and lawyers in Malaya, and her Pudu School eventually grew to have more than 1000 pupils.

After the Japanese invasion of Malaya in 1941 Foss was evacuated to Singapore. When Singapore fell she and the remaining British women were marched to Changi prison camp. She was interned for three and a half years, keeping up her own and her fellow prisoners' spirits, organizing work parties and clandestine meetings of husbands and wives. She endured punishment and interrogation as well as sickness and the endemic acute hunger. After the war the Colonial Office sent her an official commendation for the exceptional services she had rendered to her comrades in captivity. On her release she was too ill and weak to walk; she had lost almost all her hair as well as 5 stone. But former pupils from Pudu found her and cherished her back to the beginnings of renewed health.

Foss recovered slowly in post-war Britain and applied to return to Malaya, only to be told by the SPG that the bishop of Singapore (John Leonard Wilson) refused to have her back. Perhaps this was because it was no longer possible under Malayanization to have a European as headmistress, or because she had not minded that so many of her girls were not Christian. Determined to save for her fare to return independently, she went back to South Africa to teach Zulu girls for a year in Natal. She later learned that her girls' school was declared a 'whites-only' area by the Nationalist government and all the Africans forcibly displaced.

In July 1948 Foss returned to Singapore. No longer a headmistress, she had new work, training the first generation of Malaya's welfare officers. She went to hospitals, orphanages, leper settlements, and gaols and personally demonstrated the harmlessness of being a blood donor. But once the emergency of the communist insurgency began in Malaya, the government used her as an interpreter for Mandarin in the courts that were trying young Chinese suspects. She then had to trace and reunite the families of the communists willing to be repatriated to mainland China. As well as Mandarin she could speak Malay, and more than a smattering of Cantonese, Hakka, and Japanese. (In Natal she had also coped with the click language of the Zulu.) She was much happier doing welfare work again after the emergency, organizing campaigns against malaria and yaws and taking salt, clothes, and medicines by jeep and canoe, and on foot through the jungle, to inaccessible Malay villages.

Josephine Foss returned to England in 1957, and taught Malay and Mandarin to English people and English to foreigners—above all to the Japanese. 'I was determined to teach Japanese ladies to show that I had no permanent hate against them' (memoirs). She died at her home, 2 Broadlands Road, Highgate, London, on 23 July 1983.

SYBIL OLDFIELD

Sources memoirs, Bodl. RH · *The Times* (4 Aug 1983) · H. P. Thompson, *Into all lands* (1951), 650, 654 · b. cert. · d. cert. · *CGPLA Eng. & Wales* (1983)

Archives Bodl. RH, typescript of memoirs held in Society for the Propagation of the Gospel | Women's Library, London, newspaper cuttings with photographs

Likenesses photograph, Women's Library, London, biographical cuttings collection

Wealth at death under £25,000: probate, 17 Aug 1983, *CGPLA Eng. & Wales*

Fossard family (*per. c.*1080–1194?), gentry, is first represented in the historical record by **Nigel Fossard** (*d.* in or before 1128). He was one of two major Domesday tenants in Yorkshire of Robert, count of Mortain, holding extensive properties from the count in all three ridings. Indeed Nigel Fossard and the other major tenant, Richard de Sourdeval, held almost all the 114 tenant manors of Count Robert in the county and Nigel himself held about 500 carucates in Yorkshire. In the North Riding he had over 200 carucates including 25 in Guisborough, 'Middleton', and Hutton Lowcross, which later formed a castlery centred on Lythe Castle near Whitby. In the East Riding he had about 200 carucates including 13 in each of Watton, Bainton, and Birdsall and 12 in Wharram-le-Street. In the West Riding he had almost 60 carucates including 12 in Bramham. Nigel's estates were confined to Yorkshire and it has been suggested that this concentration of lands resulted from Count Robert's intention that Nigel live and work in the county. After Count Robert's rebellion and fall in 1088 Nigel Fossard's tenancy was transformed into a tenancy-in-chief, although he had already acquired that status because of a small property holding in York. The relationship between the crown and the Fossards was strengthened further in the early twelfth century when Henry I actively encouraged the development of the compact lordship around Lythe Castle as part of his plan to increase royal influence in north-east Yorkshire. Nigel was a patron of St Mary's Abbey, York, to which he gave property in Doncaster and lands and churches in York, Hutton Cranswick, Bainton, and Caythorpe. He also gave Bramham church to Ramsey Abbey.

It has been suggested that Nigel was living until at least 1120 and it is probable that he survived until nearly the end of the decade because at some point before 1129 his son and successor, **Robert Fossard** (*d. c*.1138), was having difficulties with his inheritance. Shortly before 1129 the Fossard estate was in the king's hands for reasons that are unclear and Robert is recorded as making a fine to gain their recovery. It was in that year that the Fossard lands at Doncaster were leased to the crown for twenty years, although neither Robert nor any of his immediate successors was able to redeem the property. Among the recipients of Robert's patronage was Nostell Priory, which received churches in Bramham, Wharram-le-Street, and Lythe and 3½ carucates of land in the same villages. Unfortunately Robert's gift of Bramham church was made at the expense of his father's gift of the same church to Ramsey Abbey and in a writ issued between 1126 and 1129 Henry I commanded Robert to do right to the abbot of Ramsey while confirming the church to Nostell in a separate charter. Robert's support of Nostell was, however, rather uncertain, as in 1130 another charter of Henry I referred to the fact that Robert and another man had unjustly seized land in Bramham given by Anschetill of Bulmer to the priory.

Robert was probably dead by 1138, when his son **William** [i] **Fossard** (*d*. 1168/9) was involved in the battle of the Standard against David, king of Scots. The chronicle of Richard of Hexham records that before the battle William was among those Yorkshire barons who assembled with Archbishop Thurstan at York to debate the best course of action to be taken in response to David's aggressive activities in northern England. William was still supporting King Stephen's cause in 1141 when he was captured at the battle of Lincoln. For the rest of the civil war he was probably a political satellite of William le Gros, earl of York. He made a donation to Watton Priory between 1154 and 1160, which referred to his impending journey to Jerusalem, and he may have been on crusade during the early years of Henry II's reign. It was probably this William who made a grant to the hospitallers of Jerusalem at Huntington near York and he was a generous patron of a number of East Riding religious houses including Meaux, Ellerton, and Swine. In 1166 the return of Hugh, bishop of Durham, recorded that William held one knight's fee from the bishop in the East Riding and his own return listed thirty-three and a half fees of the old and new enfeoffment. William [i] died in 1168 or 1169 when the custody of his son **William** [ii] **Fossard** (*d*. 1194?) was given by Henry II to William le Gros. In 1170 William [ii] owed a fine of 10 marks, and by 1171 he was in possession of his father's lands, as in that year he rendered account of 80 marks for

a fine of his land. The delay in paying the fine for relief may have been due to difficulties in his relationship with William le Gros. An unconfirmed story from the Meaux chronicle relates that while William [ii] was in the care of the earl he seduced his guardian's sister and had to flee abroad, where he stayed supposedly until 1179. In the meantime William le Gros received royal authority to pull down William's castle at Mountferatt in Birdsall. The fact that Henry II was willing to sanction this action suggests that there had been a deterioration in the relationship between the crown and the Fossards since the reign of Henry I. There is no evidence to suggest that William [ii] ever attended the royal court and he may well have angered Henry II by showing some sympathy for the northern rebellion of 1174. William [ii] Fossard, who was a patron of Meaux Abbey and Watton Priory, probably died in 1194, and by 1197 Robert of Thornham had obtained from Richard I the marriage of William's [ii] daughter and heir, Joan. In that year Thornham consolidated his hold on the Fossard inheritance when he redeemed the former family estate at Doncaster by paying 500 marks to the crown. JOHN WALKER

Sources P. Dalton, *Conquest, anarchy, and lordship: Yorkshire, 1066–1154*, Cambridge Studies in Medieval Life and Thought, 4th ser., 27 (1994) · W. Farrer and others, eds., *Early Yorkshire charters*, 12 vols. (1914–65), vol. 2 · H. Hall, ed., *The Red Book of the Exchequer*, 3 vols., Rolls Series, 99 (1896) · R. Hexham, 'De gestis regis Stephani et de bello standardi', *Chronicles of the reigns of Stephen, Henry II, and Richard I*, ed. R. Howlett, 3, Rolls Series, 82 (1886) · H. M. Thomas, *Vassels, heiresses, crusaders and thugs: the gentry of Angevin Yorkshire, 1154–1216* (1993)

Fossard, Nigel (*d*. in or before **1128**). *See under* Fossard family (*per. c*.1080–1194?).

Fossard, Robert (*d. c*.**1138**). *See under* Fossard family (*per. c*.1080–1194?).

Fossard, William (*d*. **1168/9**). *See under* Fossard family (*per. c*.1080–1194?).

Fossard, William (*d*. **1194?**). *See under* Fossard family (*per. c*.1080–1194?).

Foster, Ann (*d. c*.**1693**). *See under* Salem witches and their accusers (*act*. 1692).

Foster, Sir Augustus John, first baronet (**1780–1848**), diplomatist, was the second son of John Thomas Foster (*d*. 1796), MP for Ennis in the Irish House of Commons, and his wife, Lady Elizabeth Hervey (1757–1824) [*see* Cavendish, Elizabeth Christiana, duchess of Devonshire], daughter of Frederick Augustus *Hervey, earl of Bristol and bishop of Derry. He was the nephew of Lord Liverpool. Foster was born on 4 December 1780. His parents soon separated and he was reared in Devonshire House, his mother eventually marrying her lover, the fifth duke of Devonshire. After education at Drogheda and at Christ Church, Oxford, Foster travelled in France, was interned there in 1803, and released on Fox's intercession. He was secretary to the legations in Naples and Stockholm.

In January 1811 Foster was offered the sensitive position of minister-plenipotentiary in Washington, DC. His unconciliatory manner there did nothing to prevent the Anglo-American War of 1812–14 but was, equally, hardly a cause of it. In 1812 he returned from America and on Liverpool's initiative was elected for Cockermouth. He was a reluctant orator and in May 1814 was nominated minister-plenipotentiary at Copenhagen, where he remained until 1824, subsequently serving at Turin from 1825 to 1840. He was created baronet on 30 September 1831.

Having earlier courted Annabella Milbanke, Foster in 1815 married Albinia Jane (d. 28 May 1867), daughter of George Vere Hobart. They had three sons, including the philanthropist and educationist Vere Henry Louis *Foster. After retiring in 1840, Foster lived at Glyde Court, Ardee, co. Louth. His health declined, causing delirium, and on 1 August 1848, at Branksea Castle, Dorset, he cut his throat and died, the verdict being 'temporary insanity'.

H. C. G. MATTHEW

Sources GM, 2nd ser., 30 (1848), 317 · HoP, *Commons* · DNB · Burke, *Peerage*
Archives L. Cong., corresp. and papers · PRO NIre., corresp., diaries, and papers | BL, corresp. with Lord Aberdeen, Add. MSS 43232–43246 · BL, corresp. with Lord Holland, Add. MS 52003 · BL, corresp. with Lord Palmerston, Add. MSS 48471, 48474 · BL, letters to Sir George Rose, Add. MS 42794 · NRA Scotland, priv. coll., letters to John Macpherson-Grant · Sheff. Arch., letters to Lady Erne · U. Edin. L., letters to Grimr Thorkelin · U. Southampton L., corresp. with Lord Palmerston

Foster, Balthazar Walter, first Baron Ilkeston (1840–1913), physician and politician, was born on 17 July 1840 in Cambridge, the son of Balthazar Foster (1813–1862) of Beaulieu, Hampshire, and his wife, Marian (d. 1898), daughter of J. Green of Cambridge. His parents moved to Ireland in 1847 and Foster was educated at Drogheda grammar school and Trinity College, Dublin, where he studied medicine from 1857. He became prolector in anatomy at the Royal College of Surgeons in Dublin and qualified LRCSI, but had virtually abandoned hope of a medical career (and was applying for a naval commission) when he was appointed demonstrator in practical anatomy and medical tutor at Queen's College, Birmingham, in 1860. He was appointed professor of anatomy at Queen's and took his MD at the University of Erlangen in 1864. In the same year he married (25 August) Emily Martha (d. 1920), daughter of William Lucas *Sargant of Edgbaston. He became professor of medicine on the amalgamation of Queen's and Sydenham colleges in Birmingham in 1868, holding the post until 1892.

In Birmingham, where he became physician to the General Hospital, Foster was galvanized by what he later remembered as a 'new atmosphere of modern thought and scientific enterprise' (BMJ, 2 Aug 1890), in contrast to the traditionalism of Dublin. A series of articles in the medical press from 1863, covering treatment for stomach ulcers, the circulation of the blood, valvular diseases of the heart, and cyanosis, among other topics, established him as an innovative researcher. His work on premature death among diabetics from acetonaemia was the first on that subject to be published in England, but he considered his best work to be his experimental use of ether in the

Balthazar Walter Foster, first Baron Ilkeston (1840–1913), by Sir Benjamin Stone, 1897

treatment of phthisis. This, like almost all his published academic work, was undertaken before he had reached the age of thirty. In 1870 he published *Method and Medicine*, an energetic defence of the value of experimental science to a profession which he considered too ready to infer near metaphysical laws from the practice of observation. This, his only statement on medical methodology, would turn out to be his last significant scientific work, as in the 1870s he became preoccupied with the social application of medicine and questions of public health. A pamphlet on the illness of the prince of Wales in 1872 argued that the illnesses of royals, like those of their subjects, stemmed from neglect of 'the ordinary laws of health'; a more didactic publication, *How we Die in Large Towns* (1875), for a working-class audience, made the case for isolation hospitals and other preventive measures to improve urban mortality rates. He was elected FRCP in 1873.

Foster's appraisal of the public role of medicine steered him towards a political career. A speech by Gladstone in 1878, stressing the importance of the medical profession to the social politics of the future, steered him towards politicizing his vocation. His 1883 address, *The Political Powerlessness of the Medical Profession*, proved pivotal. In it he criticized the 'sickly sentimentality' which had curbed animal experimentation and which threatened to emasculate the Vaccination Acts. He called for better representation of the medical profession on the council of the British Medical Association (still dominated by the teaching hospitals and crown nominees) and urged doctors to stand for local and national office. Foster himself was already active in the Birmingham Liberal Association, working with the radical group which had rejuvenated the city under Joseph Chamberlain's leadership in the 1870s. In 1883 he was elected to Birmingham corporation on the Liberal ticket, and in the following year he was adopted by the Chester Liberals as their parliamentary candidate. He won the seat narrowly in the 1885 general election, with a programme of free education and improved housing for the poor. These were components of Chamberlain's *Radical Programme* (1885) and Foster was stigmatized as a Birmingham carpetbagger, but he did not follow Chamberlain in rejecting Irish home rule in 1886.

Foster had an Irish past and was said to have retained a 'Hibernian brogue' all his life (*BMJ*, 8 Feb 1913). He wooed Chester's Irish vote in 1885 with criticism of England's subjection of the Irish masses. As president of the National Liberal Federation from 1886 to 1890 he played a major part in keeping that Chamberlainite organization loyal to Gladstone. Childhood memories of seeing 'whole villages unroofed and the people turned upon the wayside' (*Ilkeston Advertiser*, 19 March 1887) in Ireland shaped his commitment to the victims of landlordism in rural England. His sponsorship of Collings' Allotments and Small Holdings Bill was one of Foster's few contributions to the 1885–6 parliament. This bill failed, but the Liberal government's Medical Act of 1886, which tightened the qualification requirements for practitioners and introduced direct representation for the profession on the General Medical Council, owed much to Foster's prescriptions. Following the fall of the Gladstone government in 1886 Foster was defeated at Chester, unseated by the faggot votes of the duke of Westminster's tenants. A knighthood in August 1886 suggested his retirement from politics, an impression reinforced by his election as one of the first representatives of his profession on the General Medical Council under the 1886 reforms. *The Lancet* (7 August 1886) pronounced him 'too good a physician to spend his strength on practical politics', but he returned to Westminster in 1887, winning Ilkeston in a by-election. He would hold this safe Liberal seat for twenty-three years.

For most of this period his party was in opposition, and Foster was an assiduous but invisible back-bencher, speaking only infrequently on medical matters and rural conditions, though he held the presidencies of the Allotments and Small Holdings Association and the Land Law Reform Association. On the return of the Liberals to power in 1892 he was made parliamentary secretary to the Local Government Board—'a most important appointment for the profession', in Foster's view (Foster to E. Hart, 17 Aug 1896, Wellcome L., MS 5424/19), as he became the first medic to hold a ministerial post in Britain. He was one of the better appointments in the Liberal government of 1892–5, orchestrating the successful sanitary campaign to prevent

the 1893 cholera epidemic from reaching Britain, encouraging the extension of the poor-law infirmary system, and devising the land purchase clauses of the 1894 Local Government Act. Some predicted his return to the board when the Liberals regained power in 1905, but he was passed over, ostensibly on grounds of age. The slight was exacerbated after his sixth victory at Ilkeston in January 1910, when he was asked by the Liberal leadership to vacate his seat for the defeated former minister J. E. B. Seely.

In June 1910 Foster—lifelong scourge of the aristocracy—was elevated to the peerage. He did little in the House of Lords, his political discomfort being compounded by waning health. A bowel obstruction was operated on successfully in 1911, but he died of bowel cancer at his London home, 30 Grosvenor Road, Westminster, on 31 January 1913. He was buried at Brookwood cemetery on 3 February 1913. He was survived by his wife, their son Balthazar Stephen Sargant Foster, second Baron Ilkeston (1867–1952), and three daughters, Emily Mary (b. 1865), Margaret (b. 1872), and Winifred (b. 1877). One son, Harold Balthazar Walter, died in infancy (1866–1867).

Foster's career demonstrated how easily the rationalist middle-class radicalism of the Chamberlain school could accommodate the later, socially oriented 'new Liberalism'. His intellectual roots were utilitarian and positivist and he was moved to enter politics by the belief that, with legislative power shifting from 'the trader and the mill-owner' to 'the labourer and the artisan', the impartial wisdom of the professions was needed to steer social forces into safe channels (B. Foster, *The Political Powerlessness of the Medical Profession*, 1883, 19). Foster's constructive interventionism left him sceptical of *laissez-faire*, while his rationalism distanced him—a moderate churchman—from his party's denominational disputes: he advocated free education as social policy in 1885, virtually without reference to the issue's religious implications, prompting his tory opponent to accuse him of atheism. The intellectual basis of his politics left him, though, impatient with compromise. His radicalism encompassed the abolition of the House of Lords, primogeniture, and the death penalty, as well as support for the nationalist Plan of Campaign in Ireland, universal male suffrage, salaried working-class poor-law guardians, and the eight-hour day for railwaymen and miners. Unlike many Liberals of his generation, he feared neither the emergence of the Labour Party nor Lloyd George's redistributionary finance. His last parliamentary speech, in the Lords' debate on the 1911 Parliament Bill, celebrated 'the beginning of the end of the old system' (*Hansard 5L*, 8, 1911, 771).   JOHN DAVIS

Sources J. Leyland, ed., *Contemporary medical men and their professional work: biographies of leading physicians … from the 'Provincial Medical Journal'*, 2 vols. (1888) • *BMJ* (8 Feb 1913) • *The Lancet* (8 Feb 1913) • Munk, *Roll* • Burke, *Peerage* • *Men and women of the time* (1899) • *Chester Chronicle* (1885–6) • *Ilkeston Advertiser* (1887–1913) • *Hansard* • J. L. Brand, *Doctors and the state: the British medical profession and government action in public health, 1870–1912* (1965) • WWW
Archives Wellcome L., papers | BL, letters to Sir Henry Campbell-Bannerman, Add. MSS 41234–41239, *passim* • BL, corresp. with W. E. Gladstone, Add. MSS 44493–44789, *passim*

Likenesses B. Stone, platinum print, 1897, NPG [*see illus.*] · Spy [L. Ward], lithograph, repro. in *VF* (11 Oct 1894) · photographs, repro. in *BMJ* · photographs, repro. in *The Lancet* · portrait, repro. in *ILN*, 101 (1892), 260
Wealth at death £19,305: resworn probate, 20 Feb 1913, CGPLA Eng. & Wales

Foster, (Myles) Birket (1825–1899), painter and illustrator, was born at 2 Rosella Place, North Shields, Northumberland, on 4 February 1825, fifth son of Myles Birket Foster (1785–1861) and his wife, Ann (1790–1884), daughter of Joseph King of Newcastle upon Tyne. Both parents came from prosperous north country families, staunch adherents of the Society of Friends, more commonly known as Quakers. From early childhood Birket Foster lived in London, where his father founded M. B. Foster & Sons, which became the largest firm of bottlers in the world, remaining in family ownership until 1957. Birket Foster was educated at a Quaker boarding-school in Tottenham, Middlesex, and Isaac Brown's academy, Hitchin, Hertfordshire (*c.*1835–1840), where his natural flair for drawing was encouraged. He wished to be a landscape painter, but at the age of sixteen entered the family business with little enthusiasm and near fatal results, owing to an accident with a broken bottle.

After this event, Birket Foster was placed by his kindly father in the studio of Ebenezer Landells, who had been a pupil of Thomas Bewick, the celebrated Newcastle engraver. Landells soon recognized that Birket Foster had an original talent as a draughtsman and eventually most of his time was spent in drawing on wood for engraving, including work for the *Illustrated London News*; however, signed contributions by him appeared only after he had left Landells in 1846. Many of his illustrations were engraved by Edmund Evans, a lifelong friend, with whom he travelled for an *Illustrated London News* series entitled 'The watering places of England'. Characteristic vignettes by Birket Foster appeared in *The Boys' Country Year Book* (1847) commissioned by Henry Vizetelly, engraver and publisher, who was to have an important influence on his career. In 1850 Vizetelly arranged for him to work on *Evangeline* by H. W. Longfellow: it was the success of these illustrations that set a vogue for the Birket Foster style. The critic of *The Athenaeum* praised the book, commenting that 'Mr Foster's designs in particular have a picturesque grace and elegance' (Huish, 10). Subjects for Longfellow's *Hyperion* (1852) were sketched with Vizetelly in that year, during a tour of Germany, Switzerland, and the Austrian Tyrol. *Christmas with the Poets* (1851), devised and engraved by Vizetelly and illustrated throughout by Birket Foster, was selected by the trustees of the British Museum for display at the Great Exhibition of 1851 as a fine example of contemporary illustration and printing. Birket Foster was to become the most sought after poetry illustrator of the day, associated with all the popular names, including Sir Walter Scott. His illustrations for Scott's *Lay of the Last Minstrel*, engraved by Edmund Evans, were published by A. and C. Black, for whom he also worked on a series called *Picturesque Guides*, travelling to Wales, Scotland, and the Lakes. The 1855 edition of Milton's *L'allegro and Il penseroso*, published by W. Kent, notably includes etchings on steel by Birket Foster, an interesting example of his work without the intervention of an engraver; for *The Hamlet* by Thomas Warton (1859) he etched his own designs on copper.

On 13 August 1850 Birket Foster married a cousin, Anne Spence (1825–1859), daughter of Robert Spence, banker, of Tynemouth, Northumberland. They had five children, including Myles Birket Foster (1851–1922), a musician of some note, and William Foster (1853–1924), painter and ornithologist. The couple lived in the St John's Wood area of London. Anne had always encouraged his ambition to paint, but died of tuberculosis in 1859 before his achievement in this field was recognized by his election as an associate of the Society of Painters in Water Colours in 1860. His success in this medium was instant and phenomenal. He wrote happily to his brother-in-law, 'commissions for pictures pour in and it is far more delightful working in colour' (Spence family letters, 19 Feb 1860). He further remarked that he knew his own style to be 'very peculiar', as he made a liberal use of body colour (admixture of white) and practised a dry, finely stippled technique that diverged widely from the traditional watercolour method. He had effectively pioneered a new style, one which was exactly to the taste of the public. *The Milkmaid* (1860), one of the best-known of his early watercolours (V&A), is an elaboration of an engraving in Milton's *L'allegro*: it was quite common for his watercolours to be based on previous illustrations.

1862, the year in which Birket Foster was made a full member of the Society of Painters in Water Colours, also saw publication of *Birket Foster's Pictures of English Landscape*, a series of typical countryside scenes, engraved by the brothers Dalziel. In a letter to the Dalziels, John Ruskin described the plates in this handsome book as 'peculiarly good of their class—rich, gracefully composed, exquisite book illustrations' (*The Brothers Dalziel*, 154). Many of the subjects had been sketched in the villages and lanes of Surrey, where in 1863 Birket Foster built a large house at Witley, near Godalming. This essay in the Victorian Tudor style was set in about 20 acres on an elevated site and named The Hill (dem. 1953). It was one of the first houses to be extensively decorated by the firm of Morris, Marshall, Faulkner & Co., with wallpapers and tapestries by William Morris and also stained glass, tiles, and furniture to the designs of Edward Burne-Jones and his circle. On 25 August 1864 Birket Foster married Frances Watson (1841–1921), daughter of Dawson Watson, a solicitor, and sister of the watercolourist John Dawson Watson. Although sixteen years younger than Foster, she proved a capable chatelaine for The Hill, where fellow artists were frequently entertained, including Frederick Walker and W. Q. Orchardson; Orchardson's portrait of the second Mrs Birket Foster was exhibited at the Royal Academy in 1868.

Pretty children in flowery lanes continued to be Birket Foster's most popular subjects, but a more topographical and architectural element appears in his work towards the end of the 1860s. 'The Italian Palazzi have been touched with a ready dainty hand', commented the critic of the *Art Journal*, describing Foster's *Bellagio*, which was exhibited with the Watercolour Society in 1867, following his first visit to Italy in 1866. He visited Italy again with Orchardson in 1868 and made several trips to Venice between 1871 and 1876 to execute fifty watercolour views of that city, commissioned by the MP Charles Seely for a fee of £5000. *Brittany: a Series of Thirty Five Sketches by Birket Foster* was published by the artist as a book of lithographs in 1878. In 1883 he was in Spain as part of a long continental tour; he made a final visit to France and Italy in 1887. Lithographs in *Some Places of Note in England* (1888) reflect his tours nearer home over a period of many years.

'Mine has been a very uneventful life, but one that my art has made very pleasant to me', wrote Birket Foster in biographical notes compiled in 1895 for the Royal Berlin Academy to which he had been elected an honorary member in 1874 (Archiv der Preussischen Akademie der Künste). In this reference he also lists a selection of his watercolours in order of significance, including *On the Shore, Bonchurch, Isle of Wight* (1862), *The Meet* (1869), and *The Weald of Surrey* (1870). The last two were among 110 works by Birket Foster in the important Barnet Lewis collection, auctioned at Christies on 28 February–3 March 1930. It is a comparatively recent custom to catalogue this artist under both forenames; in his lifetime, however, he always signed only as Birket Foster, or with the characteristic BF monogram. He painted few pictures in oils, mostly for exhibition at the Royal Academy, but did not care for the medium. His watercolours were much faked, usually in the form of loose copies of the numerous chromolithographs (colour prints) that featured his work.

Birket Foster sold The Hill for £10,000 in 1893 and moved to Braeside, The Heath, Weybridge, Surrey (dem. *c.*1970). Almost his entire collection of pictures was sold at Christies on 26 April 1894, including seven panels in oils by Edward Burne-Jones on the theme of St George and the dragon. He died on 27 March 1899 at Braeside and was buried on 1 April in Witley churchyard. All the leading newspapers and periodicals carried admiring tributes, but a later appreciation by the Dalziel brothers provides an apt summary: 'Birket Foster was a genuine man, kind and generous to a degree in all the ways of life. He stands as one of England's most popular landscape draughtsmen and as a painter in watercolour of great distinction' (*The Brothers Dalziel*, 138). A studio sale was held at Christies on 26–27 June 1899, after which his estate was resworn at £35,323 14*s.* 4*d.* Centenary exhibitions were held at the Laing Art Gallery, Newcastle, in 1925 and Towneley Hall Art Gallery, Burnley, in 1999. The work of Birket Foster is represented in over fifty public collections; major holdings can be found in the Victoria and Albert Museum, London, the Birmingham City Art Gallery, the Bristol Museum and Art Gallery, the Walker Art Gallery, Liverpool, and the Henry E. Huntington Art Gallery, San Marino, California.

JAN REYNOLDS

Sources register of births, Society of Friends, Newcastle upon Tyne · J. Reynolds, *Birket Foster* (1984) [with list of works] · M. B. Huish, *The life and work of Birket Foster: Art Journal*, supplement (1890) · Newcastle upon Tyne City Library, Spence family MSS, 1844–80, SL 920, CR 5584406A · Archiv der Preussischen Akademie der Künste, Berlin, election details and biographical notes, 1874, 1895 · H. M. Cundall, *Birket Foster* (1906) · *The Times* (29 March 1899) · *Morning Post* (29 March 1899) · *Daily Telegraph* (29 March 1899) · DNB · [G. Dalziel and E. Dalziel], *The brothers Dalziel: a record of fifty years' work … 1840–1890* (1901); repr. as *The brothers Dalziel: a record of work* (1978) · private information (2004) [B. Neild] · *The reminiscences of Edmund Evans*, ed. R. McLean (1967) [introduction by Ruari McLean] · M. Hardie, *Water-colour painting in Britain*, ed. D. Snelgrove, J. Mayne, and B. Taylor, 2nd edn, 3: *The Victorian period* [1968], 109–12 · review of Watercolour Society exhibition, Art Journal, 29 (1867), 147 · J. Foster, *Pedigrees of the Forsters and the Fosters* (1862) · T. Compton, *Recollections of Tottenham Friends* (1893) · m. cert., 1850

Archives Guildford Muniment Room, Guildford, corresp. · NL Scot., MS 6403 | CUL, letters to R. Dudley · Newcastle City Library, letters to Spence family, SL 920, CR 5584406A [manuscript letters, plus xerox copies and microfilm; originals of xerox copies in the Dutch Institute, Paris] · NL Scot., letters to James Tait Black · U. Cal., Los Angeles, Charles E. Young Research Library, corresp. with Polly Brown, Edmund Evans, and Edmund W. Evans

Likenesses D. W. Wynfield, photograph, *c.*1860–1869, NPG · Lock & Whitfield, woodburytype photograph, 1880, NPG · B. Foster, self-portrait, oils, 1883, Aberdeen Art Gallery · W. Hodgson, pencil and watercolour drawing, 1891, NPG · Elliott & Fry, carte-de-visite, NPG · McLean & Haes, carte-de-visite, NPG · photograph, repro. in Cundall, *Birket Foster*, frontispiece; priv. coll. · photograph (in his thirties), repro. in Reynolds, *Birket Foster*, 60; priv. coll. · photograph (aged about twenty-five), repro. in Reynolds, *Birket Foster*, 39 · woodcut, BM; repro. in *Family Friend* (1875)

Wealth at death £35,323 14*s.* 4*d.*: resworn probate, Dec 1899, CGPLA Eng. & Wales

Foster, Charles James (1818–1896), jurist, was the fourth son of Richard Foster, a nonconformist brewer, of Cambridge. He received his early schooling under Cyrus Edmunds at Cambridge before going on to University College, London. After obtaining an MA in political economy, he proceeded to the degree of bachelor of laws in 1842, at the same time winning the university law scholarship. In 1849 he received the degree of LLD. Admitted to Lincoln's Inn in 1835, he was called to the bar in November 1841. However, his progress as an equity practitioner was retarded by his occasional deafness, and he never succeeded at the bar.

At the end of 1849 Foster was appointed to succeed C. J. Hargreave as professor of jurisprudence at University College, beginning his lectures the following spring. Foster was more conscientious in this post than any professor since John Austin, whose work he taught, but which he also set out to controvert. He elaborated his own approach, which followed traditional natural law thinking, in *The Elements of Jurisprudence* (1853). Foster was not entirely happy with the nature of the London University law degree, and applied unsuccessfully for a readership at the Middle Temple in 1850 and at Lincoln's Inn in 1852. He also applied unsuccessfully for the post of parliamentary counsel in 1860. Foster eventually resigned his professorship in 1858. He remained active in the university, however. From the late 1840s he headed a committee of graduates which campaigned to obtain a representative in the House of Commons for London University, writing a pamphlet in 1851 supporting the proposal. In 1858 he was appointed to the senate of the university, and he was chairman of the new convocation of graduates from 1858 to 1863.

A Congregationalist, Foster was a prominent member of the Liberation Society, which was committed to disestablishment of the Church of England. In 1854 he became the paid chairman of its parliamentary committee, and by 1856 was the manager of all its parliamentary business. A cunning strategist, he worked tirelessly and tenaciously in his post, building up useful contacts, increasing the number of the society's friends on local parliamentary registers, and making contact with agents in Ireland seeking disestablishment. His tactics paid dividends: in 1861, he successfully marshalled nonconformist and Liberal protests against the clause of the Census Bill which required a return of religious profession. However, he resigned from the society in June 1863 after the more demagogic style of Edward Miall had come to prevail over his subtler approach.

On 15 September 1859 Foster married Mary Agnes Cavan, the only daughter of James Ogston; they had two children. In the early 1860s Foster attempted once more to revive his practice at Westminster Hall and on the Norfolk circuit, but with little success. With a family to support, he decided in 1864 to emigrate to New Zealand, settling at Christchurch, where he became a partner of J. C. Helmore. He was initially successful, being appointed legal adviser to the city council in 1866; but in 1869 he was declared bankrupt, though discharged soon afterwards. Four years later he was appointed the first law lecturer at Canterbury College, and continued to lecture to small numbers until the classes ended in 1880. In 1881 he moved to the small farming town of Geraldine, where he began to write a book on procedure. This work, *A Treatise on the Principles and Practice of the Supreme Code* (*New Zealand*), appeared in 1884. However, neither his learned works nor his practice were very successful. In 1890 he returned to Christchurch, where he made a little money by giving private tuition in Latin and mathematics. A tall, thin man, with a grey beard, he had a thoughtful but humorous demeanour. He died in Sumner, New Zealand, on 22 November 1896, having slipped into poverty.   MICHAEL LOBBAN

Sources J. Farrar, 'Dr. C. J. Foster—Canterbury's first law teacher', *Canterbury Law Review*, 1 (1980–82), 5–14 • G. W. Keeton, 'C. J. Foster: the story of a failure', *Solicitor Quarterly*, 4 (1965), 350–55 • W. H. Mackintosh, *Disestablishment and liberation: the movement for the separation of the Anglican church from state control* (1972) • G. I. T. Machin, *Politics and the churches in Great Britain, 1832 to 1868* (1977) • *The Times* (2 Feb 1897) • *Canterbury Times* [Christchurch, New Zealand] (26 Nov 1896) • *GM*, 3rd ser., 7 (1859), 418 • W. P. Baildon, ed., *The records of the Honorable Society of Lincoln's Inn: admissions*, 2 (1896), 169 • W. P. Baildon, ed., *The records of the Honorable Society of Lincoln's Inn: the black books*, 4 (1902), 258 • college correspondence, UCL • UCL, Brougham MSS • University College, London, *Annual report* (1843) • University College, London, *Annual report* (1850) • University College, London, *Annual report* (1859)

Archives UCL, Brougham MSS

Foster, Sir Clement Le Neve (1841–1904), geologist and mining engineer, was born on 23 March 1841 at Camberwell, Surrey, the second son of Peter Le Neve *Foster (1809–1879), later secretary to the Society of Arts, and

Georgiana Elizabeth (*bap.* 1817, *d.* 1885), daughter of the Revd Clement Chevallier. He was educated at the Collegiate School in Camberwell, and afterwards at the *collège communal* of Boulogne. In 1857 he graduated *bachelier ès sciences* of the French empire. In the same year he entered the School of Mines in London, where he was an outstanding student, winning many prizes, including the duke of Cornwall's scholarship. He then continued his studies at the Royal Saxon Mining Academy at Freiberg in Germany.

In 1860 Foster was appointed to the staff of the geological survey of England, and for five years he was engaged in fieldwork in Kent, Sussex, Derbyshire, and Yorkshire. This led to his first scientific publication, a memoir prepared with William Topley on the valley of the Medway and the denudation of the weald, which was published in the *Quarterly Journal of the Geological Society* (vol. 22). In 1865 he was awarded a DSc by the University of London, and in the same year he resigned his post on the geological survey to become lecturer to the Miners' Association of Devon and Cornwall and secretary to the Royal Cornwall Polytechnic Society. In 1868 he was employed by the Turkish viceroy in Egypt on an expedition to examine the mineral resources of the Sinai peninsula. In the same year he also reported on a Venezuelan goldfield, and from 1869 to 1872 he was engineer to a goldmining company in northern Italy.

In 1872 Foster was nominated inspector of mines under the new Metalliferous Mines Regulation Act, being appointed to Cornwall. In the same year he married his cousin, Sophia Chevallier, the second daughter of Arthur F. Tompson of Belton, Suffolk; they had one son and two daughters. Eight years later, in 1880, he was transferred to Llandudno in north Wales, where he remained for twenty-one years. In 1890, on the death of Sir Warington Smyth, he became professor of mining at the Royal School of Mines, an office which he held concurrently with his inspectorship. He proved to be an excellent teacher. In 1897, as inspector of mines, Foster investigated the cause of an underground fire in a lead mine at Snaefell in the Isle of Man. The cage in which he had descended with an exploring party was jammed in the shaft, and the party was subjected to a process of slow poisoning by the carbon monoxide generated by the fire. Contemporary accounts of the accident vouched for the courage with which, in the face of what seemed like certain death, Foster noted down his own sensations for the benefit of science. He never fully recovered from the damage to his heart, sustained as a result of near suffocation, and for nearly a year he was incapacitated.

Foster learned Dutch for the purpose of translating P. Van Diest's work on Banca and its tin stream works, and in 1876, with William Galloway, he published a translation from the French of J. P. Callon's treatise on mining. His principal work was a textbook, *Ore and Stone Mining* (1894), and he contributed the article on mining to the ninth edition of the *Encyclopaedia Britannica*. He was also author of a textbook, *Mining and Quarrying* (1903), and of numerous memoirs and papers in the *Proceedings* of the

Geological Society and other scientific societies and in various scientific periodicals. From 1894 he edited the mineral statistics issued by the Home Office, and the annual reports on mines and quarries. While he achieved considerable reputation as a geologist and metallurgist, it was as a miner and a mining expert that he was really eminent. Though at the beginning of his inspectorship his enthusiasm for imposing novel restrictions and in insisting on the reform and improvement of existing methods was little appreciated by the mining community, he ultimately won the esteem alike of miners and mine owners in both the districts in which he served.

Besides his official work, Foster produced numerous reports, and advised on many questions connected with mining and mining legislation. He served on various departmental committees and royal commissions, including those for the Chicago and the St Louis exhibitions. He was a juror at the Inventions Exhibition in 1885, at Paris in 1867, 1878, 1889, and 1900, also at Chicago in 1893. He received the Légion d'honneur for services at Paris in 1889, was elected a fellow of the Royal Society in 1892, and was knighted in 1903. In 1901 he resigned the inspectorship, but retained his professorship until his death. He died on 19 April 1904 at his home, 86 Coleherne Court, Earls Court, in London. He was serving on the royal commission on coal supplies at the time. He was survived by his wife.   H. T. WOOD, rev. R. C. COX

Sources The Engineer (22 April 1904), 419 · PRS, 75 (1905), 371 · Nature, 69 (1903–4) · Journal of the Society of Arts (29 April 1904) · election certificate, RS · CGPLA Eng. & Wales (1904)
Likenesses photograph, RS
Wealth at death £6560 2s. 3d.: probate, 16 May 1904, CGPLA Eng. & Wales

Foster, Elizabeth Christiana. See Cavendish, Elizabeth Christiana (1757–1824).

Foster, George (fl. 1650), millenarian and religious writer, is virtually invisible in contemporary records. Nearly everything known about him comes from two tracts of 1650. In The Sounding of the Last Trumpet, which was circulating in April Foster recorded a series of visions he had experienced in the first two months of the year, beginning on 14 January, and which he claimed had been commanded by God to be printed. In these visions God had prophesied to Foster that unequal wealth would end; that after its recent tyrannical treatment of the Levellers parliament and its forces would be overthrown by an army led by Lord Fairfax, whom Foster unsuccessfully attempted to meet on 15 January in order to deliver his prophecy; and that a period of equality in wealth and power would follow. In November, Foster published a reset but otherwise unaltered version of this tract together with The Pouring Forth of the Seventh and Last Viall, which combined the message of social levelling with a philosemitic one (Foster now signed himself Jacob Israel). The saints and converted Jews, he predicted, would in 1651 gather in Italy where they would proceed to defeat and by 1654 kill the pope, and by 1656 kill the sultan of Turkey.

This would clear the way for the founding of Sion in Jerusalem, first as a large temple resembling St Paul's Cathedral, then as a purely spiritual construction: the community of the saints. However, between April and November Fairfax had resigned his command as commander-in-chief of the parliamentary army and retired to Yorkshire; the leader of Foster's apocalyptic crusade would be an unspecified Englishman.

Foster's visions were of God revealing a fiery apocalypse to come, in which all inequality of wealth would disappear and some people would be destroyed. The very rich and very poor would respectively find their lot eroded or raised up to the level of the godly middling sort; charity would abound; and all forms of selfish behaviour would cease. Foster stated that the New Model Army was to be accepted as the instrument of God, its occupying presence in London being a way of silencing all opposition to millenarian politics. The language of these works is impeccably both prophetic and experiential. It inhabits and refashions the writings of several Old Testament prophets (notably Isaiah and Daniel), and the epistle of James, and is painstaking in its detailed account of elaborate vision sequences, and the physical fits, shakings, and tremblings that accompanied them. These would sometimes last some seven hours, and some had, in Foster's mind, musical accompaniments. Characteristically, God was experienced by Foster as an interpreter of the visions, and occasionally angels visited with divine messages. There is evidently some connection, at least in The Sounding of the Last Trumpet, with the writings of the ranters Abiezer Coppe and Laurence Clarkson, and possibly also of Digger Gerrard Winstanley, since Foster appears to repeat some of their key phrases. This suggests that Foster may have been part of the ranter circles, though in the absence of further evidence it may be that Foster simply read ranter tracts. His interest in the joining of Jews and Christians resembles in outline the vision of the prophet Thomas Tany.

Foster had a distinctive vision of the final 'revolution of all things', as he put it: a construction by God of new, non-fleshly bodies for the souls of everyone. He understood man to be an angel driven into a fleshly form at the fall, and the recovery of Eden to involve a vegetarian (indeed, vegan) paradise of subsistence on fruit, with animals brought into the universal freedom enjoyed by humans. In the fallen world, Foster claimed, the spirits of dead, wicked men possessed witches and noisy animals such as dogs and hens. This was the state of hell, which would last for the wicked until the general restitution. Finally, in the redeemed world, only one language would be spoken.

Charges for Cromwell's entertainment on 6 June 1652 from, among others, Israel Jacob, may locate Foster in Canterbury among aldermen and city officials, in more elevated company than he is usually supposed to have kept.   NIGEL SMITH

Sources Ninth report, 3 vols., HMC, 8 (1883–4) · A. L. Morton, The world of the Ranters: religious radicalism in the English revolution (1970) · C. Hill, The world turned upside down: radical ideas during the English revolution (1972) · Greaves & Zaller, BDBR · J. C. Davis, Fear, myth and *history: the Ranters and the historians* (1986) • N. Smith, *Perfection proclaimed: language and literature in English radical religion, 1640–1660* (1989) • private information (2004) [A. Hessayon]

Foster, George Carey (1835–1919), chemist and physicist, was born in October 1835 at Sabden in Lancashire, the only son of George Foster, calico printer and justice of the peace in Lancashire and the West Riding of Yorkshire. After education at private schools Foster became a student of chemistry at University College, London, in 1852. Graduating with honours and a prize in 1855 he served at the college as an assistant in Professor Williamson's chemistry laboratory. In 1857 Foster joined the British Association for the Advancement of Science (BAAS), presented his research on the nomenclature of organic chemistry at their meeting, and maintained a close involvement thereafter. From 1858 he undertook research in organic chemistry under Kekulé at Ghent, later moving to Paris and Heidelberg. Having further pursued the study of heat, light, and electricity, introduced to him by Williamson, in 1862 he was appointed professor of natural philosophy at Anderson's University in Glasgow. During three years there Foster became familiar with the student assisted research undertaken at the natural philosophy laboratory run by William Thomson at Glasgow University. He met Mary Ann Frances Muir of Greenock, whom he married in 1868; his happy marriage produced four sons and four daughters, all of whom survived him, the partnership ending with his wife's death in 1917.

University College, London, appointed Foster as professor of experimental physics (physics from 1867) in August 1865; there he became a much respected if not especially effective lecturer. Although to some extent modelled on Thomson's archetype in Glasgow, Foster's first achievement was to establish a students' physical laboratory in 1866, the first in Britain to offer systematic instruction in experimental physics to undergraduates. In the same year Foster was invited to join the BAAS committee on electrical standards, and often chaired its meetings. Working with other leading figures in physics and telegraphy such as Thomson, Wheatstone, Fleeming Jenkin, and C. W. Siemens, he acquired much expertise in precision techniques of electrical measurement, especially of resistance and determining current flow, and induction, in relation to the problems of telegraphy.

Foster was elected a fellow of the Royal Society in 1869, serving two terms as its vice-president in 1891–3 and 1901–3. He was president of section A of the BAAS in 1877 and was general treasurer of the association from 1888 until 1904. In the course of his many investigations to measure and compare standards of electrical resistance Foster adapted the Wheatstone bridge to measure small differences (rather than ratios) of resistance. This important device, known and widely used for many years as the Carey Foster bridge, was presented at one of the earliest meetings of the Society of Telegraph Engineers in 1871. Foster had been one of the founder members of this society (the Institution of Electrical Engineers from 1888) and served as its president in 1880–81. Foster's reputation as an expert in the practical aspects of physics was further

enhanced by the publication in 1875 of his preface to *Introduction to Experimental Physics*, a translation by B. Loewy of A. F. Weinhold's German original, *Vorschule der Experimentalphysik* (Leipzig, 1874).

In the thirty-two years that Foster ran his laboratory at University College his students, including W. E. Ayrton, Oliver Lodge, and J. A. Fleming, practised accurate measurement. As dean of the faculty of sciences in 1874 Foster achieved BSc status for experimental physics in 1876, and, with Fleming and Beare, the construction of purpose designed new laboratories in 1893, the physics wing of which was renamed as the Carey Foster Laboratory after he retired from the retitled Quain chair in 1898.

From the beginning of his professorship at University College, Foster had championed the higher education and equal rights of women, and his efforts were acknowledged as an inspiration and exemplar. Foster was a leading light in the movement to reconstruct University College into a University of London which taught and examined, and throughout the 1880s and 1890s he campaigned to unify its teaching and examining functions, a sensitive debate, his tact being indicated by his appointment as the first principal of University College in 1900 upon his retirement from teaching. In his four-year tenure he oversaw considerable reorganization and development of the college, substantially increasing the provision of accommodation, and cultivating growth in its intellectual and social activities.

Foster was for many years editor of the *Philosophical Magazine*, working at this task until shortly before his death. His many achievements were recognized by the granting of honorary doctorates—an LLD from Glasgow, and a DSc from Manchester. A quiet, unassuming man, somewhat nervous in manner, he was disinclined to draw attention to his wide-ranging accomplishments, hence, perhaps, his neglect by historians of physics.

Foster lived a contented private life with his family in a number of houses in London while employed at University College. After retiring in 1904 Foster and his family moved to Rickmansworth in the Hertfordshire countryside, where he became a justice of the peace and took an active interest in Liberal Party politics. Foster developed congestion of the lungs in January 1919 and died of heart failure on 9 February at his home, Ladywalk, Long Lane, Rickmansworth. He was buried next to his wife in the cemetery at Rickmansworth.

GRAEME J. N. GOODAY and COLIN A. HEMPSTEAD

Sources A. H. Fison, *JCS*, 115 (1919), 412–27 • J. Lodge, 'George Carey Foster, 1835–1919', *PRS*, 96A (1919–20), xv–xvii • O. J. Lodge, 'George Carey Foster', *London, Edinburgh, and Dublin Philosophical Magazine*, 6th ser., 37 (1919), 319–20 • *Nature*, 102 (1918–19), 4889–90 • W. P. Ker, 'Notes and materials for the history of University College', *UCL Collection* (1898), 64–9 • N. Harte and J. North, *The world of University College, 1828–1978* [1978] • H. Bellot, *History of University College, London, 1826–1926* (1929) • O. J. Lodge, *Past years* (1931) • G. J. N. Gooday, 'Precision measurement and the genesis of physics teaching laboratories', PhD diss., University of Kent, 1989 • d. cert.

Archives University of Strathclyde, Glasgow, recollections of Anderson's University, Glasgow | CUL, letters to Sir George

Stokes · UCL, corresp. with Sir Oliver Lodge · UCL, letters to Karl Pearson
Likenesses photograph, repro. in R. Appleyard, *The history of the Institution of Electrical Engineers, 1871–1931* (1939), facing p. 288 · photograph, repro. in Harte and North, *World of University College*, 80
Wealth at death £66,155 4s. 3d.: probate, 12 May 1919, *CGPLA Eng. & Wales*

Foster, Sir George Eulas (1847–1931), politician in Canada, was born in Wakefield parish, Carleton county, New Brunswick, on 3 September 1847, the seventh child of John Foster (1805–1888), a farmer, and Margaret Heine (1808–1850). His parents were both from loyalist families, his father from New England, his mother of Pennsylvania Dutch descent. He was brought up on a farm in King's county, where he attended local schools. At the age of eleven he became a committed Free Christian Baptist.

At confederation, in 1867, Foster was an undergraduate at the University of New Brunswick, where he became friends with George Parkin. After graduation in 1868, he taught for four years in as many schools. He was offered the chair of classical language and literature at the University of New Brunswick, but first spent a year at Edinburgh University and a semester at Heidelberg. There, the young member of the Sons of Temperance discovered that undergraduates '[paid] their assiduous attentions to the goddesses of beer and tobacco'. In September 1873 he assumed his teaching post, but did not recapture the happiness of earlier days.

After resigning his position in 1879 Foster embarked on a career as a prohibition lecturer, speaking occasionally on 'patriotism' as well. That year he travelled 10,600 miles throughout North America, giving 162 addresses. But by April 1882 his enthusiasm was waning and, at a friend's urging, he returned home to stand in the recently called federal election.

Facing an incumbent who shared his political philosophy and had represented King's county for a decade, Foster, having abandoned his second career, was not deterred from launching a third. He campaigned as an independent Liberal-Conservative, a native of the county, and a total abstainer and prohibitionist, and won a narrow victory.

Foster rose rapidly to political prominence. In 1885, on the recommendation of Sir Leonard Tilley, he became minister of marine and fisheries, and in 1888 he accepted the prestigious finance portfolio. Later he recalled,

and so five years and a half after my appearance in the House, I found myself in the most responsible chair in the Cabinet, after that of my chief. I was naturally elated, but did not therefore lose my head. I believed I could make good, and so embarked upon the, for me, great adventure. (Wallace, 65)

In the following year Foster embarked on another 'great adventure', either the most reckless or the most courageous of his life. On 2 July he married Addie Davies Chisholm (d. 1919), one of the founders of the Woman's Christian Temperance Union of Ontario, the daughter of Milton

Sir George Eulas Foster (1847–1931), by Bassano, 1916

Davies, a Hamilton banker, and the divorced wife of Daniel Black Chisholm, a Hamilton barrister and former member of parliament.

As finance minister until 1896, Foster reached the peak of his career. Five times he was passed over for the party leadership. Although some members of his party disapproved of his marriage, his failure to become leader had more to do with character than circumstance. Although his letters to his wife reveal a warm, even playful side, many of his colleagues found him unremittingly serious. Foster was one of seven cabinet members who, in January 1896, precipitated Prime Minister Mackenzie Bowell's resignation. In the election later that year Foster stood in York county, where he won an unprecedented majority, although the government as a whole was defeated.

In the election of 1900, following Sir Charles Tupper's strategy of attacking government ministers in their strongholds, Foster ran in St John against A. G. Blair, minister of railways and a former premier of the province, and, like his leader, was defeated. During the next four years, now settled in Toronto, he dabbled in business. In 1903 he travelled to England to participate in Joseph Chamberlain's crusade for tariff reform and imperial preference. He was elected in North Toronto the following year and became opposition finance critic; he took up his old campaigns for tariff reform or preferential trade with the empire and opposed Wilfrid Laurier's reciprocity campaign of 1911.

After the Conservative victory of 1911 Foster sought the

finance portfolio in Sir Robert Borden's government, but in the end had to content himself with the trade and commerce portfolio. Under Foster, however, the trade and commerce portfolio gained new status. His work as Canada's representative on the royal commission on imperial trade (1912–14) earned him a knighthood in 1914. In 1916, as one of four British representatives at the Allied Economic Conference in Paris, he was appointed an imperial privy counsellor. In 1918 he was created a GCMG for his wartime service, and at the end of the war was a member of the British delegation to the Paris peace conference. However, he returned home before the treaty was signed to be with his wife, who died on 17 September 1919, leaving him 'dull without and dark within' (Wallace, 202).

In 1920 Foster headed the Canadian delegation to the first assembly of the League of Nations at Geneva. There, on 9 December, he married Jessie (d. 1947), the daughter of Sir William Allan MP. After the close of the deliberations the couple sailed for Canada, where Foster took up the work of his ministry until the election of 1921 was called. He then accepted a seat in the senate.

During the next decade the Fosters travelled widely. A member of the interparliamentary union, Foster became a champion of the League of Nations, and represented Canada at its seventh (1926) and ninth (1929) conferences. He gave public lectures on its behalf, and when poor health slowed him down Lady Foster took his place. He died on 30 December 1931 at Ottawa.

A major force in the Conservative Party for more than forty years, Foster defies easy categorization. A gifted orator, he was too much the 'persistent pedagogue' to attract a large following. As one contemporary noted, 'Foster has always been an individualist; aloof, repellent, unassimilable.' Yet, he added, 'there is no man in the party or in the House with his intellectual grip on public affairs and the ability to express it' (Bridle, 221, 227). A nationalist with an imperial perspective, as finance minister Foster supported the major tenets of the national policy, while seeking to modify its structure through tariff reform and imperial preference. His outward-looking nationalism, shared by fellow intellectuals and fellow maritimers George Parkin and George M. Grant, envisaged an expanding role for Canada within the British empire.

In recognition of his contributions to Canada and the empire, Foster was awarded honorary degrees by Acadia University (1885), the University of New Brunswick (1894), Queen's, Kingston (1914), and Edinburgh (1920).

GAIL G. CAMPBELL

Sources W. S. Wallace, *The memoirs of the Rt Hon. Sir George Foster* (1933) · G. H. Theobald, 'George Foster and James Hannay: studies of the imperial idea in New Brunswick, 1883–1900', MA diss., University of New Brunswick, 1969 · A. Bridle, *Sons of Canada: short stories of characteristic Canadians* (1916) · C. Berger, *The sense of power: studies in the ideas of Canadian imperialism, 1867–1914* (1972) · *DNB*
Archives NA Canada, MSS · University of New Brunswick, account books | NA Scot., corresp. with Arthur Balfour
Likenesses F. S. Challoner, drawing, c.1915, repro. in Bridle, *Sons of Canada* · Bassano, photograph, 1916, NPG [*see illus.*] · E. Macklin, oils, 1926, repro. in Wallace, *Memoirs of the Rt Hon. Sir George Foster*

Foster, Sir (Thomas) Gregory, first baronet (1866–1931), university administrator and educationist, was born in London on 10 June 1866, the eldest son of Thomas Gregory Foster (1815–1903), barrister, of Clapham and Lincoln's Inn, and his wife, Sophie (d. 1911), daughter of John Farquhar Allday of Birmingham. He was educated at University College School and from 1884 at University College, London, where he graduated with honours in English language and literature in 1888. In 1892 he received his PhD degree from Strasbourg University for his thesis on the Anglo-Saxon poem *Judith*, his *editio princeps* of which was published in the same year. He was a sound philologist. On 15 August 1894 he married Fanny Maude (d. 1928), daughter of James Sledge of Hove; they had two sons and two daughters.

As Quain student from 1894 to 1899 and then as assistant professor from 1900 to 1904 Foster taught in the English department of University College, London. He was also professor of English language and literature at Bedford College for Women, London (1897–1900).

In 1900 Foster was appointed secretary to University College and embarked upon the administrative career which was to make his name. In 1904 he was elected principal and in 1907, when the college was incorporated into the newly reformed London University, continued to serve under the new title of provost. The new university had the difficult task of creating a sense of unity among the many diverse bodies that constituted it while addressing larger issues of what manner of institution a university for a capital city and an empire should be. Consisting as it did of internal and external sides, each with different needs and of a diverse group of constituent colleges and schools with little common identity, friction was inevitable. As provost of its most powerful constituent college, Foster had ample opportunity to demonstrate both inspiring leadership and delicate diplomacy. During his long term of office (1904–29) the college grew rapidly; many new departments were established, student numbers trebled, and buildings were added. Despite his care for the university, he always looked after his own college.

As provost, Foster took a friendly interest in the students, interviewing each of them at the beginning of each session, an increasingly heavy burden. They rewarded him with intense personal loyalty and incorporated his name in the college chant. In 1903 he visited the United States with the Mosely commission and thereafter welcomed American students in London. In 1912 he was one of the promoters of the first congress of the universities of the empire and he helped in the establishment of the Universities Bureau of the British Empire. Together with his friends Sir Israel Gollancz and William Paton Ker he welcomed English scholars visiting London; he continued to contribute to the study of English and was an editor of the Whitehall Shakespeare. Despite his personal affinity for the arts he served the sciences well, securing Rockefeller donations for the hospital and the School of Tropical Medicine.

In 1925 Foster's health almost drove him to resign his post, but he was persuaded instead to take a year's leave,

Sir (Thomas) Gregory Foster, first baronet (1866–1931), by Sir William Orpen, 1930

which he spent in South Africa. Returning to a hero's welcome from the students, Foster declined to stand for election as vice-chancellor, fearing that his connection with University College would create jealousies among the weaker constituents, and threw his considerable influence behind William Beveridge's candidacy. At this time the senate was debating the issue of a site befitting a university which served a capital city and an empire. Beveridge and Foster favoured the most central site, in Bloomsbury, which was close to many of the constituent colleges and served commuting students well through its proximity to railway stations. Others promoted majestic riverside sites or the remote but larger Holland Park site. Foster and his supporters won the Bloomsbury site, with its legacy of crowding and, some said, fragmentation, by promoting a persuasive vision of a new kind of university, nothing like Oxford or Cambridge, serving commuting students and creating a university quarter in the heart of London. Having worked at Toynbee Hall in his youth, Foster was an enthusiastic supporter of the Workers' Educational Association and further approved of Bloomsbury as an intellectual centre which would attract working people. In 1927 the site was secured for the university.

By this time Foster was suffering from continual ill health and pain, yet he was still able to take part in the college centenary celebrations of 1926. His first wife died in 1928, the same year in which he was finally elected to a two-year term as vice-chancellor of London University. He once confessed to a friend that only immense will-power kept him active: 'My motto is Safety Last' (*The Times*, 2 Oct 1931, 14). He had been knighted in 1917 and was created a

baronet in 1930. In March 1931 he married Elise Johanna Emma, daughter of George Peter William Augener. Foster died at 39 St Aubyns, Hove, Sussex, on 24 September 1931 and was buried on 1 October in St Pancras Church. His second wife died in October that year. His descendants remain baronets. Many friends and colleagues mourned his loss and the historian of University College has called him 'the virtual re-founder of University College' (Harte, 205).   ELIZABETH J. MORSE

Sources N. Harte and J. North, *The world of UCL, 1828–1990*, rev. edn (1991) • N. B. Harte, *The University of London, 1836–1986: an illustrated history* (1986) • *WWW*, 1929–40 • Lord Beveridge, *Power and influence* (1953) • *The Times* (2 Oct 1931), 14 • *The Times* (3 Oct 1931), 15 • 'Funeral and memorial services', *The Times* (2 Oct 1931), 15 • 'Wills and bequests', *The Times* (20 Nov 1931), 9 • G. Foster, *The University of London: history, present resources and future possibilities* (1922) • J. M. Crook, 'The architectural image', *The University of London and the world of learning, 1836–1986*, ed. F. M. L. Thompson (1990), 1–33 • S. Rothblatt, 'London: a metropolitan university', *The university and the city: from medieval origins to the present*, ed. T. Bender (1988), 119–49 • *Annual Register* (1931), 131 • Burke, *Peerage* (1939) • *CGPLA Eng. & Wales* (1931) • m. cert. [Fanny Maude Sledge]
Archives UCL, corresp., lecture notes, etc. | CAC Cam., corresp. with A. V. Hill • UCL, letters to Karl Pearson
Likenesses J. Russell & Sons, photograph, *c*.1917, NPG • W. Orpen, oils, 1930, UCL [*see illus.*]
Wealth at death £25,940 17*s*. 7*d*.: probate, 17 Nov 1931, *CGPLA Eng. & Wales*

Foster, Sir Harry Braustyn Hylton Hylton- (1905–1965), speaker of the House of Commons, was born in Ewell, Surrey, on 10 April 1905, the only son of Harry Braustyn Hylton Hylton-Foster, barrister, and his wife, Margaret Isobel Hammond-Smith. He had one sister. He was educated at Eton College and Magdalen College, Oxford, where he obtained a first class in jurisprudence in 1926. He was called to the bar by the Inner Temple in 1928 and in the same year was legal secretary to the first Viscount Finlay at the Permanent Court of International Justice. On 22 December 1931 he married Audrey Pellew Clifton Brown (*b*. 1908), daughter of Douglas Clifton Brown (later Viscount Ruffside), who was speaker in 1943–51. She was created a life peer in 1965. They had no children.

In the Second World War, Hylton-Foster served in the intelligence branch of the Royal Air Force volunteer reserve and was deputy judge advocate in north Africa, then in Italy. He was successively recorder of Richmond (1940–44), Huddersfield (1944–50), and Kingston upon Hull (1950–54). He was also chancellor of the dioceses of Ripon (1947–54) and Durham (1948–54). He took silk in 1947.

In 1945 Hylton-Foster unsuccessfully stood for election at Shipley, but in 1950 he was returned as Conservative member for York and held this seat again in 1951 and 1955. In 1954 he became solicitor-general and was knighted. He appeared for the crown in several important trials, one notable case being the Brighton conspiracy trial of 1958. In 1957 he was sworn of the privy council.

In the 1959 general election Hylton-Foster stood for the safer Conservative seat of the Cities of London and Westminster, a move which caused some 'local criticism' in

Yorkshire (*The Times*, 3 Sept 1965, 11). In the new parliament Hylton-Foster was supported by the Conservative government as speaker of the House of Commons, a move which became controversial as the Labour Party believed that there had been insufficient consultation between the parties. But after protests were made regarding the process Hylton-Foster was elected to the post unanimously. A later speaker, Selwyn Lloyd, commented that it set an unfortunate precedent for Hylton-Foster to 'go direct from office to Speaker's Chair' (Lloyd, 23), although he conceded that in Hylton-Foster's case the office of solicitor-general was less politically controversial than many other ministerial posts.

His immediate successor as speaker was to comment:

the characteristics which had marked his work as solicitor-general—clarity, modesty, wit, and gentleness—Hylton-Foster now showed as Speaker. The days had gone when a prime minister could say of a Speaker 'We trembled at the rustle of his gown'. Discipline now had to be evoked rather than imposed. Hylton-Foster could be strict in his rulings, but he often gave them with a light touch and a happy turn of phrase which disarmed his critics. He ruled the House with urbanity and charm, always calm and unruffled, master of the understatement. He appeared to carry the burden of his office lightly, with the saving grace of not taking himself too seriously. Only those who knew him intimately realized how sensitive he was and how deeply he was hurt when a member charged him with being unfair.   (H. M. King, *DNB*)

In the 1964 general election Hylton-Foster was opposed in his constituency by both Liberal and Labour candidates, and his share of the vote fell from 65 per cent in 1959 to 58 per cent. But Lloyd suggests that this 'was an impressive victory for a candidate who could not campaign for himself' (Lloyd, 133). He was unanimously re-elected speaker by the new parliament, with the Labour Party in office. In the following year parliament celebrated the 700th anniversary of Simon de Montfort's parliament; Hylton-Foster was host to all the speakers of the Commonwealth and in Westminster Hall presented the queen with a congratulatory address on behalf of the Commons.

Hylton-Foster was well liked and respected, and both Harold Wilson and Edward Heath paid tributes to him on his death which mentioned his 'ever-ready' and 'penetrating' wit (*The Times*, 3 Sept 1965, 10). He returned to his duties before he was physically fit following a hernia operation in the autumn of 1964. On 2 September 1965 he collapsed in Duke Street, St James, London, and was dead on arrival at St George's Hospital, Hyde Park Corner. He was survived by his wife. The funeral took place at St Barnabas, Ranmore, Dorking, Surrey, four days later.

MARC BRODIE

Sources DNB · *The Times* (3–4 Sept 1965) · WWBMP · Burke, *Peerage* · S. Lloyd, *Mr Speaker, sir* (1976) · *CGPLA Eng. & Wales* (1965)
Likenesses photograph, repro. in *The Times* (3 Sept 1965)
Wealth at death £26,285: probate, 7 Oct 1965, *CGPLA Eng. & Wales*

Foster, Henry (1796–1831), geophysicist and naval officer, born in August 1796 at Woodplumpton, near Preston, Lancashire, was the eldest son of Henry Foster, incumbent of Woodplumpton. He had two sisters and one brother. He was educated under a Mr Saul at Green Row, Cumberland.

It was his father's wish that he should take orders, but in 1812 he entered the navy as a volunteer under Captain Morton in the *York*, and was appointed sub-lieutenant on 13 June 1815. In 1815 he served in the *Vengeur* (Captain Alexander), and in 1817 in the *Eridanus* (Captain King) in the North Sea and Channel fleets. From 1817 to 1819 he served in the *Blossom* (Captain Hickey), surveying the mouth of the Columbia River to establish the boundary line between Great Britain and the United States. When in the *Creole* with Commodore Bowles in 1819 he made a useful survey of the north shore of the River Plate. In 1820 he accompanied Captain Basil Hall in the *Conway* to South America, making gravity pendulum and other observations. His next appointment, in 1823, was to the *Griper* (Captain Clavering) on her voyage with Captain Edward Sabine to the coasts of Greenland and Norway, after which in 1824 he was promoted full lieutenant and elected FRS. Foster sailed with Edward Parry on his third voyage in search of the north-west passage in 1824–5 and was responsible for the extensive series of geomagnetic and astronomical observations which were published in the *Philosophical Transactions of the Royal Society* (1826). For these papers he received the Copley medal, the highest award of the Royal Society, on 30 November 1827, and was promoted commander. From April to September 1827 he again accompanied Parry in his ill-fated attempt to sledge to the north pole.

On 12 December 1827 Foster was appointed to command the sloop *Chanticleer*, sent out by the government to the South Atlantic to determine longitudes, take gravity pendulum measurements to determine the ellipticity of the earth, and make other measurements connected with nautical astronomy, according to instructions drawn up by a committee of the Royal Society. This work was in part a continuation of that done to determine the figure of the earth by Hall and Foster in the Pacific in 1819, and by Sabine and Foster in 1823. Foster sailed from Spithead on 27 April 1828 and began the pendulum experiments on Rat Island, Montevideo. He rounded Cape Horn on 27 December, and on 5 January 1829 passed Smith Island, in the South Shetland Islands. Two days later he touched at Trinity Island, also in the South Shetlands, which he named 'Clarence Land', and of which he took possession in the name of Great Britain, not being aware of its discovery in 1599 by Dirck Gherritz, and of its inclusion on old charts as 'Gherritz Land'. From 9 January to 4 March he remained at an island in the South Shetlands which he named 'Deception Island', making astronomical and geodesic observations, then returned to Cape Horn on 25 March, and anchored in St Martin's Cove. Here he was joined on 17 April by Captain King in *Adventure*, employed on a survey of the adjacent islands. Leaving Cape Horn on 24 May Foster sailed for the Cape of Good Hope, which he reached by 16 July, and where he worked in the observatory until 13 December. He then visited St Helena, where he made further observations, and, sailing back to South America and Trinidad, he arrived at Portobelo, Panama, on 22 December 1830. By early 1831 he had measured the difference of longitude across the isthmus of Panama by means of rockets and then embarked in a canoe at Cruces on 5 February to return down the River Chagres. That evening he fell from the boat into the river and was drowned. His remains were recovered on 8 February and buried on the river bank, nearly half way between Palomatio Viejo and Palomatio Nueva. He was commemorated by a monument there, by a second raised to his memory by the officers of the *Chanticleer* in the port of San Lorenzo at Chagres, and by a third in Woodplumpton church.

Foster left a large mass of observations. A report edited by Francis Bailey, comprising a life of Foster and detailed descriptions of his equipment, experiments, and results, forms the whole of volume 7 of the *Memoirs of the Royal Astronomical Society* (1834). Other observations were edited to form the appendix to the *Narrative of a Voyage to the Southern Atlantic Ocean, in the Years 1828, 29, 30* (2 vols., 1834), based on the journal of W. H. B. Webster, surgeon of the *Chanticleer*. A French translation by A. de Lacaze appeared in 1849.

Foster's premature death robbed the navy of one of its most proficient and assiduous scientific officers. It is ironic that much of his geophysical work came to nothing because of his use of the gravity pendulum method, which was shortly afterwards found to be defective.

GORDON GOODWIN, rev. ELIZABETH BAIGENT

Sources GM, 1st ser., 101/2 (1831), 64–5 • GM, 1st ser., 102/1 (1832), 87–8 • *Navy List* • *United States Journal* (1831) • W. E. Parry, *Journal of a third voyage for the discovery of a north-west passage from the Atlantic to the Pacific* (1826) • W. E. Parry, *Narrative of an attempt to reach the north pole…* (1828) • A. Day, *The admiralty hydrographic service, 1795–1919* (1967) • private information (2004)
Archives RAS, papers relating to experiments with pendulums • RS, papers

Foster, Sir Idris Llewelyn (1911–1984), Welsh and Celtic scholar, was born on 23 July 1911 at Carneddi, Bethesda, Caernarvonshire, the elder child and elder son of Harold Llewelyn Foster, of Bethesda, and his wife, Anne Jane Roberts, both shopkeepers. He was educated at Bethesda county school and the University College of North Wales, Bangor, from which he graduated BA (Wales) with first-class honours in Welsh (with accessory Latin) in 1932 and MA (Wales) with distinction in 1935. From 1932 onwards he pursued research on the complex but fascinating and important Middle Welsh prose tale *Culhwch ac Olwen* under the guidance of Ifor Williams. The award of a University of Wales fellowship in 1935 enabled him to spend periods of study also at the National University of Ireland with Professor Osborn Bergin, and at the University of Bonn with Professor Rudolf Thurneysen: he could thus claim to have sat at the feet of possibly the three greatest Celtic scholars of the early twentieth century.

In 1936 Foster was appointed head of the department of Celtic at the University of Liverpool where he remained for eleven years, except for three and a half years (1942–5) spent at Cambridge during the Second World War in the intelligence division of the naval staff, where he worked mainly on material in Serbo-Croat. In 1947 he was elected to the Jesus chair of Celtic in the University of Oxford and a fellowship of Jesus College; on his retirement in 1978 he

was made emeritus professor of the university and honorary fellow of the college. He brought to the chair not only extraordinary erudition in the major Celtic languages and their literature but also an avid interest in a wide range of more or less kindred disciplines: history, archaeology, anthropology, art, music, and theology. Thus equipped he conferred a new lustre on Celtic studies at Oxford.

Foster's publications were sparse but uniformly learned, penetrating, and judicious: he wrote not only on Middle Welsh narrative and religious prose (for example, his chapter in *Arthurian Literature in the Middle Ages*, ed. R. S. Loomis, 1959, and his British Academy Rhys lecture of 1950, *The Book of the Anchorite*) but also on the earliest Welsh poetry (as in his chapter in *Prehistoric and Early Wales*, edited by himself and Glyn Daniel, 1965). He edited with Leslie Alcock the volume *Culture and Environment* in 1963. His interest in early poetry led to the formation of the Hengerdd colloquium which met two or three times a year under his chairmanship at Jesus College between 1972 and 1978 and which bore fruit in the volume *Astudiaethau ar yr Hengerdd / Studies in Old Welsh poetry* (ed. R. S. Bromwich and R. Brinley Jones, published in 1978 and dedicated to Foster).

Regrettably Foster's *magnum opus*, the definitive edition of *Culhwch ac Olwen*, remained unfinished at the time of his death. It was, however, in a notable act of *pietas*, completed and augmented by his friends Rachel Bromwich and D. Simon Evans in a series of four publications which appeared between 1988 and 1997. Foster's reluctance to publish was partly due to the clear priority he gave during his Oxford years to teaching. He not only lectured on a wide variety of topics within the Celtic field but also supervised the research of a long sequence of able graduate students. At one time four of the five professors of Welsh language and literature in the constituent colleges of the University of Wales were former pupils of his. His penetrating intelligence and vast learning were matched by a sustaining interest in the lives and doings of his pupils and an impish sense of humour. Short and rotund in appearance, he commanded general affection among a wide circle of friends. Although unmarried, he was particularly fond of children and they of him.

Many institutions and societies both in England and in his native Wales benefited from Foster's steadfast service. He was a member of the Royal Commission on the Ancient and Historical Monuments of Wales and Monmouthshire from 1949 to 1983, the Standing Commission on Museums and Galleries (1964–82), and the Council for the Welsh Language (1973–8). In Oxford he was successively chairman of the modern languages board and the anthropology and geography board and was a select preacher to the university in 1973–4. For many years he acted as external examiner in both Welsh and Welsh history for the University of Wales. Among other bodies he served were the Society of Medieval Languages and Literature (president, 1953–8), the Honourable Society of Cymmrodorion (editor, 1953–78), the Cambrian Archaeological Society (president, 1968–9), the Irish Texts Society (president, 1973–84), the Gwynedd Archaeological Trust (chairman, 1974–9), the Ancient Monuments Board for Wales (chairman, 1979–83), and especially the National Library of Wales (treasurer, 1964–77; vice-president, 1977–84), and the national eisteddfod of Wales (chairman of council, 1970–73; president of court, 1973–7). He was also a member of the governing body of the Church in Wales: he was a convert to Anglicanism from the nonconformity in which he had been brought up, but his strong and vital attachment to his new faith did not preclude a continuing appreciation of the virtues of the old.

Foster was appointed Sir John Rhys memorial lecturer of the British Academy in 1950; O'Donnell lecturer in the University of Edinburgh in 1960, and in the University of Wales in 1971–2; G. J. Williams lecturer at University College, Cardiff, 1973; and James Ford special lecturer in the University of Oxford, 1979. He was elected a fellow of the Society of Antiquaries in 1954 and was knighted in 1977.

Foster died on 18 June 1984 at the Caernarfon and Anglesey General Hospital, Bangor. He had retired to his native Bethesda for which his affection had never diminished throughout his forty years' exile in England. He was buried in Glanogwen parish church, Bethesda.

R. Geraint Gruffydd

Sources The Times (25 June 1984) · D. Ellis Evans, Transactions of the Honourable Society of Cymmrodorion (1984), 331–6 · WWW · R. Bromwich and R. B. Jones, eds., Astudiaethau ar yr Hengerdd / Studies in Old Welsh poetry (1978) · Culhwch ac Olwen: testun Syr Idris Foster, ed. R. Bromwich and D. S. Evans, 2nd edn (1997) · R. Bromwich and D. S. Evans, eds., Culhwch and Olwen: an edition and study of the oldest Arthurian tale (1992) · R. Bromwich and D. S. Evans, eds., Glossary to Culhwch ac Olwen (1992) · b. cert. · d. cert. · private information (2004)

Archives NL Wales, corresp. and papers | NL Wales, letters to John Glyn Davies · NL Wales, corresp. with C. A. Gresham

Wealth at death £82,401: administration, 28 Dec 1984, CGPLA Eng. & Wales

Foster, James (1697–1753), preacher and General Baptist minister, was born at Exeter on 16 September 1697 and baptized on the same day at St Mary Major, Exeter, the son of James Foster, a fuller, who had become a dissenter, although he was the son of a clergyman of Kettering, Northamptonshire. He was educated from 1702 at the free school of Exeter, where he learned grammar under Mr Thorpe, and afterwards at the academy kept there by Joseph Hallet (1656–1722).

Foster began to preach in 1718. As a student he had always rejected 'human authority in all matters of religious opinion, faith and practice. Nothing would convince him short of reason and argument' (Fleming, 8). When the orthodox dissenters at Exeter, alarmed at the apparent growth of Arianism, insisted that their ministers subscribed to the Trinity, Foster was among those who refused. As a consequence he was forced to leave Exeter. He accepted an invitation from the congregation at Milborne Port, Somerset. This congregation, however, also proved too orthodox for him, and he left to live in the house of Nicholas Billingsley, the Presbyterian minister at Ashwick, near Shepton Mallet in the Mendips. Billingsley had also adopted heterodox views and had already welcomed to his house Hubert Stogdon, a former student of

Hallett's, whose indiscretion had first made public the heterodox opinions held by a small group of younger ministers in Exeter.

Foster and Stogdon became intimate friends, and jointly served two chapels at Colesford and Wookey, near Wells; Foster's salary from both amounting to only £15 a year. While at Ashwick he published his Essay on Fundamentals (1720), arguing that the Trinity is not an essential doctrine. About this time he moved to Trowbridge, Wiltshire, where he ministered to a small congregation. His salary was so insufficient that he considered entering his landlord's trade as a glover. Robert Houlton, however, a local gentleman, employed him as domestic chaplain. After reading the work of John Gale against infant baptism, Foster, like Stogdon, rejected the practice, and was baptized by Gale in London. In 1724 he became the colleague of Joseph Burroughs at the General Baptist chapel in Paul's Alley, Barbican, a position previously occupied by Gale. Theirs was the only London pulpit after Salters' Hall to invite the Arian Thomas Emlyn to preach. A contemporary survey lists Foster and Burroughs as two of the three Socinian Baptists in London ('A view of the dissenting interest in London of the Presbyterian and Independent denominations from the year 1695 to the 25 of December 1731', DWL, MS 38.18, p. 102). In 1728 Foster was also appointed to give the Sunday evening lecture at the Old Jewry.

In 1731 Foster wrote one of his most important works, The Usefulness, Truth, and Excellency of the Christian Religion, against Matthew Tindal's Christianity as Old as the Creation (1730). Tindal is said to have admired this answer, and well he might, for in his characteristic effort to clear Christianity from contempt by purging it of corrupt doctrines and superstitious worship, Foster conceded much to the deist's position. They both agreed that the religion of nature is the greatest part of Christianity; that reason is the ultimate authority in religious matters; and that the chief design of religion is to promote morality. Between 1735 and 1737 Foster was engaged in controversy with Henry Stebbing upon heresy, in which he maintained the innocency of intellectual error. In 1744 he became pastor of the Independent church at Pinners' Hall. When William Boyd, earl of Kilmarnock, one of the rebel lords, declared himself a presbyterian, Foster administered the sacrament to him in the Tower, and was present at his execution. His published Account of Kilmarnock's behaviour (1746) was attacked in various pamphlets. It was insinuated unfairly that dissenters were willing to accept Charles Edward Stuart in order to rid themselves of the Test Act. Foster's 'tender, sympathizing spirit' was said to have been deeply affected by this affair, and his health began to decline (Fleming, 12).

Foster received the degree of DD from the Marischal College, Aberdeen, in December 1748. He is said to have declined many offers of preferment in the Irish church from Bishop Rundle. Besides separate sermons, including one preached at the funeral of Emlyn, he published Sermons on the Following Subjects (4 vols., 1744), which went through five editions by 1755. This provoked A Vindication of some *Truths of Natural and Revealed Religion* (1746) by John Brine, a Particular Baptist and high-Calvinist. Brine thought Foster's refusal to carry faith 'one jot beyond our understanding' led directly into atheism (Ivimey, 3.401). Foster's *Discourses on All the Principal Branches of Natural Religion and Social Virtue* (2 vols., 1749–52) attracted 2000 subscribers, an indication of his great contemporary reputation. His works have not retained the popularity they enjoyed in his lifetime. By the early nineteenth century they were 'nearly forgotten' (*Monthly Repository*, 1822, 104).

But it was as a preacher that Foster achieved his greatest fame, as indicated in Pope's familiar lines:

Let modest Foster, if he will, excel
Ten Metropolitans in preaching well.
(A. Pope, 'Epilogue' to the satires, 1.132–3)

It had become proverbial that 'those who had not heard Farinelli sing and Foster preach were not qualified to appear in genteel company' (J. Hawkins, *A General History of the Science and Practice of Music*, 5 vols., 1776, 5.321). When he preached at the Old Jewry, there 'was a confluence of persons of every rank, station, and quality. Wits, freethinkers, and numbers of clergy; who, whilst they gratified their curiosity had their … prejudices loosened' (Fleming, 15). Even Philip Doddridge, who had refused to let him enter his pulpit, was impressed after hearing him preach and pray. Foster's elevation of reason and the claims of private judgement was matched by a conviction that salvation depended on practical morality and benevolence rather than on doctrinal consensus.

Foster appears never to have married. He was lodging with the mother of his 'Beloved friend', Nehemiah Stokes, in St Stephen, Coleman Street, London, when he made his will (1750). He had a paralytic stroke in April 1750, and a second in July 1753. He died at Pinners' Hall, Middlesex, on 5 November 1753, and is buried in Bunhill Fields. He left the interest on £300 to both his sister, Sarah Smith, and brother, Thomas Strong, for their lives; Stokes was to receive the entire sum after their deaths.

LESLIE STEPHEN, *rev.* JIM BENEDICT

Sources C. Fleming, *A sermon preached at Pinners-Hall, on occasion of the death of the late Rev. James Foster, D.D. with memoirs of his life and character* (1753) • C. Bulkley, *A sermon preached at the evening-lecture in the Old Jewry on Sunday November 18, 1753, on occasion of the death of the late Rev. James Foster, D.D.* (1753) • W. Wilson, *The history and antiquities of the dissenting churches and meeting houses in London, Westminster and Southwark*, 4 vols. (1808–14), vol. 2, pp. 270–85 • J. V. Price, 'Introduction', in J. Foster, *The usefulness, truth, and excellency of the Christian religion*, ed. J. V. Price (1995) • J. Murch, *A history of the Presbyterian and General Baptist churches in the west of England* (1835), 158–9 • J. Ivimey, *A history of the English Baptists*, 4 vols. (1811–30), vol. 3, pp. 183–4, 215, 377–8, 399–404 • C. G. Bolam and others, *The English presbyterians: from Elizabethan puritanism to modern Unitarianism* (1968), 140, 155–74, 188–9 • M. R. Watts, *The dissenters: from the Reformation to the French Revolution* (1978), 371–82 • R. Brown, *The English Baptists of the eighteenth century* (1986), 74–6, 93, 156 • T. S. James, *The history of the litigation and legislation respecting Presbyterian chapels and charities in England and Ireland between 1816 and 1849* (1867), 704 • *Calendar of the correspondence of Philip Doddridge*, ed. G. F. Nuttall, HMC, JP 26 (1979), nos. 479–80, 512, 1173, 1178 • *Monthly Repository*, 16 (1821), 131, 573 • 'Review of *Letters of Mary Lepel, Lady Hervey*, 1821', *Monthly Repository*, 17 (1822), 104 • L.-M. Hawkins, *Anecdotes, biographical sketches, and memoirs* (1822), 164 • J. Stoughton, *Religion in England under Queen Anne and the Georges*, 2 vols. (1878), vol. 1, pp. 333–4 • will, PRO, PROB 11/805, fol. 11 • *IGI*

Archives BL, letters to Thomas Birch, Add. MS 4307, fols. 120, 122 • BL, letter to Lord Hardwicke, Add. MS 35588, fol. 319 • BL, letter to Macro, Add. MS 32557, fol. 131

Likenesses J. N. Bernigeroth, line engraving, 1750 (after J. Wills), NPG • S. F. Raveret, line engraving, 1752 (after W. Smith), BM, NPG • P. van Bleeck, mezzotint (after J. Wills), BM, NPG

Wealth at death £600: will, 1753, PRO, PROB 11/805, fol. 11

Foster, John (*bap.* 1731, *d.* 1774), classical scholar and schoolmaster, was baptized on 7 January 1731 at Windsor, Berkshire, the son of Henry Foster (*d.* 1761/2), builder and alderman, and his wife, Elizabeth. He entered Eton College in 1742, with Septimus Plumptre as his tutor, and became a king's scholar the following year. In 1748 he was admitted a scholar and matriculated at King's College, Cambridge. The university elected him Craven scholar in 1750, and included a Latin poem of his on the death of Frederick, prince of Wales, in its *Luctus* (1751). According to William Cole, Foster while still a scholar tutored Lord Montfort's heir, Thomas Bromley, who subsequently presented him to the rectory of Shrawardine, Shropshire, in 1758. From 1751 to 1758 Foster held a fellowship at King's. His founder's-day oration there was published in 1752, together with a facetious commencement poem on the topography of the human body. He graduated BA and took deacon's orders, at Ely, in 1753, returned to Eton as assistant master in 1754, and proceeded MA in 1756. His prize-winning dissertation of 1754, *Enarratio et comparatio doctrinarum moralium Epicuri et Stoicorum*, was published in 1758.

Foster's scholarly, lucid *Essay on the Different Nature of Accent and Quantity* (1762) was prompted by Henry Gally's *Dissertation Against Pronouncing the Greek Language According to Accents* (1754) and by Oxford University's decision in 1756 to stop printing accents at its press. Foster's *Essay* (which includes a chapter on English metre) defends the accentual marks in current use, showing them to be tonal, not quantitative, and conformable to ancient accounts of the tones. An enlarged second edition (1764) reviewed Gally's *Second Dissertation* (1763); a third edition followed in 1820, by which time the accents, defended in Richard Porson's *Medea* (1801), were 'secure from attack' (Clarke, 227).

On 16 December 1765 Foster succeeded Edward Barnard as headmaster of Eton, and the following May was created DD by royal mandate. Also about this time he married his wife, Mary. Cole expected that Eton's reputation would suffer 'as he is supposed to be *too profound a Critic, & more of a Scholar* than a *Gentleman* (for they should be blended in the *Character* of a *Head Master* of *such a Schole* as *Eton*)' (Cole, fol. 22r). It did indeed suffer. Foster's rigour as a disciplinarian betrayed a want of real authority, made more obvious by the continuing presence as provost of the immensely popular Barnard. Foster's troubles included the 'rebellion' of 1768, when 160 boys removed themselves to an inn at Maidenhead. By the time he resigned in July 1773 the number of boys at the school had fallen from 522 to 230.

Foster was appointed a canon of Windsor in March 1772. To recover his health, weakened first by study, then by the headmastership, he went abroad to Spa, where he died in the summer of 1774; he was survived by his wife and daughter Mary, who was born in 1770. His will, dated 6 July 1773, was proved on 30 August 1774, and he was buried at Windsor, near his father's grave, on 21 October 1774.

HUGH DE QUEHEN

Sources H. C. Maxwell Lyte, *A history of Eton College, 1440–1910*, 4th edn (1911) · R. A. Austen-Leigh, ed., *The Eton College register, 1698–1752* (1927) · W. Cole, 'Journal of tour in France', 1765–6, BL, Add. MS 5835, fol. 22 · *GM*, 1st ser., 28 (1758), 245 · *GM*, 1st ser., 44 (1774), 390 · *GM*, 1st ser., 53 (1783), 1005–6 · *GM*, 1st ser., 54 (1784), 180–82 · M. L. Clarke, *Greek studies in England, 1700–1830* (1945) · transcript of parish register, New Windsor, St George, Society of Genealogists, 7 Jan 1731 [baptism] · transcript of parish register, New Windsor, St George, Society of Genealogists, 29 Jan 1762 [burial] · transcript of parish register, New Windsor, St George, Society of Genealogists, 21 Oct 1774 [burial] · transcript of Eton College chapel register, Society of Genealogists · W. Sterry, *Annals of the King's College of Our Lady of Eton beside Windsor* (1898)

Archives Eton, letters to Lord Townshend, MS 245

Likenesses oils, Eton

Foster, John, first Baron Oriel (1740–1828), politician, was born in September 1740 and baptized on 28 September 1740, possibly at Dunleer, co. Louth, the elder son and heir of Anthony Foster (1705–1779), a barrister and politician, of Collon, co. Louth, and his first wife, Elizabeth (1708–1744), the daughter of William Burgh, of Bert, co. Kildare, the accountant-general for Ireland.

Family, estate, education, and marriage The Foster family had settled in Dunleer in or before 1666, and remained there until 1744, when they moved to a house in the village of Collon which still stood at the beginning of the twenty-first century. They were of Cromwellian, English origins. Foster's paternal grandfather, another John (1675?–1747), who was a country attorney, built up the family estate, by purchase, from extremely small beginnings. By 1750, at 6000 Irish acres, it neared its maximum extent. It had been described as 'mere waste land' that had formerly been owned by the Cistercians of Mellifont, and Anthony Foster spent something like £50,000 over a twenty-year period on improvements, which John Foster continued. In 1778 the rental of the estate approached £5000 per annum. It exceeded £10,000 in 1801, but by then Foster's debts stood at over £72,000. If the Foster family was dogged by humble origins and a burdensome estate, it was fortunate in the fact that part of the estate was located in and around a parliamentary borough, Dunleer. After a bitter struggle the Fosters established in 1735 a right of nomination to one of the two seats for the borough, and Anthony Foster sat for it from 1737 to 1760. John Foster was educated at Drogheda grammar school under the Revd Dr Richard Norris, and entered Trinity College, Dublin, in 1757. He graduated in 1760 and entered the Middle Temple in 1762; he was called to the Irish bar (where he practised little) in 1766, and became a bencher of King's Inns, Dublin, in 1784.

Foster married on 14 December 1764 his first cousin, Margaretta Emelia (1736–1824), the eldest daughter of Thomas Burgh (1696–1754), of Oldtown, co. Kildare, and

John Foster, first Baron Oriel (1740–1828), by Gilbert Stuart, *c*.1791

Anne Downes, the daughter of the bishop of Cork and Ross, Dive Downes. The marriage was a love match, and remained so until Margaretta died in 1824. The Fosters were unfortunate in the early deaths of a number of their children: four sons died young, and in the end they had one surviving son, Thomas Henry (1772–1843), who married Lady Harriet Skeffington, *suo jure* Viscountess Massereene, in 1810, and one daughter, Anna Dorothea (1774–1865), who married the second Baron Dufferin in 1800. In consideration of his political services Foster's wife was created Baroness Oriel on 5 June 1790 and Viscountess Ferrard on 22 November 1797. Oriel, or Uriel, is the name of the old Irish kingdom of which co. Louth forms a part, and Ferrard was the barony in co. Louth where most of the Foster estate was located.

Early political career, 1761–1784 On both his father's and his mother's side, Foster's family had a parliamentary and an office-holding tradition. He first entered the Irish parliament in 1761, when not quite of age, as member for Dunleer. In 1768, two years after his father's elevation to the bench, as chief baron of the Irish exchequer, he succeeded him as MP for co. Louth. The Foster estate was the best in the smallest county in Ireland, and Foster was a conscientious and popular MP. He represented the county uninterruptedly and, after 1768, without contest until his elevation to the peerage in 1821, by which time—if service in the two parliaments is aggregated—he had been for three years the father of the House of Commons at Westminster. Foster's official career was also long and uninterrupted. His entrance into the inner circle of the lord lieutenant's advisers took place in 1777, when he was appointed chair of the committee of supply and ways and means under the hard-pressed and notably inadequate administration of the second earl of Buckinghamshire (1776–80). In the absence of the English holder of the office, Foster acted as the effective chancellor of the exchequer in Ireland; his government salary took the form of another sinecure, the customership of Dublin port (1779–84). Foster gave the Buckinghamshire administration plucky and ingenious support but concentrated on pursuing the economic and financial measures which, to him, were of paramount importance. He occasionally maintained his popular credibility by paying lip-service to the less substantial constitutional reforms which were the obsession of the so-called 'patriots'. Foster was sneeringly described as a 'ministerial patriot' in June 1780. But the description was unintentionally apt. A contemporary biography of him gives examples of the measures to boost the Irish economy which he quietly effected alongside the much-publicized free trade conceded to Ireland in 1779–80. These included bounties on the export of Irish linens and sailcloth, annual grants to encourage the growth of flax-seed, and efforts to extend Ireland's trade to America. A trustee of the linen manufacture since 1779, Foster was protective of the linen trade in Ireland throughout his career. Characteristically, he thought that the associations formed to ban the importation of British goods and so blackmail the British government into conceding Irish demands 'have done us more service than the whole of the Free Trade will do these fifty years' (Malcomson, *Foster*, 50). No one on the British side of a negotiation with Foster ever doubted the strength of his Irish patriotism.

Another striking example of Foster at work comes from 1782. While others were still celebrating the winning of the so-called constitution of 1782, Foster lost no time in carrying two favourite and previously frustrated measures. The first was his Partnerships Regulation Act of 1782, 'the first attempt' in the British Isles 'to create general limited liability' (French, 15). This measure was accompanied by the act of 1782 establishing the Bank of Ireland, which, under its charter granted in the following year, 'was given a virtual monopoly of joint-stock banking in Ireland' (ibid., 26).

Foster believed not only in prosperity by act of parliament but in prosperity by act of an Irish parliament. The most famous measure sponsored by him, his eponymous corn law of 1784, was another, slightly more delayed consequence of the constitution of 1782. Foster's corn law granted bounties on the export, and imposed duties on the import, of corn, on a sliding scale determined by the home price in Ireland. It built on the foundation laid by Pownall's British corn law of 1773, and it was made possible, and successful, by the hard economic fact that Great Britain had recently become an importer, instead of an exporter, of corn. Foster's corn law was made possible by his willingness to incur unpopularity with the Dublin

journeyman and labouring classes by reducing to nothing in the years 1782–4 the much-cherished bounty on the inland carriage of corn to Dublin. For this and other reasons (including his drastic Libel Act of 1784), he was a marked man in Dublin in the period 1783–5; but his readiness to tolerate personal unpopularity in what he deemed a good cause was one of his leading political characteristics.

Chancellor of the exchequer and speaker Appointed chancellor of the exchequer in name as well as in fact on 23 April 1784, Foster withstood considerable hostility in connection with Pitt's famous commercial propositions of 1785. These had started life as a purely commercial plan of Foster's for equalizing the duties on almost all goods passing between Great Britain and Ireland, and allowing goods imported from the British colonies into Ireland to be re-exported to Great Britain. Foster wrote later (and the comment is highly revealing of his political thinking): 'My opinion always was that it was the best policy to keep the commercial subject by itself, and to leave the Imperial concerns to the general, unexplained but well understood situation in which they are' (Malcomson, *Foster*, 50). In the event, the annexation of an imperial contribution, particularly in the unpalatable form which it took, was the means of wrecking the propositions. Characteristically, Foster supported them loyally in public until it became politically impossible for him to do so or for the Irish government to persevere with the measure. At the time of the union, in 1799, Pitt severely taxed Foster with inconsistency in opposing the union after having supported the propositions. But this was unfair for two reasons. First, Foster had privately criticized the propositions because they had been encumbered by Pitt with 'imperial concerns' far less all-embracing than a union. Second, by 1799, indeed by 1793, Ireland had obtained piecemeal most of the commercial benefits which the propositions had held out.

A member of the Irish privy council since 9 July 1779, Foster was sworn of the British privy council on 6 September 1786. This marked the new political importance he had acquired when he was elected, with government support, speaker of the Irish Commons on 5 September 1785. He was twice re-elected, on 2 July 1790 and on 9 January 1798. In 1785–6 he expressed his admiration for Pitt—'a wonderful man', 'a prodigy of talents and integrity' (Malcomson, *Foster*, 385)—but his admiration was progressively chilled by the characteristic absence of any response from Pitt. In February 1789, at the time of the regency crisis, he wrote to an English opposition friend: 'There never was, that I could hear of, any attempt towards a party for Mr Pitt in this kingdom …, and the Prince's administration will be well supported. It will have my best wishes' (Foster to Lord Sheffield, 12 Feb 1789, PRONIre., T/3725/4).

The Roman Catholic question The nominal neutrality of the speakership, and the rapid recovery of the king, averted a public demonstration of his intended switch of allegiance. However, on the issue of political concessions to Irish Roman Catholics, his opposition to the policy of Pitt's government from 1791 onwards was manifest and declared. Foster had supported and contributed to the Irish Catholic relief acts of 1778 and 1782, which were largely confined to property rights and rights of worship. In 1782 he reached his *ne plus ultra*. 'He would', he said in a well-known passage, 'draw a line round the Constitution, within which he would not admit them [the Catholics] while their principles were, he would not say hostile, but certainly not as friendly to the Constitution as those of Protestants' (Malcomson, *Foster*, 66).

In 1792 the influence of Foster and the like-minded politicians who constituted the lord lieutenant's cabinet was strong enough to ensure that the relief act which passed did not extend to the Catholics either the franchise or, almost as contentious, the right to carry arms; also that it was not sponsored directly as a government measure. But in 1793 the British government, bent on rallying the Catholics behind the war effort and weaning them away from radical reform, decided to push through the Irish parliament the franchise and the right to carry arms. Having probably ascertained in advance that the Irish administration had 'the good sense' not to resent his 'maintaining an opinion which he could not yield, upon one single point', Foster openly opposed the bill in committee (Malcomson, *Foster*, 67). In his speech he warned, not altogether prudently, that men who were fit to elect MPs must be regarded as fit to be elected. Following the passing of the 1793 Catholic Relief Act on the government's terms, the battleground shifted to the right to be elected, or Catholic emancipation. With the British government and the Irish cabinet united against it, this was defeated in the Irish parliament in March 1795. But it remained a live issue, and it re-emerged in 1799–1800 to embarrass the proponents, and to divide the opponents, of the union. Had Foster not been a convinced and committed anti-emancipationist, it is possible that the anti-unionist majority in the Irish House of Commons would have held up in 1800.

Foster was a paternalist, not a bigot. He did not doubt the generally good disposition of the Catholic masses, if given proper leadership and shown proper example. When the Irish militia was set up in 1793, he strongly supported the inclusion of Catholics in the force, convinced of their loyalty to the British crown. In August 1794 he wrote: 'Our militia is in excellent state and, though the majority of men are Catholic, I believe they would all stand or fall with their officers' (*Anglo-Irish Dialogue*, 14). Although he was a leading advocate of tough measures of counter-insurrection in the period 1795–8, including in March 1798 the risky tactic of making pre-emptive arrests of the known United Irish leaders, he was not a panicky protestant. His measures for the strengthening of the Irish economy, and the primacy he accorded to economic policy, were in part his formula for killing emancipation with kindness.

The union   Foster was always going to have opposed the union of Great Britain and Ireland, but his bitter and factious response to the issue was dictated by the arrogant and ham-fisted way in which he was handled in November–December 1798, when he was excluded from discussions in London on the draft proposals for the union. In mid-December 1798 Foster reported: 'I saw Pitt yesterday, and … it was really too ridiculous when he told me he had nothing to communicate, or detain me for, nor anything to talk further upon. Think of this, after being detained a month!' (Foster to Sheffield, 18 Dec [1798], PRONIre., T/3725/12).

Too late Pitt and Foster exchanged, via intermediaries, messages of mutual esteem; Foster was given every opportunity to return to the government fold and either to contribute to the detail of the measure or just to be neutral, without being required to profess support for the principle. His refusal to make terms for himself refutes the charge of time-serving and even venality often levelled at him by contemporaries and historians. However, the fact that he was universally known to be 'the first debtor as well as the first Commoner in the kingdom' (Brodrick to Midleton, 22 March 1799, Midleton Papers, MS 1248, vol. 17, fols. 11–13) in itself exposed him to this charge; and a successful move by his fellow anti-unionists, who then abandoned it at his request, to get up a subscription for the payment of his debts only served to compromise him further. Foster was handsomely compensated for his losses resulting from the union: in addition to the automatic £7500 for his half share in the borough of Dunleer, he was given £5000 a year for life for the speakership. As with all his personal finances, Foster made a mess of this grant: he sold it for £30,000 in 1806, and then lived for a further twenty-two years.

In February 1801 Foster wrote of the union: 'even so carried, it is the law. We are bound; and … I shall not be surprised if the loyal men who opposed it by their advice shall be its supporters by their arms' (Malcomson, *Foster*, 351). On the other hand, he feared that the Catholics would soon seek to undo the union:

> They will soon feel how little they will be in Britain, how great they would be here [Ireland]. They will look to restoring the Parliament and to filling the vacancies [left] by purchased boroughs with popular elections, in which they will hope for a majority; and if this comes to pass, a Catholic government and consequent separation will be the effect. (ibid.)

Foster ceased to desire the restoration of the Irish parliament as early as 1801. Although in May 1802 he attacked the methods by which the union had been carried, he did not attack the union itself. As a typical exercise in post-union reconciliation and assimilation, he was reappointed to the Board of Trade in February 1802. However, because of mutual prejudice and distrust, he was not overeager to be wooed back into office by the post-union administration of Henry Addington. But when he did return in May 1804, as chancellor of the Irish exchequer, under Pitt and on his own terms, there was no inconsistency in his comeback, or even in his co-operation in covering up in November–December 1804 the illegal use which had been made of secret service money to carry the union.

Chancellor of the Irish exchequer, 1804–1806, 1807–1811 The financial provisions of the Act of Union had been based on the premise that, in 1800, Ireland was in too weak an economic condition to bear taxation on equal terms with Great Britain. It was accordingly enacted that the treasuries, revenues, and debts of the two kingdoms should be kept separate until Ireland was in a condition to bear equal taxation and until the debts of the two kingdoms should be in the proportion of 1 on the part of Ireland to 7½ on that of Great Britain. In the meantime, Ireland's contribution to imperial expenditure (excluding British debt charges and the civil list) was tied to British expenditure in the same proportion, subject to a revision after twenty years if, within that time, financial amalgamation had not taken place. With greater prescience and accuracy than anyone else exhibited at the time of the union, Foster had prophesied in an anti-union speech in 1800 that Ireland would be unable to meet its proportion of contribution; that the 1:7½ proportion of debts would be reached by an increase in the Irish debt, not a decrease in the British; and that one of the conditions for financial amalgamation would thus be fulfilled at a time when the other could not, because Ireland would by then be much less capable of bearing equal taxation than it had been in 1800. 'We are to increase our encumbrances', Foster had declared, 'in order to enjoy the burden of equal taxation with Britain.' Even Foster, however, had not foreseen the duration or the financial effects of the war.

At the outset, Foster tried by fairly draconian means to raise the level of Irish taxation. His 1804 budget aimed at producing 'an additional £1,250,000, mostly from additional rates of indirect taxation on articles of consumption', but the attempt 'to raise a great part of the supplies within the year' was a failure, due to the disappointing yield of the taxes at the higher rates (McCavery, 177–8, 183). There were a number of other reasons for 'the narrow limits to which taxation was reduced in Ireland' (ibid., 173). In 1800, over 85 per cent of all Irish exports were to Great Britain and 78 per cent of all Irish imports were from Great Britain. The Act of Union stipulated that Anglo-Irish trade was to be duty-free, with a few specified exceptions. This crippled potential revenue from the customs; the excise was similarly crippled by the more imprecise stipulation of the act that 'no duty could be laid in Ireland on any article not liable to one in England, nor were the duties to be higher in Ireland than in England'. Foster contravened this stipulation in a number of respects, and the conflicting legal opinions to which his taxes gave rise revealed that this part of Article 7 was, in the words of Sir Henry Parnell, fourth baronet, 'almost wholly unintelligible'. 'What was originally planned as a guarantee [to Ireland] became a liability from the point of view of Irish Chancellors' attempts to raise revenue' (ibid., 175–6).

Of all the remaining areas of potential revenue, taxing whiskey and the related articles of malt and imported spirits was by far the most promising, but during Foster's second term of office at Westminster he was consistently let down by British ministers when he made the attempt. Between June 1808 and March 1810, distillation from grain was prohibited throughout the United Kingdom, nominally to avert food shortages, but actually out of deference to the powerful West Indian sugar lobby. As the Irish taste was for corn spirits, not sugar spirits, the effect of the prohibition on Ireland was mainly to stimulate illicit distillation. The Irish way of dealing with illicit distillation, founded on legislation of the Irish parliament promoted by Foster in 1785, was to fine townlands and, if necessary, parishes where illicit stills had been discovered but the workers of them had not. Foster reactivated this system in 1807, but in March 1810 the chief secretary, home secretary, and prime minister united to persuade him to 'suspend' the imposition of townland and parish fines. The so-called suspension lasted until 1813, well after Foster's retirement from office. On balance, it appears that his policy—based on good local knowledge—was correct, and that his senior colleagues had succumbed to the special pleading of Irish MPs and county magnates who had economic reasons for wanting illicit distillation to flourish. Because of its timing, this suspension deprived the Irish revenue of much of the benefit it should have received from the lifting of the prohibition on distillation from grain.

Foiled by these various obstacles in his attempts to raise revenue, Foster was constrained to borrow, and, during his second term of office as chancellor of the Irish exchequer, borrowing was the bedrock of his budgets. In the event, Foster's enforced precipitation of financial amalgamation redounded to Ireland's advantage: when it came in 1817, its practical effect was to halve Ireland's union contribution, and equal taxation for the whole of the United Kingdom did not immediately, or in some respects ever, ensue.

Administrative reform Foster's other approach to the problem of insufficient revenue was to crank up its net yield through reform of inefficiencies and abuses in the revenue departments. In Britain, this broadly speaking had been Pitt's formula for peacetime finance between 1783 and 1793, and when Foster set up a commission of inquiry into the public offices in Ireland in 1804, with a brief to begin with the revenue, he was acting on Pittite precedent. In Ireland, the treasury board established by act of parliament in 1793, even when its role had been further defined by amending legislation in 1795, had remained largely ineffective—certainly for the intended purpose of superintendence of the revenue—and the first lordship of the treasury had remained a sinecure until Foster's appointment to it in May 1804. Pitt had hoped for an active and efficient Irish treasury board in 1793, and he meant business in appointing Foster first lord. Foster, too, seems earlier to have formed the view that the chancellorship of the Irish exchequer could not be fully effective unless that office were combined with the first lordship of the Irish treasury.

Pitt failed to make it clear, and probably was not clear in his own mind, how the prime ministerial powers implicit in the offices conferred on Foster were to be reconciled with the authority of the lord lieutenant. The lord lieutenant in May 1804 was an Addington appointee, the third earl of Hardwicke, who was retained on what amounted to probation. Pitt may have assumed that Hardwicke would be at pains to work in harmony with Foster and would set the tone in this respect for the rest of the Irish administration. But, in the event, Foster's high-handed exercise of the powers of the first lordship brought him into conflict with not only the lord lieutenant but also the lord chancellor of Ireland, the Irish law officers, and the chief commissioner of the revenue—almost everyone, in fact, except the supine chief secretary, Sir Evan Nepean. Foster was widely accused of having a despotic love of power. But the more probable explanation for his behaviour is that he knew that his reforms depended on the support of Pitt, and reckoned (rightly) that Pitt's last ministry and Pitt's health were both precarious. Foster was a man in a hurry, and behaved accordingly.

As a result, while the programme of reform and retrenchment, which he stood for, made headway, Foster himself suffered a number of political and personal defeats. Three bills essential to his programme were stopped in June 1805 on Pitt's own instructions, and there was a long hiatus between then and October 1805 during which it was unclear whether Foster was in or out of office. One of these bills was for the division of the revenue board into separate boards of customs and excise, with a view to abolishing the overmighty chief commissionership and then to dividing the customs from the excise business in each of the ports. The bill, having failed to become law in 1805, was taken up and carried by Foster's successor as chancellor of the exchequer in 1806, when Foster himself was out of office and in opposition. Likewise, the whig–Grenvillite government of 1806–7 implemented the recommendations for revenue reform made in the first report of Foster's inquiry board in December 1805. That board itself, though unpopular and seen as the vehicle for a Fosterite witch-hunt, continued in operation and even survived Foster's final retirement in 1811. Another centrepiece of his programme, the abolition of fees in the customs department, was delayed by the events of 1805–7, was rejected on a technicality in July 1807, in spite of his return to office in April, and did not become law until June 1808. So, it was a case of slow and much interrupted progress towards a more efficient and productive collection of the revenue.

The political obstacles to progress transcended Foster's allegedly despotic methods. For one thing, British and Irish administrations (with the exception of Pitt in 1804–5) were frightened of conceding to any Irish politician the authority necessary for proper superintendence of the revenue. For another, the Irish treasury board was almost entirely composed of MPs, and indeed was increasingly used as a nursery for Irish political talent; so it would have been very difficult for Foster, even if he had been reappointed first lord in 1807, to make it a working body, and impossible during the parliamentary session. Finally, though governments paid lip-service to the need for retrenchment and reform, ministerial instability was such during the period 1801–11 that, in practice, they all succumbed to political pressures in the hiring and firing

of all levels of revenue officials. It was on this very issue that Foster resigned in 1811.

Books, buildings, and gardens Outside politics (and family life) Foster had wider interests than most politicians. He was a notable bibliophile, though the most important component of his library—a collection of pamphlets on financial and economic subjects, now in the library of Queen's University, Belfast—reflected his specialisms as a public man. He was 'a great architect' (the description was sarcastic). Fairly early in his career, in 1776, he consulted James Wyatt, whom he was annoyed to find 'as difficult of access as a Prime Minister' (*Anglo-Irish Dialogue*, 3), probably about Rathescar Lodge, a house situated between Collon and Dunleer, in which Foster lived until his father died in 1779 and which has Wyatt windows. James Gandon, the architect employed to alter the Parliament House, was given a free hand with the extension to the House of Lords accommodation in 1784–9; but, when it came to the Commons extension on the Foster Place side of the building, his plans were modified and their execution in 1787–93 entrusted to others—both largely because of the interference of Foster in his capacity as speaker. When the heating system installed under Foster's aegis in the Commons chamber destroyed the dome of the building in 1792, he was said to be angered at 'the imputation on his flues' (Malcomson, *Foster*, 268). Less controversially, he was an important propagator of the Greek revival in Irish architecture. The garden house or temple which he built about 1780 in the elevated demesne above Collon village, and which came to be called Oriel Temple and used as a full-time residence, has (in addition to Wyatt-esque plasterwork) possibly the earliest Doric portico in Ireland. In 1786 he employed the watercolour painter John James Barralet to paint the Foster family on the steps of the temple—a wonderful evocation of late eighteenth-century Irish civilization. Inside, he commissioned Peter de Gree in 1788 to decorate the temple with a series of *grisailles* depicting Mercury introducing the arts and industry to Hibernia. About 1812 Edward Parke (who had been employed by Foster on the Commons building in the early to mid-1790s) designed a stable block at Oriel Temple and, much more significantly, a court house in nearby Dundalk. This latter commission he owed to Foster's position as foreman of the Louth grand jury and governor of the county; and Dundalk court house is still one of Ireland's most important Greek revival buildings.

It was, however, as a horticulturist and botanist that Foster achieved greatest renown outside the political sphere. As early as 1769, in a letter describing his success with Pensacola convolvulus seeds sent him by the English naturalist John Ellis, he described himself as 'a great planter' (Ellis Papers, Linn. Soc.). John Claudius Loudon stated that Foster and the second earl of Clanbrassill, of Tollymore Park, co. Down, and Dundalk House, co. Louth, 'were the persons who introduced by far the greatest number of trees into Ireland' during the eighteenth century, and whose arboretums, both dating from 1768, were the oldest in the country (Loudon, 1.108–9). Founder of the Dublin Society's botanic garden at Glasnevin in 1797, Foster suggested the overall scheme for the garden which made it in Loudon's day 'not only the largest in Europe, but the most comprehensive in its plan' (ibid., 1.116–17). Between Glasnevin and Mount Oriel, as Foster's 600 acre nursery and plantations round Oriel Temple were called, a great deal of mutually enriching exchanges of plants went on. Boasting more than 1700 European and American plants, 'Foster's collection at Collon was described as second only to Kew' (Lamb and Bowe, 55).

Final years, 1811–1828 Few things flourished like Mount Oriel during Foster's last years, which were 'clouded not a little' (Malcomson, *Foster*, 110). When he retired from office in 1811, no financial provision—though it was sorely needed—was made for him, nor did his repeated applications for a UK peerage bear fruit until 1821, when, on 17 July, he was created Baron Oriel. He was a poor attender at Westminster between 1812 and 1821, although he spoke prominently on the protectionist (and losing) side in a series of corn laws debates in May 1814. He can only have been dismayed when parliamentary grants for a lavish programme of Church of Ireland church and parsonage building, in effect inaugurated by him in 1808, petered out in 1823. Foster did not live to see the passing of Catholic emancipation in 1829, but he lived long enough to see his family's long-running monopoly of a seat for co. Louth almost terminated at the general election of 1826, when the Catholic freeholders of the county voted in large numbers against landlord instructions and against Foster's nephew John Leslie *Foster. A factor in this near defeat was Foster's well-known financial difficulties, which were themselves a major blight on his last years. His adored wife, Lady Ferrard, died on 20 January 1824, and Foster himself died at Collon House on 23 August 1828. He was buried at Dunleer church on 27 August.

A. P. W. MALCOMSON

Sources A. P. W. Malcomson, *John Foster: the politics of the Anglo-Irish ascendancy* (1978) • T. R. McCavery, 'Finance and politics in Ireland, 1801–17', PhD diss., Queen's University, Belfast, 1981 • R. G. Thorne, 'Foster, John', HoP, *Commons, 1790–1820* • *Irish parliamentary register*, 2 (1786) • *Walker's Hibernian Magazine* (Jan 1786) • K. Lamb and P. Bowe, *A history of gardening in Ireland* (Dublin, 1995) • E. A. French, 'The origin of general limited liability in the United Kingdom', *Accounting and Business Research*, 21/18 (1990), 15–34 • PRO NIre., Donoughmore MSS, T 3459 • PRO NIre., Stanley of Alderley / Sheffield MSS, T 3725 • Midleton papers, NL Ire., MS 8869/3 • Midleton papers, Surrey HC, MS 1248 • J. C. Loudon, *Arboretum et fruticetum britannicum*, 2nd edn, 8 vols. (1844), vol. 1 • E. McParland, *James Gandon: Vitruvius Hibernicus* (1985) • Springfield Castle MSS, incorporating some Foster / Massereene, PRO NIre., MIC 680/L • A. P. W. Malcomson, *Archbishop Charles Agar: churchmanship and politics in Ireland, 1760–1810* (Dublin, 2002) • Ellis papers, Linn. Soc. • *An Anglo-Irish dialogue: a calendar of the correspondence between John Foster and Lord Sheffield, 1774–1821* [1976]

Archives NL Ire., corresp. and papers • NL Ire., letters • PRO NIre., corresp. and papers, D/207, D/562, D/1739, D/2681, D/4084, T/2519/4, MIC/680/L | Birm. CA, letters to Matthew Boulton • BL, corresp. with third Lord Hardwicke, Add. MSS 35643–35755 • BL, letters to Sir Robert Peel, Add. MSS 40221–40335 • Ches. & Chester ALSS, letters to John Holroyd, first earl of Sheffield • E. Sussex RO, letters to John Holroyd, first earl of Sheffield • Hants. RO, corresp. with William Wickham • Linn. Soc., corresp. with John Ellis • PRO, letters to William Pitt, PRO 30/8 • PRO NIre., letters to John Holroyd, first earl of Sheffield

Likenesses N. Hone, oils, c.1765–1770, priv. coll. • engraving, c.1785, repro. in *Walker's Hibernian Magazine*, frontispiece • Barralet, group portrait, watercolour, 1786 • Irish school, line engraving, c.1790, NG Ire. • G. Stuart, oils, c.1791, Nelson-Atkins Museum of Art, Kansas City, Missouri [*see illus.*] • H. D. Hamilton, oils, 1799, Mansion House, Dublin • P. Maguire, stipple, pubd 1799 (after G. Stuart), NG Ire. • J. Sherwin, line engraving, pubd 1803 (after unfinished oil painting, c.1785), NG Ire. • engraving, 1805, repro. in Malcomson, *John Foster*, frontispiece • W. Beechey, oils, 1810, Leinster House, Dublin • F. Bartolozzi, stipple, BM, NPG • M. Gauci, lithograph (after T. Lawrence), BM, NPG • C. H. Hodges, mezzotint (after G. Stuart), NG Ire. • Irish school, stipple and line (after G. Stuart), NG Ire. • T. Lawrence, oils, priv. coll. • J. Sherwin, group portrait, sketch (*The installation banquet of the knights of St Patrick, 1783*), NG Ire. • G. Stuart, oils, second version, Clandeboye, co. Down • R. L. West, oils, Royal Dublin Society • line engraving, BM; repro. in *List of members who voted for a legislative union* (1799) • oils (after G. Stuart), NG Ire.

Wealth at death approx. £10,000 p.a., subject to debts of £70,000–£75,000: Malcomson, *John Foster*

Foster, John (1759–1827), architect and engineer, was born in Liverpool, the son of John Foster (*d.* 1801), master joiner, and his wife, Isabella. Although little known outside Liverpool, Foster's career was the archetypal tale of success in a boom town. Apprenticed as a joiner under his father, he purchased his freedom of the borough for 12 guineas in 1773.

Foster proved himself a competent, if derivative, architect, and was involved in such projects as the new gaol (1786), the Athenaeum (1799), the major modifications to the town hall (1789–92, 1795–7, 1802, 1811), and the new exchange (1807). He was also responsible for the public dispensary (1781), extensions in 1802–3 to the Theatre Royal (built 1772), St John's market (1822), and the corporation church of St Luke, begun in 1811 and completed, massively overspent, to a much altered design by his son John *Foster in 1831. However, he was more important as an early town planner: under his direction—for he gained significant political influence in the 1780s—street widening, paving, and lighting were coupled with control over building heights, spacings, and fire resistance.

In 1799 Foster was appointed dock surveyor (chief engineer) in place of Thomas Morris, who was dismissed for seeking an allegedly unreasonable pay increase. Foster, who was not a qualified engineer, was paid three times as much as Morris, who was. Such were his talents that he was able, lacking both qualifications and experience, adequately to discharge these heavy new responsibilities. Working to the advice of John Rennie (1761–1821), he doubled the area of Liverpool docks, and modernized every dock already existing when he was appointed. In 1802 he became corporation surveyor as well, by equally suspect means but with equally successful results.

A flawed genius, Foster was the master, and sometimes inventor, of almost every known form of local government corruption. His sister Jane married Matthew Gregson, who came of an old family of merchants, bankers, and manufacturers: Matthew disliked his parvenu brother-in-law and acquired some incriminating papers which give a glimpse of Foster's personality. His funding of his son John's 'archaeological' trips to Greece with C. R. Cockerell, for example, is exposed as speculation in the acquisition of antiquities for resale to the highest bidder, whether in Britain, Bavaria, or France. Ethically this equated with his property speculations in partnership with Stanistreet and Eden, the corporation solicitors, to whom Thomas Foster was articled. Insider knowledge enabled them to appropriate profits which rightly belonged to the corporation.

Foster established a dynasty which temporarily controlled the fastest-growing town and port in Britain, from offices rather than from the council chamber. His son Thomas became town clerk, William was secretary to the dock committee, and John the younger was borough architect. Corrupt as they undoubtedly were, all the Fosters were very able men, and were pioneers of the new system of employing expert local government officers to manage the corporation's large and valuable estate rather than merely to organize banquets.

Dissenting merchants engineered Foster's fall: gaining power as dock audit commissioners, they investigated his largest single project, Princes Dock, opened in 1821 at a cost of about £650,000, and found serious malpractice. The work itself was excellent, employing innovative techniques learned from Rennie, but gross overcharging by contractors connected with or related to Foster made the completed job cost at least double what it should. Among the accused was Timothy Grindrod, masonry contractor for St Luke's Church. In 1824 a compromise was reached: Foster resigned and the audit commissioners, rather reluctantly, dropped the matter. He died a rich but deeply disgraced man on 27 April 1827 at his home at Newington Bridge, Liverpool. His death was briefly noted by just two Liverpool newspapers: none carried any obituary or account of the funeral of the 'city boss'. He might have been lauded as an architect, engineer, and town planner, a key man in the growth of professional local government. His dishonesty ensured that none of these professions wished to own him: instead, recitals of his misdeeds contributed to the passage of the Municipal Reform Act of 1835.   ADRIAN JARVIS

Sources A. Jarvis, 'The interests and ethics of John Foster, Liverpool dock surveyor, 1799–1824', *Transactions of the Historic Society of Lancashire and Cheshire*, 140 (1990), 141–60 · J. Longmore, 'The development of the Liverpool corporation estate, 1760–1835', PhD diss., U. Reading, 1982 · R. Muir and E. M. Platt, *A history of municipal government in Liverpool* (1906) · An Old Stager [J. Aspinall], *Liverpool a few years since*, 3rd edn (1885) · Colvin, *Archs.* · Lpool RO, Gregson MSS · *Gore's General Advertiser* (3 May 1827) · *Gore's Directory of Liverpool* (1827)

Archives Lpool RO, accounts and minutes of Liverpool corporation | Lpool RO, Gregson MSS · Merseyside Maritime Museum, Liverpool, Mersey docks and harbour board collection

Likenesses W. Spence, marble bust, 1831, Walker Art Gallery, Liverpool

Wealth at death under £60,000 in personal property; substantial real estate: will, 1827, Lancs. RO, WCW

Foster, John (1770–1843), Baptist minister and essayist, was born on 17 September 1770 at Wadsworth Lane in the parish of Halifax, Yorkshire, the eldest son of John Foster (d. 1814) and his wife, Ann (d. 1816), both of whom were small farmers and weavers. Foster remembered himself as a contemplative and awkward child with few friends. He enjoyed reading and the study of nature. His early education was limited, and he worked alongside his parents from a young age. His father was a leading local Baptist, and at the age of about seventeen Foster became a member of the congregation at Hebden Bridge. Still working for his parents, he studied for three years at Brearley Hall under John Fawcett DD, before leaving for the Baptist college, Bristol, in September 1791. He was remembered as a hard worker, but throughout his life he lamented his own idleness.

Foster started work as a preacher in May 1792. After three months in Newcastle, he moved to Dublin in 1793. He was minister at a meeting-house in Swift's Alley for just over a year, commenting of his time there 'The congregation was very small when I commenced, and almost nothing when I voluntarily closed', a pattern which was to continue throughout his career as a minister. After several months at home, he returned to Dublin in 1795 to take charge of a classical and mathematical school, which after eight or nine months he gave up as a failure. At this time, his friendship with some of the violent Dublin democrats made him fear imprisonment. In February 1796 he returned once more to Yorkshire, and stayed there until early 1797 when he took up a post in Chichester. This lasted two and a half years, but after the Chichester Baptist Society collapsed he moved in 1799 to live with an old friend in Battersea. Here, he preached a little and helped train twenty Samoan boys for mission work. He also met Maria Snooke (1776?–1832), whom he was to marry in May 1808.

In 1800 Foster took charge of a small congregation at Downend, near Bristol, and in February 1804 of one at Sheppard's Barton, Frome. During his time here, his *Essays in a Series of Letters to a Friend* (1805) were first published. The book had been two years in the writing, and contained four essays: 'On a man's writing memoirs of himself', 'On decision of character', 'On the application of the epithet romantic', and 'On some of the causes by which evangelical religion has been rendered less acceptable to persons of cultivated taste'. It was extremely successful. By 1856 it had run to twenty editions, and the *Bristol Mirror* (quoted in the *Gentleman's Magazine*, 1843) commented: 'He paints metaphysics'.

Shortly after the book's publication Foster resigned from Sheppard's Barton, having problems with his thyroid gland which made preaching painful. He became a regular contributor to the *Eclectic Review* from 1806 until 1839, contributing altogether 184 articles, a number of which were posthumously republished in his *Contributions, Biographical, Literary, and Philosophical, to the Eclectic Review* (2 vols., 1844).

After his marriage Foster moved to Bourton in Gloucestershire, where his first son, John, was born in 1810. He did not preach regularly again until his return to Downend at the end of 1817. After six months of unpopularity, he left for Stapleton, Gloucestershire. Here, another influential essay was published, *On the Evils of Popular Ignorance* (1820).

In 1822 he began to lecture fortnightly in Broadmead Chapel, Bristol, although after two years bad health forced him to make the lectures monthly, and in 1825 he stopped altogether.

Of Foster's five children, two died in infancy, and his remaining son, John, died aged fifteen, after a lingering illness, in 1826. His wife became consumptive, and after years of declining health died in 1832. Foster wrote relatively little during this period, and from 1836 his own health began to decline. He became involved in a controversy between the Serampore missionaries and the committee of the Baptist Missionary Society, strongly siding with the missionaries. After a long illness of the lungs, he died at his home in Stapleton, where he lived alone, in the early morning of 15 October 1843. He was buried at the Downend Baptist Chapel burial-ground.

Foster's opinions were often controversial. He believed that 'churches are useless and mischievous institutions, and the sooner they are dissolved the better' (letter, 10 Sept 1828). Though a Baptist minister, he never once administered baptism; nor did he believe in eternal punishment or the rite of ordination. Politically, he was a republican, and 'never ceased to regard royalty and all its gaudy paraphernalia as a sad satire on human nature' (letter, 22 Feb 1842). He favoured parliamentary reform, Catholic emancipation, and popular education, and opposed the corn laws. The *Bristol Mirror* called him 'an unaffectedly great and good man'.

THOMAS HAMILTON, *rev.* JESSICA HININGS

Sources J. E. Ryland, ed., *The life and correspondence of John Foster*, 2 vols. (1846) · W. Landels, *Baptist worthies* (1884) · *GM*, 2nd ser., 21 (1844), 95–6 · D. M. Lewis, ed., *The Blackwell dictionary of evangelical biography, 1730–1860*, 2 vols. (1995) · J. F. Waller, ed., *The imperial dictionary of universal biography*, 3 vols. (1857–63) · R. Hall, *Reviews of the following works*, 2nd edn (1825) · T. Coles, *Letters from John Foster to Thomas Coles, MA* (1864) · *Annual Register* (1843) · *The Times* (18 Oct 1843) · Allibone, *Dict.*
Archives Bristol Baptist College, biographical material, extracts, letters, and sermons
Likenesses W. Walker, stipple, pubd 1823 (after N. Branwhite), BM, NPG

Foster, John (1787–1846), architect, was born in Liverpool, the second son of John *Foster (1759–1827), joiner, contractor, and architect, who was from 1790 surveyor to the city corporation of Liverpool, where he spent nearly all of his working life. John Foster senior's most important work was the execution of the exchange (1789–92) (now the town hall), following designs by James Wyatt. In 1795 the building was gutted by fire and restored, again by Foster senior under Wyatt's direction. Foster senior's own works were inspired by Wyatt's and in the neoclassical style. The connection between the Fosters and the Wyatt family continued when John Foster junior was placed as a pupil in the office of Jeffry Wyatt (later Sir Jeffry Wyatville) in Lower Brook Street, Mayfair (*c.*1804–1806). While there he submitted three designs to the Royal Academy summer exhibition, a design for a mausoleum in 1804, one for a museum in 1805, and one for a national gallery in 1806.

In 1809 Foster went abroad for several years, travelling in Greece with C. R. Cockerell, among others, and participating in the excavations of the temple of Athena at Aegina, and the temple of Apollo at Bassae, a record of which was later published by Cockerell. Returning to England in 1816, he entered into partnership with his brother Thomas in the family's building firm, and on his father's retirement as surveyor to Liverpool corporation in 1824 succeeded him in that post. Thomas Foster became town clerk in 1832, strengthening further the family's grip on municipal office. The rest of Foster's professional life was spent in Liverpool where he was a founder member of the Liverpool Academy of Arts in 1810. He was a considerable draughtsman, and a collection of eight of his views of monuments in Greece and Asia Minor are held in the Walker Art Gallery, Liverpool. A larger collection is in the Yale Center for British Art, New Haven, Connecticut. Three of his watercolour views of Liverpool, and one of the Irongate, Glasgow, are held in the Liverpool Record Office, Central Library, Liverpool. He was a fellow of the Society of Antiquaries. On his death, in Liverpool on 21 August 1846, he was living in Hamilton Square, Birkenhead; he was buried in St James's cemetery, Liverpool (below the present Anglican cathedral).

Foster's output was fairly large, most of it in Liverpool, and most of it in a severe and scholarly Greek style. He took over one of his father's largest projects, St Luke's Church, Luke Place (designed by Foster senior in 1802, built 1811–31). A grand exercise in a Perpendicular style, with a big west tower, this was gutted in the Second World War, and survives as a shell. Foster's most important work was the custom house on Canning Place (1828–35), once an important element in the cityscape from the Mersey, with a giant hexastyle Ionic portico and a dome, reminiscent of the work of Sir Robert Smirke. This was bombed in 1940 and subsequently demolished. Of eight churches by Foster in Liverpool, only St Andrew's, Rodney Street, and the shell of St Luke's survive. Of the former only the façade, which has an Ionic loggia and twin towers, is certainly his. At St James's cemetery, dramatically sited in a ravine which had been widened out by quarrying, Foster designed the chapel (1825–6), a small and perfect Greek Doric temple, with hexastyle porticos at either end and a noble interior with monolithic Ionic columns. His Huskisson rotunda (1836), a fine Corinthian rotunda commemorating Sir William Huskisson, the statesman killed at the opening of the Liverpool and Manchester Railway in 1830, is also in St James's cemetery.

Foster also designed in other styles: a couple of his churches were in a Gothic style, reminiscent of work by the Wyatt family. His most important Gothic work was undoubtedly a series of alterations and additions to the older (west) wing of Knowsley Hall, Lancashire, for the earl of Derby (*c.*1820). Much of this survives, notably the great dining-room and the castellated wing immediately to the west of it, though substantial alterations were carried out by William Burn in the 1840s, and the detail is no longer Foster's. He remodelled Garswood Hall at Ashton in Makerfield for Sir John Gerard (*c.*1828) in the Greek revival style, but this was entirely demolished in 1921. His grandstand at Aintree racecourse of 1829 was burnt down and replaced in 1892, and his Lime Street railway station, built for the Liverpool and Manchester Railway (1835–6), has been demolished.

Foster was the leading architect in Liverpool for most of the period c.1816–1835, when the city was at the height of its prosperity. His influence was probably a factor in ensuring Liverpool's continued allegiance to the classical style for most important commissions through the mid-nineteenth century. Sadly, only three or four of his own works survive in any recognizable condition.

STEVEN BRINDLE

Sources Colvin, *Archs.*, 373–5 · P. Fleetwood-Hesketh, *Murray's Lancashire architectural guide* (1955), 88–9 · J. A. Picton, *Memorials of Liverpool*, rev. edn, 1 (1875), 470 · *South Lancashire*, Pevsner (1969) · J. M. Robinson, *A guide to the country houses of the north west* (1991) · *DNB*

Archives Sir John Soane's Museum, London, letters from Greece, Div. I, F. 6 [copies]

Foster, Sir John Galway (1903–1982), lawyer, was born in Paris on 21 February 1903, the only child (he also had a half-brother and two half-sisters) of Brigadier-General Hubert John Foster, Royal Engineers, military attaché at the British embassy in Washington, and a woman whose surname was Galway, an Irish Canadian. No birth certificate can be found. He was educated first in France and then at Hildesheim in Germany. At the age of eight he was trilingual, and he always spoke French and German fluently. After attending A. J. Richardson's private school in Broadstairs, Kent, in 1917 he won a scholarship to Eton College, where he immediately gave evidence of his cleverness. When he left at the age of sixteen he had won thirteen school prizes. He continued his scholastic success at New College, Oxford, where he matriculated in January 1922. He achieved first-class honours in modern history in 1924 and was elected a fellow of All Souls College the same year. He remained a fellow until his death, having been advanced to a distinguished fellowship in 1980. The popular press tipped him as a future prime minister. Foster, however, was not a man with strong allegiance to any particular party. He admitted that his loyalties were to justice and the welfare of mankind in general, and felt that a conventional political career was wellnigh impossible for him.

Foster was called to the bar in 1927 (at the Inner Temple) and took silk in 1950. Before the outbreak of the Second World War he had a number of appointments, such as secretary to the Thetis inquiry, the budget leak inquiry, and the Law Reform Committee. He was a lecturer in private international law in Oxford (1934–9) and at The Hague, and recorder of Dudley in 1936–8 and of Oxford (1938–51 and 1956–64). On his ceasing to be recorder he was appointed KBE (1964).

In 1939 Foster became first secretary and legal adviser to the British embassy in Washington and later, in Supreme Headquarters, Allied Expeditionary Force, legal adviser to General Dwight Eisenhower. He was made a member of the Légion d'honneur and the American Legion of Merit, awarded the Croix de Guerre (with palms), and played a part in the Nuremberg trials. In 1944 he was accorded the rank of brigadier.

Foster was elected a Conservative member of parliament for the Northwich division of Cheshire in 1945, a seat he held until his retirement in 1974. Between 1951 and 1954 he served as under-secretary of state for Commonwealth relations, but greatly perplexed the establishment by his rapid and informal methods of administration. Do what he might, he found that he invariably finished the week's work in under twelve hours; furthermore, he was reluctant to keep minutes, considering them a waste of time.

After Gerald (later Lord) Gardiner (subsequently lord chancellor) retired from the chairmanship of the Council of Justice, Foster succeeded him in the post, which he held until his death. He was also active in bringing about the European convention on human rights. Throughout his life he fought tirelessly on behalf of the victims of persecution, be they Jews or Tamils or some unfortunate stranger who had experienced any degree of injustice.

Foster possessed a powerful brain. His mind was nimble and quick, and he used his intellect with virtuosity, perceiving connections between ideas, propositions, theories, and hypotheses with lightning speed and consummate skill. In pleading a case he showed himself both innovative and imaginative. Not altogether surprisingly some judges (and, indeed, some of his fellow members in the House of Commons) found him difficult to follow. His style was much more appreciated in the appellate courts, especially the House of Lords; a search of post-Second World War reported cases shows that Foster had been counsel in more than 160. His greatest expertise was in private international and domicile law. He was an outspoken critic of the accusatorial system of justice and would have liked to remake it, based rather on the continental mould. He greatly enjoyed his arbitration cases at the International Court of Justice at The Hague.

Foster was a most unusual and remarkable character, for his public achievement was negligible compared with his private and personal influence which was considerable in England but especially so in North America. First and foremost he was a true egalitarian. He possessed a rare combination of ebullience, cleverness, good humour, delight in the kaleidoscope of human affairs, an unselfish and practical interest in the successes and tribulations of friends and acquaintances, and the gift of combining a crystal-clear objectivity with great kindness and an infinite capacity for helping those in trouble. He possessed a fund of amusing anecdotes, which were enriched by the fact that he was a gifted extrovert. He was unmarried. He died at 20 Devonshire Place, London, on 1 February 1982.

MIRIAM ROTHSCHILD, *rev.*

Sources personal knowledge (1990) · *The Times* (2 Feb 1982) · M. Rothschild, *John Foster* (privately printed, [n.d.]) [John Foster memorial lecture, 1986] · Oxf. UA · d. cert. · *CGPLA Eng. & Wales* (1982)

Likenesses photographs, repro. in Rothschild, *John Foster*

Wealth at death £444,209: probate, 3 Dec 1982, *CGPLA Eng. & Wales*

Foster, John Leslie (1780/81?–1842), judge, was the eldest son of William Foster (d. 1797), bishop of Clogher, and his wife, Catherine Letitia Leslie (d. 1814), daughter of Henry Leslie DD. His grandfather was Anthony Foster, lord chief baron of Ireland. He was admitted to Trinity College, Dublin, on 1 March 1797, and graduated BA in 1800 and LLB in 1805; and he was granted an honorary LLD degree in 1810. He joined Lincoln's Inn, London, on 13 March 1800 and was called to the bar in Ireland in the autumn of 1803.

In 1804 Foster published an essay, *On the Principles of Commercial Exchanges, Particularly between England and Ireland*, and was soon appointed a commissioner for improving the Irish bogs. In 1806 he was unsuccessful in contesting the parliamentary seat of Dublin University against the Hon. George Knox, who was, like him, a conservative. Foster was, however, returned the following year, and retained his seat until the general election of 1812. On 19 August 1814 Foster married the Hon. Letitia Vesey Fitzgerald, daughter of James Fitzgerald; they had seven children—six sons and one daughter. His wife survived him and died on 1 February 1864.

In March 1816 Foster again entered parliament, as member for Yarmouth, Isle of Wight. He was made advocate-general in Ireland in June 1816 and counsel to the commissioners of revenue in Ireland in April 1818. At the general election of 1818 he was returned for both Armagh and Lisburn, when he elected to serve for Armagh, which he represented until 1820. He was elected for Louth at a by-election on 21 February 1824, and again at the general election in 1826. His two speeches in the House of Commons, of 24 April 1812 and 9 May 1817, on Grattan's motion respecting the penal laws against the Roman Catholics of Ireland, were published separately. On 4 February 1819 he was elected FRS; he was also at that time a member of the Royal Irish Academy and vice-president of the Dublin Society for the Improvement of Useful Arts. Foster took silk eventually, as well as acting as commissioner of the Board of Education in Ireland, and of the Irish fisheries. He was opposed to Catholic emancipation until it became inevitable under Peel's government. In 1825 he gave evidence before the House of Lords select committee on the state of Ireland. He was appointed a baron of the court of exchequer in Ireland by patent dated 13 July 1830. Finally, he was transferred to the court of common pleas, a few months before his death; he died when on circuit at Cavan on 10 July 1842.

GORDON GOODWIN, rev. SINÉAD AGNEW

Sources J. S. Crone, *A concise dictionary of Irish biography*, rev. edn (1937), 72 · Burke, *Gen. Ire.* (1912) · Burke, *Gen. Ire.* (1976), 428 · *GM*, 2nd ser., 18 (1842), 424 · *GM*, 1st ser., 100/2 (1830), 76 · *GM*, 1st ser., 84/2 (1814), 288 · Burtchaell & Sadleir, *Alum. Dubl.*, 2nd edn · W. P. Baildon, ed., *The records of the Honorable Society of Lincoln's Inn: admissions*, 2 (1896) · F. E. Ball, *The judges in Ireland, 1221–1921*, 2 vols. (1926), 268–9, 279, 287, 329–30, 345–6 · E. G. Powell, 'Foster, John Leslie', *Dictionary of political economy*, ed. H. R. I. Palgrave (1894–9) · W. B. S. Taylor, *History of the University of Dublin* (1845), 464 · [J. Watkins and F. Shoberl], *A biographical dictionary of the living authors of Great Britain and Ireland* (1816), 120 · Allibone, *Dict.* · C. J. Smyth, *Chronicle of the law officers of Ireland* (1839), 161

Archives Bodl. Oxf., accounts of his visit to Constantinople · Church of Ireland College of Education, letters · priv. coll., MSS · Royal Irish Acad., corresp. and papers | BL, corresp. with Sir Robert Peel, Add. MSS 40224–40496 · PRO NIre., letters to his uncle, John Foster

Foster, Joseph (1844–1905), genealogist and antiquary, born at Sunniside, Sunderland, on 9 March 1844, was the eldest of five sons and three daughters of Joseph Foster, a woollen draper of Bishopwearmouth, co. Durham, and his wife, Elizabeth, daughter of Emanuel Taylor. His grandfather was Myles Birket Foster (1785–1861), founder of the London bottling firm. His uncle, also named (Myles) Birket *Foster (1825–1899), a painter, had encouraged his early interest in genealogy. Educated privately, Foster began business as a printer in London. He took to genealogical research and it appears that he may have wanted to become a herald. Although he retained a close friendship with several of the officers of arms throughout his life, and was granted unreserved access to the records, he never received an invitation. Foster's first work was on his Quaker ancestry, *Some Account of the Pedigree of the Forsters of Cold Hesledon, Co. Durham* (1862). He married, on 12 August 1869, Catherine Clark, eldest daughter of George Pocock of Burgess Hill, Sussex, and they had two sons and three daughters.

In 1871 Foster privately printed *The King of Arms*, and in the meantime continued his assiduous genealogical researches, publishing extensive pedigrees and histories of several northern families, including another of his own. In 1873 the first part of his projected *Pedigrees of the County Families of England* appeared as *Lancashire County Families*, soon followed by three volumes of *Yorkshire County Families* (1874). In 1875 he published an edition of Robert Glover's *Visitations of Yorkshire*, and began the marathon task of transcribing the admission registers of the four inns of court.

In 1879, in collaboration with Edward Bellasis, Bluemantle pursuivant at the College of Arms, Foster produced the *Peerage, Baronetage and Knightage*, based upon the earlier *Lodge's Peerage*. He exposed the mythical ancestries admitted for publication by his predecessors and introduced brilliant new artwork along with a section entitled 'Chaos' dealing with baronetcies of doubtful creation. Stephen Tucker, Rouge Croix pursuivant, attacked Foster particularly over the heraldic illustrations and blazonry (*The Genealogist*, 4 1880, 64). Foster and Bellasis defended themselves in *A Review of a Review of Joseph Foster's 'Peerage'* (1880). In *Lodge's Peerage* of 1903, Foster lambasted his adversaries in a brilliant introduction which reverberates with words and the style of the renowned genealogist Horace Round, whose disdain for some of his fellow professionals knew no bounds. It is possible that Round wrote much of the piece himself: he certainly aided Foster in publishing a series entitled Collectanea Genealogica et Heraldica (1881–5), which contained much trenchant criticism and exposure of contemporary genealogical myths. In it he printed transcriptions of legal and other registers and genealogical researches. Some of the volumes, such as *Members of Parliament, Scotland, 1357–1882* (1882), were reissued separately, while others were left incomplete.

Foster's prolific transcription work was published in

Men at the Bar (1885); *The register of admissions to Gray's Inn* (1557–1859), *together with … marriages in Gray's Inn Chapel* (1889); *Index ecclesiasticus, or, Alphabetical lists of all ecclesiastical dignitaries in England and Wales since the Reformation* (1890); and several editions of *Heralds' Visitations*, among other works on heraldry and genealogy. Never averse to building upon the work of others, Foster founded much of his reputation on the transcriptions made by Colonel Joseph Lemuel Chester (1821–1882) and George Edward Cokayne, (1825–1911), which he printed and published as his own editions. The London bookseller Bernard Quaritch purchased other works of Chester and Cokayne, and prevailed upon Foster to publish the Oxford matriculation register and the bishop of London's register of marriage licences. The latter appeared as *London Marriage Licences (1521–1869)* in 1887, and the former, alphabetically arranged, under the title *Alumni Oxonienses*, of which four volumes, covering the period 1715–1886, appeared in 1887, and another four volumes, covering the period 1500–1714, in 1891. Foster had copiously supplemented Chester's work from his own researches and the university awarded him the honorary degree of MA in 1892. The next year he carried his work a stage further in *Oxford Men and their Colleges*. In later life Foster published further works on heraldry. *Concerning the Beginnings … of Heraldry as Related to untitled Persons* appeared in 1887, and *Some Feudal Coats of Arms* in 1902. The eighth Lord Howard de Walden sponsored the De Walden Library to which Foster contributed *A Tudor Book of Arms*, *Some Feudal Lords and their Seals* and *Banners, Standards and Badges* (1904). Foster's work was severely censured by Oswald Barron in *The Ancestor* for alleged lack of scholarship and knowledge, to which he replied in two pamphlets, *A Herald Extraordinary* and *A Comedy of Errors* (1902–3).

Foster died at his home, 21 Boundary Road, St John's Wood, London, on 29 July 1905. He was buried in London at Kensal Green cemetery; his name was also inscribed on a memorial stone in Bishopwearmouth cemetery. In his will (proved 10 November 1905), he left his widow £86 2*s.* 2*d.*—his entire personal estate, and a measure of the small profit he had realized from a lifetime of ardent work. His library of much annotated books and manuscripts was dispersed at his death. Four volumes of grants of arms were secured for the British Museum Library (Add. MSS 37147–37150) and subsequently edited for publication (1915–16) by W. Harry Rylands. Foster was no scholarly antiquary, but his energy as a transcriber and collector of genealogical and heraldic data has few parallels, and many of his publications remained classic resources, several of permanent value.   CECIL R. HUMPHERY-SMITH

Sources BL cat. · *The Times* (1 Aug 1905) · *Miscellanea Genealogica et Heraldica*, 4th ser., 1 (1904–5), 279 · Culleton MSS, Institute of Heraldic and Genealogical Studies · J. Titford, 'The Chester manuscripts and the Harleian Society', *Genealogists' Magazine*, 25/10 (June 1997), 401–6 · WWW, 1897–1915 · DNB · *The Ancestor*, 2 (1902) · S. Tucker, review, *The Genealogist*, 4 (1880), 64–7 · private information (1912) · *CGPLA Eng. & Wales* (1905) · d. cert. · m. cert.
Archives BL, heraldic collections, Add. MSS 37147–37150 · BL, index compiled by him to arms and monuments in Kentish churches · Bodl. Oxf., transcript by him of Jenyns ordinary · CUL, lists of English and Welsh incumbents and barristers, index to Le Neve's *Fasti* · S. Antiquaries, Lond., compilation of grants of arms before 1730 | Bodl. Oxf., letters to J. E. A. Fenwick and T. F. Fenwick · Institute of Heraldic and Genealogical Studies, Canterbury, Culleton MSS · LUL, letters to J. H. Round · U. Durham L., letters to Jonathan Backhouse
Wealth at death £86 2*s.* 2*d.*: probate, 10 Nov 1905, *CGPLA Eng. & Wales*

Foster, Marjorie Elaine (1893–1974), rifle shot and poultry farmer, was born at 107 Canfield Gardens, Hampstead, London, on 20 June 1893, the only child of Lancelot Henry William Foster, syphon manufacturer, and his wife, Mary Aldridge Leetham. Encouraged by her father who had held a commission in the East Kent regiment before his marriage, she took up small-bore rifle shooting at the age of eight and became a junior member of Camberley Rifle Club.

After leaving school Foster worked as a sculptor and during the First World War served with the Women's Legion of Motor Drivers, training other women drivers and servicing vehicles. It was here that she met Blanche Margaret Mary Badcock (d. 1957), a keen rifle shot who, after the war, became her lifelong companion and business partner in a poultry farm at Frimley in Surrey. Both women joined the South London Rifle Club at Bisley, headquarters of the National Rifle Association, the only club there that was prepared to accept female members, and during the 1920s they became highly proficient at their sport. In 1926 Badcock was the first woman to compete for the sovereign's prize, the blue riband of target rifle shooting, held at Bisley every July and restricted to past and present members of the armed forces. Marjorie Foster first took part in 1929.

In July 1930 Foster, competing against 861 male and 4 female entrants, achieved her greatest success by winning the sovereign's prize. She was the only woman to accomplish this feat in 140 years, and her achievement was not equalled until July 2000. During the three-stage event she became the first woman to reach the last 100 competitors. Her outstanding ability to concentrate and to master the unpredictable wind conditions on the Bisley range enabled her to win by a single point, scoring a bull's-eye with her final shot. Her success was commemorated by a telegram from George V, the prize of £250 and the gold medal, and, astonishingly, the presentation of a car by the residents of her home town, Frimley, as a token of their pride in her achievement. She had proved that a woman was as capable as a man of winning in the strongly militaristic and masculine world of shooting.

Foster came second in the sovereign's prize in the following year and reached the last 100 a further three times before the outbreak of war in 1939. Having continued to train drivers, largely for the First Aid Nursing Yeomanry, between the wars, she served in Auxiliary Territorial Service during the Second World War, commanding a transport company and training young riflemen in shooting. She was badly wounded during the bombing of Plymouth and was later made an MBE in recognition of her war service.

After the war Foster resumed her shooting career and

competed in the last 100 of four sovereign's prizes, culminating in her final appearance in 1961 aged sixty-eight. She represented England on ten occasions and captained a Great Britain team on a tour to Canada in 1958. She also became heavily involved in coaching both individuals and teams at national and county level, served on the council of the National Rifle Association for seventeen years, and helped to run a number of shooting clubs such as the British Commonwealth Rifle Club.

Foster was said to be a quiet, shy person with a dry sense of humour. Her outstanding ability as a rifle shot rested on her excellent powers of concentration and her judgement of wind conditions, an expertise that she passed on to the many young shots she coached over a thirty-year period. Following the death of Blanche Badcock in 1957, she retired from the poultry business and moved into a bungalow within the grounds of Bisley camp, where she continued her numerous administrative duties with rifle clubs. By 1970, however, her health had deteriorated and she seems to have suffered from Alzheimer's disease. She died at Brookwood Hospital, Woking, Surrey, on 30 March 1974.

JOYCE KAY

Sources E. Taplin, 'Marjorie Foster', unpublished essay, De Montfort University · J. Huntington-Whiteley, ed., *The book of British sporting heroes* (1998) [exhibition catalogue, NPG, 16 Oct 1998 – 24 Jan 1999] · S. Crawford, 'Shooting', *International encyclopedia of women and sports*, 3 (2001), 1006–7 · S. Cornfield, *The queen's prize: the story of the National Rifle Association* (1987) · b. cert. · d. cert. · *CGPLA Eng. & Wales* (1974)

Likenesses photograph, 1930, repro. in Cornfield, *The queen's prize*, facing p. 112 · photograph, 1934, Hult. Arch.; repro. in Huntington-Whiteley, *Book of British sporting heroes*

Wealth at death £23,550: probate, 20 May 1974, *CGPLA Eng. & Wales*

Foster, Sir Michael (1689–1763), judge and legal writer, was born at Marlborough, Wiltshire, on 16 December 1689, the second son of Michael Foster (1658–1720), a Marlborough attorney, and his wife, Sarah Coleman (*b.* 1657). The Fosters were a dissenting family. Educated at Marlborough Free School, Foster matriculated at Exeter College, Oxford, on 30 October 1705. After leaving Oxford without a degree he was admitted to the Middle Temple on 23 May 1707, and was called to the bar on 15 May 1713. Unsuccessful in London, he practised in Marlborough with some reputation, and succeeded his father as clerk of the peace. He did not abandon London, arguing a case there at least once. In 1716 he and Thomas Abney established a 'club of dissenters about the Temple' (*Diary of Dudley Ryder*, 226) to encourage dissenting bar students to resist pressure to conform to the Church of England. Foster was keen that the dissenters concentrate on securing liberty of conscience rather than on doctrinal squabbles, and in 1720 appeared his anonymous *A Letter of Advice to the Protestant Dissenters*, on the healing of their divisions. In 1725 Foster married Martha (1701/2–1758), eldest daughter of James Lyde of Stanton Wick, Somerset. They had no children.

Foster's interests soon turned from Marlborough to Bristol, and in 1731, after withdrawing his candidature for the town clerkship, Foster was an unsuccessful candidate for

Sir Michael Foster (1689–1763), by John Faber junior, 1748 (after James Wills)

the stewardship of the sheriff's court of Bristol, attributing his failure partly at least to objections to his being a dissenter. The next year Foster was one of the founding protestant dissenting deputies who co-ordinated the campaign against the Test and Corporation Acts. In 1735 appeared Foster's *An examination of the scheme of church power laid down in the 'Codex juris ecclesiastici Anglicani'*, an attack upon the ample view of the powers of the established church in Edmund Gibson's *Codex juris ecclesiastici Anglicani* (1713), a work much cited in the church–state controversies of the 1730s. The *Examination*, eagerly followed up in the press, went through two editions in 1735 and a third in 1736, and stimulated an answer by the civilian Dr John Andrew.

In 1735 Foster attained a position at Bristol when John Scrope, burdened by his responsibilities as secretary to the Treasury, resigned as recorder and *ex officio* senior alderman of Bristol, and recommended that Foster replace him. In 1736, in consequence of his recordership, Foster was created serjeant-at-law in the last general call of serjeants. His sponsors were John Scrope and Algernon Seymour, earl of Hertford, subsequently seventh duke of Somerset, who had interests in Marlborough and of whose will Foster was to be an executor. In 1739, upon the death of Thomas Coster MP, Foster offered himself as a parliamentary candidate for Bristol, but stood down in favour of Henry Combe. As recorder Foster successfully defended the city of Bristol's jurisdiction in 1741 in the prosecution of Samuel Goodere for the murder of his brother, Sir John Goodere, bt, aboard a ship in the port of

Bristol, and in *R. v. Broadfoot* (1743) upheld the legality of pressing mariners into the navy. The latter decision received favourable notice from the higher judiciary, and Foster published a report of it in 1758. In 1749 Foster was involved as recorder in the aftermath of the Bristol turnpike riots, writing to Philip Yorke, first Baron Hardwicke, elected high steward of Bristol in 1737, to explain his reluctance on legal grounds to proceed to the immediate trial of certain rioters imprisoned at Bristol and to defend the conduct of the city magistrates. Foster was involved also in the aftermath of the Bristol corn riots of 1753, corresponding with the mayor and consulting Hardwicke on behalf of the city. He was named in the special commission for the trial of the rioters, though excused from acting under it. In 1738 Foster had written to Lord Hardwicke expressing his hopes for the chief justiceship of Chester, and by 1743, aiming for higher judicial office, was taking advice on advancement from his friend Thomas Abney of the court of common pleas. A letter to Lord Hardwicke followed in November 1744, and Foster's ambitions came to fruition in his knighting on 21 April 1745 and his appointment on the following day, upon Hardwicke's recommendation, to replace Sir William Chapple in the court of king's bench.

The king's bench at this time was noted for its unanimity, and Foster generally concurred with his colleagues, though he was capable of taking a strongly independent line, as in *R. v. Midwinter and Sims* (1749) where he refused to interpret the Waltham Black Act of 1723 as denying benefit of clergy to the aider and abetter of the killing of a horse. A statute 'of so penal a nature ought to be construed literally and strictly' (M. Foster, *A report of some proceedings on the commission of oyer and terminer and gaol delivery for the trial of rebels in the year 1746 in the county of Surry, and of other crown cases*, 3rd edn, 1792, 417), a view which Foster saw 'no reason to alter' (ibid., 416) despite the opposing views of his colleagues, though William Murray, Baron Mansfield, prevented the publication of a report of the case until after Foster's death, by which time Mansfield's selective memory of the decision had assisted capital convictions in *R. v. Royce* (1767) and the *Coal-heavers' case* (1768). Foster was concerned also with the effectiveness of habeas corpus to protect those impressed into military service as the Habeas Corpus Act 1679 covered only detention on a criminal charge and the judges were said to have no power to examine the truth of returns made to the writ. Outside the provisions of the 1679 act Foster began to use habeas corpus in the vacation to release persons impressed, and convoked the king's bench judges to discuss the matter. The question was seized upon by William Pitt the elder in support of his stance as a patriot, and in 1758, in opposition to Mansfield, Pitt introduced a parliamentary bill drafted by the attorney-general, Sir Charles Pratt, to extend the scope of the 1679 act. The Commons having passed the bill the Lords asked the judges for their opinions. Foster prepared answers to the Lords' questions but avoided presenting them on the ground of his wife's recent illness and death (on 15 May 1758). The bill was

rejected, Mansfield speaking eloquently against it. Hardwicke asked the judges to draft another bill, but there was no legislation until 1816.

In 1758 Foster presided over the prosecution at the Surrey assizes of Martha Gray, a Richmond Park gatekeeper, for obstructing a common footway through the park, of which Princess Amelia was ranger. Refusing to allow the defence to rely upon technicalities, Foster summed up clearly for the prosecutors and the way was restored, giving Edward Thurlow 'great pleasure … that we have one English judge, whom nothing can tempt or frighten, ready and able to hold up the laws of his country as a great shield of the rights of the people' (Dodson, 88). In the following year Foster published *Considerations on the Statutes of 21 and 28 Hen. VIII Concerning the Residence of the Clergy* in answer to the published claims of Thomas Sherlock, bishop of London, to license non-residency. In 1762 Foster was among the commissioners of errors in the case of *Harrison v. Evans*, arising from the City of London's practice of fining dissenters who refused to stand for, or exercise, the office of sheriff, which the Corporation Act of 1661 forbade them to hold. Taking a wide view of the Toleration Act of 1688 Foster concurred in declaring the unlawfulness of the fines, a decision subsequently upheld upon writ of error in parliament. Foster's argument in the case was published in 1771 in Philip Furneaux's *Letters to the honourable Mr Justice Blackstone concerning his exposition of the Act of Toleration*, and subsequently elsewhere.

In 1762 appeared Foster's greatest work, *A report of some proceedings on the commission of oyer and terminer and [gaol] delivery for the trial of the rebels in the year 1746 in the county of Surr[e]y, and of other crown cases. To which are added discourses upon a few branches of the crown law*, which appeared in a second edition in 1776 and a third in 1792, both by Foster's nephew Michael Dodson, together with Dublin editions in 1763, 1767, and 1791. Hardwicke, who saw the work before publication, regarded it as characteristically 'full of much learning and ability' (Dodson, 43), but failed to prevent Foster publishing reports of certain cases in the House of Lords as contrary to a standing order of 1698, though at Hardwicke's request Foster suppressed his reports of two cases upon statutes of William III concerning possession of coining equipment and naval stores. Mansfield, who also saw the work before publication, read it with 'great pleasure and approbation' (Dodson, 32), but succeeded in preventing publication of Foster's report and discussion of *R. v. Midwinter and Sims*. Foster strove for accuracy in his reports, adding observations of his own to many of the cases. In the first three of his discourses, on treason, homicide, and accomplices, he aimed to elucidate principle and eradicate inconsistency and excess in the law, success in which gained his work high authority, and led Blackstone to describe him as 'a very great master of the crown law' (Blackstone, 4.2). In the fourth discourse, on kingship and succession to the throne, in answer to some of the writings of Chief Justice Hale, Foster demonstrated his whig principles, characterizing hereditary succession as simply an expedient in government. Foster's health began to decline after his wife's death, and by 1760 he was obliged to spend time in Bath. In 1763 he was rarely present in court, and died in the evening of 7 November of that year to be buried, at his direction, near his wife in the church of Stanton Drew, Somerset. His property, including houses in Pinner, Middlesex, and Bedford Row, London, was left to his three sisters for their lives and then to his nephews and nieces, with a gift of his books and manuscripts to his nephew Michael Dodson, and bequests to his friend Sir John Eardley Wilmot, and for the support of dissenting worship. A good whig, and a man of learning and integrity, to whom Lord Mansfield readily turned for advice, his reputation for justice was high: as Charles Churchill put it in his *Rosciad*, 'Each judge was true and steady to his trust, As Mansfield wise, and as old Foster just' (p. 13). And his principled concern for personal liberty led Chief Justice de Grey to describe him in 1771 as 'the magna charta of liberty of persons, as well as fortunes' (*Crosby's case*). N. G. JONES

Sources M. Dodson, *The life of Sir Michael Foster, kt* (1811) · priv. coll., Foster MSS · will, PRO, PROB 11/895/12 · A. W. B. Simpson, ed., *Biographical dictionary of the common law* (1984) · A. J. Ashworth, 'The making of English criminal law (4) Blackstone, Foster and East', *Criminal Law Review* (1978), 389–99 · E. P. Thompson, *Whigs and hunters* (1975) · J. Latimer, *The annals of Bristol in the eighteenth century* (1893) · P. Langford, *A polite and commercial people: England, 1727–1783* (1989) · H. Walpole, *Memoirs of King George II*, ed. J. Brooke, 3 (1985) · Foster, *Alum. Oxon.* · H. A. C. Sturgess, ed., *Register of admissions to the Honourable Society of the Middle Temple, from the fifteenth century to the year 1944*, 1 (1949) · Baker, *Serjeants* · W. Blackstone, *Commentaries on the laws of England*, 4 (1769) · C. Churchill, *The Rosciad*, 8th edn (1763) · *The diary of Dudley Ryder, 1715–1716*, ed. W. Matthews (1939) · W. Prest, 'Law, lawyers and rational dissent', *Enlightenment and religion: rational dissent in eighteenth-century Britain*, ed. K. Haakonssen (1998), 169–92 · W. A. Shaw, *The knights of England*, 2 (1906), 287 · memorial, Stanton Drew, Somerset

Archives priv. coll., MSS, corresp., etc. | BL, corresp. with Lord Hardwicke, MSS Hardwicke 35587, 35588, 35590, 35596–35597 · BL, Add. MSS 9828, 32703, 32719, 32732, 35586, 35592, 35635

Likenesses J. Faber junior, mezzotint, 1748 (after J. Wills), BM, NPG [*see illus.*] · attrib. T. Hudson, portrait (of Foster?; in judicial robes), Harvard U., law school · J. Neagle, line engraving (after J. Wills, 1792), BM, NPG · J. Wills, portrait (in judicial robes), repro. in J. Oldham, *The Mansfield manuscripts and the growth of English law in the eighteenth century*, 1 (1992), 52 · engraving, repro. in Dodson, *Life*

Foster, Sir Michael (1836–1907), university teacher, was born in Huntingdon on 8 March 1836, the eldest child of the three sons and seven daughters of Michael Foster (1810–1880) and his wife, Mercy Cooper. Foster was the descendant of a line of nonconformist farmers in Hertfordshire and Bedfordshire, broken by his father, who studied medicine at University College, London; he returned to Huntingdon to practise. A fervent Baptist, he was a prominent member of the small community.

Early years and education Foster was educated at the local grammar school in Huntingdon and then studied at University College, London. He graduated BA in 1854, heading the honours list in classics. He might have chosen to sit for a scholarship in classics at Cambridge, but as they did with many young dissenters of his generation the religious tests at Oxford and Cambridge precluded his attendance. His path was also typical of the secularization of the period in that he later abandoned evangelical religion for

Sir Michael Foster (1836–1907), by John Collier, 1907

agnosticism. Devoting his energies to proselytizing for science, he maintained the habits of dissenting religion without the belief.

With Cambridge barred to him Foster went on to the medical school of University College, London, where he won gold medals in anatomy and physiology, and chemistry in 1856—and attracted the attention of William Sharpey, professor of anatomy and physiology. He graduated MB (1858) and MD (1859). He had not yet taken the decision to follow a career in physiology but he joined the British Association for the Advancement of Science, and published a paper, 'The effects produced by freezing on the physiological properties of muscle', in the *Proceedings of the Royal Society of London* (1859–60). He finished his training with two years of clinical study in Paris, the traditional route for those who aspired to the upper ranks of the British medical profession.

In autumn 1860, suspecting that he had contracted tuberculosis, Foster signed on as a ship's surgeon on HMS *Union*, bound for the Red Sea to assist in the building of a lighthouse near Mount Sinai. He also hoped to be able to carry out some natural history studies but found himself limited to examination of some marine life. In the end he did not have tuberculosis, although he continued to suffer from poor health for many years, one reason for his return to Huntingdon, where he practised alongside his father until 1866. Foster married twice; both of his wives were from Huntingdon. His first marriage, on 30 April 1863 to Georgina Gregory Edmonds (1840/41–1869), daughter of

Cyrus Edmonds, brought a son, Michael George Foster (later MD, Cambridge), and a daughter, Mercy. After Georgina's death he married, on 22 August 1872, Margaret Sarah Rust, daughter of George Rust, who survived him.

In January 1867, at Sharpey's invitation, Foster moved to London as instructor in physiology and histology, rising to lecturer, then in 1869 to assistant professor, and he was appointed Fullerian professor of physiology at the Royal Institution, succeeding Thomas Henry Huxley. In this period he was one of the demonstrators in Huxley's course of elementary biology at South Kensington.

The Cambridge school of physiology At Huxley's instigation, and reportedly with the support of George Henry Lewes and George Eliot, a praelectorship in physiology was created at Trinity College, Cambridge. Foster, Huxley's choice, was appointed to the new post in May 1870. Foster was to be associated with Cambridge for the rest of his career, becoming the first university professor of physiology in 1883 until his resignation in 1903. He aimed from the beginning to establish practical courses in biology and physiology, and to ensure that all students of biology passed through his hands. Initially this was rather difficult because he had no university appointment. An honorary MA was conferred on him, but this did not grant him any official status within the university. In practice this was a large impediment since he could not sit on the board of studies and could operate only indirectly through amenable colleagues and friends. It is a tribute to Foster's tact and political skill that he was able to achieve so much from a position of such little power. Despite the fact that his appointment was only at Trinity his course was open to all university students. There is no doubt that he was a successful teacher; from 1870 to 1883 the number of students attending courses in physiology grew from 20 to 130 and in elementary biology from 45 to 80. He began teaching in a small room, and moved later to purpose-built premises in 1879 and 1891. When he became university professor in 1883 the full degree of MA was conferred on him, and from that point on he could act with authority within the university.

Foster's fame rested on his creation of the Cambridge school of physiology. His own brief research career dwelt on the problem of the heart beat. The central question was whether the heart beat was neurogenic—initiated by neural impulses—or myogenic—initiated by the cardiac muscle itself. When Foster began research in the late 1850s the neurogenic theory was dominant. His own work, which favoured a myogenic theory, was not immediately influential. None the less the heart beat problem became the core interest of the first group of researchers he gathered around him at Cambridge, many of whom later branched into other aspects of research. In addition Foster's rationale for favouring the muscle as an initiator depended, in part, on an evolutionary attitude. By analogy with other organisms, like amoebae, and the snail's heart, which were rhythmic without nervous tissue, he concluded that the mammalian heart muscle should not require differentiated nerves and ganglia. This evolutionary approach has been seen as a defining characteristic of

the Cambridge school, and an important factor in its success. Some have argued that it defined British physiology as a whole, although there are important exceptions, for example the work of Foster's Oxford colleague John Burdon Sanderson, which was not in any meaningful sense evolutionary.

Foster's students dominated the field in Britain and America. His successor in the Cambridge chair, John Newport Langley, worked on the role of the autonomic nervous system and had been one of the first generation of his students. Walter Holbrook Gaskell, who also remained at Cambridge, was noted for his studies of the heart beat; he concluded that the beat was of muscular rather than nervous origin. They formed the core of a group of researchers—the Cambridge school—which was recognized around the world. Others, like Henry Newell Martin, who became the first professor of biology at the new Johns Hopkins University in Baltimore, played an important role in spreading the influence of the school further afield. Among the most prominent later students were the Nobel prizewinners Charles Scott Sherrington and Henry H. Dale.

Social scientists have outlined three pivotal factors for the success of a research school: the personality of the leader, the research programme itself, and financial and institutional support. In large part Foster was personally responsible for the success of his research school. By all accounts he was a charismatic and inspiring leader who developed a coherent and compelling programme of research. None the less he benefited greatly from the financial and institutional support of the University of Cambridge. The university's support was effective because of the relative strength of the university, as opposed to the colleges, a result of the mid-Victorian reforms. Most importantly Foster garnered support within the university because by the 1880s Cambridge had become the destination of choice for medical students who aimed to become élite medical practitioners. Thus Foster attracted sufficient numbers of undergraduates to generate broad support within the university to finance junior positions and laboratory facilities: fundamental resources for a research school.

The maturation of British physiology Foster's importance as a teacher extended widely. He contributed the section on nerve and muscle to the *Handbook of the Physiological Laboratory*, edited by Burdon Sanderson (1873), which was a pioneering English language text for laboratory courses in physiology. It also became notorious within Britain, and was a contributing factor in the emergence of a strong antivivisectionist movement, which opposed any experimentation on live animals—the cornerstone of the new experimental physiology which had largely originated in continental Europe. With his student F. M. Balfour, Foster published *The Elements of Embryology* (1874); with the assistance of Langley he published *A Course of Elementary Practical Physiology and Histology* (1876). His *Text-Book of Physiology*, the first English language textbook of wide influence, was printed in 1877; its impact can be measured by the fact that it was translated into Russian, German, and

Italian, and remained in print through six editions, and part of a seventh. Since at the time British physiologists were struggling to establish themselves, taking as their models their continental, and particularly German, colleagues, the wide diffusion of this text is a testament to Foster's importance in the establishment of physiology as a research science in Britain.

After 1880 Foster worked mainly to organize physiology as a profession in Britain rather than as a researcher in his own right. Here he again mimicked Huxley's career trajectory. Foster was a founder of the Physiological Society; he chaired the inaugural dinner in 1876. He was the first and solo editor of the *Journal of Physiology*, which began in 1878. He remained its editor until 1894, when Langley bought it and became the editor, although Foster continued to be credited as co-editor. Foster also played a crucial role in organizing opposition to the antivivisectionist campaign which culminated in the Cruelty to Animals Act of 1876. It is no coincidence that the Physiological Society and journal were founded in the same period. An active member of the British Association, Foster rose to be secretary of its biological section (1867), deputy president of anatomy and physiology (1870), joint general secretary (1872–6), president of the physiology section (1897), and finally president of the association in 1899. Elected a fellow of the Royal Society in 1872, in 1881 he succeeded Huxley as secretary, a position he resigned in 1903. Against internal opposition he created a role for the Royal Society in confidentially advising government departments. He helped to establish the Meteorological Office and the National Physical Laboratory. Like other Victorian scientific luminaries he sat on a myriad of commissions and inquiries, including those for the prevention of malaria and tropical diseases, vaccination, the disposal of sewage, tuberculosis, and the reorganization of the University of London. On the international front he was an important organizer of the first International Congress of Physiology in Basel in 1889.

Foster owed much of his success to Sharpey and Huxley, who were more than mere patrons: his biological approach to physiology and his espousal of experimentation were drawn from their examples. Foster was one of the scientific naturalists centred around Huxley who believed that science should be the basis of reformed national institutions, and that universities should train for the professions. For physiology in particular its eventual utilitarian goal of improving medical practice was important in garnering support outside the small British research community. However, Foster himself did not display much interest in clinical medicine, and was not closely allied to medical circles.

Throughout his life Foster took great pleasure in cricket and in gardening. At University College, London, he had captained the eleven. At Cambridge he began an annual match first between students and staff, and later between teachers and assistants in the biological laboratories. Foster always captained his side, and he played until 1895. His home was located on a chalk slope of the Gog-Magog Hills about 4 miles from Cambridge. There, doing much of the physical labour himself, he created an impressive flower garden. He was a knowledgeable horticulturist who specialized in irises. He created many new hybrids and occasionally published articles in gardening and horticultural journals.

Knighthood and final years In 1899 Foster was knighted and his Oxford colleague Burdon Sanderson received a baronetcy; this recognition was celebrated at a special dinner of the Physiological Society. Foster wrote to Burdon Sanderson, 'Like you I don't care for these things—but we may both congratulate each other that our common science has received such marked recognition & it is above all things nice that *we should be* run in together.' Their honours symbolized the public triumph of experimentalism over the antivivisectionists, since Queen Victoria herself was widely believed to be an antivivisectionist. As Foster commented, 'Either common rumour as to the "old lady's" prejudices is wrong or she must have screwed up her face when she accepted Salisbury's two suggestions' (4 June [1899], John Burdon Sanderson Collection, MS ADD 179/7, fols. 224–5, UCL).

In 1900 Foster was elected MP for the University of London, and a deputy took over the duties of his Cambridge professorship, which he resigned three years later. In politics he was a Liberal, but at the introduction of Gladstone's Home Rule Bill, he joined the Liberal Unionists and supported the Conservative government. In parliament he sat initially on the government (Conservative) side of the house; unable, however, to support the government on several occasions, notably for their Education Bill of 1902, he crossed the floor of the house and joined the Liberal opposition. In 1906 he stood for election as a Liberal in the general election and was defeated by twenty-four votes. On 28 January 1907 Foster gave a lively speech in London at the meeting of the British Science Guild. He became ill that evening and died on 29 January near Fitzroy Square on the way to University College Hospital, from pneumothorax caused by the bursting of an ulcer. He was buried in the cemetery at Huntingdon; a service in his memory took place in the chapel of Trinity College, Cambridge.

TERRIE M. ROMANO

Sources G. L. Geison, 'Foster, Michael', *DSB* · G. L. Geison, *Michael Foster and the Cambridge school of physiology: the scientific enterprise in late Victorian society* (1978) · T. M. Romano, *Making medicine scientific: John Burdon Sanderson and the culture of Victorian science* (2002) · R. D. French, *Antivivisection and medical science in Victorian society* (1975) · T. M. Romano, 'Gentlemanly versus scientific ideals: John Burdon Sanderson, medical education, and the failure of the Oxford school of physiology', *Bulletin of the History of Medicine*, 71 (1997), 224–48 · *DNB* · F. M. Turner, *Between science and religion: the reaction to scientific naturalism in late Victorian England* (1974) · F. L. Holmes and G. L. Geison, eds., 'Research schools: historical reappraisals', *Osiris*, 2nd ser., 8 (1993) · R. D. French, 'Darwin and the physiologist, or, The Medusa and modern cardiology', *Journal of the History of Biology*, 3 (1970), 253–74 · K. E. Rothschuh, *History of physiology* (1973) · W. J. O'Connor, *Founders of British physiology: a biographical dictionary, 1820–1885* (1988) · *CGPLA Eng. & Wales* (1907) · d. cert. · m. cert. [Georgina Edmonds] · m. cert. [Margaret Rust]

Archives NL Scot., letters · priv. coll., letters · RS, letters · Wellcome L., lecture notes | CUL, corresp. with Lord Kelvin; corresp. with Sir George Stokes, etc. · ICL, Imperial College archives, corresp. with Thomas Huxley · King's AC Cam., letters to Oscar

Browning · Oxf. U. Mus. NH, letters and cards to Sir E. B. Poulton · RBG Kew, J. D. Hooker papers, letters · RBG Kew, W. T. Thistleton-Dyer papers, letters · UCL, John Burdon Sanderson papers, letters · W. Sussex RO, letters to A. B. Kempe · Wellcome L., corresp. with Lister Institute; letters to E. A. Sharpey-Schafer **Likenesses** H. von Herkomer, oils, 1892, Trinity Cam. · photograph, 1900, repro. in Geison, *Michael Foster and the Cambridge school* · J. Collier, oils, 1907, NPG [*see illus.*] · J. Collier, oils, second version, RS · J. Collier, portrait, priv. coll. · B. Stone, three photographs, NPG · photograph, repro. in Rothschuh, *History of physiology* · sketch, repro. in French, *Antivivisection* · three photographs, NPG **Wealth at death** £4294 7*s.* 11*d.*: probate, 23 March 1907, *CGPLA Eng. & Wales*

Foster, Peter Le Neve (1809–1879), barrister and secretary of the Society of Arts, was born on 17 August 1809 at the White House, Lenwade, Norfolk, the only son (there were also two daughters) of Peter Le Neve-Foster (1780–1829), lessee of Lenwade corn mill and a local landowner, and his wife, Grace Rebecca Osorio (*d.* 1835). The Le Neve and Foster families were both of considerable antiquity in the area; Foster's father chose to hyphenate the names though this usage was not formalized. As a young man he had travelled and lived in Portugal and France, and his wife, whom he married in Aldeburgh in 1807, was of Iberian-Jewish stock. Foster was educated at Norwich grammar school, admitted pensioner at St John's College, Cambridge, in 1826, migrated to Trinity Hall the following year, graduated BA in the mathematical tripos in 1830, and was later elected a fellow of his college. In 1836 he was called to the bar in Middle Temple and for about fifteen years he practised as a conveyancer. He married in 1837, at Gorleston, Suffolk, Georgiana Elizabeth (*bap.* 1817, *d.* 1885), the third of the five daughters of the Revd Clement Chevallier, of Great Yarmouth. They raised two daughters and eight sons, of whom six, including Sir Clement Le Neve *Foster, went into the engineering professions, one became a senior civil servant, and another a chemist.

Foster was elected in 1837 into the Society of Arts, where earlier generations of Fosters and Osorios had been active. He served as treasurer in 1850–51, and in 1853 succeeded George Grove in the prestigious and full-time position as secretary, a post he held until his death. Foster was involved, with Sir Henry Cole and Sir Charles Wentworth Dilke, with the organization of the Great Exhibition of 1851 and that of 1862, also with several of the contemporary foreign exhibitions. An enthusiastic pioneer of photography, Foster organized a series of touring exhibitions of photographs from the society's collection; he was one of the founders in 1853 of the Photographic Society, and contributed to its *Journal*. He served a term as president of the Quekett Microscopical Society. He was for a time on the council of the British Association, and for thirteen years secretary of its mechanical science section. A prolific contributor to scientific and technical journals, much of his writing in the *Journal of the Society of Arts* was anonymous; his addresses 'Aluminium' in 1859 and 'On Bonelli's electric loom' in 1860 were notable for their foresight.

Unlike his contemporaries in the field, Foster, a modest man, did not receive the honours he might have expected, though he was a knight of the Tunisian order of Iftikar and a member of the Italian order of the redemption. Under the terms of his father's will, Foster inherited the White House and an obligation to pay legacies to his sisters, but even though he sold the property after his mother died, the money was insufficient to meet the payments. He was burdened throughout his life, and after his own death his widow, who had been a Latin and French scholar, undertook translation work in order to continue paying the legacies. In 1878 an appeal was launched for a testimonial to mark his twenty-five years as secretary to the Society of Arts, but before it could be delivered, Foster suffered an unexpected heart attack and died at his house at East Hill, Wandsworth, London, on 20 February 1879.

H. T. WOOD, *rev.* ANITA MCCONNELL

Sources P. Le Neve-Foster, *The Le Neves of Norfolk: a family history* (privately printed, Sudbury, 1969) · *Journal of the Society of Arts*, 27 (1878–9), 316–17 · A. Stirling, 'Peter Le Neve Foster and photography', *RSA Journal*, 142 (Nov 1994), 67–70 · *Nature*, 19 (1878–9), 385–6 · *Engineering* (28 Feb 1879), 178 · *The Engineer*, 47 (1879), 160 · Venn, *Alum. Cant.* · H. W. Saunders, *A history of the Norwich grammar school* (1932), 331 · Boase, *Mod. Eng. biog.* · *ILN* (8 March 1879), 224–5 · *CGPLA Eng. & Wales* (1879) **Archives** Norfolk RO, papers | BL, corresp. with Charles Babbage, Add. MSS 37195–37199 · UCL, corresp. with E. Chadwick **Likenesses** photograph, repro. in Stirling, 'Peter Le Neve Foster and photography' · portrait, repro. in *ILN* **Wealth at death** under £600: probate, 25 March 1879, *CGPLA Eng. & Wales*

Foster, Sir Robert (1589–1663), barrister and judge, was the youngest son of Sir Thomas *Foster (1548–1612) of Hunsdon, Hertfordshire, a judge of the common pleas under James I, and his wife, Susan, *née* Foster (*c.*1552–1626), of Iden, Sussex. Following his father's profession, Foster entered the Inner Temple on 5 November 1604 and received his call to the bar on 27 January 1611. He married Elizabeth Harvey and in 1625 he, his wife, and their son Thomas leased the manor of Fosters (or Forsters) in Sussex from the Pelham family. On 23 November 1629 he became a bencher of the Inner Temple and on 7 May 1631 was chosen autumn reader. In January 1637 Charles I created him serjeant-at-law and in 1639 his name first appeared in connection with the house called Great Fosters at Egham, Surrey.

During this period it was alleged that Foster defended such unpopular royal policies as the billeting of troops and ship money. Charles I knighted him on 27 January 1640 and raised him to the bench of the common pleas in place of Sir George Vernon. During 1640–42 he rode the northern and western circuits, including a tumultuous summer circuit in the west in 1642, during which he encountered both advanced military preparations and growing protests against the king's commission of array. Although petitions urged him to declare against the king's commission he maintained judicial neutrality. Later that year he joined the king at Oxford where he attempted unsuccessfully to hold a court of common pleas.

On 31 January 1643 Foster received the degree of DCL from the University of Oxford. Although the *Dictionary of National Biography* described him as an 'ardent royalist', in

1643 the Commons petitioned for his continuance in office suggesting that he took his judicial neutrality very seriously. However, in 1644 he was one of the royalist judges who tried and condemned Captain Turpin. While, unlike Serjeant Glanvill, Foster was not impeached on a charge of high treason for this action, the Long Parliament in 1645 removed him from office and disabled him as though he were dead for his adherence to the king. At the close of hostilities he compounded for his delinquency, paying a substantial fine.

In the decade after the execution of Charles I on 30 January 1649 Foster lived in semi-retirement, practising only within the Inner Temple as a chamber counsel and conveyancer. On 14 October 1656 the lord protector in council granted him licence to travel to London on private business. At the Restoration he was restored to the common pleas on 31 May 1660 and displayed considerable zeal at the trials of the regicides in mid-October 1660. Upon the conclusion of these twenty-nine trials Charles II raised Foster to the position of chief justice of the king's bench on 21 October 1660. In the years 1660–63 he resumed his activities on the western circuit as assize judge. During this period he presided at the trials of Fifth Monarchists and of the Quakers Crook, Gray, and Bolton. His reputation suffered somewhat when he urged Charles II to execute Sir Henry Vane against the petitions of both houses of parliament and the king's own promise of the younger Vane's life. At Vane's trial in 1662 Foster admonished the accused for his unrepentant carriage citing it as a pretext for denying him mercy. Foster died on 4 October 1663 and was buried at Egham, Surrey, under a tomb bearing a bust in his judicial robes. He appears to have died a wealthy man, bequeathing to his two daughters marriage portions of £1000 each. His son Thomas (d. 1685) was later knighted and inherited the house of Great Fosters.   D. A. ORR

Sources DNB · Foss, *Judges*, 7.97–9 · Baker, *Serjeants*, 186, 512 · Foster, *Alum. Oxon.* · F. A. Inderwick and R. A. Roberts, eds., *A calendar of the Inner Temple records*, 2 (1898) · W. R. Prest, *The rise of the barristers: a social history of the English bar, 1590–1640* (1986), 362 · J. S. Cockburn, *A history of English assizes, 1558–1714* (1972), 240, 272–4 · *VCH Surrey*, 3.425 · *VCH Sussex*, 9.196–7 · H. Nenner, 'The trial of the regicides: retribution and treason in 1660', *Politics and the political imagination in later Stuart Britain*, ed. H. Nenner (1997), 21–42 · V. A. Rowe, *Sir Henry Vane the younger: a study in political and administrative history* (1970), 240–41 · H. H. L. Bellot, *The Inner and Middle Temple* (1902), 141
Likenesses marble bust, St John the Baptist church, Egham, Surrey

Foster, Robert (1754–1827), naval officer and benefactor, was born on 24 April 1754 in Lancaster, the eldest of the four children of Dodshon Foster (1730–1792), merchant, and his wife, Elizabeth, *née* Birket (1729–1766). He attended John Jenkinson's school at Yealand Conyers and the free school at Sedbergh, Yorkshire. Aged about eighteen, he went to sea before being appointed a storekeeper on the West Indian island of Antigua. This experience enabled him to give evidence, at William Wilberforce's request, before a select committee of the House of Commons on the slave trade in 1791. At the start of the American War of Independence Foster, despite his Quaker upbringing, joined the brig *Endeavour*, which was fitted out in Antigua to cruise against rebel American privateers. The news of his involvement in the British war effort dismayed Foster's friends and family in England. In 1778 he left the *Endeavour* and was later master's mate in the *Jupiter*. Following the death of her master Foster assumed the post, and in the following year he was appointed acting lieutenant in the *Pelican*. Later in 1779 Foster obtained leave to visit his father at Lancaster where, to the consternation of Friends, he went to Quaker meeting in his naval uniform. At that time he withstood all remonstrances, but soon after, at his maternal grandfather's request, he quit the navy. Foster became a man of peace and from then on avoided discussing his naval career. He seems to have given sufficient reassurances to local Friends and, contrary to the Quaker testimony against war, was never disowned for his violation of their principles.

On leaving the navy Foster was appointed by his grandfather Myles Birket as a manager of his estate at Hebblethwaite Hall, near Sedbergh. On 1 March 1784 he married Mary Burton (1753–1799) at Brigflatts; the couple had nine children. In the next year Foster inherited the Hebblethwaite Hall estate, as well as property near Lancaster, following his grandfather's death. He now erected a woollen mill at Hebblethwaite in which the local poor were employed in the manufacture of stockings for men in the Greenland fishery. Foster sold the merchandise himself and, new to the trade, agreed prices suggested by his customers. In addition to the mill Foster also established a school for the education of poor children and himself served in the role of physician, lawyer, and judge among his country neighbours. In 1796 he greatly enlarged his business interests at Hebblethwaite, expanding the range of cloth produced and building a second mill.

After the death of his wife Foster married (on 25 February 1802, again at Brigflatts) Margaret Burton, *née* Walker (1756–1835), widow of John Burton, his first wife's brother. The couple had no children. About 1805 Foster was visited at Hebblethwaite by William Wordsworth, who introduced him to the poet Richard Southey. Much taken with Foster, Southey wrote of 'a man worth seeing; he looked like a first assassin in *Macbeth* as to his costume' (possibly a reference to Foster's preference for wearing 'self-grey' homespun woollens). He was, Southey concluded, 'a rare man' (*Life and Correspondence of Robert Southey*, 29–30). Of dark complexion, his small and regular features and bushy eyebrows gave him a severe appearance, though his voice was pleasant and his discourse earnest, learned, and genial.

In 1812 Foster sold his estates and, with his wife and a daughter from his first marriage, he moved to Newcastle upon Tyne (near to many of his now married children), where he took a house in Northumberland Street and served as a diligent director of the Newcastle Savings Bank. From this date he frequently attended the Quaker yearly meeting in London. In 1824 he suffered a slight attack of paralysis from which he never fully recovered. His final illness was prolonged and gave great suffering.

An unorthodox yet sincere and benevolent Quaker, Foster died at Newcastle on 15 June 1827 and was buried on 20 June in the Quaker burial-ground in the town's Pilgrim Street. A memoir, written by R. Spence Watson, appeared in a study of Quakers of the north-east in 1899.

BENJAMIN S. BECK

Sources M. B. Foster, 'Robert Foster', in J. Foster, *The Fosters of Cold Hesledon* (1862), 79–83, appx · R. Spence Watson, 'Robert Foster, 1754–1827', in J. W. Steel and others, *A historical sketch of the Society of Friends … in Newcastle and Gateshead, 1653–1898* (1899), 110–17 · A. Sedgwick, *Supplement to the memorial of the trustees of Cowgill Chapel* (1870) · J. Foster, ed., *Pedigrees of the county families of England*, 1: *Lancashire* (1873) · *The life and correspondence of Robert Southey*, ed. C. C. Southey, 6 vols. (1849–50) · lieutenant's logbooks, NMM, ADM L/P/60, ADM L/J/144, ADM L/H/113 · U. Durham L., archives and special collections, Durham probate records, Robert Foster 1827 · death duty registers, PRO, IR 26 and IR 27 · Society of Friends' birth, marriage, and death registers, PRO, RG 6 · M. Hartley and J. Ingilby, 'The romance of Hebblethwaite Hall', *The old hand-knitters of the dales* (1951), 84–92 · private information (2004)
Likenesses silhouette, priv. coll.
Wealth at death under £4000: Durham probate records, Robert Foster 1827, U. Durham L.; PRO, death duty registers, IR 26 and IR 27

Foster, Samuel (*b.* in or before **1600**, *d.* **1652**), mathematician, was born in Northamptonshire. His parents' names are not known but he had an elder brother, Walter *Foster, who was also a mathematician. He was educated in Coventry before entering Emmanuel College, Cambridge, on 23 April 1616 as a sizar. He gained his BA in 1619 and his MA in 1623, after which he became usher at the grammar school in Coventry. At the same time he developed an interest in observational astronomy. On the death of Henry Gellibrand, professor of astronomy at Gresham College, London, Foster was elected to the post on 2 March 1636. He resigned eight months later on 25 November, probably for religious reasons—he was a strict nonconformist and Ward claims that he refused to kneel for communion (Ward, 1.86). His successor, Mungo Murray, vacated the professorship on his marriage in 1641 and Foster was re-elected on 26 May of that year.

During the civil war and Commonwealth Foster's rooms became the meeting place for many of London's scholars. Royalists and parliamentarians alike joined together to discuss issues of mathematics and natural philosophy, in particular the new mechanical philosophy. It was from this group that the Royal Society eventually arose.

Foster devoted much of his time to making astronomical observations, concentrating especially on solar and lunar eclipses. He also designed and modified instruments (including those of one of his predecessors, Edmund Gunter), mainly for the use of artisans and seamen, and taught the use of these instruments during his lectures. He was renowned for his expertise in dialling and the construction of sundials. Owing to almost continuous ill health he published little during his lifetime but left many manuscript treatises. He died at Gresham College in May (not in July, as Ward has it) 1652, and was buried in the church of St Peter-le-Poer in Broad Street.

According to the contemporary scholar Dr John Twysden, Foster was 'a learned, industrious and most skilful mathematician' (*Miscellanies*, preface). His works reflected the important contribution which he made to the development of mathematical instruments in the seventeenth century. The two works published in his lifetime, *The Use of the Quadrant* (1624) and *The Art of Dialling* (1638), demonstrated his ability to facilitate the work of practical mathematicians by providing relatively easy instrumental methods to avoid long calculations. This was also evident in most of the manuscripts which were published posthumously by John Twysden and Edmund Wingate and which are either concerned with describing instruments or giving instruction in dialling. It was only in the *Miscellanies, or, Mathematical Lucubrations of Mr Samuel Foster* (edited by Twysden and published in 1659) that others of his interests were represented. This collection contains several astronomical tracts and editions of Aristarchus of Samos's writings on the sun and moon and of the lemmata of Archimedes, as well as further texts on the use of instruments.

H. K. HIGTON

Sources E. G. R. Taylor, *The mathematical practitioners of Tudor and Stuart England* (1954) · I. R. Adamson, 'The foundation and early history of Gresham College, London, 1596–1704', PhD diss., U. Cam., 1976 · J. Ward, *The lives of the professors of Gresham College* (1740) · Venn, *Alum. Cant.* · *Miscellanies, or, Mathematical lucubrations of Mr Samuel Foster*, ed. J. Twysden (1659) · J. Aubrey, *Brief lives: a modern English version*, ed. R. Barber (1982)
Archives Bodl. Oxf., papers

Foster, Sir Thomas (1548–1612), judge, was born at Hunsdon, Hertfordshire, on 10 August 1548, the son of Thomas Foster (*d.* 1571?), possibly a yeoman in the queen's household, of Hunsdon, and his wife, Margaret Browning (*d.* 1585x99). Foster was admitted to the Inner Temple from Clifford's Inn on 16 October 1571, but the date of his call to the bar is uncertain; it probably occurred after his marriage on 22 July 1575 to Susan (*c.*1552–1626), daughter of another Thomas Foster, of Iden, Sussex, and certainly before he delivered a reading at Clifford's Inn in 1584. He enjoyed a thriving practice in Westminster Hall, and from 1593 Foster was retained as fee'd counsel by the city of London, where he also worked with the Company of Skinners, while serving in his native county as steward of the manor of Amwell Parva or Rusheyne. Called to the bench in January 1595, Foster delivered his reading on 32 Hen. VIII c. 32 in August 1596. In January 1600 he was among fourteen Inner Temple benchers levied for the Irish campaign, although he paid only the minimum contribution of £10.

Foster was one of those nominated as serjeants-at-law towards the end of 1601 but not actually called until May 1603, after James I's accession, when he named Robert Cecil, Lord Howard of Walden, and Lord Hunsdon as patrons. Appointed serjeant to Queen Anne in 1603, and to Prince Henry in 1604, when he was also knighted, Foster was mentioned as a possible attorney of wards in October 1605. But not until November 1607 did he gain further promotion, as puisne justice of common pleas. Foster died in London on 18 May 1612, shortly after his nomination by Thomas Sutton as one of the original governors of the

Charterhouse School, and was buried on 11 June in Hunsdon church under an elaborate tomb with full-length effigy. A manuscript treatise in Cambridge University Library (Add. MS 8945, fols. 1–27v), 'A brief declaration of the use of the law by Justice Foster', is substantially identical to the text published in 1629 as the second part of *The Lawyer's Light*, where it is attributed to John Dodderidge, although Francis Bacon has also been identified as author.

Thomas Foster's religion is unknown, but his widow was presented as a recusant before the Hertfordshire quarter sessions in the early 1620s. His youngest son, the royalist Sir Robert *Foster (1589–1663), served as a judge under both Charles I and Charles II.   WILFRID PREST

Sources W. R. Prest, *The rise of the barristers: a social history of the English bar, 1590–1640* (1986) · Foss, *Judges*, vol. 6 · Baker, *Serjeants* · R. L. Lloyd, ed., 'Admissions to the Inner Temple to 1659', typescript, 1954, Inner Temple Library, London · F. A. Inderwick and R. A. Roberts, eds., *A calendar of the Inner Temple records*, 1 (1896); 2 (1898) · *The letters of John Chamberlain*, ed. N. E. McClure, 2 vols. (1939) · J. Lambert, *Records of the Skinners of London* (1934) · *VCH Hertfordshire*, vol. 3 · H. Chauncy, *The historical antiquities of Hertfordshire*, 1 (1826); repr. (1975), vol. 1 · H. C. Gibbs, *The parish registers of Hunsdon, co. Hertford, 1546–1837* (1915) · E. Lodge, *Illustrations of British history, biography, and manners*, 2nd edn, 3 (1838), 66 · PRO, LR6/154/9; SC6/Jas. I/1646, fol. 17; SC6/Jas. I/1648 [Queen's and prince's serjeantcies] · administration of will, 26 May 1612, PRO, PROB 6/8, fol. 61r · *Calendar of the manuscripts of the most hon. the marquess of Salisbury*, 19, HMC, 9 (1965), 347 · W. B. Bannerman, ed., *The visitations of the county of Surrey … 1530 … 1572 … 1623*, Harleian Society, 43 (1899), 183

Archives BL, Add. MS 38139, fol. 104v

Likenesses effigy, Hunsdon church, Hertfordshire · portrait, Kirtlington Park, Oxfordshire

Foster, Thomas (1796/7–1826), painter, was born in Dublin. He became a pupil in the Dublin Society Schools in 1811. In 1815 he was awarded a premium of £34 2s. 6d. for entering two portraits and a subject picture to the Hibernian Society of Artists, and *The Adoration of the Shepherds* to the Hawkins Street exhibition. In 1818 he went to London and was admitted as a student of the Royal Academy Schools in March, at the age of twenty-one. Foster was a frequent visitor at the studio of Joseph Nollekens, the sculptor, where he used to model from antique heads. He was befriended by John Wilson Croker, for whom he painted numerous portraits of his family. He was also friendly with Sir Thomas Lawrence, several of whose portraits he copied for Croker. His portraits of H. R. Bishop, the musician, which were later engraved, and of Colonel Phillips (who was with Captain Cook at the time of his death) showed rapid advancement in Foster's technique. He was a regular exhibitor at the Royal Academy where he showed *Mazeppa* in 1822, and also at the British Institution until about 1825. He was one of the initial associates of the Royal Hibernian Academy but died just before its first exhibition. Foster was considered by his friends to be a painter of great potential; he was good-looking, well connected, full of energy and enthusiasm, and popular in society. However, according to the painter James Northcote all these qualities would have prevented him from becoming a great artist. His socializing occupied much of his time not spent in the studio. Foster sat for one of the murderers in Northcote's *Burial of the Princes in the Tower*. Croker had given Foster a commission to paint the scene at Carlton House when Louis XVIII received the Order of the Garter, and for this ambitious subject he made numerous studies. In March 1826 he committed suicide by shooting himself at a hotel in Piccadilly, London. He left a letter stating that his friends had deserted him, and that he was tired of life. It is uncertain whether his suicide was due to problems relating to the picture, or to a hopeless attachment to a young lady whose portrait he was painting.

L. H. CUST, *rev.* L. R. HOULISTON

Sources W. G. Strickland, *A dictionary of Irish artists*, 2 vols. (1913) · M. Arnold, *Library of the Fine Arts*, 2 (1831), 217–19 · E. Fletcher, ed., *Conversations of James Northcote RA with James Ward* (1901) · W. Hazlitt, *Conversations of James Northcote* (1830) · Redgrave, *Artists* · B. Stewart and M. Cutten, *The dictionary of portrait painters in Britain up to 1920* (1997) · Bryan, *Painters* · Graves, *RA exhibitors* · S. C. Hutchison, 'The Royal Academy Schools, 1768–1830', *Walpole Society*, 38 (1960–62), 123–91, esp. 171 · A. Le Harivel, ed., *National Gallery of Ireland: illustrated summary catalogue of prints and sculpture* (1988) · A. M. Stewart, ed., *Irish art loan exhibitions, 1765–1927*, 1 (1990) · Graves, *Artists* · A. M. Stewart and C. de Courcy, eds., *Royal Hibernian Academy of Arts: index of exhibitors and their works, 1826–1979*, 1 (1985)

Likenesses S. W. Reynolds, engraving (after watercolour drawing) · drawing, AM Oxf. · watercolour drawing, BM; repro. in Strickland, *Dictionary of Irish artists*, pl. xxv

Foster, Thomas Campbell (1813–1882), legal writer, son of John Foster of Leeds, editor of the *Leeds Patriot*, was born in Knaresborough, Yorkshire, on 6 October 1813. Beginning in journalism as sub-editor of the *Liverpool Standard* and then a parliamentary reporter for *The Times*, he was sent to Ireland during the famine as *The Times's* 'Irish Commissioner'. His trenchant articles, later expanded for separate publication, stirred up a vigorous controversy with Daniel O'Connell.

Turning to the law, Foster was admitted to the Middle Temple on 23 April 1840, called to the bar in 1846, and went on the northern and afterwards the midland, then the north-eastern circuit. He stood as a Liberal-Conservative for Sheffield in 1867, but was unsuccessful.

Red-haired, and becoming stout in middle age, Foster was a florid advocate and built a large criminal practice in Yorkshire. With N. A. Finlason he produced *Reports of Cases Decided at Nisi prius etc* (1858–67). He also wrote two books on legal subjects and a shorthand manual. In 1868 Foster was appointed revising barrister for the West Riding boroughs, resigning in 1875, on being made queen's counsel and bencher of his inn. He was recorder of Warwick from 1874. He was leading counsel for the crown at the trial of the murderer Charles Peace at Leeds in 1879. After a considerable period of bad health, he died at his home, 30 Orsett Terrace, Hyde Park, on 1 July 1882, leaving a widow, Isabella. He bequeathed a prize of 10 guineas for achievements in the bar examinations.

FRANCIS WATT, *rev.* PATRICK POLDEN

Sources *The Times* (3 July 1882) · *Law Times* (15 July 1882), 205 · *Solicitors' Journal*, 26 (1881–2), 568 · *Law Journal* (8 July 1882), 370 · Boase, *Mod. Eng. biog.* · [S. Morison and others], *The history of The Times*, 2 (1939), 9 · H. A. C. Sturgess, ed., *Register of admissions to the Honourable Society of the Middle Temple, from the fifteenth century to the year*

1944, 2 (1949) • J. H. B. Browne, *Forty years at the bar* (1916) • *CGPLA Eng. & Wales* (1882)
Wealth at death £18,248 10s. 4d.: probate, 15 Aug 1882, *CGPLA Eng. & Wales*

Foster, Vere Henry Louis (1819–1900), philanthropist and educationist, was born in Copenhagen on 26 April 1819, the third son of Sir Augustus John *Foster, first baronet (1780–1848), then British minister to Denmark, and his wife, Albinia Jane (d. 1867), daughter of George Vere Hobart. In 1824 his father became minister to Sardinia, and Vere was educated at Turin, Eton College (1830–34), and Christ Church, Oxford (1838–40), which he left without taking a degree. In 1842 he joined the diplomatic service, serving as attaché at Rio de Janeiro (1842–3) and at Montevideo (1845–7), where he met Giuseppe Garibaldi, then commanding the Uruguayan naval flotilla.

In late 1847 Foster visited the family's Irish estates in co. Louth, and with his eldest brother Frederick began a programme of famine relief and assisted emigration. After his father's death in 1848, and in the wake of a religious crisis that inclined him towards scepticism, he chose to devote himself to improving the conditions of the Irish poor. Following a period as an agricultural student at the Glasnevin model farm near Dublin, he began a campaign to promote emigration to America. Foster travelled to New York on the emigrant ship *Washington* in late 1850, and exposed the abuses on board and the exploitation of emigrants on landing in a letter later presented by his cousin Lord Hobart to the select committee on the Passengers' Acts in 1851. He made a number of extensive tours on foot of the United States, and published the pamphlet *Work and Wages* (1852), which appeared in many subsequent editions, encouraging Irish emigrants to travel to the interior and providing practical information on employment and transport. Convinced that the emigration of young single women was a priority, he established the Irish Female Emigration Fund in 1852 and later the Irish Pioneer Emigration Fund. After clerical criticism that some of his female emigrants had been 'abandoned' on arrival at New York, in 1857 Foster joined the Women's Protective Emigrant Society (established by Elizabeth Phelps, Eliza W. Farnham, and Horace Greeley to assist recent immigrants to find work inland) as an unpaid travelling agent. He was assiduous in persuading local charitable bodies in America to assist in the settlement of Irish immigrants.

As Irish emigration declined in the later 1850s Foster turned his attention to education. In 1858–9 he proposed a new mode of funding for the national school system, combining voluntary contributions and a local rate with government grants. Finding the commissioners of national education unenthusiastic, and the Catholic clergy hostile to 'vesting' in the national board the schools under clerical management, he undertook to improve the infrastructure of education by means of private subscription. Between 1859 and 1864 some 1400 schools were supplied with wooden floors as a result of his efforts, and considerable improvements were made in the housing of teachers.

He designed and organized the printing of a series of writing and drawing copybooks, which were the mainstay of Irish education for half a century. Profits from the sales of these books were channelled back into educational charities. Always concerned at the low status and insecurity of Irish teachers, Foster became their spokesman in 1867, contributed regularly to the fledgeling *Irish Teachers Journal*, and presided at the conferences of the Irish National Teachers Association from its foundation in 1868 until 1872.

With the commencement of the land war in 1879 Foster revived his emigration campaign. Although not hostile towards land transfer to the farmers, he opposed 'confiscation' by government intervention and rejected Gladstone's 1881 Land Act as 'robbery'. He believed that emigration, although no panacea, could alone provide immediate practical relief for the distressed west of Ireland. Finding his emigration fund swamped by applicants, Foster was forced to restrict aid to women aged between eighteen and thirty, who were selected in the localities by teachers and the clergy and given shipping vouchers of £2 each to cover the ocean voyage, along with other assistance. Some 18,000 were thus aided in 1880–83, with more following in 1886–9.

Foster had always used his personal resources as the foundation of his charitable activities, and spent up to £50,000 on emigration alone between 1849 and 1889. He lived frugally in Belfast from 1867, and left only £75 at his death, on 21 December 1900, at his home, 75 Great Victoria Street. He was buried in the city cemetery, Belfast. A Liberal in politics, he believed fervently that the landowning class in Ireland had a moral duty to improve the lives of the peasantry. He opposed the Home Rule Bill of 1886 as likely to lead to civil war, but favoured provincial parliaments in Ireland and regional parliaments in Scotland, England, and Wales. His last years were spent editing the correspondence of his great-grandfather Frederick Hervey, fourth earl of Bristol and bishop of Derry (1730–1803), and his grandmother Lady Elizabeth Foster, later duchess of Devonshire (1759–1824). He published a selection of these letters under the title *The Two Duchesses* (1898). PETER GRAY

Sources M. McNeill, *Vere Foster, 1819–1900: an Irish benefactor* (1971) • Boase, *Mod. Eng. biog.* • *The Times* (22 Dec 1900), 9
Archives priv. coll., MSS • PRO NIre., corresp. and papers | Merseyside RO, Liverpool, letters to Henry Body
Likenesses Kilpatrick, photograph, c.1890, NPG • photograph, repro. in McNeill, *Vere Foster, 1819–1900* • photograph, Royal Victoria Hospital, Belfast • photogravure, NPG
Wealth at death £75 10s. od. in England: Irish administration sealed in England, 16 March 1901, *CGPLA Eng. & Wales*

Foster, Walter (d. 1667), Church of England clergyman, was born in Northampton of unknown parentage, the elder brother of Samuel *Foster (d. 1652), mathematician and professor of astronomy at Gresham College. He was admitted to Emmanuel College, Cambridge, on 24 May 1614 as a scholar, graduated BA in 1618, and proceeded MA in 1621. He remained in Cambridge as a fellow of Emmanuel from 1622 to 1632, proceeding BD in 1628, the year in which he was ordained priest. Samuel Ward, writing in response to Bishop James Ussher's letter of 10 December 1630 seeking someone to make a transcript of the epistle of Ignatius in Caius College Library, reported that Foster 'is a good scholar and an honest man' (Parr, 438). He was keen to find some paid writing as he suffered from a speech impediment, and had earlier been interested in this document, but was then about to leave Cambridge and the work could not be lent out.

The problem with his speech did not prevent Foster's becoming, in 1633, rector of Aller, in Somerset, a living in the gift of Emmanuel College, where, on 8 September 1635, he married Rachel Northover. He was ejected in 1646 by the parliamentary authorities (and according to one account briefly imprisoned) but remained in the parish after his deprivation, serving as parish clerk, and as parish register (essentially the same position) from 1654, in which post he was replaced the following year, 'having absented himself' (Som., ARS, D/P/All.2/1/2). During this period he spent some time in Dorset, where he had friends and Foster relatives; he was in Sherborne in 1652 when he inherited £80 from his brother Samuel, together with Samuel's library in Gresham College. Indeed, he seems to have settled in Sherborne, where 'he was mayntained there in his private retired life by what hee had in portion with his wife' (Walker rev., 313).

Foster successfully petitioned for restoration to his living in 1660. He had been unable to do anything with Samuel's papers and had passed them to John Twysden who issued them in 1659 as *Miscellanies, or, Mathematical Lucubrations of Mr Samuel Foster*, commenting in the preface that they

> were communicated to me, by that learned Divine Mr Walter Foster, B in Divinity, skilful also in these studies; to whom of right it belonged to have raised up their seed to his deceased Brother, had not his infirm health, and domestic affaires held him in the country.

Nothing is known of Walter Foster's accomplishments in mathematics; he did not publish anything other than a verse contributed to Ralph Winterton's *Aphorisms of Hippocrates* in 1633.

Foster died at Aller in 1667. In his will, made on 31 August and proved on 6 December, he expressed the hope

> to dye as I have lived in the true doctrine of the Gospell of Christ as it is professed and maintayned in the Church of England in opposition to all Popish corruptions and fanaticall enormities so rife now amongst us (PRO, PROB 11/325, fol. 168)

and to be buried in the east end of the churchyard. His wife having predeceased him he left the majority of his estate to his widowed sisters Martha Bayes of Coventry and Elizabeth Poynter of Northampton.

ANITA McCONNELL

Sources VCH Somerset, 3.69–70 · F. W. Weaver, ed., *Somerset incumbents* (privately printed, Bristol, 1889) · E. H. Bates Harbin and M. C. B. Hawes, eds., *Quarter sessions records for the county of Somerset*, Somerset RS, 23–4, 28, and 34 (1907–19), 3.208 · R. Parr, ed., *The life of the most reverend father in God, James Usher … with a collection of three hundred letters* (1686), 438 · *Miscellanies, or, Mathematical lucubrations of Mr Samuel Foster*, ed. J. Twysden (1659), preface · parish register of Aller, Som. ARS · will, PRO, PROB 11/325, sig. 68, fols. 409r–409v · *Walker rev.*, 313

Foster, William (*b.* 1591), Church of England clergyman and writer, was born in November 1591, son of William Foster of London, barber–surgeon. After studying for two years at Merchant Taylors' School he matriculated from St John's College, Oxford, on 8 December 1609, before graduating in 1613 and proceeding MA in 1617. In 1628 he was appointed to the living of Hedgerley, Buckinghamshire, and became chaplain to Robert Dormer, earl of Carnarvon. He may have been married by this date, as the baptism of the first of eight children born in Hedgerley to Foster and his wife, Anne, was recorded in June 1629. One of his three sons, Richard, died in 1637, soon after birth, as did the last of his children, Margaret, in December 1642. During this period he seems to have served the cure of Hedgerley, his children being baptized in the parish every two years or so and his signature appearing in the parish register on several occasions.

In 1629, following a practice common among noted preachers in the early seventeenth century, Foster published a sermon he had preached at Paul's Cross on 26 May, *The Means to Keep Sinne from Reigning in our Mortall Body*. More controversially his treatise, *Hiplocrisma-spongus, or, A Sponge to Wipe Away the Weapon-Salve* (1631), argued that the alleged cure was magical and unlawful. In the dedication he acknowledged a debt to the writings of Johannes Roberti, the Belgian Jesuit. The work was immediately challenged by Robert Fludd, doctor of physic and an eminent Rosicrusian in *Doctor Fludd's Answer unto M Foster, or, The Squeezing of Parson Fosters Sponge*. Thereafter Foster seems to have abandoned writing in favour of pastoral work. The inference drawn from George Lipscomb's *The History and Antiquities of the County of Buckingham* (1847) that he was killed in 1643 is probably mistaken, though since there was considerable military activity in Buckinghamshire during the civil war, it is possible that he met a violent end; his burial is not recorded in the parish register. However, the next incumbent at Hedgerley was not inducted until 1650, so Foster may have died later in the 1640s.

JOAN A. DILS

Sources Wood, *Ath. Oxon.*, new edn, 2.573 · G. Lipscomb, *The history and antiquities of the county of Buckingham*, 4 vols. (1831–47), vol. 4, p. 508 · parish register, Hedgerley, Buckinghamshire, 1539–1805, Bucks. RLSS, PR 99/1/1 · Foster, *Alum. Oxon.* · *ESTC* · *DNB*

Foster, William (1821–1884), worsted manufacturer and merchant, was born on 2 February 1821, probably at Low Fold, Clayton, Queenshead (later Queensbury), near Bradford, Yorkshire, the eldest son of John Foster (1798–1879), worsted cloth merchant, and his wife, Ruth (1801–1882), daughter of Abraham Briggs; the Briggs family were farmers in Bradford. William obtained a modest but sound education at the local nonconformist academy of Joseph Hinchliffe at Horton House, Bradford, and in 1834 joined his father at Prospect House, Queensbury, in his successful business as a master manufacturer in the domestic worsted trade. From a warehouse adjoining Prospect House, pieces of worsted cloth, woven in the cottages of local hand-loom weavers, were stored before their sale at the piece halls of Bradford or Halifax. In the same year Abraham Briggs conveyed land to his son-in-law John Foster, including a farm at Black Dyke. From this farm the purpose-built spinning mill (opened in 1835) took its name, and became known as Black Dyke mills (later famous as the home of the brass band of that name). William's apprenticeship (1834–42) familiarized him with all the processes of production, and when he came of age his father had every confidence in making him a full partner in the business.

For the next forty years Foster was the dominant figure in the affairs of the firm, which carried the name John Foster & Son, in spite of the founder's subsequently taking three other sons into the business. By 1874 William had brought into the firm three sons from his first marriage, William Henry (b. 1848), Robert John (b. 1850), and Frederick Charles (b. 1851). They extended the wide range of commercial interests initiated by their father between 1842 and 1882. In addition to the manufacture of worsted cloth, the partnership at Black Dyke mills operated as merchants and bankers, as well as manufacturers of soap, tiles, coke, tar, and chemical dyestuffs. Profits also accrued from collieries, farms, brickworks, and building contracts.

It was, however, as a principal manufactory of worsted cloth made from cotton warps and alpaca or mohair wefts that Black Dyke mills gained an international reputation and generated massive wealth for William Foster and his family. The firm's growth during Foster's chairmanship is revealed in the extensive business archive discovered by E. M. Sigsworth, which shows that the number of spindles in use for spinning yarn was 3036 in 1842 and by 1889 had increased to 51,368. The number of power looms for weaving cloth increased from 61 in 1842 to 962 in 1875. Combing was the last sector of the worsted trade to be mechanized and the firm's six combing machines in 1852 increased gradually to fifty-seven by 1880. When the textile trade was subdued in 1880–81 Foster founded a movement to promote the weaving of ladies' fashion garments from wool. It was patronized by leading society people, including the marquess of Salisbury and the countess of Bective, after whom it was named, and enjoyed a moderate success.

In addition to his widespread textile interests, Foster was quick to realize the importance of railways. By 1864 he was a director of the West Riding and Grimsby Railway, the sale of which he personally negotiated to the Great Northern Railway in 1865, and by virtue of which he became a director of that large and successful company. He founded and chaired the Bradford and Thornton Railway Company in 1870, and in 1872 he was invited to join the board of the Lancashire and Yorkshire Railway Company.

William Foster was first married in January 1848 to Emma Elizabeth (1828–1865), daughter of Swithin Anderton, a leading Bradford manufacturer. During their seventeen-year marriage she gave birth to five sons and four daughters. From 1856 she and William lived at Harrowins House, a mansion erected by him in a commanding position at Queensbury. Foster's second marriage, in 1867, to Mary Ellen Hornby of Filey, in the East Riding of Yorkshire, produced six more children.

In 1862 Foster's father paid £205,000 for a castle and an estate of nearly 11,000 acres at Hornby, near Lancaster. In 1878, shortly before his father's death, Foster and his second wife left Queensbury to live for a while at Hornby Castle, which became their permanent home in 1882. His landed estates in Lancashire (Hornby Castle) and west Yorkshire had a gross annual value of £9098 by 1879. The Fosters took their place in the ranks of the landed gentry with further land purchases at Egton Hall (Whitby), Canwell Hall (Staffordshire), and Moor Park (Oxford). This transfer into the upper reaches of English society was reinforced by the marriages of most of William Foster's children to sons or daughters of the landed classes. Such upward social mobility was made possible by the enormous wealth created by the ever expanding manufactory at Black Dyke mills, one of the largest woollen textile mills in the world.

Foster's devotion to business matters did not preclude him from a career in public service. He sat for many years as a magistrate for Bradford, the West Riding, and Lancashire. He served as high sheriff of Lancashire in 1881, and deputy lord lieutenant of Yorkshire. A Liberal in politics, he declined to stand as the Liberal candidate for North West Lancashire in 1880 on health grounds. He became vice-president of the Bradford chamber of commerce and was a member of the Queensbury local board of health (1864–73). A prominent freemason, he was also an active member of the Anglican church in Queensbury, financing extensions to Holy Trinity Church, and acting for twenty-five years as trustee and manager of the national school there.

Foster's interests included music (he was a member of the committee that organized the Bradford Subscription Concerts) and game shooting on the family estates. He was a regular churchgoer (twice on Sundays) and enjoyed wine in moderation. Portraits and diary entries (Sigsworth, 355–64) suggest that he was forthright and decisive, but approachable and understanding when the need arose, particularly with his children. Throughout middle age he was constantly pained and irritated by bowel ulcers, inclining him to depression and melancholy. Daily application of nitric acid for his condition and, ultimately, surgery of the bowel finally took their toll and he died at Hornby Castle on 8 February 1884, only two years after his retirement, and was buried on 13 February at Holy Trinity Church, Queensbury. He was survived by his second wife.

GARY FIRTH

Sources E. M. Sigsworth, *Black Dyke mills: a history* (1958) · F. Barrett, 'Fosters of Black Dyke', *Transactions of the Halifax Antiquarian Society* (1967), 57–72 · J. H. Patchett, *The development of Queensbury* (1992) · [J. Hogg], ed., *Fortunes made in business: a series of original sketches*, 2 (1884), 3–56 · *Bradford Observer* (9 Feb 1884) · J. Bateman, *The great landowners of Great Britain and Ireland*, new edn (1879) · E. M. Sigsworth, 'Foster, William', *DBB* · J. Parker, *Illustrated history from Hipperholme to Tong* (1904), 431–47 · P. Hudson, *West Riding wool*

textile industry: a catalogue of business records from the sixteenth to the twentieth century (1975), 142–75 · *Bradford Observer* (14 Feb 1884)
Archives U. Leeds, Brotherton L., John Foster & Son, personal and business papers · W. Yorks. AS, Bradford, John Foster & Son, MSS
Likenesses engraving, repro. in Hogg, ed., *Fortunes made in business* · engraving, repro. in Sigsworth, *Black Dyke mills*, 355
Wealth at death £1,279,813 6s. 8d.: resworn probate, Dec 1884, CGPLA Eng. & Wales

Fotherby, Martin (*c*.1560–1620), bishop of Salisbury, was born in Grimsby, the second son of Martin Fotherby and his wife, Isabell. Having matriculated at Trinity College, Cambridge, at Michaelmas 1576, he graduated there in 1581, became a fellow in 1583, and proceeded MA in 1584 and DTh in 1607. In 1592 he succeeded his elder brother, Charles (later dean of Canterbury), as vicar of Chislet, Kent, and in the same year married Margaret, daughter of John Winter, a prebendary of Canterbury. His non-residence at Chislet gave rise to complaints at archidiaconal visitations that the vicarage house was left unrepaired and that he failed to distribute money to the poor. In 1594 he became rector of St Mary-le-Bow, London, but resigned the living a year later. Fotherby is said to have been both kinsman and chaplain to Archbishop John Whitgift, which may have facilitated his preferment to the eleventh prebend in Canterbury Cathedral in 1596. He was presented by the ecclesiastical lawyer Richard Cosin, another of Whitgift's protégés. He was also rector of Great Mongeham (1596–1603), of Chartham (1596–1618), and of Adisham (1601–18), all three livings being in Kent.

Under James I Fotherby became a royal chaplain and preached at least once at court. He also delivered a visitation sermon before Archbishop Richard Bancroft in 1607 in which he joined his voice to those who gave precedence to prayer and Bible-reading over hearing sermons. He was made a fellow of Chelsea College in 1610. On 26 March 1618 he was elected bishop of Salisbury. Royal confirmation was granted on 9 April and he was consecrated ten days later, letting it be known that he had not given anything for his elevation. His register for his brief episcopate contains only five folios of routine business, and he appears to have made very little impression on his diocese.

Fotherby died in London on 11 March 1620 and was buried two days later in All Hallows, Lombard Street, where his brother-in-law Francis Dee was rector. His monument (for which he left £100 in his will) did not survive the fire of London, but its inscription, describing him as learned, eloquent, and urbane, has been preserved. In his will (PRO, PROB 11/135, fols. 206r–208r), made three days before his death and proved on 24 March, Fotherby paid a warm tribute to his wife, as 'a kynde and lovinge wiefe towards mee', and left her £500 in ready money and an annuity of £80. He remembered two sons and three daughters, and showed himself particularly concerned with the education of the former. He reflected ruefully on the cost of being a bishop, 'myne estate beinge much shruncke, by the charge of my cominge unto this place, and the chargeable fashion of my livinge therein', but was still able either to make bequests or to refer to past gifts amounting to over £2500. His will also shows that he had acquired a

Martin Fotherby (*c*.1560–1620), by unknown artist, 1618

number of estates in Kent, enabling him to establish his descendants among the gentry of that county. Fotherby's intellectual legacy consisted of a treatise attacking atheism, published posthumously as *Atheomastix* (1622), and a collection of four sermons, published in 1608. There is a portrait in the South Canonry, Salisbury.

PENELOPE RUNDLE

Sources M. Fotherby, bishop's register, Wilts. & Swindon RO, D1/2/20 · LPL, register of Archbishop George Abbot 1 · S. H. Cassan, *Lives and memoirs of the bishops of Sherborne and Salisbury* (1824) · Venn, *Alum. Cant.*, 1/2.165 · W. H. Jones, *Fasti ecclesiae Sarisberiensis, or, A calendar … of the cathedral body at Salisbury* (1879) · A. Hussey, 'Visitations of the archdeacon of Canterbury', *Archaeologia Cantiana*, 25 (1902), 11–56 · W. Berry, *Pedigrees of the families of the county of Kent* (1830) · parish register, London, All Hallows, Lombard Street, GL, MS 17613 [burial] · *Fasti Angl., 1541–1857*, [Canterbury] · *Fasti Angl., 1541–1857*, [Salisbury] · P. E. McCullough, *Sermons at court: politics and religion in Elizabethan and Jacobean preaching* (1998) [incl. CD-ROM] · K. Fincham, *Prelate as pastor: the episcopate of James I* (1990) · will, PRO, PROB 11/135, fols. 206r–208r · G. S. Stephenson, ed., *The register book of the parish church of Saint James, Great Grimsby* (1889) · parish register, Great Grimsby, St James's, 20 Jan 1547 [marriage, Martin Fotherby and Isabell, parents]
Archives Wilts. & Swindon RO, register, D1/2/20
Likenesses oils, 1618; Sothebys, 31 March 1999, lot 69 [see illus.] · oils, 1618–19, Salisbury Cathedral School

Fothergill, Anthony (1685/6–1761), landowner and theological writer, was baptized on 9 December 1686 at Ravenstone, Westmorland, the youngest son of Thomas Fothergill of Brownber, Ravenstonedale, farmer. Like his forefathers and descendants for many generations, he owned the estate of Brownber and lived and died there. Though he is said to have had no 'liberal education', he published several theological works, the largest of which is entitled *Wicked Christians practical atheists … by Anthony Fothergill, a husbandman in the county of Westmoreland* (1754). The description of husbandman is no doubt an attempt at a translation of the Lake country statesman, that is to say, a landowner–farmer. *Wicked Christians*, along with the rest of Fothergill's writings, was well received by William Rose, who praised the 'honest ploughman' (*Monthly Review*, 13, 1755, 57). The work was followed by two pamphlets, one rejecting the Athanasian creed, the other discussing Arminianism. It is stated that Fothergill also wrote some pieces in verse and contributed to the *Monthly Review*. He seems to have acted as the parish lawyer. He died on 13 June 1761, aged seventy-five. The parishioners put up in Ravenstonedale church a brass plate to his memory, bearing an inscription which concludes: 'his integrity of heart, social disposition, and uncommon abilities gained him general esteem' (*GM*, 1186).

EDWIN CANNAN, rev. ADAM JACOB LEVIN

Sources *GM*, 1st ser., 72 (1802), 1186 • *Monthly Review*, 13 (1755), 57–61 • *Monthly Review*, 14 (1756), 8–10 • *Monthly Review*, 15 (1756), 677–8 • private information (1889) • J. Nicolson and R. Burn, *The history and antiquities of the counties of Westmorland and Cumberland*, 1 (1777), 518, 528

Fothergill, Anthony (*bap.* 1737, *d.* 1813), physician, the son of Anthony Fothergill and his wife, Frances Bainbridge (*b.* 1703), was born in Murthwaite, Ravenstonedale, Westmorland, and was baptized there on 12 March 1737. He was educated at nearby Sedbergh School, where he learned the classical languages then necessary for entry into the study of medicine. In 1755 he was apprenticed to his maternal cousin John Drake Bainbridge (1725–1814) of Durham, a surgeon who became an influential figure in that city, of which he was mayor five times between 1761 and 1794. Fothergill remained with him for five years and then went to the University of Edinburgh as a medical student. He joined the prestigious Royal Medical Society in 1761 and graduated MD in 1763 with a thesis on intermittent fever. The thesis was dedicated to his teacher, William Cullen, and to Sir Ralph Milbanke. Sir Ralph was a landowner in Yorkshire and Durham and had been MP for Scarborough from 1754 to 1761, but by 1763 he was the member for Richmond, Yorkshire. Sir Ralph's cousin Jane Routh married J. D. Bainbridge in 1757. In view of Fothergill's dedication, it seems likely that Sir Ralph had contributed to his education.

Soon after graduation Fothergill met Dr John Fothergill (no relation) in London and on his counsel settled in Northampton. In 1764 Anthony Fothergill was appointed physician to the general infirmary but he seems to have met with unexpected difficulties. John Fothergill wrote encouragingly from London: 'Depend more on propriety of conduct than on recommendations, though these ought not to be neglected. Have patience, be firm' (Fox, 132). Anthony Fothergill corresponded with John Fothergill throughout his years in Northampton and some of their correspondence was published by J. C. Lettsom in his memoir of John Fothergill.

In 1778 Anthony Fothergill was elected to the Royal Society; his sponsors included John Fothergill and William Hunter. The following year he became a licentiate of the Royal College of Physicians, an essential step if he was to practise as a physician in London. In 1781 he moved to London in an attempt to fill his distinguished namesake's place, and lived for a while in John Fothergill's house in Harpur Street. He became a member of the Society of Collegiate Physicians, a pressure group campaigning against the continued exclusion of licentiates who were not graduates of Oxford or Cambridge universities from the fellowship of the Royal College of Physicians. His practice, however, did not prosper and the next year Fothergill moved to Bath, where he was to spend the most fruitful years of his career. He lived at 9 Walcot Parade, a terrace of houses on the London Road. He became an active member of the Medical Society of London, contributing papers on influenza, consumption, and the treatment of epilepsy. But his main interest was in the fledgeling Royal Humane Society, founded by William Hawes and Thomas Coggan in 1774. The society was concerned with the resuscitation of persons apparently dead from drowning and in 1794 it awarded a gold medal to Fothergill for an essay on the subject. While in Bath, Fothergill wrote on lead poisoning, rabies, and the abuse of spirituous liquors, and he published a tract on the Cheltenham waters in 1798. In 1792 he had the distinction, along with J. C. Lettsom, of being elected a foreign member of the American Philosophical Society.

In 1803, at the age of sixty-six, Fothergill gave up his practice in Bath and moved to Philadelphia. He took lodgings in Walnut Street and at once took an active role in the affairs of the American Philosophical Society, contributing on bills of mortality for the United States, 'ice islands', population, and on the cold in Northampton. He was a member of committees commenting on work submitted for publication by the society. At the same time he made exhaustive daily observations on the weather, wind, and temperature and wrote on the population, longevity, and diseases of Philadelphia. This work was never published but the manuscripts are preserved in the library of the College of Physicians of Philadelphia. Fothergill enjoyed an active social life in Philadelphia, meeting distinguished medical men such as John Morgan, founder of America's first medical school. He visited Thomas Jefferson in Washington, who was president not only of the United States but also of the Philosophical Society. His letter of thanks, 'by the hand of Mr Maddison', is preserved among the Jefferson papers. In 1812 the recurrence of war between his native country and the United States made Fothergill's position in Philadelphia difficult and he returned to England. He died at St George's Place, London, on 11 May 1813. By Fothergill's own assessment he was worth £20,000. He left many individual legacies to friends and relations. J. C. Lettsom was to have received £1000 to prepare an edition of Fothergill's works but, as he died in 1815, he did not live to receive his money or to accomplish his task. There was a legacy to the Royal Humane Society, and he also left £500 to the Medical Society of London to establish a medal in his memory. The Fothergillian medal is awarded by the society triennially. He never married.

CHRISTOPHER C. BOOTH

Sources C. Lawrence, P. Lucier, and C. C. Booth, 'Take time by the forelock: the letters of Anthony Fothergill', *Medical History*, suppl. 17 (1997) [whole issue] · C. Thornton and F. MacLaughlan, *The Fothergills of Ravenstonedale* (1905) · private information (2004) [C. R. Morris] · P. J. Wallis and R. V. Wallis, *Eighteenth century medics*, 2nd edn (1988) · F. F. Waddy, *A history of Northamptonshire General Hospital, 1743–1948* (1974) · Northampton Hospital, minute books, 29 Dec 1764 · R. H. Fox, *Dr John Fothergill and his friends* (1919) · minutes of the Society of Collegiate Physicians, RCP Lond. · P. J. Bishop, *A short history of the Royal Humane Society* (1974) · A. Fothergill, MS autograph letter to George Turner, Bath, England, 10 April 1792, Library of the American Philosophical Society · Munk, *Roll* · parish register (baptism) 12 March 1737, Ravenstonedale, Westmorland, PRO, PROB 10/4119 · C. C. Booth, 'The Fothergillian medals of the Medical Society of London', *Journal of the Royal College of Physicians of London*, 15 (1981), 254–8
Archives American Philosophical Society, Philadelphia, MSS
Likenesses aquatint silhouette, 1801, Wellcome L. · silhouette, repro. in J. C. Lettsom, *Hints designed to promote beneficence, temperance and medical science*, 2, 369 · stipple, BM, NPG
Wealth at death £20,000: will, PRO, PROB 11/550, fol. 592

Fothergill, (Arthur) Brian (1921–1990), biographer, was born on 3 April 1921 at 3 Park Avenue, Lytham St Annes, the youngest of three children of John Smirthwaite Fothergill (1887–1938) and his wife, Kathleen Anderson, *née* Entwisle (1895–1957), daughter of Anderson Entwisle of Milnshaw, Lytham St Annes. The Fothergills were a wealthy, landowning family with property in Westmorland and John Smirthwaite Fothergill was able to live near Kendal on family income.

Brian Fothergill (seldom referred to as Arthur) was educated at Wycliffe College, Stonehouse, Gloucestershire, from 1931 to 1937, and at King's College, London, from 1939 to 1942. He had decided to become an Anglican priest and therefore did not sit his final degree examinations but left as an associate of King's College. He then took a pre-ordination course at Westcott House, Cambridge, from 1942 to 1944 and probably qualified for the priesthood; however, in 1944 he joined the army intelligence corps. He served in India and Malaya, where he met several people who were to become his lifelong friends, including Kenneth Williams, Stanley Baxter, and John Schlesinger. The experiences of army life apparently overturned his career plans and he never went back to the idea of becoming a priest. The army also gave him the opportunity to refine his beliefs and soon after he was demobbed in 1947 he was received into the Roman Catholic church.

Fothergill began work as a schoolteacher, with his longest spell as assistant master at St Philip's School in South Kensington, London, from 1949 to 1956. Despite struggling on for nine years, teaching never gave him any satisfaction and in 1957 he decided to devote all his time to writing. It was probably his mother's death which enabled him to break away from teaching. His father had been killed in 1938 by a train and in 1941 his mother married J. M. Somervell of Kendal. The Somervells owned K Shoes and it was said that Fothergill's mother first married into one of the oldest families in Westmorland and then into one of the richest. In 1957 Fothergill would have inherited a secure income for the rest of his life.

Nevertheless, Fothergill had trouble settling to a regular routine. The root of his problem was his homosexuality, which led to his constantly moving home—from Earls Court, to St John's Wood, to Chelsea in London; then to Brighton—and it was not until about 1970 when he bought a house in Islington, London, and met Owen Gordon, a clerk with the St John Ambulance Brigade, that he was able to enjoy a long-term relationship.

Fothergill's first book, a biography of the brother of Charles Edward Stuart (Bonnie Prince Charlie), was almost written before he left teaching and was published in 1958 as *The Cardinal King*. It was followed by six other biographies, all published by Faber and Faber. His biographies were usually about people on the margins of history with odd characteristics; some were downright eccentrics. All his work was meticulously researched, and if his subject was already written about, Fothergill usually managed to present new evidence and to rescue the person's reputation from obloquy. The most striking example of such rehabilitation was his treatment of Sir William Hamilton, previously known for little other than his willingness to live as Nelson's cuckold; Fothergill showed Hamilton to have been an outstanding diplomat, soldier, scholar, and epitome of an eighteenth-century man of taste.

Fothergill received the PEN Silver Pen award for *Sir William Hamilton* and the Heinemann award for literature for *Sir William Hamilton* and *Beckford of Fonthill*. Critical acclaim was given to all his books, although they were not bestsellers, as he himself was well aware. He once told his publisher that sales of *The Mitred Earl* might have doubled had it been called *The Belted Bishop*. He was elected a fellow of both the Society of Antiquaries and the Royal Society of Literature in 1970, and in the Royal Society of Literature he went on to become a member of the council in 1977, the vice-president in 1986, and chairman from 1986 to 1989. In 1980 he edited the society's annual *Essays by Divers Hands*.

Fothergill was a tall man who paid attention to his clothes and his appearance, although without regard to contemporary fashion. Towards the end of his life his health deteriorated quickly. He contracted tuberculosis and then had a heart bypass before being diagnosed with cancer. During these illnesses he was nursed by Owen Gordon and spent much of his time reconsidering his religious beliefs. Just before he died he gave up Catholicism and returned to the Church of England.

Brian Fothergill died on 6 August 1990 at Homerton Hospital in Hackney, London.

JOHN R. TURNER

Sources C. Monteith, *The Independent* (15 Aug 1990) · R. Fothergill, *The Fothergills: a first history* (1998) · *The Times* (15 Aug 1990) · *WWW, 1981–90* · C. D. Kinaman, ed., *Contemporary authors*, 1st rev. edn (1976), vols. 17–20
Wealth at death £707,332: probate, 21 Dec 1990, CGPLA Eng. & Wales

Fothergill, George (1705–1760), college head, was born on 20 December 1705 at Lockholme, in Ravenstonedale, Westmorland, the eldest of seven sons of Henry Fothergill of Lockholme (1670–1753), a landowner who claimed Norman ancestry, and Elizabeth (1681–1766), daughter of Richard Fawcett of Rottenmoor, Warcop. He attended the free school in Ravenstonedale, founded in 1668 by Thomas Fothergill, master of St John's College, Cambridge, and was then sent to Kendal School. On 16 June 1722 he entered Queen's College, Oxford, as a batteler.

Fothergill's parents, who had a large family to raise, were poor and for six years their son could not visit them. His dutiful letters home reveal a serious, pious youth, who attended prayers twice daily, heard two sermons on Sundays, and spent his money on books, not drink. As a servitor he received £8 a year and had to wait on gentlemen commoners at meal times; he earned an additional £5 for waking three of them for early chapel. His conscientious tutor directed him to the Hebrew lectures. In 1724 he received an Appleby scholarship and later he became a taberdar, with emoluments of £16 16s. per annum. He took the degree of BA in 1726 and of MA in 1730. He was appointed chaplain of Queen's in 1730, and in 1734 was elected to the next vacant fellowship, which he acquired in 1736. He took his BD in 1744 and DD in 1749. In 1751 the fellows of Queen's appointed him principal of St Edmund Hall and vicar of Bramley, in Hampshire. When Dr Joseph Smith, provost of Queen's, died on 23 November 1756 the fourteen votes of the fellows were equally divided between Fothergill and Dr Joseph Browne. A second vote of senior fellows only also resulted in a tie, and Dr Browne was elected, on the ground that he was the senior candidate.

Fothergill published at Oxford, during his lifetime, nine sermons, some of which reached second and third editions. At a time when the university was often accused of Jacobite sympathies these sermons show an anxiety to urge obedience to established rule, as in the *Danger of Excesses in the Pursuit of Liberty* (1737) and the *Duty, Objects, and Offices of the Love of our Country*, preached before the House of Commons on Restoration day 1758. In 1761, after Fothergill's death, his brother Thomas, provost of Queen's from 1767 to 1796, published *Sermons on Several Subjects and Occasions by George Fothergill, D.D.*; its sixteen sermons are mainly concerned with personal godliness. In 1765 this volume reappeared, with the same title, as 'vol. ii. 2nd ed.', the nine sermons mentioned above being collected together and printed as volume 1.

Fothergill, who was long afflicted with asthma, died on 5 October 1760 and was buried in the chapel of St Edmund Hall. He had forbidden any monument.

EDWIN CANNAN, *rev.* JOHN D. HAIGH

Sources C. Thornton and F. McLaughlin, *The Fothergills of Ravenstonedale: their lives and their letters* (1905) · *Hist. U. Oxf.* 5: *18th-cent. Oxf.*, 230–32, 254, 259, 264, 375, 428, 434 · A. Chalmers, ed., *The general biographical dictionary*, new edn, 32 vols. (1812–17) · A. Wood, *The history and antiquities of the colleges and halls in the University of Oxford*, ed. J. Gutch (1786), 149 · Foster, *Alum. Oxon.*

Archives Bodl. Oxf., family corresp. [copies] · Cumbria AS, Kendal, letters to parents | Queen's College, Oxford, letters to Joseph

Smith and his father, also Joseph, provost of Queen's College, Oxford

Likenesses oils, 1754, Queen's College, Oxford · oils, St Edmund Hall, Oxford; repro. in Thornton and McLaughlin, *Fothergills of Ravenstonedale*, facing p. 64

Fothergill, Jessie (1851–1891), novelist, was born on 7 June 1851 at Cheetham Hill, Manchester, the eldest child of Thomas Fothergill of Carr End, Wensleydale, Yorkshire, and his wife, Anne, daughter of William and Judith Coultate of Burnley. When she was quite young the family moved to Bowdon in Cheshire, 10 miles from Manchester. Her father came from a long line of yeomen Quakers. His marriage to a non-Quaker forced him to leave the Society of Friends, but he stayed a nonconformist all his life, as did his children. He was engaged in the cotton industry, died in 1866, and shortly after Jessie Fothergill, with her mother, sisters, and brothers, moved to Littleborough, near Rochdale. Jessie was educated first in a small private school in Bowdon, and afterwards for some years at a boarding-school in Harrogate. When her education was completed she lived quietly at Littleborough, studying the life led by the workers in the cotton mills. She paid a first visit to Germany in 1874. On her return to England she published her first novel, *Healey*, in 1875, and from that time she devoted herself to literary work. In 1877 she achieved a notable success with her third novel, *The First Violin*, which was begun during a fifteen-month stay in Düsseldorf, where she studied German and music. The novel was first serialized in *Temple Bar*, and its popularity was the beginning of a career throughout which her 'price as an author gradually rose to a very respectable £600 a novel' (Sutherland, 230). Her other works, many of which ran to several editions, included *Aldyth* (1876), *Probation* (1879), *The Wellfields* (1880), *Kith and Kin* (1881), *Made or Marred* (1881), *One of Three* (1881), *Peril* (1884), *Borderland* (1886), *The Lasses of Leverhouse* (1888), *From Moor Isles* (1888), and *A March in the Ranks* (1890).

Jessie Fothergill's novels largely depict life on the moorland, in the factories of Lancashire and Yorkshire; but she combined enthusiastic descriptions of the influence of music with the fruits of her observation of the places where her life was mainly spent. 'Cotton mills and music, manufacturing England and Germany' were the chief subjects of her pen (Gardiner, 155). Her plots were rather less satisfactorily devised than her studies of character, which were usually subtly and powerfully portrayed; her heroines are 'strong-minded and socially aware' (Blain, Clements & Grundy, *Feminist comp.*).

Jessie Fothergill suffered from a chronic lung complaint, and she often travelled for the sake of her health, largely to avoid British winters. She spent a year in the United States in 1884, and published 'Some American recollections' in *Temple Bar* in February 1886. Her novels also appeared in Indian and Australian journals. She taught herself Italian, and spent the winter of 1890 to 1891 in Rome, which formed the setting of her final novel, *Oriole's Daughter* (1893); this work centred on the relationship between a republican and his illegitimate daughter. Jessie

Fothergill died suddenly at Bern, Switzerland, on 28 July 1891. Her sister, Caroline Fothergill, also wrote novels of a similar nature and quality.

BERTHA PORTER, *rev.* REBECCA MILLS

Sources J. Crisp, *Jessie Fothergill, 1851–1891* (1980) · H. Speight, *Romantic Richmondshire* (1897), 477–9 · H. C. Black, *Notable women authors of the day* (1893), 184–97 · L. Gardiner, 'Jessie Fothergill's novels', *Novel Review*, 21 (May 1892), 153–60 · Blain, Clements & Grundy, *Feminist comp.* · J. Sutherland, *The Longman companion to Victorian fiction* (1988) · F. Hays, *Women of the day: a biographical dictionary of notable contemporaries* (1885), 71–2 · M. Sadleir, *XIX century fiction: a bibliographical record based on his own collection*, 1 (1951), 133 · W. de la Mare, 'Women novelists of the 70s', *The eighteen-seventies* (1929), 60–63, 72 · *The Dial*, 1 (1880), 135–6 · J. Fothergill, 'The first violin', *The international library of famous literature*, ed. R. Garnett and others, 20 (1899), 9739–52 · Allibone, *Dict.* · b. cert.
Likenesses photograph, repro. in Black, *Notable women*
Wealth at death £1121 9s. 6d.: resworn probate, Feb 1892, *CGPLA Eng. & Wales* (1891)

Fothergill, John (1712–1780), physician and naturalist, was born on 8 March 1712 at Carr End, a moorland farm near Bainbridge, Wensleydale, Yorkshire, the third son of eight children of John Fothergill (1676–1745), Quaker preacher and farmer, and his first wife, Margaret Hough (1677–1719), of a substantial Quaker family in Cheshire. Margaret died later in childbirth; her baby also died. The surviving children were Alexander (1709–1788), Thomas (1711–1733), John, Joseph (1713–1761), William (1714–1724), Samuel *Fothergill (1715–1772), and Ann (1718–1802). John Fothergill the elder married Elizabeth Buck in 1727; she died in 1745. The Fothergills had been members of the Society of Friends since the time of George Fox. The elder John Fothergill travelled extensively as a preacher, visiting America three times between 1706 and 1737. During his absence in 1721 Thomas Hough, the children's maternal uncle, took John and Samuel into his home in Cheshire, and sent John, and perhaps also Samuel, to the school at Frodsham. In 1724 John (possibly accompanied by Samuel) entered the distinguished grammar school at Sedbergh where John studied Greek and became fluent in Latin. In 1728 Samuel was apprenticed to a Stockport shopkeeper. After a rebellious youth Samuel experienced a religious awakening, married, settled in Warrington, and toured America as a Quaker preacher. He became guardian to John Coakley Lettsom, later John's secretary and disciple.

John was also apprenticed in 1728, to the eminent Bradford apothecary, bookseller, and Quaker minister Benjamin Bartlett, an enthusiastic botanist who encouraged his interest in natural history. In 1734 Bartlett released him from his indenture and encouraged him to pursue medical training at Edinburgh. Throughout his life Fothergill loved Bartlett and his family. At Edinburgh University Fothergill was an outstanding student. Among his professors were Charles Alston, who became a lifelong friend, and Alexander Monro primus, who encouraged him to take the daring step of obtaining his MD degree at Edinburgh. Fothergill also joined the nascent student Medical Society (later the Royal Medical Society of Edinburgh). He

John Fothergill (1712–1780), by Valentine Green, pubd 1781 (after Gilbert Stuart, 1781)

graduated in 1736 with a thesis on the use of emetics, the only MD that year. The Royal College of Physicians controlled the right to practise physic in London and fellowships in the college were normally reserved for men with Oxford and Cambridge degrees. Graduates of continental universities could seek a licence to practise, but were not considered to be members of the college, and graduates of Scottish universities were seldom able to take the licensing examination.

Fothergill sought further training at St Thomas's Hospital, London, where he studied with Edward Wilmot. In the summer of 1740 he travelled abroad, and on his return to London he rented a house at 2 White Hart Court, near the Friends' meeting-house, and practised as an unlicensed physician. Like other Edinburgh graduates he had trouble establishing himself in London, and for some time served the suburban poor, many of whom had encountered him at St Thomas's and remembered his kindness. Fothergill often walked through the city all day and returned without a fee. On 1 October 1744 he became the first English graduate of Edinburgh to be examined and licensed by the college.

In 1748 Fothergill published *An Account of the Sore-Throat Attended with Ulcers*. This important work discussed a London epidemic of an illness which is now thought to have been scarlet fever, although he included earlier reports of diphtheria epidemics, thinking they represented the same illness. He provided a comprehensive clinical description of this often fatal illness, which he attributed to a specific contagious poison, transmitted by the breath.

His emphasis on the specificity of the disease and its transmission by contagion were notable. He opposed the prevailing treatment which included bleeding, purging, and complex traditional remedies. Instead, he wrote, treatment should strengthen the patient with diet, cordials, clean air, and cinchona (the source of quinine) as a febrifuge. The book was an immediate success. The first printing sold out within weeks and several more editions appeared during Fothergill's lifetime. William Withering later credited Fothergill's therapy with saving many lives. This success helped build Fothergill's medical practice; although he never held a hospital or court appointment he soon became one of the richest physicians in England. In 1754 his sister Ann came to keep house for him and in 1765 he bought a country retreat, Lea Hall, in Cheshire. In 1767 he moved his London household to Harpur Street, Bloomsbury. In a letter to Samuel he wrote of spending seventeen hours visiting patients, climbing fifty flights of stairs in one day.

Among Fothergill's Edinburgh friends was the surgeon William Hunter, who settled in London about 1746; they collaborated on many efforts, including the formation of a society of physicians modelled on the Edinburgh Medical Society. Between 1757 and 1784 this group, which never adopted an official name, published six volumes of transactions under the title *Medical Observations and Inquiries*. Fothergill planned the journal and paid its first secretary. He also wrote or communicated more than fifty papers, about a fourth of the whole, but published some anonymously so his name would not appear too frequently. His contributions included the first clear description of tic douloureux (trigeminal neuralgia), sometimes called Fothergill's disease, and one of the earliest clinical accounts of migraine headache. He wrote two papers on angina pectoris, one of which, in 1776, referred to the 'scar-like appearance of the heart' (Booth, 90). This was the earliest published record of a cardiac infarction found during a post-mortem examination of an angina patient. He also wrote on epilepsy, *hydrocephalus internus* (tubercular meningitis), coffee, rabies, obesity, and menopause. He favoured the use of antimony: a preparation of antimony, aloes, scammony, and colocynth known as Fothergill's pill was popular for a century.

Between 1751 and 1754 Fothergill anonymously published observations on the weather and diseases of London in the *Gentleman's Magazine*. He was not, however, the author of the work entitled *Rules for the Preservation of Health, by J. Forthergell*, which was compiled by an unscrupulous bookseller from works by other authors. In 1754 Fothergill initiated an unsuccessful campaign to improve the registration of vital statistics and causes of death throughout England.

In 1767 Fothergill and Hunter tried to force the Royal College of Physicians to include licentiates in its government. The exclusion of some licentiates on 25 June led to the famous riot before the college gates. Fothergill did not participate in the riot, but he and Hunter raised a subscription to take the matter to court. Their case was thrown out in 1770. This episode led to the formation of the Society of Collegiate Physicians.

Among Fothergill's closest Quaker friends were the banker David Barclay and the merchant and botanist Peter Collinson. Collinson traded with America, and was the English patron of the American botanical collector John Bartram. Collinson was also a correspondent of the Swedish naturalist Carl von Linné, whose work he helped introduce to England. Fothergill became an enthusiastic Linnaean and in 1762 bought an estate at Upton in Essex where, in a 5 acre garden, he grew thousands of species of plants, including some 3400 species of conservatory plants. (The estate later became West Ham Park.) Unable to visit as often as he wished, he sometimes drove down after dark and toured his garden by lantern light. He introduced about a hundred plants into cultivation in England including Fothergill's lily (*Nerine curvifolia*), Fothergill's geranium (*Pelargonium Fothergillii*), and Fothergill's slipperwort (*Calceolaria Fothergillii*). Linné named a genus of American shrubs *Fothergilla*. Fothergill also acquired extensive collections of shells, corals, and insects. His collection of shells and corals was offered in his will to William Hunter, and was later placed in the Hunterian Museum in Glasgow. Fothergill was elected FRS in 1763.

It was through Collinson that Fothergill and Benjamin Franklin became acquainted. Collinson was the London agent for Franklin's Philadelphia Library. In 1745 Collinson wrote to Franklin about electrical experiments and sent him experimental equipment. The next year Franklin wrote to Collinson of his experiments. Collinson and Fothergill then arranged for the publisher of the *Gentleman's Magazine* to publish his account as a pamphlet with an unsigned preface by Fothergill. Religion also tied Fothergill to the colonies: in 1743 he became the correspondent from the English Friends' yearly meeting to the Philadelphia yearly meeting. The yearly meetings were the central deliberative bodies for the Friends. He soon became a respected political adviser to the Quaker members of the Pennsylvania assembly. In 1757 the assembly sent Franklin to London. On his arrival he fell ill and became Fothergill's patient. They became fast friends and collaborators.

In 1760 Fothergill became a trustee of the Pennsylvania Land Company, which held considerable estates. He suggested that unclaimed shares in the company be sold for the benefit of the Philadelphia Hospital and arranged for Barclay and Franklin to become agents for the hospital fund. His pamphlet *Considerations Relative to the North American Colonies* (1765) argued for the repeal of the Stamp Act. In 1775 he joined Barclay and Franklin in a last minute attempt to avert the American War of Independence. The rejection of their plan of conciliation led to Franklin's departure, but did not alter their lifelong friendship. On learning of his death Benjamin Franklin wrote 'I think a worthier man never lived' (*Works*, 501).

In 1777 Fothergill turned to Barclay for help in founding the Ackworth School in Yorkshire. In his last letter to Franklin, dated 25 October 1780, he described it as 'a school for a plain English education' for the sons and daughters of poor Friends (*Works*, 497–9). The school is Fothergill's most important monument. In the same letter he shared his dream for an international 'College of Justice' which would put an end to general warfare.

Fothergill began or joined many efforts to help the unfortunate and oppressed. He raised funds in 1771 for the foundation of the New York Hospital, and, like many Friends, he supported abolition of the slave trade. He was a very close friend of the prison reformer John Howard, and influenced the passing of the Act for Preserving the Health of Prisoners in 1774. Upon passage of the Penitentiary Act in 1779, Fothergill, Howard, and George Whatley, the treasurer of the Foundling Hospital, were appointed to establish two new national penitentiaries, but Fothergill's death frustrated this plan. He tried to improve the diet of the poor and campaigned for street improvement, for the prohibition of dangerous sugar factories within the City of London, for the removal of cemeteries, for public baths, and for aid to prisoners of war. In addition, Fothergill often gave money to individuals and reserved time for free medical care for the poor. After moving to Harpur Street he started a small dispensary in his home. He encouraged, helped, and advised many medical students as they began their careers, most notably John Coakley Lettsom. He also paid for publishing Anthony Purver's translation of the Bible. Perhaps his most important contribution of this sort was raising a subscription for the support of Joseph Priestley, who wrote to Franklin that 'without this assistance, I must have desisted altogether' from scientific work (Fox, 215).

Fothergill died at Harpur Street of a urinary retention, probably caused by prostate cancer, on 26 December 1780. He endured two weeks of acute physical misery, but confided to his sister on his deathbed that he had at last become assured of his salvation. He was buried at the Quaker burial-ground in Winchmore Hill on 5 January 1781.

Fothergill was spare and slight, with 'brilliant, acute, deeply penetrating' eyes, always neatly and soberly dressed, his manner quiet, modest, and restrained, though he had a subtle wit (*Works*, 16). Throughout his life he was a strict Friend. Fanny Burney thought him 'an upright, stern old man, … an old prig', when he came to attend to her mother, but when she herself fell ill she commented that 'he really has been … amazingly civil and polite to me … as kind as he is skilful' (*Works*, 15). His niece Betty Fothergill, who stayed in his London household in 1769–70, when she was seventeen, wrote in her journal, 'Surely, he is the first of men. With the becoming dignity of age he unites the cheerfulness and liberality of youth. He possesses the most virtues and the fewest failings of any man I know' (Fox, 265). MARGARET DeLACY

Sources R. H. Fox, *Dr John Fothergill and his friends* (1919) · *Chain of friendship: selected letters of Dr. John Fothergill of London, 1735–1780*, ed. B. C. Corner and C. C. Booth (1971) · C. C. Booth, *Doctors in science and society: essays of a clinical scientist* (1987), 84–149 · *List of the graduates in medicine in the University of Edinburgh from MDCCV to MDCCCLXVI* (1867) · J. J. Abraham, *Lettsom, his life, times, friends and descendants* (1933) · *The works of John Fothergill*, ed. J. C. Lettsom, 3 vols. (1783–4) · Munk, *Roll* · *GM*, 1st ser., 51 (1781), 165–7 · 'Dictionary of Quaker biography', RS Friends, Lond. [card index]

Archives RS, MSS · RS Friends, Lond., corresp. and MSS · Wellcome L., MSS on Siberian flora | BL, corresp. with E. M. Da Costa, Add. MS 28537 · Linn. Soc., letters to John Ellis

Likenesses oils, 1740–49, RCP Lond. · V. Green, mezzotint, 1741 (after G. Stuart), Wellcome L. · Cook, line engraving, pubd 1781, Wellcome L., BM, NPG · V. Green, engraving, pubd 1781 (after G. Stuart, 1781), AM Oxf. [*see illus.*] · mezzotint, pubd 1781, BM · F. Bartolozzi, coloured stipple, 1782 (after R. Livesay), Wellcome L., BM, NPG; repro. in Lettsom, *Works* (1783) · A. J. A. Mignerot, line engraving, 1782 (after R. Livesay), Wellcome L. · J. Hall, line engraving, 1790 (after C. Blackberd; after Mrs P. Wright), Wellcome L. · aquatint silhouette, 1801, Wellcome L. · stipple, 1825, Wellcome L. · Hogarth?, oils, RCP Lond.; repro. in Fox, *John Fothergill*, facing p. 18 · R. Livesay, portrait (after Mrs Wright), repro. in Corner and Booth, eds., *Chain of friendship* (1971), frontispiece · G. Stuart, portrait (from memory), Pennsylvania Academy of Fine Arts, Philadelphia; repro. in Fox, *John Fothergill*, frontispiece · Mrs Wright, bust (commissioned by Lettsom); plaster copies, RS Friends, Lond., and Ackworth, Yorkshire · bust on Fothergillian medal of the London Medical Society, repro. in Abraham, *Lettsom*, 219 · silhouette, repro. in A. C. Brinton, *Quaker profiles: pictorial and biographical, 1750–1850* (1964) · stipple, Wellcome L.

Wealth at death approx. £25,000; library; real estate?; legacy to Ackworth School and various relatives and friends: Fox, *Fothergill*

Fothergill, John Milner

Fothergill, John Milner (1841–1888), physician, was born on 11 April 1841 at Morland, Westmorland, the son of George Fothergill (d. 1866), a surgeon apothecary, and his wife, Sarah Milner (d. 1869). He was educated locally, first at St Bees grammar school, under the Revd Miles Atkinson, and later at Appleby grammar school. In 1853 he was apprenticed to his father and, though continuing at school during term-time, assisted him in his practice during the school holidays. He entered the University of Edinburgh in 1859 and graduated MD in 1865, in the latter year obtaining the licences of both the Royal College of Surgeons and the Royal College of Physicians of Edinburgh.

On graduating from Edinburgh Fothergill was, against his wishes, obliged by his father's ill health and poverty to return as assistant to the practice at Morland. After his father died, Fothergill successfully applied in 1869 to become senior resident medical officer at the Leeds Public Dispensary. While working there he began the experimental research into the operation of digitalis upon the heart, for which he was awarded the Hastings gold medal of the British Medical Association in 1870. Having become embroiled in a dispute with the dispensary matron and the chairman of the house committee, in 1871 Fothergill decided to leave Leeds to pursue his work on diseases of the heart on the continent. He studied at Vienna and Berlin before returning to England in 1872 with the manuscript of his first book, *The Heart and its Diseases* (1872).

Fothergill now settled in London and attempted with limited success to establish a practice. In 1872, soon after arriving, he became a member of the Royal College of Physicians. He obtained the post of assistant physician to the West London Hospital in 1874, which he retained until 1881. He also became, in 1876, a member of the staff of the City of London Hospital for Diseases of the Chest, to which he was eventually appointed physician. During the 1870s Fothergill carried out a series of experiments for the

British Medical Association on the mutual antagonism of various poisons. His discovery that belladonna (atropine) and strychnia would neutralize the effect of aconite on respiration led to his being awarded the Fothergillian gold medal of the Medical Society of London, established by his ancestor John Fothergill (1712–1780), for his essay *The Antagonism of Therapeutic Agents* (1878). The use of atropine in a normally fatal dose to revive breathing in cases of opium poisoning proved his findings, though this never became general practice.

Fothergill's reputation was largely based upon his numerous and extensive writings on a range of medical subjects, in particular gout, digestion, and diet. His early success during his first years in London was based on extensive contributions to the medical press, such as the *British Medical Journal* and the *London Medical Record*. In later years he wrote a number of successful medical textbooks and practical guides to medicine. He also published on a variety of non-medical subjects, even writing an (unsuccessful) novel, *Gaythorne Hall* (1885). Fothergill acquired great fame in the United States after he published *The Practitioners' Handbook of Treatment* in 1876, a pragmatic and useful work that proved widely influential. For many years he wrote a monthly letter for the *Philadelphia Medical Times*. He was accounted in 1878 'the English medical author best known in the United States' (*Cincinnati Lancet and Clinic*, 7 Dec 1878), next to Sir Thomas Watson, and he received a number of honours from American bodies, including an honorary MD degree from Rush College, Chicago.

Fothergill's style was vigorous and frequently contentious, as was his character:

> He was by birth and characteristics a Westmorland dalesman, witty, humorous, though somewhat unpolished in speech and rough in manner. A certain sense of personal grievance under which he laboured during a large part of his life made him often unduly aggressive … but his power, vigour and genial humour [made him many friends]. (*BMJ*, 542)

Unfortunately Fothergill's outspoken nature also offended a great many of his contemporaries; among them was the editor of the *British Medical Journal*, with whom he conducted a protracted and damaging feud. Fothergill stood out by his appearance, weighing approximately 300 lb, and was known to friends as 'the claimant' for his resemblance to the Tichborne pretender.

Fothergill married Adelaide Beatrice Hammersty on 4 November 1880 at St Thomas's Orchard, Portman Square, London. They had no children together. He died of diabetes, from which he had long suffered, at his house at 3 Henrietta Street, Cavendish Square, London, on 28 June 1888, survived by his wife.   PATRICK WALLIS

Sources 'Autobiography of the late J. Milner Fothergill M. D.', *New England Medical Monthly*, 21 (1902), 2–11 • J. Leyand, ed., *J. Milner Fothergill: a biography* (1887) • *The Lancet* (14 July 1888) • *BMJ* (7 July 1888), 51–2 • 'J. Milner Fothergill', *Cincinnati Lancet and Clinic* (7 Dec 1878) • *CGPLA Eng. & Wales* (1888) • *DNB*
Archives Wellcome L., papers
Likenesses lithograph (after Barraud and Jerrard), Wellcome L.

Wealth at death £509 10s.: probate, 7 Aug 1888, *CGPLA Eng. & Wales*

Fothergill, John Rowland (1876–1957), innkeeper and author, was born on 27 February 1876 at Kennington, Ashford, Kent, the only son of George Fothergill and his wife, Isabel Eliza (*née* Crawshay). He had two sisters. His mother died when he was two days old, and George Fothergill subsequently remarried; there was a son by this second marriage. The Fothergills were a long-established Lakeland gentry family, claiming descent from a Norman baron, and his father was both remote and stern. At the age of eleven Fothergill was sent to Old College in Windermere and endured much humiliation and beating. A year later he entered Bath College and in 1895 went up to St John's College, Oxford, where he stayed only one term, as he failed the preliminary examinations.

It would be fair to describe Fothergill during the next twenty-six years of his life as a dilettante. At Bath College, already a romantically handsome youth, he had some early initiation into homosexuality. As an undergraduate he met Oscar Wilde, and he was to become an intimate of Wilde both before his trial and later in France after Wilde had served his sentence. Fothergill was also closely associated with Robert Ross for a number of years.

After leaving Oxford Fothergill drifted for a number of years without a real vocation though, with the assistance of William Rothenstein, he opened the Carfax Gallery in Oxford in 1898. During a tour of European museums he was impressed by Greek antiquities and 'decided to learn about Greek art and to live it' (Sox, 145). At about this time Fothergill had an affair with a rich young American, Beatrice Romaine Goddard. Torn between homosexual and heterosexual attachments, Fothergill joined Edward Perry Warren's unusual group of bachelor aesthetes known as the Lewes House Brotherhood. He helped collect antiquities for the Boston Museum of Fine Arts, and continued his studies in classical archaeology. Eventually leaving this milieu, Fothergill studied at Leipzig, and then at the Slade School (1905–6), and was drawn into the circle surrounding Augustus John. During this time he was briefly married to Doris Elsa Henning.

In 1922 Fothergill abandoned the life of a dilettante and scholar. Much to the astonishment of those close to him, and at the age of forty-six, he acquired The Spreadeagle in Thame, Oxfordshire, and found his vocation. Also in 1922 he embarked on a lasting and transparently happy marriage to Kate Headley Kirby, who contributed enormously to the running of The Spreadeagle; they had two sons. In his most successful book, *An Innkeeper's Diary*, Fothergill wrote cryptically that his background and previous work disqualified him from any of the usual jobs: 'I found that I must do something for a living so I was counselled to take an inn' (Fothergill, *Diary*).

Fothergill described himself in *Who's Who* as an 'amateur pioneer innkeeper'. Before the Second World War innkeeping was an outré occupation for someone of his background, yet, virtually single-handedly, he made the profession of innkeeping smart as well as respectable. In its heyday during the latter part of the twenties, The

Spreadeagle became a haunt for the literary and artistic world, as well as for Oxford dons and well-connected undergraduates. Its patrons included writers such as G. B. Shaw, H. G. Wells, Evelyn Waugh, the Sitwells, and G. K. Chesterton, artists such as Augustus John and Paul Nash, and actors and actresses. Even heads of state such as Field Marshal Smuts were numbered among the guests.

Fothergill possessed many (though by no means all) of the essential attributes of an outstanding innkeeper: he was an excellent chef, a connoisseur of wine (though he drank very little himself), an early campaigner for 'real food', and cared passionately about the quality of the furnishings. Foodstuffs were regularly ordered from Athens, France, Norway, Jaffa, and Italy, and he also sought out the best local produce. Three local bakers produced 'three different kinds of bread made of flours that I have forced upon them, besides the breads we make ourselves', and there was 'cheese from East Harptree, salt from Malden, mustard from Newport Pagnell' (Fothergill, *Diary*, 170).

Yet the success of Fothergill's enterprise depended first and foremost on his intriguing, volatile, and provocative personality. He had a clear idea of the kind of clientele he wished to attract, and those whom he cherished felt honoured to be sharing his company. He had little compunction in showing the door to the wrong sort. 'I've determined', Fothergill wrote in his diary, 'not only to have proper and properly cooked food but to have only either intelligent, beautiful or well-bred people to eat it' (*The Times*, 29 Aug 1957). H. G. Wells described Fothergill as 'a fantastic innkeeper ... dressed in the suit of bottle-green cloth, with brass buttons and buckled shoes' (Sox, 161). Harold Acton concurred that:

> for a quiet dinner there was no alternative but to drive to Thame. At John Fothergill's ... one could be sure of good food and better wine in congenial surroundings with a host whose affability and erudition revived a more liberal age. (ibid., 161)

Fothergill was an irresistible raconteur, but if he had lacked the art of telling stories in print it is unlikely that he would still be remembered today. Fortunately, he was persuaded to write *An Innkeeper's Diary*, which was an instant best-seller when it was first published in 1931 and has been reprinted many times since as well as being dramatized for both television and radio. Like Flora Thompson's *Lark Rise to Candleford* it recalls with uncommon vividness the feel of Oxfordshire life in a former era; both writers convey the moral values that prevailed at their time and in their own social class.

The *Diary* presents an image of its author as irascible, gratuitously offensive, and an outrageous snob. He would refuse to accept guests because he disliked their notepaper or their letter-writing style. On one occasion, he recounts having charged a party who had come in for tea an extra 6*d*. per head because they were ill-shaped, ugly or ill-dressed—'surely a more praiseworthy action than charging people extra because they *are* beautiful, well-bred and dressed' (Fothergill, *Diary*, 27). He particularly detested those who came in off the streets and tried to use

his lavatories without asking. He would accost these interlopers and demand their addresses—'in case I need a pumpship when I'm passing your home' (private information).

Ten years at The Spreadeagle brought Fothergill fame but scarcely fortune. He was a poor businessman, and book royalties could not compensate for hotel losses. He was forced to sell, spent an unsuccessful year at a hotel in Ascot, and in 1934 acquired the Three Swans in Market Harborough, where he stayed until 1952. Fothergill died at St Luke's Hospital, Rugby, on 26 August 1957. While at Market Harborough he had published two more volumes of reminiscences, *Confessions of an Innkeeper* in 1938 and *My Three Inns* in 1949, but neither had the bite and raciness of *An Innkeeper's Diary*. It surpassed them as his best book, a minor classic in the annals of innkeeping.

HILARY RUBINSTEIN

Sources J. Fothergill, *An innkeeper's diary* (1931) · J. Fothergill, *Confessions of an innkeeper* (1938) · J. Fothergill, *My three inns* (1949) · D. Sox, *Bachelors of art: Edward Perry Warren and the Lewes House Brotherhood* (1991) · R. McDonall, *Daily Telegraph* (23 Feb 1973) [magazine article] · *The Times* (29 Aug 1957) · WWW · private information (1986) · CGPLA Eng. & Wales (1957) · M. Holroyd, *Augustus John: a biography*, rev. edn (1976) · b. cert. · m. cert., 1922
Archives Tate Collection, corresp. and drawings
Likenesses photograph, 1898, repro. in Sox, *Bachelors of art* · L. Falli, portrait, *c*.1899, repro. in Sox, *Bachelors of art* · R. Brooks, portrait, *c*.1905 (after photograph, 1898), repro. in Sox, *Bachelors of art* · A. John, drawing, 1906, repro. in Fothergill, *Innkeeper's diary* · J. R. Fothergill, self-portrait, 1910, repro. in Fothergill, *Innkeeper's diary* · photograph, 1923, repro. in Fothergill, *Innkeeper's diary* · H. Coster, photographs, NPG · W. Rothenstein, portrait, repro. in Sox, *Bachelors of art* · B. Thomas, caricature, repro. in *Daily Telegraph*
Wealth at death £12,966 12*s*.: probate, 1 Nov 1957, CGPLA Eng. & Wales

Fothergill, Samuel (1715–1772), Quaker minister, was born on 9 November 1715 at Carr End, near Countersett, in Wensleydale, Yorkshire, the sixth son of John Fothergill (1676–1745) and his wife, Margaret (1677–1719), daughter of Thomas and Ellin Hough of Sutton, Cheshire. His parents were devout Quakers of substantial means, his father travelling widely as a preacher. After his mother's death, and in his father's absence, he was cared for by his uncle Thomas Hough at Sutton. Precise details of Fothergill's education are unclear: he may have attended a Quaker school at Brigflatts, near Sedbergh, or have been educated with his brother John *Fothergill (1712–1780) at Frodsham and then at Sedbergh grammar school. As a bright and lively youth Samuel Fothergill rebelled against the fetters of his religious upbringing during his apprenticeship with Henry Ardern, a Stockport shopkeeper, but at the age of twenty he passed through a period of spiritual turmoil during his father's absence on a religious visit to America, and returned to the Quaker fold. He moved to Warrington in Lancashire, where initially he lived with another brother, Joseph, and set up in business there as a shopkeeper and tea merchant. One of the Quaker ministers who counselled him at this time was Susannah Croudson (1698–1773), a Warrington milliner seventeen years his senior, who was the daughter of William and Mary Croudson of Warrington. He and Susannah married on 1 August 1738; they had no children.

Fothergill became a preacher in his early twenties and, from 1739, he travelled extensively in the ministry. He was a regular attender at the regional yearly meetings in England and at the principal yearly meeting held in London. From August 1754 to July 1756 he made a religious visit to America, travelling over 8700 miles to visit most of the Friends' meetings (and some isolated Quaker families), from Massachusetts to Georgia. He encouraged Pennsylvanian Friends to maintain their pacifist principles during the French and Indian War, supporting those who refused to pay war taxes.

Fothergill was one of the leading public Friends of his generation. By the 1750s he was at the forefront of efforts to revive the declining membership of the Society of Friends through tightening its religious discipline. In 1753 he proposed the establishment of an annual meeting of ministers and elders, thus forming an inner circle to guide the society. He led the 'revival committee', appointed by the London yearly meeting in 1760 to strengthen discipline within the society, which visited monthly and quarterly meetings across the nation in 1761. He was also a member of the deputation, with the same aims, which visited Ireland during 1762, and in 1764 he travelled through Scotland on a similar, though informal, disciplinary visit. The same concern, to reawaken increasingly wealthy and worldly Friends to Quaker principles, led him to visit the homes of well-to-do London Friends in 1769. He was sought after to help to resolve disagreements within the Quaker community, as, for example, in 1766, when he acted as conciliator in a bitter dispute involving members of the society in Cumberland. On a wider front he urged his neighbours in Warrington to raise a subscription for the relief of the poor during the winter of 1756, and acted as apologist for the Quaker attitude to baptism in a pamphlet published in 1763.

Contemporaries saw Fothergill as a 'great, and eminent minister' (Frost, 66). He preached with power and conviction, even if, as another Friend complained in 1764, he sometimes assumed that only members of the close-knit ministerial élite of which he was a part had access to divine inspiration. A tall figure, cultured and grave, yet affable, he was also an eloquent speaker, his words flowing forth 'like a mighty, and impetuous stream, yet beautifully rolling along' (ibid., 67). His sermons and prayers were copied down; some were published.

Fothergill's health deteriorated after his return from America, when he suffered a period of mental exhaustion; he retired from business about 1765. By 1768 he was a changed man: 'a hollow cough, hoarse and appears very feeble' (Crosfield, 473). Towards the end of 1771 he was seized by a painful and debilitating illness. He died at his home at Sankey near Warrington, on 15 June 1772, and was buried in the Quaker burial-ground at Penketh, Lancashire, on 19 June. He was survived by his wife, who died on 8 May 1773. ANGUS J. L. WINCHESTER

Sources G. Crosfield, *Memoirs of the life … of Samuel Fothergill* (1843) · 'Dictionary of Quaker biography', RS Friends, Lond. [card index] · digests of births, marriages, burials, Lancashire quarterly meeting, RS Friends, Lond. · *The records and recollections of James Jenkins*, ed. J. W. Frost (1984) · R. H. Fox, *Dr John Fothergill and his friends* (1919) · *Chain of friendship: selected letters of Dr. John Fothergill of London, 1735–1780*, ed. B. C. Corner and C. C. Booth (1971) · *The diary of Isaac Fletcher of Underwood, Cumberland, 1756–1781*, ed. A. J. L. Winchester (1994) · *DNB* · R. M. Jones, *The later periods of Quakerism*, 2 vols. (1921)
Archives RS Friends, Lond., corresp. and sermons | RS Friends, Lond., Crosfield MS, vol. 329 · RS Friends, Lond., Robson MSS, corresp.
Likenesses silhouette, RS Friends, Lond.

Fotheringham, John Knight (1874–1936), historian and astronomer, was born on 14 August 1874 at St John's presbytery, Tottenham, Middlesex, the second son of David Fotheringham (1830–1918), a Presbyterian minister, and his wife, Jane Ross (1834–1917). A delicate child, he was to suffer much ill health later in life. He was educated at the City of London School and gained an exhibition to Merton College, Oxford, where he obtained a first class in *literae humaniores* (1896) and in modern history (1897). From 1898 to 1902 he was a senior demy at Magdalen College. In 1903 he married Mary Eleanor, the daughter of Joseph Atkinson of Crosby Garrett, Westmorland; there were no children.

Much of the research for Fotheringham's first published works was undertaken during his senior demyship at Oxford; two papers on aspects of chronology appeared in the *Journal of Philology* (1903), while an edition of *The Bodleian Manuscript of Jerome's Version of the Chronicle of Eusebius* was published by Oxford University Press in 1905. In 1904 Fotheringham was appointed lecturer in classical literature at King's College, London, a post which he held until 1909. During this period he completed and revised volume 11 (covering the period from 1801 to 1837) of Longman's *Political History of England* (published in 1906). For his work on Eusebius he was admitted DLitt by Oxford University in 1908.

In 1909 Fotheringham was appointed lecturer in ancient history at King's College and in 1912 reader in ancient history. The latter post he formally held until 1920, although it was suspended following the outbreak of the First World War. From 1909 to 1916 he was concurrently research fellow at Magdalen College, Oxford, which inevitably involved frequent commuting between London and Oxford. His main task at Oxford was the production of a definitive edition of Jerome's Latin version of the *Chronica* of Eusebius, although the First World War and his own ill health delayed completion of this major project; it was not published until 1923. Around 1909 he commenced serious research on the secular accelerations of the moon and sun, as determined from ancient observations of eclipses and other events, a study which was to become a major preoccupation with him over the next decade or so. In this work, which was published mainly in *Monthly Notices of the Royal Astronomical Society* between 1909 and 1920, Fotheringham combined his skill as a classical scholar with a depth of astronomical knowledge and expertise. In 1910 he wrote an important paper on the visibility of the crescent moon, a topic of considerable relevance to the study of certain early calendars. This paper, which appeared in *Monthly Notices*, became a model for later research on the subject and was still quoted in the literature at the end of the twentieth century.

Fotheringham's duties lapsed at King's College in 1915 and at Magdalen in 1916, leaving him without income. He was briefly employed in a government office, but after a few months he had to resign on health grounds. In 1918, after a period of convalescence, he was appointed assistant at the Oxford University observatory by Professor Herbert H. Turner. This post carried only a meagre salary. Fotheringham received much encouragement from Turner, but it would seem that in general Oxford academics were slow to recognize the value of his work. Eventually, in 1925, a readership in ancient history and chronology was specially created for him at Oxford, and he held this position—along with an honorary assistantship at the university observatory—until his death in 1936. However, a professorship eluded him. In his early years at the university observatory he completed his studies on the lunar and solar accelerations, culminating in his Halley lecture on 'Historical eclipses' (1921). In 1923 he collaborated with Professor Stephen H. Langdon and Carl Schoch in a detailed study of the Venus tablets of Ammizaduga. This research, published in 1928, led to the assignment of 1921 BC as the first year of the reign of King Ammizaduga of Babylon, fifth successor of Hammurabi. However, such an early date for Ammizaduga has been questioned by modern scholars.

In 1926 and 1927 Fotheringham published in *Monthly Notices* two papers on the apparent fluctuations in the motions of the moon, sun, and inner planets as revealed by telescopic observations extending back to the eighteenth century. This phenomenon he termed 'trepidation'. These studies brought him into conflict with Professor Ernest W. Brown. The true cause of the fluctuations, which eluded Fotheringham, was later (1939) conclusively demonstrated by Sir Harold Spencer Jones to be due to irregularities in the earth's rate of rotation.

Three years before his death Fotheringham was elected a fellow of the British Academy. He died at his home, Dunbarrow, Hids Copse Road, Cumnor Hill, near Oxford, on 12 December 1936 after a short illness, and was buried on 15 December at Aston Tirrold Presbyterian Church, where he had regularly worshipped. He was survived by his wife. Fotheringham was described by a contemporary as both a 'keen controversialist' and 'a very lovable man' (Myres, 562–3).

Fotheringham is remembered mainly for his extensive researches on the accelerations of the moon and sun as revealed by the study of ancient astronomical observations. He was the first person to make a reasonably accurate estimate of the apparent solar acceleration, and also considerably refined the adopted value for the lunar acceleration. His most outstanding paper on this subject was published in *Monthly Notices* in 1920. Here he produced an intriguing diagram showing lunar acceleration v. solar acceleration as derived from ancient eclipse observations. During the 1960s and 1970s in particular, this diagram attracted remarkable interest among geophysicists, and Fotheringham's work is still frequently quoted in geophysical literature. F. R. STEPHENSON

Sources J. L. Myres, 'John Knight Fotheringham, 1874–1936', *PBA*, 23 (1937), 551–64 • R. A. Sampson, 'John Knight Fotheringham', *Isis*, 27 (1937), 485–92 • C. Singer, *Archeion*, 19 (1937), 172–8 • W. H. M. G. [W. H. M. Greaves], *Monthly Notices of the Royal Astronomical Society*, 97 (1936–7), 270–72 • *WWW*, 1929–40 • *The Times* (14 Dec 1936) • *Oxford Mail* (14 Dec 1936) • *Oxford Times* (18 Dec 1936) • *Oxford Times* (25 Dec 1936) • *Oxford Magazine* (21 Jan 1937) • A. Pogo, 'The writings of J. K. Fotheringham', *Isis*, 29 (1938), 58–68 • City of London School, file
Likenesses W. Stoneman, photograph, 1933, NPG • photograph, repro. in Sampson, *Isis*
Wealth at death £2418 8s. 4d.: probate, 18 Feb 1937, CGPLA Eng. & Wales

Fougasse. *See* Bird, (Cyril) Kenneth (1887–1965).

Foulds, John Herbert (1880–1939), composer and author, was born on 2 November 1880 at 49 Dorset Street, Hulme, Manchester, one of the four children of Fred Foulds, a bassoonist, and his wife, Mary, *née* Greenwood, who were both members of the Plymouth Brethren. Self-educated musically, yet later an apprentice conductor to Hallé, Richter, Nikisch, Mahler, and Lamoureux, Foulds initially earned a living as an orchestral cellist in the Hallé Orchestra from 1900 to 1914 and as a practical all-round musician, lecturing, playing, arranging music, and teaching, while constantly composing music.

Foulds was soon regarded as an efficient and charming light-music composer—the *Lament* from the *Keltic Suite* (1911) remained popular long after his death—and he wrote much incidental music for contemporary plays, including Bernard Shaw's *Saint Joan* (1924). Despite championship by Granville Bantock, Elgar, and Richter, Foulds's serious works fared less well, though in 1906 Henry Wood conducted a successful Proms performance of his symphonic poem *Epithalamium*. Meanwhile he reacted against his strict religious upbringing by showing a growing interest in theosophy and the occult, which was reflected in his music; for instance, the score of the symphonic poem *Mirage* (1910) is headed by a representation of the occult symbol of a pentagram.

In 1909 Foulds married a Llandudno girl, Maud Woodcock; they had a son, Raymond, in 1911. Then in 1915 he met the charismatic violinist Maud MacCarthy (1882–1967), who shared his theosophical interests but broke up his marriage. After a period of living together they married and had a son, Patrick, and a daughter, Marybride. Maud MacCarthy was a pioneer ethnomusicologist, played many Indian instruments, and was able to pitch precisely the twenty-three *srutis*, or microtonal intervals, characteristic of Indian music. These skills influenced Foulds's experiments with quarter-tones and non-Western modes, and her profound knowledge of Indian spiritual beliefs strengthened his esoteric convictions.

The turning point in Foulds's life was conducting the first performance of his *A World Requiem* (1919–21) on armistice night 1923 to an emotional audience in a packed

Albert Hall. Encouraged by the British Legion, it was repeated annually until 1926, when it was boycotted inexplicably by both concert promoters and the emergent BBC; by the late twentieth century it had not been performed in its entirety since. Unfortunately public enthusiasm was countered by critical disdain, and there is evidence that there was a jealous conspiracy against the work, possibly because its immediate popularity was distrusted by the musical establishment; it was known in the Foulds family as the 'Wreck 'Em'. Its relegation undermined Foulds's confidence; he fled to Paris, where he earned a living as a cinema organist before returning to London in 1930.

In 1935 the whole family moved to India, and Foulds joined his wife in collecting Indian folk music. From 1937 he worked for All-India Radio while learning to play Indian instruments, and he formed an Indo-European orchestra, hoping to further his aim of a synthesis of Eastern and Western music. This goal was never realized, for he died suddenly of cholera in Calcutta on 25 April 1939.

Throughout his life Foulds had become increasingly convinced of the occult nature of musical inspiration, maintaining that sections of *A World Requiem* and the prophetically minimalist piano piece *Gandharva-Music* (1915) were clairaudiently heard. In his lively and provocative book *Music To-Day op 92* (1934) he discussed the occult effect of quarter-tones, which he first used in 1898, then later in *Mirage*, *A World Requiem*, and the fine and idiomatic *Quartetto intimo* (1931–2) and other works. He felt that another way for composers to break away from Western diatonicism lay in experimenting with Indian modes. He demonstrated their effectiveness in the set of piano pieces *Essays in the Modes* (1920–27), the piano concerto *Dynamic Triptych* (1929), and the orchestral *Three Mantras* (1919–30), which had served as preludes to each act of his lost opera *Avatara*.

Foulds's interests were alien to the English musical culture of the inter-war years, and his compositions thus remained largely unperformed until the 1980s, when they enjoyed a modest revival of interest. In 1998 an enormously enthusiastic response to a Proms performance of the *Three Mantras* seemed to indicate that Foulds's multicultural concerns were more relevant to late twentieth-century audiences than to those of his own time.

DIANA SWANN

Sources BL, John Foulds MSS, Add. MSS 56469–56483 · M. MacDonald, *John Foulds and his music*, rev. edn (White Plains, NY, 1989) · D. Swann, 'Gentlemen v. players: alienation and the esoteric in English music, 1900–39', PhD diss., U. Southampton, 1998
Archives BBC WAC, files · BL, MSS, Add. MSS 56469–56483 · NRA, priv. coll., MSS, memos, corresp.
Likenesses photographs, 1910–39, repro. in MacDonald, *John Foulds* · photograph, BL, John Foulds MSS, Add. MSS 56482

Foulger [*née* Rutherford], **Dorothea** (1787–1852), educationist, was born in 1787 (probably in November), in the London parish of St George-in-the-East, the daughter of Dr John Rutherford and his wife, Lydia Rebecca Duplex. Her mother's family were Huguenot silk weavers who settled in England in the 1760s. Little is known about her life until

she and her husband, John Foulger (1782–1850), moved to Walthamstow from east London in 1833 after their children had grown up. They had at least three children, Samuel (*b.* 1806), Arthur (1819–1851), and Mary Anne Lydia. Both John and Dorothea Foulger were active in their local Independent (Congregational) chapel, the New Meeting, in Marsh Street, Walthamstow (the chapel, which included a memorial tablet to the Foulgers, has since been demolished), where John Foulger served as a deacon and later as trustee. The New Meeting in Marsh Street had been energized by the evangelical revival, and the church strongly identified itself with the cause of foreign missions: its minister from 1837 to 1846, the Revd J. J. Freeman, had been a missionary in Madagascar and Mauritius. John Foulger, as a Cape merchant, had early contact with French missionaries in southern Africa, and the Foulgers kept an open house for missionaries of all denominations. Here, Dorothea Foulger presided over a mixed household comprising extended family, servants, and visiting missionaries. In no sense was her home merely a place for private relaxation; Dorothea Foulger's home provided missionaries a welcome respite from their labours but also served as a site of valuable social and spiritual contacts, both within the local community and the wider evangelical world. Hence, Dorothea Foulger was ideally placed to understand missionaries' anxieties about their children's education and, as a woman who believed in acting on her faith, set out to fill the perceived need.

In every sense of the word, Mrs Foulger was the moving spirit of what would become Walthamstow Hall school for missionaries' daughters. In April 1838 she pressed the home secretary of the London Missionary Society, John Arundel, for an opinion about the feasibility of opening such a school. When Arundel replied that the society thought it better to educate girls at existing schools (at reduced rates to the society), Mrs Foulger and her committee politely ignored him. She plainly believed that a non-denominational (but Christian and evangelical) school devoted to the needs of girls whose parents were missionaries was needed. The school certainly intended that its pupils should follow in their parents' footsteps; the subjects taught included: reading, writing, accounts, English language, history, geography, drawing, music, needlework, and Latin. Latin was included because, since it was assumed the girls would become missionaries, they would require a thorough grounding in the structure of language. Certainly, it provided an education which would allow its pupils to take advantage of the increasing career opportunities available to women. Of the students who left the school between 1841 and 1878, 57 became teachers, 37 wives of missionaries, 18 missionaries in their own right, 8 clerical workers, 4 nurses, and 3 doctors; the school also produced one milliner, one school matron, and one wood-engraver (Pike and Curryer, 24, 28).

When the committee formally began to run the school in August 1838, Dorothea Foulger was elected one of the two cash secretaries. In charge of the purse-strings, Mrs Foulger widened her remit to include the hiring (and, in one delicate case, firing) of teachers and matrons. She served on the furniture subcommittee and was a regular visitor to the school, reporting on its state to the committee. Nor were Dorothea Foulger's family left out of the enterprise: John Foulger was one of a committee of three men charged with finding premises for the new school (Walthamstow was seen as a particularly salubrious location for schools: there were at least six in the village in the early nineteenth century), and in 1882 the school moved to Sevenoaks, then the residence of the Foulgers' daughter, Mary Anne Lydia Pye-Smith, who maintained a lifelong interest in the school. Both Foulgers was also instrumental in the foundation of Eltham College, a school for the sons of missionaries, which opened in 1842. John was on the governing committee and Dorothea was a member of a committee of ladies who ensured the house was appropriately furnished and adapted for the needs of schoolchildren. As an administrator, organizer, and proponent of education, Dorothea Foulger put her evangelical principles into practice. Mrs Foulger remained a committee member and a secretary of Walthamstow Hall until her death at Walthamstow on 6 May 1852 from an inflammation of the lungs. She was buried on 13 May in Abney Park cemetery. L. E. LAUER

Sources M. C. Martin, 'Women and philanthropy in Walthamstow and Leyton, 1740–1870', *London Journal*, 19/2 (1995), 119–50 · *Evangelical Magazine and Missionary Chronicle*, new ser., 30 (1852), 346–8 · E. Pike and C. E. Curryer, *The story of Walthamstow Hall* (1938) · C. Witting, ed., *The Glory of the Sons: a history of Eltham College for the sons of missionaries* (1952) · 'Earliest papers file', committee minutes, Walthamstow Hall, Sevenoaks · H. D. Budden, *The story of Marsh Street Congregational Church, Walthamstow* (1923) · d. cert. · Foulger pedigree, Vestry House Museum, Walthamstow
Likenesses engraving, Walthamstow Hall, Sevenoaks, Kent; repro. in Pike and Curryer, *Story of Walthamstow Hall*

Foulis, Andrew, the elder (1712–1775). *See under* Foulis, Robert (1707–1776).

Foulis, Andrew, the younger (1756–1829). *See under* Foulis, Robert (1707–1776).

Foulis, Sir David, first baronet (*d.* 1642), court official and politician, was the son of Henry Foulis (*d.* 1571) of Colinton, an advocate, and Margaret Haldane (*fl.* 1545–1560). Between 1594 and 1602 he was sent by James VI to London six times, primarily to secure payment of the king's English pension but also, in 1601, to offer assistance against the Irish rebels. In October 1598 he was appointed keeper of the king's secret papers. He accompanied James to England in 1603, was knighted on 13 May, naturalized by act of parliament in March 1605, and created honorary MA during the court's visit to Oxford in August 1605. He was granted land in Yorkshire, including part of the Lennox estate in May 1603 and the manors of Greenhow and Templehurst in January 1604, plus a pension of £118 13s. 4d. in October 1604. He gained an interest in manufacturing alum in England in 1607 and in Scotland in 1609, and purchased further manors in Yorkshire in 1608–9, including Ingleby, his main residence. By 1632 his estate was believed to be worth more than £1000 a year. He had five sons and two daughters from his marriage to Cordelia

Fleetwood (*d.* 1631), daughter of William Fleetwood of Great Missenden, Buckinghamshire.

Foulis served as cofferer to Prince Henry and Prince Charles from 1610 until 1617, when he sold his place to Sir Henry Vane. In February 1620 he was created a baronet and by 1621 he was serving on the commission of the peace for the North Riding, acting as *custos rotulorum* in 1626–9. In 1625 he became a member of the council of the north and by 1630 he was a deputy lieutenant. In July 1630, however, Foulis, among others, was removed from the northern recusancy commission at Lord President Wentworth's request. In 1629–30 he was questioned by the privy council regarding his receipt in 1614 of the exiled Sir Robert Dudley's discourse on government.

In April 1631 Foulis was required to account for moneys he had received when cofferer to Prince Charles. His failure to do so caused auditors to examine his books, whereupon he was found to be about £5000 in arrears (Reid, 420). In July 1632 he apparently encouraged opposition to the commission for compounding for knighthood fines, claiming in addition that Wentworth had not made full payment to the exchequer; the lord president saw this as a vain attempt by Foulis to draw attention away from the investigation into his own financial affairs. Foulis also supported Sir Thomas Layton's challenge to the jurisdiction of the court at York. His attempts to curry favour with the king caused Charles to remark that Wentworth was an 'honest and a wise man, and what himself it would appear' (Strafford MSS, 12/254b). The cause of the investigation into Foulis's accounts is not known and it is not certain that Wentworth was involved, but his response to Foulis's challenge was characteristically severe.

In November 1633 Foulis, his son Henry, and Layton, sheriff of Yorkshire, appeared in Star Chamber charged with opposing the king's service, slandering the lord president, and treating the court at York with contempt. Foulis was removed from all his administrative posts, ordered to pay a fine of £5000 to the crown and damages of £3000 to Wentworth, and sent to prison following refusal to pay. Apart from a temporary release in 1636–8 due to the spread of sickness, he spent most of the next seven years in the Fleet prison. Freed by the Long Parliament, he testified against Wentworth at his trial. He died in 1642 and was buried at Ingleby. He was described by a contemporary as 'never accounted inclined to the Puritans as such, but a lover of them as Englishmen, and very kind and helpful to them in their troubles' (Cliffe, 345). His 'Declaration of the diet and particular fare of King Charles I when duke of York', detailing wage and food allowances of the duke's attendants, was printed in *Archaeologia* in 1806. FIONA POGSON

Sources DNB · *CSP Scot. ser., 1589–1603* · *CSP dom., 1603–18; 1623–5; 1629–37; 1639–40* · J. T. Cliffe, *The Yorkshire gentry from the Reformation to the civil war* (1969) · J. Graves, *The history of Cleveland* (1808) · R. R. Reid, *The king's council in the north* (1921) · J. H. Gleason, *The justices of the peace in England, 1558 to 1640* (1969) · S. R. Gardiner, *History of England from the accession of James I to the outbreak of the civil war*, 7 (1884) · *Reg. PCS*, 1st ser. · J. Pory to J. Mead, 12 Feb 1630, BL, Harleian MS 383 · Strafford papers, Sheff. Arch., Wentworth Woodhouse muniments, 12, 14, 20–21, 24–5 · *Report on manuscripts in various collections,*

8 vols., HMC, 55 (1901–14), vol. 2 · J. Rushworth, *The tryal of Thomas earl of Strafford* (1700)
Archives CKS, MSS · LPL, letters | BL, letters to Anthony Baron, Add. MS 4125
Wealth at death land sold to pay debts incurred following Star Chamber case: Cliffe, *Yorkshire gentry*

Foulis, David (**1710–1773**), composer and physician, was born on 8 October 1710 at Woodhall, Currie, Edinburgh-shire, the second of two sons and four daughters born to William Foulis (1674–1737) of Woodhall, an advocate, and his second wife, Helen Hepburn. David Foulis studied medicine at Edinburgh University under Alexander Monro from 1729 to 1732 before pursuing further medical studies in Leiden and Rheims in 1734–5. He graduated MD from Rheims on 10 October 1735 and was admitted a fellow of the Royal College of Physicians in Edinburgh on 2 August 1737. From June 1741 until his death, Foulis was employed as physician to George Heriot's Hospital, the prestigious charity school in Edinburgh, a position which he shared with his good friend Colin Drummond from 1766.

Foulis is more noteworthy as one of very few Scottish-born composers of the eighteenth century. It is unknown where he gained his musical education, but he probably learned some music as a boy before being exposed to the work of Italian composers when a student in the Netherlands and France. His compositions have been seen as expressions of the enthusiasm of Scottish musicians in the mid-eighteenth century for Italian music, widely shared in the Edinburgh Musical Society, of which he was elected a member on 8 June 1737 and was a director in 1739. His works suggest that he played the violin. As well as contributing two pieces to Niel Stewart's *Collection of Marches & Airs*, published in Edinburgh about 1761, Foulis wrote a distinguished set of six violin sonatas which were privately published about 1770 in Edinburgh as *Six Solos for the Violin with a Bass for a Violoncello or Harpsichord*. The 'Gentleman' composer was not named, but the ascription of the works to Foulis, first made by William Stenhouse in his notes printed with the 1839 edition of James Johnson's *The Scots Musical Museum*, has never been challenged. The dedicatee, Francis Charteris, a well-known patron of music in late eighteenth-century Edinburgh, may have funded the publication. Foulis would certainly have known Charteris through the Edinburgh Musical Society.

Foulis's finances seem to have run into difficulties after 1750. On 20 June 1753 he was struck off the membership list of the Edinburgh Musical Society for failing to pay his subscriptions, but later that year he negotiated a pay rise from £20 to £30 p.a. from Heriot's. His absence from the meetings of the Royal College of Physicians between January 1758 and July 1761 may suggest ill health. His situation had recovered sufficiently for him to serve as a councillor of the college from December 1764 to December 1765, but after 1 May 1770 he was in receipt of a pension of 7s. weekly from the college. It was this body that subsidized his nursing care from February 1773 (when he was lodging with Miss Paton on Castle Hill, Edinburgh) until he died, presumably in Edinburgh, at some time before 19 April

1773, when Heriot's recognized Drummond as their sole physician on account of Foulis's death. There is no record of any will, nor is Foulis's place of burial known. The biggest enigma in Foulis's life is why he should have died in such an impecunious state, only miles from the large family mansion at Woodhall, near Edinburgh. He might have expected some kind of legacy on the death of his father in 1737 (his elder brother John having died in 1732), but William Foulis's will clearly excludes David, passing all the family property to John's son William. It is possible that David had incurred the family's wrath, perhaps by continuing his studies abroad after the death of John, or perhaps through his marriage. Not even the name of his wife is known; the only record of his marriage is a handwritten family tree among miscellaneous Foulis papers in Edinburgh Central Library which states: 'David practised as a physician in Edinr and died married' (XDA 758.3 F76).

Helen Goodwill

Sources M. Brown, 'An eighteenth century Scottish composer—David Foulis', *Stretto*, 6/3 (1986), 11–30 · Edinburgh Central Library, Foulis papers, XDA 758.3 F76 · records of Heriot's Hospital, George Heriot's school, Edinburgh, 7–10 · D. Johnson, 'Dr David Foulis: medic and musician', *Edinburgh Medicine* (July 1982), 5–7 · testament of Mr William Foulis of Woodhall, advocate, 16 June 1737, NA Scot., CC 8/99 · *The account book of Sir John Foulis of Ravelston, 1671–1707*, ed. A. W. C. Hallen, Scottish History Society, 16 (1894) · Burke, *Peerage* · GEC, *Baronetage* · list of medical students at the University of Edinburgh, 1726–1762, U. Edin. · R. W. Innes Smith, *English-speaking students of medicine at the University of Leyden* (1932) · minute books, Royal College of Physicians of Edinburgh · *Williamson's directory for the city of Edinburgh, Canongate, Leith, and suburbs* (1773)
Archives Edinburgh Central Reference Library, papers

Foulis, Henry (*bap.* **1635**, *d.* **1669**), religious controversialist, was baptized at Ingleby Greenhow, in the North Riding of Yorkshire, on 5 April 1635, the second son of Sir Henry Foulis, second baronet (1607/8–1643), of Ingleby, and his wife, Mary (*d.* 1657), daughter of Sir Thomas Layton of Sexhowe and Mary Fairfax; Sir David *Foulis (*d.* 1642) was his grandfather. His father, a lieutenant-general of horse in the parliamentarian army when the royalists took Leeds, was subsequently fined and imprisoned; following his death on 13 September 1643, administration of his estates was granted in 1646 to a creditor. Sir Henry's eldest son, David Foulis, third baronet (*bap.* 1633, *d.* 1695), held local office during the 1650s and married the daughter of a leading compounding official. Henry was, as he later recalled, 'whilst a School Boy … too much sway'd to Presbytery' and having limited reading matter and 'believing with the Ignorant, all things in Print to be true, was perswaded to incline to the wrong side'. However, 'a little before his going to the University', as a result of a chance reading of George Bate's anonymously published defence of Charles I's dealings with parliament, *Elenchus motuum nuperorum in Anglia* (1649), Foulis abandoned his family's political and religious stance and became a royalist and an Anglican (Foulis, sig. b2). He matriculated from Queen's College, Oxford, on 10 November 1654, graduated BA on 3 February 1657, proceeded MA on 25 June 1659, and on 31 January 1660 was elected a fellow of Lincoln College; there he joined Nathaniel Crew, who had had a similar 'conversion'.

Foulis's *The History of the Wicked Plots and Conspiracies of our Pretended Saints* (1662), begun in 1659 and dedicated to his elder brother and sister-in-law, was a trenchant attack on presbyterians. Comparing them with the Jesuits, it traced their 'wickedness' in England and Scotland from the reign of Elizabeth onwards, with a particular indictment of their efforts to secure a conditional restoration of the monarchy. In years to come the book was popular among tories and it was 'chained to deskes in some countrey churches, to be read by the vulgar' (Ord, 433); Richard Baxter, on the other hand, thought that Foulis had written 'against the Presbyterians with as filthy a Language almost as a Man in his Wits could do' (*Calendar*, 2.206). Foulis's other published work, *The history of the Romish treasons and usurpations: together with a particular account of the many gross corruptions and impostures of the Church of Rome* (1671), showed him equally hostile to papists. He is supposed to have planned further works, but to have destroyed his notes just before he died, probably in Oxford, on 24 December 1669. He was buried at St Michael's Church, Oxford, on 26 December. His books were to be catalogued by Anthony Wood, who described him as an 'acquaintance and dear friend' (*Life and Times*, 2.178).

SARAH CARR

Sources H. Foulis, *The history of the wicked plots and conspiracies of our pretended saints* (1662) · GEC, *Baronetage* · J. W. Ord, *The history and antiquities of Cleveland*, republished (1972) · Foster, *Alum. Oxon.* · Wood, *Ath. Oxon.* · Wood, *Ath. Oxon.: Fasti* · *The life and times of Anthony Wood*, ed. A. Clark, 5 vols., OHS, 19, 21, 26, 30, 40 (1891–1900) · *IGI* [register of Ingleby Greenhow, Yorkshire] · *Hist. U. Oxf.* 4: *17th-cent. Oxf.*, 811 · M. Goldie, 'Restoration political thought', *The reigns of Charles II and James VII and II*, ed. L. K. J. Glassey (1997), 17 · A. J. Hopper, 'A directory of parliamentarian allegiance in Yorkshire during the civil wars', *Yorkshire Archaeological Society Journal*, 73 (2001), 94 · P. A. Bolton, 'Foulis, Sir David, 3rd bt', HoP, *Commons, 1660–90* · *Calendar of the correspondence of Richard Baxter*, ed. N. H. Keeble and G. F. Nuttall, 2 vols. (1991)

Foulis, James (*d.* in or before **1549**), poet and lawyer, was the son of the Edinburgh burgess Henry Foulis and a sister, possibly called Margaret, of James *Henryson of Fordell, king's advocate. His siblings, except for one sister, and parents were killed by plague in Edinburgh in the late 1490s and he was raised by his maternal uncle. His surviving sister, Isabel, married Adam Strachan or Strathauchin, who belonged to a family which produced several notaries at the period. In 1530 Foulis was described as 'eme' (a term probably designating kinship) to Robert Foulis, burgess of Linlithgow. He married Katherine Brown before 1525 and they had five sons, Henry, John, James, Adam, and Robert. He also had two natural daughters, Alison and Grizel.

A student of Robert Galbraith at the University of Paris, Foulis then studied law at the University of Orléans and became procurator of the Scots nation there in July 1512. In 1511 or 1512 he published in Paris a book of collected poems under the title *Jacobi Follosii Edinburgensis calamitose pestis elega deploratio*, bearing a dedication to James Henryson. He returned to Scotland early in 1513 and in April of the following year moved into property in the High Street

of Edinburgh; later he acquired further land within the burgh. He was a burgess of Edinburgh, acting as commissioner for the burgh to parliament in 1526 and again consistently between 1532 and 1546. In 1528 Foulis was one of the assessors of the council at the burgh's Michaelmas head court. This coincided with the busiest period of his career as an advocate before the lords of council. He was never king's advocate, although he did appear occasionally, as did other men of law, as substitute in the absence of the king's advocate, Adam Otterburn. He is known to have owned an edition of works by Bartolus printed in Lyons in 1538.

Foulis was made lord clerk register, and so became a lord of session, in March 1532, offices which he retained until his death. He and his wife acquired from the master of Glencairn in 1527 and 1529 lands in Colinton from which his family afterwards took its designation. The grant of Colinton was erected into a free barony by the king in 1533. In 1534 Foulis was instructed by the lords to create and keep a book recording constitutions of procurators by litigants. If maintained, this book has not survived. He was also charged by parliament with causing the acts of parliament to be printed by any person he should choose, though little seems to have come of this proposal. He aided in the composition of the speech of welcome made on Mary of Guise's entry into Edinburgh in 1538. In 1543 he was a commissioner to negotiate a marriage between the infant Queen Mary and Prince Edward of England. Due to his being 'febill and waik in his persoun' his son Henry was in April 1548 made his substitute as lord clerk register (Livingstone, vol. 3, no. 2716). Foulis was dead by 8 February 1549.

JOHN FINLAY

Sources acts of lords of council, NA Scot., CS 5, CS 6 · R. K. Hannay, ed., *Acts of the lords of council in public affairs, 1501–1554* (1932) · J. M. Thomson and others, eds., *Registrum magni sigilli regum Scotorum / The register of the great seal of Scotland*, 11 vols. (1882–1914), vols. 3–4 · M. Livingstone, D. Hay Fleming, and others, eds., *Registrum secreti sigilli regum Scotorum / The register of the privy seal of Scotland*, 1–4 (1908–52) · *APS*, 1424–1567 · J. Durkan, 'The beginnings of humanism in Scotland', *Innes Review*, 4 (1953), 5–24 · *The protocol book of John Foular*, ed. J. Durkan, 4, Scottish RS, new ser., 10 (1985) · *The protocol book of John Foular*, ed. W. Macleod and M. Wood, 1–3, Scottish RS, 64, 72, 75 (1930–53) · J. Kirkpatrick, 'The Scottish nation in the University of Orleans, 1336–1538', *Miscellany ... II*, 44 (1904), 45–102 · C. B. B. Watson, ed., *Roll of Edinburgh burgesses and guild-brethren, 1406–1700*, Scottish RS, 59 (1929) · G. Brunton and D. Haig, *An historical account of the senators of the college of justice, from its institution in MDXXXII* (1832) · J. Finlay, 'Professional men of law before the lords of council, c.1500–c.1550', PhD diss., U. Edin., 1997 · *DNB*

Foulis, Sir James, of Colinton, second baronet, Lord **Colinton** (*d.* **1688**), politician and judge, was the eldest son of Sir Alexander Foulis of Colinton, first baronet, and his wife, Elizabeth, daughter of Robert Hepburn of Ford, and widow of Sir John Stewart, sheriff of Bute. He graduated MA from the University of Edinburgh on 25 July 1624, and was knighted by Charles I on 14 November 1641; he succeeded his father in the baronetcy about 1670. He was a shire commissioner for Edinburgh in parliament in 1645–7, and again in 1648–51, and served as a member of the committee of war (1643, 1644, and 1646–8) and the committee of estates (1646–8), and as a commissioner to enforce acts against runaways and deficients (1644). He does not appear to have served on such bodies under the radical covenanting regimes in power from late 1648, but was appointed to the March 1651 committee for managing the army, dominated by former supporters of the engagement, and to the 1651 committee of estates. With the other members of the last-mentioned body nominated to accompany the army he was captured at Alyth by a detachment of Monck's forces, then besieging Dundee, on 28 August 1651, was taken prisoner to London, and had his lands confiscated.

After the Restoration Foulis became an ordinary lord of session and a senator of the college of justice as Lord Colinton (1661), and acted as a commissioner of supply (also in 1661) and a convenor of the justices of the peace (1663). He continued to represent Edinburgh as a shire commissioner in the parliaments and conventions of estates from 1661 to 1681, and was one of the lords of the articles in 1661, 1672, and 1681. He became a lord commissioner of justiciary when that court was established in February 1671 as the supreme criminal court in Scotland. He was named a privy councillor and commissioner of exchequer in 1674, and served as convenor of the commissioners of supply (1678) as well as a commissioner for the plantation of kirks. In December 1681, during the treason trial of the earl of Argyll, he voted against the relevancy of the indictment, and it was only carried by Lord Nairn's casting vote. On 14 February 1684 he was appointed lord justice clerk, a position he held until his death. His first wife, Barbara, was a daughter of Andrew Ainslie, merchant burgess of Edinburgh; they had two sons. His second wife, Margaret, whom he married on 1 June 1661, was daughter and coheir of Sir George Erskine of Innerteil (Inverteil) and widow of Sir John Mackenzie of Tarbet, first baronet. Colinton died in Edinburgh on 19 January 1688 and was buried in Greyfriars churchyard four days later. He was succeeded by his son, James *Foulis of Colinton.

J. A. HAMILTON, rev. ALISON G. MUIR

Sources M. D. Young, ed., *The parliaments of Scotland: burgh and shire commissioners*, 1 (1992), 261 · *APS*, 1643–86 · G. Brunton and D. Haig, *An historical account of the senators of the college of justice, from its institution in MDXXXII* (1832), 359–60 · Burke, *Peerage* (1970) · R. Douglas and others, *The baronage of Scotland* (1798), 87–8 · D. Laing, ed., *A catalogue of the graduates … of the University of Edinburgh*, Bannatyne Club, 106 (1858) · R. Douglas, *The peerage of Scotland*, 2nd edn, ed. J. P. Wood, 1 (1813), 103, 395 · J. Nicoll, *A diary of public transactions and other occurrences, chiefly in Scotland, from January 1650 to June 1667*, ed. D. Laing, Bannatyne Club, 52 (1836), 355, 428 · J. R. Young, *The Scottish parliament, 1639–1661: a political and constitutional analysis* (1996)
Archives BL, letters to duke of Lauderdale and Charles II, Add. MSS 23114–23138, 23242–23247, *passim*

Foulis, Sir James, of Colinton, third baronet, Lord Reidfurd (*c.*1645–1711), judge and politician, was the son and heir of Sir James *Foulis of Colinton, second baronet (*d.* 1688), and his first wife, Barbara (*d.* in or before 1661), daughter of Andrew Ainslie, merchant burgess of Edinburgh; he was known by the designation Foulis of Reidford until he succeeded his father on 19 January 1688. He graduated MA at Edinburgh on 14 July 1659, and also studied at Leiden. This obviously paved the way for a career in law. Foulis was admitted advocate on 8 June 1669, and on 10 November 1674 he was nominated an ordinary lord of session, taking his seat on 27 November with the courtesy title Lord Reidfurd. He married Margaret, daughter of John Boyd, dean of guild, Edinburgh; they had seven sons, James, John, Henry, David, George, Thomas, and Robert.

In January 1685 Sir James was returned as one of the parliamentary commissioners for Edinburghshire, occupying the seat previously held by his father, recently appointed lord justice clerk. He appears to have endorsed government policy against covenanters and Presbyterian dissidents. Following the revolution of 1688, despite his former politics, on 20 February 1689 Foulis again secured a place as a commissioner for Edinburghshire. In March 1689 he took his place in parliament, and signed the act declaring the convention a lawful meeting of the estates. However, he withdrew after failing to acknowledge the estates' letter to William of Orange, congratulating the prince on his success 'in delyvering us and in preserving to us the Protestant religion' (*APS*, 9.103). As a general rule even the most ardent Jacobites grudgingly subscribed the act establishing the legality of the convention, but baulked at endorsing a letter which was clearly inconsistent with their loyalty to James VII. Consequently, Foulis was fined £100 Scots for absence from parliament in July 1689, and a further £600 Scots on 25 April 1693, when his seat was declared vacant on account that he had failed to take the oath of allegiance. Evidently there was little doubt where Foulis's political sympathies lay. In 1691 his name appeared in a dispatch addressed to the earl of Mellvile, as one of a number of those in the Lothians disaffected to the government.

Following the accession of Queen Anne, Foulis—like many former Jacobites—was restored to a position in central government. He was named as a member of the privy council in 1703, and elected a commissioner of parliament for Edinburghshire the following year. In July 1704 he took and subscribed the oath of allegiance with the assurance, and endorsed the oath of parliament. In September 1705 Foulis adhered to Atholl's protestation against the proposed treaty of union. From this juncture he consistently opposed this venture.

Outside the public sphere, Foulis was involved in a complicated lawsuit with his stepmother, Dame Margaret Erskine, Lady Castlehaven, over her interest in his father's estates. The chief papers relating to this case were published under the title *An exact and faithful relation of the process pursued by Dame Margaret Erskine, against Sir James Foulis now of Collingtoun* at Edinburgh in 1690. Sir James's notes exhibit some details of Scottish aristocratic life and customs of the period. Sir James died in August 1711. He was succeeded in the baronetcy by his eldest son, James *Foulis.

DEREK JOHN PATRICK

Sources M. D. Young, ed., *The parliaments of Scotland: burgh and shire commissioners*, 1 (1992) · APS, 1689–95; 1702–7 · *State papers and letters addressed to William Carstares*, ed. J. M'Cormick (1774) · G. Brunton and D. Haig, *An historical account of the senators of the college of justice, from its institution in MDXXXII* (1832) · DNB

Foulis, Sir James, of Colinton, fifth baronet (*bap.* 1714, *d.* 1791), antiquary, was baptized in Edinburgh on 16 March 1714, the eldest son of Henry Foulis, son of Sir James *Foulis of Colinton, third baronet, judge and politician; his mother was Jean, daughter of James Foulis, an Edinburgh merchant, and the niece of Sir John Foulis, baronet, of Ravelston. James succeeded to the baronetcy after the death of his uncle, also James, the fourth baronet, in 1742. He was married to Mary, daughter of Archibald Wightman, with whom he had three daughters and two sons. As a young man Foulis served in the army but retired early and thereafter pursued the life of a country gentleman and man of letters on his estate at Colinton, near Edinburgh. In 1781 he contributed a dissertation on the origins of the Scots, based on an extensive knowledge of Gaelic, in the *Transactions of the Antiquarian Society of Scotland*. On his death at Colinton in January 1791, Foulis left manuscript memoranda of a series of investigations into the origins of ancient place names in Scotland. The baronetcy passed to his only surviving son, James; the family name changed to Liston-Foulis at the first marriage of the eighth baronet, Sir William (1812–1858).

G. B. SMITH, *rev.* PHILIP CARTER

Sources Burke, *Baronetage* · Anderson, *Scot. nat.* · IGI · GM, 1st ser., 61 (1791), 91

Foulis, Sir James, of Woodhall, seventh baronet (1770–1842), portrait painter and sculptor, was born on 9 September 1770, the son of William Foulis and his wife, whose name was Campbell. He was the great-grandson of William Foulis of Woodhall, second son of Sir John Foulis, first baronet, of Ravelston, and Margaret, daughter of Sir Archibald Primrose of Carrington. The Ravelston Foulis baronetcy had been forfeited in 1746 when the second baronet was hanged as a Jacobite; but in 1825 Foulis succeeded the last of the Colinton branch of the family in their baronetcy.

From 1790 to 1794 Foulis lived in Rome, where he studied with Alexander Nasmyth, who had married his sister Barbara in 1786, and with Archibald Skirving. He was also acquainted in Rome with Jacob More, with whom he met the banker and biographer Sir William Forbes. Forbes described him as 'very modest, and tho but an indifferent portrait painter, he is now established at Edinburgh and has painted some strong likenesses' (Ingamells, 376).

Foulis was one of the twelve artists that met in Poole's Coffee House, Edinburgh, on 1 April 1808, in an endeavour to establish an annual exhibition in Edinburgh similar to those of the Royal Academy in London. He exhibited with the Society of Associated Artists in Edinburgh from 1808 to 1811. His portrait of James Gillespie (1726–1797), founder of Gillespie's Hospital, is in the collection of the city of Edinburgh. He resigned from the Society of Artists on 23 November 1811 and in 1812 joined the Edinburgh regiment of militia.

Foulis had married on 24 August 1810, at St Cuthbert's, Edinburgh, Agnes, eldest daughter of John Grieve of Edinburgh. They had two sons and two daughters. He died on 16 April 1842 at Woodhall House, Edinburgh; he was survived by his wife and succeeded by his eldest son, Sir William Liston-Foulis. G. B. SMITH, *rev.* JILL SPRINGALL

Sources P. J. M. McEwan, *Dictionary of Scottish art and architecture* (1994) · GEC, *Baronetage* · Burke, *Peerage* · E. Gordon, *The Royal Scottish Academy of painting, sculpture and architecture, 1826–1976* (1976) · GM, 2nd ser., 18 (1842), 330 · J. Ingamells, ed., *A dictionary of British and Irish travellers in Italy, 1701–1800* (1997) · IGI
Likenesses M. Burton, portrait, repro. in *Dowells sale catalogue of paintings, drawings and prints* (6 Sept 1974), lot 162
Wealth at death £933 6s. 2d.: inventory, 23 June 1848, NA Scot., SC 70/1/68, 698–9

Foulis, Oliver. *See* Lloyd, David (1635–1692).

Foulis, Robert (1707–1776), printer and bookseller, was born in Glasgow on 20 April 1707, the son of Andrew Faulls (Faulds; *c.*1690–1742), maltman of Glasgow, and Marion Paterson. He was brought up in Glasgow, and was apprenticed there to Alexander Leggatt, barber, in 1720, and in 1727 was made free as maltman, barber, and wigmaker. In 1730 he matriculated at Glasgow University to study moral philosophy under Francis Hutcheson, under whose influence he fell, but there is no record of him taking a degree. His brother, **Andrew Foulis the elder** (1712–1775), printer, was born in Glasgow and matriculated as a student of humanity at Glasgow in 1727 under Professor Andrew Rosse; he remained there teaching Greek, Latin, and French.

Booksellers in Glasgow In 1738 Robert and Andrew travelled to England and France, where they were entertained by Andrew Michael Ramsay, known as the Chevalier Ramsay, the tutor to the sons of James Edward Stuart. Under his supervision they examined the early records of Glasgow University, then in the Scots College in Paris. On this journey they purchased many books in Paris and London, returning with 6 or 7 hogsheads of books, according to one contemporary account. They returned to Glasgow where they sold the books, and, using the capital secured through these sales, Robert returned to the continent the following year, travelling to London in 1740 to sell more continental purchases, and to survey the market for literature in England.

In 1740 Robert established himself as a bookseller within the confines of Glasgow University, issuing in that year *A Catalogue of Books Newly Imported from Abroad*, which included books in Latin and Greek, especially editions of classical authors from the scholar-presses of the continental Renaissance, but also books in various European vernacular languages. The catalogue also included manuscripts in Latin and Arabic, as well as coins and medals, indicating a desire to spread risks. Items in the catalogue could also be purchased through the Edinburgh dealer Gavin Hamilton. Throughout the next year Robert established himself on his own as a publisher of books in Glasgow, issuing twelve titles printed by a number of Glasgow printers, including Alexander Miller, the printer to the

Robert Foulis (1707–1776), by James Tassie, c.1765

university, and Robert Urie. These books began with Cicero's *De natura deorum*, and included editions of Phaedrus, Juvenal, and Terence, as well as volumes of Presbyterian sermons. The titles were also sold by the Edinburgh booksellers Gavin Hamilton and John Balfour, and by a Scottish bookseller in London, Andrew Millar. In 1742 Robert married Elizabeth Moor (d. 1750), sister of the professor of Greek at Glasgow, James Moor. In the same year his career took a significant step forward when he began to print books himself, the first of which, an edition of the *Meditations* of Marcus Aurelius, was issued in June 1742, and retailed for 3*s*. bound. There then followed a number of books on religion and editions of classical authors including Demetrius of Phalerum's *De elocutione* (1743), the first Greek text to be printed at Glasgow. The relationship between Foulis and Francis Hutcheson continued to be close, and the first of the forty separate editions of works by Hutcheson to be published by the Foulis brothers appeared in 1742. In 1743 Robert petitioned the university that he:

> hath provided himself with types both Greek and Latin of such exactness & beauty that [he] can execute printing work in either language, in such manner as will be no dishonour to one who bears the character of University-Printer, & of this he is ready to exhibit specimens: he therefore humbly petitions that he may be admitted as printer to the University of Glasgow. (U. Glas., Archives and Business Records Centre, MS 3607)

He was duly appointed by the university on condition that he referred to himself as university printer only on classical texts. The following year he was joined permanently in partnership in this business by his brother, although accounts survive from as early as 1742 recording payments to Robert and Andrew Foulis together for books bought for the university. The brothers' trade with the university continued to be a staple source of income throughout their active partnership.

Publications The partnership of the Foulis brothers marked the most significant period for Glasgow in publishing and printing during the eighteenth century. They printed some 586 editions together during their active partnership, 1744–75, producing books at a rate which varied from nine in 1764 to forty-three in 1751, an average of almost seventeen a year. Their connections with the university formed the basis of their success, with works written or edited by Glasgow professors such as Francis Hutcheson, George Muirhead, James Moor, and William Leechman dominating the British authors, and classical texts required for studies in the college such as Cicero, Xenophon, Epictetus, and the poets of the *Anacreonta*, frequently reprinted or re-edited by the brothers. The range of classical authors represented in their list was in fact very wide—sixty-three Greek and Latin authors, the majority of whom were published only once or twice, ranging from Euclid to Velleius Paterculus, but with many Greek texts with Latin translations, and a Greek grammar. Of greatest significance, however, were the four volumes of the works of Homer issued in 1756–8 in folio, described by Edward Harwood as 'One of the most splendid editions of HOMER ever delivered to the world … its accuracy is equal to its magnificence' (Harwood, 4–5). The brothers jointly won the silver medal of the Select Society of Edinburgh for the best-printed and most correct Greek book. The Homer was financed by an informal group of professors at Glasgow, led by William Rouat, who had led the establishment of a 'Society for Printing at their own expense intirely under their own direction, a compleat set of the best Greek & Latin Classicks' (Edinburgh University Library, MS La.II.511). The texts were printed in a new fount of Greek type designed and cut by the Glasgow typefounder Alexander Wilson. After three sets of corrections at the printers' expense, the text was proof-read, sheet by sheet, by professors Moor and Muirhead: the corrected proofs are now in the National Library of Scotland. Despite the importance of the edition for classical scholarship and the history of printing and publishing in the Enlightenment, the venture was a financial disaster for the brothers. In contrast 1750 saw the brothers make their sole foray into Gaelic printing, a translation of Richard Baxter's *A Call to the Unconverted*.

British literature began to feature more prominently in the Foulis brothers' published output from the end of the 1750s as they sought to exploit a more widespread market. Books in French and Italian were also published, and a series of small-format editions of the English poets retailing at 1*s*. a volume became successful. Towards the end of the active partnership of Robert and Andrew Foulis their reputation began to rely on their output of high-quality editions of British literature. Their publications of the year 1770 can be seen to demonstrate this range—Addison, Collins, Dryden, Shenstone, and Waller, in addition to the more predictable classical authors such as Anacreon and Pindar. The edition of Milton's *Paradise Lost* which they published in 1770 is a good example of the impact of their more successful books. They issued two versions, on good-quality paper of foolscap and demy size, printed with the beautiful Double Pica roman typeface; it retailed at 21s. for the demy and 13s. for the foolscap. It was well received by contemporaries: James Beattie, for example, wrote to Robert Foulis remarking that 'the Milton is wonderfully fine. It is indeed the most Magnificent Book I have ever seen, and seems to be perfectly correct' (Carnie, 'The letters of Robert Foulis', 43). James Scott, the finest bookbinder working in Scotland in the eighteenth century, chose it as a vehicle for a presentation piece to George III, intending the volume to act as a specimen of the highest-quality printing and binding that Scotland could offer.

During the 1750s Robert Foulis attempted to break the monopoly of London printers relating to printing the works of English authors, especially in the case of the works of Alexander Pope, which were the literary property of William Warburton and John Knapton. Foulis successfully negotiated with Warburton the right to print Pope's works in Scotland.

The success of the Foulis brothers' partnership was not solely due to the astute choice of authors, editors, and subject genres. The brothers paid particular attention to the details of the production process itself, and it is in this area that their reputation was enhanced in the twentieth century. Above all their typefaces were both carefully chosen and sufficiently superior to the general standards of Scottish typography at the time to stand out. The types used by the Foulis brothers were cut by the typefounder Alexander Wilson, and are of significance for the strength of the larger sizes, and in particular for the beauty and regularity of the Greek fount. Wilson based his roman and italic types on those of Caslon and Baskerville, and his Greek ones on those of the sixteenth-century French typefounder Garamond. Wilson's types in turn influenced later generations of typographers including the great Italian Dr Giovanni Madersteig.

Presswork The press operated by the Foulis brothers had first been established in a room on the ground floor of the inner quadrangle of the university. In 1747 they were forced to move from the college to seek more space in property which they acquired in a tenement situated between the west side of the High Street and the east side of Shuttle Street. It is unlikely that the office employed more than two presses and a proofing press, and consequently no more than two journeymen printers at a time. Given the emphasis placed on accuracy, and the importance of their Greek books, the Foulis press room would have employed more than one compositor, very probably one with the ability to set Greek.

The presswork was of above-average quality for the time, but did not equal that of the greatest contemporary printers such as Baskerville. The paper used by the Foulis brothers was generally also of above-average quality, although the books produced were slightly smaller than average, especially for the larger formats. They also printed books on vellum and silk, and Robert Browning owned a copy of the 1748 Epictetus printed on linen. The Editiones Minimae volumes, a series of Greek texts printed in very small formats, were in some cases issued in special editions printed on satin. The Foulis brothers also bound a proportion of their own stock. By 1770 their binder occupied two college rooms, and a distinct Foulis trade style can be discerned on bindings which cover their smaller-format works, especially on classical texts.

The partnership was also one which continued to depend to an extent on the sales of secondhand books, and of new books printed by other British printers. Their custom came principally from within the university, not only from the academic staff, but also from the wealthier students. James Douglas, later the fourteenth earl of Morton, wrote to Robert Foulis while studying law at Leiden requesting a particular edition of Grotius to be sent to him in Holland. William Hunter, the celebrated Glasgow collector, was another regular customer, purchasing almost £50 worth of books from the *Catalogue of books of various ages, languages, and sciences; to which is subjoined, a catalogue of manuscripts in the Greek, Latin, oriental and other languages* which the brothers issued in 1771. Included among these purchases was a copy of the *L'estrif de fortune* printed at Bruges by Colard Mansion between 1477 and 1484. The work is now found in only three copies, imperfect ones at Cambridge University Library and the Bibliothèque St Geneviève in Paris, and the complete copy purchased from the Foulis brothers by Hunter, now in Glasgow University Library. Robert Foulis had taken great trouble to research the book: he included a detailed description of it in the catalogue, and had shown it to Benjamin Franklin on his visit to Alexander Wilson's foundry in 1771. The brothers also sold a medieval manuscript copy of Ranulph Higden's *Polychronicon* to the Advocates' Library in Edinburgh in 1772.

Academy of Fine Arts Robert's wife, Elizabeth, died in 1750. A year later he married Euphan (*d.* 1774), a daughter of William Boutcher, a seedsman of Edinburgh, with whom he would have a son, Andrew, and a daughter, Euphemia. In 1751 Robert travelled to the continent with another brother, James, visiting Leiden and Paris and paying visits to a number of prominent Greek scholars. Partly this visit was to enable Robert to complete the preparatory work necessary for the publication of the edition of the works of Plato which was announced through the issue of proposals and a specimen of a new Greek type in 1751, although the work was never published. The other purpose for the visit was to acquire paintings, prints, and drawings which the brothers were beginning to collect for another project which they were about to embark on. In 1753–4 they established an Academy of Fine Arts in Glasgow, for which they received some initial support from the university in the form of a loan for £150 repayable over ten years. The brothers were also helped through the patronage of both the lord chancellor, the earl of Hardwicke, who assisted the brothers in passing the art collection through customs, and of Charles Yorke, the solicitor-general. The academy was based around a large collection of paintings acquired by the brothers during their European book trading visits. In 1772 they imported from Campveere in the Netherlands through the customs house in Edinburgh fifteen boxes of pictures and one box containing busts, paying a much reduced duty. The pupils included David Allan, but the concept was not financially viable, and the academy was closed down on the death of Andrew in Glasgow on 18 September 1775; the paintings were sold cheaply in London shortly afterwards. Robert died in Edinburgh on 2 June 1776, on his return from the disastrous visit to London to sell the collection of artworks. He was buried in lair 43 of the Ramshorn churchyard, Glasgow. The brothers left considerable debts behind them, largely the result of the financial liabilities of the Academy of Fine Arts.

Decline of business Andrew Foulis the younger (1756–1829), printer and bookseller, was born in Glasgow, the son of Robert Foulis and Euphan Boutcher, and matriculated at Glasgow University in 1769. Andrew inherited the printing house operated by his father and uncle, complete with Wilson's Greek type. Between 1776 and 1800 he printed 103 editions, his output peaking with sixteen in 1777 alone but gradually declining from 1790 onwards, with no books being printed in 1798 or 1799 and only one in 1800 itself. Andrew sold books in the college premises, like his father and uncle had before him, and was partnered at first by James Spottiswood, from whom he separated in 1781. The long delays which surrounded the printing of the *Catalogus impressorum librorum in Bibliotheca universitatis Glasguensis* eventually led the university to withdraw his appointment and turn him out of the college in 1795. There then followed a period of litigation instigated by Foulis.

As the fortunes of his printing and publishing business declined, Andrew Foulis the younger turned to the practice of publishing books by subscription, but without any great improvement in the finances of the operation. Partly the decline in the fortunes of his business may have been due to the high retail prices of his books. His 1795 folio of Aeschylus, for example, retailed at 3 guineas for the ordinary paper issue, and 10 guineas for the fine paper issue, which amounted to the colossal sum of £20 when the cost of the illustrative plates was included. Such prices were well in excess of trade norms for the time.

In 1791 Foulis prepared for publication 'A slight sketch of the origin of the Glasgow Press, and Academy of the Fine Arts' with which he hoped to obtain subscriptions for the failing press, to enable him 'to carry on the printing at Glasgow, upon the plan it has hitherto been conducted; the value to be repaid in books, the first productions of the press'. He intended the proposals to be sent only to 'the most liberal and discerning' but it is doubtful whether he ever issued them ('Slight sketch', 8). He issued only fourteen more titles from his press after this, the final book issued under the Foulis imprint being John Anderson's *Observations upon Roman Antiquities*, which was in all likelihood printed by Andrew Foulis in 1800, but names Edinburgh as its place of publication. By 1806 he was still trying to operate in the book trade, although he was by then little known, and had gained the reputation of being 'a troublesome and litigious man' (Edinburgh University

Library, MS La.IV.26). He continued to live in Glasgow until 1824 dealing in pictures. Andrew Foulis the younger eventually moved to Edinburgh, where he operated for a while as a picture framer. He died in 1829 in the Edinburgh poorhouse. RICHARD OVENDEN

Sources D. Murray, *Robert and Andrew Foulis and the Glasgow press* (1913) · P. Gaskell, *A bibliography of the Foulis press*, 2nd edn (1986) · *Some letters of Robert Foulis*, ed. D. Murray (1917) · J. Maclehose, *The Glasgow University Press, 1638–1931* (1931) · P. Gaskell, 'The early work of Robert Foulis and the Wilson foundry', *The Library*, 5th ser., 7 (1952), 77–110, 149–76 · *Robert and Andrew Foulis: an exhibition in the Hunterian Museum*, Hunterian Museum (1958) [exhibition catalogue, Hunterian Museum, Glasgow, 10–29 March 1958] · A. Foulis the younger, 'A slight sketch of the origin of the Glasgow Press', 1791, U. Edin. L., MS La.III.363.2 · P. Gaskell, 'Printing the classics in the eighteenth century', *Book Collector*, 1 (1959), 98–111 · *Pope's literary legacy: the book-trade correspondence of William Warburton and John Knapton*, ed. D. W. Nichol (1992) · J. Burnett, 'A note on the Foulis Homer of 1756–58', *The Bibliotheck*, 12 (1984), 330–35 · R. H. Carnie, 'Andrew Foulis the younger: some illustrative letters', *The Bibliotheck*, 6 (1971–3), 93–104 · R. H. Carnie, 'The letters of Robert Foulis to James Beattie', *The Bibliotheck*, 9 (1978–9), 33 · R. Ovenden, 'Scott bindings on the 1770 Foulis Milton', *For the love of the binding: studies in bookbinding history presented to Mirjam Foot*, ed. D. Pearson (2000), 261–9 · U. Glas., MS 3607 · E. Harwood, *A view of the various editions of the Greek and Roman classics*, 4th edn (1790) · U. Edin. L., MS La.II.511 · U. Edin. L., MS La.IV.26
Archives Mitchell L., Glas., family corresp. and MSS · U. Glas.
Likenesses J. Tassie, paste medallion, *c.*1765, Scot. NPG [*see illus.*] · oils (A. Foulis the elder), U. Glas.
Wealth at death died in debt

Foulis, Thomas (*c.*1560–1628), goldsmith, financier, and mining entrepreneur, was a younger son of Henry Foulis of Colinton (*d.* 1571), an advocate, and his wife, Margaret Haldane (*fl.* 1545–1560). He became a goldsmith of Edinburgh in 1581, after an apprenticeship to the wealthy Michael Gilbert. In 1578–9 he had visited France to study the finer points of the craft. He made some sinking irons for the royal mint in 1581 and was appointed sinker in 1584. In this office, which he retained until 1614, he helped to design coins and seals and made the matrices for them.

Foulis's career as royal financier began with James VI's impending marriage to Anne of Denmark. He became chief supplier of jewels to the court, collaborating closely with Robert Jowsie, merchant of Edinburgh, who supplied clothes. The pair were sent on the first of many shopping trips to London in July 1589. James bought from Foulis, often on credit, a total of almost £100,000 Scots worth of gold and jewels up to 1595 (when fiscal crisis forced an abrupt halt). Foulis developed an agency in London, handling the correspondence of a Scottish ambassador to Italy in 1597. English diplomats themselves used Foulis's services. The scale of his and Jowsie's debts in London was causing concern there by 1593.

In May 1591 Foulis gained responsibility for handling the subsidy paid to King James by Queen Elizabeth, amounting to about £30,000 Scots per year. Hitherto the English had sent the cash directly to Scotland, but with Foulis conducting so much royal business in London it made sense for him to receive the subsidy there. The usual envoy receiving the money was David *Foulis (*d.* 1642), who made a career as a Scottish courtier and eventually became a Yorkshire baronet.

Foulis's and Jowsie's English interests led them in 1593 to persuade James VI to create the office of conservator for Scottish merchants in Spain, and to appoint a Scottish Catholic to it. Apparently the 'Scottish' merchants keen to trade with Spain were clandestine Englishmen, and Foulis was doing a favour for his English business contacts. The scheme soon collapsed. It did Foulis's standing no lasting harm with the English, who seem to have recognized that he was guided by business rather than political interests.

Meanwhile, in 1592, Foulis began to interest himself in mining, obtaining a royal monopoly of refining of metal ores. In 1593 he bought out the proprietor of a lead mine in Lanarkshire that was then known as the Friar Muir of Glengonnar, but in Foulis's time came to be known as Leadhills; he immediately began importing foreign mining experts. The following year he obtained a 21-year lease of the mining rights from the crown. Foulis was to be involved with Leadhills for the rest of his life. At this prosperous period in his career he probably invested considerable sums in developing the mine.

In January 1594 Foulis moved into the coinage, collaborating with the burgh of Edinburgh in managing the issue of a new currency with a higher face value. The operation continued until April 1596. In September 1594 the king pledged to him a great jewel called the 'H', which in 1597–8 was to play a symbolic role in his regime. By now the king was using Foulis as a banker, paying the English subsidy and various other revenues into his account and drawing on it as needed. The account's annual turnover was over £40,000 Scots—and the king was increasingly overdrawn. This led Foulis to construct an elaborate credit empire, borrowing from large numbers of relatively humble people in order to support his lending to the king. Before his generation, the main bankers in Scotland had been Italians; Foulis was an important pioneer of domestic Scottish banking.

To solve his financial problems James turned to the Octavians, an eight-man exchequer commission appointed on 9 January 1596. They set out to make economies in spending and to improve the efficiency of revenue collection. They immediately closed the king's account with Foulis, acknowledging an outstanding debt of £51,881 Scots. They attempted to prise the English subsidy away from him but failed. Foulis formed a link with Sir George Home of Spott, leader of the chamber faction that would eventually oust the Octavians.

In March 1597 Foulis was appointed to a commission to investigate the customs. This led, in May, to a decision to impose customs duties on imported goods—a radical fiscal departure since customs had previously been levied only on exports. On 25 May collectors of the new customs for the year to come were appointed: Foulis and Jowsie. This was also the point at which Foulis's sister Margaret married one of the Octavians, Thomas Hamilton of Drumcairn, providing Foulis with an ally in the scheme that followed.

In October 1597 Foulis initiated discussions with the treasurer, Walter Stewart (the leading Octavian), about taking over the substance of the treasurership. He would leave Stewart the title of treasurer, but control of the revenues would be transferred to him. After intense negotiations this bore fruit on 29 December, when a new financial commission was appointed with Foulis as its sole executive officer. He could now ensure that his and Jowsie's debts were repaid—the arrangement allocated £30,000 Scots per year to this. He had full control over collection and disbursement of the royal revenues, and was effectively running them as his own business.

But on 17 January 1598 Foulis's scheme came crashing about his ears, and he himself suffered a nervous breakdown: he 'fell in a phrenesie, becaus he was not able to satisfie his creditors for the debt he had contracted in furnishing the king' (Calderwood, 5.673). The king ordered Foulis's commission cancelled and the treasurer resumed his office. This suggests that Foulis simply lacked the resources to sustain his scheme. But in truth, he did not just fall: he was pushed, with the connivance of the king. The royal secretary, John Lindsay of Balcarres, purchased one of the debts that Foulis owed, and on 6 January had obtained an order to arrest royal money about to be paid to Foulis on the grounds that he as creditor should receive it. This toppled Foulis's delicately balanced credit empire and forced him into bankruptcy. The king backed Lindsay's hostile move on 13 January by demanding the return of the 'H' jewel, a public indicator of loss of confidence.

Formally, therefore, Foulis was bankrupt, but the real bankruptcy was that of the crown which refused to pay him. Foulis's and Jowsie's debts in Scotland came to £160,522 Scots, equivalent to about a year's gross crown revenue from all sources. They received an order protecting them from their creditors, though they still had to pay interest, and found this difficult. In March 1598 they obtained a lease of the customs, giving them some liquidity, but it was cancelled in November. In May Jowsie got £30,000, an entire instalment of the English subsidy, apparently to pay English creditors. In June the pair received a six-year lease of the mint, being allowed to set off their annual £5000 duty to the crown against their debts. None of this came near the scale of the debt, and it was noted in February 1600 that Foulis and Jowsie 'have furnished his majesty and are thereby wracked and undone' (*CSP Scot.*, 13/2.623). Foulis's main source of liquidity at this point may have been the Leadhills mine.

Foulis made efforts to retrieve his position. On 1 May 1601 he proposed a major fiscal project (presumably a new tax), of which he hoped to be granted an eleven-year lease: it would, he said, pay off royal debts to himself and others, and at the end of the lease be worth £20,000 annually to the crown. The privy council was interested, but eventually rejected the scheme. Meanwhile Foulis and the council argued at length over the scale of his debts.

In 1603 the union of crowns transformed the Scottish finances when James and his court departed to be paid for by England. At last it began to be possible actually to repay debts instead of contracting more. In 1606 a parliamentary tax was voted, and the shire commissioners in parliament demanded that the money be applied to repaying Foulis and Jowsie. About a third of the net tax revenue, £81,880, was allocated to their creditors between 1607 and 1611. Once this money ran out, Foulis and the remaining creditors once more importuned the council, who did their best to avoid paying.

Eventually, in 1620–21, agreement was reached with the council; payments resumed, continuing until June 1625. Foulis evidently abandoned many of his legitimate claims in return for cash in hand. The debt acknowledged in 1598 had been £160,522, on most of which Foulis was due to pay interest at 10 per cent. A scheme to repay him between then and 1604 had envisaged the crown paying instalments totalling £180,000 in order to cover the interest. Yet the payments made by the crown between 1598 and 1625 totalled only £156,076. The remaining creditors were paid either out of Foulis's own pocket, or not at all.

Foulis remained active in public life. He retained a court connection through his brother-in-law Hamilton. He helped to run the Hilderstone silver mine on Hamilton's estates in 1607. In 1613 Foulis patented a new process for extracting silver from lead ore. He farmed sheep on a large scale at the Leadhills estate, and prospected for gold on nearby Crawford Muir. After his agreement with the council, he emerged as a respected elder statesman in financial matters. He signed a proclamation on bullion export in 1620, and gave advice on the subject in 1622. He advised the government on wool export in 1623, and became a justice of the peace for Lanarkshire. He backed a controversial soap monopoly in the early 1620s. His last public appearance, in 1627, was to advise on whether Dutch coins should be allowed to circulate in Scotland.

But Foulis's main occupation after 1598 was lead mining at Leadhills. His lease of the mine was converted into a heritable feu at some point; because of his bankruptcy this was usually held in the names of his nephews George and Robert Foulis and his son-in-law John Muir of Anniston, with Thomas acting either as sub-lessee or as manager. Once the debts were paid off the mine emerged as a highly profitable concern.

Foulis's first wife, Jean Francis, died in 1623. By December 1628, when Foulis died in Edinburgh, he had married Rachel Porteous (*fl.* 1628–1629). One son, Thomas, had predeceased him in 1612; the other, David Foulis of Glendorch (*fl.* 1612–1635), married Elizabeth Baillie. Of his three daughters, Margaret married John Muir of Anniston, Jean married James Lockhart, and a third married James McMath. David Foulis attempted to claim the Leadhills inheritance but it had been assigned to his father's nephew Robert Foulis (*d.* 1631), advocate. Robert's heir Anne Foulis secured it following the successful defence of her case by her advocate and (later) husband, James Hope (1614–1661). On the basis of the Leadhills fortune, their descendants became earls of Hopetoun.

JULIAN GOODARE

Sources J. Goodare, 'Thomas Foulis and the Scottish fiscal crisis of the 1590s', *Crises, revolutions and self-sustained growth: essays on fiscal history, 1130–1830*, ed. W. M. Ormrod and others (Stamford, 1999) · *Reg. PCS*, 1st ser. · *Reg. PCS*, 2nd ser. · R. W. Cochran-Patrick, ed., *Early records relating to mining in Scotland* (1873) · J. Goodare, 'James VI's English subsidy', *The reign of James VI*, ed. J. Goodare and M. Lynch (2000) · G. Burnett and others, eds., *The exchequer rolls of Scotland*, 23 vols. (1878–1908) · *CSP Scot.*, 1547–1603 · *APS* · J. M. Thomson and others, eds., *Registrum magni sigilli regum Scotorum / The register of the great seal of Scotland*, 11 vols. (1882–1914); facs. repr. (1984) · Hopetoun MSS, NRA Scotland · D. Calderwood, *The history of the Kirk of Scotland*, ed. T. Thomson and D. Laing, 8 vols., Wodrow Society, 7 (1842–9) · Lanarkshire testaments, 6 Aug 1629, NA Scot., CC 8/5/3, fols. 44r–45v
Archives NRA Scotland, papers on Leadhills, Hopetoun MSS
Wealth at death assets of £12,618 16s. 8d. Scots; debts of £54,676, excl. landed property: Lanarkshire testaments, 6 Aug 1629, NA Scot., CC 8/5/3, fols. 44r–45v

Foulkes, Isaac [*pseud.* Llyfrbryf] (1836–1904), writer and publisher, was born on 9 November 1836 at the farm Y Cwrt, Llanfwrog, Denbighshire, the son of Peter Foulkes and his wife, Frances, *née* Jones. At the age of fifteen he was apprenticed to Isaac Clarke, printer, in Ruthin; but in 1854, his apprenticeship unfinished, he entered the office of the *Amserau* newspaper in Liverpool as a compositor, and soon afterwards set up a printing business of his own in that city, which he conducted, at various locations, until his death. In 1860 he married Anna Foulkes (*d.* 1900), with whom he had two sons and three daughters.

Foulkes's miscellany of folklore, *Cymru fu*, published in three parts during 1862–4, has been referred to by Saunders Lewis as one of the most important literary events of the century. It informed the awakening working classes and furnished them with a knowledge of tradition that would underpin their patriotism. He issued in 1877–88 Cyfres y Ceinion ('the Gem Series'), a series of cheap reprints of Welsh classics which were inspired by the same populist, patriotic motive, and which gave notable stimulus to the Welsh literary revival at the end of the nineteenth century. In May 1890 he began to issue Y Cymro ('The Welshman'), a weekly Welsh newspaper intended primarily for Liverpool Welshmen, but soon read widely in Wales as well; Foulkes was both editor and publisher, and he ensured the paper's early success by persuading a friend, the novelist Daniel Owen, to serialize his new novel, *Enoc Huws* (1891), in its pages. He then encouraged the ailing novelist to persevere with his final novel, *Gwen Tomos* (1894), also serialized in Y Cymro.

Foulkes, who was known in bardic circles as Llyfrbryf ('Bookworm'), was a keen student of Welsh literature, and as author, critic, editor, and publisher devoted to this cause literary judgement and unflagging energy. Besides being a regular contributor to the Welsh press, he also published several books, including his collection of folklore, *Cymru fu* (pt. i. 1862; pts. ii. and iii. 1863–4; 2nd edn 1872), a novel, *Rheinallt ap Gruffydd* (1874), and biographies of the poet Ceiriog (1887; 2nd edn, 1902; 3rd edn, 1911) and of the novelist Daniel Owen (1903). Although inevitably lacking a sufficient degree of critical detachment, both biographies include indispensable material and display, on the whole, sound literary judgement; Foulkes's close association with both writers and his own central role in Welsh literary life ensure that they remain invaluable guides to the life and times of two of the foremost authors of Victorian Wales. Among other works which he both edited and published are *Enwogion Cymru*, a biographical dictionary of eminent Welshmen (1870), and the *Mabinogion*, with a translation into modern Welsh (1880). Editions of *Dafydd ap Gwilym*, the *Iolo Manuscripts*, and Yorke's *Royal Tribes of Wales* were also issued from his press.

Foulkes's first wife died in 1900, and on 27 February 1904 he married Sinah Owen (*b.* 1871/2), the daughter of John Owen, a farmer. Isaac Foulkes died on 2 November 1904 at Cilgwyn, Rhewl, near Ruthin, and was buried three days later in Llanbedr churchyard.

J. E. LLOYD, rev. ROBERT RHYS

Sources *Y Cymro* (10 Nov 1904), 4, 5 · *Y Cymro* (17 Nov 1904), 3 · E. V. Evans, 'Isaac Foulkes', *Y Geninen*, 23 (1905), 31–5 · *DWB* · *Bygones* (9 Nov 1904) [Oswestry] · *Brython* (25 May 1911) · private information (1912) [L. Jones] · m. cert. · *CGPLA Eng. & Wales* (1904)
Archives NL Wales, letters to T. C. Edwards
Wealth at death £808 6s. 3d.: administration, 9 Dec 1904, *CGPLA Eng. & Wales*

Foulkes, Peter (*bap.* 1676?, *d.* 1747), Church of England clergyman and classical scholar, was probably baptized at St Mary on the Hill, Chester, on 5 November 1676. He was the third son of Robert Foulkes of Llechryd, Denbighshire, then deputy baron of the court of exchequer of Chester, and Jane, *née* Ameredith, of Landulph, Cornwall. In 1690 he was admitted to Westminster School as a king's scholar, and was elected three years later to a Westminster studentship at Christ Church, Oxford. While an undergraduate he published, in conjunction with John Freind and under the auspices of Henry Aldrich, dean of the college, an edition of *Aeschines Against Ctesiphon and Demosthenes on the Crown* with a Latin translation (1696). He graduated BA in 1698 and MA in 1701. Two years later he was chosen as censor at Christ Church in preference to the poet Edmund Smith; in 1705 he served as the junior proctor and was a grand compounder for the degrees of BD and DD in 1710.

Foulkes's cousin, the regius professor of divinity, William Jane (*d.* 1707), named him residuary legatee and devisee of his property at Liskeard and Bodmin said to be worth between £10,000 and £12,000. In the year of his cousin's death, Foulkes married Elizabeth Bidgood of Rockbeare, Devon (*d.* 1737); the couple had at least two sons. Three years before, he had been appointed canon of Exeter Cathedral where he later become subdean (1723), chancellor (May 1724), and precentor (1731). He was made a canon at Christ Church, Oxford, in November 1724 and was subdean there between 1725 and 1733. In 1714 he was appointed rector of Cheriton Bishop, Devon, and two years later, vicar of Thorveton in the same county. In 1722, following the death of Andrew Davy of Medland, Cheriton Bishop, Foulkes inherited land in trust for his second son. On the death of his wife, Elizabeth, he married, on 26 December 1738, Anne, the widow of William Holwell and

daughter of Offspring Blackall, bishop of Exeter. In addition to his publication with John Freind, Foulkes published three Latin poems in 1695, 1688, and 1727, and a sermon preached in 1723 on the anniversary of the execution of Charles I. He died on 30 April 1747, survived by his wife, and was buried in Exeter Cathedral.

EDWIN CANNAN, rev. PHILIP CARTER

Sources R. Polwhele, *The history of Devonshire*, 3 vols. (1793–1806), vol. 2 · A. Wood, *The history and antiquities of the colleges and halls in the University of Oxford*, ed. J. Gutch, appx (1790) · *GM*, 1st ser., 9 (1739), 46 · *IGI* · P. Foulkes, will, PRO, PROB 11/754, fols. 220v–221v

Foulkes, Robert (*bap.* 1633, *d.* 1679), Church of England clergyman and murderer, was baptized, by his own account, on 19 March 1633 at Stanton Lacy, Shropshire. Nothing is known about his parents or his place of birth, although it is presumed that he was a native of Shropshire where he lived for most of his life. He was educated at Christ Church, Oxford, matriculating in November 1652, and subsequently became a clergyman. On 7 September 1657 he married Isabella (*b.* 1633), daughter of Thomas Colbatch, rector of Ludlow, Shropshire, with whom he had four children between 1665 and 1672. In September 1660 Foulkes became vicar of Stanton Lacy, a parish adjacent to Ludlow.

The exercise of his clerical duties brought Foulkes into a series of conflicts with his neighbours. From the late 1660s he was involved in promoting an aggressive series of legal actions in both the ecclesiastical and secular courts against certain parishioners for the withholding of tithe payments. Furthermore, Foulkes made enemies by encouraging parishioners to take legal action to settle disputes with their neighbours, and angered local officeholders by accusing them of corruption. Foulkes also became notorious in his parish and further afield for his extramarital sexual relations, especially with Anne Atkinson, of whom he seems to have been guardian. She was the unmarried daughter of his predecessor as vicar of Stanton Lacy, Thomas Atkinson (*d.* 1657). Foulkes's illicit involvement with Anne Atkinson was suspected from about 1673, although their affair may have begun much earlier, soon after Foulkes's arrival in the parish. In July 1676 Herbert Croft, bishop of Hereford, convened a special session of his audience court to consider complaints made by several parishioners of Stanton Lacy against their vicar's behaviour. The bishop summoned Foulkes before him and ordered him to abstain from Atkinson's company at all times, except in church or unless accompanied by three or four reputable people. The following month disciplinary proceedings against Foulkes were begun in the Hereford consistory court. It was alleged that he had fathered an illegitimate child on Atkinson which she had given birth to secretly in the north Shropshire village of West Felton and had put out to nurse in north Wales. However, attempts to prove these charges by the ecclesiastical authorities and a local justice of the peace, Robert Owen, proved inconclusive. Foulkes was also accused of beating his wife, whom he suspected of committing adultery with William Hopton, a bailiff employed by the earl of Craven.

These charges were bound up with allegations of professional abuse such as failure to conduct services at the appointed times, and the neglect of pastoral duties such as administering to the sick and dying and catechizing the young. However, direct evidence of Foulkes's adultery proved difficult to find and the case dragged on inconclusively for two years.

In 1678 Anne Atkinson became pregnant with Foulkes's child. In an attempt to conceal the pregnancy and possibly to seek an abortion Foulkes accompanied Atkinson to London. They took lodgings in York buildings in the Strand where, in November, Atkinson gave birth to a girl. Foulkes, who performed the delivery himself, strangled the infant and disposed of its body in a privy. Foulkes returned to Stanton Lacy alone, but was arrested and brought back to London after Atkinson revealed that he had killed the child. He was found guilty of murder at the Middlesex sessions of 15 January 1679 and sentenced to death. While awaiting execution Foulkes was visited in his prison cell at Newgate by a number of leading Anglican divines, including William Lloyd, then dean of Bangor, and Gilbert Burnet. Lloyd persuaded the bishop of London to obtain a nine-day reprieve for Foulkes during which he wrote a penitential sermon, published after his death as *An Alarme for Sinners*. It was designed to reassert the authority of the Church of England which had been damaged by his scandalous behaviour and later became highly regarded as a model of repentance. Prayers were said for Foulkes across London's pulpits on the fast day of 30 January. The following day he was executed at Tyburn and buried by night in St Giles-in-the-Fields. Details of Foulkes's crime were reported in a number of contemporary pamphlets and versions of his life continued to appear into the eighteenth century. Although in *An Alarme for Sinners* Foulkes accused Anne Atkinson of equal culpability for the crime, she avoided criminal prosecution and returned to Stanton Lacy, to the apparent distress of Foulkes's widow. She was eventually excommunicated in 1682 after William Lloyd, now bishop of St Asaph, wrote to Archbishop William Sancroft to complain that her evasion of punishment stood as a disgrace to the church.

DAVID TURNER

Sources D. Turner, '"Nothing is so secret but shall be revealed": the scandalous life of Robert Foulkes', *English masculinities: 1660–1800*, ed. T. Hitchcock and M. Cohen (1999), 169–92 · R. Foulkes, *An alarme for sinners* (1679) · *A true and perfect relation of the tryal and condemnation, execution and last speech of that unfortunate gentleman Mr Robert Foulks* (1679) · *The execution of Mr Rob. Foulks* (1679) · *The Shropshire amazement, or, An account of a barbarous and unnatural murder committed by Mr Robert Foulkes* [n.d., 1708?] · *The wonders of free grace* (1690) · Wood, *Ath. Oxon.*, new edn, 3.1195 · W. P. W. Phillimore, *Diocese of Hereford*, 4: *Stanton Lacy*, Shropshire Parish Registers, (privately printed, London, [1902]) · Foster, *Alum. Oxon.* · *Athenian Mercury*, 4/16 (21 Nov 1691) · acts of office, archdeaconry of Ludlow, 1665–86, Herefs. RO, HD4/1 box 40 · deposition book, 1660–82, Herefs. RO, HD4/2/16 · miscellaneous court papers, 1673–9, Herefs. RO, HD4/25–26 · T. Powys, estate book, 1665–70, Shrops. RRC, MS 320/1 · Middlesex sessions roll, 15 Jan 1679, LMA, MJ/SR 1556 · Bodl. Oxf., MS Tanner 35

Foulston, John (1772–1841), architect, was a pupil of Thomas Hardwick and set up practice in London in 1796.

In 1811 he won the competition for a complex of buildings in Plymouth consisting of a hotel, assembly rooms, and theatre. His success with this important commission established his local reputation, and he moved to Plymouth, where he remained for twenty-five years the leading architect of the neighbourhood. So much of Foulston's work has been lost that it is difficult to appreciate its impact, but with the backing of the ambitious mayor Edmund Lockyer he extensively transformed both Plymouth itself and its satellite towns of Stonehouse and Devonport. He was active not only as an architect, designing a further series of public buildings, stucco-faced terraces in the London manner, and attractive suburban villas, but also as a town planner, responsible for the creation of Union Street, a bold stroke of planning which united the three towns.

Most of Foulston's work was in the Greek revival style—which it was his role almost single-handedly to propagate in the area—but his best-known project was the extraordinary group of buildings erected at Ker Street, Devonport, in 1821–4, an extreme example of the picturesque stylistic eclecticism of the early nineteenth century. It consisted of a Greek Doric town hall and commemorative column, a terrace of houses in the Roman Corinthian order and a pair in the Greek Ionic, a 'Hindoo' nonconformist chapel, and an 'Egyptian' library. (The chapel and the houses have been demolished.) Foulston wrote of himself that, in designing this group:

> it occurred to him that if a series of edifices, exhibiting the various features of the architectural world, were erected in conjunction, and skilfully grouped, a happy result might be obtained. Under this impression, he was induced to try an experiment (not before attempted) for producing a picturesque effect.   (J. Foulston, *The Public Buildings, Erected in the West of England, as Designed by John Foulston, F.R.I.B.A.*, 1838, 3)

In a number of his other works, notably the proprietary library (1812; des. 1941) and St Catherine's Church (1823; dem. 1958) in Plymouth and the ballroom in Torquay (1830; dem.), the influence of Sir John Soane was strongly apparent; while his few Gothic projects, although more conventional, included a restoration in 1829 of the medieval abbey gatehouse in Tavistock. His theatre in Plymouth (dem. 1939–41) was notable for its extensive early use of cast iron.

Shortly before he retired Foulston took into partnership the architect George Wightwick, who succeeded to his practice. In his latter years he created an elaborate water garden at the *cottage orné* he had built for himself on the outskirts of Plymouth, and was wont to drive round the streets of the town in a gig disguised as a Roman war chariot, looking, in Wightwick's words '(as far as his true English face and costume allowed) like Ictinus of the Parthenon, "out for a lark"' (G. Wightwick, 'The life of an architect', *Bentley's Miscellany*, 42, 1857, 297).

In his retirement Foulston made a set of nineteen watercolour drawings of his buildings which is now in the City Art Gallery at Plymouth. His pupils were Michael Angelo

Nicholson, E. W. Gribble, C. E. Lang, and T. J. Ricauti. In 1838 he became a fellow of the Institute of British Architects. He died at his home in Plymouth on 30 December 1841 and was buried in St Andrew's new cemetery, Plymouth.   PETER LEACH, *rev.*

Sources Colvin, *Archs.* · J. M. Crook, 'Regency architecture in the west country: the Greek revival', *Journal of the Royal Society of Arts*, 119 (1970–71), 438–51 · J. Gwilt, ed., *An encyclopaedia of architecture*, 2nd edn (1851); rev. edn, rev. W. Papworth (1867); new edn (1881); new edn (1888) · F. Jenkins, 'John Foulston and his public buildings in Plymouth, Stonehouse, and Devonport', *Journal of the Society of Architectural Historians*, 27 (1968), 124–35 · *Dir. Brit. archs.* · [W. Papworth], ed., *The dictionary of architecture*, 11 vols. (1853–92)
Archives Cornwall RO, corresp. and plans for baths, hotel, and terrace in Stonehouse, Devon · RIBA, perspective of Civil and Military Library, Devonport · RIBA BAL, biography file | RIBA, nomination papers
Likenesses photograph, RIBA BAL, photographic collection

Fountaine, Sir Andrew (1676–1753), art collector, was born in Salle, Norfolk, the eldest son of Andrew Fountaine (1632–1707), a gentleman, and Sarah (*b. c.*1654), youngest daughter of Sir Thomas Chicheley of Wimpole, Cambridgeshire. At Eton College he was a king's scholar and in 1693 went to Christ Church, Oxford; he graduated BA in 1697. A gifted scholar, he later contributed to George Hickes's *Thesaurus septentrionalis* (1705) of materials for Anglo-Saxon studies. According to family tradition William Cavendish, second duke of Devonshire, a friend of his father, introduced him to court. In 1698 Henry Aldrich, dean of Christ Church, selected him to make the Latin oration to William III on his entry to Oxford, for which the young man was knighted in 1699.

Fountaine accompanied Lord Macclesfield to carry the Act of Succession to the elector of Hanover in 1701. This had the effect of launching him into the court circles of Europe, where his charming personality and ready knowledge of virtuosi interests such as coins and medals made him a court favourite. Fountaine's political mission turned into a grand tour. His travels are chiefly documented in correspondence with the German philosopher and mathematician Leibnitz (1646–1716) between 1701 and 1704. He was admitted to the Royal Society of Berlin and in 1702 travelled to Italy, where he was to establish a friendship with Cosimo (III) de' Medici, grand duke of Tuscany. Robert Nelson wrote to Fountaine's mother of her son's charms: ''tis well Sir Andrew has in the sweetness of his conversation so strong a remedy against those prejudices that might arise from his great Erudition' (Moore, 1985, 28).

Fountaine was in Holland in 1705, a member of the mission to the states general of the United Provinces, where he had further opportunity to enlarge his collection of books and coins. In February 1707 his father died and in that year he was appointed gentleman usher of the black rod, accompanying Thomas Herbert, eighth earl of Pembroke, courtier, virtuoso, collector, and newly appointed lord lieutenant of Ireland, to the opening of the Irish parliament. In Ireland Fountaine established a friendship

with Jonathan Swift, documented in Swift's correspondence and *Journal to Stella*. Fountaine was dangerously ill in the winter of 1710 but Swift correctly predicted his recovery.

Fountaine is notable for having made a second grand tour of Europe in 1714, a trip which marked his maturity as a collector. It is likely that this period saw him acting not only for himself but for friends such as the Pembrokes at Wilton, where some Italian paintings 'were bespoke when Sir And. Fountaine was in Italy' (*A Catalogue of the Paintings and Drawings in the Collection of Wilton House, Salisbury, Wiltshire, Compiled by Sidney, 16th Earl of Pembroke*, 1968, 6). The most important record of Fountaine's tour is the group portrait *Sir Andrew Fountaine and Friends in the Tribune Gallery of the Uffizi, Florence* (1715) by Giulio Pignatta (priv. coll.). He was the equal of any Italian dealer and was said by Jonathan Richardson the younger to have 'out-Italianed the Italians themselves' (W. T. Whitley, *Artists and their Friends in England, 1700–1799*, 2 vols., 1928, 1.18). His collection of majolica was the finest outside Italy, and his family seat at Narford Hall, Norfolk, became a point of pilgrimage for the breadth and variety of its collection. Its dispersal in the celebrated four-day sale at Messrs Christie, Manson, and Woods in 1884 saw the formation of the 'syndicate', whose sole aim was to purchase prize items and offer them, at the price paid, to the government.

After his return to England Fountaine seems to have concentrated on alterations at Narford (originally purchased by his father), giving true expression to his virtuosity. The library at Narford remains almost intact as a decorative scheme, as is the installation of Antonio Pellegrini's fine decorative cycle of classical subject matter in the saloon, almost certainly the gift of Lord Burlington. Fountaine was a favourite of Caroline of Ansbach, princess of Wales, and her portrait as queen still graces the staircase at Narford. Fountaine was vice-chamberlain to Caroline and tutor to her third son, Prince William Augustus, being installed for him (as proxy) knight of the Bath on 17 June 1725.

In March 1727 Fountaine became warden of the Royal Mint, succeeding Sir Isaac Newton. In 1728 Robert Morris dedicated his *Essay in Defence of Ancient Architecture* to Fountaine, naming him—together with lords Herbert and Burlington—a 'practitioner of architecture'. In 1732 or 1733 Fountaine retired from London, concentrating upon further work on Narford about 1735, this time employing Andien Clermont on further decorative schemes. The continuing regard in which he was held may be judged from a letter from Lord Leicester (undated but *c.*1750):

> I hope before my Gallery is finish'd to have your advice about it. I flatter myself you will approve of my placing my statues … Your kindness for Holkham Hall that belongs to it I am most sensible of, & that you w[ou]ld spare nothing to contribute to its beauty … I long prodigiously to see you here … to have your advice about finishing my rooms & offices. (Moore, 1985, 27)

Details of Fountaine's final years are sketchy: his death, unmarried, at Narford on 4 September 1753 marked the end of a virtuoso who was the immediate predecessor of Horace Walpole as an arbiter in matters of taste and *virtu*. He was buried at St Mary's Church, Narford.

ANDREW W. MOORE

Sources J. M. Kemble, ed., *State papers and correspondence illustrative of the social and political state of Europe from the revolution to the accession of the house of Hanover* (1857) · *The Fountaine collection: catalogue of engravings, etchings and drawings by the old masters* (1884) [sale catalogue, Christies, 7–10 July 1884] · *Catalogue of the celebrated Fountaine collection of majolica* [1884] [sale catalogue, Christies, 16–19 June 1884] · *The Fountaine library* (1996), lots 300–45 [sale catalogue, Christies, 27 Nov 1996] · sale catalogue (1902) [Sothebys, 11–14, 21 June 1902] · A. W. Moore, *Norfolk and the grand tour: eighteenth-century travellers abroad and their souvenirs* (1985) [exhibition catalogue, Norwich Castle Museum, 5 Oct – 24 Nov 1985] · B. Ford, 'Sir Andrew Fountaine: one of the keenest virtuosi of his age', *Apollo*, 122 (1985), 352–63 · A. Moore, 'The Fountaine collection of maiolica', *Burlington Magazine* (June 1988), 435–47 · A. Moore and C. Crawley, *Family and friends: a regional history of British portraiture* (1992), 31–3, 109 · G. Knox, 'Antonio Pellegrini and Marco Ricci at Burlington House and Narford Hall', *Burlington Magazine* (Nov 1988), 846–53 · J. Ingamells, ed., *A dictionary of British and Irish travellers in Italy, 1701–1800* (1997) · H. E. Pagan, *British Numismatic Journal*, 63 (1993), 114–22 · *Catalogue of pictures and objects of art from the celebrated Fountaine collection* (1894) [sale catalogue, Christies, July 1894] · *Catalogue of the Fountaine collection of porcelain* (1904)

Archives priv. coll., family MSS · V&A NAL, inventory of Narford, Norfolk

Likenesses C. Maratta, red chalk, *c*.1702, priv. coll. · G. Pignatta, group portrait, oils, 1715 (*Sir Andrew Fountaine and friends in the Tribune Gallery of the Uffizi*), priv. coll. · L. F. Roubiliac, terracotta bust, *c*.1747, Norwich Castle Museum · J. A. Dassier, copper medal, BM · W. C. Edwards, line engraving (after Armstrong), BM, NPG · L. F. Roubiliac, marble bust, Wilton House, Wiltshire · A. Selvi, copper medal, BM

Fountaine, John (1600–1671), judge, was the son of Arthur Fountaine of Wood Dalling, Norfolk, and Anne, daughter of John Stanhow. He matriculated as a pensioner at Pembroke College, Cambridge, during Michaelmas term 1613, graduated BA from there in 1618, and proceeded MA from Trinity Hall, Cambridge, in 1621. His degrees were subsequently incorporated at the University of Oxford in July 1621. Fountaine continued his education at Lincoln's Inn, which he entered on 30 October 1622, and subsequently received his call to the bar on 21 June 1629. In 1641 he served as counsel to the University of Cambridge but it was his role in the civil wars of the 1640s that first brought him to national prominence. In 1642 he distinguished himself by refusing to pay the Long Parliament's war tax and was consequently imprisoned in the Gatehouse, Westminster, on 12 October. About this time upon the death of his first wife he received four days' liberty and also successfully petitioned for liberty to attend service at St Margaret's Church. On 20 December 1642 his petition for bail was refused and he remained imprisoned in the Gatehouse.

Fountaine had regained his liberty by 1645 when he re-emerged at Oxford in association with Sir John Stawel in a scheme for uniting the freeholders of the western counties in the king's cause. The prince of Wales was appointed general of the association and went to Bristol to assume command of the newly raised forces. However, the scheme foundered and Fountaine surrendered to parliamentarian forces in the west, leaving the extent of his royalist sympathies in doubt. On 11 April 1646 Colonel Thomas Rainborowe, commanding parliamentarian forces at Woodstock Manor, was able to report that Fountaine had turned himself in and was presently at Aylesbury. Rainborowe's letter was read to the House of Commons on 25 April and the house subsequently resolved that Fountaine be imprisoned at Bristol. While at Aylesbury Fountaine allegedly composed a letter to Dr Samuel Turner at Oxford evaluating the debate on church government. The authorship of the letter, reprinted in Richard Steward's *An answer to a letter written at Oxford, and superscribed to Dr. Samuel Turner, concerning the church, and the revenues thereof* (1647), is, however, unconfirmed. It is signed 'J. T.' and the postscript reads, 'I give you commission to shew this to my Lord Dorset, (who by + and something else can guess my name) and to as many more as owne Reason and Honesty' (Steward, 8). The author criticized the *jure divino* claims of the episcopate, defended parliament's right to dispose of church lands and property as it saw fit, and called for a presbyterian form of church government as the best way of bringing peace to the kingdom.

Fountaine returned to public prominence on 17 January 1652 when the Rump Parliament appointed him to the Hale commission for the 'considering of the inconveniencies' of the law (Wood, *Ath. Oxon.*, 3.1091). The following 17 March he received full pardon for his delinquency and he later compounded for his estates at £480. This enabled Fountaine to remain active in public service for the remainder of the interregnum. On 29 April 1653 the council of state placed him on a commission to investigate the prison of the upper bench and suggest regulations for the improving of its management. On the following 13 June he joined a similar commission aimed at the inspection and improvement of public offices. In 1655 he was among a group of prominent barristers and legal officers that included Sir John Glyn, Oliver St John, and Sir John Maynard who vocally favoured Oliver Cromwell's taking the crown. Fountaine was created serjeant-at-law in November 1656, and rode the assize circuit in Oxford in the winter of 1657, the midlands circuit in the winter of 1658, and the western circuit in the summer of that year. He was also made a commissioner of the great seal on 3 June 1659 when the restored Long Parliament appointed Fountaine, John Bradshaw, and Thomas Tyrell joint commissioners for a period of just under five months. On 1 November 1659 Bradshaw delivered the seal to Bulstrode Whitelocke on order of the committee of public safety. However, the great seal was once again put in commission on 17 January 1660 with Fountaine as one of the commissioners. It remained in commission until the Restoration later that year. Charles II confirmed Fountaine's status as serjeant-at-law in June 1660 but he played no further role on the bench.

Some time after the death of his first wife Fountaine married Theodosia, daughter of Sir Edward Harrington of Ridlington, Norfolk. They had three sons, John Fountaine

(1653–1680) of Melton, Yorkshire, also a barrister of Lincoln's Inn, Thomas (1657–1709), who succeeded his brother at Melton, and Harrington, of whom little is known. His elder son John had two daughters, the second of whom married Robert Monckton and became the mother of the first Viscount Galway. Although he appears to have been, broadly speaking, a conformist in religion Fountaine exhibited sympathies with nonconformists at the Restoration. He was responsible for introducing the judge Sir Matthew Hale to the preacher Richard Baxter in 1667 and also advised the latter in 1669 on charges relating to Baxter's unofficial ministry to the parishioners of Acton in Middlesex where both Baxter and Hale lived. Possibly with Hale's complicity, Baxter was released. Fountaine, who purportedly kept chambers at Boswell Court, Carey Street, died on either 14 or 16 June 1671 after a year's illness. He was buried in the parish church at Salle, Norfolk, the original seat of his family.   D. A. ORR

Sources DNB · Foss, *Judges*, 6.430–33 · Venn, *Alum. Cant.*, 1/2.166 · Foster, *Alum. Oxon.* · Wood, *Ath. Oxon.*, new edn · Baker, *Serjeants*, 192, 512 · A. Cromartie, *Sir Matthew Hale, 1609–1676* (1995), 185–6 · S. F. Black, '*Coram protectore*: the judges of Westminster Hall under the protectorate of Oliver Cromwell', *American Journal of Legal History*, 20 (1976), 33–64 · S. F. Black, 'The courts and judges of Westminster Hall during the great rebellion, 1640–1660', *Journal of Legal History*, 7 (1986), 23–52 · JHC, 4 (1644–6), 523–4 · R. Steward, *An answer to a letter written at Oxford, and superscribed to Dr. Samuel Turner, concerning the church, and the revenues thereof* (1647), 1–8 · *Burnet's History of my own time*, ed. O. Airy, new edn, 2 (1900), 122–3

Fountaine, Margaret Elizabeth (1862–1940), lepidopterist and diarist, was born on 16 May 1862 at South Acre, near Norwich, Norfolk, the second of eight children and eldest daughter of John Fountaine, rector of South Acre, and his wife, Mary Isabella (Isobel) Lee-Warner (d. 1906). After his death in 1877, Isobel, with her six daughters and two sons, moved to Eaton Grange in Norwich. On 15 April 1878 Margaret, who was educated at home, began keeping a diary, which she continued from April to April of each year until a few months before her death. Although proud of ancestors who had come over with the Conqueror, she also brought to a strict Victorian family an unconventional spirit that often put her at odds with her relatives. As she observed in her diary on 15 April 1883, 'My ruling passion is the love of independence' (Fountaine, *Love among the Butterflies*, 28). Her unconventionality was manifested at the age of twenty-eight by her infatuation with an Irishman, Septimus Hewson, one of the paid choristers of Norwich Cathedral, though she deemed him her inferior. She followed him to Dublin, having imagined an engagement where none existed, and he remained the greatest disillusionment of her life.

After Fountaine came out socially, she dabbled in art, for which she had shown some talent, and studied singing in a desultory way. But after her uncle Edward Fountaine left her a bequest in 1891 that allowed her to travel far beyond Dublin, she found her true vocation in collecting butterflies, to which she devoted the rest of her life. She pursued this vocation worldwide, first in Europe and after 1901 often in the Middle and Near East. She refused to ride sidesaddle, and accompanied only by a guide or translator ventured intrepidly into remote areas where she felt protected by her own sense of rectitude—for, in her own words, 'There is a direct and special protection over a pure and high-minded woman, which no man however base can break through' (Fountaine, *Love among the Butterflies*, 68)—and perhaps by her size: she was unusually tall, standing 5 feet 9 inches.

Fountaine claimed to find would-be admirers almost everywhere and turned down many proposals of marriage. One suitor, the British vice-consul at Broussa, threatened her with a breach-of-promise suit after she broke the engagement she had agreed to in 1905. Despite her pride in class, which was apparently always malleable, she had formed a liaison with her Syrian dragoman, Khalil Neimy (1877–1929), which from about 1903 became a marriage in all but name. Enduring for twenty-seven years, their relationship survived her shock at learning, in 1901 after she agreed to marry him (twenty-four to her thirty-nine), that he was already married. Their various later plans to marry also fell through. Accompanied by Neimy, she travelled in 1908–9 to South Africa and elsewhere in Africa; in 1910 she visited a brother in the United States; in 1911 she travelled in Costa Rica; in 1912 in India, Ceylon, and Tibet.

From 1914 to 1917 Fountaine and Neimy made a disastrous attempt to settle in Australia as farmers, after which she went alone to the United States, until in 1919 she left for Fiji. In 1920 she rejoined Neimy in New Zealand briefly, before returning alone to the United States and then to England. In 1923 they travelled together to Burma, but since he insisted on returning to Damascus to care for his ailing mother (over Fountaine's jealous objections), she returned to England, where in 1925 she established a large studio at 100A Fellowes Road, Hampstead. For the rest of her life this was her home whenever she returned to England. Then she set off on her travels again, principally in Africa, until a commission to secure particular specimens sent her to the West Indies. After Neimy died in 1929, she went to South America, determined to bury her grief in work, and she continued her worldwide travelling, with intervals in England, until her death at Mount St Benedict, after suffering a stroke on 21 April 1940 while collecting on the island of Trinidad.

The fruit of her travels was the Fountaine–Neimy collection of about 22,000 butterflies, bequeathed to the Castle Museum in Norwich, together with twelve volumes of her diaries (1878–1939), over 1 million words long and without margins. In addition, her carefully drawn sketchbooks of larvae and pupae, many previously undescribed, repose in the Natural History Museum, South Kensington. Although she began her diary as a serial record, she later kept notes drafted into a continuous narrative instead, usually during the following year. A year's record, copied into identically bound ledger-like leather books each about the size and thickness of a London telephone directory, also notes the time required to read it, and includes a studio portrait of Fountaine herself, typically standing straight with shoulders back, barely smiling or unsmiling, eyes focused fearlessly ahead. Variations in ink colour show that before Fountaine began recording a new year, she established the reading time for a previous year's account by rereading it. The diaries' readability is considerably enhanced by the two-stage compositional methods she developed. She was a talented writer and could build up a scene or a characterization through the accretion of details or a telling phrase or mood. She never, however, violated the serial nature of a diary, refusing both the novelist's foreshadowing and the autobiographer's retrospective reflection, and remaining faithful to the ongoing record of her adventurous life.   HARRIET BLODGETT

Sources M. E. Fountaine, *Love among the butterflies: the travels and adventures of a Victorian lady*, ed. W. F. Cater (1980) [diaries 1817–1913] · M. E. Fountaine, *Butterflies and late loves: the further travels and adventures of a Victorian lady*, ed. W. F. Cater (1986) [diaries 1914–39] · H. Blodgett, 'Preserving the moment in the diary of Margaret Fountaine', *Inscribing the daily: critical essays on women's diaries*, ed. S. L. Bunkers and C. A. Huff (1996), 156–68 · Burke, *Gen. GB* [Fountaine of Narford; Lee-Warner of Tyberton Court] · b. cert.
Archives NHM, sketchbooks of pupae and larvae · Norwich Castle Museum, collection
Likenesses photographs, 1877–1912, repro. in Fountaine, *Love among the butterflies*
Wealth at death £4508 19s. 0d.: probate, 9 Oct 1940, CGPLA Eng. & Wales

Fountainhall. For this title name *see* Lauder, Sir John, second baronet, Lord Fountainhall (1646–1722).

Fountains, John of [John de Fontibus] (d. 1225), abbot of Fountains and bishop of Ely, is so called from his connection with the Cistercian monastery of Fountains, Yorkshire, where he was abbot between 1211 and 1219. However, nothing is known of his origins or his monastic career before he was blessed as abbot by the bishop of Down at Melrose on 13 December 1211. In the following year he was instructed by the Cistercian general chapter to visit his abbey's daughter house at Lyse in Norway, but appears to have appealed against this order. Two years later, with the abbot of Kirkstead, he was again told to investigate alleged ill doings at Lyse. At Fountains itself he appears to have been remembered only for having continued the building of the abbey church. In 1213 he was thanked for unspecified services by King John, perhaps as a result of the abbey's being used as a store for royal valuables. He was also occasionally employed on ecclesiastical business, most notably in 1219, when, with the archbishop of Canterbury and bishop of Coventry, he was ordered by the pope to examine and report on the life and miracles of Bishop Hugh of Lincoln, in advance of Hugh's canonization.

Fountains's contacts with Archbishop Langton may have been a factor in his becoming bishop of Ely. The death of Bishop Eustace in 1215 had led to a disputed election. At first the monks chose Geoffrey de Burgh, the brother of Hubert de Burgh, but then tried to revoke their choice, and elected Master Robert of York instead. Though never consecrated, the latter appears to have maintained himself at Ely until Pope Honorius III (r. 1216–27) between 9 June 1218 and 11 May 1219 annulled both elections. The pope referred the matter to the papal legate Pandulf, the archbishop of Canterbury, and the bishop of Salisbury,

who on 16 January 1220 reported to Henry III that they had agreed on the abbot of Fountains. The temporalities were restored on 20 January, and John was consecrated in London by Langton on 8 March, and enthroned on the 15th. His experience in the case of Hugh of Lincoln may have led to his being appointed in 1223 to head a commission to investigate the miracles attributed to William of York—William was canonized in 1227. John's involvement in secular affairs appears to have been limited. But in 1221 he was appointed with the bishop of Salisbury to investigate complaints against Richard Marsh, bishop of Durham, by the Durham monks, and in the autumn of 1223 he went on an embassy to France. He was one of many landowners in central England to find himself at odds with Falkes de Bréauté, which may help to explain his presence at Bedford on 20 July 1224, during the siege of the castle. On 11 February 1225 he was a witness at the reissue of Magna Carta.

As bishop, Fountains was several times obliged to defend the liberties of his see against the sheriff of Cambridgeshire. He is said by the Ely chronicler to have been much liked in his diocese, though there is little to show for his administration. But various deeds of enfeoffment of lands and messuages close to the castle site in Ely, and at the great hithe on the northern end of the river front, reflect the spread of commercial activity in the town, and at the same time point to the bishop's role in the city's development. In confirmation of gifts made by his predecessors, Fountains gave the Ely monks the churches of Witchford and Meldreth, to enable them to maintain hospitality, and to endow his own obit added the tithes of Hadham, Hertfordshire. He also bequeathed to the cathedral his pastoral staff and various sets of vestments. Fountains died on 6 May 1225, and his anniversary was celebrated annually on 7 May. He was originally buried near the altar of St Andrew in Ely Cathedral, but after Bishop Hugh of Northwold's rebuilding of the presbytery he was reinterred near Prior John Crauden, in front of the high altar.   DOROTHY M. OWEN

Sources [H. Wharton], ed., *Anglia sacra*, 1 (1691), 634–5 · J. Bentham, *The history and antiquities of the conventual and cathedral church of Ely*, ed. J. Bentham, 2nd edn (1812), 145–6 · E. Miller, *The abbey and bishopric of Ely*, Cambridge Studies in Medieval Life and Thought, new ser., 1 (1951), 75–112 · *Chancery records* [PRO and RC] · *CEPR letters*, 1.89, 66, 90–1 · *Curia regis rolls preserved in the Public Record Office* (1922–), vols. 10–11 · *Ann. mon.*, 1, 3 · *Rogeri de Wendover liber qui dicitur flores historiarum*, ed. H. G. Hewlett, 3 vols., Rolls Series, [84] (1886–9), vol. 2, pp. 253, 257–9 · *Memoriale fratris Walteri de Coventria / The historical collections of Walter of Coventry*, ed. W. Stubbs, 2, Rolls Series, 58 (1873), 242–3 · W. W. Shirley, ed., *Royal and other historical letters illustrative of the reign of Henry III*, 1, Rolls Series, 27 (1862), 74–5 · J. R. Walbran, ed., *Memorials of the abbey of St Mary of Fountains*, 1, SurtS, 42 (1863), 134–6 · D. Knowles, *The monastic order in England*, 2nd edn (1963), 658 · D. A. Carpenter, *The minority of Henry III* (1990), 334
Archives BL, survey of episcopal demesne manors, 1222, Cotton MS Tiberius B.ii · CUL, Ely dean and chapter, charters and cartularies

Fountayne, John (1715–1802), dean of York, was born on 12 January 1715 at High Melton, near Doncaster, West Riding of Yorkshire, the second son of John Fountayne (1684–1736), of High Melton, and his wife, Elizabeth (1688–1768), daughter of Sir Francis Carew, baronet, of Beddington, Surrey. He was admitted a pensioner at St Catharine's College, Cambridge, on 28 March 1732, where his uncle Thomas Sherlock was master. Fountayne was a fellow there from 1736 to 1741. He took the degrees of BA in 1735, MA in 1739, and DD in 1751 (the latter taken *per saltum* with a Latin sermon—or *concio ad clerum*—written for Fountayne by Laurence Sterne). He was ordained deacon on 26 February 1738, and priest in March 1739. It was a natural career path for the younger son of a family linked by kinship to others with clerical scions.

Fountayne's rapid promotion in the church owed a great deal to the support of the childless Sherlock, who appointed him prebendary of Uffculme in Salisbury Cathedral in 1739. He held the position until his death. He was further named a canon of Windsor in January 1741. Fountayne resigned this canonry in 1748, the year after he had been appointed by the crown to the deanery of York. He was recommended by Bishop Sherlock and the first marquess of Rockingham to the duke of Newcastle and was chosen in preference to Archbishop Herring's candidate, Jacques Sterne, precentor of the minster. Sherlock tried subsequently to obtain a bishopric for his nephew from Newcastle but the latter raised objections on grounds of age.

Fountayne was three times married and was left a widower from each marriage. His first wife (whom he married on 23 April 1745) was Ann, daughter of William *Bromley (*bap*. 1663, *d*. 1732) of Baginton, Warwickshire, formerly speaker of the House of Commons and secretary of state in Queen Anne's last administration, 1713–14. The couple had no children and Ann Fountayne died on 11 February 1747. His second wife (whom he married on 1 August 1749) was Frances Maria, eldest daughter of Thomas Whichcot (1700?–1776), politician, of Harpswell, Lincolnshire. She died on 22 August 1750, leaving one daughter. On 14 May 1754 Fountayne married for the third time. His new wife was Ann, only daughter of Charles Montagu MP, of Papplewick, Nottinghamshire. The couple had two sons and four daughters. Ann Fountayne also predeceased her husband, dying on 12 September 1786.

Fountayne was moderately learned, borrowing heavily from the minster library and donating some of his books to it. He published only one sermon (on Isaiah 24: 4–5), preached in York Minster on Friday 6 February 1756, the day of the general fast for the Lisbon earthquake. It was a call for sorrow and repentance, which lamented 'the great and general Decay of Religious Worship' (p. 23). At York Fountayne presided over the chapter for more than half a century, the latest in a line of men of considerable distinction to hold the deanery since the 1690s. His early years were troubled by controversies centring on Jacques Sterne and the leading ecclesiastical lawyer of the northern province, Dr Francis Topham, the latter dispute immortally captured in Sterne's allegory *A Political Romance* (1759) in which Fountayne appears as 'John, the parish clerk'. There was greater stability after Archbishop Hutton's translation to Canterbury in 1757. In 1768 the

dean's previously implicit power to nominate residentiaries was confirmed by royal letters patent, and Fountayne used it to promote colleagues whose goodwill and amicability could be relied on to facilitate chapter business. They included the poet William Mason but not the dean's Cambridge contemporary Laurence Sterne, who felt disappointed by this apparent breach of friendship. He bitterly dubbed Fountayne 'a very corrupt man—I knew him weak & ignorant—but thought him honest' (*Letters*, 147). Fountayne went into residence for three months every year at the minster, until he received a royal dispensation from this obligation dated 4 July 1800: he died in the deanery on 14 February 1802 during his period of residence. He was buried at High Melton on 23 February. Fountayne left two surviving, unmarried daughters (Ann and Catherine Judith) and was succeeded in his estate by his only surviving grandson from his third marriage, Richard Fountayne Wilson. In 1782 he had told his relative Richard Gee that 'the world is of no consequence to me now, I have lost my son' (BL, Add. MS 29599, fol. 414, 5 Sept 1782), but Fountayne soldiered on in his duties at the minster despite subsequent deaths.

Fountayne was very much the landed clergyman, 'the first ecclesiastical commoner in the county' (Burke, 2.96), having succeeded to the manor of High Melton on his eldest brother's death without surviving heirs in January 1740, aged only twenty-five. He extended and redesigned the hall in a Palladian style about 1750, built farm buildings and cottages, and donated altar prayer books and stained glass to the village church, some by Peckitt of York. In politics, Fountayne was a moderate whig, a member of the Yorkshire Association, and in favour of parliamentary reform. He was also a staunch upholder of the second marquess of Rockingham's interests in the city of York; Fountayne conducted Rockingham's funeral service in York Minster and counted 'his loss amongst the greatest of my many misfortunes' (Fountayne to Earl Fitzwilliam, 14 July 1782, Sheffield City Record Office, Fitzwilliam MSS, F63/30). If the dean's relations with Fitzwilliam (who succeeded to his uncle's Yorkshire estates in 1782) were never as close, he stayed loyal to him after the Foxite whigs lost power in 1783–4.

NIGEL ASTON

Sources GM, 1st ser., 72 (1802), 190, 299 · *Christian Observer*, 1 (1802) · J. Hunter, *South Yorkshire: the history and topography of the deanery of Doncaster*, 1 (1828), 363–71 · E. Miller, *The history and antiquities of Doncaster and its vicinity: with anecdotes of eminent men* (1804) · R. Michell, *The Carews of Beddington* (1981), 84 · E. Carpenter, *Thomas Sherlock, 1678–1761* (1936) · *Fasti Angl., 1541–1857*, [Salisbury], 81 · S. L. Ollard, *Fasti Wyndesorienses: the deans and canons of Windsor* (privately printed, Windsor, 1950), 132 · *Fasti Angl., 1541–1857*, [York], 7 · *Report on manuscripts in various collections*, 8 vols., HMC, 55 (1901–14), vol. 8, p. 171 [Wood] · *Reports on the manuscripts of the earl of Eglinton*, HMC, 10 (1885), 297 · G. Ormerod, *The history of the county palatine and city of Chester*, 2nd edn, ed. T. Helsby, 3 vols. (1882) · J. Britton, *The history and antiquities of the metropolitical church of York* (1819) · D. M. Owen, 'From the Restoration until 1822', *A history of York Minster*, ed. G. E. Aylmer and R. Cant (1977), 241–2 · *Correspondence of Thomas Gray*, ed. P. Toynbee and L. Whibley, 3 (1935), 353; repr. with additions by H. W. Starr (1971) · A. H. Cash, *Laurence Sterne: the early and middle years* (1975) · *Letters of Laurence Sterne*, ed. L. P. Curtis (1935), 147 · L. Sterne, *A political romance* (1759); repr.

(1971) [with an introduction by K. Monkman] · [E. Burke], *The correspondence of Edmund Burke*, 2, ed. L. S. Sutherland (1960), 96–7 · *Yorkshire: the West Riding*, Pevsner (1959) · M. Bloy, 'Rockingham and Yorkshire: the political, economic and social role of Charles Watson-Wentworth, the second marquis of Rockingham', PhD diss., University of Sheffield, 1986, vol. 2, pp.129–30 · I. R. Christie, *Wilkes, Wyvill and reform: the parliamentary reform movement in British politics, 1760–1785* (1962) · N. C. Phillips, *Yorkshire and English national politics, 1783–4* (1961) · C. Collyer, 'The Rockinghams and Yorkshire politics, 1742–61', *The Thoresby Miscellany*, 12, Thoresby Society, 41 (1954), 352–82 · E. A. Smith, *Whig principles and party politics: Earl Fitzwilliam and the whig party, 1748–1833* (1975) · probate register, Borth. Inst., vol. 146, fol. 24 · parish registers (baptism, marriage, and burial), High Melton

Archives Doncaster Central Library, parish church of St James, High Melton, unattributed typescript, L283 HIG · Doncaster Central Library, Doncaster Archives, Book of Common Prayer donations, P20/10/1 · York Minster, calendar of chapter acts, 11 Nov 1756 to 23 Oct 1777, H9/2/1, fols. 90–92 · York Minster, calendar of chapter acts, 1784–1807, H9/3a, fols. 222, 246 · York Minster, chapter files, D1/1740–1749/169, 173–81 · York Minster, Liber Donorum · York Minster, York Minster Library borrowers, Acc. 1988/22/5 · York Minster Library, register of loans 1, 1717–78, Acc. 1988/22 | BL, Carew MSS, Add. MS 29599, fols. 414, 426 · Bodl. Oxf., Beckwith MS, vol. 2, fol. 206 · Lincs. Arch., diocese of Lincoln, episcopal act books, 1723–1761, fol. 342 · Sheff. Arch., Fitzwilliam MSS · Sheff. Arch., corresp. with Earl Fitzwilliam · Sheff. Arch., Wentworth Woodhouse Muniments · York Minster, corresp. with archbishop [Hutton] regarding appointment of a residentiary · York Minster, William Mason commonplace book, Add. MS 25, fol. 101

Likenesses J. Downe or Downes, group portrait, 1777 (with his wife and son), priv. coll. · J. Highmore, group portrait, priv. coll. · J. Highmore, sketches (for his group portrait), Tate collection

Wealth at death under £10,000; estate to grandson at age of 21: will, Borth. Inst., probate register, vol. 146, fol. 24

Fourdrinier, Henry (1766–1854), paper manufacturer, was born on 11 February 1766 in Lombard Street, London, one of several children of Henry Fourdrinier, a wholesale stationer of Huguenot descent, and his wife, Jemima (*d.* 1781). Paul *Fourdrinier, Henry's grandfather, had gone to London in 1719 and set up as a stationer and engraver, which led to the establishment of the firm of Bloxham and Fourdrinier, paper makers and stationers, in 1759. With the exception of the younger Henry, the Fourdriniers were freemen of the Drapers' Company. Henry's marriage with Mary, whose parentage is unknown, produced a son, George Henry (*b.* 1797), and at least two daughters.

Henry and his brother, **Sealy Fourdrinier** (1773–1847), and William Bloxham were engaged in the stationery business, situated in Sherbourne Lane in the City of London, when, in 1801, they were introduced to John Gamble who had gone to London to secure an English patent on a machine for making paper in continuous rolls, devised by Nicolas Robert and patented in France in 1799. Gamble showed them samples of the paper and they bought a one-third share in his patent rights. The original machine was imported and erected at the Dartford works of John Hall, the Fourdriniers' millwright. There, a third Fourdrinier brother, Charles, worked alongside Gamble, Leger Didot, who had been involved with Robert in its creation, and Bryan *Donkin (one of Hall's former apprentices), to develop it. In 1803 they installed it in a mill at Frogmore, Hertfordshire, acquired for the purpose. Gamble remained technically and financially associated with the Fourdriniers until 1811.

Hall had no real interest in the machine and allowed Donkin to take over the project. In June 1803, at Fort Place, Bermondsey, close to Donkin's own works, the Fourdrinier brothers erected and fitted out a factory, which they rented, and from 1811, leased, to Donkin who manufactured and sold the machines. The intention was that users would pay the Fourdriniers an annual royalty, according to the size of machine supplied.

The stationery business had been yielding profits of £14,000 a year, and Henry drew on this income for the cost

Henry Fourdrinier (1766–1854), attrib. John Downman, *c.*1786 [second from left, with Sealy Fourdrinier (second from right) and other members of his family]

of buildings and development. Absorbed with the new machine, he neglected the stationery business; profits fell disastrously, and by 1809 it had lost £5635. In all, Henry expended around £60,000 in the first few years of development of the paper-making machine and the enterprise was declared bankrupt in November 1810. During these years the firm changed its identity several times. The original firm of Bloxham and Fourdrinier became Henry and Sealy Fourdrinier when Bloxham withdrew, then, early in 1809, Fourdriniers, Towgoods, and Fourdrinier, in the persons of Henry and Sealy, Matthew Towgood, senior and junior, and Charles Fourdrinier. Matthew Towgood was Henry's banker. In October 1809 it became Towgood, Fourdrinier, and Hunt (Matthew Towgood junior, Charles Fourdrinier, and Joseph Brooks Hunt), at which point Towgood moved to Sherbourne Lane and took over the Fourdriniers' stationery business.

Sales of the new machine were slow; craftsmen were opposed to the introduction of machinery and the mill owners lacked enterprise. During the first ten years only nineteen machines were made, and twenty-five during the next ten years. Few mill owners paid their patent dues and even this small revenue dried up between 1810 and 1816 because owners took advantage of the Fourdriniers' financial problems. Twelve suits were filed in chancery, which cost another £5000, though most were successful. During his visit to England in 1814, Tsar Alexander I of Russia became interested in the machines and an agreement was made that the Fourdriniers should receive £700 annually for the use of two machines for ten years. The machines were erected at Peterhof on the Gulf of Finland under the superintendence of Henry's son, George Henry Fourdrinier, but the fee was not paid, until Henry, at the age of seventy-two, made the journey to St Petersburg in company with one of his daughters and placed his petition personally in the hands of Tsar Nicholas I.

In 1837 a parliamentary select committee sat to decide to what extent the country had benefited from the Fourdriniers' faith in the eventual success of their machine. It transpired that by this time many branches of trade were prepared to testify to their individual profit. A supply of continuous paper enabled newspaper proprietors to develop rotary printing presses and sell vastly more newspapers, pottery manufacturers now had good-quality tissue paper, which was used in printing on pottery, and all trades now employed rolls of paper for wrapping, replacing the calico previously used for this purpose. Of more concern to government was the enormous rise in revenue from duty on paper arising from this increased consumption, while a secondary consideration was the fact that machine minding was less skilled than paper making by hand, which was an advantage in an industry beset with labour disputes. The report was presented to parliament with a recommendation that the Fourdriniers should receive £20,000, but over succeeding years arguments in both houses forced this down to a meagre £7000, which was agreed in 1840. Sealy Fourdrinier received a share of this award. He had married Harriot Pownall in

1800; their son James Sealy practised as an architect at Tottenham. Sealy was described as solicitor's clerk on the certificate issued at his death on 27 October 1847 at 16 Providence Street, Walworth Common.

Some years later a committee was formed to raise money by subscription to purchase an annuity on the lives of Henry Fourdrinier and his two unmarried daughters. A mere £700 was raised within the trade, but by then only Henry's daughters survived. Henry Fourdrinier spent his last years at the Old Rectory, Mavesyn Ridware, Rugeley, Staffordshire. It was a modest house but he was well regarded locally. He died there on 3 September 1854.

Henry lived to see a flourishing machine-made paper trade enabling the proliferation of cheap newspapers and books in Britain and Europe. Yet he got no reward for his persistence and died in poverty. At the time of his death, his son held Ivy House Mill at Hanley, Staffordshire, which was taken over by Brittains, makers of fine tissue paper for the pottery industry, in 1855. Thus ended the Fourdrinier family's connection with the paper trade, though the name continued for many years as Fourdrinier, Hunt & Co., stationers. ANITA McCONNELL

Sources Hansard 3 (1839), vol. 47; (1840), 43.53 · ILN (9 Sept 1854), 234 · British and Colonial Printer and Stationer (Sept 1888) · GM, 2nd ser., 28 (1847), 665 [death notice of Sealy Fourdrinier] · R. H. Clapperton, The paper-making machine: its invention, evolution and development (1967) · Drapers' Company registers · d. cert. · d. cert. [Sealy Fourdrinier]
Likenesses attrib. J. Downman, oil on copper, c.1786, NPG [see illus.] · J. F. Skill, J. Gilbert, W. and E. Walker, group portrait, pencil and wash (Men of science living in 1807–8), NPG · oils, Sci. Mus. · portrait, repro. in Clapperton, Paper-making machine

Fourdrinier, Paul (1698–1758), engraver and printseller, was born in Groningen in the Netherlands, the son of Jacques Fourdrinier and his wife, Jeanne Theroude, Huguenot refugees from Dieppe, Normandy. In the *Dictionary of National Biography* his works and career were assigned to two individuals, Peter and Paul Fourdrinier; Peter is now seen to be a fictitious individual resulting from an accidental misnaming of Paul. According to George Vertue, he studied architectural engraving in Amsterdam under Bernard Picart, then regarded as 'one of the best masters of that art in Europe' (A. Palladio, *Quattro libri dell'archittetura*, ed G. Leoni, 1715–19, 4/2, preface). He travelled to London in 1719 and on 4 October 1721 married Susanne Grolleau (1694–1746) at the French church, St Martin Orgar. They had at least five children: Paul (b. 1724), Judith (b. 1727), Marie (b. 1728), Henry (1730–1779), and Charles.

Fourdrinier had established premises at the corner of Craggs Court, Charing Cross, by 1727; his trade card, designed by William Kent in 1731, advertises 'Prints, Mapps, and Stationery Wares'. Fourdrinier engraved Kent's designs for illustrations to Homer's *Odyssey* (1725), John Gay's *Fables* (1727), James Thomson's *Seasons* (1734), and Alexander Pope's *Essays on Man* (1734). His engravings of Kent's architectural work, however, were more successful and included the triumphal arch erected in Westminster Hall for the coronation of George II and Queen Caroline (1727), *The Treasury, Whitehall* (1734), and *Queen*

Caroline's Library in St James Park (1737). Fourdrinier also engraved the architectural plans of Houghton, Norfolk, the seat of Sir Robert Walpole, in 1736; he produced a satirical print of Walpole in 1730.

Among the designs of other leading contemporary architects engraved by Fourdrinier were those of Lord Burlington, Colen Campbell, James Gibbs, Isaac Ware, and John Wood. From 1738 to 1751 his prints recorded the building of Westminster Bridge, designed by Charles Labelye, then the longest stone bridge over a tidal river. He engraved plates to James Dawkins and Richard Wood's *The Ruins of Palmyra* (1753) and to James Stuart and Nicholas Revett's *The Ruins of Balbec* (1757); he also contributed to William Chambers's *Designs of Chinese Buildings, Furniture, Dresses, Medicines and Utensils* (1757). Impressions of many of his architectural engravings may be found in the Guildhall Library, the Victoria and Albert Museum, and the British Museum.

Fourdrinier died in January or February 1758 and was buried in the Huguenot cemetery, Wandsworth; he was described in an obituary as 'an eminent engraver' (*London Magazine*, February 1758). The stationery business was continued by his sons and grandsons: Charles and his son, also Charles, maintained the shop at Charing Cross until 1811. Another son, Henry, worked in partnership with William Baker of Lombard Street from 1757. A painting of Henry and his family of about 1785 shows his daughter Jemima—the future mother of Cardinal Newman—and his sons Henry *Fourdrinier (1766–1854) and Sealy *Fourdrinier (1773–1847) [see under Fourdrinier, Henry], who, in 1807, jointly patented a machine for making continuous paper. TESSA MURDOCH

Sources F. G. Lee, 'Pedigree of Fourdrinier and Grolleau', *Miscellanea Genealogica et Heraldica*, new ser., 3 (1880), 385–6 · E. Harris and N. Savage, *British architectural books and writers, 1556–1785* (1990) · T. Clayton, *The English print, 1688–1802* (1997), 176 · T. Murdoch, ed., *The quiet conquest: the Huguenots, 1685–1985* (1985), 164–5 [exhibition catalogue, Museum of London, 15 May – 31 Oct 1985] · [S. W. Kershaw and H. Wagner], 'The Fourdrinier family and Cardinal Newman', *Proceedings of the Huguenot Society*, 8 (1905–8), 291–2, 391–2 · Redgrave, *Artists* · J. Strutt, *A biographical dictionary, containing an historical account of all the engravers, from the earliest period of the art of engraving to the present time*, 1 (1785), 304 · Vertue, *Note books*, 3.136 · F. Basan, *Dictionnaire des graveurs*, 2nd edn (1765) · *London Magazine*, 27 (1758), 100 · A. Heal, *London tradesmen's cards of the XVIII century* (1925)
Archives UCL, Huguenot Library, MSS

Fourdrinier, Sealy (1773–1847). *See under* Fourdrinier, Henry (1766–1854).

Fournier, Daniel (*c.*1711–*c.*1766), engraver and printmaker, was probably a member of a French protestant refugee family; he may possibly be linked with Daniel Fournier, the son of Nicholas Fournier and Madeleine Rossignol, who is recorded in Friedrichsdorf in Germany in 1711. Trained as a chaser, he practised that craft until at least 1748, but then turned to printmaking. An etched self-portrait bears the inscription 'à-la-mode beef-seller, shoemaker, and engraver'. He etched a survey of the Leeward Islands and engraved in mezzotint a portrait of Cuthbert Mayne, a priest executed for heresy in 1579. In the 1760s he

ran a drawing academy attended by the painter Hugh Barron; he also taught drawing and perspective at the Kensington military academy, run by a Mr Marquois.

In 1761, at about the age of fifty, Fournier wrote and published *A treatise of the theory and practice of perspective, wherein the principles of that most useful art as laid down by Dr Brook Taylor, are fully and clearly explained by means of moveable schemes properly adapted for the purpose*. Dedicated to Marquois, the treatise follows Joshua Kirby's earlier attempt to explain Taylor's abstruse publications on perspective of 1715 and 1719. Subscribers included John Muller, professor of fortification at the Royal Military Academy at Woolwich. It is said that at the time Fournier was writing it he used to draw the diagrams on alehouse tables with chalk, and was known by the name of 'the Mad Geometer'. A second enlarged edition appeared in 1764. In addition to these accomplishments Fournier is said to have made a fiddle and taught himself to play upon it. His son, also Daniel, was baptized at the Huguenot church in Spring Gardens in 1744, where the registers record his wife's name as Marie. Fournier died in Wild Court, Wild Street (later Great Queen Street), Lincoln's Inn Fields, London, about 1766. L. H. CUST, *rev.* TESSA MURDOCH

Sources F. Grose, *The Olio* (1792), 165 · City of London RO, debtors schedule index 13/4/9, Fleet prison, 5 December 1748 · D. Fournier, *A treatise of the theory and practice of perspective* (1761) · W. Minet and S. Minet, eds., *Régistres des églises de la Savoye de Spring Gardens et les Grecs*, Huguenot Society Quarto publications, 26 (1922), 89 · H. Bromley, *A catalogue of engraved British portraits* (1793), 402 · J. C. Smith, *British mezzotinto portraits*, 2 (1879), 515 · Redgrave, *Artists* · G. Benthall, 'Early art schools in London, 1635–1770', MS, V&A NAL, fol. 66
Likenesses D. Fournier, self-portrait, etching

Foveaux, Joseph (*bap.* 1767, *d.* 1846). *See under* New South Wales Corps (*act.* 1789–1810).

Fowke, Francis (1753–1819). *See under* Fowke, Joseph (1716–1800).

Fowke, Francis (1823–1865), engineer and architect, was born on 7 July 1823 at Ballysillan, Belfast, the eldest of the three children of John Fowke (1794–1851), lieutenant in the 68th regiment of foot, and his first wife, Jane (1794–1827), daughter of John Stevenson Ferguson and his wife, Ellen. He was educated at Dungannon College and at a military tutor's for two years. In 1839 he entered the Royal Military Academy at Woolwich, and came out sixth in a batch of sixteen in 1842. His pre-eminent drawing ability led to a commission with the Royal Engineers, one of only four in his year. He was made second lieutenant on 18 June 1842, first lieutenant on 1 April 1846, second captain on 17 February 1854, and captain on 23 February 1856. He married Louisa Charlotte (1822–1874), daughter of the Revd Robert Rede Rede of Ashmans, Suffolk, and his wife, Louisa, on 22 May 1845. They had five children, two of whom died in infancy. Shortly after his marriage he was sent to Bermuda, and served there for four or five years. On his return to England he was stationed in Devonport, Plymouth, where he prepared the working drawings for the Raglan barracks (built 1854–6), and received much credit for their sanitary improvements. He came up with numerous proposals for elongated shot for rifled ordnance, but had difficulty persuading the military authorities to give them a trial.

In 1854 Fowke was invited to assist in superintending the machinery section of the Paris Universal Exhibition of 1855. When the secretary to the British Control Commission, Captain Henry Cunliffe Owen, was ordered to the Crimea, Fowke was appointed in his place and resided in Paris during the year of the exhibition. He carried out a series of experiments on the strength of colonial woods, the results of which were published in the parliamentary reports on the exhibition, and which reputedly led to a huge increase in the exports of Jamaican lancewood and mahogany (*PICE*, 468). He was made a chevalier of the Légion d'honneur for his exhibition work, but was unable to wear the decoration as it was awarded for civil and not military service. He was sent to Paris again in 1858 to represent the British members of the International Technical Commission for rendering the St George's branch of the Danube navigable. An independent scheme which he proposed was unanimously adopted, but later abandoned for political and financial reasons.

Work on the 1855 exhibition led to a close association with the head of the British Commission, Henry Cole, who was inspector-general (later secretary) of the Department of Science and Art in London. Fowke joined the department's staff in summer 1856, and was officially made an inspector in 1857. By 1860 he had also been appointed architect and engineer, to which duties were added in 1862 (when he ceased to be inspector) those of superintendent of construction of the South Kensington Museum (now the Victoria and Albert Museum) and, in 1863, of science referee for the museum. Photographs taken about that time reveal a tall man with a prominent moustache and a hint of the 'melancholy and reserve' mentioned in his obituary in *The Builder*. On the department's move from Marlborough House to South Kensington in 1857, he successfully converted the iron buildings commonly known as the Brompton Boilers (by Sir William Cubitt), the adjoining old houses, and the wooden schools of design into a working unit. He then designed a picture gallery to house the Sheepshanks bequest, in association with Richard Redgrave RA, whose formula for skylights minimized the glare and reflection on paintings. It became the first public gallery to be lit at night: Fowke invented a system, approved in 1859 by a scientific commission headed by Michael Faraday, which allowed hundreds of gas burners to be lit almost instantaneously. He continued to experiment with gas lighting in the Vernon and Turner picture galleries, built to his designs in 1858-9 at very small cost. During the years 1860-65 he designed and erected several new buildings for the museum, including the north and south courts and the residences and lecture theatre surrounding the main quadrangle. His collaboration with the decorative artist Godfrey Sykes led to the exploration and use of innovative materials such as terracotta. Plans which he drew up for the completion of

the museum from the south side were ultimately superseded by those of Sir Aston Webb.

In 1859-60 Fowke produced designs for the industrial museum in Edinburgh (opened in 1866 as the Museum of Science and Art, now the Royal Museum of Scotland), as well as for the interior of a new wing for the National Gallery of Ireland, Dublin. He designed the Prince Consort Library, Aldershot, which was erected at the private cost of Prince Albert in 1860, and a drill shed in South Kensington for the 1st Middlesex volunteer engineers (a corps formed at his suggestion), which was commended by Sir Joseph Paxton as the cheapest structure he had ever seen (Cole, 'Brief notes', xii). He designed the conservatory, council chamber, and south arcade of the Royal Horticultural Society Gardens at South Kensington (since demolished). The buildings of the International Exhibition of 1862 were erected to his designs on the same site, their main feature being two gigantic glass domes. Although the exhibition buildings were considered a success in terms of lighting, ventilation, and internal arrangement, they were severely criticized for stylistic shortcomings, and Fowke was subjected to attacks (which he bore with great patience) on his lack of 'official' qualifications. At the close of the exhibition the government refused to purchase the buildings, in spite of previous plans for adapting them to permanent use, and they were largely demolished in 1864. Fowke's reputation was nevertheless restored when he was awarded first prize in a public competition to design a natural history museum on the site of the demolished exhibition buildings, but he died before the plans could be executed, and a design by Alfred Waterhouse was eventually substituted. Shortly before his death he produced a design for the Royal Albert Hall, which was erected with alterations by his successor, Major-General Henry Scott, in 1867-71.

Fowke's numerous inventions included the widely used 'bellows' camera, a portable military fire-engine (awarded a medal at the 1862 exhibition), and a collapsible canvas pontoon exhibited in Paris in 1855 and described in *Professional Papers of the Corps of Royal Engineers* (new ser., 7, 1858, 81-7) and the *Journal of the Royal United Service Institution* (4, 1860-61, 237-52). He was the author of a plan for coastal defence batteries (*Professional Papers of the Corps of Royal Engineers*, new ser., 5, 1856, 88-90) and a description of the Sheepshanks Gallery (1858). In collaboration with Henry Cole he wrote for the *Cornhill Magazine* 'The National Gallery difficulty solved' (1/3, 1860, 346-55) and 'London the stronghold of England' (1/6, 1860, 641-51). He was mistakenly assumed to be the author of *Some Account of the Buildings Designed for the International Exhibition of 1862* (1861), which was written by Cole. He died of a burst blood vessel on 4 December 1865 at his official residence in the South Kensington Museum, and was buried on 9 December at Brompton cemetery, London. The *Athenaeum* observed that 'the public has lost in this engineer and architect one of the ablest of its servants'.

H. M. CHICHESTER, *rev.* DALE DISHON

Sources H. Cole, 'Brief notes on the career of the late Captain Francis Fowke, R.E.', *Professional Papers of the Corps of Royal Engineers,* new ser., 15 (1866), ix–xv • *The Builder*, 23 (1865), 881–2 • *The Athenaeum* (9 Dec 1865), 808–9 • *The Times* (14 Dec 1865) • *GM*, 2nd ser., 23 (1845), 538 • *PICE*, 30 (1869–70), 468–70 • Lieutenant-Colonel Stokes, 'Remarks on a passage in the "Notes on the career of the late Captain Fowke"', *Professional Papers of the Corps of Royal Engineers*, new ser., 16 (1868), xv–xvi • *The museums area of South Kensington and Westminster*, Survey of London, 38 (1975) • F. Fowke, letters to H. Cole, 1855–63, V&A NAL, MS 86.JJ, box II (iv) • H. Cole, diary, 1855–65, V&A NAL, MS 55.CC [transcribed by E. Bonython] • *Army List* (1843–65) • S. Fooks and R. Fowke, Fowke family tree, www.crc.ufl.edu/genie/genie.html

Archives Sci. Mus., corresp. and papers, chiefly relating to work as director of works at South Kensington Museum • V&A NAL, family corresp. | V&A NAL, letters to Sir H. Cole **Likenesses** J. and C. Watkins, photograph, *c*.1862, V&A • Donnelly, photographs, 1862–5, V&A • Elkington & Co., gilt bronze bust (after model by T. Woolner, 1866), V&A • Minton & Co., gilded terracotta bust (after plaster model by T. Woolner, 1866), V&A • bronze bust (after model by T. Woolner?, 1866), Royal Engineers, Brompton Barracks, Chatham, Kent • wood-engraving, NPG; repro. in *ILN* (3 May 1862), 431 **Wealth at death** under £9000: administration, 25 Jan 1866, CGPLA Eng. & Wales

Fowke, John (*c*.1596–1662), merchant and politician, was the third son of William Fowke of Tewkesbury, Gloucestershire, gentleman, and his wife, Alice, daughter of George Carr of Bushley, Worcestershire. He was bound apprentice to the Haberdashers' Company in 1608 and gained his freedom in 1617. He was married twice, first to Catherine, daughter of Richard Briggs, a London haberdasher, with whom he had two sons and a daughter. His second wife, whom he married on 27 September 1638 at Hackney, was Mary (*b*. 1621), daughter of Edward Basse, a wealthy London mercer; they had a son and five daughters who died in infancy. Despite not having held any of the customary junior offices, Fowke was chosen master of the Haberdashers in 1642, following his election as alderman; he served two further terms as master, in 1652–3 and 1655.

Fowke was initially successful as an overseas merchant trading in the Mediterranean, and served on the governing bodies of the East India Company in 1625–6 and the Levant Company in 1629–54. Yet in 1627 he suffered a major setback when he joined other merchants in refusing to pay customs duties not approved by parliament, and had goods worth £5827 seized by customs officers. Continuing defiance in 1628–9 earned him a summons before privy council and subsequent imprisonment, as well as the seizure of his ship and its cargo, for which an enormous £40,000 bail was demanded. He was in further trouble in 1630 for expressing dismay about the future following the recent dissolution of parliament—in his appeal of 1641 to the Commons for compensation, he was to claim that this early opposition to Charles's government had cost him £20,000. He had also clashed with the East India Company, over penalties he had incurred as security for a defaulting merchant, and company investments, allegedly totalling £3700, had been seized. He enjoyed better relations with the Levant Company, serving on two of its committees in 1638 and 1641, yet relations with this company too were later to deteriorate.

By the late 1630s Fowke was living on Mark Lane, near the Tower, alongside other overseas merchants. However, the earlier seizures and financial penalties had probably retarded his career, as in 1640 he was given only a third ranking in his ward in a listing of citizens according to wealth. The bitter experience of those early years greatly influenced his later life when, as political influence and power fell open to him, he grasped the opportunities offered to seek recompense for his personal losses. It also led him largely to abandon trade after 1640 in favour of the new openings for investment provided by the state. His political enemies were thus able to portray him as a man moved by greed who was engaged in a cynical, and corrupt, pursuit of self-interest, but this judgement ignores his early established political convictions and his later role in securing the City for parliament.

Fowke rapidly established himself as a leading London radical in the early 1640s, drawing on his previous political record and his membership of the capital's godly network. Furthermore, his marriage to Mary Basse brought him a father-in-law who was a close London ally of Oliver Cromwell. In summer 1641 Fowke's influence among London's liveried citizens in common hall was sufficient for him to be selected as both a City delegate to Scotland to confer about trade and as a representative to support the assembly's claim to elect both London sheriffs. Characteristically, he was simultaneously addressing his first appeal to the Commons for compensation for the losses he had incurred fighting unparliamentary customs duties. In the following December he led the delegation which presented the second London root and branch petition and acted as spokesman before the house, a role he was similarly to perform on other important occasions in the 1640s when the City made its views known to parliament.

A royalist claim that Fowke was one of the newcomers to common council in the disputed elections of 1641 is almost certainly false, yet his influence in the assembly appears to have been negligible before January 1642, when he was appointed a member of the committee investigating the 1641 elections. More importantly, he became a member of the London militia committee and a keen supporter of parliament's militia ordinance. He was also elected an alderman, serving for Farringdon Within in 1642–9 and Tower in 1649–62; a term as sheriff followed in 1643–4. His parliamentarian zeal and political weight in the City were such that in January 1643 he was one of four citizens named as traitors by the king because of their responsibility for London's disaffection from him.

A supporter of an active prosecution of the war, Fowke allied in 1644 with the younger Vane and Oliver St John against the earl of Essex and later found much common ground with political independents, while at the same time endeavouring to maintain cordial relations with political presbyterians. As far as his religious convictions were concerned, Fowke was described in 1661 as a man 'not much noted for religion, but a countenancer of good ministers' (*CSP dom.*, *1660–61*, 539), but his second marriage had taken place at Hackney, where the minister was the puritan divine Calybute Downing, and Fowke was subsequently at the forefront of the campaign to abolish bishops. Almost certainly a religious presbyterian, he was prepared to serve alongside moderate Independents on the committees chosen by parishioners of St Dunstan-in-the-East in the 1640s to govern the parish. He was also sufficiently wary of giving ministers more power to be among the seven members of common council who spoke out against critics of the October 1645 ordinance for the appointment of triers to vet elders. Repelled by some of the more extreme demands of political presbyterianism, he came to side with their Independent opponents and was one of eleven members of common council in May 1646 who recorded their dissent to the City remonstrance, urging an exclusive presbyterian church settlement and suppression of gathered churches.

Fowke was earning for himself an unsavoury reputation. Appointed a commissioner of customs in 1643, he was fined and imprisoned for several months in 1645 amid suspicions of dishonesty for refusing to deliver his accounts on oath. He also took his dispute with the East India Company to the House of Lords in 1646 and obtained judgment in his favour the following year. He was eventually to be compensated from the sale of forest lands, but matters dragged on until 1658. Further opportunities for profit opened up in 1646 with his appointment as controller for the sale of bishops' lands (and later dean and chapter lands too); he was to spend nearly £4000 on acquiring property from the dioceses of Gloucester and Bristol.

During the attempted counter-revolution of 1647 Fowke was purged from the London militia committee, but he was subsequently restored to it after the army's intervention. In 1648 he helped persuade the City to yield to the army, yet having been later named a commissioner for the king's trial he joined other prominent City parliamentarians in refusing to attend or sign the death warrant. With Cromwell's backing he was elected lord mayor in 1652 but his mayoralty was blighted by clashes with the other branches of the City's government that arose from charges of nepotism, corruption, and misgovernment, and from his efforts to use the opportunity to gain parliament's support in his long-running battle with the East India Company. As lord mayor he also took an active part in the trial of the Leveller leader, John Lilburne. Further influential positions in the 1650s included a judge of probate (1653–4) and membership of committees for the regulation of trade (1650–51), relief under articles of war (1652), law reform (1652–3), sale of crown property (1653), and Irish matters (1654, 1656). Furthermore, he finally succeeded in gaining an award of £27,615 compensation for his losses over customs duties and £7000 damages against the East India Company.

During the final days of the protectorate Fowke was one of the City delegates sent on 9 December 1659 to confer with Fleetwood and on 19 January 1660 to convey thanks to Monck. In the following March he made a public declaration denying any complicity in the regicide, and later retired to his estate at Claybury in Essex. Yet he retained enough confidence in the City to be elected an MP for London in 1661, although he was a largely inactive member, being nominated to only four committees. He died in London 'of an apoplexy' on 22 April 1662.

KEITH LINDLEY

Sources E. Cruickshanks, 'Fowke, John', HoP, Commons, 1660–90, 2.352–4 · V. Pearl, London and the outbreak of the puritan revolution: city government and national politics, 1625–1643 (1961); repr. with corrections (1964), 316–20 · DNB · K. Lindley, Popular politics and religion in civil war London (1997), 102, 140–41, 144–5, 172–3, 191, 195–6, 199–200 · A. B. Beaven, ed., The aldermen of the City of London, temp. Henry III–[1912], 2 (1913), 66 · R. L. Greaves, 'Fowke (or Foulkes), John', Greaves & Zaller, BDBR, 1.297–8 · GL, MS 10091/19 (25 Sept 1638); MS 15857/1, fol. 179; MS 15860/3 (11 Nov 1608) · journals, CLRO, court of common council, vol. 40, fols. 23, 31, 39, 48, 60; vol. 41, fols. 83–4, 88–92 · The journal of Thomas Juxon, ed. K. Lindley and D. Scott, CS, 5th ser., 13 (1999), 90, 119n., 123, 410 · CSP dom., 1651–2, 416, 455; 1652–3, 205; 1660–61, 539 · R. R. Sharpe, London and the kingdom, 2 (1894), 337–8, 365, 370 · C. H. Firth and R. S. Rait, eds., Acts and ordinances of the interregnum, 1642–1660, 1 (1911), 38–40, 990, 1007, 1255, 1261 · The visitation of London, anno Domini 1633, 1634, and 1635, made by Sir Henry St George, ed. J. J. Howard and J. L. Chester, 2 vols., Harleian Society, 15, 17 (1880–83) · J. Maclean and W. C. Heane, eds., The visitation of the county of Gloucester taken in the year 1623, Harleian Society, 21 (1885) · W. J. Harvey, ed., List of the principal inhabitants of the City of London, 1640 (1886) · T. C. Dale, ed., The inhabitants of London in 1638, 2 vols. (1931) · A. W. Hughes Clarke and R. H. D'Elboux, eds., The register of St Dunstan in the East, 5 vols., Harleian Society, register section, 69, 84–7 (1939–58)

Likenesses T. Athow, wash drawing (after a contemporary portrait), AM Oxf.

Wealth at death property in Gloucestershire and Claybury in Essex, possibly London too; purchased bishops' lands: DNB; Cruickshanks, 'Fowke, John'

Fowke, Joseph (1716–1800), East India Company servant and free merchant, was born in Madras and baptized there on 22 October 1716, one of the four children of Randall Fowke (1673–1745) of the Madras council, and his wife, Anne, née May (1680–1734). Joseph probably travelled to England in 1728 with his father, who was making a short visit. He went back to Madras as a writer about 1736, rising to third in council. He returned to England in 1752. A year later he wrote of his fortune, partly acquired through trading in diamonds, as standing at £18,000 (J. Fowke to J. Walsh, 12 Jan 1753, BL OIOC, MS Eur. D546). Although nominated governor of Madras in 1754, he never took up the appointment, having failed to agree a salary with the company.

Joseph's marriage on 7 May 1750 to Elizabeth (1731–1760), the daughter of Joseph Walsh (1694–1731), a company official, and his wife, Elizabeth, née Maskelyne (d. 1734), whose cousin Margaret became Lady Clive, forged an important family link for the Fowkes. Their three children, Francis, Arthur, and Margaret, were born after they had returned to England. As a widower, Joseph married Kitty Lavinia Treacher in London on 1 September 1770. She died at St Helena in 1774. They had three children, Sophia (b. 1769), Louisa (b. 1770), and William, who was born in India. Joseph also had a natural daughter, Elizabeth (b. 1768), whose mother was Grace Croftes. There appears to have been another natural daughter, born in

India of an unknown mother, 'who cannot be publickly acknowledged' (J. Fowke to F. Fowke, [1786], BL OIOC, MS Eur. E6, item 108).

Joseph again departed for India in 1771 with his second wife and set up as a free merchant trading in diamonds, hoping to recoup the modest fortune that he had gambled away after his first wife's death. Family and political links with Clive drew him towards Warren Hastings's opponents, particularly to General Clavering and Philip Francis. In April 1775 he was found not guilty on a charge of conspiracy against Hastings although convicted of conspiracy against Hastings's associate Richard Barwell. Joseph moved to Benares to carry on his diamond trading. In 1780 Francis obtained a sinecure in Calcutta for him, but they quickly fell out, although they were later reconciled. Joseph's appointment was terminated in 1783. On his return to England in 1788 he was worth no more than £1400. He engaged in a bitter dispute with the company over his claim to a pension. Edmund Burke raised the matter in parliament, but Joseph refused the company's only offer of £700 of arrears. He died in Bath on 16 May 1800, bequeathing to the sole beneficiary of his will 'a debt due to me from the East India Company of which I have been unjustly deprived'.

Old Fowke, as he was widely known to contemporaries, was a complicated man. Hastings complained of his undeniably violent and morose temperament, yet Burke saw him as 'a man of honour even romantick; and of very great natural abilities' (Burke to Dundas, 22 April 1791, *Correspondence*, 6.251). Both were right. He was a reckless gambler, querulous with friends and relations, negligent of his children when young and a trial to their patience thereafter, but talented enough to be considered more than once for a governorship, a valued friend of Samuel Johnson, and a discerning lover of music.

Francis Fowke (1753–1819), eldest son of Joseph, was born on 22 October 1753 and baptized at St George's, Hanover Square, London, on 22 December 1753. He was sent to school at Dr Gilpin's in Cheam, Surrey, and went to Bengal as a writer in 1773. In August 1775 he was appointed resident at Benares to implement the provisions of the treaty of Fyzabad, which had been negotiated by Clavering, Colonel Monson, and Philip Francis against Hastings's opposition. After Monson's death in September 1776 Hastings regained control of the Bengal council and was able to use his casting vote to recall Francis Fowke from Benares in December 1776. Hastings was censured by the company and ordered to reinstate Fowke in 1777, orders which were ignored. A motion in council for Fowke's restoration moved by Philip Francis on 5 April 1779 failed. However, Fowke regained Benares in February 1780 as part of a short-lived truce agreed between Hastings and Philip Francis. In January 1781, a month after Philip Francis had sailed for England, Hastings again recalled Fowke and once more the company ordered his reinstatement, which was finally effected in April 1783.

In between residencies at Benares, Francis lived in Chinsura and Calcutta. He amassed a fortune of at least £70,000 founded on trade in diamonds and opium, and on government contracts. He returned to England in 1786. His natural son William, baptized in Calcutta on 17 October 1781, came back to England with him. By 1788 Francis had entered into a liaison with Mary Lowe (c.1769–1847), said to have been an actress. They had fifteen children but remained unmarried until 19 July 1813, when, apparently in some secrecy, they went through a ceremony at St Olave's, Southwark. This belated marriage took place twelve days after Francis had written a will, which, after securing an annuity of £500 to his wife, declared that all his children were born previous to his marriage but that all should share equally in his estate.

Francis lived in Wimbledon in the 1790s and commanded the Wimbledon light horse volunteers. He later lived at 41 Hertford Street, Mayfair, Westminster, commenced the building of Boughrood Castle in Radnorshire in 1817, and rented property in Worthing and near Torquay. Francis was a more equable man than his father, whom he roundly castigated for improvidence but, none the less, assisted financially. However, they seem to have shared a love of music and a taste for creating bewildering family networks. Francis died at Bochrwyd (Boughrood) on 20 October 1819.

Margaret Benn-Walsh [*née* Margaret Fowke] (1758–1836), the youngest child of Joseph and Elizabeth, was born on 13 July 1758 and baptized at St George's, Hanover Square, London, on 16 August 1758. She was a goddaughter of Lady Clive. Left motherless at an early age and forsaken by an impecunious father, she came under the guardianship of John Walsh (1726–1795), her maternal uncle, who had been a councillor in Madras and private secretary to Lord Clive. Member of parliament for Worcester from 1761 until 1780 and a fellow of the Royal Society, he was unmarried, brusque in manner, but a benefactor to all his sister's children. As a young girl Margaret was boarded out. Her carers were not always well chosen and at one time she became quite seriously mentally disturbed. She briefly attended a school in Queen Square, London, but between the ages of seven and seventeen her education was acquired in the library of John Walsh and those of the Clives and the Stracheys. At seventeen Margaret was 'a tall and large woman' (Walsh to F. Fowke, 20 April 1775, BL OIOC, MS Eur. E3, item 38), and in 1776 she embarked for Bengal, 'I suppose to get her a husband, which, she has not beauty or fortune enough to get here' (F. Fowke, sen. [uncle] to F. Fowke, 22 Nov 1775, BL OIOC, MS Eur. E3, item 44). At first she lived in Calcutta but later joined her father and brother in Benares and Chinsura. Independently minded, she was not intimidated by her domineering father, defying him, for example, over an excursion up the Ganges with friends that he considered unsuitable.

Margaret was among the first British women to take an informed interest in Indian music. She was a pioneer of the genre which was termed 'the Hindostannie air', a piece derived from an Indian original arranged in an English idiom. By 1784 she had made a collection of songs and delighted Hastings with her performance. Margaret not only organized musicians and linguists to make transcriptions and to perform the airs but she also took down the airs herself and attempted to play along with Indian musicians. She was also interested in mathematics, excelled as an equestrienne, and, by all accounts, had a compelling manner and presence.

Margaret returned to England with her brother in 1786. The following year she married John Benn (1759–1825), who had been assistant resident at Benares, where he made an estimated £80,000 trading in diamonds and opium. On the death of John Walsh in 1795 Margaret inherited all his property in trust for her as yet unborn son. After four stillborn children, a daughter was born in 1794 and a son, John Benn-*Walsh, eventually first Baron Ormathwaite, in 1798. The Benns assumed the additional name Walsh in 1795. John Benn-Walsh senior was elected to parliament in 1802 and created a baronet in 1804. He died at Cheltenham in 1825. Margaret died at Binfield Park, Berkshire, on 29 September 1836. The careers of Joseph Fowke and his eldest son and daughter not only illustrate the opportunities for acquiring wealth in eighteenth-century British India, in spite of the hazards of its volatile politics, but also show how individuals responded to Indian culture.   T. H. BOWYER

Sources BL OIOC, Fowke MSS, MSS Eur. A2, C2–C6, D10–D17, E3–E10, F2–F3, G3 · BL OIOC, Ormathwaite MSS, MS Eur. D546 · 'Memoir of Lady Walsh' (by her son), BL OIOC, Photo Eur. 32, 6 vols. · G. R. Kaye and E. H. Johnston, eds., *Catalogue of manuscripts in European languages belonging to the library of the India Office*, 2/2: *Minor collections and miscellaneous manuscripts* (1937), 64–9 · M. C. Poulter, introduction to 'A descriptive list of the Ormathwaite collection', BL OIOC, Ormathwaite MSS, 3–11 · E. Green and H. Green, *The Fowkes of Boughrood Castle: a study in social mobility* (1973) · J. Pratt, 'Fowke family', *N&Q*, 153 (1927), 424–5 · H. D. Love, *Vestiges of old Madras, 1640–1800*, 4 vols. (1913) · F. E. F. Penny, *Fort St George* (1900) · I. Woodfield, '"The Hindostannie air": English attempts to understand Indian music in the late eighteenth century', *Journal of the Royal Musical Association*, 119 (1994), 189–211 · J. Parkes and H. Merivale, *Memoirs of Sir Philip Francis*, 2 vols. (1867), vol. 2 · *The correspondence of Edmund Burke*, 6, ed. A. Cobban and R. A. Smith (1967) · *GM*, 1st ser., 57 (1787), 638 · *GM*, 1st ser., 70 (1800), 493 · *GM*, 2nd ser., 6 (1836), 555 · *Annual Register* (1825), 258 · *The letters of Samuel Johnson*, ed. B. Redford, 2 (1992) · *The letters of Samuel Johnson*, ed. B. Redford, 4 (1994) · 'Marriages at Fort St. George, Madras', *The Genealogist*, new ser., 20 (1903–4), 105 · *Bengal Past and Present*, 26 (1923), 150, 164 · *Bengal Past and Present*, 30 (1925), 113 · IGI · St George's, Hanover Square, parish registers

Archives BL OIOC, corresp. and papers, MSS Eur. A2, C2–C6, D10–D17, E3–E10, F2–F3, G3 · BL OIOC, letters, MS Eur. D 546 | BL, letters to Warren Hastings, Add. MSS 29132–29133, 29153–29154 · BL OIOC, corresp. with Philip Francis, MSS Eur. C 8, D 18, E 12–22, F 5–6 · BL OIOC, Ormathwaite MSS · NL Wales, corresp. and literary papers

Fowke, Margaret. *See* Walsh, Margaret Benn- (1758–1836), *under* Fowke, Joseph (1716–1800).

Fowke, Martha. *See* Sansom, Martha (1689–1736).

Fowke, Phineas (*bap.* 1639, *d.* 1710), physician, the son of Walter Fowke, also a physician, and his wife, Mary, was born at Bishop Burton, Yorkshire, and was baptized there on 7 January 1639. His mother was the daughter of Thomas Micklethwaite, rector of Cherry Burton, Yorkshire, and sister of Sir John Micklethwaite (1612–1682),

physician-in-ordinary to Charles II. He was admitted at Queens' College, Cambridge, on 21 April 1654, and graduated BA in 1658; and on 26 March in the same year was admitted a fellow of the college. His family connections directed him towards medicine, and he graduated MD at Cambridge in 1668. Fowke practised in London, residing in Little Britain, and was admitted a fellow of the College of Physicians on 12 November 1680. In 1684 he married Sarah, daughter of Sir Vincent Corbet, at Shrewsbury. She died on 6 December 1686.

Fowke was learned in theology as well as in medicine, and was an admirer of Seth Ward, bishop of Salisbury, whose views on passive obedience he strongly supported. In some manuscript notes on a sermon of Ward's, on the text 'And they that resist shall receive to themselves damnation', Fowke expresses his contempt of the conduct of the University of Oxford in 1688, saying, 'These great pretenders to loyalty invited the Prince of Orange. They had no patience when King James bore upon their priviledges in Oxford, but exclamed bitterly against the king and joyned with the wiggs and dissenters to bring in the Prince of Orange'. Despite this Fowke was admitted to Christ Church as a nobleman in 1689. In 1704 Fowke gave 49 books to the library of Christ Church.

Fowke retired to his paternal estate in Staffordshire, and died at Little Wyrley Hall on 21 January 1710. He was buried in the neighbouring church of Brewood, and his death is recorded on his wife's monument in St Chad's Church, Shrewsbury.

NORMAN MOORE, *rev.* MICHAEL BEVAN

Sources Munk, *Roll* · Venn, *Alum. Cant.* · original lists, RCP Lond. · S. Ward, *Seven sermons*, 2nd edn (1674) · private information (2004) [J. Curthoys]

Archives Wellcome L., notebook

Fowle, Sir Thomas (*bap.* 1637, *d.* 1692), goldsmith and banker, was baptized on 6 January 1637, the fifth son of Edward Fowle, a yeoman, and his wife, Barbara, of Stanton St Bernard, Wiltshire. The family held enough leasehold and copyhold land directly to support the two elder sons, Edward and Henry, and to provide premiums to apprentice the next three boys, Daniel, Robert, and Thomas, to London goldsmiths. Details of Fowle's education are unknown until he was apprenticed on 12 August 1652, at the age of fifteen, for eight years, to James Pewte, a 'shopkeeping goldsmith' in Tower Street. He became free of the Goldsmiths' Company in 1660, when he probably opened a shop in the vicinity of Temple Bar in Fleet Street, where he was established at the Black Lion by 1667, the year in which he became a liveryman of the company. It was this period that first saw the provision of credit accounts and the development of the clearing system which, based on the agreement of a ring of goldsmiths to accept each other's 'notes', in effect to honour third-party debts, was the vital step in the establishment of goldsmith banking. These developments can be traced in Fowle's career. His surviving '1664 daybook' charts an emerging business serving a burgeoning clientele of gentry and lawyers living both in the west of the City and beyond, towards Westminster and the court at Whitehall. Fowle's trade was diverse, and included the sale of plate and jewellery, bullion exchange, and some provision of financial services. In the summer of 1665, when the plague was at its height in the City, Fowle closed his shop; he reopened in January the following year. Trade recovered quickly, and on 9 June 1666 he married Jane, the daughter of Roger Norton of St Anne Blackfriars, a prosperous London stationer. Her marriage portion of £900 provided a significant addition to the capital of the business. In early September the great fire destroyed much of the City but stopped just short of Fowle at Temple Bar. The goldsmiths to the east were not so fortunate, for Lombard Street was reported to be 'all in dust', which must have given, at least for a while, a competitive advantage to those in Fleet Street.

After the great fire, Fowle started to sell the most fashionable plate, which was commissioned from Arthur Manwaring, a leading English silversmith, and from Wolfgang Howzer and Jacob Bodendick, two 'strangers' working in the 'new' or 'French fashion'. The pattern of his trade remained broadly similar for the next few years, his main profits being generated by the sale of plate and jewellery with a limited return on bullion dealings and interest on loans. In 1672 the 'stop of the exchequer' (when the repayment of loans to lenders was suspended) was a severe setback to a number of Lombard Street goldsmiths. Their difficulties may have helped the emerging Fleet Street goldsmith bankers such as Fowle, despite their client base being substantially different. Perhaps it is not coincidental that the first clearing accounts between Thomas Fowle and Robert Blanchard (later Child's Bank) appeared in Blanchard's ledger for 1672; the moneys cleared between them rose steadily to more than £17,000 in 1679. There were similar arrangements to accept and clear notes with other goldsmith bankers. These included most of those that kept 'running cashes' listed in the vicinity of Fleet Street in the *Little London Directory* of 1677.

Fowle's banking activities grew steadily, with net profits in the late 1670s in excess of £1000, raising to £3000 by the end of the next decade. Part of these were retained for expansion but some were used to purchase land, particularly in the west country. Despite the growth in banking activity, Fowle continued to employ a number of subcontractors and specialist craftsmen to make a wide range of plate and jewellery. In 1681 William Fowle (1658–1684), the second son of Thomas Fowle's eldest brother Edward, finished his apprenticeship with Arthur Manwaring and was established with a house and shop in Hungerford Street, off the Strand. Thomas financed his nephew's trade, taking most of his production, until William's untimely death in 1684. Prominent among William's plate were splendid toilet services, either finely cast and chased with mythological scenes, such as the Calverley set in the Victoria and Albert Museum, or flat-chased with lively chinoiseries, such as that in the Metropolitan Museum, New York. The cast and chased toilet services are considered among the finest surviving examples of Caroline goldsmithing.

Fowle was known for his strong tory sympathies and played an active role in the life of the Goldsmiths' Company and the City. In 1682 he was elected to the court of assistants of the company. In 1686 he became an alderman and was soon after chosen as sheriff and knighted. The following year he became prime warden of the Goldsmiths' Company, but was removed from this office and discharged as alderman at a time when, having dissolved parliament, James II replaced many opposed to him. On the accession of William III, Fowle was again elected prime warden, but declined to serve. However, he co-operated with the new regime, acting as a member of the committee of City financiers that negotiated loans for the government in 1690; he also lent some £20,500 himself. He was elected member of parliament for Devizes in the tory interest in March 1690, but the proceedings of the election were disputed and he was unseated on petition the following December. Although out of parliament, he was re-elected an alderman in 1691. He died 'of an apoplexy' on 11 November 1692 and was buried on the 24th in his parish church of St Dunstan-in-the-West, Fleet Street, with very considerable pomp (Luttrell, 614, 623). His wife survived him, and died on 2 January 1707.

Fowle was clearly firm in his business dealings, as he notes, for example, in his pocketbook: 'Tho. Wotton my sarvant is indebted to me By Negligence in Letting a woman cheat Him of Five Guinys' (PRO, C104/120, pt 1). Nevertheless, he was generous in his will, for, after making ample provision for his widow and his only child, Susan (who married Jonathan Cope), he left land and money to fifteen relatives and made several charitable bequests. He also left £200 to 'my old servant' Thomas Farmer, his bookkeeper, who continued to serve at the Black Lion, under Robert Fowle, the son of Thomas's brother Robert, in partnership with Thomas Wotton, his former apprentice. His nephew Robert, as residuary legatee, was left, according to a contemporary report, £10,000 'to continue that trade, with the house and shop in Fleet Street where he lived, so his dealings seems the same as if Sir Thomas was yet living' (W. Ball to Sir Cyril Wyche, 24 Jan 1693, National Archives of Ireland, Wyche MSS).

D. M. MITCHELL

Sources Fowle and Wotton exhibit, PRO, C104/107, 108, 112, 115, 117–25 • '1664 daybook', Goldsmiths' account books, July 1664–Sept 1667, PRO, C114/179 • Child & Co. customer ledgers, Royal Bank of Scotland, London, CH/194/1–3 • parish register, Stanton St Bernard, 6 Jan 1637, Wilts. & Swindon RO [baptism] • apprentice books 1 to 4, Goldsmiths' Company • court books Z and 1 to 10, Goldsmiths' Company • D. M. Mitchell, 'Mr Fowle pray pay the washwoman: the trade of a London goldsmith–banker, 1660–1692', *Business and Economic History*, 23/1 (1994), 27–38 • D. M. Mitchell, 'Dressing plate by the "unknown" London silversmith "WF"', *Burlington Magazine*, 135 (1993), 386–400 • [S. Lee], *A collection of the names of the merchants living in and about the City of London* (1677); repr. as *The little London directory of 1677* (1863) • N. Luttrell, *A brief historical relation of state affairs from September 1678 to April 1714*, 2 (1857) • NA Ire., Wyche MSS • A. B. Beaven, ed., *The aldermen of the City of London, temp. Henry III–[1912]*, 2 vols. (1908–13) • will, PRO, PROB 11/413, sig. 6

Archives PRO, corresp. and papers, C104/107, 108, 112, 115, 117–25 | Royal Bank of Scotland, London, Child & Co. ledgers

Wealth at death popularly supposed to have died 'very rich'; one son-in-law put personal estate at 'upwards of £40,000': notes from files of History of Parliament; papers of nephew Robert Fowle; will, PRO, PROB 11/413, sig. 6

Fowle, Thomas Welbank (1835–1903), theologian and writer on social issues, was born at Northallerton, Yorkshire, on 29 August 1835. He was the son of Thomas Fowle, solicitor, and of Mary Welbank, both of Northallerton. After education at Durham School (1848–53) and at Charterhouse, he entered Exeter College, Oxford. After a term's stay there he gained an open scholarship in 1854 at Oriel College, where he graduated BA in 1858 and proceeded MA in 1861. As an undergraduate he took an active part in the debates at the Oxford Union, and was president in 1858. His intimate associates included T. H. Green and Professor Albert Venn Dicey, and his sympathies, like theirs, were democratic.

After rejecting thought of the bar, Fowle took holy orders in 1859, becoming curate of Staines in Middlesex. A collection of sermons he preached there, *Types of Christ in Nature*, was published in 1864.

In 1861 Fowle married Sarah Susannah Atkinson, daughter of Richard Atkinson, who was a medical practitioner in Richmond, Yorkshire. They had seven daughters.

In 1863 Fowle was appointed vicar of Holy Trinity, Hoxton, London. Under his influence new schools were built, which, managed by a committee of churchmen and nonconformists, were the first to be governed under a conscience clause. Here in a poor and densely populated parish his advanced political ideas gathered strength, and he studied economic conditions closely. In 1868 he became vicar of St Luke's, Nutford Place, London, and in the same year he reached a wider public through an essay on 'The church and the working classes' in *Essays on Church Politics*.

In 1875 Fowle was presented to the rectory of Islip, and there he gave practical effect to his theories on social questions. He instituted and successfully managed an allotment system for agricultural labourers, and as a poor-law guardian helped to reduce outdoor relief, to which he was strongly opposed. In schools under his management he encouraged self-government by appointing a voluntary board of managers. He also instituted a clothing club, a penny savings bank, and a working men's club.

Fowle's first wife died in 1874 and in 1876 he married Mabel Jane Isaacs, daughter of Jacob Isaacs, a West Indies merchant. They had one son and one daughter.

Fowle wrote extensively on both theology and social questions. An active-minded broad-churchman, he endeavoured to reconcile new scientific discoveries with old religious beliefs in three articles on evolution in the *Nineteenth Century* (July 1878, March 1879, September 1881), as well as in the two-volume *New Analogy*, which he published in 1881 under the pseudonym of Cellarius, and *The Reconciliation of Religion and Science*. His most important contributions to social policy were an article in the *Fortnightly Review* for June 1880 advocating the abolition of outdoor relief and a concise manual on *The Poor Law* in the English Citizen series (1881; 2nd edn, 1890), a work which attracted much attention at home and abroad.

Fowle actively supported the extension of the franchise to the agricultural labourer between 1882 and 1884, most effectively as a platform speaker but also through the publication of an article in the *Fortnightly Review*, 'The third Reform Bill: why delay it?' (1883), and of his influential pamphlet *An Earnest Appeal to his Grace the Archbishop of Canterbury* (1884). He opposed Irish home rule in 1886 and for the next ten years was prominent among the Liberal Unionists. His authority on social questions was undiminished by his change of political allegiance. To his advocacy was largely due the creation of parish and district councils under the Local Government Act of 1894. In 1892 he urged the prudence of old-age pensions in a pamphlet called *The Poor Law, the Friendly Societies, and Old Age Destitution: a Proposed Solution* (new edn, 1895).

The sudden death of Fowle's only son in 1895 broke his health. He suffered a stroke in 1896 and a second in 1901 which compelled him to retire from Islip to Oxford, where he died, after further strokes, at his home, 159 Woodstock Road, on 14 January 1903. He was buried at Islip by the side of his son. His second wife survived him.

W. B. OWEN, *rev.* C. A. CREFFIELD

Sources J. Cook Wilson, *Memoir of Thomas Welbank Fowle* (1903) · *Oxford Magazine* (28 Jan 1903) · C. W. Fremantle, 'Old age pensions and pauperism', *Charity Organization Review*, 8 (1892), 321 · *St Luke's, Nutford Place, Parish Magazine* (Feb 1903) · private information (1912)

Likenesses photograph, Oxford Union

Wealth at death £973 4s. 2d.: resworn probate, July 1904, CGPLA Eng. & Wales (1903)

Fowler, Abraham (*fl.* 1568–1576), poet, was a queen's scholar at Westminster School, which he left in 1568 on being elected to Christ Church, Oxford. The university register indicates that Fowler received a BA from Christ Church in February 1572, but gives no other details of his life. Fowler contributed a thirty-six-line poem in alternate rhymes to Thomas Rogers's *Philosophicall Discourse Entituled, The Anatomie of the Minde* (1576). Rogers also had been a student of Christ Church. Fowler's verse is followed by a poem by Camden.

SIDNEY LEE, *rev.* ELIZABETH GOLDRING

Sources T. Rogers, *A philosophicall discourse entituled, The anatomie of the minde* (1576) · *Reg. Oxf.*, vol. 2 · Foster, *Alum. Oxon.* · J. Welch, *The list of the queen's scholars of St Peter's College, Westminster*, ed. [C. B. Phillimore], new edn (1852) · E. Brydges, *Censura literaria: containing titles, abstracts, and opinions of old English books*, 2nd edn, 10 vols. (1815)

Fowler, Alfred (1868–1940), astrophysicist, was born at Wilsden, Yorkshire, on 22 March 1868, the eighth and youngest child, and seventh son, of Hiram Fowler and his wife, Eliza Hill. About 1876, after the mill at which his father worked was burned down, the family moved to Keighley, where Alfred attended two elementary schools and then entered the trade and grammar school in 1880. In 1882 he was awarded a Devonshire exhibition to the Normal School of Science (later absorbed into the Imperial College of Science and Technology) at South Kensington, becoming, at the age of fourteen, probably the youngest student ever admitted there. He gained a first-class diploma in mechanics and was enabled to continue his studies through an appointment as 'teacher in training'.

His duties included acting as an assistant to J. N. Lockyer, who in 1879 had set up his solar physics observatory at South Kensington and was conducting astronomical research there in close association with spectrographic work at the college. Thus at the beginning Fowler saw astronomy and spectroscopy as two aspects of a single subject, and his subsequent work was controlled by this view.

Fowler remained with Lockyer (from 1888 onwards as demonstrator in astronomical physics) until the latter's retirement from the college in 1901, when he became assistant professor of physics and assumed charge of the astronomical work. In 1915 he was appointed professor of astrophysics and in 1923 one of the first Yarrow research professors of the Royal Society. He continued to work at the college, to his distinct relief without undergraduate teaching responsibilities, until his retirement in 1934. He once remarked in mild despair of two of his students—Richard Gregory and H. G. Wells—that they would keep stopping work to discuss socialism. In 1892 he married Isabella, daughter of John Orr, a designer of dress materials; they had two children, a son and a daughter.

During Fowler's association with Lockyer his work was merged in that of the elder man. Together they amassed much data on the successive spectra emitted by the elements as the exciting stimulus was intensified, a manifestation, in Lockyer's view, of the step-by-step dissociation of the elements into simpler forms. The idea was controversial, however, and only when Niels Bohr's theory of spectra appeared in 1913 did it become respectable. On the astronomical side Fowler spent much time in the study of the sun's atmosphere during total eclipses. He went with the British government expeditions of 1893, 1896, 1898, 1900, 1905, and 1914 to various parts of the world for this purpose. While on the way to the last of these, he was caught in the outbreak of the First World War, and only got back to England with difficulty (and without equipment).

From 1901 onwards Fowler worked on his own responsibility, and a series of papers appeared recording the identification of previously unknown celestial spectra with spectra obtained in the laboratory. By this time, American observatories were obtaining much better photographs of astronomical spectra than could be found in Britain. His excellent links led to his involvement in their interpretation. Among other achievements the absorption bands in the spectra of the red stars were traced to titanium oxide, the bands in the spectra of comets' tails to low-pressure carbon monoxide, certain bands in sunspot spectra to magnesium hydride, and the absorption at the shorter wavelength end of celestial spectra to ozone in the earth's atmosphere. Of especial importance was the laboratory production of the spectrum then attributed to 'cosmic hydrogen' and now to ionized helium: this proved of great value in establishing the Bohr theory of spectra. As that theory developed, Fowler's almost unrivalled knowledge of spectra became of increasing importance, and he displayed a natural ability in classifying spectrum lines comparable with his skill in identifying them.

Fowler played an active part in the administrative work of science both nationally and internationally. He was largely responsible for the organization of the International Astronomical Union (founded in 1919), of which he was the first secretary. He was highly successful also as a director of research. Besides British recruits he worked with a number of foreign researchers, one of whom, M. N. Saha, wrote his very important paper on the stellar spectral sequence while working with Fowler in 1920. Fowler was appointed CBE in 1935 and was elected fellow of the Royal Society in 1910. He was president of Section A of the British Association in 1926, of the Royal Astronomical Society from 1919 to 1921, and of the Institute of Physics from 1935 to 1937. His numerous other distinctions included honorary degrees from the universities of Bristol, Cambridge, Durham, and Leeds, the Bakerian lectureship of the Royal Society (1914 and 1924), the gold medals of the Royal Astronomical Society (1915) and the US National Academy of Sciences (1920), and a royal medal of the Royal Society (1918). Fowler died at 1 Montpelier Avenue, Ealing, London, on 24 June 1940; he was survived by his wife and children.

HERBERT DINGLE, *rev.* A. J. MEADOWS

Sources H. Dingle, *Obits. FRS*, 3 (1939–41), 483–97 · *The Observatory*, 63 (1940), 262–7 · *CGPLA Eng. & Wales* (1940) · personal knowledge (1949) · private information (2004)
Archives ICL, corresp. and papers · RAS, letters to Royal Astronomical Society · Royal Observatory, Edinburgh, corresp. related to solar notation · Sci. Mus., personal notebook | American Philosophical Society, Philadelphia, corresp. with Niels Bohr and S. A. Goulsmit · Nuffield Oxf., corresp. with Lord Cherwell · University of Copenhagen, Niels Bohr Institute for Astronomy, Physics, and Geophysics, corresp. with Niels Bohr
Likenesses W. Stoneman, photograph, 1933, NPG · Maull & Fox, photograph, RS · photograph, repro. in Dingle, *Obits. FRS*, facing p. 483
Wealth at death £11,191 8s. 3d.: probate, 11 Sept 1940, *CGPLA Eng. & Wales*

Fowler, Charles (1792–1867), architect, was born on 17 May 1792 in Cullompton, Devon, the son of John Fowler of Cullompton and his wife, Jane. At the age of fifteen he was apprenticed to John Powning, architect and builder, of Exeter. On the completion of his articles in 1814 he moved to London to work as an assistant in the office of David Laing, architect to the customs and excise, before setting up in independent practice there in 1818. In 1822 he won the competition for rebuilding London Bridge but the result was set aside in favour of the design by John Rennie, and the principal feature of his career, for which he gained notice on the continent as well as in Britain, was to be his speciality as a designer of large covered market buildings. One of his first commissions was the New market in Gravesend, Kent (1818–22; dem.), and three major examples followed: the Covent Garden market (1828–30) and Hungerford market (1831–3; dem.) in London, and the Lower market in Exeter (1835–7; dem.).

In these works, together with the great conservatory at Syon House (1827–30), Fowler spanned the rapidly widening gap between architecture and civil engineering. A sophisticated functionalist economy of structure, embracing on occasion a highly innovative use of cast iron, was combined with an appropriately simplified neo-classical elevational style derived from French rationalist architects such as Jean-Nicolas-Louis Durand. This rationalist approach is overtly expressed in Fowler's statement that:

> The proper excellence of architecture is that which results from its suitableness to the occasion … and this principle rightly pursued leads to ORIGINALITY without the affection of NOVELTY; but … the present enlightened epoch in architecture is woefully distinguished as having no character of its own nor any pretensions beyond that of adopting the various styles that have prevailed in all ages and nations without regard to the difference of circumstances upon which they were founded. (Taylor, 'Centenary memoir', 60)

The critic John Claudius Loudon meanwhile described Fowler as 'one of the few modern architects who belong to the School of Reason and who design buildings on fundamental principles instead of antiquated rules and precedents' (ibid., 59).

Alongside this and particularly following the Exeter commission, Fowler also maintained his connection with his native county, where he had a long-standing patron in William Courtenay, tenth earl of Devon: his works there included the Totnes Bridge (1826–8), a small group of churches, and alterations to the earl of Devon's Powderham Castle (1837–48). The churches are mainly in a conventional Gothic style but the most ambitious, that of St Paul in Honiton (1835–8), is in the neo-Norman manner. In 1835 he was one of the founder members of the Institute of British Architects, from 1836 to 1843 he was one of the institute's joint honorary secretaries, and in 1850–51 he was elected a vice-president. He also contributed a number of papers to the institute's *Transactions* and to Loudon's *Architectural Magazine* and published posthumously *A description of the plan for the revival of Hungerford market, with some particulars of the buildings proposed to be erected* (1929). Many of his designs were exhibited at the Royal Academy. James Mountford Allen and Henry Roberts were his pupils.

Fowler retired from practice in 1852 because of ill health, and moved first to Kent and then to Buckinghamshire, where he died at his home, Wester House, Great Marlow, on 26 September 1867. His son Charles Fowler (c.1823–1903), architect, studied under his father and then in Germany. He became a fellow of the RIBA and practised in London. PETER LEACH, *rev.*

Sources Colvin, *Archs.* · *The Builder*, 25 (1867), 761 · *Sessional Papers of the Royal Institute of British Architects* (1867–8) · J. Taylor, 'Charles Fowler: master of markets', *ArchR*, 135 (1964), 174–82 · J. Taylor, 'Charles Fowler: a centenary memoir', *Architectural History*, 11 (1968), 57–74 · *CGPLA Eng. & Wales* (1867)
Wealth at death under £35,000: resworn probate, May 1880, *CGPLA Eng. & Wales* (1867)

Fowler, Christopher (1613/14–1677), clergyman and ejected minister, was born at Marlborough, Wiltshire, the son of John Fowler. He entered Magdalen College, Oxford, as a servitor in 1627, matriculated on 14 October 1631 aged seventeen, and graduated BA on 9 February 1632. Having moved to St Edmund Hall he proceeded MA on 29 October 1634. It is probable that his attachment to Calvinist theology owed something to the influence of John Prideaux (d. 1650), regius professor of divinity at Oxford. Fowler was ordained in the diocese of Salisbury in 1637, as a deacon on 5 March and as priest on 24 December. He at first preached in and around Oxford but on 10 June 1640, on the presentation of his father and of Mark Fowler, of Aldbourne, Wiltshire, he was admitted rector of West Woodhay in the same county. On 3 August he was granted a licence to marry Elizabeth Burges of Marlborough, aged twenty-five, who survived him.

After the fall of Reading in April 1643 Thomas Bunbury, vicar of St Mary's, Reading, joined the king at Oxford, and Fowler may have for a short time acted in some unofficial capacity in the parish. Within a few months, however, being threatened by royalist troops, he made his way to London; there he preached at St Margaret, Lothbury, where he signed the covenant. In that parish, Wood complains, his 'odd gestures and antic behaviour … drew to his congregation a numerous crowd of silly women and young people, who seemed to be hugely taken and enamoured with his obstreporousness and undecent cants' (Wood, *Ath. Oxon.*, 3.1098). In 1645 Fowler was nominated as one of two replacements for fellows of Eton College, John Meredith and David Stokes, who had sided with the royalists. An ordinance to this effect was read and committed in the House of Lords on 20 December 1645, but appears not have been implemented. About this time Fowler returned to Reading and served as minister of St Mary's, baptizing there four sons and five daughters between 5 August 1646 and 10 May 1660; the first-born, Joseph, became chaplain and tutor in Lord Wharton's family in 1673. In 1649 Fowler refused to take the engagement to the Commonwealth but he remained in the ministry of St Mary's and following Bunbury's death was presented to the living under the great seal on 12 October 1652.

Fowler was zealous in defence of his Calvinist and presbyterian beliefs, persisting in the teeth of every change in fashion. He made many enemies in Berkshire, acknowledging in 1656 that:

> I am a person under many censures, especially passion, and rigidness, for the first I cannot justify myself, and for the other I must not condemn my self, unless this be my fault, that in my ministry I have opposed heresy for truth's sake. (Fowler, sig. A2r)

It is hard to know how well founded were the many charges of malice and bad faith raised against him. Certainly he contended in a region highly polarized by the hostilities, where radical movements were strong and extreme, and which later experienced a violent backlash. Fowler was violently attacked by Baptists and Quakers from the one side, and by the Restoration authorities from the other, in a career of polemical struggle lasting over thirty years—he later recalled a public debate on infant baptism at Hampstead Norreys, Berkshire, as early as the winter of 1645–6 and he was still contending into the 1670s. As assistant to the Berkshire commissioners in 1654 Fowler was in the front line of resistance to the forces of heresy.

The process of their ejection from the rectory of Bradbury of the Behmenist John Pordage (1607–1681) in December 1654 was defended at great length by Fowler in the first part of *Daemonium meridianum* (1655); to a second bulky instalment he appended a confutation of the millenarian Baptist John Pendarves (*d.* 1656). The Quaker Thomas Speed was imprisoned by Reading corporation, attacked by Fowler, and defended by George Fox (1624–1691). Fowler had public disputes with another Quaker, Edward Burrough, first at Reading in November 1657 and second at the nearby village of Easthampstead in November 1659. Fowler and Simon Ford worked closely with the corporation against the religious radicals, to the point where the aldermen were forced to affirm publicly that they and not the ministers were in effective charge of the town's religious policy. On the prompting of the corporation Fowler included in the second part of *Daemonium meridianum* their response to charges that they were preventing citizens of unsatisfactory views from employing apprentices; such a ban was held to be justified in cases where prospective masters 'deny the ordinances of Jesus Christ, or neglect the performance of private duties in their family' (Fowler, 56).

Throughout these extraordinary times efforts were made to continue the ordinary business of the ministry. On 31 October 1659 the town records that 'Mr Fowler is desired to perform divine service in St Mary's church every morning, six days in the week, according to Mr John Kendrick's will, and to continue the weekly Friday lecture' (*Leeds MSS*, 194). But Fowler was soon faced with less sympathetic authorities: on 17 October 1661, Humphrey Henchman (1592–1675), bishop of Salisbury, complained of 'two that will not yet conforme, one of them, Mr. Fowler, a busy turbulent man, yet these are content to submit to my appointment that at the weekly Lecture common Prayer be read' (*Calamy rev.*). But on 29 November 1661 Thomas Tuer, the rural dean, reported that Fowler was refusing to use the Book of Common Prayer (*CSP dom., 1661–2*, 161). He was ejected from St Mary's under the Act of Uniformity in August and on 11 September 1662 Peter Mews (1619–1706), the future bishop of Winchester, was admitted as his successor. In December the mayor of Reading informed John, second Baron Lovelace (1616–1670), lord lieutenant of Berkshire, that 'numerous sectaries in the town meet every Sunday at Christopher Fowler's, who instructs them contrary to law, and by these meetings the audiences in the churches are made very thin. The schismatics scorn persuasion and defy powers' (ibid., 589); on 10 December it was ordered that 'Christopher Fowler a seditious minister' be sent to Windsor Castle (ibid., 587). He cannot have been long detained. On 14 January 1663 Mews complained to Williamson about his predecessor's crowded meetings:

> the concourse thereto being so great, and he so confident of their legality … He wants to repeat the old rebellion, having formerly uttered bloody imprecations against the late King and his friends. His meetings are the greatest hindrance to reducing the place to order. (*CSP dom., 1663–4*, 11)

Five days later Fowler's meeting was raided by the mayor and constables; his hearers dispersed, 'but Fowler persisted that he would keep his house open for all who would come, and had satisfied the Lord Lieutenant', which, given the stalwart royalist record of Lovelace, may appear unlikely (ibid., 18). At length, on 23 November, a warrant was issued to the governor of Windsor Castle to receive 'Christopher Fowler for seditious and dangerous practices' (ibid., 347). Refused a writ of habeas corpus, Fowler petitioned the king on 17 February 1664: he had been imprisoned 'for reading sermons in his own house, some of his neighbours coming in to hear'; now, 'his family being numerous and his means small', he promised 'to live as a loyal subject, to remove in a quarter of a year from his dwelling at Windsor, and to hold no more such meetings'. Order was given for his release, and interestingly Lovelace was to stand security for his good behaviour (ibid., 487).

In 1669 Fowler was reported to be preaching in Wiltshire, at Ramsbury and at the court house at Aldbourne. But it is possible that he had moved to the London area after his release from prison, and there is some reason to suppose that he may have been instrumental in the founding of a presbyterian meeting at Unicorn Yard, off Tooley Street, Southwark. Certainly on 25 May 1672 he was able to secure a licence under the indulgence, as a teacher at his house in nearby Kennington, Surrey. He also applied for a licence in Reading, but this was refused, for on 16 April Sir William Armourer had written to Lord Arlington opposing any such concession in the strongest terms:

> Till the Restoration he was always the most violent man against the King, and the most malicious against all that were for him … His prayer in the pulpit for his majesty's father was … in these words, 'And as for the King, let the blood of England, the blood of Scotland, the blood of Ireland fly in his face and dog him day and night, and let him never have peace of conscience till he return to Jesus Christ and his Parliament'.

Armourer urged Arlington to 'preserve this town from such a man, who has been the author of most of the evil in it' for his licensing 'would be the ready way to set us by the ears' (*CSP dom., Dec 1671–May 1672*, 328). By this time Fowler was almost sixty. He died on 15 January 1677 and was buried at St John's, Dowgate Hill, London.

STEPHEN WRIGHT

Sources Calamy rev. · Foster, *Alum. Oxon.* · *CSP dom.*, 1661–4; 1671–2 · *The manuscripts of the duke of Leeds*, HMC, 22 (1888) · [C. Fowler], *Daemonium meridianum: Satan at noon. The second part* (1656) · Wood, *Ath. Oxon.*, new edn · *Walker rev.* · *JHL*, 8 (1645–6) · C. Coates, *The history and antiquities of Reading* (1802) · W. Wilson, *The history and antiquities of the dissenting churches and meeting houses in London, Westminster and Southwark*, 4 vols. (1808–14) · W. Cooper, *The good man perished from the earth, being a sermon preached upon the death of that eminent and faithful servant of Christ, Mr Christ Fowler* (1677) · BM, Luttrell Coll. 1.45 · *The Genealogist*, new ser., 31 (1915), 183

Fowler, Constance (*d.* 1664). *See under* Aston, Herbert (*bap.* 1614, *d.* 1688/9).

Fowler, Edward (1631/2–1714), bishop of Gloucester, was born at Westerleigh, Gloucestershire, the third son of Richard Fowler (*d.* 1681). Richard Fowler may have been exercising his ministry in Westerleigh in 1632, although

Edward Fowler (1631/2–1714), by Sir Godfrey Kneller, 1711

he is recorded as admitted to the perpetual curacy there only on 18 February 1646. Edward Fowler was educated at the College School in Gloucester under William Russell, his brother-in-law. He then followed the path of his older brothers Stephen and Samuel to the University of Oxford. On 22 November 1650 he matriculated from Corpus Christi College, Oxford, and three years later, on 14 December 1653, according to Anthony Wood, he became a 'chaplain' on account of his talent for extemporary prayer (Wood, *Ath. Oxon.*, 4.612). Fowler graduated BA on 23 December 1653. He appears to have then migrated to Cambridge University, where he was incorporated on 27 March 1656 and proceeded MA from Trinity in 1656. He was incorporated as an MA at Oxford on 5 July 1656.

Early career At some stage Fowler served as chaplain to Amabella (or Amabel), dowager countess of Kent, and it was, says Wood, through her patronage that he was admitted on 12 December 1656 as curate of Northill, Bedfordshire, a donative in the gift of the Grocers' Company. No record has yet been discovered of any ordination that Fowler may have undergone. Nor is his precise denominational affiliation in the 1650s known. From his own later writings and the hostile comments of his enemies several likely associations can be suggested. Fowler was influenced by the Cambridge Platonists and probably already knew Henry More at this time. It is likely that Fowler was subject to strong family influences: his father was by this time a presbyterian although an Arminian in theology, and his brother Stephen, rector of Crick in Northamptonshire from 1650, was sufficiently godly to assist the ejectors in that county in 1654. These connections became

important after the Restoration when the 1662 Act of Uniformity posed a dilemma for such godly ministers. Richard Fowler left his benefice before the act (probably in 1661); Stephen Fowler acquired episcopal ordination in August 1661 but seems to have been unable to bring himself to conform to the act and was ejected in late 1662, but Edward Fowler's decision is obscure. Some sources suggest that he took up to two years to conform and was not in residence at Northill until 1664: Anthony Wood disparagingly comments that 'he had wheeled about with the times' (Wood, *Ath. Oxon.*, 4.612). One of Dr John Walker's informants claimed, however, that his nonconformity 'was no longer than a days time, for hearing that the Grocers' Company were giving it to another, he came and declaring himself satisfy'd went on in the cure' (*Calamy rev.*, 209).

Religious controversialist Fowler presumably spent the 1660s exercising his ministry in Bedfordshire, close enough to Cambridge and London to be aware of political and intellectual developments, but also familiar with the everyday pastoral challenges posed by religious apathy or the attractions of dissent and sectarianism. In 1670 he suddenly launched himself into the world of religious controversy. His début was an attack on Calvinist or, as it was increasingly portrayed, 'puritan' theology. He sought to expose the irrationalism and antinomianism implicit in puritan teachings on justification by faith alone, imputed righteousness, and absolute predestination. It was aimed, noted Thomas Barlow in his own copy, 'against the zealous non-Conformists' and especially at their charge that many of those who had, like Fowler, conformed to the restored Church of England were time-servers, hypocrites, or latitudinarians. *The Principles and Practices of Certain Moderate Divines of the Church of England* (1670) argued that nonconformist accusations of apostasy against some Anglican ministers were a smokescreen. What nonconformists resented was that these younger ministers had repudiated the shibboleths of Calvinism. The moderate divines had simply demonstrated:

> that the grand designe of the gospel is to make men good: not to intoxicate their brains with notions, or furnish their heads with a systeme of opinions; but to reform mens lives and purifie their natures: which noble principle ... doth utterly overthrow the *Latitudinarianism* they are accused of. (Fowler, *Principles*, 18–19)

Fowler returned to the point the following year in an avowed sequel, *The Design of Christianity*, and provoked an onslaught from nonconformists like John Bunyan who were eager to defend their own (Calvinist) understandings of doctrines like justification. One such person believed that Fowler had substituted 'the meer morality of a Heathen' for the Christian doctrine of justification and asked Richard Baxter, another leading nonconformist, to repudiate Fowler's work as a perversion of his own teaching (Keeble and Nuttall, 2.117). Fowler and Baxter exchanged letters and discovered a mutual respect and theological outlook, although Baxter warned against intemperate replies to sincere if misguided critics. Unfortunately Fowler did not heed this advice. He responded to

Bunyan with a vicious assault, calling him a 'ranting anti-nomian', an 'ignorant fanatic', and an 'impudent malicious schismatic' (Fowler, *Dirt wip't Off*). Some have wondered whether Fowler might later have been reflected in Bunyan's unflattering portrait of 'Mr Worldly Wiseman'. A few years later Fowler turned his guns on the Quakers and exposed 'the absurd opinions of that sect' in print too.

Fowler's venture into print had the added advantage of attracting the patronage of Archbishop Gilbert Sheldon (to whom *The Design of Christianity* had been dedicated). Sheldon brought Fowler to the capital by collating him to All Hallows, Bread Street, on 25 August 1673. Fowler's next preferment was owed to Henry More, who used his connections with Anne, Lady Conway, and Lord Chancellor Finch to transfer his own claim to a prebendal stall at Gloucester to 'Mr Fowler, a good scholar and a good Christian' who 'is a very honest man indeed in all mens judgments' and 'has writ several books with very good approbation' (*Conway letters*, 423–4). On 29 February 1676 Fowler was installed in the fourth prebend in Gloucester Cathedral. More also mentioned Fowler's financial needs with five small children to support and this suggests that Fowler had already been married to Ann (*d.* 1696), daughter of Arthur Barnardiston, a master in chancery, for several years.

Fowler continued to maintain and make relationships across the denominational and ideological divides of Restoration England. In the later 1670s he was corresponding with Henry More about ghosts as evidence of spiritual philosophy: the supernatural tales he passed on were incorporated into More's *Sadduccismus triumphatus, or, Full and Plain Evidence Concerning Witches and Apparitions* (1681). He was entrusted by Dr John Worthington with the care of his children and his manuscript writings. He knew John Locke by 1678, visited Locke's master, the earl of Shaftesbury, and Thomas Firmin, the Socinian philanthropist. His initial respect for Richard Baxter was tempered to some extent by that divine's 'prescribing and imposeing, rather than reasoning' in debate (DWL, Morrice Ent'ring book Q, fol. 593). It is likely that Fowler also knew Roger Morrice, the leading presbyterian agent. Fowler's brother Stephen had taken out a licence as a presbyterian preacher at Kilsby, Northamptonshire, under the 1672 indulgence and he was still there ministering to a large congregation in 1687. Edward Fowler was a member of the Welsh Trust, an ecumenical project for propagating the gospel and educating the poor in Wales, which included churchmen like John Tillotson and Edward Stillingfleet, dissenters like Baxter, and laymen of different opinions like Firmin and Edward Harley.

Towards the end of the 1670s Fowler, in common with many ministers, turned his attention to the dangers of Roman Catholicism. At the height of the Popish Plot in June 1679, and with Fowler's encouragement, the chapter of Gloucester Cathedral 'most cheerfully voted down' as 'a vile relic of popish superstition', a stained-glass window which Fowler then ceremonially smashed. The next year Fowler brought out 'a farther pursuance of the argument

of *The Design of Christianity*' called *Libertas evangelica*. This book stated that the target of his earlier work could be reduced to three heads, 'Antinomian, Fanatical and Popish', and that this book would concentrate its fire on popish errors (sig. A8). On 31 March 1681 Fowler, having resigned his other cure of souls, was instituted to the vicarage of St Giles Cripplegate, a sprawling parish just beyond the walls of the city. On 10 June 1681 he was awarded the degrees of BD and DD by the University of Oxford.

Fowler's response to the perceived threat from popery was to urge that protestants should sink their differences and present a united front. He had consistently argued in print since 1670 that the Thirty-Nine Articles should be regarded as articles of peace rather than of faith—in other words, that those clergy who subscribed them did so as a basis for harmony rather than as a recognition that they were absolutely necessary for salvation. His well-known stance made him a natural source of advice for those troubled by conformity. In 1682 he replied to the questions about subscription put on behalf of John Osmond, fellow of Corpus Christi, Oxford, by John Wickes: by subscribing to the articles as articles of peace we are not declaring our belief in the truth of each of them but simply binding ourselves not to contradict them—as John Bramhall, William Chillingworth, and Edward Stillingfleet had all asserted—'if the Gentleman can swallow this sense of subscription, he need not trouble himself about particular articles, so long as he does not believ that any one of them contains an errour of so dangerous as that our concern for the souls of men should oblige us to preach against it' (BL, Add. MS 33498, fols. 71–2). In 1683 Fowler offered a slightly different gloss on the issue in his contribution to the London clergy's pamphlet series *Cases and other Discourses Written to Recover Dissenters to the Communion of the Church of England*: the English church:

> requires no man to believe those Articles, but at worst only thinks it convenient that none should receive Orders, or be admitted to Benefices, etc. but such as do believe then (not all as Articles of our Faith, but many as inferior Truths). (*Resolution of this case of conscience, whether the Church of England's symbolising so far as it does with the Church of Rome, makes it unlawful to hold communion with the Church of England?*, 1683: 1694 edn, 283)

Bishop Henry Compton of London was said to have allotted topics to different authors and there may be some significance in the choice of Fowler to discuss whether dissenters were right to see the Church of England as insufficiently purged of its Roman Catholic heritage.

The tory reaction By the 1680s Fowler had come a long way from the hesitant conformist of 1662: his theology was in line with the tenor of Restoration Anglicanism, he was an advocate of its prayer book-based private devotions and was offering weekly communions at St Giles, and he had demonstrated in print and action his detestation of popery and of sectarianism. But he was still out of step with the majority of churchmen in one major area: Fowler could not bring himself to join in with the persecution of dissenters; on his own admission he 'seldom dealt severely with the fanatics' that he encountered daily in his parish (Fowler, *Great wickedness*, sig A3v). Indeed he spoke of them in public and from his pulpit as 'good people, saying he could wish that those good people, speaking of such as frequent not the church at all, would come over to the church, or to the like effect' (LPL, process book D1591, fol. 115). Predictably Fowler's reputation was as one of the trimming clergy or moderate divines along with Simon Patrick, John Tillotson, Edward Stillingfleet, and others whom the tory press saw as soft on dissent. In January 1683 Narcissus Luttrell reported that some of these ministers were under threat of suspension 'by their not being so violent against the dissenters as others were' and although he did not name Fowler he did name his curate William Smythies (Goldie and Spurr, 576). The same year the parishioners of St Lawrence Jewry explicitly asked that Fowler should not be appointed to their vacant parish because of his well-known distaste for the suppression of dissent. And when that August Fowler gave a sermon before the mayor and corporation of Gloucester in the cathedral he was accused of preaching faction and sedition for dwelling upon Catholic rather than protestant treachery. Fowler became a target for the zealots of the tory reaction, the national wave of harassment and persecution directed against nonconformists and their alleged sympathizers during the early 1680s.

In his London parish of St Giles Cripplegate, Fowler was exposed to the problem of dissent and disaffection from the church. Leading figures in the parish were either half-hearted conformists or outright dissenters, but Fowler did more than simply turn a blind eye, he seems to have offered them his protection. From his arrival in the parish Fowler encouraged the election of some of these individuals as vestrymen and so gave them a role in parish government. William Smythies, who served as curate from 1674 to 1704, was reputed to have been an active whig, to have given out alms to churchgoers and nonconformists alike, and to have profited personally from his position. In 1683 Fowler protected the vestryman Randolph Watson by attesting to his conformity when his neighbours denounced him to the recorder of London for having jeered at the prayer book and the worship of the church during a parish meeting. At the visitation of 14 May 1684 Fowler sought to block the churchwardens' attempt to present a group of parishioners including the radical distiller Thomas Rawlinson and two Baptists, the physician Charles Bateman and the minister William Kiffin, for non-attendance at church: Fowler claimed 'that he was in great hopes of bringing them to the church and to the holy communion'. Later that summer Fowler gave the sacrament to two new churchwardens who had failed to attend the visitation to take their oath of office and were technically excommunicate. This gave a group of disaffected 'loyal' or tory parishioners the opportunity to bring Fowler before the church courts. Although Fowler was ready to admit the central charge of having given communion to the churchwardens, his critics were not prepared to let the case drop and it dragged on from November 1684 until December 1685. Fowler protested to Archbishop Sancroft

that this 'vexatious suit' was damaging the reputation of the whole church, that his pastoral strategy of persuasion rather than persecution had been vindicated by the numbers coming to his church, and that 'this malicious prosecution, which all London rings of' was the work of 'scandalous persons' (Bodl. Oxf., MS Tanner 31, fol. 225). Morrice reported that the 1683 incident at Gloucester was fomented by these same parishioners who had also persuaded the king that Fowler discouraged the 'loyal' and countenanced a 'seditious Factious Vestery', although this impression was subsequently corrected by the lord keeper and the archbishop (DWL, Morrice Ent'ring book P, fol. 433). On 9 December 1685 Fowler was formally suspended and required to pay £5 costs, but he was allowed to submit and was reinstated by the new year. Fowler's symbolic defeat was a coup for the tory parishioners and their backers who were determined to destroy dissent and purge local government. But events had moved on and the indefatigable Fowler was already playing a leading role in the group of London clergy who were attempting to orchestrate the propaganda and parliamentary campaign against James II's plans for repeal of the penal laws (DWL, Morrice Ent'ring book P, fol. 491).

The revolution of 1688 and after Fowler lent his pen to the cause. Once again he participated in a joint propaganda effort by the Anglican clergy and contributed to the series of anti-Catholic tracts 'Notes of the Church' and the 'Texts Cited by Papists out of the Scriptures'. He preached at the chapel in Whitehall on 4 July 1686 when the king had omitted to appoint a protestant preacher. He was out and about in London seeking legal advice and trying to organize his brethren to oppose the ecclesiastical commission, but found little support even from Bishop Compton. Fowler's various connections with dissent made him a valuable go-between for the different parties. When, for example, William Stanley, Princess Mary's Anglican chaplain, visited London in 1687 and put it about that William of Orange would maintain the Church of England and the penal laws, it was Fowler who worked assiduously among the dissenters of Cripplegate to counteract the effect of these comments. He was at the forefront of affairs in 1688 when James II put the Church of England on the spot by requiring the clergy to read the declaration of indulgence to their congregations. As the London clergy gathered to consider their response Fowler circulated a paper which he may have obtained from the dissenters on the illegality of the king's use of the suspending power and the danger of 'an unlimited toleration'. At their meeting on 13 May one speaker—thought to be Fowler—said 'he in conscience could not read it; to read it was to desire his people to obey it, which he thought unlawful' (Thomas, 61; DWL, Morrice Ent'ring book Q, fols. 255–7). This stance by Fowler and his London brethren undoubtedly strengthened the resolve of the church's episcopal leaders to oppose James II.

Fowler was well known to the Orange party and his name figured on Gilbert Burnet's December 1688 list of London ministers whose communication skills might be of use to William. Accordingly Fowler was appointed one of the new group of royal chaplains and became a powerful voice of support for the new monarchs and for the platform of religious reform with which they associated themselves. The deprivation of Bishop Robert Frampton of Gloucester as a nonjuror in 1691 opened the way for promotion: Fowler was nominated to the see on 23 April, elected on 2 July, and consecrated on 5 July 1691. He continued to hold the vicarage of St Giles *in commendam* and to preach there. His parliamentary duties kept him in London.

Fowler saw the providential revolution of 1688 as an opportunity for eirenicism and for spiritual and moral renewal. In a sermon of 16 April 1690 he spoke of the benefit of James II's reign in forcing Anglicans and dissenters 'to be united in affection, and to have more charity for each other' so that 1688 'was the most comfortable year, that ever fell within my memory'. His, of course, was an ideal of a broad inclusive national church, not a toleration. He served on the commission appointed in September 1689 to revise the prayer book so as to placate moderate dissent and broaden the Church of England. He repeatedly 'urged the putting nothing dubious into Articles, Creeds or Publick Prayers' that might offend dissenters. The Athanasian creed, which included anathemas and a disputed account of the Trinity, was a particular bugbear as:

> it would not only keepe out many Nonconformists, some of which and those they ought to be most concerned to take in[,] did thinke that it was best to expresse Creeds in Scripture language, and that if it were retained some very learned moderate Conformable Divines would turne Nonconformist, and [he] named one or two of them that had not read it of twenty yeares themselves, nor of late suffered their readers to read it.

He suggested that its use be left voluntary, but when it was decided to refer the matter to the new convocation of the clergy of the church he recognized that it was a lost cause and was satisfied that he had 'done his duty and discharged his conscience' (DWL, Morrice Ent'ring book P, fols. 646–7).

If Fowler's hopes of protestant reconciliation were not met his aspirations for moral and spiritual renewal did come closer to realization. Fowler's post-revolution sermons were full of providentialism, of exhortations to respond to this divine mercy by individual and national reform of life and piety. He became an enthusiastic proponent of the societies for the reformation of manners which sprang up in the wake of the revolution. His *A Vindication of an Undertaking of Certain Gentlemen, in order to the Suppressing of Debauchery, and Profaneness* (1692) publicized the societies and the support they were receiving from Queen Mary and from dignitaries of the church like Bishop Stillingfleet: Fowler himself sought the signatures of various bishops to a paper commending their work. He explicitly framed this reform movement within the context of an international struggle against the antichristian forces of Rome and France. In a similar fashion Fowler endorsed the religious societies—allowing a small group of *dévots* led by Edward Stephens to use St Giles for daily communion—and became a member in due course of the Society for the Propagation of Christian Knowledge. In 1699 he told John Sharp, archbishop of York, that 'our whole bench have never done the 40th part of that service and honour to our Church that these Church of England laymen have done' and he was bitterly critical of Archbishop Tenison who had deliberately sidelined Fowler from dinners at which the bishops considered how to foster the reform societies because of such criticism of their lack of enthusiasm (Hart, 179, 183, 255–6).

Only a partial picture emerges of Fowler's political and episcopal activities in these years. He defended the revolution in print: he wrote an anonymous reply to the paper of John Ashton, the Jacobite conspirator executed in 1691. But in the Lords he opposed the attainder against Sir John Fenwick. He lobbied the king for the annexation of the mastership of the Savoy to the see of Gloucester in order to improve the bishopric's revenues. On 19 December 1696 his wife, Ann, died. Together they had had three sons and five daughters, of whom Edward and Richard and three daughters survived their father. In due course Fowler remarried. His second wife, Elizabeth, was the widow of the moderate Anglican divine Hezekiah Burton and daughter of a London merchant, Ralph Trevor; she died on 2 April 1732. Most of Fowler's energies now seem to have gone into the pamphlet controversies. His unease about the Athanasian creed can be traced in his papers as early as 1680, and may have owed something to his friendship with Firmin. In 1693 Fowler published his first anonymous work on the Trinity, *Twenty Eight Propositions*, which was an attempt to reply to Socinians and refute the Arian errors. He rapidly got sucked into controversy with Stephen Nye. Other speculative ideas also embroiled the aged Bishop Fowler in debate. In 1706 he published *A Discourse of the Descent of the Man, Jesus Christ, from Heaven* in which he asserted the pre-existence of Christ's human soul, a doctrine which he owed to Henry More. In 1709 he responded to the third earl of Shaftesbury's *Letter Concerning Enthusiasm* and the furore over the French prophets, whose ecstasies he believed owed more to 'Possession, than intended Imposture or Delusion' (Fowler, *Reflections*, 56).

In 1707 Fowler lamented the emergence of high- and low-church labels, while dismissing tory claims of the church in danger, and defending his opposition to the Occasional Conformity Bill. He described how 'a grievous Malady' disrupted his personal visitation of his diocese and prevented his attendance at the House of Lords 'where I have been but once for these three years' (Fowler, *Charge*, 3–4). He managed to attend the Lords to oppose the tory peace in December 1711, but was clearly failing: Bishop Nicolson noted with some surprise in his diary for January 1712, 'Bishop of Gloucester not dead' (*London Diaries*, 576). In fact Fowler survived for another two years. He died at Chelsea on 26 August 1714, aged eighty-two, and was buried in the churchyard at Hendon, Middlesex. In 1717 his remains were reinterred in a vault in the same churchyard. A monument to his memory was erected in the chancel.

JOHN SPURR

Sources R. Morrice, 'Ent'ring book', DWL, Morrice MS P–Q [vols. 1–2] · Bodl. Oxf., MSS Tanner · BL, Add. MS 33498 · LPL, court of arches papers · E. Fowler, *The principles and practices of certain moderate divines of the Church of England* (1670) [Thomas Barlow's copy, Bodl. Oxf., 8. A. 16. Linc.] · E. Fowler, *Dirt wip't off* (1672) · E. Fowler, *The great wickedness and mischievous effects of slandering* (1685) · E. Fowler, *Reflections upon a letter concerning enthusiasm* (1709) · E. Fowler, *The charge of the bishop of Gloucester* (1707) · J. Spurr, 'Latitudinarianism and the Restoration church', *HJ*, 31 (1988), 61–82 · M. Goldie and J. Spurr, 'Politics and the Restoration parish: Edward Fowler and the struggle for St Giles Cripplegate', *EngHR*, 109 (1994), 572–96 · J. Spurr, *The Restoration Church of England, 1646–1689* (1991) · T. Claydon, *William III and the godly revolution* (1996) · T. J. Fawcett, *The liturgy of comprehension 1689* (1973) · R. Thomas, 'The seven bishops and their petition, 18 May 1688', *Journal of Ecclesiastical History*, 12 (1961), 56–70 · R. Stromberg, *Religious liberalism in 18th century England* (1953) · *Calendar of the correspondence of Richard Baxter*, ed. N. H. Keeble and G. F. Nuttall, 2 vols. (1991) · A. T. Hart, *The life and times of John Sharp, archbishop of York* (1949) · *The Conway letters: the correspondence of Anne, Viscountess Conway, Henry More, and their friends, 1642–1684*, ed. M. H. Nicolson (1930) · *The London diaries of William Nicolson, bishop of Carlisle, 1702–1718*, ed. C. Jones and G. Holmes (1985) · *Calamy rev.* · Wood, *Ath. Oxon.*, new edn, 4.612–16 · Wood, *Ath. Oxon.: Fasti* (1820), 194–5 · Foster, *Alum. Oxon.* · Venn, *Alum. Cant.* · W. Kennett, *A register and chronicle ecclesiastical and civil* (1728) · *Fasti Angl.* (Hardy), vol. 1

Archives LPL, corresp. | BL, Add. MS 33498 · Bodl. Oxf., Tanner MSS

Likenesses G. Kneller, oils, 1711, unknown collection; copyprint, NPG [*see illus.*] · J. Smith, mezzotint, 1717 (after G. Kneller), BM, NPG

Fowler, Eileen Philippa Rose (1906–2000), fitness instructor, was born on 13 May 1906 at Clyde Lodge, Clyde Road, Tottenham, north London, the daughter of Herbert Henry Charles Fowler, civil engineer, and his wife, Daisy Annie Murphy. An active child from an early age she chose the stage as a career. Her parents were unhappy with her choice but allowed the young Eileen to train in music and dance. Although Eileen did appear on the stage in the 1920s, she found the late nights, poor diet, and parties too tiring for her, and she sought fresh outlets for her talents. In the 1930s, having witnessed the damage that a poor lifestyle could do, she embarked on a new career as a fitness instructor. She became involved in the fitness craze that swept Britain and other nations during the 1930s, and became an enduring, albeit unofficial, figurehead of the Keep Fit movement. She maintained that exercise could be fun as well as good for health and that boring, repetitive drill was not necessary. She set up classes from 1934, training housewives and factory workers, and during the war she established the Industrial Keep Fit organization to provide classes for workers in Middlesex, Hertfordshire, and Essex. The Women's Auxiliary Air Force did not want her in their ranks, so as an alternative she went around the country organizing shows and pageants in consultation with the Central Council of Physical Recreation advocating general fitness as part of the war effort. During this period she met her future husband, John Morgan Carson (*d.* 1987), an electrical engineer; they were married on 17 February 1945.

After six years semi-retirement following her marriage Eileen Fowler continued her work in industry and expanded it to include the Central Council of Physical

Eileen Philippa Rose Fowler (1906–2000), by unknown photographer, 1955 [with her Keep Fit unit]

Recreation's Movement and Dance festivals at Wembley in London. In the late 1940s the popularity of such displays led to her training two hundred women from her organization, to give a display before the Football Association cup final at Wembley. Fowler believed that the growth of prosperity during the 1950s was to blame for the poor physical health of the nation after rationing was abandoned. Although her tours and displays were popular, she found lasting fame through her media work. On April fool's day 1954 she broadcast her first radio programme of exercises, which was also the BBC's first show dedicated to fitness. As many as half a million people, mainly women, were up at 6.45 a.m. to join in the exercises. The popularity of the Keep Fit movement continued throughout the 1950s, and in 1956 the Keep Fit Association was established, with Fowler among the founding members. She regularly attended its events, and taught classes at large-scale events. She remained active at an individual level, organizing her own EF Keep Fit classes at Horndon on the Hill, Essex, and later transferring these classes, in which she trained Keep Fit leaders, to Frinton-on-Sea after she and her husband moved there.

At this time Fowler was also asked by the BBC to come up with an idea for a television programme. She trained some Keep Fit pupils as fitness instructors for the programme and, with EF emblazoned on the front of their outfits and exercises such as 'skipalong' and 'swingtime', the show was a success. The first broadcast was inundated with 100,000 requests for her exercises. Her first television career ended in 1961, but she remained involved in the Keep Fit movement. A precursor to the fitness video, the long-playing record, allowed adherents to continue their routines. Fowler provided the exercises, such as 'the slipper swing', the 'rolling pin roll', and the 'book balance', while others provided advice on elegance and poise and tips on how to stay young. Fowler published her first book, *Stay Young Forever*, in 1963. In the 1970s she appeared on television again as she hosted another Keep Fit programme, along the lines of a contemporary disco dance programme. She also had an early morning slot on the *Today* programme on Radio 4; when it was threatened with the axe her devoted fans protested, and she was retained. In 1975 she was awarded the MBE.

In 1983, at the age of seventy-seven, Fowler published another book, *Keep Fit Exercises for Everyone*. At her ninetieth birthday party she performed some exercises to demonstrate the level of her fitness in old age. In that year she moved to an old people's home in Colchester, where she insisted that her fellow residents join her in a daily series of exercises. Eileen Fowler died on 7 March 2000 at Colonia Court Nursing Home, St Andrews Avenue, Colchester, Essex, from bronchopneumonia and old age. Immaculately turned out, small, and lithe, she enjoyed good health almost to the end of her life, supported by her apparently boundless vitality: she was always her own best advertisement.   JULIE ANDERSON

Sources *Daily Telegraph* (13 March 2000) · *The Independent* (16 March 2000) · *The Guardian* (11 March 2000) · b. cert. · m. cert. · d. cert. · E. Fowler, 'Keep fit with Eileen Fowler', *Physical Recreation*, 9/4 (Oct 1957), 8–12
Likenesses photograph, 1955, Hult. Arch. [*see illus.*] · portrait, repro. in *Daily Telegraph* · portrait, repro. in *The Independent* · portrait, repro. in *The Guardian*

Fowler [*married name* Felkin], **Ellen Thorneycroft** (1860–1929), novelist, was born at Summerfield, Racecourse, Chapel Ash, Wolverhampton, Staffordshire, on 9 April 1860, the elder daughter of Henry Hartley *Fowler, first Viscount Wolverhampton (1830–1911), and his wife, Ellen (1830–1911), youngest daughter of George Benjamin Thorneycroft. Her sister, Edith Henrietta Hamilton [*see below*], was also a writer. Although the household was strictly Methodist, Ellen Fowler was a member of the Church of England from childhood. She was educated at home for the most part, but at the age of seventeen attended Laleham School, Middlesex, for about one year. Until her marriage on 16 April 1903 to Alfred Laurence Felkin (1856–1942), an inspector of schools, she lived at home with her parents at Woodthorne, Wolverhampton.

Ellen Fowler's first publication, *Songs and Sonnets* (1888), was followed by *Verses, Grave and Gay* (1891), and *Verses, Wise or Otherwise* (1895). In 1898 she won public commendation with her novel *Concerning Isabel Carnaby*. This was autobiographical in origin, as it dealt with 'the contrast between Methodist domesticity and high London society' (Sutherland, 231). The novel was noticed by William Robertson Nicoll, who encouraged her to devote herself to novel writing. Her best-known books followed one another in quick succession: *A Double Thread* (1899), *The Farringdons* (1900), *Fuel of Fire* (1902), *Place and Power* (1903), and *Kate of Kate Hall* (1904), the last-named a romance written in collaboration with her husband.

Ellen Fowler was seen as a brilliant and witty conversationalist. As a novelist she was regarded as a faithful chronicler of simple society; her novels are best remembered for their lively dialogue. Her place in English fiction might have been higher had the construction of her novels been more vigorous, and their range less narrow. Although one review commented that she neglected to

Ellen Thorneycroft Fowler (1860–1929), by Bassano

address important contemporary issues such as women's suffrage in her books ('the outlook of today, though hinted at, does not intrude'; *TLS*, 15 March 1923, 178), she earned something of a feminist reputation from two of her later novels. *Miss Fallowfield's Fortune* (1908) deals with the lot of single women, and *Her Ladyship's Conscience* (1913) with an unconventional relationship between an older man and younger woman. Her last novel was *Signs and Wonders* (1926). She was a member of the Writers' Club and the Women's Athenaeum Club, and a fellow of the Royal Society of Literature.

After her marriage Ellen Fowler lived at Eltham, Kent, until 1916, when she moved to Bournemouth. During her later years failing health curtailed her writing. She died on 22 June 1929 at her home, Mershire Lodge, Marlborough Road, Bournemouth, survived only by her husband, as their marriage had been childless.

Ellen Fowler's sister **Edith Henrietta Hamilton** [*née* Fowler] (1865–1944), novelist, was born at Summerfield, Racecourse, Chapel Ash, Wolverhampton, on 16 February 1865. On 23 June 1903 she married William Robert Hamilton (1869–1954), a Church of England clergyman, at All Saints' Church, Knightsbridge, London. They had two sons: Gavin Robert Fowler Hamilton (*b.* 1905) and Henry Fowler New Hamilton (*b.* 1908). Edith's first publications were sharply amusing children's books, including *The Young Pretenders* (1895), illustrated by Philip Burne-Jones, and *The Professor's Children* (1897). Less well known than her sister, her adult novels also deal with the romantic problems of high-minded and politically active Christian members of the upper class. Her works in this vein include *For Richer for Poorer* (1905) and *Patricia* (1915). 'As in her sister's novels, the combination of snobbishness and spirituality is achieved with considerable polish' (Kemp and others, 138). She also wrote a biography of her father (1912). Edith Henrietta Hamilton died on 18 November 1944 and was survived by her husband.

M. CLARE LOUGHLIN-CHOW

Sources Blain, Clements & Grundy, *Feminist comp.* · J. Sutherland, *The Longman companion to Victorian fiction* (1988) · A. Perry, *The Fowler legacy* (1997) · S. Kemp, C. Mitchell, and D. Trotter, *Edwardian fiction: an Oxford companion* (1997) · *The Times* (24 June 1929) · [W. B. Thomas], review of *Fuel of fire*, *TLS* (3 Oct 1902), 292 · [H. H. Child], review of *Place and power*, *TLS* (4 Sept 1903), 254–5 · [H. H. Child], review of *Kate of Kate Hall*, *TLS* (7 Oct 1904), 304 · [W. J. C. Lancaster], 'In subjection', *TLS* (11 May 1906), 170 [review] · [H. H. Child], review of *Miss Fallowfield's fortune*, *TLS* (15 Oct 1908), 347 · [E. E. Mavrogordato], 'Her ladyship's conscience', *TLS* (6 Nov 1913), 515 [review] · [E. E. Mavrogordato], 'Ten degrees backward', *TLS* (7 Oct 1915), 346 [review] · [E. E. Mavrogordato], 'New novels', *TLS* (13 May 1920), 301 [incl. review of *Beauty and bands*] · [O. Williams], review of *The lower pool*, *TLS* (15 March 1923), 178 · *TLS* (11 March 1926), 180 [review] · private information (1937) · *CGPLA Eng. & Wales* (1929) · *DNB* · *WWW* · m. cert. [Edith Hamilton] · d. cert. [Edith Hamilton]
Likenesses Bassano, photograph, NPG [*see illus.*]
Wealth at death £32,985 7s.: probate, 2 Sept 1929, *CGPLA Eng. & Wales* · £2421 3s. 10d.—Edith Henrietta Hamilton: probate, 1945, *CGPLA Eng. & Wales*

Fowler, George Herbert (1861–1940), zoologist and historian, was born in Lincoln on 4 September 1861, the only child of the Revd John Fowler (1823/4–1902), headmaster of Lincoln grammar school, and his wife, Martha Bodley, daughter of William Hulme Bodley, a Brighton medical practitioner, and sister of the architect George Frederick *Bodley (1827–1907). Fowler was educated at Marlborough College, where his father had taught, and then at Eton College, as a king's scholar. In 1880 he entered Keble College, Oxford. The lectures of H. N. Moseley inspired him to turn to zoology in his final year and he obtained his BA with second-class honours in natural science in 1884. From 1884 to 1887 he held a Berkeley fellowship at the University of Manchester. For part of this time he studied under Rudolf Leuckart at Leipzig, obtaining a PhD for research on coral. On 20 August 1885 Fowler married Ursula Mary Dewes (1867–1912), but the marriage was not a success and the couple separated on 8 September 1892.

Between 1887 and 1889 Fowler acted as assistant to E. Ray Lankester at University College, London. He also taught zoology at Royal Holloway College in 1888 and 1891. The summers of 1889 and 1890 were spent in research at the recently founded Plymouth laboratory of the Marine Biological Association of the United Kingdom, and in 1890 he acted as interim director for six months at a difficult period in the institution's history (following the resignation of G. C. Bourne). He acted as the association's secretary until 1895.

In January 1891 Fowler returned to University College as an assistant, and later assistant professor of zoology, under W. F. R. Weldon who spoke highly of his energy and capability, but the routine work of the department left Fowler little time for independent research. A problem then attracting much attention in marine zoology was Alexander Agassiz's theory that plankton occurred only in the surface and deepest waters of the ocean, and not in the intermediate layers. Fowler designed a self-closing plankton net and in 1896 and 1897, and again in 1900, made cruises in HM survey ship *Research* to try it out. The results led him to propose some interesting ideas on plankton distribution but he was unable to obtain the sea time needed to develop them further.

As a zoologist Fowler was seen as competent rather than brilliant, and when Weldon left for Oxford in 1899 Fowler was passed over in favour of E. A. Minchin. These factors, and the onset of eye strain, contributed to his decision to resign from his University College post in 1909. Fowler's enduring legacy to marine science was the Challenger Society, founded with R. Norris Wolfenden in 1903, which he ran as secretary until 1910, also editing the society's influential publication *Science of the Sea* (1912). He continued to be a force in the society, not always for the good, as he campaigned against the admission of women as members.

After his retirement Fowler lived at the Old House at Aspley Guise in Bedfordshire. Its restoration led him to the study of local history which became the dominant passion of the second half of his life. In 1912 he founded the Bedfordshire Historical Record Society to publish sources (mainly medieval) for the county's history. He served as chairman of the county records committee (1913–40) and was instrumental in the setting up of the British Records Association in 1932. This work was interrupted by the outbreak of the First World War, for the duration of which he worked as a voluntary assistant in the hydrographic and naval intelligence departments of the Admiralty. His main task was preparing charts for use by submarines, covering such topics as currents and tidal streams, bathymetry, seasonal variations in density (which affected the operation of sonar), ice movements, North Sea wrecks, and coastal defences. He published *Charts: their Use and Meaning* in 1916. When the war ended he recommended that the hydrographic department should undertake oceanographic research because of its naval applications. Though his ideas were not fully adopted, some marine research was undertaken by the navy during the inter-war period as a result of this initiative.

Fowler declined the offer of a knighthood for his wartime services, but was made a CBE in 1918. After recovering from a breakdown due to overwork he returned to historical research. His output was prolific: the *Bedfordshire Bibliography* by L. R. Conisbee (1962) has no fewer than thirty-three references to editions of medieval sources and historical articles on related themes. These included a magnificent analysis and synthesis, begun during the war, of the Domesday Book for Bedfordshire (1922) and a fourteenth-century *Sheriff's Roll* (1929). Fowler was also concerned with the wider aspects of the subject and wrote *The Care of County Muniments* (1923), 'for long the only textbook in the field' (Bell, 160). As chairman of the county records committee he was responsible for setting up the Bedfordshire Record Office which became a model for local record offices elsewhere. He stood for the county council, becoming an alderman, and also helped develop the county library service.

Fowler was a man of enormous energy and diverse interests. He was a winter sports enthusiast and made regular visits to the Alps. He published a book on the history of skating, *On the Outside Edge* (1897), and *Notes on the Early History of Ski* (1909). He enjoyed working with his hands. When advised to rest from intellectual work after the war he took up silversmithing and he listed his recreations in *Who's Who* as gardening and the repair of manuscripts. In his later years he still regularly spent two days a week at the Bedfordshire Record Office. He died at the Old House, Aspley Guise, on 15 August 1940 and was cremated. He left the residue of his estate to fund studies in Old Icelandic at Oxford University.   MARGARET DEACON

Sources P. J. Bell, *Bedfordshire Magazine*, 14 (1973–5), 158–62 · M. B. Deacon, 'G. Herbert Fowler (1861–1940): the forgotten oceanographer', *Notes and Records of the Royal Society*, 38 (1983–4), 261–96 · F. J. Manning, 'In memoriam: George Herbert Fowler', *The cartulary of Bushmead Priory*, ed. G. H. Fowler and J. Godber, Bedfordshire Historical RS, 22 (1945), vi–vii · report of the Records Committee (Bedfordshire County RO), 1967, 1–6 · M. Deacon, 'British oceanographers and the Challenger Society, 1903 to 1922', *Ocean sciences, their history and relation to man: Fourth International Congress on the History of Oceanography* [Hamburg 1987], ed. W. Lenz and M. Deacon (1990), 34–40 · Bedfordshire County RO, Fowler MSS · Southampton Oceanography Centre, Archives of the Challenger Society · PRO, Admiralty MSS · Crockford (1900) [John Fowler] · Som. ARS, Hydrographic Department archive · *The Times* (17 Aug 1940) · *The Times* (22 Aug 1940) · application for professorship, UCL, Bedfordshire County RO, Fowler MSS, M13/54 · Foster, *Alum. Oxon.* · L. R. Conisbee, *A Bedfordshire bibliography* (1962), 254 · Venn, *Alum. Cant.* [John Fowler] · 'Bodley, George Frederick', *DNB* · private information (2004) [P. Bell] [D. M. Damkaer]

Archives Beds. & Luton ARS, antiquarian and genealogical notes and collections · LUL, notes and MSS collection | NHM, corresp. with Albert Gunther relating to *Encyclopaedia Britannica* · Southampton Oceanography Centre, Challenger Society archives

Likenesses two group portraits, photographs, 1896–1900, Southampton Oceanography Centre; repro. in Deacon, 'G. Herbert Fowler' · photograph, repro. in *Zur Erinnerung an die Feier des 70. Geburtstages Rudolf Leuckarts am 7. Oktober 1892* (1892) · photograph, repro. in Bell, 'Dr G. Herbert Fowler', 158

Wealth at death £28,152 4s. 8d.: resworn probate, 13 Nov 1940, CGPLA Eng. & Wales

Fowler, Henry (1779–1838), hymn writer, was born at Yealmpton, Devon, on 11 December 1779, and was apprenticed before he was twelve to a 'Mr E of Dartmouth'. He remained reticent in his autobiography about his early life, but recalled the 'carnal vigour' and 'increasing folly' (in which he included country dancing) of his youth, until he was converted by the zeal of a poor shoemaker. He began to preach occasionally in Independent meeting-houses in Devon and Bristol. In August 1813 he 'received a call' to Birmingham, where he stayed until the end of 1819. Ultimately he settled in London, becoming in July 1820 minister of Gower Street Chapel. As 'a close, searching preacher', Fowler had for some years an excellent congregation, and a fair-sized one to the close of his life. His frame of mind seemed, in general, rather gloomy; certainly his autobiography, *Travels in the Wilderness* (1839), is not cheerful reading. In addition to numerous religious tracts and biographies, he published a collection of hymns, a second edition of which appeared in 1836. Fowler died on 16 December 1838, and was buried on Christmas day at Islington.

    GORDON GOODWIN, *rev.* SARAH BROLLY

Sources H. Fowler, *Travels in the wilderness* (1839)

Likenesses R. Cooper, engraving

Fowler, Sir Henry (1870–1938), mechanical engineer and metallurgist, was born in Port Street, Bengeworth, Evesham, Worcestershire, on 29 July 1870, the eldest son of Henry Fowler, cabinet-maker, upholsterer, and house agent, and his wife, Mary Hughes. He was educated at Evesham grammar school and, from 1885 to 1887, at Mason Science College, Birmingham, where he gained the junior engineering diploma. From then until 1891 he was apprenticed under John Aspinall, chief mechanical engineer of the Lancashire and Yorkshire Railway at its Horwich works near Bolton.

In 1891 Fowler gained the first Whitworth exhibition awarded to a member of the Horwich Mechanics' Institute. He then became assistant to George Hughes, chief of the testing department, whom he later succeeded. This enabled him to pursue his appreciation and devotion to metallurgy, which had been first inspired by his mechanical engineering studies at Mason College. In 1895 he married Emma Needham Smith (1870–1934), daughter of Philip Smith. They had two sons and one daughter.

In the same year as his marriage Fowler became a gas engineer and in 1900 transferred to a similar post on the Midland Railway at Derby, where he became assistant works manager in 1905, works manager in 1907, and chief mechanical engineer in 1909. He made a major contribution to production methods in the railway's workshops and to the use of improved metallurgy, in locomotive and rolling-stock construction, as well as being an advocate of the use of super-heated steam and compound expansion to increase locomotive power and efficiency.

Shortly after the outbreak of the First World War in 1914, Fowler became secretary to the railway munitions committee and the following year was appointed director of production at the Ministry of Munitions. He became superintendent of the Royal Aircraft Factory at Farnborough in 1916 and also assistant director of aircraft production in 1917. In 1918–19 he was chairman of the inter-allied conference on standardization of aircraft components and deputy member of the Munitions Council. For his wartime work he was appointed CBE in 1917 and KBE in 1918.

Three years after Fowler's return to railway work he became deputy chief mechanical engineer of the newly formed London, Midland, and Scottish Railway (LMS) in 1923 and two years later succeeded George Hughes as chief mechanical engineer. The task of integrating the locomotive, carriage, and wagon design, and the building and repair activities of six important former companies with their own individual practices was extremely difficult. Fowler inaugurated the introduction of line production in locomotive repairs, greatly reducing time spent in workshops, and a firm standardization programme to reduce, as rapidly as possible, the 393 individual locomotive types inherited by the LMS. By 1926 new, and much more powerful, express passenger and freight locomotive designs had been prepared to his directions and, while these were nullified by opposition within a divided management structure, in 1927 the Royal Scot express locomotives were introduced for principal main-line services. In 1931 Fowler was appointed scientific and research adviser to Sir Harold Hartley, vice-president of the LMS and director of research.

Fowler was a man of great energy and enthusiasm and pursued his wide interests in many fields of engineering with great vigour. He took a keen and sympathetic interest in the education of young engineers and was a member of the governing body of the Midland Institute at Derby. He was awarded an honorary LLD by Birmingham University and an honorary DSc by Manchester. He was president of the Institution of Locomotive Engineers in 1912, the Institution of Automobile Engineers in 1921, section G of the British Association in 1923, the Institution of Mechanical Engineers in 1926–7, and the Institute of Metals in 1932–3. From 1925 he was also a member of the permanent commission of the International Railway Congress Association, in which he played a very active part, and a member of council of the Institution of Civil Engineers from 1928 to 1934.

Sir Henry Fowler died at his home, Spondon Hall, Spondon, Derbyshire, on 16 October 1938, and was buried at Nottingham Road cemetery, Derby.

GEORGE W. CARPENTER, rev.

Sources *Journal of the Institution of Locomotive Engineers*, 28 (1938), 606–8 · *Institution of Mechanical Engineers: Proceedings*, 140 (1938), 600–01 · E. S. Cox, *Locomotive panorama*, 1 (1965) · H. A. V. Bulleid, *Master builders of steam* (1963) · *The Times* (18 Oct 1938) · b. cert. · d. cert. · *CGPLA Eng. & Wales* (1938) · J. Chacksfield, *Sir Henry Fowler: a versatile life* (2000)
Likenesses photograph, repro. in *The Times*
Wealth at death £18,198 11s. 8d.: probate, 30 Dec 1938, *CGPLA Eng. & Wales*

Fowler, Henry Hartley, first Viscount Wolverhampton (1830–1911), politician, was born on 16 May 1830 in Sunderland, the only son of the prominent Wesleyan minister Joseph Fowler (1791–1851) and his third wife, Elizabeth Macneil Laing, daughter of Alexander Laing of Glasgow and stepdaughter of John Hartley of Sunderland. Henry was sent as a boarder to Woodhouse Grove, a school for the sons of Wesleyan ministers at Rawdon, near Leeds. Some years later his father was scheduled to move to Birmingham and planned to send him to King Edward's School, from which the boy dreamed of winning a scholarship to Oxford and then going on to the bar, but the Wesleyan conference unexpectedly assigned London instead. Fowler completed his education at St Saviour's School, Southwark, which had no scholarships to offer, and had to

Henry Hartley Fowler, first Viscount Wolverhampton (1830–1911), by Harry Furniss, before 1891

forgo his hopes of attending a university. His father's death in March 1851 underlined the limitations on his prospects and he was forced to settle for the lower branch of the law, being admitted as a solicitor in 1852.

From childhood Fowler had visited his uncle, John Hartley, in Wolverhampton and in 1855 the young solicitor moved to that town. Perhaps an additional attraction was Ellen (1830–1911)—his uncle's sister-in-law and the daughter of George Benjamin Thorneycroft, a prosperous ironmaster—whose acquaintance he had made on his visits. Although Ellen's family considered Fowler's social position beneath her, the couple determined to marry and eventually did so on 6 October 1857 at St Mark's Church, Chapel Ash, Wolverhampton. In that year Fowler went into partnership with his brother-in-law, Charles Corser, and the married couple moved into Summerfield, Racecourse, Chapel Ash, a house on the Thorneycroft grounds. Their two daughters, the novelist Ellen Thorneycroft *Fowler (1860–1929) and Edith Henrietta *Hamilton (1865–1944) [see under Fowler, Ellen Thorneycroft], were born there. Fowler had a home of their own built in 1867. Woodthorne, Wergs Road, Tettenhall, Wolverhampton, was the couple's main residence for the rest of their lives and it was here that their last child, Henry Ernest (1870–1943), was born.

Soon after his marriage Fowler began to give his attention to local politics. He was elected a town councillor of St Matthew's ward in 1858 and in 1860 he became an alderman. In late 1862, after only seven years' residence in the town, he became the youngest mayor in England. He was elected to the Wolverhampton school board in 1870 and became its first chairman, but in the 1873 contest he suffered the only election defeat of his life, apparently through the complacency of his supporters. During these years of local service he laboured to improve the town's sewerage facilities and water supply and assisted with the arrangements to build a new town hall.

Always a supporter of the Liberal Party, Fowler was adopted as a parliamentary candidate alongside C. P. Villiers for Wolverhampton at the 1880 election and was successful. In November 1884 Gladstone offered to appoint him civil lord of the Admiralty, but he declined—officially because he had insufficient knowledge of naval affairs, but probably in the hopes of securing a better place. Whatever the motive, the effect was advantageous: within a month he had been offered and accepted the under-secretaryship of the Home department.

When Wolverhampton was divided into three constituencies, Fowler chose to stand for the east division. He was faithfully returned by its electors in the 1885 election and thereafter, relinquishing this seat only when he was elevated to the peerage. In the brief Liberal government of 1886 he served as financial secretary to the Treasury and throughout his career he was considered proficient on financial issues. He employed his noted speaking skills on behalf of the first Irish Home Rule Bill. Gladstone rewarded his loyalty and service by arranging for him to become a privy councillor (20 June 1886). A consistent feature of his public life was his willingness to accept a political compromise—critics sometimes said he was a trimmer—and, although he sided with the home-rulers, he hoped for a way to paper over the cracks in the Liberal Party.

During the years of Conservative government which followed, among other parliamentary ventures, Fowler was the guiding force behind the Wolverhampton Corporation Act of 1891. One of the benefits secured by this measure was the corporation's right to present the freedom of the borough and on 15 February 1892 Fowler became the first recipient of this honour.

When the Liberals won the 1892 election, there was some speculation that Fowler might become chancellor of the exchequer or home secretary, so he took his place as president of the Local Government Board a disappointed man. Nevertheless, he was responsible for one of the few legislative successes of this government, the Local Government Act of 1894, a measure which extended democratic local government to rural householders (both male and female). The Parish Councils Bill (as it was commonly called) was controversial because of the perception that it was an attack on the position of the country squire and parson. It occupied 57 sittings of parliament during which 619 amendments were moved. Fowler spoke 803 times, never once moving the closure, and his patience, mastery of the ways of parliament, and willingness to compromise helped to secure its passage.

Gladstone made his last parliamentary speech during a debate on the Local Government Bill and in the cabinet reshuffle which followed his retirement in March 1894 Fowler was promoted to secretary of state for India. He supported Curzon's viceroyalty and resolutely opposed Congress demands for constitutional reform. He approved the Indian government's imposition of a duty on cotton despite influential voices in Lancashire claiming that this would be a significant blow to their own cotton industry. In February 1895 Sir Henry James led an attack on this policy in the Commons. Rosebery's government was already in a vulnerable position and some people anticipated that there would be a small rebellion on this issue which would bring it down. In this context, Fowler delivered his greatest speech, its peroration containing the arresting assertion, 'Every Member of this House, whether elected by an English, or by a Scotch, or by an Irish constituency, is a Member for India' (*Hansard 4*, 30.1321). James's motion was rejected by a large majority and, as an instance of a speech altering the outcome of a parliamentary vote, Fowler's feat has been often cited but seldom repeated.

In June 1895 Fowler was weakened by an attack of influenza and in order to facilitate his full recovery the queen, who held him in esteem, called him to Balmoral to be her minister in attendance. Before the month was over his health had been restored, but the government in which he served had suffered a terminal blow. On the same day that he gave up the seals of office, in recognition of his widely respected service in the India Office, the queen created him a knight grand commander in the Order of the Star of India and his wife a lady of the Imperial Order of the Crown of India.

The long years of opposition set in. Although as India secretary Fowler had authorized a successful military operation in the remote region of Chitral he opposed the plans of his tory successor to place this commitment on a more permanent footing and gave an influential speech on this subject in November 1897. He served as chairman of the committee on Indian currency (1898–9), which made the economically orthodox but unimaginative recommendation that a gold currency should be established. Fowler also employed his talents more widely in the private sector. In 1897 he became a director of the National Telephone Company, rising to its presidency in November 1901 and resigning only to re-enter the cabinet in 1906.

When the Liberal Party needed to find a new leader in late 1898, Fowler was seen as a well-qualified contestant but an undesirable winner. *The Times* of 17 January 1899 observed, 'We do not know why the party appear to have agreed to set aside the claims of SIR HENRY FOWLER, but the fact is plain enough.' His over-cautious nature, uninspiring moderation, and grim demeanour were probably some of the factors which made some Liberals quietly consider him ill-suited to be their chief, however much they might concede that he was a valuable lieutenant. He defended Britain's involvement in the Second South African War, and was unopposed when re-elected for his Wolverhampton seat in the 'khaki' election of September 1900. Echoing the rhetorical tactic of his celebrated cotton duties speech, he argued in one oration that the colonies of Natal and the Cape were just as much British territory as the counties of Cornwall and Kent. In February 1902, along with H. H. Asquith and Sir Edward Grey, he became one of the founding vice-presidents of Rosebery's Liberal League. Later that year he also announced his desire, shared with other Liberal Imperialists, to see the party abandon its commitment to introducing a home rule bill.

Fowler was doomed to spend what might have been his most productive years in opposition. When the Liberals finally formed a government again in late 1905 he was in his mid-seventies. Judging that he no longer had the energy for a more demanding position, he opted to take his place in Campbell-Bannerman's cabinet as the chancellor of the duchy of Lancaster. When Asquith became prime minister in 1908 he let it be known that he wished to slow down still further. The king announced that Fowler would be created a viscount. He chose to be called Lord Wolverhampton, an honour which was conferred upon him on 4 May 1908. During that summer he helped to navigate the Old Age Pensions Bill through the Lords. In October he became lord president of the privy council. A year later, on 20 October 1909, he was awarded an honorary LLD by the University of Birmingham. The government proved to have more stamina than its frail lord president. Lord Wolverhampton mustered all his strength in order to participate in the opening of parliament on 21 February 1910, but he was unable to perform his duties thereafter and finally resigned in June.

Throughout his years in the Commons, Fowler had continued to be a partner in his Wolverhampton law firm, which came to be called Fowler, Langley, and Wright and in the late twentieth century continued to exist under that name. In 1876 he also began a London partnership with another noted Methodist, Robert Perks. He served as president of the Incorporated Law Society in 1901. His branch of the profession was delighted when he, a mere solicitor, took charge as lord president of an investigation by the judicial committee of the privy council, a body which included both the current and a former lord chancellor.

Observers often commented on Fowler's stern facial expression and manner. G. W. E. Russell reported of his club life, 'Temperate to a fault, he drank one glass of sherry in a bottle of soda-water, and looked none the more cheerful for it' (Fowler, 666). He was fond of the saying 'life is earnest' and even managed to include it in the letter to Ellen in which he celebrated their recent engagement. Nevertheless, despite his will dominating their home, he won the genuine affection of his family. Although open to compromise in matters of policy, he was loyal in his associations, remaining faithful throughout his life to the political party, provincial town, and religious denomination which had served him well as a young man. An active Wesleyan, he was instrumental in the building of Trinity Church, Wolverhampton, and served as chapel steward there for many years. Nevertheless, his was the kind of Methodism that wished to stay close to the mother church: he occasionally received communion in the Church of England and was married and buried and had his children baptized and confirmed within her fold. Fowler was the first solicitor and the first Methodist to enter the cabinet or to be created a peer.

When his wife died on 6 January 1911 Lord Wolverhampton was already too ill to attend the funeral. He died of cerebral thrombosis at his home in Wolverhampton on 25 February 1911. His remains were buried at Tettenhall churchyard on 1 March 1911. TIMOTHY LARSEN

Sources E. H. Fowler, *The life of Henry Hartley Fowler, first Viscount Wolverhampton* (1912) • A. Perry, *The Fowler legacy: the story of a forgotten family* (1997) • *Wolverhampton Chronicle* (1 March 1911) • *The Times* (27 Feb 1911) • 'The change of ministry', *The Times* (15 Aug 1892) • *The Times* (17 Jan 1899) [on liberal leadership contest] • 'Sir H. Fowler on the war', *The Times* (30 Nov 1899) • 'Funeral of Viscount Wolverhampton', *The Times* (2 March 1911) • 'The freedom of Wolverhampton conferred on Mr H. H. Fowler', *Wolverhampton Chronicle* (13 Jan 1892) • *Wolverhampton Chronicle* (11 Jan 1911) [obit. of Lady Wolverhampton] • 'Mr Fowler and the Parish Councils Act', *Review of Reviews*, 10 (1894), 228–40 • *Hansard 4* (1895), 30.1285–1361, esp. 1301–21 • H. C. G. Matthew, *The liberal imperialists: the ideas and politics of a post-Gladstonian élite* (1973) • 'The late Viscount Wolverhampton', *Methodist Times* (2 March 1911)

Archives BL OIOC, corresp. and papers relating to India, MSS Eur. C 145, fol. 102, D 592 | BL, letters to Henry Campbell-Bannerman, Add. MS 41216 • BL, corresp. with W. E. Gladstone, Add. MSS 44475–44479, *passim* • BL OIOC, letters to Arthur Godley, MS Eur. F 102 • BL OIOC, corresp. with Lord Wenlock, MS Eur. D 592 • Bodl. Oxf., corresp. with Herbert Asquith • Bodl. Oxf., corresp. with Lord Kimberley • CAC Cam., letters to W. T. Stead • Cardiff Central Library, letters to Sir Hugh Owen • LPL, corresp. with Edward Benson • NL Scot., corresp., incl. with Lord Rosebery • U. Birm. L., corresp. with Joseph Chamberlain

Likenesses H. Furniss, pen-and-ink caricature, before 1891, NPG [*see illus.*] • A. S. Cope, portrait, oils, 1893, Wolverhampton town hall • A. S. Cope, portrait, exh. 1896, Law Society, London • London Stereoscopic Co., two photographs, *c.*1902, NPG • Spy [L. Ward], group portrait, chromolithograph caricature, NPG; repro. in *VF* (3 Dec 1892) • B. Stone, photograph, NPG • Whitlock & Son, photograph, repro. in Fowler, *Life of Henry Hartley Fowler* • Whitlock & Son, photograph, repro. in *Wolverhampton Chronicle* (22 June 1910) • photogravure, NPG

Wealth at death £93,967 14*s.*: resworn probate, 21 March 1911, *CGPLA Eng. & Wales*

Fowler, Henry Watson (1858–1933), lexicographer and grammarian, was born on 10 March 1858 at Tonbridge, Kent, the eldest child of the seven sons and one daughter of the Revd Robert Fowler (1820–1879) and his wife, Caroline, *née* Watson. Robert Fowler (the son of a master carpenter at Buckfastleigh, Devon) read mathematics at Christ's College, Cambridge, before becoming a fellow of the same college in 1854. He vacated his fellowship when he married in December 1856 and became an assistant master at Tonbridge School. Thereafter he owned a private school in nearby Tunbridge Wells. After his father died in 1879, Henry Fowler was to bear the main responsibility for the family. This, then, was the background of a man who in somewhat spartan circumstances in London, Guernsey, and Somerset produced the first edition of the *Concise Oxford Dictionary of Current English*, one of Britain's standard desk dictionaries, as well as a world-famous guide to modern English usage, and numerous other works of lesser interest, some of them in association with one of his brothers, Francis George Fowler.

Henry Fowler was educated at Rugby School, and was admitted to Balliol College, Oxford, as a scholar in 1877. His contemporaries at Balliol included several who later

Henry Watson Fowler (1858–1933), by unknown photographer

became distinguished scholars, men of letters, and politicians—including R. L. Poole, T. F. Tout, Arnold Toynbee, J. W. Mackail, and Lord Curzon—but apparently at that stage Fowler was best known for 'his reserve and his refinement'. The class of his degree, a second in moderations (1878) and also in *literae humaniores*, the study of Greek and Roman classical literature, philosophy, and history (1881), disappointed his friends, and doubtless left its mark on Fowler himself. Dr Jowett, the famous master of Balliol, gave him a routinely worded testimonial: 'Mr H. W. Fowler … is quite a gentleman in manner and feeling … He is a very fair scholar and has, I think, a natural aptitude for the profession of Schoolmaster' (Coulton, 101).

After leaving Oxford, Fowler taught briefly at Fettes College in Scotland, before moving to Sedbergh School in north-west Yorkshire in 1882. He remained at Sedbergh as a teacher of classics and of English literature until 1899. One of his pupils, Alexander Lawrence, later recalled that he found Fowler 'a cold mechanical machine'. He qualified this remark by adding 'I for one respected him immensely, but in those days I should have said he lacked humanity' (Coulton, 104–5). His diligence was exceptional. In term time the day began with a swim in the Strait Bridge pool. This was followed by an average ten-hour working day, teaching and reading, Sundays included. In the holidays he often went to Norway or Switzerland, walking, climbing, and skating.

Fowler left Sedbergh on a point of principle, after learning from the headmaster that if he was invited to become a housemaster he would be required to train the boys for confirmation in the Church of England. This he refused to do. He moved south to London, found modest lodgings at 14 Paulton's Square, Chelsea, and set up as a freelance writer and journalist. He lived on the £120 a year that he had inherited from his father and an average £30 a year earned from his writing. His daily routine included a morning bathe in the Serpentine, together with a jogging run 'at nine or ten miles an hour' to and from the Serpentine. His freelance writing was for the most part undistinguished. Many of his journalistic articles were later collected into volumes and published under various pseudonyms, among them *More Popular Fallacies* (1904) by Quillet, and *Si mihi —!* (1907) by Egomet (republished under his own name in 1929 as *If Wishes were Horses*).

Fowler moved to Guernsey in 1903 to join his brother Francis George Fowler, and there, in hermit-like circumstances (two adjacent granite cottages) in the parish of St Peter-in-the-Wood, the brothers embarked on a series of scholarly books. First they translated the works of the Greek writer Lucian of Samosata: this project was published in four volumes in 1905 as part of the Oxford Library of Translations. Lucian's work falls into three main categories: rhetorical essays and speeches, sophistic and philosophical problems, and satirical sketches. The Fowlers' translations, especially of the satirical sketches, barely stand the test of time. The English prose has a noticeably old-fashioned edge, and, in keeping with the spirit of the age, all passages of doubtful decency have been removed. The crucial factor, however, was that the volumes brought the brothers into contact with the scholarly engine of the Clarendon Press.

The Fowlers next turned to preparing a work for which they suggested the title 'The new solecist for literary tiros', a volume dealing with stylistic and grammatical misuse of the English language. In the ensuing extensive correspondence with the Clarendon Press several other titles were suggested, but in the end the book was called *The King's English* (1906). The nation took it to its heart and, with minor alterations, it remained a standard authority throughout the twentieth century.

In 1908, on his fiftieth birthday, Fowler married Jessie Marian Wills (1862–1930), the superintendent of a nursing home in Guernsey, and the devoted pair remained together until Jessie's death.

After completing *The King's English* the Fowler brothers turned to the compilation of a 'short dictionary', to be derived from the published sections (A–Sc) of the *Oxford English Dictionary* and, for the later letters, from other large dictionaries, such as the *Century Dictionary* (1889–91). They emphasized in their preface that the process of compiling a desk dictionary entailed more than simple reduction. Also, in order to survive in competition with the dictionaries of similar size issued by other publishers—Chambers, Collins, Macmillans, Cassells, and so on—it needed to record new words of the Edwardian period, such as aeroplane, carburettor, motorist, radioactive, rag-time, and

Zionism. *The Concise Oxford Dictionary of Current English* (*COD*) was published in 1911. The nine new editions published in the twentieth century testify to its popularity.

After a brief adventure in the armed forces in France in 1915 to 1916 (performing, they complained, only such menial or unmilitary duties as dishwashing, coal-heaving, and porterage), the Fowlers returned to England and were invalided out of the army. Francis died from tuberculosis in 1918 and Henry Fowler carried on alone, first in Guernsey and from 1925 in the village of Hinton St George in Somerset. First he completed a small dictionary derived from the *COD*, though he had found the larger dictionary 'not to be easily squeezable' (preface to *The Pocket Oxford Dictionary*, 1924). He adopted some unorthodox techniques for *The Pocket Oxford Dictionary* (*POD*): for example, the entry for ox, after its definition ('Kinds of large usually horned cloven-footed ruminant quadruped used for draught, for supplying milk, & as meat'), continues 'sex &c.: *bull, cow, bullock, calf, steer, heifer, calve, stall, byre, pasture, graze, browse, chew the cud, bellow, low, moo, charge, gore, butt, toss, moo-cow, bovine.*' Numerous other similar lists are provided, for example under 'accelerando' (other musical directions) and 'officer' (lists in descending order of seniority of ranks in the armed forces). The first edition of the *POD* was published in 1924. The eccentric lists were abandoned in later editions.

Fowler then revived the notion of what the brothers since at least 1909 had thought of as 'The idiom dictionary'. The aim was to rearrange the twists and turnings of misconstrued syntax and faulty English usage, and place them in alphabetical order in the manner of a dictionary. *A Dictionary of Modern English Usage*, one of the most celebrated reference works of the twentieth century, was published in 1926. It quickly established itself as an authoritative guide to the language, though specialists saw Fowler's work as that of a gifted amateur scholar. He remained essentially unaware of the great linguistic controversies that were being presented in monographs and learned journals throughout Europe, the New World, and elsewhere in the works of such scholars as Ferdinand de Saussure, Leonard Bloomfield, Edward Sapir, and Otto Jespersen. Fowler's work lay plainly in the area of prescriptivism, that is, of setting down rules about how features of the language are sanctioned by long usage, the passage of time, and, where appropriate, the classical rules of the languages of ancient Greece and Rome. The new wave of scholarship, conversely, tended to favour a doctrine of descriptivism.

Modern English Usage was aimed at a domestic audience. Fowler disclaimed any knowledge of American English, and by implication the varieties of English spoken and written elsewhere in the world. In a letter written to his publishers in 1911 he drew attention to further limits of his horizon:

> We have our eyes not on the foreigner, but on the half-educated Englishman of literary proclivities who wants to know Can I say so-&-so? … Is this use English? … Not but what we may be of some use to the foreigner who knows English pretty well; but the foreigner as such we must leave out of consideration.

Fowler's declining years were devoted to a plan for a dictionary provisionally called 'The quarto Oxford dictionary'. It was to have been a double dictionary, with a line across each page: above the line would be placed all words requiring literary treatment, and below it all words for which mere definition would suffice. For example, iron, oak, and window would be placed above the line, and grate (noun), okapi, and zinc below it.

By 1932 Fowler's health was failing sharply. In September 1932 his doctor found high blood pressure and albuminuria, and he died at his home, Sunnyside, Hinton St George, on Boxing day 1933. 'The quarto Oxford dictionary', was never finished.   R. W. Burchfield

Sources *The Times* (28 Dec 1933) · *Sedberghian* (March 1934) · G. G. Coulton, *H. W. Fowler* (1935) · H. W. Fowler, correspondence with his wife, 1915–16, St John Cam. · E. A. Gowers, *H. W. Fowler: the man and his teaching* (1957) · R. W. Burchfield, *The Fowlers: their achievements in lexicography and grammar* (1979) · R. W. Burchfield, *The new Fowler's modern English usage*, 3rd edn (1998) · J. McMorris, *The warden of English: the life of H. W. Fowler* (2001) · Oxford University Press, archives · *CGPLA Eng. & Wales* (1934)

Archives Oxford University Press, archives, MSS · St John Cam., corresp. with his wife

Likenesses photographs, Oxford University Press, archives [*see illus.*] · photographs, repro. in Coulton, *H. W. Fowler*

Wealth at death £3270 14s. 9d.: probate, 28 Feb 1934, *CGPLA Eng. & Wales*

Fowler, Sir James Kingston (1852–1934), physician, was born at Woburn, Bedfordshire, on 11 March 1852, the fifth son of James Fowler of Woburn, and his wife, Frances, daughter of Henry Sargeant of Bedford. After leaving school Fowler entered King's College, London, in 1870, intending to proceed to Cambridge to prepare for holy orders, but he suddenly decided to study medicine and therefore joined King's College medical school. He qualified MRCS in 1874 and was house physician to George Johnson and house surgeon to Sir William Fergusson at King's College Hospital. In 1876 he gained his LRCP and went as house physician to Addenbrooke's Hospital in Cambridge, where he also entered Gonville and Caius College as an undergraduate. He became MA in 1879 and MD in 1884.

After returning to London in 1879 Fowler was for a short period on the staff of the Westminster Hospital, but in 1880 he left on being elected assistant physician both to the Brompton Hospital for Diseases of the Chest and to the Middlesex Hospital. As pathologist and curator of the museum at the Middlesex he gained a wide experience of morbid anatomy and applied this with great success to the study of disease in the living. In 1891 he was appointed full physician. In the wards he was a successful teacher, owing to his methodical and accurate observation, and the care he used to indicate the reasoning by which he arrived at his diagnosis. He was joint lecturer in the practice of medicine from 1899 until 1913, when he was made consulting physician and emeritus lecturer.

Fowler edited *A Dictionary of Practical Medicine*, published in 1890. In collaboration with Rickman Godlee he published in 1898 the treatise *The Diseases of the Lungs*. He was thus early to recognize the importance of the close co-operation of physician and surgeon in the treatment of chest diseases. In 1921 he published a monograph entitled *Pulmonary Tuberculosis*, on the disease on which he was a recognized authority. Fowler also wrote articles on emphysema and syphilis of the lungs for C. Allbutt's *System of Medicine*, in 1898 and 1909.

Fowler played a notable part in the reconstitution of London University, in 1900. He was a senior member of the senate and afterwards dean of the faculty of medicine. When Otto Beit founded the Beit memorial fellowships, Fowler was made honorary secretary and one of the trustees of the fund.

Fowler received many professional distinctions and honours. He was a censor of the Royal College of Physicians in 1908 and 1909 and senior censor in 1913. The honorary degree of DSc was conferred upon him by Sheffield University in 1908. In the previous year he was president of the Medical Society of London. In 1910 he was appointed KCVO after his attendance with Alfred Pearce Gould on Prince Francis of Teck in his last illness. He was one of the first members of the colonial advisory medical and sanitary committee (formed in 1909) and chairman of the colonial medical appointments board. In 1913 he was made chairman of the West African yellow fever commission.

During the First World War Fowler served on the staff of the 3rd London Territorial Hospital, but in 1917 he went to the Rouen Base Hospital as consulting physician with the honorary rank of colonel, Army Medical Service. He was mentioned in dispatches, and appointed CMG in 1919; he became KCMG in 1932 on his retirement from his Colonial Office appointments.

Fowler was unmarried. He made numerous friends, mostly from outside the medical profession. Tall, always well dressed and well groomed, he was a distinguished figure in any company. Through his friendship with John, second Lord Montagu of Beaulieu, he was appointed warden of Beaulieu Abbey, and in 1911 he wrote *A History of Beaulieu Abbey*, which is well illustrated and gives details of the life of the Cistercian monks. In 1928 he published a smaller work on Hayles Abbey, Gloucestershire, of which he was custodian. After his retirement he lived in the warden's lodge at Beaulieu, where he died on 3 July 1934.

R. A. YOUNG, rev. MICHAEL BEVAN

Sources *The Times* (4 July 1934) · *BMJ* (14 July 1934), 91–2 · *The Lancet* (14 July 1934), 104 · personal knowledge (1949)
Archives U. Glas., corresp. with E. Hindle on Beit research fellowship in tropical medicine
Likenesses Elliott & Fry, portrait, repro. in *BMJ*, 91
Wealth at death £14,868 19s. 7d.: probate, 4 Oct 1934, *CGPLA Eng. & Wales*

Fowler, Jessie Allen (1856–1932). *See under* Fowler, Lydia Folger (1822–1879).

Fowler, John (1537–1579), printer, was born in Bristol and educated first at Winchester College, and then at New College, Oxford, from 1553. He became a fellow of New College in 1555 and graduated MA in 1557, but he resigned his fellowship at the accession of Elizabeth and went abroad. On 19 April 1564 he and Edward Rastell matriculated at the University of Louvain, where they were joined the following day by John Storey. On 5 May 1565 Fowler was licensed as a printer by the university, and on 29 July 1570 by the Brussels privy council. In his application for the latter licence he deposed that his work was that of an editor–publisher rather than a printer proper, and that he knew Latin, French, Italian, and Spanish as well as English, and some Flemish and Greek. From 1567 to 1573 he worked uninterruptedly as a translator, editor, and publisher in Louvain. It was probably there, and before 1571, that he married Alice (d. 1602), the daughter of fellow Bristolian John Harris, one-time secretary to Sir Thomas More. From 1568 he maintained business relations with Christopher Plantin.

From 1573 Fowler was using Antwerp printers to produce some of his publications, and in 1574 he and his family removed to Antwerp. (It is quite possible, as Southern conjectures, that some of these Antwerp imprints prior to 1576 were in fact printed in Louvain with a false address.) Antwerp briefly became his main place of residence and business. As a consequence of the Dutch revolt, Fowler moved to Douai in 1577, to Rheims in 1578, and finally to Namur, where he died on 13 February 1579. He was buried in the church of St John the Evangelist in Namur.

Fowler was the most important English Catholic publisher of the 1560s and early 1570s, having over fifty works printed in English or Latin. Much of his surviving output consists of the controversial and devotional works of William Allen, Richard Bristow, Nicholas Sander, and Thomas Stapleton, particularly theological works on issues disputed with protestants, such as the sacrifice of the mass, the invocation of saints, the veneration of images, and the nature of authority in the church, and Thomas Harding's famous replies to John Jewel (1566, 1567, 1568). Fowler also printed Stapleton's translation of Bede's *History* (1566, the first English edition), and was editor of Thomas More's *Dialogue of Comfort* (1573), Laurence Vaux's catechism (1574), Thomas à Kempis's *De Christi imitatione* (1575), and the Jesus psalter (1575). His business was continued by his widow until her death.

PAUL ARBLASTER

Sources A. C. Southern, *English recusant prose* (1950), 342–4 · Gillow, *Lit. biog. hist.*, 2.327 · A. Rouzet, M. Colin-Boon, and others, *Dictionnaire des imprimeurs, libraires et éditeurs des XVe et XVIe siècles dans les limites géographiques de la Belgique actuelle* (Nieuwkoop, 1975), 64–5 · *Matricule de l'Université de Louvain*, 4, ed. A. Schillings (1961), 674 · geheime raad Spaanse periode, National State Archives, Brussels, 1276/5 · T. F. Knox and others, eds., *The first and second diaries of the English College, Douay* (1878) · L. Antheunis, 'Engelsche drukkers in de Spaansche Nederlanden: John Fowler (1537–1579)', *Bijdragen tot de Geschiedenis*, 28 (1937), 114–27 · A. F. Allison and D. M. Rogers, eds., *The contemporary printed literature of the English Counter-Reformation between 1558 and 1640*, 2 vols. (1989–94)

Fowler, Sir John, first baronet (1817–1898), civil engineer, was born in Sheffield on 15 July 1817, the eldest of the nine

Sir John Fowler, first baronet (1817–1898), by Sir John Everett Millais, c.1868

children of John Fowler (b. 1784), land surveyor of Wadsley Hall, near Sheffield, and his wife, Elizabeth (1792–1858), née Swann. After attending Whitley Hall School, Fowler became a pupil of John Towlerton Leather, then engineer to Sheffield waterworks. He also worked for George Leather, John Towlerton's uncle, on the Aire and Calder navigation, Goole lock, and railway surveys. In 1837 Fowler began working for John Urpeth Rastrick on various railway schemes, including the London–Brighton line and the surveys for the West Cumberland and Furness Railway. When this scheme failed he accepted Leather's invitation to act as resident engineer on the Stockton and Hartlepool Railway. When the line opened in March 1841 Fowler was appointed engineer to the company.

Fowler established his practice in the Yorkshire–Lincolnshire area. In 1844, with an increasing volume of professional work, he moved to London and set up his offices and home at 2 Queen Square Place, Westminster. Many of his schemes became absorbed in the Manchester, Sheffield, and Lincolnshire Railway, of which he became chief engineer. In addition he was engineer to the East Lincolnshire Railway. As his workload expanded so did his staff and at this time several people joined him with whom he was to be associated for most of his career—William Wilson, who assisted with the design of Sheffield Victoria Station, John Whitton, who was to marry Fowler's eldest sister, and his younger brother Henry Fowler, who acted as resident engineer on the East Lincolnshire Railway. Fowler married Elizabeth Broadbent (d. 1901), of Manchester, on 2 July 1850; they had four sons. They moved from

above the office to live at Thornwood Lodge, Kensington, in 1867.

In March 1852 Fowler was appointed engineer to the Oxford, Worcester, and Wolverhampton Railway. This company had run into severe financial problems, but Fowler completed the line successfully. Further work followed in the west midlands, such as the Severn Valley Railway, and he designed two 200 foot cast-iron arch bridges across the Severn. J. D. Baldry joined Fowler's staff in 1853, and from 1855 acted as his business manager.

Fowler first came to prominence in engineering circles as a result of the refusal of the Board of Trade inspecting engineer to sanction his tubular girder bridge across the Trent at Torksey. The issue was the subject of heated discussion at the Institution of Civil Engineers (*Proceedings of the Institution of Civil Engineers*, 9, 1849–50, 232–87). Fowler's design had the overwhelming support of the engineering community. The bridge was eventually opened to railway traffic in April 1850.

Fowler's fame among the wider public stemmed from his involvement with railways in the London area. With William Wilson he designed the first Grosvenor railway bridge and Victoria Station. He also assisted George Parker Bidder with the London, Tilbury, and Southend Railway. Most important of all was his involvement with London's underground railways. In 1853 he secured parliamentary assent for the North Metropolitan Line between Edgware Road and King's Cross. He then overcame many obstacles to obtain the necessary finance, and the support of other railway companies. Construction of the Metropolitan Line eventually began in 1860, and the Metropolitan District Line, for which Fowler was also the engineer, was begun in 1863. In these lines, and their extensions to Hammersmith and elsewhere, Fowler was ably supported by staff such as T. Marr Johnson, A. G. Linn, W. Morton, and most famously Benjamin Baker. Baker became his partner in 1875. Together they acted as consultants with Greathead on the City and South London and the Central London railways.

Baker had joined Fowler's staff after the completion of the Grosvenor Bridge, at a time when Fowler was designing a bridge across the Thames at Rotherhithe as part of an outer circle of railways around London. This was the first of many long-span bridge proposals in which Fowler became involved over a period of nearly thirty years. Of these only the Forth railway bridge was built, and that is Fowler's other great achievement. Following the failure of the Tay railway bridge, work on Sir Thomas Bouch's proposed Forth Bridge design was suspended by the railway companies involved. They appointed a commission comprising Fowler, William Henry Barlow, and Thomas Elliott Harrison in 1881 to advise on the crossing, which recommended a cantilever bridge, based on the design by Fowler and Baker. This was accepted, and Fowler and Baker were appointed engineers for the bridge, one of the greatest achievements of the Victorian age and one of its most substantial surviving monuments, still in use more than a century later. Following its completion, on 17 April 1890, Fowler was created a baronet.

Fowler had already been knighted in 1885 for his services in Egypt and the Sudan. He first visited Egypt while on holiday in 1869, and was introduced to the khedive, Ishmail Pasha, and subsequently consulted about a number of engineering schemes. Although little was built, these schemes involved the most accurate survey of Upper Egypt and the Sudan then available. In 1884 Fowler lent his maps to the British government to assist in the relief of Khartoum, and was rewarded by being made KCMG.

Fowler had a long association as consultant to New South Wales railways, where John Whitton became the engineer. He also advised on railway schemes in Algeria, Belgium, France, Germany, Portugal, and the United States, and was consultant to an Indian government inquiry in 1870 into railway gauges. He reported on the Tiber floods in the 1870s and his partner Baldry was involved with a Spanish irrigation scheme.

In Britain there was hardly a significant railway company which did not seek his advice. At various times he acted as consultant to the Great Western (in succession to I. K. Brunel), Great Northern, Highland, the Manchester, Sheffield, and Lincolnshire, and Cheshire Lines railways. This involved him in the design of major stations such as St Enoch's, in Glasgow, Liverpool Central, and Manchester Central.

Fowler rapidly rose to the top of the profession, becoming president of the Institution of Civil Engineers in 1865 at the unprecedented age of forty-eight. His presidential address was one of the first to deal seriously with the education and training of engineers. Fowler was well qualified to deal with these themes, his practice being renowned for the quality of training he offered. He helped set up the ICE's inquiry into the engineering education in 1865, and the consequent report of 1870. Under his presidency a membership class for students was created. He was also president of the mechanical sciences section of the British Association in 1882.

Fowler appreciated the value of research, and encouraged innovative design in his practice. He was one of the leading advocates of the use of steel, and was a member of the committee of civil engineers set up in 1868 to investigate its engineering properties. He was also a pioneer in the use of concrete, a material extensively used in the retaining walls of Millwall docks, for which Fowler was the engineer, again in association with William Wilson. He also designed an experimental concrete arch bridge on the District Line near Cromwell Road in 1867–8. He was an early advocate of the use of photography by engineers.

Although Fowler was professionally involved almost until his death, he appreciated the value of relaxation, and from 1857, when he purchased property in Scotland, he frequently took holidays there. His estate at Braemar House, Ross-shire, was well loved by his family and many distinguished friends from all walks of life. He stood unsuccessfully for parliament in 1880 and 1885 as a Conservative. He was devoted to children, and one of the last photographs of him shows him with his eldest grandson. Fowler died at High Cliffe Hotel, Bournemouth, on 20 November 1898. His wife, who survived him, did much to assist his biographer, Thomas Mackay, to complete his work.   MIKE CHRIMES

Sources T. Mackay, *The life of Sir John Fowler* (1900) · M. M. Chrimes, 'Sir John Fowler—engineer or manager', *PICE*, new ser., 97 (1993), 135–43 · *PICE*, 135 (1898–9), 328–37 · *Engineering*, 4 (1867), 556–9 · W. Westhofen, *The Forth Bridge* (1890), 64–9 · W. Humber, ed., *A record of the progress of modern engineering*, 4 (1866) · R. A. Paxton, ed., *100 years of the Forth Bridge* (1990) · Burke, *Peerage*

Archives Inst. CE, letters etc; reports on the Nile · LMA, records of railway companies · NA Scot. · PRO · V&A NAL, corresp. and papers | Bodl. Oxf., corresp. with Sir William Harcourt · CUL, corresp. with Lord Mayo · ICL, department of civil and environmental engineering, engineers' reports on Forth railway bridge · Museum of London, Millwall docks papers

Likenesses portrait, *c*.1860, priv. coll. · J. J. E. Mayall, oils over albumen print, *c*.1865, NPG · J. E. Millais, oils, *c*.1868, Inst. CE [*see illus.*] · D. W. Stevenson, plaster bust, 1889, Scot. NPG · H. C. Fehr, bust, 1899, priv. coll.; formerly at Inst. CE · T. O. Barlow, stipple (after J. E. Millais), NPG · Lock & Whitfield, woodburytype photograph, NPG; repro. in T. Cooper, *Men of mark: a gallery of contemporary portraits* (1882)

Wealth at death £179,329 11*s*. 9*d*.: probate, 22 Feb 1899, *CGPLA Eng. & Wales*

Fowler, John (1826–1864), agricultural engineer, was born on 11 July 1826 at Melksham, Wiltshire, one of at least two sons of John Fowler, merchant. His father was a leading member of the Quakers in Melksham. Fowler was at first engaged in the corn trade, but in 1847 he entered the works of Gilkes, Wilson, Hopkins & Co. at Middlesbrough. While in Ireland in 1849 he became concerned at the cost of manual labour used in draining land, and he conceived the idea of a mechanical system. In 1850 he conducted experiments in partnership with Albert Fry at Bristol, which resulted in the completion of a patent drainage plough. It was exhibited at the Royal Agricultural Society's show at Exeter that year. This first drainage plough was worked by horses, but the implement was improved in succeeding years and adapted for steam power. In 1855 he undertook a contract for the drainage of Hainault Forest, Essex. On 30 July 1857 Fowler married Elizabeth Lucy (1833–1881), ninth child of Joseph Pease, MP for South Durham, with whom he had five children.

By the mid-1850s Fowler was turning his attention to the application of steam power to ploughing and field cultivation. After many experiments and trials, he devised a system which fulfilled all the conditions laid down by the Royal Agricultural Society, and he received at the Chester show in 1858 the prize of £500, offered 'for a steam cultivator that shall, in the most efficient manner, turn over the soil and be an economic substitute for the plough or the spade'.

Fowler's steam plough worked by indirect traction. Instead of pulling the plough behind it the steam engine remained on the headland and drew the plough across the field by windlass and steel cable. As the system was developed a second engine, on the opposite headland to the first, was substituted for the windlass. This 'double-engine' system became the most successful form of steam ploughing in Britain and in many other countries. During Fowler's lifetime his steam ploughs were sold to Egypt for work on cotton plantations, and exports to central Europe and other countries followed. The cost of a steam-ploughing set in the 1860s being £1000–2000, its purchase was beyond the means of most farmers, but through contractors the use of steam ploughs became more common.

Ransomes and Sims, of Ipswich, had been makers of some of Fowler's experimental ploughs in 1856. Other devices were made by Robert Stephenson's works at Newcastle, and it was there that the equipment with which Fowler won the prize in 1858 was produced. In 1860 Fowler entered into an agreement with Kitson and Hewitson of Hunslet, Leeds, for them to manufacture his steam ploughs. Business expanded and the new Steam Plough Works was built on neighbouring land at Hunslet. In 1863 Fowler's new firm, John Fowler & Co., was established. In 1864 more than 400 men were said to be employed. Between 1850 and 1864 Fowler took out in his own name and in partnership with other persons thirty-two patents for ploughs and ploughing apparatus, reaping machines, seed drills, traction engines, slide valves, the laying of electric telegraph cables, and the making of bricks and tiles.

By the summer of 1864 Fowler's health was suffering from overwork and he retired to Ackworth, Yorkshire, to recuperate. Being recommended active exercise he began to hunt, and in November 1864 he fractured his arm by falling from his horse; tetanus ensued, from the effect of which he died at Prospect House, Ackworth, Yorkshire, on 4 December 1864. He was survived by his wife.

JONATHAN BROWN

Sources M. R. Lane, *The story of the Steam Plough Works: Fowlers of Leeds* (1980) · T. Davis, *John Fowler and the business he founded* (1951) · *Farmer's Magazine*, 3rd ser., 35 (1869), 1–2 · *Leeds Mercury* (6 July 1864) · *Leeds Mercury* (9 July 1864) · *Leeds Mercury* (16 July 1864) · *Leeds Mercury* (7 Dec 1864) · *GM*, 3rd ser., 18 (1865), 123 · *Practical Magazine*, 5 (1875), 257–62 · d. cert. · *CGPLA Eng. & Wales* (1865) · Burke, *Gen. GB* · *DNB*

Archives U. Reading, Rural History Centre, Archives of John Fowler & Co. (Leeds) Ltd, MSS

Likenesses photographs, U. Reading, Rural History Centre, Archives of John Fowler & Co. (Leeds) Ltd, 7 FOW 7

Wealth at death under £20,000: probate, 20 Jan 1865, *CGPLA Eng. & Wales*

Fowler, John Beresford (1906–1977), interior decorator, was born on 20 June 1906 at the Old Mill House, Lingfield, Surrey, the son of Robert Richard Fowler and his wife, Blanche Beresford, *née* Forster. His father was clerk of the course at the fashionable Edwardian race course at Lingfield. The comfortable circumstances of Fowler's childhood ended in 1915 with his father's early death, and the family moved to the artistic London suburb of Bedford Park and a life of genteel poverty at 12 Woodstock Road (a house designed by Norman Shaw). There was still just enough money for Fowler to be sent to Tormore, a boarding preparatory school, and on to Felsted School, which his elder brother and father had also attended. However, his mother was compelled to remove him in 1923, at the age of sixteen. A series of humble jobs followed and, after a breakdown, he spent a year on a cousin's farm in Kent.

He enjoyed this stint, for he was a countryman at heart and deeply knowledgeable about rural ways.

Fowler made the first step towards his later career when he was taken on by Thornton Smiths, a large decorating and antique business in Soho Square. There he was given the task of painting 'Chinese' wallpapers, so fashionable at that time; he began with leaves and soon graduated to flowers and birds, for he was a natural draughtsman with a light touch and great technical skill. These papers, having been suitably distressed, were sold as genuinely of the eighteenth century. In Soho Square Fowler also learned and perfected many of the techniques, such as marbleizing and graining, that he later taught to the many craftsmen whom he employed. His next step was to join the decorative painting studio of Margaret Kunzer. She was soon asked to set up a studio for painting furniture and objects to supply the decoration department of Peter Jones (1929). There Fowler gathered around him a small band of talented assistants, and when he decided to set up on his own in 1934 he took them with him, to 292 King's Road, Chelsea—a gimcrack Regency house, part of which he rented. Existence was precarious and funds short; accounts were done on the kitchen draining board and the sewing by somebody's nanny.

Fowler's style of what he famously called 'humble elegance' was refreshingly new, and brought a breath of the country to the town. The showroom was on the first floor because the ground floor had another tenant, but a coffin-shaped showcase on wheels was trundled daily into the front garden and its fresh and unusual stock-in-trade caught the beady eyes of two well-known decorators, Mrs Somerset Maugham and Sybil *Colefax, Lady Colefax (1874–1950), who both lived nearly opposite. Both asked Fowler to join them; he chose Lady Colefax, whom he considered marginally less formidable, and joined her firm in Bruton Street in 1938. Little survives of his pre-war work, and it is hard to discern from black and white photographs why his growing band of fashionable patrons found his work so fresh and exciting.

When war came Fowler, who was hopelessly myopic, was excused call-up. He plunged into dangerous and arduous work as an air raid warden and hospital orderly; meanwhile wartime restrictions meant very little decorating, even on his one day off a week. The first years of peace were still times of privation and rationing, but the most important point in his life came when Mrs Nancy Lancaster acquired the firm, which was by then at 39 Brook Street, premises that had formerly been the office of the Gothic architect Sir Jeffry Wyatville and had been discovered by Fowler in 1944. Mrs Lancaster did not herself decorate professionally but had consummate taste; Kelmarsh, Northamptonshire, and Ditchley Park, Oxfordshire, designed by the baroque architect James Gibbs—two houses that she had decorated when married to Ronald Tree MP—were considered pinnacles of pre-war luxury and taste. She used her newly acquired business to buy at cost the wherewithal to furnish Haseley Court, Oxfordshire; more importantly she had exclusive use of the services of John Fowler, who was made a partner in the firm.

It was a stormy relationship: her aunt Lady Astor called them the unhappiest unmarried couple in England. Lancaster contributed scale and comfort, and Fowler his incomparable colour sense and eye for detail, to the splendid result. When photographs of Haseley appeared it became the wonder of the age, and the concept of decoration of country houses was changed forever.

In 1947 Fowler bought a miniature Gothic folly: the Hunting Lodge, Odiham, Hampshire. His decoration of it was the acme of simplicity, but not in the least cottagey; it had supreme elegance yet was not over-grand. When photographs of the Hunting Lodge were published it too had enormous influence, as did the remarkable garden that Fowler created around it. He advised on numerous gardens over the years, and so severe were his views on which plants were acceptable that many of his friends dared not plant anything unless it was 'Fowler approved'.

In spite of the lengthening queue of people clamouring to be 'Fowlerized', as restrictions were eased the business was chaotically run and, until more businesslike partners were taken on, scarcely prospered. Fowler himself earned a pittance. Apart from potboiling Mayfair flats, which he loathed doing, he worked on at least thirty-five grand country houses and on many lesser ones too. His favourite jobs were perhaps Daylesford, Oxfordshire (for Lord Rothermere), Tyninghame, East Lothian (for Lady Haddington), and Grimsthorpe, Lincolnshire (for Lady Ancaster). The last is open regularly to the public. Fowler called his decorating haute couture but his approach was scholarly and his knowledge of the past profound; he never forgot a detail or a date. As a young man he had haunted museums, especially the Victoria and Albert, which was often open late. In those less scientific days he relied on scrapes and intuition to reveal original colours, and he was a master of the application of paint in an aesthetically pleasing but nevertheless authentic way. Much of this expertise is enshrined in *English Decoration in the 18th Century* (1976), which he wrote in collaboration with John Cornforth.

Through friendship with some of its officials Fowler was asked quite early on to advise the National Trust, although some were suspicious of employing a fashionable Mayfair decorator. After he had retired from his firm, in 1975, he worked almost exclusively for the trust for little more than his expenses. An amazing total of thirty houses benefited from his advice. Three stand out, at two of which— Clandon Park, Surrey, and Sudbury Hall, Derbyshire, both almost completely stripped of their original contents—he created a wonderful warm atmosphere. The third, Errdig, in Denbighshire, was an untouched, almost ruined house that was saved from complete dereliction from mine subsidence as a result of Fowler's impassioned letters to the reluctant grandees of the National Trust.

In youth Fowler had been inclined to long hair, sandals, and left-wing politics. In maturity he was distinguished-looking—slim, upright of stature, and beautifully tailored—but the left-wing politics remained. He was a perfectionist and a hard taskmaster, but those whom he castigated knew that he could carry out what they had failed to do far better himself. Almost all who worked for

him became devoted friends for life. He was a brilliant teacher and a lavish host (with a superb cook) and inspired much laughter, often laughing himself until he cried. He was a good talker but listened too, and proved a reliable friend for those with troubles. He could be high-handed with clients and dismissed several in mid-job when they proved intractable, but took endless trouble for those whom he liked. He was not interested in money and turned down many of the rich and influential whom he sensed would prove incompatible.

Among official buildings that Fowler worked on are Buckingham Palace, Holyroodhouse, Chequers, Chevening, Christ Church, Oxford, and the Bank of England. He was appointed CBE in 1973. He died, after a long struggle with cancer, on 27 October 1977 at the Hunting Lodge, which he left to the National Trust; his ashes were scattered on the lake there. He never married.

STEPHEN LONG

Sources C. Jones, *Colefax and Fowler: the best of interior decoration* (1989) · J. Cornforth, *The inspiration of the past: country house taste in the 20th century* (1985) · S. Long, *Colefax and Fowler: fifty years, 1934–1984* (1984) · b. cert. · d. cert. · *The Times* (29 Oct 1977) · *The Times* (7 Nov 1977) · *The Times* (25 Nov 1977)

Wealth at death £125,307: probate, 5 June 1978, *CGPLA Eng. & Wales*

Fowler, Lorenzo Niles (1811–1896). *See under* Fowler, Lydia Folger (1822–1879).

Fowler, Lydia Folger (1822–1879), physician, author, and lecturer, was born on 5 May 1822 at Nantucket, Massachusetts, USA, the sixth child of Gideon Folger, mechanic, manufacturer, shipowner, and farmer, and his wife, Eunice Macy Folger. She received her early education in Nantucket, where she developed interests in mathematics and astronomy, and later she studied for one year at Wheaton Seminary, Norton, Massachusetts, where she taught from 1842 to 1844.

On 19 September 1844 Lydia Folger married **Lorenzo Niles Fowler** (1811–1896), phrenologist, of the burgeoning New York publishing firm Fowlers and Wells. Born in Cohocton, New York, on 23 June 1811, Lorenzo and his brother, Orson Squire Fowler, had intended to enter the ministry of the Congregational church, but as students at Amherst Academy and College in the early 1830s they became enthusiastic converts to phrenology. Subsequently they itinerated throughout the eastern states proclaiming the mental science of Spurzheim. By 1842 they had established a permanent office at Clinton Hall, New York city, where Lorenzo specialized in performing phrenological analyses for clients. Clinton Hall was to become a hub for a number of physiological and social-reform causes, including temperance, anti-smoking, vegetarianism, hydropathy, mesmerism, homoeopathy, anti-slavery, sex education, and women's rights, and Lydia Folger Fowler was to play an integral part in its operations.

In 1845 Lydia began accompanying her husband on lecture tours, and from 1847 she addressed female audiences on anatomy, physiology, and hygiene. She started her writing career the same year, publishing two books for children on physiology and phrenology; the trilogy was completed in 1848 with a work on astronomy. In November 1849 she began studying medicine at Central Medical College, Syracuse, New York, a small school committed to eclecticism. From March 1850 she was responsible for giving instruction to the female students, and upon her graduation on 5 June 1850 she became the second woman in the USA to receive the degree of doctor of medicine. During 1851–2 she held the post of professor of midwifery and diseases of women and children at the college.

Lydia Fowler went on to practise medicine in New York city throughout the years 1852–60, holding her own daily surgery oriented towards homoeopathic therapies, and conducting gynaecological examinations under the auspices of the Fowlers' phrenological depot. She actively promoted women's medical education, giving courses of private lectures and publicizing her views on the necessity for female physicians. She was also a campaigner for women's rights, acting as secretary of national conventions in 1852–3, and was a leading temperance advocate, being in February 1853 the presiding officer of the Woman's Grand Temperance Demonstration at Metropolitan Hall, New York.

In 1860–62 Lydia Fowler accompanied her husband and his business partner, Samuel Wells, on a lecture tour of Britain, where the American phrenologists' works had been published for more than a decade by their agent, William Horsell, at 492 Oxford Street, London. The popular, freethinking former Methodist minister, Joseph Barker, too, had helped to disseminate the Fowlers' doctrines, reprinting a selection of their writings in 1849–50. The tour was very successful, reviving popular interest in the science and giving it a practical and anti-elitist emphasis which was to mark its British character henceforth. Lydia Fowler's lectures to women on health were well received, and while in Europe she extended her medical education and experience, studying in Paris during the winter of 1860–61, and working in the obstetrics department of the New Hospital for Women, Marylebone Road, London, in 1861.

Lydia and Lorenzo Fowler emigrated to Britain in 1863. They opened an office in Cook's Buildings at 107 Fleet Street, London, and Lydia devoted her time to lecturing and writing, being ineligible to practise medicine under the 1858 Medical Act. In 1863 she published a temperance novel entitled *Nora: the Lost and the Redeemed*, and a series of pamphlets based on some of her lectures. She and her husband became members of the Congregational City Temple at High Holborn, and Lydia served the community as one of the Temple's district visitors. She also became involved in temperance work, holding the position of honorary secretary of the British Women's Temperance Association, an organization formed in 1876 to unite all existing women's temperance groups in the country and extend the work to new areas.

Lydia Folger Fowler died of pneumonia on 26 January 1879 at her home in London, at 62 St Augustine's Road, Camden Square. She had worked tirelessly for the interests of women in Britain and the United States, and earned much respect. The *New York Times* noted that she

was 'remarkable for the dignity of her manner'. Her published lectures show her confidence in ordinary women's ability to promote their families' physical and material well-being by acting in accordance with the divinely instituted laws of nature.

Lydia and her husband had three daughters, Amelia (*b.* 1846), Loretta (*b.* 1850), and **Jessie Allen Fowler** (1856–1932). Born on 11 July 1856 in New York, Jessie Allen succeeded her mother as honorary secretary of the British Women's Temperance Association and assisted Lorenzo in all aspects of his work. In 1896 she and Lorenzo returned to the USA, where Jessie assumed the editorship of the Fowlers' *Phrenological Journal*. Lorenzo Niles Fowler died, after suffering a stroke, on 2 September 1896 at the home of his sister, Charlotte Fowler Wells, in West Orange, New Jersey; he was buried in Rosedale cemetery, New Jersey. On Charlotte's death in 1901, Jessie became the sole heir to the firm of Fowler and Wells. The same year she completed a course in the women's law class of New York University. She remained committed to phrenology, although its popularity was waning, and maintained a high output of writing. Jessie Allen Fowler died on 15 October 1932 at her home at 843 West 179th Street, New York, and was buried on 17 October.

MARK CLEMENT

Sources M. B. Stern, *Heads and headlines: the phrenological Fowlers* (1971) · F. C. Waite, 'Dr Lydia Folger Fowler: the second woman to receive the degree of doctor of medicine in the United States', *Annals of Medical History*, new ser., 4 (1932), 290–97 · R. Cooter, *The cultural meaning of popular science: phrenology and the organization of consent in nineteenth-century Britain* (1984) · P. T. Winskill, *The temperance movement and its workers*, 4 vols. (1891–2), vol. 3 · *New York Times* (10 Feb 1879) · *New York Times* (4 Sept 1896) · *New York Times* (16 Oct 1932) · E. T. Jones, ed., *Notable American women, 1607–1950: a biographical dictionary* (1971) · L. L. Shiman, '"Changes are dangerous": women and temperance in Victorian England', *Religion in the lives of English women, 1760–1930*, ed. G. Malmgreen (1986), 193–215 · E. P. Lovejoy, *Women doctors of the world* (1957) · M. E. Lender, *Dictionary of American temperance biography: from temperance reform to alcohol research, the 1600s to the 1980s* (1984)
Archives Cornell University, MSS

Fowler, Peter Howard (1923–1996), physicist, was born on 27 February 1923 in Cambridge, the elder son and eldest of four children of Sir Ralph Howard *Fowler (1889–1944), mathematical physicist, and his wife, Eileen Mary (*d.* 1930), only daughter of Ernest *Rutherford, Baron Rutherford of Nelson. He had reached the age of only seven when his mother died after his young sister was born. By great good fortune Phyllida and Derek Cook, friends of his parents, moved into the Fowler home, Cromwell House in Trumpington. The four Fowler children (Peter, Elizabeth, Patrick, and Ruth) and the three Cook children (Lesley, Joanna, and Allison) grew up as one large, and by all accounts, happy family, with only eight years between the eldest and youngest child. Fowler's first exposure to formal education was at his nursery school, the Malting House, Cambridge. In his report for the winter term of 1927, Mr Slavson wrote:

> Peter's interest in fires still persists but we have succeeded
> both in extending that interest into other channels than
> merely bonfire and to divert it … Peter is outstandingly of an

experimental and investigatory nature, but, at the present time, these tendencies are focused around fire. (Wolfendale, 178)

All this was at the age of four! His traits of experimental skill which were to blossom in later life were already apparent.

From an early age Fowler was fascinated by the weather, and especially clouds. This interest in meteorology could well have stemmed from his ancestor Luke Howard (1772–1864), Quaker, meteorologist, and business man. Howard was credited with classifying cloud types—cirrus, nimbus, cumulus, and stratus—and inspiring Constable and indeed Goethe. At seven Fowler left the Malting House to board at his preparatory school, Summer Fields at Oxford. This was a deeply unhappy experience and in later life he vowed never to send his own children away at such a tender age. The choice of Winchester College as his public school was probably strongly influenced by his father, who had been a scholar there. He was a popular pupil, keenly interested in experimental science, an unusual attribute for Wykehamists at that time. His choice of Bristol University came about primarily because his father had a high regard for Professor Arthur Tyndall and the Bristol physics department. After two years of wartime Bristol he joined the Royal Air Force, became a radar officer, and, as he wrote, 'benefited from a course on radio physics from Professor Nevill Mott and others' (Wolfendale, 178). His time in the RAF was eventful. His notable success related to the 'Gee' navigational aid. By 1944 the allies had developed this aid to guide bombers in the raids on the continent. The Germans, in their turn, constructed a powerful radio jammer to disable it. In a very short time Fowler, as a signals officer at Dover, devised a method of locating the jamming station in a manner not foreseen by the Germans. The station, which was located on a mountain at the Feldberg, near Frankfurt, was quickly destroyed.

In 1946 Fowler was released from the RAF and returned to Bristol to resume his undergraduate studies. By this time he had already shown an interest in cosmic rays. In a letter to his grandmother, Lady Rutherford, Tyndall wrote, in February 1947:

shortly before he left, earlier in the war, my colleague Dr [Cecil] Powell had developed a new technique for studying particles from atomic nuclei by firing them into a photographic plate and measuring the minute tracks which showed up when the plate was developed. We had already given Peter, as an inquisitive student, an opportunity at that stage of measuring a few of these before he joined the RAF. His experience with photographic plates allowed him to participate in a series of experiments which led to three research papers.   (Wolfendale, 179)

All three papers were published in 1947 with Fowler as an author. This was after only one year of degree-level physics. After graduating in 1948, he was immediately appointed an assistant lecturer, and in 1951 he was appointed lecturer. He was extremely fortunate in falling for Rosemary Hempson Brown (b. 1925/6), whom he married on 23 July 1949. She was the daughter of Rear-Admiral George Herbert Hempson Brown and was herself a physicist, having obtained a first in physics in 1947. She became a research student in Cecil Powell's group and after Fowler graduated in 1948 the two worked together. She was happy to give up her research to provide him with the family life which he longed for after his years of boarding-school and the RAF. Their long and happy marriage was blessed with three daughters, who all read science at university.

Although he was very active in the Bristol work, Fowler arrived just too late to share in the glory of the discovery of the pion (by C. M. G. Lattes and others in 1947), the discovery that was to earn Powell the Nobel prize. Nevertheless, Fowler's activities were acknowledged by Powell in his Nobel address, and after her husband's death Mrs Powell gave the Fowlers his presentation copy of *The Prix Nobel* (1950). Fowler's forte was the detailed, and at times inspired, understanding of the emulsion technique. A significant discovery was that of the heavy tau meson, later termed the kaon (work carried out with his wife-to-be and others). This atomic particle decays into three pions and is now known to be one of the 'strange particles', the first of which were discovered in the elegant cloud-chamber experiments of G. D. Rochester and C. C. Butler in 1947. An early colleague of that period was D. H. Perkins, himself a distinguished nuclear emulsion physicist, and in 1959 they, with Powell, produced a major work: *The Study of Elementary Particles by the Photographic Method*. This book of over 600 pages became a bible for all those working in the field of cosmic rays—and not just those using the emulsion technique. Fowler also worked with Perkins on studies of the possible use of negative pion beams for cancer therapy, a technique that was, then, ahead of its time.

The 1950s saw Fowler produce a steady stream of papers devoted to elementary particle physics using the emulsion technique. Balloon launches with increasingly massive payloads became commonplace. However, an interest in astrophysics was developing and this led to a number of discoveries, including the demonstration that very light atomic nuclei in the cosmic radiation come from the fragmentation of heavier nuclei on collision with the nuclei of gas in the gas between the stars. From September 1956 to June 1957 Fowler was visiting professor in the University of Minnesota, where heavy nuclei in the cosmic radiation had been originally discovered. In 1958 he was offered a permanent appointment by the University of Minnesota—as a full professor—but what turned out to be a minor health problem prevented him from taking up the post. Fowler's research work was recognized by the University of Bristol in 1958 by the award of a DSc and in 1961 by his promotion to reader. Election to the Royal Society followed in 1964. An honour which gave him, and many others, particular pleasure was his appointment as Royal Society research professor in the same year.

In the late 1960s Fowler had become interested in the gas-scintillation process as yet another technique to use in his pursuit of the heavy primary cosmic rays. After development work, and a balloon-borne instrument, a detector was made for the last all-British satellite, Ariel VI. Ariel VI was launched on 24 May 1979 and the Bristol detector accumulated very significant data on the abundance of the heavy primary cosmic rays. The analysis of the data took many years, but the results turned out to be both exciting and unexpected, not least the presence of very heavy nuclei. It was with these nuclei (having charge Z > 70) that Fowler's name came to be identified; here, an exotic mechanism transcending the standard model had to be postulated. Mention should also be made of his work following the Chernobyl disaster on 26 April 1986. There were many British students reading Russian and studying in Russia at the time, mostly in the vicinity of Kiev, and thus potentially at risk. Bristol was much involved and Fowler's knowledge of radiation and meteorology was of considerable value. Discussions between the University of Bristol, Fowler, and the Nuclear Radiological Protection Board resulted in the students' being brought home about three days after the disaster.

After retiring from the university in 1988, Fowler developed an association with Rolls-Royce, where he studied the temperature of turbine blades, work which was carried out with Peter Stewart, a Rolls-Royce engineer. The principle of the method was to determine the thermal broadening of the narrow resonance lines generated when epithermal neutrons are absorbed by specific metals. Alas, for financial reasons Rolls-Royce did not proceed with the necessary funding, but the technique was of great interest. Fowler was also chairman of the Herschel House Trust in Bath for many years, on behalf of the Royal Society. The house was where William Herschel made his celebrated discovery of the planet Uranus in 1781. In many ways Fowler and Herschel were alike—both had great technical skill and both were fascinated by the cosmos.

Fowler was a great family man, devoted husband of Rosemary, and a proud father. As a younger man he had enjoyed cricket and squash, and in later life his principal relaxation, aided and abetted by Rosemary, was his garden, and their efforts were often rewarded by prizes at local flower shows. He died of heart failure at his home, 320 Canford Lane, Westbury-on-Trym, Bristol, on 8 November 1996, and was buried in Bristol. He was survived by his wife and three daughters. A memorial service was held at Bristol Cathedral on 18 April 1997.

ARNOLD WOLFENDALE

Sources A. Wolfendale, *Memoirs FRS*, 44 (1998), 177–89 · *The Independent* (14 Nov 1996) · *The Times* (18 Nov 1996) · *Daily Telegraph* (10 Dec 1996) · *WWW* [forthcoming] · m. cert. · d. cert.
Archives University of Bristol Library, MSS
Likenesses photograph, 1967, repro. in *Memoirs FRS*, 176 · photograph, repro. in *The Independent* · photograph, repro. in *The Times* · photograph, repro. in *Daily Telegraph*
Wealth at death £342,641: probate, 21 March 1997, *CGPLA Eng. & Wales*

Fowler, Sir Ralph Howard (1889–1944), mathematical physicist and weapons researcher, was born at Fedsden, Roydon, Essex, on 17 January 1889, the elder son of Howard Fowler, of Glebelands, Burnham, Somerset, and his

Sir Ralph Howard Fowler (1889–1944), by Walter Stoneman, 1943

wife, Frances Eva, daughter of George Dewhurst, cotton merchant, of Manchester. Like his father, who had represented England at rugby, Fowler demonstrated wide-ranging athletic ability. His sister Dorothy played golf for England in 1921–8. His younger brother was killed on the Somme.

Fowler was educated at home by a governess, then at a preparatory school at Horris Hill. He was elected in 1902 to a scholarship at Winchester College, of which he was to become a member of staff before the First World War, and a fellow in 1933. During this period his family moved from Essex to Norfolk. From Winchester he won an entrance scholarship at Trinity College, Cambridge, where he obtained a first class in part one of the mathematical tripos in 1909, and became a wrangler in part two in 1911 with special credit in schedule B. He was awarded a Rayleigh prize for mathematics in 1913, and the Adams prize in 1924. He represented Cambridge at golf in 1912.

After taking his degree Fowler began research in pure mathematics, at which he was exhaustive rather than brilliant. His work on the behaviour of solutions of second-order differential equations led to his election into a prize fellowship at Trinity in 1914. During the war, however, Fowler turned his attention to applied mathematics and theoretical physics, which gave him full scope both for his true mathematical powers and for his strong practical inclinations. On the outbreak of war Fowler obtained a commission in the Royal Marines; he was severely wounded in the Gallipoli campaign. While convalescing in England he began a notable collaboration with Archibald Vivian Hill, the first great influence in his career. With him at Whale Island, Portsmouth, Fowler organized the anti-aircraft experimental section of the munitions inventions department of the Ministry of Munitions. Later he became its assistant director, was promoted captain, and appointed OBE in 1918. Some of his joint researches with other members of the section in anti-aircraft gunnery afterwards became classics in ballistics. An account entitled 'The aerodynamics of a spinning shell' (*PTRS* 221 A, 1920–21 and 222, 1921–22) had a considerable influence on naval gunnery in the Second World War.

In 1919 Fowler returned to Cambridge. In 1920 he was appointed lecturer in mathematics at Trinity, and came under the second great influence in his life, Sir Ernest *Rutherford, whose daughter, Eileen Mary, he married in 1921. She died in 1930, leaving two daughters and two sons, the elder of whom was Peter Howard *Fowler, himself a distinguished physicist. The Fowler family lived at Trumpington, and Fowler also had a country house at Ashmore, Wiltshire, in his beloved west country. Fowler became a prolific researcher in the domains of statistical mechanics and atomic physics. His early collaboration with Charles Galton Darwin resulted in the publication of his Adams prize essay as the exhaustively detailed book *Statistical Mechanics* (1929). He was elected FRS in 1925 and was awarded a royal medal by the society in 1936. He delivered the Bakerian lecture in 1935. He was elected first Plummer professor of mathematical physics at Cambridge in 1932. In 1938 he was appointed director of the National Physical Laboratory, but a heart attack prevented his taking up the appointment and he retained the Plummer chair.

Before the outbreak of war in 1939 Fowler became involved with an Admiralty committee to consider the influence that air power might have on the navy. He was soon sent to Canada to co-ordinate war research there with war research in Britain; he later extended these activities to the United States, and was instrumental in establishing what became the British central scientific office in Washington, DC. For the success of this mission he was knighted in 1942. In spite of failing health he became a member of the Admiralty scientific advisory board, and chaired powerful Admiralty committees. With E. A. Milne he compared the destructive power of armour-piercing and high-explosive projectiles.

Fowler, a man of great personal charm, was remembered by contemporaries as a mathematical physicist of amazing quickness and versatility of mind. His most original work was his paper 'On dense matter' (*Monthly Notices of the Royal Astronomical Society*, 87, 1926, 114), wherein he characterized white dwarf stars in terms of quantum statistics. Astronomical interests prompted his work on Emden's differential equation (*Monthly Notices of the Royal Astronomical Society*, 91, 1931). However, he was at his best as a collaborator, and was renowned for critical insight and infectious enthusiasm. Fowler finally succumbed to his heart condition and died on 28 July 1944 at his home, Cromwell House, Trumpington; he was cremated in Cambridge on 2 August of that year.

E. A. MILNE, *rev.* ALAN YOSHIOKA

Sources E. A. Milne, *Obits. FRS*, 5 (1945–8), 61–78 · C. G. Darwin, *Cambridge Review* (14 Oct 1944), 6–8 · *The Times* (29 July 1944) · *The Times* (3 Aug 1944) · *The Times* (5 Aug 1944) · *The Times* (17 Aug 1944) · *The Times* (12 Sept 1944) · E. A. Milne, *Nature*, 154 (1944), 232–3 · S. Zuckerman, *From apes to warlords* (1978) · *CGPLA Eng. & Wales* (1945)
Archives CAC Cam., corresp. with A. V. Hill · CUL, corresp. with Francis John Worsley Roughton · IWM, corresp. with Tizard and others, with memorandum
Likenesses W. Stoneman, photograph, 1943, NPG [*see illus.*] · photograph, repro. in *Obits. FRS*, 61
Wealth at death £15,507 1s. 2d.: probate, 2 Jan 1945, *CGPLA Eng. & Wales*

Fowler, Richard (1765–1863), physician, was born in London on 28 November 1765, and, though he lived to a great age, he was of feeble health when a child. He was educated at Edinburgh and studied medicine there. While a student he visited Paris in the times before and during the revolution and became acquainted with a number of those involved, including Count Mirabeau. He returned to Edinburgh in 1790 and continued his medical studies, graduating MD on 12 September 1793 with a dissertation entitled 'De inflammatione'. He was also a member of the celebrated Speculative Society of Edinburgh, to which he contributed essays.

Fowler was admitted licentiate of the Royal College of Physicians, London, on 21 March 1796, and settled in practice at Salisbury, where he lived for the rest of his life. He was soon elected physician to the Salisbury Infirmary, and held the office until his retirement in 1847, when he was elected consulting physician. He was elected FRS in 1802, and took an active part in the meetings of the British Association for the Advancement of Science (BAAS), of which he was one of the first members. In order to attend a meeting of the BAAS and to read a paper there he made the journey from Salisbury to Aberdeen in 1859, when nearly ninety-four years of age. Fowler was successful in practice, and held a leading position in Salisbury for many years. He purchased and endowed land for the Salisbury and South Wiltshire Museum, to which he gave a large part of his books and collections in 1862. On 12 August 1805 he married Anne Bowles, the daughter of William Bowles of Heale House, sister of Sir George Bowles (1787–1876) and the granddaughter of Sir Thomas Frankland. He was elected a fellow of the Royal College of Physicians in July 1837.

Fowler always kept up an interest in science, and was well known among the scientific and literary figures of his day. When a student in Edinburgh, after his return from Paris, he became interested in Galvani's recent discoveries on electricity and made numerous experiments on the subject, which he published in 1793 as *Experiments and observations on the influence lately discovered by M. Galvani, and commonly called animal electricity.* His observations on muscular irritability caused by electricity acting over a distance on the bodies of frogs, and on conductors, were influential, and the work was later translated into German. The work also included notes on the action of opium on nerves and muscles.

Many years later, Fowler published two small books on the psychology of disabled persons: *Observations on the Mental State of the Blind and Deaf and Dumb* (1843) and *The Physiological Processes of Thinking, Especially in Persons whose Organs of Sense are Defective* (1849). The works show some reading and contain interesting observations, but are lacking in clarity and method. Fowler also wrote *On Literary and Scientific Pursuits as Conducive to Longevity* (1855)—an area he was well qualified to comment on. He died at Milford, near New Sarum, Wiltshire, on 13 April 1863, and was buried at Salisbury. He was survived by his wife.

J. F. PAYNE, *rev.* PATRICK WALLIS

Sources GM, 3rd ser., 14 (1863) · *The Lancet* (25 April 1863) · Munk, *Roll* · *Nomina eorum, qui gradum medicinae doctoris in academia Jacobi sexti Scotorum regis, quae Edinburgi est, adepti sunt, ab anno 1705 ad annum 1845,* University of Edinburgh (1846) · P. F. Mothelay, *Biographical history of electricity and magnetism* (1922) · *Salisbury and Winchester Journal* (18 April 1863) · CGPLA Eng. & Wales (1863) · Boase, *Mod. Eng. biog.* · GM, 1st ser., 75 (1805), 773
Wealth at death under £14,000: probate, 21 May 1863, CGPLA Eng. & Wales

Fowler, Robert (1724–1801), Church of Ireland archbishop of Dublin, was born on 23 December 1724, and baptized at Skendleby, Lincolnshire, the third son of George Fowler of Skendleby and his wife, Mary, daughter and coheir of Robert Hurst. He was educated at Westminster School, where he was elected a king's scholar in 1744. On 24 May of that year he was admitted to Trinity College, Cambridge, graduating BA (1748), MA (1751), and DD (1764). In 1756 he was appointed chaplain to George II, and in January 1765 became prebendary of Westminster. In the following year he married Mildred, eldest daughter of William Dealtry of Gainsborough, Lincolnshire, and coheir of her brother, also William, of Ashby, Lincolnshire. The couple had one son and two daughters.

Fowler was promoted from his prebend to the bishopric of Killaloe and Kilfenora by patent dated 29 June 1771, and on 8 January 1779 was translated to the archbishopric of Dublin, with a seat in the Irish privy council. He was, in addition, chancellor of the Order of St Patrick. The Church of Ireland clergyman and author Philip Skelton commented on Fowler's great regard for religion, his kindness and affability, accompanied by a warmth of temper, and his solemnity when reading in church, an observation also made by John Wesley.

In 1782 Fowler was one of twelve spiritual peers in the Irish House of Lords who protested against the bill for the relief of dissenters, thought likely to promote clandestine and improvident marriages. In 1789 he joined with fourteen other peers in protesting against the parliament's memorable address requesting that the prince of Wales assume the regency in Ireland. He also protested against the resolution condemning the answer of the marquess of

Buckingham, the lord lieutenant, who refused to transmit the address. Fowler died suddenly on 10 October 1801 at Bassingbourn Hall, Cambridgeshire, where he had resided for two years for his health. His son Robert was promoted to the bishopric of Ossory in 1813. The elder daughter, Mildred, married Edmund Butler, Viscount Mountgarret (later earl of Kilkenny); the younger, Frances, married Richard Bourke, later bishop of Waterford and Lismore.

B. H. BLACKER, *rev.* PHILIP CARTER

Sources Venn, *Alum. Cant.* · H. Cotton, *Fasti ecclesiae Hibernicae,* 1–5 (1845–60) · R. Mant, *History of the Church of Ireland,* 2 vols. (1840) · GEC, *Peerage* · GM, 1st ser., 71 (1801), 965, 1049 · parish register, Skendleby church, Lincolnshire, 24 March 1725 [baptism] · N&Q, 12th ser., 12 (1923)
Archives NL Ire., accounts
Likenesses J. K. Sherwin, line engraving, pubd 1803 (after his unfinished oil painting, *c.*1785), NG Ire. · W. Daniell, soft-ground etching, pubd 1809 (after G. Dance, 1795), BM, NPG · J. K. Sherwin, oils (*The installation banquet of the knights of St Patrick,* 1783), NG Ire.

Fowler, Sir Robert Nicholas, first baronet (1828–1891), banker and politician, was born at Bruce Grove, Tottenham, Middlesex, on 12 September 1828, the only child of Thomas Fowler (*d.* 1851) and his wife, Lucy Waterhouse. His father, a well-connected member of the Society of Friends, was an amiable London banker who enjoyed hunting, while his mother, more severe in her religion, came from a prosperous family of Lancashire Quakers.

Tottenham was known for its active meeting, and the nonconformist Grove House School was attended by Fowler for a short time. As a boy he was renowned for his interest in history and politics, and he was endowed with an excellent memory. Throughout life he was a perfect storehouse for quotations from Greek, Roman, and English orators and poets. In 1846 he went up to University College, London, where he took firsts in mathematics and classical honours (BA 1848, MA in mathematics 1850). On graduation he went into the family bank, Drewett and Fowler, in the City of London and became a senior partner only three years later on the sudden death of his father. The following year he negotiated a merger with Barnard, Dimsdale, and Dimsdale, also a family firm founded by Quakers. The success of Dimsdale, Fowler, Barnard, and Dimsdale rested on its appeal to a clientele which was largely upper-middle-class, nonconformist, and often related by blood or marriage to the partners. It weathered the financial crisis of 1866, moved to a more prestigious location in Cornhill, prospered, and gave Fowler the comfortable means to pursue both an active political career and the Badminton hunt. Unlike some businessmen who turned to politics, however, he never delegated to other partners his central role at the bank. From the late 1860s to the end of the bank's existence as a family firm in 1890 he took an active interest in its daily affairs—even while serving as lord mayor—and presided, as dominant partner in the 1870s and 1880s, over its continuing role as a sound, solidly based, and increasingly profitable private bank at a time when the tide was turning against small houses.

Fowler's marriage on 27 October 1852 to Sarah Charlotte

Sir Robert Nicholas Fowler, first baronet (1828–1891), by unknown engraver

Fox (1834/5–1876) of Falmouth was within the extended Quaker commercial and financial world. Nevertheless, neither he nor his bride considered themselves 'strict Quakers', and in 1858 they left the Society of Friends and later joined the Church of England. Fowler belonged to the evangelical school and was throughout his life a man of strong and deep religious feeling. Both during his mayoralty and in the years following he often preached at the theatre services which were begun at the instance of Lord Shaftesbury for the working men of London.

Inheriting his paternal grandfather's farm near Corsham in Wiltshire, Fowler extended the estate, rebuilt Gastard House, and established his family there, though business required that he keep a residence for himself in London's West End. He cultivated the brusque mannerisms and old-fashioned dress of a country squire, and his passion for hunting contrasted oddly with his support for Quaker causes and the Evangelical Alliance. His energetic toryism was also unusual in a former Quaker.

Fowler made his first, unsuccessful, attempt to enter parliament in the general election of 1865, standing as a Conservative for the then Liberal stronghold of the City of London. Another chance presented itself soon afterwards in the Cornish constituency of Penryn and Falmouth where his wife's family were prominent (though Liberals). He failed in his first attempt but succeeded in 1868. It was his fate, however, to get into parliament just as the Conservatives were swept from power, and to lose his seat in 1874 when they returned to office under Disraeli. When he re-entered the house in 1880 (for the City) the Conservatives were once again in opposition. These circumstances

naturally affected the prospects and character of his parliamentary career; he settled into the style of a confirmed opposition back-bencher, became an inveterate writer of letters to the papers, was assiduous in attendance at late-night sittings, and jealously guarded the diminishing prerogatives of the private member. Not a good speaker, 'his voice being rough and uncultured and his delivery impeded by a stammer' (*ILN*), he none the less rose often. His maiden speech on the enslavement of Kaffir children by Boer farmers in South Africa (19 February 1869) signalled a dominant object of his public life, the protection of 'natives' throughout the British empire, a commitment which, like his lay preaching in London, reflected a Quaker belief in the 'stewardship of wealth'.

In spite of his support for causes strongly associated with Liberal nonconformity, Fowler was a flamboyant tory, vigorous in local party organization in London. In 1878 he was returned unopposed as alderman for Cornhill, the ward in which his bank was located. President of the City Conservative Association and chairman of the City Carlton Club, he was well positioned to stand successfully for the City in 1880. Immediately on taking his seat his evangelical and tory principles were joined in the passionate struggle to prevent the Liberal radical and atheist Charles Bradlaugh from taking the oath. Active in the anti-Bradlaugh campaign in both the house and the City, he was personally involved in the forcible ejection of Bradlaugh into Palace Yard in August 1881.

Fowler rose within City affairs amid anxious anticipation of radical municipal reform. These fears helped create a defensive and stridently partisan undercurrent in his own mayoralty in 1883–4 and 1885. Custom prescribed elevation to the office by seniority, but in the autumn of 1883 the aldermanic court chose Fowler over the Liberal next on the list. The result was to cast a shadow over Fowler's election, though in the event he served a second term in 1885 when his successor died in office.

The event which excited most attention during Fowler's first tenure of the mayoralty was his speech at the banquet in proposing the health of her majesty's ministers. As all men knew the intensity of his opposition to Gladstone's policy, there was a good deal of curiosity to see how he would fare in proposing his health; but happily the love of Homer, shared by Fowler and Gladstone, saved the situation. A quotation from the *Iliad* (xvi.550) did justice to the great orator's fighting powers and won from Gladstone a hearty recognition of the lord mayor 'as a frank, bold, and courageous opponent in the House of Commons' (*DNB*).

The issue of 'the City in danger' touched both Fowler's self-interest as a City banker and his nostalgic toryism. A vow 'not to abandon an ancient and a venerable institution in the hour of her danger and her need' (*The Times*, 26 Jan 1884) led him to make questionable use of the resources of his office in a covert campaign against Sir William Vernon Harcourt's London Government Bill (8 April 1884). The seeming victory of the anti-reformers was followed by a personal triumph for Fowler in the general election of 1885, when he kept his seat with the largest majority in the country. He received a baronetcy from Lord Salisbury in 1885, a common honour for a former lord mayor, and in the next election, in July 1886, he was returned unopposed.

Years spent in opposition, a quirky independence bred by his devotion to out-of-doors causes, and, beneath his coarsely effusive *bonhomie*, an underlying lack of self-confidence conspired, however, to keep Fowler on the periphery of politics once his party came to power in 1886. Moreover, the last years of his life were overshadowed by the belated scandal of his partisan abuses while lord mayor. In 1887 a campaign in the Liberal press, led by the radical Henry Labouchere, greatly embarrassed Fowler and, though the select committee appointed by the Conservative government shielded him from criminal prosecution for 'malversation', the allegations of dirty tricks paid for by corporation funds were clearly substantiated.

Beyond parliament and the City there remained Gastard House in Wiltshire, which the railway made easily accessible for fox-hunting and, perhaps a secondary consideration, weekend visits to the large family which he insisted live there in rural seclusion. He and his wife, Sarah, had ten daughters and one son. After her eleventh child was born she became a semi-invalid and died at the age of forty-one a few days before Christmas 1876. Subsequently their many children were cared for by the eldest daughter, Lucy Charlotte. He never remarried.

Fowler came to enjoy the kind of foreign travel which his wealth could provide. On his return from a tour of the Far East in 1877 he published a conventional memoir, full of haphazard reflections and casual condemnation of aspects of colonial society which irritated his evangelical sensibilities. He made another world tour in 1886 with his son, Thomas, who had finished at Harrow School. It was intended that Tom take a position in the family bank, but the rapidly consolidating world of London finance dictated otherwise. In 1890 Fowler reluctantly allowed the firm to be merged with Prescott's Bank into a joint-stock business. Though he managed to get a place for his son among the many partners, there was inevitably a sense of loss and closure. The following spring he caught a bad case of influenza in Cornwall at the funeral of one of his daughters. This was compounded by his stubborn insistence on travelling back to London for the annual spring meeting of the Aborigines Protection Society. By the day of the meeting his flu had developed into pneumonia, and on 22 May 1891 he died of heart failure at 137 Harley Street, London. He was buried in the churchyard at Corsham.

Fowler died a wealthy man. Beyond the shares in Prescott's there were investments in railways, insurance, and electrical supply. But much had been poured into the Gastard estate, where he was determined to establish his son as a member of the landed gentry. Thomas was, however, unmarried when he was killed in one of the last engagements of the Second South African War in 1901. There was to be no landed dynasty built on a City fortune.

Lord Onslow once complained that Fowler 'had peculiar views on many subjects' (*Hansard 3*, 300, 1885, 1415). Seeming contradictions ran through his public and private worlds. On the one hand there is the tender and anxious conscience confided to his diary, and his daily meditation and prayer; on the other a bluff and consciously anachronistic churchman-and-tory persona which, with his large, loose frame and full beard, rough, loud voice, and cigars and good stories, led even his admiring son-in-law and biographer to assert, approvingly, that his 'talents were all of the solid kind: of what is called brilliance of intellect he possessed almost nothing at all' (Flynn, 28). Some of Fowler's opinions that seem to run counter to his philanthropic principles, such as his surprising defence of Governor Eyre or his praise for the Congo regime of Leopold II, king of the Belgians, stem from his need to discover virtue in prescriptive authority, as did the childlike joy he took in the social condescension of the duke of Beaufort. It is a mentality he shared with many other successful businessmen.

H. L. MALCHOW

Sources J. S. Flynn, *Sir Robert N. Fowler, bart., a memoir* (1893) · H. L. Malchow, *Gentlemen capitalists: the social and political world of the Victorian businessman* (1991) · L. C. Fowler and J. E. Fowler, *A short account of the Fowler family from 1550 to 1891* (1891) · *Memoirs of Robert and Rachel Fowler* (1863) · R. N. Fowler, *A visit to Japan, China and India* (1877) · *ILN* (30 May 1891) · *Hansard 3* (1885), 300.1415 · Boase, *Mod. Eng. biog.* · *CGPLA Eng. & Wales* (1892) · *DNB*

Archives Bodl. Oxf., corresp. · Bodl. RH, corresp.

Likenesses J. Sperling, chalk drawing, *c.*1840, priv. coll. · F. Holl, portrait, 1885, Pitlochry · Sheldon?, bust, 1886, Guildhall, London · H. Manesse, etching, NPG · T. [T. Chartran], caricature, watercolour study, repro. in *VF* (25 June 1881) · marble bust, Gastard, near Corsham, Wiltshire · wood-engraving, NPG [*see illus.*]

Wealth at death £114,046 5*s.* 7*d.*: resworn probate, June 1892, *CGPLA Eng. & Wales* (1891)

Fowler, Thomas (1832–1904), philosopher and college head, was born at Burton upon Stather, Lincolnshire, on 1 September 1832, the eldest son of William Henry Fowler and his wife, Mary Anne Welch. His early intellectual development owed much to his uncle by marriage Joseph Fowler of Winterton, son of William Fowler (1761–1832).

After attending Hull grammar school and the private school of R. Ousby, curate of Kirton in Lindsey, Fowler entered as a day boy, in January 1848, King William's College, Isle of Man. Among his schoolfellows were Frederic William Farrar, Edward Spencer Beesly, and the poet Thomas Edward Brown, who, although a year and a half Fowler's senior, formed with him a lifelong friendship. In half-holiday walks with Brown, Fowler began to cultivate that eye for beauty in nature which always stimulated his zest for travel. On 31 May 1850 he matriculated at Oxford, aged seventeen, as postmaster of Merton College. In 1852 he obtained a first class in mathematical, and a second class in classical, moderations; and in the final examinations of 1854 a first in classics and a first in mathematics. In the same mathematical first classes was his friend Charles Lutwidge Dodgson (Lewis Carroll); together the two read mathematics privately with Professor Bartholomew Price.

As an undergraduate, Fowler was in full sympathy with the Oxford Movement, but about 1854, when he graduated BA, he gave up his Tractarian opinions and connections, as well as the conservative political views in which he had been brought up, and adopted what became established liberal, but moderate, opinions in theology and politics. In 1855 he was ordained, and became fellow and tutor of Lincoln College. In 1857 he became its sub-rector. In 1858 he won the Denyer theological prize for an essay on *The Doctrine of Predestination According to the Church of England*.

It was during the twenty-six years of his residence in Lincoln College (1855–81) that Fowler made his name as teacher, writer, and man of affairs. He was regarded there as a man of genuine scholarship, obvious intelligence, and extreme good nature. As a teacher, he excelled in the small conversational lecture and especially in the 'private hour', to which he devoted much time with individual pupils, trying to make them read and think for themselves. One of his earliest pupils at Lincoln was John Morley. Fowler was known for the extravagant breakfasts with which he would sometimes entertain pupils, during which fish, mutton, and beef were washed down with strong beer. He was an efficient administrator and during Mark Pattison's rectorship in particular he was a very active sub-rector. Despite Fowler's respect for Pattison's intellect and sympathy for his liberal aims, there was an antipathy between the two men. Pattison had failed to be elected to the rectorship in 1851 and was antagonistic towards the college regime under which Fowler had been elected a fellow; when Fowler became tutor in 1855 it was as a result of Pattison's acrimonious resignation. In 1861 Fowler's own defeat by Pattison in the election to the rectorship caused Fowler too to feel angry. And Pattison's ally Richard Christie criticized Fowler—'essentially a commonplace man' (Green, 267)—for his presumption in standing against Pattison.

Fowler first came into close touch with university business as proctor in 1862. From then on he took a leading part in it, either as member of congregation and of the hebdomadal council, or as delegate of the Clarendon press, the university museum, and the common university fund. He was reputed to be a disinterested administrator who displayed common sense and breadth and clearness of view. His opinions on university reform were influenced by Mark Pattison. Fowler gave evidence before the University of Oxford commissioners on 26 October 1877 on lines which followed Pattison's *Suggestions on Academical Organisation* (1868), advocating a transference of the more advanced teaching from the colleges to the university. In active co-operation with Henry Liddell, J. M. Wilson, Arthur Stanley, Jowett, and others, Fowler played an effective part in promoting the important series of reforms which included the establishment of natural science as a subject of serious study in the university, the removal of tests, and the various provisions, financial and other, made by the commissioners of 1877, especially those by which a career at Oxford was opened to men willing to devote themselves to study and teaching. Fowler was public examiner in the final classical school (1864–6, 1869–70, 1873, and 1878–9); and he was select preacher (1872–4).

In 1873 Fowler became Wykeham professor of logic, a position he held until 1889. He had already published his *Elements of Deductive Logic* (1867) and *Elements of Inductive Logic* (1870), which followed the lines of Mill's *Logic* and were much used as textbooks, reaching several editions. He went on to publish editions of Bacon's *Novum organum* (1878) and Locke's *Conduct of the Understanding* (1881), as well as monographs on Locke (notable for the historical setting of philosophical ideas), Bacon, and *Shaftesbury and Hutcheson* (1882). His *Progressive Morality* (1884) is a short, popular work in which moral experience is probed and analysed, always with the practical end in view of discovering principles for the education of character. *The Principles of Morals*, a more technical work, was published in two parts (1886, 1887), the first under the joint authorship of Fowler and J. M. Wilson, the second under Fowler's name alone. Working without significant innovation in the empiricist tradition Fowler displays, like Mill, a moderate utilitarianism and offers an Aristotelian notion of welfare in place of unrefined utility.

On 23 December 1881 Fowler was elected president of Corpus Christi College, to his own surprise and that of others. It was unusual at that time for a head of house to be chosen from outside the college, and Fowler only accepted the post after consultation with a Corpus Christi fellow, possibly Henry Smith, whom he had regarded as the heir apparent. At least one person was happy with the choice: Mark Pattison confided to Meta Bradley, 'what a relief it is to me that Fowler has removed to another college' (Green, 267). Fowler piloted Corpus skilfully through the difficulties of the period of transition which followed 1882, when the statutes made by the commissioners of 1877 came into operation, and won popularity among seniors and juniors. His exhaustive *History of Corpus* was published in 1893. In 1898 he issued a less elaborate account of the college in the Oxford College Histories series. He wrote several articles for the *Dictionary of National Biography*.

From 1899 to 1901 Fowler was vice-chancellor of the university. The work of the office was exceptionally heavy and undermined his health. The Second South African War was in progress, and he as vice-chancellor, by arrangement with the War Office, was responsible for selecting young university men for commissions in the army. He was largely responsible for overcoming the opposition in Oxford, originating in hostility to the Second South African War and expressed for example by Edward Caird, to conferring the honorary degree of DCL at the encaenia of 1899 upon Cecil Rhodes.

Fowler, who retained traces of his Lincolnshire accent, was a plump man with a 'round cheerful face' and a 'rolling, ungraceful gait'. He was made FSA in 1873 and an honorary LLD of Edinburgh in 1882, proceeded to the degree of DD in 1886, and was elected an honorary fellow of Lincoln in 1900. He died, unmarried, in the president's lodgings at Corpus Christi on 20 November 1904, and was buried in the cemetery at Winterton, Lincolnshire. In the church there a choir screen, with inscription, was erected to his memory; and there is a tablet in the cloister of Corpus. By his will he was a benefactor of the three colleges—

Merton, Lincoln, and Corpus—with which he had been connected. His books were bequeathed to the Wykeham professorship and placed in the philosophy library.

J. A. Stewart, *rev.* C. A. Creffield

Sources *The Times* (21 Nov 1904) · *The Athenaeum* (26 Nov 1904), 732 · *Oxford Magazine* (23 Nov 1904) · *WW* · R. Metz, *A hundred years of British philosophy*, ed. J. H. Muirhead, trans. J. W. Harvey (1938) [Ger. orig., *Die philophischen Strömungen der Gegenwart in Grossbritannien* (1935)] · V. H. H. Green, *Oxford common room* (1957) · C. M. Blayden, *Well remembered* (1953) · private information (1912) · personal knowledge (1912)
Archives CCC Oxf., papers | NL Scot., letters to Alexander Campbell Fraser
Likenesses F. T. D. [F. T. Dalton], caricature, chromolithograph, NPG; repro. in *VF* (2 Nov 1899)
Wealth at death £57,309 4*s.* 2*d.*: probate, 11 Jan 1905, *CGPLA Eng. & Wales*

Fowler, William (1560/61–1612), writer and courtier, was the son of Jane Fisher and William Fowler (*d.* 1572), a prominent Edinburgh burgess and treasurer of the French revenues of Mary, queen of Scots. Fowler's sister was the mother of the Scottish writer William Drummond of Hawthornden. From 1574 to 1578, Fowler appears to have been a student of St Leonard's College at the University of St Andrews, graduating MA in 1578. He continued his education in Europe, possibly studying civil law at the Collège de Navarre in Paris. His prose work, *An answer to the calumnious letter and erroneous propositiouns of an apostat named M. Io. Hammiltoun*, published by John Leprevik in 1581, records a theological controversy in which he became embroiled in Paris, ending in a violent contestation between the staunchly protestant Fowler and the Scottish Jesuit John Hamilton. Fowler's *Answer* is partly a personal account of what he terms religious persecution, and partly theological polemic.

Fowler's tract prefigures the relatively controversial public role which he assumed for the next decade when Marian political sensitivities and the threat of Catholic insurgency were intensified. Despite the fierce conviction of Fowler's protestantism, he was associated with Esmé Stewart, duke of Lennox, who was exiled from Scotland before his death on account of his Catholic affiliations. Fowler was briefly imprisoned in England because of visits to the French ambassador, Mauvissière (Fowler was allegedly the first to report Lennox's death to the latter). Given Fowler's own admitted association with 'the Frenche course and the Queen of Scotts' (*Works*, 3.xvii), his religious and therefore political allegiances were on occasions uncertain. As a consequence perhaps, he embarked on a brief career of espionage, employed in the service of Francis Walsingham, and was known as 'le petit Fouler'.

By 1584 Fowler was still in contact with Walsingham and English agents, but that year also marked his formal and literary entry into the inner Scottish court circle of James VI. Francis Stewart, first earl of Bothwell, presented Fowler with the parsonage of Hawick. As early as 1581 with the publication of *An Answer*, Bothwell had served as Fowler's literary patron; this patronage continued throughout Fowler's writing life with the exception of one dedication in 1587 to Lady Jean Fleming, wife of Sir John Maitland, chancellor and secretary to James and allegedly an enemy of Bothwell; Fowler's affinity with the controversial Bothwell occasionally courted disfavour.

In 1589 Fowler participated in the marriage negotiations between James and Anne, and travelled to Denmark. In November of that year he was appointed master of requests and 'secret-depute' to Anne. In the last decade of the sixteenth century Fowler appears to have travelled extensively in Italy, notably Padua and Venice. By 1603 he was clearly an established member of the Jacobean English court. Surviving documents and letters attest his acquaintance with Arabella Stuart (1575–1615), a relationship which acquired some notoriety on the basis of a number of playful, anagrammatic love poems which Fowler sent to Arabella. Arabella Stuart is possibly the beloved Bellisa of Fowler's amatory corpus. One 'dedication' seemingly alludes to Arabella's rejection of the political power which James, as her cousin, was always conscious she potentially possessed: 'whose chastfull hands disdayned for to sweye / both sceptars crovnes' (*Works*, 1.261; Lodge, 3.170). Arabella's name is the subject of copious anagrams throughout the Hawthornden papers. Fowler's Arabella lyrics probably belong to the first decade of the 1600s. In a letter of 1603 to the earl and countess of Shrewsbury, Fowler eulogizes Arabella as 'the e[i]ght[h] wonder off the world … to the first seven' (Lodge, 3.366–7); an image repeated in one of the *Tarantula of Love* sonnets (*Works*, 1.160).

By 1608 Fowler's position as secretary to Anne, a post in which John Donne showed interest, seems increasingly tenuous as his relationship with the queen became increasingly strained. Fowler died in 1612, in London, and was buried on 20 May in St Margaret's, Westminster. Fowler had married, though there is no record of his wife's name, and was survived by four children.

Fowler's surviving body of work is substantial: an amatory and philosophical sonnet sequence, *The Tarantula of Love*, and translations of the *Trionfi* of Petrarch and of Machiavelli's *Il principe*. Stylistically and thematically, these works demonstrate the markedly Italian influence on the literature associated with James's Scottish court in the 1580s. Fowler's *Triumphs* (1587) demonstrates the rhetorical amplification of contemporary Scottish writing; the *Tarantula* shows Fowler's verbal adroitness as a petrarchist but one also committed to profound philosophical and religious exploration. Fowler also attempted a number of psalm translations, modelled on those of Theodore Beza. There is a substantial amount of unpublished manuscript material which reveals Fowler's fascination with emblem writing and the composition of anagrams, as well as a wealth of occasional, social, and funeral verse (one recipient was Sir Edward Dymok). Little of his writing was published, excluding *An Answer*, early dedicatory sonnets to James (1584) and Thomas Hudson (1584), and two funeral poems including an epitaph on the death of Robert Bowes (1597). *A true reportarie of the most triumphant, and royal accomplishment of the baptisme of the most excellent, right high, and mightie prince, Frederick Henry; by the grace of God, prince of Scotland* (1594) has been attributed to him.

S. M. DUNNIGAN

Sources NL Scot., Hawthornden MSS 2063–2065 · a copy of *The tarantula*, U. Edin. L., Drummond MSS, MS De.3.68, fols. 1–36v · presentation copy of Fowler's translation of Petrarch's *Trionfi*, U. Edin. L., MS De.1.10 · *The works of William Fowler*, ed. H. W. Meikle, J. Craigie, and J. Purves, 3 vols., STS, new ser., 6 (1914), STS, 3rd ser., 7, 13 (1936–40) · H. W. Meikle, 'The life and works of William Fowler', in *The works of William Fowler*, ed. H. W. Meikle, J. Craigie, and J. Purves, 3, STS, 3rd ser., 13 (1940), ix–xlii · J. Purves, 'Fowler and Scoto-Italian cultural relations in the sixteenth century', in *The works of William Fowler*, ed. H. W. Meikle, J. Craigie, and J. Purves, 3, STS, 3rd ser., 13 (1940), lxxx–cl · R. D. S. Jack, *The Italian influence on Scottish literature* (1972) · R. D. S. Jack, 'William Fowler and Italian literature', *Modern Language Review*, 65 (1970), 481–92 · R. D. S. Jack, 'Poetry under King James VI', *The history of Scottish literature*, ed. C. Craig, 1: *Origins to 1660*, ed. R. D. S. Jack (1987), 125–40 · E. Lodge, *Illustrations of British history, biography, and manners*, 3 (1791) · E. Cooper, *The life and letters of Lady Arabella Stuart*, 2 vols. (1866), vol. 1, p. 277 · E. T. Bradley, *Life of the Lady Arabella Stuart*, 2 vols. (1889), vol. 1, pp. 70, 174 · D. N. Durant, *Arbella Stuart: a rival to the queen* (1978) · *Scots peerage*

Archives NL Scot., MSS, MSS 2063–2067 · U. Edin. L., MSS, MSS De.1.10, De.3.68, La.II.52 | NA Scot., Warrender MSS

Wealth at death est. over £300: Meikle, Craigie, and Purves, eds. *Works of William Fowler*; E. M. Thompson, 'The daughter of Anne of Denmark's secretary', *SHR*, 19 (1921), 23–4

Fowler, William (1761–1832), architect and artist, was born at Winterton, Lincolnshire, on 13 March 1761, the eldest in the numerous family of Joseph Fowler (1734–1822) and his wife, Mary, formerly Tomlinson. Following a modest education under Mr Teanby, the village schoolmaster, he went on to run a successful enterprise as a builder and architect, with all the woodwork done at Winterton under his own eye by a large staff. He married on 23 May 1790 Rebecca Hill (1757–1820); their three sons, Joseph (1791–1882), William (1795–1815), and James (1799–1816), assisted him in the building trade. There were also two daughters, Rebecca (1793–1814) and Mary Ann (1803–1858). Fowler was strongly Wesleyan by persuasion—a chapel had been built at Winterton in 1777—but he remained faithful to the Anglican church.

By dint of working long hours Fowler produced many drawings of old buildings, tombs and brasses, stained glass, and Roman mosaic pavements. The first such pavement had been excavated at Winterton; Fowler sketched it, then another pavement uncovered nearby, then a magnificent example in Admiral Shirley's garden at Horkstow, when he was encouraged to have his drawings engraved so that copies could be distributed. The Winterton and Horkstow pavements were engraved in 1796 by his brother-in-law John Hill, a London craftsman, but Fowler taught himself to engrave and print the remainder of his output, some 114 illustrations; some of these were coloured with the help of his sister Ann. The prints were initially issued separately but in 1804 and 1809 were bound in three sets, identified as one volume and two appendices, dedicated to Sir Joseph Banks, a Lincolnshire landowner and president of the Royal Society.

In search of topics, Fowler visited ecclesiastical buildings, colleges, and stately homes across the northern and

William Fowler (1761–1832), by William Bond, 1810 (after George Francis Joseph)

midland counties, and included the mosaic fronting Thomas Becket's tomb at Canterbury. Banks carried his fame to the royal family, and he was invited to Windsor to show his drawings to the queen and princess. In 1821 he travelled via Alnwick to Edinburgh, and met Sir Walter Scott at Abbotsford.

Fowler endeavoured to obtain fidelity by working from tracings and rubbings, reducing the scale by means of a pantograph. It is said that he was the first to show the lead when illustrating stained glass. Banks remarked to the Society of Antiquaries, 'Others have shown us what they thought these remains ought to have been, but Fowler has shown us what they are; and this is what we want' (Ball). Fowler's productions were not, however, universally admired. The antiquary Samuel Lysons, who had been working on the Horkstow pavement, wrote to Banks in 1797 that he found the mosaic far better than Fowler's plate had led him to expect. Except for the chariot race, said Lysons, Fowler's plate was very inaccurate, but it contained portions since destroyed. Furthermore, Fowler had objected to Lysons making a drawing of it and seemed to regard it as his own property.

Although the first volume of Fowler's plates attracted 425 subscribers, the later volumes were less well supported, and the scarcity of prints in later years suggests that few sets were sold. After his wife's death Fowler retired to the 'Gothic Cottage' which his father had built, where he was cared for by his widowed sister-in-law. He died on 22 September 1832 and was buried at Winterton.

ANITA MCCONNELL

Sources H. W. Ball, 'Notes on William Fowler and his works', *North Lincolnshire Monthly Illustrated Journal* (April 1869) · *The Banks letters*, ed. W. R. Dawson (1958) · *Bibliotheca Lindesiana, collations and notes*, no. 2 (1883) · *GM*, 1st ser., 102/2 (1832), 389 · Colvin, *Archs.*, 379 · J. Fowler, *Wesleyan Magazine* (April 1834) · will, Lincs. Arch., Stow wills, 1831–33/56 · *The correspondence of William Fowler, of Winterton, in the county of Lincoln*, ed. J. T. Fowler (1907)
Archives Lincs. Arch., corresp. · S. Antiquaries, Lond., scrapbook of publications, sketches, brass rubbings and corresp.
Likenesses W. Bond, stipple, 1810 (after G. F. Joseph), BM, NPG [*see illus.*]
Wealth at death £200: PRO, IR 26/1290, fols. 123*v*–124*r*

Fowler, William (1828–1905), financier and politician, born at Melksham, Wiltshire, on 28 July 1828, was the fourth son of John Fowler (1792–1861) and his wife, Rebecca Hull (1799–1842), daughter of William and Jenny Hull of Uxbridge. His family were zealous members of the Society of Friends (Quakers) and his grandfather Robert Fowler (1755–1825) was for many years a Quaker minister having a 'concern' for the people of Ireland and France. In 1790 he had married Rachael Barnard (1767–1833) of Coalbrookdale. This union had provided links with the great Quaker dynasties—the Wilsons of Kendal, the Peases of Darlington, the Waterhouses of Liverpool, the Lloyds of Birmingham, and the Gurneys of Norwich.

After receiving a rudimentary education in Melksham (1836–45), in 1845 Fowler was sent to University College in London. He was always regarded as the brightest of John Fowler's five sons and in 1849 at the age of twenty obtained a BA with honours in classics and mathematics. In 1850 he graduated LLB and became a fellow of the college. He then joined the chambers of Hugh Cairns, later lord chancellor, and became an equity draftsman and conveyancer. In 1852 he was called to the bar at the Inner Temple. In 1856 he joined Cuncliffe Alexander & Co. of Lombard Street.

Alexanders, Overend and Gurney, and the National Discount Company constituted at this time the 'big three' bill brokers in the City. After 1860 Overend and Gurney became involved in a series of unfortunate transactions. There was a run on the banks, precipitated not by the size of the firm's losses but by the ensuing publicity, and they were ruined. The great crash, known as 'black Friday' came on 11 May 1866. British credit sustained a severe blow which took many years to recover. Fowler, then a partner in Alexander & Co., was at the centre of this disaster which left him financially embarrassed for many years. He published *The Crisis of 1866: a Financial Essay* (1866). On his retirement from Alexander & Co. in 1877 Fowler was appointed a director of the National Discount Company and various other City institutions.

In November 1868 Fowler stood for parliament as a Liberal candidate, and won the Cambridge seat, which he held until defeated in February 1874. He took a particular interest in the concentration of landownership; a Cobden Club essay by him on the laws affecting the tenure of land was published in 1872. His parliamentary speech on the Contagious Diseases Acts was also published (1870). He was a patron of the Howard League for prison reform.

After standing unsuccessfully for Northampton in October 1874, he regained his Cambridge seat in April 1880 but lost it again in November 1885. Declining to follow Gladstone's Irish home-rule policy, he unsuccessfully stood for Perth as a Liberal Unionist in July 1886. He remained a keen supporter of free trade. His essay on the appreciation of gold was published by the Cobden Club in 1886; an essay by him on Indian currency appeared in 1899.

Following the death in 1864 of his elder brother John *Fowler, 'father of the steam plough', William Fowler became a junior partner with his younger, unmarried brother Barnard Fowler (1833–1882) in the manufacturing business founded by John in Leeds. Their elder brother Robert Fowler (1825–1888) was senior partner. When the company became incorporated in 1886, the three brothers, together with their nephew Robert Henry Fowler (1851–1919), son of Henry Fowler (1823–1880), the eldest of the Fowler brothers, became directors. William Fowler was chairman of the company from 1888 until his death. He took little part in the day-to-day management of the company, but regularly attended board meetings and social events such as the foreman's annual dinner. His last appearance was at the company's seventeenth annual general meeting, held in Lombard Street in December 1903.

Fowler married three times. First, on 9 August 1855, he married Rachel Maria, daughter of Robert Howard of Ackworth in Yorkshire, a manufacturing chemist. Her mother was one of the Birmingham Lloyd family. They had four sons and four daughters before she died in 1868. Second, in 1871 he married Elizabeth Fox, daughter of Francis Tuckett of Frenchay, near Bristol. She died later the same year. Third, in 1875 he married Rachel, *née* Pease, widow of Charles Albert Leatham of York and daughter of Joseph *Pease MP [*see under* Pease, Edward]. Her younger sister Elizabeth Lucy Pease was the wife of William's brother John. William Fowler died in Folkestone, Kent, on 16 September 1905 and was buried in Tunbridge Wells four days later. Several obituary notices described him as a man of remarkable powers, with a tender heart.

MICHAEL R. LANE

Sources *Cambridge Chronicle and University Journal* (22 Sept 1905) · *Cambridge Daily News* (20 Sept 1905) · U. Reading, Rural History Centre, Museum of English Rural Life, family archives · priv. coll., family archives · John Fowler & Co. (Leeds) Ltd. board minute-books and other documents, priv. coll. · RS Friends, Lond. · P. H. Emden, *Quakers in commerce: a record of business achievement* (1939) · T. Davis, *John Fowler and the business he founded* (1951) · M. R. Lane, *The story of the Steam Plough Works: Fowlers of Leeds* (1980)
Archives U. Reading, Rural History Centre, collection | BL, corresp. with W. E. Gladstone, Add. MSS 44394–44488 · King's AC Cam., letters to Oscar Browning · Wellcome L., letters to John Hodgkin
Likenesses portrait, repro. in *ILN* (1888)
Wealth at death £6721 13*s*.: probate, 3 Nov 1905, CGPLA Eng. & Wales

Fowler, William Warde (1847–1921), historian and ornithologist, was born at Langford Budville, Somerset, on 16 May 1847, the second son of John Coke Fowler, stipendiary magistrate at Merthyr Tudful and afterwards at Swansea, and his first wife, Augusta Bacon, granddaughter of John Bacon RA. After two years at the school of the Revd Francis Kilvert at Bath, and tuition from his father, in 1860 he went to Marlborough College, where he was taught by Francis Edward Thompson. He entered New College, Oxford, in 1866, and after a term won a scholarship at Lincoln College, where he became the favourite and later friend of Mark Pattison, the rector, with whom he shared his interests in natural history and German scholarship. The portrait of Pattison in Lincoln College hall was Fowler's gift. He also enjoyed contact with Henry Nettleship. After being awarded a first class in classics in 1870, he became fellow of Lincoln College in 1872, and tutor and dean in 1873, teaching Roman history for his own college and Oriel. As a tutor he was highly regarded and keen to help his students to form their own opinions. Among his academic circle were Baldwin Spencer, Percy Gardner, and J. A. R. Munro. He was librarian from 1881 and in the same year was appointed as the first lay sub-rector in the history of the college, a position he held until 1904. During this period he was a central figure in the college, though he had little interest in enforcing discipline or chapel attendance. Temperamentally, Fowler was conservative, even resisting the introduction of electricity into his college rooms. Politically, he always called himself a Liberal, was initially a home-ruler, and later became a Liberal Unionist; after the First World War he declared his sympathy with the international outlook of Labour. He remained tutor until 1910, and then retired to Kingham, where, since 1873, he had enjoyed a country home and entertained his pupils. From 1899 he lived there with his sister Alice, and, after her death in 1917, with his two younger sisters, until his death, on 15 June 1921.

Fowler's interests and works were varied. His love and pursuit of music were lifelong and he published a work on Mozart, his favourite composer. By long and patient observation, overcoming defects of sight and hearing, he became an authority on birds and their migrations. He published several works on the subject, which were highly praised, including a special contribution to the life history of the marsh warbler. His *Kingham, Old and New* (1913) is an attractive record. A familiar figure in Oxford, Fowler shrank from public affairs, but enjoyed being a curator of the parks and of the botanic garden. His ideal of a university is expressed in *An Oxford Correspondence* (1903), in which he criticizes the lack of learning at Oxford and praises contemporary German methods of scholarship, a position he continued to maintain during the war.

Fowler's central interest was Rome, especially Rome of the republic, and his lectures on these subjects were very popular. His most original and convincing work is to be found in his writings on Roman religion: the *Roman Festivals of the Period of the Republic* (1899), the Gifford lectures on the *Religious Experience of the Roman People* (1911), and *Roman Ideas of Deity* (1914). These works, especially the first, established Fowler's reputation in Europe and America as an authority in this field, and he published several articles in Germany, where he was particularly well regarded. He published many other works on different areas of Roman

history and its social aspects, including *Roman Essays and Interpretations* (1920), and *Social Life at Rome in the Age of Cicero* (1908), as well as a popular life of Caesar, which relied heavily on the views of Mommsen. In later life he published three studies of the *Aeneid* (1915-19), which were respected, and *Essays in Brief for Wartime* (1916; 2nd edn, 1917). He was awarded an honorary LLD from Edinburgh and DLitt from Manchester. He was president of the Classical Association in 1920.

P. E. MATHESON, *rev.* MYFANWY LLOYD

Sources W. W. Fowler, *Reminiscences* (1921) · R. H. Coon, *William Warde Fowler* (1934) · V. Green, *The commonwealth of Lincoln College, 1427–1977* (1979), 518–22 · P. E. M., 'To W. W. F., on reading his "Death of Turnus"', *Oxford Magazine* (20 Oct 1921), 9 · E., 'William Warde Fowler', *Oxford Magazine* (20 Oct 1921), 11–12 · G. P. Gooch, *History and historians in the nineteenth century*, 4th edn (1928) · B. W. Henderson, 'Warde Fowler: a sketch', *Fortnightly Review*, 117 (1922), 148–53 · Foster, *Alum. Oxon.* · Allibone, *Dict.*
Archives Lincoln College, Oxford, papers and diaries | BL, letters to C. C. Bell and H. I. Bell, Add. MS 42711 · BL, corresp. with Macmillans, Add. MS 55121 · Bodl. Oxf., letters to Percy Gardner
Likenesses photographs, *c.*1887, repro. in Coon, *William Warde Fowler* · A. Macdonald, oils, 1907, Lincoln College, Oxford
Wealth at death £11,539 0s. 5d.: resworn probate, Sept 1922, *CGPLA Eng. & Wales* (1921)

Fownes, George (1815–1849), chemist, was born on 14 May 1815, the eldest son of John Fownes (d. 1854), glover of Coventry Street, London. Following education at Enfield and at Bourbourg near Gravelines, France, he was apprenticed to his father until 1837. However, his interests were scientific and during the early 1830s he joined the Western Literary and Scientific Institution in Leicester Square (founded 1825). There he formed a philosophical class with Thomas Everitt, Robert Murray, Henry Watts, and others for their mutual improvement. Fownes's connection with this group continued when he was a pupil of Everitt, by then professor of chemistry at the Middlesex Hospital, between 1837 and 1839. During this period Fownes worked with Justus Liebig at Giessen, where he matriculated in 1838 (he obtained his PhD there in 1841). After his return to London, Fownes was assistant to Thomas Graham at University College for a year before being appointed lecturer in chemistry at Charing Cross Hospital. This position, which he held until 1842, gave him an entrée to the London scientific community. From 1841 to 1845 he delivered a Friday evening discourse each year at the Royal Institution as well as two courses of lectures on chemistry in 1842 and 1843, the latter course being repeated at the London Institution in 1844. He was an original member of the Chemical Society (founded 1841) and one of its secretaries between 1842 and 1848.

Fownes's excellence as a lecturer and as a chemist prompted Michael Faraday, albeit as his third choice, to offer him, in 1842, the professorship of chemistry at King's College, Toronto, but he declined on the grounds of his father's ill health. Although there were few openings for chemists in academic institutions in London, the teaching hospitals, with their requirement that chemistry be taught to medical students, offered a career path for many aspiring chemists. In 1842 Fownes was appointed professor of chemistry to the Pharmaceutical Society and succeeded Everitt at the Middlesex Hospital. He held the latter position until 1845 and the former until 1846 when he became professor of practical chemistry in the Birkbeck laboratory at University College, with Watts as his assistant.

Of Fownes's five books, *Chemistry, as Exemplifying the Wisdom and Beneficence of God* won the first Actonian prize offered by the Royal Institution in 1844, and *A Manual of Elementary Chemistry, Theoretical and Practical* (1844) became an important textbook. Edited by August Wilhelm Hofmann, Henry Bence Jones, and Watts, it had gone through thirteen editions by 1883. Fownes was elected a fellow of the Royal Society in 1845 and published four out of his total of eighteen papers in its *Philosophical Transactions*, including his discoveries of benzoline and furfuramide; he received its gold medal in 1847.

From about 1844 Fownes's health declined because of pulmonary disease. Visits to Switzerland (1846) and Barbados (1847–8) were of no avail and he died in his father's house in Grange Terrace, Brompton, on 31 January 1849.

FRANK A. J. L. JAMES

Sources *Quarterly Journal of the Chemical Society*, 2 (1850), 184–7 · *Pharmaceutical Journal and Transactions*, 8 (1848–9), 449–50 · J. S. Rowe, 'The life and work of George Fownes', *Annals of Science*, 6 (1948–50), 422–35 · *The correspondence of Michael Faraday*, ed. F. A. J. L. James, 3 (1996) · *Abstracts of the Papers Communicated to the Royal Society of London*, 5 (1843–50), 882–3 · *Catalogue of scientific papers*, Royal Society, 2 (1868), 691 · database of lecturers, Royal Institution of Great Britain, London · J. S. Fruton, *Contrasts in scientific styles: research groups in the chemical and biological sciences* (1990) · *GM*, 2nd ser., 42 (1854), 534

Likenesses C. Cook, stipple and line print (after a photograph by Collins), NPG · portrait, repro. in Rowe, 'Life and work of George Fownes', following p. 422 · two photographs, RS

Fowns, Richard (1561/2–1625), Church of England clergyman and religious controversialist, was born in Worcestershire, the son of a clergyman. He was elected student of Christ Church, Oxford, in 1577. He matriculated on 20 November 1581, aged nineteen, graduated BA on 30 January 1582, and proceeded MA on 3 April 1585. On 28 February 1586 he was installed as rector of Hill Croome in his native county.

Having on 16 May 1605 proceeded BD and DD, on 10 July 1606 Fowns lectured at Oxford on 2 Thessalonians 2: 3–4. This fiercely anti-papal sermon on the Antichrist was published in the same year as *Concio ad clerum* and dedicated to Henry, prince of Wales, whose chaplain Fowns became. Further preferment came when he was presented to the rectory of Severn Stoke, Worcestershire, on 6 January 1612. Fowns later worked up his sermon into an 800-page treatise, *Trisagion, or, The three holy offices of Jesus Christ, the sonne of God, priestly, propheticall, and regall; how they ought to all his church to be received, with a declaration of the violence and injuries offered unto the same by the spirituall and Romish Babylon*, published in 1618 and reissued in 1619. The three parts of this work were dedicated to Prince Charles, to Archbishop George Abbot, and to Lord Chancellor Francis Bacon. They set out the nature of Antichrist and identified

him firmly with the Roman Catholic church, as well as looking for signs of his imminent fall in recent events at home and abroad. Fowns died in 1625 and was buried in the church at Severn Stoke on 25 November; his monument was 'miserably defaced' (Wood, 2.388–9) during the civil war.

GORDON GOODWIN, *rev.* SCOTT MANDELBROTE

Sources Foster, *Alum. Oxon.* · Wood, *Ath. Oxon.*, new edn, 2.388–9 · T. R. Nash, *Collections for a history of Worcestershire*, 2 vols. (1781–2) · *CSP dom.*, *addenda, 1580–1625* · P. E. McCullough, *Sermons at court: politics and religion in Elizabethan and Jacobean preaching* (1998) [incl. CD-ROM]

Fox, Albert (1857–1914), trade union leader and politician, was born at Farnborough, Hampshire, on 7 April 1857, the son of Charles Fox, a private in the 22nd regiment, and his wife, Marcia. He attended the board school at Farnborough until he was twelve, and in his early years was drawn towards railway life. In the early 1880s Fox got a job as an engine cleaner at the Mexborough railway depot. The Associated Society of Locomotive Engineers and Firemen (ASLEF) did not admit engine cleaners as members at that time, but in 1886 when he was promoted to fireman he immediately joined the union and played an active role, becoming secretary of the local branch. He noticed that every year some five new orphans resulted from accidental, or other, deaths of members, and in 1889, when he was member of the national executive for Yorkshire, he carried a resolution establishing an orphan fund. When Thomas G. Sunter, the union's general secretary, died on 20 September 1901, a ballot was held to determine his successor and on 8 December Fox was elected.

With new leadership there were important changes in policy. At the union's triennial conference held in Swansea in 1903 it was resolved that membership should be open to engine cleaners and electric motormen. Funds were to be centralized, and an organizing secretary was to be appointed. It was also agreed that the society should affiliate to the Labour Representation Committee and contest a parliamentary constituency. In accordance with the new forward-looking policy, Fox stood in the 1906 general election as the Labour candidate for the South Leeds constituency, where the ASLEF head office was located. In the light of his late adoption he did well to poll 4030 votes to the victorious Liberal's 6200. In a by-election in the same constituency in 1908 he did less well, being beaten into third place by the tory candidate.

Throughout his years as general secretary Fox claimed that it was essential for locomotive men to be organized separately from other railway workers. He expressed this view in evidence given to the royal commission on the railway conciliation scheme of 1907. At a conference with the Amalgamated Society of Railway Servants (ASRS) in 1903 to discuss closer co-operation he said: 'It was not merely a question of hours and wages with enginemen. There are 101 ways in which they need protection in their calling which are not known to other workers and which can only be taken in hand by themselves' (McKillop, 79). Fox's policy was summed up in the words 'Organise your craft: federate your union'. At about this time J. H. Thomas of the ASRS pointed out that his union had more locomotive grade members than ASLEF. Not surprisingly the ASRS favoured amalgamation rather than federation, and the negotiations broke down. Nevertheless, during Albert Fox's time as general secretary ASLEF membership rose steadily (from 10,502 in 1901 to 32,200 in 1913), thus strengthening the society's claim to speak for a majority of the 62,000 members of the locomotive grades.

Although ASLEF's programme before 1914 included a maximum eight-hour working day, Fox told a conference called in support of Walter Hudson's Eight Hours Bill that he had no mandate to go to the House of Commons to secure it 'since they felt that if they asked the companies they would get it' (*Report of a Conference*, 10). Fox could, however, act decisively when events required, as happened in August 1911, when the companies refused to recognize the unions and he moved the resolution at ASLEF's Liverpool conference for a national railway strike at twenty-four hours' notice.

Albert Fox was an enthusiastic leader of the locomotive engineer and fireman, but as the union's historian admitted 'he lacked the gift of directing others to share the burden of great administration' (Raynes, 161). Fox's health collapsed in 1912, and he was granted an increase in salary of £50 p.a. and three months' leave, but he failed to recover. He died of pernicious anaemia at his home at 33 Spencer Place, Leeds, on 22 March 1914, and was buried at Beeston cemetery in south Leeds on 27 March 1914. He was survived by his wife, Mary E. Fox, and by one son and one daughter.　　　　　　　　　　　　PHILIP S. BAGWELL

Sources F. Bealey and H. Pelling, *Labour and politics, 1900–1906: a history of the Labour Representation Committee* (1958) · J. R. Raynes, *Engines and men* (1921) · N. McKillop, *The lighted flame: a history of the Associated Society of Locomotive Engineers and Firemen* (1950) · P. S. Bagwell, *The railwaymen: the history of the National Union of Railwaymen*, [1] (1963), esp. chaps. 4, 6 · H. A. Clegg, A. Fox, and A. F. Thompson, *A history of British trade unions since 1889*, 1 (1964) · 'Royal commission on the railway conciliation scheme of 1907', *Parl. papers* (1912–13), 45.17, Cd 6014 · *Report of a conference on the railways eight-hour bill, summoned by the TUC*, 28 April 1911 · 'Select committee on railway servants', *Parl. papers* (1892), 16.1, no. 125; 16.123, no. 246 · *Journal* [Associated Society of Locomotive Engineers and Firemen] (1883–1914) · b. cert. · d. cert.

Archives U. Warwick Mod. RC, MSS

Likenesses photograph, Associated Society of Locomotive Engineers and Firemen, 9 Arkwright Road, London

Wealth at death £711 0s. 10d.: probate, 27 July 1915, CGPLA Eng. & Wales

Fox, (Georgiana) Caroline [née Lady (Georgiana) Caroline Lennox], *suo jure* **Baroness Holland of Holland** (1723–1774), noblewoman, was born on 27 March 1723 at Richmond House in Whitehall, London, the eldest child of Charles *Lennox, second duke of Richmond and Lennox (1701–1750), and his wife, Lady Sarah Cadogan (1706–1751), daughter of William, first Earl Cadogan. Among Caroline's eleven siblings were Emilia Mary [see Fitzgerald, Emilia Mary, duchess of Leinster], Charles *Lennox, third duke of Richmond and Lennox, Lord George Henry *Lennox, Sarah (d. 1826) [see Napier, Lady Sarah], and Louisa Augusta (d. 1805) [see Conolly, Lady Louisa Augusta]. Her upbringing reflected her status as the daughter of one of

(Georgiana) Caroline Fox [Lady (Georgiana) Caroline Lennox], *suo jure* **Baroness Holland of Holland (1723–1774)**, by Allan Ramsay, 1766

the country's premier aristocratic families. Often at court, where her father held high office, she was educated partly in French and was allowed to develop a penchant for Roman history, as well as to indulge herself in the lighter and more fashionable reading of the day. Serious in character, she displayed both the early maturity and the insecurity of the firstborn. Though the strength of her parents' marriage provided a certain stability during her adolescence, the rational tone of the Richmond household failed to assuage her deepest anxieties about the future. Marriage was, inevitably, the issue of her life; and given her position at the apex of society there was the danger that her parents might arrange a union without due regard for her feelings. Ultimately irreligious, and mistrustful of the world, she snatched at love for fear that it would pass her by.

The crucial moment for Caroline seemed to have arrived when Henry *Fox (1705–1774), an aspiring politician nearly twenty years her senior, became the focus of her feelings around 1742. A *habitué* of Richmond House for a number of years, he had watched Caroline closely as she emerged into maturity. The sincerity and strength of his passion for her were compelling, and Caroline responded in like measure. But in the eyes of her parents, and in particular of her mother, Fox was simply too much the *parvenu* to be acceptable as a son-in-law. The duchess summarily rejected his approaches on the subject of marriage in March 1744; she believed that her daughter would cool once the family moved to the rural seclusion of Goodwood for the summer. Fox, too, shared this view—he did not trust time, or Caroline, to do his work for him. He pressed her into making an immediate choice between himself and her parents, leaving her no way out but pain in greater or lesser degree. Caught between her fears, she agreed to go through with a clandestine marriage on 2 May 1744, at the home of Sir Charles Hanbury Williams, and was immediately ostracized by her own family and society at large.

Yet the first decade of Caroline's married life seemed, on the whole, to vindicate her choice of evils. Her initial uncertainties about the strength of her husband's commitment to her dissolved as children came and grew. Their illnesses certainly generated anxiety, but three of the four sons she gave birth to between 1745 and 1755 survived (among them Henry Edward *Fox), and family life at Holland House, open and casual in tone, appeared to betoken contentment. Fox's career, too, seemed to prosper, and although his ascent towards the highest reaches of government reduced the time that he could give to his family, his good humour was grounded in devotion to his wife and children. There was even a reconciliation with the Richmonds, who could not harden their hearts against a grandchild; in March 1748 Caroline was readmitted, in large measure at least, to the good graces of her parents. This mitigated some of the grief when death removed them both before the end of 1751. Caroline now had her own family, thriving and accepted, to occupy and sustain her.

But no aspect of this fulfilment survived intact beyond the mid-1750s. For one thing, Caroline had failed to repair completely her status as the eldest Lennox of her generation. Her act of disobedience in 1744, though formally forgiven, still ensured that her father's will assigned care of his three infant daughters to Caroline's younger sister Emily, now countess of Kildare. This rankled. Despite a deep affection for one another, Caroline and Emily quarrelled bitterly in 1758 and again in 1769 over the upbringing of their siblings—and in between there were reminders enough for Caroline of how her position had been permanently usurped. Even as a matchmaker she could not dominate, as in the negotiations with Gertrude Russell (née Leveson-Gower), duchess of Bedford, over the marriage of her eldest son. Then, too, her husband's political fortunes waned sharply after 1756, breeding in him a bitterness that percolated from the public realm into the home. This confirmed Caroline's aversion to the political world. While interested enough in gossip relating to it and ever prepared to listen to her husband's troubles, she had no wish to play the role of political wife, either as hostess or as private adviser. In her eyes politics, and especially Fox's political friends (for most of whom she cared little), simply drew her husband away from home. It was little, if any, consolation that, while paymaster-general in the Newcastle administration, Fox successfully sought a peerage for her, and she was created Lady Holland, baroness of Holland, on 3 May 1762. Some of Fox's enemies thought that her influence was decisive in Fox's refusal to become first lord of the Treasury in 1763, but he had more than enough reasons of his own to walk away from such a promotion. Caroline was glad enough to see him retreat from front-line politics shortly thereafter, but Fox's elevation to the Lords did nothing to temper the feelings of bitterness and betrayal that had grown steadily since the crisis of 1756 that had wrecked his career.

Ever since that year, Caroline had watched this blight from the political world eat away gradually at the life of her family. Her two eldest sons, Stephen and the precocious Charles James *Fox, felt the full effect of their father's disillusion with life. They had already had to contend with his reckless indulgence of them, and now they were further warped by being conscripted into Fox's campaign of hate and revenge against his political enemies. Caroline had not the strength to protect them against such irresponsibility. Having flouted the discipline of her own father and mother, she was in no position to fill the vacuum of parental authority created by her husband. Nor had she any beliefs of her own strong enough to counteract Fox's pervasive cynicism. She had no option but to endure the gradual spoiling of her two elder children.

Despite the foreign excursions that were possible, and indeed necessary, once Fox had retired completely from politics in the mid-1760s, Caroline's last years were a mounting torment. Despite her entreaties Stephen and Charles James could not, or would not, control the gambling that steadily squandered their father's fortune and precipitated his stroke in October 1773. Suffering from cancer, Caroline began to experience increasingly acute physical pain herself, which she tried to fight but in which, for all her intelligence, she could not find the least meaning. Even so she had to watch as her husband passed genially into oblivion, intent only on escaping easily from life while she battled vainly to find a way through her own mortal illness. His death on 1 July 1774 left her stranded, alone and badly frightened on the verge. Her final agony, measured in days, lasted until the 24th of the same month. She died at her London home, Holland House, Kensington, and was buried at Farley in Wiltshire shortly afterwards.

PETER LUFF

Sources S. Tillyard, *Aristocrats: Caroline, Emily, Louisa and Sarah Lennox, 1740–1832* (1994) · Earl of Ilchester [G. S. Holland Fox-Strangways], *Henry Fox, first Lord Holland, his family and relations*, 2 vols. (1920) · BL, Holland House papers, Add. MSS 47568, 47570 · NL Ire., Leinster papers · *Correspondence of Emily, duchess of Leinster (1731–1814)*, ed. B. Fitzgerald, 3 vols., IMC (1949–57), vol. 1 · Suffolk RO, Bury St Edmunds, Bunbury papers · W. Sussex RO, Goodwood MSS · L. Mitchell, *Holland House* (1980) · Princess Marie Liechtenstein, *Holland House*, 3rd edn, 2 vols. in 1 (1875) · GEC, *Peerage*, new edn

Archives BL, Holland House papers, Add. MSS 47568, 47570 · NL Ire., Leinster papers

Likenesses A. Ramsay, portrait, 1766, priv. coll. [*see illus.*]

Wealth at death estate subject to serious legal action over Lord Holland's pay office accounts: Earl of Ilchester, *Henry Fox*, 2.356–7

Fox, Caroline (1767–1845), diarist and correspondent, was born on 3 November 1767 at Lord Holland's house at Piccadilly, London. She was the daughter of Stephen Fox, second Baron Holland (1745–1774), and his wife, Lady Mary Fitzpatrick (1746/7–1778), sister of John, second earl of Upper Ossory. Caroline Fox was the elder of two children, her brother, Henry Richard *Fox, succeeding as third Baron Holland on the death of their father in November 1774. Her mother died in October 1778 and she was placed in the care of her step-aunt Henrietta Vernon, wife of George Greville, second earl of Warwick. Three years later she was removed to the household of Gertrude, duchess of

Bedford, her great-aunt, who had three orphaned grandsons to bring up. In 1779 her mother's sister Lady Louisa Fitzpatrick married Lord Shelburne and after 1781 Caroline Fox found more congenial society at the Shelburne house at Bowood in Wiltshire. She developed a deep attachment to her youngest step-aunt, Elizabeth Vernon, Aunt Ebey (*c*.1763?–1829). This was based partly on the shared interests of the Enlightenment, though the relationship did limit her social and political activities. Between 1804 and 1829 they lived together at Little Holland House until Elizabeth Vernon's death.

Though educated by private tutors, Caroline also learned much from her affectionate uncle, Charles James *Fox, and the savants of Bowood, who included Jeremy Bentham, P. E. Dumont, Samuel Romilly, and Jan Ingenhousz. Bentham, not her only suitor, dared to propose marriage and, though refused, retained a romantic attachment to her. Of a modest and patient disposition, she could be forthright in conversation. In politics Caroline Fox was a firm supporter of the Foxite whig party. As a young woman her opinions verged on the republican and Jacobinical. She kept the party's transcripts of the trial of the leading United Irishmen before secret committees of the Lords and Commons (1798), so that these could be compared to the official version. Her papers and commonplace books contain accounts of political negotiations and important political events associated with her family, and her correspondence, particularly with Charles James Fox and the third and fourth lords Holland, contains vignettes of politicians and lively comment. Her journals also give details of her travels in Europe.

An aristocratic outsider, 'dear little auntie' was beloved in the family for her high principles and tolerant religious views. In later life Caroline Fox gathered round her a group of women of literary and historical tastes which included Caroline Norton, Lady Callcott, Helena Blackwood, and Mary Russell Mitford. Her essay on the Abbé Sicard was printed in *Friendly Contributions* (1838), edited by Lady Mary Fox in aid of educational charities. It demonstrates her interest in the education of children, especially deaf mutes, as well as her continuing support for the Bonapartist cause. She founded and enjoyed visiting an infant school with playground in Kensington on land purchased from the Holland estate about 1840.

An intellectual woman of independent means, Caroline Fox had a stroke in June 1844; she died at Little Holland House on 12 March 1845 and was buried at Millbrook church, Bedfordshire.   V. E. CHANCELLOR

Sources Earl of Ilchester [G. S. Holland Fox-Strangways], *The home of the Hollands, 1605–1820* (1937) · Earl of Ilchester [G. S. Holland Fox-Strangways], *Chronicles of Holland House, 1820–1900* (1937) · *The journal of Elizabeth, Lady Holland, 1791–1811*, ed. earl of Ilchester [G. S. Holland Fox-Strangways], 2 vols. (1908) · *The journal of the Hon. Henry Edward Fox*, ed. earl of Ilchester [G. S. Holland Fox-Strangways] (1923) · *Letters of Lady Holland to her son, 1821–1845*, ed. Lord Ilchester (1946) · Lord Holland [H. R. V. Fox] and J. Allen, *The Holland House diaries, 1831–1840*, ed. A. D. Kriegel (1977) · J. B. Trotter, *Memoirs of the later years of the Rt. Hon C. J. Fox* (1811) · Princess Marie Liechtenstein, *Holland House*, 2nd edn, 2 vols. (1874) · review, *QR*, 135 (1873), 405–45 · *The works of Jeremy Bentham*, ed. J. Bowring, [new edn], 11 vols.

(1843–59), vol. 10 · L. Mitchell, *Holland House* (1980) · E. T. Lean, *The Napoleonists* (1970) · Burke, *Peerage* (1847) · *GM*, 1st ser., 37 (1767), 562 · BL, Holland House MSS, Add. MSS 51958–52000, 52064, 52058 · d. cert.

Archives BL, corresp., journals, and papers, Add. MSS 51958–52000 | BL, Holland House MSS, letters to C. J. Fox, Add. MS 51467 · BL, Holland House MSS, letters to third Lord Holland, Add. MSS 51731–51743 · BL, letters to fourth Lord Holland, Add. MSS 52036–52055 · CKS, corresp. with Lord Stanhope

Likenesses J. Reynolds, portrait, 1770 · E. Landseer, portrait, repro. in Mitchell, *Holland House*, facing p. 192 · portrait (in old age), repro. in *Chronicles*, facing p. 114 · three miniatures, repro. in *Chronicles*, facing p. 114

Wealth at death £6000–£8000—funds left in trust; Little Holland House and St Anne's (mortgaged): letter to fourth Lord Holland, 17 April 1845, BL, Add. MS 52064

Fox, Caroline (1819–1871), diarist, was born at Penjerrick, near Falmouth, Cornwall, on 24 May 1819, the second daughter of Robert Were *Fox (1789–1877), mineralogist, of Penjerrick, and his wife, Maria Barclay (1786–1858), daughter of Robert Barclay of Bury Hall, Surrey. She was educated privately on a plan of her parents and a tutor that included science and a modern language as well as visits to the locality, which are recorded in her earliest journal. With her brother and sister she played a part in the foundation of Falmouth Polytechnic (1833).

Caroline Fox early displayed an incisive intelligence and an attractive literary style. Her frank appraisals of contemporaries probably led her to bequeath her journals to her sister Anna Maria (*d.* 1897) and to instruct that they be destroyed after her death. This invaluable historical source was preserved in part by a relative by marriage, Horace N. Pym, who edited a version published in 1882. A two-volume edition with an appendix of letters by John Stuart Mill to her brother Barclay Fox appeared in the same year, and an edition was edited by Wendy Monk and published in 1972. Although most of the manuscript was burnt, the first volume, from the beginning of 1832 to October 1834, was discovered at Penjerrick. An educational exercise, it contains interesting glimpses of the environment and family life of the period.

Stemming from her connection with the Society of Friends, Caroline Fox steadfastly held the principles of equality and fraternity. She called herself a Quaker-Catholic (an inclusive Quaker), and she visited prisons in London with her kinswoman Elizabeth Gurney Fry (1780–1845) and supported the Anti-Slavery Society. She shared her father's interest in science, and attended meetings of the British Association for the Advancement of Science, including those at Dublin. Her acquaintances included Michael Faraday and William Whewell. In 1840 John Stuart Mill and John Sterling visited Falmouth, and she developed an attachment to the latter, by 1843 a widower, but her family may have disapproved of the match on religious grounds or on those of health. Sterling died in 1844, and she continued to take an interest in his daughters. She admired Mill but strongly disliked the cold logic of his treatise *On Liberty* (1859). By contrast her regular visits to London led to a deepening friendship with Thomas Carlyle and his wife, dating from 1840.

In her journals Caroline Fox described a great number of

literary men such as Charles Kingsley, Wordsworth, and Tennyson, and painters whom she knew included Samuel Lawrence, who drew her portrait, Holman Hunt, and Edwin Landseer, who incurred her disapproval. Partly through her friendship with T. B. Macaulay and his sister, she also recorded the talk of politicians, including that of some foreign ambassadors such as Baron von Bunsen from Prussia, François Guizot from France, and J. C. Adams from the United States. She recorded a charming meeting with Giuseppe Garibaldi at Pau in France in 1863. Caroline Fox travelled widely on the continent, making her first visit to Paris in 1838 and to Switzerland in 1846. In 1867 she visited the Paris Exhibition and Venice before going on to Hyères and Menton on the French riviera.

After 1860 Caroline Fox and her sister were occupied in rearing their four orphaned nephews. Nevertheless, her visitors at Penjerrick included the statesman John Bright and the explorer David Livingstone and she remained a lively correspondent. Entries in her journal became more sparse as chronic bronchitis took hold of her. She held Bible classes with other nonconformists in Falmouth and her paper 'Bible cases of conversion', was published posthumously in the *Friends' Quarterly Examiner* (1872). Other religious tracts, translated into Italian, were printed in Naples and Florence by Caroline and her sister Anna Maria. They included *Il mozzo Bertino*, published in Florence in 1867.

Caroline Fox died peacefully in Penjerrick on 12 January 1871 and was interred in the Quaker burial-ground at nearby Budock. Her journal usefully combines soundness of judgement and absence of scandal with perceptive comment about her contemporaries.

V. E. CHANCELLOR

Sources *The journals of Caroline Fox, 1835–1871: a selection*, ed. W. Monk (1972) · H. Willson, *Caroline Fox* (1944) · Boase & Courtney, *Bibl. Corn.* · R. J. N. Tod, *Caroline Fox: Quaker bluestocking* (1980) · R. L. Brett, 'Saved from the flames', *The Times* (18 Feb 1978) · 'Fox, Anna Maria of Penjerrick', *Cornish Echo* (1897); pubd separately [1897] · C. H. Fox, *A short genealogical account* (1864) · M. S. Fox, *Memoirs* (1874) · Burke, *Gen. GB* · C. H. Hawkin, ed., *Schimmel-Pennenck, Mary Ann* (1858) · BL, Backhouse MSS, Add. MSS 61711–61712 · d. cert.
Archives BL, Backhouse MSS, Add. MSS 61711–61712 · priv. coll., journal
Likenesses H. von Herkomer, portrait (aged twenty-seven; after a drawing by S. Lawrence), repro. in Monk, ed., *Memories of old friends*, frontispiece
Wealth at death under £7000: administration, 9 Feb 1871, *CGPLA Eng. & Wales*

Fox, Charles (1740?–1809), poet and orientalist, is of uncertain parentage and upbringing. It is most likely that he was the son of Joseph Fox, a Quaker grocer from Falmouth, though it is elsewhere suggested that he was the child of a John Fox and Rebecca, *née* Steevens, of High Wycombe. He kept a bookseller's shop and house in Falmouth, the latter being destroyed by fire. Robert Southey, writing under the pseudonym Manuel Alvarez Espriella, described how Fox, realizing that nothing could be saved, 'went upon the nearest hill and made a drawing of the conflagration—an admirable instance of English phlegm' (*Letters from England*, 3 vols., 1807, 1.6). Following the fire,

Fox pursued his interest in portrait and landscape painting. With his brother, the master of a merchant ship, he travelled to the Baltic and, accompanied only by his sketch book, made a walking tour of Sweden, Norway, and part of Russia.

Fox settled in Bristol on his return to England. Here he developed his talent for languages and began a collection of Persian manuscripts. Fox's *Poems, Containing the Plaints, Consolations, and Delights of Achmed Ardebeili, a Persian Exile* was published by Joseph Cottle in 1797. Though praised for its literary quality and scholarship, Fox's volume was far less commercially successful. Indeed, having sold the copyright—together with that for Wordsworth's *Lyrical Ballads*—Cottle found that both works had been 'reckoned as nothing' by the publisher, Thomas Longman (Cottle, 2.26). A close friend to both authors, Cottle then regained the copyrights, returning to Fox his receipt for £20.

Fox dedicated himself to poetry for much of the remainder of his life. By about 1803 he had completed a two-volume set of poems translated from Persian, though his ill health prevented this work from being taken through to publication. A man, according to the bookseller William Hone, of 'great natural genius' and 'the quickest reasoning power', Fox's weakness proved to be his eccentricity and a habit of working on 'trivial and not very interesting matters' (Hone, 1.762).

In 1792 Fox married a Miss Feniers, the daughter of a Dutch merchant. Husband and wife were renowned for their conviviality and generosity towards young literary scholars and writers, many of whom visited their house at Villa Place, Bathwick, Bath, which they shared with their parrot. It was here, for example, that the Babylonian scholar Claudius James Rich first became interested in the study of Arabic and was given ready access to Fox's excellent library. Here too Southey met the Church of England clergyman Adam Clarke, to whom Fox provided instruction in Persian during his second stay in Bristol from 1798. Clarke, in return, claimed to have turned Fox into a 'devout believer'. Following Fox's death on 1 March 1809, many of his papers, including his illustrated travel journals, fell into Clarke's possession; the details of this collection are recorded in J. J. B. Clarke's *European and Asiatic Manuscripts of Adam Clarke* (1835) and in the third volume of George Boase and William Courtney's *Bibliotheca Cornubiensis* (1874).

W. P. COURTNEY, rev. PHILIP CARTER

Sources *GM*, 1st ser., 79 (1809), 385 · R. Polwhele, *Reminiscences in prose and verse*, 3 vols. (1836) · R. Polwhele, *Biographical sketches in Cornwall*, 3 vols. (1831) · J. Cottle, *Early recollections; chiefly relating to the late Samuel Taylor Coleridge, during his long residence in Bristol*, 2 vols. (1837) · J. W. Etheridge, *The life of the Rev. Adam Clarke*, 2nd edn (1858) · J. Foster, *A revised genealogical account of the various families descended from Francis Fox of St Germans, Cornwall* (1872) · W. Hone, *The Every-day Book and Table Book*, 3 vols. (1830)

Fox, Charles (1795–1849), engraver, was born on 17 March 1795 at Costessey Park, near Norwich, and baptized there on 18 March, the second son of Robert Fox (d. 1827?), a steward to the Jerningham family on the Costessey estate, and Maria Hatton. He received lessons in drawing from Charles Hodgson (1769–1856) of Norwich, and in 1807 as Master Fox he began exhibiting with the Norwich Society of Artists. He continued to exhibit with the society until 1828. His exhibits included portraits, local views, and architectural subjects. According to the *Art Journal* (March 1849), Fox's 'early pursuits were turned to agriculture and floricultural matters', but his interest in art was greater and his father was persuaded to apprentice him to the engraver W. C. Edwards (1777–1855) of Bungay, Suffolk.

At the end of his apprenticeship in 1820 Fox moved to London, where 'he engaged himself' as an assistant to John Burnet (1784–1868) (*Athenaeum*, 233). At the time Burnet was preparing engravings of the works of David Wilkie, and Fox assisted him in completing these. He went on to engrave alone other works after Wilkie, most notably *The First Council of Queen Victoria* (1837) and *Village Recruits* (1838), as well as plates for Cadell's edition of the Waverley novels of Sir Walter Scott. In addition he engraved various illustrations for some of the other popular publications and periodicals of the day. Among the portraits he engraved was a full-length portrait of Sir George Murray after H. W. Pickersgill, which was much acclaimed when it was published. He also engraved portraits of his teachers Edwards and Burnet, the latter after a watercolour by Stephen Poyntz Denning (1795?–1864), who inspired Fox to paint portraits in watercolour, which he did mainly for his own pleasure and that of his friends. Fox exhibited a total of four portraits at the Royal Academy in 1836 and 1837 from 2 Whitehead's Grove, Chelsea, in London, and was described in the catalogue as a miniature painter. He retained his early love and knowledge of flowers, and through his friend Dr John Lindley, secretary of the Horticultural Society, he became a judge at the society's flower shows. He also reported on the merits of flowers sent for opinion to the *Gardeners' Chronicle* and *The Florist*, as well as supervising the illustrations for *The Florist*. He was highly regarded as one of the best judges of flowers and for the integrity of his judgements.

Fox appears to have had a wide circle of friends and endeared himself to all who knew him. For the last three years of his life he suffered from heart disease, and he died, apparently unmarried, on 28 February 1849 'after a painful illness of three weeks' (*The Florist*, April 1849, 89) at the home of his friend C. M. Robison of Leyton, Essex. Lindley wrote of him in his obituary: 'Alas! poor Fox! the dear kind, good, noble-minded fellow, who never had an enemy' (*Gardeners' Chronicle*, 135). Fox was buried in London in Brompton cemetery. Friends and acquaintances, 'many of them in humble life', paid for a stone inscribed to 'A Man greatly beloved', to mark the burial place (*The Florist*, April 1850, 100).   NORMA WATT

Sources *The Athenaeum* (3 March 1849), 233 · *GM*, 2nd ser., 31 (1849), 434 · B. Hunnisett, *An illustrated dictionary of British steel engravers*, new edn (1989) · Rajnai Norwich Artists Archive · *The Florist* (April 1849), 89 · *The Florist* (April 1850), 100–01 · *Gardeners' Chronicle* (3 March 1849), 135 · *Art Journal*, 11 (March 1849) · *Norwich Mercury* (10 March 1849) · d. cert.

Likenesses W. Carpenter, chalk drawing, 1848, BM

Fox, Charles (1797–1878), scientific writer, was born at Falmouth in Cornwall on 22 December 1797, the seventh son of Robert Were *Fox (1754–1818), a Quaker shipping agent and Elizabeth (1768–1849), daughter of Joseph Tregelles of Penryn. He was the younger brother of Robert Were *Fox (1789–1877), FRS. He was educated at home, before becoming a partner in the firm of G. C. and R. W. Fox & Co., merchants and shipping agents of Falmouth. Fox was also a partner in the Perran Foundry Company, engineers, at Perranarworthal, where from 1824 to 1847 he was the general manager. On 20 December 1825 he married Sarah (1800–1882), only daughter of William Hustler of Bradford. They had two daughters, the elder of whom, Juliet Mary, married Edmund Backhouse MP.

Fox was a founder member of the Royal Cornwall Polytechnic Society at Falmouth in 1833 (of which he was president in 1871–2) and in 1837 he persuaded his clerk William Jory Henwood (1805–75), later FRS, to take up a scientific career. With Sir Charles Lemon, Fox encouraged the Polytechnic Society to offer a premium of £300 for the construction of a 'man-engine', a machine to raise and lower men in Cornish mines, of which he subscribed £100; others made the fund up to £600. The result was the erection of the first such engine at Tresavean mine in Gwennap in 1842. The machine was a great success, and its invention was the means of saving miners much unnecessary labour in ascending and descending mine shafts by ladders. In 1841, in connection with the society, he founded the Lander prizes for maps and essays on geographical districts.

Along with Robert Hunt (1807–1887), FRS, Fox helped to found in 1859 the Miners' Association of Cornwall and Devon, of which he was president in 1861–3 and thereafter vice-president. He was president of the Royal Geological Society of Cornwall in 1864–7. He was also concerned in the management of several Cornish mines, and was one of the first to recognize the usefulness of boring machines, writing a paper about them in 1867. He also made communications to the three Cornish learned societies, and to the *Mining Journal* and *Hardwicke's Science-Gossip*.

He was particularly interested in such discoveries, philological and antiquarian, as tended to throw light on Bible history, in which connection he visited Palestine, Egypt, and Algiers. In all fields of natural history he was deeply read, making collections and examining microscopically the specimens of each branch.

Fox and his wife shared an interest in spiritual matters, and she published a metrical version of the book of Job (1852–4), in addition to other poetry. In 1840 Fox edited *Extracts from the Spiritual Diary of John Rutty, M.D.*, and in 1870 he wrote a small work *On the Ministry of Women*. For the last twenty-five years of his life he lived at Trebah, near Falmouth, and died there on 18 April 1878, of bronchial illness, being buried in the Quaker burial-ground, Budock, on 23 April. He was survived by his wife, who died on 19 February 1882.   G. C. BOASE, *rev.* JUSTIN BROOKE

Sources Reports of the Miners' Association of Cornwall and Devon, 1869, p. 1 • Reports of the Miners' Association of Cornwall and Devon, 1879, p. 1 • J. Foster, *The descendants of Francis Fox* (1872), 11 • Boase & Courtney, *Bibl. Corn.*, 1.160, 165, 3.1186–7, 1189 • *Records from papers and letters respecting Charles Fox of Trebah, near Falmouth* (1878), 12 • *Journal of the Royal Institution of Cornwall*, 6 (1878–81), 2–3 • *Weekly Welcome* (April 1879), 215–16 • *Transactions of the Royal Geological Society of Cornwall*, 10 (1879), x, xii-xiii
Archives priv. coll., family MSS
Likenesses portrait, repro. in *Weekly Welcome*

Fox, Sir Charles (1810–1874), civil engineer, was born in Derby on 11 March 1810 the youngest of the four sons of Francis Fox (1760–1833) and his wife, Charlotte Douglas (1771–1855). His father was a physician and in the hope that Fox too would take up medicine he was articled to his brother Douglas, who had trained as a surgeon. However, he showed more interest in mechanics, and in 1829 he joined John Ericsson and John Braithwaite who were building the locomotive *Novelty*, to be entered for the famous Rainhill trials on the Liverpool and Manchester Railway. He also worked with Ericsson in experiments on rotary engines. The following year he married Mary, second daughter of Joseph Brookhouse; they had three sons and a daughter.

After moving for a time to a Liverpool engineering firm, in 1834 Fox became one of the assistants to Robert Stephenson on the construction of the London and Birmingham Railway, working first on the Watford section and then on the extension from Camden Town to Euston. Dur-

Sir Charles Fox (1810–1874), by Charles Baugniet, 1851

ing that project he developed a new method for building skew arches, about which he read a paper to the Royal Institution, and he designed an innovatory wrought-iron trussed roof for the Euston terminus. At a period when the use of cast and wrought iron was reaching new heights of invention he became one of the leading experts in the field, known in particular for his advocacy of cast iron.

In 1839 Fox joined Francis Bramah to establish a firm of engineering contractors, Bramah, Fox & Co., which had its main works at Smethwick in the west midlands. By 1841 John Henderson had become a partner in the firm, and four years later it was renamed Fox, Henderson & Co. Under that name it became one of the best-known engineering companies in the country, specializing in railway equipment, bridges, and structural ironwork of all kinds. In the railway boom of the 1840s and 1850s many of the major station roofs were supplied by Fox Henderson, for instance at Paddington, Liverpool Tithebarn Street and Birmingham New Street. They also made roofs for market halls and at least six slipyard roofs, plus other structures, for naval dockyards. Like other ironwork firms they exported structures, including a cast-iron lighthouse to India and the iron chains for the Kiev suspension bridge. They also undertook railway contracts in Ireland, Germany, Switzerland, and Denmark.

Apart from the breadth of its work and its manufacturing capacity, the importance of Fox Henderson lay in its contribution to advances in structural design. Fox led the design side of the company while Henderson took charge

of the manufacturing processes, and through that combination they were able to offer technically innovative solutions. The firm was also a nursery of engineering talent, which had on its staff at one time or another engineers such as E. A. Cowper, R. M. Ordish, J. W. Grover, and William Siemens.

The abilities of the firm were dramatically demonstrated through its involvement in the construction of the Crystal Palace in Hyde Park for the Great Exhibition of 1851. From an early stage Joseph Paxton enlisted the help of Fox Henderson in the development of his design, and the partners submitted the winning contract for the project. As well as making structural calculations and producing working drawings, the firm took responsibility for manufacturing many of the building components and for the erection of the structure on site. Fox said that it had been his role to 'mature and realize' Paxton's idea, yet without his willingness to take the risk of developing the project the building would never have been completed in the time allowed (*ILN*). The Crystal Palace represented a major advance in prefabricated construction, combining iron, wood, and glass components mostly fabricated off-site to a standard 8 ft module. It was also a pioneering example of framed construction. Fox was knighted on 22 October 1851 for his contribution to the success of the Great Exhibition.

After the close of the exhibition Fox Henderson dismantled the Crystal Palace and rebuilt it in a more permanent form at Sydenham in south London in 1852–4. By then there were signs that the firm was overstretched, and in

1856 it went into liquidation following a loss on the construction of the Zealand Railway in Denmark. The following year Fox established himself as a consulting engineer in London and was joined by his two elder sons, (Charles) Douglas *Fox and Francis *Fox: in 1860 they formed the partnership of Sir Charles Fox & Sons. Their practice was responsible for widening the railway approach to Victoria Station, including the bridge over the Thames from Battersea, and for the engineering of railways in Queensland, South Africa, and Canada. Fox was an advocate of economy in railway construction and thus of narrow-gauge railways. In conjunction with G. Berkeley he built the first narrow-gauge railway in India.

Early in his career Fox was described as having 'the dress of a decent mechanic, the air of an educated and well-bred man, and no gloves' (Conder, 15). This combination of a gentlemanly manner with practical ability stood him in good stead, though he was also known to be ruthless. He became a member of the Institution of Civil Engineers in 1838, and was a founder member of the Institution of Mechanical Engineers. He was also a member of the British Association and the Society of Arts and a fellow of the Royal Asiatic and Royal Geographical societies. He died at his son Douglas's home at 7 Vanbrugh Terrace, Greenwich, on 14 June 1874, and was buried at Nunhead cemetery on 18 June.   ROBERT THORNE

Sources PICE, 39 (1874–5), 264–6 · F. Fox, River, road and rail (1904) · F. Fox, Sixty-three years of engineering: scientific and social work (1924) · F. R. Conder, Personal recollections of English engineers, and of the introduction of the railway system into the United Kingdom (1868) · ILN (5 July 1851), 21–2 · G. F. Chadwick, The works of Sir Joseph Paxton, 1803–1865 (1961) · H. Spencer, An autobiography, 1 (1904) · J. McKean, Crystal Palace: Joseph Paxton and Charles Fox (1994) · CGPLA Eng. & Wales (1874) · d. cert. · The Times (16 June 1874) · DNB

Likenesses C. Baugniet, lithograph, 1851, BM, NPG [see illus.] · Maull & Co., carte-de-visite, NPG · H. W. Phillips, group portrait, oils (The royal commissioners for the Great Exhibition, 1851), V&A · lithograph (after a pencil drawing by Baugniet, 1851), Inst. CE · woodengraving (after a photograph by Elliott & Fry), NPG; repro. in ILN (27 June 1874)

Wealth at death under £8000: probate, 17 July 1874, CGPLA Eng. & Wales

Fox, Charles James (1749–1806), politician, was born on 24 January 1749 in Conduit Street, London, the second son of Henry *Fox, later first Baron Holland (1705–1774), politician, and Lady (Georgiana) Caroline Lennox, suo jure Baroness Holland of Holland (1723–1774), daughter of the second duke of Richmond [see Fox, (Georgiana) Caroline, Baroness Holland of Holland]. He had an elder brother, Stephen, later second Baron Holland (1745–1774), a minor politician until his early death, and a younger brother, Henry Edward *Fox (1755–1811), who had a distinguished military career. This was a close-knit family and Fox enjoyed loving relationships with all his immediate connections. Through his mother's family he was a direct descendant of Charles II, and he was given the distinctly Stuart names of Charles and James. This was an unlikely beginning for the future leader of the whig party. There were other un-whiggish aspects to Fox's inheritance. His father was held responsible for completing the removal of

Charles James Fox (1749–1806), by Sir Joshua Reynolds, 1782

the whig party from office in 1762–3, and was never forgiven for this. Since Fox proved to be the most filial of sons, his father's enemies became his own. A son's affection also prompted Fox, throughout his political career, to defend his father's reputation and actions across a whole range of topics, notably against charges that he had embezzled huge amounts of public money while acting as paymaster-general. With some confidence Henry Fox hoped to 'build' on his son 'for many hours of Comfort' (Mitchell, Charles James Fox, 16).

The close, emotional involvement of father and son was established early. Henry Fox found Charles 'infinitely engaging & clever & pretty' (Mitchell, Charles James Fox, 4), and preferred him to all other companions at meals from the time that the boy was three years old. Accordingly little or no restraint was put on his son's whims and desires; state papers could be thrown onto the fire, watches destroyed, or garden walls built or demolished with no sanctions or punishment meted out. It was known around Europe that Charles Fox had had the most indulgent of upbringings, as evidenced in Les amours et les aventures du Lord Fox (1785, 17–18). Free of all discipline and restraint when a child, Fox in turn found it impossible to restrain others. A major failing in his political leadership was his inability to impose authority on others, particularly if they were young. It was always a maxim of his that 'he did not like to discourage the young ones' (C. Grey, The Life and Opinions of the Second Earl Grey, 1913, 11). Critics endlessly returned to the theme that Fox's own career had been blasted by the indiscipline and wilfulness that characterized so many of his actions.

Fox had dark, swarthy features and was extremely hirsute; at his birth his father had likened him to a monkey. He had a rounded face, dominated by luxuriant eyebrows; the whigs lived by nicknames and his was the Eyebrow. A dandy in youth, he was unkempt in middle age; caricaturists delighted in portraying him as unshaven, with clothes in disorder. Inclined to corpulence by nature, Fox's dissipated lifestyle did nothing to counter a tendency to be overweight. He enjoyed riding and cricket but, in the latter game, a combination of impulsiveness and too much weight led to his being run out between wickets.

Education   As in all other aspects of his upbringing Fox was given *carte blanche* about his education. By his own choice he went, first, at the age of seven, to Mr Pampellone's school in Wandsworth and then, on 22 June 1758, he enrolled in Dame Milward's House at Eton College. There he encountered such men as the second duke of Leinster, Lord John Townshend, Earl Fitzwilliam, James Hare, and the fifth earl of Carlisle, all of whom were to be lifelong friends and associates. He called them 'the Gang' (Mitchell, *Charles James Fox*, 7). He quickly established himself as a classical scholar of note, and Eton was moved to publish some of his Latin writings. In 1763 he was taken to Paris by his father. The boy was given a substantial amount of money with which to gamble and the ever-indulgent father arranged for him to lose his virginity to a certain Madame de Quallens. He briefly returned to Eton but, perhaps predictably after these experiences, he was asked to leave early in 1764, as he was 'too witty to live there—and a little too wicked' (*The World*, 3 Feb 1787).

In the autumn of 1764 Fox entered Hart Hall, Oxford, where his tutor was William Newcombe. There he took some interest in mathematics and deepened his classical repertory, but he left the university without a degree and with a mild contempt for its 'nonsenses' (Mitchell, *Charles James Fox*, 8). Of more importance were renewed visits to Paris, which he described as 'such a nurture in Education [as] was never seen' (ibid., 9). He returned there in April–May 1765, accompanied by his mother and elder brother. Between September 1766 and August 1768 he made an extensive grand tour, partly in the company of Etonian friends, which took in Paris, Lyons, Lausanne, and many Italian cities. He was interviewed by Voltaire at Ferney and stayed with Gibbon in Switzerland. More particularly he met leading figures in French society, with whom he established friendships that would, in the long term, carry the most profound political consequences. Among these were the duc d'Orléans, the marquis de Lafayette, and the duc de Lauzun. The last became co-owner with Fox of a number of racehorses. Further visits to the French capital in 1769 and 1771 confirmed Fox's place among the European élite, whose reputations were made or damned in Parisian salons. Fox returned to England in the height of French fashion, as what was called a *petit maître*, or Macaroni. Such preferences began to establish in the public mind Fox's reputation for things alien and un-English, a point of criticism that dogged him for the whole of his political life.

Private life   This distinctive upbringing led Fox to lead a private life that was considered exotic, scandalous, attractive, and larger than life. Nor was it really private. Fox was the subject of more caricatures than any other person in the late eighteenth century (N. K. Robinson, *Edmund Burke: a Life in Caricature*, 1996, 7–8). His peccadilloes and vices were paraded before the public without interruption. Journalists and pamphleteers joyfully joined the hunt. Rarely can the private life of a major statesman have been subjected to such comment and ridicule. Two aspects of his life commanded particular attention. First, Fox was properly recognized as the doyen of the gambling craze that disturbed so many family fortunes in the last decades of the eighteenth century. His winnings and losses were on a heroic scale. Between 1772 and 1774 his father was required to pay off £120,000 of debt incurred at Newmarket and at the gaming tables in Brooks's Club. Between 1781 and 1784 Fox was twice sold up as a bankrupt, to the terrible embarrassment of friends such as Carlisle, who had stood as sureties for his debts. In the 1780s he borrowed heavily from the banker Thomas Coutts. In 1793 his friends raised £61,000 to buy him an annuity but, in spite of this provision, Fox left £10,000 of debt at his death. Throughout his life his private finances were a shambles and were quite often 'more the subject of conversation than any other topic' (Mitchell, *Charles James Fox*, 101). Inevitably, too, immoderate drinking was the natural accompaniment of inveterate gambling.

Second, Fox's relationships with women had a considerable notoriety, even for a period when the mistress or the lover was an unremarkable feature of London life. On the grand tour there had been a Kitty, an Angelina, and a silversmith's wife in Nice. Having returned to London he took up with 'an Irish woman more beautiful than words', called Mrs Holmes (Mitchell, *Charles James Fox*, 12). In 1782 he had an affair with Perdita Robinson, the actress, and in 1783–4 he was probably the lover of Georgiana, duchess of Devonshire. At times these women were shared with old friends from school and politics. In 1784 or 1785, however, he met Elizabeth Bridget *Armitstead (1750–1842), a former mistress of the prince of Wales, and they began living together. They were married in secret in September 1795 but it was not until 1802 that she was acknowledged in public. Under her influence Fox's life became increasingly domesticated. His London home, in South Street, was sold in March 1798. Henceforth they lived exclusively at St Anne's Hill in Surrey, in a villa purchased in 1784. In spite of this reformation of manners Fox was remembered for his earlier excesses. It was thought that the character of Charles Surface in Sheridan's *School for Scandal* was built on his escapades, as were certain themes of Samuel Foote's *The Cozeners*.

There can be no doubt but that this history severely damaged Fox's prospects. George III regarded him as beyond morality and as the prince of Wales's tutor in debauchery. Equally, many voters refused to support a man who was so often and so openly profligate. Conversely such considerations never influenced Fox's decisions. The world within which he moved was a narrow one. Insulated by circles of admiring friends, who forgave him everything, he considered all opinion coming from outside these ranks to be nearly worthless. He rarely recognized this avalanche of moral disapproval as threatening; indeed he collected the very caricatures that showed him up in the worst possible light. For such indifference he paid a heavy penalty. As Lord Carlisle observed, 'the respect of the world was not easily retrievable, he became so callous to what was said of him, as never to repress a single thought, or even temper a single expression when he was before the public' (Mitchell, *Charles James Fox*, 14). Even before his political career had started Fox had firmly established a reputation that militated against the possibility of success.

The Hollands Of all his family Fox was closest to his niece Caroline and his nephew Henry, later third Baron Holland. After the death of their father, Stephen Fox, second Baron Holland, in 1774, Fox, although not their official guardian, appointed himself as their guide and mentor. Both children developed a keen interest in politics. They also provided an invaluable link to the first marquess of Lansdowne, who was also their uncle, a family link much exploited in 1782 and again in the 1790s. In particular Fox took great trouble with the upbringing of his nephew, the heir to the family's name and reputation. As Holland remembered, Fox 'seemed to take pleasure in awakening my ambition, and directing it, both by conversation and correspondence' (Mitchell, *Holland House*, 41). Fox determined when Holland should embark on the grand tour and arranged introductions and programmes. Since the boy also shared Fox's literary interests he received letters from his uncle that were tutorials on what it was appropriate for a whig to like and believe. The result was that Holland became his uncle's creature. It was assumed that Fox was grooming his nephew to take over the leadership of the party, a project that was thwarted by Holland's failure to overcome a speech impediment and by his controversial marriage.

In July 1797 Holland married Elizabeth, Lady Webster, whom he had met in Italy. As a divorced woman she carried a notoriety that was only sharpened by the most powerful of personalities. Macaulay described her as 'a bold looking woman, with the remains of a fine figure, and the air of Queen Elizabeth' (J. Clive, *Thomas Babington Macaulay*, 1973, 210). Fox disapproved of the match and refused to attend the wedding; in his view Holland had destroyed any chance of a prominent political career. The new Lady Holland, with some justice, pronounced herself 'extremely afraid of my Uncle Charles' (Mitchell, *Holland House*, 39). Only with difficulty were relations restored; Fox was never the sort of man who could hold on to a grievance beyond a certain time. On the other hand, to venerate Fox fitted Holland's inclinations and his wife's ambitions. Their famous uncle gave them a status which virtually every other factor in their lives would have denied them. Holland House, standing in the middle of Holland Park and within easy access of London, therefore became the centre of Foxite social life and the temple in

which Fox himself was revered. From 1797 until 1840 Holland House was a salon with a clear purpose. Holland transmitted his uncle's values into the nineteenth century, and associated new generations of the rich and talented in their trusteeship. In a real sense Fox's affection for and care of his nephew was returned in full measure.

Entry into politics, 1768–1774 Fox was elected to parliament on 10 May 1768, when only nineteen years of age and therefore technically ineligible to stand. His father had bought the representation of Midhurst in Sussex. Fox quickly established himself as someone of exceptional ability and promise. A talented orator, he allegedly addressed the Commons 254 times between 1768 and 1774. If true, this would suggest that this was the period in which Fox took politics most seriously in the whole of his career. Predictably his views were those of his father. Remembering Henry Fox's ill treatment by the Rockingham whigs, the son became a supporter of the Grafton and North ministries. At this stage his opinions were quite the opposite of those that could be expected of a future populist. He was prominent in the campaign to punish John Wilkes for challenging parliament, and both Fox and his brother were manhandled by London crowds for their pains. As he lectured the Commons on 25 March 1771:

> What acquaintance have the people at large with the arena of political rectitude, with the connections of kingdoms, the resources of national strength, the abilities of minister, or even with their own dispositions? … I pay no regard whatever to the voice of the people: it is their duty to do what is proper, without considering what may be agreeable. (*Speeches*, 1.13–14)

In these years relations between Fox and Lord North were congenial; each respected the other and they frequently met socially. Fox had been elected to The Club and to The Dilettanti. Their later collaboration in the coalition ministry of 1783–4 was built on the memory of these years. Accordingly Fox had no quarrel with North's American policies, even those which tended to the coercion of the colonists, nor with his attempt to regulate the British presence in India. It seemed that Fox could look forward to a most promising future as a ministerialist. Between 1772 and 1774, however, this easy progress was shattered. Twice Fox was appointed to government office and twice he resigned for reasons that the political world at large found hard to understand.

In February 1770 Fox was given a place on the Admiralty board. He resigned it on 15 February 1772 in protest against the passing of the Royal Marriages Act. In requiring the immediate descendants of monarchs to win the approval of the sovereign before marrying, the act cast doubt on the relationship of Fox's parents, his mother being descended from Charles II. In December 1772 he was appointed to the Treasury board, where his attention to business seemed to confirm all his earlier promise. Unfortunately he surrendered this post in February 1774, ostensibly to mark his indignation at the government's feeble response to the printers, who had shown contempt for the rules of parliamentary procedure by printing reports of parliamentary debates. In fact he and his family had felt increasingly slighted by Lord North, who had refused their persistent claims that the Holland barony should be raised to an earldom. Both resignations were therefore prompted by family considerations rather than by any sharp disagreements about major policies. At this stage of his career Fox could be said to have had no politics except family politics.

For a young man of twenty-five to take the offers of public office so lightly was critically noted. At best it was described as capricious. George III took it to be presumption. Taken in conjunction with Fox's private life doubts were expressed about whether Fox could take anything quite seriously. His later inattention to politics, involving yet another resignation and a period of secession from parliament, seemed to follow a pattern.

The making of a whig, 1774-1782 Since Fox had not been born a whig, whiggery was in a sense thrust upon him. He drifted into association with the Rockingham party as a convert. Quite when the process of conversion was complete is difficult to pinpoint. His own nephew found the question hard to answer in his history of the whig party. It was certainly a slow process, but certain factors were pushing him inexorably in that direction. The first was an antipathy to the king that grew into the most bitter suspicion; no two men could have been more different in temperament. After 1774 Fox came increasingly to accept the whig theory that George III was intent upon undermining parliamentary government in the hope of establishing an authoritarian regime based on continental models. When, in April 1780, John Dunning's resolution passed the Commons, Fox, declaring that the influence of the crown had grown so dangerously that restraints needed to be applied, thought the occasion 'glorious'. In his view:

the question now was ... whether that beautiful fabric [the English constitution] ... was to be maintained in that freedom ... for which blood had been spilt; or whether we were to submit to that system of despotism, which had so many advocates in this country. (24 April 1780, *Speeches*, 1.261)

In arriving at this position Fox owed a great deal to the ministrations of Edmund Burke, who after 1774 made a point of seeking him out. Thereafter Fox always regarded him as his mentor in politics. Inevitably these views led Fox to revise his opinion of North, who was increasingly seen as 'the blundering pilot', the real, if reluctant, abetter of George III's ambitions (26 Oct 1775, *Speeches*, 1.44).

As Fox moved away from the crown, radicals of all kinds welcomed him with enthusiasm. In July 1780 he was elected MP for the populous and prestigious constituency of Westminster, which he was to represent with only a brief interruption until his death. He acquired the title Man of the People. This new position naturally involved a greater commitment to reform politics. By temperament and education Fox had always been a friend to slaves and to religious dissenters of all kinds. Now he began to take a higher profile in debates on parliamentary reform. In public speeches he could be found advocating shorter parliaments and dramatic extensions of the franchise. Such behaviour opened up a discrepancy between his public

and private views that remained unchanged until he died. In public Fox was an advanced parliamentary reformer; in private he regarded the issue with fatalism or a mild enthusiasm. As far as it had merit reform could be used against the executive power of the crown.

Even as Fox swallowed small doses of whiggery there was still everything to play for. He retained a personal liking for Lord North, though thinking him weak. North, in turn, deeply respected Fox's abilities. Between Fox and the king there was a profound animosity but not yet of a type to provoke a royal veto on Fox's re-entering office. Between the spring of 1778 and the summer of 1780 there were several negotiations designed to facilitate this. As Fox himself observed in 1778, 'I shall be told by prudent friends that I am under no sort of engagement to any set of men, I certainly am not' (Mitchell, *Charles James Fox*, 44). There was still some distance to travel before Fox could shake off family loyalties and wholeheartedly embrace the Rockingham party.

The American issue, 1774-1782 As far as Fox did reconsider his political affiliations in these years it was the question of the American War of Independence that prompted him to do so. Connections with America became a point of family honour. After Fox's death his nephew proudly reflected on 'the predilection it is so gratifying to think that the Americans have for our name' (Mitchell, *Charles James Fox*, 26). The members of the Fox Club always wore buff and blue, the colours of the uniforms in Washington's army. Inevitably Fox's views were deeply influenced by personal connections. He occasionally corresponded with Thomas Jefferson and, on a further visit to Paris between November 1776 and January 1777, he had met Benjamin Franklin. During the war itself Fox was provided with information by General Burgoyne, who, before military adventures took him across the Atlantic, had been one of Fox's gambling cronies at Brooks's. On the general's death in 1792 Fox assumed responsibility for his children.

Fortified with these contacts Fox rapidly became associated with the American cause. In important parliamentary speeches he emerged as one of North's major critics. Within a month of his second resignation from office, in April 1774, he was to be found voting against the government's American measures on the grounds of their inexpediency. He told the Commons that he:

imputed all the present disturbances to the persisting in taxation, and said the Americans had now discovered that taxation was used as a punishment, and that it was bad policy to use power to punish with, nor was it prudent to risk more in the contest than was necessary. (6 March 1775, *Memorials and Correspondence*, 1.138)

When such policies led to violence in America, Fox was not surprised but could only take pleasure in the discomfiture of North. Lord Carlisle observed that all bad news from America was 'a great cause of amusement to Charles' (Mitchell, *Charles James Fox*, 27).

From the outbreak of hostilities Fox believed that the war would be a long-drawn-out affair and that the Americans had a real chance of emerging as victors. Neither opinion was fashionable and some regarded such views as unpatriotic, even treasonable. Taking this line, however, Fox, even as early as 1776, began to consider the granting of independence to America as the lesser evil. Joyfully he joined those attacking Sandwich and Germain for their perceived incompetence in managing warfare and, more importantly, he gradually came to see himself and his American friends as joint victims of George III. Fox began to think in Manichaean terms; perhaps the king's refusal to listen to American claims about taxation and representation was not merely a misreading of a difficult problem but rather part of an attack on the representative ideal on both sides of the Atlantic. The American issue came increasingly to be symbolic of even wider concerns and fully justified Fox in orchestrating the fall of North's government in March 1782.

The political crisis of 1782–1784: events Between March 1782 and March 1784 British politics was convulsed by a series of crises which collectively came to be the determining experience in Fox's own career. All his future decisions could somehow be traced back to the events of these years. As a point of reference, even the French Revolution never had a comparable impact on Fox's thinking.

On 25 March 1782 Fox was appointed foreign secretary in a ministry that was jointly led by Rockingham and Shelburne. From the start it was an unhappy experience and, although it was Rockingham's sudden death in July that formally dissolved the experiment, it was a ministry dead in all but name long before that. Fox believed that George III had engineered its demise. He had used Thurlow, the lord chancellor, as a royal spy in the cabinet. More seriously, he had encouraged Shelburne to thwart Rockinghamite initiatives at every turn. In particular Fox found that his representative in Paris, Thomas Grenville, who was in charge of negotiations with the French, met nothing but obstruction from Richard Oswald, Shelburne's nominee as negotiator with the Americans. It was an impossible situation, and Fox had determined to resign even before Rockingham's death brought matters to a head.

The Shelburne administration, which ran from July 1782 until February 1783, was totally preoccupied with the finalization of peace terms with America and France. When details of the treaty became known Fox felt obliged to oppose anything Shelburne suggested, after his experiences of the previous summer, while Lord North equally objected to them as reflecting unfairly on his twelve-year administration. On this single conjunction of interests was born the Fox–North coalition. Later it would become infamous, as the union of men who had vilified each other for much of the American war. Crucially, however, at the moment of its formation it was accepted without comment as the reunion of two men who had worked together, between 1769 and 1774, with mutual respect and harmony. Its birth was marked by one startling aspect, however: George III was given no role in determining who should hold any government office. After the Thurlow experience of the previous summer Fox could not allow any royal nomination.

The Fox–North coalition was in office from March to December 1783. Its ending was as dramatic as its birth. On 27 November the coalition's East India Bill, which was designed to put the administration of India onto a new footing, passed the Commons by the comfortable majority of 229 to 120. On 15 December it was defeated in the Lords by eight votes, but only because the king had intervened decisively in the legislative process. Bishops and lords of the royal household had been threatened and cajoled. Fox was appalled. He warned the Commons that 'We shall certainly lose our liberty, when the deliberations of Parliament are decided—not by the legal and the usual—but by the illegal and extraordinary exertions of prerogative' (17 Dec 1783, *Speeches*, 2.275). When the king nominated William Pitt as prime minister, Fox therefore felt justified in opposing the appointment, and government came to a standstill as he used his majority in the Commons to obstruct the new minister's measures. The crisis was resolved only in March 1784, when the king dissolved parliament. In the ensuing election Fox lost the argument decisively and Pitt was returned with a substantial majority.

The political crisis of 1782–1784: consequences There emerged sharply contrasting responses to the tangled politics of these years. In Fox's view the delinquency of George III had been proved over and over again. There was no longer any doubt about his wish to subvert parliamentary institutions. The destruction of the Shelburne–Rockingham and Fox–North ministries had been premeditated and brutally executed. Publicly and blatantly the wishes of the Commons had been overturned. So brazen had been the king's behaviour that Fox began to liken him to Stuart monarchs of unfortunate memory. Equally, the dissolving of parliament three years early, in March 1784, and the extensive manipulation of the subsequent election by John Robinson, on the king's behalf, also substantiated fears. If monarchs could always remove parliamentary obstruction by the weapon of dissolution the real power of the legislature was much compromised. In Fox's view these events had permanently overturned the long-established metaphor of the balanced constitution, whereby liberty was secured by legislative and executive checking excess in each other. George III was intent on making executive power supreme. The only possible response was to make similar claims for the House of Commons, particularly with respect to the nomination of ministers. Fox henceforth argued for a total revision of the rules of the political game.

Alternatively it could be held that it was Fox himself who was threatening the notion of balance in the constitution. The maxim of the monarch's right to nominate ministers had never been so challenged before. Nor had the right to call and dissolve parliaments been contested. Both had been seen as legitimate aspects of the executive's prerogative powers. Fox was therefore accused of twice foisting himself upon an unwilling monarch, finding allies anywhere, and snatching at any idea that might suit his purpose. In the caricatures of these months he was depicted as Oliver Cromwell, the scourge of kings, or as

Guy Fawkes, intent upon blowing up accepted usages. In particular he was accused of trying to replace monarchy with the oligarchical domination of himself and his aristocratic friends. Voters in the election of March 1784 had to decide whether liberty was more threatened by despotism or oligarchy. On this point Fox lost overwhelmingly; even leaders of the parliamentary reform movement, like John Jebb and Christopher Wyvill, voted for Pitt. In taking this decision many such men associated what looked like reckless politics with the vagaries of Fox's private life. There seemed to be a pattern linking the politician and the private individual.

Those supporters of Fox who survived the 1784 election increasingly called themselves Foxite rather than whig. The change of name betokened a new agenda in politics. There was now only one point of reference. George III wished to be a despot on the continental model. Fox referred to the king as Satan. Every point of Foxite politics had the curbing of the executive as its end. Even the Reform Bill of 1832, enacted by Charles Grey, Fox's political heir, had this as its primary objective. Fox's interpretation of the events of 1782–4 anchored the views of his followers for half a century.

Ireland As in so much else Fox's responses to the problems raised by Ireland were conditioned by family connections and by his antipathy to George III. Unlike most contemporary politicians he had visited Ireland, in the summer of 1777, accompanied by Lord John Townshend. They had toured Killarney and had a long stay in Dublin, where they met Henry Grattan and Lord Charlemont, future leaders of the volunteer movement. Another prominent patriot was the duke of Leinster, Fox's uncle. This family connection confirmed Fox's sympathies for the Irish cause, and he assured his uncle in 1780 that he 'never missed an opportunity of declaring in public as well as in private, how much I wished you success in all the points you were likely to push' (Mitchell, *Charles James Fox*, 35). The fact that the king was hesitant about meeting Irish claims merely added another reason for assisting the volunteers.

In retrospect it became a great point of pride for Fox that, although the life of the Shelburne–Rockingham government was only three months, its main legislative achievement was the granting of a limited measure of home rule to Ireland, with the establishment of parliamentary sovereignty in Dublin. It seemed that this action wisely prevented the Irish situation from developing along American lines. The 1782 settlement was, however, in Fox's view, a final one. There were to be no more concessions or revisions. Ireland was to be required to contribute to her own defence, and there was to be 'some clear understanding with respect to what we are to expect from Ireland' under this heading (Mitchell, *Charles James Fox*, 251). Further Irish issues were subordinate to the central debate in Westminster politics about George III and his nominee, Pitt. When the latter proposed a commercial treaty with the Dublin parliament Fox opposed it in a series of speeches between February and July 1785. Quite simply he was anxious to deny Pitt any legislative triumph,

even if his Irish friends suffered as a consequence. After 1785 Fox's relations with Henry Grattan and Henry Flood cooled.

Fox's sympathy for Ireland's grievances quickened again in the 1790s as part of his preoccupation with George III's intentions in government. One of the leaders of Irish patriotism was now Lord Edward Fitzgerald, Leinster's son and Fox's favourite cousin. His death in the Irish rising of 1798 affected Fox deeply and he came to be seen as a martyr of the king's despotic ambitions, which also threatened Fox himself. On the other hand Fox could not support Fitzgerald's demands for an independent Irish state. Ambivalence therefore came to characterize Fox's views. He took little part in the crisis surrounding the Act of Union in 1800, beyond supporting the general principle of religious toleration, as he always did. The mishandling of the Irish situation by Pitt and the king had, in his view, produced a situation where only extreme options were available, and thus the Foxite was left without a relevant policy.

Warren Hastings and the regency crisis After 1784 Fox was happiest when an issue could be directly related back to the debates of that year; then he was at his most sure-footed. The impeachment of Warren Hastings fitted the pattern neatly. Before 1783 Fox, unlike Burke, had shown little or no interest in Indian affairs. It so happened, however, that the Fox–North coalition government had been brought down by the defeat of its India Bill. To prove that the bill had been necessary by proving the delinquency of Warren Hastings, governor-general of Bengal, was in turn to demonstrate the malignancy of the king in destroying it. As far as Fox was concerned the impeachment of Hastings was less about India than about the crisis of 1782–4 in England. In this respect he diverged sharply from Burke, who increasingly complained about Fox's behaviour. As one of Fox's aunts observed, 'The Trial … is likely to be a party business, and, of course, no justice done' (Fitzgerald, 183). Fox was appointed one of the managers of the impeachment by the House of Commons. In February 1788 he opened the charge that Hastings had gravely misused Chet Singh, the ruler of Benares, in a speech that was widely recognized as an oratorical *tour de force*. Almost immediately afterwards he lost interest in the whole proceedings, much to Burke's discomfiture. Once the connection between the pursuit of Hastings and the death of the coalition government had been established in the public mind Fox saw the trial increasingly as tiresome and devoid of interest.

The same narrow focus determined Fox's role in the regency crisis, which ran from early November 1788 to early March 1789, during George III's supposed bout of madness. Fox was in Italy when the crisis broke and did not reach London until late November. He then became ill and was in Bath from 27 January to 21 February 1789. Essentially, therefore, his party's response to the crisis was left to Sheridan and Grey, who unfortunately offered different policies. Fox sided with the latter in demanding that the prince of Wales be given full rights of regency, with no conditions being set by the Commons. The prince, although a deep embarrassment to Fox in such matters as his secret marriage to Mrs Fitzherbert, was a true party man in his distaste for the king. His assumption of full powers would give Fox the opportunity to reverse the defeat of 1784, even if his denial of the right of the Commons to set terms sat oddly with his claims for that body enunciated only four years earlier. This inconsistency was noted by contemporaries, who accused Fox of snatching at any idea that would bring him power. Caricaturists showed him as Falstaff suborning the prince of Wales. Fox's defence lay in the fact that his absences and illness prevented him from being a central figure in the drama and in the thought that, if executive power was to be guarded against, it could be safely entrusted to the prince of Wales, if not to his father.

Fox and France Very early in life Fox pronounced himself a confirmed Francophile, and thereafter he never changed his mind. He spoke and read the language fluently and, as a young man, conspicuously dressed in the French style. He was cosmopolitan by temperament and his frequent visits to Paris had confirmed this inclination. His circle of acquaintance was wide but certain men became his particular friends; Lafayette, Noailles, Talleyrand, Orléans, and Lauzun were those he knew best and liked most. Not surprisingly, perhaps, they were all to be found in that section of the French aristocracy which welcomed the events of 1789. The first four were to become prominent politicians, the last, as duc de Biron, a leading general. Some had also fought for Washington, thereby linking in their own careers events in England, France, and America. Whenever Foxites visited Paris these men arranged their programmes. This was true of Holland's visit in 1791 and of Fox's in 1802. In particular huge numbers of Foxites poured into the French capital between 1789 and 1791 in order to witness the revolution and to bring first-hand reports back to England.

Educated in the same classical culture, polished in the same salon society, and travellers with common friends, these men came to call themselves citizens of the world. They claimed to have no substantial national loyalties. Fox called his Parisian friends 'French Whigs', while Talleyrand referred to the Foxites as 'our masters' (Mitchell, *Charles James Fox*, 109). Lafayette, in writing to Fox in 1800, appealed to 'Cette Sympathie de Liberté et de patriotisme qui Unira toujours, j'ose le dire, Certaines Ames' ('That sympathy for liberty and patriotism which will, always, I dare to say, unite certain souls'; Mitchell, *Charles James Fox and the Disintegration of the Whig Party*, 154). Citizens of the world thought of politics in simple terms. On one side were despots and intolerant churches; on the other stood the friends of representative government and toleration. In the 1770s Lafayette had fought for Washington, and Fox had supported him in the Commons. Between 1782 and 1784 Foxites had received letters of encouragement from their American and French friends. In 1789 Fox and Jefferson welcomed the fall of absolute monarchy in France. Over these years the battlefield changed but not the purpose of the battle. Lafayette assured Holland that 'Si nos deux pais peuvent avoir dans le même tems [*sic*] une

administration libérale, la cause du genre humain est gagnée' ('If our two countries could have a liberal administration, the cause of human kind is won'; Mitchell, *Charles James Fox*, 109).

Fox's loyalties were not national but were offered to people like himself at home or abroad. This carried the advantage that he would always have first-hand information about French events. But there was also the disadvantage that cosmopolitanism was suspect in the minds of those who did not share it. Very soon after 1789 the caricaturist began to show Fox in the guise of the Jacobin, certainly un-English and possibly traitorous.

The French Revolution, 1789–1792 Fox's reaction to news of the fall of the Bastille was, famously, 'How much the greatest event it is that ever happened in the world, & how much the best' (30 July 1789, *Memorials and Correspondence*, 2.361). His French friends were at last in charge of their country's affairs. The violence of the summer of 1789 was regrettable but that soon passed, and for the next two years they were intent on turning an absolute monarchy into a constitutional state. Even if American models were followed more closely than English ones Fox could only approve of a constitution, completed in 1791, that included a propertied franchise, religious toleration, and an assault on the institution of slavery. It appeared so sensible and so whiggish. All his friends who visited France in these years confirmed this interpretation. So involved was Fox in these events that he occasionally intervened directly. He decided to write to Barnave, for example, to urge continued moderation after the French king's flight to Varennes in 1791. The habit of directly interfering in the politics of other countries became a Foxite trait that, on more than one occasion, irritated Pittite governments. All of this led Fox to misunderstand the dynamic of the revolution. For him, it was essentially a French adaptation of the revolution of 1688 in England, when in fact it increasingly proved itself to be something quite different.

Predictably Fox had no sympathy with the arguments put forward in Burke's *Reflections on the Revolution in France*, published in November 1790. Burke's belief that the revolution represented a profound threat to the ideas of propertied government, organized religion, and prescriptive values in politics, bringing with it confusion and violence, seemed strangely at odds with what Fox knew of France at first hand. He read the book but found it 'in very bad taste' and 'favouring Tory principles' (Mitchell, *Charles James Fox*, 113). Both Burke and Fox had seen absolutist France as a threat to England but now the former believed that the menace had deepened, while the latter thought that it had been removed. In Fox's view there was no reason why a constitutional France should attack parliamentary England. In April 1791 Fox told the House of Commons that he 'admired the new constitution of France, considered altogether, as the most stupendous and glorious edifice of liberty'. France was now a country 'from which neither insult nor injustice was to be dreaded' (15 April 1791, *Speeches*, 4.199).

If war threatened in these years, it came from an altogether different direction. In the autumn of 1790 Fox was active in securing a peaceful outcome to a dispute with Spain over Nootka Sound, on the west coast of America. In March–April 1791 he performed a similar function in helping to resolve difficulties with Russia over the ownership of the fortress of Ochakov on the Black Sea. On this occasion he sent a personal emissary, Sir Robert Adair, to St Petersburg. A grateful Catherine the Great placed a bust of Fox in a cabinet, between those of Cicero and Demosthenes. In an immediate sense Fox could contrast the potentially disruptive nature of traditional dynastic politics with the quiet constitution making in France.

France, 1792–1799 After the overthrow of the French monarchy in August 1792 Fox's views had, of necessity, to be remodelled. Quite clearly the revolution was now taking a different path from that followed by England in 1688. He was appalled by the violence of the Jacobin republic. The September massacres disgusted him. The execution of Louis XVI, Marie Antoinette, and some of his friends, such as Biron, were examples of 'wild extravagance & unfeeling cruelty' that 'stained the noblest cause that ever was in the hands of Men' (Mitchell, *Charles James Fox*, 131). Equally the constitutional experiments of the Directory failed to impress him. He was only too well aware that they were vitiated by corruption and a lack of genuine commitment to parliamentary values. From the summer of 1792, therefore, Fox found himself in the uncomfortable position of having no option in France that he could positively favour.

In reordering his thoughts Fox first tried to apportion blame for the revolution's descent into violence, and once again his thoughts turned to the mismanagement of kings. First, as George III was a reluctant constitutionalist, so Louis XVI's 'fate was in a great degree owing to his avowed connection with the nobility of that country; a nobility whose views were hostile to the interests of the people' (25 Nov 1795, *Speeches*, 6.41). One of the principal reasons for the failure of the 1791 constitution had been Louis's refusal to play his part in good faith. His monarchical misbehaviour was compounded, in Fox's view, by the fact that his fellow rulers declared war on France in 1792–3. Despots joined in the first coalition and then attacked the revolution in order to snuff out whatever was liberal in its make-up. In doing so the war took on an ideological sharpness of focus, being despotism against constitutionalism. Fox was not surprised that Pitt and George III entered the coalition against France on 1 February 1793. Once this situation was in place Fox's choice became clear. Nothing in France attracted him but every alternative was worse. French liberty, however perverted and misdirected, had to be preferred to despotisms in arms. As he wrote to Mrs Armitstead:

> Any thing that proves that it is not in the power of Kings and Princes by their great armies to have every thing their own way is of such good example that without any good will to the French one can not help being delighted by it, and you know I have a natural partiality to what some people call rebels. (Mitchell, *Charles James Fox*, 125)

Another crucial factor in Fox's thinking that led to the same conclusion was an insistence that it was France that had been attacked; the terror was a dreadful example of defensive measures to meet a national crisis. Fox never abandoned, until the last few months of life, the notion that successive French governments really wanted peace, if only European despots would allow it. In particular the British government, by pouring subsidies into Europe, was intent on keeping the war going. In August 1795 Fox, typically, told his nephew:

> Peace is the wish of the French of Italy Spain Germany and all the world, and Great Britain alone the cause of preventing its accomplishment, and this not for any point of honour or even interest, but merely lest there should be an example in the modern world of a great powerful Republic. (Mitchell, *Charles James Fox*, 162)

If France was pacific and Britain was the aggressor it was only right to offer sympathy to the former. To many of Fox's contemporaries this was an idiosyncratic reading of events that bordered on treason.

Fox and Napoleon The establishment of Napoleonic France changed little in Fox's thinking. The new regime had originated in a *coup d'état* directed against a representative system, however defective. It was therefore 'a very bad beginning … the manner of the thing quite odious' (Mitchell, *Charles James Fox*, 166). On the other hand coalitions of despots still would give France no peace, which was what Napoleon most desired. Fox reasoned that someone who had come to power by a coup, who was faced with civil war within France itself, and who faced financial problems on a huge scale must have wanted a peace above all things. If he was to survive at all Napoleon had to be 'moderate, wise, and … pacifick' (ibid., 167); only English money and the enduring resentments of George III and Pitt kept the war going. When a peace with Napoleon was finally signed at Amiens in 1802, Fox was relieved and delighted. Controversially, in his eyes, it was none the worse for being a peace that was generous in its terms to the French:

> However it may have happened, it is an excellent thing, and I do not like it the worse for its being so very triumphant a peace for France … Bonaparte's triumph is now complete indeed, and, since there is to be no political liberty in the world, I really believe he is the fittest person to be the master. (*Memorials and Correspondence*, 3.34)

The coming of peace allowed the resumption of cross-channel visiting. Foxites flooded into Paris. Fox himself was in France from 20 July to 17 November 1802, accompanied by his wife, the Hollands, and many others. Talleyrand and Lafayette acted as hosts and introduced Fox to leading figures from the revolutionary period, such as Sieyès and Barère. Fox and his party were so fêted that their activities were kept under surveillance by officials from the British embassy. Fox had three interviews with Napoleon himself, on 2 and 3 September and 7 October. None of them went well. Conversation degenerated into arguments about how free the press should be and how useful or pernicious was the existence of a standing army in a state. Napoleon tried hard to impress his visitor but Fox saw and heard little to please him.

English caricaturists were merciless in representing this visit as yet another example of Fox's willingness to fawn on anything French. Gillray's *Introduction of Citizen Volpone and his Suite in Paris* was typical. Such criticism was damaging but unfair. Fox returned home with all his previous views confirmed: Napoleon was the enemy of representative government, and a soldier before all else. At the same time he had brought some sort of order back to France, was tolerant in religious matters, and had a creative energy that was awesome. In choosing between evils Bonaparte was the least objectionable. Fox never developed that extravagant admiration for Napoleon that soon afterwards came to flavour the politics of Holland House.

When Fox took charge of English foreign policy once more—when the 'ministry of all the talents' came into office in January 1806—he still had a firm belief that peace with France was always possible. The resumption of war in 1803 had been England's fault yet again. Peace was a matter of an hour's conversation with his old friend Talleyrand, now in charge of France's foreign relations. It was a startling and horrific experience to discover that the French were in fact anything but pacific in intention. There were protracted disputes about the future of Sicily, Switzerland, Hanover, and Malta. Mortally ill, Fox's last months were saddened by the necessity of accepting that his assessment of Bonaparte had been sadly awry. His opponents took pleasure in noting that 'Charley Fox eats his former opinions daily and even ostentatiously' (H. Sandford, *Thomas Poole and his Friends*, 1888, 2.160). In this narrow sense Fox's death, in September 1806, was a mercy; his position had begun to appear ridiculous, not least to himself. According to one critic he 'should have died, for his fame, a little sooner' (ibid.). It was an inglorious ending to an association with France that had in so many other ways proved fruitful and enriching.

Domestic politics, 1789–1794 The whig party confronted the challenges of the French Revolution in a debilitated condition. Some years before 1784 antagonisms had been engendered within the party that merely festered in the 1790s. Burke, both in the impeachment of Warren Hastings and in the regency crisis, felt himself to be the Nestor of the party, whose words and manner were increasingly ignored and even ridiculed. Sheridan, Grey, and Tierney were younger men, whose ambition was of the hurrying kind. It was Fox's responsibility, as party leader, to keep these men together. In this he failed dramatically. The years of the French Revolution graphically underlined his deficiencies as leader. He had neither the will to discipline nor the inclination to pamper. He was often absent from London, and too frequently he only intervened when a crisis was beyond repair. As early as 1791 he was talking privately of retiring from politics altogether. In 1794 he claimed to want nothing more than 'a lodge in some vast Wilderness' (Mitchell, *Charles James Fox*, 132).

The first confrontation was with Edmund Burke, whose *Reflections on the Revolution in France*, published in November 1790, argued that the French experiment, based on natural rights theory rather than prescription, was therefore subversive of all property-based politics. Whigs should consequently oppose it. Fox's interpretation, that the French were merely following English models, was untenable. In theory Fox should have been able to contain these arguments. Burke had been his tutor in whiggery and was always a respected friend. In the House of Commons itself he admitted that 'he was indebted to his right honourable friend for the greatest share of the political knowledge he possessed,—his political education had been formed under him,—his instructions had invariably governed his principles' (2 March 1790, *Speeches*, 4.72). Yet there was no cosseting of Burke. As a result, on 6 May 1791 Burke interrupted a speech in the Commons to announce that all association with Fox was at an end. Both men were in tears. Burke never spoke to Fox again, and on his deathbed in 1797 refused a last interview with his former friend. With his departure the true ownership of the whig legacy could be disputed.

On the other wing of the party Sheridan, too, was causing trouble. He had attended celebrations in London on 14 July 1790, celebrating the fall of the Bastille. More seriously, in April 1792, he and Grey founded an Association of the Friends of the People. Such activity threatened to give whiggery a populist, even democratic, reputation. Fox detested such initiatives; he had disliked Paine's writings on the revolution as much as Burke's. But such was his reluctance to discipline these young men that terrible damage to party unity was done.

In spite of these pressures Fox was able to hold the allegiance of the bulk of his party until July 1794. In particular such grandees as the duke of Portland, Earl Fitzwilliam, and the earl of Carlisle stayed with him until that late date. Until 1792 they preferred to agree with Fox that the French were merely perpetrating a strangely Gallic version of 1688 in England. After that date Fox held their allegiance by the more blatant argument that to cross to the Pittite benches would be, tacitly, to forgive Pitt for his behaviour in 1783–4. So powerful was that magic that it was not until July 1794 that Portland and his friends could confront such a possibility; but then their fear of France was stronger than their resentment about Pitt. Fox could hardly believe that they 'would disgrace' themselves in this manner (Mitchell, *Charles James Fox*, 136).

Domestic politics, 1794–1801 The defections of 1794 reduced Foxite numbers so dramatically that Fox could no longer be said to be leading a party at all. He and his friends were nothing but a talented lobby group; they had no serious pretensions to government. As recently as 1792–3 there had been semi-serious talks with the aim of Fox joining Pitt in a crisis coalition. All such language was now ruled firmly out of court.

A new situation gave Fox only limited objectives. The first was to keep alive some faint semblance of civil and political liberty. Between 1792 and 1797 Pitt enacted a series of emergency measures that effectively put many civil liberties into abeyance while the war lasted. Fox saw them in a darker context, as the permanent extinction of liberty; George III's tyranny would be established using the excuse of the war. As Fox instructed his nephew in 1795:

> There appears to me to be no device at present but between an absolute surrender of the liberties of the People and a vigorous exertion … My view of things is I own very gloomy, and I am convinced that in a few years this Government will become completely absolute, or that confusion will arise of a nature almost as much to be deprecated as despotism itself … This is a great *Crisis*. (Mitchell, *Charles James Fox*, 140)

Foxites therefore offered what assistance they could to those who were persecuted under these measures; Fox himself was a character witness for Arthur O'Connor when the latter was accused of treason in 1798. Similarly, from 1795 onwards Fox re-established contacts with Wilberforce and Wyvill, both in order to keep the reform movements alive and to co-ordinate the energies of all those who, for whatever reason, might be interested in forming a peace party.

Looking for new allies Fox also began to treat radicals like John Horne Tooke with less condescension. Although steadfastly refusing electoral alliances Fox was seen publicly to consort with radicals, notoriously at a dinner in 1798, at which the toast of 'Our sovereign lord, the people' was drunk. For this bravado Fox lost his place on the privy council. This new association with radicals must be kept in perspective, however. In private Fox never subscribed to extravagant forms of parliamentary reform, nor did he agree with radical assessments of the situation in France. His contact with radicals had altogether plainer origins. Quite simply he believed that since 1794 any middle ground in British politics had been removed; nothing was left but the possibility of royal despotism or radicalism. It was not a choice that any Foxite could relish but, if forced to choose, Fox's distaste for George III was still uppermost in his thinking. In 1796 he told his nephew, 'We as a party I fear can do nothing and the contest must be between the Court and the Democrats'. In such a situation it was prudent to offer the latter a little 'Aristocratick Leven' (Mitchell, *Charles James Fox*, 152).

Dismal prognostications such as this fortified Fox in his decision to secede from parliament. From 1797 to 1801 he rarely appeared at Westminster at all. If he had a political role in these years it was through the proxy of his nephew. Action such as this, which could be deemed to be contemptuous of parliament's claims to sovereignty, was highly controversial. Some Pittites argued for Fox's arrest. Some Foxites, such as Sheridan and Tierney, refused to follow their leader's example. But Fox himself believed that he had no choice. As far as he could see the game was up. George III had succeeded in undermining the capacity of Lords and Commons to resist the crown. Civil liberties had been abrogated. He increasingly likened himself to Brutus, the last of the Romans, defeated by the rising tyranny of Pitt as the new Augustus. Many of his own friends were, indeed, already in prison. Politics, in any meaningful sense, had come to an end.

Domestic politics, 1801–1806 Fox had not anticipated Pitt's resignation in February 1801, which, splitting the king's supporters, once more opened up politics to new configurations. Fox felt compelled to return to public life, but only on his own terms. Psychologically he perhaps never

returned. Certainly in the last five years of his life he made very few speeches and only appeared at Westminster irregularly. He still believed that George III, though taking a knock with the loss of Pitt, was ultimately the dominant force in politics. In 1804 he said of the monarchy 'There is not a power in Europe, no not even Bonaparte's, that is so unlimited' (Mitchell, *Charles James Fox*, 194). The fact that the king could appoint Henry Addington, the son of his old doctor, as prime minister proved the point. Fox's return to politics was therefore determined less by the hope of office than by the more limited ambition of giving a push to particular measures and policies. Addington, for example, could be supported as long as he promoted peace with France, and ditched immediately hostilities were resumed in May 1803. Fox had not approved of Addington's appointment or administration generally but had merely bolstered 'Addington's *accommodation* with France' (ibid., 201).

In the spring of 1804 Fox entered into a political agreement with the Grenville party. Critics once again observed that Fox apparently had little difficulty in co-operating with a man whom he had vilified for most of the 1790s. Comparisons were easily made, to Fox's disadvantage, with the coalition of 1783. In fact since 1801 the Grenvilles had shown an increasing willingness to stand up to the king and, more particularly, had become committed to both Catholic emancipation and the abolition of the slave trade. As Fox more and more saw politics in terms of single issues, these were two that were dear to his heart. There was therefore sufficient overlap of interests to make a Fox–Grenville alliance plausible. Even so it was always an association of convenience rather than of affection on both sides.

The Fox–Grenville understanding provided the basis for the 'ministry of all the talents', which took office in January 1806 and in which Fox was once again foreign secretary. Throughout his last term in office Fox was ill with the disease that would eventually kill him. As has been observed above, his conduct of foreign affairs, involving failed peace negotiations with France, was an unhappy one. It was offset to some extent by his major role in securing the abolition of the slave trade. In one of the last speeches he made in the House of Commons he had the honour of moving the appropriate motion:

> So fully am I impressed with the vast importance and necessity of attaining what will be the object of my motion this night, that if, during the almost forty years that I have had the honour of a seat in parliament, I had been so fortunate as to accomplish that, and that only, I should think I had done enough, and could retire from public life with comfort, and the conscious satisfaction, that I had done my duty. (10 June 1806, *Speeches*, 6.659)

This measure and the Libel Act of 1792 are the only pieces of legislation that can be directly attributed to Fox in a career stretching from 1769 to 1806. His long exclusion from office gave his public life a most unusual character. It only made sense, in his eyes, if taken as evidence of the true malevolence of George III.

Fox and reform Fox's attitudes to reform issues were conditioned by two factors. First, he was not born into a reforming family tradition; unlike Pitt he would have to come to reform by way of education and personal conversion. Second, as a good whig, he was libertarian in matters of individual liberty while being reverential towards institutions that had proved their worth. Predictably, therefore, his performance on reform was patchy and, to many critics, ambiguous.

As has been noted above Fox lived his own life with minimum reference to the opinion of others. He was anxious always to extend this privilege to others. In his view the state and society in general should allow as much freedom of choice and information as was consistent with stability and security. This belief was most clearly expressed in religious matters. Toleration in religion was one of his most consistent objectives. From support for the dissenters' campaign of 1773, to win admittance to Oxford and Cambridge, to their wider campaigns of the 1780s and 1790s, for full civil and political equality, Fox was always their ally. He was equally complaisant towards the claims of Roman Catholics. The Test Acts had been justified by the idea that Catholicism and dissent represented political dangers. He was clear that the passage of time had rendered them harmless. To argue otherwise was to raise an 'alarm which can be accounted for on no rational principle' (14 May 1805, *Speeches*, 6.601). More importantly still, toleration was to be argued for in the language of natural rights. Fox told the Commons that 'Toleration in religion was one of the great rights of man, and a man ought never to be deprived of what was his natural right' (19 April 1791, *Speeches*, 4.192). He was a consistent opponent of both the slave trade and of slavery itself; he told a close friend that he 'should prefer the abolition of it to any political good that can be gained or even wished, for the Party or the country' (Mitchell, *Charles James Fox*, 248). Fox's monument in Westminster Abbey is, with some justice, supported by the figure of a weeping black slave.

On issues where individual rights were less involved Fox was all ambiguity. The pupil of Burke did not undertake institutional change lightly. He had no interest in the kinds of economical reform that so intrigued Pitt. He had nothing to offer the Irish, constitutionally, after 1782. Above all his reaction to parliamentary reform was marked by an enormous disparity between public and private statements. On hustings in Westminster in the early 1780s Fox could find merit in something close to universal suffrage as an antidote to executive power. In private he thought reform might do some small good, particularly after 1784, when a purified House of Commons might be better able to constrain a rampant executive. But there was never great enthusiasm for the project. He voted for the reform bills of 1785, 1792, and 1797 but wished no success to the first, because it had been promoted by Pitt, and heartily wished that the last two had never been brought forward. With justice, committed reformers like John Jebb and Christopher Wyvill deeply suspected that Fox could not be trusted on the issue. After his death these ambiguities were lost in the hagiography that surrounded his name but in historical terms Fox was a reformer sometimes, on some issues, and in some contexts.

Fox and religion Fox had little or no connection with organized religion. He had no record of church-going and numbered few clergymen among his friends. Men such as the Revd Henry Bate or William Dickson, bishop of Down, were either rakes in priest's clothing or admirers of Fox's intelligence without religious reference. Most people of strong religious convictions never felt happy in Fox's company; it was hard for them to understand or forgive his private life or his public statements. This fact considerably compromised Fox's standing as a reformer because so many of his contemporaries approached reform with religious promptings. Christopher Wyvill, William Wilberforce, and many dissenters found it hard to work with Fox on reform issues and doubted his motives.

Above all Fox refused to allow that religious prescriptions should constrain the individual in private life, and he detested ostentatious shows of piety. In 1773 he bluntly told the House of Commons that 'Religion was best understood when least talked of' (*Memorials and Correspondence*, 1.71). Such views were inevitably controversial in a society in which the reformation of manners was very much part of the social agenda promoted by the king himself. Fox gave enormous offence, for example, as a junior minister in North's government for supporting a proposal that would have allowed divorced women to marry the co-respondents in their cases. Religion and its claims closely to regulate morality was a legacy of the seventeenth century that Fox refused to accept. In this respect neither Roman Catholicism nor dissent, as religious systems, could hold any attraction.

Fox believed that maintaining a certain distance from revealed religion had positive advantages; it was the only guarantee of well-founded toleration. The diarist Samuel Rogers recorded Fox as saying:

> The only foundation for toleration is a degree of Scepticism and without it there can be none, for if a Man believes in the saving of souls, he must soon think about the means; and if, by cutting off one generation, he can save many future ones from Hell-fire, it is his duty to do it. (Mitchell, *Charles James Fox*, 243)

The kind of mild deism that Fox affected allowed all religious systems to be given equal weight and value.

Fox had no belief in an afterlife. When his last secretary, John Trotter, suggested otherwise in a draft biography the passage was removed at the behest of Fox's surviving family. There was no priest at Fox's deathbed and no religious rites accompanied his passing, other than prayers that he allowed to be read, out of consideration for his wife.

Foxites Central to Fox's life and career was his view that 'friendship was the only real happiness in the world' (Mitchell, *Charles James Fox*, 12). It is vital to understand that Foxite politics was often merely an extension of friendship with Fox, a carrying over of activities at Newmarket and in Brooks's Club into Westminster. Fox was one of the most gifted men of the late eighteenth century. Johnson and Burke recognized him as an equal. He was highly intelligent, amusing, and only spasmodically ambitious. Subscriptions to Brooks's fell away on the infrequent occasions when Fox was called away to office, because one of the principal entertainments was no longer available. Further, Fox never used friendship to mould, influence, or discipline. Friendship never had an ulterior motive. Such passive amiability was calamitous in a party leader but made for compelling friendships. A new phrase, 'to Charley it', was coined to express the pleasure of being asked to spend a weekend at Fox's home at St Anne's Hill (Mitchell, *Charles James Fox and the Disintegration of the Whig Party*, 253).

In return Fox's followers indulged him to an outrageous degree, forgiving him for political misjudgements and personal embarrassments. Many of them became embroiled in Fox's debts but complaint was rare. Those, like George Tierney, who did remonstrate from time to time were very much the exception that underlined a general rule. Strikingly, particularly after 1794, the word 'whig' gave way to the word 'Foxite' as the appellation under which they were happy to act; as this change of title suggests their politics were simply what Fox said and thought. Foxites were generally a decade or so younger than Fox himself. Most, like Edward Bouverie, 'invariably voted in favour of almost every motion proposed by the late Charles James Fox, who was one of his dearest and most intimate friends' (J. Wilson, *A Biographical Index of the Present House of Commons*, 1806, 442). There was much in this arrangement that was warm and reassuring but it also carried dangers. Fox increasingly cocooned himself within the circle of his friendships, cutting himself off from salutary comment from other quarters. According to one critic 'The Misfortune of Fox (one misfortune) has been, that he avoids, or at least does not invite the knowledge of what is said out of his own circle' (Mitchell, *Charles James Fox and the Disintegration of the Whig Party*, 250). Foxite self-sufficiency was a distinctive, political style, whose exclusiveness was its greatest strength and its major weakness, at one and the same time.

In Foxite circles mutual affection and regard was reinforced by a consciousness of martyrdom. To follow Fox after 1794 was to suffer loss. Professional careers were blighted; sons, like Charles Grey, became embroiled in family disputes with their fathers; Michaelangelo Taylor was disinherited. At best all prospect of office disappeared for a whole generation. Quite properly they were styled 'Fox's martyrs'. Significantly though, in these trying circumstances, certain Foxites kept a skeleton party apparatus intact. James Perry and the *Morning Chronicle* remained true to Fox, as did William Adam, the party's general manager. When former friends returned to the fold in the early decades of the nineteenth century they rejoined a party that Foxites had shaped and fashioned. It was in itself no mean achievement of Fox's friends. As Lord John Russell remembered, 'There were only forty of them, but every one of them is ready to be hanged for Fox' (Lord John Russell, *Recollections and Suggestions*, 1875, 268).

Death In December 1805, just before the 'ministry of all the talents' took office, Fox began to exhibit the symptoms of serious illness. It was described as 'a dropsical

complaint' (Mitchell, *Charles James Fox*, 236); his legs and abdomen began to be distended with water. On 7 August 1806 he underwent the first of a series of tappings to remove the water but these painful operations were only palliatives. He died at 5.45 p.m. on 13 September 1806 at Chiswick House, west of London, which the duke of Devonshire had loaned him for the period of his illness. There is some doubt about his last words. His secretary recorded them as 'I die happy; I pity you.' His wife thought they were 'It don't signify, my dearest, dearest Liz' (ibid., 237). In its philosophic detachment this latter version more likely captures the truth. A post-mortem examination revealed a hardened liver, thirty-five gallstones, and no less than 7 pints of a transparent fluid in the abdomen.

By his will Fox left £250 to his nephew, Lord Holland, and to a certain Robert Stephen; there was also an annuity for a Harriet Willoughby. Both of these are assumed to be illegitimate children. Another boy, also carrying a family name, Henry, is mentioned in other sources but not in the will; quite possibly he predeceased Fox. One of these boys was deaf and mute; Fox would communicate with him by using a kind of sign language. The bulk of the estate was left to Mrs Fox.

Fox's funeral took place at Westminster Abbey on 10 October 1806. It was a private, not a public, occasion yet Fox's friends were delighted to observe that the crowds who turned out to pay their respects were at least as numerous as those which had watched Pitt's obsequies nine months earlier. Fox was buried near the west door of the abbey. A monument was commissioned from Westmacott at the enormous cost of £6000. The dying statesman is shown lying on a couch, dressed in a toga; two weeping women, also in classical draperies, stand on one side of the couch, a mourning black slave on the other.

The Fox cult in the nineteenth century The close friendships that underpinned Foxite politics gave his name a talismanic quality. The youth of so many of his adherents ensured an astonishing longevity to his influence. Whig politics in the first three decades of the nineteenth century cannot be properly understood without taking into account the enduring power of Fox's career and personality. A Fox Club was formed in London as early as 1790. In 1808 it held the first of its Fox dinners, which then became annual events marking Fox's birthday. Very quickly their proceedings became a model to be followed all over the country. Very quickly, too, the nature of the evening became ritualized. Ideally the guest of honour would be one of the 'martyrs' from the 1790s or, as Holland described them, 'the old ones of Claret and Foxite memory' (Mitchell, *Holland House*, 51). The miseries and sufferings of Fox's career would then be tearfully rehearsed, after which standard toasts associated Fox's name with reform issues he had known and with topics that had arrived on the political agenda long after his death. His name alone gave whiggish respectability to any point of view. As Grey told a Fox dinner in Newcastle in 1819 'What subject is there, whether of foreign or domestic interest, or that in the smallest degree affects our Constitution which does not immediately associate itself with the memory of Mr Fox' (*The Times*, 7 Jan 1819). The last recorded dinner took place in Brooks's Club in 1907.

The posthumous deification of Fox took many other forms as well. The bust of him by Joseph Nollekens became an indispensable adornment of whig houses. Locks of his hair and complete sets of his speeches were given as birthday presents in whig families. Portraits and busts appeared everywhere. The duke of Bedford placed a bust of Fox in the centre of his pantheon of whig worthies at Woburn Abbey and a statue in Bloomsbury Square. His portrait hung in the dressing room of Sarah Siddons. In 1811 the prince of Wales took the oaths of office as regent with a bust of Fox at his side. The names Charles or Charles James were the baptismal choices for many boys at whig christenings. In symbol Fox far outlived his natural life. The centre of this worship was his nephew's home at Holland House, whose lobby was dominated by another Westmacott statue of his uncle. Most of the first volume of Holland's *Memoirs of the Whig Party during my Time* was given over to a discussion of Fox's career and the enduring relevance of his beliefs.

By its very nature the transformation of politics into totems that can properly be called religious did not allow of doubt. The ambiguities and irregularities in Fox's career were smoothed away by the passage of time. The rough edges in his politics, of which there were many, were simply honed away. This is particularly true on reform issues. Two decades or so after his death it would have been a great heresy for a whig to argue that Fox had ever been anything but an uncomplicated friend of change. Sir James Mackintosh, who had known Fox well, could assure those at an Edinburgh Fox dinner in 1823 that 'it is said those who hold the opinions of Mr Fox are the advocates of Catholic Emancipation and Parliamentary Reform. We are the advocates of Catholic Emancipation and Parliamentary Reform' (*Morning Chronicle*, 18 Jan 1823). In historical terms he was only 60 per cent right. By the same generous effect of time passing Fox was accorded posthumous victories. In the debates of 1828–9, which finally allowed full emancipation to dissenters and Catholics, and in those of 1830–32, which finally reformed parliament, Fox's name is invoked again and again. To many whigs in those years these were the final victories in campaigns that Fox himself had initiated. The Foxite cult allowed Fox more success after death than he had ever known in his lifetime.

Literature and history Inevitably Fox is remembered largely for his role in politics. Almost certainly such an emphasis would have displeased him. Politics, for him, was an absorbing aspect of life but only one among many. Fox's response to Pitt was largely conditioned by sympathy and contempt for someone who seemed to have no life outside politics. By contrast Holland recorded that 'My Uncle Charles who is confessedly the most indulgent of Politicians is likewise the one, who has the greatest variety of occupations and amusements that bear no relation to these subjects—*Fireside Amusements*' (Mitchell, *Charles James Fox*, 178). After 1784 more and more time was spent at St Anne's Hill, where 'Nightingales, Flowers, Litterature,

History etc.' were 'good and substantial reasons for staying here' (ibid.). After the party splits of 1794 Fox's interests swung dramatically away from politics altogether, to the dismay of some of his young followers who wished to keep up the Westminster battle against Pitt.

Fox's intellectual life operated within specific categories and was far from all-encompassing. Surprisingly he had little or no interest in political or economic theory. He had not hurried to read Burke or Paine on the French Revolution; Godwin was unreadable; Rousseau's *Contrat Social* was simply 'too extravagant' to be of use to a practising politician (7 May 1793, *Speeches*, 5.115). As for the fashionable claims of political economy Fox dismissed them by telling Grey that he did not 'mind those things' (W. E. S. Thomas, *The Philosophic Radicals*, 1979, 53). He read Adam Smith's *The Wealth of Nations* but thought that half of it could have been 'omitted with much benefit to the subject'; it was, overall, 'tedious' (Trotter, 36). Fox's lack of interest in, or understanding of, financial policy was turned into myth. There was a story current by the mid-nineteenth century that 'Charles Fox never could understand what Consols were—he knew that they were things that went up and down in the City, and he was always pleased when they went down, because it so annoyed Pitt' (A. West, *Recollections, 1832–1866*, 1899, 2.297–8).

Compared to studies such as these literature was in every way preferable and, in particular, the poetry and prose of Greece and Rome, which Fox admired as a schoolboy and continued to read in their original languages for the whole of his adult life. Friendships with classical scholars such as Samuel Parr in early life, and with Gilbert Wakefield after 1796, confirmed these predilections. It was one of Fox's proudest achievements that he established dates for the Greek poet Lycophron that have never since been challenged. Fox also read Spanish, Italian, and French. Letters to his nephew were, to some extent, tutorials in the literatures of these countries. He had a particular liking for the work of Dante, Boccaccio, and Ariosto. In English literature his preferences were firmly for the Augustan poetry of the early eighteenth century. He disliked Romantic literature for its subject matter and the primacy it seemed to give to the outpouring of emotion. Wordsworth sent Fox a presentation copy of the *Lyrical Ballads* but, in return, received only the frosty comment that the great statesman was 'not of your faction' (A. Dyce, *Reminiscences and Table Talk of Samuel Rogers*, 1903, 88).

Besides literature there was history. Few political creeds were more historically based than whiggery. Many Foxites, in the long wilderness years in opposition, turned to the writing of history for consolation and vindication. Fox was no exception. In 1799 he began work on a project that would be published in 1808 as *A History of the Early Part of the Reign of James II*. It was researched in London and Paris, with many French and English friends being recruited to help with particular manuscript collections. The work was never completed. The published version deals only with the events of 1685. Fox had hoped to go beyond 1688, in order that the virtues of William III should cast the vices of James II into even greater relief.

His choice of topic was hardly accidental. James's reign pointed up a moral:

> We are taught, generally, the dangers Englishmen will always be liable to, if, from favour to a Prince upon the throne, or from a confidence, however grounded, that his views are agreeable to our own notions of the constitution, we, in any considerable degree, abate of that vigilant, and unremitting jealousy of the power of the crown which can alone secure to us the effect of those wise laws that have been provided for the benefit of the subject. (C. J. Fox, *A History of the Early Part of the Reign of James II*, 1808, 103)

For someone who had spent most of his political life opposing what he saw as tyrannical aspirations in George III, these words applied as much to his own day as they did to the circumstances of 1685.

Historiography Since Fox's views were thought to have an enduring relevance to subsequent generations the writing-up of his career has been more than usually influenced by party considerations. The careers of few men have been so totally appropriated by other generations. Fox was claimed as forerunner and guide by elements of the British left down to the twentieth century.

Predictably perhaps, in the first half-century after his death the assessment of Fox's career was a family affair. His papers passed first to his nephew, Lord Holland, who drew on them extensively to produce *Foreign Reminiscences* (1850) and *Memoirs of the Whig Party during my Time* (1852–4). They were then left to Lord John Russell, who had known Fox and who had been brought up at Holland House. As an act of piety he allegedly destroyed those papers that could in any way embarrass Fox's memory before producing *Memorials and Correspondence of Charles James Fox* (1853–7) and *The Life and Times of Charles James Fox* (1859–66). In these early years the only critical works to appear were those written by Fox's last secretary, John Trotter, namely *Circumstantial Details of the Long Illness and Last Moments of the Right Hon. Charles James Fox* (1806) and *Memoirs of the Later Years of the Rt. Hon. C. J. Fox* (1811). Both books were publicly repudiated by surviving members of the Fox family.

When whiggery shaded into Liberalism after 1850 the Fox inheritance passed to writers who were no less anxious to claim him as a progenitor of their own views. Five biographies appeared which hoped to fix Fox in the liberal tradition: they were G. O. Trevelyan's *The Early History of Charles James Fox* (1881), J. L. Hammond's *Charles James Fox: a Political Study* (1903), J. Drinkwater's *Charles James Fox* (1928), E. Lascelles's *The Life of Charles James Fox* (1936), and C. Hobhouse's *Fox* (1947). Studies which have attempted to place Fox squarely in an eighteenth-century context as a man of his time are therefore comparatively recent: they are L. Reid's *Charles James Fox: a Man for the People* (1969), J. W. Derry's *Charles James Fox* (1972), and L. G. Mitchell's *Charles James Fox* (1992).   L. G. MITCHELL

Sources L. G. Mitchell, *Charles James Fox* (1992) · L. G. Mitchell, *Charles James Fox and the disintegration of the whig party, 1782–1794* (1971) · L. Mitchell, *Holland House* (1980) · J. W. Derry, *Charles James Fox* (1972) · *The speeches of the Rt. Hon. C. J. Fox in the House of Commons*, ed. J. Wright, 6 vols. (1815) · *Memorials and correspondence of Charles James Fox*, ed. J. Russell, 4 vols. (1853–7) · Lord John Russell, *The life and times of Charles James Fox*, 3 vols. (1859–66) · H. R. Vassall, Lord Holland, *Memoirs of the whig party during my time*, ed. H. E. Vassall,

Lord Holland, 2 vols. (1852–4) · Lord Holland, *Foreign reminiscences* (1850) · *The correspondence of Edmund Burke*, ed. T. W. Copeland and others, 10 vols. (1958–78) · *The correspondence of George, prince of Wales, 1770–1812*, ed. A. Aspinall, 8 vols. (1963–71) · *The letters of Richard Brinsley Sheridan*, ed. C. Price, 3 vols. (1966) · B. Fitzgerald, *Emily, duchess of Leinster, 1731–1814: a study of her life and times* (1949) · N. B. Perry, 'The whig cult in nineteenth-century sculpture', *Past and Present*, 70 (1976), 94–105 · J. Trotter, *Circumstantial details of the long illness and last moments of the Right Hon. Charles James Fox* (1806)

Archives BL, corresp. and papers, Add. MSS 47559–47581, 51468–51475, 47584–47601, 51457–51459 · Suffolk RO, Bury St Edmunds, accounts as paymaster of widows' pensions · U. Mich., Clements L., corresp. · Yale U., Farmington, Lewis Walpole Library, letters · Yale U., Beinecke L., letters | BL, corresp. with Lord Grenville, Add. MSS 58935, 69038 · BL, corresp. with Thomas Grenville, Add. MS 41856 · BL, Holland House MSS · BL, corresp. with Sir R. M. Keith, Add. MSS 35525–35560, *passim* · BL, corresp. with William Windham, Add. MS 37843 · Bodl. Oxf., letters to Thomas Coutts · Bodl. Oxf., corresp. with Lord Macartney · Castle Howard, Yorkshire, Carlisle MSS · Chatsworth House, Derbyshire, Chatsworth MSS · N. Yorks. CRO, corresp. with Christopher Wyvill · NL Scot., corresp. with Robert Liston · Northants. RO, Milton MSS · NRA Scotland, letters to William Adam · priv. coll., letters to William Eden · priv. coll., corresp. with duke of Manchester · priv. coll., letters to Lord Shelburne · Royal Arch., letters to George III · Sheff. Arch., corresp. with Edmund Burke · Sheff. Arch., corresp. with Lord Fitzwilliam · Sheff. Arch., letters to marquess of Rockingham · Suffolk RO, Bury St Edmunds, letters to duke of Grafton · U. Durham L., letters to second Earl Grey · U. Nott. L., letters to duke of Portland · Yale U., Beinecke L., letters to Caroline Fox

Likenesses J. Reynolds, oils, 1764–5, Eton College · J. Reynolds, oils, 1782, Holkham Hall, Norfolk [*see illus.*] · T. Day, miniature, 1787, NPG · portrait, 1790–95, Palace of Westminster, London · J. Nollekens, marble bust, 1791, Hermitage, St Petersburg · J. Nollekens, marble bust, *c*.1802, V&A · S. W. Reynolds, mezzotint, pubd 1802 (after J. R. Smith), BM, NPG · J. Nollekens, marble bust, 1803, Castle Howard, North Yorkshire · J. Opie, oils, 1804, Holkham Hall, Norfolk · J. Nollekens, marble bust, 1805, NPG · T. Rowlandson, six caricatures, coloured etchings, 1806, V&A · C. Williams, caricature, coloured etching, pubd 1806, V&A · J. Nollekens, marble bust, 1808, Royal Collection · R. Westmacott, statue, *c*.1810–1815, Westminster Abbey · R. Westmacott, bronze statue, *c*.1816, Bloomsbury Square, London · H. Edridge, pencil sketch, BM · K. A. Hickel, group portrait, oils (*The House of Commons, 1793*), NPG · K. A. Hickel, oils, NPG · T. Hickey, double portrait, oils (with Edmund Burke), NG Ire. · W. Lane, group portrait, chalk (*Whig statesmen and their friends, c*.1810), NPG · J. Nollekens, terracotta bust, NPG · T. Phillips, portrait, priv. coll. · J. Sayers, caricatures, etchings, NPG · caricatures, BM, NPG · chalk drawings, NPG · plaster bust (after J. Nollekens), Scot. NPG · plaster medallion (after W. Whitley), Scot. NPG

Wealth at death debts of £10,000

Fox, Charles Richard (1796–1873), army officer and numismatist, eldest child of Henry Richard Vassall *Fox, third Baron Holland (1773–1840), and Elizabeth Vassall *Fox (1771?–1845), daughter of Richard Vassall, was born on 6 November 1796 at Brompton Park House, London, eight months before his mother's divorce from Sir Godfrey Webster and his parents' marriage in July 1797. The Hollands took him to Spain from 1802 to 1805. He was at Eton College from January to October 1808, but left to accompany his parents once more to Spain (1808–9). Debarred by illegitimacy from succession to the family peerage, he served first in the navy (1809–13), and was present at the sieges of Cadiz (1810) and Tarragona (1813). After travelling with his parents on the continent in 1814–

15, he joined the army as an ensign in June 1815. He became colonel in 1837 and general in 1863.

On 19 June 1824, Fox married Mary FitzClarence (d. 1864), second daughter of the duke of Clarence and his mistress, Dorothy Jordan. She was raised to the rank of a marquess's daughter on 24 May 1831, and was housekeeper of the state apartments, Windsor Castle (1835–45). In 1829 Fox went with his regiment to Halifax, Nova Scotia, but on his father-in-law's accession as William IV he was appointed, on 24 July 1830, equerry to Queen Adelaide and recalled. In March 1831 he was made equerry to the king but resigned over William's attempt in early May 1832 to dispense with Grey's ministry. However, the king appointed him an aide-de-camp on 28 May 1832. As a member of a prominent whig family he sat in parliament for Calne (1831–2) and Tavistock (1833–4). He was elected for Stroud in May 1835, but immediately resigned in favour of the home secretary, Lord John Russell. He stood unsuccessfully for Sandwich, in May 1841, and sat for Tower Hamlets (1841–7). He served at the Board of Ordnance under successive whig governments: as surveyor-general (a junior ministerial post, 1832–4), as secretary to the master-general (1835–41), and then as surveyor-general again (May–September 1841 and 1846–1852). In 1836 his father, as chancellor of the duchy of Lancaster, appointed him its receiver-general for life.

Possessed of scholarly and antiquarian interests, Fox was elected a member of the Society of Dilettanti in 1837. In 1843 he inherited most of the books and papers of John Allen (1771–1843), of whom he later contributed a brief memoir to Allen's *Inquiry into … the Royal Prerogative in England* (1849). His early interest in coin collecting was strengthened by his travels in Greece and Turkey in 1820 while aide-de-camp to Sir Frederick Adam at Corfu. In 1840 Sir Alexander Burnes gave him his collection of Bactrian coins. In 1851 he acquired one of the collections of Whittall of Smyrna. He also bought at the Pembroke, Thomas, and Devonshire sales, but in 1852 sold off his duplicates. He published a description of part of his collection, entitled *Engravings of Unedited or Rare Greek Coins*, part 1: 'Europe' (1856). A new edition (1862) included part 2: 'Asia and Africa'. The collection was purchased (after Fox's death) in 1873 by the Royal Museum, Berlin, the acquisition raising its coin cabinet to international status. The Fox collection consisted of 11,500 Greek coins, among which were 330 in gold, and more than 4000 in silver. It was remarkable for its many rare or unique specimens, and for their admirable state of preservation.

After the death of his first wife on 13 July 1864, Fox married, on 16 August 1865, Katharine, second daughter of John Maberly MP, who survived him. He had no children. Fox died on 13 April 1873, after a long illness, at his house, 1 Addison Road, Kensington, his home since 1827. Fox inherited his father's amiability, and displayed wit without cynicism. He endeavoured to make his house a literary centre, especially for some of the younger antiquaries. In politics he called himself 'a movement whig'.

C. J. WRIGHT

Sources Holland House MSS, BL · Earl of Ilchester [G. S. Holland Fox-Strangways], *The home of the Hollands, 1605–1820* (1937) · Earl of Ilchester [G. S. Holland Fox-Strangways], *Chronicles of Holland House, 1820–1900* (1937) · J. Allen, *Inquiry into the rise and growth of the royal prerogative in England*, ed. B. Thorpe, new edn (1849), xviii–xxv · J. Friedlaender, 'Die Fox'sche Münzsammlung', *Archäologische Zeitung*, 31 (1874), 99–103 · J. Friedlaender and A. von Sallet, *Das königliche Münzkabinet* (1877), 43–5 · *Catalogue of Greek coins … being the duplicates of the collection of … C. R. Fox* (1852) [sale catalogue] · A. Michaelis, *Ancient marbles in Great Britain*, trans. C. A. M. Fennell (1882), 64, 165 · *JHL*, 41 (1796–8), 334 [evidence in Webster Divorce Bill] · m. certs. · d. cert. · H. E. C. Stapylton, *The Eton school lists, from 1791 to 1850*, 2nd edn (1864), 61 · *DNB*

Archives BL, corresp. relating to numismatics, Add. MS 39997 · BL, family corresp., Add. MSS 51780–51793, 51966, 52057–52058, 52170–52171 · NRA, priv. coll., journals and notebooks | All Souls Oxf., letters to Sir Charles Richard Vaughan · BL, corresp. with John Allen, Add. MS 52176 · BL, letters to Lady Holland, Add. MS 52150 · Blair Adam, Kinross-shire, Adam of Blair Adam MSS · PRO, corresp. with Lord John Russell, PRO 30/22 · U. Southampton L., corresp. with Lord Palmerston

Likenesses A. Cooper?, oils, *c*.1815, repro. in Earl of Ilchester [Fox-Strangways], *Chronicles* · G. Hayter, group portrait, oils, 1833 (*The House of Commons, 1833*), NPG · C. Landseer, oils, 1836, repro. in Earl of Ilchester [Fox-Strangways], *Chronicles* · J. Doyle, pen-and-pencil, 1847, BM · J. E. Boehm, medal, 1862, BM · wood-engraving (after photograph), repro. in *ILN*, 62 (1873), 393

Wealth at death under £80,000: probate, 29 April 1873, *CGPLA Eng. & Wales*

Fox, Charles Richard Jeremy (1921–1991), writer on jazz and radio broadcaster, was born on 7 April 1921 at 4 Clarence Buildings, Weymouth, Dorset, the son of Harold Fox, at the time an electrician with HMS *Gibraltar*, and his wife, Martha Mary Warren. The family moved to Bournemouth in the mid-1930s, and Fox lived there until he moved to London in 1954. He developed an interest in jazz in his schooldays and soon began to study and write on the subject. Fox was giving regular record recitals to the Bournemouth Rhythm Club by the early 1940s, helping to formulate many local youthful tastes for jazz; he made a similar contribution in the field of modern literature, of which he was also an enthusiastic follower. Everyone who has written appreciatively of his career has noted his wide and all-embracing tastes; his outlook on both music and literature was founded on the traditional but extended to the most avant-garde. Before he was able to write for a living, he worked for Thomas Cook, the well-known travel agency. During the war years he worked in the drawing-office of the Experimental Bridging Establishment at Christchurch, where the famous Bailey bridge was conceived.

Fox moved to London in 1954, having already established a solid reputation as a jazz critic through his writing in various jazz magazines including *Jazz Forum*, published in the 1940s, and he later became a regular contributor to Albert McCarthy's *Jazz Monthly*, founded in 1955, which published some of the country's most intelligent writings on jazz until it folded in 1972. His services were soon in demand for the newly created LP sleeves, and he wrote many for the smaller jazz labels as well as for the larger EMI, Philips, and Decca groups, for the latter writing regularly for the London series Origins of Jazz. He also contributed to *The Decca Book of Jazz* (1958) and *Duke Ellington: his Life and Music* (1958) (both edited by Peter Gammond), contributing one of the best pieces in the book on Ellington (who was always one of his very special interests) and his recordings in the 1930s; he then collaborated with Peter Gammond, Alun Morgan, and Alexis Korner on *Jazz on Record: a Critical Guide* (1960). Charles Fox wrote *Fats Waller* (1960; reprinted in *Kings of Jazz*, New York, 1978) and *Jazz in Perspective* (1969); and collaborated with Valerie Wilmer on *The Jazz Scene* (1972) and with Max Harrison and Eric Thacker on *The Essential Jazz Records, Volume 1* (1984; 2nd edn, 2000). An outstanding example of his writings on jazz was 'Sit down and listen: the story of Max Roach', an article in *Repercussions: a Celebration of African–American Music* edited by Geoffrey Haydon and Dennis Marks (1985). There was a frequent strain of wit in his reviews, a good example being reprinted in Jim Godbolt's *A History of Jazz in Britain, 1950–70* (1989). But like others who have become too deeply embroiled in the more temporal forms of journalism and broadcasting, he never got round to writing the really substantial volumes on jazz that his followers would have liked him to produce, or what would surely have been welcome books on his other interests such as music-hall and cricket (he was a loyal supporter of Hampshire).

From the early 1950s Fox was a regular jazz record reviewer for *The Gramophone*, and he wrote for *Jazz News* from 1951 to 1962. He was also jazz critic at various times for the *New Statesman*, *The Guardian*, and the *Sunday Times*. He interviewed many leading jazz musicians including Benny Carter, Milt Jackson, Dizzy Gillespie, Earl Hines, and Clark Terry for BBC Radio 3's series *Jazzmen Talking* and presented a history of jazz called *Jazz in Perspective* for the same network, as well as conceiving many individual radio features, of which the most ambitious were documentaries on Jelly Roll Morton and Max Roach and a history of ragtime. From the early 1960s he was the host of the weekly record programme *Jazz Today*. In the 1970s he returned to his native Weymouth to live at 40 The Esplanade; he travelled to London each week to record the programme, keeping a 'pad' in Bayswater at the home of Alexis Korner and his wife. When Peter Clayton became ill he took over Radio 3's *Jazz Record Requests*, but Clayton briefly took over again when Charles Fox suddenly succumbed to a heart attack and died in an ambulance on his way to the Weymouth and District Hospital on 9 May 1991.

Fox's great literary interests were less known. A shared interest in poetry led to a friendship with the poet Christopher Logue, whom he first met in 1949 at a meeting of the Bournemouth Film Society. With the help of Patrick Brangwyn they produced for a short while a poetry magazine entitled *Ninepence*. Fox often contributed poems to other magazines, both jazz and literary—a typical example of his crossover interests being 'Poem for the Late Jimmy Noone' published in 1947. At this time he wrote and published a children's book. In 1958 he was involved with Logue in the experimental poetry-and-jazz

movement and produced a successful album with the backing of the Tony Kinsey Quartet.

The fostering of serious jazz interest on BBC Radio 3 was Charles Fox's natural niche; he was an erudite and scholarly man, bearded and prone to wearing the tweed jackets and woolly pullovers so characteristic of the immediate post-war years, and many may have found him a bit daunting at first acquaintance. But then one discovered a person of great warmth, charm, wit, and humour, always ready to spend generous time on any jazz or literary project. He is remembered as one of the finest writers and talkers on jazz that the British scene has produced.

PETER GAMMOND

Sources B. Kernfeld, ed., *The new Grove dictionary of jazz*, 2 vols. (1988) · *The Times* (11 May 1991) · *Daily Telegraph* (11 May 1991) · *Daily Telegraph* (16 May 1991) · personal knowledge (2004) · b. cert. · d. cert. · *CGPLA Eng. & Wales* (1991) · J. Godbolt, *A history of jazz in Britain, 1950–70* (1989)

Wealth at death under £125,000: probate, 28 Aug 1991, *CGPLA Eng. & Wales*

Fox, Sir Cyril Fred (1882–1967), archaeologist and museum director, was born at Chippenham, Wiltshire, on 16 December 1882, the first son of Charles Frederick Fox FSA, a bank official, and his wife, Henrietta Maria Paul, of Saffron Walden in Essex. His sister married Bernard Gotch, the watercolour artist. He was of Hampshire stock with roots in the Isle of Wight, and the family returned to that county during his boyhood. From a preparatory school in the Isle of Wight he went on to Christ's Hospital, then (1895–8) still in London, but though he did well his days there were arid, for he was always a countryman at heart. Diphtheria and other illness led to his leaving school at sixteen to take up market gardening at Worthing. He was already gaining an interest in the antiquities of the countryside, and in Sussex he encountered a Cambridge bacteriologist, Louis Cobbett, who obtained for him a position as a clerk at the bovine tuberculosis research station at Stansted in Essex. Removal of this institution to Cambridge in 1912 led Fox into exploring the antiquities of the Cambridge region. Having already served in the Essex yeomanry (Territorial Army), when the First World War broke out he received a commission. But further illness kept him in England and after the war he returned to the research station as superintendent of its field laboratories. However, post-war reorganization made his future there uncertain, and at thirty-six he turned to archaeology as a career.

Fox gained entry to Magdalene College, Cambridge, in 1919, as a part-time student of archaeology, at first reading for the English tripos, and was much encouraged by Professor H. M. Chadwick, who had him transferred to work for a PhD. In 1922 he had assembled his material for a thesis, which was published in 1923 as *The Archaeology of the Cambridge Region*. This was a landmark in archaeological thinking, and gave Fox an immediate standing among scholars. He was elected a fellow of the Society of Antiquaries of London in the same year, and was appointed to an assistantship in the Museum of Archaeology and Ethnology at Cambridge.

In 1924 Fox was nominated keeper of the National Museum of Ireland, but the electors' choice of an Englishman was not confirmed at higher level, a German archaeologist, Walter Bremer, being appointed. Mortimer Wheeler had, however, already persuaded Fox to apply for the keepership of archaeology under him as director at the National Museum of Wales; though Cambridge would have liked to retain him, he accepted the Cardiff position. Two years later, in 1926, he succeeded Wheeler as director, and guided the affairs of the National Museum of Wales until his retirement in 1948. Fox's time as director saw great developments. A monumental new building was in hand, and he brought to fruition the plans for the Welsh Folk Museum at St Fagans—rural craftsmanship was always dear to Fox's heart. And Fox, though he himself never spoke Welsh, achieved the unifying of the regional and local museums of the principality by affiliation to the National Museum.

Fox served with distinction on public bodies such as the royal commissions on ancient and historical monuments in Wales and in England, and on the Ancient Monuments Board of the Ministry of Works. Yet he never allowed these duties or the administration of a great national museum to slow his own impetus to pursue research. The museum had a long tradition of fieldwork to give life to its collections, and this was congenial to the countryman's outlook; Fox seized every opportunity for such activity, as the stream of publications testifies. Wales provided him with all the expanding variety of terrain and problems he needed for the rest of his long working life.

In 1932 Fox followed his Cambridge regional study with another classic, *The Personality of Britain*. In this work he carried the new trends of thinking then current in human geography into prehistory and protohistory. 'This study of Britain as an environment for Man' was produced as one of four major discourses for the International Congress of Pre- and Protohistoric Sciences in London that year. It shows Fox as an exponent of the distribution map as an archaeological tool, and many of the maps were made in fruitful collaboration with Lily Chitty. Its dual division of Britain into highland and lowland zones (sometimes called Fox's law) was not subsequently so much followed in detail, but the work had a strong influence on the thinking of a whole generation, and the concept of a Jurassic zone as a determinant through the whole of the human historical geography of Britain held its place.

Fox's archaeological studies ranged widely in time, and each is a pioneer model of its class. His many perceptive excavations of burial mounds in Wales led through individual reports to his *Life and Death in the Bronze Age* (1959). Work on the Cambridgeshire dykes led naturally to a full field survey of Offa's Dyke as the great boundary between England and Wales, the successive reports being brought together in a British Academy publication (1955). Finds of the Iron Age in Wales yielded a number of important papers and museum monographs, culminating in his *Pattern and Purpose: a Study of Early Celtic Art in Britain* (1958).

Fox's study of rural houses in Wales was also most influential. The three volumes he produced (with Lord Raglan), *Monmouthshire houses: a study of building techniques and smaller house plans from the 15th to the 17th centuries* (1951–4), did much to give a respectable scholarly status to work on such buildings among social and economic historians, and, most important, in the Royal Commission on Historical Monuments (England). The whole subject of vernacular architecture owed much to Fox.

In 1934 Fox was president of the Museums Association, and in 1935 was knighted for his services to museums. In 1940 he was elected fellow of the British Academy. He served as president of the Society of Antiquaries of London from 1944 to 1949, through the crucial post-war years, and was awarded the society's gold medal in 1952. He was an honorary DLitt of Wales (1947) and an honorary fellow of Magdalene (1952). He was held in high esteem by his colleagues, as marked by the volume of twenty essays, *Culture and Environment* (1963), in his honour.

Fox was one of the leading archaeological thinkers of a fruitful generation. He was a man of energetic enthusiasm, capable of inspiring colleagues and friends. He was a rapid worker, as the flourish of his penmanship reveals; he was not given to laboured reworking of completed tasks. He had a deep love of literature and poetry, paying great attention to the words he wrote. He had a fine visual memory, which he did not, however, allow to impede the flow of his original creative thought. Fox saw the past as a continuum leading into the present. His interests lay above all in the landscape, and in all forms of human craftsmanship. He was remembered for the humanism he brought into archaeological interpretations.

In 1916 Fox married Olive, daughter of Arthur Congreve-Pridgeon, vicar of Steyning in Sussex. She was drowned off the Gower peninsula in 1932; with her he had two daughters, Helen Felicity, an art critic, and Penelope Eames, the author of a work on medieval furniture (1977). He married second in 1933 Aileen Mary, an active archaeologist, daughter of Walter Scott Henderson, solicitor, of Surrey; they worked much together in the field. He retired to Exeter, where she held a position of university lecturer in archaeology. There were three sons of this marriage. Fox died at the Cranford Nursing Home, Cranford Avenue, Exmouth, Devon, on 15 January 1967.   E. M. JOPE, *rev.*

Sources S. Piggott, 'Sir Cyril Fox, 1882–1967', *PBA*, 53 (1967), 399–407 · W. F. Grimes, *Archaeologia Cambrensis*, 116 (1967), 208–10 · M. Wheeler, 'Homage to Sir Cyril Fox', *Culture and environment: essays in honour of Sir Cyril Fox*, ed. I. L. Foster and L. Alcock (1963), 1–6 [incl. bibliography] · personal knowledge (1981) · private information (1981)

Archives English Heritage, Swindon, National Monuments Record, corresp. · Museum of Welsh Life, Cardiff, corresp. and papers · NL Wales, corresp. and papers · U. Cam., Museum of Archaeology and Anthropology, corresp. and papers | Bodl. Oxf., letters to O. G. S. Crawford · NL Wales, corresp. with Thomas Jones · S. Antiquaries, Lond., letters to C. F. Tebbutt

Likenesses Elliott & Fry, photograph, 1931, NMG Wales, NPG · photograph, 1932, repro. in Grimes, *Archaeologia Cambrensis*, facing p. 208 · silhouette, 1933, NMG Wales · E. Walters, charcoal drawing, 1937, NMG Wales · L. Monroe, ink drawing, 1939, priv. coll. · W. Stoneman, two photographs, 1945–58, NPG · portrait, S. Antiquaries, Lond. · portrait, priv. coll.

Wealth at death £5767: probate, 3 April 1967, *CGPLA Eng. & Wales*

Fox, Sir (Charles) Douglas (1840–1921), civil engineer, was born near Smethwick on 14 May 1840, the eldest in the family of three sons and one daughter of Sir Charles *Fox (1810–1874), civil engineer, and his wife, Mary, daughter of Joseph Brookhouse, clockmaker, of Derby. He attended Cholmondeley School, Highgate School (1851–4), King's College School (1854–5), and King's College, London (1855–7), of which he became an honorary fellow in 1887.

Fox was to have gone to Trinity College, Cambridge, but that plan foundered with the sudden financial collapse in early 1857 of his father's erstwhile flourishing contracting business. Instead, he was articled to his father who, later in 1857, had begun to practise as a consulting engineer in London. In 1863 Fox joined his father in partnership. The latter had already built an international reputation in railway and allied engineering. By 1865 the new practice was involved in major projects in Britain, the USA, Canada, southern Africa, India, Australia, and South America. Douglas Fox's potential was well exercised when, from 1863 to 1866, the firm, still just father and son, masterminded the complex system of railway viaducts and bridges in Battersea, separating the lines from the east and south to Victoria from those from the south-west to Waterloo, including the widening of the Grosvenor Bridge over the Thames from two to seven tracks.

Sir Charles Fox died in 1874. His second son, Francis *Fox, had joined the partnership, which the two brothers now carried on together as Douglas Fox & Partners. Work continued to pour in, especially from southern Africa and South America, but also at home. The brothers' commitments included acting as consulting engineers to the Central Argentine Railway Company (jointly with Livesey, Son and Henderson); the South Indian Railway Company; the Southern São Paulo Railway Company; and also the Dorada (Columbia) Railway Company. In 1886 Douglas Fox and James Brunlees were knighted on completion of the first tunnel under the Mersey which, along with the railway linking Birkenhead with Liverpool, they had jointly engineered.

Among the many projects for which the firm was responsible during Fox's later years were the Liverpool Overhead Railway (the first electric elevated city railway in the world), the extension from Rugby to London of the Great Central Railway, including its Marylebone terminal, the Great Northern and City tube (with large tunnels to accommodate standard rolling stock), and the 'Hampstead tube' linking Charing Cross with Golders Green and Highgate. Abroad they included much of the Cape government railways in southern Africa, the whole Rhodesia railway system, including the 500 ft span Victoria Falls arch bridge over the Zambezi River, the Benguela railway in Angola, and several railways and other works in South America.

Fox was president of the Institution of Civil Engineers (1899–1900). He was a JP for many years. Like his father, he was of an urbane and generous disposition. Having inherited his mother's religious principles, he was strict in his observances, and not only at home, but also at his office, prayers began each day for all present. A member of the Church of England, he was active in the Church Missionary Society. In 1863 he married Mary (d. 1920), daughter of Francis *Wright, a Derbyshire industrialist of Osmaston Manor, Derby. They had one son and four daughters. His brother Francis also married a daughter of Francis Wright, whose Butterley Company manufactured railway equipment, including the cast iron for Vauxhall Bridge and Paddington Station.

Fox died on 13 November 1921 at 27 Campden House Road, Kensington, the home of one of his daughters.

RALPH FREEMAN, rev.

Sources PICE, 213 (1921–2), 416–18 · The Times (15 Nov 1921) · The Engineer (18 Nov 1921) · private information (1993) · CGPLA Eng. & Wales (1921)
Archives CUL, corresp. with Lord Kelvin
Wealth at death £45,766 8s. 2d.: probate, 20 Dec 1921, CGPLA Eng. & Wales

Fox, Douglas Gerard Arthur (1893–1978), schoolmaster and musician, was born on 12 July 1893 at Putney, London, the only son and elder child of Gerard Elsey Fox, an engineer, and his wife and first cousin, Edith Makinson Spencer. His mother, a good pianist, began to teach him the piano when he was four and was already showing signs of unusual musical talent. Gerard Fox became manager of his employer's branch in Bristol, whereupon his son entered the preparatory department of Clifton College, where Arthur Peppin was already making his name as director of music. The boy caused some consternation in the sight-reading tests by experiencing no difficulty with any of the pieces put before him. Peppin sent him for tuition to R. O. Beachcroft, a fine teacher and a pianist of distinction.

In 1907 Fox went up to the senior school and became the first holder of Clifton's newly founded music scholarship (value £24 per annum). In March 1910 he left Clifton, having won an open organ scholarship to the Royal College of Music. There he was taught by Sir Walter Parratt (organ), Herbert Sharpe (piano), S. P. Waddington and later Charles Wood (harmony and counterpoint), and Sir Charles Villiers Stanford (orchestral rehearsals). In 1911 he became an associate of the Royal College of Organists (ARCO) in January, winning the Sawyer prize, and a fellow (FRCO) in July. In 1912 he entered Keble College, Oxford, with the organ scholarship.

At Oxford, Fox came to know Hugh Allen, later Heather professor of music, and Henry Ley, organist of Christ Church and later precentor of Eton. Fox had joined the university Officers' Training Corps in May 1914 but when the First World War broke out the warden of Keble turned down his application for leave to apply for a commission with the explanation: 'Your duties here are so necessary for the College life.' Later he was able to join the 4th Gloucestershire regiment. He served in France in 1916, was sent home with trench fever, and returned to the front in 1917.

On 4 September 1917 he wrote with his left hand to Arthur Peppin: 'I was wounded on the 27th August and on the 28th they took my arm (right) off just above the elbow. Apparently they consulted very carefully before doing it, but it seems to have been hopelessly shattered, and they thought I probably should not have lived if they had left it' (*The Times*). The letter is devoid of regret, bitterness, self-pity, or despair. Sir Charles Parry wrote a few days later to Peppin: 'I don't think anything that happened in this atrocious war has so impressed me with the very malignity of cruelty as the utter destruction of that dear boy's splendid gifts.' Stanford wrote to Fox's father: 'I am sure his art will come out somehow.' When Hugh Allen, then organist of New College, heard the news he played evensong in the chapel using only his left hand and the pedals. This sort of encouragement was a major factor in helping Fox adjust to his handicap. In January 1918 Allen invited him to become president of the Oxford University Musical Club for the summer term and he returned to Oxford, immersing himself in its musical life. In that term he was offered and accepted the post of director of music at Bradfield College. This was a major turning point in his life.

Fox was director of music at Bradfield from 1918 to 1930, when he moved to the same position at Clifton College. In both posts he made an outstanding contribution to musical education. He was recognized as one of the finest teachers of his day, setting the highest standards for his pupils, and reaching them constantly himself in spite of his physical handicap. He built up a sizeable repertory for organ and piano recitals which he gave in all parts of the country and for the BBC, and he gave especially memorable performances of the Ravel concerto for the left hand. He produced a steady stream of successful candidates for scholarships at the universities and colleges of music, but perhaps his greatest achievement was to infect with his enthusiasm that larger number of boys who were not themselves performers on any instrument and whose interest was latent. His remarkable qualities were widely recognized; he was president of the Music Masters Association (1931) and of the Incorporated Society of Musicians (1958).

Fox retired from Clifton in 1957, and became organist of Great St Mary's Church, Cambridge, where he remained until 1963, making a valuable contribution to the musical life of both the city and the university. He was appointed OBE in 1958, and Bristol University conferred on him an honorary DMus in 1966. His doctorate of music at Edinburgh University in 1938 was by examination (he had become BMus at Oxford in 1920). He was made a fellow of the Royal College of Music in 1973 and he was also an honorary member of the Royal Academy of Music.

Fox died on 23 September 1978 at Cowlin House, 26 Pembroke Road, Clifton, Bristol, where he had lived for some years with his devoted sister Winifred, who survived him by three years. He was unmarried. In his address at the crowded memorial service held in Clifton College chapel on 25 November, Sir Thomas Armstrong, who had succeeded Fox as organ scholar of Keble in 1916 and later became principal of the Royal Academy of Music, said:

> Douglas stands, in a way, for the whole of that doomed generation, for all the men killed and maimed on the Somme, in the Salient, and on many fronts—the men whose hardships and joys, whose sufferings and sacrifices, he

shared. We speak of them as heroes: but heroism manifests itself in different ways: sometimes it is a matter of a moment's instinctive decision: sometimes of patient endurance, without the excitement of battle, perhaps for a lifetime: sometimes, it is a question of facing death, more often of facing life. Douglas's heroism was of the latter kind, begun in a moment of tragedy, continued in the daily problems of professional life, and ended in the recognition, freely accorded him, of a task well done.

H. G. EDWARDS, rev.

Sources W. Fox, *Douglas Fox, a chronicle* (1976) · *The Times* (28 Sept 1978) · Sir T. Armstrong, memorial service address, Clifton College, 25 Nov 1978 · personal knowledge (1986) · WWW · CGPLA Eng. & Wales (1978)
Archives SOUND BL NSA, performance recordings
Wealth at death £75,325: probate, 3 Nov 1978, CGPLA Eng. & Wales

Fox, Ebenezer (d. 1886), journalist, was born in England, and practised his profession in the north until he had nearly attained middle age. For several years he was chief reporter on the *Manchester Guardian*. His account of the great floods at Holmfirth in 1852 was widely quoted. Delicate health induced Fox to emigrate first to Australia and then in 1862 to New Zealand. He settled in Dunedin and joined the staff of the *Otago Daily Times*, the first daily newspaper in New Zealand, which had been formed in 1861 by Julius Vogel and William Cutten, the latter being replaced in 1864 by Benjamin Farjeon. In 1868, after a company had taken over *The Times*, Vogel lost the editorship and that year founded a competitor, the *New Zealand Sun*, in which he was joined by Fox. When that collapsed in 1869 the two friends moved to Auckland. Vogel joined William Fox's ministry as colonial treasurer, and Ebenezer Fox became his private secretary. In 1870 Fox was appointed confidential clerk and secretary to the treasury, which position he held until his death, being implicitly trusted by successive ministries. In the *New Zealand Times* he wrote a series of articles on deforestation which attracted much attention. Fox, whom contemporaries described as kindly but eccentric in character, died of muscular atrophy at Wellington in January 1886.

G. B. SMITH, rev. ELIZABETH BAIGENT

Sources *New Zealand Times* (9 Jan 1886) · *Phonetic Journal* (20 March 1886) · G. H. Scholefield, *Newspapers in New Zealand* (1958) · R. Dalziel, 'Vogel, Julius', *DNZB*, vol. 1 · R. Dalziel, *Sir Julius Vogel, business politician* (1986)

Fox, Edward (1496–1538), diplomat and bishop of Hereford, was born at Dursley, Gloucestershire, one of at least three children of William Fox (of a well-known Shropshire gentry family) and his wife, Joanna. According to one unreliable source he had a brother named Charles; he is more reliably reported to have had a brother named Edmund and a sister Joanne (later Joanne Austen). Fox was educated at Eton College and at King's College, Cambridge (where he was admitted on 27 March 1512), elected a fellow in 1515, graduated BA in 1517, proceeded MA in 1520, and received a doctorate in either divinity or canon law in 1532. While at Cambridge he was supposed a member of the famous White Horse tavern discussion group (perhaps being influenced by Lutheran views—he also developed an interest in conciliarist political theory). He probably vacated his fellowship between 1525 and 1527, but from 22 September 1528 to 8 May 1538 he served King's as provost, a legal position in the king's gift.

Fox's early clerical career was advanced by Cardinal Wolsey, whom he served as secretary. Wolsey conferred on Fox his first preferment as prebendary of Osbaldwick, York (8 November 1527). Later, through royal patronage (probably as rewards for his work on the divorce), he was rector of Combe Martin, Exeter (from 3 January 1528), archdeacon of Leicester (1531–5), dean of Salisbury (from May 1533), and archdeacon of Dorset (from 1533). In May 1535 he was presented to the prebend of Sts Mary and George at Windsor. He was also made master (non-resident) of Sherburn Hospital, co. Durham, in December 1528. Fox was royal almoner from c.1532, prior to his elevation to the see of Hereford (nominated 20 August 1536, temporalities restored on 2 September). He is last referred to as royal almoner in 1537, when Henry VIII made over to him for the royal alms the goods of all suicides.

As secretary to Wolsey, Fox became involved in the first crisis arising from Henry VIII's wish for a divorce, becoming one of the king's most valued agents thereafter. In 1527 he helped to recruit the services of the Hebraist Robert Wakefield, and in February 1528 he and Stephen Gardiner were sent to Orvieto in Italy, to negotiate with Pope Clement VII. They were to obtain an open decretal commission, which would allow the case to be tried and decided in England, but on 13 April they only secured a fresh dispensation for Henry to marry Anne Boleyn, and a general commission, which might be subject to appeal. Fox was on hand to meet Lorenzo Campeggi on 9 October 1528 on his arrival in England and was present at the cardinal's first audience with the king on the 22nd. A year later, in October 1529, Fox brought Thomas Cranmer back to the king's attention, after a chance meeting with Cranmer near Waltham Abbey in the previous August. In February 1530 he and Gardiner were sent to secure Cambridge's collective approval of the matter (a formal expression of opinion in favour of the divorce was signed by 200 scholars) and two months later, with John Longland and John Bell, he secured a similar declaration from Oxford. Fox was later sent to Paris (on 7 July 1530), to join John Stokesley and Reginald Pole in their negotiations with the scholars of Paris.

Alone or with other scholars Fox produced a number of polemics and books on the divorce, including the first drafts of the so-called *Henricus octavus*, a book presented in the king's name in 1529 at the Blackfriars annulment trial, and a book entitled *Gravissimae, atque exactissimae illustrissimarum totius Italiae et Galliae academiarum censurae* (1530), written with John Stokesley and Nicholas de Burgo. This was later translated into English by Cranmer and entitled *The Determinations of the Moste Famous and Mooste Excellent Universities of Italy and France* (1531). With access to this material, it is likely that Fox and Stokesley were also responsible for a further polemic on the divorce, the influential *Glasse of Truthe* (1532). Fox subsequently debated the issues with Thomas More, John Fisher, and Eustace

Chapuys, and voted in support of the divorce as prolocutor of the lower house of southern convocation. He was also very much a supporter of the royal supremacy, having carried out a great deal of research on the issue for the king. In 1537 he was among the scholars who agreed that the authority of a general council is higher than that of the pope, and later agreed that the 'bishop of Rome' has no more authority in England than any other foreign bishop. It was Fox's self-appointed task to collect further evidences in support of the supremacy. His gatherings, with those of others, were brought together to form the so-called *Collectanea satis copiosa*, while Fox also wrote an investigation and comparison of papal and royal authority entitled *De vera differentia regiae potestatis et ecclesiasticae, et quae sit ipsa veritas ac virtus utriusque*, which was printed by Berthelet in at least two editions (1534 and 1538).

Fox was a talented diplomat, and was often employed in this capacity on issues not involving Henry VIII's divorce. In 1532 he was one of the signatories to a treaty with France, and was present later when this treaty received the signatures of Henry VIII and the French ambassador. He was in France in April 1533, a commissioner to conclude a yet stricter league with François I, and in 1534 went to Scotland to arrange a similar peace treaty. His most important diplomatic missions, however, were to Germany, to negotiate both with princes and with Lutheran theologians. In 1535 he worked with Cranmer at Lambeth, discussing various points on which he would have to confer with the Lutheran divines in Germany. On 31 August he received his credentials from the king, and in October set out with Nicholas Heath to meet initially with the elector of Saxony and afterwards with other German rulers. While overseas Fox made an important address to the protestant league of Schmalkald (24 December), and secured from the elector and Philip, landgrave of Hesse, a petition known as the Christmas articles. In April 1536, again attempting to negotiate a religious agreement, Fox attended a Schmalkaldic diet at Frankfurt, and took back to England the reply of the protestant divines, known as the Wittenberg articles. The German theologians wanted the king to subscribe to the articles, which he refused to do.

Theologically, Fox was very much of a Lutheran persuasion, and indeed, Martin Bucer dedicated to Fox a treatise on the eucharist which prefaced the 1536 edition of his commentaries on the gospels. In that same year Fox tried to give a Lutheran slant, based upon the Wittenberg articles, to the book of ten articles, a formulary intended to resolve certain questions of doctrine and ceremonial, which was presented to convocation for ratification on 11 June 1536, and subsequently seen into print by Fox. Then in 1537, when the king demanded that the bishops meet again to resolve further theological difficulties, Fox similarly influenced the production of *The Institution of a Christian Man*, better known as the Bishops' Book. This new formulary was drawn up through a number of committee and synodal meetings, in which debate polarized around Fox and the very conservative Stokesley. Gardiner noted 'much stoutness' between them, but progress was still made, and the Bishops' Book was brought to publication by Fox just before his death.

As bishop of Hereford, Fox was in office too briefly, and in residence too rarely, to be truly effective. He did conduct one visitation of his diocese, which resulted in injunctions for the Augustinian abbey at Wigmore, addressing the usual monastic problems of discipline and debt. Fox died in London on 8 May 1538, and was buried in the church of St Mary Mounthaw, London. His will, which was dated to the day of his death, was proved on 20 March 1539. He left legacies of £10 apiece and cloth to friends and family members, and bequeathed money and salt (to be provided by Sir William Fitzwilliam in repayment of debts owed to Fox), to King's College, Cambridge, leaving the residue of his estate to his sister Joanne and brother-in-law John Bridget.   ANDREW A. CHIBI

Sources F. Oakley, 'Edward Foxe, Matthew Paris, and the royal *potestas ordinis*', *Sixteenth Century Journal*, 18 (1987), 347–53 • *LP Henry VIII*, vols. 1–3 • A. A. Chibi, *Henry VIII's bishops: administrators, scholars and shepherds* [forthcoming] • *CSP Spain*, *1485–1543* • *CSP Venice*, *1509–58* • G. D. Nicholson, 'The nature and function of historical argument in the Henrician reformation', PhD diss., U. Cam., 1977 • E. Surtz and V. Murphy, eds., *The divorce tracts of Henry VIII* (1988) • S. Thompson, 'The pastoral work of the English and Welsh bishops, 1500–58', DPhil diss., U. Oxf., 1984 • L. B. Smith, *Tudor prelates and politics, 1536–1558* (1953) • *State papers published under … Henry VIII*, 11 vols. (1830–52) • T. Fuller, *The worthies of England*, ed. J. Freeman, abridged edn (1952) • T. F. Mayer, 'A fate worse than death: Reginald Pole and the Parisian theologians', *EngHR*, 103 (1988), 870–91 • H. A. Kelly, *The matrimonial trials of Henry VIII* (1976) • T. F. Mayer, *Thomas Starkey and the commonweal: humanist politics and religion in the reign of Henry VIII* (1989) • N. S. Tjernagel, *Henry VIII and the Lutherans: a study in Anglo-Lutheran relations from 1521 to 1547* (1965) • C. G. Bretschneider and others, eds., *Corpus reformatorum*, [101 vols.] (1834–) • P. Janelle, *L'Angleterre catholique á la veille du schisme* (1935) • W. H. Frere and W. P. M. Kennedy, eds., *Visitation articles and injunctions of the period of the Reformation*, 3 vols., Alcuin Club, Collections, 14–16 (1910) • PRO, PROB 11/27, fol. 203v • A. A. Chibi, 'The social and regional origins of the Henrician episcopal bench', *Sixteenth Century Journal*, 29 (1998), 955–73 • A. T. Bannister, ed., *Registrum Caroli Bothe, episcopi Herefordensis*, CYS, 28 (1921) • A. A. Chibi, 'The intellectual and academic training of the Henrician espiscopy', *Archive for the Reformation* (1998)

Archives BL, Cott. MS Vitell. B. xiii • BL, Cott. MS Cleo. E, vi • CCC Cam., MS 242 • Oxford University Library, Bodley MS 282 • PRO, state papers domestic, Henry VIII, SP 1/56, 1/63

Fox, Elizabeth Bridget. *See* Armitstead, Elizabeth Bridget (1750–1842).

Fox, Elizabeth Vassall [*née* Elizabeth Vassall], **Lady Holland** [*other married name* Elizabeth Vassall Webster, Lady Webster] (**1771?–1845**), political and literary hostess, was the only child of Richard Vassall (1732–1795), the heir to three Jamaican sugar plantations, by his marriage in spring 1770 to Mary (*c.*1750–1835), daughter of Thomas Clarke of New York. Mary Vassall married secondly, in 1796, Sir Gilbert Affleck, bt (*d.* 1808). Elizabeth celebrated her birthday on 25 March and was probably born in 1771, describing herself in her journal as two years eight months older than her second husband (BL, Add. MS 51927, fol. 164v). Her place of birth has been given variously as London and Jamaica, and by 1781 her father was living on the eastern side of Golden Square, London. Left

Elizabeth Vassall Fox, Lady Holland (1771?–1845), by Robert Fagan, 1793

largely to her own devices as a child, she benefited from the cultured friendship of a neighbour in Golden Square, Anthony Morris Storer (1746–1799). As a young woman, she was also to display an interest in science.

On 27 June 1786, aged fifteen, Elizabeth Vassall was married to Sir Godfrey Webster, fourth baronet, of Battle Abbey, Sussex. Her husband, born on 25 December 1747, was over twenty years her senior and the couple were ill assorted. However, she established a close friendship with Thomas Pelham, later second earl of Chichester, Webster's political patron in the whig party. She had five children: Godfrey Vassall Webster (1789–1836), later fifth baronet; a son who died young, born in 1790; Henry Vassall Webster (1793–1847); Harriet Frances (1794–1849), later Lady Pellew; and a boy who lived for seventeen days, born in October 1795. In 1791 her husband agreed to indulge her desire for foreign travel. After a stay in Paris, they journeyed through Switzerland to Nice, where she joined the circle of the duchess of Devonshire. In 1792 the Websters visited Germany before travelling south again via Prague, Vienna, and Venice, reaching Naples in October. In 1793 they returned briefly to England but almost immediately set off again for Italy.

In Naples in 1794 Lady Webster met Henry Richard *Fox, third Baron Holland, the nephew of Charles James Fox; and in May 1795 she refused to return to England with her husband, who in August changed his name to Vassall on succeeding to his father-in-law's West Indian estates. Early in 1796 she conceived a child by Lord Holland and in

May travelled back to England with him, where their son Charles Richard *Fox was born on 6 November. On 4 July 1797 Webster divorced his wife and resumed his previous surname, retaining for life her West Indian fortune of £7000 per annum; and on 6 July, at Rickmansworth, she married Lord Holland. With him she had five further children: Stephen (1799–1800); Henry Edward *Fox (1802–1859), later fourth and last Baron Holland; Mary Elizabeth (1806–1891), later Lady Lilford; Georgiana Anne (1809–1819); and a daughter, born and died on 24 June 1812. Following Webster's suicide on 3 June 1800, Holland assumed the additional name of Vassall to safeguard his children's right to his wife's West Indian fortune.

The divorce, which meant that Lady Holland could not be presented at court, rendered her position a difficult one and her notoriety was increased by the disclosure that, to retain one at least of her Webster children, she had staged the illness, death, and fake burial of her daughter Harriet in Italy in 1796. The child was returned to her father in 1799. The story, which was widely known, received a fresh airing in Lady Charlotte Bury's *Diary Illustrative of the Times of George the Fourth* (1838). It is a testimony to her intelligence and strength of character that despite these disadvantages Lady Holland was able to establish so dominant a position in society. Wishing to enlarge her second husband's circle, 'as he, thank God, lives constantly at home', she avidly sought out new acquaintances for him. Within a short time Holland House, a Jacobean mansion at Kensington purchased by Holland's grandfather, had become one of the most brilliant centres of political and literary society in all Europe. The dazzling roll-call of her guests is recorded in her Dinner Books, 1799–1845 (BL, Add. MSS 51590–51597). Part of the attraction of the house was the contrasting characters of the Hollands themselves. Joseph Jekyll's son characterized them as resembling the opposite poles of a magnet, he attractive and she repulsive. She was certainly a demanding hostess. T. B. Macaulay described her as 'this violent, weak, imperious woman'. In 1820, at a time of unrest in southern Europe, Lady Granville joked that Lady Holland was 'the only really undisputed monarchy in Europe' (V. Surtees, ed., *A Second Self*, 1990, 140). Her regal manner was satirized by Lady Caroline Lamb in *Glenarvon* (1816), where she appears as the 'princess of Madagascar', a nickname which stuck. Most of her friendships were punctuated by quarrels occasioned by her demanding nature and forthright opinions. Her intermittent hostilities with Thomas Creevey and Charles Greville are well known, but in 1834 there was a serious dispute with Lord and Lady William Russell over her comments on their incompetent conduct of British affairs at Lisbon in 1833, and in 1835 she accused Talleyrand of being a tory in disguise.

Holland allowed her to exercise an unrestrained despotism over his household and daily life. On one occasion when Lord Grey insisted she let her husband have a slice of melon at dinner, he remarked 'Ah, Lord Grey, I wish you were always here. It is a fine thing to be Prime Minister.' In later years, if she thought he was overtiring himself, she would have the servants wheel his chair away from the dinner table while he was in mid-conversation. However, it was he who firmly dictated the politics of the house. On her marriage to Holland she had regarded the whig party, centred as it was around a few great families, as 'obsolete' but by late 1830, when the whigs came to power, Tavistock said she was acting and thinking 'as if … in the days of the Pelhams & Walpoles'. Nor did Holland permit her to interfere in significant political decisions. When in May 1827 she urged him to take office under Canning, she herself admitted 'he had requested her to leave him alone and not ever advise him one way or the other'. Contemporaries considered that, ambitious as she was for her husband, she had damaged his career. In January 1828 when she demanded of Lord John Russell why Holland had not been made foreign secretary, he retorted, 'If you must know, it is because no man will act in a Cabinet with a person whose wife opens all his letters.' In fact, however, the real reason Holland was not offered a post in the Goderich ministry was due solely to George IV's distaste for his politics.

Lady Holland was widely held to value all things foreign before anything British. She accompanied Holland on his European tours, notably to Spain (1802–5 and 1808–9), from which she was one of the first to introduce the dahlia to England. Her admiration for Bonaparte developed early. When British troops were embarked for service against France in 1800, she observed complacently 'they inspire as little alarm to their enemies as they do confidence in their countrymen'. In 1815, while travelling in Italy, she commissioned a bust of Napoleon from Canova. Her desire to visit him on Elba was frustrated only by his flight which may, ironically, have been precipitated by copies of *The Courier* she had sent him, which reported discussions at Vienna on the advisability of removing him to the south Atlantic. Despite this, she was to secure permission from the British government for herself and others to send out books and other luxuries to him on St Helena. His complaints about his custodian there, the hapless Sir Hudson Lowe, she and her husband accepted at face value. On his death in 1821, Bonaparte left her the gold snuff box presented to him by Pius VI at Tolentino in 1797; this she bequeathed to the British Museum.

Lady Holland's independence of mind also exhibited itself in a disdain for religion. This was strengthened by the presence in the Holland household from 1802 of John Allen (1771–1843), who was known as Lady Holland's atheist or 'anti-chaplain', though she discouraged as impolite any too overt expression of such views at the dinner table. She was, however, extremely superstitious. Macaulay observed that she was 'afraid of ghosts, but not of God'. She also feared death. This may partly account for her chronic hypochondria. At one point she was being treated by seven physicians. Dr Chambers's forthright observation in response to her complaints of heart and stomach pain in 1833 that as one grew older the heart naturally enlarged, she regarded as her 'death warrant'; his services were summarily dispensed with. However idle her fears may have been, they did serve to render her life miserable.

After the death of Lord Holland on 22 October 1840, Lady Holland could no longer bring herself to live at Holland House but continued to entertain as large a circle as ever, mostly at 33 South Street, which her mother had left her. In November 1843 she moved to 9 Great Stanhope Street, which she rented from Lord Palmerston. John Allen remained a member of her household until his death on 8 April 1843. Her servants (of whom the best known were the Doggett brothers, 'Harold' her page and 'Edgar' the librarian) were devoted to her but her children she succeeded in alienating. Her will was controversial, leaving to Lord John Russell for his life the income from the family's Lambeth estate. Her explanation, that this reflected Holland's intention to leave him the reversion of the Ampthill estate, was disputed. As resented, but far more justified, was her decision to leave Russell those family papers and materials for a life of Charles James Fox on which both her husband and Allen had worked. Russell published these as *The Memorials and Correspondence of Charles James Fox*, (4 vols., 1853–7). Taken ill on the 9th, Lady Holland died on 17 November 1845 at Great Stanhope Street of heart disease, and was buried at Millbrook, near Ampthill, in Bedfordshire, on 25 November. Her husband's kinsman, Lord Ilchester, edited a selection of her letters to the fourth Baron Holland, *Elizabeth, Lady Holland to her Son, 1821–1845* (1946), and extracts from her diaries, *The Journal of Elizabeth, Lady Holland* (1908) and *The Spanish Journal of Elizabeth, Lady Holland* (1910).   C. J. WRIGHT

Sources n/a, BL, Holland House Papers · *Elizabeth, Lady Holland to her son, 1821–1845*, ed. earl of Ilchester [G. S. Holland Fox-Strangways] (1946) · *The journal of Elizabeth, Lady Holland, 1791–1811*, ed. earl of Ilchester [G. S. Holland Fox-Strangways], 2 vols. (1908) · *The Spanish journal of Elizabeth, Lady Holland*, ed. earl of Ilchester [G. S. Holland Fox-Strangways] (1910) · Earl of Ilchester [G. S. Holland Fox-Strangways], *The home of the Hollands, 1605–1820* (1937) · Earl of Ilchester [G. S. Holland Fox-Strangways], *Chronicles of Holland House, 1820–1900* (1937) · S. Keppel, *The sovereign lady* (1974) · *The Greville memoirs, 1814–1860*, ed. L. Strachey and R. Fulford, 8 vols. (1938) · *The letters of Thomas Babington Macaulay*, ed. T. Pinney, 6 vols. (1974–81) · A. Bourke, *Correspondence of Mr Joseph Jekyll … (1894)*
Archives BL, corresp. and papers, Add. MSS 51520–51957 · BL, Holland House papers · NL Scot., extracts from diary and corresp. · NRA, letters | All Souls Oxf., letters to Sir Richard Vaughan · BL, corresp. with John Allen, Add. MSS 52172–52174 · BL, corresp. with C. J. Fox; family papers, Add. MSS 47565–47575 · Borth. Inst., letters to Mary Ponsonby, Countess Grey · NL Ire., letters to R. W. Fitzpatrick · PRO, letters to first earl Granville, PRO 30/29 · U. Durham L., corresp. with Charles, second Earl Grey · W. Sussex RO, letters to duke of Richmond
Likenesses R. Fagan, oils, 1793, priv. coll. [*see illus.*] · L. Gauffier, oils, 1793, repro. in Keppel, *Sovereign lady* · G. Romney, oils, before 1797, repro. in Keppel, *Sovereign lady* · E. Landseer, pen and wash caricature, *c.*1835, NPG · C. R. Leslie, oils, 1838, repro. in Keppel, *Sovereign lady*
Wealth at death £80,000: PRO, death duty registers

Fox, Eliza Florance Bridell- [*née* Eliza Florance Fox] (1823/4–1903), painter, was born in December 1823 or January 1824 in London, the only daughter and middle of the three children of William Johnson *Fox (1786–1864), Unitarian minister of South Place Chapel, Finsbury, London, and Eliza Florance (1793–1869), daughter of James Florance, barrister, of Chichester, Sussex. Known as

Tottie, Eliza had few friends; her childhood influences were her father's friends who included Harriet Martineau, Mrs Harriet Taylor, and the radical Unitarian and composer Eliza *Flower and her sister Sarah Flower Adams the poet. After their father's death in 1829, the girls became wards of William Fox, and lived with the Fox family. In 1834 Eliza Fox's parents separated. Sarah Flower married the railway engineer inventor William Bridges-Adams, while Eliza Flower moved to Craven Hill, Bayswater, and was soon joined by Fox and his daughter. Miss Flower's home became a haunt for bohemian writers, poets, artists, and actors, but in 1839 her health suffered, and together with Eliza Fox and her father, Eliza Flower moved in with William and Sarah Bridges-Adams in Queen Square, Westminster.

Eliza Fox planned to be a painter, and after she and her father moved to Charlotte Street, Bloomsbury, in 1843, she went to Henry Sass's School of Art until 1846. Eliza Flower died of tuberculosis in December 1846, and thereafter Eliza Fox looked after her father, in addition to pursuing her art career. He always encouraged his daughter both in her art and in her efforts to improve educational opportunities for women. In 1848 he lent his library once a week, and there women artists, guided by a professional teacher, could sketch the 'undraped model'; existing art schools did not offer such classes. Occasionally Eliza Fox herself tutored the students, an arrangement that lasted until 1858. She became a friend of the artist and supporter of women's rights Barbara Bodichon. In 1849 she met Mrs Gaskell, who was in London following the publication of *Mary Barton*, her first novel; Eliza became a close friend of the Gaskell family. In 1852 she paid a brief visit to Paris, and in 1857 joined the Society of Female Artists, sending pictures to their exhibitions until 1870. She persuaded Mrs Gaskell to sign Barbara Bodichon's petition for the Married Woman's Property Bill, for which William Fox, who became MP for Oldham in 1847, voted in the House of Commons. Eliza Fox was one of a group of women artists who signed a letter begging the academicians to allow women to enter the Royal Academy Schools.

In 1858, with her cousin the artist and architect George Edward Fox (1834–1908) and another friend, Fox went on a painting tour of Germany and Italy, ending in Rome, where she met Frederick Lee *Bridell (*bap.* 1830, d. 1863), a very promising artist. They became instant friends, and were married in Rome in February 1859. Her friend the poet Robert Browning gave her away, and Elizabeth Barrett Browning arranged the wedding feast. Bridell persuaded his wife to start painting historical and genre subjects; her painting *St. Perpetua and St. Felicitas*, shown in 1861 at the Society of Female Artists, which depicted St Felicitas as an African, created a stir. But Bridell's health deteriorated, and in 1863 they returned to London where he died that August. His death was followed the next year by that of her father on 3 June 1864 and, unexpectedly, of Mrs Gaskell on 12 November 1865. Barbara Bodichon invited the distraught Eliza to her house in Algiers, where she painted the colourful pictures of Arab life and landscapes that were to become her best-known works, as well as portraits. She returned to London some four years later and on 8 August 1871 married her cousin George Fox. She continued to paint and to exhibit (under the name Eliza Bridell-Fox), and to attend feminist meetings. She collected her father's letters and papers, bequeathing them to Richard Garnett, Fox's future biographer. Eliza Bridell-Fox became ill late in 1903, and died that year on 9 December at her home, 21 Campden Hill Road, Kensington. She was buried in Brompton cemetery.

BRENDA COLLOMS

Sources R. Garnett and E. Garnett, *The life of W. J. Fox, public teacher and social reformer, 1786–1864* (1910) · E. Bridell-Fox, 'Memories', *Girls' Own Paper* (19 July 1890) · C. Yeldham, *Women artists in nineteenth-century France and England*, 2 vols. (1984) · E. C. Clayton, *English female artists*, 2 vols. (1876) · *The letters of Mrs Gaskell*, ed. J. A. V. Chapple and A. Pollard, new edn (1997) · P. Dunford, *A biographical dictionary of women artists in Europe and America since 1850* (1990) · P. Gillett, *The Victorian painter's world* (1990) · P. G. Nunn, *Victorian women artists* (1987) · *Mary Howitt: an autobiography*, ed. M. Howitt, 2 vols. (1889) · D. Cherry, *Painting women: Victorian women artists* (1993) · d. cert. · 'The Society of Female Artists', *English Woman's Journal*, 1 (May 1858), 208 · 'The fifth annual exhibition of the Society of Female Artists', *English Woman's Journal*, 7 (March 1861), 59–60 · B. Bodichon, *Hester Burton* (1949) · G. D. Leslie, *The inner life of the Royal Academy* (1914)

Wealth at death £2175 18s. 3d.: probate, 9 Jan 1904, CGPLA Eng & Wales

Fox, Dame Evelyn Emily Marian (1874–1955), mental health worker, was born at Morges, Switzerland, on 15 August 1874, one of four children, of whom two died in childhood, born to Richard Edward Fox, of Fox Hall, Edgeworthstown, co. Longford (who was related to Charles James Fox and Maria Edgeworth), and his wife, Emily, daughter of Lieutenant-Colonel William Godley of the East India Company. After her father's death in 1885 Evelyn and her elder sister Adeline were brought up by their mother in Ireland and England and educated at the high school in Morges. At Somerville College, Oxford, she took second-class honours in modern history in 1898. It was not until she was thirty-two that she decided to devote herself to the cause of mentally handicapped people. In the intervening years she qualified for her future career by training at the Women's University Settlement in Southwark, London, and by undertaking work which brought her into personal touch with mentally handicapped children and their families.

In 1908 the royal commission on the care and control of the feebleminded issued a report which was to result in the Mental Deficiency Act of 1913. Evidence had been pouring in regarding the medical, social, educational, economic, eugenic, and legal aspects of the subject, and with public opinion roused the time was ripe for action. Evelyn Fox was quick to realize the extent of the work which lay ahead. A voluntary co-ordinating body appeared to be the first need, to stimulate effort and to prepare the way for the implementation of the act, in co-operation with the new statutory authorities. The Central Association for the Mentally Defective was accordingly founded in 1913 under the chairmanship of Leslie Scott, with Evelyn Fox its honorary secretary and its material assets a borrowed typewriter and the promise of £10. In response to widening demands and under her direct inspiration, the scope of the work grew rapidly and in 1922 the name of the association was changed to the Central Association for Mental Welfare. Later again, in 1946, the association amalgamated with other bodies to form the National Association for Mental Health. By 1951, when Evelyn Fox retired, the association had indeed attained national status, covering the whole field and administering some £100,000 yearly. It employed numerous paid staff including a medical director and a general secretary.

During these years of expansion Evelyn Fox was the guiding spirit. The uphill struggle, with set-backs including two world wars, called forth her fighting qualities. Many pioneer schemes then initiated later became an integral part of the National Health Service, for example community care, occupation centres, voluntary associations, and training courses for professional mental health workers. Although her work centred round the association's London office, she had occasion to travel to all parts of the country, forming personal contacts and initiating local schemes. She took an active part also in the wider movements of mental health: she became honorary secretary of the Child Guidance Council when it was first formed in England with the help of the Commonwealth Fund of America in 1927; she served on the Wood committee on mental deficiency which reported in 1929, and on the London county council mental hospitals committee from 1914 to 1924; and she gave evidence before royal commissions and read papers at many conferences at home and abroad. In recognition of her services she was appointed CBE in 1937 and DBE in 1947.

Evelyn Fox's home life was full of human ties and many interests: art, music, books, young people, the garden, and her dog. She remained a countrywoman at heart, facing a long daily journey to London from Aldbourne near Marlborough for the sake of the downs she loved. In 1945 she and her sister moved to Laughton in Sussex, accompanied by friends who looked after both sisters until they died. In appearance Evelyn Fox was short and round-faced, with rough, curly hair which was white in later life. Her voice was strident, the result perhaps of her own and her sister's deafness. Her downright manner was tempered by the merriment and devilment in her eyes. She had a fundamental concern for humanity, clearness of vision and directness of aim, ceaseless and resilient energy, thoroughness, hatred of shams and sloppiness, and a very practical administrative ability. She died at her home, The Nook, Laughton, Sussex, on 1 June 1955.

R. R. THOMAS, *rev.*

Sources WWW · Burke, *Gen. Ire.* · private information (1971) · personal knowledge (1971) · CGPLA Eng. & Wales (1955)

Likenesses J. Grant, pastels (posthumous), National Association for Mental Health, London

Wealth at death £24,372 12s. 7d.: probate, 13 Aug 1955, CGPLA Eng. & Wales

Fox, Felicity Lane-, Baroness Lane-Fox (1918–1988), philanthropist, was born on 22 June 1918 in Newton Kyme, near Tadcaster, Yorkshire, the youngest child in the family of one son and three daughters of Captain Edward Lane-

Fox JP and his wife, Enid Maud Bethell, herself later appointed MBE in 1967 for work for hospitals. Both her parents came from old Yorkshire families, her mother being the daughter of Alfred James Bethell, of Rise, and her father being the younger brother of George Richard Lane-Fox, the first and last Baron Bingley, of Bramham. At the age of two, Felicity developed periostitis, which left her with a permanently weak right arm. In 1930, at the age of twelve, on a summer holiday on the Yorkshire coast at Filey, she contracted poliomyelitis in a vicious form, which left her totally paralysed. Two years passed before she was able to sit up or to hold a cup or pencil. During this period she was living at home in the family house near Wetherby. Deprived of any formal education, she acquired knowledge by her own efforts supported by her mother's wide-ranging enthusiasms. Her mother, who lived until 1986, devoted the next fifty-five years of her life to the daily care of her disabled daughter. After her mother became incapable of looking after her, she was cared for by her sister.

When war came in 1939, Felicity Lane-Fox took on a job with the billeting officer in Wetherby. After the end of hostilities in 1945 she went into local politics as a councillor for the Wetherby division of the West Riding county council and became chairman of the local Conservative association. Her interest in politics took her from there in 1960 to an appointment as assistant at the Conservative Research Department and in 1963 she became a member of the executive of the National Union of Conservative and Unionist Associations. Through these links with the party, she became known to Margaret Thatcher, who, on becoming prime minister, offered her in 1981 a life peerage, which she was only persuaded to accept after her mother convinced her that the House of Lords would give her a forum for speaking on behalf of the disabled. This she assiduously did during the next seven years, making her maiden speech, a fortnight after taking her seat, on the integration of disabled children into ordinary schools. She was absent from the house on only three working days during her first year as a member.

Felicity Lane-Fox's work for the disabled had already won her an OBE in 1976, for in spite of her own disability, and with the indefatigable help of her mother, who combined the roles of nurse, chauffeur, and counsellor, she travelled widely, spoke frequently, and carried on a large correspondence on behalf of a number of societies and projects connected with disabled people. Among these were the Nuffield Orthopaedic Centre at Oxford, where she was a member of the house committee, and the national fund-raising committee of the Disablement Income Group, of which she was chair. In 1978 she became patron of the Handicapped Adventure Playground Association. To all these activities she paid full attention, regularly attending their meetings, to which she was driven in a specially adapted minicar into which she could be winched through the back window by her mother, who in spite of increasing age managed to propel her in the vehicle or on the ground with unflagging energy. For having learned to walk with the aid of a calliper and some

human support, Felicity in 1966 slipped on an icy patch of roadway, broke her pelvis, and was never able to walk again.

After becoming a baroness Felicity Lane-Fox accepted several further appointments to societies for the disabled, in particular becoming a member of the prince of Wales's advisory group on disability and of the committee of inquiry into arts and disabled people. But the project which was closest to her heart was the Phipps Respiratory Unit Patients' Association (PRUPA). This unit, originally established in Clapham by Dr Geoffrey Spencer to provide relief and therapy for patients suffering from breathing maladies, was, thanks to her fund-raising efforts, later moved to become part of St Thomas's Hospital in Lambeth Palace Road, where it was renamed the Lane-Fox Respiratory Unit, and is a fitting memorial to her.

Felicity Lane-Fox leavened her arduous work for the disabled by a variety of other interests. She enjoyed watching cricket, tennis, racing, drama, and documentaries on television or listening to them on the radio, as well as a game of bridge and perhaps, most of all, social intercourse and conversation with her many friends. Her life was an example of how to overcome crippling physical infirmity and use the experience of it to alleviate the plight of fellow sufferers.

The fact that Felicity Lane-Fox was chair-bound, and also possessed a mane of thick brown hair, made it appear that her head was unusually large. With a high forehead, mischievous grey eyes, a classical nose, and a magnolia complexion, which never showed signs of ageing, her face gave an impression of being poised for laughter, into which it readily dissolved. She died, unmarried, in St Thomas's Hospital on 17 April 1988; a memorial service was held at St Margaret's, Westminster, on 7 June 1988.

EDWARD FORD, rev.

Sources *The Times* (18 April 1988) · *The Times* (8 June 1988) · *The Independent* (19 April 1988) · *WW* · private information (1996) · personal knowledge (1996) · *CGPLA Eng. & Wales* (1988)
Wealth at death £200,277: probate, 11 Aug 1988, *CGPLA Eng. & Wales*

Fox, Francis (1675–1738), Church of England clergyman, was born at Brentford, Middlesex, the son of Francis Fox of Brentford. According to Thomas Hearne, Fox served six years as an apprentice mercer in London before matriculating at St Edmund Hall, Oxford, aged twenty-two, in 1698. As an undergraduate Fox was very devout, attending the sacrament every Sunday at Christ Church and having the character of a 'Sanctified Person' (*Remarks*, 1.34). Although a high-churchman, Fox's political sympathies were whig, to the consternation of Hearne, who thought anyone whose theology was high church must be a tory in politics. Fox graduated BA in 1701 and MA in 1704; he incorporated at Cambridge as an MA in 1707.

Fox served as chaplain to Sir Owen Buckingham, lord mayor of London, in 1705. His sermon *The Superintendency of Divine Providence over Human Affairs*, preached before the lord mayor on 29 May 1705, provoked Hearne to comment, 'he is a Man of great Boldness and Assurance, but has neither parts nor Learning', while recalling that Fox 'once scrupled the Oath of Abjuration, yet upon reading the preface to Volume 1 of my Lord Clarendon's *History* he immediately took the oath, without having any argument to offer for it' (*Remarks*, 1.34).

In April 1707 Hearne alleged that Fox ('commonly called Father Fox') 'is turned from his Whiggish Principles and that he has prevailed in some measure with Sir Owen Buckingham to do the same' (*Remarks*, 2.6). Hearne associated Fox with the church whigs, including Edmund Gibson, White Kennett, and Gilbert Burnet. In 1708 Burnet, as bishop of Salisbury, presented Fox to the rectory of Boscombe, in Wiltshire, where he raised money from some of his London friends, including Sir Charles Duncombe, Henry Hoare, and Robert Nelson, to repair and re-order the parish church and to provide a new set of communion silver. In 1713 Burnet presented Fox to the vicarage of Potterne, in Wiltshire, and to the prebendal stall of Wilsford and Woodford, in Salisbury Cathedral, which he exchanged for the prebend of Stratton in 1730. Fox was also chaplain to William, first Earl Cadogan.

Fox was concerned for the education of children; he published *The duty of public worship proved with directions for a devout behaviour ... and an account of the method of the common prayer by way of question and answer* in 1713 and *An Introduction to Spelling and Reading, Containing Lessons for Children*, both of which were still in the lists of the Society for Promoting Christian Knowledge in 1818. His *New Testament Explained*, in two volumes (1722), set out the parallel passages, a chronology, marginal readings, and notes on difficult texts.

In 1726 Peter, Lord King, presented Fox to the rectory of St Mary's, Reading. There he was involved in controversy over an assize sermon preached at Abingdon, entitled *Judgement, Mercy, and Fidelity: the Weightier Matters of Duties of the Law*, on Matthew 23: 23, which he published and dedicated to Lord Chancellor King. Joseph Slade, a former curate of St Mary's and lecturer at St Lawrence's, Reading, published a correspondence with Fox about the sermon, a sermon criticizing Fox's sermon, and some personal reflections on Fox in October 1727. Slade accused Fox of disregarding the importance of faith in God in favour of faith between men, and of using his text to argue that some of the duties of the church were less essential than others, including attendance at Sunday worship and partaking in the eucharist. Lancelot Carleton, rector of Padworth, subsequently published a criticism of Slade and a defence of Fox. Carleton—whose text a manuscript note (probably by Hearne) in the Bodleian copy says was amended by Fox before publication—accused Slade of imposing artificial distinctions between fidelity between Christians and faith in God, and of emphasizing involvement in ceremonies over 'an active and lively faith' (Carleton, 23). The high-church (and presumably tory) Slade's aside on electoral malpractice locates this dispute within the political context of the 1727 general election. Fox died at Reading on 6 July 1738 and was buried in St Mary's.   W. M. JACOB

Sources *Remarks and collections of Thomas Hearne*, ed. C. E. Doble and others, 11 vols., OHS, 2, 7, 13, 34, 42–3, 48, 50, 65, 67, 72 (1885–1921), vols. 1–2 • C. Coates, *The history and antiquities of Reading* (1802) • Foster, *Alum. Oxon.* • Venn, *Alum. Cant.*, 1/2 • R. C. Hoare, *The history of modern Wiltshire*, 2 (1826) • J. Hutchins, *History and antiquities of the county of Dorset*, ed. W. Shipp and J. W. Hodson, 3rd edn, 4 vols. (1861–74), vol. 2 • *Churches of south-east Wiltshire*, Royal Commission on Historical Monuments (1987) • L. Carleton, *A letter, to the Revd Mr Joseph Slade* (1727)
Archives CUL, family corresp.

Fox, Sir Francis (1844–1927), civil engineer, was born at Bellefield, near Birmingham on 29 June 1844, the second son of Sir Charles *Fox (1810–1874), civil engineer, and Mary Brookhouse. From the ages of eleven to sixteen he attended Cavendish House School, Sherwood, Nottinghamshire. After his father was seriously injured in a fall at the seaside in 1861 Francis was obliged to join the family firm. He began as his father's pupil, and in 1868 became a partner, along with his father and elder brother (Charles) Douglas *Fox (1840–1921), in the firm of Sir Charles Fox & Sons, of 8 New Street, Spring Gardens, Westminster.

Fox's first major project was as assistant to Edmund Wragge, resident engineer on the improvements to the approaches to Victoria Station including an additional railway bridge, which was erected 1864–7. Meanwhile he continued his studies by attending the lectures of Professor John Tyndall and others at the Royal Institution. Shortly after the completion of the bridge, in 1869, Fox married his first wife Selina (d. 1900), third daughter of Francis Wright of Osmaston Manor, Derbyshire. They had two sons, who were later to join the firm, and three daughters. Under his elder brother Douglas's lead the firm was largely involved in railway engineering, but Francis's own career was much more multi-disciplinary.

In 1872 Fox was appointed manager of the Huntcliff mines in Cleveland, which gave him experience in underground excavation and ventilation which was to prove invaluable in his later career. While there Fox hosted a visit from Sir Stafford Northcote, chancellor of the exchequer, and a deputation of MPs. In September 1877 Fox was party to some of the earliest telephone calls in the UK—initially from his home at Saltburn by the Sea, and subsequently over the seventeen miles between Middlesbrough and the Huntcliff mines.

In August 1882 Fox was invited by the chairman of the Manchester, Sheffield, and Lincolnshire Railway Company to act as engineer on some of their new lines. His first major work was to design a swing bridge over the Dee at Hawarden Bridge, on a line linking the north Wales coalfield to the Wirral. It was the largest such span in the country and opened in 1889. Fox was also involved in the neighbouring Mersey railway tunnel between Liverpool and Birkenhead, first proposed by his father in the 1860s. In 1879 James Brunlees and Douglas Fox & Partners were appointed joint engineers for the tunnel which was built 1880–86. As a result of these commitments Francis moved to north Wales where he lived, at Mount Alyn, Rossett, until 1893. After the completion of the tunnel in 1888 the firm was appointed joint engineers with James Henry Greathead (1844–1896) to the Liverpool Overhead Railway, one of the earliest electric railways. Fox acted as partner on the site with S. B. Cottrell.

In 1894 the firm was appointed engineers for the southern extension of the Great Central Railway (formerly the Manchester, Sheffield, and Lincolnshire Railway) between Rugby and London, including Marylebone Station. This was the last main line to be built in the country, and Fox took great care in the design of the earthworks, endeavouring to avoid the mistakes of the early railway engineers. The works were completed in 1899. While these works proceeded Fox was appointed in 1894 as the British representative on the international commission of experts on the Simplon Tunnel, completed in 1906. From 1894–6 he and his brother Douglas were engineers for the Snowdon Mountain Railway, and Francis took advantage of his visits to Switzerland to inspect the mountain railway systems in use there.

The firm's experience of tunnelling and railway engineering led to its appointment, again with Greathead, as consultants to the Great Northern and City Railway in 1892. This was a much wider diameter than the other tube railways as it was designed to take Great Northern steam locomotives into the City. Work began in 1898. The firm also designed the Charing Cross, Golders Green and Highgate Railway (now part of the Northern Line) with W. R. Galbraith as its partner. It was opened in 1907. Fox selected the sites of the stations, and at this time he designed a channel tunnel scheme.

By this time there had been major changes in the firm, which had become Douglas Fox & Partners following the death of Sir Charles Fox in 1874. The family dominated the firm until Sir Francis Fox's retirement in July 1920. Douglas's son, Francis Douglas, became a partner in 1890 and Francis's sons, Charles Beresford and Francis Henry, followed him in 1904 and 1907, although their involvement was relatively brief. In 1909 Charles Beresford left for Toronto and Francis Henry served in the First World War and did not rejoin the firm. Of greater importance to the firm's success were George Andrew Hobson, who joined in 1880 and was a partner in 1900–12 and Ralph Freeman, who played an important part in the design of the Victoria Falls Bridge and became a partner in 1912. Most influential of all was Charles Metcalfe, who had been Douglas Fox's partner in 1878 and who from 1886 acted jointly with the firm in the development of South African railways.

Francis Fox himself had seen the potential of the grouting pan devised by Greathead for tunnelling works for other applications, and became increasingly involved in the use of grouting in the restoration of historic structures. The most famous application was at Winchester Cathedral where Fox was appointed consultant in 1905. The masonry was in poor condition and this was compounded by the effects of subsidence. Fox advised the strengthening of the masonry, making use of grouting equipment, and then underpinning the foundations with concrete. Fox himself inspected the foundations using diving equipment. He realized the work there could only be done safely by a diver, and it was all carried out by the diver William A. Walker over five and a half years, being completed in 1912. Fox was consulted over many ancient buildings such as Peterborough Cathedral (1897), St Paul's

Cathedral (1912), and latterly Lincoln Cathedral (1921–4) and Exeter Cathedral. Overseas, Fox reported on St Sophia in Constantinople, and on the campanile of St Mark's, Venice.

Throughout his life Fox showed a humanitarian concern stemming from his religious beliefs and reflected in charitable and other works. On all its railway contracts his firm insisted on no Sunday working, and took steps to ensure a priest was available to the workforce. In 1870 he bought shares in the Omnibus Company to draw attention to the need for brakes to protect the horses. While employed in the Yorkshire iron mines he designed workers' cottages which took account of the miners' wishes. From the 1860s he was involved in mission work with the London City Mission and others. His eldest daughter, Selina Fitzherbert Fox MD founded the Bermondsey Hospital and Medical Mission in 1904. During the First World War he lectured to wounded troops. He became aware of a shortage of material for bandages for the wounded, and realized linen could be salvaged from the large number of drawings owned by his and other engineering firms. As a result 121 miles of material were obtained.

Fox was elected an associate of the Institution of Civil Engineers in 1870, becoming a member in 1874. He was knighted in 1912 in recognition of his restoration work. Following the death of his first wife he married Agnes Horne, younger daughter of Henry King Horne, of Guerrier, Normandy, in 1901. Aside from his engineering work he was a watercolour artist. His extensive writings, for the *Encyclopaedia Britannica* and elsewhere, were generally on engineering subjects, and included autobiographical works. From 1894 Fox lived at Alyn Bank, Wimbledon, where he developed magnificent gardens. He died there, from a duodenal ulcer and haemorrhage, on 7 January 1927, survived by his second wife. He was buried at Putney Vale cemetery.   MIKE CHRIMES

Sources F. Fox, *Sixty-three years of engineering: scientific and social work* (1924) · F. Fox, *River, road and rail* (1904) · *Engineering* (14 Jan 1927), 49–51 · *DNB* · W. T. Pike, *Contemporary biographies* (1905), 223 · *WWW* · *The Builder*, 132 (1927), 42 · *The Times* (8 Jan 1927) · *The Times* (11 Jan 1927) · d. cert.
Archives Brunel University, Middlesex, Freeman, Fox and Partners archives · Inst. CE, MSS · PRO, MSS | CAC Cam., corresp. with Channel Tunnel Co.
Likenesses Maull & Fox, carte-de-visite, *c*.1880, Inst. CE · F. A. Cooper, portrait, repro. in Fox, *River, road and rail*, 73 · Maull & Fox, repro. in Fox, *Sixty-three years of engineering*, frontispiece
Wealth at death £40,615 10s. 2d.: probate, 18 Feb 1927, *CGPLA Eng. & Wales*

Fox, George, the younger (*d.* 1661), religious writer, was born in Charsfield, Suffolk. He served in the parliamentary army, but there is no firm evidence to support the claim that he was a Leveller despite his seeming awareness of their views. As a result of George Whitehead's testimony at Mendlesham, Suffolk, in 1654, he became a Quaker and was known as 'the younger'—in 'truth' rather than in age—to distinguish him from his famous namesake, to whom he was probably unrelated. By October 1655 he was incarcerated at Bury St Edmunds for having accused the justices at the Suffolk quarter sessions of unfairly treating Whitehead and other Friends. Because he refused to find sureties he remained in prison, from whence he wrote *A Strong and Terrible Alarm* (22 September 1656), a brief prophetic work addressed to all who profess God superficially. Oliver Cromwell ordered his release the same year, and in 1657–8 he testified in the Orkney Islands and Scotland until George Monck banished him from Scotland as part of a campaign against Quaker efforts to win converts among the troops. In 1659 Fox preached in Cambridgeshire and Essex.

Fox was a prolific writer, composing at least twenty-eight tracts, mostly between 1659 and mid-1661. In *Honest, Upright, Faithful, and Plain Dealing* (May 1659) he addressed the army, claiming that God had enabled it to triumph to make way for the spread of 'truth', but that instead the army had become covetous, seizing the estates of its enemies. He encouraged the army to seek peace with other states and not to establish any religious group by force. To those who had experienced the inner workings of the Spirit before joining other sects, he implored them to return to the 'truth', in *A Visitation of Love* (1659). With George and John Whitehead he wrote *A Brief Discovery of the Dangerous Principles* (1659), refuting an attack on Quakers by the Independent John Horne and Thomas Moore. The prophetic tone so characteristic of most of his work is reflected in *A Word to the People of the World* (1659) and *The Words of the Everlasting and True Light* (1659), the latter of which prominently referred to Christ as king of the saints. Fox also found time to articulate principles of social behaviour in *An Exhortation to Families* [1659].

As he observed the contest for power between Richard Cromwell, various military factions, and parliament, Fox addressed the disputants in three important tracts. In *This is for You who are called Common-Wealths Men* (1659) he called for the establishment of the people's liberties and legal reform while denouncing ordained clergy and oppressors. Directing his message to the army in *A Few Plain Words* (1659) after it ousted Cromwell and parliament, he challenged those who contended that a new parliament must be elected if the people's rights were to be assured, arguing instead that parliaments are chosen by the oppressors and reflect their interests. Rather than calling for a wider franchise, he urged the army to rule in the ways of God and for the people's good, abolishing tithes and compulsion in religion. As Monck's army marched toward London, each member of the restored Rump Parliament received a copy of *For the Parliament of England and their Army (so called)* (January 1660), in which Fox prophesied, 'The Decree is *gone out*, and sealed against *you*, and it cannot be *recalled*' (*Collection of the Several Books and Writings*, 101). The Rump, he maintained, was not God's instrument to deliver his people.

Early in 1660 Fox was barred from Portsmouth by its governor, and by 16 May he and Robert Grassingham were imprisoned at Harwich, Essex, after Fox nearly incited a riot by criticizing the government and church. While incarcerated he wrote a series of pamphlets, including *A Noble Salutation* (16 May 1660), which offered the king advice on how to govern and included the disavowal of

revenge and the implementation of religious toleration. He also explained the Quakers' tenets, including their repudiation of violence. After Richard Hubberthorne gave Charles II a copy on 4 June, the latter reputedly promised to leave the Quakers alone as long as they did not disturb the peace. Within a year the tract had reached a sixth edition. On 21 May the House of Commons ordered that Fox and Grassingham be placed in its custody, and they were detained at the gatehouse, Westminster, where Hubberthorne visited them.

Some of Fox's prison tracts—*A General Epistle, and a Tender Greeting* (3 June 1660) and *To the Called of God* (14 July 1660)—exhorted the Friends to persevere through persecution, but in *A Message of Tender Love* (1660) he expressed concern that 'a sad day of Apostacy' had descended on many Quakers as manifested by their loss of zeal and simplicity (G. Fox, *A Message of Tender Love*, 1660, 6). Other tracts—*Honest, Plain, Down-Right-Dealing with the People called Episcopal-Men, and Presbyterians* (14 June 1660) and *A Few Queries to the Teachers of the Episcopal Society* (22 June 1660)—were addressed to the major religious groups, challenging them to support the king by dissuading him from establishing compulsory forms of worship. Who originated royal supremacy, episcopacy, surplices, baptism by sprinkling, and godparents, Fox pointedly asked? Continuing this theme in *The Testimony of God to those Rulers, Teachers and People* (28 June 1660), he warned that those who 'set themselves *in* [Christ's] *Seat … shall be broken down with dishonour*' (G. Fox, *Testimony of God*, 1660, 6). He was still in prison when he wrote *The Dread of Gods Power* (28 July 1660), in which he again urged those in authority to eschew revenge and chided them for increasing oppression.

By late August 1660 Fox and Grassingham were still in the gatehouse and had not been examined, but on 30 August the House of Commons ordered their release on bail. However, the men refused to pay fees of £50 to the clerk plus rent of 10s. per week. Their attempt to settle for a lesser amount failed, and they were still in prison on 21 September when Fox completed *A True Relation of the Unlawful and Unreasonable Proceedings*. He was apparently free by 8 October when he finished *The Breathings of True Love*, which advised Friends not to take up arms or spread false reports. In the aftermath of Thomas Venner's insurrection, Fox was among the thousands of Quakers who were imprisoned. Once again in the gatehouse at Westminster, in January 1661 he wrote *Two General Epistles* (1663) and another work entitled *To the Tribulated Flock of Christ* (2 March 1661), exhorting believers to remain faithful. Fox was not a signatory of the important Friends' declaration of pacifism the same month. He was still incarcerated on 12 March 1661, when he expounded on Quaker tenets concerning Christ, justification, resurrection, and the afterlife, in *His Faith Touching Four Particulars*. He may have been free by 13 April, when his powerful prophetic work, *Englands Sad Estate & Condition Lamented*, was printed. Most people, he declared, were idolatrous, and he likened their ministers to bands of robbers.

Fox died at Hurst (now Hurstpierpoint), Sussex, on 7 July

1661, and was buried the same month at nearby Twineham. *A Collection of the Several Books and Writings* (1662) and *Compassion to the Captives* (1662) were the first such compilations of Quaker writings, though neither contained all of his works. The popularity of his writings among Friends was attested by the Particular Baptist Thomas Hicks, who (with exaggeration) in August 1674 named *The Breathings of True Love* as one of four books the Quakers liked more than the Bible. Fox's early death deprived the Friends of one of their most vigorous critics of the government and the established church.   RICHARD L. GREAVES

Sources N. Penney, ed., *'The first publishers of truth': being early records, now first printed, of the introduction of Quakerism into the counties of England and Wales* (1907) · *The journal of George Fox*, ed. N. Penney, 2 vols. (1911) · *A collection of the several books and writings, given forth by that faithful servant of God and his people, George Fox, the younger* (1662) · A. R. Barclay, ed., *Letters, &c. of early Friends* (1841), 80–81, 231 · RS Friends, Lond., Penington MS 4, fols. 45–7 · Greaves & Zaller, *BDBR*, 302–3 · H. Barbour, *The Quakers in puritan England* (1964) · W. C. Braithwaite, *The second period of Quakerism*, ed. H. J. Cadbury, 2nd edn (1961) · H. Barbour and A. O. Roberts, eds., *Early Quaker writings, 1650–1700* (1973) · T. L. Underwood, *Primitivism, radicalism, and the Lamb's war: the Baptist–Quaker conflict in seventeenth-century England* (1997) · 'Dictionary of Quaker biography', RS Friends, Lond. [card index]
Archives RS Friends, Lond., Penington MSS

Fox, George (1624–1691), a founder of the Religious Society of Friends (Quakers), was born in July 1624 in Drayton-in-the-Clay (now Fenny Drayton), Leicestershire, the eldest of four children of Christopher Fox, a weaver, and his wife, formerly Mary Lago (d. 1673), who may have been from the neighbouring county of Warwickshire. The parish of Drayton-in-the-Clay was staunchly puritan and had been so for more than a generation before George was born. George's father served as churchwarden in the parish, winning the label 'Righteous Christer' for his rectitude. It appears that the Fox family enjoyed a prosperous life: Fox's father operated perhaps two looms while his mother probably came from a well-off family. The family was relatively wealthy, and upon the death of his father, in the late 1650s, Fox inherited a large sum of money, a legacy that freed him from future financial worries.

Early years Relatively little is known of Fox's early years because the first sixteen pages of his dictated memoir were lost or destroyed; Thomas Ellwood, who edited the memoir for publication after Fox's death, supplied some of the missing information. No record remains of Fox's formal schooling or education, although his scrawling handwriting and repetitiveness may reflect dyslexia or a neurological condition that inhibited his ability to express himself clearly in writing, not a lack of education. He was certainly able to read, amassing during his lifetime a substantial library, but his main reading remained the Bible, which he used polemically to good purpose. He remembered later that as a child he had exhibited much 'Gravity and stayedness of Mind and Spirit' (*Journal*, 1694, 2). In or soon after 1635 Fox's father apprenticed his son to George Gee, a shoemaker who lived in nearby Mancetter.

In late summer 1643, following his nineteenth birthday and after a drinking session with two other youths, Fox broke off his apprenticeship, left home, and went to London, stopping in towns on the way where parliamentary army troops were garrisoned. Plagued with periods of depression that paralysed him and led him to flee from the presence of others in the places he visited, he found no immediate satisfaction for his restlessness. After almost a year he returned home where he disputed religious issues with the scholarly Nathaniel Stephens, his parish minister and defender of the parliamentary cause.

Fox's religious experiences and message From his base in Drayton-in-the-Clay, Fox wandered the midlands over the next few years, seeking out ministers and others who might suggest remedies for his malady of spirit. He was advised to seek relief by smoking and singing but rejected both, and once again found no help from the company of others. His isolation and religious contemplation led him to reject traditional clerical structures, which in turn led to a break with his parish church about 1646. Stephens went so far as to warn Fox's relatives in the neighbouring villages that the young man was one of the 'newfangles' (Ingle, 43). Supported by income from his shoemaking skills, Fox wandered further afield, into Derbyshire and Nottinghamshire. There his anti-clericalism, coinciding with social and political upheaval in the aftermath of the civil war, attracted followers. However, he still suffered from melancholia and spiritual restlessness.

The turning point in Fox's life, as he later recalled, came some time in 1647 when he heard a voice saying, 'there is one, even Jesus Christ, that can speak to thy Condition' (*Journal*, 1694, 8). From then on Fox proclaimed the present accessibility of God who 'was now come to *Teach* his People himself' (ibid., 73). There was no need to rely on human teachers, Fox preached, for even the scriptures were less authoritative than one's inward guide. He relied on the Bible, which he knew well and whose words were prominent in his teaching and writing, but his stress on the primacy of the Spirit inevitably fed the kind of individualism that greatly hindered lasting unity among his diverse followers. Because the scriptures did not use the term and spoke nothing of it explicitly, he rejected the doctrine of the Trinity, a position bound to alarm and antagonize the orthodox. Nor did he make clear distinctions between the Father and the Son. He opposed oath-taking because he wanted to adhere to the Bible's injunction to let his 'yea' be 'yea' and his 'nay' 'nay'. He could also find no scriptural justification for paying tithes to a church with which he disagreed, let alone to a private person who might be thus enriched; resistance to the continual support of a tithing system became an important area of Quaker agitation in the 1650s. This cluster of beliefs put Fox beyond the pale of mainstream puritanism. Most of these ideas did occur in the thinking of other contemporary radical sectaries and he was not the first to make a principle of the non-payment of tithes, but he did place this stance more centrally within his teaching than other radicals did.

Fox proclaimed his message first in the midlands, where it occasioned little success. Indeed, it led him to be gaoled at Nottingham and Derby. A millenarian dimension in his teaching lent Fox a subversive air that seemed to threaten the established order in a very radical way. He was seldom very specific about long-term goals, other than calling for his followers to allow the ever-present Christ to rule in their hearts and lives. But such generalizations, particularly when uttered by someone as forthright and uncompromising as himself, might have far-reaching consequences in the hands of people newly empowered by Fox and his followers. The group that emerged first called themselves 'Children of the Light' or 'Friends of the Truth', though the preferred term ultimately became the Religious Society of Friends. Following Fox's imprisonment in Derby in 1650 on a charge of blasphemy, a local justice, Gervase Bennett, labelled his followers 'Quakers' because they shook and trembled during their meetings, and this unwanted name endured. While in Derby, Fox turned down an offer of freedom and a captaincy to fight in the campaign that shortly ended at the battle of Worcester in September 1651, an assertion of the personal pacifism that later characterized the group as a whole. It was during his incarceration that he dealt with the first serious challenge to his leadership: a group of local Quakers, led by Rice or Rhys Jones, confronted Fox about the central Quaker belief in the inward Christ, arguing that this rendered the existence of a historic Jesus unnecessary. This dispute with the 'Proud Quakers', as Jones's followers came to be known, remained unresolved for at least a decade, despite Fox's attempts to lure them back into the mainstream movement.

Once freed late in 1651, Fox walked barefoot through the December mud into Lichfield, shouting 'Woe to the bloody city of Lichfield!' and decrying the unfaithfulness of a people who had ignored a parliamentary order to tear down the city's magnificent cathedral and use its lead roof for ammunition—an episode that demonstrates some common ground between Fox's early beliefs and behaviour and those of other more spectacular Quaker prophets. Then he ventured into Yorkshire and Lancashire, tapping into local discontent. In the isolated and hidden dales of the north-west, he targeted religious seekers such as Baptists and political dissidents who disliked having their tithes appropriated for absentee landlords or to finance distant university colleges and their fellows. This campaign to bring an end to tithes without compensation led to rumours of his mounting a much wider attack on private property. Fox refused to bow or doff his hat to those who considered themselves his social superiors, and he insisted that his followers should stop paying tithes, that a university education did not qualify a person to be a minister, and that anyone, even women or children, could rightfully speak in the religious gatherings—called simply 'meetings'—in which they congregated.

Fox 'convinced'—the term used for those who saw and testified to the Quaker truth—most of the disciples prominent in the early movement: Richard Farnworth, Richard Hubberthorne, Francis Howgill, the justice Anthony Pearson, and, most important, Margaret *Fell (*née* Askew) (1614–1702), whom he later married. He also claimed among his converts James Nayler, a figure as prominent as

himself in the earliest years of the movement, although Nayler attributed his conversion to the work of God speaking directly to him, much in the manner of Fox's own conversion narrative. Following a vision on Pendle Hill, on 13 June 1652 Fox spoke with great effect to a crowd of over 1000 at Firbank Fell, between Kendal and Sedbergh; it has since become an important place for Quaker pilgrimage. Within weeks the nascent church began to take on an organized form following Fox's arrival at the end of June at Swarthmoor Hall, near Ulverston, the home of Fell and her husband, Thomas, vice-chancellor of the duchy of Lancaster. Quaker missionaries soon spread throughout the British Isles, gaining particular success in the southern part of England.

The importance of Thomas Fell as one of the movement's most prominent supporters (although he himself never converted) was quickly demonstrated when in October 1652 Fox and Nayler were summoned to appear in nearby Lancaster on charges of blasphemy brought by three local puritan ministers worried about deteriorating relations with their parishioners. Fell, one of three presiding judges, managed to have the charges dismissed on a technicality. Fox remained in and around Swarthmoor Hall until late in July 1653, when he travelled towards Carlisle. Wherever he went, he invaded churches—he disparaged them as 'steeplehouses'—and excoriated ministers as the very symbols of an apostasy stretching back to the first century (for example, *Journal*, 1694, 17). 'Deceit', whether expressed in governing, trading, praying, or professing, remained his common target, and he prophesied about an approaching but not very well defined 'Day of the Lord' that would bring an end to such empty practices (ibid., 17, 137). His preaching won converts among New Model Army soldiers stationed in the borders, and he almost set off a riot in Carlisle's St Mary's Church when, in September, the authorities again arrested him on charges of blasphemy. In this instance Gervase Benson and Pearson, two convinced Friends and judges themselves, came to his assistance even as he bombarded the authorities with radical epistles against oppression and tithing on the grounds that, as he wrote, Christ 'Redeems Men out of the *Tenths*' (ibid., 115).

Quakers and the Commonwealth By 1653 the emergence of some elements resistant to the developing discipline of the movement, such as Rhys Jones and his 'Proud Quakers' in Nottingham, led to worries about the involvement of 'Ranters' who considered themselves exempt from traditional moral and religious restraints. Fox was soon admonishing such followers to keep low in the truth and 'go not out from the spirit of God'. But in the same epistle he also averred that 'to the pure all things are pure' (*Works*, 7.38), a sentiment bound to feed the antinomianism occasioning his concern. The scattered meetings, up to this point accustomed to convening on an *ad hoc* basis in woodlands, barns, or private homes to await silently the mysterious moving of God's spirit, began to be formalized into 'monthly meetings' after one such was established for the Friends around Durham. These meetings maintained order and also saw to the needs of poor adherents in the neighbourhood; they also formed the basic discipline and decision making units of the sect.

Although the early Friends asserted the primacy of the spoken word, especially in spontaneous utterance, the movement made a very effective use of the press. In the early years there were scores of Quaker pamphlets, most prolifically and effectively from the pen of James Nayler. The first of Fox's own efforts reached London bookstalls in December 1653, followed early in the new year by the arrival of the first Quaker missionaries in the capital. Fox soon headed there himself, stopping along the way to attend general meetings which alerted the authorities enough to arrest him at Whetstone near his childhood home. From Leicester an armed guard escorted him to London, but he still proclaimed the approaching day of the Lord to all whom he met. 'The Lamb shall have the victory' (*Works*, 7.241), he confidently announced. The church, he insisted, was caught up in an apostasy going back nearly sixteen centuries, and this condition would remain until people came to 'know the scriptures by the spirit that gave them forth' (G. Fox, *This is a Controversy betwixt the Quakers and the Papists*, 1664, 2–3).

After arriving in London, Fox had an audience with a wary Lord Protector Oliver Cromwell, a reception occupying the better part of the morning of 9 March 1654. Although Fox condemned the clergy and admonished his host to rule by God's will, he made a good enough impression for Cromwell to order the release of his guest. Once freed, Fox counselled the government to exclude all the nation's clergy save the most radical, a recommendation designed to replace ordained ministers with lay Quakers. He did preach in London but otherwise spent most of eighteen months in nearby counties, leaving the metropolis to other Quakers, in particular James Nayler, who arrived there in the summer of 1655.

Controversy with James Nayler Nayler, a radiant and intelligent speaker and, because of his prominence in the capital city, widely regarded as the sect's pivotal leader, soon became Fox's chief rival. No formal theological differences divided them, although Nayler took a harder line than Fox in advising the Friends to avoid compromise with the government when they suffered arrest. Nayler began to collect a coterie of committed sympathizers, many of them women, a development that seemed to be leading to a split within the movement itself. Instead of confronting his rival, Fox left for a preaching mission in the west country late in December 1655 and by January in the following year ended up in the vindictively harsh conditions of Launceston gaol. With Fox absent, the tensions within the movement in London increased over the next six months; some followers of Nayler, in particular Martha Simmonds, disrupted Quaker meetings. In a move designed to heal the breach, a visibly troubled Nayler was persuaded by Fox's followers first to attend a meeting at Bristol and then to move on to visit Fox at Launceston, only to be intercepted and himself imprisoned at Exeter. In the meantime Simmonds arrived in Launceston to abuse Fox: 'she came singing in my face, inventing words' (RS Friends, Lond., Swarthmore MS 3.193).

Major-General John Desborough freed Fox and his companions in September. After 'tarrying' a full week following his release and preaching to large meetings in the region, Fox finally arrived at Exeter late in the month, but the reunion with the imprisoned Nayler only sharpened the personal animosity between the two. Fox gave Nayler his hand to kiss; when Nayler refused, Fox thrust out his foot for him to kiss instead, an act of submission which Nayler also refused to make. The two parted; Fox later described this as a moment of realization that 'there was now a *wicked* spirit risen amongst *Friends* to war against. I admonished him and his company' (*Journal*, 1694, 220). In the following month, after his own release, Nayler and a small group of followers, including Simmonds, entered Bristol in an unequivocal re-enactment of Christ's entry into Jerusalem. Arrested and taken to London, where he was tried by parliament, Nayler was whipped and branded, and his tongue was bored; he was returned to Bristol to be paraded and whipped before being imprisoned in Bridewell, London, where he remained until 1659. Fox was never truly reconciled with his former ally, nor did he publicly indicate that he himself bore some responsibility for these events, and he all but endorsed Nayler's harsh punishment.

Fox's activities following the sensation of Nayler's case indicate his belief that if Quakerism was to endure, he would have to give the movement's internal policy as much of his attention as other important matters, including the convincing of others through missionary activities. He extended monthly meetings to the entire nation, telling those who attended that they should search out disorder and see that 'Friends be kept in order' (RS Friends, Lond., Portfolio MS 36.140B). After 1657 there were more general meetings than usual, where Quaker leaders and others could come to hear instructions and return inspired to work against disunity. Quarterly meetings in each county with an established Quaker presence also emerged at this time. Together with the monthly meetings, this structure was designed to contain Naylerism and to ensure that power resided in the hands of a leadership willing to check the activities of those below them.

In this period, too, the second-day (i.e. Monday) morning meeting originated. Located in London, it was intended to make sure that ministers—the lay leaders recognized as likely speakers in the meetings—were evenly spread around the countryside. It amounted to a kind of executive committee of the Quaker leadership. Because it was dominated by those close to London, its growing influence meant that Swarthmoor Hall, which Margaret Fell had made the centre of the Quaker movement since 1652, was eclipsed: henceforth London would be the centre of power among Friends.

During this time Fox began to respond to rumours of sexual immorality among the Quakers, including marriage arrangements. He demanded bluntly that all 'Unrighteousness and Filthiness … be shut out' (G. Fox, *Concerning Marriage*, 1661, 5); leading Friends who engaged in illicit sexual activities had been disavowed and testified against publicly from the beginning. Having eschewed a class of pastors (or 'priests' as Fox always designated his clerical opponents), the Quakers had to find a substitute that would both confirm their own religious approach and meet the requirements of the law which, since 1653, allowed civil marriages. What Fox finally proposed was that a couple seeking marriage should appear before their local meeting, which would determine whether their marriage was acceptable; if the union was approved, the decision would be announced on a market day in the village square. The ceremony would occur during a meeting for worship in which, as always, all were free to speak. A certificate, including the promises the couple made to each other, was signed by those present to testify to what had occurred and to set the meeting's formal seal on the union. Although Fox hoped that this procedure would settle the matter once and for all, it failed to do so: as a result, he was continually faced with problems regarding marriage arrangements.

Restoration and pacifism By 1659 the republican Commonwealth was increasingly threatened by a rising tide of conservative discontent, much of it focusing on the role of those perceived to be radicals, such as the Quakers. When Fox went to Scotland in 1657, for example, and preached his unsettling message to soldiers of the New Model Army, General George Monck ordered his arrest, but Fox had already returned south. Realizing that the restoration of a Stuart monarch would probably jeopardize the movement, Fox and his group redoubled their efforts to forestall what increasingly seemed inevitable.

In 1659 Fox wrote his socially most radical pamphlet, *Fifty-Nine Particulars for the Regulating [of] Things*, an appeal to the recently reconvened Rump Parliament. In it he not only called for such nostrums as cutting the cross out of the flag but also demanded that the estates of 'great ones' be confiscated and sold for the public relief of the poor. Few, however, took his suggestions very seriously: the authorities certainly did not, or at least there was no response, and the pamphlet failed to slow the rush towards restoration. It was not republished until the twenty-first century; instead, Quakers henceforth busied themselves reprinting more obscure but politically safer theological tracts. In the meantime, other Quakers wrote broadsides and pamphlets with both veiled and open references to the dangers posed by the threatened restoration. By the end of 1659 some Quakers went so far as to toy with the idea of an armed resistance, while others recruited for the militia to protect the republic. Fox had expansively hoped that the Commonwealth would offer a chance for the Friends to replace the Church of England as the dominant religious group in the nation, whereas the Commonwealth's demise would end such dreams. Always personally rejecting participating in war himself, Fox watched events warily. Torn by indecision over the direction he should take, he was immobilized by depression in Reading for ten weeks in autumn 1659. Back in London early in 1660, he was reconciled with the recently released Nayler, who knelt before him and begged his forgiveness. It proved a poignant final meeting. Shortly afterwards

Nayler set off to rejoin his family in the north, but died following a violent robbery *en route*.

After the popular acclaim accompanying Charles II's return in May 1660, the Quakers, like other radical sectaries, were viewed as enemies of the new regime; Fox himself was gaoled for five months in Lancaster. Such governmental suspicion only increased following the thwarted Fifth Monarchist uprising led by Thomas Venner in January 1661. In response and later that same month Fox and his associate Richard Hubberthorne wrote a broadside, *A Declaration from the Harmles & Innocent People of God, called Quakers*, later known more famously as the 'peace testimony', that came to define the most long-lasting aspect of the movement. Designed to meet the political exigencies of the moment—to remove 'the Ground of Jealousie and Suspicion' towards them, as they phrased it—and to assert their understanding of what God was requiring of them, the document announced that Quakers denied 'All bloody Principles and Practices, … all outward Wars and Strife, and Fightings with Outward Weapons, for any end, or under any pretence whatsoever' (*Journal*, 1694, 233). They would never revert to practices from which Christ's spirit had called them. Although signed by twelve prominent men, the peace testimony was never promulgated by any body of Friends, but no successor body of Quakers has ever formally repudiated it.

However, the peace testimony was not immediately embraced by all Friends. For one thing, it did not settle the question of whether a Quaker should pay taxes to support a war. And it failed to address the broader question of whether war might be legitimate for the state even if Quakers would not participate. For example, Isaac Penington, son of a regicide and a leading Friend, thought the state had an obligation to use military force to protect the innocent and produced a pamphlet making this very point later that year. But Fox and the signatories ignored such attempted reconsiderations and instead moved to face the reality that their statement was signally failing in its intention of preventing parliament from taking action against political and religious dissidents such as themselves.

Restoration prosecution and Quaker consolidation Although the new king proved conciliatory to the Friends, the new parliament was not, and approved a number of measures aimed at suppressing suspected radical groups. The Quaker Act became effective in 1662; it prohibited any group of more than five persons from gathering for any religious service contrary to that of the Church of England, a law calculated to make it practically impossible for the Friends to meet legally. Their opposition to paying tithes also brought the force of the law against them. Unique among dissenters, Fox counselled open resistance to such laws; he did so knowing full well that such defiance would mean going to gaol or paying fines for violating the act. Soon Quakers were being incarcerated almost indiscriminately, their numbers overcrowding the nation's gaols, women and children alike being swept up in raids sometimes provoked by reports from paid informers. Fox found himself imprisoned in three different towns—successive terms in Lancaster and Scarborough between January 1664 and September 1666, and in Worcester between December 1673 and February 1675—usually for refusing to swear an oath of allegiance to the crown, each occasion eroding the strength of his already weakened body and psyche.

Quakers did not go quietly in the face of such prosecution. Although efforts to restrict pamphleteering were intensified, they found ways to publish leaflets and other materials. They also petitioned both the king and parliament to alert the authorities to their plight. On one occasion 7000 women from all over the country presented and then published a petition calling for an end to tithing; this effort to politicize women's voices was a striking innovation. At the same time, a belief in the need to collect accounts of Quaker sufferings and petitioning for redress further centralized the movement in London and prompted the employment of a clerk to oversee the sect's office.

Missionaries were sent to other countries: Quaker emissaries soon appeared in Ireland, Algiers, Constantinople, Rome, France, the Netherlands, northern Germany, and Poland, and there were also early forays into the English colonies of Barbados, Jamaica, and the American mainland—Fox himself visited the colonies between October 1671 and June 1673, and the first ever yearly meeting of Friends was organized in New England in 1661. Fox also addressed epistles of advice and admonition to Jews, Muslims, the Chinese people, and believers everywhere, and eagerly awaited word of Quaker successes (or setbacks) when such came back to their London headquarters. Much later, he travelled to the Netherlands and parts of Germany, encouraging those convinced earlier, and preaching to and disputing with other dissenters who flourished there.

Dissent and marriage Quakerism, however, continued to be plagued by its own dissidents. They claimed, like Nayler, that their understanding of the demands of the 'Inward Light of Christ' was as valid and controlling as Fox's. The persecution occasioned by the Restoration—four Friends, including one woman, had already been hanged in Massachusetts before King Charles intervened to put a halt to it—put a premium on Quaker unity, always crucial if Fox was to assert his authority in defining the contours of the movement. Attention to details such as church polity might not be as immediately gripping or exciting as proselytizing, but the needs of the movement demanded that Fox now devote a major amount of his time to the task. The case of John Perrot underlined the need for doctrinal uniformity.

Perrot, a Quaker missionary who had run into trouble with the Inquisition while in Rome, had returned to London in 1661 and had begun to query the practice of requiring men to take their hats off when they spoke or prayed in meeting. This raised profound questions of authority and good order within the movement and about Quakers' use of the Bible itself. Perrot insisted that the principle of equality between men and women allowed Friends to override the apostle Paul's injunction that only women

should cover their heads when they worshipped, and that if women kept their heads covered, so might men. Although Fox struggled to explain how he justified his position, by the end of 1661 he finally resorted to iterating that 'order, comeliness, and decency' (*Works*, 7.190) required him to uphold the present practice and that Perrot should submit in good order. Perrot refused, and in mid-1662 he accepted deportation to the New World, but his dispute with Fox had attracted the support of a group of Quakers led by John Pennyman, who felt the movement was becoming increasingly oligarchical. For Fox, 'the Hat' hereafter became a symbol of defiance, and he recalled as significant the fact that Nayler too had kept his head covered during prayer. Fox's victory over Perrot and his supporters—Isaac Penington prominent among them—did not end internal threats to his leadership, but it seemed to justify the need for tighter control of the movement.

Fox's allies in London took a major step in this direction in May 1666, as their leader was in prison in Scarborough Castle for refusing to swear the oath of allegiance. Donning the mantle of patriarchs and apostles, eleven Quaker leaders issued a 'Testimony from the brethren' to be sent to, and read at, all meetings with the requirement that it be kept for ready reference. It prohibited separatists like Perrot from holding office or travelling in the ministry and required all Quakers to submit their writings for approval before publication. When he was released in September, Fox saw no reason to question what his associates had done, as the 'Testimony from the brethren' clearly indicated that those with authority within the movement intended to exercise it. Instead, he immediately turned his attention to strengthening the authority of monthly meetings over those associated with Quakers, a matter he emphasized during a three-month tour of Ireland in 1669, his first trip overseas. He focused also on the still volatile question of marriage and seemed to be moving towards enhancing the role of women Friends in a new departure: in 1666 he had used an epistle to speak broadly of 'service' and 'duty' for women, but he did not at that time articulate anything very specific about what he had in mind.

Fox's determination in this regard was underscored by his planned marriage to the now widowed Margaret Fell, born ten years before him and the mother of eight living children, all but one of them active Quakers. A powerful figure within Quakerism in her own right, Fell advocated the equality of women, having published a skilfully argued pamphlet justifying female preaching. Fox approached the marriage in a matter-of-fact way more common to a business deal than a physical union; for example, in an early example of a prenuptial agreement, he won the approval of Fell's children and indicated that he had no financial interest in their mother's extensive property. The couple decided to be married on 27 October 1669 in the Quaker meeting in Bristol, a city with which neither had much direct contact. In the previous week Fox took advantage of this opportunity to illustrate the correct and evolving procedure for a Quaker marriage.

The couple, accompanied by Fell's daughters and such luminaries as the recently convinced William Penn, appeared before Bristol Friends twice and won their expected approval; Bristol's male Quakers also met with the two separately and endorsed the union.

The wedding revealed no additional role for female Friends, so either Fox had not fully decided how they might contribute or he was not yet prepared to spring his decision on an unsuspecting society. Not until two years later, while he was in Barbados, did he issue an epistle describing the new role for women as he now conceived it. He provided that one of the responsibilities of the separate disciplinary meeting for women was to interview the couple first to make sure that they were ready for marriage, and that neither had financial obstacles or other commitments that might threaten their marriage. As much as anything else, this new departure fuelled a new upsurge of dissent among Quakers, particularly those from isolated rural areas in the north-west where women's meetings had not yet been instituted; London's women meetings, in contrast, had been active for more than a decade.

Within ten days of their marriage the couple departed on their separate ways, George to London and Margaret back to Swarthmoor Hall; there was no indication that either found any hardship from the decision to deny themselves the comforts of their 'outward *Habitation*' (*Journal*, 1694, ix). But Margaret Fox may have been more bothered than she appeared to be: the following year, imprisoned behind the heavy doors in the basement of Lancaster Castle, she fell victim at fifty-five to a false or imaginary pregnancy. Fox, for whom sexual relations do not seem to have been very important, left no comments about his reactions to this development. However, this was a period of suffering for him as well; a severe depression gripped him through autumn and winter 1670. With Margaret in Lancaster's gaol, he remained in London, nursed slowly back to health by a succession of the women overseen by one of his stepdaughters-in-law.

New World journey Fit again by March 1671, Fox determined to travel to the plantations across the Atlantic, a trip that offered the opportunity not only to bolster Friends in that part of the world but also to deal with the remnants of Perrotism that had emerged when Perrot had emigrated to Jamaica—Perrot himself had died there some six years earlier. In August 1671 the thirteen-strong group of Quakers was seen off from Gravesend by Margaret Fox and William Penn. The party landed at Barbados early in October, and following a few weeks of recuperation, it was there that Fox took three momentous steps for the Society of Friends: he promulgated his decision on the role of women's meetings in overseeing marriages; he encountered African slaves for the first time and responded to the institution of slavery; and he composed another major declaration of the Quaker faith.

The new responsibility that Fox delegated to women divided Quakers into contending factions back in England, a threat that may have determined his choice of venue for his epistle. The sermon on slavery could be neither as controversial nor as radical as his decree on the role of women, but it lent the Quakers a vague reputation for opposing slavery without their doing very much to relieve Africans of their burden. Even so, Quakers in Barbados, although numerous and quite well off, bore the brunt of distrust from their neighbours because of suspicions that in encouraging their slaves to attend their religious services on an equal basis they did not fully favour the institution of slavery. It did not help their reputations, either, that they were accused of not paying their full share to defend the island colony. Preaching fewer than twenty days after he arrived on the island, Fox carefully spiritualized the issue of slavery, averring that status was determined by a person's possession of Christ. 'All are God's free people,' he asserted, 'who walk in the truth' (RS Friends, Lond., Epistle, 315, MS Q4–5). He broached but did not endorse outright the idea that a slave who had been faithful in discharging all responsibilities and who had been purchased with the master's money might be freed after thirty years; until then—and relying on the master's good judgement—slaves should remain loyal and full members of their owner's family. The sermon held out an indistinct hope for emancipation (albeit after a long time), but it also indicated that Fox believed slaves should be in some sense part of their owners' families, included in attendance at Quaker meetings.

Fox also dealt with the slave issue in his famous 'Letter to the governor and assembly of Barbados'. In the section on servitude, he attempted to lay to rest the 'lie' that Quakers encouraged slave unrest in a colony whose population was more than two-thirds African. Slave rebellions, he confessed, were abhorrent to his followers, and this was one of the reasons why Quakers encouraged slaves to attend their meetings for worship. There they learned to be sober, temperate, charitable, just, and certainly not to rebel; in fact, Fox insisted, Quakers' slaves were more apt to be law-abiding than the slaves of other masters. Let the island's authorities discard their misgivings about Quakers and their human property, he told the governor and assembly; then all would prosper together. However, Fox's letter is better remembered for dealing with Quakers' religious orthodoxy. The local 'evil slander' regarding Quaker beliefs was as bad as the attack on them for the way in which they dealt with their slaves. Fox affirmed that Friends adhered to traditional Christian views of God's creation of the universe, Jesus's virgin birth, his crucifixion for sin, and his bodily resurrection. In later centuries evangelical Quakers reasserted this dogma to position Friends squarely within the range of orthodox Christianity; the letter's only Quaker twist was Fox's affirmation that Christ 'is now come … to rule in our hearts', something he could hardly have omitted without repudiating everything for which he had already stood for nearly thirty years (Ingle, 234–5).

Three months after arriving in Barbados, Fox and his party left for Jamaica and the mainland. His seven-week visit to the island that William Penn's father had captured for the English in the mid-1650s went happily, with few signs of Perrot's residual influence; he also conferred twice with the island's governor, and started disciplinary men's and women's meetings. After a stormy passage, in April the voyagers arrived in Maryland, where the Friends were already quite influential. Fox took the opportunity to confer with the indigenous Americans, but, interestingly, he never mentioned any contacts with local slaves. The Quaker party did not stay long in Maryland but soon left for Long Island, where they were anxious to arrive in time for a half-yearly meeting late in October, especially as there was evidence of Perrotism there. Finding that their fears had been groundless, the group sailed across the sound to Rhode Island, home to every kind of dissenter because of the religious tolerance instituted by its founder, Roger Williams, who was now in his seventies. Many colonial and local officials were Quakers, a fact that elated Fox and lent his visit something of the quality of a royal progress. He stayed at the home of Nicholas Easton, the newly elected Quaker governor and attended a wedding and a general meeting, but left in July 1672 before a debate scheduled with Williams, who was an outspoken critic of the movement.

Perhaps surprisingly, Fox did not turn northwards to New England, where four Friends had been executed only a little more than a decade earlier; inspired by these martyrdoms, the Quaker numbers here had grown much larger. Instead he returned to the south, proceeding as far as North Carolina. Provincial officials came to greet him warmly everywhere he went, a contrast with his receptions on many occasions in England. In Maryland he spent a considerable time visiting Friends on both the eastern and western shores and dispatched an epistle to the governor explaining Quaker beliefs. In May 1673, firmly convinced that Friends in the colonies had a glorious future before them, Fox embarked for the voyage back to Bristol. The tour had been a good one for the Quaker leader, for it had given him a glimpse of the expansion of the faith far beyond its home island; newly established disciplinary meetings in the colonies would help shield these fledgeling groups from the influence of dissidents like Perrot's supporters and keep them within the mainstream. On his arrival in England, he set about seeing that books and pamphlets would be channelled to the colonial Quakers.

Controversy and further consolidation Fox arrived on 28 June and quickly discovered that the situation in England was not nearly as straightforward as the one he had left across the Atlantic; the increased power that Fox's colonial declarations had conferred on female Quakers had ignited controversy back home. In November 1671, with Fox only recently arrived in the New World, male Friends in Bristol acted. Prompted by a substantial businessman, William Rogers, who was himself close enough to the centre of power to have attended the Fox–Fell wedding and to have signed their certificate, the men objected when women Friends (including Isabel Yeamans, Fox's stepdaughter) had tried to organize their own separate women's meeting. The men's meeting simply decreed that there would be no women's meeting until they all, male and female, assented to one. It was the first open

challenge to the new order and reverberated sharply through the Quaker community. From his position in the midst of this controversy, Rogers emerged as the principal anti-Fox activist in the Society of Friends; his efforts made him, in fact, the initiator of what is usually known as the Wilkinson–Story dispute.

This dispute, the most serious and widespread of those that racked Quakerism in the later seventeenth century, had strong roots around Bristol and in the north-west. It presented Fox and the central Quaker leadership with a problem that lasted for a decade, but it also enabled them to define what became the basic polity of Quakers. One Friend confronted Fox directly in Wiltshire to remind him that the apostle Paul had advised women to remain silent in the church. Fox's laboured response silenced his critic, but the dissent he represented certainly did not dissipate so easily. However, Fox's position was significantly bolstered and enhanced by the influential expertise and writings of two forceful and socially prominent recent adherents to Quakerism, William Penn and the Scot Robert Barclay, both of whom took active roles in the struggle. Fox's own role, although still substantial, was none the less diminished by his imprisonment in Worcester late in 1673, not six months after he had returned from America. The Test Act, passed in March, provided for an oath recognizing the supremacy of the crown and abjuring the Catholic doctrine of transubstantiation; Fox of course refused to swear to either, and even after his wife obtained a royal pardon for him, he refused to accept it lest he indirectly admit to wrongdoing. Dragging on for fourteen months, this imprisonment weakened his body and spirit, and he left Worcester Castle in poor health.

The dispute quickly expanded from a mere discussion of women's roles. Provincial leaders in the north-west already distrusted orders that came from London; and it seemed that such orders were becoming more frequent. The 'Testimony from the brethren' (1666) had established the principle of a central authority for the movement, and with it the London leadership had begun to act. Annual sessions of London yearly meeting started in 1668. The second-day morning meeting, going back to the 1650s, reasserted its right to oversee publications of Quakers: even a proposed Fox publication on women fell victim to its constraint in 1676. In the same year the London leadership set up the 'meeting for sufferings', a quaintly named body that convened weekly in London and gradually evolved into an executive committee for British Friends. Within it, a shadowy central group of twelve oversaw financial aspects of the movement; the need for such a body underscored one aspect of the stability that Quakerism had achieved by the mid-1670s. Not surprisingly, membership of these groups was centred in London and also overlapped, creating coteries of powerful men.

In the rural, isolated, and provincial north-west Quakers saw these moves as granting Fox and his associates powers that resembled those of the pope and his curia— indeed, that very analogy was used by contemporary critics to describe the supporters of Fox and his allies. The Lancastrians John Wilkinson and John Story, whose names were somewhat incorrectly attached to the dispute as a whole, objected not only to centralization but also to the Londoners' insistence that Quakers permit 'serious sighings, sensible groaning and reverent singing' in their meetings and stand firmly against paying tithes. Liberty of conscience became their cry, to which Fox thundered in response, 'God is a God of Order, and not of Confusion' (G. Fox, *Several Plain Truths Manifested*, 1684, 26). The fundamentals of the dispute could perhaps be encapsulated in a single couplet from a dissident Quaker pamphlet:

TAKE heed, beware of Novelty,
And Female Authority.
(*Innocency Vindicated and Envy Rebuked*, 1684, 10)

The efforts in Westmorland of Margaret Fox, who had taken the lead since 1671 in defending the decrees from London, also irritated the dissenters within the movement—so much so, that Fox felt obliged to issue her with a rebuke in May 1674. Rumour and counter-rumour circulated about the words and actions of each side, becoming ever more exaggerated with each retelling. Meetings such as that at Reading (where Thomas and Anne Curtis, two of Fox's former closest colleagues, were leaders) split; some opponents of Fox reprinted tracts by Nayler and Perrot. Hints of class crept into the discussion: secessionists pointed to the wig worn by the gentrified Penn, which Fox had felt was acceptable because of hideous scarring that Penn had acquired during a youthful bout of smallpox.

Tired and ill, Fox allowed others to carry the burden of the dispute during the mid-1670s. Perhaps, too, he realized that his own teaching had laid the foundations for the dissent, something his opponents did not permit him to forget. He began assuming a rather unaccustomed pastoral role, trying to conciliate and win the opponents back for the movement, but he never shrank from supporting those who were making the rules in London. Such firmness from Fox and others eventually wore down the opposition: Story died in 1681, while Wilkinson sank into an obscurity that Fox may have believed he richly deserved; and an embittered William Rogers wrote a lengthy account of his side of the story, circulating it first in manuscript and then in print. Still, the two Reading meetings did not reunite until 1716; other aspects of the dispute lingered; and they all became part of the historical residue of Quakerism.

Fox's journal and the end of his life After Fox's release from Worcester he spent most of the mid-1670s at or near Swarthmoor Hall. Here he rested and put in order the collection of letters his wife had saved from the movement's early days. This process—accompanied by a probable destruction of some letters—became the basis for refreshing his memory as he worked to finish his memoirs, which were posthumously published in 1694 as *A journal or historical account of the life, travels, sufferings, Christian experiences and labour of love in the work of the ministry, of that ancient, eminent and faithful servant of Jesus Christ, George Fox*. Fox had begun dictating the *Journal* while still at Worcester, but had not finished by the time he was freed. His memoir has remained a classic of religious literature and

has never gone out of print. Although it is mistitled in its implication that, as a journal, it was a day-to-day account of his life, many still find its narrative compelling. As the autobiography of one who struggles with his inner uneasiness and then discovers a sense of security allowing him to transcend and overcome his wonderings, Fox's *Journal* speaks to a variety of seekers and people who simply want to understand the human condition. His central proclamations, 'the mighty *Power* of the *Lord* was over all' and '*Christ was come to teach* [his] *People himself*', served to convey his own gripping awareness of God's powerful, immediate presence, but they also remind even casual readers that they, too, can be recipients of the same grace that Fox experienced (*Journal*, 1694, 82, 72).

However, the book has distorted the history of the movement. Centring as it inevitably does on Fox, it stands as his own view of things. Some people, for example Elizabeth Hooten, the first person Fox convinced, receive no more than occasional mentions, despite the major part she played as a Quaker minister until her death in Jamaica in 1672. The *Journal* emphasizes those aspects of the movement most associated with Fox himself (the great open-air rallies and disputations) at the expense of others (the brilliantly planned and executed publicity drives and the co-ordinated tithe-strikes) in which he was less involved. It was also a product of the struggle against dissent within the movement, reflecting the period of its composition. Fox casually excluded from his narrative or played down the role of several people who had once occupied prominent positions in the movement, such as the Curtises at Reading, Wilkinson and Story, and especially James Nayler. Fox took pains to emphasize how he had always been vindicated against his opponents, either by his own victories, by the direction of events, or by God's interventions on his behalf. Its main subject can therefore come across as mean-spirited and vindictive. Moreover, Fox never concedes, much less confesses, any errors on his part: here is a man always in the right, sure of himself and his role, and convinced beyond any human doubt that he will be victorious in the end. This kind of cocksureness can easily antagonize and raises questions about whether Fox and his supporters rewrote the history of their movement in a way to justify their decisions and to deprecate their opponents. No final answers can be offered to this important question, even though circumstantial evidence suggests that Fox destroyed letters he did not wish later generations to see, and he certainly rewrote enthusiastic letters that embarrassed him as he reread them; he knew that controlling the sources would control history's verdict.

By 1680 things were looking better for those in charge of the Quaker movement. Now spending most of his time in London, where he could attend meetings for sufferings and second-day morning meetings as well as lobbying parliament when something of immediate concern arose there, Fox became more sedentary than he had been during his entire life. Even so, he did review quite a few proposed pamphlets for the benefit of the morning meeting, admonishing its members to be sure that they did not permit Ranterish publications to go to the countryside in the name of Friends. Two of Margaret Fox's daughters lived in the area, and so Fox alternated between their homes in Kingston, Surrey, and Romford, Essex, or stayed closer to the centre of things in the Quaker settlement just off Gracechurch Street.

Fox put on extra weight, his face growing full—a visitor reporting that his fingers were so puffy that he could hardly write—and took juniper berries to medicate himself for what he called 'dropsy', or congestive heart failure. On bad days he was almost totally inactive, while on good ones he had much less energy than previously. Nevertheless, streams of pamphlets, fewer of them as polemical as in the past, still flowed from his pen. He took more time overseeing his money now than he had in the past, investing some in shipping, lending some to traders, even, his opponents whispered, secreting some to avoid ubiquitous tithe collectors. After Charles II gave William Penn the grant of land in the New World that became Pennsylvania, Penn gave Fox a plot in Philadelphia, 16 acres in the suburbs, and 1250 acres in the out-country. Fox wanted all these financial matters to remain a secret lest intelligence of them sully not only his reputation but also that of the movement.

Fox went to the continent on two brief trips, one in 1677, the other seven years later. The first, which lasted three months, was the more extensive, taking him as far east as the border area close to Denmark, where a small Friends' meeting had been established in Friedrichstadt. The party included George Keith (who after Fox's death became the most prominent of all the Quaker dissidents), Penn, Barclay, and Isabel Yeamans, as well as some well-to-do Quaker businessmen seeking to make valuable economic contacts in Europe—even Fox took some iron ore from the Fell forge to show around in the hopes of making a continental sale. Fox spent some time in Amsterdam where, as he did elsewhere, he set up both men's and women's meetings and advised the recently convinced Dutch Quakers to avoid schisms by reading his books and pamphlets; he also made sure that they instituted some kind of control over publications by continental Friends. A miracle allegedly occurred during this trip when a woman Fox described as creeping on her hands and knees for fourteen years proceeded to get up and walk normally; Fox, however, claimed no credit for it. The second of the continental trips was briefer—a six-week visit to the Low Countries—but the strain of mediating the deeply divided Dutch Quaker movement proved exhausting, forcing him to recuperate for a month on his return.

In the last decade of Fox's life things began to improve for the English Quakers, partly because of changes in the religious and political climate, and partly as a result of the lobbying they did; Penn, a close friend of the Stuart monarchs, played a particularly important role in this activity. In March 1686 James II issued a pardon for all those convicted of not attending the established church, a move that elated the Friends who saw over 1600 colleagues released from prison. In the following year James high-handedly promulgated a declaration of indulgence for dissenters, prompting many Quakers, mobilized by Penn but silently repudiated by Fox, to write public letters of thanks to James; many were rewarded with appointments to borough corporations through the new corporation charters that the king was issuing. However, with the replacement of James by William and Mary in the revolution of 1688–9, the Quakers lost influence; the Toleration Act of 1689 gave them a right of free religious assembly, but nothing more. Fox was, of course, happier with this bare liberty than with the handclasp with perceived tyranny, but relations between him and the royalist-inclined Penn soured, a situation that had been threatening for some time. Fox considered his younger associate contaminated by his closeness to kingly power, even as he wondered if a time of tolerance did not present a false liberty that would foster looseness and less strictness.

Fox still found enough energy during these final years to visit the London meetings, and he donated land at Ulverston for a Friends' meeting-house close enough to Swarthmoor Hall for his wife to supervise. In October 1688 he completed his last will and testament. Margaret, now aged seventy-six, arrived in April 1690 for a visit, a journey especially wearing for her. When she returned alone to the north-west at the end of June, Fox went back to Quaker business, reading reports about which the meeting for sufferings or the second-day morning meeting wanted his advice. Six months later, on 11 January 1691, Fox attended the Gracechurch Street meeting and, as usual, preached. At the end of the meeting he complained of a coldness near his heart and went to bed at the nearby house of Henry Gouldney, a local Quaker with whom Fox had stayed several times before. To reassure the Friends who waited at his bedside, Fox repeated: 'All is well. The *Seed* of God reigns over all, and over *Death* it self' (*Journal*, 1694, 614). Two days later, about 9.45 in the evening, he died of congestive heart failure, his chin firmed up, his spirit at peace. On 16 January a procession of thousands accompanied Fox's body to Bunhill Fields, where many other dissenters were interred. The exact location of the grave site, now adjacent to Bunhill Fields meeting-house, is unknown.

Aftermath Fox's death did not end the problems Quakers faced; indeed, it marked little change at all, for he had successfully created a structure that easily survived his death. At the time of his death yet another schism was occurring among the Quakers in Pennsylvania, this time involving George Keith, who thought that the Friends there were not 'Christian' enough and wanted to compose a creedal statement for them. That most of the previous disagreements had involved the antinomian left wing rather than the theological right only underlined how far Fox had consolidated the individualistic Society of Friends into a more fundamentally stable and conservative position. Fox did leave the Society of Friends with the germs of these differences and with the likelihood that they would continue to breed discontent, but he also bequeathed the movement enough administrative machinery to deal with such problems.

To carry out their leader's wishes, the London yearly meeting's second-day morning meeting turned its attention immediately after Fox's death to compiling and completing his memoirs, assigning this task to Thomas Ellwood, a Quaker who had been a supportive friend of John Milton. Ellwood somewhat toned down its original vigour as he edited it for publication. The finished *Journal* issued from its publisher, Thomas Northcott, in 1694, containing a long preface by William Penn, as well as testimony by Fox's widow and long selections from Fox's other writings. Four years later, a second volume, consisting of selected epistles, appeared; a third volume, consisting of a collection of selected doctrinal works, was published in 1706. All three works naturally reflected the judgements of their editors. A memoir closer in time to most of the events described therein was dictated by Fox in 1664 when he was incarcerated at Lancaster; eventually published in 1925 as the *Short Journal*, it exudes more vibrancy and power in the selected events it describes after 1647.

A complete edition of Fox's voluminous writings, both published and unpublished, remains to be achieved; the closest approximation is an eight-volume edition brought out in Philadelphia in 1831. The extant and unpublished collections of documents that came to make up the *Journal* are housed in London in the library of the Religious Society of Friends; denominated the Spence manuscripts, these were edited by Norman Penney and first published in 1911. The Swarthmore manuscripts, collected only at the end of the nineteenth century, contain primarily the letters that Margaret Fell kept when she had oversight of the developing movement in the 1650s; an extremely valuable collection, they too are in the archives with the Spence manuscripts in London. A further valuable guide of major worth is the *Annual Catalogue of George Fox's Papers*, edited by H. J. Cadbury (1939), which not only provides a comprehensive catalogue but also contains sentences offering glimpses of documents long since lost or destroyed.

Fox was surely one of the most important religious figures that England produced, for his movement, although it remained small, both endured and spread worldwide, while numerous later reformers, including John Wesley and William Booth, were directly influenced either by his example or by his theological positions. The conflict that his compelling ideas occasioned during his lifetime continued (and continues) within the Religious Society of Friends; without a firmly based authority the possibility of disagreement was ever present. His life and experience also left to his followers a heritage of both a firm commitment to acting on ineffable religious insights and an assertive attitude about the rightness of their positions. Such inclinations, encapsulated in 1955 in the phrase 'speak truth to power', garnered for Quakers the 1947 Nobel peace prize, but made them, like Fox, sometimes difficult to get along with. Still, he remained a charismatic leader, almost uniquely able to articulate concretely what generations of his followers believed they themselves

needed to say, whether theologically or not. A kind of touchstone, his career and experiences continue to inspire.   H. LARRY INGLE

Sources H. L. Ingle, *First among Friends: George Fox and the creation of Quakerism* (1994) · *Journal … of George Fox*, ed. T. Ellwood (1694) · *The journal of George Fox*, ed. N. Penney, 2 vols. (1911) · *The short journal and itinerary journals of George Fox*, ed. N. Penney (1925) · *Works of George Fox*, 8 vols. (1831) · H. J. Cadbury, ed., *Annual catalogue of George Fox's papers: compiled in 1694–1697* (1939) · RS Friends, Lond., Swarthmore papers · W. C. Braithwaite, *The beginnings of Quakerism* (1912) · W. C. Braithwaite, *The second period of Quakerism* (1919) · R. Moore, *Light in their consciences* (2000) · W. Evans and T. Evans, eds., *Friends library*, 14 vols. (1837) · N. Penney, ed., *Extracts from state papers relating to Friends, 1654 to 1672* (1913) · H. J. Cadbury, ed., *Swarthmore documents in America* (1940) · W. Rogers, *Christian Quaker*, 8 parts (1680–84) · R. Barclay, *Anarchy of the Ranters and other libertines* (1676) · *Papers of William Penn*, ed. M. M. Dunn and R. Dunn, 1–4 (1981–6) · H. Barbour, *Quakers in puritan England* (1964) · J. Barclay, ed., *Letters &c. of early Friends* (1841) · H. Barbour and A. Roberts, eds., *Early Quaker writings, 1650–1700* (1973) [reissue planned for 2003]
Archives Bodl. Oxf., travel journal of trip to West Indies and New England · Bristol RO, letters · RS Friends, Lond., letters and MSS | Haverford College, Pennsylvania, Richardson MS · RS Friends, Lond., J. Penington MSS · RS Friends, Lond., Spence MSS · RS Friends, Lond., Swarthmore MSS · Swarthmore College, Pennsylvania, Half-Year's Women's Meeting in Maryland
Likenesses J. Holmes, stipple, pubd 1699 (after G. Honthorst), BM, NPG · T. Fairland, lithograph (after unknown artist), NPG

Fox, George (*bap.* 1801, *d.* 1871), topographer, a native of Pontefract, Yorkshire, was baptized in Pontefract on 15 November 1801, the son of John Fox, a bookseller and stationer, and his wife, Elizabeth. He worked in partnership with his father and was for some years a member of the corporation. He compiled a *History of Pontefract* (1827), illustrated with his own drawings. Fox died at his home, Friar Wood House, Pontefract, on 23 August 1871. He was survived by his wife, Eliza.

GORDON GOODWIN, *rev.* WILLIAM JOSEPH SHEILS

Sources *Pontefract Advertiser* (26 Aug 1871) · parish register, All Saints, Pontefract, 15 Nov 1801, Borth. Inst. [baptism] · *CGPLA Eng. & Wales* (1871)
Wealth at death under £3000: probate, 14 Oct 1871, *CGPLA Eng. & Wales*

Fox [*formerly* Fuchs], **Harold Munro** (1889–1967), zoologist, was born Harold Munro Fuchs in Clapham, London, on 28 September 1889, the elder of the two children and the only son of Georg Gotthilf Fuchs, once a captain in the Prussian army, and his wife, Margaret Isabella Campbell, daughter of Lieutenant-Colonel Andrew Munro from Sutherland, of the 19th (Yorkshire) regiment. His parents separated when he was very young; his sister, Alison Settle OBE, became the editor of *Vogue*.

From preparatory school in Henley, Fuchs, at the age of thirteen, became a day boy at Brighton College, whence he obtained a scholarship to Gonville and Caius College, Cambridge, in 1908. He graduated in 1911 with a second class in part two of the natural sciences tripos, and spent a year working at the Plymouth laboratory, followed by ten months at Naples. In 1913 he became a lecturer in zoology at the Royal College of Science, London. On the outbreak of war he joined the Army Service Corps and changed his name to Fox. He served in Egypt, Salonika, and the Balkans, and during part of the war, because of his linguistic abilities, he was attached to French and Italian units in Palestine. In 1917 he married Léonie Thérèse, the daughter of Henri Roger, an official with the Suez Canal Company.

After the war Fox returned to London for six months before becoming a lecturer at the school of medicine in Cairo. During the summer of 1919 he spent some time at the Plymouth laboratory, and discovered that the small flagellate *Bodo* could be used to detect respiratory surfaces of aquatic invertebrates. His thesis on this subject, written in Cairo, gained him a fellowship at Caius (1920). While in Cairo he paid frequent visits to the Gulf of Suez, where he observed that the regular cycle of spawning in the sea urchin *Diadema* was restricted to a few days near new moon. This led to a review of available information on lunar periodicity, and to the publication in 1928 of *Selene, or, Sex and the Moon*. After returning to Cambridge to take up his fellowship he organized an expedition to Egypt to study the fauna of the Suez Canal (1924). Experts were recruited to study the collections, and Fox pressurized them all into publishing at the same time. This study established that the Bitter Lakes acted as a barrier to the majority of animals that might migrate from the Red Sea to the Mediterranean. The true importance of this barrier was realized only much later; after the building of the Aswan High Dam the salinity of the Bitter Lakes was reduced and more animals entered the Mediterranean.

The most important of Fox's researches began in 1923, when at the Roscoff laboratory in Brittany he examined the red–green blood of the fan-worm *Spirographis*. The pigment had been called chlorocruorin by E. Ray Lankester in 1867, and some of its properties had been established, but Fox's experiments demonstrated its function and chemical nature. He returned to various aspects of this work over the next thirty years. In 1927 he was appointed to the chair of zoology at Birmingham, and after fourteen years transferred to Bedford College, London. At Birmingham and Bedford College he pioneered work on metabolic rates in various environments, and at different latitudes. Also, with H. Ramage, he made the first spectrographic analyses of the rarer elements in a variety of animals. He became an international authority on respiratory pigments. Fox and his wife separated while he was professor at Birmingham. He married, in 1931, Natalya (Natasha) Lvovna, daughter of Lev Yulevich Mertens of Saratov, Russia. There were no children of either marriage. Natasha shared with Fox a dislike of pretence, a love of travel, and considerable linguistic ability.

Fox was elected FRS in 1937 and honorary president of the Société Zoologique de France in 1955, and was appointed Fullerian professor of physiology at the Royal Institution for 1953–6. He also received the gold medal of the Linnean Society (1959), an honorary DSc from the University of Bordeaux (1965), and the Darwin medal of the Royal Society (1966).

For forty years Fox edited *Biological Reviews of the Cambridge Philosophical Society*. His own writings were concise and clear, and he would not tolerate lower standards in his authors. His teaching, like his writing, was always meticulously prepared, with an emphasis on elegance and clarity. He retired in 1954 but continued editing, and developed an interest in ostracod crustaceans, on which he published ten papers between 1962 and 1967.

When he was ten or eleven years old Fox had been run over by a horse-bus, which caused him to be a patient for almost a year in St George's Hospital, London. However, he was left with no permanent disability and became a good shot and an accomplished horseman, ballroom dancer, and swimmer. He was handsome and had great vitality, which gave him a rapidity of speech and a constantly questioning mind. He was for many years a member of the Savile Club. He remained a keen horseman throughout his retirement, and died in St George's Hospital on 29 January 1967 after suffering a heart attack while on his usual weekend ride. He was survived by his second wife.

JOHN GREEN, *rev.* V. M. QUIRKE

Sources J. E. Smith, *Memoirs FRS*, 14 (1968), 207–22 · personal knowledge (1981)
Archives ICL, corresp. and papers · Royal Holloway College, Egham, Surrey, papers · U. Lond. | CUL, letters to Charles Ogden
Wealth at death £3095: probate, 30 March 1967, *CGPLA Eng. & Wales*

Fox, Henry, first Baron Holland of Foxley (1705–1774), politician, was born on 28 September 1705 at Chiswick, the second son of Sir Stephen *Fox (1627–1716), financier, and Christian (1679–1719), daughter of the Revd Francis Hope, rector of Haceby, and afterwards of Aswarby, Lincolnshire. Thanks to the enormous wealth acquired during his father's long career as a financier his childhood was materially very comfortable. Equally important, though, were the discipline and love of parents whose quietly traditional Anglican piety had its roots in Sir Stephen's humble Wiltshire origins and Lady Fox's clerical background. It was a tory upbringing, certainly, but this was as much a matter of religious observance as of politics. Sir Stephen's essential loyalties lay with the Church of England; his toryism had never led him beyond the fringes of active political life, and he had never been a Jacobite.

Education and early career Such a background led naturally on to Eton College, whither Henry accompanied his elder brother, Stephen, in 1715. But, with a father in his eighties, it was unlikely that the security of Fox's early years would last into adolescence. The chief props fell away with the deaths of Sir Stephen in 1716 and Lady Fox in 1719. Shared grief certainly strengthened the bonds between the orphans. Fox's deepest emotional attachment, at least until his marriage in 1744, was to his elder brother; even thereafter any quarrel between them (such as that over Fox's decision to refuse the secretaryship of state in March 1754) caused anguish to both. Even so, the insecurity of an orphan of thirteen can still be detected in the care with which Fox recorded and preserved his mother's dying injunctions to serve God and obey his guardians. The most important figure among the latter was probably Edward Nicholas, MP for Shaftesbury, who shared Sir Stephen Fox's toryism and who helped to guide

Henry Fox, first Baron Holland of Foxley (1705–1774), by Sir Joshua Reynolds, 1763–4

his sons towards maturity in its spirit. Thus in February 1721 Fox matriculated at Christ Church, Oxford, where his tutor was George Wigan, who had begun to act in the same capacity to the young John Wesley the previous year. Described by Thomas Hearne as 'two pretty, modest young Gentlemen', the brothers Fox were still enveloped in a tory-Anglican atmosphere (T. Hearne, *Remarks and Collections of Thomas Hearne*, ed. C. E. Doble, 11 vols., 1885–1921, 7.242). But the charge first levelled by Chesterfield, that the younger Fox was 'by Education a Jacobite', needs to be treated with the greatest caution; the evidence that he dabbled in Jacobitism while at Oxford is very slender (BL, Stowe MS 308, fol. 13). Much more significant is the passion for politics that was kindled during his years as an undergraduate. The bursting of the South Sea Bubble in 1720–21 prepared the ground for a general election in 1722, which included a contest among university tories at Oxford. From the vantage point of Christ Church, Fox could do little more than observe until he came of age, but well before that time he was a devotee of the Cocoa Tree, the London headquarters of toryism. He remained at Oxford until the end of 1724, and moved thence (without taking a degree) to Gray's Inn with the seeming intention of pursuing a legal career. Yet the world of politics already held him.

Fox sought entry to that world almost as soon as he came of age, standing for parliament at Hindon in 1727. This attempt to exploit his family's tory, Wiltshire origins failed on petition at the hands of a Walpole ministry recently reconfirmed in power. A surprise attack on the venal borough of Old Sarum the following year also came to nothing, and he had to wait until 1735 for electoral success. In the interval he broke decisively with the tory Anglicanism of his upbringing and adopted the whig, freethinking tenets of his mature years as a career politician. This process began with a change of mentors in 1726; in that year the death of Edward Nicholas removed the guiding hand of the tory past, and Fox made the acquaintance of John, Lord Hervey. The latter was the archetype of the fashionable deist of the 1720s. His air of sophistication, his willingness to flatter, and the influence he enjoyed at court through his intimacy with Queen Caroline made him hard for a young tory to resist. But Hervey's hold over the younger Fox was never as complete as that which he enjoyed over the elder, partly because his dealings with Henry lacked the homosexual element that was almost certainly present in his relationship with Stephen. None the less, Hervey's anti-clericalism and his contempt for revealed religion had a corrosive effect on the beliefs of Fox's youth. The decade after 1726 was an unsettled period of drift, as Fox gradually turned his back on his parents and his own upbringing.

Political character Yet while Fox's Christian beliefs may have disintegrated, he did not emerge from the wreck as an unprincipled cynic. On the contrary, he chose to live by fashionable principles which did not rest on fear of divine disfavour, in particular a sociability rooted in the ethics of plain dealing. Fox was, as Waldegrave remarked, 'a warm Friend, a man of Veracity, and a Man of Honor' (*Memoirs and Speeches of … Waldegrave*, 156). He defined honesty as fighting openly and unreservedly to advance the interests of his allies. His character came to display a directness that had its own peculiar charm and which attracted a loyal circle of intimates; by the early 1730s this group already included men such as the third duke of Marlborough, Thomas Winnington, Charles Hamilton, and John Bateman. Though they did not represent the finer elements in contemporary politics they had strong ties to Fox, for whom the consolations of friendship came to replace those of religion. Yet his philosophy rested on an excessively optimistic view of human nature which meant that, in both his personal and his political relationships, Fox was far too incautious. He never distinguished accurately between relationships founded on genuine personal affection and those whose essence was no more than self-interest. He naïvely believed that loyalty on his part could lead to no harm and would inevitably be reciprocated, and those who sought his company and his good offices were seldom turned away. For many years a widening circle of acquaintances proved to be a significant source of political strength. As long as the winds of fortune seemed to be wafting him towards high office, the fact that he was undiscriminating in his choice of intimates and associates hardly seemed to matter. But when those winds turned about, the chaff scattered and Fox was genuinely hurt and bewildered at being betrayed by those he had trusted. At the end the treachery of Richard Rigby and John Calcraft revealed his shortcomings as a judge of character and robbed him of his final defences against cynicism by wrecking what was left of his faith in human nature.

Such a transition from ardent faith to bitter disillusion also characterized Fox's public career. Brought to court by Hervey, he chose to abide by the simple principle of loyal service to the head of the king's administration. His break with toryism was eased by his rejection of his Anglican past, but he found little compensating material for belief in the whiggism of the 1730s. The defence of the Hanoverian succession and its Walpolian corollary, fiscal prudence, engaged his interest but penetrated no farther into his being. He devoted himself to men, not measures; first, and perhaps most passionately, to Sir Robert Walpole before his fall from power in 1742; then to Walpole's successor as prime minister, Henry Pelham, until his death in 1754; in a secondary fashion to the duke of Cumberland; and finally, briefly, but fatally, to Thomas Pelham-Holles, duke of Newcastle. Loyalty to the administration and its leader became his political ethic, and for many years it served him well; the emphasis which Fox placed on fidelity made him a trusted ally and enhanced his value to his superiors. But the vagaries of politics were to make loyalty a far more complicated business than he could have realized when he first pledged himself to serve the prime minister of the day in the later 1730s. It was to end in a reputation for mercenary and rapacious self-interest totally at odds with the creed by which he tried, in all sincerity, to abide for twenty years.

Some of those complexities were foreshadowed at the outset of his active political career. Fox gave unswerving support to his earliest patron, Hervey, even acting as his second in a duel with William Pulteney in 1731. In return Hervey used his influence at court to advance his protégé. He exerted himself to secure Walpole's backing for Fox's candidacy at Hindon in 1733, for which constituency Fox was finally chosen at a by-election in February 1735. Hervey was also responsible for securing the lucrative court office of surveyor-general of works for Fox in 1737. Such swift promotion seemed to prove that friendship was useful as well as agreeable. But Hervey soon ceased to be his only mentor. As he established himself as a useful speaker in the lower house from 1737 onwards, Fox was drawn inexorably into the orbit of Sir Robert Walpole. For a while loyalties to Hervey and Walpole ran in parallel. The prime minister was increasingly on the defensive after the excise crisis of 1733 and the elections of 1734. Hervey was an ally at court, and the support of able young parliamentarians such as Fox was a useful counterweight to the hostility of William Pitt and others of the Cobham Cubs. As the Walpole administration ran into serious difficulties at home and abroad in 1739 Fox became an increasingly fierce partisan of the prime minister. Some of the energy with which he defended government policy may have derived from the need of a convert to prove himself, but much of it was not a matter of calculation. Had that been the case he might have been tempted to abandon a sinking ship; as it was, he stayed aboard to the end. In the process, though, he was forced to break with Hervey, who quarrelled with Walpole in the early 1740s; by now Fox regarded himself as a government man and was critical of Hervey's refusal to stand behind Walpole in a time of crisis. He did not embark on a cold and calculating exchange of patrons. But it was still the case that Hervey's political influence could not match that of Walpole even in the years of his decline, and in abandoning Hervey, Fox (not for the last time) opened himself to the charge of putting hopes of future advancement ahead of gratitude for past favours.

In fact devotion to Walpole did not necessarily hold out glittering prospects. The outbreak of war in Europe in 1740 and the reverses suffered in the general election of 1741 gravely weakened the prime minister. After the new parliament met in December 1741 his supporters engaged in a bitter and intense battle to ensure his survival. Fox was as deeply committed as any, spending long hours in the Commons as a series of closely fought election petitions began to go against the ministry, leading eventually to Walpole's demise in February 1742. These months of drama established Fox's credentials as a full member of the old corps of whigs. He found himself in the company of other rising young men (most of whom had only entered parliament in 1741) for whom whiggism seemed to be defined as the resolute defence of Walpole. Those who shared this formative experience were to furnish Fox with more close political friends for the future; they included men such as William Cavendish, marquess of Hartington and subsequently fourth duke of Devonshire, Lord Fitzwilliam, Lord Coke, Welbore Ellis, Sir Charles Hanbury Williams, Henry Legge, and young Horace Walpole.

The reign of the old corps whigs The partisan comradeship forged in the winter of 1741–2 provided the framework for Fox's political career into the 1750s. Although Walpole's young followers could not prevent their master's fall from power, for the next ten years they waged a campaign of revenge against those who had brought him down. Fox played a prominent part in this, and in the process revealed a lack of moderation which was to do him much harm. The obverse of zeal for one's friends was intransigence towards one's adversaries; it made Fox a figure to be feared, but also to be hated. He neither forgave nor forgot his opponents; even as late as 1751, in a struggle over a by-election at Westminster which evoked memories of the battle to save Walpole a decade earlier, he was to suggest harsh confinement in the Tower of London as a fitting punishment for a political opponent, Alexander Murray. A refusal to give quarter and a passion for revenge, although allowed unrestrained expression only in 1762, were already significant motifs in Fox's career in the 1740s and 1750s.

These qualities even created difficulties in Fox's relationship with Henry Pelham, who emerged as Walpole's natural successor after 1742. Pelham neither believed in nor enjoyed the politics of vendetta. For him the defeats of 1741–2 highlighted the need to extend the basis of government support beyond the old corps. He was prepared to try to tolerate new whigs such as Carteret and Bath who had been taken into office despite, or rather because of, their part in bringing about Walpole's fall. Fox chafed under such restraints, and in the early months of 1745 found himself at odds with Pelham over a Commons inquiry into the inconclusive naval battle off Toulon in 1744. Together with other 'young whigs', Fox took a prominent and passionate part in the attempt to foist all blame onto Thomas Mathews, one of the admirals concerned, largely because of Mathews's links with the new whigs. Pelham's precarious position would be weakened by further alienating the new whigs, whose leader, Carteret, by now Lord Granville, retained influence with the king despite being ousted from government in December 1744. Pelham, therefore, made repeated attempts to defuse the issue, but Fox was not to be deflected. The same tensions surfaced again after the outbreak of the Jacobite rising of 1745. As part of the military response to the growing Jacobite threat in the autumn of that year, various noblemen were granted the right to raise their own regiments. This roused the ire of Fox and other young whigs. They did not object to measures to safeguard the Hanoverian succession. But many of the noblemen in question (such as the duke of Bedford and Lord Halifax) belonged to the 'new allies', a group of former opponents of Walpole who had been brought into government in December 1744 to replace the new whigs. Pelham again took a middle line, fearful of the political consequences of a breach with the new allies. Fox had no such qualms. On 1 November he savaged the beneficiaries of the scheme in a speech which greatly hurt Pelham. Fox's opposition proved unavailing but it seemed odd behaviour in one who claimed to be a devoted supporter of the prime minister.

Fox was certainly troubled by Pelham's unwillingness to place his exclusive reliance on the old corps, but for most of the time their interests ran in parallel. Pelham was careful not to neglect his most faithful supporters even while seeking to broaden his basis of support. Thus Fox was promoted to the Treasury board in 1743, and repaid that trust by refusing to have anything to do with the attempt by Bath and Granville to replace Pelham in February 1746. As a result of that crisis Fox was promoted again, this time to the office of secretary at war, where he remained until 1754. This move marked the start of his relationship with the duke of Cumberland, the king's younger son and captain-general of the army, and Fox soon became identified in the minds of many as the political lieutenant of the rather sinister Butcher of Culloden. In fact Fox's attachment to Cumberland, while genuine and no doubt useful to him politically, may have obscured but never superseded his primary political role as an old corps loyalist. The battles that he fought on Cumberland's behalf after 1746 need to be viewed in this broader context. It was natural that, as a leading government supporter with responsibility for military matters, Fox should have piloted through the Commons the changes to the Mutiny Act which Cumberland wanted after 1748. Nor was it surprising that he supported Cumberland in his developing conflict with the duke of Newcastle and Lord Chancellor Hardwicke. In Fox's eyes Newcastle had been less than completely loyal in the final years of the Walpole

administration, and had been much too eager to deal with Walpole's enemies after his fall in 1742. But the net effect of siding against Newcastle and Hardwicke was damaging to Fox's long-term prospects; as Newcastle moved closer to the centre of power, Fox's association with Cumberland began to count against him. At the same time the value of his services to the Walpolian cause began to depreciate markedly as the Pelhamite regime entrenched itself.

This process of marginalization was accelerated by the death of Frederick, prince of Wales, in March 1751. Some provision had to be made for the possibility of a regency in case George II died before his grandson, the future George III, came of age. Newcastle's ally, Hardwicke, framed a bill which prevented Cumberland from becoming sole regent in such circumstances. In the Commons, Fox had no hesitation in attacking elements of the proposal which were an affront to Cumberland. It was easy to accuse Fox of pique at being deprived of the influence which a Cumberland regency would have brought him. More important, in fact, was his long-standing, if previously covert, antipathy to Newcastle and Hardwicke; Fox saw nothing wrong in attacking the handiwork of men whom he regarded as guilty of treachery to Walpole. But it did him damage. Fox was now numbering among his open enemies key figures within the administration rather than identifiable opponents of government. The lack of restraint with which he attacked the enemies of Walpole may have been an asset in the old corps world of the 1740s. But in the more inclusive Pelhamite atmosphere of the 1750s such fierce partisanship came to look outdated and self-seeking, and it made him powerful enemies.

This became clear in 1753 when Hardwicke brought forward a Clandestine Marriages Bill which sought to allow parents of means to prevent their offspring eloping and marrying beneath them. Since Fox had himself run off with and married Lady (Georgiana) Caroline Lennox [see Fox, Caroline (1723–1774)] on 2 May 1744 against the will of her parents, the duke and duchess of Richmond, he had reason enough to oppose the measure. But when Pelham threw the weight of government authority behind the measure Fox unwisely personalized the issue and raised the stakes to an untenable level by launching an overt attack in the Commons on Hardwicke himself. It was a serious and costly loss of self-control; Fox simply did not have the weight to sustain such a challenge to Hardwicke. He had no option but to recant in public and to endure the scathing rejection of that gesture by Hardwicke in the Lords. The breach between Fox and the Newcastle group was now visible to all, and Fox's chances of effecting a genuine reconciliation after trading insults with Hardwicke were negligible.

Political ambitions realized? Yet such a reconciliation turned out to be Fox's goal almost from the moment that Henry Pelham died on 6 March 1754. To account for this unlikely volte-face the nature of Fox's political talents and the extent of his ambitions need to be understood. Some contemporaries viewed Fox 'as the rising Minister in the House of Commons', and many more believed that he aspired to succeed Pelham as prime minister (*Memoirs and Speeches of … Waldegrave*, 155). But Fox's prominence in the lower house did not necessarily imply an ambition to dominate government. Although he never admitted it openly, the responsibility that went with sole command inspired him chiefly with apprehension. Fear of the danger of being exposed to blame for major policy failures far outweighed any desire in Fox for the kudos which went with the leadership of government. That he should have been so afraid of the risks that inevitably accompanied the premiership may be accounted cowardice, but it involved at least an equal measure of self-knowledge. Unlike Newcastle, for example, Fox was aware of his own limitations; he knew that he did not have what was required to safeguard the national welfare, and lack of confidence held him back from grasping at what was beyond his ability to conduct. But this modesty, if such it was, left him vulnerable to danger of a different sort, a danger that increased as he rose in political seniority to the front rank in 1754. Ever a follower, he needed a leader who could shield him from ultimate responsibility. With Walpole and Pelham he had been lucky. But once Pelham departed the scene in 1754 and Fox approached the heart of government, his security in high office depended on the king selecting a prime minister competent to run the country—and here fortune turned decisively against him.

In essence, then, Fox's talents and interests were more limited than many realized. His principal concern was for his status as a leading member of the House of Commons, where he was certainly a formidable presence. Waldegrave accurately captured Fox's essential strengths in this sphere: 'He has great parliamentary Knowledge, but is rather an able Debater, than a complete Orator; his best Speeches are neither long, nor premeditated; quick and concise replication, is his peculiar Excellence' (*Memoirs and Speeches of … Waldegrave*, 157). There was much of the barrister about him. The ability to think on his feet, and the speed with which he could discern and exploit inconsistencies in an opponent's argument made others wary of challenging him. Even a more naturally gifted speaker like the elder Pitt acknowledged such skills by implication when he complained of Fox in November 1755 that 'when a man has truth on his side, he is not to be overborne by quick interrogatories' (Walpole, *Memoirs*, 2.79). In addition Fox had many personal friends in the lower house and a reputation as a tried and trusted member of the old corps. Under normal circumstances he could rely on being able to play the card of partisanship to secure a favourable hearing from a majority of MPs, at least until 1756. In the lower house, his home territory, Fox felt entirely comfortable. But in contrast to Walpole, Pelham, or Pitt, he did not combine mastery of the Commons with an aptitude and enthusiasm for administration or policy making. As secretary at war and later as secretary of state he was efficient in the dispatch of business, but in neither post did he do anything more than carry out policies decided by others.

This was to prove a very significant limitation and it was reflected in the scope of Fox's ambitions after March 1754.

Pelham's death cleared the path for Fox to become the administration's leading representative in the Commons. In contemporary parlance, he aspired to be recognized as the 'leader of the house', with responsibility for co-ordinating support for government measures in the lower house and for taking the most prominent part in defending them in debate. He was quite content to leave the king to dispose of the key policy making offices of state as he saw fit, and to work under whoever was selected to fill them, provided that his own claims to pre-eminence in the Commons were recognized. It was especially unfortunate, therefore, that George II chose to ask Hardwicke to construct a new ministry in the aftermath of Pelham's death. Newcastle unsurprisingly emerged as the new first lord of the Treasury, and both he and Hardwicke viewed Fox as a dangerous rival rather than a loyal subordinate. This was quite understandable in the light of the events of the previous year, and it meant that they were bound to reject any overtures from Fox as insincere and self-seeking. Yet Fox's claim that 'he only offered, as he really meant, to serve absolutely under the Duke of Newcastle and only required sufficient powers to be able to do it, in the House, without exposing himself' was genuine (*Political Journal of … Dodington*, 255). For the sake of satisfying his limited ambitions Fox was prepared to wipe the slate clean and to act as Newcastle's political lieutenant, just as he had served Walpole and Pelham. He was therefore genuinely pleased on 12 March to receive Newcastle's offer that he should be 'Secretary of State, of course Cabinet Councellor, and at the head of the House of Commons' (Digby MSS, Sherborne Castle, Dorset).

This arrangement broke down when Newcastle made it clear that he was not prepared to entrust Fox with the information or authority which the latter felt were essential for him to carry out his tasks in the Commons. As a result he turned down the offer of the secretaryship of state. Recriminations began immediately, centring on what had, or had not, been said about the 'management' of the lower house. Fox was certainly bitter about what he regarded as Newcastle's breach of promise and evident lack of trust in him. But venting his anger on Newcastle did not solve his new dilemma; he now had to choose between continuing to seek an accommodation with Newcastle or going into opposition. For a variety of reasons, not least because success in opposition might place full responsibility for leading the government rather than just the Commons in his hands, Fox's preference was still to serve under Newcastle. His best hope of achieving this was to sit as quiet as possible and hope that events would prove to Newcastle that he could not manage the Commons without Fox's assistance. So when the elder Pitt launched his attacks on the government front bench in the lower house in November 1754, Fox sat silent; neither did he respond with any enthusiasm to the idea of an alliance with Pitt to bring down Newcastle. Pitt was a rival in the lower house, Fox's chosen arena; Newcastle was not. Fox and Pitt were certainly in contact during December 1754, but in the end Fox agreed to take a more prominent part in the defence of the government in return for nothing more than the honorific promotion to a seat on the cabinet council. In the early months of 1755 Fox exerted himself on Newcastle's behalf in the Commons over issues related mainly to Scotland, but it was not an arrangement satisfactory to either party.

Newcastle was eventually forced to concede the lead to Fox because his government's position was weakened during the summer of 1755 by the outbreak of hostilities with France. A stronger front-bench team had to be in place before parliament next met. After trying unsuccessfully for a settlement with Pitt, Newcastle was forced, reluctantly as ever, to offer Fox in September 1755 what he had refused him in March 1754: promotion to the secretaryship of state and his designation as the 'leader' of the lower house. This offer did not indicate any lessening of Newcastle's suspicions, but Fox now had his prize and he was prepared to renew his offer to serve Newcastle as a faithful lieutenant. In the short term, all appeared well. During the Commons session that began in November 1755 Fox enjoyed as complete a triumph as he could have wished, in the shape of large government majorities and a personal victory over the elder Pitt in debate. This happy state of affairs extended into the new year, and on 7 February 1756 Fox wrote to his wife in terms that suggested that all his political ambitions had been fulfilled:

> Whenever I am out [of office] I will answer for myself (but don't say so) that I would never try by opposition to get into any, or even invited come into a principal place of business again. Vanity or pride is satisfied by having been what I am, I shall not be thought to have been unequal to my station. (BL, Add. MS 51415, fol. 221)

It was an avowal of content uttered on the edge of the abyss.

The essential flaw in Fox's position lay in his readiness to leave the business of government entirely in Newcastle's hands. In the summer of 1756, as the war with France began to go badly, Newcastle's lack of leadership qualities was starkly revealed. According to the arrangement in which he had acquiesced in September 1755, however, Fox had no option but to defend the measures of a man in whom he rapidly lost all confidence. The crucial blow came with Admiral Byng's failure in May 1756 to bring relief to the besieged island of Minorca, following which this important Mediterranean naval base fell to the French. Newcastle's attempt to shift all blame for this off his own shoulders was worrying enough for Fox. Someone would have to be answerable if the rising tide of public anger was to be assuaged when parliament met. But Fox's spirit was fatally undermined by the dawning perception that while Newcastle remained at the helm things could only go from bad to worse. Self-preservation, let alone the good of the country, dictated that Fox should desert without delay. But this meant reneging on all his professions of fidelity, and abandoning the principle of loyal service on which he had chosen to ground his political career. He could not escape from the ruin of the Newcastle government with his reputation and values intact.

With autumn advancing Fox became increasingly desperate as his search for a retreat with honour led nowhere.

He floated the idea of giving up his secretaryship of state to Pitt, but the latter would not rescue an administration in its death throes. Newcastle was happy enough to see Fox replaced, but unless this could be arranged, he was not prepared to release him from the task of defending the government when parliament met. In the end this latter prospect was too much for Fox to face. He conveyed his decision to resign to George II on 15 October, but could offer no convincing defence to the charge of deserting the king and his government in a time of the acutest crisis.

Political mercenary The experience of these months conditioned Fox's conduct for the remainder of his political career. Henceforth he was averse to holding any position which carried even the appearance of genuine responsibility; having escaped bruised and battered from the snares of the Newcastle administration, he had no wish to be caught in a similar trap again. He obeyed the king's orders to seek out Pitt with a view to forming an administration at the end of October 1756, but was not disappointed when Pitt turned him down. Nor would he listen to George II's urgings that he form his own ministry. Fox's chief concern now was to defend what was left of his status. The premiership held fewer attractions than ever, now that the country was mired in a wartime crisis; as Fox had already confessed to his ally, John Campbell, on 15 July, 'though I see how fatally ill things are going, as I don't know how to mend them I am not unreasonable enough to wish for what I could not conduct' (BL, Add. MS 51406, fol. 14). Equally, though, after so many years as a prominent figure in the Commons and in government, he could not tolerate the idea of being humiliated by seeing those he regarded as lesser men in the lower house promoted over his head. He would not accept being reduced to insignificance. While he may have flirted with thoughts of higher offices, his minimum conditions were the paymastership, a post which reflected his seniority but carried no responsibility for framing policy, and a peerage for his wife. To secure these, though, he could not afford to retire completely from the fray. He had to make it worthwhile for his enemies to buy him off at the price which he deemed appropriate.

Accordingly Fox's attitude to the Pitt–Devonshire administration which took office in November 1756 seemed inconsistent. Pitt had set his face against granting Fox the position of paymaster which would have bought his acquiescence. Fox responded by making the new government's life as uncomfortable as possible in the lower house. But he never pushed matters so far as to actually bring the government down, a cautious balancing act also reflected in *The Test*, a paper which first appeared in December 1756 and which was widely assumed to be written under Fox's directions. In fact Fox had little more to do than wait, for by the beginning of March 1757 George II could bear Pitt no longer. Fox offered to come to the king's aid, but only as paymaster and only if a long list of favours for relatives and friends was granted. Any real intention to serve others wholeheartedly had vanished; he was now a political mercenary out for himself. By collecting his insurance payout in advance, it would not matter to him if the projected government failed to materialize or quickly crashed in ruins. Newcastle was wary enough not to engage in such an enterprise, but so great was the king's desperation that he dismissed Pitt on 6 April without having a replacement ministry ready to take over. For more than two months there was a vacuum as the three principal players, Pitt, Newcastle, and Fox, jockeyed for position in the formation of a new government. Fox's preferred objective throughout was the paymastership, but he also had to guard against the danger that an accommodation between Newcastle and Pitt would freeze him out completely. When this fear seemed about to materialize at the start of June, Fox had to offer to undertake the ministry himself, ostensibly to rescue the king from the intolerable Pitt, but in reality to prevent his own exclusion from any deal. His heart was never in it but as a tactic it worked. Fox's planned ministry was stillborn, and the king had to give in to the forces of Newcastle and Pitt. But George II still felt honour-bound to obtain the paymastership for Fox, and Newcastle and Pitt now decided that it was a price worth paying. On 18 June matters were settled. Fox claimed to be entirely satisfied with his office and his new role of sitting quiet in the Commons.

Fox's professions of contentment sounded increasingly hollow the more often they were repeated. The events of 1756–7 had fatally undermined his political standing. Few could now consider him worth courting as a potential prime minister, especially as by 1759 Pitt had established a complete mastery in the Commons where Fox, effectively in retirement, looked on in virtual silence. The astonishing victories of the Seven Years' War certainly made the paymastership an exceptionally lucrative office, but they were the victories of Fox's arch-rival. Nor did the consolations of the past satisfy as they had once done. His self-image of the loyal follower had been shattered by his desertion of Newcastle, and the friendships in which he had invested so much now began to fail him. In the process of attempting to pluck rewards from the ruins after October 1756 he alienated close friends such as the duke of Devonshire, and death was soon to remove Marlborough and Hanbury Williams. His personal unpopularity also became increasingly obvious and galling as Pitt's public reputation soared. A veneer of philosophical indifference to the slights of the world was no defence against all these blows. Anger and cynicism began to eat away at Fox's character; by his own standards he had always acted morally, but this had not shielded him from the disaster of 1756 and its aftermath. By the time an opportunity offered itself to strike back at a hostile world which refused to accept him at his own valuation, caution and self-restraint had vanished entirely.

That opportunity came in 1762. For all its military successes, the Pitt–Newcastle administration did not long survive the accession of a new king in 1760. George III's decision to make his favourite, Lord Bute, secretary of state in March 1761 made a further change of ministers almost inevitable, and it brought Fox into play once more.

In early 1761 Bute used Lord Fitzmaurice to establish contact with Fox with the intention of using him as a counterweight to Pitt. By now Fox's desires were largely confined to a peerage in his wife's name; this residual ambition and the opportunity for revenge made Bute's overtures impossible to resist. That it might be politically unwise, let alone irresponsible, to support a favourite who was as unsuited to high office as Newcastle had been now meant nothing to Fox; damaging an already tarnished reputation mattered far less than getting what he wanted, as an ill-judged effort to matchmake between his sister-in-law Lady Sarah Lennox and the young king in the spring of 1761 clearly demonstrated. After Pitt resigned in October 1761 Fox did whatever was required of him in support of the government in the Commons, even yielding pre-eminence there to George Grenville, on the understanding that a peerage for his wife would be forthcoming, as it duly was in May 1762. When Newcastle was forced from office in the same month it seemed that Fox had reward and revenge enough to make complete retirement from politics irresistible. Yet even now he was not sated.

Bute replaced Newcastle as head of the administration, and took upon himself the task of concluding a peace settlement. When Grenville refused to co-operate in the matter the king and Bute turned to Fox in early October 1762 and asked him to pilot the peace through the Commons. There were no obstacles for Fox in policy terms; he had sufficient of the Walpolian left in him to endorse Bute's condemnation of the German war and approval of the peace terms. There was certainly the danger that he could be used and then sacrificed; George III regarded him with obvious distaste, openly telling Grenville on 11 October that 'we must call in bad men to govern bad men' (*The Grenville Papers*, ed. W. J. Smith, 4 vols., 1852–3, 1.452). But set against this was one last opportunity for Fox to reward friends, punish enemies, make a figure in the Commons, and perhaps secure an earldom. Having carried the peace treaties through the lower house he might then escape with his gains. So, having refused outright to take the secretaryship of state and its executive responsibilities, on 13 October Fox once again accepted the role of the king's minister in the lower house. Within a month it had wrecked his relationships with Cumberland and Devonshire, and the latter's dismissal from the privy council made the breach with Fox irreparable. There were few problems in defending the peace when parliament met; on 9 December it was approved by a huge majority. Fox seized the opportunity to advocate a thoroughgoing purge of Newcastle's adherents. The 'massacre of the Pelhamite innocents', which did so much to poison the politics of the 1760s, was neither necessary nor well judged. It revealed, as Cumberland said, the 'bitterest revenge and unhumanity' in Fox (Ilchester, *Letters to Henry Fox*, 2.218). More than his desertion of Newcastle, more than the vast profits derived from the paymastership, it stained his reputation beyond hope of cleansing. It also left him completely exposed when, his nerve having failed, Bute decided to retire in March 1763. His offer of the Treasury to Fox held few attractions, and Fox chose instead to insist on his promised peerage.

Final years A barony was granted to Fox in April 1763, but at a price. Thanks to the ill judged intervention of Shelburne, Fox found that he was supposed to have agreed to surrender the pay office in exchange for becoming Baron Holland of Foxley. He fended this off and broke angrily with Shelburne, losing in the process his intimates Calcraft and Rigby. Once in the Lords, though, he was bereft of all influence and was probably lucky to retain the paymastership until May 1765, when Grenville ousted him as part of his onslaught against Bute's supposed influence with the king. Yet even then Holland could not disengage from politics: his failure to gain the earldom that would keep him on a par with Pitt rankled; he harboured too many resentments; and his enemies still pursued him, especially over the vast profits derived from the paymastership. He nurtured his feuds, yet his reach was short and satisfaction continued to elude him until his death on 1 July 1774 at his home, Holland House, Kensington, London. He was buried at Farley in Wiltshire. His most significant bequest, that of his enmities, went to his favourite son, Charles James *Fox (1749–1806), through whom Holland continued to take revenge from beyond the grave, notably against Shelburne in 1782–3. It was a bitter and destructive legacy.

A life in politics brought material rewards in plenty. Despite some evidence of gambling in the 1730s and 1750s Fox seems to have had few financial problems. From the later 1730s he had a healthy income from political office, but this was dwarfed by the profits which he derived from the paymastership during and after the Seven Years' War. These came largely from speculating (quite legally) with the vast balances of public money that passed through his hands, an opportunity which did not end in 1763 thanks to the very lengthy delays involved in auditing his accounts. As late as 1773 his indebtedness to the public was more than £500,000, and his unofficial profits as paymaster probably amounted to £400,000. Wealth on this scale was matched only by the opprobrium that followed in its train.

Involvement in politics never left much room for private pursuits. Outside of the Commons, Fox's time went first to his family. In Lady Caroline he had a perceptive and supportive companion, but she could not inoculate her two eldest sons, Charles James and Henry Edward *Fox, against her husband's inability to refuse them anything; Fox's paternal indulgence spoiled them irreparably, and they repaid him with huge gambling debts that reduced his fortune and soured his domestic life. For the rest, the political treadmill prevented much travel; Fox spent extended periods abroad only in the early 1730s and again after 1763. Shooting on the west country estates of his elder brother was his principal recreation in his younger days, an interest that was replaced in retirement by building. His passion for the construction of Gothic ruins did not console him in old age, though; they were too potent a symbol. The poet Thomas Gray sensed some consonance between an inner 'desolation' and the realization of Holland's architectural obsessions at his seaside retreat at Kingsgate on the Kent coast.

> Old and abandon'd by each venal friend,
> Here Holland took the pious resolution
> To smuggle some few years and strive to mend
> A broken character and constitution …
> Here reign the blustring north and blighting east,
> No tree is heard to whisper, bird to sing,
> Yet nature cannot furnish out the feast,
> Art he invokes new horrors still to bring;
> Now mouldring fanes and battlements arise,
> Arches and turrets nodding to their fall,
> Unpeopled palaces delude his eyes,
> And mimick desolation covers all.
> (T. Gray, *The Complete Poems*, ed. H. W. Starr and J. R. Hendrickson, 1966, 53)

Decay was congenial; spiritual ruin was given material form. Whence came, then, the breaking of this character?

Contrary to the belief of some contemporaries and historians, Henry Fox was not a prime minister *manqué*, and the chief interest of his career does not lie in his failure to attain an office to which he never seriously aspired. Rather, what needs to be explained is why the seemingly good intentions which paved his early path in politics led to a living hell in 1756 and after, and created a reputation blacker than that of almost any other figure of the era. Macaulay's *aperçu* that Fox sinned no more than his contemporaries, but simply canted less, will not do. Prior to 1756 Fox was no cynic. He believed in honouring his commitments, both to his friends and to the head of the king's administration. He was loyal and honest, ingenuous even in his willingness to please. Yet these were dangerous qualities in one who aspired to lead the government's forces in the lower house. That office carried with it responsibilities; Fox was answerable to the Commons for the framing of government policy. Yet he allowed Newcastle, whose incapacity he knew but chose to ignore, free rein in that crucial area after rescuing his administration in September 1755, and he had no excuses when that incapacity led to disaster. Blind loyalty left Fox no choice but to betray Newcastle and to suffer the consequences for nearly twenty years. After October 1756, guilty of treachery by his own standards, Fox descended to the level of a mere *condottiere*. His reputation plummeted, both because he abandoned all care for his public image and because his residual ambitions made him appear sufficiently dangerous to be worth blackening. He was without doubt the victim of his own flaws. But he was also seduced and betrayed by the culture of freethinking. The creed by which he chose to live in the 1730s taught him nothing about the defects of his own nature, and so could not shield him against them. Nor did it provide him with any antidote to the poison of disillusion which set to work after 1756. From 1762 onwards, through his own actions and those of Charles James Fox, that poison seeped into the body politic. PETER LUFF

Sources Earl of Ilchester [G. S. Holland Fox-Strangways], *Henry Fox, first Lord Holland, his family and relations*, 2 vols. (1920) · *Lord Hervey and his friends, 1726–38*, ed. earl of Ilchester [G. S. Holland Fox-

Strangways] (1950) · BL, Holland House MSS · Chatsworth House, Derbyshire, Devonshire MSS · Sherborne Castle, Dorset, Digby MSS · Dorset RO, Fox Strangways (Ilchester) papers · Yale U., Lewis Walpole Library, Hanbury Williams MSS · BL, Newcastle MSS · BL, Hardwicke MSS · Dorset RO, Calcraft papers · BL, Stowe MS 308 · *The memoirs and speeches of James, 2nd Earl Waldegrave, 1742–1763*, ed. J. C. D. Clark (1988) · H. Walpole, *Memoirs of King George II*, ed. J. Brooke, 3 vols. (1985) · Walpole, *Corr.* · Earl of Ilchester [G. S. Holland Fox-Strangways], ed., *Letters to Henry Fox, Lord Holland* (privately printed, London, 1915) · *The political journal of George Bubb Dodington*, ed. J. Carswell and L. A. Dralle (1965) · L. S. Sutherland and J. E. D. Binney, 'Henry Fox as paymaster-general of the forces', *EngHR*, 70 (1955), 229–57 · P. A. Luff, 'Henry Fox and the "lead" in the House of Commons, 1754–1755', *Parliamentary History*, 6 (1987), 33–46 · P. A. Luff, '*Mathews v. Lestock*: parliament, politics and the navy in mid-eighteenth-century England', *Parliamentary History*, 10 (1991), 45–62 · P. A. Luff, 'The noblemen's regiments: politics and the Forty-Five', *Historical Research*, 65 (1992), 54–73 · L. B. Namier, *England in the age of the American revolution*, 2nd edn (1961) · J. C. D. Clark, *The dynamics of change: the crisis of the 1750s and English party systems* (1982) · J. B. Owen, *The rise of the Pelhams* (1957) · C. G. A. Clay, *Public finance and private wealth: the career of Sir Stephen Fox, 1627–1716* (1978) · L. G. Mitchell, *Charles James Fox* (1992) · R. Halsband, *Lord Hervey* (1973) · R. R. Sedgwick, 'Fox, Henry', HoP, *Commons, 1715–54* · L. B. Namier, 'Fox, Henry', HoP, *Commons, 1754–90* · GEC, *Peerage* · BL, Add. MS 51324

Archives BL, corresp. and papers, Add. MSS 51352, 51375–51447 · Derbys. RO, corresp. relating to Ireland · Dorset RO, corresp. and letter-books · National Archives of Canada, Ottawa, corresp. and papers · Suffolk RO, Bury St Edmunds, accounts and ledgers as paymaster general, corresp., and papers | BL, letters to Peter Collinson, Add. MSS 28558, 28727 · BL, letters to Lord Hardwicke and Charles York, Add. MSS 35430, 35587–35604, *passim* · BL, letters to Lord Holdernesse, Egerton MSS 3413, 3432 · BL, corresp. with Sir Benjamin Keene, Add. MSS 43436–43439 · BL, corresp. with duke of Newcastle, Add. MSS 32699–32936 · Bodl. Oxf., corresp. with Lord Guilford · Bodl. Oxf., letters to Lady Townshend · Chatsworth House, Derbyshire, letters to dukes of Devonshire · Hunt. L., letters to Lord Loudon · Mount Stuart Trust, Isle of Bute, archive, corresp. with Lord Bute, etc. · NA Scot., corresp. with Lord Marchmont · priv. coll., letters to Lord Shelburne · Sherborne Castle, Dorset, corresp. with Digby family · Warks. CRO, letters to James West · Yale U., Farmington, Lewis Walpole Library, letters to Sir Charles Hanbury Williams

Likenesses W. Hogarth, group portrait, oils, *c.*1738 (*The Holland House group*), Ickworth House, Park and Garden, Suffolk; repro. in Ilchester, ed., *Lord Hervey* · oils, *c.*1762 (after J. Reynolds), NPG · J. Reynolds, portrait, 1763–4, priv. coll. [*see illus.*] · J. Haynes, etching, pubd 1782 (after W. Hogarth), BM, NPG · stipple, pubd 1798 (after J. E. Liotard, 1754), BM, NPG · J. G. Eccardt, oils (after J. B. van Loo), NPG · J. Macardell, mezzotint (after A. Ramsay), BM

Fox, Henry Edward (1755–1811), army officer, was born on 4 March 1755, the son of Henry *Fox, first Baron Holland (1705–1774), and his second wife, (Georgiana) Caroline *Fox, *née* Lennox, *suo jure* Baroness Holland of Holland (1723–1774), eldest daughter of Charles *Lennox, second duke of Richmond. He was the younger brother of Charles James *Fox (1749–1806), politician and gambler.

After being educated at Westminster School he was commissioned cornet in the 1st dragoon guards on 16 September 1770 and soon afterwards took one year's leave to attend the military academy at Strasbourg. He was promoted lieutenant on 4 June 1773, transferring to the 38th foot later that year and was promoted captain on 14 February 1774.

The 38th foot was stationed at Boston, and with it Fox participated in the early battles of the American War of Independence. These included operations around Boston at Concord (19 April 1775) and Bunker Hill (17 June 1775), and General Sir William Howe's campaign in New York at Long Island (27 August 1776) and White Plains (28 October 1776). Fox was appointed an aide-de-camp to Howe in 1776, and promoted major in the 49th foot on 12 July 1777. He was present during operations around Philadelphia, at the battles of Brandywine (11 September 1777) and Germantown (4 October 1777), and with the 2nd battalion of grenadiers at Monmouth (28 June 1778).

Fox was promoted lieutenant-colonel in the 38th foot on 12 October 1778, and afterwards took one year's leave of absence to go to England. Once back in America he joined the siege of Charles Town (11 February – 12 May 1780) before returning to the northern theatre of operations, where he participated in the raid on Springfield (7–23 June 1780). He was subsequently appointed to command the 2nd battalion of grenadiers. Shortly before the end of the war he was promoted brigadier (1782) and on 12 March 1783 colonel in the army and aide-de-camp to the king.

Fox was commander of the forces in Nova Scotia from 1783, and commandant of Chatham barracks from 23 December 1789. He married on 14 November 1786 Marianne (d. 1808), daughter of William Clayton and sister of Catherine, Lady Howard de Walden. They had three children: Louisa Amelia (d. 1828), who married Major-General Sir Henry Bunbury, Henry Stephen [*see* Fox, Henry Stephen (1791–1846)], who served as envoy-extraordinary and minister-plenipotentiary to the United States of America, and Caroline, who married Major-General William Napier.

On 26 September 1793 Fox was appointed quartermaster-general on the duke of York's staff in Flanders to replace Colonel James Moncrieff, recently killed; Fox arrived at the headquarters at Menin on 8 October. He was appointed colonel of the 117th foot on 3 December and promoted major-general on 20 December 1793. In April 1794, while continuing in his staff post, he assumed command of Major-General Gerard Lake's infantry brigade and was present at the battles of Tourcoing (17–18 May) and the strategically important post of Pont-à-Chin (22 May), where he brilliantly repulsed the French at a cost to them of six thousand men and seven guns. Fox assumed command of the 4th and 5th brigades of York's army on 31 August, adding the 6th brigade to his command by November. While participating in the rigours of the winter retreat through north Holland, he had a reputation for ensuring his own comfort and even had a French cook in his retinue.

Fox was appointed colonel of the 10th foot on 23 June 1795, and inspector-general of the recruiting service on 21 October 1795. After being promoted lieutenant-general on 26 June 1799, he was appointed lieutenant-governor of Minorca on 18 July, arriving there in the following November. After the death of General Sir Ralph Abercromby at the battle of Aboukir (20 March 1801) Fox was appointed on 25 July 1801 commander-in-chief of the forces in the

Mediterranean (Gibraltar excepted) and moved to Minorca with the local rank of general. Having on 9 May 1803 been appointed commander-in-chief of the forces in Ireland, he was caught badly unawares by Robert Emmet's farcical Dublin uprising (22 July) and was soon replaced by Lieutenant-General Cathcart, whose appointment was gazetted on 20 October.

Fox briefly took Cathcart's place as commander of the London district before returning to the Mediterranean in December 1804 as lieutenant-governor of Gibraltar (appointment dated 2 April 1804) and was promoted local general on 23 November. He was appointed commander-in-chief in the Mediterranean on 9 May 1806 and minister to Sicily, but his health was weak and the active command of the troops was entrusted to his deputy, Lieutenant-General Sir John Moore.

From the time of his arrival at Messina on 2 July Fox received several strong representations from the Sicilian court for an expedition to Calabria. These were resisted because sufficient strength was lacking, especially after the dispatch in March 1807 of 5900 men under Major-General Mackenzie Fraser to occupy Alexandria. Fox and Moore were angered by the political activities of Rear-Admiral Sir William Sidney Smith at the Sicilian court since these conflicted with both generals' views on military operations in Italy. Although Smith left Sicily in January 1807 to join Vice-Admiral Sir John Duckworth's squadron, Fox and Moore continued to be importuned by William Drummond, British minister at the Sicilian court, to conduct operations in Italy.

Fox was recalled by the British government in July 1807 because his continued poor health would not allow him to command troops in the field. He was replaced by Moore, whose letter to Major-General Robert Brownrigg (quartermaster-general at the Horse Guards) in February on this subject influenced the decision to recall Fox.

Having been promoted full general on 25 April 1808, Fox was appointed governor of Portsmouth two years later. He died there on 18 July 1811 after a long and painful illness due to a mortification of his leg. R. N. W. THOMAS

Sources 'Returns of officers' services, 1809–10', PRO, WO 25/745 · 'In-papers, commander-in-chief, British army on the continent, 1793–5', PRO, WO 1/166–172 · BL, Stewart papers, Add. MSS 40633–40634 · BL, Don papers, Add. MSS 46702–46706 · The correspondence of George, prince of Wales, 1770–1812, ed. A. Aspinall, 8 vols. (1963–71) · The later correspondence of George III, ed. A. Aspinall, 5 vols. (1962–70) · H. Bunbury, Narratives of some passages in the great war with France, from 1799 to 1810 (1854) · The diary of Sir John Moore, ed. J. F. Maurice (1904) · GEC, Peerage · army lists, war office · An accurate account and impartial narrative of the war by an officer of the guards, 3rd edn, 2 vols. (1796) · R. Brown, An impartial journal of a detachment from the brigade of foot guards (1795) · E. Brynn, Crown and castle: British rule in Ireland, 1800–30 (1978)
Archives BL, corresp. and papers, Add. MSS 37090, 37053, 57550–57551 · Bodl. Oxf., family corresp. · Derbys. RO, letter-book · PRO, 'In-papers, commander-in-chief, British army on the continent, 1793–5', WO 1/166–172 · Suffolk RO, Bury St Edmunds, apologia relating to conduct in Ireland and letter-book · University of New Brunswick, Harriet Irving Library, letter-book | BL, Don papers, Add. MSS 46702–46706 · BL, Add. MSS 47570, 51422, 51454, 51459, corresp. with Fox family · BL, corresp. with Lord Hardwicke, Add. MSS 35740–35743 · BL, corresp. with Sir Hudson Lowe, Add. MSS 20107, 20163, 20165–20166, 20189 · BL, letters to Lord Nelson, Add. MSS 34914–34931 · BL, corresp. with Sir Arthur Paget, Add. MS 48395b · BL, letters to Alexander Stewart, Add. MSS 40633–40634 · NAM, British army on the continent, 1793–5 · NL Ire., corresp. and papers relating to Ireland · NL Scot., corresp. with Hugh Elliot · NL Scot., corresp. with Lord Lynedoch · PRO, corresp. with Sir George Carlton, PRO 30/55 · U. Aberdeen L., corresp. with A. M. Fraser
Likenesses C. Turner, mezzotint, pubd 1805 (after T. Phillips), BM, NPG

Fox, Henry Edward, fourth Baron Holland of Holland and fourth Baron Holland of Foxley (1802–1859), diarist and diplomatist, was born on 7 March 1802 at Holland House, Kensington. He was the only surviving legitimate son of Henry Richard *Fox, third Baron Holland (1773–1840), and his wife, Elizabeth [see Fox, Elizabeth Vassall, Lady Holland (1771?–1845)]. Of a delicate constitution and lame from birth, he was educated privately. His tutors were the Revd Matthew Marsh and Joseph Blanco White. From 1811 the Revd Philip Shuttleworth, warden of New College, Oxford, took charge of his studies. He matriculated at Christ Church, Oxford, in 1819 and read widely, but he lacked interest in academic life and went down at his own request without a degree in May 1822. He enjoyed the theatre, the opera, and collecting paintings and books. His friends included Edward Cheney, Henry Greville (younger brother of the diarist), George Howard (later seventh earl of Carlisle), and John Stuart Wortley (later second Baron Wharncliffe).

From his earliest years Fox was introduced by his parents to the élite of European society. As an infant he visited Napoleon's France and Spain between 1802 and 1805. Joseph Nollekens made a bust of him in 1806. His varied travels and the intellectually sophisticated set at Holland House inculcated a sense of superiority and his diary, although not published until 1923, was known to contemporaries from its caustic characterization as 'Fox's Martyrs' (Holland, To her Son, 26). Fox was a charming man, with dark hair and regular features. He was befriended by Lord Byron, attracted the amorous attentions of Lady Caroline Lamb, and shared the favours of Countess Teresa Guiccioli. Unhappy courtships and an overbearing mother directed him to the continent with John Wortley in February 1823 and, with short intermissions, he remained there. He married in May 1833 Mary Augusta (1812–1889), daughter of the seventh earl of Coventry. Apart from a son who died at birth, they had no children. Largely at Lord Holland's instigation (he had succeeded to his father's title in October 1840), they adopted in France a daughter, Marie Fox, later Princess Liechtenstein (1850–1878).

Although reared in freethinking Enlightenment circles, Fox had a profound religious experience in Rome in December 1825. It is not clear whether he became a Roman Catholic at this date or, as was later claimed, on his deathbed. Correspondence between his widow and Lord Brougham suggests an earlier date (Fox-Strangways, Chronicles, 299–300). Fox's Catholicism may have influenced him in his refusal to take his parliamentary seat for

Horsham under the patronage of the duke of Norfolk between 1825 and 1827. He also declined offers of a peerage during the struggle for the Reform Bill of 1832, and seldom attended the House of Lords when he succeeded to his father's peerage. Despite early Bonapartist leanings, Holland opposed despotism and favoured liberal causes in Europe, but resisted the efforts of Lord Lansdowne and Lord John Russell to draw him into whig politics. Instead he drew on a wide network of international contacts including Metternich, Talleyrand, Lieven, Esterházy, and Jerome Bonaparte to further his choice of a diplomatic career.

Fox held the posts of secretary of legation in Sardinia from 1832 to 1835 (in charge 1834–5), secretary of embassy in Austria from 1835 to 1837 (minister *ad interim* in the absence of Sir Frederick Lamb), minister to the German confederation from 1838 to 1839, and minister to Tuscany from 1839 to 1846, a position to which he had long aspired. Appointed by Palmerston, who initially censured his absenteeism and ineptitude, particularly in showing confidential documents to Metternich, Fox served both whig and tory governments until dismissed by Lord Aberdeen in June 1846, and conducted delicate political and commercial negotiations. After his dismissal he continued to enjoy an elegant social life and to engage in extensive intelligence-gathering, especially among liberal émigrés from throughout Europe, a service to his country vital in revolutionary times. His sympathies with liberal movements of the continent coloured his edition of his father's *Foreign Reminiscences*, which appeared in 1850, and which was attacked by Croker in the *Quarterly Review* (March 1851). His subsequent edition of his father's *Memoirs of the Whig Party during my Time* (1852) was better received.

Holland and his wife, a notable linguist, resided in Tuscany at Casa Feroni (Palazzo Amerighi), and also leased Lorenzo de' Medici's villa at Careggi, where G. F. Watts stayed. C. R. Leslie (1841) and Watts (1843) painted portraits of Holland, and Count Alfred d'Orsay drew him in the series Men about Town (1832–48). Alterations to Holland House in 1848 proved expensive and the property was encumbered with debt. Thereafter the Hollands spent much of each year in Paris and Naples, where Lady Holland inherited an apartment in the Palazzo Roccella. Holland died there after a suddenly severe illness on 18 December 1859 and was interred in a private chapel erected by his grieving widow. He left estate valued for probate at below £50,000 to her 'will', apart from some significant legacies and annuities (*The Times*, 27 Feb 1860). With his death the barony of Holland became extinct.

V. E. CHANCELLOR

Sources *The journal of the Hon. Henry Edward Fox*, ed. earl of Ilchester [G. S. Holland Fox-Strangways] (1923) · Earl of Ilchester [G. S. Holland Fox-Strangways], *Chronicles of Holland House, 1820–1900* (1937) · *Elizabeth, Lady Holland to her son, 1821–1845*, ed. earl of Ilchester [G. S. Holland Fox-Strangways] (1946) · Princess Marie Liechtenstein, *Holland House*, 2nd edn, 2 vols. (1874) · Lord Holland [H. R. V. Fox] and J. Allen, *The Holland House diaries, 1831–1840*, ed. A. D. Kriegel (1977) · Earl of Ilchester [G. S. Holland Fox-Strangways], *The home of the Hollands, 1605–1820* (1937) · *The journal of Elizabeth, Lady Holland, 1791–1811*, ed. earl of Ilchester [G. S. Holland Fox-Strangways], 2 vols. (1908) · *The Times* (Dec 1859–Feb 1860) · J. Prest, *Lord John Russell* (1972) · L. Mitchell, *Holland House* (1980) · Boase, *Mod. Eng. biog.*

Archives BL, corresp. and papers, Add. MSS 51748, 52001–52169, 52113–52169, 63145 | BL, corresp. with Lord Aberdeen, Add. MS 43151 · BL, corresp. with John Allen, Add. MS 52175 · BL, letters to Eleanor Fazakerley, Add. MS 61937 · NL Scot., corresp. with Edward Ellice, MS 15016 · PRO, corresp. with Lord John Russell, PRO 30/22 · Shrops. RRC, letters to D. K. Sandford · U. Southampton L., corresp. with Lord Palmerston, MS 62

Likenesses J. Nollekens, bust, 1806 · C. R. Leslie, oils, 1841 · G. F. Watts, oils, 1843; damaged by fire · Count D'Orsay, drawing (Men about Town series, 1832–48), NPG · portrait, repro. in J. Saunders, *Portraits and memoirs of eminent living political reformers* (1840), 191

Wealth at death under £50,000: probate, 20 Feb 1860, CGPLA Eng. & Wales

Fox [*later* Vassall], **Henry Richard**, third Baron Holland of Holland and third Baron Holland of Foxley (1773–1840), politician and man of letters, was the youngest child and only son of Stephen Fox, second Baron Holland (1745–1774), and Lady Mary Fitzpatrick (1746/7–1778), daughter of John, first earl of Upper Ossory. Caroline *Fox (1767–1845) was his sister. He was born at Winterslow House, Wiltshire, on 21 November 1773 and baptized on 19 December. He succeeded to the title at his father's death on 26 November 1774. After his mother's death on 6 October 1778, he was brought up by his uncles John, second earl of Upper Ossory, and Charles James *Fox. Fox, whom he idolized, was the single greatest influence on his life.

Education, marriage, and change of name Educated at Loughborough House School from September 1779 and at Eton College from about 1781 to 1790, Holland matriculated from Christ Church, Oxford, in October 1790, and was created MA on 20 June 1792. During the long vacation of 1791 he travelled abroad for the first time. In Paris he met Talleyrand and Lafayette. Having imbibed his uncle's whig politics, his sympathy for the French reformers and a desire for good Anglo-French relations became his guiding principles. After leaving Oxford, Holland visited northern Europe, returning in December 1792. From March 1793 he spent nine months in Spain, before sailing to Italy in January 1794. At Naples he met Elizabeth Vassall (1771?–1845) [*see* Fox, Elizabeth Vassall], wife of Sir Godfrey Webster. He spent 1795 with her at Florence and Lucca. They returned to London in May 1796 and their eldest son, Charles Richard *Fox, was born on 6 November. Sir Godfrey divorced his wife on 4 July 1797, keeping her fortune and winning damages of £6000. She and Holland were married at Rickmansworth on 6 July. Despite Lady Holland's domineering temperament it was an extremely happy marriage. They had five legitimate children: Stephen (*b.* 18 Jan 1799, *d.* 21 Nov 1800); Henry Edward, afterwards fourth and last Baron Holland (*b.* 7 March 1802) [*see* Fox, Henry Edward]; Mary Elizabeth (*b.* 19 Feb 1806), who in 1830 married the third Baron Lilford; Georgina Anne, (*b.* 7 Nov 1809, *d.* 31 Oct 1819); and a daughter, born and died on 24 June 1812. Following Webster's suicide on 3

Henry Richard Fox, third Baron Holland of Holland and third Baron Holland of Foxley (1773–1840), by John Simpson (after Charles Robert Leslie, 1829)

June 1800, Holland assumed the name of Vassall to safeguard his children's rights to his wife's West Indian fortune.

Holland House Rejecting proposals to sell the family seat, Holland House, Kensington, for building, Holland took up residence there after his marriage and with his wife established it as one of the most brilliant centres of political and literary society in all Europe. He took his seat in the Lords on 5 October 1796, making his maiden speech on 9 January 1798 against Pitt's Assessed Taxes Bill. Although not an eloquent parliamentary orator, he soon became a leading whig speaker in the Lords. The many protests he entered in the House of Lords's *Journal* were collected as *The Opinions of Lord Holland* (1841). That made on 23 March 1801 on the bill for suppressing rebellion in Ireland was considered so subversive that the Lords ordered it to be struck from the record. During the debate on the union with Ireland, Holland moved, on 30 April 1800, for the reconsideration of the two acts barring Roman Catholics from sitting in parliament—the first time Catholic emancipation had been raised.

Following the peace of Amiens, Holland took his family to Spain, engaging as doctor for the tour John Allen, who henceforth became his unofficial secretary and confidant. Passing through Paris, Holland was presented to Napoleon on 3 August 1802. He did not return to England until 1805. An ardent Hispanophile, Holland assembled an extensive Spanish library, publishing in 1806 *Some Account of the Life and Writings of Lope Felix de Vega Carpio*; a revised edition, including a life of Guillen de Castro, appeared in 1817. However, *Three Comedies Translated from the Spanish*

(1807), usually attributed to Holland, is almost certainly not his (J. L. Whitney, *Catalogue of the Spanish Library … bequeathed by George Ticknor*, 1879, 372). He also contributed 'An account of the suppression of the Jesuits in Spain' to *Letters from Spain, by Don Leucadio Doblado* (1822, 445–60), and a letter on Godoy to the *London and Westminster Review* (3, 1836, 56–8).

Political career In 1806 Holland's uncle, Fox, became foreign secretary. Holland was sworn a privy councillor on 27 August, having on 20 August been nominated with Lord Auckland joint commissioner to negotiate with the American representatives, Monroe and Pinckney, on the right of search for enemy cargoes and the impressment of British seamen found on American ships. The draft treaty settled only the former issue and was rejected by Jefferson. Early in the summer Fox's health failed. Though piqued that Grey sent Lauderdale rather than himself as envoy to Paris on Yarmouth's recall, Holland was able to comfort his uncle's last weeks. He was present at Fox's death on 13 September, and was chief mourner at his funeral at Westminster Abbey on 10 October 1806. In 1808 he published his uncle's *History of the Early Part of the Reign of James II*. He was already collecting Fox's letters with the intention of writing his life. This he never finished, and the materials were eventually edited by Lord John Russell.

Fox had intended Holland to succeed him as foreign secretary. However, he was appointed lord privy seal on 15 October, a post he held until the ministry fell on 25 March 1807. He was to be out of office for twenty-three years. Also on 25 March 1807 Holland sat as a lord commissioner to convey the royal assent to Fox's bill abolishing the slave trade. Holland himself was an equally keen supporter of the abolition of slavery in 1833, despite its adverse effect on his West Indian income. On the French invasion of Spain in 1808, Holland, unlike most whigs, urged British intervention. Accompanied by his wife and Lord John Russell, he toured the Peninsula from November 1808 until July 1809, bombarding the British military with impracticable suggestions for supporting the defeated Spanish armies.

With the onset of George III's illness in November 1810, the prince of Wales was expected to bring the whigs into office and in January 1811 Holland was spoken of as a possible prime minister. He would, more probably, have been a member of any whig cabinet. However, the whigs' disastrous mishandling of the prince ended any such possibility. When, in November 1812, Grenville yielded the whig leadership to Grey, Grey himself offered to step down in Holland's favour, a suggestion he dismissed as 'nonsensical' (BL, Add. MS 51545, fol. 30).

Following Napoleon's abdication in 1814 Holland opposed the restoration of the Bourbons. From August 1814 to August 1815 he toured the continent. An unsatisfactory encounter with King Joachim at Naples in February 1815 led Holland to outline a constitution for the kingdom. To disprove Austrian claims that this advocated democracy, he printed it in 1818 as a *Letter to a Neapolitan from an Englishman, 1815*. After his return, his attempt to prevent Ney's execution alienated Wellington, while his opposition to the exile of Napoleon at St Helena deeply embarrassed the whigs.

Queen Caroline, Catholic emancipation, and reform In 1818 Holland inherited Ampthill, Bedfordshire, from Lord Upper Ossory. Following the settlement in 1823 of Lord Kensington's claim to the Holland House estate, Holland began to develop that property, laying out Addison Road in 1824. He also started developing his Lambeth estate. These ventures probably contributed little to his straitened finances. As a peer he attended the queen's 'trial' in 1820. He thought Caroline 'if not mad … a very worthless woman' (*Memoirs of the Whig Party*, 2.121). In denouncing the Holy Alliance in the Lords on 19 February 1821 he caused a scandal by describing Tsar Alexander I as a 'prince who ascended a throne still reeking with the blood of his father' (*Hansard 2*, 19 Feb 1821). In 1824 Metternich banned him from the Austrian dominions as a radical.

In the political vacuum caused by Liverpool's stroke on 17 February 1827, Holland's *Letter to the Rev. Dr. Shuttleworth* argued the advantages of Catholic emancipation. Unlike Grey, Holland supported the administrations of Canning and Goderich. Those whigs in office were eager to have him in the cabinet. George IV disingenuously assured Lansdowne on 1 September that Holland should fill the first vacancy. On 11 December, a month before his resignation, Goderich himself proposed this to the king.

By 1828 Holland had for twenty years been presenting petitions from dissenters for the repeal of the Test and Corporation Acts. On 26 February Russell's motion for repeal was carried despite government opposition. Holland moved the second reading of the bill in the Lords. After it had passed he again pressed for Catholic emancipation. The issue was forced by the County Clare election. Holland's fear that this might strengthen anti-Catholic feelings prompted his *Animadversions on Lord Bexley's Letter to the Freeholders of Kent* (1829). However, Wellington's government itself enacted the measure.

Holland strongly opposed Wellington's Eastern policy, and urged the establishment of a strong Greece under a constitutional monarchy, observing 'as a citizen of the World, I am sorry that the Russians had not taken Constantinople' (*Hansard 2*, 4 Feb 1830). He also attacked the government's policy of non-intervention in Portugal as favouring the conservative Miguelites against Dom Pedro and Maria II.

When Grey replaced Wellington as prime minister, he offered the post of foreign secretary to Holland. However, Holland was laid up with gout. He remarked later to Grenville that, while in 1806 too young and inexperienced for the post, 'now I am in constitution too old & in habits much too desultory & idle to be suited to it' (BL, Add. MS 51531, fol. 159v). William IV, whose daughter Mary had married Charles Richard Fox in 1824, thought Holland 'a *wild* politician' (Paget, *One-Leg*, 230) and suggested he become chancellor of the duchy of Lancaster, the office he held from 25 November 1830 until his death, except during Peel's brief first ministry.

After the 1830 election Holland remarked 'I was never a very keen *reformer* but I think reform now absolutely inevitable' (BL, Add. MS 51751, fol. 47). He regarded its aim as 'substituting constitutional improvement for disaffection & revolution'. Unlike the king and Grey, he wished to see fifty or sixty peers created to force through the bill and constitute an upper house able to work with a reformed Commons. When reform finally passed in 1832, Holland was one of six commissioners who conveyed the royal assent to the bill.

Foreign affairs and death Holland's particular interest remained foreign affairs. He was eager that Britain and France—the two liberal powers—should co-operate against the absolute monarchies. Thus, during the Belgian crisis he welcomed the Anglo-French convention of 1831 against the Netherlands. Having long argued for intervention in the Peninsula, he saw the Quadruple Alliance of 1834, between Britain, France, and the newly established constitutional governments in Spain and Portugal, as a tardy vindication of his views. At home, he opposed the refusal of Stanley, the chief secretary for Ireland, to appropriate Irish church revenues, correctly foreseeing the threat that this posed to the government. Between September and November 1832 he was confined to his room by gout and because of ill health played little part in parliament in 1833–4, though he did support bills, both lost, for removing the civil disabilities of Jews and allowing dissenters to graduate at Oxford and Cambridge.

From 1832 Holland dissuaded Grey on a number of occasions from resigning. When Grey finally did so on 8 July 1834, Holland wished him to retain some formal link with Melbourne's cabinet. The whigs were dismissed on 14 November 1834. After Peel's brief ministry Holland, with Melbourne, was one of five signatories of a letter (11 April 1835) asking Grey to be prime minister. Melbourne's resumption of office on 18 April was conditional on royal support for the appropriation of the surplus Irish church revenues. However, opposition in the Lords forced the government to abandon the bill on 24 August. Holland worked up an undelivered speech on the subject which appeared as *Parliamentary Talk* (1836).

In autumn 1838 Holland crossed the channel for the last time and was received by Louis Philippe. In 1839 the renewed outbreak of hostilities between Turkey and Mehmet Ali, the viceroy of Egypt, divided Europe. France, sympathetic to Egypt, felt excluded as Palmerston negotiated a convention with Russia, Austria, and Prussia to preserve Turkey by threatening force against Mehmet Ali. Holland, with Clarendon, led opposition in cabinet to the treaty and the likely rupture with France. However, Palmerston carried his policy by threatening resignation and Holland and Clarendon were reduced to recording their dissent in the cabinet's minute to the queen on 8 July 1840 authorizing the signing of the convention. Hostilities in the Levant and the threatening attitude of France led to further disputes in cabinet, with Holland always urging a conciliatory policy. The strain may have hastened his end. He is reported as saying: 'these Syrian affairs will be too much for me. Mehemet Ali will kill me' (Reeve's note for

23 October 1840 in his edition of Greville's diary). However, his death surprised contemporaries. Taken ill when he rose on 21 October 1840 he died at Holland House at 6 a.m. the following day, 22 October 1840, of 'obstruction of the bowels' (death certificate). He was buried at Millbrook, near Ampthill, on 28 October.

Literature and publications Holland bore a strong family likeness to Charles James Fox. Lame in the left leg, by the late 1790s he was already afflicted by the gout which plagued him for the rest of his life. Lacking religious convictions he never attended church. A brilliant conversationalist, his affability was legendary. He was the dedicatee of many literary works, including *The Parish Register* (1807) by Crabbe, his favourite poet, and *The Bride of Abydos* (1813) of his friend Byron. However, his reputation declined rapidly after his death. Thiers's praise of him in the national assembly on 28 November 1840 led to *The Times* accusing him on 7 December 1840 of leaking cabinet secrets to the French government. Even Macaulay writing in his defence was forced to concede 'the magnanimous credulity of a mind which was as incapable of suspecting as of devising mischief' (*Edinburgh Review*, July 1841).

Apart from the works mentioned above the following are either by or attributed to Holland: *Observations on the Tendency of a Pamphlet Entitled, Sound Argument Dictated by Common Sense* (1795); *Imitations* (1799), based on two satires of Juvenal; chapter 9 of the *Annual Register ... 1806* on negotiations with France—reprinted in *Memoirs of the Whig Party*, which is also attributed to John Allen (*DNB*); an edition of Joseph Townsend's *Dissertation on the Poor Laws* (1817); *A Dream* (1818); and Canto XXV and 'The Seventh Satire of Ariosto', both appended to W. S. Rose's translation of *Orlando Furioso*, 5 (1827), 277–315. His edition of the *Memoirs from 1754 to 1758 by James Earl Waldegrave, KG* appeared in 1821 and of Walpole's *Memoirs of the Reign of King George the Second* posthumously in 1846. On his death he left a great mass of manuscript material. From this his son published *Foreign Reminiscences* (1850) and *Memoirs of the Whig Party* (1852–4), and his kinsman Lord Ilchester *Further Memoirs of the Whig Party, 1807–1821* (1905). His political diary, begun in 1831, was edited by A. D. Kriegel as *The Holland House Diaries, 1831–1840* (1977). Other publications are his sonnet on the Greek question (1827) in *Notes and Queries* (18 November 1871), 414; a verse letter in William Jerdan, *National Portrait Gallery* (3, 1833); and *Eve's Legend ... 1824* (1928).

C. J. WRIGHT

Sources BL, Holland House MSS · *Hansard 2* (1821), 4.779 · *Memorials and correspondence of Charles James Fox*, ed. J. Russell, 4 vols. (1853–7) · H. R. Vassall, Lord Holland, *Memoirs of the whig party during my time*, ed. H. E. Vassall, Lord Holland, 2 vols. (1852–4) · Earl of Ilchester [G. S. Holland Fox-Strangways], *The home of the Hollands, 1605–1820* (1937) · Earl of Ilchester [G. S. Holland Fox-Strangways], *Chronicles of Holland House, 1820–1900* (1937) · Marquess of Anglesey [G. C. H. V. Paget], *One-leg: the life and letters of Henry William Paget, first marquess of Anglesey* (1961) · L. Mitchell, *Holland House* (1980) · d. cert.

Archives BL, corresp. and papers · Duke U., Perkins L., corresp. · NRA Scotland, priv. coll., travel journals and notes · RCP Lond., letters relating to illness and death of Charles James Fox and other members of Fox family | All Souls Oxf., letters to Charles Richard Vaughan · Beds. & Luton ARS, Ampthill estate MSS · Beds. & Luton ARS, letters to Samuel Whitbread · BL, corresp. with John Allen, Add. MSS 52172–52173 · BL, corresp. with Lord Broughton, Add. MS 47224 · BL, corresp. and papers relating to C. J. Fox, Add. MSS 47570–47591 · BL, corresp. with Lord Grenville, Add. MSS 58950–58952 · BL, corresp. with Thomas Grenville, Add. MSS 41857–41859 · BL, letters to Princess Lieven, Add. MS 47375 · BL, letters to Lord Morley, Add. MS 48226 · BL, letters to Lord Spencer · BL, corresp. with Lord Wellesley, Add. MSS 37296–37313 · BL, letters of him and his family to Harriet Willoughby, Add. MS 62901 · BL, letters to Sir Robert Wilson, Add. MSS 30108–30112 · BLPES, corresp. with Francis Horner · Bodl. Oxf., corresp. with Lady Byron · Bodl. Oxf., letters to H. S. Fox · Bodl. Oxf., corresp. with Napier family · Borth. Inst., letters to Countess Grey · Bucks. RLSS, letters to Thomas Grenville · Castle Howard, letters to Lady Carlisle · Devon RO, corresp. with Lord Fortescue · Duke U., Perkins L., letters to J. C. Purvis · JRL, letters to E. D. Davenport · Lambton Park, Chester-le-Street, co. Durham, letters to earl of Durham · Lpool RO, letters to Lord Stanley · N. Yorks. CRO, corresp. with Christopher Wyvill · NA Scot., letters to Sir John Dalrymple · NL Ire., letters to Lord Upper Ossary · NL Scot., corresp. with Edward Ellice · NMM, letters to George Mackinley · NRA Scotland, letters to William Adam · priv. coll., letters to Lord Lansdowne · priv. coll., letters to Lord Waldegrave · PRO, corresp. with Lord Granville, PRO 30/29 · PRO, corresp. with Lord John Russell, PRO 30/22 · PRO NIre., corresp. with marquess of Anglesey · Pusey Oxf., corresp. with Lord Radnor · U. Durham L., corresp. with second Earl Grey · U. Lpool L., corresp. with Joseph Blanco White · U. Southampton L., corresp. with Lord Palmerston · UCL, corresp. with Lord Brougham · W. Sussex RO, letters to duke of Richmond · W. Yorks. AS, Leeds, letters to Lord Clanricarde · Wilts. & Swindon RO, Fox-Holland (Ilchester) Collection · Woburn Abbey, Bedfordshire, letters to sixth duke of Bedford · Woburn Abbey, Bedfordshire, letters to seventh duke of Bedford

Likenesses F. X. Fabre, oils, 1795, NPG · F. X. Fabre, oils, 1796, Eton College · J. Nollekens, marble bust, 1804, Woburn Abbey, Bedfordshire · S. W. Reynolds, mezzotint, pubd 1806 (after J. R. Smith), BM · G. Parker, stipple, pubd 1822 (after A. Wivell), BM, NPG · G. Hayter, oils, 1823, NPG · E. Landseer, pen-and-wash caricature, c.1835, NPG · J. Francis, marble bust, 1838, Royal Collection · C. R. Leslie, oils, 1838, NPG · R. Westmacott, bust, after 1840, St Michael's Church, Millbrook · E. H. Baily, bust, 1845, Westminster Abbey, London · G. F. Watts or J. E. Boehm, statue, c.1870, Holland House · J. Doyle, caricatures, sketches and drawings, BM · G. Hayter, group portrait, oils (*The trial of Queen Caroline, 1820*), NPG · G. Hayter, group portrait, oils (*The House of Commons, 1833*), NPG · W. Lane, group portrait, chalk (*Whig statesmen and their friends, c.1810*), NPG · T. Lawrence, chalk drawing, Courtauld Inst. · J. Simpson, oils (after C. R. Leslie, 1829), NPG [*see illus.*] · A. Wivell, mezzotint (after J. R. Smith), NPG

Fox, Henry Stephen (1791–1846), diplomatist, only son of General Henry Edward *Fox (1755–1811), and his wife, Marianne (d. 1808), sister of Sir William Clayton, fourth baronet, was born at Chatham, Kent, on 22 September 1791. He was educated at Eton College and matriculated from Christ Church, Oxford, on 26 January 1809. Fox spent much time in the fashionable world, where his wit and charming manners made him popular. He inherited his family's whig views but also its weakness for gambling. Seeking a diplomatic career, Fox served as attaché with the mission to the Sicilian court from September 1814 to early 1818, first at Palermo and from summer 1815 at Naples. From 1818 until October 1824 he was an attaché at Paris. Here his financial embarrassments led to his arrest for debt and the intervention of the French government to secure his release. In 1824 he was made secretary of legation at Turin, serving as chargé d'affaires from December 1824 to June 1825, and in mid-1826 he was transferred to Naples as secretary of legation, where he stayed until June 1828, acting as chargé d'affaires from June 1827.

In February 1828 he was gazetted secretary of legation at Vienna but instead accepted the appointment as first minister-plenipotentiary and envoy-extraordinary at Buenos Aires though, because of civil war in Argentina, the Foreign Office delayed his departure for South America until 1831. He was next moved to Rio de Janeiro, where he arrived in August 1833, and thence to Washington, where he presented his credentials on 1 April 1836. Relations between Britain and the United States were bedevilled by disputes, of which those relating to the slave trade and Canada were the most serious, and war seemed likely. Fox found the posting uncongenial and became increasingly reclusive. At the beginning of 1842, to his considerable chagrin, Peel's government, alarmed by what it saw as its minister's active dislike of America and its institutions, sent Lord Ashburton on a special mission to settle the north-eastern boundary dispute. In November 1843, desiring to negotiate an equally successful treaty concerning Oregon, the government decided Fox should retire. He presented his recall in February 1844.

While in the Americas Fox had developed an enthusiasm for botany and the extensive collections in his herbarium eventually passed to his nephew, Sir Charles James Fox Bunbury. He continued to reside in Washington, where he died (unmarried) from an overdose of morphine on 13 October 1846; he was buried in the congressional cemetery on the 16th. C. J. WRIGHT

Sources Register of services, 1791–1836, PRO, FO 366/329 · BL, Add. MS 51542, fols. 132–133v [H. E. Bunbury to Lord Holland, 8 May 1822] · BL, Aberdeen MSS, Add. MS 43061 · BL, Aberdeen MSS, Add. MS 43123 · C. J. F. Bunbury, 'Notes on the vegetation of Buenos Ayres and the neighbouring districts', *Proceedings of the Linnean Society of London*, 2 (1848–55), 221 · PRO, FO 5/451, fol. 3 [R. Pakenham to Lord Palmerston, 16 Oct 1846] · Earl of Ilchester [G. S. Holland Fox-Strangways], *Chronicles of Holland House, 1820–1900* (1937) · BL, Add. MS 51480, fol. 55 · parish register, St Mary's, Chatham, CKS [baptism] · PRO, FO 5/453, fols. 102–4
Archives Bodl. Oxf., corresp. and papers · PRO, corresp. and papers relating to Canada, FO 97/16–19 | BL, corresp. with Lord Aberdeen, Add. MSS 43123, 43154–43155 · BL, corresp. with Lord Holland, Add. MS 51613 · NA Canada, corresp. with earl of Durham
Likenesses pen-and-ink caricature, after 1848 (of Fox?), BL, Add. MS 48577, fol. 55
Wealth at death under £30,000: PRO, death duty registers, IR 26/264

Fox, Henry Watson (1817–1848), missionary, was born at Westoe, co. Durham, on 1 October 1817, a younger son of George Townshend Fox (d. 1848), of Durham. He was educated at Durham grammar school and at Rugby School (1831–6), where he came under the influence of Thomas Arnold and first contemplated life as a missionary. He took his BA from Wadham College, Oxford, in December 1839 and a year later was ordained deacon with a view to entering the service of the Church Missionary Society (CMS). On 30 December 1840, at Bagborough, Somerset, he married Elizabeth (Lizzy; 1820/21–1845), daughter of

G. H. James of Wolverhampton; ten weeks later, with his new wife and the Revd Robert Noble, he embarked for Madras to found a CMS mission among the Telugu speakers of the Northern Circars.

At Masulipatam, Noble established a school for upper-caste boys while Fox experimented with street preaching. Although he devoted many hours to learning Telugu he always feared that he was unable to move his listeners' hearts, and often the enormity of the task before him overwhelmed him. In January 1843 Fox and his wife, both ill, retreated to the kinder climate of Ootacamund, from where Fox made an extensive tour through the Travancore and Tinnevelly districts. He kept a journal of his travels but his Christianizing zeal prevented him from recording the Indian scene with any sympathy. In October 1844 the Foxes returned to Masulipatam, but Lizzy was still not strong; she died of hepatitis on 31 October 1845. Fox was devastated by loneliness and feared that this was God's way of concentrating his mind on religious rather than earthly passions. He steeled himself now to part also with his beloved son and daughter and arrived home in England in March 1846 to place them with his parents. In the following October he returned to the solitary life of a preacher in the villages around Masulipatam.

Fox's stay was short-lived. In January 1848, after repeated attacks of dysentery, he left India permanently, and in the following July he was appointed assistant secretary to the CMS. Still frail he overworked himself in preparing for the society's 50th anniversary and on 14 October 1848, a fortnight before the celebrations, he died at his mother's home in Durham.

In 1850 Fox's eldest brother, the Revd George Townshend Fox, published a memoir of him which quotes copiously from his letters and journals. The book, which opens with a cherubic-featured portrait of Fox, was intended to encourage Rugby schoolboys to sign up for the missionary cause and it explicitly compared Fox with an earlier, more famous missionary who died young, Henry Martyn. It concluded with a lengthy description by Fox's sister, Isabella, of his attainment of peace in death—sufficient reward, it was implied, for a career marred by failure, doubt, and disappointment. In his memory Rugby School created the Rugby Fox mastership for a teacher at Noble's school in Masulipatam and instituted an annual sermon to raise funds for it. In 1872 the preacher was Fox's son, the Revd Henry Elliott Fox (1841–1926), secretary of the CMS from 1895 to 1910. KATHERINE PRIOR

Sources G. T. Fox, *A memoir of the Rev. Henry Watson Fox* (1850) · G. A. Solly, ed., *Rugby School register*, rev. edn, 1: *April 1675 – October 1857* (1933) · R. B. Gardiner, ed., *The registers of Wadham College, Oxford*, 2 (1895) · *WWW* · Madras ecclesiastical records, BL OIOC, N/2/24, fol. 407 · *List of tombs and monuments erected in Madras* (1898)
Archives U. Birm. L., Church Missionary Society archives
Likenesses Woodman, lithograph, repro. in Fox, *Memoir of the Rev. Henry Watson Fox*

Fox, John [*called* Tinker Fox] (*bap.* 1610, *d.* 1650), parliamentarian army officer, was baptized on 1 April 1610 at St Matthew's parish church, Walsall, Staffordshire, the son of Renold Fox of Walsall. On 24 June 1634, in the same church, he married Emma Tudman, sister of Humphrey Tudman of Walsall. His social status before the civil war is uncertain and, unlike Tudman, he was not listed in Walsall's ship money papers.

John Fox probably captained a troop of horse under Lord Brooke from February 1643, but his name is not mentioned among those parliamentarian troops defending Birmingham when it was sacked by Prince Rupert on 3 April. The accounts of Fox's garrison at nearby Edgbaston House, Warwickshire, commenced on 12 October. The rents of the house's wealthy Roman Catholic owners, the Middlemores, were confiscated and their heraldic monuments in Edgbaston church were demolished. Fox was probably also involved in the assault on the royalist garrison at nearby Aston Hall on 28 December. Royalist propaganda quickly utilized the reputation of the west midlands' prominent metalworking industry to depict Fox as a local tinker:

> one Fox, a tinker of Walsall, in Staffordshire, having got a horse and his hammer for a poleaxe, invited to his society 16 men of his brethren … marched seven miles to Birmingham in Warwickshire near which Towne they fortified a house called Edgebaston House … In this house they have nestled so long that their 16 are swollen up to 200, which rob and pillage very sufficiently.   (Thomason tract E37(1), *Mercurius Aulicus*, 24 Feb 1644)

By scorning Fox as 'the Jovial Tinker' the royalists presented and called on an image of a social subversive long established in ballads and popular culture.

In March 1644 the earl of Denbigh granted Fox a colonel's commission to raise a regiment of horse and dragoons. Fox recruited his regiment from the parliamentarian Black Country and Arden regions, and established an additional garrison at Stourton Castle, Staffordshire. On 24 March Stourton was threatened by royalists, and, attempting to relieve the castle, Fox was defeated on Stourbridge Heath on 27 March. The royalists celebrated that the 'first running rebel was the Jovial Tinker himself' (Thomason tract E42(26), *Mercurius Aulicus*, 30 March 1644).

Local parliamentarians failed to pay or supply Fox's new regiment, and, fearing mutiny, Fox informed Denbigh on 5 April 1644: 'I neede not enymyes to destroy us for this garrison will destroy itself' (Denbigh MS, CR2017/C9-76A). The regiment came to depend upon plunder and surprise raids for its maintenance. On 3 May, pretending to be commanding a disorientated troop of Rupert's horse, Fox bluffed his way into royalist Bewdley and captured the governor, Sir Thomas Littleton. By June Edgbaston House mustered 281 men, and on 13 December Fox successfully raided Dudley town only hours after its garrison had marched out. Refraining from field engagements, Fox legitimized his existence by administering excellent intelligence networks, providing swift and accurate reports of enemy activity to his superiors. In May 1645 his garrison at Hawkesley House, Worcestershire, fell to the king's main field army, but Fox held out at Edgbaston.

Both locally minded and militant, Fox was ultimately ostracized by both Denbigh and the Warwickshire county committee. In 1647 he quarrelled with his former treasurer, Robert Porter, over the Edgbaston rents, and claimed that arrears of nearly £4000 were due to him. He was accused of corruption and he resisted orders to fully disband the garrison until May 1648.

Fox was in London by the autumn, and, his first marriage having come to an end, he married Angelick, Lady Hasteville, at St Bartholomew-the-Less on 16 October. He was subsequently employed as commander of the lord president's guard during the trial of Charles I, but was himself arrested and imprisoned for debt, having to be released by a special order of the court. Several royalist reports erroneously named him the king's executioner. He was sent on the republic's business to Edinburgh, and was imprisoned there by the kirk party regime during May 1650. When the council of state secured his eventual release in July his health was broken. Fox was a minor military entrepreneur without the status, reputation, or resources to prevent his ultimate ruin. In great debt, he was described by the council of state on 21 October 1650 as 'being ready to starve' (*CSP dom.*, *1650*, 395). Nineteenth-century antiquarians embellished an inaccurate image of Fox as an illiterate bandit and low-born religious radical, but his enduring significance remains as the roundhead bogeyman of royalist propaganda. He died between 21 October and 9 November 1650, when his second wife received £10 from the council of state for his burial.

ANDREW J. HOPPER

Sources A. Hopper, '"Tinker" Fox and the politics of garrison warfare in the west midlands, 1643-50', *Midland History*, 24 (1999), 98–113 · Warks. CRO, Denbigh MS CR2017 · PRO, SP 28/182; SP 23/85/389–416 · *CSP dom.*, *1650* · M. A. E. Green, ed., *Calendar of the proceedings of the committee for compounding … 1643–1660*, 5 vols., PRO (1889–92) · A. Hughes, *Politics, society and civil war in Warwickshire, 1620–1660* (1987) · Sixth report, HMC, 5 (1877–8) · parish registers, Walsall, St Matthew, Staffs. RO [transcripts] · *The life, diary, and correspondence of Sir William Dugdale*, ed. W. Hamper (1827) · J. W. Willis Bund, 'A civil war parliament soldier: Tinker Fox', *Reports and papers read at the meetings of the Architectural Society, Worcester Archaeological Society* (1918), 373–403 · will, PRO, PROB 11/214, sig. 198 · IGI

Wealth at death died in poverty; £40 p.a. from Edgbaston estates to widow; residue and personal gifts to sons; bequests of £14: will, PRO, PROB 11/214, sig. 198

Fox, John (d. 1676×8), nonconformist minister, may have graduated BA from Clare College, Cambridge, in 1624, but this is uncertain. He proceeded MA in 1636. He appears to have been admitted vicar of Pucklechurch, Gloucestershire, in November 1657. He was ejected in 1662 and moved to Marshfield in Gloucestershire. In 1670 he published *Time and the end of time, or, Two discourses: the first about redemption of time, the second about consideration of our latter end*. Many subsequent editions were published, including a Welsh translation in 1784. In 1672 he was licensed to preach at Horningsham, Wiltshire, and Marshfield and Nailsworth in Gloucestershire. In 1676 he published *The door of heaven opened and shut …, or, A discourse concerning the absolute necessity of a timely preparation for a happy eternity*.

Describing his address as Marshfield, Fox made his will in April 1676, leaving 5s. to his wife, Elizabeth, and the rest of his estate to his daughter, also Elizabeth. Joseph Barnard of Stoford, Wiltshire, and two London clerics, Thomas Vincent and Richard Fairclough, were appointed overseers. His will was proved by his wife in January 1678.

STUART HANDLEY

Sources Venn, *Alum. Cant.* · *Calamy rev.* · will, PRO, PROB 11/356, sig. 3, fols. 24v–25 · *N&Q*, 2nd ser., 5 (1858), 438 · *CSP dom.*, 1671–2

Fox, John (1693–1763), biographer, was born at Plymouth on 10 May 1693, the son of John Fox (*d.* 1723) and Mary (*d.* 1731), the daughter of Samuel Brett of Plymouth. As a result of his father's zeal for dissent and 'the great opinion he entertained of Dissenting ministers', Fox was educated for the ministry ('Memoirs of himself', 129). He was sent first to Tavistock grammar school, where he remained two years studying Helvicus, Ovid, and Virgil, before returning to Plymouth to attend the grammar school, 'until thought fit for an academy' (ibid., 130). He then read the Greek Testament and Virgil for a few months with Nicodemus, son of Nathaniel Harding, Independent minister at Plymouth. In May 1708 they entered Joseph Hallett's academy at Exeter, where Fox quickly quarrelled with Nicodemus. He became friends with his tutor's son, Joseph Hallett (1691–1744), who was responsible for introducing Arian opinions into the academy. Hallett lent Fox a number of books about the Trinity after the class had been lectured on the subject, and as a result Fox could never afterwards accept the orthodox position.

After having passed through 'the several courses of the academy' in three years, Fox returned home to Plymouth, but 'with no great disposition of being a minister' ('Memoirs of himself', 130, 131) because of the difficulties he now faced in conscientiously subscribing to the doctrinal clauses of the Thirty-Nine Articles necessary to qualify under the Toleration Act. Arguments with his father about his reluctance to subscribe led to a coolness between them. Fox also dreaded being examined by the Exeter assembly of ministers about his doctrinal beliefs, without which he would not be permitted to preach. After some months Isaac Gilling, minister of Newton Abbot in Devon, came to Plymouth in disguise to stay with Fox's family, because a process was out against him for illegally keeping a Latin school. Gilling's mother and Fox's grandmother were sisters. Fox was allowed by his father to accompany Gilling on a journey to London, and Gilling promised to do all in his power to remove Fox's aversion to the ministry. After they arrived in London, Fox slipped out of Gilling's hands, and staying with a relative of his mother spent his time viewing the great people and visiting theatres. As a result of seeing Queen Anne at her chapel, the duke of Marlborough, and other personages, he began 'to form a very different notion of crowned heads and ministers of state from what I had been taught in the country' (ibid., 133). He was astonished by the haughty superiority displayed by the London ministers towards their country brethren, and not favourably impressed with John Shower, the only minister with whom he had an interview. At the end of two weeks Gilling felt able to return to Newton Abbot, taking Fox with

him. The sight of a letter from his father to Gilling, left perhaps by design, led Fox to realize his father's despair that he would ever become a minister, which deeply moved him. 'From that moment I determined to be a minister at all events' (ibid., 133). With this intention he remained with Gilling for three-quarters of a year (1712–13), 'the most pleasant part of my life', living 'in that charming and delightful retreat' (ibid., 133), before returning home. Gilling directed his studies, and he fell in love with Gilling's daughter, Elizabeth (1695–1762), whom he married ten years later, on 23 December 1723. In May 1713 Edmund Calamy visited the west of England and, hearing of Fox's scruples about subscribing to the Thirty-Nine Articles, made him easy by telling him confidentially that he himself had never subscribed, and that if Fox kept himself to himself the omission would never be suspected.

In October 1714 Fox went to London. It had always been intended that he should live in London before he began to preach, that 'I might have something more than the common education in the Dissenting way, and learn a little more of the world than was usual for such to know' ('Memoirs of himself', 134). He remained there until April 1716, lodging with four young ministers in Austin Friars. It has been suggested that he attended the classes of John Eames, but Fox does not mention this himself. He became an intimate friend of Secker (the future archbishop) and Samuel Chandler (who lived with Calamy), to both of whom, and especially to Secker (who kept up a regular correspondence with him until 1718), he attributed the growing freedom of his doctrinal opinions. While he was in London his father urged him to undergo his examination as a candidate for the ministry. Fox sought first the help of Calamy, but then made the mistake of approaching Daniel Williams with the same purpose, without realizing the rivalry between the two ministers. As a result the proposal had to be abandoned. His description of Williams is particularly unflattering. His friend Jeremy Burroughs (a young minister who afterwards became collector of the customs at Bristol) came to his aid, by advising him simply to take the oath of allegiance, as if he had been licensed. The 1715 Jacobite rising, when all ministers were ordered to take the oath afresh, provided the opportunity. As Fox was signing his name in the court of exchequer with the rest, Calamy 'seemed much surprised to see me there and looked very hard at me' (ibid., 195).

Fox declined to complete his studies at Edinburgh as his father had wished, believing it to be of no additional advantage, and returned to Plymouth. He decided that if he was to become a minister he should receive the sacrament. Harding admitted him without question, but suspected that he had not been licensed to preach, which Fox admitted in confidence. He preached his first sermon at Chumleigh, Devon, but there was already 'a whispering and grumbling among the ministers, who suspected I was gone to preach without examination' ('Memoirs of himself', 196). Harding denied that he was responsible for the rumour. Fox preached elsewhere, but found that his behaviour was 'being interpreted as an high contempt of the Assembly, and of the Plymouth ministers in particular' (ibid., 197). He realized that without submission to the Exeter assembly all his father's hopes that he would 'make a figure at home' as a minister would be dashed (ibid., 197). To reduce the risk of failure, he applied to be allowed to choose his own examiners. This occasioned a very warm debate at the assembly in May 1717, with the Plymouth ministers complaining in particular at Fox's behaviour in preaching without authority. The assembly wrote to Fox to persuade him to submit himself for examination. Despite his deep resentment against the assembly, to please his father he submitted himself for examination in September. The event was cleverly managed by his friends who 'gave punctual and early attendance' on the first day and elected a favourable moderator and examiners before the Plymouth ministers arrived. By his own account attempts by one examiner to discover his opinions on the Trinity were frustrated by his supporters. He was licensed to preach on 17 October 1717 after preaching at Newton Abbot before his examiners and defending a question in Latin. It proved to be little satisfaction to his father. Relations with Harding were so poor that he only once preached at the Independent meeting in Plymouth. When the Exeter controversy, concerning the orthodoxy of some of the city's younger ministers, broke out, Fox joined with the heterodox party, who refused to subscribe. As a result he preached only to 'the poor remains of a few broken congregations' (ibid., 200). All expectations of entering the ministry were at an end, and following the death of his father in May 1723, Fox gave up all pretence of becoming a minister. He conformed to the Church of England some years before 1736. He died on 22 October 1763, ten months after his wife.

Fox's main contribution was as a commentator on contemporary dissent during the first decades of the eighteenth century. His 'Memoirs' and the 'Characters' of some of his contemporaries were drawn up towards the end of his life, after he had conformed. Written with great freedom, they reveal his alienation from the ministry and from the culture of dissent, and are strongly coloured by his prejudices and dislikes. Nevertheless, his sketches are truthful if unflattering, including the positive features of even those he disliked. 'It is not too much to say that from these sketches we learn more than from any other source, respecting the inner life of the West of England and London Dissenters, during the first quarter of the last century' (Gordon, 176).

There have been at least four manuscript versions of Fox's 'Memoirs' and 'Characters', two of which were published. In 1821 the original manuscript of the 'Memoirs' with nine 'Characters' was published in the *Monthly Repository*, together with nine letters from Secker and two from Chandler to Fox. Notes were added by John Towill Rutt. The editor's promise to deposit the originals in Dr Williams's Library, London, was not fulfilled. The manuscript had been lent in 1790 by Fox's grandson, George Cleather, to James Northcote, the painter, who appears to have made two copies, one in quarto, one in folio, and both entitled 'The worthyes of Devon'. The account of John

Enty from one of the copies was used by Joshua Toulmin in his *Historical View* (1814). Extracts from Fox's 'Characters' also appeared in William Hazlitt's *Conversations of James Northcote*. The folio copy was sold after Northcote's death and acquired by the Plymouth Proprietary Library, but was destroyed by enemy action during the Second World War. It was, however, published in the transactions of the Devonshire Association (1896–7). The quarto volume was purchased by Alexander Gordon in March 1899 and is apparently the only volume extant. A fourth volume of the 'Memoirs' and eleven 'Characters' belonged to T. J. White in 1897, and before him to Stephen Tucker, Somerset herald, Rouge Croix. DAVID L. WYKES

Sources 'Memoirs of himself, by Mr John Fox … with biographical sketches of some of his contemporaries; and some unpublished letters', *Monthly Repository*, 16 (1821), 129–35, 193–200, 257–62, 270–76, 325–31, 441–6, 505–7, 569–74, 633–5, 697–8, 721–7, see also notes by J. T. Rutt, pp. 221–4, 721–7 • 'The Fox memoirs: worthies of Devon', *Report and Transactions of the Devonshire Association*, 28 (1896), 114–73; 29 (1897), 79–94 • 'Plymouth Proprietary Library manuscripts', *Report and Transactions of the Devonshire Association*, 31 (1899), 120–22 • J. Fox, 'Worthyes of Devon', JRL, Unitarian College collection • A. G. [A. Gordon], 'John Fox, the biographer', *Christian Life* (15 April 1899), 176–7 • A. Brockett, ed., *The Exeter assembly: the minutes of the assemblies of the United Brethren of Devon and Cornwall, 1691–1717*, Devon and Cornwall RS, new ser., 6 (1963) • W. Hazlitt, *Conversations of James Northcote* (1830); repr. in W. Hazlitt, *The round table, Northcote's conversations, Characteristics*, ed. W. C. Hazlitt (1884) • J. Toulmin, *An historical view of the state of the protestant dissenters in England* (1814), 569 • R. N. Worth, 'The history of nonconformity in Plymouth', *Journal of the Plymouth Institute* (1876?), 23–4 • C. W. Bracken, 'The Plymouth grammar school', *Report and Transactions of the Devonshire Association*, 76 (1944), 151 • DNB

Fox, Sir John Jacob [*formerly* Jacob] (1874–1944), analytical chemist, was born on 12 April 1874 at 6 Samuel Street, Spitalfields, London, the eldest of the five sons and one daughter of Marks Fox, furrier of London, and his wife, Hannah Jacobs. He was born Jacob Fox and added the name John in the early 1920s. He was educated in London at St Thomas Charterhouse School and entered government service in 1896 as an assistant of excise. He joined the government laboratory in 1896 and, by arrangements recently made for assistants, he attended courses in chemistry at the Royal College of Science from 1897 until 1899, but did not take a degree. After completing his course he married, on 17 October 1899, Amelia (Millie; *b.* 1874), daughter of Saul Boas, a diamond dealer. They had a son, Charles, and a daughter, Irene. Fox next attended classes at the East London Technical College, both in the evenings and during holidays, frequently working there for twelve hours at a time. He took his intermediate science examination in 1907, his BSc (by research) in 1908, and DSc (by thesis) in 1910.

Fox joined the permanent staff of the government laboratory in 1904. His abilities were soon recognized and he was chosen to assist Professor Thomas Thorpe, principal of the laboratory, on the development of 'leadless glazes' to avoid the dangers of poisoning factory workers. Fox carried out much research at East London College and at the laboratory. He became interested in ultraviolet absorption spectra, on which he carried out researches with

James Dobbie, his new principal (later termed government chemist), in the years before the First World War.

During the war Fox devised new rapid methods of analysis to increase activity without a great increase in staff. In 1920 he was appointed a superintending chemist and exercised both his encyclopaedic knowledge of organic chemistry and his administrative abilities to organize an increased work load arising from the Safeguarding of Industries Act of 1921 and from new silk duties in 1926. He also wrote *The Analysis of Pigments, Paints, and Varnishes* (1927) with T. H. Bowles, and reviewed annually between 1926 and 1933, with B. A. Ellis, all published analytical methods in the *Annual Reports on the Progress of Chemistry*. He also wrote more than sixty papers for scientific journals.

Fox continued to carry out much research after the war with Dobbie and Sir Robert Robertson, government chemist from 1920. In 1936 he was himself appointed government chemist, having been deputy from 1929. In 1940 he joined the staff of the director of scientific research in the Ministry of Supply, as chief adviser to the controller of chemical research, while retaining his duties as government chemist. His interest in chemistry continued until the end of his life, together with his ready help to staff and enquirers. He held many offices in learned societies, and was treasurer of his local church for many years.

Fox was appointed OBE in 1920 and CB in 1938, and was elected FRS in 1943. He was knighted in 1944 and died later that year, on 28 November, at 24 Hayes Crescent, a nursing home in Golders Green. His wife survived him.

P. W. HAMMOND

Sources A. G. Francis, *Analyst*, 70 (1945), 1–2 · J. T. Hewitt, *JCS* (1945), 719–22 · R. Robertson, *Obits. FRS*, 5 (1945–8), 141–57 · P. W. Hammond and H. Egan, *Weighed in the balance: a history of the laboratory of the government chemist* (1992) · m. cert. · *CGPLA Eng. & Wales* (1945) · b. cert. · d. cert.
Archives priv. coll., corresp. and notebooks · PRO, corresp. and notebooks, DSIR 26 | CUL, corresp. with Gordon Sutherland
Likenesses photographs, Laboratory of the Government Chemist, Teddington
Wealth at death £4172 15s. 9d.: probate, 30 March 1945, *CGPLA Eng. & Wales*

Fox, Joseph (1775–1816), dental surgeon and philanthropist, the only son of Joseph Fox (1733–1795), dentist, and his wife, Mary (b. 1751, d. before 1795), daughter of the Revd John Rogers, a Baptist minister of Long Lane, Southwark, was born in Crooked Lane, Lombard Street, London, on 7 November 1775. Nothing is known of his early education except that he attended a school in Tooting kept by a Mr W. Lord, and was presumably trained in dentistry by his father. In 1795–6 he was dresser to Henry Cline, the surgeon, having studied at Guy's Hospital since at least 1794, the year he was elected to its Physical Society (to which he gave a dissertation on the teeth on 3 October 1795). In 1796 he obtained the membership of the Company of Surgeons by examination, and when the company was reorganized under a new name in 1800 he consequently became a member of the Royal College of Surgeons. Fox practised at several addresses in London, mainly in Lombard Street with his cousin, John Fox, and his brother-in-law, Richard

Downing. In 1808 he married Ann (1777–1813), daughter of Joseph and Mary Gibbs. They had a daughter and a son.

In the spring of 1799 Fox began a course of lectures on the teeth to students at Guy's, and he continued as a lecturer there until his death. This was certainly the first series of lectures specifically on dentistry to be given in Britain, and probably in the world. On them he based his two books, *The Natural History of the Human Teeth* (1803) and *The History and Treatment of the Diseases of the Teeth* (1806), which were the first important dental works in English to have illustrations of operative dental procedures and of pathological dental conditions. Fox was also the first to give specific instructions for the correction of irregularities of the teeth. There were three English editions of his works, two American editions, and a French translation by Lemaire. These works were the first true textbooks on dentistry for students and practitioners, and for the next fifty years they were the most quoted ones in the English-speaking world.

Fox became a supporter of Edward Jenner after attending a meeting of the Physical Society in October 1798 at which vaccination was discussed, four months after the publication of Jenner's *Inquiry into the Cause and Effects of the Variolae vaccinae*. When the Royal Jennerian Society was established to further vaccination in January 1803, Fox became a vice-president and the first secretary, allowing part of his house to be used as a 'vaccinium' by the society. In gratitude for his services he was presented with a silver medal in June 1803.

Fox also belonged to the Askesian Society, where he met influential men of science including the chemist William Allen, whose diary is the chief contemporary source for Fox's life and who became Fox's greatest friend and an associate in his philanthropical activities. Fox became a member of the Royal Institution on 10 March 1800 but never lectured there, though he presented a copy of his *Natural History* to the library.

Although Fox's lectures and dental practice continued until his early death, his final years were dominated by his work for the organized education of poor children; indeed the burden of travel, correspondence, and committee work for this was probably a major cause of his death. In November 1807 Fox attended a lecture by Joseph Lancaster on the latter's method of providing education on Christian but non-denominational principles for large numbers of children, with the senior pupils teaching the younger. Fox immediately appreciated the simplicity and efficiency of this scheme, which became the Royal Lancasterian Society. With William Allen and William Corston, a straw-hat manufacturer with an interest in industrial schools, Fox saved the society from bankruptcy in 1808 when Lancaster owed over £6000; Fox provided £2000 immediately and drew bills upon Corston for the remainder. Lancaster agreed to the appointment of trustees, and Fox became the first secretary and Allen the first treasurer. In 1814, when Lancaster again owed over £8000, the committee took over the institution, changing its name to the British and Foreign School Society. The society developed schools both in Britain and abroad. In a debate in the House of Commons on 21 May 1816 Lord Brougham paid tribute to Fox for his salvation of the Lancasterian system of education.

In 1814 Fox became associated with Robert Owen, mill owner and socialist educationist, who wished to extend the educational and social experiments at his New Lanark Mills against the wishes of his partners. The necessary capital to buy the mills was provided by Fox (who contributed £10,000) and others, on condition that the children should receive non-denominational religious teaching.

Fox was a friend of Josiah Wedgwood II (1769–1843), and a series of letters to him in the autograph of Fox written between 1813 and 1816 is preserved in Keele University. These contain important information about the manufacture by Fox of porcelain artificial teeth, using materials supplied by Wedgwood. They reveal Fox's deep religious convictions and details of his workload, travels, and health, as well as his relations with Lancaster and Owen.

Towards the end of his life Fox suffered a series of 'spasmodic attacks'. He died suddenly from a 'rupture of the gall bladder' on 11 April 1816 at his home, 27 Argyle Street, London, and was buried on 18 April in the family vault of the Baptist meeting-house, Long Lane, Southwark.

R. A. COHEN

Sources R. A. Cohen, *Joseph Fox of Guy's (1775–1816), dentist and philanthropist: 1st Lilian Lindsay memorial lecture, 3rd June 1995* (1995) • *The life of William Allen, with selections from his diary and correspondence*, 3 vols. (1846) • letters from Fox to J. Wedgwood, 1813–16, Keele University • R. A. Cohen, 'Messers Wedgwood and porcelain dentures: correspondence, 1800–1815', *British Dental Journal*, 139 (1975), 27–31, 69–71 • J. Walker, *The Royal Jennerian Society ... its organization ... and history*, 2nd edn (1816) • Royal Jennerian Society, minutes, Wellcome L. • W. Corston, *A brief sketch of the life of Joseph Lancaster* (1840) • Guy's Hospital register of pupils and dressers, Guy's Hospital, Wills Library • examinations book of the Surgeons Company, RCS Eng. • I. Inkster, 'Science and society in the metropolis: a preliminary examination of the social and institutional context of the Askesian Society of London, 1796–1807', *Annals of Science*, 34 (1977), 1–32 • *Hansard 1* (1816), 34.633 • register book of parchment certificates from Dr Williams's Library, General Register Office • minute book (April 1816), British and Foreign School Society • register book of burials formerly kept by Independents, Colliers Rent, White Street, Southwark, General Register Office, 45, III

Archives University of Keele, letters to Josiah Wedgwood II

Wealth at death under £9000: will, PRO, PROB 11/1581, fols. 149r–153r

Fox, Leslie (1918–1992), mathematician, was born on 30 September 1918 at 9 Princess Street, Chickenley Lane, Dewsbury, Yorkshire, the elder of two children of Job Senior Fox (1892–1974), coalminer, and his wife, Annie, *née* Vincent (1896–1988). He won a scholarship to the Wheelwright Grammar School in Dewsbury, which was noted for the number of boys who went on to distinguished careers, especially as mathematicians. In 1936 he won a scholarship to Christ Church, Oxford. After taking a first-class degree in mathematics in 1939 he started research for the degree of DPhil under Professor Richard Vynne Southwell in the engineering department; most of his research was concerned with secret war work. After completing his doctorate in 1942 he joined the Admiralty computing service to work under the direction of Donald Harry Sadler

(another former Wheelwright boy). There he learned the art of making mathematical tables, and the rigour and patience necessary to ensure that the result of every calculation was correct.

In 1945 Fox moved, with a group of others, to the newly formed mathematics division at the National Physical Laboratory, where he remained until 1956. During this time one of the early computers was being built at the laboratory: Fox did not take a great interest in the detailed workings of the machine, but he realized that a great revolution in mathematical calculations was under way. These early developments convinced him of the need for those using computers for scientific calculations to have a sound understanding of the numerical methods involved, their limitations as well as their powers. When he was invited to take charge of the new computing laboratory at Oxford he seized the opportunity to begin a new career in education.

After a year at the University of California, Fox moved to Oxford in 1957. At once he began to argue vigorously and successfully for the inclusion of numerical analysis in the undergraduate mathematics syllabus. He attracted a steady stream of graduate students, many of whom went off to spread the teaching of numerical analysis at other universities. His aim was much wider than university teaching: he organized a number of summer schools, where he and his colleagues instilled good practices in scientific computation into visitors from other universities, industrial firms, and government research establishments. His interest in education also extended to schools, and he was an active member of the Oxford branch of the Mathematical Association, of which he became president. In 1963 he was appointed professor of numerical analysis, and was elected to a professorial fellowship at Balliol College. On his retirement Balliol elected him an emeritus fellow, and he maintained close ties with the college to the end of his life.

Fox wrote all or a major part of eight books and more than eighty articles. His first book, on boundary value problems, was unusual in this area in still being in print nearly forty years later. His lasting influence, on students, colleagues, and others, was more personal and at least as important. Always looking for opportunities to reach a wider audience, in 1970 he took up a one-year visiting professorship at the Open University. He wrote a good deal of course material, and made a number of radio and television programmes. In 1986 the Open University awarded him an honorary doctorate.

Fox was a fellow of the Institute of Mathematics and its Applications from its foundation, and served on its council for some years, as well as acting as editor of its journals. In 1989 he was elected an honorary fellow of the institute. He travelled widely; the most convivial of men, he made new friends wherever he went. At various times he held visiting professorships in California, Illinois, Yugoslavia, India, and Australia, as well as at the Open University.

Fox was married twice: first, on 10 July 1943, to Pauline Helen Dennis, from whom he was divorced on 4 April 1973; and second, on 20 July 1973, to Clemency Mary

Holme Clements (b. 1937), journalist, elder daughter of Thomas Fox. There were no children by either marriage.

Fox was a keen sportsman throughout his life. As a student at Oxford he played football for the university and for Oxford City Football Club. At the National Physical Laboratory he was club tennis champion and captain of the cricket team, and distinguished himself as a sprinter in the civil service championships. On his return to Oxford he joined the Barnacles cricket club. Later in life he was persuaded to take up golf; in 1979 he arranged an annual contest between the dons of Oxford and Cambridge, and was captain of the Oxford team until his death.

Following his retirement in 1983 Fox's colleagues and friends founded the Leslie Fox prize for young research workers in numerical analysis. Awarded annually, it has attracted a worldwide entry of a very high standard. The winner of the first competition, in 1985, was an American, Lloyd Nicholas Trefethen. When Fox's successor, Keith William Morton, retired in 1997 it was appropriate that Trefethen should be appointed to the professorship of numerical analysis that had been created for Fox.

Throughout his life Fox remained true to his roots, a forthright socialist and above all a Yorkshireman. After sixty years free of illness he suffered a heart attack in 1981. He was soon back at work, but decided to retire early, in 1983; sadly, his retirement was dogged by illness. Following more heart trouble he died from a ruptured aneurysm in the John Radcliffe Hospital, Oxford, on 1 August 1992. He was cremated and his ashes buried at St Nicholas's Church, Marston, Oxford, on 8 August 1992. He was survived by his second wife.   DAVID MAYERS

Sources J. Walsh and D. F. Mayers, *Bulletin of the London Mathematical Society*, 31 (1999), 241–7 · K. W. Morton, ed., *Leslie Fox, 1918–1992* (1993) · *The Times* (2 Sept 1992) · *The Independent* (11 Aug 1992) · WWW [forthcoming] · personal knowledge (2004) · private information (2004) [brother; widow] · b. cert. · bap. cert. · d. cert. · divorce cert. · m. certs. · parish register, Marston, St Nicholas, 8 Aug 1992 [burial]

Likenesses photograph, 1982, Oxford University Computing Laboratory · photograph, repro. in *The Times*

Wealth at death under £125,000: probate, 5 Nov 1992, CGPLA Eng. & Wales

Fox, Sir Lionel Wray (1895–1961), civil servant and penologist, was born on 21 February 1895 in Halifax, the son of Samuel Fox, boilermakers' draughtsman, and his wife, Minnie Wray. He was educated at Heath grammar school, Halifax, and Hertford College, Oxford, but joined the army on the outbreak of war in 1914. He served with the duke of Wellington's regiment, reached the rank of captain, was mentioned in dispatches, and was awarded the MC and the Belgian Croix de Guerre.

Having entered the civil service as top in his year Fox joined the Home Office as an assistant principal in 1919. In 1921 he married Marjorie Bailey, daughter of Charles Henry Horner of Halifax; they had one son and two daughters. From 1925 to 1934 he was secretary to the Prison Commission and there learned to put into effect the combination of exactitude of mind and deep humanity of feeling which characterized his career. In 1934 he was appointed deputy receiver to the Metropolitan Police district and he

was acting receiver in 1941–2 before returning to the Prison Commission as chairman.

Rejoining the commission in the middle of the war, Fox had to lead his service through the most arduous years in which prisons and borstals were damaged by enemy action. After the war he had to grapple with the problems of overcrowding and shortage of staff which indeed remained his preoccupations until in February 1959, in helping to compose the white paper *Penal Practice in a Changing Society*, he was able to propose and support the biggest prison building programme for a century. He did not live to see its completion or the later increased influx of prison population.

While still secretary to the Prison Commission Fox published *The Modern English Prison* (1934), in the second chapter of which he discussed the problem of deterrence and reformation. He recalled the principle set out in the Gladstone committee report of 1895 that 'prison treatment should have as its primary and concurrent objects deterrence and reformation' (Fox, 30). Remarking that experience showed that 'deterrent power lies fundamentally not in *severity* of punishment, but in *certainty* of detection and punishment' (ibid., 31) he went on to say:

> it then becomes possible, without impairment of the principle of deterrence, to remove from the prison regime any features introduced to emphasize its deterrent aspect which prove to be incompatible with the concurrent duty 'to turn the prisoners out of prison better men and women than when they came in'.   (ibid., 32)

He concluded: 'the most effective method of protection, *if it can be done*, is to reform the offender' (ibid., 32). In 1952 Fox published *The English Prison and Borstal Systems*, which for long remained a standard work. He also wrote for the *Encyclopaedia Britannica* and the *British Journal of Delinquency*.

Fox's name will be associated with the drafting of the new prison and borstal rules under the Criminal Justice Act of 1948. He also helped to institute corrective training, preventive detention, and the detention centres; and developed the open borstal and the open prison system, leaving to his successors a rich variety of both systems. He saw the beginnings of the scheme to provide prison welfare officers and he chaired the council and executive committee of the Central After-Care Association from its inception in 1949 until he retired from the Prison Commission in 1960. He then became visiting fellow of the Institute of Criminology at Cambridge.

Fox left as distinctive a mark on the service as Sir Evelyn Ruggles-Brise, who alone served longer than Fox, and his influence on prison affairs was as important as that of Sir Alexander Paterson. At a memorial service for Fox held in Wormwood Scrubs prison chapel the secretary of state, R. A. B. Butler, spoke of him as a charitable and single-minded man who succeeded to and embellished a great tradition. 'At the latter end of his life he achieved many of the reforms to the perfection of which he had devoted long years' (private information, 1981). Fox held firmly to the belief in which he grew up, feeling strongly about the unjustifiable harshness of imprisonment, to which his fiery temperament reacted. He did not volunteer information about his brother, Ralph Fox, who was killed fighting on the republican side in the Spanish Civil War, but he felt very warmly about him, as one who had shared his strength of conviction. Fox was an intimidating adversary in argument about prison matters: he had not only detailed experience but a fine mind. His many friends had to accept an awkward diction and sharpness of manner before they came to the warm-hearted and charming personality which underlay the natural reserve which he seemed to cast aside more easily abroad than at home.

Fox was held in great esteem in the international world. He was a member of the long-established International Penitentiary Commission and when its duties were taken over by the social defence section of the United Nations he rapidly became a leader in that sphere. He was president of the United Nations European consultative group on the prevention of crime and the treatment of offenders from 1951 until 1960, and was elected honorary president of the second quinquennial United Nations Congress held in London in August 1960, over which illness prevented him from presiding. He died at Westminster Hospital, London, on 6 October 1961.

Fox was appointed CB in 1948 and knighted in 1953. In 1964 the International Penal and Penitentiary Foundation published a volume of studies in penology dedicated to Fox which included tributes to his work.

BUTLER OF SAFFRON WALDEN, *rev.*

Sources L. W. Fox, *The modern English prison* (1934) · personal knowledge (1981) · private information (1981) · *The Times* (10 Oct 1961) · *WWW* · N. Morris and D. J. Rothman, eds., *The Oxford history of the prison: the practice of punishment in Western society* (1996) · CGPLA Eng. & Wales (1962)

Wealth at death £1924 15s. 0d.: probate, 12 March 1962, CGPLA Eng. & Wales

Fox, Luke (1586–1635), navigator, son of Richard Fox, seaman and assistant of the Trinity House at Kingston upon Hull, was born at Hull on 20 October 1586. Having 'beene Sea-bred from my Boyes-time' (Fox, 169) he acquired his knowledge of seamanship in voyages southward to France, Spain, and the Mediterranean, and northward to the Baltic, Denmark, and Norway, and by coastal journeys. In 1606 he offered his services as mate to John Knight, captain of a Danish expedition to Greenland, but was rejected by the promoters on account of his youth. He none the less remained determined to explore the Arctic and particularly the north-west passage. He wrote:

> At the Returnes home of all Ships from thence, I enquired of the Masters Mates and others that were that way imployed, whereby I gathered by Report and Discourse and Manuscripts how farre they had proceeded, what they had done, and what was to doe. (ibid., 169–70)

Fox's earliest patrons were the mathematician and charter member of the North-West Passage Company Henry Briggs and Sir John Brooke, who brought to Charles I's attention the 1629

> Petition of Luke Fox to the king for a small supply of money towards the discovery of a passage by the north-west to the South Sea, Hudson and Sir Thomas Button having discovered

a great way, and given great hopes of opening the rest. (*CSP col.*, 1.105)

In reply to this the Royal Navy pinnace *Charles* (70 tons) was placed at the disposal of the adventurers. Fox hoped to sail in 1630 but it was too late in the season and he instead traded in the *Charles* under letters of marque for the rest of the year. Briggs died in 1631 and the voyage might have been abandoned but for the news that the Bristol merchants had projected a rival scheme under Captain Thomas James, who left Bristol on 3 May 1631. Not wanting to be outdone several London merchants, including Sir Thomas Roe and Sir John Wolstenholme, fitted out for Fox the *Charles* with a crew of twenty men and two boys victualled for eighteen months.

Fox sailed on 30 April 1631 from the Pool below London Bridge to the Orkney Islands. Sailing from there due west on the sixtieth parallel he made land on 20 June on the north side of Frobisher Bay; two days later he sighted Cape Chidley, off the south shore of Hudson Strait. Passing Resolution Island 2 leagues south on 23 June, his crew saw signs of Captain James, who had put in there for repairs. From this date until 11 July Fox worked his way along the north shore of Hudson Strait until he reached a position between Mill and Salisbury islands. He then proceeded to the south of Coats Island until 19 July, when he began his search for the north-west passage. On 27 July he made the furthest point reached by Sir Thomas Button in 1612 on 'Sir Thomas Roe's Welcome' Island (now Roes Welcome).

Being prohibited by his instructions from proceeding to a higher latitude than 63° N in this direction, Fox turned southward along the west shore of Hudson Bay, naming a cluster of islands 'Briggs his mathematicks' after his old friend. On 27 August, when he entered the mouth of the Nelson River, he found the remaining half of an inscribed board erected by Button in 1612 or 1613, which he replaced by a new one of his own. From there he sailed east-south-east for 61 leagues until 30 August, when he met his rival, Captain James, in the *Maria* of Bristol, with whom he dined, finding his host 'no Sea-man' (Fox, 223). Fox then proceeded to 55° 14′ N, or Wolstenholme's *ultima vale*, later known as Cape Henrietta Maria, at the head of James Bay. On 3 September he turned northward until he reached Cape Pembroke on Coats Island five days later. From 15 to 20 September Fox undertook a remarkable series of observations on the channel, which was named Foxe Channel by Edward Parry some 200 years later, on the west shore of Baffin Land.

On 22 September, after reaching 'Foxe his farthest' (Fox, 239), Fox turned homeward, continuing his observations among the numerous islands and sounds off the north shore of Hudson Strait. On 28 September Fox reached Resolution Island, at the entrance to Hudson Strait. On 5 October he made Cape Chidley; two days later he wrote: 'this warmth we find in the open Ocean, doth much revive us, for truly … the most of us were ready to fall downe with the rest, that were downe already' (ibid., 243). On 31 October he 'Came into the *Downes* with all my men recovered and sound, not having lost one Man, nor Boy, nor Soule, nor any manner of Tackling, having been forth neere 6 moneths' (ibid., 244).

Fox described his voyage in the engagingly titled and written *North-West Fox* (1635). It was accompanied by an important large folded map of the Arctic, now rarely found in the book. It appeared two years later than the account of James, his Bristol rival, which stole the limelight.

Fox ended his life in poverty having had no satisfaction from his petitions for reimbursement for the cost of maintaining the *Charles* for the six months after his return. Towards the end of his book he says that he had

> washt the Black-moore these five yeares, having yet received neither sallery, wages or reward; except what som few Gentlemen hath, I know not whether in curtesie or charity bestowed upon me having to fore had my meanes taken from me in the time of warres, betwixt *France*, *Spaine*, and us. (Fox, 268)

Fox, who was a younger brother of Trinity House, died at Whitby in July 1635. He was very severely criticized during his lifetime for not wintering and continuing his explorations. This and the delay in publishing his account of the voyage have meant that he never won the acclaim he deserved. Many of the whimsical names he gave to features have also been superseded; but his entertaining account of his voyage, which also contains important information about earlier explorations, is now recognized as valuable, as is the voyage itself. The Foxe basin, channel, and peninsula all bear testimony to his achievement.

C. H. COOTE, *rev.* ELIZABETH BAIGENT

Sources T. Rundell, ed., *Voyages towards the north-west*, Hakluyt Society (1849) · BL, Add. MS 19302 · W. F. E. Morley, 'Fox, Luke', *DCB*, vol. 1 · L. Fox, *North-west Fox* (1635); repr. in M. Christy, ed., *The voyages of Captain Luke Fox of Hull, and Captain Thomas James of Bristol*, 2 vols., Hakluyt Society, 88–9 (1894) · E. S. Dodge, *North-west by sea* (1961) · L. H. Neatby, *In quest of the north-west passage* (1958)
Archives BL, journal of voyage to north-west passage, Add. MS 19302 [copy] · Thomas Gilcrease Institute of American History and Art, 1400 North 25th West Avenue, Tulsa, Oklahoma, journal and logbook of ship *Charles*
Wealth at death died in poverty: Morley, 'Fox, Luke'; *DNB*

Fox, Sir (George) Malcolm (1843–1918), army officer and advocate of physical training, was born at 7 Wardwick, Derby, on 4 March 1843, younger son of Douglas Fox (1798–1885), surgeon (elder brother of Sir Charles Fox, 1810–1879, civil engineer), and his wife, Marianne (1814–1898), daughter of Jedediah Strutt, of Green Hall, Belper. Malcolm Fox, educated at Rossall School (1854–5) and Brighton College (1858–63), was always more interested in games than books. In December 1863 an ensigncy was purchased for him in the 100th regiment, with which he served until August 1875 (lieutenant June 1865, captain June 1871). Like many officers he was appalled by the poor physical condition of recruits, particularly those from the industrial areas, and his love of boxing and other sports including cross-country running matched their perceived needs. His reputation as an organizer of competitions in such activities soon spread, especially later when he was in Malta, where they were open to the whole garrison. In 1875 he transferred as captain into the Royal Highlanders

(Black Watch), with which he went to Egypt in 1882 under Wolseley, and was wounded at Tell al-Kebir.

In April 1883 while still on sick leave Fox was appointed assistant inspector of gymnasia at Aldershot, an appointment after his own heart which he owed partly to the duke of Edinburgh, who knew his Malta achievements. In July 1883 he was promoted major. On 6 September 1881 he married Mary Rose (1858–1882), daughter of Captain William Newall, Gordon Highlanders. She died in childbirth in July 1882, on the eve of his departure for Egypt. On 23 July 1884 he married Marion Jane (1863–1957), daughter of John Remington Mills of Tolmers, Hertford, a young heiress whose fortune enabled him to widen his horizons, entertain on a grand scale, travel to study continental developments, and, later, lay out at his own expense the army athletic ground and build the gymnasium (now much enlarged) at Aldershot (1894). His immense energy and his power to arouse enthusiasm were recognized by his promotion to lieutenant-colonel in July 1888 and his appointment as inspector of gymnasia in 1890, a position he held until 1897 and again (in retirement) from 1900 to 1902. His objective throughout was to improve the physical fitness as well as the fighting skills of the soldier by introducing gymnasium-trained instructors into every regimental depot. To raise the standard of bayonet-fighting he invented a wooden 'springrifle' and instituted regimental competitions, later incorporated in the annual royal naval and military tournament, of which he was an inspiration. A pioneer of boxing in the army, where it became very popular, and also in the public schools, he organized army boxing and cross-country competitions. Distrusting the style of fencing then current in Britain and France, he went to Florence in 1893 to study the system of the Cavaliere Masiello, which so impressed him that he brought back the cavaliere and his best pupil, Magrini, to Aldershot to instruct officers and staff-sergeants at the gymnasium: all the 'sabre fencing' winners at the royal tournament in the next few years were pupils.

In 1897 Fox was appointed assistant adjutant general, north-eastern district, at York, and in 1900 he retired as colonel. He was called upon by the Board of Education to introduce improved physical training as part of the school and teacher-training college curricula, as inspector of physical training to the board (1903–10), for which he was knighted in June 1910 (in January 1909 he had been appointed a commander of the Swedish royal order of the Sword). He adopted the freer, less jerky style of the Ling system, which he had admired during his visits to Denmark and Sweden, and he successfully overcame the prejudices of some teachers, who had suspected 'militarism'. In 1903, responding to anxiety at the Second South African War rejection rate of would-be army recruits, the government reluctantly appointed the interdepartmental committee on physical deterioration, composed of officers and officials, to investigate working-class conditions relative to alleged physical deterioration. Fox was an active member of the committee, missing only one of its sittings. The recommendations of its *Report* (1904) contributed to the post-1905 Liberal social reforms including the provision of school meals and the medical inspection of schoolchildren. Fox's last achievement was, as a member of the committee on a new cavalry sword, to produce a well-balanced weapon with a good grip (for which he experimented with gutta-percha), designed for thrusting on the Masiello principle. This, the 1908 pattern sword—'the finest sword ever produced for the British Army' (Robson, 165)—was used as a combat weapon by the British cavalry in the First World War and in the last years before mechanization, and is still used for ceremonial.

In 1909 Fox suffered the first of a series of strokes, which over the years reduced him to a bedridden invalid, and he died at his home, Rustington House, Rustington, near Littlehampton, Sussex, on 10 March 1918, leaving a widow, and a daughter by each of his marriages; he was buried at Rustington churchyard on 15 March. Plainly a soldier in appearance, he stood slightly above middle height, not conspicuously muscular, and with a deceptively fierce expression.

S. G. P. WARD

Sources private information (2004) · *WW* · *The Times* (13 May 1918) · *Army List* · *WWW*, 1916–28 · E. A. L. Oldfield, *History of the army physical training corps* (1955) · G. Deghy, *Noble and manly: the history of the national sporting club* (1956) · B. Robson, *Swords of the British army*, rev. edn (1996) · J. Gordon, *My six years with the black watch, 1881–1887: Egyptian campaign, eastern Sudan, Nile expedition, Egyptian frontier field force* (1929) · Marquess of Anglesey [G. C. H. V. Paget], *A history of the British cavalry, 1816 to 1919*, 4 (1986), chap. 17 · Burke, *Gen. GB* (1937) · 'Inter-departmental committee on physical deterioration', *Parl. papers* (1904), vol. 32, Cd 2175, 2210, 2186 · B. B. Gilbert, *The evolution of national insurance in Great Britain: the origins of the welfare state* (1966) · *The syllabus of physical exercises for schools*, Board of Education (1909) · E. M. Spiers, *The late Victorian army, 1868–1902* (1992) · *CGPLA Eng. & Wales* (1918)

Likenesses A. M. de Neuville, portrait, *c*.1883, Scottish United Services Museum, Edinburgh · Spy [L. Ward], caricature, 1896, repro. in *VF*; originally in Fox Gymnasium, Aldershot · photographs, *c*.1896, NAM · St H. Lander, oils, 1910–11, priv. coll.

Wealth at death £31,244 12s. 5d.: resworn probate, 2 July 1918, *CGPLA Eng. & Wales*

Fox [Foxe], **Richard** (1447/8–1528), administrator, bishop of Winchester, and founder of Corpus Christi College, Oxford, was born at Pullocks Manor, Ropsley, near Grantham, Lincolnshire. He gave his age as seventy-nine in April 1527, indicating that he was born in 1447 or 1448.

Family and early career Fox's father, Thomas, came of an old-established freeholding family and held the manor of Pullocks at the time of Fox's birth. His mother, Helena (parentage unknown), died early; by 1465 Thomas was married to Alice. Richard Fox had a brother, John; John's son, also John, was appointed archdeacon first of Surrey (1519), then of Winchester (1520), both in Richard Fox's diocese, and was associated with Corpus. Richard Fox had at least two sisters. A niece, Anne Joyner, was married first to Edmund Mill, Fox's 'well-beloved servant', then to Lionel Norreys, one of Fox's officials and executors. Two nephews, Richard and Thomas Colson, had clerical careers assisted by their uncle.

Nothing definite is known about Fox's education. According to Thomas Greneway, president of Corpus

Richard Fox (1447/8–1528), by Joannes Corvus, 1530–32?

Christi College, writing in 1566, he studied at Magdalen College, Oxford, newly founded in 1457; a later tradition has him migrating to Cambridge to avoid an outbreak of plague and entering at Pembroke College. There is no positive evidence in either case, though Fox's later election as master of Pembroke and his importing of Magdalen men to Corpus are suggestive. He held the degree of BCL when he was ordained acolyte in Salisbury diocese on 5 April 1477, although of what university is unknown. The Salisbury connection may have come about through Grantham parish church's constituting two prebends of Salisbury Cathedral, although itself in Lincoln diocese. It seems unlikely that he was the Richard Fox, styled master and bachelor of grammar, who was admitted to the Guild of the Holy Cross at Stratford upon Avon in 1477–8. On 5 July 1479 a Master Richard Fix of Lincoln diocese was one of three Englishmen matriculated at Louvain University. His faculty was canon law, but since Fox did not acquire a canon-law degree he probably did not stay long in Louvain. In 1482 or early 1483 Fox, still BCL, became canon of Salisbury holding the prebend of Bishopstone. On 30 October 1484 he was admitted in absence to the wealthy vicarage of Stepney, diocese of London. Fox may have been employed by the crown as a civil lawyer, possibly in chancery. The connection is suggested by his founding a chantry at Pembroke in 1502 for John Dawson, dean of Salisbury (1473–85), and keeper of the hanaper in chancery (1472–9).

On 22 January 1485 Richard III ordered the bishop of London to cancel Fox's admission to Stepney, because he was 'now and at that time … with our great rebel Henry ap Tudder' (Horrox and Hammond, *British Library Harleian Manuscript 433*, 2.198–201). Historians from Edward Hall onwards suggest that Fox was a student at Paris when he joined Henry Tudor's cause; but the earlier account by Polydore Vergil is more circumspect. Fox may have left England when active plotting for a Tudor invasion began between Henry's leaving Brittany in October 1484 and his visit to Paris in January 1485.

Councillor to Henry VII Fox probably acted as secretary to Henry, drafting the letters, in royal form, sent to sympathizers in England. He took part in Henry's invasion, was present at Bosworth (22 August 1485), and the next day drew up a warrant for the arrest of Bishop Robert Stillington and Sir Richard Ratcliffe. He acquired the canonry and prebend of Norrington in Hereford on 16 September 1485, vacated the vicarage of Stepney shortly after, was 'secretary' when appointed to a keepership of a park at Windsor on 18 September, and was 'beloved secretary' on appointment as canon and prebendary of Brownswood in St Paul's, London, on 26 October 1485. In November he became keeper of the exchanges at Calais, now 'beloved councillor and secretary'. He visited Cambridge in December 1485 with Peter Courtenay, bishop of Exeter and keeper of the privy seal; both men were granted the degree of DCL. He exchanged the Salisbury prebend of Bishopstone for that of Grantham Borealis in February 1486, and was appointed protonotary in chancery; this grant was backdated to Bosworth and held jointly with the previous protonotary, Henry Sharp, until Fox surrendered it in October 1488. He entered major orders on 25 March 1486, being ordained subdeacon in Lincoln diocese. On Courtenay's translation to Winchester, Fox succeeded him, as keeper of the privy seal on 24 February 1487 and as bishop of Exeter, to which he was provided on 29 January in the same year. He was consecrated on 8 April. On 8 February 1492 he was translated to Bath and Wells.

As keeper of the privy seal Fox appears to have been, with John Morton (*d.* 1500), Henry's leading minister. Morton as chancellor remained at Westminster in term-time. Fox headed the council accompanying the king on his frequent progresses, was designated its president, and attended to its multiple undifferentiated business, including the hearing of suits, foreshadowing the later court of requests. While the business of the privy seal office was largely routine, either its authorization or the king's signature was normally necessary to initiate payments from the exchequer; Fox's office and his close relationship to the king therefore gave him an oversight of general policy. He was too occupied to visit Exeter or Wells for enthronement, although usefully available to celebrate pontifical mass at court on high feast days. Ambassadors

and rebels named him as part of the inner core of government. As commissioner for the 'benevolence' of 1491, he was credited by the London great chronicle with being more moderate in his demands than Morton. However, Erasmus attributed to Fox—*vir minime stupidus* ('a man very far from stupid')—on More's authority the persuasive device known since the early seventeenth century as 'Morton's fork', namely that while the well-dressed could obviously afford to contribute handsomely, so could those who looked impoverished, since they obviously had large savings.

Diplomacy and finance Fox was heavily involved in diplomacy. He was sent on a mission to France in March 1487. In August 1487 he went to Scotland with Sir Richard Edgcumbe to discuss a marriage alliance. A meeting of the two kings was arranged, but was prevented by the overthrow and death of James III at Sauchieburn on 11 June 1488. Fox was a member of the delegations to negotiate with Spanish and Portuguese embassies in 1488–9, concluding treaties in both cases, that with Spain providing for the marriage of Katherine of Aragon to Prince Arthur. He was sent to negotiate with the French at Boulogne and Calais during the spring and summer of 1490, and again in the spring of 1491, and in June 1492. He had prime responsibility for organizing the army and fleet for the invasion of France in September 1492. Years later he was to sympathize when Wolsey had a similar task; 'you shall have a cold stomach, little sleep, pale visage, and a thin belly, with constipation [*cum rara gestione*], all of which, and as deaf as a stock, I had when I was in your case' (*Letters*, 70). He accompanied the king on the invasion, providing an armed contingent, and headed the delegation that negotiated the treaty of Étaples in November, laying the basis of peace with France until the end of the reign. Fox remained in Calais until February 1493, involved in follow-up negotiations with Philippe d'Esquerdes, whom he would have known in 1485; he also, by the king's command, redesigned the elaborate system of water-defences at Calais.

Fox had been a member of a commission in 1488 to overhaul the management of crown lands. The commission may have initiated the move back to the Yorkist system of receivers paying direct to the king's chamber, rather than into the exchequer. Finance officers now reported direct to the king, and so acquired more independent authority when the new system came effectively into operation from about 1492, possibly reducing Fox's directing role in government. The death of Bishop John Shirwood led to Fox's translation, on 30 July 1494, to the bishopric of Durham. His role was now more a proconsular one, with responsibility for the defence of the border and for negotiations with Scotland. Fox was enthroned at Durham on 23 July 1495. In November 1495 James IV ostentatiously received Perkin Warbeck, fresh from his attempted invasion of England; in May 1496 Fox conducted unsuccessful negotiations for a marriage between James and the infant English princess, Margaret; in September that year Warbeck led a raid into England. Henry planned an invasion of

Scotland which, in the event, was foiled by the Cornish rising of June 1497. In July Fox was commissioned to negotiate for the surrender of Warbeck, if possible. However, in August 1497 James attacked Fox's border castle at Norham; the castle resisted a two-week siege, thanks to precautions already taken by Fox, and James retreated on the approach of an English army. The English invaded Scotland and on 30 September 1497 Fox concluded a seven-year truce at Ayton. Negotiations, for which William Warham was responsible, converted this into a truce for the lifetime of either king. A further incident involving Norham led to a personal interview between James and Fox at Melrose in November 1498 at which the Stewart–Tudor marriage proposal was resurrected. Fox was the sole commissioner for the subsequent negotiations in 1499, which led to a treaty of perpetual peace and the agreement for James to marry Margaret on 24 January 1502.

Fox was not concerned only with Scottish affairs during his time at Durham. He was in London in February 1496 for the negotiations leading to the *Intercursus Magnus* treaty with the Netherlands, and in September of that year he helped draft instructions for ambassadors. In May 1501 he accompanied the king to Calais for a meeting with the Archduke Philip, the ruler of the Low Countries.

Surprisingly Fox succeeded neither to the chancellorship nor to Canterbury when Morton died in September 1500. Thomas Langton of Winchester was nominated to Canterbury, but died before he could be installed. Henry Deane became chancellor and then archbishop, to be succeeded in both posts on his death in February 1503 by William Warham (d. 1532). Fox succeeded Langton at Winchester on 20 August 1501. Archbishop Matthew Parker (d. 1575) records Fox's alleged retort to Warham, 'Canterbury had a higher seat but Winchester was more succulent' (*Matthaei Parker*, 461). Winchester was the richest see in England. Still keeper of the privy seal (it was during his unprecedentedly long tenure that the designation 'lord privy seal' came into use) and now with a more accessible diocese, Fox was again heavily involved in all aspects of government. He personally planned Katherine of Aragon's journey to London after her arrival at Plymouth in October 1501, though not, as is sometimes alleged, the pageants to welcome her to London. The Yorkist pretender Edward de la Pole, earl of Suffolk, accused Fox of luring Sir James Tyrrell (suspected of complicity with Suffolk) with fine words to leave the castle of Guînes, near Calais, and surrender himself to Sir Thomas Lovell in May 1502: a safe conduct was rapidly violated. Fox negotiated with a series of embassies competing for English support. He helped negotiate a commercial treaty between England and the Netherlands which the Flemings called the *Malus Intercursus* when the Archduke Philip was accidentally detained in England in 1506. In 1507 he was in Calais to negotiate a marriage between the future Charles V (r. 1519–56) and Henry VII's daughter Mary. In 1508–9 he had long negotiations with the Spanish ambassador Fuensalida over Henry's procrastination about the promised marriage between Prince Henry and Katherine of Aragon,

now a widow. Fox himself seems to have had no doubts (possibly in contrast to Warham) about the pope's right to grant a dispensation for Henry to marry his brother's widow. He did, however, receive officially in 1505 Henry's protest that he had entered into the marriage contract while under the age of puberty, and so was not bound to it.

Fox was heavily involved in the levying of fines for alleged offences and taking of bonds for good behaviour which grew into a system of government in Henry's later years. He was himself a victim of the system: in 1504 he paid £2000 for a general pardon for alleged irregularities as custodian of episcopal lands in royal hands during vacancies, of the goods of the imprisoned Bishop Stillington, and as a collector of the clerical subsidy. He headed a commission established in 1504 to redress wrongs committed by the king; there is no evidence of any victim coming forward. His dedication to Henry's service is illustrated by a story told in Roper's *The Life of Sir Thomas More*. In 1504 More objected in parliament to Henry's demands for taxation. Some time later Fox suggested to him that 'if he would be ruled by him he would not fail into the king's favour again to restore him'. Coming away More met his friend Richard Whitford, then Fox's chaplain and later monk of Syon. Whitford begged him not to follow Fox's counsel; 'for my lord my master, to serve the king's turn, will not stick to agree to his own father's death' (Roper, 8). Roper's life of his father-in-law was not written until Mary's reign and cannot be trusted for detailed information. But it is interesting that such a story was told in the More household. Relations between Fox and More seem, in spite of Fox's patronage of humane letters, to have been distant. Fox does seem to have been particularly close to Henry VII, whom he later described as 'the king that was my maker' (*Letters*, 83), perhaps even the king's friend, in so far as that was possible.

Elder statesman Fox was one of the inner group of councillors who, at Henry VII's death, moved rapidly to arrest Sir Richard Empson and Edmund Dudley. Dudley tried in vain to speak to Fox, then sent him and Sir Thomas Lovell as those 'in whom I know their old and loving master … had as much confidence and trust as in any living man' a list of those the king had 'hardly entreated' so that restitution could be made (Harrison, 86). Fox was the leading figure among Henry's executors, appointed in person, rather than *ex officio*, and was later to be accused by Warham of using that position to establish his own power in the new regime. He remained as keeper of the privy seal, and Thomas Ruthall continued as secretary. Ambassadors were seen by Fox and Ruthall. There was talk of a cardinal's hat for Fox, and in 1510 the Spanish ambassador suggested that both Fox and Ruthall should become cardinals. Henry VIII told the ambassador that he trusted Fox more than his other councillors, but that he had none the less to be careful; Winchester was, after all, a fox.

Polydore Vergil believed that Fox and the lord treasurer, Thomas Howard, earl of Surrey, were rivals, with Surrey eager to involve the kingdom in war. The political situation was more complicated. Nevertheless Vergil's account is supported by a letter from Wolsey to Fox, dated 30 September 1511, suggesting ways to decrease Surrey's influence with the king, and deploring attempts to involve the country in a Scottish war.

Warham, still lord chancellor, was none the less overshadowed by Fox. Their relations were not good. Fox organized a protest in the Canterbury convocation of January 1510 against alleged archiepiscopal encroachments on the rights of diocesan bishops, and was threatened with an interdict in retaliation. In 1511 Fox and his colleagues took their complaints about the sweeping rights claimed by Canterbury in probate of wills to the Roman rota. Pope Julius II (r. 1503–13) referred the case back to Henry VIII, who in 1513 produced a compromise. Warham protested about Fox's influence on the king; in his absence Fox, he alleged, spread untruths, which he would not do to his face, 'for he forceth little what he sayeth' provided he 'may hinder me in any behalf'; indeed that Fox 'more regardeth his own private causes' than 'the common weal and defence of the realm' (*Literae Cantuarienses*, 3.435–7).

Fox and Ruthall were responsible for promoting Wolsey into the king's favour and by 1513 Wolsey had overtaken Fox. Wolsey organized the invasion of France. While Fox was kept busy provisioning the fleet at Portsmouth, and providing advice on a range of diplomatic problems, his was the subordinate role. He sympathized with Wolsey on his 'outrageous charge and labour' and recalled his own exertions in 1492. Fox accompanied Henry on the invasion, as did Wolsey. Fox was injured by a kick from a mule, but played a prominent part in negotiations with Maximilian and, in August 1514, in drawing up the peace treaty with France. In the same month, he was appointed, with Wolsey and John Heron, to a commission to secure the repayment of debts due to the king (Gunn, 93).

According to a report compiled soon after, and published by Robert Keilwey in 1602, Fox spoke out at the meeting called in November 1515 to resolve the crisis over attempts in parliament to curb the judicial immunities of the clergy. To the king's expressed approval of Henry Standish's defence of the secular authority Fox 'answered our lord the king in these English words: "Sir, I warrant you Dr. Standish will not abide by his opinion at his peril"', leaving Standish to ask what 'should one poor friar do alone, against all the bishops and the clergy of England?' (Pollard, 44). Warham was equally outspoken on the church's behalf. Almost immediately Warham resigned as chancellor; Fox gave up the privy seal in May 1516. It is difficult to tell whether Fox was glad to retire from politics, or whether, as Vergil claimed, he had been elbowed aside by Wolsey, and disapproved of the new policy of subsidizing the emperor and the Swiss against the Venetians that threatened the recent peace with France. Fox told Wolsey that he was glad to give up political responsibilities 'whereby I may do some satisfaction for twenty eight years negligence' of episcopal duties—the more so given his confidence in Wolsey's talents. He expressed his support for the new policy and gave Wolsey friendly advice; not to work after 6 p.m., and, out of term, 'to keep the

Council with the king's grace wheresoever he be' (*Letters*, 82–4). A year later he excused himself from attendance on the king to discuss fortifications; were he now to be involved in 'any matter concerning the war', he feared that he would not 'be in such quietness that I shall dare say mass these next five or six days'. 'Being of the age of seventy years and above, and looking daily to die' Fox might reasonably contemplate retirement (*Letters*, 92–6). But he could also indicate disapproval of current policy to the Venetian ambassador, and suggested that it was useless striving against Wolsey who was 'not cardinal but king' (*Calendar of State Papers, Venetian, 1509–1519*, 412). While Fox expressed 'no little remorse' for 'the many intolerable enormities' that he had seen in war (*Letters*, 93), he continued to urge Wolsey to pay attention to the defence of Portsmouth. Fox did not oppose war as an instrument of policy, but he evidently prided himself on the 1492 peace with France and the 1502 peace with Scotland which were destroyed by the war of 1512–14; and he had hopes of the peace of 1514 that were quickly disappointed. The French pension which (with many others) he was granted for his peacemaking in 1492, and which was renewed in 1514, is unlikely to have been the only reason for his preference.

Diocesan affairs Although never visiting Exeter or Bath and Wells as bishop, Fox appointed efficient deputies, kept tight control of major appointments, and vigorously defended his rights. At Durham he carried out ordinations, attempted some control of clerical standards, and insisted on the use of corporate revenues for the upkeep of churches. He also used excommunication to buttress secular sanctions in reducing the borders to order. At Winchester Fox was able to keep close control of the diocese even while attending to affairs of state. Archdeacons were to carry out personal visitations, with particular emphasis on clerical absenteeism and on the proper upkeep of the fabric. Fox did not carry out parochial visitations himself, nor is there any indication that he preached, but he occasionally presided at the consistory court, and up to 1520 ordained in person. He claimed in a letter to Wolsey in 1527 never to have been 'rigorous' in punishing his secular clergy, except in cases of manifest fornication or adultery; even then he had never shamed them by imposing open penance, and had not, in any of his dioceses, deprived any parsons. He dealt with major scandals in monastic houses and convents, attempting to 'restrain' nuns from 'going out of their monasteries', although regretting the impossibility of enforcing strict enclosure (*Letters*, 150–51). In 1517 he published a free translation of the Benedictine rule into English for the benefit of the nuns of his diocese. More generally, Fox aimed at a reasonable standard of observance among the religious, and displayed little interest in the fashionable reformed orders, other than in supporting an attempt by the Observant Franciscans to impose a more austere habit on their Conventual brethren. He sponsored the printing of a processional according to the Sarum use in 1501. *The Contemplacioun of Synnaris*, printed at Fox's expense in 1499, was an Anglicization of a work written in Scots by a Franciscan Observant, William Touris. While in the form of a general meditation on sin and salvation, it laid heavy stress on the duties of kings, prelates, and officers to do justice. It probably came to Fox's notice during his meeting with James IV in 1498 (the absence of any reference to James in the work makes it unlikely that it was printed as a compliment to the king). There were a few heresy trials during Fox's time at Winchester; one, that of Thomas Denys, a relapsed heretic, resulted in a burning.

Builder and patron of the arts Fox was active as a builder. The fortifications of Calais and Norham have already been noticed. He improved the hall and built a new kitchen at Durham Castle, displaying his badge of the pelican in its piety. He was probably involved in Henry VII's building work at Westminster and elsewhere, and as one of Henry's executors he had some responsibility for planning the glass at King's College chapel, Cambridge. At Winchester he took over the reconstruction of the east end of the cathedral which had been going on since the 1470s; the great east gable, the high vault, aisles, and screen of the presbytery, and his own chantry chapel complete with a carved cadaver all date from his time. He took a personal interest in the work, and probably provided much of the finance. The work is typical of early Tudor court practice, with some Renaissance detail on an essentially Gothic composition, most notably in the cornices of the presbytery screen and the chests placed above them for the bones of Anglo-Saxon kings, queens, and bishops.

Fox may have bought his copy of Lorenzo Valla's *Elegentiae*, printed at Louvain in 1476, on his visit in 1479. As Henry VII's secretary he was courted by the Italian humanists Pietro Carmeliano and Giovanni Gigli, anxious to ingratiate themselves with the new regime. Bernard André, Henry's poet laureate and court annalist, who had also arrived from France in 1485, likewise saw Fox as a notable patron, and addressed him as *Maecenas meus*. Fox purchased the large library built up over many years in Rome and elsewhere by his predecessor at Durham, John Shirwood; he failed to acquire Shirwood's Greek manuscripts, however, perhaps an indication that he had not yet realized the significance of Greek. In 1506 Erasmus dedicated to him a translation of Lucian's *Toxaris*. Andrea Ammonio produced poems in praise of Fox as model statesman and bishop as well as one in sympathy for the death of Fox's pupil 'Grastocus'—probably John, Lord Greystoke, who died of sweating sickness in August 1508. From 1511 Ammonio, now Henry VIII's Latin secretary, tried to secure Fox's patronage for Erasmus. Fox responded by teasing half-promises which were never fulfilled. However, More reported to Erasmus in December 1516 that Fox, 'a man of excellent judgement as you know' (*The Correspondence of Erasmus*, 4.171), had publicly commended Erasmus's New Testament as worth ten commentaries. It may be at Fox's initiative that Erasmus's text was used to supply the scriptural captions in the glass of King's College chapel. In 1517 Fox presented Ammonio to a rich living just before the latter's death.

Founder of Corpus Christi College, Oxford Fox was elected chancellor of Cambridge University in 1498–9, apparently

for a single year. He was master of Pembroke College, Cambridge, from 1507 to (probably) 1516. As executor of Lady Margaret Beaufort and friend of John Fisher it is likely that he was involved in the foundation both of Christ's College in 1505 and of St John's in 1511. Fox seems to have had less to do with Oxford before becoming bishop of Winchester, and therefore visitor of both New College and Magdalen. In 1504 he was appointed by Pope Julius II, with Bishop James Layburne of Carlisle, to revise the statutes of Balliol College. The new statutes produced in 1507 were Fox's work; seeking to rectify what was seen as the excessively democratic structure of the college, they were couched in the form of an elaborate organic metaphor which looks forward to the Corpus statutes. In 1507 Fox's commissary conducted a visitation of Magdalen. The college had fallen into indiscipline, and Fox had evidently arranged beforehand to bring about the resignation of the long-standing president, Bishop Richard Mayew of Hereford, who was eventually succeeded by Fox's protégé John Claymond.

In 1511 Fox was acquiring land in Oxford for a new college for the use of monks of his cathedral priory at Winchester. That was still his intention in 1513 when building started. By 1516 he had changed his mind, possibly at the instigation of Bishop Hugh Oldham of Exeter (*d.* 1519), who was to be a major benefactor of the new college. On 1 March 1517 Corpus Christi College was founded, for a president, twenty fellows, and twenty scholars (*discipuli*). Public readers (for the benefit of the university generally) were to be provided in 'humanity' and Greek, the latter the first such regular post in England, though quickly followed in Cambridge in 1518. Unlike the Collegium Trilingue founded at Louvain in 1517, Corpus made no specific provision for Hebrew, although both Erasmus and Fisher congratulated Fox on founding a trilingual college. Corpus's professed aim was the training of priests through literature and theology; the latter was to be based on scripture and the fathers rather than on authorities 'inferior in doctrine because later in time' (*Statutes of the Colleges of Oxford*, 2, 10, 51). The college was to be small, and the life of its members strictly regulated—as a beehive, both in discipline and activity. The first president was John Claymond (*d.* 1537) and there was a strong Magdalen contingent among the fellows. Building craftsmen from the royal works were employed, but the architecture was conservative in style. With its very specific emphasis on moral formation Corpus represented the most complete example of the humanist college in England. Wolsey's much larger Cardinal College (later renamed Christ Church) followed in its footsteps, and Wolsey's own public readers resided at Corpus until their accommodation was ready. Oddly, More's letter of 1518 written from the court, and reproving Oxford for its alleged hostility to Greek, makes no mention of Fox's foundation.

Last years From 1516 Fox was resident in or near Winchester. He continued to keep a very tight control of local government in Hampshire, and was active on commissions. When in 1517 he was accused of offending against the enclosure laws, Wolsey was prepared to take his word as to his own innocence and those of his officers. In 1519, in a letter unusually in Latin (and therefore presumably for public consumption), Fox congratulated Wolsey on his plans for ecclesiastical reform. The deafness that he had apparently suffered in 1492 was presumably partial or temporary, since there is no other mention of it. He became blind at some stage in his retirement, certainly by 1522. This did not prevent his being made responsible for seeing that the local commissioners for the forced loans of 1522–3 made an appropriate contribution themselves. According to Polydore Vergil, Fox and Fisher opposed unsuccessfully Wolsey's demand for clerical taxation in 1523. In December 1526 he asked to be excused 'riding … the country this winter season' about the clerical subsidy, with the implication that he had done so during the two previous years (*Letters*, 148–50). Like other diocesans, he had various clashes with Wolsey over the exercise of legatine powers. In March 1527 John Fisher dedicated to Fox his treatise on Corpus Christi; he credited Fox with having prompted Henry VII to make him a bishop. In April 1527 Fox was examined about Katherine of Aragon's marriage to Prince Arthur and the subsequent negotiations for her marriage to Prince Henry. He acknowledged Henry's protest of being under age in 1505, but affirmed his belief that this was at Henry VII's command, and that Henry did subsequently marry of his own volition. Fox at first refused to sign the statement on the grounds that, in spite of his blindness, he had not been allowed to have a counsellor present; he signed only out of deference to royal command.

Fox died on 5 October 1528 at Wolvesey Palace, Winchester, and was buried in his chantry at the cathedral. His will, drawn up on 15 February that year, omits the usual dedication to the Virgin Mary and the saints, and has an Augustinian emphasis on salvation through grace; it goes on to leave valuable bequests of tapestries and plate to his successor, the more so if that should be Wolsey, on condition he does not trouble Fox's executors; there are particular bequests to the marquess of Exeter, Lord Sandys, and Sir William Paulett (his steward, the future lord treasurer), and Fox directs that any goods not otherwise spoken for be sold for the benefit of the most needy of his tenants. Separately from the will Fox converted Robert Curteys's chantry in Grantham, for which he had been an executor, into a grammar school. He had earlier, in 1523, built a schoolhouse on the episcopal estates at Taunton, although leaving the pay of the master to be otherwise provided. Jointly with Sandys he refounded the guild and chapel with a free school at Basingstoke.

The man and his legacy Fox was a supremely competent statesman. He served the commonwealth to the best of his very considerable abilities, while recognizing a tension between his political and episcopal roles. He was a master of rhetoric, in both speech and writing, using it to convey a highly persuasive tone of gentle reasonableness, and he wrote in an attractive flowing style, in both Latin and English, neither elaborate nor obscure, with an ironical undertone; but he was a tough negotiator in the interests of the king or of the rights of his see. Unsurprisingly, he was accused of double-dealing. William Tyndale in 1530 notoriously accused Fox and Morton of betraying the secrets of the confessional to Henry VII. That testimony is naturally suspect; less so is the anecdote of his devotion to Henry VII (cited above) which was later told in the More family. Fox was protective of subordinates. He was alert to intellectual trends, coming round, after 1495, to an appreciation of the value of Greek in education, commending Erasmus's New Testament, and patronizing craftsmen working in the 1520s in the fashionable classicism of the French court. Corpus Christi College is a monument to Fox's adaptability, his attention to detail, and his determination to carry any project through to a successful conclusion, and the more surprising in its completeness given Fox's late conversion to the idea of an unequivocally humanist college to train secular priests.

Fox had no compunction about accumulating great wealth. His net income from his bishoprics ranged from some £1500 p.a. at Exeter to some £4000 p.a. at Winchester. He also looked after the interests, including patronage rights, of the absentee Italian bishops of Bath and Wells and of Worcester, until giving way to Wolsey in 1517–18. The keepership of the privy seal brought with it an official salary of £365 a year. Fox's varied services brought other rewards, including profits from wardships, and a pension from France of 1050 livres (about £120) paid most years from 1492 to 1512, and again from 1514 to 1520. His contribution of £2000 to the clerical 'loan' of 1522 (half Wolsey's contribution, and twice that of any other bishop) would suggest an income of £8000, though that would otherwise seem unlikely for the years after his retirement from politics.

Fox used his wealth in the approved manner—the maintenance of a large and dignified household, the repair and improvement of buildings, the distribution of alms, and the provision of education. He was a skilled player in the benefice game, advising Claymond in 1517 on speed and secrecy to safeguard his existing interests. His relatives, ecclesiastical and secular, benefited considerably if not ostentatiously from his patronage. For all his ironical intelligence, his extensive experience of the realities of power, and his shrewd appreciation of character, Fox was a conservative; he never questioned, at least openly, prevailing attitudes in church and state, even while preferring, whenever possible, peaceable methods. His ideals were stability and efficient administration.

C. S. L. DAVIES

Sources *Letters of Richard Fox, 1486–1527*, ed. P. S. Allen and H. M. Allen (1929) · Emden, *Oxf.* · Emden, *Cam.* · *Hist. U. Oxf.*, vols. 2–3 · M. P. Howden, introduction, *The register of Richard Fox, lord bishop of Durham, 1494–1501*, ed. M. P. Howden, SurtS, 147 (1932) · R. H. K. Carless, 'Selected aspects of the life of Richard Fox, 1446–1528', MLitt. diss., University of Bristol, 1987 · Chancery records · B. André, *Historia regis Henrici septimi*, ed. J. Gairdner, Rolls Series, 10 (1858) · J. Gairdner, ed., *Letters and papers illustrative of the reigns of Richard III and Henry VII*, 2 vols., Rolls Series, 24 (1861–3) · W. Campbell, ed., *Materials for a history of the reign of Henry VII*, 2 vols., Rolls Series, 60 (1873–7) · *LP Henry VIII*, vols. 1–4 · Calendar of state papers, Venetian, Spanish etc., PRO · *The Anglica historia of Polydore Vergil, AD 1485–1537*, ed. and trans. D. Hay, CS, 3rd ser., 74 (1950) · W. Roper, *The life of Sir Thomas More*, ed. E. V. Hitchcock, main ser., EETS, 197

(1935) • W. Tyndale, *The practice of prelates*, ed. H. Walter, Parker Society, 37 (1849) • J. B. Sheppard, ed., *Literae Cantuarienses: the letter books of the monastery of Christ Church, Canterbury*, 3 vols., Rolls Series, 85 (1887–9) [Warham's complaints about Fox] • A. H. Thomas and I. D. Thornley, eds., *The great chronicle of London* (1938) • C. J. Harrison, 'The petition of Edmund Dudley', *EngHR*, 87 (1972), 82–99 • J. Crook, ed., *Winchester Cathedral: nine hundred years, 1093–1993* (1993) • A. J. Smith, 'The family of Richard Fox', *The Pelican* [Corpus Christi College] (1986–7), 16–19 • J. G. Milne, *The early history of Corpus Christi College, Oxford* (1946) • A. F. Pollard, *Wolsey* (1929) • P. Gwyn, *The king's cardinal: the rise and fall of Thomas Wolsey* (1990) • M. Kelly, 'Canterbury jurisdiction and influence during the episcopate of William Warham', PhD diss., U. Cam., 1963 [for probate dispute, 1510–13] • *The registers of Robert Stillington, bishop of Bath and Wells, 1466–1491, and Richard Fox, bishop of Bath and Wells, 1492–1494*, ed. H. C. Maxwell-Lyte, Somerset RS, 52 (1937) • J. Greatrex, 'On ministering to "certayne devoute and religiouse women": Bishop Fox and the Benedictine nuns of Winchester diocese', *Women in the church on the eve of the dissolution*, ed. W. J. Sheils and D. Wood, SCH, 27 (1990), 223–35 • M. C. Erler, 'Bishop Richard Fox's manuscript gifts to his Winchester nuns: a second surviving example', *Journal of Ecclesiastical History*, 52 (2001), 334–7 • A. A. MacDonald, 'Catholic devotion into protestant lyric: the case of the "Contemplacioun of Synnaris"', *Innes Review*, 35 (1984), 58–87 • R. Horrox and P. W. Hammond, eds., *British Library Harleian manuscript 433*, 4 vols. (1979–83) • *The correspondence of Erasmus*, ed. and trans. R. A. B. Mynors and others, 22 vols. (1974–94), vol. 4 • *Statutes of the colleges of Oxford*, 3 vols. (1853) • *Matthaei Parker Cantuariensis archiepiscopi de antiquitate Britannicae ecclesiae*, ed. S. Drake (1729) • CCC Oxf., MS 1821 • S. J. Gunn, 'The Act of Resumption of 1515', *Early Tudor England* [Harlaxton 1987], ed. D. Williams (1989), 87–106 • C. N. L. Brooke, 'Chancellors of the University of Cambridge, c.1415–1535', *Humanism, reform and the reformation: the career of Bishop John Fisher*, ed. B. Bradshaw and E. Duffy (1989), appendix 1

Archives Devon RO, register • Hants. RO, register • U. Durham L., register | CCC Oxf., early records • CCC Oxf., corresp. with John Claymond • Hants. RO, Winchester consistory court books

Likenesses oils on wood panel, 1522, NPG • J. Corvus, oils on wood panel, 1530–1532?, CCC Oxf. [*see illus.*] • J. Corvus, portrait, second version, NPG • portrait (after J. Corvus), repro. in Allen and Allen, eds., *Letters*; formerly at LPL [lost during Second World War] • tomb effigy, Winchester Cathedral

Wealth at death immensely wealthy

Fox, Robert (1798–1843), antiquary, was born in Huntingdon on 22 March 1798, the penultimate of at least nine children of John Fox (*b.* 1748/9, *d.* in or before 1817), a cabinet-maker and upholsterer, and his wife, Frances. His early education is unknown, but probably under the influence of a family friend, the Huntingdon surgeon David Mackie, he trained for medicine and was admitted a member of the Society of Apothecaries on 3 September 1818 and of the Royal College of Surgeons on 5 March 1819. In this capacity he practised in Huntingdon, Godmanchester, and the surrounding area, being prominent in the Huntingdonshire Medico-Chirurgical Society. It was at a meeting of this society in 1835 that Fox personally experienced a lightning strike, which stimulated him to the study of electricity. He constructed for this purpose a large 'atmospheric battery' attached to his Godmanchester home and lectured widely with the aid of portable apparatus. He was effectively the founder, in 1840, of the Huntingdon Literary and Scientific Institution (the building, erected in 1842, is now a public hall).

Fox's interest in antiquarian matters probably arose from an acquaintance with Thomas Inskip of Shefford,

Bedfordshire, a watchmaker and collector of local Romano-British antiquities. On settling in Godmanchester in the 1820s he threw himself into the study of the town's history, and in 1831 he published *The History of Godmanchester*. It is one of the best town histories of its time, based on concentrated research in local and national records, and it gained Fox admission to the Society of Antiquaries. He was also a collector of antiquities, geological specimens, and coins, and in 1838 became a member of the Numismatic Society. In 1826 and 1831 he served as a bailiff of Godmanchester and he was an alderman from the creation of the new corporation in 1835. In politics a whig, in 1831–2 he successfully advanced the petition of the non-parliamentary borough to be united with Huntingdon for the purposes of the franchise, coincidentally campaigning there against the domination of aristocratic influence.

Fox was married twice. With his first wife, Jane (*bap.* 1792, *d.* before 20 Jan 1831), daughter of Edward Ashton, whom he married on 20 November 1821, he had two daughters and three sons. After her death c.1831 he married in 1832 Anne Taylor (c.1806–1877), sister of Richard Taylor, the New Zealand missionary, and they had a daughter. His second wife survived him. Fox died at his home in Post Street, Godmanchester, of heart disease on 7 June 1843, and was buried on 11 June in Godmanchester churchyard. His small but choice collection of antiquities was purchased by subscription after his death, and became the core of the Huntingdon Literary and Scientific Institution's collection. What remains of this mainly passed in 1957, at the institution's closure, to the Norris Museum, St Ives, which also possesses one literary manuscript by Fox of 1816–29. Fox's historical collections are among Godmanchester borough records in the county record office, Huntingdon. Other parts of his collection, notably of coins, are in the Cambridge University Museum of Archaeology and Anthropology.

P. C. SAUNDERS

Sources R. Fox, scrapbook, Huntingdon CRO • R. Fox, 'Satires', 1819–29, Norris Museum, St Ives, Huntingdonshire [bound with *The Lash*, 1809] • *Cambridge Chronicle and Journal* (10 June 1843) • parish registers of Godmanchester and Huntingdon St Mary and St Benedict, Huntingdon CRO • Archdeaconry of Huntingdon probate records, wills of John Fox, 1817, and Robert Fox, 1843, Cambs. AS, Huntingdon • *Edward Cassey & Co.'s history, gazetteer, and directory of Bedfordshire and Huntingdonshire* (1862) • Enumerators' schedules of 1841–81 censuses • monumental inscriptions, Godmanchester churchyard • Huntingdon Scientific and Literary Institution Shareholders' registers and minutes, Huntingdon CRO • 'Annual report for 1893–4', *Proceedings of the Cambridge Antiquarian Society*, 8 (1891–4), 390 • Cambs. AS, Cambridge, P 51/1/2

Archives Cambs. AS, Huntingdon, commonplace book and papers • Norris Museum, St Ives

Wealth at death under £1500

Fox, Robert Were (1754–1818), merchant and industrial entrepreneur, was born on 5 July 1754 in Fowey, Cornwall, the second of the five sons of George Croker Fox (*d.* 1807) and his wife, Mary. The Foxes were a Quaker family holding a long-established and significant position in Cornish commercial life. As mine owner, merchant, and shipping agent, Fox was to play a pivotal role in further enhancing this influence at a time when Cornwall had emerged as an early focus of British industrialization. He was principal partner in the family firm, G. C. Fox & Sons, from 1780 until 1810, and during this period consolidated his company's position in the rich Gwennap copper mines, notably as adventurers (shareholders) in Poldice and Wheal Unity. In partnership with John Williams of Scorrier, another local mining magnate, he also purchased the mineral rights of the duchy of Cornwall for a period of thirty-one years, operating as Fox, Williams & Co.

In 1791 Fox and Williams established the Perran foundry (on an inlet of the River Fal) to supply machinery to the Gwennap mines. Fox sought business partners among the influential group of Quakers involved in Cornish commerce, and principal shareholders were the interrelated Price and Tregelles families of Falmouth and Penryn. Although Fox was anticipating the expiry (in 1800) of Boulton and Watt's patent rights on the manufacture of steam engines, it was not until the 1830s that large Cornish engines were being built at the Perran foundry. In this earlier period, Perran concentrated on the production of smaller components, larger items being constructed at the Neath Abbey ironworks in south Wales, which the partners had acquired in July 1792. Near the Perran foundry was the Perran smelting house, a tin-smelting operation acquired by Fox between about 1802 and 1806 but abandoned by 1811.

About 1799 Fox purchased the lease on Portreath harbour, on the north Cornish coast. Between 1800 and 1805 the port was extensively reconstructed to facilitate the export of copper ore (to south Wales for smelting) and the import of coal (again from south Wales) and timber. In 1809 Fox and Williams began the Portreath-Poldice tramway, with the aim of linking the harbour to the nearby Gwennap mines. As well as establishing more efficient communications, the construction of various spurs and short branches allowed them to exercise monopolistic control over the traffic between port and mines.

Alongside his mining interests, Fox was involved in the maritime trade of Falmouth, then home of the packet service and extensive shipping business. In May 1794 he was appointed consul to the United States of America for the port of Falmouth, a position he held until succeeded by his son Robert Were Fox FRS, in 1815. Fox lived in Falmouth, at Bank House, Grove Place, and at the nearby country residence of Penjerrick. He married in 1788 Elizabeth (1768–1849), the daughter of Joseph and Sarah Tregelles of Falmouth, with whom he had six sons, the eldest being the geologist and physicist Robert Were *Fox. He died, probably in Falmouth, in 1818.   Philip Payton

Sources S. E. Gray, *Old Falmouth* (1903) · W. Tregoning Hoope, 'Summary of the history of Perran foundry', *Journal of the Royal Cornwall Polytechnic Society*, 6 (1927–30), 274 · Boase & Courtney, *Bibl. Corn.* · D. B. Barton, *Essays in Cornish mining history*, 2 (1970) · D. B. Barton, *A history of tin mining and smelting in Cornwall* (1965) · D. B. Barton, *The Cornish beam engine: a survey of its history and development in the mines of Cornwall and Devon from before 1800 to the present day*, 2nd edn (1969) · *Annual Monitor* (1820), 24 · *Annual Monitor* (1849), 122–30 · *Biographical catalogue: being an account of the lives of Friends and others whose portraits are in the London Friends' Institute*, Society of Friends (1888), 250 · J. Griscom, *A year in Europe*, 2 vols. (1823), 1.202 · will, PRO, PROB 11/1614, sig. 121

Fox, Robert Were (1789–1877), geologist and physicist, was born on 26 April 1789 in Falmouth, Cornwall, the eldest son of Robert Were *Fox (1754–1818) and his wife, Elizabeth (1768–1849), daughter of Joseph Tregelles of Falmouth. The family were members of the Religious Society of Friends and Fox remained a Quaker throughout his life, serving as an elder of his quarterly meeting for more than fifty years. He was educated at home by private tutors, but was said to have taught himself science. The Fox family had extensive business interests in and around Falmouth in shipping, banking, and industrial concerns; Fox himself was especially involved with the family's iron foundries at Perran Wharf, near Falmouth, and Neath Abbey in south Wales. In 1814 he married Maria (1786–1858), daughter of Robert Barclay of Surrey. The couple later had three children. Their daughter Caroline *Fox became a well-known diarist.

Fox started to take an interest in science at an early age, and in 1812, together with Joel Lean, he was granted a patent (no. 3621, 1812) for improvements to steam engines. In 1815 he began to investigate the high temperatures in Cornish mines, and was convinced by his experiments that these could not be caused solely by mining activity but must be due to factors deep within the earth. His first of a long series of papers on the subject was read to the Royal Geological Society of Cornwall in 1818 (published 1822), and he successfully persuaded several continental geologists (including the German geographer Baron von Humboldt, whom Fox had met in France in 1814) of the existence of heat within the earth. He was led from these studies to investigate the formation of mineral veins in the Cornish rocks, at first attributing it to electrical currents; his ideas about the nature of these currents and their effects on mineral formation changed as he continued his experiments, and can be followed in a series of papers published in various scientific journals from 1830 onwards, and summarized in a paper for the Royal Cornwall Polytechnic Society in 1836.

Fox also studied terrestrial magnetism, and its connections with electricity, and this led him to correspond with Michael Faraday. He devised an improved compass dipping needle, with the assistance of Thomas Brown Jordan, which was used by naval expeditions to determine the locations of the south and north geomagnetic poles. He also participated in magnetic surveys of the British Isles, on behalf of the British Association for the Advancement of Science (BAAS). He was assisted with grants from the BAAS in 1834, 1836, and 1838 to purchase more accurate thermometers for furthering his work on measurement of heat within the earth. He and his family regularly attended the annual meetings of the BAAS, and he came to know many of the leading men of science of the period; among those entertained at his home in Falmouth were Henry De la Beche, William Buckland, Adam Sedgwick, and William Whewell, as described by Fox's daughter Caroline (1819–1871) in her journal.

Fox was elected FRS in 1848. He and his brother Charles

*Fox (1797–1878) were also responsible for the founding of a scientific society in Falmouth in 1833—the Royal Cornwall Polytechnic Society—which was intended to encourage science and the arts through an annual exhibition and meeting. Fox donated money for a number of the prizes awarded by the society for inventions to be used in mines. He was also known and respected for his philanthropic work, including support of a Lancastrian school in Falmouth and the Bible Society; he supported religious emancipation in Britain and Spain, and the ending of slavery. His gardens at his home at Penjerrick, Budock Water, near Falmouth, were noted for their beauty, and for his collection of plants brought from all over the world. He died there on 25 July 1877, survived only by his eldest daughter, and was buried at the Quaker burial-ground, Budock, Falmouth. DENISE CROOK

Sources J. H. Collins, *A catalogue of the works of Robert Were Fox … with notes and extracts and a sketch of his life* (1878) · Boase & Courtney, *Bibl. Corn.* · R. W. Fox, 'On the temperature of mines', *Transactions of the Royal Geological Society of Cornwall*, 2 (1822), 14–18, pl. 1 · R. W. Fox, 'On the electro-magnetic properties of metalliferous veins, in the mines of Cornwall', *PTRS*, 120 (1830), 399–414 · R. W. Fox, 'Some observations on metalliferous veins', *Transactions of the Royal Geological Society of Cornwall*, 4 (1832), 21–8 · R. W. Fox, 'On mineral veins', *Annual Report of the Royal Cornwall Polytechnic Society* (1836), 32–7, 81–141 · *Memories of old friends, being extracts from the journals and letters of Caroline Fox, from 1835–1871*, ed. H. M. Pym, 2 vols. (1882) · *Barclay Fox's journal*, ed. R. L. Brett (1979) · J. Morrell and A. Thackray, *Gentlemen of science: early years of the British Association for the Advancement of Science* (1981) · L. A. Bauer, 'Life and work of Robert Were Fox', *Terrestrial Magnetism and Atmospheric Electricity*, 15 (1910), 207–8 · d. cert.

Archives RS, letters | PRO, letters to Sir Edward Sabine, BJ3 · Royal Institution of Great Britain, London, Faraday MSS · RS, Sabine MSS

Wealth at death under £25,000: resworn probate, 1878, *CGPLA Eng. & Wales* (1877)

Fox, Roy Clifton (1901–1982), trumpeter and band leader, was born on 25 October 1901 in Denver, Colorado, USA, the son of Joseph Wilbur Fox (*d.* in or before 1953), a carpenter. His parents, who were both musical, were members of the Salvation Army and were moved to a mission in Los Angeles, California, while Roy and his sister Vera were still very young. At the age of three he first sang a Salvation Army hymn, and at the age of eleven he bought his first cornet. His parents left the Salvation Army in 1908, his father resuming his career as carpenter and painter and his mother working in a bakery, while Roy did his bit to boost the family income by selling papers. His only musical education came from a shoemaker friend who taught him the rudiments of the cornet, and he was soon playing in a small orchestra that sometimes provided background music for silent films. He joined the Los Angeles Examiner Newsboys' Band and had his first professional experience playing for a Cecil B. de Mille film. Soon afterwards he changed to the trumpet and played in a number of local bands.

In 1918 Fox was asked to join a newly formed outfit led by the drummer and band leader Abe Lyman at The Sunset inn in Santa Monica; the band also included Gus Arnheim, Miff Mole, and Ray Lopez. It was during this period that he developed a distinctive soft style of playing, firstly using the song 'Whispering', a title that provided him with a trademark and subsequently a signature tune. He became a well-employed musician playing with bands in San Francisco, Los Angeles, Baltimore, Miami, New York, and elsewhere, occasionally leading groups of his own, the first at the Club Royale in Culver in 1920, and he married about 1927 Dorothea, a dress designer, who sadly turned out to be an alcoholic. The marriage somehow survived for a few years in the USA and London until the 1930s, but it never brought him much happiness. At this time he was leading a band at the Montmartre Café on Sunset Boulevard in Hollywood, which played for many pictures made by MGM, Paramount, and other studios. He became musical supervisor for the Fox film studios, lived in Beverly Hills, and became a well-known figure in the Hollywood scene, which gave him plenty of good names (he had a brief affair with the film star Jean Harlow) to sprinkle around in his autobiography *Hollywood, Mayfair and All that Jazz* (1975).

Roy Fox's reputation had clearly spread, for in 1930 he was cabled from London and asked to form a seven-piece American band for an eight-week engagement at the Café de Paris. The band opened there on 29 September 1930. Although this first band was fairly average, relying on Fox's reputation as the 'whispering cornetist', it was good enough to be taken up by E. R. Lewis of the burgeoning Decca Record Company, and its recordings, the first one made in January 1931, were successful enough to create a steady demand for more. He was now asked to form a British band, and he became musical director for Decca.

Fox relinquished his Hollywood job, sent his American musicians home, and formed a recording band which had Lew Stone as its pianist, Bill Harty as its drummer, and Al Bowlly as vocalist. The records the band made became very popular, one of the first hits being 'Peanut Vendor', recorded in February 1931, which helped to start Al Bowlly on his successful career. Fox himself played the trumpet less frequently over the years and was rarely heard on the recordings of the band.

Fox was next asked to take his band into the newly opened Monseigneur club in Piccadilly. The personnel now included Nat Gonella (trumpet) and Joe Ferrie (trombone). It was an outstanding band, and the recordings made by the Monseigneur group have always been considered classics of British dance band music. At the height of the band's popularity Roy Fox became seriously ill with pleurisy, and the pianist Lew Stone temporarily took over the leadership. When the time came to renew the contract, the management were disinclined to improve the terms offered, even though the Roy Fox band had now become a top attraction through its regular BBC broadcasts on Wednesday nights from 10.30 to 12 and also through Fox's stage shows at the Palladium and elsewhere. The result of the disagreement was that Roy Fox left and Lew Stone took over the Monseigneur contract, with most of the musicians staying with him. Roy Fox went, loyally supported by Syd Buckman, to the Café Anglais in Leicester Square. Some predicted a fall in his popularity, but his new band, built round a group of musicians from the Spider's Web Club, was as good as ever, and the Roy Fox nights on the BBC continued without a break. Roy Fox made nearly 600 recordings in his time, a lot of them sophisticated and bland, but a number in good swinging jazz mode, particularly when featuring one of his star players and singers.

On 16 January 1933 the band moved to the Kit Kat Club, owned by Gaumont-British Pictures, who were able to give it generous publicity. Among several vocalists a newcomer, Denny Dennis, made a considerable reputation for himself during this period, and the band appeared at the royal command performance at the Palladium in 1933 and accompanied Evelyn Laye. The relief band at the Kit Kat was led by Joe Loss.

In 1934 Roy Fox was back at a greatly refurbished Café Anglais. He stayed for three months, then began a period of touring the British variety halls. The band was broken up in 1938. He had regularly suffered from ill health, and his band work became more intermittent after this. He led a band in Australia during 1938, then, barred from working in Britain during the war, led small groups in New York before returning to London in 1946. During this time he had married a girl called Kay, but this marriage too was dissolved as she was unhappy living in London. On 7 February 1953 he married Eileen (formerly Helen; *b.* 1928/9), a model, daughter of William O'Donnell, a farmer, and this time marriage gave him much happiness and a son, Gary. In the same year he disbanded his final orchestra. He led a life of mixed fortunes after retiring from the band world: always hoping that a chance might come to revive his 1930s kind of music, but never having the vitality to pursue the matter when it did; giving interviews; introducing a series of programmes called *Roy Fox Remembers*; mainly running an entertainment agency and acting as personal manager to various film and television actors; and latterly surviving on memories and a few royalties. He lived for a while in Kings Road, Chelsea, but spent his last years at Brinsworth House, 72 Staines Road, Twickenham, where he died, aged eighty, on 20 March 1982.

PETER GAMMOND

Sources R. Fox, *Hollywood, Mayfair and all that jazz* (1975) · A. McCarthy, *The dance band era* (1971) · H. Francis, *Roy Fox, 1936–1938* (1975) [disc notes, World Records SHB33] · m. cert. [Eileen O'Donnell] · d. cert. · A. Clegg, *The bands that matter: Roy Fox* (1970) [disc notes, Decca ECM 2045]
Likenesses photograph, Decca Record Company, London · photographs, BBC · photographs, repro. in *Melody Maker*

Fox, Samson (1838–1903), mechanical and chemical engineer, and benefactor, born at Bowling, near Bradford, Yorkshire, on 11 July 1838, was one of three sons of James Fox, a Leeds cloth-mill worker, and his wife, Sarah Pearson. From the age of ten he worked with his father at the mill; but, showing mechanical aptitude, he was soon apprenticed to the Leeds firm of Smith, Beacock, and Tannett, machine-tool makers, where he became foreman and later traveller. While there Fox designed and patented several tools for the machine cutting of bevelled gear and for the manufacture of trenails. He married on 18 May 1859 Marie Ann, daughter of Charles and Alice Slinger. The couple had one son and two daughters. Subsequently he started with his brother and another partner the firm of Fox, Brother, and Refitt, manufacturing special machine tools at the Silver Cross engineering works.

In 1874 Fox founded the Leeds Forge Company, acting as managing director until 1896, and being appointed chairman in May 1903. In 1877 he patented the Fox corrugated boiler furnaces (by which the resisting power to external pressure was greatly increased), the plates being hammered by means of swage blocks under a steam hammer. This invention led to the practical application of triple expansion engines to marine boilers. The steamship *Pretoria*, built in 1878, was the first ocean-going steamer to be fitted with Fox's corrugated flues. Machinery for rolling in place of hammering was undertaken in 1882, and a Siemens steel plant laid down.

Fox took out, in 1886, patents for the manufacture of pressed steel underframes for railway wagons instead of the old wrought-iron frames. Demand for the improved form of rolling stock led to great extension of the business in Leeds, and to the establishment of a factory at Joliet, near Chicago. There the first pressed steel cars used in America were made, as well as the 'Fox' pressed steel bogie trucks. The American business grew rapidly and new works were erected at Pittsburgh, which were merged in 1889 to form the Pressed Steel Car Company.

Fox was the first to use water-gas on a large scale for metallurgical and lighting purposes to reduce his manufacturing costs. The plant which he set up in September 1887 was soon producing 40,000 cubic feet per hour of water-gas, which was cheaper than ordinary coal gas, and had a far greater heating and lighting power. He was made president of the British Water-Gas Syndicate upon its formation in 1888, but it went into liquidation in 1893. In 1894 he produced the first carbide of calcium for making acetylene gas by the method discovered by T. L. Willson in America in 1888. He was the pioneer of the acetylene industry in Europe, for which works were set up at Foyers, Inverness-shire.

Fox became a member of the Institution of Mechanical Engineers in 1875 and of the Institution of Civil Engineers in 1881. A member of the Society of Arts from 1879, he was awarded in 1885 the society's Howard gold medal for his invention of corrugated iron flues. An enthusiastic lover of music, he gave in 1889 the sum of £45,000 for the new buildings of the Royal College of Music, South Kensington, which were opened by the prince of Wales on 2 July 1894. His benefaction gave rise in 1897 to a prolonged libel action, in which Fox was plaintiff, against Jerome K. Jerome and the publishers of *To-Day*, for printing articles in the paper (May–August 1894 and January 1896) which reflected on Fox's conduct of his business and accused Fox of giving large sums to the college in order to give a wrong impression of his commercial prosperity. After sixteen days' trial, the verdict was found for plaintiff without costs, the defendants undertaking not to republish the libel.

Fox took a leading part in the political and municipal

life of Leeds. He lived at Grove House, Harrogate, and was for three years in succession (1889–91) mayor of that town, which he also represented on the West Riding county council. He was JP for Leeds and Harrogate, and was a member of the Légion d'honneur. On his return from a tour in Canada and America, Fox died of blood poisoning at Daisy Bank, Walsall, Staffordshire, on 24 October 1903, and was buried at Woodhouse cemetery, Leeds.

W. B. OWEN, *rev.* IAN ST JOHN

Sources PICE, 155 (1903–4), 430–31 · *The Times* (26 Oct 1903) · *Institution of Mechanical Engineers: Proceedings* (1903), 919–21 · *Journal of the Society of Arts*, 51 (1902–3), 951 · Leeds Forge Company · private information (1912) · CGPLA Eng. & Wales (1904)
Likenesses marble bust, Royal College of Music · portrait, Grove House, Harrogate, Yorkshire · portrait, Leeds Forge, Leeds, Yorkshire
Wealth at death £156,722 8s. 6d.: probate, 16 Jan 1904, CGPLA Eng. & Wales

Fox, Sir Stephen (1627–1716), financier and government official, was born in Farley, Wiltshire, the seventh of ten children of William Fox (*d.* 1652) and his wife, Margaret Pavey. His parents were of modest wealth and seem to have lived on the lower margins of gentility. Fox received some education with the support of a more prosperous great-uncle, attending the choir school in Salisbury until the age of thirteen. By his own account he had, at that age, acquired the capacity to compose Latin verse and to dance, suggesting some hopes of a gentlemanly career, but he did not attend either university or one of the inns of court. Instead he followed his brother John to court. John was a musician who had gained employment in the chapel of the prince of Wales and Fox joined him as an unpaid assistant, serving as a page-boy. It was from these humble beginnings that he rose to become perhaps the richest commoner in England, a close associate of monarchs and chief ministers, and the longest-serving Treasury commissioner of his age.

Royal service and accumulation of wealth, 1642–1673 Fox apparently found favour quickly at court and was allowed to play with the royal children on occasions. When civil war broke out in 1642 he stayed in London with the younger princes and princesses, taking over the duties of closet keeper in the chapel of St James's from his brother John who went north with the royal party. As royal fortunes deteriorated he found service with a series of royalist aristocrats including Henry, Lord Percy, with whom he was present at the battle of Cropredy Bridge in 1644. By 1646 he was serving under Percy, who was master of the horse to the prince of Wales, holding the post of gentleman of the horses, a position of some responsibility. In 1649 his total wealth was £85, all of which he lent to his brother John who needed it for the support of his wife and children. During the late 1640s Fox had been in regular attendance on the prince of Wales and he was with him in the Netherlands in 1650 when a change of regime there led to the withdrawal of support for the exiled court. This led to the sale of the prince's horses and forced Fox to return to England. The low point of his adult fortunes came in 1651, at home in Wiltshire with his brother, who

was a fugitive after the battle of Worcester, contemplating a life as a small farmer. However, during that year he met and married Elizabeth Whittle (1627–1696) and he was saved from a life of farming by the offer of service in the household of the duke of Devonshire as keeper of the duke's privy purse, an offer conveyed to him by Thomas Hobbes.

After less than a year Fox was back in royal service in France, joining the court at the nadir of its fortunes. In July 1654 the court left France supported by a pension supplied by Mazarin, anxious to be rid of the diplomatic embarrassment of hosting the exiled court. Fox was appointed to handle these moneys and his careful husbanding of the meagre resources of the court through the rest of the 1650s saved the king from serious embarrassment. In return for his services he was granted arms in 1658, taking as his motto 'Faire sans dire' ('Deeds not words'), a sentiment that seems to have guided him through his subsequent official career. Clearly, through his service in the 1640s and 1650s he had established a reputation for honesty and dependability and he was with the king when Charles stepped ashore at Dover in 1660.

Fox's hopes at the Restoration were rather disappointed. He had been the chief executive officer of the court in exile and seems to have hoped to become cofferer in the restored court. Position in the impoverished court in exile had not been subject to the same intense competition that existed back in England in the 1660s, however, and his lack of social status clearly ruled him out of the highest positions in the court. He was appointed second clerk comptroller under the board of green cloth, an office worth about £600 as compared with the £2000 promised by the cofferership. He served as clerk of green cloth until 1689, with only one interruption in 1679, but he never secured the cofferership. None the less, such a career would have been some achievement for a man from his relatively humble beginnings and whose fortunes had been at such a low ebb in the early 1650s. In addition to his household service Fox was used by the king to make secret service payments, payments to individuals which avoided the cumbersome exchequer process. This was a source of modest further profit and a further indication of the trust in which he was held.

The making of Fox was, however, the formation of the king's guards in 1661. The decision to retain a force of 3500 soldiers to protect the king was a rushed one, taken in the aftermath of the Venner rising. The position of paymaster was a new one, over which there could be no prior claims, and the appointment of Fox seems to have reflected the king's preference. As paymaster Fox developed a system of pay which led to the rapid accumulation of a vast fortune. The problem was that no funds were available specifically to meet the £123,000 bill for the guards. Like many other disbursing officials Fox was issued with exchequer tallies rather than cash, and he was forced to pledge or sell them at a discount on the money market in order to raise the money actually to pay the troops. This he did, borrowing more and more on the crown's behalf, as well as advancing some of his own money to the commanders at interest. In August 1662 the commanders sought to regularize this, proposing an 'Undertaking' whereby an individual would guarantee to advance the soldiers their full wages on time in return for 12*d*. in the pound (5 per cent) of their pay (the 'poundage'), recovering the money from the exchequer when it was available. Fox was initially an intermediary in the search for such an individual but, when no one could be found for this risky enterprise, he took it on himself. The attraction was that he received his percentage on all sums paid to the soldiers but only paid interest on what he needed to borrow. So long as he received fairly regular sums from the government he could hope to pay less in interest on borrowing to pay the soldiers than the 5 per cent that he claimed from the total bill. The government benefited because it was, effectively, borrowing to pay the soldiers without paying interest, and the soldiers received regular pay at a cost of only 5 per cent for the privilege. By the standards of the day this was not a corrupt or improper arrangement. It soon became clear, however, that the government was falling considerably in arrears and that Fox might be paying more in interest than he received in the poundage. The government agreed to pay interest on money that was more than two months in arrears, covering his borrowing costs, while still allowing the exchequer two months interest-free borrowing. This took much of the risk out of the operation and, as he accumulated profit, Fox could put more of his own money into the advances. Because he was increasingly using his own money, he thereby reduced his interest costs and further increased his profit margins. As he ploughed money back into the Undertaking during the 1660s his profit margins continually increased and the rate of his capital accumulation accelerated. Knighted in 1665 he grew rich at a dizzying rate and he was able to advance money to other departments too—to the garrisons, on a large scale to the household in 1668–9, and for troops in the Second Anglo-Dutch War. He survived the stop of the exchequer in 1672 partly because many of the government debts he held were not affected and partly because his importance to the government ensured that those that were affected were none the less honoured. A generation of financiers suffered what turned out to be terribly damaging blows to their business, but Fox was not among them. In 1673 he advanced £471,700 to the government for various purposes—a staggering sum for a man who had been worth only a few hundred pounds in 1660.

Treasury commissioner and investments The principal source of revenue which secured Fox's borrowing was the excise and in the late 1670s he was involved in a struggle for control of the receipts, a struggle which he eventually won. Between 1674 and 1676, therefore, he was the government's biggest creditor and the controller of one of the main sources of government revenue. As a result of this prominence he became centrally involved in national party politics for the only time in his life. Danby, it seems, was suspicious of this concentration of power and engineered Fox's dismissal as paymaster. Fox had been MP for

Salisbury in 1661 and Danby's role in his fall may have influenced him in supporting the impeachment of the king's minister in 1678. That intervention in politics in turn cost Fox his household position, an indication of the king's displeasure. In 1679 he was involved in a parliamentary storm over secret service payments but, having survived that, he appeared once again indispensable to the government. He was restored to the green cloth in April and to the paymastership in May, only to relinquish the post in November on his appointment to the Treasury commission. He was to serve as a commissioner until 1702, when he was seventy-five, with only two brief intermissions. This short involvement in national politics signalled his arrival as a figure of considerable significance; his appointment to the Treasury commission was followed by the abandonment of the Undertaking, perhaps on his advice—he surely knew exactly how much money could be saved thereby.

By 1680 Fox was a man of great wealth and considerable political importance. From the early 1670s he had been buying up land, particularly in Wiltshire and east Somerset, and fee-farm rents. There were, of course, standard motives in doing this, particularly the security and status offered by extensive landholdings, but the latter was probably of less significance for Fox. It seems clear that he was offered a peerage at least once, and probably more than once, but declined such elevation. In his family life, however, he was less than blessed and by 1680 it seemed that his line would not be continued. Of the seven boys born to his first wife only two reached adulthood, one of whom, William, died in 1680. At that point his only surviving son, Charles, was thought to be so corpulent that he would not produce an heir, and the prediction proved correct. This dynastic disappointment coincided with the end of his attempts to acquire a provincial estate. None the less, his rapidly increasing wealth made his daughters attractive catches: at the age of twelve his daughter Jane was wooed by the duchess of Sunderland on behalf of her son; Jane later married the even more eligible earl of Northampton. Elizabeth, her elder sister, had already married into the Cornwallis family, less wealthy but a distinguished lineage none the less. Although he was concerned to protect the interests of his wider family, particularly the relatively impecunious Cornwallis branch, Fox made no serious attempt to establish a large provincial estate after the 1680s, suggesting that his motive had initially been dynastic rather than personal glory. His financial position in 1686 was staggering—his assets were worth about £380,000, producing £23,000 per annum—but land constituted only a third of the total value.

Fox's investments in the 1680s and 1690s were more diverse and he developed a balanced portfolio of interests. One of the benefits of household and government office was the patronage to which it gave access, and he seems to have taken care to look after his relatives and friends through his disposition of the patronage which he controlled. He did not keep a particularly extravagant household: he extended his apartments in Whitehall and kept a house at Chiswick but he never took up the life of a country gentleman. His charitable endeavours were limited but significant, and they were all carried out during his life. The most significant was his important role in the establishment of the Chelsea Hospital—he both found the means to pay for it and bought the plot of land on which it stood. He also built a church and almshouse in his home village of Farley and tried, without success as it turned out, to set up a grammar school there. His legacy in 1716 was orderly and a very accurate account of his assets is possible. His total wealth at that point was £174,000, yielding about £9000 per annum. Although this was a huge sum for a village boy whose parents could not afford to send him to university or to the inns of court, it was smaller than his fortune had been in 1686, seemingly because he had alienated assets looking after his family.

Fox's wealth and governmental experience had by 1680 made him particularly expert in financial affairs. Throughout his time in government office, however, he was an administrator rather than a politician. He was not a privy councillor and although he was elected to parliament several times, serving as the member for Salisbury, Westminster, and Cricklade during his career, he seems to have been a reluctant speaker. Simply by dint of his importance in government he became embroiled in party politics in the later 1670s, and he was out of favour again following the revolution of 1688. He did not sit in the Convention Parliament, so he was not required to take a public stand on the change of monarch, but his closeness to the regime meant that he was not immediately in William III's favour. He had been, however, William's London banker since 1680, and his expertise soon proved attractive to the regime with the result that he was back on the Treasury commission by 1690, serving continuously thereafter until retirement. He was, briefly, first lord of the Treasury in 1696-7.

Retirement and assessment In 1702 Fox finally retired from public office, the change of monarch allowing him the opportunity to leave the Treasury commission without causing offence. His final dealings with the household left a rather sour taste—having suggested economies in the establishments he found that his nominees were ousted from offices by his successors and he once again failed to secure the cofferership. In 1702 he lost his parliamentary seat and the Fox influence at Cricklade seems to have dissolved by 1710. Retirement did not, it seems, suit him and it was a blessing in many ways when he married again after the death of his first wife in 1696. His 1703 marriage to Christian Hope (1679-1718) brought four children, the last born when he was eighty, and three of them—Stephen, Henry, and Charlotte—survived into adulthood. Although this did not lead him to re-energize his efforts to establish a country estate it did lead to a redistribution of his legacy in favour of his second family. His son Henry *Fox, first Baron Holland of Foxley (1705-1774), built on this fortune and did establish himself as a substantial country gentleman while Henry's son, Charles James *Fox (1749-1806), was to become more famous than his grandfather. Sir Stephen Fox died in 1716 and was buried on 7

November in the new church he had paid for in Farley where a memorial tablet still remains.

An important part of Fox's financial success appears to have been a reputation for honesty and integrity, and a personal attractiveness. Many of his private loans were made to aristocrats who found in him a courtier who knew finances, rather than a parvenu. A number of accusations have subsequently been levied against him—for example that he exploited the soldiers, or that he lent ultimately ruinous amounts of money to Sir Edward Hungerford with the intention of foreclosing on him and acquiring his lands. By the standards of the day, however, there was nothing dishonest about his conduct and, despite his prominence in government affairs over such a very long period, there were no serious accusations of corruption or abuse against him. The surviving papers do not offer as much insight into his personality as they do into his business, a fact which is in itself revealing of the man. But it seems clear from his career that he possessed a combination of virtues which fitted him for life as a financier with court connections. A portrait of Fox aged about forty-three, by Sir Peter Lely, reveals a handsome man with strong features. A court education, and command of languages, provided the gloss that made him acceptable in aristocratic circles; government connections reassured lenders in the money markets who were reluctant themselves to run the risk of dealing directly with government offices; and all those who dealt with him seem to have found him trustworthy. His vices seem to have been a sometimes pronounced wish to get his own way and a sensitivity to slights or underestimates of his qualities. In general, however, given his rise and prominence, his popularity is remarkable and most contemporary comment upon him was very positive.   MICHAEL J. BRADDICK

Sources C. Clay, *Public finance and private wealth: the career of Sir Stephen Fox, 1627-1716* (1978) · *Memoirs of the life of Sir Stephen Fox* (1717) · G. O. Nichols, 'English government borrowing, 1660-1688', *Journal of British Studies*, 10/2 (1970-71), 83-104 · G. O. Nichols, 'Intermediaries and the development of English government borrowing: the case of Sir John James and Major Robert Huntington, 1675-79', *Business History*, 29 (1987), 27-46 · G. O. Nichols, 'The development of English repayment and interest rates: an examination of government borrowing and the loans of Sir Stephen Fox, 1667-1674', *Revue Internationale de la Banque*, 30/31 (1985), 247-65 · C. D. Chandaman, *The English public revenue, 1660-1688* (1975) · H. Roseveare, *The treasury: the evolution of a British institution* (1969) · H. G. Roseveare, 'The advancement of the king's credit, 1660-1672: a study in economic, political and administrative history based mainly on the career of Sir George Downing, knight and baronet', PhD diss., U. Cam., 1962 · J. P. Ferris, 'Fox, Stephen', HoP, *Commons, 1660-90*, 2.356-9

Archives Royal Arch., papers | BL, corresp. with John Ellis, Add. MSS 28875-28894 · BL, Holland House papers, corresp., Add. MSS 51318-51336 · Castle Ashby, Northampton, letters to fourth earl of Northampton · Chatsworth House, Derbyshire, letters to granddaughter, Lady Elizabeth Compton · Dorset RO, Ilchester collection, official and business papers, D. 124 · NL Scot., accounts and corresp. with Sir James Stansfield

Likenesses P. Lely, oils, c.1670, NPG · R. Earlom, mezzotint, 1701 (after J. Baker), BM, NPG · J. Baker, oils, Royal Chelsea Hospital, London · J. Simon, mezzotint (after J. Baker), BM, NPG

Wealth at death £174,024: Clay, *Public finance*, table XII, pp. 324-5

Fox, Sydney Harry (1899–1930), matricide, was born on 2 January 1899 at Great Fransham, Norfolk, the fourth and youngest son of Rosaline Fox, *née* Rallison (1866–1929), a dressmaker, and daughter of a farm labourer. She had married William George Fox, a railway signalman, but left him for a railway porter, who was reputedly Fox's father. She seems to have been a genial woman of little intelligence or financial morality. Sydney Fox (who suffered epileptic fits until the age of seven) was educated at the parish school of Great Fransham, where he lived until the age of thirteen. Around 1910 he was birched after keeping money he had collected in a door-to-door charity collection. His illegitimacy encouraged him to indulge fantasies that he was of noble paternity.

For three years Fox worked in London as 'an angel-faced page-boy' to an elderly Irish baronet, Sir John Leslie. He became a pet of the family, and was nicknamed Cupid because of his charming looks. After making overtures to an elderly housemaid, he acquired her life savings. Next he stole some Leslie silver, together with the family bible, 'and used the signatures for his own purposes' (Leslie, 117). After this disgrace he became a ledger clerk in the Charing Cross branch of Cox's Bank but was dismissed in November 1916 for stealing a cheque book, which he used to buy meals at the Jermyn Court Hotel. As a condition of not being prosecuted, he enlisted as a storeman in the Army Ordnance Corps in December 1916, and served in southern England.

In 1917–18 Fox served three months with hard labour for obtaining money by false pretences from a Brighton grocer. A resumption of epileptic fits necessitated his hospitalization from June 1918 to February 1919. These fits (together with headaches) continued throughout the 1920s and made him unfit for regular employment, to which he was temperamentally averse. A medical report of 1920 noted his 'backward development, simple-minded[ness]', but another in 1926 judged him 'alert, anxious' (Ministry of Pensions to directorate of public prosecutions, 9 Jan 1930, PRO DPP 1/90). Having become a clerk in the Parliament Street branch of Grindlay's Bank in July 1919, '20 days later Fox commenced a series of forgeries which displayed remarkable ingenuity for so young a person' ('Antecedents of Sydney Harry Fox', 1930, PRO DPP 1/90). In consequence he served eight months' hard labour in 1919–20. Later in 1920 he was given six months for obtaining from Harrods a gold cigarette case and fine clothes by using the name of a regular customer. In 1922 he was sentenced to twelve months for fraudulently obtaining credit from a London hotel. In 1924 he was sentenced to twelve months' hard labour for larceny and fraud.

When at liberty Fox turned his homosexuality to profit, and had relations with older men. On two occasions officers were disgraced when policemen found their letters to Fox. One Scotland Yard detective, describing Fox's 'squalid and terrifying' sexual career, stated that he lived off 'men of wealth who should have known better'. The officer showed Fox's 'photograph in female dress with his beautiful eyes upturned to Heaven' to Shane Leslie: 'it was indeed the corruption of the lily' (Leslie, 117). Fox relished the gaiety of theatrical dressing-rooms and supper parties with men friends. Among his admirers was James Agate, who found him 'a charming young man, of a gay and debonair manner, and a free and open-handed disposition' (Agate, 93). In 1927 Fox became the gigolo of a middle-aged Australian married woman, Charlotte Isabel Morse, daughter of George Morgan, with whom his mother took a flat at Southsea. After insuring her life for £3000, and inducing her to make a will in his favour, he unsuccessfully attempted to gas her. When they parted, he stole some jewellery; for this crime in 1928 he was imprisoned for fifteen months. Despite his talent in charming women, he could not bear his barrister 'to think that he had ever gone with a woman save for the money he might get from her. He took a pride from the fact that his pleasure lay entirely with his own sex' (Jesse, 3).

On his release from prison, Fox rescued his mother from Portsmouth poorhouse in March 1929. They began a precarious existence, staying together in luxury hotels where they bilked their bills. Progressively they pawned their belongings until almost destitute. Occasionally he visited London (where he used the Strand Palace Hotel as a rendezvous) and probably had earnings from sexual services to men. He played the part of a devoted son, and treated Rosaline Fox well until he saw a way of improving his comforts by encompassing her destruction. On 16 October 1929 Fox took two bedrooms at the Hotel Metropole, Margate. Two life insurance policies worth £3000 existed on his mother's life. He renewed these on 21 October to expire at midnight on 23 October. On the latter evening Fox strangled his mother, lit a match to ignite newspapers piled under her armchair, and ensured that her body was found twenty minutes before the expiry of the policies. He was apparently influenced by reports of the accidental death on 11 October of Walburga, Lady Paget, and he hoped it would be thought that his mother had suffocated in an accidental fire. Suspicions hardened after he claimed on the insurance policies: having been charged with murder on 9 January, he was tried at Lewes before Sir Sidney Rowlatt (12–21 March 1930). The prosecution was led by the attorney-general, Sir William Jowitt. The circumstantial evidence was powerful: Fox's testimony on 19 March irreparably harmed his case. There were no grounds for appeal. He was hanged on 8 April 1930 at Maidstone prison.   RICHARD DAVENPORT-HINES

Sources PRO, DPP 1/90 · F. Tennyson Jesse, ed., *Trial of Sidney Harry Fox* (1934) · S. Leslie, *The film of memory* (1938) · J. Agate, *Ego 9: concluding the autobiography of James Agate* (1948) · D. G. Browne and E. V. Tullett, *Bernard Spilsbury: his life and cases* (1951), 336–43 · R. Wild and D. Curtis-Bennett, *"Curtis"* (1937), 262–6 · b. cert. · d. cert.

Archives PRO, DPP 1/90–94

Likenesses photograph, 1930, repro. in Tennyson Jesse, *Trial of Sidney Harry Fox*

Fox, Terence Robert Corelli (1912–1962), chemical engineer, was born in London on 2 May 1912, the only son of Corelli Fox, electrical engineer, and his wife, Mabel Ballard;

he had two sisters. He was educated at Regent Street Polytechnic Technical School, and in 1930 he entered Jesus College, Cambridge, to study for the mechanical sciences tripos. In that examination he had unparalleled success, getting a starred first in 1933, with all possible prizes. Fox's tripos result may have coloured his later views: he retained a perhaps unwarranted faith in the efficacy of examinations.

Fox then spent four years as a technical assistant in the Billingham division of ICI. In 1937 the professor of mechanical sciences, Charles Inglis, persuaded Fox to return to Cambridge to take up a junior position as a demonstrator in the engineering laboratory; he became a fellow of King's College in 1941, and a lecturer in 1945. He was an outstanding teacher. His lectures were vividly given, for he had histrionic gifts: the laws of mechanics were sometimes illustrated by practical demonstrations involving the dynamics of the lecturer, as when he propelled himself across the floor on a chair by the swinging action of his legs which did not touch the ground.

Fox's great opportunity came in 1945 when Cambridge University accepted the offer from Shell of about £450,000 for a chemical engineering department. His appointment in 1946 as Shell professor caused a stir in the small world of chemical engineers, as it was then. The appointment was in many ways remarkable: Fox had published no research papers, nor did he ever; he was not at that time an established member of the chemical engineering profession.

Fox immediately took to his job with enthusiasm, spending the first year in the United States where the subject was well established; he returned to plan the Cambridge course for which the first students were accepted in 1948. Fox's course included enough of the existing technological material to be acceptable to industrialists, but the technology was taught in such a way as to illustrate the application of basic scientific principles. He took a similar approach to the style of teaching experiments. In their gift, Shell had allowed for the purchase of large equipment, but Fox insisted on keeping the capital, using the interest for research and for small experiments to teach principles rather than practice.

The building to house the Shell department was largely designed by Fox, whose engineering and artistic talents would have made him an admirable architect. Though he did not publish any papers himself, he promoted research in his department; he gave shelter and encouragement to Francis T. Bacon with his fuel-cell team at a crucial stage in the development of the cell which eventually went to the moon; he supervised a number of research students, who were devoted to him; and he actively encouraged his staff to do research, though it was a little bizarre to be told, on having derived some new piece of theory, that 'it would make a good tripos question'. Most of the books published from the Shell department owed something to Fox.

His desire for rigour often made him a trying colleague. He found it difficult to delegate fully, and it was said that he would use as much effort in spending 10s. as £10,000.

These traits naturally led to strain and he suffered a succession of nervous breakdowns in the early 1950s which caused his resignation from the Shell chair in 1959.

Fox was tall and slender with fine-drawn, dark good looks that indicated his Italian ancestry. He had all the outward marks of a brilliant King's man: widely read, and an entertaining conversationalist. But he was a reserved man with few close friends. He never married. He died in the National Hospital for Nervous Diseases, Queen Square, London, on 5 October 1962.   J. F. DAVIDSON, *rev.*

Sources *The Times* (6 Oct 1962) · personal knowledge (1981) · *WWW* · *CGPLA Eng. & Wales* (1963) · d. cert.
Likenesses photograph, repro. in *Chemical Engineer* (Dec 1984), 45
Wealth at death £12,067 15s.: administration, 25 Nov 1963, *CGPLA Eng. & Wales*

Fox, Sir Theodore Fortescue (1899–1989), medical editor, was born on 26 November 1899 at Strathpeffer spa, Ross and Cromartyshire, the youngest in the family of two sons and three daughters of Dr Robert Fortescue Fox, a rheumatologist at the spa hospital, and his wife, Catharine Stuart McDougall. After Leighton Park School, Robbie, as he was known, served with the Friends' Ambulance Unit in 1918, and then in 1919 won a scholarship to Pembroke College, Cambridge, where he achieved a second class in part one of the natural sciences tripos (1921). He then obtained his LRCS and MRCP at the London Hospital in 1924. After one appointment as a houseman at the same hospital, he became a ship's surgeon before joining *The Lancet* in 1925. There he remained until 1964, except for his service in the Royal Army Medical Corps from 1939 to 1944. He became BChir in 1926, proceeded MD in 1936, and was elected FRCP in 1946, two years after becoming editor of *The Lancet*.

Fox was an excellent medical editor. He wrote well, could readily reduce a full-length book to a three-page article, and conducted negotiations with wit and urbanity. The rate at which his assistant editors came and went reflected his exceptionally high standards. Fox's *Lancet* crucially influenced two major medical issues: the equitable delivery of health care, and publishing and interpreting breakthroughs in medical research. During negotiations (1944–8) about the setting up of a national health service his low-key editorials balanced the advantages and disadvantages, and eventually helped to persuade the profession to join the scheme. So esteemed then were Fox's contributions, both publicly and behind the scenes, that he was offered a knighthood, but he declined lest he compromised *The Lancet*'s independence. He thought that any state system might threaten the doctor–patient relationship, something he had found in the USSR in 1936 and recorded in *The Lancet* and his MD thesis; this theme resurfaced in post-war accounts of visits to the USA, China, and the USSR again, as well as in major lectures (including the Harveian oration of the Royal College of Physicians in 1965). *The Lancet*'s scientific articles reported many post-war revolutionary discoveries, including the antibiotic explosion and unrecognized childhood conditions from adverse influences during pregnancy, such as thalidomide or X-irradiation. Fox judged papers without asking for expert opinions, a challengeable policy, but he took only a few days to decide whether to publish a piece, and, equally attractively, *The Lancet* printed articles within a few weeks of receipt.

Fox recruited experts to explain difficult concepts in editorials (whose anonymity also challenged current practices), which were then rewritten for non-experts. His *Lancet* also had space for debate, for developing new hypotheses, and for reminding readers that the traditional killers, such as famine, still co-existed with diseases of affluence. Unlike many editors, Fox insisted that campaigns should be short and crisp—to bore readers was to risk losing everything. He explained these policies in his Heath Clark lectures in 1963 (published in 1965 as *Crisis in Communication*), suggesting that the literature explosion could be contained by dividing journals into archival and newspaper forms.

All this made Fox's *Lancet* acknowledged as the best medical journal in the world, a most readable and prestigious exemplar, a fact that was reflected by the highest citation rate of any journal. Moreover, his public persona as a fighter of causes, and as an engaging after-dinner speaker enabled him to promote new concepts (such as universal family planning, health centres, and postgraduate medical education) in other ways. Fox was prominent in the Royal College of Physicians and, uniquely for a non-clinician, was a (narrowly defeated) candidate for the presidency in 1962. Knighted in 1962, and given honorary degrees by the universities of Birmingham (DLitt., 1966) and Glasgow (LLD, 1958), after retirement in 1964 he was director of the Family Planning Association (1965–7).

Tall and thin, with a slight stoop, Fox had an attractive mild stammer, often (like his lifelong friend Russell Brain) speaking after a disconcerting and lengthy silence, but then with good sense and wit. A puritan in most things, particularly clothes, food, and drink, his main interests after *The Lancet* were genealogy, the countryside, and his garden in Rotherfield, Sussex. As prizes for his pre-war intellectual parlour games he produced old copies of the rival *British Medical Journal* still in their wrappers.

In 1935 Fox married Margaret Eveline, daughter of William McDougall, Presbyterian minister. They had four sons, the youngest of whom, Robin, became editor of *The Lancet* in 1991. His wife died in 1970 and his second and eldest sons died in 1970 and 1983 respectively. He died at Rotherfield on 19 June 1989.   STEPHEN LOCK, *rev.*

Sources *The Guardian* (22 June 1989) • *The Times* (23 June 1989) • *BMJ* (1 July 1989), 47–9 • *The Lancet* (1 July 1989) • private information (1996) • personal knowledge (1996) • *CGPLA Eng. & Wales* (1989)
Wealth at death under £100,000: probate, 2 Oct 1989, *CGPLA Eng. & Wales*

Fox, Timothy (1629/30–1710), clergyman and ejected minister, was born in Birmingham, the son of Edward Fox, and educated at Aston and at Birmingham, under John Bryan and Mr Billingsley. On 23 March 1647, aged seventeen, he was admitted to Christ's College, Cambridge. He matriculated in the following year but appears not to have taken a degree. On 6 July 1650 he was presented under

great seal to the rectory of Drayton Bassett, Staffordshire; he was ordained by Thomas Porter, at Whitchurch in Shropshire, and compounded for the first fruits at Drayton on 24 February 1651, surety being given by Thomas Fox of Tamworth. He refused, however, to take the engagement. By the time of his ejection in 1662 under the Act of Uniformity Fox had a wife, Frances (who survived her husband), and five young children to support, but having settled in nearby Tamworth, 'by his Pen, and help of Relations, he had a comfortable Livelihood until the Oxford Act, which forc'd him to remove and rent a Farm in Derbyshire' (Calamy, *Abridgement*, 2.626). In 1672 he was licensed to preach at his home in Ticknall, Derbyshire. From May to November 1684 Fox was held prisoner in Derby gaol, not, as Calamy reports, for any religious activity, but merely for visiting his son, then an apprentice in that town. At the time of the Monmouth rebellion in 1685 he was imprisoned again, this time in Chester gaol, without cause stated, and was released after a month only on bond of £600. In 1689 his house in Cauldwell, Derbyshire, was certified as a place of worship and during 1690–91 he appears to have been preaching at Hartshorne and other locations in Derbyshire, and once a month at Appleby in Leicestershire. Fox's will of 1707 was signed as of Cauldwell; he died on 30 May 1710 and was buried at Tamworth. An inventory valued his goods at £312 6s. 6d. Of his children, it seems that Jane was his favourite, since Fox bequeathed her £100 in money and a share in his property—more than his eldest son, Samuel; Lettice, Joseph, and Thomas were either provided for earlier, or they must have displeased him, for each received only £5.

GORDON GOODWIN, *rev.* STEPHEN WRIGHT

Sources *Calamy rev.* • Venn, *Alum. Cant.* • A. Gordon, ed., *Freedom after ejection: a review (1690–1692) of presbyterian and congregational nonconformity in England and Wales* (1917) • will and inventory, Lichfield RO, B/C/11/1710 • E. Calamy, ed., *An abridgement of Mr. Baxter's history of his life and times, with an account of the ministers, &c., who were ejected after the Restauration of King Charles II*, 2nd edn, 2 vols. (1713) • E. Calamy, *A continuation of the account of the ministers ... who were ejected and silenced after the Restoration in 1660*, 2 vols. (1727) • *The nonconformist's memorial ... originally written by ... Edmund Calamy*, ed. S. Palmer, [3rd edn], 3 vols. (1802–3) • J. Peile, *Biographical register of Christ's College, 1505–1905, and of the earlier foundation, God's House, 1448–1505*, ed. [J. A. Venn], 1 (1910)
Wealth at death £312 6s. 6d.: will and inventory, Lichfield RO, B/C/11/1710

Fox, Uffa (1898–1972), naval architect and boat builder, was born on 15 January 1898 at East Cowes in the Isle of Wight, the only son and second of the three children (another son and daughter died in childhood) of Arthur Walder Fox, a skilled carpenter engaged on the construction of Osborne House, and his wife, Lucy Cobbold, a housekeeper to Queen Victoria in one of the annexes to Osborne House. He was educated at the nearby village school of Whippingham until the age of fourteen when he became a boat-building apprentice at Cowes with S. E. Saunders, builder of fast motor boats, hydroplanes, and flying boats. He studied naval architecture and mathematics at evening school. As a youth his interests were those of the countryside and the sea, particularly Sea Scouting. His favourite sport was cricket and as a chorister at St James's Church he developed a love of music which lasted throughout his life. In the First World War he served in the Royal Naval Air Service for nearly two years.

After the war Fox had a variety of jobs, sailed twice to the United States, and started work on his own as a boat builder. In 1925 he married Alma Philips, whose father ran the Old East Medina Mill on the Isle of Wight. She divorced him in 1939 and he married Laura Louisa, Mrs Enoch, a widow from Bembridge, Isle of Wight, who divorced him in 1945. In 1956 he married Yvonne, daughter of Édouard Bernard, of Paris, the widow of a French industrialist, who survived him. There were no children from any of the marriages.

Fox's first major successes as a designer were in the 14 foot racing dinghy class. He concentrated on trying to produce a fast planing boat. Ariel, his first design, won every race in her class in Cowes week in 1925. Rodicut, his second design, although not yet carrying out his intention, was second in the race for the Prince of Wales cup in 1927. In 1928 Avenger, the initiator of the planing dinghies, captured fifty-two firsts, two seconds, and three thirds out of fifty-seven starts. With the deep V-shaped hull for the first third of her length Fox introduced a new feature into such boats which greatly increased their speed. This was widely copied and made him world famous. All these triumphs were greatly assisted by the fact that he was himself a first-class helmsman. He used his experience with these dinghies in designing the canoe in which he won both the American championship for paddling and sailing and the New York international canoe championship in 1933. It was the first occasion on which the latter trophy had left the United States since fifteen presentations in 1866.

In the Second World War Fox's main contribution to the war effort was the design and construction of the first parachuted airborne lifeboat which proved to be of great value in air–sea rescue work. Much of his time was taken up with organizing the Local Defence Volunteers, who became the Home Guard on 22 July 1940, of which he was a lieutenant in the Isle of Wight. When peace was restored Fox returned to designing dinghies. His 12 foot Firefly won the Royal Yachting Association design competition and was selected as a class for the 1948 Olympics. He then turned his attention to the creation of a planing keel-boat. The result was the Flying Fifteen—15 feet on the waterline, 20 feet overall with a draught of 2 feet 6 inches—a successful boat with which he achieved all his ambitions. It became well known not only to the sailing fraternity but also to the general public. The town of Cowes presented *Coweslip*, a Flying Fifteen, to Prince Philip, duke of Edinburgh, who sailed her with Fox, as later did Prince Charles, and she and the class were soon established as popular favourites.

In 1968 Fox designed the 22 foot Atlantic row boat *Britannia*, in which John Fairfax rowed across the Atlantic, and *Britannia II*, in which he crossed the Pacific in 1970, with both drawing on his wartime experience with the airborne lifeboat. Throughout his life he produced many one-off designs for individual clients, wrote a considerable number of articles, and published some ten books on maritime matters, including his reminiscences in two volumes, *Joys of Life* (1966) and *More Joys of Living* (1972). He was appointed a royal designer for industry in 1955 and made a CBE in 1959.

Uffa Fox is widely remembered as a naval architect—membership of the Royal Institution of Naval Architects was conferred on him in 1952, thus crowning the achievements of a boy denied the full formal education for this profession—but among his friends, who included members of the royal family, and those who lived in the Isle of Wight, he will be recalled as 'a character', one whose traits were often attractive but sometimes lacking in taste. At home he was always hospitable—he loved good food and wine, the latter sometimes a little too much so—and was invariably amusing. His ebullient nature displayed itself both in a jovial heartiness and in an explosive temper which at times he found difficult to control. At dinner parties he would launch into a sing-song which included his rendering of various sea shanties, some not well known, a number of which he recorded. He was free with wise advice to fellow sailors and showed innumerable kindnesses to those less robust than himself. Yet his attitude to others who dared to question his views or his actions, the well-known and unpleasant complications of his domestic life, his handling of his precarious and unpredictable financial affairs, and his abrasive attitude towards those in authority and those who were in his employment lost him some of the admiration and affection which his inventiveness, skill, determination, and honesty deserved. He died on 26 October 1972 at Alvechurch, Worcestershire.   EDWARD HEATH, rev.

Sources U. Fox, *Joys of life* (1966) · U. Fox, *More joys of living* (1972) · personal information (1986) · *The Times* (27 Oct 1972) · WWW · *CGPLA Eng. & Wales* (1973)
Archives FILM IWM FVA, actuality footage · IWM FVA, news footage | SOUND BL NSA, 'interview', BBC, 1971, 29 E BBC REC111M S1C7 · BL NSA, performance recordings
Wealth at death £49,786: probate, 10 Jan 1973, *CGPLA Eng. & Wales*

Fox, William (1736–1826), founder of the Sunday School Society, was born at Clapton, Gloucestershire, on 14 February 1736, the youngest of the eight children of James Fox (*d.* 1738/9), tenant farmer on Clapton Manor estate. Left fatherless, the eldest son took over the farm, while William was employed there by his elder brother to scare birds. His education was scanty, but when one of his brothers saw some verses he had written he decided that the boy should be given the opportunity to learn a trade. There are two versions of the next stage of his life: Joseph Ivimey, who knew Fox in later years, says that he was apprenticed in 1752 to a draper at Oxford, whereas the anonymous 'Memoir' in the *Sunday School Teachers' Magazine* (1830) says that the brother who saw the verses lived at York and apprenticed him to a draper of that city. Both writers then relate the somewhat unlikely sequel: that Fox, whose family were pious Baptists, so impressed his master that before his apprenticeship was completed his

William Fox (1736–1826), by Samuel Freeman, pubd 1827

after some years of decline it was absorbed into the Sunday School Union.

In 1787 Fox moved to Colchester, but the climate disagreed with his wife's health and after two years they moved to Islington, before moving once more in 1795, when Fox purchased the manor of Clapton, where two of his brothers still lived, and rented a house near by. He set up a free day school, and gave generously to the poor of the district, but had sold the estate by 1805. When the Baptist Society in London for the Encouragement and Support of Itinerant and Village Preaching (known from 1822 as the Baptist Home Missionary Society) was founded, Fox was its treasurer. In 1807 he bought the manor of Lechlade, where he resided until the deaths of his wife and a daughter. He passed his last years in Cirencester, where, deaf and infirm, he died on 1 April 1826; he was buried, alongside his wife and daughter, at Lechlade.

ANITA McCONNELL

Sources P. B. Cliff, *The rise and development of the Sunday school movement in England, 1780–1980* (1986) · J. Ivimey, *Memoir of William Fox esq., founder of the Sunday School Society* (1831) · 'Memoir of Mr William Fox, founder of the Sunday School Society', *Sunday School Teachers' Magazine*, new ser., 1 (1830), 258–67 · *VCH Gloucestershire*, 6.60; 7.112, 120 · W. T. Whitley, *A history of British Baptists* (1923) · T. W. Laqueur, *Religion and respectability* (1976)

Likenesses S. Freeman, stipple, pubd 1827, NPG [*see illus.*]

master transferred to Fox his house and shop, together with goods valued at £4000.

Fox married in 1761 the elder daughter of Jonathan Tabor, a merchant of Colchester, and three years later moved to London, where he established himself as a wholesaler, first in Leadenhall Street and later in Cheapside. As a wholesale merchant Fox travelled widely and this brought home to him the lack of education and spiritual poverty of the rural population. Fox, who by this time had been made a deacon of the Particular Baptists' Prescot Street Chapel, spoke at the monthly meetings of the Baptist Society in London, and had originally intended to set up day schools, but the magnitude of the task discouraged both clergy and laity. His endeavours to lobby members of parliament were similarly unproductive, but gradually he became aware of others who were campaigning on similar lines, notably Robert Raikes, whose establishment of Sunday schools had met with considerable success.

Recognizing that Raikes's scheme was both workable and economical, Fox called a meeting in London to canvass support for a society which would not evangelize, but would raise money for schools, bibles, and textbooks. His proposals were supported by Raikes and by other philanthropists, including Jonas Hanway, and the Sunday School Society was founded in September 1785, with the earl of Salisbury as president. The society's aims as set out by Fox were the prevention of vice, the encouragement of industry and virtue, and 'to make that part of the community, the country poor, happy—to lead them in the pleasant paths of religion … [and] to prepare them for a glorious eternity' (Laqueur, 34), an aim undertaken by twenty-four officers and governors drawn from the Church of England and the various dissenting bodies. The society flourished in its early years, but it was too centralized to develop and

Fox, Sir William (1812–1893), premier of New Zealand, born at Westoe, co. Durham, in June 1812, was the third of the five surviving sons of George Townshend Fox, deputy lieutenant of co. Durham, and his wife, Ann Stote, *née* Crofton. He was admitted commoner of Wadham College, Oxford, on 28 April 1828, and graduated BA on 23 February 1832 and MA on 6 June 1839. He was called to the bar from the Inner Temple on 29 April 1842. On 3 May that year he married Sarah Halcomb (*d.* 1892), the daughter of a Wiltshire landowner, and six weeks later emigrated with her to New Zealand. There in 1843 the New Zealand Company appointed him their resident agent at Nelson, in succession to Captain Arthur Wakefield, killed in a settler foray against Maori who were resisting a survey of tribal land. Five years later Governor George Grey made him attorney-general for the southern region of the colony; but Fox, who had thrown himself into the agitation for self-government, then at its height, soon resigned his post as a protest against the governor's dilatory action in the matter. The New Zealand Company then made him their principal agent in the colony, and the settlers of the central districts chose him to represent them on a mission to London to urge at Downing Street their demands for a constitution. The Colonial Office, however, refused to receive him, and he returned to New Zealand after travelling in the United States, Canada, and Cuba. Having been elected to a seat in the second New Zealand parliament, on 20 May 1856 Fox ousted the short-lived Sewell ministry and took office, only to be himself ejected thirteen days afterwards by Edward Stafford. Five years later he turned the tables on his opponent, and this time retained the premiership for thirteen months (1861–2). He also went on to a third period of office (1863–4). He was thus in power through much of the period of the New Zealand wars. Although in contemporary politics he was thought of as leader of the 'peace' party, it is now clear that Grey was the dominant force in Maori policy and that Fox shared many of the views of his opponents about the inevitability of a European future for the country.

In June 1869, after again defeating Stafford, Fox formed a ministry with Julius Vogel as treasurer. Fox endorsed Vogel's economic policy of borrowing abroad for development, but was not always easy with the scale of borrowing or Vogel's tendency to ignore criticism. The ministry lost power briefly in September 1872 and on its restoration Fox did not take the leadership. He returned as premier for the last time during a political crisis in February–March 1873. He remained a member of parliament until defeated in the 1879 general election, was re-elected in a by-election in 1880, and ended his political career when he lost his seat in 1881.

In the early 1880s Fox was appointed as joint commissioner with Francis Dillon Bell to investigate the tangle of Maori land claims in the southern Taranaki district. Fox and Bell found unjustified land confiscations and broken promises and recommended that about a fifth of the confiscated land be returned to the original owners.

As a young man Fox, who was an active person of untidy appearance, made some notable exploratory journeys in the South Island. He had an eye for landscape, and his romantic watercolours of places he visited in New Zealand and America and of the countryside around his home in the Rangitikei are significant contributions to nineteenth-century colonial art. Pledged to a life of temperance from the 1840s, he devoted much of his time in the 1880s to temperance and its associated reforms, such as women's suffrage and banning women from work in hotel bars. In 1887 he and Lady Fox moved from their country estate, called Westoe after his birthplace, to Auckland.

Fox had been made KCMG on 24 May 1879. His active career was marked chiefly by the part he took in gaining self-government for New Zealand, by the support he gave to provincial institutions, and by his vigorous defence of the New Zealand colonists against the charges made against them in England of forcing on wars with the Maori in order to grab their lands. His chief book, *The War in New Zealand* (1860), is not only a warm vindication of his fellow colonists from these accusations, but a trenchant, and in places caustic, criticism of the conduct of the wars by the British military leaders. Another volume, *The Six Colonies of New Zealand* (1851), was written as an anti-government polemic but has some value as a brief sketch of the colony. Fox was also a prolific journalist who used his newspaper columns to launch vitriolic attacks on his opponents, and he published a number of political pamphlets.

Fox's death, at his home in Symonds Street, Auckland, at the age of eighty-one on 23 June 1893, followed a year after that of his wife. He was buried at Purewa, Auckland. His generous nature and quick, impulsive temperament made him an impatient critic alike of Sir George Grey's devious tactics and of the slow-moving policy of the Colonial Office. The same qualities caused him to show to better advantage as the fighting leader of an opposition than when on the defensive as minister. Lacking a clear vision of the future, Fox tended to let others make policy. Nevertheless he was fond of power, and from 1856 until 1873 he and Stafford were the colony's two leading politicians.

W. P. REEVES, *rev.* RAEWYN DALZIEL

Sources R. Dalziel and K. Sinclair, 'Fox, William', *DNZB*, vol. 1 · B. J. Poff, 'William Fox: early colonial years, 1842–8', MA diss., University of Canterbury, New Zealand, 1969 · E. Bohan, *Sir Edward Stafford: New Zealand's first statesman* (1994) · R. M. Allan, *Nelson: a history of early settlement* (1965) · R. Dalziel, *Julius Vogel, business politician* (1986) · J. Rutherford, *Sir George Grey, KCB, 1812–1898: a study in colonial government* (1961) · Reports of the West Coast Commission, appendices to the journals of the House of Representatives, 1880, G-2; 1881, G-5; 1882, G-5, G-5A; 1883, G-3 · d. certs.
Archives Canterbury Museum, Christchurch, Godley MSS · NL NZ, Turnbull L., Vogel, McLean, Hall MSS · PRO, NZ, Company MS, CO 208
Likenesses photograph, *c.*1872, NL NZ, Turnbull L. · oils, City Art Gallery, Auckland, New Zealand · wood-engraving, NPG; repro. in *ILN* (23 Nov 1861)

Fox, William Johnson (1786–1864), preacher and politician, was born on 1 March 1786 at Uggeshall Farm, Wrentham, Suffolk, the eldest child of six sons and three daughters of Paul Fox (1753?–1812) and his wife, Mary. Paul Fox farmed a small property for his widowed mother, though he had prudently absented himself for a two-year stay in London (as a clerk to the lottery, having won a share of a prize on his arrival) to escape the suspicion of Sir Thomas Gooch, bt (1745–1814), the game-preserving squire at Wrentham, that he was a poacher. After Gooch relented, Fox returned and married Mary, the eldest of five daughters of a village barber, probably named William Johnson, given the contemporary conventions of nomenclature. Looking back on his life, Fox thought that the 'sluggish tenacity of brain' he inherited from his father was offset by a 'nervous irritability' derived from the 'delicate and sensitive' nature of his mother (Garnett, 4).

Apprenticeship and ministry At some point in 1788 or 1789 the family moved to Norwich, where the father worked as a shopkeeper, as a handloom weaver—the entry in the register of St George's Chapel for the baptism of Sarah Johnson Fox in November 1791 notes that her father was 'not able to pay the duty'—and from 1800 to his death as a master in the chapel school. Educated in that school, William assisted his father at the loom, worked as an errand-boy, and in 1799 became a clerk in the banking firm of Kebb and Back. There his arithmetical facility brought a rise in salary from £20 to £60, and with it the possibility of buying books and the formulation of a seven-year plan of self-education, primarily mathematical. He entered essay competitions and had some verse published in *The Iris*, a local radical paper; his first poem was in praise of the rifle that came with his service in the volunteers.

The Foxes were strict Calvinists, and the young man's attainments brought encouragement to enter the ministry. In September 1806 he enrolled in the Independent

William Johnson Fox (1786–1864), by Eliza Florence Bridell, *c.*1863

academy at Homerton, near London, headed by the formidable John Pye Smith (1774–1851). Despite the sense of isolation that seems to dominate his recollections, he and his fellow students surreptitiously played cards and went to the theatre, though on one occasion, when he walked to London to see a Shakespeare play and found a modern comedy playing instead, he walked back again. There was a degree of intellectual liberality at Homerton, but the divinity course increased in credal stringency towards its conclusion.

A year or so before his formal leave-taking from Homerton in April 1810, Fox became minister to an Independent congregation in Fareham, Hampshire, and during that time studied the much agitated and many-sided controversy over the Trinity. He had read Locke's *Essay Concerning Human Understanding* while working at the bank, in time economized from the dinner hour, and had already been made aware of Unitarianism by some of his radical Norwich friends; the question must have been canvassed as well among Homerton students, some of whom were persuaded to the Unitarian side, as in time was Fox. He withdrew to an unsuccessful Secessionist chapel in Fareham and in mid-1812 was invited to the Unitarian congregation in Baffin's Lane, Chichester. He signalized his conversion by publishing *Letters to the Rev. John Pye Smith* (1813), attacking the sacrificial view of the atonement as biblically and morally insupportable.

In Chichester, Fox continued his studies, in literature as well as theology, and improved his oratory. He also formed an attachment to Eliza (1793–1869), the eldest of thirteen children of James and Charlotte Florance; James

Florance (1770?–1838) was a Unitarian barrister and founder of the town's public library. A 'semi-engagement' was called off in 1815. Fox's growing reputation as a controversialist and a spellbinding preacher led to his being called to London in 1817 to succeed William Vidler (1758–1816) at the once Universalist, but by then Unitarian, chapel in Parliament Court, Bishopsgate, at a salary of £200, raised to £300 the next year. In February 1824 the congregation moved to a new chapel in Finsbury, formally the Finsbury Unitarian Chapel, but generally known from its location as South Place.

Minister of the South Place chapel Fox and Eliza Florance had continued to correspond, and, following her removal to London as a pupil teacher, they drifted into a misguided marriage on 20 April 1820 in the parish church of St George-in-the-East. Two sons and a daughter were born: Florance (*b.* 1821) was a deaf mute who, despite his handicap, worked from 1841 to 1866 at the office of the registrar-general; Eliza, nicknamed Tottie, became, as Eliza Bridell (later Bridell-Fox), a well-known painter [*see* Fox, Eliza Florance Bridell-].

The tightly knit Unitarian community in London had been galvanized into newly forceful action by Robert Aspland, a convert from the Calvinistic Baptists; other prominent figures with whom Fox associated were Thomas Southwood Smith, another former Baptist who had abandoned his Unitarian pulpit in Yeovil for a medical and public career in London, and John Bowring, a merchant and *littérateur* from an old Unitarian family in Exeter. Fox's immediate introduction to the Benthamite circle to which Smith and Bowring belonged came about, however, through Henry Southern, who edited periodicals in which some of Fox's work had appeared and who became co-editor with Bowring of the *Westminster Review*. Fox wrote the opening article in the first issue of that journal in January 1824, turning a review of a poem, *Men and Things in 1823*, into a radical manifesto. He declined Bowring's invitation to edit Bentham's *Not Paul but Jesus*, a task then taken on by Francis Place. Fox played a crucial role in founding the British and Foreign Unitarian Association in 1825, serving for a time as its secretary for foreign correspondence. In the early 1830s he helped to found the London domestic mission.

In 1826 Aspland handed over the editorial conduct of the *Monthly Repository*, which he had begun in 1806, to a committee of the association, and Fox was brought in as sole editor in 1827. He broadened the contents of the journal beyond the theological discussions and denominational exchanges that had been its stock-in-trade and brought in a new and stellar band of contributors. His best-known find was the young Harriet Martineau (1802–1876), whose apprenticeship as a writer he oversaw and who remained forever grateful for his encouragement. In 1831 Fox purchased the copyright of the journal from the Unitarian Association, spun off denominational matters to a short-lived *Unitarian Chronicle* (1832–3), and made the *Repository* a largely literary magazine. Fox himself took responsibility for dramatic criticism as well as other literary matters, and it is a tribute to his perspicacity that he early recognized the genius of Tennyson and was the first critic to perceive the promise of Robert Browning.

Fox's house in Stamford Hill became an important gathering place for intellectuals. Worried about its effects on his sister Harriet, James Martineau (1805–1900) called them a 'free-thinking and free-living clique' (Martineau abstracts, 5 May 1830). The circle was more than that, however. Not only was it a clearing-house for ideas and opinions, but it opened opportunities in the burgeoning press, much as the more famous household of John Chapman, with George Eliot's commanding and recording presence, was to do in the early 1850s.

At one remove from the group was John Stuart Mill, whose friend Harriet Taylor belonged to Fox's congregation at South Place. Mill contributed to the *Repository* and regularly defended Fox and his friends to an unconvinced Thomas Carlyle. He called Fox to the attention of the Saint-Simonians in Paris, and if the Saint-Simonian 'missionaries' Gustave d'Eichthal (1804–1886) and Charles Duveyrier (1803–1866) visited Stamford Hill in 1831–2, the ground would have been well prepared. 'Harriet is full of Saint-Simonism', noted James Martineau some months earlier; Fox was about to pay a visit to Dublin, and she had urged her brother to 'set him agoing' on the subject (Martineau abstracts, 24 March 1831).

After his letters to Pye Smith in 1813, Fox's theological interests gradually gave way to his role as an aggressive and eloquent champion of the extension of full civil rights to dissenters and of the broadest interpretation of toleration: he precipitated a considerable intramural fuss in the *Repository*, when the radical journalist Richard Carlile (1790–1843) was imprisoned for blasphemy in 1819, by publishing a sermon urging Unitarian sympathy with the fullest freedom for deists. With the repeal of the Test and Corporation Acts in 1828 and the granting of Catholic emancipation the next year, Fox and his friends threw themselves into the campaign for the Reform Bill. He made use of the *Repository*, of course, and he had connections with the political unions, appearing regularly at public meetings in Leicester Square and notably at the great demonstration in Lincoln's Inn Fields on 31 October 1831. He was, said Francis Place, 'the bravest among us!' (Saunders, 71).

Illness and scandal At that point, a personal crisis sharply altered the direction of Fox's life. Early in 1822 he had suffered a complete physical and mental collapse and was unable to preach for a year. Strains in the marriage may have contributed to and certainly worsened his illness, but the trouble was soon compounded by a friendship between the Foxes and the family of the well-known radical printer Benjamin Flower, who in 1820 had settled in nearby Dalston with his two daughters, the composer Eliza [see Flower, Eliza (1803–1846)] and the poet Sarah, known after her marriage as Sarah Flower Adams. In the autumn of 1823, when Fox had been invited to preach in Edinburgh, Southwood Smith, who had been minister there, arranged a tour of the highlands which included Fox and the Flower family. Shortly after, Eliza Flower became Fox's assistant and amanuensis, and common

interests drew them into more than friendship—they always celebrated the anniversary of their ascent of Ben Lomond on 8 September—though Fox maintained that the relationship was never more than platonic. On Benjamin Flower's death in 1829, Fox was named trustee for his two daughters.

Matters might have remained in that ambiguous state had Fox not written an article in the *Repository* in 1833 on the question of dissenters' marriages, in which he advocated divorce on grounds of incompatibility, bringing a sharp response from prominent Unitarians, ministerial and lay. By 1834 the scandal had spread beyond the few members of South Place in whom Eliza Fox had confided. A protest from one segment of the congregation provoked Fox's resignation, withdrawn when a vote showed him to possess the confidence of a majority. The minority withdrew from the congregation, and in January 1835 Fox and Eliza Flower set up a household in Craven Hill, Bayswater. In the following spring the organization of nominally Presbyterian but actually Unitarian ministers in London and the vicinity voted to expel Fox. The expulsion brought a sympathetic response from James Martineau, who, while not extenuating the domestic situation, was strengthened in a growing dislike for formal and official Unitarianism that led in time to his leadership of the 'new school' that transformed the denomination in mid-century (Martineau to Fox, 30 May 1835, Speck collection).

The new domestic arrangement—in a succession of residences before a permanent settlement in 1844 in Charlotte Street, Bedford Square—was accepted by some old friends but brought estrangement from others. Harriet Martineau broke with them but in time began writing to Eliza Flower, and eventually, after some awkward exchanges over conflicting principles, resumed the correspondence with Fox until 1853, when she cut ties over his refusal of her request to return her letters.

Fox had adhered increasingly loosely to denominational ties, but once freed from them he gave up the title of Reverend and abandoned biblical texts for his sermons, which he supplemented with lectures on both secular and broadly religious themes, the most notable a series on religious ideas delivered in 1849. His inclination to heterodoxy was reinforced by Philip Harwood, his assistant in 1840–41, who first called respectable attention to the corrosive mythical understanding of Christianity advanced in Germany by David Friedrich Strauss (1808–1874).

Faced with the loss of Unitarian subscribers, Fox gave up the *Repository* in 1836 to R. H. Horne (1803–1884), who the next year was succeeded by Leigh Hunt (1784–1859), its last editor. Meanwhile, Fox had turned to newspaper writing, at first in the *Sunday Times* and then in the *True Sun*, both owned by Daniel Whittle Harvey (1786–1853). From 1839 to 1843 he was a leader writer for the *Morning Chronicle*, as he was, briefly, for the *Daily News* on its inception in 1846. He also continued to open doors for others: in 1843 his introductions for Harwood began a journalistic career that culminated in the editorship of the *Saturday Review*.

Lecturer and member of parliament But Fox had another string to his bow besides South Place and the press, as a popular lecturer. In 1844–6 he delivered an extensive series of well-received and long-admired lectures to the working classes at the National Hall in London, although Crabb Robinson found them 'full of claptrap and vulgar radicalism' (Robinson, diary, 3 Nov 1844). From 1843 he lectured for the Anti-Corn Law League, at £10 or £20 a performance. While he had gradually emancipated himself from the need for a written text, it was less easy to overcome the handicap of his unimpressive appearance. Very short and, for his height, very stout, with a massive head, long grey hair parted in the middle, and sombre clothes, he struck one observer as looking like 'a sturdy but truncated Puritan' (*Daily News*, 6 June 1864). But all that was forgotten when he began to speak. The modern historian of the league concedes his effectiveness while finding his language 'highly pretentious' and his letters 'insufferably sanctimonious and glib' (McCord, 185). Contemporaries reacted differently. An earlier historian who heard him at Drury Lane described his performance as superb with epigram and sarcasm, delivered in a rich, deep voice 'so beautifully articulated … that his stage whisper might have been heard at the farthest extremity of the gallery … [and] with a beauty of elocution which Macready … might have envied'. Fox appealed powerfully to the emotions of his audience, bringing 'thousands starting on their feet, with arms extended, as if ready to swear extinction to monopoly' (Prentice, 2.59–60). A more detailed description of his platform technique appears in John Saunders's memoir of Fox in the *People's Journal* in early 1847. In addition, between October 1844 and March 1846 Fox contributed to *The League*, the league's newspaper, a series of letters on the corn laws from 'A Norwich weaver-boy'.

After the death of Eliza Flower in December 1846, Fox took up a candidacy for a parliamentary seat at Oldham that had been under discussion for some time. He was, moreover, relieved from financial anxiety and constant newspaper writing by a lifetime annuity of £400 begun in 1847 by the great silk manufacturer Samuel Courtauld (1793–1881), cementing a relationship with the principals of the firm that had begun in Chichester in 1812 with William Taylor (1755–1843), then a traveller for Courtaulds and the father of Samuel Courtauld's partner and Fox's close friend Peter Alfred Taylor (1790–1850). He regularly contributed, however, to the *Weekly Despatch* from 1846 to 1863. His role at South Place had steadily diminished, and his last six addresses were given there in 1852. The ministries of two successors almost sent the congregation under, but it was revived after 1863 by Moncure Daniel Conway (1832–1907), an American whose twenty-year tenure began its later transmutation into the South Place Ethical Society.

At Oldham, one of the sitting MPs, the famous factory reformer (and Unitarian) John Fielden, had alienated a segment of his supporters who found Fox's free-trade radicalism particularly appealing. But in the Chartist decade Fielden remained popular with many non-voting working men; the campaign in July 1847 was violent, and Fox had

on occasion to be protected by troops. Returned at the head of the poll, he was unseated briefly in 1852 only to be re-elected when the holder of the other Oldham seat suddenly died. He was again thrown out in 1857, amid the jingoistic excitement called forth by the war with China (begun by his old associate John Bowring), to which his more famous colleagues Richard Cobden and John Bright were also sacrificed. Again returned for an unexpected vacancy in the same year, he represented Oldham until his resignation in 1862. His style of speaking was not suited to the House of Commons, and his parliamentary effectiveness was reduced by declining health, but he supported extension of the suffrage and was particularly identified with national education, on which he introduced an unsuccessful bill in 1850.

Fox was reconciled to his wife some time after Eliza Flower's death. He died in London on 3 June 1864 of inflammation of the bladder and was buried in Brompton cemetery. A memorial service was conducted at South Place by M. D. Conway on 12 June.   R. K. WEBB

Sources R. Garnett and E. Garnett, *The life of W. J. Fox, public teacher and social reformer, 1786–1864* (1910) · F. E. Mineka, *The dissidence of dissent: the Monthly Repository, 1806–1838* (1944) · F. Fox, ed., *Memoir of Mrs. Eliza Fox* (1869) · S. K. Ratcliffe, *The story of South Place* (1955) · M. Parnaby, 'William Johnson Fox and the *Monthly Repository* circle, 1832–1836', PhD diss., Australian National University, 1980 · R. K. P. Pankhurst, *The Saint Simonians, Mill and Carlyle: a preface to modern thought* (1957) · J. Saunders, 'W. J. Fox', *People's Journal*, 3 (1847), 68–73 · *Christian Reformer, or, Unitarian Magazine and Review*, 5 (1838), 504, 673–5 · *Daily News* (6 June 1864) · register of the Independent church, Wrentham, PRO · register of the Congregational church, Norwich (Old Chapel), PRO · abstracts of Harriet Martineau's letters, Harris Man. Oxf. · A. Prentice, *History of the Anti-Corn-Law League*, 2 (1853), 59–60 · N. McCord, *The Anti-Corn Law League, 1838–1846* (1958) · H. Martineau, letter to W. J. Fox, U. Cal., Berkeley, Bancroft Library, R. S. Speck collection of Harriet Martineau · J. Martineau, letter to W. J. Fox, 10 May 1835, U. Cal., Berkeley, Bancroft Library, R. S. Speck collection of Harriet Martineau · H. C. Robinson, diary, DWL · J. Foster, *Class struggle and industrial revolution: early industrial capitalism in three English towns* (1974) · documents relating to W. J. Fox, 1834, DWL, MS 24.86 · *Harriet Martineau's autobiography*, ed. M. W. Chapman, 3 vols. (1877) · G. Wallas, *William Johnson Fox (1786–1864)* (1924) [Conway memorial lecture]

Archives BL, letters · PRO NIre., diary, D 2009 | Co-operative Union, Holyoake House, Manchester, Co-operative Union archive, letters to G. J. Holyoake, HM/96636/1–12 · DWL, corresp. with Henry Crabb Robinson · U. Cal., Berkeley, Bancroft Library, R. S. Speck collection of Harriet Martineau

Likenesses J. R. Wildman?, oils, 1825, South Place Ethical Society, London · D. Maclise, group portrait, 1844 (*Dickens reading The Chimes to his friends*), V&A · E. Fox, engraving, 1847, repro. in Saunders, 'W. J. Fox', 68 · S. Bellin, group portrait, pubd 1850 (*Meeting of the council of the anti-corn law league*; after J. R. Herbert, 1847), BM, NPG · J. Doyle, pen-and-pencil caricature, 1851, BM · E. F. Bridell, oils, c.1863, NPG [*see illus.*] · F. Bridell, oils, NPG

Wealth at death under £600: probate, 16 June 1864, CGPLA Eng. & Wales

Fox, William Tilbury (1836–1879), physician and dermatologist, was a son of Luther Owen Fox (1811/12–1879) MD FRCS, of Broughton, Hampshire. He is usually referred to as Tilbury Fox; his brother, Thomas Colcott Fox (1849–1916), also became a dermatologist. Fox entered University College Hospital (UCH) medical school in 1853. In 1857 he graduated MB with the gold medal and scholarship in medicine at the University of London. He obtained the MD in 1858.

At UCH Fox became house physician to Sir William Jenner (physician in charge of the newly formed skin department), and learned about skin diseases. He then became resident house surgeon at the Lambeth General Lying-in Hospital, London, and for a short time he was in general practice with Mr Tapson in Bayswater. He then chose midwifery as his speciality and was appointed physician-accoucheur to the Farringdon General Dispensary. He wrote on post-partum femoral deep vein thrombosis, and, while still at the dispensary, published *Skin Diseases of Parasitic Origin* (1863), which dealt with parasitic and fungal skin diseases, and in particular with ringworm, but Fox was unaware of the wide range of different fungi. The first edition of his major book, *Skin Diseases: their Description, Pathology, Diagnosis and Treatment with a Copious Formulary* (1864), listed his appointments as senior physician to St John's Hospital for Skin Diseases and physician to the Farringdon General Dispensary. At that time these hospital appointments were unpaid, but helped a physician build up his private practice.

In 1864, probably on the recommendation of Erasmus Wilson of UCH, Fox travelled to Egypt, the Middle East, and India with the earl of Hopetoun and became ill, perhaps with rheumatic fever. These travels were the basis of his contributions to tropical dermatology and the *Scheme for obtaining a better knowledge of endemic skin diseases in India, prepared with T. Farquhar, for the India Office* (1872). On his return Fox settled in Sackville Street, Piccadilly, London, and soon built up a large private practice in dermatology. In 1866, shortly after he had failed to become assistant physician at Charing Cross Hospital, he was appointed physician to the skin department, which had been formed for him. In 1868 he returned to UCH where he headed the skin department and collected funds for a wide range of medicinal baths. Fox was a good teacher: two of his students became founder members of the American Dermatological Association.

In 1875 Fox extended Robert Willan's *Atlas of Skin Diseases*, which had been previously edited by Thomas Bateman. This established his reputation. His books were translated and he became well known outside Great Britain; one of his obituaries even appeared in German. Fox was a prominent member of the editorial staff of *The Lancet* and made many helpful friends in this role. As a member of convocation of London University he opposed the admission of women to degrees.

Fox strove to put British dermatology on a scientific basis. His writing was eclectic and combined the British interest in treatment, French interest in theory, and German and Austrian interest in histology. Fox used his great energy and geniality to promote dermatology as a speciality, and emphasized the importance of general medicine to the dermatologist. With Erasmus Wilson he played an important role in establishing dermatology as a sub-speciality at the British Medical Association's annual meetings. Fox would have been the first president, but died shortly beforehand. Fox gave an early description of urticaria pigmentosa as distinct from other forms of urticaria. He also provided original descriptions of dermatitis herpetiformis, and of impetigo contagiosa streptogenes. Fox also made contributions to tropical dermatology, where he narrowed the clinical picture of leprosy and recognized 'oriental sore' as a single disease (cutaneous leishmaniasis) with different names in different countries.

About 1873 Fox developed aortic valve disease with frequent angina; he died at the Hôtel Continental, Paris, on 7 June 1879 following an anginal attack while on a brief holiday. He was buried at Willesden cemetery, London, on 14 June 1879. His father died fourteen days after him. Fox was married, with a family; his wife, Sophia Campbell Fox, survived him. A religious man, Fox wished his obituary to include the statement 'I die a Christian' (*The Lancet*).

GEOFFREY L. ASHERSON

Sources *The Lancet* (14 June 1879), 865–6 · *BMJ* (14 June 1879), 915–16 · *Medical Times and Gazette* (14 June 1879), 662 · 'Nekrologe', *Vierteljahresschrift für Dermatologie und Syphilis*, 2 and 3 (1879), 506–7 [translation in *The Lancet* (1 Nov 1879), 675] · J. T. Crissey and L. C. Parish, *The dermatology and syphilology of the nineteenth century* (1981) · M. P. English, 'William Tilbury Fox and dermatological mycology', *British Journal of Dermatology*, 97 (1977), 573–6 · W. R. Merrington, *University College Hospital and its medical school: a history* (1976) · A. Rook, 'William Tilbury Fox (1836–79): his contribution to tropical dermatology', *International Journal of Dermatology*, 20 (1981), 140–42 · H. Schadewaldt, 'Geschichte der Dermatologie: die ersten Mitteilungen über Urticaria Pigmentosa', *Hautarzt*, 11 (1960), 177–80 · *DNB* · *CGPLA Eng. & Wales* (1879) · *The Lancet* (21 June 1879), 900

Likenesses Beynon & Co., group portrait, lithograph (*Building and famous alumni of University College Hospital, London*), Wellcome L. · portrait, repro. in A. Rook, 'William Tilbury Fox'

Wealth at death under £18,000: probate, 16 July 1879, *CGPLA Eng. & Wales*

Fox, Wilson (1831–1887), physician, the son of Charles Fox, a manufacturer, of a well-known Quaker family, was born at Wellington, Somerset, on 2 November 1831. He was educated at Bruce Castle, Tottenham, and University College, London, and graduated BA in 1850, MB in 1854, and MD in 1855. After a year spent as house physician at the Edinburgh Royal Infirmary he passed some time in Paris and Vienna, and then for two further years he was a pupil of Rudolf Virchow in Berlin. Here Fox made important observations on the degeneration of the gastric glands.

On 20 April 1859 Fox married Emily Anne Doyle (*d.* 1870), daughter of Captain Wellesley Doyle, and settled at Newcastle under Lyme, where he became physician to the North Staffordshire Infirmary. In 1861, supported by Virchow's strong recommendation, he was appointed professor of pathological anatomy at University College, London, and soon afterwards he was made assistant physician to University College Hospital. In the following year he became a member of the Pathological Society and in 1866 he was elected a fellow of the Royal College of Physicians. In 1867 he became full physician to his hospital and Holme professor of clinical medicine. In 1870 he was appointed physician-extraordinary to Queen Victoria and was elected FRS. He afterwards became physician-in-ordinary to the queen and frequently attended her majesty in Scotland. He acquired a large practice, and was an active member of the leading medical societies and of the

Royal College of Physicians. His first wife died in 1870 and on 30 July 1874 he married Evelyn Laura (*b.* 1843/4), daughter of Admiral Baldwin W. Walker, baronet, and widow of Captain Hugh Burgoyne. From the late 1870s he was honorary librarian to the Royal Medical and Chirurgical Society, and he was vice-president of the Pathological Society from 1875 to 1877.

In personal appearance Fox was tall, spare, and erect, with a refined expression. Although he was somewhat reserved in manner, his sincerity and earnestness made a strong impression on those with whom he came into contact. He was a man of great benevolence, and often placed his house at Rydal in the Lake District at the disposal of the bishop of Bedford during the summer months, for the use of invalided East-End clergymen and their families. He enjoyed walking, riding, cricket, racket sports, music, and climbing.

Equally as a teacher and as an investigator and writer Fox ranked high. His cases were thoroughly studied, with special attention given to the mental and emotional state of his patients, in whom he inspired great confidence. Fox was the first physician to save life in cases of rheumatic fever where the temperature was excessively high, by placing the patient in baths of iced water. Fox's lectures were highly valued by his students, and an important characteristic of his teaching was its emphasis on pathological facts as a basis for practical diagnosis and treatment. All his writings were the product of great research and labour, and showed an encyclopaedic knowledge of their subjects. Fox spent many years preparing a treatise on diseases of the lungs and an atlas of their pathological anatomy, works that were nearly complete at his death.

Fox's principal writings were: 'On the origin, structure, and mode of development of cystic tumours of the ovary' (*Medico-Chirurgical Transactions*, 1864, 47, 227–86); 'On the artificial production of tubercle in the lower animals' (lecture, Royal College of Physicians, 1864); 'On the development of striated muscular fibre' (*Philosophical Transactions*, 156, 1866); *On the Diagnosis and Treatment of the Varieties of Dyspepsia* (1867), which was enlarged in a third edition in 1872 and also published under the title *The Diseases of the Stomach*. This was substantially a reproduction of Fox's articles in John Reynolds's *System of Medicine* (vol. 2, 1868), in which Fox also contributed the article on pneumonia, and an article entitled 'On the treatment of hyperpyrexia by means of the external application of cold' (*System*, vol. 3, 1871).

In April 1887 Fox was suddenly summoned to the deathbed of his eldest brother, at Wellington. From there he went north towards his house at Rydal Mount for a rest, but he caught pneumonia on the way and died on 3 May at the Park Hotel, Preston, Lancashire. He was buried in Taunton on 6 May 1887.

G. T. BETTANY, *rev.* KAYE BAGSHAW

Sources *The Lancet* (7 May 1887), 939–40 • *The Lancet* (14 May 1887), 1011–13 • *BMJ* (7 May 1887), 1021–22 • Munk, *Roll* • m. certs. • d. cert. • W. R. Merrington, *University College Hospital and its medical school: a history* (1976), 219

Likenesses V. Prinsep, oils, exh. RA 1889, RCP Lond. • Beynon & Co., lithograph (*Buildings and famous alumni of University College Hospital, London*), Wellcome L. • bust, Shire Hall, Taunton, Somerset • lithograph, Wellcome L. • photogravure, Wellcome L.
Wealth at death £25,609 5*s.* 8*d.*: resworn probate, April 1888, *CGPLA Eng. & Wales* (1887)

Foxcroft [*née* Whichcote], **Elizabeth** (1600–1679), theosophist, was born at Stoke, Shropshire, the daughter of Christopher Whichcote of Whichcote Hall, Stoke, and his wife, Elizabeth, *née* Fox. Some time before 1629 she married George Foxcroft, London merchant and subsequently agent for the East India Company at Fort St George. It was through her brother, Benjamin Whichcote (1609–1683), sometime provost of King's College, Cambridge, and her son Ezekiel [*see below*] that she became acquainted with Henry More, a leading member of the group known as the Cambridge Platonists. It was probably through More that she came to know the philosopher Lady Anne Conway (1631–1679). During the absence of her husband in India, from 1666 to 1672, Elizabeth Foxcroft lived with Anne Conway as companion and amanuensis, residing at the Conway home, Ragley Hall, Warwickshire. Her correspondence with More and with John Worthington (1618–1671), husband of her niece Mary, shows that she shared Anne Conway's interests, especially in religious matters. It was probably for her that More wrote his treatise on the thought of the German mystic Jakob Boehme, his *Philosophiae Teutonicae censura*. Worthington bequeathed to her his books on Boehme and the Flemish prophet Hendrik Niclaes. A few letters to her survive, but, as far as is known, no writings by her. She died in 1679 and was buried at Clapham on 25 August 1679.

Ezekiel Foxcroft (*bap.* 1629, *d.* 1674), mathematician and alchemist, son of George and Elizabeth Foxcroft, was born in London and baptized at St Stephen, Coleman Street on 29 October 1629. He was educated at Eton College and matriculated at King's College, Cambridge, in 1649. He graduated BA in 1652/3, was elected fellow of King's in 1652, and proceeded MA in 1656. He lectured in mathematics at King's College, and served as senior proctor of the university in 1673.

Foxcroft was affiliated to the circle of the Cambridge Platonists, whom he came to know through his uncle, Benjamin Whichcote, and through John Worthington, who bequeathed books to Foxcroft as well as to his mother. Foxcroft knew Robert Boyle, and as 'a great Chymist' was linked to the circle of Samuel Hartlib. His main claim to fame is his masterly translation of Johann Valentin Andreae's *Chymische Hochzeit* (1616) which was published posthumously with the English title of *The Hermetick Romance, or, The Chemical Wedding* (1690). Foxcroft's translation of this Rosicrusian text links him with the educational aims of the Hartlib circle, as well as with the Platonic and religious ideals of the Cambridge Platonists. His interest in Rosicrusianism may be linked with his mother's interest in Boehme. In 1666 Foxcroft witnessed and defended the cures effected by the Irish healer Valentine Greatrakes. He was also one of the likely sources for Isaac Newton's knowledge of alchemy. Foxcroft did not marry, and remained in Cambridge until his death in 1674. SARAH HUTTON

Sources *The Conway letters: the correspondence of Anne, Viscountess Conway, Henry More, and their friends, 1642–1684*, ed. M. H. Nicolson, rev. edn, ed. S. Hutton (1992) · *The diary and correspondence of Dr John Worthington*, ed. J. Crossley and R. C. Christie, 2 vols. in 3, Chetham Society, 13, 36, 114 (1847–86) · Venn, *Alum. Cant.* · J. W. Montgomery, *Cross and crucible: Johann Valentin Andreae (1586–1654), phoenix of the theologians*, 2 vols. (1973) · W. Sterry, ed., *The Eton College register, 1441–1698* (1943) [Ezekiel Foxcroft] · B. J. T. Dobbs, *The foundations of Newton's alchemy, or, The hunting of the greene lyon* (1975) [Ezekiel Foxcroft] · IGI [Ezekiel Foxcroft]
Archives PRO, SP 29/177/61 | BL, Harley MS 6486 · BL, More, Add. MS 23216

Foxcroft, Ezekiel (*bap.* 1629, *d.* 1674). *See under* Foxcroft, Elizabeth (1600–1679).

Foxcroft [*formerly* Jones], **Helen Charlotte** (1865–1950), historian and literary editor, was born on 12 December 1865 at Hinton House, Hinton Charterhouse, Somerset, the eldest of the seven surviving children (two sons and five daughters) of Edward Talbot Day Jones (1837–1911) of Hinton House and his wife, Wilhelmina Colquhoun (1841–1910), daughter of Robert Robertson-Glasgow of Montgreenan, Ayrshire, and Mary Campbell. In 1868 Edward Jones adopted the name of Foxcroft on inheriting the Foxcroft property of Halsteads, in Ingleton, Yorkshire.

Like many daughters of Victorian gentry Helen Foxcroft was educated at home but by 1886 she had enrolled for 'instruction by correspondence' at Newnham College, Cambridge. From these modest beginnings she developed a passion and a gift for historical research, which in the early 1890s she focused on the life and writings of the Restoration statesman George Savile, first marquess of Halifax (1633–1695), 'the Trimmer'. She was an unusually quick and efficient researcher. Though only a private scholar, in two years she amassed from public and private archives a huge body of material, with the ambitious objective not only of completing a 'Life and letters' of Halifax but an edition, too, of his writings, of which the best known are *The Character of a Trimmer, A Letter to a Dissenter, Advice to a Daughter*, and *A Character of King Charles the Second*.

It was difficult to find a publisher for such an undertaking; during 1894–6 Foxcroft negotiated with John Murray, Macmillan, and the Clarendon Press, but all declined. At last Longmans, Green & Co., to their credit, took it on, and in September 1898 they published in two volumes *The life and letters of Sir George Savile, bart., first marquis of Halifax &c. With a new edition of his works now for the first time collected and revised*. Longmans, Green & Co. soon found (1901) that this already old-fashioned example of a 'life and letters' was slow to sell. The book's complex documentation, and perhaps the elevated formality of Foxcroft's style, deterred the common reader; more than half the 1000 copies printed were eventually remaindered or destroyed. But her work was welcomed by scholars. Even before publication Thomas Seccombe made substantial use of her manuscript for his article on Halifax in the *Dictionary of National Biography*. C. H. Firth reviewed it in the *English Historical Review* (vol. 14, January 1899). He recognized that it would not attract the general public but he judged it 'a contribution of very great value to the history of the later Stuarts and the Revolution' and noted 'much hitherto unpublished or uncollected material'. An example of this was Halifax's record of conversations with William III, discovered by Foxcroft in the Spencer archives. Over the years she continued to receive friendly encouragement from Firth.

Though not easy to come by, Foxcroft's edition of Halifax's writings (265 pp. in part 2 of the *Life and Letters*) held its own for ninety years as the standard edition, textually superior to the editions by Raleigh (1912) and by Kenyon (1969). It has now been superseded by Mark N. Brown's edition of the works (3 vols., 1989), which incorporates extensive new material unknown to Foxcroft, from drafts in Halifax's hand.

As a biographer of Halifax, Foxcroft believed in the greatness of her subject, though not uncritically. The occasionally distorting effects of this predisposition in Halifax's favour have been demonstrated, and amply offset, in Brown's own commentaries in his edition. Nevertheless the biography has not been superseded as the quarry for others that she intended it to be. The 'short life' of Halifax that she published in her old age, *A Character of the Trimmer* (1946), is essentially a condensation of the original work, with some updating.

Foxcroft was also an authority on the historian and bishop Gilbert Burnet, Halifax's one-time ally and correspondent. In her *Supplement to Burnet's History of my Own Time* (1902), still important, she revealed what was gained and lost when Burnet revised his manuscript memoirs of the 1680s for his later history. She edited Burnet's letters to Halifax (1907) and contributed a major part to a life of Burnet (1907), with T. E. S. Clarke.

Helen Foxcroft spent almost all her life at Hinton Charterhouse, where her strong sense of civic duty led her to give much time to political and welfare causes. She supported her brother Charles Talbot Foxcroft, MP for Bath, as speech-writer and researcher, from 1919 until his death in 1929. A devoted Conservative, she lectured and wrote widely on political subjects. She served as a magistrate from 1930 to 1945, and for forty-five years worked for the Soldiers', Sailors' and Airmen's Families Association. A neighbour who knew her well thought her 'a fine lady, but reserved, not a gossip; and absent-minded' (private information). She was in many ways eccentric: determined to fly, she found an airman to pilot her round Salisbury Plain in 1913. She loved Somerset, its history, its countryside, and its people. Losing her sight towards the end, she died, unmarried, at Hinton House on 6 July 1950; she was buried on 8 July at the church of St John the Baptist, Hinton Charterhouse. BASIL GREENSLADE

Sources Som. ARS, Robertson–Glasgow papers, DD/RG · Burke, *Gen. GB* (1969), 2.247–8 · *The Times* (15 July 1950) · *Bath and Wilts Chronicle and Herald* (7 July 1950) · private information (2004) · parish register, Hinton Charterhouse, St John the Baptist, 21 Jan 1866

[baptism] · parish register, Hinton Charterhouse, St John the Baptist, 8 July 1950 [burial]

Archives Som. ARS, Robertson–Glasgow papers, MSS mainly related to research and anti-socialism, incl. corresp. with publishers, DD/RG

Likenesses photograph, repro. in *Bath and Wilts Chronicle and Herald*

Wealth at death £23,921: probate registry, York YO1 7EA · father's wealth 2474 acres, value £3162 p.a. gross; passed to subject and four younger daughters (incl. one who married) after brother's death; bought cottages in Hinton Charterhouse 1910; never well off; wrote in order to augment family funds: John Bateman, *The great landowners of Great Britain and Ireland*, rev. edn (1883), 174

Foxe, John (1516/17–1587), martyrologist, was born at Boston, Lincolnshire. His father, who may have been related to Henry Foxe, an affluent merchant who became mayor of the town in 1551, died while John Foxe was very young. John's mother subsequently married Richard Melton, a prosperous yeoman of the nearby village of Coningsby. John Hawarden, a fellow of Brasenose College, became rector of Coningsby in 1533, and about 1534 John Foxe entered Brasenose College, where his room-mate was Alexander Nowell, the future dean of St Paul's. The natural assumption that Hawarden paved the way for Foxe's entry into Oxford is confirmed by the fact that Foxe, three decades later, dedicated a work to Hawarden, and in it thanked him for making his university career possible.

Magdalen College Although Foxe took his bachelor's degree on 17 July 1537 it is not clear how long he remained at Brasenose. He may have studied for a time at Magdalen College School, and he certainly became a probationer fellow at Magdalen College in July 1538. He was elected a full fellow in July 1539. In 1539–40 Foxe was one of the college lecturers in logic and in July 1543 he proceeded master of arts. While at Oxford, Foxe became a committed evangelical. Among Foxe's papers is the draft of a letter he wrote to Owen Oglethorpe, the president of Magdalen, defending himself against unnamed detractors who accused Foxe of not attending mass or any church services. Foxe claimed that his actions were being monitored by some of the masters who suspected him of belonging to a 'certain new religion' (*novae cuiusdam religionis*) because of his zealous study of scriptures. Foxe added that there were other young men in the college who shared his beliefs, particularly Robert Crowley and Thomas Cooper, and that they were being persecuted by the same enemies (BL, Lansdowne MS 388, fols. 53r–58r). Though he may have exaggerated for rhetorical effect, it is clear that Foxe belonged to an evangelical minority at Magdalen, and one under pressure from the conservative majority. This pressure was taking its toll on Foxe—in a letter of 1545 he called Magdalen a prison—and it undoubtedly contributed to Foxe's decision to leave Magdalen.

The primary reason for this decision, however, was a college statute requiring every fellow to take priest's orders within one year of completing his obligatory regency (a one-year period of public lecturing in the university) as a master of arts. In Foxe's case, this meant that he had to

John Foxe (1516/17–1587), by unknown artist, 1587

enter holy orders by Michaelmas 1545. He was unwilling to do this; in a letter to one friend he explained that he could not remain at Magdalen 'unless I castrate myself and leap into the priestly caste' (*nisi in sacerdotale genus memet castrari ac praecipitare velim*). To another friend he declared flatly that 'I do not intend to be circumcised this year' (*neque libet mihi hoc anno circumcidi*; BL, Lansdowne MS 388, fols. 80v, 117r). Foxe resigned his fellowship in 1545.

Although this was a disappointing end to a promising academic career, the years at Magdalen were not without benefits or achievements. In autumn 1544 Foxe wrote his first surviving literary work, *Titus et Gesippus*, a Latin comedy based on one of Boccaccio's tales. More importantly, Foxe had become part of a network of Oxford evangelicals. Other protestants who were Foxe's contemporaries at Magdalen (Robert Crowley, Henry Bull, and Laurence Humphrey in particular) were later among his closest friends. Now, suddenly without a livelihood, Foxe turned to his evangelical connections for help.

The lean years, 1546–1548 Although Foxe sowed a plentiful crop of pleading letters he initially reaped a meagre harvest: a small gift of money, a lot of advice, and an invitation to stay with the great Hugh Latimer. Eventually Foxe secured a position as tutor in the household of Sir William Lucy, one of Latimer's friends, at Charlecote, Warwickshire. There he married Agnes Randall on 3 February 1547. Shortly afterwards, for reasons that remain unclear, Foxe left the Lucy household.

The next period of Foxe's life is obscure, illuminated only by the brief and occasionally confusing memoir of him written by his son Simeon *Foxe in 1611 and first published in the 1641 edition of *Acts and Monuments*. According to Simeon, John Foxe stayed with his wife's family in Coventry and then returned home to Coningsby.

Simeon Foxe claimed that John's relations with his stepfather, who apparently remained Catholic, were strained and, perhaps as a result, Foxe moved to London in the summer or autumn of 1547. Simeon relates a dramatic and oft-repeated story of his father sitting destitute in St Paul's when a stranger came up to him, gave him some money, and told him that he would be employed within a few days. Within three days an offer came from the duchess of Richmond inviting Foxe to be tutor to the children of her brother, the earl of Surrey, who had been executed in January 1547. The few available facts undermine this colourful tale. Some time in 1547 Foxe's translation of a sermon of Martin Luther (ESTC 16983) was published; in the dedication of this work Foxe declared that he lived in Stepney. This must have been before Foxe became tutor to Surrey's children and indicates that he lived in London for some time before he was employed by the duchess. The leisure for translation also suggests that Foxe was not desperate; in fact, Luther's sermon was one of three translations Foxe made for the evangelical printer Hugh Singleton in 1547–8. Foxe dedicated the third of these works, a translation of Urbannus Regius, *An Instruction of the Christian Faith* (ESTC 120847), to Richard Melton. This dedication, in which Foxe thanks Melton for his kindnesses, may indicate that Foxe's break with his stepfather was exaggerated by Simeon. It is even possible that Foxe received some financial support from his family during the first months of his stay in London. At the same time Foxe may have been introduced to Singleton by evangelical friends and someone must have recommended him to the duchess of Richmond; Foxe was not bereft of useful friends.

An Edwardian reformer, 1548–1553 Foxe's pupils were Surrey's three eldest children—Thomas, later the fourth duke of Norfolk; Jane, afterwards countess of Westmorland; and Henry, afterwards earl of Northampton—and later Charles Howard, the future commander of the English fleet against the Spanish Armada. At first Foxe dwelt at Mountjoy House, the duchess of Richmond's London residence. Later he and his pupils resided at the duchess's manor at Reigate. The post of tutor not only provided Foxe with the first financial security he had known since leaving Oxford, but it also led to his forging a strong bond with Thomas Howard that was later invaluable.

Moreover, the duchess's patronage further facilitated Foxe's entry into the ranks of England's protestant élite. He was ordained deacon by Nicholas Ridley on 24 June 1550, staying in the duchess of Suffolk's house before the ceremony. He met John Hooper and became friends with William Turner and John Rogers; he also attracted the support of William Cecil. Most importantly, in spring or summer 1548 Foxe met John Bale at Mountjoy House. This was more than the beginning of a beautiful friendship; during Edward VI's reign Bale loaned Foxe valuable manuscripts and certainly encouraged, very probably guided, Foxe in the composition of his first martyrology.

This project came to fruition only later, and meanwhile Foxe waded into the turbulent waters of religious controversy. In 1548 he brought out a tract, *De non plectendis morte adulteris consultatio* (ESTC 11235), arguing that adultery should not be a capital crime. This was a controversial stand, and in 1549 the veteran reformer George Joye published a vehement and effective rebuttal of Foxe's work: *A Contrary to a Certain Mans Consultation* (ESTC 14822). While Foxe had argued against imposing the death penalty on adulterers, he had also recommended that clerical sanctions, including excommunication, should be imposed on them. One of Joye's counter-arguments was that excommunication had fallen into desuetude. Foxe's next published work, his *De censura sive excommunicatione ecclesiastica rectoque eius usu* (ESTC 11233), called for its revival.

Foxe's *De censura* (1551) went further, calling for the revival of a system of ecclesiastical discipline and for a new code of canon law. It can only be understood as an attempt to encourage, and possibly influence, the commission for reforming the ecclesiastical laws, which finally met in October 1551. It is significant that Foxe claimed that he had discussed *De censura* with Ridley and that the bishop had spurred him on and authorized the work, and, even more noteworthy, that the work was dedicated to Cranmer, the sponsor and director of the proposed revision of canon law. In 1553 the canon-law revision foundered on the rocks of parliamentary opposition, but in later years Foxe tried to salvage Cranmer's great project.

During his stay in Reigate tutoring members of the Howard clan Foxe rounded out his evangelical credentials by suppressing the cult attendant upon a shrine of the Virgin Mary at Ouldsworth, which had been credited with miraculous healing powers. This round of congenial activities—teaching, writing, and iconoclasm—came to an end with Mary's accession in July 1553. The third duke of Norfolk was released from the Tower and regained custody of his grandchildren. The heir to the dukedom was placed in Stephen Gardiner's household. Although his employment was terminated, Foxe stayed in London. At the end of January 1554 Foxe wrote pessimistically to a friend, Peter Deleen, a minister of the Dutch Strangers' Church in London, about the future and his reluctance to leave England. Yet some time in the late winter or early spring of 1554 he set sail from Ipswich with his pregnant wife. After a stormy passage the Foxes arrived in Nieuwpoort.

Exile The couple stayed for a few days at Nieuwpoort, then journeyed on to Antwerp. After a detour to Rotterdam, to visit Erasmus's birthplace, Foxe pressed on to Frankfurt and then to Strasbourg, which he reached in July 1554. There, from the press of Wendelin Rihelius, he printed *Commentarii rerum in ecclesia gestarum*. The dedication to the work (in a fruitless attempt to secure patronage, it was made to Duke Christopher of Württemberg) was dated 31 August 1554. *Commentarii* is a history of the true church—largely, though not entirely, in England—and the persecutions it suffered from Wyclif to Reginald Pecock and Savonarola. Although only an octavo of 212 leaves, *Commentarii* was a forerunner of *Acts and Monuments*; indeed, much of the former work would be incorporated into the latter. It was also the result of research that had been directed and inspired by John Bale, who must have lent Foxe his unique copy of *Fasciculi zizaniorum*, one of the major sources for *Commentarii*.

In the autumn of 1554 Foxe returned to Frankfurt where he resided with Anthony Gilby, later the puritan sage of Ashby-de-la-Zouch. The English exiles in Frankfurt had split into two factions: one, headed by John Knox, used a liturgy based on a revised version of the 1552 prayer book, while a second, headed by Thomas Lever, followed the 1552 prayer book without revision. Attempts at compromise failed, and in late March 1555 the second faction, now led by Richard Cox, persuaded the Frankfurt authorities to expel Knox from the city and to enforce the use of the unrevised prayer book by the English congregation. Foxe had himself supported Knox, and believed he was unjustly treated. When printing a letter from Ridley in *Acts and Monuments* Foxe deleted passages in which the bishop criticized Knox's activities at Frankfurt. Moreover, sixteen years later Foxe initiated his own plan to revise the Book of Common Prayer.

On 27 August 1555 Whittingham, Foxe, and nearly twenty other former members of Knox's faction wrote to the English congregation, declaring their intention of departing. Their request for arbitration accomplished nothing, and by 22 September 1555 Foxe had arrived in Basel. On that day his infant daughter Christina was baptized there, with Thomas Bentham, the future bishop of Coventry and Lichfield, as her godfather. In Basel, Foxe was reunited with Bale and resided with him in a former convent which the English exiles rented from the city.

Foxe went to work for the Basel printers. During seven months in 1557–8 Foxe and his assistants received £15 from Hieronymus Froben for preparing a new Latin edition of Chrysostom's works. Most of Foxe's work was done, however, for Johann Oporinus as a proofreader. This was not lucrative, and Foxe, with a growing family to support, supplemented his income with small sums from fellow exiles, including Grindal and James Haddon. He also wrote to Thomas Howard, now duke of Norfolk, appealing for an allowance. (Characteristically, in the same letter, Foxe also exhorted the duke to stand steadfastly with the true religion and admonished him not to neglect his study of scripture.)

Yet although his work in the great Basel print-shops brought him little money, it had advantages for Foxe. For one thing, it placed Foxe at the centre of networks of protestant scholarship. This range of contacts was extended by Bale, who introduced Foxe to Conrad Gesner and also to Alexander Ales (Alesius), who later supplied Foxe with information about the Henrician reformation. Also moving in Bale's circle was Heinrich Pantaleon, a protestant physician, whose own martyrology later became intertwined with Foxe's. Bale was indeed remarkably generous to Foxe, not only lavishing praise on him in his own great work, *Scriptorum illustrium maioris Brytanniae … catalogus*, but even giving him credit for work based on Bale's own research.

The continental protestant scholar with much the greatest influence on Foxe's work was Matthias Flacius, whose seminal *Catalogus testium veritatis* was published by Oporinus in 1556; undoubtedly Foxe helped to assist in its publication. This work posited a true church consisting of isolated groups of faithful Christians through the ages, united only by the Holy Spirit and having neither institutions nor personnel in common; it powerfully influenced Foxe's ecclesiology and provided him with a rich source of information incorporated into *Acts and Monuments*. Extracts from another historical work, edited anonymously by Flacius, *Joannis Hus et Hieronymi Pragensis confessorum Christi historia et monimenta*, later appeared in Foxe's second Latin martyrology; much larger extracts from the work were reprinted in *Acts and Monuments*.

Foxe's employment in the print-shops also facilitated publication of his own works. Oporinus printed Foxe's *Christus triumphans*, an allegorical drama in Latin verse of the history of the church, in March 1556. It attracted some contemporary attention, being performed at Cambridge, and probably Oxford, in the 1560s and translated into French in 1562 and into English in 1579. Its major interest, however, lies in its providing the first evidence of what became a major preoccupation of its author, one certainly nurtured and stimulated by his friendship with Bale: a profound interest in the history of the church as an ongoing fulfilment of prophecies contained in Revelation.

Two minor works by Foxe were printed by Oporinus in March 1557. The first, *Locorum communium tituli*, was a structured commonplace book, designed to systematize study and develop the memory, and as such was a project Foxe revived later in his career. The second work, *Ad inclytos ac praepotentes Angliae proceres … supplicatio*, was a Latin appeal to the English nobility to end the persecution of protestants in England. Predictably the work had no effect on events in England, but it drew both commendations and the gift of a gold coin from Thomas Lever, now the minister of the English congregation at Aarau. In a letter to Lever, written in the winter of 1557–8, Foxe made the first of the complaints of ill health which became a regular feature of his letters in later life.

Foxe's poor health may have been aggravated, if not caused, by overwork. In addition to his work for Oporinus and Froben, and the writing of numerous relatively minor works, Foxe was busy with two major projects. One was a translation into Latin of Thomas Cranmer's attack on Gardiner, *An Answer … unto a Crafty Cavillation* (ESTC 5991). This task had been pressed upon Foxe by Pietro Martire Vermigli (known as Peter Martyr), and Foxe had already complained to Peter Martyr of the difficulties involved, in April 1555. By summer 1556 Foxe had a draft of the translation ready, but Cranmer's controversial eucharistic theology made it impossible to find a printer for it in Germany or Switzerland. Even though Christopher Froschauer, the eminent Zürich printer, had agreed to print

Foxe's translation by March 1558, the book was never published.

Foxe's second Latin martyrology The other project eventually came to fruition as Foxe's second Latin martyrology, but it was originally designed as part of an even more ambitious undertaking. The idea was formed, probably by Edmund Grindal, who seems to have informally headed the project, for two parallel editions of a *martyrum historia* (the phrase is Grindal's), one in English, the other in Latin. The Latin edition was entrusted to Foxe, while a team of exiles gathered data and prepared the English language edition. From the outset, however, despite Grindal's insistence that the two martyrologies be as similar as possible, Foxe seems to have envisioned a work different from the one Grindal had in mind, covering not only the Marian persecution, but also (and here Bale's influence can be discerned) Lollards and pre-Marian reformers.

Grindal had hoped to have both editions ready for publication soon after the summer of 1556, but this proved a wildly over-optimistic estimate. Foxe, who devoted himself increasingly to the Latin martyrology as the Cranmer translation foundered, nevertheless did not finish it until the late summer of 1559 and then only by abridging drastically its intended scope. The English martyrology was never completed at all. The work of Grindal's team was not, however, fruitless. They amassed a considerable collection of documents which were passed on to Foxe and were printed in his second martyrology.

Meanwhile, on 8 September 1558, Foxe's daughter Dorcas was baptized. Soon afterwards, on 17 November, Queen Mary died. When the news reached the continent Grindal wrote to Foxe to recommend that he delay publishing his martyrology until 'we are able to obtain more accurate and more detailed information from England' (BL, Harley MS 417, fol. 102r–v). Foxe, however, ignored Grindal's advice and pressed on with his project, interrupting his labours to compose a tract, *Germaniae ad Angliam gratulatio*, printed by Oporinus in January 1559. In this Germany congratulates England on the restoration of the gospel and Foxe thanks the Germans for their hospitality to the English, before concluding with an epilogue addressed to the duke of Norfolk. The latter responded with a letter in early March warmly extending his patronage and expressing his eagerness to see his former tutor.

Norfolk had to wait for over half a year for his reunion. Foxe remained in Basel working on his martyrology, though he was anxious to return home. He restricted his work (with the important exceptions of Jan Hus and Jerome Prague) to English men and women who died for the gospel. Nevertheless, as the full title of his *Rerum in ecclesia gestarum … commentarii* makes clear, with its reference to a Europe-wide persecution (*per Europam persecutionem*), Foxe planned a further volume or volumes on the sufferings of the godly on the continent, and never ceased to see the English Reformation in its larger European context.

Rerum … commentarii, which was printed in Basel in August 1559 by Oporinus and his fellow printer Nicholas Brylinger, was a folio of about 750 pages, divided into six books. The first book was largely a reprint of Foxe's 1554 martyrology with some additions. The second book covered the reigns of Henry VIII and Edward VI, from the death of Richard Hunne in 1515 to the execution of the duke of Somerset in 1552. Foxe's two basic sources for this book were first Bale's *Catalogus* and then Edward Hall's chronicle. He supplemented these sources with Alesius's *Of the Auctoritie of the Word of God*, Bale's edition of John Lambert's treatise, and Bale's *Examinations of Anne Askew*, all reprinted (in Latin) in *Rerum*. Foxe also relied on accounts sent to him by eyewitnesses; among these were the vivid description of Somerset's execution and, in a triumph of precisely directed enquiry, the extraordinarily accurate account of William Gardiner's martyrdom. With Edward VI's reign Foxe came into his own, but for events before the reign he was almost totally dependent on Bale's research, writings, and contacts.

The final four books of *Rerum* were devoted to the Marian persecution. Book 3, which covered the first eighteen months of Mary's reign and ended with the martyrdoms of John Rogers and John Hooper, was almost entirely a collage of print or manuscript treatises, including the letters of Jane Grey, Stephen Gardiner's examination of Sir James Hales, and two works by Hooper never subsequently reprinted: an appeal to the English nobility and a treatise on the eucharist. Where he had previously built on Bale's foundations, Foxe now relied on material gathered by Grindal and Bullinger.

The final three books, covering the period up to Cranmer's death in March 1556, are also based on the research of Grindal and his team, and probably represent what Grindal's planned martyrology would have looked like had it been written. They consist almost entirely of the writings of the martyrs themselves, generally their letters and their accounts of their examinations. Martyrs for whom such materials did not exist were simply listed unless informants supplied accounts of their sufferings. The final four pages of *Rerum* merely list the martyrs of the final two and a half years of Mary's reign, along with the dates and locales of their executions; by now Oporinus wanted the work finished in time for the Frankfurt book fair, while Foxe wanted to return home. *Rerum* appeared, with a warm dedication to the duke of Norfolk, in September 1559.

Although it was rushed and truncated, *Rerum* was also Foxe's first great literary success. Jean Crespin expressed interest in printing a French translation of *Rerum*; ultimately he simply paid Foxe the compliment of plagiarizing it liberally (Foxe responded in kind). Oporinus bestowed an equally backhanded compliment on his former employee by pestering him for the second part of the martyrology (eventually provided by Heinrich Pantaleon), while the great Bullinger wrote congratulating Foxe on the work.

Foxe had left England in 1554 penniless and relatively unknown. He returned home in October 1559 not much richer, but with a substantial reputation. He also returned with a goal: the completion, on his own terms, of the martyrology that he had started. Like Aaron's serpent, this project swallowed all the other concerns in Foxe's life, in a task that preoccupied him for the next decade.

The first edition of *Acts and Monuments* Foxe wasted no time in starting work on his new martyrology. On 10 November 1559 he published one of the last letters Nicholas Ridley wrote, as *A Friendly Farewell which Master Doctor Ridley did Write* (ESTC 21051), and in an epilogue announced that this was just a sample from the larger work he was preparing on the martyrs. The *Friendly Farewell* was printed by John Day. There is no indication that Foxe knew Day before Elizabeth's reign; this was the first of Foxe's books that Day published. It is striking that within a month of his return, Foxe had enlisted Day's support for his great project.

Day issued another of Foxe's works, this one published anonymously, in September 1560. *A Solemne Contestation of Divers Popes* is a first-person oration, placed in the mouth of the papal Antichrist, describing how he rose to power over the princes of Christendom and how he abused this power. It is composed entirely of quotations from papal bulls, books of canon laws, and historical works, giving it an appearance of authenticity. (Although the quotations were accurate, they were often brutally twisted out of context.) This tract, which was reprinted in *Acts and Monuments*, demonstrated that the scope of Foxe's research already extended beyond England and before Wyclif.

In the meantime Foxe had been staying at the duke of Norfolk's mansion in Aldgate. On 25 January 1560 he was ordained priest by Grindal. There is evidence that in the summer of 1560 Foxe was offered the deanery of Christ Church, Oxford; if so, he must have declined it. Instead he left London in autumn 1560 and went to Norwich, where he lived with his friend John Parkhurst, now bishop of Norwich. He preached in the diocese, and also conducted archival and oral research there, whose fruits appeared in the first edition of *Acts and Monuments*. Foxe returned to London by August 1562 where he once more lived in Norfolk's Aldgate mansion while commuting to Day's printshop, where he supervised the printing of his martyrology.

On 20 March 1563 the first edition of *Acts and Monuments* (immediately and universally referred to as Foxe's 'Book of martyrs') was published by John Day. A massive folio volume, containing about 1800 pages, it is about three times the length of *Rerum*. Part of the reason for its length was its increased chronological and geographic scope. The bulk of the work covers church history from Wyclif until the accession of Elizabeth but an introductory section provides an overview of church history, particularly papal history, from the year 1000. And while English history predominates, considerable attention is given to continental history.

The second reason for the size of the work was the range of sources on which it was based. Foxe drew even more extensively from already favoured authors like Bale and Flacius, while also extracting large sections from books he used for the first time, for instance Johannes Cochlaeus's history of the Hussite wars and various martyrological

works by Jean Crespin. Foxe also expanded his already formidable reprintings of the writings of the Marian martyrs, while his use of oral testimony and eyewitness accounts increased geometrically. But the great difference between this book and Foxe's previous martyrologies was its reprinting of archival material. Here, for the first time, Foxe advanced on the methodology of Bale. Foxe's most important archival sources were the London episcopal registers, which he quarried systematically, working backwards as far as the 1520s—that Foxe was forced to publish before he had completed his research was due to Day's pressure on him to publish the work quickly. He also drew on ecclesiastical records from the diocese of Norwich, while friends sent him extracts from the episcopal registers for Coventry and Lichfield. Limited as this documentary base was, in comparison to later editions of *Acts and Monuments*, in 1563 its range was unprecedented in English historical writing.

Despite its massive size, *Acts and Monuments* must have been a financial success, for Day and Foxe very quickly decided to produce a second edition. (In Henry Bull's *Certain most Godly … Letters of such True Saintes and Martyrs* (ESTC 5886), published a year later by John Day, a marginal note on page 46 promises that more information would be forthcoming on a particular subject 'in the next edition of the boke of martyrs'.) Of course, part of Foxe's readiness to undertake a second edition was his desire to correct the flaws in the first. The translations had been done by others, sometimes unsatisfactorily, and for lack of revision the text sometimes contradicted the message that Foxe was trying to convey. Nevertheless, Day would not have agreed to print a second edition if he had not been encouraged by the sales of the first.

Shipton Another indication that the first edition of *Acts and Monuments* had succeeded was Foxe's appointment to the prebend of Shipton in Salisbury Cathedral. Valued at just under £40 a year, it was the only ecclesiastical living that Foxe held for any significant period and it provided most of his income for the rest of his life. The appointment's timing is interesting. Peter Vannes, the previous incumbent, died some time between 28 March and 30 April 1563. Foxe was presented to the living on 22 May. It looks very much as though Foxe was granted the first suitably remunerative benefice that became available after *Acts and Monuments* was published in the second half of March.

Foxe's handling of the responsibilities attached to his position reflected his ideas on the proper role of the clergy. He took no interest in his duties as a canon of Salisbury Cathedral, and in fact never visited it. At least once he was pronounced contumacious for his non-attendance, and he was also cited for refusing to donate a tithe of his income towards repairing the cathedral. On the other hand, he was entitled to appoint the vicar of Shipton under Wychwood and his choice was William Masters, a former Marian exile, who was unusually well educated for the position. On one occasion Foxe even gave Masters permission to cut and sell the timber of the vicarage, an offer so generous that Masters demurred at taking advantage of it, and one showing that while Foxe would not contribute towards the upkeep of Salisbury Cathedral he would pay lavishly to keep a godly and qualified, indeed overqualified, preacher in his parish.

Minor works and major controversies, 1563–1566 Plague broke out in London in summer 1563 and Foxe remained in the city to minister to the afflicted. He also composed *A Brief Exhortation … in this Heavy Tyme at Gods Visitation in London* (ESTC 11230) which was not only intended to comfort the dying and bereaved but also contained a forceful plea to London's civic élite for money to aid the sufferers. The plague may also have visited Foxe's household. Bishop Parkhurst wrote a letter to Foxe in January 1564, offering condolences for an unspecified bereavement; possibly one of Foxe's daughters had died.

In November 1563 Foxe lost a mentor when John Bale died. Bale's influence on Foxe's martyrologies had been profound. Both of the Latin ones had been based to varying degrees on research by Bale, who also wrote sections of the first edition of *Acts and Monuments*. He had inspired Foxe, encouraged him, and placed the fruits of his research at Foxe's disposal. Above all, it was essentially Bale's interpretation of history as a fulfilment of the prophecies in Revelation that Foxe adopted and made the keystone for his own thought. That even Foxe's earliest historical works had ranged back into the middle ages, and that Foxe wove the Lollards and other medieval heretics into the tapestry of protestant history was largely due to Bale.

Yet Bale's death may also have been somewhat liberating for his junior colleague. Bale was a forceful personality and towards the end he may have been stifling Foxe's development as much as stimulating it. It is noteworthy that both Bale and Foxe had previously announced that Foxe would edit a complete edition of Wyclif's works, an immense project which clearly reflected Bale's interests. Nothing now came of this project, and in future Foxe took on projects that dealt with concerns, notably pastoral concerns, that were far removed from Bale's interests.

Foxe's partner in a number of these projects was Henry Bull, whose *Certain most Godly … Letters of such True Saintes and Martyrs* was published in 1564. (The work was edited anonymously and has previously been attributed to Miles Coverdale, who wrote an introduction to it. Susan Wabuda, however, has conclusively demonstrated that Bull edited *Letters of the Martyrs*.) Bull's research apparently began independently of Foxe's but by 1562 or 1563 the two men were exchanging information. But while Bull made use of material gathered by Foxe (or gathered by Grindal and others for Foxe), Foxe made even greater use of the material Bull had gathered; eventually much of *Letters of the Martyrs* was incorporated in *Acts and Monuments*. Yet when Foxe reprinted Bull's text, he generally followed without changing the considerable emendations Bull made to the original letters. Once again, a substantial section of *Acts and Monuments* was not written by Foxe, but was the work of another author.

Foxe wrote only two minor works, apart from his response to the plague, in the period immediately following the publication of the first edition of *Acts and Monuments*. The first of these was a translation into Latin of Grindal's sermon on the death of the emperor Ferdinand. The other was *Syllagisticon* (ESTC 11249), a collection of theological arguments on the eucharist formulated as syllogisms. It was preceded by a long exhortatory letter to Catholics, in which Foxe urged them to read the work and see for themselves the logical and theological absurdity of the doctrine of transubstantiation.

Most of Foxe's energy was consumed with research for the second edition of *Acts and Monuments*, but he also found himself drawn into the controversy over vestments. Foxe's desire to purge the English church of what he considered to be 'popish' abuses had been apparent when he supported Knox at Frankfurt and it had not abated since. Foxe's name appeared on a list presented to Lord Robert Dudley between 1561 and 1564 of twenty-eight 'godly preachers which have utterly forsaken Antichrist and all his Romish rags' (Magd. Cam., Pepys Library, 'Papers of state', 2.701). On 20 March 1565 he was one of twenty clergymen who appealed to the ecclesiastical commissioners to be allowed to follow their consciences on wearing vestments. But when Archbishop Parker none the less moved to enforce compliance, his efforts centred on London, and since Foxe did not hold a benefice in the city, his defiance went unpunished.

Indeed, Foxe may have gained an unofficial position as a minister from the controversy. In spring 1566 Robert Crowley (a friend of Foxe from their days at Magdalen College) was placed under arrest and suspended from his livings for his outspoken opposition to Parker's vestiarian policies. Crowley remained suspended for some time and there is much evidence that Foxe acted as an unofficial surrogate for him in the London parish of St Giles Cripplegate during this period. It is noteworthy both that Foxe moved into the parish towards the end of the decade, and that John Field, who assisted Foxe in researching the second edition of *Acts and Monuments*, became curate of St Giles about the same time.

Preparing the second edition of *Acts and Monuments* Internal evidence reveals that Foxe had begun writing the second edition of *Acts and Monuments* no later than 1566. The section on which Foxe was working in that year dealt with the history of the Ottoman empire, a topic he had not discussed in any of his previous martyrologies. Its composition at this time indicates that Foxe planned to make the second edition radically different from its predecessors. Other circumstances occurring at about the same time compelled Foxe to make further alterations in the contents of the new editions.

In January 1566 a quarto volume of six dialogues, totalling about 1000 pages, was published at Antwerp under the descriptive title *Dialogi sex, contra summi pontificatus, monasticae vitae, sanctorum, sacrarum imaginum oppugnatores, et pseudomartyres*. Although published under the name of the Catholic exile Alan Cope, it was written by Nicholas Harpsfield, archdeacon of Canterbury in the previous reign. Most of the work is an attack on the Magdeburg centuriators, and to a lesser extent on John Jewel and Johann Sleidan. But the sixth and longest dialogue, totalling about 250 pages, is an attack on Foxe's martyrology. Catholic scholars, notably Thomas Harding and Thomas Stapleton, had attacked Foxe's first edition but, though occasionally effective, these had consisted of isolated passages in works devoted to other topics. Harpsfield's was the first sustained and systematic assault on Foxe's work and, indeed, the only one written during the martyrologist's lifetime.

Dealing with Harpsfield's criticisms was a painful but instructive experience for Foxe. Where these were demonstrably accurate, Foxe quietly removed the offending passages from the second edition. Where the criticisms could be rebutted, he mounted a vigorous counter-attack, seeking to crush his opponent under piles of documents. Thus Harpsfield's two (quarto) page attack on Foxe's account of the Lollard 'martyr' Sir John Oldcastle was answered by a thirty-four (folio) page reply which reprinted a number of parliamentary statutes. In short, Foxe reacted to Harpsfield's challenge like the commander of a besieged city, abandoning what could not be defended and fortifying what could. Harpsfield drove Foxe to more intensive and extensive research and made his martyrology a more impressive, although not necessarily more accurate, work of scholarship.

Work on the second edition of *Acts and Monuments* progressed. Meanwhile Agnes Foxe gave birth, on 2 February 1568, to a second son, who was named Simeon. The child was born in the duke of Norfolk's London house, where the Foxe family still resided, but soon afterwards the family moved to a house in Grub Street, in the parish of St Giles Cripplegate, where Foxe spent the rest of his life. One reason for the move may have been Foxe's increasing activity in the parish of St Giles. The new residence also had the advantage of being closer to Day's print-shop. But the move probably stemmed from the catastrophe that befell the duke of Norfolk.

In summer 1569 Foxe wrote a remarkably frank letter to Norfolk reporting that rumours of the duke's plans to marry the queen of Scots were flying around London, and bluntly warning him 'that in case you take this way to marry with this Lady in our Queens days, it will in the end turne you to noe great good' (BL, Harley MS 416, fol. 154r). This excellent advice was not heeded. Norfolk was sent to the Tower on 8 October 1569, and ultimately, on 16 January 1572, in the wake of the Ridolfi plot, he was condemned to death. On the day after Norfolk's conviction, the duke's gaoler reported that his prisoner 'longethe muche for Mr Foxe his old scholemaister, to whome he muche desyres to performe that faithe which he first grounded him in' (PRO, SP 12/85/13). Throughout the spring Foxe, together with his former room-mate Alexander Nowell, now dean of St Paul's, ministered to the spiritual needs of the condemned man. On 2 June 1572, when Norfolk was executed, Foxe and Nowell were with him on the scaffold. In his final instructions to his heirs Norfolk directed that Foxe be paid £20 a year; Simeon Foxe declared that the payments were faithfully made to his father.

The second edition of *Acts and Monuments* In the meantime the second edition of Foxe's *Acts and Monuments* was printed, in two volumes, in 1570. Although it incorporated much of the first edition, it was rewritten so thoroughly as to constitute a separate and distinct work. For one thing the scope was considerably extended; it now began with the apostolic era, and the first volume covered the history of the pre-Reformation church. Although English history still predominated, a real effort was made to cover events in Europe. The new edition was also transformed by the breadth of the research on which it was based. Foxe printed more extracts out of standard protestant histories like the Magdeburg Centuries (*Historia ecclesiae Christi*), Flacius's *Catalogus testium veritatis*, and Sleidan's *Commentaries*. Where it could not be avoided, Foxe similarly exploited the works of such Catholic historians as Pope Pius II and Johannes Cochlaeus. In addition to these great plinths of text, Foxe embellished his work with reprints of scores of pamphlets, tracts, and sermons. Moreover, most of the letters of the martyrs gathered by Bull, supplemented with others gathered by Foxe, were printed in this edition.

Yet Foxe's second edition also far surpassed any previous English historical work in the range of medieval chronicles and histories on which it was based. Foxe had the immense good fortune to be able to consult the vast collection of historical manuscripts gathered by Archbishop Matthew Parker. Although the primate and the martyrologist had their differences, which later became manifest, Parker saw an opportunity to use Foxe's *Acts and Monuments* to demonstrate his own interpretation of history in which an apostolic English church was corrupted by the papacy, in a process that began with Augustine of Canterbury's mission and became more virulent as foreign bishops like Lanfranc and Anselm were foisted on the English church after 1066. This in turn led to the establishment in the English church of such popish 'abuses' as transubstantiation, clerical celibacy, and auricular confession.

Parker used Foxe's *Acts and Monuments* as a means of conveying this message, and the research that supported it, to a wider audience than it would normally reach. In particular, Parker's most substantial achievement to date, *Testimonie of Antiquitie* (ESTC 159), was reprinted in Foxe's martyrology. In return, Parker placed his collection at the martyrologist's disposal and Foxe took full advantage of the opportunity. His single most important source for medieval history was Matthew Paris's *Chronica majora*, which he obtained from the archbishop, as he also did the Anglo-Saxon Chronicle and Gervase of Canterbury's chronicle. The archbishop also supplied Anglo-Saxon lawcodes and ecclesiastical documents. Through Parker, moreover, Foxe came into contact with a group of antiquarian scholars working loosely under the archbishop's aegis. He became friends with William Lambarde (whose *Archianomia* was also reprinted in *Acts and Monuments*), and while his relations with John Stow were markedly poorer, at Parker's behest the two shared resources, notably the great chronicle of London. Parker even seems to have put some of his researchers to work refuting specific charges made by Catholic critics of Foxe's first edition; for example, there is evidence that Parker's manuscripts were combed for proof that King John was poisoned by a monk, a claim made by Foxe and indignantly (and correctly) denied by Stapleton.

There was also a geometric expansion of the archival sources consulted for the 1570 edition. Foxe had finished his work on the London diocesan records and he proceeded to exploit the diocesan registers for Canterbury with equal thoroughness. He worked extensively on ecclesiastical records from the dioceses of Hereford, Lincoln, and Rochester, as well as adding to the material he had already drawn from the records of Coventry and Lichfield. Copies of isolated extracts from the episcopal records of Bath and Wells, Chichester, Durham, and York were also sent to Foxe. He also made systematic use for the first time of the Royal Archives, particularly the Tower records.

But perhaps the most significant development in Foxe's use of sources was his greater reliance on oral evidence. Some of this was gathered by Foxe himself, who pumped even casual acquaintances for information. William Maldon, who was one of these sources, left a vivid account of Foxe at work:

> I with another chanced to goe in the company of mr Foxe, the gatherer together of these grete boke, and he desired us to tell hym if wee knewe of any man that had suffered persecution for the gospell of Jesus Christ, to the end that he myght add it unto the boke of marters. Then said I that I knewe one that was whipped in king Henryes time for it, of his father. Then he enquired of me his name. Then I bewrayed and said it was I myself … Then I promysed him to wryght it. (BL, Harley MS 590, fol. 77r)

But after the publication of the first edition, personal testimonies poured in on Foxe without solicitation as people sought to exonerate themselves and accuse or eulogize others.

While this new material was being absorbed into the second edition, a great deal of material from the first edition was not reprinted. (Contrary to common belief, a considerable amount of very significant material in the early editions of Foxe's book was not carried over either to the later editions or to the Victorian editions which were largely based on the 1583 edition.) One obvious reason for these cuts was to make space for new material. Another, resulting from the attacks by Harpsfield and other Catholics on the first edition, was Foxe's determination to airbrush any polemical blemishes, particularly of protestants holding schismatic or heretical beliefs, out of his history.

Authorship of *Acts and Monuments* Despite these cuts Day's printing operation buckled under the task of publishing the second edition. The most serious problem was that Day underestimated the size of the new edition, which ultimately ran to about 2300 pages, and consequently ran out of paper. Day had to paste together smaller sheets of paper to finish the volume. (It was because of this problem

that Foxe's ambitious plans for an appendix on the continental protestant martyrs was never printed.) All of this underscores Day's commitment to the publication of *Acts and Monuments* and Foxe's extraordinary good fortune in finding a printer ready to support his mammoth project. Day made considerable sacrifices to publish *Acts and Monuments*. In particular it was he who underwrote woodcut illustrations for *Acts and Monuments*; the edition of 1563 contained over fifty, the edition of 1570 three times that number. Admittedly Day received concessions from William Cecil which facilitated his task: permission to exceed the legal quotas for hiring foreign workmen and lucrative monopolies for printing primers and the metrical psalms. Yet Day risked a great deal in printing *Acts and Monuments* and if he made money and increased his prestige in doing so (Day's epitaph would boast that he was the printer of *Acts and Monuments*), he more than earned it. Without Day *Acts and Monuments* would have been a much smaller book, with considerably fewer illustrations or none at all.

Acts and Monuments was essentially a collaborative undertaking. It was built on material collected by Bale, Grindal, Bull, and Parker, as well as on Foxe's own researches, in which, too, the martyrologist had the assistance of copyists as well as of the many people who did fieldwork for him, poring over local records or interviewing their neighbours. In fact the word 'author' needs to be used with some care in discussing Foxe and *Acts and Monuments*. If by author one means the person who actually wrote the words of a particular text, then Foxe was not the author of much of *Acts and Monuments*, whole sections of which were written by others. But as the person who shaped the text and controlled its messages, Foxe is the undisputed author of *Acts and Monuments*.

Even a brief comparison of the first and second editions shows how completely and systematically their shared passages were rewritten. Similarly, anyone comparing the original version of a text printed in *Acts and Monuments* with Foxe's version is likely to notice Foxe's complete readiness to alter even the tiniest details of the former. There are factual inconsistencies in *Acts and Monuments*, with much repetition, chronological inaccuracy, and faulty organization, but the themes of the work are presented without a scintilla of doubt, hesitation, or ambiguity; the text says exactly what Foxe wishes it to say and nothing else. This is particularly true of the 1570 edition, which was rigorously proof-read and impeccably cross-referenced. Even more remarkably, isolated errors were corrected by hand in the individual copies after printing but before they left the print-shop. No effort was spared to ensure that all error, doctrinal and typographical, was excised from this edition.

Celebrity Even when every allowance is made for the considerable assistance that Foxe received in writing and printing *Acts and Monuments*, the energy he invested in this Herculean task is astonishing. In fact, his health seems to have been undermined by the effort. Foxe had started to complain of ill health during his exile, and the strain of a decade spent striving to complete his *magnum opus* only aggravated his condition. In the dedication of the 1570 edition, Foxe claims that he has spent his health on his martyrology. Foxe's son Simeon, a physician, claimed that as a result of his father's mind being 'over-strained' by the composition of his martyrology, he 'fell into that withered leannesse of body in which many afterward saw him, never again returning to that pleasing and cheerfull countenance which he had before' (*Acts and Monuments*, 1641, vol. 2, sig. B2r).

In compensation, *Acts and Monuments* made Foxe England's first literary celebrity. The clearest evidence of this is the letters written to him from complete strangers, which are extant among his papers, asking his advice on theological and pastoral issues. The renown Foxe won as a martyrologist fuelled, and was fuelled by, his reputation as an extraordinarily popular and influential London minister. A condemned prisoner wrote to Foxe, asking him and Nowell to raise money on his behalf so that he could bribe a courtier to obtain a royal pardon, and declaring that he has turned to them for help because 'I know … your influence to work powerfully among all the ministers of London' (BL, Harley MS 416, fol. 165r).

Much of Foxe's reputation in London was based on his alms-giving. Simeon Foxe declared that 'there was nothing that so much won to Master Fox the love of people as the pity he usually shewed to all sorts of men in distresse' and added that wealthy individuals entrusted Foxe with large sums of money to be spent on charitable causes (*Acts and Monuments*, 1641, vol. 2, sigs. B3v, B6v). Possessed of a potent charisma derived from his personality and writings rather than his office, Foxe was the forerunner of such godly divines as Richard Greenham and William Bradshaw, whose influence and authority likewise far outstripped their ecclesiastical rank. His consequent freedom from institutional constraints made Foxe an alarming prospect for the church authorities, and when he looked like adding to his independent authority they slapped him down.

In 1570 Foxe further burnished his reputation with a sermon preached at Paul's Cross on Good Friday. The Paul's Cross sermon on the holiest day in the Christian calendar would have been a major event in any year but it held special significance in 1570 because Pius V's bull excommunicating and deposing Elizabeth had been promulgated only a month before. Foxe's *Sermon of Christ Crucified* contrasted Catholicism with true religion, but like both his previous *Syllogisticon* and many of his later works, a major purpose of this sermon was to convert Catholics to the gospel. The sermon proved very popular, being published in English in six editions during Foxe's lifetime and translated into Latin in 1571.

Reformatio legum ecclesiasticarum It is significant that Foxe's first major project after the publication of the second edition of *Acts and Monuments* was editing the code of ecclesiastical law drawn up by Archbishop Cranmer in 1552. Foxe's interest in canon law reform went back twenty years to his *De censura*, and his publication of Cranmer's law code was an attempt to implement the new code of canon law which he had championed decades

before. Yet the title Foxe gave to his edition of Cranmer's law code, *Reformatio legum ecclesiasticarum*, hints that Foxe's plans went further than reviving Cranmer's work. The introduction to *Reformatio* explicitly calls for the revision of the Book of Common Prayer and in fact the publication of *Reformatio* was part of a complicated scheme involving Thomas Norton to have parliament decree the removal of 'popish remnants' from the liturgy. The plan failed, however, and neither the canon-law code nor the revision of the prayer book were enacted.

Foxe's efforts to revise the prayer book cannot have been appreciated by Archbishop Parker, but the primate was perhaps mollified by Foxe's composition of a laudatory preface to an edition of the gospels printed in Anglo-Saxon characters, which was published under Parker's auspices in 1571 as *The Gospels of the Fower Evangelistes* (ESTC 2961).

Foxe resurrected another old project in 1572, expanding and restructuring *Locorum communium tituli* and publishing it as *Pandectae locorum communium* (ESTC 11239). Unlike its predecessor, this work enjoyed enough popularity to be reprinted once, in 1585, although it cannot be said to have had any lasting impact. Both *Locorum communium tituli* and *Pandectae locorum communium* were, as Foxe makes clear in his detailed introduction to the latter, designed as manuals to enable the reader to develop and improve his memory through systematic study. These books further demonstrate what is readily apparent in *Acts and Monuments* and *Syllogisticon*: Foxe's abiding interest in the twin arts of rhetoric and logic.

In autumn 1572 Foxe received his final preferment. Almost certainly through the efforts of James Pilkington, a fellow exile at Basel and now bishop of Durham, Foxe was presented to a prebend in Durham Cathedral. He was installed by proxy on 14 October 1572, but resigned the stall a year later. Foxe appears to have fallen victim to an effort by the Durham chapter to purge non-residents from their ranks; Thomas Lever, now archdeacon of Coventry, resigned a prebend there at exactly the same time.

Practical divinity and spiritual healing Foxe had promised in the second edition of *Acts and Monuments* that he would edit a collection of the works of William Tyndale, John Frith, and Robert Barnes; this duly appeared in January 1573. This book neatly combines two concerns that preoccupied Foxe for the remainder of his life. One of these concerns might be labelled apologetic: it was the desire to produce logical and theological arguments, buttressed by historical examples, which would induce Catholics and Jews to abandon their 'superstitions' and embrace the gospel. In the introduction to his edition of Tyndale, Frith, and Barnes, Foxe expresses the hope that those who 'be not yet wonne to the worde of trueth, setting aside all partialitie and preiudice of opinion, woulde with indifferent iudgementes, bestow some reading and hearyng likewise of these [three authors]' (*The Whole Workes of W. Tyndall, John Frith, and Doct. Barnes*, 2 vols., 1572–3, sig. A3v).

In his introduction Foxe also claims that the edition offered spiritual guidance to readers of all ages, advising young readers to study Frith, middle-aged readers Tyndale, and older readers Barnes (*Whole Workes*, sig. A2v). Behind his publication of the writings of reformers and martyrs lay his desire to supply models from the past for godly readers in the present; to supply practical divinity, as it were, by historical precedent. This pastoral concern underlies a remarkable series of translations edited by Foxe and colleagues, notably Henry Bull.

The first, and most important, of these was a translation of Luther's commentary on Galatians into English—*A Commentarie ... upon the Epistle to the Galathians* (London, 1575; ESTC 16965). Foxe's involvement is established by the introduction, extolling Luther as a comforter of troubled consciences, which closely paraphrases statements Foxe had made in *Acts and Monuments* and also comments he had made twenty-five years before in a translation of one of Luther's sermons. Luther's commentary met a need; there were six editions in Elizabeth's reign, and its popularity and iconic status only increased in the seventeenth century.

Henry Bull died in 1577, leaving among his papers a translation of Luther's commentary on the psalms of ascent (*A Commentarie upon the Fifteene Psalmes*, 1577; ESTC 16975). Foxe encouraged its publication and provided an introduction, again extolling Luther as a great spiritual physician. Spiritual comfort, too, is stressed in Bull's edition of John Hooper's commentary on four psalms—*Certeine Comfortable Expositions* (1580; ESTC 13743). The introduction to this work, recommending it to 'the sorrowing soule, which gronest for releife' (sig. ¶4r), was written by 'A.F.', probably Foxe's wife, Agnes. John Foxe also contributed a commendatory preface to a translation by William Gace of some of Luther's sermons, published in 1578, as he did in the same year for William Hilton's translation of Urbannus Regius, *The Sermon which Christ Made on his Way to Emaus* (ESTC 20650). All these works were intended to serve a pastoral purpose, and show Foxe as an organizer, if not the organizer, of a series of works by earlier reformers, most notably Luther, designed to comfort afflicted consciences. Just as the young Foxe's translations of sermons or treatises by Luther, Oecolampadius, and Regius were meant for the edification of his friends, so the older, successful Foxe devoted his time and energy, and invested his prestige, in providing translations intended to give spiritual comfort to those in need.

If this activity was a continuation of interests that the martyrologist had held for decades, it was also an extension of Foxe's activities as a spiritual physician in London. Simeon wrote of his father:

> There repaired to him, both Citizens and strangers, Noblemen, and Common-people of all degrees, and almost all for the same cause, to seek some salve for a wounded conscience. At length, some who were likewise sick in body, would needs be carried to him, but this to stop rumors, he would not suffer to be used. For because they were brought thither, they were by some reported to be cured. (*Acts and Monuments*, 1641, vol. 2, sig. B2r)

Yet if Foxe refused to attempt to cure ordinary diseases, he was active in healing those who were believed to suffer from that most extraordinary affliction, demonic possession.

Foxe's most notable success in this field was with his dispossession of a lawyer named Robert Briggs, who had fallen into despair of his sinfulness and the impossibility of his attaining salvation. Briggs repeatedly attempted suicide and then, in April 1574, fell into mysterious seizures during which he would hold conversations with Satan and also with angels. It is evident from repeated references which Briggs made to Foxe in these colloquies that the martyrologist had been counselling the lawyer, and on 24 April Foxe visited Briggs in the Temple during one of his seizures. He led a group of bystanders in prayer, commanding the devil to depart in the name of Jesus, and Briggs immediately regained his senses. A few days later Briggs suffered another seizure, accompanied by the loss of his sight, but was restored to full health when the bystanders prayed, using a prayer which Foxe had presciently left behind for just such an emergency. Briggs's seizures ceased after 1 May and he was considered cured. The case created a sensation; four manuscript accounts of it survive, and there were other manuscript accounts which are now lost. These accounts of Foxe's success influenced the dispossessions of John Darrell and other early modern English exorcists.

A few months later, in July 1574, demons were allegedly cast out of two London girls named Agnes Briggs (no relation to Robert) and Rachel Pinder. This case also created a sensation and a pamphlet, *A Verie Wonderfull Straunge Miracle*, was published within a few weeks of the dispossession. Although he had not conducted the actual dispossession, Foxe had been involved in the treatment of the two girls. With Foxe's reputation swelled by two 'miraculous' cures, Archbishop Parker intervened. The primate claimed to be concerned by the prospect of fraud and disorder; he was probably at least equally motivated by fears of a vast increase in the prestige and charisma of as independent and potentially troublesome a figure as Foxe. Parker had the two purported demoniacs interrogated, and imprisoned the mother of one of them, while copies of *A Verie Wonderfull Straunge Miracle* were called in. On 15 August 1574 the girls did penance at Paul's Cross, publicly confessing that their possessions and cures had been fraudulent. But Parker was after bigger game. A book, *The Disclosing of a Late Counterfeyted Possession* (ESTC 3738), was published under the archbishop's auspices shortly afterwards. Foxe was not named in its preface, which rebuked those who deluded the people 'for the maintenaunce of their owne estimation' (*Disclosing*, sig. A2r). But he was clearly and explicitly named in the text of the work, so this constituted a stinging rebuke. Parker went so far as to deny the authenticity of all demonic possessions, denouncing as sorcerers those who claimed to expel demons.

The exposure of Briggs and Pinder as frauds, coupled with Parker's blanket condemnation of all possessions as frauds, ended Foxe's dramatic expulsions of evil spirits from demoniacs, but his extensive ministry among the spiritually afflicted continued. Foxe's organization of the translations of Lutheran works and his casting out of demons may seem to be unrelated activities but they were actually two facets of Foxe's work as a spiritual physician.

The third edition of *Acts and Monuments* In 1576 John Day's son Richard returned from Cambridge, where he had been a divinity student, and began working for his father. It seems to have been Richard Day who was in charge of printing the third edition of *Acts and Monuments*; perhaps this was intended to be a baptism of fire for him. In the event, the decision to publish a new edition seems to have been made suddenly, with little advance planning by either John Day or Foxe. Hence the prevalence of basic typographical errors and a clear absence of any proofreading, let alone the meticulous corrections of the previous edition. The rush to publish may have limited the amount of money Day could raise to print the edition; the edition, its colophon dated 27 June 1576, was printed in smaller type and on poorer quality paper than its predecessors. And Foxe, atypically, does not seem to have done extensive research for it. Nevertheless, Foxe did make his contribution to this edition, which did not merely reprint that of 1570. Although there was no substantial deletion from the earlier text, information from oral sources was added to the sections dealing with Mary's reign and the beginning of Elizabeth's. Some of the additional material, notably John Hale's admonitory oration to Elizabeth, printed for the first time in this edition, was undoubtedly intended to spur Elizabeth and those in authority to thorough reformation of the church. The edition of 1576 is the high water mark of Foxe's radicalism, and subsequent events cooled his ardour for ecclesiastical reform.

Samuel Foxe and Magdalen College Samuel Foxe (1560–1630), who was born in the bishop's palace at Norwich on 31 December 1560, had been tutored in the duke of Norfolk's house. In October 1572, when he was almost twelve years old, Samuel entered the Merchant Taylors' School in London. Two years later he entered Magdalen, his father's old college. John Foxe wrote to his old friend Laurence Humphrey, the president of the college, asking him to take Samuel under his wing. Humphrey obliged and Samuel was elected a demy. Humphrey continued to take a close interest in Samuel's progress; at one point the president was personally coaching Samuel in Greek. Yet Humphrey's mentorship had its drawbacks; opposition to the president from more radical members of the college was mounting. The close association between Samuel Foxe and Humphrey made the martyrologist's son a target for the president's opponents.

A sign of trouble came in spring 1577, when John Foxe wrote to Humphrey, asking that his son's tutor, one of the most outspoken radicals in the college, be replaced with another tutor. In December 1577 Samuel Foxe left suddenly for France without obtaining a leave of absence. John Foxe persuaded his son to return and his intervention secured Samuel's readmission to the college without the imposition of any disciplinary measure. In 1579 the college elected Samuel a probationer fellow and he became a full fellow the next year. But in 1581 Samuel was

expelled from his fellowship. His father, in a letter to a bishop, denounced those responsible for Samuel's expulsion as 'those factious puritans' and 'thrice pure puritans'. Claiming that Samuel was expelled not for any fault of his own but simply because he was Humphrey's supporter, John Foxe warned his correspondent that the faction that expelled Samuel threatened all bishops and indeed the very stability of the church (BL, Harley MS 416, fols. 152r–153r).

This letter indicates how deep a chasm Samuel's troubles at Magdalen had opened between Foxe and the radicals. In part this was a generational conflict between men like Foxe and Humphrey, who had once been in the vanguard of reform, and their more extreme successors. In Foxe's case, this conflict was sharpened by his anger at the treatment of his son. The result was a muting, even a cessation, of John Foxe's calls for the further reformation of the church. An indication of how sharply Foxe's views had altered came in a letter that he wrote to Archbishop Whitgift in 1584. Thirteen years earlier Foxe had fought for revision of the Book of Common Prayer, but now, though he could not bring himself to approve fully of Whitgift's programme of mandatory subscription to the prayer book, he saw it as an understandable reaction to young and factious agitators.

John Foxe's frenetic lobbying, which included appeals to Cecil and Grindal, ultimately saw Samuel restored to his fellowship by royal command. The latter, however, still felt uncomfortable at Magdalen where the tensions between Humphrey and his opponents were far from resolved, and in December 1582 he obtained a year's leave of absence to study overseas. He left England in spring 1583, and after obtaining a number of extensions to his leave, he stayed abroad, travelling and studying in Germany, Switzerland, Italy, and France, until he returned to England in June 1586.

Heretics, Catholics, and Jews, 1575–1583 If one of Foxe's preoccupations was responding to the pastoral needs and afflicted consciences of the godly, another was trying to convert those who had not embraced the gospel. This second preoccupation dominated the works written in the final decade or so of his life. In April 1575 a conventicle of Flemish Anabaptists was arrested in London. Some of them recanted and others were banished from the realm, but others remained in prison under sentence of death. Possibly at the request of the Dutch Strangers' Church, Foxe intervened energetically on behalf of the condemned men. He wrote to the queen, Lord Burghley, the privy council, and one of the commissioners who had condemned them, urging that their sentences be commuted. Foxe also wrote to the Anabaptists, pleading with them to abandon their detestable opinions, and adding a long discourse on the humanity of Christ (which these Anabaptists had denied) to his letter. Despite his efforts, two Anabaptists were burnt at Smithfield on 22 July 1575; Foxe and his former protégé John Field were present.

In the letters he wrote on behalf of the Anabaptists, Foxe's deep abhorrence of the death penalty for heresy shines through. But this sentiment should not be confused with toleration. Foxe despised the Anabaptists' doctrines and was determined to eradicate such heresies from England. He approved of the banishment of the Anabaptists and urged exile, imprisonment, flogging, or branding as alternatives to execution. Most importantly, his fundamental argument for sparing the lives of the Anabaptists was his conviction that, if they were given enough time, they could be persuaded to recant their errors. Along with Foxe's determination to eliminate false religion went a profound conviction that it should, and could, be eliminated by persuasion rather than by force.

In 1563 Hieronymo Osorio da Fonseca, the bishop of Sylva, Portugal, had written a widely admired book urging Elizabeth to embrace Catholicism. Walter Haddon, a celebrated Latinist, responded in 1563, and Osorio replied in 1567. Haddon's second response was interrupted by his death in 1572. At Burghley's behest Foxe took up Haddon's pen and completed the work, in the end writing five-sixths of it. In doing so, Foxe followed his own agenda. In contrast to Haddon's point-by-point rebuttal of Osorio, Foxe dealt only with selected issues, but discussed them at enormous length. Thus a six-folio declaration by Osorio that Luther's teachings had led people to despair of their salvation was answered by a forty-one-folio discourse by Foxe on justification. Foxe's book was consequently less a rebuttal of Osorio than a treatise on theological issues in which he was particularly interested.

On 1 April 1577 Foxe preached a sermon at the baptism of a convert from Judaism at All Hallows, Bread Street. An expanded version of this sermon was printed in Latin in 1578 as *De oliva evangelica* (ESTC 11236). In his previous *Sermon of Christ Crucified* Foxe had contrasted the Catholic church with the true church. Now he not only made the same contrast between Judaism and the gospel, he also equated Judaism with Catholicism. Both were dominated by a priestly caste, both persecuted the followers of Christ, and both had replaced faith with a slavish addiction to law and ceremony. Just as Foxe had appealed to Catholics to accept the gospel, so he now appealed to Jews to do the same. It was typical of Foxe that he ended *De oliva evangelica* with an appeal to Christians to remove idols and superstitions (like the mass, purgatory, and clerical celibacy) from the church; these, he claimed, prevented the Jews from converting to Christianity.

In 1580 Foxe continued his attack on Catholicism, albeit anonymously, with his *Papas confutatas* (ESTC 11240). The work is divided into two parts, the first directed against the papal Antichrist, the second a treatise on the doctrinal errors of the Catholic church. Both parts were substantially compilations from earlier writings. Three years later he published his last work of anti-Catholic propaganda, *De Christo gratis justificante* (ESTC 11234). Ostensibly a further reply to Osorio, it was probably also a response to Edmund Campion's *Decem rationes*, as well as being directed to Foxe's favourite religious constituency, that of Christians afflicted in conscience. Revealingly, and remarkably, Foxe gave a copy of this treatise to Edmund Plowden, the eminent recusant lawyer. Throughout his dealings with Anabaptists, Jews, and Catholics, Foxe retained a remarkably positivist belief that they would be impressed by his arguments and a remarkably optimistic conviction that they were ripe for conversion.

The fourth edition of *Acts and Monuments* In October 1583 the fourth edition of *Acts and Monuments* was printed. Unlike the previous edition, this one had been planned well before publication. As word circulated about the new edition Laurence Humphrey passed on to Foxe suggestions he had received for improving it. These included the use of better paper and more legible type, more extensive references, and the inclusion of all the material deleted from the previous editions (BL, Harley MS 416, fols. 203r–205r). Foxe and Day followed some of these suggestions. The new edition, which ran to about 2100 pages, was indeed printed on better paper and in larger type. Some of the material excised from earlier editions was restored but a great deal of it was not, and material was deleted. Offsetting this Foxe brought in more archival material, drawn from further research in the Tower records and in the registers of the privy council, and additional oral testimony. A highly personal addition, and one which adumbrated Foxe's next major project, was a digression in the narrative, 'The mysticall numbers in the Apocalyps opened', in which Foxe applied the chronology of events in Revelation to human history (Foxe, *Acts and Monuments*, 1583, 101).

Yet despite its enhanced size, improved physical appearance, and careful preparation, this edition was hurriedly printed. One document added to the text was dated 25 July 1583, only months before the edition was published. The reason for the haste was Day's failing health; for both personal and financial reasons he was anxious to see the edition completed. Day succeeded in this (he died on 23 July 1584), but at a certain cost to the edition. The proofreading and correction processes were non-existent while the cross-references, which had hitherto been updated in each succeeding edition, were not revised, with the result that the notes in the fourth edition referred readers to the relevant pages in the third edition.

The fourth edition was the last edition of *Acts and Monuments* to appear in Foxe's lifetime. Five further unabridged editions of the work appeared in the next 101 years. Each contained significant additions of material (largely accounts of Catholic or prelatical 'atrocities' and introductory materials) reflecting the different agendas of its editors. *Acts and Monuments* remained a living and evolving text long after Foxe was dead.

Foxe's final years, 1583–1587 In June 1586 Samuel Foxe finally returned from abroad, and sought to secure the 'lawyer's place' among the fellows at Magdalen College. Despite Lord Burghley's support, he was unsuccessful, although he obtained the lesser 'physician's place'. Meanwhile John Foxe took steps to secure his son's future. His brother-in-law Thomas Randall, who had leased Foxe's prebendal lands and tithes, died in 1585. John Foxe manoeuvred to have these leases settled on Samuel, so that the income from the prebend would remain with the Foxe family even after John's death. There was a difficulty in that Bishop John Piers of Salisbury, having already obtained the right to nominate Foxe's successor from the queen, had promised the prebend to his domestic chaplain (who was also his son-in-law). Foxe appealed to Whitgift for help and consequently Piers renounced his interest in the prebend. The leases were bestowed on Samuel Foxe and they remained in the hands of his descendants until 1761.

Despite his position at Magdalen College, Samuel stayed in London assisting his father with his last great project, a massive Latin commentary on Revelation. John Foxe died, at his house in Grub Street in the parish of St Giles Cripplegate, while the work was in progress, on 18 April 1587, and Samuel published the incomplete book later that year and dedicated it to Whitgift. The *Eicasmi, seu, Meditationes in sacram Apocalypsim* (ESTC 11237) ran to 396 quarto pages even though it extended only to the seventeenth chapter of Revelation. It owes its length to its function as a systematic and historically detailed exegesis of Revelation along lines pioneered by John Bale, who maintained that the events described in this last book of the Bible as preceding the second coming of Christ were prophecies of events in human history, most of which could be identified as having already taken place. The framework of Foxe's commentary on Revelation rested on the foundations of *Acts and Monuments*. Thus Foxe's commentary on Revelation 8: 7 is followed by a six-page description of the first ten persecutions of the church, which is essentially a précis of the first section of *Acts and Monuments*. And, in a splendid example of the wheel's coming full circle, in order to support his novel identification of Jan Hus and Jerome of Prague as the two witnesses described in Revelation, Foxe reprinted nearly forty pages from *Acts and Monuments* which, in turn, were reprinted from Flacius's work on Hus. To Foxe the *Eicasmi* was not only a guide to understanding the events in Revelation, it was a guide to understanding the events in *Acts and Monuments* as well.

John Foxe was buried in St Giles Cripplegate on 20 April 1587, with a memorial recording that he had died aged seventy. His widow, Agnes, continued to live in their house on Grub Street and a letter addressed to her there, from her son Samuel and dating from 1592 or 1593, survives among the Foxe family papers. She was almost certainly the Mother Foxe buried at St Giles Cripplegate on 22 April 1605.

Samuel Foxe and his father's papers   Samuel Foxe prospered after his father's death. In 1587 he entered the service of Sir Thomas Heneage, the queen's vice-chamberlain, and became his steward. It was thanks to Heneage's patronage that Samuel became MP for Midhurst in 1589 and for Knaresborough in 1593, and that he accumulated a substantial estate. On 15 August 1589 he married Anne Leveson (*d.* 1630), a kinswoman of Sir Thomas, and in a letter of 1628 was able to boast that he had spent £1000 in providing marriage portions for his two daughters, and that his estate was unencumbered by debt. He settled at Warlies, near Waltham Abbey, Essex, and died there in January 1630. In his will he made provision for a younger son, Robert, but the bulk of his property was bequeathed to his widow and eventually passed to his elder son, Thomas.

Samuel's greatest bequest, however, was made, indirectly, to posterity. On John Foxe's death Samuel came into possession of his father's library and his papers. Samuel was shrewd enough to see their value and dispersed them with care. At least some, perhaps all, of John Foxe's printed books were either sold or given to Archbishop Whitgift, who also acquired a number of manuscript works which had belonged to the martyrologist. An important collection of John Foxe's manuscripts, source materials for *Acts and Monuments*, and Bull's *Letters of the Martyrs* was given to Emmanuel College, Cambridge, some time between 1584 and 1597; whether this gift was made by John Foxe or Samuel Foxe is unknown. Other manuscripts were sold by Samuel to Lord William Howard of Naworth. In 1614, in celebration of Thomas Foxe's graduating MA at Magdalen, Samuel Foxe gave fourteen manuscript works formerly owned by his father to the college that had once expelled him. Samuel retained and conserved the greatest part of his father's papers, however, including all of his father's extant correspondence. These manuscripts remained in the hands of Samuel Foxe's descendants until the historian John Strype acquired them from Sir Thomas Willis, Samuel Foxe's great-grandson. Strype sold most of these manuscripts to Edward Harley, earl of Oxford; the remainder passed into the Lansdowne collection. Both sets of these manuscripts are now in the British Library.

Foxe's historical reputation   In his lifetime John Foxe was one of the most prominent members of the Elizabethan church. His translation of Luther's commentary on Galatians and his commentary on Revelation were both highly influential and popular for over a century after his death. He was a significant figure in the development of practical divinity and spiritual healing in England. Nevertheless all these achievements were overshadowed by *Acts and Monuments*, and Foxe's reputation after his death was completely intertwined with that of his great work. The romantic picture of people from all sections of English society devoutly studying *Acts and Monuments* in their parish church needs to be modified in the light of the limits of both early modern book production and early modern literacy. No sixteenth-century book could hope to be read by more than a minority of the population, and the diffusion of Foxe's work into the parish churches did not get seriously under way until the seventeenth century, reaching its height in the immediate aftermath of the civil war, just when his reputation was on the verge of a precipitous decline. Nevertheless through the first half of the seventeenth century *Acts and Monuments* was not merely a remarkably popular book but was one of immense, almost unquestioned, authority. It was also a work of direct relevance to its readers on a range of theological, apologetic, homiletic, and even political issues of central concern.

By the end of the seventeenth century, however, there was only one way in which *Acts and Monuments* could be of interest to large numbers of readers: as a compendium of atrocities, real and imagined, committed by Catholics against protestants and as a knife to twist in the wound of sectarian hatred. The last early modern unabridged edition of the work was printed in 1684 at the height of the exclusion crisis. In the future, however, editors did not even bother to reprint the entire work, but preferred to cut away the sections of it that did not suit their purposes, retaining only sensational episodes of torture and death, which, when taken together with equally sensational illustrations, gave Foxe's work a lurid quality which was certainly far from the author's intention. Fresh examples of such episodes, such as the Irish massacre of 1641, were added to these editions. The process of abridging Foxe's book and of adding material to it had begun almost immediately after his death. But between 1684 and 1832 the only editions of Foxe published were, through both abridgement and enlargement, works that bore little relation to the original and were merely topical anti-Catholic screeds. The Victorian unabridged editions of the work, first published in 1832, were similarly motivated by the desire both to stem increasing toleration of Catholicism and to bolster the evangelicals against the rising tide of high-church Anglicanism.

Foxe's reputation suffered greatly as a result of this partisan appropriation of his martyrology. On the one hand, fierce attacks, inspired by religious motivations, were launched in the first half of the nineteenth century against the accuracy of *Acts and Monuments* by Bishop John Milner, William Cobbett, William Eusebius Andrews, and, most importantly, Samuel R. Maitland. At the same time, the production of the new unabridged editions of Foxe, as well as the defence of the credibility of these editions and of Foxe himself, was undertaken by people of impeccable evangelical credentials but limited scholarship and ability. Maitland, who spearheaded the criticism of these new editions, which rapidly blossomed into a full-scale assault on Foxe's veracity and his abilities as a historian, was a learned and often perceptive critic, and his criticisms, while inspired by a deep aversion to low-churchmanship in all its forms, were not infrequently well founded. So complete was Maitland's victory over Foxe's nineteenth-century champions that, in the words of a Victorian Catholic writer, 'no one with any literary pretensions has since ventured to quote Foxe as an authority' (Trenow, 12).

The tide eventually turned in 1940 with the publication of J. F. Mozley's biography of Foxe. While overly sympathetic to his subject, Mozley nevertheless persuasively challenged many aspects of the dominant, excessively negative, evaluation of Foxe's work and initiated a rehabilitation of Foxe as a historian which has continued to this day. In 1963 William Haller produced a very influential study of the reception and impact of *Acts and Monuments* which, while poorly researched and surprisingly ill-informed about Foxe's text, did succeed in establishing the seminal influence of Foxe's work in early modern England.

Current scholarship has formed a more complex and nuanced estimate of the accuracy of *Acts and Monuments*

than is afforded either by the hypercriticism of Maitland or the overestimation of Mozley. Foxe's great work is too large and the product of too many contributors to allow any unequivocal generalization on the subject. It would be rash to forget that Foxe not only was himself an assiduous researcher into oral and documentary sources, but he was in addition able to draw on the work of other scholars and on networks of informants. But it would also be imprudent to overlook that Foxe was an accomplished rhetorician with powerful motives for shaping and editing his material. It was rare, though not unknown, for him to invent material. But he edited, amended, and even rewrote his sources with alacrity. Perhaps he may be most profitably seen in the same light as a barrister pleading a case for a client he knows to be innocent and whom he is determined to save. Like the hypothetical barrister, Foxe had to deal with the evidence of what actually happened, evidence that he was rarely in a position to forge. But he would not present facts damaging to his client, and he had the skills that enabled him to arrange the evidence so as to make it conform to what he wanted it to say. Like the barrister, Foxe presents crucial evidence and tells one side of a story which must be heard. But he should never be read uncritically, and his partisan objectives should always be kept in mind.

The importance of *Acts and Monuments* is currently uncontested. It is at once both the most important narrative source for the English Reformation and a work that helped to shape its later development. Nevertheless serious study of this mighty work is still in its infancy. Foxe's manuscript collections have gone largely unexplored; indeed, their true extent was established only in the 1990s. And the immense size of the various editions, together with the variations between them, along with the readiness of modern scholars to rely on accessible but grossly deficient Victorian editions, have meant that a great deal of Foxe's martyrology remains practically unknown. At the beginning of the third millennium—a juncture Foxe would have been surprised to see humanity reach—it can at least be said that historians have become aware of the problems involved in understanding his methods, purposes, and achievements, as well as of the labour likely to be needed to solve them.

THOMAS S. FREEMAN

Sources Foxe's correspondence, BL, Harley MSS 416–417 • Simeon Foxe's memoir of his father and Foxe's letters from his days at Magdalen College, BL, Lansdowne MS 388 • personal papers of John Foxe, BL, Harley MSS 418–426, 590, 716, 783 • personal papers of John Foxe and his family, BL, Lansdowne MSS 335, 353, 389, 679, 819, 1045 • S. Foxe, biographical memoir of John Foxe, in J. Foxe, *Acts and monuments*, 2 (1641) • J. Foxe, *Christ Jesus triumphant*, trans. R. Day (1607) [ESTC 11232; the dedication to this edition, and only this edition, contains valuable biographical detail on John Foxe] • J. G. Nichols, ed., *Narratives of the days of the Reformation*, CS, old ser., 77 (1859) • W. Nicholson, ed., *The remains of Edmund Grindal*, Parker Society, 9 (1843) • J. F. Mozley, *John Foxe and his book* (1940) • D. Loades, ed., *John Foxe and the English Reformation* (1997) • D. Loades, ed., *John Foxe: an historical perspective* (1999) • G. Bray, ed., *Tudor church reform: the Henrician canons of 1535 and the Reformatio legum ecclesiasticarum*, Church of England Record Society, 8 (2000) • *Two Latin comedies by John Foxe the martyrologist: Titus et Gesippus and Christus* *triumphans*, ed. J. H. Smith (Ithaca, NY, 1973) • S. Wabuda, 'Henry Bull, Miles Coverdale, and the making of Foxe's Book of martyrs', *Martyrs and martyrologies*, ed. D. Wood, SCH, 30 (1993), 245–58 • T. Freeman, '"The Good Ministrye of Godlye and Vertuouse Women": the Elizabethan martyrologists and the female supporters of the Marian martyrs', *Journal of British Studies*, 39 (2000), 8–33 • T. Freeman, 'John Bale's book of martyrs?: the account of King John in *Acts and monuments*', *Reformation*, 3 (1998), 175–223 • P. Collinson, 'Truth and legend: the veracity of John Foxe's book of martyrs', *Elizabethan essays* (1994), 151–77 • T. Freeman, 'Texts, lies and microfilm: reading and misreading Foxe's "Book of martyrs"', *Sixteenth Century Journal*, 30 (1999), 23–46 • J. Facey, 'John Foxe and the defence of the English church', *Protestantism and the national church in sixteenth century England*, ed. P. Lake and M. Dowling (1987), 162–92 • B. Gregory, *Salvation at stake: Christian martyrdom in early modern Europe* (Cambridge, MA, 1999) • R. Bauckham, *Tudor apocalypse* (1978) • K. Frith, *The apocalyptic tradition in Reformation Britain* (1979) • P. Christianson, *Reformers and Babylon: English apocalyptic visions from the Reformation to the eve of the civil war* (Toronto, 1978) • T. Betteridge, *Tudor histories of the English Reformations, 1530–83* (1999) • W. Haller, *Foxe's book of martyrs and the elect nation* (1963) • R. Helgerson, *Forms of nationhood: the Elizabethan writing of England* (Chicago, 1992) • J. R. Knott, *Discourses of martyrdom in English literature, 1563–1694* (1993) • H. White, *Tudor books of saints and martyrs* (Madison, WI, 1967) • T. S. Freeman, '"The Reformation of the Church in this Parliament": Thomas Norton, John Foxe and the parliament of 1571', *Parliamentary History*, 16 (1997), 131–47 • T. S. Freeman, 'The importance of dying earnestly: the metamorphosis of the account of James Bainham in *Foxe's Book of Martyrs*', *The church retrospective*, ed. R. N. Swanson, SCH, 33 (1997), 267–88 • T. Freeman, '"The Reik of Maister Patrick Hammyltoun": John Foxe, John Winram and the martyrs of the Scottish Reformation', *Sixteenth Century Journal*, 27 (1996), 23–46 • T. Freeman and M. Borges, '"A grave and heinous incident against our holy Catholic faith": two accounts of William Gardiner's desecration of the Portuguese royal chapel in 1552', *Historical Research*, 69 (1996), 1–17 • T. Freeman, 'Notes on a source for John Foxe's account of the Marian persecution in Kent and Sussex', *Historical Research*, 67 (1994), 203–11 • T. Freeman, '"A solemne contestation of divers popes": a work by John Foxe?', *English Language Notes*, 31 (1993–4), 35–42 • C. Davies and J. Facey, 'A Reformation dilemma: John Foxe and the problem of discipline', *Journal of Ecclesiastical History*, 39 (1988), 37–65 • M. Murphy, 'John Foxe, martyrologist and "editor" of Old English', *English Studies*, 49 (1968), 515–23 • J. G. Rechtien, 'John Foxe's *Comprehensive collection of commonplaces*: a renaissance memory system for students and theologians', *Sixteenth Century Journal*, 9 (1978), 83–9 • P. S. Dunkin, 'Foxe's *Acts and monuments*, 1570, and single-page imposition', *Library*, 5th ser., 2 (1947), 159–70 • V. Norskov Olsen, *John Foxe and the Elizabethan church* (Berkeley, CA, 1973) • W. W. Wooden, *John Foxe* (Boston, 1983) • W. Winters, *Biographical notes on John Foxe the martyrologist* (1876) • C. M. Dent, *Protestant reformers in Elizabethan Oxford* (1983) • HoP, *Commons, 1558–1603*, 2.155–6 • J. Woolfson, 'The Paduan sojourns of Samuel and Simeon Foxe', *Quaderni dell' Università di Padova*, 30 (1997), 111–24 • D. Trenow, *The credibility of John Foxe, the 'martyrologist'* (1868) • GL, MS 6419/1, fol. 95r • parish register, Waltham Abbey [Samuel Foxe, burial]

Archives BL, Add. MS 19400 • BL, corresp. and papers, Harley MSS, Lansdowne MSS • Emmanuel College, Cambridge, MSS 260–262 | BL, Harley MSS 416–426, 590, 783 • BL, Lansdowne MSS 335, 353, 388, 389, 819, 1045 • Inner Temple, London, Petyt MSS

Likenesses oils, 1587, NPG [*see illus.*] • S. de Passe, line engraving, pubd 1620 (after unknown artist), BM, NPG • G. Glover, line engraving, BM, NPG; repro. in J. Foxe, *Acts and monuments* (1641) • W. and M. van de Passe, line engraving, BM, NPG; repro. in H. Holland, *Herōologia* (1620)

Wealth at death well off; Samuel Foxe: will, BL, Lansdowne MS 819, fol. 32r

Foxe, Richard. *See* Fox, Richard (1447/8–1528).

Foxe, Samuel (1560–1630). *See under* Foxe, John (1516/17–1587).

Foxe, Simeon (1569–1642), physician, was the younger of the two sons of John *Foxe (1516/17–1587), the martyrologist, and Agnes Randall (1519–1599/1605) of Coventry, who was said to have been fifty at the time of her son's birth on 2 February 1569 in the house of the duke of Norfolk, Aldgate, London. Samuel *Foxe (1560–1630), the diarist, was his brother. He was educated at Eton College, and on 24 August 1583 was admitted a scholar at King's College, Cambridge. He became a fellow on 24 August 1586, but in the same year wrote a letter to his father expressing his disgust with academic logic and dialectics. He explained that the study of natural philosophy was much more congenial to his mind, and would better serve his wants in old age, strongly suggesting that he may have been thinking already of a medical career. No doubt he was also influenced by the ejection of his elder brother Samuel from his fellow's place at Magdalen College, Oxford, between 1581 and 1585. If he was not inclined to follow an academic career, Foxe none the less proceeded BA in 1587 and MA in 1591, and continued as a fellow until 1592.

Writings from his early student years reveal Foxe to be a serious young man and personally devout. His friend and admirer Baldwin Hamey later wrote that Foxe was serious without being morose, and religious without being superstitious. Bishop Piers promised him a prebend, but Foxe preferred to study medicine. After leaving college he lived for some time with Archbishop John Whitgift. He saw military service with Sir John Norris and the earl of Southampton, in Ireland and the Low Countries, and is said to have been taken prisoner and detained for a time at Dunkirk. He was in Padua and Venice between 1602 and 1604, studying medicine, but also gathering information for the English government. He was fluent in Italian. Foxe reached London in 1605, and shortly afterward commenced to practise medicine with great success. At some point he must also have incorporated his foreign degree at an English university, but the dates for his Padua MD and the incorporation remain a mystery.

Foxe was admitted a candidate of the London College of Physicians on 30 September 1605, and a fellow on 25 June 1608. He was censor in 1614, 1620, 1621, 1623, 1624, 1625, 1631, and 1632. He was elected registrar on 20 November 1627; treasurer on 3 December 1629; anatomy reader in 1630; elect on 22 December 1630; president from 1634 to 1641; and consiliarius, also in 1641.

Foxe is probably best known as the friend and physician of the dean of St Paul's, John Donne. The striking funerary monument of Donne in St Paul's was commissioned largely at the expense of Foxe, who preserved his anonymous benefaction during his lifetime. Foxe is also now generally accepted as the author of a memoir of his father's life, which first appeared in 1641 in a new edition of John Foxe's *Acts and Monuments*. If true (and the case is a very strong one), this would reveal a hidden revolutionary side to Foxe, since the republication of his father's great work was largely directed against the increasing ritualization of the Anglican church under Archbishop William Laud, as a reminder to Englishmen of the threat of Roman Catholicism.

Foxe's greatest monument may be his tenure as college president from 1634 to 1641. Never married, Foxe was devoted to the College of Physicians and enjoyed enormous popularity and respect among the fellows, who would not let him resign the office, despite the fact that Foxe was, by 1641, over seventy years of age. Foxe dealt with numerous and serious college problems during his presidency, problems that would have sapped the energy of a far younger man. The greatest of these involved the apothecaries of London who were chafing under the control of the physicians, and were clamouring for their recognition as practitioners in their own right. All of this occurred in the politically charged atmosphere that was the prelude to the civil war, which did not make Foxe's job any easier, as he was responsible for deciding the appropriate college response to contemporary events and pressures. Foxe was a stickler for enforcing college rights and privileges. One of these cherished rights was the censorship of any medical book published in England. In 1641, in one of his last acts as president, Foxe allowed the publication of Roger Drake's vindication of William Harvey's theory of the circulation of the blood. As college president Foxe would officially neither approve nor disapprove of the book's publication. His personal view was much more positive. Initially sceptical, Foxe eventually became a strong supporter of Harvey. It is likely they had been friends all along. Both were products of Cambridge and Padua, had begun practice in London, and had entered the College of Physicians at approximately the same time. Harvey was elected a fellow in 1607 and in the following year, 1608, had cast one of the votes that made Foxe a fellow as well. The two physicians were often paired in college business and seemed to have an excellent working relationship.

Foxe was a long-time resident of Carter Lane in the parish of St Martin Ludgate but also had rooms in the college house on Amen Corner, Paternoster Row, where he died at two in the morning on 20 April 1642. In his will dated 21 October 1641 and proved by his nephew Thomas *Foxe, Foxe requested a 'Christian burial within the Cathedral Church of St Paul in London, as near to the monument of Doctor Linacre as conveniently may be', while also bequeathing £20 to the maintenance of the cathedral (PRO, PROB 11/189/51). Thomas Linacre was the first president of the London College of Physicians in the early sixteenth century and Foxe identified closely with the humanist physician, not the least in his devotion to Galen, whom Linacre edited and translated. Foxe was buried on 24 April 1642, also leaving the college £40, to which his nephew added another £60. Thomas Foxe also wrote an epitaph for his uncle and erected a monument to his memory in St Paul's, long since lost. In 1656, at the urging of Baldwin Hamey, the college placed Foxe's bust in the new Harveian Museum, all of which was destroyed by the great fire of 1666. His portrait was saved from the fire, but has since disappeared.　　　　WILLIAM BIRKEN

Sources B. Hamey, 'Bustorum aliquot reliquiae ...', RCP Lond. · J. F. Mozley, *John Foxe and his book* (1940) · J. Foxe, *Actes and monuments*, 8th edn, 3 vols. (1641) · *The acts and monuments of John Foxe*, new edn, ed. G. Townsend, 8 vols. (1843–9); facs. edn (1965) · W. Winters, 'John Foxe, the martyrologist and his family', *TRHS*, 5 (1877), 28–82 · W. D. Macray, *A register of the members of St Mary Magdalen College, Oxford*, 8 vols. (1894–1915), vol. 3 · annals, RCP Lond. · Munk, *Roll* · E. Gosse, *The life and letters of John Donne, dean of St Paul's*, 2 vols. (1899) · BL, Harley MS 416 · M. A. E. Green, ed., *Calendar of the proceedings of the committee for advance of money, 1642–1656*, 3 vols., PRO (1888) · J. McConica, 'Scholars and commoners in Renaissance Oxford', *The university in society*, ed. L. Stone, 1 (1974), 151–81 · G. Keynes, *The life of William Harvey* (1966) · J. Woolfson, *Padua and the Tudors* (1998)
Archives BL, Harley MS 416

Foxe, Thomas (1592–1662), physician, was the eldest of two sons of Samuel *Foxe (1560–1630) [see under Foxe, John], eldest son of John *Foxe, the martyrologist, and Anne Leveson (d. 1630), the daughter of Sir John Leveson of Eastwell, Kent. He was born at Havering atte Bower, Essex, on 14 February 1592. His earliest years were spent at Havering and in the neighbourhood of Warlies, in Waltham, Essex, where the family eventually settled. Nothing is known of his earliest schooling.

Foxe matriculated from Magdalen Hall, Oxford, on 19 June 1607. He was elected demy at Magdalen College in 1608 and remained demy until 1613. He graduated BA in 1611, but was admonished by college authorities for disrespectful behaviour at divine service in 1612 and 1613. None the less, he was elected fellow of Magdalen in 1613 and remained as such until 1630. He was praelector in logic at the college from 1613 to 1615. He graduated MA in 1614. On 2 November 1615 he was allowed to divert his studies to medicine. He also practised medicine for at least four years after this date. He took a year's leave of absence from the college in 1621, but was elected junior proctor for Oxford in late 1621 and bursar at Magdalen in 1622. It is likely he took his MD at Magdalen in the latter year. On 24 December 1622 he was deprived some days at commons for angry words to another fellow, Peter Heylin, the future Laudian apologist and historian. He took his second leave of absence in 1623.

On 23 May 1623 Foxe appeared in London for examination at the College of Physicians where his uncle Simeon Foxe was then censor. He was referred to in the annals of the college as 'Dr. Fox, junior'. He was elected a candidate in the college on 25 June 1623, but never pursued a fellow's place and dropped out of college records until 1635. He took another leave of absence from Magdalen in 1624, but was elected bursar again in 1625, before taking another leave of absence in 1626. Family evidence places him at Warlies in early 1627. He resumed his fellowship of Magdalen in this year and served continuously there until 1630.

In 1628 Thomas and Samuel Foxe were planning a lucrative marriage for the son, but these plans fell through. His father died in 1630 and his mother died later that year. By Samuel Foxe's will of 29 June 1622 Thomas would inherit his estate after the death of his mother. The elder Foxe was especially proud that his substantial estate would pass to his son entire, unencumbered by any debt. With the sale of his resigned Magdalen fellowship in 1630 and his inheritance in the same year, Thomas Foxe busily set to work expanding his holdings and wealth in and around the parish of Waltham church. Another important source of income was that from the clerical living of Shipton under Wychwood in Oxfordshire, which Elizabeth I had bestowed on his grandfather. The Foxe family was also thriving in London where his uncle Simeon Foxe, whose medical career had no doubt influenced his nephew, was elected president of the College of Physicians in 1634. By 1632 Thomas Foxe had married Anne (1588–1648), daughter of Robert Honywood of Charing, Kent, and Marks Hall, Essex, and the granddaughter of Mrs Mary Honywood, a good friend of John Foxe. Their only child, Alice, was born on 22 February 1637. The marriage may have been another factor that impelled Foxe to resume his medical practice in London. He is listed as a 'licentiate' residing within the jurisdiction of the college. By 1638 the family were living in the parish of St Botolph's, Aldersgate, where their house was rated the fifth most valuable dwelling in a parish of more than 200 householders.

Foxe and his uncle Simeon were easily confused by both contemporaries and later historians. Both were 'Dr Ffox' and associated with the College of Physicians, and both lived in close proximity to the College House in Amen Corner. A privy council letter to one of them survives from 1639, and an even more intriguing last letter from the condemned earl of Strafford to Charles I was carried by 'Mr. Doctor Ffox' to the royal court on 4 May 1641. Testifying to the closeness of uncle and nephew at this time was Simeon's will of 21 October 1641. Naming Thomas Foxe the will's sole executor, the old physician also bestowed £1000 towards the dowry of Alice Foxe, his nephew's four-year-old daughter, and left the remainder of his estate to Thomas Foxe after various disbursements to friends and relations. In the early morning hours of 20 April 1642, with his nephew at his bedside, Simeon Foxe died in his rooms at the College of Physicians. Thomas Foxe proved his uncle's will on 29 April, and dutifully carried out its provisions. With the college's permission, he occupied his uncle's rooms there for several months after his death.

On 11 September 1643, his own estate increasing from his uncle's legacies and his advantageous marriage into the Honywood family, Thomas Foxe received an assessment of £1000 from the parliamentary committee for the advance of money, for the war effort against Charles I. As with all those assessed, he finally settled with a lesser payment later. But his initial assessment was still significant. It was five times greater than that of most fellows of the College of Physicians and more commensurate with the income of a landed gentleman than a working physician. His estate increased again in 1646 with the death, without heirs, of his younger brother, Robert Foxe, a captain in the navy.

Thomas's wife died on 26 May 1648, and was buried with her family at Charing. Foxe continued to reside in London until at least 1650. By 1654 he seems to have given up his London residence though continuing to visit the City.

Some indication of his wealth came in the request that year of a loan of £500 to his friend, James Hay, earl of Carlisle and lord of Waltham Abbey. Foxe sold Warlies after 1630, but continued to live in Waltham where he now seems to have retired. He lived to see his daughter married well to Sir Richard Willys, bt, of Fen Ditton, Cambridgeshire; the birth of his first grandchild, Ann Fox Willys, in February 1660; and the birth of a grandson, Thomas Fox Willys, on 30 June 1661. Foxe died on 20 November 1662 in Waltham and was buried in Waltham church six days later. His actual medical practice remains an enigma beyond his observation that his grandson was born 'bereft of his wits' (Winters, 58) in 1661. This same grandson died in a lunatic asylum in 1701. Foxe's will of 1662, executed by his daughter, makes no mention of a medical career.

WILLIAM BIRKEN

Sources W. Winters, 'John Foxe, the martyrologist and his family', *TRHS*, 5 (1877), 28–82 · W. D. Macray, *A register of the members of St Mary Magdalen College, Oxford*, 3 (1901) · annals, RCP Lond. · BL, Lansdowne MS 679 · BL, Harley MS 416 · B. Hamey, 'Bustorum aliquot reliquiae …', RCP Lond. · will of Simeon Foxe, PRO, PROB 11/189, sig. 51 · J. F. Mozley, *John Foxe and his book* (1940) · LPL, MS 272 · M. A. E. Green, ed., *Calendar of the proceedings of the committee for advance of money, 1642–1656*, 3 vols., PRO (1888) · L. Stone, ed., *The university in society*, 2 vols. (1974) · M. Zell, ed., *Early modern Kent, 1540–1640* (2000) · will, PRO, PROB 11/309, sig. 140
Archives BL, Harley MSS 416–426 · BL, Lansdowne MSS, papers, 388, 679, 819

Foxley, Barbara (1860–1958), educationist and campaigner for women's rights, was born on 20 August 1860 at Market Weighton in the East Riding of Yorkshire, the second daughter of the Revd Joseph Foxley (1827–1911), vicar of that parish, and his wife, Lucy Allen. She was educated privately at home, then at schools in Manchester and London, before going up to Newnham College, Cambridge, in 1879. She took a second class in the historical tripos in 1881, but this was at a time before Cambridge awarded degrees to women. She then gained a teaching certificate and later obtained an MA from Trinity College, Dublin. She did not receive her MA degree from Cambridge until 1949, following the university's decision to open its degrees to women in the previous year.

A small, delicately featured woman, Foxley possessed an incisive intellect and was a talented linguist and an impressive public speaker. She made important contributions to education, women's rights, and public life in south Wales. She held various teaching posts and by the age of twenty-five obtained her first headship at Dewsbury church school but it was her appointment as headmistress of Queen Mary's High School, Walsall, which marked a decisive step in her career. She placed a very high value on the education of girls and in Walsall her work attracted wide attention. Her reputation led to a position in the education department at Manchester University as 'mistress of method', where she produced a translation into English of Jean Jacques Rousseau's seminal text *Émile* for the Everyman's Library edition (1911). She was appointed to a position at University College, Cardiff, in

1911, where four years later she succeeded Millicent Mackenzie as professor of education: Cardiff at this time had separate education departments for women and men students. Her forceful, but likeable, personality, her organizational ability, and her dedication to her work ensured that her years in Cardiff, where she remained until her retirement in 1925, were extremely successful. As she modestly put it, 'The College seemed to like me' (*Western Mail*).

Professor Foxley was a dedicated campaigner for women's suffrage and an advocate of women's rights, pressing, in particular, for women to enter public life. She was a member of the executive committee of the very effective Cardiff and District Women's Suffrage Society, where she worked alongside Mary Collin, headmistress of Cardiff High School for Girls. By 1913 the Cardiff Society, which was affiliated to the moderate National Union of Women's Suffrage Societies (NUWSS), was the largest society outside London. In 1919, when the NUWSS was renamed the National Union of Societies for Equal Citizenship, following the partial enfranchisement of women in 1918, she was elected to its national executive committee.

Foxley consistently urged women to stand for public office. Politically she was a liberal and in 1924 she stood as official Liberal candidate for the Cathays ward in a by-election to Cardiff city council. She won the seat, polling almost twice the number of votes as the Labour candidate. As a councillor she took particular interest in education, housing, and issues relating to women. In religion she was a Unitarian and was a frequent and eloquent preacher at Cardiff's Unitarian church. In later years she continued to live a very active life, travelling widely. She spent much of her retirement in Cardiff before moving to the spa town of Llandrindod Wells, Radnorshire, for health reasons, where she died at the Spa Nursing Home on 26 August 1958.   DEIRDRE BEDDOE

Sources *The Times* (28 Aug 1958) • *Western Mail* [Cardiff] (27 Aug 1958) • A. Mee, ed., *Who's who in Wales* (1921), 147 • Glamorgan RO, Cardiff and District Women's Suffrage Society records

Archives Glamorgan RO, Cardiff, Cardiff and District Women's Suffrage Society records, election publicity and suffrage activity material

Likenesses portrait, 1924, Glamorgan RO [election leaflet] • photographs, Glamorgan RO [newspaper clippings]

Wealth at death £575 8s. 4d.: probate, 20 Oct 1958, CGPLA Eng. & Wales

Foxwell, Herbert Somerton (1849–1936), economist and bibliographer, was born at Shepton Mallet, Somerset, on 17 June 1849. He was the eldest of the four sons of Thomas Somerton Foxwell (1806–1886), of Shepton Mallet, who had a considerable and lucrative business as an ironmonger and later as a slate and timber merchant, and his second wife, Jane Handcock (1824–1878), who was of Irish and Channel Islands descent. Herbert Foxwell was educated at the Wesleyan Collegiate Institute (later Queen's College), Taunton, and graduated BA of London University in 1867. He proceeded in the Lent term of 1868 to St John's College,

Cambridge, where he was senior in the moral sciences tripos of 1870 and was elected a foundation scholar of his college, being awarded the Whewell scholarship in international law in 1872.

Foxwell, although spending much of his time in London, lived at Cambridge throughout his adult life, first at St John's, and then, after his marriage in 1898, at 1 Harvey Road, a few doors from John Neville Keynes. His wife was Olive May (1878–1930), eldest daughter of William Edward Dorrington, a Manchester shipper. They had two daughters. Foxwell usually spent the summer at Barmouth, where he was an energetic walker and mountaineer. He died at his home in Harvey Road on 3 August 1936.

Foxwell's university work was threefold: at Cambridge; at University College, London; and at the London School of Economics and Political Science. His interests were: political economy in general; banking; the formation of a library of economic literature; and the compilation with W. R. Scott and Henry Higgs of a definitive bibliography of economic literature. Beginning with extension lecturing, he was in 1874 appointed examiner at Cambridge in the moral sciences tripos and elected a fellow of St John's, where he was first a lecturer and later (1912) director of economic studies; he remained closely associated with the college for sixty years. Two of his younger brothers were also members of the college: Edward Ernest Foxwell (1851–1922), later a professor of economics in Japan and an authority on railways, and William Arthur *Foxwell (1853–1909), a physician.

During the absence from Cambridge (1877–85) of Alfred Marshall, Foxwell took the main share in the honours teaching of economics in the university. He was also appointed to succeed W. S. Jevons as professor of political economy at University College, London, in 1881, and he did not retire until 1927. Until 1902 the only scope afforded for the study of economics in London University was as a compulsory subject for the MA degree in philosophy and as an optional one for the DSc. For many years Foxwell had the whole range of economics as his field. He lectured on banking and currency from the first session of the London School of Economics (1895/6) until his retirement in 1922. In 1907 he and Edwin Cannan were appointed professors of political economy in the University of London.

From 1878 Foxwell was a fellow of the (Royal) Statistical Society, and in 1882 he was elected an honorary member of the Political Economy Club. In the late 1880s he was active, if not the prime mover, in the foundation in 1890 of the British Economic Association (later the Royal Economic Society) and the establishment of the *Economic Journal*. He was the society's president from 1929 to 1931. He was elected a fellow of the British Academy in 1905.

When Foxwell began lecturing in 1874, the economic teaching of J. S. Mill was dominant in England, but a new and wider approach was already appearing in the work of a brilliant group of men born in the period from 1835 to 1855, which included W. S. Jevons, A. Marshall, William Cunningham, Arnold Toynbee, Charles Wicksteed, and J. N. Keynes. Foxwell described 'The economic movement in England' in a very important contribution to the second volume of the *Quarterly Journal of Economics* (October 1887). Here he argued that economics is not a self-contained science, the 'laws' of which are normative and universal, as was implied by the followers of Ricardo and Mill, but is part of the wider study of the development of institutions and governments, which dominates the economic ideas of each nation and generation, continually growing as conditions change. Although not opposed to pure analysis, when properly limited and defined—for he was a wholehearted admirer of Jevons and appreciated Marshall, who had been his teacher—Foxwell's bent was historical. Partly for this reason, he was in opposition to the trend of 'orthodox' British economics, especially in his strong support in the 1880s and early 1890s for bimetallism and in his partial sympathy with the movement towards imperial preference and tariff reform (about 1903). He had an early interest in the development of socialism, illustrated in his long historical introduction to the English translation of Anton Menger's *The Right to the Whole Produce of Labour* (1899). He was one of the first British economists to appreciate the importance of Marx. He was also ahead of his contemporaries in recognizing the social costs of unemployment, the subject of his lecture 'Irregularity of employment and fluctuations of prices', published in *The Claims of Labour* (1886).

Although Foxwell never lost his interest in general economics, the subject of which he was complete master was banking. In his university lectures and in those delivered to many public bodies he showed a close personal knowledge of the practice of banking, both at home and abroad, and its relation to industry, based on continual contact with bankers and other business people. During more than a generation there can have been few people seriously interested in the wider problems of banking and currency who did not come under his influence. Unfortunately, the only book which he published on any subject, *Papers on Current Finance* (1919), relates only to the period from 1909 to 1917, except that reprinted in it is an article of 1888 on the inevitability of the growth of monopoly under competition.

Largely because of his reluctance to publish, Foxwell is best-known not for his economic teaching but for the libraries which he formed on economic and allied subjects, covering the period from about 1740 to 1848. The first, containing 30,000 items, was purchased by the Goldsmiths' Company in 1901, and presented in 1903 to the University of London. With further purchases and gifts, the collection has subsequently been substantially increased. Immediately after the disposal of this first library was completed, Foxwell started upon a second collection. In 1929 this was sold to Harvard University, 4000 volumes at once and the remainder to be delivered after his death. By 1939 it formed a very important part of the Kress Library of Business and Economics at the Harvard business school. It then contained some 42,000 books and pamphlets, and, as compared with the Goldsmiths' library, was particularly strong on the historical side.

Foxwell's charm won him a wide circle of friends, and his apparent immunity from fatigue enabled him to indulge his passion for books without ever neglecting his duties. In discussion temperate, but in business intractable, he was embittered in his later years by many obstacles in the transfer of his first library and by disappointment in failing to attain the chair of political economy at Cambridge in 1908 after Marshall's retirement.

A. L. BOWLEY, *rev.* RICHARD D. FREEMAN

Sources J. M. Keynes, 'Herbert Somerton Foxwell, 1849–1936', *PBA*, 23 (1937), 470–86 · C. E. Collet, *Economic Journal*, 46 (1936), 589–619 [incl. bibliography] · A. G. D. Foxwell, *Kress Library of Business and Economics*, 1 (1939) · personal knowledge (1949) · A. Kadish and R. D. Freeman, 'Foundation and early years', *A century of economics*, ed. J. D. Hey and D. Winch (1990)

Archives BLPES, corresp. relating to Royal Economic Society · Harvard U., Baker Library, corresp. and papers · LUL, corresp. and papers, book accounts · priv. coll., MSS | Bishopsgate Institute, London, letters to George Howell · BL, corresp. with Macmillans, Add. MS 55196 · BLPES, letters to Edwin Cannan · Col. U., letter to Edgar Seligman · CUL, letters to Francis Jenkinson · King's AC Cam., letters to Oscar Browning · King's AC Cam., letters to John Maynard Keynes · St John Cam., letters to Joseph Larmor · U. Cam., Marshall Library of Economics, letters to John Neville Keynes · University of Toronto, corresp. with James Mavor

Likenesses W. Stoneman, photograph, 1917, NPG · C. Hopkinson, oils, Harvard Graduate College of Business Administration, Cambridge, Massachusetts · A. Shore, oils, St John Cam. · portraits, repro. in *Economic Journal*

Wealth at death £23,451 18s. 1d.: probate, 18 Feb 1937, *CGPLA Eng. & Wales*

Foxwell, William Arthur (1853–1909), physician, born at High Street, Shepton Mallet, Somerset, on 13 July 1853, was the third son of Thomas Somerton Foxwell (1806–1886), an ironmonger, of Shepton Mallet and Weston-super-Mare, and his second wife, Jane (1824–1878), daughter of William Handcock of Jersey. His elder brother Herbert Somerton *Foxwell (1849–1936) was professor of political economy at the University of London. After Queen's College, Taunton, Foxwell graduated BA in 1873 at London with honours in English and moral science. In 1874 he matriculated from St John's College, Cambridge, where he read natural sciences and graduated in 1877. He then pursued his medical education at St Thomas's Hospital, London. In 1881 he became MRCS. He graduated MB with a first class in medicine at Cambridge in 1883, and he proceeded MA and MD in 1891, with a thesis entitled 'The heart in debility'. He became LRCP (1881), MRCP (1885), and FRCP (1892).

After holding the posts of house physician at St Thomas's Hospital (1881), clinical assistant at the Brompton Hospital (1882), and junior resident medical officer at the Manchester Children's Hospital, Pendlebury (1882–3), Foxwell was elected as resident pathologist at Birmingham General Hospital (1884) and was honorary assistant physician there from 1885 to 1889. During the winter of 1887–8 he studied at Vienna, chiefly on diseases of the throat and ear, and travelled to many health resorts in Switzerland, France, and Germany. In 1889 he became honorary physician at the Queen's Hospital, Birmingham, where he became senior honorary physician upon the retirement of Sir James Sawyer. During his period with the hospital, and newly interested in the effects of climate on disease, Foxwell persuaded hospital staff to construct a roof ward, only partially covered in and otherwise open to the air, in which considerable success was obtained in the treatment of various diseases except those of a tubercular nature.

In addition to the post he held at the Queen's Hospital, Foxwell was also for a time pathologist to the Birmingham Hospital for Women, demonstrator in medical pathology in the Queen's faculty of medicine at Mason College, Birmingham, and from 1896 to 1898 examiner in medicine at the University of Cambridge. From 1887 to 1901 he was honorary librarian at the Medical Institute, Birmingham, of which he was president at his death, and from 1886 to 1888 he edited the *Birmingham Medical Review*. In 1906, following the resignation of A. H. Carter, he was appointed professor of therapeutics in the new Birmingham University and received the degree of MSc.

Foxwell's chief publication was *Essays on Heart and Lung Disease* (1895), which comprises many important articles that helped to establish him as an authority on heart disease. In Birmingham in 1892 he read his Ingleby lecture, entitled 'The condition of the vascular system in anaemic debility'; this was followed in 1895 by his paper 'The enlarged cirrhotic liver', which was presented to the Birmingham and midland branch of the British Medical Association in order to facilitate diagnosis of the condition. Foxwell was also, in 1899, Bradshawe lecturer of the Royal College of Physicians, and he presented a paper entitled 'The causation of functional murmurs', in which he attributed the condition to a dilatation of the pulmonary artery immediately beyond the valve, rather than to a change in the viscosity of the blood as was hitherto widely accepted. Over a short but productive career he wrote numerous other articles, many of which appeared in the *Birmingham Medical Review*.

Foxwell was twice married. His second marriage, in 1889, was to Eliza Selina (*b.* 1850?), daughter of Charles Hollins of Torquay and widow of Robert Pollock of Birmingham. From 1895 until his death he lived at The Grange, Northfield, Worcestershire, with his wife, their daughter, Florence, and three stepsons. Of a shy and reserved nature and already in poor health, Foxwell died in the Warneford Hospital, Leamington Priors, Warwickshire, on 4 August 1909, as the result of severe injuries to the head and spine sustained in a cycling accident near Warwick three days earlier. On 7 August his body was interred in the Franciscan burial-ground in Olton. A memorial tablet and bust designed by his stepson Courtenay Pollock was placed in the Queen's Hospital, Birmingham, and an annual prize for a clinical essay—open to qualified residents at the Queen's Hospital, at Birmingham General Hospital, and at the children's hospital— was endowed in his memory. Foxwell was survived by his wife.   E. M. BROCKBANK, *rev.* JONATHAN REINARZ

Sources Munk, *Roll* • *The Lancet* (14 Aug 1909) • *BMJ* (14 Aug 1909), 425–6 • J. T. J. Morrison, *William Sands Cox and the Birmingham medical school* (1926) • *Birmingham Gazette and Express* (4 Aug 1909) • *Birmingham Daily Post* (5 Aug 1909) • *Birmingham Gazette and Express* (9 Aug 1909) • b. cert. • d. cert. • *CGPLA Eng. & Wales* (1909) • Venn, *Alum. Cant.* • private information (1912)

Likenesses C. Pollock, marble bust, *c.*1910, Queen's Hospital, Birmingham

Wealth at death £5581 10s. 8d.: administration, 2 Oct 1909, *CGPLA Eng. & Wales*

Foy, Nathaniel (1648–1707), Church of Ireland bishop of Waterford and Lismore, was born at York, the son of John Foy MD (*d.* 1660). He was educated at Dublin Corporation Free School, and from 1663 at Trinity College, Dublin, graduating MA (1671), and BD and DD (both 1682), and where he was elected a fellow in 1684. He was ordained priest in 1670, and in the same year was installed as a canon of Kildare. On 20 December 1678 he was appointed minister of the parish of St Bride, Dublin. While James II was in Ireland, Foy defended the established church, most of its bishops having fled the country. Crowds assembled at St Bride's on alternate Sundays to hear his replies to sermons delivered at Christ Church Cathedral on preceding Sundays by a doctor of the Sorbonne in the presence of the king. This task he accomplished by means of abstracts of his antagonist's arguments supplied to him by gentlemen who wrote shorthand. He was prevented from preaching on several occasions, and his firmness in supporting the protestant faith led to his being imprisoned in July 1689, together with the future archbishop William King and other clergymen.

After the battle of the Boyne he was rewarded by William III who, on the recommendation of Gilbert Burnet, bishop of Salisbury, promoted Foy to the united sees of Waterford and Lismore by letters patent on 13 July 1691. Along with bishops King and Anthony Dopping, he vainly attempted to initiate a programme of church reform. In December 1695 he was 'imprisoned' in Dublin Castle for three days by order of the House of Lords, but was, in fact, well looked after by Capel, the lord lieutenant. His offence was to protest against the rejection of a bill for the union and division of parishes. The bill would have addressed the problems of clerical pluralism, non-residence, patronage on a political basis, and the appointment of reformers to the Irish episcopal bench. In May 1702 he travelled to London with Thomas Lindsey, bishop of Killaloe, to lobby the House of Lords on behalf of the Irish bishops, seeking the insertion of a clause in the Act of Resumption to enable profits from forfeited Jacobite estates in Ireland to be used for the repair and rebuilding of churches. In his own diocese he enforced strict ecclesiastical discipline, especially in his insistence that a uniform system of examination be used for candidates for the diaconate. He encouraged schemes for ecclesiastical book buying and proposed in parliament that wealthy pluralists should make refunds to poorer clergymen.

Foy's only publication was *A sermon preached in Christ's Church, Dublin, on 23 Oct. 1698. Being the anniversary thanksgiving for putting an end to the Irish rebellion, which broke out on that day 1641. Before the House of Lords* (1698). It advocated 'a mission "to reduce ... The Irish nation" to Protestant, Anglicized civility, analogous to the mission of St Paul to the pagans', and 'urged renewed efforts to bring a Protestant education to the children of the natives' (Hayton, 179, 168). During his lifetime he expended £800 on the improvement of the episcopal palace at Waterford, and built apartments there for the widows of clergymen through the generosity of his predecessor at Waterford, Bishop Hugh Gore, who had bequeathed £1200 for the project. By his own will he established and endowed the free school at Grantstown, which opened just prior to his death. He died, unmarried, in Dublin on 31 December 1707 and was buried at the west end of Christ Church Cathedral, Waterford, in St Saviour's Chapel.

THOMPSON COOPER, *rev.* J. FALVEY

Sources W. G. Carroll, *Succession of clergy in the parishes of S. Bride, S. Michael le Pole and S. Stephen, Dublin* (1884) · W. King, correspondence, TCD, Lyons collection, MSS 1995–2008 · Representative Church Body Library, Dublin, Rennison MSS · W. H. Rennison, ed., *Succession list of the bishops, cathedral and parochial clergy of the dioceses of Waterford and Lismore* (1920) · *CSP dom.*, 1690–97 · M. Quane, 'Bishop Foy School, Waterford', *Journal of the Cork Historical and Archaeological Society*, 2nd ser., 71 (1966) · R. W. Jackson, 'Bishop Foy of Waterford', *Old Foyonian* (1957) · D. Grogan, 'Bishop Foy and the cause of reform', ed. J. Falvey, *Decies: Journal of the Old Waterford Society*, 50–51 (1994–5) · J. J. Falvey, 'The Church of Ireland episcopate in the eighteenth century', MA diss., University College, Cork, 1995 · H. Cotton, *Fasti ecclesiae Hibernicae*, 1–5 (1845–60) · D. Hayton, 'Did protestantism fail in early eighteenth-century Ireland …', *As by law established* …, ed. A. Ford, J. McGuire, and K. Milne (1995), 166–86 · Burtchaell & Sadleir, *Alum. Dubl.*, 2nd edn

Archives TCD, corresp. with William King and account of his stand in House of Lords

Foyle [*married name* Batty], **Christina Agnes Lilian** (1911–1999), bookseller, was born on 30 January 1911 at 35 Estelle Road, Highgate, London, one of the two daughters and three children of the booksellers William Alfred *Foyle (1885–1963) and his wife, Christina Tulloch (1880/81–1976). William Foyle and his brother Gilbert (1886–1971) were proprietors of a successful bookshop in Charing Cross Road, London. Christina, who survived tuberculosis when seven, went to a boarding-school in Hertfordshire and a finishing school, Aux Villas Unspunnen, at Wilderswil, near Interlaken, in Switzerland. A good-looking and self-assured young woman, she returned to London in 1928 and immediately joined the family firm. W. and G. Foyle Ltd moved into purpose-built premises at 119 Charing Cross Road in 1929. With an estimated 30 miles of shelving, it was for some decades the biggest bookshop in existence.

One day, working behind the counter, Christina Foyle recommended *The Forsyte Saga* to a customer who turned out to be its author, John Galsworthy. Excited by this encounter with a cultural celebrity, she had the idea of hosting parties where book lovers might meet their favourite writers in a setting less formal than a lecture. Her father challenged her to arrange an event, and the first of Foyle's literary luncheons took place at the Holborn Restaurant in October 1930, with Lord Darling and Gerald du Maurier, plus 250 diners paying 4s. 6d. each. Thereafter, Christina organized ten luncheons per year (monthly except for January and August), held latterly at the Dorchester or Grosvenor House Hotel. Attendance

often exceeded a thousand. Speakers included novelists as varied as H. G. Wells and Barbara Cartland and luminaries ranging from Emperor Haile Selassie to Bud Flanagan. Present at 662 of the 664 luncheons during her lifetime, Christina Foyle was a fixture of the London literary scene, acquiring a fund of anecdotes. Arthur Conan Doyle told her about séances, and Arnold Bennett showed her the dirty £5 note which he had been carrying around for twenty years as a gift for the first person he saw reading one of his novels. She liked to relate how she had written to Hitler, offering to buy Jewish books destined for burning. No one doubted her flair as a publicist, aided by her associate Ben Perrick. With her father she established the Book Club in 1937, an art gallery, and a lecture agency.

On 29 January 1938 Christina Foyle married Ronald Frederick James Batty (*d.* 1994), who worked in the shop's antiquarian division. They had no children, and she was still always referred to in business as Miss Foyle. With her sister Winifred giving up work when she married and her brother Richard dying in 1957, she assumed an ever expanding role in running the firm, of which she was a director from 1940. Foyle's became the largest mail-order supplier of books in the world in the 1950s.

When her father died in 1963, Christina Foyle succeeded him as managing director, inheriting both a majority shareholding in W. and G. Foyle Ltd and Beeleigh Abbey, his large house beside the River Chelmer in Essex. Its fine library meant much to her, as did the extensive garden and, above all, her myriad dogs, cats, budgerigars, peacocks, and tortoises. A full staff of servants made credible her boast that she did not know how to boil an egg—this despite her nominal authorship of a recipe book for the busy working woman. Few ever dared contradict Miss Foyle, who insisted that she read an entire book each day and drank nothing but champagne. Her high-pitched little voice, inscrutable smile, steely grey-blue eyes, and genteel, if not regal, demeanour all conveyed that she expected deference. She sat on the council of the Royal Society of Arts (1963–9) and received an honorary doctorate in 1975 from the University of Essex. *So Much Wisdom* (1984) reproduced her favourite inspirational quotations.

Christina Foyle ruled her bookshop as an autocrat, and was scarcely an enlightened one. Setting her face firmly against change, she forbade the use of cash registers, computers, and calculators: even in 1990, Foyle's assistants relied on mental arithmetic or pencil and paper to add up bills. Anyone attempting to place an order by telephone would be told to write or visit. When warned about turning away business, Miss Foyle sometimes answered that she was too rich to need worry about money—yet her reluctance to spend any on maintenance was only too apparent from the worn linoleum, tatty notices, and general shabbiness of the premises. Whims and prejudices often seemed to govern her choice of staff. An essential qualification for working at Foyle's was readiness to accept low pay and poor conditions. Forty women in the postal department were dismissed in 1956 for talking too loudly. In summer 1965 employees went on strike to demand a living wage and union recognition. Beyond a small core of old retainers, a high proportion were transient foreign students, hence the story of the customer who asked for *Ulysses* and was told that he had gone to lunch.

On the positive side, Miss Foyle's refusal to discard old stock ensured that the shop accumulated an unrivalled range of titles. No inventory was kept, however, and the arrangement of books on shelves was notoriously idiosyncratic. Foyle's infuriated many customers with a complex sales system reminiscent of communist eastern Europe: the purchaser needed to take a book to a sales desk to get an invoice, go to another desk to pay and have the invoice stamped, and then return to collect the book. The idea was to limit the number of staff handling money. Disregard of normal accounting procedures meanwhile allowed major fraud to persist undetected.

Weakened by a chest infection, Christina Foyle died at Beeleigh Abbey on 8 June 1999, leaving her fortune to a charitable trust. She was cremated at Chelmsford. The shop passed to her nephews. The infamous inefficiencies that eroded Foyle's reputation as 'the world's greatest bookshop' had only enhanced her claim to be Britain's best-known bookseller.   JASON TOMES

Sources *Daily Telegraph* (10 June 1999) · *The Times* (10 June 1999) · *The Independent* (11 June 1999) · *The Guardian* (10 June 1999); (11 June 1999) · J. Davies, 'The chaos Christina left behind', *The Times* (31 July 2001) · C. Foyle, *So much wisdom* (1984) · b. cert. · m. cert. · d. cert. **Archives** University of Bristol Library, corresp. and papers relating to trial of *Lady Chatterley's lover* | CUL, corresp. with Samuel Hoare **Likenesses** Becker, double portrait, photograph, 1938 (with Ronald Batty), Hult. Arch. · H. Coster, photographs, 1938, NPG · photograph, repro. in *The Times* (10 June 1999) · photograph, repro. in *Christina Foyle's party book* (1968), 7 **Wealth at death** £59,029,581: probate, 26 Nov 1999, *CGPLA Eng. & Wales*

Foyle, William Alfred (1885–1963), bookseller, was born on 4 March 1885 in Shoreditch, London, one of the eight children (six sons and two daughters) of William Henry Foyle, a wholesale grocer, and his wife, Deborah Barnett. Foyle was also the seventh child of a seventh child of a seventh child, and it was to this that he attributed visionary and intuitive gifts. He was educated at Dame Alice Owen's School, Islington, London. At the age of fifteen he sat for, and failed, the civil service entrance examination; undaunted, he enrolled for a short course at King's College, London. His first working post, in 1902, was as a clerk with Edward Marshall Hall KC, who collected old silver and frequently sent his young employee to the salerooms. Here Foyle learned the techniques of buying and selling, but books were his personal interest and he took the opportunity of bidding at the salerooms for any interesting lots.

Foyle started trading as a bookseller by selling his own school books second-hand as soon as he had no further use for them. In 1903, at the age of eighteen, he opened, with his brother Gilbert, a bookshop in Islington, north London, moving on shortly to Peckham, south London, and in 1904 to Cecil Court, off Charing Cross Road, in central London, where in many shops and on roadside barrows second-hand books were the chief commodity. Three years later the business moved to Charing Cross Road itself, where, with many extensions, it remained in his lifetime. William bought in stock wherever he could find it—in salerooms, from individuals, and from other second-hand bookshops. One shop he visited often, in New Oxford Street, in London's West End, was run by Christina Tulloch, the daughter of William Tulloch, a watchmaker, and his wife, Helen Gifford, both children of seafaring people from the Shetland Islands.

Thinking Foyle a poor student, Miss Tulloch let him have the books very cheaply. The interest went beyond books; he persuaded her to become his business partner and his wife. They married on 14 August 1907 and had one son, who predeceased his parents, and two daughters, one of whom, Christina *Foyle, became a director of the bookselling business as it expanded. She was to achieve renown later with literary luncheons, developed from lectures by leading authors which William Foyle had started in the early 1920s, introducing to the public, among others, the Sitwell brothers and sister, Arthur Conan Doyle, T. H. Hall Caine, and Walter de la Mare.

Foyle concentrated single-mindedly on the business of books. He seldom forgot a title, and went to endless trouble to track down unusual or rare books for customers, so that the shop's reputation grew. Its move in 1907 to Charing Cross Road allowed it to stock books on a wider range of subjects: art, theology, music, education, and other matters of popular interest. 'Foyles of Charing Cross Road' became a mecca for booklovers. Foyle also became an authority on the lives of booksellers of the past, and modelled himself on Thomas Guy, a seventeenth-century bookseller whose philanthropy in later affluence led to the foundation of Guy's Hospital, London, and James Lackington, who had named his eighteenth-century bookshop the Temple of the Muses.

Foyle was determined to create the greatest bookshop in the world, and in due course used the phrase in the firm's advertising, when there were few to contradict the claim. The business was founded on buying and selling second-hand books and existed for nine years before it began to trade in new books in 1912, when the first publisher to give him credit terms was William Heinemann. With the stock regularly increasing, the shop always needed more space. Dickensian premises in Manette Street, off Charing Cross Road, were bought from the Revd Basil Bourchier, then vicar of St Anne's, Soho, and in 1929 a splendid four-storeyed building was opened by the lord mayor of London, Sir J. E. Kynaston Studd.

In every major development of the bookselling trade Foyle strove to be among the first in the field. He began the Book Club in 1937; it enrolled a quarter of a million members and added hugely to the turnover of the retail business. He foresaw the increased demand for books that would result from the extension of further education in the 1930s and the subsequent shortages in the Second World War years, and was ready to meet it.

Outwardly, Willie Foyle was an enigmatic man. An adored if neglectful parent, overflowing with high spirits, mischievous, seldom serious, he displayed to few strangers the acute mind that lay behind the sense of fun and ready laughter. Extremely sensitive, he was a considerable amateur artist and pianist, an individualist, and no lover of committees. The few clubs he belonged to were of the bohemian variety, where he met unconventional friends such as Pino Orioli, a noted Florentine bookseller, and A. J. A. Symons, with the latter of whom he started the First Edition Club, boasting elegant premises in London's stylish Bedford Square. Through Symons he also met the solitary and eccentric fellow bookseller Christopher Millard, who was devoted to exploring the estuaries of the rivers Blackwater and Crouch in his own dinghy. This inspired Symons and Foyle to acquire a 7 ton yacht of their own, sailing the Essex rivers, and the experience led Foyle to make his home near the town of Maldon, buying in 1945 the twelfth-century Premonstratensian abbey of Beeleigh, situated on the River Chelmer. In this beautiful setting he was able to indulge his passion for collecting rare books, and formed a great library. Among his acquisitions were incunabula from William Caxton, Wynkyn de Worde, and Koberger; Shakespeare folios; and a superb collection of fourteenth- and fifteenth-century illuminated manuscripts.

Although not preoccupied with money, Foyle died a very wealthy man, a circumstance due in some degree to his cautious daughter Christina, who in the earlier days of the business had learned many hard lessons from facing creditors, and also to her extraordinarily able husband, Ronald Batty, who played a vital role in the business. Foyle died at Beeleigh Abbey on 4 June 1963.

CHRISTINA FOYLE, rev. G. R. DAVIES

Sources private information (2004) [Christina Foyle] · *The Times* (6 June 1963) · personal knowledge (2004) · [W. and G. Foyle Ltd], *Foyles fifty years, 1904–1954* (1954) · *The Bookseller*, no. 2998 (8 June 1963), 2098 · m. cert.
Likenesses A. Dellow, photograph, 1955, Hult. Arch. · T. C. Dugdale, portrait, Beeleigh Abbey library, Maldon, Essex · photographs, NPG · photographs, W. and G. Foyle Ltd, London
Wealth at death £118,989 1s. 7d.: probate, 5 Sept 1963, *CGPLA Eng. & Wales*

Fradelle, Henry Jean Baptiste Victoire (1778–1865),

historical genre painter, was born at Lille in France. Of his parents, nothing is known. He studied in Paris, and afterwards in Italy. He settled in London in 1816, and sent to the Royal Academy in the following year *Milton Dictating 'Paradise Lost' to his Daughter*. He then resided at 4 Nassau Street, Middlesex Hospital. He also contributed thirty-six pictures, many illustrating scenes from the works of Shakespeare and Sir Walter Scott, to the British Institution, and two to the Society of British Artists in Suffolk Street, between 1817 and 1854. In this latter year his address was 5 Brecknock Crescent, Camden New Town. He exhibited at the Paris Salon between 1827 and 1837, and in 1834 won a third class medal at the Salon. He also produced portraits in oil, and miniature portraits including one of Miss Stephens as Susanna in *The Marriage of Figaro*.

On 19 February 1832, at All Souls, Marylebone, Middlesex, Fradelle married Maria Elizabeth Latilla. Their son,

Henry John Charles Fradelle, was baptized in the same church on 25 May 1833. He also became an artist.

Among Fradelle's best paintings, *Mary Queen of Scots and her Secretary Chatelar* was engraved by both V. Rogers and A. Duncan, and *The Earl of Leicester's Visit to Amy Robsart at Canmore Place* by Charles Turner in 1826. The preparatory drawing for the latter, in black chalk, is in the British Museum, London. His *Othello Relating the Story of his Life to Brabantio and Desdemona* (exh. RA, 1824) is now in the Royal Shakespeare Gallery, Stratford upon Avon. He died at his home, 36 Weymouth Street, Portland Place, London, on 14 March 1865.   L. A. FAGAN, rev. JOHN-PAUL STONARD

Sources Thieme & Becker, *Allgemeines Lexikon* · Bénézit, *Dict.* · G. Meissner, ed., *Allgemeines Künstlerlexikon: die bildenden Künstler aller Zeiten und Völker*, [new edn, 34 vols.] (Leipzig and Munich, 1983–) · Graves, *RA exhibitors* · Graves, *Artists* · Redgrave, *Artists* · artist's file, archive material, Courtauld Inst., Witt Library · *CGPLA Eng. & Wales* (1865) · IGI · H. Blättel, *International dictionary miniature painters / Internationales Lexikon Miniatur-Maler* (1992)
Wealth at death under £200: probate, 25 July 1865, *CGPLA Eng. & Wales*

Fraenkel, Eduard David Mortier (1888–1970),

classical scholar, was born in Berlin on 17 March 1888, the son of a wine merchant, Julius Fraenkel, who was a first cousin of Ludwig Traube and an uncle of Ernst Fraenkel, and his wife, Edith Heimann. He attended the Askanisches Gymnasium, where the classical teaching was of a high order, but on entering the University of Berlin in 1906 he enrolled as a student of law. An unbaptized Jew had little chance of obtaining a professorship, and Fraenkel was unwilling to become a schoolmaster. He greatly profited from his training in Roman legal science, in which he never lost his interest. But the famous public lectures given by Wilamowitz, and also a long conversation when he asked the great man to advise him how he might spend his time on his first visit to Italy, impelled him at all costs to become a student of classical philology. In Berlin he learned much from Diels, Eduard Meyer, Norden, Schulze, and above all Wilamowitz; but in 1909 he transferred to Göttingen, where he greatly profited from the teaching of Leo and Wackernagel, and in 1912 took his degree with a thesis about middle and new comedy which showed great promise.

After working for two years on the Latin thesaurus in Munich, Fraenkel habilitated in Berlin in 1917, and was appointed *Privatdozent*; in 1920 he became professor *extraordinarius*. Two years later appeared the most remarkable of all his books, *Plautinisches im Plautus*. Other scholars, especially since the important papyrus discoveries of Menander, had studied Plautus chiefly for what he could teach them about his Greek originals; Fraenkel loved him for himself, and did much to make clear the nature of his own specific contribution to his adaptations of Greek plays.

In 1923 Fraenkel became full professor at Kiel; in 1928 he moved to Göttingen, and in 1931 to Freiburg im Breisgau. He became a leading figure in his profession, and helped to found the periodical *Gnomon*; he often visited Italy, and kept in touch with Giorgio Pasquali in Florence. In 1928 he published *Iktus und Akzent im lateinischen Sprechvers*; although he later disowned the main conclusions of this learned book, it contains much valuable matter. In 1931 appeared *Kolon und Satz*, the most substantial product of his lifelong interest in the order of words. In the summer of 1933, the year when the National Socialists came to power, Fraenkel was forbidden to teach, and the next year he moved to Oxford. In August 1934 he was elected to a Bevan fellowship at Trinity College, Cambridge, but in November he applied for the Corpus chair of Latin at Oxford, and largely through the influence of A. E. Housman, Fraenkel was elected. He was naturalized in 1939.

Fraenkel found it difficult to settle down in an environment so different from what he was accustomed to, and at first and for long after alienated many well-wishers by his tactlessness and insensitivity. But although he terrified many of his pupils, his teaching from the first made a profound impression. He lectured effectively on Catullus, Virgil, and Horace; but he exerted special influence through his famous seminars on Aeschylus's *Agamemnon*, in which he went through the play in almost as much time as it took Agamemnon to capture Troy. In 1950 he brought out an edition of the *Agamemnon* in three volumes, containing the most detailed commentary ever devoted to a Greek text. Although some of the author's judgements may be questioned, it makes a massive contribution to Greek scholarship.

As time passed, Fraenkel became accustomed to English life, and radically revised his attitude. He found that although Oxford undergraduates were ignorant of secondary sources, by comparison with German students they often knew their texts thoroughly, and were thus excellent subjects for the instruction he could impart. The affection for Oxford and the English which he had developed was heartily reciprocated by his pupils and his younger colleagues; and when he retired from his chair under the age limit in 1953 he was elected an honorary fellow of Corpus Christi College, given a large room in which to keep his books, and enabled to continue to hold his famous seminars. After the Second World War he resumed his connections with the continent. He was in touch with many German scholars; but the country he loved most was Italy, where he often taught and lectured and where he received the freedom of the city of Sarsina, birthplace of Plautus.

In 1957 Fraenkel published a learned and humane book on Horace; in 1962 a short book about another favourite author, Aristophanes; and in 1968 an important study of Latin word order and prose rhythm; a two-volume selection from his many learned articles appeared in 1964. He remained active in teaching and research until his death.

Fraenkel was one of the most learned classical scholars of his time. In an age when few dared to attempt excellence in Greek and Latin, he was eminent in both, and was also well acquainted with metric, linguistics, Roman legal science, and the monuments of ancient art. Above all he was an interpreter of texts, and brought to the work the entire apparatus of modern learning. He was denied the

gift of divination, and he had little sympathy with any literature or art which might be considered decadent; thus his *Horace* suffered from his failure to appreciate Hellenistic poetry, together with his inability even to entertain the notion that the regime of Augustus was not in all ways admirable. But with his vast learning he combined a deep love for Mediterranean life and an imaginative sympathy with almost all its manifestations which gave his teaching an exhilarating quality. Like his master Wilamowitz he was first and foremost a teacher and only in second place a writer, hard though this is to credit for those acquainted only with his vast output of learned work. As a teacher he had certain defects. He was not quick on the uptake, and could seldom elicit suggestions from his hearers; he tended to extremes of praise or blame, and many of his pupils found him frightening. But all this was nothing in the face of his boundless enthusiasm for the study of the ancient world, his tireless eagerness to help anyone whom he supposed in any way to share it, and his imaginative sympathy with the writers and the civilizations which were the objects of his study.

Fraenkel was a fellow of the British Academy (1941–64), and was awarded the Kenyon medal in 1965. He received honorary degrees from the universities of West Berlin, Urbino, St Andrews, Florence, Fribourg, and Oxford.

In 1918 Fraenkel married Ruth von Velsen, who gave up a promising academic career for his sake, and sustained him with unfailing love and loyalty. They had three sons and two daughters. On learning of the death of his wife, Fraenkel chose not to survive her and died at his home, 1 Kybald Street, Oxford, on 5 February 1970.

HUGH LLOYD-JONES, *rev.*

Sources S. Timpanaro, *Atene e Roma*, new ser., 15/fasc. 2–3 (1970), 89–103 · H. Lloyd-Jones, *Gnomon*, 43 (1971), 634–40 · G. Williams, 'Eduard Fraenkel, 1888–1970', *PBA*, 56 (1970), 415–42 · personal knowledge (1981) · d. cert.
Archives AM Oxf., notebooks and papers · Bodl. Oxf., Society for the Protection of Science and Learning MSS; home office files
Likenesses photograph, repro. in Williams, 'Eduard Fraenkel', facing p. 415 · photograph, repro. in Lloyd-Jones, *Gnomon*, facing p. 636
Wealth at death £20,025: probate, 9 Dec 1970, *CGPLA Eng. & Wales*

Fraigneau, William (1717–1778), Church of England clergyman, was born in London, the son of John Fraigneau, who belonged to a Huguenot family. He became a queen's scholar at Westminster School in 1731 and was admitted a pensioner to Trinity College, Cambridge, on 24 June 1736, aged nineteen. Having graduated BA in 1740 and MA in 1743 he took holy orders; he was elected a fellow of his college in 1742. He was professor of Greek in the university from 1742 until 1750, when he resigned the position. He then accepted the post of tutor to the family of Frederick St John, second Viscount Bolingbroke, and in March 1758 was presented by Bolingbroke to the vicarage of Battersea. His patron later presented him to the rectory of Beckenham, Kent, which he was allowed to hold conjointly with Battersea after a dispensation was passed in 1765.

Fraigneau, who was described by the Cambridge antiquary William Cole as 'a little man of great life and vivacity', married Catherine, by the time he drew up his will on 3 March 1764. He died in Brighton on 12 September 1778.   ALSAGER VIAN, rev. S. J. SKEDD

Sources Venn, *Alum. Cant.* · *Old Westminsters* · *Fasti Angl.* (Hardy) · O. Manning and W. Bray, *The history and antiquities of the county of Surrey*, 3 (1814), 341 · E. Hasted, *The history and topographical survey of the county of Kent*, 4 vols. (1778–99), vol. 1, p. 88 · Nichols, *Lit. anecdotes* · will, PRO, PROB 11/1046, sig. 400

Frail, John (1804–1879), election agent, was born on 1 May 1804 at Shrewsbury. A hairdresser by trade, he advanced himself through his own talents for organization, hard work, and venality. He began electioneering about 1830, under the tory whip William Holmes, among a dozen agents working to relate constituencies more closely to party. His specialities were the tedious but productive processes of voter registration and election petitions, but his other skill was 'the dirty work' ('Select committee on the Derby election', 1840; *VCH Shropshire*, 3.337) of bribery and influence. Under him, Conservatives topped the Shrewsbury polls for twenty years (1832–52), with two returned in 1835 and 1841. Disraeli benefited in 1841, although he had to protest sharply to Holmes about Frail's attempt to extract more than the pre-arranged payment. Frail was also clerk of Shrewsbury and five other racecourses (1842–79), and revitalized meetings with innovations such as handicapping and race-trains. He survived scandals over kick-backs and became the most important Conservative in Shrewsbury.

From 1847 to 1848 Frail undertook party 'business' for William Beresford, the protectionist whip. Often this was undocumented, since it involved much covert negotiation, for which Frail (once an actor) sometimes assumed aliases and disguises. He acknowledged managing successful petitions against Liberals elected in 1847 at Carlisle and Derby, the resulting by-elections, and withdrawal of petitions against Conservatives at Colchester and Essex North (Beresford's own seat). From 1849 to 1852 he was the party's salaried agent at £300 a year plus expenses, with two London locations, Cecil Street and 391 Strand. He managed elections and petitions in the City of London, Westbury, Devizes, Kidderminster (1849), St Albans (1850), and Aylesbury (1851). At the Derby election of 1852, however, his own agent, Thomas Morgan, was arrested for bribery, with £300 and a letter of instructions from Beresford to Frail. At a select committee hearing in December, Frail's impassive denial of involvement undoubtedly contributed to Beresford's (qualified) exoneration, but both were removed from party management in 1853.

Unofficially, Frail continued to supply information and advice, but his role in later elections was less detectable and, at Shrewsbury at least, less successful. Possibly he developed interests with Liberals; possibly, as he complained to Disraeli in 1859 and Corry in 1868, local associations were neglected for 'more expensive' boroughs (Frail/Corry, 26 Oct 1868, MS Hughenden B/IX/G/36) by the party organization centralized under Philip Rose and Markham Spofforth.

Frail was married and had at least two sons, Charles Simpson Frail, a solicitor, and John Ernest Frail, both of whom succeeded him as clerks of the Shrewsbury racecourse. He died at Claremont Hill, Shrewsbury, on 9 March 1879, soon after becoming mayor. Even those who despised his tactics and sneered at his original social status admitted his 'sheer electioneering genius' (Sir Henry Lucy, *Sixty Years in the Wilderness*, 1912, 64). The extent of his activities indicates that statistics of party efficiency and organization in the post-Reform Bill decades still owed much to bribery, compromise, and self-interest.

MARY S. MILLAR

Sources Boase, *Mod. Eng. biog.* · *The Times* (18 March 1879) · J. F. A. Mason, 'Parliamentary representation, 1832–85', *VCH Shropshire*, 3.308–42 · M. J. Angold and A. T. Gaydon, 'Horse-racing', *VCH Shropshire*, 2.177–83 · *Benjamin Disraeli letters*, ed. J. A. W. Gunn and others (1982–), vols. 3–4 · Bodl. Oxf., Dep Hughenden B/XXI/T/151, ff.; B/IX/G/36; B/XX/Bd/70; B/I/B/18, ff.; B/XXI/P/244 · d. cert. · *VCH Shropshire*, 3.337 [1840] · 'Select committee on the Derby election', *Parl. papers* (1852–3), 12.165 ff., no. 78
Likenesses photograph, repro. in *VCH Shropshire*, 3 (1979), facing p. 193 · photograph, repro. in *Sporting Times* (24 July 1875), 396 · photograph, repro. in *Illust[rated] Sp[orting (?)] and Dr[ ] News*, 6 (1877), 419 · photograph, repro. in *Illust[rated] Sp[orting (?)] and Dr[ ] News*, 10 (1879), 627
Wealth at death under £4000: probate, 29 April 1879, *CGPLA Eng. & Wales*

Fraizer, Sir Alexander, first baronet (1607?–1681), physician and courtier, was the son of Adam Fraser, second son of Thomas Fraser of Durris in Kincardineshire; his mother belonged to the family of Duff of Drummure. Educated at Aberdeen, his Montpellier MD (1635) was incorporated at Cambridge on 9 March 1637. Fraizer was admitted a candidate of the College of Physicians of London on 30 March 1640, and a fellow on 23 November 1641. He became an elect on 26 July 1666. He lost his position as a fellow before 1 March 1653 but was restored on 22 December 1658.

In the autumn of 1645 Fraizer attended Prince Charles in the west of England as his physician. He appears to have taken a message somewhat earlier from Charles I to the imprisoned James Hamilton, duke of Hamilton. In January 1646 he was assisting Culpeper in the latter's fruitless negotiations with Hamilton. On 27 December 1647 Charles I, then at Carisbrooke, granted Fraizer a pension of £300, with remainder to his wife; this was probably as a reward for assistance in negotiating the engagement signed on 26 December. Fraizer was certainly one of the principal London correspondents of William Hamilton, earl of Lanark and from 1649 duke of Hamilton, and was engaged in forwarding his correspondence with the king. Fraizer is reported to have been arrested about 17 May (Bodl. Oxf., MS Clarendon 31, fol. 85b), but appears to have been released and to have fled to the continent soon afterwards.

In November 1649 Fraizer was in Paris. He accompanied Charles II to Jersey as his physician. He continued to be a partisan of Hamilton, and is said by Clarendon to have played a significant part in organizing Charles II's expedition to Scotland, on which he accompanied him. Fraizer's role in the 'Start' of 4 October 1650 led to his being banished from Scotland and he returned to The Hague. Fraizer's subsequent movements are uncertain. In August 1653 he was attending Charles II as his physician in Paris. Until this time Fraizer had been on friendly terms with Sir Edward Hyde, but in December he joined in an intrigue against him. Fraizer accompanied the king to Cologne, and in the spring of 1656 he was sent to Paris to arrange an interview between Charles II and Henrietta Maria. He brought letters from the queen to Charles at Bruges in May, but by July he was out of favour. In December 1657 Fraizer was in Paris trying to obtain, through Sir William Lockhart, a pass to return to England. He was in the country soon after and associating with Buckingham. In January 1661 he treated Princess Henrietta for measles.

On 28 May 1664 Fraizer received a warrant for the place of principal physician to the king. In August 1668 he was given permission to go to Scotland for two months, and in 1670 he was sending newsletters there to Lord Lauderdale. Fraizer received many small grants, including an annual pension of £100. He was knighted in 1660 and on 2 August 1673 he was created a baronet. He had purchased the land at Durris which had formerly belonged to his family. In March 1677 Fraizer was granted a plot of land to build apartments in Greencloth Yard, part of Whitehall Palace.

Fraizer was married twice. His first wife was Elizabeth Dowchly, from near Bristol; they had two sons, Alexander and Charles, and a daughter, Elizabeth. Charles became a fellow of Trinity College, Cambridge; graduated BA (1670) and MA (1674); and was made MD by royal mandate in 1678. He was appointed physician-in-ordinary to Charles II in 1677 and, as such, was admitted a fellow of the Royal College of Physicians in 1684. About 1658 Frazier married Mary (d. 1695), widow of Dudley Wylde of Canterbury and fourth daughter of Sir Fernando Carey (d. 1638), and his wife, Phillipa, daughter of Sir William Thockmorton. Mary was a woman of the bedchamber and dresser to the queen from June 1662. Fraizer's daughter from his second marriage became Carey Mordaunt (d. 1709) after her marriage to Charles Mordaunt, Lord Mordaunt, later earl of Peterborough (1658–1735).

Few records of Fraizer's medical practice remain, although enough survive to give some indication of the scope of his professional activities within the royal household. Most of the available details are recorded in the diary of Samuel Pepys, including mention of the illness and death from smallpox of the princess royal at Christmas 1660, for which Fraizer and the other royal physicians had been criticized, as they had apparently disagreed as to whether the princess was suffering from measles, spotted fever, or smallpox. Multiple consultation was integral to medical practice, and at times hindered diagnosis and treatment. Although differential diagnosis was difficult, much of the criticism probably related to Fraizer's apparent high regard in a court where he also had enemies. Fraizer also seems to have been involved in the trepanning of the skull of Prince Rupert, although he did not carry out the surgery himself (a high-ranking physician would not perform such operations if a competent, but lower ranking surgeon were available—in this case James Mullins of St Thomas's Hospital). He may also have been consulted during the severe illness of Queen Henrietta Maria in 1663, when, in extremis, her head was shaved and live pigeons tied to her feet. Fraizer was more closely involved in the treatment of the unfortunate dukes of Cambridge and Kendal, infant sons of the duke of York, both of whom died in 1667, the duke of Kendal at the age of eleven months, apparently from infantile convulsions. The duke of Cambridge had apparently been 'full of spots about his body' (Pepys, 8.192) and Fraizer was unsure how to treat him. Samuel Pepys wrote (19 September 1664) that

> Fraizer is so great with Lady Castlemayne and Steward, and all the ladies of the court, in helping them to slip their calfes when there is occasion, and with great men in curing them of their claps, that he can do what he pleases with the King in spite of any man, and upon the same score with the prince—they all having more or less occasion to use him. (Pepys, 5.275)

Fraizer died at Whitehall on 28 April 1681, in his seventy-fifth year, and was buried at Durris on 28 July. His widow was buried at Fulham, Middlesex, on 22 December 1695.

HELEN M. DINGWALL

Sources Munk, Roll • Pepys, Diary • J. Robertson, Book of bon-accord, or, A guide to the city of Aberdeen (1839) • J. Menzies, A sermon preached at the funeral of Alexander Fraiser (1681) • L. Hutchinson, Memoirs of the life of Colonel Hutchinson, ed. N. H. Keeble (1995) • E. Walker, Historical discourses upon several occasions (1705) • GEC, Baronetage • DNB • private information (2004) • Venn, Alum. Cant. • The manuscripts of his grace the duke of Portland, 10 vols., HMC, 29 (1891–1931), vol. 1, p. 333 • G. Burnet, The memoires of the lives and actions of James and William, dukes of Hamilton and Castleherald (1677) • S. E. Hoskins, Charles the Second in the Channel Islands, 2 vols. (1854) • E. Hyde, earl of Clarendon, The history of the rebellion and civil wars in England, 3 vols. (1702–4) • T. Birch, Letters between Colonel Robert Hammond and the committee at Derby House (1764), 51 • W. A. Shaw, ed., Calendar of treasury books, 1, PRO (1904); 5 (1911); 7 (1916) • CSP dom., 1650; 1663–4; 1680–81
Wealth at death see abstract of will, Herald and Genealogist, vol. 4, pp. 138–9

Frame, Sir Alexander Gilchrist [Alistair] (1929–1993), engineer and businessman, was born on 3 April 1929 at 16 Burns Street, Dalmuir, Dunbartonshire, Scotland, the eldest son in the family of four children of Alexander Frame, industrial chemist, and his wife, Mary Gilchrist, née Fraser. Known throughout his life as Alistair, he was educated at Broxburn high school, graduated from Glasgow Technical College with a first-class degree, and won a Shell scholarship to Fitzwilliam College, Cambridge, to read chemical engineering. He graduated with an upper second-class degree in 1952. On 27 June 1953 he married Sheila Isabel Dingwall Mathieson (b. 1927/8), shorthand typist and daughter of Thomas Barclay Mathieson, electrical engineer; they had one daughter.

Frame joined the UK Atomic Energy Authority (UKAEA) in 1954 in Risley, Cheshire, where Sir Christopher Hinton was head of the atomic energy production division. At this time the government decided to set up a fast-breeder research programme at Dounreay, on the north coast of

Scotland, to see whether fast-breeder reactors were a suitable power source for generating electricity. The Dounreay fast reactor was functioning by 1959, and Frame became director of the UKAEA reactor and research group in 1964. He was in charge of building Britain's first prototype fast reactor at Dounreay, where work began in 1966: this was supplying electricity to the national grid from 1975.

In 1968 Frame was appointed chief engineer of Rio Tinto-Zinc Corporation Ltd (RTZ), the international group of mining companies formed in 1962 out of the merger of the Rio Tinto Company and Consolidated Zinc. The chairman, Sir Val Duncan, put him in charge of the building of a nuclear power station linked to an aluminium smelter at Holyhead, Anglesey, a project approved and subsidized by the government, which wanted Britain to build up its own aluminium industry. Frame demonstrated his ability to pick a team of engineers and managers of the highest calibre, and showed that he could meet deadlines, and move a large-scale project forwards. The smelter was completed on time, and under cost.

Frame's next project was the channel tunnel. He was appointed managing director of Rio Tinto-Zinc Development Enterprises Ltd (RTZ-DE), formed by RTZ to be responsible for the planning, financing, and construction of large-scale projects worldwide. RTZ-DE was appointed project manager by the British Channel Tunnel Company, in which RTZ held 20 per cent of the shares, in 1971, and was given the responsibility for carrying out new studies on the feasibility of constructing a tunnel under the English Channel. Frame took expert advice on tunnel design and construction, estimated the cost and time-scale of the project and its economic benefits, and proposed a new route for the tunnel on the British side, which would shorten its length by 2 miles, save £7 million in construction costs, and reduce the annual operating costs by £300,000. During the two years of the study Frame built up a close rapport with his French counterpart, Jean Gabriel, project director of the Société Française du Tunnel sous la Manche. On the basis of his final report to the government in June 1973, the government decided to go ahead. By the end of the year a bill had passed through parliament; an agreement between the British and French governments and the tunnel companies had been signed (the English signatories were Frame and Lord Harcourt, chairman of the British Channel Tunnel Company) in which they agreed to construct the initial tunnel works, 2 kilometres of pilot tunnel from both the British and French coasts, to be completed by the middle of 1975; and the British foreign secretary and French foreign minister had signed a treaty. Work began on both sides of the channel at the end of 1973, with Frame, newly elected to the board of RTZ, in charge of the management of the channel tunnel project on the English side. Following the defeat of the Conservative government in the February 1974 general election, and the death of the French president, Georges Pompidou, in April of the same year, the channel tunnel project was cancelled by the new Labour government, as an unnecessary use of public money, in January 1975. It was revived by the Conservative government in 1982, and the tunnel that opened in 1994 followed the RTZ design. Frame joined the board of Eurotunnel in 1990.

Frame was appointed RTZ's first technical director in 1975, and was chief executive and deputy chairman from 1978 to 1985. Knighted in 1981, he succeeded Sir Anthony Tuke as chairman of RTZ in 1985, at a time when the company was under fire for stripping valuable resources from Namibia, where it had been operating a uranium mine at Rossing since the late 1960s. As chairman Frame oversaw the company's expansion in other directions, including investment in the oil and gas industries, at the same time acquiring interests in many of the world's major mineral deposits. His greatest success was the acquisition in 1989 of British Petroleum's mineral interests, including Kennecott, the large American copper company. This made RTZ the world's largest mining company. Nevertheless he wanted it to be seen as a diversified industrial company rather than a mining finance house; this would have the added benefit of diverting attention from its involvement in politically sensitive areas. Frame resigned as chairman in 1991, but was asked to remain as a non-executive director.

Frame was chairman of the Council of Mining and Metallurgical Industries from 1983; he was appointed an honorary fellow of Fitzwilliam College, Cambridge, in 1985, and awarded an honorary DSc from the University of Glasgow in 1990. He helped to found the Major Projects Organization for the development and exchange of ideas at Templeton College, Oxford. He became chairman of the CBI National Manufacturing Council in 1992, of Wellcome in 1992, and of British Steel in 1993, but had to resign after a few months because of ill health. He died of bronchopneumonia and aortic stenosis, at his home, Pine Cottage, Church Hill, Holmbury St Mary, Dorking, Surrey, on 26 December 1993. He was survived by his wife and daughter. His funeral was on 6 January 1994 at Holmbury St Mary parish church and a memorial service was held at St Paul's, Knightsbridge, on 25 March 1994.

ANNE PIMLOTT BAKER

Sources D. Hunt, *The story of the channel tunnel, 1802–1994* (1994) · R. Heller, 'Sir Alistair Frame: a retrospective', *RTZ Review*, 29 (March 1994), 3–4 · M. Bonavia, *The channel tunnel story* (1987) · T. Jepson, *Rio Tinto-Zinc in Namibia* (1976) · *The Times* (30 Dec 1993) · *Financial Times* (31 Dec 1993) · *The Times* (17 June 1985) · *WWW* · b. cert. · m. cert. · d. cert.
Archives Rio Tinto plc, London, MSS
Likenesses photograph, repro. in *The Times* (30 Dec 1993) · photographs, repro. in Hunt, *Story*
Wealth at death £1,213,271: probate, 19 Dec 1994, CGPLA Eng. & Wales

Frampton, Sir George James (1860–1928), sculptor and craftsman, was born at 91 Brook Street, Lambeth, London, on 18 June 1860, the second son of James Frampton, a journeyman stonemason, of London, and his wife, Teresa, *née* Llanfield. He received his first artistic training in 1880–81

Sir George James Frampton (1860–1928), by Meredith Frampton, 1919

at the South London Technical Art School under the sculptor William S. Frith, and between 1881 and 1887 he studied at the Royal Academy Schools, while producing decorative and ornamental sculpture for a variety of clients. His first entrance into the sculptural profession came in 1878 when he worked as a stonemason on the hôtel de ville (town hall) in Paris. He first exhibited at the Royal Academy in 1884, showing *Socrates Teaching the People in the Agora*; in 1887 *An Act of Mercy* won for him the academy gold medal and travelling studentship.

From 1888 to 1889/90 Frampton studied sculpture in Paris under Antonin Mercié, at the time a master of far-reaching influence, and painting under P.-A.-J. Dagnan-Bouveret and Gustave Courtois. On his return to London he worked briefly as an assistant to the important establishment sculptor Sir Joseph Edgar Boehm. Frampton's first love was architecture and he provided decoration for a number of buildings in London in the 1880s, notably the façades of the Chelsea Conservative Club (c.1885) and the Constitutional Club in Northumberland Avenue (1885–6), both destroyed. That he turned to sculpture, however, was due to his having looked at the monuments in Westminster Abbey. His *Angel of Death* gained him a medal at the Paris Salon of 1889. The last notable work of his early manner is a group, *The Children of the Wolf* (Victoria Museum, Calcutta), the plaster of which was shown at the 1892 Royal Academy exhibition (bronze version 1893). In April 1893 he married the painter Christabel Cockerell (1863–1951), daughter of George Russell Cockerell, of London; they had one son, Meredith Frampton (1894–1984) [*see* Frampton, (George Vernon) Meredith], also a painter.

At the beginning of the 1890s Frampton felt a powerful attraction to the arts and crafts movement, and he soon began to produce works in which the element of craftsmanship is strongly accentuated, often managing to fuse the decorative arts with the fine arts. He also felt the influence of contemporary European symbolism, as is apparent in his bas-relief *Mysteriarch* (1893, Walker Art Gallery, Liverpool) which was awarded the *médaille d'honneur* at the Paris Exhibition of 1900. He exhibited with the symbolists on a number of occasions, notably at the Venice Biennale of 1897, La Libre Esthétique in Brussels, and the first Vienna Secession in 1897.

Frampton was closely associated with the art magazine *The Studio* from its inception in 1893, and he contributed to it several articles on subjects such as enamelling, goldsmiths' work, wood-carving, and polychromed sculpture. More particularly through *The Studio* he wielded very great influence on the rise of the late nineteenth-century style of decorative design in Germany, which, from the title of the magazine which sponsored it, has become known as *Jugendstil*. Peculiarly characteristic of Frampton from this time onward is the combination of different materials in one work: for instance, bronze and marble in his 1897 statue (one of his best works) of Dame Alice Owen (d. 1613) for Owen's School in Islington, London (now in Potters Bar, Hertfordshire); and ivory and bronze adorned with jewels in his bust *Lamia* (1900, Royal Academy of Arts, London).

Frampton's career was one of almost unbroken and resounding success: he was elected an ARA in 1894 and an RA in 1902, his diploma work a marble bust of the marchioness of Granby (his intention was to execute it in lavish polychromy); in 1908 he was knighted; and he received numerous other honours—he was created an honorary LLD at St Andrews University (1894), was made master of the Art Workers' Guild (1902), was one of the founding signatories of the Society of British Sculptors (1904), becoming its president in the year it became a royal society (1911–12), and was a member of the Royal Fine Arts Commission from its foundation in 1924. The work for which Frampton is perhaps best-known is his statue of Peter Pan (1912) in Kensington Gardens, London.

His other important works include a series of statues of Queen Victoria in Calcutta, Southend, St Helens, Newcastle upon Tyne, Leeds, and Winnipeg, Canada; and several public monuments in London, notably statues of Quintin Hogg (1906) in Langham Place and Edith Cavell (1920) in St Martin's Place—the latter being dismissed by critics at the time—and a characteristic bronze bas-relief memorial to Sir W. S. Gilbert (1913) in the Victoria Embankment wall on the north side of Waterloo Bridge. He also executed the sculptures (1909) in the spandrels of the main entrance of the Victoria and Albert Museum and the two couchant stone lions (1914) in front of the Edward VII wing of the British Museum. Among other noteworthy works are the portrait busts of George V and Queen Mary in the Guildhall, London; the sculptural decoration on the front of the Lloyd's Register building in the City; the saints on the chantry of William of Wykeham in Winchester Cathedral; some figures on the spire of St Mary's Church, Oxford; the figure of St George on the Second South African War memorial at Radley College, Oxfordshire; the statue of Edward VI at Giggleswick School, Yorkshire; the monument to the shipbuilder Charles Mitchell at Newcastle upon Tyne; the sculptural decoration on the façade of the Glasgow Art Gallery and Museum; and the statues of Queen Mary in the Victoria Memorial Hall, Calcutta, and Government House, Delhi. The Tate collection has a bronze bas-relief portrait of the illustrator Charles Keene, cast after Frampton's death. Among the medals which Frampton modelled are the City Imperial Volunteers medal for the corporation of the City of London (1901) and the Coronation Medal of Edward VII (1902). He also made a number of fine enamelled pieces of arts and crafts jewellery, chiefly as gifts to his wife but shown at the Royal Academy in 1898. Frampton died on 21 May 1928 at his home at 91 Carlton Hill, St John's Wood, London; he was survived by his wife.

TANCRED BORENIUS, rev. ANDREW JEZZARD

Sources A. Jezzard, 'The sculptor Sir George Frampton', PhD diss., U. Leeds, 1997 · A. Jezzard, '"An all-round craftsman": George Frampton's church monuments', *Journal of the Church Monuments Society*, 11 (1996) · A. Jezzard, 'George Frampton: art worker/medallist', *The Medal*, 24 (1994) · S. Beattie, *The New Sculpture* (1983) · B. Read, *Victorian sculpture* (1982) · T. Stevens, 'George Frampton', *Patronage and practice: sculpture on Merseyside*, ed. P. Curtis (1989), 74–85 · *CGPLA Eng. & Wales* (1928) · b. cert. · d. cert. · *The Times* (22 May 1928)
Archives Henry Moore Institute, Leeds, photographs · V&A NAL, corresp. and papers
Likenesses G. J. Frampton, self-portrait, pencil drawing, 1894, NPG · G. C. Beresford, two photographs, 1902, NPG · M. Beerbohm, pencil drawing, 1908, U. Texas, Texas · M. Frampton, oils, 1919, NPG [*see illus.*] · W. Stoneman, photograph, 1924, NPG · B. Partridge, pencil drawing, 1927, NPG · S. J. Solomon, portrait, exh. RA 1928 · W. Strang, portrait, Art Workers' Guild, London
Wealth at death £70,316 4s. 2d.: probate, 30 June 1928, *CGPLA Eng. & Wales*

Frampton, John (*fl.* 1559–1581), merchant and translator, was a member of a company of Bristol-based merchants trading in Andalusia who was arrested in 1559 by the Spanish Inquisition, and had his property confiscated. He was released from captivity in 1562, but he was not forgotten and in 1571 Archbishop Grindal, along with Frampton's fellow merchants John Mershe and Thomas Aldarsey, appealed to William Cecil to have Frampton's cause remembered. In 1577 Frampton appealed once again to Cecil, together with two other merchants, to be reimbursed for more than £2200 that they had lost in Spain, with money to be taken from Spanish subjects under arrest in England.

At about this time Frampton began to translate out of Spanish into English a number of books on the subjects of trade, seamanship, and exploration. Between 1577 and 1581 he published translations of Monardes's *Joyfull Newes out of the Newe Founde Worlde* (1577); *A Briefe Description of the Portes, Creekes, Bayes, and Havens, of the West Indies* (1578), from Martin Fernandez de Enciso; *Travels*, from Marco Polo (1579); *A Discourse of the Navigation which the Portugales Doe Make* (1579), from Escalante; *A Discoverie of the Countries of Tartaria, Scithia & Cataya* (1580); and *The Arte of Navigation*

(1581), from Pedro de Medina. All of these but the *Discoverie* of 1580 were dedicated to Edward Dyer. The *Joyfull Newes* went through two other editions, in 1580 and 1596.

CHRISTOPHER BURLINSON

Sources L. C. Wroth, 'An Elizabethan merchant and man of letters', *Huntington Library Quarterly*, 17 (1953–4), 299–314 · *CSP dom.*, 1547–80 · P. Croft, *The Spanish Company*, London RS, 9 (1973) · *STC*, 1475–1640 · D. H. Sacks, *The widening gate: Bristol and the Atlantic economy, 1450–1700* (1991) · J. Parker, *Books to build an empire: a bibliographical history of English overseas interests to 1620* (1965) · Tanner, *Bibl. Brit.-Hib.*

Frampton, Mary (1773–1846), diarist and botanist, was born on 7 June 1773 at Moreton, Dorset, the daughter of James Frampton (*d.* 1784) and his second wife, Phillis, *née* Byam (*d.* 1829), who had been previously married to Dr Charlton Wollaston. Mary Frampton during the earlier part of her life went with her parents to London once every two years, and was present at the Gordon riots, the Warren Hastings trial, and the thanksgiving service for the recovery of George III in 1789. About two years after her father's death Mary Frampton and her mother settled at Dorchester. Her mother was evidently an accomplished person, with a wide circle of well-connected relations and friends, and she and Mary formed a centre for the society of the county.

Mary Frampton's *Journal … from the Year 1779 until the Year 1846*, edited with notes by her niece Harriot Georgina Mundy, was published in 1885. It begins in 1803, prefaced by reminiscences from 1779, and incorporates a large correspondence from friends and acquaintances, together with much additional information supplied by the editor. Mary Frampton's views were those of a strong tory, and the edited journal forms an interesting picture of the times, and gives, in particular, a good deal of information about the court. The Framptons became acquainted with the family of George III during his frequent visits to Weymouth, and their correspondents supplied them with many stories about the prince regent and his relations with Mrs Fitzherbert, Lady Jersey, and Caroline of Brunswick, and also about Princess Charlotte, whose governess Mrs Campbell was a great friend of the Framptons. The book deals with public affairs and society talk, giving anecdotes about Mrs Montagu, 'Mary of Buttermere', Archbishop Sumner, Maria Edgeworth, Napoleon and his widow, the empress Maria Louisa, Charles X of France, and Baron Stockmar. It also touches on events such as the outbreak of the French revolution, the French invasion of Wales in 1797, the visit of the allied sovereigns to London in 1814, and the riots and Swing fires of 1830.

In addition to her journals, Mary Frampton occupied her time at Dorchester with an intensive study of the county's flora. She produced five volumes of drawings of Dorset plants, which were left in the possession of her family at the time of her death. Plant records from her were acknowledged by T. B. Salter in his botanical appendix to J. Sydnham's *History of Poole* in 1839.

Mary Frampton died, unmarried, at Dorchester on 12 November 1846.　　　　L. C. SANDERS, rev. REBECCA MILLS

Sources *The journal of Mary Frampton, from the year 1779 until the year 1846*, ed. H. G. Mundy (1885) · Desmond, *Botanists*, rev. edn · index of deaths (microfilm), 1846, General Register Office for England · *The Athenaeum* (7 Nov 1885), 597–8 · *Saturday Review*, 60 (1885), 621–2 · *The Spectator* (10 April 1886), 485–6 · C. J. Robinson, 'The journal', *The Academy* (7 Nov 1885), 301–2

Frampton, (George Vernon) Meredith (1894–1984), painter, was born in St John's Wood, London, on 17 March 1894, the only child of Sir George *Frampton (1860–1928), one of the leading sculptors of his day, and his wife, Christabel Annie Cockerell (1863–1951), a painter. He was educated at Westminster School, London, and attended St John's Wood Art School and then (1912–15) the Royal Academy Schools. During the First World War he worked on the western front in a field survey company and in interpretation of aerial photographs. He was one of the most accomplished of the many inter-war European painters who represented the observed world with pronounced clarity. From 1920 to 1945 he showed in the Royal Academy summer exhibition in all but four years, being elected ARA in 1934 and RA in 1942.

The majority of Frampton's paintings are portraits (many of them commissions, both private and institutional). His sitters, who included the duke of York, later George VI, in 1929, were active in imaginative and intellectual pursuits—art, architecture, music, theatre, literature, science, and public service. He specially admired the French sculptor Jean-Antoine Houdon (1741–1828) for the directness with which he conveyed a sitter's presence and personality without obtruding himself between subject and viewer. Unusually for his generation, Frampton was an heir to this tradition. Early portraits employed austere backgrounds, but he increasingly revealed unusual skill in realizing the appearance of three-dimensional objects with almost *trompe-l'œil* verisimilitude, as well as a keen sense of the texture and even the feel of any depicted substance. Carefully chosen attributes both explained a sitter's work and interests and provided a satisfying interplay of forms, within which shapes were made to rhyme in curious and subtle ways. Like his pure essays in the genre, these images proved Frampton a master of still life, with a relish for the particular which embraced test-tubes, matchboxes, skulls, autograph scores, and even a can of weed-killer. For all his love of tradition, both the enigmatic stillness of his paintings of commonplace objects and his interest in purity of form in an abstract sense were peculiarly expressive of the modern era.

In 1951 Frampton married Hilda Norman, daughter of the architect James Bow Dunn. They had no children. In 1953 he was placed at his own request on the Royal Academy's retired list. Perfectionist in all things, he declined to continue painting once a slight deterioration in eyesight precluded the extreme clarity he sought. But his retirement was into anything but inactivity. A member for sixty-nine years of the Art Workers' Guild, he had inherited from his father a strong feeling for materials and a commitment to meticulous workmanship. He retired to the striking hilltop house (in Monkton Deverill,

(**George Vernon) Meredith Frampton** (1894–1984), self-portrait, 1923

Wiltshire) he had designed in the 1930s, its style reminiscent of the architecture of seventeenth-century France. Here he created (and from his studio-cum-workshop maintained for forty years) an interior remarkable for its beauty and its well-thought-out detail, from the mechanism of clocks to the ingenious adaptation of items of furniture.

After 1945 Frampton's dignified, thoroughly realized art virtually disappeared from public consciousness for thirty years. He was eighty-eight when in 1982 he held his first one-man exhibition, a retrospective at the Tate Gallery, London. To his surprise and delight, members of a younger generation found inspiration in his work and he was able to die knowing that his art would not be forgotten. Prudent and orderly, uncompromising in his views on life and art, and instinctively reserved in a post-war world which contradicted them extensively, he was a man of humour, courtesy, and charm who unbent when he sensed that his deep feeling for beauty, order, and sound technique was shared. Shortly after moving to Mount Pleasant, Castle Hill Lane, Mere, Wiltshire, he died there on 16 September 1984.   RICHARD MORPHET, *rev.*

Sources *Meredith Frampton* (1982) [exhibition catalogue, Tate] · personal knowledge (1993) · *CGPLA Eng. & Wales* (1984)
Archives IWM, papers · Tate collection, papers | Hunt. L., corresp.
Likenesses G. V. M. Frampton, self-portrait, 1923, priv. coll. [*see illus.*]
Wealth at death £186,342: probate, 13 Nov 1984, *CGPLA Eng. & Wales*

Frampton, Robert (*bap.* 1622, *d.* 1708), bishop of Gloucester and nonjuror, was baptized on 26 February 1622 at Pimperne, near Blandford, Dorset, the youngest of eight children of Robert Frampton, a farmer, and his wife, Elizabeth Selby. Frampton was educated at the free school at Blandford before matriculating at Oxford in 1637 the age of fifteen. He studied at Corpus Christi College before moving to Christ Church, graduating BA on 25 June 1641. The English civil war began before he could proceed MA and his refusal to sign the covenant prevented him from continuing his studies. Though the civil war interrupted his education Oxford University honoured him with the degree of DD on 8 July 1673.

After leaving Oxford in 1641 Frampton served as tutor to the children of a widow at Farnham, Dorset, where he also set up a private school. He joined the Clubmen of Dorset, a neutralist movement that sought an end to the war between the king and parliament, and participated in a battle with the New Model Army on 5 August 1645 at Hambledon Hill, near Blandford Forum in Dorset. Later he became the master of the free school at Gillingham, Dorset, teaching approximately one hundred boys. While teaching at Gillingham he was encouraged by the local pastor, Dr Davenant, to take holy orders, and Robert Skinner, bishop of Oxford, privately ordained him at Gillingham. Frampton then succeeded Davenant as pastor at Gillingham, where he boldly continued to use the proscribed liturgy of the Church of England. When this led to trouble he became the chaplain to the earl of Elgin, who allowed him to use the liturgy in the family chapel at Ampthill, Bedfordshire.

Frampton gained note as a preacher, preaching often in London during this period, but his royalist sympathies and commitment to the church's liturgy gained him 'both admiration and disgust' among his contemporaries (Evans, 19–20). He escaped further trouble by accepting an offer to become chaplain for the Levant Company at Aleppo, Syria. The company knew of Frampton's royalist views and believed that he would keep the factory 'steady to the crown and church' (ibid., 20). After informing the earl of Elgin of his decision he left England in 1655, aboard the *Antelope*, preaching every Sunday and reading the liturgy when asked. A storm broke the main mast and forced them back to Falmouth, where they stayed until leaving five months later. While serving as chaplain at Aleppo he learned Arabic and studied the archaeological remains in the region. His linguistic ability, which included knowledge of Italian, German, and Arabic, gave him access to the local leaders, including the mufti of Aleppo, a relationship that allowed Frampton to help his friends. He also took advantage of his time in the Middle East to visit the Holy Land, including Jerusalem, at Easter 1660. At the end of 1666 he returned to England, not long after the great fire of London.

After his return from Aleppo, Frampton married Mary Caning (*c.*1632–1680) of Foxcote, Warwickshire. There is some confusion as to the date of their marriage. The licence seems to have been issued on 29 January 1667.

Robert Frampton (*bap.* 1622, *d.* 1708), attrib. Robert More, 1691

However, the wedding is recorded in the parish register of St Paul's, Covent Garden (out of sequence, among 1667 marriages), as having taken place on 10 May 1666. They had met before his departure for Aleppo and corresponded during his tenure there. Mary Frampton died on 11 October 1680 and was buried in a chapel of Gloucester Cathedral. Their daughter was to be a source of support to her father during his years of adversity.

Soon after his marriage, in 1667, Frampton received word of a plague in Aleppo. He returned there and served in Syria until 1670. Before he left he endowed a charity and then travelled overland to England, stopping in Rome, where he preached for the brother of the Catholic duke of Norfolk, Lord Henry Howard. He arrived back in England in May 1671, his wife joining him in London. After his return to London he was appointed a preacher at the rolls and served as chaplain to the lord keeper, Sir Orlando Bridgeman. Bridgeman presented him with prebends at Gloucester and Salisbury in 1672. Henry Howard, for whom he had preached in Rome, also obtained for him the rectory of Oakford Fizpain, in Dorset.

Already a noted preacher during the interregnum, Frampton's reputation continued to grow after the Restoration. John Evelyn and Samuel Pepys both spoke highly of his abilities. Writing in 1667, at the time of Frampton's furlough in London, Pepys commented upon hearing him preach that he gave the best sermon that he had ever heard: 'The truth is, he preaches the most like an apostle that ever I heard a man. And was much the best time that ever I spent in my life at church' (Pepys, 8.21). Evelyn wrote that Frampton 'was not only a very pious and holy man, but excellent in the pulpit; for the moving affections' (Evelyn, 3.629). In 1673 Charles II appointed him to the deanery of Gloucester, after hearing him preach twice at the court, once after the naval defeat at Sole Bay. Though he was renowned for his preaching, none of his sermons was published.

After his installation as dean of Gloucester on 6 May 1673 Frampton divided his time between Gloucester, where he wintered, and Dorset, where he spent the summers. In 1681 he was nominated to succeed the recently deceased bishop of Gloucester, John Pritchett, and was 'joyfully elected by the chapter' (Evans, 126). After his consecration as bishop of Gloucester on Palm Sunday, 27 March 1681, he was licensed to hold his livings and the prebend of Torleton *in commendam* along with his see. He resigned the livings in 1683 at the request of Archbishop William Sancroft. However, apparently to provide for his old age, his friend Philip Sherd of Hampton obtained for him the rectory of Avening, Gloucestershire. He gave up this living a year later, taking instead the vicarage of Standish, which was in his patronage as bishop of Gloucester.

Frampton preached often as bishop at the court at Whitehall, as James II considered him, along with Thomas Ken, among the best preachers in England. However, he incurred the king's displeasure after preaching against Roman Catholicism in the king's chapel. Frampton angered him further by his refusal to install the candidate of Magdalen College's Catholic president in the living of Slimbridge in Gloucester. These actions led the king to complain without success to Archbishop Sancroft about the bishop's behaviour.

In 1688 Frampton opposed James's indulgence for Catholics and nonconformists and the requirement that the indulgence be read from the church's pulpits. Sancroft wanted Frampton to join the delegation that took the bishops' petition to the king, but a travel delay prevented him from joining the six envoys to the king, sparing him imprisonment in the Tower. Though not arrested Frampton showed his solidarity with his colleagues by his constant attendance at the prison during their incarceration.

Although opposed to the papist policies of James II, Frampton refused to take the oaths to William and Mary. After their accession to the throne he withdrew to the country and awaited his deprivation. He was suspended from his position from 1 February until 1 August 1689, when the seven bishops who refused the oaths were deprived. Like Thomas Ken, he was a moderate nonjuror. He did not actively participate in the nonjuring activities of some of his fellow nonjuror bishops, strongly disapproving of the consecrations of George Hickes and Thomas Wagstaffe as bishops in a new nonjuring line. Unlike Hickes he did not consider the established church to be schismatic. Though he could not take the oaths he still considered himself a member of the established church. Therefore, while no longer able to serve as bishop, he was allowed to return to his living at Standish, Gloucestershire, officiating there as his conscience allowed, reading the service, preaching, and catechizing the young.

Although he refused to say prayers for the reigning monarchs he was not an active Jacobite. None the less, his attempts to raise funds to assist nonjuring clergy put him under suspicion in 1696 after a plot to assassinate William III was discovered; he was arrested and imprisoned in the Tower and then released soon after when no evidence was found of his complicity in the plot.

After the death of James II, Queen Anne sought to bring Frampton back into the episcopate by appointing him to the see of Hereford. Frampton declined, insisting that he be allowed to resume his duties as bishop of Gloucester, as he had never accepted his deprivation as lawful. In addition, he did not feel that he could take the new oaths any more than he could the old ones. Already near seventy at his deprivation he remained in relatively good health until his death at eighty-six, though the frailty of age kept him confined to his home at Standish. Six months before he died, he fell and broke two ribs. Then in mid-March of 1708 he developed a fever, which led to his death at his home on Tuesday 25 May 1708. Later that week he was buried on the north side of Standish church.

ROBERT D. CORNWALL

Sources T. Evans, *The life of Robert Frampton, bishop of Gloucester* (1876) · Foster, *Alum. Oxon.* · J. L. Chester and J. Foster, eds., *London marriage licences, 1521–1869* (1887) · Wood, *Ath. Oxon.*, new edn · J. H. Overton, *The nonjurors: their lives, principles, and writings* (1902) · C. J. Abbey, *The English church and its bishops, 1700–1800*, 2 vols. (1887) · W. E., 'Frampton, bishop of Gloucester', *N&Q*, 6 (1852), 349 · Pepys, *Diary* · Evelyn, *Diary* · N. Luttrell, *A brief historical relation of state affairs from September 1678 to April 1714*, 6 vols. (1857) · S. R. Gardiner, *History of the great civil war, 1642–1649*, new edn, 4 vols. (1893); repr. (1965) · E. H. Plumptre, *The life of Thomas Ken*, 2 vols. (1888) · 'Frampton, bishop of Gloucester', *N&Q*, 3rd ser., 11 (1867), 278 · *Fasti Angl., 1541–1857*, [Bristol] · W. H. Hunt, ed., *The registers of St Paul's Church, Covent Garden, London*, 3, Harleian Society, register section, 35 (1906)

Archives BL, biography, Add. MS 32010

Likenesses attrib. R. More, portrait, 1691, Flaxley Abbey, Gloucestershire [*see illus.*] · oils, bishop's palace, Gloucester; repro. in Evans, *Life*

Frampton, Tregonwell [*called* the Father of the Turf] (*bap.* 1641, *d.* 1728), racehorse trainer, was baptized on 3 April 1641 at Moreton in Dorset, the fifth son of William Frampton (*bap.* 1608, *d.* 1643), lord of the manor of Moreton, and his wife, Katharine Tregonwell (1602–1665) of Milton Abbas. Nothing is known of his childhood or education, but it is clear that early in his life he developed a taste for field sports of all kinds, including horse-racing, hare coursing, cockfighting, and hawking. By about 1670 he was regarded as the most active pursuer of falconry in the west country. Shortly afterwards he moved to Newmarket where he acquired a house, later named Gogmagog Stable, and began to keep horses in training. In 1674 his horse Nutmeg beat the duke of Albemarle's Black Buttocks in a match. The following year Nutmeg won again, beating Lord Montagu's Bay Lusty in a race on which £2000–£3000 was bet; it was recorded that 'Mr. Frampton, a gentleman of some £120 rent, is engaged £900 deep'.

Thereafter there are many records of Frampton's running his horses both at Newmarket, where he was one of the first commoners to do so, and elsewhere. In 1676 Sir

Tregonwell Frampton (*bap.* **1641,** *d.* **1728**), by John Faber junior, *c.*1730–40 (after John Wootton)

Robert Howard ran his son's horse against one of Frampton's for £1000, and the following week Frampton was engaged in another match at Salisbury, again for £1000. He was also deeply involved in cockfighting, winning a great cocking match against Lord Ross in 1698.

Frampton won more races than he lost, but he was not always scrupulous in his methods. A match with Sir William Strickland, a Yorkshire baronet, was seen as an important contest between the north and the south, and may have given rise to a song which begins:

Four and twenty Yorkshire knights
Came out of the north countree
And they came down to Newmarket
Mr. Frampton's horses to see.

With large sums wagered on the outcome, Frampton suggested a secret trial before the race itself, which Strickland's horse, Old Merlin, won by about a length. Frampton was pleased with this result, having secretly arranged for his horse to carry 7 lb more than had been agreed. Confident that his horse would easily win the race itself he bet accordingly, but his scheme was foiled because Strickland, as unscrupulous as Frampton himself, had made Old Merlin carry 7 lb overweight also. Not surprisingly Old Merlin again won by about a length. Frampton lost heavily as a result, and it may have been this reverse that led him

to sell the family estate in Dorset, which he had inherited from his brother William in 1689, to his cousin Giles for £5000. However the exact dates of both the race and the transfer of property are not known, although the latter certainly took place before 1702. On another occasion, when Frampton was running one of William III's horses, a dispute over an alleged false start led to litigation between the king, in the person of Frampton, and the duke of Devonshire, who won the case after two trials in the court of common pleas in 1698 and 1699.

Although Frampton was clearly guilty of chicanery on these and other occasions it is almost certain that, contrary to legend, he did not deliberately maltreat his horses. The basis for this charge lies in the story that after his celebrated horse Dragon had beaten a mare in a race for 1000 guineas the owner of the mare declared he would race her against any other mare or any gelding the next day for 2000 guineas, whereupon Frampton had Dragon gelded and raced him again the next day while still bleeding from the operation; Dragon duly won the race but then dropped down dead at the winning post. This story appears to have had its genesis in an avowedly fictional account by John Hawkesworth a quarter of a century after Frampton's death, wherein Hawkesworth stated that he remembered 'this horrid narrative' to be true. However, neither Frampton nor Dragon was named in the work, and Frampton's association with the story seems to have come about wholly by chance in that, in order to boost sales, an enterprising print seller had the story engraved and placed at the bottom of a print of Frampton's portrait. This print sold well and was subsequently copied by other engravers, most notably John Jones in 1791. These prints did enormous damage to Frampton's reputation. John Lawrence, for example, described Frampton as 'brutal and callous-hearted' and possessed of all the characteristics of 'the lowest blackguard retainer of the stable' (Lawrence, 2.213). Lawrence recounted an unsubstantiated story that irons resembling instruments of torture were found in Frampton's house. No contemporary source hints at any deliberate cruelty on Frampton's part, and although he is known to have run a horse called Dragon in several matches in 1712–13 no details or results of these races have survived, other than the notice in the *Daily Courant* of their having taken place.

It is unclear when Frampton first became engaged as the keeper of the king's running horses, or royal racehorse trainer. He may have held minor office under Charles II, but it is more likely that he began to run horses on the king's behalf under William III. In 1695 he won the Newmarket Town Plate with one of the king's horses against the earl of Sunderland and the same year he is recorded as having received payment from the king for 'settling the Establishment of the Race Horses'. William III was a regular visitor to Newmarket and Frampton both bought and ran horses on his behalf as well as his own. At the Newmarket meeting in April 1698, for example, he ran three horses, Cricket, Turk, and Stiff Dick; Turk is described as being the king's horse, and the following year Frampton sold Cricket, together with another horse, to the king for £107 10s. In 1700 he received payment of £1000 from the king as supervisor of the racehorses at Newmarket, for the maintenance of ten stable lads and for the provision of hay, oats, bread, and all other necessaries for ten race-horses. From then until his death he regularly received a salary, which fluctuated from year to year but which seems to have been based on the rate of £100 per horse per year.

Frampton continued to train horses for Queen Anne and made challenges on her behalf. One was to the dukes of Devonshire, Rutland, and Somerset to select any six horses of theirs to run against any six of the queen's in a series of matches run over seven days. However, he also sought to ensure that the conditions were in his favour, for he specifically excluded the duke of Somerset's best horse, Windham, from the challenge, and also stated that he would decide whether the distance of the races was to be 4 or 6 miles, and whether the weights should be 8 stone 7 lb or 10 stone.

A visitor to Newmarket at this time described Framp-ton as:

the oldest, and, as they say, the cunningest jockey in England; one day he lost 1000 guineas, the next he won 2000, and so alternately. He made as light of throwing away £500 or £1000 at a time as other men do of their pocket money, and was perfectly calm, cheerful, and unconcerned when he had lost a thousand pounds as when he had won it. (Whyte, 1.398)

A less favourable view was given by Sir George Etherege in the couplet:

I call a spade a spade, Eaton a bully,
Frampton a pimp, and brother John a cully.

Frampton was an acknowledged misogynist, and his clothes were described as uncouth and old-fashioned. He never changed his style of dress, and would turn up at court dressed in his normal clothes, enquiring in the most familiar manner for the king or queen. Queen Anne is said to have referred to him as Governor Frampton. At the twelfth night festivities at court he was a conspicuous person, and was usually the winner in the gambling that took place on that occasion in the apartment of the groom porter.

As well as training and running Queen Anne's horses, Frampton exercised on her behalf the function of turf arbiter at Newmarket, a duty which during the reign of Charles II had been carried out by the king himself. The post, which gave him considerable power, was equivalent to that of senior steward of the Jockey Club. He retained his title as keeper of the running horses under George I, and it was probably during this period that he acquired the nickname Father of the Turf. Towards the end of his life he appears to have devoted more of his time to the duties of turf arbiter and to have cut back on the number of horses he had in training. Between 1723 and 1726 there are no records of any of his horses having run either at Newmarket or elsewhere, and it is also noticeable that

during the last ten years of his life he appears to have lost more races than he won. He died, unmarried, on 12 March 1728 in Newmarket, and was buried in All Saints' Church. A mural monument of black and white marble was erected to his memory, but this was destroyed during later renovation of the church in the 1870s and replaced by a small and inconspicuous inscription.   JOHN PINFOLD

Sources J. P. Hore, *The history of Newmarket and the annals of the turf*, 3 vols. (1885–6) · J. P. Hore, *Sporting and rural records of the Cheveley estate* (1899) · F. Siltzer, *Newmarket: its sport and personalities* (1923) · J. B. Muir, *W. T. Frampton and the 'Dragon': a refutation of the charge made by his critics* (1895) · J. C. Whyte, *History of the British turf*, 2 vols. (1840) · J. Hutchins, *The history and antiquities of the county of Dorset*, 3rd edn, ed. W. Shipp and J. W. Hodson, 1–2 (1861–3) · R. C. Lyle, *Royal Newmarket* (1945) · R. Onslow, *Headquarters: a history of New-market and its racing* (1983) · W. Chafin, *Anecdotes and history of Cran-bourn Chase*, 2nd edn (1818) · J. Lawrence, *A philosophical and practical treatise on horses*, 2 vols. (1798) · N. Luttrell, *A brief historical relation of state affairs from September 1678 to April 1714*, 6 vols. (1857) · J. Haw-kesworth and others, *The adventurer*, 1 (1752), 220–21
Archives Dorset RO, family MSS
Likenesses J. Wootton, portrait, 1728, Jockey Club, Newmarket · J. Faber junior, mezzotint, c.1730–1740 (after J. Wootton), BM, NPG [*see illus.*] · by or after J. Wootton, oils, NPG
Wealth at death see will, Siltzer, *Newmarket*, 167

Framyngham, William (1512–1537), scholar and author, was born on 23 February 1512 at Norwich, and educated at the local grammar school, where he was contemporary with John Caius. From Norwich he went to Pembroke College, Cambridge, where he graduated BA in 1530. From 1530 until his death he was a scholar of Queens' College, where he proceeded MA in 1533. He was bursar for three years from 1534. He died in Norwich on 29 September 1537. He left all his books to his friend and schoolfellow John Caius, who states that along with Framyngham he wrote dissertations and notes upon them, but could never recover them from those in whose care he left them when he went to Italy in 1539. Long afterwards, in 1570, Edmund, bishop of Rochester, professed to know of them, but Caius apparently did not follow up the clue and all of Framyngham's works remain lost.

Caius describes his friend as 'a man of tenacious memory, fertile wit, [and] infinite reading, indefatigable in work and diligence' (Caius, fol. A3r–v). He also attests to his eloquence, learning in Greek and Latin, and ability in poetry, history, and theology. Framyngham's diligence and learning are shown by the range of the seven works which, according to Caius, he had completed before his death aged twenty-five. These included two prose books on continence, a poem in heroic verse on the burning of the Sodomites 'owing to the awfulness of their crimes and obscene liberality', and a poem in pentameters and hex-ameters in which the author consoles himself for his blindness, brought on by immoderate study while at Cam-bridge. The attribution to Framyngham by Caius of a poem on the martyrdom of St Laurence carries potential political connotations, owing to the execution in 1535 of the Carthusian monk Robert Lawrence for his refusal to swear the oath of supremacy, particularly when placed in conjunction with another poem ascribed to Framyngham by Caius, on the controversial topic of idolatry. The inventory of Framyngham's goods confirms his devotion to learning and fondness for music (which Caius also mentions): he left over 100 books, worth £17, compared to £7 19s. worth of non-literary chattels, which included a pair of virginals and a lute in a box. CATHY SHRANK

Sources J. Caius, *De libris propriis* (1570) · wills, vol. 1, 1501–58, CUL, department of manuscripts and university archives · inventories, 1498–1546, CUL, department of manuscripts and university archives, vice-chancellor's court, inventories, bundle 1 · Tanner, *Bibl. Brit.-Hib.* · Cooper, *Ath. Cantab.* · N. Carlisle, *A concise description of the endowed grammar schools in England and Wales*, 2 vols. (1818) · D. H. Farmer, *The Oxford dictionary of saints*, 4th edn (1997) · *DNB*
Wealth at death more than 100 books, valued at £17; non-literary chattels, including a pair of virginals and a lute in a box, worth £7 19s.: will, 1537, Cambridge University Archives

Francatelli, Charles Elmé (1805–1876), chef and writer on cookery, was born in London, an Englishman of Italian descent. His father was Nicholas Francatelli, a steward. He trained in Paris under Antonin Carême, the founder of French *haute cuisine*, returning to England at a time when it was becoming fashionable to employ French cooks. He worked for many years as *chef de cuisine* to the earl of Chesterfield, and his subsequent employers included Lord Kinnaird at Rossie Priory, in Perthshire, and the Melton Club in London. He took over from Louis Ustache Ude as *maître d'hotel* at Crockford's, the gambling club in St James's Street, London, and from there he became chief cook and *maître d'hotel* to the royal household from 1841 to 1842. He may have left after such a short period because of Queen Victoria's lack of enthusiasm for French cuisine: it was well known that she and Prince Albert preferred plain food. Following a period at the Coventry Club, Francatelli was appointed *chef de cuisine* at the Reform Club in 1854 to run the famous kitchens designed by its first chef, Alexis Soyer. Despite continual battles with the steward over the hiring and firing of kitchen staff, Francatelli remained there until 1861. He managed the kitchen at St James's Hotel in London's Berkeley Street from 1863 to 1870, and that of the Freemasons' Tavern from 1870 to 1876.

Like his contemporary Alexis Soyer, Francatelli was a successful writer of cookery books, starting with *The Modern Cook* (1846), which ran to twenty-nine editions and was described by a reviewer as 'a cookery book which may truly be called *supreme*' (*Literary Gazette*). In this, as well as including recipes for English dishes such as boiled pork *à l'anglaise* and lark pudding *à la* Melton Mowbray, Francatelli introduced many new recipes, including salmis of snipes *à la* Talleyrand and stewed peas *à la française*, and there was a section on how to serve wine in the French manner. He also suggested menus for every season of the year, and in the 1853 edition printed the bills of fare for many of the dinners served to Queen Victoria, including a dinner party with seventy dishes. In the preface he deplored the state of English cooking, despite the fine ingredients, and the fact that the English felt the need to bring in foreigners to prepare their feasts, and exhorted English cooks and their employers to treat cookery as 'an art by which refined taste is to be *gratified*, rather than a coarse appetite *satisfied*'.

Although this was written for the well-to-do, Francatelli was always concerned with economy in cooking: his remark that he could feed a thousand families a day on the food that was wasted in London alone was much quoted. Just as Soyer, in his *Poor Man's Regenerator* (1847), had turned his attention to the poorer classes, so Francatelli brought out *A Plain Cookery Book for the Working Classes* (1852), with recipes for economical dishes such as cowheel broth, ox-cheek soup, sheep's pluck, and stuffed bullock's heart, as well as instructions on making large quantities of nourishing soups suitable for serving in soup kitchens. In *The Cook's Guide and Housekeeper's and Butler's Assistant* (1861), which included recipes for American drinks such as gin sling, mint julep, and cock-tail, he honoured Florence Nightingale with his new version of kedgeree, 'Rice *à la* Sœur Nightingale'. This went through three editions in six months. His last book was *The Royal English and Foreign Confectioner* (1862).

Francatelli married Elizabeth Cooke, daughter of William Cooke, hotel keeper, on 2 August 1870, at St John the Evangelist, Notting Hill, London. He died on 10 August 1876 at 1 Cavendish Place, Eastbourne, Sussex.

ANNE PIMLOTT BAKER

Sources *Chef to Queen Victoria: the recipes of Charles Elmé Francatelli*, ed. A. M. Currah (1973) · A. Hayward, *The art of dining* (1883), 75–6 · L. A. Fagan, *The Reform Club: its founders and architect* (1887), 105 · P. Pullar, *Consuming passions: a history of English food and appetite* (1970), 179–80 · *Literary Gazette* (18 April 1846), 354–5 · *ILN* (19 Aug 1876) · *Annual Register* (1876) · 'Celebrated chefs: Charles Elmé Francatelli', *The Chef*, 1/2 (14 Dec 1895), 1–2 · S. Mennell, *All manners of food: eating and taste in England and France from the middle ages to the present* (1985) · *DNB* · *The Times* (16 Aug 1876) · *CGPLA Eng. & Wales* (1876) · m. cert.
Likenesses J. Brown, engraving, repro. in C. E. Francatelli, *The cook's guide* (1861), frontispiece · A. Hervien, engraving (engraved by S. Freeman), repro. in C. E. Francatelli, *The modern cook* (1846), frontispiece · stipple, NPG
Wealth at death under £800: probate, 26 Aug 1876, *CGPLA Eng. & Wales*

France, Sir Arnold William (1911–1998), civil servant, was born on 20 April 1911 at St John's Road, Knutsford, Cheshire, the only son, and oldest child, of William Ernest France (1880–1939), bank manager, and his wife, Catherine Moncrieff, *née* Ames (1879–1963), teacher of dancing. He was a boarder at Bishop's Stortford College (1924–8). In 1929 he followed his father into the District Bank, where he worked for eleven years in the Manchester area, sometimes looking after small branches in the Peak District. On 27 April 1940 he married Frances Margaret Linton Palmer (1913–1998), whom he had met on a walking tour in Austria. She was the daughter of Dr J. C. L. Palmer.

It was during the Second World War that France first began to show distinction. Conscripted into the Royal Corps of Signals in 1940, he served for three years with the Sudan defence force. Transferred to Cairo, and on the basis of his banking experience, he was seconded to be deputy economic and financial adviser to the minister of state, Middle East. He made such an impression that in 1945 he gained a place at the Treasury as a principal. He was then assigned mainly to overseas finance and became assistant secretary in 1948 and under-secretary in 1952. He became third secretary in 1960, and worked with Edward Heath on Britain's abortive application to join the European Common Market.

Transferred to the Ministry of Health as deputy secretary in 1963, at a time when an expensive recasting of the National Health Service was being considered, France was permanent secretary between 1964 and 1968. The system of primary health care had rested on individual medical practices and standard payments to doctors. Under the 1966 charter of general practice a range of special payments encouraged the development of group practice, the building of new and well-equipped surgeries, and the hiring of ancillary nursing staff. As right hand man to Kenneth Robinson, the minister of health, and with the authority of an ex-Treasury official France was crucial to the successful outcome of the negotiations with the medical profession. He was appointed KCB in 1965. Between 1968 and 1972 he was chairman of the Board of Inland Revenue. As chairman he focused on management and staff relations, rather than on detailed tax policy, and oversaw the opening of the Inland Revenue's first computer centre at East Kilbride. He was advanced to GCB in 1972.

After retiring from the public service in 1973 France was a director of Pilkington Brothers (1973–81), Tube Investments (1973–81), and the Rank Organization (1973–83). He lived at Lingfield, Surrey, from 1948 until his death. Between 1973 and 1981 he was chairman of the board of management of Lingfield Hospital school, where the needs of multi-handicapped children with epilepsy were very close to his heart. He was a committed Anglican, and for many years churchwarden and treasurer of his local church. Between 1973 and 1978 he was chairman of the Church of England's central board of finance, presenting sets of figures in a way even the least numerate could follow. In all his activities he worked towards consensus by listening and persuading, but succeeded in getting effective and timely results.

France was a devoted family man, with four daughters, and, towards the end of his life, seven grandchildren. He died on 2 January 1998 at Ashurst Park, Fordcombe Road, Langton Green, Tunbridge Wells, Kent, following a stroke. The funeral and cremation were on 12 January 1998 at St John the Evangelist, Blindley Heath, Surrey, where his ashes were later interred. His widow died on 22 December 1998. They were survived by their four daughters.

ARTHUR GREEN

Sources *The Times* (19 July 1968); (23 Jan 1998) · *Church Times* (23 Jan 1998) · memorial address, 12 Jan 1998, St John the Evangelist, Blindley Heath · *WWW* · private information (2004) [Bishop's Stortford College, Mrs J. J. Wheeler] · b. cert. · d. cert.
Likenesses photograph, repro. in *The Times* (27 Jan 1998)
Wealth at death under £180,000: probate, 8 April 1998, *CGPLA Eng. & Wales*

Frances, Juanita [*née* Juanita Frances Lemont; *married name* Juanita Frances Schlesinger] (1901–1992), feminist activist and organizer, was born on 5 October 1901 in Adelaide, Australia. Her mother, whose name was Lemont, was a shop assistant; her father, who was in the navy, was unknown to her, but is described on her marriage certificate as Timothy Lemont, master mariner. Her early education and professional training as a nurse took place in Adelaide. However, by the late 1920s she had moved to London, where she worked first as a nurse and then embarked on a brief stage career as a dancer and a conjuror's assistant.

On 16 April 1934 Juanita Lemont married Gerald Leonard Schlesinger (1889–1965), a divorced banker, with whom she had two daughters. The marriage ended in divorce in 1947, whereupon she took the name Juanita Frances (although she was known in some circles as Frances). As a young married woman living in west London, she became involved in charitable work with women in North Kensington. A meeting with Flora Drummond, veteran feminist and chair of the Women's Guild of Empire, launched her on what was to become a lifelong career of feminist activism in pursuit of married women's rights. While working for the guild in North Kensington she soon became acquainted with the small circle of feminists campaigning in London at the time. Her organizational potential was spotted by Dorothy Evans, secretary of the Six Point Group, who asked her to join a new committee on the housewife. In 1938, with Frances as its chair, the committee broke away from the Six Point Group to become the Married Women's Association (MWA). Although concerned to retain links with old feminism, Frances was keen to develop a new feminist organization which would bring to the foreground issues relevant to the lives of young married women and mothers. Hence her early decision to drop the term 'feminist' from the MWA's literature was an attempt to attract the support of young women, many of whom had not previously been politically active.

As chair of the MWA, Juanita Frances steered the association through the first ten years of its life, playing a prominent role in its development and, at the same time, making a major contribution to the shape of post-war 'new' feminism. So called because of its emphasis on equality in difference, 'new' feminism focused in particular on the legal and economic rights of the married woman and housewife. Under Juanita Frances's leadership and in close association with the Labour MP Edith Summerskill, the MWA demanded recognition of the housewife as an equal worker and marital partner entitled to half the male wage and property of a marriage.

In the late 1940s and 1950s, a period when women were widely thought to have achieved equality, and feminism was often viewed as redundant, Juanita Frances struggled, often against the wishes of branch members, to ensure that the association remained committed to her feminist vision of legal and economic equality for women on the home front. As editor of the MWA's monthly journal, *Wife and Citizen*, she sought to maintain what was in the late

1940s and 1950s one of the only published forums for feminist debate.

Although she was committed to cross-party women's politics, Juanita Frances's own sympathies lay with the Labour Party, particularly in the immediate post-war years. By the 1950s and 1960s, her political interests and energies were committed to working at a national rather than at a local branch level. With the aim of turning the MWA into a pressure group for married and divorced women's rights, she worked hard during this period to generate support from a range of high-profile figures. Her ability to court and attract attention to the MWA was a key factor in the association's emergence as a leading women's pressure group in the 1960s.

During the 1960s piecemeal legal reforms such as the Married Women's Property Act (1964) and the Matrimonial Homes Act (1967) began to address MWA concerns. Acknowledging that 'the door to the economic rights of a wife during marriage has been opened', the MWA retained its commitment, as it does to this day, to joint ownership of all marital income and property (Blackford, 'Ideas and structures of feminism', 222).

Although towards the end of her life failing health prevented her from playing a major role in the MWA, Juanita Frances remained committed to the association, a familiar figure at its lunch parties in the houses of parliament. She died of heart failure on 25 November 1992, in the Royal Free Hospital, Camden, and was cremated at Golders Green on 3 December. CATHERINE BLACKFORD

Sources C. Blackford, 'Ideas, structures and practices of feminism, 1939–64', PhD diss., University of East London, 1996 · C. Blackford, 'Wives and citizens and watchdogs of equality', *Labour's promised land? Culture and society in labour Britain, 1945–51*, ed. J. Fyrth (1995) · m. cert. · d. cert. · certificate of making decree nisi absolute, no. 14239/45
Archives University of East London, MSS
Wealth at death £52,062: resworn probate, *CGPLA Eng. & Wales*

Franchi, Gregorio (1769/70–1828), art collector, was born in Portugal to Loreto Franchi, an Italian singer employed at court. William Beckford met him during his stay in Portugal in 1787, when he was invited to hear the seventeen-year-old play Haydn in the Patriarchal College, and gained his father's consent (as a letter testifies) to take him back to England and to provide for the young man's future well-being. The talented and artistic youth gradually grew to be indispensable within Beckford's entourage at Fonthill, and took a leading part in furnishing the new abbey buildings, the grandest of the eighteenth-century 'Gothic' style mansions, with paintings, tapestries, furniture, silver, and *objets d'art*. He married in Portugal in 1795, but after the birth of a daughter he left his family in Lisbon and returned to England.

As Beckford became a leading collector in Europe, Franchi acted as his agent, visiting auctions and salerooms in England and abroad, buying and selling on his behalf, negotiating wartime blockades, commissioning new works; he also became his artistic collaborator, designing new *objets d'art* to suit the fantasy of the 'Romantic interior'. Franchi and Beckford corresponded daily, even while living in the same house, Beckford writing over a thousand extant letters in Italian in a racy, intimate, at times salacious style, Franchi replying in Portuguese; a selection of the letters, in translation, was published by Boyd Alexander under the title *Life at Fonthill, 1807–1822*. Recent work by curators of the Victoria and Albert Museum, which bought a number of items belonging to Beckford at the Fonthill and Hamilton Palace sales in the nineteenth century, has identified a number of drawings by Beckford, or by Franchi, initialled by Beckford, that served as patterns for leading silversmiths commissioned to carry them out, as well as supporting documents. A number of examples are in the Victoria and Albert Museum, and still more in Brodick Castle in Scotland, a charming small castle on Arran Island that houses some silver and other items Beckford's daughter Susan brought with her when she married the tenth duke of Hamilton in 1811 or later inherited on Beckford's death in 1844; some other items are in the National Museum of Scotland. Some of the most exquisite are small spoons with 'oriental' or 'Renaissance' motifs. Franchi appears to have been on good terms with Beckford's daughters, not only Susan, but also Maria Margaret, whom Beckford had turned out for making a runaway love match with Major James Orde, and he continued to work for the tenth duke, who built up his own collections. In 1797 Beckford made his last journey to Portugal, where he had arranged for the order of Christ to be bestowed on Franchi, giving him the title of chevalier. Franchi's way of bringing the best out of the craftsmen is illustrated by a comment by William Gibbs Rogers, a woodcarver:

> Mons Franchi, a man of taste. He would come into the carvers workshop with a volume of Holbein or Aldegreve, select a spoon or handle and have them executed in ivory or ebony as high as he could get talent to bring them, would watch the progress of work day by day and the question would often be 'if you spent another day on it could it get finer'.

As Franchi's Portuguese letters relating to the detail of the works in hand have only just been translated, we can expect to know a good deal more about his role in the joint labours of commissioning, designing, procuring, and execution.

At about the time of the sale of Fonthill in 1822, however, Franchi and Beckford fell out; the exact circumstances are not known, but Beckford was unforgiving. Franchi had built up his own small collection while working for Beckford, and when it was sold at the time of his death the excellent taste of the items was noted. His will, made in Rome in 1825, showed his care in recording 'objects of curiosity' he had stored in various locations and settling any small debts. He left an annuity to his wife, and to his daughter Isabella he left that portion of his property in Portugal that belonged to him, to come to her only after the death of his wife and her mother. He also left a remembrance to Miss Catherine Hillman and Miss Randall, both of 74 Upper Berkeley Street and Portman Square, with whom he had lodged. He instructed that

Beckford's letters to him be returned, and the rest destroyed. He died in early August 1828 and was buried in the cemetery of St Marylebone on 9 August, with a headstone provided by Susan, duchess of Hamilton.

ELINOR SHAFFER

Sources will, PRO, PROB 11/1745, sig. 534 · B. Alexander, ed., *Life at Fonthill, 1807–1822* (1957) · Beckford's Portuguese journals · W. Beckford, *Recollections of a journey to Alcobaça and Batalha* (1835) · C. Wainwright, *The Romantic interior: the British collector at home, 1750–1850* (1989) · M. Baker and M. Snodin, *William Beckford and Portugal* (1987) [exhibition catalogue, 'A Viagem de uma paixão', Palácio de Queluz] · *A taste for magnificence: William Beckford* (New York, 2001) [exhibition catalogue, Bard Centre for the Decorative Arts] · B. Alexander, *From Lisbon to Baker Street: the story of the Chevalier Franchi, Beckford's friend* (Lisbon, 1977) · M. Baker and M. Snodin, 'William Beckford's silver', *Burlington Magazine*, 122/932 (Nov 1980), 735–48; 122/933 (Dec 1980), 820–34 · St Mary Marylebone parish register, City Westm. AC, 9 Aug 1828 [burial] · unpublished letters of Franchi, priv. coll.

Francia, François Louis Thomas (1772–1839), watercolour painter and printmaker, was born on 21 December 1772 in Calais, the son of Louis Charles Francia, director of the military hospital there, and his wife, Marie-Madeleine, *née* Mancel (d. 1772). Although intended for a legal career, Francia was allowed to study part-time at the Académie de Dessin, Calais, where he was awarded numerous prizes. He moved to England in 1790 and found employment as a teacher in Hampstead even though he spoke little English, and from 1792 he taught at Joseph Charles Barrow's drawing school. Francia concentrated initially on topographical scenes, many made for reproduction, and it was with one of these that he made his début at the Royal Academy in 1795, the first of eighty-five exhibits there. The majority were in watercolour, and his commitment to the medium was encouraged by the growing market for topographical views of Britain and the burgeoning reputation of specialist practitioners. From 1795 he was a regular visitor to the 'academy' held in the home of the collector Dr Thomas Monro, and he was a founder member in 1799 (along with Thomas Girtin), and later secretary, of The Brothers, a society of professional and amateur watercolourists who gathered together to sketch from literary sources. He also joined the second of the specialist watercolour exhibition societies, the Associated Artists in Water Colours, and showed 103 works from its foundation in 1808 until 1812, latterly as its secretary. Although Francia suffered professional disappointments during his time in England—he failed to be elected an associate of the Royal Academy following the display in 1816 of two of his oil paintings of shipwreck subjects (Norwich Castle Museum)—he was made painter in watercolours to the duchess of York in 1811. In 1800 he married the artist Maria Child, from whom he was later estranged.

Few of Francia's early works survive, but those from after 1800, such as *Benet's Abbey, Norfolk* (1802; Cecil Higgins Gallery, Bedford), typically display a debt to Girtin in terms of their sombre palette, the use of broad washes, and the creation of simplified forms. These features are especially apparent in moorland scenes such as *Mousehold Heath, Norwich* (1808; Yale U. CBA), which often employ the panoramic format pioneered by Girtin. Such spacious compositions are among the most powerful evocations in these years of dramatic weather and light effects. After 1810 Francia increasingly turned to coast and river scenery for his subject matter, producing watercolours for William Bernard Cooke's *Views on the Thames* (1818–22) and a set of lithographs entitled *Marine Studies* (1822), and it was as a painter of shipping, wrecks, and working ports that he returned to Calais in 1817. The views of Calais and the nearby coast he produced during the remainder of his career retain much of the breadth of his earlier work, but, although he continued to study avidly from nature—the watercolour *Greenwich Park*, dated 1826 (Museé des Beaux-Arts, Calais) shows him sketching—his work lost some of its spontaneity, and his style came to appear thoroughly old-fashioned in his later years. However, he continued to tour, and in the 1830s he was one of the first artists to visit Brittany and Pont Aven.

Much of Francia's energy went into teaching, and he published two distinguished drawing manuals during his time in England. *Studies of Landscapes* (1810) includes more than fifty hand-coloured soft-ground etchings after sketches by Thomas Gainsborough, John Varley, Girtin, and others, and this was followed by *Progressive Lessons* (1813), which concentrates on the 'process of Sketching' and its relation to 'Painting … in Watercolours'. Francia is remembered, however, for his influence on young professional watercolour painters, particularly after his return to Calais, when he was able to pass on up-to-date ideas from London to a new generation of French artists. He gave lessons to William Wyld (1806–1889), Olivier Isaac (1802–1868), his own son, Alexandre (1813–1884), and many others, including, for a short time, Richard Parkes Bonington, whose watercolours of coastal views, in particular, display Francia's influence. Just as importantly for young watercolour painters, Francia had excellent connections with patrons and with art circles in Paris, Calais, and London, and, typically, he remained a friend and supporter of Bonington throughout his life.

Francia continued to exhibit after his move to Calais, showing at various institutions in the provinces, as well as organizing a one-man show in his home town in 1828. He may also have exhibited sixteen works at the Salon in Paris from 1836 onwards—only the surname Francia is given in the catalogue, perhaps reflecting a growing sense of isolation; certainly, his letters suggest that he was still plagued with professional frustrations, and he maintained a thoroughly irascible manner. His correspondence also reveals, however, a knowledgeable man with varied interests in addition to local art politics and painting. On his return to Calais he acted as secretary to the British consul, and he was an active member of numerous societies relating to antiquarian studies, agriculture, science, education, and public welfare. In addition he contributed numerous articles to the local press on a range of subjects. Francia died on 6 February 1839 in his long-term home in the rue de la Poissonerie and was buried in Calais. Alexandre, his sole surviving son, continued to work in his father's style.

GREG SMITH

Sources A. Reed and C. S. Smith, *Louis Francia (1772–1839) and his son Alexandre* (1985) · M. Pointon, *The Bonington circle: English watercolour and Anglo-French landscape, 1790–1855* (1985) · M. Pointon, *Bonington, Francia and Wyld* (1985) · P. Le Nouene, ed., *Louis Francia* (Calais, 1989) [exhibition catalogue, Musée des Beaux-Arts, Calais, 15 Oct 1988 – 9 Jan 1989] · J. E. Grislain, *Lumières d'Outre-Manche* (Calais, 1998)
Archives Archives Municipale, Calais, MSS | V&A, papers of the Associated Artists in Water Colours
Likenesses A. Francia, lithograph (after bust by A. Isaac, *c*.1842)

Francillon, James (1802–1866), judge and legal writer, was born on 21 November 1802, the sixth son of Francis Francillon and Frances Brook, daughter of Thomas Fennings, both of Harwich, Essex. He was descended on his father's side from a Huguenot family settled in England since 1685. Educated at the King's School, Rochester, he became an articled clerk in East Stonehouse, Devon, and in 1824 joined the firm of Wiltons in Bristol as conveyancing clerk, later being admitted an attorney. In November 1828 he entered Gray's Inn, and was called to the bar in 1833.

Francillon went on the Oxford circuit, enjoying a fair practice, but as an able conveyancer was chiefly employed in chamber work. In 1838 he married Lucy, daughter of Thomas Augustus Gale. In 1847, when the modern county courts were constituted, he was appointed judge for the Gloucestershire district, later becoming also a magistrate for Gloucestershire and Wiltshire, and deputy chairman of the Gloucestershire quarter sessions. While living in Cheltenham he attended the Unitarian chapel and was a friend of the Unitarian social reformer Henry Solly.

Francillon was regarded as one of the best of the original county court judges. A selection of his early judgments was published between 1850 and 1852. His *Lectures, Elementary and Familiar, on English Law* (first and second series, 1860–61), written in a popular style, had some reputation in its day.

Francillon died of cholera at Ouchy, near Lausanne in Switzerland, on 3 September 1866. He left, with other children, a son, Robert Edward, also of Gray's Inn, who became a prolific writer, mostly of novels and short stories. FRANCIS WATT, *rev.* PATRICK POLDEN

Sources *GM*, 4th ser., 2 (1866), 559 · *Law Times* (15 Sept 1866) · Boase, *Mod. Eng. biog.* · J. Whishaw, *Synopsis of the members of the English bar* (1835) · J. Foster, *The register of admissions to Gray's Inn, 1521–1889, together with the register of marriages in Gray's Inn chapel, 1695–1754* (privately printed, London, 1889) · *CGPLA Eng. & Wales* (1866) · Holdsworth, *Eng. law*, vol. 15 · [F. G. B. Wills], ed., *The Roffensian register ... from 1835 ... to 1930*, 4th edn (1937) · Allibone, *Dict.* · H. Solly, *'These eighty years', or, The story of an unfinished life*, 2 vols. (1893)
Archives Glos. RO, diary
Wealth at death under £5000: probate, 22 Sept 1866, *CGPLA Eng. & Wales*

Francis, Alban [*name in religion* Placid] (*d.* 1715), Benedictine monk, was born at an unknown date in Middlesex and was professed as a monk at the English abbey of Stss Adrian and Denis at Lamspringe in the prince-bishopric of Hildesheim on 9 May 1670. He took the name Placid in religion.

It was while working on the English mission in Cambridge that Francis attracted brief national notoriety; he was at this time acting as chaplain to Joshua Basset, master of Sidney Sussex College. On 7 February 1687 James II addressed a mandatory letter under his signet manual to John Peachell, master of Magdalene College and vice-chancellor of the University of Cambridge, commanding him to admit Francis to the degree of master of arts 'without administering unto him any oath or oaths whatsoever, or tendering any subscription to be made by him' (*DNB*). This letter was laid before a congregation of the university on 21 February 1687 and the senate advised that the king should be petitioned to revoke his mandate; Francis could be admitted to the degree provided he would swear as the law required. He refused, insisting upon a royal dispensation. On the same afternoon the heads of houses agreed to send a letter to the duke of Albemarle and another to the earl of Sunderland, secretary of state, through whose hands the mandate had passed. A second letter from the king dated 24 February was read in the senate on 11 March. The senate persisted in its refusal to comply with the royal letters; consequently, the vice-chancellor and the senate (by its deputies) was cited to appear before the ecclesiastical commission at Whitehall. The lord chancellor, Jeffreys, declared himself deeply concerned for the university (of which he was a member) that Peachell should be so incompetent. On 12 May Peachell was deprived of the office of vice-chancellor and was suspended from his mastership; the deputies of the senate were also subsequently reprimanded by the lord chancellor. A new vice-chancellor was elected, but Francis never received his degree.

Following the revolution of 1688 Francis withdrew to Lamspringe for a time, and then returned to the mission. He is said to have been committed to Newgate on 7 March 1691 when Jacobite documents were found on him; his confinement seems to have been short. In 1697, he was elected *in absentia* to the abbacy of Lamspringe; however, the election was immediately contested, and the abbacy eventually went to the rival candidate, Maurus Knightely. Francis died in the south province of England on 27 July 1715.

THOMPSON COOPER, *rev.* DOMINIC AIDAN BELLENGER

Sources A. Allanson, *Biography of the English Benedictines* (1999) · P. Cunich and others, *A history of Magdalene College, Cambridge, 1428–1988* (1994) · J. Twigg, *The University of Cambridge and the English Revolution, 1625–1688* (1990) · D. Lunn, *The English Benedictines, 1540–1688* (1980) · *The life and times of Anthony Wood*, ed. A. Clark, 3, OHS, 26 (1894), 221, 356 · B. Whelan, 'A disputed election at Lambspring', *Downside Review*, 78 (1960), 274–85 · *CSP dom.*, 1686–7, 360, 373, 382

Francis [*née* Gittins], **Ann** (*bap.* 1738, *d.* 1800), classical scholar and poet, was baptized on 7 April 1738 in South Stoke, near Arundel, Sussex, the daughter of Jane Sapp (*bap.* 1718, *d.* 1779) and the Revd Daniel Gittins, rector of South Stoke and vicar of Leominster. Her education was unusually extensive: her father taught her Latin, Greek, and Hebrew, interests she pursued throughout her life. As a young girl she began a history of Frederick the Great, but abandoned it on her father's death. On 25 October 1764 she married the Revd Robert Bransby (or Brainsby) Francis (*bap.* 1740), rector of Edgefield, near Holt, Norfolk, and lived there the rest of her adult life. She was recognized as an accomplished classics scholar and a versatile poet whose publications testify to her learning as well as her knowledge of and facility with current literary trends.

In 1781 Francis published by subscription *A poetical translation of the 'Song of Solomon', from the original Hebrew, with a preliminary discourse, and notes, historical, critical, and explanatory*. As the title suggests, this was a scholarly work of serious intent, recasting the biblical text as a Pindaric drama focusing on the triangle of Solomon, the Spouse, and the Jewish Queen; it is psychologically astute as well as technically impressive. In her preface Francis indicates her awareness that her audience may question the propriety of the translation:

[it may] be thought an improper undertaking for a woman [since] the learned may imagine it a subject above the reach of my *abilities*; while the unlearned may incline to deem it a theme unfit for the exercise of a *female* pen.

In emphasizing the 'feebleness' of her pen even as she demonstrates her wide learning and contextualizes the poem by extensive reference, Francis illustrates the predicament facing learned women in the late eighteenth century: how to reconcile deep learning with cultural expectations of female weakness? That she dedicates the work to John Parkhurst, the author of a Hebrew lexicon, may further indicate her attempt to reconcile learning with decorum.

Francis's subsequent publications are wide-ranging and continue to reflect both her learning and her attention to the requirements of her own society: in 1785 she published *The Obsequies of Demetrius Poliorcetes: a Poem*, a retelling of Plutarch, again with notes; in 1788 came the *Poetical Epistle from Charlotte to Werther*, which emphasizes female subjectivity while also defending Goethe; in 1790 appeared *Miscellaneous Poems, by a Lady*, which was printed privately and sold mainly in Norwich and Norfolk; and in 1798 she published *A Plain Address to my Neighbours*, a broadside ballad arguing against the values of the French Revolution and reflecting fears of a French invasion.

The scholarly bent of Francis's poetry suggests a mind comfortable with the display of learning, a point of view supported by her frequent favouring of the female voice: the Jewish Queen, Charlotte, Dido, and Anna (in her *Miscellaneous Poems*). In addition, her *Miscellaneous Poems* mainly explores female experience, concentrating on friends, family, and the privacy of her intimate circle. Her many elegies to dead friends, and especially those to her mother (who died in 1779), are balanced by playful and teasing poems on dead pets. The *Poems* especially reflect Francis's attentiveness to the literary trends of the 1780s, including translations, sonnets, and poetical celebrations of George III's return to health. However, what emerges from her work most strongly is a sense of contradiction. Given that her first publication was not until 1781, when she was forty-three, one suspects that she devoted her earlier years to her family, and began to publish only once her domestic duties had been completed. And yet, as her work makes clear, she was very well read, deeply interested in scholarship and literature.

Francis may be said to embody the dilemma of the conservative intellectual woman of the late eighteenth century, who accepts neither her own cultural relegation to the margins nor the need for a 'revolution in female manners' (M. Wollstonecraft, *Vindication of the Rights of Woman*, 1792, chapter heading). On her death she was praised as a daughter, wife, and mother as well as for her 'mental acquirements', as her obituary phrased it (Lonsdale, 447). As her body of work demonstrates, Francis was remarkable for her simultaneous political conservatism and her evident belief in the intellectual equality and social prominence of women. She died on 7 November 1800, probably at Edgefield.   JACQUELINE M. LABBE

Sources J. Todd, ed., *A dictionary of British and American women writers, 1660–1800* (1984) · Blain, Clements & Grundy, *Feminist comp.* · 'Ann Francis', *Eighteenth-century women poets: an Oxford anthology*, ed. R. Lonsdale (1989), 447; pbk edn (1990) · IGI · DNB

Francis, Enoch (1689–1740), Particular Baptist minister, the son of Francis David Francis, was born at Pantyllaethdy on the Teifi, between Llanllwni and Llanybydder. He began to preach in 1707 at Llanllwni. The date of his ordination is not known, but it was before 1721, as he was invited to preach at the Baptist Association meeting at Hengoed in 1722. He was a popular preacher and for many years made an annual preaching tour through south Wales. In 1729 he published two Welsh sermons, *Gwaith a gwobr ffyddlon weinidogion yr efengyl* ('The work and reward of faithful ministers of the gospel') and a sermon on Isaiah 55:2 written in verse. When his cousin, Abel Francis, embraced Arminianism, he published a defence of Calvinism in 1733 entitled *Gair yn ei bryd* ('A word in season').

Francis married Mary Evans (1690–1739) from Blaenrhymni, near Hengoed, about 1718 and went to live at Capel Iago in Llanybydder. They had six children, two daughters and four sons. One son, Benjamin Francis, later trained for ministry, and after settling at Horsley published poems and hymns in English and Welsh. By 1733 Enoch Francis was living in Pen-y-gelli, near Newcastle Emlyn, and was preaching to several congregations meeting in the area. His wife died on 23 August 1739 and he died on 4 February 1740, after being taken ill while preaching at Fishguard on his return from Llangloffan. He and his wife were buried at Cilfowyr.   KAREN E. SMITH

Sources DWB, 269–70 · T. Rees, *History of protestant nonconformity in Wales* (1861), 338–9 · T. R. Roberts, *Eminent Welshmen: a short biographical dictionary* (1908), 127–8 · J. Thomas, *A history of the Baptist Association in Wales* (1795) · T. M. Bassett, *The Welsh Baptists* (1977) · *Trafodion Cymdeithas Hanes Bedyddwyr Cymru* (1911–12), 20–51

Francis [formerly Morgan], **Francis** (1822–1886), writer on angling, born at Seaton, Devon, was the son of Captain Morgan RN; his mother, Sarah, was the only daughter of Henry Robinson *Hartley, who founded the Hartley Institution at Southampton. He changed his name to Francis on coming of age (1843) and inheriting property. After being educated at various private schools, and with several tutors, he qualified as a civil engineer, but soon abandoned this profession for that of a sports writer. He moved from being paid £2 a column to an annual salary of £200 as angling editor of *The Field*, a position which he held for more than a quarter of a century.

Francis's life was enthusiastically devoted to angling. No kind of fishing, from gudgeon to salmon, came amiss to him, and he speedily made himself familiar with every mode of catching fish. His ardour never flagged; a lifetime of fishing found him, when he reeled up his last line at Houghton, Hampshire, as enthusiastic as when in his boyhood he caught his first fish. For several years Francis was naturalist director of the Brighton aquarium, where he had special opportunities of observing fish and making experiments on their culture. It was on his plan that the National Fish Culture Association was established. He was always enthusiastic about the improvement of English streams and founded the Thames Rights Defence Association. He was a member of the commission on oyster culture (1868–70), set up in response to the decline in freshwater oysters caused by river pollution. He helped to introduce the ova of the English brown trout to the New Zealand and Tasmanian streams. He wrote extensively on fishing, its principles, practice, and management. His most famous work, *A Book on Angling*, was first published in 1867 and was enlarged and reissued several times, thus instructing and educating a whole generation of anglers. The memoir to him prefixed to the sixth edition (1885) stated: 'His memory is the memory of a man who spent his life not merely in selfish amusement, but in contributing largely to the amusement of others.' (Francis) He was also a fair classical scholar and published several novels.

In 1851 Francis married Mary Cole of Oxford. He suffered a stroke in 1883, from which he recovered, but he succumbed to the recurrence of a cancer of the tongue, for which he had undergone two operations. Francis died on 24 December 1886, at his home, The Firs, Twickenham, Middlesex, where he had lived for many years, and was buried in Twickenham. His wife survived him.

M. G. WATKINS, rev. WRAY VAMPLEW

Sources F. Francis, *A book on angling*, 6th edn, with memoir (1885) · *Fishing Gazette* (1 Jan 1887) · *The Field* (1 Jan 1887) · M. G. W., *The Academy* (1 Jan 1887), 9–10 · Boase, *Mod. Eng. biog.* · T. Westwood and T. Satchell, *Bibliotheca piscatoria* (1883) · J. Lowerson, *Sport and the English middle classes, 1870–1914*, new edn (1995)
Wealth at death £3182 17s. 8d.: probate, 2 Feb 1887, *CGPLA Eng. & Wales*

Francis, Sir Frank Chalton (1901–1988), museum director and librarian, was born on 5 October 1901 in Liverpool, the only child of Frank William Francis, provision broker, who died in 1914, and his wife, Elizabeth Chalton, furrier; both parents were from Liverpool. He was educated at the Liverpool Institute; at Liverpool University, where he took a first in classics; and at Emmanuel College, Cambridge, where he spent two years (1923–5) engaged in research on early Greek philosophy, and of which he became an honorary fellow in 1959.

In 1925–6 Francis taught at Holyhead county school, but in the latter year entered the British Museum as an assistant keeper in the department of printed books. He remained in the museum for the rest of his career. His work lay in the routines of the department, including, from 1930, the revision of the general catalogue, but like many of his colleagues he was also required to perform special language duties. For this purpose he acquired a knowledge of Swedish through classes at University College, London. In 1936 he joined the Bibliographical Society and in the same year became editor of its transactions, *The Library*. Francis served as secretary of the British Museum from 1946 to 1947, and in the following year was appointed keeper of printed books. He had already served as chairman of the Library Association's committee on central cataloguing, and played a major part in the establishment of the *British National Bibliography*, which was first issued in 1950. He was also largely responsible for terminating the revision of the museum's published general catalogue, and replacing it with a photolithographically produced edition of the working copy of the catalogue. This was published between 1960 and 1966, when Francis had already become (in 1959) director and principal librarian of the museum (posts he held until 1968).

Within the Bibliographical Society, Francis's editorship of *The Library* (until 1953) was combined with the honorary secretaryship, which he held jointly or solely from 1938 to 1964, guiding the society through the Second World War, and editing its *Studies in Retrospect* (1945). His position in the museum, his willingness to advise others, and his knowledge of historical bibliography involved him in the reconstruction and cataloguing of a number of older libraries, notably Lambeth Palace Library and the cathedral libraries. He lectured in historical bibliography at University College, London, from 1945 to 1959.

The British Museum had been severely damaged during the Second World War, and as director Francis continued the work of his predecessors in restoring galleries and in opening new ones (notably the Duveen gallery for the display of the Elgin marbles in 1962). He was particularly concerned to make the museum's collections more accessible to the public, and a feature of his directorship was the expansion of the museum's design, educational, and publication services. A notable example of the new attitude towards display was the Greek and Roman life room (1960). The museum's collections were greatly enriched, and one for which he had particular enthusiasm was the Ilbert collection of clocks (1958). Exhibitions were also brought in from outside the museum. The growth and improved display of both library and antiquities made the museum's need for more space imperative.

In line with his wish to make the collections of antiquities more accessible, Francis was also sympathetic to the growing demands that the museum's library should serve a wider public than its traditional clientele of scholars who sought manuscripts and older books in the humanities. In particular, a need had been voiced for a greatly improved reference service in the natural sciences. He believed that this must be met with the aid of the museum's existing privilege of legal deposit, and without jeopardizing the unity of the museum's library collections.

The British Museum Act of 1963, upon which Francis had a direct influence, embodied much of this thinking.

Besides changing the composition of the body of trustees, it empowered them to house parts of the collections outside the museum buildings, thus enabling the transformation of the department of ethnography into the Museum of Mankind, creating a legal basis for a new library, and permitting the establishment of the National Library of Science and Invention. The integration of the Patent Office library into the department of printed books, as the basis of the new scientific service, was one of the landmarks of his directorship. Francis also initiated serious planning for a new library building. Architects were engaged, and plans for a new building on the south side of Great Russell Street had reached an advanced stage when in 1967 the government revoked the decision to build on the Bloomsbury site. Thus the establishment of the universal library for which he had worked was set back, though not permanently, by the government's ruling, and by the subsequent setting up of the national libraries committee.

On his retirement in 1968 Francis moved to Nether Winchendon near Aylesbury, while maintaining his links with the bibliographical and library worlds, and in particular with facsimile publishing. He continued to visit the United States, where he was highly regarded and had many friends. He was president of the Association of Special Libraries and Information Bureaux (1965–6), Bibliographical Society (1964–6), Library Association (1965), Museums Association (1965–6), and International Federation of Library Associations (1963–9). Honorary degrees were awarded by Oxford and Cambridge, and by other universities in Britain, Ireland, and North America. He was appointed CB in 1958 and KCB in 1960.

In appearance Francis was strong of profile, of medium height, and heavily built. He was handicapped by arthritis in later life. Genial and hospitable in private, he could be forceful and indeed dominating in public and official life. He married in 1927 Katrina Florence (Kitty; d. 1991), daughter of Thomas McLennon, warehouseman. They had two sons and one daughter. Francis died on 15 September 1988 at Chilton House, Chilton, Buckinghamshire, and was buried at Nether Winchendon.

R. JULIAN ROBERTS, rev.

Sources The Times (16 Sept 1988) · The Times (15 Dec 1988) · The Independent (20 Sept 1988) · personal knowledge (1996, 2004) · private information (1996, 2004) · CGPLA Eng. & Wales (1989) · P. R. Harris, A history of the British Museum Library, 1753–1973 (1998)
Archives BM · priv. coll., papers | Bodl. Oxf., corresp. with Graham Pollard
Likenesses J. Ward, drawing, BM; repro. in Harris, History, pl. 103 · double portrait, colour wash drawing (with his daughter, Jane), priv. coll.
Wealth at death £93,399: probate, 6 Jan 1989, CGPLA Eng. & Wales

Francis, (Bertram) Frederick (1919–1998), engineer and businessman, was born on 15 October 1919 at 30 Sumatra Road, Hampstead, London, the only child of Walter Henry Francis (b. 1892), businessman, and his wife, Florence Eleanor Dell (b. 1898). Fred, as he was usually known, was educated at Finchley Catholic grammar school, though he belonged to the Church of England. He left at the age of fourteen and took a job at an electrical engineering company, moving on in 1934 to the office of a shopfitter's, where he learned administrative skills. In 1939 he founded his own tool-making business in Mill Hill, and the company operated twenty-four hours a day to provide supplies for the war. It was his intention to join the RAF—he had already obtained his pilot's licence—but he felt better employed in production. After the war, he took a flight in a light aircraft, and was hooked; within three weeks he had bought his own plane, and he remained passionate about flying for the rest of his life.

His firm thrived after the war, but Francis became bored and turned to making toys, which he had wanted to do since his childhood. He founded Minimodels in 1947, and demand became so great for the tin-plate toys that in 1953 the company moved to a purpose-built factory in Havant, Hampshire. This also allowed him to sail, and for a time he lived aboard his 46 foot yacht, Yvalda, which was moored in Chichester. In 1952 Francis had patented a keyless clockwork winding mechanism, and now he placed it in a range of metal-bodied model racing cars: these 'Scalex' cars, and the complementary 'Startex' range, were very popular—perhaps in response to the scarcity of toys during and immediately after the war—but the toy trade proved capricious and demand soon collapsed.

In 1956, however, Francis saw a demonstration by Victory Industries of 'rail racing'—battery-powered model cars, guided by the raised edges of a roadway. An exceptional engineer, he quickly adapted his Scalex models to take an electric motor; he also devised a track system with metal rails carrying an electric current in two parallel grooves, along which players could guide the cars. Since the name of Scalex was well established but the cars were now electrically powered, the new product was called Scalextric; it was unveiled in January 1957 at the annual Harrogate toy fair. It was a sensation. The price for the most basic set was £5 19s. 6d., and by 1958 demand was far greater than production capability—and even the North American market, for a long time impenetrable to British toys, began to ask for more. He felt that the availability of layouts in shops for public use ensured the toy's rapid success. On 1 November 1958 Francis sold Minimodels to the Lines Brothers Group, the world's largest toy manufacturer.

Francis decided to return to London, where he dabbled with pile-driving in the Thames and invested in a company that towed wood pulp, Tough-Henderson, which by 1965 was very profitable. But he again decided to move on, sensing that the company would suffer with the emergence of container vessels. A great Francophile who frequently sailed in and around that country, Francis set off for the Mediterranean in his new boat, Fredela. On his return, he accepted an invitation from Victory to join the company as a technical adviser; in 1966 their slot-racing game was voted the best on the market by Which? magazine. The following year, when he returned to Chichester, he met Diane Elizabeth Haines (b. 1945); they married on 3 April 1978 and had two daughters, Catherine and Julia. This was his second marriage, an earlier marriage in 1956 to a woman named Hazel having lasted only a few months.

During the 1960s and 1970s Francis also spent time thinking about winches. He had been unhappy with their performance during the building of *Fredela*, and had made a fully enclosed electric winch himself; it pleased him so much that in 1963 he marketed a commercial version. Although it preceded the mass-produced yacht, and although many in the industry mistrusted electricity on boats, it soon became well known and he later developed a new model, of which a modified version was used by the Royal National Lifeboat Institution. He sold the company when it was doing well, but in 1977 he saw the market expanding and returned to business with a third generation of the 'Francis winch', which the lifeboat institution also adopted.

Meanwhile there was still a demand for Scalextric. Sales had decreased at the end of the 1960s because of inflation, but the game, its basic design virtually unchanged, remained in production, now competing against the appeal of the home computer. Francis also entertained children by talking at local schools about the birth of Scalextric and its success.

In 1985 Francis was diagnosed with cancer of the lymph system and was given a year to live; he survived for thirteen years. He sold his winch-building company, but spent time restoring old motorbikes and continued to sail in his beloved *Fredela*. He died peacefully on 6 January 1998 after a viral infection forced him into St Richard's Hospital, Chichester. Ten days later he was buried near his home, in St James's Church in Birdham, Sussex. His wife, Diane, and their two daughters survived him.

DANIEL CREWE

Sources G. Butler, 'Reminiscences by Fred Francis: the man who invented Scalextric', unpublished manuscript, priv. coll. • private information (2004) [Diane Francis, widow; Graham Butler; Geoff Dell, funeral tribute] • *Daily Telegraph* (11 Feb 1998) • A. Slade, 'An history of Scalextric', www.nscc.co.uk/history.htm • d. cert.

Archives Havant Museum, Hampshire, original tin plate Scalextric toys

Wealth at death £131,420—gross; £122,203—net: probate, 28 Sept 1998, *CGPLA Eng. & Wales*

Francis, George Grant (1814–1882), antiquary, was born in Swansea, Glamorgan, on 4 January 1814, the eldest son of John Francis (d. 1841), coach-builder, of Swansea, and his wife, Mary Grant. John Deffe Francis (1815–1901), a minor painter and art collector, was his younger brother. Francis was educated at Swansea high school, after which he joined his father's flourishing coach-building firm, which he sold after the latter's death in February 1841. Until within a few years of his own death Francis took a very prominent part in every question affecting the interest of his native town. 'Whatever his hand found to do' wrote a contemporary, 'he did it with a might which certainly deserved success, though it by no means uniformly commanded it. … As with many other men of a similar temperament, his enthusiasm ran away with him'. Thus his numerous schemes for local improvements were not always appreciated. In 1835 he helped to found the Royal

Institution of South Wales, and presented it with his large collections of local fossils, antiquities, coins, and seals, together with one of the best libraries of works relating to Wales of its time, of which he compiled and printed a catalogue, afterwards adding a supplementary volume. On 29 October 1840 he married Sarah, eldest daughter of John Richardson of Swansea, and of Whitby Lodge, Northumberland; they had three sons.

Francis was elected FSA on 16 January 1845, was its honorary secretary for south Wales, and was also a corresponding member of the Society of Antiquaries of Scotland and of the Welsh Manuscripts Society. He shared in the formation of the Cambrian Archaeological Association in 1846, and frequently contributed to its journal, *Archaeologia Cambrensis*. To the volume for 1848 he sent for insertion the original contract of affiance between Edward of Caernarfon, prince of Wales, and Isabella, daughter of Philip the Fair, king of France, dated at Paris 20 May 1303, which he had discovered in Swansea Castle. It was printed separately the same year. He was active in restoring to public use the ancient grammar school of Bishop Gore, Swansea, of which he was for many years chairman and one of the trustees. His connection with it enabled him to collect materials for his book, *The Free Grammar School, Swansea; with brief memoirs of its founders and masters, and copies of original deeds* (1849). By the town council he was entrusted with the restoration and arrangement of their neglected and scattered muniments. His effort brought a warm tribute from Lord Campbell in the court of queen's bench. He afterwards privately printed one hundred copies of *Charters Granted to Swansea* (1867).

The preservation and restoration of Oystermouth Castle, near Swansea—one of the many ancient ruins pertaining to the house of Beaufort, lords of Gower and Kilvey—also owed much to Francis's exertions, for which he was presented with a piece of plate. In 1851 he was selected to represent the Swansea district as local commissioner at the Great Exhibition. During the same year the British Association appointed him secretary to its department of ethnology when holding its meeting at Swansea. Francis was mayor of the borough in 1853–4, and was also colonel of the 1st Glamorgan artillery volunteers, a corps raised by his exertions in 1859. In 1867 he communicated to the Swansea newspaper, *The Cambrian*, 'as the earliest organ of the copper trade', some curious papers which he had discovered in the record office on the metallurgy of the district. These papers excited considerable interest, and Francis printed a limited run of fifty copies as *The smelting of copper in the Swansea district, from the time of Elizabeth to the present day* (1867). So numerous were the enquiries for the book that he published it in 1881 as a quarto volume, supplemented with material from the Gnoll MSS of Neath, and illustrated with autotype portraits of men connected with the copper trade and sketches of places historically associated with it. From a large mass of original documents extant among the Gnoll papers at Neath, Francis was able to add to this second edition many new and important facts, while he personally examined each of the copper-smelting works described in the book. Subsequent work has partially suspended the book, which none the less remained of use over a century later. Francis wrote many other monographs on Welsh history and topography including: *Original Charters and Materials for a History of Neath* (1845, fifty copies privately printed); *The value of holdings in Glamorgan and Swansea in 1545 and 1717, shown by rentals of the Herbert family* (1869, twenty-five copies printed); and *Notes on a gold chain of office presented to the corporation of Swansea in … 1875, … together with a list of [mayors] from 1835 to 1875* (1876). Many other scholars benefited from his wide and varied knowledge of the Swansea district.

Francis died at his London house, 9 Upper Phillimore Place, Kensington, on 21 April 1882, and was buried on 26 April in Swansea cemetery.

GORDON GOODWIN, *rev.* BETI JONES

Sources *Swansea and Glamorgan Herald* (26 April 1882) · *Swansea and Glamorgan Herald* (3 May 1882) · T. Nicholas, *Annals and antiquities of the counties and county families of Wales*, 2nd edn, 2 (1875), 628 · G. Williams, 'Swansea's great gracious foreman', *Country Quest*, 26/4 (Sept 1985), 27–8 · m. cert. · *DWB*
Archives U. Wales, Swansea, corresp. and historical notes; corresp. and papers | Bodl. Oxf., corresp. with Sir Thomas Phillipps · NL Wales, letters to J. M. Traherne
Likenesses portrait, repro. in G. G. Francis, *Charters granted to Swansea* (1867)

Francis, George William (1800–1865), botanist, was born in London. He was apprenticed to the internationally famous Loddiges nursery in Hackney, and in 1835 he published his *Catalogue of British Flowering Plants and Ferns*, which went through five editions by 1840. From 1841 to 1845 he edited the *Magazine of Science and School of Arts*. His family was increasing and he emigrated to South Australia, arriving in the colony in September 1849. Shortly after his arrival he took a lease on the old botanical garden, north of the Torrens River, as a yearly tenant. While in England he had established a minor reputation as writer of a number of elementary scientific textbooks and of a *Dictionary of Arts, Sciences and Manufactures* (1846). He was a member of the Botanical Society of the British Isles and a fellow of the Linnean Society. In 1855 he was appointed the first director of Adelaide Botanic Garden, a position he held until his death. He died after a long illness, of dropsy, on 9 August 1865, and was buried the next day. He left a widow and ten children.

B. D. JACKSON, *rev.* ALEXANDER GOLDBLOOM

Sources Desmond, *Botanists*, rev. edn · G. Bridson, *The history of natural history* (1994) · B. J. Best, *The life and works of George William Francis* (1965) · *South Australian Register* (10 Aug 1865)
Archives NHM · State Library of South Australia, Adelaide
Likenesses portrait, repro. in Best, *Life and works of George William Francis*

Francis, James Bicheno (1815–1892), hydraulic engineer, was born on 18 May 1815 at South Leigh, Oxfordshire, the son of John Francis, a railway builder and superintendent, and his wife, Eliza Frith Bicheno. He attended school at Radleigh Hall and Wantage Academy, leaving at fourteen to work under his father on the construction of canal and harbour works. In the spring of 1833 he emigrated to

America and found work on the construction of the Stonington railroad in Connecticut. A year later he moved to Lowell, Massachusetts, and by 1837 was chief engineer to the proprietors of the locks and canals on the Merrimack River. On 12 July that year Francis married Sarah Wilbur Brownell of Lowell; they had six children. About 1841 Francis began a series of measurements to determine the amounts of water drawn off by each of the mills along the canal, and these led to the development of the well-known Francis formula for the flow of fluids over weirs. The proprietors then decided to exploit the water-power potential of the river, and Francis designed a turbine based on the Howd patent but with the vanes reshaped to give a combination of radial and axial flow. This type, known as the mixed flow or Francis turbine, became the one most generally used for medium head hydro-electric installations. The results of his experimental work, conducted with his characteristic emphasis on thoroughness and accuracy, were published in *The Lowell Hydraulic Experiments* (1855). Francis joined the American Society of Civil Engineers at its first meeting in 1852 and was elected president in 1880. He retired in 1885 and died at Boston on 18 September 1892. He was survived by his wife.

RONALD M. BIRSE

Sources C. W. Mitman, 'Francis, James Bicheno', *DAB* · R. Porter, ed., *The Hutchinson dictionary of scientific biography*, 2nd edn (1994), 248–9

Francis, James Goodall (1819–1884), politician and entrepreneur in Australia, was born in London on 9 January 1819, son of Charles Francis and his wife, Anne, *née* Smith. In 1834 he arrived in Van Diemen's Land. He obtained work in a hosiery shop in Hobart Town and in 1837 became a partner to James Hamilton, a storekeeper in Campbell Town. He returned to Britain in 1840, but went back to Van Diemen's Land in 1847 and with a former acquaintance, Duncan McPherson, took over the firm of Boyes and Poynter in Hobart Town. In 1853 Francis and Macpherson opened a branch establishment in Victoria; Francis became its managing partner and moved to Melbourne. IIe rapidly grew in influence as he became a director of the Bank of New South Wales in Melbourne, of the Victorian Sugar Company, and of the Melbourne Underwriters' Association, and president of the chamber of commerce. He also had gold mining and pastoral interests. From 1859 to 1874 he represented Richmond in the Victorian legislative assembly, holding cabinet office three times, in particular being commissioner of trade and customs in 1863–8 and treasurer in 1870–71 under Sir James McCulloch.

Francis introduced the protectionist revision of the tariff of 1865–6 and at an intercolonial conference in 1870 refused to lower duties at the behest of New South Wales. But he was only a moderate protectionist and, faced with falling revenue in 1871, he proposed a property tax rather than higher duties, a proposal which wrecked the ministry. After a spell of radical government and the imposition of 20 per cent duties, Francis succeeded in regaining office as premier in 1872. That year, his ministry promoted the important Education Act which provided for the first time in Victoria compulsory, free, and non-sectarian primary education, and removed state aid from church schools. Apart from that, the government hastened railway development, stopped assisting immigration, passed the first factory legislation, namely the Supervision of Workrooms and Factories Act of 1873, and an act to reduce mining accidents. But Francis's proposals to widen the franchise and deal with inter-house disputes by double dissolutions and joint sittings aroused opposition, and a dangerous attack of pleurisy caused his resignation. On recovery, he paid a long visit to England. In 1878 he re-entered political life, amid another constitutional crisis arising from another inter-house parliamentary deadlock. At his third attempt he was elected to the legislative assembly, and in 1880 he briefly took office again without portfolio; but in 1883 ill health compelled him to retire into private life and to his vineyard at Sunbury.

Francis was a poor speaker, but a good administrator, and his integrity gave him great influence in the assembly. As premier he avoided constitutional strife or sensational appeals to the people and his practical good sense and level-headed independence were widely appreciated. He died at Queenscliff, Victoria, on 25 January 1884, leaving an estate of £178,000, and survived by his wife, Mary Grant, *née* Ogilvie, and their eight sons and seven daughters. He was buried privately at Queenscliff, according to the wishes of his family, on 28 January.   A. G. L. SHAW

Sources *AusDB* · K. Thompson and G. Serle, *A biographical register of the Victorian parliament, 1859–1900* (1972) · A. S. Kenyon, 'The James Hamilton letters', *Victorian Historical Magazine*, 15 (1933–5) · *The Argus* [Melbourne] (26 Jan 1884) · C. M. H. Clark, ed., *Select documents in Australian history, 1851–1900* (1955), 286–91 · *DNB*
Wealth at death £178,000—in Australia: *AusDB*

Francis, John (1780–1861), sculptor, is believed to have been born in Lincolnshire on 3 September 1780. He was brought up to be a farmer in his native county, then moved to Thornham in Norfolk where he settled with his wife, Mary Evetts (*b*. 1779), a miller's daughter from the village. His talent for sculpture caused friends to persuade him into a change of career and in 1810 he went to London where he worked first under Samuel Joseph and then under Francis Chantrey. About 1815 he came to the notice of the famous agriculturist Thomas Coke, later earl of Leicester, who introduced him to various friends in the whig party which was to provide him with many of his patrons. He still had to struggle to establish himself and had to return to his farm more than once to earn his living. The key to his eventual success was royal patronage. A chance incident brought him to the attention of the duke of Sussex who formed a high opinion of him, both as an artist and as a man, and commissioned small, cabinet-size busts of his own family and political associates. Francis is also said to have become a favourite artist of William IV; the favour was continued by Queen Victoria and Prince Albert, who entrusted him with private commissions, executed under the prince's close supervision. In 1844 Francis modelled a bust of Albert's father, Duke Ernst I of Saxe-Coburg and Gotha, but it was accidentally smashed and the sculptor had to provide a replacement for it. Shortly afterwards he made a model of the prince's favourite greyhound, Eos, which was twice cast in bronze, once for the dog's grave at Windsor, and again for Osborne House, Isle of Wight (Royal Collection). Francis exhibited frequently at the Royal Academy from 1820 until 1857. The bulk of his exhibits were the portrait busts, mostly in marble, which formed his basic stock in trade; he also showed a few statues, in full and cabinet size. In 1837 he exhibited a figure of *Il Penseroso* after Milton but this venture into the world of the imagination seems to have had no sequel. He also made a few church monuments.

Francis died at his home, 56 Albany Street, Regent's Park, London, on 30 August 1861 and was buried in Highgate cemetery. Examples of his work are in the National Portrait Gallery, London, the National Gallery of Victoria in Melbourne, Australia, in the Mansion House, City of London, and in a number of private collections, particularly the Royal Collection and that of the dukes of Norfolk at Arundel Castle, Sussex. His pupils included Joseph Durham, Matthew Noble, and Thomas Thornycroft, who married his daughter Mary [see Thornycroft, Mary], herself a sculptor.   L. A. FAGAN, *rev.* ADAM WHITE

Sources R. Gunnis, *Dictionary of British sculptors, 1660–1851* (1953); new edn (1968) · Graves, *RA exhibitors* · E. Manning, *Bronze and steel: the life of Thomas Thornycroft, sculptor and engineer* (1932), 1–58 · E. Manning, *Marble and bronze: the art and life of Hamo Thornycroft* (1982), 21–4, 39 · R. Ormond, *Early Victorian portraits*, 1 (1973) · J. Roberts, *Royal artists: from Mary queen of Scots to the present day* (1987), 116–17 · *Art Journal*, 23 (1861), 312 · Redgrave, *Artists* · *CGPLA Eng. & Wales* (1862)
Archives Courtauld Inst., Conway Library, photograph file | Henry Moore Institute, Leeds, Hamo Thornycroft MSS · Henry Moore Institute, Leeds, Thomas Thornycroft MSS
Likenesses daguerreotype, *c*.1837, Henry Moore Institute, Leeds · N. J. Crowley, watercolour, repro. in Manning, *Marble and bronze*, 22 · daguerreotype, repro. in Manning, *Bronze and steel*, 8
Wealth at death £15,000: probate, 4 April 1862, *CGPLA Eng. & Wales*

Francis, John (1811–1882), publisher, was born in Bermondsey, London, on 18 July 1811. His father, James Parker Francis (1777?–1850) of Saffron Walden, Essex, where he was apprenticed to a leather dresser, had married Elizabeth (1774/5–1868), daughter of Thomas Perkins, a gunflint maker of Ware, and settled in Bermondsey, where John Francis and his two sisters grew to adulthood (Francis, 1.2). For twenty-five years James Francis was secretary of the Leather-dressers' Trade Union, and the family attended a small nonconformist church meeting at Collier's Rents under the pastorate of James Knight (ibid., 3). First educated at a dame-school in Long Lane, then by F. Painter in Bermondsey, John Francis then attended a nonconformist school in Unicorn Yard, Tooley Street, Southwark. John Cooper, the school's secretary, helped him in 1823 to apprentice himself to E. Marlborough, a well-known newspaper agent at 4 Ave Maria Lane.

In August 1831, having completed his full time, John Francis responded to an advertisement in *The Athenaeum* and was hired by Charles Dilke and James Holmes, the owners, as a junior clerk in the office of *The Athenaeum*; he lived at 2 Catherine Street until the journal moved to 20

Wellington Street, Strand. Because of his exceptional ability by 4 October he became business manager and publisher of the paper.

At fourteen Francis had begun teaching in the Sunday school of John Rippon's chapel, Carter Lane, Southwark, and when Rippon moved to New Park Street in May 1833, Francis became superintendent of the Sunday school and secretary to the visiting association for the neighbourhood poor. As secretary to the south London branch of the Sunday School Union, he worked for the repeal of the corn laws. In 1849 Francis joined the new Bloomsbury Chapel, under the pastorate of William Brock; as superintendent of the Sunday school there, he sought free education of the people, and served ably as a district visitor in St Giles-in-the-Fields for eleven years, and as superintendent for nearly ten. When Francis moved to Canonbury (1861–8) and to Dr Allon's congregation at Union Chapel, he again paid district visits. His move to 11 Burghley Road, Highgate Road, in 1868 made it possible for him to attend Bloomsbury Chapel until 1877, when a Baptist chapel was completed in Highgate Road.

As early as 1830 Francis had begun to oppose the heavy newspaper taxes; he was Liberal in politics, and rather relished being styled a radical. In 1838 Francis, keen to support the plan of his friend Sir Rowland Hill to issue penny-stamped covers for letters, had the 28 April issue of *The Athenaeum* printed on Dickenson's 'peculiar paper' to demonstrate how postal forgery could be thwarted. While Milner Gibson fought the battle in parliament, Francis insisted on visiting MPs in their homes in the early morning or late at night. *The Athenaeum* became the first paper systematically to wage war against 'taxes on knowledge', under Francis's energetic leadership (Francis, 1.15); the main targets were the duty of 1s. 6d. on each advertisement, the stamp duty of 1d. on each newspaper, and the paper duty of 1½d. per pound, which were successively repealed in 1853, 1855, and 1861. Although he served as treasurer of the committee for the repeal of advertising duty formed in 1849, Francis was its founder and most active member; he visited Edinburgh and Dublin with John Cassell and Henry Vizetelly in support of the cause. In 1863 his services were rewarded with a testimonial from both the press and the Association for the Repeal of the Taxes on Knowledge.

Francis wrote 'The progress of periodical literature from 1830 to 1860' for the *Bookseller* of 26 April 1861 (pp. 215–16) and 'The literature of the people' for *The Athenaeum* of 7 January 1870, as well as 'The forthcoming school board elections' for the Baptist *Freeman* of 8 September 1876. Largely at his instigation, the price of *The Athenaeum* was reduced from 4d. to 3d. to enhance circulation, and on 15 October 1831 the first gratis supplement, containing eight pages of reading matter, increased the size to twenty-four pages for 4d. During the three years in the 1840s when Charles Wentworth Dilke was manager of the *Daily News*, Francis assisted in the commercial department and controlled the subscription list. He provided newsvendors with names of nearby subscribers so that they could supply copies directly. He managed the commercial

affairs of *Notes and Queries* from 1872. In 1881 *The Athenaeum* noted his fifty years as publisher, declaring it unprecedented in London journalism.

Firm yet gentle, sincere, and generous, Francis was the unfailing friend and best adviser of all who knew him. After missing work only once owing to illness in thirty years, increasing ill health in 1881 forced his move to his old rooms above the office in Wellington Street. He died there of cancer on 6 April 1882 and was buried in Highgate cemetery on 18 April, near the grave of Faraday. In his memory two pensions were founded in connection with the Newsvendors' Benevolent and Provident Institution. His wife, Charlotte, *née* Collins, had predeceased him, on 7 December 1879, aged seventy-one.

Francis's elder son, John Collins Francis, succeeded him as publisher of *The Athenaeum*, and produced *John Francis, Publisher of 'The Athenaeum': a Literary Chronicle of Half a Century* (1888), an extraordinary compilation based on the periodical's contents. John Francis's younger son, Edward James Francis, acted as printer for *The Athenaeum*, *Notes and Queries*, and other publications. He also served as manager of the *Weekly Dispatch* from 1875 until his death on 14 June 1881. In 1911 John Collins Francis inherited the paper from Sir Charles Dilke, along with his cousin, J. Edward Francis, who had served as printer after the death of Edward James Francis.

BARBARA QUINN SCHMIDT

Sources J. C. Francis, *John Francis, publisher of 'The Athenaeum': a literary chronicle of half a century*, 2 vols. (1888) · C. W. Dilke, ed., *The papers of a critic: selected writings by Charles Wentworth Dilke*, 2 vols. (1875) · *The Athenaeum* (15 April 1882), 476 · *Nation and the Athenaeum* [centenary supplement] (21 Jan 1928), 602–14 · L. A. Marchand, *The Athenaeum: a mirror of Victorian culture* (1941) · P. Chalmers, *Mr Francis, of 'The Athenaeum', on the plan of Sir Rowland Hill*, 2nd edn (1889) · H. R. Fox Bourne, *English newspapers: chapters in the history of journalism*, 2 (1887), 211–36 · H. J. Nicoll, *Great movements and those who achieved them* (1881), 269–337 · H. Vizetelly, *Glances back through seventy years: autobiographical and other reminiscences*, 2 vols. (1893) · W. Garrett, *William Charles Wentworth Dilke* (1982), 137 · Boase, *Mod. Eng. biog.* · d. cert.

Archives BL, Dilke MSS, Add. MSS 43910–43913 · BL, letters to Hepworth Dixon, Add. MS 38794

Likenesses portrait, repro. in Francis, *John Francis*, vol. 1

Wealth at death £981 6s. 9d.: probate, 7 June 1882, *CGPLA Eng. & Wales*

Francis, Peter William (1944–1999), vulcanologist, was born on 28 December 1944 in Mufulira Hospital, Northern Rhodesia (now Zambia), the first of two sons of Richard James Francis (1909–1984), a retail pharmacist, and his wife, Blanche Maude (1908–1991), a nurse. After his family resettled in England, he attended Bournemouth grammar school and Reading School, and then studied at Imperial College, London, where he earned a first-class honours degree in geology in 1966. While at Imperial, Francis attended a talk for the college's expeditions society on the subject of a 'ghost' mining town in the Bolivian Andes. The lecture fired the imagination of a small group, which assembled an expedition to the region. Francis joined as equipment officer, and the group travelled to South America by sea in July 1966. Before long Francis was to enjoy his first taste of remote volcanoes. Francis remained at Imperial to carry out doctoral research, completed in 1969, on the structural geology of the Outer Hebridean island of Barra. His growing flair for organizing fieldwork in remote and harsh environments was put to use on a further expedition to the Andes in 1970, this time to northern Chile, leading to an early paper on ignimbrites published in the *Geologische Rundschau* in 1974. Recruited as a lecturer to the department of earth sciences of the Open University in 1971, Francis initiated geochemical studies of Andean volcanic rocks and made further contributions to the understanding of pyroclastic flows.

Always excited (if often frustrated) by new technology, Francis was quick to recognize the potential of the newly available Landsat satellite images for mapping vast and arid terrains, such as the central Andes. By this means, he was the first to describe Cerro Galan, in north-west Argentina, as the core of a giant caldera. He subsequently led an Anglo-Argentinian expedition to the volcano in 1982. The project received military support, and was the last joint operation between the British and Argentine armies before the Falklands War.

Flying above the freshly emplaced deposits of the 1980 Mount St Helens eruption, the ravaged landscape reminded Francis of the hummocky terrain apparent in satellite images of many Andean volcanoes. This led him to make important contributions to the understanding of the catastrophic collapses of volcanoes that result in giant debris avalanches. These included the first description of one of the world's best-preserved debris avalanche deposits at Socompa volcano in Chile.

Francis had a long connection with NASA and paid many extended visits to the USA, first as senior visiting scientist at the Lunar and Planetary Institute in Houston, Texas (where he studied images of Martian volcanoes), and later as visiting professor at the University of Hawaii. Francis was a member of the vulcanology team for NASA's major earth system enterprise mission (but did not live to see its launch in December 1999). It was while in Washington, DC, for a NASA meeting that he met Mary Elizabeth Brown, *née* George (b. 1948), then working at the British Embassy; he married her in London on 14 June 1991.

By the mid-1980s a new generation of improved Landsat satellites was in orbit. While surveying Andean volcanic summits for signs of activity using the new images, Francis made the chance discovery of an infrared 'glow' within the summit crater of Láscar in Chile. A year later the volcano's lava dome exploded, showering the distant town of Salta in Argentina with ash. Francis's observations heralded the modern era of volcano monitoring from space.

In the early 1990s Francis turned his attention to volcanic gas emissions, and to the possibility of monitoring them remotely (and hence safely) using compact infrared spectrometers. Francis pioneered the application of this technology through field campaigns on Mount Etna and Vulcano in Italy. He later set up the gas surveillance programme at Montserrat Volcano Observatory, where he carried out three tours of duty as deputy chief scientist following the reawakening of Soufrière Hills volcano on

the Caribbean island in 1995. He was respected for the considered and equitable way in which he engaged in scientific debate on the volcanic crisis, and for his decision making, always informed by a profound understanding of how volcanoes work.

Francis had a major impact on the teaching of earth sciences at the Open University. Always an innovator, he launched their first earth system science course. In 1998 he was awarded the title of professor of vulcanology. With a gift for lucid and accessible writing and a drive to communicate science to the wider audience, Francis popularized vulcanology and planetary science through books and magazine articles. His first book, *Volcanoes* (1976), was widely read and enjoyed. He revised and expanded it for Oxford University Press in 1993.

In his spare time Francis was an amateur pilot, yachtsman, bookworm, and enthusiastic walker and jogger. He died of a heart attack during a visit to Paris on 30 October 1999, and was buried at St Michael's Church, on the campus of the Open University, on 16 November 1999.

CLIVE OPPENHEIMER

Sources S. Self and others, *Bulletin of Volcanology*, 62 (2000), 143–5 · C. Oppenheimer, *Memoir 21* (2002) [GS Lond.] · *Electronic Telegraph* (13 Nov 1999) · private information (2004) [Michael Francis, brother] · m. cert.
Wealth at death £258,441: probate, 2000, *CGPLA Eng. & Wales*

Francis, Philip (1708–1773), translator and writer, was born on 19 July 1708, and was baptized on 21 July at St Mary's Church, Mary Street, Dublin, the son of John Francis (d. 1724), dean of Lismore, who at the time of Philip's birth was rector of St Mary's parish, and his wife, Anne (d. in or after 1724). Two other sons, Richard *Francis (1698x1700–1742) and Tench, and three daughters lived to maturity. Philip attended a school in Capel Street conducted by Thomas Sheridan, the friend of Swift, before entering Trinity College, Dublin, in April 1724 at the age of fifteen. He took a BA degree in 1729, was later ordained in the established church, and was briefly a curate in St Peter's parish, Dublin. In 1739 he married Elizabeth Rowe (c.1710–c.1741), but she died not long after, leaving him a son, Philip *Francis (1740–1818).

It appears that Francis had taken holy orders because his father in his will had so desired, and not from any solid commitment to the reformed faith. Indeed, he belonged to a cluster of Anglican clerics in Dublin at this time (including Thomas Sheridan, James Sterling, Matthew Pilkington, James Eyre Weeks, and William Dunkin) who, perhaps taking their cue from another noted cleric, Jonathan Swift, were more interested in a career in literature and political journalism than in their priestly duties. Francis was on particularly friendly terms with Dunkin, and, on the occasion of the publication in Dublin in 1742 of the first volume of his translations of Horace, he was profuse in his acknowledgement of his indebtedness to 'this honest and good man' whose friendship he had enjoyed for many years (*Memoirs*, xix).

About 1744, soon after the death of his wife, Francis moved to England, where an appointment to the rectory of Skeyton in Norfolk was soon abandoned for the prospects of a literary career in London. But to help out, while he was awaiting literary success, he took to schoolmastering at Esher in Surrey, teaching being then another favoured alternative occupation for Anglican clergy. Gibbon was for a short while a pupil, but was removed by his parents when it was found that Francis was more interested in socializing in London than in conducting a school.

As well as translating into English verse the works of Horace, Francis was also interested in playwriting, and in pursuance of this aim he cultivated the acquaintance of such leading theatrical luminaries as David Garrick and Colley Cibber. But in spite of Garrick's playing a leading part, a prologue by him, and an epilogue by Cibber, his first play, *Eugenia*, was not a success when produced at Drury Lane in February 1752. Its failure may have been due to the use of blank verse and to an English audience's preference for tragedies with plenty of bloodshed, a commodity which Francis's play lacked. In any event his attempt to transform what had been a French comedy by Madame Grasigny into an English tragedy did not come off. A further play by Francis, *Constantine*, produced at Covent Garden in February 1754 and again based in part on a French piece, was even less successful, and was taken off after the fourth night. His translation the *Orations of Demosthenes*, published in two volumes in 1757, proved a sore disappointment when it was adjudged inferior to other translations of Demosthenes.

Francis signalled his entrée to the political world with an appointment *c*.1754 as chaplain in the household of Lord Holland, a post which involved tutoring Lord Holland's younger son, Charles James Fox, the future statesman. Apropos of this appointment the poet Charles Churchill dubbed Francis 'the atheist chaplain of an atheist lord' (Churchill, 2.138). In 1756 Lord Holland secured a place for Francis's son, Philip, then aged sixteen, in what was to become the Foreign Office: it was to be the first step in a distinguished career as a public servant and Indian statesman.

Domesticated in such a political family, it was to be expected that Francis would become involved behind the scenes as a journalist and pamphleteer, but the extent of his work in that sphere is indeterminate, since it was necessarily anonymous. It appears fairly certain, however, that he was the author of *Mr Pitt's Letter Versified*, in which he attacked Pitt the elder following his resignation from office in 1761. In the follow-up pamphlet *A Letter from the Anonymous Author of Mr Pitt's Letter Versified* he continued to be highly critical of Pitt. Though a nominal whig, Francis supported men rather than policies. Thus, in *The Political Theatre* (1764) he championed the tory Lord Bute against the new Grenville government and satirized Pitt as the modern Cleon.

Francis's appointment to the vicarage of Chilham in Kent in June 1761 was short-lived. However, his connection with Lord Holland secured for him in 1762 the rectory of Barrow in Suffolk and in 1764 the chaplaincy of Chelsea Hospital for old soldiers. He was to draw an income from both these posts, most of the time as an absentee, until his death. A recommendation in 1764 for a crown pension of £300 per annum does not appear to have materialized. Francis was to show the extent of his gratitude to his patron when he quarrelled with Lord Holland because he was not made an Irish bishop.

Francis's chief, and perhaps only, claim to fame rests on his translations into English verse of the works of Horace, which were first published in four volumes between 1742 and 1746. Many English poets before Francis had produced translations of Horace, but no less a judge than Samuel Johnson pronounced that Francis had 'done it the best; I'll take his, five out of six, against them all' (*Boswell's Life of Johnson*, 2.253), although, Johnson added, the lyrical part of Horace never can be perfectly translated. And, accepting that poetry is by definition untranslatable, Francis's renderings of Horace surely must at times depart significantly from the original. Francis himself tacitly admits as much when he states that he had endeavoured not only to give Horace's general meaning but also to preserve 'that force of expression in which his peculiar happiness consists' (*Memoirs*, xv). Indeed it appears axiomatic that the better a translation is *qua* English verse—and Francis's translations often reach heights by any standard memorable—the more likely it is that the excellence in English has been achieved at some lack of fidelity to the original. If one were to single out a few of his translations for special mention, the following would arguably appear on such a list: 'To Delius' (*Odes*, ii. 3), 'To the Romans' (*Odes*, iii. 6), 'To Lollius' (*Odes*, iv. 9), 'To Maecenas' (*Odes*, iv. 29), and 'To Melpomene' (*Odes*, iv. 30).

The involvement of William Dunkin in Francis's translations has already been alluded to, and it is important to quantify Dunkin's involvement in order to demonstrate Francis's overwhelming contribution. In the earlier editions of Francis's translations of Horace, Dunkin's translations are duly attributed, and it is evident that he was responsible for the translation of 15 out of 120 odes, 3 out of 18 satires, and 2 out of 22 epistles. The translation of *Ars poetica* and *Carmen Seculare*, both lengthy pieces, is the work of Francis. It can be concluded, then, that about ten per cent of these translations is the work of Dunkin and the remaining ninety per cent or so the work of Francis. It should be added that many of Dunkin's translations are light, playful, inconsequential pieces, such as the hilarious 'To Lydia' (*Odes*, i. 25).

Francis's health began to deteriorate from 1766 onwards. In 1767 he was struck severely by palsy and a paralytic stroke followed in 1771. From about 1767 he lived in Bath, where he was to die on 5 March 1773, a sad wreck of a man in very straitened circumstances.

PATRICK FAGAN

Sources parish register, Dublin, St Mary [baptism], 21 July 1708 · Betham's abstracts of wills, NA Ire. · will, dated 25 Sept 1770, PRO, PROB 11/986, fols. 26v–27 · *DNB* · J. Parkes and H. Merivale, *Memoirs of Sir Philip Francis*, 2 vols. (1867), vol. 1 · Burtchaell & Sadleir, *Alum. Dubl.*, 2nd edn · P. Fagan, ed., *A Georgian celebration: Irish poets of the eighteenth century* (1989), 128–34 · P. Francis, 'preface', in *A poetical translation of the works of Horace*, 5th edn, 1 (1753) · *GM*, 1st ser., 43 (1773), 155 · *GM*, 1st ser., 55 (1785), 245 · *Boswell's Life of Johnson*, 2 vols. (1906); repr. in one vol. (1976), 253 · C. Churchill, *Poems* (1766), 2.138–9

Wealth at death insubstantial; income from chaplaincy of Chelsea Hospital, and rectory at Barrow, Suffolk; leasehold property in Harlequin Row, Bath; furniture and fittings; also books: will, dated 25 Sept 1770, PRO, PROB 11/986, fols. 26v–27

Francis, Sir Philip (1740–1818), politician and political writer, was born in Dublin on 22 October 1740, the only son of the Revd Philip *Francis (1708–1773), translator and writer, and Elizabeth Rowe (*c*.1710–*c*.1741). His paternal grandfather, John Francis (*d*. 1724), had been dean of Lismore. His father was a good classical scholar, educated at Trinity College, Dublin. He moved to England soon after his son's birth and opened a small school at Esher, attended for a short time by Edward Gibbon. His son was left behind in Dublin at school with Mr Roe, but was brought to England in the early 1750s and entered at St Paul's School in March 1753. His companions there included Philip Rosenhagen and Henry Sampson Woodfall. He made a reputation in classics and was school captain in 1756. Meanwhile his father had obtained the patronage of Henry Fox, for whom he wrote pamphlets and squibs, and by whom he was appointed private chaplain to Lady Caroline Fox. According to his son Dr Francis 'almost lived at Holland House' (Parkes and Merivale, 1.360).

Early career Francis junior did not go to university but on leaving school was given a clerkship in the secretary of state's office. Next he went as secretary to General Thomas Bligh on the ill-fated expedition to Cherbourg in 1758. His administrative apprenticeship continued in 1760 when he served as secretary to Lord Kinnoul's mission to Portugal and on his return acted as private secretary to William Pitt the elder. In summer 1761, according to his own testimony, he was present at the peace discussions between Pitt and the French envoy, Bussy (Cobbett, *Parl. hist.*, 29.958). The network of patronage through his father, Robert Wood, and John Calcraft held out promising prospects. But his early marriage, on 12 February 1762, to Elizabeth Macrabie (*d*. 1806) of Fulham, a pleasant woman without rank or fortune, caused a temporary estrangement from his father. In December 1762 Welbore Ellis, another of Fox's friends, became secretary at war, and appointed Francis chief clerk at the war office. With his immediate superior, Christopher D'Oyly, the deputy secretary, Francis was soon on terms of close friendship. The next few years saw him much occupied with his new job, and as an affectionate and attentive husband and father, with a considerable circle of convivial friends, among them Thady Fitzpatrick and Philip Rosenhagen. He was also beginning to write and to take part in anonymous newspaper warfare. As 'One of the People' in 1763 he defended Fitzpatrick in the *Public Ledger* in the noisy dispute with David Garrick over ticket prices at Drury Lane. In 1766 he sent a long memorandum on Portuguese affairs, based on the Kinnoul visit, to the duke of Richmond, secretary of state in the Rockingham ministry. Anonymous letters under Tandem (*Public Advertiser*, 1 August 1766) and Lusitanicus (*Public Advertiser*, 2, 13, 24

Sir Philip Francis (1740–1818), by Thomas Goff Lupton, pubd 1817 (after James Lonsdale, 1806–10)

January 1767), all concerned with Portuguese matters, may reasonably be attributed to him, and to his second wife he confided in later years that 'he scarcely remembered when he did not write'. With the virtual retirement of Fox after his resignation from the paymastership in 1765 Francis's main hopes rested with John Calcraft. In his fragment of autobiography, composed about 1775, Francis traced in some detail the eclipse of Fox and the recriminations which accompanied it, complaining that it had deprived his father of the chance of an Irish bishopric. Of himself he wrote: 'I had no hope of advancement but on the line of Opposition'. Open opposition by a senior government clerk was both difficult and hazardous, but an anonymous newspaper campaign held out possibilities. The expulsion of John Wilkes after the Middlesex election of 1768 was the issue which enabled Calcraft to bring about the reconciliation of Chatham, Temple, and George Grenville, and Francis wrote: 'I was convinced that the Ministry could never stand the consequences of the Middlesex election' (Parkes and Merivale, 1.361).

The Junius letters On 6 February 1768 a correspondent signing himself 'C' wrote to Grenville offering advice on taxation policy, and claiming 'a number of late publications'. On 3 September he wrote again, claiming 'a multitude' of other letters, including those signed Lucius, and one on the commission of trade. A month later he wrote a third time, claiming 'Atticus', 'The Grand Council', and 'almost everything that, for two years past, has attracted the attention of the publick'. Under the signature 'C', he published letters in the *Public Advertiser* on 5 April, 12 April, 6 May, 19 July, and 23 July 1768, the first and third attacking the ministry over its handling of the Wilkes issue

(Cannon, 517–18). It seems certain that Francis knew of these letters. His father was at Bath recovering from a stroke, and his family and friends kept him supplied with pamphlets and newspaper items. On 3 September 1768 Dr Francis asked his son 'whose is that famous letter signed Lucius?', and on 27 November 'what a spirit has our friend "C"'. Calcraft wrote on 20 October to Dr Francis commending Atticus. On 21 November a letter attracting little notice appeared in the *Public Advertiser* defending Wilkes and signed Junius. On 21 January 1769 the first of the acknowledged *Junius letters appeared. When Junius opened a private correspondence with Henry Sampson Woodfall, printer of the *Public Advertiser*, he signed himself 'C'.

The authorship of the Junius letters has been the subject of innumerable publications of various merit. The case for Philip Francis, first proposed by John Taylor in 1816, has established itself as by far the most probable, though categorical proof is still not forthcoming. There were in the letters frequent references to war office matters and, under the name of Veteran, Junius in 1772 seemed much agitated at the resignation of Francis, launching a series of attacks upon Lord Barrington, secretary at war and Francis's superior in the years 1765–72. Francis attended parliamentary debates and in his fragment of autobiography claimed that he had taken down Chatham's speech of 22 November 1770 on the Falkland Islands, 'and had it published in a few days' (Parkes and Merivale, 1.363). We know that Francis was present at debates on 10 December 1766, 9 January 1770, 22 January 1770, 2 February 1770, 22 November 1770, and 10 December 1770. Junius (as Philo-Junius) claimed to have been present at the debate of 10 December 1766; quotes (as Philo-Junius) from the debate of 9 January 1770, refers to 22 January 1770, and quotes (as Phalaris) from the debate of 10 December 1770. If Francis was not Junius we have to envisage them, by a strange coincidence, sitting side by side in the Lords on at least four occasions. Moreover, for the debate of 10 December 1770 Francis claimed to have supplied Chatham (through Calcraft) with the gist of a legal argument, a claim confirmed when the Chatham correspondence was published in 1838. Junius (as Phalaris) quoted Chatham's remarks in the debate.

There is also a close correspondence between the political views of Francis and those of Junius. Francis gambled on the probability of war with Spain, which, in his view, would bring Chatham and the opposition back to power, 'when I might have commanded anything'—an extravagant opinion for a chief clerk to hold. He was bitterly disappointed when war did not come, and, into the bargain, he lost £500 on stock market speculation, which deterred him 'from entering into such traffic again'. Junius took a parallel course, attacking the ministry, telling Woodfall in 1771 that war was inevitable, and by January 1773 plunged into despair—'all alike, vile and contemptible'. He devoted his last letters (Veteran, Nemesis) to ridiculing Anthony Chamier, who had replaced Francis's friend D'Oyly as deputy secretary, as 'a little whiffling broker'. In his autobiography Francis included a long paragraph on Woodfall's trial for publishing Junius's letter to the king.

Some account of the whereabouts of Junius can be constructed from his private letters to Woodfall, some of which can be dated to a few hours. There is nothing in Francis's movements to clash with these dates. There is, for example, a gap in Junius's communication with Woodfall between May 1772 and January 1773, when Woodfall resumed with a long letter, appearing to bring Junius up to date with events. Francis left for a continental holiday on 8 July 1772, returning on 14 December, one week before Woodfall resumed signalling in the *Public Advertiser*. Nor is there anything in the inferred characters of the two to create difficulty. It would not be unfair to Junius to describe him as clever, arrogant, rancorous, and occasionally prosy, through a desire to parade his legal and classical knowledge. Such a description fits Francis, but few of the rival candidates, with some comfort.

There remains corroborative evidence. Handwriting and linguistic evidence has been exhaustively examined but strongly disputed. Other evidence strains scepticism to reject. Lady Francis, Sir Philip's second wife, related that her husband's wedding gift was a copy of the *Letters of Junius*, and that he left her another inscribed copy when he died. The contents of Francis's library reveal a deep interest in the pamphlet and newspaper warfare of the period, often with written notes and corrections. The evidence of Miss Giles's letters at Bath and the identification in the French archives of Francis and Fitzpatrick as collaborators in the letters adds weight to an already powerful case. If the attribution of the *Letters of Junius* to Francis is correct, it confirms the impression of his ability and capacity for work, while doing little to make him appear more amiable.

India Francis's upward progress, frustratingly slow to himself, suffered two severe blows in 1772. First, his friend D'Oyly resigned from the war office and Francis's claim to succeed him fell through, possibly because of discontent with the financial arrangements. Francis accordingly resigned, whereupon Junius commenced a ferocious press campaign against Lord Barrington, the secretary at war. In the course of 1772 Calcraft died, leaving Francis distracted: 'the place I was not in always seemed preferable to my actual situation. I felt I was a burthen to my friends as well as to myself.' Calcraft's bequest of £1000 with an instruction to his executors to bring Francis into parliament for his borough of Wareham was little consolation—'I was not much disappointed'. Francis filled in his time by translating a treatise on circulation by Isaac de Pinto, and contemplated emigrating to America, where he had purchased frontier lands in Pennsylvania. From this disagreeable situation he was rescued by a piece of great good fortune. On 4 June 1773 he learned that John Cholwell, nominated to the supreme council in India at a salary of £10,000 p.a., had declined to serve. Applying through D'Oyly and Barrington he approached Lord North and was appointed. No doubt the danger from the climate and the voyage, both of which claimed many victims, had discouraged more powerful contenders, and Francis admitted that the lateness of Cholwell's decision must have helped his cause. There was no opposition in parliament to his nomination and the king wrote approvingly that he was 'allowed to be a man of talent' (*Correspondence of King George the Third*, 2.496, 498). During the summer he was given advice and information on Indian affairs at Walcot and Oakley by Lord Clive, and made himself agreeable to the Clive family. He left for India on the *Ashburnham* on 30 March 1774, leaving behind detailed and slightly peremptory instructions to his wife on the upbringing of their children. He arrived in Calcutta with the two other new councillors on 19 October 1774.

The convulsions and animosities which characterized East India Company rule at this time stemmed mainly from personal struggles for patronage and precedence, but there were three aspects of the settlement that North had carried in 1773 which made for instability. The supreme council consisted of five members, the governor-general having a casting vote: continuity of policy was at the mercy of death and absences. The supreme court, which had been established under Sir Elijah Impey, was independent of the council and was soon perceived as a rival centre of power. Thirdly, control from afar was divided between the government and the company itself. When Lord North resolved in 1776 to recall the governor-general, Warren Hastings, the company refused to do so.

Francis claimed later that he went out to India with friendly opinions of Hastings. If so they did not last long. Within a few weeks he was reporting that 'corruption is no longer confined to the stem of the tree, or to a few principal branches: every twig, every leaf is putrified' (Parkes and Merivale, 2.18). The discovery of Hastings's role in the Rohilla war appears to have been decisive. In part North may have been to blame for the clash, since Francis recorded that before he left the first minister told him 'we are to be armed with extraordinary power to correct enormous abuses' (ibid., 1.367). Such extravagant language to an ambitious and overbearing man was unwise. Francis was soon engaged in bruising and protracted struggles at council with Hastings, challenging every decision, a war of minutes and memoranda. At first the three new members had the upper hand, but the death of George Monson in September 1776 restored Hastings's supremacy. Francis was buoyed up by assurances from his friends in England that Hastings would be recalled and that he would succeed him as governor-general. He lived in considerable style, surrounded by swarms of servants, most of them, as he complained, quite useless, and his ability at cards—one of the main pastimes of the British community—helped him to amass a modest fortune worth £3000 p.a. His subventions home allowed his wife to live with some elegance and to purchase a better house in London's Harley Street.

But the great game was slipping from Francis's grasp. With events in America going from bad to worse ministers had little time for Indian disputes, and his long and impassioned communications were unwelcome. His prospects at home were not improved when two of his patrons left office, D'Oyly in February 1778, Barrington in December. Two further events did him no good. In December 1778 he

was found in compromising circumstances at night in the house of Mme Grand, a nubile sixteen-year-old, and the enraged husband obtained damages against him in the supreme court. In August 1780 relations with Hastings were so bad that they fought a duel, in which Francis was seriously wounded. Three months later he left India, reaching Dover after a difficult voyage on 19 October 1781.

The political situation Francis found was very different to the one he had left in 1774. North's government, about to receive news of the surrender at Yorktown, was on its last legs. North advised the king to give Francis a civil reception, partly as a courtesy to his rank, partly because 'he has it in his power to do considerable mischief' (*Correspondence of King George the Third*, 5.292, 293). Francis had not given up hope of being sent back as governor-general. He intended to bring himself into parliament but Calcraft's promise of a seat for Wareham had outlived its date. In the meantime he began a vigorous campaign in the newspapers denouncing Hastings's administration. Since 1773 Francis had been in friendly though infrequent correspondence with Edmund Burke, who had obtained in February 1781 a select committee on Indian affairs: a rival secret committee had also been established under the auspices of Henry Dundas, moving towards the domination of Indian matters which he was to hold for more than twenty years. After some hesitation Francis threw in his lot with the opposition. By March 1782 he was supplying Burke with evidence to support the campaign against Hastings. But though his new allies took office when North resigned, they were unable to carry Francis's nomination to the governor-generalship. In an acrimonious cabinet on 1 June 1782 Rockingham and Fox clashed with Shelburne, who had the king's support for Lord Cornwallis. Within a month Rockingham was dead and Fox had resigned, and though the latter resumed office in 1783 in the coalition with North, the appointment of Francis was not pursued. He was obliged to be content with a studied encomium from Burke, introducing the ill-fated India Bill, who praised him as 'the man, whose deep reach of thought, whose large legislative conceptions, and whose grand plans of policy make the most shining part of our report, from whence we have learned all our lessons' (ibid., 6.50–51; Cobbett, *Parl. hist.*, 23.1368–9).

Parliamentary career Francis accordingly bought himself a seat in parliament for Yarmouth, Isle of Wight, at the general election of 1784. He was heard in the house with respect but his parliamentary career was not a success. He was neither a fluent speaker nor a ready debater, and his carefully prepared interventions took the form of long lectures. He was also at first very much a one issue man, and that issue, the government of India, was far from fascinating to most members. Windham, a popular speaker at home in the house, commented that 'about my performances, a great fuss is made, while of his nobody speaks a word' (*Windham*, 1.86). Disappointment sat heavily upon Francis. To the censoriousness apparent in his early fragment of autobiography he added deceit. To his friend Edward Wheler he wrote in January 1782 categorically denying that he had employed William Macintosh, author of *Travels in Europe, Asia and Africa* (1782), which had liberally praised him: however, his private cash book showed three payments to the printer John Almon in 1782–3 on behalf of Macintosh, worth more than £1000. To Sir John Day in India he wrote in November 1781 congratulating him warmly on his victory over the supreme court: to Chambers in India he wrote the following month that Day 'hangs but by a thread … Many who censure the court are far from approving of his conduct or admiring his learning' (Parkes and Merivale, 2.205–6, 212, 214).

Since the coalition had been dismissed in December 1783 over its India Bill it followed that Indian business would be prominent in the new house, where Francis's friends were in a minority. His early efforts were ill-co-ordinated. On 16 June 1784 he warned the house that the directors of the East India Company were optimistic in believing that the war against Tipu Sultan would soon be over, and moved for papers: he was not supported and was forced to withdraw. When, on 2 July, he made a major effort it misfired: he clashed at first with his own leader, Fox, 'at which the Treasury bench laughed'. He then launched into an imprudently long survey of Indian affairs, concluding with a sustained attack upon Hastings, to whom, he insisted, he retained no spark of personal animosity (Cobbett, *Parl. hist.*, 24.1038–9, 1042–58; *Commons Journal*, 40.212). The one triumph he helped to engineer, the impeachment of Hastings in 1787, did Francis little good. The house voted by 96 to 44 not to include him with Burke, Richard Brinsley Sheridan, and others among the managers of the impeachment, on the grounds that he was an evident partisan. All his friends could do was to sign a round robin regretting the house's decision and promise to consult him constantly. For the opposition as a whole the impeachment was a disaster, diverting energy and zeal for seven years, and ending with the acquittal of Hastings on all charges. Incredibly Francis continued to believe for a further decade that his friends would appoint him governor-general when they achieved power—'the only real reparation that can be offered me for all my suffering in that country, and for the slight and injustice I have met with in England from the year 1781 to this hour' (*Correspondence of George, Prince of Wales*, 5.350). Half buried beneath the personal vendettas against Hastings and Impey were Francis's larger views on the government of India—sensible, but characteristically negative. On 21 December 1790 he argued that the overriding policy should be peace, that Britain should not seek territorial extensions, nor make entangling alliances with Indian princes. In 1793 he insisted, against Dundas, that the company ought to be confined purely to trade and have no part in the government of India: 'a trading company is unqualified for sovereignty' (Cobbett, *Parl. hist.*, 28.1183–5, 30.685–700).

In 1790 Francis contested the seat of Hindon without success, but bought in at £4200 for the borough of Bletchingley, Surrey. The shadow of the French Revolution was already changing the face of British politics. When the

whig party began to split Francis remained with Fox, pursuing an increasingly radical line, while his friendship with Burke cooled. A harbinger of the future was a sharp exchange in 1791 when Burke showed him the draft of his *Reflections on the Revolution in France*. Francis was much more sympathetic towards the revolution and told Burke bluntly that his famous description of Marie Antoinette was pure foppery: Burke retorted that he had written it with tears streaming down his face. When the book came out Francis wrote again, denying that France had ever enjoyed an effective constitution, and maintaining that the revolution had been against 'intolerable oppression' (*Correspondence of Edmund Burke*, 6.85–92, 150–55). In April 1791 he spoke strongly and effectively in support of William Wilberforce's motion for the abolition of the slave trade. In August 1792 Lord Auckland dined with Francis and thought him 'in general very republican', condemning the lack of assistance given to the Poles in resisting the partition of their country (*Journal and Correspondence*, 2.472). He was a founding member of the Friends of the People the same year, and took an active part in petitioning for reform of parliament, speaking for Charles Grey's motion of 6 May 1793 for parliamentary reform. He attacked Windham for using the French Revolution to block change of any kind, and concluded with a flourish that corruption 'has increased, was increasing, and ought to be diminished'. He persevered with the Friends, drawing up, after consultation with William Smith, the dissenting MP, and Christopher Wyvill, organizer of the 1780 Association movement, a plan of reform which was adopted in May 1795. It urged the abolition of rotten boroughs with compensation, extension of the representation to large towns, a uniform inhabitant householder franchise, single member constituencies, and payment of members. Wyvill, drawing on his experience of the 1780s, tried gently to dissuade Francis from so comprehensive a plan, which would undoubtedly be denounced as totally destructive. By the time Grey presented the scheme to parliament in May 1797 Francis was no longer in the house; it was rejected by 256 votes to 91. In November 1795 he was one of Fox's dwindling band of supporters who divided against the Seditious Meetings Bill, and in February 1796 he divided with Fox and the minority on Grey's motion for a negotiated peace with France.

Francis's electoral arrangements gave trouble at the general election of 1796. He was unable to obtain a safe seat and joined Peter Moore, a colleague in the Hastings trial, in a hazardous attack upon Tewkesbury, where the Martin and Dowdeswell interests usually prevailed. Francis and Moore stood upon an inhabitant householder franchise, but their votes were rejected, and their petition failed. The effort left Francis sued for debt by a local publican and out of parliament. The extra time at his disposal was devoted to London society, to writing arch and stilted letters to his female acquaintances, and to attending the court of the prince of Wales. This placed considerable strain on his income, which was not large, and he acquired a reputation for parsimony. He served under Fox, he told the duchess of Devonshire, 'not only without pay, but without hope' (Parkes and Merivale, 2.307).

In 1802 Francis resumed his parliamentary career, brought in for Appleby, Westmorland, without a contest by Lord Thanet, a Foxite peer. In summer 1802 he took advantage of the peace to visit France, where he won some celebrity for telling Napoleon that the prospects for continued peace depended upon him. With the resumption of war with France, Francis changed his tune, as did many others, pledging support for Henry Addington in a national struggle. He continued to intervene on Indian matters and on 5 April 1805 attacked the thirst for conquest in India in a speech which he printed and distributed. This led to suspicion that he intended a campaign against Lord Wellesley, the retiring governor-general. In the debate of 10 March 1806 he denied the rumours: 'I will never be concerned in impeaching any body. The impeachment of Mr Hastings has cured me of that folly. I was tried, and *he* was acquitted' (Cobbett, *Parl. hist.*, 6.394).

The accession of Fox and Grenville to power in February 1806 after the death of Pitt was the last chance for Francis to attain high office. The situation was complicated by the fact that news of the death of the new governor-general, Lord Cornwallis, was received at exactly the same time. Few people thought it would be wise to send Francis to India to throw a vigorous expansionist policy into full reverse. On 18 February Grenville told Windham that 'the appointment of Francis will not be urged even by his warmest friends' (*Correspondence of George, Prince of Wales*, 5.349). Fox was particularly lukewarm and Francis quarrelled with him publicly in the debate of 31 March. Speaking pointedly from the opposition benches Francis complained that he had been 'dismissed and discarded' by Fox: the new secretary of state retorted that he had never given Francis any encouragement (Cobbett, *Parl. hist.*, 6.609, 610). The best that was offered Francis was the governorship of the newly acquired Cape of Good Hope at £10,000 p.a. This he declined, seeing it, not unreasonably, as 'no better than a cruel banishment', and asked for a peerage (*Correspondence of George, Prince of Wales*, 5.349–50). In the end he settled for a knighthood in the Order of the Bath. Even for that he was obliged to wait until after Fox's death in September 1806 (ibid., 5.349–50, 359–60). In October there was some discussion about sending Francis to Buenos Aires as governor, but it came to nothing. So did hopes of the governorship of Jamaica in January 1807.

Francis was re-elected at Appleby in December 1806. Some of his hopes were transferred to his son, Philip, now thirty-eight, who contested Bridport, an open borough where money talked, in 1806 and again in 1807, but without success. Francis's own parliamentary career was plainly over. The semi-independent line he took in the Commons during the 'ministry of all the talents' seems to have irritated his patron, Lord Thanet, who thought he had behaved shabbily, and was 'glad to be rid of him' at the general election of 1807, when he did not stand. His last reported speech in the Commons on 25 March 1807 was inevitably on India, when he rose to ask a question

and went on to make so long a speech that the speaker asked him to sit down (Cobbett, *Parl. hist.*, 9.191–3).

Final years Out of parliament and in his seventies Francis loitered off-stage. He continued to attend the prince regent, complaining to Thomas Creevey 'well, I am invited to dinner today, and that is perhaps all I shall get after two and twenty years service' (Maxwell, 149). In 1810 he published on the circulation of paper money and the following years *Thoughts on the Regency Question*. He declined to be involved with Major John Cartwright in a new campaign for parliamentary reform, dismissing it as 'a hopeless enterprise … the mass of the English population is inert' (Cartwright, 2.4). When, at the start of the regency in 1811, the whigs hoped to return to power, Francis wrote to the prince asking for any employment, suggesting the chief secretaryship in Ireland, a post which normally went to bright young men. The only further recognition came in 1815 when he was made GCB.

Painful illness in Francis's last years did not prevent a second marriage, in December 1814, to a young lady forty years his junior, Emma, daughter of the Revd Henry Watkins of York. He continued to visit country houses, a tall, austere, and somewhat forbidding guest, but apparently well received. In 1814 he published *Letter to Earl Grey*, protesting against the transfer of Norway from Denmark to Sweden and the blockade of Norway to bring it about. In 1816 in his discursive *Letter Missive to Lord Holland*, he urged that the Roman Catholic clergy in Ireland should be given state salaries and the peasantry relieved from tithes to a protestant church which they disliked, in order to reduce grievances and promote stability. Francis appeared at his best in private life. He had been on good terms with his father, whom he supplied with money. His first wife, never strong, had become a semi-invalid, treated by Francis with consideration: his second wife regarded him with awe. He was on particularly affectionate terms with most of his five daughters, two of whom, Harriet and Elizabeth, died in 1803 and 1804, to their father's great grief. In his younger days he romped with his male friends, and in 1799, in a last letter to Rosenhagen, dispatched to India to redeem a ramshackle life, he wrote: 'Oh, Philip Rosenhagen! Philip Rosenhagen! you ruined my morals' (Parkes and Merivale, 2.278). But in public life he was overcombative, caustic, and severe. Colonel Watson, who called upon him at the war office in his early days, found him a 'pompous, haughty coxcomb', full of the insolence of office (Spencer, 2.125). Lady Holland, in the 1790s, paid tribute to his skill in writing state papers and petitions, but added: 'his temper is irritable to madness: indeed, he is more or less always in a passion, for if he begins temperately, the ardour of his imagination works him to rage before the sentence closes'. Francis, she remarked, was 'very vain, and any distinction quite turns his head, especially from people he rather calls great folks' (Ilchester, *Journal … Lady Holland*, 1.268–9). Nathaniel Wraxall did not deny him 'talents such as are rarely dispensed to any individual', but added that he was 'bursting with bile' and that 'acrimony distinguished and characterised him in everything' (Wheatley, 3.439–40). He never changed. Sir James

Mackintosh, who dined with him in the last year of his life, noted 'the vigorous hatreds which seem to keep Francis alive' (Mackintosh, 2.342). He died peacefully in London on 23 December 1818 and was buried, as he wished, with little ceremony at Mortlake in the grave of his daughter Elizabeth. JOHN CANNON

Sources DNB • R. G. Thorne, 'Francis, Philip', HoP, *Commons, 1790–1820* • L. S. Sutherland, 'Francis, Philip', HoP, *Commons, 1754–90* • J. Parkes and H. Merivale, eds., *Memoirs of Sir Philip Francis*, 2 vols. (1867) • Cobbett, *Parl. hist.* • *The correspondence of King George the Third from 1760 to December 1783*, ed. J. Fortescue, 6 vols. (1927–8) • *The correspondence of George, prince of Wales, 1770–1812*, ed. A. Aspinall, 8 vols. (1963–71) • [P. Francis], *The Francis letters*, ed. E. Keary and B. Francis, 2 vols. (1901) • S. Weitzman, *Warren Hastings and Philip Francis* (1929) • C. Wyvill, ed., *Political papers chiefly respecting the attempt ... to effect a reformation of the parliament of Great Britain*, 6 vols. (1794–1804) • J. A. Cannon, ed., *The letters of Junius* (1978) • A. Spencer, ed., *Memoirs of William Hickey*, 4 vols. (1913–25) • *The historical and the posthumous memoirs of Sir Nathaniel William Wraxall, 1772–1784*, ed. H. B. Wheatley, 5 vols. (1884) • R. J. Mackintosh, ed., *Memoirs of the life of Sir James Mackintosh*, 2 vols. (1835) • W. Windham, *The Windham papers*, 2 vols. (1913) • *The Creevey papers*, ed. H. Maxwell, 2 vols. (1903) • *The life and correspondence of Major Cartwright*, ed. F. D. Cartwright, 2 vols. (1826) • L. S. Sutherland, W. Doyle, and J. M. Rogister, 'Junius and Philip Francis: new evidence', *BIHR*, 42 (1969), 158–72 • R. W. Davis, *Dissent in politics: the political life of William Smith* (1971) • *The Grenville papers: being the correspondence of Richard Grenville ... and ... George Grenville*, ed. W. J. Smith, 4 vols. (1852–3) • J. Wade, ed., *The letters of Junius*, 2 vols. (1855) • *The journal and correspondence of William, Lord Auckland*, ed. [G. Hogge], 4 vols. (1861–2) • *The correspondence of Edmund Burke*, ed. T. W. Copeland and others, 10 vols. (1958–78) • D. Grant, ed., *The poetical works of Charles Churchill* (1956) • *The later correspondence of George III*, ed. A. Aspinall, 5 vols. (1962–70) • *The manuscripts of J. B. Fortescue*, 10 vols., HMC, 30 (1892–1927), vols. 1–2 • *JHC* • J. N. M. MacLean, *Reward is secondary: the life of a political adventurer and an inquiry into the mystery of 'Junius'* (1963) • *Diaries and correspondence of James Harris, first earl of Malmesbury*, ed. third earl of Malmesbury [J. H. Harris], 4 vols. (1844) • *The journal of Elizabeth, Lady Holland, 1791–1811*, ed. earl of Ilchester [G. S. Holland Fox-Strangways], 2 vols. (1908) • H. R. Vassall, Lord Holland, *Memoirs of the whig party during my time*, ed. H. E. Vassall, Lord Holland, 2 vols. (1852–4) • J. C. Hobhouse, Lord Broughton, *Recollections of a long life*, 6 vols. (1909–11) • J. Taylor, *The identity of Junius* (1816) • *The journal of the Hon. Henry Edward Fox*, ed. earl of Ilchester [G. S. Holland Fox-Strangways] (1923) • L. S. Sutherland, *The East India Company in eighteenth-century politics* (1952) • K. Feiling, *Warren Hastings* (1966) • C. H. Philips, *The East India Company, 1784–1834* (1961) • P. J. Marshall, *Trade and conquest: studies on the rise of British dominance in India* (1993)
Archives BL, corresp. and papers, Add. MSS 27775–27788, 34287, 40756–40765, 47781–47783 • NRA, account books | BL, corresp. with Lord Holland, Add. MS 51405 • BL, letters to Lord North, Add. MS 61865 • BL, letters to William Windham, Add. MSS 37882–37886, *passim* • BL OIOC, corresp. and papers, incl. corresp. with Edmund Burke, MSS Eur. C 7–8, D 18–25, E 12–47, F 4–17, G 4–8 • BL OIOC, Home misc. series, corresp. and papers relating to India • BL OIOC, letters to William Harwood, MS Eur. D 566 • Morgan L., letters to Philip Baggs • Morgan L., letters to Alexander Mackrabie • NRA, letters to Lady Downshire • Sheff. Arch., corresp. with Edmund Burke • U. Aberdeen L., letters to Eliza Fraser • U. Birm. L., corresp. with Sir John Clavering • U. Birm. L., corresp. and papers relating to Junius
Likenesses portrait, pastel, 1777, repro. in Francis, *Francis letters* • J. Smart, miniature, 1781, V&A • J. Sayers, caricature, etching, pubd 1788, NPG • caricature, 1788, repro. in Parkes and Merivale, eds., *Memoirs*, vol. 2 • J. Sayers, caricature, etching, pubd 1794, BM • J. Hoppner, portrait, 1811, repro. in Francis, *Francis letters*, vol. 1 •

T. G. Lupton, mezzotint, pubd 1817 (after J. Lonsdale, 1806–10), BM, NPG [*see illus.*] • J. Lonsdale, oils, NPG
Wealth at death approx. £3000 p.a.: Parkes and Merivale, eds., *Memoirs*

Francis, Richard (1698×1700–1742), lawyer and legal writer, was born in Dublin, of Anglo-Irish descent, the eldest child of Dr John Francis (*d.* 1724), rector of St Mary's Church, Dublin, and dean of Lismore, a prominent Church of Ireland clergyman, and his wife, Anne (*d.* in or after 1724). Richard had two younger brothers, Tench and Philip, and two younger sisters, Mary and Ann. Tench Francis emigrated to America and became recorder of Philadelphia, while Philip *Francis (1708–1773) was a clergyman, writer, and translator, and father of Sir Philip *Francis (1740–1818), often regarded as the author of the letters of Junius.

Richard was educated at Mr Chamberlaine's school in Dublin; he entered Trinity College, Dublin, on 16 May 1715, but did not take a degree. He was admitted to the Middle Temple in London on 30 June 1719 to begin the study of law, and he was called to the bar on 15 May 1724. He practised law in London, living in the parish of St Andrew, Holborn. In 1727 the first edition of his book *Maxims of Equity* was published in London; it was a slim folio of under 100 pages, but was the earliest book on the principles of equity jurisprudence. The success of this work is attested to by the fact of its reappearance in several later editions; a third edition appeared in London in 1746, and a fourth in 1812. The last edition was published in 1823 in Richmond, Virginia, edited by William Waller Hening.

Francis emigrated to Virginia and became prominent in the practice of law in Williamsburg. The first notice of 'Richard Francis, esquire, barrister at law' found in Virginia is his appointment on 9 November 1738 by the council to examine an applicant for admission to practise law in the general court of Virginia. There were similar appointments in 1740, 1741, and 1742. On 15 October 1741 he was appointed clerk of the council, a position of great prestige. There is an order signed by him as clerk of the council on 26 July 1742. On 15 October 1742 his successor in the office was appointed, and on 31 December 1742 his widow, Susannah (it is not known when they married), took administration of his estate in London, he having died in Yorktown, Virginia. Thus it appears that he died some time between 26 July and 15 October 1742, at the age of forty-two or forty-three. There is no evidence that Francis and his wife had any children. W. H. BRYSON

Sources D. E. C. Yale, 'Francis, Richard', *Biographical dictionary of the common law*, ed. A. W. B. Simpson (1984), 189–90 • J. Parkes and H. Merivale, *Memoirs of Sir Philip Francis*, 2 vols. (1867), vol. 1, pp. xxxv, 1–2 • Burtchaell & Sadleir, *Alum. Dubl.*, 2nd edn • H. A. C. Sturgess, ed., *Register of admissions to the Honourable Society of the Middle Temple, from the fifteenth century to the year 1944*, 1 (1949), 284 • 'Francis, Philip', *DNB* • 'Francis, Sir Philip', *DNB* • consistory of London register, LMA, Dodson (1720–51), fol. 88 • *Executive journals of the council of colonial Virginia*, 4, ed. H. R. McIlwaine (1930), 429 • *Executive journals of the council of colonial Virginia*, 5, ed. W. L. Hall (1945), 38, 69, 81, 87, 95, 97 • *Virginia Magazine of History and Biography*, 10 (1902–3), 412–13 • *Virginia Magazine of History and Biography*, 14 (1906–7), 227 • *Virginia Magazine of History and Biography*, 15 (1907–8),

377 · *Virginia Magazine of History and Biography*, 17 (1909), 266 · Holdsworth, *Eng. law*, 12.188–90 · T. Jefferson, *Reports of cases* (1829), 66

Francis, Sir Richard Trevor Langford (1934–1992), broadcasting executive and public servant, was born at the Imperial Nursing Home, Harrogate, Yorkshire, on 10 March 1934, the son of Eric Roland Francis (1902–1987), production engineer, and his wife, Esther Joy Todd (1906–1999). He was educated at Malsis Hall, Crosshills, Yorkshire (1944–8), and Uppingham School (1948–53) before going to University College, Oxford, on an open scholarship to read natural sciences. In his second year, he switched from chemistry to politics, philosophy, and economics. At Oxford he acted with the Oxford Experimental Theatre and the Oxford University Dramatic Society. He graduated with a third-class degree in 1956. After two years' national service, commissioned in the Royal Artillery, he entered the BBC as a general trainee—a highly competitive entry system which was one of the most prized undergraduate career entry schemes.

After developing one of the BBC's first successful afternoon programmes, *Table Talk*, Francis graduated to *Panorama*, working with Britain's first-rank television reporters such as Richard Dimbleby, Ludovic Kennedy, and Robin Day. Apart from his command of the studio, he made some elegant films on subjects as diverse as Albert Schweitzer in Lambarene and the struggle for black emancipation in the southern states of America. Typically, matching his physical appearance (he could have been taken for a rugby international) he played a sturdy role in internal debates about *Panorama*—then the BBC's leading television current affairs programme, but under threat from heavy competition from ITV. In a cogently argued memorandum to Paul Fox, the BBC's head of public affairs broadcasting, he said:

> Panorama is losing its status ... faced with increasing competition, we are no longer indispensable. The concept of the studio as the House of Richard Dimbleby has become dull and predictable. We must get more contracted experts as reporters in the fields of Defence, the Communist Block, Science. (BBC WAC, 732/1, 191/9, 11 Aug 1964)

This was the beginning of a long, almost theological debate about the role and structure of *Panorama* in the 1960s.

Francis became assistant editor of the BBC's late evening programme *24 Hours* in 1966, and ran the BBC's general election coverage in 1970 (and the coverage of the US presidential election in 1972). 'General Elections are to television as wars are to the aircraft industry—they force development and invention', he said (*The Independent*, 29 June 1992). The 1970 election programme was the first to use computer online processing. This complex, leading-edge studio responsibility was built on Francis's experience as the producer of global live coverage of the extraordinary American Apollo space programme (including the landing on the moon in July 1969). He was known to lapse frequently into NASA space communication language—and once was presented with 400 feet of negative film when

he responded to a question about its possible inclusion with the word 'negative' instead of 'no'.

After a period as assistant head of BBC current affairs Francis became in 1973 BBC controller, Northern Ireland. This followed his production in 1971 of a special programme on Northern Ireland called *The Question of Ulster* which, he said, was 'designed to be a long, cool programme of talk, not action' (*The Independent*, 29 June 1992)—giving considered background and context to the daily diet of news film of the troubles which had broken out in August 1969. The then home secretary, Reginald Maudling, urged the BBC not to transmit. The governors discussed the issue and decided to go ahead with the broadcast on 5 January 1972. Over two-thirds of the population of Ulster watched the programme, chaired by Lord Devlin. The dire warnings that had preceded the programme proved unfounded. As controller, Northern Ireland, Francis was courageous and clear, and 'established clear and effective ground rules' (Hussey). His five years covered a period of great trouble in Northern Ireland, and he won the admiration of his staff and the BBC management for his carefulness and calmness when faced with many conflicting political and social pressures. He deployed his Yorkshire determination in defence of high editorial standards. In a speech at Chatham House in February 1977 he said:

> The experience of broadcasting in Northern Ireland, for all the threats to society and to human life, suggests that the practice of free speech within a well tested framework of responsibility is the best—if not the easiest—way to cover extraordinary circumstances. I believe we have a contribution to make to the maintenance of democracy both by providing a forum where harsh differences of opinion can be aired, and by reporting and courageously investigating the unpalatable truths which underlie the problems in our midst. I am sure that if and when the communities of Northern Ireland reconcile their conflicts, it will be by understanding them rather than by ignoring them. (Francis, 'Broadcasting')

In 1977 Francis gained a seat on the BBC board of management, as director of news and current affairs. He guided a disparate group of news and current affairs producers, many of whom saw his role as a touch bureaucratic (as did some other members of the board). He construed his role as one of trying to set common standards, and as being a spokesman for policy. A speech at the Royal Television Society in 1981 captured the essence of his views:

> Any really democratic society is vulnerable to its own openness. That is, perhaps, the paradox with which all of us, as citizens and broadcasters, have to grapple. There are those who, for the best and most honourable of motives, believe that this very openness contains the seeds of democracy's self destruction. I cannot believe that our democracy is so fragile a thing that it has neither the will nor the strength to identify and withstand the pressures upon it. (Francis, 'Television')

During the Falklands War, he incurred the displeasure of Margaret Thatcher for saying, in a speech in Spain (about broadcasters' responsibilities in covering the conflict), that 'the widow of Portsmouth is no different from the widow of Buenos Aires'—stressing the need for impartiality to underpin a reputation for telling the truth (Francis, address). The chairman of the BBC, Marmaduke Hussey, later said that 'Dick Francis set standards for BBC journalists while arguing a persuasive case for editorial freedom. His reward was the respect of both journalists and politicians—chafing communities who rarely applaud the same man' (Hussey).

Francis's career towards what some saw as the possible prize of the BBC's director-generalship took a step further when he became managing director, radio, in 1982. To some he was something of a technocrat, with more of a stubborn determination than a nimble, lightfooted wit. But he saw the BBC as a cause, and when he gave his loyalty to a task, he didn't let go. As managing director, radio, he embraced local radio and its separate management structure. (He had already shown his enthusiasm in Northern Ireland, by establishing Radio Ulster.) He also fought for the redevelopment of the Langham Hotel—a prime property owned by the BBC for many years and sold by the governors (to the surprise of many staff) as part of a deal to buy the White City racetrack site. He involved many members of staff in helping to develop the architect Norman Foster's plans for the Langham Hotel. His deputy, Charles McLelland, said:

> More than anything else, this gave everybody working in Radio, the feeling that they had a boss who cared not just for the future of Radio, but for them as individuals. For the first time in many years they felt they were part of a dynamic future. (*The Guardian*, 29 June 1992)

Francis's determination in the interests of local radio and the Langham redevelopment led him to be seen as something of a problem on the BBC board of management. He had the capacity to be relentless in his point of view. He was engineered out of the BBC, to the dismay of many, in 1986. (His departure set a blueprint for further sudden removals from high office a year or so later.) The process upset him badly. Like some others on the board of management, he had not realized that the BBC was beginning to be in the grip of forces which almost resented the public service successes of its past, and which needed to associate that past with managerial failure to justify its new accountancy-led, market-orientated thinking.

Within a very short period of his departure from the BBC Francis became director-general of the British Council. He had bounced on the trampoline and emerged higher than the point from which he fell. In his five years as director-general, he managed to extend the council's programme by 20 per cent in real terms, and to increase its grant from the government each year. He introduced new planning mechanisms and efficiency savings, being 'convinced that the best way to protect the Council's independent but complementary role [to the Foreign Office] and its traditional values was to prove its worth by business criteria' (Orr, *The Times*, 3 July 1992). He travelled frequently—as he had done with the BBC, where his reputation for enjoying jet travel and the comforts of the VIP lounge was legendary. Some British Council staff thought that he spent too much time away from base, but he believed in walking his global ship (in his interests in *Who's Who* he listed 'off-shore sailing and listening to music six miles high'. Others admired his stamina and were energized by the excitement with which he reported on local achievements. He wanted to expand the council's activities in eastern Europe and, at home, he successfully relocated half the council's staff to new premises in Manchester—a demanding managerial challenge. He was a doughty promoter of the English language and wanted to see the best of British art in all its forms exhibited abroad. The British Council was well served by him, and his own artistic enthusiasms for good music, opera, and photography underpinned what was to be his last professional achievement. 'His representation of the Council, at home and abroad, has lifted its standing throughout the world', said Marmaduke Hussey in his appreciation in *The Times*.

Francis was professionally self-assertive, and was well-versed in the art of presentation. He was implacable in his consistency for what he believed to be right. He was, above all, a public servant. His career began at a time when Britain strongly embraced the concept of the public services. It ended as that world, which was assaulted by Prime Minister Thatcher, had begun to crumble. In many ways, he was an intrepid figure, with great enthusiasms masking an inner shyness. His was a life of achievement in a competitive environment. He took risks, and could keep calm under the greatest pressure—a characteristic that made him one of Britain's top (and pioneering) live studio television directors, and that served him well when he was responsible for all global television coverage outside the USA of the Apollo space programme which landed man on the moon. Equally, he brought his cool head to technically complex general election television programmes, as well as to the complexities of Northern Ireland as the BBC controller during a critical and dangerous period for journalists and staff. He conducted his hobby of offshore sailing with the energy (and occasional insouciance to danger) that marked his professional career. Privately, he was a kind and generous friend—with little of the pomposity that some professional observers felt was characteristic.

Francis was married twice: first, on 22 December 1958, to Beate Ella Paula Stientje Ohlhagen (*b.* 1931), air hostess, daughter of Karl Wilhelm Ohlhagen, from whom he was divorced in 1973; and second, on 1 October 1974, to Elizabeth Penelope Anne Fairfax-Crone (*b.* 1945), a television researcher and producer, daughter of Fairfax Chinnery Fairfax-Crone. There were two sons by each marriage.

Francis was at various times a member of the 'D' Notice Committee and of the Press Complaints Commission, the Media Law Group, the UK–Japan 2000 Group, and the Franco-British Council; a council member of the Royal College of Art and of Voluntary Service Overseas; a governor of Westminster College; a trustee of the Charities Aid Foundation; a vice-president of the Royal Institute of Public Administration; and a deputy chairman of Visnews and of the International Press Institute. He was elected a companion of the British Institute of Management in 1984, honorary president of the Radio Academy in 1986, and a fellow of the Royal Society of Arts in 1988. He was made KCMG in 1989 and a fellow of Kings College, London, in 1991. He died, following a heart attack, at Queen Mary's University Hospital, Roehampton, on 26 June 1992, and was buried in Queen's Road cemetery, Richmond, on 3 July. His memorial service was held in St Paul's Cathedral on 17 November 1992 under the auspices of the two organizations he had served so well. It was attended by over a thousand people, and the BBC Symphony Orchestra played Elgar's 'Nimrod' and Richard Strauss's *Also sprach Zarathustra* (which he had used for his Apollo space programmes). The music linked this quintessential Englishman with the creative inventiveness and expansive style that had marked his life.   ROBERT ROWLAND

Sources personal knowledge (2004) · private information (2004) [family] · *WWW*, 1991–5 · *The Times* (27 June 1992) · *The Independent* (29 June 1992) · *The Guardian* (29 June 1992) · M. Hussey, *The Times* (1 July 1992) · D. Orr, *The Times* (3 July 1992) · BBC WAC · D. Orr, 'Sir Richard Francis', *Connect* (Aug 1992) · R. Francis, 'Broadcasting to a community in conflict: the experience in Northern Ireland', speech to Royal Institute of International Affairs, 22 Feb 1977 · R. Francis, 'Television: the evil eye', speech to Royal Television Society, 14 July 1981 · R. Francis, address to 31st general assembly of International Press Institute, Madrid, 11 May 1982 · b. cert. · m. cert. · d. cert.
Archives BBC WAC | FILM BFI NFTVA, documentary footage
Likenesses photograph, repro. in *The Times* · photograph, repro. in Hussey, *The Times* · photograph, repro. in *The Independent*
Wealth at death £139,315: probate, 30 Oct 1992, *CGPLA Eng. & Wales*

Francis, Thomas (*c*.1519–1574), physician, was born in Chester and educated at Christ Church, Oxford, as a member of which he was admitted BA on 19 June 1540 and MA on 7 July 1544. Following this, he studied theology for some time, but transferred to medicine in August 1550. By 1552 he was acting as regius professor of physic, apparently as a temporary deputy for John Warner. A contemporary described Francis as 'a man of distinguished learning' (Lewis, 231).

Francis was admitted MB and received his licence to practise on 9 March 1555. He took his MD on 29 July 1555. On 21 May 1554 he succeeded Warner and became regius professor of physic in his own right. He resigned this office in 1561 to become provost of Queen's College. This was not a popular appointment, and 'serious disturbances' took place at his inauguration (letter of Francis, Calfhill, and others to Cecil, dated from Oxford, 11 May 1561, *CSP dom.*, *1547–80*). He retired from the provostship in 1563.

Francis had been admitted a fellow of the College of Physicians on 21 October 1560, at the *comitia* specially convened for that purpose, and became censor in 1561 and in the three following years. He was provisionally named elect on 30 September 1562 in place of John Clement, who had gone abroad, and was definitely appointed to that office on 12 May 1564. He was president of the college in 1568, and consiliarius in 1571. While president, he came into conflict with Eliseus Bomelius, whom he prosecuted for practising physic without a licence from the college. Bomelius in his letters to Cecil threatened to expose Francis's ignorance of Latin and astronomy, but eventually apologized for having circulated such palpably false statements. Francis was physician-in-ordinary to Queen Elizabeth, and, according to Wood, much respected by her.

Francis lived in Silver Street, in the parish of St Olave, London, where he was buried on 15 April 1574. His will, dated 8 April and proved on 9 November 1574, left his wife, Anne, comfortably provided for, but he was more solicitous for the welfare of one 'Edwarde Marbecke alias Fraunces, a yonge childe, nowe or late withe me in house dwellinge'. He names as his executors Roger Marbeck and John Riche.

GORDON GOODWIN, rev. SARAH BAKEWELL

Sources Munk, *Roll* · Foster, *Alum. Oxon.* · G. Lewis, 'The faculty of medicine', *Hist. U. Oxf.* 3: *Colleg. univ.*, 213–56, esp. 231–4 · Emden, *Oxf.* · private information (2004) [A. H. Nelson]

Franciscus à Sancta Clara. *See* Davenport, Christopher (*c*.1595–1680).

Francis-Williams. For this title name *see* Williams, Edward Francis, Baron Francis-Williams (1903–1970).

Franck, Richard (*c*.1624–*c*.1708), travel writer, appears to have been born in Cambridge. Nothing at all is known about his parentage or early childhood, and although he alludes to his education having been at the university there is no independent corroboration to support this suggestion. Because he is referred to as 'Captain' in an approving poem prefixed to his principal publication, there is reason to think that he saw service in the civil wars of the 1640s. Moreover, his unembarrassed enumeration of six great patriots of the English nation—Ireton, Vane, Nevill, Marten, Marvell, and Cromwell—makes it almost certain that this must have been with the parliamentarian forces. He has been plausibly identified with the man who was quartermaster of Thornhaugh's Nottinghamshire cavalry regiment by July 1647. The regiment was one which formed part of the English occupying army in Scotland from early 1652 to the spring of 1654, and again between March 1658 and the spring of 1659. It seems probable, from internal evidence, that it was during the first of these tours of duty that he undertook a lengthy and difficult journey from Glasgow to Caithness and then back through Aberdeen and Edinburgh to England. Thereafter he set himself to writing an account of his experiences on the road, producing an extraordinary work which was probably written about 1658 but not finally printed until 1694.

Northern Memoirs is a most unusual narrative, marked by Franck's eclectic interests and given ripe flavour by his often highly colourful judgements. In the first instance it is possible to take this simply as a generally appreciative assessment of the people, landscape, and heritage of Scotland not inconsistent with the growing body of travel literature on that country over the next 100 years which would culminate in the acute observations of Thomas Pennant and Samuel Johnson. Indeed at times Franck appears to anticipate these later visitors with his awestruck response to Scotland's natural beauties and architectural curiosities. Thus the highlands 'represent a part of the creation left undrest' (Franck, 215), Dunnottar is 'this gawdy fortress' (ibid., 230); there is unfeigned feeling in his description of 'Disconsolate Dundee' (ibid., 235), and obvious pleasure in encountering unexpectedly the 'fair imbellishments' of the old royal palace at Falkland (ibid., 240). His aesthetic joy in discovering the fecundity and untamed wildernesses of northern Scotland is also particularly noteworthy, the traveller expressing his delight at seeing Loch Ness, 'whose streams are strewed with eel and trout, whilst her deeps are saluted with the race of salmon', and claiming, with engaging hyperbole, that its 'fertil banks and shining sands are hourly moistned by this small Mediterrane' (ibid., 201).

But Franck also has other preoccupations which regularly cut across the narrative of his journey, revealing priorities and commitments which plainly distance him from subsequent generations of English travellers. To start with, he is fired by an idiosyncratic religiosity which further reinforces the notion that he had spent his formative adult years in the puritan environment of the parliamentary army. He is essentially Independent in contemporary ecclesiastical affiliation; but his outlook is marked also by flashes of intense personal piety and mysticism: the early praise for 'the evangelical sweets of reason and religion' (Franck, xxxiii) effectively alerts the reader to this peculiarity. It is plain, moreover, that Franck strongly disapproves of what he interprets as the declining moral and theological standards of his own day, frequently insinuating that modern English religion has departed from its pristine Reformation original.

Franck is also, somewhat incongruously, an enthusiastic angler. Observations on local aquatic life and recondite disputes about fishing techniques intrude so frequently as to unbalance the narrative, creating a sense that Franck, with probably a very limited formal education, possessed little or no intellectual discipline. Certainly he found it quite impossible to organize his idiosyncratic material into a coherent literary work. This tendency was not wholly disadvantageous, for it allowed him *inter alia* to become the first author to describe salmon fishing in Scotland, and to offer his readers a pioneering account of fly-fishing for trout. But the most substantial and notorious of these many piscatorial diversions is a passage recounting his confrontation with Izaak Walton, the century's most famous angler, at Stafford. The two men had had an angry exchange about Walton's assertion in *The Compleat Angler* that pike are generated by the pickerel weed, but the impression ultimately given by Franck's relation of this episode, and by his relentless side-swipes at Walton, is less one of the latter's deficient understanding of piscine reproduction than of the former's vengeful and boorish hostility towards him (Franck, 176–7).

Little is known of Franck after his return from Scotland, though he seems to have settled in Nottinghamshire, presumably regularly fishing the Trent. He signed letters in support of General John Lambert in his expulsion of the restored Rump Parliament in October 1659, and was duly cashiered by Monck in early 1660. As one of the 'Lambertonians' (Hutchinson, 298) he was under suspicion after the Restoration, and it was reported that he was arrested about October 1663, though it is not clear when he was released. It is evident that during the 1680s he went out to the American colonies where he wrote a second and much less noteworthy work, *A Philosophical Treatise of the Original and Production of Things* (1687), a rare volume of which a copy exists in the British Library. On the basis that it purports to be the work of Philanthropos, a pseudonym (albeit common at this time) which Franck had already used in *Northern Memoirs*, as well as because of a suspiciously chaotic and splenetic literary style, he has also been suspected as the author of *The Admirable and Indefatigable Adventures of the Nine Pious Pilgrims … to the New Jerusalem* (1708).

The date and place of Franck's death is unknown. However, as he would have been of an advanced age by the time of this last publication and may well have died shortly afterwards, 1708 is the conventional approximation.   DAVID ALLAN

Sources R. Franck, *Northern memoirs … by Richard Franck, Philanthropus*, ed. W. Scott (1821) · C. H. Firth, 'Franck's *Northern memoirs*', *SHR*, 25 (1927–8), 230–33 · L. Hutchinson, *Memoirs of the life of Colonel Hutchinson*, ed. N. H. Keeble (1995)

Francklin, Richard (*d.* 1765), printer and bookseller, may have been the apprentice bound to the London printer William Hunter on 2 February 1719; if so, his father was Richard Franklyn, a yeoman from Otterington, Yorkshire. Francklin's first publication dates from 1718 by which time he was already associated with the oppositional whig and Oxford wit Nicholas Amhurst, whose works he published and who was a major influence on his publishing career.

Francklin was presumably married in 1720 or earlier as his son, Thomas *Francklin, was born in 1721; the name of his wife is unknown. Francklin's business was based at the sign of the Sun in Fleet Street from 1720; by 1726, however, his shop was located under Tom's coffee-house in Covent Garden, where he remained until 1758. From 1726 until 1731 Francklin was closely involved in the publication of *The Craftsman*, a weekly whig periodical edited by Amhurst which ran from 1726 to 1750. Through this association Francklin came into contact with William Pulteney, later earl of Bath, and Henry St John, Viscount Bolingbroke. The journal became one of the most controversial political prints of its century between 1726 and 1737, with several prosecutions for seditious libel being brought against it. Francklin himself was tried and acquitted in 1729, but in 1731 he was arrested following the periodical's publication of the so-called Hague letter which concerned the treaty of Seville (1729). The year 1731 was particularly busy for publications related to *The Craftsman*, many of which were published by Francklin himself, and at least two anti-*Craftsman* tracts appeared with Francklin's own name in their imprints, a sign either of a willingness to publish for the other side or that his name was so intimately linked with *The Craftsman* as to be worth falsifying. Despite some initial problems about the jury, Francklin was tried and convicted by king's bench in December 1731.

The case proved relatively notorious and the proceedings were printed in London, Edinburgh, and Dublin.

Francklin was imprisoned for a while but was able to keep a hand in the running of the business; a contemporary observer drew a parallel between Francklin's predicament and that of the imprisoned New York newspaper printer John Peter Zenger: 'he like Zenger prints on, and leave[s] those concerned to make the best of it'. Francklin's publishing output fell markedly, and apparently some compensation was raised for him by a number of noblemen and gentlemen. However, he was able to draw on the assistance of his journeyman, Henry Haines, who between 1732 and 1736 published a number of Francklin's publications in his own name; Haines even went so far as to set up a new printing shop elsewhere in Covent Garden. While not an utterly false imprint, the house of Haines was assuredly a front designed to protect Francklin from further court action while still publishing works critical of government policy. However, Haines ran afoul of the authorities himself, spending two years in prison from 1737 for libel.

During the 1740s and 1750s Francklin increasingly turned to safer publications, including poetry, drama, and a number of works by his son, Thomas, as well as relying on a few steady sellers such as the English translation of Noel Antoine Pluche's *Spectacle de la nature, or, Nature Display'd* and some of Bolingbroke's political works. Even after the split between Bath and his quondam oppositional allies in 1742, Francklin maintained his connections with most of them, and it was rumoured that he paid for Amhurst's tomb in 1742. From 1747 Francklin acquired a country house on Horace Walpole's property which, given *The Craftsman*'s stance against Sir Robert Walpole, provided an irony not lost upon Francklin's new landlord: 'can there be an odder revolution of things?' he wrote in 1755 (Walpole, 35.237).

In 1761 Francklin's wife died, and he himself died on 1 February 1765. As he had destined his son for the clergy rather than the book business, his trade was carried on by a former apprentice, William Bunce. Little is known of his appearance, although an account of him included in *The Craftsman* in 1730 described him as 'very diminutive … a plain, quiet, common bookseller' (Sichel, 257 n. 5).

J. J. CAUDLE

Sources Walpole, *Corr.* · D. F. McKenzie, ed., *Stationers' Company apprentices*, [3]: *1701–1800* (1978) · *London Magazine* (30 Aug 1761), 505 · *London Magazine* (1 Feb 1765), 157 · *GM*, 1st ser., 54 (1784), 238 · H. R. Plomer and others, *A dictionary of the printers and booksellers who were at work in England, Scotland, and Ireland from 1668 to 1725* (1922) · H. R. Plomer and others, *A dictionary of the printers and booksellers who were at work in England, Scotland, and Ireland from 1726 to 1775* (1932) · A. Chalmers, ed., *The general biographical dictionary*, new edn, 32 vols. (1812–17) · B. Lillywhite, *London signs* (1972) · B. Lillywhite, *London coffee houses* (1963) · W. Sichel, *Bolingbroke and his times: the sequel* (1901–2); repr. (1968)

Francklin, Thomas (1721–1784), Church of England clergyman and writer, was born in London, the son of Richard *Francklin (d. 1765), bookseller near the piazza in Covent Garden, who printed William Pulteney's paper *The Craftsman*. Thomas was educated at Westminster School from 1735 and at Trinity College, Cambridge, from 1739; he graduated BA (1743), and proceeded MA (1746) and DD (1770). In 1745 he was elected to a minor fellowship at Trinity; the following year he was promoted to socius major and he resided in college until the end of 1758. On Pulteney's advice and encouragement he was educated for the church but he received no preferment from Pulteney. He was ordained deacon at Ely in May 1746 and priest at Rochester on 6 March 1747 but he did not accept a ministerial appointment until 1759. He spent some time as usher in his old school, and on 27 June 1750 was elected professor of Greek at Cambridge. Later that year, together with some other former pupils of Westminster, he became involved in a heated dispute with the university proctors over late-night revelry in a tavern in the town. The incident came before the vice-chancellor's court but Francklin seems to have escaped with no serious censure.

On 2 January 1759 Francklin was instituted to his college living of Ware, Hertfordshire, which he held together with the lectureship of St Paul's, Covent Garden, and a proprietary chapel in Queen Street, London. On 20 January 1759 at St Paul's, Covent Garden he married Mary Venables (d. 1796), daughter of a London wine merchant. Their eldest son was the orientalist William *Francklin. As a popular preacher his services were often in demand; he was appointed king's chaplain in November 1767 and was selected to preach the commencement sermon at St Mary's, Cambridge, on the installation of the duke of Grafton as university chancellor in 1770. Through the influence of Frederick Cornwallis, archbishop of Canterbury, he was presented to the rectory of Brasted in Kent, whereupon he vacated the living at Ware.

For the greater part of his married life Francklin was compelled, by the need to earn a sufficient income to support his family, to write for the press and the stage. In 1757 he brought out a periodical entitled *The Centinel*, which was intended as a continuation of *The World*, but it failed to attract a wide circulation and was dropped after the twenty-seventh issue. He also contributed to Tobias Smollett's *Critical Review*; one of his reviews so derided the author, Arthur Murphy, that Murphy rushed to defend his reputation in *A Poetical Epistle to Samuel Johnson, AM*, and Francklin was obliged to resort to the law to prevent Murphy from further maligning his character. Francklin's stage plays were far from innovative but two of them, *The Earl of Warwick* (1766) and *Matilda* (1775), proved financial successes, due more to the excellence of the acting rather than the quality of the writing. Both were adapted, without acknowledgement, from works by the French dramatist La Harpe. *The Contract* (1776), a feeble comedy about two people attempting to extract themselves from a marriage contract, which opened at the Haymarket on 12 June 1776, was more original but failed to win public approval. Francklin's play *Mary Queen of Scots* existed in manuscript only and was never performed. In conjunction with Smollett he lent his name to a translation of Voltaire's works but he appears to have contributed only *Orestes*, performed at Covent Garden Theatre on 13 March 1769 for the benefit of Mary Ann Yates, and *Electra*, produced at Drury Lane on 15 October 1774. His theatrical endeavours brought him into contract with major figures in literary and artistic circles such as Dr Johnson and Sir Joshua Reynolds, who used their influence to secure his appointment in 1768 as chaplain to the Royal Academy.

Francklin's most significant works were on classical literature. His first venture was an anonymous version of a treatise by Cicero, *On the Nature of the Gods* (1741), which, after revision by C. D. Yonge, formed one of the volumes in Bohn's Classical Library. In 1749 he published *The Epistles of Phalaris Translated from the Greek*; his translation of the tragedies of Sophocles, published in two volumes in 1759, was long considered the best in the English language. Equally well received was his translation *The Works of Lucian* (2 vols., 1780; 2nd edn, 1781), the whole of which was dedicated to the politician Richard Rigby, and its parts inscribed to other prominent figures such as Johnson, Reynolds, Edmund Burke, and John Douglas, later bishop of Salisbury.

Francklin published numerous other works, most of little value, but one, his humorous *Letter to a Bishop Concerning Lectureships*, drew attention to the manner of election to lectureships and the poor pay attached to them. He published several single sermons and a collection, *Sermons on the Relative Duties* (1765), which reached a fourth edition by 1788. He died at his home in Great Queen Street, London, on 15 March 1784. His death was lamented by one obituarist as a 'considerable loss to the republic of letters' (*GM*, 54.239). Three volumes of his sermons were published posthumously, in 1785 and 1787, primarily to provide financial assistance for his children and for his widow, who died on 24 May 1796.   M. J. MERCER

Sources *GM*, 1st ser., 29 (1759), 45 · *GM*, 1st ser., 54 (1784), 238–9 · *GM*, 1st ser., 66 (1796), 446 · J. Aikin and others, *General biography, or, Lives, critical and historical of the most eminent persons*, 10 vols. (1799–1815) · Venn, *Alum. Cant.*, 1/2.175 · Allibone, *Dict.* · C. Knight, ed., *The English cyclopaedia: biography*, 6 vols. (1856–8) [suppl. (1872)] · Genest, *Eng. stage*, 5.119–20, 242–6, 441–7 · Nichols, *Lit. anecdotes*, 2.594; 6.425 · *IGI* · *DNB*
Archives V&A NAL, corresp. with David Garrick
Likenesses C. Haghe, lithograph (after O. Humphrey, 1782), NPG

Francklin, William (1763–1839), orientalist, was born in 1763, the eldest son of the classical scholar and dramatist Thomas *Francklin (1721–1784) and his wife, Mary (*d.* 1796), the daughter of a wine merchant named Venables. He was educated at Westminster School from 1777 to 1781 and at Trinity College, Cambridge (1781–2). He was admitted as a cadet in the service of the East India Company in 1782 and appointed ensign of the 19th regiment of Bengal native infantry on 31 January 1783. By 1814 he had risen to the rank of lieutenant-colonel in both his regiment and the Bengal army. On being invalided on 1 October 1815 he was made regulating officer at Bhagalpur. He retired in India in December 1825, and died there on 12 April 1839, aged seventy-six.

A distinguished officer, Francklin also enjoyed considerable reputation as an oriental scholar. In 1786 he made a tour of Persia, in the course of which he lived at Shiraz for eight months as the close friend of a Persian family, and was thus able to write a fuller account of Persian customs

than had before appeared. This was published as *Observations Made on a Tour from Bengal to Persia* (Calcutta, 1788) and was translated into French in 1797. His publications also include a compilation of the memoirs of George Thomas (1756–1802), the military adventurer in India; translations from Persian; archaeological remarks on the plain of Troy, seeking to corroborate the existence of an ancient city there; historical, political, geographic, economic, and religious essays on parts of India. His religious writings include a discussion of the worship of the serpent in various parts of the world. He also maintained a learned correspondence with William Vincent (1739–1815), who was second master at Westminster during the time he was there, and Francklin was one of the few people to whom Dean Vincent acknowledged obligations in the preface to the *Periplus* (1800–05). Francklin was a member, and during the later years of his life, librarian and member of the council, of the Royal Asiatic Society. He was also member of the Asiatic Society of Bengal.

GORDON GOODWIN, *rev.* PARVIN LOLOI

Sources W. Francklin, 'Preface', in T. Francklin, *Mary queen of Scots*, ed. W. Francklin (1837) · J. Welch, *The list of the queen's scholars of St Peter's College, Westminster*, ed. [C. B. Phillimore], new edn (1852), 407, 414–15 · Dodwell [E. Dodwell] and Miles [J. S. Miles], eds., *Alphabetical list of the officers of the Indian army: with the dates of their respective promotion, retirement, resignation, or death … from the year 1760 to the year … 1837* (1838), 102–3 · *Journal of the Royal Asiatic Society*, 5 (1839), ii–iii [annual report, 11 May 1839] · *East-India Register* · *Asiatic Journal*, new ser., 29/2 (1839), 80 · Venn, *Alum. Cant.*

Frank, Sir (Frederick) Charles (1911–1998), physicist, was born on 6 March 1911 in Durban, South Africa, the eldest of the three sons of Frederick Frank (1877–1970), farmer, and his wife, Medora Celia Emma (1876–1966), daughter of Charles Read, of Brundish Hall, Suffolk, and his wife, Emma. Frederick's father, Charles Henry Frank of Poslingford, was a Suffolk farmer, like Medora's father, but an impoverished one, and a number of his seventeen children emigrated to Canada or South Africa in search of a better life. Frederick himself became a merchant seaman, and sailed more than once around the Horn before enlisting in the 3rd South African light horse (Kitchener's horse) during the Second South African War. After the war he joined two of his elder brothers in a business in Durban, and in 1910 he married Medora, who had nursed him in hospital ten years earlier. In 1911, when their son Frederick Charles was only ten weeks old, the family moved back to England, eventually settling at Abbot's Farm, Denham Abbots, Suffolk, where Charles Frank (he never used the forename Frederick) spent his childhood.

Frank's early schooling, until the age of nine, was at a tiny village school near Denham Abbots, run by a Mrs Petley. He then went as a boarder first to Thetford grammar school from 1920 to 1926 and, after the family had moved from Denham Abbots to Cavendish, to Ipswich School from 1927 to 1929. There he took part in school plays—in the part of Mrs Hardcastle in *She Stoops to Conquer* he is said to have fondled, scolded, and complained in turn with equal skill and energy—and school debates, in one of which he eloquently opposed a motion, proposed by his younger brother John, that scientists should be kept in their place. There, too, he learned chemistry and gained an open scholarship to Lincoln College, Oxford, and a state scholarship. At Oxford from 1929 he coxed, rowed, punted, and pursued the study of chemistry, gaining a first in 1933. He then became nominally an engineer, earning a DPhil in 1937 for work on dielectrics carried out in the Oxford engineering laboratory. Part of his later strength as a theoretical physicist lay in the breadth of his background: from 1936 to 1940 he worked successively as a physicist with P. J. W. Debye in Berlin, as a colloid chemist with Eric Rideal in Cambridge, and (in the early days of the war) as a chemist at Porton, before finding his wartime métier with R. V. Jones in Air Ministry intelligence. He had met Jones at Oxford, and they became lifelong friends. The story of their wartime collaboration is well told in Jones's book *Most Secret War* (1978), which includes several stories of the inspired common sense with which Frank managed to interpret the confused scraps of information coming from occupied Europe, and the extraordinary observational powers which enabled him to detect enemy radar stations from the tiny blurred images on aerial reconnaissance photographs, and which led to the successful Bruneval raid in 1942. For this work he was appointed OBE in 1946.

In the same year Frank moved to the physics department in the University of Bristol, where he worked until long past his retirement in 1976, becoming a professor in 1954 and head of department in 1969. He spent his 1964–5 sabbatical year in the USA, and he was also frequently consulted by American organizations. With publications spanning sixty years, he was remarkable for the sheer breadth of his contributions to science. Though his main work was in dislocation theory he also made major contributions to our understanding of cold fusion, liquid crystals, alloy structures, polymers, earthquakes, and continental drift. Soon after Frank's arrival in Bristol, Cecil Powell and his group there discovered the pi-meson, and this led Frank to look for other possible explanations of what Powell had found, and to his brilliant realization that a mu-meson might catalyse nuclear fusion by enabling two nuclei to approach very close to each other. (A year or so later, Andrey Sakharov made the same suggestion independently.) Fifty years later muon-induced fusion continued to be an active field of study, and Frank's original paper continued to be widely quoted.

But this was by way of a digression for Frank: his main field of work for many years was the study of dislocations, those imperfections in crystal structure which profoundly influence the mechanical strength of metals and other materials, and which are therefore of great technological importance. There his contributions were manifold and of fundamental significance: they included the laws governing dislocation branching, the existence and properties of dislocation networks, and the Frank–Read mechanism for the generation of dislocations. The idea for this mechanism came simultaneously and independently in 1950 to Frank and to Thornton Read, working at Bell Laboratories in the United States, and they published

it jointly. A year earlier Frank had shown that accepted theories failed by an enormous factor to account for the observed growth rates of crystals, but that these could readily be explained if the growth face contained a screw dislocation, and that this mechanism would produce 'growth spirals' on the growth face. This theory was dramatically confirmed when he presented it at a conference: a member of the audience rose to say that he had recently observed just such spiral features, and produced photographs of them illustrating exactly what Frank had predicted.

The diversity of other fields in which Frank made significant contributions can be illustrated by choosing (almost at random) three characteristically short and incisive papers: one on asymmetry in nature (1953), which anticipated population dynamics studies, one on liquid crystals (1958), which stimulated a vast amount of subsequent work on these materials, and one on island arcs (1968)—those curved chains of islands which occur particularly in the Pacific—which drew a delightful analogy between the earth's crust and a ping-pong ball. If one pushes one point on a ping-pong ball inwards, it will form a saucer-shaped dimple with a sharp rim, and he showed that island arcs are probably formed by a similar deformation of the earth's crust.

In his retirement Frank continued to publish until well into his eighties. In particular he undertook the substantial task of editing the Farm Hall transcripts—the secretly made recordings of the conversations of a group of eminent German physicists who were detained at Farm Hall in Cambridgeshire between June and December 1945, including their reactions to the dropping of the first atomic bombs. He had himself visited and talked with them in November 1945; now, almost fifty years later, he was able to correct errors in the transcripts, and to elucidate their contents, which made a fascinating story.

Frank was one of the outstanding physicists of his generation. In all his work he showed deep physical insight, an easy mastery of the relevant mathematics, great originality, and an incisive clarity of presentation. For his many scientific achievements he was elected FRS in 1954, and was awarded the Copley medal, the Royal Society's highest honour, in 1994. He served as a vice-president of the society from 1967 to 1969, and was knighted in 1977. His many other academic honours included seven honorary degrees. For over sixty years, he contributed profoundly to our understanding of nature, not only through his own 200 publications but also through endless conversations with all the colleagues who came to seek his help and advice in understanding their work. But his interests were not confined to science: they included languages and etymology, the history of science, and the theatre, music, and art; and he served for many years as a governor of two of Bristol's schools: Queen Elizabeth's Hospital and Badminton School.

Of middle height, with an impressive head, Frank was gruff but even-tempered, warm-hearted but unsentimental, and habitually rigorous in his thinking. He could be counted on to express lively, stimulating, and well-argued views, not only on scientific matters but on almost any issue worthy of debate. So too, on non-scientific matters, could his wife. In December 1939, he had met (Maia) Maita Marianne Asché (b. 1918), the lively and delightful daughter of Boris Asché, a professor of engineering in St Petersburg. Her family was Finnish and she had been born in Finland, but through the accidents of revolution and civil war she had been brought up in Czechoslovakia, and she was staying with Walter Adams (the secretary, and later the director, of the London School of Economics) in Cambridge when Frank met her. They married on 28 April 1940, and were a splendidly matched couple, who together contributed greatly to the social life of both the University of Bristol and the city.

In his later years Frank became increasingly infirm physically, though his clarity of mind and his phenomenal memory remained practically unimpaired, and he bore his infirmities with stoic patience. A few hours before he died, on 5 April 1998 (at Southmead Hospital, Bristol, of internal bleeding), he was busy reading, and vigorously discussing with his friends, a new book on geophysics. He was survived by his wife; they had no children. His remains were cremated on 16 April at Canford crematorium, Bristol. R. G. CHAMBERS

Sources F. C. Frank, unpublished autobiographical note, 10 Aug 1984, University of Bristol, Frank archive · M. M. M. Frank, transcript of tape-recorded interview with J. F. Nye, 1 March 1999, University of Bristol, Frank archive · F. R. N. Nabarro and J. F. Nye, *Memoirs FRS*, 46 (2000), 177–96 · R. G. Chambers and others, eds., *Sir Charles Frank, OBE, FRS: an eightieth birthday tribute* (1991) · R. V. Jones, *Most secret war* (1978) · J. Friedel, *Graine de mandarin* (1994) · *The Guardian* (10 April 1998) · *The Independent* (15 April 1998) · *Daily Telegraph* (24 April 1998) · *The Times* (27 April 1998) · m. cert. · WWW [forthcoming] · d. cert.

Archives University of Bristol, archive | FILM Bristol University archive, videotape of a lecture on 'Snowflakes' given at Bristol in 1995

Likenesses R. A. Philpott, photograph, 1976, University of Bristol · J. Hicks, oils, 1985, University of Bristol, H. H. Wills Physics Laboratory

Wealth at death £548,173: probate, 1 July 1998, *CGPLA Eng. & Wales*

Frank, Mark (*bap.* 1612, *d.* 1664), college head and theologian, was baptized on 29 December 1612 at Little Brickhill, Buckinghamshire, the son of Humfrey Frank, rector there, and his wife, Elizabeth. Nothing is known about his early education, but on 4 July 1627 he went up to Pembroke College, Cambridge, an institution that was to play a central part in his life. He began as a sizar, and became a scholar in 1630, before graduating BA in the following year, and proceeded to a fellowship on 8 October 1634, the year of his graduation as MA. He was ordained in 1639 to serve in the college, graduated BD in 1641, and took his turn as junior treasurer in 1641–2 and senior treasurer in 1642–3.

Frank's sermons, published in 1679, are notable for having something of the characteristics of Lancelot Andrewes, a former master of Pembroke; they are vivid in style, imaginative in interpreting scripture, and strong on the sacraments in the life of the church, but his preaching also embodies the simpler style that was coming into vogue. One sermon was preached at Paul's Cross on 4 May 1642 before the lord mayor and aldermen, in which he made his enthusiastic views on the monarch and the customs of the Church of England clear: 'the King's preminence is expressly part of your oath of allegiance ... Bishops are fathers by their title' (*Sermons*, 2.433). He was cited twice by the House of Commons for this sermon. Not surprisingly he refused to take the solemn league and covenant, and was ejected from his fellowship on 13 March 1643. At this time he also befriended Nicholas Ferrar and the religious community at Little Gidding, which was suppressed in 1646. Nothing is known about him from his ejection until his reinstatement after the Restoration, on 10 August 1660, but the long time of deprivation was rewarded by significant preferments. He was appointed chaplain to the archbishop of Canterbury, William Juxon, and continued as chaplain to Juxon's successor, Gilbert Sheldon. On 19 December 1660, Frank was made canon treasurer of St Paul's Cathedral and archdeacon of St Albans, then part of the diocese of London. He was also made a DD by royal mandate in 1661, along with other distinguished churchmen who had sided with the royalists during the interregnum. On 23 August 1662 he was elected master of Pembroke College, and also rector of Barley, Hertfordshire, succeeding another prominent theologian and preacher, Herbert Thorndike.

It was during Frank's mastership that the new chapel was built, through the munificence of another Pembroke man, Matthew Wren, bishop of Ely, to the designs of his nephew, the architect Christopher Wren. Frank's was not a passive role, for he took an active interest in the need for the foundations to be solidly built, and in the endowment of the chapel from the profits of the manor of Hardwick, which Bishop Wren had arranged. Frank died in 1664, some time before 7 June, a year before the consecration of the chapel, and was buried near the entrance to the north door of St Paul's Cathedral. He never married. Among the engravings by William Dolle is one of Frank, in the possession of Pembroke, which indicates two character traits that come as no surprise, thoughtful eyes and a determined mouth. Frank's preaching quotes freely from the early church fathers, and even pleads a special place for the Virgin Mary, when this would have been both unusual and controversial. He ends a Christmas sermon with a reference to the eucharist, another characteristic of Andrewes: 'do but make room for him, and we will bring him forth, and you shall look upon him, and handle him, and feed upon him' (*Sermons*, 1.90). As the Anglican theologican A. M. Allchin remarked, 'for long neglected, Frank is attracting more attention from scholars as a creative thinker' (Allchin, 70). KENNETH W. STEVENSON

Sources Venn, *Alum. Cant.* · private information (2004) [J. Ringrose, Pembroke College, Cambridge] · *The sermons of Mark Frank*, 2 vols., Library of Anglo-Catholic Theology (1849) · *Fasti Angl., 1541–1857*, [St Paul's, London] · A. M. Allchin, *The joy of all creation: an Anglican meditation on the place of Mary*, 2nd edn (1993), 70–96 · R. Greenacre, *Mark Frank (1613–1664): a Caroline preacher* (1994) · *Walker rev.* · will, PRO, PROB 11/314, fols. 146v–147r · G. B. Morgan, ed., *The tombs, monuments, &c, visible in S. Paul's Cathedral (and S. Faith's* *beneath it) previous to its destruction by fire* A.D. *1666* (1885) • parish registers, Little Brickhill, Bucks. RLSS

Likenesses W. Dolle, line engraving, BM; copies, NPG

Wealth at death books to Pembroke College, Cambridge; £100 to Pembroke College, Cambridge, for armouring the gateway: will, PRO, PROB 11/314, fols. 146v–147r

Frankau, Gilbert (1884–1952), novelist and poet, was born on 21 April 1884 in Gloucester Terrace, London, the eldest of three sons and one daughter of Arthur Frankau (1849–1904), a principal partner of the firm of J. Frankau & Co., wholesale cigar merchants, founded originally in 1837 to import leeches from France. His mother, Julia *Frankau (1859–1916), daughter of Hyman Davis, was a successful novelist under the pen-name Frank Danby. Gilbert Frankau attended St Michael's preparatory school, Westgate-on-Sea, and, having won a scholarship to Harrow School, he turned it down to attend Eton College, his mother's favourite. He took his first step towards becoming a writer while still a schoolboy, when he launched and edited *The X* magazine, with Lord Turnour (later Earl Winterton) as his assistant editor. The magazine, too outspoken about the masters, was suppressed by the headmaster after only four numbers. Heavily influenced by Kipling and claiming to have 'never attempted originality in either verse or prose' (G. Frankau, 54), Frankau immediately found a fresh outlet for his talent with a volume of satiric verse entitled *Eton Echoes* (1901).

Frankau decided, however, to go into the family business and left school shortly afterwards to become a cigar merchant. He went to Hamburg to learn German, and his aptitude for learning languages was remarkable; in time he had an equal fluency in French, Italian, and Spanish, then turned to learning Turkish. With concentrated application he quickly acquired a thorough knowledge of the cigar business and became managing director of the family firm at the age of twenty-one, after his father's death in 1904. His activities took him to Havana, then on a two-year world tour, in an effort to restore the fortunes of the business. On 12 December 1905 Frankau married Dorothea Frances Markham Drummond-Black (1874–1945); they had two daughters, Ursula and the novelist Pamela Sydney *Frankau (1908–1967). Pamela was to write of her difficult relationship with her father in *Pen to Paper* (1961). Writing was not altogether neglected. Frankau produced pieces for journals and magazines, and in 1912 he published *One of Us*, a novel in *ottava rima* as used by Byron in *Don Juan*, and followed this up with a dramatic poem, *Tid'apa* (1915), reprinted from the *English Review*.

On the outbreak of the First World War in 1914 Frankau abandoned the cigar business and joined up at once; he was commissioned in the 9th battalion of the East Surrey regiment in October, but transferred to the Royal Field Artillery five months later and served at Loos, Ypres, and the Somme, where he composed war poetry collected in *The Guns* (1916) and *The City of Fear* (1917). In October 1916 he was sent to Italy as a staff captain to undertake special duties to counter German propaganda against Britain. His activities involved a press and film campaign which he handled most effectively. But delayed symptoms of shell-shock led to his being invalided out of the army in February 1918. Frankau decided to seek an income from more commercial writing; it was his intention to write a book that 'sells a hundred thousand copies' (P. Frankau, 180). His first prose novel, *The Woman of the Horizon*, was published in 1917. With *Peter Jackson, Cigar Merchant* (1920), a Kiplingesque story of a civilian soldier, he attained both popular acclaim and prosperity. Each book was planned with the utmost care, and regular hours were assigned to its writing. His study was his office and he would brook no interruption: no telephone calls were accepted; crises, no matter how grave and pressing, had to wait until he emerged.

By 1919 Frankau was divorced, and sought a rest cure in Rutland, where he learned to hunt. On 2 February 1922 he married an actress, Aimée (b. 1883/4), the daughter of Robert de Burgh, and the former wife of Leon Fred Quartermaine. In the same year Frankau made a dramatic plea for divorce law reform in *The Love-Story of Aliette Brunton*. Books now appeared with clockwork regularity, and a number of his plays were produced, if not wholly successfully. A 1920 dramatization of his mother's novel *The Heart of a Child*, starring Aimée de Burgh, was a failure. In 1921 *The Seeds of Enchantment*, in which he attacked indiscipline and proclaimed the superiority of the white above the black and Asian races, was published. In 1924 his speeches took a political turn. In spite of his Jewish descent his sympathies were with the extreme right, and traces of fascist sensibility can be found in *Gerald Cranston's Lady* (1924).

In 1926, with the publication of *Masterson*, a story of the cruelty of fashionable society, Frankau undertook a long and strenuous tour of the United States, which he evoked vividly and entertainingly in *My Unsentimental Journey* (1926). There he described a disregard for Hollywood, although several of his novels were later adapted for the screen. An unhappy venture into journalism, his first since he was at Eton, came in 1928 when he launched and edited *Britannia*, a sixpenny weekly with a strongly emphasized imperialist note. It was not a success. The fees paid to contributors made even the recipients gasp. Advertisers held aloof and after ten issues Frankau returned to novel writing.

During this time Frankau also embarked on an ill-advised venture as vice-chairman of an advertising agency. The pressure was too much for his wife, and the marriage was dissolved; he married Susan Lorna Harris (b. 1902/3) on 14 July 1932. Of his later novels, which lacked the energy of his previous output, *Christopher Strong* (1932), *Three Englishmen* (1935), and *Son of Morning* (1949) may be singled out. Frankau remained committed to his anti-socialist political beliefs as the Second World War approached, but upon its outbreak he was commissioned in the Royal Air Force Volunteer Reserve, and was promoted squadron leader in April 1940. His last book, considered by some as being among his best, was *Unborn Tomorrow* (1953), a vision of the future. Although he was aware that death was near, his iron resolve and self-discipline enabled him to finish it just before he died of lung cancer at his home, 4A King's Gardens, Hove, on 4

November 1952. He had always 'inclined towards Rome', and had converted to Catholicism a few months before his death. His wife survived him.

Always something of an exhibitionist, Frankau had adopted an aristocratic bearing. Kindness he professed to regard as sloppy, but all through his life his deeds were far kinder than his words. Many found Frankau's arrogance insufferable, but he prided himself on being like the heroes in his books—dashing and tough. As a story-teller he had considerable talent. His narrative style was compelling, his characters often larger than life, his imagery inclined to be lavish. One of the most widely read novelists of the 1920s and 1930s, Frankau, in his own view 'never for a minute [lost] sight of his public' (P. Frankau, 186). He treated writing as a business and believed his public, which his daughter said comprised 'housewives and ex-soldiers and tired business-men', deserved their money's worth: 'length, sex, colour, pace, action' (ibid.).

R. J. MINNEY, *rev.* CLARE L. TAYLOR

Sources G. Frankau, *Self-portrait: a novel of his own life* (1940) · P. Frankau, *Pen to paper: a novelist's notebook* (1961) · *The Times* (5 Nov 1952) · personal knowledge (1971) · m. certs. · d. cert.
Archives BL, corresp. with Society of Authors, Add. MS 56704 · Ransom HRC, corresp. and MSS · Ransom HRC, MSS
Likenesses F. Lion, oils, 1923, NPG · H. Coster, photographs, NPG · Elliott & Fry, photograph, repro. in P. Braybrooke, *Novelists: we are seven* [1926]
Wealth at death £9715 9s. 11d.: probate, 18 Feb 1953, *CGPLA Eng. & Wales*

Frankau [*née* Davis], **Julia** [*pseud.* Frank Danby] (1859–1916), novelist, was born in Dublin on 30 July 1859, the sixth of eight children of Hyman Davis (1824–1875), dentist and later portrait photographer, and his wife, Isabella (1824–1900). Both parents were Jewish (Reform synagogue). When her father returned to London in 1864, they lived in Bruton Street, Mayfair, London, and then in Warrington Crescent in Maida Vale. With her younger sister Eliza, later to write *Mrs Aria's Diary*, a weekly column in *Truth*, she went to Miss Belisario's strictly Orthodox Jewish school. Later she was educated at home, first by a tutor and then by Mme Laura Lafargue, eldest daughter of Karl Marx. Formal education ended with her father's death, but was continued informally in the company of her brother James, a musical comedy librettist, who had a circle of artistic friends including George Moore and Oscar Wilde.

On 28 March 1883 Julia Davis married Arthur Frankau (1849–1904), a partner in a well-established firm importing leaf tobacco. They lived in London, first in Weymouth Street, Marylebone, and later in Mayfair. They had three sons and two daughters, one of whom died in infancy. Their eldest son, Gilbert *Frankau (1884–1952), became a novelist and poet. Arthur, an assimilated Jew by upbringing, had briefly satisfied his future mother-in-law by being received into the Jewish Reform synagogue before his marriage. But when he refused to have his son circumcised two years later, both he and his wife were expelled and their connection with religious Judaism ended. Her ability to employ nannies, governesses, and servants

Julia Frankau (1859–1916), by George Charles Beresford

allowed Frankau to develop her interest in eighteenth-century prints and to pursue her enthusiasm for the theatre and other interests. Meanwhile she established herself in literary and artistic society, helped by her good looks, wit, and human sympathy.

Using the pseudonym Frank Danby, Frankau's first book, *Dr Phillips*, was published by Vizetelly, the radical publisher of Zola, in 1887. It is the story of the eponymous Jewish doctor who practises in the Jewish community in Maida Vale. Frankau contrasts the narrow, uncultured Jews in their over-furnished and ornate homes, whom she saw as 'worshipping a single Deity, Gain' (*Dr Phillips*, 15), with Phillips's gentile mistress, Mary Cameron, whose rooms are decorated in simple Liberty style. Faced with the danger of losing Mary, Dr Phillips kills his wife with an overdose of morphine. The publication was considered scandalous: the Jewish community, from which Frankau wanted to distance herself, found it offensive; while Phillips's life with his mistress and their child outraged conventional morality. Nevertheless it was twice republished, in 1887 and again in 1912.

By 1889 Frankau had published two more novels. But she temporarily abandoned fiction and wrote three scholarly books on eighteenth-century engravers and their methods. These were published under her own name. Then, according to her own words in *Who's Who*, she 'relapsed into novel writing'. She had by this time established a routine of writing every morning, forbidding callers until after lunch. This self-discipline enabled her to write nine more novels, many of which were reprinted and went into several editions.

Many factors contributed to Frankau's success. Powerful story-telling captured the reader's imagination and densely packed plots drove the stories on. The plots themselves were conventionally romantic but, although the proprieties were observed and conventional sexual morality was preserved, there were titillating temptations on the way to the happy ending. Readers were invited into the milieus of the aristocracy and the upper middle classes. The first of these works was *Pigs in Clover* (1903) in which Frankau returned to a Jewish subject, distinguishing between 'good' and 'bad' Jews. This was successful without being scandalous. The novels were set in her world and reflected her interests: gambling in *Baccarat* (1904); the theatre in *The Heart of a Child* (1908); racing in *When the Roof Fell in* (1910); a gallery of colour prints provided the setting for the seduction scene in *Concert Pitch* (1913).

Frankau's most popular novel was the overtly daring *Joseph in Jeopardy* (1912). From the first chapter the reader knew that the hero was not in love with his wife, but his faithfulness was not in question until towards the end when, subverting the norm, a woman was the seducer. The attempted seduction aroused his 'manhood' and, although he resisted temptation, it was made clear that he had become aware of his sexuality.

After her husband died in 1904, Frankau became a keen traveller and chauffeur-driven motorist, while her social life was expanded by holding afternoon salons frequented by, among others, George Moore, Max Beerbohm, Arnold Bennett, Somerset Maugham, and William Nicholson. Her sister Eliza's lover, Henry Irving, was also a frequent visitor.

Undeterred by diabetes compounded by tuberculosis, both of which she knew to be incurable, Frankau completed the semi-autobiographical novel *Twilight*, which was published in the year of her death. Julia Frankau died on 17 March 1916 at her home in Hay Hill, Mayfair, London. Her ashes were buried in her husband's tomb in Hampstead general cemetery, London.

ELIZABETH ECCLESHARE

Sources E. Aria, *My sentimental self* (1922) · G. Frankau, *Self portrait* (1939) · *WW* (1916) · M. Salaman, 'A personal tribute', *Jewish Chronicle* (24 March 1916) · M. Strickland, 'Literary woman behind the man', *Jewish Chronicle* (22 Feb 1996), suppl. · T. M. Endelman, 'The Frankaus of London', *Jewish History U.S.A.*, 8/1–2 (1994), 117–15 · tombstone, Hampstead general cemetery, London · m. cert.
Likenesses G. C. Beresford, platinotype print, NPG [*see illus.*] · O. Small?, drawing, repro. in Aria, *My sentimental self*, facing p. 58; destroyed · photograph, repro. in *Jewish Chronicle* [supplement] (23 Feb 1996) · photograph, priv. coll.
Wealth at death £34,068 16s. 8d.: probate, 23 May 1917, CGPLA Eng. & Wales

Frankau, Pamela Sydney (1908–1967), novelist, was born on 3 January 1908 at 14A Great Cumberland Place, London, the younger of the two daughters of Gilbert *Frankau (1884–1952), novelist, and his first wife, Dorothea Frances Markham Drummond-Black (1874–1945). Gilbert's mother, Julia *Frankau (whose pseudonym was Frank Danby) also wrote novels, giving Pamela a strong Jewish literary inheritance. Gilbert had small time for the home and less for the nursery; his departure from the family in 1919 when he left to marry an actress had no immediate effect on Pamela. In later years, however, being the

Pamela Sydney Frankau (1908–1967), by Bassano, 1935

stronger of the two sisters, she found herself having to give support, both financial and emotional, to her mother. Pamela's inability to remain solvent derived partly from her addiction to the gambling table, but mostly from her need to pay her mother's debts as well as her own, and her extreme generosity. After private lessons in the Old Rectory, Honiton, Devon, she and her sister, Ursula, were sent as boarders to Burgess Hill School for Girls, Sussex, from 1919 to 1924. Memories of this time are chronicled with her accustomed wit in the first part of the autobiographical *I Find Four People* (1935).

Slight and dark, with the look of Walt Disney's Bambi, and blessed with powerful attraction, a ready wit, and a passionate concern for others as well as herself, Pamela stood out in school as she did all her life. Her early hope was to go on the stage, but writing took over, and her first novel, *Marriage of Harlequin*, published in 1927 when she was nineteen, brought her much press notice, on the lines of 'talented daughter of a famous father'. She wrote tirelessly—before she was thirty-two she had published twenty novels, only three of which she cared to remember: *She and I* (1930), *I was the Man* (1932), and *Tassell-Gentle* (1934). All the early books, however, show traces of her idiosyncratic turn of phrase and her perception, foreshadowing what was to come. Her great-aunt, Eliza Aria, a well-known journalist and society hostess, introduced her to many of the famous of her time: John van Druten, G. B. Stern, and Rebecca West, with whom she was to have a close but stormy relationship; a rift of nine years was finally mended.

Pamela's affair with Humbert *Wolfe, poet and civil servant, whom she met in 1931, so absorbed her that his sudden death from heart failure in 1940 after a birthday dinner (he was born on 5 January 1885) cut her life in two. Married with a daughter, Wolfe was known for his many attachments, but his love for Pamela was real, if not consistently faithful. Three weeks after his death she left for the United States; after some months there in emotional disarray she returned to England via Lisbon in November 1940, at the height of the blitz. A spell in the Ministry of Food, editing *Food Facts* (as she claimed, her largest seller), ended when she joined the Auxiliary Territorial Service in February 1942.

Pamela was troubled always by an ambiguous sexuality, and her next love was a fellow woman officer, who became her sponsor when in 1942 she was received into the Roman Catholic church. However, on 30 October 1945 she married Marshall Dill Jr (b. 1916), an American who was then in navy intelligence. In 1946 she gave birth to a son who lived only a few days. The marriage foundered, ending in divorce in 1951. But after a silence of nine years she had begun to write again, and returned to England with the manuscript of *The Willow Cabin* (1949) which, drawing as it did on the experience of her love for Humbert Wolfe, was to become a Book Society choice and her most successful novel. Her books now, combining her early wit and agility of mind with a depth of experience, commanded a wide readership, both in Britain and in the United States. They speak with her own voice, her particular use of language, her lightness of touch. This is both their strength and their weakness; a surface dazzle can sometimes obscure her profound understanding of the human condition. In her obituary Rebecca West wrote that 'none of her novels, though they are better than most, was as good as she was' (*The Times*, 9 June 1967). Pamela's own favourite was *The Bridge* (1957), concerned as it was with the imperatives of the Roman Catholic faith. *Ask me No More* (1958) showed the unacceptable face of Humbert Wolfe in the guise of Geoffrey Bliss, a playwright whose love life has a cat's-cradle complexity.

Though Pamela was not one to have at any time a tranquil life, the last ten years had a semblance of calm, producing steady and successful work, and a last attachment, Margaret (Peggy) *Webster (1905–1972), daughter of Dame May Whitty, and a theatrical director of standing. They lived together at 55 Christchurch Hill, Hampstead, London; a telegram addressed to '55 Christ Churchill' brought from Pamela the comment 'with those two characters on our side, how can we lose?'

In 1964 Pamela was operated on for breast cancer; the disease returned in the form of cancer of the bone. She endured much pain, and faced the future with courage and humour. She died on 8 June 1967, at her home in Christchurch Hill, her sister Ursula and Peggy with her. She was buried in Hampstead cemetery, where Ursula now lies with her. Her last work, *Colonel Blessington*, a thriller, concerning a confusion of sexual identity, unfinished at her death, was completed by the undersigned, and published in 1968.   DIANA RAYMOND

Sources personal knowledge (2004) · P. Frankau, *I find four people* (1935) · P. Frankau, *Pen to paper: a novelist's notebook* (1961); American edn (1962) · P. Frankau, *The willow cabin* (1949) · G. Frankau, *Self-portrait* (1939) · R. West, *The Times* (9 June 1967) · D. Raymond, *Pamela Frankau: a life* [forthcoming]
Archives BBC WAC · Boston University · Ransom HRC, letters and MSS | University of Tulsa, Oklahoma, McFarlin Library, Rebecca West collection | SOUND BBC Broadcasting House, London
Likenesses photographs, 1928–37, Hult. Arch. · J. Wolfe, portrait, c.1931, priv. coll. · Bassano, photograph, 1935, NPG [*see illus.*] · photograph, c.1940, priv. coll. · P. Chandler, photograph, c.1960, priv. coll. · L. Ginnett, portrait, priv. coll.
Wealth at death £21,460: probate, 15 Aug 1967, *CGPLA Eng. & Wales*

Frankel, Benjamin

Frankel, Benjamin (1906–1973), composer, was born on 31 January 1906 at 705 Fulham Road, Hammersmith, London, the second of three children of Charles Frankel (c.1871–1935) and his wife, Golda Dora Adler (c.1869–1958). His father, born in Warsaw, served in the tsarist army before settling in London as a tobacconist, later becoming a synagogue beadle; his mother was born in the Polish town of Tarnopol, then part of the Austro-Hungarian empire. Like his elder brother and younger sister, Frankel demonstrated a considerable early talent for music, but he was alone in pursuing it seriously.

Frankel was educated at the Latymer foundation school, Hammersmith, leaving to become a watchmaker's apprentice at fourteen. A year later he began studying the violin and the piano at Trinity College of Music, London; he subsequently concentrated on the piano under the American virtuoso Victor Benham, who taught him for two years at no cost, latterly in Cologne and Berlin. After returning to England in 1923, Frankel earned a living for many years as a jazz violinist, pianist, and arranger, for Carroll Gibbons and Henry Hall among others. His formal training continued with Orlando Morgan on a composition scholarship (1929–34) from the Worshipful Company of Musicians at the Guildhall School of Music in London, where later he became principal composition teacher (1946–57).

Frankel was a leading committee member of the International Society for Contemporary Music from 1952 to 1955, serving as a vice-president during 1954–5. A leading and prolific film composer from 1934, he composed 104 film scores including music for *The Seventh Veil* (1945), *The Man in the White Suit* (1951), *The Importance of being Earnest* (1952), *Night of the Iguana* (1964), and *Battle of the Bulge* (1965). During the 1930s and 1940s he was also musical director for shows by C. B. Cochran, Noël Coward, and others in London's West End.

Frankel's earliest surviving concert work dates from 1926, but he gained recognition with his clarinet trio (1943), first sonata for solo violin (1945), and first four string quartets (1944–9), their introspective lyricism revealing an individual style. His violin concerto (1951)—commissioned by the violinist Max Rostal for the Festival

Benjamin Frankel (1906–1973), by Lida Moser, 1953

of Britain—was his first major work and cemented his reputation. Inscribed 'to the Six Million', it was a heartfelt lament for the victims of the Holocaust.

Frankel was a member of the Communist Party of Great Britain for twelve years; and works by him such as *May Day* (1947) indicated his political affiliations. In 1952, however, outraged by the show trials and summary executions of alleged spies in Prague, he publicly resigned from the party in a letter to the *New Statesman and Nation* (published on 13 December 1952). A secular Jew who none the less identified absolutely with his roots, Frankel was drawn late in life to Roman Catholicism, though he never converted.

Always dapper, Frankel had a strong personality and an imposing, high-domed forehead which disguised a diminutive stature. He was married three times. His first marriage, on 13 February 1932, to Joyce Stanmore Rayner (*b.* 1908), was dissolved in 1944. They had two sons and one daughter. The second, on 14 October 1944, was to Phyllis Anna Leat (1905–1967). His third marriage, to Xenia Hamilton-Kennaway, *née* Szladkowska (*b.* 1926), a musician, took place in 1972.

After leaving the parental home at 190 Hammersmith Road on his marriage, Frankel was itinerant for many years, eventually settling at 17 Soho Square, London, with his second wife, then at Rodmell Hill, Rodmell, near Lewes, from 1953 to 1957, where he entertained a lively artistic circle that included the poet Cecil Day Lewis, the film director Anthony Asquith, and the political writer Leonard Woolf (his neighbour). He settled in 1958 in Locarno, initially at Verbanella Alta, Minusio (1958–63), then at via ai Monti 31 (1963 onwards).

After adopting Schoenbergian serialism (broadly, the use of all twelve musical pitches in predetermined order), Frankel began his important cycle of eight symphonies 'that crystallised his position as one of the major English symphonists of our time' (*Daily Telegraph*, 13 Feb 1973).

These works were completed in the period 1958–71: no. 1 in 1958; no. 2 in 1962; no. 3 in 1964; no. 4 in 1966; no. 5 in 1967; no. 6 in 1969; no. 7 in 1970; and no. 8 in 1971.

Other significant works by Frankel included his viola concerto (1967) and his last work, the opera *Marching Song* (1971–3), after the play by John Whiting and to a libretto by Hans Keller. He left many chamber works, of which the piano quartet (1954), clarinet quintet (1956), and fifth string quartet (1965) are outstanding examples, as well as song cycles, orchestral overtures, and an instrumental mass. Many works were commissioned for the Cheltenham Festival. He also broadcast many stimulating talks for BBC radio.

The onset of heart disease in 1959 led to a long and courageous battle against severe odds, as when Frankel continued writing his sixth symphony while critically ill in hospital. His final years were divided between his house in Locarno and long visits to London for medical treatment and musical engagements. Despite the increasing success of his music, Frankel was frequently in debt on account of his generosity, lack of financial acumen, heavy medical bills, and love of the good life. He left debts approaching £50,000 (though these were eventually settled by posthumous royalties).

Frankel died, following a coronary thrombosis, in New End Hospital, London, on 12 February 1973. His ashes were buried in Golders Green crematorium, London, on 13 March 1973.   E. D. KENNAWAY

Sources priv. coll., personal papers of Benjamin Frankel · E. D. Kennaway, 'Benjamin Frankel: a reappraisal', ed. B. Tschaikov, *Musical Performance*, 2/1 (1998), 75–89 · B. Orr and E. D. Kennaway, *The music of Benjamin Frankel*, ed. J. Williams (1996) · C. Mason, 'Frankel, Benjamin', Grove, *Dict. mus.* (1954) · R. Palmer, *British music* (1947), 95 · *WW* (1973), 1133 · B. Frankel, 'Reactions to Prague', *New Statesman and Nation* (13 Dec 1952), 718 · *Daily Telegraph* (13 Feb 1973) · *MT*, 114 (1973), 414 · b. cert. · m. cert. [Joyce Stanmore Rayner] · m. cert. [Phyllis Anna Leat] · d. cert. · E. Lutyens, *A goldfish bowl* (1972) · private information (2004) · records of Golders Green crematorium, London

Archives FILM BFI NFTVA, documentary footage | SOUND BBC WAC · BL NSA, *The BBC archive*, BBC Radio 3, 26 June 1988, H10080/2 · BL NSA, *Composer of the week* (2 parts), BBC Radio 3, June 1996, H7400/2, H7400/3 · BL NSA, current affairs recording · BL NSA, 'Frankel and the symphony', M398R BD1 · BL NSA, recorded talks

Likenesses Von Löwenstein, bronze head, *c.*1950, priv. coll. · L. Moser, photographs, 1953, NPG [*see illus.*] · M. Cosman, three studies, crayon?, priv. coll. · photographs, Lebrecht collection, London

Wealth at death insolvent to amount of approx. £50,000: subject's sole legatee and executor (widow), 1973

Frankel, (Sally) Herbert (1903–1996), economist, was born on 22 November 1903 at Carlton Terrace, Johannesburg, Transvaal Colony, the first of three children of Jacob Frankel (1866–1930) and his wife, Mathilde, *née* Buxbaum (1876–1960). His parents, both Orthodox Jews, were born in Germany; his father emigrated to South Africa in 1896 and worked in the grain trade. Frankel went first to the Deutsche Schule and then to St John's College, Johannesburg. Despite achieving only a third class in his school-leaving exam he was able to enter the University of the

Witwatersrand, and there flourished, moving with distinction from a BA honours in economics to an MA. His MA dissertation was published in London as *Cooperation and Competition in the Marketing of Maize in South Africa* (1926).

In 1923 Frankel began attending lectures at the London School of Economics, and later enrolled there for a PhD on railway freight rates, a topic he had started to investigate at the request of the Transvaal chamber of mines. The dissertation was successfully submitted in 1927 and published as *The Railway Policy of South Africa* (1928). This study, like the one on maize, was notable for its painstaking attention to detail, and the strength, directness, and clarity of its criticisms of government policies exercised through monopolistic agencies without regard to the true economic costs. The hostility to government intervention in economic matters expressed in these early studies was to remain a distinctive feature of Frankel's thinking throughout his life. While in London, Frankel visited his relatives in Frankfurt and met his cousin, Ilse Jeanette Frankel. They were married in Wiesbaden, Germany, on 19 June 1928. They had one son and one daughter.

In 1930 Frankel was appointed to the chair of economics and economic history at the University of the Witwatersrand. His publications during his remaining years in South Africa included a major investigation of the role of capital in the economic development of Africa, *Capital Investment in Africa: its Course and Effects* (1938), and a pioneering study of the national income of South Africa since 1918. He served on many official inquiries, and was very active as a personal economic adviser to Sir Ernest Oppenheimer. He also had a close and long-standing relationship with Jan Hofmeyer, and advised him when he was minister of finance during the Second World War. Frankel's deep commitment to free market economics and his lifelong opposition to racial discrimination were expressed in his contribution to a liberal manifesto, *Coming of Age* (1930), with contributions also by Hofmeyr, Edgar H. Brookes, and others. Although too radical to be acceptable to the vast majority of white South Africans, the policies advocated were seen by many Africans as offering only a token advance, especially on the crucial issue of the franchise.

In 1945 Frankel was invited to take up a new chair of colonial economic affairs, established at Oxford to further the training of colonial service officers. He immediately informed Hofmeyr, hoping with all his heart that he would be told, 'Don't go, there's a job for you here, I've work for you here.' But Hofmeyr made no such response and Frankel accepted the Oxford offer (Frankel, 185; endorsing the account by Alan Paton, *Hofmeyr*, 1964, 256). He took up the chair and an associated fellowship at Nuffield College in 1946, and held this until retirement in 1971, though the title was twice changed, finally becoming the chair of the economics of underdeveloped countries. Frankel's strongly expressed free market convictions were no more popular in his new community than they had been in South Africa, and this, together with his strong distaste for abstraction and theory, left him somewhat isolated from the mainstream of British economics.

He preferred more practical work leading to advice for governments, even when he knew that it was unlikely to be accepted. He served on numerous committees and commissions, including a working party on the east African groundnut scheme (what better example could there be of the folly of government intervention?), and the royal commission on east Africa (1953–5). His inaugural lecture, and some of his main essays and articles from his early period in Oxford—all more general and reflective than his pre-war studies—were published in 1953 as *The Economic Impact on Under-Developed Societies*.

Frankel was a man of great charm and many friendships. He found congenial company among fellow liberals in the Mont Pelerin Society formed under the leadership of F. A. Hayek, and was twice elected a vice-president. He served as president of the Oxford Jewish congregation, and from 1971 to 1989 was first chairman of governors of the Oxford Centre for Postgraduate Hebrew Studies. He travelled widely in Africa, the United States, and Israel, and from 1967 to 1974 was regularly a visiting professor at the University of Virginia.

Frankel died at his home, 62 Cutteslowe House, Park Close, Oxford, on 11 December 1996. He was survived by his son and daughter, his wife, Ilse, having predeceased him in 1994.   CHARLES H. FEINSTEIN

Sources S. H. Frankel, *An economist's testimony: the autobiography of S. Herbert Frankel* (1992) · *The Independent* (30 Dec 1996) · *The Times* (1 Jan 1997) · *Daily Telegraph* (4 Jan 1997) · WWW
Likenesses photograph, repro. in Frankel, *Economist's testimony* · photograph, repro. in *The Independent*
Wealth at death £215,695: probate, 19 Aug 1997, CGPLA Eng. & Wales

Frankel, Sir Otto Herzberg (1900–1998), agricultural scientist, was born on 4 November 1900 in Vienna, Austria, the third of four sons of Ludwig Herzberg-Frankel, lawyer, and his wife, Thérèse, *née* Sommerstein, daughter of a Galician estate-owning family. His paternal grandfather, an author, adopted the hyphenated name Herzberg-Frankel (Herzberg being his mother's maiden name) but Frankel reverted to the family name after his father's death. The affluent Jewish family into which he was born suffered relative impoverishment as a consequence of the First World War.

Frankel received private tuition, and was then educated classically at the Piaristen Staatsgymnasium, Vienna, from the age of ten to eighteen. He taught himself chemistry before being admitted to Munich University in 1919 to study chemistry, physics, and botany. He left after only three semesters, but with a determination to become involved in agriculture. After a short period at the Agricultural Institute of the University of Giessen and some practical experience of farming at the estate of his aunt Ann in Galicia, he completed his formal education at the Agricultural University of Berlin. There he developed a particular interest in genetics and studied under the supervision of Professor Erwin Baur. He was awarded a doctorate of agriculture in 1925 for research on genetic linkage in *Antirrhinum majus*. He married Mathilde (Tilli) Donsbach (1899–

1989) the same year. There were no children of the marriage.

Frankel worked for two years as a cereal breeder on a large estate at Dioseg in Bratislava before transiently joining a team of scientists in Palestine who were establishing a plant and animal breeding programme supported by the Empire Marketing Board. During this period he developed his interest in cytogenetics and he pursued this when he moved briefly to the Plant Breeding Institute in Cambridge. In 1928 he accepted a post as plant breeder and geneticist at the newly established Wheat Research Institute (WRI) at Lincoln College, near Christchurch, New Zealand, where he arrived in March 1929 and remained for twenty-two years. WRI was funded through the New Zealand department of scientific and industrial research (DSIR), as well as receiving financial support from wheat growers, millers, and bakers. During his time at the institute Frankel was outstandingly successful in introducing a sequence of widely grown new varieties that elevated the yield and baking quality of New Zealand wheat. He also pursued his interests in cytogenetics, publishing revisions of the taxonomy of species in the *Hebe–Veronica* complex and investigating the nucleolar cycle in *Fritillaria* species following encouragement from C. D. Darlington while on a short visit to the John Innes Institute, Bayfordbury, England. In wheat he also deployed his skills as a cytogeneticist in making a detailed analysis of the meiotic behaviour of two inverted duplications he identified as the cause of abnormal progeny in one of his crosses.

In 1935, six years after arriving in New Zealand, Frankel made a visit to Europe and, in addition to spending time at the John Innes Institute, also visited Nicolai Vavilov in Leningrad, USSR. This contact was the inspiration for his acclaimed work on genetic conservation after his official retirement. His first marriage having ended in divorce in 1937, on 8 December 1939 he married Margaret Anderson (1902–1997), a potter, painter, and teacher from a Christchurch family, who shared his interest in architecture and gardening, and with whom he enjoyed fifty-eight happy years of marriage; they had no children. During the late 1930s and early 1940s, Frankel was active in assisting with the immigration to New Zealand of Jewish refugees from Europe, and also began to take a wider interest in the management and politics of research.

In 1942 Frankel was appointed chief executive officer of WRI in succession to his mentor F. W. Hilgendorf, and following a merger between WRI and the DSIR agronomy division he became director of the crop research division based at Lincoln in 1950. His contributions to plant breeding and genetics had been recognized in 1948 when he was elected a fellow of the Royal Society of New Zealand. Nevertheless, after a short time, he became frustrated by resistance to the direction in which he wished to develop the division and to his attempts to build a high-quality scientific research group. In 1951 he left New Zealand to become chief of the division of plant industry (DPI) of the Commonwealth Scientific and Industrial Research Organisation (CSIRO), Australia, based in Canberra. In 1953 he

was elected a fellow of the Royal Society and in 1954 a fellow of the Australian Academy of Sciences. Over ten years he rejuvenated the DPI by emphasizing the need for high quality, fundamental science, recruiting talented staff, and investing in new facilities. In 1960 Frankel became a member of the CSIRO executive based in Melbourne, a post he held until his official retirement six years later, when he was knighted.

Over the next thirty years Frankel embraced a second career, publishing more after his retirement than in the preceding forty years. With the status of honorary research fellow in the DPI he researched into the genetics of floral morphogenesis and fertility in wheat, while devoting a significant proportion of his time to the affairs of the International Genetics Federation. However, following in Vavilov's footsteps, his most enduring contribution was to promote conservation of biodiversity among the world's crops and their relatives. He did this by catalysing the international community into action, bringing together the International Biological Programme (IBP) and the Food and Agriculture Organisation (FAO) of the United Nations in the common cause of halting 'genetic erosion' and conserving 'genetic resources'. He was prominent in moves to establish a network of regional genetic resource centres under the aegis of the Consultative Group on International Agricultural Research, and the subsequent formation of the International Board for Plant Genetic Resources. In 1974 he presented a paper to the Thirteenth International Congress of Genetics in California entitled 'Genetic conservation: our evolutionary responsibility', which was considered by many to be one of his most influential works. For a further twenty years he continued to write and debate about the science and politics of what became known as biodiversity, and played no small part in placing the issues of genetic conservation on the international agenda.

For his international efforts on behalf of genetic conservation Frankel was honoured by the French Academy of Agricultural Science in 1969, by the Pacific Science Association in 1979, by the Japan Academy in 1983, and by the United States National Academy of Science in 1988. In 1995 he co-authored with A. H. D. Brown and J. J. Burdon a landmark volume, *The Conservation of Plant Biodiversity*. He died in Australia on 21 November 1998.   IAN CRUTE

Sources L. T. Evans, *Historical Records of Australian Science*, 12 (1998–9); repr. online: www.science.org.au/academy/memoirs/frankel. htm; repr. in abridged form in *Memoirs FRS*, 45 (1999), 167–81 • *The Times* (10 Dec 1998) • Burke, *Peerage* • WWW
Archives NL Aus., MSS | FILM Australian Academy of Science
Likenesses photograph, repro. in *The Times* • photograph, repro. in Evans, 'Sir Otto Frankel', www.science.org.au/academy/memoirs/frankel.htm • photograph, repro. in *Search*, 21/2 (1990), 47

Frankfort de Montmorency. For this title name *see* Montmorency, Raymond Harvey de, third Viscount Frankfort de Montmorency (1835–1902).

Frankland, Sir Edward (1825–1899), chemist, was born on 18 January 1825 at Churchtown, Garstang, Lancashire, the son of Margaret Frankland (1797–1881), daughter of John

Sir Edward Frankland (1825–1899), by Lock & Whitfield, pubd 1880

Frankland (1770–1811), calico printer, and his wife, Molly (*née* Dunderdale). Frankland's father, to whom his mother was not married, was Edward Chaddock Gorst (1803–1859), who later changed his name to Lowndes and who became deputy clerk of the peace for Lancashire. One of Gorst's legitimate children was the Conservative Party politician, Sir John Eldon *Gorst. Margaret Frankland later married William Helm, a Lancaster cabinet-maker; they had two sons who died in infancy. Frankland's illegitimacy cast a shadow over all his life since he was pledged to silence as to the identity of his natural father, though a handsome annuity was paid to his mother.

Early life and education Frankland was educated at eight schools in Lancashire, of which that run by James Willasey in Lancaster was the most enlightened, the pupils being encouraged to acquire firsthand knowledge of nature and even to conduct experiments. The final phase of his education, at Lancaster grammar school, appears to have been almost entirely unproductive. From there he was apprenticed in 1840 to a local pharmacist, Stephen Ross. Though he later wrote disparagingly of his six years with Ross it is probable that he acquired many useful skills at the shop, not least that of handling chemicals with care and precision. At this time he also borrowed books from the mechanics' institute, attending classes there and in a makeshift cottage laboratory made available to local apprentices and other young men by a local doctor, James Johnson. Others in that youthful circle were the scientific writer Robert Galloway (also apprenticed to Ross) and the anatomist William Turner.

With support and encouragement from Johnson, Frankland acquired in 1845 a place in the Westminster laboratory of Lyon Playfair, which was then part of the Office of Woods and Forests but soon became the Museum of Economic Geology. There he undertook analyses of coal, minerals, and coal gas, learning rapidly on the way. The following year Playfair accepted the additional role of professor at the Putney College of Engineering, and took Frankland with him as lecture assistant. Playfair's lecture course was attended by Frankland; at the end of it he passed the examination—the only written one he ever sat.

At Westminster and Putney, Frankland encountered another of Playfair's assistants, Hermann Kolbe (1818–1884), with whom he began a lifelong friendship. Kolbe had obtained his PhD under Bunsen at Marburg and inherited a belief that organic compounds were composed of radicals (identifiable groups of atoms). A current concern of many was to isolate such radicals if possible, or at least demonstrate their persistence through a series of reactions. Frankland was caught up in Kolbe's enthusiasm and together they commenced a study of aliphatic nitriles (alkyl cyanides), hoping to confirm the presence of hydrocarbon radicals in the fatty acids. Their successful hydrolysis of ethyl cyanide to propionic acid achieved this goal, by showing the presence of the ethyl radical, and the results were communicated to the Chemical Society in April 1847. Next month the two friends set off on an extended visit to Marburg, where Frankland followed his success with nitriles with an attempt to isolate the ethyl radical by treating its cyanide with potassium. Though unsuccessful in this respect he did obtain evidence of another reaction, leading to kyanethine (a pyrimidine derivative). The three-month stay was also marked by his first acquaintance with Sophie Fick (1821–1874), whom he was later to marry.

This first Marburg period was immediately followed by a spell as teacher of chemistry at Queenwood School, Hampshire, a progressive institution run by the Quaker educationist George Edmondson. After his arrival in September 1847 Frankland soon formed a firm friendship with another teacher, John Tyndall, with whom he taught one of the first laboratory-based science courses in England. To his lectures in elementary chemistry at Queenwood, Frankland added a course for residents of the nearby village of King's Somborne, whose vicar was Richard Dawes, a pioneer in popular science education. Despite a heavy teaching load Frankland managed to find time for further research, again hoping to isolate ethyl. He used potassium to disengage it, not from ethyl cyanide but from ethyl iodide. Deterred by an explosion from using this highly reactive metal he replaced it by zinc, heating the reagents in a sealed tube. As there was no eudiometer in which to examine the gaseous products, he left the tubes unopened. Then, a combination of mismanagement, indiscipline, and lack of resources at the school caused him to resign in October 1848, but not before he and Tyndall had spent a month's holiday in France together, Frankland himself being caught up in the June uprising in Paris.

In October 1848 Frankland, accompanied by Tyndall, made his second journey to Marburg. This time the visit was longer and serious research was commenced at once. After some abortive experiments with chloroform he determined to try the action of sodium on fatty acids, apparently obtaining some radicals as methyl (though in reality their dimers as ethane). Then, in the following February, he opened under water one of the sealed tubes he had brought from Queenwood. The evolution of gas was as spectacular as it was significant. Among the gaseous products was one that seemed to be the long-sought ethyl (actually butane). These and other results were incorporated in the 45-page thesis which he successfully submitted in July 1849 for his degree of PhD.

In his last month at Marburg, Frankland found that, among the tubes brought from Hampshire, a liquid product from the zinc/ethyl iodide reaction contained zinc, and was thus an organic compound containing a metal. He had discovered a new branch of chemistry in which metals are linked to carbon; he called it 'organometallic chemistry', and it has since become a major branch of the science. Following a few months' work in Liebig's laboratory at Giessen, and Christmas at Sophie Fick's home in Kassel, he returned hotfoot to England with the promise of a new job—professor of practical chemistry at Putney.

First professorships Frankland's return to Putney in 1850 enabled him to embark on an ambitious teaching programme, including a comprehensive course on applied chemistry. It also gave him new opportunities for research. Concerned to examine the action of light on the reactions between metals and alkyl halides, he took advantage of a flat place on the roof of his chemistry laboratory on which such experiments could be conducted as daylight increased with the advancing spring. The outcome was the formation of a range of wholly new organometallic compounds (involving zinc, tin, mercury, and so on), thus firmly establishing this new branch of chemistry. Even more important was a deduction he made from the new data. As he contemplated the regularity of their formulae he gradually realized that each element had a limit to the number of radicals that could be attached to it, concluding that each had a definite combining power. From novel and highly obscure compounds he had discovered one of the great principles of all chemistry, which came to be known as valency. Although others, particularly August Kekulé, claimed priority for this discovery, Frankland was certainly the first to articulate the concept of what he called 'combining power'. The results he later communicated to the Royal Society, and they were read to the society's meeting on 10 May 1852. This important paper was subsequently published as 'On a new series of organic bodies containing metal' (*PTRS*, 142, 1852, 417–44).

Frankland remained at Putney for only one year as, on 2 January 1851, he was appointed the first professor of chemistry at the new Owens College, Manchester (later to become Manchester University). Before leaving London

he married Sophie Fick on 7 February 1851 at St Martin-in-the-Fields. They subsequently had three children in Manchester: Margaret (*b.* 1853), Frederick (*b.* 1854), and Sophie (*b.* 1855). His first major task at Owens College was the design of new laboratories, but he maintained his own programme of research into organometallic chemistry. Using the new Mancunian technique of heating under pressure in iron digesters, borrowed from his friend the Manchester industrialist James Nasmyth, he prepared zinc alkyls in large quantities, isolating a few new products. His work in this field was recognized by his election as FRS in 1853 and the award of the Royal Society's royal medal in 1857. He had several able young men to assist his research, including W. J. Russell, Frederick Guthrie, and James Wanklyn.

At the same time Frankland's concentration on a growing number of industrial consultancies, to a degree hitherto unheard of in other universities, helped to establish in Manchester a strong tradition of applied chemistry. He advised industry on an immense range of topics, including the purity of water, new processes for gas making, the design of gas burners, the use of nickel ores (for the duke of Argyll), the purification of spirits, agricultural chemistry, coal analysis, and the manufacture of alkalis among other things. During this period he had his first experience of being an expert witness in litigation about chemical matters, a process with which he was to become increasingly familiar. Despite a heavy teaching load his lectures on chemistry had an unprecedented breadth of coverage; they included elementary chemistry, organic chemistry, and technological chemistry, and laboratory instruction was also included. Fortunately examination papers, syllabi, and even his lecture notes survive.

The early years of Owens College were so clouded by general mismanagement, students of indifferent quality, and falling numbers that in the mid-1850s it nearly closed. Sharing in the general discontent Frankland decided to move, preferably to London, and in July 1857 was appointed lecturer in chemistry at St Bartholomew's Hospital. His place at Manchester was taken by Henry Enfield Roscoe.

London to 1868 The Frankland family settled at Haverstock Hill in north London. A fourth child, Percy Faraday *Frankland, was born in 1858; a fifth child died in infancy. Frankland's post at St Bartholomew's Hospital gave few opportunities for research, though he was able to use the better laboratory facilities at the Royal College of Chemistry in Oxford Street, then headed by A. W. Hofmann. Within two years Frankland obtained an additional post, teaching chemistry at the East India Company's military college at Addiscombe. He remained there until the dissolution of the college in 1861. Following the retirement that year of Michael Faraday, Frankland commenced working for the Royal Institution, at first on a temporary basis and then, holding a tenured post, from May 1863 to November 1868. For part of one year (1861) he thus held three appointments simultaneously. From 1865 to 1868 he also acted as temporary replacement for Hofmann, who was in

Germany on three years' leave from the Royal College of Chemistry.

The first years of Frankland's return to London were marked by a dramatic drop in industrial consultancies, a continuation of heavy teaching commitments, a surge in research output, a new involvement in the scientific societies, and his first major work in water analysis. Industrial research was restricted by the distance from heavy chemical manufacture, though in his early years in London, Frankland did some work on illuminating gases, researched on time-fuses, gun cotton, and other aspects of the explosives industry, and began investigations into atmospheric pollution (including the formation of acid rain). Teaching, meanwhile, at four institutions increased his awareness of the inadequacy of traditional approaches to chemistry that equally ignored its industrial relevance and eschewed modern interpretations (including valency). Again, his surviving lecture notes indicate the new emphases. When, in 1865, he acted as Hofmann's temporary replacement he inherited from the latter an examinership of the papers set by the Department of Science and Art. Rapidly transforming the trends of these papers he introduced modern concepts almost at once, and in 1866 published his *Lecture Notes for Chemical Students*. This influential book expounded the doctrine of valency and also introduced a modern notation representing atoms by their letters and joining them with 'bonds' (a word also introduced in the book). Though originating with Crum Brown the system became known as Frankland's notation. It is in universal use today and constitutes a major contribution to chemical theory and education.

At first Frankland's research was limited to some more work in organometallic chemistry, though when he was joined by B. F. Duppa in 1860 there followed the most sustained research effort he had ever made. A new field of organoboron chemistry, including the intensely reactive trialkylborons, was opened up by allowing zinc alkyls to react with boron trihalides. They (or a mixture of zinc and alkyl halide) were also treated with diethyl oxalate, leading to the formation of new substituted lactic acids. These in turn could be dehydrated to new unsaturated acids. Finally, the work by Frankland and Duppa in acetoacetic ester chemistry led to further discoveries of ketones and acids and to the formulation of the ester in its keto form. By virtue of the many new compounds discovered, the systematic use of familiar reagents in new contexts, and the arguments used to determine constitution, this experimental programme established Frankland as a founder of synthetic organic chemistry.

Frankland's research interests were surprisingly wide. Several projects were initiated by an adventure in mountaineering, a sport of which he was extremely fond. On 20 August 1859 he and Tyndall ascended Mont Blanc, their party being the first to spend a night on its summit. He showed that candles burned at the same rate at that height as in the valley, but gave out less light. This led to a series of investigations on illuminating power in which he differed from the classical explanation by Davy, that luminosity arises from unburned solid particles, and suggested instead that it is because of dense hydrocarbon vapours. Another mountain ascent (though not by himself) was concerned to examine the origins of muscular power and it led Frankland to a study of the energy derived from different kinds of foodstuffs. His research, reported in 1866, was the first quantitative study of food combustion and of what came to be called calorific values. It was also his interest in mountains that prompted him to views on glaciers which, however, soon proved to be incorrect. He assumed they arose from evaporation of ocean water, followed by condensation in the cold upper atmosphere. In 1861 he was experimenting with the spectroscope and, together with Norman Lockyer in 1868, observed a new bright line in the spectrum of a solar prominence. They had discovered helium.

During these years of intense research and teaching Frankland found support within the metropolitan scientific community. He served on the council of the Chemical Society (1858–9), was vice-president in 1860, and foreign secretary from 1861. He was also a member of the Royal Society's council in the periods 1857–9 and 1865–7. In 1859 he delivered the society's Bakerian lecture. From its formation in 1864 he became one of the nine members of the X-Club, an informal but exclusive pressure group centred on T. H. Huxley, that was concerned with the interests of its members, the advancement of British science, and the promotion of scientific naturalism. The club embodied a religious scepticism that was characteristic of Frankland's own public stance, though private papers suggest this was exaggerated. He certainly passed from Anglicanism through Congregationalism to Unitarianism in his formal allegiances.

A momentous event in Frankland's life occurred when, on joining the Royal College of Chemistry, he found himself also the heir to Hofmann's post as analyst for the London water supply. Confronted with an endemic problem of water-borne disease, yet without the later knowledge of pathogenic micro-organisms, he urgently sought for chemical means of detecting noxious impurities in water. Within months he had developed a new method of analysis for carbon and nitrogen content with assistance from H. E. Armstrong, and in 1867 he advanced the contentious suggestion that previous sewage contamination (and therefore unsuitability for domestic use) could be detected by measuring the nitrate concentration.

The Royal College of Chemistry, 1868–1885 In 1868 Frankland's temporary appointment at the Royal College of Chemistry was transformed into a permanent post, Hofmann having at last decided to remain in Germany. Within the year Frankland also resigned from his professorship at the Royal Institution and foreign secretaryship at the Chemical Society. By the end of 1871 the college had relocated at South Kensington and the Frankland family had also moved to nearby Lancaster Gate. Here Sophie Frankland's health seriously deteriorated—she was suffering from tuberculosis—and she was sent to Davos in Switzerland for convalescence, but she died there in 1874. The next year, on 11 May, Frankland married his second wife, Ellen Frances Grenside (1848–1899) of Wimbledon. Two daughters were born of this marriage.

From now on research had to take second place to teaching, though the 1870s saw Frankland's last researches on both acetoacetic ester and organoboron compounds, together with some measurements of solar intensity. The completion of his research career was signalled in 1877 by publication of his *Experimental Researches*, a huge volume of collected papers, heavily edited to conform to the conventions of the time, yet an impressive monument to the research output of one man. Within a year of his appointment to the college he was calling for laboratory training to be part of the Department of Science and Art chemical courses. Since most teachers were without training in laboratory skills he began, in 1869, courses of practical laboratory instruction for any teachers who cared to come. His methods were summarized in a short book *How to Teach Chemistry* (1875), containing details of 109 lecture experiments. Meanwhile he had published a second edition of his *Lecture Notes* (1870–72); a third edition followed in 1881.

There was one exception to Frankland's retirement from academic research. That was in the field of water quality. Between 1868 and 1876 he published papers on analyses of gases formed in water analysis, on river pollution by sewage, on fungi in potable water, on the purification of sewage and of foul water from both factories and mines, on the softening of hard water, and on analysis of potable waters. Relentlessly pursuing the quest for safe drinking-water he led the campaign against supplies that failed to meet his standards, thereby making enemies of several chemists representing the water companies. He became a world leader in this field, and analysed waters from far and near. So demanding was his consultancy practice that students and college authorities remarked on his frequent absence. In 1882 he set up his own laboratory at Grove House, for a time in collaboration with his son Percy.

During the 1870s Frankland's rising profile in the scientific community led to his return to the council of the Royal Society (1875–7) and to his appointment as vice-president (1868–70) and president (1871–2) of the Chemical Society. His concern to raise both the status of the chemist in society and standards of chemical practice led him to embark on a crusade for professionalization of chemistry. This led directly, in 1877, to creation of the Institute of Chemistry, the world's first professional organization for scientists. He became its first president and was thereafter tireless in activity on its behalf.

Closing years In 1885 Frankland took early retirement at the age of sixty, being unwilling to bear official criticism for his lucrative preoccupations with water analysis. By now he had moved his home to The Yews, a large house on Reigate Hill and the first one he had owned. Here he established his private laboratory and, aided by several assistants, continued to undertake water analyses from all over the world. He carried out some research on electric storage batteries, and was increasingly involved in litigation on behalf of industrial firms. A fourth term of membership of the Royal Society council (1886–8) was followed by the award of its prestigious Copley medal in 1894 and in the following year by appointment as its foreign secretary (which post he held for the rest of his life). He maintained his membership of the X-Club until it finally disintegrated in 1892. In 1887 he was made a JP for Reigate, and in the jubilee honours of 1897 was made KCB. He also held honorary doctorates from Oxford and Edinburgh and honorary memberships of over a dozen scientific societies, most of them overseas.

From about 1888 Frankland's home life was marred by a quarrel with his son Percy, then professor of chemistry at Dundee. This began with a dispute about payment for water analyses and continued, with mutual recrimination, for ten years. Then, in January 1899, his second wife, Ellen, died and the breach with Percy was healed. In July he started a holiday in Norway, a favourite place for vacations. Accompanied by his secretary, Jane Lund, he continued the practice of the previous year or two by spending the mornings dictating the notes of his autobiography. Shortly afterwards he was taken ill with severe pains in the neck, became delirious, and died on 9 August 1899 at Golaa Gudbrandsdal, Norway, before any of the family could reach him. He was buried at Reigate churchyard on 22 August.

Edward Frankland was tall (5 ft 10¾ in.), and had weak eyesight and a tendency to dyspepsia but otherwise he enjoyed good health, enabling him to walk long distances for almost all his life. His chemical achievements are startlingly diverse. His foundation of organometallic chemistry, discovery of the phenomenon of valency, recognition of the chemical 'bond', and pioneering work in organic synthesis put him at the forefront of theoretical chemists of any country. As a scientific educator he was instrumental in facilitating practical classes, teacher training, and (by means of his books and examinerships) the widespread use of modern symbols. As founding president of the Institute of Chemistry he played a leading role in the professionalization of science. By more than three decades of work in water analysis he ensured much safer drinking-water for urban populations, thus helping to prevent a pandemic of water-borne disease. He was for many the leading British chemist of the nineteenth century.   COLIN A. RUSSELL

Sources E. Frankland, *Sketches from the life of Edward Frankland*, ed. M. N. W. and S. J. C. (privately printed, London, 1902) · C. A. Russell, *Lancastrian chemist: the early years of Sir Edward Frankland* (1986) · C. A. Russell, *Sir Edward Frankland: chemistry, controversy and conspiracy in Victorian England* (1996) · H. McLeod, 'Edward Frankland', *JCS*, 87 (1905), 574–90 · H. E. Armstrong, 'First Frankland memorial oration of the Lancastrian Frankland Society', *Chemistry and Industry* (25 May 1934), 459–66 · *The Times* (14 Aug 1899) · *Chemist and Druggist* (19 Aug 1899) · *PICE*, 139 (1899–1900), 343–9 · *Chemical News* (18 Aug 1899) · *Nature*, 60 (1899), 372 · *Memoirs of the Literary and Philosophical Society of Manchester*, 44 (1899–1900), xxxviii–xlii · C. A. Russell, *The history of valency* (1971) · C. A. Russell, 'Edward Frankland—the first president', *Chemistry in Britain*, 13 (1977), 4–7, 20 · CGPLA Eng. & Wales (1899)

Archives Linn. Soc., botanical papers · Open University, Milton Keynes, MSS · priv. coll., corresp. and papers · Royal Institution of

Great Britain, London, letters · RS, diary and lecture notes · U. Lpool, letters | CUL, letters to Sir George Stokes · CUL, Darwin MSS · Deutsches Museum von Meisterwerken der Naturwissenschaft und Technik, Munich, letters to H. Kolbe, etc. · ICL, H. E. Armstrong MSS · ICL, corresp. with Thomas Huxley · University of Exeter Library, letters to Sir Norman Lockyer **Likenesses** photograph, *c.*1870, RS · J. Adams-Acton, plaster medallion, NPG · Lock & Whitfield, woodburytype photograph, NPG; repro. in T. Cooper, *Men of mark: a gallery of contemporary portraits* (1880) [*see illus.*] · Maull & Polyblank, photograph, RS · photographs, Royal Society of Chemistry, London · photographs, priv. coll. · photographs, Royal Institution of Great Britain, London **Wealth at death** £138,627 3*s.* 11*d.*: probate, 27 Sept 1899, *CGPLA Eng. & Wales*

Frankland [*née* Toynbee], **Grace Coleridge** (1858–1946), bacteriologist, was born on 4 December 1858 at Beech Holme, Wimbledon, Surrey, the youngest daughter and ninth child of Joseph *Toynbee (1815–1866), a celebrated aural surgeon, and his wife, Harriet, daughter of Nathaniel Reynolds Holmes. Little is known about her early life except that she was educated at home, in Germany, and for one year at Bedford College, London. Her scientific predilections seem to have developed seriously after her marriage on 17 June 1882 to Percy Faraday *Frankland (1858–1946), second son of Sir Edward *Frankland; a chemistry lecturer (later professor), he shared her special interest in bacteriological problems, particularly where these impinged upon matters concerning public health.

Grace was one of the British women scientists who made notable contributions to research in the medical sciences during the late nineteenth century, a time when opportunities for women to study science were limited. She achieved success for her independent contributions as well as her collaborative work. Her first publication, in 1887, was a study of micro-organisms in air, and was the outcome of work she and her husband undertook. This was followed in 1888 by their joint studies of micro-organisms in water and soil. Other joint papers published in British scientific journals in 1889 and 1890 included a study of nitrification, of the chemical reactions which occurred in fermentation processes, and of the possibility of using fermentation processes to prepare chemically pure substances. A bacteriological appendix which she compiled appeared in another joint publication on sugar fermentation in 1892. She was also co-author of two volumes, *Micro Organisms in Water: their Significance, Identification and Removal* (1894) and the biography *Pasteur* (1898). Percy Frankland was magnanimous in his praise of his wife, dedicating his book *Our Secret Friends and Foes* (1882) to 'the companion whose sympathy and invaluable assistance have so greatly enhanced the enjoyment of scientific work' (*JCS*, 1998).

Independently, Grace Frankland was probably best-known for her monograph *Bacteria in Daily Life* (1903). She was also a regular contributor of original research papers to a number of journals, especially *Nature*; the subjects covered included typhoid fever epidemics in America, bacteria and carbonated waters, and Dr Yersin and the plague virus. Elected a fellow of the Royal Microscopical

Society in 1900, and one of the first twelve women scientists admitted to the Linnean Society of London, in December 1904, her petition for entry into the Chemical Society in October 1904 was unsuccessful.

Grace and Percy Frankland had one son, Edward Percy; they were a popular couple whose home, which exuded a heady atmosphere of scientific adventure, was always open to visitors. They moved to Loch Awe in Argyll after Percy retired in 1919, and spent much of their time enjoying music, gardening, and travelling. Grace Frankland died at Loch Awe on 5 October 1946, a victim of senility, and was buried in the churchyard of Glenorchy, Argyll. Her husband died three weeks later.

SUSAN L. COHEN

Sources M. R. S. Creese, *Ladies in the laboratory? American and British women in science, 1800–1900* (1998), 150–51 · W. E. Gather, *JCS* (1948), 1996–2000 [obit. of Percy Faraday Frankland] · W. E. Gather, *Obits. FRS*, 5 (1945–8), 697–715 [obit. of Percy Faraday Frankland] · P. Phillips, *The scientific lady: a social history of women's scientific interests, 1520–1918* (1990) · minutes, Chemical Society, London, 21 Oct 1904 · A. T. Gage, *A history of the Linnean Society of London* (1938) · M. Rayner-Canham and G. Rayner-Canham, *Women in chemistry: their changing roles from alchemical times to the mid-twentieth century* (1998) · Royal Holloway College, Egham, Surrey, Bedford College archives · b. cert. · m. cert. · d. cert. · WW **Likenesses** Maull & Fox, cabinet print, Linn. Soc. **Wealth at death** £1250 19*s.* 5*d.*: confirmation, 24 April 1947, *CCI*

Frankland [*née* Trappes; *other married name* Saxey], **Joyce** (1531–1587), educational benefactor, was the daughter of Robert Trappes, a London goldsmith who came from a Lancashire family, and his wife, Joan. Robert Trappes may have bought property in Surrey, for at Banstead in that county on 15 August 1549 Joyce married her first husband, Henry Saxey, a clothworker and citizen of London. The couple raised a son, William, almost certainly the William Saxse admitted to Gray's Inn on 21 November 1576. By this date, Henry Saxey had died, and Joyce's second husband, William Frankland, also a clothworker, was near his life's end. In his will, proved in 1577, William Frankland left to his wife a jointure of the manor of Thele, Stanstead St Margaret's, and rights also to Rye House (scene of the famous plot), in Stanstead Abbots, both in Hertfordshire. Having lost two husbands, it was now Joyce Frankland's lot to lose her only son. In 1581, on a journey from Rye House to London, William Saxey was thrown by his horse; on 22 August he died from his injuries.

Alexander Nowell, dean of St Paul's, recalled the impact of the tragedy:

> The mother fell into sorrows uncomfortable, whereof I, being of her acquaintance, having intelligence, did with all speed ride to her house near Hoddesdon to comfort her the best I could, and I found her crying, or rather howling, continually 'Oh my son, my son!'. And when I could by no comfortable words stay her from that cry and tearing of her hair, God I think, put me in mind at the last to say 'Comfort yourself good Mrs Frankland, and I will tell you how you shall have 20 good sons to comfort you in these your sorrows … if you would found certain fellowships and scholarships to be bestowed upon studious young men, who should be called Mrs Frankland's scholars, they would be in love towards you as dear children … and they and their

successors after them, being still Mrs Frankland's scholars, will honour your memory for ever and ever'.   (Venn, 3.229)

It might be wondered whether Nowell's speech was inspired by the spirit of divinity or of opportunism, but it appears to have affected Joyce Frankland most profoundly.

Henry Saxey and William Frankland were both London tradesmen, but at least one of them must have acquired, and settled upon Joyce, very substantial property, mainly outside London. She now set out to use her considerable wealth in the cause which Nowell had advocated. Her mother's example may also have persuaded her to this course; in 1568 Joan Trappes had founded four scholarships at Lincoln College, Oxford, and Joyce contributed to their augmentation. More substantial were the lectureships, fellowships, and scholarships of her own endowment, including a lectureship in Hebrew at Gonville and Caius College, Cambridge, founded in 1585.

Joyce Frankland died in 1587 at Aldermanbury in London and was buried at the church of St Leonard, Foster Lane. Gonville and Caius was one of the chief beneficiaries of her will, dated 20 February 1587: endowments to the value of more than £2000 provided for the founding of a chaplaincy there and for 'six fellowships, to be called my fellows and William Saxies'. She contributed also £400 to Emmanuel College, Cambridge, for the endowment of fellowships and scholarships. To Brasenose College, Oxford, she left substantial property in Kensington, Suffolk, Berkshire, and Kent, amounting to £1840 in capital value, together with much valuable plate. Her bequests provided generously for the college table, for the foundation of four new scholarships, and for increases in the stipends of the Bible clerk and the under-reader of the logic lecture. It had been reported to Joyce Frankland by Jeffrey Nightingale of Gray's Inn and Newport, Essex, that the place of his origin, 'a great and poor town', lacked a school. Although never visiting Newport, she assigned properties valued at £470 to remedy the deficiency, stipulating that the appointment of masters was to be controlled by Gonville and Caius College. The school was established in the upper part of a building donated in 1554 by Robert Driver for use as a guildhall.

It has been estimated that the educational benefactions of Joyce Frankland, during her lifetime and in her will, totalled £4840, a huge sum in the 1580s. There are portraits of Joyce and both her parents in the combination room of Gonville and Caius, and two more of herself at Brasenose College. The image in the hall of Brasenose depicts her with a ruff, a jewelled cross, and an open watch; the date 1586 is inscribed above a shield bearing the motto 'Suffer and Serve'; a Latin inscription appears at the right hand corner. This portrait was engraved and appears in Churton's *Life of Alexander Nowell* of 1809.

STEPHEN WRIGHT

Sources J. Venn and others, eds., *Biographical history of Gonville and Caius College*, 1: 1349–1713 (1897) • *Brasenose College quatercentenary monographs*, 1, OHS, 52 (1909), monographs iv–vii; 2/1, OHS, 53 (1909), monographs ix–xi • W. K. Jordan, *The charities of London, 1480–1660: the aspirations and achievements of the urban society* (1960) • R. Churton, *The life of Alexander Nowell, dean of St Paul's* (1809) • A. Wood, *The history and antiquities of the colleges and halls in the University of Oxford*, ed. J. Gutch (1786) • R. Clutterbuck, ed., *The history and antiquities of the county of Hertford*, 3 vols. (1815–27) • J. E. Cussans, *History of Hertfordshire*, 2/2 (1874) • J. Foster, *The register of admissions to Gray's Inn, 1521–1889, together with the register of marriages in Gray's Inn chapel, 1695–1754* (privately printed, London, 1889) • *VCH Hertfordshire*, vol. 3 • *VCH Essex*, vol. 2 • will, PRO, PROB 11/70, sig. 17 • will, PRO, PROB 11/77, sig. 7 • F. Lambert, *Registers of Banstead, Surrey*, Parish Register Society, 1 (1896) • *DNB*

Likenesses oils, 1586, Gon. & Caius Cam.; version, Brasenose College, Oxford • portrait, Brasenose College, Oxford; repro. in Churton, *Life of Alexander Nowell*

Wealth at death est. at over £4000: Jordan, *The charities of London*, 402

Frankland, Percy Faraday (1858–1946), chemist, was born at 42 Park Road, Haverstock Hill, Hampstead, on 3 October 1858, the second son and fourth child of Sir Edward *Frankland (1825–1899) and his first wife, Sophie Fick (1821–1874). His father's fundamental contributions to chemistry established his reputation as one of the leading scientists of the nineteenth century and brought him high office in the Chemical and Royal societies. As a result, the young Frankland was given the opportunity of meeting many of the famous scientific personalities of the day.

Frankland was educated at University College School and in 1875 became a student in the Royal School of Mines. His choice of a career would have been medicine and he secured a Brackenbury scholarship at St Bartholomew's Hospital but he was overruled by his father who persuaded him to embark on the study of chemistry. He spent two years at the University of Würzburg on organic chemistry research under the influence of Wislicenus and took his PhD on diazo-coupling of naphthalene derivatives with salicylic acid. On his return to England in 1880 he was appointed a demonstrator at South Kensington under his father, with whom he made investigations on water analysis, and he graduated BSc at London University in 1881. He also carried out independent bacteriological researches in his private laboratory. On 17 June 1882 he married Grace Coleridge (1858–1946) [see Frankland, Grace Coleridge], youngest daughter of Joseph *Toynbee, the celebrated ear specialist.

In 1888 Frankland left London to become professor of chemistry at University College, Dundee, where he continued his work on bacteriology and started research on stereochemistry, which was ultimately to form his main scientific interest. In his investigations on the culture of bacilli he was much helped by his wife, and they published jointly a volume, *Micro-Organisms in Water*, in 1894 and a life of Pasteur in 1898. Frankland also published *Our Secret Friends and Foes* (1893), an early popular introduction to germ theory. His researches on the chemical reactions occurring during fermentation and on the chemistry of optically active compounds were recognized by his election as FRS in 1891.

In 1894 Frankland became professor of chemistry at Mason College, later the University of Birmingham. Over the years he developed a very strong school of chemistry.

As dean of the faculty of science from 1913, his considerable organizing abilities were soon to be put severely to the test. During the difficult wartime years the new university buildings at Edgbaston, including the chemistry laboratories, were commandeered as a military hospital and work had to revert to the unsuitable accommodation previously occupied in Edmund Street. Despite these difficulties, between 1914 and 1918 he carried out research on synthetic drugs, on explosives intermediates, and on mustard gas, and he was responsible with W. J. Pope for the adoption of Guthrie's method for the manufacture of mustard gas. He was a member of the Admiralty inventions board and of missions sent to France and Italy.

Frankland's early bacteriological investigations and those on the purification of water were of great practical importance. In conjunction with his father's chemical approach to the problem they helped to ensure that public water supplies were free from noxious pollutants. He discovered new bacteria and studied the variation in their activity on changing the media in which they grew. He was the first after Pasteur to isolate pure, optically active compounds from processes of fermentation. The isolation of these substances led naturally to his stereochemical researches.

Before he left Dundee, Frankland had commenced his studies on the optical rotations of fairly simple compounds, such as glyceric acid. He proceeded to examine the effects on optical rotation of different substituents attached to an asymmetric centre. At that time one of the most mysterious phenomena of organic chemistry was the sequence of changes known as the Walden inversion, which raised acute problems about the steric configurations of quite simple molecules. To this Frankland gave much attention in his Birmingham years. It was perhaps his misfortune to have selected a number of research topics to which he doggedly adhered yet for which the techniques and instrumentation then available were quite inadequate. He himself believed that although these researches did not lead to comprehensive generalizations, they revealed a number of interesting regularities; these regularities have since secured an important place in the framework of structural organic chemistry.

Like his father, Percy Frankland became president of both the Chemical Society (1911–13) and the [Royal] Institute of Chemistry (1906–9). In the latter capacity he materially helped to further the profession of chemistry and to enhance its place in national life. His particular strength was in emphasizing the importance of the institute's examinations. He tirelessly pressed the case for their wider recognition, setting up a permanent board of examiners to maintain standards of excellence. As early as 1899 he had successfully proposed an examination in biological chemistry and he served as censor of the institute from 1906 to 1921.

In 1919 Frankland was made an officer of the order of SS. Maurizio e Lazzaro of Italy and the following year he was appointed CBE. He received honorary doctorates from the universities of St Andrews (LLD, 1902), Dublin (ScD, 1912), Birmingham (LLD, 1924), and Sheffield (DSc, 1926), and was awarded the Davy medal of the Royal Society in 1919.

Frankland was fond of wild country and spent his vacations on his sheep farm at Ravenstonedale in Westmorland and in travelling throughout Europe. He retired in 1919 to the House of Letterawe on Loch Awe, where he spent twenty-seven leisured years—with boating and other cultural pursuits occupying much of his time. He remained there until his death on 28 October 1946, a few weeks after that of his wife. He was buried at Glenorchy. There was one son of the marriage, Edward (1884–1958), who abandoned a chemical career owing to ill health and devoted himself to his property in Westmorland and Yorkshire, and to the writing of novels.

Frankland was keenly interested in antiquities, history, and music, but did not appreciate modern music and art. Sir D'Arcy Thompson said of him that he was 'a man of singularly high principle, of unusual integrity and simple goodness'. Under a superficial irascibility there lay a kindly disposition, a keen interest in his students, and an eagerness to combat injustice of any kind. He was considered by those who knew him in Dundee and in Birmingham to be one of the great teachers of his time. He expected a very high standard of teaching from his staff, and he was very critical of carelessness of experiment, speech, or thought in his students.

Certain temperamental difficulties may have contributed to an estrangement from his father that apparently began with a dispute about water analysis fees in the late 1880s. The relationship was a complex one, and neither side appears blameless. There was probably an element of resentment at the dominating influence of Edward Frankland and there were strong differences of opinion as to the relative merits of chemical and biological analysis. Ultimately, however, the issue appears to have been financial. The rift was healed in 1899, after the death of Edward Frankland's second wife and only a few months before Edward himself died. But of the strength and influence of the scientific tradition that Percy Frankland had inherited, symbolized by his second forename, there can be no doubt. W. E. GARNER, rev. COLIN A. RUSSELL

Sources W. E. Garner, *Obits. FRS*, 5 (1945–8), 697–715 · C. A. Russell, 'Percy Frankland: the iron gate of examination', *Chemistry in Britain*, 13 (1977), 425–7 · L. H. Lampitt, *First P. F. Frankland memorial lecture* (1949) · C. A. Russell, *Edward Frankland: chemistry, controversy and conspiracy in Victorian England* (1996) · d. cert. · E. Frankland, *Sketches from the life of Edward Frankland*, ed. M. N. W. and S. J. C. (privately printed, London, 1902)

Archives priv. coll. | priv. coll., Edward Frankland MSS [on microfilm at Open University]

Likenesses B. Munns, portrait, 1919, U. Birm. · cartoon, repro. in *The Mermaid* [Birmingham University], 1/1 (1904) · photographs, Royal Society of Chemistry Library, London · photographs, Edward Frankland Archives

Wealth at death £23,914 11s. 4d.: confirmation, 24 April 1947, *CCI*

Frankland, Richard (1630–1698), nonconformist tutor, was born on 1 November 1630, at Rathmell, Giggleswick,

Richard Frankland (1630–1698), by unknown artist

Yorkshire, the son of John Frankland (*d.* before 1650). Between 1642 and 1648 he was educated at Giggleswick grammar school, before being admitted on 18 May 1648 at Christ's College, Cambridge. He took his BA in 1652 and proceeded MA in 1655. Meanwhile, he had begun to preach at Hexham in Northumberland, and then at Houghton-le-Spring and Lanchester. He was ordained by presbyters at St Nicholas's, Durham, on 14 September 1653. About 1655 he left Lanchester and became chaplain to John Brook at Ellenthorp Hall, near Boroughbridge in Yorkshire. He then became curate at Sedgefield in co. Durham. Oliver Cromwell's plans for a college in Durham included a post for Frankland, but the patent for establishing the college, issued in May 1657, was never put into effect.

On 11 October 1658 Frankland married Elizabeth (1627–1706), daughter of Samuel Sanderson of Hedley Hope, co. Durham, and his wife, Barbara Liddell. They had three sons and four daughters. At some point before August 1659 Frankland was presented to the living of St Andrew's, Bishop Auckland, by its patron Sir Arthur Hesilrige. Following the Restoration a local attorney named Bowster demanded of him 'publicly before the congregation' (*DNB*) whether he intended to conform. Frankland responded that he would take this decision when the terms of conformity were settled and that meanwhile the king had dispensed with conformity in his declaration of 25 October 1660. Bowster and a neighbouring clergyman then obtained the keys to the church and locked Frankland out. Frankland turned to the law for redress, having the perpetrators indicted for riot at the quarter sessions. The defendants had the case moved up to the assizes where it was dismissed on a technicality, there being a flaw in the indictment. Bishop Cosin offered to institute him at

Bishop Auckland if he would receive episcopal ordination, but Frankland was unwilling to renounce his ordination by presbyters or to receive an episcopal ordination in private.

Following his ejection Frankland returned to Rathmell, where his daughter Barbara was buried in August 1662 and other children were baptized in 1664, 1666, and 1668. He lived modestly, his house being rated for two hearths in the 1665–6 hearth tax returns. By 1672–3 it had increased to three hearths. It may be from this period that the story dates of Frankland's going to London and using his contacts with the old presbyterian lord chamberlain, the earl of Manchester (*d.* 1671), to meet and chastise the king 'to reform your life, your family, your kingdom, and the church', to which a somewhat startled monarch replied 'I will do what I can', before saying 'I thank you sir', and retreating into the council chamber (BL, Add. MS 4460, fol. 49).

Frankland opened his first dissenting academy at Rathmell on 8 March 1670. It taught 'logic, metaphysics, somatology, pneumatology, natural philosophy, divinity and chronology' (*DNB*). Morning prayers were at seven, lectures finished by noon, private study continued until prayers at six. Under the declaration of indulgence he was licensed to preach at Rathmell on 22 July 1672. Between February and May 1674 he moved to Natland, near Kendal, where he continued to teach until the middle of 1683. During this time Frankland assisted at the first nonconformist ordination in Yorkshire on 10 July 1678. The increasing persecution of nonconformists brought problems and in March 1681 Oliver Heywood recorded that Frankland had been excommunicated in the ecclesiastical court, although he later received absolution. Natland's proximity to Kendal made Frankland's academy vulnerable under the Five Mile Act, and by 20 June 1683 he had moved his school to Calton Hall in Kirkby Malham, the seat of the Lambert family, 7 miles from Skipton. Late in 1683 he moved again, to Dawson Fold, Crosthwaite, near Kendal, which he left in September 1684 for Hartborough, near Cartmel in Lancashire. Hartborough had the advantage of being on the Lancashire–Cumberland border and hence it was easier to avoid a writ issued in either county by simply crossing into the other.

By 8 November 1686 Frankland had moved to Attercliffe, near Sheffield, taking advantage of James II's religious policy of toleration and obtaining a dispensation at a cost of 50s. Following the revolution of 1688 Frankland registered Rathmell as a meeting-house on 8 October 1689. However, while the Toleration Act protected him as a minister, it did not prevent attacks upon his dissenting academy. The authorities were particularly agitated by his continued training of students for the ministry, for which he received grants from the Presbyterian Fund from 1690. On 2 February 1691 Frankland was excommunicated for not appearing before the chancellor of the archbishop's court in York in answer to a citation of May 1690. With the support of Philip, Baron Wharton, and Sir Thomas Rokeby, a judge in the court of common pleas, who approached the secretary of state, Viscount Sydney,

Frankland was able to get the sentence reversed. The absolution was publicly read in Giggleswick church. Frankland was one of the Yorkshire nonconformist clergymen who met at Wakefield on 2 September 1691 to consider the 'heads of agreement' sent from London to promote union between presbyterians and Independents. Attempts to suppress the academy by the clergy in Craven in 1692 through a petition to the new archbishop of York, John Sharp, were unsuccessful. Sharp asked Archbishop Tillotson for guidance but in the end seems not to have made use of his advice not to mention nonconformity but instead explain the objections to licensing the academy on the grounds that there was already a school in the parish and that Frankland was breaking his university oath by teaching outside the universities. A meeting between Sharp and Frankland followed at which Frankland was shown the petition against him, but Sharp did not greatly pursue it and seemed more interested in the deficiencies of the local clergy, which Frankland was only too happy to discuss. Frankland also faced prosecution in London, but this was quashed on 14 February 1695.

In 1697 Frankland published his only work, *Reflections on a letter writ by a nameless author to the reverend clergy of both universities*. Frankland was increasingly subject to ill health, writing on 25 October 1697 that he was 'afflicted with gravel and wind' (Nicholson and Axon, 188–9). He died 'of the stranguary, or a universal decay' (ibid., 189) on 1 October 1698, and was buried on the 5th in Giggleswick church. He was survived by his wife and three of his daughters. His will of 27 September 1698 gave his wife £30 per annum and made his three daughters his executors, with four 'yeomen' as overseers. One of his daughters died in 1700, followed by his wife in 1706. The other daughters, Elizabeth (1664–1739) and Margaret (1672–1718) married one Hill and Samuel Smith, respectively.

STUART HANDLEY

Sources Venn, *Alum. Cant.* · *Calamy rev.*, 211–12 · F. Nicholson and E. Axon, *The older nonconformity in Kendal* (1915), 113–98 · I. Parker, *Dissenting academies in England* (1914), 64–8 · A. Gordon, ed., *Freedom after ejection: a review (1690–1692) of presbyterian and congregational nonconformity in England and Wales* (1917), 267–8 · *The Rev. Oliver Heywood … his autobiography, diaries, anecdote and event books*, ed. J. H. Turner, 4 vols. (1881–5) · [J. Hunter], ed., *Letters of eminent men, addressed to Ralph Thoresby*, 1 (1832), 171–5 · *IGI* · G. F. Nuttall, 'Assembly and association in dissent, 1689–1831', *Councils and assemblies*, ed. G. J. Cuming and D. Baker, SCH, 7 (1971), 301 · *DNB*

Likenesses oils, DWL [*see illus.*]

Frankland, Thomas (1632/3–1690), impostor and antiquary, was born in Lancashire; his parents' names are not known. He matriculated from Brasenose College, Oxford, in June 1649, aged sixteen, and graduated BA in February 1653. He was elected a fellow of Brasenose in 1654 and proceeded MA in 1655. The next year he was incorporated MA at Cambridge, but remained at Brasenose, where he was junior bursar in 1657–8, and in the university was elected senior proctor in 1662 when the sequence of office between colleges broken during the interregnum was restored. He proceeded BD the following year after initially having three graces, preliminary to receiving his degree, refused, and apparently finally being granted it only because he had taken holy orders. He turned his studies to medicine and went on to hold further college posts—senior bursar in 1664–5 and vice-principal in 1667–8. But on 8 March 1668 he resigned his fellowship and shortly afterwards, having renounced holy orders, he went to London to practise medicine. He married and settled in the parish of St Vedast, Foster Lane, where he buried his first wife, Mary, on 19 April 1670. Nine months later, on 31 January 1671, he married Ruth Burcher in the Temple Church: four of their children were baptized—and two buried—in St Vedast between January 1672 and August 1676.

In London, Frankland claimed to be an MD of Oxford and Cambridge by turns when challenged by graduates of either university. Frankland applied for membership of the College of Physicians, and in December 1671 was admitted as a candidate on the strength of a certificate of his doctorate which he himself had written and sealed. His professional conduct passed scrutiny well enough for him to be elected a fellow of the college on 29 July 1675, and beyond that to become junior censor. The attainment of office proved fatal to Frankland's ambitions. Anthony Wood described him as 'a proud, haughty man, scornfull and undervaluing', and his manner towards his juniors in the profession proved so oppressive that a group of them instigated an inquiry in Oxford into the authenticity of his degree (*Life and Times*, 2.393). Frankland's riposte that he was a graduate of Cambridge was in turn exposed as a technicality, his doctorate there having been granted *ad eundem* on the strength either of his forged certificate or of mere assertion. Even so his fall from grace was not resounding. The authorities in Oxford merely reported in November 1677 that there was no record of his doctorate, and took no further action; his membership of the college was suspended, but he was not formally expelled until the summer of 1682, by which time he had found other expedients. In the meantime he had been accused of accepting bribes to protect other empirics from the attentions of the college, a delict in which he may not have acted alone. Wood believed that the delay in his ejection was a matter of college politics, which is likely enough. It also reflects some of the perplexities and anomalies in the practice of medicine which persisted for more than another century.

Before his expulsion Frankland had turned to history, and compiled and published *The Annals of King James I and King Charles I*, which appeared anonymously in 1681. It was a work of substantial industry, and as it consists largely of parliamentary reports and public documents might be regarded as looking forward to the archival publications of the eighteenth century. He seems also to have compiled *The honours of the lords spiritual asserted, and their privileges to vote in capital cases in parliament maintained by reason and precedent* (1679). Ten years later he received £800 of secret service money, which was a perilous resource for one of his habits, whether or not he had, as Wood reported, also forged a will. By one route or another he came at last to the Fleet prison, and died there in 1690. He was buried in the old vault of the church of St Vedast, Foster Lane, on 14

April, where the clerk who compiled the parish register, at least, continued to recognize him as 'Doctor in Physicke' (Littledale, 2.236). G. H. MARTIN

Sources DNB · Foster, *Alum. Oxon.* · Wood, *Ath. Oxon.*, new edn, 4.289–90 · *The life and times of Anthony Wood*, ed. A. Clark, 1–2, OHS, 19, 21 (1891–2) · Munk, *Roll* · W. A. Littledale, ed., *The registers of St Vedast, Foster Lane, and of St Michael le Quern, London*, 2, Harleian Society, register section, 30 (1903), 236 · [C. B. Heberden], ed., *Brasenose College register, 1509–1909*, 2 vols., OHS, 55 (1909), 186 · IGI · receipt book for payments out of secret service money for William III, 1689–90, Bodl. Oxf., MS Rawl. A. 306

Frankland, Sir Thomas, fifth baronet (1718–1784), naval officer and politician, was born on 26 June 1718 'in the East Indies', presumably India (PRO, ADM 107/3, p. vii). He was the second son of Henry Frankland (*d.* 1738) of Mattersey, Nottinghamshire, and Mary (*d.* 1783), daughter of Alexander Cross, merchant. His father, the fourth son of the second baronet Sir Thomas Frankland of Thirkleby, was a servant of the East India Company, and became governor of Bengal, where he died on 23 August 1738. Possibly influenced by his uncle's appointment to the Board of Admiralty in 1730, the younger Thomas entered the navy on 11 May 1731 as a volunteer per order in the *York* (Captain Philip Vanbrugh), and he later spent three-and-a-half years in the *Scarborough* (Captain Thomas Durell) in the West Indies and North America and then over a year in the *Oxford*. He passed for lieutenant on 3 November 1737 and on 23 February 1738 was appointed to the *Chatham*, again with Captain Philip Vanbrugh, in home waters, and then in March 1740 briefly to the *Cumberland*, before his promotion to captain on 15 July 1740 in the *Rose*.

Frankland took Governor Tinker to the Bahamas and remained on that station until 1746. During that period he was able to make a number of prizes, some being privateers or Spanish *guarda-costas*, including one commanded by the man who is alleged to have cut off Robert Jenkins's ear, Juan de Leon Fandino, who in June 1742 made a resolute defence. One prize, however, had a very rich cargo. Returning home in late 1746 Frankland was appointed to the *Dragon*, again in the West Indies, which he commanded until the peace. On 31 July 1755 he was appointed to command the Leeward Islands station as a commodore, though he was very soon after promoted to flag rank. In the *Winchester* he arrived on his station in October. He attempted with the small means at his disposal to counter the piracy and privateering which was increasing as the threat of war with France approached, and achieved some success. His command was, however, marked by disputes, firstly with his predecessor, Commodore Thomas Pye, who, being junior to Frankland, had committed the mistake of keeping his broad pennant flying in Frankland's presence, and was 'excessively angry' that Frankland would not allow it. He had also, in Frankland's opinion, been guilty, during the time of his command, of several gross irregularities, which Frankland officially reported, and which, on Pye's return to England, were inquired into by a court martial. In this matter Frankland may have been moved by a personal dislike of Pye rather than by zeal for the service. However, while his account may have been rendered more harsh, it is consonant with the general tenor of his service and character. His letters, written in a vigorous but obscure and not overly literate style, give the impression of an able but unpolished and cantankerous personality.

Frankland's determination to maintain his own rights is best illustrated by his reply to an official letter indicating the wish of the first lord of the Admiralty with respect to some patronage which Frankland, after his promotion to the rank of rear-admiral, conceived to belong to himself as commander-in-chief. 'You will please', he wrote to the secretary of the Admiralty on 12 May 1757, 'to acquaint Lord Temple that I have friends of my own to provide for; … it is a privilege I never have or can give up' (PRO, ADM 1/306). Frankland also fell out with the governor of Antigua over the privateer question and with the local naval agent, though these disagreements may have arisen from Frankland's efforts to check abuses, such as those in the naval hospital at Antigua and in the dockyard at English Harbour. However, even before the letter quoted above, on 5 May 1757, the Admiralty had appointed a successor, Commodore John Moore, and Frankland returned to England in October, not to be employed again, though rising in due course to vice-admiral and then admiral. Later the Treasury opened an action against him for money from prizes he had, they believed, wrongfully retained, and eventually he had to return £30,000.

In 1747 Frankland had been returned as member of parliament for the family borough of Thirsk, Yorkshire, which he continued to represent until 1780, when he retired, apparently seeking the governorship of Greenwich Hospital. Having failed in this objective he resumed the seat in 1784. In general, he supported the government, but he later became less reliable, for example, over the Wilkes affair. He spoke occasionally, mostly on naval matters, and deplored an alleged decline in discipline. On 24 May 1743 he had married Sarah (1724–1808), daughter of Joshua Rhett, a justice and sometime acting governor of South Carolina. They had many children—sources disagree between thirteen and nineteen—and those mentioned in his will numbered three sons and six daughters, but some evidently died in infancy, as his heir was his second son. He succeeded to the family baronetcy in 1767 on the death of his elder brother, Sir Charles Henry Frankland, sometime consul-general in Lisbon. It seems probable that he also inherited money and estates from his father and from the baronetcy, to which he clearly added prize money. He held land in Thirkleby and around Thirsk in the North Riding of Yorkshire and had a London house in Old Bond Street, but he sold Mattersey. While he clearly benefited by family interest, Frankland seems to have been a competent officer, but he was apparently too rigid in his relations with others. He died at Bath on 21 November 1784 and was survived by his wife, who died on 20 September 1808. A. W. H. PEARSALL

Sources DNB · R. Pares, *War and trade in the West Indies, 1739–1763* (1936); repr. (1963) · R. Pares, *Colonial blockade and neutral rights, 1739–63* (1938) · J. Charnock, ed., *Biographia navalis*, 5 (1797), 18 · R. Beatson, *Naval and military memoirs of Great Britain*, 3 vols. (1790) ·

GEC, *Baronetage* · M. M. Drummond, 'Frankland, Thomas', HoP, *Commons, 1754–90* · letters, PRO, ADM 1/306 · passing certificate, PRO, ADM 107/3, 316 · muster books, PRO, ADM 36/525 *Chatham*, 3395 *Scarborough*, 4735 *York* · *GM*, 1st ser., 54 (1784), 879 · will, PRO, PROB 11/1124, fols. 164r–166r

Wealth at death property in Yorkshire and London: will, PRO, PROB 11/1124, fols. 164r–166r

Franklin, Benjamin (1706–1790), natural philosopher, writer, and revolutionary politician in America, was born in Boston, Massachusetts, New England, on 6 January 1706 and baptized later that day. His parents were Josiah Franklin (1657–1745), a tallow chandler and soap maker who had emigrated from England in 1683 to practise his puritan faith, and his second wife, Abiah (1667–1752), the daughter of Peter *Folger of Nantucket Island, Massachusetts. Josiah had eighteen children, seven by his first wife and eleven by his second. Benjamin was the ninth child born to Josiah and Abiah.

Early years: Boston, Philadelphia, and London, 1706–1726

Franklin had only two years of formal education. He studied at a traditional grammar school (probably in 1714–15), and at an English school during the following year. He then worked for his father, but disliked the trade. In 1718 his brother James set up a printing shop in Boston. Since Franklin loved to read and write poetry his father apprenticed him to James, and in that year the twelve-year-old Franklin signed a nine-year indenture. After reading everything in his father's small library he borrowed books from his friends. Having purchased an odd volume of *The Spectator*, Franklin taught himself composition by making notes on the essays, then jumbling the notes, and later constructing them in his own words. He compared these with the originals and corrected his.

In 1721 James Franklin started his own newspaper, the *New England Courant*, which became America's first witty, daring, literary, and anti-establishment journal. To Benjamin his brother's printing shop served as a miniature republic of letters where groups of James's friends met daily to discuss the materials they were writing for the *Courant*. Benjamin set the contents in type, printed and delivered the journal to the customers, and heard their comments. At sixteen he emulated his brother's friends and wrote for the paper, in what became the first essay series in American literature, under the pseudonym Silence Dogood:

> But being still a Boy, and suspecting that my Brother would object to printing any Thing of mine in his Paper if he knew it to be mine, I contriv'd to disguise my Hand and writing an anonymous Paper I put it in at Night under the Door of the Printing-House. (*Autobiography*, 17–18)

Between 12 June and 7 July 1722 Benjamin took charge of the *Courant* while his brother served a prison term for suggesting that local officials had deliberately delayed sailing out to resist pirates. After James had further offended the authorities, in January 1723, the Massachusetts general assembly narrowly agreed to prohibit him from publishing the newspaper without prior review. James defied the order, printed the *Courant*, and hid from the authorities between 24 January and 12 February, leaving Benjamin

Benjamin Franklin (1706–1790), by Joseph Siffred Duplessis, 1778

once more in charge. In this capacity the adolescent gave 'our Rulers some Rubs in it' (ibid., 19).

Notwithstanding their professional co-operation the siblings often quarrelled, and James, who 'was otherwise not an ill-natur'd Man', sometimes beat his apprentice. Benjamin ran away and on 25 September 1723 sailed for New York, which had the nearest printing establishment. Failing to find work there he went on to Philadelphia, the only other town in English speaking North America with a printing press, arriving on the morning of 6 October with 1 Dutch dollar and about 20 pence in copper. Franklin then went to work for Samuel Keimer in his recently opened printing shop. Seven months later, befriended by Pennsylvania's governor, William Keith, who promised to give him a contract for the public printing, Benjamin returned to Boston to ask his father for a loan to start a printing shop but was refused. Back in Philadelphia, Keith pledged to lend Franklin the money to buy the press and types but suggested he go first to London to make the purchases and to arrange for supplies from the stationers, booksellers, and printers. At this time Franklin was courting Deborah Read (1705?–1774), his landlady's daughter, and they planned to marry, but her mother insisted they wait until Franklin's return. He sailed for London on 5 November 1724, by chance with Thomas Denham, a Quaker merchant. In London, Franklin learned that Governor Keith had deceived him and had 'no Credit to give' (*Autobiography*, 41). Without money or prospects Franklin found work at Samuel Palmer's London printing shop, 54 Bartholomew Close. There, in February 1725, he set in type the third edition of William Wollaston's *Religion of Nature Delineated*, and wrote an ironic rejoinder, *A Dissertation on Liberty and Necessity, Pleasure and Pain*. With no publisher, no author, and no bookseller indicated, the pamphlet was archetypal clandestine literature. It won him notoriety among London libertines, and the friendship of William Lyons, who had spent six months in gaol for expressing freethinking views in his own book; via Lyons he also met Bernard Mandeville, author of the infamous *Fable of the Bees*, and it is Franklin who provides us with the only description of the author's personality. Later that year Franklin left Palmer's printing house for John Watt's larger printing establishment and in spring 1726 Thomas Denham encouraged Franklin to return with him to Philadelphia and work as his clerk and shopkeeper while learning the mercantile business. Franklin agreed and left England on 23 July 1726.

Printer in Philadelphia, 1726–1748 Franklin attended to Denham's business 'diligently, studied Accounts, and grew in a little Time expert at selling' (*Autobiography*, 52). However, following a severe bout of pleurisy he left Denham (who died in July 1728 after a lingering illness) and returned to work as the manager of Samuel Keimer's printing shop in March 1727. In the following spring he and an associate, Hugh Meredith, borrowed money from Meredith's father to set up their own printing shop and a year later Franklin published his first political pamphlet, *A Modest Inquiry into the Nature and Necessity of a Paper Currency* (1729). Partly because of its influence the Pennsylvania assembly passed a paper currency bill. In autumn 1729 the partners bought the failing *Pennsylvania Gazette* 'for a Trifle' from Samuel Keimer. Franklin immediately revived its fortunes by writing an editorial analysis of the current controversy between Governor William Burnet and the Massachusetts assembly. The paper's circulation was boosted further after October 1735, when he was appointed Philadelphia's postmaster. 'Tho' the Salary was small', the position 'facilitated the Correspondence that improv'd my Newspaper, increas'd the Number demanded, as well as the Advertisements to be inserted, so that it came to afford me a very considerable Income' (ibid., 101).

In August 1725 Franklin's former betrothed, Deborah Read, had married John Rogers. He proved a poor husband who was rumoured to have another wife, and Deborah soon left him to return to live with her mother. Rogers absconded in December 1727. On 1 September 1730 Franklin and Deborah Read Rogers joined together in a common-law marriage, and set up a home with Benjamin's illegitimate son, William *Franklin, who according to his own correspondence was born in 1730 or 1731 but whose ensign commission (June 1746) may suggest a birth date of about 1729; firm details of William's mother are unknown (*Papers*, 3.474n.). In October 1732 Deborah gave birth to a son, Francis Folger Franklin, who died of smallpox aged four. Eleven years after the birth of Francis, Franklin's third and last child, Sarah, was born on 31 August 1743. Deborah was a member of Philadelphia's Anglican Christ Church, where both Francis Folger and Sarah were baptized and where Francis was buried. Franklin subscribed for seats for his family in the church and supported its projects, but never became a member.

Admitted a freemason in January 1731 Franklin was elected grand master on St John's day, 24 June 1734, the first indication of his rise to local prominence. In July 1731 he organized the Library Company of Philadelphia and during the autumn he sponsored Thomas Whitemarsh as his printing partner in Charles Town, South Carolina. By 1732 Franklin had taught himself to read and write German and he subsequently studied French, Spanish, Italian, and Latin, attaining a reading knowledge of them all. Later that year Franklin started his own almanac, *Poor Richard*, to which he contributed and with which he achieved commercial success, selling almost ten thousand copies annually. Even after his retirement from printing in 1748 Franklin supplied the copy for *Poor Richard* until 1757, when he wrote the last almanac, *Poor Richard Improved … 1758*, on his voyage to England. The preface of that work, reprinted under the title *The Way to Wealth* (initially as *Father Abraham's Speech*), became his best-known writing until the posthumous publication of his *Autobiography* (see below). Additional work followed his appointment in October 1736 as clerk of the Pennsylvania assembly. The position allowed him to keep up his interest 'among the Members, which secur'd to me the Business of Printing the Votes, Laws, Paper Money, and other occasional jobs for the Public, that on the whole were very profitable' (*Autobiography*, 100).

In addition to new publishing ventures and political responsibilities Franklin was now also engaged in self-improvement. By 1 July 1733 he had devised a scheme of thirteen useful virtues and a chart listing the violations which he recorded in the second part of the *Autobiography*. Franklin's proposed virtues were intended to correct his particular faults, though he thought the method of attaining the virtues might be useful to others. The morning question on his chart of the day began, 'What Good shall I do this Day' and the evening question was 'What Good have I done to day' (*Autobiography*, 83). Discussing the project in the *Autobiography*, he concluded that though he fell short of the ideal envisioned, 'Yet I was by the Endeavour made a better and a happier man than I otherwise should have been' (ibid., 87).

Self-improvement also coincided with Franklin's growing interest in, and reputation for, scientific enquiry and experimentation. In the edition of the *Pennsylvania Gazette* for February 1735, for example, he publicized the importance of fire-fighting (this followed his proposal for a fire protection society to his Philadelphia debating club, the Junto), and on 7 December 1736 he organized Philadelphia's first fire company. To hinder counterfeiting of paper currency he devised a new printing technique (reproducing images of plant leaves) and used it for the New Jersey paper currency of 1736. On 21 October 1743 Franklin intended to observe an eclipse of the moon but was prevented by bad weather. He found that the eclipse was observed in Boston and that a hurricane, which had passed over Philadelphia on the 21st, had struck there later. That observation led him to speculate that though the hurricane had blown from the north-east the storm itself had moved up from the south. Fascinated by the whirling winds in the great storms he analysed the nature of whirlwinds and waterspouts, correctly theorizing that they had vacuums at their centre, and ingeniously comparing their motion to the circular motion of water draining from a tub. During winter 1740–41 he designed a superior stove and in 1744 he wrote a pamphlet to popularize his invention which conserved wood while proving more efficient: 'My common Room, I know is made twice as warm as it used to be, with a quarter of the Wood I formerly consum'd' (*Papers*, 2.437). The pamphlet was translated into various languages and gave him an international reputation. Though offered a patent on the stove, the practical idealist refused it, saying that since he enjoyed 'great Advantage from the Inventions of Others, we should be glad of an Opportunity to serve others by an Invention of ours' (*Autobiography*, 116).

In 1743 Franklin published *A Proposal for Promoting Useful Knowledge*, the founding document for the precursor of America's first scientific society, the American Philosophical Society. In April 1745 the London merchant Peter Collinson, a member of the Royal Society, sent the Library Company a pamphlet describing the new German investigations in electricity. Franklin and several friends practised the existing experiments with the Leyden jar (an early capacitor) and designed their own tests. On 25 May 1747 Franklin sent Collinson a letter explaining how the capacitor worked. Franklin proved that there were not two kinds of electricity (the current theory) but only one, to which he applied the terms *plus* and *minus*, or *positive* and *negative*. Franklin demonstrated that in electrifying objects nothing new was created or lost, rather that the electricity was rearranged. For the Nobel prize-winning physicist R. A. Millikin, Franklin's law of the conservation of charge was 'the most fundamental thing ever done in the field of electricity' (Millikin, 38).

Finally, these fruitful years also witnessed Franklin's emerging political conscience and spirit of activism. In 1747 French and Spanish privateers attacked ships and settlements in the Delaware River, and the French and Indians assaulted Pennsylvania's frontiers. The authorities were unable to raise a military as the Pennsylvania assembly was controlled by Quakers, many of whom were pacifists. On 17 November 1747 Franklin published a 24-page pamphlet entitled *Plain Truth* in which he outlined the province's defenceless and alarming situation, and urged private citizens to organize themselves as a defensive force if the government would not. On the verso of the title-page he printed America's first political cartoon with the moral that God helps those who help themselves. He proposed a militia association, which proved successful and made him a popular hero, provoking the jealousy of Pennsylvania's main proprietor, Thomas Penn. When King George's War (1740–48) concluded the militia association dissolved.

The retired printer, 1748–1757 On 1 January 1748 Franklin formed a partnership with his journeyman David Hall and retired as a printer, so acquiring more time for electrical experimentation. In April 1749 he theorized that clouds became electrified and that lightning was electrical in nature, and in July of the following year he devised an experiment to test his hypothesis. By this date Franklin had also proposed the idea of lightning rods (March 1750). In London, Franklin's letters on electricity were gathered by the physician John Fothergill and published as *Experiments and Observations on Electricity* in February 1751. The brief book was translated into French, and Franklin's experiment was successfully carried out in France on 10 May 1752. Before learning of the French proof Franklin speculated that he might also be able to test his hypothesis by flying a kite at the approach of a thunder storm, and in June 1752 he tried the experiment. Franklin ran a hemp string from the kite to a Leyden jar, insulating himself with a silk ribbon attached to the string. When the fibres on the string stood out, he knew the experiment had succeeded, thus proving electricity to be a basic element of nature. His work made Franklin the most famous natural philosopher since Isaac Newton: 'The Prometheus of modern times', as Immanuel Kant put it in 1756 (*Papers*, 20.490).

In October 1748 the common council of Philadelphia had chosen Franklin to be a councilman. On 3 June of the following year he was named a justice of the peace for Philadelphia, and in 1751 he was elected to the Pennsylvania assembly. Because Franklin had been the assembly's clerk since 1736 he was intimately familiar with its workings and was immediately assigned to the most important committees. Known as a superior writer he authorized the replies to the governor's messages. His public offices culminated in his being appointed, on 10 August 1753, joint deputy postmaster-general of North America.

In 1749 Franklin projected an academy in Philadelphia, raised funds for it, supervised its construction, and served as its first chairman of the board of trustees. It became the Academy and College of Philadelphia and later the University of Pennsylvania. In 1751 his friend Thomas Bond attempted to raise funds for a hospital in Philadelphia. He enlisted Franklin, who wrote two essays on the subject in the *Pennsylvania Gazette* and raised subscriptions. When these proved insufficient Franklin petitioned the Pennsylvania legislature for funds. The county legislators objected that it would benefit only the city and claimed that even Philadelphians were not really supporting the plan. Franklin then devised the first matching grant. He proposed a bill making the grant conditional: when the hospital's subscribers had raised £2000 then the legislature would add an additional £2000. Subscriptions increased and the Pennsylvania Hospital, America's first, opened on 6 February 1752. Franklin's varied activities brought recognition. In 1753, while journeying through New England on post office business, he received honorary MAs from Harvard (25 July) and Yale (12 September). On 30 November he was awarded the Copley medal of the British Royal Society, at that time the most distinguished prize for scientific achievement in the world. The Royal Society unanimously elected him to membership on 29

April 1756. On another post office tour to Virginia, William and Mary College granted him its first honorary master's degree (20 April 1756) and on 1 September he became a corresponding member of London's Society of Arts.

Among his contemporaries Franklin's scientific achievements eclipsed his literary output. However, by the mid-eighteenth century he had also established an international reputation as a writer. During the 1730s he had written numerous essays, news note jokes, and hoaxes, among them 'A witch trial at Mount Holly' (22 October 1730) which he published in the *Pennsylvania Gazette*. His salacious 'Old mistresses' apologue, or, Reasons for preferring an old mistress to a young one' (25 June 1745) circulated widely in manuscript. 'The speech of Miss Polly Baker, before a court of judicature, at Connecticut in New England, where she was prosecuted the fifth time for having a bastard child' (17 April 1747) created a publishing sensation, appearing in seven English newspapers and the two most popular English magazines within three weeks of its first appearance. Much of his work, like 'The speech of Miss Polly Baker', appeared anonymously or under a pseudonym. Other pieces, such as his grotesque poem, 'An apology for the young man in gaol, and in shackels, for ravishing an old woman of 85 at Whitemarsh, who had only one eye, and that a red one', first appeared in a rival's newspaper, while Franklin's epitaph (1729), his mock biblical parables (1755), and numerous letters, like the one of 6 June 1753 to Joseph Huey on the contest of faith versus good works, circulated privately in manuscript in England and America before being printed.

In addition to belletristic writings Franklin was also increasingly celebrated for the high quality of his pro-American propaganda. The hoax 'Rattlesnakes for felons' (9 May 1751) proposed sending rattlesnakes to Great Britain in return for the transported convicts shipped to America. His essay 'Observations concerning the increase of mankind, peopling of countries, &c.' (1751) was intended as a response to the British Acts of Trade and Navigation. It roused a young John Adams to contemplate the future independence of what became the United States, as well as influencing the theories of Adam Smith on capitalism and Thomas Malthus on population. Alarmed by the French incursions into the Ohio valley and along the Pennsylvania and Virginia frontiers, on 4 May 1754 Franklin wrote an editorial in which he urged unification of the colonies, printing it under a cartoon which depicted a snake cut into pieces, with the caption: 'JOIN OR DIE', the first symbol of the unified American colonies. That summer, representing Pennsylvania, he attended the Albany conference called by Westminster to urge the Iroquois or Six Nations to remain with the British and to arrange a common defence of the frontier against the French troops and their American Indian allies. Franklin drafted a plan of union as he journeyed to the conference. On 2 July 1754 the conference voted to form a union of the colonies, and on 10 July, it adopted, with revisions, Franklin's plan (*Papers*, 5.374–87). However, the colonies rejected it because they thought it gave too much power to the British authorities, while the British Board of Trade rejected it because of fears that a union could lead to independence.

In December 1754 the Board of Trade put forward its own proposals for union about which Franklin consulted William Shirley, governor of Massachusetts. Franklin objected that the British plan did not give the colonists the right to choose their own representatives and also protested against the proposal to have parliament tax Americans. On 4 December he wrote that it was 'an undoubted Right of Englishmen not to be taxed but by their own Consent given thro' their Representatives' (*Papers*, 5.444). On 22 December, in reply to Governor Shirley's suggestion that the colonists elect members of parliament, Franklin argued that if all the past Acts of Trade and Navigation, were repealed and if the colonies were given 'a reasonable number of Representatives' then the colonists might be satisfied. Such preferences were, Franklin claimed, certainly due to 'those who have most contributed to enlarge Britain's empire and commerce, encrease her strength, her wealth, and the numbers of her people, at the risque of their own lives and private fortunes in new and strange countries' (*Papers*, 5.451). Franklin's defiant Americanism struck a new chord in eighteenth-century political discourse. Years later James Madison wrote that Franklin's letters to Shirley 'repelled with the greatest possible force, within the smallest possible compass' Britain's claim to govern America (Farrand and Hutson, 3.540n.).

London, 1757–1762 Pennsylvania's governors refused to assent to tax bills unless the proprietors' land was exempted, prompting the Pennsylvania assembly to petition the British authorities. The assembly voted Franklin its agent, and on 3 February 1757 he accepted, thereafter spending the period 1757 to 1762 in England, where he lodged with his son, William, at 7 Craven Street, Strand, London. His wife, Deborah, fearing the voyage, remained in Philadelphia. Shortly after arriving in London Franklin met the president of the privy council, Lord Granville, who told him (27 July 1757) that George II's instructions to the governors were law: 'the King is the Legislator of the Colonies' (*Autobiography*, 167). Franklin disagreed. He found the British public and the authorities ignorant about America and began a campaign to enlighten them. His 'A defence of the Americans', which appeared in the *London Chronicle* (12 May 1759), was the grandest statement of Americanism in the colonial period. Franklin's subsequent pamphlet, arguing for the economic and strategic importance of Canada to the colonies and to Great Britain (*The Interest of Great Britain Considered*, 1760), was partly responsible for convincing the British authorities to retain Canada rather than Guadeloupe at the conclusion of the Seven Years' War (1756–63).

Following instructions Franklin consulted the London physician and friend of Pennsylvania's Quaker leaders, John Fothergill, who advised him to try for an accommodation with the proprietors before appealing to the British authorities. That negotiation dragged on inconclusively but in Pennsylvania on 17 April 1759 the governor passed a tax bill that included the proprietors' estates. The

Penn family tried to have the act disallowed and, despite the arguments of lawyers hired by Franklin, the Board of Trade recommended on 24 June 1760 that it be annulled. Franklin appealed to the king in council, and, after personally guaranteeing that the proprietary estates would be taxed with perfect equity, won the case. The Penns, however, continued to oppose acts taxing their lands.

During this first mission to England, Franklin frequently attended two informal clubs. One—consisting primarily of scientists, philanthropists, and explorers (including, on occasions, the navigator, James Cook)— met on Mondays; the other, dubbed the Club of Honest Whigs, met on Thursdays, and included dissenting ministers such as Joseph Priestley and Richard Price, as well as James Boswell. Franklin also regularly attended meetings of the Royal Society, the Associates of Dr Bray (a small philanthropic organization which Samuel Johnson visited on 1 May 1760 while Franklin was its chairman), and the Society of Arts. Time permitting Franklin continued his scientific interests when in Britain, inventing a clock with only three wheels; experimenting with an early form of air conditioning (17 June 1758); designing a damper for stoves and chimneys (2 December 1758); and gradually improving his new musical instrument, the glass armonica (13 July 1762). As in America, Franklin's scientific work was acknowledged by British universities, and he received an honorary degree of doctor of laws from St Andrews (12 February 1759) and from Oxford a doctorate of civil law (30 April 1762).

Philadelphia and London, 1762–1775 Franklin left England in late summer 1762 and arrived back in Philadelphia on 1 November. He found troubles at home following the murder in Lancaster, Pennsylvania, of a group of Christian American Indians by a mob (the Paxton boys). Franklin wrote a scathing denunciation of the act in *A Narrative of the Late Massacres*, published on 30 January 1764. When the Paxton boys marched on Philadelphia to kill the Christian Indians there the government floundered. Franklin organized Philadelphia's defence, met the leaders of the rioters, and persuaded them to present a list of their grievances and disperse.

On 26 May 1764 Franklin was elected speaker of the Pennsylvania house of representatives, as news of the impending Stamp Act reached the colonies. On 13 June the Massachusetts house of representatives asked colonial assemblies to oppose the act. Franklin presented the request to the Pennsylvania assembly on 12 September. This promptly instructed Pennsylvania's London agent, Richard Jackson, to resist the proposed act and to argue that only the Pennsylvania legislature had the right to impose taxes in the colony.

Before the Pennsylvania election of 1763 Franklin was exposed to a series of allegations by his political opponents that he coveted the governorship; that he had bilked the public moneys while he was the assembly's agent in England; that William Franklin's mother was his maidservant Barbara whom he mistreated and had buried in an unmarked grave; that he was prejudiced against Germans; and that he was overly sympathetic to the cause of the American Indians. The most bitterly contested assembly election in colonial Pennsylvania began at 10 a.m. on 1 October 1764, and continued until 3 p.m. on the following day. Franklin lost by eighteen votes (*Papers*, 11.390–91). However, the anti-proprietary party retained its majority and appointed Franklin, on 26 October 1764, to join Richard Jackson as the assembly's agent to England.

The purpose of Franklin's second mission to Britain (1764–75) was to petition the new king, George III, for a change from proprietary to royal government in Pennsylvania. But British imperial politics intervened. After Franklin reached London he was immediately immersed in attempts to reject Grenville's Stamp Act. He now began a series of essays and letters to the London newspapers opposing the Stamp Act and distributed a satirical cartoon to members of parliament. Franklin's efforts were, however, in vain. The Stamp Act passed the Commons on 27 February 1765 and received the royal assent on 22 March, to take effect, on 1 November. Franklin had lost, but he supposed the Stamp Act could be tolerated. On 11 July 1765 he wrote to the young Philadelphia patriot Charles Thomson: 'I took every step in my Power, to prevent the Passing of the Stamp Act', but 'We might as well have hinder'd the Sun's setting'. Franklin accepted defeat before hearing of Virginia's Stamp Act resolves. On 30 May 1765 Virginia's house of burgesses denied that Britain had the right to tax Virginians. Emboldened by the Virginia resolves other colonies followed its line and local mobs threatened the stamp distributors. Because of rumours that Franklin had supported the Stamp Act his Philadelphia home was surrounded on the night of 16 September. Deborah armed herself, ready to fight and defend their home, though the threat came to nothing. On 1 November, the day the Stamp Act was to take effect, courts throughout the colonies refused to convene. American colonial administration collapsed.

On 13 February 1766 Franklin attended a parliamentary committee of the whole house to testify against the Stamp Act. His answers to MPs constituted a triumphant display of political knowledge and of pro-Americanism. To the suggestion that military forces should be sent to America he asserted, 'They will not find a rebellion; they may indeed make one' (*Papers*, 13.142). Publication of his *Examination* confirmed Franklin's reputation as the pre-eminent spokesman for the American colonies. On 11 April 1768 the Georgia assembly appointed him its agent: on 8 November 1769 New Jersey did the same; and on 24 October 1770 the Massachusetts assembly followed suit, making him the agent for four colonies.

Between 1764 and 1775 Franklin wrote a series of spirited pro-American essays, among them the 'Grand leap of the whale over Niagara Falls' (3 May 1765), 'Rules by which a great empire may be reduced to a small one' (11 September 1773), and 'An edict by the king of Prussia' (22 September 1773). A treasonous manuscript, 'Remarks on Judge Foster's arguments in favor of the right of impressing seamen', probably written about 1770, also circulated clandestinely. According to Franklin it was George III not the poor sailor who deserved impressment, for 'I am not satisfied of the Necessity or Utility' of the 'Office of King' in Great Britain (*Papers*, 35.500). Though Franklin predicted American independence, he said that every year brought America increasing strength. If there must be war, it was he believed better to postpone it for as long as possible.

The mounting political crisis and his reputation as a critic of the British government did not lessen Franklin's appetite for self, social, and scientific observation. In 1771, while staying at Twyford with the bishop of St Asaph, he wrote, in the form of an open letter to his son William, an account of his life to 1731. This later formed the first part of what was commonly known after Franklin's death as his *Autobiography*, a remarkably candid and influential study in the genre. In 1766 he visited Germany and journeyed to France in 1767 and 1769. In 1771 he toured Ireland and Scotland with Richard Jackson, staying with David Hume in Edinburgh and with Lord Kames at Blair Drummond. Conditions in Ireland depressed him: there were a few rich 'Landlords, great Noblemen and Gentlemen, extremely opulent, living in the highest Affluence and magnificence', while the majority were 'extremely poor, living in the most sordid Wretchedness in dirty Hovels of mud and Straw, and cloathed only in Rags'. He wrote on 13 January 1772

> That in the Possession and Enjoyment of the various Comforts of Life, compar'd to these People every Indian is a Gentleman: and the Effect of this kind of Civil Society seems only to be, the depressing Multitudes below the Savage State that a few may be rais'd above it.

In May 1768 Franklin, as natural philosopher, had experimented on the relationship between canal water depths and the speed of canal boats. In July of that year he devised a phonetic alphabet and corresponded in it; in the autumn he had maps of the Atlantic engraved which contained the course of the 'river in the ocean', the gulf stream. Franklin also supervised publication of the revised and enlarged fourth English edition of his *Experiments and Observations on Electricity* (1769). In August 1772 the Académie Royale des Sciences in Paris elected him a foreign associate at a time when he was engaged in repeated experiments concerning the interaction of oil and water, correctly determining 'the scale of magnitude of molecular dimensions, the first person ever to do so, but he did not recognize it' (Tanford, 80).

While in London Franklin learned that British repressive tactics had been encouraged by the Massachusetts governor, Thomas Hutchinson, and by his lieutenant-governor Andrew Oliver. Franklin sent their correspondence to Massachusetts, hoping that the letters would lessen the rage of the radicals against the British authorities. Instead the correspondence exacerbated the strife between the governor and the Massachusetts assembly, which petitioned for Hutchinson's and Oliver's removal. At the same time Hutchinson obtained a copy of Franklin's 7 July 1773 letter urging the colonial assemblies to resolve never to 'grant aids to the Crown in any General War till' the rights of Americans:

> are recogniz'd by the King and both Houses of Parliament. ... Such a Step I imagine will bring the Dispute to a Crisis; and whether our Demands are immediately comply'd with, or compulsory Means are thought of to make us Rescind them, our Ends will finally be obtain'd.   (*Papers*, 17.282)

Hutchinson sent the copy to Lord Dartmouth, the colonial secretary, who judged it treasonable. On Dartmouth's instruction General Thomas Gage, military commander-in-chief in America, sought unsuccessfully to obtain the original so that Franklin could be prosecuted.

The Hutchinson–Oliver letters were published in Boston in June 1773. To prevent a duel over the source of the letters on 25 December Franklin published the statement, 'I alone am the person who obtained and transmitted to Boston the letters in question'. He also forwarded to Lord Dartmouth the Massachusetts petition to remove Hutchinson and Oliver. A preliminary hearing took place on 11 January 1774. News of the Boston Tea Party reached London on 20 January and further infuriated the British authorities with Massachusetts and its agent. The hearing on the Massachusetts petition before the privy council took place in the cockpit on 29 January. In an hour-long diatribe, the British solicitor-general, Alexander Wedderburn, excoriated and denounced Franklin, demanding that he be marked and branded as a criminal. Britain's greatest officials, many of whom Franklin knew well, sneered and snickered while he stood silent, America's scapegoat.

On 31 January 1774 Franklin was dismissed as deputy postmaster-general for North America. The American post office had never been profitable before Franklin took it over and it never has been since. During 1774 and early 1775, even as he petitioned against the Boston Port Bill (which became law on 31 January, closing Boston's port), Franklin satirized the British government's handling of American politics while still attempting to reconcile Great Britain with the colonists. In an effort to forestall the bill he personally guaranteed payment of the cost of the tea dumped in Boston harbour. His efforts, including his collaboration with William Pitt, earl of Chatham, in January 1775, came to nothing. He left London on 20 March, his second mission, like his first, a failure. He was being prosecuted in court, and on 13 May 1775 the sheriff of Middlesex was ordered to arrest him.

Philadelphia, 1775–1776 While Franklin was at sea the battles of Lexington and Concord (17 and 18 April 1775) started the War of American Independence. He arrived at Philadelphia on 5 May and on the following day the Pennsylvania assembly unanimously chose him as a delegate to the second continental congress. His draft 'Articles of confederation' (written before 21 July 1775) asserted America's sovereignty and gave greater powers to the central government than did the United States constitution in 1787. But congress was not yet ready. On 23 July John Adams reported that Franklin 'does not hesitate at our boldest Measures, but rather seems to think us, too irresolute, and backward' (*Diary and Autobiography*, 1.253). In the autumn he was appointed by congress to a committee to confer with General George Washington in Massachusetts and, on 29 November, as the chair of a standing committee of secret correspondence to deal with foreign affairs. In effect Franklin was now the first secretary of state. His propagandist writings of the period included the satiric song 'The King's Own Regulars' (27 November 1775), which George Washington enjoyed, and the hoax 'Bradshaw's epitaph' (14 December 1775), which concluded with the words that Thomas Jefferson adopted as his personal motto: 'Rebellion to Tyrants is Obedience to God'.

In congress Franklin again argued for an 'Instrument of confederation' (16 January 1776), a document giving articles of confederation for the union, but was defeated. Instead Franklin, along with Charles Carroll of Carrollton, Samuel Chase, and Father John Carroll, was appointed a member of the commission to convince the Canadians to join the Americans against Britain. Though now seventy and suffering from ill health Franklin undertook the arduous mission (26 March to 30 May), which failed. After his return he served on the committee to draft the Declaration of Independence. Thomas Jefferson chaired the committee and decided to compose the document himself, though Franklin added to and revised it. Congress voted for independence on 2 July, and then debated, altered, and finally adopted the declaration on 4 July 1776. Elected to the Pennsylvania state convention on 8 July, Franklin was chosen its president on the 16th.

Drafting the Pennsylvania declaration of rights Franklin made the bold assertion that the state had the right to discourage large concentrations of property and wealth in single individuals as a danger to the happiness of the majority (*Papers*, 22.533). However, the Pennsylvania convention rejected his radical economic suggestion. During congressional debates on the articles of confederation (30 July to 1 August 1776) he unsuccessfully advocated that representation be proportional to population, rather than equal by states. Congress appointed Franklin, Adams, and Edward Rutledge to a committee to confer with Lord Howe on Staten Island. At the meeting, which took place on 11 September, Howe stated that he felt for America and would lament her fall as a brother would, to which Franklin replied with 'a Bow, a Smile and all the Naivetee which sometimes appeared in his conversation, … "My Lord, We will do our Utmost Endeavours, to save your Lordship that mortification"' (*Diary and Autobiography*, 3.422). In the autumn Franklin drafted his 'Sketch of propositions for a peace', suggesting that Britain cede Canada to an independent United States. Elected by congress as a commissioner to France with Silas Deane and Arthur Lee he sailed from Philadelphia on 27 October 1776.

Minister to France, 1776–1785 Franklin arrived in France on 3 December 1776 and proceeded to Paris, where he met secretly with the comte de Vergennes, French foreign minister. The American commissioners formally requested French aid on 5 January 1777, and on the 13th they received a verbal promise of 2 million livres. From his knowledge of Voltaire's *Lettres philosophiques* (1734) and Montesquieu's *L'esprit des lois* (1748) Franklin understood the French association of Pennsylvania and Quakerism

with virtue and simplicity and dressed and presented himself accordingly. (His readiness to discard his wig was also due to a scalp irritation from which he then suffered.) On 8 February 1777 he wrote to his friend Emma Thompson:

> Figure me … very plainly dress'd, wearing my thin grey strait Hair, that peeps out under my only Coiffure, a fine Fur Cap, which comes down my Forehead almost to my Spectacles. Think how this must appear among the Powder'd Heads of Paris.

John Adams testified that Franklin was idolized while in France:

> His name was familiar to government and people, to kings, courtiers, nobility, clergy, and philosophers, as well as plebeians, to such a degree that there was scarcely a peasant or citizen, a *valet de chambre*, coachman or footman, a lady's chambermaid or a scullion in a kitchen, who was not familiar with it, and who did not consider him as a friend to human kind. (*Works of John Adams*, 1.659)

From the French finance minister, Turgot, there came the famous epigram: 'Eripuit coelo fulmen, sceptrumque tyrannis' ('He snatched the lightning from the skies and the sceptre from the tyrants'; Aldridge, 124).

On 21 October 1778, following France's decision to send a minister plenipotentiary to the United States, congress responded by electing Franklin to a similar position. To facilitate the production of passports, loan certificates, promissory notes, and other documents he purchased a press and types and printed such items, as well as a number of his bagatelles. As minister plenipotentiary Franklin's duties were numerous. He borrowed funds from France for the expenses of congress, issued letters of marque for American privateers, managed the interests of the continental navy overseas, and oversaw the purchase and shipping of arms and other supplies for the continental army. He negotiated for the humane treatment and exchanges of American prisoners of war and helped hundreds of escaped American prisoners. On Tuesdays he attended the royal court with his fellow ministers, entertained Americans at dinner on most Sundays and cultivated good relations with a host of influential French intellectuals and politicians. Though his multifarious duties precluded extensive scientific experimentation Franklin nevertheless encouraged it among others and was able to write selective papers himself. Thus learning that ships used in the salt trade lasted longer than others he conceived a method for prolonging the life of lumber by seasoning it in salt. He devised a test for the conductivity of metals; a magnificent display of the aurora borealis (3 December 1778) prompted him to write a series, 'Suppositions and conjectures', on the phenomenon. His description of a new technological device, bifocal glasses, came on 23 May 1784.

In June 1781 congress appointed Franklin, Henry Laurens, and Thomas Jefferson to join John Jay and John Adams as commissioners to negotiate peace following General Cornwallis's surrender to George Washington at Yorktown on 19 October 1781. From March to June 1782 Franklin negotiated with the British emissary Richard Oswald, a London merchant with American sympathies and an old friend of the American minister. On 18 April

Franklin suggested that Britain should cede Canada to the United States. Had Franklin been the only commissioner, he might have been able to settle the peace then and to have secured Canada. But when John Jay arrived in Paris on 23 June he insisted on prior recognition of American independence as a condition for formal peace negotiations, thus delaying the talks while the war at sea slowly changed to favour the British.

On 10 July 1782 Franklin proposed to Oswald the 'necessary' terms for peace, ignoring congress's instruction to act only with the knowledge and concurrence of France. Oswald's new British commission (21 September 1782) effectively recognized the United States and overcame Jay's hesitation. A draft of the articles for the treaty was prepared and sent to Britain, again without informing the French. John Adams arrived in Paris on 26 October and joined the negotiations, and on 30 November, Oswald and the American commissioners signed the preliminary articles of peace. In December, when the comte de Vergennes complained of America's failure to consult the French, Franklin diplomatically admitted the impropriety, expressed gratitude to France, and asked for another loan. Vergennes assured him of a further 6 million livres. Franklin, Adams, and Jay signed the definitive treaty of peace on behalf of the United States on 3 September 1783.

On 12 May 1784 the formal ratification of the peace treaty with Great Britain was exchanged, and on the next day Franklin requested to be relieved from his post to return home. Jefferson arrived in Paris on 30 August to join Franklin and Adams in attempting to make treaties with the European nations and the Barbary States. On 2 May 1785 Franklin received permission to leave France. 'I shall now be free of Politicks for the Rest of my Life. Welcome again my dear Philosophical Amusements' (*Writings*, ed. Smyth, 9.318). He left Passy on 12 July 1785 at a time when a bladder stone was causing him pain. None the less Franklin spent most of the voyage writing pieces such as his *Maritime Observations*, which suggested a number of improvements for convenience, safety, and swiftness in sailing.

Philadelphia, 1785–1790 Franklin arrived at Philadelphia on 14 September 1785 to the largest ceremony and reception that city had ever displayed. He was elected to the supreme executive council of Pennsylvania on 11 October, chosen its president on the 18th, and served in that position (in effect, governor) for three years. These years also saw a final flourish of experimentation and invention. In January 1781 he fashioned an instrument for taking down books from high shelves which he followed with a series of chairs with a seat that unfolded to become a ladder, with a writing arm on one side (now a staple feature of university lecture theatres) and a rocking chair with an automatic fan. From 28 May to 17 September 1787 he served in the constitutional convention. Though he had previously argued, and initially continued to advocate, that representation should be proportional to population, on 3 July he moved the 'Great Compromise' whereby representation was proportional in the house of delegates but equal by state in the senate. On 7 and 10 August he

argued that the right to vote should be extended as widely as possible, and condemned property qualifications as necessary either for the franchise or for office-holding. His closing speech supporting the constitution was the most effective propaganda for its ratification. Aged seventy, he had been the oldest signer of the Declaration of Independence in 1776, and now, aged eighty-one, he again achieved that position with regard to the United States constitution.

On 14 October 1788 Franklin ended his service as president of the supreme executive council of Pennsylvania, terminating his career in public office. Despite suffering from gout and a bladder stone, he still, as of 25 November 1788, enjoyed 'many comfortable Intervals, in which I forget all my Ills, and amuse myself in Reading or Writing, or in conversation with Friends, joking, laughing, and telling merry Stories' (*Writings*, ed. Smyth, 9.683). On 23 April 1787 he had been elected president of the Pennsylvania Society for Promoting the Abolition of Slavery and on 12 February 1789 he wrote and signed the first remonstrance against slavery addressed to the American congress, though congress said it had no authority to interfere in the internal affairs of the states. His final work, published on 20 March 1790, was a brilliant satire on a defence of slavery. In these final months Franklin also returned to his autobiographical essay. Between his starting the project in England in 1771 and his final period of writing he had added two further sections. The first composed in France in 1784 was a dozen-page survey on his method of self-discipline, and was followed during 1788–9 when he carried his account down to his arrival in England in 1757. The final section, written in bed, provided a brief sketch of Franklin's English agency from 1757 to 1762.

To the man who had written that 'nothing can be said to be certain except death and taxes' (to Jean Baptiste Le Roy, 13 Nov 1789) life's second great inevitability came about, from pleurisy, on 17 April 1790 in Philadelphia. Franklin, who was then eighty-four, was buried four days later at Philadelphia's Christ Church burial-ground beside his wife, Deborah, who had died on 19 December 1774, and their son Francis. On hearing of the news of Franklin's death the French assembly voted to wear mourning for three days. The United States house of representatives passed, but the senate defeated, a motion to wear mourning for a month. Franklin was survived by his son William, from whom he had been alienated following the latter's support for the British during the revolution; among other members of his family to survive him were William's illegitimate son, William Temple Franklin, William Temple Franklin's illegitimate daughter, Ellen Franklin, and his daughter, Sarah, who had married Richard Bache in October 1767. Months after his death the first part of Franklin's unfinished autobiographical essay (to 1731) was published in France. Two versions of this first part, anonymously retranslated into English, appeared in 1793 and were thereafter much reprinted, usually as *The Life of Benjamin Franklin, Written by Himself*. In 1817 Franklin's grandson, William Temple Franklin, brought out the first three parts of the original English version and in an 1848 edition the work was first called the *Autobiography*; John Bigelow's edition of 1868 included Franklin's fourth and final section, again under the title of *Autobiography*, the name by which the text is now best-known. From the eighteenth century to the present it has proved one of the world's most popular autobiographical studies, remarkable for its frank account of the author's misadventures and for an ability to inspire numerous individuals with its account of self-discipline and motivation.

Reputation During the 1730s Franklin became known as the most successful newspaperman and writer in the colonies. In the 1740s he was celebrated as Philadelphia's most public-spirited citizen. He became the world's best-known living scientist through his design, in 1744, of a stove more efficient than any previous one, and his proof in 1752 that lightning was electrical in nature. During the 1750s he also became the dominant Pennsylvania politician. From 1757 to 1764 and again from 1764 to 1775 he lived in England, where he was America's spokesperson and unofficial ambassador. He was the best-known American before George Washington's rise to prominence during the revolution. During the 1770s and 1780s he was famous as a revolutionary and then as a statesman. At his death in 1790 he was celebrated as a patriot and founding father, being the only person to sign all three fundamental documents of American statehood: the Declaration of Independence (1776), the peace treaty with Britain (1783), and the constitution of the United States (1787). His contemporaries often commented on his egalitarianism (Thomas Penn called him a 'Tribune of the People' in 1748; *Papers*, 3.186) and on his metaphysical scepticism (Condorcet thought him a Pyrrhonist). Throughout the latter part of his life he was renowned for his self-motivation. Without education he had become one of the most learned persons of his time. Without inherited money he had become wealthy. Without prospects as a young man he had become famous.

Five aspects of Franklin's reputation endure. His standing as a public-spirited citizen has been kept alive by his *Autobiography* and by the institutions that he founded—among them the Library Company of Philadelphia, the American Philosophical Society, and the University of Pennsylvania. His reputation as a scientist is confirmed by the existence of every lightning rod. The best-known period of Franklin's life, the French years (1777–85), authenticates his position as a statesman. David Hume's 1763 description of Franklin as a 'Great Man of Letters' (*Papers*, 10.81) and the inclusion of his writings in almost all anthologies of American literature attest to his ability as a writer. The poverty and obscurity of his family background, coupled with his later fame as a scientist, statesman, and writer, continue to make Franklin the single most famous example of a self-made man.

Posthumously three major elements have been added to his reputation: materialist, philistine, and rake. The three supposed characteristics say more about later times and

the naïvety of the writers than about Franklin. The popularity of *The Way to Wealth* (a name later given to the preface for the *Poor Richard* almanac of 1758) identified Franklin with getting and saving money. This aspect of Franklin's posthumous reputation was reinforced by Max Weber's influential identification of him with 'The Spirit of Capitalism' and by Franklin's picture on the United States $100 bill. However, instead of spending his life in the acquisition of wealth, Franklin retired aged forty-one to produce 'something for the common Benefit of Mankind' (*Papers*, 3.317). He dedicated thousands of hours to public-spirited causes without expecting or receiving any material reward. He turned down a patent for his stove design which would have made him a fortune and he offered to pay for the tea dumped into the harbour at the Boston Tea Party, though to have done so would have impoverished him. Few men of any time were as idealistic as Franklin.

Arising in great part because of Franklin's identification with materialism, but also because he belonged to no religious sect, the idea of Franklin as philistine, without idealism or spirituality, has been presented most forcefully in D. H. Lawrence's characterization in his *Studies in Classic American Literature* (1923). Lawrence, like some other critics, identified Franklin as the embodiment of an acquisitive American culture. But, again, such judgements are misleading. Franklin wrote more about religion and virtue than any other colonial American layman. He contributed money to every religious society of Philadelphia. He devoted his time and money to more idealistic causes throughout his life than almost any of his contemporaries. Even in his will he tried to help the young artisans of Boston and Philadelphia.

Finally comparatively frank details of his interest in sex in the *Autobiography*, the knowledge that he had an illegitimate son, and a number of his risqué writings, such as 'Old mistresses' apologue' and 'The Elysian Fields' have contributed to the idea of Franklin as a womanizer, a view that became increasingly popular during the twentieth century. But after he married Deborah Read, at the age of twenty-four, there is no evidence whatever that he had any other sexual relations. His affectionate lifelong relationships with several women in America, England, and France during his mature years bespeak, in many cases, delightful flirtation and, in all cases, devoted friendship.

Franklin's reputation during his own lifetime was well founded. Besides dozens of general biographies numerous books are devoted to various aspects of Franklin—as businessman, economist, printer, postmaster, philosopher, politician, scientist, theologian, statesman, writer, private citizen, friend—and to numerous specialized topics within these and other general subjects. Franklin's great ability and drive were exceeded only by his interests and achievements. Every study of Franklin must be selective and none can do him justice.

Perhaps Franklin would have wished to be remembered for his concern for the 'common Good of Mankind' (*Papers*, 9.229). He wanted to become an *amicus humani generis*. Numerous contemporaries thought he realized that ambition (Edmund Burke called him the 'friend to mankind'; *Correspondence*, 4.419). When thanked for aiding a stranger Franklin replied, on 6 June 1753: 'the only Thanks I should desire is, that you would always be equally ready to serve any other Person that may need your Assistance, and so let good Offices go round, for Mankind are all of a Family' (*Papers*, 4.504). Near the end of his life he wrote, 'God grant, that not only the Love of Liberty, but a thorough Knowledge of the Rights of Man, may pervade all the Nations of the Earth, so that a Philosopher may set his Foot anywhere on its Surface, and say, "This is my Country"' (*Writings*, ed. Smyth, 10.72).

J. A. LEO LEMAY

Sources *The papers of Benjamin Franklin*, ed. L. W. Labaree and others, [35 vols.] (1959–) · *The autobiography of Benjamin Franklin: a genetic text*, ed. J. A. L. Lemay and P. M. Zall (1981) · *B. Franklin: writings*, ed. J. A. L. Lemay (1987) · J. A. L. Lemay, *The canon of Benjamin Franklin, 1722–1776: new attributions and reconsiderations* (1986) · B. Franklin, *The writings*, ed. A. H. Smyth, 10 vols. (1905–7) · C. Van Doren, *Benjamin Franklin* (1938) · *Diary and autobiography of John Adams*, ed. L. H. Butterfield and others, 1–4 (1961), vol. 3 · *Papers of John Adams*, ed. R. J. Taylor and others, 10 vols. (1977–96), vol. 1 · L. H. Butterfield and others, eds., *Adams family correspondence*, 1 (1963–) · *The works of John Adams*, ed. C. F. Adams, 10 vols. (1850–56) · *The papers of Thomas Jefferson*, ed. J. P. Boyd and others, 27 vols. (1950–) · G. Hunt, ed., *Journals of the continental congress*, 20 (1912) · M. Farrand and J. Hutson, eds., *Records of the federal convention of 1787*, 4 vols. (1966–87) · A. O. Aldridge, *Franklin and his French contemporaries* (1957) · *Autobiography of Joseph Priestley* (1970) · *The correspondence of Edmund Burke*, ed. T. W. Copeland and others, 10 vols. (1958–78) · R. A. Millikin, 'Benjamin Franklin as a scientist', *Meet Dr Franklin*, ed. R. N. Lokken (1981) · C. Tanford, *Ben Franklin stilled the waves* (1989)

Archives American Philosophical Society, Philadelphia, corresp. and papers · BL, corresp. · Hist. Soc. Penn., corresp. and papers · Hunt. L. · L. Cong. · University of Pennsylvania, Philadelphia · University of Strathclyde, Glasgow, MSS · Yale U. | Glos. RO, corresp. with Granville Sharp · NA Scot., letters to Lord Kames · Sheff. Arch., corresp. with Edmund Burke · U. Mich., Clements L., letters relating to British politics

Likenesses D. Martin, 1766, White House, Washington, DC · J. B. Nini, medallion, 1777, Smithsonian Institution, Washington, DC · plaster replica, 1777 (after medallion by J. B. Nini), Scot. NPG · J. S. Duplessis, portrait, 1778, Metropolitan Museum of Art, New York [*see illus.*] · Houdon, bust, 1778, Metropolitan Museum of Art, New York · oils, Scot. NPG · plaster replica (after medallion by unknown artist), Scot. NPG

Wealth at death among wealthier persons in Philadelphia at death: will, inventory, City Hall, Philadelphia · left lands in Nova Scotia, Philadelphia, Ohio, Boston, and Georgia to son, William Franklin, to daughter, Sarah Franklin Bache, and to their children, with numerous bequests to other friends, relatives, and institutions; left £1000 to Boston and £1000 to Philadelphia for loans to young artificers; personal property, mainly the furnishings of home, valued at £22,554 9s. 10d. Pennsylvania currency; plus £3500 sterling; plus cash in the hands of French and English bankers: *Writings*, ed. Smyth, vol. 10, pp. 493–510

Franklin, Charles Samuel (1879–1964), radio telecommunications engineer, was born in Walthamstow, Essex, on 23 March 1879, the thirteenth child of James Charles Franklin, a carpenter and builder, and his wife, Martha Bulbeck. He received his engineering and scientific training under Silvanus P. Thompson at Finsbury Technical College, after which he worked briefly in Manchester and

Norwich. In 1899, at the age of twenty, he joined the Wireless Telegraph and Signal Company (later Marconi's Wireless and Telegraph Company), with which he remained associated until his retirement in 1939.

During the Second South African War, Franklin helped to introduce wireless communication in South Africa for military use, returning to Britain in 1902 to act as wireless operator for Guglielmo Marconi. Thus began a long personal association with Marconi, to whom he remained devoted throughout his life. They sailed across the Atlantic to demonstrate the reception of wireless messages up to a range of 1550 miles from the Poldhu transmitting station in Cornwall. From 1904 to early 1906 Franklin demonstrated radio equipment in Russia. From 1908 to 1916 much of his work was done in isolated wireless stations along the coast, and during this period Franklin was at his happiest. He worked in the short-wave, ultra-short, and micro-wave spectra, and had many important patents.

By 1913 Franklin had patented techniques of using a thermionic valve as a radio frequency generator. He had devised a photographic method of recording radio signals and designed a regenerative receiver of high sensitivity. From 1916 to 1920, working with Marconi, he developed the short-wave beam principle which led to the first beamed short-wave system. He designed efficient reflectors which concentrated radiation into a narrow searchlight-like beam, and he built a special short-wave transmitter employing tubes of his own design. At Inchkeith in Fife a rotating parabolic reflector station, transmitting on a wavelength of 6 metres, demonstrated the possibilities of a radio beacon for navigation. Franklin designed a special spark transmitter operating in compressed air, and his inductance capacity oscillator (the 'Franklin drive') formed an essential part of the short-wave beam communication system. On 19 September 1918 Franklin married Catherine, daughter of John Griffiths, a lime and coal merchant, of Caernarfon. They had no children.

During 1923 and 1924 Franklin installed a short-wave station at Poldhu. He and Marconi conducted tests between it and Marconi's yacht, *Elettra*, chiefly to determine the day and night ranges and reliability of signals transmitted on wavelengths of 97 metres or less, with and without reflectors, and also to investigate the angle and spread of the beam. On 97 metres and 12 kW, daylight signals were received across 1250 nautical miles, and night signals at a range of 2320 nautical miles. Later, reception was reported in the USA and Australia. The beam transmitter and flat grid aerial system designed by Franklin (the Franklin beam aerial) formed the basis of worldwide short-wave communication. A necessary part of the system was Franklin's invention of the concentric feeder for the transmission of the very high frequency currents to and from the aerial arrays, the forerunner of the coaxial cable.

In 1922 Franklin assisted in the design and installation of the transmitter and aerial system of 2LO, London's first broadcasting station, and his team was responsible for running it initially. Later he designed the transmitters and aerial system for the BBC station at Alexandra Palace, which transmitted the world's first regular television service in 1936. He retired from the Marconi Company in 1939, but acted as a research consultant to them for some years afterwards.

Among the awards which Franklin received were the Morris Liebmann memorial prize of the Institute of Radio Engineers (New York) in 1922; the James Alfred Ewing medal of the Institution of Civil Engineers in 1936; and in 1949, the Faraday medal of the Institution of Electrical Engineers for 'his distinguished work in radio engineering, and more particularly for his development of the beam aerial and other devices that made long-range high-frequency communication a practical possibility'. Also in 1949 Franklin was appointed CBE.

Franklin was a small, frail, diffident, modest man, who seldom spoke unless spoken to, and was happiest working in seclusion. During his Poldhu days, when told of a problem which had baffled his colleagues, he would wander off alone across the headland. Suddenly, he would squat down motionless upon the cliff-top, remain there for perhaps an hour or more, oblivious of wind and weather, then return and state exactly where the fault lay. He would be right.

When he retired from the Marconi Company in 1939, Franklin moved back to Mullion Helston, near Poldhu, where his wife died in 1946. Later he returned to the home counties and lived at 19 Victoria Road, Buckhurst Hill; he died of heart failure at 1A Manor Road, Ilford, Essex, on 10 December 1964. ELEANOR PUTNAM SYMONS, rev.

Sources Marconi Company archives, GEC Marconi Ltd, The Laurels, Victoria Rd, Chelmsford · 'Notes by Mr Franklin', GEC Marconi Ltd, The Grove, Warren Lane, Stanmore, London, Marconi Company Archives [unpublished typescript] · *Nature*, 205 (1965), 652–3 · *The Times* (16 Dec 1964) · W. J. Baker, *A history of the Marconi Company* (1970) · private information (1981) [B. D. S. Lock] · m. cert. · d. cert.
Wealth at death £23,118: probate, 30 April 1965, *CGPLA Eng. & Wales*

Franklin, Eleanor Anne. *See* Porden, Eleanor Anne (1795–1825).

Franklin [*née* Montagu], **Henrietta** [Netta] (1866–1964), educationist and suffragist, was born on 9 April 1866 in London, the first of the eleven surviving children of Samuel *Montagu, later first Baron Swaythling (1832–1911), foreign-exchange banker and Jewish philanthropist, and his wife, Ellen Cohen (1848–1919). Her brother Edwin *Montagu was sometime secretary of state for India. She was educated at home, at Doreck College, and at King's College for Ladies, London. On 7 October 1885 she married her cousin Ernest Louis Franklin (1860–1950), financier son of the banker Ellis Franklin and Adelaide Montagu, in the New West End Synagogue, Bayswater. Between 1886 and 1903 she gave birth to four sons and two daughters.

The decisive, inspiring experience for Henrietta Franklin and her life's work was her encounter, in 1890, with the educational reformer Charlotte Mason, founder of the child-centred Parents' National Education Union (PNEU), which focused on liberal pre-school and primary education as a collaborative effort by mothers and teachers. Henrietta Franklin was honorary organizing secretary for the PNEU, 1894–1964, and in 1892 started the first PNEU school in London. The movement affirmed every child's right to be respected as a unique personality (its motto being: 'I am, I can, I ought, I will') and to have access to a 'generous curriculum' including nature study, poetry, religion, art, carpentry, gymnastics, and music. A tireless publicist and organizer for the validity of Charlotte Mason's educational philosophy and praxis as a teacher trainer, it was Henrietta Franklin who ensured that the PNEU achieved national and international exposure, not least through her writing and public lecture tours (which included most of the capitals of Europe, North America, and, in 1923, South Africa), as well as through her gift for consolidating the national network and by means of her own personal wealth.

In religion Henrietta Franklin differed from her Orthodox father and husband and supported her sister Lily *Montagu in the establishment of a Liberal Jewish path that focused on the spirit rather than on the letter of the law. This Liberal Judaism, influenced by the thought of Claude Montefiore, stressed ethics as the core of Jewish life and inaugurated a new form of religious service in which men and women sat together, prayers and hymns were in English, and which eventually enabled Lily Montagu to officiate as the first woman lay minister and preacher at a Liberal Jewish service. Together with her sister Lily, Henrietta Franklin published *Daily Readings from the Old Testament* in 1922, stressing those psalms and passages in Isaiah, Ezekiel, Job, and Zechariah that affirm the unity of man and peace as the culmination of the religious ideal.

Henrietta Franklin's feminism was manifest not only in her Liberal Judaism but also in her political activism. She was an early member of the National Council of Women, and became both its vice-president and its president. She was a committed suffragist, being on the executive committee of the Jewish League for Woman Suffrage formed in 1912 and later chair of the National Council for Equal Citizenship. In 1915 she served on the executive committee of the Women's Municipal Party which encouraged the candidature of women for the London county council and London borough councils. During the First World War Henrietta Franklin was one of the courageous, unpopular 'pacifist feminists' who supported the Women's International Congress at The Hague in 1915, aiming firstly to demand that international disputes should in future be settled by some other means than war and, secondly, to claim that women should have a voice in the affairs of the nations. She was also a signatory to the open Christmas letter to German women drafted by Emily Hobhouse in December 1914, and a financial supporter of the Women's International League for Peace and Freedom.

Henrietta Franklin, or Netta, was a very able woman of immense force of character and phenomenal, restless energy. Rather than being content to become a mere society hostess, she gave herself totally to many causes of liberal progress. She could never feel that she had learned enough or had filled a day to the uttermost. For the last fifty-three years of her life she had had to fulfil all her commitments with an artificial leg. 'Well, I would sooner lose a leg than an arm,' she said. In 1950 she was made CBE. Henrietta Franklin died on 7 January 1964 at her home, 88 Carlton Hill, St John's Wood, London. Her monument is the longevity of the PNEU. SYBIL OLDFIELD

Sources M. Gibbon, *Netta* (1960) · E. Cholmondeley, *The story of Charlotte Mason* (1960) · *The Times* (8 Jan 1964) · E. Umansky, *Lily Montagu and the advancement of Liberal Judaism* (1983) · L. G. Kuzmack, *Woman's cause: the Jewish woman's movement in England and the United States, 1881–1933* (1990) · *The Times* (13 Jan 1964)
Likenesses photographs, 1869–c.1928, repro. in Gibbon, *Netta* · J. S. Sargent, portrait, 1898, repro. in Gibbon, *Netta*, frontispiece; formerly in Walker Gallery, Liverpool
Wealth at death £220,710: probate, 10 April 1964, *CGPLA Eng. & Wales*

Franklin, Hugh Arthur (1889–1962), women's activist, was born on 27 May 1889 at 28 Pembridge Villas, Notting Hill, London, the fourth of six children of Arthur Ellis Franklin (1857–1938), a senior partner in the banking firm of A. Keyser & Co., and his wife, Caroline Jacob (1863–1935), who was an active supporter of women's enfranchisement, eventually being elected to the executive committee of the Jewish League for Woman Suffrage. His elder sister, Alice Franklin, was an energetic feminist. Another sister, Helen Caroline *Bentwich, spent many years in Palestine and was later prominent in the London county council. Hugh Franklin's parents were Jewish, and he was brought up in the Jewish faith.

Franklin was educated at Clifton College, and from 1908 at Gonville and Caius College, Cambridge, where he initially read engineering, later changing to economics and sociology. He joined the Independent Labour Party and the Fabian Society, and in 1909 he became actively involved with the women's suffrage movement, joining the Men's League for Women's Suffrage, and organizing meetings at Cambridge for the constitutional suffragists Millicent Garrett Fawcett and Lady McLaren. However, his main sympathies lay with the militants of the Women's Social and Political Union, and when in 1910 the Men's Political Union for Women's Enfranchisement was formed by Victor Duval as its male affiliate, he immediately joined it. Also, at this time Franklin abandoned Judaism and declared his intention of leaving Cambridge, although he was persuaded to stay for finals. None of this met with the approval of his father, who allegedly offered money (which was refused) to Victor Duval as an inducement to him to persuade Hugh Franklin to leave the Men's Political Union. Hugh Franklin's involvement with suffrage activity, particularly in organizing the Women's Social and Political Union procession 'From Prison to Citizenship', which took place on 18 June 1910, made him miss several of his finals papers, and at the end of June he went down for good from Cambridge. With some reluctance, he accepted employment as private secretary to Sir Matthew

Nathan, then secretary to the Post Office and a prominent member of the Anglo-Jewish 'cousinhood'.

In the 'black Friday' suffrage demonstration of 18 November 1910 Franklin was arrested, but not charged; he was outraged by police tactics, and on 26 November 1910 he attempted to whip Winston Churchill, whom as home secretary he believed to be responsible. For this he was sentenced to six weeks' imprisonment in Pentonville, where he went on hunger strike; also, he was dismissed from Nathan's employment. On 8 March 1911 he was again arrested for trying to break Churchill's windows, again refused food, and was forcibly fed. Thereafter he travelled the country speaking on behalf of women's suffrage, particularly protesting against the treatment in prison of the male suffragist William Ball. He then set fire to an empty railway carriage at Harrow Station, and promptly went into hiding above Henderson's bookshop (popularly known as 'the Bomb Shop' because of its supposed anarchist clientele) at 66 Charing Cross Road. He was arrested in February 1913, and sentenced to nine months' imprisonment. Again he went on hunger strike, and was forcibly fed, apparently more than 100 times, until his release on licence under the Prisoners (Temporary Discharge for Ill-Health) Act, commonly called the 'Cat and Mouse Act'. Like most 'mice', he disappeared immediately on release, adopting the alias Henry Forster, and with his fiancée, the militant suffragette Elsie Diederichs Duval (1893?–1919), sister of his Men's Political Union colleague and friend Victor Duval, he escaped first to Dresden, then to Belgium, where he remained until the outbreak of war, and the amnesty on women's suffrage offences in August 1914.

Hugh Franklin was disqualified for war service on the grounds of poor eyesight, and served on the staff of the ordnance factories at Woolwich. On 28 September 1915 he married Elsie Duval at the West London Synagogue. He supported anti-war movements, particularly favouring Sylvia Pankhurst. His wife, whose health had already been undermined by hunger striking and forcible feeding, died of influenza on 1 January 1919 at her father-in-law's house.

After the war Hugh Franklin was set up in the timber trade, at which he was ultimately unsuccessful. He appears to have married again in 1921. His second wife was Elsie Constance Tuke, known as Bunny. This marrying out of the Jewish faith may explain why Franklin's father cut him out of his will. Despite being disinherited, he does not seem to have needed to work for a living, and in 1931 he gave up business for writing. He joined the Labour Party, in whose interest he unsuccessfully contested the parliamentary seats of Hornsey in 1931 and St Albans in 1935, finally winning a seat on the Middlesex county council in 1946. He was treasurer of the National Council for Civil Liberties from 1934 to 1939. He also held office on committees of the London county council, the Metropolitan Water Board, the New Fabian Research Bureau, the Labour Party national executive council, and on boards of governors of schools and on hospital management committees. His experiences of imprisonment led him not only to join the Howard League for Penal Reform, but also to write a play (never produced) entitled 'On Remand'.

Hugh Franklin in later life appeared a typical unremarkable resident of Hampstead Garden Suburb, though with an active, albeit impractical, interest in inventing. Tall, thin, with long legs, he was always tinkering with an antique motor car, and to his nephews and nieces seemed great fun. He died of heart failure at New End Hospital, Hampstead, on 21 October 1962, leaving no issue. He was survived by his second wife.   DAVID DOUGHAN

Sources Women's Library, London, Franklin / Duval MSS • B. Harrison, 'Interviews from 20th century women's movement' (sound tapes; interviews with Colin and Charlotte Franklin, and with Norman and Jill Franklin), Women's Library, London • E. Crawford, *The women's suffrage movement: a reference guide, 1866–1928* (1999) • Museum of London, Suffragette Fellowship collection • A. V. John and C. Eustance, eds., *The men's share? Masculinities, male support and women's suffrage in Britain, 1890–1920* (1997) • H. Bentwich, *If I forget thee* (1973) • b. cert. • d. cert.
Archives Women's Library, London, corresp. and papers | Museum of London, Suffragette Fellowship collection |SOUND Women's Library, London, Harrison tapes
Likenesses photograph on postcard, Women's Library, London
Wealth at death £626 2s. 0d.: probate, 22 March 1963, *CGPLA Eng. & Wales*

Franklin, Jacob Abraham (1809–1877), newspaper proprietor and editor, was born on 2 February 1809 in Portsmouth, the eldest of twelve children (including two daughters) of Abraham Franklin (1784–1854), a silversmith and licensed navy agent of Bath Square, Broad Street, and his wife, Miriam (1789–1870), nicknamed Polly, daughter of Jacob and Alice Aaron. Immediately following the Napoleonic wars the family moved from Portsmouth to Liverpool, settling from 1822 in Manchester. There Franklin's father, the British-born son of an immigrant Hebrew teacher from Breslau, built up a business in the West Indies trade and branched out into money-changing and stockbroking. Raised in a pious Jewish household, Jacob Franklin imbibed a lifelong reverence for traditional (Orthodox) Judaism, and was a competent Hebraist. While still in his teens he organized religion classes in his parental home on the junction of Broughton Lane and Bury New Road for children of Manchester Jewry, sharing the teaching with his sister Sarah (1810–1847). Out of that initiative emerged Manchester's first Jewish school, over which their brother Isaac (1812–1880) eventually presided. Franklin evidently also helped to found the Manchester Mechanics' Institute, one of the earliest such institutes in the country. He took classes there, reflecting his clear mathematical bent and his interest in science and philosophy; he became one of the institute's directors and an honorary teacher of mathematics.

Franklin practised successfully as an optician in St Ann's Place, Manchester, involving himself also in his father's West Indian business. In 1840 he retired on an annuity and went to London, where he involved himself in the campaign for Jewish political emancipation. He also represented the Manchester Jewish community on the Board of Deputies of British Jews. From premises in Throgmorton Street he practised as a public accountant and became a recognized authority on financial matters, developing a certain expertise in the finances of India. He argued that international monetary values should be secured by notes representing fixed proportions of gold and silver, and tirelessly advocated Britain's adoption of the metric system and decimal coinage. Among his clients were French, Indian, and Brazilian railway companies. Upon the recommendation of Baron Lionel de Rothschild he was selected by Prince Albert to prepare digests of accounts for an investigation into the Provident Savings Bank.

Franklin was a pioneer of Anglo-Jewish journalism. Although in 1836 Morris Raphall (1798–1868) had briefly run a literary periodical, the *Hebrew Review*, Anglo-Jewry had no newspaper of its own. The sensational Damascus affair of 1840, when the mysterious disappearance of a Catholic priest and his servant provoked a ritual murder charge against Syrian Jews and the imprisonment and torture of their leaders, convinced Franklin of the need for an authoritative organ to represent Jewish opinion. This conviction was reinforced by his gathering unease at the burgeoning Reform Jewish movement in London, which he as an observant traditionalist rejected as an inauthentic and dangerous travesty. He wanted a newspaper which would both take up the cudgels on behalf of Jewry and defend traditional Judaism, 'the model system Divinely revealed' which entailed 'the duties and privileges of their national vocation as "a Kingdom of Priests and a Holy Nation"' (*Voice of Jacob*, 11 Sept 1846). He deplored the indifference to Judaism of Jewish youngsters who, owing to 'the neglect of parents and elders' and 'the liberalism of the day', esteemed social parity with non-Jews above 'the spiritual rank assigned by Providence' (ibid.).

Accordingly, during 1840 Franklin discussed plans for a newspaper with several communal activists and intellectuals, receiving financial backing from Sir Moses Montefiore as well as from Baron Lionel de Rothschild. It was anticipated that Franklin would direct the business side of the enterprise, leaving the editorial role to others. But when the two men (one of whom was Raphall) selected as joint editors proved unable to take up their positions he assumed the editorship himself, but was also responsible for the financial running of the paper until relieved of the latter task by his brother Ellis (1822–1909).

The resultant publication, issued by the Anglo-Jewish Press from offices at 27 Camomile Street, St Mary Axe, London, was launched on 16 September 1841, two months before the initial, short-lived series of the *Jewish Chronicle* started: Franklin might well have been unaware that this rival venture was being planned until too late to back out of his own. Entitled the *Voice of Jacob*, an obvious play upon its editor's name and House of Jacob, a generic name for the Jewish people, it avowed 'the Promotion of the Spiritual and General Welfare of the Jews … the Dissemination of Intelligence on Subjects affecting their Interests and … the Advocacy and Defence of their Religious Institutions' (*Voice of Jacob*, 16 Sept 1841). Arguably the most scholastically distinguished of its contributors was the Manchester

Hebraist Tobias Theodores, rivalled by future *Jewish Chronicle* editor Abraham Benisch, newly arrived from Bohemia. Franklin had no desire to attract a non-Jewish readership; indeed, he endeavoured to prevent non-Jews placing subscription orders. Nevertheless, there were from the beginning a number of Christian subscribers, pre-eminently the philosemitic duke of Sussex (1773–1843), whose patronage Franklin was proud to acknowledge.

There were, as he feared, many conversionists among the paper's non-Jewish subscribers, but Franklin gradually came to realize that, like the duke, there were also genuine philosemites whose aim was to learn more of Jews and Judaism in a spirit of tolerance. As he frequently emphasized, the outstanding figure among them was Charlotte Elizabeth Tonna (1790–1846), editor of the *Christian Lady's Magazine*. So zealously in her pages did she use what she read in his periodical to plead for justice for Jews at home and abroad that an abiding friendship blossomed between the two editors, and to their mutual embarrassment a false rumour spread that they were husband and wife. Impressed with her efforts, which had no ulterior motives attached, he reached out to non-Jewish readers, acknowledging that his paper could serve as a valuable vehicle for influencing non-Jewish opinion and dissipating prejudice and misunderstanding. Thus in 1843 he gave 'relations … towards the Gentile world' as one of the paper's main guiding considerations. Another notable non-Jew with whom he became friendly was Colonel George Gawler (1796–1869), an early 'gentile Zionist' who outlined his vision of Jewish agricultural settlement in Palestine in the *Voice of Jacob*.

Almost from the outset it was evident that the *Voice of Jacob* was not commercially viable. In the first issue it was announced as 'a fortnightly publication' but the second issue did not appear for a full month. Despite his best efforts Franklin was unable to obtain a wide circulation. A very sizeable proportion of its Jewish subscribers were in the British colonies, especially in the West Indies, where he had influence. Except for those cast in a mould resembling his, communal leaders failed to give his newspaper the support it deserved. The more squeamish among the Anglo-Jewish élite objected to his forceful and forthright approach, fearing that he might antagonize non-Jews with some of the items he carried. But he was unrepentant. If Christians took offence, it could not be helped: 'we shall always bear in mind the peculiarities of our national position' (*Voice of Jacob*, 4 Feb 1842). Making a profit had not been Franklin's motive, and he consoled himself by observing 'we labour not to sell but to serve' (ibid.). He poured his own money into the undertaking, which was in some respects run on a shoestring, with his brother Ellis helping with the proofs and a younger sibling, Henry (1826–1907), while still a schoolboy, contributing articles on biblical themes. But with the relaunch in 1844 of the more moderate and successful *Jewish Chronicle*, the paper became less viable. In the issue of 11 September 1846 Franklin announced his withdrawal from the enterprise, contemplating what he had accomplished in a spirit of satisfaction, not least its role in forging cordial contacts

with Christians, but resenting the apathy, even animosity, encountered from so many of his fellow Jews. A notice signed by Haim Guedalla, treasurer of the Anglo-Jewish Press, announced that 'a Committee of Influential Gentlemen' (headed by a brother of Sir George Jessel, the future solicitor-general and master of the rolls) would secure the paper's future. It continued under Guedalla's editorship until its final issue, dated 1 September 1848.

Franklin spent the rest of what his close associate Abraham Benisch called 'an active and bustling life' (*Jewish Chronicle*, 10 Aug 1877) in various communal endeavours: urging the establishment of a college for the training of Anglo-Jewish rabbis, writing a column in the *Jewish Chronicle* that was marked by his characteristically clumsy, convoluted style, and compiling invaluable and copious statistical material for the principal communal charity, the Jewish Board of Guardians. It was his weakness, as Benisch observed, that an unsurpassable divide existed between 'the warmth and vividness' of his 'lofty aims' (ibid.) and his ability to stimulate enthusiasm for them in others. His difficult personality brooked no compromise, but the welfare of the Jewish people was always uppermost in his heart. He was a founder of the Anglo-Jewish Association, formed in 1871 to advance the status of oppressed Jewries overseas. Unusually for a religious Jew he never married. The orphaned young daughter and son of his brother Abraham Gabay Franklin (1821–1870) became his wards. He died of Bright's disease at his home, 24 Westbourne Park Villas, Paddington, London, on 3 August 1877, and was buried in the Willesden cemetery of the United Synagogue. He left several bequests in the cause of Jewish religious education.

HILARY L. RUBINSTEIN

Sources A. Benisch, *Jewish Chronicle* (10 Aug 1877) • A. L. Emanuel, Portsea, letter, *Jewish Chronicle* (17 Aug 1877) • *Jewish Chronicle* (13 Nov 1891) • A. E. Franklin, ed., *Records of the Franklin family and collaterals* (1935) • U. Southampton, Hartley Library, MS 120/2/1–2 and MS 225/17/1 • H. L. Rubinstein, 'A pioneering philosemite: Charlotte Elizabeth Tonna (1790–1846) and the Jews', *Jewish Historical Studies*, 35 (1996–8), 103–18 • will, 24 Dec 1873, Principal Registry of the Family Division, London, with codicils • D. Cesarani, *The Jewish Chronicle and Anglo-Jewry, 1841–1991* (1994) • J. M. Shaftesley, ed., *Remember the days: essays on Anglo–Jewish history presented to Cecil Roth* (1966) • *Voice of Jacob* (1841–6) • *Christian Lady's Magazine* • d. cert. • *CGPLA Eng. & Wales* (1877)
Archives U. Southampton L., papers relating to the *Voice of Jacob* and the Jacob Franklin Trust
Likenesses photograph
Wealth at death under £35,000: will with two codicils, 22 Aug 1877, *CGPLA Eng. & Wales*

Franklin [*née* Griffin], **Jane, Lady Franklin** (1792–1875), traveller and promoter of Arctic exploration, was born in London, the second of the three daughters of John Griffin, a London silk merchant, and his wife, Mary Guillemard, both of Huguenot descent. Her mother died when Jane was four years old and the sisters grew up in close companionship with their father, in London and on his frequent journeys in Europe. Among their extensive London acquaintance were the Arctic explorer John *Franklin (1786–1847) and his wife, Eleanor [*see* Porden, Eleanor Anne]. Eleanor Franklin died in 1825, leaving a baby

Jane Franklin, Lady Franklin (1792–1875), by Amélie Romilly, 1816

daughter, and on 5 November 1828 John Franklin and Jane Griffin were married. Franklin was knighted in 1829.

Never idle herself, Lady Franklin liked to see all around her busy, and was much irked by the three years immediately following her marriage before her husband was again at sea. As he sailed she wrote urging him to be on the alert for future employment and expressing the 'unmingled satisfaction I feel at having been forced out of our career of vanity and trifling idleness' (letter of 8 Dec 1830, Rawnsley, 68–9). While her husband was away Lady Franklin travelled in the eastern Mediterranean, encountering discomforts and dangers only partially alleviated by her lady's maid and the flea-proof iron bedstead which accompanied her on all her journeys, even to the top of a Hawaiian volcano.

In 1836 Sir John was appointed lieutenant-governor of Van Diemen's Land, later renamed Tasmania, at Lady Franklin's suggestion, and they set sail, accompanied by her stepdaughter Eleanor and her niece by marriage Sophia (Sophy) Cracroft. Sir John intended Eleanor to be as a daughter to his childless second wife, and to know her only 'by the endearing appellation of Mamma' (letter of 11 Nov 1828, Woodward, 160). In fact relations between them were never close and later flared into open warfare on Eleanor's engagement, when Lady Franklin, insisting that after his disappearance her husband's fate was still uncertain, refused to release to Eleanor money due on his death. A settlement but no reconciliation was reached. It was Sophy Cracroft who was as a daughter to her. Lady Franklin was an energetic governor's lady; an acquaintance and admirer of Elizabeth Fry, she took an intelligent and kindly interest in women convicts. Although Sir John's enlightened views on prison reform and his wife's 'busyness' had their critics, the couple were generally popular. They encouraged the social and intellectual development of Tasmania, establishing a scientific society, which became the Royal Society of Tasmania, and a school. Lady Franklin took every opportunity of exploring Australia and New Zealand as well as Tasmania.

Sir John was recalled in 1844, and critics of his progressive views may have prejudiced the further employment for which he and his ambitious wife were eager. After pressure from both, he was appointed commander of the Admiralty expedition to look for the north-west passage. He set sail in 1845. When two years had passed with no news, Lady Franklin demanded that steps be taken to find the missing ships. She bombarded the Admiralty with pleas and suggestions for routes. Her persistence and her willingness to court useful friends and spend the money she had inherited from her father won the respect of many at the Admiralty. Between 1850 and 1857 she helped fit out five ships for the search. The last, the yacht *Fox* (Captain Leopold McClintock), launched after the official search had been called off, traced the expedition's story to its tragic end. For her role in the search the Royal Geographical Society awarded Lady Franklin the patron's medal for 1860, the first and for many years the only woman it so honoured. Sir Roderick Murchison, president of the society, was one of the main champions of her cause, realizing that it coincided neatly with his wish to promote Arctic exploration for commercial as well as scientific ends.

After the ordeal of the search Lady Franklin disdained the expected retirement. With Sophy Cracroft, who had become as experienced a traveller and keeper of the record as herself, she travelled extensively, although her later journeys were more formal and less adventurous than her earlier ones. She was received with deference in America, Japan, India, and elsewhere. She had an audience with Pope Pius IX, 'having ascertained that there would be no nonsense about it—no kneeling I mean', recorded Miss Cracroft (Woodward, 349). She discussed Arctic research with the emperor of Brazil, met Brigham Young at Salt Lake City, and made friends with Queen Emma of Hawaii. She hoped through Murchison to persuade Queen Victoria to stand godmother (with herself as proxy) to Queen Emma's son, with the aim of asserting British influence and thus thwarting American and French designs on the islands. Although the child died before the elaborate ceremony planned could take place, the friendship persisted, and in 1865 Lady Franklin arranged for Queen Emma, now childless and a widow, to visit Britain.

From 1862 Lady Franklin and her niece maintained a house in London, its walls hung with portraits of men who had shared the ordeal of the Franklin search. From here she supervised the preparation of memorials to her husband. She died on 18 July 1875 at 45 Phillimore Gardens, London, and was borne to her grave in Kensal Green cemetery by six naval officers, all Arctic men.

DOROTHY MIDDLETON

Sources F. J. Woodward, *Portrait of Jane* (1951) • *The life, letters and correspondence of Jane Lady Franklin, 1792–1875*, ed. W. R. Rawnsley (1923) • L. P. Kirwan, *The white road: history of polar exploration* (1959) • A. L. Korn, *The Victorian visitors* (1958) • S. Cracroft, *Lady Franklin visits Sitka, Alaska, 1870*, ed. R. N. De Armond (1981) • R. A. Stafford, *Scientist of empire: Sir Roderick Murchison, scientific exploration and Victorian imperialism* (1989)
Archives BL, letters [copies] • NL Aus., corresp. and diaries • Scott Polar RI, corresp., journals, and MSS • University of Hawaii Library, Manoa, corresp., journal, and MSS relating to Hawaii | BL, letters to J. Barrow, Add. MSS 35306–35309 • BL, letters to Sir Roderick Murchison, Add. MS 46126 • BL, corresp. with Robert White relating to Franklin expedition • CAC Cam., corresp. with Robert White, papers relating to Franklin expeditions • NL NZ, Turnbull L., corresp. and papers relating to Sir John Franklin's estate • RGS, corresp. with RGS, Sir E. Omanney, and Sir G. Black • Scott Polar RI, letters to William Scoresby
Likenesses attrib. T. Bock, 1815?, Victoria Museum, Launceston, Tasmania • A. M. Romilly, chalk drawing, 1816, NPG [*see illus.*] • marble bust, 1877 (after A. M. Romilly), RGS
Wealth at death under £14,000: resworn probate, April 1876, *CGPLA Eng. & Wales* (1875)

Franklin, Sir John

Franklin, Sir John (1786–1847), naval officer and Arctic explorer, was born on 16 April 1786 in Spilsby, Lincolnshire, the ninth of the twelve children of Willingham Franklin (*d.* 1824), a mercer, and his wife, Hannah Weekes. He had four brothers and seven sisters, and was educated at a preparatory school in St Ives, Huntingdonshire, and, from the age of twelve, at Louth grammar school, near Spilsby.

Early years Franklin remained at Louth grammar school a mere two years before the lure of the sea led him to persuade his father to send him on a merchant vessel from Hull to Lisbon. It has been suggested that Franklin's father hoped a taste of sea-faring life would bring his son back to his intended career in the church, but if this was the case it misfired, and Franklin requested that an appointment be secured for him as a first-class volunteer in the Royal Navy. In October 1800 he joined the *Polyphemus*, which, within six months, played a role in the battle of Copenhagen. Franklin's second appointment was as a midshipman on *Investigator*, under the command of his uncle Captain Matthew Flinders. *Investigator* circumnavigated Australia before being abandoned as unseaworthy. Her scurvy-weakened crew set sail for home in *Porpoise*, which sank, leaving them stranded on a sandbank for six weeks until Flinders was able to secure help.

Franklin's next commission was with *Bellerophon*, on which he saw action at the battle of Trafalgar in 1805. He continued war duty on *Bedford*, and was promoted lieutenant on 11 February 1808. In September 1814 *Bedford* sailed for New Orleans, where Franklin was slightly wounded. The Napoleonic Wars were drawing to an end, and, after a short commission on *Forth*, Franklin was discharged on half pay. This might have been a severe blow to his considerable ambitions, but in 1818 the Royal Navy elected to resume its exploration of the Arctic, at the instigation of John Barrow, second secretary of the Admiralty and an accomplished traveller, who was convinced that there was a north-west passage, a navigable sea route between

Sir John Franklin (1786–1847), by unknown photographer, 1845

the Pacific and Atlantic oceans. Not only was this exploration an important part of an expanding empire, but it was a practical way to employ idle naval personnel in peacetime. Franklin's war record and experience of exploration aboard *Investigator* secured him the command of the small brig *Trent*.

First Arctic experiences Two Arctic expeditions left England in 1818. The first, under Commander John Ross, aimed to seek a north-west passage through the archipelago to the north of Canada. The second, under Commander John Buchan, aimed to cross the Arctic Ocean in the barque *Dorothea* in company with *Trent*. Buchan and Franklin were forced to return to Barrow with nothing more to report than that the pack ice north-west of Spitsbergen formed an impenetrable barrier.

Barrow was undeterred, and in 1819 another two expeditions were sent out. The first, under William Edward Parry, was to seek an entrance to the north-west passage from Baffin Bay through Lancaster Sound, while the second, under Franklin, was to explore the north coast of the American continent east of the Coppermine River. This was no mean task for Franklin. The coast had been sighted only twice before (once in 1771 by Samuel Hearne, and once in 1789 by Alexander Mackenzie). The plan was for the Hudson's Bay Company (HBC) and the North West Company (NWC) to convey Franklin to Hudson Bay and to equip him for his overland expedition. However, the area Franklin was to explore was far to the north of the two companies' normal supply lines, and communications were at best tenuous.

After only three months' preparation the expedition set

sail, on 23 May 1819, on the HBC's supply ship *Prince of Wales*. Franklin's crew included the midshipmen George Back and Robert Hood, the surgeon–naturalist John Richardson, and the seaman John Hepburn, all of whom were to earn Arctic fame. They reached York factory on Hudson Bay on 30 August, and, after a difficult journey along part of the HBC's regular trading route, wintered at Cumberland House in what became Saskatchewan. In midwinter, Franklin, Back, and Hepburn travelled to the NWC post at Fort Chipewyan, in what became Alberta. The next stage of the journey began on 18 July 1820, after Franklin had discovered that the supplies and men he had been so confidently offered by the trading companies were not forthcoming. The party left Fort Chipewyan and headed towards Fort Providence, an NWC post on the Great Slave Lake, under the command of Willard Wentzel. Wentzel and Akaitcho, a Copper chief, agreed to accompany Franklin into the unexplored territory along the Yellowknife River. A second winter was spent at Fort Enterprise.

It was at Fort Enterprise that the problems of inadequate supplies and unwilling guides began to tell. Back had to snowshoe back to Fort Chipewyan for supplies, and Franklin's aggressive response to the problems alienated both the Indians and the voyageurs. The situation was resolved temporarily when Back returned with replenishments. The third, and most arduous, part of the expedition began on 14 June 1821; the party travelled down the Coppermine River, reaching the sea on 18 July, after which Wentzel and the Indians returned to Fort Providence. Franklin's party of twenty men set out to explore the coast east of the Coppermine River in two small Indian canoes. Progress, however, was painfully slow, provisions were critically low, winter was approaching, and there was unrest among the voyageurs. They turned back at Turnagain Point on the Kent peninsula on 18 August. One canoe was so badly damaged that it had to be abandoned, and the party was forced to return overland to Fort Enterprise. On the way they were reduced to eating lichens, and cold and exposure took a huge toll. Nine men died, and it was suspected that Michel, one of the voyageurs, was eating the bodies of his fallen comrades. Michel shot Hood, and was in turn executed by Richardson.

It was a pathetic party that struggled into Fort Enterprise, only to find that it had not been restocked with provisions as promised. They existed on bones, scraps of vegetation, and deer skins for another three weeks until some Indians arrived and took them to Fort Providence. Eleven men of the party of twenty had died of starvation or exposure, or at the hands of their comrades.

Franklin spent another winter in the north before returning to London in September 1822. He went home a hero, having displayed great courage during three years of almost unimaginable hardship and privation. He was hailed triumphantly as 'the man who ate his boots', although no reference was made to the spectre of cannibalism that was the cause of the deaths of Michel and Hood. At a time when Britain was hungry for heroes and tales of *noblesse* in the face of terrifying danger and hardship, Franklin was perfect. His *Narrative of a Journey to the Shores of the Polar Sea, in the Years 1819, 20, 21, and 22* (1823) was immensely popular and was regarded as something of a classic in travel literature.

The traders, however, and particularly George Simpson of the HBC, told a different story, noting in Franklin an inability to adapt, and a rigid adherence to orders when better results might have been obtained with flexibility. They also resented his antagonism to them during the winter at Fort Enterprise, and they accused him of taking sides in the trade wars between the HBC and the NWC. In reality, Franklin was a diffident man in many respects, though his peers found him knowledgeable in his own field. The governor-in-chief, Lord Dalhousie, wrote in 1827 that he was endowed 'with slow, clear perception, with a dignified & impressive good sense, sound judgement & presence of mind' (Ramsay). This description suggests that Franklin was neither the dashing naval hero beloved by the British public nor the irrational weakling projected by Simpson.

Regardless of the grumblings of disgruntled traders and voyageurs, and the appalling deaths on an expedition that offered little in the way of scientific or geographical achievement, the Royal Navy was well pleased with Franklin. He had been made a commander in his absence (on 1 January 1821), and was promoted post captain on 20 November 1822. He was also elected fellow of the Royal Society. Despite this public acclaim, Franklin remained a modest man, and was awkward at social gatherings. He married the poet Eleanor Anne *Porden (1795–1825) on 19 August 1823, and his daughter, Eleanor Isabella, was born on 3 June 1824, when he was already laying plans for his next expedition.

Later Arctic experiences Franklin had learned a hard lesson, and his next expedition was supplied by the Royal Navy, with the HBC providing transport. The first supplies, two strong boats, and a party of seamen were sent in advance to ensure that they arrived in time. Franklin and the main body of the second expedition, which included Richardson and Back, left on 16 February 1825. On his arrival in New York he learned that his wife, ill since the birth of their daughter, had died shortly after he had left.

The expedition forged north-west, arriving at Cumberland House on 15 June and establishing winter headquarters at Fort Franklin on Great Bear Lake in August. The winter was spent comfortably with ample supplies, and the expedition set out north in four boats on 22 June 1826. On 4 July, at the Mackenzie delta, the party split, and Franklin and Back travelled west, intending to rendezvous with *Blossom* under the command of Frederick William Beechey, at Icy Cape (later in Alaska). Progress was slow, and with the onset of winter Franklin abandoned the journey, and prudently decided to return to Fort Franklin. Ironically, a boat dispatched from *Blossom* was waiting for him the day he turned back: had he known, he would have pressed on. Meanwhile, Richardson and midshipman Edward Nicholas Kendall had travelled east, and had completed their survey of the coast eastwards to the Coppermine River. They arrived back at Fort Franklin almost three weeks before Franklin.

The second winter passed as comfortably as the first, and the expedition was back in Liverpool on 26 September 1827. In contrast to his return from his first Arctic expedition, Franklin's second homecoming was happy in the knowledge that he had made a significant contribution to Arctic geography. A sizeable portion of the coast of Arctic North America had been surveyed, and important data on geology, meteorology, topology, and magnetism had been collected. Franklin set to work on his second book, *Narrative of a Second Expedition to the Shores of the Polar Sea, 1825, 1826, and 1827* (1828), which was written in the same, somewhat arid, laboured style as the first.

For the next two years Franklin was fêted as Arctic hero. He received a knighthood on 29 April 1829, and was awarded a gold medal from the Société de Géographie de Paris and an honorary DCL from Oxford University. He married Jane Griffin [see Franklin, Jane (1792–1875)], a friend of his dead wife, in London on 5 November 1828. Biographers of John and Jane Franklin have commented on his shyness in the courtships of his wives, although both marriages appear to have been perfectly satisfactory.

Franklin's career suffered an unexpected blow when, after working on plans with the Admiralty for further Arctic exploration, he was informed that the Royal Navy's operations in that area were no longer required. In 1830 he was given command of the frigate *Rainbow*, and was stationed in the Mediterranean during the Greek War of Independence. For his services there he received the order of the Redeemer of Greece and the Royal Hanoverian order. After returning home in 1833 Franklin was unemployed until April 1836, when he was offered the lieutenant-governorship of Van Diemen's Land.

Lieutenant-governor of Van Diemen's Land Between 1823 and 1836 the colony at Van Diemen's Land had been under the rule of Sir George Arthur, whose social reforms had alienated members of the small community. On his arrival in Hobart on 6 January 1837, Franklin quickly realized that he had inherited a gravely split and uneasy command. Although he was a deeply religious man who strove fervently to improve conditions among the convicts, Franklin's inexperience in administration hampered him severely. His steps to introduce a representative assembly to the colony were considered inappropriate by the British government in what was largely a penal station, and his preoccupation with improving social and educational facilities was unpopular with the Colonial Office. The situation was not improved by Lady Franklin, who undertook reform and education with a zeal that rendered her insensitive to or dismissive of the ominous rumblings of outrage against her husband from other government officials.

The outcome was that, when Franklin's period of office expired, he was not invited to continue, and he left Hobart on 3 November 1843. From the government's point of view, Franklin's six-year appointment was at best unsuccessful and at worst disastrous. The petty factions that had arisen from Arthur's rule had festered, goaded by the sly political manoeuvrings of the colonial secretary, Lord Stanley. But Franklin's sense of justice and compassion had made him a popular figure among many Hobart colonists, settlers and convicts alike. He had established a scientific society, and founded (and largely financed) a school, for which Dr Arnold of Rugby was requested to select a headmaster. He even attempted to prevent the extinction of the few surviving Aborigines, but what he could do was too little and far too late.

Franklin's last voyage and its aftermath Franklin returned to England in June 1844, his confidence shattered by the Van Diemen's Land experience. During his absence the search for the north-west passage had been renewed, and expeditions under the command of Peter Dease, Thomas Simpson, Back, and James Clark Ross had mapped most of the Arctic coast of mainland North America. Of the north-west passage, a route winding through the frozen islands had been established, with the exception of a 300 mile stretch between Barrow Strait and the mainland. The Admiralty began to discuss the possibility of an expedition to explore this last tantalizing section of the passage.

Franklin's depression at his perceived failures in Van Diemen's Land lifted instantly. With the support of fellow Arctic explorers William Edward Parry, Richardson, and Ross, he began to petition to be allowed to lead the proposed expedition. His enthusiasm prevailed, and he was given the commission on 7 February 1845. Franklin, perhaps because he was not flamboyant, egotistical, or abrasive, was a man well liked by his colleagues, his men, and his seniors at the Admiralty. He was reliable and honest, and it may have been his affability, coupled with knowledge that this pleasant, likeable man had been hurt by his unfortunate experiences in Hobart, that prevailed over the Admiralty's doubts about his age (he was fifty-nine when the expedition left). These were not, perhaps, the soundest of reasons for choosing a man to command an arduous journey, since there were other, younger, and equally appropriate men who might have been chosen.

Franklin's ships, *Erebus* and *Terror*, were bomb-vessels powered by high-pressure steam engines with the latest boilers. Their keels were extended to obtain a more advantageous vertical alignment and to protect their interiors, and their sterns redesigned to allow the raising and lowering of new propellers. But they were only part of what was to be the best-equipped, best-prepared Arctic expedition ever mounted. The expedition took advantage of the latest technology in food preservation and canning, the most recent advances in Arctic land travel, and crews that were the cream of the Royal Navy. Supplies—which included handsome silverware, fine cut glass, and an extensive library—were expected to last for three years, though it was believed that the expedition would have solved the question of the north-west passage long before that and returned home in a blaze of glory.

Erebus and *Terror* sailed down the River Thames on 19 May 1845. Shortly before departure, daguerreotypes were taken of Franklin and his officers. Franklin sits in full uniform, a large man tending to fat with heavy jowls, his baldness concealed by his hat. It seems that he had changed little since 1827, when Lord Dalhousie described him as having 'dark complexion & hair, his head very round, bald, with thick curled short hair' (Ramsay). Franklin's orders were to sail to Lancaster Sound, and search either southwest from Barrow Strait towards the mainland (where he had explored on his first two expeditions) or north and west through Wellington Channel. On 26 July 1845 they were hailed by whalers in Baffin Bay, after which John Franklin was never sighted again.

At first the failure of the expedition to return provoked no response from the Admiralty: it was equipped to survive three years, the ships and men were the best the Royal Navy could provide, and their leader was the reliable, responsible Franklin. But when no word of the expedition had been heard by 1847, the families and colleagues of the crew, and especially Lady Franklin, began to agitate for the Admiralty to begin a search. Between 1847 and 1859 some thirty expeditions were sent to discover the fate of Franklin, most sponsored by the Admiralty, but some by Lady Franklin herself or by the wealthy American merchant Henry Grinnell, whose interest was roused by Lady Franklin's appeal to the president of the United States. Unaware of Franklin's fate, the Admiralty promoted him rear-admiral in October 1852.

Gradually, the search expeditions began to piece together what had happened to Franklin's expedition. In 1850 Horatio Thomas Austin and William Penny found his 1845–6 wintering site at Beechey Island in Barrow Strait. Four years later, HBC explorer John Rae heard accounts from the Inuit that white men had died on King William Island, and he found relics indicating that the bodies he found were unquestionably those of the crews of *Erebus* and *Terror*. Rae wrote that, 'From the mutilated state of many of the corpses and the contents of the kettles, it is evident that our wretched countrymen had been driven to the last resource—cannibalism—as a means of prolonging existence' (J. Rae, letter to the Admiralty, 29 July 1854, cited in *The Times*, 23 Oct 1854).

Rae's claim outraged the British public, who dismissed his findings and allegations with scorn, refusing to believe that Englishmen of her majesty's navy would eat each other. The search continued, and in 1859 Leopold McClintock and William Hobson found, along with more bodies and relics, two written messages. The first, dated 28 May 1847, stated that Franklin was commanding the expedition and all was well. The second, dated 25 April 1848, was written by Franklin's second in command, Francis Rawdon Moira Crozier, and reported that *Erebus* and *Terror* had been abandoned on 22 April, and that the remaining crew was intending to walk to Back's Fish River. Franklin, Crozier wrote, had died on 11 June 1847. He did not say how Franklin met his death, and, since it is likely that he was buried in the ice, only the discovery of his body will reveal the truth.

The final part of the Franklin expedition tragedy was as clear as it would ever be. After wintering at Beechey Island, the ships had circumnavigated Cornwallis Island and then sailed south through Peel Sound and Franklin Strait, where they had been beset in an area which has some of the thickest sea ice in the world. After Franklin's death and Crozier's abandonment of the ships, the party, weakened by starvation and scurvy, struggled towards the Adelaide peninsula, some dying on the way, others when they reached the mainland at Starvation Cove. Not one of the 129 members of the expedition survived. But, by reaching the Adelaide peninsula, the expedition essentially completed the discovery of the north-west passage, despite rival claims by leaders of the search expeditions.

The aura of mystery about and the horrifying fate of Franklin's final expedition, together with the fame and honour he had earned for his first land expedition, meant that biographers had difficulty making fair judgements of Franklin for many years after his disappearance and death. Assessments have oscillated between emphasizing his reliability, deep sense of morality, and courage, and his apparent inflexibility, inability to adapt to new conditions, and unquestioning following of orders. But, as with Robert Falcon Scott more than half a century later, the brave naval officers who died carrying out their duty for England, no matter how misguided or flawed, attained an exalted position with the British public. In Franklin's case, this is not wholly unwarranted: he was not the most innovative or successful of Arctic explorers, but his charting of the North American coast was accurate and extensive, his governorship of Van Diemen's Land was just and compassionate, and his personal qualities and characteristics were admirable.

B. A. RIFFENBURGH

Sources R. J. Cyriax, *Sir John Franklin's last expedition* (1939) · C. S. Houston, ed., *Arctic ordeal: the journal of John Richardson, surgeon-naturalist with Franklin, 1820–1882* (1984) · C. S. Houston, ed., *To the Arctic by canoe, 1819–1821: the journal and painting of Robert Hood* (1974) · C. S. Houston, ed., *Arctic artist: the journals and paintings of George Black, midshipman with Franklin, 1819–1822* (1994) · R. Owen, *The fate of Franklin* (1978) · A. H. Markham, *Life of Sir John Franklin and the north-west passage* (1891) · P. D. Sutherland, ed., *The Franklin era in Canadian Arctic history* (1985) · G. F. Lamb, *Franklin—happy voyager—being the life and death of Sir John Franklin* (1956) · A. Cooke and C. Holland, *The exploration of northern Canada, 500 to 1920* (1978) · K. Fitzpatrick, *Sir John Franklin in Tasmania, 1837–1843* (1949) · P. Nanton, *Arctic breakthrough: Franklin's expeditions, 1819–1847* (1971) · E. Ramsay [ninth earl of Dalhousie], *The Dalhousie journals*, ed. M. Whitelaw, 2 vols. (1978–82)

Archives Bexley Local Studies and Archive Centre, account of a search to find him in the Arctic · BL, personal and family corresp. and papers, Add. MSS 22613, 40666, 45545, 46868, 47768–47772, 56233 · Derbys. RO, corresp., journal · Lincs. Arch., MISC DON 430; 447/1–2 · McGill University, Montreal, McCord Museum, corresp. · Mitchell L., NSW, corresp. relating to Van Diemen's Land · NMM, lunar observations · PRO, letters to Sir Edward Sabine, BJ 3 · PRO, CO 6/15–16 · PRO NIre., corresp. and papers of him and Lady Franklin · RGS, corresp. and papers · Scott Polar RI, corresp., journals, letter-books, and papers · University of Tasmania Library, corresp. and papers of him and Lady Franklin | BL, corresp. with Charles Babbage, Add. MSS 37183–37200, *passim* · Lincs. Arch., letters to Booth family · NMM, letters to Mary Anne Kay · NMM, letters to Mary Kendall and Edward Kendall · Scott Polar RI, letters to George Back · Scott Polar RI, corresp. with Robert Brown · Scott

Polar RI, letters to W. H. Fitton · Scott Polar RI, corresp. with John Richardson · Scott Polar RI, letters to James Clark Ross
Likenesses W. T. Fry, stipple, 1823 (after T. Wageman), BM, NPG; repro. in *New European Magazine* (1823) · G. R. Lewis, pencil, pen and ink drawing, *c*.1823, Scott Polar RI · T. Phillips, oils, 1828, NPG · D. D'Angers, bronze plaque, 1829, Scott Polar RI · P. J. D. D'Angers, bronze plaque, 1829, NPG · P. J. David, wax bust, 1829, priv. coll. · W. Derby, watercolour drawing, *c*.1830, NMM · W. Brockedon, chalk drawing, 1836, NPG · S. Pearce, oils, *c*.1837 (after J. M. Negelen?), Scott Polar RI · daguerreotype, 1845, Scott Polar RI · photograph, 1845, NMM [*see illus.*] · C. Bacon, bronze statue, 1861, Spilsbury, Lincolnshire · plaster relief plaque, 1861 (after J. S. Westmacott), Scott Polar RI · M. Noble, statue, 1866, Waterloo Place, London · M. Noble, marble bust on monument, 1875, Westminster Abbey, London · A. C. Lucchesi, bronze bust, 1898, NPG · L. Haghe, lithograph (after Negelen), BM, NPG · S. Pearce, group portrait, oils (*The Arctic council, 1851*), NPG

Franklin, Lilian Annie Margueretta (1882–1955), commanding officer of the FANY, was the only daughter (there was also one son) of William Franklin (1852–1920) of Horsham, Sussex, a wholesale merchant, and his wife, Louisa (1845–1923). The family lived for a number of years at Cecil Lodge in Hook, Surrey.

In 1909 Lilian Franklin joined the First Aid Nursing Yeomanry (FANY) corps, an all-women uniformed organization which had been founded two years earlier by 'Captain' Edward Baker and which was an initial success. The women, aged from eighteen to thirty, provided their own horses and bought their own uniform as well as paying a 10*s*. enrolment fee and 6*s*. a month subscription. They went on a weekend camp, appeared at the royal tournament, and were trained by the guards. A photograph of 1909 shows Lilian Franklin in frogged red jacket and navy skirt, mounted sidesaddle, recruiting in Whitehall. In 1910 dissatisfaction with Baker caused a split, leading to the formation, by Mabel St Clair Stobart, of the rival Women's Sick and Wounded Convoy Corps which was later incorporated into the voluntary aid detachments.

Baker and his daughter Kitty left the corps shortly afterwards. Lilian Franklin was one of six women to remain with the FANY and it was largely due to her that it survived. After inspecting the FANYs at their Pirbright camp in July 1914 Surgeon-General Woodhouse recommended their usefulness to the War Office. At the outbreak of war the following month they offered their services for the war effort, but to no avail. However, the Belgians and the French were not so dismissive and for the next four years the FANYs ran hospitals and casualty stations, and drove ambulances and supply cars, for the two armies all along the western front. Finally, on 1 January 1916, the British military authorities capitulated and a convoy was formed at Calais base under the command of Lilian Franklin, the first women to drive officially for the British army.

The women, initially housed in tents on the beach, transported the dead and wounded from the casualty clearing stations, the ambulance trains, and the barges to hospitals or hospital ships. In 1920 an unnamed Royal Artillery officer recalled the gallant role played by Franklin on 25 April 1917. On that night, he noted, there was a bombing raid on a camp at Audruicq, which housed many German prisoners-of-war as well as supplies; an ammunition dump was hit and there were many casualties. Franklin arrived with the first ambulance:

> The Boche was crumping them down all over the place, most unhealthy. Franklin just stood there, out in the open, helping to load the ambulances … She had a cheery word for everyone. The bombs were continuous, and shrapnel was raining down, but she never went for shelter and she never flinched. (FANY archives)

The officer described her as the bravest woman that he had ever met. She was mentioned in dispatches in 1917 and appointed OBE in 1918; she also received Belgian gallantry awards.

After the war, when most of the other women's services were demobilized, the FANY continued to train, although recruitment was much reduced. Franklin became the first corps commandant in 1924 when the FANY was reorganized along more formal lines. She was succeeded by Mary Baxter Ellis in 1932. Franklin was a tall, strong-featured, wiry woman, variously described as dour, dedicated, and unflappable. She was often affectionately caricatured in FANY magazines with her long cigarette holder and battered First World War topi. She never married and died on 8 January 1955, aged seventy-three, at her home, 94 Rushams Road, Horsham, Sussex, of a cerebral thrombosis. She was buried in a family grave at St Paul's Church, Hook, Surrey. LYNETTE BEARDWOOD

Sources Duke of York's HQ, Mercury House, London, FANY archives · I. Ward, *FANY invicta* (1955) · H. Popham, *FANY, the story of the women's transport service* (1984) · IWM, Grace McDougall papers · private information (2004) [M. C. Bone, archivist, St Paul's Church, Hook, Surrey] · E. Baker, recollections, in *Women and war*, vol. 1, June 19, Duke of York's HQ, Mercury House, London, FANY archives · *CGPLA Eng. & Wales* (1955) · d. cert. · parish register, Hook, St Paul, [n.d.] [burial]
Archives Duke of York's HQ, Mercury House, London, FANY archives, corresp. and minutes
Likenesses five photographs, 1909–20, Duke of York's HQ, Mercury House, London, FANY archives
Wealth at death £9781 10*s*. 1*d*.: probate, 1955, *CGPLA Eng. & Wales*

Franklin, Mary (1800–1867), schoolmistress, was born, probably in Coventry, on 5 August 1800, the eldest child and first daughter of Francis Franklin (1772–1852), Baptist minister, and his wife, Rebecca, *née* Dyer. Her father had been pastor of the Cow Lane Chapel, Coventry, since 1799, with a stipend of £40 p.a. on which he and his wife worked hard to bring up ten children, three of whom died in infancy. Like so many of her female contemporaries in similar situations, Mary looked to school-keeping for her own support. After attendance then work as an assistant at a school in Bocking in Essex, she began to take pupils in her parents' parlour, at first little boys, including the young Charles Bray, the future ribbon manufacturer, as well as little girls. Soon she combined forces with her sister Rebecca [*see below*] and they rented a house in Hertford Street, Coventry, allowing them to take older girls as boarders, as well as day girls.

The enterprise flourished and they moved several times more within Coventry, to a house called Nant Glyn in Warwick Row, then to Hertford House, and finally to Little

Park Street. Mary supplied the motherly warmth and the organizing ability, Rebecca the cultivated style and dramatic presence. Pupils came from as far away as India and the USA, but also from London and the surrounding countryside. These included Mary Anne Evans, the future novelist George Eliot, who boarded with them from 1832 to 1835.

The curriculum was the conventional female one: English, arithmetic, history, and drawing, with French, German, and music as extras. The last three were taught by visiting masters of a high standard, and all the teaching was marked by an exemplary rigour. Mary's niece, Rebecca Franklin Hine, recalled that her aunts'

> system of training was undoubtedly that of the strictly rigid, somewhat despotic regime—repression of evil rather than eliciting the good. … Their teaching on all subjects was the very reverse of the present style of veneer—thorough to the lowest foundations, from Holy Scripture to the correct Parisian accent   (Supplement, *Coventry Herald*, 5)

although she confirmed that Aunt Mary's mathematics stopped short of algebra and geometry.

Both Mary and Rebecca were committed supporters of their father's chapel, to which their pupils were taken on Sundays. The physical description of the character Rufus Lyon and his surroundings in George Eliot's novel *Felix Holt* is acknowledged to be a vivid picture of the Revd Francis Franklin and the courtyard of the Cow Lane Chapel. The Franklins were General rather than Particular Baptists. The essential Calvinism of their creed was buttressed by extensive good works and the support of the Baptist Missionary Society, of which Mrs Franklin's brother, John Dyer, was secretary, and for which another sister, and a brother who died in training, set out to work. Such charitable work provided a pattern and some occupation for George Eliot in the first years after she left school. The sisters retired to live at 13 White Street, Coventry, where Mary Franklin died on 4 December 1867 of dropsy following bronchitis.

Rebecca Franklin (1803–1873), schoolmistress, was born in Coventry on 30 November 1803, the third daughter of Francis and Rebecca Franklin. With her cousin Eliza Dyer she attended a school in Paris for a year and on her return began to take pupils in one of the Sunday school rooms at Cow Lane. Soon she combined forces with Mary and they moved to Hertford Street. Rebecca considered all things literary and the deportment and cultivation appropriate to ladies her especial provinces. The girls were encouraged to read widely among the English poets and were not forbidden novels. She laid stress on speaking in harmonious tones and in finished, even studied, sentences. Indeed, her niece recalled that a 'sort of intangible, diffusive, and yet exquisite elaboration of diction clothed all her ideas, clothed them in fact in such multiform circumlocution, and yet precision of detail, as made it a perfect puzzle to catch her real meaning' (Supplement, *Coventry Herald*, 5). Rebecca encouraged George Eliot to eliminate her midland accent, to pitch her voice low and evenly, and to strive always to speak in well-formed sentences.

The affection between teacher and pupil was real and enduring: contact was maintained after George Eliot left school and she condoled with Rebecca on her periodic bouts of ill health. Rebecca in turn was deeply distressed by George Eliot's loss of faith. She endeavoured to find a minister of appropriate stature and learning to debate with her; in 1842 she joined those pleading with Robert Evans to behave more humanely in face of his daughter's intellectual and emotional turmoil. Sadly Rebecca Franklin's mind gave way in her last years and she died on 29 May 1873 at 13 White Street, Coventry.

GILLIAN SUTHERLAND

Sources *The George Eliot letters*, ed. G. S. Haight, 9 vols. (1954–78) · *Coventry Herald* (7–8 Nov 1919) [George Eliot centenary suppl.] · I. Morris, *Three hundred years of Baptist life in Coventry* (1925) · Cow Lane Chapel records, Leics. RO · *Coventry Standard* (May 1873) [Rebecca Franklin]

Archives Coventry Local Studies Library, George Eliot Collection

Likenesses photograph (Rebecca Franklin), repro. in *Coventry Herald*

Wealth at death under £2000—Rebecca Franklin: probate, 23 June 1873, CGPLA Eng. & Wales

Franklin, Rebecca (1803–1873). *See under* Franklin, Mary (1800–1867).

Franklin, Robert (1630–1703), Presbyterian minister, was born in London on 16 July 1630 of unknown parents. As a young child he was sent to Suffolk to live with his aunt, Mrs Browning, and shortly after, at the age of eight, he began to attend the grammar school at Woodbridge. Here, as he confessed, he was bad-tempered and vain, spent too much time at sport, and often tried to lie his way out of trouble. He was taught writing and accounts in order to take up a London apprenticeship, but the schoolmaster's belief in his academic ability convinced the boy's guardians to send him to Cambridge. He was admitted to Jesus College as a sizar in March 1647, and matriculated from Queens' College in the same year but did not graduate. Franklin's tutor was Samuel Bantoft (d. 1692), whom he is reported to have succeeded in that post. But within a short time, having impressed the leading parishioners in a preaching contest against a Dr Brooks, Franklin was admitted in August 1651 to the appropriate rectory of Kirton, Suffolk, taking the engagement to the Commonwealth on 20 August. This inaugurated a career in which his efforts to find adequate maintenance were repeatedly disappointed. At Kirton it proved impossible to survive on an income of 50s. per annum, so Franklin set up a school. This proved very popular, but local parents were most often unable to pay and Franklin took up the curacy at Bramfield. He must have regretted this decision, for here, as he recounts, he received nothing at all, and a further move to the living of Blythburg, on the presentation of Lady Elizabeth Brooke of Cockfield Hall, proved equally unsatisfactory. Yet another benefice was found for him, at Westhall, Suffolk, where his fortunes at last improved. The aged incumbent, 'very old and rendered speechless by the palsy', and his wife paid him '10s. per week and … £4 per annum' (*Nonconformist's Memorial*, 3.292–3). The incumbent soon resigned and Franklin was formally admitted on 4 August 1658, compounding for the first fruits the following month.

Franklin was ejected under the Act of Uniformity in 1662, and for six months during the following year he acted as a private chaplain in the household of Sir Samuel Barnardiston (1620–1707) at Brightwell Hall, near Ipswich. From there he went to London and was given lodging by a Mr Eastland. He preached in the city during the plague, and was reported to be giving sermons at Blue Anchor Lane soon after the fire in 1666. That event made a deep impression upon Mary Smith (*d.* 1713), who was 'an eye witness of it, and forced to move all on the Lord's day'; afterwards she 'grew out of love with company that were vain and light' (Gravenor, 28). About this time she met Robert Franklin, and they married in 1669. In that year he was reported to be preaching, again at Blue Anchor Lane, to 100 persons. In 1670 he was arrested for preaching at Colnbrook, Buckinghamshire, and committed to Aylesbury gaol, where he exchanged letters with Mary. The couple buried five children at Bunhill Fields, but at least two daughters, Joanna and Sarah, survived infancy. It seems that a building adjoining their house in Blue Anchor Lane was used for meetings, and Franklin was licensed as a Presbyterian teacher in April 1672.

In 1682 'Mr Robert Franklyn, of St Giles without Cripplegate clerk' was fined £60 for attending two unlawful conventicles at the Blue Anchor on 8 October and of 'having taken it upon himself to preach and teach the persons assembled' (Jeaffreson, 4.172). The following January he was in Newgate prison, where he was visited by Oliver Heywood, and his goods were sold. Calamy tells us that Franklin was arrested while preaching in Glovers' Hall, 'and carried before the Lord Mayor, and on refusing the corporation oath … was committed to Newgate for half a year' (Calamy, *Continuation*, 806). After his release the Franklin family moved to Goat Alley, near Bunhill Fields. However, soon after their move Franklin was seized 'at ten a clock at night … and carried to New Prison; and when released, was forced to appear at every session, and give in bail: and so was perpetually almost harassed till the time of King James's liberty' (ibid.). Perhaps it was on one of these occasions that, as Calamy remembered, 'justices, informers, constables and soldiers … were fierce and noisy, and made great havoc' (Calamy, *Historical Account*, 1.89). On 23 November 1691 Franklin contributed £5 to the Common Fund of presbyterians and congregationalists. In 1695 he was preaching to a congregation which met at Plasterers' Hall in Addle Street near Cripplegate, London. He died in London in 1703 and was buried at Bunhill Fields on 12 October.   ALSAGER VIAN, *rev.* STEPHEN WRIGHT

Sources Calamy rev. · *The nonconformist's memorial … originally written by … Edmund Calamy*, ed. S. Palmer, [3rd edn], 3 vols. (1802–3) · E. Calamy, *A continuation of the account of the ministers … who were ejected and silenced after the Restoration in 1660*, 2 vols. (1727) · A. Gordon, ed., *Freedom after ejection: a review (1690–1692) of presbyterian and congregational nonconformity in England and Wales* (1917) · Venn, *Alum. Cant.* · *Congregational Historical Society Transactions*, 1 (1901–4), 345–52 [printed letters, unsigned introduction] · J. T. Cliffe, *The puritan gentry besieged, 1650–1700* (1993) · E. Calamy, *An historical account of my own life, with some reflections on the times I have lived in, 1671–1731*, ed. J. T. Rutt, 2 vols. (1829) · B. Gravenor, *The dissolution of the earthly house of this tabernacle* (1713) · J. C. Jeaffreson, ed., *Middlesex county records*, 4 vols. (1886–92)

Franklin, Rosalind Elsie (1920–1958), crystallographer, was born at Chepstow Villas, Notting Hill, London, on 25 July 1920, the elder daughter and second of the family of five children of Ellis Arthur Franklin (1894–1964), merchant banker of London, and his wife, Muriel Frances Waley (1894–1976). Both parents came from established Anglo-Jewish families; Helen *Bentwich (Labour chairman of the London county council, 1956–7) was her aunt; Herbert *Samuel, Viscount Samuel (Liberal politician and first high commissioner for Palestine) was her great-uncle; Arthur *Waley (translator of oriental literature) was her mother's cousin. From 1932 to 1938 Rosalind was a scholar at St Paul's Girls' School and went on to Newnham College, Cambridge, where she read natural sciences, taking her part two in chemistry in 1941. Wartime constraints made her time at Cambridge austere and directed her PhD to an industrial problem with the Coal Utilisation Research Association (CURA), while also burdening her with duties as a London air raid warden.

At CURA Franklin worked on cokes and chars. She found that, although the total volume of the pores in such material increases with increasing temperature, their accessibility decreases. She showed this by a series of ingenious experiments in which, finally, even gaseous helium molecules are unable to penetrate the material. She realized that to reach an understanding of the internal structure of coals and chars it was necessary to use X-ray diffraction methods and these she learned when she moved in 1947 to the Laboratoire Centrale des Services Chimiques de l'État in Paris, where she was employed as a *chercheur* of the Centre National de la Recherche Scientifique. These were personally happy years for her and scientifically very productive. She learned, and improved, X-ray techniques for dealing quantitatively with substances of limited internal order, which presented much more difficulty than the highly ordered crystals which the X-ray crystallographers of the day were more familiar with. In a series of beautifully executed investigations Franklin discovered the fundamental distinction between chars that turned into graphite on heating and those that did not, and further related this difference to the chemical constituents of the material from which the chars were made. These results later proved to be highly relevant for the development of carbon fibres, materials of industrial importance which are made of rolled up parallel sheets of graphite layers.

The combination of these X-ray analytical techniques with chemical preparatory skill attracted the attention of others, and in 1950 Franklin was invited by John Randall to build up an X-ray diffraction laboratory at King's College, London, for the purpose of studying the structure of DNA. She accepted, and started work in January 1951 as a Turner and Newall research fellow of London University. Although DNA is now almost a household word, at that

Rosalind Elsie Franklin (1920–1958), by Elliott & Fry, 1946

Franklin in 1950 makes it clear that on 'the experimental X-ray effort there would be for the moment only yourself and Gosling'.

Within the first year Franklin transformed the state of the field. By drawing thinner fibres of DNA she was able to enhance the alignment of the molecules within the specimen, and these, together with finer collimation of the X-ray beam, produced much better X-ray patterns. Moreover, by introducing methods to control and vary the water content of the specimens, she showed that two forms of the DNA molecule, which she called A and B, existed, and defined conditions for the transition between them. It became clear that previous workers had been working, unbeknown to them, with a mixture of the two forms, or at best of poorly oriented specimens of the B form. In May 1952 she obtained the superb patterns of the B form which later graced the textbooks, and which J. D. Watson saw early in 1953. Inspection of this helical pattern, together with the distribution in December 1952 of a report by Franklin of her work, gave crucial information to Watson and Crick for the final building of their DNA model in February–March 1953.

However, despite her discovery of the simpler B pattern, Franklin's attention was mostly directed to the A form, because here the molecules are not in random rotational positions, as in B, but packed in a crystal lattice. The X-ray pattern thus shows sharp crystalline 'spots' and offered the possibility of an objective crystallographic analysis because of the greater wealth and precision of the diffraction data available. In retrospect this may look a misjudgement, but it was a reasonable decision because, if correctly interpreted, the A pattern would yield more precise information about the DNA molecule, though, of course, any model for DNA must be capable of forming either structure A or B. In fact, the analysis ran into an impasse and in January 1953 Franklin turned to the B form, the X-ray pattern which was characteristic of some kind of helical structure.

By March 1953 Franklin had carried the quantitative analysis of her B form patterns to the point where the paths of the backbone chains were determined, and she wrote up her work in a typescript dated 17 March, that is, one day before news of the Watson and Crick structure reached King's. The draft contains all the essentials of her later paper (with Gosling) in *Nature* in April, together with one by Wilkins and his colleagues, which accompanied Crick and Watson's paper announcing their model for the structure of DNA. In Franklin's draft, it is deduced that the phosphate groups of the backbone lie, as she had long thought, on the *outside* of the two coaxial helical strands whose configuration is specified, with the bases arranged on the inside. Her notebooks show that she had already formed the notion of interchangeability of the two purine bases with each other, and also of the two pyrimidines. The step from base interchangeability to the specific base pairing postulated by Crick and Watson is a large one, but there is little doubt that she was poised to make it. The notebooks also show that she had grasped that the A form

time it was not at all clear, despite Avery's great paper of 1944, that it was the hereditary substance itself, and certainly no one, not even Crick and Watson, who finally solved its double helical structure, suspected that the three-dimensional structure itself would point to a direct conclusion on how genes replicated themselves. (The crucial feature of the structure of DNA is not the double helical arrangement of the two phosphate sugar backbones, but the unique pairing of the heterocyclic bases projecting from each of these two strands. It means that each strand is complementary to the other so that, when the two come apart, each can be used to assemble a duplicate of its former partner.) In 1950 DNA was only known to be an important chemical constituent of the chromosomes of the cell nucleus, but that it alone carried the genetic information, irrespective of the protein constituents, was not generally accepted by biochemists.

Work on DNA at King's had been begun by M. H. F. Wilkins who, before 1951, together with a research student, R. G. Gosling, had succeeded in obtaining well-orientated fibres of the long DNA macromolecules, which showed a higher degree of crystallinity, as judged by the X-ray diffraction pattern, than specimens produced by earlier workers. Franklin was asked by Randall to undertake a systematic X-ray study of DNA fibres and Gosling was placed under her supervision. Randall left an unfortunate ambiguity about the respective positions of Wilkins and Franklin which later led to dissension about the demarcation of the DNA research at King's, but a letter of his to contained two chains or strands which ran in opposite directions, but had not understood the exact relation between the two forms, namely that the A form is a somewhat more tightly wound form of the B double helix in which the bases change their tilt direction considerably, thus obscuring the helical structure underlying the A form X-ray pattern. In a second paper to *Nature* in July 1953 Franklin and Gosling showed this conclusively, and indeed this paper stands as the first analytical demonstration of the correctness of the Watson–Crick model.

In mid-March 1953 Franklin moved to Birkbeck College, London, at the invitation of Professor J. D. Bernal. Here her main work was on tobacco mosaic virus, taking up its X-ray study where it had been left in the work of Bernal and Fankuchen, fifteen years before. Watson had put forward the hypothesis that the large rod-shaped virus particle was composed of a helical arrangement of small protein molecules (or subunits). Franklin showed that this was, in essence, correct. Using her improved techniques, she was able to obtain spectacular, and beautiful X-ray patterns of the virus, of such clarity that she could begin a quantitative analysis of the structure. In four short years, together with a small devoted group of students and collaborators, she determined the precise helical geometry of the protein units, and above all showed that the ribonucleic acid (RNA) of the virus, the carrier of the infectivity, in other words of the genetic information, formed a long single chain embedded deeply within the protein framework.

On 16 April 1958 Franklin died of cancer at the Royal Marsden Hospital, Chelsea; she was buried at the Jewish cemetery, Willesden, London. Franklin was initially struck by cancer in 1956; she bore her illness bravely, never complaining, and worked as much as possible to the very end. She was cut off tragically at the height of her powers and her early death was a great loss to science. But her mark was made. The results of her work on two major biological problems, as well as the techniques used to obtain them, helped lay the foundations of structural molecular biology. In 1962 Watson, Crick, and Wilkins were awarded a Nobel prize for their work on DNA. The prize is not given posthumously so the practical question of whether Franklin should have been included did not arise. However, since Franklin's contributions, and indeed her actual X-ray data, were crucial to the total achievement, it is difficult to see how she could have been denied a share.

The impression sometimes given in writing or film in which Franklin figures is of an absolutely dedicated woman. This is only part of her character. She was single-minded and uncompromising in her work, so that she sometimes was bound to provoke exasperation among her colleagues, a feeling immediately tempered by the admiration they felt. But she was not austere, she had a sense of fun, and was a woman of wide culture, at home in several European countries and the USA. She loved travel, took walking and cycling holidays abroad, and was a good mountain climber.

As a scientist she was not merely a gifted experimentalist, but possessed a good analytical mind. Had she lived she would surely have gone on to further heights, but she will be remembered as one of the select few who made crucial contributions to one of the most important discoveries of the twentieth century.   AARON KLUG

Sources J. D. Watson, *The double helix* (1968) · A. Klug, 'Rosalind Franklin and the discovery of the structure of DNA', *Nature*, 219 (1968), 808–10, 843–4 · A. Klug, 'Rosalind Franklin and the double helix', *Nature*, 248 (1974), 787–8 · J. Glynn, 'Rosalind Franklin, 1920–1958', *Cambridge women: twelve portraits*, ed. E. Shils and C. Blacker (1996), 267–82 · A. Sayre, *Rosalind Franklin and DNA* (1978) · H. F. Judson, *The eighth day of creation: the makers of the revolution in biology* (1979) · personal knowledge (2004) · private information (2004) · *CGPLA Eng. & Wales* (1958) · Randall to Franklin, 4 Dec 1950, CAC Cam., Franklin MSS
Archives CAC Cam., scientific corresp. and papers · priv. coll.
Likenesses Elliott & Fry, photograph, 1946, NPG [*see illus.*] · photograph, 1950–51, NPG
Wealth at death £11,278 10s. 9d.: probate, 30 June 1958, *CGPLA Eng. & Wales*

Franklin [Frankelin], **William** (b. *c.*1610), self-proclaimed reincarnation of Christ, seems to have been born at Overton, near Andover, in Hampshire, about the year 1610. It was to be said of him that he became an apprentice rope-maker in London and that he married about 1634. In 1650 he was reported to have a wife and three children living in Stepney. If so, he may be identified with the William Franklin, rope-maker of Ratcliffe Highway, who had four children by his wife, Margery, baptized in the parish of St Dunstan, Stepney, between January 1639 and October 1642. Franklin was accounted a 'civil man', 'well esteemed' for his zealous and constant observance of gospel ordinances. He was a member of a gathered congregation (perhaps that presided over by William Greenhill) and regarded by the godly as an 'eminent Saint'. In 1646, having been 'much afflicted' by the plague and apparently 'somewhat distracted in his brain', Franklin was bled 'divers times' by a surgeon (Ellis, *Pseudochristus*, 6). During his sufferings he was alleged to have blasphemed, 'saying, *That he was God, that he was Christ*'. Upon his recovery Franklin repented, declaring that he had been seduced by the wiles of Satan. Afterwards, however, he 'plunged' deeper still into 'such spiritual delusions', pretending that he had 'received some Revelations and Visions'. He may have become acquainted with those that denied 'Ordinances, Scriptures, Christ', and supposedly claimed that he had the gift of prophecy. In addition, he imagined that he could 'speak with new Tongues' and would 'babble out words' which neither he nor others were able to understand. Franklin was also said to have ceased carnal relations with his wife and 'to keep company with other women'. For 'all which evils' he was excluded by his congregation (ibid., 7).

Some time in 1649 Franklin was introduced to **Mary Gadbury** (b. *c.*1619), the wife of James Gadbury, by a woman living with Gadbury. Mary Gadbury may have been the Mary Pakeman who, aged about eighteen, married James Gadbury by licence in the parish of St Gregory by St Paul's, London, in September 1637. In 1643 or there-abouts, James Gadbury had deserted his wife and gone to the Netherlands with a servant; Mary had pursued her husband across the sea but to no avail. On her return she lived with a daughter in London, mainly in Watling Street, finding employment as a seller of 'Laces, pins, Band-strings, and other trifles for Gentlewomen'. A 'frequent hearer of the Word', Mary Gadbury gadded 'chiefly' to the sermons of John Goodwin and Henry Jessey (Ellis, *Pseudochristus*, 8). After their meeting with Franklin, Gadbury and her introducer began to sing joyously. Gadbury, moreover, confessed that she was possessed by 'certain Fits' which would 'set her whole body in a trembling' (ibid., 9, 10). She also acknowledged that a voice within began to speak to her in 'Parables', saying that 'the Lord would send his Son to raign in the person of a man'. Soon after Franklin arrived at Gadbury's house and convinced her that he was the Son of God come to earth in 'a new body' (ibid., 11). Franklin later stayed the night with Gadbury, perhaps lying in 'the same bed' as her, for which she was accused by her neighbours of keeping a 'naughty house' (ibid., 13). It was probably about this time that Gadbury heard 'the Voyce' of the Lord 'bid her sell what she had, and follow him'. She obeyed and departed with Franklin to Hampshire—'the Land of *Ham*' of Psalm 105: 23 (ibid., 13, 14).

In November 1649 Franklin and Gadbury arrived in Andover on the wagon that travelled weekly between there and London. While lodging at The Star inn Franklin began to preach. His obscure yet seemingly spiritual words, delivered with 'a very plausible and affected (though slow) manner of speech', began to attract attention (Ellis, *Pseudochristus*, 17). Thereupon, Franklin departed for London. In his absence Gadbury spread a rumour that she had seen Christ 'in the person of a man'—her account of 'a plaine man in gray cloaths' answered to Franklin's description (ibid., 18, 19). Gadbury, moreover, perhaps now pregnant with Franklin's illegitimate child, declared that she was like 'a woman in travail' (ibid., 20). At her trial she reportedly claimed that

> shee was ye bride & ye Spouse ye lambes wife … ye Virgin Mary yt bare Christ & yt shee was deliured … of a fiery flyeing serp[an]t and of ye old dragon w[hi]ch shee had sent unto ye place of perdition. (Clarke MS 18, fols. 27v–28r)

A disciple likewise affirmed that he had seen her 'delivered' of 'a Dragon', suggesting that her initial hope of pro-creating the saviour of the world was transformed by the ensuing misshapen stillborn (Ellis, *Pseudochristus*, 22).

Franklin returned from London on 8 December only to find a cold welcome at The Star inn. Warned 'to depart', he and Gadbury left Andover bound for the village of 'Crooxeason' (Crux Easton). There they were entertained for six weeks or so by the local minister, William Woodward, and his wife, Margaret (Ellis, *Pseudochristus*, 25). While at Crux Easton Franklin began to preach at Woodward's house, declaring that he was 'ye Christ crucified without ye gates of Jerusalem ye son of god & saviour of ye world', 'the Lion of the Tribe of Judah' that had 'the key of the bottomlesse pit' 'and yt he was come to gather ye elect' (Clarke MS 18,

fol. 27v; Ellis, *Pseudochristus*, 31). He soon attracted followers to whom he assigned 'offices and titles'. One was John the Baptist, 'sent forth to tell that *Christ was come upon the earth*'. Another was a 'destroying' angel 'sent forth to curse the earth' (a figure from the Revelation). Another still was usually a 'healing' angel, but at other times 'one of the two Witnesses' (of Revelation 11: 3; Ellis, *Pseudochristus*, 31–2).

Franklin and three of his adherents were apprehended by warrant and brought to Winchester on 27 January 1650. Witnesses were examined before two justices of the peace and a recantation drawn up and offered to Franklin. To this he subscribed his name. Gadbury proved more obdurate and was dispatched to 'the house of Correction' (Ellis, *Pseudochristus*, 44). Chastened and whipped, she recanted by subscribing her mark. While imprisoned the pair were questioned by Humphrey Ellis, a minister of the cathedral church of Winchester. Ellis, who had previously preached a sermon warning of 'the abundance of heresies, and the great increase of false christs, false teachers, and deceivers amongst us', found Franklin 'very ignorant' in the 'Principles' of religion (Ellis, *Two Sermons*, 30; Ellis, *Pseudochristus*, 48). Ellis supposed that Franklin had 'sucked' his 'wicked Principles' from 'the Familists', though he added that Franklin was 'sometime a zealous Professor [of] *Anabaptism*' (Ellis, *Pseudochristus*, 48, 60, 59). Franklin and Gadbury were subsequently tried at the assize (western circuit) beginning on 7 March 1650 before Lord Chief Justice Henry Rolle. Franklin was sentenced to remain in gaol 'till he give good security for his good behaviour'. Gadbury received further 'correction' before eventually being released at the quarter sessions held the week after Easter (ibid., 51, 52). On 22 April she left Winchester on the wagon that travelled weekly between there and London. Nothing else is known of her.

In May, Ellis published his relation of the 'Grand Impostures' of William Franklin and Mary Gadbury. It was entitled *Pseudochristus*. After the Restoration, Thomas Comber used Ellis's account in his denunciation of the 'Several Kinds of Inspirations and Revelations Pretended to by the Quakers'. Comber's index referred his readers to 'Frankelin … and the Hamp-shire Revealers' (Comber, title-page, index). The number of Franklin's followers, however, remains unknown (contemporary estimates of 500 or 600 converts appear exaggerated). In June 1666 William Woodward, having previously had his Hampshire living 'sequestred from him', was deprived of his living of Trottescliffe, Kent (Ellis, *Pseudochristus*, 52). Woodward had been charged with uttering profane and blasphemous speeches: that the Lord's prayer was not commanded to be used, that the Church of England might as well be called the Church of Rome, that he had attained such perfection that he could not sin, and that one 'William Frankelin', a rope-maker who had lived with him, was the Christ and Saviour.

ARIEL HESSAYON

Sources H. Ellis, *Pseudochristus* (1650) · Worcester College, Oxford, Clarke MS 18, fols. 27v–28v · C. Gilbert, *The libertine school'd* (1657), 26 · T. Comber, *Christianity no enthusiasm* (1677), 94 and index · 'Return of appeals … to the high court of delegates, 1533–

1832', *Parl. papers* (1867–8), 57.20–21, no. 199 • H. Ellis, *Two sermons: the first, concerning the last times* (1647)

Franklin, William (1730/31–1813), colonial governor, was born after November 1730 in Philadelphia, the eldest child of Benjamin *Franklin (1706–1790), inventor and statesman, and either his common-law wife, Deborah Read Rogers (1705?–1774), the daughter of John Read and his wife, Sarah, or a mistress. He grew up above his father's printing shop on lower Market Street with his siblings Francis and Sarah.

Franklin was educated locally at Annand's classical academy, Philadelphia, from 1738 to 1743, then, thwarted in his wish to go to sea, in 1746 enlisted for a military campaign in Canada. Later he joined an Indian treaty expedition in the Ohio territory. He no longer lived in the Franklin household, and Deborah publicly and 'in the foulest terms' was heard to call him 'the greatest Villain upon Earth' ('Diary of Daniel Fisher', 276)—unlikely maternal sentiments. He studied law, and in the early 1750s, when Benjamin Franklin was elected to the Pennsylvania assembly, he turned over to his son its clerkship and, later, other colonial offices. Franklin became grand secretary of Philadelphia's masonic lodge. In 1752 he joined his father in the famous kite experiment with electricity, and in 1754 accompanied him to the Albany conference on colonial defence and the following year to confer with General Braddock, whom Franklin assisted in procuring military provisions.

Firm opponents of Pennsylvania's proprietors, Franklin and his father departed for London in 1757 on the elder's mission to counter them. The Franklins lodged at 7 Craven Street, Strand. After studying at the Middle Temple, Franklin was called to the bar on 10 November 1758 and then travelled with his father through Britain and Europe. When his father received an honorary doctorate from Oxford on 30 April 1762, Franklin was awarded an honorary MA, being described as 'learned in municipal law' (*Papers*, 10.76). Tall and handsome, he plunged into social life, one result being the birth of a son, William Temple Franklin, probably in 1760, to an unknown mother. When his father left for Philadelphia in 1762, he remained in London and received the royal governorship of New Jersey, probably through the agency of the earl of Bute. He took the oaths on 9 September 1762, five days after marrying Elizabeth Downes (*bap.* 1728, *d.* 1777).

The governor and his wife arrived in America in February 1763 and settled in Burlington, New Jersey. Caught between the demands of London and those of his colony, Franklin erroneously believed that the 1765 Stamp Act could 'be quietly carried into Execution throughout' New Jersey (PRO, CO 5/987), while, later, he was castigated by London for not thwarting local action against the Townshend Acts. Vigorously using his position to forward private enrichment schemes, in 1766 he led the way in forming the Illinois Company, which vainly sought a massive grant of land from the crown. He built a grand house facing the Delaware River and farmed 600 acres outside Burlington. He practised his Anglican faith as religiously as befitted his position and in 1772 was elected a member

of the London-based Society for the Propagation of the Gospel.

For several years Franklin provided his father, now back in England, with colonial intelligence. As he continued to oppose Pennsylvania's proprietors, Franklin was challenged to a duel—which never took place. In 1768 he attended the Fort Stanwix conference, where the representatives of the Six Nations named him Sagorighweyoghsta: 'dispenser or arbiter of justice'. From 1772 onwards his relations with the New Jersey assembly deteriorated, and he began lobbying for the governorship of Barbados. However, with Lord Dartmouth's appointment as head of the Board of Trade, London became far less critical of him: he had, said Dartmouth, 'kept his Province in good Order, during Times of Difficulty' (*Papers*, 19.360). He owed much of his advancement to the influence of his father, who in 1771 had addressed his *Autobiography* to Franklin. Yet by 1774 Franklin was steering a course that placed an unbridgeable gulf between them. His fervent support of parliament's policy towards Massachusetts in the wake of the Boston Tea Party caused his father to call him 'a thorough Courtier' who saw 'every thing with Government Eyes' (*Papers*, 21.287).

When the Continental Congress met in Philadelphia in September 1774, Franklin began sending highly secret intelligence to Lord Dartmouth. Remaining steadfastly at his post while other governors fled, he became the *bête noire* of American radical leaders. He was a 'madman', who might well be tarred and feathered (Reed MSS, 4.1). When in January 1776 he prepared a further confidential report, it was intercepted and his house was broken into. By June he was arrested as an 'enemy to the liberties of this country' (*Minutes of the Provincial Congress*, 456). 'New Jersey have dethroned Franklyn', reported one gleeful member of the Continental Congress (Smith, 4.210). To his tormentors he firmly restated his loyalty to the king: '*Pro Rege et Patria* was the Motto I assumed when I first commenced my Political Life, and I am resolved to retain it till Death' (Revolutionary Era MSS). He was held captive in Connecticut for over two years, on one occasion beaten, on another nearly hit by musket shot. When his wife, now in British-controlled New York city, became seriously ill, he was refused permission to visit her, and she died 'broken hearted' in July 1777 (*Papers*, 25.553).

Late in 1778 Franklin was freed. In New York, where he was awarded an annuity from the British Treasury, he was the acknowledged leader of the American loyalists, for whom he struggled to secure aid. He also built up an unofficial yet active spy network. Deeply embittered and seeking revenge, he was appointed in 1780 president of the Board of Associated Loyalists, which organized bands to plunder rebel areas. This created havoc in official British relations with the rebels and was disbanded, and a discredited Franklin departed for London in August 1782.

In England, Franklin sought to ensure that the peace settlement provided recompense for loyalist losses in America. His father, however, was a chief negotiator of the treaty, and his hatred of loyalists in general, and the leading role played by his son in particular, was unyielding. Parliament in 1788 granted Franklin but a fraction of his claims. Mortified, he made unavailing attempts to recoup moneys he had earlier sunk into western land schemes and faded from the political scene.

On 14 August 1788 Franklin married his Irish-born London landlady, Mary D'Evelyn (c.1753–1811). Two years after she died, on 3 September 1811, Franklin, suffering from angina pectoris and influenza, died, aged eighty-two, at his home, 28A Norton Street, Marylebone, on 16 November 1813. He was buried in the churchyard of St Pancras Old Church on 25 November. Effectively disinherited by his father, with whom he had never been reconciled, his bequests totalled about £600.

BOYD STANLEY SCHLENTHER

Sources The papers of Benjamin Franklin, ed. L. W. Labaree and others, [35 vols.] (1959–) · S. Skemp, William Franklin: son of a patriot, servant of a king (1990) · L. R. Gerlach, Prologue to independence: New Jersey in the coming of the American Revolution (1976) · P. H. Smith and others, eds., Letters of delegates to congress, 1774–1789, 26 vols. (1976–2000) · M. B. Norton, The British Americans: the loyalist exiles in England, 1774–1789 (Boston, 1972) · C. Van Doren, Secret history of the American Revolution (1941) · L. R. Gerlach, William Franklin: New Jersey's last royal governor (1975) · C. A. Lopez and E. W. Herbert, The private Franklin: the man and his family (1975) · W. S. Randall, A little revenge: Benjamin Franklin and his son (1984) · PRO, Colonial Office records, series 5 (North America) · D. S. Shields, Civil tongues and polite letters in British America (1997) · B. H. Newcomb, Franklin and Galloway: a political partnership (1972) · W. H. Mariboe, 'The life of William Franklin', PhD diss., University of Pennsylvania, 1962 · C. Fennelly, 'William Franklin of New Jersey', William and Mary Quarterly, 6 (1949), 361–82 · The writings of Benjamin Franklin, ed. A. H. Smyth, 10 vols. (1905–7) · The autobiography of Benjamin Franklin, ed. L. W. Labaree and others (1964) · V. O. Stumpf, 'Who was Elizabeth Downes Franklin?', Pennsylvania Magazine of History and Biography, 94 (1970), 533–4 · 'Extracts from the diary of Daniel Fisher, 1755', Pennsylvania Magazine of History and Biography, 17 (1893), 263–78 · GM, 1st ser., 83/2 (1813), 510 · Minutes of the provincial congress and the council of safety of the state of New Jersey (1879) · New Jersey Historical Society, Newark, Revolutionary Era MSS · parish register, London, Old St Pancras, LMA [burial] · American Philosophical Society, Philadelphia, Franklin MSS · New-York Historical Society, New York, Reed MSS

Archives American Philosophical Society, Philadelphia · L. Cong., political corresp. and papers · New Jersey Historical Society, Newark, Revolutionary Era MSS · PRO, corresp., PRO 30/55 · PRO, Colonial Office records, series 5 (North America) · Yale U., Sterling Memorial Library | American Philosophical Society, Philadelphia, Bache collection · Hist. Soc. Penn., Gratz collection · U. Mich., Clements L., Clinton MSS · U. Mich., Clements L., corresp. with Thomas Gage

Likenesses M. Brown, oils, c.1790, priv. coll.

Wealth at death about £600 in bequests: will

Franklyn, William (1480/81–1556), dean of Windsor, was born in 1480 or 1481 at Bledlow, Buckinghamshire, and educated at Eton College, where he was admitted scholar in 1496, and King's College, Cambridge, where he graduated BCnL in 1504–5. He took orders—he is recorded as vicar of Thurleigh, Bedfordshire, in February 1510—and in 1514 Bishop Ruthal appointed him chancellor of the diocese of Durham and receiver of episcopal revenues. In 1515 he became archdeacon of Durham, and in the same year rector of Easington and master of the hospital of St

Giles, Kepier, both in co. Durham. In this and the following years Franklyn was active in directing border warfare. His headquarters were at Norham, and a grant of arms was made to him for recovery of this castle by his 'prowes and pollice' (Longstaffe, 31). On 21 February 1518 he was installed prebendary of Haydour-cum-Walton in Lincoln Cathedral. From 1518 to 1528 he was prebendary of Howden Minster. By 1522 he was rector of Houghton-le-Spring, Durham; he also held the prebend of Eveston in the collegiate church of Lanchester in the same county.

On Wolsey's being provided to the bishopric of Durham in commendam in 1523, Franklyn was assiduous in devising plans for increasing the revenues of the see. In the most notable of his many letters to Wolsey (11 April 1523), he advised how his collieries and lead mines might be more profitably worked, and recommended obtaining parliamentary confirmation of certain palatine rights. He drew attention to muniments at Durham Place in London which would support the commendatory's claims. He apparently offered to yield the chancellorship to Wolsey's existing steward, retaining for himself the surveyorships of Yorkshire and the bishopric, despite a loss of 40 or 50 marks in his income; he wrote 'I am yonge inow and maye take payne and labour being of full myend to applie my self to do your grace the most honour plesure and service that may lie in my power' (Hutchinson, 1.405). But Wolsey confirmed Franklyn in the chancellorship, which he retained under Bishop Tunstall.

In 1525 Franklyn was retained as counsellor to the duke of Richmond, the king's illegitimate son, on his being made president of the north. Franklyn described his new superior as 'a chylde of excellent wisdome and towardnes', for whose 'good and quyk capacitie, retentyve memorie, vertuous inclinasion to all honor, humanitie and goodness' it would be hard to find 'any creature lyving of twise his age hable or worthy to be compared to hym' (Nichols, xxix). On 13 February 1526 Franklyn was installed prebendary of Stillington in York Minster, which he held for life, and where in 1532 he proposed to undertake a formal period of residence. In 1527 he became president of Queens' College, Cambridge, but was succeeded by Simon Haynes in the summer of 1528. He continued to work chiefly in the north. In October 1528 he was a commissioner to treat for peace with James V, king of Scots, and in 1531 was again serving in Scotland. He had a hand in the negotiations which led to the peace concluded at Holyrood on 31 July 1534. In that year he was licensed to exchange his archdeaconry of Durham for that of York, but this was not effected. In 1535 he was one of the council of the north commissioned to tax the clergy, and during that year became prebendary of Auckland in the college of that name, for which he would receive a pension of £3 on its dissolution.

On 17 December 1536 Franklyn was appointed dean of Windsor, being installed on the 19th. He also held the associated posts of register of the Order of the Garter and dean of Wolverhampton. By 1537 he was rector of Stanmore, Middlesex, where he retreated when plague struck

Windsor. On 15 November 1540 he acquired the rectory of Chalfont St Giles, Buckinghamshire, resigning his Lincoln prebend. As dean of Windsor he assisted at the baptism of the future Edward VI, and at the funeral of Queen Jane, in 1537. From about 1540 he was frequently absent through illness. St George's Chapel was in consequence without firm leadership, which may have contributed to the development of radicalism there in 1543. Foxe tells a story of his failing to discipline one of the inferior clergy for mild insubordination, concluding that Franklyn was 'a timorous man' (*Acts and Monuments*, 5.469); but this is an unworthy judgement on a man honoured for gallantry. Nevertheless, his last years were inglorious. He surrendered most of his benefices, including on 14 January 1545 the hospital of Kepier. He was obliged to alienate much property of St George's Chapel to the crown. In August 1552 his continuing illness impeded the work of Edward VI's commissioners. Shortly after Mary's accession he resigned, a successor being named on 8 February 1554. Franklyn retired to Chalfont St Giles, where he died in January 1556 and was buried in the church. His will, which does not survive, was subsequently challenged because of its provision for Catholic devotional purposes.

C. S. Knighton

Sources W. Hutchinson, *The history and antiquities of the county palatine of Durham*, 1 (1785), 404–6 • S. Bond, ed., *The chapter acts of the dean and canons of Windsor: 1430, 1523–1672* (1966), 11 • D. S. Boutflower, ed., *Fasti Dunelmenses: a record of the beneficed clergy of the diocese of Durham*, SurtS, 139 (1926), 47 • *Heraldic visitation of the northern counties in 1530, by Thomas Tonge*, ed. W. H. D. Longstaffe, SurtS, 41 (1863), 31 • *The acts and monuments of John Foxe*, new edn, ed. G. Townsend, 5 (1846), 468–9 • *Fasti Angl., 1300–1541*, [Lincoln], 69 • *Fasti Angl., 1066–1300*, [York], 80, 113 • J. G. Nichols, ed., 'Inventories of the wardrobes … etc. of Henry Fitzroy, duke of Richmond', *Camden miscellany, III*, CS, 61 (1855), xxiii–xxiv, xxix • J. Strype, *Ecclesiastical memorials*, 3 vols. (1822), vol. 2, pp. 9, 12 • *LP Henry VIII* • M. Bateson, ed., *Grace book B*, 1 (1903), 200, 204, 205, 220 • G. Lipscomb, *The history and antiquities of the county of Buckingham*, 4 vols. (1831–47), vol. 2, p. 69; vol. 3, p. 232 • Cooper, *Ath. Cantab.*, 1.141, 547 • *CSP dom., 1547–53*, no. 691 • Bodl. Oxf., MS Ashmole 1123, no. 11 (fol. 183v) • *CPR, 1553–4*, 157–8 • *DNB* • *CEPR letters*, 17/2.471; 18.292

Franks, Barbara Mary, Lady Franks (1907–1987). *See under* Franks, Oliver Shewell, Baron Franks (1905–1992).

Franks, Sir John (1769–1852), judge in India, was born at Loher Cannon, near Tralee, co. Kerry, the second son of Thomas Franks (1729–1787), lawyer, of Ballymagooly, co. Cork, and his wife, Catherine, daughter of the Revd John Day and sister of Robert Day, MP for Ardfert in the Irish parliament. He was educated at Trinity College, Dublin, from 1783 (BA, 1788; LLB, 1791). He was called to the Irish bar in 1792. He went on the Munster circuit, and had a good practice as chamber counsel. He took silk on 25 November 1822. In 1825 the Board of Control, on the recommendation of his friend William Conyngham Plunket, then Irish attorney-general, appointed him a judge of the supreme court at Calcutta. Before departure he received the customary knighthood on 20 April 1825. He held office until the effect of the climate on his health brought about his resignation in 1834. On his return he resided at Roebuck, near Dublin. He became a bencher of King's Inns, Dublin, in 1840.

Franks was thrice married. He married first his cousin Catherine (d. 1812), daughter of Thomas Franks of Carrig, co. Cork; they had two sons and three daughters. He married second his cousin Jane, daughter of John Marshall of Gurteen, co. Cork, and widow of George Sandes of Kilcavan. Third, in 1849, he married Sarah Wollaston, daughter and coheir of William O'Regan, barrister. His heir was his eldest son, John Franks (1803–1881) JP, of Ballyscaddane, co. Limerick.

Franks was popular, both as advocate and as judge. He was a close friend of John Philpot Curran, and had 'peculiar aboriginal wit, quiet, keen, and natural to the occasion, and, best of all, never malignant' (*GM*, 409).

Franks died at St Bridget's, Clonkeagh, co. Dublin, on 11 January 1852.   Francis Watt, *rev.* Roger T. Stearn

Sources *GM*, 2nd ser., 37 (1852), 408–9 • Burtchaell & Sadleir, *Alum. Dubl.*, 2nd edn • Burke, *Gen. Ire.* (1958) • Boase, *Mod. Eng. biog.* • T. W. Moody and others, eds., *A new history of Ireland, 4: Eighteenth-century Ireland, 1691–1800* (1986) • R. F. Foster, *Modern Ireland, 1600–1972* (1989)

Franks, Oliver Shewell, Baron Franks (1905–1992), philosopher and public servant, was born on 16 February 1905 at Woodbrooke settlement, Selly Oak, Birmingham, the elder son and oldest of four children of the Revd Dr Robert Sleightholme *Franks (1871–1964), scholar and theologian, and his wife, Katharine (Kitty; 1875–1971), daughter of Joseph Shewell, of Redcar, Yorkshire, an engineer and iron bridge builder. Profoundly reasonable and publicly austere, a figure of immense moral authority, Oliver Franks lived an exceptional life. He did not seek his various careers of don, mandarin, diplomat, banker, provost, pillar of state. They sought him. He did not collect committees, as some men do. Committees collected him. He did not pine for public recognition. Recognition came to him. He bore an uncanny resemblance to Aristotle's magnanimous man, 'moderately disposed towards wealth, power, and every kind of good and bad fortune, however it befalls him'. Franks was made for magnanimity:

> He does not enter for popular contests, or ones in which others distinguish themselves; he hangs back or does nothing at all, except where the honour or the feat is a great one. The tasks he undertakes are few, but grand and celebrated. (Quoted in Danchev, *Oliver Franks*, 195)

Religion and politics Franks was a philosopher king with a nonconformist conscience. 'The Establishment smites the Establishment', proclaimed a commentator on one of his multifarious Franks reports (Danchev, *Oliver Franks*, 198), a fine phrase but a doubtful verdict. When it came to establishments he was in them but not of them. In a life almost coterminous with the century—he was highly attuned to the patterns of the past, especially to the *longue durée* of Fernand Braudel, his favourite historian—Franks swam peaceably in the two streams of English dissent that were his birthright: the Congregational church and the

Oliver Shewell Franks, Baron Franks (1905–1992), by Yousuf Karsh

Religious Society of Friends. His father was a Congregational minister, like his father before him; his mother was a Quaker from a family of Quakers. His upbringing was uplifting. A mettlesome air of intellectual enquiry pervaded the entire household. Oliver and his sisters and brother were expected to think—think hard—for themselves. Mealtimes were feasts of conversation. Robert Franks did not read the newspaper at breakfast; the family talked—talked about everything from the flowers in the fields to the Channel Fleet. They weighed words and knew their meaning. They analysed articles in *The Times*. On Sundays they dissected the sermon they had heard. The opinions were sensible, but the talk was unrestrained. This was a liberal household in more senses than one.

Politically they were staunch believers in the unimpeachable virtue of Mr Gladstone—in moments of hilarity, the GOM (Grand Old Man). They voted Liberal, always; the children followed suit. Young Oliver, aged five, sported a loyal rosette at the general election of 1910. Old Oliver was not so ostentatious. In the 1930s he was politically engaged, briefly, in the Oxford Movement for the Propagation of Peace, a comprehensively lost cause. In the 1940s and 1950s he attended meetings of XYZ, a clandestine dining club of Labour supporters and sympathizers in the City, whose stalwarts included Hugh Dalton, Evan Durbin, Hugh Gaitskell, Douglas Jay, and the self-styled liberal–socialist economist James Meade, a close friend. XYZ had a strong Fabian flavour, and there was indeed something of the Fabian about Oliver Franks. He would build a new Jerusalem; and he would repine for its soul.

Typically, he was not an XYZ member as such, more a benevolent assessor. In party political terms, during the period of his most active public service he was concerned to preserve his status as 'a neuter' as he put it (Danchev, *Oliver Franks*, 174). Ennobled in 1962, he took the Liberal whip, as expected, though in unmistakable cross-bench fashion his sponsors were a civil servant and a judge. Thereafter he permitted himself the occasional foray into national politics, chairing election meetings of the Oxford Liberals in 1963 and 1964, and addressing a Liberal Party rally at the Oxford Union in favour of a decisive vote to remain in the EEC in the referendum of 1975. In later life he was given to describing himself as 'an unreconstructed Gladstonian Liberal'; in playful mood he might even suggest that he and Lord Gladwyn (the former Gladwyn Jebb) were the only ones left, a conceit in which the latter was happy to share. Just how Liberal he was, or became, is a moot point. Unquestionably party meant little to him. Party politics was too much of a game, too often trivial or reprehensible—not serious. There was a touch of disdain in Franks's contemplation of the political stew. During the intervals of his Falklands inquiry in 1982 he would sit back and listen as 'the parliamentarians cracked their silly parliamentary jokes' (Danchev, *Oliver Franks*, 28–9). It was an attitude reminiscent of Demodocus on the Milesians:

Milesians are not stupid, I aver;
But they behave the same as if they were.

Franks was a mugwump. He disliked labels, but it may be appropriate to adapt the one he gave himself. He was, if anything, an unreconstructed Liberal internationalist.

Mods and Greats In 1910 the Franks family moved from Birmingham to Bristol, where Oliver's father became principal of the Western College, and Oliver became a west countryman. After a couple of dismal dame-schools he went to Bristol grammar school (1915–23). His progress offers no crumb of comfort to those who like their great men to be school dunces. Every year with monotonous regularity he carried off the form prize. He departed the classical sixth with prizes in English literature, Latin, and Greek testament. Inevitably, he was school captain. At his second attempt, to the delight of the whole family, he won an open scholarship in classics to Queen's College, Oxford (1923–7).

To his fellow students he was Father Franks, preternaturally wise, solemn, seclusive, masterful. At the outset, however, he was not so secure, intellectually or financially. 'At Oxford in the 1920s we were either rich or poor', wrote Douglas Jay, a near contemporary (Danchev, *Oliver Franks*, 16). Franks was poor. He did not join the Oxford Union because he could not afford to. He went to the occasional free concert, and once a term to the sixpenny seats in the cinema. He took up rowing, frugally, and persevered, despite 'much *algō ton orron* [pain in the arse]' (ibid., 16). On Sundays he went, 'all good', to chapel at Mansfield College, almost a family foundation. Two years into his degree came the event which confirmed him to himself: moderations—the first public examination in *literae humaniores*—fifteen papers in everything from Aristophanes to Virgil. He prepared himself for this test with exemplary thoroughness. 'With the approach of Mods', reported his old school magazine, 'Mr Franks has withdrawn into an anchorite's seclusion, whence he only occasionally emerges, wearing the most remarkable stockings.' The results were spectacular: fourteen alphas and a solitary beta in Latin prose, some of the highest marks in the whole university, and the best first at Queen's since the First World War. 'Did not Mr Franks collect innumerable alphas in his recent encounter? Does he not now read paperbacks upon the river? Is not that the manifestation of real genius?' (Danchev, *Oliver Franks*, 17–18).

After that Franks never looked back. Moderations were followed by Greats—two years of philosophy and ancient history. Franks read prodigiously, as usual, encouraged by his father's example and conversation:

> Mr Franks has become almost a legendary figure. There appear to be some doubts of his tangible existence at Queen's. One fact only has penetrated to us. Mr Franks, with characteristic wisdom, is reading St Thomas Aquinas for that most soul-destroying of all ordeals, Greats. We commend his example, for here is balm for the tortured spirit. (Danchev, *Oliver Franks*, 19)

In 1927, in swift succession, the wise Mr Franks took a congratulatory first, a fellowship at Queen's, and a year's leave of absence, 'to go to Europe and grow older'. He travelled in Germany, Austria, and Italy, where he was arrested by Mussolini's police in possession of Plato's *Republic*—the very book in which Socrates makes the argument that 'there will be no end to the troubles of states, or indeed … of humanity itself, till philosophers become kings in this world, or till those we now call kings and rulers really and truly become philosophers' (quoted in Danchev, *Oliver Franks*, 24). The arrest of the tyro philosopher by the myrmidons of *Il Duce* is a fine thing to contemplate.

Philosophy and friendship Back in Oxford, Franks began plying his trade. He wrote almost nothing, but he was an outstanding college tutor. One of his first pupils was a woman from Lady Margaret Hall—Barbara Tanner—reading the new combination of philosophy, politics, and economics (a combination which Franks did much to make academically respectable). It so happened that she and Franks were already acquainted. Their relationship developed, as it were, philosophically. They married at Redland Friends' meeting-house in Bristol on 3 July 1931, and remained the best of friends for nearly sixty years. It was a friendship of an appropriately Aristotelian cast.

Barbara Mary Franks (1907–1987) was the eldest child and only daughter of Herbert George Tanner (1882–1974), of Llanfoist, Clifton Down, Bristol, businessman and magistrate, and Agatha Mary Gales (1877–1957), daughter of a Liberal electoral agent and peace activist. Barbara had been weaned on good organization and good causes. The Tanners were teetotallers, vegetarians, non-smokers, pacifists, nonconformists, and Liberals. Her mother was a Quaker by upbringing; her father became one by conviction after the war. Barbara herself had been to Sidcot, the co-educational Quaker school at Winscombe, Somerset, where her grandparents had been (and where Franks's parents settled in retirement). In youth as in maturity she had both sense and sensibility. She also had a keen social conscience, and an impulsion to act. Her commitment to public service antedated that of her husband; in this respect, as perhaps in others, it was he who learned from her. Already in the 1930s she was serving on the committee of the Eye Hospital in Oxford, and organizing the Plantation Club for poor girls in the Gorbals, Glasgow. She also acted from time to time as research assistant to Sir George Clark, the historian. During the Second World War she worked first for the press research department of the Foreign Office, and then for the Women's Voluntary Service. After the war family movements enforced a break in such activities, but no sooner were they re-established in Oxford in the 1950s than she began an intensive involvement in the social provision of the city. Signally, she was a magistrate for twenty-two years, by common consent an outstanding chairman of the city bench, compassionate, expeditious, and fair. She also served as a member of the board of governors of Aylesbury and Oxford prisons, Huntercombe borstal, Campsfield detention centre, and a local probation hostel; chairman of the local Citizens' Advice Bureau and of Age Concern; a trustee of Oxfam; an independent member of two wages councils; and chairman of the management committee of the Nuffield Orthopaedic Hospital.

Oliver Franks and Barbara Tanner were fundamentally compatible people. They shared the same values in life and the same belief in religion as relevant to the living of it. For Franks that was what was most important in the marriage. At the heart of this was a certain simplicity, evident in the pastimes they shared: gardening, reading, walking, shrimping in the Isles of Scilly. Franks was proud of his wife's distinction on the bench, proud that she held the same office as her father and grandfather before her. It appealed to his sense of the fitness of things. They both took great pleasure in the generational continuity, and in the more equal opportunity it betokened. There was a mutual respect between them. If she was not his intellectual equal, in human terms he was if anything overmatched. In general she ranged further than he. Her Quaker sympathies were deeper, her pacifist leanings stronger. In middle age she lost her shyness but retained her modesty. She practised yoga and tai chi. She liked to meditate. At seventy-five she learned to stand on her head. She was her own woman, an expression she would probably have deplored. At the same time she supported her husband in everything he did, just as he supported her. This was not a matter of form, but a grave moral obligation. In the last ten years of her life she took up painting, with amazing success. She sought technical instruction and went on painting holidays in the south of France, revelling in the warmth and colour of the late summer. He supported her in that, making tea and chatting amiably to the assorted amateur artists who appeared in the house or set up their easels in the garden, before resuming his reading.

Franks consulted her on anything of consequence. Together they determined that he should not become Oxford-bound. It was decided that he should apply for the first available (and interesting) philosophy post in the UK. This happened to be the chair of moral philosophy at Glasgow, a chair previously occupied by none other than Adam Smith. It was the only job for which he ever made unsolicited application. The application was successful. They left Oxford in 1937. The new professor of moral philosophy was thirty-two. He was not long for the life of the mind.

Whitehall and war Franks had been at Glasgow for barely a year when he received a terse enquiry from Whitehall. 'Do you undertake to go wherever you are sent in the event of a national emergency?' He replied in the affirmative. The question prompted some reflection, but no crisis of conscience. For Franks the Second World War was not a good war, but it was a necessary one. As he saw it, 'Hitler had to be squashed' (Danchev, *Oliver Franks*, 39). If conscripted, he would have served. In the event he was immured for the duration in the Ministry of Supply (1939–46). After that, as he later remarked, life was not the same. Squashing Hitler launched Franks into a new orbit. By the end of the war, in spite of his amateur status, he was permanent secretary, a feat equalled only by John Maud (later Baron Redcliffe-Maud) in the Ministry of Food. Success brought recognition. It was in these years that he made his reputation as an adjudicator, his most natural and effective role on the public stage. Stuart Hampshire has written:

> The work of practical reason is never finished, never final and secure. Surveying any tract of history, and looking into our own minds, we see the ebb and flow of contrary passions and interests needing to be reconciled; in the mind by that form of inner adjudication which is called reflection, and in the state by the literal and visible adjudication of parliaments and law courts, (Danchev, *Oliver Franks*, 43)

and, one might add, Oliver Franks.

In consequence Franks became hot property. He was besought to remain at the Ministry of Supply; coveted by the Board of Trade and the Ministry of Works; offered the National Coal Board, the flagship of the nationalized fleet. He wanted none of these. Approached with some trepidation, the new world of Whitehall had proved compelling, and in many ways congenial. Yet his kinship remained in some measure provisional. He was a temporary permanent secretary, as he liked to say, and he was in need of a restorative. The nationalized industries failed to light a spark. More than once in the post-war period he considered the possibility of working at the grindstones of politics and administration, most excruciatingly as governor of the Bank of England, only to reject it (after some hesitation) every time. In 1946 (the year in which he was made KCB), happily, he was offered a position he did want—the only one, he said, that he ever really wanted—a position for which he was apparently predestined, if not actually pre-elected, since before the war: provost of Queen's College, Oxford (1946–8).

Diplomacy and dollars Free at last, Franks spent a year, in his words, 'frisking like a lamb in green pastures' (Danchev, *Oliver Franks*, 57). Then came another summons. On 30 June 1947 he was given leave of absence from the college, 'to prepare a scheme for the comprehensive restoration of the economy of Europe on the lines adumbrated by Mr Marshall, the United States Secretary of State' (ibid., 57). The scheme was to be submitted by 1 September 1947. It was surely the largest long-vacation task ever undertaken.

The summons had come from the foreign secretary. Any explanation of Franks's galvanic influence on the international transformations of the mid-twentieth century must begin with his role as the special agent of Ernest Bevin. The tall, spare don and the short, squat docker were an unlikely combination, as Bevin himself pointed out. 'You, Oliver, 'ad a university experience. My experience is in the 'edgerows of life' (Danchev, *Oliver Franks*, 52). The dissimilarity mattered not at all. Bevin had encountered Franks during the war, as minister of labour. He liked this sure-footed scholar, who could be of such help to him. One could rely on Franks, without obligation. He had no history. He was at once judicious and resourceful, masterly and discreet. For Bevin this was an extremely attractive proposition. On Franks's side the chemistry was simple. He approved of Bevin, and of what he was trying to do. He made no allowance for him, as so many did. He even joked about him, an unusual public sign of affection. 'The Secretary of State', he once informed the waiting Dean Acheson, 'is doing his own version of hurrying to the meeting' (ibid., 53).

It was Bevin who seized Marshall's lifeline and organized a collective response; Bevin who mooted a conference in Paris to determine how Europe should respond; Bevin who fingered Franks to get the job done; Bevin who left him to it. As chairman of the new-found Committee for European Economic Co-operation (the CEEC, later the Organization for European Economic Co-operation, OEEC, later still the OECD) and leader of the British delegation, Franks was given plenipotentiary powers and virtually no instructions. Essentially he had to shoehorn sixteen nations into one report, 'European availabilities and requirements', for the four years 1948–51 in a matter of six weeks.

The exercise was a sore trial to all concerned (Austria, Belgium, Denmark, France, Greece, Iceland, Ireland, Italy, Luxembourg, the Netherlands, Norway, Portugal, Sweden, Switzerland, Turkey, and the UK), regardless of the bounty it might bring. Among other things it called for figures and forecasts of a sophistication well beyond most national capabilities. At bottom, however, the problem facing the CEEC was not econometric but diplomatic. In William Diebold's words, 'the main job in Paris was finding some numbers that would pass muster in Washington' (Danchev, *Oliver Franks*, 71): a problem of palatability, and hence of persuasion. That was where Father Franks came in.

The numbers initially produced in Paris, by census and aggregation, were highly unpalatable. For the sixteen countries plus western Germany they showed an accumulated balance of payments deficit of $29.2 billion over the four-year period in question—the headline figure of dollar aid required, in the CEEC's estimation, for a sustainable European recovery programme. Of this global deficit no less than $28.2 billion was with the American continent: $8.1 billion in 1948 reducing annually to $5.8 billion in 1951. These numbers were shocking, not only because of their order of magnitude, but also because of their pessimistic outlook. $29 billion was a colossal sum, far exceeding Britain's aggregate international lending throughout the nineteenth century. For the United States it was out of the question, as the imperious undersecretary of state, William Clayton, immediately informed Franks. Marshall planners might not know the size of the Marshall plan, but they knew it had to be smaller than that. As disturbing was the clear intimation that the aid programme would not be sufficient to restore equilibrium after four years, as Washington hoped and expected. A deficit would remain, and with it the prospect of further importunings. When would the Europeans finally be able to stand on their own thirty-two feet?

Franks now had the measure of the problem. He held all the threads in his hands. Huddling separately with a small executive committee of the CEEC, a trusted member of Bevin's inner circle (Edmund Hall-Patch), and—very privately—key US officials offering 'friendly aid', he set about the necessary revising and recasting. With the help of a short postponement, this intensive diplomacy bore fruit. Miraculously the CEEC did produce a report, to which everyone was prevailed upon to subscribe. As to numbers, it was marvellously murky. The report dealt in dollar deficits. Dollar aid, it declared disingenuously, was a matter for the US. The 'tentatively estimated deficit' with the American continent had shrunk to an accumulated total of $22.4 billion over the four-year period: $8 billion in 1948 reducing to $3.4 billion in 1951. If most capital equipment were shown (and financed) separately, as agreed, then the numbers became $19.3 billion, $7.1 billion, and $2.8 billion respectively. Moreover there was a 'tentatively estimated surplus' with the rest of the world of $2.8 billion over the same period. For technical reasons the report doubted the possibility of offsetting this surplus against the dollar deficit, but merely to mention it was enough for enticingly small net figures to swim before the eyes.

These numbers passed muster on at least two counts. First and foremost, their order of magnitude was no longer scary. In Franksian parlance the European antithesis to Marshall's thesis was $19.3 billion. The administration's synthesis was $17 billion. The European recovery programme was presented for congressional approval in December 1947. In April 1948 a first tranche of $5 billion was made available for an initial twelve-month period. Of this the UK received no less than $1.24 billion, an unexpected satisfaction owing something to the calming presence of Franks. Second, the CEEC's numbers provided at least a fig leaf of cover for the future. The report concluded with the positive reassurance that the Americans demanded: 'Certainly the deficit after the end of 1951, on these assumptions, should be of dimensions which will be manageable without special aid' (Danchev, *Oliver Franks*, 83). On this occasion, perhaps, Franksian principles were overborne.

The long vacation was over. The lines adumbrated by Marshall had been substantiated by Franks. It was a remarkable achievement. The foreign secretary's special agent had secured the first great transatlantic bargain of the post-war period.

Greeks and Romans Franks was not allowed to rest, but was offered instead the plum of the Washington embassy (1948–52). The prime minister himself made the call. Franks accepted only after prolonged hesitation. He was loath to part with Queen's; Barbara was reluctant to leave Oxford. Yet they went. His own explanation is characteristic. 'In the end, the obvious dawned. Unless there is a proper objection of conscience, there are things it is not appropriate to refuse' (Danchev, *Oliver Franks*, 89). The Stoic technical term for this is *kathekon* or appropriate action. Franks was a lapsed philosopher, but he consciously attended to the philosopher's question—how should one live? He returned a Stoic answer. To live well was to live virtuously. Franks was a virtuous man who did not cultivate virtue, except perhaps to take a quiet pride in his own power of right judgement. He did what he thought right: that is, in Cicero's words, honourable and seemly. It would not have been seemly to refuse Clement Attlee, or for that matter Ernest Bevin.

Franks was sent to Washington with a specific purpose in mind. Bevin's attention had shifted from economic to military security. What he sought was an 'Atlantic pact' of mutual assistance among the Western democracies. Here too the Europeans needed help. An Atlantic pact required an American commitment, ultimately a commitment to use force. For the heirs of George Washington to make such a commitment it was axiomatic that some moral stiffening would be needed. Who better than Franks to provide it?

The Atlantic pact became in due course the north Atlantic treaty (later the North Atlantic Treaty Organization, NATO), signed with great fanfare in Washington in April 1949. It was the outcome of nine months of gruelling international negotiation. The principal negotiators were the ambassadors of Belgium, Canada, France, Luxembourg, the Netherlands, and the UK, partnered by the US secretary of state. In spite of his relative youth Franks swiftly attained a unique position in this company, becoming the unofficial moderator of the ambassadors, and ultimately the guarantor of the treaty on the European side—a tribute to his qualities and his accomplishment. He was now a committee man of unbeatable experience. He had chaired not only the CEEC, but also the governing body of an Oxford college, compared to which, he observed, the Europeans were child's play.

The crux of the treaty was the pledge, the provision for collective defence against armed attack: one for all and all for one. The form of words embodying this provision evolved through a number of sinuous but significant compromises, and occasioned the most rancorous (and fundamental) disputes between the Europeans and the Americans. The basic elements were well stated by the Canadian diplomat Escott Reid:

> The firmer the pledge, the greater the effect the treaty might be expected to have in deterring the Soviet Union and in restoring in Western Europe the confidence necessary for its recovery. The weaker the pledge, the less reluctant the senate would be to ratify the treaty. (Danchev, *Oliver Franks*, 100)

The Europeans tended to emphasize the first consideration, the Americans the second. By February 1949, after seven months of negotiation, they arrived at an impasse. Those who wanted a treaty (a majority) despaired of a strong pledge; those who wanted a strong pledge (another majority) despaired of a treaty. At this juncture the incoming secretary of state, Dean Acheson, made his famous 'unorthodox proposal' to Franks:

> On an experimental basis I suggested that we talk regularly, and in complete personal confidence, about any international problems we saw arising. Neither would report or quote the other unless, thinking it would be useful in promoting action, he got the other's consent and agreement on the terms of a reporting memorandum or cable. ... We met alone, usually at his residence or mine, at the end of the day before or after dinner. No one was informed even of the fact of the meeting. We discussed situations already emerging or likely to do so, the attitudes that various people in both countries would be likely to take, what courses of action were possible and their merits, the chief problems that could arise. If either thought that his department should be alerted to the other's apprehensions and thoughts, we would work out an acceptable text setting out the problem and suggesting approaches. (ibid., 104)

In this spirit Franks and Acheson re-examined the pledge from first principles. They disassembled all the pieces and together constructed a new form of words—'a bit of redrafting to ease the constitutional sensibilities of the Congress', as Franks put it later (ibid., 104). It read:

> The Parties agree that an armed attack against one or more of them in Europe and North America shall be considered an armed attack against them all; and consequently that, if such an armed attack occurs, each of them in exercise of the right of individual or collective self-defence recognized by article 51 of the Charter of the United Nations, will assist the Party or Parties so attacked by taking forthwith such action including the use of armed force, individually and in concert with the other parties, as it deems necessary to restore and assure the security of the North Atlantic area. (Danchev, *Oliver Franks*, 105)

This bit of redrafting did the trick. The impasse was broken. The negotiations were swiftly concluded. With one minor transposition, the draft concocted à deux by Franks and Acheson became the keystone of the North Atlantic treaty. It has remained in place ever since.

An entangling alliance had been created, against the weight of history. As Bevin reported to the cabinet, American readiness 'to enter into a commitment to defend Europe in time of peace marked a revolutionary step in their policy' (Danchev, *Oliver Franks*, 107). Appropriately enough, it was the old firm of Bevin and Franks who

signed for the UK. Bevin was exuberant. The North Atlantic treaty was his crowning achievement as foreign secretary. It was the second great transatlantic bargain of the post-war period. It too was secured by Franks.

Just as Franks had been an amateur mandarin, so he was an amateur diplomat. It was a career refrain. He might have been a professional philosopher, but in retrospect the message is clear: philosophy was not enough. Franks was a lifelong layman—the most distinguished of his day. He seems to have relished that status. He was interested in the subject at hand, whatever it was. He was unlearned but educable. He was knowledgeable on cognate matters. He was inquisitive, purposive, co-operative. He had a remarkable talent for finding the right level of detail. He was flexible (not biddable), and generally unprejudiced. He listened to what he was told; his opinions, however, were his own. This whole profile was immensely reassuring, in London and Washington alike. The consummate Dean Acheson, for one, was not easily impressed; but his unorthodox proposal tells its own story. The quality and scope of the relationship between Franks and Acheson, as ambassador and secretary of state, is unparalleled in American history, and likely to remain so. It meant that Franks could become a participant in internal American deliberations; it was in fact the hard currency of the much mythologized special relationship. Franks reflected:

> The special relationship was not a mystique of the shared inheritance of the English-speaking peoples. It arose out of common aims and mutual need of each other; it was rooted in strong habits of working together on which there was supervened the sentiments of mutual trust. (Danchev, *Oliver Franks*, 121)

He had no time for the patronizing game played by so many of his countrymen, the game of Greeks and Romans. Acheson and his advisers were not lacking in Greek wisdom. What they required was efficacy. 'In the Anglo-American relationship', Franks observed wisely, 'British policy has to pass the test: can the British deliver?' (ibid., 88).

Franks was as efficacious as any. It was very largely on his urging and his argument—'the Americans will to some extent ... test the quality of the partnership by our attitude to the notion of a token ground force'—that the British government overcame its reluctance and committed a brigade group to Korea in 1950, as 'a valuable contribution to Anglo-American solidarity' (Danchev, *Oliver Franks*, 127). It was his formulations, delphic as they were, which governed nuclear consultation between the two countries, and which became part of the essential grammar of Anglo-American relations during the cold war. With regard to the delicate question of US bases in the UK, for example, he provided the 'joint decision' formula of 1951: 'The use of these bases in an emergency would be a matter for joint decision by His Majesty's Government and the United States Government in the light of the circumstances prevailing at the time.' From the British point of view these transactions surely left something to be desired, yet no one, not even Winston Churchill, was able to improve upon them. As Acheson's special assistant remarked of the joint decision formula, 'the agreement was as precise as anyone could make it—as precise as anyone wanted it to be—but there was still … ambiguity there that served everybody's interests … and needs' (ibid., 134).

Great and good Franks chose to depart the diplomatic life in 1952. He was pressed to become the first secretary-general of NATO, a natural transition, but at length accepted a more unexpected offer, the chairmanship of Lloyds Bank, the largest of the London clearing houses (1954–62). Franks offered Lloyds his moral eminence, in Gordon Richardson's phrase, and his administrative gift. Lloyds offered Franks a vantage point from which to observe the world. It paid handsomely—far more than any other position he ever held—and it allowed full scope for his burgeoning practice of public adjudication. This took the characteristic form of an official inquiry, followed by a report. Soon he appeared to be in session almost continuously. He chaired two major inquiries—on administrative tribunals and inquiries (1955–7) and on Oxford University (1964–6)—and played a leading part in a third, on the working of the monetary system (1957–9), under Lord Radcliffe. More followed. In 1971–2, at the request of the home secretary, Franks inquired into the controversial catch-all section 2 of the Official Secrets Act of 1911; and in 1982–3, at the request of the prime minister, into the government's handling of the Falklands conflict. In between, he kept his hand in with a number of smaller, solo productions on the development of India and Pakistan (1960), British business schools (1963), the Committee of London Clearing Bankers (1974), and a register of immigrants' dependants (1976). In 1975 he was briefly but happily reunited with Radcliffe on the publication of ministerial memoirs.

Franks did not write these Franks reports, yet he was their author. They excelled in exposition. They exhibited a drive for clarity, rationality, efficiency. The reforms they invariably advocated were enlightened, ameliorative, improving in the sense that Gladstone understood. Franks's affinity for the fundamental meant that little was overlooked. Often he confronted taboos of various kinds: national sovereignty, official secrecy, college autonomy. Reasoned discussion of the taboo is already an enlightened step. The radical undertow of the reports is easy to miss. With the exception of official secrets legislation, moreover, Franks left nothing as he found it. Perceptions changed even when institutional practice did not.

Franks had as much influence on people as on events. He was a natural exemplar. Clement Attlee's unreserved judgement was a representative one: for the majority of those who encountered him, Franks was the ablest man they ever met. There was a period, extending from the mid-1940s to the mid-1960s, when it seemed to his contemporaries that he could do almost anything—chancellor of the exchequer or governor of the Bank of England, as Rab Butler put it. But these were paths not taken. Franks forswore further influence on policy making. After Lloyds he retreated once more to his beloved Oxford, becoming provost of Worcester College (1962–76) and

Lockean under-labourer in the college garden. In the end he offered no lessons to others except that of a life well led. He died at his home, Blackhall Farm, Garford Road, Oxford, on 15 October 1992. A memorial service was held at the university church of St Mary the Virgin, on 13 December. He was survived by his two daughters, Caroline (b. 1939) and Alison (b. 1945).

'He was a man of the greatest reticence, but with nothing to conceal; a man of intensely "private life", but wholly transparent': Franks attained what T. S. Eliot self-referentially admired in Spinoza. The hallmark of his intensely private life was his simplicity—a Quaker tenet. 'We nearly all of us have something of the sailor or gardener in us', he told the Pilgrim Society in 1948 (Danchev, *Oliver Franks*, 196). John Locke presented his patron, Lord Shaftesbury, with a delightful little volume of his own composition, *The Growth of Vines and Olives*. Perhaps if things had fallen out differently Franks might have done likewise for his patron, Bevin. In every sense, he stood squarely in the tradition of looking after the garden he inherited. It is sometimes said that he was not creative. In diplomacy he was highly creative. Complex international negotiation suited Franks's temperament. Always deliberate, he could be deliberately cautious or deliberately adventurous as the need arose. Caution was what Franks sufficiently possessed to be able (judiciously) to throw it to the winds. It is true that the Marshall plan and the Atlantic pact were 'given' to him, but these were flying saucers—grand ideas as yet unformed. Franks supplied the *phronesis*, the practical wisdom, to make them real. It was as if Marshall and Bevin sat, massively, on the bough of history while Franks worked the wood. He was not alone in this endeavour, but his coadjutors were few. Franks was one of the founders of the post-war world.

ALEX DANCHEV

Sources A. Danchev, *Oliver Franks: founding father* (1993) • P. Boyle, 'Oliver Franks and the Washington embassy, 1948–52', *British officials and British foreign policy*, ed. J. Zametika (1990), 189–211 • N. Henderson, 'The Franks way—then and now', *The Times* (17 Jan 1983) • O. Franks, *Falkland Islands Review* (1992) [1983] • *The Times* (17 Oct 1992) • *The Independent* (17 Oct 1992) • WWW • Burke, *Peerage* • A. Balazs, 'Oliver Franks' Washington embassy', MLitt diss., U. Oxf., 1994 • A. Danchev, 'Taking the pledge: Oliver Franks and the negotiation of the North Atlantic treaty', *Diplomatic History*, 15 (1991), 199–219 • *Hist. U. Oxf.* 8: *20th cent.*
Archives Worcester College, Oxford, MSS | Bodl. Oxf., corresp. with William Clark • Bodl. Oxf., Round Table Add. MSS | FILM BFI NFTVA, news footage | SOUND BL NSA, current affairs recording
Likenesses Y. Karsh, photograph, 1948, repro. in Danchev, *Oliver Franks* • Y. Karsh, photograph, Camera Press Ltd, London [*see illus.*] • photograph, repro. in *The Times* • photograph, repro. in *The Independent* • photograph, repro. in *The Independent* (19 Oct 1992) • photograph, repro. in *The Times* (28 Oct 1992)

Franks, Robert Sleightholme (1871–1964), theologian, was born on 1 April 1871 at Redcar, North Riding of Yorkshire, the eldest son of the Revd William James Franks, Congregational minister, and his wife, Ann Eliza, daughter of Robert Sleightholme of Whitby. He was educated at Sir William Turner's Grammar School, Redcar, and St John's College, Cambridge, where he graduated in mathematics in 1893. Later he studied theology at Mansfield

College, Oxford, under A. M. Fairbairn. After a brief period as tutor in the college, Franks was ordained at Prenton Road Congregational Church, Birkenhead, in 1900. He married in 1902 Katharine (1872–1971), daughter of Joseph Shewell of Redcar, and they had two sons and two daughters. In 1904 he became lecturer in theology at Woodbrooke, Selly Oak; then in 1910 he went to what was to be his life's work as principal of the Western College, Bristol, where he remained until 1939, devoting his life to training young men for the Christian ministry. He received an honorary LLD from Bristol University in 1928.

It was as a theologian that Franks was chiefly known. His most notable book was *A History of the Doctrine of the Work of Christ*, first published in two volumes in 1918 and subsequently republished in a single volume in 1962. It was for this work that Franks was awarded the DLitt by Oxford in 1919. It is a historical study of ecclesiastical doctrine. The subject is presented as a microcosm of Christian doctrine, and four syntheses or total views of doctrine are enumerated: Greek, medieval, protestant orthodoxy, and modern protestant. Around these points the historical study turns. The whole massive work was to some extent a development of a small earlier work, *The New Testament Doctrines of Man, Sin and Salvation* (1908).

Some years later Franks presented his own interpretation of this doctrine in *The Atonement* (1934). The method as well as the conclusion were alike remarkable, for Franks argued for the Abelardian view of the atonement and sought to prove it by the method of Anselm. He aimed to show that love rather than life was the key word in the doctrine; and he hoped that the method adopted would provide theology with a metaphysical basis.

Years later, while in his eighties, Franks published *The Doctrine of the Trinity* (1953), a most lucid historical survey, in which, after an examination of the New Testament 'matrix' of the doctrine, he traced its development in the patristic period, and with remarkable balance and proportion outlined subsequent thought from Aquinas to Karl Barth.

Although predominantly a theologian, Franks was profoundly interested in the philosophy of religion and especially in its metaphysic. In 1929 he published *The Metaphysical Justification of Religion*, lectures delivered at King's College, London. Reared in the Ritschlian school of theology, he quickly came to see the need for a firmer metaphysic through studying both Ernst Troeltsch and F. D. E. Schleiermacher, whose *Christian Faith* (1821) supported an experiential theology with a philosophical basis. As the King's College lectures show, Franks carried his quest for a metaphysic of religion through the works of C. H. Weisse, whose fundamental motive was to show the congruence of Christianity with reason largely understood.

Franks published several shorter pieces either in learned journals or symposia. He was a contributor to the *Dictionary of Christ and the Gospels* and other works edited by James Hastings. Although he represented the best of a theological liberalism later out of fashion, he was unusual in that, unlike most protestant theologians of the period, he valued the work of the medieval scholastics. Not only

in his main book but also in an essay contributed to *Amicitiae corolla* (1933) can be seen—especially in his treatment of Alexander of Hales—how deep his learning in this period was. Franks found in Alexander a more sympathetic spirit than in Aquinas, believing that the experientialism of Alexander lived in the mystics, Quakers, pietists, and Moravians, leading to Schleiermacher, until Karl Barth, like a new Aquinas, challenged the whole method.

Throughout his long life Franks held to his conviction that the subjective element in Christianity is somehow fundamental and that it could be given a sound philosophical basis. This meant that he was at odds with the theology of Barth, which he regarded as altogether unsatisfactory.

Essentially a scholar, Franks was a shy, devout, and kindly man, a sound mathematician and a keen musician. He lived long enough to be in the gallery to see his elder son, Oliver Shewell *Franks, take the oath as a life peer in 1962. He died in the Chesterfield Nursing Home, Clifton Hill, Bristol, on 20 January 1964.

JOHN HUXTABLE, *rev.*

Sources *The Times* (21 Jan 1964) · private information (1981) · personal knowledge (1981) · A. Danchev, *Oliver Franks: founding father* (1993) · *CGPLA Eng. & Wales* (1964)

Wealth at death £4930: probate, 2 March 1964, *CGPLA Eng. & Wales*

Franks, Sir Thomas Harte (1808–1862), army officer, was the second son of William Franks of Carrig Castle, near Mallow, co. Cork, and his wife, Catherine, eldest daughter of William Hume, MP for the county of Wicklow. He was commissioned ensign in the 10th (North Lincolnshire) regiment on 7 July 1825, and was promoted lieutenant on 26 September 1826 and captain on 1 March 1839, serving with his regiment in Portugal, Corfu, and elsewhere.

In 1842 Franks accompanied his regiment for the first time to India. He was promoted major on 29 December 1843, and lieutenant-colonel on 28 March 1845. He took part in the First Anglo-Sikh War (1845–6), when the 10th regiment was one of those which were called up to help to fill the gap caused by the heavy losses at Mudki and Ferozeshahr. At the battle of Sobraon, Franks was wounded, and had a horse shot under him. He was rewarded by being made a CB. In the Second Anglo-Sikh War (1848–9) Franks's regiment was the first British one to come up to the siege of Multan, and Franks, as one of the senior officers with the besieging force, held many independent commands. After the siege he joined Sir Hugh Gough on 10 February 1849, and served with great distinction at Gujrat. He was promoted colonel on 20 June 1854, and was appointed to the command of the Jullundur brigade on 11 May 1855. He had handed over his command, and was just going home on sick leave, when the 1857 mutiny broke out. He refused to go to England, and remained at Calcutta until his health was sufficiently restored to enable him to take the field.

In January 1858 Franks was appointed to command the 4th infantry division in the field, with the rank of brigadier-general. This division was ordered by Governor-General Lord Canning to march across the north-eastern frontier of Oudh, driving the mutineers before it, and then to meet Sir Jang Bahadur, prime minister of Nepal who had promised to bring a force of Gurkhas to the assistance of the British, after which the two corps together were to co-operate in Sir Colin Campbell's operations against Lucknow. The junction with Jang Bahadur's Gurkhas was cleverly effected, and on 19 and 23 February Franks inflicted two severe defeats on the rebel leader, Muhammad Hussein Nazim, at Chanda, and between Badshahganj and Sultanpur respectively. The effect of these victories was, however, minimized by the severe set-back which he received in an attempt to take Dohrighat. Sir Colin Campbell was much incensed at this defeat, and after the final capture of Lucknow refused to give Franks another command in the field. This was a severe blow to Franks, who at once returned to England, where he was promoted major-general on 20 July 1858, made a KCB, and given the thanks of parliament.

Franks was first married to Matilda, daughter of Richard Kay and widow of the Revd W. Fletcher, and later to Rebecca Constantia Elizabeth, widow of Samuel Brewis of Langley House, Prestwich, Lancashire. Franks's health was ruined by his exertions, and he died, after a lingering illness, at his residence, Ibstone House, Ibstone, Oxfordshire, on 5 February 1862, survived by his second wife.

H. M. STEPHENS, rev. ALEX MAY

Sources Army List · A. Lee, The history of the 10th foot, the Lincolnshire regiment, 2 vols. (1911) · R. Cannon, ed., Historical record of the tenth, or the north Lincolnshire, regiment of foot (1847) · L. Shadwell, The life of Colin Campbell, 2 vols. (1881) · J. W. Kaye, A history of the Sepoy War in India, 1857–1858, 9th edn, 3 vols. (1880) · G. B. Malleson, History of the Indian mutiny, 1857–1858: commencing from the close of the second volume of Sir John Kaye's History of the Sepoy War, 3 vols. (1878–80) · C. Hibbert, The great mutiny, India, 1857 (1978) · GM, 3rd ser., 12 (1862), 385, 513–14 · CGPLA Eng. & Wales (1862)

Archives Royal Lincolnshire Regiment Museum, Lincoln, letters to Sir Denham Norreys

Wealth at death under £4000: probate, 13 March 1862, CGPLA Eng. & Wales

Franks, Sir (Augustus) Wollaston (1826–1897), collector and museum keeper, was born at Geneva on 20 March 1826, the eldest of six children (two sons and four daughters) of Frederick Franks (d. 1844), naval officer, and Frederica Anne (d. 1864), daughter of Sir John Saunders Sebright and his wife, Harriet Crofts. His godfather was William Hyde Wollaston, a friend of his mother's family. His mother was the sister of his father's first wife and the marriage, although not illegal, was voidable and considered improper. It may be for this reason that Franks's father chose to live abroad (he had relatives—the Gaussens—in Geneva). Franks's family moved to Rome in 1828 and did not return to London until 1843.

Franks was well connected and comparatively rich. His mother was an heiress; her father had married an heiress; and Franks's cousin was the third earl of Harewood. His father came from a banking family: his great-grandfather had married a Pepys, while his grandmother was of rich Huguenot descent (her father had been a director of the Bank of England and governor of the East India Company). On both sides of the family there were collectors;

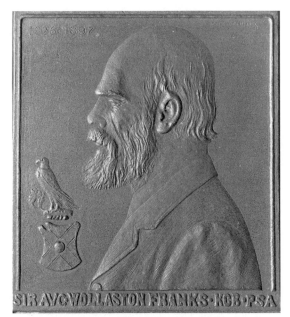

Sir (Augustus) Wollaston Franks (1826–1897), by Charles J. Praetorius, c.1898

his father collected pictures and his mother minerals, and he was even distantly related to that other benefactor of the British Museum, Richard Payne Knight.

Franks was educated at Eton College (1839–43) and at Trinity College, Cambridge (1845–9). His father having died and left him a 'sufficient fortune' by the time he went up to university, he decided to read for an ordinary degree and devoted his time to antiquarian studies. He was one of the founders of the Cambridge Architectural Society and a member of the Ray Society and of the Cambridge Antiquarian Society. Franks published, while still an undergraduate, an account of a palimpsest brass at Burwell (1847), an extensive paper on the Freville family (1847), and a small and much quoted book on medieval glazing quarries illustrated from his own drawings (1849). All this work showed the influence of the Cambridge Camden Society (later the Ecclesiological Society), of which he was a member, and foreshadowed many of his later interests.

Franks moved to London in 1849, and became very influential in the newly founded Archaeological Institute, where he organized the annual exhibitions and gained a deep knowledge of European antiquities. He was honorary secretary to the organizing committee of the medieval exhibition held at the Royal Society of Arts in 1850, and, as a result of this work, was appointed to a newly established post at the British Museum to oversee the establishment of a collection of British antiquities, which had been recommended by a royal commission in 1850. Under the supervision, and with the support, of Edward Hawkins, keeper of antiquities, and with the encouragement of his successor, Samuel Birch, Franks set about the creation of a collection that was ultimately to result in the formation of five of the departments of the present-day British Museum (medieval and later, prehistoric and Romano-

British, ethnography, oriental, and Japanese). In 1866 he became keeper of the newly created department of British and medieval antiquities and ethnography.

Franks already had a formidable reputation as a scholar. He wrote many pithy notes in the *Archaeological Journal*, and had published books on oriental glass and enamels (1861) and on Arabian inscriptions (1863), but his most important work was his contribution to Kemble's *Horae ferales*, which in 1858 broke new ground in prehistory, for example by recognizing for the first time the La Tène culture. The breadth of his interests and knowledge increased throughout his life and he wrote papers and books on subjects as diverse as Indian sculpture, Japanese prehistoric flints, Hans Holbein, Anglo-Saxon rings, Chinese paintings, book-plates, megalithic monuments in the Netherlands, and many more.

This output reflected his collecting interests, both personal and public. Because of his wealth he could afford to buy with his own money for the museum, often with the purpose of encouraging the trustees to spend their money on similar material. Typical of his *modus operandi* was the way in which he persuaded the museum to collect Italian maiolica. Within a few months of his arrival at the museum, he purchased for himself twenty-one maiolica dishes from the collection of the Abbé James Hamilton; he then purchased another two major items, so that when the great Bernal collection came on to the market in 1855 he was able to offer his pieces to the museum as bait so that the trustees could approach the Treasury for a grant to buy maiolica and much else at the sale (the trustees received £4000 for this purpose). Later he was to do this on a grander scale, offering, for example, to give the museum material equivalent in value to the grant they had applied for (£3000) to purchase items at the Fountaine sale of pottery and porcelain in 1884. In the case of the royal gold cup of the kings of France and England, his most prestigious acquisition, he made the purchase for £8000 and then appealed to friends to help him with cash so that he could give the cup to the museum. Throughout his long life he built up his own collections and enriched the museum from his own generosity. On his death he bequeathed the whole of his collection—some 3300 objects—to the British Museum. He also gave or steered other objects to other museums, and particularly to the Victoria and Albert Museum. He gave two paintings to the National Gallery and his great collection of brass rubbings to the Society of Antiquaries of London.

Franks also attracted gifts, the most important of which was the great collection of Henry Christy, which in effect formed the foundation of the British Museum's ethnographic collection. This was left in trust to a small body of men, of whom one was Franks, who steered it to the museum. At first it was housed in Victoria Street and Franks paid out of his own pocket for its first curator, Charles Hercules Read, and for an illustrator. He also added to this collection at his own expense (he reckoned to have spent £5000 on American and Asian items) and out of a small fund left by Christy; particularly splendid were

his additions of the pre-Columbian turquoise masks and Afro-Portuguese ivories.

Other great collections came in similar ways. They included: the glass of Felix Slade; the Indian sculpture collection of Hindoo Stuart from the Bridge family; the clocks and scientific instruments of Octavius Morgan; his own collection of armorial book-plates (which incorporated part of the de Tabley collection); the residue of the Meyrick collection; the playing cards of Lady Charlotte Schreiber (better known as Lady Charlotte Guest); the Bähr collection of Livonian antiquities; and the India Museum's sculpture collection. Smaller collections were also acquired, such as that of the Danish state antiquary J. J. A. Worsaae, the medieval collections of the architect William Burges, and many more.

Two or three major objects given by Franks to the museum deserve special mention. The 'Franks Casket', recovered by a Paris dealer from a kitchen drawer in Auzun, is one of the most important runic-inscribed objects of the Anglo-Saxon period. Dated to the eighth century, it is made of whalebone and is carved with scenes from a universal history in a style otherwise unknown in Britain. The 'Treasure of the Oxus' is one of the most intriguing of his donations. Buried perhaps about 200 BC, the largest part of it is considered to be an accumulated temple treasure of the Achaemenian Persians, consisting of silver and gold plate (much of it decorated with fabulous beasts), and some 1500 gold and silver coins. Franks also acquired the museum's only serious piece of prehistoric Japanese Haniwa sculpture.

Although a lifelong bachelor, Franks was a sociable—if shy—man. He attached great importance to his club (the Athenaeum) and moved in the governing circles of his day. He was well known abroad and was a fervent supporter of the International Congress of Archaeology and Anthropology and attended most of its early meetings. He travelled widely in Europe (but apparently not outside it), and his travels fed his collections. He was a leading authority on European heraldry and might well be described as the first professional prehistorian. He was much sought after to sit on international committees, and was director (and later president) of the Society of Antiquaries, to which he left many books. He was created KCB in 1894, was an honorary doctor of both Oxford and Cambridge, a fellow of the Royal Society, antiquary to the Royal Academy, and (after his retirement in 1896) he was made a trustee of the British Museum and a member of its standing committee.

Despite his apparent worldliness, Franks in personal terms remains an enigma. He was neatly bearded and dapper, and was a neat dresser, but he hated public appearances and public speaking, and few descriptions of him survive. Dame Joan Evans's childhood memory of being given a piece of lapis by Franks; a description of him weeding the lawn outside his residence in the British Museum, while the children of other keepers played cricket on the other lawn; a Christmas in Brussels with Lady Charlotte Schreiber, with whom he visited the dealers in that town: these provide rare glimpses of his private life. Little is known of his relationship to his family, but he looked after his sister Frederica and she was buried with him in his grave. Joan Evans, whose father, John Evans, was one of Franks's oldest friends, provides us with a neat word-portrait:

He was … a grey dreamy person, with an unexpected dry humour and an incurable habit of addressing himself to his top waistcoat button. These buttons, indeed, served as a barometer of enthusiasm. If he were looking at an antiquity he liked very much indeed, he fingered the top button; if very much the next; if moderately the next and so on down the scale. There were few objects of antiquity which failed to evoke a response of some sort, for his knowledge was incredibly wide. (Evans, 143)

Franks was conservative in thought, a traditionalist, deeply dedicated to the museum and particularly to the department that he had created. This was so much the case that he refused the principal librarianship of the British Museum in 1874 and the directorship of the South Kensington Museum twice. Although he had friends in the museum (Sir Charles Newton, for example), he was clearly aloof from many of his younger colleagues, with the exception of Read, who was his successor as keeper and the executor of his estate. He was very friendly with John Evans and through him presumably knew many of the intellectual aristocracy of the mid-Victorian period. He also knew and corresponded with his foreign contemporaries, Lartet, Worsaae, Lindenschmidt, Nilsson, Khanikoff, Vogt, and Schliemann. But despite his extended and deep interest in archaeology and anthropology, he was clearly more at home with his fellow rich or aristocratic collectors, including Charlotte Schreiber, Lord Londesborough, W. E. Gladstone, Sir John Lubbock, and Baron Ferdinand de Rothschild.

In many respects Franks was the second founder of the British Museum. Through his energy and dedication he created the core of its non-classical or eastern Mediterranean collections of antiquities. He fought skilful battles against reluctant and parsimonious trustees and Treasury protectionism. He seized the opportunity of the move of the Natural History Museum to South Kensington to install the collections under his care more spaciously. Writing at the end of his life, he was able to quantify his contribution to the museum's growth:

When I was appointed to the Museum in 1851 the scanty collections out of which the department has grown occupied a length of 154 feet of wall cases, and 3 or 4 table cases. The collections now occupy 2250 feet in length of wall cases, 90 table cases and 31 upright cases, to say nothing of the numerous objects placed over the cases or on walls. (Franks)

To this are to be added the archaeological and other reserve collections and Franks's own collection, which was to come to the museum in 1897 as his bequest. He was a professional museum man as well as a distinguished scholar, aware of the importance of records and inventories (although curiously little of the documentation of his own collections survives). He was experienced in exhibition technique and was consulted both in Britain and abroad on museum matters. He was keen on publication of the collections in his area and himself wrote a number of catalogues.

Franks's own tastes in collecting tended to shape the collecting policy of the British Museum for the next century. He was very much a collector of material from dealers, particularly single items or small collections of portable material. For the museum he would acquire larger collections, but very much of the same sort of material. With the exception of ethnographic material he collected little sculpture, apart from the great Indian collections, which clearly fascinated him at a period when they were of little interest to anybody else. He left all European sculpture collecting to the South Kensington Museum. They also collected furniture and the British Museum consequently has none. He put a lot of energy into collecting pottery and porcelain on a historical basis and much of his material was less than fifty years old when he bought it. He did not buy prestige pieces, Berlin or St Petersburg porcelain vases for example, but left this to South Kensington. He collected historic silver and gold plate with great discernment, and his interests in archaeology meant that the museum acquired vast ranges of excavated material from throughout Europe. He was one of the earliest museum collectors to recognize the importance of ethnographic material and he bought in this area almost exclusively for the museum and not for himself, although he spent a lot of his own money on it. He was deeply knowledgeable about the material culture of the Far East and collected widely and well, including the earliest Japanese porcelain to be imported into Europe at the time of the Edo opening up of trade to the West.

Franks died of cancer of the bowel on 21 May 1897 at 11 Duchess Street, Portland Place, London, and was buried in Kensal Green cemetery. His name is today known to only a few specialists, yet he was as important to the museums of Britain (and particularly to the British Museum) as was Bode to Berlin and the German national collections.

DAVID M. WILSON

Sources 'A. W. Franks', *Nineteenth-century collecting and the British Museum*, ed. M. Caygill and J. Cherry (1997) · D. M. Wilson, *The forgotten collector: Augustus Wollaston Franks of the British Museum* (1984) · *DNB* · J. Evans, *Time and chance: the story of Arthur Evans and his forebears* (1943) · A. W. Franks, 'The apology of my life', unpubd MS, BM · *WWW* · parish register, Geneva, English chapel, 1820, GL [baptism] · d. cert. · *CGPLA Eng. & Wales* (1897) · D. M. Wilson, *The British Museum: a history* (2002)

Archives BM · S. Antiquaries, Lond., heraldic collections and drawings | BL, letters to S. G. Perceval, Add. MS 41494 · Salisbury and South Wiltshire Museum, Salisbury, letters to A. H. L. F. Pitt-Rivers · U. Newcastle, Robinson L., letters to Walter Trevelyan · V&A NAL, letters to Sir Henry Cole

Likenesses C. J. Praetorius, bronze plaque, c.1898, BM, NPG [see illus.] · C. J. Praetorius, related plaque, S. Antiquaries, Lond. · C. W. Sherborn, book-plate etching, BM, NPG · photograph, priv. coll. · stipple, NPG

Wealth at death £120,316 1s. 4d.: probate, 13 July 1897, *CGPLA Eng. & Wales*

Fransham, John (bap. 1670, d. 1753?), linen draper and writer, was born in Norwich and baptized there at St Peter Mancroft on 22 May 1670, the youngest son of Robert Fransham (d. 1718), a linen draper, and his wife, Susannah or

Susan. He was the brother of the attorney Isaac Fransham (1660–1743) and a distant relative of the scholar John Fransham (*bap.* 1730, *d.* 1810). He was probably the John Fransham who married Philippa Stevenson at St Mary in the Marsh, Norwich, on 29 April 1701. He was apprenticed to his father, and by the early 1700s seems to have been running the family business. On 3 May 1708 he was admitted a freeman of the city of Norwich. He was a friend of Daniel Defoe, with whom he maintained a regular correspondence from 1704 to 1707. These letters show that Fransham was a leading figure in 'polite coffee-house society' in Norwich and that in politics he was a staunch whig, an ardent supporter of the protestant succession, and an opponent of attempts to introduce an occasional conformity bill (*N&Q*, 5th ser., 3.261). He is believed to have been rent agent to Horace Walpole.

Fransham was the author of a number of topical works and a contributor to the *Gentleman's Journal*, a monthly periodical published in London in the early 1690s. In 1710 he published a short discourse in praise of latitudinarianism, entitled *The Criterion, or, Touchstone, by which to Judge of the Principles of High and Low Church*, which was republished as *A Dialogue between Jack High and Will Low*. Two other works have been attributed to him: *An Exact Account of the Charge for Supporting the Poor of Norwich, Compiled by J. F.* (1720) and *The World in Miniature, or, The Entertaining Traveller* (2 vols., 1740). Fransham probably died in 1753, the year in which his will was proved in the consistory court of Norwich.   M. J. MERCER

Sources *N&Q*, 2nd ser., 2 (1856), 467–8 · *N&Q*, 5th ser., 2 (1874), 37 · *N&Q*, 5th ser., 3 (1875), 261–3, 282–4 · P. Milligan, *The register of the freemen of Norwich, 1548–1713* (1934), 95 · *Index of wills proved in the consistory court of Norwich*, Norfolk RS, 34 (1965), 78; 38 (1969), 76 · IGI

Archives priv. coll., corresp. with Daniel Defoe

Fransham, John (*bap.* 1730, *d.* 1810), scholar and teacher, was baptized on 19 March 1730 in the parish of St George of Colgate, Norwich, the first of the two children of Thomas Fransham, parish clerk or sexton, and his wife, Isidora Stangroom. The surviving memoirs of Fransham were written by men who did not know him before the 1780s and who certainly did not plan to write his biography while he was alive. Their accounts of Fransham's early life rely on recollections of what Fransham had told them and are accordingly doubly muddled and unreliable. He was intellectually precocious as a child and his talents were early recognized and supported by various members of the Norwich intelligentsia, most notably John Taylor (1694–1761), minister of the Octagon Chapel. His parents were poor, however, and unable to support any formal plan of study beyond sending him to an elementary school in Norwich. Consequently, between *c.*1745 and *c.*1750 Fransham worked variously as an apprentice cooper, an attorney's clerk, a veterinary surgeon's assistant, an actor, a soldier, and a weaver. He continued his intellectual pursuits and about 1750 began acting as a tutor. His fees were exceptionally low—providing the main reason for his relative success—and he continued to tutor in French, classics, and mathematics until the final

year of his life, at times in a private, but mainly in a public capacity when he had as many as twenty pupils at a time. He appears to have had no particular political or religious allegiances and at different times he worked for both the high-churchman Samuel Cooper (1738–1800) and the Arian nonconformist minister Samuel Bourn (1714–1796). His most remarkable pupils were William Saint, who taught mathematics at the Royal Military Academy between 1807 and 1810, and who assembled a *Memoir* of Fransham, and James Stark (1794–1859), who became a leading Norwich school artist. Except for one brief period, Fransham lived continuously in or near Norwich, though he frequently changed address. He never married. He was for much of his life extremely poor and took great pride in frugality; in the 1770s he claimed to be living on a farthing's worth of potatoes a day; later in life he lived chiefly on tea and bread and butter. Such money as he earned he liked to spend on books.

As a scholar Fransham's main interests were mathematics, and philosophy. As a mathematician he was largely concerned with adopting positions: he championed the ancient over the modern mathematics, and geometry over algebra. In philosophy he idolized David Hume, but developed strong Platonic leanings, which were already evident in his *Essay on the Oestrum, or, Enthusiasm of Orpheus*, published in Norwich in 1760. Fransham was known chiefly as a polytheist, though it is doubtful whether he ever had settled theological views. Rather, his Humean critique of religion led him to take a psychological interest in the earliest myths and legends, especially those in the Greek tradition. In maintaining that these contained truths which had been subsequently lost—the superiority of the classical to the modern age is the most consistently reiterated theme in Fransham's writings—he found himself championing a polytheistic world-view. In 1767 he accompanied one of his pupils to London, and took with him his philosophical writings, hoping to find a publisher. In this he was largely unsuccessful, though he did manage to publish anonymously *Two anniversary discourses: in the first of which the old man is exploded, in the second the new man is recognised* (1768), a bizarre work of which the first part is an ironic attack on Socrates, the second an ironic celebration of Ben Jonson's character Bartholomew Cokes. His more substantial impact on literary London was less fortunate. He came to the attention of the playwright Samuel Foote and was caricatured as Johnny Macpherson in the latter's immensely successful comedy *The Devil upon Two Sticks* (1768). Fransham's fondness for wearing a plaid inspired his portrayal as a Scot; Foote also shows him as quarrelsome, proud of his understanding, filled with naïve indignation at the ways of the world, and boasting of his 'threepence an hour for larning Latin to a physician in the ceety' (Foote, 44). His London experiences subdued Fransham's literary ambitions. After his return to Norwich he continued to revise and add to his manuscripts, which were circulated among his acquaintances, but he appears to have made no further attempt to publish them.

It is clear from his published and unpublished writings that Fransham was a gifted and original scholar, as well as

that Fraser is best known. In 1882 he turned his attention to Locke, writing the article on him for the ninth edition of the *Encyclopaedia Britannica*, followed by *Locke* (1890), a companion volume to his *Berkeley* in the Blackwood series. In 1894 he produced a heavily annotated edition of Locke's *Essay* complete with lengthy biographical, critical, and historical prolegomena. Two slighter volumes followed: *Thomas Reid* (1898), and *Berkeley and Spiritual Realism* (1908), a very brief synopsis of what Fraser took to be the enduring lessons of Berkeley's philosophy. Hume, however, he had little sympathy for, calling the *Treatise* a 'scarecrow' (*Reid*, 61) and referring to Hume's philosophy as 'the suicide of intelligence' (ibid., 60) and 'metaphysical nihilism' (*Berkeley*, 72n.).

Fraser was an influential, but not very careful, editor. His edition of the *Works* revived serious interest in Berkeley's philosophy; and his edition of Locke's *Essay* remained the standard one for decades. Even so, he modernized Locke's text, left words out (and inserted others), was haphazard in his record of variants, and even confused different editions. In Berkeley's *Works* (both editions) he printed pages of the *Commonplace Book* in the wrong order.

Fraser's *Berkeley*, *Locke*, and *Reid* were all intended for student use. In each a brief introductory account of the subject's philosophy is inserted into a biographical format. All make use of unpublished materials. In keeping with the idealism that dominated late nineteenth-century philosophy in England, Fraser is critical of his authors' empiricism. This is most striking in his interpretation of Berkeley. He minimizes Berkeley's early sensationalism: he frequently describes the *Principles* as 'juvenile'. Instead, he emphasizes the later writings, especially *Siris*, which he perversely took to be a much deeper and more satisfactory work. In it, he said, 'Berkeley's thought culminates, not in a paradox about Matter, but in the conception of God as the concatenating principle of the universe' (Berkeley, *Works*, 1901 edn, 1.x). In this way, he thought, Berkeley was able to avoid the 'disintegrative tendency' of Locke's empiricism which, he said, 'must end incoherently' in scepticism (*Locke*, 283).

Like Berkeley, Fraser thought that matter was 'really mental experience' (*Philosophy of Theism*, 2 vols., 1895–7, 1.125), but such experiences were causally inert, for only minds were capable of agency. Individual selves were real, and active in the world, but the sensible world as whole was the product of God's agency. It was, he said, 'a system of mind-dependent sense-signs' (ibid., 131), which were 'symbolic of a truer reality' (*Berkeley*, 163). This position, which he called 'spiritual realism', informs even his earliest essays. It was also the one he attributed to the later Berkeley.

For many years Fraser's philosophy was expressed only in his commentaries on other philosophers and in the annotations he supplied in editing their writings. An invitation to give the Gifford lectures for 1894–6 gave him the opportunity to present his thought at greater length and resulted in *Philosophy of Theism* (2 vols., 1895–7), the only extended statement of his position.

Although Fraser did not retire until he was seventy-two, much of his writing dates from his retirement. His university duties left him little time for writing. In addition to his chair, he was dean of the faculty of arts (1859–91) and he represented the senate at the university court (1877–91)— all this during a period of exceptional change and growth at the university. He was an excellent teacher: seven of his students subsequently held philosophy chairs in Scotland, and another nine in other countries. Indeed it is as an educator, rather than as an original philosopher, that he is important. Significantly his first two books, *Essays in Philosophy* and *Rational Philosophy*, both include material on the teaching of philosophy.

On 30 April 1850 Fraser married Jemima Gordon Dyce (d. 1907) of Cuttlehill, Aberdeenshire; they had at least one son, and two daughters. Fraser received honorary degrees from several universities including Glasgow (1871), Oxford (1883), Edinburgh (1891), and Aberdeen (1906); he was made a member of the Royal Society of Edinburgh in 1858 and of the British Academy in 1903. In 1904 he published a very readable autobiography, *Biographia philosophica*. On retirement he moved from Edinburgh to Gorton House, near Hawthornden, but after his wife's death he lived at 34 Melville Street, Edinburgh. He died at his home on 2 December 1914, and was buried three days later in Lasswade churchyard.   Nicholas Griffin

Sources A. C. Fraser, *Biographia philosophica: a retrospect* (1904) · A. S. Pringle-Pattison, 'Alexander Campbell Fraser, 1819–1914', *PBA*, [6] (1913–14), 525–38 · A. S. Pringle-Pattison, *Mind*, new ser., 24 (1915), 289–325 · *WWW, 1897–1915* · *DNB*
Archives NL Scot., corresp. and MSS · NL Scot., notes on lectures · U. Edin., notebooks | NL Scot., corresp. with Blackwood's
Likenesses D. O. Hill and R. Adamson, photographs, 1843–8, NPG [*see illus.*] · W. Hole, etching, 1884, NPG; repro. in W. Hole, *Quasi cursores: portraits of the high officers and professors of the University of Edinburgh at its tercentenary festival* (1884) · G. Reid, oils, U. Edin.
Wealth at death £6225 7s. 3d.: confirmation, 20 Jan 1915, *CCI*

Fraser, Alexander Garden (1873–1962), educationist and missionary, was born on 6 October 1873 at Tillicoultry, Clackmannanshire, the son of Sir Andrew Henderson Leith *Fraser KCSI (1848–1919), of the Indian Civil Service, and his first wife, Agnes Archibald (d. 1879) of Tillicoultry; his grandfather the Revd A. G. Fraser was a Presbyterian missionary in India for sixty years and his father while in the Indian Civil Service also served as moderator of the Presbyterian church assembly in India. Fraser was educated at Merchiston Castle School in Edinburgh and at Edinburgh University and Trinity College, Oxford. At Oxford in 1892, with his friends J. H. Oldham, W. E. S. Holland, and Temple Gairdner, he pledged himself to become a missionary under the influence of the visiting evangelists J. R. Mott and R. E. Speer who were campaigning for 'The evangelization of the world in this generation' (E. A. Livingstone, *The Evangelization of the World in this Generation*, 1900). On graduating he worked with the Student Volunteer Missionary Union in which he fell in love with a Cambridge student, Beatrice Glass (1873–1970), who was committed to work with the Church Missionary Society (CMS) in Uganda. The Presbyterian Fraser impetuously became an Anglican, joined the CMS and followed his fiancée in 1900 to Uganda where they were married in the following year. They had two sons and three daughters.

In Uganda characteristics of Fraser's later educational policies emerged. He encouraged his pupils to undertake manual labour by leading them through the swamplands, carrying mud on his head, to the building site of the new cathedral. He persuaded the CMS, despite the reluctance of some colleagues, to establish Kings School, Budo, as an élite secondary boarding-school for sons of chiefs and future ordinands with a resident European staff. Before he could take charge of this project he had to return to Britain in 1903 on the breakdown of his wife's health and to a lesser extent of his own. He next took a course in theology at New College, Edinburgh. One of the few overseas posts of the CMS to which the doctors would now allow his wife to accompany him was in the highlands of Ceylon. In 1904 Fraser was appointed principal of the society's Trinity College, Kandy, and held the position until 1924.

At the time of Fraser's arrival the college was suffering from severe absenteeism and breakdown of discipline. There had been six principals in four years. Fraser revived the college by raising money to enable personally hand-picked graduates from Oxford and Cambridge to be recruited to the staff. Prefects were appointed, staff became resident, and a community spirit was fostered through social service schemes in which staff and students together built shelters for rickshaw pullers, visited hospitals, and made a social survey of the Kandy slums which shamed the authorities into action. More controversially Fraser introduced study of the vernacular languages at the expense of Latin, Greek, and French. He was eventually ordained as a priest in the Church of England at the age of forty-two but was rebuked by the Anglican bishop for allowing ministers of other denominations to preach at the school. His modernization of the curriculum, his ecumenical practices, his love of horseplay, and his expressed sympathy for the aspirations of Ceylonese nationalists scandalized many other missionaries, sixty of whom petitioned the CMS for his recall. Though a candidate, he failed to be appointed bishop of Colombo.

His tenure was interrupted by service with the YMCA and as an army chaplain in France during the First World War. After returning to Trinity he served as chairman of a commission on village education which visited India in 1919. During this investigation he was highly critical of European missionaries for having failed to protest against the massacre of Amritsar.

In 1924, at the suggestion of his brother-in-law J. H. Oldham, Fraser was appointed the first principal of the government secondary school at Achimota in the Gold Coast. This was the favourite project of the colony's governor, Sir Gordon Guggisberg, who saw it as the key to the training of local people who would eventually take over all government posts from expatriates. Before setting out Fraser preached a sermon in Westminster Abbey attacking the Kenya government so fiercely for its oppression of African labour that the Kenya legislature adjourned in protest

against such misuse of the abbey's pulpit. While this incident could have jeopardized his appointment, it was probably a calculated indiscretion to demonstrate that, although he would be a government official as principal of Achimota, his sympathies were with African aspirations.

Fraser took with him on his staff the well-known African-American educationist J. E. K. Aggrey who did much to win the support of African nationalists. This support was continued after Aggrey's death when Fraser persuaded the government to make Achimota an independent institution with a governing body of which Africans were members. As at Trinity, he brought in talented Oxford and Cambridge graduates and on their arrival made them study local languages and culture. Here too he introduced the practice of voluntary social service in the community. The college became co-educational and its activities included not only arts and science but also agriculture and engineering; it came to provide a full ladder from infant education to external university degrees. When later Gold Coast became the first British colony in Africa to achieve independence, many of its ministers and senior civil servants were Achimotans. Fraser, however, alienated his most important ally, Guggisberg, by getting hold of a government file in a department which had nothing to do with Achimota and writing a pungent minute in it. In 1926 and 1927 he visited Nigeria to report to the government on the state of education there. His report was so critical and trenchantly phrased that it was not published. With Guggisberg he wrote *The Future of the Negro Race*, published in London in 1929.

Fraser left Achimota in 1935. He spent an uncomfortable period as warden of a new adult education centre, Newbattle Abbey, in Dalkeith, Scotland, from 1937 to 1940, as his powers were restricted by his governing body. Intermittently between 1940 and 1948 he served as assistant chaplain of Gordonstoun School, warmly sympathizing with the ideas of its founder, Kurt Hahn. From 1941 to 1943 he was principal of an American Quaker teacher training college, Highgate, in Jamaica. Here again, though he won the affection of his students and staff, he had an uneasy relationship with his governing body. Returning to England, he served in 1944–6 as curate at Goring by Sea, where his son-in-law was the incumbent. His final enthusiasm was for the Moral Re-Armament movement in whose house in Berkeley Square, London, he spent his last years.

Fraser was widely recognized as the greatest colonial headmaster of his time. He was deeply religious, though to the dismay of some of his fellow missionaries he saw his duty not as to proselytise but rather to help to bring in the kingdom of God by whatever means. Christianity he saw as linked to national independence, and high-quality educational institutions as a prelude to decolonization. He was a resolute and successful opponent of the colour bar. His charisma inspired devotion and admiration from staff and pupils but his impulsiveness and fiery temper limited his wider influence. He was openly contemptuous of officialdom and used to quote Kierkegaard to the effect that there is nothing so repellent to God as an official because God is personal and the official is a negation of personality, though in 1930 he accepted the appointment as CBE. In a sermon in Oxford in 1940 Fraser compared the British treatment of Africans in the Rhodes era with that of the Poles and Jews by Hitler. Yet in retirement he was surprised by and resented his exclusion from committees which advised the colonial secretary on educational policies.

Fraser was a handsome man and at his most charming when silently expressing his regret for his impulsive and wounding utterances, though he hated to apologize in words. A colleague, Lord Hemingford, described him as an imperious democrat, a romantic realist, a hard hitting mystic, and irrepressibly naughty (BBC interview 1962). Fraser died aged eighty-nine in Trinity House Nursing Home, 26 Church Road, St Leonards, Sussex, on 27 January 1962.   RICHARD SYMONDS

Sources Bodl. RH, Fraser MSS, MS Brit. Emp. s.283 · W. E. F. Ward, *Fraser of Trinity and Achimota* (1965) · C. K. Williams, *Achimota: the early years, 1924–1948* (1962) · V. L. O. Reimann, *History of Trinity College, Kandy* (1922) · A. C. Fraser and G. Guggisberg, *The future of the negro race* (1929) · *CGPLA Eng. & Wales* (1962) · *WWW* · private information (2004)
Archives Bodl. RH, papers | Bodl. RH, corresp. with Lord Lugard · Bodl. RH, C. Kingsley Williams MSS, Brit. Emp. s.283 · Trinity College, Kandy, Sri Lanka, archives · U. Birm. L., Church Missionary Society archives | SOUND Bodl. RH, Fraser papers, audiotape of BBC programme *The Chief*, 1982, interviews with Fraser and those who knew him
Likenesses photographs, repro. in Ward, *Fraser of Trinity and Achimota*
Wealth at death no value given: confirmation, 1962, sealed

Fraser, Alexander George, sixteenth Lord Saltoun of Abernethy (1785–1853), army officer, was the elder son of Alexander, fifteenth Lord Saltoun of Abernethy in the peerage of Scotland, and Margery, daughter and heir of Simon Fraser of Newcastle, a director of the East India Company. He was born in London on 22 April 1785, baptized at Marylebone, and educated at Eton College. On 13 September 1793 he succeeded his father when still a minor. He entered the army as an ensign in the 35th regiment on 28 April 1802, and was promoted lieutenant on 2 September of that year and captain on 7 September 1804. On 23 November 1804 he exchanged into the 1st, with which he served continuously for many years. In September 1806 he accompanied the 3rd battalion to Sicily, where it formed part of the guards brigade under Major-General Henry Wynyard, and in October 1807 he returned to England with it.

In September 1808 Saltoun again left England, as lieutenant and captain of the light company of the 3rd battalion of the 1st guards, and his battalion was one of the two comprising the guards brigade of Major-General Henry Warde which landed at Corunna, with the army under Sir David Baird. From Corunna Baird marched to meet Sir John Moore at Mayorga-de-Campos, and in the terrible winter retreat which followed the guards distinguished themselves by their good order. Saltoun was present throughout the severe campaign, and at the battle of Corunna with his light company. In 1809 his battalion formed part of Major-General Disney's brigade of guards in the

Walcheren expedition, and in 1811 it was sent to Cadiz, but too late to be present at Barossa.

At the close of 1812 Saltoun joined the 1st battalion of his regiment with the main army before Burgos, and from that time he went through the Peninsular campaigns with the 1st brigade of guards. He commanded the light infantry company of his battalion throughout the campaigns of 1813 and 1814, and was present at the battle of Vitoria, the battle of the Pyrenees, the forcing of the Bidassoa, the battles of the Nivelle and the Nive, and at the operations before Bayonne, especially in the repulse of the sortie. He was promoted captain and lieutenant-colonel on 25 December 1813, and posted to the 3rd battalion, but as it was in England he obtained leave to continue to serve with Lord Wellington's army in the Peninsula. He returned to England, and joined his former battalion on the conclusion of peace in 1814.

On 6 March 1815 Saltoun married Catherine Thurlow (*d.* 9 July 1826), an illegitimate daughter of Edward, Lord Chancellor *Thurlow, and in the following May he was again ordered on foreign service. At the battle of Quatre Bras he commanded the light companies of the 2nd brigade of guards, and at the battle of Waterloo he held the garden and orchard of Hougoumont against all the onslaughts of the French, while Sir James Macdonell of the Coldstream Guards held the farmhouse itself. Saltoun had four horses killed under him during this day's fighting, and lost two-thirds of his men. When the guards made their famous charge on the French old guard, the light companies were led on by Saltoun, who also received the sword of General Cambronne when he surrendered.

For his bravery in this great battle Saltoun was made a CB, a knight of the orders of Maria Theresa of Austria and of St George of Russia, and in 1818 he was made a KCB. He had been a representative peer of Scotland since 1807, and as a consistent tory he received the post of a lord of the bedchamber in 1821, in which year he was also made a GCH. On 27 May 1825 he was promoted colonel; in 1827 he became lieutenant-colonel commanding the 1st battalion of the Grenadier Guards, and on 10 January 1837 he was promoted major-general.

In 1841 Saltoun received the command of a brigade in the First Opium War under Sir Hugh Gough, which he commanded at the battle of Chinkiang (Zhenjiang) and in the advance on Nanking (Nanjing). On Gough's departure from China, Saltoun succeeded him in the command-in-chief of British troops there, a post which he held until 1843. For his services in the war he received the thanks of parliament, and in 1846 he was appointed colonel of the 2nd (or Queen's) regiment. He was promoted lieutenant-general in 1849, and made a KT in 1852.

Saltoun had a high reputation as a gallant soldier; Wellington once described him as a pattern to the army both as a man and a soldier. He was also an accomplished musician and a musical enthusiast, and was at the time of his death president of the Madrigal Society of London and chairman of the Musical Union. He died of dropsy at Auchroath, his shooting box near Rothes, on 18 August 1853, and was buried at Fraserburgh, Aberdeenshire. He was succeeded as seventeenth Lord Saltoun by his nephew, Major Alexander Fraser.

H. M. STEPHENS, *rev.* JAMES LUNT

Sources *Hart's Army List* · *GM*, 2nd ser., 40 (1853) · J. Philippart, ed., *The royal military calendar*, 3rd edn, 5 vols. (1820) · Foster, *Alum. Oxon.* · F. W. Hamilton, *The origin and history of the first or grenadier guards*, 3 vols. (1874) · H. T. Siborne, ed., *Waterloo letters* (1891) · Fortescue, *Brit. army*, vols. 10, 12 · A. Fraser, *The Frasers of Philorth*, 3 vols. (1879) · Burke, *Peerage* · GEC, *Peerage*
Archives U. Aberdeen L., family and military corresp. and papers | BL OIOC, letters to Lord Tweeddale, Ms Eur. F 96 · NA Scot., letters to Lord Melville · PRO, letters to Ann Carter, J 90/946 · PRO, letters to Henry Pottinger, FO 705 · W. Sussex RO, letters to duke of Richmond
Likenesses T. Lawrence, oils, *c.*1809; formerly, United Service Club, London, in care of Crown Commissioners · C. Baugniet, lithograph, BM, NPG · W. Salter, group portrait, oils (*Waterloo banquet at Apsley House*), Wellington Museum, Apsley House, London · W. Salter, oils (study for *Waterloo banquet at Apsley House*), NPG · G. Zobel, mezzotint (after T. Lawrence), BM

Fraser, Alexander George (1786–1865), genre and domestic painter, was born in Edinburgh on 7 April 1786. He studied painting under John Graham (1754–1817) at the academy of the trustees for the board of manufactures and fisheries in Edinburgh. His fellow pupils included William Allan (1782–1850), John Burnet (1784–1868), and David Wilkie (1785–1841). In 1809 he exhibited at the Associated Society of Artists, Edinburgh, *Playing at Draughts*, which established his reputation as a painter of Scottish genre. Fraser began exhibiting at the Royal Academy in 1810 with *A Green Stall* and sent further works, *The New Coat* and *Preparing for Fish Market*, in 1812 before moving to London in 1813. By 1813 Fraser's former fellow pupil Wilkie was well established in London, where he employed Fraser as an assistant to paint details and still life in his pictures. Fraser's hand is recognizable in, for example, Wilkie's *The Irish Whiskey Still* (1840; NG Scot.). Fraser also received commissions passed on from Wilkie which the latter had no time to undertake. He continued besides to paint independently. The National Gallery of Scotland possesses two unidentified male portraits by Fraser; one is dated 1816 and the other belongs stylistically to the same period. These portraits are fairly uncouth and raw and this earthy quality reveals that Fraser's paintings are close in character to the works of his compatriot Walter Geikie (1795–1837). Fraser's colours tend towards rich brown hues which enhance the down-to-earth quality of the overall image. On 30 June 1826 Fraser married, in Edinburgh, Janet William Moir; their son Alexander *Fraser also became a painter.

Fraser's *A Highland Sportsman* (1832; NG Scot.) captures the appearance of the cottage interior but is devoid of the feelings of intimacy evoked by a similar painting of the subject by Alexander Carse (1770–1843): *The Return from the Hunt* (priv. coll.). Fraser's pictures show a tendency towards Victorian sentimentality. *A Highland Sportsman* was engraved by C. Cousen; other paintings by Fraser that were engraved include *The First Day of Oysters*, by W. Greatbach; *The Moment of Victory*, by C. Rolls; and *The Cobbler at*

Lunch, by William Howison. These engravings indicate the popularity of Fraser's genre paintings.

Many of Fraser's paintings were humorous and on a small scale, for example, *The Scotch Fair* (*c.*1834; McManus Gallery, Dundee) or *Music Makers* (Bukowski Gallery, Stockholm). Of Wilkie's many followers Fraser was the most capable. In 1840 he was elected an associate of the Royal Scottish Academy, an institution he had helped to found. In 1842 his *Naaman Cured of the Leprosy* obtained the premium at the British Institution for the best picture of the year. From 1848 Fraser was prevented by ill health from painting and ceased to exhibit at the Royal Academy. He died at Wood Green, Hornsey, London on 15 February 1865. L. H. CUST, *rev.* LUCY DIXON

Sources D. Macmillan, *Scottish art, 1460–1990* (1990) · P. J. M. McEwan, *Dictionary of Scottish art and architecture* (1994) · K. Andrews and J. R. Brotchie, *Catalogue of Scottish drawings* (1960) · J. Caw, *Scottish painting past and present, 1620–1908* (1908); repr. (1990) · Graves, *Brit. Inst.* · W. D. McKay and F. Rinder, *The Royal Scottish Academy, 1826–1916* (1917) · Graves, *RA exhibitors* · D. Irwin and F. Irwin, *Scottish painters at home and abroad, 1700–1900* (1975) · [J. Lloyd Williams], *National Gallery of Scotland: concise catalogue of paintings* (1997) · *Catalogue of the permanent collection of paintings, drawings, and sculpture*, Dundee Museums and Art Galleries Dept [1973] · J. Halsby and P. Harris, *The dictionary of Scottish painters, 1600–1960* (1990) · R. Billcliffe, ed., *The Royal Glasgow Institute of the Fine Arts, 1861–1989: a dictionary of exhibitors at the annual exhibitions*, 4 vols. (1990–92) · *GM*, 3rd ser., 18 (1865), 652 · *IGI*
Archives NL Scot.

Fraser, Alexander Mackenzie (1758–1809), army officer, was born at Tore, Ross-shire, the fourth and posthumous son of Colin Mackenzie of Kilcoy and his wife, Martha (1727–1803), eldest daughter of Charles Fraser of Inverallochy, Aberdeenshire. Mackenzie was tutored at home, and then attended ordinary classes at Aberdeen University before entering the Edinburgh counting-house of Sir William Forbes & Co. In 1778 he accepted Lord Macleod's offer of a lieutenancy in the 73rd (later 71st) highlanders and was soon appointed adjutant. While serving at Gibraltar during the great siege, he took part in the famous sortie of 26–7 November 1781 as a supernumerary aide-de-camp, and distinguished himself during the destruction of the Spanish floating batteries on 13 September 1782, when he was wounded. Promoted captain on 13 January 1781, Fraser returned to Britain in 1783 and went on half pay. Having retired from the army in 1784, on 27 April 1785 he married Helen Anne (1764–1802), daughter of Major William Mackenzie and sister of Francis Humberston *Mackenzie (from 1797 Lord Seaforth), and bought an estate at Belmaduthy, Ross-shire. They had two sons and two daughters.

In 1793, on the outbreak of war with France, Mackenzie's brother-in-law F. H. Mackenzie, raised the 78th highlanders and appointed Mackenzie his major. The 78th was sent to garrison Guernsey later that year, and on 10 February 1794 Mackenzie was placed in command as lieutenant-colonel. He led the 78th to the Low Countries in September 1794 and joined the duke of York's army on the River Waal. During a successful sortie at Nijmegen on 4 November, he took command when General de Burgh was wounded, and on 5 January 1795, after the 78th had repulsed a determined French assault on Geldermalsen, he was publicly thanked by General Sir David Dundas: 'Colonel Mackenzie, you and your regiment have this day saved the British army' (*Royal Military Calendar*, 3.310). Retreat was nevertheless inevitable, and in appalling winter conditions the British, with the 78th as part of the rearguard, fell back across the Rhine and embarked for home from Bremen.

Francis Humberston Mackenzie had meanwhile raised a second battalion of the 78th and, after his brother-in-law's return from the continent, arranged for him to become its lieutenant-colonel commandant. At the end of 1795, however, the two battalions were ordered to be amalgamated, and although F. H. Mackenzie agreed to go on half pay, leaving Alexander Mackenzie to succeed as sole colonel commandant (gazetted 3 May 1796), friction arose when F. H. Mackenzie realized the extent of his brother-in-law's financial advantage.

In March 1796 Alexander Mackenzie sailed for the Cape of Good Hope where, in June, the two battalions of the 78th were united, and he then took his 1300-strong regiment on to India. The 78th spent most of 1797 stationed at Berhampur before moving in December to Benares; it afterwards helped provide the escort to the governor-general, Sir John Shore, when he went to Lucknow to enforce the deposition of Wazir Ali as nawab of Oudh. In February 1798 Mackenzie led a force to occupy the fort at Allahabad, newly ceded by Oudh. He then served under Sir James Craig in the Maratha country before returning to Lucknow when unrest in Oudh appeared imminent. On 1 January 1800 he embarked at Calcutta for England.

In 1802 Mackenzie was promoted major-general and entered parliament as MP for Cromarty, a seat placed at his disposal by Henry Dundas. He supported Pitt's ministry. In 1806 he was returned for Ross-shire on Seaforth's interest, and represented it until his death. After his mother's death in 1803 he inherited the Inverallochy estate, taking by royal licence her maiden name of Fraser in addition to his own. In the same year he was appointed to the staff in the south of England, commanding a brigade of militia. In December 1805 he was sent with Lord Cathcart's short-lived expedition to Hanover and, after his return, was sent to Sicily in June 1806 to serve under General Henry Fox. When, soon after, a breach with Turkey appeared likely, the British government, anxious to forestall any French reoccupation of Egypt, ordered Fox to send a force to seize Alexandria. Because Egypt was riven by factions, Fox was told to select as commander of the expedition a man with political as well as military talents. Sir John Moore, who had recent experience of Egypt, should have been sent, but Fox chose Fraser. Colonel Henry Bunbury, quartermaster-general on Sicily, had misgivings: 'A fine specimen of an open, generous, honourable highland chieftain … everyone in the army loved Mackenzie Fraser, but no one deemed him suitable for a separate and difficult command' (Bunbury, 287). And so it proved.

Although Alexandria capitulated readily enough on 21 March 1807, within two days Fraser was informed by the British resident, Major Ernest Misset, that unless he advanced into the Nile delta and occupied Rosetta and Rahmanieh, Alexandria's population would starve for want of provisions. This placed Fraser in a quandary: his 5000-strong force was intended solely as a garrison for Alexandria, yet he was also directed to make use of Misset's local knowledge. He decided to send two regiments under General Wauchope to occupy Rosetta, but Wauchope was killed and his men repulsed with nearly 500 casualties. Against his better judgement, and urged on by Misset who promised the support of the warrior mamelukes of Upper Egypt, Fraser renewed the attempt, sending Brigadier Stewart and 2500 men. The siege of Rosetta lasted a fortnight until 21 April when, instead of the mamelukes, Albanian troops loyal to the Turkish viceroy Mohammed Ali, arrived in overwhelming strength, annihilated a British detachment at al-Hamed, and compelled Stewart's withdrawal. Fortunately, the arrival of 2000 reinforcements from Sicily and the presence of the navy offshore safeguarded Fraser's position, and it proved possible to hold Alexandria as a bargaining counter in peace negotiations with the Turks until its evacuation in September 1807.

Although the enterprise had been mismanaged, Fraser escaped official censure. He pointed out in self-justification that much of his command consisted of unreliable foreign regiments—with the Royal Sicilians by far the worst—and that if he had not been fever-stricken at the time he would have led the second attack on Rosetta personally. None the less, he had allowed himself to be misled by Misset, whose ambition to see Britain play a wider role in Egypt's internal affairs Fraser failed to recognize (it had soon become evident that the failure to occupy the Nile delta did not, as Misset claimed, lead to famine in Alexandria). His handling of the military situation was also open to criticism. Rather than sending detachments to Rosetta, Sir John Moore believed that Fraser should have used his entire force. 'Fraser … is a very excellent man', Moore wrote confidentially to Thomas Graham on 24 May 1807; 'he was not, however, up to the job, and the disasters which have befallen were owing to the bad measures he adopted, and to the worse manner in which they were executed' (C. Oman, *Sir John Moore*, 1953, 412).

In October 1807 Fraser sailed for England from Sicily with 7000 troops under Moore. Having been promoted lieutenant-general on 25 April 1808, he accompanied Moore on the abortive expedition to Sweden the following month, and was with him when the same force landed in Portugal in August. When Moore advanced into Spain, Fraser was given command of a division. After the terrible retreat to Corunna, he endorsed Moore's decision not to negotiate with the French for a peaceful evacuation, and in the subsequent battle (on 16 January 1809) his division protected the British right flank. Fraser's contribution to victory at Corunna was recognized with the award of the army gold medal.

Back in England, Fraser accepted command of the 4th division for the expedition to Walcheren in July 1809. He captured Fort Ter Haak, the town of Ter Veere, and Fort Ramakins, but having joined the siege of Flushing, his health, already precarious, broke completely. 'Walcheren fever' complicated an existing inflammation of the lungs and, after returning to England, he died aged fifty-one on 13 September 1809 while convalescing at the home of his brother-in-law, Sir Vicary Gibbs, the attorney-general, at Hayes Common, Kent. In accordance with Fraser's wishes, he was buried near where he died, at Hayes, Kent.

ALASTAIR W. MASSIE

Sources U. Aberdeen, Mackenzie Fraser MS 3470 · J. Philippart, ed., *The royal military calendar*, 3 (1816), 307–15 · J. Philippart, ed., *The royal military calendar*, 3rd edn, 4 (1820), 101–9, 217–24 · H. Bunbury, *Narratives of some passages in the great war with France, from 1799 to 1810* (1854) · *The diary of Sir John Moore*, ed. J. F. Maurice, 2 vols. (1904) · J. MacVeigh, *The historical records of the 78th highlanders* (1887) · P. Mackesy, *The war in the Mediterranean, 1803–1810* (1957) · 'Notes of an expedition to Alexandria in the year 1807', *United Service Journal*, 3 (1837), 183–92, 481–8; 1 (1838), 44–9; 2 (1838), 15–28 · G. C. Bond, *The grand expedition: the British invasion of Holland in 1809* (1979) · L. Smiley, *The Frasers of Castle Fraser* (1988) · A. Mackenzie, *History of the Mackenzies, with genealogies of the principal families of the name*, new edn (1894) · W. F. P. Napier, *History of the war in the Peninsula and in the south of France*, 1 (1892) · D. R. Fisher, 'Mackenzie (afterwards Mackenzie Fraser), Alexander', HoP, *Commons, 1790–1820*
Archives U. Aberdeen L., corresp. and papers, MS 3470 | BL, corresp. with Sir James Willoughby Gordon, Add. MS 49495 · BL, letters to J. R. Mackenzie, Add. MSS 39195–39199 · NA Scot., letters to Lord Seaforth, GD 46
Likenesses H. R. Cook, stipple (after R. Cosway), BM; repro. in *Royal Military Panorama* · H. Raeburn, oils, Dunecht House, Aberdeenshire; repro. in Smiley, *The Frasers*, 7

Fraser, Sir Andrew Henderson Leith (1848–1919), administrator in India, was born at Bombay on 14 November 1848, the eldest son of Dr Alexander Garden Fraser, Presbyterian missionary, and his wife, Joanna Maria, daughter of John Shaw, a minister in Skye descended from a Perthshire family. After education at the Edinburgh Academy and at Edinburgh University, where he gained his MA in 1868, Fraser joined the Indian Civil Service. In 1871 he was posted to the Central Provinces, where he worked for the next twenty-seven years, becoming a commissioner in 1891. He was called to the bar at the Middle Temple in 1874.

The civilians of the Central Provinces prided themselves on their empathy with peasant India—on knowing the vernacular and being accessible to ordinary villagers. They were a tight-knit, sociable bunch and often their wives had more scope for partnership with their husbands than in the metropolitan provinces. Fraser married, in 1872, Agnes W. Archibald (*d.* 1879), daughter of Robert Archibald of Devonvale, Tillicoultry, with whom he had a daughter and a son, the missionary Alexander Garden *Fraser (1873–1962). He married, second, in 1883, Henrietta Catherine Lucy, daughter of Colonel Henry Ibbetson Lugard of the Indian army. Henrietta, who knew Hindustani, often assisted Fraser in his official dealings with women, especially aristocratic women in purdah.

In 1898 Fraser was nearing the end of a solid, if unspectacular, career when the new viceroy, Lord Curzon,

Sir Andrew Henderson Leith Fraser (1848–1919), by Lafayette, 1906

appointed him to officiate as home secretary and then, in November 1899, made him chief commissioner of the Central Provinces. In March 1902 Curzon offered him the presidency of an all-India commission into the police. Having toured every province, Fraser produced a report which unflinchingly catalogued evidence of inefficiency and corruption, and recommended immediate improvement in the pay, training, and status of the Indian subordinates in the police.

Curzon promoted Fraser to the lieutenant-governorship of Bengal in November 1903, at which time he was also made KCSI. Although one of the most senior civilians, he was not an obvious choice for the job: Bengal's administrative style was much less personal than that of the Central Provinces, and Fraser was unused to having a city within his jurisdiction, let alone one as politically advanced as Calcutta. Curzon's preference for him over the acting incumbent, John Bourdillon, was almost certainly determined by their respective attitudes to the partition of Bengal. There had been talk for years of reducing Bengal to a more manageable size, and while chief commissioner of the Central Provinces, Fraser himself had set the ball of administrative realignment rolling by recommending, on the grounds of linguistic affinity, the transfer of Sambalpur to Orissa in Bengal. Also, as president of the police commission, Fraser had been shocked to see how out of touch Bengal's administrators were with the people, often unable to speak Bengali fluently and only touring the districts infrequently. He thought the situation particularly bad in the eastern districts of the province and he suggested to Curzon that these be given over to Assam to create a new eastern Bengal and Assam service which, as in the Central Provinces, would pay heed to the local peasantry rather than to Calcutta's urban sophisticates. Bourdillon was annoyed at the slur on Bengal's administrators and crossly rejected talk of partition, a reaction which probably cost him the lieutenant-governorship.

In October 1905 the partition took effect, unleashing a storm of protest from Bengali Hindus. Fraser was one of its principal architects and backed it unreservedly, impatiently rejecting any interpretation of it as an attempt to set the Muslim majority of East Bengal against the Hindu majority in the west. Confronted by a rising tide of terrorism, Fraser resisted the clamour for repressive measures. He was a small, trim man, with close-cropped hair and sharp features. He did not appear physically strong and critics misinterpreted his restrained approach as weakness, even though it actually required considerable courage to resist both the vitriol of Calcutta's expatriate community and repeated attempts on his life. To Fraser, however, it was obvious that mass repression was unnecessary. Even though he could write feelingly on the injustice of submitting Oriya speakers to a Hindi-speaking administration, he was unable to believe that the issue of Bengali nationalism inspired more than a few fanatics. The Indians whom he knew and loved were loyal and, in his view, untainted by terrorism and conspiracy. His solution was a long-term one—the promotion of Indian industry and with it employment for Calcutta's misguided youth. The anti-partition agitation dominated Fraser's lieutenant-governorship. He was also kept busy implementing Curzon's numerous beautification projects for Calcutta. A devout churchman, in 1907 he was proud to be chosen moderator of the Presbyterian church assembly in India.

In November 1908 Fraser retired to Scotland. In 1911 he published a book of reminiscences, *Among Indian Rajahs and Ryots*, which was staunch in its defence of the partition of Bengal. He became a member of the continuation committee of the World Missionary Conference and founder chairman of the ecumenical Women's Christian College of Madras. In 1919 he gave a qualified and hesitating approval to the Montagu–Chelmsford scheme of constitutional reform. He could not envisage India as a nation, but allowed that some form of provincial self-government might eventually prevail as long as the politicians were elected from constituencies based on class, religion, and profession rather than territory.

Fraser died at 58 Melville Street, Edinburgh, on 26 February 1919 and was buried in Dean cemetery, Edinburgh,

on 3 March. He was survived by his second wife, dedicatee of his memoirs, their three sons, and the son and daughter of his first marriage.   KATHERINE PRIOR

Sources A. H. L. Fraser, *Among Indian rajahs and ryots* (1911) • correspondence, BL OIOC, Curzon MSS • A. H. L. Fraser, letters and confidential memoranda, BL OIOC, Morley MSS • S. Sarkar, *The swadeshi movement in Bengal, 1903–08* (1973) • *India Office List* (1908) • *The Times* (27 Feb 1919), 1, 8 • ecclesiastical records, BL OIOC • [T. Henderson and P. F. Hamilton-Grierson], eds., *The Edinburgh Academy register* (1914) • *The administration of Bengal under Sir Andrew Fraser, K.C.S.I.* (1903–1908) (1908) • *Bombay Calendar and General Directory for the Year 1849* (1849) • *WWW*, 1916–28 • O. S. Crofton, ed., *List of inscriptions on tombs or monuments in the Central Provinces and Berar* (1932) • BL OIOC, Women's Christian College of Madras collection

Archives BL OIOC, Curzon collection and Women's Christian College of Madras collection • BL OIOC, letters to Lord Minto and Lord Morley, MS Eur. D 573 • CUL, corresp. with Lord Hardinge

Likenesses group portrait, photograph, c.1905, repro. in Fraser, *Among Indian rajahs* • Lafayette, photograph, 1906, V&A [*see illus.*] • L. Jennings, bust, c.1910, Dundee City Art Gallery

Wealth at death £5206 1s. 0d.: confirmation, 8 Oct 1919, CCI

Fraser, Angelica Patience (1823–1910), social reformer, was born on 25 January 1823 at 56 Marischal Street, Aberdeen, the seventh daughter and twelfth child of Alexander Fraser (1775–1840), merchant and lord provost of Aberdeen, and his wife, Agnes Dingwall Fordyce (1781–1834), the sixth daughter of Dr Arthur Dingwall Fordyce of Culsh. She was educated at a school run by a Mrs Kilch in Union Street, Aberdeen, until the age of fourteen, when she was sent to Miss Crymble's boarding-school at 15 Royal Circus, Edinburgh. On the death of her father in 1840 the family moved to Union Terrace, Aberdeen, and subsequently to 26 Bon Accord Terrace. Her sister Jessy married Alexander Thomson, a leading lay member of the Free Church in Scotland, in 1825, and Angelica, with other members of the family, spent a great deal of time at his house in Banchory, near Aberdeen.

The death of her mother when Angelica was only eleven was said to have affected her profoundly, leading her to seek comfort in religion. Throughout her childhood years her health was delicate, and after an unhappy love affair at the age of nineteen she was sent to Ventnor on the Isle of Wight, as her family feared she was suffering from consumption. When she returned a year later she began what was to be a lifetime's active involvement in social reform, encouraged no doubt by her brother-in-law. From 1848 to 1879 she lived in Edinburgh, first with her brother Arthur and her sister Agnes at 36 Great King Street, and later at 3 Athol Place. She worked as a district visitor among the poor, attached to the mission of Free St George's Church at Fountainbridge.

In her early thirties, through the influence of Dr Hood Wilson, who had been appointed to Fountainbridge church in 1853, Angelica Fraser began a lifelong crusade to improve the working conditions of tailors. Motivated by a belief that 'make him a self-respecting man and the tailor will bring about his own social and economic emancipation' (Askew, 108), she organized a group of women, known as lady readers, to read the scriptures to tailors as they worked. By 1875 similar groups had been established in other Scottish cities and extended to Belfast, Liverpool, and London.

In 1879 Angelica Fraser moved to London to keep house for her brother Alexander and joined the Marylebone Presbyterian Church. She organized shop reading to tailors in the West End of London and, concerned to improve their working conditions, in March 1880 called a Conference of Tailors to discuss issues of practical concern. In 1885 she raised over £1000 in six months to establish an institute for London tailors, known as Tailors' Hall, which was based in Mill Street, Conduit Street. Built with a lecture hall and reading-room, it was intended 'to meet the social, intellectual, technical and physical needs of the members' (Askew, 162). In 1906 an endowment fund was set up for the Tailors' Hall to mark fifty years of her work for tailors. Her success and influence over the tailors were said to be due 'to the unerring judgement and tender sympathy with which she handled men of all ages, types and temperaments' (Askew, 153), and she was known among them as the Florence Nightingale of Tailors.

Angelica Fraser was also involved in the temperance movement. In 1875 she helped to establish the Edinburgh Tailors' Abstinence Union, and co-founded the Scottish Ladies' Temperance Society a year later. She was also a long-serving member of the Free Church of Scotland's Women's Foreign Missionary Society, which she first joined in 1850. In 1865 she was appointed a visitor to the Free Church normal school in Edinburgh, and her work there led to the formation in 1872 of the Teachers' Private Prayer Union. Angelica Fraser relaxed by pursuing interests in archery and botany. She was also a fine singer and a good organ player. In 1910, on her eighty-seventh birthday, she received a brooch from Edward VII, who had been petitioned by the Association of London Master Tailors to recognize her work among tailors. She died on 27 November 1910 at her home, 10 Upper Westbourne Terrace, London, having attended her last meeting at Tailors' Hall on 9 November; she was buried in Kensal Green cemetery.

SERENA KELLY

Sources W. D. Askew, *Angelica Patience Fraser* (1923) · *The Times* (29 Nov 1910) · *In Memoriam: an Obituary of Aberdeen and Vicinity* (1911) · Register of births, NA Scot.
Likenesses charcoal drawing, 1843, repro. in Askew, *Angelica Patience Fraser* · photographs, 1862–90, repro. in Askew, *Angelica Patience Fraser*
Wealth at death £8788 12s. 8d.: probate, 26 Jan 1911, *CGPLA Eng. & Wales*

Fraser, Angus (c.1800–1870). *See under* Fraser, Simon (1773–1852).

Fraser, Archibald Campbell, of Lovat (1736–1815), politician, was born on 16 August 1736, the son of Simon *Fraser, eleventh Lord Lovat (1667/8–1747), Jacobite leader, and his second wife, Primrose Campbell (1710–1796). He was educated at a school at Petty, Inverness-shire. He was present at Culloden during the battle, and following his father's execution for high treason in 1747 he was sent to Glasgow, where he was educated at the university between 1750 and 1752. After attending a London academy in the following year, he returned to Glasgow, where, on a

Archibald Campbell Fraser of Lovat (1736–1815), by James Tassie, 1795

small annual maintenance from the forfeited Lovat estates, he set up as a merchant. In 1763 he married Jane Fraser, daughter of William Fraser of Leadclune, Inverness; they had five sons, all of whom predeceased their father.

Fraser later served as a diplomat; he was British consul at Tripoli and, from 1766 to 1774, at Algiers. He inherited the restored family estates in 1782, on the death of his elder half-brother Lieutenant-General Simon *Fraser (1726–1782), whom he also succeeded, unopposed, as MP for Inverness-shire; he held his seat until 1784. In parliament he supported the lifting of the ban on wearing highland dress, and opposed Fox's East India Bill, emerging in 1784 as a follower of the Pitt administration.

Fraser was known for his traditional values and eccentricity, an example of which included the erection of a monument to himself listing his extensive public service in both foreign and domestic affairs. His achievements overseas included the conclusion of peace in 1764 between Denmark, Venice, and the Islamic states of Africa, and his efforts to prevent British subjects' being taken into slavery. In Scotland he undertook a survey of the west-coast fishing industry; encouraged the production of wool, hemp, and flax; was an ardent agrarian improver who raised standards of dairy production and improved highland cattle breeds; and, by providing employment for returning highland soldiers, prevented emigration and thus preserved the indigenous population. He also claimed to have put down an insurrection, *bliadhna na coarach* ('the year of the sheep'), on 10 August 1792, an assertion that, along with some others, remains unsubstantiated.

Fraser died on 8 December 1815, and was buried in the churchyard at Kirkhill, Inverness-shire. All his sons had died before him, and the Lovat estates passed, according to an entail executed in 1808, to his fifth cousin three times removed, Thomas Alexander Fraser (1802–1875), who was created Baron Lovat in 1837, and restored as twelfth Lord Lovat in 1857. Fraser's eldest son was **John**

Simon Frederick Fraser (1765–1803), politician and soldier. He was educated at Wadham College, Oxford, where he matriculated on 4 July 1786. He entered Lincoln's Inn, London, in 1789, and while there published *Reports of Proceedings in Law of Contested Elections* (1790), before moving to the Inner Temple three years later. Between 1796 and 1802 he was MP for Inverness-shire, and was a supporter of Pitt. He also served as the regimental commander of the Fraser fencibles in Ireland in 1798. He died, unmarried, the father of one son, at Lisbon, on 6 April 1803.

ROBERT CLYDE

Sources GEC, *Peerage*, new edn · E. Haden-Guest, 'Fraser, Archibald Campbell', HoP, *Commons* · J. Anderson, *Account of the family of Frizell or Fraser* (1825) · J. Hill-Barton, *Life of Simon, Lord Lovat* (1845) · D. R. Fisher, 'Fraser, John Simon Frederick', HoP, *Commons, 1790–1820*
Likenesses J. Tassie, two paste medallions, 1795, Scot. NPG [*see illus.*] · plaster medallion, 1795 (after J. Tassie), Scot. NPG

Fraser, Bruce Austin, Baron Fraser of North Cape (1888–1981), naval officer, was born in Acton, Middlesex, on 5 February 1888, the younger son (there were no daughters) of General Alexander Fraser CB of the Royal Engineers, and his wife, Monica Stores Smith. He was educated at Bradfield College, Berkshire, before passing into HMS *Britannia* in September 1902. He completed his cadetship with distinction, and was appointed a midshipman in HMS *Hannibal*, a battleship with the Channel Fleet, in January 1904.

Gunnery specialist In the years that followed, Fraser served in a succession of battleships and destroyers in home waters, being promoted sub-lieutenant in September 1907. In 1911, having determined to become a gunnery specialist, he was posted to HMS *Excellent* at Whale Island. Fraser passed out top of the course. He acted as gunnery officer in the cruiser *Minerva* (1914–16), and saw action in the Dardanelles. He spent some months of 1916 on the senior staff of HMS *Excellent*, thus missing Jutland. At the end of the year, he was posted to the new battleship *Resolution*, in which he became commander in 1919. Ironically, for an officer who had shown exceptional leadership and technical capabilities, Fraser was obliged to end the war without experiencing a major action in a modern warship.

In April 1920 he suffered a bizarre misfortune. Because he was on poor terms with his captain in *Resolution*, he sought escape by responding to a call for Mediterranean Fleet volunteers to travel to Baku and assist the White Russian fleet against the Bolsheviks. He arrived in command of his detachment of thirty-one men, just in time to be caught up in a local Bolshevik coup. The British party was imprisoned in wretched conditions until freed in November, when Fraser came home to spend a further two years on the staff of *Excellent*.

Despite favourable reports and widespread acceptance as a popular and able officer, Fraser's career thus far had been sluggish. But from 1922 onwards he was plainly marked for high rank, earning the commendation of the Admiralty board in 1924 for his work on a new fire control

Bruce Austin Fraser, Baron Fraser of North Cape (1888–1981), by Bassano, 1946

installation. As fleet gunnery officer in the Mediterranean (1925–6) and as a captain in the Admiralty tactical division (1926–9), he worked close to the heart of the navy's gunnery development. From 1929 to 1932 he held his first seagoing command in the cruiser *Effingham* in the East Indies. As director of naval ordnance (1933–5), he devised the armament for Britain's last generation of battleships, the 14 inch King George V class.

In 1936–7 Fraser commanded the aircraft-carrier *Glorious*. In January 1938, just short of his fiftieth birthday, he was appointed rear-admiral, and chief of staff to Sir A. Dudley Pound, commander-in-chief, Mediterranean. It was in this role that he forged the close relationship with Pound that continued in the Second World War, when Pound was first sea lord.

In March 1939 Fraser became controller of the navy and third sea lord. In this role, for three testing years he bore responsibility for the navy's construction and repair programme, perhaps above all for the creation of the corvette, mainstay of the Atlantic convoy escort system. He also played an important part in the development of warship radar. In May 1940 he became vice-admiral.

Fraser won the confidence of Winston Churchill in this period at the Admiralty, and never lost it for the remainder of the war, despite periodic differences of opinion, for instance when the controller opposed Churchill's enthusiasm to build a new battleship. In June 1942 Fraser was sent to sea once more, as second in command of the Home

Fleet under Sir John Tovey. He arrived just before the tragedy of convoy PQ17, one of the darkest naval episodes of the war.

Commander-in-chief, Home Fleet By 8 May 1943, when Fraser was appointed to succeed Tovey as commander-in-chief, Home Fleet, he could claim wide experience of both naval operations at sea, and their strategic direction ashore. A bluff, cheerful, straightforward officer with much shrewdness and technical knowledge but no pretensions to intellectualism, he was committed throughout his career to making inter-service co-operation a reality. He had shown remarkable gifts for winning the confidence of his peers and political masters at home, while commanding the affection and loyalty of subordinates afloat. Essentially a simple man who used to declare without embarrassment that he had never read a novel in his life, a bachelor who had made the Royal Navy his life's work, he was acknowledged as one of the outstanding naval professionals of his generation. His elevation was widely welcomed.

Yet in the strategic situation in the summer of 1943, it seemed unlikely that Fraser would be granted the opportunity to conduct a major fleet action. The Russian victory at Stalingrad, and the consequent shift in the balance of advantage against the Germans, diminished the importance of the western allies' Arctic convoys. These now offered a lure to the three German capital ships based in Norwegian waters—*Tirpitz*, *Scharnhorst*, and *Lützow*—but it seemed unlikely that the Germans would consider the bait worth the hazard to their remaining fleet. Correspondingly, the British Home Fleet had been weakened by the transfer of ships to the Mediterranean. *Anson* and *Duke of York*—in which Fraser flew his flag—were now the only British battleships at Scapa.

Yet in September, to the surprise of the British, *Tirpitz* and *Scharnhorst* sortied for two days to bombard Spitsbergen. This was a negligible feat, yet sharply reminded the Royal Navy of the difficulties of keeping effective watch on the German ships. A fortnight later, a substantial British success was gained, when midget submarines successfully crippled *Tirpitz* in Kaafiord. She was rendered unfit for active operations for six months. Four days afterwards, *Lützow* escaped into the Baltic. *Scharnhorst* was now alone.

As a succession of allied convoys sailed to Russia that autumn, almost unmolested but shadowed by units of the Home Fleet, Fraser, having declined an offer by Churchill to become first sea lord, continued to believe that *Scharnhorst* would sooner or later come out. Earlier in the war, the German battle cruiser had inflicted major damage upon British shipping. On 19 December British Ultra decrypts revealed that *Scharnhorst* had been brought to three hours' readiness for sea. Fraser's force 2, led by the cruiser *Jamaica* and the *Duke of York*—the only British ship with the armament to match that of *Scharnhorst*—sailed from Icelandic waters at 11 p.m. on 23 December. Fraser had carefully briefed his captains, and carried out repeated exercises in identifying and engaging hostile

ships by radar, given the almost permanent Arctic darkness.

On the afternoon of 24 December 1943, in atrocious weather, the British convoy JW55B was ordered to slow to 8 knots because force 2 was 400 miles behind, too distant for comfort when the convoy was only the same distance from *Scharnhorst* in Altenfiord. *Scharnhorst* sailed to attack JW55B at 7 p.m. on 25 December, commanded by Rear-Admiral Erich Bey.

Engagement with *Scharnhorst* Eight hours later, this news was passed to Fraser, whose ships were still struggling through mountainous seas to close the gap with the convoy. Fraser accepted the risk that *Scharnhorst* would turn away if he broke wireless silence, and ordered JW55B to turn northwards, away from the Germans. Bey was still searching in vain for the convoy at 7.30 a.m. on 26 December, when the 8 inch cruiser *Norfolk*, a unit of force I, led by Vice-Admiral R. L. Burnett, located *Scharnhorst* on radar at 33,000 yards. The British ship, with her 6 inch consorts *Belfast* and *Sheffield*, opened fire at 9.29. They strove to close the range speedily, and avoid the sort of mauling *Graf Spee* had inflicted upon a British cruiser squadron four years earlier. At this early stage, *Norfolk* damaged *Scharnhorst*'s radar. Bey, as the British had expected, at once withdrew at 30 knots.

The British now suffered almost three hours of acute apprehension, having lost touch with *Scharnhorst*, and being fearful that she might break away into the Atlantic. Only at 12.20 did *Belfast* triumphantly report the battle cruiser once more in sight. Bey had turned north, still searching for JW55B. Burnett's cruisers and destroyers lay between the Germans and the convoy.

In the second 21 minute cruiser action, the British ships suffered significant damage before *Scharnhorst* broke away unscathed. Yet Bey now hesitated fatally. He knew that a British battle group was at sea. But he believed it was too distant to harm him. Only at 2.18 p.m. did he abandon the attempt to engage the convoy and turn for home, independent of his destroyer escort.

Fraser was now racing to cut across *Scharnhorst*'s southward track. At 4.17 p.m., *Duke of York*'s 14 inch guns opened fire at 12,000 yards, and straddled their target—clearly illuminated by starshell—with the first broadside. Critics subsequently suggested that *Scharnhorst* might have been destroyed at this stage of the battle, had Fraser not delayed ordering in his destroyers. He was fearful that a premature torpedo attack would drive the German ship away north-eastwards, beyond his grasp.

Under fire from *Duke of York*, *Scharnhorst* turned away at full speed first north, then east. By 5.13 p.m., when at last Fraser loosed his destroyers, he had left it too late. The enemy was outrunning both the British cruisers and destroyers. Only *Duke of York*'s guns were still within range. At 6.20 p.m., an 11 inch shell from *Scharnhorst* temporarily severed the flagship's radar cables, blinding her gunners. For a few terrible minutes, Fraser believed that victory had been snatched from him.

Yet just before the British ship was hit, although *Scharnhorst* had succeeded in opening the range to 20,000 yards, a shell from *Duke of York* burst in her no. 1 boiler room, abruptly cutting the ship's speed to 8 knots. Power was restored soon afterwards. But the brief crisis allowed three of Fraser's destroyers to close. Four of the twenty-eight torpedoes which they launched hit *Scharnhorst*, drastically reducing her power and ensuring her destruction. At 7.45 p.m., after enduring concentrated gunfire and torpedo attacks for almost three hours more, *Scharnhorst* sank. Her guns continued firing almost to the last. Out of her complement of 1803, thirty-six survivors were plucked from the Arctic darkness.

Duke of York's gunnery had plainly been the decisive factor in the victory. For all the undoubted British advantage of strength, the entrapment and destruction of *Scharnhorst* had been a considerable achievement, ensuring Fraser's perpetual celebrity in the annals of the Royal Navy, alongside that of the Norwegian North Cape beyond which the battle was fought.

The end of the war Fraser's remaining service with the Home Fleet was dominated by the conduct of further Russian convoys. But with the shift of strategic attention from the Mediterranean to north-west Europe, force was now available to provide massive escorts, and allied losses declined steeply. On 16 June 1944 Fraser relinquished command. He was now assigned to become commander-in-chief, Eastern Fleet. In November he became commander-in-chief, Pacific Fleet.

Fraser's task in the Pacific was delicate. The American navy dominated the theatre, and the Royal Navy's contribution seemed not merely modest, but even unwelcome. The Americans were deeply suspicious of British imperial motives in the eastern hemisphere. It is a tribute to Fraser's competence and transparent good nature that he achieved an amicable working relationship with the Americans. He believed passionately in the need to develop—and to perpetuate post-war—Anglo-American co-operation. Such gestures as volunteering to adopt American navy signalling procedures went far to encourage trust.

His command continued to suffer from lack of resources, and it was only in the last weeks of the war that its forces achieved real weight. The British were hampered by the acute discomfort of their ships in tropical conditions. But the fleet made a useful contribution to the last stages of the Pacific war. It was Fraser who signed the Japanese surrender document for Britain, aboard the battleship *Missouri* in Tokyo Bay on 2 September 1945.

Final years On his return home in 1946, Fraser was saddened to be denied the succession as first sea lord. He was appointed commander-in-chief, Portsmouth, in May 1947, and at last gained the first sea lordship in September 1948, together with promotion to admiral of the fleet a month later.

Fraser's tenure at the Admiralty embraced a series of cold war crises, and finally responsibility for British naval participation in the Korean war. For all the affection and respect that he commanded as an old 'sea-dog', Fraser was considered by some critics to possess too limited an intellect to distinguish himself at the summits of power. He retired from the Royal Navy in April 1952, and passed the next twenty-eight years in almost uneventful retirement.

A barony was conferred upon him in 1946. He was appointed GCB in 1944 (KCB, 1943; CB, 1939); KBE in 1941 (OBE, 1919). He was first and principal naval aide-de-camp to the king (1946–8), and held honorary degrees from the universities of Oxford (DCL, 1947), Edinburgh (LLD, 1953), and Wales (LLD, 1955). He held the American DSM. He was a member of the Russian order of Suvorov and of the grand order of Orange Nassau (Netherlands); was a chevalier of the Légion d'honneur and holder of the Croix de Guerre with palm (France); and held the grand cross, order of St Olav (Norway). A lifelong bachelor, he died in London on 12 February 1981, when the barony became extinct.

MAX HASTINGS, rev.

Sources R. Humble, *Fraser of the North Cape* (1983) · S. W. Roskill, *The war at sea, 1939–1945*, 3 vols. in 4 (1954–61) · *CGPLA Eng. & Wales* (1981) · F. H. Hinsley and others, *British intelligence in the Second World War*, 3 (1984–8) · J. Winten, *The forgotten fleet* (1969) · S. Roskill, *Churchill and the admirals* (1977) · *The Times* (13 Feb 1981)

Archives NMM, papers | FILM BFI NFTVA, current affairs footage · BFI NFTVA, news footage · IWM FVA, 'The Royal Navy in northern and Atlantic waters', Admiralty, 1943 · IWM FVA, actuality footage · IWM FVA, news footage

Likenesses W. Stoneman, photograph, c.1940–1949, NPG · O. Birley, oils, c.1945–1948, Royal Naval College, Greenwich · Bassano, photograph, 1946, NPG [see illus.]

Wealth at death £178,022: probate, 24 April 1981, *CGPLA Eng. & Wales*

Fraser, Catherine (1786–1868), penal reformer, was born on 26 June 1786 at the High Street, Wapping, the only surviving child of James Fraser (1749–1825), merchant, and his wife, Ann, *née* Thatcher. James Fraser had premises in Wapping and later became a biscuit baker. In August 1794 Ann died and James remarried, having another eight children. Not long after moving his family to North Terrace, Camberwell (1823), James Fraser died, on 11 September 1825, leaving trust funds for all his children to finance good education and comfortable lifestyles. Catherine Fraser and her half-sisters, Harriet and Elizabeth, remained spinsters and continued to live in North Terrace.

On 19 March 1832 Catherine Fraser joined Elizabeth Fry's British Ladies Society for promoting the reformation of female prisoners, although she was not a Quaker, but a member of the Church of England. By September of that year she was an active member; a frequent visitor to Newgate prison, she was appointed with three other women to confer with Robert Fowler on the ignorant and neglected state of female prisoners awaiting trial in Newgate. In 1834 she was appointed, with four others, to visit all the convict ships and to distribute useful articles, including sewing materials and reading matter, to the women prisoners. Later that year she was asked to visit Tothill Fields prison as well as Newgate. From 16 September 1838 until October 1854 she kept a diary of her prison visiting.

In 1836 a prison inspectors' report argued that the lady visitors were well-meaning but easily exploited and inclined to regard themselves as being in charge of the women's side of Newgate prison. Catherine Fraser was part of the subcommittee called to look at several material points which had been raised. The British Ladies took the report seriously and tried very hard to remedy the situation so they could continue visiting the prison. Newgate was never lost to them, but from then on Elizabeth Fry transferred her attentions to crusades abroad, especially in France.

After Elizabeth Fry's death in 1845 Catherine Fraser became one of the most prominent members of the British Ladies Society. Her main interest was in the convict ships, which she continued to visit until transportation was abolished in the 1850s. Subsequently she became a member of her local emigration society and was keen to help any of the convicts emigrate after their sentences. She also visited several women who were sentenced to death, the most notorious being Maria Manning, who with her husband, Frederick Manning, was convicted of, and executed for, the murder of Patrick O'Connor in 1849.

After her diaries end in October 1854 it is known that Catherine Fraser continued her work with the British Ladies, encouraging her half-sister Elizabeth to join the society. By October 1856 one side of Newgate had been closed to female prisoners so Catherine Fraser began to visit Millbank prison. In 1857 she brought up the subject of individual patronage to discharged prisoners, as Sir Joshua Jebb, surveyor-general of convict-prisons, and Lady Jebb had brought it to her attention that not enough was being done to assist women with employment or accommodation on their discharge from prison. In 1859, at the age of seventy-two, Catherine Fraser was still visiting Newgate, and in 1861 she was appointed to visit Horsemonger Lane prison. By December 1867 she had ceased the monthly meetings of the British Ladies, although they were still in contact with her, relying on her expertise.

Catherine Fraser died at her home, 6 North Terrace, Camberwell, London, on 3 December 1868, following a stroke. She asked for her remains to be placed in the family vault in St Giles, Camberwell. At their meeting on 21 December the British Ladies Society recorded her passing, praising her 'indefatigable labours of love' and 'her ready pen, her clear head, her good judgement and her Christian piety' (British Ladies Society meeting minutes, 21 Dec 1868). AMANDA PHILLIPS

Sources British Ladies Society meeting minutes, 12 May 1823–16 March 1835, Hackney RO, London · British Ladies Society meeting minutes, 17 Dec 1855–6 May 1891, Hackney RO, London · C. Fraser, diaries, 1838–54 · parish register (birth), Wapping, St John, 26 June 1786 · parish register (baptism), Wapping, St John, 16 July 1786 · d. cert. · will of C. Fraser, proved London, 18 Dec 1868 · records for St John's Church, Wapping, LMA
Wealth at death under £4000: probate, 18 Dec 1868, CGPLA Eng. & Wales

Fraser, Charles (*bap.* 1823, *d.* 1886), missionary and educationist, was baptized in Aberdeen on 29 July 1823, the son of Hugh Fraser, merchant, and his wife, Christina McAllan. He attended Aberdeen grammar school (1833–8) and

then Marischal College, Aberdeen, from which he graduated MA in 1845. He then studied divinity at Christ's College, Aberdeen, and, in 1846, at New College, Edinburgh. After brief missionary work to Scottish textile workers in Brittany, Fraser was ordained in 1855 and sent by the colonial committee of the Church of Scotland to Canterbury, New Zealand (a province founded by Anglicans). He arrived with his wife, Jane Bissett (*d.* 1869), in April 1856, to minister at St Andrew's Church, Christchurch, which was opened in February 1857. Fraser played a central part in the swift establishment of Presbyterianism in the area, travelling long distances to set up charges in the hinterland. Canterbury presbytery was established in 1873. Fraser's integrative approach, liberal theology, and interest in Darwinism led to difficulties with evangelicals, and in 1861 there was a secession from his congregation.

Fraser played an active part in the development of the intellectual life of Christchurch and was secretary of its Philosophical Institute (1868–9). He was energetic in founding schools and advocated, from 1867, the foundation of a university of New Zealand; he taught at Canterbury Collegiate Union (later Canterbury College) and served on the senate of the University of New Zealand, 1879–83. He edited and published the *New Zealand Presbyterian* (1866–7) and the *Canterbury Presbyterian* (1873–4).

Fraser's wife died, childless, in 1869. In January 1883 he was controversially deposed for sexual misconduct. On 21 March 1883, at Christchurch, he married Margaret Anna Blyth and retired to his farm, ministering in a small church built for him by a sympathetic supporter. He died on 25 August 1886, an interesting example of the Scottish church diaspora. H. C. G. MATTHEW

Sources DNZB, vol. 3 · T. R. Elder, *The history of the Presbyterian church in New Zealand, 1840–1940* (1940) · G. M. Miller, *Centennial history of St Andrew's Presbyterian church, Christchurch* (1956)
Likenesses photograph, Canterbury Museum, New Zealand

Fraser, Claud Lovat (1890–1921), artist and designer, was born in London on 15 May 1890, the elder son of Claud Fraser, solicitor, and his wife, Florence Margaret Walsh, harpist and watercolour artist. He was baptized Lovat Claud Fraser, following the family tradition of naming the eldest son Lovat; later he changed the order of his names, generally signing himself C. Lovat Fraser.

Lovat Fraser was educated at Charterhouse School, Surrey, from 1904 to 1907 and joined his father's City firm in 1908, despite his own reservations about being suited for a career in law. Having acquired his father's love of theatre and his mother's talent for art he drew and painted from an early age. A letter home from school in 1903 noted that he was writing three plays and requested a toy theatre to design their settings. His passion for art was irrepressible and even while working as an articled clerk he filled his court notebooks with sketches of people. He sold two pictures in 1909, and in January 1911 six of his caricatures were privately printed in a limited edition. In 1911 he enrolled at the Westminster School of Art, where he studied etching with Walter Sickert, but, deciding to develop his imaginative style independently, he left after six months to set up his own studio in London. A charming man, he made friends in the worlds of art, literature, and theatre. These included the painters Albert Rutherston and Paul Nash; Haldane MacFall, who wrote the article 'The art of Lovat Fraser' in the *Art Chronicle* (12 November 1911); and Edward Gordon Craig, who recruited Lovat Fraser to the committee of the Society of Theatre. Lovat Fraser's first one-man show (1913) included drawings of theatrical characters and scenes, and decorations for chapbooks and broadsides, which were published in 1913 under the title *Flying Fame*. He was an authority on the news and ballad sheets, known as broadsides, from the seventeenth to the nineteenth century and in his own work he recognized the importance of visualizing design and type as an inseparable whole.

Despite poor health Lovat Fraser was commissioned in the army in 1914 but he was invalided home in 1916 to work on visual propaganda and army records. In February 1917 he married the American singer Grace Inez Crawford, with whom he had one daughter. Having been demobbed in 1919 he held a successful exhibition that September at London's Mansard Gallery, featuring designs for settings and costumes for *As You Like It* and *La serva padrona*, executed for productions by Nigel Playfair at the Lyric Theatre, Hammersmith. Lovat Fraser was one of the first designers to turn his attention to designing for a small stage, and his witty and innovative designs for *The Beggar's Opera* at the Lyric in 1920 were considered by James Laver 'to have inaugurated a new era in stage design' (*Oxford Companion to the Theatre*, 4th edn, 305). From 1920 onwards he produced innumerable theatre designs, textile designs, and book illustrations. In 1921 he began work on a one-man exhibition at the Leicester Galleries (December 1921), which became his memorial exhibition following his death, at the Bevan Hospital Nursing Home, Sandgate, Kent, on 18 June 1921. He was buried in Layston churchyard, Buntingford, Hertfordshire.

A. D. RUTHERSTON, rev. CATHERINE HAILL

Sources C. L. Fraser, *John Drinkwater and Albert Rutherston* (1923) · C. L. Fraser, *Grace Lovat Fraser* (1969) · I. Rogerson, ed., *Claud Lovat Fraser* (1984) [exhibition catalogue, Manchester Polytechnic Library, autumn 1984, and North East London Polytechnic Library, spring 1985] · G. L. Fraser, *Claud Lovat Fraser* (1970) [exhibition catalogue, V&A, 11 Sept – 28 Dec 1969] · *Claud Lovat Fraser* (1919) [exhibition catalogue, Mansard Gallery, London, Sept 1919] · C. L. Fraser, introductory note to 'Old broadside ballads', *The Chapbook* (Sept 1920) · CGPLA *Eng. & Wales* (1921) · W. Gaunt, 'Curtain-raiser of the 1920s', *The Times* (21 May 1968)
Archives Bryn Mawr College, Massachusetts, corresp., diaries, and MSS · V&A, letters to his family · Yale U., Beinecke L., MSS
Likenesses G. C. Beresford, two photographs, 1911, NPG · P. Nash, pencil drawing, AM Oxf.
Wealth at death £761 1s. 0d.: administration, 24 Dec 1921, CGPLA *Eng. & Wales*

Fraser, Donald (1826–1892), minister of the Presbyterian Church of England, born at Inverness on 15 January 1826, was the second son of John Fraser (d. 1852), a merchant and shipowner of Inverness and provost of the burgh, and his wife, Lillias, daughter of Donald Fraser (d. 12 July 1836), minister of Kirkhill, near Inverness. He was educated by private tutors, and in his twelfth year became a student at the King's College, Aberdeen, residing at the boarding-

school of George Tulloch at Bellevue House, Aberdeen. He graduated MA in March 1842, and in the autumn sailed for North America in the brig *Retrench*, joining his father at Sherbrooke in Lower Canada. For a short time he tried commerce, but on the failure of a firm in which he was junior partner he found himself without an occupation. Having become increasingly absorbed in religious work, he entered Knox Theological Academy, Toronto, in the autumn of 1848 to prepare for the ministry, and took his third session in theology at New College, Edinburgh.

After returning to Canada in 1851, Fraser was licensed as a preacher by the presbytery of Toronto, and on 8 August was ordained to the Free Church, Coté Street, Montreal. His marriage on 28 February 1852 at Kingston in Canada to Theresa Eliza Isabella, fourth daughter of Lieutenant-Colonel A. Gordon, brought them four sons and a daughter. Fraser remained in Montreal until 1859, when he accepted a call to the Free High Church of Inverness. In 1870 he moved to the Marylebone Presbyterian Church, London, where he ministered until his death. For more than twenty years he took a leading part in the Presbyterian church of England, and he was moderator of the synod in 1874 and in 1880. He was also prominently connected with many missions and charities, and was a vice-president of the British and Foreign Bible Society. In 1872 he received the honorary degree of DD from the University of Aberdeen.

In addition to his sermons Fraser was the author of many works on theology, notably *Synoptical Lectures on the Books of Holy Scripture* (2 vols., 1871–6), a work especially praised by C. H. Spurgeon. In 1892 he published a commentary on the Thirty-Nine Articles. He wrote a memoir of Thomas Chalmers in *Men Worth Remembering* (1881) and a biography of Mary Jane Kinnaird (1890). His autobiography was unfinished at his death on 12 February 1892 at 3 Cambridge Square, Hyde Park, London, and was edited for publication (1892) by J. O. Dykes. Fraser was buried near his mother in the chapel yard at Inverness on 19 February 1892, his wife surviving him.

E. I. CARLYLE, rev. H. C. G. MATTHEW

Sources *Autobiography of the late Donald Fraser*, ed. J. O. Dykes (1892) · *The Times* (15 Feb 1892) · *The Scotsman* (15 Feb 1892) · *Inverness Courier* (16 Feb 1892)
Likenesses woodcut, NPG
Wealth at death £4040 13s. 7d.: administration, 6 May 1892, CGPLA *Eng. & Wales*

Fraser, Donald (1870–1933), missionary, was born on 1 June 1870 at Lochgilphead, Argyll, the fourth of eight children of William Fraser (1824–1892), the local Free Church of Scotland minister, and his wife, Violet Ferguson. He was educated at Glasgow high school, and at Glasgow University, which he entered in 1886 at the age of sixteen. He then attended the Free Church Hall to train for the Christian ministry. During this period Fraser was greatly influenced by the spirituality of the Keswick Convention, and by the American student volunteer movement. Fraser was one of the founders of the Student Volunteer Missionary Union of Great Britain and Ireland (SVMU) in 1892, and became its travelling secretary in

1893. He was also instrumental in the foundation of the Inter-University Christian Union (later the Student Christian Movement) in 1894. The SVMU expanded rapidly, and in January 1896 a major conference of students interested in mission took place in Liverpool, with the theme 'Make Jesus king'. Fraser was chairman of this conference, and made a deep impact by the effectiveness of his leadership. During these years he travelled to the USA and widely in Europe, and was already becoming well known in international student Christian circles.

Fraser was ordained as a minister of the Free Church of Scotland in June 1896, and soon afterwards set out as a missionary to British Central Africa. For most of the next thirty years Fraser worked among the Ngoni people of northern Malawi—first at Ekwendeni, then, from 1902, at Loudon (Embangweni). There he developed a very distinct style of mission, of which the large sacramental convention and missionary itineration over large areas were key features. The sacramental conventions were based on the highland communion seasons with which his father, William, was closely associated in Scotland; but to the sacrament of the Lord's supper (eucharist) Fraser added mass baptisms. Soon these gatherings were attracting many thousands of Ngoni each year. In addition Fraser spent a large proportion of each year travelling (at first on foot, and later by motor cycle) to encourage and supervise local Christians. Fraser also encouraged the composition of indigenous church music, and took a more positive attitude than many of his colleagues to the promotion of indigenous leadership—female as well as male—and to African culture in general. His views on the relationship of mission to culture are best expressed in his 'The evangelistic approach to the African' (*International Review of Missions*, 1926).

For much of his African career Fraser was aided by his wife, Agnes Renton Robson, a medical doctor, who not only supervised the mission hospital at Loudon but effectively ran the station during her husband's long absences on tour. They married in 1901 and had four children—Violet, George, Catherine, and Donald.

Fraser published six books on Africa and Christian mission, of which the most influential was *Winning a Primitive People* (1914), an account of pioneer missionary work among the Ngoni. In addition, he wrote a large number of articles for a range of Christian journals including the *International Review of Mission*, the *Scots Observer*, and the *Free Church of Scotland Monthly*. Throughout his life he remained an outstanding and influential speaker and preacher, both in English and in ChiTumbuka.

After the First World War, Fraser spent an increasing amount of time away from Africa, as organizer of a major missionary campaign for the Scottish churches (1921–2), and moderator of the United Free Church of Scotland (1922–3). Having returned to Nyasaland in 1924 he was recalled in 1925 to become the mission secretary of the United Free Church. He left Nyasaland reluctantly and largely out of loyalty to church headquarters. The return to Britain did, however, enable him to play a more prominent role in national and international church affairs. In

1926 he was chairman of the international conference held at Le Zoute in Belgium on 'The Christian mission in Africa', and he took an active role in defending the interests of the church against what he saw as colonial encroachments in the field of mission education in Africa. In 1929 he was appointed a chaplain to George V. He maintained and developed relationships with such leading figures in the ecumenical movement as Joseph H. Oldham and John R. Mott.

Fraser died on 20 August 1933 at his home, 40 Highburgh Road, Glasgow, of complications following surgery for the removal of his gall bladder. He was cremated two days later, and his ashes returned to Nyasaland by his widow, Agnes. In 1935 his ashes were buried at Loudon, where he had spent most of his missionary career.

T. Jack Thompson

Sources T. J. Thompson, *Christianity in northern Malawi: Donald Fraser's missionary methods and Ngoni culture* (1995) · A. Fraser, *Donald Fraser of Livingstonia* (1934) · J. McCracken, *Politics and Christianity in Malawi* (1977) · T. J. Thompson, 'Donald Fraser', *Biographical dictionary of Christian missions*, ed. G. H. Anderson (1998) · *DNB* · T. Tatlow, *The story of the Student Christian Movement* (1933) · *CCI* (1933) · private information (2004)
Archives National Archives of Malawi, Zomba, Livingstonia MSS · NL Scot., notebooks and papers · NL Scot., Livingstonia MSS · priv. coll. · SOAS, International Missionary Council archives, Le Zoute Conference MSS | Yale U., divinity school, Day Missions Library, John R. Mott MSS
Likenesses photograph, *c.*1895, repro. in Tatlow, *Story of the Student Christian Movement* · photographs, *c.*1900–1920, National Archives of Malawi, Zomba, Malawi · Annan (Glasgow), photograph, 1920, repro. in Fraser, *Donald Fraser* · W. Pratt, oils, *c.*1934, Church of Scotland Offices, Edinburgh
Wealth at death £1381 4s. 9d.: confirmation, 6 Oct 1933, *CCI*

Fraser, Francis Charles (1903–1978), zoologist and museum administrator, was born on 16 June 1903 at Glenturret, Station Road, Dingwall, Ross-shire, Scotland. He was the youngest of the six sons (there were also four daughters) of James Fraser (*d.* 1910/11), master saddler and blacksmith, and his wife, Barbara Anne Macdonald. He was educated at Dingwall Academy and Glasgow University (1921–1924), from where he graduated with a BSc (honours) in zoology. His first job was demonstrator in the department of geology at Glasgow University from 1924 to 1925.

Fraser's academic potential, coupled with a good nature and ready humour, secured him, in 1925, a position as zoologist with the Colonial Office's *Discovery* investigations committee to quantify, using scientific methodology, the whale stocks around the Falkland Islands. On finding out Fraser's first name Stanley Kemp, the director of research, told him: 'we've got one of those already; you'll be Jimmy' (*Memoirs FRS*, 289). Between 1925 and 1933 Jimmy Fraser travelled to the Antarctic three times and, in 1942, he was awarded the polar medal. Much of his research concentrated on the biology of the species on which baleen whales fed; his first major publication was 'On the development and distribution of the young stages of krill (*Euphausia superba*)' in *Discovery Reports*, volume 14 (1936).

In 1933 Fraser was appointed assistant keeper in the

Francis Charles Fraser (1903–1978), by Godfrey Argent

mechanism for determining the age of cetaceans by counting the number of concentric rings in the wax plugs in their ears. With his assistant, Peter Ernest Purves, he elucidated the hearing mechanism of marine mammals using pioneering techniques. The result was a series of papers, co-authored with Purves, and culminating in a major review, 'Hearing in cetaceans' in *Bulletin of the British Museum (Natural History)*, zoology series, volume 7 (1960). Fraser was elected FRS in 1966 for this work, but his relationship with Purves had become strained. He retired from the museum in 1969 but continued his research until shortly before his death from stomach cancer at Beckenham Hospital in Kent on 21 October 1978. His wife survived him.

In the course of his career Fraser published nearly eighty scientific papers. In particular he produced for the museum four *Reports on Cetacea Stranded on the British Coasts* for the years 1927–66 (published 1934–74) and wrote (with H. W. Parker) *Guide for the identification and reporting of stranded whales, dolphins, porpoises and turtles on the British coasts*, first published in 1949. With J. R. Norman, another museum zoologist, Fraser wrote one popular work: *Giant Fishes, Whales and Dolphins* (1937).   ANN DATTA

Sources N. B. Marshall, *Memoirs FRS*, 25 (1979), 287–317 • A. J. E. Cave and others, 'Appreciations of the scientific work of Francis C. Fraser CBE, FRS, 1903–1978', *Journal of Zoology*, 190 (1980), 441–6 • R. J. Harrison, 'F. C. Fraser', *Nature*, 277 (1979), 334–5 • L. H. Matthews, 'Dr Francis C. Fraser, CBE', *Polar Record*, 19 (1978–9), 404 • J. Clutton-Brock, 'Dr Francis C. Fraser', *Antiquity*, 54 (1980), 169 • J. G. Sheals, *The Times* (25 Oct 1978) • W. T. Stearn, *The Natural History Museum at South Kensington: a history of the British Museum (Natural History), 1753–1980* (1981) • departmental staff file: Fraser, F. C., NHM, archives, DF208/51 1933–1945 • departmental staff file: Fraser, F. C., NHM, archives, DF208/93 1947–1980 • personnel file: Fraser, F. C., NHM, archives, DF1005/33 1931–1967 • personal knowledge (2004) • private information (2004)

Archives NHM, archives • NHM, specimens • Southampton Oceanography Centre, Discovery investigation archives

Likenesses G. Argent, photograph, repro. in Cave and others, 'Appreciations' • G. Argent, photograph, RS [*see illus.*] • photograph, repro. in Marshall, *Memoirs FRS*

Wealth at death £13,152: probate, 20 Dec 1978, *CGPLA Eng. & Wales*

department of zoology at the British Museum (Natural History). He was put in charge of the osteological room, the mammalian skeletal material and marine mammal collections. Thereafter his research was mainly devoted to cetology (study of whales). He was actively involved in choosing public exhibits for the New Whale Hall and, in particular, installing the 93 ft long life-size model of the blue whale in 1938.

In 1936 Fraser was awarded the DSc from Glasgow University. On 30 June 1938 he married Anne Nuttall (*b.* 1906); they had no children. During the Second World War he was seconded to the Admiralty. Shortly after rejoining the museum he participated in the Danish Atlantide expedition to west African waters from 1945 to 1946. It was from this time that Fraser became involved with identifying the animal remains from archaeological excavations in Britain leading to the museum's becoming a major repository. But it was Fraser's efficient re-organization of the skeletal collections as well as his scholarly publications that brought him to the attention of the museum's managers, and he was promoted to deputy keeper of zoology in 1948 and keeper of zoology in 1957. He was an effective administrator, yet sensitive to the needs of the staff at a time when the museum was undergoing expansion, and in 1962 he was made CBE.

Fraser relinquished the keepership in 1964 to concentrate on whale research. He took immense pleasure in talking about cetaceans not only to colleagues but whenever answering enquiries from the public. He discovered a

Fraser, Sir Francis Richard (1885–1964), university professor, was born in Edinburgh on 14 February 1885, the seventh child of Sir Thomas Richard *Fraser (1841–1920), professor of medicine, and his wife, Susannah Margaret Duncan. He went from Edinburgh Academy to Christ's College, Cambridge, where he obtained a first class in part one of the natural sciences tripos in 1907; he then gained his MB with honours at Edinburgh University in 1910. He proceeded MD in 1922. While a hospital resident in 1911 he was host on behalf of his indisposed father at a private dinner to Abraham Flexner, the American medical educationist. This facilitated his appointment in 1912 as assistant in medicine at the Rockefeller Institute, New York. He was thus among the first young British medical graduates to seek research training in the United States in preference to central Europe. He worked on poliomyelitis and on the action of digitalis. In 1914 he became an instructor in medicine under W. T. Longcope in Columbia University at the Presbyterian Hospital, New York, where he was also assistant physician. In 1915 he relinquished this post to volunteer for service in the Royal Army Medical Corps in which he worked first as a pathologist and later as a physician on active service in France. In 1919–20, now lieutenant-colonel, he was consulting physician to the army of the Rhine. In 1919 he married Mary Claudine Stirling, daughter of Colin Donald and widow of his second cousin, Captain J. A. Fraser. They had one son.

Following the Haldane report of 1913 recommending the creation of university clinical units, Sir Archibald Garrod had been appointed professor of medicine at St Bartholomew's Hospital medical school in 1920; Fraser was appointed assistant director and succeeded his chief as professor and director later that year. These were exciting times, with an upsurge of scientific standards in clinical studies, for which Fraser set an example by enlisting the co-operation of the leading respiratory physiologists, J. S. Haldane and Joseph Barcroft, in research on breathlessness in heart disease. In 1925 and in 1928 Fraser travelled widely, visiting the medical schools of North America and Australia.

In 1934 Fraser was appointed the first professor of medicine in the new British postgraduate medical school at Hammersmith. To date the full-time university academic units had not always had complete autonomy within the voluntary hospitals, so Fraser ensured that all the medical beds at the new centre were under the control of his academic assistants. He was highly skilled at perceiving academic promise, and young doctors on his staff who were still in their twenties were given every opportunity to deploy their talents as clinical teachers and investigators. With the help of his colleague in pathology, E. H. Kettle, the new school became a Mecca for the training of medical teachers: the joint staff rounds for the exchange of experience along with final analyses in clinico-pathological conferences became quite famous. Later there was hardly a centre in the English-speaking world which did not owe something to the spirit created by Fraser at Hammersmith. This achievement was due entirely to the exemplary personal attributes of all concerned, for the slump of the 1930s had left the projected buildings incomplete and the new centre was created in extremely cramped quarters.

With the outbreak of war in 1939, Fraser was seconded to the Ministry of Health as consultant adviser on the organization of civilian hospitals in wartime. Even facing a severe depletion of civilian doctors, Fraser ensured the maintenance of standards by building up a skeleton clinical pathological service in all areas of the country. In September 1941 he became director-general of the Emergency Medical Service; he was knighted in 1944. During this disturbed and strenuous period, he never lost touch with the need to think ahead to the end of the war and the future of postgraduate training. Many meetings and discussions took place to bring together the school at Hammersmith with the famous London specialist hospitals (beginning with the Maudsley, Queen Square, Great Ormond Street, and Moorfields hospitals) as the embryo

British Postgraduate Medical Federation. Fraser recommended the appointment of postgraduate medical deans in all the medical schools of Great Britain to meet the needs of returning Royal Army Medical Corps personnel. His foresight was remarkable and the university postgraduate deans held the first of many conferences in the month the European war ended.

Fraser had realized from the beginning of his career in postgraduate medical education that the Hammersmith school was only the initiator in a wider movement which must, to be effective, spread to many thousands of general practitioners. To help this movement he ensured the involvement of other general hospitals in London, thus paving the way for the later growth and creation of postgraduate teaching centres in the larger district hospitals in the rest of the country. All the functions of such centres were written into the charter of the University of London's British Postgraduate Medical Federation, of which Fraser became the first director in 1946; he held this post until 1960.

During Fraser's professional life, medicine was in transition, and his own response was to give it vigorous and far-sighted leadership. Through his deep involvement in academic medicine and his experience in the Emergency Medical Service, he influenced the creation of a high standard of service to the sick, on a pattern subsequently developed in the National Health Service. Tireless in his work, he would leap from a night train in the early morning with a bundle of journals already digested. His lectures became personal tutorials. He left the rostrum and strode up and down the gallery, popping questions to his alerted listeners. His list of headings was ostentatiously torn up at the end of each session, so that he never repeated his presentations in the same way. In ward teaching he exemplified thoroughness by spending at least an hour on the details of one patient. 'Never let a student ever see you do anything second-rate', was his exhortation to his juniors.

Fraser was quite unflappable in a crisis and never revealed exasperation. He thought carefully through every major problem and arrived at meetings with a solution, persuading others to agree with him. With all this drive he combined a sympathy and an understanding which helped many individuals through their human dilemmas and difficulties.

Fraser's research experience and interests spread into many fields, including poliomyelitis, heart failure, thyroid disease, and disorders of neurohumoral transmission; his contribution to the last of these revolutionized physiological thinking in the late 1930s. He held many honorific lectureships—Goulstonian, Croonian, Harveian, and Flexner, among others. His services to the Pharmacopoeia Commission extended over twenty years. From 1947 to 1949 he was deputy vice-chancellor of the University of London. Edinburgh and London universities conferred on him the honorary degree of LLD and in 1948 he was appointed commander of the order of Orange-Nassau for his war services to the Netherlands.

In his youth Fraser was a rugby player. His holidays were

usually spent fishing near a family home in Argyll at the southern end of Loch Shiel. Interested in ornithology and botany, even his relaxations were directed to continuous occupation of his active mind. His warm-hearted, unflagging idealism was blended with an austere belief that idleness is a sin. Fraser, who lived latterly at 9 Melina Court, Grove End Road, London, died in Hammersmith Hospital, London, on 2 October 1964.   JOHN MCMICHAEL, *rev.*

Sources *BMJ* (10 Oct 1964), 950–51 · *The Lancet* (17 Oct 1964) · *CGPLA Eng. & Wales* (1964) · personal knowledge (1981)

Wealth at death £8964: probate, 30 Dec 1964, *CGPLA Eng. & Wales*

Fraser, George Sutherland (1915–1980), poet and literary scholar, was born on 8 November 1915 in Glasgow, one of the two children of George Sutherland Fraser (1885–1942), a member of the legal staff of Glasgow corporation, and his wife, Ada Grace, *née* Jones (1887–1952). The latter is described by William Hall as having been 'a talented musician' (Hall, 51); she was a descendant of the same Johnson family that produced Samuel Johnson, the hymn-writer, and which was collaterally connected with Dr Samuel Johnson. Fraser attended the primary section of Glasgow Academy, but when the family moved to Aberdeen in 1924 (the father was appointed depute town clerk, and promoted town clerk in the following year) he went to Aberdeen grammar school.

To Fraser, Glasgow and Aberdeen were respectively 'romantic' and 'classic' cities, symbolic of the two aspects of his own temperament. In his autobiography, *A Stranger and Afraid* (posthumously published, 1983), he wrote that 'the relaxing air of Glasgow' encouraged in him 'a sad and helpless dreaminess', while 'the brisk, cold air of Aberdeen' woke him up and 'brisked' him 'into an unaccustomed alertness' (p. 37). For his poetry, however, Aberdeen was the more significant. In poems such as 'Social Pleasures', 'Problems of a Poet', 'A Letter to Anne Ridler', 'A Winter Letter', and especially in 'Home Town Elegy', the Aberdonian environment provided exactly what Fraser needed to fulfil his aim (expressed in a letter to David Daiches) of exploring 'personal and local themes in a mood of gently restrained lyricism' (*THES*).

In 1933 Fraser went to St Andrews University as a bursary student, and in 1937 took a joint honours degree in English and history, although he also acquired a love for moral philosophy, which he had to take as part of the more general preparation for an honours degree required by the Scottish university system. While still an undergraduate he made something of a reputation for himself as a writer and student journalist, and on returning to Aberdeen he became a cub reporter on the *Aberdeen Press and Journal*. At the outbreak of war in 1939 he volunteered for the army and joined the Black Watch—motivated by a patriotism which, as his poem 'Meditation of a Patriot' suggests, was distinctly non-jingoistic, and perhaps also by the example of his father, who had been an officer in the Highland light infantry during the First World War. Fraser, however, was anything but a man of military cast; he belonged to nature's 'awkward squad' and could never master the intricacies of drill. He was transferred to the

George Sutherland Fraser (1915–1980), by John Waller

RASC, and spent most of his service in the Middle East as a warrant officer carrying out journalistic and editorial duties, first with the army public relations directorate in Cairo (1941–2), and then in Eritrea in charge of the *Eritrean Daily News* (1942–4). He was posted back to Cairo in 1944, and then returned to London where he was demobilized in December 1945. Poems such as 'Egypt' and 'Monologue for a Cairo Evening' came out of this experience.

Fraser's first volumes of poetry belong to the 1940s, including *The Fatal Landscape* (1943), *Home Town Elegy* (1944), and *The Traveller has Regrets* (1948). At this time he also became involved with the 'New Apocalypse' movement centred on J. F. Hendry and Henry Treece. Fraser became their critical spokesman and he wrote the introduction to the movement's 1941 anthology, *The White Horseman*. He argued that New Apocalypse was a flexible philosophy 'which hardly dictates to anyone how he is to write or feel' (p. 6); its controlling ideal was 'the living completeness of man', reflected in a balanced art form in which 'intellect and will' were as necessary as the creatively potent outpourings from the unconscious more obviously associated with a cult of the 'apocalyptic' (p. 3). Although this was very much a young man's manifesto, and the movement itself one with which Fraser associated himself only for a short time, the desire to reconcile emotional upheaval and rational structures remained with him throughout his life.

After the war Fraser returned, not to Aberdeen, but to a flat in Beaufort Street, Chelsea, London, where his mother and sister, Jean (to whom he was most closely attached), had moved after his father's death in 1942. The life to which he dedicated himself now was that of poet and writer, existing, often precariously, on reviews and articles for literary journals, including the *TLS*, the *New Statesman*, and the 'quality' Sunday newspapers, and broadcasts for the BBC Third Programme. Another inhabitant of Beaufort Street was a young woman, Eileen Lucy (Paddy) Andrew (*b.* 1918), daughter of Melville and Evelyn Andrew. Paddy, who had taken an English degree at St Anne's College, Oxford, and was then working at the Board of Trade, shared Fraser's passion for poetry, and it was not long before they fell in love and were married, on 30 August 1946. Their house in Great Ormond Street, Bloomsbury, soon became a kind of unofficial cultural centre for young, aspiring writers.

Among other commissions undertaken by Fraser at this time were two travel books on Scotland and *News from South America* (1949), an account of a journey to Brazil, Uruguay, Argentina, and Chile made as a member of a cultural mission sponsored by the Hudson Institute. In Buenos Aires he had interviews with Borges and Perón, and attended a political rally addressed by both Evita and General Perón. The country which most impressed him, however, was Chile. He liked Santiago with its 'affectionate flavour of use' (*News*, 167) and its spectacular backdrop of the Andes; but the deepest impression was made by his encounter with Pablo Neruda, at whose house he stayed. Neruda was for Fraser a type of the heroic man of action conjoined with the uncompromising man of letters. Although his own position as an uncommitted liberal set him aside from the dangerous extremism of Neruda, he was one of the first to recognize the outstanding quality of the Chilean writer's work; and this meeting led Fraser to translating Neruda's poetry.

In 1953 Fraser's first major critical work was published—*The Modern Writer and his World*. This was the fruit of his being appointed in 1950 to succeed William Empson as cultural attaché to the British embassy in Japan. In the preface he describes it modestly as an attempt 'to provide Japanese students of English literature, who had been cut off from contact with us during the war, with a fairly clear guide-book to modern tendencies' (*The Modern Writer*, 7). It is more than that, however. Ranging from the late nineteenth-century symbolists to mid-twentieth century literature, it offers a highly readable survey which manages to be both just to individual writers and perceptive in its treatment of their relation to their times.

Impressions of Japan and other Essays (1952) and *Three Philosophical Essays* (n.d.) also belong to the Japan visit. In the latter Fraser confesses that he would have liked to become a philosopher, but realized that he did not have a sufficiently abstract frame of mind. These essays are concerned with the exploration of personality and Sartrean existentialism, but drift towards the anecdotal mode which became increasingly characteristic of Fraser's later writings. He puts the emphasis on social interaction rather than logical analysis, and typically concludes that 'truth, like personality, is made actual in the response of one mind to another, and like human life itself it is a developing project' (Fraser, *Three Philosophical Essays*, 52).

In 1958 Fraser exchanged his absorbing, but insecure,

literary life in London for a post in the English department of the newly chartered University of Leicester. The young poet was turning into the middle-aged family man (he and Paddy had three children: the eldest, Helen, was born in 1949, the second, George, in 1951, and the third, Katie, in 1952); and his growing domestic responsibilities made a regular income and the more settled pattern of life offered by a provincial city both necessary and desirable. University life offered him the chance to focus on the critical work that now seemed to be his main strength, and to pursue his fascination with modern writers in greater depth. A number of volumes followed including *Vision and Rhetoric* (1959), *Lawrence Durrell* (1968), *Metre, Rhythm, and Free Verse* (1970), *Essays on Twentieth Century Poets* (1977)—which overlaps considerably with *Vision and Rhetoric: Alexander Pope* (1978)—and the posthumously published *A Short History of English Poetry* (1981). All are informed with that balanced awareness of 'romantic' and 'classic', visionary and rationally moderate, which runs as a theme throughout Fraser's life, but there is an undeniable decline in the forcefulness and originality of the later work. Although he was interested in the various manifestations of literary theory which British universities eagerly adopted from France and America in the 1960s and 1970s, and which his philosophical interests particularly qualified him to analyse and assess, his own work continued in an earlier vein of warm appreciation illuminated with passages of practical criticism.

In 1963 Fraser was appointed reader in poetry at Leicester, and he spent part of the following year as visiting professor at the University of Rochester in New York state. Increasingly, his vocation was becoming that of a teacher; in 1975 he said of himself: 'Poetry is my main gift. But to earn a living I became first a literary journalist, then a university teacher, and now teaching, especially the teaching of poetry, has become as true a vocation as writing poetry' (King and Smith, 13). His lectures, though on occasion inclined to the rambling and diffuse, were most often a blend of inspired, off-the-cuff analysis and wide-ranging literary reference (he seemed to have read everything, and to be able to deliver an astute judgement on any author or subject). But his forte was the seminar and, still more, private or after-dinner conversation, where his penchant for anecdote and reminiscence had full scope.

Despite the predominance of critical work and teaching, Fraser did have the fortune to experience a late resurgence of his talent for poetry. A new volume, *Conditions*, appeared in 1969, and he continued to write occasional poems in the 1970s. These were gathered with the previously published work in *Poems of G. S. Fraser*, edited by his friends Ian Fletcher and John Lucas (1981). The later poems continue the formal neatness and rhymed precision of the earlier ones, but the themes are less parochial and the verse movement more colloquially liberated. Although the need for balance is still their underlying concern, they are also more coolly discursive than the plangently elegiac earlier poems, more cosmopolitan, and more urbane.

Illness overshadowed Fraser's life in the late 1970s. He

retired from the University of Leicester in 1979, but after little more than six months of leisure he died, at his home, 19 Guilford Road, Leicester, of heart disease on 3 January 1980. He was buried in Leicester. In later years his hair, and his appearance generally, was often untidy in a rumpled, academic way; he had a broad forehead, thick eyebrows, dreamy but slightly ironic, bespectacled, hazel eyes, and rubicund cheeks. His voice, long since Anglicized, nevertheless still carried a hint of the lilting, Scottish intonation. Fraser was survived by his wife.   R. P. Draper

Sources G. S. Fraser, *A stranger and afraid* (1983) · *Poems of G. S. Fraser*, ed. I. Fletcher and J. Lucas (1981) · G. S. Fraser, introduction, *The white horseman*, ed. J. F. Hendry and H. Treece (1941) · G. S. Fraser, *News from South America* (1949) · G. S. Fraser, *The modern writer and his world* (1953) · G. S. Fraser, *Vision and rhetoric* (1959) · G. S. Fraser, *Conditions* (1969) · G. S. Fraser, *Three philosophical essays* (Tokyo, 1952) · W. Hall, 'G. S. Fraser: poet and critic', *Cauld Kail Het: a Grampian English Views anthology*, ed. [D. Morrison] (1985) · R. P. Draper, 'G. S. Fraser: the poetry of exile', *Northern visions*, ed. D. Hewitt (1995), 99–109 · B. Bergonzi, 'Poets of the 1940s', *The myth of modernism and twentieth century literature* (1986), 129–42 · C. King and I. C. Smith, eds., *Twelve more modern Scottish poets* (1986), 13–14 · D. Daiches, review of *A short history of English poetry* and *Poems of G. S. Fraser*, THES (26 June 1981) · private information (2004)
Archives NL Scot., corresp. and papers; literary papers · Ransom HRC, MSS and letters
Likenesses J. Waller, photograph, repro. in Fraser, *News from South America*, frontispiece [*see illus.*] · photograph, repro. in Fraser, *News from South America* · photograph, repro. in King and Smith, eds., *Twelve more modern Scottish poets*

Fraser, Gordon (1911–1981), greetings card publisher, was born (lame in one leg) on 26 February 1911 at Ben Wyvis, North Park Grove, Roundhay, Leeds, the son of Kenneth Fraser, managing director of the Yorkshire Copper Works, and his wife, Alice Gertrude Fraser, *née* Woodall. His father was of Scottish descent.

Following education at Oundle School and St John's College, Cambridge, with some 'topping up' at Munich University, the London School of Economics, and Pitman's College, Gordon Fraser set up in 1935 as a bookseller in Portugal Place, Cambridge. On 9 April the following year, four days before Easter, he married a merchant's daughter, Nancy Katharine Jones, at the Presbyterian church, Downing Street, Cambridge. The couple had two children: a son, Ian Gordon Fraser, and a daughter, Margaret Alice Fraser (later Moss).

Fraser combined his bookshop with a small gallery of fine art prints, and began publishing books himself on a modest scale. The latter included finely printed works on vorticism and the Bodleian Library exhibits, and a selection of classics. In 1938 he introduced his first Christmas greetings cards, blending good design with high-quality printing and a price that would not deter customers.

The Second World War caused Fraser's career to take a new turn. On its outbreak, he became a full-time member of the Cambridgeshire civil defence, and a year later joined the army and trained at Sandhurst. This prepared him for a wartime role as an officer in the intelligence corps, using his knowledge of French and German. His assignments took him first to Palestine, then to the western desert. One of the highlights of his army career was when he was dropped into Yugoslavia as a member of Fitzroy Maclean's British military mission and became a link between allied forces and such high-ranking partisan leaders as Velebit and even Tito himself.

After the war Fraser was appointed director of UNESCO's radio division in Paris, and it was not until 1954 that he was able to return and resume full control of his business. It was then that he broadened his range of greetings cards. His first birthday cards appeared in 1955 and he subsequently added Easter, Valentine, mother's day, father's day, and other cards appropriate for a wide range of occasions. A further development was fine art cards, with reproductions of old masters, themselves followed by postcards, notepaper, stationery, and gift wrapping to suit all tastes.

Throughout this period and up to his death, Fraser personally selected his gallery designs, opening a London office as a base to interview artists and overseas buyers. The gallery itself had by then moved to Bedford, where it remained thereafter, with Ian Fraser succeeding his father as art editor. In 1978 the company acquired the Roundwood Press in Warwickshire to meet all its printing requirements.

On 27 June 1981 Fraser was killed in a car accident while driving on the M6 south of Preston, Lancashire. His Jaguar sports car exploded in flames, and he died instantly. The cause of the accident was never established, and a subsequent coroner's inquest recorded a verdict of death by misadventure. He was survived by his wife.

Fraser undoubtedly revolutionized greetings card design and quality, and he maintained a house style that was widely imitated. By the time of his death his cards were selling at a rate of over 100 million a year in eighty-five countries, with associated companies in France, Switzerland, Canada, Australia, and the United States. The Gordon Fraser Gallery's annual turnover at this time was running equally impressively, around £10 million. Fraser was a colourful personality who made his mark wherever he went. Practically his sole methods of relaxation were books—he was a discriminating reader and a devoted follower of F. R. Leavis—and an annual skiing holiday at Davos, Switzerland.   Adrian Room

Sources *The Times* (2 July 1981) · *The Times* (23 Sept 1981) [report of coroner's inquest] · *Cambridge Evening News* (31 Jan 1986) [account of firm's 50th anniversary] · b. cert. · m. cert.
Wealth at death £478,366: probate, 14 Dec 1981, *CGPLA Eng. & Wales*

Fraser, Helen Charlotte Isabella. *See* Vaughan, Dame Helen Charlotte Isabella Gwynne- (1879–1967).

Fraser, Helen Miller. *See* Moyes, Helen Miller (1881–1979).

Fraser, Hugh, lord of Lovat (*d.* in or before **1440**). *See under* Fraser family (*per. c.*1300–*c.*1500).

Fraser, Hugh, first Lord Lovat (*d.* **1501**). *See under* Fraser family (*per. c.*1300–*c.*1500).

Fraser, Hugh, first Baron Fraser of Allander (1903–1966), department store owner and businessman, was born at

Hugh Fraser, first Baron Fraser of Allander (1903–1966), by Sir James Gunn, 1964

Glencaple, Partickhill Road, Partick, Lanarkshire, on 15 January 1903, the only son of Hugh Fraser (d. 1927), drapery warehouseman, and his wife, Emily Florence, *née* McGown. He was educated at Glasgow Academy and Warriston School, near Moffat. His mother was influential in allowing him to leave school in 1919. She wanted him to train as an accountant, but after a few months he had his way and entered his father's business, Fraser, Sons & Co., a large emporium at the foot of Buchanan Street, Glasgow. He learned the business from the bottom, by trial and error, but to such purpose that his father made him managing director in 1924 when he was only twenty-one. Three years later on his father's death he became chairman. The young chairman had ideas for expansion, but he bided his time until 1936 when he defied economic depression and began to extend his business by acquiring other stores in Glasgow: Arnott & Co., Robert Simpson & Sons, and Thomas Muirhead & Co. His finances became stretched but credit was forthcoming from banks impressed by his remarkable qualities of vision, imagination, shrewdness, and, above all, integrity.

Periods of recession made acquisition easy for those such as Fraser who were willing to gamble on a future upturn in their particular line of business. During the Second World War he acquired Peter Allan of Edinburgh in 1940, Gordon and Stanfield of Perth and Muir, Simpson Ltd of Glasgow, and Alexander Ewing & Co. of Dundee in 1941, and Dallas and The Colosseum, both of Glasgow, in 1942. During the post-war years he acquired D. and A. Prentice of Greenock and Logie & Co. of Stirling in 1945,

and McLachlan and Brown of Stirling, and D. and A. Wallace of Perth, and William Small of Edinburgh in 1946. Many other Scottish stores followed, the most important acquisitions coming in 1951 with his purchase of a majority stake in the Scottish Drapery Corporation.

Fraser's business prospered to such an extent that in 1948 he was able to float the House of Fraser Ltd as a public company with a capital of £1 million. At the same time he formed a private company, Scottish and Universal Investments Ltd (SUITS), which was his vehicle for acquisitions other than retailing. The original shareholders saw the value of their investment multiplied tenfold in a few years. This success was due to two things: first, Fraser's thorough knowledge of the drapery business, which enabled him to see and grasp opportunities for improving the profits of businesses which he acquired; and second, his idea, probably adopted from the speculative house-building trade, of purchasing land, then mortgaging the land and buildings erected thereon, in order to finance further developments. Fraser first used this method in 1936 when he mortgaged 14–16 Buchanan Street to meet the cost of its purchase, and used it frequently thereafter.

Fraser first 'invaded' London by acquiring the John Barker group in 1957. Here he had won the confidence and support of the directors. He had to battle to win control of Harrods, then London's largest department store, since the board was hostile and there was another competitor. Fraser's success in 1959 was regarded as a Pyrrhic victory by those who thought he had paid too much and who did not know their man. By this time the House of Fraser had perhaps larger interests in the length and breadth of England than in Scotland, but Fraser's office in Buchanan Street remained his headquarters to the end, even if he had constantly to go to London and occupy his suite in the Savoy Hotel. Twice his bids for Scottish companies failed. In the first, his wish to help friends who wanted to keep control of Scottish Motor Traction in Scotland could not allow him to make a financially unjustifiable offer. In the second he was frustrated by the determined directors of the knitwear company Lyle and Scott and certain circumstances of which they took legal advantage. But when an attempt was made in 1964 to gain control of the *Glasgow Herald*, he did fight successfully to acquire the newspaper, through SUITS, and keep its control in Glasgow.

Fraser was a Glasgow town councillor for eight years from 1938, but while he took his share of committee work, the slow pace of business irritated him. He was happier in 1959 when he applied himself with vigour to the expansion of the tourist industry in the Scottish highlands. Fraser himself sat on the Scottish Tourist Board. The House of Fraser held a one-third stake in Highland Tourist (Cairngorms) Development Ltd, which built the Aviemore Centre, and its complex of skiing and other facilities testified to his vision and enterprise.

SUITS was converted to a public company in 1960 and acquired by Lonrho in 1979. In memory of his mother in 1960 Fraser created the Hugh Fraser Foundation, with a capital of over £2 million. Fraser realized that trusts had often been created to meet a contemporary need and were later in difficulties because that need had been met and they were unable to devote funds to other causes. Consequently, with unexampled generosity and foresight, he gave power to his trustees to make payments in their sole discretion to any person, fund, institution, or society, whether in Scotland or elsewhere.

As well as holding numerous other honours and honorific positions, Fraser was an honorary LLD of St Andrews (1962) and was created a baronet in 1961 and a baron in 1964. He spoke once in the Lords, but not very effectively. He was no orator and he disliked public appearances. He was secretly a benefactor to many who were old, infirm, or sick. Unlike other successful millionaires he made and kept friends; he did not want power so much as to succeed: he was not one to bury his talent in the ground.

Slim, unostentatiously but well groomed, with a trim moustache and a flower in his buttonhole, an endless smoker of cigarettes, with a Scots voice perhaps rather rough when first heard, he was highly strung, a warmhearted man who enriched the life of all who knew him. He liked to be at home at weekends to play snooker with his doctor and then to have a four at bridge where he was as shrewd as he was bold. He enjoyed a flutter at Monte Carlo and other continental casinos where, as he said, he was very lucky. Some would say that he was lucky in business too, but there his success was based on knowledge, on hard work, on careful and accurate calculations, and above all on his shining integrity.

Fraser was always a family man. He had the great good fortune in 1931 to found a happy home for himself by marrying, on 2 April, Kathleen (Kate) Hutcheon, daughter of Sir Andrew Jopp Williams Lewis, shipbuilder, former lord provost of Aberdeen. From her he had support, inspiration, and advice for the rest of his life. Fraser's home was his refuge in days of difficulty and disappointment, and his greatest delight in success and triumph was to share it at his own fireside. The couple had a daughter, Ann, and a son, Sir Hugh *Fraser, second baronet (1936–1987), who succeeded his father as chairman of the House of Fraser and other companies. In March 1965 Fraser suffered a massive heart attack in his suite at the Savoy Hotel. He was confined there for several weeks but insisted that the public should not be aware of his condition. He recovered, but died at his home, Dineiddwg, Mugdock, near Milngavie, Stirlingshire, on 6 November 1966. Survived by his wife, he was given a funeral service in Glasgow Cathedral. His son succeeded to the baronetcy but after holding it for a short time disclaimed the barony.

Fraser allowed his stores to maintain their individuality but always saw himself as a patriarch, caring for his numerous employees, many of whom felt a strong loyalty to him. He always gave his occupation as 'warehouseman'. The *Glasgow Herald* of 7 November 1966 reported the words of Sir Alec Douglas Home: 'He was a great citizen of Glasgow, and a pioneer of business enterprise in Scotland'. The *Herald*'s obituarist declared 'Like Wolfson and Clore … he has always combined managerial skill with business acumen'. His biographer wrote 'As a businessman he was first of all a warehouseman and secondly a financier' (Pottinger, 178). The figures were there to confirm this judgement: when Fraser took over as managing director in 1924 turnover was £165,000; in 1965 turnover of the House of Fraser was £100 million.

T. M. KNOX, *rev.* IAIN F. RUSSELL

Sources M. Moss and A. Turton, *A legend of retailing … House of Fraser* (1989) · G. Pottinger, *The winning counter* (1971) · DSBB · *Glasgow Herald* (7 Nov 1966) · *Glasgow Herald* (3 April 1931) · b. cert. · d. cert. **Archives** U. Glas., Archives and Business Records Centre, House of Fraser archives **Likenesses** J. Gunn, portrait, 1964, Scot. NPG [*see illus.*] · F. Eastman, portrait · J. Gunn, portrait, probably Harrods, London · A. Sutherland, portrait, House of Fraser · cartoon, repro. in Moss and Turton, *A legend of retailing*, 168 **Wealth at death** £2,085,454 18s. 10d.: confirmation, 21 March 1967, CCI

Fraser, Sir Hugh, second baronet (1936–1987), businessman, was born on 18 December 1936 in Bearsden, Dunbartonshire, the only son and younger child of Hugh *Fraser, first Baron Fraser of Allander (1903–1966), businessman, and his wife, Kathleen Hutcheon (Kate or Katie), *née* Lewis, daughter of Sir Andrew Jopp Williams Lewis, shipbuilder and lord provost of Aberdeen. His father, the chairman and managing director of the House of Fraser, was made a baronet in 1961, and a peer in 1964. Fraser was educated at St Mary's School, Melrose, and Kelvinside Academy, Glasgow, before leaving school at sixteen to go into the family business, which he joined on his seventeenth birthday, starting work in the McDonalds store in Buchanan Street, Glasgow.

Fraser worked closely with his father, who made him a director at the age of twenty-one and gave him overall responsibility for the stores in Scotland, to prepare him for the time when he would take over the whole business, although his father had no intention of losing control himself: he told journalists in 1961, 'in due course he will overtake me, but he will never take me over' (Moss and Turton, 200). Fraser became assistant managing director in 1960. On 26 April 1962 he married Patricia Mary Bowie (b. 1938/9), radiographer, and daughter of John Bowie, dyer and cleaner, of Milngavie, Dunbartonshire. They had three daughters, but the marriage ended in divorce in 1971, and in 1973 Fraser married an international showjumper, Aileen Margaret Ross (d. 1984), daughter of George Paterson Ross. This marriage was dissolved in 1982.

Determined to move away from the old-fashioned image of the group's stores, Fraser converted the original Fraser store in Glasgow into a high-class fashion shop for well-to-do young women, and began to introduce boutiques into other stores, including the Frank Usher boutique in Watt and Grant of Aberdeen, and the His and Hers Chelsea Boutique in the Fraser store in Buchanan Street, Glasgow. He also converted Simpson Hunters in Glasgow into a Young World shop, devoted to children's wear. Following his father's heart attack in 1965, Fraser was appointed deputy chairman. After his father's death in 1966, Fraser was elected chairman of the House of Fraser and of Scottish and Universal Investments Ltd, his father's investment company, just before his thirtieth birthday. He renounced the peerage, but was unable to disclaim the baronetcy. He was the fourth Hugh Fraser to head the family business, which his father had built up from a group of drapery stores in Scotland into a chain of seventy-five department stores, headed by Harrods Ltd, which the House of Fraser had acquired in 1959.

Faced with the formidable task of taking on this large enterprise, Fraser embarked on a policy of expansion and modernization, introducing a more youthful style into existing stores. In 1966 he staged a 'Youthquake' at Barkers of Kensington, where models wearing the latest clothes by young designers danced along the catwalk to pop music before a large audience of young people. He continued to open boutiques, shops within department stores, in an effort to revolutionize the sale of fashion wear in department stores and attract the fashion-conscious. 'Way-In' opened in Harrods in 1967, followed by the 'Hi-Street West Eight' boutique in Barkers, and 'Impact' opened in McDonalds in Glasgow in 1969. He resumed his father's policy of acquisition in 1969, when he bought J. J. Allen Ltd, the Bournemouth group of stores. He went on to acquire Guy and Smith of Grimsby in 1969; E. Dingle & Co., a group of stores in the south-west, in 1971; and James Howell & Co. in Cardiff in 1972. At the same time he was closing some stores, mainly in Scotland, but he also closed Pontings, in London, in 1970. As the supermarket chains began to sell clothing, he pursued a policy of trading up, aiming to make the House of Fraser the best store in every large town in Britain.

Between 1966 and 1973 sales doubled to over £200 million, and profits doubled to over £10 million. Fraser was chosen as the Young Business Man of the Year by *The Guardian* in 1973, acknowledging how he had restructured and expanded the family business, and the new and exciting style he had brought in to the stores. But the House of Fraser was fighting against competition from smaller specialist chains such as Laura Ashley and Mothercare, and when the recession began to bite in 1973 Fraser was ready to give up the House of Fraser, partly because he had no son to whom to pass on the business, but also because he was tired of the relentless pressure of his hectic business life, having devoted all his time and energy since leaving school to the House of Fraser and Scottish and Universal. He resigned as managing director of the House of Fraser, and when Boots Ltd proposed a merger, Fraser supported the idea, intending to give up the chairmanship of the House of Fraser and concentrate on developing Scottish and Universal. But when the Monopolies and Mergers Commission allowed Boots to pull out of the proposed merger in 1974, Fraser decided to stay on.

The failure of the merger with Boots proved the turning point in Fraser's career. The years after 1974 were difficult. He had tried to prove himself a worthy successor to his father, and to turn the House of Fraser into a successful modern corporation, but he was hampered by the worldwide recession following the rise in oil prices, and by the return of government control, with restrictions on profits, and the decline in consumer demand. In an attempt to cut down on his responsibilities Fraser had given up the chairmanship of Harrods, because he no longer wanted to divide his time between London and Glasgow, headquarters of the House of Fraser. He continued to buy department stores, including in 1975 the Hide group of thirteen stores, in an effort to strengthen the House of Fraser presence in the south of England. But he became increasingly addicted to gambling, playing for high stakes; a stock exchange inquiry in 1976 revealed that he had been selling House of Fraser shares to finance his gambling. In 1976 he was fined £600 under the Companies Act for the misclassification of a loan, and for improper share dealings.

Lonrho, the international trading company, first became involved in the fortunes of the House of Fraser in 1977, when in an attempt to increase its holdings in Britain it acquired nearly 30 per cent of the shares, and Roland Walter (Tiny) Rowland, the managing director, and Lord Duncan-Sandys, the chairman, joined the board of directors. Lonrho gained control of Scottish and Universal in 1978 after buying Fraser's personal stake, and in 1980 turned its attention to acquiring the House of Fraser, and especially Harrods. In 1980 Lonrho started to harass the House of Fraser board, questioning decisions and sending circulars to shareholders. After Fraser and Rowland were reconciled in January 1981, Fraser lost the support of the directors, and he was removed as chairman at the end of January. He subsequently resigned from the chairmanship of Harrods, which he had just resumed. Lonrho then launched a takeover bid for the House of Fraser, which was turned down by the Monopolies and Mergers Commission in December 1981. Fraser resigned from the board in February 1982.

After 1981 Fraser spent most of his time in Scotland, where he settled into a quieter business life once he had severed his connections with the House of Fraser. He built up a chain of menswear shops—the Sir Hugh and Sir group, which he later sold—and he held a number of directorships, mainly in Scotland, as well as the chairmanship of Dumbarton Football Club. He was popular in Scotland. He worked hard on behalf of the Hugh Fraser Foundation, the charitable trust set up by his father, to give substantial amounts of money to medical research in Scotland. Through the trust he bought the island of Iona for the National Trust of Scotland as a memorial to his father, and he gave his Mugdock estate near Glasgow to form the Mugdock Country Park. Although he was little interested in politics, he joined the Scottish National Party in 1974, and he served for a time on the Scottish Development Council. In 1985 he was awarded an honorary doctorate by the University of Stirling. He died from lung cancer on 5 May 1987 at his mother's home in Mugdock, near Milngavie, Dunbartonshire. A memorial service was held at St Paul's, Milngavie, on 18 May 1987.

ANNE PIMLOTT BAKER

Sources M. Moss and A. Turton, *A legend of retailing: House of Fraser* (1989) · *The Guardian* (22 Feb 1973) · *The Times* (5 Jan 1981) · *The Times* (6 May 1987) · *The Times* (19 May 1987) · *The Times* (20 May 1987) · Burke, *Peerage* · *WWW*, 1981–90 · b. cert. · m. cert.

Archives U. Glas., Archives and Business Records Centre, House of Fraser archives
Likenesses photographs, 1951–80, Hult. Arch. · double portrait, photograph, c.1958 (with his father), repro. in Moss and Turton, *Legend of retailing* · photographs, repro. in *The Times* (6 May 1987)

Fraser, Sir **Hugh Charles Patrick Joseph** (1918–1984), soldier and politician, was born on 23 January 1918 in Westminster, the third of five children and younger son of Simon Joseph *Fraser (1871–1933), soldier, the fourteenth (sometimes reckoned sixteenth) Lord Lovat, of Beaufort Castle, Beauly, Inverness-shire, and his wife, Laura (1892–1965), second daughter of Thomas *Lister, the fourth and last Baron Ribblesdale (1854–1925). He was educated at Ampleforth College, the Sorbonne, and Balliol College, Oxford. He led the school debating society. As head of St Oswald's House, Fraser declined his headmaster's invitation to become head boy, preferring to study in Paris before going up to Balliol as an exhibitioner. As chairman of the Oxford University Conservative Association, he was less hostile to Neville Chamberlain's foreign policy than was his college contemporary Edward Heath, whom he succeeded as president of the Oxford Union in 1939. Fraser was proud to preside over the reversal in debate of the notorious 'king and country' resolution of 1933. His patrician manner and grandiloquent debating style, both in the union and later in the House of Commons, were lightened by wit and self-mockery. He gained a second class in modern history in 1939.

At the start of the Second World War, Fraser was with the family yeomanry regiment, the Lovat Scouts, but he soon sought more adventurous service with Phantom (general headquarters, liaison regiment) and the Special Air Service regiment. After the battle of Arnhem (1944) he took part in the Pegasus operation for the rescue of stragglers. In one night, as joint beach-master with Airey Neave—then also serving with intelligence school no. 9—he took part in saving 138 evaders from across the Rhine. Nicknamed Fearless Fraser, he was appointed MBE (military division, 1945) and became a chevalier (with palm) of the Belgian order of Leopold II. He was also awarded the Belgian Croix de Guerre and the Netherlands order of Orange Nassau.

Fraser was twenty-seven when he won Stone in the general election of 1945. He was the sole successful Conservative candidate in Staffordshire, and one of only four Roman Catholic tories elected. He compared the 'nightmare' of his maiden speech to 'a descent by parachute behind the enemy line'. Early on he displayed his independent judgement by going against the opposition whips and voting against the Washington loan agreement. In 1950 the seats of Stafford and Stone were united. So, until his return in the general election of that year, Fraser shared the constituency with a Labour MP, Stephen Swingler.

From 1951 to 1954 Fraser was parliamentary private secretary to the colonial secretary, Oliver Lyttelton. Together they toured Malaya during the communist insurgency, once crash-landing at Penang, and visited Kenya during the period of the Mau Mau uprising. In 1956, after the seizure of the Suez Canal Company, Fraser was vehement for military action against Nasser's Egypt; but he did not belong to the Suez group of tory critics of the government's failure to complete the Suez operation.

In 1958 Fraser joined the succeeding ministry headed by Harold Macmillan as parliamentary under-secretary of state and financial secretary to the War Office. He held those posts until 1960. In 1962 he became, successively, parliamentary under-secretary of state for the colonies and the last secretary of state for air and a privy councillor. From April to October 1964 he was minister of defence for the Royal Air Force in the new ministry that had absorbed the three service departments. After the Conservative electoral defeat that year Fraser was dropped from the shadow cabinet. Temperamentally different from Edward Heath, he opposed joining the European Common Market. In 1967 Fraser's fire was directed against another Balliol contemporary, Denis Healey, for the cancellation of the TSR 2.

Fraser never held office again, although he kept his seat until his death. To some contemporaries he seemed at times to have lost a sense of political purpose. But he espoused causes out of conviction, irrespective of party policy or establishment opinion. In 1968 he was one of those who, like Enoch Powell and Michael Foot, opposed the reform of the House of Lords on lines drawn, in part, by the Labour peer, the seventh earl of Longford, Francis Aungier Pakenham, whose daughter Antonia (b. 1932) he had married in London on 25 September 1956. They had three sons and three daughters. The marriage was dissolved in 1977.

Fraser called for the return of conscription. The romantic appeal of Zionism and his own assessment of British interests in the Middle East made him a consistent and eloquent partisan of the state of Israel. This involved some financial loss because of disagreement on the Arab–Israel question with business associates. Fraser also championed, and visited, the largely Roman Catholic people of eastern Nigeria during their struggle for the independent state of Biafra, at a time when the integrity of the Nigerian federation was the common policy of Labour government and Conservative opposition. Ever loyal to friends, Fraser backed Jonathan Aitken MP, then a young journalist, when he was prosecuted under the Official Secrets Act in connection with a *Sunday Times* article he wrote on Biafra. Fraser demanded his own prosecution, but the attorney-general did not oblige and Aitken was acquitted.

At the party leadership election of 1975 Fraser stood in the first round. Margaret Thatcher was the successful candidate. That same year Fraser was shocked and distressed when an Irish terrorist bomb intended for him killed a neighbour instead. But he spoke out all the more against the IRA. Knighted in 1980, he was a gallant cavalier descended from Jacobite Frasers who turned from rebellion to the wars of empire. He was a charming and entertaining companion with a high sense of the ludicrous. He could jest about the sacred; but faith and family were very dear. A traditional Roman Catholic, he sympathized with

Anglicans resentful of liturgical innovation; and he spoke in the Commons against the Church of England measure of 1974 as ousting parliamentary 'power and responsibility' for the established church. Having undergone surgery, Fraser died on 6 March 1984 in St Thomas's Hospital, London.   JOHN BIGGS-DAVISON, *rev.*

Sources personal knowledge (1990) · *The Times* (7 March 1984) · *The Times* (15 March 1984) · Burke, *Peerage* (1999) · *CGPLA Eng. & Wales* (1984)
Likenesses O. Bowey, portrait, 1966, priv. coll.
Wealth at death £193,179: administration, 7 Nov 1984, *CGPLA Eng. & Wales*

Fraser, (William Jocelyn) Ian, Baron Fraser of Lonsdale (1897–1974), promoter of the welfare of blind people, was born in Eastbourne, Sussex, on 30 August 1897, the elder son (his brother died in infancy) and eldest of three children of William Percy Fraser (1849–1925) of Johannesburg, a prospector and financier, who had been one of the original Rand pioneers, and his wife, Ethel Maude (*d.* 1930), daughter of Joscelyn Percy Cooke of Escourt, Natal.

Fraser's early enthusiasm was for 'soldiering'. He joined the cadet corps at Marlborough College at the age of fourteen, became the youngest cadet to gain 'certificate A', passed on to Sandhurst in 1915, and enlisted in the King's Shropshire light infantry. After two months of fighting on the Somme in 1916, and one month short of his nineteenth birthday, he was wounded by a German sniper whom he was attempting to dislodge from behind an iron loophole plate. The bullet traversed both eyes without damaging the lids or rendering him unconscious. On his retirement from the army in 1917 he was promoted captain. While in hospital in London he was contacted by St Dunstan's, a hostel and training centre for blinded servicemen founded and run by Sir (Cyril) Arthur Pearson, who was also blind. In September 1916 Fraser went to stay in one of its annexes, 21 Portland Place, where Pearson himself lived. He also met Pearson's assistant, Irene Gladys (*d.* 1978), the daughter of George Frederick Mace of Chipping Norton, Oxfordshire, and married her on 23 July 1918. She was appointed CBE for her work for blind people. They had one daughter.

As assistant and, from 1921, successor to Pearson as chairman of St Dunstan's, Fraser devoted his life to the welfare of blind people. He mastered technical devices and soon set about his chosen task of easing the existence of blind people by improving the braille system then in use and, after long experiments with recording devices, by instigating the 'talking book' project.

Fraser was a commanding figure, tall and handsome, and a forceful speaker, with a prodigious memory. He entered the London county council in 1922 and served for three years as a Conservative member for North St Pancras. He was elected to parliament in 1924, for the same constituency, which he represented until 1929 and from 1931 to 1936, when he resigned. From 1940 to 1950 he was the member for Lonsdale, Lancaster, and from 1950 to 1958 for Morecambe and Lonsdale, Lancaster. During the whole of this period he was the ex-servicemen's champion in and out of parliament, fighting tirelessly for their

(William Jocelyn) Ian Fraser, Baron Fraser of Lonsdale (1897–1974), by Elliott & Fry, 1942

pensions to be increased. A founder member of the Royal British Legion, he was for eleven years its national president (1947–58). He also served for thirty years on the council of the Royal National Institute for the Blind, whose vice-president he became, and for two terms (1936–9 and 1941–6) as a governor of the BBC. He qualified as a barrister (Inner Temple, 1932) and became director and chairman of many companies (including his own family business in South Africa); but always his major concern was for the blinded ex-servicemen of St Dunstan's, thinking up schemes for its development and extension, which culminated in the opening of their renovated home at Ovingdean, later known as Sir Ian Fraser House.

Fraser had a great zest for life, was impatient with bureaucratic delays (although endlessly patient with his blind protégés), and he was something of a showman, which indeed helped to advertise the projects near to his heart. His hobbies included fishing, riding, and bridge, and (as he readily admitted) arguing; indeed he was proud of his Scottish descent, and especially of a turbulent ancestor, Simon Fraser, eleventh Lord Lovat, who was hanged, drawn, and quartered for his part in the 1745 Jacobite rising. He published an autobiography, *Whereas I was Blind*, in 1942 and *My Story of St. Dunstan's* in 1961.

Fraser was appointed CBE in 1922 and CH in 1953. In 1934 he was knighted and in 1958 he became a life peer. He also held several foreign awards. He died in a London hospital on 19 December 1974.   P. D. TREVOR-ROPER, *rev.*

Sources *The Times* (21 Dec 1974) · I. Fraser, *Whereas I was blind* (1942) · I. Fraser, *My story of St. Dunstan's* (1961)
Archives Borth. Inst., papers concerning political and commercial interests in South Africa · NRA, priv. coll., corresp. and MSS | FILM BFI NFTVA, news footage
Likenesses photographs, 1928–51, Hult. Arch. · Elliott & Fry, photograph, 1942, NPG [*see illus.*] · W. Bird, photograph, 1963, NPG · R. Coleman, photograph, St Dunstan's, London · Fayer, photograph, St Dunstan's, London
Wealth at death £102,506 in England and Wales: probate, 30 May 1975, *CGPLA Eng. & Wales*

Fraser, Sir Ian James (1901–1999), surgeon, was born on 9 February 1901 at 211 Albertbridge Road, Belfast, the only child of Robert Moore Fraser (1856–1952), general practitioner, and his first wife, Margaret (d. 1903), daughter of Adam Boal Ferguson, farmer. His mother died when he was two but he grew up in a happy home with his father, stepmother (Alice, *née* Cuthbert, daughter of Dr Alexander Cuthbert of Londonderry), and younger half-sister, Margaret. In 1913 he entered the Royal Belfast Academical Institution (from a local private school, Miss Wylie's intermediate school and kindergarten, Knock), where he showed the keen intelligence and remarkable memory which never left him, and which earned him many prizes. He entered Queen's University, Belfast, in 1918, and was placed first in each subject in his final degree examinations in 1923 and in both parts of the Irish surgical fellowship (FRCSI, 1926), with commendation in the MD from Queen's in 1932. His first consultant post was in 1927 to the Royal Belfast Hospital for Sick Children, and by the outbreak of the Second World War he was among the leaders of Ulster surgeons. With a notable academic record, including twenty-four medical journal publications between 1930 and 1939, he was elected FRSE in 1939. By then, as commissioner of the new Northern Ireland (Ulster) District St John Ambulance Brigade, he had reinvigorated the organization; he was appointed OBE (1940) in recognition, and progressed to high office in the order (becoming bailiff grand cross in 1974), regularly attending chapter-general meetings until he was ninety-four.

The war enlarged Fraser's now confining Ulster stage. He volunteered and was posted to west Africa, where he became Royal Army Medical Corps consultant surgeon to the four British west African colonies. In 1941 he was withdrawn to lead a team in trials, under battlefield conditions in north Africa, of the first batches of penicillin, which successfully established the drug's efficacy after trauma, especially if used early. He was in the Sicilian campaign; was appointed to the DSO at Salerno; was posted home after serious diphtheria; waded onto the Arromanches beaches on D-day plus 2; undertook marathon operating sessions under fire; commanded a tented hospital at Bayeux; and was promoted brigadier and posted to general headquarters central command, Agra, India.

On demobilization Fraser returned to his consultant post at the Royal Belfast Hospital for Sick Children and was also appointed consultant at the Royal Victoria Hospital, a post which had twice eluded him. In 1947 he was invited to apply for the vacant chair of surgery at Queen's University, Belfast, but declined: he was too gregarious for the library and laboratory; too fond of animals (especially dogs) to sacrifice them even for science. His path now lay in clinical practice through the National Health Service until his retirement in 1966, and in extensive private practice, in both of which he excelled.

Among his professional and academic honours Fraser was president of the Royal College of Surgeons in Ireland (1954–6), of the Association of Surgeons of Great Britain and Ireland (1958), of the Ulster Medical Society (1967), and of the British Medical Association (1962–3). He was a founder of the Ulster Surgical Club; a frequent external examiner; visiting lecturer to many academic and medical bodies worldwide; and the recipient of numerous honorary degrees. He was knighted in 1963 and received many foreign distinctions. Within Northern Ireland he was honorary colonel to two Territorial Army units, served the Royal Belfast Academical Institution as a governor and Queen's University in many capacities, notably as a member of its governing body until he was nearly ninety, was sometime surgeon-in-ordinary to the governor of Northern Ireland, and was a deputy lieutenant for Belfast. He was chairman of the police authority (Royal Ulster Constabulary) from 1970 to 1976, was associated with many charitable bodies, and was a director of a major Irish commercial bank (Allied Irish Banks).

Fraser's main interests in retirement were the history of surgery and its Irish practitioners, institutions, and memorabilia, Irish silver and antiques, sport, and cultural activities. Always an inspiring teacher, brilliant raconteur, and committed professional he was in wide demand as a speaker and representative, even after his triple coronary by-pass at eighty-seven, and he was a perceptive and engaging memoirist. He was unquestionably ambitious but not predatory; warm-hearted and gregarious, with infectious charm and sophisticated humour, he exuded irrepressible vitality and was generous and unfailingly courteous to all and especially helpful to juniors. He had married on 2 September 1931 Eleanor Margaret Mitchell (1902–1992), and although his son John died aged two, the other two children, Mary-Alice and Ian Marcus Moore (Mark), survived him. When nearly ninety he wrote, 'I have had … a very happy home life, entirely due to my wife and our two children' (Fraser, *Blood, Sweat and cheers*, 143). Irked by the physical restrictions which he suffered, especially after his wife's death, he remained intellectually alert with memory undimmed until his death at his home, 19 Upper Malone Road, Belfast, on 11 May 1999. He was buried at Drumbeg parish church, Belfast, two days later.

PETER FROGGATT

Sources Royal Victoria Hospital, Belfast, Fraser Archive • P. Froggatt, 'Sir Ian Fraser', *Ulster Medical Journal*, 68 (1999), 49–53 • I. Fraser, *Blood, sweat and cheers* (1989) • J. B. Lyons, *An assembly of Irish surgeons* (1984) • I. Fraser, 'Penicillin: early trials in war casualties', *BMJ* (22–9 Dec 1984), 1723–5 • I. Fraser, 'Random recollections of World War II', *Ulster Medical Journal*, 63 (1994), 201–13 • *The Independent* (29 May 1999) • *The Times* (21 May 1999) • P. G. Parks, 'Tribute to the late Sir Ian Fraser', *Journal of the Irish College of Physicians and Surgeons*, 29 (2000), 118–19 • personal knowledge (2004) • private information (2004) • *Belfast Street Directory*

Archives priv. coll., family MSS • Royal Victoria Hospital, Belfast

Likenesses portraits, priv. coll.

Wealth at death £1,348,875: probate, 21 Oct 1999, *CGPLA NIre*

Fraser, (Walter) Ian Reid, Baron Fraser of Tullybelton (1911–1989), judge, was born in Glasgow on 3 February 1911, the only child of Alexander Reid Fraser, stockbroker, and his wife, Margaret Russell MacFarlane. He was educated at Repton School, where he distinguished himself academically. He then became a scholar of Balliol College, Oxford, and, after taking a first-class honours degree in philosophy, politics, and economics (1932), completed his education at the University of Glasgow, where he graduated LLB in 1935. The following year he was admitted to the Faculty of Advocates and soon demonstrated the remarkable breadth of his legal quality both in practice and in lecturing in constitutional law, first at Glasgow University (1936) and, after the Second World War, at the University of Edinburgh (1948). His book, *Outline of Constitutional Law* (1st edn 1938; 2nd edn 1948), became one of the standard textbooks of the law degree courses in Glasgow and elsewhere, and was a work which readily found its place in the libraries of practitioners. He was intellectually agile, clear and simple in his use of language, and, although not the outstanding advocate of his generation, excelled in debate and in appellate work, particularly in those cases which appealed to his academic cast of mind. In 1939 his legal career was interrupted by the war. On its outbreak he was a subaltern in a Territorial Army anti-aircraft battery commanded by a fellow member of the faculty. He joined the Royal Artillery, reached the rank of major, and served in Burma, becoming deputy assistant adjutant-general in 1945. After the war, in spite of the fact that his practice was almost exclusively civil, he accepted service as an advocate depute, finally becoming home depute, the senior figure in the crown office under the law officers. In 1953 he took silk, and in 1959 was elected dean of the Faculty of Advocates, an office which he held until 1964, when he became a senator of the college of justice in Scotland (until 1974), with the judicial title of Lord Fraser.

As a judge Fraser was not only respected but also liked by the bar, and in both the outer house and the inner his acute intellect, coupled with the inherent diffidence of his quiet personality, was matched by his invariable courtesy, charm, and a healthy appetite for hard work. In 1974 he became a lord of appeal in ordinary, privy councillor, and life peer, and in the eleven succeeding years in which he sat on the appellate committee of the House of Lords (until 1985) and in the privy council, he made a notable contribution to the development and clarification of the law, delivering many lucid speeches on Scots appeals to the House of Lords. For example, in 1980 he clarified the duty of care owed by the occupier of premises to firemen fighting a fire there, and in 1983 declared that the Court of Session's supervisory jurisdiction over decisions of administrative bodies was not enjoyed by the sheriff court.

While he was an advocate Fraser was active in politics and unsuccessfully contested the East Edinburgh constituency as a Unionist in the general election of 1955. He became a member of the Law Reform Committee (Scotland) in 1954, and of the royal commission on the police (1960–62). After he entered the House of Lords he was much concerned with legislation, especially with bills dealing with the administration of justice. When he retired from full-time judicial work he became chairman of the university commissioners, dealing with university and college constitutions which had been affected by the Education Reform Act of 1988.

Fraser was a member of the queen's bodyguard for Scotland (Royal Company of Archers). In 1975 he became an honorary master of the bench at Gray's Inn, and in 1981 he was elected an honorary fellow of Balliol. He also became an honorary LLD of Glasgow (1970) and Edinburgh (1978).

Fraser was a competent yachtsman but his main hobbies were shooting and walking, which he undertook on his small estate at Tullybelton in Perthshire. On foot, indeed, the normal pace of his tall, spare frame over the ground was too rapid for most of his friends, who preferred to meet him when he had come to rest. Shy and reserved, he loved music and conversation. On 8 November 1943 he married (Mary Ursula) Cynthia Gwendolen, the only daughter of Colonel Ian Harrison Macdonell, of the Highland light infantry. They had one son. Fraser died in a road accident on 17 February 1989 en route from Tullybelton House in Bankfoot to Edinburgh, on the M90 between Perth and Edinburgh. He had been driving his car in blizzard conditions.   EMSLIE, *rev.*

Sources Lord Kilbrandon, *Balliol College Annual Record* (1989), 26–8 · records of the Faculty of Advocates, Parliament House, Edinburgh, Advocates' Library · *The Times* (20 Feb 1989) · *The Independent* (23 Feb 1989) · personal knowledge (1996)

Fraser, James, of Brae (1639–1699), Church of Scotland minister, was born in the parish of Kirkmichael, Ross-shire, on 29 July 1639, the son of Sir James Fraser of Brae (*d.* 1649), who held considerable estates in the north-west of Scotland and had sat in the Glasgow assembly of 1638, and Dame Beatrix Wemyss (*b. c.*1610, *d.* in or after 1685). Though initially a sickly infant he grew into a boisterous child who frequently played truant from his grammar school and—in an incident he later attributed to the workings of providence—only narrowly escaped from drowning after tumbling into a deep well.

His father's premature death, in 1649, robbed Fraser of a guiding influence and threw the administration of the family estates into utter chaos. Though he graduated MA from Marischal College, Aberdeen, in 1658 he was increasingly beset by crippling debts and became enmeshed in a bitter cycle of litigation against his own relatives. Having lost both his fortune and his reputation he experienced a protracted spiritual crisis in 1665–6, which led him to abandon his ambitious plans to study law and to seek, instead, consolation from his 'natural Melancholly' in religion (*Memoirs*, 155–7, 187). Though initially tempted by Quakerism he turned violently against that sect and in 1672 received ordination at the hands of those Church of Scotland ministers who had been forced out of their livings by the re-establishment of episcopacy. On 31 July that year he married Isobel, widow of William Hamilton, an Edinburgh merchant, and daughter of Sir William Gray of Pittendrum. They had two daughters, but Isobel died as the result of a sudden fever at the end of October 1676. Her death profoundly shocked Fraser, who dedicated the most tender and personal passages of his *Memoirs* to her virtues and untimely fate.

Fraser conceived of himself as a 'Watchman' or a 'keeper of men'—entrusted with safeguarding the souls of his fellow countrymen—and began a punishing schedule of open-air preaching and home visits in the southern shires of Scotland. Ministering to 'several Hundreds in the

Cities, and Thousands in the Country' (*Memoirs*, 336) in defiance of the ecclesiastical legislation of 1662, Fraser before long came to the attention of the authorities. A reward of 1000 merks was offered for his capture on 4 June 1674, and—having failed to present himself to the privy council—he was outlawed on 5 August 1675. He appeared alongside Donald Cargill at a 'numerous' field conventicle held on successive Sundays at Dovan Muir, Fife, on 4 and 11 June 1676, but his luck deserted him after he attempted to preach in Edinburgh. Betrayed by a serving maid he was taken captive on Sunday 28 January 1677 when a party of soldiers raided the town house in which he was conducting a service. Brought before the Scottish privy council and found to be 'a person of the most dangerous and pernicious principles and practises', Fraser was ordered to be transferred from the Tolbooth to the prison on the Bass Rock on 1 February 1677 (*Reg. PCS, 1676–8*, 104). He remained there until July 1679, using his time to study Hebrew, Greek, and Oriental languages. He also wrote the 'Treatise of faith' and some other miscellanies which were posthumously published as *A Treatise Concerning Justifying or Saving Faith* (Edinburgh, 1722) and *Good Tidings of Great Joy to All People* (London, 1873).

Having repeatedly petitioned the privy council for his release Fraser was lucky to secure the patronage of Sir Hugh Campbell of Caddell, who raised the bail of 10,000 merks required as surety before he might be released. Freed on 18 August 1679 Fraser was at pains to promise his future good conduct and distanced himself from those 'rash and unwarrantable' covenanters who had sought recourse to armed insurrection (*Memoirs*, 333). It was this refusal to involve himself in violent actions that later saved him from a far harsher fate. He did, however, return immediately to preaching illegally and by the winter of 1681 warrants had once more been issued for his arrest. Not wishing his friend to be heavily fined Campbell of Caddell brought him to answer the charges before the Scottish privy council. Sentenced to another term of imprisonment on 22 December 1681 Fraser was now subjected to a far harsher regime and was kept under close supervision at Blackness Castle. On 16 March 1682 he appealed again to the privy council and accepted an offer to go into exile upon the payment of a bond of 5000 merks.

Fraser sailed for England at the end of May 1682 and arrived in London on 16 June, then began to work as an unlicensed private preacher at the rate of 10s. per sermon. Informed against after preaching at the Glovers' Hall he was arrested on 21 July 1683 and was interrogated by the English privy council on 22–3 July. Though he criticized the murder of Archbishop Sharp he said that he had never borne arms against the king or taken the covenant, and denied being in contact with whig plotters in their 'Cabals or Coffee-houses'. He still refused to take the oaths of allegiance and supremacy. As a result of this, on 14 January 1685 he was committed to Newgate gaol. Surprisingly, Fraser found Newgate relatively congenial in comparison with his Scottish prisons and, though he rowed with the Quaker inmates and 'Free-willers', he wanted for nothing and declared that the other captives and the turnkeys were extremely civil (*Memoirs*, 384). Released after several months he returned to Scotland in early 1687 and lived quietly in Lothian and Tweeddale until the revolution of 1688–9 transformed his fortunes.

Fraser took over the running of the parish of Culross on 3 January 1689, depriving the former incumbents—who had refused to pray for the new sovereigns William and Mary—of their stipends. However, this action ignited a bitter feud within the region and earned him the enmity of the local magnate, Alexander Bruce, third earl of Kincardine. While Fraser attempted to claim the local church, as well as the meeting-house he had been allotted, the former ministers seized the parish plate and records. Matters came to a head in June 1689, when Kincardine attempted to lock Fraser out of the church. Hearing of this, soldiers from Lord Kenmure's regiment and local villagers forcefully reinstalled him, breaking down the door, and having Fraser preach to them 'in it all day' (*Reg. PCS, 1688–9*, 444–5). As an enthusiastic supporter of the new government the reconstituted Scottish privy council found in favour of Fraser and he was duly rewarded with custody of the church building, records, and plate. Thereafter he wrote a stout defence of the convention of estates in which he demonstrated how James VII and II had abdicated his throne—and he provided straw and oats for the horses of the garrison of Inverness. He was a member of the assembly of the Church of Scotland in both 1690 and 1692, and in January 1691, together with Campbell of Caddell, he successfully negotiated a reduction in the taxes levied on Inverness-shire.

On 22 October 1695 Fraser was elected to the presbytery of Inverness after a hotly disputed contest. However, his stipulation that one of the town's churches should be set aside for his exclusive use so that he might preach twice a day, both 'forenoon and afternoon' (*Fasti Scot.*, 6.461), led to a renewal of controversy and his eventual decision to remain at Culross. Fraser's second wife, Christian, formerly widow of Alexander Carmichael, minister of Pettinain, and daughter of John Inglis, minister of Hamilton, died childless about 1696. Fraser himself died at Edinburgh on the evening of 13 September 1699, having witnessed an eclipse of the sun that morning and having confided to his friends that he was 'full of the consolations of Christ' (*Memoirs*, ii). He left behind him a considerable number of unpublished theological works and reflections, which were assiduously harvested over the next 200 years by his adherents. These reveal him to have been a combative polemicist (see *Lawfulness and Duty of Separation*, 1744, and *Prelacy an Idol*, 1713) and a learned theologian (see *Meditations on Several Subjects in Divinity*, 1721). Despite his ultra-Calvinism he still managed to propose in his writings that redemption might be universal. This was enough to cause a major re-evaluation of his thought and career in the mid-eighteenth century and threw the Cameronian sect into grave dispute over his continued worth. However, Fraser's chief fame rests upon the publication of his memoirs (Edinburgh, 1738), which chart his spiritual development and which were intended to serve as a guide to the road to salvation.   JOHN CALLOW

Sources Memoirs of the life of the very Reverend Mr. James Fraser of Brea, minister of the gospel at Culross (1738) · Fasti Scot., new edn, vols. 5–6 · Reg. PCS, 3rd ser., vols. 4–7, 10, 13 · A. Whyte, James Fraser laird of Brea (1911) · CSP dom., 1683–5 · R. MacGregor, Memorials of the Bass Rock (1881) · J. Walker, The theology and theologians of Scotland (1872) · R. Wodrow, The history of the sufferings of the Church of Scotland from the Restauration to the revolution, 2 vols. (1721–2) · R. Douglas, The peerage of Scotland (1764), 5.531 · M. Grant, No king but Christ (1988)
Archives BL, Harley MSS 6543–6544, Add. MS 37996 · U. Edin., New Coll. L., sermon notes, MSS Box 53.8
Wealth at death over £1000; by 1680s Fraser had amassed £900 and had provided dowries for sisters; estate at Brae seems to have been the only one he continually maintained and in 1685 the lands round Inverness were valued at £100 p.a.: Reg. PCS, 1684–5, p. 525; Memoirs, 148–56, 310

Fraser, James (1645–1731), book dealer, was born in the manse at Petty, Inverness-shire, on 28 September 1645, the third son of nine children of the minister, Alexander Fraser (c.1606–1683?), of Kiltarlity, and his wife, Marjory or Margaret Clogie. From Inverness grammar school Fraser proceeded to King's College, Aberdeen, graduating MA in 1664. His next years are unclear; Professor Ker, his contemporary biographer, believed Fraser left for London directly.

In 1675 Fraser became tutor to Charles Beauclerk, Lord Burford, and Charles II's son by his mistress Nell Gwyn; from 1678 he was tutor (on John Evelyn's recommendation), to Charles, son of John, Lord Berkeley of Stratton; by 1682 he was fulfilling the same role with the children of the earl and countess of Yarmouth. Fraser accompanied family parties under official passes overseas (in 1683 to the Netherlands; in 1698 to France). By now established with annuities he married, on 18 September 1682, Mary Nourse, daughter of the squire of Woodeaton, Oxfordshire, and niece of the countess of Yarmouth. They had four children: James, William, Mary, and Martha.

Fraser held many commissions from Charles II to George I. He served as secretary and register of the Royal Chelsea Hospital for almost forty years from its foundation in 1682. The post was created for Fraser in lieu of settling a royal debt that Charles II owed Nell Gwyn. The post was undemanding as Fraser's book trade prospered, directed from his hospital apartments, his various Haymarket lodgings, and the coffee-house venues of hectic book auctions, where habitués like Robert Hooke gathered.

From 1688 until 1692 Fraser acted as licenser at Stationers' Hall. This position ended abruptly when he licensed Basilikon Doron, the work being ascribed not to James I but to a reviser. The royalist outcry necessitated Fraser's resignation. The publisher, John Dunton, considered that Fraser was 'kind and impartial', 'his compass of Learning was very large, his judgement correct and moderate, his imagination lively'; there was 'no Honester Licenser' (Life and Times of Anthony Wood, 4.44–50; Dunton).

Twenty letters between Fraser and his patron, Henry Hyde, second earl of Clarendon, show Fraser's industrious versatility. As Clarendon's London-based man of affairs, Fraser digested and relayed the news from London to Clarendon at Cornbury. Fraser reported on matters relating to the church, court, and parliament; Irish, French, and Dutch affairs; their East India Company investments; plus the social round and gossip. Characteristically, a letter of October 1690 closed with book news—the late duke of Lauderdale's giant library was to be auctioned; the manuscript catalogue was promised. Fraser's two letters to an unknown correspondent described the final hours of Charles II with great feeling. His single letter to Jean Le Clerc summarized British affairs tartly. Robert Wodrow, the Scottish churchman and antiquary, meticulously collected Fraser's letters over thirty years; Fraser guided Wodrow's religious histories through the presses, acting as his expediter, networker, and bookman.

Fraser's own library included rare classics on China, Tartary, Siam, Australia, and America. His ethnobotanical interests showed in letters: the 'Manga-paka tree', Sloane's beans, the heath pea or Karemyle (now Lathyrus linifolius) are discussed. Karemyle intrigued Fraser and Sir Robert Sibbald. Sibbald's great encyclopaedia, Scotia illustrata (1684), gave it more attention than any other Scottish species. Traditionally, during crop failures communities used Karemyle tuberules instead of foodstuffs and survived. Sibbald and Fraser urged further experimentation.

Letter writing remained Fraser's forte and enduring interest. A substantial archive was deposited by Fraser at King's College after its removal from Whitehall. Only at the beginning of the twenty-first century was it gradually becoming accessible to scholars. Some material indicates that Fraser was royal librarian. John Ker's Frasereïdes (1732), a classical funeral panegyric, noted him as royal librarian to James II, as did a letter from Fraser to Southwell (22 October 1685) in which he anticipated custody of the Whitehall Library. Yet there is more: the inscribed Fraser escutcheon in King's College Chapel noted him as royal librarian in 1724. A letter in Aberdeen brought Fraser a report on economic intelligence in Carolina from Jean Boyd, Huguenot refugee and Carolinan assemblyman. Addressed 'A Monsieur Fresur Bibliothecaire de la M[ajes]te Britannique a Londres', Fraser added '1691' (Aberdeen UL, MS K 257/9).

Evidence is also provided by the newly accessed Aberdeen catalogue. A sheaf of documents is headed 'Catalogue of all the mapps, draughts, designs[,] plans of towns, harbours, ports, citadells[,] sea-cards, journalls[,] itineraries, and other unprinted MSS in his ma[jes]tys closet at Whitehall. April. 27. 1685'. The catalogue is carefully classified in Fraser's best hand—including the titles of 568 books (Aberdeen UL, MS K 257/4). These five pieces of evidence make the case for Fraser the royal librarian when none was known.

Fraser donated numerous 'valuable', 'fine' books to King's College (1051 books are named, with several 'large parcels'; Pickard, 104), and the money for building its new library (c.£1600; completed 1725). Both King's and Whitehall libraries burnt down (c.1772/3 and 1698 respectively);

Fraser's achievement has been obscured by their destruction.

Fraser was also benefactor to the newly founded Society in Scotland for Propagating Christian Knowledge. Led by James Kirkwood it planned to print and distribute three thousand bibles in Irish and establish libraries in all highland parishes. Fraser funded the Inverness Library, its librarian / schoolmaster, and endowed twelve bursaries— all for Frasers or Invernessians. This library, the Inverness Kirk Session Library, survives in the town. Commemorating Fraser's sustained generosity to King's College, Aberdeen, the degree of *juris utriusque doctor* was conferred on him on 19 July 1725. Ker and David Mallet panegyrized the achievement in *Donaïdes* (1725).

Book trading and collecting always preoccupied Fraser. Delayed consignments reveal book orders for the king, nobles, and Fraser himself. Using tutorial tours and official passes he attended auctions where he examined and bought. Among those who gave Fraser commissions were Ashmole, Boyle, Clarendon, Evelyn, Hooke, Pepys, and Petty. Moving in court circles and on the fringes of the Royal Society, in 1687 Fraser donated a 'cappercail or cock of the wood' to the society museum (Ker, *Frasereïdes*, 51–3).

Fraser died in London on 26 May 1731, and he was buried in St Martin-in-the-Fields. In his will, dated 10 September 1730, Fraser made bequests to his family (excluding his estranged son-in-law, Grangehill), King's College, the burgh of Inverness, and charity schools. His massive library of 3612 books was auctioned in 1732.

BRIAN MOFFAT

Sources J. R. Pickard, 'Dr. James Fraser—library's administration, 1722–31', *A history of King's College Library, Aberdeen, until 1860* (1987), 44–155 · J. M. Henderson, 'James Fraser, 1645–1731', *Aberdeen University Review*, 25 (1937–8), 138–46 · C. Innes, ed., *Fasti Aberdonenses … 1494–1854*, Spalding Club, 26 (1854) · P. J. Anderson, 'Note on heraldic representations at King's College, Old Aberdeen', *Proceedings of the Society of Antiquaries of Scotland*, 23 (1888–9), 80–86 · N. Hodgson and C. Blagden, *The notebook of Thomas Bennet and Henry Clements: with some aspects of book trade practice* (1956) · O. Payne, *A catalogue of the library of the very learned James Fraser, JUD, lately deceased* (1732) · M. J. Cormack, *Inverness Kirk Session Library* (1979) · A. Fergusson, ed., *Major Fraser's manuscript: his adventures … with Simon Fraser, Lord Lovat, 1696–1737*, 2 (1889) · *CSP dom., 1666–1704* · Aberdeen UL, Special Collections, MSS K 257/1–52 · will, PRO, PROB 11/644, sig. 119 · P. J. Anderson, ed., *Officers and graduates of University and King's College, Aberdeen, MVD–MDCCCLX*, New Spalding Club, 11 (1893) · P. J. A. [P. J. Anderson], *Historical notes on the libraries of the Universities of Aberdeen* (1893) · R. S. Rait, *The universities of Aberdeen: a history* (1895) · J. Ker, *Donaïdes* (1725) · J. Ker, *Frasereïdes* (1732) · *The correspondence of Henry Hyde, earl of Clarendon, and of his brother Lawrence Hyde, earl of Rochester*, ed. S. W. Singer, 2 (1828) · R. T. Gunther, *Early science in Oxford*, 10: *The life and work of Robert Hooke* (1935), 117, 142, 147, 166, 170, 175, 183 · *The diary of Robert Hooke … 1672–1680*, ed. H. W. Robinson and W. Adams (1935), 322, 393, 426 · *The correspondence of the Rev. Robert Wodrow*, ed. T. M'Crie, 3 vols., Wodrow Society, [3] (1842–3) · N. Macpherson, 'On the chapel and ancient buildings of King's College, Aberdeen', *Archaeologia Scotica* (1890), 416, 437–8 · *GM*, 1st ser., 2 (1732), 586–7 · *The life and errors of John Dunton*, [rev. edn], 1, ed. J. B. Nichols (1818), 266–7 · *The life and times of Anthony Wood*, ed. A. Clark, 4, OHS, 30 (1895) · *Seventh report*, HMC, 6 (1879), 531–6 [letters of Robert, earl of Yarmouth, 1669–1683] · *The manuscripts of the House of Lords*, 4 vols., HMC, 17 (1887–94), vol. 1, pp. 145–6 · *Report on the manuscripts of the earl of Egmont*, 2 vols. in 3, HMC, 63 (1905–9), vol. 2, pp. 145–51 · *Manuscripts of the earl of Egmont: diary of Viscount Percival, afterwards first earl of Egmont*, 3 vols., HMC, 63 (1920–23), vol. 1, pp. 9, 92–5 · *Report on the manuscripts of the marquis of Downshire*, 6 vols. in 7, HMC, 75 (1924–95), vol. 1, pp. 147–8 · *Report on the manuscripts of Allan George Finch*, 5 vols., HMC, 71 (1913–2003), vol. 4, pp. 391, 462 · C. G. T. Dean, *The Royal Hospital Chelsea* (1950) · D. Ascoli, *A village in Chelsea: an informal account of the Royal Hospital* (1974) · W. H. Godfrey, *The parish of Chelsea*, ed. P. Norman and others, 4, Survey of London, 11 (1927) · P. J. A. [P. J. Anderson], *The grammar school and Royal Academy of Inverness* (1907) · A. Mitchell, ed., *Inverness Kirk: session records, 1661–1800* (1902) · R. L. Emerson, *Professors, patronage, and politics: the Aberdeen universities in the eighteenth century* (1992) · J. J. Carter and J. H. Pittock, eds., *Aberdeen and the Enlightenment* (1987) · S. Gleissner, 'Reassembling a royal art collection for the restored king of Great Britain', *Journal of the History of Collections*, 6 (1994), 103–15 · *The Petty–Southwell correspondence, 1676–1687*, ed. marquis of Lansdowne [H. E. W. Petty-Fitzmaurice] (1928) · S. Thurley, *Whitehall Palace: an architectural history of the royal apartments, 1240–1698* (2000) · T. Birch, *The history of the Royal Society of London*, 4 vols. (1756–7), vol. 4, p. 549 · C. Blagden, *The Stationers' Company: a history, 1403–1959* (1960)

Archives U. Aberdeen L., MSS K 257/1–52 | BL, letters to James Petiver, MSS 3321, fols. 130, 215; 4066, fol. 344 · BL, letters to Sir Hans Sloane, MSS 4036, fols. 224, 250; 4039, fol. 38 · BL, letters to Lady Yarmouth, MSS 36988, fols. 197, 227; 27448, fol. 128v · NL Scot., Robert Wodrow collection, copy-letter to Sibbald, Adv. MS 33. 5. 19 · U. Glas., corresp. with the earl of Clarendon, MS Hunter 73 (T. 3. 11)

Likenesses oils, 1726, U. Aberdeen; repro. in Dean, *Royal Hospital* · portrait, repro. in Mitchell, ed., *Inverness Kirk*, facing p. 196; formerly, High Church Hall, Inverness, 1904

Wealth at death over £1450: will, PRO, PROB 11/644, sig. 119

Fraser, James (1700–1769), Church of Scotland minister and theologian, was born at the manse of Alness in Ross-shire, where his father, **John Fraser** (d. 1711), was minister from 1696 until his death. The father, a native of the highlands, graduated at Aberdeen in 1678. He attended dissenting meetings in London, while lodging with an Anabaptist, and was seized with Alexander Shiels in 1684. He was sent to Leith and then, chained with Shiels, to Edinburgh. On 18 May 1685 he was imprisoned at Dunnottar Castle, near Aberdeen. After three months of terrible suffering he and his wife, Mrs Jean Moffat, were among a hundred people shipped to New Jersey, where they were to be disposed of for the benefit of the laird of Pitlochie. On arrival Fraser was set free, Pitlochie and his wife having died of fever during the voyage. He went to New England and preached as a licentiate at Waterbury, Connecticut. He returned to Scotland after the revolution of 1688 and was ordained on 23 December 1691 as the minister of Glencorse, near Edinburgh, moving in 1695 to Alness. He died at Alness on 5 November 1711.

James Fraser, his son, was a man of considerable theological learning, a conscientious minister (though noted more for preaching the law than for providing consolation), and an able biblical critic. He was remembered as a humble man, a good friend, and a faithful counsellor. He was licensed by the presbytery of Chanonry on 6 November 1723 and was ordained on 17 February 1726, becoming minister of Alness. Local lairds organized opposition to his settlement, and, the church doors being locked against him, his ordination service took place in a corner of the churchyard. He married Jean Macleod (d. 1778), 'a cold, unfeeling, bold, unheeding worldly woman' (Kennedy, 37) who all but starved him, leaving Fraser to pick up food that a friend would leave for him at a secret place on one of his walks.

In 1774 Fraser published at Edinburgh *The Scripture Doctrine of Sanctification*, a very copious exposition of chapters 5-7 of the epistle to the Romans. He contended that John Locke misunderstood chapters 5 and 6 to be addressed to gentile converts only, and chapter 7 to be addressed to Jewish converts only. In making his case he embarked upon an elaborate refutation of the Arminian views of Grotius, Henry Hammond, Locke, Daniel Whitby, and others. The burden of his complaint was that Locke failed to implement his stated policy of reading the intention and scope of biblical books as wholes. The subtext was Fraser's defence of evangelical orthodoxy against the encroachments of moderatism. His book retains historical significance as an able and elaborate example of Calvinist biblical interpretation. Fraser was a regular correspondent of the ecclesiastical historian Robert Wodrow, to whom he suggested the preparation of his work on witchcraft. He died on 5 October 1769.

W. G. BLAIKIE, *rev.* ALAN P. F. SELL

Sources *DNB* · A. Fraser, 'A short account of the author', in J. Fraser, *The scripture doctrine of sanctification* (1774) · J. Kennedy, *The days of the fathers in Ross-shire*, 2nd edn (1861); repr. (1979) · *Fasti Scot.* · A. P. F. Sell, 'John Locke's highland critic', *Records of the Scottish Church History Society*, 23 (1987-9), 65-76; repr. in A. P. F. Sell, *Dissenting thought and the life of the churches* (1990), chap. 8 · A. P. F. Sell, 'Fraser, James', *DSCHT*

Fraser, James (1712/13-1754), East India Company servant and collector of oriental manuscripts, was the second son of Alexander Fraser (*d.* 1733) of Reelig, near Inverness, and his wife, Catherine, daughter of Hugh Fraser of Belladrum. Fraser was appointed a writer to the East India Company's Bombay presidency in 1730. He served for some ten years at the company's trading posts at Mocha in the Yemen and at Cambay and Surat, in western India, where he seems to have spent most of his time. Clearly a gifted linguist, Fraser not only mastered the vernacular languages used around the Arabian Sea, but took lessons in literary ones as well, in Avestan from Parsis, Sanskrit from Brahmans, and Persian from learned Muslims. He made a large collection of manuscripts, coins, and miniatures, a set of which, consisting of royal portraits, was presented to Alexander Pope, who passed it on to the Bodleian Library at Oxford.

Fraser returned to Britain about 1740 and worked up some of his material into a book published in 1742 as *The history of Nadir Shah, formerly called Thamas Kuli Khan, the present emperor of Persia; to which is prefixed a short history of the Moghol emperors*. It contains a map of the Mughal empire and part of Tartary. It was the first book in English treating of the Persian ruler Nadir Shah, 'the scourge of God', who had invaded India in 1737-8. It is important not only for a first-hand account of contemporary events probably written by William Cockill, who had served in Persia, but also for historical texts and original documents translated from Persian by Fraser.

Having married Mary (*d.* 1795), only daughter of Edward Satchwell, of Warwickshire, on 21 February 1742, Fraser applied to return to India. He was appointed to the company's council at Surat and, in view of his linguistic skill, was given special responsibility for negotiating at the court of the Mughal governor of the city. Fraser was in India during the Jacobite uprising of 1745, in which his elder brother Alexander was charged with being a captain in the Jacobite forces; he himself was accused of Jacobitism on his return from India but was exonerated by the government. His last years at Surat were turbulent ones. He became embroiled in bitter quarrels with his colleagues and with the company's governor at Bombay. He was accused of forming a cartel with the Indian merchant who acted as his agent and an official at the governor's court to fix prices to the disadvantage of other traders at Surat. He made vigorous counter-accusations, but was dismissed from the service in 1748 and returned to Britain the following year.

Although he complained that he had lost heavily through his premature recall, Fraser had still succeeded in 'improving his fortune by trade' (*Scots Magazine*) and was able to build 'a very pretty box' on his family land at Easter Moniack (*Highlands and Islands*, 211). He died there on 21 January 1754, leaving ambitious plans for further translations unfulfilled. He left a widow, a son, and three daughters.

After his death Fraser's collection of about 200 oriental manuscripts, including Avestan and Sanskrit, which he had purchased at Surat, Cambay, and Ahmadabad, was bought from his widow for the Radcliffe Library at Oxford; it was transferred to the Bodleian Library on 10 May 1872. His claim that his forty-one 'Sanskerrit' manuscripts 'formed the first collection of that kind ever brought into Europe' ('A catalogue of manuscripts', appended to Fraser, *History of Nadir Shah*, 37-9) appears to be valid, though single Sanskrit manuscripts had reached England and France even earlier. It was in order to inspect Fraser's Avestan manuscripts that the famous French orientalist Anquetil Duperron visited Oxford in 1762, when brought as a prisoner of war to England.

A. A. MACDONELL, *rev.* P. J. MARSHALL

Sources J. Fraser, *The history of Nadir Shah* (1742), preface · L. Lockhart, *Nadir Shah* (1938), 304-6 · W. Irvine, 'Note on James Fraser, author of *The history of Nadir Shah* (1742)', *Journal of the Royal Asiatic Society of Great Britain and Ireland* (1899), 214-20 · J. Fraser to the directors, 18 Nov 1747, BL OIOC, E/4/461, 95-110 · Bombay public consultations, 19 Jan 1748, BL OIOC, P/341/15 · J. Fraser's petition, 15 Oct 1742, BL OIOC, E/1/31, no. 9 · committee of correspondence report on petition, 4 Nov 1742, BL OIOC, D/20, fol. 59 · A. Mackenzie, *History of the Frasers of Lovat* (1895) · J. Fraser to J. Cleland, [n.d.], Bodl. Oxf., MS Top. Oxon b.43 · J. Fraser's memorial, 12 Jan 1750, BL OIOC, E/1/35, nos. 162-5 · *Scots Magazine*, 16 (1754), 50-51 · *Highlands and islands*, Pevsner (1992) · Burke, *Gen. GB* (1914) · BL, Add. MSS 35447-35448

Archives LPL, catalogue of MSS · NRA Scotland, priv. coll., papers | BL OIOC, corresp. series, petitions, letters, and MSS, E/1, E/4

Likenesses Panton, portrait, 1750, priv. coll.

Fraser, James (*b.* in or after **1805**, *d.* **1841**), publisher, was from an Inverness family. Through shrewd application, his business prospered at 215 Regent Street, London. Early in 1830 William Maginn, a disgruntled former contributor to *Blackwood's Edinburgh Magazine*, and Hugh Fraser, a wealthy if briefless barrister, brought their proposal for a new tory literary miscellany, modelled on *Maga*, to James Fraser who had at that time also been considering establishing a magazine. The first monthly issue of *Fraser's Magazine for Town and Country* appeared in February 1830 with Maginn as editor (until September 1836) and chief contributor, writing 'for almost every issue' to December 1840 (Houghton, 309). Asserting its superiority in independence, wit, and intelligence in opposition to sentimentalism, it became the most talked-about magazine in London, and regally nicknamed itself Regina, the queen of the magazines. The first year's circulation of 8700 copies was as large 'as that of any half-crown periodical of the day' (Thrall, 14).

Until his death James Fraser served on the editorial committee, solicited articles, established payment rates (including occasional pay to poor authors for work never to be published), and became 'proprietor by purchase' (Gulliver, 67). He took risks on works such as *Sartor Resartus*, which he serialized in ten numbers of the magazine but at a reduced rate of pay, after rejecting it as a book. Thomas Carlyle felt contempt for his British publisher for a time, finally regretting his death, at 'no more than thirty-five years old' (Kaplan, 269), because of his consequent reduced earnings with Chapman and Hall. Regular contributors to *Fraser's Magazine* gathered periodically round the table in the publisher's back room 'to wine and dine and exchange ideas' (Mannin, 153), creating its rollicking style of personal attack and high-spirited joking. Daniel Maclise's well-known portrait of the Fraserians, for the most part men like Maginn, 'if less brilliant and less scurrilous' (Houghton, 309), appeared in the January 1835 issue, omitting women contributors but portraying Southey, Coleridge, Lockhart, and David Brewster, who contributed little or nothing. John Galt, James Hogg, David Moir, Percival Banks, T. C. Croker, Abraham Heraud, Thomas Wright, Barry Cornwall, and Robert Willmott appeared along with Carlyle and William Makepeace Thackeray, whose first regular means of support was the magazine. Over a twenty-year period (1834–53) Thackeray contributed numerous articles and serials including 'The Yellowplush Papers' and 'The Luck of Barry Lyndon'. Two contributors also served as editors: Francis Mahony (Father Prout) (1836–7) and E. V. Kenealy (1838–41). Maginn's ongoing series (1830–38) of caricatures, the Gallery of Illustrious Literary Characters, in which he wrote the letterpress for Daniel Maclise's pen-and-ink drawings, was to foreground 'for the first time in publishing history, a large number of contemporary figures (81) sketched in portrait and prose' (Houghton, 305). The collection was last reproduced in volume form in 1883.

Maginn's editorship ended as a result of his savage review of Grantley Berkeley's novel *Berkeley Castle* and concomitant marital difficulties. On 3 August 1836 Berkeley sought the name of the anonymous reviewer and reported Fraser as saying 'it was not his custom to reveal

the names of his contributors … I will deliberate on your request, and write to you my determination' (Berkeley, 56). For this, Berkeley severely beat Fraser with a weighted whip. Cross actions were tried, with Fraser obtaining £100 damages for assault, and Berkeley obtaining 40s. for libel; both paid court fees. Fraser died on 2 October 1841 at Argyll Street, London, after a lingering illness, which had resulted from the beating.

As a publisher, Fraser was liberal and straightforward in business transactions and had good literary taste and judgement. G. W. Nickisson succeeded him as proprietor and probably editor in late 1841 or early 1842. In 1847 *Fraser's Magazine* was transferred to John W. Parker of West Strand with the younger Parker serving as editor from July. In October 1882 *Fraser's* was subsumed by *Longman's Magazine* when the firm was sold.

BARBARA QUINN SCHMIDT

Sources M. M. H. Thrall, *Rebellious Fraser's: Nol Yorke's magazine in the days of Maginn, Thackeray, and Carlyle* (1934) · [W. E. Houghton], 'Fraser's Magazine for Town and Country, 1830–1882', *Wellesley index*, 2.303–19 · J. D. Vann, 'Fraser's Magazine', *British literary magazines*, ed. A. Sullivan, [2]: *The Romantic age, 1789–1836* (1984), 171–5 · W. Bates, *The Maclise portrait-gallery of 'illustrious literary characters'* (1883) · J. A. Froude, *Thomas Carlyle: a history of the first forty years of his life, 1795–1835*, 2 (1906) · G. F. Berkeley, *My life and recollections*, 2 (1865) · W. Jerdan, *The autobiography of William Jerdan: with his literary, political, and social reminiscences and correspondence during the last fifty years*, 4 vols. (1852–3), vol. 3 · H. S. Gulliver, *Thackeray's literary apprenticeship*, reprint of 1934 edn (1969) · E. Mannin, *Two studies in integrity: Gerald Green and the Rev. Francis Mahony ('Father Prout')* [1954] · *The letters and private papers of William Makepeace Thackeray*, ed. G. N. Ray, 1 (1945) · P. L. Shillingsburg, *Pegasus in harness: Victorian publishing and W. M. Thackeray* (1992) · D. R. Dean, 'John W. Parker', *British literary publishing houses, 1820–1880*, ed. P. J. Anderson and J. Rose, DLitB, 106 (1991), 233–6 · P. Leary, 'Fraser's Magazine and the literary life, 1830–1847', *Victorian Periodicals Review*, 24 (1994), 105–26 · *The collected letters of Thomas and Jane Welsh Carlyle*, ed. C. R. Sanders, K. J. Fielding, and others, [30 vols.] (1970–) · J. Turpin, 'Daniel Maclise, Disraeli, and *Fraser's Magazine*', *Éire–Ireland*, 15/1 (1980), 46–63 · W. J. Graham, *English literary periodicals* (1930) · F. Kaplan, *Thomas Carlyle: a biography* (1983)

Likenesses D. Maclise, group portrait, pen-and-ink lithograph, 1835 (*The Fraserians*), BM; repro. in Thrall, *Rebellious Fraser's*, frontispiece · portrait, repro. in Thrall, *Rebellious Fraser's*, 12

Fraser, James (1818–1885), bishop of Manchester, was the eldest son of James Fraser, a retired Indian merchant, of a branch of the family of Fraser of Durris and his wife, Helen (d. 1880), a daughter of John Willim, solicitor, of Bilston, Staffordshire. He was born on 18 August 1818 at Prestbury, Gloucestershire. His father lost money in ironstone mines in the Forest of Dean, and dying in 1832 left his widow and seven children poorly provided for. Fraser's early years were chiefly spent at his maternal grandfather's at Bilston, but when his father removed to Heavitree, Exeter, he was sent to school there. In 1832 he was educated at Bridgnorth School, Shropshire, and from 1834 to 1836 at Shrewsbury School. Though entered at Balliol, and an unsuccessful competitor for scholarships at Corpus Christi College, Oxford, he was elected a scholar of Lincoln College and matriculated on 16 March 1836, and went into residence in January 1837. He was a strong athlete, and had a passion for horses, but he had no money for

James Fraser (1818–1885), by Sir John Everett Millais, 1880

the latter. As an undergraduate he lived a very reclusive life, and no doubt acquired then his remarkable self-mastery. In 1837 he failed to win the Hertford scholarship, but in 1838 he almost won, and in 1839 did win, the Ireland scholarship. In November 1839 he took a first class in final honour schools, graduated BA on 6 February 1840, and was elected a fellow of Oriel. At this time he appeared to his friends as shy and immature. At the end of his year of probation at Oriel he became reader of sermon notes, and he was also tutor from 1842 to 1847; he graduated MA on 18 May 1842, and in January 1844 became subdean and librarian. Though in no respect a great tutor, his sympathies gave him unusual popularity among the undergraduates.

On 18 December 1846 Fraser took deacon's orders and, having indulged himself with a last fortnight's hard hunting in Leicestershire, forswore that pleasure for the rest of his life. He was involved in some parochial work in Oxford, was ordained priest in 1847, and in July 1847 accepted the college living of Cholderton, Wiltshire, which on this occasion was made tenable with a fellowship. He took pupils until 1856, and for twenty years was occasionally an examiner at Oxford and elsewhere. On 12 December 1851 he preached his first sermon as select preacher at Oxford, and was select preacher subsequently in 1861, 1871, 1877, and, though he did not preach any sermon, in 1885. In 1854 he became examining chaplain, and subsequently in 1858 chancellor, to W. K. Hamilton, bishop of Salisbury. Several of his sermons at Salisbury were published. On Bishop Hamilton's recommendation

he was appointed assistant commissioner to the royal commission on education in 1858 for a district of thirteen poor-law unions. In 1860 he resigned his fellowship, on accepting the rectory of Ufton Nervet, Berkshire. In this parish, where he accomplished many parochial improvements, he developed his great capacity for business and for leadership. In March 1865 he was appointed a commissioner to report on education in North America, and was in Canada and the United States from May to October. His report, made in 1866, stamped him as a man who was destined for ecclesiastical promotion, and in that year Lord Cranborne made him the offer of the bishopric of Calcutta, which he declined. In 1867 he prepared for the commission on the employment of children in agriculture, on the recommendation of the home secretary, a masterly report on the south-eastern district. On 3 January 1870, expressly on the grounds of his authority on educational questions, Gladstone offered him the bishopric of Manchester; he was consecrated on 25 March.

Fraser's new sphere was the most difficult of its kind in the kingdom. It was almost a new diocese. Its first bishop, James Prince Lee, had lived a retired and a comparatively inactive life. The machinery of diocesan organization was defective, and little was being done for church extension. During Fraser's episcopate 99 new churches were consecrated, 20 churches were rebuilt, 109 new district parishes were created, and the whole fabric of diocesan machinery—conferences, Board of Education, and building society—was created and brought to working order.

In addition to the usual episcopal duties Fraser threw himself into almost every social movement of the day. He was to be seen going about the streets on foot, his robe-bag in his hand; he addressed meetings several times a day; he spoke to workmen in mills and to actors in theatres; he was diligent in attending his diocesan registry; he was a member of the governing bodies of Manchester and Shrewsbury grammar schools and of Owens College, visitor of the high school for girls and of the commercial school, and president of the College for Women. 'Omnipresence', said his foes, 'was his forte, and omniscience his foible.' He earned for himself the name of 'bishop of all denominations'. In 1874 he was chosen to arbitrate between the employers and employees in the Manchester and Salford painting trade, and his award, made on 27 March, secured peace for the trade for two years. He was again arbitrator in March 1876; in 1878, during the great north-east Lancashire cotton strike, the employees offered to refer the dispute to him, but the employers refused. He always protested against the unwisdom of strikes and lockouts, and sought to make peace between the disputants. He was the first person outside the co-operative body to draw attention to that movement, having described the Assington Agricultural Association in his report on agriculture in 1867. When the Co-operative Congress was held in Manchester in 1878, he presided on the second day, and appeared in 1885 at the congress held at Derby.

Fraser was never a professed theologian, but his views were on the whole of the old high-church school. He had little sympathy with the Tractarian high-churchmen, and in all matters of practice he was extremely liberal, and more disposed to take a legal than an ecclesiastical view of such matters. His first appearance in convocation was to second Dean Howson's motion in favour of the disuse of the Athanasian creed; his first speech in the House of Lords was on 8 May 1871, in support of the abolition of university tests. He said, characteristically, to his diocesan conference in 1875: 'If the law requires me to wear a cope, though I don't like the notion of making a guy of myself, I will wear one.' Yet he was fated to appear as a religious persecutor, to his own infinite distress. When first he went to Manchester the extreme protestant party looked to him for assistance in suppressing ritualism in the diocese. For some time he succeeded in pacifying them, and it was not until after the Public Worship Regulation Act was passed in 1874, of the policy of which he approved, that strife began. In 1878 complaint was made to him of the ritual practice of the Revd S. F. Green, the incumbent of Miles Platting. He disregarded this, but the Church Association forced him into action, Green being eventually, in 1881, imprisoned for contempt of court. Gladstone's initiative behind the scenes led to his release. This famous case continued with a further suit against Fraser, decided in his favour by Baron Pollock on 10 and 11 December 1883.

On 24 April 1880 Fraser's mother, who had hitherto lived with him, died. Three months before, he had married Agnes Ellen Frances Duncan (to whom he had become engaged in 1878), daughter of John Shute Duncan of Bath, sometime fellow of New College, Oxford. In September 1885 Fraser suffered from congestion of the veins of the neck, caused by a chill. He was obliged to curtail his work, and was thinking of resigning his bishopric when, on 22 October, he died suddenly in the bishop's palace, Manchester. He was buried at Ufton Nervet in his mother's tomb on 27 October. His death was universally lamented. Nonconformists of all denominations, with the Jewish and Greek congregations of Manchester, sent flowers to his funeral. Huge crowds attended a memorial service in Manchester on the day of his burial.

J. A. HAMILTON, rev. H. C. G. MATTHEW

Sources T. Hughes, *James Fraser, second bishop of Manchester: a memoir, 1818–1885* (1887) · J. W. Diggle, *The Lancashire life of Bishop Fraser* (1887) · *Manchester Guardian* (23–9 Oct 1885) · *The Guardian* (28 Oct 1885) · J. Bentley, *Ritualism and politics in Victorian Britain: the attempt to legislate for belief* (1978) · Gladstone, *Diaries* · C. Bullock, *The lives of three bishops* (1889)
Archives Manchester, Chetham's Library, sermons, notes, and MSS | BL, corresp. with W. E. Gladstone, Add. MSS 44388–44389 · LPL, corresp. with Lord Selborne · LPL, corresp. with A. C. Tait · Notts. Arch., corresp. with Harry Cowgill
Likenesses J. E. Millais, oils, 1880, Man. City Gall. [*see illus.*] · T. Woolner, statue on monument, 1887, Albert Square, Manchester · Debenham & Gabell, photograph, repro. in Diggle, *Lancashire life of Bishop Fraser* (1889) · J. Forsyth, recumbent effigy on monument, Manchester Cathedral · J. Galloway, lithograph (after G. E. Tilson), BM · Lock & Whitfield, woodburytype photograph, NPG; repro. in T. Cooper, *Men of mark: a gallery of contemporary portraits* (1878) · W. Wontner, oils, Oriel College, Oxford · photogravure, NPG · prints, NPG
Wealth at death £89,724 1s. 6d.: resworn probate, Feb 1886, CGPLA Eng. & Wales (1885)

Fraser, James Baillie (1783–1856), traveller and artist, was born on 11 June 1783 in Edinburgh, the eldest of six children of Edward Satchwell Fraser (1751–1835) and his wife, Jane, daughter of William Fraser of Balnain. James was brought up on the Scottish family estate at Reelig, near Inverness, and tutored for his later education in Edinburgh. From 1799 until 1811 he was in Guiana overseeing the family's sugar plantation at Berbice, apart from a return home from 1806 following illness.

In January 1813 Fraser sailed for India. Though shipwrecked off Madras, he reached Calcutta by October. His intention was to help pay off family debts, but his initial trading partnership in Calcutta failed after only a year. In January 1815 he left for Delhi to meet his brother William *Fraser (1784–1835), political and recruiting agent for the British forces engaged in the Nepal War. They met at Nahan, and for the following months James became engrossed in sketching the scenery of the Himalayas, at that time little known to Europeans. He toured the region, seeking the sources of the rivers Jumna and Ganges. Twenty of his landscapes were published as coloured aquatints in London in 1820 under the title *Views in the Himala Mountains* and an account of his journey was published concurrently as *Journal of a tour through part of the snowy range of the Himala mountains and to the sources of the rivers Jumna and Ganges*. He also employed Indian artists from Delhi to make portrait drawings of local recruits and Gurkhas. These, which he collected with the co-operation of his brother, are now regarded as the finest of the company school genre. On his return to Calcutta in 1816 Fraser joined another partnership in the shipping business, but it was his artistic activities which he took more seriously under the guidance of the professional artists William Havell (1782–1857) and George Chinnery (1744–1852). By 1820 he had completed the drawings for *Views of Calcutta and its Environs*, published in London, with twenty-four coloured aquatints, between 1824 and 1826. In 1820 he crossed India via Delhi and Rajputana to Bombay, sketching and gathering geological information with a view to publication.

From Bombay, Fraser accompanied the East India Company diplomat Dr Andrew Jukes to Persia, sailing to Bushehr and thence via Shiraz to Esfahan, where Jukes died late in 1821. Fraser proceeded alone, traversing lawless and difficult territory on his way between Tehran, Mashhad, Tabriz, and finally home via Tiflis, reaching London in 1823. At every stage he sketched and gathered information, much of it included in his *Narrative of a Journey into Khorasan in the Years 1821 and 1822* (1825) and *Travels and Adventures in the Persian Provinces of the Southern Banks of the Caspian Sea* (1826).

On 4 September 1823 Fraser married Jane Tytler, daughter of Alexander Fraser Tytler, Lord Woodhouselee. In succeeding years he wrote a series of historical novels, among them *The Kuzzilbash, a Tale of Khorasan* (1828), *The Persian Adventurer* (1830), *The Highland Smugglers* (1832), and *Tales of the Caravanserai* (1833). In 1834 he contributed *An Historical and Descriptive Account of Persia* as volume 15 of the Edinburgh Cabinet Library.

drawing, 1833, NPG [see illus.] • W. Drummond, lithograph (after E. U. Eddis), BM, NPG

James Baillie Fraser (1783–1856), by William Brockedon, 1833

When Russian moves in Turkey caused British alarm in 1833, the Foreign Office chose Fraser to travel to Persia to report on Russian influence in the region. Between December 1833 and May 1835 he travelled over 10,000 miles, mostly on horseback, the real purpose of his mission kept secret. After submitting memoranda to the Foreign Office on the Russian threat, Fraser was appointed companion to three Persian princes making an official visit to London in 1836. This done, he accompanied them homeward as far as Constantinople. Fraser published lengthy accounts of his experiences with the princes and of his former Persian travels, and two romances: *Allee Neemro, the Buchtiaree Adventurer* (1842) and *The Dark Falcon* (1844). His last publication, in 1851, was the *Military Memoir of Lieut. Col. James Skinner, C. B.*, an account of the life of Skinner, of Skinner's horse fame, based on their conversations years previously in Delhi and on Skinner's own journal.

Fraser spent his last years carrying out improvements on his Scottish estate. He died there, childless, on 23 January 1856.   TOBY FALK

Sources Fraser of Reelig MSS • M. Archer and T. Falk, *India revealed: the art and adventures of James and William Fraser, 1801–35* (1989) • D. Wright, 'James Baillie Fraser: traveller, writer and artist, 1783–1856', *Iran*, 32 (1994)
Archives NRA Scotland, priv. coll., corresp. and papers | NA Scot., letters to Sir John McNeill • NL Scot., letters to Blackwood & Sons • U. Durham L., letters to Viscount Ponsonby
Likenesses H. Raeburn, oils, *c.*1799, repro. in Archer and Falk, *India revealed*, fig. 9; priv. coll. • W. Brockedon, black and red chalk

Fraser, James Stuart, of Ardachy (1783–1869), army officer in the East India Company, was the youngest son of Colonel Charles Fraser of that ilk (*d.* 1795), of Ardachy, Inverness-shire, a scion of the house of Lovat, who fought as a marine officer under Admiral Hawke, and afterwards entered the Madras army, and died a colonel in command of a division at Masulipatam on 5 May 1795. Charles Fraser married Isabella Hook, and they had six sons and three daughters; the eldest son, Hastings Fraser, distinguished himself as a king's officer in India, and died a general and colonel 86th (Royal County Down) regiment in 1854. James Stewart Fraser (as his baptismal register has it) was the youngest child, and was born at Edinburgh on 1 July 1783. He was educated in a school at Ham, Surrey, and afterwards at Glasgow University, where he showed a predilection for languages and astronomy. A Madras cadet of 1799, he was posted as lieutenant to the 18th Madras native infantry on 15 December 1800.

Fraser served in 1807 as assistant to Colonel Marriott on an escort conveying the Mysore princes to Bengal, and was aide-de-camp to Sir George Barlow, governor of Madras, at the time of the 1809 mutiny of the Madras officers. He became a regimental captain on 6 November 1809, and private secretary to the government of Madras on 9 May 1810. He accompanied the Madras division in the expedition against the Île de France (Mauritius) in the same year, as deputy commissary, and was on the personal staff of Colonel Keating, 56th regiment, in the landing at Mapou and the advance on Port Louis. He was subsequently appointed barrack-master at Fort St George (29 March 1811), town-major of Fort St George and military secretary to the governor (21 May 1813), and commandant at Pondicherry (28 October 1816). In 1816–17 he was commissioner for the restitution of French and Dutch possessions on the Coromandel and Malabar coasts. This duty was facilitated by his ability to speak French and he was thanked and commended by the government for his role in the long negotiations. He became major on 10 December 1819, and lieutenant-colonel on 1 May 1824.

While commanding at Pondicherry, Fraser married, at Cuddalore, on 18 May 1826, Henrietta Jane (*d.* 1860), daughter of Captain Stevenson, Admiralty agent for the eastern coast of India, and grandniece of General Stevenson, who commanded the nizam's subsidiary forces at Assaye and Argaon. She was twenty years Fraser's junior; they had a large family. In 1828 Fraser was deputed to discuss the claims of the French at Mahé, and the same year was appointed special agent for foreign settlements. He became brevet colonel on 6 November 1829. On 12 February 1834 he was appointed secretary to the government in the military department. He was present in several actions during the conquest of Coorg, and carried out the negotiations that brought the war to a close. He was appointed resident at Mysore and commissioner of Coorg on 6 June 1834, and assumed charge of the Mysore residency in October following. On 26 September 1836 he was appointed regimental colonel 36th Madras native infantry (his previous regimental commissions had been in the 18th native infantry). He was appointed resident at Travancore and Cochin (5 January 1836), and officiating resident at Hyderabad (1 September 1838), and was repeatedly thanked by government for his services. He appears, however, to have interfered in the disputes of the Syrian Christians at Travancore and afterwards, and so to have incurred the Madras government's displeasure. On 28 June 1838 he became a major-general, an exceptional case of rapid promotion by seniority.

On 31 December 1839 Fraser was appointed resident at Hyderabad, and was vested with a general superintendence over the post offices and post roads of the nizam's territory. In 1842 he successfully suppressed sepoy insubordination at Secunderabad. He remained at Hyderabad, which he considered the political centre of India, for fourteen years. Repeatedly, but with little success, he urged the Indian government to be firmer with the nizam over intrigue, corruption, and mismanagement. However, latterly he dissented from the high-handed measures of Lord Dalhousie as governor-general. His strained relations with Dalhousie led Fraser to resign his Hyderabad appointment in 1852 and return to Britain. He later revisited India, but held no further public appointment. He became lieutenant-general on 11 November 1851, and general on 2 June 1862. Except for the war medal, he received no mark of distinction for his long and distinguished services.

Fraser was tall (over 6 feet 3 inches) and spare-built. He was cultured, a good rider, and a keen sportsman. His official acts apparently showed scrupulous integrity. Fraser, who for some time had been totally blind, but otherwise retained his faculties, died at his home, Verandah House, Twickenham Park, Middlesex, on 22 August 1869.

H. M. CHICHESTER, rev. ROGER T. STEARN

Sources Memoirs and correspondence of General J. S. Fraser, ed. H. Fraser (1885) • The Times (29 Aug 1885) • review, The Athenaeum (21 Feb 1885), 244–5 • private information, 1889 [India office] • Burke, Gen. GB • T. A. Heathcote, The military in British India: the development of British land forces in south Asia, 1600–1947 (1995) • P. Lawson, The East India Company (1993) • Boase, Mod. Eng. biog. • S. Wolpert, A new history of India (1993) • CGPLA Eng. & Wales (1869)
Archives NA Scot., letters to Lord Dalhousie | PRO, corresp. with Lord Ellenborough, 30/12
Likenesses portrait, repro. in Fraser, ed., Memoirs and correspondence
Wealth at death under £14,000: probate, 15 Sept 1869, CGPLA Eng. & Wales

Fraser, John (d. 1609), theologian, was the fourth son of Alexander Fraser and grandson of Sir William Fraser of Philorth. He was probably a Queen Mary scholar in Paris when in 1578 he was given licence to be ordained by the local bishop. He enrolled in the university in 1586 and became prominent in its affairs, as proctor of its German nation in 1595 (a position he held for the fifth time in 1605), as quaestor (bursar) in 1588 and 1607, as dean of the nation in 1607, and as assistant dean in 1608. He suggested new procedural rules for elections to the rectorship, and

himself held that office in 1597; a fine coat of arms decorates the entry recording this in the Paris proctor's book. He had taken the degree of bachelor of divinity by 1598, and became prior of St Nicolas in Noyon, north of Paris. As prior he was present at James Leith's marriage in 1605, and for a time he acted as preceptor in the household of Nicolas Viole, formerly a maître des requêtes in the king's government. As rector Fraser welcomed Henri IV returning from the wars. He also cultivated the papal diplomats Innocenzo del Bufalo and Matteo Barberini, composing a congratulatory address to the former in 1604, and in the following year dedicating to the latter a poem hailing the election of Pope Paul V, and he helped poor Roman Catholics taking refuge in Paris. Two papal subsidies were paid him as he made strenuous efforts to win over protestant Scots, one of whom, a son of the earl of Mar, was transferred out of harm's way to Orléans. Fraser probably died about Easter 1609, as George Strachan wrote about the loss to the Scottish Catholics in Paris in April that year, and again in 1610. He wrote at least two polemical works arguing against protestantism: the one, published in Paris in 1604 and reprinted in a revised edition in the following year, was addressed to 'a Gentleman of Qualitie'; the other, perhaps printed at Paris and published in 1605, was directed to 'the ministers of Great Britanie'. The commentaries on Aristotle attributed to him by Dempster probably circulated only in manuscript. Fraser was buried at the church of St François in Paris.   JOHN DURKAN

Sources A. Fraser, The Frasers of Philorth, 3 vols. (1879) • CSP Rome, 1572–8, no. 777 [ordination licence, 1578] • Bibliothèque Nationale, Paris, MS Lat. 9956, fol. 20v [incorporated 1586]; MS Lat. 9957, fol. 10 [coat of arms] • Archives Nationales, Paris, H3 2589, fols. 215, 224, 227, 228, 246 • Archives Nationales, Paris, H3 2590, fols. 153, 219, 228 • C. E. Du Boulay, Historia universitatis Parisiensis, 6 (Paris, 1673), 896, 904 • Archives Nationales, Paris, Y, 135/4066, 144/2549 • B. Barbiche, ed., Correspondance du nonce en France Innocenzo del Bufalo, évêque de Camerino (1601–1604) (Rome, 1964), 238, 563, 586, 593, 778 • G. Levi della Vida, George Strachan: memorials of a wandering Scottish scholar of the seventeenth century, Third Spalding Club (1956), 9ff.

Fraser, John (d. 1711). See under Fraser, James (1700–1769).

Fraser, John (bap. 1750, d. 1811), botanist, was born in Inverness-shire, Scotland, where he was baptized at Tomnacross near Kiltarlity on 14 October 1750, the fourth of seven children of Donald Fraser Down, a grounds officer to Simon Fraser, master of Lovat. 'Down' is said to be a self-designated patronymic that indicated the father's hair colour. It had no legal status and was never used by John. His mother was probably Mary, née McLean of Cragganmore, Inverness-shire. Fraser moved to London between 1770 and 1776, married Francis Shaw in 1778, and settled as a hosier and draper at Paradise Row, Chelsea. The Frasers had two sons, John (bap. 1780) and James Thomas (bap. 1782), both of whom were involved in their father's botanical efforts in the 1800s.

Having acquired a taste for plants from visiting the Chelsea Physic Garden of the Society of Apothecaries, Fraser visited Newfoundland and collected plants there between 1783 and 1786. From September 1786 until January 1788, he explored Georgia and the Carolinas, where he travelled briefly with the French botanist André Michaux, obtained many new plants for importation into England, and worked closely with Thomas Walter, an amateur botanist from South Carolina. On his return to London, he arranged the publication of Walter's *Flora Caroliniana* (1788), the first regional flora from eastern North America to use the Linnaean binomial Latin system for scientific nomenclature.

After a brief visit to Paris in 1789, where he sold his new American plants to scientists such as Charles L'Heritier and to aristocrats such as the duke of Orléans, Fraser returned to Chelsea and established his American nursery on King's Road at Sloane Square. He then made his third, fourth, and fifth visits to North America in 1790, 1791, and 1796, on each occasion returning through Charleston, South Carolina, which served as the base of his explorations of the south-east. From 1791 until at least 1800, he and his brother James (*bap.* 1753) shipped plants to England from their growing gardens at Charleston and on nearby Johns Island. Having introduced various American pines, oaks, azaleas, rhododendrons, and magnolias, in 1796 he visited St Petersburg, where Catherine II purchased a collection of plants from him. He then introduced into England the Tartarian cherries. Revisiting Russia in 1797 and 1798, he was appointed botanical collector to the tsar Paul I. Believing the tsar had commissioned him to collect plants in America, he returned to the United States in 1800, taking with him his elder son, John. After an extended trip through Virginia, Kentucky, and Tennessee, they sailed to Cuba, where in 1801 they were assisted by the botanists Alexander von Humboldt and Aimé Bonpland.

When Fraser returned to Russia, Alexander I declined to reimburse him for the America expedition; he was finally paid 6000 roubles for his American plants in 1803, after he had made two journeys to Russia to petition for remuneration. In conjunction with his sister, Christy (*bap.* 1756), he then introduced to England the weaving of hats from the leaves of a Cuban palm, an industry that was supported by Queen Charlotte and that was for a time successful. By 1807 he had begun his seventh and last visit to America, again taking his son John. During this sojourn, they discovered Catawba rhododendron in bloom on Roan Mountain along the Tennessee–North Carolina border. Their introduction of this hardy plant into England formed the basis for many of the best hybrid rhododendrons subsequently developed by British horticulturists. While returning from the Carolina Mountains to Charleston, Fraser was thrown by his horse and broke several ribs, an injury from which he never recovered. He returned, with many new plants, in 1810 to his Chelsea nursery, which, however, was never very successful. He died at Sloane Square on 26 April 1811 and was buried in the old burial-grounds of St Luke's, Chelsea.

Fraser's herbarium, which also contained many of Thomas Walter's plant specimens, was presented in 1849 to the Linnean Society by his son; the collection is now at the Natural History Museum in London. Fraser's name is commemorated in a number of American plants, such as the Fraser magnolia and the Fraser fir. Described as enterprising, indefatigable, and persevering, Fraser was an enthusiastic self-promoter, ardent explorer, and important botanical collector. Many of the plants he introduced into England were described and illustrated in Curtis's *Botanical Magazine* and in Edwards's *Botanical Register*.

G. S. BOULGER, *rev.* MARCUS B. SIMPSON JUN.

Sources R. Hogg, *Journal of Horticulture*, 8 (22 July 1852), 250–51 · W. J. Hooker, 'Biographical sketch of John Fraser, the botanical collector', *Companion to the Botanical Magazine*, 2 (1836), 300 · J. C. Loudon, *Arboretum et fruticetum Britannicum, or, The trees and shrubs of Britain*, 1 (1838) · B. Henrey, *British botanical and horticultural literature before 1800*, 2 (1975) · parish register (baptism), Kiltarlity, Inverness, 14 Oct 1750 · parish register (burial), Chelsea, St Luke's, 1811 · M. B. Simpson, S. Moran, and S. W. Simpson, 'Biographical notes on John Fraser (1750–1811): plant nurseryman, explorer, and royal botanical collector to the czar of Russia', *Archives of Natural History*, 24 (1997), 1–18 · Old parochial registers, General Register Office for Scotland, Edinburgh · marriage records, St Luke's parish, Chelsea, LMA · *GM*, 1st ser., 81/1 (1811), 596–7 · private information (2004)

Archives Academy of Natural Sciences, Philadelphia, herbarium · Musée National d'Histoire Naturelle, herbarium · NHM, MSS · Russian Academy of Science, St Petersburg, herbarium | Linn. Soc., J. E. Smith herbarium · NHM, Thomas Walter herbarium

Likenesses J. Hoppner, portrait, repro. in Simpson, Moran, and Simpson, 'Biographical notes on John Fraser (1750–1811)' · lithograph (after portrait by H. Raeburn?), repro. in Hooker, 'Biographical sketch'

Fraser, Sir John (1760–1843), army officer, was the second son of William Fraser of Park, near Fraserburgh, factor to George Fraser, fourteenth Lord Saltoun, and his wife, Katherine, daughter of John Gordon of Kinellar. On 29 September 1778 Fraser was appointed lieutenant in the 73rd highlanders, afterwards the 71st Highland light infantry. He was later on board Rodney's fleet with a second battalion (afterwards disbanded) of this regiment during the actions with the Spanish Caraccas fleet under Don Juan de Langara and at the relief of Gibraltar. He served at the defence of Gibraltar in 1780–82, until the loss of his right leg, his second wound during the defence, compelled him to return home.

Fraser was captain of a garrison invalid company at Hull in 1785–93, and at the outbreak of the French Revolutionary War raised men for an independent company. He became major on 28 August 1794, and lieutenant-colonel, royal garrison battalion, on 1 September 1795. He served at Gibraltar in 1796–8, part of the time as acting judge advocate and civil judge. On 1 January 1800 he was appointed colonel of the Royal African Corps, composed of military offenders from various regiments pardoned on condition of life-service in Africa and the West Indies (see *N&Q*, 3rd ser., 8, 1865, 134). With this corps he served on the west coast of Africa in 1801–4, and made a brave but unsuccessful defence of Goree in Senegal, against a superior French force from Cayenne. Goree was compelled to surrender on 18 January 1804, but not before the enemy's loss exceeded the total strength of the defenders at the outset.

After his exchange Fraser was appointed to command an expedition against Senegal, which never started. He became a major-general in 1808, served in Guernsey in 1808–9, and in the latter year he was appointed to the staff at Gibraltar. Fraser commanded that garrison until the arrival of General Campbell. He was then sent to negotiate for the admission of British troops into the Spanish fortress of Ceuta (on the Moroccan coast opposite Gibraltar); afterwards he commanded the British garrison there until his return to England on promotion to lieutenant-general in 1813. In 1809, in recognition of its distinguished conduct in the West Indies, the Royal African Corps was reorganized as the Royal York rangers, another Royal African Corps being formed in its place. Fraser retained the colonelcy of the rangers until the regiment was disbanded after the peace. He was made lieutenant-governor of Chester Castle in 1828, and GCH in 1832, and was a member of the consolidated board of general officers. He became general in 1838.

Fraser married, first, on 15 April 1790, Everilda, daughter of James Hamer of Hamer Hall, Lancashire, and they had one son and two daughters, one of whom, Everilda (d. November 1840), married General Francis Rawdon Chesney (1789–1872). His second marriage, about three years before his death, was to Miss A'Court. Fraser was described by his kinsman Lord Saltoun as a brave, chivalrous, upright old soldier. He died at Campden Hill, Kensington, London, on 14 November 1843 and was buried at St Barnabas' Church, West Kensington.

H. M. Chichester, rev. Roger T. Stearn

Sources J. Philippart, ed., *The royal military calendar*, 3rd edn, 2 (1820) · A. Fraser, *The Frasers of Philorth*, 3 vols. (1879) · *GM*, 2nd ser., 21 (1844) · T. C. W. Blanning, *The French revolutionary wars, 1787–1802* (1996) · M. Harding, ed., *The Victorian soldier: studies in the history of the British army, 1816–1914* (1993)

Fraser, John. *See* Frazer, John (*c.*1809–1852).

Fraser, John Simon Frederick (1765–1803). *See under* Fraser, Archibald Campbell, of Lovat (1736–1815).

Fraser, Lindley Macnaghten (1904–1963), broadcaster and economist, was born on 14 August 1904 in Edinburgh, the son of Norman Fraser, a minister of the United Free Church of Scotland, and of his wife, Cecilia Craigie Fraser. His schooling started at George Watson's College, Edinburgh, and after the family moved to Liverpool in 1913 he went to the Liverpool Institute High School. He was a classical exhibitioner at Balliol College, Oxford, where he took a first class in honour moderations in 1924 and a first class in *literae humaniores* in 1926. In 1925 he was elected treasurer of the Oxford Union Society, becoming librarian and then president in 1926. Later that year he was awarded the Procter visiting fellowship at Princeton University in the USA and in 1927 the Eastman fellowship at Brookings School of Economics in Washington.

In 1928 Fraser became a fellow and praelector in economics at Queen's College, Oxford. For his first book, *Protection and Free Trade* (1932), Brookings awarded him a doctorate of philosophy. Among his pupils at that time was Harold Wilson, later prime minister. An Oxford contemporary recalled Fraser as 'a man of most acute mind and versatile gifts' (McCallum, 314). His ten years as an Oxford

don were remarkably successful and, together with Oliver Franks, 'these two brilliant but very different tutors carried all before them' (ibid., 315).

On 5 December 1932 Fraser married Elspet Mackenzie (*b.* 1907/8), the daughter of Dr Samuel Ridley Mackenzie of Montreal. They had two daughters. The marriage was dissolved in 1945. Fraser became the Jaffrey professor of political economy at Aberdeen University in 1935 and two years later his second book was published: *Economic Thought and Language*, which offered a systematic critique of the terminology used in economic analysis. The work was translated into several foreign languages.

Fraser's career changed fundamentally in 1940 when his friend and former Oxford colleague Sir Frederick Ogilvie, then director-general of the BBC, persuaded him to join the staff of the BBC's German Service on secondment from Aberdeen University. Although he had never before even seen the inside of a broadcasting studio, he had been invited in December the previous year to do a talk in German for the German Service, which had been set up only in September 1938. It turned out that he talked German very clearly but with a distinct accent—R. B. McCallum recalled his 'strong, clear, Edinburgh German' (McCallum, 314). This was perfectly acceptable to the BBC, which believed that the German public suspected people speaking from London with too good an accent. They thought of them as German refugees—which meant, from their point of view, traitors to Germany. Fraser joined the staff as a German news commentator on 13 February 1940. When George VI visited the BBC external services shortly afterwards, he asked Fraser how he had qualified to broadcast to the Germans. There was widespread laughter at Fraser's reply, 'By teaching economy to the Aberdonians'.

Later that year Fraser started working with the German news Electra House liaison unit, more formally known as the department for enemy propaganda. That body was subsumed in 1942 into the political warfare executive. Having close links with the BBC, it moved into Bush House, in London, the base for the BBC German Service. Fraser's regular commentaries became a feature of the BBC German Service programmes throughout the war years, commanding an ever more attentive and appreciative audience in Germany. He believed not merely that there was no need for bitterness towards Germans as such, but also that by stressing the point some might be persuaded at least to join in the struggle against the common enemy. Fraser maintained that attitude throughout the war.

After the war Fraser decided to resign his chair at Aberdeen University and to remain with the BBC. He became the German Service director in October 1947 and head of German programmes in February 1948. His frequent visits to the Federal Republic of Germany and his continued, regular broadcasts made him widely known and respected throughout the German-speaking countries of Europe. He was made an OBE in 1958. On 21 March 1959 he married Elizabeth Scott, *née* Marks (*b.* 1914/15), a sculptor.

All his adult life Fraser had a deep love of music. He was a keen and talented amateur pianist; he set Shakespeare's sonnets to music and was a well-informed critic of the opera. He was a most enjoyable companion: fond of good living (especially good beer), of hard and honest argument, good jokes, and above all of people. It was this character, with its intellectual integrity, its humanity, and high-spirited humour, that made up Fraser's broadcasting personality.

Fraser died of lung cancer at St Thomas's Hospital, Lambeth, London, on 10 March 1963. RICHARD HEWLETT

Sources A. Briggs, *The history of broadcasting in the United Kingdom*, 3 (1970) · G. Mansell, *Let truth be told* (1982) · M. Tracey, *A variety of lives* (1983) · *BBC handbook* (1961) · staff files, BBC WAC · *The Times* (11 March 1963) · *WWW, 1961–70* · *Ariel* [BBC staff magazine] (March 1963) · d. cert. · m. certs. · R. B. McCallum, 'Lindley Macnaghten Fraser', *Oxford Magazine* (23 May 1963)

Archives BBC WAC, MSS | FILM IWM FVA, performance footage | SOUND IWM SA, performance recording

Likenesses photograph, pubd 1941, Hult. Arch.

Wealth at death £10,725 15s. 0d.: probate, 29 July 1963, *CGPLA Eng. & Wales*

Fraser, (William) Lionel (1895–1965), merchant banker, was born on 15 June 1895 in London, the second of the four children of Harry and Alice Fraser (*d*. after 1931). His father, a Scot, was butler to Gordon Selfridge, founder of Selfridges department store.

Fraser's schooling began and ended at St Mary Abbots higher grade church school, Kensington, although he periodically attended other schools as his parents moved around the country. Thanks to a scholarship, he enrolled, at the age of thirteen, at Pitman's School where he received an intensive commercial training, studying French, German, Spanish, shorthand, typing, and accounts.

Fraser's working life began in June 1911, aged sixteen, when he joined Bonn & Co., a small bank that specialized in foreign exchange transactions. He handled correspondence and bookkeeping at a salary of £70. A member of a territorial regiment, he was mobilized on the outbreak of war and commissioned in 1915, before being invalided out because of a knee injury sustained during a game of football. For the rest of the hostilities, he worked in naval intelligence.

The early 1920s saw turbulent conditions in the foreign exchange market, providing lucrative opportunities for astute operators. In 1921, following the acquisition of Bonn & Co. by Helbert, Wagg & Co., he was made head of Helbert, Wagg's foreign exchange department. With George Bolton, later a leading figure at the Bank of England and elsewhere in the City of London, as his second in command, Fraser established Helbert, Wagg as a leading participant in the London foreign exchange market, much enhancing the firm's standing. In the mid-1920s, he switched to UK equities, both trading and underwriting, and soon developed a formidable reputation as a corporate financier. He was made a director of Helbert, Wagg in 1934. In 1931, aged thirty-six, he married Cynthia Elizabeth Walter and they had two sons and a daughter. A devoted family man, he lived at home looking after his mother until his marriage.

In the Second World War, sponsored by Montagu Norman, governor of the Bank of England, whose personal investments he managed, Fraser worked at the Treasury, his responsibilities including liaison with the governments-in-exile of occupied countries. He was created CMG in 1945 for his services. These connections led to his appointment as the Bank of England's representative to the State Bank of Morocco.

Returning to Helbert, Wagg after the war, Fraser was appointed deputy chairman in 1946. The same year, he also became chairman of the newly formed Issuing Houses Association. In 1954, he was made chairman of Helbert, Wagg. A highly regarded figure in the City, his reputation sprang from his expertise in the provision of advice about corporate finance. He played an influential role in a number of take-overs. For instance, he was called upon to act as an impartial mediator in the negotiations that followed Sears's controversial hostile take-over bid for Watneys in 1959.

Fraser received many invitations to sit on outside boards. His directorships included the engineering firm Tube Investments, Royal Exchange Assurance, and also Spicers, the paper makers. In 1950 he became chairman of boiler-makers Babcock and Wilcox, a Helbert, Wagg client. He devoted up to a third of his working time to the Babcock chairmanship, which he held until 1960.

In the 1950s Fraser also served as chairman of Thomas Tilling, of which he had been a director since 1942. This appointment stemmed from the untimely demise of his predecessor, Frederick Heaton, in May 1949. Just before his death, Heaton had negotiated the sale of Tilling's bus and garage interests, its major business, to the government body charged with the nationalization of British transport. It fell to Fraser to deploy these resources to develop Tillings into a new entity, a diversified industrial holding company, then a relatively novel concept in the UK. By 1962, when he stepped down, the activities of Tillings's thirty or so main subsidiaries were indeed diversified, comprising building supplies, electrical wholesaling, engineering, glassware manufacture, textiles, insurance, vehicle distribution, and publishing. A small and specialized head office staff provided guidance and supervision, especially in relation to finance and strategy. But hands-on management was decentralized, being conducted at subsidiary level. This textbook conglomerate structure proved successful, Tillings's business expanding rapidly and profitably.

Although not the originator of the proposal for a merger between Helbert, Wagg and Schroders, Fraser actively pursued the idea. There is no doubt that he expected to become deputy chairman of the new entity and was disappointed when Gordon Richardson was appointed in May 1962. He resigned a few months later, having been recruited to set up the London subsidiary of the French merchant bank Paribas.

At a height of 6 feet 4 inches, Fraser never went unnoticed. The newspaper publisher Hugh Cudlip described him in a thumbnail sketch as a tall, straightforward, handsome, commanding figure. He had a forceful and energetic personality and a strong will to win, sometimes earning him enemies. But among his friends, including his obituarist in *The Times*, he was cherished for a 'warm heart, a gift for friendship, and a gay attitude to life ... He was an ardent Christian Scientist and his deep religious convictions added a fundamental integrity and seriousness of character. All these things made him an inspiring leader' (*The Times*, 6 Jan 1965).

Business absorbed most of Fraser's time and energy, although in 1945–50 he served as a Conservative member of Chelsea borough council and toyed with the idea of standing for parliament. He and his wife were keen collectors of abstract art, and Fraser served as a trustee of the Tate Gallery. He enjoyed club life, being a member of six clubs, including the Garrick, the Travellers', and White's. Lionel Fraser died of bronchial pneumonia and cancer on 2 January 1965 at his residence, 30 Charles Street, Westminster, London, aged sixty-nine.

RICHARD ROBERTS

Sources W. L. Fraser, *All to the good* (1963) · R. Roberts, *Schroders: merchants and bankers* (1992) · C. Shaw, 'Fraser, William Lionel', *DBB* · *The Times* (6 Jan 1965) · d. cert.
Likenesses photograph, Banque de Paris et des Pays-Bas, London · photographs, repro. in Fraser, *All to the good*
Wealth at death £136,983: probate, 31 March 1965, *CGPLA Eng. & Wales*

Fraser, Louis (*fl.* 1831–1866), naturalist and museum curator, is of unknown birth and parentage. The form of his education is likewise obscure, but from his writings he appears to have been a careful naturalist with limited scope and ambitions. He married Mary Ann Harrison on 17 February 1844; no record of their son Oscar's birth can be found, but a daughter, Laura, was baptized at Manchester Cathedral in August 1869, apparently twenty-five years after the Frasers married (and possibly after Fraser's death). He worked for some fourteen years in the museum of the Zoological Society of London, from where in 1839 his earliest extant letter was sent (to the anatomist Richard Owen, accompanying preparations of the anuses of emu and rhea).

Fraser left to become naturalist to the Niger expedition of 1841–2; he spent time on the island of Fernando Po afterwards, where he collected many new species. Fraser then returned to the Zoological Society, from where he corresponded frequently with Edward Smith Stanley, thirteenth earl of Derby—who owned an extensive private menagerie and museum at Knowsley Hall, near Liverpool—concerning the purchase of live animals. In 1846 Fraser left the Zoological Society's employ when Lord Derby sent him to north Africa to collect specimens, a trip frustrated by the weather and by bandits. In 1848 Fraser became temporary conservator at Knowsley, and set to work compiling extensive catalogues of Derby's magnificent zoological collections. In November 1850, through his aristocratic patron, he received the appointment of consul at Ouidah, west Africa (he was also vice-consul for the kingdom of Dahomey), later moving on to collect in South America in 1857–9.

Fraser returned to England and became a dealer in bird specimens, opening shops successively at Knightsbridge and in Regent Street; but these proved unsuccessful. He next obtained employment at Woodward's Gardens at San Francisco, which he reportedly quitted for some unknown occupation on Vancouver Island. Later he returned to England, as it is known that he was living in London in June 1866. His son, Oscar L. Fraser, was in 1888 recorded as being an assistant in the Indian Museum, Calcutta.

In addition to numerous papers for the Zoological Society, of which he was elected a corresponding member in 1857, Fraser was the author of *Zoologia typica* (1849), which included figures of twenty-eight mammals and forty-six birds, all newly described. It was his intention that the work should appear at regular intervals, but financial circumstances compelled him to bring it to a premature close. Fraser was also responsible for the *Catalogue of the Knowsley Collections*, of which he published the first (and only) part in 1850. He wrote the type descriptions of many new mammals and birds himself, among which was that of *Palaeornis derbyana*, the Derbyan parakeet, which he named after the thirteenth earl. Fraser himself was honoured by other naturalists, who named a squirrel, a lizard, and a small bird after him. The date and circumstances of his death are not known but nothing is heard of him after 1866.

CLEMENCY THORNE FISHER

Sources birds and mammals archives, Liverpool Museum · letters to Richard Owen, NHM · National Museums and Galleries on Merseyside, Archives department, Edward Smith Stanley, thirteenth earl of Derby MSS · Liverpool Central Library, Edward Smith Stanley, thirteenth earl of Derby MSS · Knowsley Hall Library, Edward Smith Stanley, thirteenth earl of Derby MSS · *Thacker's 1888 Indian Directory*, 210 · IGI
Archives Liverpool Museum, birds and mammals archives | Knowsley Hall Library, thirteenth earl of Derby MSS · Liverpool Central Library, thirteenth earl of Derby MSS · National Museums and Galleries on Merseyside, Archives dept., thirteenth earl of Derby MSS · NHM, letters to Richard Owen

Fraser, Marjory Kennedy- (1857–1930), folklorist, was born at 50 High Street, Perth, on 1 October 1857, the daughter of David *Kennedy (1825–1886), a great singer of traditional Scots songs, and his second wife, Elizabeth Fraser (b. 1827); their family eventually numbered eleven children. The Kennedys were originally from Rannoch, settled in Perth, moved to Edinburgh and then lived in London, 1862–6. In 1866 they began a series of tours in Britain, Australia, New Zealand, Canada, the United States, and South Africa to take traditional Scots songs to emigrants and their descendants; they often travelled under fairly primitive conditions by coach or wagon, owing to the expense of taking such a large party by rail. Marjory trained as a piano accompanist in Edinburgh and made her first public appearances at Lanark in 1870, and the Music Hall, Edinburgh, in 1871. Visits for vocal training were made to Milan and Paris, where she was also taught the piano by Mathilde Marchesi. Disaster struck when three of the youngest members of the family died in a fire at the Théâtre des Italiens at Nice on 23 March 1881, a blow from which their father never recovered—he died at Stratford, Ontario, on tour in October 1886. Meanwhile

Marjory Kennedy-Fraser (1857–1930), by John Duncan

Marjory, whose maternal grandfather had spoken Gaelic in his youth, developed an interest in Gaelic songs, and, encouraged by Professor J. S. Blackie, took lessons in Gaelic and Gaelic songs from the poetess Mary MacKellar, who was then living in Edinburgh. In the spring of 1887 she married a cousin of her mother's, Alexander (Alec) Fraser, soon to be appointed headmaster of Alan Glen's Technical School at Glasgow; his health gave way from overwork and he died on 9 November 1890, leaving her with two children, David and Patuffa. She earned her living by teaching music in Edinburgh and as music critic for the *Edinburgh Evening News*. She had a special interest in Wagner and Richard Strauss and visited Bayreuth in 1899. With her close associate, Professor Frederic Niecks, she founded the Edinburgh Musical Education Society in 1900.

In 1895 Marjory Kennedy-Fraser was asked to give a lecture recital on Celtic music, which involved presenting examples of the music of the various Celtic peoples. One work that impressed her was Ducoudray's collection of traditional Breton songs, which had been commissioned by the French government. In 1905, the last year of the life of the celebrated folklorist Father Allan McDonald, she paid what became a famous visit to the island of Eriskay, which lies in the sound between South Uist and Barra. She went at the urging of John Duncan the artist, and perhaps partly because an American folk-song collector, Evelyn Benedict, was already visiting the island, and another, Amy Murray, was expected to come in the autumn. She returned to Eriskay in 1907 and in that year gave her first recital based on her researches. She took with her to Eriskay 'a very small and easily portable graphophone' and

recorded songs on wax cylinders. In 1907–8 and subsequently she recorded on Barra. The outcome of Mrs Kennedy-Fraser's visits to the Outer Hebrides were the three volumes of *Songs of the Hebrides* (1909, 1917, 1921), *Sea Tangle* (1913), *From the Hebrides* (1925), and *More Songs of the Hebrides* (1929). All except the last were compiled with the help of Kenneth MacLeod, a young theological student from the island of Eigg, who was found for her by Professor Donald MacKinnon as Gaelic amanuensis. MacLeod told the writer of this memoir that when he saw what she was doing to the songs he had wanted to withdraw from the collaboration, but that MacKinnon had persuaded him to continue. Her last visit to Barra was made in 1927.

Songs of the Hebrides established Marjory Kennedy-Fraser's reputation; lecture tours and recitals in London and the United States followed. In 1911 she was given a civil-list pension to enable her to continue her work. She wrote the libretto for Granville Bantock's opera, *The Seal Woman*, and sang the part of Mary Macleod in it. Patronized by W. B. Yeats and Lady Gregory, the friend of Patrick Geddes and John Duncan, she became a central figure in the Celtic revival, and *Songs of the Hebrides* is one of its enduring monuments. *Songs of the Hebrides* took such a hold on the public mind that any criticism of it was considered almost an act of *lèse-majesté*, and Mrs Kennedy-Fraser was wrongly given the credit of having saved the songs from oblivion. For a long time the only criticism of her method was made in a paper, 'Half a century of vocal Gaelic music', read by Malcolm MacFarlane to the Gaelic Society of Inverness on 27 March 1925:

> Mrs Kennedy Fraser's Collection is marred by the tunes being adapted to English words and by the liberties taken with their original forms; and they have, in cases, to be timed anew for the Gaelic singer. Also, the new words are often conceived in a false Gaelic spirit for which there is no valid excuse. Miss Frances Tolmie's excellent collection of Skye airs can be relied on as giving the tunes in accordance with the forms in which she found them. This collection is also too little used by singers. It was not, like some recent publications, conceived in a mercenary spirit for upper and middle class English consumpt, but was given for preservation to the English Folksong Society. It is Number 16 of that Society's Transactions. (*Transactions of the Gaelic Society of Inverness*, 1927)

It must be said in Mrs Kennedy-Fraser's favour that her *Songs of the Hebrides* did bring about an appreciation among English speakers of the beauty of the hitherto despised oral tradition of the highlands and islands.

In 1929 Marjory Kennedy-Fraser published a lively autobiography, *A Life of Song*. She was operated on for breast cancer in 1925 and died, from a recurrence of it, at 6 Castle Street, Edinburgh, on 22 November 1930.

J. L. CAMPBELL

Sources M. Kennedy-Fraser, *A life of song* (1929) • personal knowledge (2004) • E. Bassin, *The old songs of Skye: Frances Tolmie and her circle* (1977) • J. L. Campbell, *Scots Magazine*, 68 (1958), 307–14 • F. Collinson, 'Songs of the Hebrides', *The Scotsman* (6 Jan 1958) • J. L. Campbell and F. Collinson, *Hebridean folksongs*, 3 vols. (1969–81) • M. F. Shaw, *Folksongs and folklore of South Uist*, 2nd edn (1977) • b. cert.

Archives U. Edin. L., corresp. and papers | SOUND J. L. Campbell Recordings, Isle of Canna

Likenesses J. Duncan, oils, 1931, Scot. NPG · J. Duncan, oils, Scot. NPG [*see illus.*]
Wealth at death £5436 18s. 6d.: probate, 26 Feb 1931, CCI

Fraser, Olive (1909–1977), poet, was born on 20 January 1909 at 160 Victoria Road, Torry, Aberdeen, the daughter of Roderick Fraser, the son of a Flemington ironmonger and farmer, and Elizabeth Jane King, also from a farming family. Olive Fraser was brought up in the north-east coast seaport of Nairn, for the most part by her beloved great-aunt, Ann Maria Jeans; her parents had emigrated to Australia in the years soon after her birth. She was educated in Nairn at Millbank School and at Rose's Academical Institution, where she distinguished herself in practically all subjects (except mathematics).

In 1927 Olive Fraser went to Aberdeen University to study English at King's College, and in her first year there (and again in her fourth) she was winner of the prestigious Calder prize for English verse. In 1933, two years after leaving Aberdeen with her honours MA, she took up a scholarship to Girton College, Cambridge. In Cambridge, the first inklings of what would turn out to be years of ill health made it even harder for the 24-year-old to settle to an undergraduate discipline. In 1935 she sealed her charismatic reputation as carefree poet and rather too fascinating personality—'she wasted the time of promising young scholars' (Shire, 8), her tutor grudgingly said of her time at Girton—by becoming the first woman to win the chancellor's medal for English verse, with her poem 'The Vikings'.

Poor health, and a thyroid condition that for much of the next four decades went misdiagnosed, were to shape the rest of Olive Fraser's life. The years following her education are a catalogue of pennilessness, recurring terrible illness, and a variety of day jobs, ranging from training polo ponies to making furniture. During the Second World War, Fraser joined the cipher department of the Royal Navy, and worked as a watch officer in Liverpool and as a landgirl in Nairn. In 1952 she denied her Presbyterian roots and converted to Roman Catholicism. After short stints as a librarian (one of them at the Bodleian in Oxford, which she left under a cloud), she spent the fifties, sixties, and seventies moving from temporary home to temporary home, and spending a great deal of time in hospitals between London and the north-east of Scotland, suffering miserable health and diagnosed as schizophrenic. Finally in 1968, at Cornhill Hospital in Aberdeen, she was correctly diagnosed as having hypothyroidism, myxoedema, and for the first time in thirty years her condition improved, leaving her enjoying 'wonderful years of good health' (Shire, 29) before her death in 1977.

Along with her two gold medals, Olive Fraser won more than twenty literary prizes. She shared a national award for Scots verse lyrics with Alexander Scott and Sydney Goodsir-Smith in 1951. She dealt with severe penury as well as illness, publishing poems where she could and surviving on what employment she could get and what small money her work brought in, when she wasn't too ill to write. Her collected poems were lovingly assembled and edited, as *The Wrong Music*, twelve years after Fraser's

death by her friend Helena Mennie Shire, after Shire had edited a selection in 1980, *The Pure Account*.

It is in Shire's biographical introduction to *The Wrong Music* that the quite daunting spirit of Olive Fraser is best preserved, alongside the loss and frustration of her years spent at the mercy of illness and poverty. The version of Fraser as someone buckled under by such stress gives way to one of her as a battler, a friend, and an inspirer of a great network of loyal and helpful friendships, a fine mind always fighting to get to the next poem. Shire's memoir of the first half of her life gives us Fraser's childhood spent 'running about climbing trees and pushing (schoolboy) classical scholars into rivers at an age when girls in the south would be painting their faces and having boy-friends' and Fraser as a vibrant, charismatic student and poet, 'notably good-looking, rosy-cheeked, yellow-haired and with a penetrating blue gaze'. She is remembered as someone 'full of life and fun', who 'gave the men a run for it' and seems to have charmed or alarmed everybody she came in contact with (Shire, 3–4).

'As a person she was life-enhancing' as one friend later put it (Shire, 9). She was a woman of immense strength who at one point in her life forced Cambridge University to rethink its codes and try to find a way round the problem of presenting a gold medal to a woman in the Senate House when women were still not allowed to be university members and to wear the prescribed Senate House garb of gown and mortar, 'a kind of quasi-academic dress had to be devised' (Shire, 9). In one of her final poems, after all the years lost to bad health and medical institutions, Olive Fraser was still inciting her readers to reach for the stars, 'because you can' (Shire, 201). Olive Fraser died on 9 December 1977 after surgery for cancer of the bladder, in Cornhill Hospital, Aberdeen.   ALI SMITH

Sources H. M. Shire, ed., *The wrong music: the poems of Olive Fraser, 1909–1977* (1989) · *The pure account: poems of Olive Fraser* (1981) · d. cert. · b. cert.
Archives U. Aberdeen L., personal and literary papers

Fraser, Patrick, **Lord Fraser** (1817–1889), jurist and judge, third son and the fourth of at least eight children of Patrick or Peter Fraser (c.1777–1850) flax dresser, of Perth, and his wife, Ann Fraser (c.1790–1854), also a flax dealer, was born at Perth on 18 September 1817. He was educated at Perth Academy and was then employed in the offices of Messrs Wedderspoons, writers in Perth. Fraser next moved to Edinburgh, and entered the office of William Fraser, clerk to the burgh of Canongate, and he also studied in law classes at Edinburgh University from 1836 to 1839. He then served in the firm of Tod and Hill, writers to the signet, at 59 George Street, Edinburgh. On 2 December 1843 he was admitted to the Faculty of Advocates, and three years later he published *The Law of Personal and Domestic Relations*, which dealt at length with the law of husband and wife, parent and child, and master and servant. In subsequent editions, it was split into three independent works, each of which was the leading work on its subject until into the twentieth century. Fraser also wrote for the *North British Review*, notably an article in 1848 criticizing Patrick Fraser Tytler's *History of Scotland* as a tory and episcopalian view of its subject. Fraser himself was a Liberal and a Free Churchman, but his own historical studies of marriage law are marred by an insistence that before the Reformation Scotland enjoyed its own system of canon law.

On 27 March 1851 Fraser married Margaret Ann Sharp (1825–1899), daughter of William Sharp of Larches, merchant of Birmingham and Manchester, and his wife, Margaret Stock. They were to have one son and four daughters. In 1854 Fraser chaired a committee of the Faculty of Advocates set up to consider the qualifications of intrants, and he is said to have largely written its report, which contained extensive comparative, and in particular German, material. Fraser's expertise in family law was deployed not only in a number of significant cases on irregular marriage and succession but also in drafting the Marriage (Scotland) Act 1856, which imposed residence requirements regulating 'Gretna Green' marriages, and the Conjugal Rights Amendment (Scotland) Act 1861, which changed the law on the consequences of judicial separation and divorce. In 1857 he was one of the founders, with John McLaren and William Guthrie, of the *Journal of Jurisprudence*, and he was awarded an LLD by Edinburgh University in 1871 in recognition of his juristic contribution. Fraser was appointed sheriff of Renfrewshire in 1864 and, after two unsuccessful candidacies, was elected dean of faculty in 1878. His deanship was notable for his vigorous defence of the faculty's interests and those of an independent Scottish legal system, and he was appointed queen's counsel in 1880. On 8 February 1881 he was appointed a lord of session, and he acted as a lord ordinary in the outer house until his death.

Contemporaries believed that Fraser had been appointed to the bench too late to make as major a contribution as a judge as he had as an author. He died suddenly of heart disease on holiday at Gattonside House, near Melrose, on 27 March 1889, shortly after returning from a walk. An omnivorous reader with wide knowledge and extensive recall, Fraser played a significant role in the development of Scottish legal literature in its post-institutional nineteenth-century phase, as well as being, despite genuinely humble origins, one of the leading advocates of his day.   HECTOR L. MACQUEEN

Sources H. Goudy, *Juridical Review*, 1 (1889), 178–83 · *Journal of Jurisprudence*, 33 (1889), 259–65 · *Scottish Law Review*, 5 (1889), 88–9 · *The Scotsman* (29 March 1889) · *The Times* (29 March 1889) · *Perthshire Advertiser* (29 March 1889) · Old parish registers, Perth · Register of births, deaths and marriages · J. F. Mitchell and S. Mitchell, *Monumental inscriptions (pre 1855) in North Perthshire* (1975) · matriculation roll, U. Edin. L., special collections division, university archives, Morgan transcripts, 1116, 1135, 1143 · *The Post Office Edinburgh and Leith directory* (1842–89) · F. J. Grant, ed., *The Faculty of Advocates in Scotland, 1532–1943*, Scottish RS, 145 (1944) · M. Ash, *The strange death of Scottish history* (1980), 118–21 · J. W. Cairns, 'Laws of Scotland', *Stair memorial encyclopedia*, 13, 1267–85 · W. D. H. Sellar, 'Marriage by cohabitation with habit and repute', *Comparative and historical essays in Scots law*, ed. D. L. Carey Miller and D. W. Meyers (1992), 117–36 · A. F. Rodger, 'Scottish advocates in the 19th century: the German connection', *Law Quarterly Review*, 110 (1994), 563–91 · S. P. Walker, *The Faculty of Advocates, 1800–1986* (1987) · OPR Perth, 387/17 · d. cert., REG BDM 378/4 · d. cert., REG BDM 799/2

Likenesses J. H. Lorimer, oils, exh. 1877?, Faculty of Advocates, Parliament Hall, Edinburgh · photograph, repro. in *Juridical Review*, facing p. 179 · photograph, repro. in *Perthshire Advertiser* (12 Aug 1929), 67
Wealth at death £47,916 6s. 9d.: confirmation, 29 April 1889, CCI · £450: additional estate, 24 June 1892, CCI

Fraser, Peter (1884–1950), prime minister of New Zealand, was born on 28 August 1884 in the highland village of Fearn, Ross-shire, the fifth of six children of Donald Fraser, the village shoemaker, and his wife, Isabella McLeod. Peter left the local board school for a carpentry apprenticeship when he was fourteen, already with an interest in politics inherited from his father, who was a leading member of the local branch of the Liberal Association. This was further stimulated by reading the British socialist writers of the time. In spite of his bad eyesight this marked the beginning of Fraser's lifelong self-education through reading which was to give him a wide knowledge of literature and history. The bad eyesight ended his apprenticeship and after a period of intermittent work in London, where he became a member of the Independent Labour Party, in 1910 he sailed for New Zealand, attracted by the country's reputation for social advancement.

Having arrived in New Zealand at a time when labour was becoming increasingly restive, Pat Fraser, the name by which he was then known, found employment first as a labourer and then on the wharves in Auckland. After joining the Socialist Party, he was also elected president of the Auckland General Labourers' Union. He was a tall, thinnish, red-headed man, with thick spectacles which gave him a scholarly air. Fraser soon made his mark among an emerging group of militant labour leaders. An effective and powerful orator, sarcastic and quick with words when necessary, he was also an effective organizer. Direct action by unions revealed its limitations in the outcome of the bitter miners' strike at Waihi in 1912. Fraser, as a representative of the 'red federation' of labour, recognized the absence of any general support for the miners and—accepting defeat—sought a settlement. At the second Unity Conference in July 1913, which sought to bring together the disparate labour groups, Fraser, by this time working on the wharves in Wellington, became secretary-treasurer of the short-lived Social Democratic Party, formed (alongside the United Federation of Labour) to represent the political side of the labour movement. The fragile nature of this unity was demonstrated by further strikes organized by militants later in 1913. The outbreak of the First World War sharpened the divisions. Fraser was among those labour leaders who saw it as an 'imperialist war' and strongly opposed it.

In July 1916 the New Zealand Labour Party was formed. Fraser was elected to its national executive and remained a member until the end of his life. Ideas of direct action and the general strike gave way to those of parliamentary action. The immediate challenge was the government's decision to introduce conscription. Fraser's opposition was not absolute. He was not a pacifist, but argued that conscription should only be introduced if accompanied by 'conscription of wealth'. In December he was arrested

Peter Fraser (1884–1950), by Elliott & Fry, 1942

and convicted of sedition for advocating the repeal of the law. Sentenced to twelve months' imprisonment, he served the full term.

After his release from prison Fraser for a time edited the *Maoriland Worker* and continued to write for it and its successor, the *New Zealand Worker*, through the 1920s. He also revealed his political skills in organizing the successful by-election campaign of H. E. Holland, the party leader. This was followed, in October 1918, by his own success in a by-election for the Wellington Central seat. He was to represent this constituency for the rest of his life. During the great post-war influenza epidemic, Fraser displayed great courage and organizing ability, and he built up a reputation as a tireless and respected constituency worker. On 1 November 1919 he married Janet Henderson (1883–1945), daughter of William Munro, a Glasgow storeman, and his wife, Mary. They had no children, though Janet had a son from her previous marriage to Frederick George Kemp. Until the election of the Labour government Fraser and his wife were both active in municipal politics. Not only did Janet bring Fraser great domestic happiness; her ability and interests, especially in health issues, added to his influence in the labour movement.

As an opposition MP from 1919 to 1935 Fraser played a very considerable role in the parliamentary Labour Party. In the formulation of policy he and Walter Nash were the chief influences, leading the party away from socialism to humanitarian welfare, while Fraser became the party's most devastating debater and a master of parliamentary tactics and procedure. In addition, he played an important role in the administration of the party, and dealt firmly with party dissidents. In 1933, on H. E. Holland's death, Fraser was elected deputy to the new leader, Michael Joseph Savage. Two years later, when the coalition government was swept from power, Fraser took education and health, key portfolios for labour, as well as marine and police. An outstanding minister of education, he came to the job well prepared by long study and was strongly committed to the importance of education in social reform.

When war broke out in 1939 Savage was dying, and Fraser assumed the direction of New Zealand's war effort from the outset. In April 1940, after Savage's death, he became prime minister and brought to the position great skills as a leader, dominating government in a way which reflected his unrivalled ability as well as his temperamental compulsion to do everything himself. He recognized that war meant the involvement not merely of the armed services, but of the whole nation, and he sought closer collaboration between the two political parties. Ultimately he was able to persuade neither his own party nor the opposition, whose new leader S. G. Holland appeared to place party advantage before national unity. In the end it was through the small war cabinet, in which J. G. Coates, eschewing party politics, played a prominent role, that the prime minister ran the war effort.

The course of the war raised crucial questions about the deployment and control of New Zealand forces. Especially after the disastrous campaign in Greece and Crete in 1941 Fraser was determined to have a voice in these decisions. A key to this was his relationship with General Bernard Freyberg, commanding officer of New Zealand's second expeditionary force. Fraser spelt out to the British authorities Freyberg's responsibility to report fully to the New Zealand government on any plans for actions involving New Zealand troops. The role he played at this time did much to clarify the concept of dominion status in wartime. Perhaps his most difficult decision followed Japan's entry into the war and rapid advance into south-east Asia and the Pacific. Fraser had to wrestle with the question of whether to recall the New Zealand division from the Middle East and commit it to the Pacific theatre, following Australia's decision to do so, or to acquiesce to Churchill's request that it remain where it was. Having decided that the division should stay where it was, Fraser, with remarkable political skill, persuaded a divided government and parliament to give their full support.

That decision notwithstanding, Fraser was determined that New Zealand should have a voice in the direction of the Pacific war and in the political decisions which would shape the post-war world. Direct diplomatic relations were established with the United States, while the Canberra pact of 1944 sought to ensure that Australian and New Zealand interests in the Pacific would not be overlooked. At the San Francisco conference, and at meetings of the United Nations general assembly, Fraser assumed international stature as a leader of the 'small nations' opposing the granting of veto rights to the great powers. He chaired the committee which led to the establishment of the Trusteeship Council and played an important part in elevating the status of the Economic and Social Council to that of a principal body of the United Nations.

Leadership of a country at war, with its unremitting pressure, took its toll. Fraser's exhaustion and recurring ill health seemed paralleled by those of his party. The wartime general election in 1943 saw its majority reduced, and in 1946 it only narrowly survived. After that election Fraser added Maori affairs to his responsibilities, developing a long-held interest and building on the close links he had forged with Maori leaders during the war. But the government had lost its drive. It faced growing attacks from militant trade unions, notably the watersiders and the carpenters. Increasingly isolated, Fraser gave little encouragement to young members and new ideas. Popular support for the party dwindled. Fraser judged that compulsory military training must be introduced if New Zealand was to contribute effectively to Commonwealth defence. He committed the full weight of government to supporting its approval in a referendum. It was a courageous move but it left the party split and in disarray.

Fraser's government was decisively defeated in the general election held soon afterwards, in December 1949. A year later, on 12 December 1950, he died in Lewisham Hospital, Wellington. He was buried on 15 December 1950 in Karori cemetery, Wellington. His wife had predeceased him in 1945. He had become a member of the privy council in 1940 and was appointed a Companion of Honour in 1946. He received the freedom of a number of cities, including London, and several honorary degrees.

Fraser was not alone among Labour leaders of his generation in moving from youthful militancy to conservative old age. Through all the changes he maintained his superb gifts as a politician, revealed above all during his years in government: his acute and penetrating judgement and his remarkable political intuition. These gifts, the foundation of his dominance in the party, were matched by others: an intolerance of opposition and a ruthlessness in maintaining his authority. Fraser could be devious and secretive, ready to take the expedient course, and he disliked publicity in all its forms. Yet there was another side to him. His commitment to educational reform never waned—though neither did his mistrust of academics and intellectuals. He was responsible for the first government initiatives in support of the arts in New Zealand, including the founding of the national orchestra, and he found time to go to the theatre regularly. On international questions especially, he sought to ground his views in moral principles. He then held to those views tenaciously. However, Fraser's style and his political strengths did not make him a popular politician. The passionate voice of his early years, the soaring oratory heard again at San Francisco, was rarely heard in his later years in New Zealand, where it had given way to a dreary and ineffective delivery. He never had a place in the public's affection comparable to that of Savage, and few in New Zealand recognized his stature in the wider world.

Many of those who worked closely with Fraser came both to respect him and to be thoroughly exasperated by him. He worked very long hours but had no idea of organizing his time. He preferred oral to written reports. Talking was his way of conducting business and his chief recreation, and if conversation revealed his immense range of knowledge it could also be a highly inefficient way of reaching decisions. Possibly the lack of formal education explains how a mind in many ways so remarkable should have lacked discipline and order.

A man of complications, of vision, and of pettiness, Fraser has none the less a claim to greatness. It lies above all in his leadership of New Zealand during the war. He faced enormous responsibilities and coped with impossible situations. Above all he was a realist. At the same time he revealed a determination to place national interests as he saw them before those of his party. Some in the party never forgave him for this, yet it is clear to historians that Fraser was one of New Zealand's most able prime ministers.   T. H. Beaglehole

Sources M. Clark, ed., *Peter Fraser: master politician* (Palmerston North, 1998) • A. McIntosh, 'Working with Peter Fraser in wartime: personal reminiscences', *New Zealand Journal of History*, 10 (1976) [abridged version repr. in M. Clark, ed., *Peter Fraser* (1998)] • F. L. W. Wood, *The New Zealand people at war: political and external affairs* (Wellington, 1958) • B. Gustafson, *From the cradle to the grave: a biography of Michael Joseph Savage* (Auckland, 1986) • I. McGibbon, ed., *Undiplomatic dialogue: letters between Carl Berendson and Alister McIntosh, 1943–1952* (Auckland, 1993) • J. Thorn, *Peter Fraser* (1952) • K. Sinclair, *Walter Nash* (Auckland, 1976) • P. J. O'Farrell, *Harry Holland: militant socialist* (Canberra, 1964) • E. Olssen, *The red feds* (Auckland, 1988) • N. M. Taylor, *The New Zealand people at war: the home front*, 2 vols. (Wellington, 1986) • M. McKinnon, *Independence and foreign policy: New Zealand in the world since 1935* (Auckland, 1993) • M. Bassett and M. King, *Tomorrow comes the song: a life of Peter Fraser* (Auckland, 2000) • b. cert. • d. cert.

Archives FILM BFI NFTVA, news footage • New Zealand Archives, news footage | SOUND BL NSA, current affairs recording

Likenesses photograph, 1940, Hult. Arch. • Elliott & Fry, photograph, 1942, NPG [*see illus.*] • Karsh of Ottawa, photograph, 1948 • A. Stones, bronze statue, *c.*1987, Victoria University law school, Wellington, New Zealand, forecourt

Fraser [*née* Jupp], **Rhoda Mary Napier** [*pseud.* Crae Ritchie] (1918–1970), communist and peace campaigner, was born on 23 February 1918 in Edinburgh, the second of three children of George Jupp, clerk to the board of works, and his wife, Ethel Ritchie. She was educated in Edinburgh and chose nursing as a career. Her first involvement in organized protest occurred while she was matron of a children's nursery in Glasgow during the Second World War. When closure was threatened she led a mothers' pressure group which was successful in keeping it open. Rhoda Jupp joined the Communist Party of Great Britain in her early twenties and in 1944 became Scottish women's organizer. After marrying Louis Fraser, a *Daily Worker* reporter, on 24 August 1945, she lived in Shawlands, Glasgow, and belonged to the Shawlands Communist Party branch for twelve years.

Rhoda Fraser led Communist Party campaigns for more nursery schools, better housing and maternity services, equal pay and improved conditions for women workers. In 1947 she wrote an open letter to John Strachey, minister of food, protesting at increased food prices, while also leading demonstrations in opposition to the right-wing Housewives' League. Now secretary of the Scottish Communist Party's women's advisory committee, she travelled throughout Scotland, recruiting women into approximately fifty 'women's sections', and initiated the party's first women's weekend and residential schools which proved very popular. She forged strong links with the Women's Co-operative Guild, but her major achievement was the organization of the first Scottish National Assembly of Women held in Glasgow on 8 March, international women's day, 1953, on the theme 'The world we want for our children'. Attended by 400 delegates it represented an impressive cross-section of women's organizations nationwide.

An active peace campaigner, Rhoda Fraser was inspired by the World Congress for Peace in Paris in April 1949 to organize the 'peace bus'. Decorated with a banner depicting Picasso's dove of peace and given a rousing send-off by Helen Crawfurd-Anderson, it toured throughout Scotland in June, alerting people to the dangers of nuclear warfare. In 1950 Rhoda Fraser collected Scottish signatures to the Stockholm peace petition and during the Korean War she worked with Monica Felton to bring home prisoners of war and support their families. She was involved with cultural events organized by the Communist Party, including a successful series of children's Christmas holiday lectures in 1954 on poetry, history, and music. A poet herself, she had two books of poems published under her pen-name, Crae Ritchie.

In 1956 Rhoda Fraser began to criticize Communist Party policy and after the Hungarian uprising she left the party and returned to Edinburgh with her husband. In the 1960s she worked for the Scottish Council of Social Service and was in charge of the geriatric department, administering welfare for the elderly. Her work for peace continued, however. She joined the Campaign for Nuclear Disarmament in 1958, and regularly sold CND papers on Edinburgh's main streets at weekends thereafter. She became honorary secretary of the Edinburgh branch of the Peace in Vietnam Committee. Her last act of protest was reported in the press in 1969 when she suddenly appeared amid Edinburgh dignitaries at a hotel reception for the South Vietnamese ambassador and courageously spoke out in direct conflict with his views.

Tragically, Rhoda Fraser died at the early age of fifty-two. She was found dead from an overdose of drugs on Murray-field golf course in Edinburgh on 9 March 1970 after suffering severe depression. She was survived by her husband.

In appearance Rhoda Fraser was slim, fair-haired, and attractive. Remembered for her 'passionate compassion' (*Glasgow Herald*, 23 March 1970) in the cause of peace, she also spoke on other issues with feeling and conviction. When asking the Scottish Communist Party congress in 1955 to remember 'our other army of allies … the half-a-million women workers in Scotland', she challenged 'Do you want a man's party or a mass party?' (Report of Scottish Congress of Communist Party, 26–27 March

1955). An extremely capable organizer, she enjoyed working together with women and made a significant and lasting contribution to their organization and development, both in the Communist Party and the broad labour movement in Scotland.   AUDREY CANNING

Sources Scottish committee of Communist Party, reports on women's work, 1944–56, Gallacher Memorial Library, Scottish communist party archive · private information (2004) · 'Biographical preface', C. Ritchie, *Confrontation* (1973) · *Glasgow Herald* (23 March 1970) [memorial service report] · Mrs R. Fraser, 'Control food prices', *Scotland Demands*, CP Special (1947) · R. Fraser, 'New perspectives for Scottish Women', *World News and Views* (28 Nov 1953), 560 · R. Fraser, 'Towards a real democracy', *Scottish Bulletin* (1946) · 'Millions sign for peace', *Peace Pictorial*, 2 [n.d., 1950?] · M. Henery, 'A Scottish women's school', *World News* (26 March 1955), 254 · R. Fraser, 'They taught us', *World News* (4 Sept 1954), 706 · *The Scotsman* (27 Sept 1969) · Scottish Congress of Communist Party, 26–7 March 1955, Gallacher Memorial Library, Scottish communist party archive · m. cert. · d. cert.
Archives Scottish Poetry Library, Edinburgh, MSS | Caledonian University, Glasgow, Gallacher Memorial Library, Scottish communist party archive · Mitchell L., Glas., MSS
Likenesses portrait, repro. in C. Ritchie, *Confrontation* · portrait, Mitchell L., Glas., Arts department · portrait, Scottish Poetry Library, Edinburgh

Fraser, Robert (1798–1839), poet, the son of a sailor, was born at Pathhead, Fife, on 24 June 1798. He was educated at local schools, and in 1812 was apprenticed to a wine merchant. In 1817 he became a clerk to an ironmonger, and two years later entered into partnership as an ironmonger in Kirkcaldy. He married Ann Cumming on 20 March 1820, and they had nine children. In 1833 he went into business alone but lost his fortune in 1836 through having become financial surety to a friend, after which his health declined. He learned several foreign languages and contributed original pieces and verse translations from German, Spanish, and other languages to the *Edinburgh Literary Gazette*, the *Edinburgh Literary Journal*, and various newspapers. In 1838 he became editor of the *Fife Herald*, and moved to Tarvit Mill, near Cupar, where he died on 27 May 1839, survived by his wife. He was buried at Kirkcaldy parish cemetery. A selection of his poetry was edited by his friend David Vedder, soon after Fraser's death.

WILLIAM BAYNE, *rev.* SARAH COUPER

Sources *Poetical remains of the late Robert Fraser*, ed. D. Vedder (1839) · M. F. Conolly, *Biographical dictionary of eminent men of Fife* (1866), 192–3 · Chambers, *Scots.* (1835) · C. Rogers, *The modern Scottish minstrel, or, The songs of Scotland of the past half-century*, 3 (1856), 252 · Irving, *Scots.* · Anderson, *Scot. nat.* · d. reg. Scot.

Fraser, Sir Robert Brown (1904–1985), first director-general of the Independent Television Authority, was born on 26 September 1904 in Adelaide, South Australia, the elder son (there were no daughters) of Reginald Fraser, an Adelaide businessman, and his wife, Thusnelda Homberg. He was educated at St Peter's School, Adelaide, Trinity College, Melbourne (1924–6), where he obtained a third-class honours degree in classics, and at the London School of Economics (1927–30), where he obtained a BSc (Econ.) with second-class honours. At the London School of Economics his political leanings as an intellectual socialist caught the attention of Hugh Dalton, whose literary executor he became, and of Harold Laski. In 1930, on the advice of Laski, he became leader writer for the *Daily Herald*, where he stayed until 1939. Fraser married in 1931 Betty, daughter of George Harris, a government scientist. They had one daughter. Fraser stood unsuccessfully as Labour candidate at York in 1935.

On the outbreak of war Fraser joined the empire division of the Ministry of Information (MOI). In 1941 he became director of the publications division and was responsible for the enormously successful series of MOI booklets about major aspects of the war. Despite Dalton's urging that he stand for parliament in 1945, he elected to continue with the MOI, where he was appointed that year as controller of production. In the following year he became director-general of the newly formed central office of information (COI). This proved a demanding post, calling for the creation of a new organization largely out of the remnants of the MOI, many of whose senior staff had departed with the ending of the war. When he left it eight years later, the COI was established as a permanent part of the government's publicity machinery and the ground rules which distinguished between publicity for government activity and that of a politically partisan kind had been clearly defined.

In August 1954 the Independent Television Authority (ITA) was set up by statute to run a new advertising-supported television service. In September Fraser was appointed its first director-general. Within weeks he was able to work out with the art historian Kenneth Clark, the ITA chairman, and other members of the authority a framework for the operations of the private companies which would provide the programmes to be broadcast by the ITA. (In Fraser's time there were to be fifteen companies, in addition to a central news company.)

In 1963 Lord Hill of Luton became ITA chairman, determined that the authority should play, and be publicly seen to play, a more commanding role in the supervision of the programmes. Fraser's relationship to Hill's two predecessors had been that of a chief executive with influential, but non-executive, chairmen. Now, as he himself said, it became more analogous to that of a civil service permanent secretary with his minister. The new relationship worked well and Fraser must share the credit for the fact that when Hill went to the BBC as chairman in 1967 the public standing of ITV had been greatly improved. (Its standing with the viewing audience had never been in doubt, and remained consistently high.) Fraser's leadership of the authority's staff and his management of its operations were notable. The authority's responsibilities included the planning and provision of the network of stations transmitting the independent television programmes. When Fraser retired in 1970, the authority had completed virtual national coverage in black and white signals from a network of nearly fifty transmitters and was already, from a further dozen stations, providing two-thirds of the population with higher standard and colour transmissions, which had begun the previous year. After retiring from the ITA Fraser was independent chairman of Independent Television News for three years from 1971 to 1974.

Fraser was invariably elegant in writing, in public speaking, and in dress. He had great mental and physical stamina and the absorptive capacity of the first-rate civil servant. He was decisive and not prepared to fudge on important issues. Only his close associates knew the immense amount of careful thought and sheer hard work which went into his mastery of any subject and into his decisiveness. In spite of his own high standards, he was tolerant—sometimes perhaps over-tolerant—of the shortcomings of others. He had an intense dislike, surprising in so prominent a figure in the communications world, for the personal publicity which his position occasioned. Although his appointment as ITA director-general in 1954 gave rise to criticism in some newspapers because of his socialist past, his earlier political sympathies were by then no longer evident. He was always punctilious, to the point of being over-cautious, about questions of political impartiality arising in ITV programmes.

Fraser was appointed OBE in 1944 and was knighted in 1949. He was an honorary fellow of the London School of Economics (1965) and a life member of the Royal Institute of Public Administration (1975). He died in London on 20 January 1985. His wife died the following day.

ANTHONY PRAGNELL, rev.

Sources B. Sendall, *Origin and foundation, 1946–62* (1982), vol. 1 of *Independent television in Britain* (1982–90) · *The Second World War diary of Hugh Dalton, 1940–1945*, ed. B. Pimlott (1986) · personal knowledge (1990) · private information (1990) · *The Times* (21 Jan 1985) · *CGPLA Eng. & Wales* (1985)

Wealth at death £60,369: probate, 26 March 1985, *CGPLA Eng. & Wales*

Fraser, Robert William (1810–1876), Church of Scotland minister and writer, the son of Captain Robert Fraser, sometime of the household of the prince regent, and Helen Buchanan, was born at Perth on 10 July 1810. He was probably educated at Edinburgh University and proceeded MA in 1836. On 25 August 1828 he married Margaret (d. 1890), daughter of Andrew Buchanan of Ringwood Lodge, in co. Wexford; they had three daughters and four sons. He was licensed to preach by the Edinburgh presbytery in 1840, and in September 1843 was presented to the parish of Burntisland, Fife, where he distinguished himself as a preacher. In 1844 he was chosen to succeed Thomas Guthrie (1803–1873) as minister of St John's Church, Edinburgh, where he attracted a large congregation. Fraser was best known as the author of many works including *Moriah, or, Sketches of the Sacred Rites of Ancient Israel* (1849), *Turkey, Ancient and Modern: a History of the Ottoman Empire* (1854) and *Elements of Physical Science* (1855). He edited, among other works, *Ebb and Flow: the Curiosities and Marvels of the Seashore: a Book for Young People* (1860) and *The Seaside Naturalist* (1868). He died on 10 September 1876 in Edinburgh and was survived by his wife.

J. M. RIGG, rev. ROSEMARY MITCHELL

Sources *The Scotsman* (12 Sept 1876) · *Fasti Scot.* · Boase, *Mod. Eng. biog.* · *CCI* (1876)

Wealth at death £1777 5s. 7d.: confirmation, 7 Dec 1876, *CCI*

Fraser, Sir Simon (*c*.1270–1306), rebel, was the son of Sir Simon Fraser of Oliver Castle, by Tweedsmuir, and his wife, Mary. The elder Simon, who had been keeper of the forests of Traquair and Selkirk, died in 1291, by when his son was of age. The younger Simon swore fealty to Edward I in 1291 and attested King John's homage to the English king at the end of 1292. Having fought against Edward at Dunbar, Fraser swore fealty to him again in October 1296, and in 1297, to gain release from English prison, he agreed to campaign with Edward in Flanders. He was rewarded with the return of his lands. He impressed the king while he was abroad and returned to Scotland in 1298 almost certainly as keeper of Selkirk Forest. In the aftermath of the battle of Falkirk he was involved in fighting with the Scots in that forest, and at the end of the year he was ordered to join an expedition for the relief of Stirling Castle. In 1299, however, doubts were again expressed about his loyalty. Edward's sheriff asserted that, when the Scots launched an expedition in the south-east, Fraser met them on the best of terms. There is a strong suggestion that the Scots were able to use Selkirk Forest precisely because Fraser was Edward's warden there. Yet in August 1299 the guardians appointed Sir Robert Keith to be their warden of the forest, and Fraser spent the period from 4 September 1299 to 12 June 1300 in a Scottish prison. This served to convince Edward of his loyalty, and on his release Fraser returned to English service and to his forest wardenship.

In March 1301 Fraser received his fee and robes in person at Lincoln, but by September he had changed sides. This volte-face was probably caused by his having been replaced as warden of Selkirk Forest by Sir Hugh Audley, as well as by a disillusionment over the scarcity of wage payments. He then employed his undoubted energy in trying to expel the English from south-east Scotland, leading a force against the garrison at Roxburgh early in 1303, moving on to the new peel at Selkirk, which he captured, attacking Linlithgow, which he failed to take, and finally defeating Sir John Seagrave's force at Roslin on 24 February. By June, Fraser and Sir Edmund Comyn were raiding south of the border. Nevertheless, most Scots submitted to Edward I early in 1304. As one who had personally betrayed the king, Fraser could submit only by agreeing to undergo three years' exile from Edward's lands in both England and France. He declined the offer and was outlawed, together with William Wallace, at the parliament of March 1304. At the same time the pair were 'discomfited' at Hopperew, on Fraser's own lands. Fraser probably submitted soon afterwards, since on 25 July he and others were ordered to prove their loyalty by capturing Wallace. Although he was allowed to buy back his lands, his exile had been increased to four years, subject to recall. He was still in Scotland in April, when he was given leave to go to Berwick to discuss 'the state of Scotland' (*CDS*, 5, no. 492, xvii), but he soon joined Robert Bruce in his rebellion and was captured shortly after the battle of Methven. Fraser was taken to London and there hanged, drawn, and beheaded on 7 September 1306; his head was stuck on a pole beside that of Wallace. He and his wife, Mary, had two daughters, possibly called Margaret and Joanna. Sir Simon's death brought to an end the Tweeddale line of the family after which the Fraser descent continued through the Stirling Touch-Frasers [*see* Fraser family (*per. c.*1300–*c*.1500)].

FIONA WATSON

Sources A. Makenzie, *History of the Frasers of Lovat* (1986) • *Scots peerage*, vol. 7 • *CDS*, vols. 1–5 • J. Stevenson, ed., *Documents illustrative of the history of Scotland*, 2 (1870) • F. Palgrave, ed., *Documents and records illustrating the history of Scotland* (1837) • G. W. S. Barrow, *Robert Bruce and the community of the realm of Scotland*, 3rd edn (1988) • W. Gibson-Craig, ed., *Facsimiles of national manuscripts of Scotland*, 2 (1870) • Andrew of Wyntoun, *The orygynale cronykil of Scotland*, [rev. edn], 2, ed. D. Laing (1872) • *The chronicle of Walter of Guisborough*, ed. H. Rothwell, CS, 3rd ser., 89 (1957) • J. Topham, *Liber quotidianus contrarotulatoris garderobae: anno regni regis Edwardi primi vicesimo octavo* (1787) • Chancery records

Fraser, Simon, eleventh Lord Lovat (1667/8–1747), Jacobite conspirator, army officer, and outlaw, was the second but first surviving son of Thomas Fraser (1631–1699), sometimes styled 'of Beaufort' (the third son of Hugh Fraser, seventh Lord Lovat), and Sybilla Macleod (*d*. 1682), fourth daughter of John Macleod of Macleod. The age printed on his coffin and in his own statements indicates that he was born in 1667 or 1668. He was probably born at a small house in Tannich, Ross-shire, where his father was living. His father joined the Jacobite rising under John Graham of Claverhouse, Viscount Dundee, in 1689, for which he suffered imprisonment. In 1690 Thomas Fraser served with the Jacobite general Thomas Buchan, and six years later he allied with James, Lord Drummond (later second duke of Perth) and other nobles in an attempt to capture Edinburgh Castle for James VII and II.

A disputed inheritance Initially educated in Latin, French, and English by his Macleod uncle, Simon Fraser graduated MA from King's College, Aberdeen, in 1683. He accepted a commission in the regiment of John, Lord Murray, later first duke of Atholl. By 1696 he had risen to captain in the regiment. That year he travelled with his colonel (made earl of Tullibardine in July) and his cousin Hugh Fraser, ninth Lord Lovat. During the trip Fraser suborned Lovat into disinheriting his daughter Amelia and granting the estates and title to his father. The deed, dated 20 March 1696, settled the estates on Thomas Fraser of Beaufort for his life, with Simon Fraser receiving 5000 merks Scots, assuming that Lovat died without male heirs. Soon after his return from London, Lord Lovat died (14 September). Beaufort then styled himself tenth Lord Lovat, and Fraser assumed the courtesy title master of Lovat. However, his cousin Amelia, eldest daughter of the ninth Lord Lovat, assumed the title Lady Lovat. His colonel, Tullibardine (now lord high commissioner of Scotland), backed Amelia's claim, leading Fraser to seek marriage to Amelia in order to secure the Lovat inheritance. He entrusted Fraser of Teniechel with persuading Amelia to elope with him. Instead his agent brought her back to her mother, Amelia Murray (1666–1743), the sister of Tullibardine. The dowager Lady Lovat now arranged a marriage treaty with Alexander Fraser, master of Saltoun.

Fraser now let ambition overcome prudence. He raised some clansmen and captured Saltoun and Tullibardine

Simon Fraser, eleventh Lord Lovat (1667/8–1747), by William Hogarth, pubd 1746

after they had left Castle Downie, outside Inverness, and took them as prisoners to the island of Aigas on the River Beauly. Fraser captured Castle Downie, but discovered that his potential bride had gone. More out of annoyance than sense he forced the dowager Lady Lovat to marry him. The staunch presbyterian Duncan Forbes of Culloden supported him in this act, laying the foundations for Fraser's good relations with Culloden's heir John and his younger son Duncan, lord president of the court of session from 1737. In a dramatic scene, Fraser brought the Revd Robert Munro of Abertarf into the dowager's chamber, and had his bagpipers play to stifle her screams as the marriage proceeded. His wife apparently suffered physical and mental collapse afterwards while she resided with him on Aigas. However, he seems eventually to have charmed her (as he did many women) into giving him affection. To protect himself he initially asserted that she had called for Abertarf, and it was later rumoured that she had requested a second minister in order to have a more seemly marriage. However, with the passage of time and the failure of the marriage to gain Fraser any advantage he treated it as a practical joke without legal validity, and they separated in December 1697; he married twice more before Amelia Murray's death on 6 May 1743, without seeking divorce.

Tullibardine treated the affair from the start as a matter

of dishonour to his sister requiring revenge. Fraser and his followers were charged with rape and treason. In December 1697 the dragoons of Colonel William, Lord Forbes, rescued the dowager Lady Lovat and defeated Fraser. On 19 August 1698 the Scottish parliament ordered Fraser and his father to be tried. The court of justiciary found them guilty in their absence of high treason on 6 September and sentenced them to death. Fraser moved his father to Skye, where he died in his wife's ancestral home, Dunvegan Castle, in May 1699. Fraser immediately took the title of eleventh Lord Lovat. For months he wandered with a band of followers in the northern highlands, eluding his pursuers and sometimes inflicting heavy losses on them. In the midst of his traversing the wild landscape he opened communications with Archibald Campbell, first duke of Argyll, and played on his rivalry with the Murrays of Atholl. By autumn 1700 Argyll had persuaded William II and III to grant Lovat a remission. On the duke's advice he travelled to London, but missed William, who had gone to the continent.

Jacobite intrigue Disappointed in his wish to make contact with the protestant king, Lovat decided to renew his family's relations with James VII. John Murray, marquess of Atholl and father of Tullibardine, but a Jacobite sympathizer, had alleged that Lovat's Jacobitism was insincere. Lovat visited France, where he twice called on the Jacobite court at St Germain. His powers of persuasion led the exiled king to promise the extermination of the Atholl Murrays after his restoration. Lovat then travelled to Het Loo, where he met William, having obtained permission from James to make peace with the *de facto* British government to preserve his clan. He charmed William so much by a play of loyalty that the king granted him 'an ample and complete pardon for every imaginable crime' (*Genuine Memoirs*, 105). For the king's mercy to become effective various civil servants had to draft the remissions. In the course of that bureaucratic trail the Scottish privy council learned that William limited his leniency to crimes against the state and refused to extend it to offences involving private citizens. Thus Tullibardine once again had Lovat cited for his outrage against the dowager Lady Lovat. Summoned before the high court of justiciary, Simon failed to appear and was outlawed on 17 February 1701. On 19 February 1702 the lady presented a petition for letters of intercommuning (dealings with a proscribed person) against him, which was granted. Following William's death, and on the advice of Argyll, Lovat fled to France for his personal safety, arriving in July.

Argyll must have hoped that Lovat would remain loyal to the revolution settlement in Scotland, but instead Lovat offered his services, and those of some other Scottish peers and clan chiefs, to the Jacobite court. To gain access to the royal courts in France, Lovat converted to Catholicism, obtaining the papal legate Gualterio as an intermediary with Louis XIV. As a result he had audiences with the dowager Jacobite queen Mary of Modena (regent for her son, titular James VIII and III) and with Louis. The king gave him a valuable sword and other objects of esteem. Madame de Maintenon characterized him as 'un homme ravissant' (Lenman, 74). At St Germain he allied himself with the duke of Perth's faction in opposition to the party of Charles Middleton, second earl of Middleton. Lovat suggested a Jacobite rising in Scotland, where the Scottish Jacobites would raise 12,000 men, if the French landed 5000 troops at Dundee and another 500 at Fort William. Louis looked favourably on the proposal, but the Scottish Jacobites at St Germain sensed that Lovat was acting more from expediency than from conviction. To investigate matters further the Jacobite court decided to send him to Scotland in 1703 with Captain John Murray (a naturalized Frenchman and the brother of the laird of Abercairny), who would validate Lovat's actions and information. Murray concentrated on the lowland peers and gentry, while Lovat met the clan leaders. The clan leaders suspected Lovat's intentions, and the Jacobite George Lockhart of Carnwath (and other Scottish tories) later stated that Lovat was all the time an agent of whig dukes of Argyll (John Campbell, second duke) and Queensberry (James Douglas, first duke).

Whether Lovat genuinely had arrived in Scotland as a Jacobite agent became immaterial when he found the highland leaders unimpressed by his pleas and realized the possibility for revenge against Tullibardine, now duke of Atholl. Queensberry, seeking to secure his position in Scottish politics by implicating Atholl, the duke of Hamilton, the earls of Home, Seafield, and Cromarty, and the marquess of Tweeddale as Jacobites, found Lovat a more than useful ally. Lovat showed Queensberry an encouraging letter from Mary of Modena that might have been meant for any Scottish noble, but which he suggested was meant for Atholl. Such niceties as to whom the letter was actually addressed signified little to Queensberry, who now possessed the end of a rope that could trip up his political rivals. Lovat received a pass from Queensberry to return to the continent to gather evidence against Atholl and others. Bent on revenge, Lovat would have manufactured any material that could lead to Atholl's downfall, but the entrance of Robert Ferguson, the plotter, defused his schemes. Lovat later justified his conduct by claiming that he knowingly named non-Jacobites to Queensberry in order to obtain revenge and use Queensberry's power to gain the Lovat estates. Ferguson's revelations brought an end to the Scots plot, the fall of Queensberry, and the disgrace of Lovat among the Jacobites in France. Thanks to his pass, Lovat safely reached the Netherlands. After a risky journey he arrived in Paris, where fatigue brought on a serious illness that confined him to bed for three weeks. To save his reputation with the Jacobites he sent the dowager queen an account of his mission ('Memorial to the queen of all that my Lord Lovat did in his voyage to England and Scotland by her majesty's orders', published in Macpherson, 1.641–50). However, Lovat was arrested following Captain Murray's disclosure of his activities as a double agent to the French. Initially he was confined for thirty-two days in a dark and unhealthy dungeon at the Bastille, before being transferred to the castle of Angoulême for three years. He had his liberty restricted to the

city of Saumur for the next seven years. Allegations that he became a Jesuit and curé of St Omer are questionable.

Meanwhile Amelia Fraser, the heiress of the ninth Lord Lovat and the object of Lovat's initial marital plans, had married Alexander Mackenzie (subsequently of Fraserdale), son of Roderick Mackenzie, a judge of the court of session as Lord Prestonhall. With his father's legal advice, Alexander, in Lovat's absence, received on 2 December 1702 a decree from the court of session for the estate and title for his wife, with entail in favour of issue from their marriage. Fraserdale (as he had become) obtained a subsequent deed, dated 23 February 1703, permitting the heirs to bear the name Mackenzie in place of Fraser. This insult to the honour of the clan led the Fraser lairds to cabal against the *de facto* Lady Lovat and her husband. In 1713 they sent Major Fraser of Castle Leathers to France to locate their exiled chief and bring him home. Lovat and the major unsuccessfully pleaded with James VIII for the former's release. The duo duped Lovat's custodians into thinking that he had received a commission from the Pretender, James Stuart, and managed their escape from France. After arriving in London, they were arrested in their lodgings in Soho Square, then detained in a sponging house. However, the intervention of the northern whigs John Sutherland, sixteenth earl of Sutherland, John Forbes of Culloden, and others secured their liberty and provided bail of £5000. On 24 November 1714 Lovat asked Culloden to sign a petition for remission for his crimes. In the Inverness-shire parliamentary election of February 1715 Lovat, in London, delivered the votes of the Fraser barons to Culloden in opposition to Fraserdale in return for aid in regaining his estates. The moment had arrived for a significant improvement in Lovat's affairs, and the Jacobites unknowingly provided the spark.

The Jacobite rising of 1715 While Lovat was in London the 1715 Jacobite rising began. Argyll persuaded Lovat to support George I and not join his former allies. Lovat may have acted more from the desire to regain his estates and title than from harbouring revenge against the Jacobites for his treatment in France. In any case his allegiance to the house of Hanover seriously weakened the Jacobite party in northern Scotland. When the rebellion erupted Fraserdale could only muster half of the 800 Lovat Frasers, because the others regarded Lovat as the real chief. The rival parties further set the scene for Lovat's meteoric rise when the Jacobites seized Inverness and the earl of Sutherland raised 2000 men to oppose them. On 24 September Dr James Wellwood helped Lovat gain permission to travel to Scotland, which he soon did disguised as a servant. On 15 October in Dumfries the magistrates seized Lovat as he made his way north. The lord lieutenant of Dumfriesshire, William Johnstone, first marquess of Annandale, quickly obtained his freedom, allowing him to continue homeward. In early November he joined Culloden and his brother Duncan Forbes at Leith, and they sailed north. With the Forbes brothers Lovat raised the siege of Culloden House, then raised the Frasers for King George, warning the clan leaders to obey or be handed over to the government as traitors and be evicted by him.

Lovat next dispersed the Jacobite levies of clan Chattan, and intimidated MacDonald of Keppoch's 300 men into retreating. Seeing the revolution of fortune in favour of the Hanoverians, the Grants rose for the government and allied with Lovat. Their joint force marched on Inverness, and the Jacobite governor Sir John Mackenzie of Coull evacuated the burgh, allowing the whigs to regain it and forcing some of the Jacobite clans to concentrate on their own defence rather than strengthening the army at Perth. After taking Inverness on 12 November Lovat sent a messenger to the Frasers at Perth who were in the Jacobite army ordering them home, and they obeyed. Subsequently, he campaigned in the Inverness-shire lands of William Mackenzie, fifth earl of Seaforth, controlling them for George I and occupying at least one of Seaforth's homes. On 10 March 1716 Lovat proposed to General William Cadogan, commander of the government forces, that the best means of extirpating Jacobitism would be to transplant the rebels and make the leading clansmen hostages for good behaviour. He also suggested the raising of a force of 1500 loyal highlanders (for which he promised 300 men) to suppress Jacobite inclinations.

The reversal of Lovat's fortunes was at hand. The earl of Sutherland (whom Lovat slighted in his account of whig successes in the north) and others sent the king a memorial requesting a full pardon, which the king granted on 10 March 1716. On 27 March Archibald Campbell, earl of Ilay, brother of Argyll, wrote to Lovat saying he had permission to attend the court, where he had an audience with George I on 23 June. In June the king made him governor of Inverness and captain of Captain Robert Munro's independent foot company. From 16 February 1716 he had been a deputy lieutenant of Morayshire, Nairnshire, Ross-shire, and Cromarty. On 23 August he received a royal warrant (largely thanks to the intercession of Brigadier-General Alexander Grant of Grant with Robert Walpole, and the support of Sir David Dalrymple, Colonel Robert Munro, Duncan Forbes, and Lord Cowper) granting him the goods and life rent of the traitor Fraserdale and his fine of £500; the House of Commons approved this on 20 June 1717. Meanwhile on 4 April 1716 Cadogan had allowed Lovat to take possession of Fraserdale's silver (worth £150) that had been found in the house of the provost of Inverness. A permanent grant of the barony's lands required either a special act of parliament or a court settlement in Lovat's favour. The fall of Argyll from government favour in the summer blighted Lovat's hopes of a rapid success. Lovat's close connection with Argyll is shown by Argyll's support for Lovat's marriage on 12 December 1716 to Margaret (d. 1729), sister of Brigadier-General Grant and daughter of Ludovic Grant of Grant. They had five children: Georgina (bap. 1719), who died young; Simon *Fraser, master of Lovat (1726–1782); Alexander (1729–1762), who joined the army and rose to the rank of brigadier-general; Janet (d. in or after 1762), who married Ewen *Macpherson of Cluny; and Sybilla (d. 1755), who died unmarried.

On 11 March 1717 Lovat received orders to disband his independent company, eliminating sources of both income and power. In April he requested a payment of £4222 for keeping 800 Frasers in arms for the government. Lovat's financial problems inspired the Jacobite agent Campbell of Glendarule to hope that he might switch sides. Later Glendarule told the exiled John Erskine, earl of Mar, leader of the 'Fifteen, that while Lovat might be a whig his men were Jacobites. However, Lovat reported to Culloden in January 1717, 'I have fully reconciled myself to all my kindred on both sides, except Dunbalah's brothers' (Warrand, 2.143). The report of Donald Macdonald of Clanranald, that the settlement against Fraserdale had cemented Lovat's ties to the whigs, showed a good appreciation of the situation. In March–April 1717 the presbyteries of Inverness, Elgin, Forres, and Strathbogie underscored his conversion to the protestant side by issuing Lovat testimonials on his behalf. That November the Jacobite agent John Menzies reported that Lovat 'is the veriest rogue alive' and that secretly he attended mass (while privately abhorring it) in order to seduce women (*Stuart Papers*, 5.222). While maintaining control of his clan Lovat also found time to make visits to Bath, London, and Edinburgh between 1716 and 1719.

Recognition as Lord Lovat Lovat always professed a special relationship with the house of Argyll, which he claimed to represent in northern Scotland. However, while he was ostensibly a whig he continued from time to time to intrigue with Jacobites. As early as 1719 he wrote to Seaforth promising his support in the cause of the Pretender. The government learned of his potentially disastrous reversion and forced Lovat to visit London to explain himself. Before leaving he ordered his clan to take the field for the government. Given the pathetic episodes of the 1719 rising, under George Keith, tenth Earl Marischal, Lovat showed himself a shrewd analyst of the situation. With a charm that never deserted him until the last days, Lovat managed to convince George I of his loyalty and obtained the monarch's agreement to be godfather to his daughter Georgina. Colonel William Grant of Ballindalloch acted as the king's proxy.

However, full restoration eluded Lovat, as he was painfully reminded in 1721 when his proxy produced at the election of representative Scottish peers was protested against on the ground that Amelia, Lady Lovat, held the title by decree of the court of session. He found his vote objected to in 1722 and 1727 for the same reason. To maintain himself Lovat became involved in extraction industries and sold salmon to Inverness burgesses for resale. Legal problems absorbed a portion of his time, too. In January 1722 he had to deal with criminal letters issued against him, Munro of Foulis, Munro of Cullcairn, Rose of Kilravock, Duncan Forbes, and the laird of Castlehill. In March 1723 he arranged compensation for his brother John's burning of the tower of Fraser of Kynneries at Fanellan in 1702. Two years later he was feuding with his former chamberlain Alexander Fraser of Phopachy, who had succeeded in gaining a judgment in debt against him. However, in the matter of the Lovat peerage he eventually triumphed. In 1730 he commenced an action for reversing the previous judgments against him. On 30 July the court of session decided (by eight judges to seven) that Lovat's father Thomas had been rightful heir in 1696 according to the great seal charter of 26 March 1539 giving precedence to heirs male of the name of Fraser before others. As eldest son of Thomas, Simon was declared rightful Lord Fraser of Lovat (this being, strictly, the full form of the title). However, the litigation continued as Hugh Mackenzie (also known as Hugh Fraser), the deposed Lady Lovat's son, disputed the settlement. Apparently the intervention of Norman Macleod of Macleod (cousin to both Lovat and Hugh) persuaded the younger man to renounce his claims to the honours and estate of Lovat on 13 March 1734 for £12,000.

Lovat's wife Margaret had died in 1729, and three years after her death he unsuccessfully courted Marim Dalrymple, daughter of Sir Robert Dalrymple of Castleton. On 26 June 1733, at Rosneath, Dunbartonshire, he married Primrose (1710–1796), daughter of John Campbell of Mamore and his wife, Elizabeth Elphinstone, and thus a cousin of the duke of Argyll and the earl of Ilay. Lovat engineered the marriage by cajoling Primrose to enter a house in Edinburgh, which he then told her was a notorious whorehouse, and he threatened to expose her as a *habituée* unless she complied with his desires. They had one son, Archibald Campbell *Fraser (1736–1815), who succeeded his half-brother Simon as chief of the Frasers. The couple had separated by the time of Lovat's death in 1747.

Lovat's adventurous life appealed to the clan and secured him a certain popularity. He strove to use all his skills to impress on the clan that the chief stood above them and deserved obedience. He maintained a rude court at Castle Downie, where he kept several public tables. He encouraged the concept of common kinship between all his followers, who received cuisine according to their importance. Lovat's style reflected an individual approach that combined sentimental kinship with savage punishments, and formal ceremony with lewd jokes and orgies. That it was financially taxing appears from his decision in February 1738 to move to Inverness burgh, in order to save money by not holding his court. In 1704 the *de facto* Lady Lovat had secured the territory of Lovat as a regality. Lovat inherited this concession, which allowed him to hold regality courts that dealt with all justice save the four pleas of the crown. He was appointed sheriff of Inverness in his own right. These jurisdictional rights allowed him to exercise his remarkable talents in spreading his influence across the north of Scotland. In 1724 he sent the king a 'Memorial concerning the state of the highlands' (printed in Burt, 2.254), again recommending the establishment of independent highland companies commanded by chiefs. When the government accepted his idea, he received command of one of the first three companies, as much for strengthening his political power as for economic gain.

The Jacobite rising of 1745 Lovat's individual approach to affairs appeared in an incident in the 1733 parliamentary election in Moray, when he broke with Ilay, Alexander Brodie of Brodie, and his brother-in-law Grant by failing to give adequate support to the last's candidacy. Still he remained within the embrace of the whig establishment

until the late 1730s. By May 1737 the government knew that Lovat had again started plotting with the Jacobites. Alliance with the whigs had not brought him the rewards that he sought. In the 1690s James VII had promised to make him lieutenant-general of the highlands; furthermore, the Pretender might be willing to elevate him to a dukedom. In 1739 Lovat was the first to join the association formed to invite the Pretender to land in Scotland; his allegiance was secured by the promise of a patent of a dukedom. The government's awareness of his plotting led it to relieve Lovat of his sheriffdom and his company. In a less than equal exchange, letters patent for the title of duke of Fraser in the Jacobite Scottish peerage were drafted on 14 March 1740 but retained in Rome; Lovat never used the ducal title. In 1740 the association sent William MacGregor of Balhaldy to Rome asking that Prince Charles Edward Stuart (Bonnie Prince Charlie), the Pretender's eldest son, be sent to lead a rising. In the following year Lovat, with James Drummond, Jacobite third duke of Perth, Donald Cameron of Lochiel, and others, promised the Pretender they would rise if the French landed. However, as the French expedition sailed around the Firth of Forth in 1744, Lovat kept to his bed with a feigned sickness. In May 1745 the receipt of a letter from Charles Edward roused Lovat's wrath. These incidents suggest that plotting for its own sake might have inspired his actions. Certainly, Lovat's actions of later that summer indicate that an active role against the government gave the 78-year-old pause for thought. The Jacobite heir apparent reached western Scotland on 25 July and set 19 August at Glenfinnan for the initial muster of his forces. Perhaps, like some Scottish Jacobites, Lovat thought that absence of French troops removed his obligation to act, or he may have bided his time to see whether the rising would resemble the fiasco of 1719 or the near successes of 1689 and 1715. A further alternative is that he refused to act until the patent of the dukedom was in his hands. In any case the Lovat Frasers failed to appear on the 19th; Lovat's continuance of friendly correspondence with the whig lord president Duncan Forbes of Culloden covered him in case the Jacobite effort fizzled out. Certainly, the Jacobites later blamed Lovat's deliberate acts as prejudicial to the success of the endeavour.

Charles offered Lovat commissions as lord lieutenant of the north and lieutenant-general in the Jacobite army. On 29 August Lovat sent Charles a message at Invergarry saying that he would join the rising and urged a march on Inverness. However, the Jacobite army headed south towards Edinburgh, which it captured before defeating the government forces under General John Cope at Prestonpans on 21 September. Duncan Forbes of Culloden, representing the government in the highlands, offered Lovat an independent company in September, which was declined, but on 25 September he dined at Culloden House, and as late as 5 October Culloden and his ally John Macleod of Macleod still thought they could secure Lovat's neutrality at least. The news of Prestonpans electrified Lovat, and on 9 October he ordered Fraser of Foyers to muster the clan at Beaufort. Still reluctance delayed him, as he spent more than a week (7–16 October) dithering as to whether to act alone or only in concert with Sir Alexander MacDonald of Sleat and Macleod (who had already decided to remain loyal). The Frasers appear to have been in arms on 15 October, and the next day Foyers led them in an attack on Culloden House. Lovat maintained his friendly correspondence with Culloden and with John Campbell, fourth earl of Loudoun, who had raised a Highland regiment for the government. Lovat persuaded Culloden that his son Simon, master of Lovat, was the real spark behind the clan. The decades of good relations between Lovat and the Culloden family required some time before Culloden accepted the complicity of the former in the rising. The master of Lovat reluctantly led the clan. He thought the rising nonsensical, but more importantly was a committed whig. However, his father threatened to strip him of his inheritance and make him a cowherd in Strathfarrar if he disobeyed. Thus, on 1 December the master found himself leading the clan against the government garrison at Fort Augustus. Ten days later Loudoun, government commander in the north, marched on Castle Downie and seized Lovat, taking him to confinement in Inverness. Lovat escaped, probably with considerable assistance from inside the burgh as he was not missed for fifteen hours, on 2 January 1746. Afterwards he wrote to his son telling him that his correspondence with Culloden had been a sham, and that he expected great things from his heir when he led the clan to the prince's army. He told his son to obtain the patent of the dukedom, without which Lovat would not raise his sword. His reasoning here was specious as the clan was already out, and Lovat at nearly eighty was unlikely to make a significant difference in a campaign. When the news reached him of the Jacobite retreat from Derby he began temporizing again, and suggested to the master that he should abandon the enterprise. However, his son recognized that in the government's eyes the Lovat Frasers were too deeply implicated for an eleventh-hour retraction.

After the Jacobite defeat at Culloden on 16 April 1746, portions of the army, including Prince Charles Edward, retreated past Gortuleg, where Lovat was residing at the home of one of his gentry. Lovat met the prince and gave him dinner and advice. Having seen his hopes of a dukedom wrecked with the Jacobite army and his status shattered, Lovat promised the prince men and urged him to follow the example of his worthy forebear Robert the Bruce, who, beaten eleven times, took the field for another battle and won Scotland. The next morning the prince fled westwards, while Lovat sought refuge in a bolthole on Loch Muilly. On his way he may have witnessed the blaze of Castle Downie, fired by the soldiers of William Augustus, duke of Cumberland, in punishment for its owner's treason. Feeling deflated, Lovat fled another 70 miles west to Loch Morar on the west coast. Since he possessed the only boat on the loch, he thought himself secure. However, sailors from a warship towed a boat over the peninsula that separated the loch from the sea, and launched it on the loch. As he was preparing to say confession to the Roman Catholic bishop Hugh MacDonald,

Lovat saw the approaching boat and hid in the hollow of a tree. Unfortunately, the flannel muffling his legs betrayed his presence and he fell prisoner. Too debilitated to ride, he was carried in a litter to Fort William and by 18 June was closely confined in Fort Augustus. From there he was moved slowly to London. At the White Hart, St Albans, he had an interview with William Hogarth, whom he knew from his visits to London, and who then made the famous portrait sketch of him. Prints of Hogarth's sketch were in high demand. Lovat's appearance was described by the *Gentleman's Magazine*:

> Lord Lovat makes an odd figure, being generally more loaded with clothes than a Dutchman with his ten pair of breeches; he is tall, walks very upright considering his great age, and is tolerably well shaped; he has a large mouth and a short nose, with eyes very much contracted and down-looking, a very small forehead, almost all covered with a large periwig; this gives him a grim aspect, but upon addressing any one he puts on a smiling countenance. (*GM*, 1st ser., 16.339)

Trial and execution On reaching London Lovat was lodged in the Tower. On 15 August 1746 the House of Commons impeached him for high treason. He was tried before the House of Lords in December. The letters captured on him by Captain John Fergussone of HMS *Furnace*, and the treacherous testimony of his secretary Hugh Fraser and the prince's secretary John Murray of Broughton, secured his conviction on 18 March 1747. According to the procedures for cases of high treason, Lovat received legal counsel only on points of the law. His age and physical infirmity did not prohibit him from making a stirring defence. Much of the evidence used in his case was legally questionable. His speeches exhibited the great tact and shrewdness for which he was known, one of his former whig friends writing that he 'behaved with spirit at the Bar of the House of Lords' (Warrand, 5.143). When asked by the lord high steward whether he had anything further to say, he replied, 'Nothing except to thank your lordship for your goodness to me. God bless you all, and I wish you an eternal farewell. We shall not meet again in the same place; I am sure of that' (*State trials*, 18.840). Lovat's amazing life story, and probably his advanced years, attracted a huge crowd to witness the execution. Before his death a scaffold fell, killing several people. Before putting his head on the block, to sustain his noble reputation, he repeated Horace's line 'Dulce et decorum est pro patria mori' ('It is sweet and proper to die for one's country'), then turned to moralizing by quoting Ovid's 'Nam genus et proavos, et quae non fecimus ipsi, Vix ea nostra voco' ('For those things, which were done either by our fathers or ancestors, and in which we ourselves had no share, I can scarcely call our own'). He was beheaded at the Tower on 9 April 1747, one of four peers among 120 Jacobites executed in the rising's aftermath. His former associate Alexander Brodie of Brodie noted he had died 'with courage and decency, forgiving all Mankind' (Warrand, 5.169). In a note delivered to the sheriff he stated that he died 'a true, but unworthy Member of the Holy Catholick, Apostolick Church' (*Candid and Impartial Account*, 30). Lovat's will specified that all the pipers from John o' Groats to Edinburgh should be asked to play at his funeral; but events having made that impossible, he asked to be buried at his tomb at Kirkhill with some highland women singing a dirge. Although he died with this expectation, and the body was given to the undertaker with this aim, the government had it brought back to the Tower and buried near the bodies of other noble traitors in St Peter ad Vincula in order to prevent his grave becoming a focus for Jacobites in the Inverness area.

Lovat's betrayer John Murray of Broughton wrote, 'Lord Lovat all the World knows to have been the most abandon'd and most detested man in his Country, and one who never acted a fair part either in publick or private life' (*Memorials*, 323). Another contemporary noted, 'he was certainly a great Master in the Science of Craft' (*Genuine Memoirs*, 56). Lovat's character at first might appear a complexity of contradictions. He was both the traditional highland chief and a skilled courtier and a Jacobite conspirator who for long periods was in the confidence of Scotland's whig leaders. His ability to straddle divergent political cultures helped establish him as one of the most dominant highland chiefs of the early eighteenth century, overcoming a disputed succession by a mixture of brutality and shrewd political bargaining. In the end, his failure to predict the outcome of the 1745 rising combined with his sense of frustrated ambition in old age to bring about his downfall and the end of the Lovat hegemony he had carefully built up in Inverness-shire.

EDWARD M. FURGOL

Sources APS, 1696–1707 · R. Forbes, *The lyon in mourning, or, A collection of speeches, letters, journals … relative to … Prince Charles Edward Stuart*, ed. H. Paton, 3 vols., Scottish History Society, 20–22 (1895–6) · *Calendar of the Stuart papers belonging to his majesty the king, preserved at Windsor Castle*, 7 vols., HMC, 56 (1902–23) · *State trials*, vols. 14, 18 · *A candid and impartial account of the behaviour of Simon Lord Lovat* (1747) · *GM*, 1st ser., 16 (1746) · *GM*, 1st ser., 17 (1747) · *Genuine memoirs of the life of Simon Lord Fraser of Lovat* (1746) · D. Warrand, ed., *More Culloden papers*, 5 vols. (1923–30) · *Memorials of John Murray of Broughton*, ed. R. F. Bell, Scottish History Society, 27 (1898) · W. B. Blaikie, ed., *Origins of the 'Forty-Five*, Scottish History Society, 2nd ser., 2 (1916) · *Letters relating to Scotland in the reign of Queen Anne by James Ogilvy, first earl of Seafield and others*, ed. P. Hume Brown, Scottish History Society, 2nd ser., 11 (1915) · GEC, *Peerage*, new edn, vol. 8 · *Scots peerage*, vol. 5 · A. I. Macinnes, *Clanship, commerce and the house of Stuart, 1603–1788* (1996) · B. Lenman, *The Jacobite risings in Britain, 1689–1746* (1980) · *The letter-book of Bailie John Steuart of Inverness, 1715–1752*, ed. W. Mackay, Scottish History Society, 2nd ser., 9 (1915) · W. B. Blaikie, ed., *Itinerary of Prince Charles Edward Stuart*, Scottish History Society, 1st ser., 23 (1897) · E. Burt, *Letters from a gentleman in the north of Scotland*, 5th edn, ed. R. Jamieson (1818) · J. J. MacPherson, ed., *Original papers; containing the secret history of Great Britain*, 2 vols. (1775) · K. Thomson, *Memoirs of the Jacobites of 1715 and 1745*, 3 vols. (1845–6)

Archives BL, corresp. and papers, Add. MSS 31249–31253 · NL Scot., corresp. · NRA, priv. coll., letters · Royal Arch., corresp. and papers · U. Edin. L., letters | BL, letters to Lord Milton, Add. MS 24156 · Herts. ALS, letters to first Earl Cowper · Hunt. L., letters to earl of Loudoun · NA Scot., letters to the Grant family · NL Scot., corresp. with Forbes family · NL Scot., letters to Donald Fraser · NL Scot., legal corresp. with John Macfarlane · NRA, priv. coll., letters to Lochiel · Royal Arch., Stuart papers · U. Edin. L., letters to William Fraser

Likenesses W. Hogarth, portrait, before 1745 · attrib W. Hogarth, drawing, 1746, Harris Museum and Art Gallery, Preston · W. Hogarth, etching, 1746, BM · W. Hogarth, etching, 1746, BM · W. Hogarth, etching, pubd 1746, NPG [*see illus.*] · oils, 1746 (after W. Hogarth), NPG · J. Simon, mezzotint (after Le Clare), BM · engraving, repro. in Thomson, *Memoirs of the Jacobites*

Fraser, Simon, master of Lovat (1726–1782), army officer and politician, the eldest son of Simon *Fraser, eleventh Lord Lovat (1667/8–1747), and his first wife, Margaret Grant (d. 1729), was born at Castle Downie near Inverness on 19 October 1726 and baptized in the Church of Scotland at Kiltarlity parish church on 30 October.

In 1737 it was rumoured that Fraser's father intended to send him to France. In order to demonstrate his innocence of the charge, Lord Lovat was forced to turn him over instead to Lord Ilay, the brother and heir of the duke of Argyll. Ilay initially sent him to Glasgow University, but at Lovat's insistence he went to Edinburgh in 1739 and was studying law at St Andrews University when he was summoned home by his father to lead the clan Fraser contingent during the Jacobite rising of 1745–6. Afterwards Fraser claimed to have been extremely reluctant to do so, and his recorded participation in the rising certainly displays a marked lack of enthusiasm. Too late to join the Jacobite army for the advance to Derby, both he and his men—in common with much of the army—ran away at the outset of the battle of Falkirk on 17 January 1746. Subsequently he succeeded in avoiding taking part in the battle of Culloden altogether. Another battalion of Lord Lovat's men, led by Lieutenant-Colonel Charles Fraser of Inverallochie, did fight there on 16 April 1746, but Simon Fraser's own battalion was apparently still marching towards the battlefield when it was met by the first of the fugitives. At that point he immediately turned his men around and returned to Inverness with his colours still flying and pipes playing. There he proposed to defend the bridge over the River Ness, but was dissuaded by the townspeople. However, it is uncertain whom he intended to hold it against. A Jacobite officer, James Johnstone, recorded hearing a short but intense burst of firing in the town shortly before the British army arrived and there is also an interesting local tradition of a fight for the bridge involving the highlanders of the loyalist Argyll militia. In fact none of the militia reached the town before the first of the pursuing cavalry and it is possible, therefore, that Simon Fraser changed sides that afternoon and actually tried to hold the bridge not against the British army but against his former Jacobite colleagues. While this must remain a matter for speculation it would certainly go some considerable way to explaining Fraser's remarkable political rehabilitation which followed.

Both Simon Fraser and his father were named in the act of attainder passed on 4 June 1746, but while Lord Lovat was captured a few days later and ultimately executed in London on 9 April 1747, Simon's treatment was very different. In November he voluntarily surrendered himself and significantly was not sent to London for trial with other Jacobite leaders of similar rank but held instead in Edinburgh Castle. There, while still a prisoner, he very sensibly threw his weight behind the government's preferred candidate, Norman Macleod, against his own uncle, Ludovick

Grant, the laird of Grant, in what was to all appearances a hotly contested parliamentary election for the Inverness-shire seat. In return for his assistance in this matter, and perhaps also in recognition of his curious behaviour at Culloden, Simon was released on 15 August 1747 to continue his law studies at Glasgow and received a full pardon in 1750. When petitioning to have the family estates restored in 1771 Fraser claimed to have turned down the offer of a regiment in the French service. This, however, seems extremely unlikely and certainly overstates his importance to the dying Jacobite cause.

Instead Fraser was admitted as an advocate on 25 July 1752, and proceeded to emphasize his commitment to the government interest (and to his patron, Ilay, now third duke of Argyll) by assisting in the prosecution of James Stewart of Aucharn in the infamous Appin murder trial two months later. Afterwards he moved to London and practised for a time at the English bar. At the outset of the Seven Years' War his assiduous adherence to Argyll led to his being granted letters of service to raise and command a regiment, the 63rd foot or 2nd highland battalion, on 5 January 1757. This regiment, subsequently renumbered as the 78th foot in 1759, was largely raised in Inverness-shire and, like Fraser himself, the greater number of its officers were former Jacobites. Notwithstanding this circumstance, James Wolfe later commended the regiment to Lord George Sackville for its usefulness and courage. Initially granted the rank of lieutenant-colonel commandant, Fraser was promoted to the brevet rank of colonel in North America on 22 January 1758. He then commanded his regiment at the successful siege of Louisbourg on Cape Breton Island in 1758 and in the following year under Wolfe in the campaign to take Quebec. There he was wounded in a minor skirmish near the village of Beaumont on 26 July 1759. According to Captain John Knox of the 43rd foot, both Simon Fraser and Captain James MacPherson of the 78th were shot by the same bullet. Consequently Fraser missed both the disastrous Montmorency operation which followed and the climactic battle on the Plain of Abraham—his regiment being commanded there by a Captain James Campbell. Afterwards, however, Fraser was appointed a brigade commander and was wounded again in the defeat at St Foy outside Quebec on 28 April 1760 before taking part in the final advance on Montreal later that year.

It is unclear when Fraser left North America, but in 1762, while his regiment went to the Caribbean and took part in the capture of Havana, he himself went to Portugal with a British expeditionary force. There he was appointed a temporary major-general in the Portuguese service and, according to an 'official return of lists of members of parliament', had been promoted to the rank of lieutenant-general in that service by 1768. On 25 May 1772 he also became a major-general in the British army. In the previous year he petitioned for the return of his family's forfeited estates, but although they were restored to him in 1774 on payment of a sum of £20,983 (to cover all costs and debts incurred by the government's commissioners since

1746) the Lovat title itself was not revived until 1837. Fraser's original regiment was disbanded after the peace of Paris in 1763, but the outbreak of the American War of Independence led to his being granted fresh letters of service, on 25 October 1775, authorizing him to raise a new two-battalion Highland regiment. While a contemporary, Mrs Grant of Laggan, rather perceptively described him as being hard and rapacious under a polished exterior—a harsh verdict more than amply justified by his career—he was for the most part highly regarded as a hero, whose regiment had in large measure rehabilitated the highlands. This time numbered as the 71st foot, Fraser's Highlanders served with some distinction in America before one battalion was destroyed at the battle of Cowpens and the other was captured at the surrender of Yorktown in 1781. Survivors of both disasters served on in the garrison of Charles Town, South Carolina, until the end of the war in 1783 when the regiment was formally disbanded.

Despite being promoted to lieutenant-general on 29 August 1777 Fraser was not offered an active command during the war, but instead sat in parliament, having been elected to the Inverness-shire seat in May 1761. During the early years of his parliamentary career Fraser's military appointments in Portugal kept him away from the Commons. In the mid-1760s he sided with the Grenville interest and later supported Lord North's administration, during which he made his first recorded parliamentary speech (22 November 1775) and played an active part in Philip Francis's campaign against the then governor-general of Bengal, Warren Hastings. While in Portugal (1765?) Fraser had married Katherine (1738/9–1835), daughter of the MP John Bristow of Quidenham Hall, Norfolk; the couple had no children. He died at his house in Downing Street, London, on 8 February 1782 and was survived by his wife, who died on 14 February 1835, aged ninety-six.

STUART REID

Sources DNB · B. Lenman, *The Jacobite clans of the Great Glen* (1984) · J. Anderson, *Historical account of the family of Frisel or Fraser* (1825) · E. Haden-Guest, 'Fraser, Simon', HoP, Commons, 1754–90 · GEC, *Peerage* · D. Stewart, *Sketches of the character, manners, and present state of the highlanders of Scotland: with details of the military service of the highland regiments*, 2 vols. (1822) · S. Reid, *1745: a military history of the last Jacobite rising* (1996) · *Army List* (1757–82) · J. Knox, *An historical journal of the campaigns in North America, for the years 1757, 1758, 1759, and 1760*, ed. A. G. Doughty, 3 vols. (1914–16) · J. M. Bulloch, *Territorial soldiering in north-east Scotland* (1914) · bap. reg. Scot.

Archives U. Edin. L., corresp. | Hunt. L., letters to earl of Loudoun · NRA, priv. coll., letters to Gordon of Cairnfield · NRA, priv. coll., letters to Norman Macleod

Likenesses line engraving (after wax model), BM · portrait (of Fraser?), priv. coll.; photograph, National Museums of Scotland

Wealth at death estate redeemed from crown in 1774 at cost of £20,983 and entailed at death: will, 25 June 1782, PRO

Fraser, Simon (1729–1777), army officer, was born at Balnain, Inverness-shire, the youngest son of Hugh Fraser of Balnain, and his wife, a daughter of Fraser of Forgie. Little more is known of his early life. He began his military career at an early age in Dutch service. He was wounded in 1747 at Bergen-op-Zoom while serving in the earl of Drumlanrig's regiment of the Scots brigade. On 31 January 1755 he was appointed a lieutenant in the 62nd (later the 60th) regiment, the Royal Americans. He transferred in 1757 to the 78th regiment, Fraser's Highlanders, as a captain-lieutenant. He served at Louisbourg in 1758 and was promoted captain on 22 April 1759. He fought gallantly under James Wolfe at Quebec in 1759. On 15 March 1761 he was promoted brevet major while serving in Germany on the staff of Ferdinand of Brunswick. Given command of a light infantry unit (Fraser's chasseurs) in 1761, Fraser fought many skirmishes and battles. On 8 February 1762 he was commissioned a major in the 24th regiment and was posted for a time in Gibraltar.

In the 1760s Fraser's regiment was stationed in Ireland, where he served as principal aide-de-camp to George, fourth Viscount Townshend, the lord lieutenant. Acting as a confidential liaison officer between Townshend and Whitehall, he impressed his superiors as an 'intelligent and prudent man' (Townshend to Viscount Weymouth, 18 Aug 1769, *Calendar of Home Office Papers*, 3.493). He was promoted lieutenant-colonel of the 24th regiment in 1768 and two years later was appointed Irish quartermaster-general. He maintained an active and intelligent interest in his profession, studying new infantry tactics and applying them in regimental drills. He made friends with John Burgoyne and William Phillips, two officers under whom he later served in America. On 14 October 1769 he married a divorced woman, Mrs Grant, probably a relative of Colonel Van Phan, Dutch commandant at the Cape; they had children.

In 1776 Fraser was ordered to America to help put down the colonial rising. He sailed from Cork for Quebec in early April, in immediate charge of six British regiments, and arrived on 18 May. Given command by Guy Carleton of a brigade, composed of the 24th regiment and the grenadier and light infantry companies of the army, he was posted on the south side of the St Lawrence River. Ordered to Trois-Rivières with four battalions in early June, he was attacked on the 8th by continental forces under William Thompson and Anthony Wayne. He routed the rebels and hotly pursued them until, much to his dismay, Carleton directed him to halt the following day. On 10 June Carleton promoted Fraser to the local rank of brigadier-general, giving him command of the advanced corps and ordering him to help in cutting off the Americans' retreat from Canada. Through no fault of his, the enemy escaped, and he spent the summer screening British shipbuilding activities on Lake Champlain. On 11–12 October Carleton destroyed Benedict Arnold's fleet and advanced Fraser's corps to Chimney Rock, 12 miles from Fort Ticonderoga. Thereupon, again to Fraser's dismay, Carleton withdrew to Canada for the winter.

In June 1777 Fraser joined Burgoyne, who had replaced Carleton as army commander, in the continuing campaign against upstate New York. In early July, at the head of the advanced corps, he helped dislodge the rebels from Fort Ticonderoga. On the 7th he surprised an American force under Seth Warner at Hubbardtown, Vermont. In a sharp skirmish he distinguished himself and drove off the enemy, but at a high cost in casualties. In the battle of Freeman's Farm on 19 September he commanded the right wing, which consisted of 3003 men. Although he led four companies in a successful attack on Daniel Morgan's riflemen, he mostly was an observer of the fighting. On 7 October, in the battle of Bemis Heights, he was mortally wounded by an American rifleman, Timothy Murphy, while gallantly leading the 24th regiment. He was taken to the quarters of Baroness von Riedesel, wife of the brigadier-general commanding the German allied force, in Saratoga, where he died the following morning at eight o'clock. Later that day he was buried with military honours in the Great Redoubt on the battlefield.

PAUL DAVID NELSON

Sources 'Gen. Fraser's account of Burgoyne's campaign on Lake Champlain and the battle of Hubbardton', *Proceedings of the Vermont Historical Society, 1898* (1899), 139–47 · *Baroness von Riedesel and the American Revolution: journal and correspondence of a tour of duty, 1776–83*, ed. and trans. M. L. Brown (1965) · H. Rogers, 'Appendix no. 9: Brig. General Simon Fraser', in J. Hadden, *A journal kept in Canada…* (1884) · P. D. Nelson, *General Sir Guy Carleton, Lord Dorchester: soldier-statesman of early British Canada* (2000) · R. J. Hargrove, *General John Burgoyne* (1983) · M. M. Mintz, *The generals of Saratoga: John Burgoyne and Horatio Gates* (1990) · R. M. Ketchum, *Saratoga: turning point of America's revolutionary war* (1997) · J. H. Smith, *Our struggle for the fourteenth colony: Canada and the American Revolution*, 2 vols. (1907) · J. Anderson, *Historical account of the family of Frisel or Fraser, particularly Fraser of Lovat* (1825) · J. Redington and R. A. Roberts, eds., *Calendar of home office papers of the reign of George III, 3: 1770–1772*, PRO (1881), 493 · *DNB* · R. Blanco, ed., *The American revolution, 1775–1783: an encyclopedia*, 2 vols. (1993), vol. 1

Likenesses W. Nutter, group portrait, stipple, pubd 1791 (after J. Graham, *The burial of General Fraser*), NPG

Fraser, Simon (1737/8–1813), army officer, the son of a clan Fraser tacksman, was commissioned an ensign in Fraser's 78th Highlanders on 21 July 1757. Over the next two years he saw action at Louisbourg and Quebec, and was promoted lieutenant on 21 September 1759. He was slightly wounded during the defeat at Ste Foy (25 April 1760) before witnessing the final surrender of the French at Montreal five months later. Having been placed on half pay at the peace, in 1765 he joined his protector, General Simon Fraser, in the Portuguese service. There he remained until 1775, when, on the outbreak of the American War of Independence, General Fraser raised the 71st Highlanders and gave his namesake the senior captaincy. Fraser was shot in the face during the Danbury (Connecticut) raid in April 1777 and lost the sight of an eye but he recovered sufficiently to be present at the battles of Brandywine, Germantown, and Monmouth. Promoted major on 14 October 1778, in December he served as deputy quartermaster-general (DQMG) with the Georgia expedition. He was at the capture of Charlestown, South Carolina, in April 1780, and subsequently acted as DQMG to both Lord Cornwallis and Lord Rawdon in the Camden district. When the British evacuated the American south in 1782 Fraser went as DQMG to Jamaica, and after his return to Britain was promoted lieutenant-colonel (22 August 1783) before going on half pay.

With the onset of the French Revolutionary Wars Fraser was made brevet colonel (1 March 1794) and authorized to raise the 133rd foot. Though his regiment was drafted in 1796 Fraser was promoted major-general and, that

November, sent to Portugal to serve under Sir Charles Stuart. He commanded an auxiliary force of French exiles there until 1801. In 1803 he was appointed to the staff of the northern district, England, and promoted lieutenant-general on 23 September; he served on the staff in Scotland between June 1804 and November 1806. Having been colonel of the 6th West India regiment from 26 May 1806 he died, aged seventy-five, on 21 May 1813.

H. M. CHICHESTER, *rev.* ALASTAIR W. MASSIE

Sources Simon Fraser, statement of service, 1809, PRO, WO 25/745, fol. 7 · D. Stewart, *Sketches of the character, manners, and present state of the highlanders of Scotland: with details of the military service of the highland regiments*, 2 vols. (1822) · *GM*, 1st ser., 83/1 (1813), 591

Fraser, Simon (1773–1852), editor of traditional music and composer, was born at Ardachie, near Fort Augustus, Inverness-shire. His father, Captain John Fraser, son of Angus Fraser of Errogie, served with the 78th (Highland) regiment (the Black Watch) and 'scaled the heights of Abram, with his relative [brother-in-law], Brigadier-General Fraser' (S. Fraser, *Airs*, [1816], 3) during the battle for Quebec. Fraser's mother, Janet, was the daughter of Thomas Fraser of Gorthleck, in the parish of Stratherrick; no sibling is known. As a child, Simon Fraser notes in *Airs* (n.d., 107), she had seen Prince Charles Edward Stuart, who visited her home the night of the Jacobites' final defeat at Culloden in 1746.

Fraser was probably educated locally, later joining the Fraser fencibles (1795–1802), serving in Ireland and recruiting others, 'his enthusiasm as a Highlander and his passion for the native Celtic music being highly captivating' (*Inverness Courier*, 22 July 1852, 1). He returned to a tenancy at Knockie, near Errogie, Stratherrick, his father's family home, marrying Jane Fraser in 1802. They had one son, Hugh, in 1803. Fraser and Catherine Watson already seem to have had another son, **Angus Fraser** [*formerly* Watson] (*c*.1800–1870), considered illegitimate. The couple married in 1815 (after Jane's presumed death) and had two daughters, Catherine (*b*. 1816) and Jamesina (*b*. 1822). Angus grew up near Inverness, and may have lived at Gorthleck, close to his father. He 'used his father's surname at least from the age of fourteen, when he travelled to Edinburgh to join the army as an ensign in [his grandfather's old regiment] in 1814' (Gill, 7); he later became colour sergeant in the 1st Royal Scots.

In 1795 Simon Fraser published *Thirty Highland Airs, Strathspeys &c.*, most his own compositions. A Gaelic speaker, he published *Airs and Melodies Peculiar to the Highlands of Scotland and the Isles* (assisted by Nathaniel Gow), a valuable source of Gaelic tunes based on his father's and grandfather's 'work as collectors and singers of Gaelic and Jacobite melodies' (Alburger, 155), including music for well-known Gaelic poems, and his own melodies. Believing his collection 'the most authentic' (S. Fraser, *Airs*, [1816], 3), and worried about financial losses, he criticized Patrick MacDonald's *A Collection of Highland Vocal Airs* (1784), and engaged rival collector Alexander Campbell, author of *Albyn's Anthology* (1816), in acrimonious dispute. However, neither reputation suffered greatly and both works went into several editions (Fraser's most recently in 1982). But an ambitious project to sell *Airs* in America was a failure, since the volumes were apparently pirated before his editions could be sold.

In 1817, having lost the Knockie tenancy, Fraser moved to near Inverness. In 1820, although in 'an impaired state of health' (*Inverness Courier*, 10 Aug 1820, 1), he advertised a second volume of *Airs*, with songs from Sir Walter Scott's *The Lady of the Lake* 'adapted to native melodies' (ibid.); Scott did not approve, and the work never appeared. In 1828, living at 25 Rose Street, Inverness, with Hugh, Catherine, and Jamesina, Fraser made his will, describing Angus as 'the only person belonging to my family that is in any way possessed of the taste or talent necessary for issuing the canon of my life' (Gill, 7). Angus, who was living with Simon by 1845, edited and published volume 2 of *Airs* (n.d., but after 1852) and prepared a new edition of the 1816 work, published posthumously in 1874. His music manuscripts, including some pages of his father's, are now at Edinburgh University. 245 tunes from the manuscript, described at its rediscovery in the 1960s as 'the most important collection of Scottish Gaelic … music to be recovered in the past hundred years' (ibid., 2), have been published as *The Angus Fraser Collection of Scottish Gaelic Airs* (1996).

Simon Fraser's likeness, found in John Glen's *Glen Collection* (1891), shows a poised figure, with a thin and intelligent face and a broad forehead, holding a violin and pen. Said to make the fiddle '*speak Gaelic*' so beautifully, Fraser's 'real value lay in being the son and grandson of musical gentlemen [who realized] the importance of their Gaelic and Jacobite musical repertoire' (Alburger, 154), the publication of which became 'the canon of his life' (Gill, 7). Simon Fraser died at 25 Rose Street, Inverness, on 4 July 1852, 'having been long confined to the house, and frequently to bed, by a gradual but general decay of his physical powers, through which, however, he was sustained by cheerful and well-grounded Christian hope' (*Inverness Courier*, 22 July 1852). His worth at death was £11, including 'One half of manuscript sheet of Gaelic and Dance tunes' and 'A violin belonging to deceased' (will). Angus Fraser died in Inverness on 4 February 1870 from 'hemiplegia and general exhaustion' (Gill, 7).   MARY ANNE ALBURGER

Sources M. A. Alburger, *Scottish fiddlers and their music* (1983); repr. (1996) · D. Baptie, ed., *Musical Scotland, past and present: being a dictionary of Scottish musicians from about 1400 till the present time* (1894) · A. F. [A. Fraser], ed., *The airs and melodies of the highlands & islands of Scotland compiled by the late Captain Simon Fraser*, 2 [4 July 1852–4 Feb 1870] · S. Fraser, ed., *The airs and melodies peculiar to the highlands of Scotland and the isles*, rev. W. Mackay and A. Fraser, new edn (1874); repr. with several additions from the 1816 volume (Sydney, NS, 1982) · C. I. Fraser, *The clan Fraser of Lovat*, 2nd edn (1966) · S. Fraser, ed., *The airs and melodies peculiar to the highlands of Scotland and the isles* (privately printed, Edinburgh, [1816]) · S. Fraser, *The Wellington march* (1815) · S. Fraser, *Thirty highland airs, strathspeys, etc.* (1794–5) · R. H. S. Gill, 'An introduction and complete index to the Angus Fraser manuscript', MA diss., U. Aberdeen, 1997 · J. Glen, *The Glen collection of Scottish dance music*, 1 (1891) · A. Martin and C. Martin, eds., *The Angus Fraser collection of Scottish Gaelic airs* (1996) · D. Warrand, *Some Fraser pedigrees* (1934) · *Inverness Courier* (10 Aug 1820) · *Inverness*

Courier (22 July 1852) · b. cert. · m. cert. · bap. reg. Scot. · inventory and will, proved, 14 Dec 1857, NA Scot., SC 29/44/10
Archives U. Edin. L., papers and family papers | Blair Castle, Perthshire, corresp. with James Hamilton, secretary of the Highland Society of London [copies] · NL Scot., letters to Sir Walter Scott
Likenesses engraving, repro. in Glen, *Glen collection*
Wealth at death £11: inventory and will, proved 14 Dec 1857, NA Scot., SC 29/44/10

Fraser, Simon (1776–1862), explorer and fur trader, was born on 20 May 1776 at Mapletown, Hoosic township, New York, the youngest of the ten children of Simon Fraser (1725?–1779?) of Culbokie and Guisachan (a cadet branch of the highland Frasers of Lovat), a farmer, and his wife, Isabella Grant (1735–1814?) of Daldreggan. His parents had migrated in September 1773 with other highland Roman Catholics to America. During the American War of Independence his loyalist father was captured at the battle of Bennington and died a prisoner in Albany gaol; in 1784 his widowed mother fled with her family to Canada.

Simon Fraser's uncle John Fraser, a prominent Montreal judge, secured for his nephew some limited schooling and, in May 1792, a clerical position with the fur-trading North West Company. A year later he was sent to Canada's far north-west to learn his trade at the isolated Athabascan posts. By 1802 he had been appointed a partner.

In 1805 Fraser was selected to expand the company's trade beyond the Rockies and to explore an imperfectly known river route which the company hoped to use to ship its goods to the Pacific Ocean. Between 1805 and 1807 he founded the first trading posts west of the Rockies, on the newly discovered MacLeod, Stuart, and Fraser lakes, and at Fort George. He named this new wilderness domain New Caledonia.

On 28 May 1808 Fraser left Fort George with two clerks, sixteen voyageurs, and two Native American guides, hoping to discover a new river route to the Pacific. The mouth of the Columbia River had been discovered earlier, and then in 1793 Alexander Mackenzie of the North West Company discovered a river to the west of the Rockies believed to be the Columbia. As the company desperately needed an outlet for its Athabascan and New Caledonian furs and an incoming route for trade goods and supplies, Fraser was directed to explore the 'Columbia' to its mouth. Their gruelling 520 mile expedition took them via wild waters and hair-raising cliff-side portages. At the river's mouth, Fraser was disappointed to learn that they had not after all been following the course of the Columbia River, but that of a second river further to the north, which became known as the Fraser. Worse, hostile coastal natives forced their return, but the party managed to make their way back safely under Fraser's remarkable leadership.

Fraser returned to his duties with the company. From 1810 to 1814 he supervised the Mackenzie River district. Although he was determined to retire from the fur trade in 1815, because of the increasing conflicts with the Hudson's Bay Company he was persuaded to return to oppose them in Athabasca for one more winter. In 1816 he was among the partners arrested by Lord Selkirk at Fort William and charged with complicity in the Seven Oaks massacre. In 1818 all were acquitted. Fraser immediately retired and settled at St Andrews West, Upper Canada (now Ontario), where he farmed and operated mills. On 7 June 1820 he married Catherine (1790–1862), the daughter of Captain Allan Macdonell of Leek; they had nine children but one daughter died in infancy. He also had several children with Native American 'country' wives. His businesses did not flourish, and he was hampered by a knee injury received during the 1837–8 uprising. He died, impoverished, at St Andrews West on 18 August 1862, and his wife died the following day. They were buried on 21 August, in a single grave, in the Roman Catholic cemetery at St Andrews.

Because the route to the Pacific which he discovered was useless as a trade route, Fraser and others initially regarded his exploration as a failure; however, the trading links he set up established British claims to the land which in 1859 was claimed as British Columbia. Fraser's name and feat became widely celebrated in British Columbia, not least by Simon Fraser University.

BARBARA JOY ROGERS

Sources W. K. Lamb, ed., *The letters and journals of Simon Fraser, 1806–1808* (1960) · W. K. Lamb, 'Fraser, Simon', *DCB*, vol. 9 · parish register, RC Church of St Andrews West, Ontario · Simon Fraser University, Fraser MSS · NA Canada, Richard W. Scott collection
Archives NA Canada, MSS · Provincial Archives of British Columbia, Victoria · Public Archives of Ontario, Toronto · Simon Fraser University, Vancouver, MSS · Toronto Public Library · U. Cal., Berkeley, Bancroft Library
Likenesses Robert McCausland Co., stained-glass window, *c*.1928, Canadian Memorial Church, Vancouver, British Columbia, Canada, British Columbia Window · J. Hawes, photograph (after portrait), repro. in A. G. Morice, *The history of the northern interior of British Columbia* (1905), facing p. 54 · J. Innes, oils, Simon Fraser University; on loan · J. Innes, oils, Hudson's Bay Company Museum Coll. · J. Innes, oils, David Spencer Ltd, Vancouver, Canada · C. W. Jefferys, pen and black ink over pencil on wove paper, NA Canada · J. Stobart, portrait (exploring the Fraser River in 1808), repro. in W. Meyers, 'Via the Fraser canyon', *Beaver Magazine* [winter edition] · charcoal sketch (as a young man; after portrait), Simon Fraser University Archives · pencil drawing, Vancouver City Archives, Canada, Bruce McKelvie Finding Aid Box 2, File 4, Add MSS 1170 · photograph, University of British Columbia, Canada, Special Collections and Archives · photograph, Vancouver City Archives, Canada · photograph (after pastel by G. Schipper or W. Berczy?), NA Canada · portrait, Vancouver Public Library, Canada · portrait, priv. coll. · portraits, British Columbia Provincial Archives, 655 Belleville, Victoria, Canada · watercolour?, repro. in *The Columbian* (1 Oct 1908)

Fraser, Simon Augustine, master of Lovat (1939–1994). *See under* Fraser, Simon Christopher Joseph, fifteenth Lord Lovat and fourth Baron Lovat (1911–1995).

Fraser, Simon Christopher Joseph, fifteenth Lord Lovat and fourth Baron Lovat (1911–1995), army officer and landowner, was born in Scotland on 9 July 1911, the elder son and oldest of the five children of Simon Joseph *Fraser, fourteenth Lord Lovat and third Baron Lovat (1871–1933), and his wife, Laura, *née* Lister (1892–1965), second of the three daughters of Thomas *Lister, fourth and last Baron Ribblesdale (1854–1925). His younger brother, Sir

Simon Christopher Joseph Fraser, fifteenth Lord Lovat and fourth Baron Lovat (1911–1995), by unknown photographer, 1944

Hugh Charles Patrick Joseph *Fraser (1918–1984), was Conservative MP for the Stone division of Staffordshire (from 1950 the Stafford and Stone division, and from 1983 Stafford) from 1945 to 1984. As the master of Lovat (as he was styled in his father's lifetime), Fraser was educated at Ampleforth College and Magdalen College, Oxford (1929–32), graduating with a fourth-class degree in modern history. On 18 February 1933 his father died after watching him compete in a point-to-point race near Oxford, and he succeeded to the title and chiefship of clan Fraser and an estate of 190,000 acres in Inverness-shire. The chiefs of clan Fraser are known by their Gaelic title of MacShimidh, but their early male ancestry is Norman-French: Celtic blood came from maternal ancestors of highland stock. Simon Fraser, the eleventh Lord Lovat, a Jacobite, was the last peer to be beheaded in the Tower of London.

After leaving school Lovat had worked for a period on a coffee and cattle ranch in South America, and after leaving Oxford he served in the Scots Guards from 1932 to 1937. On 10 October 1938 he married Rosamund Broughton (b. 1917), the only daughter of Sir Henry John Delves (Jock) *Broughton, eleventh baronet (1883–1942) [see under Hay, Josslyn Victor], who was acquitted in Kenya of the murder of his wife's lover, Josslyn Victor Hay, the twenty-second earl of Erroll, in 1941. They had six children: Simon Augustine (b. 1939) [see below], Fiona Mary (b. 1941), Annabel Térèse (Tessa), (b. 1942), Kim Maurice (b. 1946), Hugh Alastair Joseph (b. 1947), and Andrew Roy Mathew (b. 1952).

On the outbreak of war in 1939 Lovat joined the Lovat scouts, a regiment his father had raised to fight in the Second South African War (1899–1902). Three of his uncles had been killed in the First World War, as had also his godfather, Julian Henry Francis Grenfell, author of the poem 'Into Battle', and this made him all the more anxious to get to grips with the enemy at the earliest possible moment, so he joined the newly formed commandos in 1941. In the same year he took part in the commando raid on the Lofoten islands, where one of their targets was the fish-oil processing station from which the Germans were obtaining glycerine for the manufacture of explosives. The commandos destroyed eighteen factories, sank eleven ships, and burnt 800,000 gallons of petrol and oil. They also brought back an Enigma machine which proved invaluable to the code-breakers at Bletchley Park. Before leaving, with German prisoners and Norwegian volunteers, Lovat used the local post office to send an offensive telegram to Hitler. This raid was followed by similar ventures at Spitsbergen and Vaagso, which had the effect of making Hitler think that Norway was being reconnoitred for an allied invasion and causing him to station 300,000 troops in that country instead of using them more efficiently elsewhere.

Lovat's no. 4 commando, which he had trained extensively in Ayrshire and Dorset, was the most successful unit in the ill fated raid on Dieppe on 19 August 1942. Lovat, who refused to blacken his face or camouflage himself for the raid, on which he carried his Winchester rifle, led his commandos through defended barbed-wire defences up to the German battery at Varengeville, which they destroyed after a brisk fight: this helped to reduce the casualties, already heavy, on the main landing force. He was awarded a DSO to add to the MC he had earned in an earlier reconnaissance raid on Boulogne. On D-day (6 June 1944) he was in command of no. 1 Special Service brigade, which landed at Sword Beach, near Ouistreham, and fought its way ashore for 6 miles up to the Orne Bridge, which had recently been captured and which it was essential to preserve against a German counter-attack. On arrival Lovat marched across Pegasus Bridge accompanied by his piper, apparently indifferent to enemy fire but in fact well aware of the danger he was confronting. After four days' heavy fighting, in which a third of his brigade had become casualties, he was severely wounded. While being evacuated on a stretcher he sent a message to his men: 'I can rely on you not to take a single step back.' Nor did they.

When Lovat had recovered from his wounds Churchill sent him with a parliamentary delegation to Moscow, and added a personal message to Stalin that he was sending him 'the mildest-mannered man that ever scuttled a ship or cut a throat'. After his return Lovat was appointed under-secretary of state for foreign affairs, but he withdrew from politics after Churchill's defeat in 1945. He then returned to the family seat at Beaufort Castle, Inverness-shire, where he bred shorthorn Aberdeen Angus, highland cattle, and sheep, and also reclaimed and reseeded much ground. At one time his farming unit extended to 35,000 acres. He was chairman of the Anglo-

Scottish Cattle Company and travelled extensively, sometimes judging, as at the Sydney Royal Show, and always learning from his observations of practices in countries ranging from Canada and Argentina to South Africa and Australia. As a very conscientious clan chief he also made various overseas visits on clan business and welcomed clan visitors at Beaufort. He was also a renowned big-game hunter and was chairman of the Shikar Club for thirty-five years. In spite of his travels and sporting interests he found time to be a deputy lieutenant, a JP, and a member of Inverness county council for forty-two years.

Athletic, debonair, extremely courageous, and an inspiring leader, Shimi Lovat was also ruthless and intolerant of inefficiency in his army career. He was also erudite, intelligent, humorous, and shrewd. In addition to his British decorations he was awarded the Croix de Guerre avec palme, appointed to the Légion d'honneur, and received the Norway liberation cross. In 1978 his memoir *March Past* was published by Weidenfeld and Nicolson.

In 1970 Lovat had handed over Beaufort Castle and most of his estates to his oldest son, **Simon Augustine Fraser**, master of Lovat (1939–1994). Born on 28 August 1939, and educated at Ampleforth, Simon Augustine Fraser served briefly as a lieutenant in the Scots Guards before studying agriculture at Cirencester Agricultural College. Following his father's transfer of the Beaufort Castle estate, he embarked on a series of enterprises designed to improve the estate's finances, including a bottling plant for Lovat spring water, and a new salmon fishery. Not all of these enterprises were successful, and in 1990, to the consternation of many, he was forced to sell off 30,000 acres of deer forest and a stretch of river. On 21 February 1972 he married Virginia Grose, daughter of David Grose, of Chelsea, a Lloyds underwriter. They had four children: Violet (*b.* 1972), Honor (*b.* 1973). Simon (*b.* 1977), and Jack (*b.* 1984). Simon Augustine died of a heart attack on 26 March 1994, in the grounds of Beaufort Castle, while riding with the Old Dounie Hunt.

Simon Augustine Fraser's sudden death was the second blow within a fortnight for his father, following as it did the news that Lovat's youngest son, Andrew, had died on safari in Tanzania, after being gored by a buffalo. The fifteenth Lord Lovat himself died, peacefully in his sleep, at his home, Balblair House, Beauly, Inverness-shire, on 16 March 1995. He was buried alongside his two sons in the graveyard of St Mary's, Eskadale, Inverness-shire on 21 March. He was survived by his wife, his two remaining sons, and his two daughters, and was succeeded in the barony and clan chiefship by Simon Augustine Fraser's elder son, Simon, then aged eighteen. The combination of death duties and business losses left the family with crippling debts of £7.4 million, including £2.7 million to the Inland Revenue.
　　　　　　　　　　　　　　　　　　　　　PHILIP WARNER

Sources *Debrett's Peerage* · Burke, *Peerage* · *WWW*, 1991–5 · *Daily Telegraph* · *The Times* (17 March 1995) · *The Independent* (20 March 1995) · private information (2004) · Lord Lovat [Simon Fraser, fifteenth Lord Lovat], *March past: a memoir* (1978) · M. L. Melville, *The story of the Lovat scouts* (1981) · C. Messenger, *The commandos, 1940–46* (1991) · R. Butler, *Hand of steel: the story of the commandos* (1980) · R. Neillands, *The raiders: the army commandos, 1940–1946* (1990) · *The Times* (28 March 1994) · *The Times* (22 March 1995)
Likenesses photograph, 10 Oct 1938, Hult. Arch. · photograph, 1944, repro. in *The Times* (17 March 1995) [*see illus.*] · photograph, 1994 (Simon Augustine Lovat), repro. in *The Times* (28 March 1994) · photograph, repro. in *The Times* (22 March 1995) · photograph, repro. in *The Independent* · photographs, IWM · photographs, repro. in Lovat, *March past*
Wealth at death £1,917,999.25: confirmation, 15 Aug 1995, Scotland

Fraser, Simon Joseph, fourteenth Lord Lovat and third Baron Lovat (1871–1933), army officer and landowner, was born at his ancestral home, Beaufort Castle, Beauly, Inverness-shire on 25 November 1871, the second son of Simon Fraser, thirteenth Lord Lovat and second Baron Lovat (1828–1887), and his wife, Alice Mary, fifth daughter of Thomas Weld-Blundell of Ince Blundell, Lancashire. He was educated at home until the age of eleven, then went to the Roman Catholic Benedictine monastery at Fort Augustus. In 1888 he moved to the Oratory School, Edgbaston, before proceeding to Magdalen College, Oxford in 1890. Following the death of his father in 1887 he inherited both the titles and the extensive estates since his eldest brother had died in infancy. In 1883 the estates had amounted to 181,791 acres, which made his father one of the twenty-eight noblemen possessing more than 100,000 acres in the United Kingdom, tenth in order of acreage but twenty-fifth in order of income. The major part of his estates consisted of heather-clad hills of little commercial agricultural value and profitable only for preserving grouse and deer or for afforestation. He later joined an influential committee whose proceedings were reviewed in *The Grouse in Health and Disease* (2 vols., 1911). In 1892 he became forty-first Mac Shimidh, chief of the clan Fraser.

From 1894 to 1897 Lovat served in the first Life Guards but, disillusioned with the ceremonial duties which kept the regiment at London or Windsor, he became a major in the 4th (volunteer) battalion of the Cameron Highlanders. In 1899 he returned from an expedition to the Blue Nile with stuffed specimens of sixteen hitherto unknown species of animals, one of which bears his name. During the Second South African War he raised and eventually commanded the Lovat scouts. This was a corps of highlanders who played a significant part in the conflict: their fieldcraft shattered the legend of Boer invisibility. In 1903 Lord Lovat became lieutenant-colonel and was created CVO.

Lovat continued to be involved with military affairs for much of the next two decades. At a meeting in Oxford in 1902 he advocated the formation of an Officers' Training Corps; and in 1904 he initiated a campaign to draw attention to military shortcomings and the need to pursue a more systematic policy of national defence. He was firmly committed to the Territorial Army, and became chairman of the Inverness Territorial Force Association in 1908. He raised two yeomanry regiments that were part of the Highland mounted brigade, which he commanded from the rank of temporary colonel (1908–13). In 1910 he

Simon Joseph
Fraser, fourteenth
Lord Lovat and
third Baron Lovat
(1871–1933), by
Elliott & Fry

attended early meetings of the Round Table, and promoted cotton production in the Sudan. His marriage to Laura (1892–1965), second daughter of Thomas *Lister, fourth Baron Ribblesdale, took place on 15 October that year; they had two sons and three daughters. Their younger son was the conservative politician Sir Hugh *Fraser (1918–1984).

Lovat and his two younger brothers played an active part in the First World War; but his brother Hugh Joseph Fraser, a major in the Scots Guards, was killed in October 1914. In 1915 Lovat commanded the Highland mounted brigade in Gallipoli, where his other brother, Alaistair Thomas Joseph Fraser, also served as a major. After being invalided home Lovat took charge of the 5th mounted division, responsible for defending the east coast of England from invasion. Following his return to France he held various posts, the most significant of which was the directorship of forestry on the western front. His work was recognized by the French with the award of the Ordre du Mérite Agricole and the Légion d'honneur.

During the land boom following the end of the First World War, Lovat embarked upon an extensive programme of rationalization of his estates. He sold large areas—particularly the deer parks and grouse moors—in order to reduce his mortgage to a manageable size. He became the first chairman (1919–27) of the Forestry Commission and organized the First Empire Forestry Conference, held in Canada in 1923. At the end of that year he was part of a mission invited by the Brazilian government to examine how to enlist British capital in developing the country, and became a founder member of the board of Parane Plantations Ltd. He was also under-secretary of state for the dominions (1927–8) and chairman (1928–9) of the Overseas Settlement Committee and first chairman of the Highlands Reconstruction Association. He was the first convenor of Inverness county council under the Local Government (Scotland) Act of 1929. In 1932 he was appointed chairman of the committee which reported on the economic rationalization of the Scottish municipal administration.

Lovat died suddenly on 18 February 1933 at Little Tew, near Chipping Norton, Oxfordshire, after watching his son win the New College and Magdalen College old members' point-to-point steeplechase challenge cup. His wife survived him. He was buried on 22 February at Eskadale, Inverness-shire. Lovat's position as a member of the House of Lords, large Scottish landowner, and head of a leading Scottish Catholic family enabled him to play a key role in a number of diverse ways, both nationally and internationally. In Scotland he played an important role in the regeneration of the economy. His military reputation was firmly established by Sir Francis Lindley's biography, published shortly after his death, especially with regard to his raising of the Lovat scouts. The fact that Lovat did not achieve higher military office can be attributed at least partly to his lack of pomposity, his critical turn of mind, and keen sense of humour, which did not always find favour with his superiors. He was succeeded, as fifteenth Lord Lovat, by his eldest son, Simon Christopher Joseph *Fraser. JOHN MARTIN

Sources F. Lindley, *Lord Lovat: a biography* (1935) · *The Times* (20 Feb 1933) · *The Times* (28 Feb 1933) · N. D. G. James, *History of English forestry* (1981) · J. Foster, *Oxford men and their colleges* (1893) · G. Donaldson and R. S. Morpeth, *Who's who in Scottish history*, pbk edn (1996) · W. Bennett, *Absent-minded beggars: volunteers in the Boer War* (1999) · *DNB* · *CGPLA Eng. & Wales* (1933)

Archives priv. coll., MSS | NRA, priv. coll., corresp. with Sir John Ewart | FILM BFI NFTVA · IWM FVA, documentary footage · IWM FVA, news footage | SOUND BL NSA · BL NSA

Likenesses Elliott & Fry, photograph, NPG [*see illus.*] · S. Macdonald, portrait, Beaufort Castle · photographs, repro. in Lindley, *Lord Lovat*

Wealth at death under marriage settlement his son, Hugh, was to receive £10,000, and his three daughters £6000 each; in the event of his children going in for a religious career, he wished £2000 to go to Hugh and £1000 each to any of the girls: *The Times* (28 Feb 1933)

Fraser, Thomas (1911–1988), politician, was born at Noonday Cottage, Blackwood, a mining village close to Lesmahagow, Lanarkshire, on 18 February 1911, the son of Thomas Fraser, a coalminer, and his wife, Mary Christie Brown. His parents had married the previous November at Blythswood, Glasgow. He attended local schools and started work in the mines at the age of fourteen, just before the general strike. On 31 December 1935 he married Janet Muncie Scanlon, a domestic servant, the daughter of James Robertson Scanlon, a coal hewer, of Turfholm, Lesmahagow. They had a son and a daughter.

Fraser, who remained an underground coal worker throughout this period, was a branch official of the National Union of Scottish Mineworkers from 1938 to 1943, when he was selected as the Labour Party candidate for parliament at a by-election in Hamilton, a seat which had been held by Labour since 1918. His nomination was supported by the miners' union, which had nominated and financially supported the previous MP. Fraser won the election, in January 1943, with a handsome majority against a local independent (the Conservatives did not contest the seat), and declared that the victory indicated his constituency's message of support to 'our fighting men in the forces' at a time of national crisis. Unusually young for a miners' MP, he thought himself insufficiently qualified to enter parliament and had been unwilling to accept the candidature, as he told Hugh Dalton, who found him 'pleasant, though curiously unassertive', with a sense of humour, and a non-drinker who 'might go quite some way' (*War Diary*, 702–3, 3 Feb 1944). In 1944 Fraser was appointed parliamentary private secretary to Dalton, then president of the Board of Trade in the wartime coalition government, whose responsibilities included the preparation of plans for the post-war reconstruction of British industry. His department took the major lead in ensuring the passage of the Distribution of Industry Act (1945), which introduced government controls on the location of new industry in the regions previously affected by the structural decline in the older industries of coal, iron, and steel.

In 1945 Fraser was appointed joint parliamentary under-secretary of state at the Scottish Office, a position he held until Labour's defeat in the 1951 election, serving Joseph Westwood, Arthur Woodburn, and Hector McNeil as Scottish secretaries in turn. Throughout his period in office he held the development brief, promoting the policy of industrial reconstruction generally and pressing the United Kingdom's 'economic' ministries on the need to relocate industry from the midlands and south of England specifically. Throughout 1946 he took a leading part in securing government support for the siting of Scotland's first new town at East Kilbride. He was greatly concerned that the life of the Lanarkshire coalfield was limited and that by the mid-1950s an estimated 20,000 miners would be either unemployed or required to migrate elsewhere to find work. His concern was so great that he consistently advocated in the cabinet's distribution of industry committee that the state should take active steps to initiate and manage new industry in the regions if private concerns refused the government's financial inducements to move.

Although ultimately unsuccessful, Fraser's dogged pursuit of regional policy and the needs of the Lanarkshire coalfield led to Harold Wilson, the president of the Board of Trade in 1950, agreeing to support the establishment of a subsidiary factory for Rolls-Royce at East Kilbride. It was a move that secured the town's industrial base and created an image of a new town firmly wedded to engineering and new technology.

In opposition between 1951 and 1964, Fraser's pragmatic and open style of politics led him to identify with the right wing of the Labour Party, taking a strongly anti-Bevan line in March 1955. From the autumn of 1955 he was consistently elected to the shadow cabinet, the only Scottish MP to achieve that position. Not surprisingly he took a lead in parliamentary debates on the economic reconstruction of Scotland, most notably between 1957 and 1958 over the government's eventual decision to site an integrated strip steel mill at Colvilles, Motherwell, a decision that secured the future of 5000 steelworkers on the Clyde.

On the return of the Labour government in 1964, Harold Wilson appointed Fraser minister of transport. The ministry came under considerable pressure from Labour MPs who believed firmly that the government should introduce an integrated transport plan based on the railway network. However, Fraser's acknowledgement that private transport, particularly the motor car, held greater public support led to the erosion of back-bench support. His failure during 1965 to produce a plan for the co-ordination of transport contributed to his downfall. He continued the Beeching plan of rail closures, though he was reluctant to permit the closing of lines in major conurbations, in isolated rural areas, or where alternative bus services could not be provided. Former Bevanites within the government, such as Barbara Castle and Richard Crossman, wrote disparagingly of his abilities, unfairly regarding him as a union hack. After he supported the view that nationalized railway workshops should not be allowed to compete for outside business, Castle commented that he was 'too ready to accept the inherited arguments of the civil service' (*Castle Diaries, 1964–70*, 22, 22 March 1965), while Crossman thought his performance 'pretty disastrous' (*Diaries*, 1.204, 18 April 1965).

Fraser's political position was further weakened by the support he gave Sir Frank Soskice, the home secretary, on the introduction of random breath tests to control drink-driving. In fact Fraser believed that this was an infringement of liberty and would offend a significant part of the middle class, whose support Labour required if it was to win the next election. Like Wilson he preferred the use by the police of selective testing on the basis of a related motoring offence. In the event, although the cabinet supported a white paper on drink-driving and the introduction of a 70 m.p.h. speed limit, Wilson sacked Fraser in a reshuffle of ministers in December 1965 ahead of the 1966 election (Soskice being moved to another ministerial post).

In 1967 Fraser resigned his Hamilton seat, which he had held continuously since 1943, to become part-time chairman of the Highlands and Islands Electricity Board, a post he held until 1973. He combined it with part-time membership of the Highlands and Islands Development Board until 1970, when he refused to be considered for a further term. He believed that the latter board wasted considerable public funds on projects with little long-term benefit to employment. His other posts included membership of the royal commission on the reform of local government in Scotland (1966–9) and chairing the committee that oversaw the transfer of staff between authorities consequent on local government reform in 1975. In 1973 he was appointed chairman of the local government commission set up to deal with the transfer of staff involved in the reform of local government.

Fraser was generally well liked by those with whom he came into contact. Unusually, perhaps, for a miners' MP in an area known for its political radicalism, he conducted public office with an open mind and a sense of reaching the 'right decision' based on practical politics. His obvious sense of duty towards the party derived from a deep sense that the labour movement needed to remain united if it was to avoid the deep schisms of the early 1930s, but it also created a view that he lacked the enterprise and drive necessary to maintain ministerial support. He died after a short illness at Law Hospital, Carluke, Lanarkshire, on 21 November 1988. His wife predeceased him.

IAN LEVITT

Sources WW · *Glasgow Herald* (1 Feb 1943) · *Glasgow Herald* (23–4 Dec 1967) · *Glasgow Herald* (22 Nov 1988) · *The Times* (23 Dec 1965) · *The Times* (23 Nov 1988) · *The Guardian* (24 Nov 1988) · I. Levitt, *The Scottish office, 1919–1959* (1995) · I. Levitt, 'New towns, new Scotland, new ideology, 1937–57', *SHR*, 76 (1997) · I. Levitt, 'Britain, the Scottish covenant movement and devolution, 1946–50', *Scottish Affairs*, 22 (1998) · I. Levitt, 'Scottish air services, 1933–75, and the Scottish new towns, 1943–75: a guide to records at the National Archives of Scotland', *Scottish Archives*, 5 (1999) · I. Levitt, 'Scottish papers submitted to the cabinet, 1945–66: a guide to records held at the Public Record Office and National Archives of Scotland', *Scottish Economic and Social History*, 20/1 (2000) · private information (2004) [Scottish office civil servants] · b. cert. · m. cert. · d. cert. · *The Second World War diary of Hugh Dalton, 1940–1945*, ed. B. Pimlott (1986) · *The Castle diaries, 1964–1970* (1984) · R. H. S. Crossman, *The diaries of a cabinet minister*, 1 (1975) · T. R. Gourvish, *British railways, 1948–73: a business history* (1986)
Archives Bodl. RH, corresp. on colonial issues
Wealth at death £9847.97: confirmation, 27 June 1990, *CCI*

Fraser, Sir Thomas Richard (1841–1920), pharmacologist, born in Calcutta on 5 February 1841, was the second son of John Richard Fraser, Indian civil servant, and his wife, Mary Palmer Fraser. He was educated at various Scottish public schools before entering the University of Edinburgh. He graduated MD in 1862 with a gold medal for his thesis, 'On the characters, actions and therapeutic uses of the ordeal bean of Calabar'. A brilliant student, he was taken up by Robert Christison, professor of materia medica at Edinburgh, as his research assistant from 1864 until 1870 when he became an extramural lecturer in materia medica and therapeutics at Surgeons' Hall, Edinburgh. Fraser was appointed assistant physician to Edinburgh Royal Infirmary from 1869 to 1874.

During these years Fraser's researches and papers into the antagonism of poisons established his reputation as one of the foremost pharmacologists in Britain. He became a leading figure in the change from older, empirical, pharmacological methods where the action of remedies was studied through their administration in disease, to the newer scientific approach of first defining the pathological nature of the disease before accurately supplying substances to remedy it. His outstanding work on physostigma, later utilized in ophthalmology, and strophanthus, in cardiology, had its roots in this period and brought him the Bargbier prize of the French Academy for his paper, 'The physiological action of the Calabar bean' in 1868. Fraser was working closely with Alexander Crum-Brown (later professor of chemistry) and in 1868–9 they shared the Royal Society of Edinburgh's biennial Makdougall Brisbane prize for their joint paper, 'The connection between chemical constitution and physiological action'. He had been elected a fellow of the Royal Society of Edinburgh in 1867, and was elected a fellow of the Royal

Sir Thomas Richard Fraser (1841–1920), by Barraud

College of Physicians, Edinburgh, in 1869. Thus, at the early age of twenty-eight, he was already invested with many of the honours coveted by scientific men.

Changes in perception and methodology conspired to bring Fraser into conflict with established personalities. Fraser was a member of the Edinburgh committee of a British Medical Association investigation into the action of mercury as a cholagogue. In 1871 Fraser publicly dissociated himself from the findings of the committee's reporter and convenor, Professor J. Hughes Bennett, which were printed in the *British Medical Journal*, by publishing a 'Sketch of the present state of our knowledge respecting the action of mercury on the liver' in the *Edinburgh Medical Journal*, which was seen by many as a minority report. The quarrel rumbled on throughout the early 1870s.

In 1874 Fraser married Susannah Margaret Duncan, daughter of the Reverend R. Duncan; they had four sons and three daughters. Their seventh child was Sir Francis *Fraser (1885–1964), later professor of medicine at the British postgraduate medical school. Soon afterwards he took the unusual step of leaving Edinburgh, resigning his academic and medical posts, to become medical officer of health for mid-Cheshire, but he remained external examiner in materia medica in the universities of Edinburgh and London. Three years later the situation was remedied when he was recalled to Edinburgh in 1877 to succeed Sir

Robert Christison as professor of materia medica and clinical medicine. By all accounts Fraser was an admired lecturer clothing the sometimes dry subjects with interesting facts: borne out by an affectionate cartoon in the *Quasi cursores* (1884) which showed Fraser in an elegantly nonchalant pose gazing at a specimen held aloft in one upstretched hand with the thumb of his other hand hooked casually into his waistcoat. He had a keen eye, and during his Royal Infirmary years paced the corridors and wards missing nothing and noting everything.

After his position was assured in 1877 Fraser accumulated many establishment appointments, beginning with admiralty adviser on the outbreak of scurvy in Sir George Nares's Arctic expedition in 1877 and his appointment as physician to the Edinburgh Royal Infirmary in 1878. In 1881 he presided over the pharmacology and materia medica section of the International Medical Congress, London. Fraser inherited Christison's role of consulting physician to the Standard Life Assurance Company, and became medical adviser to the Prison Commission in Scotland. In 1898 he was appointed chairman of the Indian plague commission. He was elected president of the Royal College of Physicians, Edinburgh, 1900–02 and received a knighthood in 1902 for his services in India. In 1907 he was appointed honorary physician-in-ordinary to the king in Scotland. Numerous academic honours from British and European universities were heaped on Fraser before and after he retired through ill health in 1917.

In his private life Fraser enjoyed fishing, shooting, and photography, mainly at his country estate at Acharacle, Argyll. He died on 4 January 1920 at his town home, 13 Drumsheugh Gardens, Edinburgh. His funeral service was conducted at the cathedral church of St Mary, Edinburgh, on 8 January, following which he was buried in the Dean cemetery. Fraser was survived by his wife.

BRENDA M. WHITE

Sources *BMJ* (17 Jan 1920), 100–01 · *The Lancet* (10 Jan 1920), 122–3 · A. R. C., *Edinburgh Medical Journal*, 3rd ser., 24 (1920), 122–6 · correspondence and editorial comment, *BMJ*, 422–3, 482, 503 · J. Bell, 'Introductory address delivered at Surgeons' Hall, Edinburgh, at the opening of the medical session, November 1870', *Edinburgh Medical Journal*, 16 (1870–71), 577–90, esp. 579 · J. H. Gaddum, 'The development of materia medica in Edinburgh', *Edinburgh Medical Journal*, 3rd ser., 49 (1942), 721–36, esp. 721–7 · R. M. Birse, *Science at the University of Edinburgh, 1583–1993: an illustrated history to mark the centenary of the faculty of science and engineering, 1893–1983* (1994) · W. B. Hole, *Quasi cursores: portraits of the high officers and professors of the University of Edinburgh at its tercentenary festival* (1884) · W. S. Craig, *History of the Royal College of Physicians of Edinburgh* (1976) · *Medical Directory* (1902) · *WWW*, 1916–28

Archives Royal College of Physicians of Edinburgh, lecture notes · U. Edin. L., lecture notes

Likenesses W. Hole, etching, 1884, Wellcome L. · R. Home, oils, 1919, U. Edin. · Barraud, photograph, Wellcome L. [*see illus.*] · W. Hole, cartoon, NPG, Royal College of Physicians of Edinburgh; repro. in Hole, *Quasi cursores* · T. M. Ronaldson, oils, Royal College of Physicians of Edinburgh, Duncan Room · A. Swan, photograph, repro. in *BMJ* (17 Jan 1920), 1

Wealth at death £19,364 10*s.* 7*d.*: confirmation, 10 April 1920, *CCI*

Fraser, William (*d.* 1297), bishop of St Andrews, was the son of Sir Gilbert Fraser, sheriff of Traquair, and his wife, Christina, and was perhaps born at Oliver Castle in Peeblesshire. William's brother Simon held the same shrieval office and was father of Sir Simon *Fraser (*d.* 1306). He was probably at Oxford in 1256–7 and was a master by 1271, when he was dean of Glasgow; by 1277 he was parson of Ayr, by which time he was certainly chancellor of Alexander III—he may have held that office since 1273. His advancement was presumably due to the king's patronage, which finally secured him election to the see of St Andrews on 4 August 1279; he was consecrated by the pope at Rome on 19 May following. He ceased to be chancellor about this time, and he is not known to have been politically active in the following six years; indeed he seems to have been at the curia again in 1284–5.

On the sudden death of Alexander III on 19 March 1286, Fraser was cast into a leading role in the assemblies at which the Scots sent an embassy to Edward I, swore to preserve the royal dignity for the rightful heir, and chose six guardians, including the bishops of St Andrews and Glasgow, for a time which was originally that of the queen's pregnancy, but, when the infant was stillborn or died, stretched out for six and a half years. The guardians successfully put down a rebellion by the Brus family in the winter of 1286–7, and so consolidated their control that by 1289 negotiations to winkle the heiress Margaret, the Maid of Norway, out of the possession of her father, Erik II of Norway, had been successfully concluded, while a marriage treaty with England incorporating protection of a Scotland 'free in itself and without subjection' (Stevenson, 1.167) was concluded at Northampton on 28 August 1290. For all this Bishop William visited England several times and maintained contact with Edward I by messenger; he was clearly the leading protagonist of this alliance among the guardians (now four in number after the deaths in 1289 of the earls of Buchan and Fife).

On 7 October 1290 the bishop sent a famous letter from Leuchars in Fife to Edward I, reporting rumours of the death of Margaret in Orkney, and sinister military moves by Robert (V) de Brus. He asked Edward to speak with Balliol should he visit him, and ended with a plea: if the Maid had indeed died 'let your excellency deign to approach the border, for the consolation of the Scottish people and for avoiding the shedding of blood, so that the faithful men may keep their oath [of 1286] inviolate and set over them for king him who of right ought to have the succession, if so be that he will follow your advice' (Stones and Simpson, 2.3–4). The last nine words so contradict the oath that they may be the result of miscopying by a clerk, for Fraser showed himself a determined upholder of the freedom of the kingdom; he still thought that Edward I presented the best guarantee of that.

The demand for overlordship made by Edward I was accepted in obscure circumstances, including the condition that the guardians remain in office with an associate appointed by Edward; from mid-June 1292 the bishop and others certainly swore fealty to Edward as overlord for the time of adjudication. In the Great Cause Fraser acted as one of the forty judges or assessors named by John de Balliol, and on 6 November 1292 was the first of the

Scottish eighty assessors to approve Edward's judgment in Balliol's favour over the claim of Brus. Final judgment for Balliol on 17 November was followed by the guardians giving him sasine [seisin] of the kingdom.

As early as 1288 Bishop William had been sued by John Mazun, a Gascon wine merchant, over the debts of Alexander III, and this case was still *sub judice* in February 1293; by then his action as guardian for the heir to the earldom of Fife in denying sasine of certain lands to Macduff, a relative of the late earl, was on its way through the Scottish courts. King John's parliament of February 1293 upheld the bishop, and Macduff's appeal to King Edward was ultimately the *casus belli* in 1296. On 2 January 1293 Fraser and three lay magnates had protested to Edward against the hearing of appeals outside Scotland, so that the king's determined assertion of his lordship by hearing appeals steadily alienated Bishop William and other supporters of King John's rights.

With the outbreak of Anglo-French war in 1294 their opportunity came. In 1295 King John was subjected by the Scottish community to direction by a council of twelve, certainly including Bishop Fraser, who was appointed an envoy to France at Stirling on 5 July 1295, and who concluded the Franco-Scottish treaty at Paris on 23 October. Still in France during the Scottish collapse between April and July 1296, he did not return thereafter, dying at Auteuil, just outside Paris, on 20 August 1297. He was buried in the Dominican friary there, though his heart was later buried at St Andrews.

Fraser had been one of the misguided who believed that Edward I was a fair man who would choose the rightful king of Scots and secure the acceptance of that king by rival Scots, all without any advantage to the English crown. Robert Wishart, bishop of Glasgow, stood up to Edward in 1291, but William Fraser took longer to realize the purpose of Edward's policy. When he did, his response was as robust as Wishart's, for he was no less patriotic. In the sharing of leadership among the guardians the two bishops seem to have been pre-eminent, at least after the deaths of the two earls in 1289. A. A. M. DUNCAN

Sources J. Dowden, *The bishops of Scotland … prior to the Reformation*, ed. J. M. Thomson (1912), 19–21 · D. E. R. Watt, *A biographical dictionary of Scottish graduates to AD 1410* (1977) · G. W. S. Barrow, *Robert Bruce and the community of the realm of Scotland*, 3rd edn (1988) · E. L. G. Stones and G. G. Simpson, eds., *Edward I and the throne of Scotland, 1290–1296*, 2 vols. (1978) · W. Gibson-Craig, *Facsimiles of the national manuscripts of Scotland*, 1 (1867), no. 70 · J. Stevenson, ed., *Documents illustrative of the history of Scotland*, 2 vols. (1870)
Likenesses cast of seal, NA Scot. · seal, Durham DGC, misc. ch. nos. 1296, 1305, 740

Fraser, William, twelfth Lord Saltoun of Abernethy (1654–1715), landowner and politician, was born on 21 November 1654, the second son of Alexander Fraser, master of Saltoun (*c.*1630–1682), and his first wife, Lady Anne Kerr (1631–1658), eldest daughter of William *Kerr, earl of Lothian (*c.*1605–1675). Both he and his elder brother, Alexander, matriculated at King's College, Aberdeen, in 1667. Following the death of Alexander in December 1672 Fraser was much involved in his father's lawsuits. He went to France in 1679 and stayed until he was recalled by his

grandfather in September 1680. On 29 October 1681 the duke of York procured a commission for him as a captain in the earl of Mar's regiment, but he resigned his commission following his father's death in November 1682. Now master of Saltoun he married, on 11 October 1683, Margaret (*d.* 1734), second daughter of James *Sharp (1618–1679), archbishop of St Andrews. They had three sons and four daughters. Despite a marriage portion of 40,000 merks he still had to sell land in 1689 and 1690.

Fraser succeeded his grandfather, Alexander Fraser, as Lord Saltoun on 11 August 1693, and took his seat in parliament on 7 May 1695, where he joined the grouping around Sir John Dalrymple. In August 1697 Saltoun initiated a plan to marry his eldest son, Alexander, to Emilia Fraser, the heir of Hugh Fraser, Lord Lovat, but he reckoned against the determination of the residual heirs, Thomas Fraser of Beaufort and his son, Simon, to thwart the match. They warned Saltoun not to enter Inverness-shire without their permission, and when Saltoun paid a visit to the dowager Lady Lovat they kidnapped and imprisoned him on 6 October 1697 and threatened him with the gallows. Saltoun fell prey to dysentery and was released after signing a paper promising not to pursue the marriage. If that marriage was designed to pay off his creditors Saltoun found another way and by judicious land sales he cleared his estates from debt.

In the 1698 parliament Saltoun was accounted an opposition peer and in 1700 he signed the opposition's petition asking that parliament meet at the time to which it had been adjourned. In the 1700–01 session he supported an act asserting Scotland's right to Darien, rather than the preferred option of an address to the crown. He also voted against a standing army. He did not attend the parliament in 1702. Saltoun opposed the union with England, voting against the ratification of the treaty on 16 January 1707. He came under suspicion when a Jacobite invasion threatened in 1708, a warrant being ordered for his arrest on 8 March, but it was respited on 13 May owing to ill health, he giving bond of £3000 to 8 November.

Saltoun died on 18 March 1715 and was buried in the family vault at Fraserburgh. He was survived by his wife, who died in Edinburgh on 29 August 1734, and was succeeded by his son Alexander (1684–1748).

STUART HANDLEY

Sources GEC, *Peerage* · A. Fraser, *The Frasers of Philorth*, 3 vols. (1879) · *Scots peerage* · C. Dalton, *The Scots army, 1661–1688* (1909) · P. Hopkins, *Glencoe and the end of the highland war* (1986) · *The manuscripts of the House of Lords*, new ser., 12 vols. (1900–77), vol. 8, pp. 87, 111, 199 · P. W. J. Riley, *King William and the Scottish politicians* (1979) · J. R. N. MacPhail, ed., *Papers from the collection of Sir William Fraser*, Scottish History Society, 3rd ser., 5 (1924) · P. W. J. Riley, *The union of England and Scotland* (1978) · C. Innes, ed., *Fasti Aberdonenses … 1494–1854*, Spalding Club, 26 (1854)
Likenesses oils, repro. in Fraser, *Frasers of Philorth*, vol. 2, p. 192

Fraser, William (1784–1835), administrator in India, second son of Edward Satchwell Fraser (1751–1835) and his wife, Jane, was born on the family estate at Moniack, near Inverness, on 6 September 1784. The estate was heavily mortgaged as a result of poor investments in Guiana, and William went to India in 1801 expressly to repair the family's fortunes. All four of his brothers followed him, but only the eldest, James Baillie *Fraser (1783–1856), survived to return home.

William arrived in Calcutta in February 1802 and attended Fort William College, where he won a succession of prizes. From 1805 to 1814 he served in various subordinate capacities to the resident at Delhi, initially David Ochterlony and then Archibald Seton. Fraser thrived at Delhi. His Indian lifestyle, gruff temperament, and notoriously scant regard for physical danger were soon the stuff of local legend.

In 1808–9 Fraser accompanied Mountstuart Elphinstone on his expedition to Kabul. In 1814–15 he served as the political agent for the Anglo-Nepal War, in which capacity he rallied a force of 6000 irregular troops, among them many Gurkha defectors who went on to serve in the first two British Gurkha regiments established after the war. In May 1815 he was directed to begin the settlement of Garhwal and with his brother James he made an extensive tour of the Himalayan foothills, hitherto largely unexplored by Europeans. In 1820 he was appointed deputy superintendent of the Delhi territory and in July 1821 was further promoted to become the second member of the board of commissioners in the ceded and conquered provinces. In 1825, as a major in Skinner's horse, he fought at the siege of Bharatpur, drawing the high praise from Skinner that 'a better soldier than [William] never drew cold steel in the world'. In January 1830 he was appointed resident and agent to the governor-general at Delhi, a post he held until his death. On the evening of 22 March 1835 he was shot dead while riding towards his Delhi home. He was buried the next day in the burial-ground at Delhi; his remains were subsequently removed to a marble tomb in the churchyard of St James's Church, Delhi. The tomb was destroyed in 1857. The murder of such a prominent and popular civilian shocked Delhi's population, Indian and European alike. The assassin was identified as one Karim Khan, hired by the young nawab of Firozpur, Shams al-Din, whose affections Fraser had alienated during his settlement of a rancorous inheritance dispute between him and his younger brothers. Both Karim Khan and Shams al-Din were tried and hanged.

Fraser never married (at least in the eyes of the church), but he maintained several Indian mistresses. His favourite *bibi*, Amiban, appears in several of the paintings he and his brother James commissioned from Delhi artists. He had several children but James failed to persuade him to send any of them to him in Scotland.

KATHERINE PRIOR

Sources M. Archer and T. Falk, *India revealed: the art and adventures of James and William Fraser, 1801–35* (1989) • M. Irving, *A list of inscriptions on Christian tombs or monuments in the Punjab, North-West Frontier Province, Kashmir, and Afghanistan*, ed. G. W. de Rhé-Philipe, 2 (1912), 114–15 • M. M. Kaye, ed., *The golden calm* (1980) • writers' petitions, company servants' bonds, Bengal administrations, East India Company documents, BL OIOC • J. Lawrence, 'Murder of Commissioner Fraser, Delhi, 1835: a tale of circumstantial evidence', *Blackwood*, 113 (1878) • W. Dalrymple, *City of djinns* (1993)

Archives NRA Scotland, priv. coll., corresp. and papers | BL OIOC, East India Company documents

Likenesses H. Raeburn, oils, *c*.1801, repro. in Archer and Falk, *India revealed*, fig. 5 • R. Home?, watercolour, *c*.1806, priv. coll. • Lallji or Hulas Lal, miniature on ivory, 1815, priv. coll. • watercolour, *c*.1830, priv. coll. • portrait, after 1835, Indar Pasricha collection • portraits, repro. in Archer and Falk, *India revealed*, figs. 6, 11, 15, 17

Wealth at death £60,000 p.a., according to brother: Archer and Falk, *India revealed*, 56

Fraser, Sir William (1816–1898), genealogist and archivist, was born at Links of Arduthie, by Stonehaven, Kincardineshire, on 18 February 1816. Though his father, James (*d*. 1834), and grandfather William were stonemasons, Fraser's paternal forebears came of farming stock in Strathspey and Stratha'an, in Banffshire. His mother, Ann Walker (*d*. 1821), was a farmer's daughter from Fetteresso, Kincardineshire. She had three children, William, John, and Ann, but died when William (the eldest) was only five. John died young, and William and Ann lost their father in 1834. In 1830 William, having been schooled privately, was apprenticed to a firm of writers (solicitors) in Stonehaven. Almost archetypally the 'lad o' pairts', he sought his fortune in Edinburgh in 1835, joining the well-established firm of Hill and Tod, writers to the signet. He attended classes in the University of Edinburgh, including Scottish law and conveyancing. Dry as these subjects must have been, they fired young Fraser's enthusiasm for the study of Scottish history and the documents on which that history must be based. His capacity for familiarizing himself with a remarkably wide range of document collections in public custody and also in private ownership was clearly phenomenal. Already by 1847, when he was enlisted to edit the Dryburgh Abbey cartulary for the Bannatyne Club, John Spottiswoode wrote of 'his intimate acquaintance with old writings' and 'his zeal and intelligence in antiquarian research' (*Liber S. Mariae de Dryburgh*, 1847, page inserted before the preface). For that work Fraser had investigated the contents of no fewer than fourteen family collections of muniments.

By 1851 Fraser had gained the status of solicitor before the Supreme Court, and might have looked forward to a lucrative career in private practice, not only in litigation over property but also in peerage cases. However, he took the decisive step in the following year of accepting appointment as assistant keeper of the register of Sasines (the official record of all conveyances of land and other real estate in Scotland). Politically motivated appointments blocked Fraser's further promotion for many years, but at last in 1880 he was made deputy keeper of the records—effectively head of all offices in the Register House—and held the post until his compulsory retirement in 1892.

As a solicitor, Fraser had served as clerk to notable advocates, among them the eminent medievalist Cosmo Innes. Another was Charles Baillie, later a judge as Lord Jerviswoode. With him Fraser was involved in settling a Renfrewshire boundary dispute which he must surely have found congenial, involving as it did essentially medieval procedures of perambulation and the testimony of the oldest local gamekeepers, shepherds, and farmers. A lengthy minute of the case, 'drawn by William Fraser', was elaborately printed at Edinburgh in 1852, accompanied by a large hand-coloured map (*Duchall Muir Marches*). In the 1840s and 1850s Fraser, especially while partner in the firm of Gibson and Fraser, provided expert advice in peerage cases and published genealogical material which presaged his later family histories. Some of this related to the north Ayrshire family of Makdougall Brisbane of Brisbane, one of the three landowning families in the boundary dispute already mentioned.

The earliest Fraser family history was *The Stirlings of Keir and their Family Papers* (1858), produced, as was to be the case with all subsequent histories, at the expense of the family. Fraser was lucky in two respects. He hit upon exactly the right formula for his enterprise, with memoirs of the family clearly separated from the documents, charters, letters and so on illustrating the family fortunes. He caught precisely the moment when romanticism, family pride, Scottishness, and a heightened awareness of national identity (greatly boosted by Queen Victoria), combined with advances in editorial scholarship (in which the Scottish publishing clubs had set a notable example) to generate a spirit of emulation among the titled landowners of Scotland. The Montgomeries, earls of Eglinton, Stirling Maxwells of Pollok, Carnegies, earls of Southesk, Colquhouns of Luss, Frasers of Philorth (lords Saltoun), Grants of Grant, Steuarts of Grandtully, Wemyss of Wemyss, Melvilles, earls of Melville, and Leslies, earls of Leven (the list is not exhaustive), all vied with each other to ensure that their family annals appeared in the red bindings with gilt Gothic lettering, in stout, expensive volumes which were to become familiar. Fraser was not always successful. He got nowhere with the dukes of Atholl, Gordon, Hamilton or Roxburghe, and the earl of Haddington protested at his financial demands. Although he carried out searches at Inveraray with a view to producing a 'Campbell book', no such work appeared. His biggest catch was the fifth and sixth dukes of Buccleuch and Queensberry, for whom after much delay Fraser edited *The Scotts of Buccleuch* (2 vols., 1878) and the massive *Douglas Book* (4 vols., 1885). He was on friendly terms with the ninth marquess of Lothian and his father, but never completed a history of the Kerrs of Ferniehirst and Newbattle. His last work was devoted to the lords Elphinstone, Balmerino, and Coupar; it appeared in two volumes in 1897, shortly before the author's death. Altogether, over forty years, Fraser chronicled twenty-four families in forty-nine volumes. This astonishing achievement was made possible by a capacity for hard work, a salaried office which demanded a fairly short working day, a memory which never failed, and strong, clear handwriting, all which qualities marked his output to the end. Fraser was ahead of his contemporaries in publishing facsimiles of many of the records he edited. After his death his trustees published 288 of these, with a summary catalogue (1903).

When the Historical Manuscripts Commission was set up in 1869, the distinguished record scholar John Stuart was put in charge of its Scottish activities. Fraser was an obvious choice first to assist Stuart (1870), then to succeed him (1877). His labours as a family historian helped him

greatly as an inspector of historical record in private hands, and vice versa. Indeed, sometimes the manuscripts to be reported on were actually in his own custody. Many of the reports and appendices in the commission's folio volumes were Fraser's work, often dealing with collections he already knew well.

It is noteworthy that Fraser was able to persuade the families whose history he compiled to pay for the printing and production of the volumes, although he himself retained most of these (usually limited to a few hundred) and sold them for relatively high prices. The resulting income, fees for peerage cases and other legal work, shrewd investments, and ingrained habits of thrift made Fraser a wealthy man. An inveterate snob, he dearly loved a lord and liked nothing better than hobnobbing with the landed classes. With many of them his relations were warm and friendly, and in middle life his skill as a shot made him a welcome addition to shooting parties on ducal and other grouse moors. Handsome and affable, Fraser was a great favourite with the ladies, but he never married and his sister, who was also single, kept house for them both from 1846 until her death three months before his own.

In 1860 Fraser acquired 32 Castle Street, Edinburgh, the house in which Kenneth Grahame, author of *The Wind in the Willows*, had been born the previous year. This was to be his home until his death there on 13 March 1898. He was buried in Dean cemetery, Edinburgh. To the last he retained a fondness for the volumes he had edited, his 'red remnants' as he calls them in a letter accompanying a copy of the *Cartulary of Cambuskenneth* (1872) which he gave in January 1898 to Dr Heron Watson, the physician who had attended his sister just before her death. Even in this letter Fraser could not resist referring to the 'young Lord' (Elphinstone) to whom he had some days earlier given a copy of his last family history. His contribution to the publication of Scottish historical record had been formally recognized in the 1880s: in 1882 the University of Edinburgh conferred the honorary degree of doctor of laws; three years later Gladstone, as Liberal prime minister, made him a CB; and in 1887 Gladstone's Conservative successor, Lord Salisbury, informed Fraser that the queen had been pleased to confer the knight commandership of the Bath, an honour which obviously gave Fraser immense satisfaction.

At his death Fraser left estate worth over £104,000, a very considerable sum at the time, of which £25,000 was to go to Edinburgh University to endow a chair in 'what may be considered my life work', but unfortunately his will called this 'ancient history'. After taking legal advice the university diverted a sum sufficient to fund a lectureship in classical history, the remainder being enough to endow the Sir William Fraser chair of Scottish history, which was first filled by Peter Hume Brown. Other provisions required the building and maintenance of the Fraser homes, originally intended for indigent authors and artists; and there were generous gifts to the university library and the Royal Infirmary of Edinburgh.

William Fraser was not a profound interpreter of the

past, nor did he have the imagination or breadth of vision which makes the true historian. But he possessed in abundance the attention to factual detail which is essential for the scholar whose *métier* is to edit and produce source material. In terms of the sheer volume of family histories and editions of original charters and other documents, published over a period of more than half a century, he has had no rival among Scottish antiquaries and genealogists.   G. W. S. BARROW

Sources G. Donaldson, *Sir William Fraser* (1985) · J. R. N. MacPhail, ed., *Papers from the collection of Sir William Fraser*, Scottish History Society, 3rd ser., 5 (1924) · *The Scotsman* (15 March 1898), 7 · Fraser trustees minute books, priv. coll. · GEC, *Peerage*, new edn, vol. 9 · W. Fraser to P. H. Watson, 7 Jan 1898, priv. coll.
Archives Lyon Office Library, notes on deputy keepers of the records of Scotland and papers relating to patents of peerage and Berwickshire families · NA Scot., collection of deeds and papers · NA Scot., corresp. and papers · NA Scot., historical notes, transcripts, corresp., GD397 · NA Scot., jottings on first visit to London, GD237/21/58 · NL Scot., corresp. and papers, MSS 90, 3553, 5406, 8902–8906 · NRA Scotland, priv. coll., corresp. and MSS relating to Douglas Barony · PRO, corresp. as HMC inspector, HMC1 · Tods, Murray and Jamieson, W.S., Edinburgh, Fraser Trustees, private MSS · U. Edin. L., lecture notes | BL, corresp. with W. E. Gladstone, Add. MSS 44388–44521, *passim* · NA Scot., corresp. with duke of Buccleuch, GD224/197/1003 · NA Scot., corresp. with Lord Lothian, etc., GD40/9 · NA Scot., letters to Lord Polwarth, GD 157 · NL Scot., corresp. incl. with Lord Rosebery · NL Scot., letters to Lord Tweeddale, MS 14465 · U. Edin. L., corresp. with David Laing
Likenesses W. Crabb, oils, 1869, U. Edin. · C. Laurie, engraving, 1886 (after photograph?), repro. in Macphail, ed., *Papers from the collection of Sir William Fraser*, frontispiece · T. Faed, oils, 1887 (after photograph?), Merchants' Hall, Hanover Street, Edinburgh · photograph, 1887, repro. in Donaldson, *Sir William Fraser* · Debenham of Edinburgh, photograph, NPG · mezzotint, BM
Wealth at death £104,728 17s. 1d.: Donaldson, *Sir William Fraser*, 61

Fraser, William (1817–1879), educationist, was born at Cullen in Banffshire about the end of 1817. He was educated at the Edinkillie parish school, attended Belfast College for a term, and then proceeded to the Glasgow Normal Seminary, where he became a master and disciple of David Stow. He appears to have attended Glasgow University, but did not take a degree. Together with Stow and most of the teaching staff, Fraser left the Normal Seminary in 1843 after the Disruption of the Scottish church. Meeting initially in tents, Stow and his followers established the Glasgow Free Church Normal College, where Fraser taught for several years. He was deeply influenced by Stow's educational philosophy, especially by his belief in the integrity of mental and moral development and by his faith that schooling could overcome the effects of a deprived home.

Fraser left the college to study theology at New College, Edinburgh. He was ordained in 1848 and in 1849 became pastor of the Free Middle Church, Paisley, where he remained until his death. In 1854 he married Isabella Harriet Pollock of Dublin, some years his junior, and they had a large family.

In 1857 Fraser toured Great Britain and Ireland to collect information that would assist in establishing a national educational system for Scotland. His findings reinforced his conviction that non-denominational education neglected the spiritual development of children, even supposing it could be achieved in a sectarian society. His work *The State of our Educational Enterprises* (1858) established his reputation as an educationist and several of his suggestions were incorporated in the Education Bill for Scotland. Fraser's other writings included his adulatory and influential *Memoir of the Life of David Stow* (1868).

Since 1850 Fraser had conducted a class for Sunday school boys, out of which grew the Paisley Young Men's Bible Institute. Their Sunday evening discussions pondered the challenges to faith posed by contemporary developments in science, archaeology, and textual criticism. From these discussions emerged Fraser's most personal work, *Blending Lights, or, The Relations of Natural Science, Archaeology, and History, to the Bible* (1873). In his belief that modern discoveries need not jeopardize faith, Fraser accepts the compromise originally propounded by Sir Francis Bacon that distinguished between the word of God, as enunciated in the Bible, and the works of God, knowable through empirical observation. His boldest assertion was that the ordinary reader has both the right and the duty to submit the Bible to critical scrutiny. Although modest in its intentions and ultimately cautious on the subjects of man's origins and evolution, the work reveals Fraser as a generous and fair-minded teacher applying Stow's principle of the compatibility of mental and spiritual development.

In 1857 Fraser revived the Paisley Philosophical Society, becoming its president about 1864. He made collections which later formed the basis of the museum and worked to establish a free library and museum for Paisley. In 1867 he announced on behalf of the wealthy thread manufacturer Sir Peter Coats the donation of a site and buildings for both the library and museum. Fraser also drew up a list of about 3000 volumes and raised £1000 to set up a reference library in addition to the free lending library. Also under Fraser's direction the Philosophical Society tried to serve the educational needs of both the middle and working classes in Paisley.

Fraser served twice on the Paisley school board. In 1872 he received an honorary LLD from the University of Glasgow. By 1878 his health was failing, and he died at his residence, the Free Middle Church manse, Paisley, on 21 September 1879, survived by his wife and eight children. He was highly respected in Paisley, a cheque for 2000 guineas being presented to him on behalf of the community shortly before his death. Large crowds attended his funeral and followed the procession to Woodside cemetery. He is remembered today as the biographer who recorded Stow's life with the passion of a disciple and for his contributions to Paisley's educational institutions, especially the museum and public library.

ELIZABETH J. MORSE

Sources Irving, *Scots.* · W. Ewing, ed., *Annals of the Free Church of Scotland, 1843–1900*, 1 (1914) · *Memorial volume of the proceedings in connection with the establishment of the Free Library and Museum, Paisley* (1871) · 'Churches … and their ministers: Free Middle—now St

John's', *Paisley and Renfrewshire Gazette* (10 Sept 1953) • W. M. Metcalfe, *A history of Paisley, 600–1908* (1909) • *The John Neilson Institution: its first fifty years* (1902) • W. I. Addison, *A roll of graduates of the University of Glasgow from 31st December 1727 to 31st December 1897* (1898) • R. Brown, *The history of the Paisley grammar school* (1875) • Boase, *Mod. Eng. biog.* • *DNB* • *CCI* (1880) • obituaries, Central Library, Paisley, Local Studies Library

Likenesses photograph, Paisley Museum and Art Galleries, Lantern Slide Collections • portrait, Paisley Museum and Art Galleries; in poor condition

Wealth at death £565 16s. 1d.: confirmation, 12 May 1880, *CCI*

Fraser, Sir William Augustus, of Ledclune, fourth baronet (1826–1898), politician and author, born on 10 February 1826, was the eldest son of Colonel Sir James John Fraser, third baronet (*d.* 1834), of the 7th hussars, who was on the staff at Waterloo, and his wife, Charlotte Anne, only child of Daniel Craufurd, and niece of Major-General Robert Craufurd. Succeeding to the baronetcy as a child, Fraser left Eton College in 1844, and after three years at Christ Church, Oxford (graduating BA 1849, MA 1852), was gazetted a cornet in the 1st Life Guards on 4 June 1847. He left the army, shortly after obtaining a captaincy in 1852, to enter politics. A staunch Conservative, he became a familiar figure at the Carlton Club, where he was known pre-eminently as a raconteur of stories about Wellington and Waterloo, and latterly of Disraeli and Napoleon III. He was a great hero-worshipper, and was especially fascinated by the spectacle of great and successful ambition concealed beneath a mask of melancholy impassivity. On Wellington he gradually became a considerable authority. He practically decided the vexed question as to the place where the Waterloo ball was held, and he preserved many little details of the great duke, which but for him would have been lost. His results were printed in a very loosely compacted volume of anecdotes called *Words on Wellington* (1889), followed by *The Waterloo Ball* (1897). Similar volumes of personal gossip, with a large admixture of autobiography promiscuously huddled together in paragraphs, were *Disraeli and his Day* (1891) (an important and influential source), *Hic et ubique* (1893), and *Napoleon III* (1896).

Fraser's zeal as a collector of old maxims, relics, and *bons mots* accorded well with his political views. He believed, with Disraeli, that the Garter and election at White's were the two culminating peaks of human ambition. His parliamentary hero was Disraeli, though he also, surprisingly, admired Richard Cobden. The ups and downs of his own political career were somewhat remarkable. In 1852 he was returned as a Conservative at the head of the poll for Barnstaple, but the election was declared void for bribery, and the constituency, a notoriously corrupt one, was disfranchised for two years. At the election of 1857 Fraser, who had in the meantime been defeated at Harwich, stood again at Barnstaple, and was again returned at the top of the poll. He was, however, defeated in 1859, coming out this time at the bottom of the poll. In 1863 he was chosen without opposition at a by-election at Ludlow, but he held this seat for no more than two years, and then remained out of parliament until 1874, when he was

returned for Kidderminster. This constituency he represented until the general election of 1880, when he retired. In 1877 Fraser rendered a great service to historical research by moving (on 9 March) for a return relative to members of the House of Commons from 1295 to 1696 to be printed as a supplement to the return from 1696 onwards, printed in 1876. This was accomplished in 1878. He was elected FSA on 11 December 1862, and during the later years of his life was a member of Queen Victoria's bodyguard for Scotland.

From his anecdotes it might be assumed that Fraser was only less susceptible to beauty than to wit and valour, but he maintained Disraeli's opinion that a man in chambers was the only true master of the universe, and he died a bachelor in the Albany, Piccadilly, on 17 August 1898. He bequeathed his large fortune to his nephew, Sir Keith Alexander, eldest son of General James Keith Fraser, formerly colonel of the 1st Life Guards, who succeeded to the baronetcy. He left his splendid collection of Gillray's caricatures to the House of Lords, a similar collection of H. B.'s caricatures to the House of Commons, and a unique set of portraits of former speakers to the House of Commons, the chairs of Thackeray and Dickens respectively to the Travellers' Club and the Athenaeum, Nelson's sword to the United Service Club, Byron's sofa to the Garrick, the manuscript of Gray's 'Elegy' to Eton College Library, and the duke of Marlborough's sword to the Scots Guards at St James's Palace. The chief portion of his library was auctioned by Sothebys from 22 to 30 April 1901.

Besides the works mentioned Fraser published anonymously in 1867 and 1869 two little volumes of verse, and issued (in 1876) 300 copies of some annotations on Pope by Horace Walpole from a copy in his possession. He also issued *London Self-Governed* (1866), a plea for more centralized municipal bodies for London, with an amusing denunciation of the Metropolitan Board of Works.

THOMAS SECCOMBE, *rev.* H. C. G. MATTHEW

Sources *The Times* (18 Aug 1898) • *The Scotsman* (20 Aug 1898) • *The Guardian* (24 Aug 1898), 1283 • W. F. Monypenny and G. E. Buckle, *The life of Benjamin Disraeli*, 6 vols. (1910–20)

Likenesses Ape [C. Pellegrini], caricature, watercolour study, repro. in *VF*, 13 (9 Jan 1875)

Wealth at death £450,166 13s. 11d.: probate, 13 Oct 1898, *CGPLA Eng. & Wales*

Fraser, William Milligan, first Baron Strathalmond (1888–1970), oil industrialist, was born on 3 November 1888 in Glasgow, the second of the eight children of William Milligan Fraser (1852–1915), who founded and became managing director of the Pumpherston Oil Company, and his wife, Janet Loch. He was educated at Glasgow Academy (*c.*1899–1906) and then at the Royal Technical College, Glasgow, where he worked in the department of technical chemistry which had been endowed by Dr James Young, founder of the Scottish shale-oil industry.

After finishing his education, Fraser remained in Glasgow in a close-knit community of business and family connections. In 1909 he joined the Pumpherston Oil Company, which was the largest of the Scottish shale-oil enterprises, and made his first visit to North America on commercial and technical investigations. In 1913 he was appointed a director of the company and that same year he married Mary Roberton (d. 1963), daughter of Thomson McLintock, who in 1877 had founded the Glasgow accountancy firm that bore his name and who in 1913 was also chairman of the Pumpherston Oil Company. In 1915 Fraser became a director of that company, after the death of his father. By that time the First World War had broken out and Fraser was devoting much effort to the pressing need for increased domestic oil production. He went to the USA as chairman of the inter-allied petroleum specifications commission which had the task of co-ordinating supplies of oil for the allies. In 1918 he was appointed CBE for his wartime work.

However, as the war drew to a close it was clear that the Scottish shale-oil industry could not survive unchanged. The extraction of oil from the solid, clay-like shale, which had first to be dug from the earth, was far more expensive than the production of liquid petroleum, which was increasing world-wide. In 1918, with shale oil facing growing competition from liquid petroleum, Fraser was instrumental in creating the Scottish Oil Agency, a joint marketing organization for the separate Scottish shale-oil companies. In 1919 he went further, merging the separate companies into Scottish Oils Ltd, which later in the year was acquired by the Anglo-Persian Oil Company, which Fraser joined.

This was a most important move in Fraser's working life. The Anglo-Persian had been formed in 1909 to exploit a major oil discovery which had been made in Persia in 1908, marking the beginning of the Middle East oil industry. Since its formation, the Anglo-Persian, in which the British government held a majority shareholding, had expanded very rapidly and was on its way to becoming one of the world's biggest companies, a member of the famed 'seven sisters' which were to dominate the international oil industry for much of the twentieth century. Joining such a company, which operated internationally in a vitally important strategic industry, opened up far wider horizons than those of the comparatively parochial Scottish shale-oil industry in which Fraser had spent his earlier career.

On 1 April 1923 Fraser, who had yet to reach his thirty-fifth birthday, became a director of Anglo-Persian, at the same time as Sir John Cadman. For a while Fraser continued to live in Glasgow, but after Cadman became Anglo-Persian's chairman in 1927 he persuaded Fraser to move closer to London. With some reluctance, for Fraser was strongly attached to his Scottish roots, Fraser and his family moved to Surrey and in 1928 he was appointed deputy chairman of Anglo-Persian.

For the next thirteen years Fraser remained as deputy chairman under Cadman, with whom he formed a happy and effective working relationship based on their complementary characteristics. Cadman was by background and temperament a man who moved with ease between the worlds of business and government, displaying consummate diplomatic skills in his dealings with representatives of governments, whether they were British ministers or rulers of Middle East states. Under Cadman, Fraser was the linchpin of the business, a practical manager with technical knowledge, a great grasp of detail, and a quick commercial mind. But he was not at all gregarious and, though said to be humorous and warm-hearted by those close to him, his tall figure could seem remote, taciturn, and somewhat dour to those who were not his confidants.

As deputy chairman of Anglo-Persian (renamed Anglo-Iranian in 1935, after Persia changed its name to Iran), Fraser was involved in some of the most important developments in the international oil industry in the late 1920s and 1930s. For example, he played a part in formulating the proposals for the famous 1928 Achnacarry agreement, by which the world's largest oil companies tried to protect themselves from surplus production and competition by forming an international cartel to divide up international oil markets. Fraser was also active in the formation of Shell-Mex and BP Ltd, in which Anglo-Persian and Royal Dutch–Shell merged their UK marketing activities from 1932. In that same year, the shah of Persia cancelled Anglo-Persian's oil concession in his country. Fraser was closely involved in the negotiations in Tehran, which resulted in a new concession agreement being reached in 1933. In the meantime, he was active in the development of the oil industry in Iraq, where oil was discovered in 1927 and from where exports commenced in 1934. He was also concerned with the negotiations with the sheikh of Kuwait that resulted in Anglo-Persian and Gulf Oil Corporation jointly obtaining an oil concession in that country in 1934. Four years later, the joint company discovered the great Burgan oilfield which gave birth to the Kuwaiti oil industry. As the 1930s approached their end, Fraser was awarded a knighthood in the 1939 birthday honours, announced only a few months before the outbreak of the Second World War. Some two years later, in 1941, he succeeded Cadman as Anglo-Iranian's chairman.

The elevation to the chairmanship added a new dimension to Fraser's responsibilities, in that he now had to spend much more time on political and diplomatic matters, which previously had been handled largely by Cadman. This was not, on the whole, a role that came easily to Fraser, who never succeeded in winning the confidence of ministers and civil servants. They variously described him as secretive and autocratic and at times questioned his suitability for the chairmanship of a company of such national importance.

The most dramatic event in Fraser's chairmanship came in 1951 when after abortive negotiations to revise Anglo-Iranian's oil concession in Iran, the Iranian government nationalized the company's assets in that country. The company's operations there were brought to a halt as the crisis quickly escalated into a major international diplomatic crisis, in which the British and American governments became deeply involved. Round after round of negotiations took place in search of a settlement of the dispute, which was finally ended in 1954 when a consortium of international oil companies, in which Anglo-Iranian had a 40 per cent share, took over the operations which before the crisis had been conducted by Anglo-Iranian on its own. During the negotiations, Fraser's tough, uncompromising stance caused him to be heavily criticized by diplomats from both sides of the Atlantic and it was thought by some that he ought to be ousted. But he hung on and under his aegis Anglo-Iranian expanded and developed other sources of oil supply to make up for the loss of its supplies from Iran during the crisis. As a result, the company came out of the dispute in good shape and afterwards adopted a new name: British Petroleum.

In 1955 Fraser was raised to the peerage, characteristically choosing a Scottish title, Baron Strathalmond, of Pumpherston, Midlothian. The next year he retired. His commitment to British Petroleum had left him little time for public activities and other business interests. From 1935 to 1955 he was petroleum adviser to the War Office and in 1951–2 he was chairman of the oil supply advisory committee of the Ministry of Fuel and Power. In 1946 he was awarded the first Cadman memorial medal by the Institute of Petroleum and in 1951 an honorary LLD was conferred upon him by Birmingham University. He was also a director of the Burmah Oil Company from 1939 to 1955, and a director of Great Western Railway and of the National Provincial Bank.

In his younger years Fraser was a fine footballer and tennis player. He later took up shooting and golf as his main sports. His wife predeceased him in 1963. They had one son and one daughter. Strathalmond died in London on 1 April 1970, forty-seven years to the day after he had joined the board of Anglo-Persian. J. H. BAMBERG

Sources J. H. Bamberg, *The history of the British Petroleum Company*, 2: *The Anglo-Iranian years, 1928–1954* (1994) · DNB · *BP Shield* (April 1970) · *The Times* (2 April 1970) · *Daily Telegraph* (2 April 1970) · *The Naft* (Oct 1941) [company magazine, BP Archives] · R. Winsbury, *Thomson McLintock & Co.: the first hundred years* (1977) · U. Warwick Mod. RC, BP Archives

Archives U. Warwick Mod. RC, BP Archives

Likenesses J. Gunn, oils, Britannic House, London

Wealth at death £155,669: probate, 13 Aug 1970, *CGPLA Eng. & Wales*

Fraser, Winifred (b. 1872, d. in or after 1923?), actress, was born in London on 29 February 1872, of unknown parentage. She was educated in Hampstead and made her professional début in 1888 as Sophia in an adaptation of Oliver Goldsmith's *The Vicar of Wakefield* alongside William Farren junior. After a period of touring, first in the classical repertory, in the company managed by Ben Greet, and later in more modern works, including *Jim the Penman*, by Sir Charles Young, and *The New Magdalen*, by Wilkie Collins, she made her first appearance in the West End in November 1889, as Alice Fairfax in *Her Own Witness*. She then played several small roles in major London productions, including Rosie in Lady Bancroft's *My Daughter* and Lucy in the same author's *A Pair of Spectacles*.

Winifred Fraser's first major success seems to have been as Hedvig in the first London production of Ibsen's *The Wild Duck*, at the Royalty Theatre in May 1894. The power of her acting at this period is well caught by a first-night review of this production:

> Miss Winnifred [*sic*] Fraser, who had the fascinating but extremely difficult part of Hedwig [*sic*] the fourteen-year-old girl, showed rare qualities in so young an actress. Though actually a woman, she had the charm of childhood, and yet power. She possesses the rare gift of holding a house when saying nothing, but merely thinking and wondering, yet there was no visible effort or pulling of faces. (Theatre Museum, London)

This role was one of many that she was offered in the late 1890s, a period in which she seems to have been in constant demand, working with many of the leading figures in the London theatre, including Olga Nethersole, Ben Greet, E. S. Willard, and Sir Augustus Harris, and doing much touring, notably in *Under the Red Robe* (1897).

By 1900 Winifred Fraser had been invited to become part of Mrs Patrick Campbell's company—once more at the Royalty—in, among others, the first London production of Edmond Rostand's *Les Romanesques*, '[f]reely done into English verse' (programme, Theatre Museum) as *The Fantasticks*, by George Fleming. She played Sylvette, the lover of Campbell's principal-boy hero Percinet, in a production also notable for the performance of the young George Du Maurier as the 'Bravo' Straforel, and according to a review she 'interpret[ed] the naïve heroine's sentimental passages with exceptional charm and pathos' (Theatre Museum). In 1903 she made her first acquaintance with the title role of J. M. Barrie's *Little Mary*, understudying Nina Boucicault; she subsequently made the part her own, playing it in many revivals at Wyndham's Theatre, and in 1905–6 touring it, with other leading roles, around Australia. In 1907 she took part in another major tour, in the leading female roles of R. B. Sheridan's *The School for Scandal* and Oscar Wilde's *The Importance of being Earnest*. This period of travel culminated, in 1910, in her first visit to the United States, where she played Barbara Pennymint in *Pomander Walk*, by Louis N. Parker, at Wallack's theater in New York, and in the following two years toured the role around the remainder of the country.

From this point Winifred Fraser's career seems to have been entirely based in the States. She returned to classical repertoire in 1913, taking the role of Good-Dedes in a production of *Everyman* at the New York Children's Theater, and later in that year made her first appearance in Chicago—as Nellie Heron in *The Necessary Evil*. She remained in the USA for the duration of the First World War, and, by this time in her forties, carved out a niche for herself in New York playing the many middle-aged matrons who populate turn-of-the-century melodramas, among them Mrs Greville in *Hush*, at the Little Theater in October 1916; Mrs Torrance in *The New Word*, at the Empire in May 1917; and Mrs Martha Van Zile in *Polly with a Past*, by G. Middleton and G. Bolton, at the Belasco Theater in September 1917. She maintained her home in America—as well as her penchant for these roles—when the war ended, and spent the 1920s on Broadway playing—among many other roles—Mrs Morland in J. M. Barrie's *Mary Rose* (at the Empire in December 1920), Mrs Smallwood in *The Enchanted Cottage*, by Sir Arthur Pinero (at the Ritz Theater in March 1923), and Mrs Considine in *Mary, Mary, quite Contrary*, by St John Ervine (at the Belasco in September 1923). Her marriage to the actor-manager George Foss (1859–1938) had by this time ended, without children, so that she seems—ironically enough given her frequent impersonation of middle-aged mothers—to have remained single and childless throughout these years. The date of her death, which probably occurred in the USA, is not known. STEPHEN FOLLOWS

Sources J. Parker, ed., *The green room book, or, Who's who on the stage* (1909) • Adams, *Drama* • F. Gaye, ed., *Who's who in the theatre*, 14th edn (1967) • reviews and programmes, Theatre Museum, London

Frasi, Giulia (*fl.* **1740**–*c*.**1772**), singer, probably came from Milan, where she was taught by Giuseppe Ferdinando Brivio. A soprano, she sang in 1740 in her teacher's *La Constanza in trionfo* at Lodi and in Giovanni Colombri's *Il Bajazet* at Alessandria. She then appeared in Bergamo and Modena before joining the opera company at the King's Theatre, London, in autumn 1742, where her first appearances were in the pasticcios *Gianguir* (2 November 1742) and *Mandane* (4 December 1742), both of which included music by Brivio. According to Charles Burney, 'Frasi was at this time young, and interesting in person, with a sweet and clear voice, and a smooth and chaste style of singing' (Burney, *Hist. mus.*, 4.449). She became the lover, by 1743, of Charles Churchill (1720/21–1812), an army officer, and by 22 July 1744 she had given birth to an illegitimate daughter, who soon died. Horace Walpole reported that the MP Thomas *Winnington (1696–1746) referred to the baby as the '*opéra comique*' (Walpole, *Corr.*, 18.481), because the mother was an opera girl and Churchill was the illegitimate son of the actress Anne Oldfield. A year later Walpole was gossiping that Frasi and Winnington were lovers.

Frasi appeared in all except one of the fifteen seasons when Italian operas were performed at the King's Theatre between her début there and 1760–61. In addition to many operas by minor Italian composers, she sang in Christoph Willibald Gluck's *La caduta de' giganti* (1746) and in three operas with music by Handel, *Rossane* (1743, a version of his *Alessandro*), the pasticcio *Lucio Vero* (1747), and *Admeto* (1754). She was never a star singer in the opera company, but became Handel's choice as a leading soprano in his Lent oratorio seasons. Frasi sang arias from Handel's oratorios at concerts for the Decayed Musicians' Fund in 1746 and 1747, and was then employed by the composer to sing in his revival of *Judas Maccabaeus* in 1748. By this time Burney was her singing teacher, and he tells of how Frasi informed the composer that she was going to study hard and learn thoroughbass, so that she could accompany herself. Handel, 'who well knew how little this pleasing singer was addicted to application and diligence', said 'Oh—vaat may we not expect!' (Burney, *An Account*, 36). She worked hard at her English, however, for according to Burney she pronounced the language, when singing, more clearly and articulately than English singers. Over the next four years Frasi created the title roles in Handel's *Susanna* (10 February 1749) and *Theodora* (16 March 1750), Pharaoh's daughter in *Solomon* (17 March 1749), and Iphis in his last oratorio, *Jephtha* (26 February 1752). She sang in the composer's oratorio seasons until his death in 1759, appearing in every one of his oratorios except *Semele* (although Semele's aria 'Oh Sleep' was in her concert repertory) and took part in performances of *Messiah* at the Foundling Hospital. Frasi performed Handel's music at the Three Choirs meetings from 1756 to 1764 and at music festivals in Oxford and Salisbury. She was engaged at Ranelagh Gardens in 1751 and 1752, and sang in Thomas Arne's *Alfred* in 1753, his *Eliza* in 1756, and his *Artaxerxes* at her own benefit in 1769. Frasi was one of the singers in John Christopher Smith's oratorio *Paradise Lost* in February 1760.

Giulia Frasi's brother John (*c*.1730–1795) also settled in England, working first as an embroiderer; he was declared bankrupt in 1768 but by the time of his death had established himself as a dentist, 'having acquired considerable dexterity in the art of making and fixing artificial teeth' (*GM*, 1795). He was not the hypothetical singer 'Signor Frasi' mentioned by some music historians, the parts attributed to whom were those of Giulia Frasi herself. About 1764 the young R. J. S. Stevens heard her singing at Haberdashers' Hall in one of the Castle concerts organized by John Stanley: 'she was a short fat woman, and had a remarkably clear voice; and (which attracted my notice considerably) she had on a pair of very fine brilliant earrings' (*Recollections of R. J. S. Stevens*, 7)—perhaps similar to those she is depicted wearing in an anonymous engraving, the *Musical Lady*. She continued to sing in concerts and in the Covent Garden Lent oratorios, for she appeared in *Judas Maccabaeus* for her benefit at the Haymarket in May 1770, and a rhyming alphabet published in the January 1772 *Gentleman's Magazine* listed 'Frasi, whose singing delights' among the female performers of Covent Garden. About this time she fell into serious debt, brought about, according to Burney, by her over-generous hospitality towards Italians who came to London. She fled to Calais, where she was dependent on annual pensions of 5 guineas from about a dozen English music-lovers. Her income dwindled as her benefactors died, and she died in Calais, in miserable poverty, many years after her departure from the stage.

OLIVE BALDWIN and THELMA WILSON

Sources A. H. Scouten, ed., *The London stage, 1660–1800*, pt 3: 1729–1747 (1961) • G. W. Stone, ed., *The London stage, 1660–1800*, pt 4: 1747–1776 (1962) • C. Sartori, *I libretti italiani a stampe dalle origini al 1800*, 7 vols. (Cuneo, 1990–94) • C. Burney, *An account of the musical performances … in commemoration of Handel* (1785) • Burney, *Hist. mus.*, vol. 4 • C. Burney, 'Frasi, Giulia', in A. Rees, *Cyclopaedia*, 15 (1819) • Walpole, *Corr.*, 9.16, 18.481 • W. Dean, *Handel's dramatic oratorios and masques* (1959) • O. E. Deutsch, *Dokumente zu Leben und Schaffen*, vol. 4 of (1985) *Händel-Handbuch*, ed. W. Eisel and M. Eisel (1978–85) • *Recollections of R. J. S. Stevens*, ed. M. Argent (1992) • D. Lysons and others, *Origin and progress of the meeting of the three choirs* (1865) • D. J. Reid, 'Some festival programmes of the eighteenth and nineteenth centuries [pt 1]', *Royal Musical Association Research Chronicle*, 5 (1965), 51–79 • D. J. Reid and B. Pritchard, 'Some festival programmes of the eighteenth and nineteenth centuries', *Royal Musical Association Research Chronicle*, 8 (1970), 23–33 • *Music and theatre in Handel's world: the family papers of James Harris, 1732–1780*, ed. D. Burrows and R. Dunhill (2002) • D. Burrows, 'Handel's performances of *Messiah*: the evidence of the conducting score', *Music and Letters*, 56 (1975), 319–34 • D. Burrows, 'The autographs and early copies of *Messiah*:

some further thoughts', *Music and Letters*, 66 (1985), 201–19 · M. Sands, *Invitation to Ranelagh* (1946) · R. Fiske, *English theatre music in the eighteenth century* (1973) · *GM*, 1st ser., 42 (1772), 39 · *GM*, 1st ser., 65 (1795), 255

Likenesses mezzotint, Harvard TC

Wealth at death none; died in poverty, having fled to France because of debt: Burney, 'Frasi, Giulia'

Fraunce [France], **Abraham** (1559?–1592/3?), poet and lawyer, was born in Shropshire and went to Shrewsbury School, where his name is on the register for January 1572. He matriculated as a pensioner at St John's College, Cambridge, on 20 May 1575. On 8 November 1575 he was made a Lady Margaret scholar of his college; he graduated BA in 1580 and in the same year was elected one of its fellows. He commenced MA in 1583. In 1578 and 1579 he acted in 'Hymenaeus' (author unknown, although some have suggested Fraunce himself; Nelson, 2.906) and in Thomas Legge's trilogy 'Richardus tertius'. At some time before 1583 he wrote 'Victoria', a Latin comedy modelled on Luigi Pasqualigo's *Il fedele* (1576).

Immediately after his university studies Fraunce began the study of law, having enrolled on 5 June 1583 at Gray's Inn; on 8 February 1588 he was called to the bar. He then returned to Shropshire, where he practised at the court of the marches of Wales (this prerogative court for the border areas, established by Henry VIII, was located in Shrewsbury). There is a letter (BL, Harley 6995, item 35) of 11 August 1590, in which Henry Herbert, second earl of Pembroke, has written to the lord treasurer, recommending Fraunce as the queen's solicitor in the court, but the suit was unsuccessful.

While a student, and later while working in the law, Fraunce was also a prolific author, skilled at summarizing or re-presenting the work of classical or continental writers to an English audience. His works of poetry, philosophy, emblematics, and mythology are all popularizations, yet imaginative and creative none the less. All his writing was dedicated to members of Sir Philip Sidney's circle: Sidney himself, his sister Mary and brother Robert, Mary's husband the earl of Pembroke, or their friend Edward Dyer. The patronage may have had its origins at Shrewsbury School, to which Philip Sidney had also gone. It was cemented by Sidney's generosity to Fraunce in his years at university; in the letter of 1590 Pembroke says of Fraunce that 'he was bred up by my brother *Sir Phillip Sidney* long in *Cambridge*'. The manuscript of the play 'Victoria' is dedicated to Sidney (it is on deposit from Penshurst at the Kent Archives as MS, U1475/Z15). In addition there is, also with Sidney as the named recipient, a 'Tractatus de usu dialectices', with 'Emblemata varia, ad principes Europae et rem historicam spectantia, calamo bene depicta, et versibus latinis illustrata' (Bodl. Oxf., MS Rawl. D. 345). The first part is a short treatise on dialectic, closely following the work of Pierre de la Ramée (Petrus Ramus), the French philosopher whose work was very much in vogue in the Sidney circle, to some extent because of Fraunce's own writing. The second part is a series of devices of well-known historical figures, with discussion; this follows the work of Paolo Giovio, the Italian

bishop and scholar. Another manuscript (BL, Add. MS 34361) is dedicated to Edward Dyer:

> The sheapheardes logike conteyning the praecepts of that art put downe by Ramus; examples fet owt of the Sheapheards kalinder; notes and expositions collected owt of Bourhusius, Piscator, Mr Chatterton; and divers others. Together with twooe general Discourses, the one touchinge the prayse and ryghte use of logike: the other concernynge the comparison of Ramus his logike, with that of Aristotle.

This work is also an abbreviated attempt to explain the dialectic of Ramus, this time using literary examples from Spenser's *Shepheardes Calender* (1579).

Fraunce's first published work, a translation of Thomas Watson's *Amyntas* (1585), was *The lamentations of Amuntas for the death of Phillis; paraphrastically translated out of Latine into English hexameteres* (1587). This work, which neglects to name Watson as the author, was more popular than the original work and went through at least four editions before 1600. It, and all Fraunce's subsequent English verse, was written in verse form imitative of the classical hexameter. The experiment in hindsight seems doomed but at the time it was considered by many writers to be an interesting direction. In 1588 Fraunce published his *Insignium, armorum, emblematum, hieroglyphicorum, et symbolorum, quae in Italia imprese nominantur, explicatio: quae symbolicae philosophicae postrema pars est* (entered in the Stationers' register, 20 May 1588). This was dedicated to Robert Sidney. It is, as the title correctly describes it, a treatise on the nature of emblems and other devices, and follows an interest established in the Rawlinson manuscript. There is an addendum, possibly an additional part, which is in manuscript: 'Symbolicae philosophiae liber quartus et ultimus' (on deposit from Penshurst as MS U1475/Z16, Kent County Archive Office).

The Arcadian rhetoric, or, The precepts of rhetorike made plaine by examples Greeke, Latin, English, Italian, French, Spanish (1588; entered in the Stationers' register, 11 June) is a text on stylistic devices and uses many literary examples to exemplify them. In this Fraunce quotes from Spenser's unpublished *Faerie queene: the lawiers logike, exemplifying the praecepts of logike by the practice of the common lawe* (1588; entered in the Stationers' register, 20 May) and follows the same Ramist method that he had used in his manuscripts, of providing literary examples to demonstrate principles of logic. Here, however, he expands the approach by using common law cases from Plowden and others.

There is a slight hiatus in Fraunce's publishing between 1588 and 1591. In the latter year appeared *The countesse of Pembrokes Emanuel, conteining the nativity, passion, buriall, and resurrection of Christ: togeather with certaine psalmes of David, all in English hexameters*, dedicated to Mary Sidney, countess of Pembroke. Then follows, also in 1591, *The countesse of Pembrokes Yvychurch, conteining the affectionate life, and unfortunate death of Phillis and Amyntas: that in a pastorall; this in a funerall: both in English hexameters* (entered in the Stationers' register, 9 February). This work, as the title hints, is in two parts, the first a translation, somewhat modified, of Tasso's pastoral play *Aminta*, the second a modified and slightly expanded version of Fraunce's translation of Watson's *Amyntas*. Both works have been adjusted to make room for the countess of Pembroke to appear as a character. After this work comes what may be Fraunce's most imaginative work, *The third part of the countesse of Pembrokes Yvychurch. Entituled, Amintas Dale, wherein are the most conceited tales of the pagan gods in English hexameters, together with their auncient descriptions and philosophicall explications* (1592). This is a series of explications of mythological narratives from Ovid's *Metamorphoses*, presented in a lively frame narrative that again features the countess of Pembroke. The work concludes with an amusing tale of three brothers who have offended the gods by their astrological predictions—possibly a satire of Richard, John, and Gabriel Harvey, all celebrated figures at Cambridge.

Fraunce's writings were well known to his contemporaries. His attempt to import classical verse forms into English brought scorn from Ben Jonson, who said to William Drummond of Hawthornden that 'That Abram Francis in his English Hexameters was a Foole' (Jonson, *Works*, ed. C. H. Herford and P. Simpson, 1925–52, 1.133). Richard Barnfield parodies his style in the concluding section of his *Affectionate Shepheard* (1594). Yet, others were more positive: Robert Greene openly imitates him in his *Philomela* (1592), Nashe commends him as 'sweete Maister France' in his preface to Robert Greene's *Menaphon* (1589, sig. B2r), and even Gabriel Harvey, who may not have yet known of the satire in *Amintas Dale*, names Fraunce as one of those 'commendably employed in enriching, and polishing their native Tongue' (G. Harvey, *Foure Letters*, 1592, sig. F4v). He is believed to be Corydon in Spenser's *Colin Clouts Come Home Again* (1595). In Francis Meres's *Palladis tamia* (1598) he is said to be, after Sidney but in company with Spenser, Richard Barnfield, and others, 'amongst … the best' (248r) in pastoral.

Because of an inaccurate report in Joseph Hunter's 'Chorus vatum' (BL, Add. MS 24488, fol. 350) it was long believed that Fraunce lived out his years in Wales and died in 1633. But it appears that he was dead by 1593, for in the induction to his *Phillis* (1593, sig. Blr; cancelled in many copies) Thomas Lodge refers to two recently deceased poets 'who in theyr Swan-like songes *Amintas* wept', a probable allusion to Fraunce and the poet Thomas Watson (the authors of *Amyntas*). It seems likely that Fraunce died in or near Shrewsbury in late 1592 or early 1593.

WILLIAM BARKER

Sources G. C. Moore Smith, introduction to *Victoria, Materialen zur Kunde des älteren englischen Dramas*, ed. W. Bang, 14 (Louvain, 1906) · Venn, *Alum. Cant.* · Cooper, *Ath. Cantab.* · A. H. Nelson, ed., *Cambridge*, 2 (1989), 901, 926, 944–5 · M. G. Brennan, 'The date of the death of Abraham Fraunce', *The Library*, 6th ser., 5 (1983), 392–2

Fraunceys, Adam (*c.*1310–1375), merchant and mayor of London, is of uncertain origin. His parents were called Adam and Constance, but who they were and where they lived is unknown. It is unlikely that the family came from London, and possible that Adam was born in Yorkshire, in view of his close relationship with Simon Fraunceys [*see below*], and of the precautions which he took in 1369 to avoid identification with two felons from that region who shared his name. His exact date of birth is not known, but it must have been during or about the first decade of the fourteenth century, and in youth he was probably sent to London to be apprenticed. By 1339 he was already a merchant of some means, operating in Bruges, and able to offer the king the substantial loan of £100. Details of his business dealings are sparse, but like most wealthy merchants of the period he exported wool, and by the 1340s had become a supporter of the various syndicates of customs farmers which prevailed for most of that decade. At the same time Fraunceys lent large sums of money to the nobility and gentry, military men embarking on service overseas, fellow citizens, religious houses, and not least the crown and members of the royal family.

So successful had Fraunceys become as a merchant and financier that in 1352 he was elected in quick succession alderman of Queenhithe ward (removing in 1356 to Lime Street) and then mayor, holding office for two consecutive years. In November 1352 he was appointed, possibly *ex officio*, to investigate alleged corruption by collectors of the fifteenth granted in 1348 and 1352. Between 1357 and 1359 he sat on a commission to inquire into the failure to enforce the Statute of Labourers in London, and in February 1364 both he and his close associate John Pyel were among those sent on a mission to Calais to deal with complaints by the staplers against the government, which resulted in the reorganization of the administration there. He represented London in parliament at least six times, more than most citizens of his day, and his career seems to reflect a clear sense of civic pride and responsibility. He was co-founder of a college of chantry priests at Guildhall in 1356, and in his will he established two chantries in the church of St Helen, Bishopsgate, in whose precinct he had lived for a number of years and where he chose to be buried. If he was not a Londoner by birth, he certainly devoted his energies wholeheartedly to his adoptive city, showing little interest in his native town, wherever it may have been. By 31 May 1359 he had married Agnes, whose surname is unknown.

In common with other members of London's mercantile élite Fraunceys was an assiduous purchaser of land. A high proportion of his acquisitions were in London itself, but he also busied himself creating estates outside the city, mostly in the neighbouring counties of Essex and Middlesex. In February 1349, at the height of the plague, he bought the manor of Wyke in Middlesex, comprising lands in Hackney Wick, Old Ford, and Stepney, from his fellow mercer John Causton, and later added to this collection, apparently through local clerical agents who bought small parcels of land on Fraunceys's behalf. In 1357 he bought the manor of Chobhams in West Ham, and in 1359 that of Ruckholts in Leyton. Meanwhile he was buying up lands in North Middlesex, in Enfield, Tottenham, and Edmonton, mostly in partnership with Peter Favelor, a retainer of William de Bohun, earl of Northampton. In 1361 he acquired the manor, and shortly afterwards, probably around 1363, the lordship, of Edmonton, which was to be the centrepiece of his estates. It was at this time, and no doubt to mark this important occasion, that he had an impressive cartulary of his properties drawn up, and it was on the manor of Edmonton that his descendants were settled.

Adam Fraunceys died in London on 4 May 1375 and was buried at St Helen's, Bishopsgate. He was survived by his widow, Agnes, who was still living in 1394, his son, Adam, knight of the shire (d. 1417), and daughter, Maud, later countess of Salisbury (d. 1424) [see Montagu, Maud].

Simon Fraunceys (d. 1358), merchant and mayor of London, was born in the late thirteenth century. He appears to have come from Pontefract, Yorkshire, and, like Adam Fraunceys, may have come to London as a boy apprentice. In 1311 his son, John, was apprenticed to Simon Paris, mercer, for seven years. His civic career began when, though not yet an alderman, he was elected sheriff in 1328. In 1336 he was made alderman of Langbourn ward, and in 1339 alderman of Cheap. Fraunceys was chosen to succeed John Oxenford as mayor when the latter died in office in June 1342, and was re-elected the following October. He served as mayor once again for the year 1355-6, towards the end of his life. He was summoned to represent the king's council and parliament six times between 1339 and 1352, and served on other royal commissions. A wealthy merchant and financier he died holding lands in Essex, Middlesex, Bedfordshire, and Kent. He was closely associated with both Adam and Ellis Fraunceys, executors of his will, although it cannot be said with any certainty that a blood tie existed between them. He died on 4 July 1358, leaving a widow, Maud, and a son, Thomas.   STEPHEN O'CONNOR

Sources S. J. O'Connor, ed., *A calendar of the cartularies of John Pyel and Adam Fraunceys*, CS, 5th ser., 2 (1993) · S. J. O'Connor, 'Finance, diplomacy and politics: royal service by two London merchants in the reign of Edward III', *Historical Research*, 67 (1994), 18–39 · S. J. O'Connor, 'Adam Fraunceys and John Pyel: perceptions of status among merchants in fourteenth-century London', *Trade, devotion and governance: papers in later medieval history* [Manchester 1989], ed. D. J. Clayton and others (1994), 17–35 · A. B. Beaven, ed., *The aldermen of the City of London, temp. Henry III-*[1912], 2 vols. (1908–13) · *CIPM*, vol. 10 · will of Adam Fraunceys, CLRO, HR 103/79 · R. R. Sharpe, ed., *Calendar of letter-books preserved in the archives of the corporation of the City of London*, [12 vols.] (1899–1912)
Archives Hatfield House, Hertfordshire, Hatfield MSS, cartulary, CP 290
Wealth at death substantial, but impossible to quantify: *CIPM*, 10; will, *CLRO*, HR 103/79

Fraunceys, Simon (d. 1358). *See under* Fraunceys, Adam (c.1310–1375).

Frauncis, Elizabeth (c.1529–1579). *See under* Essex witches (act. 1566–1589).

Fraxino, Simon de. *See* Freine, Simund de (d. before 1228?).

Frazer, Alastair Campbell (1909–1969), pharmacologist and food scientist, was born at Fairhaven, Lower Road, Farnborough, Orpington, Kent, on 26 July 1909, the second son of Wilson Ray Frazer, civil servant in the Local Government Board, and his wife, Grace Haldane, *née* Robbs. He was educated at Lancing College, of which he was a scholar, and from 1926 at St Mary's Hospital medical

school, University of London, where he graduated in medicine and surgery in 1932. He taught physiology and pharmacology at the medical school for ten years, and for two periods was acting head of the department of physiology. In 1942 he was appointed independent reader in pharmacology in the University of Birmingham, being promoted professor of pharmacology in the following year. He married Hilary (b. 1924/5), younger daughter of Ralph Eddowes Garrod, a chemist, on 14 August 1943. They had three sons and a daughter.

From 1937 to 1945 Frazer held a Sir Halley Stewart research fellowship. He received a London DSc in 1945, having achieved a Birmingham MD in 1943 and a London PhD in 1941. At St Mary's Hospital medical school Frazer had developed a special interest in the mechanism of the absorption of fat from the gut and in the physical chemistry of emulsions of fat, and both in London and in Birmingham he gathered around him a group with a lively interest in these subjects. The study of sprue, a tropical disease in which absorption from the gut is defective, led to a growing interest in the chemistry and biochemistry of food, and in nutrition in general, while as a pharmacologist Frazer was naturally concerned with toxic substances, in both food and drugs. In 1953 an honours degree course in medical biochemistry was started by Frazer in the department of pharmacology at Birmingham, and an alteration of name, both of the chair and of the department, from 'pharmacology' to 'medical biochemistry', which was instituted in 1956, illustrated an important development in Frazer's interests.

For many years Frazer was an adviser to the government on overseas developments, and in this connection he travelled widely in the Caribbean area and in Africa. In 1955 he chaired a committee on medical health policy in Uganda, and in 1961 was chairman of a commission to advise on research in east Africa. His concern with nutrition and toxicology involved him nationally and internationally in bodies set up to advise about the control of food and drugs. When the Ministry of Health set up a committee on the safety of drugs in 1963 Frazer was appointed a member, and shortly before his death he had been made chairman in succession to Sir Derrick Dunlop. He was a member of the Agricultural Research Council for many years.

Frazer was a lucid and compelling speaker and was widely invited to take part in conferences and to give lectures, both at home and abroad. He possessed to a remarkable degree the ability to move from a subject of medical and scientific significance, which had no obvious or direct practical importance, to one of industrial consequence. He was much in demand as a consultant in industry, where he was able to advise on the possible practical application of an observation which at first appeared to be of academic interest only. At the time of his death he was president both of the British Food Manufacturing Industries Research Association and of the British Industrial Biological Research Association.

Frazer's resignation from his university post in 1967 to become the first director-general of the newly established British Nutrition Foundation was surprising to many but not totally unexpected to those who appreciated the width of his interests. The foundation had been recently set up by a group of academic scientists and industrialists to promote co-operation between industry and non-industrial bodies in all aspects of nutrition, and particularly in research. Frazer's appointment involved a move from Birmingham to London, and the building up of an entirely new institution, a duty which he tackled with zest and effectiveness.

Frazer was a large man whose beard added to his striking appearance. He radiated good humour and friendliness and much enjoyed the good things of life and endeavoured to ensure that those around him could do likewise. He delighted to travel to distant parts and had friends in many countries. He was an honorary foreign member of the Gastroenterological Society of Belgium, of the Royal Academy of Belgium, and of the Société Philomathique de Paris. He was appointed CBE in 1962. He was the author of many medical and scientific publications; his monograph, *Malabsorption Syndromes*, was published in 1968. He died suddenly at his home, 28 Montpelier Street, Westminster, London, on 14 June 1969.   F. G. YOUNG, *rev.*

Sources *The Lancet* (28 June 1969), 1323–4 · *The Times* (17 June 1969), 10h · *The Times* (21 June 1969), 10g · *The Times* (24 June 1969), 10g · personal knowledge (1981) · *Nature*, 222 (1969), 1309 · *Who's who in science* (1968), 601 · b. cert. · m. cert. · d. cert.
Wealth at death £24,782: probate, 24 Oct 1969, *CGPLA Eng. & Wales*

Frazer, Andrew (1739?–1792), army officer and military engineer, was the son of George Frazer, a deputy surveyor of excise in Scotland, and was probably the Andrew Frazer born on 18 March 1739 in St Cuthbert's parish, Edinburgh, the son of George Frazer and his wife, Christian Paterson. He was appointed practitioner engineer, with the rank of ensign in the train, on 17 March 1759, and sub-engineer, with the rank of lieutenant, in 1761. In 1763 he was ordered to Dunkirk and served as assistant to Colonel John Desmaretz, the British commissary appointed to observe the demolition of the works there in accordance with treaty obligations. On 18 October 1767 he succeeded Desmaretz in that office, and he retained it until the break with France in 1778. In the British Library manuscripts are two reports from Frazer: 'A description of Dunkirk' of 1769 (Add. MS 16593), and 'Report and plans of Dunkirk' of 1772 (Add. MS 17779, fol. 82). A letter from Frazer to David Murray, seventh Viscount Stormont, British ambassador at Paris in 1777 (Add. MS 24164, fol. 172), indicates that he discharged consular functions at Dunkirk. He became engineer-in-ordinary and captain in 1772, brevet-major in 1782, and regimental lieutenant-colonel in 1788. In 1784 he served in Dominica. He designed St Andrew's parochial church, Edinburgh, built in 1785. He married on 2 September 1773 at St Martin-in-the-Fields, Westminster, Charlotte, daughter of Stillingfleet Durnford, of the engineer department, and granddaughter of Colonel Desmaretz; their son was Sir Augustus Simon *Frazer (1776–1835). Frazer, who had not long retired from the service, died on his way to Geneva in July 1792. According to an item in the *Gentleman's Magazine*, he had left the army following his

court martial 'for doing, though he followed precedent, what he certainly was not justified in doing, and wasting the public money, but not to his own emolument' (*GM*), and had left the country rather than dishonour his comrades by naming those who had sought to enrich themselves.   H. M. CHICHESTER, *rev.* ROGER T. STEARN

Sources *Army List* · J. Redington and R. A. Roberts, eds., *Calendar of home office papers of the reign of George III*, 4 vols., PRO (1878–99) · BL, Add. MSS 16593; 17779, fol. 82; 24164, fol. 172 · *Scots Magazine*, 54 (1792), 413 · W. Porter, *History of the corps of royal engineers*, 1 (1889) · *GM*, 1st ser., 62 (1792), 766, 1053 · IGI
Likenesses J. Kay, group portrait, caricature, etching, BM, NPG

Frazer, Sir Augustus Simon (1776–1835), army officer, the only son of Colonel Andrew *Frazer (d. 1792), Royal Engineers, and his wife, Charlotte, daughter of Stillingfleet Durnford, of the Ordnance office, was born at Dunkirk on 5 September 1776. His father was at that time employed as a commissioner for superintending the destruction of the fortifications. For a short time Frazer attended Edinburgh high school. In August 1792 he joined the Royal Military Academy, Woolwich, and on 18 September 1793 he was gazetted second lieutenant, Royal Artillery.

In December 1793, though only seventeen years old, Frazer was ordered to the duke of York's army in Flanders, and in January 1794, the month he was promoted first lieutenant, he was attached with two guns to the battalion of the 3rd guards. With the guards he served throughout the retreat before Pichegru, and was present at the battles of Mouveaux, Cateau Cambrésis, Tournai, and Boxtel, and at all the other principal actions until the departure of the infantry from the continent. In May 1795 he was attached to the Royal Horse Artillery, and in 1799, when he was promoted captain-lieutenant, he served in the expedition to The Helder and the battles of Bergen. On 12 September 1803 he was promoted captain, and appointed to the command of a troop of horse artillery. In 1807 he commanded all the artillery employed in the expedition against Buenos Aires, and was present in the disastrous assault on that city in July.

Frazer next remained for some time on ordinary garrison duty in England, and he was promoted brevet major on 4 June 1811. In November 1812 he exchanged troops of horse artillery with Major Bull, whose health had broken down in the Peninsula, and he joined the allied Anglo-Portuguese army in its winter quarters at Freneda. In April 1813, when he had been but a short time with the army, Wellington determined to have an officer on his staff for the general command of all the horse artillery in the field, and offered the post to Frazer, as senior horse artillery officer with the army. In this capacity he served on the staff throughout the rest of the Peninsular campaigns, and was present at the affairs of Salamanca and Osma, the battle of Vitoria, the siege of San Sebastian, at which he commanded the right artillery attack, at the passage of the Bidassoa, the battles of the Nivelle and the Nive, the investment of Bayonne, and the battle of Toulouse. He soon became a favourite with Wellington, and was well rewarded for his services. He was promoted brevet lieutenant-colonel on 21 June 1813; granted a gold cross and one clasp for the battles of Vitoria, San Sebastian, Nivelle, Nive, and Toulouse; and made one of the first KCBs (2 January 1815) on the extension of the Order of the Bath. Promoted lieutenant-colonel in the Royal Artillery on 20 December 1814, he was appointed to command the artillery in the eastern district.

In 1815, when Bonaparte escaped from Elba, Frazer at once took his old position, commanding the Royal Horse Artillery on Wellington's staff in Belgium. He was now allowed to bring nine-pounders into action instead of six-pounders, a change which certainly had a great deal to do with the effective fire of the British guns at Waterloo. When the war was over Frazer was appointed British artillery commissioner for taking over the French fortresses, and on 20 June 1816 he was elected FRS. For some time he commanded the Royal Horse Artillery at Woolwich; in October 1827 he was appointed assistant inspector, royal carriage department, Woolwich arsenal, and in July 1828 replaced Sir William Congreve, second baronet, as director of the Royal Laboratory, Woolwich. He was promoted colonel in the Royal Artillery in January 1825, and died at Woolwich on 11 June 1835.

H. M. STEPHENS, rev. ROGER T. STEARN

Sources E. Sabine, ed., *Letters of Colonel Sir Augustus S. Frazer, KCB …* (1859) · F. Duncan, ed., *History of the royal regiment of artillery*, 2 vols. (1873) · A. J. Guy, ed., *The road to Waterloo: the British army and the struggle against revolutionary and Napoleonic France, 1793–1815* (1990) · R. Muir, *Britain and the defeat of Napoleon, 1807–1815* (1996) · J. Haydn, *The book of dignities: containing rolls of the official personages of the British empire* (1851) · *GM*, 2nd ser., 4 (1835) · O. F. G. Hogg, *The Royal Arsenal: its background, origin, and subsequent history*, 2 vols. (1963)
Archives Royal Artillery Institution, Woolwich, London, MSS
Likenesses R. J. Lane, lithograph, 1859, NPG

Frazer, Sir James George (1854–1941), social anthropologist and classical scholar, was born in Blythswood Square, Glasgow, on 1 January 1854, the eldest of the four children of Daniel F. Frazer (1821–1900), leading partner in the long-established firm of chemists Frazer and Green, and his wife, Katherine (d. 1899), daughter of John Brown, merchant. He was educated at Springfield Academy and Larchfield Academy in Helensburgh, and from 1869 he attended the University of Glasgow, where he graduated MA in 1874. His Scottish education, which included philosophy, literature, and natural science, was considerably broader than its English counterpart, but was not as intensely focused on Latin and Greek. As Frazer had shown ability in classics, it was understood that he would complete his academic preparation in England. As the Frazers were staunch members of the Free Church of Scotland, his father was unwilling to send him to Oxford because of the lingering aura of the Oxford Movement, so he went instead to Trinity College, Cambridge, perhaps the single place in the kingdom most embodying the spirit of irreligion that his father feared. In 1878 he was placed second in the first class of the classical tripos. In 1879, on the strength of an essay on Platonic epistemology, he was elected to a college fellowship; renewed twice, it became tenable for life. In 1882 he was called to the bar in the Middle Temple, but he never practised.

Sir James George Frazer (1854–1941), by Lafayette, 1926

Frazer's interest in anthropology and religion had two sources: E. B. Tylor's epochal *Primitive Culture* (1871), which offered an evolutionary perspective on the development of culture, and his friendship with the Scottish biblical scholar William Robertson Smith, whom he met at Trinity. For introducing the methods and results of German higher criticism to Britain in his capacity as editor of the ninth edition of the *Encyclopaedia Britannica*, Smith had become the defendant in a series of celebrated heresy trials within the Free Church of Scotland, which resulted in his 'exile' to England. Smith's pioneering work, *Lectures on the Religion of the Semites* (1889), opened Frazer's eyes to the possibility of applying comparative ethnographic methods to the study of ancient religion. In 1888 Smith commissioned him to write the articles on 'Taboo' and 'Totemism' for the *Encyclopaedia*; Frazer never looked back. At the same time that Frazer embarked on the research that produced the first edition of his best-known work, *The Golden Bough* (2 vols., 1890; 2nd edn, 3 vols., 1900; 3rd edn, 12 vols., 1911–14), he continued with classical scholarship in the form of a six-volume translation and commentary on the ancient Greek traveller Pausanias (*Pausanias's Description of Greece*), which appeared in 1898. Throughout his life Frazer continued to work on classical projects in which he could employ his anthropological knowledge to advantage, the most considerable of these being an edition of Apollodorus, *The Library* (1921), in the Loeb classical series, and a five-volume edition of Ovid, *Fasti* (1929).

From the start Frazer always thought of himself as a servant of the facts, regardless of where they might take him. He frequently changed his mind in print, although never about the merits of either evolutionary theory or the comparative method for understanding human behaviour. He digested an immense number of accounts of the religious beliefs and practices of 'savages' written by explorers, soldiers, missionaries, and traders that were then streaming into London and other imperial capitals; perhaps the greatest novelty in *The Golden Bough* was Frazer's willingness to analyse the religious life of classical antiquity in the same way as he did that of contemporary 'savagery', and thus to compare the shining Greeks and Romans with the filthy 'primitives'. In that sense his work may be seen as the final phase in the dethroning of classical culture that had been going on in Europe for two centuries.

The nominal subject of *The Golden Bough* is an explanation of a strange rite that took place from time to time in Nemi, outside ancient Rome. In a grove sacred to Diana a runaway slave would take on all comers in single combat in order to claim the title of 'king of the wood'. To comprehend this little drama fully, Frazer invoked the concept of sacred kingship, which in turn led him to a survey of the principal religions of classical antiquity, in all of which (he believed) that institution existed. In these he discerned a central ritual pattern, in which the priest–king impersonates the god who embodies the spirit of vegetation; the latter dies in the autumn only to revive in the spring. He then scoured the world's religions and myths, ancient and contemporary, for innumerable examples of analogous belief and practice, to demonstrate the universality of this theme. By this point the king of the wood has long been forgotten, as Frazer himself acknowledges in the preface to the final volume of the third edition of *The Golden Bough*; in fact he was always only a lay figure, a pawn in a much larger game. Frazer's true subject is nothing less than humanity's long upward struggle towards an understanding of itself and the world. In Frazer's view that movement towards the light began in earliest times with the priest–king employing magic to compel the gods to do his bidding, followed by a religious stage in which humans admit their powerlessness and now beseech rather than command the gods. Thus for Frazer religion is a necessary stage in mental evolution, but one that is based on mistaken premisses; it has now in turn been superseded by a world-view based on rationality: positive science.

In focusing on the pattern of the dying and reviving god that lay at the heart of the religions of the ancient Mediterranean, while never mentioning Christianity, Frazer was more than a little disingenuous. In truth he was engaged all the while in a covert campaign against religion in general and Christianity in particular and may perhaps be seen, along with H. G. Wells, as the most important exponent of secularism in the twentieth century. Although from the start his reductionist view of religion received harsh criticism from other scholars, the educated public, adrift and eager for intellectual clarity in post-Darwinian Britain, seems to have drawn other conclusions. The three editions of *The Golden Bough*, and especially the one-volume epitome that he published in 1922, sold in their tens of thousands. Impressed by the quantity of the information he adduced and by the elaborate style in which he presented it, many readers concluded that Christianity represented a survival of an outlook that was now superseded. The Frazer files at Trinity contain many letters from readers thanking him for having lifted the scales from their eyes regarding the 'true' (that is, mistaken) nature of Christianity.

Frazer often compared his position in Cambridge, compiling and synthesizing the findings of observers working throughout the world, to that of a spider at the centre of its web, remaining quite still but sensitive to all external movement. He often insisted that only a library worker such as himself could see the entire phenomenon of mental evolution and not be seduced or bemused by the details of any one specific culture or epoch. His Nazarene-like devotion to scholarship came to an end when he married, on 22 April 1896, Elisabeth Johanna de Boys [see Frazer, Lilly, Lady Frazer], daughter of Sigismund Adelsdorfer, a French merchant, and widow of Charles Baylee Grove, a master mariner with whom she had two children. To the forceful Mrs Frazer, known as Lilly, her husband's shyness meant that he would always be passed over for fame and academic preferment unless she acted as his advocate. Along with this role she also took upon herself that of doorkeeper, deciding who might and who might not gain admission to him. A difficult woman, her presence had the unfortunate effect of exaggerating Frazer's isolation. Although she antagonized many people, it should be said that she and Frazer were devoted to one another lifelong.

Frazer's work brought him many honours: among the most notable, in 1908 he was named to the first chair of social anthropology in Britain, at the University of Liverpool; in 1914 he received a knighthood, in 1920 induction into the Royal Society, and in 1925 membership in the Order of Merit. He was an original member of the British Academy. Perhaps most gratifying to him, in 1922 his friends and admirers established the Frazer lectureship in anthropology, given each year in one of the four universities (Cambridge, Oxford, Glasgow, Liverpool) with which he had had a relationship over his scholarly career. His marriage consolidated his favourable reputation in France, where he received several honours, including associate membership of the Institut de France.

After the First World War the Frazers left Cambridge for London and then led a wandering existence in the 1920s. Long subject to eye trouble, Frazer suddenly went blind in 1931. With the aid of amanuenses he kept working until he died at Fen Causeway in Cambridge, on 7 May 1941, of natural causes; Lilly Frazer died several hours later. They were buried side by side in St Giles's cemetery, Cambridge. ROBERT ACKERMAN

Sources R. Ackerman, *J. G. Frazer: his life and work* (1987) · T. Besterman, ed., *A bibliography of Sir James George Frazer* (1934) · J. B. Vickery, *The literary impact of 'The golden bough'* (1973) · R. Ackerman, 'Frazer on myth and ritual', *Journal of the History of Ideas*, 36 (1975), 115–34 · J. G. Frazer, 'Speech on receiving the freedom of the city of Glasgow', *Creation and evolution in primitive cosmogonies* (1935) · *CGPLA Eng. & Wales* (1941)

Archives BL, notebooks, Add. MSS 45442–45496 · Trinity Cam., travel journals; corresp. and papers · U. Oxf., Pitt Rivers Museum, letters from Sir W. B. Spencer and notes relating to Spencer's last journals | BL, corresp. with Macmillans, Add. MSS 55134–55155 · Bodl. Oxf., corresp. with J. L. Myres · King's AC Cam., letters to Oscar Browning · Royal Anthropological Institute of Great Britain and Ireland, London, letters to C. W. Hobley and MS introduction to Hobley's book · Trinity Cam., corresp. with Sir Joseph John Thomson · U. Leeds, Brotherton L., letters to Sir Edmund Gosse · UCL, letters to Sir Francis Galton

Likenesses L. Monod, crayon drawing, 1907, Scot. NPG · L. Monod, drawing, 1907; in FM Cam., 1959 · E. A. Bourdelle, bronze bust, 1922, NPG; version, Trinity Cam. • W. Stoneman, two photographs, 1924–36, NPG • W. Rothenstein, sanguine drawing, 1925, NPG • Lafayette, photograph, 1926, NPG [see illus.] • H. M. Raeburn, oils, U. Lpool • W. Rothenstein, portrait, repro. in W. Rothenstein, *Twenty-four portraits* (1920) • photographs, repro. in Ackerman, *J. G. Frazer*

Wealth at death £7333 1s. 0d.: probate, 29 Aug 1941, *CGPLA Eng. & Wales*

Frazer [Fraser], **John** (*c.*1809–1852), poet and Irish nationalist, was born in Birr, King's county, but almost nothing is known of his parentage or early life. A protestant of Huguenot and Scots descent, he was by trade a cabinet-maker. A 'steady and unassuming workman' Frazer suffered from chronic (if unspecified) ill health, 'which ultimately incapacitated him for profitable employment' (*Dublin University Magazine*, 92).

Frazer's poems were published over the aliases J. de Jean, J., F., Ff., Maria, J. Robertson, Z, and Y in numerous Irish radical journals in the 1840s, and he was eventually taken up by a Dublin circle, probably featuring a Mrs Smith of Upper-Fitzwilliam Street, Dublin, to whose memory his *Poems* (1851) is dedicated 'in warm acknowledgment of the long and unvarying friendship, with which she laboured to promote the interest, and improve the literary taste of the author' (p. v).

Frazer had been fired to write by the agitation for repeal of the union in July 1843. He dedicated *Poems for the People* (1845) to 'The Irish People', in 'Admiration and Honor of their Enduring Resistance to Oppression, and of their Present Sublime Effort for Legislative Independence and National Regeneration' (p. iii). The poems bore 'strong proofs of a hurried composition', but 'the few hours an operative mechanic could snatch from repose or recreation, after thirteen or fourteen hours of toil, were those only which the author could devote to shewing, that his heart was with his country'. He wrote 'for his countrymen alone—and not for every generation of them—but merely for the present—as his first and most imperative duty', to sustain 'the spirit of the people in their contest for their unquestionable right to self-government' (pp. vii–viii).

Repeal was the most important theme for the poets of *The Nation* which published approximately 300 poems in its first year (October 1842–3). Its circulation of 10,000 copies reached an estimated 250,000 readers. Frazer, who also wrote for the *Freeman's Journal* and the *Weekly Register* was regarded as prolific, but was not represented in the first part of *The Spirit of the Nation* (1843), though four of his verses were collected in the second part, published in November of that year. *The Nation* was suppressed in the summer of 1848 along with other militant papers such as the *Irish Felon* (where Frazer also published as late as 22 July). It was the Irish famine of the late 1840s, however, that inspired Frazer's starkest images. 'The Three Angels' was perhaps the longest visionary poem on that subject:

Some gathered their kith to a fugitive band,
And sought the stars of a happier land;—
Themselves and their kindred through, thro' sheer despair,
Some slew, in belief that *to slay* was *to spare*!—

A cannibal fierceness but ill-suppressed
In many—made some—we must veil the rest!
(*Poems 1851*, 131)

Two of Frazer's children, Robert Alexander (aged twelve), and Louisa (aged sixteen) died during the 1849 cholera epidemic. Touching poems in their memory are included in his collected *Poems* (1851), which was selected and arranged by friends who knew that Frazer's politics commended him to some of the book's subscribers and antagonized others. Frazer, in 'hopeless ill-health', could not attempt to revise poems the defects of which were apparent to him as he surveyed them *en masse*. Moreover, his preface apologized 'for publishing at all, when every interest in the community is involved in such distress' (p. vii).

Frazer died in Dublin in March 1852, and 'a respectable collection was formed for objects which must have been very near and dear to the poor fellow in his last days', while the profits from a new edition of his poems (never published) were promised for the same (doubtless political) purpose (*Dublin University Magazine*, 1854, 90–91). When his hitherto unpublished poem *Blanche* was posthumously printed, an anonymous if fiercely unionist commentator noted that Frazer had 'dignified disaffection' by 'genius' in the 'ignoble heats of 1848', writing 'with a sincere and direct hostility to the English interest in Ireland' (ibid., 90–91). As, indeed, he had.

WARWICK GOULD

Sources 'Blanche—a poem by the late J. De Jean Frazer', *Dublin University Magazine*, 43 (1854), 90–101 [incl. fiercely Unionist commentary on this hitherto unpublished poem, and notice of his life and works] • D. J. O'Donoghue, *The poets of Ireland: a biographical dictionary with bibliographical particulars*, 1 vol. in 3 pts (1892–3) • K. MacGrath, 'Writers in *The Nation*, 1842–5', *Irish Historical Studies*, 6 (1948–9), 189–223 • *Irish Book Lover*, 13 (1921–2), 140 • *Irish Book Lover*, 6 (1914–15), 79–80; 7 (1915–16), 32 • C. Morash, ed., *The hungry voice: the poetry of the Irish famine* (1989) [with introduction by T. Brown] • C. M. Collins, ed., *Celtic Irish songs and song-writers: a selection* (1885), 96–7 [Frazer] • C. Morash, 'Literature, memory, atrocity', *'Fearful realities': new perspectives on the famine*, ed. C. Morash and R. Hayes (1996), 110–18

Archives NL Ire., letters

Frazer [*other married name* Grove], **Lilly**, **Lady Frazer** [*née* Elisabeth Johanna de Boys Adelsdorfer] (1854/5–1941), writer and translator, was born in Alsace, the daughter of Sigismund Adelsdorfer, a merchant; nothing is known of her mother. After a convent education she married Charles Baylee Grove, a British master mariner, with whom she had two children, Lilly Mary and Charles Grenville. Upon Grove's death she found herself in Britain with two teenaged children and little money; accordingly she turned to writing. Although she had no special knowledge of the subject, she managed to secure a commission from the Badminton Library to compose *Dancing* (1895), the first encyclopaedic survey of its kind in English and as such a landmark in dance history. In this connection, seeking information about 'dance among the primitives', in December 1894 she met James George *Frazer (1854–1941), a fellow of Trinity College, Cambridge, the then little-known author of the first edition of *The Golden Bough* (1890); on 22 April 1896 they married, in Cambridge.

Frazer was an unworldly man of retiring disposition, and Lilly Frazer, who was neither unworldly nor retiring, soon concluded that he had been passed over by his university and by the world of letters. She quickly took charge of his life, stationing herself outside his study and deciding who might, and who might not, gain access. In 1903 she opened a second front, the objective being to make his work as well known in France as it was in Britain. She proceeded to recruit translators for the numerous volumes of *The Golden Bough* as they appeared, supervising their work closely for the next twenty years; she herself translated *Adonis* in 1921 and the one-volume epitome of *The Golden Bough* in 1923.

Lilly Frazer's own literary career began as a reaction to the dismal way that French was taught in schools in Britain. With an entrée to the progressive Perse School for Boys in Cambridge she became an early advocate of the aural-oral method of teaching modern languages and pioneered the use of the phonograph in education. She also wrote many stories and playlets in French for classroom use. Notable among her other productions was *First Aid to the Servantless* (1913), a witty and indeed prophetic description of middle-class life without servants, and *Leaves from the Golden Bough* (1924), a collection of tales culled from her husband's immense work and retold for children. During the First World War she also translated several volumes of anti-German propaganda produced in France.

Although Lilly Frazer was generally regarded by academic Cambridge as a 'difficult' woman, even her detractors agreed that she cared for her husband deeply and that everything she did was in furtherance of his career. The conduct of her social relationships was not enhanced by her deafness, however, which had become nearly total by 1910 and which accentuated her tendency to see conspiracies everywhere. None the less, she had a large circle of her own friends, especially abroad, with whom she conducted a spirited correspondence. Always regarding Cambridge as provincial, she had long pressed her husband to agree to move to London, a wish that was granted in 1914. Although he had no interest in awards and prizes, she was gratified by the various marks of public recognition that her husband's work then began to attract, especially the knighthood in 1914, which permitted her to style herself Lady Frazer. During the 1920s they travelled widely in Europe; in 1931, however, Frazer, who had long suffered from eye trouble, suddenly went blind, which both ended their peripatetic existence and caused an unwanted return to Cambridge.

In the depression her husband's royalty income plunged drastically; characteristically resourceful, Lilly Frazer succeeded in securing grants-in-aid from several public and private bodies to permit them to live comfortably in their last years. During the 1930s she had a series of respiratory illnesses but soldiered on, her sole *raison d'être* being to keep her husband alive. He died in Cambridge on

7 May 1941, and she died several hours later, on 8 May, aged eighty-six, and was buried beside him in St Giles's cemetery, Cambridge.   ROBERT ACKERMAN

Sources Trinity Cam., Frazer MSS · R. Ackerman, *J. G. Frazer: his life and work* (1987) · R. A. Downie, *Frazer and the 'Golden bough'* (1970) · d. cert.
Archives Trinity Cam., papers | BL, Macmillan papers, Add. MS 55134 ff.
Likenesses L. H. Monod, crayon drawing, 1907, Scot. NPG · photograph, 1930, repro. in Ackerman, *J. G. Frazer*, following p. 126
Wealth at death £9260 17s. 8d.: probate, 5 Sept 1941, CGPLA Eng. & Wales

Freake, Edmund (*c*.1516–1591), bishop of Norwich and of Worcester, was probably born in Essex, since by the age of twelve (when he helped with the prior's alchemy experiments) he was a canon of the Augustinian priory of Leighs. On the surrender of that house he transferred to the neighbouring abbey of Waltham, where he remained until that too surrendered (23 March 1540), receiving a pension of £5. On 19 December 1544 he was ordained deacon in London by John Hodgkin, suffragan bishop of Bedford, to the title of his crown pension. On 12 January 1545 he was licensed to receive the priesthood from any bishop, and on 18 January he was so ordained, again by Hodgkin. There is no further record of Freake for almost twenty years; he must have graduated MA at Cambridge about 1550. Possibly the marriage he contracted at this time brought some supplement to his pension—this could in part explain Cicely Freake's dominating role in their partnership. In 1562 Freake was presented to the rectory of Fowlmere, Cambridgeshire, by the earl of Oxford. Court patronage must explain his subsequent rapid advance into the ranks of the higher clergy, which began with his appointment to a canonry of Westminster on 8 March 1564. On 1 May he was further elected as the abbey's *lector theologiae*.

On 18 November 1565 Freake preached at Paul's Cross, and in Lent 1566 at court. On 13 July 1567 he was instituted to the rectory of Purleigh, Essex, at the crown's presentation. He was seemingly designated a canon of Canterbury; but Archbishop Matthew Parker wrote disapprovingly (29 March 1568) of his suit to receive the full emoluments despite intended non-residence, and the appointment was not made. On 10 June 1570, at Cecil's request, the University of Cambridge voted to confer the degree of DTh on Freake, by then the queen's chaplain. Freake's attendance at court prevented his receiving the degree until 20 August, when he was presented for it by John Whitgift. On 22 December following Freake was appointed dean of Rochester, where he was installed on the 24th. On 1 August 1571 he was appointed a commissioner for Rochester Bridge; on the same day he was further presented to the deanery of Salisbury, being installed and admitted to residence on 18 September.

On 11 February 1572 Queen Elizabeth authorized Freake's election as bishop of Rochester. He was consecrated in the chapel of Lambeth Palace on 9 March and enthroned by proxy on 22 April. He thereby vacated his two deaneries and other benefices, but held the archdeaconry of Canterbury *in commendam* during his tenure of the see. By 29 March 1572 he was lord high almoner, being then granted the customary disposal of deodands (causes of accidental deaths, which were forfeited to the crown) and the goods of suicides (with effect from 26 February).

On 4 November 1575 the queen assented to Freake's translation to Norwich; proxies for his enthronement there were appointed on 22 November. This promotion must have been of the queen's devising: he was not on Parker's shortlist of candidates. So far as can be judged, Freake had hitherto favoured reform, and before the watershed of 1566 represented by Parker's *Advertisements* had supported toleration for nonconformity. His later critics denounced him as a turncoat. He may well have trimmed his opinions in the interests of advancement. The only key to his opinions while still at Rochester is a letter he wrote to Bishop Parkhurst of Norwich (13 June 1574), responding to inquiries about the lawfulness of the 'exercises', the self-regulating conferences favoured by radical clergy. Freake had heard no order for their suppression in his diocese or that of London, so he and Bishop Grindal would allow them to continue 'to the comforte of Gode's church [and] encrease of knowledge in the mynisterie' (*Letter Book of John Parkhurst*, 246). When Freake succeeded Parkhurst at Norwich, however, he proceeded to stifle dissent, having clearly been instructed by the queen or by Parker, or perhaps both, to remedy the effects of his predecessor's laxity. This predictably provoked conflict not only with the puritan clergy but with their supporters among the gentry.

Norfolk and Suffolk, where native independency was now flavoured with religious sentiment, had since 1572 been without the dominating influence of a Howard duke. With no senior peer in the region, competing factions among the gentry jostled to fill the county leadership, and the bishop of Norwich's position was of enhanced significance. Parkhurst had allied himself with the 'godly' gentry. Freake, with no previous local connections, of necessity made his friends among the conservatives, which naturally brought accusations that he was himself a crypto-Catholic. He began by putting as many conservatives on the county benches as he could. At his primary visitation in 1576 a direct assault was made on radical preachers in Norwich, many of whom were deprived. The ejected men had friends at court, chiefly through the intervention of Nathaniel Bacon, the son of Lord Keeper Nicholas Bacon. The privy council, worried that Freake was acting too severely, arranged a royal progress through Suffolk and Norfolk in August 1578, during which recusant gentry were publicly humiliated and supporters of reform were rewarded. The bishop himself was obliged to reach accommodation with some of the ejected ministers. Others, however, had been driven permanently outside the established church. Victims of Freake's purge would be leading figures in the presbyterian movement later centred at Dedham; some would seek yet more radical alternatives.

In Suffolk the bishop's policies had some support from those whom the evangelicals had irritated; but here again there was prolonged discord, perhaps most notably at Bury St Edmunds in 1582–3. Freake's greatest irritant was, however, his own chief officer John Becon, whom he had appointed chancellor on his arrival in the diocese, apparently not realizing that he favoured those whom he would be required to discipline. By 1577, when a further visitation was in prospect, the bishop's gentry allies were campaigning to have Becon removed; Sir Thomas Cornwallis offered him cash to go away. When Becon refused to resign, Freake simply undercut his jurisdiction by reviving the defunct episcopal court of audience, and appointing the former chancellor William Masters to preside there. This ploy did not amuse the privy council, which told the bishop to restore the conventional processes. In July 1578 a truce was agreed between bishop and chancellor before the council at Greenwich. But during the queen's progress in the following month a scheme Becon advanced for remodelling the diocesan structure was favourably received, to Freake's further indignation. Once the royal party had left his diocese he revoked Becon's patent and had him physically prevented from officiating. The council professed themselves incredulous of these proceedings, and on 9 October 1578 they appointed a commission of local gentry to examine the whole affair. The resulting inquiry produced a welter of accusations against the bishop, his officials, household servants, familiars, and, most famously, his wife. Mrs Freake's control of her husband and his diocese was said to be *vox populi* throughout Norfolk; according to one deponent the bishop had tearfully admitted that if he did not do whatever she wished, 'she wold make hym weary of his liffe' (PRO, SP 15/25, no. 119).

It is chiefly because of these depositions that Freake is remembered as a feeble-minded man. But the stories all come from hostile sources, and Freake was eventually successful in obtaining Becon's removal by threatening his own resignation; he called the chancellor 'an instrument to woorke my continewall troble' and would have no reconciliation (PRO, SP 12/126, no. 6). The privy council had Becon moved to another diocese, and Freake restored the sympathetic Masters as chancellor in April 1580. It was not the end of the bishop's troubles; he and his officers were repeatedly accused of avarice, unseemly conduct, and, above all, toleration of recusancy; Catholic prisoners (it was said) were indulged, while information against 'semynaryes and massemongers' was ignored (*Papers of Nathaniel Bacon*, 2.276).

Since 1578 Freake had been telling his friends that he wanted a quieter (and, according to his opponents, richer) diocese. To encourage him to stay Cornwallis (again) offered him money. In 1579 it was proposed that he change places with Thomas Cooper of Lincoln, but the latter was unenthusiastic for the very reasons that Freake wished for release. It was then proposed that he should replace Cox at Ely, but Freake refused to grant the pension Cox asked for. Once again Freake achieved his purpose by offering resignation; on 29 August 1583 he told Lord

Burghley that unless the queen agreed to move him from his present 'continuall crossing and overthwarting', he wished to be altogether discharged (BL, Lansdowne MS 38, fol. 204). His absence from a commission of oyer and terminer (directed against recusants) in March 1584 was recognized as a signal of his impending departure. He was translated to Worcester on 26 October 1584, being enthroned there by proxy on 7 February 1585.

Freake's last episcopate was troubled by debts, but no great controversy. In January 1589 he wrote to the queen asking to be excused attendance at parliament, explaining that the local roads were too bad for coaches, and that his physician had advised him not to ride lest it bring on an attack of the stone, with which he had previously been 'moste grievouslie visited' (PRO, SP 12/222, no. 36).

Freake died on 21 March 1591, and was buried in Worcester Cathedral. His widow survived until 15 July 1599; she was buried at Purleigh. Their son John, who died in 1604, was likewise buried there, having succeeded his father first at Fowlmere in 1571 and then at Purleigh in 1575; he was also made archdeacon of Norwich by his father in 1581. John is not mentioned in the bishop's will, where his other son Edmund is named executor (an office he refused), sharing the estate with his sister Martha (who married Nathaniel Cole, fellow of Trinity College, Cambridge) and their mother. Freake published a translation of a presumed work of St Augustine, *An Introduction to the Love of God* (1574; STC 935), turned into verse by Robert Fletcher (1581?; STC 936).   C. S. KNIGHTON

Sources LP Henry VIII, 15, no. 393 (2) • CPR, 1563–6, 85, 366; 1566–9, 27; 1569–72, 20, 249, 278, 378, 379, 394, 440, 450, 466, 478; 1575–8, 35, 386–7, 388 • CSP dom., 1547–80, 382, 601–4, 606–7; 1581–90, 575; addenda, 1566–79, 548, 551–2 • state papers domestic, Elizabeth I, PRO, SP 12/126, no. 6; 12/222, no. 36; 15/25, no. 119 • will, PRO, PROB 11/77, sig. 26 • BL, Lansdowne MS 38, fol. 204 • BL, Egerton MS 1693, fols. 87–9, 98–100 • Fasti Angl., 1541–1857, [Canterbury], 15, 51, 54 • Fasti Angl., 1541–1857, [Salisbury], 6, 96 • Fasti Angl., 1541–1857, [Ely], 37, 80, 106 • J. Venn, ed., Grace book Δ (1910), 238 • The letter book of John Parkhurst, bishop of Norwich, ed. R. A. Houlbrooke, Norfolk RS, 43 (1974–5), 54–5, 245–6 • The papers of Nathaniel Bacon of Stiffkey, ed. A. H. Smith, G. M. Baker, and R. W. Kenny, 1: 1556–1577, Norfolk RS, 46 (1979), 236; 2: 1578–1585, Norfolk RS, 49 (1983), 16, 22–3, 223–4, 225–6, 274–6, 286 • Correspondence of Matthew Parker, ed. J. Bruce and T. T. Perowne, Parker Society, 42 (1853), 319, 477 • Registrum Matthei Parker, diocesis Cantuariensis, AD 1559–1575, ed. W. H. Frere and E. M. Thompson, 3 vols., CYS, 35–6, 39 (1928–33), 162–3, 328–31 • J. E. Oxley, The Reformation in Essex (1965), 57, 239 • A. Hassell Smith, County and court: government and politics in Norfolk, 1558–1603 (1974), 208–25 • D. MacCulloch, Suffolk and the Tudors: politics and religion in an English county, 1500–1600 (1986), 193–200 • F. Heal, Of prelates and princes: a study of the economic and social position of the Tudor episcopate (1980), 251, 299 • Calendar of the manuscripts of the most hon. the marquis of Salisbury, 2, HMC, 9 (1888), 195–8 • C. S. Knighton, ed., Acts of the dean and chapter of Westminster, 2 (1999), 14 • P. McGrath and J. Rowe, 'The recusancy of Sir Thomas Cornwallis', Proceedings of the Suffolk Institute of Archaeology, 28 (1958–60), 226–71, esp. 241–3 • P. Collinson, The Elizabethan puritan movement (1967), 202–4 • Bodl. Oxf., MS Tanner 50, fols. 27v–29 [notes of sermon at St Paul's Cross, 1565] • W. C. Waller, 'An Essex alchemist', Essex Review, 13 (1904), 22–3 • A parte of a register [1593] • DNB

Archives CKS, episcopal registers (Rochester) • Norfolk RO, reg/13/19, fols. 216–17 • PRO, SP12 and 15 • Worcs. RO, b.716.093-BA.2648/10(i), fols. 62–70, 96–7, 123–38

Wealth at death debts: will, 1591, PRO, PROB 11/77, sig. 26

Fream, William (1854–1906), agriculturist and writer, was born in Gloucester, the second son in the family of four sons and three daughters of John Fream, builder and contractor, and his wife, Mary, *née* Grant. As a boy he was a chorister of Gloucester Cathedral, and he was always devoted to music. He was educated at Sir Thomas Rich's Blue Coat Hospital, whence he entered the employment of a Gloucester corn and seed merchant. However, in 1872 he gained a royal exhibition at the Royal College of Science, Dublin. He studied there for three years, receiving prizes in botany, practical chemistry, and, with special distinction, in geology. He also made a number of long botanical walking tours in Ireland, particularly in Connemara. Fream became an associate of the Royal College by diploma. He also graduated in science with honours in chemistry at the first University of London BSc examination in 1877.

From 1877 to 1879 Fream was professor of natural history at the Royal Agricultural College, Cirencester. Following a brief period as a temporary lecturer and demonstrator in botany at Guy's Hospital medical school, and a winter studying zoology at the Royal School of Mines in London, in 1880 he joined Professor John Wrightson in establishing the College of Agriculture at Downton, Wiltshire. He taught natural history there and instituted a series of field classes and laboratory demonstrations.

Fream paid visits to Canada in 1884, 1888, and 1891, to examine agricultural conditions there, describing his findings in a series of papers. These include the pamphlet *The Gates of the West* (1892), *Across Canada: a Report on Canada and its Agricultural Resources*, written for and published by the government of Canada (1885), and, in two parts, 'Canadian agriculture', which appeared in the *Journal of the Royal Agricultural Society* in 1885. In 1888 Fream received an honorary LLD from McGill University, Montreal.

In 1890 Fream became the first Steven lecturer in Edinburgh University on agricultural entomology, a then novel subject which he had included in his curriculum at Downton. In the same year he was appointed editor of the *Journal of the Royal Agricultural Society of England*, an office he held until 1900.

For twelve years, from January 1894 until his death, Fream was agricultural correspondent of *The Times*, writing useful weekly articles on agriculture and special annual reports on crop returns. His articles showed an intense love of country life and an intimate knowledge of wild flowers. He was a chief examiner in the principles of agriculture under the Department of Science and Art, South Kensington.

Apart from his writings on Canada, and his journalistic work, Fream edited exhaustively the thirteenth and fourteenth editions of *Youatt's Complete Grazier* (1893 and 1900). His most widely read book was *The Elements of Agriculture*, published for the Royal Agricultural Society of England in 1891 (7th edn, 1902). Before his death some 36,000 copies had been sold.

Fream lived largely at Downton, but he also had working quarters in London, where he was said to be popular in congenial society. He died, unmarried, at Downton on 29

May 1906, and was buried in Gloucester cemetery. A Fream memorial fund, subscribed by leading agriculturists, was entrusted to the Board of Agriculture and Fisheries, the income to be awarded annually as prizes under special regulations.

ROBERT WALLACE, *rev.* ALEXANDER GOLDBLOOM

Sources *The Times* (31 May 1906) · *CGPLA Eng. & Wales* (1906) · **Wealth at death** £14,656 2s. 6d.: probate, 4 Aug 1906, *CGPLA Eng. & Wales*

Freame, John (1665–1745), banker and lobbyist, was probably the second son in the family of at least three children of Robert Freame, a Gloucestershire clothier. In 1681 his father was one of the 'first purchasers' of Pennsylvania and some members of the Quaker Freame family emigrated there to escape religious persecution by the Gloucestershire magistrates.

The young John Freame sought refuge in London: he was apprenticed in 1683 to Job Boulton, a leading Lombard Street goldsmith. Boulton was also an influential member of the Friends' Committee on Sufferings, one of the first lobby groups in British politics. Freame completed his apprenticeship in 1690 and set up as a banker in partnership with another young Quaker, Thomas Gould. He married Gould's sister Priscilla (1673/4–1727) in 1697 and they had seven children. The Freame–Gould business partnership (cemented also by Gould's marriage to Freame's sister, Hannah) lasted until Thomas Gould's death in 1728; Gould's own son set up an independent bank which went bankrupt in 1730.

The Freame bank was one of the few seventeenth-century banks to survive well into the next century. Others among this select few (like Hoares or Coutts) evolved into West End banks for gentlemen, while Freame and Gould's business seems to have focused on the City's merchant community. They financed links not only with the English provinces but with Quaker traders in the American and Caribbean colonies and the Baltic. Among the enterprises in which they participated financially were the Enfield turnpike, Atlantic trading ventures, the Pennsylvania Land Company, the London Lead Company, and the Welsh Copper Company. The latter two Quaker-dominated companies developed the reverberatory furnace for lead smelting, which was financed by a £500 loan at 6 per cent interest from Freame and Gould; the bank also owned shares in the company and dealt in its by-product, silver, for the Royal Mint.

Freame's career was clearly built on the religious connections forged during his apprenticeship. The Friends deposited their 'national stock' (that is, their central funds, amounting to £1100 in 1695) in his bank from an early stage, and he knew the Quaker luminaries of the day intimately. He was frequently called upon to arbitrate in Quaker business (as well as religious) matters and served as clerk to the Friends' supreme body, the yearly meeting, in 1711. The year after that he published *Scripture Instruction*, a textbook of morals much reprinted for over a century and used in the schools of the Quaker educational

pioneer Joseph Lancaster. Freame was one of those Quakers who helped to entrench toleration after 1689 by diplomatically, but relentlessly, wringing from a reluctant Anglican establishment small cumulative concessions on matters such as affirmation (in place of the oaths of which they disapproved) or summary prosecution before magistrates (rather than the more vexatious church courts), thus reconciling his faith's many tender consciences to the requirements of civil society.

Freame's daughter Priscilla married in 1723 the Quaker merchant David *Barclay (1682–1769) whose son joined Freame's son, Joseph, in 1733 as a partner with a quarter share in the Lombard Street bank. The bank was a pioneer of the rediscounting of provincial bankers' bills in London and held large reserves at the Bank of England to support this position. John Freame spent more time on Quaker affairs after his son entered the bank. He also reconstructed the London Lead Company (of which he became governor), following revelations in the later 1720s of misuse of its funds by Quaker fraudsters in the South Sea Bubble affair. He died in 1745, his wife having predeceased him in 1727; his funeral at Winchmore Hill, in the burial-ground of the Quaker meeting-house near his country home, Bush Hill, north of London, was the Friends' equivalent of a Westminster Abbey interment. Apparently a man of self-effacing modesty, his quiet effectiveness had enabled him to become one of the more successful bankers, political lobbyists, and religious leaders of his generation.

LESLIE HANNAH

Sources RS Friends, Lond., archives · Swarthmore College, Pennsylvania, USA, Quaker archives · will of John Freame, PRO, PROB 11 742/271 · M. Ackrill and L. Hannah, *Barclays: the business of banking, 1690–1996* (2001) · **Archives** Barclay's Bank Archives, Wythenshawe, Manchester · GL, poll tax assessments and apprenticeship records | Tyne and Wear Archives Service, London Lead Co. MSS

Frece, de. For this title name *see* Tilley, Vesta [Matilda Alice de Frece, Lady de Frece] (1864–1952).

Frece, Sir (Abraham) Walter de (1870–1935), music-hall entrepreneur and politician, was born on 7 October 1870 at 90 Salisbury Street, Everton, Liverpool, the eldest son of Henry de Frece, music-hall manager, and his wife, Marian Rowe. He was born into a prominent Liverpool theatrical family and although, after completing his education at Liverpool Institute and in Brussels, he was initially apprenticed to an architect, he ultimately followed all three of his brothers into the theatre. Jack and Ben became music-hall managers and Lauri was an actor.

De Frece wrote songs for many top music-hall performers, including Dan Leno, for whom he wrote 'The Shopwalker', and Vesta *Tilley (1864–1952). He married the latter on 16 August 1890: her real name was Matilda Alice Powles, and she was the daughter of Henry William Powles, comedian. Vesta Tilley specialized in male roles, including Burlington Bertie. They had no children.

It was as a music-hall manager and company director

that de Frece had his greatest success. His music-hall interests expanded rapidly during the 1890s and especially after the turn of the century, and by 1909 he owned or controlled around fifteen theatres, mainly located in northern industrial towns. He was one of the first music-hall entrepreneurs to appreciate the opportunities presented by the rapidly expanding leisure market in seaside resorts and also controlled a number of theatres on the south coast.

In 1910 de Frece went into partnership with Sir Alfred *Butt, through the formation of the Variety Theatres Controlling Company Limited (VTCC). This merger provided de Frece with access to the lucrative metropolitan market and, he hoped, with the opportunity to resist the spiralling wage demands of variety performers. It also constituted the first real challenge to the predominance of Moss Empires (with whom de Frece had been briefly allied during 1909) within the music-hall industry. After the conclusion of a 'triple alliance' between the VTCC, Charles Gulliver (of the London Theatres of Varieties Limited), and Oswald Stoll in 1912, de Frece became one of the most powerful men in the music-hall business.

During the First World War, de Frece organized theatrical and cinematic entertainments for the troops and to raise money for wounded veterans. In 1918 he was appointed a trustee of the King's Fund for Disabled Officers and Men and in 1919 he was knighted in recognition of his war work. After the war de Frece and Vesta Tilley withdrew from active involvement in the music-hall business. In 1919 de Frece sold his interest in the VTCC to Charles Gulliver, although he remained chairman of the company. In the same year he floated the Alliance Film Company.

Increasingly, however, de Frece and his wife dedicated themselves to public life. He was elected the Unionist MP for Ashton under Lyne in February 1920, his success in this contest being widely attributed largely to his wife's ability to mobilize the newly enfranchised female electorate. As *The Times* (14 February 1920, 15) noted, 'the most significant fact of the election is the further example it has supplied of the influence of woman in politics and the power of the women's vote.' De Frece stood down as the representative for Ashton under Lyne after being sued by an unsuccessful Labour candidate whom he branded as a Bolshevik sympathizer, but was immediately re-elected to represent Blackpool. He continued in parliament until 1931, when he retired on account of the ill health of his wife. While an MP, de Frece championed the cause of the theatrical business. He campaigned vigorously for the abolition of the entertainments tax imposed during the First World War, and in 1924 was elected founding chairman of the House of Commons entertainment industry committee. He served as a deputy lieutenant of Berkshire, and was also honorary colonel of the 9th battalion of the Manchester regiment.

Sir Walter and Lady de Frece retired to Monte Carlo, where they lived until his death from pneumonia and a fever on 7 January 1935 at the Park Palace. His recreations included racing, golf, and motoring, and he cultivated a debonair image, dressing in the fashion of 'a man about town rather than one of large business enterprises' (*Daily Telegraph*, 8 Jan 1935). He was survived by his wife.

ANDREW CROWHURST

Sources *Daily Telegraph* (8 Jan 1935) · *The Times* (8 Jan 1935) · Lady de Frece, *Recollections of Vesta Tilley* [1934] · S. Maitland, *Vesta Tilley* (1986) · A. Crowhurst, 'The music hall, 1885–1922: the emergence of a national entertainment industry in Britain', PhD diss., U. Cam., 1992 · *The Times* (14 Feb 1920), 15 · WWW · b. cert. · m. cert. · d. cert. · *CGPLA Eng. & Wales* (1935)
Wealth at death £69,620 9s. 3d.: probate, 30 April 1935, *CGPLA Eng. & Wales*

Fréchette, Louis Honoré (1839–1908), poet and journalist, born at Lévis, Quebec, Canada, on 16 November 1839, was the eldest son of Louis Fréchette, a contractor, whose family was originally established on the Île de Ré, Saintonge, France. His mother was Marguerite Martineau de Lormière. Fréchette's early education was somewhat sporadic, as, being two or three years older than his classmates, he resented the rules of the institutions he attended. He passed from the Petit Séminaire de Québec to the Collège de Ste Anne-de-la-Pocatière, before finishing the sixth form at the Séminaire de Nicolet (rhetoric). In September 1860, despite the fact that he had not completed his *baccalauréat-ès-arts* (he did not take the final two years of philosophy), he was accepted into a leading law firm in Quebec City. He went on to attend law courses at Laval University in Quebec City and published his first volume of poetry, *Mes loisirs*, in 1863. He also studied at McGill College and Queen's University. He was called to the bar of Lower Canada in 1864 and opened a law office at Lévis, but never practised law seriously, though it was not until 1879 that he actually retired from the profession.

In April 1865 Fréchette was one of the founding editors of *Le Journal de Lévis*, but he had to leave it after eight months for unknown reasons. He was later to blame the religious leaders of his parish for a blow to his prospects, but it has also been posited that 'as an outspoken opponent of the proposed confederation of the British North American colonies, he may have disclosed the local defence system to a Fenian spy, thus arousing the suspicions of the political authorities' (*DCB*, 359).

In November 1866 Fréchette went to Chicago and there devoted himself for five years to journalism. He then edited *L'Amérique*, a Republican Party paper for the city's French population, and was for a time corresponding secretary of the Illinois Central Railway. His poetic reputation was enhanced by *La voix d'un exilé*, published in three instalments in the leading Quebec Liberal newspapers (1867, 1868, 1869) and in volume form in Chicago. This work showed the strength both of his French patriotism and of his clerical antipathies. In 1871 he moved to New Orleans. There, while the siege of Paris was in progress, he showed his devotion to France by fighting a duel with a retired German officer whom he had offended in a theatre by avowing his French sympathies; he had never used a sword before. In late February 1871 he returned to Quebec.

Turning to politics, Fréchette unsuccessfully contested

his native town, Lévis, at the general election of 1871 in the Liberal interest; but in 1874, when Alexander Mackenzie came to power, he won the seat. On 10 July 1876 he married Emma, the second daughter of Jean-Baptiste Beaudry, a merchant and banker of Montreal. Fréchette continued to be a consistent supporter of Mackenzie's Liberal government. He failed to retain his seat in 1878 and 1882, and henceforth devoted to journalism all the energies that he spared from poetry. He edited his *Journal de Québec*, contributed largely to *L'Opinion Publique*, and during 1884–5 was editor of *La Patrie*. He wrote frequently, too, for the American magazines *The Forum*, *Harper's*, and *The Arena*. Fréchette continued to campaign for the Liberal Party, and in 1887 Honoré Mercier, a Liberal, became premier of Quebec. When Fréchette was not awarded his desired post of Quebec chargé d'affaires in Paris, he became angry at what he perceived to be ingratitude for his fifteen years of work for the party, and thus left for France, with his family, on 9 May 1887. It was there that he completed and published his best-known work of poetry, *La légende d'un peuple* (1887), in which he commemorated with skill, vigour, and variety the history of the French race. He also lectured in France, but after a bout of depression returned to Canada in December 1887. In 1889 Mercier awarded him the post of clerk of the legislative council, and Fréchette had also begun to write again for *La Patrie* in October 1888. In addition to this he became an editor for *Le Canada Artistique* and the radical magazine *Canada-Revue*. Not one to shy away from controversy, his polemical articles in these papers have been credited with influencing the federal election of 1896 and the Quebec provincial election of 1897, both won by the Liberals.

Meanwhile Fréchette had published further volumes in verse between 1877 and 1891, among which *Les fleurs boréales* and *Les oiseaux de neige* (1879) were crowned by the Académie Française in 1880. Fréchette was also the recipient of the first prix Montyon for that year. He was the first Canadian citizen to receive this honour, and the reaction to it was mixed. The delight of his supporters was mitigated by his enemies' accusations of plagiarism and their pointing to his ideological support for the Third Republic as the underlying reason for the award. Further honours followed, however. He was made an officier d'Académie lauréat of the Institut de France. The leading Canadian universities conferred honorary degrees upon him (LLD at McGill College, Montreal, and Queen's University, Kingston, in 1881, and at Toronto University in 1900; DLitt at Laval University in 1888), and in 1897, the year of Queen Victoria's diamond jubilee, he was created CMG. In 1898 he became honorary president of the École Littéraire de Montréal. He was furthermore, in 1900, chosen as president of the Royal Society of Canada.

Besides poetry, Fréchette published prose works, including *Lettres à Basile* (1872), *Histoire critique des rois de France* (1881), and *Originaux et détraqués* (1892), the last the most lively and original of his prose compositions. A collection of tales, *La Noël au Canada*, appeared in both English and French versions (1899–1900). In 1900–01 *Le Monde*

Illustré (Montreal) serialized his recollections of his childhood, which were reprinted sixty years later as the appealing *Mémoires intimes*. Fréchette also attempted drama in *Félix Poutré* (1871), *Papineau*, and *Véronica* (1903), but these, though vigorously written, lack dramatic instinct. At his death he had in preparation an authoritative edition of his poetry. It appeared posthumously in Montreal in 1908 (three series) and contained all the poems by which he desired to be remembered. Age had softened his antipathy towards the church, and consequently the unclerical verses of *La voix d'un exilé* found no place in this final edition. Fréchette died of a stroke at Montreal on 31 May 1908. He was survived by his wife and three children, Louis-Joseph, Jeanne, and Louise.

As a poet Fréchette owed much to Victor Hugo, both in the mechanism of his lines and in the logical method of developing his themes. If he lacked Hugo's vibrant lyrical quality, he was by no means his unsuccessful imitator in patriotic verse, perhaps best seen in *La légende d'un peuple*. In contrast to the poet William Henry Drummond, whose French types show no resentment against English rule, Fréchette presents the kind of French-Canadian sentiment which failed to reconcile itself to the events which brought British control over Quebec in 1759. His literary work has been held in high esteem in Canada, particularly in Quebec. One commentator perceptively summed up his influence:

> He became the prime force, in his day, in the creation of French-Canadian literature by his pioneering in poetry and drama, his success as a pamphleteer and short-story writer, and his contributions to many periodicals and cultural or literary societies in Quebec, France, and the United States. ... Fréchette gave legitimacy to working in the field of literature. (*DCB*, 361)

PELHAM EDGAR, *rev.* M. CLARE LOUGHLIN-CHOW

Sources *WWW*, 1897–1915 · J. G. Bourinot, *Canada* (1897) · *The Times* (2–25 June 1908) · J. Blais, 'Fréchette, Louis', *DCB*, vol. 13 · D. M. Hayne, 'Fréchette, Louis', *The Oxford companion to Canadian literature*, ed. W. Toye (1983)
Likenesses L.-P. Hébert, bronze bust, *c*.1895, National Gallery of Canada, Ottawa · portrait, repro. in Bourinot, *Canada*, 441

Frecheville, Sir Peter (1513–1558). *See under* Frescheville family (*per*. 1518–1682).

Frecheville, Peter (1534–1582). *See under* Frescheville family (*per*. 1518–1682).

Frecheville, Sir Peter (1575–1634). *See under* Frescheville family (*per*. 1518–1682).

Frederica Charlotte Ulrica Catherina, duchess of York (1767–1820). *See under* Frederick, Prince, duke of York and Albany (1763–1827).

Frederick V, count palatine of the Rhine and elector of the Holy Roman empire (1596–1632). *See under* Elizabeth, Princess (1596–1662).

Frederick, Colonel. *See* Frederick, Felice (1725?–1797).

Frederick, Prince, duke of York and Albany (1763–1827), army officer and bishop of Osnabrück, was the second son of *George III and Queen *Charlotte. He was born at St

Prince Frederick, duke of York and Albany (1763–1827), by Sir David Wilkie, 1822–3

James's Palace, London, on 16 August 1763, and on 27 February 1764 was elected to the bishopric of Osnabrück through his father's influence as elector of Hanover. On 1 November 1780 he was gazetted a colonel in the army. In the following year he went to Hanover to study French and German, and visited the Austrian and Prussian military manoeuvres. He was appointed colonel of the 2nd Horse Grenadier Guards on 23 March 1782; was promoted major-general on 20 November 1782; and was made lieutenant-general on 27 October 1784, when he became colonel of the 2nd or Coldstream Guards. On 27 November 1784 he was created duke of York and Albany in the peerage of Great Britain, and earl of Ulster in the peerage of Ireland. He retained the bishopric of Osnabrück until 1803.

In 1787 the duke of York, always his father's favourite son, returned to England. He took his seat in the House of Lords on 27 November 1787, and on 15 December 1788, on the question of the regency in opposition to Pitt's Regency Bill, he made a speech which attracted attention, as it was held to convey the sentiments of the prince of Wales. On 26 May 1789 he fought a duel on Wimbledon Common with Colonel Lennox (afterwards duke of Richmond), who was aggrieved by some of the duke's remarks. The duke coolly waited for Lennox's shot, and then fired in the air. His courage and his refusal to use his rank to decline the challenge were much applauded.

In January 1791 a marriage was arranged for York with **Frederica Charlotte Ulrica Catherina** [Princess Frederica of Prussia] (1767–1820), eldest daughter of Frederick William II, king of Prussia, and his first wife, Elizabeth of Brunswick. The couple had met in Berlin and the marriage

was celebrated there on 29 September 1791, and at Buckingham House (later Palace) on 23 November. There were no children of the marriage; husband and wife soon separated, and the duchess of York retired to Oatlands Park, near Weybridge, Surrey. A modest, self-effacing woman, she cared little for London society, preferring the company of her pet dogs, and attending church every Sunday. Her sympathy with the estranged princess of Wales and her daughter Charlotte incurred the prince regent's resentment, but she was liked and respected by the rest of the family. She died on 6 August 1820, of consumption, and was buried in Weybridge church on 14 August.

On the outbreak of war in 1793 George III insisted that York should take command of the English contingent dispatched to Flanders to co-operate with the Austrian army under the prince of Coburg. The campaigns of 1793, 1794, and 1795 in Flanders served to prove that the English army was unable to cope with the enthusiastic French republicans, and that York was not a born military commander. His staff were chiefly responsible; the duke showed himself brave but inexperienced, and there is much truth in Gillray's caricatures and Peter Pindar's squibs, which represented him as indulging too freely in the prevalent dissipation of his officers. In 1793 the allied army drove the French army out of Belgium, defeated it at Tournai and Famars, and took Valenciennes on 26 July. Then came a difference between the generals; the prince of Coburg wished to march on Paris, while York was ordered to take Dunkirk. The armies separated, and Carnot at once concentrated the French troops in an attack on the duke near Dunkirk. After severe fighting at Hondschoten on 6 and 8 September the English had to fall back, and, after the defeat of the Austrians at Wattignies, finally joined them at Tournai, where both armies went into winter quarters. In February 1794 the duke joined the headquarters of the army in Flanders, and the new campaign opened with some successes at Château Cambrésis, Villers-en-Cauchies, and Troixville. But in May the French army under Pichegru attacked the English army at Tournai. In the last engagement the English were defeated, and York himself was nearly taken prisoner. After this defeat the English army steadily fell back, in spite of the arrival in July of ten thousand fresh troops under the earl of Moira, and the duke was driven out of Belgium. There followed the winter retreat of 1794–5, which concluded the unsuccessful campaign. York shared the perils of the retreat up to the beginning of December, when he returned to England.

The duke's reputation had not been raised. Nevertheless George III promoted him to be a field marshal on 18 February 1795, and made him commander-in-chief of the army on 3 April 1798. Amherst, the retiring commander-in-chief, had allowed countless abuses in the discipline and administration of the army. The duke by his rank was considered to belong to no party; he was in a position to put down much of the jobbery which had disgraced his predecessor's tenure of office, and determined to remove some of the abuses he had seen in Flanders. In 1799 he was appointed to command an army destined to invade Holland in conjunction with a Russian army corps. The vanguard of this army captured several Dutch ships in The Helder; but when the main force arrived under the duke on 13 September disaster followed. Generals Brune and Daendaels's army, though defeated three times, managed to keep the English and Russians penned on the narrow strip of land seized by Abercromby, and on 17 October the duke signed the convention of Alkmaer, by which the 'victors' could leave Holland on condition that eight thousand French prisoners of war were released. This failure confirmed the general opinion that the duke was unfit to command an army in the field.

Public attention now focused on the state of the army; money was not spared by parliament, and the duke devoted himself to the task of weeding out incapable officers, and encouraging the competent. However, on 18 March 1809 York was forced to retire from his post of commander-in-chief. He had become involved with the adventuress Mary Anne *Clarke, who made money out of her affair with the duke by promising promotion to officers, in return for payment. This matter was raised in the House of Commons by Colonel Wardle on 27 January 1809, and referred to a select committee, which proved that York had been careless in his dealings with Mrs Clarke, but he could not be convicted of receiving money himself, and he was acquitted of corruption. Sir David Dundas, who succeeded the duke as commander-in-chief, continued his policy, and the prince regent's reinstatement of his brother at the head of the army in May 1811 was generally approved. The duke had seen for himself how much the army suffered from poor, outdated organization and inefficient officers. He helped to introduce a system whereby more men were promoted on merit, rather than through purchase or nepotism. In order to improve the officers' training, he founded the Royal Military Academy, Woolwich, and a military school at High Wycombe which was the forerunner of Sandhurst. Among his innovations were improvements to the style and provision of the clothing of soldiers on active duty.

In 1818, on the death of Queen Charlotte, the duke was appointed official guardian of his mentally ill father, George III. The death of the king made York heir-presumptive to the throne. He looked forward to becoming king. 'By God! I'll have everything the same at mine!' he exclaimed in admiration at *George IV's coronation in 1821. The new king's affection for the duke made him an important person at court, but he took little interest in politics. He opposed Catholic emancipation, and on 25 April 1825, in the House of Lords, passionately affirmed his protestant convictions in a speech which was understood to reflect the king's views. In July 1826 he was attacked with dropsy, and died at the duke of Rutland's house, Arlington Street, London, on 5 January 1827. On 19 January he was buried in St George's Chapel, Windsor.

York's conduct as commander-in-chief had considerable influence on the history of the British army. He supported the commanders' efforts to revive military spirit with some success; he looked after the soldiers and their comforts, and sternly put down the influence of personal favouritism. Despite his involvement in the Mary Anne Clarke scandal, he did much to eradicate political jobbery in military appointments, and systematic corruption. The irony has been noted that, despite his contribution to the nation's defence and his improvements to the army, 'the Duke is now chiefly remembered in the public mind as a man who marched his army up and down a hill and ran it as a commercial proposition, with the aid of his mistress' (GEC, *Peerage*).

H. M. STEPHENS, rev. JOHN VAN DER KISTE

Sources R. Fulford, *Royal dukes: the father and uncles of Queen Victoria*, rev. edn (1973) · P. Fitzgerald, *Dukes and princesses of the family of George III*, 2 vols. (1882) · J. Van der Kiste, *George III's children* (1992) · A. H. Burne, *The noble duke of York* (1949) · *The Times* (6 Jan 1827) · GEC, *Peerage* · *The Times* (14 Aug 1820) · *The Times* (15 Aug 1820)
Archives Royal Arch.
Likenesses J. Zoffany, group portrait, 1770 (*George III and family*), Royal Collection · C. Lochée, Wedgwood medallion, 1787, Nottingham City Art Gallery and Museum · J. C. Lochée, marble bust, c.1787, Royal Collection · J. Reynolds, oils, c.1790, Royal Collection · R. Cosway, miniature, 1792, Royal Collection · mezzotint, 1794 (after unknown portrait), NPG · J. Nollekens, marble bust, 1813, Royal Collection · Canton, hand-coloured engraving, pubd 1815 (after his portrait), NPG · T. Lawrence, oils, exh. RA 1816, Royal Collection · G. Swendale, portrait, 1822 (after T. Lawrence), NPG · D. Wilkie, oils, 1822–3, NPG [*see illus.*] · J. C. Bromley, mezzotint, pubd 1828 (after R. Bowyer), NG Ire. · R. Westmacott, statue, 1834, The Mall, London · S. W. Reynolds, mezzotint, 1835 (after J. Reynolds), NPG · F. Chantrey, marble bust, 1837, Royal Collection · W. Beechey, oils, Waddesdon Manor, Buckinghamshire · T. Campbell, marble bust, Hopetown House, Lothian region · J. De Veaux, wax medallion, NPG · attrib. I. Francis, bust, Royal Collection · G. Hayter, group portrait, oils (*The trial of Queen Caroline*, 1820), NPG · J. Meyer, two miniatures, Royal Collection · I. Parkes, silver medal, National Museum of Ireland, Dublin · S. W. Reynolds and S. Cousins, mezzotint (after J. Jackson), BM, NPG · F. Vincent, mezzotint and stipple (after H. Brock), NPG · J. Zoffany, oils, Royal Collection · oils (after J. Jackson), NPG · portraits, NPG; repro. in R. Walker, *Regency portraits* (1985) · silhouette (with George IV), NPG · two sculptures, NPG

Frederick Lewis, prince of Wales (1707–1751), was born at the Leine Palace, Hanover, on 20/31 January 1707, the first child of George Augustus (Georg August), electoral prince of Hanover or Brunswick-Lüneburg, later *George II, king of Great Britain and Ireland (1683–1760), and *Caroline (1683–1737), daughter of Johann Friedrich, margrave of Brandenburg-Ansbach. He was baptized Friedrich Ludwig, after his godparents, his great-uncle King Friedrich I of Prussia and his grandfather Georg Ludwig, elector of Hanover, later *George I, king of Great Britain and Ireland. At his birth Frederick was fourth in line to the English throne, after his great-grandmother Sophia, dowager electoress of Hanover, his grandfather, and his father, according to the terms of the Act of Settlement of 1701 which limited the succession to her crown to Sophia and the protestant heirs of her body. The Act of Union between England and Scotland in that year extended the Hanoverian succession to the new throne of Great Britain.

The young prince in Hanover Frederick spent his early childhood as a focus of attention at the Hanoverian court.

Frederick Lewis, prince of Wales (1707–1751), by Philip Mercier, *c*.1735–6

His development was closely supervised by his grandfather, who in September 1713 appointed Johann Friedrich Grote, of a senior Hanoverian court family, as his governor and senior tutor, and a Latin scholar, Nikolaus Ernst von Neubour, as sub-tutor. This regime remained in place after 1714, when most of the royal family moved to their new home in Great Britain. Frederick was left behind in Hanover as a representative of the electoral family. The choice of a seven-year-old boy as George I's representative was not a difficult decision to take; George I wanted to emphasize that the direct line of the dynasty was not abandoning Hanover, and the option of leaving his son George Augustus there would have been unwise, destabilizing the dynasty in both Britain and Germany by apparently excluding the new prince of Wales from the political and social life of the London court, while allowing him opportunities for independent action on the continent that could have made a breach between father and son more perilous than disagreement on British soil. George I's youngest brother, *Ernest Augustus, also remained in Germany to ensure that the dynasty's interests were protected and that government was not entirely left to ministers.

Frederick acted as the ceremonial head of the Hanoverian court during the long absences of George I, where he received visiting diplomats and royal and aristocratic travellers. Care was taken that he learned English, under a French protestant tutor, Mr Hanet, and during his grandfather's reign he met several British ministers, including John, Baron Carteret, and Charles, Viscount Townshend, and some young noblemen who diverted to Hanover

while on the grand tour, such as John Hervey, later Lord Hervey.

Frederick was involved as far as possible in the process of making the Hanoverian royal family British, despite his residence in Hanover. In 1716 both he and his great-uncle Ernest Augustus, by this time reigning bishop of Osnabrück, were made knights of the Garter at a ceremony at the Leine Palace. In Britain Frederick was known in this period as the duke of Gloucester, even though he was never actually given this title either in a royal warrant or letters patent; however, this title identified him with a previous boy protestant heir, William, son of Queen Anne, who had died aged eleven in 1700, and so Frederick became the embodiment of a lost promise that could in his person be fulfilled. Ragnhild Hatton suggested that among the strongest support for the removal of Frederick to Britain was that which came from English clergy who hoped to be able to educate Frederick in the principles of the established church in Oxford or Cambridge. If this was a wish for a monarch brought up in the Church of England like Queen Anne, they were to be disappointed; George I may well have wished his grandson to avoid becoming embroiled in the intellectual disputes of the established church at an impressionable age. However, as he grew older he was kept informed of British affairs. In 1723 he was recorded as receiving a packet of reports of parliamentary proceedings, probably a regular occurrence, and in the same year he received models of British warships to study.

George I was an early advocate of inoculation for smallpox, a cause also supported by Frederick's mother, Caroline. Both had supported Charles Maitland's experiments with smallpox inoculation at Newgate prison in 1721, and in 1723 Maitland was commissioned (with a fee of £1000) to visit Hanover and inoculate Frederick. Maitland reported that although uncomfortable from the eruption, Frederick was still able to entertain his attendants 'with that pleasant facetious humour, which is easy and natural to him' (BL, Sloane MS 4076, fol. 98), and although he complained of soreness on his skin Maitland did not expect there to be any lasting scars.

Frederick was not forgotten in his grandfather's iconography, for his portrait was included in the painted hall at Greenwich Hospital by Sir James Thornhill, derived from sketches made on a visit by the painter to Hanover in 1719. Yet, as his parents became established as prince and princess of Wales without him, his German upbringing had no part to play in their emphatically British shadow monarchy. Family relationships were broken. Frederick occasionally corresponded with his eldest sister, *Anne, but they do not seem to have developed a close bond, and from 1721, when Caroline produced a healthy, British-born prince, *William Augustus, the prince and princess of Wales were able to show physical evidence on British soil of the permanence of the protestant succession. Frederick and William were made British peers at the same time in 1726, Frederick becoming duke of Edinburgh, and William duke of Cumberland, but the fact that Frederick was nineteen and William five at the time of their ennoblement could have already suggested how William's profile was being enhanced at Frederick's expense. George I is said to have arranged, informally, Frederick's first engagement, to his cousin Wilhelmine, daughter of his aunt Sophia Dorothea, who had married Friedrich Wilhelm I of Prussia, and according to Wilhelmine's memoirs the wedding was to take place in Hanover in summer 1727, but was cancelled following the death of George I at Osnabrück on 11/22 June 1727.

No moves were made to bring Frederick to London on the accession of George II; Frederick was able to lead the mourning at his grandfather's funeral, and act as the focus of Hanoverian celebrations for George II's coronation, without interference or guidance from Britain. At Westminster Abbey, Frederick was forgotten as his six-year-old brother William walked in state as the embodiment of the continuance of the protestant succession. The issue of Frederick's removal to London was left unresolved, perhaps because negotiations were continuing for the marriage of Frederick to his cousin Wilhelmine of Prussia, although without enthusiasm from either George II or Friedrich Wilhelm I, and George II and the British government were reluctant to give Frederick an establishment before the terms of his marriage were finalized.

Frederick's maturity led him to test his capacity for wielding authority in Germany; his position was enhanced by the death of Ernest Augustus in August 1728, which left him the only male representative of the dynasty on German soil. It was rumoured that he visited Berlin that summer in order to meet Wilhelmine and revive negotiations for their marriage. This story was untrue, but he did meddle in the relations between Hanover and Prussia by accelerating marriage negotiations between his cousins Princess Frederica of Prussia and Wilhelm Friedrich, margrave of Brandenburg-Ansbach, without involving George II. This insult to his parents may have been intended to emphasize that he was an independent actor and force a speedy resolution to the issue of his marriage, but instead it alienated the kings of Great Britain and Prussia from each other, removed any real prospect that he might marry Wilhelmine, terminated the alliance between Hanover and Prussia carefully maintained by George I, and allowed Prussia to secure the reversion of the Rhineland duchies of Berg and Jülich, enhancing Prussia's power in northern Germany at Hanover's expense. Following this disaster, George II decided that his son would be more dangerous in Hanover than in London. On 4 December 1728 Frederick was abruptly taken from a ball in Hanover by emissaries from his father and almost secretly conducted to Great Britain, to the bewilderment of most British diplomats.

Prince of Wales Following Frederick's arrival in London on 7 December 1728 os, he was created prince of Wales on 8 January 1729. Frederick was at first placed in the queen's apartments with his younger brothers and sisters; this was both a reprimand from George and Caroline, and a reminder that he was in tutelage as a British prince. None the less he was an adult male, in contrast to his favoured younger brother, and this had to be acknowledged: on 21 January 1729 Frederick took his seat in the Lords, and so demonstrated the dynasty's participation in British institutions. Frederick's early social calendar allowed him to affirm his espousal of the protestant cause that justified his family's place on the British throne. The audience Frederick gave to a Quaker delegation associated him with toleration, while his investiture as chancellor of the University of Dublin emphasized his and the dynasty's commitment to the established church.

Frederick's parents had reaped little political advantage from their period of estrangement from George I, and they had no intention of allowing their son to try to do better. Frederick was kept on a tight rein. His income was restricted to £2000 per month out of George II's receipts from the civil list, plus £9000 per annum from the revenues of the duchy of Cornwall. No application was made for a separate parliamentary grant as had been enjoyed by George II when prince of Wales. Frederick carried over £100,000 of debts from Hanover, which was not a recommendation to a frugal administration, nor to a British court that prided functionality before ostentation. His income was sufficient to provide for a household of his own, assembling a coalition of former employees of George I, young men that he had met in Hanover such as Henry Brydges, marquess of Carnarvon, and nominees of the government. Frederick's independence was real, but limited; his small court was established as a satellite of his parents' establishment and of the Walpole ministry. When George II left for his first visit as king and elector to Hanover in May 1729, Frederick was passed over as regent in favour of his mother, an action repeated on subsequent occasions, and interpreted as a snub. During the king's absence Frederick made several public appearances and visits to the nobility at their town and country houses, usually in the company of his mother and siblings so that he seemed to be largely under his mother's wing. He also began to advertise his cultural interests, organizing at least one theatrical performance at Richmond in 1729.

Frederick's financial situation may have tempted him, in summer 1730, to consider a marriage with a British heiress: many decades later, Horace Walpole reported that Sarah Churchill, duchess of Marlborough, had offered Frederick £100,000 if he would marry her granddaughter Lady Diana Spencer. Frederick wrote of his passion for a 'ldy Dye' (Suffolk RO, Ickworth papers 941/57/1, quoted in Vivian, chap. 13) about this time, but however 'unprecedentedly cordial' (F. Harris, 281) the relationship between the duchess of Marlborough and Frederick's parents, it was unlikely that they would have allowed the marriage of their eldest son to a commoner, or that Frederick would have closed off the opportunity, however remote it then seemed, for a more prestigious marriage with a European princess.

Frederick's closest friend in his early years in Britain was John, Lord Hervey, Queen Caroline's protégé and from 1730 vice-chamberlain to the royal household. Friends and courtiers, such as Hervey and John, Baron Ashburnham, his lord of the bedchamber, could advise him on artistic tastes as well as the political landscape.

Frederick's early efforts to demonstrate his independence from his parents took the form of house-building. The aforementioned visits of 1729 led to Frederick's making the acquaintance of patrons such as Richard Boyle, third earl of Burlington, and also William Kent, who became Frederick's architect. In 1730 Frederick leased a house and grounds at Kew from Lady Elizabeth St André, sister of William Capel, third earl of Essex, one of Frederick's early hosts in London and an enthusiast for the arts. Kent extensively remodelled the house, adding two new wings and drastically altering the remainder. The house, known as the White House, was adjacent to the Dutch House, retained for Frederick's sisters, and so maintained Frederick's close association with the rest of the royal family, while at the same time emphasizing his individual connoisseurship. The house included a chimneypiece by Michael Rysbrack and carvings by John Boson, who had worked for Burlington at Chiswick. Frederick also acquired 50 acres at Kew to use as a farm; he thus reinvented himself as a country gentleman in miniature within easy reach of London.

Frederick also began to build his art collection. With the house at Kew, Frederick took possession of the extensive collection of seventeenth-century portraits assembled by Lady Elizabeth's great-aunt Dorothy (née Bennet), Lady Capel of Tewkesbury (d. 1721), including many by Anthony Van Dyck. The acquisition may have sparked an interest in seventeenth-century painting, if it did not already exist, that led Frederick to acquire many paintings by Van Dyck, Rubens, and others, many of which had once belonged to Charles I but had been dispersed under the Commonwealth. Frederick's first principal painter was Philip Mercier, who held the post from 1729 to 1736. As well as painting two portraits of Frederick, and three versions of *The Music Party*, which depicted Frederick playing the cello in the company of his sisters Anne, *Amelia, and *Caroline [see under Amelia, Princess], he bought pictures and books for Frederick's collection, although Mercier's contribution to its final shape seems to have been minor. Frederick's patronage of Mercier, a follower of Watteau, has been used to show Frederick as an early British supporter of the rococo style, but Frederick bought very little rococo work, except the silverware of George Wickes, and his other portrait commissions were from painters who exhibited a variety of differing influences. A more dramatic display was the barge designed by Kent that Frederick first used on the Thames on 15 July 1732. 67 feet long, surmounted by marine carvings, and with its own 'state house' for a cabin, it was both aesthetically more pleasing and faster in the water than any of the king's barges. It continued to be used by the royal family into Queen Victoria's reign, and in the early twenty-first century was still enjoying a distinguished retirement at the National Maritime Museum, Greenwich. Construction was supervised by Charles Calvert, fifth Baron Baltimore, who had succeeded Ashburnham as Frederick's lord of the bedchamber in 1731. Baltimore also acted as a buyer for Frederick, travelling to Paris in 1735.

A mistress, music, and a garden Frederick made other conspicuous assertions of majesty-in-waiting in 1732. One was the birth of his first child, Cornwall Fitz-Frederick, on 5 June 1732. The boy's mother was Anne *Vane (d. 1736), one of Queen Caroline's maids of honour, daughter of Gilbert Vane, second Baron Barnard, and Mary, née Randyll. Lord Hervey and William Stanhope, first Baron Harrington, disputed the parentage, but Frederick was sufficiently certain of his fatherhood to set Anne Vane up in a series of impressive town houses and appoint Fitz-Frederick warden of the stannaries and master of Dartmoor Forest. Frederick's relationship with Vane marked the end of his friendship with Hervey. Hervey had once expressed the hope that their friendship could rival the passion Hervey enjoyed with Stephen Fox, and he regarded Frederick's liaison with Vane as a betrayal. Frederick also took George Dodington as his political adviser about this time, further aggravating the eclipsed Hervey. Dodington, like Hervey, held office from the crown (as a lord of the Treasury), but he was not as closely identified with the court as was Hervey. The last fruit of the friendship between Frederick and Hervey was a play, *The Modish Couple*, which opened at Drury Lane, London, on 10 January 1732. It was credited to Charles Bodens, an army officer, but was probably written by Hervey and Frederick. Frederick appeared on the third performance, the author's benefit, but the play was unpopular and on the fourth night was booed from the stage.

Frederick's other blow to assert his independence in 1732 was his sponsorship of the Opera of the Nobility, established as a rival to the Haymarket season presided over by Handel. This was a natural development of Frederick's interest in theatre and music. Hervey presented it as a deliberate attempt to polarize society between supporters of the court, who continued to attend Handel's operas, and supporters of Frederick attending the Opera of the Nobility, but the case was not clear-cut, and in the first and last of the four seasons between 1733 and 1737 in which Handel and the new opera company presented rival productions, each company received Frederick's £250 bounty. It may have sometimes suited Frederick to identify himself wholly with the younger generation of aristocrats who supported the new opera, but he could not afford to offend Britain's greatest composer or his clientele for very long.

Frederick's political education had been furthered by Dodington, who knew the levers of patronage from the vantage point of a borough patron as well as that of a courtier. Frederick's new town residence, Carlton House, acquired from Burlington in March 1733, was adjacent to Dodington's home in Pall Mall, and the two properties were joined by a connecting passage, which critics said was used for Frederick to visit prostitutes procured by Dodington. In contrast to the rebuilding of the White House at Kew, Frederick seems to have sanctioned little rebuilding beyond the remodelling of some interiors (including a library) and the building of a new façade. The house's purchase cost £6000, a sum that Frederick borrowed from his treasurer, John Hedges, and was paid off with £1000 from Frederick's own resources and a further £5000 loan from Dodington.

Carlton House's importance for Frederick lay in its potential for display. Its location at St James's was an attraction, as it could be presented as part of a complex of royal residences, both an extension of and in opposition to St James's Palace. It came with a large garden alongside St James's Park, which was extensively replanned by Kent. The garden at Carlton House may have been the first formal garden in Britain to eschew a geometric plan: Sir Thomas Robinson, a near neighbour, wrote that 'it has the appearance of beautiful nature, and without being told, one would imagine art had no part in the finishing' (Coombs, 154); Kent was applying similar ideas to the grounds of Stowe, the Buckinghamshire seat of Richard Temple, Viscount Cobham, at the same time. Kent added a garden building, the octagon, in which paintings from Frederick's collection were displayed. Peter Scheemakers and Michael Rysbrack were among the sculptors who were commissioned to provide garden ornaments, Rysbrack contributing the two busts of Alfred the Great and Edward, the Black Prince, that were installed at the entrance to the octagon in 1736. During his lifetime Frederick planted over 15,200 trees in the garden, and despite its 9 acres, the garden at Carlton House has been claimed as the ancestor of the garden squares that were to grow up in London.

Frederick's plans for his residences and the expansion of his collection of art and books placed a great strain on his resources. His allowance from the civil list still languished at £24,000 a year, and his father's failure to find him a wife helped push him further towards outright opposition. The excise crisis of 1733 tempted him to come out in open opposition to the Walpole administration, but he was persuaded not to by Dodington, and in the following year he did not use his patronage of borough seats to shape an opposition party in the Commons. By this time he had new political advisers: his new equerry George Lyttelton, the first of Frederick's advisers to be younger than the prince, and (at Lyttelton's suggestion) Philip Dormer Stanhope, fourth earl of Chesterfield. Despite the opposition of both to the Excise Bill, they wished Frederick to bide his time. Frederick had also been courted by other opposition groups. It was believed by John Perceval, first earl of Egmont, that the tory leader Henry St John, Viscount Bolingbroke, had advised his followers to try to build a coalition around Frederick. For the moment Frederick remained connected to the court; his presidency of St George's Hospital, adopted in 1734, can be viewed in these terms as much as expressing Frederick's interest in voluntary institutions, as the hospital's founders included court physicians, and the wards were named after members of the administration.

Marriage Frederick regarded the wedding of his sister Anne to William, prince of Orange, in 1734 as an insult; the message conveyed by the union was that Anne, not Frederick, was to be first relied upon to secure the protestant succession. Following his sister's marriage Frederick formally requested that his parents redress the snub by finding him a bride. While he waited, his resentment at his parents' treatment of him was expressed in a satire, the *Histoire du Prince Titi*, published in 1736; it was probably at least co-written by Frederick, and depicts its prince as a hero of the people who replaces his narrow-minded father on the throne after the king tries to exclude him from the succession—reflecting the lingering wish of George and Caroline that their eldest son should never be king of Great Britain. Eventually, in 1735, on George II's next visit to Hanover, the king selected Princess *Augusta of Saxe-Gotha (1719–1772) as the prospective princess of Wales. This news provided Frederick with a reason finally to repudiate Anne Vane, whom he had neglected following the birth of their short-lived daughter Amelia in 1733, and who (apparently without Frederick's knowledge) had renewed her old affair with Hervey. Both Fitz-Frederick and Vane were dead by the end of March 1736, providing Frederick with, if not a clean slate, then at least no unwanted family responsibilities to disturb his marital plans. Frederick had also by this time acquired a new female companion whom his enemies described as his mistress; if so, Frederick was more discreet about the sexual nature of their relationship. Lady Jane Hamilton (d. 1753) was the youngest daughter of James Hamilton, sixth earl of Abercorn, and his wife, Elizabeth Reading, and was the third wife of Lord Archibald Hamilton, younger brother of George Hamilton, first earl of Orkney, hence her usual style of Lady Archibald Hamilton. (Orkney, a friend of George I, had been visited by Frederick at Cliveden in 1729.) They were frequently seen in each other's company and she perhaps also fulfilled the role of slightly older mentor figure previously enjoyed by Hervey and Dodington.

Augusta landed at Greenwich on 25 April 1736; Frederick sailed down the Thames in his barge to meet her at the Queen's House before dining with her in public. Frederick's journey down the Thames with Augusta to the Tower of London was calculated to arouse attention, although his plan for Augusta to travel to St James's in a carriage with a guard of honour was vetoed by George II. The wedding, on 27 April 1736 at the Chapel Royal, St James's Palace, was a public-relations triumph for Frederick, despite the ceremonial being less grand than that enjoyed by his sister. Handel provided a new anthem, 'Sing unto God', for the wedding service, and also celebrated the marriage with the opera *Atalanta*. The couple appeared devoted to one another, and Augusta declared her wish to follow Frederick's wishes in everything; she even persuaded George II to sanction the appointment of Lady Archibald Hamilton as her mistress of the robes and keeper of her privy purse. The king also raised Frederick's allowance to £50,000.

Opposition to Walpole Among the speeches in the Commons congratulating Frederick on his marriage were two from George Lyttelton and William Pitt, arguing that the wedding had been forced on George II and Walpole by popular demand. The speeches implicitly flattered Frederick by depicting him as a people's hero, and represented part of a bid by the group of 'Cobham's cubs'—the young opposition whigs sponsored by Frederick's fellow gardening enthusiast Viscount Cobham—to make Frederick their ally and an important weapon in their battle against Walpole. Frederick's favour was also sought by older whigs. When in February 1737 Frederick went to the Commons in a bid to force his father to increase his allowance, William Pulteney, not Lyttelton or Pitt, proposed the motion demanding that £100,000 be settled on the prince.

Frederick may have felt that as the threat of outright opposition had brought him his marriage, more systematic acts of defiance would win a more comfortable financial settlement. This was the assumption of the king and the ministry. In anticipation of the opposition motion, Walpole persuaded George II to settle £50,000 on the prince as an independent allowance, as well as giving Augusta a separate jointure, also of £50,000, bringing their joint income to the level enjoyed by George II and Caroline when prince and princess of Wales. Frederick's response was to declare that 'the Affair was now out of his Hands, and therefore he could give no Answer to it' (GM, 7.483), thereby placing his faith in the efforts of the opposition and not the Walpole ministry's proposals. The motion was defeated; some of Frederick's erstwhile allies, such as Dodington and his followers, voted with the government rather than be identified with a strategy that cut into the royal prerogative.

Frederick's next act forced a decisive breach with his parents' court and the ministry. On the evening of 31 July 1737, while the royal family was residing at Hampton Court, Augusta went into labour. Despite the protestations of his staff, including Lady Archibald Hamilton, Frederick insisted on leaving immediately for St James's, where there were few servants and no bed prepared; Augusta gave birth to a daughter there before midnight. The episode was greeted with incredulity by the court, but Frederick insisted in his letter to Queen Caroline on 1 August that he had always intended that Augusta should lie in at St James's, and had already told the queen and his sisters so. The birth of an heir in London meant that Frederick could more easily act as the focus of metropolitan celebrations of the birth, and distance George and Caroline from the securing of the protestant succession in a further generation. George II maintained a show of decorum until after the baptism of Frederick's daughter, also Augusta [see below], on 29 August, after which the king and queen refused to see Frederick. On 10 September Frederick was ordered to leave St James's Palace with his family as soon as it was safe for his wife to travel; the guard was withdrawn from Frederick's residences; furthermore, anyone who held office from the king was barred from entering Frederick's presence. Frederick left St James's on 12 September to the acclaim of the crowd, whom he hailed with the words 'God bless the King and God bless the poor' (Hervey, 3.822). He could now plausibly present himself as a people's prince, on whom the king had turned his back. The death in November of Caroline, who the court had once hoped would act as an intermediary between king and prince, did nothing to help

matters, Caroline confirming her hatred of her son on her deathbed.

The separation of the households lost Frederick those officers who preferred the security of government employment, and confirmed his alignment with the opponents of Walpole. He met Pulteney, Carteret, and Sir William Wyndham at Kew in October, formally appointed Lyttelton as his secretary that month, and in February 1738 made William Pitt a groom of the bedchamber. Pitt's brother Thomas Pitt became assay master of the stannaries in March 1738 and Frederick's election manager, with the intention of returning opposition candidates in the boroughs where Frederick, through the duchy of Cornwall, was the dominant property owner. Bolingbroke returned to Britain from France in July 1738 in the hope that Frederick would take a more outspoken role. This was unlikely, however, given that Frederick still needed to be able to rebuild his relationship with George II should he cease to be a proscribed person. Furthermore, opposition rhetoric militated against Frederick becoming a party man. Bolingbroke's *The Idea of a Patriot King* circulated in manuscript about this time, and for the more idealistic of Frederick's political allies the document expressed their hope that Frederick would become a virtuous king who would restore the mixed constitution, corrupted by Walpole's domination of the monarch and the executive's control of the legislature. This message appealed to disenchanted whigs and proscribed tories alike; Frederick commissioned a miniature of Charles I in 1738, and was happier than either his father or grandfather to be seen as the heir of the Stuarts. Behind the rhetoric, the opposition leaders manoeuvred to gain ascendancy over Frederick while waiting for the moral revolution.

Without his apartments in St James's, and with a growing family, Frederick needed a town residence that was larger than Carlton House, and late in 1737 acquired the lease of Norfolk House, the town residence of the duke and duchess of Norfolk in St James's Square. Frederick extensively refurbished the house, consuming more of his slender resources. It was at Norfolk House that Frederick's second child and eldest son, the future *George III, was born on 24 May 1738. Frederick also needed a country house that was larger than the White House at Kew. In 1738 he began to make quarterly payments for Cliveden, which he rented from Anne O'Brien, *née* Hamilton, *suo jure* countess of Orkney, daughter of the earl, who had died in 1737, and her husband, William O'Brien, fourth earl of Inchiquin. Unlike Norfolk House, Cliveden did not undergo any major alterations. In 1739 he additionally bought Park Place, near Henley-on-Thames, Oxfordshire, from Lord Archibald Hamilton, which became a base for hunting.

Excluded from court, Frederick found that much more of his time was his own. A visit to Bath in October and November 1738 helped him to show that he and his wife were determined to be part of the modern, fashionable world, and provided a spectacle in which Frederick, at the centre of fireworks and illuminations, could profess his loyalty to the king and to the patriot whig causes of English trade and English liberty. In November he prohibited his courtiers from wearing fabrics that were not made in England. He had assumed patronage of racing at Epsom, where he kept stables, and in 1739 took the lease on a house there, called Durdens, from one of his gentlemen of the bedchamber, Francis, seventh Baron North. As well as racing, Frederick was an enthusiastic huntsman (he commissioned several paintings of hunting scenes from John Wootton) and also captained cricket sides for Surrey and London.

In January 1739 Frederick voted in the House of Lords for the first time, against the convention of Pardo with Spain, which failed to meet the demands of one of his constituencies, the City of London merchants; Pitt had led the attack in the Commons. When war with Spain broke out in October, Frederick appeared in the City to toast the crowd. The parliamentary diarist William Hay thought that Frederick entirely turned himself over to the tories, led by Wyndham, during 1739, but Frederick's court remained broadly composed. He visited Lord Cobham at Stowe in July 1739, where he was welcomed into the heart of patriot whig imagery, Stowe landscape gardens. His major contribution to patriot propaganda was his commissioning of *Alfred*, a masque written by James Thomson and David Mallet, with music by Thomas Arne, staged at Cliveden on 1 August 1740. The event projected Frederick as the successor to Alfred the Great, depicted as 'piously English' and advised by 'an ancient hermit living in a cave by the Athelney marshes' (Gerrard, 135). The masque was performed by the Covent Garden company in the small amphitheatre in Cliveden's gardens, and included 'Rule, Britannia!', which remains Frederick's most obvious contribution to Britain's self-image.

Reconciliation with George II The general election of 1741 provided Frederick with a substantial parliamentary party of about twenty-five. Frederick's members helped bring Walpole's majority down to twenty-six, and assisted in forcing Walpole from office early in 1742. His conduct once Walpole fell revealed his lack of political surefootedness. After allowing his allies in January 1742 to negotiate with Walpole, in February he supported demands that tory leaders should be included in the new ministry, and opposed Pulteney for making easy terms with the court. Pulteney then met Frederick and emerged as his new advocate, negotiating an agreement with George II that gave Frederick £100,000 per annum as an independent allowance; George II agreed to it reluctantly and after much wavering the sum passed the Commons in May 1742 only with the stipulation that it should be paid last from the exchequer.

During the Wilmington administration Frederick seems to have tried to keep as many friends as possible from his former opposition colleagues while remaining faithful to his reconciliation with his father; although many of his allies were happy to be found offices in the government at Frederick's request, others, particularly Pitt and Lyttelton, disagreed with both the men and the measures of the new ministry. Ayscough wrote in August 1742 that 'The Prince has neither Power, Influence, or Credit—His interfering for any one is the sure way of ruining their Interest—Undone with his own Party—neglected by the Court' (R. Harris, 393). Frederick admired both Pitt and Lyttelton and tried to keep them loyal to him. He affected neutrality on the issue of British subsidies to Hanoverian troops which the Cobhamites opposed throughout the early 1740s; Frederick, however, maintained ties to Hanoverian courtiers and was defensive of the interests of the electorate.

The reconciliation with George II had even less success on a personal level than it had on a political one. Without the diplomacy and interest of Caroline to break the boulders in a rocky relationship, Frederick was an even more semi-detached member of the court than he had been before 1737. Frederick had been a focus of the movement that had forced Britain to go to war, but was marginalized once the War of the Austrian Succession began. He was refused permission to take up arms and add practical experience to the military theory he had learned in Hanover, and instead had to see his brother Cumberland be compared by versifiers in the press to the Black Prince and Henry V, antecedents who Frederick had once thought would be his exclusively. The most Frederick could do was commission paintings of battles from the War of the Spanish Succession from John Wootton for Leicester House. During the Jacobite rising of 1745–6, Frederick was reduced to staging a mock siege of Carlisle Castle as part of a dessert, ridiculing the military campaign that was bringing his brother a heroic reputation in London. Furthermore, Frederick's political alliances had continued to disintegrate. Lyttelton joined the ministry in December 1744 as part of the reconstruction that excluded Carteret; as Frederick admired Carteret as a war minister, Lyttelton was dismissed as Frederick's secretary. Pitt joined a ministry dominated by Henry Pelham and other old enemies of Frederick in February 1746, and also lost his place in the prince's household. Another long-term adviser, the prince's mistress Lady Archibald Hamilton, had resigned her place with the princess the previous summer.

Frederick seems to have had no further mistress and instead remained faithful to his wife. Despite his political marginalization, Frederick's and Augusta's large family ensured their significance in dynastic terms. Their first two children were followed by *Edward Augustus (1739–1767); Elizabeth Caroline (1740–1759); *William Henry (1743–1805); *Henry Frederick (1745–1790); Louisa Anne (1749–1768); and Frederick William (1750–1765). In 1743 Frederick acquired the lease on Leicester House, his parents' home when prince and princess of Wales, which provided better accommodation for his growing family than Norfolk House. A painting commissioned from Barthélémy du Pan in 1746 showed the children playing in the garden at Carlton House, incorporating the children into Frederick's iconography. Frederick maintained his reputation for philanthropy by accepting the presidency of Bath General Hospital in 1746.

Frederick had hoped that he would be able to support the ministry 'as a Son, and not as a Courtier' (R. Harris,

394); this translated into respect from his father coupled with a decisive voice in parliament and the ministry. Frederick never received the first and he lacked the ability to establish the second. The election of 1747, called early in apprehension of Frederick's disenchantment with the ministry, was calculated to raise a Pelham-dominated Commons; anticipation of the election's intended result confirmed Frederick's return to opposition.

Leader of the opposition Frederick again worked on coalition-building, issuing the 'Carlton House declaration' on 4 June 1747. This offered the tories an end to 'Distinctions of Party' as well as place and militia bills, a civil list fixed at £800,000 a year rather than one that fluctuated with the hereditary revenues of the crown, and a £300 p.a. qualification for JPs. This document was not accepted by the tory leaders until the following February, and then with suspicion, but it became the basis for a developing commitment to co-operation between Frederick and the tories. Frederick had maintained his core following in the Commons at the general election of 1747, again managed for him by Thomas Pitt and Francis Ayscough, although he had not advanced, as former allies, such as Hugh Boscawen, Viscount Falmouth, in Cornwall, supported the Pelham ministry. The prospect of Frederick's imminent accession, as George II entered his late sixties, probably encouraged government supporters to defect. The most prominent of these was John Perceval, second earl of Egmont, who had been returned as a ministerialist at the election but soon afterwards joined Frederick, becoming his principal political adviser. George Dodington also rejoined Frederick's household, taking up a specially invented post as Frederick's treasurer of the chamber. The dominance of the reversionary interest also helped suppress the differences in political outlook between the different factions among Frederick's supporters. Frederick's own views often diverged from those held by the majority of his followers: he opposed the treaty of Aix-la-Chapelle in 1749, for example, arguing that Britain would have gained more by pursuing the war with France, a war the City had tired of. Meanwhile he irritated the ministry by unsuccessfully competing with the duke of Newcastle for the position of chancellor of Cambridge University, a contest which dragged on throughout 1748.

Much of the effort of Frederick's advisers was concentrated on the succession. Egmont prepared a detailed plan for the first few weeks of Frederick's reign which would have enabled bills for the civil list and settlements on the putative Queen Augusta and Prince George to be quickly piloted through parliament by Frederick's ministers while the Pelhams and their friends were just as rapidly to be expelled from office. Another document, prepared by Egmont in 1749 and regularly updated by him and Frederick, charted the intended composition of the House of Commons. With it was a list of politicians that Frederick and Egmont intended should be kept from the house, including major talents such as Henry Fox, William Pitt,

and George Grenville, all of whom had alienated Frederick in one way or another, or were reckoned too formidable opponents by Frederick and his supporters. Among the prince's party, Egmont admitted he knew 'not one man qualified to take that great and supreme part upon him which it is absolutely necessary some man should do' (Newman, 'Leicester House politics', *Camden Miscellany*, 185).

Frederick's plans also included a strong dynastic element. He knew of the intention of George I that Britain and Hanover should be divided, but had been unwilling to assent to George II's variant of this plan, that Frederick should succeed to Hanover while the duke of Cumberland should become king of Great Britain. He proposed that his eldest son, George, should surrender Hanover to his second son, Edward. His third son, William, was to marry Frederick's niece Carolina of Orange, then the heir to the hereditary stadholderate of the United Provinces, and live at The Hague. His eldest daughter, Augusta, was also intended to make a dynastic marriage, to the heir to the duchy of Brunswick-Wolfenbüttel. The most imaginative fate was reserved for his fourth son, Henry, who was to live in the West Indies as head of a new colony, 'be entirely dedicated to the sea' (Newman, 'Leicester House politics', *Camden Miscellany*, 193), and be duke of Virginia, living on £20,000 raised from the North American colonies. Prince George was to be appointed lord high admiral on Frederick's accession, which Frederick considered safer than his eldest son being 'bred among Troops' (ibid., 175), and thereby disposed to support the standing army Frederick was pledged to disband. Frederick left a message for his eldest son urging Prince George to adopt his proposals should Frederick not survive George II. Something of this plan was rehearsed in the prologues and epilogues spoken by Frederick's older children in their performance of Joseph Addison's *Cato* at Leicester House in January 1749, where Prince George declared his love for liberty and England, Lady Augusta accepted that she:

> must wed a foreigner,
> And cross the sea—the lord knows where
> (*GM*, 19.37)

and Edward looked forward to military command. Frederick had a paternal as well as a dynastic concern for his children; his surviving correspondence with them shows he emphasized reading—''tis only by that one forms ones self' (Royal Archives, Windsor Castle, RA GEO 54133–54134)—the study of history, and proficiency in French and German, but also displays his great affection for them, including his supposedly neglected eldest son.

Frederick worked hard to secure his party through personal contact. In late summer 1750, while George II was absent in Hanover, he made two journeys around the south and west of England, partly to meet supporters such as Lord Bathurst, but also to show himself to the people as a conscientious king; events were selectively reported in the newspaper Frederick sponsored, *The Remembrancer*. His younger sons joined him for part of the trip, and were taken sea-bathing near Southampton. In Gloucestershire he was publicly entertained on the Severn by Richard

Cambridge and gave money to an innkeeper whose premises had been destroyed by lightning. Despite Frederick's attempts to make himself personally known to his supporters, there remained suspicion between the tories and the opposition whigs in the alliance. There was also rivalry between leaders; the theorist Egmont and the realist Dodington were at loggerheads. Furthermore, there were no great issues of the day on which to unite and expand the opposition. The Pelham ministry actually increased its average majority between 1748 and 1750. By early 1751 Frederick was renewing his connections with William Pitt and the duke of Newcastle, of whose foreign policy, based on subsidies to continental powers and the encirclement of France, he approved.

A king in waiting Frederick furthered a number of extra-parliamentary projects during his second period in opposition. Perhaps the most enduring resulted from the return of his attention to Kew, where between 1749 and 1751 he acquired over 70 more acres, and where he began an extensive scheme to introduce exotic plants, to be accompanied by ornamental buildings, many of which were to be Chinese in design. Frederick corralled his household into participating in the physical labour at Kew. He also extended his protection of British trade. In November 1748 he reissued his prohibition of foreign fashions—explicitly French ones—from his court. In 1750 he took the lead in establishing the British Herring Fishery Company, dedicated to the better exploitation of British fishing reserves against Dutch imports, and in October was installed as its governor. Frederick also combined his philanthropic and musical interests by attending the Handel concert at the Foundling Hospital in May 1749; 'the custom of standing up for the "Hallelujah" chorus may have originated with the Prince of Wales on this occasion' (Burrows, 300) as there is no evidence that George II ever attended a performance.

Frederick made or planned major initiatives in the arts. From 1749 he employed George Vertue as his art adviser, and commissioned him to make lists of the royal art collections at the prince's residences and at the king's, as well as making copies of the inventories of the collections of Charles I and their sale by the Commonwealth. Vertue's notes reveal that Frederick had already succeeded in building a collection of sixteenth- and seventeenth-century paintings, including French, Italian, and Dutch work, that included some works owned by Charles, but suggest what a royal collection might have looked like had the English monarchy not been overthrown in 1649. Frederick was also intending to support an academy for British painters, but his death prevented the scheme reaching fruition.

Frederick did not have presentiments of death. Apart from his political and gardening plans he had been discussing commissioning a sculpture of himself from William Hoare of Bath. However, in March 1751 he was taken ill after superintending his workmen at Kew, 'complaining of a violent pain in his side' (Newman, 'Leicester House politics', *Camden Miscellany*, 195); he suffered this,

with feverishness and fainting, for two weeks. On Wednesday 20 March 1751 he was pronounced 'quite safe' (ibid., 198) by his physicians, but about 9.30 p.m., at Leicester House, he felt ill again and soon afterwards 'laid his head upon his pillow and without a convulsion sigh or groan or the least movement—rattled in his throat and was dead in three minutes' (ibid.). His death was subsequently blamed on a burst abscess in one lung, perhaps the result of an old sporting injury, from which has arisen the legend that Frederick died soon after being hit by a cricket or tennis ball. He was buried in Henry VII's chapel, Westminster Abbey, on 13 April 1751. At the time of his death, Augusta was pregnant with *Caroline Matilda (1751–1775), afterwards queen of Denmark.

Legacy and assessment Frederick's political party died with him. Augusta and Egmont supervised the destruction of all Frederick's political papers and made their peace with the court; Egmont's copies survived. Very little of Frederick's dynastic policy was carried out, and Frederick's eldest daughter, **Augusta**, duchess of Brunswick-Wolfenbüttel (1737–1813), consort of Charles II, suffered accordingly. As Frederick had intended, Augusta married Charles, hereditary prince of Brunswick-Wolfenbüttel (1735–1806). The ceremony took place at the Chapel Royal, St James's Palace, on 16 January 1764. George III, obsessed with economy, had no wish for his sister and her husband to be a drain on national finances by remaining in London as his father had wished, and they left for Germany soon after the wedding; the public adulation that the couple received on their appearances at the theatre, in contrast to the mob's dislike of George III, probably confirmed the king in his intentions. Augusta and her husband had seven children: Augustina (1764–1788); Charles (1766–1806); *Caroline (1768–1821), later the wife of George IV; George (1769–1811); Augustus (1770–1820); Frederick William, duke of Brunswick-Wolfenbüttel (1771–1815); and Amelia (1772–1773). The marriage, however, was unhappy, as Charles was insensitive and unfaithful. Augusta was visited by her mother in 1768, but was only allowed to return to Britain in 1772 when her mother was dying. Her husband became duke of Brunswick-Wolfenbüttel in 1780. The crisis of the revolutionary wars with France, and her daughter's marriage to George, prince of Wales, in 1795, gave Augusta the opportunity to spend more time in Britain, and she eventually took a house in Hanover Square, London, where she died on 23 March 1813. She was buried in St George's Chapel, Windsor.

Despite his aversion to his father's plans for his family, many of George III's activities as king owed something to Frederick's intentions. George was advised by his father's fellow enthusiast for botany, John Stuart, third earl of Bute: the tories were readmitted to court, the civil list was fixed at £800,000, and the whig oligarchy that Frederick had distrusted was broken. In establishing the Royal Academy, George III was also putting one of his father's schemes into effect; and although he lacked his father's devotion to art, George III continued to buy paintings of the kind his father had favoured. The visits that George III began to make in the middle of his reign, to Portsmouth, the west country, and the south coast, owed more to Frederick's tours than to the occasional appearance at a military parade made by George II; Frederick's belief that the monarch, or the monarch in waiting, should show himself regularly to his subjects eventually became an accepted feature of the practice of monarchy in Britain.

> Here lies Fred,
> Who was alive and is dead:
> Had it been his father,
> I had much rather;
> Had it been his brother,
> Still better than another;
> Had it been his sister,
> No one would have missed her;
> Had it been the whole generation,
> Still better for the nation:
> But since 'tis only Fred,
> Who was alive and is dead,—
> There's no more to be said.

The rhyme, quoted by Horace Walpole, was a commonly used scurrilous epitaph that had been used for others besides 'Fred'. None the less, it came to encapsulate Frederick's status as a forgotten and misunderstood figure. Partly this was because his legacy to George III was not wholly beneficial; George III was still paying off Frederick's debts well into his reign. He was also an example of filial disloyalty, a stance that his grandson George IV took to extremes. The nineteenth century, influenced by Hervey and Horace Walpole, found little good to say of him. John Doran assessed him as 'a child in character, pretty as a child, and even as self-willed as pretty children generally' (Doran, 482), and Thomas Finlayson Henderson, writing for the *Dictionary of National Biography* in 1889, thought him a representative of the vices of the age, financially and sexually debauched, and wrote: 'Though he affected to patronise the arts and literature, his tastes were not otherwise refined, and in their pursuit he was not too regardful of his dignity.' Frederick's reputation improved in the twentieth century; Sir George Young, in his biography *Poor Fred: the People's Prince* (1937), saw Frederick's political career as an attempt to revitalize the political class against a corrupt and inefficient leadership, and hoped to draw lessons from Frederick's activities for the benefit of Edward VIII. In the second half of the century scholarly work on the royal collection by Sir Oliver Millar and others drew attention to Frederick's contribution towards royal patronage of the arts and the image of the monarchy in general, a contribution brought to the attention of a wider audience by the inclusion of Frederick in a BBC television series about royal patrons of the arts, *Royal Heritage* (1977). Analysis of parliamentary politics also helped to build a greater appreciation of Frederick's position as a prince attempting to hold his position in a factional political system. By the close of the century scholarship was starting to bring together the characters of Frederick the patron of the arts, Frederick the politician, and Frederick the focus of literary productions from patriot

writers; the traditional view that Frederick was, politically, an 'empty space' (Colley, 242) was balanced by awareness that he carefully manipulated his image and was a discriminating and intelligent connoisseur.

In 1738 Frederick was dedicatee of a new edition of Sir Charles Cornwallis's life of Henry Frederick, prince of Wales. Henry Frederick had asserted his prerogatives as an independent figure in the state, enjoying a special relationship with the king and with parliament. This might suggest the sort of figure Frederick had hoped to be, but even if he had enjoyed the charisma, the insight, or the determination to make more of a political impact, it is unlikely that he would have succeeded; the mixed court and parliamentary politics of mid-eighteenth century Britain did not allow for a junior king, only for an heir apparent who was expected not to make too much trouble for his father and the administration. Perhaps Frederick's problem was that he expected too much; but while attempting to gain the near impossible goal he thought he deserved, he was able to provide a focus for the evolving concept of opposition and also strengthen the foundations of the Hanoverian dynasty in Britain.

MATTHEW KILBURN

Sources F. Vivian, unpublished MS biography of Frederick Lewis, prince of Wales, priv. coll. • C. Gerrard, *The patriot opposition to Walpole: politics, poetry, and national myth, 1725–1742* (1994) • A. Newman, ed., 'Leicester House politics, 1750–60, from the papers of John, second earl of Egmont', *Camden miscellany, XXIII*, CS, 4th ser., 7 (1969), 85–228 • A. N. Newman, 'Leicester House politics, 1748–1751', *EngHR*, 76 (1961), 577–89 • A. N. Newman, 'The political patronage of Frederick Lewis, prince of Wales', *HJ*, 1 (1958), 68–75 • L. Colley, *In defiance of oligarchy: the tory party, 1714–60* (1982) • R. Harris, ed., 'A Leicester House political diary, 1742–3', *Camden miscellany, XXXI*, CS, 4th ser., 44 (1992), 375–411 • *GM*, 1st ser., 6 (1736), 230 • *GM*, 1st ser., 7 (1737), 483 • *GM*, 1st ser., 19 (1749), 37 • *GM*, 1st ser., 21 (1751), 99–101, 184 • Frederick Lewis, correspondence, Royal Arch., RA GEO 52809–52823, 54034–54070, 54127–54236, 52808, 54024–54126, 73956–73995 • John, Lord Hervey, *Some materials towards memoirs of the reign of King George II*, ed. R. Sedgwick, 3 vols. (1931) • R. Halsband, *Lord Hervey: eighteenth-century courtier* (1973) • K. Rorschach, 'Frederick, prince of Wales (1707–51) as collector and patron', *Walpole Society*, 55 (1993), 1–76 • [S. Jones], *Frederick, prince of Wales and his circle* (1981) [exhibition catalogue, Gainsborough's House, Sudbury, Suffolk, 6 June – 26 July 1981] • R. Hatton, *George I, elector and king* (1978) • J. B. Owen, *The rise of the Pelhams* (1957) • S. Taylor and C. Jones, eds., *Tory and whig: the parliamentary papers of Edward Harley, third earl of Oxford, and William Hay, MP for Seaford, 1716–1753*, Parliamentary History Record Series, 1 (1998) • D. Coombs, 'The garden at Carlton House of Frederick prince of Wales and Augusta princess dowager of Wales', *Garden History*, 25/2 (1997), 153–77 • I. Kramnick, *Bolingbroke and his circle* (1968) • F. Harris, *A passion for government: the life of Sarah, duchess of Marlborough* (1991) • Philip, earl of Hardwicke, account of the quarrel between the prince of Wales and George II, BL, Add. MS 35870, fols. 18–36 • 'Declaration to the opposition', 1747, BL, Add. MS 28094, fols. 195–6 • C. Maitland, account of Frederick's inoculation for smallpox, 1723, BL, Sloane MS 4076, fol. 96 • R. Desmond, *Kew: the history of the Royal Botanic Gardens* (1995) • R. Browning, *The duke of Newcastle* (1975) • *The political journal of George Bubb Dodington*, ed. J. Carswell and L. A. Dralle (1965) • C. Taylor, 'Handel and Frederick, prince of Wales', *MT*, 125 (1984), 89–92 • D. Burrows, *Handel* (1994) • *The Remembrancer* (7 July–18 Nov 1750) • J. Robinson, account of Frederick's establishment, 1780, BL, Add. MS 37836, fol. 97 • C. Delafaye, diplomatic correspondence, 1728, PRO, SP 78/188; SP 78/196 • D. Underdown, *Start of play: cricket and culture in eighteenth-century*

England (2000) · G. Young, *Poor Fred: the people's prince* (1937) · J. Doran, *The book of the princes of Wales, heirs to the crown of England* (1860), 476–95 · *GM*, 1st ser., 18/1 (1813), 294

Archives BL, account book · Duchy of Cornwall RO, London, household account books · Royal Arch., corresp. | BL, corresp. with second earl of Egmont, Add. MS 47012 A, fols. 1–24 · BL, corresp. with George II, Add. MS 61467, fols. 11–13b, 16 · BL, corresp. and papers relating to opposition group at Leicester House, Add. MS 47012 A, fols. 27–90b

Likenesses E. Paletta, oils, 1707, Gripsholm Castle, Stockholm · R. A. Constantin, oils, 1716, V&A · P. Mercier, oils, *c.*1716, St David's School, Ashford, Middlesex · M. Maingaud, oils, *c.*1720, Royal Collection · attrib. G. W. Fountain, oils, 1723, Niedersächsisches Heimatsmuseum, Hanover · A. Pesne, *c.*1724, priv. coll. · G. Vertue, line engraving, 1725 (after C. Boit), BM · J. Kayser and J. A. Klyter, oils, 1727, Royal Collection · P. Mercier, oils, 1729, Shire Hall, Hertford · C. F. Zincke, enamel miniature, *c.*1729, Royal Collection · attrib. C. Philips, group portrait, oils, *c.*1730–1735, Royal Collection · C. Philips, oils, 1731–2, Yale U. CBA · B. Dandridge, oils, *c.*1732, NPG · C. Philips, group portrait, oils, 1732, Royal Collection · P. Mercier, group portrait, oils, 1733 (*The music party*), NPG; variants, *c.*1733; Cliveden, Buckinghamshire, Royal Collection · J. Wootton and W. Hogarth (?), group portrait, oils, 1734, Royal Collection · J. Amigoni, oils, 1735, Royal Collection · J. Amigoni, oils, 1735, priv. coll. · J. Amigoni, oils, 1735, Raby Castle, co. Durham · P. Mercier, oils, *c.*1735–1736, Beningbrough Hall, North Yorkshire [*see illus.*] · J. Richardson, drawing, 1736, BM · J. Richardson the elder, oils, 1736, Warwick Castle · attrib. W. Hogarth, oils, *c.*1736–1737, Royal Collection · C. Philips, oils, *c.*1737, Royal Collection · J. Wootton, two group portraits, oils, 1737, Royal Collection · J. Wootton, group portrait, oils, 1740, Royal Collection · T. Frye, mezzotint, pubd 1741 (after his oil painting, 1736, destroyed 1940), NG Ire. · T. Frye, oils, 1741, Royal Collection · J. Highmore, oils, *c.*1742, Royal Collection · J. B. van Loo, oils, 1742, Royal Collection · T. Hudson, oils, 1745–8, TCD · F. Hayman, oils, *c.*1750, Royal Albert Memorial Museum, Exeter · T. Hudson, oils, 1750, Cliveden, Buckinghamshire · D. Morier, oils, *c.*1750, Royal Collection · W. Aikman, group portrait, oils, Chatsworth House, Derbyshire · T. Burford, mezzotint (after C. Philips), BM, NPG · J. Faber junior, mezzotint (after Franken), BM, NPG · J. Faber junior, mezzotint (after J. Ellys), BM, NPG · J. Faber junior, mezzotint (after J. Davison), BM, NPG · I. Gossett, wax medallion, Royal Collection · W. Hogarth, group portrait, oils, Royal Collection · W. Hogarth, group portrait, oils, NG Ire. · attrib. P. Scheemakers, marble bust, Royal Collection · J. Simon, mezzotint (after P. Mercier), BM, NPG · van Werdlen, mezzotint (after G. Hansson), BM, NPG

Wealth at death £92,968 12*s.* 1*d.* in debt; excl. sums borrowed from Germany: BL, Add. MS 61860, fol. 75

Frederick, Sir Charles (1709–1785), politician and antiquary, was born on 21 December 1709 in Madras, the third son of Sir Thomas Frederick (1681–1730), at that time a member of the council of Fort St George, on the east coast of India, and of Mary Moncrieff (*c.*1689–1767), his wife. He was educated at Westminster School and at New College, Oxford, where he matriculated on 19 March 1725; he entered the Middle Temple on 1 February 1728. Frederick was elected a fellow of the Society of Antiquaries in 1731 and of the Royal Society in 1733. In January 1736 he was chosen director of the Society of Antiquaries and served until 1738, when he resigned the office in order to travel abroad. With his elder brother John he travelled to Italy, and from Italy went as far east as Constantinople. He returned by way of Paris and was back in London by January 1741, when he again took up his post as director of the Society of Antiquaries. He declined re-election the following year after his election to parliament. Some of his

reports on, and illustrations of, excavated antiquities remain with the society. His drawings of architectural antiquities survive in the three volumes, *Ancient Buildings … Drawn by Smart Lethuillier, Esq., … and by Charles Frederick, Esq.*, which came into the hands of Horace Walpole and are now in the British Library. He was something of an amateur architect as well, for he designed the monument to Lucy, Lady Lyttelton, in Hagley church, Worcestershire, and the monument to Thomas Miller, bishop of Waterford, in Highclere church, Hampshire.

Frederick was elected member of parliament for New Shoreham in 1741 and served until 1754, when he was elected for Queenborough, where the Ordnance office, for which he was by then working, had great influence. He sat for Queenborough until 1784, voting consistently for the government until 1782, when he followed North out of office, and confining his few interventions to matters relating to the Ordnance department. He was created knight of the Bath on 23 March 1761.

In 1746 Frederick was appointed comptroller of the royal laboratory at Woolwich and clerk of the deliveries, the most junior of the 'great officers' who made up the membership of his majesty's honourable Board of Ordnance. There is some evidence that he owed his entry into the office to the patronage of the second duke of Montagu, a fellow member of the Society of Antiquaries and master-general of the Ordnance. As comptroller he was responsible for the firework display on 27 April 1749 in celebration of the peace of Aix-la-Chapelle, for which Handel's 'Music for the Royal Fireworks' was composed. He was appointed to the post of surveyor-general, the second most senior of the civilian members of the board, on 10 April 1750, a post he held, along with the comptrollership of the laboratory, until 1782. As surveyor he was responsible for the procurement of military supplies, and can loosely be described as the technical member of the board. Almost his first action was to report to the board in June 1750 the 'many unaccountable Irregularities with which the Small Gun Office hath heretofore abounded' (PRO, WO 55/1816, 7–8) and under his direction 'A System and a Proposed Regulation for carrying on the Business for the future in the Surveyor General's Branch' was approved in January 1751. It laid down the records that were to be kept and the checks that were to be carried out to ensure that equipment supplied was in accordance with the specification, before any bills submitted could be approved for payment. This system lasted in its essentials until methods were changed under pressure of the needs of the wars against France at the end of the century.

Frederick seems to have taken considerable interest in the design of small arms, and among other details personally approved the design of a new carbine for the officers of the Royal Artillery in 1750 as well as the pattern of firearms made especially for presentation to the Iroquois in North America in 1753. Unfortunately all the official letter-books of the surveyor-general's department have been lost, the only exception being one covering the years 1761–7, in the New York Public Library, which seems to have been used intermittently when Frederick was away from the office. It shows him involved in the details of gun salutes in honour of the king's coronation, in equipping military expeditions, and in negotiating supplies to such foreign clients as Algiers and Portugal. The deliveries to Portugal that began in 1762 marked the beginning of more than 130 years' imitation by Portugal of British arms design. The only non-ordnance entries are a few relating to government or other official posts in his constituency of Queenborough, part of the care expected of any member of parliament.

On 18 August 1746 Frederick married Lucy Boscawen (1710–1784), eldest daughter of Hugh Boscawen, first Viscount Falmouth, and his wife, Charlotte Godfrey. They had six children: four sons, three of whom, Charles, Thomas Lennox, and Edward Boscawen, survived their father, and two daughters, Augusta and Lucy. His principal residence in London was in Berkeley Square. He also had a villa in landscaped gardens on the banks of the Thames at Hammersmith, bought for him out of money left for the purpose in the will of his grandfather, Thomas Frederick, and for many years he rented a 'shooting-house' near Boston in Lincolnshire.

When Frederick lost his post at the fall of Lord North's ministry in 1782, he petitioned for a pension, pleading extreme poverty. This was granted by the Fox–North coalition, and he did not stand for parliament in 1784. He died at his villa in Hammersmith on 18 December 1785. His will ordered that he should be buried in the family vault in St Olave Jewry, London. An obituary appeared in the *Gentleman's Magazine* of December 1785 and, by the terms of his will, his 'library and museum' were sold by auction in July 1786, and his Hammersmith villa in May 1787.

D. W. BAILEY

Sources *GM*, 1st ser., 55 (1785), 1010 · E. H. Fellowes, *The family of Frederick* (1932) · J. Evans, *A history of the Society of Antiquaries* (1956) · E. W. Brabrook, 'On the fellows of the Society of Antiquaries of London who have held the office of director', *Archaeologia*, 62 (1910–11), 59–80, esp. 62–80 · minutes of the board of ordnance, PRO, WO 47/34–100, WO 55/1816 · will, 20 Sept 1784, PRO, PROB 11/73 [with codicil 19 Jan 1785, proved 7 Jan 1786] · C. Aspinall-Oglander, *Admiral's wife* (1940) · O. F. G. Hogg, *The Royal Arsenal: its background, origin, and subsequent history*, 2 vols. (1963) · A. St H. Brock, *Pyrotechnics: the history and art of firework making* (1922) · Walpole, *Corr.* · Foster, *Alum. Oxon.* · J. Ingamells, ed., *A dictionary of British and Irish travellers in Italy, 1701–1800* (1997) · HoP, *Commons* · Burke, *Peerage* · IGI · Colvin, *Archs.* · W. A. Shaw, *The knights of England*, 1 (1906), 170

Archives NYPL, letter-book · S. Antiquaries, Lond., drawings and reports

Likenesses A. Casali, oils, 1738, AM Oxf. · J. Northcote, oils, 1784; Sothebys, 12 Nov 1997, lot 74 · J. Amigoni, oils; Christies, 17 Nov 1989, lot 47 · C. Phillips, group portrait (with his family); Christies, 21 Nov 1986, lot 38A

Wealth at death see will, 20 Sept 1784, PRO, PROB 11/73

Frederick, Felice [*known as* Colonel Frederick; *alias* Frederick de Neuhoff] (1725?–1797), writer on Corsica, was according to his children born in 1725. From the late 1750s he claimed to be the son of Theodor Stefan von *Neuhoff (1694–1756), the Westphalian adventurer who briefly

ruled as king of Corsica, but there is no independent evidence for this claim and considerable reason for suspecting it. Neuhoff, in his voluminous surviving correspondence, never mentions a son, though his relations with Frederick were good; and when Frederick names Neuhoff in his early letters and petitions he does so without any reference to a relationship (although this would have helped his case). Certainly Frederick cannot have been the son of Neuhoff's Irish wife, as he expressly claimed, since she was abandoned in 1720 and apparently died in 1724. The matter may be simply resolved if dispatches sent by the Genoese minister in London in October 1758 can be believed: according to these Frederick was a known Polish confidence trickster called 'Vigliawischi' (Genoa, Archivio di Stato, archivio segreto, 'Ribellione di Corsica', 15–3013). The surname intended may be Wielewicki or Wielewiejski. In the 1750s and 1760s his petitions and letters to prominent individuals were signed 'Felice Frederick' but he seems to have preferred to use the name Frederick alone where possible in later life.

The uncertainty of Frederick's identity throws serious doubt over all aspects of his life story as propagated by himself. This was partly published in his books, but largely related privately and set down after his death by his friend the oculist and writer John Taylor in the *Annual Necrology for 1797–8* (1800) and later in *Records of my Life* (1832). According to this account Frederick was born in Spain and received a good classical and military education. He served Frederick the Great of Prussia in a secretarial capacity and then obtained a post in the household of the duke of Württemberg before going to fight in Corsica, with two locals called Colonna and Buttafuoco; but Pasquale Paoli, the Corsican leader, rejected their services. His wife, a maid of honour at the Viennese court, died after only a few years of marriage, leaving him a son and a daughter. Having arrived in England about 1754, Frederick supported himself by teaching Italian; among his pupils were David Garrick, Charles Macklin, and Alexander Wedderburn, later (as Lord Loughborough) lord chancellor. He also claimed to be a close friend of Stanisław Poniatowski (later king of Poland), and that he had played host to him when he visited London.

Most of this is hard to assess. Certainly Frederick's first appearance on the scene in London was in the mid-1750s, as one of Neuhoff's more frequent and solicitous visitors in debtors' gaol. He was rewarded with the order of Redemption, or Deliverance, the gift of which was the last piece of Corsican crown prerogative remaining to Neuhoff. As soon as Neuhoff died, or perhaps slightly earlier, Frederick began to address petitions to the duke of Newcastle and others connected with the administration advocating a British take-over in Corsica, and requesting to be sent there himself. He enclosed what purported to be copies in translation of letters to him from Paoli, but these are thin and insubstantial offerings, and must be regarded as suspect. There is no evidence that Paoli regarded him as of any significance. There was some official British interest in intervention, but as Newcastle noted: 'There does not seem to be any necessity for trusting Sig^r. Frederick with the knowledge of what the Government may think proper to do' (BL, Add. MS 32866, fol. 240). He does not appear to have raised the matter again after 1762.

In 1768 Frederick published *Mémoires pour servir à l'histoire de Corse*, of which an English version came out the same year as *Memoirs of Corsica*. Dedicated to the duke of Württemberg and with a preface explaining that it was originally written at the request and for the use of the recently deceased Prince Edward, duke of York, it is largely based on the work of Antonpietro Filippini, but it adds much to the account of King Theodore that cannot be accepted. It claims, for example, that after forming the plan to sail to Corsica, but before enacting it, he travelled to Turkey and there agreed with Prince Rákóczi (the exiled ruler of Transylvania) to allow the island to be used as a base for a Moorish invasion of Italy, in return for Turkish support.

In London Frederick, never in funds and frequently in debt, lodged at first near Charing Cross, and then, for the last twenty years of his life at least, in Northumberland Street. His dark, healthy features and tall, slim figure were well known in the coffee houses of the area. He had a military bearing and, after one trip to the continent, he returned dressed in a green uniform of German style (once mistaken for a footman's livery) with an unidentified decoration around his neck. His colonelcy was explained as a brevet rank in the Württemberg army, and he allowed it to be believed that he operated as an unofficial agent for that duchy in London, claiming to have arranged for the supply of several regiments of Württemberg and Hohenlohe troops for the British campaign in America in 1777, and thereby incurred considerable expenses when the order was cancelled at the last moment. He mounted an unsuccessful campaign for reimbursement from successive British ministries until his death; though fully documented in the *Annual Necrology for 1797-8*, the affair does not feature in government records, nor is there any mention of Frederick as a representative of the Württemberg government in the archives of the duchy in Stuttgart.

In 1795 Frederick published his *Description of Corsica*. This consists of a very abbreviated geographical and historical account of the island down to the seventeenth century, and a confused relation of the rebellions of the 1750s and later, centring on Paoli, of whom it gives a far from entirely flattering picture, especially in relation to his motives for advocating union with Britain. These criticisms are, if anything, reinforced in the copy marked up for a second edition in the author's hand which survives in the British Library. Neuhoff is not mentioned at all, and more than sixty pages are given over to documents illustrating the British take-over of 1794. An appendix gives in full a petition presented to the French national assembly in 1790 advocating exploitation of the island's forests.

Whether Frederick did marry as he claimed is unknown, but it seems certain that he had two children: a son, Anthony Frederick, who was killed as an ensign in the British 15th regiment of foot at the battle of Germanstown in America in 1777; and a daughter who married a customs official named Clark and was the mother of several children including Emily *Clark, an occasional poet, author, and exhibitor of miniatures at the Royal Academy.

Oppressed by debt and, it was claimed on his behalf, deceived into guaranteeing a large bill for a friend who defaulted, Frederick committed suicide by shooting himself on the evening of 1 February 1797, in the west porch of Westminster Abbey. Initial reports that he had been murdered, although given wide publicity, were found to be groundless at the coroner's inquest, and the jury returned a verdict of lunacy. He was buried on 6 February 1797 next to his supposed father, Neuhoff, in the churchyard of St Anne's, Soho, beneath a tablet paid for by a subscription organized by Lady James. For the benefit of his daughter a new edition of Charles James's poem *Suicide Rejected* was published the same year, with a supplementary essay by James Fordyce. The subsisting doubts over Frederick's paternity were reported in a footnote by the *Gentleman's Magazine* (1797, 172), but the deceased's own version of this and other aspects of his life soon prevailed.

C. E. A. CHEESMAN

Sources *Annual necrology for 1797-8* (1800), 323-61 · J. Taylor, *Records of my life*, 2 (1832), 222-7 · A. le Glay, *Théodore de Neuhoff, roi de Corse* (1907), 383-91 · *GM*, 1st ser., 67 (1797), 172-3 · Frederick [F. Frederick], *Memoirs of Corsica* (1768) · BL, Add. MSS 32866, 32872, 32874-32875, 32887, 32933 · J. P. J. Entract, 'Colonel Frederick', MSS, Oxford University Press, Oxford DNB archives
Archives BL, Newcastle papers
Wealth at death none; heavily in debt: *Annual necrology*; Taylor, *Records*

Fredericus (d. 838), bishop of Utrecht and supposed saint, was supposed by John Bale to be an Englishman, though there is no reason to believe that he was English by either birth or descent. Bale followed William of Malmesbury, who claimed, in his *De gesta pontificum*, that Fredericus had been a nephew and disciple of St Boniface. It seems clear, however, that Malmesbury misapprehended the eleventh-century *Acta sancti Frederici* by Oetbert, mistaking the name of Ricfrid, a ninth-century bishop of Utrecht, for Winfrid, Boniface's original name. The hagiologist Miraeus stated that Fredericus was born in 'Sexberum', near Franeker in the Low Countries, and the Bollandists convincingly put his death in 838. There is an extant poem addressed to him by the ninth-century poet Hrabanus Maurus. He cannot therefore have been a relative or disciple in the literal sense of Boniface, who died in 754. Since Boniface hailed from Crediton, Bale assumed that this would also have been the birthplace of his 'nephew', Fredericus (or Fridericus), and so bestowed upon him the surname Cridiodunus, from Cridiandún, an archaic spelling of Crediton. He appeared under this name in works by Pits, Dempster, and Tanner. The notion of an English origin for Fredericus was finally and convincingly laid to rest by Henry Bradley in his article for the *Dictionary of National Biography*.

MARIOS COSTAMBEYS

Sources Bale, *Cat.*, vol. 2 · *Willelmi Malmesbiriensis monachi de gestis pontificum Anglorum libri quinque*, ed. N. E. S. A. Hamilton, Rolls Series, 52 (1870) · Oetbert, 'Acta sancti Frederici', *Acta sanctorum: Julius*, 4 (Antwerp, 1725), 452-71 · A. Miraeus, *Fasti Belgici et Burgundici*

(1622) • 'Hrabani Mauri Carmina', *Poetae Latini aevi Carolini*, ed. E. Dümmler, MGH Poetae Latini Medii Aevi, 2 (Berlin, 1884), no. 17 • J. Pits, *Relationum historicarum de rebus Anglicis*, ed. [W. Bishop] (Paris, 1619) • T. Dempster, *Historia ecclesiastica gentis Scotorum* (Bologna, 1627) • Tanner, *Bibl. Brit.-Hib.* • *DNB*

Free, Edward Drax (1764–1843), Church of England clergyman, was born on 23 December 1764 in Lambeth or in Newington, Surrey, the fifth of the six children of John Free (1711–1791), clergyman and schoolmaster, and his second wife, Mary. He attended Merchant Taylors' School, London, from 1775, and went in 1781 as a Sir Thomas White scholar to St John's College, Oxford, where he graduated BA in 1785. As a fellow of the college he followed the prescribed clerical route, eventually taking the DD degree in 1799, and becoming in 1801 vicar of St Giles', Oxford, a living he was permitted to hold along with his fellowship. An avaricious and appallingly bad-tempered man, he soon alienated the vestry of that parish by failing to offer any account of how sacrament offerings had been spent, and by failing to return documents dealing with benefactions that he had removed from the parish chest. This was behaviour that his long-suffering college had grown familiar with, for, by the beginning of 1808, St John's was seriously considering his expulsion for a physical assault on the bursar, verbal assaults on others, including the president, and his general refusal to submit to authority.

The college must have been delighted, therefore, with Free's agreement later in 1808 to resign his fellowship in order to become rector in the Bedfordshire village of Sutton, a college living situated some 60 miles from Oxford. Any hopes that they had seen or heard the last of him soon evaporated, however, for not only did he contrive to divert to other uses money given by the college for improvements to the rectory at Sutton but he also illegally pocketed money raised by felling timber on the glebe land. He also quickly alienated many of his parishioners by insisting that additional fees be paid for baptisms and burials, refusing the vestry the use of the church, using the churchyard as a farmyard for his livestock, attempting to wring the last penny out of his tithe-rights and his glebe tenants, selling the lead off the church roof and appropriating the proceeds, and failing, often for lengthy periods, to offer the customary church services. One reason for his absences was that he was often in trouble with the law—poaching, assault, and theft charges were at various times levelled against him. Another was that his sexual activities took up time. Between 1810 and 1823 he seduced a succession of female housekeepers, mostly recruited from the poorer areas of London, producing five illegitimate children with three of them, as well as causing another to miscarry.

Free's biggest mistake, however, was to offend Sutton's chief landed proprietors, the Burgoynes, and it was a member of that family, Montagu Burgoyne (1750–1836), who successfully engineered his prosecution and loss of living. This legal process, which began before the archdeacon of Bedford in 1823, dragged its way through the court of arches, king's bench, the exchequer chamber, the House of Lords, and two courts of delegates before eventually, in 1830, Free was formally removed from his benefice. The extraordinarily protracted case was widely reported and figured prominently in the report made to parliament in 1832 by the commissioners appointed two years earlier to inquire into the practice and jurisdiction of the ecclesiastical courts, a body that became preoccupied, because of Free's case, with the question of how to prosecute and remove from office scandalous clerics. Parliaments thereafter made frequent attempts to bring in bills that would facilitate such removals, but it was not until 1840, ten years after Free's deprivation, that the Church Discipline Act was passed. In those intervening years he plagued St John's and the college's visitor, the bishop of Winchester, with innumerable petitions and with litigation in king's bench seeking readmission to his Oxford fellowship. His death in the Royal Free Hospital, London, on 17 February 1843, following a traffic accident in Gray's Inn Lane, must have relieved his embarrassed college, its visitor, and those inhabitants of Sutton who had to put up with his outrageous behaviour for so long.   R. B. Outhwaite

Sources R. B. Outhwaite, *Scandal in the church: Dr Edward Drax Free, 1764–1843* (1997) [incl. bibliography] • Mrs E. P. Hart, ed., *Merchant Taylors' School register, 1561–1934*, 2 vols. (1936) • Nichols, *Lit. anecdotes*, vol. 5 • Foster, *Alum. Oxon.* • *The Times* (21 Feb 1843) • d. cert.
Archives Beds. & Luton ARS, legal documents • BL, legal documents • Hants. RO, legal documents • Lincs. Arch., legal documents • LPL, case of *Burgoyne v. Free*, Court of Arches H427/1–56 • LPL, legal documents • Oxfordshire archives, Oxford, legal documents • St John's College, Oxford, legal documents

Free [Fre, Freas], **John** (*c.*1430–1464/5), humanist scholar, spelled his name Fre or Free; it was Latinized in the fifteenth century to Frea(s), and in the early sixteenth to Phrea(s). His birthplace was Bristol according to William Worcester, who seems to have known him personally, or London according to John Burton, fellow of Balliol *c.*1467, and he may have had his schooling in either city. Free probably went up to Balliol College, Oxford, in 1445, since his supplication for BA in December 1448 specifies that he had studied three years there. Admitted in June 1449 and determined in 1450, he was dispensed in June 1453 and incorporated MA on 11 April 1454. On 21 March 1450 Free had been ordained acolyte at St Frideswide's Priory, Oxford; he was in priest's orders not later than 1456; and in April 1459 was admitted *in absentia* rector of Kelshall, Hertfordshire. In May, as clerk in the diocese of Bath and Wells and holder of benefices in the dioceses of Ely and Lincoln, he was granted extraordinary papal dispensation to hold supplementary benefices; and in July 1464 admitted by proxy rector of St Michael-in-Monte, Bristol.

By March 1450 Free was a fellow of Balliol. In autumn 1456 he left Oxford for study in Italy at the expense of William Gray, bishop of Ely. Like Gray, he went to Guarino da Verona, at Ferrara, where he was already on 22 October 1456. Free is one of five English pupils commended by name in Lodovico Carbone's funeral oration on Guarino, the others being Gray, John Gunthorpe, Robert Flemming, and John Tiptoft, earl of Worcester. Assimilating Guarino's methods of study and composition, Free began to write the new humanist hand, and to learn Greek, as Guarino encouraged his students to do. Evidence for Free's supposed Hebrew studies is negligible. Among his humanist friends and correspondents from Ferrara were Girolamo Castiglione, Carbone, and the Hungarian Janus Pannonius.

Free had been provided with money by Gray on setting out, and Gray had promised more; a year later this had not arrived and Free had to pawn books and clothes. Gray was then indulgent enough for Free, in autumn 1458, to ask for an extra sum to buy Greek books, which he could begin to translate. Some time after this he passed to Padua, where he still was in early 1461, being styled *doctor artium* in a university document of 22 March. There he became friends with Ognibene da Lonigo and the Greek Andronico Callisto. The presentation manuscript of his last surviving work (Vatican City, Biblioteca Apostolica Vaticana, MS Vat. lat. 3713) makes him MD; Worcester and John Leland credit him with the degree of DCL in addition.

At Padua, Free probably first encountered Tiptoft; certainly their time there coincided. For Tiptoft he seems to have acted as secretary, making transcripts himself and probably commissioning others to do so, as well as advising the earl in acquiring books even after Tiptoft's return to England, and perhaps aiding Tiptoft in composition. He made corrections, additions (sometimes in Greek), and annotations in some of Tiptoft's manuscripts. Copies made by Free for Tiptoft of Tacitus's *De oratoribus* and Suetonius's *De grammaticis* (BL, Harley MS 2639) are most likely the first manuscripts of these texts to have reached England in post-classical times. His Latin poems, dedicated to Tiptoft, are now lost. Free's best-known work, his Latin translation of Synesius of Cyrene's *Laus calvitii* ('A praise of baldness'), completed by 9 July 1461, was also dedicated to Tiptoft. A handsome manuscript, with the prefaces of Ognibene and Free himself, illuminated in the contemporary Paduan style and bearing the arms of Thomas Beckington, bishop of Bath and Wells, has corrections in Free's hand (Bodl. Oxf., 80). Beatus Rhenanus praised Free's translation and included it, with his own commentary, in editions of Erasmus's *Praise of Folly* (Basel, Froben, 1515–32); the first English translation, by Abraham Fleming in 1579, used both Free's version and the commentary.

Free's copies of late antique grammatical pieces discovered in 1433, his notes from Guarino's lectures on Virgil's *Georgics* and other ancient texts, and drafts of his letters to Gray and his chaplain Elias Cliderow, Pannonius, Guarino, and others (1456–8) are preserved in 'Free's Notebook', a codex later also used by Gunthorpe (Bodl. Oxf., 587). Others of his notes are in a manuscript later in Worcester's possession; his excerpts from Pliny's *Natural History* and the copy he made of Poggio Bracciolini's Latin *Diodorus Siculus*, attributed to Free by Worcester, its later owner, and initially by Leland, also survive (Balliol Oxf., MS 124). A miscellany volume of Greek tragic and other poetry, also once owned by Worcester, has annotations by Free (Bodl. Oxf., Auct. F. 3. 25). Others of Free's books passed to Gunthorpe, who was in Italy when Free died.

The date and place of Free's death are not precisely documented. Leland writes that he had been in Florence and in Rome and reports a rumour that he was poisoned by a rival. The only evidence for Free's death in Rome is the sole surviving manuscript of his second Latin translation from Synesius's *De insomniis* ('On dreams'), dedicated to Pope Paul II (elected 30 August 1464), presumably in the hope of patronage (MS Vat. lat. 3713). The presentation manuscript is in Free's autograph, with decorated initials in the contemporary Roman style; Free was therefore alive in late summer 1464. Worcester's report that he was provided by the pope to the see of Bath and Wells but died within the month is repeated by Leland; the provision is not in the papal registers. If Free was so favoured, he must have died after the death of Beckington on 14 January 1465 and before the provision of Robert Stillington on 30 October 1465.

Free was the first Englishman to make himself a professional humanist on the Italian Renaissance model. Though not to be compared with the best of his Italian contemporaries, he was outstanding in the generation before that of Grocyn and Linacre as Latin stylist, Greek scholar, and translator. The circumstances of his life—he had not, as Leland believed, enriched himself by medical practice—and his death out of England, however, made him less directly influential in Oxford and on English humanists than his contemporaries Flemming and perhaps even Gunthorpe.

J. B. TRAPP

Sources Emden, *Oxf.*, 2.724–5 · [A. C. de la Mare and R. W. Hunt], eds., *Duke Humfrey and English humanism in the fifteenth century* (1970) [exhibition catalogue, Bodl. Oxf.] · *Duke Humfrey's Library and the divinity school, 1488–1988* (1988) [exhibition catalogue, Bodl. Oxf., June–Aug 1988] · R. A. B. Mynors, *Catalogue of the manuscripts of Balliol College, Oxford* (1963), 102–3 · J. Delz, 'John Free und die Bibliothek John Tiptofts', *Italia medioevale e umanistica*, 11 (1968), 311–16 · A. C. de la Mare and B. C. Barker-Benfield, eds., *Manuscripts at Oxford: an exhibition in memory of Richard William Hunt (1908–1979)* (1980), 99–101 [exhibition catalogue, Bodl. Oxf.] · R. Weiss, *Humanism in England during the fifteenth century*, 3rd edn (1967), 106–23, 195 · E. Garin, ed., *Prosatori latini del Quattrocento* (1952), 399 · R. J. Mitchell, *John Free: from Bristol to Rome in the fifteenth century* (1955)
Archives Balliol Oxf., MS 124 · Biblioteca Apostolica Vaticana, Vatican City, MS Vat. lat. 3713 · BL, Harley MS 2639 · Bodl. Oxf., MSS 80, 587, MS Auct. F. 3. 25

Free, John. *See* Freeth, John (1731–1808).

Freebairn, Alfred Robert (1794/5–1846), engraver and etcher, was the son of the landscape painter Robert *Freebairn (1764–1808) and probably the brother of the sculptor Richard G. Freebairn (1797–1825). Alfred Freebairn etched and published his father's *Outlines of Lancashire Scenery* in 1815. He entered the Royal Academy Schools in 1817 aged twenty-two and began to make his name with steel-engravings for the annuals, including *The Keepsake* and *Jennings' Landscape Annual*. He also worked for Samuel Carter Hall's *Book of Gems*. Among the numerous vignettes and illustrations he engraved were plates after David Roberts, Samuel Prout, John Sell Cotman, and James Duffield Harding. His later work was confined largely to the production of engravings by the mechanical process invented by John Bate known as the Anaglyptograph. This device, which was a development of the ruling machine, converted objects with raised surfaces, such as coins, medals, and reliefs, into patterns of printed lines which suggest the contours of the original. Freebairn produced a large number of engravings by this process, some of which were published in the *Art Union* (1846). The most important examples include, in 1838, *A Salver of the Sixteenth Century*, by Jean Goujon, and eight large-scale engravings on steel of John Flaxman's imaginative reconstruction of *The Shield of Achilles*, from Homer's description in *The Iliad*. These were copublished with Ernest Gambart in March 1846, and sold at 2 guineas. Freebairn joined the Artists' Annuity Fund in 1823. He died aged fifty-two, a few days after his mother, on 21 August 1846, and was buried in Highgate cemetery. In 1847 the sculptor Charles Harriot Smith offered, without profit to himself, to erect a monument over his grave.   L. H. CUST, *rev.* GREG SMITH

Sources *Art Union*, 8 (1846), 14, 161, 264 • B. Hunnisett, *A dictionary of British steel engravers* (1980) • B. Hunnisett, *An illustrated dictionary of British steel engravers*, new edn (1989) • S. C. Hutchison, 'The Royal Academy Schools, 1768–1830', *Walpole Society*, 38 (1960–62), 123–91, esp. 170 • G. H. Bushnell, *Scottish engravers* (1949)
Archives BM, department of prints and drawings • V&A, department of prints and drawings

Freebairn, Robert (1764–1808), landscape painter, was born in London on 16 March 1764 according to details given in the register of the Royal Academy Schools. He was apparently of Scottish descent. He is said to have been the last pupil, briefly, of Richard Wilson RA; he was articled to Philip Reinagle, from 1782 to 1785, and it was from Reinagle's studio that he sent his pictures to the Royal Academy between 1782 and 1785. On 2 April 1782 he entered the Royal Academy Schools when his age was given as eighteen on '16 last March' (Hutchison, 146). He continued to exhibit landscapes up to 1786. From Easter 1787 to March 1791 he was in Italy, where he studied the work of Jacob More and sent views of Roman scenery to the Royal Academy. In 1791 he sent two views of the *Via Mala* in the Grisons, Switzerland; in the same year the lawyer Whaley Armitage visited his studio on 10 March, and thought his landscapes 'equal to any of de Loutherbourg's' (Ingamells, 382). He brought back to England a storehouse of material, on which he drew during the rest of his life, his productions being mainly representations of Italian scenery. Many Roman views were engraved and published in his *English and Italian Scenery*. Up to and including his last year of exhibition at the Royal Academy in 1804, he exhibited fifty-four landscapes and thirty-three Italian subjects, mainly of Rome or its vicinity; others were of Naples, Verona, Genoa and Rimini. His work was also exhibited at the British Institution between 1806 and 1813. When in Italy he was patronized by Lord Powis, and on his return to England by Lord Suffolk and Mr Penn of Stoke Park, Buckinghamshire. His compositions were noted for their elegance rather than for grandeur, and were pleasing enough to enable him to secure sufficient patronage and commissions for his pictures.

Freebairn occasionally painted views of Welsh and Lancashire scenery 'in an Italian spirit' (Waterhouse, *18c*

painters, 130). Waterhouse concluded that 'his best work is distinguished'. Some of his drawings were published in aquatint. Freebairn died in London at Buckingham Place, New Road, Marylebone, on 23 January 1808, leaving a widow and four children, one of whom was Alfred Robert *Freebairn (1794/5–1846), etcher and engraver. *Outlines of Lancashire scenery, from an unpublished sketch-book of the late R. Freebairn, designed as studies for the use of schools and beginners, and etched by the younger Freebairn* was published in 1815.   L. H. CUST, *rev.* RUTH STEWART

Sources J. Ingamells, ed., *A dictionary of British and Irish travellers in Italy, 1701–1800* (1997) • W. G. Constable, *Richard Wilson* (1953) • *GM*, 1st ser., 78 (1808), 94 • Redgrave, *Artists* • T. Wright, *Some account of the life of Richard Wilson* (1824) • Graves, *Artists* • Waterhouse, *18c painters* • S. C. Hutchison, 'The Royal Academy Schools, 1768–1830', *Walpole Society*, 38 (1960–62), 123–91
Archives BL

Freeburn, James (1808–1876), army officer and inventor of shell fuses, was born in the parish of St Cuthbert's, Midlothian. At an early age he was apprenticed to a baker. At the age of seventeen he enlisted in the 7th battalion of the Royal Artillery, and for a time served as gunner and driver. In December 1827 he was made bombardier, in May 1831 corporal, in January 1835 sergeant, and in April 1844 sergeant-major. From May 1837 to September 1840 he served in the West Indies. On his return home he experimented with explosives, and during 1846, the year he was commissioned quartermaster of the 10th battalion Royal Artillery, he invented an elaborate series of metal and wood fuses for exploding live shells, both on concussion and by time. In 1847 he improved his original idea, and his fuses were approved by the master-general of the ordnance and adopted. He continued in the Royal Artillery until 21 April 1856, when he retired with the honorary rank of captain, on retired half pay of 10s. per day. He died at his residence, 43 Hanover Road, Plumstead, Woolwich, on 5 August 1876, survived by his wife, Sarah. His rise from humble origins was unusual in the army of his day.
                                         JAMES BURNLEY, *rev.* JAMES LUNT

Sources Royal Artillery Institution, Woolwich, London, records • Boase, *Mod. Eng. biog.*
Archives Royal Artillery Institution, Woolwich, London
Wealth at death under £300: probate, 7 Dec 1876, *CGPLA Eng. & Wales*

Freedman, Barnett (1901–1958), artist and designer, was born in the East End of London on 19 May 1901, the son of Louis Freedman, a journeyman tailor, and his wife, Reiza Ruk, both Jewish immigrants from Russia. Since he suffered from persistent ill health, Freedman's only formal education was at an elementary school in London, and from the age of nine he spent most of his time in hospital; there he educated himself by wide reading and also taught himself the violin and how to draw and paint. By the time he was fifteen his health had improved sufficiently for him to work, initially as an office boy. From this he quickly turned to draughtsmanship, at first with a monumental mason and later in an architect's office. A strong interest in letterforms grew out of his everyday work, and this led to his becoming one of the most distinguished, if unconventional, practitioners of that art. While in full employment he attended evening classes at St Martin's School of Art. Although he was unsuccessful in his attempts to win a London county council scholarship, William Rothenstein, then principal of the Royal College of Art, was so impressed by his work and obvious potential that he used his influence with the county council to enable Freedman to be admitted to the college as a full-time student.

After leaving the college in 1925 Freedman experienced poverty while trying to earn his living as a painter. He had married secretly, on 14 June 1924, a fellow student, Beatrice Claudia Guercio (1904–1981), the daughter of Vincenzo Guercio, a shipping agent. After receiving her parents' approval they were married again on 13 April 1930. Having been introduced to Faber and Faber, for whom he illustrated Laurence Binyon's *Wonder Night* (1927) in the publisher's Ariel Poems series, he designed a large number of book jackets for the firm over a period of twenty-five years. Nearly all were auto-lithographed on stone with hand-drawn lettering. During this period Freedman carried out a wide range of jobs for other publishers and worked extensively also on package design. For a firm of biscuit manufacturers his brief extended to the decoration of its motor vehicles. Faber and Faber gave him a free hand to design and illustrate Siegfried Sassoon's *Memoirs of an Infantry Officer* (1931). Now recognized as one of the most outstanding examples of twentieth-century book design, the volume reveals that Freedman had, by that time, developed almost total mastery of the difficult medium of auto-lithography, where the artist draws his own designs onto the stones without the intervention of trade craftsmen or photomechanical means. Freedman's unpretentious cockney manner and his dogged down-to-earth application endeared him to workers at the Curwen Press, the Baynard Press, and Chromoworks, where he received a welcome not generally extended to artists. His stamp designs for the 1935 silver jubilee commemorative issue were responsible for bringing him to the attention of a wider public.

In 1936 Freedman was invited to illustrate George Borrow's *Lavengro* (1936) for the Limited Editions Club of New York. Although the book was not well received by the members of this upmarket book club, the club's owner, George Macy, admired Freedman's work to such an extent that he awarded him contracts which included the prestigious productions of Tolstoy's *War and Peace* (1938) and *Anna Karenina* (1951). These were fine examples of total book design and ensured Freedman an honoured place in the history of book production. For Macy's Heritage Press Freedman illustrated Dickens's *Oliver Twist* (1939), Emily Brontë's *Wuthering Heights* (1941), and Charlotte Brontë's *Jane Eyre* (1942). Freedman was also employed by Ealing Films to produce publicity material for its cinema productions, and this steady stream of commercial design lifted him into relative affluence. During the Second World War he held a temporary commission in the armed forces as an official war artist. The Imperial War Museum holds an extensive range of scenes and portraits, mainly executed in watercolour; other examples are held by the National Maritime Museum. As a member of the Double Crown Club and the Athenaeum, Freedman was an endearing conversationalist, never slow to express a contentious view. When he returned to the Royal College of Art as an instructor in still life he was regarded by many of his students as an inspiring, if unpredictable, teacher who had little regard for those whom he regarded as time-wasters.

Freedman never ceased to regard himself, first and foremost, as an easel painter, and, although recognition was slow in coming, his canvases and drawings attracted the attention of private collectors, many of whom were faithful to him. To discerning book lovers the inimitable style of his book jackets and book illustration were a constant attraction, and to the general public he became known through his posters for London Transport and Shell. Freedman was also responsible for overseeing the production of the Lyons lithographs, a superb series of colour prints which were displayed in Lyons teashops throughout Great Britain and which, in retrospect, are regarded as a major achievement in bringing the work of contemporary artists before the general public. In 1946 he was appointed CBE and in 1949 he received the Royal Society's highest award, the title of Royal Designer for Industry. Freedman died of cardiac failure on 4 January 1958 in his studio at 59 Cornwall Gardens, Kensington, and was cremated at Golders Green. He was survived by his wife and son, Vincent.

IAN ROGERSON

Sources *The Times* (6 Jan 1958) · *The Times* (8 Jan 1958) · *The Times* (9 Jan 1958) · *The Times* (10 Jan 1958) · *The Times* (17 Jan 1958) · J. Mayne, *Barnett Freedman* (1948) · A. Horne, *The dictionary of 20th century British book illustrators* (1994) · I. Rogerson and S. Hoskins, *Barnett Freedman* (1990) · Manchester Metropolitan University, Barnett Freedman archive · P. Gilmour, *Artists at Curwen* (1977) · private information (2004) [V. Freedman and K. Freedman] · *DNB* · *WWW* · m. cert. · d. cert.
Archives Manchester Metropolitan University | Tate collection, corresp. with Lord Clark | SOUND BBC, various talks, discussions
Likenesses A. Spalding, lithograph, 1940–49, NPG · B. Freedman, self-portrait, lithograph, repro. in L. Tolstoy, *War and peace* (1938), vol. 6, p. 278 · W. Rothenstein, oils, Tate collection
Wealth at death £4029 2s. 6d.: administration, 11 Aug 1958, *CGPLA Eng. & Wales*

Freeling, Sir Francis, first baronet (1764–1836), postal administrator and book collector, was born at Redcliffe Hill, Bristol, on 25 August 1764. Freeling began his career in the Bristol post office, where he witnessed the successful trial, in 1784, of John Palmer's scheme for a mail coach service. In 1785 he was appointed principal, and resident surveyor in London to assist Palmer, now surveyor and comptroller-general of the mails, to develop the service; and in 1797 rose to the office of joint secretary to the Post Office. He became sole secretary in 1798, and served in this capacity as the permanent head of the Post Office until his death.

Freeling's administration saw many reforms, including the growth of local penny posts, the reorganization of London's service, a move from road to rail for transporting the mail, and the transition from sail to steam in the

Irish packet service. A baronetcy was conferred upon him for his public services on 11 March 1828. In a debate in the House of Lords, in 1836, the duke of Wellington stated that the Post Office under Freeling's management had been better administered than any post office in any other country. Freeling possessed 'a clear and vigorous understanding … and the power of expressing his thoughts and opinions, both verbally and in writing, with force and precision' (*DNB*). Freeling had been a warm admirer of Pitt, but he allowed no political partisanship to affect his administration of the Post Office.

Freeling's leisure was devoted to the formation of a curious and valuable library. He was elected a fellow of the Society of Antiquaries in 1801, and was one of the original members of the Roxburghe Club, founded in 1812. He was married three times. He and his first wife, Jane, daughter of John Christian Karstadt (whom he married about 1788), had two sons. The surname of his second wife, whom he married in 1800, was Newbury, and she died in January 1804, but nothing else is known about his later marriages. Freeling died at his residence in Bryanston Square, London, on 10 July 1836. A marble monument was erected to him in the church of St Mary Redcliffe, Bristol, with an inscription commemorating his services.

Freeling was succeeded in the baronetcy by his elder son, **Sir George Henry Freeling** (1789–1841), who matriculated at New College, Oxford, on 17 March 1807. He was private clerk to his father from 1808, and assistant secretary from 1810 until his father's death in 1836; and subsequently became commissioner of customs (1836–41). He died on 30 November 1841 at 7 Hyde Park Gardens, London, leaving a number of children.

G. B. SMITH, *rev.* JEAN FARRUGIA

Sources Post, 1/14 · Post, 1/18 · Post, 58/4 · Post, 59/26 · H. Joyce, *The history of the Post Office from its establishment down to 1836* (1893) · Foster, *Alum. Oxon.* · *GM*, 1st ser., 70 (1800), 282 · *GM*, 1st ser., 74 (1804), 91 · *St Martin's-le-Grand* [Post Office magazine], 12 (1902), 415–18 [at Post Office Archives, 7] · d. cert. [Sir George Henry Freeling] · Post, 92

Archives Haringey Archive service, letters and diaries · priv. coll., corresp. · Royal Mail Heritage, London, corresp. and papers · Yale U., Beinecke L., corresp. | BL, corresp. with Lord Liverpool and R. Willimott, Add. MSS 38248, 38286–38288, 38367, 38474 · BL, corresp. with Sir Robert Peel, Add. MSS 40186–40402, *passim* · BL, letters to Earl Spencer · NL Scot., corresp. with Blackwoods · NL Scot., letters to Sir Walter Scott · W. Sussex RO, letters to duke of Richmond · W. Yorks. AS, Leeds, corresp. with George Canning
Likenesses G. Jones, oils, *c*.1830, Post Office Archives, London · C. Turner, mezzotint, pubd 1834 (after G. Jones), BM, NPG · Miss Jones, lithograph, BM

Freeling, Sir George Henry, second baronet (1789–1841). *See under* Freeling, Sir Francis, first baronet (1764–1836).

Freeman, Alexander (1838–1897), astronomer and teacher of mathematics, was born on 28 January 1838 in Blackheath, Surrey, the son of John Freeman, a chemist and druggist, and his wife, Mary Ann. From Merchant Taylors' School, London, he entered St John's College, Cambridge, in 1857. He won a scholarship in 1860, graduated fifth wrangler in 1861, and gained the chancellor's legal prize and was elected a fellow in 1862. In 1864 he proceeded MA and was elected a fellow of the Royal Astronomical Society (RAS). His first 'brilliant' career was as a teacher of mathematics (*The Times*, 15 June 1897, 9), but astronomy was 'the great love of his life' (*Monthly Notices of the Royal Astronomical Society*, 58, 1897–8, 136), and he always hoped for an appointment. Also a pragmatist, he was ordained priest in 1867.

Freeman published astronomical papers in the *Messenger of Mathematics* (1862–73), *Proceedings of the Cambridge Philosophical Society* (1880–83), *Monthly Notices of the Royal Astronomical Society* (1872–8, 1891–4), and *The Observatory* (1888–92). In 1878 he published with notes a translation of Fourier's work as *Analytical Theory of Heat* and in 1883 an edition of Cheyne's *Planetary Theory*. A private tutor with a profound knowledge of applied astronomy, he was moderator for the mathematics tripos in 1874 and examiner in 1875, president of the board of mathematical studies in 1876 and 1877, and twice examiner for the Smith's prize. He deputized and gave formal astronomy lectures for the Plumian professor in 1880–82.

From beneath the kindly, retiring, and amiable nature that later made him a favourite in his rectory, deep feelings erupted. Provoked by conflict in the RAS about refusing its 1871 gold medal to J. Norman Lockyer for solar research, Freeman published *Solar Fictions: a Free Enquiry into the Received Astronomical Doctrines and Popular Opinions Concerning the Sun* (1871), a work noted neither by his RAS nor his college obituarists. Addressed to 'all freethinkers', this essay set out dozens of inconsistencies and foibles to ridicule the precision and conclusions claimed by observing and theoretical astronomers and the degradation of conforming to received astronomy based on 'Newtonian bondage' (*Solar Fictions*, 56). With the RAS acrimoniously splitting over state endowment for science, he attacked the Royal Greenwich Observatory as 'an odious Stuart relic … a blot' and, swiping at the astronomer royal, George Airy, 'a Garrison of Absolutism, on its haughty eminence' so that 'the sponge of liberalism must wipe it out' (ibid., 57–8). Freeman taught astronomy by giving the student critical choice so that all should submit to reason, adding, 'Modern astronomy and medieval astrology must be … treated as one' (ibid., 48). A long appendix showed how sceptics used his reasoning similarly against biblical truth, thereby showing that Freeman rejected dogma.

That this did not immediately affect his career is probably because Freeman published little between 1874 and 1887, but devoted himself to university teaching and administration and two books useful to them. That earned him his pension. He resigned his fellowship to marry Eva Elizabeth, the youngest daughter of Colonel Paterson, on 4 October 1882. St John's immediately presented him to the small country living of Murston (880 souls, worth £500), and this began his third career. In 1891 he became rural dean of Sittingbourne.

The parish could scarcely fulfil a freethinker not subscribing to the dogma. In 1893, aged fifty-five, Freeman applied for the Savilian chair of astronomy at Oxford (worth £1000 per annum) to succeed Charles Pritchard, a teacher and cleric who had taken office at the age of sixty with less experience than he had. But he offered no plan of work, and his astronomical referees were damningly brief; 1871 had not been forgotten, and the RAS ensured that H. H. Turner, chief assistant at Greenwich, was appointed.

In 1888 Freeman had built an observatory with a 6 inch refracting telescope. In 1892 he succeeded N. E. Green as acting director and in 1893 as director of the Saturn section of the British Astronomical Association, where he remained until 1895, and to which he contributed twenty papers between 1890 and 1893—his last in November 1893. After two years with heart disease he died, aged fifty-nine, at his rectory on 12 June 1897. He was survived by his wife and four children.   ROGER HUTCHINS

Sources *Monthly Notices of the Royal Astronomical Society*, 58 (1897–8), 136–7 · *Journal of the British Astronomical Association*, 7 (1896–7), 464 · letters and testimonials relative to candidacy for the Savilian professorship of astronomy, 1893, Oxf. UA, MS 184E 153 (11) · *The Eagle*, 20 (1899), 226 · *The Times* (15 June 1897), 9 · Crockford · Venn, *Alum. Cant.* · *CGPLA Eng. & Wales* (1897) · d. cert.
Wealth at death £3450 7s. 4d.: probate, 2 Aug 1897, *CGPLA Eng. & Wales*

Freeman, (Ralph) Anthony (1946–1998). *See under* Freeman, Sir Ralph (1911–1998).

Freeman, Edward Augustus (1823–1892), historian, the youngest child of John Freeman, colliery owner, and Mary Anne, *née* Carless, was born at Mitchley Abbey in Harborne, south-west of Birmingham, on 2 August 1823. The death of both his parents fifteen months later left him to the care of his paternal grandmother, the guardianship of an uncle (the Revd Joseph Freeman), the society of the elderly, and the expectation of £600 a year from the family's coal pit. He was a precocious and awkward child, and a succession of private schools did little to correct his peculiarities. In 1829 his grandmother moved from Weston-super-Mare to Northampton, where he attended a school kept by the Revd T. C. Haddon. At fourteen he was sent away to the Revd W. Browne's school at Cheam in Surrey; and when sixteen, at his own wish, he moved to a private tutor well known to the family, the Revd Robert Gutch, at Seagrave rectory in Leicestershire, to be coached for an Oxford scholarship. Endowed with a sharp mind, confident, and adventurous, he read widely and became a sound classical scholar, although James Bryce was to consider that he never showed an aptitude for the refinements of the subject (Bryce, 498). He taught himself Hebrew on the side. By independent thought, so he claimed, he reached a religious position similar to that of the Tractarians. He despised all games and sports, and walking became his favourite recreation: all his life he remained an indefatigable 'rambler', although his peculiar gait earned him the nickname of 'Hoppy-skippy'.

After failing to get a scholarship at Balliol College in November 1840 (beaten in the contest by Matthew Arnold), Freeman secured one at Trinity in the following June. The atmosphere there was congenial: the moral tone was so high that there were college fellows who

Edward Augustus Freeman (1823–1892), by Frear, pubd 1886

abstained from dinner in hall on Fridays. As an undergraduate he courted Eleanor Gutch (*bap.* 1818), later 'dearest Nelly', the daughter of his former tutor, in letters which seem confined to doctrinal and religious enquiry. As soon as he came of age (2 August 1844), overriding the objections of his grandmother and uncle, he made by post a successful offer of marriage.

Freeman's academic record was undistinguished. He won no university prizes and took only a second class in *literae humaniores* at Easter 1845. In May, however, to his great delight, he was elected by examination to a probationary fellowship at his college. As this had to be vacated on marriage, although he was of independent means he gave much thought to the choice of a career. After hesitating for some months between holy orders and architecture, Freeman decided to become a historian and resumed his studies with a fresh ardour. In 1846 he tried for the chancellor's English prize essay, his subject being 'The effects of the conquest of England by the Normans'. He did not win the prize, but, maintaining the same positions, devoted the next thirty years to proving the chancellor wrong. But first, on 13 April 1847, despite continuing opposition from his guardians, he married Eleanor at Seagrave. For a year they lived at Littlemore, near Oxford; in 1848 they moved to a house called Oaklands near Dursley in Gloucestershire. In 1855 they transferred to Lanrumney Hall, near Cardiff, and in 1860 to Somerleaze, a house with a small park near Wells in Somerset, where they settled for life.

Character, habits, and opinions The marriage was fruitful: Freeman's eldest daughter, Margaret, who was later to help him with his work, especially by indexing, was born on 17 October 1848; and he was eventually survived by two sons and four daughters. Family life seems to have been very happy: Freeman was kind and soft-hearted with those close to him, and Bryce thought that he had a genius for friendship (Bryce, 508). Freeman's biographer, the Revd W. R. W. Stephens, dean of Winchester, regarded him as

> essentially Teutonic in his whole personality, physical, as well as moral and mental; in his square sturdy frame, his ruddy hair, his fair complexion, his plain and simple habits of life, no less than in his love of truth, and straightforwardness in deed and word.   (Stephens, 2.464)

For Bryce he was 'a singularly simple and truthful man' (Bryce, 501). Sometimes he called himself a 'Zummerzet freeholder', and he did indeed share some of the interests of country gentlemen (Stephens, 1.253). He rode every day, and loved animals; at Lanrumney he kept a good number of them, some of which were butchered for his table. But he disliked and campaigned against fox-hunting, and 'drove out hunters' (from his fields or park) is a frequent entry in his diary. For similar reasons, although he could appreciate the possible medical benefits of vivisection, in 1884 he opposed the establishment of a physiological laboratory at Oxford. Likewise, Freeman hated 'the British army more than any institution in being', and regarded 'the man-slaying trade' as ignoble (Stephens, 2.198). Nevertheless, he took a full part in local government, and became a JP and a member of several local government boards. He made repeated attempts to enter parliament and a seat in the house always remained one of his major ambitions.

Although brought up as a tory, Freeman developed into an independent radical and a staunch supporter of Gladstone. He believed in liberty and democracy, home rule for Ireland, and the disestablishment of the Irish church. He hated tyrants, especially the Turks and Ottoman rule in Europe. He was proud of his role as an early 'atrocitymonger' in what became the campaign against Turkish atrocities in Bulgaria and loathed Disraeli's policy on the 'Eastern Question'. In religion he abandoned his youthful high-church position, and, while remaining a believer, assumed a tolerant, non-dogmatic stance.

Freeman's racial prejudices were, however, extreme: Stephens wrote, 'For the pure Celt he entertained a kind of natural antipathy, mingled with something like contempt, which often manifested itself in odd and amusing ways' (Stephens, 2.464). In general he believed that the French—the 'Gal-Welsh' and 'Rum-Welsh' as he called them in his letters—were as hateful as the Celts. In 1861 he wrote to William Stubbs after a trip abroad, 'We liked the Normans much, the Picards somewhat less, Paris, of course, is as beastly as ever' (Stephens, 1.295–6). He supported the Germans in the Franco-Prussian War of 1870. In 1877 he commented on a meeting with Sir Richard Burton in Trieste, 'He has killed more men than most people; but they were mainly Turks' (ibid., 2.154). In 1880 he wrote, 'I am yearning to … knock down a Jew, or anything that might be for the public good' (ibid., 2.173–4, cf. 428). His

triumphant visit to America in 1881–2 was, for him, marred by the presence of black people, whom he regarded as apes: 'This would be a grand land', he wrote, 'if only every Irishman would kill a negro, and be hanged for it' (ibid., 2.242). But to the Germans, particularly the German-speaking Swiss, his admiration remained constant. In Switzerland, he believed, primitive Germanic institutions had been preserved pure and intact. He also liked the Greeks, the spiritual companions of his childhood: Greek and Roman history was the subject of many of the articles he contributed to periodicals in 1855–60; and he became much involved in the politics of the emerging Greek kingdom.

These views, some of which Freeman expressed mainly in private within a network of scholars, were characteristic of certain sections of Victorian society. He claimed that as a rule he was an impartial observer of events and the dramatis personae, and that on controversial issues, he could see some good on both sides; indeed, he often displayed sturdy common sense. But even his friends conceded that he could be rough and rude, even fierce, in both speech and writing. And he made enemies: he was a savage critic of historians who he thought were untruthful or careless, and hounded J. A. Froude for twenty years in the *Saturday Review* on account of alleged inaccuracies in his work. His prejudices strongly affected his own historical writing, both in style and interpretation. His vehemence and his growing aim to purge his vocabulary of all foreign words, thereby reverting to a plain Germanic idiom, increasingly disfigured his prose. As for his partialities, for instance, in a letter to Stubbs in 1858, he referred to that relatively fair-minded Anglo-Norman chronicler William of Malmesbury as a 'lying affected French scoundrel' (Stephens, 1.241), whom he could hardly bring himself to read.

Scholarly activity This violence of expression is in contrast—and possibly in reaction—to the ordered life that Freeman achieved at Somerleaze, surrounded by women anxious to serve. He made himself a daily timetable and kept to it faithfully. His industry was phenomenal and his output extraordinary. Besides working on big projects and sidelines such as histories for children, he did much reviewing, journalism, and pamphleteering, for he was very involved in all the great political issues in England and Europe as well as Oxford matters. Between 1860 and 1869 he wrote for the *Saturday Review* 391 reviews and 332 miscellaneous articles as well as contributing to 'all possible Quarterlies'. When he broke with the '*Saturday Reviler*' in 1878 over the Eastern question, he sacrificed some £500–700 a year. His private correspondence was considerable. As a writer of political history adorned with geography, he spanned all ages from the Hebrews and ancient Greeks to his own times: as he noted in 1899, 'my parish is a big one, taking in all civilized Europe and America' (Stephens, 2.406). He regarded their civilizing role as the fostering of Christianity and the repulse of invaders from Asia. Especially he was interested in the political institutions and the internal and external politics of this

vast society. He often remarked that history was past politics, politics present history (ibid., 1.309).

The longest of Freeman's works, the best remembered
and the most influential, *The History of the Norman Conquest,
its Causes and Results*, was begun on 7 December 1865, when
he was forty-two, at the height of his physical and mental
powers. He wrote to Hook, 'I have actually sat down to
make a distinct *History of the Norman Conquest*, which I can
do easier than anybody else, as I have worked so much at
the subject for twenty years past' (Stephens, 1.333). The
massive demy octavo volumes appeared in rapid succession, with the fifth and last (except for the general index)
in 1876. As he progressed, he revised and expanded the
earlier volumes, using interleaved copies. The rejected
prize essay of 1846 had been inflated to gigantic proportions. Primary sources for the subject had become readily
available since the appearance of Domesday Book in four
large folios in 1783–1816: the texts and calendars published by the record commissioners, the Rolls Series of
chronicles and memorials, and the individual contributions of J. M. Kemble and Benjamin Thorpe. Also valued by
Freeman were the works of Augustin Thierry, Sharon
Turner, Sir Francis Palgrave, and J. M. Lappenberg. All
these and many more he purchased and consulted in his
study at Somerleaze, for he disliked public libraries, hated
London, and never once entered the British Museum Library or the Public Record Office; he rarely visited even the
Bodleian Library at Oxford. Hence he was criticized for his
neglect of manuscript sources. But he did not work in isolation: he corresponded regularly with scholars, both
British and foreign. His friendship with Stubbs (his junior
by two years), J. R. Green (from 1862), James Bryce, W. F.
Hook, dean of Chichester, W. R. W. Stephens, his biographer, and many others created a fruitful seminar. In this
circle William Stubbs was the expert. He had all the
answers, and Freeman admired him enormously, often
saying that Stubbs's books were real German books
(although privately he thought them a little dull). In 1874
he wrote significantly to Hook that he was busy translating Stubbs 'into thunder and lightning' (Stephens, 2.88).
Green was the beloved and sometimes wayward disciple,
the Johnny, *Johanunculus homunculus meus*, of their playful
relationship. Each 'trumpeted' the others: as the doggerel
went,

See, ladling butter from alternate tubs
Stubbs butters Freeman, Freeman butters Stubbs.
(W. H. Hutton, *Letters of William Stubbs*, 1904, 149)

Freeman had at least an adequate technical equipment
for writing a history of the Norman conquest: a good
knowledge of languages, including Anglo-Saxon, and an
interest in field archaeology and architecture, with the
ability to sketch buildings and their features. He was
much involved in politics and not unreasonably regarded
participation in government as useful training for a historian, although his statement to Bryce in 1867 that certain passages in the first volume of *The Norman Conquest*
'arose wholly out of Quarter Sessions debates' is hardly
reassuring (Stephens, 1.387). Above all, he had tremendous zest. His travels throughout England and Europe,

including wild and dangerous areas, when the railway system was still rudimentary, in order to inspect all places
and buildings relevant to the work in progress and capable of providing *Baedeker* adornment, and his industry at
his writing tables were amazingly productive. But he had,
as critics and even friends were going to point out, some
weaknesses. He could be provocative and dogmatic, and
he neglected anything he considered irrelevant to his specialities—general literature, poetry (apart from ballads,
which he wrote), the arts (except architecture), philosophy, and theology.

Freeman believed in the basic continuity of English history from the Germanic settlements in Britain in the fifth
century until his own times. There was no 'Saxon period':
it was always (Old) English history. And he imagined that
there was a gradual beneficial elaboration of the political
institutions introduced by the invaders from their Germanic homelands, so that, for example, moots, in which
Earl Godwin and other patriotic Englishmen were able to
debate the vital issues of the day, developed into the parliaments held by Edward I at the end of the thirteenth century. Inevitably, the Norman conquest made some
changes. But William the Conqueror was also the Great
Conservator; and even the hateful feudalism that came in
with the reign of his dreadful son Rufus merely gave a
twist to the steady evolution of the essentially Germanic
society. Moreover, the Norman conquest was good for
England: it was a fire which did not destroy, but only purified. The England of old 'came forth with her ancient laws
formed into shapes better suited to changed times, and
with a new body of fellow-workers in those long-
estranged kinsmen whom birth on her soil had changed
into kinsmen once again' (Freeman, 1.1–2; 5.650).

This view of English history, which Freeman shared
with his despised William of Malmesbury and most of his
Oxford friends, such as Stubbs, is undoubtedly tenable as
a panorama, and still finds exponents. It was Freeman's
treatment of the theme which from the start aroused hostile responses. His increasingly 'Germanic' vocabulary, his
restoration of the old spelling of proper names—the
Eadwards and Eadgyths—the pedantry and prolixity
repelled some, and led to a breach with Leslie Stephen
over the spelling of Saxon names in the first volume of the
Dictionary of National Biography. His pugnacity invited
retaliation. Most devastating of all were the onslaughts of
J. H. Round, a pupil of Stubbs at Oxford, an antiquary and
genealogist, a scholar with a temper as difficult as Freeman's and a worse character. Round believed that Freeman handled his sources in a cavalier fashion (a scissors-
and-paste man) and drew attention to inaccuracies; but of
greater importance was his challenge to Freeman's fundamental thesis of continuity across 1066. In the index to
Round's *Feudal England*, a collection of his articles centred
on 1066, which was first published in 1895, three years
after Freeman's death, a derisive column and a third are
devoted to 'Freeman, Professor'. Complaining about 'the
unscrupulous attacks' made on him by Freeman's supporters, Round declared, 'But truth cannot be silenced,
facts cannot be obscured. I appeal, sure of my ground, to

the verdict of historical scholars, awaiting, with confidence and calm, the inevitable triumph of the truth' (Round, 394). Round indeed scored many points, but whether he won the contest remains a moot point.

Last years Freeman received some notable honours while and after bringing out *The Norman Conquest*. He was granted honorary degrees by Oxford in 1870, when Bryce presented him in a short and witty Latin oration, and Cambridge in 1874. In 1875 the king of the Hellenes made him a knight commander of the Greek order of the Saviour; in 1876 he was elected a corresponding member of the Imperial Academy of Science at St Petersburg; in 1877 he received the order of Takova from the prince of Serbia and the order of Danilo from the prince of Montenegro. Some of these awards were in gratitude for his hostility to the Turks and his fund-raising for Christian victims of their atrocities. In 1880 he was elected an honorary fellow of his Oxford college. But his ambition to obtain a professorship at Oxford, like his hope to enter parliament, was several times disappointed, even though his range was so wide that he could be a candidate for the Camden chair of ancient history (1861) as well as for those in modern history (1858, 1862). At last, when Stubbs became bishop of Chester in 1884, Gladstone, an admirer, was able to overcome the queen's doubts over Freeman's suitability to succeed him in the regius chair of modern history, for which Freeman, perhaps uniquely, proposed himself. Gladstone hoped Freeman 'would give a powerful impulsion to historical study in Oxford' (Gladstone, *Diaries*, 11.114), but this was not to be.

Unfortunately, by 1884 the prospect had ceased to charm: Freeman had suffered since 1845 from gout and, after 1877, from bronchitis, a serious handicap. He disliked the necessary absences from Somerleaze, and found Oxford much changed for the worse. He soon realized he was not to be a success: the chair gave him no power in the school of history. He was not considered a good teacher, and his lectures were no more popular than Stubbs's had been. In 1891 he wrote, 'I have tried every kind of lecture I can think of, and put my best strength into all, but nobody comes' (Stephens, 2.429).

Despite all the difficulties, Freeman continued to write and travel indefatigably. He intended to continue his history of the Norman conquest on the same scale until at least the death of Henry I. In 1882 appeared, in two volumes, *The Reign of William Rufus*. In its 1356 pages he covered not only Rufus's thirteen years as king but also Henry's first six, and concluded with a prospectus of the remainder. It is essentially a political history, based on the chronicles, and presented chronologically. Freeman regarded the reign 'as a period of the highest interest and importance' (Stephens, 1.4). Rufus was both a true English king and the real consolidator of the conquest. Freeman's interpretation of the events is in general plausible; there are relatively few factual errors; and he tries his best to be fair to the characters, even to the 'sultan-like' Rufus, whom he abhorred (ibid., 1.332). But his remark on the trial of William of St Calais in 1088—that 'the tale … is long, perhaps in some of its stages it is wearisome'

(ibid., 1.117)—can be applied to the whole work. Freeman had a well-stocked mind, and most events suggested parallels drawn from either ancient or modern history. In one sentence Rufus is compared with both Bonaparte and Sulla (ibid., 1.150). The leisurely progress and the touristic visits to the places *en route*, the halts to recapitulate or generalize become hard to bear. Although he declares that 'into the details of the private life of Rufus it is well not to grope too narrowly' (ibid., 1.159), he rambles interminably while attempting to convey to the worldly-wise in allusive language that the king was a homosexual. In short, Freeman had become a bore.

Freeman followed *The Reign of William Rufus* with a relatively short biography of William the Conqueror in 1888, and he began to publish collections of his lectures. In 1891 he paid the last of his many visits to Normandy in preparation for writing a full history of the reign of Henry I. In 1891–2 the first three volumes of his *History of Sicily* were published. In February 1892, with his wife and their two youngest daughters, Freeman visited Spain in search of warmth. He fell ill at Valencia on 7 March of what was to be diagnosed as bronchitis and smallpox. He pushed on to Alicante on the 9th, died there on the 16th, and was buried the next day in its protestant cemetery.

Freeman died a disappointed man. But despite the spate of criticism which had embittered his last years, he had in fact made an influential contribution to English historiography. He had not only established the concept of the early appearance and unbroken continuity of a purely English political identity, but also proclaimed, with typical Victorian optimism, the evolutionary improvement of English institutions down the ages.

FRANK BARLOW

Sources W. R. W. Stephens, *The life and letters of Edward A. Freeman*, 2 vols. (1895) · E. A. Freeman, *The history of the Norman conquest of England*, 2nd edn, 6 vols. (1870–79) · Gladstone, *Diaries*, 11.113–4 · J. Bryce, 'Edward Augustus Freeman', *EngHR*, 7 (1892), 497–509 · J. H. Round, *Feudal England: historical studies on the eleventh and twelfth centuries* (1895) · W. Page, 'Memoir of J. H. Round', in J. H. Round, *Family origins and other studies*, ed. W. Page (1930), ix–xlviii [vol. incl. bibliography of J. H. Round] · J. W. Burrow, introduction, in E. A. Freeman, *The history of the Norman conquest of England* (1974), xi–xxxi · R. T. Shannon, *Gladstone and the Bulgarian agitation, 1876* (1963) · P. B. M. Blaas, *Continuity and anachronism* (1978) · H. A. Cronne, 'E. A. Freeman', *History*, new ser., 28 (1943), 78–92 · M. E. Bratchel, *E. A. Freeman and the Victorian interpretation of the Norman conquest* (1969) · *IGI*

Archives Arundel Castle, West Sussex, corresp. and papers relating to Fitzalan Chapel · Bath Central Library, papers relating to Glastonbury Abbey · Bodl. Oxf., corresp. and papers · JRL, corresp. and papers, incl. MS of *The history of the Norman conquest of England* · Manchester Metropolitan University, corresp. with J. T. Denson · University of Manchester, Freeman's library presented to Owen's College | BL, letters to G. C. Boase, Add. MS 35073 · BL, corresp. with W. E. Gladstone, Add. MSS 44377–44786, *passim* · BL, corresp. with Macmillans, Add. MSS 55049–55053 · Bodl. Oxf., corresp. with Lord Bryce · Ches. & Chester ALSS, corresp. with Lord De Tabley · DWL, letters to Henry Allon · Jesus College, Oxford, letters to W. B. Dawkins · NL Scot., letters to Alexander Campbell Fraser · Som. ARS, letters to W. A. Jones relating to antiquarian matters · Som. ARS, letters to Sir Edward Strachey · U. Durham L., letters to J. T. Fowler, etc. · U. Hull, Brynmor Jones L., letters and cards to Edith Thompson · U. Mich., letters to Charles Henry Hart

Likenesses Frear, photograph, pubd 1886, NPG [*see illus.*] · H. Vos, oils, 1889, Trinity College, Oxford · wood-engraving, pubd 1892 (after photogravure by Hills & Saunders), NPG · Hills & Saunders, photogravure, NPG · engravings, repro. in Stephens, *Life and letters* · wood-engraving, NPG; repro. in *ILN* (1892)

Wealth at death £5041: probate, 9 July 1892, *CGPLA Eng. & Wales*

Freeman, Flora Lucy (*bap.* 1869, *d.* 1925?), philanthropist and writer, was baptized on 20 May 1869 at St Martin-in-the-Fields, London, the daughter of William Henry Freeman and his wife, Emily, *née* Carrack. She founded and organized clubs for working-class girls and a pioneering Roman Catholic Girl Guide company, and wrote advice manuals about these activities. She was also the author of three moral tales, three devotional books, and three moral advice books for girls. Her childhood memories included hating needlework but also 'the joy' of reading Scott's novels aloud to her old nurse (Freeman, *God's Golden Gifts*, 58). Her books, notably *A Chain of Thought for the Church's Year* (1905), which cites authors as diverse as Isaac Williams, Jeremy Taylor, Matthew Arnold, and Cardinal Newman, indicate that she was well read, if not well educated, and had travelled in Europe. Unmarried, she dedicated *A Chain of Thought* to her 'dear mother', and wrote of the 'gift of friendship' (Freeman, *God's Golden Gifts*, 65–79).

Freeman, who had been brought up a high-church Anglican, started her work with clubs for working-class girls when aged twenty-one, in London, where she was living. By 1901 she had also run clubs for 'rough girls' and laundry workers in a 'large seaside town', as well as an 'Evening Home for Rough Girls' in London for many years (Freeman, *Religious and Social Work*, 70–85, 90–93). In 1903 she dedicated *The Sunshine of Everyday Life* 'to my many girl friends, especially those belonging to St Saviour's Pimlico, and St Barnabas' Hove'.

In *Religious and Social Work Amongst Girls* (1901) Freeman drew on her own extensive experience to give practical advice to girls of the 'upper and leisured classes' as to how to run working-girls' clubs. In her view, their primary aim was religious, and her advice about how to introduce the subject, and give religious instruction (in the Anglo-Catholic tradition), suggests that she was a gifted teacher. She also advised on how to find a suitable room, organize enjoyable activities, and finance such clubs, noting that 'Our (annual) London Club sale' (staffed by club committee girls) 'is always most successful' (p. 142). The sections on visiting indicate that Freeman took a personal interest in her club members. She referred to district visiting in south London slums, in 'one of the poorest of our London riverside parishes' (p. 90), to visiting a south London women's settlement, and to working in the East End, besides helping with church missions.

Freeman urged upper- and middle-class girls that it would bring them real happiness to use their talents and energy for the good of the poor. The dedication of the semi-autobiographical *Polly: a Study of Girl Life* (1904) to 'S. A. D. In Remembrance of Many Happy days spent together in the East End' suggests she did find this herself, although she described her virtual 'agony of shyness' when beginning conversations about religion (Freeman, *Religious and Social Work*, 28). While she believed that working-class girls would benefit from the refining influence of the upper classes, the latter were admonished as to the need for understanding, tact, and sensitivity and reminded how much they could learn. A review of *Religious and Social Work* in 1909 by 'E. E. O' stated that 'Every page is a record of living experience. No detail is too insignificant for careful and deliberate attention, and we can well believe this is the secret of Miss Freeman's wonderful success in being a friend to working girls' (*Girls' Club Journal*, 1/1, 1909, 21).

Our Working Girls and How to Help Them (1908), written after seven more years of work with girls' clubs, was also favourably reviewed. In it, Freeman admitted that experience had tempered her optimism, but she reiterated the value of such clubs as a place to give working girls recreation after a hard day's work, and to prevent them from 'falling', through having nowhere to go in their time off. Club workers were advised to help girls find the best kind of work available and to assist those who were being exploited in service. This book discussed issues such as possible difficulties with other club workers and ways to encourage purity, including how to teach the facts of life. Her article 'Notes for a lesson on purity' was printed in the *Girls' Club Journal* of 1912.

Freeman clearly had links with extensive networks of voluntary organizations, such as the Factory Girls' Country Holiday Fund, preventive homes and penitentiaries, and the National Vigilance Association. *The Patience of Perla* (1906) was dedicated to 'my dear friend, Grace Valentine Stephenson', club leader of St Mary's girls' club, Southwark, in 1913, and of the Girls' Guild, Kingsway Hall, from 1913 to 1916. In 1917 and 1921 Stephenson was secretary of the London Girls' Club Union, founded by the Hon. Maude Stanley in 1880.

In 1906 Freeman established the Brighton Girls' Club Union, a non-denominational association, initiated by approaching the vicar of each parish, and also the local rabbi. The aim was to bring together those working with girls in the area for mutual support, and to raise the standard of club work by holding annual competitions. Her account of this was printed in the *Girls' Club Journal* of October 1909, presumably as a model for others. She was still secretary in 1917 (but not in 1921). By 1917, with eleven other regional unions, the Brighton union was affiliated to the Federation of Working Girls' Clubs, founded as the Factory Helpers' Union in 1886.

Freeman's books note the influence of Maria Havergal, the daughter of an evangelical clergyman, but primarily of (often controversial) ritualist slum parsons. *Religious and Social Work* was dedicated to 'The Revd Father Black, to whom I owe so much in my Endeavours to Serve my Sisters', almost certainly William Black, curate of St Saviour's, Pimlico, from 1892 to 1910, who had been a Cowley Father. The preface was by the Revd R. R. Dolling, vicar of St Saviour's, Poplar, from 1898 to 1902, previously at St Agatha's, Portsea, whose sermons and retreats she had attended, and who was clearly in sympathy with Freeman's work. While slightly poking fun at inexperienced curates, Freeman paid tribute to the effective ministry and 'faithful friendship' of some experienced 'Priests' (Freeman, *God's Golden Gifts*, 70, 72; *Religious and Social Work*, 74, 113, 130). *The Clouds of Life* (1911) was dedicated 'by special permission' to another controversial London Anglo-Catholic, the Revd Arthur Stanton.

The Sunshine of Everyday Life (1903) and *The Clouds of Life* were addressed to the girls themselves, and contained rigorous advice about religious practice and moral behaviour. Like *Polly*, they were enthusiastically prefaced by the Revd C. H. Sharpe, Anglican diocesan missioner in Gloucester from 1893, who became a Roman Catholic in 1916. *A Chain of Thought for the Church's Year* (1905) and *The Patience of Perla* (1906), a tale of an exemplary working-class girl, set in a seaside town, were prefaced by Anglo-Catholic Brighton clergy, including the Revd Arthur Cocks, who by 1913 was the Roman Catholic priest of Hove. In 1911 and 1917 Freeman's address was 10 Cromwell Road, and in 1923, 3 Ranelagh Villas, both in Hove.

By 1916, when *Spiritual Papers* and *God's Golden Gifts* were published, Freeman had clearly become a Roman Catholic. She wrote of the 'gift' of conversion, and compared the chaotic state of the Anglican church with the certainties offered by the Church of Rome. The preface to the latter work was by Monsignor Hugh Benson (1871–1914), another convert.

In 1916 Freeman initiated Roman Catholic guiding in the Brighton area, and she remained captain of the 6th Hove company until March 1923. Like the 11th and 23rd Brighton guide companies, this was one of the eight companies already affiliated to the Catholic Women's League Girl Guides, affiliated to the guide movement, when the league's standing committee of guide leaders was launched in 1920. It was clearly an active and successful company. In February 1921 the Brighton Catholic Women's League branch (founded in December 1908) reported, 'It is very gratifying to learn that the splendid work done by Miss Freeman in connection with the Girl Guides has been publicly recognized by the local Commissioner' (*Catholic Women's League Magazine*, no. 112, 1921, 4).

On the Right Trail: Friendly Counsel for Catholic Girl Guides (1921) was very favourably reviewed in the *Girl Guides Gazette* and in the *Catholic Women's League Magazine* of January 1922. It was prefaced and recommended by Cardinal Bourne, archbishop of Westminster, who had taken a particular interest in promoting Catholic Girl Guides. Although it was the first book to incorporate the moral principles of guiding within a Roman Catholic devotional context, it was apparently considered as helpful for all guides. Like *God's Golden Gifts* (dedicated to Monsignor Connelly), this work was dedicated to the current Roman Catholic parish priest of Hove—another convert, the 'Right Rev Monsignor Canon Thomas Ottley, to whose ever-ready help and sympathy I owe so much'.

In April 1919 the Brighton Catholic Women's League branch reported 'with pleasure' the reopening of the girls' club (founded in 1909) 'under Miss Freeman—who is so well known for her good work among girls' (*Catholic Women's League Magazine*, no. 90, 1919, 7). Club members' activities (like those of Freeman's guides) included drilling, first aid, gardening, ethnic dancing, and the production of plays and an operetta, which were so successful financially that the club often presented cheques to the Catholic Women's League branch. The girls' club also successfully entered the competitions of the Brighton and Hove Girls' Club Union.

By 1925 Freeman was a member of the third order of St Francis, a Roman Catholic lay order, affiliated to the mainstream order for monks. *Thoughts from St Francis of Assisi* (1925), the third of a series published by Burns, Oates, and Washbourne, was also well reviewed in the *Catholic Women's League Magazine*. This work had a foreword by Father Cuthbert of the order of St Francis Capuchin, who was superior of the Capuchin house in Oxford. By contrast with Freeman's earlier works, all the commentaries were by Roman Catholics.

Through practical action and writing, Freeman made an important contribution to the creation of a nationwide organization, the National Organization of Girls' Clubs (founded in 1911), which was renamed the National Association of Girls' Clubs and Mixed Clubs in 1945. That Freeman's club and guide work was appreciated by contemporaries is indicated by the comments of clergy and frequent references and advertisements in the *Girls' Club Journal* from 1909 to 1914 and the *Catholic Women's League Magazine* from 1919 to 1925. The case studies cited by Freeman indicate that at least some working-class girls did enjoy and benefit from her clubs and her personal care for them.

Apart from dedications to her mother, 'S. A. D.', 'my girl friends', and Grace Stephenson, Freeman's books suggest that some of her most important relationships were with clergy, both Anglo-Catholic and Roman Catholic. She was one of a number of Roman Catholic women writers around the turn of the century and is listed in *The Guide to Catholic Literature*. Her places of residence and contacts reflect the strength of Anglo-Catholicism and Roman Catholicism in London and Brighton and on the south coast.

MARY CLARE MARTIN

Sources F. L. Freeman, *Religious and social work amongst girls* (1901) • F. L. Freeman, *Our working girls and how to help them* (1908) • F. L. Freeman, *God's golden gifts* (1916) • *Girls' Club Journal: the Organ of the Federation of Working Girls' Clubs*, 1/1 (1909), 21 • *Girls' Club Journal: the Organ of the Federation of Working Girls' Clubs*, 1/2 (1909), 39, 47 • *Girls' Club Journal: the Organ of the Federation of Working Girls' Clubs*, 1/3 (1909), 60–62 • *Girls' Club Journal: the Organ of the Federation of Working Girls' Clubs*, 2/4 (1910), 2, 24 • *Girls' Club Journal: the Organ of the Federation of Working Girls' Clubs*, 3/7 (1911), 7–8, 38–9 • *Girls' Club Journal: the Organ of the Federation of Working Girls' Clubs*, 3/9 (1911), 69 • *Girls' Club Journal: the Organ of the Federation of Working Girls' Clubs*, 4/10 (1912), 8–9, 25 • *Girls' Club Journal: the Organ of the Federation of Working Girls' Clubs*, 4/12 (1912), 74 • *Girls' Club Journal: the Organ of the Federation of Working Girls' Clubs*, 6/16 (1914), 24 • *Federation of Working Girls' Clubs: handbooks on club work, no. 1: The club leader, the club member and the club* (1917), 12 • *Catholic Women's League Magazine*, 90 (1919), 7 • *Catholic Women's League Magazine*, 101 (1920), 1; 102 (1920), 1–2; 103 (1920), 14; 105 (1920), 6; 106 (1920), 6; 110 (1920), 4 • *Catholic Women's League Magazine*, 112 (1921), 4; 121 (1921), 13 • *Catholic Women's League Magazine*, 123 (1922), 18; 124 (1922), 3; 129 (1922), 8 • *Catholic Women's*

League Magazine, 160 (1925), 16; 163 (1925), 15 · *The guide to Catholic literature, 1888–1940* (1940) · warrant returned by Miss F. L. Freeman, captain of 6th Hove C.W.L., 12 March 1923, Guide Association, archive dept, WR 12.6.24 · F. L. Freeman, *A chain of thought for the church's year* (1905) · F. L. Freeman, *The sunshine of everyday life* (1903) · F. L. Freeman, *The clouds of life* (1911) · F. L. Freeman, *On the right trail: friendly counsel for Catholic Girl Guides* (1921) · F. L. Freeman, *Thoughts from St Francis of Assisi, selected and arranged for every day in the year* (1925) · *A handbook on club work* (1921), 27, 31 · *Annual Report* [Federation of Working Girls' Clubs] (1914), 25 · *Annual Report* [Federation of Working Girls' Clubs] (1921), 27 · *Girls' clubs directory: National Organisation of Girls' Clubs*, 3rd edn (1913), 24, 32, 38–9 · *Catholic Directory* (1913–14); (1916); (1920) · *3rd report of the Catholic Women's League for 1910*, 19, 36 · Crockford (1901) · Crockford (1906) · Crockford (1910) · Crockford (1913) · Crockford (1926) · private information (2004) [Joan Bond] · H. P. Adam, *Women in council: the jubilee book of the National Council of Women of Great Britain* (1945), 97–9 · M. Rooff, *Youth and leisure: a survey of girls' organisations in England and Wales* (1935), 186

Wealth at death £4043 4s. od.: probate, 20 Nov 1925, *CGPLA Eng. & Wales*

Freeman, Gage Earle (1820–1903), Church of England clergyman and writer on falconry, born on 3 June 1820 at Tamworth, Staffordshire, was the son of Captain Charles Earle Freeman of the 69th regiment and his wife, Mary Parsons. After a private education he was admitted a pensioner at St John's College, Cambridge, in 1840; he graduated BA in 1845, and proceeded MA in 1850.

Ordained deacon in 1846 and priest in 1847, Freeman held a curacy at Geddington, Northamptonshire, from 1846 to 1854. On 5 January 1848 he married Christiana (d. 1886), daughter of John Slade of Little Lever, Bolton-le-Moors, Lancashire; they had a family of eight sons and two daughters. From 1854 to 1856 he held the perpetual cure of Emmanuel Church, Bolton-le-Moors. In 1856 he was presented by the earl of Derby to the living of Macclesfield Forest with Clough, Cheshire, where he was incumbent until 1889, when he became vicar of Askham, Westmorland (near Penrith), and private chaplain to the earl of Lonsdale. This living he held until his death. In later life he won at Cambridge four Seatonian prizes for poems on sacred subjects, 'The Transfiguration' (1882), 'Jericho' (1888), 'Damascus' (1893), and 'The Broad and the Narrow Way' (1894).

Through life Freeman devoted his leisure to hawking, having been introduced to the sport by William Brodrick of Belford, Northumberland, afterwards of Chudleigh, Devon. Having begun with a kestrel, he soon progressed to more demanding raptors. He successfully trained sparrowhawks and merlins for hunting blackbirds and pigeons, and larks and ring ousel respectively. He had his best sport while in his Cheshire parish, hawking grouse with peregrines on Buxton Moor and Swythamley, the property of his friend Philip Brocklehurst of Swythamley Park, Staffordshire. Next to peregrines, Freeman preferred goshawks, with which he hunted hares and rabbits. Lord Lilford affirmed that Freeman did more to keep English falconers in the right way than any of his contemporaries (preface to *Lord Lilford on Birds*, 1903). Indeed, his expertise and insight were much referred to in falconry literature.

Freeman contributed articles on falconry to *The Field* for

a quarter of a century over the signature Peregrine. These were mostly concerned with the training of merlins and game-hawking with eyas peregrines. In collaboration with Francis Henry Salvin he produced *Falconry: its Claims, History, and Practice* (1859), a handbook for beginners. Freeman's *Practical Falconry: and How I Became a Falconer* (1869) was slightly more discursive but highly regarded. Freeman's essay 'On the desirability of attempting to revive the sport of falconry by its practice at Alexandra Park' (1871) won the second prize (the first being taken by Captain C. Hawkins Fisher of Stroud) in a competition held by the Barnet committee for promoting the opening of Alexandra Park. The essay questioned the very basis of public exhibitions of hawks and the claim of such exhibitions to constitute falconry proper.

Following the death of his first wife, Freeman was married again in April 1891, this time to Mary, daughter of Francis William Ashton, cotton spinner and calico printer, of Hyde, Cheshire. He died at the vicarage, Askham, on 15 December 1903, and was buried at Macclesfield Forest Chapel.

G. Le G. Norgate, *rev.* Gordon T. Mellor

Sources *The Field* (19 Dec 1903) · *The Times* (16 Dec 1903) · *Penrith Observer* (22 Dec 1903) · *Mid Cumberland and North Westmorland Gazette* (19 Dec 1903) · *The Eagle*, 25 (1904), 197–8 · G. Lascelles, *The art of falconry* (1892) · R. Upton, *A bird in the hand* (1980) · R. Upton, *O for a falconer's voice* (1987) · E. B. Michell, *The art and practice of hawking* (1900) · J. E. Harting, *Bibliotheca accipitraria: a catalogue of books ... relating to falconry* (1891) · J. Maurogordato, *A hawk for the bush* (1960) · C. H. Fisher, *Reminiscences of a falconer* (1901) · Venn, *Alum. Cant.*

Likenesses photograph, repro. in Upton, *O for a falconer's voice*, 52 · photograph, repro. in Upton, *Bird in the hand*, 27 · photograph, repro. in Fisher, *Reminiscences of a falconer*, 55

Wealth at death £642 17s. 11d.: probate, 11 Feb 1904, *CGPLA Eng. & Wales*

Freeman, John (d. 1614). *See under* Freeman, John (c.1560–1596).

Freeman, John (c.1560–1596), divine, is first recorded at Michaelmas 1575, when he matriculated sizar at Trinity College, Cambridge. Admitted scholar in 1580, he graduated BA in 1581, became a fellow in 1583, proceeded MA in 1584, and died at Trinity twelve years later. An inventory of his goods and a bond obligatory, resulting from a grant of letters of administration and signed by four kinsmen— Edward, Thomas, John, and George Freeman—survive among the probate archives of Cambridge University, dated 24 July 1596.

On the basis of this slender evidence it was assumed by Thompson Cooper that this John Freeman was identifiable with the John Freeman who was town preacher of Lewes, Sussex, and dedicated to the congregation there his treatise *The Comforter, or, A Comfortable Treatise, Wherein are Contained Many Reasons Taken out of the Word, to Assure the Forgiveness of Sinnes to the Conscience that is Troubled with the Feeling Thereof, &c* (1591). Later editions dating from 1600, 1606, and 1622 are extant. As a result of this attribution it was further assumed that he must have been the author of two sermons on Romans 8: 2–28 and 11: 2–8, both apparently published separately in 1611 but no longer extant.

The lost sermons, however, were undoubtedly written by **John Freeman** (d. 1614), perhaps the man of that name who matriculated sizar from Peterhouse at Easter 1578 and/or the John Freeman who signed the above-mentioned bond obligatory. He was instituted vicar of Felsted, Essex, on 6 March 1595 on the presentation of Robert, third Lord Rich. Since Rich was the foremost patron of godly preachers in Essex it seems more likely that this John Freeman, and not John Freeman of Trinity, was the author of *The Comforter*.

Freeman established a friendship with George Manning, headmaster of Felsted School, and became involved in school activities. Unlike other Rich protégés he chose to conform in the aftermath of the Hampton Court conference (1604), and in 1609 the printer Nathaniel Butter brought out his *Apologie for the Conformable Ministers of England, for their Subscription to the Present Church Government*. It was dedicated to Richard Bancroft, archbishop of Canterbury, and Thomas Ravis, bishop of London.

Freeman made his will as vicar of Felsted on 7 April 1614. He mentions no children. His wife and executrix, Elizabeth, was to discharge family legacies, two of them to be paid 'out of that money which Mr Butter, stationer of London, oweth me for books if she can recover the same of him' (PRO, PROB 11/124, fols. 221v–222). He had died by 11 July, when his successor was instituted to Felsted, and the will was proved in the prerogative court of Canterbury on 13 August.   BRETT USHER

Sources inventory and bond obligatory resulting from grant of administration to relatives of J. Freeman, 1596, CUL, department of manuscripts and university archives, vice-chancellor's court · Venn, *Alum. Cant.*, 1/2.177 · Cooper, *Ath. Cantab.*, 3.59 · exchequer, first-fruits and tenths office, bishops' certificates of institution, PRO, E 331/London/7, m.2 [institution to Felsted] · M. Craze, *A history of Felsted School* (1955) · will, 1614, PRO, PROB 11/124, sig. 93
Archives CUL
Wealth at death minimal; only effects of a Cambridge don; no property

Freeman, John (*fl. c.*1660–*c.*1732), painter, had some repute as a history painter in the reign of Charles II and was considered to be the rival of Isaac Fuller. In early life he went to the West Indies, where there was an attempt on his life by poisoning, which he survived. He returned to England, and was much employed, although it is stated that his narrow escape from death had an adverse effect on his subsequent work (Vertue, *Note books*). He was commissioned to paint a staircase at Belvoir Castle in 1686; however it is uncertain if this was completed as the castle was rebuilt in 1801. He also drew in Kneller's academy. A John Freeman was recorded as a scene painter to the playhouse in Covent Garden. However, this would indicate that either he was still active when that new playhouse opened in 1732, or that this was a different Freeman. Some plates in R. Blome's *History of the Old and New Testament* are probably from his designs.

L. H. CUST, *rev.* SARAH HERRING

Sources E. Croft-Murray, *Decorative painting in England, 1537–1837*, 1 (1962), 45–6, 219b–220a · E. K. Waterhouse, *The dictionary of British 16th and 17th century painters* (1988), 91 · Highfill, Burnim & Langhans, *BDA*, 5.408 · [B. Buckeridge], 'An essay towards an English

school', in R. de Piles, *The art of painting, with the lives and characters of above 300 of the most eminent painters*, 3rd edn (1754), 354–439; facs. edn (1969), esp. 373 · Redgrave, *Artists*, 2nd edn, 161 · H. Walpole, *Anecdotes of painting in England … collected by the late George Vertue, and now digested and published*, 3 (1763), 7 · Vertue, *Note books*, 2.147–8 · *The manuscripts of his grace the duke of Rutland*, 4 vols., HMC, 24 (1888–1905), vol. 2, p. 108

Freeman, John (1665/6–1736), singer, was a soloist in Henry Purcell's dramatic opera *The Fairy Queen* at Dorset Garden Theatre, London, in May 1692, and he remained one of Purcell's leading singers until the composer's death in November 1695. His name appears in Purcell's manuscripts for high tenor solos in his 1692 *Ode for St Cecilia's Day* and his 1695 *Ode on the Birthday of the Duke of Gloucester*. Freeman sang in Purcell's dramatic operas *The Prophetess, or, The History of Dioclesian*, with a libretto by Thomas Betterton from the play by Francis Beaumont and John Fletcher, in 1694 (and perhaps in its 1690 première), and *The Indian Queen*, where John Dryden was librettist (1695). In *The Prophetess*, Thomas D'Urfey's *Don Quixote*, part 2 (1694), and George Powell's *Bonduca* (1695) Purcell gave him martial songs with trumpet obbligato, and Daniel Purcell later wrote similar pieces for him. John Freeman sang in Jeremiah Clarke's *Ode on the Death of Mr. Henry Purcell* and remained a solo singer in the theatre until the end of the 1699–1700 season. He also taught singing and performed in concerts. Freeman joined the Chapel Royal choir in December 1700 and became a vicar-choral at St Paul's Cathedral in January 1702. He had been a lay vicar at Westminster Abbey in 1692–3 and rejoined the choir there in 1715, thereafter continuing as a member of all three choirs until his death. His name appears in manuscripts of church music by William Croft and of Handel's 1727 coronation music. A few songs composed by Freeman were published in the 1690s, and the tune of his popular success 'Pretty Parrot Say' was used for the air 'Pretty Polly Say' in *The Beggar's Opera*. Freeman married Avis Wallet (1671/2–1732) at the chapel of the Charterhouse, London, on 13 October 1692; their daughter Elizabeth became the wife of the organist and composer James Kent in 1738. John Freeman died on 10 December 1736 and was buried four days later in his wife's grave in the west cloister of Westminster Abbey; his memorial tablet gives his age at death as seventy.

OLIVE BALDWIN and THELMA WILSON

Sources W. Van Lennep and others, eds., *The London stage, 1660–1800*, pt 1: *1660–1700* (1965) · A. Ashbee, ed., *Records of English court music*, 2 (1987); 5 (1991) · A. Ashbee and J. Harley, eds., *The cheque books of the Chapel Royal*, 2 vols. (2000) · F. B. Zimmerman, *Henry Purcell, 1659–1695: an analytical catalogue of his music* (1963) · O. Baldwin and T. Wilson, 'Purcell's stage singers: a documentary list', *Performing the music of Henry Purcell* [Oxford 1993], ed. M. Burden (1996), 275–81 · C. L. Day and E. B. Murrie, *English song-books, 1651–1702: a bibliography with a first-line index of songs* (1940) · D. Hunter, *Opera and song books published in England, 1703–1726* (1997) · A. Ashbee and D. Lasocki, eds., *A biographical dictionary of English court musicians, 1485–1714*, 1 (1998) · O. Baldwin and T. Wilson, 'Alfred Deller, John Freeman and Mr Pate', *Music and Letters*, 50 (1969), 103–10 · W. Croft, 'Praise God in his sanctuary', Bodl. Oxf., MSS Mus. b. 15, f. 32 · W. Croft, 'I will always give thanks', BL, Add. MS 17847 · H. Purcell, 'Who can from joy refraine?', BL, Add. MS 30934 · G. F. Handel, music for the coronation of George II, 1727, BL, RM 20.h.5. ·

W. Croft, 'Come all ye tuneful sisters', Royal College of Music, London, MS 995 · F. Collins, ed., *The registers and monumental inscriptions of Charterhouse chapel*, Harleian Society, Register Section, 18 (1892) · J. L. Chester, ed., *The marriage, baptismal, and burial registers of the collegiate church or abbey of St Peter, Westminster*, Harleian Society, 10 (1876) · parish register, St Bride, Fleet Street, 11 Oct 1699 · administration, PRO, PROB 6/113 · memorial tablet, Westminster Abbey **Wealth at death** see administration, PRO, PROB 6/113

Freeman, John Frederick (1880–1929), poet and businessman, was born on 29 January 1880 at 5 Pownall Road, Haggerston, London, the eldest son of John Jacob Freeman, a commercial traveller, and his wife, Catherine Esther, *née* Botham, granddaughter of a captain in a regiment of guards. His father, whose family came from Wiltshire and Sussex, was born in London and lived there all his life. Freeman was a sickly child. At three he suffered from an attack of scarlet fever which his friends and family identified as the cause of his later heart trouble. He went to school in Hackney until just before his thirteenth birthday. He was then sent to work as a junior clerk in the head offices in Southampton Row, London, of the Liverpool Victoria Friendly Society, one of Britain's largest health insurance companies in the days before the National Health Service. In the early years of his working life Freeman continued his education on his own. He taught himself to read classical Greek and became very knowledgeable about English poetry—especially that of Swinburne, Coventry Patmore, and Matthew Arnold. At eighteen he began to write his own poetry. On 30 June 1902 Freeman married Gertrude Frances Farren, daughter of Samuel Farren, a picture-frame maker, originally of Colchester and later of Dalston; the couple lived in south London at 29 Weighton Road, Anerley, near Crystal Palace, and had two daughters.

Freeman published his first volume of poetry, *Twenty Poems*, in 1909 and *Fifty Poems* in 1911, but his reputation was made with *Stone Trees* in 1916. He kept his business and literary careers strictly separate and few of the many writers with whom he corresponded were aware of his work at the Liverpool Victoria. He was part of a circle of Georgian poets, including Walter de la Mare and Alice Meynell, who were influential in inter-war literary circles. He published ten books of poetry including *Memories of Childhood* (1919), *Poems New and Old* (1920), which won the Hawthornden prize, *Music* (1921), and *The Grove* (1924). *Solomon and Balkis* is a fantasy based on the legends of the queen of Sheba and King Solomon. His *Collected Poems* was issued in 1928. Freeman lived in London all his life but his poetry was exclusively pastoral; his writing is lush and lyrical and he has a characteristic trick of repeating a word or phrase in order to emphasize the rhythm. Many of his poems use the natural world—especially trees, fire, and weather—as an extended metaphor for the human condition, as in 'Stone Trees':

> Last night a sword-light in the sky
> Flashed a swift terror on the dark.
> In that sharp light the fields did lie
> Naked and stone-like; each tree stood
> Like a tranced woman, bound and stark.

This, however, is treated in a relatively abstract way, and none of his poems deals with society or politics. Freeman was a lifelong Methodist and also a local preacher, and his religious interests found their way into his only play, *Prince Absalom* (1925). A critic for *The Academy*, the *New Statesman*, and the *London Mercury*, he wrote four volumes of literary criticism including *Portrait of George Moore* (1922) and *Herman Melville* (1926).

Freeman worked for the Liverpool Victoria Friendly Society all his life, beginning at the lowest possible position and rising rapidly through the organization until finally, in 1927, he was promoted to secretary and director. During an exceptional career he supervised the operations of over 7000 staff and contracts and funds of £20 million. His friend Sir John Squire described him as being 'more like a clerkly poet than a director' (*Letters*). He was a tall, slightly stooping man who moved rather slowly. His face was small and full-lipped and he wore glasses. He was a private man who, despite his large correspondence, disliked talking about himself; his letters are full of chatter, ruminations, and views on literature but they contain few personal details about either himself or his family.

For the last sixteen years of his life Freeman suffered from a weak heart and on 23 September 1929 he died at his home of heart failure. His wife survived him. He was buried, at his request, in the country churchyard of Thursley, Surrey. The National Trust maintains a field adjoining the churchyard dedicated by his friends to his memory.

Another volume of poetry, *Last Poems*, and a collection of letters were published posthumously. Freeman was never widely known either during his lifetime or afterwards but he was well regarded by contemporary critics.

SOPHIA CRESWELL

Sources *John Freeman's letters*, ed. G. Freeman and J. C. Squire (1936) · J. Freeman, *Last poems* (1930) · J. Freeman, *Collected poems* (1928) · *The Times* (26 Sept 1929) · *The Observer* (29 Sept 1929) · J. Freeman, *English portraits and essays* (1924) · *The insurance mail yearbook* (1930) · private information (2004) · J. A. Vickers, ed., *A dictionary of Methodism in Britain and Ireland* (2000) · b. cert. · m. cert. · d. cert.
Archives State University of New York, Buffalo, MSS and letters | BL, corresp. with Macmillans, Add. MS 55011 · Indiana University, Bloomington, Mottram MSS · NL Scot., letters to Alexander Gray · Somerville College, Oxford, letters to Percy Withers and family
Likenesses L. Knight, charcoal drawing, *c*.1928, NPG; repro. in Freeman, *Collected poems* · W. Rothenstein, portrait, repro. in J. Freeman, *Music* (1921)

Freeman, John Peere Williams- (1858–1943), archaeologist, was born on 13 April 1858 at Hamble Cliff, near Southampton, the youngest son of Frederick Peere Williams-Freeman (1815–1870), landowner, of Greatham, Sussex, and his wife, Augusta Sarah (*d.* 1897), daughter of Captain Henry Edward Napier RN FRS. He was educated at Haileybury College and at the Royal Military Academy, Woolwich (1876–8). He obtained a commission in the Royal Artillery, but resigned it soon afterwards for family reasons and studied medicine, first in London at University College Hospital and then at Durham University, taking the degree of MB in 1885 and MD in 1888. From 1889 until 1928 he practised at Weyhill, Hampshire, and held also several clinical appointments. On 16 November 1897

Williams-Freeman married his cousin, Mabel Christiana, daughter of Charles George Napier; they had one son and five daughters, the son and one daughter dying in infancy. On retirement he went to live at Botley, Hampshire, but eventually returned to his former region, living at Thruxton, near Andover.

Although of no mean standing in the medical profession, it was as an archaeologist that Williams-Freeman earned his chief claim to recognition. From youth onwards his interests were widespread; he was a clear and original thinker and an accurate observer. In 1901 he met a near neighbour, Percy Farrer, who stimulated his growing interest in the prehistoric earthworks around Weyhill. Other contacts followed and in 1915 he published his book *Field Archaeology as Illustrated by Hampshire*, a model of its kind. It was the first book to attempt to set prehistoric man in his natural environment of vegetation, a method that in time became standard procedure.

Williams-Freeman did no excavation but was first and foremost a field archaeologist, having himself invented that term. In the course of his medical practice he was able to observe the countryside and its natural features. He particularly noted the reaction of the crops to silted-up prehistoric ditches and the like, and realized, before air photography, how informative air photographs would be to the prehistorian. He often discussed these matters with O. G. S. Crawford, and when eventually chance put before him a set of air photographs of his own region, he showed them to the latter, to whom it fell to develop an important new technique. Crawford's works *Air Survey and Archaeology* (1924) and *Air Photography for Archaeologists* (1929) followed.

Williams-Freeman was essentially an alert-minded countryman, bringing to bear upon archaeology a good brain well disciplined by professional training. Although one of the last and best of the amateur, that is, part-time, archaeologists of the nineteenth century, he belonged rather to the twentieth in his methods and outlook, which were those of modern professional archaeologists. He died at his home, Tarvers, Thruxton, on 20 December 1943.   O. G. S. CRAWFORD, rev. MARK POTTLE

Sources *Papers and Proceedings of the Hampshire Field Club and Archaeological Society* (1944) · Burke, *Gen. GB* (1952) · personal knowledge (1959)
Archives Sussex Archaeological Society, corresp. and research papers relating to Chichester · Winchester Museums Service Historic Resources Centre, corresp. and papers, incl. MS chapters of unpublished work on field archaeology | Winchester Museums Service Historic Resources Centre, corresp. with G. H. M. Summer
Wealth at death £7512 13s. 3d.: probate, 1944, *CGPLA Eng. & Wales*

Freeman, Philip (1818–1875), Church of England clergyman, was born on 3 February 1818 at The Cedars, Combs, Suffolk, the son of Edmund Freeman and his wife, Margaret, daughter of William Hughes of Wexford, Ireland. He attended Dedham grammar school, Essex, under Dr George Taylor before matriculating at Trinity College, Cambridge, in October 1835. Elected to a college scholarship in 1837, he was awarded Sir William Browne's medals for a Latin ode and epigrams and a Craven university

scholarship in 1838. He graduated BA as senior classic in 1839 and, after being chosen fellow and tutor of Peterhouse, in 1842 took his MA degree. He was ordained deacon (Norwich) in 1842 and priest in 1844.

Freeman was a stalwart member of the Cambridge Camden Society. He published *Thoughts on the Dissolution of the Camden Society* (1845), arguing dissolution was preferable to dilution of the society's Christian principles. He married Ann, youngest daughter of the Revd Henry Hervey *Baber, at Stretham, Ely, on 18 August 1846. Ann was born on 11 February 1821 and survived her husband. They had two sons and two daughters.

Freeman was chosen by Ashurst Turner Gilbert as principal of the Theological College, Chichester, and served from 1846 to 1848. As an Anglo-Catholic, Freeman saw the purpose of a theological college as cultivating the holy vocation, rather than practical training or theological study. He published his views in *A Plea for the Education of the Clergy* (1851). A feature of his successful principalship at Chichester was the admission of non-graduate candidates for the ministry. He was a canon and a reader in theology in Cumbrae College (the college built by the earl of Glasgow in the island of Cumbrae, Buteshire) from 1853 to 1858, having at the same time charge of the episcopal church on the island.

Freeman was presented by the dean and chapter of Exeter to the vicarage of Thorverton, Devon, in 1858; he was appointed a prebendary of Exeter Cathedral in November 1861 and one of the four residentiary canons in 1864 by Bishop Philpotts, to whom he acted as examining chaplain. He was appointed archdeacon of Exeter in April 1865. He spent considerable time and money on the restoration of the cathedral at Exeter and his parish church at Thorverton. He was an authority on liturgical questions. Together with other ecclesiologists he assisted in the publication of *Directorium Anglicanum* (1858), an attempt to demonstrate the legality of medieval ornaments in the Anglican church. He also contributed articles to *The Guardian*, the *Christian Remembrancer*, and *The Ecclesiologist*. In 1869, at the meeting of the British Association in Exeter, he protested in energetic language against some of the views propounded by Professor T. H. Huxley on Darwinism. In 1871 he described Darwinism as 'the most easily refuted sophism of the day' (*The Guardian*, 1871, 681). In 1866 he also engaged in a controversy with Archdeacon Denison as to the real presence. After an accident in alighting from a train at Chalk Farm Station, London, Freeman died from his injuries at the residence of Thomas Gambier, surgeon, 1 Northumberland Terrace, Primrose Hill, London, on 24 February 1875. He was buried in Thorverton churchyard on 2 March.

G. C. BOASE, rev. ELLIE CLEWLOW

Sources *The Times* (26 Feb 1875), 8 · *The Times* (1 March 1875), 8 · *ILN* (6 March 1875), 223 · *ILN* (13 March 1875), 257–8 · *ILN* (24 April 1875), 403 · *Trewman's Exeter Flying Post* (3 March 1875), 5 · private information (1889) · T. A. Walker, ed., *Admissions to Peterhouse or St Peter's College in the University of Cambridge* (1912) · Venn, *Alum. Cant.* · J. F. White, *The Cambridge movement: the ecclesiologists and the Gothic revival* (1962) · A. Haig, *The Victorian clergy* (1984) · B. Heeney, *A different kind of gentleman: parish clergy as professional men in early and mid-*

Victorian England (1976) • O. Chadwick, *The Victorian church*, 2 (1970) • *The Guardian* (3 March 1875)
Wealth at death under £25,000: probate, 9 April 1875, *CGPLA Eng. & Wales*

Freeman, Sir Ralph (*d.* 1667), government official and author, was the son of Martin Freeman, of the parish of Betchworth, Surrey, and of Elizabeth Laurence. Admitted to the Middle Temple in 1606, it is only from 1618 that Freeman comes more clearly into focus. By then he was knighted; married to Catherine Brett, a near relative of George Villiers, the future duke of Buckingham; and appointed in succession to Sir Richard Naunton, one of the masters of requests in ordinary. In the following year he was a commissioner to appoint manufacturers of starch. Thereafter he was to enjoy mixed fortunes: in 1624 he failed to become ambassador to Venice; in 1625 he did not gain the provostship of Eton College; and in 1639 he was outdone in his bid to succeed as master of the rolls (a prize which was to cost Sir Charles Caesar, son of Sir Julius, no less than £15,000). On the other hand, in 1622 he gained with George Bingley the reversion of one of the two auditorships of the imposts in the exchequer and one of the two auditorships in the mint; and both these posts he went on to exercise, despite the opposition in respect of the former of Sir Giles Mompesson. Subsequently, aided by Buckingham, Sir Ralph was elected MP for Winchelsea in 1625 and again in 1628. As one of the few members who were also gentlemen of the bedchamber, he was entrusted with carrying messages from the House of Commons to the king. By now a man of substance, Freeman purchased in 1627 the rectory and parsonage impropriate of Leigh, Surrey, with its capital messuage; and then, in 1629 for £1080, in the same county, the manor of East Betchworth. On this he built Betchworth Place.

In 1635 he was made one of the newly instituted searchers and sealers of all foreign hops imported into England and a commissioner for the master-workership at the mint. This office, worth £500 per annum, he shared with Sir Thomas Aylesbury, a fellow master of requests, with whom he had already served in 1627 as commissioner for the seizure of French goods and ships in England and was to serve again in 1636 as commissioner to oversee the execution of the proclamations for the regulation of gold and silver thread. In the following year Freeman petitioned Charles I for permission to recover concealed lands in Denbigh and on 20 June 1639 gained with others, in return for a down payment of £20,000, a grant on impositions levied on coal shipped from the Tyne.

In the civil war Freeman was a royalist, travelling to Oxford in 1643, forfeiting his post at the mint, and subsequently being fined by parliament. On his London house, in St Martin-in-the-Fields, the committee for the advance of money assessed him at £400 while the committee on compounding demanded £800, with an additional £530 for his interest on coal. It was not until 1650 that his whole fine was paid and his estate discharged. Precisely what Sir Ralph's movements were during these years is not very clear. But, according to his own account in a petition to Charles II, he served in Ireland under Ormond and then in

the Isles of Scilly where he was captured at sea and taken prisoner to Portsmouth. Released, so he said, under the articles of 23 May 1651 (though the order to this effect went out from the council of state on 17 August 1650), his participation in the unsuccessful engagement at Worcester (3 September) forced him into exile. Subsequently he obviously returned to England, for he was obliged in 1655 and 1656 to obtain licences to go up to and reside in London; but then, once again, he returned to the continent. On 12 May 1660 Pepys recorded his being in the channel aboard the frigate *Lark*, 'going from the King to England'.

At the Restoration (Aylesbury then being dead), Sir Ralph became sole master worker at the mint and was to remain so until 1662 when Henry Slingsby, his deputy, became joint patentee. Though undoubtedly it was Slingsby who then became senior partner, having principal responsibility for the new method of coin production by mill and press, Freeman remained in touch, keeping the mint informed of events at court.

In addition to making his mark at court, in the mint, and elsewhere, Freeman was notable for his publications: two translations into English from Seneca, the *Booke of Consolation to Marcia* (1635) and the *Booke of the Shortnesse of Life* (1636), and *Imperiale*, on which Langbaine opined that, though he did not know if it had ever been performed, 'it far better deserv'd to have appear'd on the Theatre than many of our modern Farces that have usurp'd the Stage' (p. 226). Although this tragedy first appeared in print in 1639 it did so seemingly without Freeman's knowledge, for in his dedication of the 1655 edition he was subsequently to claim that it had never been intended for 'the open world' and was only then appearing through the 'importunity of some friends … to prevent a surreptitious publication intended from an erroneous copy'.

Freeman's will was dated 1 June 1667; on 12 June he was described as 'late'. According to his will, which was proved on 29 August, he was to be buried in Betchworth church, in his own vault next to his wife and relatives. His elder son and heir, Ralph, had two sons both of whom died without issue. Through the marriage of Elizabeth, daughter and heir of Ralph, East Betchworth passed to the family of Bouverie. Sir Ralph's other son, George (*d.* 1678), to whom he left all his plate, pictures, and household possessions, was the father of Ralph, MP for Reigate in 1679 and 1681.

C. E. CHALLIS

Sources *CSP dom.* • M. A. E. Green, ed., *Calendar of the proceedings of the committee for compounding … 1643–1660*, 5 vols., PRO (1889–92) • M. A. E. Green, ed., *Calendar of the proceedings of the committee for advance of money, 1642–1656*, 3 vols., PRO (1888) • C. E. Challis, 'Mint officials and moneyers of the Stuart period', *British Numismatic Journal*, 59 (1989), 157–97 • APC • J. K. Gruenfelder, 'The lord wardens and elections, 1604–1628', *Journal of British Studies*, 16/1 (1976–7), 1–23 • G. Langbaine, *An account of the English dramatick poets* (1691) • R. C. Johnson and others, eds., *Proceedings in parliament, 1628*, 5 (1983) • *VCH Surrey*, vol. 3 • [E. S. de Beer], '*DNB*: Sir Ralph Freeman', *BIHR*, 17 (1939–40), 46 • PRO, PROB 11/324 • J. S. Crosette, 'Freeman, Ralph (*c.*1655–86)', HoP, *Commons* • *STC, 1475–1640* • R. Freeman, *Imperiale* (1655) • *The visitation of London, anno Domini 1633, 1634, and 1635, made by Sir Henry St George*, 1, ed. J. J. Howard and J. L. Chester, Harleian Society, 15 (1880) • Pepys, *Diary*, 1.135

Archives PRO, official papers, PRO E 351, PRO AOI

Freeman, Sir Ralph (1880–1950), civil engineer, was born on 27 November 1880 at 88 Rendlesham Road, West Hackney, London, the third son of George James Freeman, a cigar manufacturer, and his wife, Edith Marion Henderson. He was educated at the Haberdashers' Aske's School, Hampstead, and in 1897 won a Siemens scholarship to the Central Technical College in Kensington, where he was an outstanding student. He was not only an Institute's scholar and a Samuel scholar but on leaving in 1900 was awarded the Siemens medal in civil and mechanical engineering. The following year he joined Sir Douglas Fox & Partners, consulting engineers, London. On 14 July 1908 he married Mary Lines (*b.* 1883/4), the second daughter of Joseph Lines, a toymaker, of Stoke Newington, London, and his wife, Jane Fitzhenry. They had three sons, including Sir Ralph *Freeman (1911–1998), and a daughter.

In his early years with Fox, Freeman was involved in parliamentary work regarding London's underground railways, and with railways in the environs of Manchester and Cork. In 1903 he assisted G. A. Hobson in the design of the braced-steel arch bridge over the Zambezi at the Victoria Falls, completed in 1905. He was engaged in the construction of the Cleveland Bridge and Engineering Company's factory and, upon his appointment as consulting engineer to the Beit Trust in 1906, he designed and supervised the construction of the Alfred Beit Bridge, and later the Otto Beit and Birchenough bridges, in Northern and Southern Rhodesia. He was responsible, too, for railways in both Africa and Brazil. He became a partner of the firm in 1912 and assumed responsibility for works as varied as a harbour at Beira in Mozambique and a ropeway 50 miles long in Colombia, and for reporting on railways in Illinois. During the First World War he supervised the construction of railways and other works at Nobel's Explosive Company factory, the building and equipping of a cordite factory for the Admiralty, the Furness shipbuilding yard, and the Royal Naval Propellant factory. He became a senior partner in Fox in 1921; in 1938 the firm changed its name to Freeman, Fox & Partners and he remained in active control until his death.

Freeman's most important work was in connection with the Sydney harbour bridge. He was retained in 1922 by the Cleveland Bridge and Engineering Company to prepare designs for the bridge but, on the death of the company's chairman the following year, its tendering for the project was abandoned. However, Dorman, Long & Co. tendered with designs prepared by Freeman and G. C. Imbault, the company's chief engineer, and upon being awarded the contract Freeman was appointed their consulting engineer. His designs had secured the contract for Britain in the face of world competition. Dorman Long established a department under Freeman in London to produce all the detailed drawings and calculations needed to construct and erect the bridge. It was of the two-hinged spandrel braced-arch type with a clear span of 1650 feet and a deck 160 feet wide to accommodate four railway tracks, a roadway 57 feet wide, and two footways each 10

Sir Ralph Freeman (1880–1950), by Elliott & Fry, 1949

feet wide. It was the heaviest bridge yet built, weighing 50,000 tons; its building involved the use of structural members of unprecedented weight and dimensions. After eight years' work it was completed in 1932.

A series of papers describing the Sydney harbour bridge was given to the Institution of Civil Engineers (ICE) in 1934. Freeman's paper dealt with the design of its structure and foundations. The ICE awarded him both a Telford gold medal for the paper and the first Baker gold medal in recognition of the development in engineering practice as described by the paper. With co-author Lawrence Ennis, director of constructional operations in Sydney, another published paper on the manufacture of the structural steelwork and erection of the bridge received a Telford premium. Freeman had a long association with the ICE, joining as a student member in 1898. He was awarded a Miller prize for his 1906 paper, 'The design of a two-hinged spandrel-braced steel arch'. He became an associate member in 1907, transferring to full membership in 1917, and he served on its council from 1937 to 1942. He was also a member of the American Society of Civil Engineers.

For several years in the 1920s Freeman gave series of lectures on structural engineering to fourth-year students at the Central Technical College in London and on long-span bridges to the University of London. He was elected a fellow of the City and Guilds Institute in 1932 and, in the same year, became one of the first nine fellows of the Imperial College of Science and Technology in London. He was president of the Institute of Welding from 1942 to 1944 and a member of the Royal Fine Arts Commission from 1939 to 1948. During the Second World War he was chairman of the structural engineering committee of the Advisory Council on Scientific Research and Technical Development of the Ministry of Supply, and he acted as an assessor to the committee on armaments development. In 1947 Freeman received a knighthood. Prior to his death he was engaged on designs for the River Severn suspension bridge, with a span of 3300 feet, and a 3500 foot long bridge across Auckland harbour in New Zealand, as well as buildings for the forthcoming Festival of Britain. Ralph Freeman died at his home, Graden, Hendon Avenue, Finchley, Middlesex, on 11 March 1950. He was survived by his wife.   ROBERT SHARP

Sources personal knowledge (1959) [*DNB*] · private information (1959) · *WWW* · *The Times* (14 March 1950), 9e · *Journal of the Institution of Civil Engineers*, 34 (1949–50), 276 · *The Engineer* (17 March 1950), 334 · *Engineering* (17 March 1950), 302 · b. cert. · m. cert. · d. cert. · *CGPLA Eng. & Wales* (1950)
Likenesses Elliott & Fry, photograph, 1949, NPG [*see illus.*]
Wealth at death £44,695 9s. 7d.: probate, 23 Sept 1950, *CGPLA Eng. & Wales*

Freeman, Sir Ralph (1911–1998), civil engineer, was born on 3 February 1911 at Graden, Hendon Avenue, Church End, Finchley, Middlesex, the eldest son among the three sons and one daughter of Sir Ralph *Freeman (1880–1950), civil engineer, later senior partner in the firm of Freeman, Fox & Partners, consulting engineers, and his wife, Mary, *née* Lines (*b.* 1883/4, *d.* in or after 1950). His father was consulting engineer for the Sydney harbour bridge, completed in 1932. He was educated at Uppingham School and at Worcester College, Oxford, where he graduated in 1932 with a second in engineering science. During his university vacations he worked for the steel fabricators Dorman, Long & Co. on the construction of Lambeth Bridge, and the widening of Putney Bridge, over the Thames, and in 1932 he joined the firm as a construction engineer. During the 1930s he worked on three important bridges: in Southern Rhodesia he was involved in the construction of the Otto Beit Bridge, a suspension bridge across the Zambezi, with a span of 1050 feet, and the Birchenough Bridge over the Sabi River, an arch bridge with a 1080 foot span. His father had done the engineering calculations for both of these. In Denmark he worked on the Storstrøm Bridge, a 2 mile multi-span railway bridge. He worked briefly, from 1936 to 1937, for Braithwaite & Co. on an oil pipeline jetty in the Medway River. In 1939 he married Joan Elizabeth, elder daughter of Colonel J. G. Rose of Wynberg, Cape, South Africa: they had two sons and one daughter.

In 1939 Freeman left Dorman Long to join Freeman, Fox & Partners in order to work on the design and construction of the Royal Naval propellant factory in Caer-went, Monmouthshire. He was commissioned in the Royal Engineers in 1943, and was posted as a captain to the experimental bridging establishment in Christchurch, Hampshire, where he helped to develop a special military suspension bridge, with a 400 foot span, using Bailey bridge components, a bridge later widely used in Burma.

After the Normandy landings, in July 1944 he was seconded to the Twenty-First Army group as bridging adviser, to advise on the construction of Bailey bridges for the allied advance into north-west Europe, and he was responsible for the design and construction of three large high-level Bailey bridges across the Rhine, including the 'Freeman bridge' at Dusseldorf. He was appointed MBE in 1945. After the war he served in the Territorial Army volunteer reserve, and held the post of commanding officer of the engineer and railway staff corps from 1969 to 1974.

Freeman rejoined Freeman, Fox after the war, and became a partner in 1947 and senior partner in 1963. In 1949 Freeman, Fox & Partners were appointed consulting engineers for the building of the Dome of Discovery, an aluminium dome with a diameter of 365 feet, designed by Ralph Tubbs, which was the centrepiece of the South Bank exhibition, part of the Festival of Britain (1951). The firm was then put in charge of co-ordinating all the structural work for the exhibition upstream of Waterloo Bridge, to be ready to hand over to the display designers by late 1950. Following his father's sudden death in March 1950, Freeman took over responsibility for the project, and by keeping to the very tight timetable ensured that the exhibition opened on time, in May 1951. His appointment in 1952 as CBE was in recognition of this achievement.

As Freeman, Fox & Partners expanded during the 1950s the firm won important contracts as consulting engineers in Britain and abroad. They were responsible for a series of power stations, beginning with Castle Donington, a thermal power station, and including power stations at High Marnham, Aberthaw B, and Rheidol, and the pumped storage hydroelectric power station at Ffestiniog in north Wales. In 1960 the firm joined with the American firm of traffic engineers Wilbur Smith Associates to form a separate company, in order to undertake the London traffic survey for the Ministry of Transport and the Greater London council. Freeman Fox, Wilbur Smith Associates was then asked to carry out the Hong Kong mass transport study in 1965, and following its report in 1967, Freeman Fox won the contract to act as consulting engineers for the first line of the Hong Kong mass transit railway, which opened in 1979. Freeman Fox was also responsible for the M2 and M5 motorways, and parts of the M4, and the rebuilding of Cannon Street Station, and it oversaw the construction of steerable dish radio telescopes in Canada and Australia.

But the firm's most important work, and the area in which Freeman himself specialized, was the construction of large bridges, beginning with the 3348 foot Auckland harbour bridge in New Zealand, completed in 1959. Freeman Fox went on to act as consulting engineers for the Forth road bridge, completed in 1964, the first major suspension bridge to be built outside the United States, and as joint consulting engineers for the Severn Bridge, opened in 1966, a suspension bridge with a main span of 3240 feet, over 1 mile of water, linking London and south Wales. This was the first suspension bridge to be built with hollow steel box girders, superseding the use of trussed girders to stiffen the deck, and it led to a revolution in the construction of suspension bridges. The Severn Bridge was followed by the Erskine Bridge across the River Clyde in Scotland, opened in 1971. Freeman had been a member of the team of engineers investigating the partial collapse of the Second Narrows Bridge while under construction in Vancouver, Canada, in 1958, and when the Haven Bridge, in Milford Haven, Pembrokeshire, and the Yarra Bridge, in Melbourne, Australia, both steel box girder bridges designed by Freeman Fox, collapsed in 1970 in the course of construction, Freeman set in motion strengthening works on existing bridges, following the recommendations of the Merrison report in 1973. But despite public concern over the safety of box girder bridges, he applied the same principles to the design of the Bosphorus Bridge, a suspension bridge linking the Black Sea and the Sea of Marmara, which was completed in 1973, and to the Humber Bridge over the Humber estuary, near Hull, Britain's last major unbridged estuary, linking north and south Humberside. Freeman's father, inspired by the Golden Gate Bridge in San Francisco, had first proposed a suspension bridge in 1935, as the crossing posed particular engineering problems because of the fast-flowing currents and frequent changes in the river-bed levels, and it took eight years to build; it opened in 1981, two years after Freeman's retirement. With a span of 1410 metres, it remained for seventeen years the longest single-span suspension bridge in the world.

Freeman was appointed consulting engineer for the Sandringham estate in Norfolk by George VI, and he held this post until 1976. Responsible for a complete overhaul of the central heating system, he used to describe himself as the queen's plumber. He was created CVO in 1964. A fellow of the Institution of Civil Engineers from 1946, he served on the council from 1951 to 1955, and from 1957 to 1961, before a period as vice-president from 1961 to 1966, and as president from 1966 to 1967. He was chairman of the Association of Consulting Engineers from 1975 to 1976, and president of the Smeatonian Society of Civil Engineers in 1978. He served on several public bodies, including from 1966 to 1969 the Ministry of Defence Advisory Council on Scientific Research and Development, which became the Defence Scientific Advisory Council in 1969, after which he served another three years. He was knighted in 1970 for services to engineering.

As well as keeping an interest in civil engineering after his retirement, Freeman continued to play golf, sail, and do wood- and metalwork. He died on 24 August 1998 at his home, Ballards Shaw, Ballards Lane, Limpsfield Chart, Oxted, Surrey, and was cremated.

His eldest son, **(Ralph) Anthony Freeman** (1946–1998), structural engineer, was born on 29 March 1946 at 4 Sherman Court, East Hill, Oxted, Surrey. He was educated at Tonbridge School and at Worcester College, Oxford, where in 1967 he was awarded a first in engineering science. His first job was with the consulting engineers Maunsell, working on the design of the elevated A40 (M) motorway, the Westway, in west London. From there he

joined the contracting engineers Fairfield Mabey, and developed his lifelong passion for large steel bridges while working on the mile-long Avonmouth Bridge, a steel box girder bridge carrying the M5 motorway over the River Avon. On 15 April 1972 he married Julie Mary (b. 1947/8), a midwife, daughter of Alan Howard Burtenshaw, a youth officer: they had one son and two daughters. He joined Freeman, Fox & Partners in 1974, and after playing a part in the strengthening work following the 1970 bridge collapses, he went to Hong Kong in 1976 to work on the mass transit railway. After two years in Germany, working for Maschinenfabrik Augsburg Nürnberg in their steel structures design office, Freeman rejoined Fairfield Mabey to work on the steel road deck for the Britannia rail bridge across the Menai Strait in north Wales. He went on to design two steel headframes at Thorpe colliery in south Yorkshire, and was appointed chief engineer of the firm in 1982.

With an international reputation as an expert on steel and suspension bridge construction, and renowned for his ability to find solutions to the most complex structural problems, Freeman left Fairfield Mabey in 1984 to set up as an independent consultant. After working on the Rama IX Bridge across the Chao Praya River in Bangkok in 1985, he formed his own practice, 3F Engineering Consultants, with its office in Bangkok. He built the cable-stayed bridge across the Hooghley River in Calcutta, and other projects included the construction of heavy lifting equipment and gantries for the erection of bridges. After returning to Britain in 1992, Freeman was elected a fellow of the Royal Academy of Engineering. He rejoined Maunsell, but in 1996 was asked to work on the construction of the Ting Kau cable-stayed bridge in Hong Kong.

Throughout his career Freeman maintained a very close relationship with his father, and after his retirement, his father installed a fax machine at home in order to be able to send and receive drawings and sketches. Always happiest when working on a construction site rather than in an office, Freeman was advising on the cable-stayed section of the Vasco da Gama Bridge over the Tagus in Lisbon, Portugal, in April 1997 when he suffered serious head injuries after a piece of equipment fell from the bridge, taking him and several workers with it. He did not recover, and died on 15 July 1998 in Townlands Hospital, Henley-on-Thames, Oxfordshire. His wife survived him.

ANNE PIMLOTT BAKER

Sources M. Banham and B. Hillier, eds., *A tonic to the nation: the Festival of Britain, 1951* (1976), 91–3 · W. C. Brown, M. F. Passons, and H. G. G. Knox, *Bosporus Bridge: design and construction* (1976) · *Bridging the Humber* (1981) · *The Humberside connection: the Humber Bridge, a commemorative handbook* (1981) · *The Independent* (1 Sept 1998) · *The Times* (2 Sept 1998) · *Daily Telegraph* (10 Sept 1998) · *The Guardian* (14 Sept 1998) · *The Independent* (13 Aug 1998) · *Daily Telegraph* (19 Aug 1998) · *The Times* (27 Aug 1998) · *WW* · b. certs. · m. certs. · d. certs. · *Oxford University Calendar*
Likenesses photograph, repro. in *Daily Telegraph* (10 Sept 1998) · photograph (Anthony Freeman), repro. in *Daily Telegraph* (19 Aug 1998)

Freeman, Richard Austin [*pseud.* Clifford Ashdown] (1862–1943), writer, was born on 11 April 1862 at 27 Thayer

Street, Marylebone, London, the youngest of the five children (four of them sons) of Richard Freeman (1822/3–1890), a journeyman tailor who rose to become the manager of a bespoke tailoring business, and his wife, Ann Maria Dunn. Virtually nothing is known of Freeman's early years; he shrouded his early life in great mystery and the details of his secondary schooling—which apparently took place at a boarding-school in north London—remained unknown even to his closest relatives. On leaving school he worked in a chemist's shop and he later qualified as an apothecary (LSA) in 1886. At eighteen he entered Middlesex Hospital, qualifying as MRCS in 1886.

In 1887 Freeman married Annie Elizabeth (d. 1948), daughter of Thomas Edwards, a master plumber of St Pancras Road, London: they went on to have two sons. But newly married and impecunious, Freeman entered the colonial service as assistant colonial surgeon in Accra in the Gold Coast Colony, where he landed in June 1887, remaining for four years. The Gold Coast was notable for the high mortality rate suffered by Europeans, and in 1891 he contracted blackwater fever and was invalided home. Freeman's continuing ill health prevented the establishment of a successful medical practice in London, and in 1896 he retired to Broadstairs to become a writer. From 1902 he lived in Gravesend, where he both wrote books and practised medicine.

In 1902 Freeman became the co-author of the first of his fictional works to become well known, *The Adventures of Romney Pringle*, written under the pseudonym of Clifford Ashdown, and the fruit of Freeman's collaboration with the physician John James Pitcairn. In 1907, now working on his own, Freeman produced the first of the Doctor Thorndyke stories, the novel *The Red Thumb Mark*, whose plot revolved around the forgery of a set of fingerprints by an ingenious mechanical device. Thorndyke, both barrister and physician, was the first of the fictional 'scientific detectives'. In 1912 Freeman published a new series of Thorndyke short stories in *Pearson's Magazine*, starting with 'The Case of Oscar Brodski', which made secure his important place in detective fiction. 'Brodski' was the first 'inverted' detective story ever written—that is, one in which the identity of the criminal is known to the reader at the outset and the plot concerns the efforts of the detective to ascertain his identity. Between 1907 and 1942 Freeman produced forty Thorndyke short stories and twenty-one Thorndyke novels, to great critical acclaim. The best stand comparison with those of Arthur Conan Doyle.

After the First World War (in which he served as a captain in the Royal Army Medical Corps, stationed in Maidstone, Kent) Freeman increasingly became involved in the eugenics movement, producing a lengthy work on the ills of society, *Social Decay and Regeneration*, in 1921. He believed that machinery and urban life had ruined modern life, and advocated what he termed the 'voluntary segregation of the fit' to live and breed in a utopian community of farmers and skilled craftsmen. Freeman was closely associated with the Eugenics Society from the First World War until the end of his life.

In mature life Freeman was a large, distinguished-looking man with a walrus moustache; he was noted for his humour and self-effacement. Freeman died at his home, Rosemount, 94 Windmill Street, Gravesend, Kent, on 28 September 1943. W. D. RUBINSTEIN

Sources N. Donaldson, *In search of Dr Thorndyke* (1971) • O. Mayo, *R. Austin Freeman: the anthropologist at large* (1980) • C. Steinbrunner and O. Penzler, eds., *Encyclopedia of mystery and detection* (1976), 157–9, 387–8 • W. D. Rubinstein, 'Charles Dickens, R. Austin Freeman, and the spirit of London', *Elites and the wealthy in modern British history* (1987) • b. cert.
Likenesses photographs, repro. in Donaldson, *In search of Dr Thorndyke* • photographs, repro. in Mayo, *R. Austin Freeman*
Wealth at death £6471 5s. 11d.: probate, 22 Jan 1944, CGPLA Eng. & Wales

Freeman, Samuel (1773/4–1857), engraver, was a charter member of the Artists' Benevolent Fund, and as such was involved in the creation of a mutual assurance society for artists who were not members of the Royal Academy. Early evidence of his promise as an engraver of historical and literary subjects is seen in his portrait of the actor David Garrick, after Sir Joshua Reynolds, in the *Monthly Mirror* (1807), engraved in stipple on steel. His engravings can be organized into three major categories: after old master paintings, after the work of contemporary or near contemporary painters, and after paintings of religious subjects. His engravings after old masters began with those which appeared in Henry Tresham's *British Gallery of Pictures* (1815–18), notably that after Raphael's *Madonna of the Diadem*. For James Dallaway's edition of Horace Walpole's *Anecdotes of Painting in England* (1826–8) he engraved *The Marriage of Henry VI and Margaret of Anjou*; he also contributed to *The National Gallery of Pictures by Great Masters* (2 vols., 1836), published by [Richard] Jones & Co., Henry Fisher's *National Portrait Gallery*, Otto von Kotzebue's *New Voyage Round the World in the Years 1823–1826* (2 vols., 1830), E. Lodge's *Portraits of Illustrious Personages of Great Britain* (4 vols., 1821–34), James Browne's *A History of the Highlands and of the Highland Clans* (4 vols., 1835–8), and G. Bell's edition of David Hume and Tobias Smollett's *The History of England … to the Reign of George the Third*. E. Baines's *History of the County Palatine and Duchy of Lancaster* (4 vols., 1836) offers two portraits, with that of John of Gaunt, after George Vertue, being the most memorable, inspiring the later *John of Gaunt … Duke of Lancaster* for G. N. Wright's *Lancashire: its History, Legends, and Manufactures* (1843).

Freeman also began engraving the work of contemporary painters, for example, his steel-engraving in 1827 of Thomas H. Shepherd's *Statue of Achilles in Hyde Park* for James Elmes's *Metropolitan Improvements, or, London in the Nineteenth Century* (1827), and portraits of contemporary literary figures: the poet Letitia Elizabeth Landon, after Joseph Wright, for the *New Monthly Magazine* (May 1837); Lord Byron, after a cut-paper silhouette by Mrs Leigh Hunt, which appeared as the frontispiece to Leigh Hunt's *Lord Byron and Some of his Contemporaries* (1828), with the silhouette in white on a black background (the reverse of the original); and Lady Anne Byron for the *Court Journal* (January 1833). Robert Chamber's *Biographical Dictionary of Eminent Scotsmen* (4 vols., 1835) contained fifteen plates by

Freeman, mostly after Lawrence, Raeburn, and Reynolds. Impressions of these and 245 other engravings by Freeman may be found in the department of prints and drawings at the British Museum.

Freeman produced four plates on religious subjects, after Northcote, Opie, Rembrandt, and Rubens, for *Historic Illustrations of the Bible*, issued in four parts by [Henry] Fisher, Son & Co. between 1840 and 1843. Soon his engravings after Lawrence and da Vinci appeared in G. N. Wright's *The Gallery of Engravings* (3 vols., 1845–6); his engravings on New Testament subjects after these two artists were published in *The Imperial Family Bible* (1844). He engraved further religious paintings, after Rubens and Northcote, for John Kitto's *The Gallery of Scripture Engravings, Historical and Landscape* (3 vols., 1846–7). Freeman lived in his last years at 22 Jeffrey's Street in Kentish Town, where he died on 27 February 1857, aged eighty-three. He was buried in Highgate cemetery on 7 March. He presumably married Mary Freeman (*d*. 1864), who was buried in the same grave, together with other members of the Freeman family, some of whom were probably the children of Samuel and Mary. Even after his death, Freeman's engravings continued appearing, notably his *Sir Walter Scott*, after J. W. Gordon, in James Caw's *The Scott Gallery* (1903).

PAUL J. deGATEGNO

Sources B. Hunnisett, *A dictionary of British steel engravers* (1980) · B. Hunnisett, *An illustrated dictionary of British steel engravers*, new edn (1989) · *Engraved Brit. ports.* · A. M. Hind, *A history of engraving and etching*, 3rd edn (1923); repr. (1963) · J. Turner, ed., *The dictionary of art*, 34 vols. (1996) · J. H. Slater, *Engravings and their value*, rev. F. W. Maxwell-Barbour, 6th edn (1929) · *Redgrave, Artists* · d. cert. · Highgate cemetery grave records, for grave no. 7930 · *Boase, Mod. Eng. biog.*

Freeman, Susanna. *See* Centlivre, Susanna (*bap*. 1669?, *d*. 1723).

Freeman, Thomas (*bap*. 1590, *d*. in or after 1614), poet, was baptized on 23 August 1590, in Bourton on the Hill, Gloucestershire, the son of Thomas Freeman, 'of the same family with those of Batsford and Todenham near to Morton in Marsh' (Wood, *Ath. Oxon.*, 155). He became a student of Magdalen College, Oxford, in 1607, and took his degree of BA on 10 June 1611.

After relocating to London, Freeman published in 1614 a collection of 200 epigrams in two parts, dedicated to Thomas, Lord Windsor, who had already privately perused a large proportion of the text. *Rubbe and a Great Cast: Epigrams* contains examples of anti-puritan satire, catalogues of contemporary sins, and tributes to Shakespeare, Spenser, George Daniel, John Donne, George Chapman, Thomas Heywood, John Owen, the popular epigrammatist, and Thomas Nashe. One piece, 'Encomion Cornubiae', is reproduced in G. Ellis's *Specimens of the Early English Poets* (3 vols., 1803, 3.113–15).

A. H. BULLEN, *rev.* ELIZABETH HARESNAPE

Sources Wood, *Ath. Oxon.*, new edn, 2.155–7 · *Foster, Alum. Oxon.* · R. R. Dubinski, *English religious poetry printed 1477–1640: a chronological bibliography with indexes* (1996) · W. P. Holden, *Anti-puritan satire, 1572–1642* (1954), 82 · R. C. Bald, *John Donne: a life*, ed. W. Milgate (1970), 283 · A. M. Clark, *Thomas Heywood: playwright and miscellanist*

(1931), 67 · R. Atkyns, *The ancient and present state of Glostershire*, 2nd edn, 2 pts in 1 (1768), 133 · *IGI*

Freeman, Thomas Birch (1809–1890), missionary and colonial official, was born on 6 December 1809 at Twyford, near Winchester, of an African father, Thomas Freeman, a farmer, and an English mother, Amy Birch. He adopted the name Freeman in youth, perhaps from his father who may have been a freed slave. Little is known of his upbringing except that it was in poverty, or of his education, save that he could write with elegance.

As a young man Freeman rose to become head gardener and botanist to Sir Robert Harland at Orwell Park, near Ipswich. Freeman joined the Wesleyan Methodists, became a lay preacher, and lost his employment for refusing to return to the Church of England. He thereupon volunteered as a Methodist missionary to west Africa, where the first white missionaries had all died within weeks of arrival. Freeman's offer was thus welcomed, in the false belief that as an African he was racially protected against tropical diseases. On 17 October 1837 he married Elizabeth Boote, housekeeper to his former employer; she died of fever in February 1838, within weeks of their arrival on the Gold Coast. On 25 November 1840, while on his first leave in England, Freeman married Lucinda Cowan, daughter of a Methodist minister; she died on 25 August 1841, within seven months of landing in Africa. Some years later he married an educated African, who bore him a son, also named Thomas Birch Freeman.

Freeman was one of the most successful Christian missionaries of his age, founding the Methodist churches of the Gold Coast and Nigeria. His faith was transparently sincere and he was a skilled diplomat, who impressed both the British colonial representatives and rulers of African kingdoms; these included the powerful interior kingdom of Asante which he visited in 1840. His converts were looking for greater self-expression than their own societies permitted; Methodism allowed Freeman to place literate Africans as lay preachers and ministers, thus spreading the organization of the church rapidly. In 1842 he visited Badagri in south-west Nigeria, and then Abeokuta, where large numbers of slaves liberated by the Royal Navy were returning home, who proved fertile soil for conversion. From 1842 he supervised an expanding number of Methodist congregations in the Gold Coast and Nigeria, visited the kingdom of Dahomey in 1843 when it threatened Abeokuta and Badagri, and made further visits to Asante in 1848 with the British governor of the Gold Coast.

Freeman's very success as an evangelist led to his resignation in 1857, for he was naïve in his financial administration, expecting that God would provide funds for each expansion. An accounting in 1857 revealed that while Freeman had been scrupulously honest he had presided over chaotic finances. He was at once given employment by the colonial government as civil commandant of Accra district, and he remained in the colonial service for the next sixteen years. In 1873 he returned to the Methodist

Thomas Birch Freeman (1809–1890), by T. A. Dean (after Marshall Claxton)

ministry in a purely pastoral role, retiring in 1885 to live in Accra. He died in the Methodist mission circuit house there, in his eighty-first year, on 12 August 1890.

JOHN FLINT

Sources T. B. Freeman, *Journal of various visits to the kingdom of Ashanti, Aku and Dahomey* (1844) · A. W. Birtwhistle, *Thomas Birch Freeman* (1949) · R. M. Wiltgen, *A Gold Coast mission history, 1471–1880* (1965) · J. F. A. Ajayi, *Christian missions in Nigeria, 1841–1891* (1965) · G. G. Findlay and W. W. Holdsworth, *The history of the Wesleyan Methodist Missionary Society*, 5 vols. (1921–4) · C. P. Groves, *The planting of Christianity in Africa*, 4 vols. (1948–58) · F. D. Walker, *Thomas Birch Freeman* (1929) · m. certs.

Archives SOAS, journals and papers · SOAS, archives of Methodist Missionary Society | PRO, Colonial Office MSS, Gold Coast corresp.

Likenesses T. A. Dean, engraving (after M. Claxton), NPG [*see illus.*] · photograph, repro. in Birtwhistle, *Thomas Birch Freeman*, frontispiece

Freeman, (Thomas) Walter (1908–1988), geographer, was born on 27 December 1908 in Congleton, Cheshire, the eldest of the three children of Thomas Ernest Freeman (1872–1957), a Methodist minister, and his wife, Mary Gibson (c.1875–1960). The family moved frequently, and lived variously in Colwyn Bay (1909–12), Great Yarmouth (1912–15), Creswell, Derbyshire (1915–19), Nantwich, Cheshire (1919–22), and Bridgend in south Wales. Between 1922 and 1926 Freeman attended grammar schools in Nantwich and Bridgend. The variety of south Wales landscapes evoked a lifelong enthusiasm for field research, regional geography, and the history of civilization.

In 1927 Freeman entered the University of Leeds and in 1930 graduated with a first-class honours degree in geography, followed in 1931 by a diploma of education. His undergraduate dissertation was on pre-Norman Glamorgan. During his student years he developed a strong interest in the League of Nations and international peace: 'In those days we thought in terms of the world, its major areas and problems, and international affairs were constantly discussed' (Freeman, 'A geographer's way', 92)—hence the broad-ranging theme of his MA thesis (Leeds, 1932) on modern migrations from Asia. In 1931, at the School of International Studies in Geneva, he witnessed growing 'tensions between French and Germans, forebodings of an imminent civil war in Spain, the deep regret of many Americans that they were outside the League of Nations, even the aggression of a picked group of Fascist Italian students' (ibid.).

'The shadow of the First World War hung over our childhood', Freeman recalled, 'and by the mid-1930s few doubted that another war must follow, sparked off by some real or manufactured crisis' (Freeman, 'A geographer's way', 93), but he never became cynical; 'the earlier teaching in geography combined with the evolutionary approach of geology gave a vision of one human world that could lapse into barbarism or advance towards universal peace' (ibid.). A devout Christian, he contemplated entering the ministry, but realized by the early 1930s that he could no longer be a Methodist. In July 1932 he was received into the Church of England, a move which caused substantial difficulties in the family, but one which he never regretted. Throughout his life he contributed to local church life.

Freeman's first appointment was to an assistantship in the department of geography at Edinburgh University (1933–6), where he met scholars such as Alan Ogilvie and Arthur Geddes, who became lifelong friends. In 1934 he assumed some editorial responsibilities for the *Scottish Geographical Magazine*. In January 1936 he moved to Trinity College, Dublin, where he initiated an honours course in geography and began research on Ireland, particularly on nineteenth-century population patterns. On 9 December 1941 he married Olive Elizabeth Aykroyd (1913–1991), a colleague at Trinity College and the youngest daughter of a well-established Dublin wool merchant and Methodist family. She was a devoted wife, keenly interested in painting and the natural world. She returned to work as a cytologist when their three children, Michael (b. 1943), John (b. 1945), and Mary (b. 1948), had grown up.

Freeman's fourteen years in Ireland were challenging and productive:

> I walked, cycled, joined any possible student tour, used holidays to acquire some understanding of a country that seemed to me different from Scotland, Wales or England. There was a heavy teaching programme … but there were some responsive students. And life in Dublin was very entertaining and enjoyable. (Freeman, 'Some personal recollections')

'I am sure that I learned more about geography when accompanying him on his excursions', his pupil Joe Haughton wrote, 'than from any textbook' (Haughton, 117). His research spanned historical and contemporary subjects. He discovered a wealth of archival material on nineteenth-century Ireland and began work on *Pre-Famine Ireland*, a work which was completed only in 1957. 'Writing *Pre-Famine Ireland* was pure joy. I never enjoyed anything more' (Freeman, 'Some personal recollections'). At the same time he initiated a comprehensive land-use survey of the Dublin region. During the war (1941–5) he worked part-time at the Scott Polar Research Institute in Cambridge as assistant to P. M. Roxby, who was preparing Admiralty handbooks on China. Having received the sad news in 1942 that the ship on which his sister Margaret was travelling had been torpedoed off the African coast, he threw himself into writing his famous book *Ireland: a Regional Geography* (1950, repr. 1965, 1969, and 1971), which was dedicated to her. He was active in the Geographical Society of Ireland and edited the *Bulletin of the Geographical Society of Ireland* (later *Irish Geography*). It was to this society, and to the department of geography at Trinity College, that Freeman left the collection of books and papers now known as the Freeman library at Trinity College, Dublin.

In 1950 Freeman became reader in geography at Manchester University, where he remained until his retirement in 1976, and where he wholeheartedly engaged with applied geography or planning. The need for such work had been impressed on him during his student years at Leeds: 'I walked for miles through the poorest areas of the town, through quarters inhabited by poor Irish, Jews and others and saw the tentative moves to make a more humane environment through building new estates' (letter to author, 4 Nov 1980). From this period came three important works, *Geography and Planning* (1958), *The Conurbations of Great Britain* (1959), and *Geography and Regional Administration* (1968), in which he argued that the geographer could 'induce people to see the life of people in terms of environment, in terms of home and workplace and the journey between them, in terms of recreation, land conservation, and those amenities providing adequate living conditions for an increasing population' (Freeman, 'A geographer's way', 97). Later, however, he was critical of planning in Britain. 'Can it be that as a reaction to the baleful congestion of people and workplace central city areas are becoming human deserts?' he asked. 'Each solution to a problem appears to raise new difficulties unforeseen in the earlier flush of hope' (ibid.). 'Slum clearance has been followed by some disastrous experiments in re-housing; in the 1950s the status symbol of an enterprising municipal authority was the multistorey block of flats, but how many people want them now?' (ibid., 100).

The Manchester years were not altogether happy. Freeman found there 'nine people doing less work than Joe Haughton and I were doing in Dublin' (letter to author, 9 July 1980). He was promoted to professor only in 1974, but on his retirement in 1976 the senate and council of Manchester University applauded his 'sustained literary output' and noted his 'strong sense of social responsibility outside the University' (University of Manchester, 1976).

Soon after his retirement Freeman and his wife moved to Abingdon, near Oxford. Now most of his time and energy was devoted to his long-standing interest in the history of geographical thought. The British Association committee established in 1947 to study the growth of modern British geography had invited him to write *A Hundred Years of Geography* (1961). This was followed by *The Geographer's Craft* (1968), *The Writing of Geography* (1971), and *A History of Modern British Geography* (1980). From 1968 to 1988 he was secretary and treasurer of the newly formed Commission on the History of Geographical Thought, and editor of its series Geographers: Biobibliographical Studies, twelve volumes of which he saw through the press.

Throughout his life Freeman loved to travel, preferably on foot or by bicycle. He recalled vividly his first international geographical congress in Amsterdam in 1938:

> It was good to realize that there were interested colleagues all over the world, and to get to know some of them as friends. … One had no illusions about the near future of Europe and it was perhaps the last chance to travel before the lights went out. (Freeman, 'A geographer's way', 94)

Conference-going, however, lost its lustre in post-war days: 'in the end scholarship depends on isolation, on contemplation, on silence as well as on debate and discussion' (ibid.).

Freeman identified field work as the single most influential factor in his work. He was also impressed by mentors who projected visions of a better world, including Roxby, Arthur Geddes, Halford Mackinder, and Dudley Stamp. His hope was to inspire students to take up research where he had left off or to channel their reforming zeal 'into practical activity through some profession helpful to society' (Freeman, 'A geographer's way', 98).

Freeman died of cancer of the liver on 11 March 1988, and his remains were cremated on 17 March at the Oxford crematorium. He was survived by his wife and their three children. A tireless researcher, a generous correspondent, and an eager traveller, Freeman was the embodiment of the liberal and compassionate scholar. He was outspoken, frank, and at times quite formidably critical. Geography was his vocation, music, religion, and long country walks his inspiration, and writing his favourite activity:

> Geography … recognizes the changes made currently as well as in past time on the face of the earth and studies the physical mechanisms as well as the human decisions through which they occur. And if such a study leads at least some geographers to hope that they may in some small way contribute to the making of a better world, at least through giving others a better understanding of it, their work will be more than a dream and a shadow. (Freeman, 'A geographer's way', 101)

ANNE BUTTIMER

Sources T. W. Freeman, 'A geographer's way', *The practice of geography*, ed. A. Buttimer (1983), 90–102 · video interview with T. W. Freeman recorded in March 1979 at Audio-Visual Services, Manchester University, dialogue project transcript series G7, Lund University [also available at RGS] · private information (2004) · J. Haughton, 'Thomas Walter Freeman, 1908–1988: an appreciation', *Irish Geography*, 21 (1988), 117–18 · K. M. Davies, 'A bibliography of Mr W. T. Freeman's contributions to the geography of Ireland', *Irish Geography*, 6 (1973), 529–31 · B. Rodgers, *Transactions of the Institute of British Geographers*, new ser., 14 (1989), 237–40 · G. L. Davies, *This protean subject: the geography department in Trinity College,*

Dublin, 1936–1986 (1986) • resolution passed at the meetings of senate and council held on 27 Sept 1976 and 16 Nov 1976, University of Manchester • G. L. Davis, 'Thomas Walter Freeman and the geography of Ireland: a tribute', *Irish Geography*, 6 (1973), 521–8 • T. W. Freeman to A. Buttimer, priv. coll. • T. W. Freeman, 'Some personal recollections', 1977, priv. coll. • P. M. Roxby, ed., *China proper*, 3 vols. (1944–5) [naval intelligence division, geographical handbook]
Archives RGS, corresp. and papers • TCD, department of geography |FILM Lund University, video interview recorded in March 1979 at Audio-Visual Services, Manchester University [also in RGS]
Wealth at death £60,172: probate, 5 Aug 1988, *CGPLA Eng. & Wales*

Freeman, Sir Wilfrid Rhodes, first baronet (1888–1953), air force officer, was born at 103 Westbourne Terrace, London, on 18 July 1888, the third son of William Robert Freeman (*d.* 1925), stone merchant, and his wife, Anne Farquharson Carr Dunn, the daughter of an Aberdeen advocate. Educated at St Christopher's School, Eastbourne, Rugby School (1902–6), and the Royal Military College, Sandhurst (1906–7), he was gazetted in February 1908 to the Manchester regiment, in which he became captain and brevet-major.

In 1913 Freeman privately learned to fly in France and after obtaining his pilot's licence on 21 July he joined the Central Flying School at Upavon, Wiltshire. On qualifying in April 1914 he became a flying officer with 2 squadron, the Royal Flying Corps (RFC), and he accompanied the squadron to France on 13 August 1914 as part of the first RFC contingent to cross the channel. In September, during the battle of Mons, a major structural failure in his aircraft compelled him to land in enemy-held territory. For two days he successfully avoided German search parties and pickets, finally swimming the River Aisne to return unscathed to his squadron. His example, perhaps the earliest recorded wartime escape and evasion by an airman, has since been followed by many thousands of other air crews.

Posted to 9 squadron in October 1914, Freeman quickly displayed a keen aptitude for developing the technical capabilities of military aviation. The squadron was the first to be equipped with wireless apparatus, and Freeman soon became an accomplished wireless operator, regularly directing artillery fire on to the German gun batteries. Assigned the post of flight commander in March 1915, he received one of the first MCs to be awarded to an RFC officer for his flying during the battle of Neuve Chapelle. He returned to England in May 1915, and in June he was posted as an instructor at the new Flying Training School at Shoreham. Shortly after his return to Britain he married, on 5 June 1915, Gladys, daughter of John Mews, barrister; they had a daughter and a son.

During the first six months of 1916 Freeman commanded 14 squadron in Egypt, but he resumed training duties in Britain in July before returning to France in December. Promoted lieutenant-colonel, he commanded the Tenth Army wing during the battle of Arras in the early spring of 1917 and the third battle of Ypres later that year—a particularly difficult period in which the German air force, flying technically superior aircraft, inflicted heavy casualties on the RFC. In October 1917 Freeman was commanding the 9th (headquarters) wing; his squadrons actively participated in the battle of Cambrai in November and in operations against the German offensive in March 1918. Posted back to Britain in April, he was attending the staff officers' course at the Royal Naval College at Greenwich when the First World War ended. He was appointed to the DSO in 1916, awarded the Légion d'honneur, and thrice mentioned in dispatches. Gazetted to the Royal Air Force on its formation on 1 April 1918 with the rank of lieutenant-colonel, he was granted a permanent commission on 1 August 1919 as wing commander.

Between the end of the First World War and the beginning of large-scale air rearmament in the mid-1930s, the majority of Freeman's RAF postings were training appointments. From November 1921 to April 1925 he was an instructor at the RAF Staff College with the rank of group captain (January 1923), and was later promoted to the post of assistant commandant. Between April 1925 and January 1927 he commanded the Central Flying School at Upavon. He held one Air Ministry post, deputy director of operations and intelligence, from January 1927 to October 1928, when he became commanding officer of the Fleet Air Arm training base at Leuchars. In July 1929 he was promoted air commodore and appointed senior air staff officer of the UK Inland Area; in September 1930 he was posted to the Middle East, where he served as chief staff officer of the Iraq command for a short time (October–December 1930) before being appointed air officer commanding, trans-Jordan and Palestine (December 1930–October 1933). As the RAF was at that time the chief military arm of British interests in the strategically vital Middle East, this was an immensely important post, with considerable political responsibilities. The appointment reflected Freeman's outstanding ability and the unanimous opinion of his superiors—repeatedly noted in his record of service—that he was an exceptionally capable officer; it was yet another positive step in his relentless advance towards the top echelons of the RAF high command. Yet at a personal level there was a heavy price to pay, for the posting exposed irreconcilable tensions within his marriage. He separated from his wife in 1931 and his first marriage was eventually dissolved in 1935. In the same year (17 April 1935) he married Elizabeth, daughter of Ernest Tatham Richmond, director of antiquities in Palestine (1927–37). They had two daughters.

In July 1933 Freeman was promoted air vice-marshal, and from January 1934 until March 1936 he was commandant of the RAF Staff College at Andover. Deeply committed to training, he took a close personal interest in the progress of individual students. Yet it is clear that he was being groomed for still higher appointments, for he was also required to attend the meetings of the chiefs of staff and, from 1935, of the special air parity subcommittee, which determined the initial scale of British air rearmament.

It was the onset of rearmament in the mid-1930s that finally brought Freeman to the very summit of his RAF career. In April 1936 he was appointed to the Air Council as air member for research and development. In this post he was responsible for both the selection and the development of new types of service aircraft, an exceptionally demanding task given the dramatic changes then taking place in aircraft technology. Much of his time was spent pressing forward the development of equipment that had already been ordered, such as the Vickers Wellington bomber, the Rolls-Royce Merlin engine, and radar, and he deserves much of the credit for their readiness by the outbreak of war. Nevertheless, he also quickly displayed a remarkable aptitude for identifying new designs with particularly promising potential, and was directly responsible for the selection of virtually all Britain's most famous wartime aircraft. Shortly after assuming his new duties he recommended placing the first production order for the Supermarine Spitfire, despite pressure from his colleagues to restrict fighter production to the Hawker Hurricane. He also initiated the development of the first four-engined bombers, the Short Stirling and the Handley Page Halifax, and of A. V. Roe's Manchester, which later became the Lancaster—the mainstay of Bomber Command during the strategic air offensive against Germany. Other models which he ordered in prototype form in this period and which were destined to give sterling service in the Second World War included the Hawker Typhoon and the Bristol Beaufighter.

In spring 1938 British rearmament was accelerated, and in June 1938 Freeman, already promoted full air marshal (January 1937), became responsible for aircraft production as well as research and development. He brought in Arthur Tedder as director-general of research and development, one of his two deputies in helping to manage 'one of the largest state-sponsored military enterprises in British history' (Ritchie, 1). As air member for development and production (AMDP) from 1938 to 1940 Freeman personally orchestrated the construction of Britain's wartime aircraft economy, organizing enormous expansion programmes for the Vickers Wellington bomber and the Merlin engine, and longer-term schemes for the large-scale production of heavy bombers, which came to fruition during the second year of the war. He also broadened the base of aircraft production by compelling manufacturers to subcontract their work, and by allocating aircraft contracts to leading manufacturing companies from beyond the professional aircraft industry, such as English Electric and Ford. And he created the essential supporting infrastructure for the industry by enlarging the output of aluminium and aircraft equipment. Most of all, in consecutive stages, he increased the output of Hurricane and Spitfire fighters, so ensuring abundant deliveries of both aircraft during the battle of Britain. Yet he never became so engrossed in production matters that he ignored development, understanding all too well that the fighting efficiency of the RAF depended on the co-ordination of quantity *and* quality. During this period he actively encouraged the development and production of Whittle's jet engine and ordered the De Havilland Mosquito, dismissing the objections of several of his colleagues and subordinates (who dubbed it Freeman's Folly). It proved to be one of the

most outstanding combat aircraft of the Second World War.

When Churchill became prime minister in May 1940, Freeman's department was transformed into a separate Ministry of Aircraft Production, under Lord Beaverbrook. Serving under a minister who in effect removed procurement from his control, and who disrupted the long-term planning of 'the bloody Air Marshals' (as Beaverbrook habitually described the chiefs of air staff), made for an uneasy working relationship. As a result of policy disagreements Freeman, who was promoted air chief marshal in May 1940, twice requested a transfer (in August and September), but continued in the ministry throughout the battle of Britain, receiving a tribute from Beaverbrook as the person 'who, more than any other man, gave the Royal Air Force the machines whose superior quality won the vital battles of the summer' (Richards, 218). Freeman returned to the Air Ministry in November 1940 to become vice-chief of air staff (VCAS), under Air Chief Marshal Sir Charles Portal, who wanted him as his right-hand man. In this capacity Freeman was responsible for administering the RAF's wartime expansion, leaving Portal free to concentrate on operational matters. Among his many achievements in these years his pivotal role in the creation of a Pathfinder force within Bomber Command is of particular note.

Although Freeman enjoyed the closest relations with Portal, dining regularly with his chief and giving him candid advice on appointments, he felt himself miscast as VCAS, believing that his most valuable talents lay in the field of aircraft procurement, and it was in procurement that he continued to make his greatest contribution to the war effort—albeit behind the scenes. In 1940, while he was still AMDP, Freeman had ordered a single-engined fighter from the American manufacturer North American, which was christened the Mustang by the RAF. He also arranged for the Merlin engine to be built in the USA. During 1942 Rolls-Royce installed a Merlin into the Mustang airframe and discovered that the combination produced a fighter significantly superior in performance to any other allied or axis model. Alerted to the potential of this formidable union, Freeman then played a crucial role in persuading the American authorities to order the Merlin Mustang, and to increase the planned volume of Mustang production. Entering service in 1944, this remarkable aeroplane rapidly inflicted crippling losses on the Luftwaffe and established air supremacy for the allies in the west European theatre. It was to Wilfrid Freeman, more than any other man, that the Merlin Mustang owed its existence.

In October 1942 Freeman retired from the RAF and was appointed chief executive of the Ministry of Aircraft Production. He immediately instituted sweeping changes in a ministry that had been poorly managed since his departure in 1940, establishing a more reliable basis for production planning, and tackling with his customary vigour a variety of industrial problems that were impeding key projects such as the jet engine. Under his dynamic direction Britain's aircraft economy achieved its peak wartime level of output and efficiency without sacrificing the qualitative improvements so vital to the operational effectiveness of the RAF. When Freeman finally relinquished his position in 1945, Britain's first jet fighter, the Gloster Meteor, was in full production, and the development of a jet bomber had been initiated. In time this emerged as the Canberra, an aeroplane still in service with the RAF at the end of the twentieth century.

Although, to the public, the name of Wilfrid Freeman was little known, he was ranked by his RAF contemporaries alongside Lord Trenchard and Lord Portal as one of the great men in British military aviation. He could be cynical, critical, and intolerant, and was incapable of suffering fools gladly, but one of his most prominent colleagues also remembered him as 'a cultured, civilised man with a warm and human understanding leavened with a remarkably alert mind and an insistence upon quality in all endeavour' (DNB). The energy, determination, and decisiveness that characterized his service throughout the rearmament and wartime years were matched by few other commanders or administrators. His achievements played a vital part in bringing victory to the allies. Appointed CB in 1932, he was promoted KCB in 1937 and GCB in 1942, and created a baronet in July 1945. After the war he became a director of the textile manufacturer Courtaulds. He died in London on 15 May 1953, and was survived by his wife. He was succeeded as second baronet by his son from his first marriage, John Keith Noel Freeman (1923–1981).

SEBASTIAN RITCHIE

Sources A. Furse, *Wilfrid Freeman: the genius behind allied survival and air supremacy, 1939–1945* (1999) · S. Ritchie, *Industry and air power: the expansion of British aircraft production, 1935–1941* (1997) · DNB · D. Richards, *Portal of Hungerford* (1977) · J. Terraine, *The right of the line: the Royal Air Force in the European war, 1939–1945* (1985) · [Lord Tedder], *With prejudice: the war memoirs of marshal of the Royal Air Force, Lord Tedder* (1966) · J. C. Slessor, *The central blue: recollections and reflections* (1956) · CGPLA Eng. & Wales (1953)
Archives Courtaulds Group, archives department, business papers · priv. coll., family letters · PRO, AIR and AVIA classes MSS | IWM, corresp. with Tizard | FILM BFI NFTVA, news footage · BFI NFTVA, record footage · IWM FVA, actuality footage · IWM FVA, news footage | SOUND IWM SA, oral history interview
Likenesses W. Stoneman, photograph, 1941, NPG · H. Coster, photographs, NPG · T. C. Dugdale, portrait, priv. coll.
Wealth at death £12,078 2s. 11d.: probate, 11 Sept 1953, CGPLA Eng. & Wales

Freeman, William Peere Williams- [*formerly* William Peere Williams] (**1742–1832**), naval officer, grandson of William Peere *Williams, and son of Frederick Williams (*d.* 1746), prebendary of Peterborough, was born in Peterborough on 6 January 1742. His mother was Mary, daughter of Robert *Clavering, bishop of Peterborough, and Mary Freeman, sister of John Cook Freeman of Fawley Court, Buckinghamshire. Williams was educated at Eton College, and in June 1757 his name was entered on the books of the 100-gun *Royal Sovereign*, guardship at Spithead. He first went to sea in August 1759, in Lord Howe's 74-gun *Magnanime*, in which he took part in the battle of Quiberon Bay on 20 November 1759.

In September 1762 Williams followed Howe to the 80-gun *Princess Amelia*, and then joined the *Romney* (50

guns) on the Halifax station in August 1763. On 18 September 1764 he was promoted to lieutenant of the 40-gun *Rainbow* on the Virginia station, and on 26 May 1768 he was made master and commander of the *Thunder* bomb vessel. He became a post captain on 10 January 1771, with his appointment to command the *Renown* (50 guns), and moved to the 28-gun *Active* on 21 March. Shortly after, on 20 June, he married Henrietta Wilts (*d.* 1819), with whom he had two sons, one of whom was also named William Peere Williams.

Like so many others on that station Williams became sick while taking the *Active* to the West Indies. Apparently, he used his interest to get his ship sent to Newfoundland; his health did not, however, improve there, and on 11 October Rear-Admiral John Montagu gave him command of the *Lively* (20 guns), which he brought home and paid off in February 1774.

Williams's next appointment was on 10 March 1777, as captain of the 36-gun frigate *Venus*, in which he joined Lord Howe's squadron in North America, and he was with Howe at the encounter with D'Estaing's fleet off Rhode Island on 10 August 1778. Perhaps again suffering ill health, on 18 September Williams exchanged with Captain James Ferguson and took Ferguson's 32-gun frigate *Brune* back to England.

In April 1780 Williams took command of the *Flora*, a new 36-gun frigate carrying six 18-pounder carronades in addition to her main armament of 18- and 9-pounders. Cruising off Ushant on 10 August, the *Flora* fell in with a French frigate, the 32-gun *Nymphe* (Captain du Rumain). *La Nymphe* was the bigger ship, but the *Flora* was better armed, and in a hard-fought action which demonstrated the power and utility of the carronade, the *Flora* had 9 men killed and 17 wounded, while the French lost 55 killed and 81 wounded. A French attempt to board the *Flora* was repulsed, and Williams's men eventually boarded and took their prize.

In March 1781 Williams, still in the *Flora*, sailed with George Darby's fleet to the relief of Gibraltar. Returning on 30 May after escorting a convoy to Minorca, and in company with the *Crescent* (28 guns, Captain Thomas Pakenham), Williams attacked two Dutch vessels off Ceuta, the *Flora* taking on her equal in the 36-gun *Castor*, and the smaller *Crescent* engaging the *Briel*. After a 2¼-hour battle, the *Castor* struck to Williams's ship, but in the meantime, the *Crescent* had been forced to strike to her Dutch opponent. The *Flora*, however, came to her assistance and chased off the *Briel*, and the two British vessels, with their prize, set off for England. Unfortunately for them, on 19 June they encountered two French 32-gun frigates, *Friponne* and *Gloire*; jury-rigged and with only 300 unwounded men (out of a full complement of 700) spread between his three vessels, Williams was in no condition to take on the French frigates, and chose to escape with the *Flora*, leaving the other two to be captured. On 30 June 1781 Lord Mulgrave described how Williams had done 'everything that courage could wish' but had been 'deficient in seamanship and abilities' which 'one would wish, both from his gallantry and connexions, not to appear publicly' (Lord Mulgrave to earl of Sandwich, NMM, SAN/F/26/116).

In April 1782 Williams retired to his country estates at Henley-on-Thames and Hoddesdon, adding Freeman to his name in November 1821 as a condition of his inheriting the Fawley Court estate in Buckinghamshire. Assisted in later life by his eponymous son, he amused himself in his retirement by waging an acrimonious and litigious war on his neighbours and tenants over the terms of their tenancies and the condition of their lands.

Williams-Freeman had continued to progress through the flag ranks, as was the custom, by sheer dint of survival, becoming rear-admiral on 12 April 1794, vice-admiral on 1 June 1795, and admiral on 1 January 1801. On 28 June 1830, on William IV's accession, he was promoted to admiral of the fleet. He died at his home on his Hoddesdon estate on 11 February 1832, and was buried in the family vault at Broxbourne, Hertfordshire. RANDOLPH COCK

Sources DNB · W. L. Clowes, *The Royal Navy: a history from the earliest times to the present*, 7 vols. (1897–1903); repr. (1996–7), vols. 3–4 · commission and warrant books, PRO, ADM 6/20, 21 · J. Gorton, *A general biographical dictionary*, 3 vols. (1841) · *Annual Register* (1780), 289 · *Annual Register* (1781), 249 · Glos. RO, Strickland MS D1245, fols. 21–8
Archives Glos. RO, corresp. and MSS of case in king's bench against Sir William Strickland and V. H. E. Strickland
Likenesses G. Romney, oils, Man. City Gall.

Freer, Ada Goodrich (1857–1931), folklorist and psychical researcher, was born at Uppingham on 15 May 1857, the daughter of George Freer, a veterinary surgeon, and his wife, Mary, *née* Adcock. Throughout her life she concealed her origin, giving the impression of coming from Yorkshire with connections to the landed gentry and the Scottish highlands. Under the patronage of F. W. H. Myers she became active in the Society for Psychical Research. She wrote papers on her psychical experience under the pseudonym of Miss X which Myers read to the society (collected in *Essays in Psychical Research*, 1899). From 1893 to 1897 she was assistant editor (to W. T. Stead) of *Borderland*, again writing as Miss X. In 1894 she was, on Myers's recommendation, given charge of the society's inquiry into second sight in the highlands and islands. On her second visit to the Hebrides, in 1895, she met Father Allan McDonald and gained access to his extensive and important collection of Hebridean folklore. From 1897 she published a substantial part of it under her own name, initially in articles in *Folklore*, acknowledging McDonald's help but falsifying the character of her own work (she did not speak Gaelic in 1895 and her knowledge of the language was never more than rudimentary).

Miss Freer became involved in the contentious cases of the Clandon House haunting (1895), the Burton letters (1895–7), and the ghost hunt at Ballechin House, Perthshire (1897). She was severely criticized by J. Callendar Ross in *The Times* (8 June 1897) and was subsequently disowned by the society. With Lord Bute, who had paid for the Scottish 'second sight' inquiry, she wrote *The Alleged Haunting of B[allechin] House* (1899), defending the ghost hunt. She abandoned psychical research and focused on folklore. In December 1901 she went to Jerusalem, where she finished *Outer Isles* (1902; her chief work and most substantial plagiarism of McDonald), wrote *Inner Jerusalem* (1905), and married an American, the Revd Hans Henry Spoer, in 1905. Her husband believed her to be almost twenty years younger than her age. She subsequently published other works on the Near East, accompanied her husband to Britain in 1909–11, and lived in Cairo from 1911. She moved to Detroit in 1923, to Sycamore, Illinois, in 1926, and to New York in 1927, where her husband was chaplain to the New York Mission Society. She died at St Luke's Hospital, New York, on 24 February 1931 (her death certificate giving her name as Adela Monica Spoer), survived by her husband. Her laudatory obituary in *Folklore* (vol. 41, 1931) made no mention of Father McDonald.

J. L. CAMPBELL

Sources J. L. Campbell and T. H. Hall, *Strange things* (1968) · T. H. Hall, *The strange story of Ada Goodrich Freer* (1980) · J. L. Campbell, *Fr Allan McDonald of Eriskay*, 2nd edn (1956) · J. L. Campbell, 'The late Fr Allan McDonald, Miss Goodrich Freer and Hebridean folklore', *Scottish Studies*, 2 (1958), 175–88 · J. Oppenheim, *The other world: spiritualism and psychical research in England, 1850–1914* (1985) · d. cert. (USA) · b. cert.
Likenesses photograph, repro. in Campbell and Hall, *Strange things*

Freer [*married name* Robinson], **Martha Walker** (1822–1888), biographer, was born in Leicester on 25 October 1822, the eldest daughter of John Booth Freer, MD. Very little is known of her life. On 8 August 1861, at St George's, Hanover Square, she married the Revd John Robinson, a widower, who had served as the rector of Widmerpool, near Nottingham, from 13 June 1831; he died on 13 November 1869. She died at 2 Brock Street, Bath, on 28 June 1888.

Martha Freer's first publication was the *Life of Marguerite d'Angoulême, Queen of Navarre* (2 vols., 1854). In this work, she attempted to present the sister of Francis I of France as an ideal Victorian lady, a project which was not without some difficulties, as she was obliged to excuse her subject's authorship of the often ribald *Heptameron* and to explain her failure to offer more substantial support to the protestant cause in France. Generally recognized as the first full biography of Marguerite, it was reviewed favourably, although there was some criticism of the length of the book. The critic of *The Athenaeum* commented that the inclusion of extraneous material meant that the biography 'which might have been a work of the most attractive character becomes a thousand pages of hard reading' (*Athenaeum*, 1854), while the reviewer in the *Literary Gazette* felt that this 'interesting and well-written biography' would have been 'improved by condensation' (*Literary Gazette*, 669). The following year, Martha Freer published a biography of Marguerite's daughter, Jeanne of Navarre, a more plausible protestant heroine. Both biographies reached second editions, and they were the most popular and best-known of her works. Later works included *Elizabeth de Valois, Queen of Spain, and the Court of Philip II* (2 vols., 1857)—the portrait of 'a faithful wife, a devoted mother and an affectionate daughter' (2.371)— *History of the Reign of Henry IV, King of France and Navarre* (4 vols., 1860–61), and *The Regency of Anne of Austria* (2 vols., 1866). All her works were published under her maiden name.

Martha Freer's work was clearly inspired by biographical studies of royal women by writers such as Agnes and Elizabeth Strickland and Mary Anne Everett Green, and by the recent publications of Julia Pardoe on French court history. She included much, often tedious, detail about court life and ceremonies, although she never neglected the wider political and religious events of the period, on which, indeed, she increasingly dwelt. She claimed to have access to unpublished material in the French and Spanish archives, and although she made more use of collections of state papers published by European scholars than she indicates, she obviously had contacts in both countries who provided her with archival information. Her attempts to make her subjects conform to Victorian stereotypes prevented her from producing any original conclusions, and her style was verbose and repetitious. Nevertheless, the verdict of Elizabeth Lee, the writer of her entry in the *Dictionary of National Biography*, describing her works as 'mere compilations', is unnecessarily harsh.

ROSEMARY MITCHELL

Sources Allibone, *Dict.* · Boase, *Mod. Eng. biog.* · review, *The Athenaeum* (14 July 1888), 66–7 · review, *The Athenaeum* (19 Aug 1854), 1015–16 · review, *Literary Gazette* (22 July 1854), 667–9 · DNB
Wealth at death £2377 9s. 3d.: probate, 25 June 1889, CGPLA Eng. & Wales

Freeth, Francis Arthur (1884–1970), industrial chemist, was born at 9 Eaton Road, Birkenhead, on 2 January 1884, the elder son of Edward Henry Freeth, master mariner, and his wife, Catherine Hinde. F. A. Freeth, who was an intensely patriotic man, was proud of his military connections. His great-grandfather, General Sir James Freeth, was a Peninsular War veteran and later quartermaster-general (1851–4), and his grandfather and two great-uncles were major-generals. His father was commissioned in the Royal Naval Reserve; he himself became a major in the Territorial Army in the Cheshire regiment and his son served in the Royal Navy.

In Freeth's young days there was little money to spare for non-essentials. His schooling was local, first at Yardleys in Birkenhead and later at Audlem grammar school where in 1897 the Cheshire county council had installed a small chemical laboratory. This, in his own words, 'fired me off properly; there was nothing but chemistry for me'. Through the goodwill of an aunt the possibility of a university career became open to Freeth and his brother, and after a preliminary failure, due to a lack of the necessary mathematics and the loss of a year through illness, Freeth was admitted to the University of Liverpool in 1902. Here he came under the influence of F. G. Donnan who had become professor of physical chemistry in 1904. After obtaining a first class in chemistry in 1905 Freeth worked with Donnan and obtained an MSc a year later. He then worked for a year with Hignetts tobacco factory as an analyst and in September 1907 joined Brunner Mond & Co., the alkali manufacturers at Northwich, a company which later became one of the leading partners in the amalgamation of 1926 which formed ICI.

Freeth rapidly made his mark as a physical chemist in the rich scientific soil of Brunner Mond, and by 1909 was chief chemist. Through correspondence he built a close relationship with the world-famous Dutch school of physical chemists, and himself became a world authority on a rather recondite but important branch of physical chemistry, the phase rule, which governs the equilibria and behaviour of soluble salts. The data he collected and tabulated on this subject, helped by an able team of assistants, who always remembered him with affection, was of immediate practical value to Brunner Mond and was still in demand fifty years later.

On 5 February 1910 Freeth married Ethel Elizabeth (*b.* 1886/7), daughter of George Newton Warbrick, of Thwaites, Cumberland. They had one son and two daughters. When the First World War broke out he was mobilized, on 4 August 1914. He went to France in February 1915 and was recalled in March. Characteristically he refused at first to return but was told that if he did not obey he would be put under arrest.

Freeth and other chemists were summoned home because of a grave crisis caused by the shortage of high explosives. Ammonium nitrate, an essential constituent, was in short supply and Britain lacked the manufacturing capacity to produce it in the quantities required. Freeth and his brother-in-law, H. E. Cocksedge, were among the few who understood the complex chemistry involved, and were in fact able to devise no fewer than three processes for its manufacture from the available raw materials. For his war work Freeth was rewarded, modestly but in keeping with his rank, with the OBE.

After the war, as the great increase in chemical research got under way, Freeth was in the van of events in Brunner Mond, recruiting men from the universities, making scientific contacts abroad, and setting up an industrial laboratory second to none in ability and equipment. His insistence on technique and on quality stamped itself on the company and set the pattern which in later years was to help ICI on the road to world pre-eminence. Freeth's standing was acknowledged by the academic world: he received a doctorate from Leiden (1924) and a DSc from Liverpool (1924) and, in 1925, became FRS. Later came many other distinctions, and he served as president, vice-president, and member of council of several learned societies.

After the formation of ICI, Freeth was separated from his beloved laboratory and set on a different road which ill suited him. He was not at ease in the area of research policy discussions, his health suffered, he began to drink heavily, and in 1937 he broke down. ICI pensioned him and retained him as a consultant. However, with his usual spirit, Freeth, with his brother's help, pulled himself round, stopped drinking, and during the Second World War was able to engage in some secret experimental work on special weapons and operational devices. As a suitable end to a distinguished career Freeth, fully recovered in health, was re-engaged by ICI in 1944 and remained with the company for eight happy years. His work concerned research liaison for the company and in this period he devised and introduced the ICI fellowship scheme for post-doctoral research at universities.

Freeth's accomplishments in the scientific world, which served his country and his employers so well, were more than balanced by his success in the human sphere. He believed passionately in service to the nation and to science. His faith in science and what it could and did achieve under his leadership was ceaselessly preached and ultimately accepted by the company he worked for and by a host of others in industry. He had a profound effect on the fortunes of Brunner Mond and of ICI, not only by the application of his own doctrines but also by his choice of young men who became the leaders of the chemical industry. A larger proportion of early ICI executive directors were 'Freeth men' than came from any of the other founding companies—thirteen out of the first fifty-five. Freeth was a good judge of potential, though, like anyone else, he had his failures. He was also wonderfully good with young people; he never talked down to them and always gave the impression that he was really interested in what they had to say. He did not always insist on the highest academic performance if recruits had ideas which promised to be first class.

Freeth's style in conversation, an art he loved, was often vehement to the point of extravagance. An excellent example is his comment upon the Brunner Mond directors: 'What are they doing, examining last month's costs with a microscope when they should be surveying the horizon with a telescope?' In his farewell speech in ICI he said, on receiving a presentation: 'I am told that somebody has accused me of saying that if the Ministry of Fuel and Power were boring for coal and they went through a layer of gold nine feet thick they would throw it away because they wouldn't know what to do with it. Sir, I only said four feet thick.' In talk Freeth was full of ideas; they poured forth, brilliant, sound, unsound, even crackpot. But on reflection self-criticism was applied and the seething cauldron would simmer down.

Freeth had great energy and sometimes worked himself excessively hard. He had an immense host of friends and acquaintances, although he was something of a snob; he was always ready and able to help one by knowing the right man to approach. He was amazingly good company. He was an artist, a wide and deep thinker in spite of his verbal fireworks, an actor manqué perhaps, vain, eager for praise and renown, sensitive, easily hurt, basically humble. Sir Cyril Hinshelwood once spoke of Freeth's fundamental optimism: 'He spoke ill of very few and well of many.' Perhaps one might end with Freeth's own words: 'I have always observed that it is the cheerful people who get things done and that in dark times one must tell oneself that tomorrow will be a better day.' Freeth died at White House Nursing Home at Church Crookham, Hampshire, on 15 July 1970. He was survived by his wife.

PETER ALLEN, rev.

Sources P. Allen, *Memoirs FRS*, 22 (1976), 105–18 • personal knowledge (1981) • private information (1981) • m. cert. • d. cert.
Archives Ches. & Chester ALSS, experimental notebooks, report | King's Lond., Liddell Hart C., corresp. with Sir B. H. Liddell Hart
Wealth at death £8957: probate, 9 Feb 1971, *CGPLA Eng. & Wales*

Freeth, John [*pseud.* John Free] (1731–1808), innkeeper and political ballad writer, was born at the Bell tavern, Philip Street, Birmingham, the son of Charles Freeth, landlord of the Bell, and his wife, Mary. Nothing is known of Freeth's education or of his early years, although it seems that he was once an itinerant street ballad singer. Where and when Freeth married is not known. His wife's name was Sarah and she was five years his junior. By 1768 John Freeth had become landlord of the Leicester Arms, on the corner of Bell Street and Lease Lane, Birmingham, where he remained until his death in 1808. Freeth's Coffee House, as the Leicester Arms was known, became one of the most celebrated taverns in England, and Freeth became known as 'the Birmingham poet'.

It was Freeth's custom to write songs—setting his words to popular tunes—about remarkable events in local and national news, and to sing them nightly to the company assembled at his coffee house. The habit was profitable: it crowded the place with patrons, attracted eminent visitors, and, since Freeth wrote as a determined radical and nonconformist, created a political meeting-place. The interest aroused by his songs encouraged Freeth to publish them, and the words of nearly 400 songs appeared in more than a dozen collections between 1766 and 1805; John Baskerville (1706–1775) was among his printers. The most substantial of these collections was *The Political Songster* (1790).

Freeth usually sang about feats of war, national emergencies, and affairs of state, such as the victories of Earl Howe and Lord Nelson, and the activities of Charles James Fox, Lord North, and William Pitt. To those ballads he added a substantial leavening of others that were complimentary, jocular, and satirical. Although unsophisticated, many of his patriotic songs have a stirring lilt; on politics he wrote with indignation, rough good humour, and an effective turn of phrase that earned him the reputation of being one of the best political ballad writers in the kingdom. From 1771 until 1785 Freeth used the pen-name John Free in punning allusion to his beliefs. His songs offer a significant insight into the popular politics of the late eighteenth century.

To draw attention to the hospitality provided at his inn Freeth issued printed invitation cards, written in verse. In some fifteen lines, he extends his invitation, comments forcefully on an item of news, and indicates the fare offered. With these cards Freeth originated an unusual, possibly unique, kind of trade card.

In late Georgian Birmingham, Freeth was an outstanding figure, respected for his probity and the warmth of his friendships. A notable group portrait was painted by Johann Eckstein entitled *John Freeth and his Circle* (1792). Freeth died, possibly of Paget's disease, in Birmingham on 29 September 1808, and was buried at the Old Meeting-

House, Birmingham. He was subsequently reinterred at Witton cemetery, Birmingham, in 1882. His wife, Sarah, died on 25 November 1807. Of their nine children, one son and seven daughters were mentioned in Freeth's will.

JOHN HORDEN, *rev.*

Sources J. Horden, *John Freeth (1731–1808): political ballad-writer and innkeeper* (1993)
Archives Birm. CL
Likenesses J. Eckstein?, pastels, 18th cent., repro. in Horden, *John Freeth* · oils, 18th cent., Birmingham Museums and Art Gallery · oils, 18th cent., Birmingham Reference Library; copy, 19th cent., Birmingham Reference Library · pastels, 18th cent., Birmingham Museums and Art Gallery · J. Millar, oil on wood panel, *c*.1790, Birmingham Museums and Art Gallery · J. Eckstein, group portrait, oils, 1792 (*John Freeth and his circle*), Birmingham Museums and Art Gallery · J. Bisset?, oils, Birmingham Museums and Art Gallery

Freind, John (1675–1728), physician, was born at Croughton, Northamptonshire, the third and youngest son of the Revd William Freind (1634–1689), rector at Croughton, and his wife, Anne Smith (*d.* 1722). Robert *Freind (1666/7–1751) and William *Freind (1668/9–1745) were his brothers. Freind and his brothers were educated at Westminster School under its famous headmaster Richard Busby and at Christ Church, Oxford. Freind matriculated at Christ Church on 7 July 1694, and received the BA on 4 June 1698, MA on 12 April 1701, BM on 1 June 1703, and DM (by diploma) on 12 June 1707.

Freind's skill in Latin, as well as his high tory politics (his brother Robert had accompanied the deposed James II to Paris), attracted the attention of the dean of Christ Church, Henry Aldrich. Aldrich assigned him, with P. Foulkes, the task of editing a new edition with Latin translation of the Greek orations of Aeschines and Demosthenes, which was published in 1696. Also in that year appeared Freind's edition of Ovid's *Metamorphoses*. While at Christ Church, Freind became friends with Francis Atterbury, then a tutor, and studied mathematics with the Newtonian David Gregory. He also became involved in the *Phalaris* controversy, taking, like Aldrich, the side of Charles Boyle against Richard Bentley.

Medicine and natural philosophy soon superseded literature for Freind, although in his medical works, written mostly in Latin, he sustained his reputation as a Latin stylist. In 1699 he sent to Hans Sloane an account of his dissection of a hydrocephalic child, which was published in the *Philosophical Transactions* (256, 1699). In the same journal in April 1701 appeared his account of a strange case of convulsions among several young people in Oxfordshire; he denied the existence of any supernatural agency and attributed the spasms to the irregular motion of the animal spirits. In 1703 he published his first major work, *Emmenologia*, a treatise on menstruation, which Freind described largely in terms of hydraulics, following the theories of the Newtonian Archibald Pitcairne. But Freind also included much learned reference to classical authors. He dedicated the book to the noted anatomist James Douglas.

Freind was closely associated with Gregory and with his students James and John Keill, who were investigating

John Freind (1675–1728), by Michael Dahl, *c.*1720–30

Newton's theory of matter. In 1704 Freind was appointed professor of chemistry at Oxford, and delivered a series of lectures which were published in 1709 as *Praelectiones chymicae*. In these he attempted to explain chemical phenomena in terms of atoms and a Newtonian short-range force, following the work of John Keill.

Freind accompanied the earl of Peterborough to Spain as a physician to the army in 1705. On his way home two years later he stopped in Rome to visit the eminent physicians Giorgio Baglivi and Giovanni Maria Lancisi. Upon his return to Britain, Freind wrote a pamphlet defending the conduct of his patron, whose military actions had been criticized. His *Account of the Earl of Peterborow's Conduct in Spain* (1707) reached a third edition within a year and elicited several responses. Meanwhile he received his DM degree and entered medical practice in London. On 3 December 1709 at St Anne's, Westminster, he married Anne Morice or Morrice (*d.* 1737), daughter of Thomas Morice, paymaster to the English forces in Portugal. They had one son, John. It is probable that Anne Morice was related to William Morrice, who married Atterbury's daughter Mary in 1715.

A second edition of Freind's *Praelectiones chymicae* was published in Amsterdam in 1710, leading to a critical review in the Leipzig *Acta Eruditorum*. Freind replied in a Latin letter in the *Philosophical Transactions* in 1711 in which he defended Newton's theory of matter. The German criticism was part of the wider debate between partisans of Newton and Leibniz on the origins of the calculus. Freind's defence of the Newtonian position undoubtedly paved the way for his election to the Royal Society in

March 1712. In that year he issued an English translation of *Praelectiones chymicae* which included his reply.

Shortly after his election to the Royal Society, Freind again left for the battlefront, this time as the duke of Ormond's physician in Flanders, where he remained for nearly a year. After his return he settled into London practice and was admitted a candidate of the Royal College of Physicians on 30 September 1713 and a fellow on 9 April 1716, on the same day as his friend and rival Richard Mead. Freind rapidly became among the most successful of London's physicians.

As his position in the *Phalaris* debate indicated, Freind supported the ancients in the 'battle of the books' of the 1690s. Yet his wholehearted defence of Newtonianism indicated that, in natural philosophy, he was a modern. He attempted to reconcile these apparently conflicting positions in his 1717 edition of books 1 and 3 of the *Epidemics* of Hippocrates, in Greek with a Latin translation. He dedicated the book to Richard Frewin. Freind accompanied the edition with nine commentaries of his own upon fevers, in which he argued that modern, Newtonian theory and practice had confirmed many of the observations of Hippocrates. Truth, explained Freind, was eternal and God-given, and God gave the privilege of understanding it only to certain individuals in each generation. Hippocrates was one of these; Newton was another. The nine commentaries covered the usual therapies, including bleeding, sweating, and vomiting. The commentary on purging included letters to and from Richard Mead and other physicians on the value of purging in smallpox. Freind advised purging after the second fever, a practice some derided as coming too late to be effective, while others questioned the value of purging over emetics.

Freind's controversial views on purging led to a vicious pamphlet war which raged for several years. The physician John Woodward attacked Freind in his 1718 *The State of Physick: and of Diseases*, arguing against Freind's hydraulic physiology as well as his method of cure. Newton had expelled Woodward from the Royal Society in 1710 after a quarrel with Hans Sloane. Woodward therefore had little sympathy for Newton's followers. Freind replied in a Latin letter to Mead, and in a satirical pamphlet, *A Letter to the Learned Dr Woodward by Dr Byfield*, both published in 1719. The 'Dr Byfield' of the latter work was a well-known empirical physician, but it was generally recognized that Freind was the author. Several other pamphlets, mostly anonymous, appeared on both sides of the debate. Woodward himself responded in *The Two Sosias, or, The True Dr Byfielde at the Rainbow Coffee-House, to the Pretender in Jermyn-Street* (1719). In the same year the apothecary John Quincy, a protégé of the late Archibald Pitcairne, defended Freind in his *Examination of Dr Woodward's State of Physick and Diseases*, but pamphlets continued to fly until at least 1722.

The Royal College of Physicians, under the presidency of Sloane, demonstrated its support of Freind by naming him Goulstonian lecturer in 1717; he was made a censor on 30 September 1718, and he delivered the Harveian oration

on 18 October 1720. In 1722 Freind was elected to parliament as a member for Launceston in Cornwall. His tory politics were well known, and he was often critical of Walpole's policies in the house. His close association with Atterbury had already led to suspicions of Jacobitism. In the controversy surrounding Defoe's 1714 pamphlet *The Secret History of the White Staff*, which named Atterbury as the mastermind of a Jacobite conspiracy, Freind's name emerged as a co-conspirator, along with George Smalridge, another Christ Church man. They were named in an anonymous pamphlet, *A Supplement to the Secret History of the White Staff, &c. containing, I: Dr Freind's Character of the Staff, II: Dr Atterbury's Character of the Purse, III: Dr Smalridge's Character of the Mitre* (1715).

Freind became involved in the Atterbury plot of 1722. For some time he had been in touch with the Stuart court in Rome and in 1720 had engaged a nurse for the newly born Young Pretender. On 30 March 1722 the Pretender wrote to Lord Strafford, who was to command the rising in the north:

> I think you have done very well to let Dr. Freind into the secret of our present affair. He is a most worthy man and out of good will to me would have quitted both his practice and his country to have attended me if I would have allowed him, which is a sufficient proof of his sincere attachment to me and the cause. (HoP, *Commons*, 53)

By April, Freind appears to have been in charge of the military chest. He escaped arrest when the other conspirators were held in August and September because, although he had been mentioned frequently in intercepted correspondence under the name of Clinton, the government decipherers had been unable to identify him. However, when the nurse he had engaged for the Young Pretender returned to England in March 1723 she admitted to her interrogators that her expenses had been paid by Freind and that she had delivered letters from him to others in the Pretender's service. Freind was arrested the next day. He was committed to the Tower on 15 March 1723 and released on bail on 21 June, with Drs Mead, Hale, Hulse, and Levett providing his sureties. According to an anecdote, Mead had been consulted by Walpole and refused to prescribe for him until his friend was released. Another story stated that Mead, who had assumed Freind's practice during his imprisonment, presented him with 5000 guineas on his release, representing the fees paid to him by Freind's patients. This sum is wildly exaggerated; Mead himself, the most successful physician in London, made that much over the course of a year. The charges against Freind were dismissed on 28 November 1723.

While in the Tower, Freind wrote a short treatise on smallpox, in the form of a letter addressed to Mead, which was published in 1723. Mead had sent him the new edition of Daniel Leclerc's *Histoire de la médecine* (1723, first published 1702). Leclerc's revision included a new section on 'modern' medicine in which he extolled Paracelsus. Freind disagreed with Paracelsian ideas and thought that Newton had been far more important to the development of true medical theory. Before his release from the Tower, Freind began to outline what would be his greatest work,

The History of Physick from the Time of Galen to the Beginning of the Sixteenth Century. This work, also addressed to Mead and published in three parts in two volumes in 1725–6, displayed to the fullest Freind's classical learning. The first part surveyed classical authors after Galen, and remains a masterful survey of late antique medical practice. As in his earlier work on Hippocrates, he separated theory from practice, noting that much could be learned from ancient medical practice, even if its theories were erroneous. However, as examples Freind chose practices which conformed to his own Newtonian theories.

The second part discussed medieval Arabic medicine and the third, medieval English medicine up to the time of Thomas Linacre in the sixteenth century. Throughout, Freind argued that medical practice had indeed progressed over the centuries, but medical theory had seen little progress until his own time. He characterized the physician as the possessor of a God-given talent, and the parallel between this characterization and the divinely ordained monarch of the Jacobites was not coincidental. He made this parallel clear in his discussion of the 'King's touch', whose efficacy was affirmed by 'undoubted authorities' (*History of Physick*, 2.274–5).

The History of Physick proved to be very popular, reaching a third edition within a year. Freind's criticisms of Daniel Leclerc were answered by his brother Jean Leclerc in his journal *Bibliothèque Ancienne et Moderne* (1726), who was in turn answered by John Baillie in a 1728 pamphlet. Baillie's pamphlet also replied to a 1726 critique by 'C. W. M. D.' whom Baillie identified as William Cockburn. Cockburn, who had made his fortune from a proprietary cure for dysentery, was stung by Freind's remark that such nostrums were the mark of a quack; apart from his own pamphlet, he also translated and published Jean Leclerc's critique, to which he added a preface.

These criticisms had little effect on the success of the book or on Freind's flourishing career. Soon after his release from the Tower he was named physician to the children of the prince and princess of Wales, and on the accession of George II in 1727 he was named one of the physicians to Queen Caroline. Some comment arose from these appointments, both that they were awarded to someone of Freind's political beliefs, and that he accepted them. His brother Robert, in the preface to Freind's collected works, complained of 'murmurings' against him. But Atterbury, by then in exile, dedicated to Freind his *Reflections on the Character of Iapis in Virgil* (1728), a discussion of the attributes of an ideal physician, which would seem to indicate that he held no ill feeling toward the doctor. The Royal College of Physicians also continued to display its confidence in Freind, who presented to the House of Commons the college's 1725 'Representation against the pernicious use of strong spirituous liquors'.

At the height of his career Freind fell ill and died of a fever, on 26 July 1728, aged fifty-two. He was buried in the church at Hitcham, Buckinghamshire, where he had purchased an estate in 1700. An inscription was placed in the church to mark his resting place. In London he had lived in Albemarle Street. A monument to the doctor was erected in Westminster Abbey, which included a long Latin epitaph by his brother Robert, half of which, according to lines attributed to Pope, 'will never be believ'd, the other never read'.

John Freind was one of the most successful physicians of his era. His *History of Physick* was much admired and remained a standard reference for many years. His writings on medical theory and practice, along with those of Richard Mead and other Newtonian physicians, established a new basis for medical thinking. Although these new theories proved to be short-lived, in their time they were highly significant and contributed to the turbulent and controversial atmosphere of medicine in early eighteenth-century London. As a friend and associate of Atterbury and a member of parliament, Freind also played a role, however minor, in some of the major political events of the 1720s.

Freind's will, written on 12 March 1727 and confirmed on 29 May 1728, named as his executors his brother Robert, John Law, and Captain Mordaunt Cratherode. He left to his wife, Anne, the income from £4000, or £200 per annum, as she preferred. She lived until 1737 and was buried next to her husband. The remainder of the estate, apart from some minor bequests, passed to their son, John, then a minor. John died unmarried in 1750.

ANITA GUERRINI

Sources J. Wigan, 'Praefatio', in *Joannis Freind medicinae doctoris opera omnia medica* (1773) · *Biographia Britannica, or, The lives of the most eminent persons who have flourished in Great Britain and Ireland*, 3 (1750) · T. M. Brown, 'The mechanical philosophy and the "Animal oeconomy": a study in the development of English physiology in the seventeenth and early eighteenth century', PhD diss., Princeton University, 1968 · A. Guerrini, 'Newtonian matter theory, chemistry, and medicine, 1690–1713', PhD diss., Indiana University, 1983 · R. J. J. Martin, 'Explaining John Freind's *History of Physick*', *Studies in History and Philosophy of Science*, 19 (1988), 399–418 · HoP, *Commons, 1715–54* · *DNB* · Munk, *Roll* · *IGI* · will, PRO, PROB 11/623, sig. 235

Archives BL, Sloane MSS, prescriptions, MS 3984 · BL, Sloane MSS, corresp., MSS 4026, 4047, 4059, 4066, 4068 · BL, corresp., Add. MS 32686 · Christ Church Oxf., corresp. · RCP Lond., corresp. · RS, classified MSS

Likenesses M. Dahl, oils, c.1720–1730, Bodl. Oxf. [see illus.] · P. Fourdrinier, line engraving, 1725 (after M. Dahl), Wellcome L. · G. Vertue, line engraving, 1730 (after M. Dahl), BM, NPG, RCP Lond., Wellcome L. · J. Bluck, coloured aquatint, 1811 (*John Freind's monument*; after H. Villiers), Wellcome L. · M. Dahl, oils, second version, RCP Lond. · F. St Urbain, copper medal, BM · boxwood medallion, RCP Lond. · line engraving (after M. Dahl), Wellcome L. · medal, RCP Lond.

Wealth at death £4000 (£200 p.a.) to wife; also bequests of £1–£200 to friends and relatives; houses in London and Hitcham: will, PRO, PROB 11/623, sig. 235

Freind, Robert (1666/7–1751), headmaster, was born at Croughton, Northamptonshire, the eldest of the three sons and one daughter of the Revd William Freind (1634–1689), rector of Croughton, and his wife, Anne (d. 1722), daughter of Francis Smith of Worcestershire. His brothers were William *Freind (1668/9–1745), Church of England clergyman, and John *Freind (1675–1728), physician. Robert was admitted to Westminster School, London, in 1680,

The most significant event of Freind's time at Westminster, however, was the controversy surrounding plans to build a new dormitory for the scholars in the college garden. This proposal, which first surfaced in 1710, received new impetus with the appointment of Francis Atterbury as dean in 1713. Atterbury secured George I's approval for the new dormitory and obtained a substantial contribution from him towards the building costs. Freind and several members of the chapter, however, objected to the plan on the grounds that it would be detrimental to their own properties, which abutted on the intended site for the building. The dispute passed through chancery and the House of Lords before finally being decided in Atterbury's favour. Freind accepted defeat with a good grace and did what he could to forward the work. He continued as headmaster until his resignation in May 1733. On 8 May 1731 he had been installed as a prebendary of Westminster, and he retained this position for a further ten years, in spite of also obtaining a canonry at Christ Church, Oxford, to which he was admitted on 29 March 1737.

Freind had married Jane, daughter of Dr Samuel de L'Angle, prebendary of Westminster, on 21 May 1713. They had four children, three of whom did not survive beyond childhood. The career of the fourth, William *Freind (*bap.* 1715, *d.* 1766), who ultimately became dean of Canterbury, was a frequent cause of concern to his father who, in his letters to the duke of Newcastle (the letters survive in the British Library), frequently solicited the duke's patronage on behalf of his son. In 1734 Freind resolved to resign the rectory at Witney in his son's favour, but could not do so without the permission of Bishop Benjamin Hoadley, which he doubted would be forthcoming. Hearing of his desire, however, Dr Hoadley is said to have replied: 'If Dr Freind can ask it, I can grant it' (Nichols, *Lit. anecdotes*, 5.87).

Freind's published output was small. His Latin poetry, which was superior to his English verse, included (in addition to the Oxford pieces already mentioned) two pieces published in *Musarum Anglicanarum* (1698), a Latin ode to the duke of Newcastle in the *Gentleman's Magazine* of 1737 (7.631), and verses on the death of Queen Caroline printed in *Pietas academiae Oxoniensis* (1738). Freind had previously written a dedication to the queen to preface the medical works of his brother John, published in 1733. The edition of Cicero's *De oratore* which Freind is alleged to have published in 1724 does not appear in the *English Short-Title Catalogue*. Freind was, however, a prolific author of Latin epigrams and monumental inscriptions. The best-known of the latter adorns the monument of Philip Carteret, younger brother of Lord Carteret, in the north aisle of Westminster Abbey. Freind's facility with Latin epitaphs was satirized in lines attributed to Pope (who was generally reckoned to be the master of the same form in English):

> Freind, for your epitaphs I'm grieved,
> Where still so much is said,
> One half will never be believ'd,

ROBERTUS FREIND. S.T.P.
SCHOLÆ. WESTMON: PER XXI ANNOS
ARCHIDIDASCALUS.

Robert Freind (1666/7–1751), by John Michael Rysbrack, 1738

and as a king's scholar doubtless participated in the traditional salutation of the monarch by the Westminster scholars at the coronation of James II in 1685. Four years later, while a student at Christ Church, Oxford, whence he had matriculated in 1686 aged nineteen, Freind wrote English verses celebrating the inauguration of William and Mary which were printed in *Vota Oxoniensia* (1689), the university's poetic tribute to the joint monarchs.

Freind graduated BA in 1690 and proceeded MA in 1693. In 1698 he served as proctor for the university, and in the same year was involved in the dispute between Charles Boyle and Richard Bentley concerning the authenticity of the 'Letters of Phalaris'. Most of the criticism which formed the body of Boyle's *Dr Bentley's Dissertations on the Epistles of Phalaris* (1698) has been attributed to Freind and Francis Atterbury (Nichols, *Lit. anecdotes*, 5.86). In 1699 Freind returned to Westminster School as under-master in succession to the classical scholar Michael Maittaire. He graduated BD and DD in 1709 and the following year preached before the House of Commons at St Margaret's, Westminster, the sermon being afterwards published. At about the same time he obtained the valuable rectory of Witney, Oxfordshire, where he frequently resided.

On 9 August 1711 Freind was appointed headmaster of Westminster School, in succession to Thomas Knipe. The school flourished under his direction. An energetic man of social gifts as well as a good scholar, he numbered among his friends not only literary figures such as Jonathan Swift and Matthew Prior but also political leaders—for instance, the earl of Peterborough and Robert Harley. Westminster's pre-eminence as the favourite place of education for the aristocracy became undisputed during his mastership.

The other never read.

Freind died on 7 August 1751, aged eighty-four, presumably in Witney; he was survived by his widow. He was buried in the chancel of Witney church, where a monument commemorates him and several other members of his family. In his will he bequeathed to his son William the advowson of his father's old parish of Croughton and made bequests to the poor of that parish and of Witney. He left instructions that his papers should be destroyed.

TONY TROWLES

Sources *Old Westminsters* · Nichols, *Lit. anecdotes*, 5.86–90 · J. Sargeaunt, *Annals of Westminster School* (1898) · *DNB* · S. Smith, 'The Westminster dormitory', *Lord Burlington: the man and his politics*, ed. E. Corp (1998), 51–70 · J. L. Chester, ed., *The marriage, baptismal, and burial registers of the collegiate church or abbey of St Peter, Westminster*, Harleian Society, 10 (1876) · *GM*, 1st ser., 21 (1751), 380

Archives BL, letters to duke of Newcastle, Add. MSS 32687–32714, *passim*

Likenesses oils, *c*.1729, Christ Church Oxf. · J. M. Rysbrack, marble bust, 1738, Christ Church Oxf. [*see illus.*] · M. Dahl, oils, Christ Church Oxf. · portrait, Westminster School, London

Wealth at death over £375; plus furniture and chattels: will, PRO, PROB 11/790/59

Freind, William (1668/9–1745), Church of England clergyman and lottery winner, was born probably at Croughton, Northamptonshire, where his father, William Freind (1634–1689), was rector; his mother was Anne Freind, *née* Smith (*d*. 1722). Robert *Freind (1666/7–1751) and John *Freind (1675–1728) were his brothers. He was educated at Westminster School, where he was elected king's scholar in 1683, and at Christ Church, Oxford, where he matriculated on 15 July 1687, aged eighteen, and took his BA in 1691 and MA in 1694. The date of his ordination is unknown, but he was curate of Croughton in 1699. On 18 November 1706, at Langley Marish, Buckinghamshire, he married Bridget (1684/5–1721), daughter of William Glover (*d*. 1707), vicar of Burnham, Buckinghamshire, and his wife, Mary (*d*. 1711). William and Bridget had three daughters.

Freind was instituted as one of the two rectors of Woodford by Thrapston, Northamptonshire, on 21 February 1711 and succeeded his brother Robert as rector of Turvey, Bedfordshire, in 1714. He resided in neither parish and employed curates. He came to wide notice when newspapers reported that on 14 February 1715 he had won the first prize, of £20,000, in 'The Adventure of £1,400,000' by statute 13 Anne c. 18, a kind of state lottery. The 'Adventure' was in fact a government loan baited with prizes: all subscribers won an annuity proportionate to their subscription, or, in the case of prize winners, the value of the prize. The lump sum of the prize was retained by the government on the understanding that it would eventually be repaid; meanwhile interest would be paid for thirty-two years. Freind therefore had won an annuity of £800 p.a. until 1747, while both the annuity and the capital value of the prize provided security for heavy borrowing.

Bridget Freind dispensed some of this fortune in charities around Burnham before her early death on 25 August

1721, and Freind's own charities included donations totalling £400 to augment two poor livings—Biddlesden, in Buckinghamshire, and Ampthill, in Bedfordshire—so that their incumbents could obtain grants from Queen Anne's Bounty, but it seems that his major outlay was in establishing himself as a country gentleman. He bought the manor of Hitcham, near Burnham, and for a while provided lavish hospitality, sometimes for royal guests, but was evidently short of money when his brother John left him £100 p.a. in a will dated 12 March 1727. Hitcham had been sold to John by then. Perhaps Freind had compounded his financial difficulties by converting his annuity into South Sea stock, as was provided for in the 'Adventure' act of 13 Anne c. 18, and then losing heavily when the bubble burst in September 1720.

There are few traces of Freind after 1727. A newspaper report of 2 May 1730 on the marriage of his eldest daughter, Anne, to the son of Bishop George Smalridge refers to Freind as 'him who got the great prize' (Nichols, *Lit. anecdotes*, 5.92). A newspaper of about 1736 advertised the forthcoming publication, in 150 weekly 2*d*. numbers, of a biblical narrative by Freind entitled *The Sacred Historian* (ibid., 5.697) but no such work has been traced, nor has *The Christian Minister Absolutely Necessary to be in Every Family*, attributed to Freind in the *Dictionary of National Biography*. By October 1742 he was a prisoner for debt in the king's bench. Laetitia Pilkington (*c*.1709–1750) describes him conducting divine service for prisoners every Sunday in the neighbouring Marshalsea prison, like Orpheus playing to wolves and bears: 'so fine an Orator, a Gentleman! and, by all Accounts, only undone by boundless Generosity and Hospitality' (*Memoirs of Laetitia Pilkington*, 1.206).

In 1742 Freind was appointed chaplain of a ship of 100 guns by favour of Daniel Finch, eighth earl of Winchilsea and third earl of Nottingham (1689–1769); he then resigned his living of Woodford by Thrapston but, it seems, retained Turvey until his death. It is unlikely that the septuagenarian chaplain saw active service or, indeed, full liberty. More likely he remained a privileged prisoner, receiving clerical income and lodging in the 'rules'—the streets neighbouring the prison. Certainly he died in such lodgings, in Blackman Street, Southwark, on 15 April 1745. Bishop Thomas Newton's story that Freind won two huge lottery prizes is probably apocryphal, despite corroborative detail added by John Nichols.

JAMES SAMBROOK

Sources Nichols, *Lit. anecdotes*, 5.85, 90–92, 102, 697 · L. Pilkington, *Memoirs of Laetitia Pilkington*, ed. A. C. Elias, 2 vols. (1997), vol. 1, pp. 205–6; vol. 2, pp. 589–90 · *Works of the Rt. Rev. Thomas Newton* (1782), vol. 1, p. 125 ['Some account of the author's life ... written by himself'] · C. L. E. Ewen, *Lotteries and sweepstakes* (1932), 140–41 · A. Luders and others, eds., *Statutes of the realm*, 11 vols. in 12, RC (1810–28), vol. 9, pp. 936–60 · W. A. Shaw, ed., *Calendar of treasury books*, 29, PRO (1957), 511, 803–5, 808 · monument, St Peter's Church, Burnham, Buckinghamshire [Bridget Freind] · J. Ecton, *Thesaurus rerum ecclesiasticorum*, 2nd edn (1754), xvii · W. M. Harvey, *History and antiquities of the hundred of Willey* (1872–8), 199–200 · *Old Westminsters*, vols. 1–2 · G. Baker, *The history and antiquities of the county of Northampton*, 1 (1822–30), 601–2 · G. Taylor, *The sea chaplains* (1978), 503 · A. J. Jewers, 'Pedigree of the family of Freind', *The Genealogist*, new ser., 30 (1914), 230–31, 236–7 · J. Bridges, *The history and antiquities of Northamptonshire*, ed. P. Whalley, 2 (1791), 268–9 ·

E. A. Irons, *Northamptonshire and Rutland clergy*, 16: *Addenda and corrigenda* (1952), 60 · parish registers, Woodford by Thrapston [bishop's transcripts] · J. Carswell, *The South Sea Bubble* (1960) · R. D. Richards, 'The lottery in the history of English government finance', *Economic History*, 3 (1934–7), 57–60 · *VCH Buckinghamshire*, 3.233 · Foster, *Alum. Oxon.* · *IGI* · J. Innes, 'The king's bench prison in the later eighteenth century', in J. Brewer and J. Staples, *An ungovernable people* (1980), 250–98

Freind, William (*bap.* 1715, *d.* 1766), dean of Canterbury, was baptized in Westminster Abbey on 10 March 1715, the son of Robert *Freind (1666/7–1751), headmaster of Westminster School, and his wife, Jane, daughter of Samuel de L'Angle, prebendary of Westminster. Admitted on the foundation at Westminster School in 1727, he matriculated at Christ Church, Oxford, in 1731, where he proceeded BA in 1735, MA in 1738, and BD and DD in 1748. He was instituted to the valuable rectory of Witney, Oxfordshire, on 4 April 1739, upon the resignation of his father, and in the same month he married Grace, second daughter of William Robinson of Rokeby Park, Yorkshire, and sister to Richard Robinson (1709–1794), later archbishop of Armagh. She died on 28 December 1776. They had one daughter, Elizabeth, married to Duncan Campbell, a captain in the marines, and three sons: Robert, William Maximilian, and John, all of whom followed their father and grandfather to Christ Church. The youngest, as Sir John Robinson, eventually succeeded to the estates of the archbishop, his maternal uncle.

On 17 October 1744 Freind succeeded his father again, this time as prebendary of Westminster, and in the same year he became chaplain-in-ordinary to George II. In 1747 he was presented to the rectory of Islip, Oxfordshire, which he held together with Witney. Freind resigned his Westminster prebend upon promotion to a canonry at Christ Church, where he succeeded David Gregory on 15 March 1756, and his unconditional surrender of this preferment is said to have secured for him the deanery of Canterbury, where he was installed on 14 June 1760. In the following year he was appointed prolocutor of the lower house of convocation and delivered the customary *concio ad clerum* (on Galatians 5: 1), which was regarded as 'elegant and animated' (Hasted, 12.44). Apart from this, Freind published little: a Latin ode on the death of Queen Caroline appeared in an Oxford collection of verses in 1738, and in 1755 he was invited to print an unremarkable sermon delivered before the House of Commons on the anniversary of the death of Charles I. However, he was well regarded at Canterbury, where it was said that 'few deans have been more esteemed than Dr Freind … he possessed a most benevolent heart, and he was modest and unassuming' (Todd, 222). He was also remembered as a lover of music, who arranged frequent well-attended concerts during his time at the deanery, and as a scholar and connoisseur. Having inherited the greater part of the fortune of his uncle, John Freind MD (1675–1728), he was able to afford items of the finest quality, such as a bust by Rysbrack of his father, which he left to the library at Christ Church. His valuable collections of books, paintings, and prints attracted much interest when they were sold by

auction in 1767. Freind died at Canterbury on 26 November 1766 and was buried at Witney, where a short inscription to his memory was placed upon the monument to his father and his mother in the church there.

RICHARD SHARP

Sources E. Hasted, *The history and topographical survey of the county of Kent*, 2nd edn, 12 (1801), 44–5 · H. J. Todd, *Some account of the deans of Canterbury* (1793), 220–24 · J. M. Cowper, *The lives of the deans of Canterbury* (1900), 174–7 · *GM*, 1st ser., 36 (1766), 599 · Nichols, *Lit. anecdotes*, 5.89, 104–5 · *Old Westminsters*, 1.353 · Foster, *Alum. Oxon.* · *DNB*
Archives BL, corresp. with duke of Newcastle, Add. MSS 32703–32971, *passim* · Hunt. L., letters to Elizabeth Montagu
Likenesses T. Worlidge, drypoint etching, BM, NPG · oils, deanery, Canterbury; repro. in Cowper, *Lives of the deans of Canterbury*, facing p. 174

Freine, Simund de [Simon de Fraxino] (*d.* before **1228**?), poet, from a family connected with Sutton Freen, Herefordshire, was a canon of Hereford by *c.*1190 and bore the title *magister*. Two poems were addressed by him to Gerald of Wales in, perhaps, 1194–7 (extant in LPL, MS 236, folios 166–166b; the texts are also in BL, Cotton MS Vitellius E.v (sixteenth-century), and Cambridge, Corpus Christi College, MS 400, page 119, which give thirty-one lines omitted in the Lambeth manuscript). One poem urges Gerald to stay in Hereford, commending the extensive studies of its cathedral school; one warmly defends him against Abbot Adam of Dore's criticism. Simund wrote two substantial Anglo-Norman poems in heptasyllabic lines. His adaptation of Boethius's *Consolation of Philosophy*, *Le roman de philosophie*, is extant in BL, Royal MS 20 B.xiv, folios 68v–77v; Bodl. Oxf., MS Douce 210, folios 51v–59v; and BL, Add. MS 46919, folios 107–16. Simund's life of St George, *La vie de Saint Georges* (Paris, Bibliothèque Nationale, MS Fr. 902, fols. 108–17), was perhaps written for Archbishop Baldwin's preaching of the third crusade in 1188. Both poems include Simund's acrostic signature in their first twenty lines. They were probably written under the patronage of Bishop William de Vere who may be the provenance of extra information in the anti-Muslim *Georges*. If so, any further writings by Simund between de Vere's death in 1198 and his own, implicit in a charter datable to 1224×8, are unknown.

JOCELYN WOGAN-BROWNE

Sources *Les oeuvres de Simund de Freine*, ed. J. E. Matzke (Paris, 1909) [incl. two Anglo-Norman poems] · *Gir. Camb. opera*, 382–4, 385–7 [edn of LPL, MS 236, fols. 166–166b] · R. W. Hunt, 'English learning in the late twelfth century', *TRHS*, 4th ser., 19 (1936), 19–42, esp. 36–7; repr. in R. W. Southern, ed., *Essays in medieval history* (1968) · J. Barrow, 'A twelfth-century bishop and literary patron: William de Vere', *Viator*, 18 (1987), 175–89 · M. D. Legge, *Anglo-Norman literature and its background* (1963); repr. (1978), 183–7 · J. C. Russell, 'Dictionary of writers of thirteenth century England', *BIHR*, special suppl., 3 (1936) [whole issue], esp. 149–50 · Bale, *Index*, 412 · M. R. James, *A descriptive catalogue of the manuscripts in the library of Corpus Christi College, Cambridge*, 2 (1912), 266 · R. Bartlett, *Gerald of Wales, 1146–1223* (1982) · J. E. Matzke, 'The legend of St George', *Publications of the Modern Language Association of America*, 17 (1902), 464–535; 18 (1903), 99–171, esp. 165–6 · D. Royce, ed., *Landboc, sive, Registrum monasterii beatae Mariae virginis et sancti Cenhelmi de Winchelcumba*, 2 (1903), 262 · W. W. Capes, ed., *Charters and records of Hereford Cathedral*, Cantilupe Society (1908), 38 · J. Barrow, ed., *Hereford, 1079–1234*, English Episcopal Acta, 7 (1993), 175, 249, 277 · R. Sharpe, *A* *handlist of the Latin writers of Great Britain and Ireland before 1540* (1997), 614

Archives Bibliothèque Nationale, Paris, MS Fr. 902, fols. 108–17 · BL, Cotton MS Vitellius E.v · BL, Royal MS 20 B.xiv, fols. 68v–77v · Bodl. Oxf., MS Douce 210, fols. 51v–59v · CCC Cam., MS 400, p. 119 · LPL, MS 236, fols. 166–166b | Balliol Oxf., MS 271, fol. 87v · BL, Arundel MS 19, fol. 31 · Bodl. Oxf., MS Rawl. B392, fol. 54

Freke, Elizabeth (1642–1714), autobiographer, was born on new year's day 1642 in Westminster, the eldest surviving child of Raphe Freke of Hannington, Wiltshire (*bap.* 1596, *d.* 1684), and Cicely (*bap.* 1610, *d.* 1651), daughter of Sir Thomas Culpeper of Hollingbourne, Kent. After her mother's early death Freke and her three sisters were raised by her father and her maternal aunt. In contrast to her sister Frances *Norton, Lady Norton, and her niece Grace *Gethin, Lady Gethin, who published devotional works, Freke's autobiographical memoir is an almost entirely secular account of a propertied gentlewoman's complex and unhappy marriage. She recorded her life in two manuscript versions now in the British Library (Add. MSS 45718–45719). In 1913 Lady Mary Carbery published Freke's memoir, blending elements from the two manuscripts and integrating selections from other parts of the manuscripts which included accounts, memoranda, and recipes.

Freke begins her autobiography with her secret marriage to her cousin Percy Freke (*c.*1643–1706), son of Arthur Freke of Youghal, co. Cork, on 14 November 1672 at St Paul's, Covent Garden. Her title sets the theme of her account: 'Some few remembrances of my misfortunes which have attended me since I was married'. Although she suffered the miscarriages, periods of ill health, and dangers to children commonplace among women of her time, the bulk of the misfortunes she reports were financial, caused, she asserts, by her husband's mismanagement and greed. Despite Raphe Freke's earlier opposition to the match, after the couple were married again in his presence on 26 July 1673 at St Margaret's, Westminster, he gave Elizabeth a substantial cash dowry and by gifts and loans supported the couple's acquisition of interests in Leeds Castle, Kent, the manor of West Bilney, Norfolk, and Rathbury Castle, Cork, and other properties. By Elizabeth's account Percy mishandled their finances and made repeated demands on her for cash. Tension between them arose as well because of Percy's desire to live at Rathbury and her preference for Bilney, which she regarded as her own estate, settled on her by her father at the time of purchase to descend to the couple's son, Raphe (*b.* 1675), their only child. After moving back and forth between Wiltshire, Ireland, London, and Norfolk, the couple lived separately for many years.

Elizabeth gradually accumulated quite substantial investments in government securities, carefully recorded in her commonplace book. Although financially ambitious she was also socially hard-headed and opposed the marriage of her son to a daughter of the earl of Drogheda as too grand; as she observed, there was 'Nothing to be objected butt her quality, which I thought too much for a Gentleman; And I cared nott to be a servant to any one In

my Old Age' (*Diary*, 41). She did however eventually help her son to acquire a baronetcy. While she gave in to almost all of her husband's demands for cash she determinedly retained West Bilney, vigorously enforcing her rights as landlord and as holder of the advowson (and indeed claiming the title of 'parson' when naming a curate for the parish). Her imperious exploitation of her estate led to violent conflicts with tenants and neighbours and legends of 'terrible tyrant' Mistress Freke persisted into the twentieth century (ibid., 18–19). Although she believed herself betrayed by Percy her narrative of his death on 2 June 1706 while staying at Bilney is one of the most emotionally explicit bereavement accounts of the period. Increasingly isolated and querulous, suffering from asthma and pleurisy, she died in Westminster on 7 April 1714 while visiting London, and was buried in the south aisle of Westminster Abbey five days later.   BARBARA J. TODD

Sources Freke's notebooks, BL, Add. MSS 45718–45720 · *Mrs. Elizabeth Freke her diary, 1671–1714*, ed. M. Carbery [also pubd in *Cork Historical and Archaeological Society Journal*, 16–19 (1910–13)] · Mary Carbery, collection on Freke, BL, Add. MS 45721 · J. Freke, R. Freke, and W. Freke, *A pedigree, or genealogye, of the family of the Frekes: for near 200 years* (1825) · PRO, PROB 11/539, fol. 184v [probably the will of Elizabeth Freke] · PRO, PROB 11/489/101 [Percy Freke] · A. M. Burke, ed., *Memorials of St Margaret's Church, Westminster* (1914) · W. H. Hunt, ed., *The registers of St Paul's Church, Covent Garden, London*, 3, Harleian Society, register section, 35 (1906) · H. F. Westlake and L. E. Tanner, eds., *The register of St Margaret's, Westminster, London, 1660–1675*, Harleian Society, register section, 64 (1935) · J. L. Chester, ed., *The marriage, baptismal, and burial registers of the collegiate church or abbey of St Peter, Westminster*, Harleian Society, 10 (1876)

Archives BL, corresp., commonplace books, diaries, and papers, Add. MSS 45718–45721

Wealth at death see will, PRO, PROB 11/539, fol. 184v (probably the will of Elizabeth Freke)

Freke, John (1652–1717), lawyer and conspirator, was born in Hilton, Dorset, on 18 March 1652 and baptized at All Saints' Church, Hilton, on 17 April 1652, the eldest of the three sons and two daughters of John Freke (*d.* in or before 1658) and his wife, Margaret Knightly, of Winterborne Stickland, Dorset. An eighteenth-century family pedigree mistakenly identified him as the son of Robert Freke. He matriculated from Wadham College, Oxford, on 2 April 1669, entered the Middle Temple in the same year, and was called to the bar on 5 May 1676.

Even before being called to the bar John Freke appears to have been committed to a radicalism that would lead the authorities, his second cousin Elizabeth *Freke recalled, 'three severall times' to seek his hanging (*Remembrances*, 45). The first incident involved the authorship of an intemperate political poem variously entitled *The History of the Insipids* and *The Chronicle*. A heavy-handed satire that culminates in the exhortation 'Let's pull all brutish tyrants down' prompted a warrant for his apprehension. Brought before the king's bench on 6 June 1676, he was released on bail because of insufficient witnesses but remained under the threat of prosecution for high treason until September. Within a year he was linked with the first earl of Shaftesbury; soon he also became a member of the Green Ribbon Club, a group of whigs who gathered at the King's Head tavern on Fleet Street. His association with the supporters of Shaftesbury, if not his presence in the earl's inner circle, is further implicit in his signature on a 1679 petition for a new parliament and his role in the Rye House plot of 1683. Freke was among those sought by the privy council in July 1683 for furthering the uprising against the crown encouraged by such men as Lord Russell, Algernon Sidney, and Robert Ferguson. Though Freke admitted only that as Ferguson's counsel he had advised him to flee if guilty, others implicated in the plot characterized him as a conduit for money and a link with the western gentry. Two years later, in May 1685, officials again took him into custody for his alleged efforts in the western counties to assist the duke of Monmouth's rebellion. Released on bail, Freke went to Tunbridge, then joined other exiles in Europe.

In the Netherlands, Freke formed a warm and enduring friendship with the philosopher John Locke. The correspondence between the two men that began in November 1686 reveals a close personal and political relationship. Over time Freke advised Locke about legal affairs, commented on the books and manuscripts the philosopher shared with him, and helped supervise some of his publications. By November 1694 Freke and their mutual friend Edward Clarke were members of Locke's 'College', the centre of a limited and informal group intent upon influencing political policies. In the next two years Locke particularly relied upon Clarke's position as a member of parliament and Freke's friendship with the lord chancellor, John Somers, to promote his concerns about censorship, recoinage, and banking. Gradually the need for 'the College' diminished and the correspondence waned; the friendship, however, continued until the philosopher's death in 1704: Locke's will entrusted 'my good Freind John Freke of the Middle Temple' with the disposal of £100 (*Correspondence of John Locke*, 8.424–5). During the 1690s Freke was one of the whig reformers associated with the Grecian Coffee House in Devereaux Court in the Strand; and by 1701, identified as a propagandist for so-called junto whigs, he and Clarke were mocked as the impersonations E. C. and J. F. in *The Taunton Dean Letter* and *Letter from the Grecian Coffee-House*.

Once Freke moved away from the centre of London politics, he became entrusted with the legal affairs of his second cousin Elizabeth Freke and figured prominently in her unpublished memoirs. Her complaints about his handling of her financial and legal affairs in Ireland and England provide some sense of the lawyer's life in the years 1702 to 1713. Little else is certain. His will was signed on 25 June 1717 and proved on 8 August 1717, though the date and place of burial are unknown. Having never married Freke left his sister Elizabeth and her three children part of the estate; the bulk, which the Freke genealogy estimated at £7000 or £8000, went to his sister Anne Broadrepp. RAYMOND A. ANSELMENT

Sources *The correspondence of John Locke*, ed. E. S. de Beer, 8 vols. (1976–89) · F. H. Ellis, 'John Freke and *The history of insipids*', *Philological Quarterly*, 44 (1965), 472–83 · *The remembrances of Elizabeth Freke*, ed. R. A. Anselment (2001) · *CSP dom.*, 1675–6, 567; 1676–7, 133, 318; 1683, 92; 1685, 157 · J. Freke, R. Freke, and W. Freke, *A pedigree, or genealogye, of the family of the Frekes: for near 200 years* (1825) [apparently based on Bod. Eng. misc. MS c. 203] · *The manuscripts of the Marquess Townshend*, HMC, 19 (1887) · J. A. Downie, *Robert Harley and the press* (1979) · M. S. Zook, *Radical whigs and conspiratorial politics in late Stuart England* (1999) · Ford, Lord Grey, *The secret history of the Rye-House plot: and of Monmouth's rebellion* (1754) · W. Carstares, *The deposition of Mr. William Carstares* (1684) · G. de F. Lord and others, eds., *Poems on affairs of state: Augustan satirical verse, 1660–1714*, 7 vols. (1963–75), vol. 7 · R. L. Greaves, *Secrets of the kingdom: British radicals from the Popish Plot to the revolution of 1688–89* (1992) · *The manuscripts of S. H. Le Fleming*, HMC, 25 (1890) · parish register, Hilton, All Saints, 18 March 1652 [birth] · parish register, Hilton, All Saints, 17 April 1652 [baptism] · will, PRO, PROB 11/559, sig. 154 · will, PRO, PROB 11/278 [John Freke senior], sig. 360 · Foster, *Alum. Oxon.* · H. A. C. Sturgess, ed., *Register of admissions to the Honourable Society of the Middle Temple, from the fifteenth century to the year 1944*, 1 (1949) · *IGI*

Archives Bodl. Oxf., letters and MSS, MSS Locke, b. 3, c. 6, c. 8

Wealth at death over £8000: Freke, Freke, and Freke, *A pedigree*; will, PRO, PROB 11/559, sig. 154

Freke, John (1688–1756), surgeon and natural philosopher, son of John Freke (*d.* 1717), also a surgeon, was born in London, was apprenticed to Richard Blundell, and was elected assistant surgeon to St Bartholomew's Hospital, London, in 1726. Soon afterwards he was appointed the first curator of the hospital museum, which was then located in a single room under the cutting ward. The calculi which the surgeons had before been accustomed to place in the counting-house when they received payment of their bills for operations were placed in this room, and probably arranged by Freke. In 1727 a minute records that

> through a tender regard for the deplorable state of blind people the governors think it proper to appoint Mr. John Freke one of the assistant-surgeons of this house to couch and take care of the diseases of the eyes of such poor persons as shall be thought by him fitt for the operation, and for no other reward than the six shillings and eightpence for each person so couched as is paid on other operations.

He was elected surgeon on 24 July 1729, and held office until 1755, when gout and infirmity compelled him to resign. Besides being one of the chief surgeons in the city of London he acquired a reputation as a man of parts, learned in science, a judge of painting and of music. He thought Hogarth superior to Vandyck, but was adversely criticized by Hogarth when he put Dr Maurice Greene, organist of St Paul's, above Handel as a composer. He was elected FRS on 6 November 1729; in the *Philosophical Transactions* of 1736, he described a case of bony growth seen in a boy aged fourteen years at St Bartholomew's Hospital, and on 23 June 1743 he read before the Royal Society a description of an instrument he had invented for the reduction of dislocations of the shoulder joint. He was dexterous with his hands and carved a chandelier of oak, gilt, which was hung in the steward's office of the hospital, bearing the inscription 'Johannis Freke hujusce nosocomii chirurgi, 1735'.

Freke made experiments in electricity and published in 1748 *An essay to show the cause of electricity and why some things are non-electricable, in which is also considered its influence in the blasts on human bodies, in the blights on trees, in the damps in mines, and as it may affect the sensitive plant*. Freke supposed that the cause of the closing of the leaves of the sensitive plant when touched was that it discharged electricity, and he devised an experiment to illustrate this, in which a small tree was placed in a pot upon a cake of resin and then electrified. He found that the leaves stood erect, falling down as soon as the electricity was discharged by touching the plant. He further conjectured that pollen was attracted from the stamen of one plant to the stigma of another by electricity. The phosphorescence of the sea, which he had observed himself, he attributed to the same cause, and went on to the still wilder suppositions that the insects in blighted leaves come there in electric currents, and that electricity is the cause of acute rheumatism. This essay with two others was republished in 1752 as *A Treatise on the Nature and Property of Fire*. Henry Fielding seems to have known Freke, and twice mentions him, once with his full name, in *Tom Jones*. 'We wish Mr. John Fr— or some other such philosopher would bestir himself a little in order to find out the real cause of this sudden transition from good to bad fortune' (*Tom Jones*, 1st edn, book 1, 74), and in the fourth book, where the contagious effect of the blows of Black George's switch is described, 'to say the truth, as they both operate by friction, it may be doubted whether there is not something analogous between them of which Mr. Freke would do well to enquire before he publishes the next edition of his book'.

In 1748 Freke published *An essay on the art of healing, in which pus laudabile, or matter, and also incarning and cicatrising, and the causes of various diseases are endeavoured to be accounted for both from nature and reason*. He had accurately observed the difficulty of extirpating all infected lymphatics in operations for cancer of the breast and the danger of not removing them. In the book Freke recommended early paracentesis in empyema. His method was to divide the skin and muscles with a knife, to break through the pleura with his finger, and to insert a cannula in the wound. He married Elizabeth, eldest daughter of his teacher, Richard Blundell. She died on 16 November 1741 and he obtained formal leave from the governors of St Bartholomew's to bury her in the church of St Bartholomew-the-Less. When he resigned the office of surgeon he asked permission to be buried there when he died, and after dying on 7 November 1756, was entombed beside his wife under the canopy of a fifteenth-century tomb, the original owner of which was forgotten.

NORMAN MOORE, *rev.* MICHAEL BEVAN

Sources minute book of St Bartholomew's Hospital, London · private information (2004) · inscription on tomb, church of St Bartholomew-the-Less, London · W. S. Church, 'Our hospital pharmacopoeia and apothecary's shop', *St Bartholomew's Hospital Reports*, 22 (1886), 1–55 · W. Wadd, *Nugae chirurgicae, or, A biographical miscellany* (1824) · *GM*, 1st ser., 26 (1756), 595
Likenesses bust, St Bartholomew's Hospital Library, London · red chalk drawing, NPG

Freke, William (1662–1744), theological and mystical writer, was born at Hannington Hall, Wiltshire, the younger son of Thomas Freke and Cicely Hussey. He attended school at Somerford, Wiltshire. On 5 April 1677 he matriculated as a gentleman commoner from Wadham

College, Oxford, but after two or three years he left without taking a degree, having been admitted to the Middle Temple on 20 November 1677. Though called to the bar on 29 May 1685 he seems never to have practised law. Thomas Hearne describes him as 'a whimsical man', which is evident from his life and writings (*Remarks*, 1.338). Freke himself comments on the 'Irregularities and Offensiveness of my studies and Actions, quite eccentrick to the common Rules and Practices of the World' (W. Freke, *Lingua tersancta*, 1703, vii). On 19 March 1688 a licence was issued for his marriage to Elizabeth Harris, with whom he had twelve children. From 1696 he lived in Hinton St Mary, Dorset, where from about 1720 he was a justice of the peace.

Freke's first publication was *A Vindication of the Unitarians* (1687), which he wrote in response to an unknown 'reverend author on the Trinity'. Claiming to be an Arian but not a Socinian he denied the Trinity because it did not correspond to reason, was not stated in the scriptures, and did not date back to the earliest traditions of the church. This was followed in 1689 with *Essays towards a Union between Divinity and Morality, Reason, or Natural Religion, and Revelation*, in which he argued that revelation and natural reason are equally the law and will of God but that true revelation cannot contradict reason.

Freke published a second edition of his *Vindication of the Unitarians* in 1690. The reason for its reissue is unknown but John Wallis, professor of geometry at Oxford, clearly thought that it was directed against him and he responded to it, and to a Socinian attack on him, with *A Fourth Letter, Concerning the Sacred Trinity* (1691). Freke replied with *The Arrian's Vindication of Himself* (1691). In 1693 he returned to the subject with *A Dialogue by Way of Question and Answer, Concerning the Deity*, in which he described trinitarianism as idolatrous, polytheistic, and antichristian. According to Anthony Wood, as a publicity stunt Freke sent copies of his book to members of both houses of parliament in the hope that 'it might be burnt and so sell the better' (*Life and Times*, 3.437). It worked. Both houses, thinking that it was the work of a Quaker, proceeded to vote it an infamous libel (13 December 1693 and 3 January 1694, respectively) and ordered it to be burnt by the common hangman. But Freke's success was fleeting: on 12 February 1694 he was arraigned at the court of king's bench for blasphemy. On 19 May he was found guilty and sentenced to pay a fine of £500, to make a recantation in the four courts of Westminster Hall, and to find security for good behaviour for three years.

Despite such unorthodox views Freke affirmed in his next book, *A Full Enquiry into the Power of Faith* (1693), that it was right for a state to have one established church to which all must assent (if not worship in) and support through taxation, and that it was important to have unity in public worship. He also set down a dream that he had had in May 1681, 'upon my recovery from the Small-Pox' (p. 54). This was the first mention of his visions, a subject with which he would become increasingly obsessed.

Nothing more was heard from Freke until 1702, when he published *The New Jerusalem*, an exegesis on chapters 21 and 22 of Revelation. In this work he also announced that he was now a master of prophetic discourse, 'having Monitions and Foresights without bounds' (p. 28). In the same year he published *A General Idea of Allegorick Language*, in which he declared his wish to make available to the world his insight into divine monitions and prophecy. This was followed in 1703 with *The Divine Grammar … of Dreams, Visions and Apparitions* and *Lingua tersancta, or, A … Compleat Allegorick Dictionary to the Holy Language of the Spirit*. In *The Great Elijah's First Appearance* (1709 and 1710) he renounced his Arianism and declared himself the great Elijah, a new prophet, and secretary to the lord of hosts. His subsequent writings, all on visions and prophecy, betray a growing eccentricity. After 1719, however, he does not seem to have published. He died at Hinton St Mary at the end of December 1744, and was buried there on 2 January 1745.

MARTIN GREIG

Sources R. B. Gardiner, ed., *The registers of Wadham College, Oxford*, 1 (1889), 316 • Foster, *Alum. Oxon., 1500–1714*, vol. 2 • *DNB* • *The life and times of Anthony Wood*, ed. A. Clark, 5 vols., OHS, 19, 21, 26, 30, 40 (1891–1900) • *Remarks and collections of Thomas Hearne*, ed. C. E. Doble and others, 11 vols., OHS, 2, 7, 13, 34, 42–3, 48, 50, 65, 67, 72 (1885–1921) • H. A. C. Sturgess, ed., *Register of admissions to the Honourable Society of the Middle Temple, from the fifteenth century to the year 1944*, 1 (1949), 196

Fremantle, Sir Edmund Robert (1836–1929), naval officer, the fourth son of Thomas Francis *Fremantle, first Baron Cottesloe (1798–1890), and his wife, Louisa Elizabeth (d. 17 Aug 1875), eldest daughter of Field Marshal Sir George *Nugent, first baronet, was born in London on 15 June 1836. Admiral Sir Thomas Francis *Fremantle (1765–1819) was his grandfather, and William Henry *Fremantle (1831–1916) was his brother. Having a grandfather and two uncles in the navy, he felt himself 'bound to enter the naval service'. After attending Mr Tabor's school at Cheam in Surrey, he obtained a nomination from the first sea lord, Sir James Whitley Deans Dundas, and passed his entrance examination at Portsmouth in 1849.

Fremantle's first appointment was to the *Queen* (116 guns, Captain Charles Wise), flagship of Admiral Sir William Parker, the 'last of Nelson's captains'. After three years in the Mediterranean, he returned to Britain and was appointed to the frigate *Spartan* (26 guns, Captain Sir William Hoste), for service on the China station. There he first experienced war, in the Second Anglo-Burmese War of 1852.

The six years' service then required to qualify for mate's rank were completed by Fremantle in June 1855. In December 1855 he was made acting lieutenant, but was not confirmed lieutenant until 14 January 1857. The *Spartan's* commission lasted five and a half years: Hoste remained in command throughout. During this long service Fremantle acquired a taste for serious reading which included Gibbon, Shakespeare, Byron, and James's *Naval History*.

On his return to Britain in 1857 Fremantle spent eight months on half pay. In July 1858 he was appointed flag-lieutenant to his uncle Admiral Sir Charles Fremantle, then commanding the channel squadron, and served with his flag in the *Renown* (July–October 1858) and the *Royal Albert* (October 1858–October 1860). On 25 October 1860 he was appointed as fifth lieutenant to the *Neptune* in the Mediterranean, later commanded by Captain Geoffrey Thomas Phipps Hornby. In August 1861 Fremantle was promoted commander and, as a necessary consequence, owing to the excess of commanders over commands for that rank, spent a long period on half pay. This time was not, in his opinion, wasted, for he took the opportunity to study steam engineering, mathematics, and nautical astronomy; later, as captain, he also studied gunnery. He then made the acquaintance of that distinguished naval thinker Captain Philip Howard Colomb, and attended lectures at the Royal United Service Institution; thus he kept in touch with both the technique and the theory of naval science.

In 1864, when the New Zealand wars were in progress, Fremantle read that the commander of the *Eclipse* had been severely wounded, and he went to London and applied for the vacancy. A few days later he received notice of his appointment and joined his ship in New Zealand in April 1864. The *Eclipse* (4 guns) was a 700 ton steamer, barque-rigged; Fremantle commanded her for three years, and although he 'saw little real fighting' in the New Zealand wars he had a commission of varied and valuable experience in command. In 1866 he married, at Sydney, Barberina Rogers (d. 5 May 1923), eldest daughter of the Hon. Robert McIntosh Isaacs, of Sydney. They had six sons, the fourth of whom died as a child.

After returning home in February 1867, Fremantle was promoted to captain in April. Appointments for captains were few, and he now spent six years on half pay. This was a very hard time for a married officer with scanty private means and a large family; but he lived in a small house of his father's at Swanbourne, in Buckinghamshire, and devoted his time to local interests, to taking part in discussions at the Royal United Service Institution, and to writing on naval subjects. This 'had its uses in keeping me in touch with the service', but he observed that in the navy there was some prejudice against officers writing to the papers. He spent some time in 1871–2 at the Royal Naval College at Portsmouth, where he passed the examination in gunnery—an unusual thing for a captain, for which he received the thanks of the Admiralty. It was not, however, until March 1873 that he obtained the command of the paddle-steamer *Barracouta*.

In May 1873 the ports in the Gold Coast Protectorate were threatened by an Asante army, and the *Barracouta* was sent with a reinforcement of 100 marines for Cape Coast Castle, where Fremantle found himself senior officer of a squadron of seven small vessels. He took part in the operations for the defence of Elmina, in protecting Cape Coast Castle and Sekondi, Dixcove, and Axim, and in various affairs on the coast, including Sir Garnet Wolseley's first operations. He was severely wounded in the advance on Kumasi. In November a severe bout of fever obliged him temporarily to leave the coast to recover at St Helena; and he returned home in May 1874. He was made CB and CMG in that year, and was mentioned in the vote of thanks in parliament.

In September 1874 Fremantle took command of the frigate *Doris* (32 guns), one of a detached squadron cruising under sail. After paying her off in September 1876, he spent nine months on half pay, again attending lectures and writing articles for naval and other papers. On 15 May 1877 he was appointed to command the ironclad *Lord Warden* (7800 tons) in the channel squadron, but saw little sea service in her, as she passed into the reserve in the following year. The command lasted until November 1879, when he transferred to the ironclad *Invincible* (6000 tons), one of the squadron in the Mediterranean under Admiral Hornby. While in command of these ships he saved life on two occasions. When leaving Plymouth Sound in June 1877 he jumped overboard after a boy who had fallen from aloft, and in Alexandria harbour in February 1880, with his ship already under way, he dived off the bridge and rescued a man who had fallen overboard. For the first rescue he received the Royal Humane Society bronze medal and for the second the Stanhope gold medal for 1880, the Royal Humane Society silver medal, and the Shipwrecked Fishermen and Mariners' Royal Benevolent Society gold medal. In 1880 he was awarded the gold medal of the Royal United Service Institution for a prize essay, 'Naval tactics'.

In January 1881 Fremantle was appointed senior naval officer at Gibraltar. There he spent three years, 'probably the most pleasant service of my career', although it galled him to witness, as an onlooker, the transports and men-of-war on their way to the war in Egypt. His next ship was the *Dreadnought* (10,800 tons), which he commanded from August 1884 until April 1885, when he became rear-admiral, aged nearly forty-nine: he was then, except for the duke of Edinburgh, the youngest officer on the flag list. Fifteen months on half pay followed. Shortly before this time the torpedo boat had made its appearance, and a school of French naval thought, which had adherents also in Britain, contended that the days of great ships were over. Fremantle strongly opposed this in his 'Ironclads and torpedo flotillas' and 'Are ironclads doomed?' in the *Nineteenth Century* and *Blackwood's Edinburgh Magazine* respectively. Later he maintained the same view in the controversy in *The Times* in 1920–21 on whether the submarine had made obsolete the battleship. The problems of shipbuilding policy in relation to strategical needs were, in fact, the unceasing study of his active mind. His view, in 1903, was that 'we should build battleships of medium size, not more than 11,000 or 12,000 tons … which would be far more useful than our 15,000 ton battleships'. He wrote much in these years on the problems of trade defence and the need which it imposed for extensive cruiser forces ('Our food supply and raw material in war', *Fortnightly Review*, February 1903; 'Oversea trade in war', *Navy League*, 1909).

From August 1886 until August 1887 Fremantle flew his flag on the *Agincourt* as second in command of the channel

squadron. In February 1888 he was appointed to command the East India station, with his flag on board the *Bacchante* and, later, the *Boadicea*. The Salisbury government ordered a blockade (1888–9) of the east African coast, ostensibly to suppress the Arab slave trade, but in fact primarily for political reasons concerning Anglo-German relations. However, Fremantle aimed wholeheartedly to end the slave trade: 'the admiral was serious about the slave trade … while the governments were using the anti-slavery terminology largely as rhetoric' (Howell, 198). With a stronger naval force than ever before used in the region, Fremantle—despite friction with the Germans and with the British consul, C. B. Euan-Smith—thoroughly enforced the blockade and so effectively ended the slave trade. In January 1890, during the colonial dispute with Portugal, his command was increased by vessels from the Cape, Australia, and China, but action proved unnecessary. In 1889 he was made KCB (GCB 1899, GCVO 1926).

Witu, inland from the Kenya coast, was ruled by a local warlord, Fumo Bukari, the 'sultan' of Witu, had been claimed by Germany, and by the 1890 Anglo-German (Heligoland) treaty became British. Bukari's followers had killed nine Germans, and the Salisbury government ordered a punitive expedition which, Salisbury privately admitted, was 'to satisfy German opinion' (Howell, 205). After Bukari refused to hand over the Germans' killers, Fremantle organized a force of seamen, marines, Imperial British East Africa Company Indians and askaris, and porters, and in October 1890 himself led it against Witu. After some fighting, Bukari's force abandoned Witu, which Fremantle's force destroyed before withdrawing without the loss of a single man.

In February 1892 Fremantle was appointed commander-in-chief in China, flying his flag successively on the *Impérieuse* and *Centurion*. He held the command until July 1895. During the Sino-Japanese War of 1894–5 he had the delicate task of preventing as far as possible British trade with China. In June 1896 he succeeded Admiral Sir Algernon Lyons as commander-in-chief at Devonport, and held the post the customary three years. In October 1896 he was promoted admiral. On 15 June 1901, having reached the age limit, he retired. During his retirement he both read and wrote on current naval matters. His principal contributions to naval literature were his prize essay on 'Naval tactics on the open sea with the existing types of vessels and weapons' (1880), the lives of Hawke and Boscawen in John Laughton's *From Howard to Nelson* (1899), and his autobiography, *The Navy as I Have Known It* (1904). Fremantle died at his home, 44 Lower Sloane Street, London, on 10 February 1929, and was buried at Swanbourne.

H. W. RICHMOND, rev. ROGER T. STEARN

Sources E. R. Fremantle, *The navy as I have known it* (1904) · Admiralty record of service, PRO · *Navy List* · private information (1936) · W. L. Clowes, *The Royal Navy: a history from the earliest times to the present*, 7 vols. (1897–1903), vol. 7 · A. Lloyd, *The drums of Kumasi: the story of the Ashanti wars* (1964) · B. Bond, ed., *Victorian military campaigns* (1967) · R. C. Howell, *The Royal Navy and the slave trade* (1987) · R. Gardiner and A. Lambert, eds., *Steam, steel and shellfire: the steam warship, 1815–1905* (1992) · *WWW* · Burke, *Peerage* · GEC, *Peerage*

Archives NMM, corresp. and papers | CAC Cam., letters to A. Hurd · Surrey HC, letters to his sister Augusta Mary Brodrick **Likenesses** W. Stoneman, photograph, 1917, NPG · Pat, cartoon, chromolithograph, NPG; repro. in *VF*, 26 (29 Nov 1894), pl. 605 · portrait, repro. in *ILN*, 114 (1899), p. 748 · portrait, repro. in *ILN*, 118 (1901), p. 491 **Wealth at death** £51,046 5s. 7d.: resworn probate, 7 March 1929, *CGPLA Eng. & Wales*

Fremantle, John Walgrave Halford, fourth Baron Cottesloe (1900–1994), arts administrator, was born on 2 March 1900 at Holton Park, Wheatley, Oxford, the second son and third child in the family of four sons and four daughters of Thomas Francis Fremantle, third Baron Cottesloe (1862–1956), landowner and public servant, and his wife, Florence Annie Alexandra (d. 1956), daughter of Thomas Tapling. He was from an old Buckinghamshire family. His great-great-grandfather Sir Thomas Fremantle captained the *Neptune* at Trafalgar. His great-grandfather, the first Baron Cottesloe, was a minister under Peel and then for many years chairman of the customs board; his elder brother, Thomas (1897–1915), died of wounds received in action in Flanders. He was educated at Eton College and at Trinity College, Cambridge, where he rowed in the winning eight in the boat race in 1921 and 1922 and was awarded a third in mechanical sciences in 1921. He then practised as a civil engineer. On 16 February 1926 he married Lady Elizabeth Harris (1906–1983), only daughter of James Edward Harris, fifth earl of Malmesbury. They had a son, John (b. 1927), and a daughter, Ann (b. 1930).

During the Second World War Fremantle (who had already served in the Territorial Army) was a senior staff officer and military liaison officer in the anti-aircraft command and lieutenant-colonel commanding the 21st anti-aircraft regiment. After the war he took on many public responsibilities, sitting as a member of the London county council for the borough of Hampstead from 1945 to 1955 and serving on the committee of the Port of London Authority from 1947 to 1967. He was vice-chairman in 1956–7 and was concerned especially with the docklands. An art collector, he was a trustee of the Tate Gallery from 1953 to 1960, serving as chairman from 1959 to 1960, and from 1953 to 1972 he was chairman of the Advisory Council and Reviewing Committee on the Export of Works of Art. He was a governor of the Old Vic and Sadler's Wells Trust from 1957 to 1960. On 19 July 1956 he succeeded to the barony. In recognition of his public work he was appointed GBE in 1960. His first marriage having ended in divorce in 1944, on 26 March 1959 he married Gloria Jean Irene Dunn, adopted daughter of W. E. Hill, of Barnstaple, Devon. They had a son, Edward (b. 1961), and two daughters, Elizabeth (b. 1962) and Flora (b. 1967).

Cottesloe followed Sir Kenneth Clark as chairman of the Arts Council in 1960, and turned his attention to the question of the building of a national theatre, a project that had been revived in 1949 with the passing of the National Theatre Bill. The London county council had earmarked a site on the South Bank, next to County Hall, but the government was beginning to have doubts about whether it should be built at all. Cottesloe was a strong supporter of the national theatre project, and liked Olivier's plan to combine the Old Vic and Royal Shakespeare Company into one big National Theatre Company, an idea that was not, however, welcomed by Peter Hall, director of the Royal Shakespeare Company. When Selwyn Lloyd, chancellor of the exchequer, announced in 1961 that there would be no government money available to build a theatre to house the National Theatre Company, Cottesloe persuaded the London county council to offer £1.3 million if the government were to contribute £1 million. He then won round the chancellor, who agreed to contribute the £1 million promised in the National Theatre Bill of 1949, after Cottesloe had assured him that a theatre, and an opera house as a home for the Sadler's Wells Company, could be built for £2.3 million.

In 1962 the National Theatre Board was set up, Laurence Olivier was appointed director of the National Theatre Company, which gave its opening performance in October 1963 at the Old Vic, and Cottesloe became chairman of the South Bank Theatre and Opera House Board, set up to supervise the building of the theatre and opera house. Denys Lasdun was chosen as the architect, and after two years produced a plan for twin buildings with outdoor terraces facing each other across a piazza. Cottesloe did not specify a budget, assuming that the government would find the money to build it. But by the time Cottesloe announced, in the spring of 1965, that the complex would cost £9.5 million, a Labour government was in office, control over the Arts Council had been transferred from the Treasury to the Department of Education and Science, and Jennie Lee had been appointed minister for the arts; instead of renewing Cottesloe's appointment at the Arts Council for a further five years, Lee appointed her close friend Arnold Goodman as chairman in May 1965, although Cottesloe remained chairman of the South Bank Theatre and Opera House Board. With growing opposition to the cost of the new complex, and the danger that the whole project would be abandoned, Lee and Goodman came to the conclusion that the National Theatre would be built only if the opera house was dropped from the scheme.

In 1967 the government agreed to the building of the theatre, the site was moved downstream, and the board became the South Bank Theatre Board, with Cottesloe retained as chairman. Lasdun was asked to submit a new design for one building containing three theatres. A new National Theatre Bill was passed in 1969, and building began in the expectation that the theatre would open in 1973, but it was seven years before it was completed. Cottesloe had to steer the project through continual crises, including labour shortages, escalating costs, and the danger of confrontation with the unions. Eventually parliament passed another National Theatre Bill in 1974, removing the ceiling on the government's contribution so that the building could be completed. The National Theatre opened on 25 October 1976, and the Cottesloe Theatre, a small experimental studio theatre, delayed because of lack of money, opened on 4 March 1977. With the opening of the National Theatre, the South Bank Theatre Board disbanded: the total cost of the project had been £16 million. That the National Theatre was built at all was largely due to Cottesloe's persistence. A shy, quiet man who avoided confrontation, he was a very effective committee chairman, and he liked to get things done through his many social contacts, rather than relying on bureaucratic channels.

With the completion of the National Theatre, Cottesloe was able to devote more time to his hospital and medical committees: he remained on the committee of the British Postgraduate Medical Federation (he had been chairman from 1958 to 1972), and he was a governor of the King Edward VIII Hospital Fund for London and of the Northwick Park Hospital advisory committee. A crack shot (like his father), Cottesloe won the match rifle championship at Bisley six times, represented England thirty-seven times, captained the English eight from 1956 to 1979, and was chairman of the National Rifle Association from 1960 to 1972. A keen oarsman in his youth, he was a steward and judge at Henley from 1947, and president of the Leander Club from 1957 to 1962. He died on 21 April 1994 in Kingston Hospital, Surrey, and was cremated on 29 April at Putney Vale crematorium; his ashes were interred at Swanbourne, Milton Keynes, Buckinghamshire. Cottesloe was survived by his second wife, Gloria, their three children, and the two children of his first marriage. He was succeeded as fifth baron by his elder son, John, a commander in the Royal Navy. A memorial service was held at St Swithun's, Swanbourne, on 9 June 1994.

ANNE PIMLOTT BAKER

Sources J. Elsom and N. Tomalin, *The history of the National Theatre* (1978) · A. Sinclair, *Arts and cultures* (1995), chap. 5, pp. 134–9 · P. Hollis, *Jennie Lee: a life* (1997) · A. Goodman, *Tell them I'm on my way* (1995) · *The Times* (23 April 1994) · Burke, *Peerage* · *WWW*, 1991–5 · *Cambridge University Calendar* · b. cert. · *CGPLA Eng. & Wales* (1995)
Likenesses W. Bird, photograph, 1959, NPG · J. Ward, group portrait, oils, 1973–6 (*A meeting of the Society of Dilettanti at the St James's Club in 1973*), Brooks's Club, London, Society of Dilettanti · F. Belsky, bronze head, 1976, National Theatre, London · photograph, repro. in *The Times*
Wealth at death £757,321: probate, 10 July 1995, *CGPLA Eng. & Wales*

Fremantle, Sir Thomas Francis (1765–1819), naval officer, third son of John Fremantle (d. 1784) of Aston Abbots in Buckinghamshire, and his wife, Frances, daughter of John Edwards of Bristol, was born on 20 November 1765. At the age of twelve he entered the navy on the frigate *Hussar*, on the coast of Portugal. Two years later he was moved into the *Jupiter*, and shortly afterwards into the *Phoenix* with Sir Hyde Parker. He was in the *Phoenix* when she was lost on the coast of Cuba in the hurricane of October 1780. He subsequently served in many different ships on the Jamaica station, where, in March 1782, he was promoted lieutenant, and where he remained until December 1787. During the Spanish armament in 1790 he was again with Parker, in the *Brunswick*, and in the following year was promoted to command the sloop *Spitfire*.

At the beginning of the war in 1793 Fremantle commanded the *Conflagration*, and in May was promoted captain of the *Tartar* just in time to sail with Lord Hood for the Mediterranean. For the next four years, in the *Tartar*, *Inconstant*, or *Seahorse*, he was attached to the Mediterranean Fleet, and was especially associated with Nelson, who formed a high estimate of his professional character and abilities. In the *Tartar* he led the way into Toulon when Hood occupied it on 27 August 1793, and was afterwards, in 1794, engaged under Nelson in the capture of Bastia.

In the action off Toulon, on 13 March 1795, the *Inconstant* (36 guns) took more than a frigate's part, following up the French 80-gun ship *Ça Ira* and so hampering her retreat as to lead to her capture. The *Inconstant* was afterwards attached to the squadron under Nelson, on the coast of Genoa, taking part in these extended operations, and more particularly in the capture of a number of gunboats at Languelia on 26 August 1795, in the capture of the corvette *Unité* on 20 April 1796, in the evacuation of Leghorn on 27 June 1796 (the success of which Sir John Jervis officially attributed to Fremantle's 'unparalleled exertions'), and in the capture of Elba on 10 July 1796. Fremantle was then sent to Algiers to negotiate with the dey, and to Smyrna in charge of convoy, returning in time to assist in the capture of Piombino on 7 November, and to be left as senior officer in those waters when Jervis drew down to Gibraltar.

Fremantle married, on 12 January 1797, Elizabeth (d. 2 Nov 1857), daughter of Richard Wynne of Falkingham, Lincolnshire; they had a large family.

After the *Inconstant* was ordered home, Fremantle exchanged on 1 July 1797 into the *Seahorse* (38 guns), one of the inshore squadron off Cadiz, under Nelson, and Fremantle himself was with Nelson on the 10th when, during a bombardment of the city, Nelson's barge was attacked by a Spanish boat carrying twice the number of her crew. A few days later the *Seahorse* was one of the ships detached with Nelson to Tenerife, where, in the attack on Santa Cruz on the morning of the 25th, Fremantle was severely wounded. On rejoining the fleet, Nelson hoisted his flag on board the *Seahorse* for a passage to England, the wounded admiral and captain being both together taken care of by Mrs Fremantle, who had accompanied her husband, and under her kindly nursing both were convalescent when the ship arrived at Spithead on 1 September. In August 1800 Fremantle was appointed to the *Ganges* (74 guns), in which, in the following year, he went up the Baltic and took a full part in the battle of Copenhagen.

When the war was renewed in 1803 Fremantle again commanded the *Ganges* in the channel, and in May 1805 was appointed to the *Neptune* (98 guns). In her he joined the fleet off Cadiz and fought at Trafalgar, the *Neptune* being the third ship in the weather line, the *Téméraire* alone coming between her and the *Victory*. After the battle Fremantle remained under the command of Collingwood until December 1806, when he returned to England, having been appointed to a seat at the Admiralty. In the following March, however, he was appointed to the yacht

William and Mary, in which he continued until his promotion to flag rank on 31 July 1810. A month later he was appointed to a command in the Mediterranean, and in June 1812 was sent into the Adriatic in charge of the squadron there. For the next two years he was engaged in a series of detached operations, including the capture of Fiume on 3 July 1813 and of Trieste on 8 March 1814. When, shortly after this, he left the Adriatic, he was able to write:

> Every place on the coasts of Dalmatia, Croatia, Istria, and Friuli had surrendered to some part of the squadron under my orders, the number of guns taken exceeded a thousand, and between seven hundred and eight hundred vessels were taken or destroyed during my command.

Fremantle's services were recognized not only by his own government, which nominated him a KCB, but also by allied governments. He was made a baron of the Austrian empire (November 1816), knight of Maria Theresa, and knight of St Ferdinand and Merit. In 1818 he was made a GCB and appointed to the command-in-chief in the Mediterranean, but he held it for little more than eighteen months. He died at Naples, after an illness of only two days, on 19 December 1819, 'of an inflammation in the bowels' (*GM*, 87). He was buried at Naples on 23 December.

Fremantle's ships were notable for their gunnery. He also had a reputation as a disciplinarian. In the very first years of the nineteenth century, when in the *Ganges*, he inaugurated a system of petty courts of inquiry formally held by the officers for the examination of defaulters. He wrote of it as having worked most satisfactorily, but added that he had felt obliged to give it up in deference to the opinion of his brother officers. It was over sixty years before the Admiralty prescribed a somewhat similar system, which remained in force for some time.

Fremantle's eldest son, Thomas Francis *Fremantle (1798–1890), was created a baronet in 1821, in acknowledgement of his father's services, and in 1874 was raised to the peerage as Lord Cottesloe. The second son, Admiral Sir Charles Howe Fremantle GCB (1800–1869), served with distinction in the Crimean War, and was afterwards commander-in-chief at Plymouth. Sir Edmund Robert *Fremantle (1836–1929), also an admiral, was Sir Thomas's grandson.

J. K. LAUGHTON, rev. ROGER MORRISS

Sources W. James, *The naval history of Great Britain, from the declaration of war by France in 1793, to the accession of George IV*, [5th edn], 6 vols. (1859–60) • *GM*, 1st ser., 90/1 (1820), 87 • *The dispatches and letters of Vice-Admiral Lord Viscount Nelson*, ed. N. H. Nicolas, 7 vols. (1844–6) • J. Foster, *The peerage, baronetage, and knightage of the British empire for 1880*, [2 pts] [1880] • private information (1889) • J. Ralfe, *The naval biography of Great Britain*, 4 vols. (1828) • A. B. Rodger, *The war of the second coalition: 1798–1801, a strategic commentary* (1964) • P. Mackesy, *The war in the Mediterranean, 1803–1810* (1957) • R. Muir, *Britain and the defeat of Napoleon, 1807–1815* (1996) • GEC, *Peerage* • Burke, *Peerage* • Boase, *Mod. Eng. biog.*
Archives Bucks. RLSS, corresp. and papers • NMM, logbooks and papers; letter-book | Hunt. L., letters to Grenville family • NA Scot., letters to Lord Melville • U. Nott. L., letters to Lord William Bentinck

Likenesses C. Picart, stipple, pubd 1810 (after Pellegrini), NPG • E. Scriven, stipple, pubd 1822 (after E. Bristow), BM • oils, NMM

Fremantle, Thomas Francis, first Baron Cottesloe, and Baron Fremantle in the nobility of the Austrian empire (1798–1890), politician and civil servant, eldest son of Vice-Admiral Sir Thomas Francis *Fremantle (1765–1819) and his wife, Elizabeth (d. 1857), daughter and coheir of Richard Wynne of Falkingham, Lincolnshire, was born in London, in Bolton Row, Piccadilly, on 11 March 1798. His mother and his sisters were Roman Catholics. He matriculated at Oriel College, Oxford, on 19 March 1816, and graduated BA in 1819, taking a first class in mathematics and a second in classics. On 14 August 1821 he was created a baronet, out of respect to the memory of his father, who died in 1819, and in 1822 he was authorized by royal licence to use his father's Austrian title of baron. On 27 November 1824 he married Louisa Elizabeth (d. 17 Aug 1875), eldest daughter in the Roman Catholic family of Field Marshal Sir George Nugent and his wife, Maria. They had three daughters and four sons, including William Henry *Fremantle (1831–1916), Sir Charles William Fremantle (comptroller of the Royal Mint, 1890–94), and Admiral Sir Edmund Robert *Fremantle (1836–1929).

From 1827 until 1846 Fremantle was MP for Buckingham, sitting as a Conservative. In the session of 1829 he made some strong speeches condemning the pauperizing influence of the poor laws. In 1833 he chaired a select committee on bribery at the Stafford election, and he succeeded in carrying a disfranchising bill in the face of much opposition. During Peel's minority government of 1834–5 Fremantle was a government whip and in 1837 he became chief Conservative whip and a member of Peel's inner circle, though F. R. Bonham remained the chief influence on party organization. His great moment came when he whipped the tories in defeating Melbourne's government by one vote on 5 June 1841. With Bonham, Fremantle planned the consequent general election and helped Peel plan his administration. He resumed his office of chief government whip. He was known for his large whiskers.

In 1844 he became secretary for war, and in January 1845 became chief secretary for Ireland. Fremantle was a curious choice for so critical a post, and he was in fact the third candidate Peel considered. In 1845 he helped to see the highly contentious Maynooth College Bill through the Commons. As the potato famine spread in Ireland, Fremantle acted competently. In January 1846 he introduced the Irish Public Works Bill, and he procured the expenditure of £50,000 for the construction of small piers and harbours, with the view of extending the fisheries of Ireland. But he lacked the buccaneering approach which would have been necessary significantly to affect the course of the famine.

In 1846 Fremantle resigned his seat at Buckingham and was appointed deputy chairman of the board of customs. He was subsequently appointed chairman of this department, a post which he held until 1873. He worked with Gladstone both as chancellor and prime minister to make the tariff structure simple and non-protectionist. In the

Thomas Francis Fremantle, first Baron Cottesloe and Baron Fremantle in the nobility of the Austrian empire (1798–1890), by William Holl (after George Richmond, 1863)

dissolution honours in 1874 Gladstone obtained a peerage for him. The first title that he chose was that of Lord Chiltern, but this was discarded in favour of the name of the hundred in which his seat of Swanbourne was situated, and he became Baron Cottesloe of Swanbourne. Though a frequent attendee in the upper house he spoke only rarely. He raised the alarm about import penetration by the United States in 1879, thus contributing to the demands for 'fair trade'. In 1880 Cottesloe was a member of the select committee of the Lords on intemperance. Other subjects in which he was warmly interested included measures for increasing the safety of railway travel and the Deceased Wife's Sister's Bill—the latter forming one of the 'liberal shadows' on his Conservatism which some of his friends deplored. As a county magnate, churchman, and patron of the Church Missionary Society he was extremely popular in Buckinghamshire, and in later years was venerated as the father of the House of Lords and patriarch of Buckinghamshire society.

Cottesloe celebrated the completion of his ninetieth year by inviting a number of his oldest friends to take communion with him at St Michael's, Chester Square; about sixty responded, including the Brodricks, Julian Halls, Nugents, and Verneys, and also his neighbour Sir Harry Verney, himself then eighty-seven years old. His declining years were clouded by the death of his wife in 1875, from accidental self-poisoning. He died at Swanbourne on 3 December 1890, and was buried there on 9 December. He was then nearly ninety-three. Cottesloe had attended the House of Commons on budget night from

1827 to 1889 without a break. He was one of the most notable, if also perhaps the most colourless, of Victorian public servants.

THOMAS SECCOMBE, rev. H. C. G. MATTHEW

Sources GEC, *Peerage* · *The Times* (4 Dec 1890) · *The Times* (8 Dec 1890) · *The Times* (10 Dec 1890) · *The Guardian* (17 Dec 1890) · Gladstone, *Diaries* · A. R. G. Griffith, *The Irish board of works, 1831–1878* (1987) · N. Gash, *Sir Robert Peel: the life of Sir Robert Peel after 1830* (1972) · C. S. Parker, ed., *Sir Robert Peel: from his private papers*, 3 vols. (1891–9)

Archives Bucks. RLSS, family MSS and corresp. | BL, corresp. with W. E. Gladstone, Add. MSS 44135–44782 · BL, corresp. with Sir Robert Peel, Add. MSS 40397–40609 · Bodl. Oxf., letters to Benjamin Disraeli · Cumbria AS, Carlisle, corresp. with Sir James Graham · Durham RO, letters to Lord Londonderry · Hunt. L., letters to Grenville family · Lpool RO, letters to fourteenth earl of Derby · U. Southampton L., letters to first duke of Wellington

Likenesses G. Hayter, group portrait, oils (*The House of Commons, 1833*), NPG · W. Holl, stipple (after G. Richmond, 1863), BM, NPG [*see illus.*] · Spy [L. Ward], cartoon, watercolour, NPG; repro. in *VF* (22 July 1876), 58 · engraving (after photograph), repro. in *ILN*, 97/2695 (13 Dec 1890), 740

Wealth at death £78,838: GEC, *Peerage*

Fremantle, Sir William Henry (1766–1850), politician and courtier, the youngest son of John Fremantle of Aston Abbots, Buckinghamshire, was born on 28 December 1766. At an early age he entered the army, and attained the rank of captain of infantry. He was on the staff of the duke of Wellington, and in 1782 he went to Ireland as aide-de-camp to the lord lieutenant, the marquess of Buckingham. Subsequently he was appointed private secretary to Lord Buckingham, and he officiated in that capacity until Buckingham retired from the Irish viceroyalty. The intimate knowledge that Fremantle acquired of Irish affairs caused him to be named resident secretary for Ireland in 1789, and he remained in Dublin until 1800, when the resident Irish secretaryship was abolished. He was also deputy teller of the exchequer, 1792–1806.

Fremantle had rendered valuable service during a very critical period and he considered his compensation for the secretaryship inadequate. When the 'ministry of all the talents' was formed by lords Grenville and Grey in 1806, Fremantle was appointed joint secretary to the Treasury, and entered parliament for Enniskillen, in 1806, moving to Harwich the same year and to Saltash in 1807. He left office with Lord Grenville. He was MP for the Tain burghs from 1808 to 1812. In the latter year he was elected for Buckingham, and retained the seat until 1827, when he resigned it in favour of his nephew, Sir T. F. Fremantle, bt. For the fifteen years during which he sat for Buckingham, Fremantle took part in all the principal debates in the House of Commons, acquiring a considerable reputation as a speaker. He usually acted with the Grenville whigs, and he was a cordial supporter of Catholic emancipation and other political and social reforms. In 1821–2, he negotiated for the Grenvilles with the government; he was sworn a privy councillor and became a commissioner of the India board, an office he held until 1826, when George IV made him treasurer of the royal household. When the mutiny at Barrackpore occurred in 1825, and the conduct

Sir William Henry Fremantle (1766–1850), by Edward Scriven, pubd 1822 (after Abraham Wivell, *c*.1820)

of Lord Amherst, governor-general of Bengal, was severely criticized in parliament, Fremantle defended the suppression of the mutiny.

As treasurer, Fremantle gained great favour with the king, to whom he had long been personally known. After performing special services in connection with the visits of several European sovereigns, he was knighted on 31 October 1827, with the grand cross of the Royal Guelphic Order of Hanover. On the accession of William IV, Fremantle was reappointed treasurer of the household, and later became deputy ranger of Windsor Great Park. He was thus brought into constant relations with the court, and was held in high esteem by the king. When the king died in 1837, Fremantle retired from the household, but retained his position of deputy ranger of Windsor Park under the rangership of Prince Albert. The park was much improved during his term of office, which continued until his death.

Fremantle married, on 12 January 1797, Selina Mary, only daughter of Sir John Elwill, bt, and widow of Felton Lionel Hervey, grandson of John Hervey, first earl of Bristol, with whom she had had five children. Lady Fremantle died on 22 November 1841 at Brighton. Fremantle died on 19 October 1850.   G. B. SMITH, *rev.* H. C. G. MATTHEW

Sources HoP, *Commons* · *GM*, 2nd ser., 35 (1851), 92–3 · *Windsor and Eton Express* (26 Oct 1850) · J. E. Cookson, *Lord Liverpool's administration: the crucial years, 1815–1822* (1975)

Archives Bucks. RLSS, family MSS and corresp. | BL, corresp. with Lord Grenville, Add. MSS 58966–58967 · Hunt. L., letters to Grenville family · Hunt. L., letters to Charles O'Conor · NL Scot., corresp. with William Elliott · NL Wales, letters to C. Watkin Williams Wynn

Likenesses E. Scriven, stipple, pubd 1822 (after A. Wivell, *c*.1820), BM, NPG [*see illus.*] · P. Audinet, line engraving (after Yellowly), NPG

Fremantle, William Henry (1831–1916), dean of Ripon, was born in Swanbourne, Buckinghamshire, on 12 December 1831. He was the second son of the politician Thomas Francis *Fremantle, first Baron Cottesloe (1798–1890), and his wife, Louisa Elizabeth (*d*. 1875), daughter of Field Marshal Sir George *Nugent, first baronet. Sir Edmund Robert *Fremantle (1836–1929), the admiral, was his younger brother. His uncle, the Revd William Robert Fremantle (1807–1895), then rector of Claydon, near Swanbourne, and William Henry's predecessor as dean of Ripon, was an important early influence, instilling him with an early evangelicalism and a lifelong love of children and games.

Fremantle's education was conventionally classical yet unusually progressive. At Cheam School he came under the influence of Charles Reiner, later tutor to Prince Albert Edward, a German liberal exile whom he described as 'without exception the best teacher I have ever known' (*Recollections*, 10). The way in which Reiner was obeyed without recourse to punishment persuaded Fremantle that a 'nation [so] ruled would have few rebellious subjects' (ibid., 11). This was a lesson he subsequently sought to apply far beyond the confines of the nation state. In Dr Hawtrey's Eton College his gregariousness won him the chairmanship of Pop, while his studiousness secured the Newcastle medal in 1849. That same year he went up to Balliol College, Oxford, where he first encountered his lifelong mentor, intermittent colleague, and inconstant patron, Benjamin Jowett. Chastened by a second in classical honours moderations, Fremantle's undergraduate career nevertheless ended in triumph with a first in *literae humaniores* and the university prize for an English essay on the subject 'The influence of commerce on Christianity', both in 1853. The following autumn he was elected to a prize fellowship at All Souls College.

Oxford also grounded Fremantle in the liberal theology that marked him for the rest of his life. In this Jowett was a direct, if oblique, influence; Arthur (later Dean) Stanley, professor of ecclesiastical history from 1856, a more profound inspiration. However Fremantle's own reading in German biblical criticism, his extensive foreign travels—Italy provoked a profound anti-papism—and his broad-ranging sympathies, especially with the French Huguenots, led if not to original conclusions then certainly to contentiously idiosyncratic emphases in his doctrine. He identified church and nation, arguing that the church was organized in the state for civic purposes and through ecclesiastical institutions for religious worship; indeed, it was commonly observed that the only part of his teaching which was obscure was 'the doubt whether the Prime Minister ought to be *ex officio* Archbishop of Canterbury, or the Archbishop of Canterbury *ex officio* Prime Minister' (Anson, 11). Yet in so doing, he effectively subordinated clerical to lay authority; hence Tractarians suspected him of Erastianism. This also opened his establishment to all theists, including nonconformists, and that was distasteful to many other Anglicans. On the other hand his belief in the fact, but not the miracle, of the virgin birth—similarly, his insistence that the resurrection of Christ represented no violation of natural law—convinced evangelicals that he was dogmatically unsound. Finally, his profession of *The Gospel of the Secular Life* (1882), which understood Christianity to be no more (nor less) than the faithful fulfilment of common duties best expressed in terms of service to society generally and its victims particularly, may have nurtured a great Balliol tradition of Christian social thought, traceable from Arnold Toynbee to R. H. Tawney, but it simultaneously outraged the sensibilities of most contemporary protestant Englishmen.

Fremantle was a strikingly good-looking man: tall, well-built, long-faced, with a high forehead and distinguished by luxuriant sideburns. He was mild of manner and temperamentally guileless. Despite or perhaps because of this, he pursued a continually controversial career. Ordained in 1855, then placed in a college living in Lewknor, he soon began proceedings against All Souls for its failure to implement the competitive principle in fellowship elections set down by the university ordinance of 3 April 1857. Appealing first unsuccessfully to the visitor and then through queen's bench, Fremantle and his co-plaintiffs, Godfrey Lushington and Arthur Watson, won their case in 1864, effectively forging the prize fellowship which endures to this day. Whatever the college thought of this act of principled defiance, Bishop Tait of London was impressed. Accordingly, in 1861 he invited Fremantle to become resident chaplain at Fulham Palace. He also encouraged the young cleric to furnish historical justification for his own, similarly principled, support of the vindicated defendants in the famous *Essays and Reviews* case brought before the privy council. The result (jointly edited with George Brodrick) was *A collection of the judgments of the judicial committee of the privy council in ecclesiastical cases relating to doctrine and discipline* (1865), an enduring contribution to scholarship.

On 6 August 1863 Fremantle married Isabella Maria (*d.* 1901), daughter of Sir Culling *Eardley, third baronet, the founder of the Evangelical Alliance. They had three sons and two daughters. Two years later he was appointed rector of St Mary's, Bryanston Square, London, a crown living. His seventeen years there, dedicated to achieving practical form for the ideal of a Christian community, either by doing good works among the poor with Octavia Hill or in the establishment of a parish council, both encouraging the widest local participation in general religious life, were probably the happiest of his career. At any rate, if he was honoured by his appointment as canon of Canterbury in 1882, he was compromised by his contemporaneous election as chaplain, fellow, and tutor of Balliol. In persuading Fremantle to assume these offices, Jowett intended to blunt Tractarian domination of the new theology school. At least in Balliol, he succeeded. Fremantle, in turn, hoped to build up liberal theology in the university. Active opposition from the 'Pusey House' wing of the faculty, coupled with Jowett's sly indifference,

ensured that he failed. His Bampton lectures for 1883, published as *The World as the Subject of Redemption* (1885), fell on deaf ears. His article 'Theology in its changed conditions' (*Fortnightly Review*, March 1887, 442–59) was denounced from the university pulpit. He was debarred from lecturing on the English Reformation as one of the official theology faculty lecturers, and even forbidden by the rural dean of Oxford from holding an informal conference of theological tutors to promote religion among the undergraduates.

It was accordingly with relief that Fremantle accepted the deanery of Ripon in 1895. Here, to a degree at least, he prospered. With the active support of his bishop, Boyd Carpenter, he was able to turn the cathedral city into a liberal protestant stronghold. More still, he became something of a link between the broad-church theology of mid-nineteenth-century Oxford and the emerging modernist movement of early twentieth-century Anglicanism. He was a founder member of the Churchman's Union (For the Advancement of Liberal Religious Thought) in 1898, and contributed suitably modernist articles to house journals such as the *Church Gazette* (launched that year), the *Liberal Churchman* (from 1904), and the *Modern Churchman* (after 1911). He also organized the first Conference of Modern Churchmen, held appropriately enough at Ripon, in July 1914. All the while his writings continued alternately to stimulate and outrage: most notably a lecture 'Natural Christianity', delivered in 1902 and published in a longer version nine years later, which led to his being denounced in the *Daily Express*.

As if this was not enough, Fremantle now increasingly pursued an informal third career as chief Anglican spokesman for international peace, a quest first begun with *Pleading Against War* (1885) and subsequently continued through numerous exhortations, pamphlets, and campaigns. He became an advocate for the international arbitration of disputes and a champion for mutual reductions in arms. His all too obvious failure in 1914 caused him great pain. Following the death of his first wife, he married, on 16 April 1903, Sophia Frances, daughter of Major T. G. Stuart. Fremantle died at his London home, 25 Barkston Gardens, South Kensington, on 24 December 1916, and was buried in Essendon, Hertfordshire, three days later. He was survived by his second wife and four of his children, who included Sir Francis Edward Fremantle (1872–1943), a medical officer of health and Conservative MP.

S. J. D. GREEN

Sources *Recollections of Dean Fremantle, chiefly by himself*, ed. W. H. Draper (1921) · P. Hinchliff, *Benjamin Jowett and the Christian religion* (1987) · P. Hinchliff, *God and history: aspects of British theology, 1875–1914* (1992) · A. M. G. Stephenson, *The rise and decline of English modernism* (1984) · J. S. G. Simmons, 'All Souls reformed, 1850–1914', All Souls Oxf. · W. R. Ward, *Victorian Oxford* (1965) · H. Anson, *Thomas Banks Strong* (1949) · C. Harvie, *The lights of liberalism* (1976) · W. Benham and R. T. Davidson, *Life of Archibald Campbell Tait*, 2 vols. (1891) · *The Times* (26 Dec 1916) · *The Times* (28 Dec 1916) · Crockford (1915) · *WWW*, 1929–40 · Burke, *Peerage* · *Wellesley index*

Archives Bodl. Oxf., sermons · LPL, corresp. relating to Anglo-Continental Society | Balliol Oxf., Jowett MSS · BL, letters to W. E. Gladstone, Add. MSS 44465–44524 · LPL, corresp. with A. C. Tait

Likenesses A. G. Gabell, photograph, repro. in Draper, ed., *Recollections of Dean Fremantle*, frontispiece · W. W. Ouless, oils, Bedwell Park, Hertfordshire

Wealth at death £15,331 19s. 10d.: probate, 12 April 1917, *CGPLA Eng. & Wales*

French, Annie (1872–1965). *See under* Glasgow Girls (*act.* 1880–1920).

French, Evangeline Frances (1869–1960), missionary, was born in Medea, Algeria, on 27 May 1869, the daughter of first cousins, John Erington French, a gentleman of private means, and his wife, Elizabeth French. Her younger sister, **Francesca Law French** (1871–1960), missionary and writer, was born in Bruges, Belgium, on 12 December 1871. After an early childhood in St Omer, France, they moved to Geneva, where they were educated at the *école secondaire*. Both women were later to acknowledge those years as a major influence, where they came into contact with a wealth of political and religious ideas. In the late 1880s the family returned to England, settling at Southsea, near Portsmouth, but the sisters found this provincial life unbearably stifling after their continental youth. Evangeline (Eva) suffered a nervous collapse in consequence, but a chance meeting with the wife of an American missionary inspired her to follow a similar vocation in the China field. After a period of training at the China Inland Mission in Liverpool she set off for China in 1893.

On arrival in Shanghai she was sent to Pingyao in Shanxi province, where she spent the next six years travelling to local villages, preaching the gospel and devoting herself particularly to women's education. In 1900 Eva was caught up in the Boxer uprising, as Shanxi bore the brunt of anti-foreign aggression, and she only narrowly escaped death. Initial newspaper and intelligence reports had listed her among those killed. After a period of furlough in England she returned to China, to Huozhou in Shanxi, as soon as it was safe to do so. She was soon joined by the novice missionary (Alice) Mildred *Cable (1878–1952), and from this point on their lives were inextricably bound together.

Francesca French in the meantime had moved briefly to Dublin to join her elder sister, Nora, after the death of their mother in 1905, and there she underwent brief training as a nurse. When Cable and Eva returned for furlough to England it was decided that she would join them in China. From this time on they became known in missionary circles as the Trio, as they were to remain for the rest of their lives.

The Trio continued their work in women's education in Shanxi until 1923, whereafter they felt a need to establish a Central Asian Mission in Jiuquan, in Gansu province, in north-west China. Apart from periods of furlough in England they spent the years until 1936 travelling by mule cart across the Gobi Desert, evangelizing among the mixed population of that part of China and central Asia. They shared an admiration for the Salvation Army and, although never members of that church, they adopted many of its methods: music and taking the gospel to the people formed the basis of their preaching style. In 1925,

in Jiuquan, they formally bought a young deaf mute girl of mixed Mongolian–Tibetan parentage, to redeem her from a life of cruelty as a servant to a local family. They called her Ailian (Love Bond) Gai (the Chinese pronunciation of Cable), and gave her the nickname Topsy. Her story was told by Cable and Francesca French in *The Story of Topsy* (1937).

The Trio were all fluent in both spoken and written Chinese and throughout their China years they wore Chinese dress and adopted the customs of the local population. They also learned Uighur, the Turkic language of northwest China's large Muslim population, and ate no pork, in order to evangelize more effectively.

After the closure of the China mission field in 1937 the Trio, together with Topsy (or Eileen Guy as she was officially known upon British naturalization), returned to Britain and involved themselves in the work of the Bible Society. Eva served on the committee of the China Inland Mission and also the Zenana and Bible Medical Mission, while Francesca was on the London committee of the Indian Ludhiana College and Hospital and president of the Girl Crusader Union. With Cable they visited Australia, New Zealand, India, and Brazil, and all three devoted themselves to the care and education of Topsy.

Evangeline French died, aged ninety-one, at her home, Willow Cottage, Stour Row, Shaftesbury, Dorset, on 8 July 1960 and was cremated on 12 July; Francesca died less than a month later, on 2 August at Troutstream Hall, Chorleywood Road, Rickmansworth, Hertfordshire. She was cremated on 5 August at Golders Green crematorium, Middlesex. Their estate passed on to Eileen Guy to be held in trust on her behalf until her death, whereafter it was willed jointly to the Salvation Army and the British and Foreign Bible Society. Eileen Guy died in London on 26 January 1998.

All evidence suggests that the many letters and journals kept during their years in China and afterwards were destroyed by the French sisters' and Cable's shared solicitor in an act of senility rather than malice, but the biographer is in consequence largely dependent on the eighteen books co-written by Cable and Francesca French for whatever information there is to be gleaned about their lives.

G. H. TIMMERMANS

Sources W. J. Platt, *Three women* (1964) · A. M. Cable and F. French, *Something happened* (1934) · B. McCredie, 'The wild, wild Gobi', 1994, SOAS, China Inland Mission Archive · P. East, 'Cart tracks across the Gobi', 1994, SOAS, China Inland Mission Archive · M. Cable and F. French, *The Gobi Desert* (1942) · private information (2004) · M. Warner, 'Introduction', in M. Cable and F. French, *The Gobi Desert* (1984), xi–xxi · E. H. Edwards, *Fire and sword in Shansi* (1903) · M. Broomhall, ed., *Martyred missionaries of the China Inland Mission, with a record of the perils and sufferings of some who escaped* (1901) · *CGPLA Eng. & Wales* (1960) · d. cert.

Archives British and Foreign Bible Society, Swindon, Wiltshire, archive · CUL, British and Foreign Bible Society archive · Overseas Missionary Fellowship archive, Sevenoaks, Kent · SOAS, China Inland Mission Archive

Likenesses H. Wrightson, group portrait, photograph, *c.*1935, priv. coll. · H. Howse, group portrait, photograph, repro. in 'Trekking with the gospel in central Asia', China Inland Mission meeting advertisement, 1932 · Vaughan & Freeman, group portrait, photograph, repro. in 'In town today (1)', China Inland Mission notice of meeting, 1935 · group portrait, photograph, repro. in Platt, *Three women*, frontispiece · group portrait, photograph, repro. in '3 women faced Gobi terrors for 15 years', *Evening Standard* (16 Jan 1943) · photograph, repro. in M. Cable and F. French, *The story of Topsy* (1937), following p. 16

Wealth at death £7816 1s. 4d.: probate, 14 Sept 1960, *CGPLA Eng. & Wales* · £10,337 18s. 11d.—Francesca Law French: 14 Sept 1960, *CGPLA Eng. & Wales*

French, Francesca Law (1871–1960). *See under* French, Evangeline Frances (1869–1960).

French, George Russell (1803–1881), genealogist and architect, was born in London. After being educated privately, he became an architect. Between 1821 and 1832 he exhibited at the Royal Academy from Wanstead, Essex, but by 1836 he was living in Leytonstone. In the 1840s he practised from London, and he was for many years surveyor and architect to the Ironmongers' Company; between 1861 and 1869 he prepared a catalogue of the antiquities and artworks exhibited in the Ironmongers' Hall. His executed works were all in the Gothic style and included Westmarsh church, Kent (1841), and All Saints' Church, Shrub End, near Colchester (1844–5). In 1835 he unsuccessfully entered a Tudor Gothic design for the new houses of parliament.

According to Howard Colvin, French's architecture was 'certainly not remarkable' (Colvin, *Archs.*, 382); he was far more significant as an antiquary. He was long an active member (and subsequently vice-president) of the London and Middlesex Archaeological Society. In 1841 he published an account of the ancestry of Queen Victoria and Prince Albert, which was followed by *The Royal Descent of Nelson and Wellington* (1853). After detailed and painstaking research he published *Shakespeareana genealogica* (1869): the first part attempted to identify the *dramatis personae* in Shakespeare's history plays, with observations on characters in *Macbeth* and *Othello* and notes on Warwickshire people and places; the second part traced exhaustively the descent of the Shakespeare and Arden families. French's thirteen tables of Shakespeare descent have not been superseded.

French was a keen temperance reformer and in 1879 published a work entitled *Temperance or Abstinence*. He died in London at his home, 6 Henrietta Street, Brunswick Square, on 14 October 1881.　　MICHAEL ERBEN

Sources Boase, *Mod. Eng. biog.* · Allibone, *Dict.* · Colvin, *Archs.* · *DNB* · S. Schoenbaum, *Shakespeare's lives*, new edn (1991)

Wealth at death £3962 17s. 7d.: probate, 21 Nov 1881, *CGPLA Eng. & Wales*

French, Gilbert James (1804–1866), writer and draper, was born on 18 April 1804 in Edinburgh, the son of James French, a manufacturer, and his wife, Janet Meikle. Following a basic education he was apprenticed to a draper. French moved from Edinburgh to Sheffield, and then to Bolton, where he settled and ultimately developed a considerable trade in the textile industry, providing fabric for clergymen and general ecclesiastical uses. He developed an interest in archaeology, particularly ecclesiology, forming an extensive library and becoming a member of

the London Society of Antiquaries and a corresponding member of the Society of Antiquaries in Scotland. In addition to presenting papers before the Archaeological Association of Great Britain, he published a variety of pamphlets. These included *Practical Remarks on some of the Minor Accessories to the Services of the Church* (1840), *The Tippets of the Canons Ecclesiastical* (1850), *Hints on the Arrangement of Colours in Ancient Decorative Art* (2nd edn, 1850), and *Bibliographical notices of the church libraries at Turton and Gorton, bequeathed by Humphrey Chetham* (1855). In 1856 French published *An Enquiry into the Origin of the Authorship of some of the Earlier Waverley Novels*, using new facts and illustrations to develop the old theory, revived by W. J. Fitzpatrick in 1856, that Walter Scott's brother Thomas and his wife were the authors of the earlier Waverley novels.

In 1852 French promoted the establishment of the Bolton Free Library, and while president of the Bolton Mechanics' Institution (1857–8) he published *Remarks on the Mechanical Structure of Cotton Fibre* (1857) and *An attempt to explain the origin and meaning of the early interlaced ornamentation found on the ancient sculptured stones of Scotland, Ireland, and the Isle of Man* (1858). French also delivered several lectures, two on the life of Samuel Crompton, inventor of the spinning mule. These he expanded into a biography, *The Life and Times of Samuel Crompton, Inventor of the Spinning Machine Called the Mule* (1859), which revived Crompton's reputation. French contributed generously to the support of Crompton's surviving son in his old age, and raised a subscription of £200 to erect a monument over Crompton's grave in Bolton parish churchyard on 29 January 1861.

French himself died at Newport Square, Bolton, on 4 May 1866. He was survived by his wife, Sarah Ann. A presentation copy of French's biography of Crompton, his most famous work, is displayed in the study of Crompton's former home in Bolton, Hall-in-the-Wood, which is now a museum. A second edition was published in 1860, and a facsimile reprint in 1970.　　EMMA PLASKITT

Sources 'French, Gilbert James', *DNB* · 'Crompton, Samuel', *DNB* · private information (1889) · *IGI* · G. French, *An enquiry into the origin of the authorship of some of the earlier Waverley novels* (1856) · G. French, *The life and times of Samuel Crompton, inventor of the spinning machine called the mule* (1859) · www.boltonmuseums.org.uk · *CGPLA Eng. & Wales* (1866)

Archives Bolton Central Library, corresp. relating to Crompton · NL Scot., collections relating to Scott's Waverley novels

Wealth at death under £12,000: probate, 27 July 1866, *CGPLA Eng. & Wales*

French, Harold Arthur George (1900–1997), actor and director, was born on 23 April 1900 at 6 Herne Hill Road, Brixton, the son of Irish parents, William Joseph French, a journeyman optician, and his wife, Gertrude Lucy Brady. He was educated at Edge Hill College, Wimbledon. After answering an Italia Conti advertisement he was soon promoted from understudy to déb—t as Mamillius in *The Winter's Tale* (1912) at London's Savoy Theatre, followed by a role in *Twelfth Night* as a black page. He appeared with Noël Coward and Gertrude Lawrence at the Liverpool Playhouse and with Lewis Casson and Sybil Thorndike at the Gaiety, Manchester, before a Christmas revival of *Where* *the Rainbow Ends* (1913) as Crispian Gray, which he reprised for the next two years. Numerous minor roles followed, including nine months with the Birmingham repertory, before he was called up in 1917, joining the Royal Flying Corps.

After demobilization French was soon back on the stage, as both Athos and the Baron de Casterae in *Cyrano de Bergerac* (1919) at the Garrick. Throughout the 1920s he was a familiar face, mostly in London but occasionally on tour, appearing chiefly in inconsequential light or musical comedy such as *The Blue Lagoon* (1920) at the Prince of Wales, *The Bird of Paradise* (1922) at the Garrick, and *Good Gracious, Annabelle!* (1923) at the Duke of York's. He toured in *By-the-Way* (1924) before appearing in it also at the Apollo and then in New York. And he appeared again with Gertrude Lawrence—a favourite co-star in such fare—as Jimmy Winter, in the Gershwins' *Oh, Kay!* (1927) at His Majesty's. On 3 February 1927 he married Phyllis Marie Symondson (1901/2–1941), who acted under the name Phyl Arnold. They had a daughter, who was killed on her first flight as an air hostess. There were more light leading roles into the 1930s, including *The Gay Princess* and *Marriage à la mode* (both 1931), *Whose Baby are You* and *Night of the Garter* (both 1932), and finally *Among Friends* (1933) for the Overture Players at the Piccadilly. Having made his film début in *Land of Mystery* (1920), by the 1930s he was appearing as an equally lightweight lead actor on screen, although perhaps only *Night of the Garter* (1933), a reprise of his stage role, *How's Chances?* (1934), directed by Anthony Kimmins, and *The Girl in the Crowd* (1935), directed by Michael Powell, are really worth remembering.

By now it was 'abundantly clear to him that neither his talents nor his inclinations fitted him for performing on the stage' (*The Times*, 24 Oct 1997) and French switched to directing for the stage, commencing with *Youth at the Helm* (1934). His first major success was *French without Tears* (1936) at the Criterion. For some time its preparation and rehearsal seemed destined to fail but, coming together so well on opening night, it was a triumph, not least for its young author, Terence Rattigan. There was a greater certainty to French in front of the stage, and he directed another ten plays in the next five years, including *Ladies and Gentlemen* (1937), Coward's *Design for Living* (1939), and S. N. Behrman's *No Time for Comedy* (1941). This latter title was sadly apt: his wife Phyllis was killed during the blitz in that year.

French also gave up film acting, turning firstly to co-scriptwriting—*Accused* and *Crime over London* (both 1936), *Jump for Glory* (1937)—and then to directing, making a good début with *The Cavalier of the Streets* (1937). His films were very English and, while making no masterpiece, he maintained a high standard of 'pleasing, unassuming, skilful entertainment' (Quinlan), partly thanks to his using the talents of such scriptwriters as Anatole de Grunwald, Terence Rattigan, and Roland Pertwee. Uncredited (as was David Lean), he co-directed *Major Barbara* (1941) for its named director, Gabriel Pascal. Particular successes after this included the romantic comedy *Jeannie* (1941), the excellent spy drama *The Day will Dawn* (1942), *Mr Emmanuel*

(1944), and *White Cradle Inn* (1947). The last was good but a box-office flop, but a big commercial success was the well-crafted *My Brother Jonathan* (1947). Also successful were 'several warm and cosily amusing portraits of middle-class British family life' (ibid.): *Dear Octopus* (1943), *English without Tears* (1944), *Quiet Weekend* (1947), and *Isn't Life Wonderful!* (1952). He directed segments of three portmanteau films based on stories by Somerset Maugham, *Quartet* (1949), *Trio* (1950), and *Encore* (1952), and was the unlikely director of *Rob Roy, the Highland Rogue* (1953), a rather wooden version of the Scottish story for Disney. Although some television work followed into the 1960s, his last film was *The Man who Loved Redheads* (1955), a final screen collaboration with Rattigan, who said of him, 'he had the kind of manners that are so good they are never noticed, intense liveliness of disposition, and as keen a sense of humour as I have ever encountered' (*The Times*, 28 Jan 1998).

French now returned to the stage, commencing with the melodrama *Tabitha* (1956); at this time he directed Australian actress Mary Parker (*d.* 1993) who later became his second wife. Among his later plays were *Waltz of the Toreadors* (1958) from Anouilh's French original, *When in Rome* (1959), *The More the Merrier* (1960), and *A Public Mischief* (1965). As late as 1971 French was touring in South Africa with *The Winter's Tale* and *The Merchant of Venice*, himself playing Shylock in the latter. In later life he wrote two well-received volumes of autobiography, *I Swore I Never Would* (1970) and *I Thought I Never Could* (1973). As a younger man he had enjoyed golf, swimming, and punting. French died on 19 October 1997 at Charing Cross Hospital, Fulham.   ROBERT SHARP

Sources I. Herbert, ed., *Who's who in the theatre*, 1 (1981) • *The Times* (24 Oct 1997), 23 • *The Times* (28 Jan 1998), 4 • www.uk.imdb.com, 29 Sept 2001 • D. Quinlan, *The illustrated guide to film directors* (1983) • H. French, *I swore I never would* (1970) • H. French, *I thought I never could* (1973) • b. cert. • m. cert. [Phyllis Marie Symondson] • d. cert. • *The Guardian* (24 Oct 1997)
Likenesses photograph, 1930, repro. in *The Guardian* • group portrait, photograph, *c.*1941 (with Barbara Muller and Michael Redgrave), Hult. Arch. • group portrait, photograph, *c.*1941 (with Michael Redgrave and Kay Hammond), Hult. Arch. • photograph, *c.*1955, repro. in *The Times*, 23
Wealth at death £379,709: probate, 31 Dec 1997, CGPLA Eng. & Wales

French, Sir Henry Leon (1883–1966), civil servant, was born at Brunswick Road, Southsea, Hampshire, on 30 December 1883, the third son of Frederick Edward French, leather seller, and his wife, Eliza Mingay. He was educated privately at Southsea and later at King's College, London. In 1901 he joined the civil service by open competition and was appointed as a second-division clerk to the Board of Agriculture. He married, in 1903, Zenobia Clare (*d.* 1954), daughter of Charles Grimes FRGS, of Southsea; they had one daughter. The marriage was dissolved by divorce in 1929, when French married Violet (*d.* 1975), daughter of G. R. Huntley, of Streatham.

French was promoted to the first division of the Board of Agriculture as an assistant head of branch in 1909. During the First World War his main concern was with agricultural policy and production. In 1917–19 he was general secretary of the food production department of the Board of Agriculture, having been secretary to Lord Milner's departmental committee on home food production and joint secretary to Lord Selborne's committee on agricultural policy. He was promoted to assistant secretary in the newly constituted Ministry of Agriculture and Fisheries in 1920, principal assistant secretary in 1929, and second secretary in 1934. It was not until 1936, when he was seconded to the Board of Trade as director of the food (defence plans) department, that French became concerned with food rather than agriculture.

In 1939 French became permanent secretary of the Ministry of Food, where he remained until September 1945. His reputation as a strong administrator rested upon the remarkable success of the ministry during the Second World War. His long career with the Ministry of Agriculture proved to be of considerable value during this period, when the acute shortage of shipping placed increasing importance upon the production of food within the United Kingdom. The relationship between the two ministries became strained in 1940 and 1941 owing to wide differences of opinion about production policy. French had much to do with the concordat reached between the two ministers (R. S. Hudson and Lord Woolton), which settled policy for the rest of the war.

The success of the Ministry of Food during the war was due to the combination of highly expert knowledge of the food industries throughout the world, a flexible and imaginative approach to new problems and opportunities, strong leadership and public relations, and sound administration. French contributed in varying degrees to these factors.

The food rationing system, fair and efficient and well enforced, reflected strong administration, which was remarkable for a wartime ministry whose staff exceeded 55,000 at one time, with a mere handful of permanent civil servants and a very wide mixture of imported talent. French attached high importance to good organization to ensure efficient operation. To some his insistence on formal channels of communication was excessive and restrictive, especially when speed of decision was essential, but it was not surprising in a man who had been principal establishment officer of a large department during the inter-war years when promotion was desperately slow, who was already fifty-six when war broke out, and who had spent thirty-eight of those years in one department.

At certain key moments, however, French showed surprising flexibility. For example, when Lord Woolton made it clear that he opposed the dual direction of the commodity divisions of the ministry (a trade director and a civil servant side by side) French altered the organization immediately so that each division had only one head (usually the trade director). Likewise, he accepted the appointment of a commercial secretary virtually in parallel with himself as permanent secretary. He told Woolton at the time that he 'hated' the new arrangement, but a year later

confided to his chief that he was now in favour of it. In spite of French's initial apprehensions about Woolton, a genuine and lasting friendship developed between the two men.

Unhappily, these bursts of flexibility rarely extended to those aspects of administration termed 'establishment matters'. French's formal, rigid attitude to such matters, which certainly reflected his own career between the wars, was exemplified most clearly by his failure to come to terms with E. M. H. Lloyd, a brilliantly imaginative man, impatient to the point of irresponsibility as it must have seemed to a civil servant as orthodox as French. Lloyd had made a great contribution to the work of the Ministry of Food in 1917–19. His ideas, often novel and unconventional, found expression in much of the early work of the food (defence plans) department and of the Ministry of Food. The failure of the two men to work together was a matter of concern: when Lloyd persuaded some outstanding men to join the ministry on the outbreak of war, French refused to endorse the appointments because they had not gone through the proper establishment channels.

On the other hand, French's selection of trade advisers and other staff from the food industries, most of which was settled well before the outbreak of war, contributed greatly to the success of the ministry. Every section of the food industries—manufacture, distribution, import, storage, transport—agreed to release their senior management to the ministry and many of the men were party to the pre-war planning. The result was that when war came the Ministry of Food came into existence almost fully grown and able to execute quickly the plans already in existence. The trade advisers and their staff worked with dedication and determination for as long as war lasted. French's choice of people was amply justified.

The strong leadership and good public relations of the ministry came, however, mainly from ministers and especially Lord Woolton. Fortunately, the qualities of the two men were mainly complementary. French, never strong in negotiation or in weighing up the views of the other party, left major issues of policy increasingly to the minister and the strong central staff which was built up after 1941. Lend-lease, which virtually ended Treasury control of the ministry for the duration of the war, at least as far as overseas purchasing was concerned, was left almost entirely to the food mission in Washington and the central staff in London. Likewise, French contributed little to the constant struggle for shipping space to meet food import requirements. He showed little interest in the problems of feeding Europe after the war or in the work of the United Nations Relief and Rehabilitation Administration and the Food and Agriculture Organization. Once the ministry was firmly established and its strength both in Whitehall and overseas clear, French seemed to feel that he had made his major contribution and could now leave more and more to others.

To some people French was unapproachable and vain. He made up his mind about people quickly and rarely changed it. Like many civil servants, the war brought him an eminence which he had never expected to attain. He quoted frequently the reported remark of an Indian minister after French's visit to India in August–September 1944: 'French, this is the greatest day in the history of India.' And he seemed to believe it.

Despite these weaknesses, French made a real contribution to the success of the Ministry of Food, which owed much to the sound foundations he laid in 1936–9 as director of the food (defence plans) department. Before the outbreak of the war he purchased on behalf of the British government all of the Norwegian supplies of whale oil. It was a vital acquisition, denying the Germans an important commodity, the shortage of which had significantly undermined the German war effort in 1917–18 (*Memoirs of … the Earl of Woolton*, 237).

After his retirement from the civil service in 1946 French occupied a number of posts in the film industry into which his close personal relations with the Rank family took him. He brought to the industry his continued interest in good organization and sound administration. In 1948 he led the British side in negotiations with the American film industry over the vexed issue of the quota of American films that were allowed to be screened in Britain. Though accused of a nationalistic attitude by the Americans, French was clear that for economic reasons Britain must maintain its quotas, and he proved a tough and determined defender of the British industry. But again he found it more than difficult to come to terms with the creative people. From 1946 to 1957 he was director-general of the British Film Producers Association and he was president from 1957 to 1958. During the same years he was director-general of the Commonwealth Film Corporation and chairman of the Film Casting Association Ltd.

French was associated with the Festival of Britain in 1951 and was first chairman of the Festival Gardens Ltd. Though he quickly made a programme of festival gardens operative, this was achieved at a cost greatly in excess of that estimated, and in parliament on 3 April his resignation as chairman was announced, part of a reorganization of the senior management of the project. He was chairman of the UNESCO co-operating body on mass communications (1946–53) and attended UNESCO conferences in 1947 and 1950. He was appointed OBE (1918) and CB (1920), KBE (1938), KCB (1942), and GBE (1946). He died at 20 Devonshire Place, London, on 3 April 1966.

JOHN WALL, *rev.* MARK POTTLE

Sources *The Times* (10 Jan 1948) • *The Times* (21 Feb 1948) • *The Times* (1 July 1948) • *The Times* (4 April 1951) • *The Times* (4 April 1966) • personal knowledge (1981) • private information (1981) • *The memoirs of the Rt Hon. the earl of Woolton* (1959) • b. cert. • *CGPLA Eng. & Wales* (1966)
Likenesses W. Stoneman, two photographs, 1938–57, NPG
Wealth at death £7816: probate, 20 July 1966, *CGPLA Eng. & Wales*

French, James Murphy. *See* Murphy, James (1725–1759), *under* Murphy, Arthur (1727–1805).

French, John (*c.*1616–1657), physician, was born at Broughton, near Banbury, Oxfordshire, the son of John French (d.

1657), yeoman, of Broughton. In 1633 he entered New Inn Hall, Oxford, where he graduated BA on 19 October 1637, and MA on 9 July 1640. Thereafter he seems to have studied medicine, and was persuaded by his mentor, Lord Saye and Sele of Broughton Castle, to enter the parliamentary army of Sir Thomas Fairfax, as a physician. At the end of the first civil war he was employed by the state as physician to the Savoy Hospital, London. He was granted an Oxford MD on 15 April 1648, and shortly afterwards was examined for membership of the College of Physicians, though there is no record of his having been finally admitted. In an era in which conventional approaches to the study and practice of medicine were under considerable attack, French seems to have aligned himself firmly with the cause of reform. In particular, he was a keen advocate of the chemical methods pioneered by Paracelsus and Van Helmont, whose ideas, and those of their followers, he attempted to popularize in the 1650s through original works and translations. From the late 1640s he was also closely associated with the circle of Samuel Hartlib, and was well respected by many, including Robert Boyle, for his expertise in the practical side of chemistry and mineralogy. According to Hartlib, French knew 'all the places for Minerals in England, and hath a great store of all manner of Oares' ('Ephemerides of Samuel Hartlib', 1648, Hartlib MS 31/22/32A). Such was French's devotion to the new science of chemistry that in his *The Art of Distillation* (1651) he dubbed it the 'true naturall philosophy' which, he suggested, ought to replace 'that empty naturall philosophy which is read in the Universities' (French, *Art of Distillation*, sigs. A2v–A3r). In addition, as physician to the Savoy Hospital, he would appear to have encouraged the implementation of various new approaches to medical training and practice, including the use of spa water treatments for maimed soldiers (his *The Yorkshire Spaw* appeared in 1652), and anatomical dissection. Thomas Wharton, for example, addressed himself to French as to an 'amico plurimum colendo' for allowing him access to dissections carried out at the Savoy (Wharton, sig. A3v). In religious and political terms, French seems to have been fully committed to the Cromwellian regime, and was particularly sympathetic to the plight of religious minorities, even Roman Catholics, all of whom, he believed, should be left to practise their faith in peace according to 'their own light' (French, *Yorkshire Spaw*, 123). According to Anthony Wood, French died in October or November 1657, at or near Boulogne in France, where he was serving as physician to the English army under the command of Sir John Reynolds (Wood, 3.436–7; *CSP dom.*, 1656–7, 593). French's widow, Mary, subsequently petitioned for relief. His father's will, dated January 1657, refers to a grandson, John, the son of John French. French's brother, William, was also a physician; he served the parliamentary army in Scotland, where he died in 1650.

PETER ELMER

Sources Wood, *Ath. Oxon.* • C. Webster, *The great instauration: science, medicine and reform, 1626–1660* (1975), 279, 297, 299, 302, 304 • T. Wharton, 'To the reader', *Adenographia, sive, Glandularum totius corporis descriptio* (1656), sig. A3v • annals, RCP Lond., 4.6–7 • *CSP dom.*, 1656–7, p. 593; 1657–8, p. 218 • will of John French senior, 1657,

PRO, PROB 11/264/195 • 'Ephemerides of Samuel Hartlib', 1648, Sheffield University, Hartlib MS 31/22/32A • J. French, *The art of distillation* (1651) • J. French, *The Yorkshire spaw* (1652)

French, John Denton Pinkstone, first earl of Ypres

(1852–1925), army officer, was born at Ripple Vale, near Deal in Kent, on 28 September 1852, the son of a retired naval officer, Commander John Tracy William French (*d.* 1854), a justice of the peace and deputy lieutenant for Kent, and his wife, Margaret Eccles (*d. c.*1865). Charlotte *Despard, feminist and socialist reformer, was an elder sister. French liked to think of himself as Anglo-Irish though his branch of this old Roscommon family had not lived in Ireland since the eighteenth century. French's father died in 1854 and his mother, suffering from insanity, in 1867. French was brought up, therefore, by his six elder sisters, who eventually agreed to his following his father's career. Having briefly attended a Harrow preparatory school and Eastman's naval academy at Portsmouth, French joined the *Britannia* at Dartmouth in August 1866, passing out as a midshipman in January 1868. However, he found he disliked the seagoing life and resigned in November 1870 to take a commission in the Suffolk artillery militia, a militia commission being a recognized back door to an army career without the necessity of attending either Sandhurst or Woolwich. He was gazetted a lieutenant in the 8th hussars on 20 February 1874, transferring in March to the 19th hussars.

Early career (1880–1902) French followed a conventional regimental career, serving as regimental adjutant from June to October 1880 and receiving his promotion to captain on 11 October 1880. He also had a spell as adjutant to the Northumberland hussars, a yeomanry regiment, from April 1881 to September 1884, in the course of which he was promoted major in April 1883. Cavalry life clearly suited French, who was an accomplished horseman and polo player. Despite the claims of later contemporaries such as the later official historian, James Edmonds, that French eschewed study of his profession, he appears to have read widely at this stage of his career. Certainly he knew Sir Edward Hamley's *Operations of War* (1866) well enough to recall Hamley's emphasis on the importance of not being trapped in a fortress when the possibility of retreating into Mauberge presented itself in August 1914. French, however, also displayed two characteristics early in his career that later caused him constant difficulties. The first was his enthusiastic pursuit of women and, indeed, on 23 June 1875 French married Isabella Soundy, a merchant's daughter, in Richmond. It was highly unusual for an officer to marry so young and French appears to have kept the marriage secret, securing a divorce in June 1878 with the assistance of the husband of one of his sisters, John Lydall. On 10 August 1880 French was married again, this time to Eleanora (*d.* 1941), daughter of Richard Selby-Lowndes, a prosperous Buckinghamshire landowner. French appears to have been devoted to Eleanora, with whom he had two sons and two daughters, one of whom died in infancy from a tragic accident. Yet French did not refrain from marital infidelities, which Eleanora appears to have borne with extraordinary patience. One

John Denton Pinkstone French, first earl of Ypres (1852–1925), by John Singer Sargent, *c.*1919–22

noted mistress was Mrs Winifred Bennett (*née* Youelle), a diplomat's wife, with whom French took up late in 1914, writing to her almost daily while in France and seeing her almost daily when he returned to the home forces command in 1916. Subsequently Mrs Bennett's visits to Vice-regal Lodge when French was lord lieutenant of Ireland aroused considerable comment.

The second trait was French's inability to keep his spending in check, few of his frequent risky financial ventures succeeding. One particularly disreputable business friend of French's was a wealthy American railway magnate, George Moore, with whom he shared a house at Lancaster Gate from 1910 until Moore's return to the United States in 1921, an arrangement conducive to both these ardent womanizers.

French's first experience of active service came when his regiment joined Lord Wolseley's expedition in the attempt to relieve Gordon at Khartoum. French served with Sir Herbert Stewart's desert column, seeing action at Abu Klea and Metemmah, and coming to the notice of Sir Redvers Buller during the column's retreat to Korti. French was rewarded with a brevet lieutenant-colonelcy on 7 February 1885. He succeeded to the command of the 19th hussars in early 1888, receiving his brevet colonelcy in February 1889 and taking his regiment to India. There he was noted by the inspector-general of cavalry, Sir George Luck. One of French's sexual indiscretions saw him placed on half pay in February 1893, but Luck, now inspector-general of cavalry at home, and Buller, now adjutant-general, came to the rescue. In August 1895, therefore, with substantive rank as colonel, French was appointed to the War Office as assistant adjutant-general, tasked with revising the manual *Cavalry Drill*. He was appointed to the 2nd cavalry brigade at Canterbury on 1 May 1897, remaining there until appointed to the 1st cavalry brigade at Aldershot on 12 January 1899, where Buller now held overall command. His new brigade-major was Douglas Haig. In a transaction at least liable to misinterpretation Haig loaned his superior £2000 with which to pay off his mounting debts.

The outbreak of the Second South African War saw French and Haig dispatched to the Cape, French with the rank of temporary major-general as Buller's choice to command the cavalry in Natal. Subsequently, however, it was decided that French should command the cavalry division as a whole and he was made a local lieutenant-general on 9 October 1899. Initially, however, French and Haig did join Sir George White's field force in Natal, where French distinguished himself in the sharp action at Elandslaagte on 21 October 1899, commanding a mixed force, which drove the Boers off two kopjes. Many of the Boers were caught in the open and ridden down by the 5th lancers and 5th dragoon guards. Small affair though it proved, the action got French noticed in the national press. With White forced back into Ladysmith, French and Haig were ordered out on the last train on 2 November 1899 before the Boers sealed off the town. Buller's original campaign plan had been rendered untenable by the siege of Ladysmith and the Boer encirclement of both Kimberley and Mafeking to the west. While Buller himself went to Natal to try to relieve Ladysmith and Lord Methuen to try to relieve Kimberley, French's division was concentrated near Colesberg to cover Cape Colony. After the triple defeat of Methuen at Magersfontein, Lieutenant-General Gatacre at Stormberg, and Buller at Colenso in the 'black week' in December 1899 Field Marshal Lord Roberts was sent out to take over command in South Africa.

French, who had enjoyed considerable success in covering the gap between the commands of Methuen and Gatacre, was ordered by Roberts to spearhead an attempt to turn the Boer left on the Modder River, the new commander-in-chief having resolved to concentrate his efforts on the relief of Kimberley. With the attention of the Boers distracted by Methuen at Modder River station, French's 4000 men marched south to cross the Riet River and then advanced rapidly to the north, crossing the Modder at Klip Drift and charging through the Boer positions on 15 February 1900, reaching Kimberley that evening. In reality, Klip Drift was not quite the spectacular cavalry success it appeared since French had broken a thinly held sector with the assistance of supporting artillery fire and the cover of considerable clouds of dust. Moreover the exertions of the operation took a terrible toll of the cavalry's horses, as did the pursuit of the retreating Boers, in which French managed to prevent the main Boer field army escaping across the Modder at Paardeburg.

Having forced the surrender of the Boers at Paardeburg, Roberts advanced on Bloemfontein, ordering French once more to outflank the Boers at Poplar Grove. French, of course, was closely associated with Buller (and, therefore, the 'Wolseley ring') rather than those who surrounded Roberts. It is also clear that from the beginning French enjoyed a poor relationship with the austere Kitchener, who had come out to South Africa as Roberts's chief of staff. As well as reinforcing Roberts's prejudice against cavalry and his predilection for mounted infantry, Poplar Grove soiled French's relationship with both men. It was essentially the poor state of the cavalry's horses and a critical lack of fodder which prevented French from cutting off the Boers on 7 March, but Roberts blamed him for the failure, though Bloemfontein fell on 13 March. French did not enjoy particular success during the subsequent advance on Pretoria and towards the frontier of Portuguese Mozambique at Koomati Poort. In July 1900, however, his operations led to the capture of Middelburg and in September he took Barberton. As the war took on the appearance of a prolonged guerrilla conflict he commanded first in the Johannesburg district in November 1900 and then, in June 1901, in Cape Colony. French was rewarded for his services with promotion to substantive major-general after the fall of Pretoria in 1900 and the KCB. He was further promoted substantive lieutenant-general on 22 August 1902, also being created KCMG. Even more significantly he received the prestigious Aldershot command on 15 September 1902.

Aldershot and the War Office (1902–1914) Whatever the frustrations of the later stages of the Second South African War, French's reputation had been made as a 'fighting general' and he had been one of only three general officers to serve in South Africa throughout the war. Moreover while giving evidence to the Elgin commission on the conduct of the war in July 1903, he favourably impressed the influential Lord Esher. Esher, indeed, wanted French appointed to his War Office (reconstitution) committee in 1904, but failed to persuade the prime minister, Balfour, of his suitability. One of the key recommendations of the Esher committee when it reported in February and March 1904 was the abolition of the post of commander-in-chief, to which Roberts had succeeded in January 1901, and its replacement with a chief of the general staff (CGS). Again both Esher and his committee colleague, Admiral Sir John Fisher, saw French as the leading candidate for CGS, not least because French was rather more open-minded than most soldiers towards naval opinion and, particularly, amphibious operations.

It has been argued that French showed little consistency in his strategic ideas, and at various times was prepared to consider operations in the Baltic as readily as in Belgium, which was the preferred theatre of war for most of his military colleagues in the event of war with Germany. It has been suggested, therefore, that he never fully made up his mind and, at a celebrated meeting of the war council on 5 August 1914, happily proposed ignoring the entire mobilization scheme and sending the British expeditionary force (BEF) to Antwerp rather than Mauberge as long planned. More recently it has been suggested that French was a significant influence on pre-war strategic planning, postulating a genuine compromise between a 'maritime' and a 'continental' strategy, by which the so-called 'Belgian option' offered Britain a more independent role in keeping with its national interest in safeguarding the channel ports. Thus there was consistency in his preference for transferring the BEF from the Aisne to Flanders in the autumn of 1914 and, while committed to the war on the western front, to his idea in December 1914 and January 1915 of unleashing Territorial and New Army divisions on the Belgian coast to seize Zeebrugge.

Esher recognized French's intellectual limitations, writing, 'I daresay that he is not the cleverest man, but he is the most successful soldier we could find. *He has never failed*' (Royal Archives, W39/21, Esher to Knollys, 16 Jan 1904). It was assumed that the CGS would become the commander-in-chief in the field in the event of war and it was important to Esher, too, that a CGS should have a clear idea of the direction in which he wished to lead the army. He was to write after observing French presiding over the annual autumn manoeuvres as inspector-general in 1907 that:

> It was generally remarked that it was a comfort to find a Leader, who, whether right or wrong, invariably knew his own mind, and possessed the force of character to stick to his opinions, and the force of intellect to defend them.
> (ibid., W40/128, Esher to king, 26 Sept 1907)

French, who took Esher's son on his military staff at Aldershot, remained the only soldier for whom Esher acknowledged a clear preference. In the event the king vetoed the appointment and French, who had not wished to go to the War Office, remained at Aldershot. He became, however, a member of the committee of imperial defence on the nomination of Esher in December 1905 with limitless tenure. He was again considered as a possible CGS amid the growing dissatisfaction with the first incumbent, General Sir Neville Lyttelton, but he remained cool towards the idea of a War Office appointment. He was promoted general on 12 February 1907 and created GCVO. On 30 November that year he left Aldershot to take up the appointment of inspector-general of the forces. French also held the appointment of aide-de-camp to the king from June 1911 to June 1913.

At Aldershot, French had come to be considered a cavalry theorist of some prominence. He had worked on *Cavalry Drill*, of course, and demonstrated the success of cavalry in a traditional role to his own satisfaction in South Africa. In fact his pronouncements on cavalry were limited, one being the preface he wrote to the English translation of Friedrich von Bernhardi's *Cavalry in Future Wars* in 1906. French, however, saw little reason to alter his views as to the efficacy of sword and lance in the face of the criticism of advocates of mounted riflemen such as Roberts and Erskine Childers. To be fair to French and other cavalry traditionalists, the actual lessons of the Second South African War had not been as clear cut as generally supposed. French's influence, however, reinforced the general emphasis on drawing moral rather than technical lessons from the experience of South Africa and subsequent conflicts such as the Russo-Japanese War, and

upon the value of the offensive over the defensive. Yet, while he was conservative in terms of cavalry, his role at Aldershot and as inspector-general consolidated his reputation as a dynamic modernist. Ultimately, therefore, he became chief of the Imperial General Staff (CIGS) on 15 March 1912, and was promoted field marshal in June 1913. French had become regimental colonel of the 19th hussars in February 1907 and that of the Royal Irish regiment in March 1913.

French's tenure as CIGS was overshadowed by the looming Irish home-rule crisis. Amid a series of apparent misunderstandings in March 1914 officers of Brigadier-General Hubert Gough's 3rd cavalry brigade and others stationed at the Curragh camp outside Dublin made it clear, when offered a hypothetical choice by the general officer commanding in Ireland, General Sir Arthur Paget, that they would resign their commissions rather than participate in any coercion of Ulster into accepting home rule. Always politically naïve, French had seriously underestimated the true depth of feeling within the army with regard to Ulster and he was not inclined to compromise on discipline. With Gough and his leading subordinates summoned to London, French was roundly abused by Roberts among others and came under increasing pressure. Thus when the secretary of state for war, J. E. B. Seely, gave a written undertaking to Gough on 23 March that the army would not be used to coerce Ulster, both French and the adjutant-general, Sir John Spencer Ewart, initialled it. The cabinet repudiated an agreement it had not authorized and, with more pressure being applied, French and Ewart both resigned on 30 March 1914. The affair not only paralysed government policy towards Ulster, but also had serious repercussions within the army, poisoning personal relationships. Many such as Gough blamed French for not standing up to the politicians. To Winston Churchill in July 1914, French appeared a 'broken man' (Churchill, 83).

Western front (August 1914–December 1915) While French believed his career over, he was once more appointed inspector-general on 26 July 1914 and he remained the obvious choice to command the BEF if Britain found itself at war amid the deteriorating diplomatic situation in Europe. French was informed that he would indeed command on 30 July. On 14 August he landed with his staff at Boulogne at the head of one cavalry and four infantry divisions. The BEF advanced to its concentration area around Mauberge, where it was to act in conjunction with General Lanrezac's French Fifth Army. Somewhat unexpectedly the BEF came into contact with the German First Army around Mons on 23 August. French's 2nd corps, commanded by the newly arrived General Sir Horace Smith-Dorrien, took the brunt of the German assault. With news that Lanrezac was in retreat and the realization that the BEF faced envelopment, French was forced to abandon plans for a further advance and ordered a retirement on 24 August. In the retreat 2nd corps became separated from Haig's 1st corps and, pressed hard, Smith-Dorrien took the decision to make a stand at Le Cateau on 26 August. At the time, French approved Smith-Dorrien's decision, which effectively saved the BEF from extinction by inflicting a sharp check on the German pursuit. Later it was to become a matter of controversy between French and Smith-Dorrien and at the time, French had clearly feared that 2nd corps would be lost altogether. Indeed French planned to withdraw the BEF to the coast at St Nazaire, a decision that resulted in Kitchener, who had been appointed secretary of state for war, crossing to France on 1 September in field marshal's uniform to order French to conform with the plans of the French commander-in-chief, Joseph Joffre.

The German First and Second armies were themselves becoming separated and Joffre ordered a counter-attack on 5 September on the Marne. The BEF advanced on 6 September into the gap between the two German armies, forcing them to retire to the Aisne. French endeavoured to cross the river, but stalemate ensued. Both sides now attempted a series of outflanking movements known as the 'race to the sea', the BEF being transferred to Flanders between 1 and 19 October 1914. 2nd corps became heavily engaged at La Bassée on 14 October at the start of what was to become the first battle of Ypres. The BEF held a series of increasingly heavy German attacks, not least on 30 and 31 October, the British line being restored at the most critical moment by the charge of a single battalion, the 2nd Worcesters, at Gheluvelt. French's mood fluctuated considerably during the battle, which came to an end in mid-November, but he was more optimistic by the spring that he could break the German lines, his command having grown to First and Second armies in December 1914.

French's first attempt to break through came at Neuve Chapelle on 10–13 March 1915, an innovative assault that made some progress before the limited technical means at the BEF's disposal brought it to a halt. The Germans themselves then launched the second battle of Ypres on 22 April, using chlorine gas to break through the French lines. Second Army helped plug the gap, but Smith-Dorrien further exacerbated the tensions between himself and French by arguing for a withdrawal from the salient held at such cost during the first battle. Arguing that Smith-Dorrien was over-pessimistic, French withdrew all troops from his command on 30 April 1915, and Smith-Dorrien resigned on 6 May. French, meanwhile, pressed an attack of his own on Aubers Ridge on 9 May and others at Festubert from 15 to 27 May and at Givenchy on 15 June. All failed, French being convinced that the reason for this was a lack of sufficient artillery shells, for which he blamed Kitchener. Indeed French had made his dissatisfaction known to the military correspondent of *The Times*, Charles à Court Repington, who publicized the claim on 14 May. The ensuing crisis helped bring down Asquith's government, but Kitchener remained at the War Office in the new coalition despite the attack on him being sustained by the Northcliffe press.

French's own position, however, was being steadily undermined by Haig, now commanding First Army, and Sir William Robertson, who had become chief of staff at general headquarters (GHQ) in December 1914. The king,

too, was losing confidence in French. Against this inauspicious background, French was compelled by allied political considerations to undertake a new offensive at Loos on 25 September 1915. It provided the first real test of Kitchener's New Army divisions and also saw the first British use of gas. There was disagreement between French and Haig, whose army carried out the assault, over the placing of reserves to exploit any breakthrough. French believed they should be held back for possible use on the second day of operations rather than being brought further forward. In the event the reserves were committed too late and the attack failed. Haig lost no time in conveying his displeasure at French's handling of the issue, making full use of a visit to France by the king while French himself was absent in London. Asquith let French know that he must go, and his letter of resignation as commander-in-chief of the BEF was formally received on 6 December 1915, French's departure being eased by appointment to the post of commander-in-chief of home forces and his elevation to the peerage as Viscount French of Ypres and of High Lake, co. Roscommon.

Home forces and Ireland Warfare on the western front had proved a steep learning curve, but French did grasp something of the nature of the tactical changes which were to occur, particularly the growing significance of artillery in what he increasingly recognized as large-scale siege operations. This realization did not mean that French readily saw any solution to the deadlock evident by the end of 1914, but it is arguable that his approach was marginally more flexible than that of Haig, who remained wedded to a view of the immutability of the battlefield and to a highly deterministic concept of battle as a structured series of events.

French was not only compelled to confront new technical and managerial difficulties in the conduct of war, but also to take account of troublesome allies since Britain was initially the junior military partner of France and Russia. French's relations with Joffre were often uneasy and he took an instant dislike to Lanrezac. Moreover Kitchener's appointment as secretary of state for war brought about a marked deterioration in French's relationship with the British government. French never forgave Kitchener for appearing in France in field marshal's uniform in September 1914 and Kitchener rather than Asquith had been the real target of French's manipulation of the shells scandal. While more experienced than most of his subordinates, French had not commanded more than a division in the field before 1914 and he was always somewhat ambivalent towards staff training with his choice of personal staff inspiring little confidence. Moreover GHQ was something of a hotbed of intrigue with the personal animosities revealed by the Curragh incident given further free rein. French's own temperament was always suspect, as evidenced by his deteriorating relationship with Smith-Dorrien. They had fallen out back in 1909 when, as French's successor at Aldershot, Smith-Dorrien had taken a more critical view of the cavalry and French had criticized Smith-Dorrien's performance at that year's autumn manoeuvres. Admittedly Smith-Dorrien had a violent temper, but he was a capable soldier and French's increasing hostility towards him was unworthy. Whatever his relationship with his immediate subordinates, however, French's preference was for old-style high visibility at the front and he generated much affection among ordinary soldiers. His wartime letters to Mrs Bennett also reveal that he was pained by the casualties incurred and tormented by the loss of friends, writing on one occasion that his room was 'becoming thick with the spirits of my friends' (IWM, French MSS, 75/46/1, French to Mrs Bennett, 24/25 Feb 1915).

French reorganized the somewhat chaotic structure of home defence arrangements, and made recommendations to improve anti-aircraft defences around London. At the same time, however, he became an unofficial strategic adviser to Asquith's successor as prime minister, Lloyd George, pushing the concept of an allied supreme war council in the autumn of 1917, as well as favouring the 'Pétain option' of closing down large-scale operations on the western front and awaiting the arrival of the Americans. Ireland, however, was to become an increasingly intractable problem. With the outbreak of the Easter rising in Dublin on 24 April 1916, French sent reinforcements and recommended General Sir John Maxwell for the Irish command. He himself was then sent out as lord lieutenant by Lloyd George in May 1918.

French now believed home rule the only realistic option for Ireland and set out to destroy the nationalist Sinn Féin in order to create the circumstances in which home rule could be safely introduced. Post-war demobilization reduced the troops at French's disposal and he endeavoured to raise the status and pay of the Royal Irish Constabulary (RIC), also approving the raising of the Black and Tans and the auxiliary division, RIC, from former soldiers on the mainland. French also pressed for the introduction of martial law. In December 1919 he narrowly escaped assassination when the IRA ambushed his motorcade at Kelly's Corner, Dublin. As violence increased so the supremacy of the lord lieutenant was reduced within the Irish administration and, though martial law was eventually imposed in December 1920, the government increasingly moved towards finding a political settlement. Lloyd George indicated in March 1921 that French would be succeeded by Lord Edmund Talbot, who, as a Catholic, would be more acceptable to Irish opinion. French resigned on 30 April 1921.

French's period as lord lieutenant had also been marked by the opening of the controversy over the conduct of the war. His unreliable and highly partisan memoir, 1914—first published in serial form in the Daily Telegraph in April 1919 and then as a book in June 1919, while he was still technically a serving soldier—was effectively the first such memoir by any leading participant. Heightening the impact of the book, which had been largely compiled by The Times journalist Lovat Fraser from conversations with French, was the seeming candour in revealing wartime disputes at the highest levels. It was also remarkable for the vigour with which French attacked both Kitchener and, more indirectly, Asquith, though the most extreme statements were reserved for Smith-Dorrien. French's book raised a serious question as to the degree to which policy makers should or could be restricted from publishing matters which might be regarded as subject to the somewhat indistinct interpretation of what constituted official secrets. Smith-Dorrien, who was himself still serving as governor of Gibraltar, was denied the opportunity to reply to French's charges in public, but French's version of events was savaged by the royal librarian, the Hon. John Fortescue, who claimed 1914 the 'work of a monomaniac' (Beckett, Judgement of History, xi), only to be promptly dismissed as an official historian. Smith-Dorrien himself was in correspondence with many sympathizers, circulating private memoranda in his own defence, and ultimately he was vindicated in the relevant volume of the official history published in 1925. French's second son, Gerald, continued to fire off further salvoes in the 'battle of the memoirs' until 1960, but considerable damage had been done to French's reputation, the king in particular being angered by the 'un-English and ungenerous' nature of 1914 (Royal Archives, Geo V, O.1470/10, Wigram to Smith-Dorrien, 13 June 1919). Not unexpectedly, most other leading participants took an uncharitable view of French's abilities, a trend still evident in the historiography in the 1960s.

French was created earl of Ypres for his Irish services in June 1922. He spent much of his time thereafter in France until appointed captain of Deal Castle in August 1923. He made his home at the castle and died there from cancer of the bladder on 22 May 1925, being buried at Ripple five days later. He was survived by his second wife, Eleanora.

Significance Undoubtedly a gifted cavalry leader, French was very much the product of the nineteenth century and intellectually and temperamentally unsuited to meeting the challenges of the new conditions pertaining in warfare. Yet he was neither a butcher nor a bungler, and in many respects French was the best the system could produce at that time and place. Others, after all, did no better and moreover lacked the more endearing qualities of the beau sabreur.

French has often seemed in the past, from his very physical appearance, the 'archetypal First World War General, more familiar with the comfortable routine of a château than with the rigours of the trenches, cheerfully nailing British manhood to the cross of the Western Front' (Holmes, Little Field-Marshal, 1). In fact, with the passing years, French has become a less controversial figure than Douglas Haig, who succeeded him as commander-in-chief of the BEF in France and Flanders in December 1915 and with whom he was almost inextricably linked in the minds of previous generations. French as much as Haig once stood condemned as one of the 'donkeys' who sent the 'lions' of the British army to their deaths. But with greater public attention being paid to the campaigns of 1916 and 1917 from the 1960s onwards Haig rather than French has become the more representative 'donkey' in popular memory. Indeed, while few would suggest the mercurial French was one of the 'great captains', his reputation has enjoyed a minor renaissance to the extent that he is now viewed rather more sympathetically.

IAN F. W. BECKETT

Sources R. Holmes, *The little field-marshal: Sir John French* (1981) · R. Holmes, 'Sir John French and Lord Kitchener', *The First World War and British military history*, ed. B. Bond (1991), 113–40 · I. F. W. Beckett, ed., *The judgement of history: Sir Horace Smith-Dorrien, Lord French and 1914* (1993) · I. F. W. Beckett, 'Haig and French', *Haig: a reappraisal 70 years on*, ed. B. Bond and N. Cave (1999), 51–63 · P. Bryant, 'The recall of Sir John French', *Stand To* (1988), 22.24–9, 23.32–8, 24.22–6 · W. Philpott, 'The strategic ideas of Sir John French', *Journal of Strategic Studies*, 12 (1989), 458–78 · G. Casser, *The tragedy of Sir John French* (1985) · Viscount French of Ypres [J. D. P. French], *1914* (1919) · *The despatches of Lord French* (1917) · G. French, *The life of FM Sir John French* (1931) · G. French, *Some war diaries, addresses and correspondence of FM the earl of Ypres* (1937) · G. French, *French replies to Haig* (1936) · G. French, *The Kitchener–French dispute: a last word* (1960) · D. French, 'The military background to the Shell crisis of May 1915', *Journal of Strategic Studies*, 2 (1979), 195–205 · I. F. W. Beckett, ed., *The army and the Curragh incident, 1914* (1986) · I. F. W. Beckett, 'Buller and the politics of command', *The Boer War: direction, experience and image*, ed. J. Gooch (2000), 41–55 · I. F. W. Beckett, 'King George V and his generals', *Leadership in conflict, 1914–18*, ed. M. Hughes and M. Seligmann (2000), 247–64 · I. F. W. Beckett, 'Selection by disparagement: Lord Esher, the general staff and the politics of command, 1904–14', *The British general staff: reform and innovation*, ed. D. French and B. Holden Reid (2002) · A. Clark, *The donkeys* (1961) · R. B. Brett, second Viscount Esher, letter to Francis Knollys, 16 Jan 1904, Royal Arch., W39/21 · R. B. Brett, second Viscount Esher, letter to King George V, 26 Sept 1907, Royal Arch., W40/128 · W. S. Churchill, *Great contemporaries* (1937) · French to Mrs Bennett, 24/5 Feb 1915, IWM, French papers, 75/46/1 · Wigram to Smith-Dorrien, 13 June 1919, Royal Arch., Geo V, O.1470/10 · *CGPLA Eng. & Wales* (1925)

Archives Brenthurst Library, Johannesburg, diary · IWM, diaries, corresp., and military and official MSS, 75/46 · NL Ire., diary · priv. coll. | BL, corresp. with Arthur James Balfour, Add. MS 49726, *passim* · BL, corresp. with Lord Northcliffe, Add. MS 62159 · Bodl. Oxf., corresp. with H. Asquith; corresp. with H. A. Gwynne; corresp. with Lord Selborne · CAC Cam., corresp. with Lord Esher · HLRO, corresp. with D. Lloyd George; corresp. with A. Bonar Law · IWM, B. Fitzgerald MSS, letters relating to appointment as British expeditionary force commander-in-chief · NAM, letters to E. Roberts · NL Scot., corresp. with Lord Haldane · NRA, priv. coll., corresp. with B. Fitzgerald · Nuffield Oxf., corresp. with Lord Mottistone · PRO, corresp. with Lord Kitchener, PRO 30/57; WO 159 · Wilts. & Swindon RO, corresp. with Viscount Long | FILM BFI NFTVA, news footage · IWM FVA, actuality footage · IWM FVA, documentary footage · IWM FVA, news footage | SOUND IWM SA, oral history interview · IWM SA, recorded talks

Likenesses oils, 1908, NAM · J. St H. Lander?, oils, *c*.1910–1915, Cavalry and Guards Club, London · F. Dodd, charcoal and watercolour drawing, 1917, IWM · W. Stoneman, photograph, 1918, NPG · J. S. Sargent, oils, *c*.1919–1922, NPG [*see illus.*] · J. S. Sargent, group portrait, oils, 1922 (*General officers of World War I*), NPG; charcoal study, Corcoran Gallery of Art, Washington, DC · G. D. G., chromolithograph, caricature, NPG; repro. in *VF* (12 July 1900) · J. Russell & Sons, photograph, NPG · J. Simpson, pencil and wash drawing, IWM · Spy [L. Ward], chromolithograph, caricature, NPG; repro. in *VF* (29 Nov 1900) · bronze bust, Cavalry and Guards Club, London · memorial tablet, Canterbury Cathedral · monument, Ypres Cathedral · portrait, Mansell Collection, London; repro. in Holmes, *Little field-marshal*

Wealth at death £25,161 1s. 6d.: probate, 7 Aug 1925, *CGPLA Eng. & Wales*

French, Nicholas (1604–1678), Roman Catholic bishop of Ferns, was born at Wexford. He was educated for the priesthood in the Spanish Netherlands at the Irish secular college at Louvain, of which he later became president. In or after 1625 he returned to Ireland and was appointed parish priest in his native town. In 1630 he wrote a Latin treatise of philosophy. He probably attended a meeting of Catholic clergy at Kilkenny in 1642. He took an active share in the deliberations of the first supreme council of the confederates and was a bitter opponent of the marquess of Ormond.

French was consecrated bishop of Ferns in November 1645, the month in which Giovanni Rinuccini arrived in Ireland, and became an important link between the factions which supported and those which opposed the papal nuncio and his mission. Rinuccini himself spoke highly of French's zeal for the Catholic cause, describing him as distinguished by his constant devotion for the church rather than by the temporizing and factionalism which tainted others. In August 1646 French became chancellor and chairman of the congregation of the Catholic clergy convened at Waterford which backed Rinuccini in his condemnation of the confederates' treaty with Ormond. He took a prominent part in the new confederate council founded in the wake of the excommunication and imprisonment of the Ormondists, but the following January it was largely at the urging of French and Nicholas Plunkett that the nuncio was reconciled with his opponents. In August 1647 Colonel Preston blamed the bishop for urging him to fight the English forces under the command of Colonel Michael Jones at Dungan's Hill outside Dublin. The ensuing military catastrophe secured the parliamentarians' grip on the Irish capital and the pale, further deepening the suspicions, recriminations, and mutual jealousies which wracked the confederacy. French was one of those sent by the supreme council to seek the military assistance of the O'Neill in the wake of Preston's rout, placing the confederates in a position of dependence on the Ulstermen which the Old English among them disliked intensely.

In February 1648 the bishop of Ferns was sent to Rome as part of the two-pronged diplomatic campaign by which the confederates hoped to shore up their weakening position. While Viscount Muskerry, Geoffrey Browne, and the marquess of Antrim went to Paris to negotiate directly with the queen and the marquess of Ormond, French and Plunkett went to Rome to treat with Pope Innocent X. (A third mission, to Spain, although entrusted to Sir Richard Blake, appears never to have got off the ground.) Officially, French and Plunkett were to seek papal mediation in the Parisian treaty between the confederates and the queen, and, in order to make such a treaty easier to conclude, to obtain the pope's permission to limit as much as possible the conditions for the religious settlement, by asking principally whether any religious concessions must be publicly agreed to, and specifically whether it was necessary to insist on the appointment of a Catholic viceroy. In the last resort they were to ask Innocent X to assume the protectorate of Ireland should the queen approve of such a plan. But French and Plunkett also travelled to Rome with private instructions from Rinuccini himself, whose priorities clearly ran quite contrary to the majority on the supreme council. The nuncio insisted that the two men first ask the pope to become Ireland's protector. Should he decline, French and Plunkett were to stress that it was their negotiation in Rome which took priority over any talks in Paris, and that their priority was to ensure, inasmuch as it was possible, that any agreement with the queen contain adequate guarantees that the religious and material rights of Catholics should be guaranteed. French and Plunkett were graciously received at Rome, where Plunkett was honoured with the title of papal knight. But their negotiation was compromised from the beginning. Having arrived in the Holy See on 23 April, some time after talks had begun in Paris, they failed to overcome the pope's resistance to formal approval of terms for peace between Catholics and their protestant ruler, a reluctance much fortified by the rumours coming from Paris of the imminence of Ormond's return to Ireland. Worse still, from the point of view of the unfortunate ambassadors, was the ripening of the talks for a truce between Lord Inchequin and the nuncio's enemies in the supreme council. When, during the absence of the two men, Rinuccini effectively pulled down the confederation around his own ears with his censure of 27 May 1648, French and Plunkett were completely at a loss as to what to do. After wending their uncertain way back to Ireland, on arrival they threw in their lot with the nuncio's opponents and French helped to undermine what little credit Rinuccini still had by reporting that opinion was divided at Rome as to the validity of his censure of the confederates.

French was also instrumental in securing the support of his fellow bishops for the second treaty with Ormond, finally concluded on 17 January 1649, by which the confederation was dissolved and the Catholics accepted the authority of the lord lieutenant. Subsequently the ground was cut from under the treaty, not only by military defeat but also by the Dunfermline declaration of 16 August in which Charles II repudiated the 1649 treaty and condemned the Irish 'rebels' as the price of his Scottish crown. In 1650 French attended the ecclesiastical assembly held at Jamestown and signed the declaration attacking the proceedings of Ormond. In 1651 French was sent to Brussels to obtain the assistance of the duke of Lorraine for the newly reformed confederacy, offering the duke the protectorate of Ireland. Their negotiations were broken off in 1652, but not before seriously damaging the reputation of the Irish clerical party among the ever wary Stuarts exiled at Paris. When French attempted to wait on Charles II in 1652 the king refused to see him.

For some years afterwards relatively little is known of the bishop's movements. He has been credited with authorship of a tract written by 'N. N.' entitled *The Polititians Catechisme* and published at Antwerp in 1658. Subsequently French certainly went to Spain, where he officiated as coadjutor to the archbishop of Santiago de Compostela in Galicia. During this time he wrote a protest and supplication addressed to the chief minister, Luis de Haro, on behalf of the Irish Catholics in the kingdom,

which was published at Seville in 1659. In 1666 French removed to San Sebastian with the intention of proceeding to Ireland, as Father Peter Walsh had procured from the duke of Ormond a licence for his return. But French forfeited the lord lieutenant's favour by sending him an insolent letter justifying the actions of the assembly at Jamestown sixteen years earlier. His licence for Ireland revoked, French went instead to France, where he became coadjutor to the archbishop of Paris. In 1667 he published, at Cologne, *In nomine sanctissimae Trinitatis vera descriptio moderni status Catholicorum in regno Hiberniae, et preces eorum, ad Sanctissimum Dominum Clementem Papam nonum*. French next went to Flanders, where, through the good offices of the internuncio Airoldi, he thoroughly reconciled himself to the court of Rome, which until then had not forgiven him his support for the 1649 treaty with Ormond. French subsequently became coadjutor to the bishop of Ghent.

French's years of exile were spent in writing and publication. In *A Narrative of the Earl of Clarendon's Settlement and Sale of Ireland*, published at Louvain in 1668, French condemned the Irish Restoration land settlement, inveighing much against Clarendon and Ormond, on whom he blamed the failure to reward the wartime loyalty of Irish Catholics. The same theme was pursued in *The Unkinde Desertor of Loyall Men and True Frinds* (1676). The attack on Ormond mounted in the latter of these two prompted Clarendon to reply with his *History of the Rebellion and Civil Wars in Ireland* (not published until 1719). French crossed swords with Andrew Sall in 1674 with the publication of *The Dolefull Fall of Andrew Sall, a Jesuit of the Fourth Vow, from the Roman Catholick Apostolick Faith, Lamented by his Constant Friend*, which reflected on the former Jesuit's abjuration of the Society of Jesus and his entry into the Church of Ireland as the prebendary of Cashel. Sall's reply drew from French *The Bleeding Iphigeneia* (1675). French died at Ghent in the Spanish Netherlands on 23 August 1678 and was buried in Ghent Cathedral. His *Narrative of the Settlement* was reprinted in 1685, so the archbishop of Armagh, Michael Boyle, noted, 'to serve a turn and make the people mad' (Ohlmeyer, 31). It was reprinted, with some additions, under the title *Iniquity Display'd, or, The Settlement of the Kingdom of Ireland*, in 1704.

THOMPSON COOPER, *rev.* SEAN KELSEY

Sources DNB · T. W. Moody and others, eds., *A new history of Ireland*, 3: *Early modern Ireland, 1534–1691* (1976) · P. J. Corish, 'Bishop Nicholas French and the second Ormond peace', *Irish Historical Studies*, 6 (1948–9), 83–100 · J. H. Ohlmeyer, *Political thought in seventeenth-century Ireland* (2000)

French, Peter (d. 1693), Dominican friar and missionary, was a native of Galway. On completion of his studies in Andalusia in the 1640s he travelled to Spanish America. There he worked for thirty years among the native peoples of Mexico. His command of one of the local languages was so accurate that he compiled a vernacular catechism, known by its Latin title *Catechismus, seu, Expositio fidei Christianae*. If it was printed no copy of it is known to have survived. According to John O'Heyne's *Epilogus* (1706) he was honoured with the title preacher-general by the

Dominican province of Mexico. He later returned to Ireland and was a member of the Galway community by the year 1682. In October of that year the provincial chapter proposed him as preacher-general for the convent of Galway and by September 1685 he had been formally installed in that position. He appears to have remained in the Galway house until his death in 1693.

THOMPSON COOPER, *rev.* THOMAS O'CONNOR

Sources T. S. Flynn, *The Irish Dominicans, 1536–1641* (1993) · private information (2004) [Dr H. Fenning]

French, Robert (1716–1779), landowner and politician, was the eldest son of Patrick French (*d.* 1744), barrister, and Jane Digby, the daughter of Simon Digby, successively bishop of Limerick and Elphin. The Frenches, of Anglo-Norman origins, had settled originally in the port of Galway, where they were regarded as one of the dominant 'tribes'. This branch of the family had acquired lands in the county centred on Monivae. Patrick French became a barrister and conformed to the established church in 1709. Robert, after entering Trinity College, Dublin, in 1734, where he graduated BA in 1737, followed his father into the law. He was admitted to the Middle Temple in 1736 and to the King's Inns in Dublin in 1742. On inheriting Monivae at his father's death in 1744 he virtually ceased legal practice and devoted himself to the improvement of his patrimony and public affairs. In April 1746 he married Nicola Acheson (*d.* 1762), the younger daughter of Sir Arthur Acheson, fifth baronet (*d.* 1749), MP, and Anne Savage, of Market Hill in co. Armagh. He was a JP for co. Galway from 1745, and in 1753 he was elected to parliament for the same county. At first a *protégé* of the government manager, Archbishop Stone, he soon adopted an independent stance. In 1761 he transferred to the less prestigious borough seat of Carrick-on-Shannon, and in 1767 he was returned for the city of Galway, which his father had represented between 1713 and 1715. In parliament, while upholding the intimate constitutional link with Great Britain, he criticized the insensitive attempts by British ministers and Irish lords lieutenant to subordinate Ireland and curtail the powers of the Irish parliament. His views were summarized in the ostensibly anonymous pamphlet of 1770 *The Constitution of Ireland*. He actively forwarded, both in parliament and his locality, endeavours aimed at material and ethical betterment, himself serving in the Incorporated Society of Dublin and from 1769 on the linen board.

French's Galway estate was praised by Arthur Young as a model of enlightened innovation. He had inherited rentals reduced by the agricultural depressions of the 1740s, and he invested heavily to attract skilled bleachers, weavers, and spinning-masters. As well as enlarging and modernizing his own mansion he rebuilt much of Monivae, adding a protestant church, charter school, and housing for tenants. He put into effect some of what he had noted during an extended trip to England during 1751. A slump in the market for Irish linens in 1773 made him reconsider his strategy. Only in the 1760s had his spending on capital improvements yielded significantly higher rentals, and by the 1770s accumulated debts restricted his activities. He did not seek re-election to parliament in 1774, but encouraged his son-in-law, Sir Lucius O'Brien, to continue his philanthropic and utilitarian interests. After his wife's death in 1762 he conducted an affair with a servant, Winifred Higgins; they had several children. French died in 1779. His eldest son, Acheson French, had predeceased him and so the estate was inherited by Acheson's son, Robert French.

TOBY BARNARD

Sources NL Ire., French of Monivae MSS · R. French, journal of trip to England, NL Ire., French MSS, MS 7375 · R. French, letters to L. O'Brien, NL Ire., Inchiquin MSS, folder 2788 · account books, NL Ire., MSS 4918, 4919 · E. Keane, P. Beryl Phair, and T. U. Sadleir, eds., *King's Inns admission papers, 1607–1867*, IMC (1982), 179 · D. A. Cronin, *A Galway gentleman in the age of improvement: Robert French of Monivae (1716–1779)* (1995) · T. C. Barnard, 'The worlds of a Galway squire: Robert French of Monivae, 1716–1779', in G. Moran and R. Gillespie, *Galway history and society: interdisciplinary essays on the history of an Irish county* (1996), 271–96 · A. Young, *A tour in Ireland*, 2 vols. (1780)

Archives NL Ire., account books, MSS 4918–4919 · NL Ire., French of Monivae MSS · NL Ire., journal of trip to England, MS 7375

French, Thomas Valpy (1825–1891), bishop of Lahore, was born on 1 January 1825 at The Abbey, Burton upon Trent; he was the eldest child of Peter French, vicar of Holy Trinity with Stretton, Burton upon Trent, and his wife, Penelope Arabella (*née* Valpy). Educated at Reading grammar school, Burton grammar school, and Rugby School, he matriculated from University College, Oxford, in 1843, graduating BA in 1846 and MA in 1849. In 1848 he won the chancellor's prize for a Latin essay, and in the same year was elected a fellow of University College. He was ordained deacon by the bishop of Ripon in 1848, and priest by the bishop of Lichfield in 1849.

In 1850 French offered his services to the Church Missionary Society and was sent to India to be principal of St John's College, Agra. In 1852 he married Miss M. A. Janson in Calcutta. For most of his career in India she lived in England, raising funds for missionary work and caring for their eight children. In 1858 he came home, but in 1861 returned to India to found the Derajat mission on the Indian frontier. In 1863 he came to England again, and from 1865 to 1869 was vicar of St Paul's, Cheltenham. He then returned to India and founded the Lahore divinity school. After short incumbencies at Erith in Kent and St Ebbe's, Oxford, he was consecrated first bishop of Lahore on 21 December 1877, having received the degree of DD from Oxford University on 11 December.

Known as the 'seven-tongued Padri' for his knowledge of classical and Indian literary languages, French hoped to build an indigenous, multi-racial Indian church rather than merely to reproduce the English church in India. But his efforts to train learned Indian clergymen who would exert Christian influence on Indian élites ultimately impeded the spread of Christianity in the Punjab. His curriculum for the Lahore divinity school, which emphasized Greek, Hebrew, and Urdu, was later abandoned as unsuited to the practical needs of the Indian church. He was greatly disappointed by the unfavourable reception of his revised Urdu prayer book (1881), which contained many Arabic and Persian terms unfamiliar to Indian Christians. French's forceful assertion of episcopal authority strongly influenced the administrative structure of the diocese of Lahore and left it unprepared for the rapid growth of Christianity among Punjabi-speaking, untouchable village labourers.

In 1887 French celebrated the opening of Lahore Cathedral, received the DOL from Punjab University, and resigned his see to embark on travels in Persia and the Middle East. In 1891 he went as a simple missionary to Muscat, Arabia, where he died on 14 May 1891. He published a number of sermons in English and Urdu, and shorter works in Hindi and Pashto.

A. R. BUCKLAND, rev. JEFFREY COX

Sources H. A. Birks, *The life and correspondence of Thomas Valpy French, first bishop of Lahore*, 2 vols. (1895) · *Church Missionary Intelligencer*, 42–4 (1891–3) · *Register of missionaries … from 1804 to 1904*, Church Missionary Society (privately printed, *c.*1905) · A. A. Powell, *Muslims and missionaries in pre-mutiny India* (1993) · M. E. Gibbs, *The Anglican church in India, 1600–1970* (1972) · *CGPLA Eng. & Wales* (1891) · d. cert.
Archives LPL, letters to Charles Golightly · LPL, letters to W. Sadler · LPL, letters to A. C. Tait · U. Birm. L., Church Missionary Society archive
Likenesses photograph, repro. in Birks, *Life and correspondence*, frontispiece
Wealth at death £11,457 12s. 4d.: resworn probate, Dec 1891, *CGPLA Eng. & Wales*

French, William (c.1786–1849), college head, was the son of Thomas French, a wealthy yeoman at Eye in Suffolk. He was sent to Ipswich grammar school, where the Revd Mr Howarth was headmaster. In 1807 he entered Gonville and Caius College, Cambridge, and he came out in 1811 as second wrangler and Smith's prizeman; he graduated BA in 1811 and MA in 1814. In 1811 he was elected fellow and tutor of Pembroke College, and he became a university proctor in 1816.

French was only thirty-four years old in 1820 when he was appointed master of Jesus College by Dr Bowyer Sparke (1759–1836), bishop of Ely, in whose family he had been a private tutor. In the following year he married Elizabeth Maria, daughter of John Wythe of Eye, and was made DD by royal mandate, and served the office of vice-chancellor. He held this position again in 1834, when he also acted as one of the syndics appointed to superintend the building of the Fitzwilliam Museum. He was presented by the lord chancellor to the living of Moor Monkton, Yorkshire, in 1827, and through his old patron, Dr Sparke, he became a canon of Ely Cathedral in 1832. He discharged his various functions with urbanity and integrity but also with a forbidding formality of manner. An accomplished mathematician, French was a candidate for the Lucasian chair of mathematics in 1826. To classical scholarship he added a considerable knowledge of oriental languages. In collaboration with a fellow of Jesus College, the Revd George Skinner (d. 1871), he published translations of the book of Psalms (1830; new edn, 1842) and the Proverbs (1831).

French managed the affairs of his college so as greatly to improve its finances, and his name is connected with the remarkable restoration of Jesus College chapel, begun under his direction by his gift of coloured glass for the east window. Reviewing the numbers of students admitted and their academic achievements, the historians of the college have, however, judged the period of French's mastership as one of 'gradual and melancholy decline' (Gray and Brittain, 151). He died at Jesus lodge, Cambridge, on 12 November 1849, in his sixty-third year, and was buried at Brockdish in Norfolk four days later.

ROBERT HARRISON, rev. M. C. CURTHOYS

Sources *GM*, 2nd ser., 32 (1849), 655–6 · Venn, *Alum. Cant.* · R. Willis, *The architectural history of the University of Cambridge, and of the colleges of Cambridge and Eton*, ed. J. W. Clark, 2 (1886), 151; 3 (1886), 199 · A. Gray and F. Brittain, *A history of Jesus College, Cambridge*, rev. edn (1979)
Archives CUL, corresp.
Likenesses oils, Jesus College, Cambridge

Frend, William (1757–1841), religious writer and actuary, was born on 22 November 1757 at Canterbury, the second son of George Frend, wine merchant, alderman, and twice mayor of the city, and his wife, Catherine (d. 1763). His mother died when he was five years old, and his father married, on 25 September 1764, Jane Kirby. He attended the King's School, Canterbury, until 1771.

By way of preparing him to enter the family business Frend was sent to St Omer to learn French and then to Quebec, where he was recruited briefly to the British army at the beginning of the American War of Independence. On returning to England, Frend matriculated at Christ's College, Cambridge, in 1776, where William Paley was one of his tutors. He graduated as second wrangler in 1780, and was ordained deacon and elected to a fellowship at Jesus College. He received priest's orders in 1783. Besides teaching mathematics and philosophy at Jesus, Frend held the livings of two parishes near Cambridge, Long Stanton and Madingley, where he founded a Sunday school.

At first Frend was zealous in his academic and religious callings (he declined the lucrative post of tutor to the Grand Duke Alexander of Russia), but his study of the Hebrew language and acquaintance with Cambridge dissenters such as Robert Tyrwhitt, Robert Robinson, and George Dyer encouraged him to question his orthodox beliefs. A long walking tour through France and the Alps in summer 1786 only postponed his crisis of conscience, and by June 1787 he had ceased to officiate in the Church of England. He resigned his two livings later that year, and in 1788 published an outspoken defence of his unitarianism in *An Address to the Inhabitants of Cambridge*, in which he declared the trinity to be 'rank nonsense' and trinitarians 'highly criminal'.

In the years following Frend was active in publishing and lecturing at Cambridge, arguing against the requirement to subscribe to the Church of England in order to graduate from the university. He first visited the Essex Street Unitarian Chapel in London on 30 December 1787, and this initiated his friendship with eminent Unitarians of the time such as Theophilus Lindsey and Joseph Priestley. His *Thoughts on Subscription to Religious Tests*, published

William Frend (1757–1841), by A. Birrell, pubd 1793 (after Sylvester Harding, 1789)

in 1788, resulted in dismissal from his tutorship (but not yet his fellowship) at Jesus (29 December 1788) but brought warm praise from Priestley: 'I like Mr. Frend's Second Address no less than his first,' Priestley told Lindsey in January 1789; 'I greatly admire his spirit and ability, and hope much from him' (Roe, *Wordsworth*, 95). Frend was to contribute the Old Testament books for Priestley's new translation of the scriptures, although his manuscript was burned in the 1791 riots which destroyed Priestley's home and laboratory at Birmingham.

In February 1793 Frend published *Peace and Union Recommended to the Associated Bodies of Republicans and Anti-Republicans*. His pamphlet appeared at a critical moment, coinciding with the outbreak of war between France and Britain. In his pamphlet Frend sought to moderate between the 'contending parties' in the increasingly acrimonious debate about the French Revolution, 'bringing them together, to consult for the common good' (Frend, ii). But, as Frend later said, in the heated climate of Cambridge in 1793 the pamphlet 'excited no small sensation' (Frend to Lady Byron, 7 Jan 1838, Lovelace–Byron deposit, 71, fol. 114). Within ten days of the pamphlet's appearance the master and fellows of Jesus denounced Frend, and initiated proceedings which led to his trial by the university authorities in May 1794. He defended himself ably, and was loudly supported in the court by undergraduates including the young Samuel Taylor Coleridge, but on 30 May he was banished from the university for offending against the statute *De concionibus*. After an unsuccessful appeal he was forced to quit Jesus College on 27 September, when the college gates were chained to prevent him

from entering. In two pamphlets, *An Account of the Proceedings in the University of Cambridge Against William Frend* (1793) and *A Sequel to the Account* (1795), he defended his religious and political beliefs, so that, although he had been forced to move to London, his opinions and influence persisted at Cambridge. Frend nevertheless remained a member of the university, and received the income from his fellowship until his marriage.

Frend lived at first in chambers in the Inner Temple, and he became prominent among the intellectual leaders of the reformist London Corresponding Society and a close associate of leading radicals of the day such as John Thelwall, William Godwin, Thomas Holcroft, and George Dyer. On 27 February 1795 William Wordsworth first met Godwin at Frend's residence in Buckingham Street, off the Strand. Later that year, on 7 December, Frend joined Thelwall on the tribune at the last mass meeting of London's citizens called by the Corresponding Society, and spoke against the 'two bills' or 'Gagging Acts' then being proposed by the government. The artist Joseph Farington, who attended this meeting, described Frend in his diary as 'a gentlemanlike looking Man: of good stature and bulk ... Dark hair witht. powder ... He was dressed in blue with a white waistcoat; and seemed in appearance ill suited to those about him' (Farington, *Diary*, 2.428).

Frend's pamphlet *On the Scarcity of Bread* (1795) and an article dealing with the causes and remedies of the scarcity and the high price of provisions show that the demise of the reform movement, which discouraged many of Frend's associates, did not diminish his own concern with social issues. In 1803, following the resumption of hostilities between France and Britain, Frend supported the call for volunteers to resist a French invasion. Among his other publications at this time were his *Principles of Algebra* (1796–9) and *Principles of Taxation* (1799). His series of volumes on the night sky, *Evening Amusements, or, The Beauty of the Heavens Displayed*, proved so popular that it ran from 1805 to 1824. His main source of income was teaching mathematics to the children of aristocratic families, among them Annabella Milbanke, who in January 1815 married Lord Byron. Their lifelong friendship was accompanied by an extensive correspondence which is an important source of information about Frend's life and opinions.

In 1806 Frend became actuary at the Rock Life Assurance Company, a post he held for twenty years; life insurance was then a new business, and Frend had an influential role in organizing the company. Two years later he married Sara Blackburne, daughter of Revd Francis Blackburne of Brignall in Yorkshire and granddaughter of Archdeacon Francis Blackburne. They had seven children; the eldest of them, Sophia, recalled in her book *Three Score Years and Ten* (1895) her father's many acquaintances, including Charles Lamb, Coleridge, Dyer, and William Blake. In the autumn of 1837 Sophia married the mathematician Augustus De Morgan.

In addition to his business interests and family life, Frend continued to voice his political and religious views in numerous contributions to the Unitarian journal the

Monthly Repository. Encouraged by Sir Francis Burdett, his protests of 1810 against flogging in the army were influential in helping to bring about the prohibition of the punishment. In later life his interest in educational progress and reform reflected his earlier experiences as a dissenter at Cambridge University. His *Plan of Universal Education* (1832) described his characteristically liberal ideas for a school system, to be funded by taxing the income of the Church of England. Although he was approaching his seventy-fifth birthday, he was strenuously active in supporting the Reform Bill which was eventually passed on 4 June 1832. Two strokes, in January 1837 and late in 1838, left Frend severely incapacitated, and he died at his home at 36 Tavistock Square, London, on 21 February 1841. After hearing the news his old friend George Dyer also passed away, and both men were buried in Kensal Green cemetery. The obituary in the *Gentleman's Magazine* praised Frend as 'a warm and steady advocate of every measure tending to benefit or improve mankind' (*GM*, 543). Recent studies of London radicalism in the 1790s have recovered Frend's prominence in literary and political circles of the time.

NICHOLAS ROE

Sources F. Knight, *University rebel: the life of William Frend* (1971) · N. Roe, *Wordsworth and Coleridge: the radical years* (1988) · N. Roe, *The politics of nature* (1992) · S. De Morgan, *Three score years and ten* (1895) · H. Gunning, *Reminiscences of the university, town, and county of Cambridge, from the year 1780*, 2 vols. (1854) · E. P. Thompson, *The making of the English working class*, new edn (1968) · *GM*, 2nd ser., 15 (1841), 541–3 · W. Frend, *An account of the proceedings in the University of Cambridge against William Frend* (1793), ii · Lovelace–Byron MSS, Bodl. Oxf., ref. 71, fol. 114 · Farington, *Diary*
Archives CUL, corresp. and papers · Jesus College, Cambridge | BL, letters to Joseph Hunter and others · Bodl. Oxf., corresp. with Noel, Byron, and Lovelace families
Likenesses A. Birrell, stipple, pubd 1793 (after S. Harding, 1789), BM, NPG [*see illus.*] · portrait, repro. in Knight, *University rebel*

Frendraught. For this title name *see* Crichton, James, first Viscount Frendraught (*c*.1620–1664/5).

Freneau, Philip Morin (1752–1832), revolutionary poet and journalist in America, was born on 2 January 1752 on Frankford Street, New York city. He was the first of two children of Pierre Fresneau (1718–1767), wine factor and land speculator, and his wife, Agnes (1726–1817), daughter of Richard Watson, planter, from Freehold, New Jersey; her later married name was Kearny. His father moved the family to New Jersey, where Philip attended Mattisonia grammar school in Manalapan. He learned quickly and in 1768 entered the sophomore class at the College of New Jersey. Collaborating with his classmate Hugh Henry Brackenridge, Freneau wrote his first significant poem, *The Rising Glory of America*, which Brackenridge read at their commencement in 1771 and which was published in the following year. The poem paid homage to the spirit of Great Britain and anticipated the day when the British spirit would shine throughout America. In a few more years, however, Freneau, along with most American colonists, changed his attitude drastically: for later editions of *The Rising Glory* Freneau revised or expurgated lines praising Great Britain. Throughout the revolutionary

period no poet more staunchly defended the cause of American independence.

After graduation Freneau was briefly employed as a schoolteacher yet made no long-term career plans. Instead he spent the majority of his time doing what he loved most: writing verse. With the start of the American War of Independence, Freneau's literary activities took on an energetic fervour and he published much satirical verse in 1775, the best taking as its subject the British general and then governor of Massachusetts, Thomas Gage: *General Gage's Soliloquy* and *General Gage's Confession*. Another of his revolutionary verses, 'Libera nos, domine', has been described by Moses Coit Tyler as 'a slashing, contemptuous, and fierce litany for total and final deliverance from every shred of British rule and contact' (Tyler, 1.425). While Freneau's vitriolic poetry contributed much to his colonial reputation, it did little for his pocketbook. He therefore soon accepted a position as private secretary to a prominent planter at Santa Cruz in the Danish West Indies, where he wrote such poems as 'The Beauties of Santa Cruz', 'The House of Night', and 'The Jamaica Funeral'.

After returning home, in July 1778 Freneau enlisted as a private in the New Jersey militia, served as a scout, and was promoted to sergeant. By no means did his military duties hinder his writing, and in that year he produced a strongly anti-British study, *American Independence*. Before the year's end he began serving on a coastal privateer and, while ferrying tobacco to St Eustacia in May 1780, he was captured by a British man-of-war and imprisoned for six weeks on the *Scorpion* anchored in the Hudson River. The experience prompted him to write *The British Prison-Ship* (1781), a bitter poem cataloguing the horrors of life on board. He also wrote many vigorous poems and essays satirizing British generals and celebrating the American patriots. His elegy, 'To the Memory of the Brave Americans under General Greene, in South Carolina, who Fell in the Action of September 8, 1781', is one of the best poems to come from the late revolutionary period. Sir Walter Scott called it 'as fine a thing as there is of the kind in the language' (Duyckinck, 1.349). Scott, however, did not acknowledge that he borrowed a line from Freneau's poem for his *Marmion*. Freneau first collected his verse as *The Poems of Philip Freneau Written Chiefly during the Late War*. After the conclusion of hostilities he wrote his best-remembered non-political poems, 'The Wild Honey Suckle' (1786) and 'The Indian Burying Ground' (1788). These, too, attracted the attention of British readers. The poet Thomas Campbell (1777–1844) liked the second so well that he borrowed a line from it for 'O'Connor's Child'.

The post-war years led Freneau to a variety of pursuits. In the 1780s he worked briefly as a postal clerk in Philadelphia and in 1784 he returned to the Caribbean as captain of his own brig. Six years later, having become dissatisfied with the seafaring life, he returned to Middleton Point, New Jersey, where on 15 April 1790 he married Eleanor Forman, the daughter of a local farmer. Together they had four children. Finally, in 1791 Freneau turned to journalism and briefly edited the New York *Daily Advertiser*. Later that year the US secretary of state, Thomas Jefferson, offered him the post of translating clerk for the department of state. Freneau accepted and returned to Philadelphia, where he also became editor of the *National Gazette*, a paper he established in confidence with Jefferson to counter the federalist tendencies of the *Gazette of the United States*. Following Jefferson, Freneau saw the federal government backsliding to aristocratic tendencies and filled the paper with harsh invective against the prevailing governmental policies. Later describing the importance of the editorial work he did for the *National Gazette*, Jefferson asserted that Freneau 'saved our Constitution, which was galloping fast into monarchy' (*Writings*, 1.231). To George Washington, who disapproved of Freneau's essays and his editorial policy, he was 'that rascal Freneau', a memorable epithet commonly associated with the poet. Following Jefferson's loss of the secretaryship of state, Freneau was also required to resign his office and suspend publication of the *National Gazette*.

Freneau next edited a series of local New Jersey newspapers, none for very long and few with much impact. For the most part he spent the remainder of his life in obscurity. He continued to write verse defending democratic principles, and he lived long enough to witness a new generation of American littérateurs led by Washington Irving, who was then being lionized in London literary circles. Freneau took Irving's behaviour as a slap in the face, a deliberate betrayal of the literary and democratic principles Freneau had represented throughout his life. In 'To a New England Poet' (1823), written during the last decade of his life, Freneau took Irving to task. Though Freneau had lived to see the American colonies achieve political independence, establishing cultural independence was another thing entirely. Freneau, the 'Poet of the Revolution', died on 19 December 1832 while returning in a severe blizzard to his home at Mount Pleasant, Monmouth county, New Jersey; he was buried there two days later. After his death Mrs Freneau sold their property at Mount Pleasant and moved to New York, where she lived until her death on 1 September 1851.   KEVIN J. HAYES

Sources L. G. Leary, *That rascal Freneau: a study in literary failure* (1941) · *The poems of Philip Freneau, poet of the American revolution*, ed. F. L. Pattee, 3 vols. (1902–7) · J. Axlerad, *Philip Freneau, champion of democracy* (1967) · M. C. Tyler, *The literary history of the American revolution, 1763–1783*, 2 vols. (1897) · E. Wertheimer, 'Commencement ceremonies: history and identity in "The rising glory of America", 1771 and 1786', *Early American Literature*, 29 (1994), 35–58 · *The last poems of Philip Freneau*, ed. L. G. Leary (1945) · E. A. Duyckinck, *Cyclopaedia of American literature*, 2 vols. (1855) · *The writings of Thomas Jefferson*, ed. P. L. Ford, 10 vols. (1892–9)
Archives Hist. Soc. Penn. · Princeton University, New Jersey · Rutgers University, New Brunswick, New Jersey
Likenesses F. Halpin, engraving, repro. in P. M. Freneau, *Poems relating to the American revolution*, ed. E. A. Duyckinck (1865)

Freney, James (*d.* 1788), highwayman and burglar, was born in Inistiogue, co. Kilkenny, the son of John Freney, a servant and bailiff, and Alice Phelon, a servant. He was educated privately. He married some time after 1742, and

using his wife's dowry he set up a public house in Waterford city. When this failed he took to highway robbery and housebreaking in Kilkenny and adjoining counties. Southern Kilkenny was one of the most lawless areas in eighteenth-century Ireland, and Freney took up with the survivors of a previous criminal group, the Kellymount Gang. Nicknamed Captain Freney, his criminal career lasted from 1745 to 1749, its length possibly due to a certain amount of protection from some of the gentry of Kilkenny with whom he remained on good terms. His crimes and pursuit were reported in the Dublin press, and he was proclaimed an outlaw in June 1747, with a reward of £100 for his capture. A further reward was offered at the Kilkenny assizes in July 1748. He was eventually captured and sentenced to be hanged at the Wexford assizes in August 1749 for breaking and entering the house of Thomas Palliser in Portobello, co. Wexford, in 1747. The sentence was not carried out as Freney turned king's evidence and testified against most of his associates in return for his freedom.

Freney's fame is due to his autobiography, *The Life and Adventures of James Freney, Written by Himself*, which was first published in Dublin in 1754 with a list of subscribers including the earl of Carrick and Richard Baldwin, the provost of Trinity College, Dublin. It is a somewhat fictionalized account, adding some episodes of heroism and chivalry to otherwise technical descriptions of housebreaking and disposal of stolen goods, and it later achieved enormous popularity in chapbook form. In 1766 Freney was appointed a tidewaiter in New Ross, co. Wexford, and he held this position until his death in 1788.

         NIALL Ó CIOSÁIN

Sources *The life and adventures of James Freney, written by himself* (1754) · Gilbert Library, Dublin, Robinson MSS · *Faulkner's Dublin Journal* (Aug 1749) · customs salary books and establishments (Ireland), PRO

Frere [*formerly* Reeves], **Alexander Stuart** (1892–1984), publisher, was born on 23 November 1892 at 1 Derby Villas, Grove Vale, Dulwich, London, the only child of Alexander Wilfred Reeves, an auctioneer, and his wife, Mary Stewart Frere. As a young man he adopted the surname Frere-Reeves and in middle age he dropped the Reeves; Frere *tout simple* became among friends his forename as well as his surname. He was educated at a local school in Southampton. In August 1914 he enlisted in the Royal East Kent yeomanry and in 1915 he fought at Gallipoli. In 1916 he was seconded to the Royal Flying Corps but he was invalided out in 1917 after his plane crashed. His education was completed at Christ's College, Cambridge, where he read economics and in 1920–21 edited *Granta*. He obtained a third class in part one of the economics tripos in 1921.

After a short spell with the *Evening News* Frere accepted a job offered by the American publisher F. N. Doubleday who on the sudden death of its founder had bought William Heinemann Ltd. In 1926 Frere was made a director of Heinemann and when after the Wall Street crash Doubleday sold his shares, he became managing director in 1932 under the chairmanship of C. S. Evans. Their relationship was often strained but together they presented a remarkable list, which included John Galsworthy, Richard Aldington, J. B. Priestley, John Masefield, W. Somerset Maugham, Thomas Wolfe, and Graham Greene.

Frere's and Evans's tastes were happily complementary, Frere being more in tune with younger, more 'advanced' writers—early on he was in serious trouble for telling people at a cocktail party that Galsworthy, then the firm's star author, went about erecting stiles in order to help lame dogs over them. Frere's personal and publishing lives were intertwined, several of his authors becoming intimate friends. He was equally at home at soirées given by Lady Cunard as he was drinking Pernods at the Dôme or Coupole or demonstrating his remarkable skill as a tap-dancer.

In 1930 Frere married Jessica, daughter of Henry Rayne, shoemaker. He married in 1933 Patricia Marion, daughter of (Richard Horatio) Edgar *Wallace, novelist, playwright, and journalist. An experienced journalist herself, she shared in much of Frere's life as a publisher. They had two sons and a daughter. For most of the Second World War he was director of public relations at the newly formed Ministry of Labour and National Service, where he worked closely with Ernest Bevin. On Evans's death in 1944 he returned to Heinemann to become, for the next seventeen years, its chairman.

Under Frere's guidance Heinemann opened four Commonwealth offices. A major acquisition was a controlling interest in Secker and Warburg. Among authors published during the post-war years were Nevil Shute, Olivia Manning, Anthony Powell, and Pamela Frankau; non-fiction titles included books by Clement Attlee, Aneurin Bevan, and General Dwight D. Eisenhower. In Frere's day the Heinemann list was eclectic, allowing room for frankly commercial best-sellers, such as the historical romances of *Angelique*, as well as the journals of James Boswell.

Frere was very opposed to what he called 'publishing by committee'. Trusting his own, often idiosyncratic, judgement, he encouraged his editors to do likewise. His belief in his authors was confirmed when he courageously stood trial on a criminal charge of publishing an obscene libel. By the standards of the early 1950s *The Image and the Search*, a novel by Walter Baxter (1953), was undoubtedly sexually frank, but Frere told the court that he felt 'publishers owed a duty to such gifted writers and to the public to ensure that their creative work was not stillborn'. After two successive jury disagreements, at a third trial the crown offered no evidence and the jury was directed to return a verdict of not guilty. It was a sensational victory and Frere was its hero. The verdict helped pave the way to the more tolerant Obscene Publications Act of 1959.

Despite the excellence of the list, shortage of working capital led Frere to approach his friend Lionel Fraser, head of the powerful conglomerate Thomas Tilling Ltd; eventually Heinemann became its wholly owned subsidiary. After an abortive attempt to sell Heinemann to McGraw-Hill in New York relations between Frere and Tillings

soured and he was 'kicked upstairs' to be president. Soon after this he felt obliged to resign—a sad end to a brilliant career. Even so, he became an adviser to the Bodley Head to which some of his most established and faithful authors followed him; they included Graham Greene, Georgette Heyer, and Eric Ambler.

Frere was short of stature and had a debonair, aristocratic presence aided by a fine Wellingtonian nose. While much loved by his authors and most of his staff, his talent for dry, humorous sarcasm also made enemies. He was an active freemason, reaching the exalted rank of grand superintendent. He was appointed CBE in 1946 and a chevalier of the Légion d'honneur in 1953. Frere died on 3 October 1984 at St Saviour's Hospital, Hythe, Kent, after a fall in which he had fractured his femur.

JOHN ST JOHN, rev.

Sources *The Times* (6 Oct 1984) · personal knowledge (1990) · b. cert. · d. cert. **Archives** U. Birm., letters to Jessica Brett Young **Wealth at death** £324,902: probate, 17 Dec 1984, *CGPLA Eng. & Wales*

Frere, Bartholomew (1776–1851), diplomatist, was born on 30 November 1776, the fifth son of John *Frere, FRS (1740–1807), MP for Norwich, and his wife, Jane, *née* Hookham (1746–1813); he was the brother of the Rt Hon. John Hookham *Frere (1769–1846), William *Frere (1775–1836), and James Hatley *Frere (1779–1866). After attending Felsted and Harrow schools, he took his BA at Trinity College, Cambridge, in 1799, and MA in 1806. In 1801 he was appointed secretary of legation at Lisbon, whence he was transferred in the same capacity to Madrid in 1802 and Berlin in 1805. In June 1807 he became secretary of embassy at Constantinople, but spent three months on a man-of-war, and returned unreceived. In 1808 he returned to Spain as secretary of embassy, his brother being ambassador, and acted as minister-plenipotentiary *ad interim* at Seville from November 1809 to January 1810, and at Cadiz from 29 January to 2 March. Gazetted secretary of embassy at Constantinople in March 1811, he and his chief, Robert Liston, did not proceed to their posts until the following year, when in June they relieved Stratford Canning from his responsibility as minister-plenipotentiary. From 1815 to 1817, and again from 1820 to 1821, Frere took charge of the embassy at the Porte as minister-plenipotentiary *ad interim*. In 1817 he married, by proxy, Cecilia Barbara, daughter of Don Pedro Creuse y Ximenes, of Minorca; she died in Spain before meeting him.

In August 1821 Frere finally retired on a pension, which he enjoyed for thirty years until his death at 23 Old Burlington Street, London, on 29 May 1851, aged seventy-four. He was a useful public servant of ordinary abilities.

STANLEY LANE-POOLE, rev. H. C. G. MATTHEW

Sources Foreign Office registers, PRO · Boase, *Mod. Eng. biog.* · Venn, *Alum. Cant.* **Archives** Balliol Oxf., corresp. with David Morier · BL, corresp. with Lord Holland and Lady Holland, Add. MS 51615 · NL Scot., corresp. with Robert Liston · priv. coll., Morier MSS

Frere, Sir (Henry) Bartle Edward, first baronet (1815–1884), colonial governor, was born at Clydach, Brecknockshire, on 29 March 1815, the sixth son of the nine sons and five daughters of Edward Frere (1770–1844), an ironmaster, and his wife, Mary Anne, *née* Greene (*d.* 1846).

Family background and early years The Freres were an old East Anglian family with some reputation for parliamentary service. Both Bartle Frere's paternal grandfather, John *Frere (1740–1807), a second wrangler at Cambridge in 1763, and his maternal grandfather, James Greene, were MPs. More important, John Frere's eldest son, John Hookham *Frere, an uncle with whom Bartle Frere was to have important contacts, followed his powerful friend George Canning as under-secretary for foreign affairs and was later minister-plenipotentiary to the central junta in Spain during the Peninsular War. Like John Frere, Hookham was an author of some note, as well as being a founder of the Royal Geographical Society. The family example of scholarship and statesmanship was therefore before the young Bartle Frere in 1832, when he left the grammar school in Bath, to which he had been sent at an early age, for the East India College, Haileybury. After passing out top of his year, he was posted to a writership in the Bombay civil service in 1834.

It was in character that the young man—tall, slim, fair, keen-eyed, and with a growing interest in geography and exploration—should choose to risk the much-questioned overland crossing through Egypt to India. After a month of scholarly and political discourse with his uncle Hookham at Malta, a visit to Egyptian Thebes, a trip by camel across the desert to the Red Sea, and hair-raising adventures in an Arab dhow, an almost starving Frere reached Bombay on 23 September 1834.

Over the next eight years, beginning as assistant in the revenue department at Poona, Frere served his apprenticeship in Indian administration. But in this old capital of the Maratha Peshwas he began also his close study of the languages, human geography, history, and customs of the peoples of the Bombay presidency—a body of knowledge which came later to be, in the judgement of his biographer, W. B. Worsfold, 'unrivalled' (Worsfold, 13). In association with Henry Goldsmid, Frere and his young companions helped in devising the revenue survey and assessment system which was afterwards spread, with beneficial results to the cultivators, throughout western India. In 1838 he succeeded to Goldsmid's place as assistant revenue commissioner and supervisor of the revenue collectors, a post which took him into almost every district of the Bombay presidency.

During these years Frere also developed into a sportsman of some renown. He was a champion marksman over 1000 yards and on one occasion killed with a revolver shot a tiger that had leapt on top of his elephant. On horseback he was a fearless but controlled rider. These qualities of the hunter's steady hand and eye, the capacity for endurance, and the courage to take independent and measured risks were to show themselves during important episodes in Frere's later life.

Sir (Henry) Bartle Edward Frere, first baronet (1815–1884), by Sir George Reid, 1881

The ladder of distinction In 1842 Frere was appointed private secretary to the incoming governor of Bombay, Sir George *Arthur. Soon he had the latter's complete confidence. At the same time he familiarized himself with the higher administration of the Bombay presidency, especially during the consolidation after the annexation of Sind. On 10 October 1844 he further strengthened ties with the Arthur family by marrying the governor's second daughter, Catherine (*d.* 1899). Shortly afterwards the couple departed from India on one of only two spells of leave—in both cases sick leave—which Frere took during his thirty-three years in India. Having returned in November 1846, he briefly occupied an interim post in the customs before being appointed political resident to the Maratha state of Satara in April 1847.

Here the political situation was soon complicated by a succession problem, which turned, somewhat typically, on the adoption of an heir by a childless ruler. As the declared policy of the forceful governor-general of India, Lord Dalhousie, was against the recognition of such adoptions and in favour of the absorption of vulnerable princely states into British India, Frere's sympathy and defence of the raja's action was an inconvenience which could have affected his career. But, instead, his independent stance was respected; and after he had duly deferred to the will of his superiors in accepting the annexation of the state, he was continued at Satara in the new position of commissioner.

Although Frere gained the goodwill of the local Indian

community by his stand on its behalf, his relations with it had not always been amicable. On one notorious occasion the slaying of a cow for sanitary reasons had brought an incensed mob of Brahmans to surround his residency. Frere handled the matter fearlessly by addressing, fining, and then dispersing his would-be intimidators—but without calling in the help of nearby garrison troops. Conversely, he was to show a lively concern for his Indian charges in the public works he undertook, especially the improvement of water supplies, education, and local government, and in the restoration of ancient monuments, not least those of the old but ruined capital of Bijapur. This energetic career in Satara assured him of higher distinction; so in January 1851 he arrived in Karachi to take up the commissionership of Sind, a turbulent territory which had been recently appropriated, without authorization, by Sir Charles Napier.

At first there was some surprise that a military man had not been nominated to bring the troublesome dispossessed amirs of Sind and resentful peoples such as the Sayyids under control. But Lord Dalhousie and Lord Falkland, now the governor of Bombay, wanted a special civilian—Frere—'that gentleman … whose firmness of purpose, mild disposition and conciliatory manners cannot but insure … the ready co-operation and respect of the military authorities' (DNB). It was a prescient view; for not only in the way Frere co-operated with his military commander, General John Jacob, in the pacification of the frontier peoples, but also in the far greater crisis of the Indian mutiny, he was to demonstrate how closely he could work with the soldiers.

The Frere–Jacob system of weaning the tribes of the borderland from their traditional turbulence was based on the premise that the frontier should not be a zone of 'know-nothing' extrusion but, rather, an area of informed interaction. As F. V. Emery has shown, this approach grew out of Frere's studies in the human geography of imperial expansion. From these he concluded that it was better to control and positively to develop civilized relationships on British frontiers as a prelude to further inevitable expansion than to leave them to chance and the probable sporadic hostilities that stemmed from unbenign neglect. As part of this policy he opened relations with the khan of Kalat and established fairs at Sukkur and Karachi. At these the frontier tribes could mingle with those under company rule and learn that there was a benevolent side to the intruding British administration. This 'great game' of diplomatic probing beyond the north-western frontier was subsequently dubbed 'interventionist' and perceived to be a factor leading up to the disastrous entanglement in Afghanistan in the late 1870s. But at this early stage in the consolidation of Sind it was probably a sensible and statesmanlike approach. It complemented Frere's internal policy of befriending and pensioning off potentially troublesome amirs.

As in Satara, so in Sind—but on a far larger scale—Frere turned his attention to public works to stimulate the economy and convert what was still in parts a tribal society into a modern commercial urban sector and an industrious peasantry producing cash crops such as indigo, sugar cane, rice, and wheat for internal consumption or for export. To achieve this he pursued three main complementary objectives: irrigation, transport, and harbour works. Consequently he initiated the transformation of the minor coastal port of Karachi into a deep-water facility, with wharves, piers, and warehouses. By 1859, when Frere left, the sea-borne trade had trebled, and Karachi was almost the equal of Madras. From this growing metropolis the railway duly snaked inland to Kotri as a result of Frere's representations to the government of India. Linking with it was a road system of some 6000 miles, for the construction of which Frere was ultimately responsible. Finally, near Rohri, the 'supply channel' was built to bring water to a network of canals extending some 300 miles from the point where the water first left the Indus. The gain in material prosperity duly led to the doubling of Sind's public revenues during Frere's administration.

In addition, Frere's energy was devoted to matters that went beyond the purely material. He established a library and museum at Karachi and gave it and nineteen other towns municipal institutions. The founding of village schools, the development of a judicial code, and the conversion of Sindi into a written language were further achievements.

Under this labour of consolidation Frere eventually felt the need to recruit his health, so departed for England in 1856. His wife and two small daughters, May *Frere and Katey, preceded him. A son, also Bartle, had been born in October 1854, and there would be two further daughters. For the year of overseas leave the family was reunited.

Frere and the Indian mutiny Leaving his wife and children behind, Frere returned to Karachi on 18 May 1857. He was greeted on arrival by the news that the Indian mutiny had broken out at Meerut a week earlier. Rising to the occasion, he took the momentous decision as a civilian administrator to half order, half persuade the local army commander to dispatch the only available British regiment, the 1st fusiliers, to secure the key fortress of Multan, on the route to the endangered Punjab. His principle being 'when the head and heart are threatened, the extremities must take care of themselves', he sent virtually all remaining regular troops on whom he could rely, barring 178 Europeans, out of Sind to the assistance of the Punjab. At the same time he co-ordinated intelligence on the progress of the rebellion so that frontier commanders in the west and regiments on the high seas could be directed to crucial points. By raising volunteer detachments and putting on a calm face at his headquarters, he kept up the morale of Sind and suppressed the three minor local insurrections. Insisting, too, that Peshawar should be held, he further won the admiration of Sir John Lawrence, chief commissioner of the Punjab—as well as the accolade 'that probably there is no Civil Officer in India who, for eminent exertions, deserves better of the Government than Mr H. B. E. Frere' (Worsfold, 24). As virtual saviour of British government in western India, he received the thanks of parliament both in January 1858 and April 1859, and on the latter occasion was knighted KCB.

Frere left Sind in October 1859 to take up a key position in the supreme government of India at Calcutta as member of the council of the viceroy, Lord Canning. He was the first 'Bombay civilian' to receive the honour. 'Clemency' Canning leaned much on Frere's knowledge of India and on his ability to explain the viceroy's post-mutiny policy of crown control, reconciliation, and legislative innovation to the European and, more particularly, the Indian communities. Consequently, the progressive members of the latter group were taken up into the hospitality of Frere and his gracious wife, Catherine, and much was done to ease tensions caused by the mutiny. Not without some reservation Frere co-operated in the financial work of the council with the British experts, James Wilson and Samuel Laing, who were sent out to restore the shattered finances. At times he even deputized temporarily for them. In the process he gained insight into the shortcomings of the system of rule in India by an overriding supreme viceregal council at Calcutta and subordinate regional governments at the presidencies of Madras and Bombay. When Frere returned to western India on 22 April 1862, by the first train to cross India from sea to sea, he was sworn in as governor of Bombay.

Here Frere's work paralleled on a greater scale his achievements in Sind. Thus the city's municipal institutions were inaugurated. The demolition of the ancient fortifications and the clearance of this land for public buildings designed by Sir Gilbert Scott improved the physical facilities. Such developments opened the way for municipal sanitary measures, which so lowered the death-rate that Florence Nightingale herself complimented Frere. As the demand for Indian cotton rose during the American Civil War and the export of this commodity from western India trebled, partly through Frere's efforts, he undertook the improvement of Bombay harbour through a special board in much the same way as he had earlier reconstructed Karachi. Inland, he initiated the building of railways and roads to Rajputana and even Delhi for this increasing trade—and, *sotto voce*, for strategic purposes following the mutiny. The only large complication in this period of prosperity was the tardiness with which sanction for local action could be wrung from the supreme government of India. It led to some friction between Frere and the new viceroy, Sir John Lawrence, though the main problems were actually those between the Bombay government and the fussy Bengal 'civilians' who mainly served the supreme government and who refused to give more than lip-service to the policy of regional governmental devolution which Canning's reforms had envisaged.

After Canning's departure in 1862, Frere became the most prominent local champion of this policy of making the legislative councils more representative and accountable in terms of the act of 1861. Non-official British and Indian nominees were brought in and debates made public. The state service was opened, and strenuous efforts were made—not least by Frere—to enlist the goodwill of the Indian population for the new crown, as distinct from

company, government. As part of this campaign, he was able to associate many of the Indian merchant class (who had surplus wealth to spend during the cotton boom) with the private initiation of public projects relating, especially, to education. English and vernacular schools sprang up all over the presidency; with Frere as chancellor, the University of Bombay acquired its main buildings; and the education of females was begun. Indeed, Frere and his wife positively encouraged prominent Indian families to imitate their own hospitable example. Soon the wives of prominent Indians were engaged in the public social support of their husbands in a way that would have been unthinkable a short while before.

In 1865–6, however, there was to be an unfortunate setback to the relatively smooth course of Frere's governorship: the bubble of the cotton export boom burst with the resumption of American shipments to Lancashire. Frere and his legislature had taken some precautions, such as passing the Time Bargains Bill of 1864 against speculation in futures. However, he and his administrators had reacted somewhat tardily to warnings from London on the need to curb other irregularities and the necessity for government to impose control over the Bank of Bombay, rather than exercise mere influence through their two *ex officio* directorships. Consequently, the bank crash of 1866 brought some censure on Frere. Nevertheless, when he retired from India in March 1867 to take up a seat on the Indian Council in London, the conferment of the GCSI by the crown and an honorary DCL by Oxford University saluted his overall achievement.

The acclaimed empire builder at home and abroad For the next ten years Frere's work on the Council of India at home and during his two missions abroad, to curb the Zanzibar slave trade (November 1872–June 1873) and to accompany the prince of Wales around the Indian empire (October 1875–April 1876), brought further acclaim and an ever-growing reputation as a great statesman of empire.

While in London, Frere lived first at Princes Gardens and then at Wressil Lodge, Wimbledon. His duties on the Council of India were not onerous and left him time for his work in learned societies. While he did not write major monographs, he penned numerous articles and pamphlets on academic and imperial subjects. He was elected president of the Royal Asiatic Society on three occasions, a fellow of the Royal Society, and, perhaps most important, president of the Royal Geographical Society (1873–4). Geographical exploration was linked in Frere's mind with 'the vital springs of national life'—that is, with the extension of British prestige throughout the world. For this reason the missionary and explorer David Livingstone was a friend whose example Frere particularly invoked. Endearing him to imperialists and humanitarians alike, such scholarly pronouncements made Frere an oracle on most issues of Britain's eastern empire. Along with his Zanzibar expedition, this preoccupation caused his mind to range further into the interlocking imperial strategic interests along the whole line of the western Indian Ocean, from Afghanistan in the north to the Cape of Good Hope in the south. Few of the imperial statesmen of that generation had defined their philosophy of empire, but Frere's thought was of such a nature that a twentieth-century scholar has seen him as a harbinger of the future geopolitics of Halford Mackinder (Emery, 349).

Frere's angry withdrawal from negotiation with the sultan of Zanzibar, Sayid Burgash, and threat of naval interdiction proved sufficient to secure the permanent closure of the island slave market in June 1873. Although Frere's ultimatum was typically unilateral, he was much praised and duly received a privy councillorship, freedom of the City of London, and an honorary LLD from Cambridge University.

Frere's other mission, the elaborate stage-management of the prince's tour around India, went off without a hitch. From it he gained the friendship of both queen and prince—a somewhat rare combination—and received in reward a baronetcy and the GCB. While in India, too, he advised the British government, especially Lord Salisbury (the Indian secretary), that a recognized mission should be established in Afghanistan. Concluding that the amir at Kabul, Sher Ali, was innately hostile, Frere recommended that he be brought to a clear understanding of his position between the British and Russian empires and that further recalcitrance should be neutralized by the conclusion of alternative alliances at Kandahar and Herat. Embodied in an earlier open letter addressed to Sir John Kaye, this Afghan policy was later the subject, along with South Africa, of Gladstone's condemnation. But in 1876 Frere's star rode ever higher. He attended the Brussels International Africa Conference, and the prince of Wales lent him his seat at Birk Hall. Here, in October, he received the fateful invitation of Lord Carnarvon, the colonial secretary, to assume the governorship of the Cape Colony.

Preparations for South African confederation The offer of Cape Colony did not at first attract Frere. But in 1875 Carnarvon had embraced a policy of confederation for South Africa for purposes that are obscure even today: competing and complementary aims include imitating his Canadian example of 1867, strategic consolidation, the imperatives of the South African mineral revolution, and securing uniformity of 'native policy'. Publicly he attributed his policy to the last reason; and certainly Frere would use this in justifying his own actions. Suffice it to say that Carnarvon had a mission which he had found he could not carry out from London: Frere was therefore cast as agent on the spot of the cause of confederation. Beyond the mere governorship he could employ his position as commander-in-chief of military forces more actively than was customary; he would be high commissioner for all South Africa with diplomatic leverage over the whole subcontinent instead of, as in the case of former incumbents, only the north-eastern Cape frontier; a special imperial grant of £2000 would supplement his salary; and, if he succeeded in carrying confederation, he would have a peerage and could stay on in the new dominion for a year or two as governor-general. Here, then, was a proposal to elevate Frere to the equivalent of the viceroyalty of India—which had been denied him by his background as

an Indian official and by the relative failure of the experiment of appointing Sir John Lawrence from his post in the Punjab to be viceroy in 1863–9. Thus Frere came to look on the 'special duty' of confederation in a different light to an ordinary governorship (Carnarvon MSS, PRO, 30/6/33, fol. 3). On 31 March 1877 he duly arrived with his wife and three daughters at the Cape.

Meanwhile a portentous development was taking place. Partly on Carnarvon's earlier initiative, and without consultation with Frere himself, Sir Theophilus *Shepstone annexed the Transvaal from Natal only days after the new high commissioner's arrival. Frere therefore confronted a situation in the north which demanded his immediate attention. But, before he could act, the Cape Frontier War broke out in August 1877 with the Sarhili's ('Kreli's') Gcaleka (Xhosa) beyond the eastern border. It soon spread back, as a rebellion, among Sandile's Ngqika Xhosa of the colony. Having established his headquarters at Kingwilliamstown, Frere therefore attempted to co-ordinate the direction of the war through his imperial military commander, Sir Arthur Cunynghame, the Cape premier, J. C. Molteno, and the young colonial minister, J. X. Merriman. But the two colonists proved jealous of their perceived military powers under the colonial self-governing constitution of 1872 and were soon at odds with Frere and Cunynghame over their relative responsibility for the conduct of hostilities. In February 1878 Frere took one of his typically independent decisions by dismissing his colonial ministry. Although constitutional, this was an action almost unprecedented in self-governing colonies. It also created the core of a resentful parliamentary opposition to Frere and his newly nominated premier, J. Gordon Sprigg. Ominously, the dismissal enabled Molteno and Merriman to join forces with the Cape Dutch MPs under J. H. Hofmeyr, who disapproved of the annexation of the Transvaal and were increasingly opposed to confederation.

Without perceiving the emerging overall pattern in Frere's thought, historians analysing this dispute have tended to concentrate too much on the issue of military command. Hostilities on the eastern frontier, in fact, opened up two further important possibilities. On the one hand, they pointed towards the post-war acquisition and consolidation of the whole long band of still-tribal Transkeian territories between the Cape and Natal in the form of a grand imperial province 'on Indian lines' under the high commissioner. On the other hand, they provided a justification for bolstering the armed forces in South Africa. To carry the wider scheme of confederation, it seemed to Frere, additional reinforcements of imperial soldiers were necessary; yet Molteno and Merriman had obstructed his request for two further regiments on the grounds that the colonial commandos could alone win the minor frontier war. This was the other, unstated, reason for dismissing the Cape ministers: they had become an impediment to Frere's mission.

Beyond the moderate problem of the eastern frontier, Frere's mind was already grappling with a much larger conundrum. To join the Cape territorially with Natal would not bring confederation until he could persuade Sprigg's wavering majority that a political link with the smaller colony would not burden them with its Zulu border problem. Simultaneously, both Natal and the Transvaal, which were now in a sense 'one government' after the latter's annexation, themselves needed reassurance that their common frontier with the Zulu was secure. All therefore turned on neutralizing the threat embodied by Cetshwayo's Zulu kingdom and the 40,000 warriors that his system of age-grade *amabutho* regiments could put into the field. As C. F. Goodfellow has argued, to meld together the white-ruled elements of confederation required a definitive solution of the black problem originally identified by Carnarvon. This was the unerring conclusion to which Frere's logical and resolute mind took him. But he was now launched on a risky course alone; for his ally and mentor, Carnarvon, had resigned over the Eastern question in January 1878. The latter's successor at the Colonial Office, Sir Michael Hicks Beach, might defer to Frere, but he was not dedicated to confederation; nor could he shield the high commissioner from cabinet and, afterwards, parliamentary criticism. Locally, too, obstacles accumulated.

The middle part of 1878 was spent in elaborating the outworks of the confederal structure. Minor rebellions in Griqualand East and West were suppressed. The Transkeian scheme went forward, and Port St Johns was annexed to help secure the eastern coastline. On the west coast, too, Walvis Bay was appropriated. North of the frontier of Griqualand West—itself scheduled for incorporation in the reluctant Cape—the tribal Keate award district came under high commission supervision. The ties of subordination between the proconsul and the Transvaal administrator and the lieutenant-governor of Natal were also strengthened. In September 1878 all was therefore ready for Frere to travel to Natal and afterwards the Transvaal to ensure that the Zulu, and then the Boers, ceased to obstruct the confederal design.

Frere's apologists, such as W. B. Worsfold, have contended, first, that Hicks Beach's private correspondence shows full agreement with the diplomatic campaign which Frere prosecuted against Cetshwayo in the latter part of 1878 and, second, that the incidents taking place in the disputed Natal–Zulu borderland fully justified this campaign. There is some justice in the first argument, but the second is false. The incidents were typical of what had characterized that border for decades: in 1878 neither the lieutenant-governor of Natal nor the white colonists saw in them a *casus belli*. Indeed, the finding of the commission on the disputed part of the border from the Buffalo River northwards to the Transvaal was favourable to the Zulu claim. Moreover, J. P. C. Laband's investigation of Zulu intentions has found Cetshwayo to be fundamentally pacific and determined to fight only if so compelled. Thus Frere's portrayal of border incidents as symptomatic of imminently hostile Zulu purposes must be seen as the stalking horse of a deliberate high commission design to remove, by overriding diplomatic-military threat or, perhaps preferably, by war itself, a perennial obstacle to the success of confederation—the Zulu military system. This

was the burden of the ultimatum which Frere suffixed to the border award in December 1878. But meanwhile the British cabinet had itself begun to show cold feet in a flurry of last-minute restraining communications. In spite of the six weeks still involved in transmission, these in effect saddled Frere with the onus of solving the Zulu problem by rapid and consummate victory—or bearing the unpleasant consequences.

Disaster, decline, and death Alas for Frere's future and reputation, a strange concatenation of military errors, for which he was responsible only in an indirect sense, led to the disaster which obliterated the 1st / 24th Imperial regiment and its colonial supports at Isandlwana on 22 January 1879. By it, confederation suffered a mortal stroke, though it would be some time in the dying.

Frere's action in calming and fortifying Natal after Isandlwana was reminiscent of experiences during the Indian mutiny and endeared him to many colonists. After the British had regrouped, the high commissioner could at last set out in March 1879 to the Transvaal. Here he met the assembled Boer malcontents. By both confronting them with the permanence of the imperial annexation and conciliating them with his own plan for a constitution embodying some self-government, he was able to bring about the dispersal of the Kleinfontein camp and ward off rebellion for the moment. But on his way back to Cape Town the real blow fell. Embarrassed by Bishop J. W. Colenso's championship of Cetshwayo and the wave of British parliamentary and public criticism after Isandlwana—not to mention the later death of the French prince imperial—Disraeli's government with some justification made Frere the scapegoat. Not only was he censured, but Sir Garnet Wolseley was created governor of Natal and the Transvaal, and the high commission was split into eastern and western halves. Thus Wolseley took responsibility for the eastern subcontinent and for the post-war settlement of 1879 in defeated Zululand on the 'sadly aborted' basis of 'divide and don't rule' (Frere to Hicks Beach, 23 Aug 1880; St Aldwyn MSS, Glos. RO, PCC 3/17).

Frere was bitterly disappointed at this partial supersession, but the pleas of his friend the prince of Wales, and his own obsession with confederation, kept him at what was now an impossible task. Based narrowly on the Cape alone, he was forced into compromises with the Sprigg government over an alternative district-by-district incorporative plan for the Transkei and a dangerous project for disarming the frontier chiefdoms which backfired into the 'Gun War' in Basutoland after his departure. All attempts to draw Wolseley into his design failed; and that 'modern major-general' proceeded arrogantly to undo all the conciliatory work so painstakingly undertaken with the protesting Transvaal Boers. Instead, two of their leaders, Paul Kruger and Piet Joubert, came southwards to lobby the Cape opposition into more forceful obstruction of confederation in the colonial parliament. They then departed to foment the First South African War, which broke out in late 1880, after Frere had left.

Meanwhile, Disraeli's Conservative government had

succumbed in April 1880 to Gladstone, whose Midlothian philippics against Frere had seemed to make dismissal inevitable. But the belief that there was some faint hope of achieving confederation caused the incoming Liberals to keep him on, though they insulted him by ending his imperial grant and removing even the Keate award district from his 'Cape' high commission. The floating vote in the colonial parliament read the auspices and hearkened to the Molteno–Merriman–Hofmeyr opposition. Thus the proposal of June 1880 for a conference on confederation was withdrawn in anticipation of its certain rejection. The British Liberal government took the cue and in August 1880 recalled Frere. A great career had crashed in denigration and defeat.

Although Frere was to receive marks of friendship and respect from many continuing admirers, royalty not least, the magic of his name was gone and his attempts at apologia were largely ignored. With health impaired, he contracted a serious chill in early 1884. He succumbed to its complications on 29 May at his home, Wressil Lodge, with the sad dying words that 'they must understand' if they looked at 'The Further Correspondence' (Worsfold, 336). He was buried in the crypt of St Paul's Cathedral.

The fall of Bartle Frere is the stuff of classical tragedy. Around the turn of the twentieth century he enjoyed some historiographical rehabilitation in the writings of the imperial school of John Martineau, W. B. Worsfold, Lord Milner, and others. But the verdicts of scholars in the era of decolonization, in particular on the causes and consequences of the Anglo-Zulu War, have brought the wheel full-circle back to Gladstone's and Colenso's condemnation of Frere's 'imperialist' capacity for independent, logical, yet ruthless action. Charm, dedication, ability, courtesy, and civilized scholarship concealed this steely inner core—though in South Africa it proved to be brittle with age rather than resilient with youth. But Frere so nearly scaled the great heights. JOHN BENYON

Sources J. Martineau, *The life and correspondence of Sir Bartle Frere*, 2 vols. (1895) [incl. list of works by Sir Bartle Frere] · W. B. Worsfold, *Sir Bartle Frere: a footnote to the history of the British empire* (1923) · C. F. Goodfellow, *Great Britain and South African confederation, 1870–1881* (1966) · P. Woodruff [P. Mason], *The men who ruled India, 2: The guardians* (1954) · *Journal of the Royal Asiatic Society* (1884) · *The Times* (30 May 1884) · C. W. de Kiewiet, *The imperial factor in South Africa* (1937) · V. Hicks Beach, *The life of Sir Michael Hicks Beach (Earl St Aldwyn)*, 1 (1932) · A. Hardinge, *The life of Henry Howard Molyneaux Herbert, fourth earl of Carnarvon, 1831–1890*, ed. Elisabeth, countess of Carnarvon, 3 vols. (1925) · J. P. C. Laband, *Kingdom in crisis: the Zulu response to the British invasion of 1879* (1992) · J. A. Benyon, *Proconsul and paramountcy in South Africa: the high commission, British supremacy and the sub-continent, 1806–1910* (1980) · J. Guy, *The destruction of the Zulu kingdom* (1979) · J. Morley, *The life of William Ewart Gladstone*, 3 vols. (1903) · J. Guy, *The heretic: a study of the life of John William Colenso* (1983) · F. V. Emery, 'Geography and imperialism: the role of Sir Bartle Frere (1815–84)', *GJ*, 150 (1984), 342–50

Archives BL OIOC, corresp. and papers, MSS Eur. D 710, F 81 · Bodl. Oxf., family corresp. · LUL, notes on African affairs · National Library of South Africa, Cape Town, corresp. and MSS · PRO, corresp., CO 959 · PRO, MSS, CO 48, CO 159 · U. Durham, memorandum on Zulu war | BL, letters to Colonel Bruce, Add. MS 43991 · BL, corresp. with Lord Carnarvon, Add. MS 60797 · BL, corresp. with W. E. Gladstone, Add. MSS 44170–44472, *passim* · BL,

corresp. with Florence Nightingale, Add. MS 45780 · BL, letters to Sir Stafford Northcote, Add. MS 50030 · BL, corresp. with Lord Ripon, Add. MS 43617 · BL OIOC, corresp. with Sir George Clerk, MS Eur. D 538 · BL OIOC, letters to Lord Elgin, MS Eur. F 83 · BL OIOC, letters to Lord Elphinstone, MSS Eur. F 87–89 · BL OIOC, corresp. with John Jacob, MS Eur. F 75 · BL OIOC, corresp. with John Laurence, MS Eur. F 90 · BL OIOC, corresp. with Lord Napier, MS Eur. 7490 [copies] · BL OIOC, letters to Sir Lewis Pelly, MS Eur. F 126 · BL OIOC, letters to Sir Richard Temple, MS Eur. F 86 · BL OIOC, corresp. with Sir Philip Wodehouse, MS Eur. D 726 · Bodl. Oxf., letters to Henry Wentworth Acland · Bodl. Oxf., letters to John William Dodson · Bodl. Oxf., letters to Lord Kimberley · CUL, corresp. with Lord Mayo · Glos. RO, St Aldwyn MSS, corresp. · Glos. RO, corresp. with Sir Michael Hicks Beach · Lpool RO, corresp. with Lord Derby · NAM, letters to Lord Chelmsford · Natal Archives Depot, letters to Sir Evelyn Wood · NRA Scotland, priv. coll., letters to the duke of Argyll · priv. coll., corresp. with David Livingstone · PRO, corresp. with Lord Carnarvon, PRO 30/6 · Rhodes University, Grahamstown, South Africa, Cory Library for Historical Research, corresp. with Sir John Sprigg · SOAS, corresp. with John Jacob · Suffolk RO, Bury St Edmunds, corresp. with Bishop Colenso [copies] · U. Hull, Brynmor Jones L., corresp. with Thomas Perronet Thompson · University of Cape Town, corresp. with Henry de Smidt

Likenesses S. Cousins, mezzotint, pubd 1859 (after H. W. Phillips), BM, NPG · G. Reid, oils, 1881, NPG [*see illus.*] · T. Brock, statue, *c.*1888, Thames Embankment, London · S. P. Hall, group portrait, oils (*The duke and duchess of Teck receiving officers of the Indian contingent, 1882*), NPG · A. R. Hayward, oils (after G. Reid), Johannesburg Art Gallery, South Africa · Lock & Whitfield, woodburytype photograph, NPG; repro. in T. Cooper, *Men of mark: a gallery of contemporary portraits* (1876) · W. E. Miller, portrait, Brenthurst (Oppenheimer) Coll. · Spy [L. Ward], caricature, chromolithograph, NPG; repro. in *VF* (20 Sept 1873) · G. J. Stodart, stipple (after W. E. Miller; Grillion's Club series), BM, NPG · L. Toucher, bust, Kimberley Public Library, South Africa · J. Watkins, carte-de-visite, NPG · T. Woolner, marble statue, Bombay town hall, India · T. Woolner, plaster bust, NPG · T. Woolner, statue on monument, Victoria Embankment, London · bust, city hall, Pietermaritzburg, Natal, South Africa · carte-de-visite, NPG · photograph, Cape Archives, Cape Town, South Africa · photograph, NPG · photographs (as a young man), repro. in Woodruff, *Men who ruled India* · photographs (in later life), repro. in Worsfold, *Sir Bartle Frere* · portrait, National Library of South Africa, Cape Town, South Africa, South African Houses of Parliament and Fairbridge Coll.

Wealth at death £23,605 16s. 5d.: probate, 19 Aug 1884, *CGPLA Eng. & Wales*

Frere, James Hatley (1779–1866), writer on prophecy, was born on 6 February 1779 at Roydon Hall, near Diss, Norfolk, and was the sixth son of John *Frere (1740–1807), antiquary, and his wife, Jane (1746–1813), the daughter and heir of John Hookham, merchant, of London. John Hookham *Frere, William *Frere and Bartholomew *Frere were his brothers. Frere was educated at Felsted (1788–92) and at Dr Barrow's school in Soho Square, London (1792–5), after which he was enrolled in the Woolwich Royal Military Academy. In 1797 he served as a lieutenant of artillery in the force that was sent to strengthen the British position in Ireland after the attempted French invasion. A military career was never likely to appeal to a young man who even then was regarded affectionately by the rest of his talented family as something of an oddity. In 1799 he suffered a nervous breakdown and it was with some relief that his family found a position for him in 1805 in the army pay office. At one stage in his uncertainty he thought of being ordained, but his marriage on 16 June 1809 to Merian (d. 1863), the second daughter of Matthew Martin of Poets' Corner, Westminster, and his consequent move to Maida Hill brought him a degree of stability. In 1820 he was attending a dissenting chapel and in 1826 he was described by S. T. Coleridge as 'a pious and well-meaning but gloomy and enthusiastic Calvinist' (B. S. Frere, 192).

As with so many of his contemporaries, Frere's study of biblical prophecy dated from the cataclysmic events in revolutionary France. Following in the tradition of writers such as the younger Robert Fleming, who in 1701 had predicted the fall of the French monarchy 'at least before 1794', Frere published *A Combined View of the Prophecies of Daniel, Esdras and St John* (1815). This was the first of six books (the last one appearing in 1850) in which he argued that the prophecy of Daniel 8:14 was a prediction of the downfall of the papacy in 1847 and that the establishment of Christ's millennial kingdom would occur in 1867. His views attained some popularity in the 1820s and 1830s when apocalyptic expectancy was at its height. Some of Frere's opinions appeared in Henry Drummond's *Dialogues*, which purported to be an account of the Albury conference on prophetic matters which Frere attended in 1826. Although Edward Irving was probably the most eloquent adherent of his views, Frere remained in the evangelical mainstream and was never identified with the Irvingite or Catholic Apostolic movement.

In 1830 Frere moved to Blackheath when he secured the post of principal clerk in the army pay office, but this was almost a sinecure and he was not surprised when the position was abolished in 1836. From then on he particularly devoted himself to the needs of the blind, for whom he opened a school and for whom in 1838 he pioneered a bi-directional reading system, with a phonetic alphabet consisting of lines, circles, arcs, and angles, details of which he published in *The Art of Teaching to Read by Elementary Sounds* (1840). He also devised a cheap method whereby these characters, made from copper wire, were soldered to a tin printing plate which could successfully reproduce on paper the embossed script for tangible reading. Frere's script was energetically promoted by the London and Blackheath Association, but it was never widely adopted, though Louis Braille's dot-matrix did not become anything like universal for another fifty years or more. Frere's stereotyping method influenced William Moon of Brighton, whose raised alphabet was still in use at the end of the twentieth century.

Three years after his wife's death on 2 October 1863, and shortly before the year for which he had predicted the inauguration of the millennial reign of Christ, Frere died on 8 December 1866 at Shillington vicarage, Bedfordshire, the home of the Revd John Alexander Frere, the third of his five sons. He was buried in the family vault at Finningham, Suffolk.   TIMOTHY C. F. STUNT

Sources H. Frere, *Pedigree of the family of Frere of Roydon in Norfolk and Finningham in Suffolk* (1874), 13 · B. S. Frere, *A record of the family of Frere of Suffolk and Norfolk* (1982), 176–98 · L. E. Froom, *The prophetic faith of our fathers*, 4 vols. (1946–54), 3.385–90 · H. J. Wagg, *A chronological survey of work for the blind* (1932) · J. M. Ritchie, *Concerning the blind* (1930)

Archives priv. coll. · Royal National Institute for the Blind Library, examples of Frere's typeface for the blind

Wealth at death under £16,000: probate, 11 Feb 1867, *CGPLA Eng. & Wales*

Frere, John (1740–1807), landowner and antiquary, was born at Westhorpe, Suffolk, on 10 August 1740, the eldest son of Sheppard Frere (1712–1780), landowner, of Thwaite, Suffolk, and his wife, Susanna (1709/10–1779), daughter of John Hatley of London and Kirby Hall, Essex. He was educated at a private school kept by the Revd Mr Steggal in Wyverstone and in 1758 admitted pensioner to Gonville and Caius College, Cambridge. He graduated BA in 1763, proceeded MA in 1766, and was elected to a fellowship of his college. He was also admitted to the Middle Temple on 3 April 1761, but did not practise law other than by serving as justice of the peace for Norfolk and Suffolk, and high sheriff of Suffolk in 1766.

On 12 July 1768 Frere married Jane (1746–1813), only child of John Hookham of Beddington, Surrey, at St Peter-le-Poer, London. They lived at 26 Bedford Row and in 1780 succeeded to Roydon Hall in Norfolk, the home of Sheppard Frere since 1766. The couple had eight sons (two of whom died in childhood) and two daughters. Four of their sons, John Hookham *Frere, William *Frere, James Hatley *Frere, and Bartholomew *Frere, are noticed separately; Edward Frere (1770–1844) trained as an engineer and became an ironmaster of Clydach, Brecknockshire, and Temple Frere (1781–1859) was rector of Finningham, Roydon, and Burston, and canon of Westminster from 3 November 1838. Their elder daughter, Jane (1773–1829), married Sir John Orde, and the younger, Susanna (1778–1839), died unmarried.

Frere was elected fellow of the Royal Society on 6 June 1771, and of the Society of Antiquaries on 23 March 1775. He was vice-president of the Marine Society (a charity to apprentice poor boys to the Royal Navy) from 1776 to his death. Edward King's *Proposals for Establishing, at Sea, a Marine School* (1785) were addressed to Frere, and resulted in the commissioning of the world's first pre-sea training ship on 13 September 1786. In 1786 Frere purchased the improved steam engine of Watt and Boulton to equip the first steam-driven flour mill, at Albion Mill, London. This enterprise was managed by his son Edward and excited opposition from existing millers, and the local populace. It burnt down (possibly owing to arson) on 2 March 1791, and the family finances were badly damaged by the fire. Frere published a short factual pamphlet justifying the activities of his mill.

Frere was also widely respected for his knowledge of antiquities, and assisted his brother-in-law John Fenn in the publication of the Paston letters, acting as intermediary with London publishers. Few of his writings survive, but his 'Account of flint weapons discovered at Hoxne in Suffolk', read to the Society of Antiquaries in 1797 (published in *Archaeologia*, 12, 1800, 204), was 'a landmark in the development of prehistory' in its recognition of the remote origins of man (Evans, 203). Frere entertained a 'disinterested attachment to monarchical government, and to the doctrines of the established church' (W. Frere, xxi), and became interested in politics during the 1790s. In 1799 he was invited to stand as ministerial candidate for Norwich. He was elected, somewhat to his surprise, but at considerable cost. He stood again, together with William Windham, in the general election of 1802, but although the two men spent £8000 on their campaign, neither was re-elected.

Frere retired to Roydon in July 1802, with debts of £30,000, and in September had a slight stroke. Another followed in the spring of 1804, and he died at East Dereham on 12 July 1807, having cleared his debts, and leaving his family with an income of £4600. In 1999 a memorial to Frere was erected in Finningham church, where he was buried, describing him as 'the first to realise the immense antiquity of mankind' (Wymer and West, 4). Frere was 'tall, and handsome, with bright blue eyes … His temper was quick, but his disposition was affectionate, and his manners were singularly charming' (Festing, 4).

DAVID STOKER

Sources B. S. Frere, *A record of the family of Frere of Suffolk and Norfolk* (1982) · Burke, *Gen. GB* (1865–72) · W. Frere, 'Advertisement containing notices of the life of Sir John Fenn', in J. Fenn, *Original letters … by various persons of rank and consequence*, 5: *Original letters, written during the reigns of Henry VI, Edward IV, Edward V, Richard III, and Henry VII*, ed. W. Frere (1823), vii–xxxviii · D. Stoker, '"Innumerable letters of good consequence in history": the discovery and first publication of the Paston letters', *The Library*, 6th ser., 17 (1995), 107–55 · W. E. Frere and B. Frere, 'Memoir', *The works of John Hookham Frere in verse and prose*, 2 vols. (1872) · G. Festing, *John Hookham Frere and his friends* (1899), 3–5 · C. B. Jewson, *The Jacobin city: a portrait of Norwich in its reaction to the French Revolution, 1788–1802* (1975), 115–16 · J. Evans, *A history of the Society of Antiquaries* (1956), 202–3 · *Albion Mill state of facts* (1791) · Walpole, *Corr.*, 16.246–7; 42.97, 100; 43.221 · *Anecdotes of the life of Richard Watson*, ed. R. Watson (1817) · Nichols, *Lit. anecdotes*, 8.158 · Nichols, *Illustrations*, 5.175–7 · 'The Marine Society: a brief history', www.marine-society.org.uk/history.html, 14 May 2000 · A. Aspinall, 'Frere, John', HoP, *Commons, 1790–1820* · J. Fenn, autobiography, Norfolk RO, SO 50/4/13 · J. J. Wymer and R. G. West, 'A memorial to John Frere', *Past: the Newsletter of the Prehistoric Society*, 33 (1999), 3–5

Archives BL, Add. MSS 27452–27454 · Norfolk RO, corresp. relating to Thomas Martin's collections · priv. coll., MSS | Norfolk RO, Colman MSS · Norfolk RO, Norfolk and Norwich Archaeological Society deposit

Wealth at death £4600 p.a.; also estate: Frere, *A record*

Frere, John Hookham (1769–1846), diplomatist and author, was the eldest son of John *Frere (1740–1807) of Roydon Hall, near Diss, Norfolk, and his wife, Jane (1746–1813), only child of John Hookham of Beddington, Surrey, a rich London merchant; Bartholomew *Frere (1776–1851), James Hatley *Frere (1779–1866), and William *Frere (1775–1836) were his brothers. He was born in London on 21 May 1769, and in 1785 went from a preparatory school at Putney to Eton College, where he formed a lifelong friendship with George Canning. In the following year the two friends joined with Robert Percy Smith and some other schoolfellows in starting the *Microcosm*, the first number of which appeared on 6 November 1786, and the last on 30

John Hookham Frere (1769–1846), by Henry Edridge, c.1800

July 1787. It ran through forty numbers, which were subsequently published in collected form with a dedication to Dr Davies, the headmaster. Frere contributed five papers to this periodical (*Works*, 2.3–22). From Eton he went to Gonville and Caius College, Cambridge, where he graduated BA in 1792 and MA in 1795. At college he won several prizes for classical composition, but was prevented by illness from going in for honours. He was fellow of Gonville and Caius from 1793 to 1816, and in 1792 won the members' prize for the Latin essay. Frere entered the Foreign Office and at a by-election in November 1796 was returned for the pocket borough of West Looe in Cornwall, which he continued to represent until June 1802, giving his silent support to the government.

In 1797 he joined with Canning in the publication of the *Anti-Jacobin*, the first number of which appeared on 20 November in that year. William Gifford was the editor, and many of the pieces were written in concert by Canning, George Ellis, and Frere. Frere's contributions are collected in his *Works* (2.57–161). After a brilliant career of eight months the *Anti-Jacobin* was brought to a close on 9 July 1798. On 1 April 1799 Frere succeeded his friend Canning as under-secretary of state in the Foreign Office. In October 1800 he was appointed envoy-extraordinary and plenipotentiary at Lisbon, and in September 1802 was transferred to Madrid, where he remained for nearly two years. There, the meddling in court politics of his mistress, Lady Erroll, caused complications. In August 1804

Frere was recalled 'in consequence of circumstances having occurred that made it impossible for him any longer to communicate personally with the Prince of Peace [Godoy]' (Hathaway, 4.383). The ministry, however, signified their approval of his conduct by granting him a pension of £1700 a year, and on 14 January 1805 he was sworn of the privy council.

In June 1807 the duke of Portland appointed Frere envoy and minister-plenipotentiary at Berlin, but owing to the treaty of Tilsit the mission had to be abandoned. On 4 October 1808 Frere was sent out to Spain as minister-plenipotentiary to the Central Junta. Affairs on the Peninsula were then in a very critical state, and his position as the British minister was one of heavy responsibility. In November, Napoleon commenced his march upon Madrid. Sir John Moore, the commander of the British forces in the north of Spain, was inclined to retreat through Portugal. Frere, however, confident that Napoleon might be anticipated, urged Moore to advance upon Madrid, or, if retreat was inevitable, to retire through Galicia. Moore yielded, and, after the disastrous retreat to Corunna, Frere was greatly blamed for the advice he had given. Although Ponsonby's motion in the House of Commons, on 24 February 1809, for an inquiry 'into the causes, conduct, and events of the late campaign in Spain', was defeated by 220 to 127 (Hansard 1, 12, 1809, 1057–119), the government determined to recall Frere, and on 29 April 1809 Marquess Wellesley was appointed as his replacement. Frere left in August, having been created 'Marquez de la Union' by the Central Junta, 'as a mark of their acknowledgement of the zeal with which he had laboured to promote the friendly union and common interest of the two countries'.

With his second mission to Spain, Frere's public career ended. He afterwards declined the post of ambassador at St Petersburg, and twice refused the offer of a peerage. On the death of his father in 1807 Frere succeeded to Roydon Hall and the other family estates in the eastern counties, with £2000 p.a. On 12 September 1816 he married his long-time mistress Elizabeth Jemima, dowager countess of Erroll, the widow of George Erroll, fourteenth earl of Erroll, and a daughter of Joseph Blake of Ardfry, co. Galway. In 1818 his wife became ill. After trying many changes of climate for the benefit of her health they went to Malta, where they took up their permanent residence. Here he amused himself with literary work, translating Aristophanes and the poet Theognis, and learning Hebrew and Maltese. In August 1827 Canning died. Talking over the loss of his friend with his niece two years afterwards, Frere said: 'I think twenty years ago Canning's death would have caused mine; as it is, the time seems so short, I do not feel it as I otherwise should' (Works, 1.209). His wife died in January 1831, and in November of that year Sir Walter Scott paid him a visit in Malta. Scott found him 'a good Tory as ever … the most entertaining man I know'. He died at the Pietà Valletta, Malta, on 7 January 1846, in the seventy-seventh year of his age, and was buried beside his wife in the English burial-ground overlooking the Quarantine Harbour.

From before the start of his diplomatic career, Frere was

a sparkling writer of humorous poetry, especially as a translator of Aristophanes. He printed his renderings of the plays on the government printing press in Malta in 1839, and they were published in England in 1840 (in 1829 he had given S. T. Coleridge, whom he helped financially, a handwritten copy of these translations). His *Ode on Aethelstan's Victory* was written while he was at Eton and was admired by Sir James Mackintosh and Scott. He also published on King Arthur and the round table (1817) and on Theognis (1842). Byron's *Beppo* (1818) was written in imitation of him and in 1819 he formed one of Byron's 'cursed puritanical committee', which decided against the publication of the first canto of *Don Juan*.

He was one of the founders of the *Quarterly Review*, though he wrote only one article for it (on Aristophanes in July 1820), signed 'W', for Whistlecraft, his *nom de plume*. He helped Robert Southey with his history of the Peninsular War (though he had pilloried him earlier in the *Anti-Jacobin*). Frere was a better man of letters than diplomatist, but it was to the latter calling that he gave the best of his life.

G. F. R. BARKER, *rev.* H. C. G. MATTHEW

Sources G. Festing, *J. H. Frere and his friends* (1899) · *The works of the Right Honourable John Hookham Frere in verse and prose*, ed. W. E. Frere and others, 2nd edn, 3 vols. (1874) · *The letter-journal of George Canning, 1793–1795*, ed. P. Jupp, CS, 4th ser., 41 (1991) · *The speeches of William Pitt in the House of Commons*, ed. W. S. Hathaway, 4 vols. (1806) · HoP, *Commons* · L. A. Marchand, *Byron: a biography*, 3 vols. (1957) · *Byron's letters and journals*, ed. L. A. Marchand, 12 vols. (1973–82)

Archives Bodl. Oxf., prize essay · NAM, corresp. and papers · NL Scot., corrections to *Theognis restitutus* · PRO, memorandum for the admiralty relating to Spanish shipping, PRO 30/8/1; 37/83–86 | BL, corresp. with Lord Holland, Add. MS 51615 · BL, letters to John Moore, Add. MS 57540 · BL, corresp. with Lord Wellesley, Add. MSS 37286–37288 · NMM, letters to Lord Nelson

Likenesses H. Edridge, pencil drawing, c.1800, NPG [*see illus.*] · J. Hoppner, oils, 1808, National Gallery of Canada, Ottawa · F. Chantrey, marble bust, 1818, National Gallery of Canada, Ottawa · M. A. Shee, oils, 1820, NPG · F. Chantrey, pencil drawing, NPG

Frere, Margaret (1863–1961), welfare worker, was born on 12 August 1863, at 45 Bedford Square, Bloomsbury, London, the only child of Bartle John Laurie Frere, solicitor, and his wife, Adelaide Ellen, *née* Rowe. In the 1890s she was a school manager of the elementary school at Great Tower Street, in the impoverished London district of Seven Dials. Like many other schools at this time, it provided poor children with dinners, clothing, and boots, to help them to come to school and to benefit from their lessons. In 1898 she and another manager of her school determined to find out why children remained underfed and badly clothed, even when they had been provided by the school with meal tickets and other material help. They visited the homes of all the children who appeared on dinner lists and this led them to conclude that the problem lay in the home. 'Only by getting to know and helping the parents', said Miss Frere, 'could the sufferings of the children be relieved' (Williams, Ivin, and Morse, 41). By so doing, she said, it would be possible to give them advice and encouragement and to check up on their home conditions.

In January 1899 the managers and teachers of Miss

Frere's school set up the Charitable Funds Committee to concern itself with everything affecting the welfare of the schoolchildren. They visited families in connection with boots and clothing, physical defects, holidays, and employment on leaving school. In 1902 the committee's name was changed to Children's Relief Committee and then to Children's Care Committee. The officials of the school board for London observed that Miss Frere's school was the happiest and cleanest of the poor schools in London, even though most of them had voluntary relief committees.

In 1904, when responsibility for London's schools was transferred from the school board for London to the London county council (LCC), all relief committees were brought together under the auspices of a joint committee on underfed children. This was developed by the LCC in 1907 into the school care service, a network across London of care committees based in elementary schools, which were charged with the task of making sure that poor pupils were sufficiently fed and clothed to benefit from their schooling (which had been compulsory in London since 1871). Each committee was modelled on Miss Frere's Children's Care Committee, with the explicit aim of creating a link between home and school. Care committees were staffed by women volunteers, local school managers, teachers, school attendance officers, and other interested outsiders, who were co-opted from bodies such as the Country Holiday Fund Visitors.

Miss Frere was co-opted a member of the LCC education committee in 1907 and in 1909 she published a little book called *Children's Care Committees: How to Work Them in Public Elementary Schools*. She served as a member of the children's care sub-committee of the LCC from 1909 until it was disbanded in 1925, and was its vice-chairman from 1910 to 1914. In 1925 she retired from these committees but continued to do voluntary work for the school care service for many years. Ill health prevented her from attending the jubilee celebration of the service at the Festival Hall in London in 1958, but she sent a letter in which she observed, 'What a fine oak has grown from the little acorn I planted.' Miss Frere did not marry and died on 14 March 1961 at her home, Shangri-La, Beech Drive, Sawbridgeworth, Hertfordshire. By the time of her death the school care service had become firmly rooted in the life of London's elementary schools and lasted until 1970, when it was merged with the school attendance service to form the education welfare service. Throughout its existence the service was underpinned by Miss Frere's philosophy that 'We must unite the home with the school education. Education means growth in grace and in the formation of character, and this cannot be if the home and the school are opposed' (M. Frere, *Children's Care Committees*, 1909, 2).

SUSAN WILLIAMS and TENDAYI BLOOM

Sources A. S. Williams, P. Ivin, and C. Morse, *The children of London: attendance and welfare at school, 1870–1990* (2001) • *The Times* (20 March 1961) • b. cert. • d. cert.

Wealth at death £7979 8s. 2d.: probate, 1 June 1961, CGPLA Eng. & Wales

Frere, Mary Eliza Isabella [May] (1845–1911), writer on India, was born on 11 August 1845 at Bitton rectory in Gloucestershire, the eldest of the four daughters and one son of Sir Bartle *Frere (1815–1884) and his wife, Catherine (d. 1899), daughter of Lieutenant-General Sir George *Arthur. May Frere, as she was known, was educated privately in Wimbledon; she learned easily and extended her knowledge through wide-ranging reading. Although she was a talented amateur actress and artist, it was her literary interests that predominated.

India provided the material through which these were to find public acclaim. In 1863 May Frere went with her mother to Bombay, where her father was governor, remaining there until his return to England in 1867. She was deeply interested in all aspects of Indian life, and in 1865–6 accompanied her father on an official tour through the Maratha territories. Her only constant female companion on the three-month journey was her Indian ayah, whom she persuaded to narrate the fairy stories and fables which had been told her as a child by her grandmother. She transcribed twenty-four of these in simple, expressive English, publishing her collection as *Old Deccan Days* in 1868. The work, illustrated by May's sister Catherine, was an immediate success, and by 1889 had gone through four editions, with translations into German, Hungarian, and Danish, and retranslations into Indian languages, including Mahratti, Hindustani, and Gujarati. Several of the stories were included in subsequent anthologies for children, but the appeal of the collection was also to a wider audience. Its publication helped stimulate the growing interest in comparative mythology; and the recording of largely unknown material encouraged the scholarly exploration of the riches of Indian folklore. May Frere was careful to respect the integrity of her material; as her ayah narrated her story, she made notes, and then read back to her the written version to ensure every detail was correct. So effective was this procedure, and so strong the Indian oral tradition, that the philologist and Sanskrit scholar Max Muller said that in one instance a story read like the direct translation of a recently discovered Sanskrit original.

As the author noted, the stories cast a new light on traditional Indian culture. Many of the themes were remarkably similar to those in European folklore. Women were also unexpectedly presented as manipulators of events and as individuals in their own right. In this way, and in giving her ayah a distinctive voice of her own in narrating, in the introduction, the story of her life, May Frere helped introduce a new perception of Indian women's experience.

This May Frere also personally explored in Bombay, where she visited women in the zenana. In the difficult years after the 1857 Indian mutiny, she played an effective part in trying to maintain an atmosphere of cordiality and understanding, and in her mother's absence in England was accounted an accomplished hostess for her father. Sir George Birdwood noted that 'Hindus, Muslims and Parsis still look back to the Governorship of Sir Bartle Frere as the Golden Age of frank and hearty discourse, on equal

Mary Eliza Isabella [May] Frere (1845–1911), by unknown photographer, 1882

with an interval in Egypt; at Nablus she acquired a number of texts and manuscripts to add to her library of Semitic and Jewish works. This collection she subsequently left to the library of Girton College, Cambridge. Known as the Mary Frere Hebrew Library, it has continued to be an important resource for scholars, the marriage contracts in some cases being of particular interest.

May Frere's later years were marked by declining health. She died in her sleep of heart failure on 26 March 1911 at the Edinburgh Hotel, St Leonards, Sussex, where she had gone to recuperate. She was buried at Brookwood cemetery, Surrey, on 31 March.

ROSEMARY CARGILL RAZA

Sources H. Loewe, *Catalogue of the printed books and of the Semitic and Jewish MSS in the Mary Frere Hebrew Library at Girton College, Cambridge* (1916) [with biographical note by Georgina Frere, pp. v–xii] · *The Athenaeum* (15 April 1911), 419–20 · *Cambridge Daily News* (5 April 1911) · *South Africa* (8 April 1911) · *DNB* · private information (2004) · d. cert.
Likenesses photograph, 1882, Girton Cam. [*see illus.*]
Wealth at death £4702 12s. 1d.: resworn administration, 13 May 1911, CGPLA Eng. & Wales

terms, between Europeans and Indians' (*The Athenaeum*, 15 April 1911), and saluted her contribution.

May Frere showed the same ability to bridge cultural and racial divides in South Africa, where she accompanied her parents on her father's appointment as governor of the Cape and high commissioner in South Africa in 1877. Here she made many friends among both the Dutch and British colonists, and took a deep interest in the customs and traditions of the African peoples. On her return to England in 1880, she and a sister were received by Queen Victoria at Windsor.

Although May Frere continued to write throughout her life, her publications were few. In 1869 *Love's Triumph*, a play in the Elizabethan manner, was published anonymously to critical acclaim. One or two short poems also appeared anonymously in *The Spectator*, and in 1890 she published under her own name three poems on patriotic and religious themes. On the whole, however, she was too critical of her own writing to launch it into the public domain.

After her parents' deaths, May Frere settled in Cambridge, but travelled widely in England and Europe and pursued her many interests in history, literature, and religion. The latter came to dominate her life, and she became deeply immersed in Biblical scholarship, learning Hebrew in order to study the Old Testament in the original. For eighteen months from late 1906 she travelled in Palestine,

Frere, Philip Howard (1813–1868), agriculturist, was born on 6 August 1813 in Grundisburgh, Suffolk, the eldest son of William *Frere (1775–1836) and his wife, Mary (d. 1864), daughter of Brampton Gurdon Dillingham. He was educated at Eton and Trinity College, Cambridge, graduating in the first class in the classical tripos (1836). The following year he was elected a fellow of Downing College, and in 1839 became tutor and bursar. Frere's residence on his father's estate at Balsham, Cambridgeshire, had equipped him well for the bursar's task of managing Downing's endowments, which mainly consisted of agricultural lands. On 2 August 1859 he married Emily (d. 1870), daughter of Henry Gipps, canon of Carlisle Cathedral, and vicar of Crosthwaite, Keswick. They had three sons, including Arthur (b. 1860) and Walter Howard *Frere (1863–1938), and two daughters.

Widely travelled, Frere's combination of foreign languages and agricultural knowledge led to his becoming editor of the *Journal of the Royal Agricultural Society of England* in 1860. Frere was not the first choice of the agricultural community (who favoured the *de facto* editor, J. C. Morton), and his appointment reflected the society council's distance from its membership. Frere steered the journal through a period of uncertain direction, contributing papers until his sudden death at Paston House, Cambridge, on 12 May 1868. He was buried at Balsham.

VICTORIA MILLAR

Sources private information (1889) · *Journal of the Royal Agricultural Society of England* · Venn, *Alum. Cant.* · Boase, *Mod. Eng. biog.* · N. Goddard, *Harvests of change: the Royal Agricultural Society of England, 1838–1988* (1988), 84, 111–12, 114–15 · G. E. Mingay, ed., *The Victorian countryside*, 1 (1981), 250 · report of the Royal Agricultural Society of England general meeting, 22 May 1868
Wealth at death under £6000: probate, 5 Oct 1868, CGPLA Eng. & Wales

Frere, Walter Howard (1863–1938), bishop of Truro and liturgical scholar, was born on 23 November 1863 at 56

Regent Street, Cambridge, the third (and younger surviving) son (two daughters followed) of Philip Howard *Frere (1813–1868), fellow of Downing College, and his wife, Emily Gipps (d. 1870). He was orphaned in early childhood and was brought up by relatives. He won scholarships to Charterhouse School and to Trinity College, Cambridge, where he took a first in the classical tripos in 1885. After a further year in Cambridge devoted to theological studies, he proceeded in 1886 to Wells Theological College, and in 1887 to ordination and a curacy in the parish of Stepney.

In 1892 Frere took what he certainly saw as the crucial decision of his life: he was one of the six original members of the Community of the Resurrection founded by Charles Gore in Pusey House, Oxford, which in 1898 found a permanent home at Mirfield in the West Riding of Yorkshire. In 1902, following Gore's withdrawal from the community in order to accept a bishopric, he was elected superior, holding this office until 1913 and again from 1916 to 1922. Thus he led the community at the most formative stage in its history; within a year of his taking office it had both begun its work in South Africa and opened a theological college at Mirfield for the training of candidates for the priesthood who could not otherwise afford it.

Frere had long been identified with the movement for prayer book revision, and liturgical scholarship was still virtually unrepresented on the bench of bishops. It was undoubtedly this that led Archbishop Randall Davidson to press for Frere's appointment to the see of Truro in 1923, an office for which his learning, administrative experience, and spiritual stature fully qualified him. He agreed with reluctance, insisting on remaining a full member of the community and having a branch house in his official residence; its lifestyle was simple but hospitable (he was reputed to clean his guests' shoes). The first years of his episcopate were overshadowed by the sheer labour and the frustrations involved in the production (and eventual rejection) of the revised prayer book. He supported the version of 1927, but resisted the amendments proposed to appease the opposition in 1928. As a diocesan he was non-partisan and consistently supportive of his clergy.

Frere took a significant part in the Malines conversations of Anglicans and Roman Catholics presided over by Cardinal Mercier in 1921–5. In another direction, the contacts that he had established with Orthodox churchmen in Russia before the revolution were renewed after the First World War with the Russian expatriate community in Paris. The triptych painted in Orthodox iconic style which now faces his tomb commemorates the relationship.

Frere's scholarship—historical, liturgical, and musical—was always at the service of the church. His *New History of the Book of Common Prayer* (1901) remained a standard textbook for many decades; much else was addressed to current needs and was consequently ephemeral. But *au fond* he was a scholars' scholar, and his most enduring work was in the production of *instrumenta studiorum*. To the analysis and editing of documents he brought a head for detail, wise critical judgement, beautifully clear minuscule handwriting, and the ability to sustain work on a variety of projects in spare moments over many years. They included, in the field of Tudor ecclesiastical history, *Visitation Articles and Injunctions of the Reformation Period* (3 vols., 1910) and his edition of the register of Archbishop Matthew Parker (3 vols., 1928–33); and, in liturgy, a long series of edited texts of which *The Use of Sarum* (2 vols., 1898–1901) and *The Hereford Breviary* (with L. E. G. Brown, 3 vols., 1904–15) may stand as representative. His expertise in early liturgical music bore fruit in *The Winchester Troper* (1894) and in facsimile editions of the Sarum gradual (1894) and antiphonal (1901–25). His masterpiece of critical scholarship, internationally acclaimed, was the three-volume *Studies in the Early Roman Liturgy*, published near the end of his life (1930–35).

The early death of Frere's parents left its mark in a certain solitariness of spirit. His one relaxation was music, by no means limited to the period associated with his scholarship. 'Who is that man with a face like St Bruno, singing passionate Breton love songs?' asked a fellow guest in an episcopal house (Wilkinson, 77). With friends who shared this enthusiasm, or could enter fully into his scholarly pursuits, he showed a lighter side to his personality: gaiety, charm, humour, a 'lilting walk' are among the characteristics recalled by them. His spiritual quality was recognized by Friedrich von Hügel. In 1935 Frere resigned his see on account of failing health and he returned to Mirfield, where he died on 2 April 1938. His funeral followed on 6 April and on 2 May his ashes were solemnly interred in the newly completed community church.

H. BENEDICT GREEN

Sources C. S. Phillips and others, *Walter Howard Frere, bishop of Truro: a memoir* (1947) · A. Wilkinson, *The Community of the Resurrection: a centenary history* (1992) · *Walter Howard Frere: his correspondence on liturgical revision and construction*, ed. R. C. D. Jasper (1954) · B. Barlow, 'A brother knocking at the door': the Malines conversations, 1921–25 (1996) · E. K. Talbot, 'Frere, Walter Howard', *A dictionary of English church history*, ed. S. L. Ollard and others, 3rd edn (1948) · Borth. Inst., Mirfield deposit, letters of Emily Frere to Ellen and Stephen Spring-Rice · *DNB* · private information (2004) · *CGPLA Eng. & Wales* (1938) · d. cert. [Emily Frere] · m. cert. [Philip Howard Frere and Emily Gipps]

Archives LPL, corresp. relating to Community of the Holy Cross | Borth. Inst., corresp. and papers · CUL, letters to H. F. Stewart · LPL, letters to Arthur Cayley Headlam · LPL, corresp. with Edwin James Palmer · LPL, letters to Athelstan Riley

Likenesses A. V. Soord, pastels, 1913, House of the Resurrection, Mirfield, West Riding of Yorkshire · H. Knight, oils, 1933, Lis Escop, Feock, Truro; copy, House of the Resurrection, Mirfield, West Riding of Yorkshire · Opie Ltd, photograph, 1933, NPG · W. Stoneman, four photographs, 1941, NPG · H. M. Guick, charcoal on paper cartoon (in early years of episcopate), House of the Resurrection, Mirfield, West Riding of Yorkshire

Wealth at death £1536 15s. 2d.: resworn probate, 12 July 1938, *CGPLA Eng. & Wales*

Frere, William (1775–1836), serjeant-at-law and college head, was born on 28 November 1775, the fourth son of the antiquary John *Frere (1740–1807) of Roydon, Norfolk, and Jane, daughter of John Hookham of Beddington, Surrey. He was the younger brother of the diplomatist and author John Hookham *Frere. Educated at Felsted School and Eton College, in 1796 he obtained a scholarship at Trinity College, Cambridge. In the same year he was elected to the Craven scholarship, and subsequently won several university honours, among them the senior chancellor's medal. He graduated fifth senior optime in 1798, and in 1800 became a fellow of the newly founded Downing College.

Frere was called to the bar at Lincoln's Inn and joined the Norfolk circuit in 1802. He was serjeant-at-law in 1809, and three years later was elected master of Downing College, his appointment being unsuccessfully contested at law. He was made recorder of Bury St Edmunds in 1814, and in 1819 became vice-chancellor of Cambridge University. He took the degrees of LLD at Cambridge in 1825 and DCL at Oxford in 1834.

On 4 May 1810 Frere married Mary (d. 1864), daughter of Brampton Gurdon Dillingham, with whom he had some six or seven children, including the agriculturist Philip Howard *Frere. Largely thanks to his wife, Downing College became something of a social centre during Frere's mastership.

Frere finally resigned from the bar in 1826, and divided his time between Downing College and his estate at Balsham, Cambridgeshire. He was the editor of *Reports of Cases* by Baron Glenbervie, and of the sixth volume of *The Paston Letters*, from the manuscripts of his uncle Sir John *Fenn.

Frere died at Downing College on 25 May 1836, and was buried at Balsham.

ALSAGER VIAN, rev. JONATHAN HARRIS

Sources GM, 2nd ser., 6 (1836), 214–15 · F. S. Moller and others, eds., *Alumni Felstedienses: being a list of boys entered at Felsted School, May 1564 – September 1931*, 6th edn (1931), 30 · Venn, *Alum. Cant.*

Archives Borth. Inst., family corresp. · Norfolk RO, collection relating to history of Norfolk | Downing College, Cambridge, catalogue to the Bowtell MSS

Likenesses G. Clint, oils, 1827, Downing College, Cambridge

Frescheville [Frecheville] **family** (*per.* **1518–1682**), gentry, was of Norman origins, deriving its name from Freulleville, near Dieppe. Some advantageous marriages brought baronial status in the thirteenth century, but political miscalculations led to the loss of important properties, and from the mid-fourteenth century the family lands were centred upon Staveley, in the north-east of Derbyshire, with Staveley Hall remaining the principal residence of the Freschevilles until the extinction of the family in 1682.

The Tudor family Such was the estate inherited in 1518 by **Sir Peter Frecheville** (1513–1558), aged only five. As a young man he served in the army during the Scottish campaign of 1544 when, under the command of the earl of Hertford, the English army smashed the pier at Leith Haven and captured the merchant ships lying in the harbour. According to Robert Thoroton, Peter was knighted by Hertford at Leith. As a substantial landowner Sir Peter took every opportunity to consolidate his inheritance, and by a fine dated 1545 acquired the remaining one-third moiety of the manor and advowson of Staveley. There is no evidence that Sir Peter resisted any of the religious alterations of the period 1534–59, while his descendants were to be loyal to the Church of England as established

under Elizabeth. With his wife, Elizabeth, daughter of Sir Richard Tempest, he had seven surviving children (who married into local gentry families such as the Barleys and Columbells); he was succeeded by his son and heir, **Peter Frecheville** (1534–1582).

Like his father, Peter Frecheville was keen to add to his estate, and in 1568/9 was able to purchase the manor of Palterton for £800 from William Segrave, who had inherited it from a Frecheville forebear. His name appears as a Derbyshire landowner in a list of 1570, in which year he also served as sheriff. With his first wife, Elizabeth, daughter of Sir Gervase Clifton, he had two daughters, the eldest of whom, Frances, in 1574 married Sir Gervase Holles (whose grandson was the noted civil war royalist and antiquary of the same name). He and his second wife, Margaret, daughter of Arthur Kaye, had four children, and soon after her husband's death she acquired Hazelbarrow Hall and land in Jordanthorpe from William Selioke for £800 which their younger son John (d. 1610) was to inherit. In 1589 she is recorded (as 'Mrs ffrechewell of Staley') as paying a forced loan of £25 to the queen, and she was to endow Staveley Netherthorpe grammar school in the year before her death in 1592.

Consolidation Margaret's son **Sir Peter Frecheville** (1575–1634) inherited the family estate and was educated at St John's College, Cambridge (1587), and at the Middle Temple (1591). He was already of sufficient standing among the county gentry to be invited by the earl of Shrewsbury to meet King James I when he stayed at Worksop Manor, 10 miles east of Staveley, on 20 April 1603 on his way south to London for his coronation. Shrewsbury spared no expense in his entertainment of the king and his entourage, and Frecheville was knighted by James on that occasion. He had already paid a forced loan of £30 to the queen in 1597, but when Charles I requested a 'benevolence' in 1626 Sir Peter was one of ten Derbyshire justices who wrote to the privy council stating that most people in the county had declined to subscribe to such demands except 'by way of Parliament', although he himself—a firm royalist—offered to pay £30.

As befitted a leading member of local society Sir Peter Frecheville was a justice of the peace from 1604 onwards, a member of parliament for the county in 1601 and 1621, sheriff in 1601 (having unsuccessfully petitioned to be allowed to decline that office because of his election as an MP), and deputy lieutenant from 1613. He founded an almshouse in Staveley Woodthorpe in 1632 for the accommodation of four poor men and four poor women, and set up an endowment to support the apprenticeship of two poor boys and girls. In his will (made on 16 March 1632) he directed that he be buried in the choir of Staveley church, and bequeathed, *inter alia*, £50 to St John's College, Cambridge, for the purchase of books to furnish the new library recently built there, and left his son John a gold chain which was his father's, and a diamond ring which had belonged to his grandmother. His character was summed up by Gervase Holles as:

an honest and worthy gentleman of good erudition and a great lover of learning and learned men. He was a good housekeeper, and the best landlord to his tenants (I think I may truly say) in England, and the person of most principal account and had the greatest power of any of the gentry in the county. (Wood, 52)

In 1604 he remodelled his ancestral home at Staveley in considerable style (it was assessed at 30 hearths in the hearth tax returns of 1670), but this building (as well as the heraldic glass in the nearby parish church) suffered considerably during the civil war. Only a fragment of the house remains today.

Courtier and cavalier With his first wife, Joyce, widow of Sir Hewett Osborne and daughter of Thomas Fleetwood, Sir Peter Frecheville had a son and heir, John Frescheville (as he usually came to spell his name). **John Frescheville**, Baron Frescheville of Staveley (1606–1682), was the last and most distinguished representative of the family (Sir Peter's second marriage, to Isabel Neville, was childless). John was educated at Magdalen Hall, Oxford, and at the Middle Temple (1624); he was elected a member of parliament for the county in 1628–9 and 1661–9 (during which he served on a number of parliamentary committees). He was a deputy lieutenant in 1639–42 and again from 1660, was a justice of the peace from 1660, and was made a gentleman of the privy chamber (1639–45). John Frescheville's first marriage, to Bruce, daughter of Francis Nicholls of Ampthill in Bedfordshire, had been brief and ended when his wife died childless on 10 April 1629, aged only eighteen. In the following year, while he was at court, he married his second wife, Sarah, daughter and heir of Sir John Harrington, a maid of honour to Queen Henrietta, of whom Gervase Holles caustically remarked:

> from Court he married her, whence she brought him no portion but Court legacies—pride, passion, prodigality. He hath tolde me (and shee hath owned it) that she has lost him five hundred poundes in cardes in one night. But now they say she gaines by it having got the knacke of game (as gamesters call it), but others call it cheating. (Wood, 53–4)

Among the Derbyshire gentry there was a marked reluctance to take up arms on the king's behalf at the start of the civil war, but when Charles I reached Nottingham in August 1642 John Frescheville and his neighbour Henry Hunloke of Wingerworth arrived with troops of horse to support him. Having already served as a young cornet of horse in the disastrous Scottish war of 1639, John went on to serve under Prince Rupert at Powicke Bridge (1642) and at the first battle of Newbury on 20 September 1643, when he was slightly wounded. Thereafter he left the royalist army to raise two regiments of horse for the king in Derbyshire. The cost of raising and maintaining troops of horse was formidable, and only the wealthiest gentry could afford it.

From 1643 John Frescheville was engaged in a series of skirmishes against parliamentary forces in Derbyshire under the command of Sir John Gell. His own house at Staveley was garrisoned for the king, but was attacked and taken shortly afterwards. He recaptured it and held it until 12 August 1644, when he agreed to surrender it to Major-General Crawford and retired to London. Despite some doubts as to his continuing allegiance he was, however, soon back in arms, and after the earl of Newcastle, hitherto the foremost royalist commander in the midlands, had fled abroad, Frescheville was appointed colonel-general of Derbyshire (29 August 1644). He then joined the indomitable royalist garrison at Newark, Nottinghamshire, and after troops from the garrison had retaken Welbeck Abbey he was made governor (16 July 1645) and entertained the king there the following month. With the royalist cause now seemingly lost, he retired to the Netherlands in November 1645.

Although John Frescheville had to compound for his estate like other royalists, the amount demanded was 'something mitigated by friendship of some of the adverse party' (Wood, 59) and he was fined only a modest £287 10s. 4d. plus an annuity of £33 10s. payable to the minister of Holmesfield chapel. He was also excused from paying the 'decimation tax' (1655). He returned to Derbyshire some time before 1659 and began co-ordinating plans for a royalist uprising in support of Booth's rising in Cheshire. After the proclamation of Charles II as king the following spring, Frescheville was appointed governor of York.

Decline and fall For generations Derbyshire gentry in the north-west of the county had profitably exploited the lead beneath their estates. From the seventeenth century ironstone began to be mined in central and north Derbyshire, and the local gentry such as the Hunlokes of Wingerworth and Leakes of Sutton began building iron furnaces. The most successful entrepreneur among gentry families was George Sitwell of Renishaw (3 miles to the north of Staveley) who rapidly became a professional ironmaster when other local families were beginning to lease their ironworks. It is known that an ironworks belonging to John Frescheville was in operation at Staveley by 1639, and that in the 1650s Sitwell was leasing the furnace and forge on Frescheville's Staveley estate, while a decade later (after the lease had terminated) he was actively mining ironstone at Staveley on which he paid Frescheville a royalty of 8s. 6d. per ton. For Frescheville, however, mineral exploitation was simply another component of his rental income (and, as such, largely devoted to the royalist cause), but it foreshadowed the growing industrialization of Derbyshire the following century.

In 1644, by virtue of his services to the royal cause and partly (according to Holles) as a result of his wife's nagging, John Frescheville had petitioned the king for a barony. A warrant was obtained but it never passed the great seal, so that after the Restoration he petitioned for its implementation. On 16 March 1665 he was created Baron Frescheville of Staveley with remainder to his heirs male only. There were, however, no male heirs but only three daughters, all of whom died without surviving children. Sarah Frescheville died in June 1665, barely three months after her husband's elevation to the peerage, and in the following year he married Anna Charlotte de Vic. There were no children of the marriage. By this time Lord Frescheville was facing financial ruin, the cumulative result of the enormous expense of raising and maintaining troops for the royalist cause (even if his composition was relatively light), generous dowries to his two elder daughters, and his wife Sarah's extravagance and gambling debts. He was therefore obliged in 1680 to sell the reversion of his Staveley estate (by then less than 2000 acres in extent) for £2600 to the third earl of Devonshire, his long-standing friend and royalist supporter, in whose family much of it remains to this day.

When news of this eventually reached the ears of Colonel Thomas Colepeper (1637–1708), a tetchy but erudite man who in 1662 had eloped with John's youngest daughter, Frances (1638–1698), he immediately entered a lawsuit to try to prevent the transfer and obtain a share of the Frescheville estate for his wife (who had been left only an annuity by her father). Despite extensive litigation he failed, and the cost ruined him. John Frescheville died in London on 31 March 1682 in his seventy-sixth year, when his peerage became extinct; he was buried at Staveley on 9 April. His tomb (erected by his widow and with his name curiously spelt 'FFrecheville') comprises a florid standing wall-monument with a marble sarcophagus surmounted by two putti, behind which is an impressive window of heraldic glass commissioned in 1676 by Frescheville himself from the York glazier Henry Gyles (1645–1709) and containing the family arms—'azure a bend between six escallops argent'—together with the arms of families with whom they were allied. The motto adopted by this steadfast royalist was 'Qui aime le Roy aime sa patrie', an eloquent testimony to his life.

From the sixteenth century until their extinction in 1682 the Freschevilles were among the most influential of the gentry families of Derbyshire. Playing their traditional role in society as justices, deputy lieutenants, sheriffs, and members of parliament, they conserved and expanded their estate at Staveley, and latterly began to exploit its mineral resources. They were considerate landlords, supported the Anglican church, founded almshouses, and were benefactors of the local grammar school. Loyalty to their sovereign in the civil war contributed to their financial ruin, as it did to a number of their Derbyshire contemporaries. But to such families their cause—as all would have asserted—was the only just and patriotic one open to them. GLADWYN TURBUTT

Sources GEC, Peerage, new edn, 5.574–9 · A. C. Wood, 'John, Lord Frescheville of Staveley', Journal of the Derbyshire Archaeological and Natural History Society, 53 (1932), 51–63 · J. T. Brighton, Royalists and roundheads in Derbyshire, Bakewell and District Historical Society (1981) · W. Swift, 'Staveley Hall and its occupants', The Reliquary, 3 (1862), 149–58 · B. Stone, Derbyshire in the civil war (1992) · George Sitwell's letterbook, 1662–66, ed. P. Riden, Derbyshire RS, 10 (1985) · D. N. Durant, Arbella Stuart: a rival to the queen (1978), 117 · J. C. Cox, Three centuries of Derbyshire annals, 2 vols. (1890) · H. J. H. Garratt and C. Rawcliffe, Derbyshire feet of fines, 1323–1546, Derbyshire RS, 11 (1985), no. 1337 · D. G. Edwards, Derbyshire hearth tax assessments, 1662–70, Derbyshire RS, 7 (1982) · HoP, Commons, 1558–1603, 2.159–60 · R. Thoroton, The antiquities of Nottinghamshire (1677), 44 · HoP, Commons, 1509–58, 2.172–3 · C. Jamison, G. R. Batho, and E. G. W. Bill, eds., A calendar of the Shrewsbury and Talbot papers in the Lambeth Palace Library and the College of Arms, 2, HMC, JP 7 (1971) · will, PRO, PROB 11/165, sig. 42 [Sir Peter Frecheville]

Frescheville, John, Baron Frescheville of Staveley (1606–1682). *See under* Frescheville family (*per.* 1518–1682).

Freshfield family (*per.* 1800–1918), lawyers, were partners in the City of London firm of solicitors which since 1800 has always used the Freshfield name in its title. Eight members of the Freshfield family, spanning four generations, held this position.

The Freshfield family's origins are obscure until the mid-eighteenth century when James [i] Freshfield, born at Newport, Isle of Wight, in 1727, is recorded as working in London as a watchcase maker. He was not, apparently, very successful since he was declared bankrupt twice, in 1755 and in 1774, and, to the mortification of his grandson, spent some time in the Fleet prison. The son of James [i], James [ii] (1751–1803), was a watchmaker and from 1774 until his death a freeman of the Clockmakers' Company. In 1775 this James Freshfield married Elizabeth Snow of Windsor. Their eldest son (the first of nine children, not all of whom survived) was **James Joseph William Freshfield** (1775–1864), the first member of the family to enter the legal profession.

Of James Joseph William's early life and education nothing is known. In 1790, at fifteen, he was articled to a London attorney and in 1795 he was admitted to the profession. Freshfield practised on his own, first at New Inn and then in Aldermanbury, until early in 1800. In that year he joined, as a partner, the firm then known as Winter and Kaye at 29 St Swithin's Lane. The firm, whose origins can be traced to a partnership in the early eighteenth century, was in 1800 one of the most significant in the City. It counted among its clients not only the Bank of England, a connection dating back almost to the establishment of the bank, but also the Royal Exchange Assurance and the banking houses of Smith, Payne and Smith (in London, Nottingham, and Hull). The Smiths, notably Robert Smith (1752–1838), created Baron Carrington by William Pitt in 1796, were closely connected with the Wilberforce and Thornton families and belonged to the influential evangelical group within the Church of England. James Joseph William was an active member of the Church Missionary Society in its early years—it was established by the evangelicals in 1799—and it is likely that this connection helped him, an able and ambitious young man of humble origins, to join such a prestigious firm. Freshfield soon formed a close working relationship with Joseph Kaye, one of the two senior partners, and in 1808 the partnership between Kaye and Winter was dissolved. Winter and his two sons established themselves separately in practice and Kaye and Freshfield retained most of the clients including the highly prized business of the Bank of England.

On 27 February 1799 Freshfield had married Mary Blackett (or Blacket; 1776–1819), daughter of John and Abigail Blackett of West Smithfield. Born into a respectable non-conformist family, it seems unlikely that she brought either wealth or connection to the marriage; John Blackett came of a well-established dissenting Durham family of farmers involved in the wool trade. James Joseph William and Mary Freshfield had a family of eleven children, nine of whom survived to adulthood. Of their four surviving sons, three became solicitors. Their eldest son, **James William** [i] **Freshfield** (1801–1857), was sent at the age of five to a dissenting academy in St Neots, Huntingdonshire, most probably through his mother's connections in that part of the world. From 1809 until 1816 he attended Dr Heathcote's school in Hackney. Until 1813 the Freshfields and their growing family lived in Hackney but in that year Freshfield senior bought the Manor House (also known as Abney House) in Stoke Newington, an old and spacious house set in considerable grounds. In 1816 his son James William completed his schooling and joined the firm as an articled clerk. He was admitted as a solicitor in 1822 and became a partner in the firm in 1824. The retirement of Joseph Kaye in 1823 and the departure, in 1825, of his son Charles Kaye when his dubious financial transactions, amounting in effect to fraud against his partners, were discovered left the firm in the hands of the Freshfields. **Charles Kaye Freshfield** (1808–1891) and **Henry Ray Freshfield** (1814–1895), James William's younger brothers, were both educated at Charterhouse School and joined the firm in 1825 and 1830 respectively; they did not, however, become partners until 1835 and 1839. The burden of running the firm in the 1820s and 1830s therefore fell very much on James William, who, unlike his brothers, enjoyed the confidence of his father who embarked during this time on an attempt, unusual for a solicitor at that time, to become a member of parliament.

In 1819 James Joseph William's first wife, Mary, had died. Two years later he married his second wife, Frances Sims, for some time a friend of the family. In 1825, probably through his connection with William Manning, a West Indies merchant and former governor of the Bank of England, Freshfield was invited to stand for election in the constituency of Penryn, then a notorious Cornish rotten borough. He failed to be elected in 1826 but stood again—this time successfully—in 1830. Freshfield, a Peelite tory (the Peels were clients of the firm), unsuccessfully contested the constituency of Falmouth and Penryn in 1832, but was its MP from 1835 to 1841 and again from 1852 to 1857; he was also MP for Boston for a year, 1851–2. In Cornwall he was actively involved in the struggle to keep the mail packet trade at Falmouth and he introduced and piloted through parliament a measure to reform rates. He continued to be, at least in name, senior partner of the firm until 1840 when he finally retired. He died on 27 June 1864.

In 1828 James William had married Mary Anne Dawes (1800–1875), daughter of Thomas Dawes, a well-known and respected City solicitor who counted among his many clients the Rothschild banking house. Between 1829 and 1837 six children were born at New Bank Buildings, where the couple lived in accommodation over the firm's offices. Two of their sons, **William Dawes Freshfield** (1831–1903) and **Edwin Freshfield** (1832–1918), became solicitors. James William was effectively in charge of the firm from

the 1830s and was senior partner from 1840 until his sudden and premature death on 19 May 1857. He did much of the work for the firm's aristocratic and wealthy clients, who included the Peels, the Carringtons, and the Gladstones, as well as the Bank of England. He was highly regarded by the bank's governor and directors; their tribute to him spoke, in terms not used of any other solicitor before or since, of his integrity, the extent of his legal knowledge, and the 'almost irreparable' loss sustained by the bank (Bank of England court minutes, 21 May 1858, Slinn, 94).

James William's younger brothers Charles and Henry took over at the firm after his death. Both were by then married, Charles (in 1834) to Elizabeth Sims Stephenson (d. 1849), daughter of Daniel Stephenson, an elder brother of Trinity House, Henry (in 1840) to Jane Crawford, daughter of William Crawford, an East India merchant well connected in the City of London, which he represented as its MP from 1833 to 1841, and a director of the Alliance Assurance Company. Charles had two sons who both died young and Henry had one son, Douglas William *Freshfield, who became better known as a traveller and mountaineer. The future of the firm, therefore, lay in the hands of their nephews, William Dawes and Edwin, both educated at Winchester College and at Trinity College, Cambridge. They both became partners in 1858 but it was not until the 1870s that their uncles retired. Charles went in 1870; he was MP for Dover from 1865 to 1868 and from 1874 to 1885 and died on 5 June 1891. Henry retired from the firm in 1877, spending his retirement at Kidbrooke Park, a house and estate in Sussex he had bought three years before. He was active in local affairs as a JP and as high sheriff of Sussex in 1885 (his father had held the same office for Surrey in 1850). Henry Freshfield died on 8 February 1895 and, like his brother Charles, left a considerable personal estate.

On 19 August 1903 William Dawes Freshfield died suddenly. The year before, the only surviving son born to him and his wife, Elizabeth Catherine, née Borrer, **James William** [ii] **Freshfield** (1877–1952), had been admitted to the firm as a partner. From 1903 until 1918 the firm's senior partner was Edwin Freshfield. In 1861 he had married Zoe Charlotte Hanson, daughter of J. F. Hanson, the Levant Company's representative in Smyrna. Edwin's travels in that part of the world, which he first visited in 1854–5 after he left Cambridge, and his marriage gave him a lifetime interest in Greece and the surrounding areas. He was awarded a doctorate from Cambridge for a treatise on the laws of the late Roman empire. He and his wife had one son, **Edwin Hanson Freshfield** (1864–1948), who, after Winchester and Trinity College, Cambridge, joined the firm in 1888, and married Mary Lee Riddell in 1905. Like his father, he had considerable antiquarian and scholarly interests. Edwin Freshfield died on 1 September 1918; Edwin Hanson Freshfield retired from the firm three years later, and spent most of his retirement travelling in the Near East; he died in May 1948. In 1927 the last member of the Freshfield family to be a partner, James William, whose interest in the law had never been strong, also retired. The firm continued to flourish under the leadership of Sir William Leese, brought in by Edwin Freshfield in 1906, and in the second half of the twentieth century developed into one of the leading City law firms.

JUDY SLINN

Sources J. Slinn, *A history of Freshfields, the firm* (1984) · Venn, *Alum. Cant.* · *IGI*
Archives Freshfields, London, partnership agreements · priv. coll., family MSS | BL, corresp. with R. Peel, Add. MSS 40428–40609
Likenesses portrait (James William [ii] Freshfield) · silhouette (James William [i] Freshfield), priv. coll.

Freshfield, Charles Kaye (1808–1891). *See under* Freshfield family (*per.* 1800–1918).

Freshfield, Douglas William (1845–1934), geographer and mountain explorer, was born at Hampstead, Middlesex, on 27 April 1845, the only son of Henry Ray *Freshfield (1814–1895) [*see under* Freshfield family], solicitor to the Bank of England, and his wife, Jane Quentin, the daughter of William Crawford, MP for the City of London. He was educated at Eton College (1859–63) and at University College, Oxford, from where he matriculated in 1863 and graduated BA in 1867 and MA in 1870. He was called to the bar by the Inner Temple in 1870 but, having private means, he never practised. On 27 November 1869 at the Church of the Holy Trinity, Brompton, he married Augusta Charlotte (1847–1910), the eldest daughter of William Ritchie, advocate-general of Bengal, and the sister of Sir R. T. W. Ritchie. They had one son and four daughters, one of whom, Eleanor, married Arthur, son of Arthur Hugh *Clough. It was a largely happy marriage, though the two drifted further apart after the death of their son, Hal (1877–1891), from meningitis.

Freshfield played a major role in the advancement of geography, especially through the Royal Geographical Society, of which he was a fellow from 1869. He was elected to council in 1870, and was honorary secretary (jointly with Clements Markham) from 1881 to 1894, and president from 1914 to 1917. He was also vice-president for three periods (1906–10, 1911–14, and 1917–24). He was an efficient and innovative administrator, and a founder of the *Geographical Journal*. It was largely a result of his initiative that J. S. Keltie was commissioned in 1884 to report on geographical teaching in Europe. The poor state of the subject in Britain, compared especially with that in Germany, led to the encouragement of geographical teaching in Oxford, and later Cambridge—financial support being given by the Royal Geographical Society for geography at Oxford from 1888 and Cambridge from 1903. The teaching of geography eventually spread to many other universities in the country. Freshfield's interest in the subject was undoubtedly inspired by his admiration for the beauty of the natural environment, especially mountains, and the need for scientific study of such environments in relation to human habitation. He received the Founder's medal of the society in 1903, and was elected a trustee in 1924. Freshfield was also a strong supporter of the Geographical Association, of which he was president from 1879 to 1911.

Douglas William Freshfield (1845–1934), by unknown photographer [detail]

It was largely due to his advocacy, in the face of strenuous opposition, that women were admitted to the fellowship of the Royal Geographical Society (for a very short period in 1892–3, but then permanently from 1913).

His summer travels in Italy and Switzerland with his parents gave Freshfield a passion for mountain travel as an aspect of serious exploration. While still a schoolboy he ascended Mont Blanc, and in the 1860s and 1870s made at least twenty first ascents, chiefly in the lesser-known Italian Alps. He edited several editions of *Hints to Travellers* and from 1872 to 1880 the *Alpine Journal*. From 1893 to 1895 he was president of the Alpine Club, having been elected a member in 1864. Second only to his love of mountains was his interest in classical life and lore (exemplified by his service as treasurer of the Hellenic and Roman societies), in consequence of which he also travelled widely over the regions of classical civilizations in the Near East. In 1868 he explored, together with Charles Tucker, Adolphus Moor, and his lifelong friend François Devouassoud, the central Caucasus, which, except for the lower heights, were then unknown. He made the first ascent of Kazbek (16,546 ft), Elbrus (18,470 ft), and several other peaks, and recorded the existence of large glaciers in the regions between them. After returning to the Caucasus in 1887 and 1889 he published his *Exploration of the Caucasus* (1896), which was for a time a standard work. In 1899 he visited India, Burma, and Ceylon, and made, with Dr Edmund Johnston Garwood, the circuit of Kanchenjunga through unmapped territory in Sikkim and Nepal, recorded in *Round Kanchenjunga* (1903). Lastly, in 1905, at the age of sixty, he tried, with A. L. Mumm, to ascend Ruwenzori in Uganda, then known as the Mountains of the Moon, but was stopped by bad weather and mud at 12,000 ft. Later in life he visited many mountains, including the Pyrenees and the Japanese Alps, and was planning an expedition to Chinese Turkestan (Sinkiang or Xinjiang) in 1914. He made a world tour in 1913.

Freshfield's quick and penetrating wit made him a champion of the causes which he embraced, and, although essentially a Victorian in outlook, he fought traditional and conservative views whenever he felt that they hindered progress. His numerous books include several privately printed volumes of verse. He was a cultivated man and a friend of Tennyson. The honorary degree of DCL was conferred on him by the universities of Oxford (1916) and Geneva (1923), the latter in connection with his study of a famous Swiss geologist in his joint book *Life of Horace Benedict de Saussure* (1920), and he was elected an honorary fellow of University College, Oxford, in 1925. He was a justice of the peace for Sussex, and a conservator of Ashdown Forest. He died at his home, Wych Cross Place, Forest Row, Sussex, on 9 February 1934 and was buried at Brookwood cemetery, Surrey, beside his wife and son. A full length biography appeared in 2001, entitled *From a Tramp's Wallet*, after his privately printed collection of notes and poems of that name.

R. N. RUDMOSE BROWN, *rev.* ROBIN A. BUTLIN

Sources *The Times* (10 Feb 1934) · H. Fisher, *From a tramp's wallet: a life of Douglas William Freshfield* (2001) · T. G. Longstaff, 'Douglas Freshfield, 1845–1934', *GJ*, 83 (1934), 257–62 · D. Middleton, 'Douglas W. Freshfield, 1845–1934', *Geographers: biobibliographical studies*, 13, ed. G. J. Martin (1991), 23–9 · M. J. Wise, 'The Scott Keltie report, 1885, and the teaching of geography in Great Britain', *GJ*, 152 (1986), 367–82 · H. R. Mill, *The record of the Royal Geographical Society, 1830–1930* (1930) · A. L. Mumm, *The Alpine Club register*, 2 (1925) · D. I. Scargill, 'The RGS and the foundations of geography at Oxford', *GJ*, 142 (1976), 438–61 · [Mrs H. Freshfield], *Alpine byways, or, Light leaves gathered in 1859 and 1860, by a lady* (1861) · D. R. Stoddart, *On geography and its history* (1986) · K. J. Garwood, *Alpine Journal*, 46 (1934), 175–6 · D. R. Stoddart, 'The RGS and the foundations of geography at Cambridge', *GJ*, 141 (1975), 216–39 · L. J. Jay, 'Douglas Freshfield's contribution to geographical education', *Historical perspectives on geographical education*, ed. W. E. Marsden (1980), 43–53 · *The Eton register*, 2–3 (privately printed, Eton, 1905–6) · Foster, *Alum. Oxon.*
Archives Alpine Club, letters | BLPES, corresp. with Violet Markham · CUL, letters to W. M. Conway · King's AC Cam., letters from him and his wife to Oscar Browning · RGS, letters to H. R. Mill [163] · RGS, corresp. with Royal Geographical Society [101]
Likenesses Hills & Saunders, photograph, 1880, RGS · J. Thomson, photograph, 1903, RGS · Johnston & Hoffmann, photograph, 1904, RGS · photographs, RGS [*see illus.*]
Wealth at death £147,610 1s. 10d.: probate, 12 March 1934, CGPLA Eng. & Wales

Freshfield, Edwin (1832–1918). *See under* Freshfield family (*per.* 1800–1918).

Freshfield, Edwin Hanson (1864–1948). *See under* Freshfield family (*per.* 1800–1918).

Freshfield, Henry Ray (1814–1895). *See under* Freshfield family (*per.* 1800–1918).

Freshfield, James Joseph William (1775–1864). *See under* Freshfield family (*per.* 1800–1918).

Freshfield, James William (1801–1857). *See under* Freshfield family (*per.* 1800–1918).

Freshfield, James William (1877–1952). *See under* Freshfield family (*per.* 1800–1918).

Freshfield, William Dawes (1831–1903). *See under* Freshfield family (*per.* 1800–1918).

Fresson, (Ernest) Edmund (1891–1963), airline executive, was born at Fairholme, Dennington Park Road, Hampstead, London, on 20 September 1891, the son of Ernest Mitchell Edward Fresson, a stockbroker, and his wife, Marian Kathleen Robins. Edmund (as he was known) was educated at Framlingham College in Suffolk, after which he was sent, in 1911, to Shanghai as a trainee engineer with Jardine Engineering. With the outbreak of the First World War he intended to return to Britain to join the Royal Flying Corps, but illness delayed his return until 1917. Eventually, having learned to fly in Canada, he served on coastal patrols, and as a flying instructor. In 1919 Fresson left the Royal Air Force (RAF) with the rank of captain and returned to China with his new wife, Dorothy Olive Cuming, whom he had married on 28 July, and who died tragically the following year. He continued his association with aircraft and resigned from Jardines in 1923 to set up an aircraft factory in Shanxi province. A prototype of an aircraft suitable for Chinese conditions was constructed, but by 1925 the German Junkers company had gained the initiative in Shanxi and, after receiving compensation for his efforts, Fresson abandoned the enterprise and returned to England in 1927.

After a short spell with Berkshire Aviation Tours, Fresson founded the North British Aviation Company with a number of associates. In March 1929 the company, which was based near Liverpool, began offering 'joy-rides' and short flights to the public in two aged Avro 504K aircraft. In the summer of 1931 Fresson flew one of the Avros across the Pentland Firth from northern Scotland to the Orkney Islands, and immediately recognized the potential of a regular air link across this turbulent stretch of water. After surveying routes and selecting the necessary landing sites, he raised capital of £2675 from local professional and business interests in Inverness. In May 1933 his new airline, Highland Airways Ltd, began fare-paying operations from Inverness via Wick to Kirkwall with a small three-passenger Monospar ST4 aircraft, Fresson himself being both managing director of the new venture and its chief pilot. The network was soon extended to include Thurso on the northern coast of Caithness.

Highland Airways' potential for success lay in the tremendous time saving that air transport offered over northern Scotland's circuitous surface communications: the one and a half hour air trip from Inverness to Kirkwall compared to a journey of around nine hours by train and ferry. In this early era of air transport the delivery of time-sensitive freight such as newspapers was almost more important than the carriage of passengers, and the new Highland Airways service meant that Orkney islanders received their copy of *The Scotsman* a full day earlier than before. Fresson's aircraft also flew regular air ambulance services, carrying patients from the outlying Orkney Islands to the hospital at Kirkwall.

Before the end of its first year Highland Airways had acquired a larger De Havilland DH 84 Dragon and additional pilots and staff. In the absence of profits, the funds required for the new aircraft came in the form of an additional capital injection from a somewhat surprising source: the North of Scotland Orkney and Shetland Steam Navigation Company. This important local shipping line judged that air travel was going to be a permanent feature in the north of Scotland and decided that participation in the new airline was the best way to minimize its effects on steamship traffic. In 1934 Highland's income was boosted with a Post Office contract to deliver mail between Inverness and Kirkwall, and the first unsurcharged air mail service in Great Britain began in May. The route network was also expanded, both within the Orkneys from Kirkwall to the islands of Hoy, Stronsay, Sanday, Westray, and North Ronaldsay, and southwards to Aberdeen, where Fresson encountered competition from fellow entrepreneur, Eric Gandar Dower, and his recently formed Aberdeen Airways. As these two aviators were both determined to develop communications to the Orkney and Shetland islands it was inevitable that intense rivalry would develop between Fresson, based at Inverness, and Gandar Dower at Aberdeen. Unfortunately, this seems to have included a mutual unwillingness to allow the other's aircraft to land at their airfields. They also had to cope with initial hostility from the railway companies, which felt threatened by the new airlines. For a while the London, Midland, and Scottish Railway (LMS) and the London and North Eastern Railway (LNER), both of which had lines in the region, used boycott tactics to prevent travel agents from accepting bookings with Highland Airways.

Fresson married in 1934 Gwendolyne Holloway (or Simons): they had one son. In 1935 Highland's lack of profits forced him to reconsider the wisdom of continuing as an independent airline. Although the terrain favoured air transport in principle, the absence of a significant tourist trade or any other major industry in the north of Scotland meant that there was insufficient revenue, and while the richer Aberdeen Airways could absorb the losses, Fresson could not. In London, Clive Pearson's United Airways had been formed with the backing of the Whitehall Securities group and soon merged with Hillman Airways and Spartan Air Lines to form British Airways Ltd. In May 1935 Highland Airways was taken over by United, and later became a British Airways subsidiary, although it continued to operate under its own name and Fresson's management. The move further expanded the airline's capital base and allowed the acquisition of two De Havilland DH 89A Dragon Rapide aircraft, as well as the northwards extension of the airline's network to Sumburgh in the Shetland Islands.

By 1938 Highland Airways had six aircraft and eight pilots as well as Fresson himself, who had now given up regular flying to concentrate on the airline's management. However, profits still eluded it and further amalgamation took place when Highland Airways and Northern Airways were taken over by the newly formed Scottish Airways Ltd, the main shareholders of which were British Airways and LMS. Northern Airways had been founded in 1934 by the former bus operator, George Nicholson. Its west Scottish routes, based on Glasgow, were now joined to those of Highland Airways. Fresson remained with Scottish Airways as a director, in control of Highland's routes and continuing its record of reliability, although it was no longer his own company. Highland Airways ceased operations in August 1938 and was wound up in 1940.

During the Second World War Fresson happily returned to flying duties when his younger colleagues joined the RAF. He worked with the associated airways joint committee, flying the Scottish Airways routes under Air Ministry control and maintaining services despite the occasional skirmish with German intruders. In recognition of this work he was appointed OBE in 1943.

After the war Scottish Airways enjoyed a brief revival until all independent British domestic airlines, apart from Channel Islands Airways, and Eric Gandar Dower's Allied Airways, were absorbed into British European Airways (BEA) in February 1947. Fresson assumed responsibility for the northern sector of the new corporation's Scottish division, but was profoundly disillusioned with the change. As an independent spirit, who had built his own company on the northernmost frontier of British aviation, he was ill-suited to the role of manager in a nationalized undertaking and found it difficult to take orders from what he saw as an overstaffed and bureaucratic headquarters in far-away London. His career ended sadly with his dismissal from BEA after he had been reprimanded for making an unauthorized ambulance flight in February 1948. Many of the destinations in the outlying Orkney Islands which he had painstakingly established with Highland Airways in the 1930s were abandoned by BEA and were to remain without regular air services until the 1960s.

Fresson belonged to that generation of British air transport pioneers whose members gained their early flying experience in the First World War, and which includes such names as Herbert Brackley, Sholto Douglas, and George Woods-Humphery. Apart from being a businessman and energetic publicist for his airline, he was an accomplished and intrepid pilot. Commercial flying in the 1930s was a fairly primitive affair at the best of times; it is a tribute to Fresson's skill and courage that Highland Airways' services were carried on with a remarkable degree of safety and regularity through some of the most appalling weather conditions in Europe and, to begin with at least, entirely without the benefit of common navigational aids such as direction-finders and radio beacons.

In November 1948 Fresson took up a position in Kenya with the subsidiary of a Scottish brewer. He later returned to Inverness to run a small charter airline, but his great work in bringing air transport to the people of the highlands and islands of Scotland was never repeated. He died on 25 September 1963 in the Northern Infirmary, Inverness.   PETER J. LYTH

Sources *Report on the progress of civil aviation*, Air Ministry, Directorate of Civil Aviation (HMSO, 1933–8) · R. E. G. Davies, *Rebels and reformers of the airways* (1987), 215–27 · A. J. Robertson, 'The new road to the isles: Highland Airways and Scottish Airways, 1933–39', *Journal of Transport History*, 3rd ser., 7 (1986), 48–60 · *DSBB* · d. cert. · m. cert. [Dorothy Olive Cuming] · b. cert.
Wealth at death £14,169: *DSBB*

Freston, Anthony Brettingham (1757–1819), Church of England clergyman and author, was the son of Robert Brettingham of Norwich, who was probably a worsted weaver, whose father was Matthew *Brettingham (1699–1769), architect, of Norwich. As a child he took the name of Freston in pursuance of the will of his maternal uncle William Freston of Mendham, Suffolk, who died in 1761, and left him estates in Norfolk and Suffolk. He matriculated as a commoner at Christ Church, Oxford, on 26 December 1775, aged eighteen, and graduated BA in 1780. On 25 July 1783 he was ordained priest by the bishop of Norwich to the title of Gayton Thorpe, Norfolk. In the same year he became a fellow-commoner of Clare College, Cambridge, where he was incorporated BA and immediately proceeded MA. Also in 1783 he married Anne (d. 1828), the widow of Thomas Hyde of Cambridge. In 1784 he contributed to the debate about means of improving the stipends of poor livings, in an anonymous pamphlet, *Provisions for the More Equal Maintenance of the Clergy*. In 1787 he published *An Elegy* and *Poems on Several Subjects*, which included some juvenilia and some slightly *risqué* verse. In 1792 he presented himself to the perpetual curacy of Needham, Norfolk, the patronage of which he had inherited from his uncle, and published anonymously *An Address to the People of England*.

In 1801 a college friend presented Freston to the rectory of Edgeworth in Gloucestershire. George Huntingford, bishop of Gloucester, subsequently appointed him rural dean of Stonehouse. In 1807 Freston published *A Collection of Evidence for the Divinity of the Lord Jesus Christ*, which he dedicated to the bishop of Gloucester: this was a defence of the divinity of Christ against Unitarianism, and showed him to be well read in seventeenth- and eighteenth-century Anglican theology. He followed this in 1809 with *Six Sermons on Some of the Most Important Doctrines of Christianity, to Which are Added Five Sermons on Occasional Subjects*. Dedicated to Spencer Perceval, then chancellor of the exchequer, it congratulated him on his 'Attention ... paid to the Melioration of the state of the inferior Clergy' and noted that 'the Non-residence of an established Ecclesiastic, either Rector, Vicar, or Curate is an Evil attended with the worst consequences to the Interests of Religion and Morality', thus showing his continuing concern for the well-being of the clergy. Freston's sermons showed possible evidence of evangelical influence, and strongly reflected the contemporary concern that the teaching of the established church should support civil obedience and duty.

Freston died on 25 December 1819, and was buried in the chancel of Edgeworth church, where he was commemorated by a mural monument. His wife died on 16 May 1828.

W. M. JACOB

Sources Foster, *Alum. Oxon.* • Venn, *Alum. Cant.* • Colvin, *Archs.* • inscription, Edgeworth church, Gloucestershire • *IGI* • A. Freston, *Six sermons on some of the most important doctrines of Christianity* (1809) • *DNB*

Likenesses Cooke of Gloucester, mural monument, Edgeworth church, Gloucestershire

PICTURE CREDITS

Flaxman, John (1755–1826)—© National Portrait Gallery, London

Fleck, Alexander, Baron Fleck (1889–1968)—© National Portrait Gallery, London

Flecker, (Herman) James Elroy (1884–1915)—© Bodleian Library, University of Oxford

Fleetwood, Charles, appointed Lord Fleetwood under the protectorate (c.1618–1692)—Society of Antiquaries of London

Fleetwood, William (1656–1723)—© Copyright The British Museum

Fleming, Sir Alexander (1881–1955)—© National Portrait Gallery, London

Fleming, Amaryllis Marie-Louise (1925?–1999)—Getty Images - Thurston Hopkins

Fleming, Sir (John) Ambrose (1849–1945)—Science Museum / Heritage Images

Fleming, Ann Geraldine Mary (1913–1981)—© Cecil Beaton Archive, Sotheby's; collection National Portrait Gallery, London

Fleming, Caleb (1698–1779)—by permission of Dr Williams's Library

Fleming, David Hay (1849–1931)—© National Portrait Gallery, London

Fleming, Sir George, second baronet (1667–1747)—© National Portrait Gallery, London

Fleming, George (1833–1901)—*Veterinary Record* (27 April 1901), 594–5

Fleming, Ian Lancaster (1908–1964)—© Cecil Beaton Archive, Sotheby's; collection National Portrait Gallery, London

Fleming, Marjory (1803–1811)—Trustees of the National Library of Scotland

Fleming, (Robert) Peter (1907–1971)—© National Portrait Gallery, London

Fleming, Robert (1845–1933)—© reserved; collection Robert Fleming Holdings; photograph National Portrait Gallery, London

Fleming, Sir Sandford (1827–1915)—Scottish National Portrait Gallery

Fleming, Sir Thomas (c.1544–1613)—© National Portrait Gallery, London

Fletcher, Andrew, of Saltoun (1653?–1716)—private collection; photograph © National Portrait Gallery, London

Fletcher, Charles Montague (1911–1995)—© Nick Sinclair; collection National Portrait Gallery, London

Fletcher, John (1579–1625)—private collection, on loan to Plymouth Art Gallery; © reserved in the photograph

Fletcher, John William (*bap.* 1729, *d.* 1785)—The New Room, John Wesley's Chapel, Bristol / Photograph by David Roberts

Fletcher, Mary (1739–1815)—© National Portrait Gallery, London

Flew, (Robert) Newton (1886–1962)—© Estate of Frank O Salisbury 2004.

All rights reserved, DACS; Wesley House, Cambridge

Flicke, Gerlach (*d.* 1558)—© National Portrait Gallery, London

Flight, (Walter) Claude (1881–1955)—courtesy Michael Parkin

Flinders, Matthew (1774–1814)—© National Portrait Gallery, London

Flood, Henry (1732–1791)—Birr Scientific and Heritage Foundation, courtesy of the Earl of Rosse. Photograph: Photographic Survey, Courtauld Institute of Art, London

Florey, Howard Walter, Baron Florey (1898–1968)—© National Portrait Gallery, London

Florio, John (1553–1625)—© National Portrait Gallery, London

Flower, Cyril, Baron Battersea (1843–1907)—© National Portrait Gallery, London

Flower, Sir William Henry (1831–1899)—reproduced by kind permission of the President and Council of the Royal College of Surgeons of London

Flowers, Thomas Harold (1905–1998)—Universal Pictorial Press

Fludd, Robert (*bap.* 1574, *d.* 1637)—© National Portrait Gallery, London

Fogerty, Elsie (1865–1945)—© reserved; reproduced by courtesy of Central School of Speech and Drama, Embassy Theatre, London

Foley, Thomas (1617–1677)—© National Portrait Gallery, London

Foliot, Gilbert (c.1110–1187)—The British Library

Folkes, Martin (1690–1754)—© The Royal Society

Follett, Sir William Webb (1796–1845)—© National Portrait Gallery, London

Fonblanque, Albany William (1793–1872)—© National Portrait Gallery, London

Fonteyn, Dame Margot (1919–1991)—© Alan Bergman from the Alan Bergman archives; collection National Portrait Gallery, London

Foot, Sir Dingle Mackintosh (1905–1978)—© National Portrait Gallery, London

Foot, Hugh Mackintosh, Baron Caradon (1907–1990)—© National Portrait Gallery, London

Foot, Jesse (1744–1826)—© National Portrait Gallery, London

Foote, Lydia (1843–1892)—© National Portrait Gallery, London

Foote, Samuel (*bap.* 1721, *d.* 1777)—© National Portrait Gallery, London

Forbes, Alexander, fourth Lord Forbes of Pitsligo (1678–1762)—private collection

Forbes, Alexander Penrose (1817–1875)—© National Portrait Gallery, London

Forbes, Archibald (1838–1900)—© Hamburger Kunsthalle / Photographer: Elke Walford, Hamburg

Forbes, Sir Charles Morton (1880–1960)—© National Portrait Gallery, London

Forbes, Duncan (1685–1747)—in the collection of the Faculty of Advocates; photograph courtesy the Scottish National Portrait Gallery

Forbes, Edward (1815–1854)—Scottish National Portrait Gallery

Forbes, James David (1809–1868)—Scottish National Portrait Gallery

Forbes, Dame (Katherine) Jane Trefusis (1899–1971)—© reserved; photograph courtesy of the Trustees of the Royal Air Force Museum

Forbes, John (1570/71–1606)—© Copyright The British Museum

Forbes, Patrick, of Corse (1564–1635)—© National Portrait Gallery, London

Ford, Sir (Richard) Brinsley (1908–1999)—by permission of the Trustees of the will of the late Sir Richard Brinsley Ford. Photograph: Photographic Survey, Courtauld Institute of Art, London

Ford, Charles Edmund (1912–1999)—Godfrey Argent Studios

Ford, Ford Madox (1873–1939)—by permission of the E. O. Hoppé Trust, Curatorial Assistance, Inc., Los Angeles; collection National Portrait Gallery, London

Ford, James (1779–1850)—The President and Fellows of Trinity College, Oxford

Ford, (Edward) Onslow (1852–1901)—© National Portrait Gallery, London

Forde, Florrie (1876–1940)—private collection

Fordham, Sir Herbert George (1854–1929)—The Royal Geographical Society, London

Fordyce, James (1720–1796)—Scottish National Portrait Gallery

Foresythe, Reginald Charles (1907–1958)—Collection Stephen Bourne

Forman, Henry Buxton (1842–1917)—© reserved; Keats House, London Borough of Camden

Formby, George (1904–1961)—© Science & Society Picture Library; photograph National Portrait Gallery, London

Forrest, Edwin (1806–1872)—Garrick Club / the art archive

Forrest, John, first Baron Forrest (1847–1918)—The Royal Geographical Society, London

Forster, Edward Morgan (1879–1970)—© National Portrait Gallery, London

Forster, (Johann) Georg Adam (1754–1794)—by permission of the National Library of Australia / The Rex Nan Kivell Collection

Forster, William Edward (1818–1886)—© National Portrait Gallery, London

Fortescue, Chichester Samuel Parkinson-, Baron Carlingford and second Baron Clermont (1823–1898)—© National Portrait Gallery, London

Fortescue, Frances Elizabeth Anne Parkinson- (1821–1879)—© National Portrait Gallery, London

Fortescue, Sir John William (1859–1933)—© National Portrait Gallery, London

Fortescue, William (*bap.* 1687, *d.* 1749)—© National Portrait Gallery, London

Fortnum, Charles Drury Edward (1820–1899)—Ashmolean Museum, Oxford

Forwood, Sir Arthur Bower, first baronet (1836–1898)—© National Portrait Gallery, London

Foskett, Daphne (1911–1998)—in a private collection on loan to the Scottish National Portrait Gallery

Foster, Balthazar Walter, first Baron Ilkeston (1840–1913)—© National Portrait Gallery, London

Foster, Sir George Eulas (1847–1931)—© National Portrait Gallery, London

Foster, Sir (Thomas) Gregory, first baronet (1866–1931)—The College Art Collections, University of London

Foster, John, first Baron Oriel (1740–1828)—The Nelson-Atkins Museum of Art, Kansas City, Missouri. (Purchase: Nelson Trust) 30-20

Foster, Sir Michael (1689–1763)—© National Portrait Gallery, London

Foster, Sir Michael (1836–1907)—© National Portrait Gallery, London

Fotherby, Martin (c.1560–1620)—photograph by courtesy Sotheby's Picture Library, London

Fothergill, John (1712–1780)—Ashmolean Museum, Oxford

Foulis, Robert (1707–1776)—Scottish National Portrait Gallery

Fourdrinier, Henry (1766–1854)—© National Portrait Gallery, London

Fowler, Edward (1631/2–1714)—© National Portrait Gallery, London

Fowler, Eileen Philippa Rose (1906–2000)—Getty Images - Hulton Archive

Fowler, Ellen Thorneycroft (1860–1929)—© National Portrait Gallery, London

Fowler, Henry Hartley, first Viscount Wolverhampton (1830–1911)—© National Portrait Gallery, London

Fowler, Henry Watson (1858–1933)—® reserved

Fowler, Sir John, first baronet (1817–1898)—courtesy of the Institution of Civil Engineers Archives

Fowler, Sir Ralph Howard (1889–1944)—© National Portrait Gallery, London

Fowler, Sir Robert Nicholas, first baronet (1828–1891)—© National Portrait Gallery, London

Fowler, William (1761–1832)—© National Portrait Gallery, London

Fox, (Georgiana) Caroline [Lady (Georgiana) Caroline Lennox], *suo jure* Baroness Holland of Holland (1723–1774)—© reserved

Fox, Sir Charles (1810–1874)—© National Portrait Gallery, London

Fox, Charles James (1749–1806)—by kind permission of the Earl of